August 12–16, 2012
Portland, Oregon, USA

Association for
Computing Machinery

Advancing Computing as a Science & Profession

SIGIR'12 Vol. 2 of 2

The Proceedings of the International ACM SIGIR Conference on
Research & Development in Information Retrieval

Sponsored by:

ACM SIGIR

Supported by:

Microsoft Research, Baidu, Google Research, Yahoo! Labs,
IBM Research, eBay, Oracle, Morgan & Claypool Publishers,
Springer, Cambridge University Press,
University of Oregon Applied Information Management Prorgram,
Now Publishers, and Oregon Health & Science University

Association for
Computing Machinery

Advancing Computing as a Science & Profession

The Association for Computing Machinery
2 Penn Plaza, Suite 701
New York, New York 10121-0701

Notice to Past Authors of ACM-Published Articles
ACM intends to create a complete electronic archive of all articles and/or other material previously published by ACM. If you have written a work that has been previously published by ACM in any journal or conference proceedings prior to 1978, or any SIG Newsletter at any time, and you do NOT want this work to appear in the ACM Digital Library, please inform permissions@acm.org, stating the title of the work, the author(s), and where and when published.

ISBN: 978-1-4503-1658-3 (Digital)

ISBN: 978-1-4503-2001-6 (Print Vol.2)

Additional copies may be ordered prepaid from:

ACM Order Department
PO Box 30777
New York, NY 10087-0777, USA

Phone: 1-800-342-6626 (USA and Canada)
+1-212-626-0500 (Global)
Fax: +1-212-944-1318
E-mail: acmhelp@acm.org
Hours of Operation: 8:30 am – 4:30 pm ET

ACM Order Number: 606121

Printed in the USA

Welcome from the General Conference Chair

Welcome to Portland, Oregon, USA for the 35th Annual ACM SIGIR Conference on Research and Development in Information Retrieval. SIGIR is the premier international forum for the presentation of new research results and the demonstration of new systems and techniques in the field of information retrieval, also known as search. My colleagues and I from Oregon Health & Science University (OHSU) are pleased to be hosting this year's SIGIR, and we hope that you enjoy your stay in Portland as well as the technical and social programs that we have arranged.

Successfully organizing a conference of the size and scope of SIGIR would not be possible without the dedicated work of a great many individuals. First and foremost, I thank the Program Committee Chairs, Jamie Callan, Yoelle Maarek, and Mark Sanderson, who together with Posters & Demos Chairs Falk Scholer, Mark Smucker, and Andrew Turpin put together an excellent main technical program. I also thank Henning Müller, who organized our slate of tutorials; Eugene Agichtein and Vanessa Murdock, who organized the workshops; Udo Kruschwitz and Su-Lin Wu, who organized the industry track; Maarten de Rijke and Mounia Lalmas, who organized the doctoral consortium; Doug Oard, who served as mentoring chair; and ChengXiang Zhai, who chaired the outstanding paper awards committee. Collectively, these individuals were largely responsible for the technical events that most SIGIR participants will attend, and I thank them for their tremendous efforts.

Many other individuals worked largely behind the scenes to ensure that SIGIR 2011 would be a success, including treasurer, Javed Mostafa; publicity chair, Jayashree Kalpathy-Cramer; publications chair, Elmer Bernstam; and local arrangements chair, Justin Fletcher. I also thank Aaron Cohen, who coordinated sponsorship, and Chris Weldon, who served as the webmaster.

Finally, I am indebted to others for the invaluable help and advice they have provided, especially James Allan, SIGIR Chair, and Ian Soboroff, SIGIR Treasurer.

SIGIR 2012 is, of course, sponsored by ACM, but has also received generous support from numerous companies and organizations. Microsoft Research, Baidu, and Google were all particularly generous with support at the Gold level, with Yahoo! Labs providing support at the Silver level and eBay, IBM Research, and Oracle providing support at the Bronze level. In addition, Morgan & Claypool, Springer, Cambridge University Press, the University of Oregon Applied Information Management Program, and Now Publishers all made arrangements to support and exhibit at the conference. The organization of SIGIR 2012 also would not have been possible without the support of the Department of Medical Informatics & Clinical Epidemiology at OHSU. Finally, logistical aspects of the conference were handled with excellence by Kim Lepin of the Division of Continuing Medical Education at OHSU.

Welcome to Portland, and I hope that you enjoy the conference and your stay in Oregon.

William Hersh
SIGIR 2012 Conference Chair
Oregon Health & Science University
Portland, Oregon, USA

Welcome from the Program Chairs

We are delighted to welcome you to the 35th edition of SIGIR, the ACM International Conference on Research and Development in Information Retrieval. The conference continues its tradition of being the premier forum for research and development information retrieval, the computer science discipline behind what many call "search". The high number of submitted papers, this year again, demonstrates both the breadth and depth of the research being done in this vibrant field, both in academia and industry. We have done our best to ensure that these papers meet high standards of quality in terms of technical contribution, innovation, presentation, reference to previous work, and methodology. At the same time, we have tried to be flexible in the application of these criteria in order to consider papers describing novel and innovative work that may be somewhat unconventional.

The conference received 483 full paper submissions this year. Examining the country code of the paper's contact author, we found that 185 (38%) come from the Americas; 158 (33%), Asia and Pacific region; and 140 (29%) from Europe, the Middle East and Africa. Of these, 98 (20%) were accepted, essentially the same as last year's acceptance rate and up from the 16.7% rate of the year before. There was almost no difference in the acceptance rates across the three broad regions. The top five countries in terms of accepted papers were the U.S.A. (36), China (14), the U.K. & Spain (both 7), and the Netherlands (6). In addition, 208 short papers were submitted to the poster track, of which 76 (36.5%) were accepted. In the other categories, there were 17 (47.2%) demonstrations, 4 workshops, and 16 tutorials accepted. The top five technical areas (as inferred from the primary keyword assigned by the authors) covered by the accepted papers, were queries and query analysis (18%), retrieval models and ranking (14%), web IR & social media search (13%), document representation and content analysis (11%), and users and interactive IR (9%). This was a small re-ordering of the topics from last year.

SIGIR this year again used a two-tier double-blind reviewing approach. In a first stage, at least three reviewers read every paper and provided ratings and comments. Then, in a second stage, the primary and secondary Area Chairs ensured the quality of the reviewing process by studying, validating, and summarizing these reviews, and adding their own feedback and ratings. When required, Area Chairs initiated a discussion among the reviewers to resolve any controversial issues or significant differences of opinion. Once the discussion stage was completed, the two Area Chairs made the final decisions for nearly all submitted papers. At the program committee meeting held in Haifa, Israel, the Program Chairs and the attending Area Chairs went over the reviews, verified the process, gathered additional input, and made decisions in the few cases for which assistance had been requested.

The success of the conference depends on the numerous volunteers who, every year, devote large amounts of their time to reviewing and assisting in the organization of the program. We would like to acknowledge the tremendous work of the 200 general program committee members, representing more than 30 countries, and the effort and dedication of the 47 Area Chairs. They should be credited for the high quality of the program this year.

We also acknowledge the tremendous job done by the Posters Chairs in handling the short papers, and the great work done by the other Chairs with their tasks. We thank the general chair Bill Hersh, who was a wonderful partner in getting this program together. We are grateful to Yahoo! Labs for graciously hosting the Program Committee meeting in Haifa and to Thomas Preuss for his support of the ConfMaster system throughout the entire reviewing process.

Finally, we are in debt to the authors and attendees. They are the ones who make this conference possible. We hope that you will find this program interesting and thought-provoking. Our goal is not only to give you the opportunity to share ideas with other researchers and practitioners from around the world, but also to foster new research and innovation in this fascinating and ever-evolving domain.

Jamie Callan
Program Chair
Carnegie Mellon University

Yoelle Maarek
Program Chair
Yahoo! Research, Israel

Mark Sanderson
Program Chair
RMIT University, Australia

Table of Contents

Session 2A: Evaluation 1

Session 2B: Structured Data

Session 2C: Recommender Systems 1

Session 3A: Users 1: Personalization and User Modeling

Session 3B: Architectures 1

Session 5A: Users 2: Exploratory Search

Session 5B: Multimedia 2

Session 5C: Recommender Systems 2

Session 6A: Query Expansion and Reformulation

Session 6B: Social Media 1

Session 8B: Entities

Session 8C: Learning to Rank

Session 9A: Community QA

Session 9B: Federated Search

Session 9C: Diversity 2

Session 10A: Evaluation 2

Session 10B: Representation

Session 10C: Classification

Doctoral Submissions

Demonstrations

Industry Talk Abstracts

Poster Abstracts

Tutorial Presentations

SIGIR 2012 Organizing Committee

General Chair: William Hersh *(Oregon Health & Science University, USA)*

Program Chairs: Jamie Callan *(Carnegie Mellon University, USA)*
Yoelle Maarek *(Yahoo! Research, Israel)*
Mark Sanderson *(Royal Melbourne Institute of Technology, Australia)*

Treasurer: Javed Mostafa *(University of North Carolina-Chapel Hill, USA)*

Posters & Demos Chairs: Falk Scholer *(Royal Melbourne Institute of Technology, Australia)*
Mark Smucker *(University of Waterloo, Canada)*
Andrew Turpin *(University of Melbourne, Australia)*

Tutorials Chair: Henning Müller *(University of Applied Sciences Western Switzerland, Switzerland)*

Workshops Chairs: Eugene Agichtein *(Emory University, USA)*
Vanessa Murdock *(Yahoo! Research, Spain)*

Industry Track Chairs: Udo Kruschwitz *(University of Essex, United Kingdom)*
Su-Lin Wu *(Yahoo! Labs, USA)*

Doctoral Consortium Chairs: Mounia Lalmas *(Yahoo! Research, Spain)*
Maarten de Rijke *(University of Amsterdam, The Netherlands)*

Mentoring Chair: Douglas Oard *(University of Maryland, USA)*

Best Papers Chair: ChengXiang Zhai *(University of Illinois - Champaign-Urbana, USA)*

Publications Chair: Elmer Bernstam *(The University of Texas Health Science Center at Houston, USA)*

Local Arrangements Chair: Justin Fletcher *(Oregon Health & Science University, USA)*

Publicity Chair: Jayashree Kalpathy-Cramer *(Oregon Health & Science University, USA)*

Sponsorships Chair: Aaron Cohen *(Oregon Health & Science University, USA)*

Webmaster: Chris Weldon *(Oregon Health & Science University, USA)*

SIGIR 2012 Committees

Senior Program Committee

Jamie Callan *(Carnegie Mellon University - USA) – Chair*
Yoelle Maarek *(Yahoo! Research - Israel) – Chair*
Mark Sanderson *(RMIT University - Australia) – Chair*

Eugene Agichtein *(Emory University - USA)*
James Allan *(University of Massachusetts Amherst - USA)*
Sihem Amer-Yahia *(QCRI and CNRS - France)*
Ricardo Baeza-Yates *(Yahoo! Research - Spain)*
Andrei Broder *(Yahoo! Research - USA)*
Peter Bruza *(Queensland University of Technology - Australia)*
David Carmel *(IBM Research - Israel)*
Ben Carterette *(University of Delaware - USA)*
Carlos Castillo *(Qatar Computing Research Institute - Qatar)*
Tat Seng Chua *(National University of Singapore - Singapore)*
Charles L. A. Clarke *(University of Waterloo - Canada)*
Kevyn Collins-Thompson *(Microsoft Research - USA)*
Nick Craswell *(Microsoft - USA)*
W. Bruce Croft *(University of Massachusetts Amherst - USA)*
Fernando Diaz *(Yahoo! Research - USA)*
Susan Dumais *(Microsoft Research - USA)*
Evgeniy Gabrilovich *(Google - USA)*
Eric Gaussier *(Université Joseph Fourier - France)*
Shlomo Geva *(Queensland University of Technology - Australia)*
Djoerd Hiemstra *(University of Twente - The Netherlands)*
Xian-Sheng Hua *(Microsoft - USA)*
Gareth Jones *(Dublin City University - Ireland)*
Franciska de Jong *(University of Twente - The Netherlands)*
Vanja Josifovski *(Yahoo! Research - USA)*
Diane Kelly *(University of North Carolina at Chapel Hill - USA)*
Wessel Kraaij *(Radboud University Nijmegen and TNO - The Netherlands)*
Oren Kurland *(Technion - Israel)*
Mounia Lalmas *(Yahoo! Research - Spain)*
Elizabeth D. Liddy *(Syracuse University - USA)*
Wei-Ying Ma *(Microsoft Research Asia - China)*
Donald Metzler *(USC/ISI - USA)*
Isabelle Moulinier *(Thomson Reuters - USA)*
Edleno S. Moura *(UFAM - Brazil)*
Marc Najork *(Microsoft Research - USA)*
Tao Qin *(Microsoft Research Asia - China)*
Maarten de Rijke *(University of Amsterdam - The Netherlands)*
Ian Ruthven *(University of Strathclyde - UK)*
Tetsuya Sakai *(Microsoft Research Asia - China)*
Fabrizio Silvestri *(Information Science and Technology Institute - Italy)*
Andrew Trotman *(University of Otago - New Zealand)*
Ellen Voorhees *(NIST - USA)*
Arjen P. de Vries *(Centrum Wiskunde & Informatica - The Netherlands)*
Ryen White *(Microsoft Research - USA)*
Yiming Yang *(Carnegie Mellon University - USA)*
Elad Yom-Tov *(Yahoo! Research - USA)*
Yi Zhang *(University of California at Santa Cruz - USA)*
Ming Zhou *(Microsoft Research Asia - China)*

Program Committee

Omar Alonso *(Microsoft - USA)*
Gianni Amati *(Fondazione Ugo Bordoni - Italy)*
Avi Arampatzis *(Democritus University of Thrace - Greece)*
Jaime Arguello *(University of North Carolina at Chapel Hill - USA)*
Javed A. Aslam *(Northeastern University - USA)*
Leif Azzopardi *(University of Glasgow - UK)*
Peter Bailey *(Microsoft - USA)*
Krisztian Balog *(Norwegian University of Science and Technology - Norway)*
Hannah Bast *(University of Freiburg - Germany)*
Nicholas J. Belkin *(Rutgers - The State University of New Jersey - USA)*
Ron Bekkerman *(LinkedIn - USA)*
Michael Bendersky *(University of Massachusetts Amherst - USA)*
Klaus Berberich *(Max-Planck Institute for Informatics - Germany)*
Bodo Billerbeck *(Microsoft - Australia)*
Roi Blanco *(Yahoo! Research - Spain)*
Toine Bogers *(Royal School of Library and Information Science - Denmark)*
Edward Bortnikov *(Yahoo! Labs - Israel)*
Mohand Boughanem *(University Paul Sabatier - France)*
Martin Braschler *(Zurich University of Applied Sciences - Switzerland)*
Eric W. Brown *(IBM Research - USA)*
Chris Buckley *(Sabir Research - USA)*
Stefan Buettcher *(Google - USA)*
B. Barla Cambazoglu *(Yahoo! Research - Spain)*
Yunbo Cao *(Microsoft Research Asia - China)*
Jaime Carbonell *(Carnegie Mellon University - USA)*
James Caverlee *(Texas A&M University - USA)*

Raman Chandrasekar *(Evri - USA)*
Kevin C. Chang *(University of Illinois at Urbana-Champaign - USA)*
Yi Chang *(Yahoo! Labs - USA)*
Longbin Chen *(Microsoft - USA)*
Ye Chen *(Microsoft - USA)*
Pu-Jen Cheng *(National Taiwan University - Taiwan)*
Ed H. Chi *(Google Research - USA)*
Paul Clough *(University of Sheffield - UK)*
Michael Cole *(Rutgers University - USA)*
Jack G. Conrad *(Thomson Reuters - Switzerland)*
Gordon V. Cormack *(University of Waterloo - Canada)*
Ingemar Cox *(University College London - UK)*
Marco Cristo *(FUCAPI - Brazil)*
J. Shane Culpepper *(RMIT University - Australia)*
Altigran S. da Silva *(Universidade Federal do Amazonas - Brazil)*
Brian D. Davison *(Lehigh University - USA)*
Gianluca Demartini *(University of Fribourg - Switzerland)*
Ludovic Denoyer *(University Pierre et Marie Curie - France)*
Debora Donato *(Yahoo! Labs - USA)*
Gideon Dror *(Yahoo! Research - Israel)*
Gregory Druck *(Yahoo! Research - USA)*
Georges Dupret *(Yahoo! Labs - USA)*
Miles Efron *(University of Illinois - USA)*
David Eichmann *(University of Iowa - USA)*
Hui Fang *(University of Delaware - USA)*
Henry Feild *(University of Massachusetts Amherst - USA)*
Dennis Fetterly *(Microsoft Research - USA)*
Marcus C Fontoura *(Google - USA)*
Luanne Freund *(University of British Columbia - Canada)*
Ophir Frieder *(Georgetown University - USA)*
Ingo Frommholz *(University of Bedfordshire - UK)*
Norbert Fuhr *(Universität Duisburg-Essen - Germany)*
Patrick Gallinari *(Universite Pierre et Marie Curie - France)*
Bin Gao *(Microsoft Research Asia - China)*
Fredric Gey *(University of California at Berkeley - USA)*
C. Lee Giles *(Pennsylvania State University - USA)*
Aristides Gionis *(Yahoo! Research - Spain)*
Ayse Goker *(City University London - UK)*
Sreenivas Gollapudi *(Microsoft Research - USA)*
Marcos Goncalves *(UFMG - Brazil)*
Gregory Grefenstette *(3DS Exalead - France)*
Jiafeng Guo *(Chinese Academy of Sciences - China)*
Qi Guo *(Emory University - USA)*
Maxim Gurevich *(Google - USA)*
Cathal Gurrin *(Dublin City University - Ireland)*
Karl Gyllstrom *(Katholieke Universiteit Leuven - Belgium)*
Sanda M. Harabagiu *(University of Texas at Dallas - USA)*
Donna Harman *(NIST - USA)*
Claudia Hauff *(Delft University of Technology - The Netherlands)*
David Hawking *(Funnelback and Australian National University - Australia)*
Daqing He *(University of Pittsburgh - USA)*
Qi He *(IBM Almaden Research Center - USA)*
Marti Hearst *(University of California at Berkeley - USA)*
Monika Henzinger *(University of Vienna - Austria)*
Katja Hofmann *(University of Amsterdam - Netherlands)*
Eric Horvitz *(Microsoft Research - USA)*
Jimmy Huang *(York University - Canada)*
Jing Jiang *(Singapore Management University - Singapore)*
Thorsten Joachims *(Cornell University - USA)*
Hideo Joho *(University of Tsukuba - Japan)*
Joemon M. Jose *(University of Glasgow - UK)*
Jaap Kamps *(University of Amsterdam - The Netherlands)*
Noriko Kando *(National Institute of Informatics - Japan)*
Evangelos Kanoulas *(Google - Switzerland)*
Jussi Karlgren *(Gavagai - Sweden)*
Gabriella Kazai *(Microsoft Research Cambridge - UK)*
Irwin King *(The Chinese University of Hong Kong - Hong Kong, SAR)*
Jinyoung Kim *(University of Massachusetts Amherst - USA)*
Marijn Koolen *(University of Amsterdam - The Netherlands)*
Yehuda Koren *(Yahoo! Research - Israel)*
Alexander Kotov *(Emory University & Georgia Tech - USA)*
Giridhar Kumaran *(Microsoft - USA)*
Wai Lam *(The Chinese University of Hong Kong - Hong Kong, SAR)*
Birger Larsen *(Royal School of Library and Information Science - Denmark)*
Martha Larson *(Delft University of Technology - Netherlands)*
Ray R. Larson *(University of California at Berkeley - USA)*
Dawn Lawrie *(Loyola University Maryland - USA)*
Matthew Lease *(University of Texas at Austin - USA)*
Miro Lehtonen *(University of Helsinki - Finland)*
Jochen L. Leidner *(Thomson Reuters Global Resources - Switzerland)*
Anton Leuski *(University of Southern California - USA)*
David D. Lewis *(David D. Lewis Consulting - USA)*
Hang Li *(Microsoft Research - China)*
Yuefeng Li *(Queensland University of Technology - Australia)*
Edo Liberty *(Yahoo! Research - Israel)*
Christina Lioma *(University of Copenhagen - Denmark)*
Chao Liu *(Microsoft Research - USA)*
Tie-Yan Liu *(Microsoft Research Asia - China)*
David Losada *(University of Santiago de Compostela - Spain)*
Jie Lu *(IBM Research - USA)*
Robert W. P. Luk *(The Hong Kong Polytechnic University - Hong Kong, SAR)*
Hao Ma *(Microsoft Research - USA)*
Craig Macdonald *(University of Glasgow - UK)*
Andrew MacFarlane *(City University London - UK)*
Eren Manavoglu *(Yahoo! Labs - USA)*
R. Manmatha *(University of Massachusetts Amherst - USA)*
Stephane Marchand-Maillet *(University of Geneva - Switzerland)*
Yosi Mass *(IBM Research Haifa - Israel)*
James Mayfield *(Johns Hopkins University - USA)*
Paul McNamee *(Johns Hopkins University - USA)*

Additional Paper Reviewers

Alvaro Barreiro *(University of A Coruña - Spain)*
Jennifer Bayzick *(Lehigh University - USA)*
Wladmir Brandao *(Federal University of Minas Gerais - Brazil)*
Guillaume Cabanac *(University of Toulouse - France)*
Ethem F. Can *(University of Massachusetts Amherst - USA)*
Bin Cao *(Microsoft Research Asia - USA)*
Maria Christoforaki *(Polytechnic Institute of NYU - USA)*
Costas Dimopoulos *(Polytechnic Institute of NYU - USA)*
Christos Diou *(Centre for Research and Technology Hellas - Greece)*
Matt Ekstrand-Abueg *(Northeastern University - USA)*
Victor Fresno *(UNED - Spain)*
Yan Fu *(Beijing Normal University - China)*
Peter Golbus *(Northeastern University - USA)*
Liangjie Hong *(Lehigh University - USA)*
Vivian Hu *(York University - Canada)*
Somayeh Khatiban *(City University London - UK)*
Haiming Liu *(University of Bedfordshire - UK)*
Qiang Lu *(Kore Federal - USA)*
Wei Lu *(Wuhan University - China)*
Pavel Metrikov *(Northeastern University - USA)*
Jun Miao *(York University - Canada)*
Sergey Nepomnyachiy *(Polytechnic Institute of NYU - USA)*
Virgil Pavlu *(Northeastern University - USA)*
Maria-Hendrike Peetz *(University of Amsterdam - Netherlands)*
Anisio Lacerda *(Federal University of Minas Gerais - Brazil)*
Joaquin Perez-Iglesias *(UNED - Spain)*
Shahzad Rajput *(Northeastern University - USA)*
Marco Tulio Ribeiro *(Federal University of Minas Gerais - Brazil)*
Calum Robertson *(Sirca Ltd - Australia)*
Alvaro Rodrigo *(UNED - Spain)*
Nuzhah Gooda Sahib *(Queen Mary, University of London-UK)*
Rodrygo Santos *(University of Glasgow - UK)*
Yue Shi *(Delft University of Technology - Netherlands)*
Adriano Veloso *(Federal University of Minas Gerais - Brazil)*
Zaihan Yang *(Lehigh University - USA)*
Zheng Ye *(York University - Canada)*
Jeonghee Yi *(Microsoft - USA)*
Ismet Zeki Yalniz *(University of Massachusetts Amherst - USA)*
Jianwen Zhang *(Microsoft Research Asia - USA)*
Jessie Zhao *(York University - Canada)*
Arkaitz Zubiaga *(City University of New York - USA)*

Poster Committee

Falk Scholer *(RMIT University - Australia) – Chair*
Mark D. Smucker *(University of Waterloo - Canada) – Chair*
Andrew Turpin *(University of Melbourne - Australia) – Chair*

Eytan Adar *(University of Michigan - USA)*
Mikhail Ageev *(Moscow State University - Russian Federation)*
John Akinyemi *(University of Waterloo - Canada)*
Elif Aktolga *(University of Massachusetts Amherst - USA)*
Omar Alonso *(Microsoft - USA)*
Robin Aly *(University of Twente - Netherlands)*
Peter Anick *(Brandeis University - USA)*
Jaime Arguello *(University of North Carolina at Chapel Hill - USA)*
Azin Ashkan *(University of Waterloo - Canada)*
Javed Aslam *(Northeastern University - USA)*
Hany Azzam *(Queen Mary, University of London-UK)*
Niranjan Balasubramanian *(University of Massachusetts Amherst - USA)*
Krisztian Balog *(Norwegian University Science and Technology - Norway)*
Alberto Barrón - Cedeño *(Universidad Politécnica de Valencia - Spain)*
Paul N. Bennett *(Microsoft Research - USA)*
Gerald Benoit *(Simmons College - USA)*
Roi Blanco *(Yahoo! Research - Spain)*
Eric Brown *(IBM Research - USA)*
Rui Cai *(Microsoft Research, Asia - China)*
Silvia Calegari *(University of Milan - Bicocca - Italy)*
Fazli Can *(Bilkent University - Turkey)*
Robert Capra *(University of North Carolina at Chapel Hill - USA)*
Annalina Caputo *(University of Bari - Italy)*
Mark Carman *(Monash University - Australia)*
Ben Carterette *(University of Delaware - USA)*
Marc - Allen Cartright *(University of Massachusetts Amherst - USA)*
Carlos Castillo *(Qatar Computing Research Institute - Qatar)*
Yi Chang *(Yahoo labs - USA)*
Francine Chen *(FX Palo Alto Laboratory - USA)*
Yi Chen *(Dublin City University - Ireland)*
Yun Chi *(NEC Laboratories America - USA)*
Paul Clough *(University of Sheffield - UK)*
Michael Cole *(Rutgers University - USA)*
Kevyn Collins - Thompson *(Microsoft Research - USA)*
Gao Cong *(Nanyang Technological University - Singapore)*
Eli Cortez *(Federal University of Amazonas - Brazil)*

Bin Cui *(Peking University - China)*
Sally Jo Cunningham *(Wakaito University - New Zealand)*
Altigran da Silva *(UFAM - Brazil)*
Na Dai *(Lehigh University - USA)*
Lorand Dali *(Jožef Stefan Institute - Slovenia)*
Jeff Dalton *(University of Massachusetts Amherst - USA)*
Kareem Darwish *(Microsoft Research - Egypt)*
Emanuele Di Buccio *(University of Padova - Italy)*
Giorgio Maria Di Nunzio *(University of Padova - Italy)*
Debora Donato *(Yahoo! Labs - USA)*
Georges Dupret *(Yahoo! Labs - USA)*
Miles Efron *(University of Illinois - USA)*
Koji Eguchi *(Kobe University - Japan)*
David Eichmann *(U. Iowa - USA)*
David Elsweiler *(Friedrich - Alexander Universitaet Erlangen - Germany)*
Jianping Fan *(UNC - Charlotte - USA)*
Fabio Faria *(University of Campinas - Brazil)*
Shaolei Feng *(Siemens Corporate Research Labs - USA)*
Nicola Ferro *(University of Padova - Italy)*
Ingo Frommholz *(University of Bedfordshire-UK)*
Xin Fu *(Microsoft - USA)*
Norbert Fuhr *(Universität Duisburg - Essen - Germany)*
Atsushi Fujii *(Tokyo Institute of Technology - Japan)*
Bin Gao *(Microsoft Research Asia - China)*
Wei Gao *(Qatar Computing Research Institute - Qatar)*
Susan Gauch *(University of Arkansas - USA)*
Shima Gerani *(University of Lugano - Switzerland)*
Shlomo Geva *(Queensland University of Technology - Australia)*
Fredric Gey *(University of California, Berkeley - USA)*
Brigitte Grau *(LIMSI - CNRS & ENSIIE - France)*
Mark A. Greenwood *(University of Sheffield - UK)*
Daniel Gruhl *(IBM Research - USA)*
Cao Guihong *(Microsoft - USA)*
Qi Guo *(Emory University - USA)*
Karl Gyllstrom *(K.U. Leuven - USA)*
Stephanie Haas *(University of North Carolina at Chapel Hill - USA)*
Preben Hansen *(Swedish Institute of Computer Science - Sweden)*
Donna Harman *(NIST - USA)*
Morgan Harvey *(University of Erlangen - Nuremberg - Germany)*
Claudia Hauff *(TU Delft - The Netherlands)*
Daqing He *(University of Pittsburgh - USA)*
Jiyin He *(Centrum Wiskunde & Informatica - The Netherlands)*
Ben He *(Graduate Univ. of Chinese Academy of Sciences - China)*
Andreas Henrich *(University of Bamberg - Germany)*
Djoerd Hiemstra *(University of Twente - Netherlands)*
Katja Hofmann *(University of Amsterdam - Netherlands)*
Frank Hopfgartner *(International Computer Science Institute - USA)*
Vivian (Qinmin) Hu *(York University, Canada - Canada)*
Jimmy Huang *(York University, Toronto, Ontario, Canada - Canada)*
Alvaro Francisco Huertas - Rosero *(University of Glasgow-UK)*
Yoshiyuki Inagaki *(Yahoo! Labs - USA)*
Giacomo Inches *(University of Lugano, USI - Switzerland)*
Diana Inkpen *(SITE, University of Ottawa - Canada)*
Jagadeesh Jagarlamudi *(University of Maryland - USA)*
Adam Jatowt *(Kyoto University - Japan)*
Jiwoon Jeon *(Google - USA)*
Jing Jiang *(Singapore Management University - Singapore)*
Daxin Jiang *(Microsoft Research Asia - China)*
Rong Jin *(Michigan State University - USA)*
Hideo Joho *(University of Tsukuba - Japan)*
Leszek Kaliciak *(Robert Gordon University - UK)*
Jaap Kamps *(University of Amsterdam - The Netherlands)*
Noriko Kando *(National Institute of Informatics - Japan)*
Nattiya Kanhabua *(L3S Research Center - Germany)*
Evangelos Kanoulas *(Google - Switzerland)*
Sarvnaz Karimi *(CSIRO - Australia)*
Maryam Karimzadehgan *(University of Illinois at Urbana - Champaign - USA)*
Mostafa Keikha *(University of Lugano - Switzerland)*
Diane Kelly *(University of North Carolina Chapel Hill - USA)*
Jinyoung Kim *(University of Massachusetts, Amherst - USA)*
Seokhwan Kim *(Institute for Infocomm Research - Singapore)*
Jin-Dong Kim *(Database Center for Life Science - Japan)*
Donald Kraft *(Department of Computer Science - USA)*
Anagha Kulkarni *(Carnegie Mellon University - USA)*
Giridhar Kumaran *(Microsoft Corporation - USA)*
Oren Kurland *(Technion - Israel)*
Dmitry Lagun *(Emory University - USA)*
Mounia Lalmas *(Yahoo! Research - Spain)*
Ni Lao *(Carnegie Mellon University - USA)*
Guy Lapalme *(Université de Montréal - Canada)*
Ray Larson *(University of California, Berkeley - USA)*
Neal Lathia *(University of Cambridge - UK)*
Matthew Lease *(University of Texas at Austin - USA)*
Gary Geunbae Lee *(POSTECH - Republic of Korea)*
Jung-Tae Lee *(Korea University - Republic of Korea)*
Teerapong Leelanupab *(University of Glasgow-UK)*
Miro Lehtonen *(University of Helsinki - Finland)*
Elizabeth Liddy *(iSchool, Syracuse University - USA)*
Xia Lin *(Drexel University - USA)*
Christina Lioma *(University of Copenhagen - Denmark)*
Ting Liu *(Harbin Institute of Technology - China)*
Nathan Liu *(HKUST - Hong Kong, SAR)*
Robert Luk *(The Hong Kong Polytechnic University - Hong Kong, SAR)*
Yuanhua Lv *(UIUC - USA)*
Hao Ma *(Microsoft Research - USA)*
Andrew MacFarlane *(City University London - UK)*
Takuya Maekawa *(Osaka University - Japan)*
Prasenjit Majumder *(DAIICT - India)*
Yi Mao *(Microsoft - USA)*
Ilya Markov *(University of Lugano - Switzerland)*
Paul McNamee *(Johns Hopkins University - USA)*
Edgar Meij *(University of Amsterdam - Netherlands)*

Donald Metzler *(USC/ISI; USA - USA)*
Einat Minkov *(University of Haifa - Israel)*
Mandar Mitra *(Indian Statistical Institute - India)*
Stefano Mizzaro *(University of Udine - Italy)*
Marie - Francine Moens *(Katholieke Universiteit Leuven - Belgium)*
Alistair Moffat *(University of Melbourne - Australia)*
Yashar Moshfeghi *(University of Glasgow - UK)*
Vanessa Murdock *(Yahoo! Research - Spain)*
Preslav Nakov *(Qatar Computing Research Institute - Qatar)*
Michael Nelson *(Old Dominion University - USA)*
Charles Nicholas *(UMBC - USA)*
Jian - Yun Nie *(DIRO - University of Montreal - Canada)*
Tae - Gil Noh *(Heidelberg University - Germany)*
Jahna Otterbacher *(Illinois Institute of Technology - USA)*
Virgil Pavlu *(Northeastern University - USA)*
Jan Pedersen *(Microsoft - USA)*
Fuchun Peng *(Microsoft - USA)*
Karen Pinel - Sauvagnat *(IRIT - France)*
Tamara Polajnar *(University of Glasgow - UK)*
Luca Pretto *(University of Padova - Italy)*
Xiaoguang Qi *(Lehigh University - USA)*
Filip Radlinski *(Microsoft-UK)*
Hema Raghavan *(IBM Research - USA)*
Edie Rasmussen *(University of British Columbia - Canada)*
John Riedl *(University of Minnesota - USA)*
Adam Roegiest *(University of Waterloo - Canada)*
Haggai Roitman *(IBM Research Lab, Haifa - Israel)*
Dan Rose *(A9.com - USA)*
Jun Sakuma *(University of Tsukuba - Japan)*
Fabrizio Sebastiani *(Consiglio Nazionale delle Ricerche - Italy)*
Kazuhiro Seki *(Kobe University - Japan)*
Jangwon Seo *(Google Inc. - USA)*
Chirag Shah *(Rutgers University - USA)*
James G. Shanahan *(Church and Duncan Group Inc. - USA)*
Milad Shokouhi *(Microsoft - UK)*
Gianmaria Silvello *(University of Padova - Italy)*
Fabrizio Silvestri *(Information Science and Technology Institute - Italy)*
Khe Chai Sim *(National University of Singapore - Singapore)*
David Smith *(University of Massachusetts Amherst - USA)*
Padmini Srinivasan *(The University of Iowa - USA)*
Vassilios Stathopoulos *(University College London-UK)*
Juliane Stiller *(Humboldt Universitaet zu Berlin - Germany)*
Aixin Sun *(Nanyang Technological University - Singapore)*
Mingxuan Sun *(Georgia Institute of Technology - USA)*
Shanu Sushmita *(University of Glasgow - UK)*
S.M.M. Tahaghoghi *(Microsoft - USA)*
John Tait *(johntait.net Ltd. - UK)*
Bin Tan *(Amazon - USA)*
Carla Teixeira Lopes *(University of Porto - Portugal)*
Simone Teufel *(University of Cambridge - UK)*
Ulrich Thiel *(Fraunhofer - Germany)*
James Thom *(RMIT - Australia)*
Paul Thomas *(CSIRO - Australia)*
Paul Thompson *(Dartmouth College - USA)*
Qi Tian *(University of Texas at San Antonio - USA)*
Anastasios Tombros *(Queen Mary, University of London-UK)*
Ricardo Torres *(University of Campinas (UNICAMP) - Brazil)*
Andrew Trotman *(University of Otago - New Zealand)*
Sarah Tyler *(University of California, Santa Cruz - USA)*
Sumithra Velupillai *(Stockholm University - Sweden)*
Vitaliy Vitsentiy *(Ternopil National Economic University - Ukraine)*
Stephen Wan *(CSIRO - Australia)*
Xiaojun Wan *(Peking University - China)*
Taifeng Wang *(Microsoft Research Asia - China)*
Changhu Wang *(Microsoft Research Asia - China)*
Lidan Wang *(University of Maryland, College Park - USA)*
Xin - Jing Wang *(Microsoft Research Asia - China)*
Mengqiu Wang *(Stanford University - USA)*
Wouter Weerkamp *(University of Amsterdam - Netherlands)*
John Whissell *(University of Waterloo - Canada)*
Tak - Lam Wong *(The Hong Kong Institute of Education - Hong Kong, SAR)*
Jun Xu *(Microsoft Research Asia - China)*
Xiaobing Xue *(University of Massachusetts, Amherst - USA)*
Grace Hui Yang *(Georgetown University - USA)*
Jiang - Ming Yang *(Microsoft - China)*
Emine Yilmaz *(Microsoft Research Cambridge - UK)*
Minoru Yoshida *(University of Tokyo - Japan)*
Xiaojun Yuan *(University at Albany, SUNY - USA)*
Dell Zhang *(Birkbeck, University of London - UK)*
Zhongfei Zhang *(State University of New York at Binghamton - USA)*
Min Zhang *(Tsinghua University - China)*
Peng Zhang *(Robert Gordon University, Aberdeen - UK)*
Lanbo Zhang *(University of California, Santa Cruz - USA)*
Dong Zhou *(Trinity College Dublin - Ireland)*
Guido Zuccon *(CSIRO - Australia)*

Additional Poster Reviewers

Marco Bressan *(University of Padova - Italy)*
Peter Golbus *(Northeastern University - USA)*
Xiang - Fei Jia *(University of Otago - New Zealand)*
Anne - Laure Ligozat *(LIMSI - CNRS & ENSIIE - France)*
Xian - Ming Liu *(Harbin Institute of Technology - China)*
David Milne *(CSIRO - Australia)*
Xinmei Tian *(University of Science and Technology of China - China)*
Wengang Zhou *(University of Texas at San Antonio - USA)*

Demonstrations Committee

Falk Scholer *(RMIT University - Australia) – Chair*
Mark D. Smucker *(University of Waterloo - Canada) – Chair*
Andrew Turpin *(University of Melbourne - Australia) – Chair*

Mikhail Ageev *(Moscow State University - Russian Federation)*
John Akinyemi *(University of Waterloo - Canada)*
Omar Alonso *(Microsoft - USA)*
Hany Azzam *(Queen Mary, University of London - UK)*
Alberto Barrón-Cedeño *(Universidad Politécnica de Valencia - Spain)*
Steve Beitzel *(Applied Communication Sciences - USA)*
Kevyn Collins-Thompson *(Microsoft Research - USA)*
Silviu Cucerzan *(Microsoft Research - USA)*
Sally Jo Cunningham *(Wakaito University - New Zealand)*
Giorgio Maria Di Nunzio *(University of Padova - Italy)*
Debora Donato *(Yahoo! Labs - USA)*
Georges Dupret *(Yahoo! Labs - USA)*
Jianping Fan *(UNC Charlotte - USA)*
Jiyin He *(Centrum Wiskunde & Informatica - Netherlands)*
Ben He *(Graduate University of Chinese Academy of Sciences - China)*
Vivian (Qinmin) Hu *(York University - Canada)*
Jiwoon Jeon *(Google - USA)*
Joemon Jose *(University of Glasgow - UK)*
Leszek Kaliciak *(Robert Gordon University - UK)*
Nattiya Kanhabua *(L3S Research Center - Germany)*
Jinyoung Kim *(University of Massachusetts, Amherst - USA)*
Giridhar Kumaran *(Microsoft - USA)*
Jochen Leidner *(Thomson Reuters - Switzerland)*
Christina Lioma (*University of Copenhagen - Denmark)*
Ting Liu *(Harbin Institute of Technology - China)*
Vibhu Mittal *(Root-1 - USA)*
Filip Radlinski *(Microsoft - UK)*
Edie Rasmussen *(University of British Columbia - Canada)*
Chirag Shah *(Rutgers University - USA)*
Rao Shen *(Yahoo! - USA)*
Milad Shokouhi *(Microsoft - UK)*
Juliane Stiller *(Humboldt Universitaet zu Berlin - Germany)*
Bin Tan *(Amazon - USA)*
Carla Teixeira Lopes *(University of Porto - Portugal)*
Ulrich Thiel *(Fraunhofer Gesellschaft - Germany)*
Anastasios Tombros *(Queen Mary, University of London- UK)*
Ricardo Torres *(University of Campinas - Brazil)*
John Whissell *(University of Waterloo - Canada)*
Jiang-Ming Yang *(Microsoft - China)*
Minoru Yoshida *(University of Tokyo - Japan)*
Dell Zhang *(Birkbeck, University of London - UK)*

Tutorial Committee

Henning Müller *(HES-SO, Sierre - Switzerland) - Chair*

Paul Clough *(University of Sheffield – United Kingdom)*
Allan Hanbury *(Technical University of Vienna - Austria)*
Preben Hansen *(SICS, Stockholm - Sweden)*
Jaap Kamps *(University of Amsterdam – The Netherlands)*
Liadh Kelly *(Dublin City University – Ireland)*
Birger Larsen *(Royal School of Library Science Copenhagen – Denmark)*
Jochen Leidner *(Linguit Ltd. - USA)*

Workshop Committee

Eugene Agichtein *(Emory University - USA) – Chair*
Vanessa Murdock *(Yahoo! Research - Spain) – Chair*

Best Paper Awards Committee

ChengXiang Zhai *(University of Illinois at Urbana-Champaign - USA) – Chair*

Tat-Seng Chua *(National University of Singapore - Singapore)*
Evgeniy Gabrilovich *(Google - USA)*
Shlomo Geva *(Queensland University of Technology - Australia)*
Paul B. Kantor *(Rutgers University - USA)*
Iadh Ounis *(University of Glasgow – United Kingdom)*
Luo Si *(Purdue University - USA)*
Ellen Voorhees *(NIST - USA)*
Arjen P. de Vries *(Centrum Wiskunde & Informatica - The Netherlands)*

Doctoral Consortium Committee

Maarten de Rijke (*University of Amsterdam - Netherlands*) - Chair
Mounia Lalmas (*Yahoo! Research - Spain*) - Chair

Peter Bruza (*Queensland University of Technology, Australia)*
Kevyn Collins-Thompson *(Microsoft Research - USA)*
David Hawking *(Funnelback and Australian National University - Australia)*
Gareth Jones *(Dublin City University - Ireland)*
Joemon Jose *(University of Glasgow – United Kingdom)*
Noriko Kando *(National Institute of Informatics - Japan)*
Oren Kurland *(Technion - Israel)*
Wai Lam *(The Chinese University of Hong Kong - Hong Kong, SAR)*
Prasenjit Majumder *(DAIICT - India)*
Isabelle Moulinier *(Thomson Reuters - USA)*
Jian-Yun Nie *(Université de Montréal - Canada)*
Tetsuya Sakai *(Microsoft Research Asia - China)*
Luo Si *(Purdue University - USA)*
Andrew Trotman *(University of Otago - New Zealand)*
Ellen Voorhees *(NIST - USA)*
Arjen P. de Vries *(Centrum Wiskunde & Informatica - The Netherlands)*
Cong Yu *(Google Research - USA)*
Yi Zhang *(University of California Santa Cruz - USA)*

Mentoring Committee

Douglas W. Oard *(University of Maryland - USA)* - Chair

Avi Arampatzis *(Democritus University of Thrace - Greece)*
Jimmy Lin *(University of Maryland - USA)*
Charles K. Nicholas *(University of Maryland, Baltimore County - USA)*

SIGIR 2012 Sponsors & Supporters

Sponsors

SIGIR
Special Interest Group
on Information Retrieval

Association for
Computing Machinery
Advancing Computing as a Science & Profession

Corporate Supporters

Gold Supporters

Microsoft® Research

Baidu 百度

Google™

Silver Supporter

YAHOO! LABS

Bronze Supporters

ebaY Research Labs

IBM Research

ORACLE®

Friends

Other Supporters

Automatic Suggestion of Query-Rewrite Rules for Enterprise Search

Zhuowei Bao
University of Pennsylvania
Philadelphia, PA 19104, USA
zhuowei@cis.upenn.edu

Benny Kimelfeld
IBM Research – Almaden
San Jose, CA 95120, USA
kimelfeld@us.ibm.com

Yunyao Li
IBM Research – Almaden
San Jose, CA 95120, USA
yunyaoli@us.ibm.com

ABSTRACT

Enterprise search is challenging for several reasons, notably the dynamic terminology and jargon that are specific to the enterprise domain. This challenge is partly addressed by having domain experts maintaining the enterprise search engine and adapting it to the domain specifics. Those administrators commonly address user complaints about relevant documents missing from the top matches. For that, it has been proposed to allow administrators to influence search results by crafting query-rewrite rules, each specifying how queries of a certain pattern should be modified or augmented with additional queries. Upon a complaint, the administrator seeks a semantically coherent rule that is capable of pushing the desired documents up to the top matches. However, the creation and maintenance of rewrite rules is highly tedious and time consuming. Our goal in this work is to ease the burden on search administrators by automatically suggesting rewrite rules. This automation entails several challenges. One major challenge is to select, among many options, rules that are "natural" from a semantic perspective (e.g., corresponding to closely related and syntactically complete concepts). Towards that, we study a machine-learning classification approach. The second challenge is to accommodate the cross-query effect of rules—a rule introduced in the context of one query can eliminate the desired results for other queries and the desired effects of other rules. We present a formalization of this challenge as a generic computational problem. As we show that this problem is highly intractable in terms of complexity theory, we present heuristic approaches and optimization thereof. In an experimental study within IBM intranet search, those heuristics achieve near-optimal quality and well scale to large data sets.

Categories and Subject Descriptors: H.3.3 [Information Storage and Retrieval]: Query formulation

General Terms: Algorithms, Performance, Theory

Keywords: Query reformulation, query-rewrite rules, enterprise search

SIGIR'12, August 12–16, 2012, Portland, Oregon, USA.

1. INTRODUCTION

While search engines on the Web are highly successful in content retrieval, enterprise search remains an important living challenge [2, 11, 12]. The retrieval community identified various sources of difficulty [5, 7, 10, 11], including the sparseness of link structure and anchor text, low economic incentive of content providers to promote easy search access, and a strong presence of dynamic, domain-specific terminology and jargon. Another practical difficulty lies in the fact that enterprise search deployments are typically managed by administrators who are domain experts but not search experts. Hence, although these administrators well understand the specific content and search needs of the domain, translating that knowledge into tuning the underlying retrieval model is a nontrivial (and sometimes impossible) task.

To address the above challenges, research and industrial groups [8, 9, 21] advocated the design of search architectures that are *(1)* easily comprehensible (featuring fairly transparent ranking mechanisms), and *(2)* easily customizable through intuitive *runtime rules* to program domain knowledge. One important type of runtime rules is that of *query-rewrite rules* (or *rewrite rules* for short) that, in essence, introduce human-controlled *query reformulation* [18, 19] at runtime. By augmenting or modifying the posed search query, rewrite rules enable administrators to easily satisfy a wide range of maintenance needs such as: adaptation of terminology (e.g., produce a query where green card is replaced with permanent residency), query specialization (e.g., h5n1 instead of seasonal flu, or issi,[1] the company's software installation tool, instead of download), query generalization (e.g., intranet account management instead of intranet password change), noise removal (e.g., elimination of web page from a query like james allan web page), and so on.

This work is motivated by a deployment of the above architecture in the IBM internal search. There, the type of tasks that dominate the effort of administrators is that of pushing up relevant documents for specific search queries. Such a task is typically triggered by an employee complaint mentioning a specific query and a relevant document (URL) missing from the top results (e.g., the first page). For example, such a complaint can be that http://issi.ibm.com/lnotes[2] is missing from the top results for lotus notes download. In turn, the administrator can phrase a rewrite rule to accommodate the potential mismatch between the query and the document. Those rewrite rules are in the spirit of (actually, a generalization of) the "query template" rules [1, 20]. In

[1]IBM Standard Software Installer.

[2]We replaced each example URL with a simplified variant.

particular, a rule is usually applicable to multiple queries (rather than to just one), and it usually results in *augmentation* (rather than *replacement*) of the query by the newly generated query. For example, the administrator can introduce the rule download → issi that, in effect, incorporates the results for lotus notes issi into those for lotus notes download whenever the latter query is posed. In Section 2 we describe our engine architecture and rules in more detail.

Manually formulating rewrite rules to handle complaints is an extremely tedious and time consuming process. First, the administrator needs to inspect the specified document in order to come up with relevant rules. For each relevant rule, a rough estimation is made on its effect on other queries (and for that, query logs may be consulted). Next, the administrator tries out her rule of choice (in a sandbox environment). If the desired effect (pushing up the desired match) is not realized, this process is repeated with alternative rules, sometimes until the conclusion that the problem lies in the ranking algorithm and/or the backend analytics. In this work, we seek to aid administrators of enterprise search by automatically producing rewrite-rule suggestions that are already validated as problem solvers. Towards this goal, we need to overcome two major challenges, which are the subject of this paper. These challenges are generic to essentially every search system that features administration by rewrite rules, and we confront these challenges in a level of abstraction that departs from our specific testbed.

Challenge 1: Generating Intuitive Rules. A straightforward approach towards suggesting rewrite rules is to generate candidates from the desired document (or specific parts thereof), and filter out the candidates that fail to achieve the desired effect. However, the number of possible rules obtained in this way can be overwhelmingly large. For example, in our experimentation over real data (within IBM intranet search), our automation often reaches around 100 suggestions, and in some cases around 1000. More importantly, the vast majority of the suggested rules do not make sense to the administrator; that is, they are not rules of the kind she would devise or perceive as intuitive. For illustration, Figure 1 shows some of the suggestions we obtained. In the top part of the table in the figure, relating to seasonal flu, the top two are reasonable but the other hardly make sense. Note, however, that determining what "reasonable" or "sense making" means may require domain knowledge. As an example, IBM uses SCIP for consulting on organizational reconstruction; thus, the top rewrites for change management in the bottom part of Figure 1 make sense. Yet one can hardly accept the other rules in that part.

We refer to a rule that makes sense as *natural*. Formulating natural rules is necessary, as administrators should be confident in the semantic justification of each rule. Put differently, comprehensiveness, which is at the heart of the architecture philosophy, is violated if rules are inconsistent with human judgment. (This problem does not arise in online query reformulation/expansion [4] that affect only the internals of the search process.) Thus, crucial to realizing automatic rule suggestion is a component that classifies rules into natural and unnatural ones. In Section 3 we present a machine-learning approach to realizing such a component.

A related problem is that of recommending query alternatives to end users [3,13,22]. However, a query alternative applies just to the user-posed query, hence is different from a rewrite rule. Furthermore, the techniques there are heavily based on query logs and/or anchor text, which may be sparse in the enterprise Intranet. The same holds true for the work of Kraft and Zien [14], aiming to find reformulations that are "closely related" to the original query. Moreover, in these works a recommendation (or reformulation) has no effect beyond the specific engine-user interaction at hand; it is not the case here, as we discuss in the next challenge.

s	t
seasonal flu	avian flu
seasonal flu	h5n1
seasonal flu	flu employee
seasonal flu	and IBM h5n1
seasonal	avian
seasonal	h5n1
seasonal	flu
seasonal	you and IBM
...	...
change management	scip
change management	strategy & change internal practice
change management	welcome to strategy
change management	welcome strategy
change management	strategy change & internal
change management	to strategy change internal practice
management	internal
management	index pages
management	internal practice scip
...	...

Figure 1: Automatically generated rules $s \rightarrow t$

Challenge 2: Cross-Query Effect. As a rewrite rule can affect multiple queries, its inclusion may actually reduce the overall search quality. Further, a rule can cancel the positive effects achieved by previous rules. To illustrate, in the example of Figure 4 (which we discuss in detail throughout Section 4) the rule spreadsheets → symphony rewrites spreadsheets download into symphony download, resulting in the document d_2 being a top match. Following a complaint on the query lotus notes download, we introduce the rule r_1: download → issi. However, r_1 also affects our previous spreadsheets download by pushing the desired d_2 below d_1.

To address the above problem, the search administrator maintains a representative benchmark of queries and desired matches (possibly weighted by popularity) that includes those indicated in past complaints. To estimate the effect of a candidate rule, search quality is evaluated (using a quality estimator of choice, e.g., DCG) by running the engine against the benchmark. If a negative effect is detected, the administrator can avoid the rule, consider a new rule, or just accept the loss in quality. But here, automation can contribute significantly in terms of both effort and quality. We can allow the system to automatically suggest the selection of a subset of the rules to optimize quality (w.r.t. the underlying estimator). Moreover, the administrator can then choose *multiple* rules (instead of just one) to address a specific complaint, and thereby enrich the search space for the system. In the above example, for instance, if the system had the rule notes download → notes issi at its disposal, it could suggest to use it instead of r_1, and thus maintain the top results for both spreadsheets download and lotus notes download. In Section 4, we formalize this idea as a combinatorial optimization problem. Unfortunately, this problem turns out to be computationally hard (NP-hard), and even hard to approximate within any nontrivial ratio. Nevertheless, we propose greedy heuristics and optimizations thereof.

A related optimization problem has been recently studied by Ozertem et al. [19], where one is given a collection of

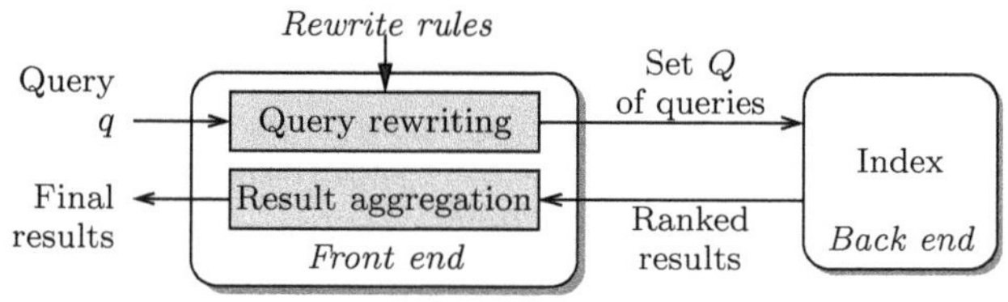

Figure 2: Search-engine architecture

query reformulations (each applying to one query) to select from, and the goal is to maximize the probability of a click in a user model built from the query log.

Organization. The rest of the paper is organized as follows. In Section 2 we briefly describe our search architecture. We study the above two challenges in Sections 3 and 4, respectively. In Section 5 we present an experimental study within IBM intranet search, and we conclude in Section 6.

2. SEARCH-ARCHITECTURE OVERVIEW

In this section, we outline the architecture of the engine deployed in IBM intranet search [21], to the extent needed as background for this work.[3] Figure 2 depicts a simplified description of the conceptual runtime flow. The front-end takes the input search query q and, by applying rewrite rules, produces a set Q of queries. In turn, the queries in Q are evaluated against the index, resulting in a list of results for each query. The results are then aggregated together to produce the final ranked list.

Similarly to existing search methodologies [6,15,23], this engine leverages structural information from Web pages (such as links, anchor text, headers and titles) in retrieval. The basic idea is to produce high-quality *fields* associated with each document, and at runtime use these fields for ranking.

Rewrite rules program the *query rewriting* component of Figure 2 to affect the search as needed. The rewrite rules in our engine are in the spirit of the *query-template* rules [1, 9, 20]. Rather than giving an elaborate specification of the rule language, we give examples (in a simplified language). The following rule fires when the query is of the form x info, where x is belongs to a dictionary of products; it introduces a new query with the term info removed.

$$EQUALS\text{: } x[\text{in PRODUCT}] \text{ info} \rightarrow x$$

The next rule, involving a regular expression, fires when the query *contains* the word lotus followed by either presentations or spreadsheets; it introduces a new query with the two words replaced by lotus symphony.

$$CONTAINS\text{: } \text{lotus } x(\text{presentations}|\text{spreadsheets}) \rightarrow \text{lotus symphony}$$

The next rule fires when the query contains msn search, and introduces a new query with msn search replaced by bing.

$$CONTAINS\text{: } \text{msn search} \rightarrow_{+} \text{bing}$$

The plus sign in $\rightarrow_{+}$ assigns *preference* to the new query (containing bing) over the original query (containing msn search). In effect, results for the new query are rewarded compared to those for the original query. We do not discuss here the details of this reward, as they are of low importance to this work.

To simplify our study, this work is restricted to rewrite rules of the form *CONTAINS:* $s \rightarrow_{+} t$, which we denote simply as $s \rightarrow t$, where s and t are terms. We focus on this particular type of rules since, besides their simplicity, we found that they are the most commonly used in our enterprise. Moreover, with this restriction the problems we consider are already challenging. While some of our contributions can be easily extended to more general rules, others require nontrivial future effort.

[3]More details on this search engine can be found in the IBM page of *Infrastructure for Intelligent Information Systems* http://www.almaden.ibm.com/cs/disciplines/iiis.

3. RECOGNIZING NATURAL RULES

In this section, we consider the first challenge discussed in the introduction, where we explained the intuition underlying the notion of *natural* rewrite rules and their importance to the realization of automatic rule suggestion in enterprise search. Our approach is to first generate a (possibly large) set of candidate rules by pure syntactic means, and then to classify them through (supervised) machine learning.

Candidate generation. The use case we consider involves a query q and a desired match (document) d that is missing from the top results. Our generation of candidate rules $s \rightarrow t$ is fairly straightforward: we produce a set S of left-hand-side candidates, a set T of right-hand-side candidates, and output the Cartesian product $S \times T$. The set S consists of all the n-grams (subsequences of n tokens) of q, where n is bounded by a constant (5 in our implementation). In principle, we could similarly choose T as the set of all n-grams of d (which could result in a huge number of candidates, even if n is bounded). But in our implementation, T consists of the n-grams just from the high-quality fields of d (produced during back-end analysis). Recall that those fields were discussed in Section 2. As an example, suppose that q is the query "change management info" and one of the considered fields is "welcome to scip strategy & change internal practice." The following are among the candidate rules.

- management → scip
- change → strategy & change internal
- change management → scip strategy

Even with the restriction to high-quality fields, the above step may generate a large number of candidate rules, most of which are unnatural (hence, useless to the administrator), as illustrated in Figure 1. We address this problem by taking a machine-learning approach: we identify a set of features and learn classification models from manually labeled data to classify rules into natural and unnatural ones.

Features. Table 1 lists the feature set we use for classifying rules. These features fall into three categories: syntactic features, features based on query-log statistics, and features based on corpus statistics. Next, we briefly discuss the features in each category. We denote the examined rule as $s \rightarrow t$, where s and t are strings of words.

The syntactic features can be indicative of the syntactic coherence of a rule. For example, using the Boolean features $beginSW(r)$ and $endSW(r)$ follows our observation that when s or t begins or ends with stop words, the rule is rarely deemed natural. We consider two types of stop words: those from conventional (English) dictionaries and those from domain-specific dictionaries (including words like "welcome," "index" and "homepage").

Table 1: Features for natural-rule recognition; the considered rule is $s \to t$, and u refers to either s or t

Syntactic	
$beginSW(r)$	Whether u begins with a stop word
$endSW(r)$	Whether u ends with a stop word
$\|r\|$	Number of tokens in u
Query-Log Statistics	
$\log refFreq(s,t)$	Log. of the s-to-t reformulation frequency
Corpus Statistics	
$\log freq(u)$	Log. of the frequency of u
$\log freq(s \wedge t)$	Log. of concurrence frequency of s and t
$\log HQfreq(u)$	Log. of the frequency of u in titles

The category of query-log statistics has the single feature $\log refFreq(s,t)$, representing common wisdom on query reformulation. In our case, we analyzed the query log of (four months of) intranet search at IBM. For a pair q_1 and q_2 of queries, $refFreq(q_1, q_2)$ is the number of sessions that begin with q_1 and contain q_2 (posed later than q_1 in the session).

Under the category of corpus statistics we have numerical statistics on s and t drawn from our engine index. The number $freq(u)$ counts the documents containing u as an n-gram (where u is s in one feature, and t in another). Similarly, $freq(s \wedge t)$ counts the documents containing both s and t as n-grams. We use $\log freq(u)$ and $\log freq(s \wedge t)$ to capture the popularity of s and t as well as correlation thereof. Finally, $HQfreq(u)$ is the frequency of u in our high-quality fields, which roughly reflects the popularity of u in titles.

Classification models. We implemented two classification models over our vector $\vec{f}$ of features. The first model is simply a linear classifier, which we trained on manually labeled data via SVM. The second model, which we found to provide a significant improvement over the first, generalizes the first by incorporating a *Decision Tree* (DT for short). More specifically, the second model is a restricted version of a DT with linear-combination splits [16, 17], and we call it *rDTLC* for short. Given the vector $\vec{f}$ of features, a DT with linear splits has a condition $\sum a_i f_i \leq \tau$ in each node (where the a_i and τ are to be learned in training). Our rDTLC restricts this family by *(1)* bounding the depth (by 3 in our implementation), *and (2)* having univariate splits (i.e., one-variable comparisons to thresholds) in all but the bottommost levels. Figure 3 illustrates our rDTLC. Note that here we essentially follow Kraft and Zien [14], who studied a problem of a similar flavor, that used a linear classifier and a standard decision tree (rather than rDTLC).

Using an algorithm for learning a linear classifier (e.g., SVM), learning an rDTLC can be done straightforwardly by selecting thresholds from the feature values in the training data, trying out every combination of the upper-level thresholds τ_i, and taking the combination that minimizes the classification error. For efficiency sake, we implemented a fix-and-optimize heuristic where we optimized one threshold at a time while fixing the others.

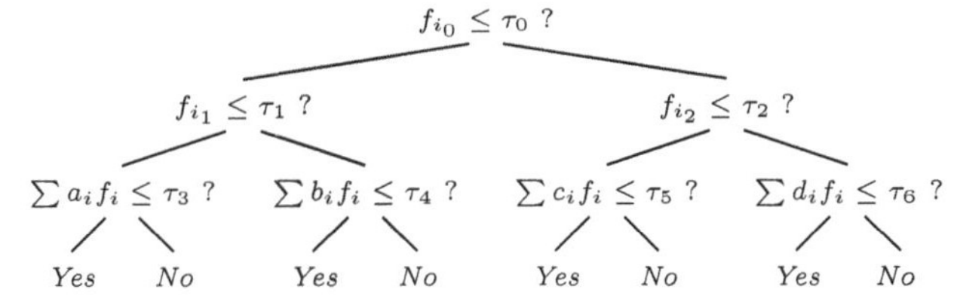

Figure 3: An rDTLC

4. OPTIMIZING MULTI-RULE SELECTION

We now consider the second challenge discussed in the introduction: selecting a set of rewrite rules from a large set of previously defined rules, so as to maximize the overall quality of search results. We formalize this task as a combinatorial optimization problem, discuss its (intractable) complexity, and propose heuristic solutions.

4.1 Administration Settings

A *rule-administration setting* (or just *administration setting* for short) is essentially an abstraction of the search-engine's interplay between queries, rewrite rules, and documents. It consists of a set R of rewrite rules and a graph G that we call the *rule-administration graph* (or just *administration graph* for short). A rule in R transforms an input *user query* q into a *rewritten query* q'. For brevity and clear distinction between the two types of queries, we refer to q (the user query) simply as a *query*, and to q' (the rewritten query) as an *r-query*. A query and an r-query are simply finite sequences over an infinite alphabet of tokens (words), and a rule $s \to t$ in R is defined similarly to the previous sections (i.e., it replaces s, a subsequence of tokens in q, with a sequence t). The administration graph is a tripartite graph describing the relationships between queries, r-queries and documents. Before we give the precise definitions, we introduce our running example for this section.

EXAMPLE 4.1. Figure 4 shows an administrator setting (R, G). The set R is depicted in the top of the figure and the graph G is depicted in the bottom. □

Formally, an administration graph is a directed, edge-weighted graph $G = (V, E, w)$, where:

- V is the union of three disjoint sets of nodes: V_{q} is a set of queries, V_{r} is a set of r-queries, and V_{d} is a set of documents.
- E is the union of three disjoint sets of edges: $E_{\mathrm{qr}} \subseteq V_{\mathrm{q}} \times V_{\mathrm{r}}$ is a set of *reformulations*, $E_{\mathrm{qd}} \subseteq V_{\mathrm{q}} \times V_{\mathrm{d}}$ is a set of *query matchings*, and $E_{\mathrm{rd}} \subseteq V_{\mathrm{r}} \times V_{\mathrm{d}}$ is a set of *r-query matchings*.
- $w : E \to \mathbb{R}_{+}$ assigns a positive score to each matching in $E_{\mathrm{qd}} \cup E_{\mathrm{rd}}$, and is zero on all the edges of E_{qr}.

EXAMPLE 4.2. Consider again our running example. Each side of the tripartite graph G is surrounded by a dashed rectangle. Let $q \in V_{\mathrm{q}}$ be the query lotus notes download. The outgoing edges of q include the (zero-weight) reformulation to the r-query q' = lotus notes issi in V_{r}, and the query matching to the document $d_1 \in V_{\mathrm{d}}$ (which, for presentation sake, is associated with the URL http://issi.ibm.com/lnotes). The weight of the latter edge is 2, representing the extent to which the engine scores the matching of d_1 to q. A higher score (namely 5) is assigned to the matching of d_1 to q', as indicated by the weight of the r-query matching (q', d_1). □

In principle, the same string can be represented by two distinct nodes: a query in V_{q} and an r-query in V_{r}. So a

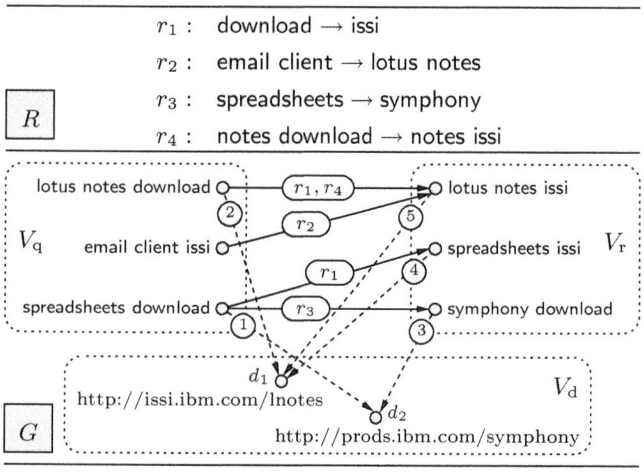

Figure 4: The administration setting (R, G) of the running example

node in $V_q \cup V_r$ should have an *identifier*, which we omit from the formal model to simplify the presentation.

Let G be an administration graph, and let $q \in V_q$ be a query. Observe that a path in G from q to d consists of either one edge (in E_{qd}) or two edges (one in E_{qr} and the other in E_{rd}). If G has a path (of length one or two) from the query q to the document d, then we denote by $\text{score}(d|q)$ the maximal weight of a path from q to d. For a query q and a natural number k, we denote by $\text{top}_k[q|G]$ the series of k documents with the highest $w(q,d)$, ordered in descending $w(q,d)$; if fewer than k documents are reachable from q via directed paths, then $\text{top}_k[q|G]$ is restricted to only the reachable documents (hence, $\text{top}_k[q|G]$ may have fewer than k documents). We implicitly assume an underlying linear order among the documents to resolve ties.

EXAMPLE 4.3. Consider again our running example (Figure 4). Let q be the query spreadsheets download. There are two paths from q to the document d_2: a direct edge, and through the r-query symphony download. Since the latter has the maximal weight, 3, among all the paths from q to d_2, we get that $\text{score}(d_2|q) = 3$. We can similarly verify that $\text{score}(d_1|q) = 4$. In particular, $\text{top}_1[q|G]$ is the series (d_1), and $\text{top}_2[q|G]$ (as well as $\text{top}_3[q|G]$) is the series (d_1, d_2). □

For a rewrite rule r and query q, let $r(q)$ denote the r-query that is obtained from q by applying r. An *administration setting* is a pair (R, G), where R is a set of rewrite rules and G is an administration graph, such that the set E_{qr} of reformulations of G is the set $\{(q, r(q)) \mid q \in V_q \wedge r \in R\}$. For a reformulation $e = (q, q') \in E_{qr}$, the set of rules $r \in R$ with $r(q) = q'$ is denoted by $R(e)$.

EXAMPLE 4.4. Consider again the administration setting (R, G) of our running example. For the edge e_1 from q_1 = lotus notes download to q'_1 = lotus notes issi we have $R(e_1) = \{r_1, r_4\}$ (where the r_i are specified in the top of the figure). Similarly, for q_2 = email client issi and the reformulation $e_2 = (q_2, q'_1)$ we have $R(e_2) = \{r_2\}$. □

4.2 Abstract Rule Optimization

Consider an administration setting (R, G). Given a subset R' of R, we denote by $G_{R'}$ the administration graph that is

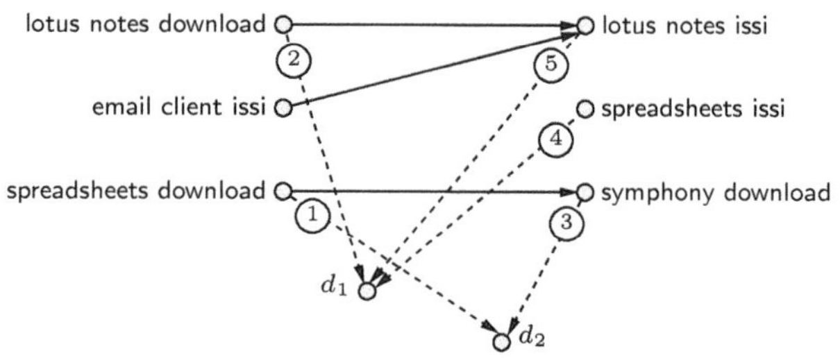

Figure 5: The graph $G_{R'}$ for $R' = \{r_2, r_3, r_4\}$

obtained from G by removing from E_{qr} every reformulation e that is produced by none of the rules in R' (i.e., $R'(e) = \emptyset$).

EXAMPLE 4.5. Consider again our running example (Figure 4), and let R' be the set $\{r_2, r_3, r_4\}$ (i.e., $R \setminus \{r_1\}$). The graph $G_{R'}$ is depicted in Figure 5. Observe that unlike G, the graph $G_{R'}$ has no edge from the query q_1 = spreadsheets download to the r-query q'_1 = spreadsheets issi, because $R'(e_1) = \emptyset$, where e_1 is the edge (q, q') of G (recall that $R(e_1) = \{r_1\}$). However, there is an edge from the query q_2 = lotus notes download to the r-query q'_2 = lotus notes issi since, although for $e_2 = (q_2, q'_2)$ the set $R'(e_2)$ lost r_1, this set still contains r_4. □

Let G be an administration graph. A *desideratum* is a function $\delta : V_q \rightarrow 2^{V_d}$ that maps each query $q \in V_q$ to a set $\delta(q) \subseteq V_d$ of *desired matches*. A *quality measure* μ determines a quality score[4] for each query q based on the series $\text{top}_k[q|G]$ and the set $\delta(q)$, for a natural number k of choice. We denote this score by $\mu(\text{top}_k[q|G], \delta(q))$. As an example, *precision at k* is the following μ:

$$\mu(\text{top}_k[q|G], \delta(q)) = \begin{cases} \frac{|\text{top}_k[q|G] \cap \delta(q)|}{|\text{top}_k[q|G]|} & \text{if } \text{top}_k[q|G] \neq \emptyset; \\ 0 & \textit{otherwise}. \end{cases} \tag{1}$$

As another example, DCG_k (without labeled relevance scores) is the following μ:

$$\mu(\text{top}_k[q|G], \delta(q)) = \sum_{i=1}^{j} \frac{2^{a_i} - 1}{\log_2(i+1)}, \tag{2}$$

where $\text{top}_k[q|G] = (d_1, \ldots, d_j)$, and each a_i is 1 if $d_i \in \delta(q)$ and 0 otherwise.

The *top-k quality* of G, denoted $\mu_k(G, \delta)$, is obtained by summing up the scores across all the queries:

$$\mu_k(G, \delta) \stackrel{\text{def}}{=} \sum_{q \in V_q} \mu(\text{top}_k[q|G], \delta(q)) \tag{3}$$

For readability, we may omit $\delta(q)$ and δ from the term $\mu(\text{top}_k[q|G], \delta(q))$ and $\mu_k(G, \delta)$, respectively, when δ is clear from the context.

EXAMPLE 4.6. Consider the following desideratum δ for our running example:

- δ(lotus notes download) = δ(email client issi) = $\{d_1\}$
- δ(spreadsheets download) = $\{d_2\}$

The reader can verify that $\text{top}_1[q|G] = (d_1)$ for all three queries q in V_q. Thus, for each of the functions μ of Equations (1) and (2) we get $\mu_1(G) = 1 + 1 + 0 = 2$.

[4]In principle, μ can represent a utility function that is not necessarily a vanilla quality measure, such as ad benefits [18].

Algorithm G-Greedy$((R, G), \delta, k)$

1: $S \leftarrow \emptyset$
2: $\Delta \leftarrow 1$
3: **while** $\Delta > 0$ **do**
4: $\quad r \leftarrow \text{argmax}_{r \in R \setminus S} \left(\mu_k(G_{S \cup \{r\}}) - \mu_k(G_S)\right)$
5: $\quad \Delta \leftarrow \mu_k(G_{S \cup \{r\}}) - \mu_k(G_S)$
6: $\quad$ **if** $\Delta > 0$ **then**
7: $\qquad S \leftarrow S \cup \{r\}$
8: **return** S

Figure 6: The globally greedy algorithm

Now, consider the graph $G_{R'}$ of Figure 5 (discussed in Example 4.5). There we have $\text{top}_1[q|G] = (d_1)$ for $q =$ lotus notes download and $q =$ email client issi, but $\text{top}_1[q|G] = (d_2)$ for $q =$ spreadsheets download. In particular, $\mu_1(G_{R'}) = 3$ for the two aforementioned functions μ. □

Abstract rule optimization is the following problem. We are given an administration setting (R, G), a desideratum δ, and a natural number k. The goal is to find a subset S of R that maximizes $\mu_k(G_S)$; that is, S is such that $\mu_k(G_S) \geq \mu_k(G_{R'})$ for every subset R' of R. Such S is an *optimal solution*. A weaker goal is to find an *α-approximate optimal solution*, where $\alpha \geq 1$ is either a number or a numeric function of the input; such a solution is a set $S \subseteq R$ that satisfies $\alpha \cdot \mu_k(G_S) \geq \mu_k(G_{R'})$ for all $R' \subseteq R$.

EXAMPLE 4.7. Suppose that μ is one of the functions of Equations (1) and (2), and consider again the administration setting (R, G) of our running example (Figure 4). Suppose that the input for abstract rule optimization contains, in addition to (R, G), the desideratum δ of Example 4.6 and $k = 1$. In Example 4.6 we discussed the graph $G_{R'}$ of Figure 5 (where $R' = \{r_2, r_3, r_4\}$). As $\mu_1(G_{R'}) = 3$ is clearly optimal, R' is an optimal solution in this case. □

To simplify the discussion on computational complexity, we assume that μ is fixed (i.e., not part of the input), and that $\mu(\text{top}_k[q|G])$ is computable in polynomial time. Next, we show that abstract rule optimization is hard to approximate. We make the following assumption on the quality measure μ: there is a positive constant c, such that for all queries q, if $\delta(q)$ consists of *exactly one* document then $\mu(\text{top}_1[q|G]) = c$ if $\text{top}_1[q|G] = \delta(q)$, and $\mu(\text{top}_1[q|G]) = 0$ otherwise (i.e., if $\text{top}_1[q|G]$ does not contain the single document in $\delta(q)$). Note that this assumption holds in standard measures that are parameterized by a restriction to the top-k results (assuming that different results are not weighted by different levels of relevancy), such as DCG_k, normalized DCG_k, and precision at k. We say that a function with this property is *reasonable at one*. The following theorem states that abstract rule optimization is extremely hard (to even approximate), no matter which quality measure μ is used, as long as μ is reasonable at one. The proof is in the appendix.

THEOREM 4.8. *Whenever μ is reasonable at one, abstract rule optimization is NP-hard to approximate by any constant factor, or even by $|V_q|^{1-\epsilon}$ for every $\epsilon > 0$.*

Algorithm L-Greedy$((R, G), \delta, k)$

1: $S \leftarrow \emptyset$
2: $T \leftarrow \{(q, d) \in V_q \times V_d \mid d \in \delta(q)\}$
3: **for all** $(q, d) \in T$ **do**
4: $\quad r \leftarrow \text{argmax}_{r \in rel_k(q,d)} \left(\mu_k(G_{S \cup \{r\}}) - \mu_k(G_S)\right)$
5: $\quad$ **if** $\mu_k(G_{S \cup \{r\}}) > \mu_k(G_S)$ **then**
6: $\qquad S \leftarrow S \cup \{r\}$
7: **return** S

Figure 7: The locally greedy algorithm

Due to the inherent hardness of our problem, in the following section we present heuristic approaches (that are explored experimentally in Section 5).

4.3 Greedy Heuristics

In this section, we devise two simple heuristic algorithms, each following a greedy approach. We call the first algorithm *globally greedy* and the second *locally greedy*. The reasons for the algorithm names will be clear from their descriptions. Later, we discuss the optimization of these algorithms.

4.3.1 The Globally Greedy Algorithm

The globally greedy algorithm, depicted in Figure 6 under the name G-Greedy, applies the following very simple approach. It initializes an empty solution $S \subseteq R$ (line 1), and iteratively adds to S the best missing rule r (found in line 5). The *best* rule r is such that the difference Δ between the quality obtained by adding r, namely $\mu_k(G_{S \cup \{r\}})$, and the current quality, namely $\mu_k(G_S)$, is maximal. The algorithm terminates (and returns S) once Δ is non-positive (hence, no improving rule can be found).

In our experiments we found that the globally greedy algorithm performs very well in terms of the quality of the returned solution S. However, this algorithm is extremely slow, due to its inherent cubic time: the loop of line 3 can take up to $|R|$ iterations, and then line 4 (finding r) entails traversing over all $r \in R \setminus S$ and computing $\mu_k(G_{S \cup \{r\}})$, which requires computing $\text{top}_k[q|G]$ (and summing up the $\mu(\text{top}_k[q|G])$) for all queries $q \in V_q$. Later, we discuss optimizations of this algorithm. But even the optimized version of this algorithm hardly scales up. Therefore, we consider the next, lower complexity algorithm.

4.3.2 The Locally Greedy Algorithm

The locally greedy algorithm, L-Greedy, is depicted in Figure 7. Similarly to the globally greedy algorithm, the locally greedy one initializes an empty solution S (line 1) and incrementally adds rules (lines 2–6). The main difference between the algorithms is that in the main loop of the locally greedy one, we search for the rule r (to add to S) in a practically tiny subset of the set R of rules (rather than in all of R).

More specifically, line 2 constructs the set T of all *tasks*, where a task is a pair (q, d) such that q is a query (in V_q) and d is a desired document for q (i.e., $q \in \delta(d)$). Then, the main loop (line 3) traverses all tasks in an arbitrary order. For a considered task (q, d), we define $rel_k(q, d)$ to be the set of all the rules r that are relevant to the task, that is: *(1)* r is on a path from q to d, or more formally, for some $q' \in V_r$

we have $e = (q, q') \in E_{\rm qr}$, $r \in R(e)$, and $(q', d) \in E_{\rm rd}$, and *(2)* taken alone r can push d to the top-k results of q, or more formally, $d \in \text{top}_k[q|G_{\{r\}}]$. In line 4, a rule r that maximizes $\mu_k(G_{S\cup\{r\}}) - \mu_k(G_S)$ is added to S, provided that this maximum value is positive.

4.3.3 *Optimization*

In both the globally greedy and the locally greedy algorithms, a significant portion of the computation takes place on computing the quality of the system on intermediate sets of rules (that is, the computations of $\mu_k(G_S)$ and $\mu_k(G_{S\cup\{r\}})$ in line 4 of Figure 6 and line 4 of Figure 7). This computation is done to obtain the difference $\mu_k(G_{S\cup\{r\}}) - \mu_k(G_S)$, where S is the current set of rules and r is a considered candidate rule. Let $\Delta(S, r)$ denote that difference. We can optimize the computation by observing that $\Delta(S, r)$ is affected by only a few of the queries, namely those on which r fires.

Formally, consider a query q, a rule r and a set $S \subseteq R$. Define $\Delta(q, S, r) = \mu(\text{top}_k[q|G_{S\cup\{r\}}]) - \mu(\text{top}_k[q|G_S])$. From (3) we get that $\Delta(S, r) = \sum_{q\in V_{\rm q}} \Delta(q, S, r)$. Denote by $V_{\rm q}(r)$ the set of queries $q \in V_{\rm q}$, such that $r \in R(e)$ for some edge $e \in E_{\rm qr}$ emanating from q. An easy observation is that $\Delta(q, S, r) = 0$ whenever $q \notin V_{\rm q}(r)$, and therefore $\Delta(S, r) = \sum_{q\in V_{\rm q}(r)} \Delta(q, S, r)$.

The optimization is as follows. During the computation we maintain each $\mu(\text{top}_k[q|G_S])$ for the current S. (So, at the beginning we compute $\mu(\text{top}_k[q|G_\emptyset])$.) When a rule r is considered, we iterate over the queries in $V_{\rm q}(r)$ and compute $\mu(\text{top}_k[q|G_{S\cup\{r\}}])$, thus obtaining $\Delta(q, S, r)$. We sum up all these $\Delta(q, S, r)$ into $\Delta(S, r)$ to be used in the next steps. Hereafter, the optimized versions of G-Greedy and L-Greedy are denoted by G-Greedy-opt and L-Greedy-opt, respectively.

4.4 Weighted Queries

In realistic scenarios, queries may carry different levels of importance, which may be expressed by means of query weights. For instance, this weight can be the frequency in which the query is posed. In the experimental study of the next section, we use as weights frequencies derived from query logs. The abstraction presented in this section can incorporate weighted queries in a straightforward manner. In particular, the abstract model assigns a weight $w(q)$ to each query $q \in V_{\rm q}$, and in the definition of $\mu_k(G)$ (see (3)), each addend $\mu(\text{top}_k[q|G])$ is multiplied by $w(q)$. The greedy algorithms automatically adjust to weights by using the weighted μ_k. An intuitive traversal order on T in the locally greedy algorithm (Figure 7) is by decreasing $w(q)$; we indeed apply this order in the experiments of the following section.

5. EXPERIMENTAL EVALUATION

In this section, we describe an empirical evaluation of our proposed solutions over the IBM intranet search engine, with datasets provided by the company's search administrators.

More specifically, our dataset was obtained from a list of 1894 suggested matches provided by IBM CIO Office, where a *suggested match* consists of a query q and a document d desired as a top match for q. Generally, the queries involved in the suggested matches are frequent, and hence are recorded for quality maintenance. Note that a query can be matched against multiple documents, and a document may be suggested for multiple queries. As mentioned in Section 3, by analyzing the high-quality fields (e.g., titles and URLs) of desired documents, we generated for each suggested match a set of query-rewrite rules, each of which, in the absence of any other rule, is capable of pushing the desired document up to the top-5 results for the given query. This produced a total of 11907 rules. Our methodology for extracting input from these suggested matches and rules will be described in the following sections. Our experiments ran on a Linux SUSE (64-bit) server with eight 4-core Intel Xeon (2.13GHz) processors and 48GB of memory. The algorithms were implemented in Java 1.6 and ran with 12GB allocated memory.

5.1 Recognizing Natural Rules

We first evaluated the classification models of Section 3 for recognizing natural rules. Among all generated rules, we randomly selected and manually labeled 1187 rules as either natural or unnatural. Such labeling is subject to human judgment; moreover, labeling often required domain-specific knowledge, and for that we needed to inspect the pages relevant to the terms involved in the rule. Using this labeled dataset, we evaluated the accuracy of the classifiers SVM and rDTLC. The results reported in this section were consistently obtained by performing a 5-folder cross validation.

We also explored the question of how the classifiers perform on rules for more *popular* suggested matches. We analyzed the query logs of four months of intranet search at IBM and estimated the popularity of each suggested match by counting the number of sessions that have a click on the suggested document for the corresponding query. Therefore, each quality measure has two versions—the *unweighted* version is denoted by uw and the *weighted* version is denoted by w. In addition, we retrained the two classifiers by incorporating the weights on rules, thereby obtained a third version denoted by wt (*weighted training*). Whether or not to train the classifier with weights is a matter of a choice that depends on the specific scenario, and for that reason we evaluated both the w and the wt versions.

Figure 8 reports the accuracy (ratio of correctly classified rules) for SVM and rDTLC. As shown, when trained without weights rDTLC outperforms SVM by about 10% for both the unweighted and weighted measures. When the classifiers are trained with weights, rDTLC has a smaller improvement (about 3%) and both classifiers achieve high accuracy.

Even with classification, the number of natural rules may still be large. An administrator may be interested in only the top-k rule suggestions for some k. We explored the naive strategy of ranking the top-k candidate rules by decreasing confidence of the classifier at hand. We leave for future work the exploration of more sophisticated *learning to rank* strategies for this task. Nevertheless, we observe that this naive approach is already beneficial compared to a random selection of k candidates (a strategy denoted as *RND*). Specifically, Figure 9 gives the Mean Reciprocal Rank (MRR) of the different rankers. Figures 10 and 11 give the normalized Discounted Cumulative Gain at the top-k results (nDCG$_k$) where $k = 1, 3, 5$ for the unweighted and weighted cases, respectively. We can see that when the classifiers are not retrained with weights, rDTLC performs significantly better than SVM (and RND), but its advantage over SVM disappears when they are retrained with weights; in particular, when trained with weights both are almost always capable of suggesting natural rules for all $k = 1, 3, 5$.

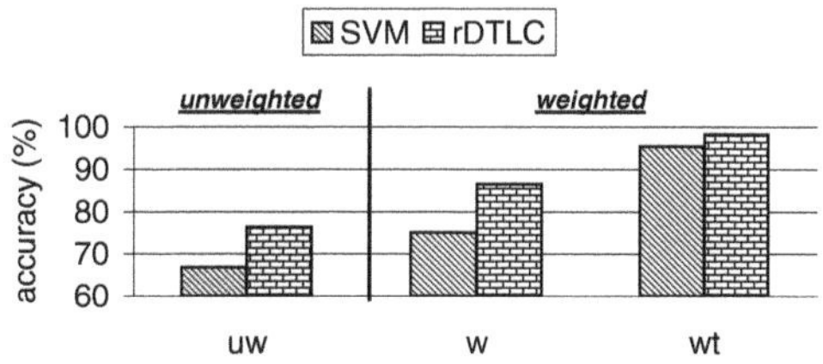

Figure 8: Accuracy of rule classification

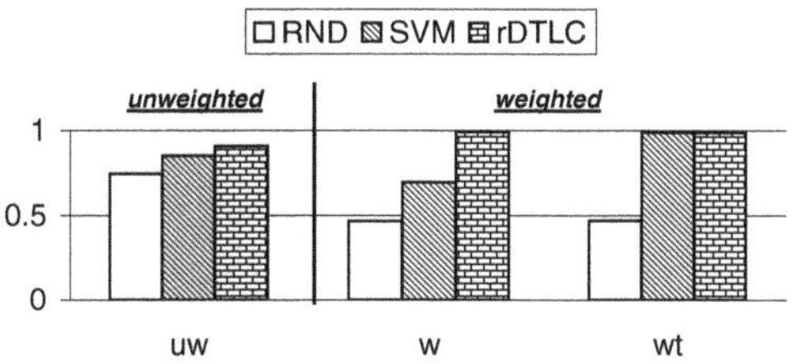

Figure 9: MRR for rule ranking

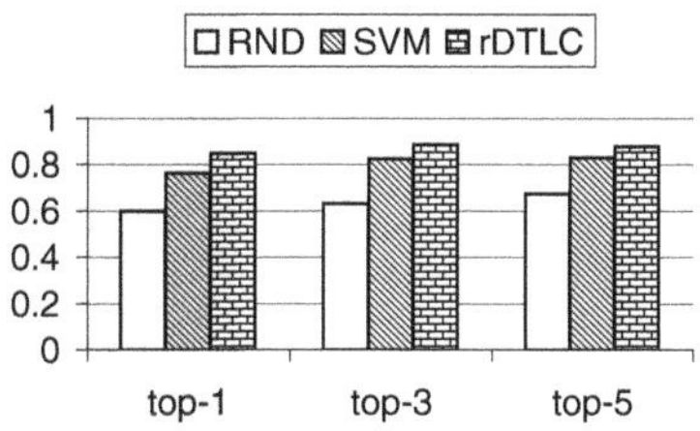

Figure 10: nDCG$_k$ (unweighted) for rule ranking

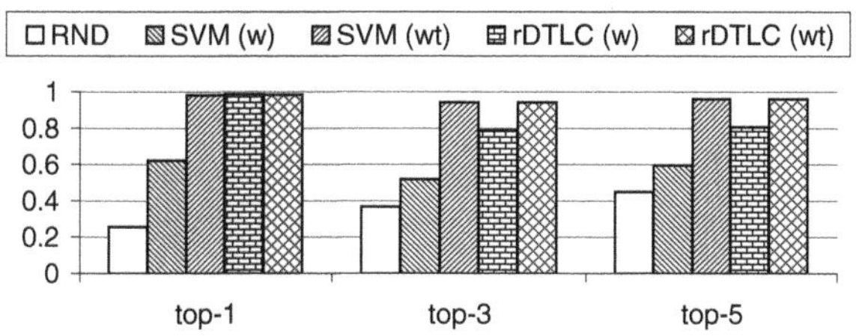

Figure 11: nDCG$_k$ (weighted) for rule ranking

5.2 Optimizing Multi-Rule Selection

We now present an experimental study of our solutions for the abstract rule optimization problem (Section 4).

Datasets. We constructed several datasets from our collection of suggested matches. Each dataset is an administration setting constructed by selecting a subset M of the suggested matches, and a subset R of the rules automatically created for M. (Observe that M implies a desideratum δ.) Later, we will explain how exactly M and R are selected for each dataset. Once M and R are selected, the administration graph G is constructed as follows. The queries in M form the set V_{q} of queries. The set V_{r} of r-queries is obtained by applying the rules in R to the queries in V_{q}. The set V_{d} of documents contains all the documents in M, as well as the top-5 results for each query and r-query in $V_{\mathrm{q}} \cup V_{\mathrm{r}}$, as obtained by invoking our search engine without rewrite rules. The edges of G are defined in the obvious manner.

Algorithms. We compared the G-Greedy and L-Greedy algorithms and their optimized versions G-Greedy-opt and L-Greedy-opt, as described in Section 4.3. We also considered several baseline algorithms: G-Random, L-Random and AllRules. G-Random and L-Random are similar to their greedy

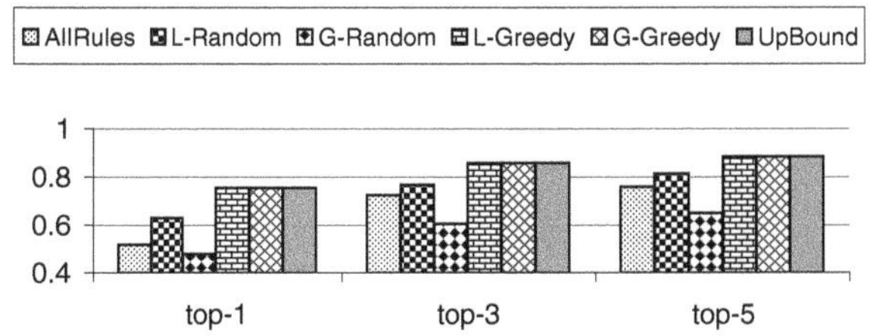

Figure 12: nDCG$_k$ (unweighted) for the labeled dataset

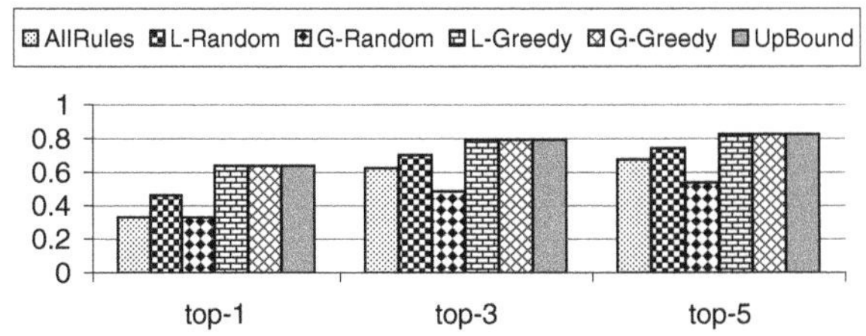

Figure 13: nDCG$_k$ (weighted) for the labeled dataset

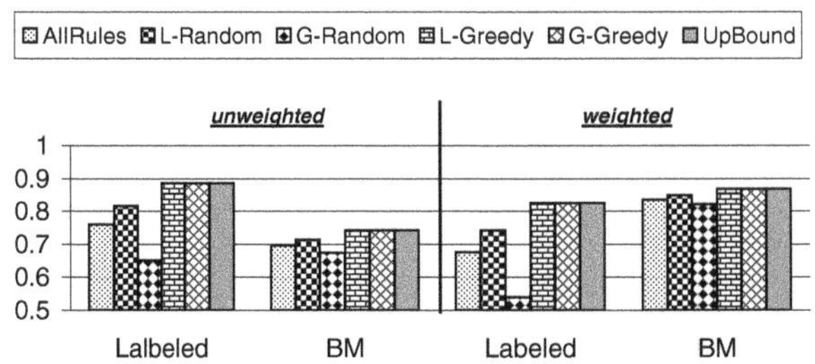

Figure 14: MRR for the labeled dataset

counterparts, except that their selection of rules is random. More precisely, G-Random selects a random subset of rules among all the rules, and L-Random randomly selects an effective rule for each suggested match. The algorithm AllRules simply selects all the rules.[5]

Measures. We consider two quality measures μ: the normalized Discounted Cumulative Gain at the top-k results (nDCG$_k$), and the Mean Reciprocal Rank (MRR). Since our administration graph is restricted to the top-5 matches for each query and r-query, MRR is restricted to the top-5 results as well (as it would not make sense otherwise).

To estimate the gap between the solution provided by each of the algorithms and the optimal solution, we computed an upper bound on the optimum for each quality measure μ, as follows. We evaluated the sum of Equation (3), where each addend $\mu(\mathrm{top}_k[q|G], \delta(q))$ is computed as if each suggested match is ranked as high as possible using a rule from the our collection. So, in principle, we allow this bound to place two documents in the same rank. Note that this number is not smaller than, and may be strictly larger than, the optimum (namely $\mu_k(G_S)$ for an optimal solution S).

Weights. We used both unweighted and weighted quality measures. In the weighted version, each query is weighted by the number of sessions where it is posed, as recorded in the aforementioned four months of query logs. For the unweighted version, the algorithms L-Greedy, L-Greedy-opt and L-Random iterate over the suggested matches (which

[5] Albeit straightforward, AllRules represents a common practice of our search administrators.

Table 2: Running time

Alg.	Labeled	BM	Extended
μ = MRR, $k = 5$ (ms)			
G-Greedy	25193	82566	> 24 hours
G-Greedy-opt	2911	7719	> 24 hours
L-Greedy	404	3517	1648137
L-Greedy-opt	39	110	87484
μ = nDCG, $k = 1$ (ms)			
G-Greedy	26356	82595	> 24 hours
G-Greedy-opt	2638	6896	> 24 hours
L-Greedy	399	3462	3522894
L-Greedy-opt	38	112	124613

form the set T in Figure 7) in a random order obtained by applying a random permutation thereof. For the weighted version, iteration over the suggested matches is ordered by decreasing weight of the involved queries.

5.2.1 *Evaluation on the Labeled Dataset*

In the first set of experiments, we used the *labeled dataset* obtained by taking as M the suggested matches that were used for labeling rewrite rules (see Section 5.1), and as R the set of rules that are manually labeled as natural. The resulting administration graph contains 135 queries, 300 r-queries, 423 documents, and a total of 1488 edges. Note that only a small portion of the suggested matches were used for labeling; the others, for which the rules are not labeled, will be used later in Section 5.2.2.

We first examined the quality of solutions produced by each of the algorithms. Figures 12 and 13 report the nDCG$_k$, with $k = 1, 3, 5$, for the unweighted and weighted cases, respectively. Figure 14 reports the MRR for both unweighted and weighted cases. (The groups labeled with BM will be discussed later.) Observe that on all quality measures, L-Greedy and G-Greedy score significantly higher than the other alternatives. In fact, they already reach the upper bound, and hence provide optimal solutions.

The goal of the next experiment is to explore the solutions in the presence of suggested matches that hit the top search results without requiring rules (yet, they can be affected by introducing rules). This setting represents a typical scenario where a search administrator needs to address problematic queries without compromising the overall search quality. For that, we enhanced the set M, from the construction of the labeled dataset, with 373 such suggested matches that are used as a *benchmark*. The groups of bars labeled with BM in Figure 14 report the MRR for both the unweighted and the weighted cases. Note that the greedy algorithms get better scores than the other alternatives, and again reach the upper bound. But now, the other alternatives get high scores as well, since many suggested matches in the benchmark are not affected by the rules in R. The results for nDCG$_k$ show a similar picture, and are therefore omitted.

Next, we compare the execution cost of the algorithms. AllRules, G-Random and L-Random entail a negligible running time (less than 0.2 ms). We focus on the globally and locally greedy algorithms, and examine the contribution of the optimization. Table 2 summarizes the running times for two different combinations of μ and k. The columns entitled "Labeled" and "BM" refer to the labeled dataset and the one enhanced with the benchmark, respectively. (The columns entitled "Extended" will be discussed later.) Observe that the locally greedy algorithms are over one order of magnitude faster than their globally greedy counterparts. In addition, the optimized versions are generally over one order of magnitude faster than their unoptimized counterparts. In particular, the optimized version of our locally greedy algorithm is capable of finding an optimal solution in real time for the typical usage scenarios.

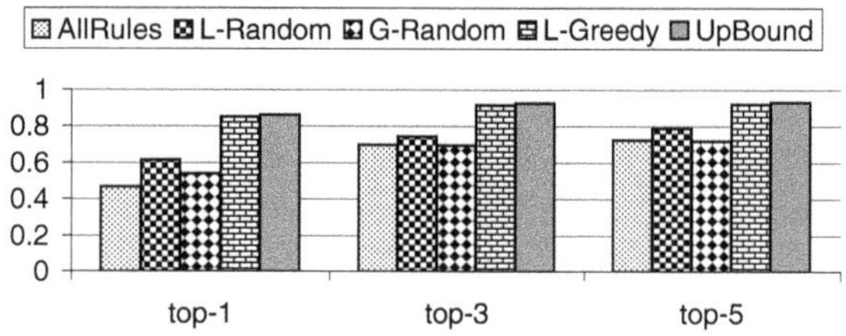

Figure 15: nDCG$_k$ (unweighted) for the extended dataset

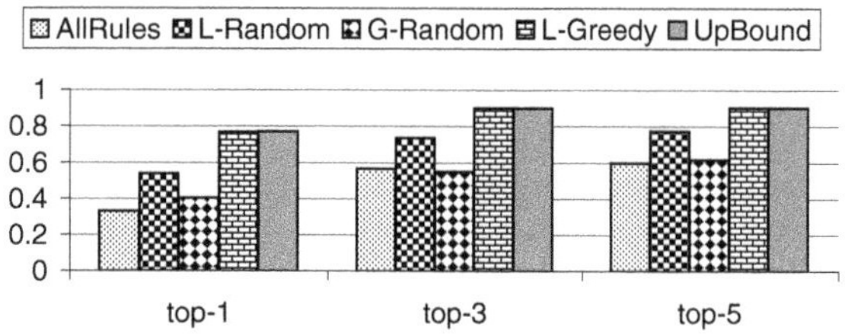

Figure 16: nDCG$_k$ (weighted) for the extended dataset

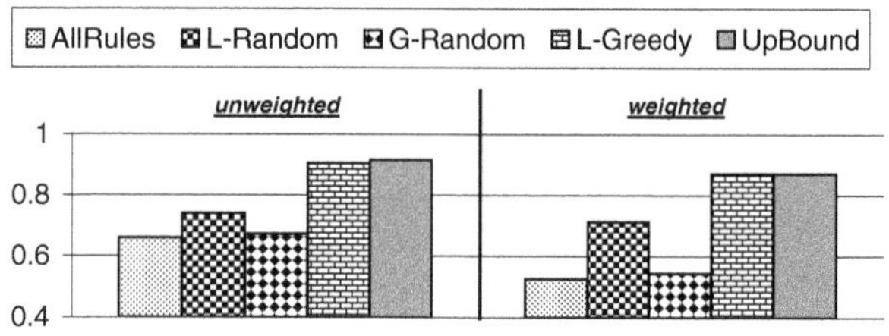

Figure 17: MRR for the extended dataset

5.2.2 *Evaluation on the Extended Dataset*

The results of the previous experiments demonstrate the effectiveness and feasibility of the greedy algorithms. To further evaluate the scalability of the greedy algorithms, we constructed a larger *extended dataset*. To create this dataset, we used as M the set of *all* the suggested matches, and as R the set of *all* the rules automatically generated for them (including those that are not labeled). The resulting administration graph contains 1001 queries, 10990 r-queries, 4188 documents, and a total of 36986 edges.

Again, the running times for two different combinations of μ and k are shown Table 2, now by the columns entitled "Extended." The globally greedy algorithms (including the optimized one) do not scale to the extended dataset. For the locally greedy algorithms, the improvement achieved by the optimization is again by over an order of magnitude.

Finally, we evaluated the quality of the solutions over the extended dataset. Figures 15 and 16 report the nDCG$_k$, with $k = 1, 3, 5$, for the unweighted and weighted cases, respectively. Figure 17 reports the MRR for both unweighted and weighted cases. Consistently with the previous experiments, L-Greedy outperforms the other alternatives. The gap between L-Greedy and the upper bound is generally around one percent, and is barely notable in the figure. These results demonstrate that even in the extreme case where the administrator adopts all candidate suggestions, L-Greedy-opt can find a practically optimal solution within a reasonable amount of time (around 2 minutes).

6. CONCLUDING REMARKS

The rule-based architecture aims to provide search administrators with the means of adapting the search engine to the content and dynamics of the enterprise. In this paper, we explored the incorporation of automation in the manual practice of administrators. Specifically, we studied the problem of suggesting natural rewrite rules, and proposed corresponding machine-learned classifiers for rules. We also studied the problem of selecting rules, from a given collection, with the goal of optimizing the quality on a benchmark. We presented a theoretical model that captures this task as a combinatorial optimization problem, analyzed its theoretical complexity, and proposed heuristic algorithms to accommodate its hardness. Experiments on a real enterprise case (IBM intranet search) indicate that the proposed solutions are effective and feasible.

While the testbed for this work has been the IBM internal search, the two challenges we studied hold in essentially every search system that supports administration by rewrite rules. Moreover, the setting and solutions we proposed are at a level of abstraction that hardly ties them to our specific testbed. In future work, we plan to focus on extending our techniques to handle significantly more expressive rules.

7. REFERENCES

[1] G. Agarwal, G. Kabra, and K. C.-C. Chang. Towards rich query interpretation: walking back and forth for mining query templates. In *WWW*, pages 1–10, 2010.

[2] O. Alhabashneh, R. Iqbal, N. Shah, S. Amin, and A. E. James. Towards the development of an integrated framework for enhancing enterprise search using latent semantic indexing. In *ICCS*, pages 346–352, 2011.

[3] R. A. Baeza-Yates, C. A. Hurtado, and M. Mendoza. Query recommendation using query logs in search engines. In *EDBT Workshops*, volume 3268 of *Lecture Notes in Computer Science*, pages 588–596, 2004.

[4] B. Billerbeck, F. Scholer, H. E. Williams, and J. Zobel. Query expansion using associated queries. In *CIKM*, pages 2–9, 2003.

[5] A. Z. Broder and A. C. Ciccolo. Towards the next generation of enterprise search technology. *IBM Systems Journal*, 43(3):451–454, 2004.

[6] N. Craswell, D. Hawking, and S. E. Robertson. Effective site finding using link anchor information. In *SIGIR*, pages 250–257, 2001.

[7] P. A. Dmitriev, N. Eiron, M. Fontoura, and E. J. Shekita. Using annotations in enterprise search. In *WWW*, pages 811–817, 2006.

[8] R. Fagin, B. Kimelfeld, Y. Li, S. Raghavan, and S. Vaithyanathan. Understanding queries in a search database system. In *PODS*, pages 273–284, 2010.

[9] R. Fagin, B. Kimelfeld, Y. Li, S. Raghavan, and S. Vaithyanathan. Rewrite rules for search database systems. In *PODS*, pages 271–282, 2011.

[10] R. Fagin, R. Kumar, K. S. McCurley, J. Novak, D. Sivakumar, J. A. Tomlin, and D. P. Williamson. Searching the workplace web. In *WWW*, pages 366–375, 2003.

[11] D. Hawking. Challenges in enterprise search. In *ADC*, volume 27 of *CRPIT*, pages 15–24, 2004.

[12] D. Hawking. Enterprise search - the new frontier? In *ECIR*, volume 3936 of *Lecture Notes in Computer Science*, page 12, 2006.

[13] R. Jones, B. Rey, O. Madani, and W. Greiner. Generating query substitutions. In *WWW*, pages 387–396, 2006.

[14] R. Kraft and J. Y. Zien. Mining anchor text for query refinement. In *WWW*, pages 666–674, 2004.

[15] Y. Li, R. Krishnamurthy, S. Vaithyanathan, and H. V. Jagadish. Getting work done on the web: supporting transactional queries. In *SIGIR*, pages 557–564, 2006.

[16] W.-Y. Loh and Y.-S. Shih. Split selection methods for classification trees. *Statistica Sinica*, 7:815–840, 1997.

[17] W.-Y. Loh and N. Vanichsetakul. Tree-structured classification via generalized discriminant analysis. *Journal of the American Statistical Association*, 83:715–728, 1988.

[18] A. Malekian, C.-C. Chang, R. Kumar, and G. Wang. Optimizing query rewrites for keyword-based advertising. In *EC*, pages 10–19, 2008.

[19] U. Ozertem, E. Velipasaoglu, and L. Lai. Suggestion set utility maximization using session logs. In *CIKM*, pages 105–114, 2011.

[20] I. Szpektor, A. Gionis, and Y. Maarek. Improving recommendation for long-tail queries via templates. In *WWW*, 2011.

[21] S. Vaithyanathan. Building search systems for the enterprise, 2011. SIGIR'11 industrial track keynote.

[22] Z. Zhang and O. Nasraoui. Mining search engine query logs for query recommendation. In *WWW*, pages 1039–1040, 2006.

[23] H. Zhu, S. Raghavan, S. Vaithyanathan, and A. Löser. Navigating the intranet with high precision. In *WWW*, pages 491–500, 2007.

[24] D. Zuckerman. Linear degree extractors and the inapproximability of max clique and chromatic number. *Theory of Computing*, 3(1):103–128, 2007.

APPENDIX

Proof of Theorem 4.8. We show a reduction from the *maximum clique* problem: given an undirected graph H, find a clique of a maximum size, where a *clique* is a set C of nodes such that every two members are adjacent. Zuckerman [24] showed that for all $\epsilon > 0$, it is NP-hard to approximate this problem to within $n^{1-\epsilon}$, where n is the number of nodes.

Given an undirected graph H, we construct the administration setting (R, G) as follows. For each node v of H, let $N(v)$ denote the set of neighbors of v, and we define two unique words a_v and b_v. For each such v, R contains the rule $a_v \to b_v$, G has the query q_v that consists of a_v followed (in some order) by all the a_u where $u \notin N(v)$, and G has two unique documents d_v^{gd} and d_v^{bd}. The r-queries of G are all those obtained by applying a rule in R to a query of G. Let q' be an r-query of G. If q' begins with a_v, then G has the r-query matching (q', d_v^{bd}) with the weight 2; and if q' begins with b_v, then G has (q', d_v^{gd}) with the weight 1. There are no query matchings in G. Finally, the desideratum δ maps each q_v (where v is a node of H) to the singleton $\delta(q_v) = \{d_v^{\mathrm{gd}}\}$.

Observe the following for a subset R' of R and a node v of H. If R' contains a rule $a_u \to b_u$ for some node $u \notin N(v)$, then q_v is reformulated into an r-query that begins with a_v and thus matches d_v^{bd} with the weight 2, implying $\mathrm{top}_1[q_v|G_{R'}] = (d_v^{\mathrm{bd}})$. If R' contains $a_v \to b_v$ but no rule $a_u \to b_u$ where $u \notin N(v)$, then q_v is reformulated only into an r-query that begins with b_v and thus matches d_v^{gd} with the weight 1, implying $\mathrm{top}_1[q_v|G_{R'}] = (d_v^{\mathrm{bd}})$. If R' contains none of $a_v \to b_v$ and $a_u \to b_u$ ($u \notin N(v)$), then $\mathrm{top}_1[q_v|G_{R'}] = \emptyset$. From this observation, the correctness of the reduction is proved straightforwardly: for each subset $R' \subseteq R$, if $\mu_1(G_{R'}) = c \cdot m$ (where c is taken from the definition of *reasonable at one*), then we can obtain from $G_{R'}$ (in polynomial time) a clique of size m in H; on the reverse direction, from each clique of size m in H we can construct a subset $R' \subseteq R$ with $\mu_1(G_{R'}) = c \cdot m$. $\square$

Time-Sensitive Query Auto-Completion

Milad Shokouhi
Microsoft Research
Cambridge, UK
milads@microsoft.com

Kira Radinsky
Technion, Israel Institute of Technology
Haifa, Israel
kirar@cs.technion.ac.il

ABSTRACT

Query auto-completion (QAC) is a common feature in modern search engines. High quality QAC candidates enhance search experience by saving users time that otherwise would be spent on typing each character or word sequentially.

Current QAC methods rank suggestions according to their past popularity. However, query popularity changes over time, and the ranking of candidates must be adjusted accordingly. For instance, while *halloween* might be the right suggestion after typing *ha* in October, *harry potter* might be better any other time. Surprisingly, despite the importance of QAC as a key feature in most online search engines, its temporal dynamics have been under-studied.

In this paper, we propose a time-sensitive approach for query auto-completion. Instead of ranking candidates according to their past popularity, we apply time-series and rank candidates according their *forecasted frequencies*. Our experiments on 846K queries and their daily frequencies sampled over a period of 4.5 years show that predicting the popularity of queries solely based on their past frequency can be misleading, and the forecasts obtained by time-series modeling are substantially more reliable. Our results also suggest that modeling the temporal trends of queries can significantly improve the ranking of QAC candidates.

Categories and Subject Descriptors

H.3.3 [**Information Search and Retrieval**]: Information Search and Retrieval—*Search Process, selection process*

General Terms

Algorithms, Measurement, Experimentation

Keywords

Query auto-completion, temporal ranking, time-series

1. INTRODUCTION

Query auto completion (QAS) is a feature incorporated in essentially every search engine, where the goal is to save user time by predicting user's intent and suggesting possible other queries matching the first few keystrokes typed. The filtering of related candidates (query suggestions) is typically based on string matching, and the ranking is ideally based on the likelihood of the filtered candidate being the query which the user has in mind. The latter challenge (ranking) is the focus of this paper, for which the goal is to sort queries according to their expected popularity. The common practice is to use past frequencies as proxy for future popularity [2, 8]. However, those approaches assume that user intent is static and does not change over time. Simple aggregation can overshadow the temporal trends that could potentially provide valuable signals for better ordering of QAC candidates.

Consider the example in Figure 1 where a user has typed *di* in Google query box on *Sunday*, February 12th, 2012. At the first glance, knowing that *dictionary* is generally a more frequent query than *disney*, it might be difficult to notice how the ranking might be improved. However, looking at the daily trends for these queries in Figure 2 reveals that *disney* is more popular on weekends. Hence, given that the first snapshot was taken on a Sunday, swapping *disney* and *dictionary* could lead to a better ranking at the time of this query. Similar observations can be made for different granularity of time-spans. For instance, previous work [4] has shown that users are more likely to search for entertainment-related queries at night, while queries related to personal finance are more common in the morning. Therefore, the ranking of QAC candidates can vary dynamically even according to the time of the day.

In this paper, we add time-sensitivity to ranking auto-completion candidates. We consider the temporal variations of query popularity in ranking QAC suggestions, that are normally shadowed by aggregation. Rather than summarizing the entire query history in one aggregated number as expected popularity, we rely on shorter but more frequent aggregation of data, and model the overall query trends by time-series. We show that the expected popularity values produced by our time-sensitive approaches are closer approximations to what will be observed later in the logs, and are more effective for ranking QAC suggestions.

The contributions of this work are three-fold: First, we study the shadowing problem that is caused by ignoring the temporal variations of query frequency in data aggregation. We investigate several aggregation options and show that query popularity predictions based on shorter but more recent data are more accurate than those produced based on aggregation over longer periods. This simple and counter-

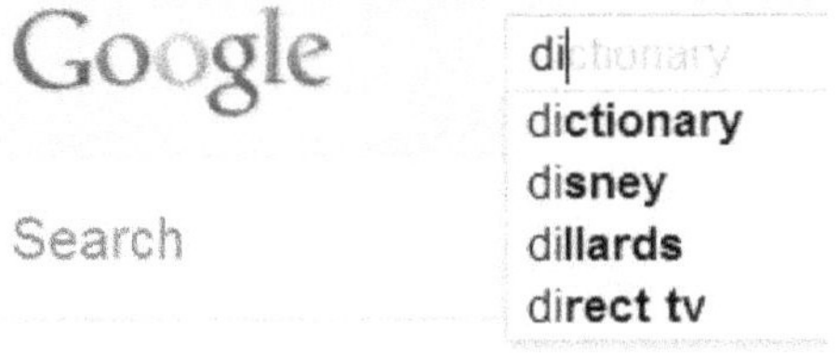

Figure 1: Google auto-completion candidates after typing *di* on Sunday, February 13th, 2012.

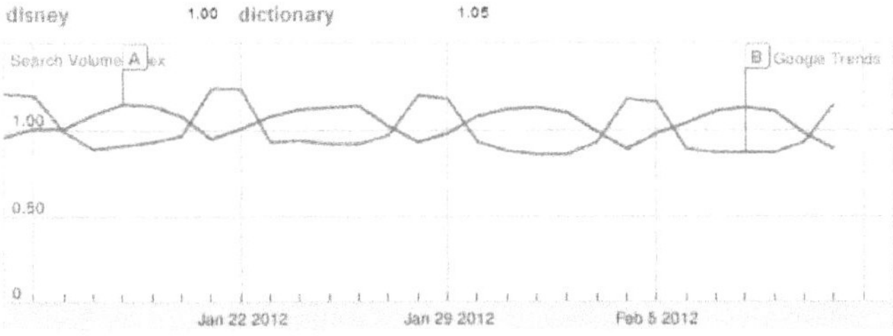

Figure 2: Daily frequencies for queries *dictionary* (red) and *disney* (blue) during January 2012 according to Google Trends (the snapshot was taken on Monday, 13-Feb-2012). Among the two queries, *disney* is more popular on weekends, while *dictionary* is issued more commonly by users on weekdays.

intuitive finding, can be useful in scenarios where applying more sophisticated time-series models is feasible. Second, we introduce a time-sensitive query auto-completion model in which the expected popularity of each query suggestion is forecasted by time-series, and dynamically varies depending on the time of query. Finally, we perform a large scale analysis over 4.5 years of sampled log data, and evaluate our predictions on daily and monthly intervals. Our experimental results indicate that accurate query popularity forecasts are essential in generating high quality QAC rankings.

2. RELATED WORK

Query auto-completion. Auto-completion during typing is a familiar feature and has been utilized in several applications ranging from early UNIX Shells to modern text editors and web browsers.

Previous work on auto-completion can be grouped into two main categories; the first group (also referred to as *predictive* auto-completion [8]) deploys information retrieval and NLP techniques to generate and rank candidates on the fly as the user enters new words and characters [13, 18, 27]. For instance, Grabski et al. [18], and Bickel et al. [6] studied sentence completion based on lexicon statistics of text collections. Fan et al. [17] ranked AC candidates according to a generative model learned by Latent Dirichlet Allocation (LDA) [7]. White and Marchionini [33] developed a real-time query expansion system that produces an updated list of candidates based on the top-ranked documents as the user types new words in the search box.

In the second group of AC techniques — including this work — candidates are pre-generated and stored in tries and hash tables for efficient *lookup*. The list of candidates is updated by new lookups with each new input from the user. The filtering of candidates in this group is typically on the basis of exact prefix matching.[1]

The ranking in *lookup* techniques is based on static scores that are assigned to candidates according to their importance. For example, in a product engine such as `amazon.com` with products names as candidates, static scores can be assigned according to popularity, price or the review scores of products [8]. In the context of web search, the most conventional approach is to rank candidates (query suggestions) according to their past popularity. In the most related study to our work, Bar-Yossef and Kraus [2] referred to this baseline as *MostPopularCompletion* (MPC) and suggested that it can be regarded as an approximate maximum likelihood estimator. The authors also proposed a context-aware technique in which the default static scores for the candidates are combined with contextual-scores based on recent session history to compute the final ranking.

We also take MPC [2] as our QAC ranking baseline and show that it can be improved significantly by considering the temporal characteristics of queries. Our work is orthogonal to all aforementioned techniques; for instance, using error-tolerant data structures that support fuzzy matching [8, 20] can expand the list of candidates that are eligible for our temporal modeling. Our work can be also combined with the *hybrid* framework of Bar-Yossef and Kraus [2] to improve the ranking of candidates with no or little context.

Time-sensitive search. The world is constantly changing and the dynamics of daily life are reflected on the web in the forms of fresh content and new information needs. Different aspects of freshness in web search have been explored; Jones and Diaz [21] and Li and Croft [24] extended the language modeling framework to incorporate the time extracted from document time-stamps. Berberich et al. [5] matched explicit temporal expressions in queries with the time-stamps mentioned in documents in a query likelihood approach for ranking. Their work was extended by Kanhabua and Nørvåg [22] that used the content of top-ranked documents for approximating the most related time-interval for the query.

Elsas and Dumais [16] showed that there is a strong connection between the rate of content changes in a document and its relevance. They proposed a probabilistic ranking model in which the term weights vary according to their temporal characteristics. Relatedly, Efron [15] investigated using linear time-series models for term weighting. Dai and Davison [11] introduced a time-sensitive version of PageRank based on multiple crawls and showed that it can be used as an effective static score for document ranking. Dong et al. [14] and Dai and Davison [12] integrated freshness in learning to rank by introducing new ways of optimizing for both freshness and relevance.

Kulkarni et al. [23] classified queries into different categories based on their change of popularity over time. The authors showed that monitoring the query popularity and content updates can reveal useful signals for detecting the change in query intent. Metzler et al. [26] classified queries with *implicit* temporal intent (e.g. halloween) according to their previous occurrences in the logs along with explicit temporal expressions (e.g. halloween 2010). Shokouhi [31]

[1]Recently, Chaudhuri and Kaushik [8] and Ji et al. [20] proposed flexible fuzzy matching models that are tolerant to small edit-distance differences between the query (prefix) and candidates.

leveraged time-series decomposition techniques for classifying seasonal queries.

Chien and Immorlica [9] demonstrated that queries with similar temporal patterns (e.g. halloween and pumpkin) can be semantically related despite no lexical overlap. Liu et al. [25] introduced a unified model for forecasting query frequency in which the forecast for each query, is influenced by the frequencies predicted for similar and correlated queries. Vlachos et al. [32] developed a compressed representation for time-series and proposed a model for detecting significant bursts in query frequencies. Baraglia et al. [3] investigated the impact of aging on *query flow graphs* and in the presence of evolving query trends. They argued that generating the graphs from scratch may not be feasible and described an incremental approach for more efficient updates. Alfonseca et al. [1] clustered queries according to their frequency time-series. They suggested that their approach can be used for query suggestion and query categorization. Zhang et al. [34] reranked documents based on their time-stamps in snippets and suggested that their approach can improve search effectiveness for temporal queries.

Radinsky et al. [29] have performed an analysis of predictability of different user behaviors (such as query clicks, URL clicks and query-URL clicks) using time-series analysis and a learning model. Similarly, Cho and Varian [10] and Shimshoni et al. [30] study the general applicability of time-series analysis for modeling query trends. However, those studies have been performed on small sets of queries ($\approx$10,000 queries) and of short periods of time (6 months), disallowing identification of long term yearly seasonality. In our work, we perform rigorous analysis of a large scale corpus of 846K queries over a period of 4.5 years for the purpose of better query suggestions.

While it is clear that freshness has been considered in several areas of web search, to the best of our knowledge, this is the first time that the temporal trends of queries are modeled and used for QAC ranking.

3. TIME-SENSITIVE AUTO-COMPLETION

In a typical QAC scenario, the user is presented with a list of query suggestions that their prefix matches the text entered in the search box. In this paper, we refer to the latest text in the search box as *prefix* (e.g. "di" in Figure 1). The prefix is updated as the user enters new characters and will eventually match the final query once the query is submitted. For each prefix $\mathcal{P}$, the list of candidates $\mathcal{C}(\mathcal{P})$ consists of all previous queries that start with $\mathcal{P}$.[2] The list of candidates is dynamically updated at run-time with each new character typed by the user.

Ideally, the candidates should be ranked based their likelihood of matching the query that the user has in mind. In the absence of any contextual information, this likelihood can be set according to the wisdom of crowds by using the general frequency in the past as a proxy for the *expected* popularity in future. The most common approach is to *aggregate* the query frequencies over a query log, and use these *aggregated* values for ranking QAC suggestions. Bar-Yossef and Kraus [2] referred to this general form of QAC ranking as *MostPopularCompletion* (MPC) where,

[2]Without the loss of generality we ignore more advanced fuzzy matching techniques [8, 20] in our work.

$$MCP(\mathcal{P}) = \arg\max_{q \in \mathcal{C}(\mathcal{P})} w(q), \quad w(q) = \frac{f(q)}{\sum_{i \in \mathcal{Q}} f(i)} \tag{1}$$

here, $f(q)$ denotes the number of times the query q occurs in a previous search log $\mathcal{Q}$. Under the MPC model, the candidate scores do not change as long as the same query log $\mathcal{Q}$ is used. Each query is represented by a single value as its popularity which is computed by counting the number of times that it has occurred in the past. As long as $\mathcal{Q}$ is not replaced by a fresher log, the assumption is that the aggregated frequencies can be regarded as reasonable approximations for future popularity. However, as mentioned earlier, the query popularity may change over time and the candidate lists must be adjusted consequently to account for recent changes.

While frequent updates of query statistics may address the freshness problem to some extent, it is not clear how often the logs must be updated to provide the best approximations for future popularity. Without the right update policy, trend effects will be disregarded. For example, a query such as *Sarah Burke* that gained high popularity in January 2012, but was not queried as often in the past, might get lower ranking if compared to the query *Sarah Palin*, which has high volume, since it was queried for many years, despite being relatively less popular in January 2012. Furthermore, aggregation methods ignore seasonal effects. For instance, at the time of this writing on 13th February 2012 – a day before the *Valentine's day* – Google suggests *verizon wireless* as top candidate for *v* and does not suggest any Valentine's related candidate in the QAC ranking (the top plot in Figure 3). The query frequency trends in the bottom plot of Figure 3 however clearly show that *valentines day* is temporally more relevant for suggestion. As another example, weekly patterns such as those shown in Figure 2 for *disney* and *dictionary* disappear in monthly aggregations. In summary, the past is not always a good proxy for future particularly for trendy and seasonal queries. Today's frequency for query *dictionary* is not necessarily the best estimate for its frequency tomorrow.

We propose TS, a time-sensitive QAC ranking model in which the default *aggregated* candidate scores in Equation 1 are replaced with *forecasted* values computed by time-series modeling of query history. Here, the score of each candidate at time t is determined according to its predicted value calculated using time-series models that capture trend, seasonality. Hence, our time-sensitive QAC ranking model can be formalized as,

$$TS(\mathcal{P}, t) = \arg\max_{q \in \mathcal{C}(\mathcal{P})} w(q|t), \quad w(q|t) = \frac{\hat{y}_t(q)}{\sum_{i \in \mathcal{Q}} \hat{y}_t(i)} \tag{2}$$

where $\mathcal{P}$ is the entered prefix, and $\mathcal{C}(\mathcal{P})$ represents its list of QAC candidates, and $\hat{y}_t(q)$ denotes the estimated frequency of query q at time t. As a result, the quality of a candidate list generated by our TS model is directly influenced by the accuracy of predictions obtained by time-series modeling. Note that, our time-sensitive model becomes similar to the context-sensitive QAC ranking of Bar-Yossef and Kraus [2] if one considers time as "context". The focus of our work is on the time-sensitivity of query suggestions, and on how we can enhance QAC to handle this aspect. We leverage techniques from time-series analysis to model temporal query behavior

Figure 3: (Top) The auto-completion candidates ranked by Google on 13th February 2012, a day before Valentine's. (Bottom) The query frequencies for *valentines day* vs. *verizon wireless* since 2004.

(Section 3.1), and demonstrate how these models can be learnt from query logs to do better QAC ranking (Section 3.2).

3.1 Time-Series Analysis & Forecast

A *time-series* consists of a sequence of data points in successive time order and with uniform intervals. Hence, annual salaries, the daily rate of CO2 emissions and any other sequence of numbers collected at uniform intervals can be represented by a time-series. In practice, time-series analysis is often used to model the temporal changes in data and to forecast future trends.

At any given time, the *Exponential smoothing* methods [19] apply a weighted average over the frequencies of previous data points to forecast the upcoming trends. In the simplest form — also known as *Single exponential smoothing* — the time-series is smoothed as follows,

$$\bar{y}_t = \lambda y_t + (1 - \lambda)\bar{y}_{t-1} \tag{3}$$

where y_t and $\bar{y}_t$ respectively denote the actual and smoothed values for the data at time t, and λ is the *smoothing parameter* ranging between 0 and 1. The recursive equation above can be also used to provide the forecast for the next interval ($\hat{y}_{t+1}$). That is,

$$\hat{y}_{t+1} = \bar{y}_t \tag{4}$$

While single exponential smoothing may produce reasonable forecasts for stationary time-series, it performs poorly in the presence of a *trend* in time-series. To remedy this problem, *Double exponential smoothing* methods extend the previous model by introducing a trend variable F_t,

$$\bar{y}_t = \lambda_1 y_t + (1 - \lambda_1)(\bar{y}_{t-1} + F_{t-1}) \tag{5}$$
$$F_t = \lambda_2(\bar{y}_t - \bar{y}_{t-1}) + (1 - \lambda_2)F_{t-1} \tag{6}$$

Here, parameter F_t models the linear trend of time-series at time t, while λ_1 and λ_2 are smoothing parameters. As in previous equations, y_t and $\bar{y}_t$ represent the actual and smoothed values at time t. The forecast for the next interval based on double exponential smoothing can be obtained by:

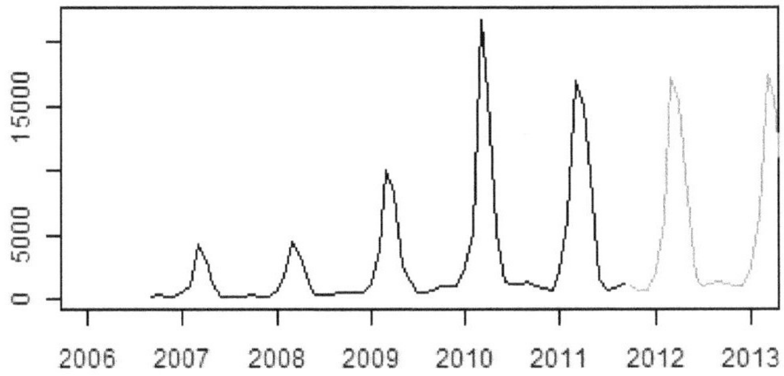

Figure 4: The black line shows monthly frequency values for query *spring flowers* between Sep'06–Jun'11. The green curve depicts the predicted values for the next 24 months (Jul'11–Jun'13) based on triple exponential smoothing. Data from `bing.com`.

$$\hat{y}_{t+1} = \bar{y}_t + F_t \tag{7}$$

That is, the value of the next data point at time $t + 1$ is predicted by linear combination of the smoothed value at time t and the latest trend parameter F_t. Hence, a negative F_t sets a smaller predicted value for the next time interval $(t + 1)$, compared to the most recently observed value y_t.

Double exponential smoothing does not capture the frequency variations due to potential seasonality (periodicity) in the data. *Triple exponential smoothing* generalizes the previous techniques by explicitly modeling the seasonality. The updated model — also known as HoltWinters smoothing — is often expressed as:

$$\bar{y}_t = \lambda_1(y_t - S_{t-\tau}) + (1 - \lambda_1)(\bar{y}_{t-1} + F_{t-1}) \tag{8}$$
$$F_t = \lambda_2(\bar{y}_t - \bar{y}_{t-1}) + (1 - \lambda_2)F_{t-1} \tag{9}$$
$$S_t = \lambda_3(y_t - \bar{y}_t) + (1 - \lambda_3)S_{t-\tau} \tag{10}$$
$$\lambda_1 + \lambda_2 + \lambda_3 = 1 \tag{11}$$

where S_t captures the seasonality of data at time t, and τ specifies the length of periodic cycle (e.g. 12 for annual cycles when the data points represent monthly frequencies). The smoothing parameters λ_1, λ_2, and λ_3 vary between 0 and 1 and can be optimized using standard techniques such as maximum likelihood. The forecast for the value of the time-series at the next interval is given by:

$$\hat{y}_{t+1} = (\bar{y}_t + F_t)S_{t+1-\tau} \tag{12}$$

Figure 4 illustrates an example of applying triple exponential smoothing for forecasting future trends. The underlying data comprises of monthly frequency values for query *spring flowers* sampled from logs of `bing.com` between September 2006 and June 2011. The green curve shows the forecast for July 2011 – June 2013 ($\tau = 12$).

3.2 Parameter Estimation and Forecasting

In this work we utilize a hill-climbing optimization technique called limited-memory BFGS (L-BFGS), which is a limited memory variation of the Broyden-Fletcher-Goldfarb-Shanno (BFGS). The technique estimated the direction by solving the following Newton equation:

$$B_k \mathbf{p}_k = -\nabla f(\mathbf{x}_k) \quad (13)$$

where B_k is the approximation of the Hessian matrix at step k, and $f = \sum \epsilon^2$ is the sum of the prediction error rates. The initial values B_0 and x_0 are guessed, and a line search in the direction at step k is then used to find the next point x_{k+1}, and a new value of the matrix B_{k+1} is estimated [28].

4. EVALUATION

Our first set of experiments focuses on forecast accuracy while in the second part we evaluate the effectiveness of QAC rankings. For each task, we borrow a couple of metrics from information retrieval and statistics for measurement.

Forecast accuracy. *Mean absolute error* (MAE) is widely used in statistics to measure the accuracy of forecasts and is defined as follows,

$$MAE = \frac{1}{n}\sum_{i=1}^{n}|\hat{y}_i - y_i| \quad (14)$$

where y is the true value and $\hat{y}$ is the prediction. MAE is an unbounded measure and is not strongly resilient to outliers. Therefore, its is often used along with other metrics such as *Symmetric mean absolute percentage error* (SMAPE) to diagnose the forecast variation. SMAPE is defined as,

$$SMAPE = \frac{1}{n}\sum_{i=1}^{n}\frac{|\hat{y}_i - y_i|}{\hat{y}_i + y_i} \quad (15)$$

In contrast to mean absolute error, SMAPE is bounded between 0 and 1, although it penalizes under- and over-estimations unequally.

QAC quality. In the absence of any contextual and personalized information, the ground-truth QAC ranking for a prefix $\mathcal{P}$ is the list of all queries that start with $\mathcal{P}$ (or are somehow filtered for the prefix) ordered according to their *true* popularity. At any given time t, the true popularity values are set according to the observed query frequency values at that time. Obviously, this information is not available to QAC ranking models at runtime, and they have to rely on historical data at time $t-1$ and before to rank candidates as close as possible to this unobserved ground-truth ($\mathcal{G}$).

We measure the quality of QAC lists by computing their *Spearman correlation* (ρ) against this gold standard $\mathcal{G}$. We also employ MRR to specifically measure the mean reciprocal rank of the *best* ground-truth candidate (top-ranked in $\mathcal{G}$) in QAC rankings.

Small differences in query frequency can cause significant changes in the ordering of QAC candidates. Both MRR and Spearman correlation penalize swapping two queries with similar frequencies the same way they penalize swapping a pair with a substantial gap in popularity. Consider a scenario where the user has typed *hall* in the search box in October, and the QAC model has to rank the following candidates: *halloween*, *halloween party games*, and *halloween party ideas*. The first candidate is orders of magnitude more popular than the other two which more or less have similar frequencies. Clearly, pairwise swappings that involve the first candidate should be rewarded or penalized more heavily than the pairwise swapping of the other pair.

To make our evaluation more robust against the potential noise caused by insignificant differences, we first take a log of — true/predicted — query frequencies and then round them to the closest integer across all our QAC ranking evaluations.

5. DATA

Our experimental data comprises of all queries that were submitted to `bing.com` by users – with a US-based IP address – between January 1st, 2007 and June 30th, 2011. We dropped queries that never appeared more than 28 times in at least one of the months during this period. In total 846,432 queries and their daily frequencies were extracted.

The quality of QAC candidates can vary depending on the amount of historical data available for each query. The effectiveness of time-series techniques for modeling the query trends is also sensitive to the amount of training data and the length of seasonal cycle (τ in Equation 12). Therefore, we use our sampled query statistics to construct two testbeds with distinctive characteristics.

Daily buckets, weekly cycles (D-W). Our first testbed is generated from daily query frequency values between January 2nd, 2011, and June 30th, 2011 (180 days). For each query at time (day) t, we use the frequencies at all previous intervals (previous daily frequencies) to fit the time-series models. We consider the last 30 days (June 2011) as our testing period for reporting the results. We set the τ value in time-series models to 7 which would allow them to capture potential weekly cycles in query frequency.

Monthly buckets, annual cycles (M-A). We aggregated the daily frequency values between January 2007 and June 2011 in monthly buckets . Hence, the history of each query is represented by 54 data points one for each month covered during our sampling time-frame. We report our evaluation results on the first 6 months of 2011. Here, we set the τ parameter in our time-series models to 12, to allow modeling of potential annual cycles.

Compared to the previous testbed, there are fewer data points for time-series modeling of query trends, and there is less variance and sparsity in query frequencies.

6. PREDICTING QUERY POPULARITY

In an oracle list of QAC suggestions, candidates are sorted in descending order of their *true* popularity. Since this ground-truth information is unavailable at runtime, QAC ranking models order candidates according to their *expected* (predicted) popularity inferred from previous logs.

Our TS auto-completion method models the entire query history by time-series and forecasts the future popularity accordingly. The MCP method [2] that we use as our baseline assumes that the aggregated frequency of a query over past search logs is a reasonable approximation for its future popularity. Surprisingly, little is known about the validity of this assumption and its impact on the ranking of QAC candidates. Furthermore, the trade-off between the recency (and size) of the query log used for aggregation, and the accuracy of outcome predictions has not been investigated.

In this section, we evaluate the accuracy of various methods for predicting the future query popularity, and in the

Table 1: The forecast error rates obtained by different methods on the D-W testbed. The query frequencies are predicted once for each of the 30 days in the testing period (June 2011). The best performing method in each row is specified by an underline. All (TS vs. P_*) and (TMS vs. P_*) pairwise differences are detected as statistically significant by the t-test ($p < 0.01$).

	P_1	P_3	P_6	P_{12}	P_h	TS	TMS
MAE	14.02	23.37	23.62	24.05	23.12	10.57	10.50
SMAPE	0.277	0.272	0.273	0.275	0.270	0.228	0.251

Table 2: The forecast error rates obtained by different methods on the M-A testbed. The query frequencies are forecasted once for each of the 6 months in the testing period (Jan–Jun 2011). The best performing method in each row is specified by an underline. Except for (MAE, $k = 1$), all (TS vs. P_*) and (TMS vs. P_*) pairwise differences are detected as statistically significant by the t-test ($p < 0.01$).

	P_1	P_3	P_6	P_{12}	P_h	TS	TMS
MAE	338	1065	1108	1189	1012	343	323
SMAPE	0.168	0.330	0.346	0.381	0.313	0.179	0.164

next section we measure the impact of these predictions on the quality of QAC rankings.

Forecast quality. MCP considers the past query frequency as expected popularity for future. For this, the query frequencies are aggregated over a past query log. We explore several aggregation options by averaging the query frequencies over the last k intervals ($k \in \{1, 3, 6, 12\}$), and also over the entire query history. We refer to latter form of aggregation as P_h and denote the others by P_k where k is the number of previous intervals used for averaging. We study the accuracy of these aggregated baselines in predicting future query popularity, and compare them against the forecasts produced by our time-series modeling of query trends (TS).

Table 1 includes the forecast error rates of different methods on the D-W testbed. The frequency of each query is forecasted once for each of the 30 days in our testing period (June 2011). At each time t, the P_k baselines use the average frequency of the past k days as their prediction. P_h computes the average over the entire query history before t. The TS model also uses the entire previous history but produces its forecasts by triple exponential smoothing ($\tau = 7$). For now, ignore the TMS column as we will get to it later. The numbers show that our TS predictions are better than all aggregated baselines on both metrics; all differences are detected as statistically significant by the t-test ($p < 0.01$). Among the aggregated baselines, MAE favors P_1 while SMAPE picks P_h as the best model. The discrepancy suggests that averaging over the entire history provides more robust predictions overall but may fail more noticeably on outliers.

We take a closer look at the daily error rates produced by the best three methods (P_1, P_h, and TS) in Figure 5. The results are consistent with the overall numbers; the MAE rates have higher variance and P_h is more robust than P_1 although it may produce greater absolute errors. P_h performs worst over the weekends and P_1 errors are highest on Saturdays and Mondays. This can be explained by the fact that search traffic is generally lower on the weekends, and grows again on Mondays. P_1 is constantly one step behind to react to these changes and P_h is too stale in general.

We repeated our analysis on the M-A testbed and summarized the results in Table 2. All methods produce 6 forecasts for each query, one for every month in our testing period Jan–June 2011. The P_k baselines use the average frequency of the past k months as their forecast while P_h computes the average over the entire query history since January 2007. The TS model also uses the entire previous history but produces its forecasts by triple exponential smoothing ($\tau = 12$). Once again, ignore the values under the TMS column as they will be described later. The numbers show that with the exception of P_1, our TS predictions are better than all aggregated baselines on both metrics; all differences are detected as statistically significant by the t-test ($p < 0.01$). The difference between P_1 and TS is statistically significant on SMAPE but not so according to MAE. The competitive performance of P_1 on this testbed can be explained by several reasons; compared to the daily frequency values used the in D-W testbed, the data here is aggregated in monthly partitions. The monthly query frequencies are less sparse and have lower variance. Furthermore, the TS model has about 6 times more data points in the D-W testbed which allows it to fit the query trends better.

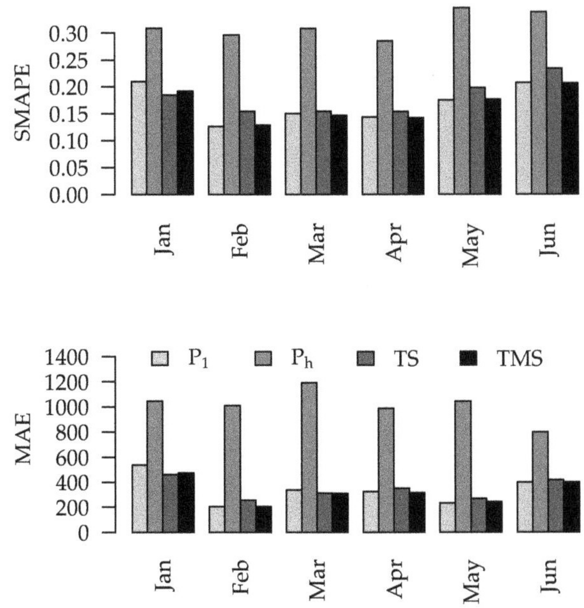

Figure 6: Daily SMAPE (top) and MAE (bottom) rates for P_1, P_h, TS and TMS predictions on the M-A testbed (January–June 2011).

Figure 6 illustrates the monthly error rates for different methods. While the trends are consistent with the overall numbers, it is interesting to note the higher error rate of P_1 for January which is due to the change of year and end of holiday season.

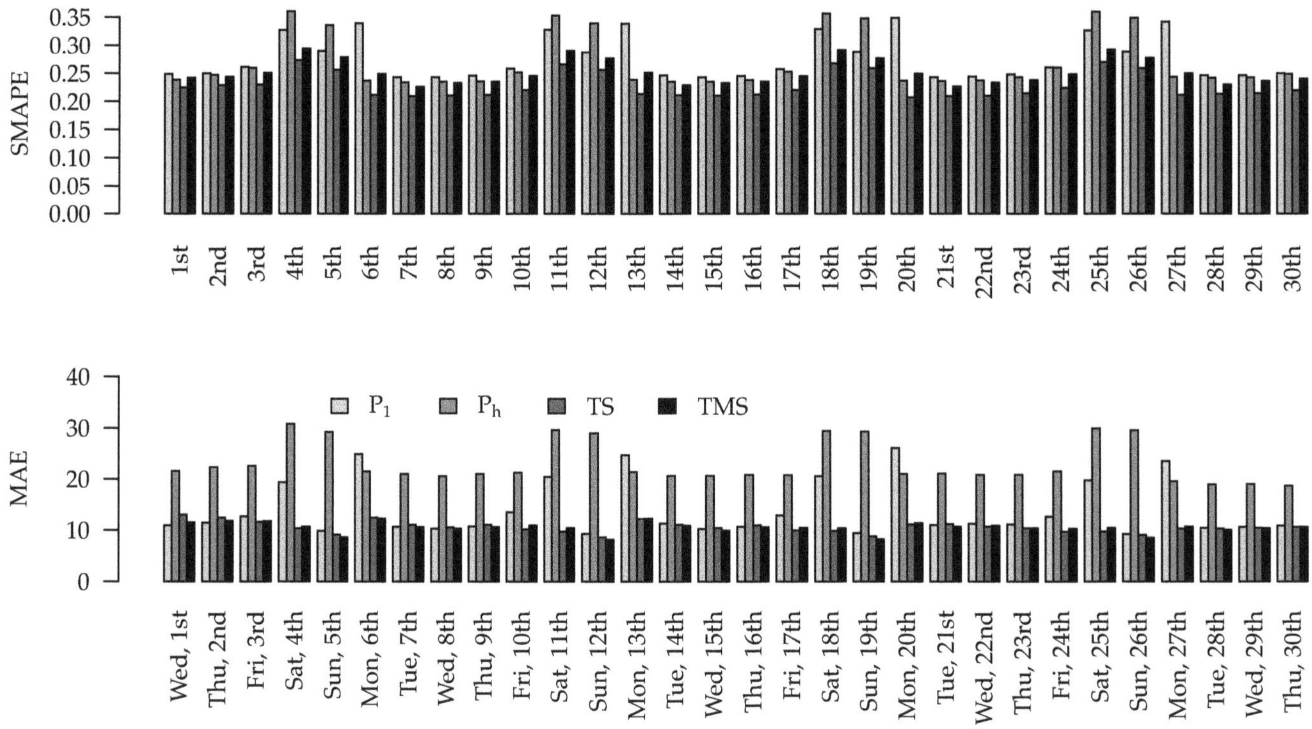

Figure 5: Daily SMAPE (top) and MAE (bottom) rates for forecast models on the D-W testbed (June 2011).

Success & Failure Analysis. We picked P_1 and TS as the two most effective methods according to the overall metrics and inspected their performance on per-query basis.

On the D-W testbed, lower error rates for TS versus P_1 are most apparent in queries with highly periodic frequency trends. Figure 7 depicts the actual and predicted frequencies for queries *nascar* and *irish lottery* as two examples from this category. The P_1 gains over TS often come from queries that were either periodic and highly popular but suddenly lost their demand (e.g. recently ended tv shows), or those that face an unexpected spike in popularity (e.g. celebrity names). Figure 8 shows two of these examples for queries *american idol* and *ginger lee*.

We also grouped the TS *weekday winners* by extracting the queries that their TS predictions are better than P_1 on those weekdays, consistently over the entire testing period (June 2011). The top winners for each day are listed in Table 3.[3] As expected all these queries have periodic trends and are related to intents that have weekly cycles. The list is dominated by queries related to lottery (e.g. euromillion), tv shows (e.g. zero punctuation) and those targeting weekly deals (e.g. dominos) or updates (e.g. week in pictures). There were no *weekday losers* apart from queries that were related to *americal idol* and *dancing with the stars*, the two tv shows that their latest series ended in May 2011, just before the start of our testing time period.

Similar patterns can be observed on the M-A testbed. TS is more effective in predicting the frequency of queries with seasonal trends, while it fails to adapt quickly when there is a sudden change in the query popularity. Figures 9 and 10 contain four examples of significant wins and losses for TS versus P_1.

[3]For presentation purposes, we excluded queries that have high overlap with those already included in the list. For example, *abc family* is dropped when *abc* is already included.

Table 3: A sample of queries where TS performs substantially better than P_1 consistently on certain weekdays during the testing period (June 2011).

Mon	dear prudence; fedex tracking; gmail; ···
Tue	euromillion; abc; daily show; dominos ···
Wed	mega millions; publix; zero punctuation ···
Thu	louisiana lottery; footy tips; olg; ···
Fri	week in pictures; nascar; cinemex ···
Sat	irish lottery; wclc; toto; ···
Sun	wisconsin unemployment; mail on sunday; ncesc; ···

Temporal model selector (TMS). Our results so far have shown that when it comes to query frequency forecast models, there is no one size fits all method that always wins. For queries with an unexpected spike in particular, the time-series models tend to overfit when trying to optimize their *smoothing* parameters. Motivated by this observation, we propose a *temporal model selector* that dynamically decides which forecast model to choose at each time-interval for the query. For this purpose, we consider a segment of query history as the *validation period* and decide between different models according to their performance on this segment. The validation process can be designed in different ways. For instance, one can pick the model that has the lowest error rate on the entire validation set. Alternatively, it is possible to train a classifier that takes in monthly error rates and other features for supervised model selection. We decided to take a simple approach and left more sophisticated

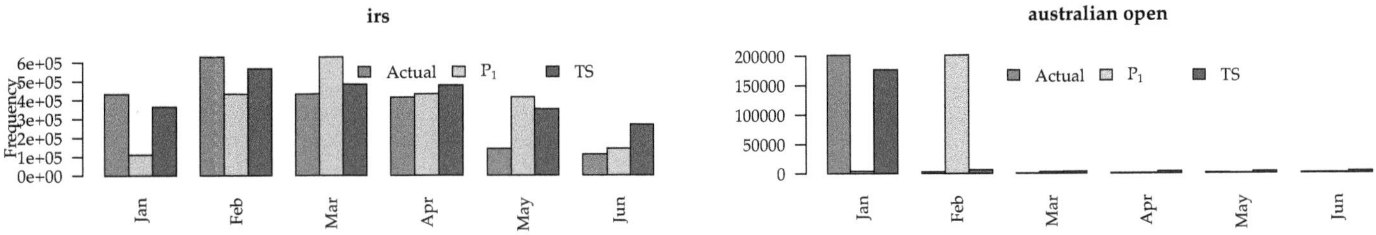

Figure 9: (left) The actual daily frequencies and the predicted values by P_1 (SMAPE ≈ 0.26) and TS (SMAPE ≈ 0.18) for query *irs* between Jan–Jun 2011. (right) Same data for query *australian open* by P_1 (MAE ≈ 0.52), and TS (SMAPE $\approx$ 0.49). TS is more successful in predicting the frequency of queries with seasonal trends.

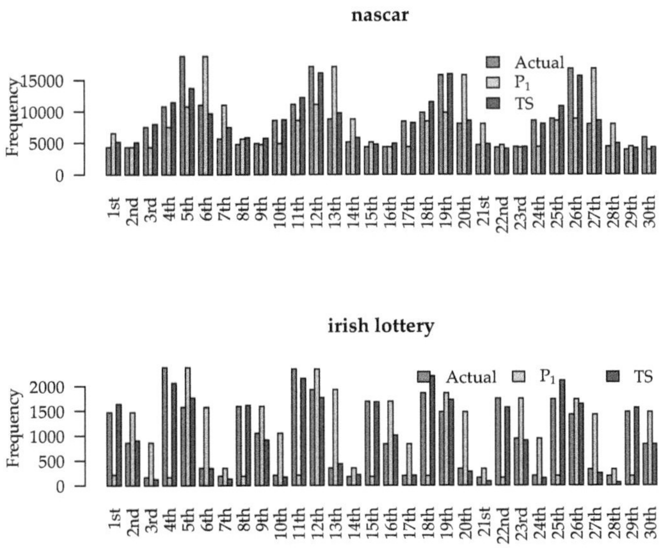

Figure 7: (Top) The actual daily frequencies and the predicted values by P_1 (SMAPE ≈ 0.19) and TS (SMAPE $\approx$ 0.06) for query *nascar* in June 2011. (Bottom) Same data for query *irish lottery* by P_1 (SMAPE ≈ 0.52), and TS (MAE $\approx$ 0.09). TS is more successful in modeling the periodic trends.

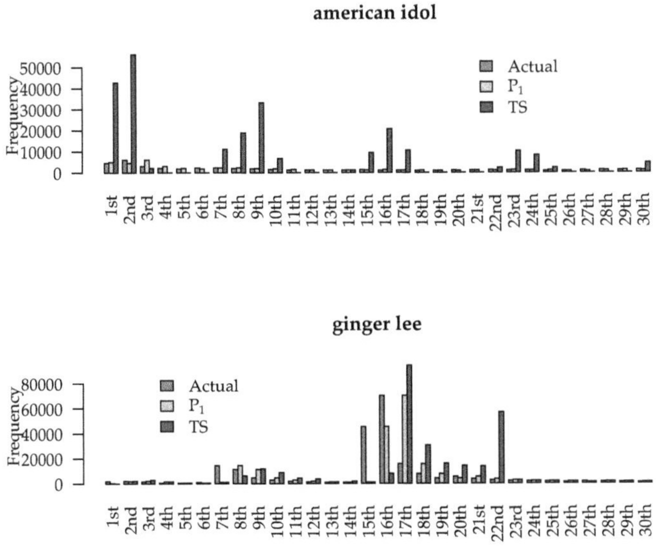

Figure 8: (Top) The actual daily frequencies and the predicted values by P_1 (MAE ≈ 0.08) and TS (MAE ≈ 0.81) for query *american idol* in June 2011. (Bottom) Same data for query *ginger lee* by P_1 (SMAPE ≈ 0.26), and TS (SMAPE $\approx$ 0.40). P_1 reacts to quick changes of popularity more effectively.

models for future work. At each time interval t, we test the performance of — P_1 and MS — forecast models at times $t-\tau, t-2\tau, ..., t-k\tau$ as long as they are included in the validation segment. We then pick the model that wins more often on the selected months. We break any tie by backing off to the model that has lower SMAPE on the entire validation set. In nutshell, the validation step reduces the risk of using time-series forecast models that overfit their smoothing parameters to fit an unexpected recent burst. Note that the corrections achieved by model selection still cannot cover the opposite cases such as *american idol* where the popularity suddenly drops.

On the D-W testbed, we used the daily frequencies in May 2011, and on the M-A testbed we used the monthly values between 2009–2010 as our validation sets. The overall error rates obtained by TMS on these testbeds can be respectively found in Tables 1 and 2. On the M-A testbed, temporal selection boosts both metrics. On the D-W testbed TMS leads to further improvements in MAE but it negatively affects SMAPE. The daily and monthly error rates in Figures 5 and 6 are consistent with the overall numbers.

In summary, our experiments suggest that despite the common assumption, aggregated query frequencies may not provide a good proxy for future popularity. Although aggregation based on fresher data is generally more effective, it still fails to predict the popularity of periodic queries. Our forecasts based on time-series analysis, and temporal model selection consistently outperform the aggregated baselines on both testbeds. In the next section, we show how improvements in forecast accuracy leads to better QAC ranking.

7. TIME-SENSITIVE QAC RANKING

We pick P_1 as the best aggregated model to form the best case for *MostPopularCompletion* (MCP) [2] baseline in our QAC experiments. At each time t (day/month), we rank the QAC candidates according to their frequency at time $t-1$ and compare them against the oracle ranking generated by the true frequency values at time t. We also use the forecasts produced by the TS and TMS models to generate two time-sensitive QAC rankings for each query.

QAC Candidates. We extract the QAC prefixes and candidates from the same query log described in Section 4. For each prefix $\mathcal{P}$ at time t, we match all the queries that start with $\mathcal{P}$ and rank them according to their true frequency at time t to generate the ground-truth ranking. We filter out all prefixes that have fewer than 3 characters, and those that have less than 5 candidates. For each forecast method at time t, we rank the top-20 ground-truth candidates based on the data available at time $t-1$ and before. Those ground-truth candidates that are observed for the first time in the logs at time t and did not exist before are omitted.

Results. Table 4 contains the evaluation results for ranking QAC candidates based on different prediction models. On the D-W testbed 30 rankings are generated for each prefix, one for each day in June 2011. Similarly, on the M-A testbed, each prefix is used to generate 6 QAC rankings, one for each month during January–June 2011. The numbers in the table are averaged across all queries and over the entire testing period. All pairwise differences are detected as statistically significant for both evaluation metrics.

The MRR and Spearman (ρ) results in Table 4 closely follow patterns to observed for SMAPE error rates in our previous experiments. On the D-W testbed in Table 5 we saw that TS had lower error rates than TMS and they both produced significantly more accurate predictions compared to P_1. The same can be observed when comparing the QAC lists generated based on their forecast values. TS has the edge over TMS while P_1 performs significantly poorer than both. Similarly, the SMAPE numbers in Table 6 suggested that TMS produces the most accurate forecasts on the M-A testbed. Here the results in Table 4 confirm that indeed these more accurate forecasts lead to higher quality QAC rankings.

We also computed the Pearson coefficient (r) between the average forecast error rates of the top five QAC suggestions and the final ρ and MRR values computed for those rankings. As expected, the Pearson coefficient suggests a negative correlation between the quality of QAC rankings and the average forecast errors of the top five candidates ($r \approx -0.17$ for SMAPE-Spearman and $r \approx -0.21$ for SMAPE-MRR).

Once again, time-series modeling is a key factor for better QAC ranking. Time-sensitive models such as TS and TMS are able to choose between *big east conference* and *big east tournament*, or between *when to plant tulips* and *when to plant tomatoes* depending on the time of query, while methods based on aggregated data constantly fall behind.

8. CONCLUSIONS

We proposed a new time-sensitive query auto-completion model in which the ranking of query suggestions varies according to their predicted popularity at the time of query.

Table 4: The effectiveness of QAC rankings produced according to different forecast models on the D-W (left) and M-A (right) testbeds. The best performing method in each experiment is specified by an underline. All pairwise differences are detected as statistically significant by the t-test ($p < 0.01$).

	D-W Testbed		M-A Testbed	
	Spearman (ρ)	MRR	Spearman (ρ)	MRR
MCP(P_1)	0.569	0.763	0.607	0.867
MCP(TS)	<u>0.623</u>	<u>0.803</u>	0.597	0.868
MCP(TMS)	0.611	0.796	<u>0.618</u>	<u>0.873</u>

We leveraged time-series techniques to predict the query popularity and showed that such methods consistently outperform different baselines that use aggregated data. We also demonstrated that predictions based on aggregated frequency over a long period are usually worse than those made on smaller but more recent data. Finally, we showed that using more accurate query popularity predictions produced by time-series modeling leads to higher quality auto-completion query suggestions.

As feature work, a mixture model produced by fitting several time-series models simultaneously (with different values of τ) may improve the quality of predictions. Last but not least, similar analysis can be done for different levels of granularity such as hourly intervals.

9. REFERENCES

[1] E. Alfonseca, M. Ciaramita, and K. Hall. Gazpacho and summer rash: lexical relationships from temporal patterns of web search queries. In *Proc. Conf. Empirical Methods in NLP*, pages 1046–1055, Singapore, 2009.

[2] Z. Bar-Yossef and N. Kraus. Context-sensitive query auto-completion. In *Proc. WWW*, pages 107–116, Hyderabad, India, 2011.

[3] R. Baraglia, F. M. Nardini, C. Castillo, R. Perego, D. Donato, and F. Silvestri. The effects of time on query flow graph-based models for query suggestion. In *Proc. RIAO*, pages 182–189, Paris, France, 2010.

[4] S. M. Beitzel, E. C. Jensen, A. Chowdhury, D. Grossman, and O. Frieder. Hourly analysis of a very large topically categorized web query log. In *Proc. SIGIR*, pages 321–328, Sheffield, United Kingdom, 2004.

[5] K. Berberich, S. Bedathur, O. Alonso, and G. Weikum. A language modeling approach for temporal information needs. In *Proc. ECIR*, pages 13–25, Milton Keynes, UK, 2010.

[6] S. Bickel, P. Haider, and T. Scheffer. Learning to complete sentences. In *Proc. ECML*, pages 497–504. 2005.

[7] D. M. Blei, A. Y. Ng, and M. I. Jordan. Latent dirichlet allocation. *J. Mach. Learn. Res.*, 3:993–1022, Mar. 2003.

[8] S. Chaudhuri and R. Kaushik. Extending autocompletion to tolerate errors. In *Proc. SIGMOD*, pages 707–718, Providence, Rhode Island, USA, 2009.

[9] S. Chien and N. Immorlica. Semantic similarity between search engine queries using temporal correlation. In *Proc. WWW*, pages 2–11, Chiba, Japan, 2005.

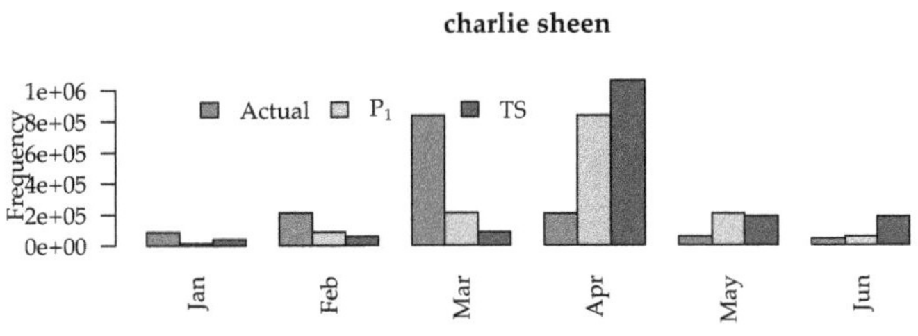

Figure 10: (left) The actual daily frequencies and the predicted values by P_1 (SMAPE ≈ 0.51) and TS (SMAPE ≈ 0.60) for query *charlie sheen* between Jan–Jun 2011. (right) Same data for query *royal wedding* by P_1 (MAE ≈ 0.58), and TS (SMAPE $\approx$ 0.59). P_1 reacts to quick changes of popularity more effectively.

[10] H. Cho and H. Varian. Predicting the present with google trends. Technical report, Google Inc, April 2009.

[11] N. Dai and B. D. Davison. Freshness matters: in flowers, food, and web authority. In *Proc. SIGIR*, pages 114–121, Geneva, Switzerland, 2010.

[12] N. Dai, M. Shokouhi, and B. D. Davison. Learning to rank for freshness and relevance. In *Proc. SIGIR*, pages 95–104, Beijing, China, 2011.

[13] J. J. Darragh, I. H. Witten, and M. L. James. The reactive keyboard: A predictive typing aid. *Computer*, 23:41–49, November 1990.

[14] A. Dong, R. Zhang, P. Kolari, J. Bai, F. Diaz, Y. Chang, Z. Zheng, and H. Zha. Time is of the essence: improving recency ranking using twitter data. In *Proc. WWW*, pages 331–340, Raleigh, North Carolina, USA, 2010.

[15] M. Efron. Linear time series models for term weighting in information retrieval. *J. Am. Soc. Inf. Sci. Technol.*, 61, July 2010.

[16] J. L. Elsas and S. T. Dumais. Leveraging temporal dynamics of document content in relevance ranking. In *Proc. WSDM*, 2010.

[17] J. Fan, H. Wu, G. Li, and L. Zhou. Suggesting topic-based query terms as you type. In *Proc. APWEB*, pages 61–67, Washington, DC, 2010.

[18] K. Grabski and T. Scheffer. Sentence completion. In *Proc. SIGIR*, pages 433–439, Sheffield, United Kingdom, 2004.

[19] C. C. Holt. Forecasting seasonals and trends by exponentially weighted moving averages. *International Journal of Forecasting*, 20(1):5–10, 2004.

[20] S. Ji, G. Li, C. Li, and J. Feng. Efficient interactive fuzzy keyword search. In *Proc. WWW*, pages 371–380, Madrid, Spain, 2009.

[21] R. Jones and F. Diaz. Temporal profiles of queries. *ACM Trans. Inf. Syst.*, 25, July 2007.

[22] N. Kanhabua and K. Nørvåg. Determining time of queries for re-ranking search results. In *Proc. ECDL*, 2010.

[23] A. Kulkarni, J. Teevan, K. M. Svore, and S. T. Dumais. Understanding temporal query dynamics. In *Proc. WSDM*, pages 167–176, Hong Kong, China, 2011.

[24] X. Li and W. B. Croft. Time-based language models. In *cikm*, pages 469–475, 2003.

[25] N. Liu, J. Yan, S. Yan, W. Fan, and Z. Chen. Web query prediction by unifying model. In *Proc. IEEE Int. Conf. Data Mining Workshops*, pages 436–441, Washington, DC, USA, 2008.

[26] D. Metzler, R. Jones, F. Peng, and R. Zhang. Improving search relevance for implicitly temporal queries. In *Proc. SIGIR*, pages 700–701, Boston, MA, USA, 2009.

[27] A. Nandi and H. V. Jagadish. Effective phrase prediction. In *Proc. VLDB*, pages 219–230, Vienna, Austria, 2007.

[28] P. L. R. Byrd and J. Nocedal. *SIAM Journal on Scientific and Statistical Computing*, 16(5):1190–1208, 1995.

[29] K. Radinsky, K. M. Svore, J. Teevan, S. T. Dumais, A. Bocharov, and E. Horvitz. Learning and predicting behavioral dynamics on the web. In *Proc. of WWW*, pages to-appear, 2011.

[30] Y. Shimshoni, N. Efron, and Y. Matias. On the predictability of search trends. Technical report, Google Inc, August 2009.

[31] M. Shokouhi. Detecting seasonal queries by time-series analysis. In *Proc. SIGIR*, pages 1171–1172, Beijing, China, 2011.

[32] M. Vlachos, C. Meek, Z. Vagena, and D. Gunopulos. Identifying similarities, periodicities and bursts for online search queries. pages 131–142, Paris, France, 2004.

[33] R. W. White and G. Marchionini. Examining the effectiveness of real-time query expansion. *Inf. Process. Manage.*, 43:685–704, May 2007.

[34] R. Zhang, Y. Chang, Z. Zheng, D. Metzler, and J.-y. Nie. Search result re-ranking by feedback control adjustment for time-sensitive query. In *Proc. NAACL-Short*, pages 165–168, Boulder, Colorado, 2009. Association for Computational Linguistics.

A Generalized Hidden Markov Model with Discriminative Training for Query Spelling Correction

Yanen Li, Huizhong Duan and ChengXiang Zhai

Department of Computer Science, University of Illinois at Urbana-Champaign, Urbana, IL 61801
{yanenli2, duan9, czhai}@illinois.edu

ABSTRACT

Query spelling correction is a crucial component of modern search engines. Existing methods in the literature for search query spelling correction have two major drawbacks. First, they are unable to handle certain important types of spelling errors, such as concatenation and splitting. Second, they cannot efficiently evaluate all the candidate corrections due to the complex form of their scoring functions, and a heuristic filtering step must be applied to select a working set of top-K most promising candidates for final scoring, leading to non-optimal predictions. In this paper we address both limitations and propose a novel generalized Hidden Markov Model with discriminative training that can not only handle all the major types of spelling errors, including splitting and concatenation errors, in a single unified framework, but also efficiently evaluate all the candidate corrections to ensure the finding of a globally optimal correction. Experiments on two query spelling correction datasets demonstrate that the proposed generalized HMM is effective for correcting multiple types of spelling errors. The results also show that it significantly outperforms the current approach for generating top-K candidate corrections, making it a better first-stage filter to enable any other complex spelling correction algorithm to have access to a better working set of candidate corrections as well as to cover splitting and concatenation errors, which few existing method in academic literature can correct.

Categories and Subject Descriptors

H.3.3 [**Information Storage and Retrieval**]: Information Search and Retrieval—*Query Alteration*

Keywords

Query Spelling Correction, Generalized Hidden Markov Models, Discriminative Training for HMMs

1. INTRODUCTION

The ability to automatically correct potentially misspelled queries has become an indispensable component of modern search engines. People make errors in spelling frequently. Particularly, search engine users are more likely to commit misspellings in their queries as they are in most scenarios exploring unfamiliar contents. Automatic spelling correction for queries helps the search engine to better understand the users' intents and can therefore improve the quality of search experience. However, query spelling is not an easy task, especially under the strict efficiency constraint. In Table 1 we summarize major types of misspellings in real search engine queries. Users not only make typos on single words, (insertion, deletion and substitution), but can also easily mess up with word boundaries (concatenation and splitting). Moreover, different types of misspelling could be committed in the same query, making it even harder to correct. Unfortunately,

Table 1: Major Types of Query Spelling Errors

Type		Example	Correction
In-Word	Insertion	esspresso	espresso
	Deletion	vollyball	volleyball
	Substitution	comtemplate	contemplate
	Mis-use	capital hill	capitol hill
Cross-Word	Concatenation	intermilan	inter milan
	Splitting	power point	powerpoint

no existing query spelling correction approaches in the literature are able to correct all major types of errors, especially for correcting splitting and concatenation errors. To the best of my knowledge, the only work that can potentially address this problem is [24] in which a Conditional Random Field (CRF) model is proposed to handle a broad set of query refinements. However, this work considers query correction and splitting/merging as different tasks, hence it is unable to correct queries with mixed types of errors, such as substitution and splitting errors in one query. In fact splitting and merging are two important error types in query spelling correction, and a major research challenge of query spelling correction is to accurately correct all major types of errors simultaneously. On the other hand, while modern industrial systems such as Google can handle this problem relatively well, it's unclear what they have done, especially what resources they have employed in order to solve the challenges.

Another major difficulty in automatic query spelling correction is the huge search space. Theoretically, any sequence of characters could potentially be the correction of a misspelled query. It is clearly intractable to enumerate and evaluate all possible sequences for the purpose of finding the correct query. Thus a more feasible strategy is to search in a space of all combinations of candidate words that are in a neighborhood of each query word based on editing distance. The assumption is that a user's spelling error of each single word is unlikely too dramatic, thus the correction is most likely in the neighborhood by editing distance. Unfortunately, even in this restricted space, the current approaches still cannot enumerate and evaluate all the candidates because their scoring functions involve complex features that are expensive to compute. As a result, a separate filtering step must first be used to prune the search space so that the final scoring can be done on a small working set of candidates. Take [7] as a two-stage method example, in the first stage, a Viterbi or A* search algorithm is used to generate a small set of most promising candidates, and in the second stage different types of features of the candidates are computed and a ranker is employed to score the candidates. However, this two-stage strategy has a major drawback in computing the complete working set. Since the filtering stage uses a non-optimal objective function to ensure efficiency, it is quite possible that the best candidate is filtered out in the first stage, especially because we cannot afford a large working set since the correction must be done online while a user is entering a query. The inability of searching the complete space of candidates leads to non-optimal correction accuracy.

In this paper, we propose a generalized Hidden Markov Model (gHMM) for query spelling correction that can address deficiencies of the existing approaches discussed above. The proposed gHMM can model all major types of spelling errors, thus enabling consideration of multiple types of errors in query spelling correction. In the proposed gHMM, the hidden states represent the correct forms of words, and the outcomes are the observed (potentially) misspelled terms. In addition, each state is associated with a type, indicating merging, splitting or in-word transformation operation. The proposed HMM is generalized in the sense that it would allow adjustment of both emission probabilities and transition probabilities to accommodate the non-optimal parameter estimation. Unfortunately, such an extension of HMM makes it impossible to use a standard EM algorithm for parameter estimation. To solve this problem, we propose a perceptron-based discriminative training method to train the parameters in the HMM.

Moreover, a Viterbi-like search algorithm for top-K paths is designed to efficiently obtain a small number of highly confident correction candidates. This algorithm can handle splitting/merging of multiple words. It takes into account major types of local features such as error model, language model, and state type information. The error model is trained on a large set of query correction pairs from the web. And web scale language model is obtained by leveraging the Microsoft Web N-gram service [1].

We conducted extensive evaluation on our proposed gHMM. For this purpose, we have constructed a query correction dataset from real search logs, which has been made publicly available. Experimental results verify that the gHMM can effectively correct all major types of query spelling errors. It also reveal that the gHMM can run as efficient as the common used noisy channel model, while it achieves much better results for obtaining the candidate space of query corrections. Therefore, in addition to being used as standing alone query correction module, the proposed gHMM can also be used as a more effective first-stage filtering module to more effectively support any other complicated scoring functions such as those using complex global features.

2. RELATED WORK

Spelling correction has a long history [8]. Traditional spellers focused on dealing with non-word errors caused by misspelling a known word as an invalid word form. A common strategy at that time was to utilize a trusted lexicon and certain distance measures, such as Levenshtein distance [13]. The size of lexicon in traditional spellers is usually small due to the high cost of manual construction of lexicon. Consequently, many valid word forms such as human names and neologisms are rarely included in the lexicon. Later, statistical generative models were introduced for spelling correction, in which the error model and n-gram language model are identified as two critical components. Brill and Moore demonstrated that a better statistical error model is crucial for improving a speller's accuracy [3]. But building such an error model requires a large set of manually annotated word correction pairs, which is expensive to obtain. Whitelaw *et al.* alleviated this problem by leveraging the Web to automatically discover the misspelled/corrected word pairs [12].

With the advent of the Web, the research on spelling correction has received much more attention, particularly on the correction of search engine queries. Many research challenges are raised, which are non-existent in traditional settings of spelling correction. More specifically, there are many more types of spelling errors in search queries, such as misspelling, concatenation/splitting of query words, and misuse of legitimate yet inappropriate words. Research in this direction includes utilizing large web corpora and query log [4, 5, 2], training phrase-based error model from clickthrough data [10] and developing additional features [7]. However, two important challenges are under addressed in these approaches, i.e., correcting splitting and concatenation errors, and ensuring complete search in the candidate space to evaluate an effective scoring function.

Query alteration/refinement is a broader topic which naturally subsumes query spelling correction. Beside correcting the misspelled query, query alteration/refinement also need to modify the ineffective query so that it could be more suitable for the search intent. For this purpose, many research topics have been studied. Query expansion expands the query with additional terms to enrich the query formulation [14, 15, 16]. Query segmentation divides a query into semantically meaningful sub-units [17, 18]. Other query reformulation methods intend to replace the inappropriate query terms with effective keywords to bridge the vocabulary gaps [19]. Particularly, there is research attempt [24] to use a unified model to do a broad set of query refinements such as correction, segmentation and even stemming. However, it treats query correction and splitting/merging as separate tasks, which is not true for real world queries. Also, it has very limited ability for query correction. For example, it only allows one letter difference in deletion/insertion/substitution errors.

Query spelling correction also shares similarities with many other NLP tasks, such as speech recognition and machine translation. In many of these applications, HMM has been found very useful [21, 20]. Our generalized HMM model for query spelling correction is novel in that it models all the major types of misspellings in a unified framework. A discrete training method is also proposed to train the parameters in the model. It is demonstrated that the gHMM model we use is very effective for the task of query spelling correction.

3. PROBLEM SETUP AND CHALLENGES

Formally, let Σ be the alphabet of a language and $L \subset \Sigma^+$ be a large lexicon of the language. We define the query spelling correction problem as:

Given a query $q \in \Sigma^+$, generate top-K most effective corrections $Y = (y^1, y^2, ..., y^k)$ where $y^i \in L^+$ is a candidate correction, and Y is sorted according to the probability of y^i being the correct spelling of the target query.

It is worth noting that from a search engine perspective, the ideal output Y should be sorted according to the probability of y^i retrieving the most satisfying results in search. However, in practice it is very difficult to measure the satisfaction as unlike in *ad hoc* retrieval where the query is given in its correct form, here the real query is unknown. As a result, different corrections could simply lead to queries with different meanings and it would be very subjective to determine which query actually satisfies the user. In this paper, we are mostly concerned with the lexical and semantic correctness of queries with the assumption that correction of mis-spelled query terms most likely would lead to improved retrieval accuracy.

The problem of query spelling correction is significantly harder than the traditional spelling correction. Previous researches show that approximately 10-15% of search queries contain spelling errors [5]. First, it is difficult to cover all the different types of errors. The spelling errors generally fall into one of the following four categories: (1) in-word transformation, e.g. insertion, deletion, misspelling of characters. This type of error is most frequent in web queries, and it is not uncommon that up to 3 or 4 letters are misspelled; (2) mis-use of valid word, e.g. "persian golf" → "persian gulf". It is also a type of in-word tranformation errors; (3) concatenation of multiple words, e.g. "unitedstatesofamerica" → "united states of america"; (4) splitting a word into parts, e.g. "power point slides" → "powerpoint slides". Among all these types, the splitting and concatenation errors are especially challenging to correct. Indeed, no existing approaches in the academic literature can correct these two types of errors. Yet, it's important to correct all types of errors because users might commit different types of errors or even commit these errors at the same time. A main goal of this work is to develop a new HMM framework that can model and correct all major types of errors including splitting and concatenation.

Second, it is difficult to ensure complete search of all the candidate space because the candidate space is very large. The existing work addresses this challenge by using a two-stage method, which searches for a small set of candidates with simple scoring functions and do re-ranking on top of these candidates. Unfortunately, the simple scoring function used in the first stage cannot ensure that the nominated candidate corrections in the first stage always contain the best correction, thus no matter how effective the final scoring function is, we may miss the best correction simply because of the use of two separate stages. In this paper, we address this challenge by developing a generalized HMM that can both be efficiently scored to ensure complete search in the candidate space and accurately correct all types of errors in a unified way.

4. A GENERALIZED HMM FOR QUERY SPELLING CORRECTION

Our algorithm accepts a query as input, and then generates a small list of ranked corrections as output by a generalized Hidden Markov Model (gHMM). It is trained by a discriminative method with labeled spelling examples. Given a query, it scores candidate spelling corrections in a one-stage fashion and outputs the top-K corrections, without using a re-ranking strategy. Other components of our algorithm include a large clean lexicon, the error model and the language model. In this section we will focus on the gHMM model structure, the discriminative training of it, as well as the efficient computation of spelling corrections.

4.1 The gHMM Model Structure

We propose a generalized HMM Model to model the spelling correction problem. We call it a generalized HMM because there are several important differences between it and the standard HMM model which will be explained later. Without loss of generality, let an input query be $q = q_{[1:n]}$ and a corresponding correction be $y = y_{[1:m]}$ where n, m are the length of the query and correction, which might or might not be equal. Here we introduce hidden state sequence $z = z_{[1:n]} = (s_1, s_2, ..., s_n)$ in which z and q have the same length. An individual state s_i is represented by a phrase corresponding to one or more terms in correction $y_{[1:m]}$. Together the phrase representing z is equal to y. Therefore, finding best-K corrections $Y = (y^1, y^2, ..., y^k)$ is equivalent to finding best-K state sequences $Z = (z^1, z^2, ..., z^k)$. In addition, there is a type t associated with each state, indicating the operation such as substitution, splitting, merging *etc.* Also, in order to facilitate the merging state we introduce a NULL state. The NULL state is represented by an empty string, and it doesn't emit any phrase. There can be multiple consecutive NULL states followed by a merging state. Table 2 summarizes the state types and the spelling errors they correspond to. Having the hidden states defined, the hypothesized process of observing a mis-spelled query is as follows:

1. sample a state s_1 and state type t_1 from the state space Ω and the type set T;
2. emit a word in q_1, or empty string if the s_1 is a NULL state according to the type specific error model;
3. transit to s_2 with type t_2 according to the state transition distribution, and emit another word, or multiple words in $q_{[1:n]}$ if s_2 is a merging state;
4. continue until the whole (potentially) mis-spelled query q is observed.

Figure 1 illustrates our gHMM model with a concrete example. In this example, there are three potential errors with different error types, e.g. "goverment" → "government" (substitution), "home page" → "homepage" (splitting), "illinoisstate" → "illinois state" (concatenation). The state path shown in Figure 1 is one of the state sequences

Table 2: State Types in gHMM

State Type	Operation	Spelling Errors
In-word Transformation	Deletion	Insertion
	Insertion	Deletion
	Substitution	Substitution
Mis-use	Transformation	Word Mis-use
Merging	Merge Multiple Words	Splitting
Splitting	Split one Word to Multiple Words	Concatenation

that can generate the query. Take state s_3 for example, s_3 is represented by phrase *homepage*. Since s_3 is a merging state, it emits a phrase *home page* with probability $P(home\ page|homepage)$. And s_3 is transited from state s_2 with probability $P(s_3|s_2)$. With this model, we are able to come up with arbitrary corrections instead of limiting ourselves to an incomprehensive set of queries from query log. By simultaneously modeling the misspellings on word boundaries, we are able to correct the query in a more integrated manner.

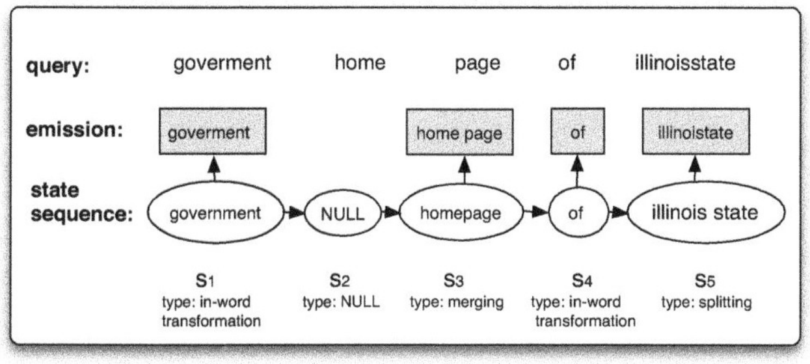

Figure 1: Illustration of the gHMM Model

4.2 Generalization of HMM Scoring Function

For a standard HMM [23], let $\theta = \{A, B, \pi\}$ be the model parameters of the HMM, representing the transition probability, emission probabilities and initial state probabilities respectively. Given a list of query words $q_{[1:n]}$ (obtained by splitting empty spaces), the state sequence $z^* = (s_1^*, s_2^*, ..., s_n^*)$ that best explains $q_{[1:n]}$ can be calculated by:

$$z^* = \arg\max_z P(z|q_{[1:n]}, A, B, \pi) \qquad (1)$$

However, theoretically the phrase in a state can be chosen arbitrarily, so estimating $\{A, B, \pi\}$ is such a large space is almost impossible in the standard HMM framework. In order to overcome this difficulty, the generalized Hidden Markov Model proposed in this work generalizes the standard HMM as follows: (1) gHMM introduces state type for each state, which indicates the correction operations and can reduce the search space effectively; (2) it adopts feature functions to parameterize the measurement of probability of a state sequence given a query. Such treatment can not only map the transition and emission probabilities to feature functions with a small set of parameters, but can also add additional feature functions such as the ones incorporating state type information. Another important benefit of the feature function representation is that we can use discriminative training on the model with labeled spelling corrections, which will lead to a more accurate estimation of the parameters.

Formally, in our gHMM model, there is an one-to-one relationship between states in a state sequence and words in the original query. For a given query $q = q_{[1:n]}$ and the sequence of states $z = (s_1, s_2, ..., s_n)$, we define a context h_i for every state in which an individual correction decision is made. The context is defined as $h_i =< s_{i-1}, t_{i-1}, s_i, t_i, q_{[1:n]} >$ where $s_{i-1}, t_{i-1}, s_i, t_i$ are the previous and current state and type decisions and $q_{[1:n]}$ are all query words.

The generalized HMM model measures the probability of a state sequence by defining feature vectors on the context-state pairs. A feature vector is a function that maps a context-state pair to a d-dimensional vector. Each component of the feature vector is an arbitrary function operated on (h, z). Particularly, in this study we define 2 kinds of feature vectors, one is $\phi_j(s_{i-1}, t_{i-1}, s_i, t_i), j = 1...d$, which measures the interdependency of adjacent states. We can map this function to a kind of transition probability measurement. The other kind of feature function, $f_k(s_i, t_i, q_{[1:n]}), k = 1...d'$ measures the dependency of the state and its observation. We can consider it as a kind of emission probability in the standard HMM point of view. Such feature vector representation of HMM is introduced by Collins [22] and successfully applied to the POS tagging problem.

Specifically, we have designed several feature functions as follows: we define a function of $\phi(s_{i-1}, t_{i-1}, s_i, t_i)$ as

$$\phi_1(s_{i-1}, t_{i-1}, s_i, t_i) = logP_{LM}(s_i|s_{i-1}, t_{i-1}, t_i) \qquad (2)$$

to measure the language model probabilities of two consecutive states. Where $P_{LM}(s_i|s_{i-1})$ is the bigram probability calculated by using Microsoft Web N-gram Service [1]. The computation of $P_{LM}(s_i|s_{i-1})$ may depend on the state types, such as in a merging state.

We have also defined a set of functions in the form of $f_k(s_i, t_i, q_{[1:n]})$, which are dependent on the query words and state type, measuring the emission probability of a state. For example, we define

$$f_1(s_i, t_i, q_{[1:n]}) = \begin{cases} logP_{err}(s_i, q_i) & \text{if } q_i \text{ is in-word transformed to } s_i \textbf{ and } q_i \notin \text{Lexicon } L \\ 0 & \text{otherwise} \end{cases} \qquad (3)$$

as a function measuring the emission probability given the state type is in-word transformation and q_i is out of dictionary. e.g. "goverment" → "government". $P_{err}(s_i, q_i)$ is the emission probability computed by an error model which measures the probability of mis-typing "government" to "goverment". (see Section 5.2).

$$f_2(s_i, t_i, q_{[1:n]}) = \begin{cases} logP_{err}(s_i, q_i) & \text{if } t_i \text{ is splitting } \textbf{and } q_i \in \text{Lexicon } L \\ 0 & \text{otherwise} \end{cases} \qquad (4)$$

to capture the emission probability if the state is of splitting type and q_i is in dictionary. e.g. "homepage" → "home page".

$$f_3(s_i, t_i, q_{[1:n]}) = \begin{cases} logP_{err}(s, q_i) & \text{if } t_i \text{ is Mis-use} \\ & \textbf{and } q_i \in \text{Lexicon } L \\ 0 & \text{otherwise} \end{cases} \tag{5}$$

to get the emission probability if a valid word is transformed to another valid word.

Note that in Equation (3), (4), and (5), we use the same error model $P_{err}(s_i, q_i)$ (see Section 5.2 for detail) to model the emission probabilities from merging, splitting errors *etc.* in the same way as in-word transformation errors. However we assign different weights to the transformation probabilities resulted from different error types via discriminative training on a set of labeled query-correction pairs.

Overall, we have designed a set of feature functions that are all relied on local dependencies, ensuring that the top-K state sequences can be computed efficiently by Dynamic Programming.

After establishing the feature vector representation, the log-probability of a state sequence and its corresponding types $logP(z, t|q_{[1:n]})$ is proportional to:

$$Score(z,t) = \sum_{i=1}^{n}\sum_{j=1}^{d} \lambda_j \phi_j(s_{i-1}, t_{i-1}, s_i, t_i) + \sum_{i=1}^{n}\sum_{k=1}^{d'} \mu_k f_k(s_i, t_i, q_{[1:n]}) \tag{6}$$

where λ_j, μ_k are the component coefficients needed to be estimated. And the best state sequence can be found by:

$$z^* t^* = \arg\max_{z,t} Score(z,t) \tag{7}$$

Note that the form of $Score(z,t)$ is similar to the objective function of a Conditional Random Field model [26], but with an important difference that there is no normalization terms in our model. Such difference also enables the efficient search of top-K state sequences (equivalent to top-K corrections) using Dynamic Programming, which will be introduced shortly.

4.3 Discriminative Training

Motivated by ideas introduced in [22], we propose a perceptron algorithm to train the gHMM model. To the best of our knowledge, this is the first attempt to use discriminative approach to train a HMM on the problem of query spelling correction. Now we describe how to estimate the parameters λ_j, μ_k from a set of <query, spelling correction> pairs. The estimation procedure follows the perceptron learning framework. Take the λ_j for example. We first set all the λ_j at random. For each query q, we search for the most likely state sequence with types $z^i_{[1:n_i]}, t^i_{[1:n_i]}$ using the current parameter settings. Such search process is described in Algorithm 2 by setting $K = 1$. After that, if the best decoded sequence is not correct, we update λ_j by simple addition: we promote the amount of λ_j by adding up ϕ_j values computed between the query and labeled correction y', and demote the amount of λ_j by the sum of all ϕ_j values computed between the query and the top-ranked predictions. We repeat this process for several iterations until converge. Finally in step 11 and 12, we average all $\lambda_j^{o,i}$ in each iteration to get the final estimate of λ_j, where $\lambda_j^{o,i}$ is the stored value for the parameter λ_j after i's training example is processed in iteration o. Similar procedures can apply to μ_k. The detailed steps are listed in Algorithm *1*. Note that in step 7 and 8 the feature functions $\phi_j(q^i, y'^i, t'^i)$ and $f_k(q^i, y'^i, t'^i)$ depend on unknown types t'^i that are inferred by computing the best word-level alignment between q^i and y'^i.

Algorithm 1: Discriminative Training of gHMM

input : A set of <query, spelling correction> pairs $q^i_{[1:n_i]}, y'^i_{[1:m_i]}$ for $i = 1...n$
output: Optimal estimate of $\hat{\lambda}_j, \hat{\mu}_k$, where $j \in \{1, ..., d\}, k \in \{1, ..., d'\}$

1 Init Set $\hat{\lambda}_j, \hat{\mu}_k$ to random numbers;
2 **for** $o \leftarrow 1$ **to** O **do**
3   **for** $i \leftarrow 1$ **to** n **do**
    /* identify the best state sequence and the associated types of the i'th query with the current parameters via Algorithm 2: */
4     $z^i_{[1:n_i]}, t^i_{[1:n_i]} = \arg\max_{u_{[1:n_i]}, t_{[1:n_i]}} Score(u,t)$
    /* where $u_{[1:n_i]} \in \mathbb{S}^{n_i}$, $\mathbb{S}^{n_i}$ is all possible state sequences given $q^i_{[1:n_i]}$ */
5   **if** $z^i_{[1:n_i]} \neq y'^i_{[1:m_i]}$ **then**
6   update and store every λ_j, μ_k according to:
7       $\lambda_j = \lambda_j + \sum_{i=1}^{n_i} \phi_j(q^i, y'^i, t'^i) - \sum_{i=1}^{n_i} \phi_j(q^i, z^i, t^i)$
8       $\mu_k = \mu_k + \sum_{i=1}^{n_i} f_k(q^i, y'^i, t'^i) - \sum_{i=1}^{n_i} f_k(q^i, z^i, t^i)$
9   **else**
10   Do nothing

/* Average the final parameters by: */
11 $\hat{\lambda}_j = \sum_{o=1}^{O} \sum_{i=1}^{n} \lambda_j^{o,i} / nO$, where $j \in \{1, ..., d\}$
12 $\hat{\mu}_k = \sum_{o=1}^{O} \sum_{i=1}^{n} \mu_k^{o,i} / nO$, where $k \in \{1, ..., d'\}$
13 **return** parameters $\hat{\lambda}_j, \hat{\mu}_k$;

This discriminative training algorithm will converge after several iterations. Here we state the following theorem on its convergence:

Theorem 1: For any training example (q^i, y'^i) which is separable with margin δ, then for Algorithm 1:

$$\text{Number of mistakes} \leq \frac{R^2}{\delta^2}$$

where R is a constant satisfying

$$\forall i, \forall z \in \{G(q^i) - \{y'^i\}\} : ||\Phi(q^i, y'^i, t'^i) - \Phi(q^i, z^i, t^i)|| \leq R,$$

where $G(q^i)$ is a set of predictions generated by Algorithm 2, and the Φ functions can be calculated from *Eq.* (6) by ignoring λ and μ. The proof of **Theorem 1** is not shown due to the space limitation.

4.4 Query Correction Computation

Once the optimal parameters are obtained by the discriminative training procedure introduced above, the final top-K corrections can be directly computed, avoiding the need for a separate stage of candidate re-ranking. Because the feature functions are only relied on local dependencies, it enables the efficient search of top-K corrections via Dynamic Programming. This procedure involves three major steps: (1) candidate states generation; (2) score function evaluation; (3) filtering.

At the first step, for each word in query q, we generate a set of state candidates with types. The phrase representations in such states are in Lexicon L and within editing distance δ from the query word. Then a set of state sequences are created by combining these states. In addition, for each state sequence we have created, we also create another state sequence by adding a NULL state at the end, facilitating a (potential) following merging state. It is important to note that if the δ is too small, it will compromise the final results due to the premature pruning of state sequences. In this work $\delta = 3$ is chosen in order to introduce adequate possible state sequences.

At the score function evaluation step, we update the scores for each state sequence according to *Eq.* (6). The evaluation is different for sequence with different ending state types. Firstly, for a sequence ending with a NULL state, we don't evaluate the scoring function. Instead, we only need to keep track of the state representation of its previous state. Secondly, for a sequence ending with a merging state, it merges the previous one or more consecutive NULL states. And the scoring function takes into account the information stored in the previous NULL states. For instance, to $\phi_1(s_{i-1}, t_{i-1} = NULL, s_i, t_i = merging)$, we have

$$\phi_1(s_{i-1}, \text{NULL}, s_i, \text{merging}) = logP_{LM}(s_{i-2}|s_i) \tag{8}$$

i.e. skipping the NULL state and pass the previous state representation to the merging state. In this way, we can evaluate the scoring function in multiple consecutive NULL states followed by a merging state, which enables the correction by merging multiple query words. Thirdly, for a sequence ending with a splitting state, the score is accumulated by all bigrams within the splitting state. For example,

$$\begin{aligned} &\phi_1(s_{i-1}, t_{i-1}, s_i, t_i = splitting) \qquad (9) \\ &= logP_{LM}(w_1|s_{i-1}) + \sum_{j=1}^{k-1} logP_{LM}(w_{i+1}|w_i) \end{aligned}$$

where $s_i = w_1 w_2 ... w_k$. On the other hand, the evaluation of $f_k(s_i, t_i, q_{[1:n]})$ is easier because it is not related to previous states. The error model from the state representation to the query word is used to calculate these functions.

At the final step, we filter most of the state sequences and only keep top-K best state sequences in each position corresponding to each query word. In sum, we have proposed and implemented an algorithm via Dynamic Programming (see Algorithm 2) for efficiently computing top-K state sequences (corrections). If there are n words in a query, and the maximum number of candidate states for each query word is M, the computational complexity for finding top-K corrections is $O(n \cdot K \cdot M^2)$.

Algorithm 2: Decoding Top-K Corrections

input : A query $q_{[1:n]}$, parameters $\vec{\lambda}$, $\vec{\mu}$
output: top K state sequences with highest likelihood

/* $Z[i, s_i]$: top K state sequences for sub-query $q_{[1:i]}$ that ending with state s_i. For each $z \in Z[i, s_i]$, *phrase* denotes the representation and *score* denotes the likelihood of z given $q_{[1:i]}$. */
/* $Z[i]$: top state sequences for all $Z[i, s_i]$. */
Init $Z[0] = \{\}$
for $i \leftarrow 1$ **to** n **do**
  /* for term q_i, get all candidate states */
  $S \leftarrow s_i, \forall s_i : edit\_dist(s_i, q_i) \leq \delta$, s_i has type $s_i.type$
  for $s_i \in S$ **do**
    for $z \in Z[i-1]$ **do**
      $a \leftarrow$ new state sequence
      $a.phrase \leftarrow z.phrase \cup \{s_i\}$
      update $a.score$ according to $s_i.type$ and *Eq.* (6), *Eq.* (8) and *Eq.* (9)
      $Z[i, s_i] \leftarrow a$
    /* delay truncation for $NULL$ states */
    if $s_i.type \neq NULL$ *and* $i \neq n$ **then**
      sort $Z[i, s_i]$ by *score*
      truncate $Z[i, s_i]$ to size K
sort $Z[n]$ by *score*
truncate $Z[n]$ to size K
return $Z[n]$;

5. OTHER COMPONENTS

Besides the gHMM model and its discriminative training, our spelling correction algorithm also relies on other important components, such as a large trusted lexicon, the error model, and the language model. In this section we will describe these components.

5.1 A Large-scale Trusted Lexicon

As mentioned in Section 3, how to define a proper lexicon L is important to a successful speller. We find that with a clean vocabulary, it will significantly improve the performance of spelling correction. However, to obtain such a clean vocabulary is usually difficult in practice. To do this, we make use of the Wikipedia data. Particularly, we select the top 2 million words from Wikipedia by their word frequencies, and automatically curate the obtained words by removing those frequent but illegitimate words from the vocabulary. This curate process involves checking if the word appears in the title of a Wikipedia article, comparing the bigram probability of other words etc. Finally we obtained 1.2 million highly reliable words in the vocabulary. Please note that all words in this vocabulary are unigrams; numbers and punctuations are not included. And no stemming and other forms of modification are conducted.

5.2 Error Model Training

Error Model. The feature functions $f_k()$ depend on an error model, which measures the probability that one word is misspelled into another. Previous studies have shown that a weighted editing distance model trained with a sufficient large set of correction pairs could achieve a comparable performance with a sophisticated n-gram model [6]. Meanwhile, a higher order model has greater tendency to overfit if the training data is not large enough. Given these considerations, we adopt the Weighted Edit Distance (WED) to estimate the error model. More specifically, we first compute the best character-level alignment of two words, and the WED between these two words is the summation of the WED of all aligned character pairs. We model the character-level WED as the character transformation probability. In addition, null character is included in the vocabulary to accomodate the insertion and deletion operations. In order to compute such a probability, a large set of query-correction pairs is obtained by leveraging the spelling services from Google and Bing; and then this probability is estimated as the expected number of transformation from one character to another in these aligned pairs. The training queries are from the MSN search query log released by the Microsoft Live Labs in 2006 (6.5 million queries). They are submitted to the spelling ser- vices, and the corrections are recorded once consensus is reached.

5.3 Use of Web N-gram Model

Another important factor in selecting and ranking the correction candidates is the prior probability of a correction phrase. It represents our prior belief about how likely a query will be chosen by the user without seeing any input from the user. In this work we make use of the Web n-gram service provided by Microsoft [1]. Web n-gram model intends to model the n-gram probability of English phrases with the parameters estimated from the entire Web data. It also differentiates the sources of the data to build different language models from the title, anchor text and body of Web pages, as well as the queries from query log. In our study, we find the **title** model is the most effective for query spelling correction. We hypothesize that this may be because the training data for query model is much noisier. Particularly, misspelled queries may be included in the training data, which makes it less effective for the task of spelling correction. Despite trained with the Web data, Web n-gram model may also suffer from data sparseness in higher order models. To avoid this issue, we make use of the **bigram** model in building our spelling system.

6. EXPERIMENTS AND RESULTS

In order to test the effectiveness and efficiency of our proposed gHMM model, in this section we conduct extensive experiments on two web query spelling datasets. We first introduce the datasets, and describe the evaluation metrics we use for evaluation. Then we compare our model with other baselines in terms of accuracy and runtime.

6.1 Dataset Preparation

The experiments are conducted on two query spelling correction datasets. One is the TREC dataset based on the publicly available TREC queries (2008 Million Query Track). This dataset contains 5892 queries and the corresponding corrections annotated by the MSR Speller Challenge [1] organizers. There could be more than one plausible corrections for a query. In this dataset only 5.3% of queries are judged as misspelled.

We have also annotated another dataset that contains 4926 MSN queries, where for each query there is at most one correction. Three experts are involved in the annotation process. For each query, we consult the speller from two major search engines (i.e. Google and Bing). If they agree on the returned results (including the case if the query is just unchanged), we take it as the corrected form of the input query. If the results are not the same from the two, as least one human expert will manually annotate the most likely corrected form of the query. Finally, about 13% of queries are judged as misspelled in this dataset, which is close to the error rate of real web queries. This dataset is publicly available to all researchers.

We divide the TREC and MSN datasets into training and test sets evenly. Our gHMM model as well as the baselines are trained on the training sets and finally evaluated on the TREC test set containing 2947 queries and MSN test set containing 2421 queries.

6.2 Evaluation Metrics

We evaluate our system based on the evaluation metrics proposed in Microsoft Speller Challenge [1], including expected precision, expected recall and expected F1 measure.

As used in previous discussions, q is a user query and $Y(q) = (y^1, y^2, , y^k)$ is the set of system output with posterior probabilities $P(y^i|q)$. Let $S(q)$ denote the set of plausible spelling variations annotated by the human experts for q. Expected Precision is computed as:

$$precision = \frac{1}{|Q|}\sum_{q\in Q}\sum_{y\in Y(q)} I_p(y,q)P(y|q) \qquad (10)$$

where $I_p(y, q) = 1$ if $y \in S(q)$, and 0 otherwise. And expected recall is defined as:

$$recall = \frac{1}{|Q|}\sum_{q\in Q}\sum_{a\in S(q)} I_r(Y(q),a)/|S(q)| \qquad (11)$$

where $I_r(Y(q), a) = 1$ if $a \in Y(q)$ for $a \in S(q)$, and 0 otherwise.

Expected F1 measure can be computed as:

$$F1 = \frac{2 \cdot precision \cdot recall}{precision + recall} \qquad (12)$$

6.3 Overall Effectiveness

We first investigate the overall effectiveness of the gHMM model. For suitable query spelling correction baselines, especially approaches that can handle all types of query spelling errors, we first considered using the CRF model proposed in [24]. This method aims at a broad range of query refinements and hence might be also applicable to query correction. However, we decided not to compare this model for the following reasons. Firstly, we communicated with the authors of [24] and knew that the program is un-reusable. Secondly, as mentioned in Section 1 this work suffers from several drawbacks for query spelling correction: (1) it is unable to correct queries with mixed types of errors, such as substitution and splitting errors in one query, because the model treats query correction and splitting/merging as different tasks; (2) this model only allows 1 character error for substitution/insertion/deletion. And the error model is trained on the <query, correction> examples that only contain 1 character error. Such design is over simplified for real-world queries, in which more than 1 character errors are quite common. In fact, within the queries that contain spelling errors in the MSN dataset, there are about 40.6% of them contain more than 1 character errors. Therefore it is expected model in [24] will have in inferior performance

Because of the reasons stated above, the best baseline method that we can possibly compare with is the system

[1] http://web-ngram.research.microsoft.com/spellerchallenge/

that achieved the best performance in Microsoft Speller Challenge [25] (we call it Lueck-2011). This system relies on candidate corrections from third-party toolkits such as hunspell and Microsoft Wrod Breaker Service [11] , and it re-ranks the candidates by a simple noisy channel model. We communicated with the author and obtained the corrections by running the Web API of this baseline approach. We also include a simple baseline called *Echo*, which is just echoing the original query as the correction response with posterior probability 1. It reflects the basic performance for a naive method. Experiments are conducted on TREC and MSN datasets.

We report the results of all methods in Table 3. In this experiment up to top 10 corrections are used in all approaches. The results in Table 3 indicate that gHMM outperforms Lueck-2011 significantly on recall and F1 on the TREC dataset. Lueck-2011 has a small advantage on precision, possibly due to the better handling the unchanged queries. On the MSN dataset which is considered harder since it has more misspelled queries, gHMM also achieves high precision of 0.910 and recall of 0.966, which are both significantly better than that of the Lueck-2011 (0.896 and 0.921). On another important performance metric, which measures the F1 on misspelled queries (F1 Mis), gHMM outperforms Lueck-2011 by a large margin (0.550 vs. 0.391 on TREC and 0.566 vs. 0.363 on MSN). These results demonstrate that gHMM is very effective for handling all types of spelling errors in search queries overall.

Table 3: gHMM Compared to Baselines

Dataset	Method	Precision	Recall	F1	F1 Mis
TREC	Echo	0.949	0.876	0.911	N/A
	Lueck-2011	**0.963**	0.932	0.947	0.391
	gHMM	0.960	**0.976**	**0.968**	**0.550**
MSN	Echo	0.869	0.869	0.869	N/A
	Lueck-2011	0.896	0.921	0.908	0.363
	gHMM	**0.910**	**0.966**	**0.937**	**0.566**

6.4 Results by Error Types

Further, we also break down the results by error types that are manually classified so that we can see more clearly the distribution of types of spelling errors and how well our gHMM model addressing each type of errors. We present the results of this analysis in Table 4, only with our model on both datasets. Top 40 corrections are used since it achieves the best results. The breakdown results show that most queries are in the group of "no error", which are easier to handle than the other three types. As a result, the overall excellent performance was mostly because the system performed very well on the "no error" group. Indeed, the system has substantially lower precision on the queries with the other three types of errors. The concatenation errors seem to be the hardest to correct, followed by the splitting errors, and the in-word transformation errors (insertion, deletion and substitution, word mis-use) seem to be relatively easier.

6.5 gHMM for Working Set Construction

Since the gHMM can efficiently search in the complete candidate space and compute the top-K spelling corrections in a one-stage manner, it is very interesting to test its effectiveness for constructing a working set of candidate corrections to enable more complex scoring functions to be used for spelling correction. For this purpose, we compare gHMM with the common used noisy channel model, whose parameters, namely error model probabilities and bigram language probabilities are estimated by the procedure mentioned in previous sections. We use recall to measure the completeness of the constructed working set, because it represents the percentage of true corrections given the number of predicted corrections. Table 5 shows the recall according to different number of outputs. It indicates that the recall of gHMM is steadily increasing by a larger number of outputs. By only outputting top-5 corrections, gHMM reaches recall of 0.969 in TREC and 0.964 in MSN. In contrast, the noisy channel model has a substantial gap in term of recall compared to gHMM. This result strongly demonstrates the superior effectiveness of gHMM in constructing a more complete working set of candidate corrections, which can be utilized by other re-ranking approaches which could further improve the correction accuracy.

Table 4: Results by Spelling Error Type

Dataset	Error Type	% Queries	Precision	Recall	F1
TREC	no error	94.9	0.990	0.982	0.986
	transformation	3.3	0.388	0.840	0.531
	concatenation	1.3	0.348	0.877	0.498
	splitting	0.5	0.500	0.792	0.613
MSN	no error	86.9	0.978	1.0	0.989
	transformation	11.1	0.493	0.762	0.599
	concatenation	1.7	0.150	0.600	0.240
	splitting	0.6	0.429	0.571	0.490

Note: % of queries might sum up to more than 100% since there might be multiple types of errors in one query.

Table 5: gHMM vs. Noisy Channel Model on Recall

Dataset	Method	1	5	10	20	40
TREC	N-C	0.869	0.896	0.899	0.901	0.902
	gHMM	**0.887**	**0.969**	**0.976**	**0.981**	**0.983**
MSN	N-C	0.866	0.870	0.873	0.876	0.886
	gHMM	**0.920**	**0.964**	**0.966**	**0.9667**	**0.967**

Note: N-C refers to the noisy channel model

6.6 Efficiency

The runtime requirement of query correction is very stringent. Theoretically, the gHMM with local feature functions can search top-K corrections efficiently by our proposed tok-K Viterbi algorithm. Here we make a directly comparison between the runtime of gHMM and a basic noisy channel that only needs to compute the error model probabilities and bigram language probabilities. Such a basic model is also implemented with Viterbi algorithm. It is run on a Windows server equipped with 2 Quad-core 64 bit 2.4 GHz CPUs and 8 GB RAM. All necessary bigram language probabilities are crawled from Microsoft Web N-gram Service and cached in local memory. We plot the runtime per query (in milliseconds) according to the number of predicted corrections in Figure 2. According to Figure 2, the computation of top-1 correction by gHMM is fast (34 ms) if the number of output is set to 1. It increases as the number of output increases because the search space is increased. Interestingly, the runtime of gHMM and the noisy channel model is of the same order of magnitude. This empirical evidence confirms the theoretical result that top-K spelling corrections can be computed efficiently via our proposed top-K Viterbi algorithm.

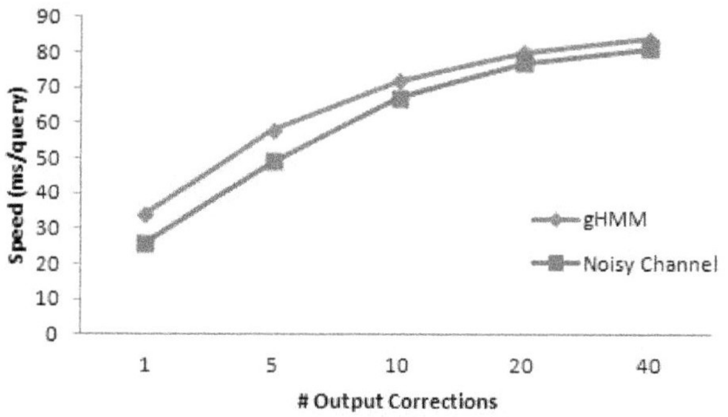

Figure 2: Runtime Comparison

7. DISCUSSION

Finally we discuss how the proposed gHMM model behaves according to the variation of important factors. Such as the number of spelling corrections in the output and the size of lexicon L *etc.*

7.1 Number of Predicted Corrections

Our datasets include all plausible corrections for a query. However it's unknown that how many corrections an algorithm should output to achieve a perfect recall. In this section we investigate how the number of predicted spelling corrections affects the precision and recall. We have carried out experiments on five correction sizes (1,5,10,20,40) on both datasets. Figure 3 summarizes the results. As expected, a bigger number of corrections leads to higher recall, and the most drastical increase of recall lies from 1 correction to 5.

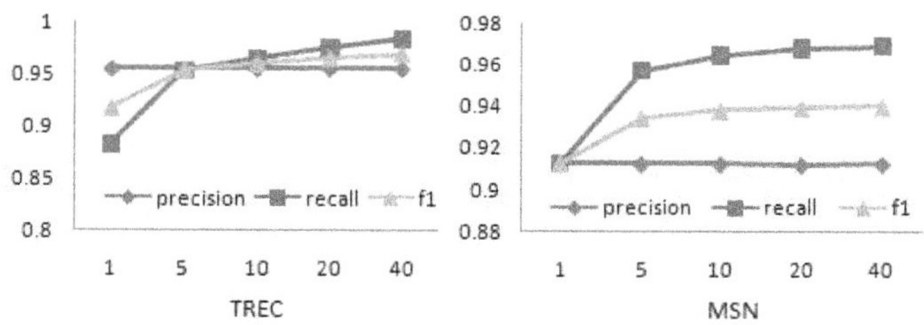

Figure 3: Results by Number of Corrections

7.2 Effect of the Lexicon Size

The size of the trusted lexicon is an important factor influencing the speller correction result. In order to investigate the effect of lexicon size, we conducted a set of experiments on both datasets using different lexicon sizes (ranging from 100,000 to 900,000). Results in Figure 4 show that the effect of lexicon size is significant on precision: the precision increases as the lexicon size increases. However the recall is not sensitive to the lexicon size.

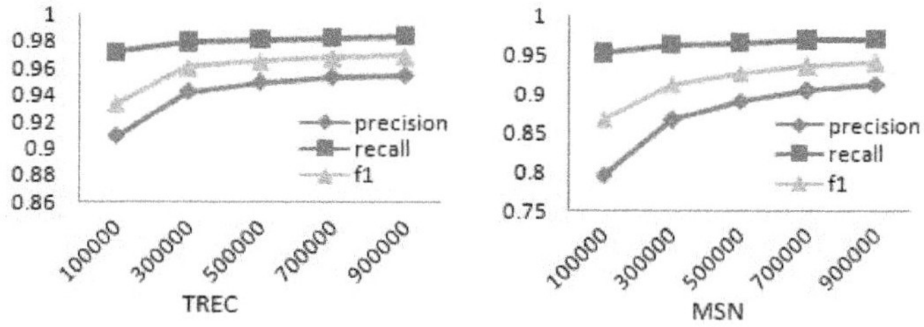

Figure 4: Correction Results by Lexicion Size

7.3 Clean vs. Noisy Lexicon

In Table 6, we show the effects of using a clean lexicon for improving the precision and recall of the spelling system. We can see that for both test sets, there is noticeable improvement in precision. By removing the noise in the automatically constructed lexicon, our system is able to find matches for candidate queries more precisely.

Table 6: Clean vs. Noisy Lexicon

Dataset	Lexicon Type	Precision	Recall	F1
TREC	clean lexicon	0.960	0.983	0.971
	noisy lexicon	0.950	0.984	0.966
MSN	clean lexicon	0.910	0.967	0.938
	noisy lexicon	0.896	0.967	0.930

Note: maximum corrections are set to 40 in this experiment

8. CONCLUSIONS AND FUTURE WORKS

In this paper, we presented a novel generalized hidden Markov model (gHMM) for query spelling correction that can address two major deficiencies of previous approaches to query spelling correction, i.e., inability of handling all the major types of spelling errors, and inability of searching efficiently in the complete candidate space. We have also proposed a novel discriminative training method for the gHMM model which enables us to go beyond regular HMM to incorporate useful local features for more effective query spelling correction. Experiment results on two query correction datasets show that gHMM can effectively handle all the major types of spelling errors and outperforms a state-of-the-art baseline by a large margin.

Moreover, our generalized HMM, equipped with the discriminative training, scores the query corrections directly and output a final ranked list of spelling corrections, without needing a filtering stage to prune the candidate space as typically required by an existing method. We have demonstrated that as an efficient one-stage approach, the proposed gHMM can also be used as a filter to construct a more complete working set than the existing noisy channel filter, making it possible to combine it with any complicated spelling correction methods to further improve accuracy. In other words, the proposed gHMM model can serve as a better candidate generation method in a two-stage framework where any sophisticated and potentially more effective spelling correction method can be applied to re-rank the generated candidates for more accurate corrections. In addition, we have also curated a large spelling correction dataset from real-world queries and made it available to the research community.

In this work, we only focused on local feature functions in order to ensure efficient evaluation of all the candidates in the search space. However, some global features, such as the overall editing distance, frequency of the query in a query log can be potentially utilized to further improve the correction accuracy. How to add the global features to the gHMM model, while still ensuring efficient search and evaluation of all the candidates in the search space, is an interesting direction for future work.

9. ACKNOWLEDGMENTS

This paper is based upon work supported in part by a Microsoft grant, the National Science Foundation under grant CNS-1027965, and MIAS - the Multimodal Information Access and Synthesis center at UIUC, part of CCICADA, and a DHS Center of Excellence.

10. REFERENCES

[1] http://research.microsoft.com/en-us/collaboration/focus/cs/web-ngram.aspx.

[2] F. Ahmad and G. Kondrak. Learning a spelling error model from search query logs. In *HLT/EMNLP*. The Association for Computational Linguistics, 2005.

[3] E. Brill and R. Moore. An improved error model for noisy channel spelling correction. In *Proceedings of the 38th Annual Meeting of the Association for Computational Linguistics*, Hong Kong, 2000.

[4] Q. Chen, M. Li, and M. Zhou. Improving query spelling correction using web search results. In *EMNLP-CoNLL*, pages 181–189. ACL, 2007.

[5] S. Cucerzan and E. Brill. Spelling correction as an iterative process that exploits the collective knowledge of web users. In *EMNLP*, 2004.

[6] H. Duan and B.-J. P. Hsu. Online spelling correction for query completion. In *Proceedings of the 20th international conference on World wide web*, WWW '11, pages 117–126. 2011, ACM.

[7] J. Gao, X. Li, D. Micol, C. Quirk, and X. Sun. A large scale ranker-based system for search query spelling correction. In C.-R. Huang and D. Jurafsky, editors, *COLING*, pages 358–366. 2010.

[8] K. Kukich. Techniques for automatically correcting words in text. *ACM computing surveys*, 24(4), 1992.

[9] M. J. D. Powell. An efficient method for finding the minimum of a function of several variables without calculating derivatives. *The Computer Journal*, 7(2):155–162, 1964.

[10] X. Sun, J. Gao, D. Micol, and C. Quirk. Learning phrase-based spelling error models from clickthrough data. In *Proceedings of the 48th Annual Meeting of the Association for Computational Linguistics*, ACL '10, pages 266–274, Stroudsburg, PA, USA, 2010.

[11] K. Wang, C. Thrasher, and B.-J. P. Hsu. Web scale nlp: a case study on url word breaking. In *Proceedings of the 20th international conference on World wide web*, WWW '11, pages 357–366, New York, NY, USA, 2011. ACM.

[12] C. Whitelaw, B. Hutchinson, G. Chung, and G. Ellis. Using the web for language independent spellchecking and autocorrection. In *EMNLP*, 890–899. ACL, 2009.

[13] Levenshtein, V I. Binary codes capable of correcting deletions, insertions, and reversals. In *Soviet Physics Doklady, 10(8), 707-710*, 1966.

[14] Jinxi Xu and W. Bruce Croft. Query expansion using local and global document analysis. In *Proceedings of the 19th annual international ACM SIGIR conference on Research and development in information retrieval*, SIGIR '96. ACM, New York, NY.

[15] Yonggang Qiu and Hans-Peter Frei. Concept based query expansion. In *Proceedings of the 16th annual international ACM SIGIR conference on Research and development in information retrieval*, SIGIR '93. ACM, New York, NY, USA, 160-169.

[16] Mandar Mitra, Amit Singhal, and Chris Buckley. Improving automatic query expansion. In *Proceedings of the 21st annual international ACM SIGIR conference on Research and development in information retrieval*, SIGIR '98.

[17] B. Tan and F. Peng. Unsupervised query segmentation using generative language models and wikipedia. In *Proceeding of the 17th international conference on World Wide Web*, WWW '08, pages 347–356. 2008.

[18] Y. Li, B.-J. P. Hsu, C. Zhai, and K. Wang. Unsupervised query segmentation using clickthrough for information retrieval. In *Proceedings of the 34th international ACM SIGIR conference on Research and development in Information Retrieval*, SIGIR '11, pages 285–294. 2011.

[19] Xuanhui Wang, ChengXiang Zhai. Mining Term Association Patterns from Search Logs for Effective Query Reformulation. In *CIKM'08*. 479-488.

[20] Stephan Vogel, Hermann Ney, and Christoph Tillmann. HMM-based word alignment in statistical translation. In *Proceedings of the 16th conference on Computational linguistics*, Volume 2 (COLING '96). Stroudsburg, PA, USA, 836-841.

[21] B.H. Juang. Hidden Markov models for speech recognition. In Technometrics, Vol. 33, No. 3, 1991.

[22] M. Collins. Discriminative training methods for hidden markov models: theory and experiments with perceptron algorithms. In *EMNLP '02*, pages 1-8, Stroudsburg, PA, USA, 2002.

[23] L. R. Rabiner. A tutorial on hidden markov models and selected applications in speech recognition. In *Proceedings of the IEEE*, pages 257–286, 1989.

[24] J. Guo, G. Xu, H. Li, and X. Cheng. A unified and discriminative model for query refinement. In *Proceedings of the 31st annual international ACM SIGIR*, SIGIR '08, pages 379–386. 2008.

[25] G. Luec. A data-driven approach for correcting search quaries. In *Spelling Alteration for Web Search Workshop*, July 2011.

[26] J. Lafferty, A. McCallum, and F. Pereira. Conditional random fields: Probabilistic models for segmenting and labeling sequence data. In *Proceedings of the 18th International Conference on Machine Learning*, pages 282–289, San Fransisco, 2001. Morgan Kaufmann.

Learning to Predict Response Times for Online Query Scheduling

Craig Macdonald[1], Nicola Tonellotto[2], Iadh Ounis[1]
[1] University of Glasgow, Glasgow G12 8QQ, UK
[2] National Research Council of Italy, Via G. Moruzzi 1, 56124 Pisa, Italy
{craig.macdonald, iadh.ounis}@glasgow.ac.uk[1], {nicola.tonellotto}@isti.cnr.it[2]

ABSTRACT

Dynamic pruning strategies permit efficient retrieval by not fully scoring all postings of the documents matching a query – without degrading the retrieval effectiveness of the top-ranked results. However, the amount of pruning achievable for a query can vary, resulting in queries taking different amounts of time to execute. Knowing in advance the execution time of queries would permit the exploitation of online algorithms to schedule queries across replicated servers in order to minimise the average query waiting and completion times. In this work, we investigate the impact of dynamic pruning strategies on query response times, and propose a framework for predicting the efficiency of a query. Within this framework, we analyse the accuracy of several query efficiency predictors across 10,000 queries submitted to in-memory inverted indices of a 50-million-document Web crawl. Our results show that combining multiple efficiency predictors with regression can accurately predict the response time of a query before it is executed. Moreover, using the efficiency predictors to facilitate online scheduling algorithms can result in a 22% reduction in the mean waiting time experienced by queries before execution, and a 7% reduction in the mean completion time experienced by users.

Categories and Subject Descriptors: H.3.3 [Information Storage & Retrieval]: Information Search & Retrieval

Keywords: Dynamic Pruning, Query Efficiency Prediction

1. INTRODUCTION

Large-scale information retrieval (IR) systems – such as Web search engines – are not just concerned with the quality of search results (also known as *effectiveness*), but also with the speed with which the results are obtained (*efficiency*). These aspects form a natural tradeoff, in that many approaches that increase effectiveness may have a corresponding impact on efficiency due to their complex nature [31].

Hence, as users exhibit preferences for faster search engines [6], to deploy techniques to improve effectiveness, search engines need to identify other opportunities for efficiency optimisations. One such technique is the use of caching, either of the search results for a query, or the posting lists of terms from the inverted index [3]. Increasingly, caching is being used for the posting lists of all terms, such that retrieval occurs from *in-memory* indices, and thus all expensive disk I/O operations are avoided [12, 15].

The exhaustive scoring of every document that contains at least one query term also degrades efficiency unnecessarily, because very few of these documents will make the top retrieved set of documents that the user will see. Dynamic pruning strategies such as MAXSCORE [30] and WAND [5] address this by omitting (*pruning*) the scoring of documents that cannot make the top-K retrieved documents set.

Of course, more than one machine is typically involved in answering a query to a Web search engine [7, 12]. For instance, more than one *query server* can service queries for a *replicated* index, thereby improving overall response time. However, no previous work has examined the most effective way to schedule queries across the query servers. In this paper, we argue that scheduling algorithms that take into account the queued workload for that server can be used to ensure efficient use of query servers resources.

However, accurate scheduling requires estimations of the execution times of queries. Yet, as we will show in this paper, one query may take substantially longer than another query with apparently similar statistics. Indeed, we explain why some queries are difficult to prune, whereby many documents are fully scored before later being expelled from the retrieved set by other documents. Hence, the difficulty is determined by how early the final top documents are retrieved when traversing the posting lists, to allow successful pruning. Accurately estimating this difficulty and hence the response time of a query will permit the efficient scheduling of queries in a replicated setting.

In this paper we propose a framework of *query efficiency predictors* that can estimate the execution time of a given query. Experiments using 10,000 queries from a Web search engine query log demonstrate the accuracy of these predictors. Moreover, we show how query efficiency prediction can be used to reduce query response time by the improved scheduling of queries across replicated query servers. Indeed, scheduling while making use of efficiency predictions can result in a 22% reduction in the average waiting time experienced by queries, and a 7% reduction in the average query completion time experienced by users.

The remainder of this paper is as follows: Section 2 introduces background material on efficient search engines; Section 3 details the contributions of this work; Section 4 contains the experimental setup common to all experiments; Section 5 examines the response times of various retrieval strategies; Section 6 defines our query efficiency prediction framework; Section 7 shows how query efficiency predictors can be used to improve the scheduling of queries to replicated query servers; Concluding remarks follow in Section 8.

SIGIR'12, August 12–16, 2012, Portland, Oregon, USA.

2. BACKGROUND

To spread the retrieval load of a large document corpus on a search engine, the inverted index can be partitioned into shards and *distributed* across multiple *query servers*, and/or identical indices *replicated* across query servers [12]. For distributed settings, queries arriving at the front-end server or *broker* are sent to multiple query servers, while the broker collates the results. For replicated settings, queries arriving at the broker are routed to the next available query server [7]. However, we know of no work that discusses different approaches for the routing or scheduling of queries across replicated query servers. Indeed, to the best of our knowledge, this is the first work addressing the scheduling of queries across replicated query servers.

Next, while the inverted index was traditionally stored on disk, with the predominance of inexpensive memory, search engines are increasingly caching the entire inverted index in memory, to assure low latency responses [12, 15].

Despite these optimisations, the matching of documents still uses the classical inverted index data structure to score and rank documents [12]. Moreover, due to its data bound nature, this represents the largest contribution to the time for a search engine to retrieve documents in response to a query. Indeed, to create a ranking of documents for a query, the posting lists for each query term must be traversed [23].

Various techniques that prune documents that are unlikely to be retrieved have been devised to improve efficiency. Some rely on pre-sorting the posting lists of different terms by the impact of the postings [2], or by removing documents that are unlikely to be retrieved (with possible loss of retrieval effectiveness) [4]. However, we focus on techniques that are *safe-to-rank-K* – i.e. cannot degrade retrieval effectiveness to a given rank K – and use docid sorted posting lists, as deployed by at least one major search engine [12]. In particular, *dynamic pruning* strategies aim to avoid the scoring of postings for documents that cannot make the top K retrieved set. All state-of-the-art safe dynamic pruning strategies [5, 28, 30][1] aim to avoid scoring parts of the posting lists, to save disk access, decompression and score computation costs. This is implemented by maintaining additional information during retrieval, namely: a *threshold* τ, which is the minimum score that documents must achieve to have a chance to be present in the final top K results; and for each query term, a *term upper bound* $\sigma(t)$, which is the maximal contribution of that particular term to any document score. The upper bound is usually obtained by pre-scanning the posting lists of each term at indexing time, to record the maximum score found in each posting list [10].

We use two such dynamic pruning strategies that score postings in a document-at-a-time (DAAT) manner, namely MaxScore [30] and Wand [5]. Compared to the scoring of every posting of every document (which we refer to as Full), both strategies can efficiently score documents while being-safe-to-rank K, and do not require impact-sorted posting lists. Instead, the postings for every term have the same global ordering, such that they can be read in parallel.

MaxScore achieves efficient retrieval by omitting the scoring of postings for documents that will not make the final retrieved set. In contrast, Wand takes a different approach, by repeatedly calculating a *pivot term*. The next document containing the pivot term is the *pivot document*, which will be the next document to be fully scored. A major benefit of Wand over MaxScore is that skipping [24] forward in posting lists can be used by Wand, which reduces posting list decompression overheads, and can reduce IO, with resulting improvements in efficiency [15, 22]. Indeed, Wand represents the state-of-the-art in dynamic pruning. Moreover, both MaxScore and Wand can equally be applied to inverted indices stored on disk or in-memory [15].

Moffat et al. [23] stated that the response time of a query is related to the posting list lengths of its constituent query terms. However, as we will show in Section 5, dynamic pruning causes queries with similar surface properties (e.g. query terms, posting list lengths) to widely vary in the time required to process. Hence, to have a better estimation of a query's response time, we propose a novel framework for query efficiency prediction. Moreover, we investigate the advantages of query efficiency prediction when applied to improved online scheduling of queries to replicated query servers. The notion of query efficiency prediction first appeared in [29], where initial experiments for disk-based indices showed some promise. In contrast, this work performs a more detailed study into efficiency prediction for in-memory indices, and uses efficiency prediction for enhancing replicated retrieval architectures.

We contrast query efficiency prediction with works from the literature on query *performance* prediction that have tried to predict the effectiveness of a query [17], either before retrieval commences (pre-retrieval prediction) [18], or by inspecting the scores or contents of retrieved documents (post-retrieval prediction) [1, 11]. Performance predictors have also been combined using machine learning [19, 21]. However, no previous work has attempted the different task of efficiency prediction. This work defines pre-retrieval efficiency predictors, and applies these to the scheduling of queries in a replicated retrieval setting.

3. CONTRIBUTIONS

The major contributions of this paper are:

- We demonstrate and explain the varying nature of response times for dynamic pruning strategies with in-memory indices.
- We propose a framework for query efficiency prediction, and instantiate various predictors within that framework.
- We conduct experiments to determine the accuracy of the query efficiency predictors for retrieval with in-memory indices.
- We propose the use of online scheduling algorithms to reduce the overall query response time when routing queries to replicated query servers.
- We show how query efficiency predictors can be used within online scheduling algorithms.

In the following, we firstly introduce the experimental setup deployed in this paper (Section 4), before experimentally investigating the pruning behaviour of dynamic pruning strategies (Section 5) and then defining and evaluating the query efficiency predictors (Section 6). The proposed query efficiency predictors are applied to online query scheduling in Section 7.

[1]We omit the database-focused algorithms of Fagin et al. [14] - these assume random access on the posting list, which is generally not possible when compression is used.

Length	1	2	3	4	5	6+	All
Train	3,888	2,717	1,387	637	185	-	8,314
Test	3,387	2,781	1,395	534	181	-	8,278
Total	6,775	5,498	2,782,	1,171	366	203	16,775

Table 1: Breakdown of the query log used in experiments by query length.

4. EXPERIMENTAL SETUP

All of the experiments in the following sections are conducted using a 50 million document corpus called TREC ClueWeb09 category B. We index this corpus using the Terrier IR platform [26][2], applying Porter's English stemmer, and removing standard stopwords. In the posting lists of the inverted index, docids are encoded using Elias Gamma-encoded deltas and term frequencies using Elias Unary [13]. Each posting list also includes skip points [24], one every 1,000 postings. The resulting inverted index size is 22GB.

For testing retrieval efficiency, we extract a stream of user queries from a real search engine log, and measure the query response time and the number of postings scored when retrieving with all index data structures loaded in memory. Experiments are made using a dual quad-core Intel Xeon 2.6GHz, with 8GB RAM. In particular, we select the first 16,775 queries of the MSN 2006 query log [9], applying Porter's English stemmer and removing standard stopwords (empty queries are removed). This amounts to 10,000 queries of more than one term (single term queries cannot be pruned). Table 1 shows the distribution of queries by length[3]. Moreover, this sample exhibits the expected power law distributional of query occurrences: e.g. 1 query occurs 88 times, and 6,279 queries occurred once.

During retrieval, we apply three retrieval strategies: an exhaustive DAAT Full, where all postings for each document are exhaustively scored; MAXSCORE [30]; and WAND [5]. Moreover, as our inverted index is larger than the available RAM, we discard the posting lists of terms that do not occur in the 16,775 queries. This is justified as it simulates an in-memory index environment without having to partition the index across multiple servers. Hence, while our query response times may be larger than would suffice for an interactive environment, this does not detract from the validity of the experiments. Documents are ranked for each query using BM25, with Terrier's default parameter settings, while the number of documents retrieved is set to $K = 1,000$.

5. ANALYSIS OF RESPONSE TIMES

To predict the efficiency of queries, we must first understand the characteristics of response times given by various retrieval strategies. While Moffat et al. [23] claimed that the main components of a query's response time are related to the number of terms in the query, and the length of the term's posting lists, there is some other anecdotal literature evidence that the response time of a dynamic pruning strategy can vary widely, even for queries with the same total number of postings to consider [3]. While Gan & Suel [16] assumed that the total postings was a sufficiently accurate estimation for caching decisions, Ozcan et al. [27] instead used actual response times, due to the variation in response times. In this section, we fully analyse and explain the variation in response times of different retrieval strategies. We also show that the total number of postings does not accurately predict the response times of all pruning strategies.

Figures 1(a)-(d) show the response time distributions for different query lengths and different strategies, for 10,000 queries with more than one query term. Ideally, most queries should have small response times – indicated by the highest frequency of response time being small, i.e. towards the left.

From Figure 1, we can see that different retrieval strategies exhibit different response time distributions. Indeed, while MAXSCORE shows only a small improvement w.r.t. Full, WAND markedly improves the response times for any query length, as it has the most number of queries with low response times, despite having to traverse the same posting lists of the same length as the other strategies. Moreover, a clear variance in the response times of queries for each strategy can be observed, even across queries of the same length. This is expected, as different queries have different numbers of postings that must be traversed.

Yet, due to their pruning behaviour, the number of postings to process does not fully depict the retrieval times of all pruning strategies. To illustrate this, Figure 2 shows scatter plots for total postings and response time for Full, MAXSCORE and WAND. From Figure 2(a), a strong correlation between the total number of postings and the query response times can be observed for Full, independently from the number of terms in the query. This correlation is explained by the fact that the strategy scores every posting for each query term, without any pruning. However, the correlations observed in Figure 2(b) & (c) for the MAXSCORE and WAND strategies are weaker. In particular, the response time for a query with a given number of postings can be markedly lower than another query with the same number of postings – for instance, queries with 2 million postings usually take between 1.8 to 3.2 seconds with MAXSCORE, and 0.9 to 2.0 seconds for WAND. Hence, the amount of pruning possible varies between queries, even for those same length and number of postings. Moreover, as WAND is able to prune some queries more aggressively than MAXSCORE, its exhibits less correlation between total postings and response times.

To explain why different queries vary in their pruning difficulty, we turn to Figure 3. This shows the distribution of weighting model scores for two example queries, each with two query terms occurring in two documents, where the top $K = 1$ ranked document is required. Vertical arrows denote the scores of postings, with the upper bound $\sigma(t)$ for each term represented by a horizontal dashed line. The threshold τ after scoring each document is shown. As this is a DAAT process, the postings lists of all terms for a query are processed in parallel. After scoring the first document in query 1, the threshold (score of the Kth retrieved document) is $\tau = 7$. Hence, for the second document, after scoring the posting for the first term, MAXSCORE can assert that each document will not reach the retrieved set, as $score(t_1) + \sigma(t_2) = 2 + 2 < 7$. Hence the posting for the second query term of that document is pruned (dotted). In contrast, for query 2, all postings must be considered for the second document, as the score of the first term's posting for that document is not low enough that it cannot be retrieved - i.e. $score(t_1) + \sigma(t_2) = 3 + 3 \geq 6$. We say that the query 1 is easier to prune than query 2.

We now quantify the pruning difficulty for both MAXSCORE and WAND. In particular, for the 10,000 queries with more than one query term, we compute the pruning ratio p, defined as the percentage of total postings for a query that were actually scored by the dynamic pruning strategy. For

[2] `http://terrier.org/`

[3] As there are very few queries with 6 or more terms, we omit these in the following experiments, and hence they do not appear in the train and test sets.

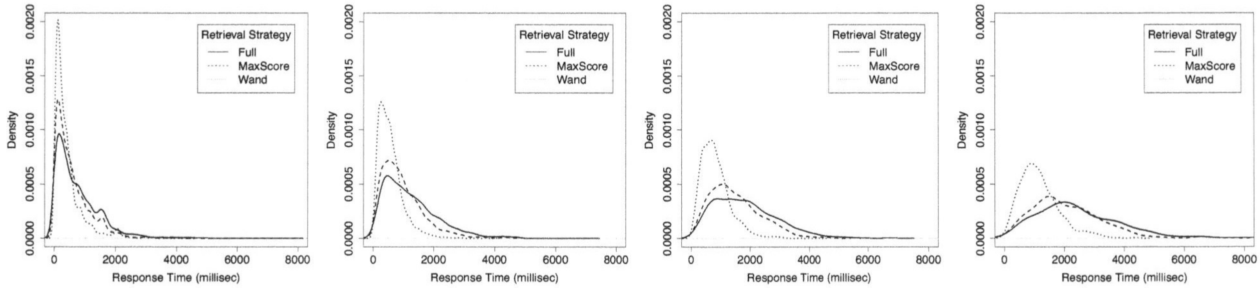

(a) 2 terms (b) 3 terms (c) 4 terms (d) 5 terms

Figure 1: Response time distributions for different query lengths and different pruning strategies.

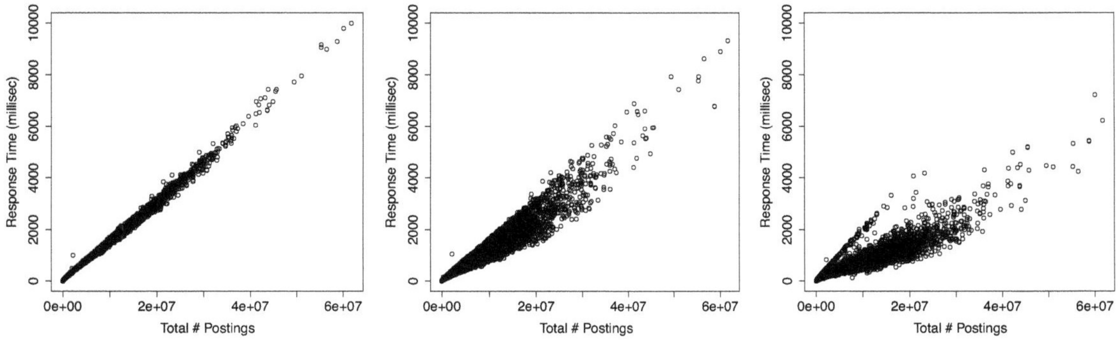

(a) Full (b) MaxScore (c) Wand

Figure 2: Total postings vs. response times for different retrieval strategies.

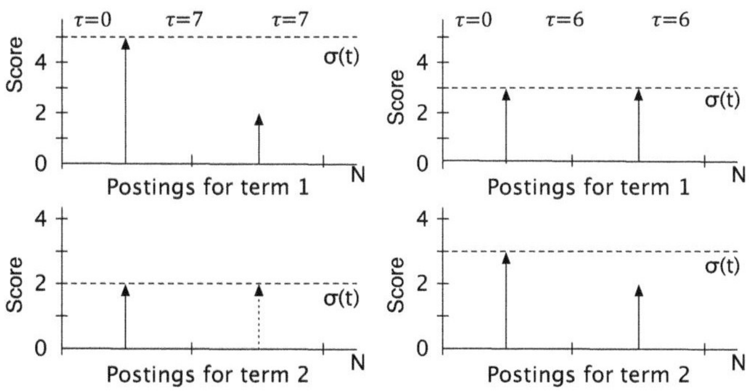

(a) Query 1: Easy to prune (b) Query 2: Difficult to prune

Figure 3: Two example queries with different pruning difficulties, each with two query terms with the same number of postings.

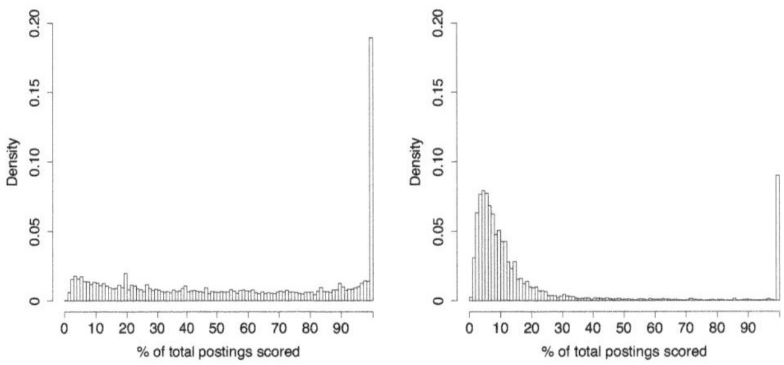

(a) MaxScore (b) Wand

Figure 4: The bucketed pruning ratios for two dynamic pruning strategies using 10,000 queries with more than one term.

instance, a value of $p = 35\%$ means that 35% of the total number of postings of the query were actually scored, while the remaining 65% of the postings were pruned. The pruning ratios of the 10,000 queries have been bucketed in buckets with size 1%. The distribution of these results are reported in Figure 4, for both MaxScore and Wand.

In both cases, a large percentage of queries are not pruned at all (i.e. $p = 100\%$, right extremes of Figure 4) ($\sim 20\%$ for MaxScore and $\sim 10\%$ for Wand). On closer inspection, we find that most of these unpruned queries consist of two query terms. This pruning difficulty has two main causes. Firstly, most of these queries have a very small total number of postings, so it is difficult to process enough of them to achieve a high enough threshold to start pruning. Alternatively, when the total number of postings is large, one of the two terms has a very low discriminative power, i.e. a term with a very low IDF and consequently a very low maximum score. In this case, the strategy is forced to behave like for single term queries (where no pruning is possible), where the single term is the most discriminative (high IDF) one, with the other just adding some background noise.

Overall, while in Figure 4(a) MaxScore does not exhibit a strong pruning ability (e.g. the pruning ratio distribution is evenly distributed among the queries), in Figure 4(b) Wand performs very well. In fact, most queries have a small pruning ratio, i.e. less than 30%, which shows that Wand is often able to score only a small portion of the total number of scored postings, thereby attaining higher efficiency.

Therefore, due to their pruning nature, we argue that the total number of postings may not be enough to predict Max-

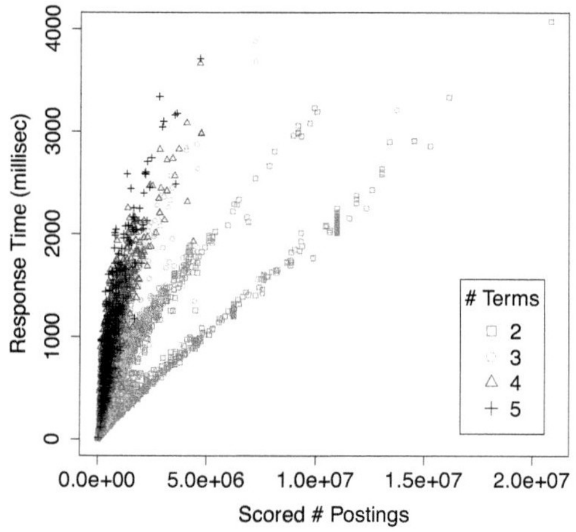

Figure 5: Scored postings vs. response times for WAND, broken down by query lengths.

SCORE or WAND's scored postings and hence the query response time. In fact, Figures 2 (b) & (c) show that, for the same total number of postings, the query response time varies markedly, particularly for WAND. Instead, the number of *scored* postings is the central statistic to be predicted that defines the resulting response time. Indeed, Figure 5 shows that, for different query lengths, the number of scored postings is correlated to the query response times. However, the pruning ratio or the number of scored postings cannot be obtained before retrieval commences. We posit that various statistics of the query terms that are available offline can be used to predict the response time of a query before retrieval commences. In the next section, we propose a framework for query efficiency prediction, and evaluate various efficiency predictors within this framework. We then show one novel application of the query efficiency prediction framework, namely the online scheduling of queries to replicated query servers.

6. PREDICTING QUERY EFFICIENCY

Having an accurate estimate of the efficiency of a query can be useful to a search engine in many ways. For instance, in a replicated setting, if the availability of query servers can be predicted by the broker, then a new query could be scheduled to the query server expected to be idle soonest.

To be of use, efficiency predictors must be pre-retrieval - i.e. available before retrieval for a query has commenced, and easily obtained at retrieval time (similar to some query performance predictors [18]). Indeed, a post-retrieval efficiency predictor is of no use, as the response time of the query is known after retrieval has occurred. Hence, our efficiency predictors are based on the available statistics of the query terms (frequency, number of postings, IDF etc). We note that some pre-retrieval query performance predictors (e.g. AvPMI [17]) use the joint probability of a pair of query terms. However, calculation of the joint probability requires n-gram language models, or posting list scans. We avoid such pair statistics, even though some search engines may record additional posting lists for some phrases [12].

In the remainder of this section, we propose a framework for query efficiency prediction, and define many predictors (Section 6.1). These predictors are evaluated compared to the response times of 10,000 queries (see Section 6.2 for prediction experimental setup), both individually (Section 6.3), and in combination (Section 6.4).

	Term Statistics $s(t)$
1.	Arithmetic mean score
2.	Geometric mean score
3.	Harmonic mean score
4.	Max score
5.	Approximation of max score [22]
6.	Variance of score
7.	# Postings
8.	# Maxima
9.	# Maxima greater than average score
10.	# Postings with max score
11.	# Postings within 5% of max score
12.	# Postings with score within 5% of final threshold
13.	Promotions into K
14.	IDF
	Aggregators $\mathcal{A}()$
a.	Maximum
b.	Variance
c.	Sum

Table 2: All tested term-based efficiency prediction statistics and aggregators.

6.1 A Query Efficiency Prediction Framework

As we have shown in Section 5, pruning difficulty varies between queries, and hence the response time of a query cannot be directly predicted. Moreover, as it is infeasible to generate offline features for the universe of possible queries, we instead use statistics that are computed for each term. These are then aggregated (e.g. sum, max) across all of the constituent terms of a query, to form different features for a given query. In this manner, a query efficiency prediction feature $f_{ij}(Q)$ is defined by a term-level statistic $s_j(t)$ for a query term t, and an aggregation function $\mathcal{A}_i$:

$$f_{ij}(Q) = \mathcal{A}_i(\{s_j(t)\ \forall t \in Q\}) \qquad (1)$$

We use a learning framework to obtain predictions for response times given a set of input features. In particular, we deploy linear regression [8] as our learning framework, both for single and multiple features. Linear regression has previously been successfully used for combining query performance predictors [17].

In terms of features, we rely on more than the frequency counts and IDFs of the query terms that have been traditionally applied by query performance predictors. In particular, recall that dynamic pruning strategies require an upper bound $\sigma(t)$ on the weighting model score for each term. This is normally identified at indexing time, by scoring the posting lists of all terms [10]. This provides an opportunity to calculate other term-based statistics, such as the maximum, mean and standard deviation of the weighting model scores observed for each posting list, as well the number of documents that would be inserted into the top K documents set, if there was only a single query term in that query.

For each term-based statistic, we create several query efficiency predictors by aggregating using three different statistical functions: sum, max and variance. The top part of Table 2 lists all used term statistics, while the bottom part lists the functions that are used to aggregate the term statistics into features for a given query. From Table 2, we highlight some representative term statistics:

Arithmetic, geometric, harmonic score means : Means of the weighting model scores from the term's postings.

Max of score: The exact upper bound $\sigma(t)$ of the scores in the posting list.

Approximation of max score: An approximation of $\sigma(t)$, using the maximum observed term frequency [22].

 # Postings: The number of postings in a term's posting list. The sum of this statistic is the number of postings scored by Full, and the upper bound on that which can be scored by dynamic pruning strategies.
 # Maxima: The number of times that the maximum score occurs. A term that has fewer maxima in the score distribution may be easier to prune.
Promotions into K: If this query term was the only query term, how many documents containing this term would make it into the top K retrieved documents. A term with a low number of promotions probably has its highest scored documents towards the start of the posting list.
 # Postings with score within 5% of the final threshold: This takes into account the number of postings that attain a score very close to the Kth scored document for a query containing only that term.
IDF: The inverse document frequency of the term. IDF and other similar statistics are the basis of several query performance predictors (e.g. AvICTF [18]).

The proposed statistics and aggregation functions listed in Table 2 are not exhaustive – while others may exist, for reasons of brevity, we focus on those listed above. Moreover, while not all predictors are likely to highly correlate with query response time, in the remainder of this section, we show that some predictors can be of use within linear regression, both in isolation, and when combined.

6.2 Prediction Experimental Setup

In the following, we address two research questions:
1. What are the most accurate efficiency prediction features when used separately in linear regression (Section 6.3)?
2. Can features be combined within linear regression for increased accuracy (Section 6.4)?

To address these research questions, we use the 10,000 queries with more than one query term (the prediction of the efficiency of single term queries is trivial as no pruning takes place). Table 1 provides the distribution of queries w.r.t. query length. We form training and testing subsets, by splitting the query sets of each length into two equal sets chronologically[4]. The training set will be used to train the regression models in the following sections, while all results are reported on the testing set. Accuracy is measured by the Pearson's correlation r ($-1 \leq r \leq 1$: 1 is a perfect correspondence; -1 is a reversed correspondence) and the Root Mean Square Error (RMSE) between the predicted and actual response times (as obtained in Section 4) for all queries.

6.3 Results: Single Predictors

To test the most accurate efficiency predictors based on single features, we compute the correlation and the RMSE between the predicted and actual response times on the test queries, after training on the corresponding training set with the same query length. The five most accurate efficiency predictors for each retrieval strategy, and their respective correlations and RMSE values for various query lengths are reported in Table 3. Sum # Postings (i.e. total number of postings) is the baseline prediction feature. Statistically significant differences in term of Pearson correlation from this baseline – according to a Fisher Z-transform – are denoted with an asterisk (*).

We firstly analyse the results in Table 3 for each retrieval strategy in turn. For Full, the most accurate efficiency predictor is the total number of postings (Sum # Postings), as each posting is scored. Some other predictors, namely Sum # Maxima and Sum # Maxima > average score exhibit similar accuracies. This is easily explainable, as a docid-sorted index typically has no trend on score distribution, so the maxima are evenly distributed along the scores of a postings list, and the number of maxima tends to be half of the total number of entries.

For the MaxScore retrieval strategy, which does prune, the baseline predictor of Sum # Postings is less accurate than for Full. However, the best predictors are the baseline predictor and, again, Sum # Maxima and Sum # Maxima > average score, mostly because MaxScore cannot prune many queries (as shown in Figure 4(a)). For Wand, the predicted vs. actual response time correlations of the baseline predictor feature are again overall lower, as Wand prunes more aggressively than MaxScore (Figure 4(a) & (b)), and is also the only pruning strategy able to skip whole portions of postings lists. For these reasons, the observed lower correlation with number of postings is expected. Instead, the Sum # Maxima > avg and Sum # Maxima features are promising, but not significantly better than the baseline.

Finally, we note that no feature based on IDF appeared in the top prediction features in Table 3. This suggests that query efficiency is a different task from query *performance* (effectiveness) prediction, with different statistics required.

Overall, we conclude that the Sum # Postings is a good single predictor for Full and MaxScore, exhibiting errors of less than 0.25 seconds. For Wand, some other efficiency predictor features show promise, but do not significantly improve over the baseline. We consider that the proposed efficiency features are 'weak features'. Hence, in the next section, we show how significantly improved efficiency prediction can be achieved by combining multiple prediction features within the regression, instead of only a single feature.

6.4 Results: Combined Predictors

Table 4 reports the correlations and RMSEs between predicted and actual response times observed on the test query set when combining all efficiency prediction features within a linear regression[5]. On analysing the results, we find that for the Full retrieval strategy, the learned model possibly overfits, and cannot outperform the baseline Sum # Postings feature. Similarly, the fact that MaxScore cannot prune many queries (see Figure 4(a)) ensures that the baseline feature is the most appropriate. However, for Wand, the regression model combining all 42 features is significantly more accurate at predicting response times than the baseline for all query lengths, and markedly improves the RMSEs values (approx 25%-30% reduction, with a prediction error of less than 0.2 seconds observed for queries of length ≥ 3).

Overall, we conclude that the proposed framework for efficiency prediction is accurate for predicting the response times of the state-of-the-art Wand strategy, where the total number of postings is not a sufficiently good predictor. For Full and MaxScore, no or little pruning occurs, and hence the total number of postings is sufficient.

[4]Other experiments using 5-fold cross validation gave similar conclusions.

[5]Predicted negative times are set to 0.

Features		Query Length							
Agg.	Term Statistic	2		3		4		5	
		r	RMSE	r	RMSE	r	RMSE	r	RMSE
Full									
Sum	# Postings	**0.920**	**0.274**	**0.945**	**0.261**	**0.957**	**0.258**	**0.963**	**0.256**
Max	# Maxima	0.879*	0.329	0.889*	0.361	0.896*	0.392	0.902*	0.407
Max	# Maxima > avg	0.870*	0.340	0.884*	0.369	0.892*	0.400	0.899*	0.413
Max	# Postings	0.879*	0.328	0.890*	0.361	0.896*	0.392	0.902*	0.408
Sum	# Maxima	**0.919**	**0.274**	**0.945**	**0.261**	**0.957**	**0.258**	**0.963**	**0.256**
Sum	# Maxima > avg	0.914	0.283	0.941	0.270	0.954	0.268	0.960	0.266
MaxScore									
Sum	# Postings	**0.871**	**0.279**	**0.891**	**0.292**	**0.910**	**0.301**	**0.922**	**0.304**
Max	# Maxima	0.837*	0.310	0.835*	0.352	0.858*	0.372	0.870*	0.387
Max	# Maxima > avg	0.832*	0.314	0.833*	0.353	0.857*	0.373	0.871*	0.387
Max	# Postings	0.837*	0.310	0.835*	0.352	0.858*	0.372	0.870*	0.388
Sum	# Maxima	**0.871**	**0.278**	**0.891**	**0.291**	**0.910**	**0.300**	**0.923**	**0.303**
Sum	# Maxima > avg	**0.870**	**0.281**	**0.890**	**0.292**	**0.910**	**0.301**	**0.922**	**0.304**
Wand									
Sum	# Postings	0.812	0.287	0.840	0.253	0.857	0.249	0.870	0.249
Max	# Maxima	0.780*	0.309	0.777*	0.294	0.782*	0.301	0.793*	0.308
Max	# Maxima > avg	0.786*	0.305	0.782*	0.291	0.785*	0.299	0.797*	0.306
Max	# Postings	0.778*	0.310	0.776*	0.294	0.781*	0.302	0.792*	0.309
Sum	# Maxima	0.814	0.285	0.841	0.252	0.858	0.247	0.871	0.248
Sum	# Maxima > avg	**0.822**	**0.280**	**0.846**	**0.249**	**0.861**	**0.245**	**0.874**	**0.246**

Table 3: Pearson correlations and RMSE values (in seconds) on the test query set of the best single predictor features for different query lengths and retrieval strategies. Significantly different Pearson correlations from Sum # Postings are denoted *.

	# Feat.	Query Length							
		2		3		4		5	
		r	RMSE	r	RMSE	r	RMSE	r	RMSE
Full									
Sum # Post.	1	**0.920**	**0.274**	**0.945**	**0.261**	**0.957**	**0.258**	**0.963**	**0.256**
Combination	42	0.885*	0.323	0.926*	0.301	0.942*	0.299	0.949	0.299
MaxScore									
Sum # Post.	1	**0.871**	**0.279**	**0.891**	**0.292**	**0.910**	**0.301**	**0.922**	**0.304**
Combination	42	0.841*	0.306	0.875	0.311	0.892	0.329	0.902	0.339
Wand									
Sum # Post.	1	0.812	0.287	0.840	0.253	0.857	0.249	0.870	0.249
Combination	42	**0.912***	**0.200**	**0.922***	**0.181**	**0.921***	**0.188**	**0.928***	**0.189**

Table 4: Pearson correlations and RMSE values (in seconds) on the test set queries when using all prediction features. Significantly different Pearson correlations from Sum # Postings are denoted *.

7. APPLYING QUERY EFFICIENCY PREDICTION TO QUERY SCHEDULING

While in general the main retrieval efficiency measure is the average time required to process the queries (*average response time*), when a stream of queries is received by a search engine, it might not be possible to start processing a new query as soon as it arrives. Instead, when the system is busy processing a query, subsequent queries are queued [7]. Therefore, the actual time delay experienced by a user while waiting for search results (*completion time*) is given by the execution time (response time) of the query, plus the time the query spent waiting to be processed (*waiting time*).

Classically, queued queries have been processed in a FIFO manner (i.e. first-come first-served) [7]. However, this only results in minimising queueing time if each query has an equal response time [20]. Instead, we propose that queues of queries can be scheduled to execute out of arrival order, by deploying specific *scheduling algorithms* [20]. In this way, for instance, quick queries may be scheduled between longer queries, to reduce the mean time delay experienced by the user population of the search engine.

As mentioned in Section 2, an oft-deployed approach to increase query throughput and reduce the average completion time is to replicate the number of query servers available for a given index shard. Hence, a new query arriving at the broker is sent to a query server that is idle, or least loaded. However, as the number of CPU cores in each query server is finite, it is natural that queries are queued until the query server is able to process them. In this manner, we propose two possible architectures for such a replicated retrieval system, as illustrated in Figure 6 for a single index shard. In the *broker queue* architecture, newly arrived queries are queued by the broker, before routing to the next available query server. In contrast, in the *queue per server* architecture, each new query is routed directly to a query server, which queues that query until it can be processed. In both architectures, there are potentials to improve the overall efficiency by the appropriate online scheduling of queries.

For instance, in the broker queue architecture, the queue can be sorted to balance throughput. For queue per server, a query can be sent to the query server with the lowest loading, for instance by measuring the number of queries it has queued to process. However, as shown in Section 5, different queries can take different amounts of time to complete, dependent on the nature of the pruning experienced by the query. As a result, a newly arrived query can be scheduled onto a query server that already has a queue of

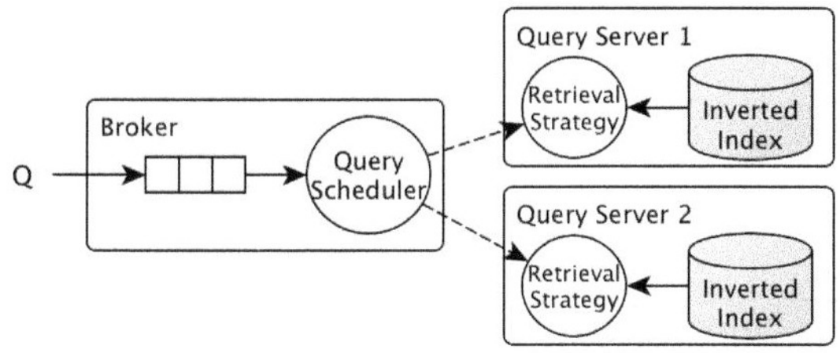

(a) Broker queue

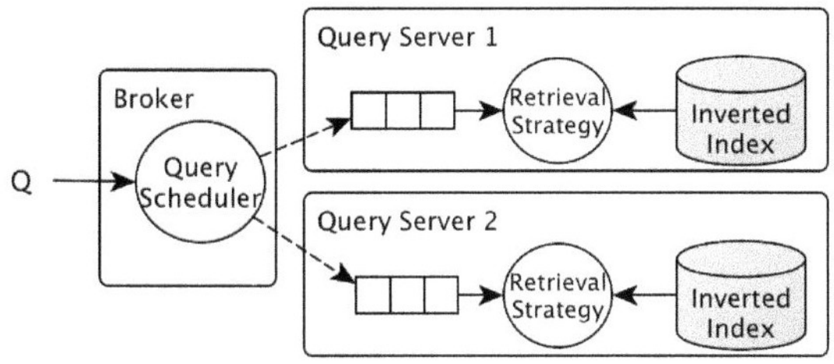

(b) Queue per server

Figure 6: Architectures for replicated query servers.

expensive queries, rather than another server which has a queue of inexpensive queries, resulting in poor load balancing across query servers. Instead, in this section, we show how query efficiency predictors can be used to improve the online scheduling of queries to distribute load across query servers, and result in improved mean completion time.

In the following we test different methods of online scheduling of queries across replicated query servers, both with a single broker queue and with a queue per server. For the former, we consider three scheduling methods [20]:

FIRST COME FIRST SERVED (FCFS): Incoming queries are kept sorted in arrival order, and as soon as a server is idle, it starts processing the first query in the queue [7]. FCFS does not need any information about the execution time of a query, and hence forms our baseline.

ACTUAL SHORTEST JOB FIRST (ASJF): Incoming queries are kept sorted in increasing order of expected service time, and scheduled to the servers in that order. ASJF assumes knowledge of the actual execution time a query will take, and hence represents scheduling with perfect knowledge, forming an oracle. ASJF is the optimal schedule to reduce the mean queueing time experiences by each query [20].

PREDICTED SHORTEST JOB FIRST (PSJF): As ASJF, but uses predicted execution times provided by our framework from Section 6 instead of actual times.

When the queue per server architecture is used, an incoming query is dispatched by the broker to a server as soon as it arrives, and then queued by that server until retrieval can commence. In this scenario, we test three methods for dispatching queries to server:

QUEUE LENGTH (QL): Queries are scheduled onto the query server with the shortest queue length. This represents our baseline.

ACTUAL EXECUTION (AE): Queries are scheduled onto the query server with the smallest queue duration time, assuming that the actual execution times of the queued queries are known a-priori. This represents scheduling with perfect knowledge, forming an oracle.

PREDICTED EXECUTION (PE): Queries are scheduled onto the query server with the smallest queue duration time, using predicted execution times provided by our framework from Section 6.

Comparing the two architectures, there are likely advantages in deploying the queue per server architecture, as this does not require the broker to know the predicted response time of a query, which uses statistics likely to be stored with the index. However, scheduling quality might be degraded by the use of multiple queues [25].

7.1 Simulation Experimental Setup

In the following, we perform simulation experiments to address the following research questions:
3. Can scheduling improve the average completion time of queries in a replicated query servers setting?
4. Can query efficiency prediction improve over Sum # Postings when scheduling queries for WAND?
5. Which replicated retrieval system architecture, broker queue (Section 7.2) or queue per server (Section 7.3), produces lower average completion times?

We devise an experiment that simulates the execution of query processing across multiple query servers, using the actual query arrival times of the 8,278 test queries from the MSN query log for various pruning strategies. This query set includes the original test set of 5,000 multi-term queries used in previous section, as well as single term queries from the same time period (approximately the 2nd 2.5 hours of May 1st 2006). The arrival rate of new queries varies between 20 and 100 per minute.

Predicted and actual query response times are as obtained from the experiments in Section 6 - i.e. for Full and MAXSCORE, we use the Sum # postings, while, for WAND, to show the benefit of our efficiency prediction framework, we compare Sum # postings and the 42 feature regression model. Hence, in the following experiments, the suffix (1) denotes the Sum # postings predictor, while (42) denotes the 42 feature regression model. For single term queries, no pruning is possible, and hence we use # postings to predict the response time of all retrieval strategies.

Simulation has previously been shown to accurately model distributed and replicated search engine architectures [7]. Our simulation experiments do not model the cost of computing an efficiency prediction. Indeed, as all features for each query term are in memory, the floating point operations to compute the predicted response time require very few CPU cycles. We also fix the number of cores per server to 1, such that contention for memory bandwidth within query servers need not be modelled. However, the number of replicated query servers is varied in the range 1..4.

Finally, following scheduling practises [20], we measure the scheduling success by comparing average wait times (AWTs) and average completion times (ACTs), as measured from the queries' arrival times.

7.2 Results: Broker Queue

Table 5 reports the ACTs and AWTs in seconds, for different scheduling strategies, pruning strategies and number of servers in the broker queue architecture. The optimal results are obtained when every query is served as soon as it arrives, i.e. they represent the average response times, with no waiting time. Other results are reported for other scheduling algorithms. In addition to executing queries in their arrival order (FCFS), three variants of shortest job first are deployed: ASJF represents the best case scheduling, when the broker's queue is sorted by the known response time of each query; in PSJF(1), queries are scheduled by their total num-

Scheduling Algorithm	Full		MaxScore		Wand	
	ACT	AWT	ACT	AWT	ACT	AWT
$+\infty$ query servers						
Optimal	0.691	0	0.573	0	0.401	0
1 query server						
FCFS	309.514	308.822	119.603	119.030	10.748	10.347
ASJF	68.379	67.688	24.540	23.967	2.674	2.274
PSJF(1)	71.460	70.769	26.596	26.023	5.314	4.913
PSJF(42)	-	-	-	-	3.230	2.829
2 query servers						
FCFS	2.005	1.314	1.012	0.439	0.524	0.123
ASJF	1.224	0.533	0.822	0.249	0.488	0.087
PSJF(1)	1.226	0.535	0.829	0.256	0.516	0.115
PSJF(42)	-	-	-	-	0.492	0.091
3 query servers						
FCFS	0.821	0.130	0.641	0.068	0.424	0.023
ASJF	0.776	0.085	0.621	0.047	0.419	0.018
PSJF(1)	0.777	0.086	0.621	0.048	0.423	0.022
PSJF(42)	-	-	-	-	0.420	0.019
4 query servers						
FCFS	0.723	0.031	0.588	0.015	0.406	0.005
ASJF	0.713	0.022	0.585	0.012	0.405	0.004
PSJF(1)	0.714	0.022	0.586	0.013	0.406	0.005
PSJF(42)	-	-	-	-	0.405	0.004

Table 5: Average completion time (ACT) and average waiting time (AWT) for different scheduling strategies, pruning strategies and number of servers, for broker queue architecture.

ber of postings; in PSJF(42), queries are scheduled by their predicted response time using all 42 prediction features.

On analysing Table 5, we firstly note that, as expected, MaxScore and Wand improve over the efficiency of the exhaustive Full. Next, on analysing the scheduling strategies, we find that FCFS performs very poorly when applied to a single server. This is a well-known problem of FCFS [20]: a query requiring a long time to process will delay all subsequent queries that, even if they require a short time to process, must wait for the long query to complete. Nevertheless, AWTs are decreased when dynamic pruning strategies are used: for example, Wand gives a benefit of 97% to the average completion time of FCFS on a single server (309.514 to 10.748 seconds). Moreover, dynamic pruning also helps in reducing the average completion time with FCFS scheduling when multiple servers are used.

Next, we compare the scheduling FCFS and ASJF, and observe that in all cases, ASJF results in markedly reduced ACTs and AWTs. This in line with our expectations from the scheduling literature [20]. The margin of improvement decreases as more servers are added, as there is less contention for query servers, and hence scheduling has less effect. Indeed, the query load within this query set is adequately handled by four query servers, as the results are very close to the optimal completion time, i.e. no queries are queued and average waiting times are close to 0. Nevertheless, the overall reduced AWTs and ACTs exhibited by ASJF allow us to conclude that there is the potential for scheduling to improve the efficiency of both non-replicated and replicated retrieval settings.

Finally, we examine the use of predicted execution times instead of actual ones (i.e. PSJF). In particular, as expected, for Full and MaxScore, the performance of PSJF(1) is almost the same as ASJF scheduling. However, PSJF(1) – i.e. Sum # Postings – does not produce accurate estimations of response time for the considerably more efficient Wand. Indeed, using the learned model with all 42 prediction features Wand results in ACT and AWTs that are much closer to the best case ASJF performances – e.g., for Wand, PSJF(42) results in a 70% reduction in ACT for a single query server compared to FCFS (from 10.748 seconds to 3.230 seconds).

Scheduling Algorithm	Full		MaxScore		Wand	
	ACT	AWT	ACT	AWT	ACT	AWT
$+\infty$ query servers						
Optimal	0.691	0	0.573	0	0.401	0
2 query servers						
QL	2.186	1.495	1.150	0.577	0.593	0.192
AE	2.054	1.363	1.047	0.474	0.540	0.139
PE(1)	2.055	1.363	1.058	0.485	0.593	0.192
PE(42)	-	-	-	-	0.551	0.150
3 query servers						
QL	0.935	0.244	0.715	0.142	0.461	0.060
AE	0.845	0.158	0.654	0.081	0.430	0.029
PE(1)	0.853	0.161	0.656	0.083	0.458	0.057
PE(42)	-	-	-	-	0.433	0.032
4 query servers						
QL	0.774	0.082	0.622	0.046	0.422	0.021
AE	0.733	0.042	0.594	0.021	0.408	0.007
PE(1)	0.734	0.043	0.596	0.022	0.419	0.018
PE(42)	-	-	-	-	0.409	0.008

Table 6: Average completion time (ACT) and average waiting time (AWT) for different scheduling strategies, pruning strategies and number of servers, for queue per server architecture.

Hence, these results attest the usefulness of the proposed query efficiency prediction framework, and its benefits for the online scheduling of replicated query servers.

7.3 Results: Queue per Server

We now study scheduling in the queue per server architecture. In particular, Table 6 reports the ACTs and AWTs in this architecture[6]. Three different scheduling methods are tested for measuring the outstanding queue for a query server: Queue Length (QL) – baseline, Actual Execution (AE) – best-case scheduling – and Predicted Execution (PE), which uses predicted response times from the query efficiency prediction framework. Two variants of PE are employed, one using total number of postings alone (1) and one using all 42 prediction features (42). A particular advantage of PE in the queue per server architecture is that the broker does not require the predicted response time of a query, but instead only the predicted response times of the queries already queued on that server.

From Table 6 we draw several observations. Firstly, choosing the query server for the next query using QL is worse than AE, across different numbers of servers. Moreover, PE produces results that are only slightly worse than the best-case AE, and in all cases better than QL. Indeed, with more than three servers, AWTs reduce towards 0 across all pruning strategies. As expected, the PE(1) results are good for Full and MaxScore, however for Wand, PE(42) results in ACTs and AWTs that are much closer to AE than PE(1). Indeed, for two query servers, PE(42) results in a 22% reduction in AWT for Wand compared to QL (from 0.192 seconds to 0.150 seconds), and a 7% reduction in ACT (0.593 to 0.551 seconds). Once again, this shows the accuracy of the query efficiency framework at encapsulating Wand's pruning behaviour.

Lastly, we compare Tables 5 & 6 to address our final research question on the two replication architectures. In general, response times are slightly lower using the broker queue architecture. For instance, the ACT of Wand with three query servers using PSJF(42) is 0.420, while PE(42) is slightly higher at 0.433. This is explainable in that the bro-

[6]We omit the results for the single server scenario, as these results are equivalent to FCFS in Table 5.

ker queue can be appropriately sorted by expected execution length, while in queue per server, the scheduling of queries is less refined [25]. However, we recognise that queue per server does not require the broker to be able to predict execution times. This is likely beneficial for fully distributed retrieval settings, when the index is sharded across multiple query servers and multiple servers serving each shard, where it is unlikely that the broker can know the predicted response times of all shards.

Overall, we conclude that the online scheduling of queries to query servers can improve the average wait and completion times of queries - indeed, PSJF improved over FCFS for the broker queue architectures, and PE improved over QL for the queue per server architecture. Moreover, such scheduling is made possible by our proposed novel framework for query efficiency prediction, particularly for the most efficient WAND dynamic pruning retrieval strategy.

8. CONCLUSIONS

Dynamic pruning techniques can improve the efficiency of queries, but result in different queries taking different amounts of time. We empirically investigated the efficiency of different queries for in-memory inverted indices, and showed how and why the amount of pruning that could be applied for a query can vary. Next, we proposed a framework for predicting the efficiency of a query, which uses linear regression to learn a combination of aggregates of term statistics. Experiments for 10,000 queries retrieving from an in-memory index of the TREC ClueWeb09 collection (50 million documents) showed that our learned predictors encapsulating 42 features could successfully predict the response time of the state-of-the-art WAND dynamic pruning retrieval strategy.

Moreover, we proposed the online scheduling of queries across replicated query servers, driven by predicted response times of queries. Two different scheduling architectures were proposed, differing in the location of the queueing. Simulation experiments showed not only the advantages of scheduling, but also the benefit of more accurate predicted response times within the scheduling algorithms.

We believe that there are many applications for the proposed query efficiency framework. For instance, we will investigate the application of query efficiency predictors for query routing across multi-shard indices. The efficiency predictors may also be used for controlling the efficiency/effectiveness tradeoff (e.g. achieved by diluting the top K safeness requirement or reducing the term upper bounds [5]).

Acknowledgements

Craig Macdonald and Iadh Ounis acknowledge the support of EC-funded project SMART (FP7-287583).

9. REFERENCES

[1] G. Amati, C. Carpineto, and G. Romano. Query difficulty, robustness, and selective application of query expansion. In *Proc. ECIR 2004*, pp 127–137.

[2] V. N. Anh and A. Moffat. Pruned query evaluation using pre-computed impacts. In *Proc. SIGIR 2006*, pp 372-379.

[3] R. Baeza-Yates, A. Gionis, F. P. Junqueira, V. Murdock, V. Plachouras, and F. Silvestri. Design trade-offs for search engine caching. *ACM Trans. on Web*, 2:20:1–20:28, 2008.

[4] R. Blanco. *Index compression for information retrieval systems*. PhD thesis, University of A Coruna, 2008.

[5] A. Z. Broder, D. Carmel, M. Herscovici, A. Soffer, and J. Zien. Efficient query evaluation using a two-level retrieval process. In *Proc. CIKM 2003*, pp 426–434.

[6] J. D. Brutlag, H. Hutchinson, and M. Stone. User preference and search engine latency. In *Proc. ASA Joint Statistical Meetings 2008*.

[7] F. Cacheda, V. Plachouras, and I. Ounis. Performance Analysis of Distributed Architectures to Index One Terabyte of Text. In *Proc. ECIR 2004*, pp 394–408.

[8] J. M. Chambers and T. J. Hastie. *Statistical Models*. Wadsworth & Brooks, 1992.

[9] N. Craswell, R. Jones, G. Dupret, and E.Viegas, editors. *Proc. Web Search Click Data Workshop at WSDM 2009*.

[10] W. B. Croft, D. Metzler, and T. Strohman. *Search Engines – Information Retrieval in Practice*. Addison-Wesley, 2009.

[11] S. Cronen-Townsend, Y. Zhou, and W. B. Croft. Predicting query performance. In *Proc. SIGIR 2002*, pp 299–306.

[12] J. Dean. Challenges in building large-scale information retrieval systems: invited talk. In *Proc. WSDM 2009*.

[13] P. Elias. Universal codeword sets and representations of the integers. *Transactions on Information Theory*, 21(2):194–203, 1975.

[14] R. Fagin, A. Lotem, and M. Naor. Optimal aggregation algorithms for middleware. *J. of Computer & System Sciences*, 66(4):614–656, 2003.

[15] M. Fontoura, V. Josifovski, J. Liu, S. Venkatesan, X. Zhu, and J. Zien. Evaluation strategies for top-k queries over memory-resident inverted indexes. *Proc. VLDB Endowment 2011*, 4(12):1213–1224.

[16] Q. Gan and T. Suel. Improved techniques for result caching in web search engines. In *Proc. WWW 2009*, pp 431–440.

[17] C. Hauff. *Predicting the Effectiveness of Queries and Retrieval Systems*. PhD thesis, Univ. of Twente, 2010.

[18] B. He and I. Ounis. Inferring query performance using pre-retrieval predictors. In *Proc. SPIRE 2004*, pp 43–54.

[19] K. Kwok, L. Grunfeld, H. Sun, P. Deng, and N. Dinstl. TREC 2004 robust track experiments using PIRCS. In *Proc. TREC 2004*, pp 191–200.

[20] J. Y-T. Leung, editor. *Handbook of Scheduling*, Chapman & Hall, 2004.

[21] S. Luo and J. Callan. Using sampled data and regression to merge search engine results. In *Proc. SIGIR 2002*, pp 19–26.

[22] C. Macdonald, I. Ounis, and N. Tonellotto. Upper bound approximations for dynamic pruning. *ACM Trans. on Information Systems*, 29(4), 2011.

[23] A. Moffat, W. Webber, J. Zobel, and R. Baeza-Yates. A pipelined architecture for distributed text query evaluation. *Information Retrieval*, 10(3):205–231, 2007.

[24] A. Moffat and J. Zobel. Self-indexing inverted files for fast text retrieval. *ACM Trans. on Information Systems*, 14(4):349–379, 1996.

[25] P. Morse. Queues, Inventories and Maintenance: The Analysis of Operational Systems with Variable Demand and Supply. Dover, 2004.

[26] I. Ounis, G. Amati, V. Plachouras, B. He, C. Macdonald, and C. Lioma. Terrier: A high performance and scalable information retrieval platform. In *Proc. OSIR Workshop 2006*, pp 18–25.

[27] R. Ozcan, I. S. Altingovde, and O. Ulusoy. Cost-aware strategies for query result caching in web search engines. *ACM Trans. on Web*, 5:9:1–9:25, 2011.

[28] M. Persin. Document filtering for fast ranking. In *Proc. SIGIR 1994*, pp 339-348.

[29] N. Tonellotto, C. Macdonald, and I. Ounis. Query efficiency prediction for dynamic pruning. In *Proc. LSDS-IR 2011 at CIKM 2011*.

[30] H. Turtle and J. Flood. Query evaluation: strategies and optimizations. *Information Processing and Management*, 31(6):831–850, 1995.

[31] L. Wang, J. Lin, and D. Metzler. Learning to efficiently rank. In *Proc. SIGIR 2010*, pp 138–145.

Prefetching Query Results and its Impact on Search Engines

Simon Jonassen
Norwegian University of Science and Technology
Trondheim, Norway
simonj@idi.ntnu.no

B. Barla Cambazoglu
Yahoo! Research
Barcelona, Spain
barla@yahoo-inc.com

Fabrizio Silvestri
ISTI - CNR, Italy; and
Yahoo! Research, Barcelona
f.silvestri@isti.cnr.it

ABSTRACT

We investigate the impact of query result prefetching on the efficiency and effectiveness of web search engines. We propose offline and online strategies for selecting and ordering queries whose results are to be prefetched. The offline strategies rely on query log analysis and the queries are selected from the queries issued on the previous day. The online strategies select the queries from the result cache, relying on a machine learning model that estimates the arrival times of queries. We carefully evaluate the proposed prefetching techniques via simulation on a query log obtained from Yahoo! web search. We demonstrate that our strategies are able to improve various performance metrics, including the hit rate, query response time, result freshness, and query degradation rate, relative to a state-of-the-art baseline.

Categories and Subject Descriptors

H.3.3 [**Information Storage Systems**]: Information Retrieval Systems

General Terms

Design, Performance, Experimentation

Keywords

Web search engine, result caching, prefetching

1. INTRODUCTION

Commercial web search engines are expected to process user queries under tight response time constraints and be able to operate under heavy query traffic loads. Operating under these conditions requires building a very large infrastructure involving thousands of computers and making continuous investment to maintain this infrastructure [7]. Optimizing the efficiency of the web search systems is important to reduce the infrastructure costs. Even small improvements may immediately translate into significant financial savings for the search engine.

SIGIR'12, August 12–16, 2012, Portland, Oregon, USA.

Recent research has shown that result caching [5, 15] is a viable technique to enhance the overall efficiency of search engines. The main idea in result caching is to store the results of frequently or recently processed queries in a large cache and readily serve subsequent occurrences of queries by the cache. This way, significantly more expensive computations at the backend query processing system are avoided, leading to important efficiency gains in the form of reduction in query response latencies and backend query workloads.

Unlike earlier works that have a focus on limited-capacity caches [5, 15], more recent works assume result caches with infinite capacities [11]. The main reason behind this infinite cache assumption is the cheap availability of storage devices that are large enough to store the results of all previous user queries issued to the search engine. Under the infinite cache assumption all future queries can be served by the cache except for compulsory misses which have to be served by the search backend. However, an infinite result cache suffers from the staleness problem [11]. The dynamic nature of web document collections requires frequent index updates, which may render some cache entries stale [1, 8]. In some cases, the search results served by the cache may not be fresh enough in terms of their content and this may degrade the user satisfaction.

In practice, an effective solution to the freshness problem is to associate every result entry in the cache with a time-to-live (TTL) value [2, 11]. In this technique, a cache entry is considered stale once its TTL expires. The hits on the expired entries are treated as misses and are processed by the backend, leading to fresh results. This way, the TTL approach sets an upper bound on the staleness of any search result served by the cache. Unfortunately, it sacrifices some of the efficiency gains achieved by means of result caching. Since the cache hits on the expired cache entries are treated as cache misses, the query traffic volume hitting the backend search system significantly increases with respect to a scenario where no TTL value is associated with the cache entries. In general, the increased backend query volume leads to an increase in the query response latencies and more backend resources are needed to handle the query traffic. Moreover, there is a higher risk that the spikes in the query volume will lead to an overloaded backend, in which case certain queries may have to be processed in the degradation mode, i.e., search results are only partially computed for these queries and the user experience is hampered.

The above-mentioned negative consequences of the TTL approach can be alleviated by combining it with a prefetching[1] strategy that has the goal of updating results of cache entries that are expired or about to be expired before a user requests them [11]. An ideal prefetching strategy would have all queries be readily served by the cache. In practice, there is no perfect knowledge of queries that will be issued in the future. Hence, prefetching strategies can only be heuristics.

The observations made before form the main motivation of this paper. In particular, we aim to devise strategies to identify cache entries that are likely to be requested when they are expired. We proactively fetch the associated search results using the idle compute cycles of the backend. The main challenge associated with prefetching is to predict when an expired cache entry will be requested. The predicted times can be used to select queries whose results are worth prefetching and to prioritize them to obtain the highest performance benefit. Although related ideas on cache freshness [11] and batch query processing [12] appear in the literature (see Section 7), our work is novel in terms of the following contributions.

- We quantify the available opportunity for prefetching (i.e., the amount of backend capacity that can be used for prefetching) and the potential benefit (i.e., the amount of requests for expired cache entries), using a query workload obtained from Yahoo! web search. To best of our knowledge, these were not reported before.
- We propose offline and online strategies to select and prioritize queries that will potentially benefit from prefetching. The offline strategy relies on the observation that the queries tend to repeat on a daily basis and applies query log mining to identify queries whose results are to be prefetched. The online strategy relies on a machine learning model that predicts the next occurrence time of issued queries. Prefetching operations are then prioritized based on these expected times.
- We conduct simulations to observe some important performance metrics, including the hit rate, query response time, freshness, and query degradation rate.

The rest of the paper is organized as follows. In Section 2, we discuss our system model and motivate the result prefetching problem through observations made over a real-life web search query log. In Sections 3 and 4, we present the proposed offline and online prefetching strategies, respectively. We provide the details of our data and experimental setup in Section 5. The experimental results are presented in Section 6. We provide the related work in Section 7. The paper is concluded in Section 8.

2. PRELIMINARIES

System architecture. In this work, we assume the search engine architecture shown in Fig. 1. User queries are issued to the search engine's main frontend, which contains an infinite result cache where the entries are associated with a TTL value. Queries whose results are found in the cache and not yet expired are readily served by the result cache. Otherwise, they are issued to the frontend of a selected backend search cluster, which is composed of many nodes that host a large index build on the document collection (only one cluster is displayed in the figure). After a query is processed at the backend cluster, the computed results are cached together with the time of the computation so that the expiration time can be determined. The query prefetching module interacts with both the search engine frontend and the search cluster frontend. This module is responsible for selecting a set of queries that are expired or about to be expired (from the query logs or the result cache) and issuing them to the search cluster's frontend, which issues them to the backend. The results computed by the backend are then cached like regular user queries.

[1]The term prefetching is used in [13, 16] differently to imply requesting the successive results pages for a query.

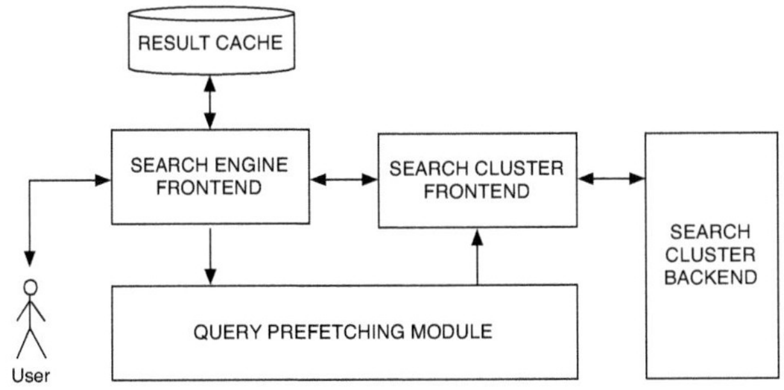

Figure 1: The sketch of a search engine architecture with a query prefetching module.

Query prefetching problem. Our focus in this work is on the query prefetching module. The idea behind this module is to avoid, as much as possible, potential cache misses by proactively computing, i.e., prefetching, the results of queries that are about to expire before they are requested by the users. At first glance, the problem of prefetching looks trivial as it seems easy to identify queries that are expired or about to be expired. The problem, however, is quite challenging because not all prefetching operations are useful and prefetching the results of a query consumes backend resources. In particular, if the results of a query are prefetched, but the prefetched results are not requested before they are expired, prefetching leads to waste of resources.

The most important benefit of prefetching is the increase in the cache hit rate [11]. This immediately corresponds to reduced average query response times as more queries can be served by the cache. In addition, the freshness can also be improved if unexpired cache entries are prefetched.[2] Finally, the fraction of queries whose results are computed in the degraded mode can be reduced if prefetching can decrease the amount of processing at peak query traffic times. In summary, the benefits expected from prefetching are reduced query response time, improved result freshness, and reduced query result degradation.

The query results need to be prefetched, as much as possible, when the user query traffic volume is low so that the user queries are not negatively affected from the query processing overhead incurred due to prefetching. Hence, the feasibility of prefetching depends on the availability of the low traffic hours. This raises the question whether the low traffic periods are long enough to prefetch sufficiently many query results. Moreover, the fraction of queries that can benefit from prefetching needs to be quantified. Finally, the potential risk for query result degradation needs to be identified.

[2]It is interesting to note that prefetching only expired cache entries results in increased staleness. In fact, cache staleness not necessarily impacts on results freshness as some expired results might not be retrieved in the future.

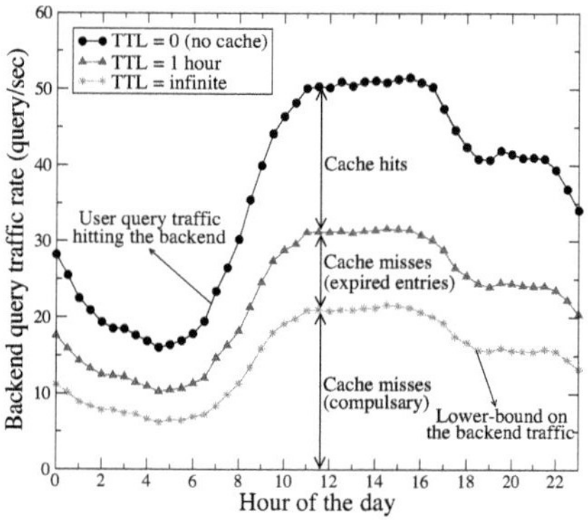

Figure 2: The user query traffic hitting the backend under different TTL values.

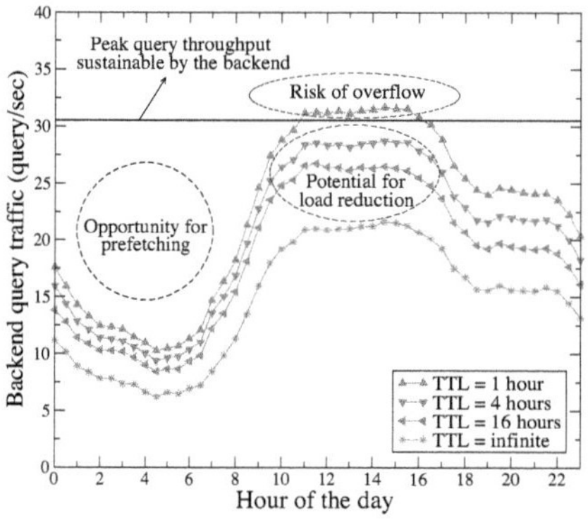

Figure 3: The variation in the user query traffic distribution within a day and its implications.

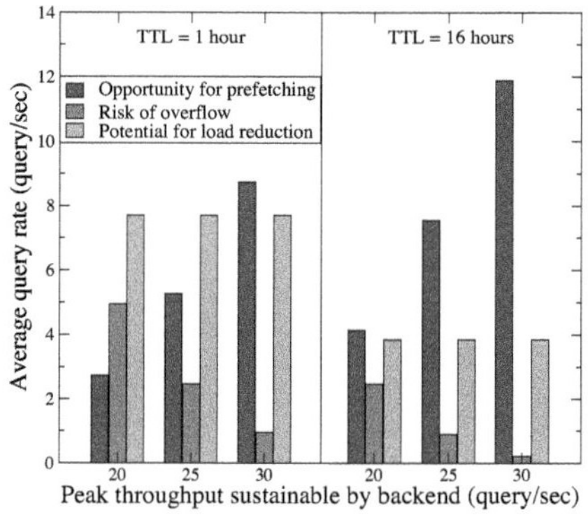

Figure 4: The opportunity, risk, and potential benefit (quantified as query per second).

We will look into these issues in what follows by analyzing a sample taken from the query traffic received by Yahoo! web search during a particular day.

Motivating observations. The upmost curve in Fig. 2 shows the user query traffic received by the search engine, i.e., the traffic that would hit the backend if there was no result cache. The bottom curve indicates the backend traffic in case of an infinite result cache with an infinite TTL, i.e., only the compulsory cache misses hit the backend. The curve in between shows the backend traffic volume when the TTL is set to one hour. We observe that, during the peak hours, a significant amount of cache misses (about one-third) are due to expired cache entries.

According to Fig. 3, there is a good amount of opportunity for prefetching (especially during the night) when compared to the amount of requests on expired cache entries. We observe that the traffic volume reaches its peak from 11AM to 4PM, resulting in a risk for query result degradation in scenarios where the backend traffic rate is comparable to the peak sustainable throughput (PST) of the backend (e.g., when the TTL is one hour). In general, the backend query load decreases with increasing TTL values, but the potential for reduction in the query load due to prefetching also decreases since there are fewer expired queries.

In Fig. 4, we try to quantify the existing opportunity for prefetching, the risk of overflow, and the potential for load reduction, assuming two different TTL values and three different PST values. The reported values are in terms of queries per second, averaged over the entire day. As an example, with a TTL of one hour and a PST of 20 query/sec, the overflow rate is about five queries per second.

Prefetching strategies. We evaluate two alternative types of prefetching strategies. The first set of techniques are offline and rely on query log mining. In these strategies, the prefetched queries are selected from the previous day's query logs. The second set of prefetching strategies are online. The idea here is to predict the next occurrence times of cached queries and try to prefetch expired or about-to-expire cache entries before they are requested while being in an expired state. Both types of strategies have two phases: the selection phase, where the queries whose results are to be prefetched are determined, and the ordering phase, where the selected queries are sorted in decreasing order of their importance and are prefetched in that order.

3. OFFLINE STRATEGIES

There is a high correlation between the repetition of some queries and the time of the day, i.e., some queries are more likely to be issued around the same time of the day. According to Fig. 2 in [10], a large fraction of queries are submitted about 24 hours after their latest submission. Hence, a reasonable strategy is to prefetch certain queries in the previous day's query logs. This strategy is based on query log mining and is completely offline. Hence, the query selection process does not incur any overhead on the runtime system.

3.1 Offline Query Selection

Let T denote the TTL of the result cache. Let τ denote the current time point and τ' denote the time point exactly 24 hours before τ. Assume that the time interval $[\tau', \tau)$ is split into N time intervals, each interval having a length of $s = (\tau - \tau')/N$ time units. Let $\langle \delta_1, \delta_2, \ldots, \delta_N \rangle$ be a sequence of N time intervals, where $\delta_i = [\tau' + (i-1) \times s, \tau' + i \times s)$. Each time interval δ_i is associated with a query bucket b_i that stores the queries issued to the search engine within the respective time interval. The queries to be prefetched during a particular future time interval $[\tau + (i-1) \times s, \tau + i \times s)$ are limited to those in the set of buckets $\langle b_i, b_{i+1}, \ldots, b_{i+\lfloor T/s \rfloor} \rangle$, i.e., the queries issued within the past time interval $[\tau' + (i-1) \times s, \tau' + (i-1) \times s + T)$. Hence, the prefetched queries are selected as

$$\mathcal{Q}_i = \bigcup_{j=i}^{i+\lfloor T/s \rfloor} b_j. \qquad (1)$$

At the end of a time interval δ_i, we switch to the next query set $\mathcal{Q}_{i+1}$ and start prefetching results of queries in that set.

3.2 Offline Query Ordering

Since it may not be possible to prefetch all queries associated with a time interval, the queries need to be ordered based on their importance, i.e., the benefit that can be achieved by prefetching a query. While ordering the queries, the past frequency of a query plays an important role. Herein, we discuss three simple strategies to determine the importance of a query.[3] The strategies differ in the way the past query frequency is weighted. In what follows, $w(q)$

[3]It is possible to come up with variants of these strategies.

represents the weight of a query q and $\mathcal{S}$ is the sample of queries considered in the selection phase mentioned above.

Unit-weighted frequency. This strategy assumes that a query's importance is equal to its frequency in $\mathcal{S}$, i.e.,

$$w(q) = \sum_{q_j \in \mathcal{S}} 1, \quad (2)$$

where q_j denotes an occurrence of q in the query sample $\mathcal{S}$. This strategy simply prefers prefetching frequent queries as an attempt towards increasing the likelihood of prefetching a query that will repeat again.

Workload-weighted frequency. This strategy assigns a heavier weight to those queries appearing during high-traffic periods, i.e., those that are issued when the backend query traffic volume is higher. The motivation here is to prefetch more queries from busy traffic hours so that the number of queries hitting the search cluster backend is reduced in those hours. We compute the weight of a query as

$$w(q) = \sum_{q_j \in \mathcal{S}} v(q_j), \quad (3)$$

where $v(q_j)$ represents the backend query traffic volume in queries per second when q_j is observed. This strategy aims at reducing the backend query volume at busy hours and, indirectly, it also aims at reducing the number of degraded query results.

Time-weighted frequency. This strategy give a higher priority to queries that occurred closer in time to τ'.

$$w(q) = \sum_{q_j \in \mathcal{S}} (\tau' + T - t(q_j)), \quad (4)$$

where $t(q)$ denotes the time at which q_j is issued. The assumption here is that the likelihood of prefetching a repeating query will increase.

4. ONLINE STRATEGIES

Online strategies are designed to identify queries that are already expired or about to expire and are going to be issued to the backend due to a TTL miss. Those queries are processed beforehand, possibly when the load at the backend is low. The key feature of this strategy is the prediction of the next time point (e_q) at which query q will be issued while its cached results are in an expired state.

In the rest of the section, we use the following notation. We denote by l_q the latest request time and by u_q the latest computation time of the results of query q. As in the previous section, τ denotes the current time and T denotes the TTL. We denote by s the selection period (i.e., we update the prefetching queue at every s time units) and by f_q the number of occurrences of q up to τ.

To estimate e_q, each time q is submitted, we predict the time to its next appearance, n_q. Under the assumption that q appears every n_q seconds, e_q can be calculated as $l_q{+}k{\times}n_q$, where k is the smallest natural number greater than 0 that satisfies $u_q{+}T{<}l_q{+}k{\times}n_q$, i.e., $k{=}\lfloor\frac{u_q+T-l_q}{n_q}\rfloor + 1$.

The value for n_q is computed through a machine learning model using the features given in Table 1. Temporal features are based on when a query is submitted. Query string features are based on the syntactic content of the query. Result page features capture the characteristics of the results returned by the search engine. Frequency features are based on counters associated with terms of the queries. We use gradient boosted decision trees to train our model [14].

Table 1: The features used by the learning model

Feature type	Feature	Description
Temporal	`hourOfDay`	Hour of submission
	`timeGap`	Time since last occurence
Query string	`termCount`	No. of terms in query
	`avgTermLength`	Avg. term length
Result page	`pageNo`	Requested result page no
	`resultCount`	No. of matching results
Frequency	`queryFreq`	No. of occ. of query
	`sumQueryTF`	Sum
	`minQueryTF`	Minimum
	`avgQueryTF`	Average
	`maxQueryTF`	Max. term query log freq.
	`sumDocTF`	Sum
	`minDocTF`	Minimum
	`avgDocTF`	Average
	`maxDocTF`	Max. term document freq.

4.1 Online Selection

The key point in the online strategy is to prefetch queries satisfying $\tau < e_q \leq \tau{+}T$ when there is processing capacity. As a naïve method of query selection, one could scan the list of queries in the cache and pick those with e_q values that satisfy the constraint. In practice, this is not feasible as the cost of scanning the cache for every submitted query is prohibitive. Hence, we resort to use a bucket data structure where each bucket stores queries with e_q values within a time-period $[t, t+s)$. Insertions and deletions in the bucket list can be realized in $O(1)$-time.

As illustrated in Fig. 5, the prefetching module maintains a list of buckets. Each time a query is requested, we remove it from the current bucket, modify e_q and place it back in a new bucket. In particular, we have two situations. If the request is a hit, we modify e_q and potentially move the query into another bucket. Otherwise, if it is a miss, we delete it from its current bucket and issue it to the backend. Once it has been processed, we update e_q and eventually insert q in the bucket list. Finally, once in every s seconds we select queries having $e_q \in (\tau, \tau{+}T]$ from the corresponding buckets and place these in the prefetching queue.

4.2 Online Ordering

To prioritize the queries in the prefetching queue, we evaluate the following three methods:

Based on age-frequency. A query is assigned a weight

$$w(q) = (\tau - u_q) \times f_q.$$

In other words, older and more frequent queries get a higher priority. This strategy tends to favor frequent queries that were refreshed long time ago. The goal of this method is to optimize the freshness of the results.

Based on age-frequency and degradation. We extend the weight function to include degradation.

$$w(q) = (\tau - u_q) \times f_q \times (1 + d_q).$$

This strategy favors older and degraded queries. The goal of this method is to optimize the freshness of the results and reduce the degradation.

Based on processing cost and expected load. Each query is prioritized according to its expected processing cost

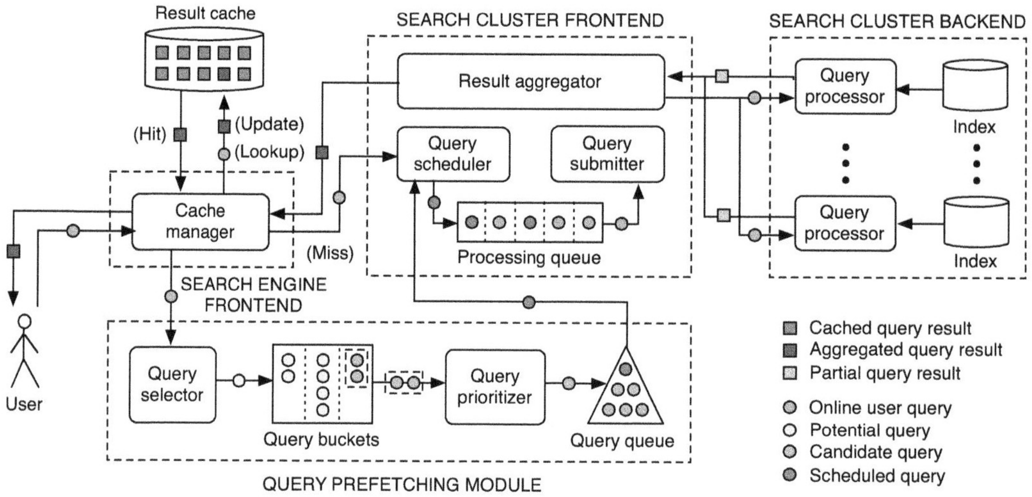

Figure 5: The proposed search engine architecture with query prefetching capability.

times the expected difference in the backend load.

$$w(q) = \rho(q) \times L(e_q),$$

where $\rho(q)$ is the estimated processing cost and $L(e_q)$ is the backend load that is observed 24 hours prior to e_q. This strategy aims at reducing the query response time and increasing the throughput.

5. DATA AND SETUP

Prefetching strategies. We evaluate a number of competing strategies. The first type of strategies are baseline strategies that do not employ any prefetching. These are `no-ttl`, which assumes that there is an infinite result cache with no TTL for entries so that any repetition of a query is a hit, and `no-prefetch`, which assumes that there is an infinite result cache with a TTL, but the prefetching logic is not activated. The second type of strategies are the offline strategies discussed in Section 3: `off-freq`, `off-vol`, and `off-time`. The third type of strategies are the online strategies discussed in Section 4: `on-age`, `on-agedg`, and `on-load`. The fourth type are the oracle versions of online strategies in which the exact next occurrence times of queries are assumed to be known. Following the convention in naming the online strategies, we refer to the oracle strategies as `oracle-age`, `oracle-agedg`, and `oracle-load`. The last implementation is an interpretation of the age-temperature refreshing strategy [11], which we refer to as `age-temp`.

The original `age-temp` strategy maintains a two-dimensional bucket structure, where one of the dimensions corresponds to the result age and the other dimension corresponds to the query frequency (temperature). In our implementation of this strategy, each age bucket is defined by the selection interval s and the temperature is computed as $\log_2(f_q)$, where f_q is the number of times a query is seen since the beginning of the first day. Each time a query is requested, we increase its frequency and potentially move it to a bucket corresponding to a higher temperature. Each time a query is processed, we move it to the bucket with the same temperature but the age dimension corresponding to τ. Furthermore, in our experiments, the temperature of a query cannot decrease. As an alternative, we have evaluated the use of a sliding time-window to dynamically maintain the number of occurrences. However, we have observed that with a window of reasonable size, e.g., 24 or 48 hours, the hit rate tends to be lower. Therefore, in our experiments, we count occurrences starting from the beginning of the first day. Further, we prioritize buckets by the corresponding age $\times$ temperature value and restrict selection to the first 30,000 queries satisfying a minimum age requirement, which prevents too fresh queries from being repeatedly refreshed. We denote the minimum result age as R and use it as the limiting factor for queries selected also by the other methods. Finally, among the selected queries, we give a higher priority to expired queries instead of unexpired ones.

In the `offline` strategies, the only cache state information that is made available to the prefetching module is whether an entry is older than R or not. Other information relies only on the query log from the past day and includes nothing about the current cache state. In the `online` strategies, the decisions are made based on the current cache state and the prediction model mentioned before. As predicting, based on a limited query log, the arrival times of queries that request expired entries is a challenging problem, we allow an entry to be prefetched up to two times without being hit in between.

We use the `oracle` strategies to show the effect of accurate prediction of the next request for an expired entry. The oracle strategies have no information about future hits, neither the number of occurrences nor the time at which they will occur. Nevertheless, they demonstrate that accurate prediction of the next requests for expired entries is enough to achieve good performance. Note that, in our results, we report only the results for the `oracle-agedg` strategy since it always outperforms the other two alternatives.

Simulation setup. We sample queries from five consecutive days of Yahoo! web search query logs. The queries in the first three days are used to warmup the result cache. No prefetching is done in these days. At the end of the third day, we start allowing queries into our data structures. The age-temperature baseline starts with queries collected from the first three days. The offline strategies start with queries collected during the third day. The online strategies use the first three days to create a model. As no predictions are

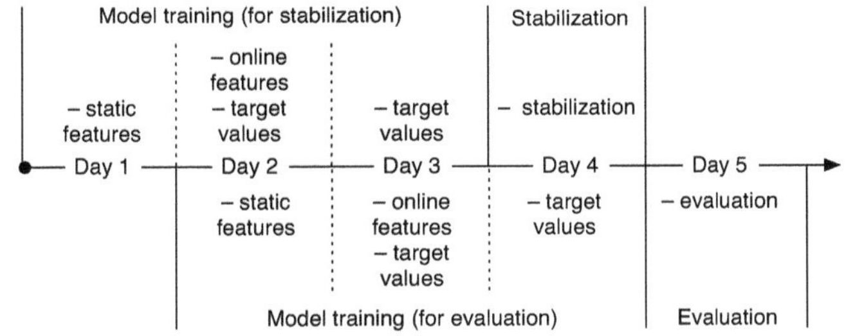

Figure 6: Temporal splitting of the query log with respect to the tasks.

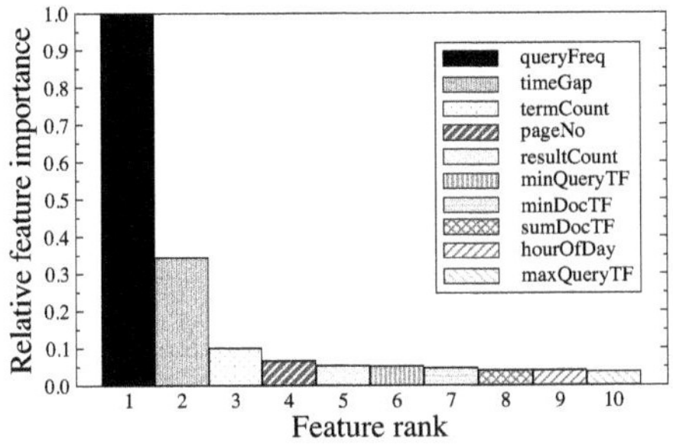

Figure 7: Feature importance.

made before the beginning of the fourth day, we use average inter-arrival times to initiate the bucket structure at the end of day three. We assume that the prefetching logic is activated at the beginning of the fourth day. Finally, for all of the techniques, we use the fourth day to stabilize the performance and the fifth day for the performance evaluation.

For the prediction model used by the online strategies, the first day of the training period is used to compute the static features (e.g., query and term frequencies).[4] The instances for which the next arrival times are tried to be predicted are extracted from the second day. The target values (i.e., the next arrival times that are tried to be predicted) are obtained from the second and third days. This setup is illustrated in Fig. 6. The importance values for the features used by the model are displayed in Fig. 7. As expected, the query frequency and the time gap between the two consecutive occurrences of a query turn out to be the most important features. For the fourth and fifth days, we train a learning model using the preceding three days.

System parameters and query processing logic. The experiments are conducted using a discrete event simulator that takes as input the user queries along with their original submission timestamps. We simulate a system with K compute nodes and P query processors, which allows up to P queries to be concurrently processed with a speedup proportional to K. We assume that the entire inverted index is maintained in the memory. In all experiments, we set the TTL (T) to 16 hours, which is chosen by an analysis of the opportunity, risk, and potential benefits of prefetching shown in Fig. 4. We fix P to 8 and vary K to create three different scenarios corresponding to poor ($K = 850$), medium ($K = 1020$), and high performance ($K = 1224$) systems. With 850 nodes, both `no-prefetch` and `no-ttl` experience a degradation of efficiency at peak performance. With 1020 nodes (20% above the first scenario), `no-ttl` reaches the peak sustainable throughput only marginally. With 1224 nodes (20% above the second scenario), both `no-prefetch` and `no-ttl` perform well.

If more than P queries are concurrently issued to the backend, the most recent queries are put into a processing queue. To prevent the queue from growing indefinitely, we monitor the processor usage P_l over the last minute. When $P_l > 0.95 \times P$, we degrade the currently processed query by P/Q_τ, where Q_τ is the number of queries being processed at the backend at that time.

[4]We use a document collection containing several billion documents to compute the features that rely on the document frequencies of terms.

Since prefetching happens while user queries are scheduled, we monitor the average number of user queries being processed over the last minute Q_l and maintain a budget of $B = \lfloor f \times P - Q_l \rfloor$ processors to be used for prefetching. By default, we use $f = 0.875$ to keep the processor utilization around 87.5 percent. To prevent the system from prefetching recently processed queries, we restrict the minimum age of queries being selected with a parameter R. In our experiments we use three different values, TTL/2, TTL/4 and TTL/8. Finally, the prefetching queue is updated/reset once in every $s = 10$ minutes.

Evaluation metrics. We evaluate the performance using five different metrics. The metrics are cache hit rate, query response time, average hit age, degradation rate, and backend query traffic rate. The hit rate reflects how good the prefetching algorithm is at having query results available at request. The change in response time reflects the real improvement from prefetching versus its overhead. The upper bound for both metrics is limited by the number of compulsory misses and corresponds to the hit rate and latency of `no-ttl`. The average hit age reflects how good the prefetching method is at keeping cached results fresh. The degradation rate reflects the amount of degraded results being served to the user and is defined as the total degradation divided by the number of queries being answered by the frontend. The total degradation is the sum of the relative degradations of the results returned by the frontend. Finally, the average backend query traffic measures the average number of queries issued to the backend. The lower bound on this number is again defined by `no-ttl`.

6. EXPERIMENTS

In this section, we present the results of our experiments. Our first observation is that in all the cases that we analyze (except for one), the best possible results are obtained, as expected, by the `oracle-agedg` strategy (the last line in the tables). Obviously, not being feasible in practice, the oracle strategy is presented only as an upper bound to the results that can be attained by the other techniques. Indeed, as the prediction accuracy gets closer to that of the oracle, we should get better and better results.

Note that, in the sole case of the average hit age results reported in Table 6, the `oracle-agedg` strategy leads to suboptimal results. This behavior can be explained by observing that the age decreases as we increase the number of times an entry is subject to prefetching. The oracle, instead, minimizes the amount of prefetching and thus some entries (especially those requested further in the future) tend to have higher ages.

Table 2: **Cache hit rate**

Strategy	$K=850$			$K=1020$			$K=1224$		
	$R=T/8$	$R=T/4$	$R=T/2$	$R=T/8$	$R=T/4$	$R=T/2$	$R=T/8$	$R=T/4$	$R=T/2$
`no-prefetch`	0.493	–	–	0.494	–	–	0.494	–	–
`no-ttl`	0.600	–	–	0.600	–	–	0.600	–	–
`age-temp`	0.517	0.517	0.516	0.533	0.533	0.533	0.542	0.542	0.543
`off-freq`	0.512	0.512	0.510	0.515	0.515	0.514	0.517	0.518	0.517
`off-vol`	0.511	0.511	0.509	0.514	0.514	0.513	0.516	0.517	0.517
`off-time`	0.511	0.511	0.509	0.515	0.515	0.515	0.519	0.521	0.521
`on-age`	0.534	0.535	0.533	0.546	0.547	0.547	0.549	0.550	0.553
`on-agedg`	0.534	0.535	0.533	0.546	0.547	0.547	0.549	0.550	0.553
`on-load`	0.493	0.493	0.494	0.494	0.494	0.495	0.494	0.494	0.497
`oracle-agedg`	0.597	0.596	0.592	0.599	0.599	0.600	0.600	0.600	0.600

Table 2 shows the cache hit rate of different strategies for various parameters. The `no-prefetch` and `no-ttl` strategies are the two extreme cases. The `no-prefetch` strategy does not involve prefetching and relies only on the TTL to cope with staleness problem. The `no-ttl` strategy correspond to an infinite cache scenario, where only the compulsory misses incur a cost. In between these two extremes, by varying the K and R parameters, we observe that, in all cases, the offline strategies perform worse than the `age-temp` baseline. Our online strategies, however, outperform the baseline. In particular, we compare the hit rate performance of a strategy A versus that of B by computing the relative hit rate improvement with respect to `oracle-agedg` as $I=\frac{\mathsf{HR}_A-\mathsf{HR}_B}{\mathsf{HR}_O-\mathsf{HR}_B}$, where HR_A, HR_B, and HR_O are the hit rates of the A, B, and `oracle-agedg` strategies, respectively. The improvement towards the oracle of our `on-age` versus the baseline `age-temp` ranges from 12% of `on-age` with $K=1224$ and $R=T/8$ to 22.78% of `on-age` with $K=850$ and $R=T/4$ with an average of 19.23%. Fig. 8 shows the hit rate trend of four different strategies: `no-prefetch`, `no-ttl`, `on-agedg`, and `oracle-agedg`. According to the figure, our method consistently outperforms the `no-prefetch` strategy.

In Table 3, we report the response time of our system by varying the simulation parameters. Query response time and hit rate are related and results confirm this behavior. As in the case of hit rate, we report the improvement with respect to the oracle that are similar to those of hit rate figures. The improvement towards the oracle of our `on-age` versus the baseline `age-temp` ranges from 12.4% of `on-age` with $K=1224$ and $R=T/8$ to 27.5% of `on-age` with $K=850$ and $R=T/8$ with an average of 21.1%. The hourly trend for the average response time is shown in Fig. 9, where the effect of peak load reduction is evident. From 11AM to 6PM, the peak load response time is greatly reduced. Therefore, in this case, the user experience should be greatly improved.

Another important aspect to consider when evaluating prefetching strategies is the load we put on the backend (Table 4). If we do not adopt any prefetching strategy, the load on the backend would certainly be affected only by the hit rate. Indeed, the higher the hit rate the less the number of queries hitting the backend. This is confirmed by the numbers in Table 4 as the `no-prefetch` strategy is the one attaining, in all cases, the minimum amount of workload at the backend. We remark that our goal is to optimize the exploitation of the infrastructure, i.e., to increase the overall load by keeping the amount of degraded queries as low as possible. Numbers in Table 4, thus, are more explanatory if read in conjunction with the results presented in Table 5. Disregarding the case $K=1224$, in which the computational capacity is too high to be overloaded even by a great number of prefetching operations (with the exception of `on-load` which tries to prefetch expensive queries first), in all cases, `on-age` and `on-agedg` attain the greatest reduction in terms of degraded queries, despite the average backend query traffic is greater than the baseline. Figs. 10 and 11 confirm the results reported in the tables and show even more remarkably the effect of prefetching on the backend query traffic, which results to be roughly flattened and far apart from the `no-cache` case. The degradation (Fig. 11) is also greatly reduced during the peak hours. In this case, we report degradation of query results for the case $K=850$ instead of $K=1020$ as in the other cases. This is because, for $K=1020$, the degradation is negligible.

We also report the average hit age measured in number of minutes passed since the last update. It is worth being pointed out that measuring the average hit ratio does not say much about the quality or staleness of results in the cache. In fact, if the majority of entries are updated but requested after a period of time very close to the TTL, the ideal strategy would not update them. Indeed, this would make the average hit age increase when those queries are actually requested only slightly before their expiration. We report these results in Table 6 and Fig. 12.

Finally, we measure the accuracy of prefetching methods. We define the accuracy as the fraction of correct prefetching actions. That is, the average between the fraction of prefetching operations never followed by a hit with respect to the total number of prefetching operations and the fraction of compulsory misses relative to the number of misses. As illustrated in Table 7, while performing less prefetching, the offline techniques have in general higher accuracy. In addition, it is worth to note that there is a high potential for improvement. If we compare prefetching accuracy with that of `oracle-agedg`, we can observe that we are still far from being close to the maximum. On the other hand, the worst accuracy is achieved by `on-load`, which illustrates that prioritizing frequent queries maximizes the probability of useful prefetching. We note that the `age-temp` baseline performs poorly with respect to our strategies.

In what follows, we enumerate what we retain to be the take away messages from this work. First, the baseline relies only on the knowledge of the past frequency and the current age. This approach cares about keeping popular entries fresh and does not care if they will be used again in the future. Second, the offline strategies rely only on the information about the queries submitted in the previous day. Even though they are worse than the baseline, they perform surprisingly well, given that they use only one day of history. Third, the online strategies rely on predicted future query expirations. This prediction task is very difficult to

Table 3: Average query response time (in ms)

	$K=850$			$K=1020$			$K=1224$		
Strategy	$R=T/8$	$R=T/4$	$R=T/2$	$R=T/8$	$R=T/4$	$R=T/2$	$R=T/8$	$R=T/4$	$R=T/2$
no-pefetch	309.1	–	–	157.5	–	–	112.5	–	–
no-ttl	183.6	–	–	122.0	–	–	95.5	–	–
age-temp	278.1	277.4	277.4	153.8	153.7	153.9	119.0	119.0	119.0
off-freq	280.5	279.9	280.1	157.2	156.2	155.3	120.3	117.8	114.8
off-vol	280.1	280.6	282.3	157.6	156.9	155.9	120.6	118.6	116.3
off-time	280.9	283.0	285.5	157.8	157.1	156.9	120.6	118.8	117.2
on-age	257.8	255.5	257.5	148.1	147.9	147.9	116.6	116.5	116.4
on-agedg	253.8	254.8	257.3	147.9	147.7	147.7	116.6	116.5	116.4
on-load	316.2	311.2	312.4	173.3	173.2	171.2	133.7	133.3	132.5
oracle-agedg	189.7	189.8	191.2	129.5	129.0	128.9	99.7	99.4	99.0

Table 4: Average backend query traffic rate (query/sec)

	$K=850$			$K=1020$			$K=1224$		
Strategy	$R=T/8$	$R=T/4$	$R=T/2$	$R=T/8$	$R=T/4$	$R=T/2$	$R=T/8$	$R=T/4$	$R=T/2$
no-prefetch	18.34	–	–	18.34	–	–	18.34	–	–
no-ttl	14.50	–	–	14.50	–	–	14.50	–	–
age-temp	23.48	23.44	23.41	27.28	27.09	26.93	32.75	32.44	32.07
off-freq	23.01	21.00	19.97	25.22	22.62	20.74	29.03	24.67	21.65
off-vol	22.98	20.97	19.95	25.19	22.59	20.83	29.00	24.97	22.23
off-time	23.04	21.18	20.08	25.15	22.73	21.28	29.23	25.50	22.92
on-age	25.11	24.93	24.33	30.34	30.03	29.15	36.99	36.43	35.26
on-agedg	25.07	24.86	24.28	30.35	30.03	29.15	36.99	36.43	35.26
on-load	18.95	19.03	19.24	19.53	19.60	19.88	20.78	20.86	21.17
oracle-agedg	20.92	20.49	19.85	22.47	21.63	20.74	23.99	23.19	21.62

Table 5: Average degradation rate ($\times 10^{-4}$)

	$K=850$			$K=1020$			$K=1224$		
Strategy	$R=T/8$	$R=T/4$	$R=T/2$	$R=T/8$	$R=T/4$	$R=T/2$	$R=T/8$	$R=T/4$	$R=T/2$
no-prefetch	166.9	–	–	1.398	–	–	0.000	–	–
no-ttl	7.2	–	–	0.003	–	–	0.000	–	–
age-temp	76.6	79.0	95.0	0.485	0.412	0.418	0.000	0.000	0.000
off-freq	87.9	88.2	89.8	0.645	0.731	0.849	0.000	0.000	0.000
off-vol	88.8	87.8	87.9	0.632	0.606	0.645	0.000	0.000	0.000
off-time	94.0	91.1	93.4	0.807	0.661	0.689	0.000	0.000	0.000
on-age	50.3	48.8	51.3	0.319	0.223	0.118	0.000	0.000	0.000
on-agedg	50.6	49.5	49.6	0.201	0.169	0.284	0.000	0.000	0.000
on-load	233.2	241.5	175.4	173.3	173.2	171.3	133.7	133.3	132.5
oracle-agedg	5.7	5.7	6.4	0.000	0.000	0.000	0.000	0.000	0.000

Table 6: Average hit age (in minutes)

	$K=850$			$K=1020$			$K=1224$		
Strategy	$R=T/8$	$R=T/4$	$R=T/2$	$R=T/8$	$R=T/4$	$R=T/2$	$R=T/8$	$R=T/4$	$R=T/2$
no-prefetch	357	–	–	356	–	–	356	–	–
no-ttl	4737	–	–	4735	–	–	4734	–	–
age-temp	342	356	375	170	209	289	137	170	246
off-freq	222	255	322	139	172	239	111	147	227
off-vol	222	254	327	138	172	329	111	148	226
off-time	226	259	329	144	179	242	118	155	232
on-age	217	255	333	135	163	235	114	148	222
on-agedg	216	254	333	135	163	235	114	148	222
on-load	356	356	353	356	356	355	352	352	360
oracle-agedg	272	291	336	258	280	324	265	287	332

Table 7: Prefetching accuracy

	$K=850$			$K=1020$			$K=1224$		
Strategy	$R=T/8$	$R=T/4$	$R=T/2$	$R=T/8$	$R=T/4$	$R=T/2$	$R=T/8$	$R=T/4$	$R=T/2$
age-temp	0.529	0.525	0.514	0.550	0.543	0.533	0.543	0.535	0.523
off-freq	0.543	0.593	0.629	0.551	0.586	0.610	0.534	0.563	0.592
off-vol	0.537	0.588	0.622	0.546	0.580	0.602	0.531	0.556	0.573
off-time	0.534	0.573	0.601	0.542	0.572	0.586	0.533	0.554	0.561
on-age	0.599	0.592	0.594	0.597	0.587	0.588	0.570	0.560	0.557
on-agedg	0.599	0.593	0.595	0.597	0.587	0.588	0.570	0.560	0.557
on-load	0.412	0.441	0.528	0.417	0.451	0.516	0.419	0.475	0.495
oracle-agedg	0.842	0.846	0.855	0.798	0.799	0.804	0.723	0.720	0.726

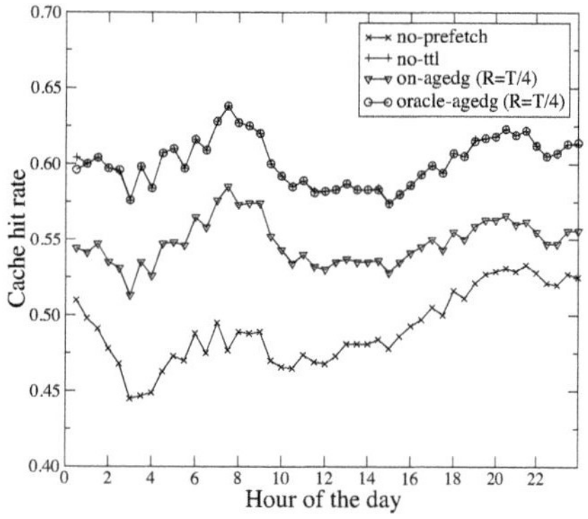

Figure 8: Result cache hit rate ($K = 1020$).

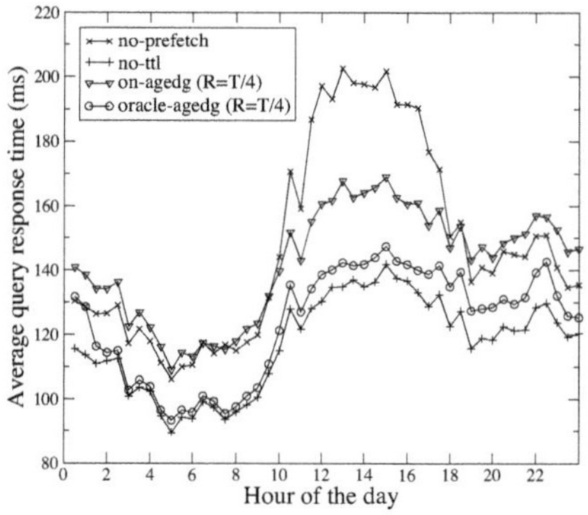

Figure 9: Average query response time ($K = 1020$).

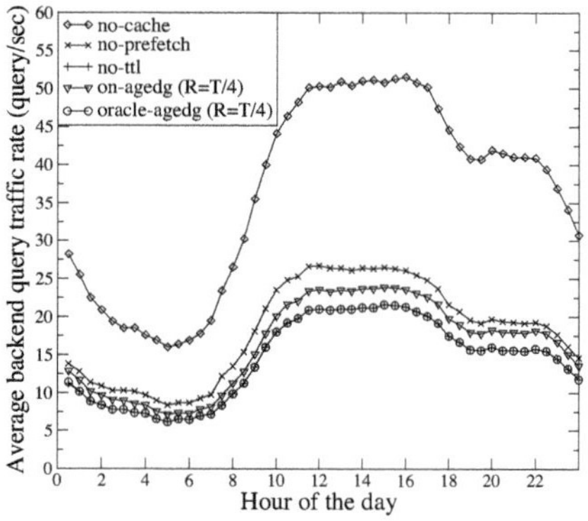

Figure 10: Backend query traffic rate (only user queries, $K = 1020$).

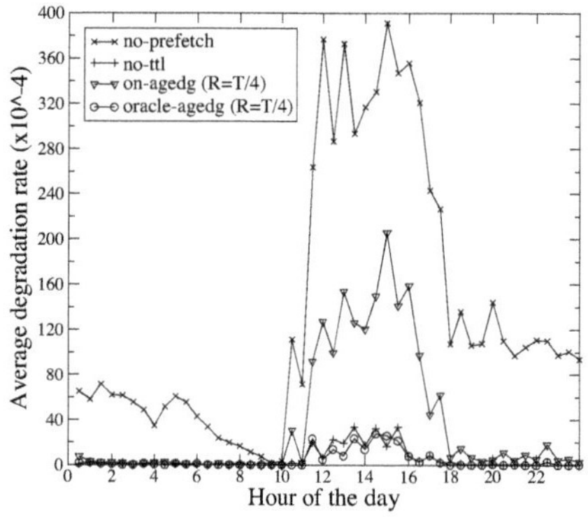

Figure 11: Average degradation rate ($K = 850$).

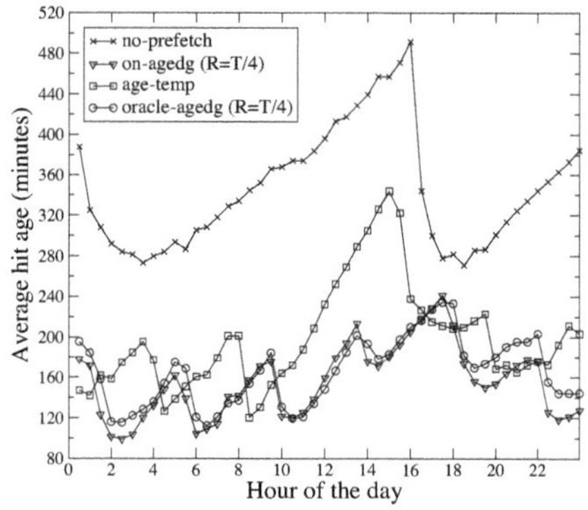

Figure 12: Average hit age ($K = 1020$).

carry out, as experiments show, yet a mildly good prediction policy gives very good results in terms of search backend exploitation, low query degradation, and hit-ratio. Fourth, even if oracle has a perfect knowledge of all the future misses, it does not have all the information needed to order the queries in the best possible way to reduce the number of misses, for instance. However, we use the oracle strategies as an upper bound to the effectiveness of prefetching with respect to the cache content. Finally, in Figs. 8–12, we observe that, during the peak hours, the benefits of prefetching are greatly amplified thus confirming our initial hypothesis, i.e., prefetching has a great potential for improving search engine utilization and peak-load performance.

7. PREVIOUS WORK

Herein, we survey the previous work on result caching, freshness, and batch query processing. Interested readers may refer to [10] for a broader survey on search efficiency.

Result caching. So far, a large body of research focused on increasing the result cache hit rates [4, 20] or to reduce the query processing cost of backend search systems [15, 21]. Depending on how the cache entries are selected, static [6], dynamic [22], or hybrid [13] caching strategies are followed. The earlier works assumed limited-capacity caches, where the main research issues are admission [5], prefetching [16], and eviction [20], whereas the recent works mostly adopted an infinite cache assumption [11]. A number of proposals are made to combine other layers of caching with result caching, resulting in two-level [3, 22], three-level [17, 18], or even five-level [19] caching architectures.

Cache freshness. The most recent works deal with result caching in the context of maintaining the freshness of the results served by the cache [1, 8, 9, 11]. In this line of research, the cache entries are associated with TTL values that are fixed for all queries. In [2], each query is associated with a different TTL value depending on its freshness requirements. In several works, the TTL approach is coupled either with more sophisticated techniques such as invalidation of potentially stale cache entries [1, 8, 9], where the goal is to predict the stale cache entries by exploiting certain information obtained during index updates. The search results whose freshness is potentially affected by the updates are then marked as invalid so that they are served by the backend system in a successive request, rather than by the cache. The approach followed in [11], on the other hand, relies on proactive refreshing of cached search results. In this approach, the indexing system does not provide any feedback on staleness. Instead, some presumably stale search results are selected and refreshed based on their likelihood of being requested in future and also depending on the availability of free processing cycles at the backend search system. Our work proposes strategies that are alternative to that in [11] and also focuses on different performance metrics.

Batch query processing. In [12], some efficiency optimizations are proposed for batch query processing in web search engines. Those optimizations (e.g., query reordering) are orthogonal to ours and, in case of a partially disk-resident index, they may be coupled with our prefetching techniques. Since we assume an in-memory index, however, we did not consider those optimizations in our work.

8. CONCLUSIONS AND FURTHER WORK

We investigated the impact of prefetching on search engines. We showed that an oracle strategy that has a perfect information of future query occurrences can achieve the best attainable results. We made an attempt to close the gap with the oracle by testing two alternative set of prefetching techniques: offline and online prefetching. We showed that the key aspect in prefetching is the prediction methodology. Furthermore, we showed that our accuracy in predicting future query occurrences is only about a half of the best that can be done. We plan to extend this work in several directions. First, we are going to design more effective techniques for predicting the expiration of a query. Second, we are going to evaluate the economic impact of prefetching on the search operations. Finally, we would like to design speculative prediction techniques that will be able to prefetch queries that were not even submitted. This would reduce the number of compulsory misses that form an upper bound on the cache performance.

9. ACKNOWLEDGMENTS

Simon Jonassen was an intern at Yahoo! Research and supported by the iAd Centre, Research Council of Norway and NTNU.

10. REFERENCES

[1] S. Alici, I. S. Altingovde, R. Ozcan, B. B. Cambazoglu, and O. Ulusoy. Timestamp-based result cache invalidation for web search engines. In *Proc. 34th Int'l ACM SIGIR Conf. Research and Development in Information Retrieval*, pages 973–982, 2011.

[2] S. Alici, I. S. Altingovde, R. Ozcan, B. B. Cambazoglu, and O. Ulusoy. Adaptive time-to-live strategies for query result caching in web search engines. In *Proc. 34th European Conf. Information Retrieval*, pages 401–412, 2012.

[3] I. S. Altingovde, R. Ozcan, B. B. Cambazoglu, and O. Ulusoy. Second chance: a hybrid approach for dynamic result caching in search engines. In *Proc. 33rd European Conf. Information Retrieval*, pages 510–516, 2011.

[4] R. Baeza-Yates, A. Gionis, F. Junqueira, V. Murdock, V. Plachouras, and F. Silvestri. The impact of caching on search engines. In *Proc. 30th Annual Int'l ACM SIGIR Conf. Research and Development in Information Retrieval*, pages 183–190, 2007.

[5] R. Baeza-Yates, F. Junqueira, V. Plachouras, and H. Witschel. Admission policies for caches of search engine results. In N. Ziviani and R. Baeza-Yates, editors, *String Processing and Information Retrieval*, volume 4726 of *Lecture Notes in Computer Science*, pages 74–85. Springer Berlin / Heidelberg, 2007.

[6] R. Baeza-Yates and F. Saint-Jean. A three level search engine index based in query log distribution. In M. A. Nascimento, E. S. de Moura, and A. L. Oliveira, editors, *String Processing and Information Retrieval*, volume 2857 of *Lecture Notes in Computer Science*, pages 56–65. Springer Berlin / Heidelberg, 2003.

[7] L. A. Barroso, J. Dean, and U. Hölzle. Web search for a planet: the Google cluster architecture. *IEEE Micro*, 23(2):22–28, 2003.

[8] R. Blanco, E. Bortnikov, F. Junqueira, R. Lempel, L. Telloli, and H. Zaragoza. Caching search engine results over incremental indices. In *Proc. 33rd Int'l ACM SIGIR Conf. Research and Development in Information Retrieval*, pages 82–89, 2010.

[9] E. Bortnikov, R. Lempel, and K. Vornovitsky. Caching for realtime search. In *Proc. 33rd European Conf. Information Retrieval*, pages 104–116, 2011.

[10] B. B. Cambazoglu and R. Baeza-Yates. Scalability challenges in web search engines. In M. Melucci, R. Baeza-Yates, and W. B. Croft, editors, *Advanced Topics in Information Retrieval*, volume 33 of *The Information Retrieval Series*, pages 27–50. Springer Berlin Heidelberg, 2011.

[11] B. B. Cambazoglu, F. P. Junqueira, V. Plachouras, S. Banachowski, B. Cui, S. Lim, and B. Bridge. A refreshing perspective of search engine caching. In *Proc. 19th Int'l Conf. World Wide Web*, pages 181–190, 2010.

[12] S. Ding, J. Attenberg, R. Baeza-Yates, and T. Suel. Batch query processing for web search engines. In *Proc. 4th ACM Int'l Conf. Web Search and Data Mining*, pages 137–146, 2011.

[13] T. Fagni, R. Perego, F. Silvestri, and S. Orlando. Boosting the performance of web search engines: Caching and prefetching query results by exploiting historical usage data. *ACM Trans. Information Systems*, 24(1):51–78, 2006.

[14] J. H. Friedman. Stochastic gradient boosting. *Comput. Stat. Data Anal.*, 38:367–378, February 2002.

[15] Q. Gan and T. Suel. Improved techniques for result caching in web search engines. In *Proc. 18th Int'l Conf. World Wide Web*, pages 431–440, 2009.

[16] R. Lempel and S. Moran. Predictive caching and prefetching of query results in search engines. In *Proc. 12th Int'l Conf. World Wide Web*, pages 19–28, 2003.

[17] H. Li, W.-C. Lee, A. Sivasubramaniam, and C. L. Giles. A hybrid cache and prefetch mechanism for scientific literature search engines. In *Proc. 7th Int'l Conf. Web Engineering*, pages 121–136, 2007.

[18] X. Long and T. Suel. Three-level caching for efficient query processing in large web search engines. In *Proc. 14th Int'l Conf. World Wide Web*, pages 257–266, 2005.

[19] M. Marin, V. Gil-Costa, and C. Gomez-Pantoja. New caching techniques for web search engines. In *Proc. 19th ACM Int'l Symp. High Performance Distributed Computing*, pages 215–226, 2010.

[20] E. P. Markatos. On caching search engine query results. *Computer Comm.*, 24(2):137–143, 2001.

[21] R. Ozcan, I. S. Altingövde, and O. Ulusoy. Cost-aware strategies for query result caching in web search engines. *ACM Trans. Web*, 5(2):9:1–9:25, 2011.

[22] P. C. Saraiva, E. Silva de Moura, N. Ziviani, W. Meira, R. Fonseca, and B. Riberio-Neto. Rank-preserving two-level caching for scalable search engines. In *Proc. 24th Annual Int'l ACM SIGIR Conf. Research and Development in Information Retrieval*, pages 51–58, 2001.

Online Result Cache Invalidation for Real-time Web Search

Xiao Bai
Yahoo! Research
Barcelona, Spain
xbai@yahoo-inc.com

Flavio P. Junqueira
Yahoo! Research
Barcelona, Spain
fpj@yahoo-inc.com

ABSTRACT

Caches of results are critical components of modern Web search engines, since they enable lower response time to frequent queries and reduce the load to the search engine backend. Results in long-lived cache entries may become stale, however, as search engines continuously update their index to incorporate changes to the Web. Consequently, it is important to provide mechanisms that control the degree of staleness of cached results, ideally enabling the search engine to always return fresh results.

In this paper, we present a new mechanism that identifies and invalidates query results that have become stale in the cache online. The basic idea is to evaluate at query time and against recent changes if cache hits have had their results have changed. For enhancing invalidation efficiency, the generation time of cached queries and their chronological order with respect to the latest index update are used to early prune unaffected queries. We evaluate the proposed approach using documents that change over time and query logs of the Yahoo! search engine. We show that the proposed approach ensures good query results (50% fewer stale results) and high invalidation accuracy (90% fewer unnecessary invalidations) compared to a baseline approach that makes invalidation decisions off-line. More importantly, the proposed approach induces less processing overhead, ensuring an average throughput 73% higher than that of the baseline approach.

Categories and Subject Descriptors

H.3.3 [**Information Search and Retrieval**]: Search process

General Terms

Algorithms, Experimentation, Performance

Keywords

Web search engine, real-time indexing, result cache, cache invalidation

1. INTRODUCTION

Large-scale Web search engines rely on one or more cache elements of previously computed results to serve user queries. Frequent queries issued to a search engine are directly served from its result cache, reducing both the average query response latency and the overall workload of the search backend. The cache hit ratio, as shown in the literature, reaches around 50% [2], depending on cache strategies, and even the classical cache strategy ensures a hit ratio of 30% [18]. As such, result caching has been used as an important optimization step in modern Web search engines.

An underlying assumption of using cache in search engines is that the same query, once repeated, always results in the same result. In practice, however, this is not the case. Modern Web search engines update their index periodically to incorporate changes to the Web. As a result, the search result of a query may change accordingly as the corpus of a search engine evolves.

Search engines can update their index in batch mode, incremental mode, or real-time mode, according to the freshness requirements for the search results. In batch mode, when documents are added, modified, or deleted, the search engine produces a new version of the index and rolls out this new version, superseding the previous one. The interval to produce a new version is often related to the size of the document collection, and typically varies from hours to days. Incremental mode is often used when it is desirable to bring down the time to introduce documents into the index to minutes or hours. With incremental indexing, we merge changes to the live index periodically, and each subsequent batch of documents is an increment to the previous index. When a search node finishes processing a new increment, it is used to produce a small index. This small index is then merged back into the live index. With real-time mode, a search node receives a continuous stream of individual documents and introduces them into the index in an online fashion to reduce the latency between fetching a document and making it searchable. The main difference between incremental and real-time modes according to our terminology is whether we merge the index on a per document basis.

It has been recently argued that, if the index is updated incrementally in a search engine using large result cache, the freshness of cached results becomes an issue since stale results potentially hurt user satisfaction [5, 9]. This issue might become even more severe for applications that require real-time index updates. Specifically, for applications like news search and social media search, new content (*e.g.*, news articles and tweets) are generated continuously, resulting in frequent change of query results. Moreover, in such applications, users are likely to issue same queries related to emerging events within short periods, increasing the hit ratio of the cache and thus the risk of serving stale results to users.

To highly benefit from real-time index updates, result caches are ideally managed in such a way that only the queries whose results do not change with respect to index update are served from the cache, and the queries whose results have changed are invalidated from the cache and re-evaluated against the updated index.

A simple approach to invalidate cached queries is to rely on their time-to-live in the cache [9]. A result is considered stale only if its time-to-live has expired. This approach makes its invalidation decisions independently of index update and results in a large number of stale results served to users. Alternatively, another approach, called CIP (Cache Invalidation Predictor) [5], invalidates cached queries whenever there are changes to the index. CIP is document-driven. It first generates for each new (or modified) document a synopsis, composed of a list of terms it contains as well as their TF-IDF (or BM25) scores. It then computes the relevance of this document to every query in the cache. A query is invalidated if its relevance to the new (or modified) document is larger than the least relevant document in its cached result. This approach is effective to ensure the freshness of the served results but is impractical to implement since each index update requires intensive computation that is linear to the cache size. Moreover, the high fraction of unnecessary invalidations increases the workload on the search engine by processing redundant queries against its index.

Contributions. In this paper, we propose *online cache invalidation*, a practical solution to invalidate cached queries with respect to real-time index update. More concretely,

- We propose a query-driven cache invalidation framework. An invalidation decision occurs only when there is a cache hit, which is key to its efficiency since no redundant invalidations occur for queries that are not issued any more. Basically, recent changes occurred in the index are consistently maintained in a subindex to evaluate the queries that lead to cache hits. A query is invalidated if its result from the subindex is more relevant than its cached result.

- We propose a pre-judgment mechanism for early pruning unaffected queries from invalidation, which limits the negative impact of online cache invalidation on query response time. To this end, we maintain the generation time of cached queries and the update time of the posting lists in the index. Only queries that have been inserted in the cache for a long time and whose related inverted lists have changed after their insertion to the cache are evaluated against subindex.

- We evaluate the online invalidation approach in a realistic setting. Different from the evaluation of CIP [5] where a static cache was used against a synthetic workload, we apply a dynamic cache over real document and query streams submitted to the Yahoo! News search engine during several weeks. The experimental evaluation conveys the efficiency of the online invalidation approach. Despite its overhead on search latency upon cache hits and memory usage, it improves the overall throughput by 73% and reduces the redundant invalidations and the stale results by 90% and 50% respectively with well-selected parameters.

Roadmap. The remainder of the paper is organized as follows. Section 2 details the proposed online cache invalidation approach. Section 3 discusses the experimental setup and reports the results. Section 4 surveys related work and Section 5 concludes the work.

2. ONLINE CACHE INVALIDATION

2.1 System model

Fig. 1 illustrates the search systems that we assume in this work. Generally, a crawler continuously updates the document collection of the search engine by discovering and fetching new and modified documents from the Web, and deleting documents that are no longer available. A search node is in charge of indexing a subset of documents from the entire document collection, *i.e.,* document-based partition of index, and processing queries over the local index it possesses. When a user issues a query, the query broker inside a broker node first checks if the query result is available in the cache. If it is the case, the result is immediately returned to the user. Otherwise, the query broker forwards the query to the corresponding search nodes, merges the local results from those nodes to form the final result, and add the query and its final result to the cache. The use of cache enables a short average latency for query processing and reduce workload imposed on the backend query processors.

The index, however, evolves in real time as new documents are fetched and old documents are modified or deleted. Cached results consequently become stale, since they no longer reflect the most recent document collection of the search engine. More specifically, a query result is stale if its top-k relevant documents after an index update are different from those before the index update. As a consequence, to keep the freshness of results served from the cache, the search engine needs to effectively and efficiently detect the stale queries and invalidate them from the cache.

In this work, we use a component, called *online invalidator*, to perform invalidations. The online invalidator is inside the broker node. This design choice is the same as that for CIP [5], and we also assume that indexer within each search node is able to communicate with the online invalidator about the latest changes in the index. With online invalidator, an invalidation occurs upon a cache hit and cache hits considered stale at query time are forwarded to the query processors. We detail in the following the mechanisms of online invalidator to invalidate stale query results from the cache.

2.2 Cache invalidator architecture

In this work, a query result is considered stale if its top-k relevant documents differ from those in the cache in either document IDs or in their ranking order [1]. In fact, document additions, modifications or deletions may make a cached result stale:

- When a document is added, if it is more relevant than the kth document in a query's top-k result, it should enter the result of that query.
- When a document is modified, if it contains more terms after the modification, it may become relevant to

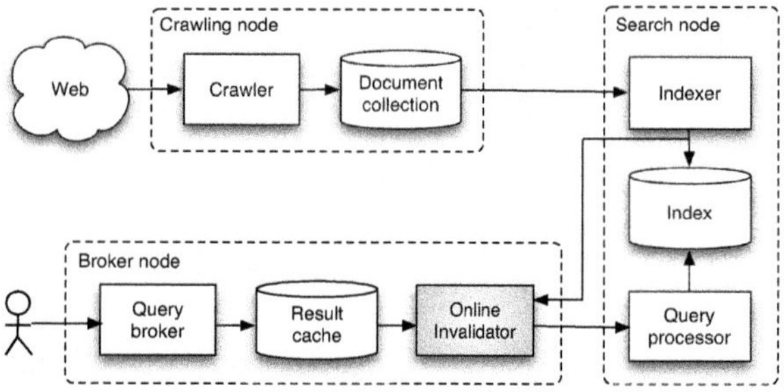

Figure 1: Search system model.

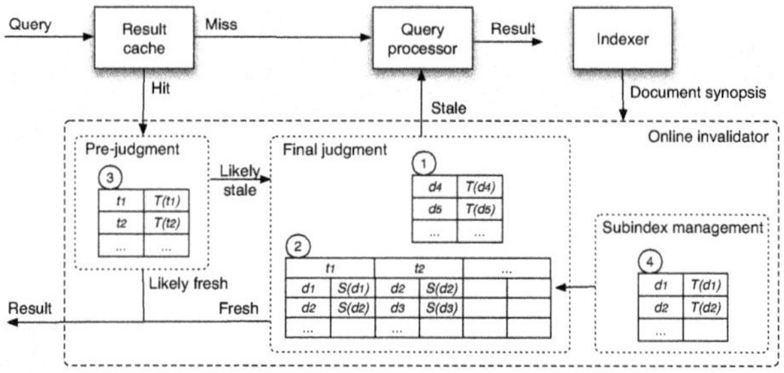

Figure 2: Online cache invalidation architecture.

a query for which the terms no overlap with the terms of the document. If a document contains fewer terms after the modification, it may become not relevant to a query for which it was previously in the top-k results. In fact, modifications also change the frequency of terms in a document and consequently the ranking of the document even if it remains in the top-k results of some queries.

- When a document is deleted, if it is in the top-k result of a query, it needs to be replaced by other relevant document in the result of that query.

We assume a basic scoring function that solely relies on content-based features like TF-IDF or BM25, to rank the top-k result of each query. A document is relevant to a query only if it contains all the query terms. This is to keep our design and experiments comparable with those in [5]. To efficiently detect the staleness caused by the above reasons and invalidate queries to keep the freshness of results, the online invalidator maintains four data structures (Fig. 2):

- The first data structure (①) maintains, for each deleted document, its document ID d and the timestamp $T(d)$ when it is deleted, in the form of pair $\langle d, T(d)\rangle$. This is necessary to make invalidation decisions upon document deletion.
- The second data structure (②) is a subindex of documents that are added to or modified in the main search index in the search nodes. This index is used to estimate if the top-k result of a query has changed due to the addition or modification of some documents in the system and will be detailed in Section 2.4.
- The third data structure (③) maintains, for each term t in the subindex, the timestamp $T(t)$ corresponding to the latest update of its posting list in the main search index, in the form of pair $\langle t, T(t)\rangle$. This information is used to eliminate unnecessary detection of stale results over the subindex.
- The last data structure (④) maintains, for each added or modified document, its document ID d and the latest timestamp $T(d)$ when it is added or modified, in the form of pair $\langle d, T(d)\rangle$. This information is used to control the size of the subindex.

Fig. 2 illustrates the architecture of the online invalidator. The online invalidation is made upon cache hit. For each cache hit, a triple $\langle q, T(q), R(q)\rangle$ is transmitted to the online invalidator. $T(q)$ indicates when query q is added to the cache and $R(q)$ is the top-k result of q. This triple is first passed to the *pre-judgment* component that estimates the likelihood of a hit result to be fresh, relying on the age of this triple in the cache and the update time of the subindex. If the hit result is likely to be stale, the triple is passed to the *final judgment* component that evaluates the impact of index change on $R(q)$ through the presence of all the top-k documents and the appearance of new relevant documents. A query is forwarded to the backend query processors only if it is considered stale after the final judgment. The invalidation process is detailed in Section 2.3. The synopsis of all the added and modified documents are transmitted to the query broker, but it is impractical and unnecessary to keep all of them in the subindex. Therefore, only a limited number of documents are maintained in the subindex by the *subindex management* component as we will see in Section 2.4.

2.3 Invalidation strategy

As seen in Fig. 2, the online cache invalidation is accomplished in two steps. The pre-judgment makes a preselection of queries and only passes the queries whose results in the cache are likely to be stale to the final judgment based on the following two observations:

- The top-k results of a query are likely to remain the same if the query is resubmitted within short time periods, denoted as δT.
- The top-k results of a query remains the same if not all the posting lists corresponding to the query terms have been updated since its last cache hit.

Algorithm 1 depicts the online invalidation process with its pseudo-code. In the pre-judgment, when there is a hit on query q at time $T_i(q)$, if $T_i(q) - T(q) < \delta T$, the cached set of top-k results $R(q)$, obtained at $T(q)$, is considered fresh and returned to user. This operation has $O(1)$ complexity. Otherwise, for each query term, the update time of its posting list $T(t_j)$ (maintained in ③) is compared to $T_i(q)$. If there exists a term t_j in q, $T(t_j) < T(q)$, $R(q)$ has certainly not changed. This is because a document can impact a query result only if it contains all the query terms, resulting in $T(t_j) > T(q)$ for all t_j in q. Otherwise, the final judgment is performed. This operation has $O(|q|)$ complexity, where $|q|$ is the number of terms q contains.

Note that we may return stale results to users with the first pre-judgment that compares the query time to its time in the cache. Returning stale results in this case is a consequence of the decision being independent of the index. Any change to the index during this time interval may change the set of results. The second pre-judgment, however, is accurate in the sense that only the cached results that are indeed fresh are returned to users. This argument comes from the observation that a query result does not change if not all posting lists affecting the query have changed.

Algorithm 1 Online cache invalidation process

Input: query q issued at $T_i(q)$ &
its cached top-k result $R(q)$ computed at $T(q)$
Output: Invalidation decision on q

Pre-judgment:
if $T_i(q) - T(q) < \delta T$ **then**
  return invalidation $\leftarrow$ false
for each t in q **do**
  if $T(t) < T(q)$ **then**
    return invalidation $\leftarrow$ false

Final judgment:
for each d in $R(q)$ **do**
  if d is deleted & $T(d) \geq T(q)$ **then**
    return invalidation $\leftarrow$ true
process q against subindex and obtain top-k' result $R'(q)$
for each d' in $R'(q)$ **do**
  if $d' \notin R(q)$ & $Score(q, d') > Score(q, d_k)$ **then**
    return invalidation $\leftarrow$ true
return invalidation $\leftarrow$ false

In the final judgment, the invalidator first examines if the set $R(q)$ has changed due to the deletion of some documents it contains. In this step, we check if each document in $R(q)$ is in the list of deleted documents (①). If there is such a document, and it has been deleted after $R(q)$ is computed (*i.e.*, $T(d) \geq T(q)$), $R(q)$ is invalidated from the cache and q is forwarded to the backend query processors as a cache miss. Otherwise, query q is processed against the subindex using the same ranking function as the query processors in the search nodes to obtain the top-k' result in the subindex $R'(q)$. If there is a document d' in $R'(q)$ that is not in $R(q)$ and its relevance score to q ($Score(q, d')$) is larger than that of the kth document in $R(q)$ ($Score(q, d_k)$), d' (or another document that is more relevant to q than d') should be included in the top-k results of q instead of the original kth document d_k. $R(q)$ is thus considered stale and invalidated from the cache. Then query q is forwarded to the query processors.

The invalidation due to document deletion in the final judgment is accurate and can be achieved in $O(k)$.The query processing using the subindex in the worst case is linear on the total length of the query related posting lists, *i.e.*, $O(|q| \times L)$, where L is the maximum length of the posting lists. The comparison of $R'(q)$ and $R(q)$ requires at most k^2 operations. The query processing on the subindex thus dominates the time required for making invalidation. However, the invalidation time can be controlled by limiting the number of documents maintained in the subindex. Moreover, as we show in Section 3.3, the lightweight pre-judgment significantly improves search performance by reducing the number of cache hits that require final judgment and thus the query response latency.

2.4 Subindex management

We describe in this section how we build and maintain the subindex. This is a process running in the backend, independent of query processing. The subindex is built in the same way as the main search index and is also updated in real time when the online invalidator receives a document synopsis from the indexer (Fig. 2). The synopsis of a document is generated as in the CIP work [5] and it consists of pairs of the form $\langle t, S(d) \rangle$, where t is a term in the document d and $S(d)$ is the relevance score of d for t. Since we focus on basic

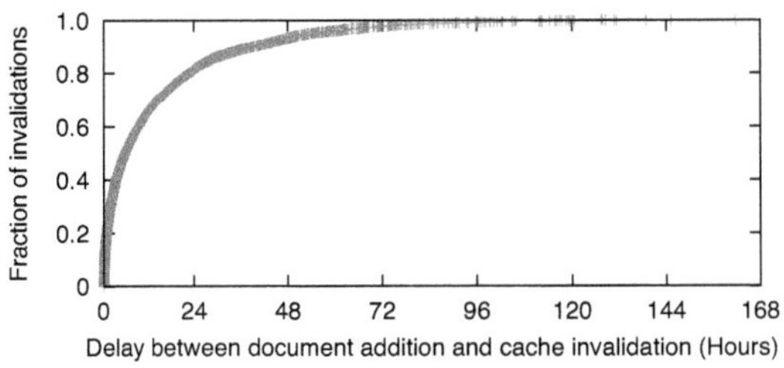

(a) Distribution of cache invalidation delay.

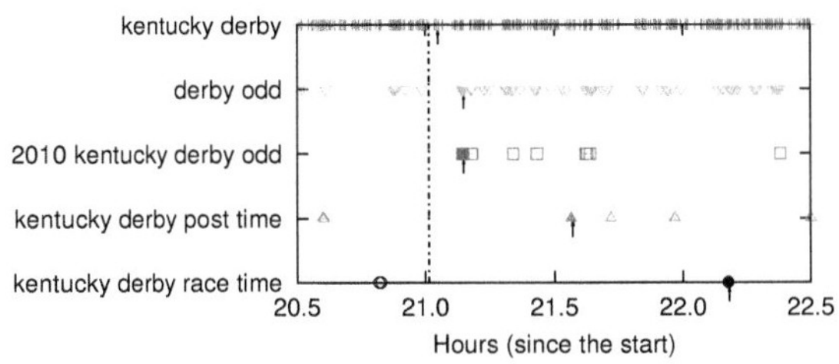

(b) Example of cache invalidation delay.

Figure 3: Rationale behind limiting subindex size.

ranking functions (*e.g.* TF-IDF and BM25) to compute the query results, $S(d)$ is also a TF-IDF or BM25 score.

In the subindex, for each term, an inverted posting list is maintained. Each posting in the list of term t corresponds to a document that contains t and its relevance score to t (TF-IDF or BM25). The postings are ranked in descending order of relevance scores. An arriving synopsis can be easily inserted to the relevant posting lists and ranked accordingly using the same mechanisms of the indexer. If a received synopsis corresponds to a document deletion, the document is inserted to the list of deleted documents with the timestamp when it is deleted (①). The update time of the corresponding posting lists are updated with this timestamp (③). If a received synopsis corresponds to a document addition or modification, the timestamp when the operation occurs is updated for each term appearing in the document (③).

The subindex cannot grow without bounds. Documents that are less likely to have impact on the results of future queries should be evicted from the subindex to keep its size moderate. One natural choice here is to fix the size of the subindex by keeping only the documents that are recently added or modified. Intuitively, if a document has been added or modified a long time ago, it is likely that the queries that include this document in their top-k results have been processed against the index, and thus have fresh cached results. Fig. 3 illustrates the intuition underlying our design choice. Fig. 3(a) depicts the distribution of necessary time for a query to be invalidated from the cache after a relevant document is added to the search index. (The setup of this experiment is detailed in Section 3.1.). We observe that more than 80% of queries can be timely invalidated if each document is maintained in the subindex for 24 hours. Therefore, we only keep in the subindex the S document that are newly added or modified.

To make the eviction of documents from the subindex efficient, when a document is added to the index, it is added to the list of added and modified documents with the corresponding timestamp (④). When a document is modified, its timestamp in the list is updated. When a document is deleted, it is removed from the list. This list is kept sorted in ascending order of timestamps. Once the size of the subindex becomes larger than the pre-defined size S after an insertion, the document in the head of the list is removed from subindex. This operation does not affect the update time of posting lists (③) and the latter are only updated when the main search index changes.

Limiting the size of subindex may lead to stale results. Consider the example in Fig. 3(b), where a document is added to the search index in the $21st$ hour of the experiment (vertical line) and each point in a horizontal line represents the occurrence time of a query. The point pointed to by arrow on a horizontal line (*i.e.*, the first point on the right of the vertical line) shows the time when a query is invalidated due to the addition of this document. We observe that more frequent queries require less time to incorporate a new document into its result set. As a result, if a query is rarely issued, when a document that impacts its result is removed before a new query occurrence, the cache invalidator is unable to realize the change to the main search index. A solution around this problem is to use a TTL-based invalidation [9] prior to our online invalidation. We discuss further the impact of the size of the subindex in Section 3.2.

3. EVALUATION

We report in this section the performance of the online cache invalidation with respect to accuracy, efficiency, and its overall impact on the search engine. Section 3.1 details the setup of our experiments. Section 3.2 and Section 3.3 qualitatively and quantitatively evaluate the online cache invalidator through comparison with the state-of-the-art CIP approach [5]. In the experiments, we implement CIP with its best-case setting, *i.e.*, entire synopsis ($\eta = 1$) and score thresholding ($1_s = true$).

3.1 Experimental setup

Dataset. In the experiments, we use a sample of the document history and query logs from the Yahoo! News search engine obtained in May 2010. We used the documents sampled from the first 3 weeks of this period to build the search engine index. This collection contains roughly 1.4M unique documents. The documents and queries sampled from the last week of this period are used to emulate the update of index and the arrival of queries.

In the document set, there are 488,441 (97.1%) additions, 13,562 (2.7%) modifications and 881 (0.2%) deletions. The amount of additions dominates the changes to the collection. Fig. 4 depicts the arrival rate of document changes during the experiment. We observe that the arrival rate of document additions remains relatively stable and occasionally presents spikes due to emerging events. Document modification mainly occurs in the first two days, following a weekly recurring pattern that we do not show in this figure. This is due to the periodically re-crawl of existing pages in the index. Document deletion rarely happens and they are spread over time.

The queries we use in the experiments is a sample of queries searching for news articles extracted from the query logs of the Yahoo! search engine. The resulted query set contains 113, 943 queries, out of which 34, 121 are unique and their frequency follows a power-law distribution (Fig. 5(a)). Fig. 5(b) illustrates the arrival rate of these queries in the search engine. We observe that the arrival of queries follows a periodic pattern and the peak area corresponds to the daytime of each evaluation day.

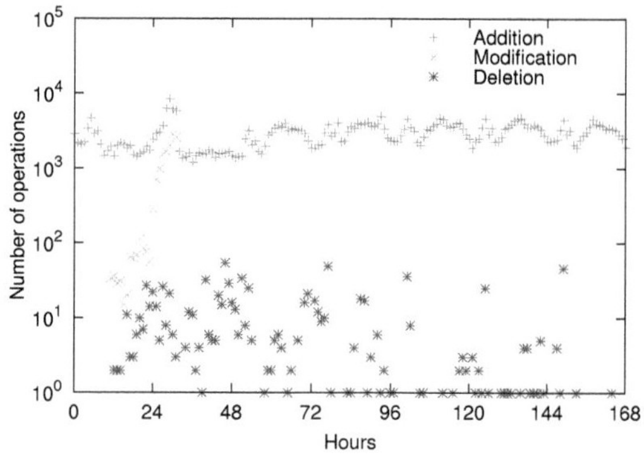

Figure 4: Document dynamics.

Setup. We build the search system on top of a proprietary platform for vertical search developed in Yahoo!. Two servers with Quad-core 2.4GHz CPU, 48G RAM and four 1.8T disks are used and they are inter-connected through a local area network of 1Gbp/s speed. One server acts as the search node: it hosts the main search index and processes the queries. The index is created and updated in real time so that any change to the document collection is reflected into the index in an online fashion. The other server acts as the query broker node: it is in charge of managing the cache, making invalidation decisions, and forwarding queries to the search node in case of cache misses. The subindex used by the online invalidator is also maintained in the query broker node.

3.2 Qualitative performance

Methodology and metrics. We examine the cache invalidation strategies over a dynamic cache of *unlimited size* in a much finer grained manner than that used in the evaluation of CIP [5]. Neither admission nor eviction is necessary and a query is removed from the cache only upon invalidation. Instead of generating a new index periodically and evaluating the same queries repeatedly against different versions of the index, we preserve the full arrival history of documents and queries, and replay them in parallel according to their original timestamps. Note that we only preserve the relative order of arrival. The documents and queries are processed at the maximum speed the system admits.

The index is updated in real time once a document is added, modified, or deleted. Once a search engine returns results for a query, we process the same query against the main search index to obtain the ground truth (its ideal set of results).

With our online cache invalidation strategy, we execute an invalidation procedure upon every hit. This decision is accurate if a stale query result is correctly invalidated or a fresh query result is returned to the user without forwarding it to the backend query processors (*i.e.*, the search node). A decision may be false positive, indicating that a query is invalidated while its result in the cache is still fresh. A decision may also be false negative, indicating that a query result is considered fresh but it has changed due to updates to the index. A false negative leads to a stale query and hurts result quality. A false positive has no impact on result quality, but it requires forwarding the query to the backend and processing it against the search index, which induces a higher load against the backend nodes. Consequently, we target lower rates of both false negatives and false positives

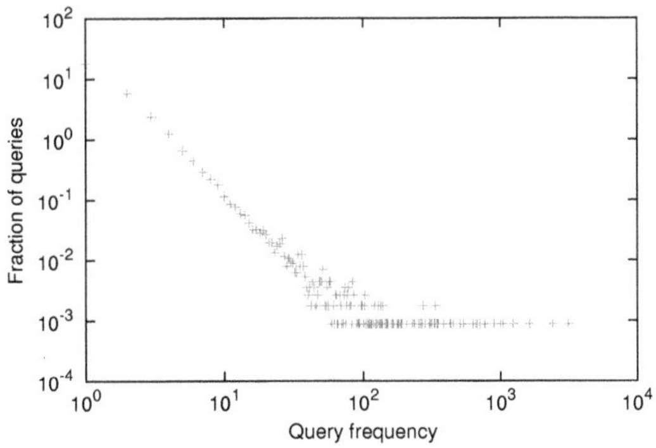

(a) Query frequency distribution.

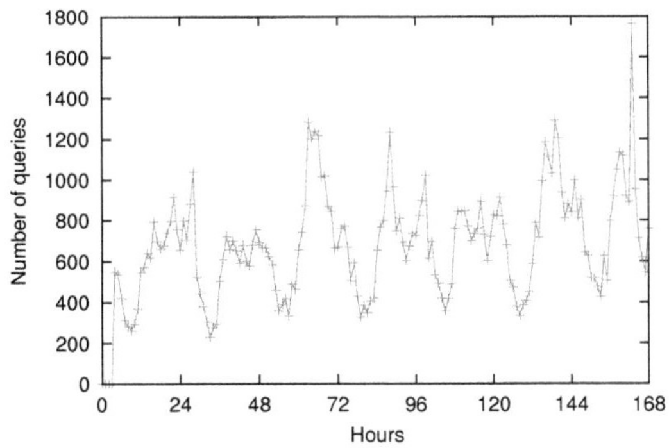

(b) Query dynamics.

Figure 5: Query characteristics.

with the invalidation process. After we process each query q, we evaluate whether its top-10 results are stale or the invalidation is a false positive by comparing this result set against the ideal top-10 obtained from the main search index. The *stale ratio* and *false positive ratio* are measured after each query as the cumulative fraction of stale queries and the cumulative redundantly processed queries over all the queries that have been answered.

Impact of subindex size. We start by evaluating the results obtained with different sizes of the subindex in the online invalidator to quantify its impact. In this experiment, we do not use pre-judgment in the online cache invalidation process to assess the stale ratio due to the final judgment step alone.

In the final judgment step, we first use different values of k' to obtain top-k' results from the subindex to make invalidation decisions. Table 1 compares the quality of the online invalidation through the stale ratio and the false positive ratio obtained at the end of the experiment. We observe that as we increase the number of results retrieved from the subindex, the number of stale results served to users drops, which is a consequence of the following. For a given k' ($\leq k$), when all the top-k' results from the subindex are present in the cached top-k results, then the cached top-k result set is considered fresh. The cached result set is not fresh in the case, for example, of a new document ranked in the $k' + 1$ position of the subindex being more relevant than the kth result in the cache. A larger value of k' implies that fewer relevant documents are omitted by the online invalidator. Increasing the number of retrieved results from the subindex, however, has negligible impact on the false positive ratio. In the following experiments, we retrieve the top-10 results from subindex in the final judgment step to guarantee the best result quality.

Table 1: Impact of results retrieved from subindex.

		Online		
	CIP	top-1	top-5	top-10
Stale ratio	0.0055	0.0089	0.0025	0.0003
False positive ratio	0.0356	0.0048	0.0048	0.0048

Fig. 6 illustrates the quality of the online invalidation using stale ratio and false positive ratio. The values for each metric are displayed with respect to the number of queries that have been returned. The size of subindex is denoted by S; $S = \infty$ corresponds to the ideal case where all the updates on the search index are maintained in the subindex.

Generally, fewer results are stale if the online invalidation is used (Fig. 6(a)). A small size of the subindex leads to a high stale ratio as we have discussed in Section 2.4. However, even if only 25K documents are maintained in the subindex, accounting for 5% of all the index updates, the stale ratio is still lower than CIP at the early stage of the experiment and is very similar toward the end. Note that the stale ratio is not zero for $S = \infty$, since invalidations are based upon the existence of more relevant documents in the subindex, ignoring order. Further comparison between the top-k in the cache and that in the subindex can ensure a stale ratio of zero, but imposes additional computation and the size of the subindex cannot be unlimited. Note that compared to CIP, our online cache invalidation strategy significantly decreases the false positive ratio (Fig. 6(b)). Only 0.5% of queries are processed redundantly with the online cache invalidation, where it increases to 3.6% with CIP. As we see in Section 3.3, this is key to efficiency.

As we have seen, the size of subindex has almost no impact on the false positive ratio, and the subindex of 100K documents guarantees a fairly good stale ratio. Consequently, we focus on a subindex of 100K documents for the following experiments.

Impact of pre-judgment. The pre-judgment of the online cache invalidation is used to reduce the number of cache hits that require query processing over the subindex. We first evaluate its impact on search result quality and invalidation accuracy in this section and then its impact on search efficiency in Section 3.3.

As we have explained in Section 2.3, the pre-judgment comprises two mechanisms. The first mechanism makes the judgment according to the recency of a query. A cached result is returned to the user if it is issued within the time interval δT. The second mechanism makes the judgment according to the update time of the posting lists corresponding to query terms, for a given query. Fig. 7 compares the performance of the online cache invalidation with each of the mechanisms as well as their combinations. We use 1_u to indicate if the second mechanism of pre-judgment is applied. $\delta T = 0$ means the first mechanism is not applied. Otherwise, the value of δT is measured in seconds.

We observe from Fig. 7(a) that using the first mechanism increases the stale ratio. A larger value of δT gives us a higher stale ratio. The differences are only significant at the early stage of the experiments, though, and become negligible as more queries are processed. We also observe from Fig. 7(a) that the second mechanism has no impact on the stale ratio. This confirms our analysis in Section 2.3 that it

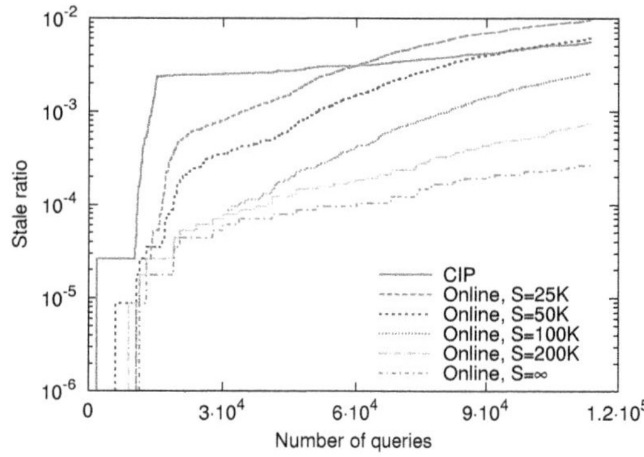

(a) Stale ratio.

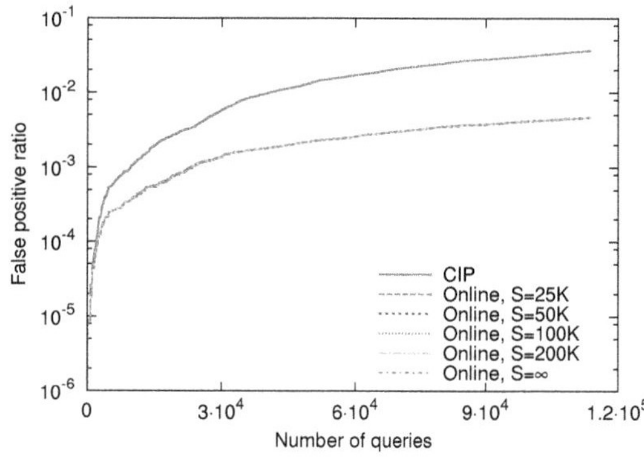

(b) False positive ratio.

Figure 6: Impact of subindex size on invalidation.

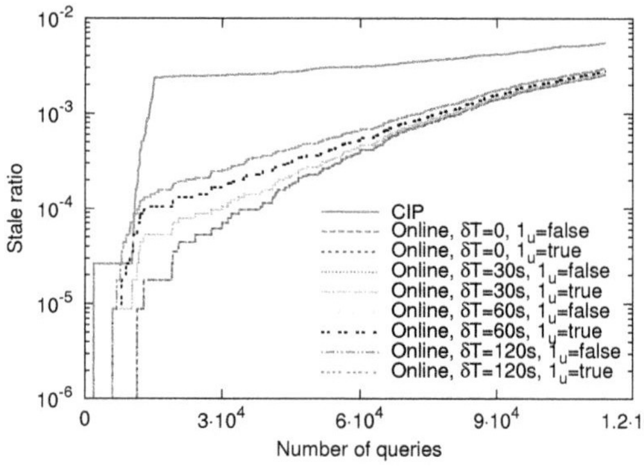

(a) Stale ratio.

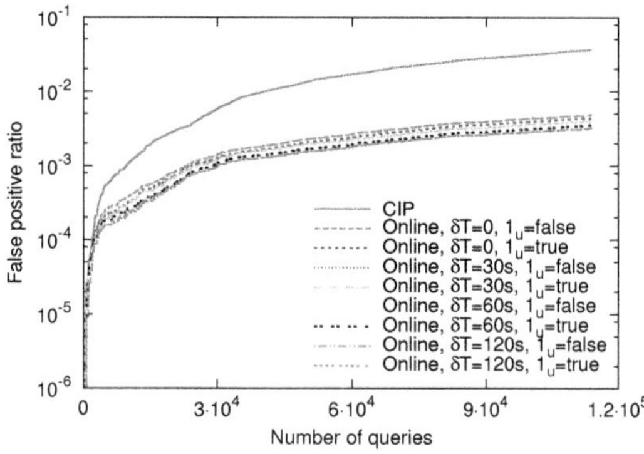

(b) False positive ratio.

Figure 7: Impact of pre-judgment on invalidation.

ensures only skipping results that indeed have not changed from final judgment.

Fig. 7(b) depicts the evolutions of false positive ratio with different pre-judgment mechanisms. Using larger δT and setting $1_u = true$ reduce the false positive ratio as more queries are eliminated from final judgment. This ensures the false positive ratio is always lower than with CIP.

In the above experiments, we assume that once a query result is added to the cache, it is only removed upon an invalidation. Considering that the CIP approach can be augmented with an age-based strategy, we also compare the performance of the online cache invalidation in this context. More specifically, each query in the cache is associated with an expiration period (TTL) and its result is considered stale at the end of this period. The invalidation decision of the online invalidator is only made upon cache hits with respect to TTL.

Fig. 8 illustrates the impact of pre-judgment through the relationship between stale ratio and false positive ratio with respect to various TTL values. The ratios are obtained at the end of each experiment. For the sake of presentation, only the cases using both mechanisms for pre-judgment are shown as the differences on stale ratio and false positive ratio between using and not using the second mechanism are negligible (Fig. 7). In Fig. 8, the points on the same curve from left to right correspond to decreasing TTL values. In all cases, a small value of TTL results in low stale ratio and high false positive ratio, since a large number of queries are invalidated independent of the changes to the index. For instance, when TTL is set to 24 hours, compared to the case where no TTL is used, the stale ratio decreases by 83% for CIP and 86% for online invalidation with $\delta T = 60$ seconds and $1_u = true$, but the false positive ratio increases by 67% for CIP and 500% for online invalidation with the same setting. Compared to CIP, our online invalidation strategy consistently outperforms it in both false positive ratio and stale ratio, with TTL values not smaller than 12 hours. The trade-off between search result quality and search efficiency can be controlled through carefully tuning the value of δT with the online invalidation.

3.3 Quantitative performance

We have seen that the online cache invalidation outperforms the CIP approach in both search result quality (wrt. stale ratio) and invalidation accuracy (wrt. false positive ratio). Since a primary goal of this work is to derive a practical scheme for cache invalidation, we further compare the efficiency of the online invalidation against CIP and discuss their memory consumption in this section.

Methodology and metrics. A key difference between the online invalidation and CIP is the underlying procedure to make invalidations. In the online invalidation approach, we perform invalidation lazily, only upon a cache hit. This invalidation scheme increases the response time in case of a cache hit. It enables fresher results by decreasing the stale ratio as we have seen in Section 3.2. When the index is updated, referring to a document addition, modification or deletion, only the four data structures described in Section 2.2 need to be updated accordingly. In the CIP approach, no additional time is needed upon a cache hit. Once the index is updated, however, it performs invalidations eagerly. This process requires extensive computation on query and document pairs to identify all the cached queries whose results may have changed. In our experiment, we implement the

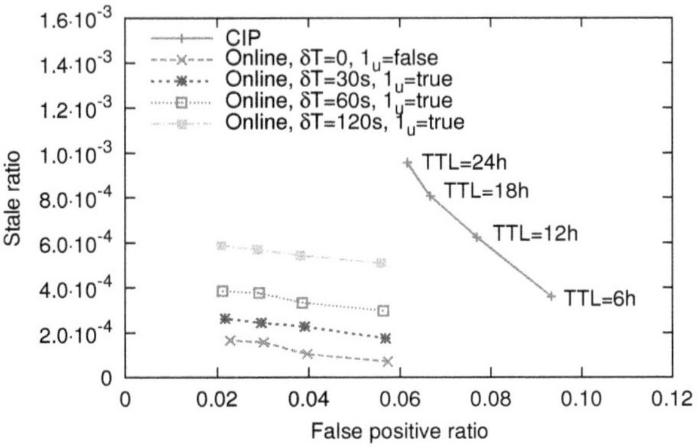

Figure 8: Impact of pre-judgment wrt. different TTL.

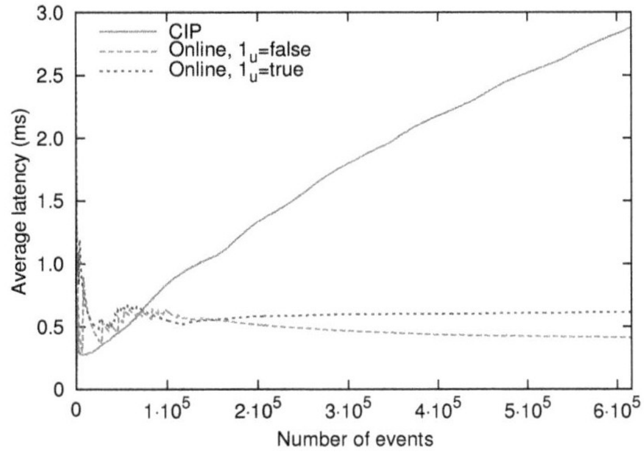

Figure 9: Efficiency of document processing.

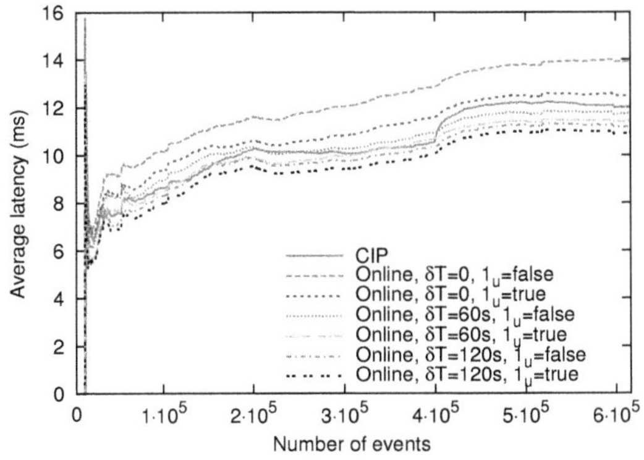

Figure 10: Efficiency of query processing.

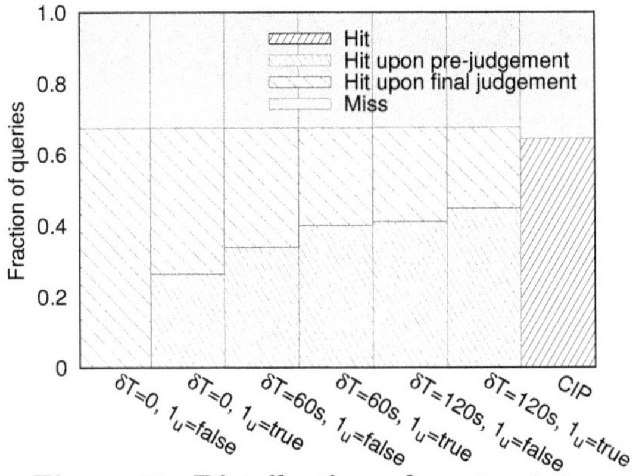

Figure 11: Distribution of query status.

CIP approach with an inverted index of the cached queries to make this process efficient [6]. We measure the efficiency of these approaches through the average latency to process a document synopsis, the average latency to respond to a query and the average throughput of the search engine.

Document processing efficiency. Fig. 9 shows the average latency for processing an index update (*i.e.*, a document synopsis) as a function of the number of incoming events, including both queries from users and document synopses from indexers. The reason for considering both kinds of events is that the latency of CIP depends on the number of queries in the cache while the latency of online invalidation depends on the number of documents in the subindex.

We observe that the latency of invalidations with CIP increases linearly with the number of arriving events. With CIP, each index update requires scanning all the queries in the cache that contain at least one term in the document, and consequently latency increases with the cache size. On average, 2.8 milliseconds are required after 600K events are issued to the query broker. In contrast, with the same number of events, only 0.6 milliseconds are enough to make the necessary processing according to an index update with online invalidation. The latency for online invalidation converges and remains stable after 200K events. Once the size of subindex reaches its limit (100K in this experiment), the latency for updating the subindex with a document does not vary much. This figure also shows the latency when the second mechanism of pre-judgment is not used. As the invalidator does not need to maintain the update time of each posting list in the subindex (*i.e.*, data structure ③ in Section 2.2), the latency is about 30% less than if it is used.

Search efficiency. Fig. 10 compares the average latency for answering a query with online invalidation against that of CIP. Since this latency depends on the size of the subindex with online invalidation, we also show its value as a function of the number of incoming events. We observe that if no pre-judgment is used ($\delta T = 0$ and $1_u = false$), the latency with online invalidation is up to 20% more than that with CIP. Pre-judgment, however, enables a significantly drop of the query processing time by reducing the number of hits that need final judgment. For instance, with online invalidation, $\delta T = 60$ seconds and $1_u = true$, the average latency for processing a query is about 5% less compared to CIP. Increasing the value of δT further reduces latency.

Fig. 11 depicts the fraction of queries that are served from the cache after pre-judgment (cache hit upon pre-judgment), served from the cache after final judgment (cache hit upon final judgment) and processed against the main search index (cache miss). We observe that online invalidation produces fewer cache misses than CIP, since there are fewer false positives (Fig. 7(b)). Moreover, the use of pre-judgment significantly reduces the number of queries that require final judgment. In online invalidation with $\delta T = 60$ seconds and $1_u = true$, only 41% of cache hits need final judgment to make the invalidation decision. These observations explain the efficiency of online invalidation for query processing.

Throughput. As we have explained in Section 2.1 (Fig. 1), the cache invalidator resides in the query broker node. Therefore, the query broker node is in charge of both processing queries and making invalidation decisions. We finally measure the overall performance of the online invalidation approach through the average throughput of the query

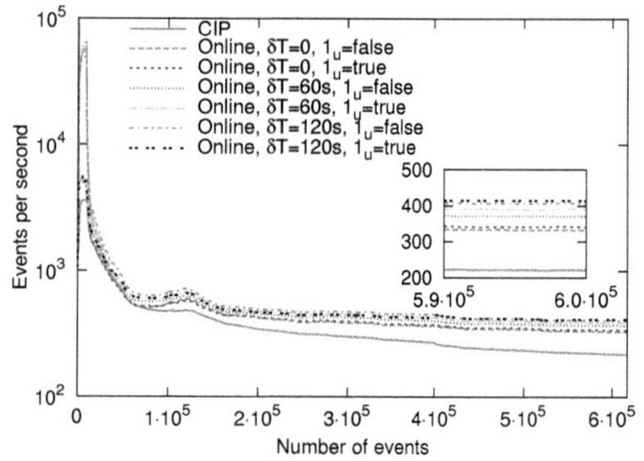

Figure 12: Throughput of query broker.

broker node. In other words, we are interested in the number of events, including incoming queries and document synopsis that the query broker node can handle per second.

Fig. 12 reveals that the online invalidation consistently outperforms CIP by coping with more events per second. Moreover, the difference in throughput increases as more events arrive in the system. This is due to the computationally intensive invalidation steps of CIP (Fig. 9). The query broker node running the online invalidation with $\delta T = 60$ seconds and $1_u = true$ can processes more than 73% events than that running CIP after 600K events arrive.

Memory footprint. The online cache invalidator maintains four data structures to make invalidation decisions (Section 2.2). In our experiments, the subindex of 100K documents maintains 214K inverted lists with 19.4M postings. As a document ID is 16 bytes and a relevance score is 4 bytes, the subindex requires 388M memory. Maintaining the update time of each posting list (*i.e.*, data structure ③ in Section 2.2) requires 856K memory as a timestamp is 4 bytes. Maintaining the timestamp for each document in the subindex (④) requires 2M memory. The memory consumption for deleted documents (①) is negligible compared to other data structures due to the limited number of deleted documents (Fig. 4). With CIP, the index of cached queries consumes 2.2M with 16K per term list of queries where the average length of a query is 20 bytes. Online cache invalidation requires much more memory than CIP to maintain its subindex. Yet, this accounts for less than 1% of 48G RAM of a modern server. To convey the scalability of the online invalidation, we conduct a separate experiment that replays the same documents and one time more queries as in the previous experiments, resulting in a cache with twice the original size. With a subindex of 100K documents, the stale ratio and false positive ratio remain stable, *i.e.*, 0.0024 and 0.0037 respectively with respect to 0.0025 and 0.0047 in the original setting (Fig. 6). This experiment confirms that the online invalidation is practical to implement in a search engine as increasing the size of cache does not require larger subindex to fit in memory.

Our experimental evaluation shows that with carefully selected parameters, *e.g.*, $\delta T = 60$ seconds and $1_u = true$, the proposed online cache invalidation ensures higher result quality (wrt. 50% lower stale ratio) and makes more accurate invalidation (wrt. 90% lower false positive ratio) than the state-of-the-art CIP approach. The online invalidation is also practical to implement in a Web search engine, given its moderate memory use and efficiency, which guarantees high throughput.

4. RELATED WORK

Caching has been widely used in Web search engines to shorten the average query response time and reduce the workload on search servers. Generally, both search results [4, 12, 13, 18] and posting lists [17, 20] can be cached with different trade-offs [3]. A seminal work on result caching in search engines has been the one of Markatos [18] comparing several basic cache replacement policies. Followup work has addressed issues including eviction [12, 18, 19], admission [4] and pre-fetching [13, 14, 16], to optimize either hit ratio or computational cost.

This body of work is based on a common assumption that the cache has limited capacity and thus queries in the cache have to be well selected to ensure good performance. However, modern search engines might store their cache entries on disk, enabling a very large cache [9]. In such cases, maintaining the freshness of cached results becomes very important.

A search engine index is not static and is continuously updated according to document additions, modifications, and deletions on the Web that are gradually captured by crawlers. Such changes may lead to inconsistencies between results in the cache and results computed on an updated index. Basically, there are three ways to update a search index [15]: in-place update, index merging, and complete re-build. The complete re-build approach periodically builds a new index with all the available documents and replaces the live index once the new index is ready. The index merging approach (incremental indexing) [11, 5], generates delta indexes with the changes regarding to the previous index and merges them to the live index within short periods. The in-place update approach (real-time indexing) directly performs changes to the live index in an online manner to make the new documents searchable shortly after being crawled. We focus in our work on real-time indexing as it ensures best freshness of the search index that is important for applications like news and social media search.

One way to keep the freshness of query results is to anticipate the future occurrence of cached queries and refresh them before they are issued to the search engine again. In [10], several cache refreshment policies are proposed based on either recency or frequency of cached queries. This work confirms the findings in [7] that frequency-based policies significantly improve the fraction of fresh hits compared to recency-based policies. A more recent work that follows this research line was proposed in [9]. In this work, the frequency of access is combined with the age of an entry in the cache to selectively refresh the cached results, and it is shown to achieve higher hit rate compared to recency-based refresh.

Another way to keep the freshness of query results is to simply invalidate results that have changed from the cache without refreshing. This is mainly motivated by the fact that issuing queries to the back end query processors without explicit user requests may incur unnecessary computational cost. An existing approach to invalidate cached results in search engines is CIP [5]. CIP invalidates queries upon updates to the index. Once a document d is added to or modified in the index, its relevance to every query in the cache is computed and queries for which top-k results are less relevant than d are invalidated. This approach is computationally expensive since the cost for computing the relevance is linear with the size of the cache. To make the invalidation more efficient, in the work of Bortnikov *et al.* [6], cached queries are organized as an index of query terms, and a document update is processed as a query against this index to identify the queries to invalidate. Another approach that reduces the computational cost of CIP was proposed by Alici *et al.* [1]. The basic idea of this work is to maintain and compare the generation time of query results against the update time of the search index to decide if query results need to be invalidated. Despite being efficient, this approach degrades the freshness of the served results due to the approximation made at invalidation time, and requires up to 20 times more backend communication compared to CIP. In our work, we make cache invalidation at query time as in the work of Alici *et al.*. Our online cache invalidation strategy achieves better invalidation accuracy compared to CIP without inducing a high communication overhead to the backend as the approach of Alici *et al.*. In fact, the same amount of backend communication as CIP is enough for making our online cache invalidation.

5. CONCLUSION

Real-time indexing in Web search engines makes it challenging to keep the freshness of query results served from their cache. In this work, we propose a practical approach that relies on a subindex of recent changes to the search index to invalidate the stale cached queries. A pre-judgment based on generation time of cached queries and update time of search index is applied before the evaluation of queries against the subindex to improve the efficiency of invalidation. Through a realistic evaluation on top of a search engine implementation, we show that our approach ensures higher result quality and invalidation accuracy compared to CIP, a previous approach to invalidation, as it results in lower stale ratio and lower false positive ratio. We show that our approach is efficient, which is an important step towards a practical implementation in commercial search engines.

Our approach in this paper relied upon term-based ranking functions that require periodic updates of global statistics to ensure the accuracy of invalidation. We leave for future work the investigation of cache invalidation approaches that use advanced ranking functions leveraging link-based features like PageRank.

6. ACKNOWLEDGMENTS

This work was supported by the COAST project (ICT-248036), funded by the European Community, and the Torres Quevedo Program from the Spanish Ministry of Science and Innovation, co-funded by the European Social Fund.

7. REFERENCES

[1] S. Alici, I. S. Altingovde, R. Ozcan, B. B. Cambazoglu, and O. Ulusoy. Timestamp-based result cache invalidation for web search engines. In *Proceedings of the 34th international ACM SIGIR conference on research and development in Information Retrieval*, pages 973–982, 2011.

[2] R. Baeza-Yates, A. Gionis, F. Junqueira, V. Murdock, V. Plachouras, and F. Silvestri. The impact of caching on search engines. In *Proceedings of the 30th annual international ACM SIGIR conference on research and development in information retrieval*, pages 183–190, 2007.

[3] R. Baeza-Yates, A. Gionis, F. P. Junqueira, V. Murdock, V. Plachouras, and F. Silvestri. Design trade-offs for search engine caching. *ACM Trans. Web*, 2:1–28, October 2008.

[4] R. Baeza-Yates, F. Junqueira, V. Plachouras, and H. F. Witschel. Admission policies for caches of search engine results. In *Proceedings of the 14th international conference on string processing and information retrieval*, pages 74–85, 2007.

[5] R. Blanco, E. Bortnikov, F. Junqueira, R. Lempel, L. Telloli, and H. Zaragoza. Caching search engine results over incremental indices. In *Proceedings of the 33rd international ACM SIGIR conference on Research and development in information retrieval*, pages 82–89, 2010.

[6] E. Bortnikov, R. Lempel, and K. Vornovitsky. Caching for realtime search. In *Proceedings of the 33rd European conference on advances in information retrieval*, pages 104–116, 2011.

[7] L. Breslau, P. Cao, L. Fan, G. Phillips, and S. Shenke. Web caching and zipf-like distributions: Evidence and implications. In *Proceedings of the 18th Annual Joint Conference of the IEEE Computer and Communications Societies*, pages 126–134, 1999.

[8] S. Büttcher, C. L. A. Clarke, and B. Lushman. Hybrid index maintenance for growing text collections. In *Proceedings of the 29th annual international ACM SIGIR conference on research and development in information retrieval*, pages 356–363, 2006.

[9] B. B. Cambazoglu, F. P. Junqueira, V. Plachouras, S. Banachowski, B. Cui, S. Lim, and B. Bridge. A refreshing perspective of search engine caching. In *Proceedings of the 19th international conference on World Wide Web*, pages 181–190, 2010.

[10] E. Cohen and H. Kaplan. Refreshment policies for web content caches. *Comput. Netw.*, 38:795–808, April 2002.

[11] D. Cutting and J. Pedersen. Optimization for dynamic inverted index maintenance. In *Proceedings of the 13th annual international ACM SIGIR conference on research and development in information retrieval*, pages 405–411, 1990.

[12] Q. Gan and T. Suel. Improved techniques for result caching in web search engines. In *Proceedings of the 18th international conference on World Wide Web*, pages 431–440, 2009.

[13] R. Lempel and S. Moran. Predictive caching and prefetching of query results in search engines. In *Proceedings of the 12th international conference on World Wide Web*, pages 19–28, 2003.

[14] R. Lempel and S. Moran. Optimizing result prefetching in web search engines with segmented indices. *ACM Trans. Internet Technol.*, 4:31–59, February 2004.

[15] N. Lester, J. Zobel, and H. E. Williams. In-place versus re-build versus re-merge: index maintenance strategies for text retrieval systems. In *Proceedings of the 27th Australasian conference on computer science*, volume 26, pages 15–23, 2004.

[16] H. Li, W.-C. Lee, A. Sivasubramaniam, and C. L. Giles. A hybrid cache and prefetch mechanism for scientific literature search engines. In *Proceedings of the 7th international conference on Web engineering*, pages 121–136, 2007.

[17] X. Long and T. Suel. Three-level caching for efficient query processing in large web search engines. In *Proceedings of the 14th international conference on World Wide Web*, pages 257–266, 2005.

[18] E. Markatos. On caching search engine query results. *Computer Communications*, 24(2):137–143, 2001.

[19] P. C. Saraiva, E. Silva de Moura, N. Ziviani, W. Meira, R. Fonseca, and B. Riberio-Neto. Rank-preserving two-level caching for scalable search engines. In *Proceedings of the 24th annual international ACM SIGIR conference on research and development in information retrieval*, pages 51–58, 2001.

[20] Y. Tsegay, A. Turpin, and J. Zobel. Dynamic index pruning for effective caching. In *Proceedings of the sixteenth ACM conference on information and knowledge management*, pages 987–990, 2007.

Learning to Rank Social Update Streams

Liangjie Hong* †, Ron Bekkerman§, Joseph Adler§, Brian Davison†
† Dept. of Computer Science and Engineering, Lehigh University, Bethlehem, PA, USA
§ LinkedIn Corp., Mountain View, CA, USA
{lih307,davison}@cse.lehigh.edu, {rbekkerman,jadler}@linkedin.com

ABSTRACT

As online social media further integrates deeper into our lives, we spend more time consuming social update streams that come from our online connections. Although social update streams provide a tremendous opportunity for us to access information on-the-fly, we often complain about its relevance. Some of us are flooded with a steady stream of information and simply cannot process it in full. Ranking the incoming content becomes the only solution for the overwhelmed users. For some others, in contrast, the incoming information stream is pretty weak, and they have to actively search for relevant information which is quite tedious. For these users, augmenting their incoming content flow with relevant information from outside their first-degree network would be a viable solution. In that case, the problem of relevance becomes even more prominent.

In this paper, we start an open discussion on how to build effective systems for ranking social updates from a unique perspective of LinkedIn – the largest professional network in the world. More specifically, we address this problem as an intersection of learning to rank, collaborative filtering, and clickthrough modeling, while leveraging ideas from information retrieval and recommender systems. We propose a novel probabilistic latent factor model with regressions on explicit features and compare it with a number of non-trivial baselines. In addition to demonstrating superior performance of our model, we shed some light on the nature of social updates on LinkedIn and how users interact with them, which might be applicable to social update streams in general.

Categories and Subject Descriptors

H.4 [**Information Systems Applications**]: Miscellaneous; H.3.3 [**Information Storage and Retrieval**]: Information Search and Retrieval

General Terms

Algorithms, Experimentation, Theory

*Part of this work was done when the first author was on an internship at LinkedIn Corp.

Keywords

Social network, Social Stream, Learning to rank, Collaborative filtering

1. INTRODUCTION

In the current Web ecosystem, social media services are ubiquitous. With the rise of websites like Facebook, Twitter, and LinkedIn, millions of users are connecting and communicating with each other over rich multimedia content, including text, images, video, and audio. The content forms streams of social updates, which allow users to get instantly informed on the latest news. When aggregated, the social update streams become a powerful tool for monitoring the geopolitical situation in various regions. For instance, social update streams have been heavily used to disseminate information during the "Arab spring". In addition, social update services become the ultimate platform for collecting information in natural disasters, such as earthquakes and tsunamis [20].

Although social update streams provide a unique opportunity for users to obtain fresh information, users commonly acknowledge two issues that prevent current social streams from being sufficiently relevant, which causes deterioration of user experience and engagement. First of all, while facing a large number of updates from their social connections, users simply cannot consume them in an effective and efficient way. This is known as the problem of *information overload* (see, e.g., [3, 12]). Furthermore, social updates for a user are usually limited in scope to their social circle, induced from their connections. Thus, it is very difficult for a user to obtain information distributed outside of their circle, even though it might match their interests. In order to obtain relevant information, users spend long hours searching social media (see, e.g., [2, 21]). We call this problem *information shortage*. To address both these problems, social media monitoring systems are being built, which filter and recommend social updates to users based on numerous signals. This area has recently attracted close attention of academic and industrial research communities.

The task of filtering and recommending social updates can be approached from various perspectives. From the Information Retrieval (IR) perspective, constructing personalized social streams can be cast into the classic ranking problem: the task is to rank social updates by descending order of user interest. It may be true that some existing IR techniques could be potentially applied to social stream ranking. However, user's interests in social streams are not represented in terms of a search query. Instead, queries are implicit and have to be inferred. The absence of a search query distinguishes the social stream ranking problem from many classic IR tasks. In addition, social information needs are more diversified compared to traditional IR scenarios. Although traditional IR tools do not appear to be directly applicable to ranking in social streams, some of recently developed *learning to rank* approaches are very appealing to be used in the new setting.

From the perspective of Recommender Systems (RecSys), building a list of relevant social updates can be viewed as recommending relevant items to users. Thus, many collaborative filtering techniques are applicable to the task of social stream ranking. However, social stream systems are much more dynamic than traditional recommender systems: many new updates can be pushed into the system every second. Therefore, the cold start problem becomes even more severe in social stream systems. The traditional collaborative filtering paradigm needs to be adjusted to ranking social streams.

Surprisingly, little prior research work has been done to tackle the problem of social stream ranking from the point of view of building an effective system. This is partially due to the fact that no real-world dataset of social updates is openly available to the research community – due to obvious reasons related to user privacy. Most commercial ranking algorithms (e.g., the one used by Facebook) are proprietary. Indeed, a successful content ranking system on social streams will not only provide more relevant information to users and improve user engagement, but also shed the light on patterns of user behavior and social trends, which might be strong signals for behavioral targeting in computational advertising – the driving power of most Web 2.0 venues.

In this paper, we start an open discussion on how to build effective systems for social stream ranking (SSR). To the best of our knowledge, we are the first group of researchers to elaborate technical details for such a system. More specifically, we address the problem as an intersection of learning to rank, collaborative filtering and clickthrough modeling, while leveraging ideas from information retrieval and recommender systems. Our contributions are three-fold:

1. Analyze social streams (based on LinkedIn data) and provide some insights on users' behavior;

2. Propose a novel probabilistic latent factor model with regressions on explicit features; integrate the idea of learning to rank and collaborative filtering

3. Demonstrate the superior performance of our model by comparing with several non-trivial real-world baselines.

The rest of the paper is organized as follows. In Section 2, we compare SSR with other related research areas. As we will point out, SSR is a unique setup to which existing techniques cannot be applied directly. In Section 3, we review the problem of social stream ranking in the context of LinkedIn. In Section 4, we introduce our ranking model step by step and compare it with some existing IR and collaborative filtering techniques. In Section 5, we evaluate our model against a number of non-trivial baselines. We conclude our paper in Section 6.

2. RELATED WORK

In this section, we briefly overview three research directions related to social stream ranking: (a) learning to rank, (b) recommender systems, and (c) clickthrough models. Some of the approaches to tackle these problems are relevant to SSR and can be adapted. Along with their similarities to SSR, we also reveal their significant differences from SSR, and discuss the uniqueness of SSR as a new research field.

Learning to Rank (LtoR): In IR, a generic task is to construct a ranked list of documents relevant to a query issued by a user. Although ranking is a fundamental problem in IR and has been studied for decades, it still remains challenging. Instead of proposing carefully designed ranking models based on heuristics or traditional probabilistic principles, a recent trend is to apply machine learning techniques to learn ranking functions automatically, i.e., LtoR [19]. In the standard LtoR setting, a typical training set consists of queries with their associated documents represented by feature vectors as well as corresponding relevance judgements. A machine learning algorithm is employed to learn the ranking model, which can predict the ground truth label in the training set as accurately as possible – in terms of a loss function. In the test phase, when a new query comes in, the learned model is applied to sort the documents according to their relevance to the query, and return the corresponding ranked list to the user as the response to the query. Depending on different hypotheses, input spaces, output spaces and loss functions, approaches to LtoR can be loosely grouped into three categories: point-wise, pairwise, and list-wise.

Although the goal of LtoR is to provide a ranked list of documents (items) for users – a similar aim as of SSR – it is different from SSR in three aspects. First, social stream systems usually do not have explicit queries and users do not have to specify any explicit input in order to obtain relevant output from the systems. Second, each user's social stream is highly dependent on their social context. Therefore, compared to IR, social streams are intrinsically personalized. The second difference leads to the third fundamental distinction between SSR and LtoR: relevance judgements are difficult to obtain in SSR and the notion of relevance can be hard to define. Nevertheless, some strategies and insights developed in LtoR can be borrowed for SSR.

Recommender Systems (RecSys): As we will see, RecSys plays a key role in many online services, improving user experience and engagement. In the simplest form, RecSys aim to present a user with a list of items in the hope that these items would match the user's interests to some extent. Content-based methods and neighborhood methods are widely used in RecSys. Content-based methods convert the problem of recommendation into an IR problem by constructing user profiles and item profiles. A user profile serves as a query to an index of item profiles. Similarity measures (e.g., cosine similarity, Jaccard coefficient) are utilized to match users and items. In contrast, neighborhood methods usually explore the notion of *topical locality*, assuming that the interaction between users and items can be predicted solely upon observations of "neighboring" users or items. That is, a user's interest in an item is approximated by the average of neighboring observations. Although content-based methods and neighborhood methods are popular due to their simplicity, they cannot exploit hidden interactions between users and items. Recently, another class of methods called *latent factor models* has gained increasing attention. These methods are highly accurate and can easily incorporate various biases. However, compared to content-based methods and neighborhood methods, latent factor models are more vulnerable to the appearance of new items and new users, i.e., to the cold-start problem. Therefore, these three approaches are complementary to each other in practice (e.g., [17]). In a general sense, SSR may be considered as RecSys, however, SSR usually does not have item ratings, and user feedback to SSR is often implicit.

Click-through Model (CM): both IR (see, e.g., [14, 9]) and RecSys [25, 31] researchers have noticed that users' feedback is vital for learning a high-quality model. In order to derive users' preferences and model users' clickthrough data, a variety of CMs have been proposed. The most common approach to clickthrough modeling is to construct a generative model aiming to explain the training data (see, e.g., [33, 13]). Other models that derive users' preferences have been proposed as well (see, e.g., [25, 5, 31, 18]). While generative models are specifically designed to understand clickthrough data, it is difficult to incorporate them into current IR or RecSys frameworks, partially due to the fact that generative models are hard to adapt to optimizing a non-probabilistic objective. Indeed, it is easier to first obtain user preferences from clickthrough data analysis and then adapt existing IR/RecSys tools to using these preferences (e.g., [25, 5, 31]). Our paper is inspired from this idea.

In addition to these three directions, some efforts have been made to directly tackle the problem of SSR. For instance, Chen et al. [8] discussed the problem of recommending content on Twitter by considering many dimensions, including content sources, topic interests of users and social voting. However, their study focused on empirical validations of several features (signals) and the dataset used is significantly smaller than ours. Their later work [7] goes beyond single Tweet recommendation to conversation recommendation. Duan et al. [11] noticed that the ranking problem of Twitter can be treated as an application of learning to rank. Their dataset is also small and relationships between recipients and senders are not explored. As we have discussed, SSR is not simply a LtoR problem. Choudhury et al. [10] argued that SSR should consider the problem of "diversity" and they tested their greedy algorithm on 67 employees from a large technology corporation. Our work differs from all this related work in three significant ways: 1) we test our proposed method on a large-scale, real-world dataset; 2) we propose a principled way to address SSR in the context of LtoR, CF and CM; and 3) we conduct comprehensive evaluation of our model against several models that underlie state-of-the-art recommender systems and report a consistent improvement in performance.

3. OVERVIEW OF LINKEDIN

Founded in December 2002 and launched in May 2003, LinkedIn[1] is primarily used for online professional networking. As of March 2012, LinkedIn has more than 160 million registered users in more than 200 countries and territories. On LinkedIn, user profiles play a central role for establishing professional existence and personal brand. Users can update their professional profiles to include a spectrum of content types (e.g., position descriptions, publications, patents, open source projects, skills, etc.). In addition, LinkedIn offers collaborative platforms to help users consume relevant news stories (e.g., LinkedIn Today[2]), seek answers to questions on professional issues (e.g., LinkedIn Groups[3]), and share useful content (e.g., LinkedIn Signal[4]). On the left-hand side of LinkedIn's homepage, a typical user will see a list of content items that come from their professional connections. This update stream consists of a wide range of types of updates including changes on their profiles (e.g., changes in their employment), shares of information (e.g., news articles, blog posts), and Twitter updates. These updates compose a social stream for the user. A snapshot of a user's homepage is shown in Figure 1.

As we have discussed in previous sections, delivering truly relevant social updates to users is a very difficult task. Information overload is certainly a serious problem for users who have hundreds of connections. In contrast, for newly joined users who do not have a sufficient number of connections, a system could recommend potentially useful updates to make the user adapt to the service more smoothly and quickly.

[1]http://www.linkedin.com
[2]https://www.linkedin.com/today/
[3]https://www.linkedin.com/myGroups
[4]https://www.linkedin.com/signal/

Figure 1: A typical example of LinkedIn homepage where the social stream of a user is highlighted by a red rectangle, shown on the left hand side of the screen.

From the LinkedIn point of view, it is important to attract users to consume their social content and interact with their social streams as it is a clear indicator of a healthy engagement pattern. A steady, but badly delivered social stream may distract the user and make them lose interest in the service. A weak social stream for new users may make them question the benefits of the service. On the other hand, if a user interacts with the social stream frequently, clicking "Like" buttons or making comments to others' updates, the user is likely to become more and more engaged.

4. SOCIAL STREAM RANKING

In this section, we will discuss the ingredients of our proposed model step by step, from a simple linear model to a much more involved tensor factorization based latent factor model. We start our discussion from why the problem of SSR cannot simply be treated as a rating prediction problem, which is a classic setting in RecSys.

4.1 Evaluation Metrics

In traditional RecSys settings where the entities are users and items (e.g., the famous Netflix competition[5]) forming a matrix of users by items, the main goal is to predict or recover missing values in this matrix – if we treat existing ratings as observed values and non-existing ratings as missing values of the matrix. The performance of recommender systems is evaluated by how accurately a system can predict these values. For instance, in the Netflix Prize, Rooted Mean Squared Error (RMSE) is used to measure the accuracy of rating predictions. RMSE is defined as $\sqrt{\frac{1}{N}\sum_{i}^{n}(x_i - \hat{x}_i)^2}$ where x_i is the ground-truth rating for rating i, $\hat{x}_i$ is the predicted value and N is the total number of ratings to be tested. Although it

[5]http://www.netflixprize.com/

might be an appropriate evaluation metric for movie recommendation tasks where multiple levels of ratings are available, two crucial issues will arise while using it as an evaluation metric to SSR.

First of all, as we see in Figure 1, the final presentation of a social stream is a list of items shown on the computer screen. Due to the limited space on the screen, users can only see a portion of the list which usually only consists of a handful of updates. Although users can always scroll down the list and even go to additional pages, not all of them do that in practice. Thus, even if the accuracy of predictions is important, we certainly wish to have higher-accuracy items on the top of the list rather than to have the whole list slightly more accurate. This ordering information cannot be easily captured in accuracy-based metrics, like RMSE. In addition to the reason that accuracy-based metrics may not be appropriate, in the practical sense, a system optimizing accuracy might fail to produce reasonable results. As we will see, the users rarely interact with the *majority* of the updates. In other words, users are only interested in a small number of items. An accuracy-optimized system may overfit non-interacted items and yield good performance overall but might not match the small portion of clicked updates. Indeed, this drawback of accuracy-based metrics is also discussed in the collaborative filtering literature (e.g., [25, 18, 31]).

Based on this discussion, we adopt rank-based metrics to evaluate the effectiveness of SSR systems. Rank-based metrics are widely used in the IR community. In this paper, we borrow Mean Average Precision from the traditional IR. We define the "precision" at position k (Precision@k) of a social stream as $(\#$ of clicks in top positions$)/k$. Then, an average measure across all top m positions (Average Precision) for user u is defined as $(\sum_{k=1}^{m}$ Precision@k$\times l_k)/(\#$ of clicks for ranked list of user $u)$ where l_k is a binary indicator whether the position k has been clicked or not and m is the total number of positions evaluated. Note that the Average Precision is evaluated per user. We can average it across all users, resulting in the Mean Average Precision (MAP) measure.

4.2 Dataset

Before discussing the details of our dataset, we introduce the concept of *impression*. Every time a user logs in LinkedIn's homepage, the system generates a list of candidate social updates from many sources, mainly based on the user's social connections. This list of updates can be small or large, depending on the user's social circle. If the number of updates in the list exceeds a certain threshold (e.g., $10 - 15$), these updates cannot be shown on a single screen, and the user will need to scroll down. An impression is a list of updates that a user has actually seen on the screen. Given historical data, we can "replay" the users' activity while analyzing impressions. Note that social updates are not distinct: one specific update produced by a user or a company can be shown to many users.

Since our experimental setting is "simulation" (details will be discussed in Section 4.1), we discard all impressions without any clicks because these impressions do not change our experimental results (as measured by MAP). Note that there is a deeper argument on this decision. Remember that one issue associated with social streams is their sparsity. Indeed, only a small number of impressions attract users and a handful of clicks is performed on such impressions, compared to the large amount of impressions produced in total. Thus, it might be useless for any model to fit these non-interacted impressions. Focusing on impressions that actually matter reduces the training set significantly and produces better results, which we saw in our empirical studies. Thus, only impressions with at least one click remain in our dataset. In our experiments, we also filter out impressions with less than five items.

Data Summary	April, 2011	September, 2011
Impressions	3M-4M	10M-20M
Updates	30M-40M	100M-200M
Clicked Updates	3M-4M	10M-20M
Non-clicked Updates	27M-36M	90M-180M
Distinct Updates	10M-20M	20M-30M
Recipients	1M-2M	4M-5M
Producers	4M-5M	6M-7M

Table 1: The basic statistics about the dataset."M" means million. The numbers are obfuscated due to commercial reason.

We report on two datasets of LinkedIn's social update stream. Both are subsamples of the actual social stream collected by LinkedIn's engineering team. The first dataset was taken from April, 2011 stream, while the second was taken from September, 2011 stream. The basic statistics on the two datasets are shown in Table 1. The reason why we take two datasets that are not consequent in time is to demonstrate that the performance of different algorithms is indeed consistent over different time periods.

4.3 Linear Models

In this section, we will discuss several simple linear models to tackle the problem of SSR. Given a social update, a user can choose to respond to this update or not. For simplicity, we treat all kinds of responses as a "click" event and no response as a "non-click" event. Thus, we focus on binary responses in this work. We denote $\mathbf{y}$ as a vector of responses to all social updates, across all impressions. This way, we concatenate updates from all impressions together and drop the notion of an impression. The ordering of elements in $\mathbf{y}$ does not matter as we only care about the correspondence: the response y_i corresponds to the i-th update in the entire dataset and f_i represents the estimation of y_i from the models described later. In addition, we define the following auxiliary functions: $r(i)$ is the recipient of update i, $s(i)$ is the sender of update i, $t(i)$ is the type of update i, and $c(i)$ is the sender type. Let $\mathcal{R}$ be the set of recipients, $\mathcal{S}$ be the set of senders, $\mathcal{T}$ be the set of types, $\mathcal{I}$ be the set of social updates.

Feature Model (FM): One straightforward model is linear estimation, which predicts the response by a linear combination of features. For a specific update i, we collect their corresponding features. Let $\boldsymbol{\phi}$ be a feature vector – we use subscript to indicate its corresponding type. For instance, $\boldsymbol{\phi}_{r(i)}$ represents the feature vector (e.g., profile) for the recipient user of update i. A simple prediction of y_i – a linear combination of user features and update features – can be defined as:

$$f_i^{(1)} = \boldsymbol{\beta}_{r(i)}^T \boldsymbol{\phi}_{r(i)} + \boldsymbol{\alpha}_{r(i)}^T \boldsymbol{\phi}_i \quad (1)$$

where $\boldsymbol{\beta}_u$ and $\boldsymbol{\alpha}_u$ are per-user coefficients to be learned from the training set. This model is essentially equivalent to the one where user features and update features are combined into a single feature vector and a per-user coefficient to be learned. Note, an even more simpler model could be also considered where a universal coefficient is used, instead of per-user coefficients. However, this model would be too restricted and personalization cannot be applied.

Latent Bias Model (LBM): Here, we introduce a linear model to explain the clicks on items. We start with an assumption that whether a new item i will be clicked by a user depends on the average click rate: $f_i = \mu$ where μ is the average click rate across all items and all users. Certainly, this estimation is too coarse and inaccurate because, as we mentioned before, the majority of items are not clicked. We can extend this base estimation by incorporating a wide range of biases: 1) type (category) bias, 2) item bias, 3) recipient bias, 4) sender type bias and 5) sender bias. Adding these biases is very intuitive. Certain types of updates (e.g., notifications about changes in user profiles, including changes in job titles etc.) receive more attentions than others. Users tend to respond (e.g., click "Like" button or make comments) more often on these types of updates than on others. In addition, some individual items are more popular than others as their content might be more interesting (e.g., breaking news, unexpected stories). From the perspective of senders and recipients, biases are also significant. For instance, some updates are coming from companies that inform their followers about their new products and services – those updates are far more popular than status updates from individual users. Moreover, certain users are more engaged than others which introduces user biases. Therefore, all these biases (i.e., prior knowledge) can capture a wide range of effects of interactions. Let b denote biases and the subscript to indicate the type of biases. Also, the subscript can be an index for a feature. Therefore, we can have the following linear estimation:

$$f_i^{(2)} = \mu + b_i + b_{t(i)} + b_{r(i)} + b_{c(i)} + b_{s(i)} \tag{2}$$

Note that these biases are generally unknown. We treat them as latent variables to be learned from the dataset. Comparing with LR, which depends on feature vectors some of which might be difficult to calculate and update (e.g., graph-based features, content based features), this model is appealing since no extra information is needed for learning, besides requiring indicators.

Combining FM and LBM: It is straightforward to consider combining FM and LBM together. Thus, the combined model will enjoy the freedom that different parts of the model will explain a variety of user behaviors. The combined model is simply:

$$f_i^{(3)} = f_i^{(1)} + f_i^{(2)} \tag{3}$$

Note, this is essentially a linear feature model with biases decomposed into many aspects.

Incorporating Temporal Effects: Social streams are temporally sensitive in nature. Users focus on fresh information and interact with them while they often do not bother to look at old updates. We model the temporal effects of updates by a simple feature: $t_{\text{recency}} = t_{\text{imp}} - t_{\text{upt}}$ where t_{imp} is the numerical time when a user sees a particular impression and t_{upt} is the numerical time when an update is produced. These feature values would be different for different updates. Even for the same update, depending on when recipients access their update streams, the feature value can vary greatly. Incorporating this feature into our estimation can be as follows:

$$f_i^4 = f_i^{(*)} + \zeta \times t_{\text{recency}} \tag{4}$$

where $f_i^{(*)}$ can be any estimator defined in Equations (1, 2 and 3) and ζ is a free parameter, indicating the importance of recency of updates. Note that ζ can be learned from the training set and can also be treated as another personalized parameter. However, we fix it across all users and manually tune this parameter mainly because of two reasons. Firstly, since not all users interact with social streams regularly and new users are coming all the time, we need to provide reasonably relevant social updates for these users. Under these circumstances, explicit features might not be available (e.g., new users) and biases are not learned reliably from the training set (e.g., not enough interactions before). Therefore, a safe choice is to rank items chronologically. In addition to that, users who are heavily engaged with their social streams are familiar with existing ranking schemes which are primarily based on recency. We do not want to suddenly change their expectations on their future impressions. Hence, we set ζ such that the temporal effect can always be an important factor and indeed the learned coefficients and biases will dominate the estimation only when it is necessary.

Since responses are binary, we impose a logistic loss on predictions and true values, yielding learning procedures of the logistic regression flavor. All these linear models can be learned effectively by minimizing the following objective function for each update i:

$$l_1(y_i, f_i^{(*)}) = \log\Big[1 + \exp(-y_i f_i^*)\Big] \tag{5}$$

where $y_i \in \{\pm 1\}$ is the ground-truth response and f_i^* is the estimated response from the models defined above. In common practice, in order to avoid overfitting the training set, we also use L_2 regularizer to shrink all parameters towards zero. Taking Equation (4) as an example, the final objective function is:

$$L_1 = \sum_i l_1(y_i, f_i^4) + \lambda_1\Big(\sum_i ||b_i||^2 + \sum_{t(i)} ||b_{t(i)}||^2 + \sum_{c(i)} ||b_{c(i)}||^2 + \sum_{r(i)} ||b_{r(i)}||^2 + \sum_{s(i)} ||b_{s(i)}||^2\Big) + \lambda_2 \sum_u \Big(||\boldsymbol{\beta}_u||_F^2 + ||\boldsymbol{\alpha}_u||_F^2\Big)$$

where λ_1 and λ_2 are two regularization parameters to be manually tuned. Many methods are available to optimize the objective function above. Here, we adopt the Stochastic Gradient Descent (SGD) method, a widely used learning method for large-scale data, to learn parameters. SGD requires gradients, which can be effectively calculated as follows:

$$\frac{\partial L_1}{\partial b_*} = -\sum_i \Big[1 - \sigma(y_i f_i^4)\Big] y_i + 2\lambda_1 \sum_* b_*$$

$$\frac{\partial L_1}{\partial \boldsymbol{\beta}_{r(i),k}} = -\sum_i \Big[1 - \sigma(y_i f_i^4)\Big] y_i \boldsymbol{\phi}_{r(i),k} + 2\lambda_2 \boldsymbol{\beta}_{r(i),k}$$

$$\frac{\partial L_1}{\partial \boldsymbol{\alpha}_{i,k}} = -\sum_i \Big[1 - \sigma(y_i f_i^4)\Big] y_i \boldsymbol{\phi}_{i,k} + 2\lambda_2 \boldsymbol{\alpha}_{i,k}$$

where b_* represents any bias terms, $\boldsymbol{\beta}_{r(i),k}$ and $\boldsymbol{\alpha}_{i,k}$ represent k-th element of coefficient for user $r(i)$ and update i respectively. Note that $\sigma(x) = \frac{1}{1+\exp(-x)}$.

4.4 Latent Factor Models

Although linear models are efficient, they are usually oversimplified and cannot capture interactions between different effects. Latent Factor Models (LFM) are widely used in recommender systems (e.g., [17, 29, 31, 30]) and have proven effective in many scenarios (e.g., [17]). Specifically, LFM can model the interactions between different types of entities such as user-user and user-item, discovering their latent relationships. In this section, we discuss two types of LFM: matrix factorization and tensor factorization, and see how they can be applied to the task of SSR.

Matrix Factorization: In traditional CF, matrix factorization techniques are used to exploit user-item interactions. A straightforward idea would be to directly apply matrix factorization methods to user-update matrix. However, this idea is not practical. As discussed above, social streams have new updates arriving all the time, and existing updates are only consumed by a small number of users. Thus, cold-start problems are much more severe here, compared to traditional CF where the user base and the item base are relatively stable. Here, we impose a latent factor $\boldsymbol{\eta}_u \in \mathbb{R}^k$ for each recipient and producer and factorize the recipient-producer matrix to predict

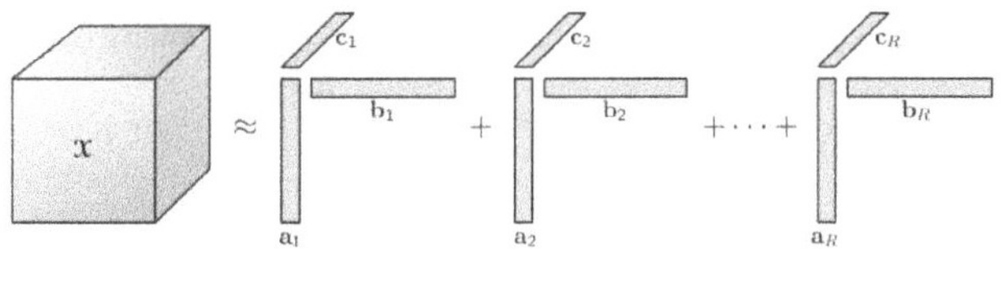

Figure 2: CANDECOMP/PARAFAC decomposition of a tensor, a three-way array. The dimensionality of three latent factors is the same.

the actions on updates. We describe the model in a probabilistic way:

$$\boldsymbol{\eta}_u \sim P(\boldsymbol{\eta}_u \,|\, \mathbf{0}, \sigma^2\mathbf{I}) \quad u \in \{\mathcal{R}, \mathcal{S}\}$$
$$y_i \sim P(y_i \,|\, \boldsymbol{\eta}_{r(i)}, \boldsymbol{\eta}_{s(i)}, b_*, \mu)$$

where b_* is any biases introduced in Section (4.3), $\mathcal{R}$ and $\mathcal{S}$ are the set of recipients and producers respectively. For $P(\boldsymbol{\eta}_u \,|\, \mathbf{0}, \sigma^2\mathbf{I})$, it is usually assumed to be Gaussian or Laplace, corresponding to L_2 or L_1 regularization on latent factors respectively. Here, we use a multivariate Gaussian assumption. For $P(y_i \,|\, \boldsymbol{\eta}_{r(i)}, \boldsymbol{\eta}_{s(i)}, b_*, \mu)$, we assume:

$$y_i \sim P(y_i \,|\, f_i)$$
$$f_i = \mu + b_i + b_{t(i)} + b_{r(i)} + b_{c(i)} + b_{s(i)} + \boldsymbol{\eta}_{r(i)}^T \boldsymbol{\eta}_{s(i)} + \epsilon$$

where ϵ allows a Gaussian distribution. Thus, the final generative process also follows a Gaussian distribution. This formalism is similar to the one introduced in [17]. The model described here is very intuitive. Whether a user u_1 is going to click on an update from a user/company u_2 depends on u_1's and u_2's affinity.

Tensor Factorization: As social streams have different entities like recipients, producers and categories, it would be natural to directly model the multi-way data interaction, rather than concentrating on two-way relationships. It has been shown that high-order relational modeling can improve the performance of CF systems in many scenarios, for instance in social tag recommendations [24, 26].Here, we focus on one particular three-way relationship: recipient-producer-category of the update. We associate latent factors $\boldsymbol{\eta}_x \in \mathbb{R}^k$ for these three types of entities. Similar to the matrix case, we define the following generative procedures:

$$\boldsymbol{\eta}_x \sim P(\boldsymbol{\eta}_x \,|\, \mathbf{0}, \sigma^2\mathbf{I}) \quad x \in \{\mathcal{R}, \mathcal{S}, \mathcal{T}\}$$
$$y_i \sim P(y_i \,|\, f_i)$$

where f_i is defined as:

$$f_i = \mu + b_i + b_{t(i)} + b_{r(i)} + b_{c(i)} + b_{s(i)} + \sum_k \eta_{r(i),k} \eta_{s(i),k} \eta_{t(i),k} + \epsilon$$

where $\eta_{*,k}$ represents the k-th element in the vector and ϵ again follows a Gaussian distribution. This particular form of tensor decomposition is known as CANDECOMP/PARAFAC (CP) decomposition [16], depicted in Figure 2. There are two important properties about CP decomposition. Firstly, it is a direct analogue to factorization methods in two-way array (matrix) data where latent factors share the same latent space. Secondly, CP decomposition has a nice yet surprising property that it has a unique solution of decomposition where matrix factorization does not enjoy this result [16]. This property indeed provides a theoretical guarantee to the decomposition and may be a reason for better performance.

We are aware of other forms of tensor factorization as well. For instance, Tucker decomposition [16], where the dimensionality of different latent factors varies, is widely used in many applications and applied to social media as well (e.g., [24, 29]). However, we do not choose the Tucker decomposition for our settings because not only it requires to pre-specify the dimensionality of all factors separately, but also does not guarantee uniqueness of the decomposition result.

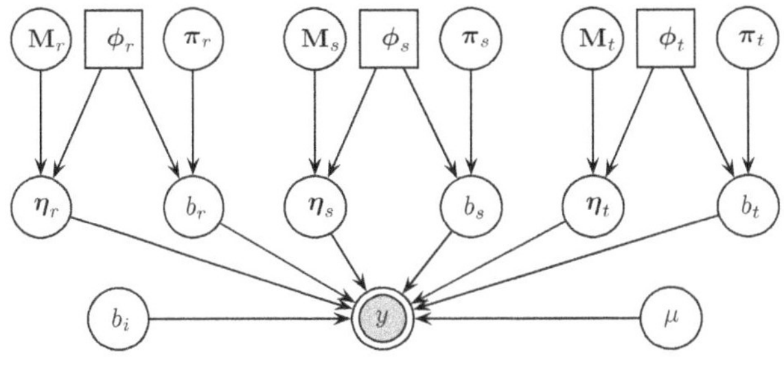

Figure 3: A graphical representation of regression-based tensor factor model. Square nodes represent features and circled nodes represents unknown variables. The response y in the middle is observed in the training set but to be predicted in the test set.

Incorporating Features: Both matrix factorization and tensor factorization discussed above do not directly incorporate explicit features. Here, we introduce features into the model by employing two levels of regression models. The basic idea is that latent features will depend on explicit features and final responses are derived from latent features. The first level regression models are defined as:

$$\boldsymbol{\eta}_{x(*)} = \mathbf{M}_x \boldsymbol{\phi}_{x(*)} + \epsilon_x \qquad x \in \{\mathcal{R}, \mathcal{S}, \mathcal{T}\}$$

where $\boldsymbol{\phi}_{x(*)}$ represents a feature vector for entity x and $\mathbf{M}_x$ is a transformation matrix to be learned. If ϵ_* follows a zero-mean k-dimensional Gaussian distribution, latent factors $\boldsymbol{\eta}_*$ indeed follow multivariate Gaussian distribution with the mean of a transformation of explicit feature vectors. This way, explicit feature space is mapped to latent feature space.

In addition to binding latent factors to explicit features, other biases may also have the same prior distributions:

$$b_{x(*)} = \boldsymbol{\pi}_x^T \boldsymbol{\phi}_{x(*)} + \epsilon_{b_x}$$

where $\boldsymbol{\pi}_x$ is a regression coefficient for entity x. If the error term ϵ_{b_x} follows a Gaussian distribution, biases $b_{x(*)}$ will also follow a Gaussian distribution centered at a transformation from explicit features. Note that this two-level regression scheme can be applied to matrix factorization as well as tensor factorization. The idea to use regression priors for matrix factorization has been explored by [1, 30] but not yet discussed on multi-way data relations like tensors. The final graphical representation of the model is shown in Figure 3.

In addition to the method described here to incorporate features, we are aware of other possibilities, such as [23] where latent factors and explicit features are treated as same set of features.

Like linear models from Section 4.3, LFM (with features) can also be learned through a Maximum A Posterior (MAP) estimation. Taking Tensor Factorization with Features as an example, the problem of minimizing the negative log posterior of the model boils down to the following objective:

$$L_2 = \sum_i L_1(y_i, f_i) + \sum_{x\in\{\mathcal{R},\mathcal{S},\mathcal{T}\}} \lambda_x \sum_{x(i)} ||\boldsymbol{\eta}_{x(i)} - \mathbf{M}_x \boldsymbol{\phi}_{x(i)}||_F^2$$
$$+ \sum_{x\in\{\mathcal{I},\mathcal{R},\mathcal{S},\mathcal{T},\mathcal{C}\}} \lambda_{b_x} \sum_{x(i)} ||b_{x(i)} - \boldsymbol{\pi}_x^T \boldsymbol{\phi}_{x(i)}||^2$$
$$+ \sum_{x\in\{\mathcal{I},\mathcal{R},\mathcal{S},\mathcal{T},\mathcal{C}\}} \Big(\lambda_{\pi_x} ||\boldsymbol{\pi}_x||_F^2 + \lambda_{M_x} ||\mathbf{M}||_F^2\Big)$$

where all constant terms are ignored and all λ terms are manually tuned regularization parameters. For both matrix factorization and CP decomposition, a number of techniques are available to solve the objective function. For instance, the alternating least squares (ALS) method is the "workhorse" [16] for both matrix and tensor factorization. However, here, we still adopt a SGD method, which can scale to the dataset with which we are working. In order to use SGD, the gradients of latent factors can be derived. Firstly, we focus on latent factors:

$$\frac{\partial L_2}{\partial \boldsymbol{\eta}_{r(i),k}} = -\sum_i \Big[1 - \sigma(y_i f_i)\Big] y_i \boldsymbol{\eta}_{s(i),k} \boldsymbol{\eta}_{t(i),k} + 2\lambda_r \Big(\boldsymbol{\eta}_{r(i),k} - \mathbf{M}_{r[k]} \boldsymbol{\phi}_{r(i)}\Big)$$
$$\frac{\partial L_2}{\partial \boldsymbol{\eta}_{t(i),k}} = -\sum_i \Big[1 - \sigma(y_i f_i)\Big] y_i \boldsymbol{\eta}_{r(i),k} \boldsymbol{\eta}_{s(i),k} + 2\lambda_t \Big(\boldsymbol{\eta}_{t(i),k} - \mathbf{M}_{t[k]} \boldsymbol{\phi}_{t(i)}\Big)$$
$$\frac{\partial L_2}{\partial \boldsymbol{\eta}_{s(i),k}} = -\sum_i \Big[1 - \sigma(y_i f_i)\Big] y_i \boldsymbol{\eta}_{r(i),k} \boldsymbol{\eta}_{t(i),k} + 2\lambda_s \Big(\boldsymbol{\eta}_{s(i),k} - \mathbf{M}_{s[k]} \boldsymbol{\phi}_{s(i)}\Big)$$

where $\boldsymbol{\eta}_{*,k}$ is the k-th element of the vector and $\mathbf{M}_{*[k]}$ is the k-th row of the matrix. For all biases, gradients $\frac{\partial L_2}{\partial b_{*(i)}}$ are as follows:

$$-\sum_{i\in b_{*(i)}} \Big[1 - \sigma(y_i f_i)\Big] y_i + 2\lambda_{b_*} \Big(b_{*(i)} - \boldsymbol{\pi}_*^T \boldsymbol{\phi}_{*(i)}\Big)$$

where $*$ means a particular type of bias and $i \in b_{*(i)}$ represents the updates those bias type match the type of interests. The gradients $\frac{\partial L_2}{\partial M_{x[k,m]}}$ for matrix M_x can be derived as:

$$2\lambda_x \sum_{x(i)} \Big(\boldsymbol{\eta}_{x(i),k} - \mathbf{M}_{x[k]} \boldsymbol{\phi}_{x(i)}\Big)\Big(-\boldsymbol{\phi}_{x(i),k}\Big) + 2\lambda_{M_x} \mathbf{M}_{x[k,m]}$$

where $\mathbf{M}_{x[k,m]}$ is the (k,m)-th element in the matrix $\mathbf{M}_x$. And finally, the gradients for regression coefficients $\frac{\partial L_2}{\partial \boldsymbol{\pi}_{x,k}}$ can be computed as:

$$2\lambda_{b_x} \sum_{x(i)} \Big(b_{x(i)} - \boldsymbol{\pi}_x^T \boldsymbol{\phi}_{x(i)}\Big)\Big(-\boldsymbol{\phi}_{x(i),k}\Big) + 2\lambda_{\pi_x} \boldsymbol{\pi}_{x,k}$$

4.5 Pairwise Learning

So far, we have demonstrated two different types of models: linear models and latent factor models. Both of them minimize certain errors in the learning process. As discussed in Section 4.1, a ranking-based evaluation metric, MAP is used in our experiments. Thus, it is more reasonable to directly optimize this ranking metric. However, it is difficult to optimize ranking measures directly [32, 6, 22] due to their discrete nature. Although some techniques (e.g., [6, 22]) have been developed to derive smoothed surrogate functions to approximate these ranking measures, including MAP, they are usually complicated and expensive to apply to large scale scenarios. Here, we use a much simpler approach: derive pairwise preferences from users' impressions and learn a pairwise ranking function.

First, let $\mathcal{O}_i$ be the set of updates in the impression i, $\mathcal{O}_{i,+}$ be the set of updates clicked by the user and $\mathcal{O}_{i,-}$ be the set of updates not clicked by the user. Remember that we eliminate impressions without any clicks (see 4.2). Therefore, we guarantee that the method described here can be applied to all impressions in our dataset. For any pair of updates (m, n) where $m \in \mathcal{O}_{i,+}$ and $n \in \mathcal{O}_{i,-}$, we can always construct a preference label $l_{m,n} = 1$, meaning that update m is favored over update n in impression i. Under this setting, we have the new objective function for impression i:

$$l_2(i, \mathbf{f}) = \frac{1}{|\mathcal{O}_{i,+}||\mathcal{O}_{i,-}|} \sum_{m\in\mathcal{O}_{i,+}} \sum_{n\in\mathcal{O}_{i,-}} \sigma\Big(f_m - f_n\Big) \quad (6)$$

where σ is a logit function. This new objective function is no longer to fit a single observed label (click or not) but to optimize a pairwise preference induced from impressions. Similar ideas are also explored in [25, 31, 18]. With this new objective function, we can replace the original loss function defined in Equation (5) in both linear model learning and factor model learning. Gradients are omitted due to space limits.

4.6 Summary & Discussion

We discussed several issues related to our proposed methods in this sub-section: 1) parameter tuning, 2) scalability and 3) feature treatment. For parameter tuning, while it is not a significant problem for Linear Models, as they can be trained efficiently, it might be prohibitively expensive to tune a Latent Factor Model. In this work, we do not heavily tune parameters and only wish to see whether these proposed approaches work in principle. One way to deploy a "parameter-free" model might be to consider a Bayesian treatment of Latent Factor Models, like [27, 29]. However, the sheer amount of data and its continuous nature prevent us to explore Bayesian treatment in this work and leave it to the future work. In terms of scalability, we conduct experiments on a single machine in this work but we do notice that SGD can be paralleled [34]. Thus, we can scale our model to even larger datasets. The way we integrate explicit features and latent factors is through regression models. However, this is not the only way to deal with this kind of problem. For instance, matrix co-factorization (see, e.g., [28]) and tensor co-factorization can be another paradigm of combining explicit features and hidden features.

5. EXPERIMENTAL RESULTS

In this section, we demonstrate the effectiveness of our model, through a comprehensive comparison with non-trivial baselines. The dataset used in our experiments is described in Section 4.2. Before we go into the details of the experimental results, we first discuss our experimental setting in Section 5.1 and then all developed models in Section 5.2.

5.1 Experimental Setting

Two standard settings are available to evaluate the effectiveness of systems for SSR. One is to test each model against an existing system in a online setting where both systems run in parallel for a similar audience in a reasonable period of time. After this, the effectiveness of both systems can be calculated using certain measurements, like error rate or ranking metrics. This is a classic A/B testing scenario. The advantage of A/B testing is obvious: it provides a real comparison between models. However, it might be

Models	Comments
Baseline (BL)	LinkedIn
Feature Model (FM)	Section 4.3
Latent Bias Model (LBM)	Section 4.3
Feature Bias Model (FBM)	Section 4.3
Matrix Factorization (MF)	Section 4.4
Tensor Factorization (TF)	Section 4.4
Matrix Factorization with Features (MF2)	Section 4.4
Tensor Factorization with Features (TF2)	Section 4.4

Table 2: All models used in our experiments.

Features	Comments
Seniority	the seniority level of a user
Visiting	how frequently a user visits LinkedIn
PageRank	discretized PageRank scores
Connectedness	how well a user is connected to others
Social strength	how tight a user's connections is
Professional	how professional an update's language is
Recency	the freshness of an update (see Section 4.3)

Table 3: All features used in our experiments.

Training/Testing	BL	FM	LBM	FBM
4_01(Tr.)/4_08(Te.)	0.5278	0.5317	**0.5943**	0.5520
4_08(Tr.)/4_15(Te.)	0.5435	0.5509	**0.6040**	0.5574
4_15(Tr.)/4_22(Te.)	0.5218	0.5246	**0.5823**	0.5235
9_01(Tr.)/9_10(Te.)	0.4829	0.4911	**0.5457**	0.4984
9_10(Tr.)/9_18(Te.)	0.4779	0.4798	**0.5432**	0.4915
9_18(Tr.)/9_25(Te.)	0.4768	0.4803	**0.5329**	0.4886

Table 4: The comparison between linear models. The best performance is shown in bold.

Type Description	Bias b_t
Job Seeker Product Update	0.5765
Joining Sub-Group	0.5407
Company News	0.4592
Joining Group	0.2625
Profile Picture Update	0.2516
Initiating Direct Ads Campaign	0.2253
Profile Update	0.1394

Table 5: Example of highly ranked types of updates

time-consuming and even impossible to compare many models in a batch. In addition, some models require tuning parameters, which may risk the business of the service a company offers. Thus, we do not use A/B testing in this paper and leave it to the future work.

In this paper, we simulate real settings of SSR, conducting offline experiments. More specifically, we gather historical data from LinkedIn user logs, which capturing all impressions users have consumed. Since we know which updates are clicked in each impression, it is easy to replay all these impressions and reorder the updates. Thus, we can produce a "new" impression for users in the dataset. The drawback of this approach to experiments is that we cannot show "new" ordering of impressions that are not clicked by users at all because whether users would have clicked them or not is impossible to test. This is another reason why we drop all impressions without any clicks (Section 4.2).

The dataset for one month is divided into weeks. We train our models on one week and test them on the following week. This setting results in more than 70% items being new in test data each week, which is an evidence to the fact that SSR is different from RecSys and IR.

5.2 Models & Features

We compare several models in our experiments. All models used in the following experiments are shown in Table 2. The baseline is a proprietary system currently deployed in the product of LinkedIn homepage. FM, LBM and their combination (FBM) are examples of simple linear models while MF, TF with their feature enhanced extensions (MF2 and TF2) are examples of latent factor models. For all models, a point-wise loss function (Equation (5)) and a pairwise loss function (6) are both tested. Without stating it explicitly, all models include the temporal effect feature discussed in Section (4.3) while the parameter ζ, the balance between recency and relevance, is manually tuned. All regularization parameters are simply set to 1. We understand that this may not be an optimal choice. For tuning a reasonable learning rate in SGD and ζ, we use the first day in the test week as a "validation" day and choose the parameter setting that can provide the optimal performance on the day. We fix the parameters for the remaining days in the test week.

Some of linear models and latent factor models require explicit features. In this paper, we include several important features to enhance our models. Note that we are aware of many other possible features. However, it is not our goal to study the effectiveness of a particular feature in this work. All features are shown in Table 3. "Seniority" measures the seniority level of a user's job title. "Visiting" measures how well engaged a user is (our assumption is that a frequent visitor is likely to interact with his/her social stream). "PageRank" (details in [4]) and "Connectedness" measure how a user connects with other users. Presumably, a highly respected and well connected user can attract others to interact with their update streams. "Social strength" is a proprietary product used in LinkedIn, measuring the connection closeness between two users. "Professional" measures how likely an update is similar in its language to professional profiles of LinkedIn users (i.e. how professional an update is). The assumption is that users may favor professional updates over non-professional updates on LinkedIn because it is a professional social network.

5.3 Results on Linear Models

In this sub-section, we focus on the comparison between the baseline and all linear models. In this Subsection, we focus on the comparison between the baseline and all linear models. The results are shown in Table 4. The first column indicates how models are trained and tested. For instance, the first number "4_01" means the models are trained on the week of April 1st and tested on the week of April 8th (8-th is the date for validation of parameter tuning) where "Tr." and "Te." are shorthand for "Training" and "Testing", respectively. We conduct experiments on two separate months to avoid some seasonal fluctuations on the data. The numbers shown on the right part of the table are MAP scores.

Our first observation is that the baseline of MAP in September is lower than its in April, implying that updates in the lower positions in the lists get clicked more often over time. One possible explanation is that users become familiar with their social streams and start to find interesting updates manually, looking at more items down the list. The second observation is that all linear models, including FM, LBM and FBM, perform better than the baseline, consistently on two-month datasets. However, for FM, which only depends on explicit features, the performance is very close to the baseline. This is reasonable because only a handful of features are used in our experiments and we do expect that these features are not likely discriminative. On the other hand, LBM, a model only depending on implicit feedback, has consistently $5\% - 6\%$ absolute improvements on MAP over the baseline. This confirms that it is vital

Training/Testing	MF	TF	MF2	TF2
4_01(Tr.)/4_08(Te.)	0.5955	0.6258	0.5951	**0.6336**
4_08(Tr.)/4_15(Te.)	0.6079	0.6228	0.6088	**0.6535**
4_15(Tr.)/4_22(Te.)	0.5962	0.6014	0.5991	**0.6312**
9_01(Tr.)/9_10(Te.)	0.5511	0.5766	0.5523	**0.6003**
9_10(Tr.)/9_18(Te.)	0.5412	0.5833	0.5449	**0.6109**
9_18(Tr.)/9_25(Te.)	0.5359	0.5799	0.5362	**0.5992**

Table 6: The comparison between latent factor models. The best performance is shown in bold.

to exploit different aspects of users' feedbacks and capture them through bias modeling (e.g., [17, 15]). Indeed, FBM gives the most improvements over the baseline in all our experiments. The idea is simple and easy to implement. For the combination of a pure feature-based model FM and a pure implicit-feedback-based model LBM, FBM does perform as someone might expect. It is significantly worse than LBM and almost identical to FM, which might indicate that simply integrating explicit features with biases may not be a good choice and more sophisticated approaches are needed.

LBM can also reveal some interesting patterns from the dataset, which might not be easily identified by other methods. For instance, we can figure out the effective popularity of different types of updates by looking at the values of b_t. The positivity or negativity of these values indicate whether a particular type of update correlates with clicks or non-clicks, while the magnitude of these values means how strongly this correlation might be. We show some samples of top ranked types in Table 5, which are positively correlated with clicks. From the table, we see that job related updates, company-related updates are comparatively attractive. In addition, users pay attention to profile changes of their connections and new connections established by their friends. Note that the value shown in the table is "automatically" normalized in the sense that SGD only updates corresponding parameters when the algorithm meets such type of updates. Also, the ratio of positive examples of a particular type will drive the parameter to strong positive numbers. Thus, no post-processing steps are required. This is an example of how our model can be used in simple data analysis tasks.

5.4 Results on Latent Factor Models

As we discussed earlier, latent factor models are widely used and have been proven to be superior to linear models. We conduct the same experiments as linear models and show their results in Table 6. Here, we compare between pure factorization-based models (MF and TF) and feature-enhanced factor models (MF2 and TF2). Note that all these models are built upon LBM and therefore the performance should at least match LBM. The second column of the table shows the results from MF, which is essentially to factorize the recipient-sender matrix and uncover latent structures. Unfortunately, the gain of performance of MF over LBM is marginal and even not observable. On the other hand, TF offers significant improvements and leads another $3\% - 4\%$ absolute boost for MAP on average. As we discussed before, social stream data is much more complex than traditional recommender system data (in various CF scenarios). Users may interact with certain updates because their senders are famous people or because the type of updates (e.g., news or twitter updates) is of a particular interest. Thus, tensor factorization can model multi-way relationships better than matrix factorization models them via a decomposition to multiple two-way relationships. Indeed, bias terms of recipients and senders in LBM might capture the basic relationship between them and a matrix factorization does not provide any additional benefits. Furthermore, we have already discussed why we do not employ the user-item

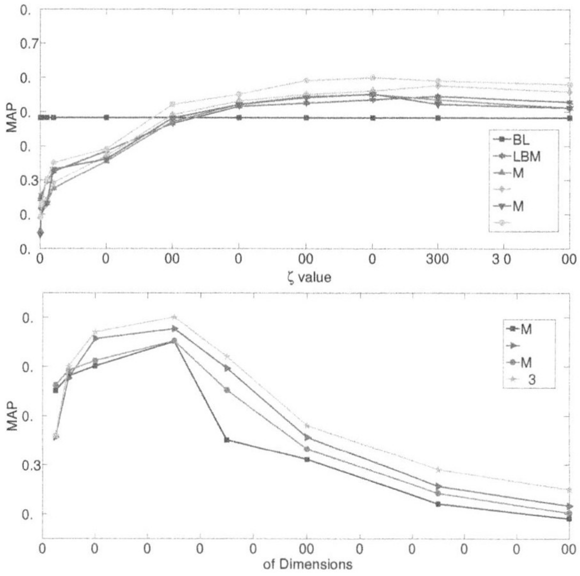

Figure 4: Parameter Sensitivity Analysis: 1) the effect of ζ (top) and 2) # of dimensions in latent factor models (bottom).

Training/Testing	LBM	MF	MF2	TF	TF2
4_01(Tr.)/4_08(Te.)	0.6169	0.6033	0.6151	0.6358	**0.6532**
4_08(Tr.)/4_15(Te.)	0.6188	0.6168	0.6188	0.6528	**0.6641**
4_15(Tr.)/4_22(Te.)	0.5897	0.6104	0.6191	0.6014	**0.6402**
9_01(Tr.)/9_10(Te.)	0.5644	0.5716	0.5723	0.5966	**0.6207**
9_10(Tr.)/9_18(Te.)	0.5593	0.5621	0.5607	0.5999	**0.6183**

Table 7: The effects of pair-wise learning. The best performance is shown in bold.

matrix in our setting: new items are much more common in social streams, compared to other recommender system setups. Thus, it is very interesting to see that well-established matrix-based factor models do not work equally well on social streams as they do in traditional CF scenarios. We believe that a more thorough investigation on this issue is desired.

For latent factor models with features, it is noticeable that MF2 failed to outperform LBM again while TF2 has gained additional $2\% - 3\%$ absolute improvement over TF consistently. This is a yet another signal that matrix factorization does not work well in SSR. For TF2, the increase of MAP can be explained by the two-level regression structure, that explicit features will help create latent features when new items or new users come into the system, effectively mitigating the cold-start problem. The performance of TF2 also validates that regression-based latent factor models are an effective approach to integrate explicit features with latent features.

We also study the sensitivity of parameters, especially the temporal balance weight ζ and the number of dimensions in latent factor models. Taking the first week of September as an example, the effects of both parameters are shown in Figure 4. The first observation is that both parameters are vital to the final performance and they are very sensitive if they are out of certain ranges. For ζ, the optimal performance is achieved when it is around $250 - 300$ while for dimensionality, the results suggest that a reasonable number $(20 - 50)$ is the key to success.

5.5 Results on Pairwise Learning

The results demonstrated so far focus on point-wise learning procedure. In other words, the objective function imposed by models is still error-based loss function. Here, we focus on how to improve performance by switching the objective function to pairwise preferences learning. More specifically, we conduct similar experiments as previous ones and report results on LBM, MF, TF MF2 and TF2, shown in Table 7. Other models are omitted due to their poor performance. First of all, we notice that almost all models can benefit from pairwise learning, even for the methods which did not show significant gains in previous experiments, such as MF and MF2. However, on another perspective, the overall improvement of a pairwise learning is not huge, usually yielding $1.5\% - 2\%$ improvement on MAP. One possibility is that the pairwise learning here is still naïve. More sophisticated session enabled learning procedures (e.g., [31]) are to be investigated in the future.

6. CONCLUSION & FUTURE WORK

In this paper, we investigate the problem of ranking social updates from a unique perspective of LinkedIn, the largest professional social network in the world. More specifically, we address the task as an intersection of learning to rank, collaborative filtering and click-through modeling, leveraging ideas from information retrieval and recommender systems. We propose a novel probabilistic latent factor model with regressions on explicit features, comparing a number of non-trivial baselines and gaining an approximately 10% improvement on MAP over the baseline. In addition to superior performance demonstrated in the paper, we shed some light on social updates on LinkedIn and how users interact with them, which might be applicable for social streams in general. For future work, it is interesting to see whether it is possible to develop efficient Bayesian treatment of latent models. In addition, other models might be explored as we demonstrate that state-of-the-art CF models do not provide comparable success in SSR. We also wish to extend our work by considering the diversity of information users wish to consume.

Acknowledgements

This material is based upon work supported in part by the National Science Foundation under Grant Numbers IIS-0545875 and IIS-0803605.

7. REFERENCES

[1] D. Agarwal and B.-C. Chen. Regression-based latent factor models. In *KDD 2009*, pages 19–28.

[2] F. Benevenuto, T. Rodrigues, M. Cha, and V. Almeida. Characterizing user behavior in online social networks. In *SIGCOMM 2009*, pages 49–62.

[3] C. Borgs, J. T. Chayes, B. Karrer, B. Meeder, R. Ravi, R. Reagans, and A. Sayedi. Game-theoretic models of information overload in social networks. In *Workshop on Algorithms and Models for the WebGraph 2010*, pages 146–161.

[4] S. Budalakoti and R. Bekkerman. Bimodal invitation-navigation fair bets model for authority identification in a social network. In *WWW 2012*, pages 709–718.

[5] B. Cao, D. Shen, K. Wang, and Q. Yang. Clickthrough log analysis by collaborative ranking. In *AAAI 2010*.

[6] O. Chapelle and M. Wu. Gradient descent optimization of smoothed information retrieval metrics. *Information Retrieval*, 13:216–235, 2010.

[7] J. Chen, R. Nairn, and E. Chi. Speak little and well: recommending conversations in online social streams. In *CHI 2011*, pages 217–226.

[8] J. Chen, R. Nairn, L. Nelson, M. Bernstein, and E. Chi. Short and tweet: experiments on recommending content from information streams. In *CHI 2010*, pages 1185–1194.

[9] N. Craswell, O. Zoeter, M. Taylor, and B. Ramsey. An experimental comparison of click position-bias models. In *WSDM 2008*, pages 87–94.

[10] M. De Choudhury, S. Counts, and M. Czerwinski. Identifying relevant social media content: leveraging information diversity and user cognition. In *Hypertext and Hypermedia 2011*, pages 161–170.

[11] Y. Duan, L. Jiang, T. Qin, M. Zhou, and H.-Y. Shum. An empirical study on learning to rank of tweets. In *COLING 2010*, pages 295–303.

[12] L. Hong, O. Dan, and B. D. Davison. Predicting popular messages in twitter. In *WWW 2011*, pages 57–58.

[13] B. Hu, Y. Zhang, W. Chen, G. Wang, and Q. Yang. Characterizing search intent diversity into click models. In *WWW 2011*, pages 17–26.

[14] T. Joachims. Optimizing search engines using clickthrough data. In *KDD 2002*, pages 133–142.

[15] N. Koenigstein, G. Dror, and Y. Koren. Yahoo! music recommendations: modeling music ratings with temporal dynamics and item taxonomy. In *RecSys 2011*, pages 165–172.

[16] T. G. Kolda and B. W. Bader. Tensor decompositions and applications. *SIAM Review*, 51:455–500, August 2009.

[17] Y. Koren. Factor in the neighbors: Scalable and accurate collaborative filtering. *ACM TKDD*, 4:1:1–1:24, January 2010.

[18] Y. Koren and J. Sill. OrdRec: an ordinal model for predicting personalized item rating distributions. In *RecSys 2011*, pages 117–124.

[19] T.-Y. Liu. Learning to rank for information retrieval. *Foundations and Trends in Information Retrieval*, 3(3):225–331, 2009.

[20] S. Muralidharan, L. Rasmussen, D. Patterson, and J.-H. Shin. Hope for haiti: An analysis of facebook and twitter usage during the earthquake relief efforts. *Public Relations Review*, 37(2):175 – 177, 2011.

[21] M. Naaman, J. Boase, and C.-H. Lai. Is it really about me?: message content in social awareness streams. In *CSCW 2010*, pages 189–192.

[22] T. Qin, T.-Y. Liu, and H. Li. A general approximation framework for direct optimization of information retrieval measures. *Information Retrieval*, 13:375–397, 2010.

[23] S. Rendle. Factorization machines with libFM. *ACM Transactions on Intelligent Systems and Technology (TIST)*, 3(3):57:1–57:22, 2012.

[24] S. Rendle, L. Balby Marinho, A. Nanopoulos, and L. Schmidt-Thieme. Learning optimal ranking with tensor factorization for tag recommendation. In *KDD 2009*, pages 727–736.

[25] S. Rendle, C. Freudenthaler, Z. Gantner, and S.-T. Lars. BPR: Bayesian personalized ranking from implicit feedback. In *UAI 2009*, pages 452–461.

[26] S. Rendle and L. Schmidt-Thieme. Pairwise interaction tensor factorization for personalized tag recommendation. In *WSDM 2010*, pages 81–90.

[27] R. Salakhutdinov and A. Mnih. Bayesian probabilistic matrix factorization using markov chain monte carlo. In *ICML 2008*, pages 880–887.

[28] A. P. Singh and G. J. Gordon. A unified view of matrix factorization models. In *ECML 2008*, pages 358–373.

[29] L. Xiong, X. Chen, T.-K. Huang, J. Schneider, and J. G. Carbonell. Temporal collaborative filtering with bayesian probabilistic tensor factorization. In *SDM 2010*, pages 211–222.

[30] S.-H. Yang, B. Long, A. Smola, N. Sadagopan, Z. Zheng, and H. Zha. Like like alike: joint friendship and interest propagation in social networks. In *WWW 2011*, pages 537–546.

[31] S.-H. Yang, B. Long, A. J. Smola, H. Zha, and Z. Zheng. Collaborative competitive filtering: learning recommender using context of user choice. In *SIGIR 2011*, pages 295–304.

[32] Y. Yue, T. Finley, F. Radlinski, and T. Joachims. A support vector method for optimizing average precision. In *SIGIR 2007*, pages 271–278.

[33] Y. Zhang, W. Chen, D. Wang, and Q. Yang. User-click modeling for understanding and predicting search-behavior. In *KDD 2011*, pages 1388–1396.

[34] M. Zinkevich, A. Smola, M. Weimer, , and L. Li:. Parallelized stochastic gradient descent. In *NIPS 2010*, pages 1–9.

Collaborative Personalized Tweet Recommendation

Kailong Chen, Tianqi Chen, Guoqing Zheng, Ou Jin, Enpeng Yao and Yong Yu
Dept. of Computer Science and Engineering, Shanghai Jiao Tong University
No. 800, Dongchuan Road, Shanghai, China 20024
chenkl,tqchen,gqzheng,kingohm,yaoenpeng,yyu @apex.sjtu.edu.cn

ABSTRACT

Twitter has rapidly grown to a popular social network in recent years and provides a large number of real-time messages for users. Tweets are presented in chronological order and users scan the followees' timelines to find what they are interested in. However, an information overload problem has troubled many users, especially those with many followees and thousands of tweets arriving every day. In this paper, we focus on recommending useful tweets that users are really interested in personally to reduce the users' effort to find useful information. Many kinds of information on Twitter are available for helping recommendation, including the user's own tweet history, retweet history and social relations between users. We propose a method of making tweet recommendations based on collaborative ranking to capture personal interests. It can also conveniently integrate the other useful contextual information. Our final method considers three major elements on Twitter: tweet topic level factors, user social relation factors and explicit features such as authority of the publisher and quality of the tweet. The experiments show that all the proposed elements are important and our method greatly outperforms several baseline methods.

Categories and Subject Descriptors

H.4.0 [**Information Systems**]: Information Systems Applications—*General*

Keywords

Twitter, Tweet Recommendation, Collaborative Ranking, Personalization

1. INTRODUCTION

Twitter is the most popular microblogging service and an important social network with over 200 million users as of 2011. It allows users to share information with their friends or the public by posting text messages of up to 140 characters, which are called tweets or statuses. Most users update their Twitter messages frequently and over 200 million tweets are generated per day. Users can access a filtered timeline of tweets from specific persons by explicitly following them. The retweet mechanism allows users to share information with their followers and accelerate the spread of information in the social network. On Twitter, users follow celebrities, friends or anyone else they care about and benefit greatly from the fresh information from these followees.

However, as a result of the rapidly increasing number of tweets, most Twitter users encounter a serious problem of information overload. It has been reported that Twitter users follow 80 people on average [22], which leads to hundreds or even thousands of tweets posted to each user every day. This bothers the active users more seriously, because they may have many more followees than regular users. The freshness of tweets is considered most important and all followees' tweets are shown to users in chronological order. Informative and useful tweets for the user may be flooded by other tweets that the user does not care about at all. For example, some followees update travel information so frequently that their tweets may prevent users from seeing important tweets such as international news. It is rather inconvenient for users to scan all the tweets posted in the last several hours or days to find useful information. A basic assumption on Twitter is that all the followees' statuses are considered equally important and they are posted to all followers sequentially. However, this assumption fails under many circumstances because users may consider only some specific aspects of the followees worth their attention.

Recommending useful tweets to a user is an important challenge and the focus of this paper. Intuitively, a tweet is useful to a user, if the user is interested in or willing to read the tweet. Whether a user is interested in a tweet is determined by many factors, such as the quality of the tweet and the authority of the publisher . Personal interest is also an important factor to decide whether a tweet is personally useful. Traditional methods analyze the content of users' posted or retweeted statuses to discover the topics of interest for Twitter users. However, profiling users' personal interests in this way is very difficult. Most users' personal preferences are related to tweets, which are short, informal, ungrammatical and noisy. Directly applying text mining and analyzing techniques designed for and tested on a traditional corpus of long text often leads to poor results [17].

Besides the user's own tweet history, there are many other kinds of important information available on Twitter. For example, the retweet history of other users can be used with the current user's tweet history to improve recommendation. In another direction, social relations between users can also greatly influence behavior. In order to fully utilize such information, we propose a framework based on collaborative ranking to capture the personal interests. Collaborative filtering and collaborative ranking are promising technologies for recommender systems. Collaborative ranking is a ranking version of collaborative filtering and provides item ranking results according to relative preference rather than user rating estimation. It works by discovering the correlation between users and items based on observed user preferences so that unobserved user preferences can be inferred from the observed ones. In personalized tweet recommendation, tweets are regarded as items, and the preferences of users on the tweets are the correlation between users and items. Our approach generalizes the traditional collaborative ranking approach by incorporating Twitter features such as content information, and social relation information, so our model fully utilizes the information mentioned on Twitter and can do better personalized recommendations.

The major contributions of the paper are as follows: (1) We use topic level latent factors of tweets to capture users' common interests over tweet content, which helps us to solve the problem of information sparsity in users' retweet actions. This allows us to adjust the collaborative filtering technique to solve the recommendation problem. (2) We introduce latent factors to model users' social relations, which greatly affect users' decisions in a social network. (3) Our model incorporates explicit features such as authority of the publisher and quality of the tweet, which can help further improve the recommendation results. The experimental results show the listed contributions can help improve tweet recommendation performance, and the combination of all the elements makes up a final model that greatly outperforms several baseline methods.

The remainder of this paper is organized as follows. Related work is discussed in Section 2. Some preliminaries to our work are introduced in Section 3. In Section 4 we describe the collaborative ranking method for tweet recommendation. Section 4.2 introduces the features of Twitter incorporated in our model. Experimental results are presented in Section 5. Finally, we conclude the paper in Section 6.

2. RELATED WORK

2.1 Recommender Systems on Twitter

As Twitter has become a popular social medium and had great impact, plenty of research focuses on analyzing the personal interest of users and building recommender systems according to that. Wu introduces a system to generate personalized tags for Twitter users to label their interest by extracting keywords from tweets [33]. Twopics [19], an entity-based profiling approach, aims to discover the topics of interest for Twitter users by examining the entities they mention in their Tweets. Recommending influential Twitter users is also a major research direction of Twitter recommender systems. Kwak [13] proposes three methods to estimate the influence of users on Twitter: the number of followers, PageRank and the number of retweets. Twittomender [9, 8] builds a followee recommender system for Twitter by profiling Twitter users by tweets and the relationships of their Twitter social graphs. TwitterRank [32], an extension of Pagerank, measures the influence of users in Twitter taking both the topical similarity between users and the link structure into account.

Some recommendation systems based on tweet recommendations have been proposed. Chen [4] studied URL recommendation on Twitter as a means to better direct user attention in information streams. Sun [31] constructs a diffusion graph to select a small subset of micro-blogs as recommended emergency news feeds for regular users. Duan [7] studies three types of features and proposes a tweet ranking strategy by applying a learning to rank algorithm. Naveed [20] used a learning approach based on pure content features to predict the probability of a message being retweeted. However, their work does not consider personalization and suggests tweets by considering only tweet quality and authority of the publisher. Also, their framework calculates the relevance between tweets and users' queries for retrieval, which requires a query to be provided in order to do recommendation. Kapanipathi [11] presents a Semantic Web approach to filter public tweets matching interests from personalized user profiles based on the generated profiles. Ramage [23] presents a scalable implementation of Labeled LDA that maps the content of the Twitter feed into dimensions. This helps improve methods for finding new users and for filtering tweets in the meanwhile. However, all their methods use only content based recommendation methods for suggesting tweets without considering the collaborative view. Moreover, they do not consider social relations between users in their approach. Cui [5] proposed a matrix factorization approach for item-level social influence modeling and devised an efficient projected gradient method to solve it. Yang [34] established a joint friendship-interest propagation model, FIP, to address recommendation and link prediction in a unified framework. But their work does not integrate specific characteristics of the Twitter platform like asymmetric social relations and is not trivial to adapt to tweet recommendation. Zaman [35] uses Matchbox, a large scale online Bayesian recommendation method to predict retweets. However, their method does not incorporate global features which are independent of users and items and more flexible for prediction. Also they do not take advantage of relative preferences to adapt to the ranking scenario of recommending tweets naturally. Our method takes advantage of relative preferences and collaborative ranking to learn user preferences based on the Twitter community data, and integrates tweet content, user social relations and other explicit features like publisher authority to greatly improve the personalized recommendation performance.

2.2 Collaborative Filtering and Collaborative Ranking

Collaborative filtering aims to build a recommender system by learning users' preferences based on the community data. In contrast to content-based methods, it does not require creation of explicit user profiles and specific domain knowledge. In domains such as movies, news, and advertisements, the content of documents is so short and limited that users' preferences cannot always be explicitly described using the terms or topics extracted by analyzing the content. So much research uses collaborative filtering for recommender systems. In recent years, collaborative filtering has attracted great attention and has been implemented in many large commercial systems, such as Google News [6] and Amazon [15]. Collaborative Filtering can be broadly divided into two categories, neighborhood-based approaches [28, 29] and model-based approaches [12, 24]. The former recommends items from the perspective of similarity of its neighbors, while the latter emphasizes latent factors using a probabilistic latent factor model or matrix factorization methods to solve problems.

Based on these widely used approaches, collaborative ranking, a ranking-oriented collaborative filtering method, is used to adapt the learning to rank scenarios. Collaborative ranking predicts a preference ordering over the yet unrated items by using a collaborative filtering method. Just like the pairwise models of learning to rank [3, 10], Pessiot [21] proposed a pairwise preference error minimization framework to optimize the item ranking. Rendle [25] proposed a Bayesian probabilistic ranking model. In the work of EigenRank[16], first user-user similarity is measured by the correlation between their rankings.

In another direction, some external information besides user-item interaction such as contextual information, user profiles and item descriptions is involved to improve recommendation. Stern [30] presents Matchbox, a large scale recommender system integrating meta data features to deal with cold start problem. Agarwal [1] proposes a regression-based latent factor model simultaneously incorporating features and past interactions. Rendle [26] proposes a context-aware factorization machine to take contextual information into account to enhance predictions. Li [14] proposes to leverage information extraction techniques to help recommender systems to train better context-aware recommendation models. In our approach, we explore the specific features of Twitter and integrate the significant ones into our collaborative ranking model to improve recommendation performance.

3. PRELIMINARY

3.1 Personal Interest Indicator

The goal of personalized tweet recommendation is to estimate the value of a tweet for each user. On Twitter, users follow many celebrities, friends, media organizations and other information sources. Tweets posted by all the publishers are pushed to users without any filtering. However, not all the information in these tweets caters for the users' personal interests, and not every aspect of his followees is worth paying attention to. For example, many people follow Obama in order to learn policies released by the White House. However, sometimes Obama will publish tweets about his interviews in other countries, which can not catch the interests of these followers. For them, a tweet recommender system should suggest the political tweets of Obama with higher priority than others.

How to detect personal interest is the key problem to be solved in this paper. There are three kinds of important user behaviors on Twitter: following another user, publishing a tweet, and retweeting a status posted by a followee. By analyzing these user behaviors, we are able to find users' personal interests. In the example mentioned above, if a person is interested in economic policy, it is more likely that he will follow some economic commentators or that tweets discussing economics will be published or retweeted by him. In our method, this information is represented as features and there is substantial evidence that the features predict a tweet's utility for a particular user.

However, the informativeness and usefulness of a tweet for a user cannot be directly measured by analyzing the tweet or the user's public Twitter profile. The main obstacle which raises the difficulty of evaluation for personalized tweet recommendation is that we must have enough user-specific relevant judgement data. These data for a particular user can only be decided by the user himself in the user experience study. In some work, Twitter users were asked to rate the quality of posts from users they follow [23]. However, this requires a great deal of time and effort, and becomes infeasible when the data set is large. Fortunately, some user actions indirectly reflect users' judgements of the usefulness. These actions include replying to a tweet, retweeting followees' statuses and tagging tweets as favorites. Because getting details of replying and tagging actions need the users' authorization, we only consider the retweeting action. For evaluation, we make an assumption below:

Assumption *Users' retweeting actions reflect their personal judgement of informativeness and usefulness.*

Intuitively, if a tweet is retweeted by a user, it means that the user has carefully read the tweet rather than just taking a short glance at it. Retweeting is a rough measure of personal usefulness. Of course, it's also true that a lack of retweeting does not necessarily mean the user is not interested in the tweet. However, to the best of our knowledge, this is a common problem for evaluation approaches for personalized tweet recommendation without user-specific judgement data.

We consider tweet recommendation in relation to the personal interests of a user. Given a collection of posted tweets by followees, we try to rank these tweets in order to put tweets which the user is likely to be interested in on top.

3.2 Why Collaborative Ranking

One important assumption underlying collaborative ranking and collaborative filtering is that users who agreed in the past are likely to agree again in the future [27]. This assumption allows us to take user preference histories and predict items which they might enjoy by analyzing similar users. In personalized tweet ranking, we can also make a similar assumption:

Assumption *Users who have retweeted similar statuses in the past are likely to retweet similar statuses in the future.*

This assumption makes collaborative ranking applicable to personalized tweet ranking. Collaborative ranking has advantages over content-based methods when it is difficult to analyze the content of tweets. Semantic relatedness of tweets which is not detected by content-based methods can be inferred using collaborative ranking. For example, a user interested in economic policies may have retweeted many statuses of president Obama. With a content-based method, it is difficult to be aware of this user's interest in other economic commentators' tweets when we lack sufficient word co-occurrence information for calculating tweet similarities. However, by analyzing other users' tweets, it can be found that people who have retweeted Obama's statuses are more likely to retweet statuses of other economic commentators.

And this implicitly detects users' probable interest in economics without analyzing the content of tweets. To adapt to the scenario that rank results of tweets are presented to users, a collaborative ranking method is better than collaborative filtering for different optimization criterion.

4. COLLABORATIVE RANKING METHOD FOR TWEET RECOMMENDATION

4.1 Optimizing Ranking Criterion for Tweet Recommendation

Here we introduce optimizing the ranking criterion for personalized tweet recommendation. Collaborative ranking is an extension of the latent factor model with ranking optimization criterion . In the latent factor model, each user u and item i have a low dimensional representation $p_u \in R^d$ and $q_i \in R^d$ in the latent feature space. The rating score is predicted by measuring the affinity between user and item:

$$\hat{y}_{u,i} = \mu + b_u + b_i + p_u^T q_i \tag{1}$$

Where y is the predicted preference of user u for item i. μ is the overall average rating, and b_u and b_i are user bias and item bias on rating score.

To adapt to the scenario of tweet ranking, we modify the model for the collaborative ranking setting according to ranking optimization criterion. Give a user u and two tweets k and h the pairwise ranking model for tweet preference is defined as follows:

$$P\left(r(k) > r(h)|u\right) = \frac{1}{1 + e^{-(\hat{y}_{u,k} - \hat{y}_{u,h})}} \tag{2}$$

Where $\hat{y}_{u,k}$ is the predicted preference of user u for tweet k, r is short notation for rank order. Equation 2 models the probability of item pairs' rank orders for a given user. We can get preference pair of items for a given user by assuming a user prefer the tweets he retweeted to the rest of tweets. Formally, we define rank preference set $\mathcal{D}$ as follows:

$$\mathcal{D} = \{< u, k, h > | k \in Re(u), h \notin Re(u)\} \tag{3}$$

Where $Re(u)$ is the set of tweets user u retweeted. Because the number of possible choices of negative sample h is large, we use sampling techniques to get negative samples in the training procedure. To learn the model, we maximize the log-likelihood over the $\mathcal{D}$ to estimate parameters. The maximizing procedure is converted to solve the objective below:

$$\min \sum_{<u,k,h> \in \mathcal{D}} \ln\left(1 + e^{-(\hat{y}_{u,k} - \hat{y}_{u,h})}\right) + \text{regularization} \tag{4}$$

L2 regularization is used as the default choice of regularization term. It can be consider as involving the prior probability for model parameters in a Bayesian view.

4.2 Incorporating Twitter Features for Recommendation

In tweet recommendation, tweets are regarded as items and rated by users according to usefulness. When users and tweets are characterized by a single latent factor, it is difficult to capture the details such as content of tweets, or followees of users. This leads to extreme sparsity of information for analyzing users and tweets, which is the main obstacle for recommendation. In our model, user and item factors can be decomposed into combinations of latent factors of related components, such as words, publisher, followee, etc. This helps involve all the related information in a latent factor model. On the other hand, we also try to incorporate contextual information into the system. Some user-independent variables, such as length of tweets and the number of times something is retweeted, can affect the preferences independent of the personal interests of the user. User-dependent contextual variables contain the number of times the publisher is mentioned and the similarity between tweet content and user profile. These contextual variables are converted into explicit features in our model. We can enrich user features to better describe user preferences, and add more item features to describe tweets' properties. Explicit features are directly related to users' preference for the tweets because the describe the contextual information.

In the following sections we describe the latent factor features and explicit features for tweet recommendation in our model. They will influence the recommendation through the factorization part. Explicit features are elements that contribute to the bias effect of users' decisions. Contextual information can be encoded as explicit features to improve recommendation.

4.3 Topic Level Decomposition of Tweets

As discussed in the previous section, directly applying the basic latent factor model to tweet recommendation encounters a serious problem of data sparsity due to the lack of retweet data. We use information on the content of tweets to solve this problem. A tweet is mainly composed of several words at the content level. We decompose the latent factors of a tweet into a combination of latent factors of words, to get the following factorization model:

$$\hat{y}_{u,i} = bias + p_u^T \left(\frac{1}{Z} \sum_{w \in T_i} q_w\right) \tag{5}$$

Here *bias* is used to indicate any form of possible bias to simplify the equation, T_i is the term set of tweet i, Z is the normalization term for features. This strategy actually converts the problem to asking whether the user is interested in the words or topics, rather than directly asking whether he is interested in the tweet. This decomposition gets more opinions from users at topic level, which helps collaborative filtering based methods get better performance. Moreover, at topic level we do not have to collect a large set of user data to have enough opinions on tweets. This helps reduce the number of users involved in the collaborative ranking algorithm and makes the process more scalable.

4.4 Incorporating Social Relations

Besides considering the content of tweets, we also try to incorporate the social relation between the user and the publisher in our model. Intuitively, if a user's interests are similar to a publisher's tweet topics, the user is more likely to retweet the publisher's tweets. So we measure the possibility of retweeting a status by considering the affinity of the user and the publisher's latent factors. Equation 6 gives a model that takes social relation into account.

$$\hat{y}_{u,i} = bias + p_u^T d_{p(i)} \tag{6}$$

$d_{p(i)}$ is a latent factor of the publisher of tweet i. This strategy incorporates the prior probability of retweeting a specific followee's statuses without considering the content of the tweet. This is reasonable under certain circumstances. For instance, a fanatical basketball fan may retweet any statuses of LeBron James even when he does not read the content. This also caters for the simple assumption that a user is more likely to retweet the statuses of a publisher who he has retweeted many times before. Furthermore, we can incorporate social relation information together with tweet content information. The modified model can be shown by the following equation.

$$\hat{y}_{u,i} = bias + p_u^T \left(\frac{1}{Z} \sum_{w_j \in T_i} q_{w_j} + \alpha d_{p(i)} \right) \quad (7)$$

Where λ indicates the importance of the publisher's latent factor relative to the words'.

4.5 Explicit Features

Besides the latent factors, information such as tweet quality, and publisher authority can be indicated as features. These features explicitly reflect the possibility of retweeting a status. We use a linear combination of these features to get retweet prediction:

$$\hat{y}_{u,i} = \sum_j b_j \gamma_j \quad (8)$$

Where b is a weight parameter vector and γ is an explicit feature we extracted. We further incorporate these explicit feature into the latent factor model described in Equation 7, to get our final predictor:

$$\hat{y}_{u,i} = \sum_j b_j \gamma_j + p_u^T \left(\frac{1}{Z} \sum_{w_j \in T_i} q_{w_j} + \alpha d_{p(i)} \right) \quad (9)$$

We can incorporate explicit features into our framework by redefining γ. In the following subsections, we will describe in detail the explicit features we use. The features are divided into four categories according to their sources.

4.5.1 *Relation Features*

Relation features refer to those features which represent the relation between the user and the publisher. A user is likely to prefer tweets posted by specific users, such as their intimate friends, celebrities, or people who share common interests. Relation features describe the relationship between the user and the publisher by analyzing their communication and social networks.

- Co-follow Score: This feature estimates the similarity of followee sets of the user and the publisher. If two users follow many identical publishers, it is likely that they share many common interests. Given a user U and a publisher P we use Jaccard similarity to measure this score:

$$Jaccard(U, P) = \frac{|Followee(U) \bigcap Followee(P)|}{|Followee(U) \bigcup Followee(P)|} \quad (10)$$

  where Followee(U) refers to the followee set of user U.

- Mention Score: This feature measures the number of times user U has mentioned publisher P in his previous tweets. If U has mentioned P many times before, it means that P gets much attention from U and U is likely to consider P's tweets useful.

- Friend: On Twitter, it is often observed that two users follow each other [32]. They are considered to be friends because they may know each other well. This type of relationship is like the ones in social networks like Facebook. This feature is binary. It is 1 when the publisher of a tweet is a friend of the follower and 0 otherwise.

4.5.2 *Content-relevance Features*

Content-relevance features measure the relevance between a tweet and a user by analyzing the content of tweets. The statuses posted or retweeted by a user previously reveal his personal interests to a degree. If a tweet is similar to a user's posts, it is likely that the user will consider the tweet to cater for his concerns.

- Relevance to Status History: This feature estimates the relevance between a tweet T and the posting history of a user U. We calculate similarity scores between T and every single post in the user's history and sum the scores to get the relevance score:

$$Relevance(T, U) = \sum_{T_i \in Tweets(U)} TweetRel(T, T_i) \quad (11)$$

  Tweets(U) represents the set of tweets posted by U. $TweetRel(T, T_i)$ measures the relevance between two tweets. Here we represent the tweets as vectors by term frequency and calculate the inner product as the result.

- Relevance to Retweet History: This feature estimates the relevance between a tweet T and the retweeted history of a user U. Similarity scores between T and every post retweeted by U are calculated and summed to get the relevance score:

$$Relevance(T, U) = \sum_{T_i \in Retweets(U)} TweetRel(T, T_i) \quad (12)$$

  ReTweets(U) refers to the set of tweets retweeted by U.

- Relevance to Hash Tags: Tweet Publisher is able to insert hash tags to emphasize the key words of a tweet. Intuitively, these hash tags are a summary of a user's personal interests. This feature estimates the count of words ever appeared as hash tags through the user's posting history for a tweet.

4.5.3 *Tweets' Content-based Feature*

Some content-based features can be used to measure the quality and popularity of a tweet. Based on the assumption that a user will prefer a high-quality tweet without considering personal interests, we introduce these features to predict whether a user considers a tweet useful.

- Length of Tweet: This feature estimates the number of terms in a tweet. A long tweet is more likely to be an informative one because it contains more information than a short one. Intuitively speaking, the user has put more effort into and spent more time editing longer tweets. This may help the tweet become popular and get more attention.

- Hash Tag Count: if a tweet has inserted hash tags, it is considered to be more informative and useful. Intuitively, the publisher spends time on tagging the tweet because he thinks the tweet may be useful. The number of hash tags in a tweet is measured by this feature.

- URL Count: On Twitter, publishers often include a URL as a supplement in their tweets. This is because the publisher cannot summarize their information in 140 characters and they use a URL to point to fuller information on another web site. The number of URLs in a tweet is estimated by this feature.

- Retweet Count: Twitter records the number of times a tweet has been retweeted. A tweet retweeted more times is more likely to be a useful one, because many other people have suggested the tweet and recommended it to their followers. This feature is an objective way to estimate the popularity of a tweet because the evaluation is from the general public. It is often used in other recommender systems as substantial evidence of the utility of a tweet and the authority of a user.

4.5.4 *Publishers' Authority Feature*

Intuitively speaking, a user is likely to prefer a tweet published by an authoritative user over others. Moreover, if a tweet is published by an authoritative user, it is more likely to be a high-quality tweet. Some features are substantial evidence of a user's authority. They can also be used to predict the popularity of a tweet.

- Mention Count: This feature estimates the times the publisher is mentioned in tweets. If a publisher has been mentioned frequently, it means he is influential and popular on Twitter.

- Followee Count: This feature records the number of people who follow the publisher. It is an objective measure of the popularity of a user based on public opinion.

- Follower Count: Users who have more followers are likely to be active on Twitter. Intuitively, active users will get more attention than inactive ones.

- Status Count: This feature measure the number of tweets ever posted by a user. Similar to follower count , this feature is also a substantial measure of activeness.

4.6 Parameter Estimation

A local minimum of the objective function given by Eq.4 can be found by performing stochastic gradient descent. To learn the collaborative ranking model, once we get a tuple $< u, k, h >$ in preference set $\mathcal{D}$, we calculate the descent of the related parameters as below and update the parameters by moving in the direction of negative gradient:

$$\frac{\partial \mathcal{L}}{\partial p_u} = \hat{e}\left(\frac{1}{Z_s^+}\sum_{s\in k} q_s - \frac{1}{Z_s^-}\sum_{s\in h} q_s + \alpha(d_{p(k)} - d_{p(h)})\right) - \lambda_1 p_u \quad (13)$$

$$\frac{\partial \mathcal{L}}{\partial q_w^+} = \frac{1}{Z_j^+}\hat{e}p_u - \lambda_2 q_w^+, \frac{\partial \mathcal{L}}{\partial q_w^-} = -\frac{1}{Z_j^-}\hat{e}p_u - \lambda_2 q_w^- \quad (14)$$

$$\frac{\partial \mathcal{L}}{\partial d_{p(k)}} = \alpha\hat{e}p_u - \lambda_3 d_{p(k)}, \frac{\partial \ell}{\partial d_{p(h)}} = \alpha\hat{e}p_u - \lambda_3 d_{p(h)} \quad (15)$$

$$\frac{\partial \mathcal{L}}{\partial b_j} = \hat{e}(\gamma_j^+ - \gamma_j^-) - \lambda_4 b_j \quad (16)$$

$$(17)$$

Here $\hat{e} = 1 - P(r(k) > r(h)|u)$ is the difference between the truth and predicted possibility of rank order. o^+ denotes the parameters for user u and tweet k while o^- denotes the parameters for user u and tweet h, where o is a placeholder. Then the algorithm loops over all the data in rank preference set $\mathcal{D}$ and updates the parameters by moving in the direction of negative gradient. This algorithm is computationally efficient and easy to implement. The complexity of the algorithm is discussed in section 5.6.

5. EXPERIMENTS

5.1 Dataset

To create the Twitter data set, we began with a randomly selected user and expanded the user-base by following their followers and followees' links. After following several steps of links, we got 8059 users in our base and downloaded all the statuses they had posted. As there is no API to directly get followees' posts for each user without authorization, we collected 1048 users who have over fifteen followees in our base and regarded the tweets posted by followees in the base as the scanned tweets of the users. The retweeted tweets are regarded as positive samples and the others are negative samples in experiments. To simulate the timeline of a user, we get one positive sample with another four negative samples from the scanned tweets and sort them in chronological order. We performed standard data preprocessing including stop word removal and stemming on the raw text. Finally we obtained a simulated scanned timeline of Twitter users in our sample; each of them had about 490 messages on average. Then the first four fifths of scanned tweets of each user is put in the training set and the others in the test set. Finally the dataset is split into a training set with 409680 tweets and test set with 102457 tweets. Figure 1 shows the number of tweets with specific retweet count in the dataset. The data is plotted on a log-log scale, the number of tweets that have not been retweeted is 102650 and is not shown in the figure due to the log-log plot style. From the figure, we see that most tweets are not retweeted or are only retweeted a few times, which shows the sparsity of the dataset. This fact coincides with the discussions in the previous sections, and motivates us to use as much information as possible to solve this problem. More discussion about sparsity is in section 5.5.

5.2 Evaluation Metrics

In the context of tweet recommendation, tweet ratings are considered binary in our scenario. Retweeting a tweet corresponds to a 1 rating, not -retweeting to a 0 rating. We use

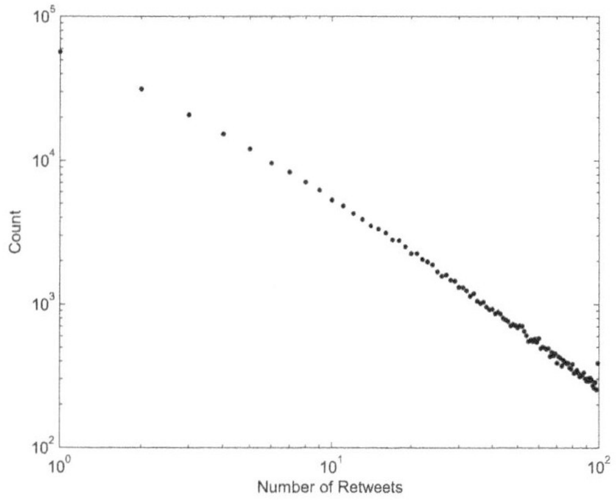

Figure 1: Sparsity of Retweets Data

Mean Average Precision (MAP), a popular rank evaluation method to evaluate the proposed approach. For a single user, average precision is defined as the average of the $P@n$ values for all retweeted tweets:

$$AP = \frac{\sum_{n=1}^{N} P@n \times retweet(n)}{|R|} \tag{18}$$

where n is the number of tweets; $|R|$ is the total number of retweeted tweets for the given user; $retweet(n)$ is a binary function to describe whether the user has retweeted the nth tweet in the result list. Finally, MAP can be obtained by averaging the AP values of all the users. $P@n$ is also used as our affiliated evaluation measure.

5.3 Method Comparison

We have compared our models to several others. The detailed implementations are listed below:

- CHRONOLOGICAL: The tweets are ranked in chronological order. Without any interventions by algorithms, this strategy indicates the default user experience on Twitter.

- RETWEETED TIMES: Retweeted Times is an objective estimate of the popularity of a tweet. This ranking strategy ignores personalization and assumes the user's interests are the same as general public's.

- PROFILING: This ranking strategy calculates the similarity between a tweet and the user's profile and shows the tweets sorted by similarity score. Profiles are simply treated as collections of words from users' posted tweets and retweeted tweets as follows:

$$\begin{aligned} Profile(U) =& Frequency(Tweets(U)) \\ &+ w * Frequency(Retweets(U)) \end{aligned} \tag{19}$$

  w measures the importance of the retweeted tweets for profiling a user, we tune the parameter to report the best result. We use Frequency(Tweets), a simple frequency count as the term weighting function, so that the profile vector can be represented as the frequency counts of the various words used in the posted and retweeted tweets. Then we calculate the inner product of the profile vector and tweet vector as the similarity measure.

- LDA: LDA[2] is a generative topic model and each document is viewed as a mixture of topics. We regard tweets as general documents here and learn an LDA model from tweets. After getting the topic distribution of each tweet, given a user U and a tweet T, the relevance score is calculated as below:

$$y_{U,T} = \sum_{T_0 \in Tweets(Followee(U))} \alpha^{\mathrm{I}(U,T_0)} D_{KL}(T_0 \| T) \tag{20}$$

  Here $D_{KL}(T_0\|T)$ calculates the symmetric KL-divergence between the topic distribution of two tweets, the indicator function $\mathrm{I}(\cdot)$ is equal to 1 if the user has retweeted T_0 and equal to 0 otherwise.

- RANKSVM: Using a Support Vector Machine to do ranking, the RankSVM algorithm[10] effectively integrates a bag of features in a model for learning retrieval functions. We use explicit features described in Section 4.5 and train RankSVM on the training data. Finally, the model is evaluated by the test data. The regularization parameter is tuned to 0.1 and the other parameters use the default settings.

- JOINTMF: The joint matrix factorization method jointly minimizes the loss functions of collaborative filtering and link prediction to get a better representation for users and items for prediction. It is similar to some other social recommendation methods such as FIP [34], and Sorec [18]. This method is to solve the following objective:

$$\begin{aligned} \min \lambda_y \sum_{<u,i>\in \mathrm{Y}} \ell(y_{u,i}, \hat{y}_{u,i}) + \lambda_s \sum_{<u,v>\in \mathrm{S}} \ell(s_{u,v}, p_u p_v) \\ + regularization \end{aligned} \tag{21}$$

  Here Y and S are records of retweet interactions and following interactions, $y_{u,i}$ and $s_{u,v}$ are the observed ratings and follower-followee relationships in the training data. $\hat{y}_{u,i}$ is the factorization model of topic level decomposition.

- CTR: Collaborative tweet ranking model integrating topic level features, social relations and explicit features proposed in this paper. Stochastic gradient descent is used for parameter estimation. In experiments, the number of latent factors is set to 200, as the bigger number will bring little improvement on performance shown in our experiments. The normalization term Z for term factors is set as $|T_i|^{\frac{1}{2}}$ according to the experimental results.

Figure 2 shows the results of P@n and MAP on the test set. Chronological strategy gets 0.3082 MAP. Not surprisingly, as whether a user would like to retweet a status depends on his personal interests rather than on time, the performance of the chronological strategy is close to a random strategy, which can be estimated by the proportion of positive samples. Also ranking by the number of times something is retweeted performs poorly with 0.3365 MAP. This means that there is still a wide gap between personal interests and the focus of public attention, which indicates that personalization is very important on Twitter. The profiling method is a classic content-based method and gives much

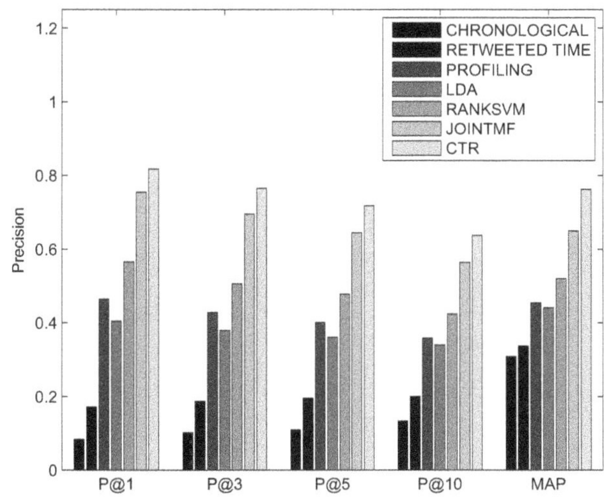

Figure 2: Evaluation Result of Compared Methods

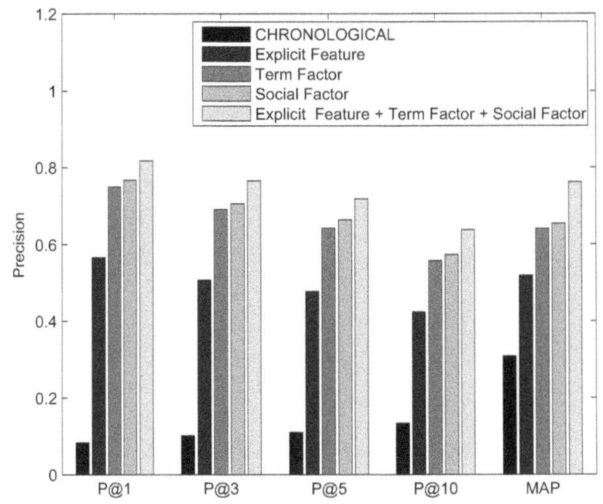

Figure 3: Comparison of CTR Components

Matrix	User-Tweet	User-Term	User-Followee
SPARSITY	0.1059%	0.7561%	0.7829%
MAP	0.3138	0.6403	0.6540

Table 1: Observed Sparsity of Data

better performance with 0.4538 MAP. The method based on an LDA topic model performs a little worse than the profiling method with 0.4408 MAP. This means that it is not a good choice to build a topic model on tweets for some specific reasons like the length of tweets. The RankSVM only considers the explicit features, and gets 0.5194 MAP. Finally, the joint matrix factorization method gets 0.6496 MAP and performs the best of the baseline methods. In comparison, the CTR model assimilates content based models by describing the information as features, and gives a 0.7627 MAP. Also, it takes advantage of collaborative filtering based methods by considering other users' opinions shared on Tweets in a global view. It achieved 46.84% and 17.41% improvements compared with RankSVM method and joint matrix factorization method in terms of MAP.

From the above results, we conclude that our proposed method gives a great improvement in recommendation performance. The result can be explained by the fact that the model includes more parameters to describe the personal interests, the attributes of tweets and user social relations,and this helps detect the detailed preferences of users.

5.4 Effectiveness of Feature Components

In the previous subsection, we have shown that our proposed CTR method greatly improves the recommendation performance. Because our CTR model consists of three major components — tweet topic latent factors, user social relation factors and explicit features — we would like to know the effectiveness of each component. We therefore conducted several experiments on CTR with only one of the components. The results are shown in Figure 3.

Figure 3 shows the P@n and MAP results of different component models. Performance of the chronological method is shown for reference. RankSVM is used to generate predictions using only the explicit features, and CTR is used to generate the predictions of the other three models. RankSVM givess comparatively low performance with 0.5194 MAP, since the model becomes a simple linear model for prediction and does not take advantage of collaborative filtering. However, it still performs better than the chronological strategy, which shows that explicit features are indeed useful. The models considering topic level factors or social factors get 0.6403 and 0.6540 MAP respectively. The two models outperform the explicit feature model by 16%. This result shows that introducing latent factors can help improve the recommendation, which supports the idea of applying collaborative filtering methods for tweet recommendation. Using topic level factors or social factors gives similar performance, which shows both parts are important to our final results. Finally, all the factors and explicit features are combined to get the highest performance with 0.7627 MAP. We conclude that all three components are effective and combining them will greatly improve tweet recommendation performance.

5.5 Data Sparsity

We also study the sparsity of our data. Traditional collaborative filtering methodsl regard the tweets as items and the retweet actions as interactions between users and items. From this point of view, the observed sparsity of the user-tweet interaction matrix is only 0.1059% and the collaborative ranking method only gets 0.3138 MAP, shown in table1. However, when the user-term interactions and user-followee interactions are taken into consideration, the data sparsity is greatly reduced. The observed sparsities of the user-term interaction matrix and user-followee interaction matrix are 0.7561% and 0.7829% respectively, which helps get better MAP performance. Our method is to alleviate data sparsity, as shown in Figure 1, by integrating all these elements and some other explicit features together to get better recommendations.

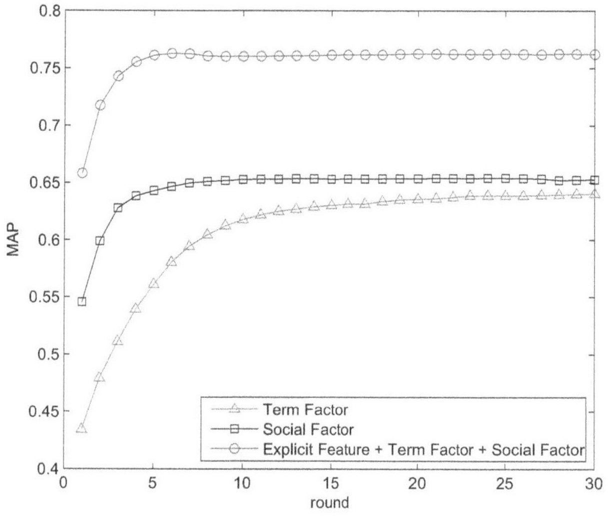

Figure 4: Runtime Convergence of CTR Models

5.6 Complexity and Runtime Convergence

In this subsection, we discuss the computation cost of the CTR model. The computational complexity of training our proposed CTR model is $O(kLNS)$. k is the number of latent factors. L is the average number of non-zero features in each training instance. N is the number of stochastic gradient descent steps. S is the amount of training data , which means the size of the rank preference set. The parameters k and L are determined by model settings, while the number of iterations N is not yet determined during model design. We can get N through runtime performance analysis. Figure 4 shows the runtime MAP of different latent factor CTR models mentioned in the previous subsection. We take ten iterations over the training set as one round, and calculate test mean average precision in each round. We find that all the models converge to a maximum value after 30 rounds. The result shows that our algorithm is stable and we only need to run the training algorithm for sufficient rounds to get the desired prediction.

6. CONCLUSION AND FUTURE WORK

In this paper, we propose a collaborative ranking model, CTR, for recommending useful tweets to Twitter users. Our approach takes advantage of collaborative filtering based recommendation by collecting preference information from many users. Moreover, extra contextual information helpful for detecting personal interests is incorporated in our model by careful design of features. Our final method makes use of tweet content, user social relations and other explicitly defined features. Experiments on real-world data show all the information used can help improve the recommendation performance, and our final method outperforms several baseline methods.

One future direction is to take more information into account such as the user's viewing history and tags of the tweet. We can also consider change of users' interests over time. Since our CTR method is generic, it is easy to incorporate more information by adding extra features.

The cold start problem is another tricky issue to deal with. In our experiments, we have assumed that each user has retweeted a sufficient number of statuses to reveal his personal interests. However, new users or inactive users have few explicit actions for our method to detect their interests. To address this, we can build a system involving an interview process, where users are asked for their opinions on certain chosen tweets to express their interests explicitly. This will be another direction of our future research.

7. ACKNOWLEDGEMENT

We thank the anonymous reviewers for their valuable and constructive comments and NSFC-RGC joint research project 60931160445 for generous support. We also thank Shenghua Bao from IBM Research China for his comments and discussions. Finally, we thank Sandy Harris from Shanghai Jiao Tong University for his carefully reading and revising our paper to correct grammatical errors.

8. REFERENCES

[1] D. Agarwal and B. Chen. Regression-based latent factor models. In *Proceedings of the 15th ACM SIGKDD international conference on Knowledge discovery and data mining*, pages 19–28. ACM, 2009.

[2] D. Blei, A. Ng, and M. Jordan. Latent dirichlet allocation. *The Journal of Machine Learning Research*, 3:993–1022, 2003.

[3] Y. Cao, J. Xu, T. Liu, H. Li, Y. Huang, and H. Hon. Adapting ranking svm to document retrieval. In *Proceedings of the 29th annual international ACM SIGIR conference on Research and development in information retrieval*, pages 186–193. ACM, 2006.

[4] J. Chen, R. Nairn, L. Nelson, M. Bernstein, and E. Chi. Short and tweet: experiments on recommending content from information streams. In *Proceedings of the 28th international conference on Human factors in computing systems*, pages 1185–1194. ACM, 2010.

[5] P. Cui, F. Wang, S. Liu, M. Ou, S. Yang, and L. Sun. Who should share what? item-level social influence prediction for users and posts ranking. In *Proceedings of the 34th international ACM SIGIR conference on Research and development in Information*, pages 185–194. ACM, 2011.

[6] A. Das, M. Datar, A. Garg, and S. Rajaram. Google news personalization: scalable online collaborative filtering. In *Proceedings of the 16th international conference on World Wide Web*, pages 271–280. ACM, 2007.

[7] Y. Duan, L. Jiang, T. Qin, M. Zhou, and H. Shum. An empirical study on learning to rank of tweets. In *Proceedings of the 23rd International Conference on Computational Linguistics*, pages 295–303. Association for Computational Linguistics, 2010.

[8] J. Hannon, M. Bennett, and B. Smyth. Recommending twitter users to follow using content and collaborative filtering approaches. In *Proceedings of the fourth ACM conference on Recommender systems*, pages 199–206. ACM, 2010.

[9] J. Hannon, K. McCarthy, and B. Smyth. Finding useful users on twitter: twittomender the followee

recommender. *Advances in Information Retrieval*, pages 784–787, 2011.

[10] T. Joachims. Optimizing search engines using clickthrough data. In *Proceedings of the eighth ACM SIGKDD international conference on Knowledge discovery and data mining*, pages 133–142. ACM, 2002.

[11] P. Kapanipathi, F. Orlandi, A. Sheth, and A. Passant. Personalized filtering of the twitter stream.

[12] Y. Koren. Factorization meets the neighborhood: a multifaceted collaborative filtering model. In *Proceeding of the 14th ACM SIGKDD international conference on Knowledge discovery and data mining*, pages 426–434. ACM, 2008.

[13] H. Kwak, C. Lee, H. Park, and S. Moon. What is twitter, a social network or a news media? In *Proceedings of the 19th international conference on World wide web*, pages 591–600. ACM, 2010.

[14] Y. Li, J. Nie, Y. Zhang, B. Wang, B. Yan, and F. Weng. Contextual recommendation based on text mining. In *Proceedings of the 23rd International Conference on Computational Linguistics: Posters*, pages 692–700. Association for Computational Linguistics, 2010.

[15] G. Linden, B. Smith, and J. York. Amazon. com recommendations: Item-to-item collaborative filtering. *Internet Computing, IEEE*, 7(1):76–80, 2003.

[16] N. N. Liu and Q. Yang. Eigenrank: a ranking-oriented approach to collaborative filtering. In *Proceedings of the 31st annual international ACM SIGIR conference on Research and development in information retrieval*, SIGIR '08, pages 83–90, New York, NY, USA, 2008. ACM.

[17] X. Liu, S. Zhang, F. Wei, and M. Zhou. Recognizing named entities in tweets. In *Proceedings of the 49th Annual Meeting of the Association for Computational Linguistics: Human Language Technologies (ACL-HLT 2011)*.

[18] H. Ma, H. Yang, M. Lyu, and I. King. Sorec: social recommendation using probabilistic matrix factorization. In *Proceeding of the 17th ACM conference on Information and knowledge management*, pages 931–940. ACM, 2008.

[19] M. Michelson and S. Macskassy. Discovering users' topics of interest on twitter: a first look. In *Proceedings of the fourth workshop on Analytics for noisy unstructured text data*, pages 73–80. ACM, 2010.

[20] N. Naveed, T. Gottron, J. Kunegis, and A. Alhadi. Bad news travel fast: A content-based analysis of interestingness on twitter. 2011.

[21] J. Pessiot, T. Truong, N. Usunier, M. Amini, and P. Gallinari. Learning to rank for collaborative filtering. In *9th International Conference on Enterprise Information Systems*. Citeseer, 2007.

[22] Z. Qu and Y. Liu. Interactive group suggesting for twitter. In *Proceedings of the 49th Annual Meeting of the Association for Computational Linguistics: Human Language Technologies: short papers-Volume 2*, pages 519–523. Association for Computational Linguistics, 2011.

[23] D. Ramage, S. Dumais, and D. Liebling. Characterizing microblogs with topic models. In *International AAAI Conference on Weblogs and Social Media*. The AAAI Press, 2010.

[24] S. Rendle. Factorization machines. In *Proceedings of the 2010 IEEE International Conference on Data Mining*, ICDM '10, 2010.

[25] S. Rendle, C. Freudenthaler, Z. Gantner, and S.-T. Lars. Bpr: Bayesian personalized ranking from implicit feedback. In *Proceedings of the Twenty-Fifth Conference on Uncertainty in Artificial Intelligence*, UAI '09, 2009.

[26] S. Rendle, Z. Gantner, C. Freudenthaler, and L. Schmidt-Thieme. Fast context-aware recommendations with factorization machines. In *Proceedings of the 34th international ACM SIGIR conference on Research and development in Information*, pages 635–644. ACM, 2011.

[27] P. Resnick, N. Iacovou, M. Suchak, P. Bergstrom, and J. Riedl. Grouplens: an open architecture for collaborative filtering of netnews. In *Proceedings of the 1994 ACM conference on Computer supported cooperative work*, pages 175–186. ACM, 1994.

[28] B. Sarwar, G. Karypis, J. Konstan, and J. Reidl. Item-based collaborative filtering recommendation algorithms. In *Proceedings of the 10th international conference on World Wide Web*, WWW '01, pages 285–295, New York, NY, USA, 2001. ACM.

[29] Y. Shi, M. Larson, and A. Hanjalic. Exploiting user similarity based on rated-item pools for improved user-based collaborative filtering. In *Proceedings of the third ACM conference on Recommender systems*, RecSys '09, pages 125–132, New York, NY, USA, 2009. ACM.

[30] D. Stern, R. Herbrich, and T. Graepel. Matchbox: large scale online bayesian recommendations. In *Proceedings of the 18th international conference on World wide web*, pages 111–120. ACM, 2009.

[31] A. Sun, J. Cheng, and D. Zeng. A novel recommendation framework for micro-blogging based on information diffusion. In *Proceedings of the 19th Workshop on Information Technologies and Systems*, 2009.

[32] J. Weng, E. Lim, J. Jiang, and Q. He. Twitterrank: finding topic-sensitive influential twitterers. In *Proceedings of the third ACM international conference on Web search and data mining*, pages 261–270. ACM, 2010.

[33] W. Wu, B. Zhang, and M. Ostendorf. Automatic generation of personalized annotation tags for twitter users. In *Human Language Technologies: The 2010 Annual Conference of the North American Chapter of the Association for Computational Linguistics*, pages 689–692. Association for Computational Linguistics, 2010.

[34] S. Yang, B. Long, A. Smola, N. Sadagopan, Z. Zheng, and H. Zha. Like like alike: joint friendship and interest propagation in social networks. In *Proceedings of the 20th international conference on World wide web*, pages 537–546. ACM, 2011.

[35] T. Zaman, R. Herbrich, J. Van Gael, and D. Stern. Predicting information spreading in twitter. In *NIPS Workshop on Computational Social Science and the Wisdom of Crowds*, 2010.

Exploring Social Influence for Recommendation - A Generative Model Approach

Mao Ye Xingjie Liu Wang-Chien Lee
Department of Computer Science and Engineering, The Pennsylvania State University, PA, USA.
{mxy177,xzl106,wlee}@cse.psu.edu

ABSTRACT

Social friendship has been shown beneficial for item recommendation for years. However, existing approaches mostly incorporate social friendship into recommender systems by *heuristics*. In this paper, we argue that *social influence* between friends can be captured quantitatively and propose a probabilistic generative model, called *social influenced selection*(SIS), to model the decision making of item selection (e.g., what book to buy or where to dine). Based on SIS, we mine the social influence between linked friends and the personal preferences of users through statistical inference. To address the challenges arising from multiple layers of hidden factors in SIS, we develop a new parameter learning algorithm based on expectation maximization (EM). Moreover, we show that the mined social influence and user preferences are valuable for group recommendation and viral marketing. Finally, we conduct a comprehensive performance evaluation using real datasets crawled from last.fm and whrrl.com to validate our proposal. Experimental results show that social influence captured based on our SIS model is effective for enhancing both item recommendation and group recommendation, essential for viral marketing, and useful for various user analysis.

Categories and Subject Descriptors

H.3.3 [**Information Search and Retrieval**]: Information Filtering; J.4 [**Computer Applications**]: Social and Behavior Sciences

General Terms

Algorithms, Experimentation.

Keywords

Recommender Systems, Social Networks.

1. INTRODUCTION

Recommendation systems have attracted a lot of attention in the past decade and have been successfully deployed in many e-commerce websites, such as Amazon and Netflix. Two widely adopted approaches for recommendation systems are collaborative filtering (CF) and content-based filtering [1]. Collaborative filtering [4, 9] recommends items for a given user by referencing item ratings from other similar users, while content-based filtering techniques [23] make recommendations by matching a user's personal interests (or profiles) with item content (e.g., item description or tags).

Recent development of social media and social networking systems brings new opportunities for recommender systems. Several research works find that there is a correlation between items selected by a user and those selected by her friends (i.e., friends share some common interests) and propose to exploit the correlation for item recommendations [12, 16, 17, 18, 19, 6]. The basic idea behind these techniques is that, since a user's friends may share common interests, recommendations can be made to the user by considering interests of her friends. For example, [32] makes recommendations by assigning weights to friends based on the similarity of item selection behavior (in terms of the number of commonly selected items) and similarity of social friendship (in terms of the number of their common friends). In addition, [12, 16] employ the random walk approach [30] to incorporate user's social relationship in item recommendation. This approach fundamentally assumes that friends exhibit similar behavior and thus aims to incorporate the friendship into the random walking process. However, due to the lack of quantified strength in friendship, equal weights have been assigned to social links from a user to her friends. This uniform weight assignment obviously does not truthfully capture the role of friendship played in the item selection process and thus is not expected to be effective for recommendations.

Some prior works avoid the aforementioned problem by integrating users' social trust network into their recommendation techniques. Assuming that trust intensities among users and their friends are handily available and that users and friends exhibit similar behaviors, the trust intensities among friends are used as the basis to assign more similarity weight to trusted friends when making recommendations [17, 18]. In [19], the authors learn a user's preference from the aggregated preferences of her friends. More specifically, they add additional regularization term in the matrix factorization approach to impose the constraints that user's latent topic vector should be similar to the average or weighted average of her friends' latent topic vectors. Recently, [6] explores a notion of *social correlation* to capture the correlation/similarity in the item selection behavior of social friends, i.e., two friends with very similar item selection behavior have very high social correlation. The authors adopt latent factor model to learn the social correlation among friends from their social network and a user-item accessing matrix. Experimental result shows that social correlation is able to improve recommendation performance.

All of the above mentioned research works obtained varied performance improvement over conventional item recommendation techniques, demonstrating the advantages taking the social friendship in item recommendation. It's not

SIGIR'12, August 12–16, 2012, Portland, Oregon, USA.

surprising that recommendation techniques that exploit the similar item selection behavior of friends have achieved a certain degree of success, as several research studies on social network analysis have indicated that a user's behavior indeed often correlates to the behavior of her friends [8, 29]. The question, nevertheless, is whether the success can be truly attributed to the ideas behind those aforementioned techniques? We argue that, while the general idea of incorporating the item selection behavior of friends is in the right direction, the *heuristics* adopted in these existing works do not exactly capture the core factors and thus cannot be fully accounted for the claimed success.

In this paper, we take the view of "social influence" from friends to explain the decision making of item selection by a user. Social influence here refers to the phenomenon that a user adopts a suggestion from friends, which may or may not deviate from her own preferences.[1] In our daily life, besides our own preference, we usually turn to our friends for opinions of books, movies or restaurants. Obviously, friends play a role in our decision making of many daily activities and events and thus impose some influence on us. Nevertheless, the influences from different friends are not equal. We do not take friends' opinions/suggestions purely based on our "trust" or "similarity" in preferences. Moreover, some friends with different interests and expertise may be very influential to us, while some other friends with very similar interests may not contribute that much in our decision making. Therefore, the notion of social influence discussed here is fundamentally different from the social correlation, trust intensity, or the various measures of friend similarity based on different heuristics.

To systematically exploit social influences from friends for item recommendation, we aim to quantitatively capture the social influence to a user from each of her friends by leveraging information embedded in the user social network, user behavior and item content. To meet our goal, we propose to adopt the *probabilistic generative model* as a methodology to model the decision making of item selection, e.g., deciding which restaurant to dine. We attribute an item selection decision by a user *probabilistically* to her own preference or the preferences of her friends (due to social influence). Assuming a set of latent topics existing in the targeted application domain[2], we propose the *social influenced selection (SIS)* model, which captures (1) the distribution of social influence from friends for each user, (2) the distribution of personal preference over the latent topics for each user, (3) the distribution of generated items for each topic, (4) the distribution of generated content for each topic; and thus enables a seamless integration of social influence, user behavior and item content for item recommendation.

Based on SIS, we aim to mine the model parameters listed above from the social network of users and the access transactions of users on items (as well as their content) through statistical inference based on *expectation maximization* (EM). In a typical EM algorithm, the E-step is used for computing the posterior of a latent variable. The multiple layers of variables we have in SIS bring new challenges. For example, the latent variables and other associated factors need to be processed together in a very large joint-variable space, which mandates development of a new and efficient learning algorithm. Assuming that the social influence exists only between friends instead of arbitrary users, we address the scalability issue by devising a new model learning algorithm which handles two layers of latent variables at the same time. In addition, to explore the flexibility and applicability of SIS, we explore the social influence and user preferences mined based on SIS for group recommendation, viral marketing and various user analysis. The primary contributions made in our research are summarized as follows.

- We point out the conceptual difference between the social influence introduced in this paper and the ideas behind other existing recommendation techniques that incorporate social friendship. We argue for using social influence along with user preference in item recommendation and we propose a probabilistic generative model, namely *social influenced selection*, that explicitly quantifies and incorporates social influence from friends to a user, along with user preference and item content in the item selection process.
- We develop a new model parameter learning algorithm to infer two layers of latent variables, including influential friends and latent topics, seamlessly in the learning process. The algorithm exploits the social networks among friends to address the scalability issue resulted from the joint-variable space.
- We demonstrate that the social influence mined based on SIS is valuable for supporting group recommendations, viral marketing, and various user analyses.
- We conduct a comprehensive performance evaluation on two real datasets crawled from last.fm and whrrl.com. Experimental results validate our ideas and show that social influence is effective for enhancing both item recommendation and group recommendation. We also find that users in whrrl.com is more likely to get influenced by friends than those in last.fm.

The remainder of this paper is organized as follows. Section 2 summarizes the related work. Section 3 introduces our SIS model which seamlessly captures social influence along with user behavior and item content. Section 4.1 proposes a new group recommendation method using the social influence obtained and discusses its potential application for viral marketing. Section 5 reports the experimental results and findings in our performance evaluation. Finally, Section 6 concludes the paper the points out the future direction.

2. RELATED WORK

In this section, we review some related works, including recommender systems, recommendation techniques enriched by social networks, and group recommendation.

Item recommendation is a crucial service for e-commerce and web services (e.g. netflix.com and amazon.com). The goal is to recommend a list of items that a targeted user may be interested in. Collaborative filtering and content-based techniques are two widely adopted approaches for recommender systems [1]. Both of them discover users' personal interests and utilize these interests to find relevant items. Collaborative filtering techniques [4, 9, 28] automatically predict relevant items for a given user by referencing item rating information from other similar users. Content-based techniques [23] make recommendations by matching a user's personal interests (or profile) to descriptive information of items. Recommender systems using pure collaborative filtering approaches tend to fail when little knowledge about the user is known or when no one has similar interests with the user. For example, if a user has little item rating/selection history or his interests are uncommon to others, then the

[1]Note that social influence is a very general term related to many different phenomena. For example, Herbert Kelman identified three broad varieties of social influence including compliance, identification and internalization [14]. In this paper, we consider the social influence quantitatively as the probability that a user adopts a suggestion from friends.

[2]The term *topic*, from topic models, represents a genre of items in this paper. Take movies as an example of the items, a topic could be action, thriller, romantic or even a latent genre that cannot be expressed literally.

item rating/selection history of other users cannot help. Although content-based methods is able to cope with the issue of lacking knowledge, it fails to account for community endorsement. For example, while a user is known to be interested in Chinese restaurants, content-based methods may possibly recommend a bad Chinese restaurant to him without considering the tendency or consensus among those with similar item selection behavior to the targeted user. As a result, there has been a continuing research interests and effort in combining the advantages of both collaborative filtering and content-based methods [3, 26]. Our proposal not only is able to take into account user behavior and item content but also incorporate the social influence from friends into the recommendation process.

We term the techniques that exploit observations and properties of social networks for recommendation as social recommendation techniques. As reported in the literature, social friendship is shown to be beneficial for recommendation [19, 18, 17, 12, 16, 32, 31, 6]. To incorporate social friendship to the recommender system, [32] propose a collaborative recommendation framework which linearly combines conventional user-based collaborative filtering with friend-based collaborative filtering (i.e., only friends are considered during the collaborative filtering approach). In addition, [12, 16] employ the random walk approach [30] to incorporate user's social network in item recommendation. There are also some model-based approaches to provide recommendation by incorporating social friendship or social trust network [17, 18, 19, 6]. In [17, 18, 19], the authors propose to use matrix factorization method to learn the user latent vectors and item latent vectors. Accordingly, they integrate the users' social trust network into their models through a linear combination [17, 18] or as a regularization term [19]. In [6], the social correlation among friends is learned with the condition that latent user space and latent item space are given. Notice that the social correlation aims to capture the similarity among friends. Thus, the social correlation among friends could reach 1 if they have identical item access patterns. In our study, we are interested in social influence. Intuitively, we believe that a user make decisions mainly based on her own preferences, even though friends' preferences and influence may contribute to her decisions.

In this paper, we also explore the potential use of social influence for group recommendation. Here we review a number of group recommendation techniques. Group recommendations have been designed for various domains such as web/news pages [25], tourism [22], music [21, 7], and TV programs and movies [24, 33]. In summary, two main approaches have been proposed for group recommendation [13]. The first one creates an aggregated profile for a group based on individual profiles of its group members and makes recommendations based on the aggregated group profile [21, 33]. The second approach *aggregates* the recommendation results for individual members into a single group recommendation list. In other words, recommendations (i.e., ranked item lists) for individual members are created independently and then aggregated into a joint group recommendation list [2], where the aggregation functions could be based on average or least misery strategies [20]. Different from these prior works, our approach exploits the preferences of group members and their influence on each other to reach the final decision. Evaluation from real datasets demonstrates a significant improvement from the our proposal of using social influence alone over the state-of-the-art methods.

3. SOCIAL INFLUENCED SELECTION

In this section, we propose a probabilistic generative model to capture the various factors contributing to the decision making of item selection. Motivated by reported empirical evidence of influence propagation via on-line social links [12, 16], one important factor we argued for, along with user preference, is the social influence. Instead of trying to capture exactly how social influence takes effect in the decision making process[3], we assume the existence of social influence and aim to capture quantified social influence among friends for use in recommender systems. In the following, we first introduce our *social influenced selection (SIS) model* and then present our approach to statistically inference a number of model parameters valuable for recommendation services and other applications.

3.1 The SIS Model

In addition to personal preference of certain items and their specific content features, we believe that social influence from friends also contribute to one's item selection decision. For example, Alice went for a movie "Kung Fu Panda" because she likes funny cartoon animations and Bob, a fan of Chinese martial art stories, had recommended it to her. In this example, we attribute the decision of watching Kung Fu Panda over other choices to Alice's own preference and Bob's (as well as other friends') suggestions. Notice that several factors are involved here, including (i) Alice's tastes of movies as well as her friend's possible preferences; (ii) Alice's independence in decision making; and (iii) influences from Alice's friends. We argue that the decision is made implicitly in accordance with the collective preferences of Alice's and her friends'. Thus, the decision making is similar to drawing a preference from the above-mentioned collection based on Alice's independence in decision making and her friend's influence. Consequently, a preference common to Alice and her friends has a higher probability to be drawn than an uncommon preference from some friend (which may have a lower probability but still possible, as evident by abnormal selection behavior sometimes made by people).

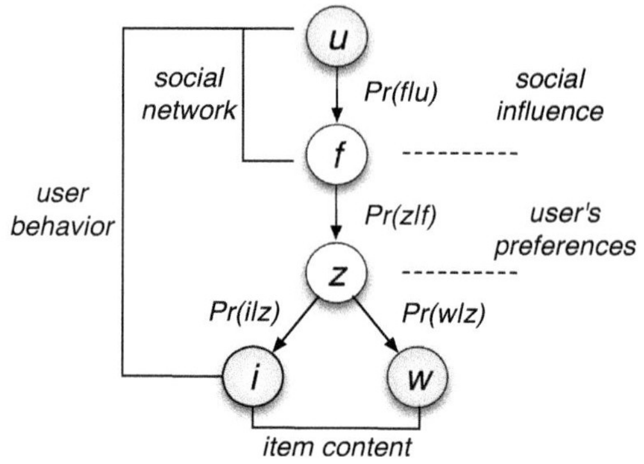

Figure 1: The SIS model

In the proposed SIS model, as shown in Figure 1, we follow the ideas of [11, 26] to represent user preferences in terms of a number of latent topics and to correlate the items (and their content) with users through these latent topics. Let $U = \{u_1, u_2, \cdots, u_N\}$ and $I = \{i_1, i_2, \cdots, i_M\}$ be the user set and item set, respectively. Each item $i \in I$ is associated with a set of tags/words $W_i = \{w_1, w_2, \cdots\}$. A latent topic set $Z = \{z_1, z_2, \cdots, z_K\}$ is employed to capture the latent user interests (i.e., preferences) and to characterize the items and their content. The SIS model assumes that a decision made by a user $u \in U$ to select an item $i \in I$ (associated with a tag $w \in W_i$) is attributed to a preference (i.e., one of the latent topics $z \in Z$) due to the user's independent choice and the social influence from friends. For instance, in

[3]How other people affect one's beliefs, feelings and behaviors (i.e., the study of social influence) has been the focus of social psychology research in the past 50 years [14]

the example discussed earlier, Alice's decision to see "Kung Fu Panda" attributed to funny cartoon animation (her own preference) or Chinese martial art (Bob's preference), both of which may be considered as the latent topics in our model. Obviously, our goal (and the novelty of SIS) lies in qualitatively capturing the social influence, which along with other model parameters of SIS such as user preference, is shown later to be valuable for recommendations and various applications. Thus, we introduce another variable f to represent the friends in SIS. Let $F(u) \subseteq U$ denote the friend list of a user u. The social influence to u from one of her friends ($f \in F(u)$) is depicted as how likely f's personal preference has contributed to the item selection decision. As discussed earlier, the probability for a friend of u's to affect the item selection is in proportional to the social influence of this friend. Notice that u's independence in decision making and her personal preference play a similar but even more important role as the social influence and friends' preferences. In SIS, for simplicity, we assume u is a special friend of herself (i.e., $u \in F(u)$). Therefore, the SIS model, as illustrated in Figure 1, are depicted as follows. A decision of item selection made by user u is probabilistically determined based on the preference of a friend (including herself) $f \in F(u)$. If $f = u$, the selection is attributed to u's own preference; otherwise ($f \neq u$), the decision is influenced by f at this time (i.e., the selection follows f's interests rather than u's own tastes). As shown in the figure, we define a parameter *social influence distribution* $\Pr(f|u)$ as the probability for u to be influenced by a friend f. Once f is picked based on $\Pr(f|u)$, we randomly draw a topic z from f's preference based on probability $\Pr(z|f)$. Then, the topic z in turn generates an item i and a tag w according to the topic's item distribution ($\Pr(i|z)$) and topic's content distribution ($\Pr(w|z)$), respectively. Note that the selection behavior of user u on both item i and its content $w \in W_i$ is probabilistically captured in a coherent fashion by the generative process of SIS. Thus, SIS is able to comprehensively incorporates various information, including social influence, user behavior and item content, in the model.

3.2 Parameter Learning Algorithm

The problem of recommending new (previously unaccessed) items to a user u can addressed by estimating the probability for u to select an item i (i.e., $\Pr(i|u)$). Candidate items with the highest aforementioned probability are recommended to u. Note that $\Pr(i|u)$ can be computed as

$$\Pr(i|u) = \frac{\Pr(u,i)}{\Pr(u)} \propto \Pr(u,i) \quad (1)$$

According to the SIS model, we have

$$\Pr(u,i) = \sum_{f \in F(u)} \sum_{z \in Z} \sum_{w \in W_i} \Pr(u,f,z,i,w) \quad (2)$$

Similar to [26], we assume items and contents are independently conditioned on the topics. As a result, the joint probability distribution over all factors is:

$$\Pr(u,f,z,i,w) = \Pr(u)\Pr(f|u)\Pr(z|f)\Pr(i|z)\Pr(w|z) \quad (3)$$

where $w \in W$ and W is the space of all item content.

The key observations from this model as shown in Figure 1 are 1) u and z are independently conditioned on f, and 2) f, w and i are independently conditioned on z. To model the item selection probability in terms of f and z, we transform Equation (3) into the following form:

$$\Pr(u,f,z,i,w) = \Pr(z)\Pr(u|f)\Pr(f|z)\Pr(i|z)\Pr(w|z)$$

Notice that we will need to obtain a number of model parameters, including $\Pr(z)$, $\Pr(u|f)$, $\Pr(f|z)$, $\Pr(i|z)$, $\Pr(w|z)$ in order to compute $\Pr(u,f,z,i,w)$ and $\Pr(u,i)$. Among them, $\Pr(u|f)$ captures the social influence from friend f to user u and $\Pr(f|z)$ depicts a user f's preference, i.e., $\Pr(z|f) = \frac{Pr(z,f)}{Pr(f)} \propto \Pr(z,f)$, where $\Pr(z,f) = \Pr(z)\Pr(f|z)$. We will show how these parameters can be used to facilitate various applications in Section 4.

In this study, we employ *expected maximization (EM)* to learn those model parameters from the user-item-content history H, i.e., $\langle u,i,w \rangle \in H$, where $u \in U$, $i \in I$, and $w \in W_i$ (i.e., W_i denotes the tag/word set associated with item i). Note that an item may contain multiple tags/words. For a history record of a user u selecting an item i where $W_i = \{w_1, w_2, \cdots\}$, we have $\langle u,i,w_k \rangle \in H$, $k = 1,2,\cdots$. Note that existing expected maximization (EM) algorithms mostly handle a single latent variable. Thus, it brings new challenges when there are multiple variables, i.e., z and f, in the model and thus mandates a new and efficient learning algorithm. To address this issue, we have performed a detailed mathematical derivation to develop an new EM algorithm in order to learn the model parameters by statistical inference. Our model parameter learning algorithm is based on the idea of maximizing the log-likelihood of $\mathcal{L}(\theta)$.

$$\mathcal{L}(\theta) = \sum_{\langle u,i \rangle \in H} \log(\Pr(u,i|\theta)) \quad (4)$$

where θ denotes the model parameters, i.e., $\Pr(z)$, $\Pr(u|f)$, $\Pr(f|z)$, $\Pr(i|z)$, $\Pr(w|z)$, in our model.

The derived EM algorithm iterates over the following steps.In E-step, instead of computing the expectation of the log-likelihood for individual latent variables (i.e.,, z and f separately), we propose to compute the expectation of the log-likelihood for $\langle z,f \rangle$ jointly. More specifically, we calculate

$$\Pr(z,f|u,i,w) = \frac{\Pr(z)\Pr(f|z)\Pr(u|f)\Pr(i|z)\Pr(w|z)}{\sum_{z \in Z}\sum_{f \in F(u)} \Pr(z)\Pr(f|z)\Pr(u|f)\Pr(i|z)\Pr(w|z)}$$

Note that we only need to compute the posteriors of those triples $\langle u,i,w \rangle \in H$, because the expectation to be maximized only weights on the observed user-item-word triples. While the friend space could potentially be the entire user space, the averaged number of friends per user is limited.[4] The total size of parameters $\Pr(z,f|u,i,w)$ for each record $\langle u,i,w \rangle$ is estimated by $|z| \cdot |F(u)|$.

In EM algorithms, the E-step is to calculate the expected value of the log likelihood function, with respect to the conditional distribution of latent variables, under the current estimate of the model parameters. In our algorithm, z and f are considered jointly in E-step. This is very important because, if we consider only a one latent variable, say z, the M-step cannot estimate the parameter $\Pr(f|z)$, which depends on the joint probability of z and f.

In M-step, model parameters are computed to maximize the expected log-likelihood found on the E-step as below.

$$\begin{aligned}
\Pr(i|z) &\propto \sum_{\langle u',i,w' \rangle \in H} \sum_{f' \in F(u')} \Pr(z,f'|u',i,w') \\
\Pr(w|z) &\propto \sum_{\langle u',i',w \rangle \in H} \sum_{f' \in F(u')} \Pr(z,f'|u',i',w) \\
\Pr(u|f) &\propto \sum_{\langle u,i',w' \rangle \in H \wedge f \in F(u)} \sum_{z' \in Z} \Pr(z',f|u,i',w') \\
\Pr(f|z) &\propto \sum_{\langle u',i',w' \rangle \in H \wedge f \in F(u')} \Pr(z,f|u',i',w') \\
\Pr(z) &\propto \sum_{\langle u',i',w' \rangle \in H} \sum_{f' \in F(u')} \Pr(z,f'|u',i',w')
\end{aligned} \quad (5)$$

[4]In our collected real data sets, the averaged number of friends per user is less than 10.

where $\sum_{i \in I} \Pr(i|z)$, $\sum_{w \in W} \Pr(w|z)$, $\sum_{u \in F(f)} \Pr(u|f)$, $\sum_{f \in U} \Pr(f|z)$ and $\sum_{z \in Z} \Pr(z)$ are all 1. By repeating the E-step and M-step, the EM Algorithm improves the model parameters iteratively until they converge to a local log-likelihood maximum.

4. APPLICATIONS OF SOCIAL INFLUENCE

In this section, we discuss how social influence learned from SIS benefits other applications such as group recommendation and viral marketing.

4.1 Group Recommendation

Given a group of people G, group recommendation aims to identify items that are welcomed by the whole group instead of individual group members, e.g., find romantic restaurants for a couple or movies for a family with kids. Although the SIS model targets on item recommendation for an individual user, the social influence learned based on SIS is very useful for group recommendation. In this section, we first briefly introduce the *aggregation-based group recommendation* strategies and then discuss our new strategy, called *social influence based group recommendation* (SIG).

For group recommendation, a widely adopted approach is to apply some aggregation strategies to obtain a "consensus" group ranking/score for a candidate item. Two popular aggregation strategies, namely *average* and *least misery*, are proposed in [20].Using the item access probability estimation $\Pr(i|u)$ as the score of item i to u, the average strategy calculates the group score of an item i to a group G as

$$S_{\text{average}}(G, i) = \frac{\sum_{u \in G} \Pr(i|u)}{|G|} \quad (6)$$

On the other hand, the least misery strategy calculates the the group score for an item i to a group G as the *smallest* predicted rating for item i in the group, specifically

$$S_{\text{misery}}(G, i) = \min_{u \in G}\{\Pr(i|u)\} \quad (7)$$

Basically, the item least disliked by each individual member shall has the highest group score for recommendation.

Note that $\Pr(i|u)$ can be calculated based on our generative model by incorporating user behavior (UB) and item content (IC). These two aggregation-based group recommendation approaches capture a group consensus of item ranking by assuming all the decisions made by users are independent and equally important. However, in a group activity, people interact with and influence each other. Thus, we take social influence into account to reach a group consensus.

Intuitively, a user in a group activity selects an item due to two possible reasons: 1) her own preference of the item, 2) influence from other group members. One direct extension of the existing aggregation-based group recommendation strategies is to is to incorporate social influence in the calculation of probability value $\Pr(i|u)$.

$$\Pr(i|u) \propto \Pr(u, i) \approx \sum_{f \in (F(u) \cap G)} \Pr(u, f, i) \quad (8)$$

where

$$\Pr(u, f, i) = \sum_{z \in Z} \Pr(z) \Pr(u|f) \Pr(f|z) \Pr(i|z) \quad (9)$$

can be easily obtained from the model parameters of SIS. Note that $\Pr(u, f, i)$ denotes the probability for u to select i under influence of f. If $f = u$, it estimates the probability that the user u's own preference in this item. This newly derived $\Pr(i|u)$ is applicable to Average (Equation (6)) and Least Misery (Equation (7)) for group recommendation.

An alternative idea is that users in a group will listen to others' opinions, i.e., social influence (instead of personal preferences) is given the highest priority to get a consensus score for the group. SIS can naturally support the group recommendation as a group selection activity, i.e., u is influenced by other group members to jointly select item i. Consider a "two-member" group $G_2 = \{u_1, u_2\}$. To select an item for the group, user u_1 may influence user u_2 and vice versa. Therefore, we define the score for recommending an item i to the group G_2 as

$$S_{\text{influence}}(G_2, i) = Pr(u_1, u_2, i) + Pr(u_2, u_1, i) \quad (10)$$

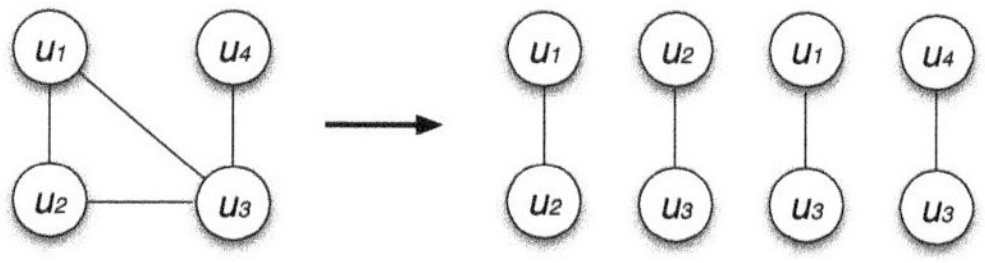

Figure 2: Decompose an arbitrary group into a set of two-member groups.

The ideas described above can be generalized for groups with more than two members by decomposing such a group into a set of two-member groups based on the friendship of members (see the example in Figure 2 for illustration). To make a group recommendation, we assume the social influence only happens between friends. Intuitively, if most pairs of friends in the group prefer a particular item, it would be a good candidate for recommendation to the group. Let G denote a group with arbitrary cardinality. The score for recommending an item i to G is defined as the sum of $S_{\text{influence}}(G_2, i)$ score over all possible friend pairs in the group. Formally,

$$S_{\text{influence}}(G, i) = \sum_{\forall \langle u, f \rangle \in G \times G, u \neq f, f \in F(u)} S_{\text{influence}}(\{u, f\}, i) \quad (11)$$

The ranking of items for group recommendation is based on the sorted group scores of items as defined above. We find superior performance of our social-influence strategy over the two aggregation strategies (to be shown in Section 5.6).

4.2 Viral Marketing

Recently, the phenomenon of influence propagation in social networks and its application in viral marketing have attracted tremendous interest. The idea is that when a user sees her social contacts performing an action such as purchasing a product, that user may decide to adopt the purchase as well [27, 15, 5, 10]. Obviously, social influence is important for viral marketing. In this section, we demonstrate how the social influence and user preference derived from our SIS model can be applied in the viral marketing study. Although the user-item selection process in SIS does not capture the causality in influence propagation, we assume that the social influence learned from our model may approximate the probability for a user to adopt the product given that her friend adopts the product.

Conventional research of viral marketing are mainly based on the social influence probability from f to u, i.e., $\Pr(u|f)$. We argue that, in addition to social influence, the personal preferences of users are also very important for viral marketing. Note that, as discussed earlier, a friend f showing high social influence to a user u doesn't necessarily implies that f and u are highly similar in terms of their item access behaviors. Intuitively, whether a product will be adopted by a user is dependent on user preference of the product itself, even though we fully agree that social influence is important for viral marketing. In short, we argue that both user's preference and social influence are critical ro viral marketing. If solely based on social influence, a product marketing plan may likely to target on a user with high social influence and high interest in the product (even if his friends are not interested in the product based on their own preferences). As a result, the aforementioned conventional viral marketing plan based purely on social influence could fail.

Here, we adopt the popular Threshold Model [15] as a case study to demonstrate how to utilize the social influence and user preferences obtained based on SIS for viral marketing strategy design. Note that, in a viral marketing study, each individual user is assumed to be either active (an adopter of the product) or inactive. We assume a setting where each user's tendency to become active increases monotonically as more of her friends become active and focus on the case where users only switch from being inactive to being active, instead of switching in the other direction. In the model, the probability for a user u to an item i is denoted as $\Pr_{VM}(i|u)$, which is calculated as follows. Let $F(u)$ denote the friend set of user u and $F'(u) \subset F(u)$ denote the subset including all active friends.

$$\Pr_{VM}(i|u) = \begin{cases} 0 & |F'(u)| = 0 \\ \alpha \Pr_{VM-self}(i|u) + (1-\alpha)\Pr_{VM-friend}(i|u) & \text{Otherwise} \end{cases}$$

where α is a weighting factor between 0 and 1. $\alpha = 1$ means users' decision is solely based on their personal preferences; while $\alpha = 0$ means users' decision is only based on the social influence, i.e., the case of conventional viral marketing study.

$$\begin{aligned} \Pr_{VM-self}(i|u) &= \Pr(i,u) \\ &= \sum_z \sum_w \Pr(z|u)\Pr(i|z)\Pr(w|z) \end{aligned} \quad (12)$$

where $\Pr(z|u), \Pr(i|z)$ and $\Pr(w|z)$ are model parameters learned from our proposed model. And

$$\Pr_{VM-friend}(i,u) = \sum_{u' \in F'(u)} \Pr(u|u') \quad (13)$$

where $\Pr(u|u')$ is the social influence parameter learned from our generative model.

Each user u has a threshold θ_u. Once $\Pr_{VM}(i|u)$ exceeds the threshold θ_u, user u will turn to active. The process of viral marketing starts with an initial set of users S. Users in S get to know the item i by advertisement. Thus, a seed user $s \in S$ has a initial probability $\Pr_{VM}(i|s) = \alpha \Pr_{VM-self}(i|s)$. Of course, for viral marketing, we always want to select users interested in the items as the seed users. The diffusion process unfolds deterministically in discrete steps: in step t, all users who were active in step $t-1$ remain active; and we update the value of $\Pr_{VM}(i|u)$ for each inactive user u and activate any user u' for which its $\Pr_{VM}(i|u') \geq \theta_{u'}$.

5. PERFORMANCE EVALUATION

In this section, we conduct a comprehensive performance evaluation using two real datasets, one from *last.fm* and the other from *whrrl.com*. We develop web crawlers to collect theses two datasets, which include user-item accessing history, users' friendship network and tags associated with each item. Besides, we collect group check-in history data from whrrl.com to validate our group recommendation approach. In our evaluation, we adopt the memory-based collaborative filtering approach (denoted as CF) as a baseline and propose to study the effectiveness of various factors (i.e., social influence (SI), user behavior (UB) and item content (IC)) considered in our SIS model. The different configurations of factors included in our evaluation are: 1) user behavior (UB) [11], which is taken as the second baseline, 2) both user behavior and social influence (UB+SI), 3) user behavior and item content factors (UB+IC) [26], which is the third baseline, and 4) all of the user behavior, social influence and item content factors (UB+SI+IC), i.e., our SIS model. In this evaluation, we conduct an extensive set of experiments for item recommendation, group recommendation, viral marketing, and various user analysis studies.

5.1 Dataset Description

Here we first discuss the datasets, i.e., *last.fm* and *whrrl.com*, used in our experiments. Last.fm is an on-line music radio web service and whrrl.com is a location-based social network web service. The last.fm dataset contains music access history of 3,143 users over 23,467 unique songs; while whrrl.com dataset includes the check-in history of 7,145 users to 74,217 unique places. It is worth noting that the whrrl.com dataset includes 17,587 *group* check-in records which are very valuable for evaluating the group recommendation approaches. Additionally, both datasets have their user social networks available. The basic statistics of these two datasets are summarized in Table 1.

	last.fm	whrrl.com
Number of Users	3,143	7,145
Number of Items	23,467	74,217
User-Item Matrix Density	8.02×10^{-3}	2.3×10^{-4}
Average Friends per User	1.91	9.08
Average Tags per Item	4.92	2.73
Average Group Size	N/A	2.93

Table 1: Datasets statistics

Note that the effectiveness of recommendation service provisioned with sparse dataset (i.e., low-density user-item matrix) is usually not high. For example, the reported precision in [32] is 0.05 over a preprocessed dataset with 2.72×10^{-4} density. Thus, in our experiments, we focus on comparing the relative performance of algorithms instead of their absolute effectiveness measures, which are expected to improve over time as the number of social network users continues to grow. Specifically, we use UB as the reference to compare the relative effectiveness measures, which are calculated as $\frac{X}{\text{UB}}$, where X are CF, UB+SI, UB+IC or SIS.

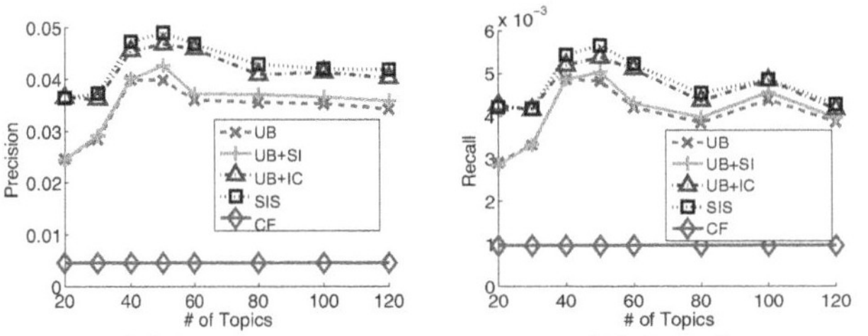

(a) Precision (b) Recall

Figure 3: Testing topic sizes (last.fm)

5.2 Item Recommendation

Item recommendation serves as the primary test case for our evaluation. For the various configurations degenerated from SIS, we use log-likelihood as model converge indicators and terminate the EM algorithms when an additional EM

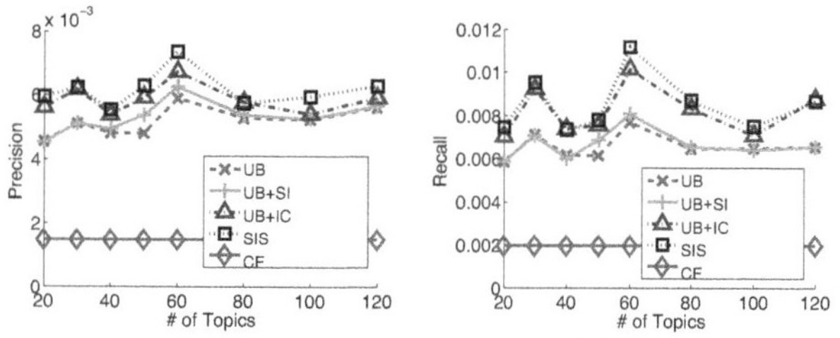

(a) Precision (b) Recall

Figure 4: Testing topic sizes (whrrl.com)

iteration cannot improve the training data's log-likelihood by 0.0001 or when the maximum iteration threshold (empirically set with 50) is reached. We adopt the cross-validation method to obtain the precisions and recalls of item recommendation. For both datasets, we mark off 30% of item assess history corresponding to each user for testing. In other words, the rest 70% of user-item pairs are used as the training data to infer model parameters. After each model is learned, we use the model parameters to find $\forall i, \Pr(i|u)$ for all users. The precision and recall for top n recommendations are used as the evaluation metrics, where $n = 5, 10, 20, 50$ (5 is the default value).

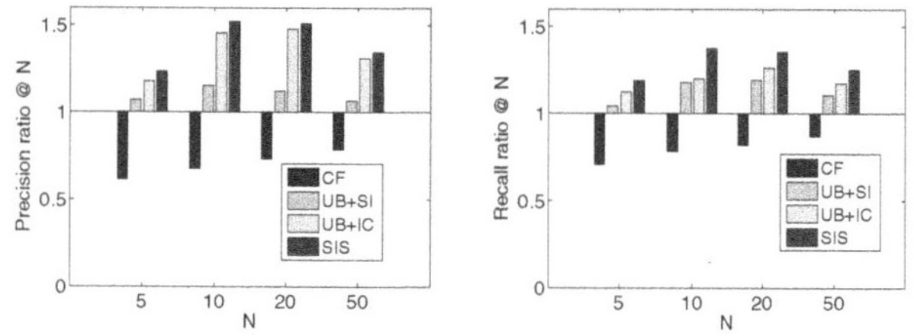

(a) Precision ratio (b) Recall ratio

Figure 5: Performance comparisons (last.fm)

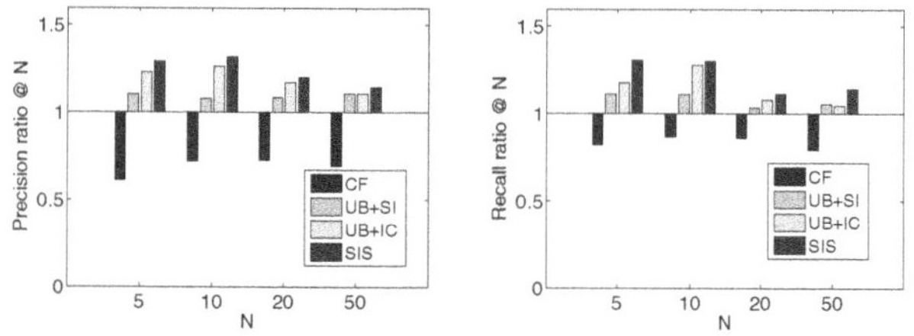

(a) Precision ratio (b) Recall ratio

Figure 6: Performance comparisons (whrrl.com)

Figure 3 and Figure 4 show the precision and recall of top 5 item recommendations for last.fm and whrrl.com by varying $|Z|$, the size of latent topics. We find that social influence indeed improves the recommendation performance, for both UB+SI against UB and SIS against UB+IC. The result shows that the best recommendation performance is reached when the chosen topic size is around 60. Therefore, we set the default value of the latent topic size to 60 for the remaining experiments.

Figure 5 and Figure 6 compare the performance of various item recommendation approaches, using last.fm and whrrl.com, respectively. Note that UB's performance is used as the reference and these two figures demonstrate the performance ratio against the UB. As shown, all the model-based approaches clearly outperform the conventional memory-based collaborative filtering (CF), i.e., values of CF are smaller than 1 while all other ratio values are greater than 1. Again, we find that leveraging the social influence indeed improves the performance (i.e., values of UB+SI are greater than 1 and values of SIS are greater than those of UB+IC). Most importantly, SIS (which integrates user behavior, social influence and item content) achieves the best performance.

5.3 Topic Analysis

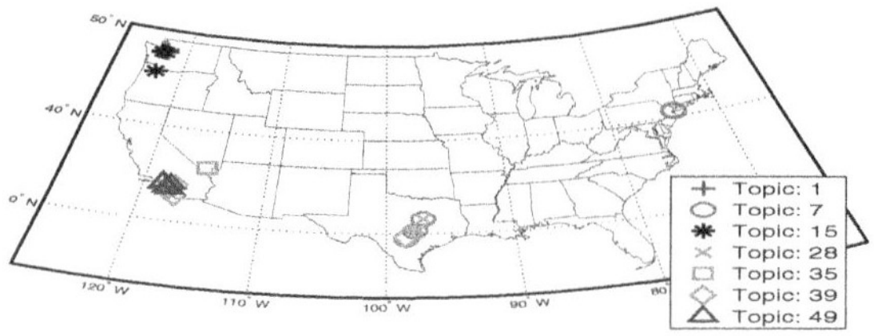

Topic No.	Representative Tags
Topic 1	coffee, shops, theater, live performance, movie
Topic 7	sports, retails, recreation, food, store
Topic 15	bars, clubs, subs, pub, wine
Topic 28	restaurant, subs, sandwich, cafe, steak
Topic 35	store, service, grocery, retail, accessory
Topic 39	movie, museum, galleries, lodging, theater
Topic 49	restaurant, bars, Americans, Mexican, wine

Figure 7: Example topics learned from whrrl.com dataset, based on SIS

Here, we study the latent topics learned from our SIS model. Notice that, in SIS, a latent topic is represented by a joint distribution of item and content. Figure 7 shows some latent topics learned from the whrrl.com dataset. As shown, places located in distance tend to belong to different latent topics (e.g., places in topic 15 and topic 49), while categorical tags with very different semantics also tend to belong to different latent topics (e.g., representative tags in topic 39 and topic 49). Obviously, in the whrrl.com dataset, the content and locations of places both have an important role in determining the latent topics. We find that several latent topics have similar representative tags, e.g., topic 15 and topic 49, but located in distance. On the other hand, some latent topics that are clustered at the same areas, e.g., topic 1 and topic 15, have quite different tags. Moreover, items (even with similar contents) in different spatial clusters tend to be in different latent topics, which confirms that the learned latent topics from our SIS model are distributions over both items (which exhibit strong locality in whrrl.com dataset) and their content.

Topic No.	Representative Tags
Topic 1	80s, Bon Jovi, Robbie Williams, Guns N Roses, American
Topic 10	Rock, Guitar Virtuoso, Roxette, English, New Wave
Topic 16	Punk, Rock, 70s, Ramones, American
Topic 20	Alizee, French, alternative rock, Italian, Lorie
Topic 27	Usher, RnB, hip-hop, Craig David, urban
Topic 35	JAY-Z, hip hop, Kanye West, rap, east coast hip hop
Topic 49	jazz, Bill Evans, jazz piano, Bebop, saxophone

Figure 8: Example topics learned from last.fm dataset, based on SIS

Figure 8 shows some latent topics learned from the last.fm dataset. Topic 1 discovers popular American rock stars in

80's, except for Robbie Williams who is an English singer. However, since the topic is discovered from users' listening history, this may indicate that users like Bon Jovi may also like Robbie Williams. Topic 10 represents another genre in rock music with extensive guitar practice, e.g., Roxette is one of the representative bands. Topic 20 has two French female singer Alizee and Lorie, and indicates the topic may be related to Italian singers. Topic 27 contains genre related to R&B and two well known singers Usher (the king of R&B) and Craig David. Topic 35 discovers topic related to hip hop music, with representative singers Jay-Z and Kanye West. And topic 49 demonstrates music related to jazz and music instruments related to jazz (piano and saxophone).

5.4 Social Influence Study

In this section, we study the social influence between friends. Instead of investigating how social influence improves the recommendation performance, here we analyze the role of user influence in different application domains (i.e., music listening vs. location check-in). We plot the distributions of social influence probabilities, denoted as $\Pr(u|f)$, among all friend-pairs in Figure 9(a). Additionally, we also consider the probability for a user u to make independent selection (denoted as $\Pr(u|u)$) and plot the distributions of independent selection probabilities in Figure 9(b). Intuitively, we believe users making decisions mainly based on their own preferences, although friends' opinions may affect the decision making to certain degree, i.e., the probability for a user to follow an uncommon preference of his friends is relatively small. Here, our experiments based on the dataset last.fm and whrrl.com confirm this intuition.

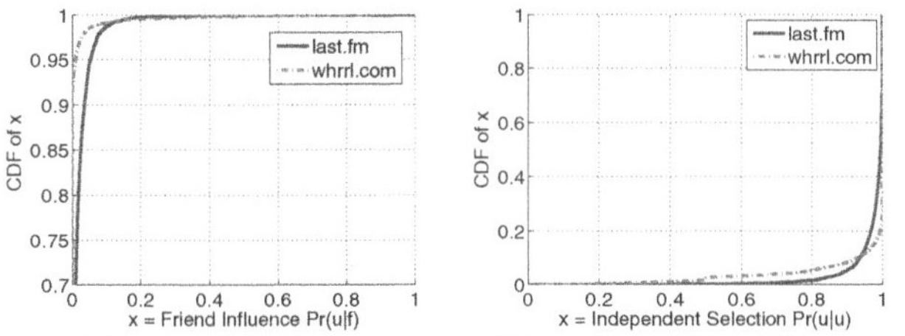

(a) Friend Influence (b) Independent Selection

Figure 9: Social influence analysis

By comparing results between last.fm and whrrl.com datasets, we find that the friend influence in whrrl.com is smaller than that in last.fm. As shown in Figure 9(a), 95% (for last.fm) and 99% (for whrrl.com) of friend-pairs have friend influence values less than 0.05, respectively. This is probably because users in whrrl.com have more friends than users in last.fm (i.e., average 9.08 friends in whrrl.com vs. 1.91 friends in last.fm). Usually not all friends are influential and, very often, a small number of friends take the most part of social influence. From Figure 9(b), we find that although both datasets suggest significant independent selection probabilities, users in whrrl.com have smaller independent selection probabilities than those in last.fm. As shown in Figure 9(b), 5% (for whrrl.com) and 1% (for last.fm) of users have independent selection probability smaller than 0.8, respectively. Generally speaking, the social influence of users in location check-in activities is more significant than those in music listening activities. One explanation is that location check-ins are inherently social activities while music listening is usually for self-entertainment.

5.5 User Profile Analysis

Both user preference of a user and social influence from her friends can be learned through our SIS model to build

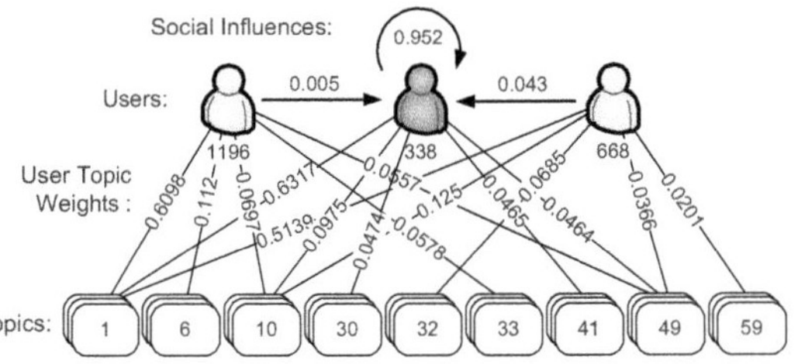

Figure 10: Example user profiles and social influence learned from last.fm dataset, by using SIS

user profiles. In this section, we analyze two user profiles to facilitate a better understanding of user behaviors. In Figure 10, we show the profile of user 338 (consisting of her preference of latent topics and influence from friends) from last.fm dataset. As shown, user 338 is influenced by user 1196 and user 668, with the influence probability values 0.005 and 0.043, respectively (other friends with lower influences to user 338 are omitted). Also, the top 5 topics of users' preferences are also shown, where the probabilities representing users' interests in the topics are labeled in the corresponding edges. Notice that there are 4 overlapped topics for user 1196 and user 338; while there are 3 overlapped topics between user 668 and user 338. In terms of common interests, user 1196 is more similar/correlated to user 338 than user 668. However, we find that user 668 exhibits more social influence upon user 338 than user 1196 does. Notice that the notion of social influence in our SIS model is able to capture the "abnormal" behavior of a user due to influence from her friends. Figure 10 confirms that friends with high correlation/similarity or share a lot common items do not necessarily exhibit strong social influence, while friends with less overlapped interests may still be quite influential, as some friends may have some special knowledge useful to others.[5]. Similarly, we study the user profile discovered from whrrl.com dataset. Figure 11 shows a user profile for user 8, consisting of his top ranked topics and social influence from two most influential friends, i.e., user 65 and user 2175. As shown, user 65 and user 2175 have the same influence on user 8 (who is relatively weak in independent selection) although they have different degrees of overlapped topics with user 8. Again, social correlation and similarity between friends do not reflect the social influence between them.

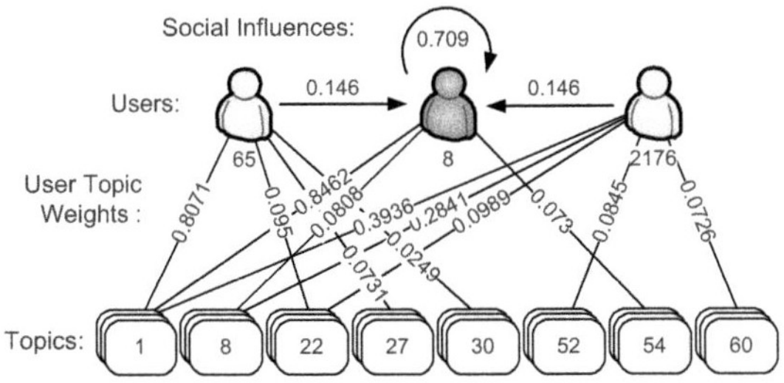

Figure 11: Example user profiles and social influence learned from whrrl.com dataset, by using SIS

5.6 Group Recommendation

Next, we report our findings in evaluating group recommendation algorithms, including the SIG algorithm we proposed, along with two aggregation-based strategies. We use

[5]As discussed in the Introduction, the ideas and assumptions made in many existing work contradict this observation.

the 17,587 group check-in records in whrrl.com in our experiment, where we consider a group check-in record (i.e., the ground truth) at a time and take the average of tested records. Notice that a record indicates a group of people visiting a place. An effective group recommendation algorithm should have this place ranked high among all the places recommended. Therefore, we propose a metric called *relative ranking* to evaluate the performance of the group recommendation algorithms. Suppose that a given algorithm returns a ranked list of m items (i.e., all places in this experiment). If the actual visited place is ranked in the l-th position of the returned recommendation list, the relative ranking is calculated as $\frac{l}{m}$. For example, if an actual visited place is ranked 10th among a total of 100 items returned by a group recommendation algorithm, the relative ranking is $10/100 = 0.1$).

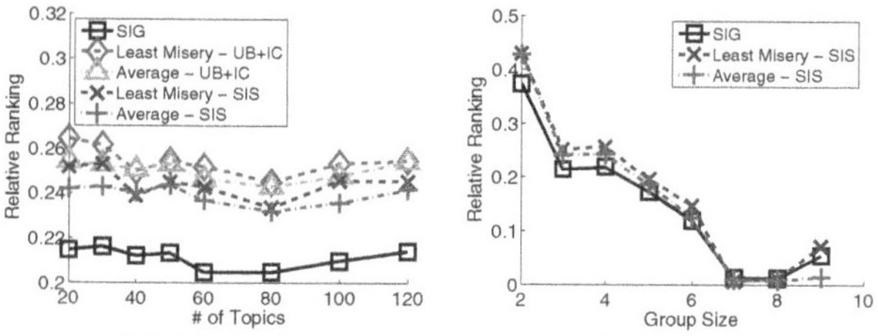

(a) Topic Size (b) Group Size

Figure 12: Group recommendation (whrrl.com)

Figure 12 compares the performance of SIG, Average and Least Misery. The values in Y-axis represent the relative rankings of actual visited places (the lower the better). The conventional Average and Least Misery strategies are devised based on user behavior (UB) and item content (IC). Here we also implement both algorithms using the model parameters discovered based on our SIS model. The result shown in Figure 12(a) indicates that SIG always outperforms the other four and reach its optimal point when the topic size is around 60. Besides, we also observe that our SIS model enhances the performance of both Average and Least Misery algorithms. Recall that the SIG algorithm only takes into account the social influence (without considering the user preference) in making group recommendation. The result is surprising as we may think that both preferences and social influence of group members are important for a group of whrrl users to decide where to go. However, this experimental result may hint that people tend to listen to other people's opinions, by compromising their own preference, in group activities. Thus, social influence based group recommendation shows the best performance.

In Figure 12(b), we find that SIG outperforms the Average-SIS and Least Misery-SIS strategies for most group sizes (the result for conventional implementations are not shown for clarity of presentation). However, as the group size growing larger, the improvement obtained from SIG decreases. This finding implies that for smaller groups, the social influence among group members plays a major role in item selection for the group. However, for larger groups, the group consensus aggregated from individual preferences may dominate the group decision, as it probably becomes too complicated to communicate with all members when the group is large. This finding is consistent with our experience in activity planning, i.e., for a smaller group, one or two influencing members may significantly determine the activity venue. On the other hand, for a large group, the social influence from individuals may become difficult to take effect on the entire group. As a result, the group's common interest dominates.

5.7 Viral Marketing

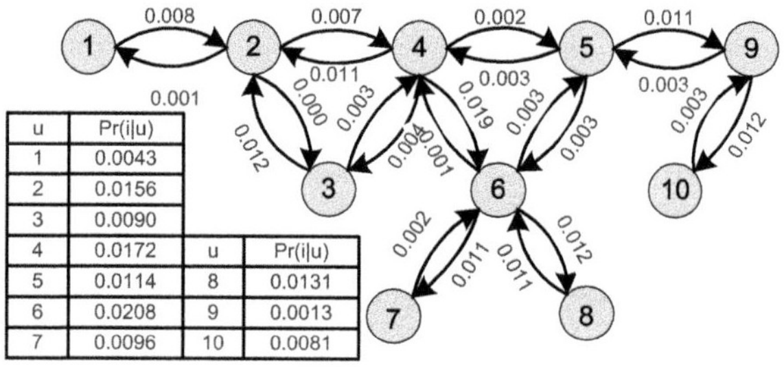

Figure 13: A subgraph of social network labeled with social influence and user preference.

To validate our idea about using social influence together with user preference for viral marketing study, we present a case to demonstrate that our approach can identify good targets for marketing. Here, we extract a small social graph from the last.fm dataset as shown in Figure 13. The social influence learned from SIS are labeled as the weight of social links in the figure. Here we select an item 2940 from last.fm as the marketing item for our case study. We also list each user's preference to item 2940 on the left-lower corner of Figure 13. In this study based on the Threshold Model, we compare the effect of viral marketing with two different approaches: 1) a conventional method (baseline), solely based on the social influence; and 2) our proposal, which combines both user preference and social influence. In the experiments, we set the threshold θ_u as 0.01 and the weight between user's preference to item 2940 and the influence from friends as 0.5. As such, these two methods execute for 10 iterations. For each seed user s, the corresponding effect of viral marketing V_s (i.e., final number of activated users) are shown in Table 2, indicating our proposal is expected to be more effective than (or at least complementary to) the baseline.

our proposal	s	5	2	4	6	8	1	3	7	9	10
	V_s	7	6	6	3	3	0	0	0	0	0
baseline	s	4	6	5	2	8	1	3	7	9	10
	V_s	6	3	2	1	1	0	0	0	0	0

Table 2: Comparison of viral marketing strategies

We also use the different seed selection made in both methods to illustrate the importance of taking into account both the user preference and social influence for viral marketing. Notice that our proposal suggests to start with seed user 5 but the baseline method suggests user 4. Obviously, user 4 is chosen by the baseline because i) she has high social influence to her neighbors, and ii) she is at the center of the social network. Under this reasoning, user 5 or 6 are inferior to user 4 because they have lower influence, comparing to the hub user 4. Actually, user 5 is the best choice in our proposal because, even though user 5 may not influence user 4 directly, user 4 can still get activated easily since she likes the item 2940 (i.e., she has a great interest in 0.0172). Therefore, our proposal targets on user 5.

6. CONCLUSION

In recent years, the so-called "social influence" has been incorporated into recommender systems based on various heuristics, e.g., assign extra similarity weight to friends in collaborative filtering. In this paper, we discuss the differences between social influence and social correlation/similarity and argue that the phenomenon of social influence can be captured quantitatively for use in various recommendations and applications. We propose a probabilistic generative model, called *social influenced selection*(SIS) model, to capture the the social influence between linked friends and user preferences and develop an efficient algorithm to discover those valuable information from real datasets through statistical inference. A novel contribution of this work is a coherent approach which facilitates seamless integration of social network, user behavior and item content for recommendation. Additionally, the social influence and user preference extracted based on SIS can be used for a variety of applications, including group recommendation, viral marketing, user analysis, and topic analysis. Moreover, through a comprehensive set of empirical experiments using datasets collected from last.fm and whrrl.com, a number of interesting findings are obtained, including: 1) the social influence is beneficial for recommender systems and item recommendation made based on SIS (which integrates user behavior, social influence and item content) achieves the best performance; 2) user behavior (in form of location check-ins) in whrrl.com shows the spatial clustering phenomenon, and items (even with similar contents) in different spatial clusters tend to belong in different latent topics; 3) users making decisions mainly based on their own preferences, although friends' opinions may affect the decision making to certain degree, i.e., the probability for a user to follow an uncommon preference of his friends is relatively small; 4) friends with high correlation/similarity or share a lot of common items do not necessarily exhibit strong social influence, while friends with less overlapped interests may still be quite influential; 5) in group activities, people tend to listen to other people's opinions, by compromising their own preference; and 6) combining both user preference and social influence (our strategy for viral marketing) is expected to be more effective than (or at least complementary to) the conventional approach solely based on social influence.

As for the future work, we would like to further extend the SIS model to capture social influences with respect to latent topics. In addition, we also plan to conduct field study to demonstrate the advantages of our proposed viral marketing strategy. Finally, instead of relying on the learned knowledge from SIS (which for individual item selection) to make recommendations for a group, we plan to develop a new generative model to capture the item selection process for group activities.

7. REFERENCES

[1] G. Adomavicius and A. Tuzhilin. Toward the Next Generation of Recommender Systems: A Survey of the State-of-the-Art and Possible Extensions. *IEEE TKDE*, 17(6):734–749, 2005.

[2] L. Baltrunas, T. Makcinskas, and F. Ricci. Group recommendations with rank aggregation and collaborative filtering. In *RecSys*, pages 119–126, 2010.

[3] C. Basu, H. Hirsh, and W. W. Cohen. Recommendation as classification: Using social and content-based information in recommendation. In *AAAI/IAAI*, pages 714–720, 1998.

[4] J. S. Breese, D. Heckerman, and C. M. Kadie. Empirical analysis of predictive algorithms for collaborative filtering. In *UAI*, pages 43–52, 1998.

[5] W. Chen, C. Wang, and Y. Wang. Scalable influence maximization for prevalent viral marketing in large-scale social networks. In *KDD*, pages 1029–1038, 2010.

[6] F. C. T. Chua, H. W. Lauw, and E.-P. Lim. Predicting item adoption using social correlation. In *SDM*, pages 367–378, 2011.

[7] A. Crossen, J. Budzik, and K. J. Hammond. Flytrap: intelligent group music recommendation. In *IUI*, pages 184–185, 2002.

[8] T. L. Fond and J. Neville. Randomization tests for distinguishing social influence and homophily effects. In *WWW*, pages 601–610, 2010.

[9] D. Goldberg, D. Nichols, B. M. Oki, and D. Terry. Using collaborative filtering to weave an information tapestry. *CACM*, 35:61–70, December 1992.

[10] A. Goyal, F. Bonchi, and L. V. S. Lakshmanan. Learning influence probabilities in social networks. In *WSDM*, pages 241–250, 2010.

[11] T. Hofmann and J. Puzicha. Latent class models for collaborative filtering. In *IJCAI*, pages 688–693, 1999.

[12] M. Jamali and M. Ester. *TrustWalker*: a random walk model for combining trust-based and item-based recommendation. In *KDD*, pages 397–406, 2009.

[13] A. Jameson and B. Smyth. The adaptive web. chapter Recommendation to groups, pages 596–627. Springer-Verlag, Berlin, Heidelberg, 2007.

[14] H. Kelman. Compliance, identification, and internalization: Three processes of attitude change. *Journal of Conflict Resolution*, 2:51–60, 1958.

[15] D. Kempe, J. M. Kleinberg, and É. Tardos. Maximizing the spread of influence through a social network. In *KDD*, pages 137–146, 2003.

[16] I. Konstas, V. Stathopoulos, and J. M. Jose. On social networks and collaborative recommendation. In *SIGIR*, pages 195–202, 2009.

[17] H. Ma, I. King, and M. R. Lyu. Learning to recommend with social trust ensemble. In *SIGIR*, pages 203–210, 2009.

[18] H. Ma, M. R. Lyu, and I. King. Learning to recommend with trust and distrust relationships. In *RecSys*, pages 189–196, 2009.

[19] H. Ma, D. Zhou, C. Liu, M. R. Lyu, and I. King. Recommender Systems with Social Regularization. In *WSDM*, 2011.

[20] J. Masthoff. Group modeling: Selecting a sequence of television items to suit a group of viewers. *User Modeling and User-Adapted Interaction*, 14:37–85, February 2004.

[21] J. F. McCarthy and T. D. Anagnost. Musicfx: an arbiter of group preferences for computer supported collaborative workouts. In *CSCW*, pages 363–372, 1998.

[22] K. McCarthy, M. Salamó, L. Coyle, L. McGinty, B. Smyth, and P. Nixon. Cats: A synchronous approach to collaborative group recommendation. In *FLAIRS Conference*, pages 86–91, 2006.

[23] R. J. Mooney and L. Roy. Content-based book recommending using learning for text categorization. In *DL*, pages 195–204, 2000.

[24] M. O'Connor, D. Cosley, J. A. Konstan, and J. Riedl. Polylens: a recommender system for groups of users. In *CSCW*, pages 199–218, 2001.

[25] S. Pizzutilo, B. De Carolis, G. Cozzolongo, and F. Ambruoso. Group modeling in a public space: methods, techniques, experiences. In *Proceedings of the 5th WSEAS International Conference on Applied Informatics and Communications*, pages 175–180, 2005.

[26] A. Popescul, L. H. Ungar, D. M. Pennock, and S. Lawrence. Probabilistic models for unified collaborative and content-based recommendation in sparse-data environments. In *UAI*, pages 437–444, 2001.

[27] M. Richardson and P. Domingos. Mining knowledge-sharing sites for viral marketing. In *KDD*, pages 61–70, 2002.

[28] B. M. Sarwar, G. Karypis, J. A. Konstan, and J. Riedl. Item-based collaborative filtering recommendation algorithms. In *WWW*, pages 285–295, 2001.

[29] P. Singla and M. Richardson. Yes, there is a correlation: - from social networks to personal behavior on the web. In *WWW*, pages 655–664, 2008.

[30] H. Tong, C. Faloutsos, and J.-Y. Pan. Fast Random Walk with Restart and Its Applications. In *ICDM*, pages 613–622, 2006.

[31] M. Ye, P. Yin, and W.-C. Lee. Location Recommendation in Location-based Social Networks. In *GIS*, pages 458–461, 2010.

[32] M. Ye, P. Yin, W.-C. Lee, and D. L. Lee. Exploiting Geographical Influence for Collaborative Point-of-Interest Recommendation. In *SIGIR*, 2011.

[33] Z. Yu, X. Zhou, Y. Hao, and J. Gu. Tv program recommendation for multiple viewers based on user profile merging. *User Modeling and User-Adapted Interaction*, 16:63–82, March 2006.

See-To-Retrieve: Efficient Processing of Spatio-Visual Keyword Queries

Chao Zhang Lidan Shou Ke Chen Gang Chen
College of Computer Science
Zhejiang University, China
{chaozhang,should,chenk,cg}@zju.edu.cn

ABSTRACT

The wide proliferation of powerful smart phones equipped with multiple sensors, 3D graphical engine, and 3G connection has nurtured the creation of a new spectrum of visual mobile applications. These applications require novel data retrieval techniques which we call What-You-Retrieve-Is-What-You-See (WYRIWYS). However, state-of-the-art spatial retrieval methods are mostly distance-based and thus inapplicable for supporting WYRIWYS. Motivated by this problem, we propose a novel query called *spatio-visual keyword* (SVK) query, to support retrieving spatial Web objects that are both visually conspicuous and semantically relevant to the user. To capture the visual features of spatial Web objects with extents, we introduce a novel visibility metric which computes object visibility in a cumulative manner. We propose an incremental method called *Complete Occlusion-map based Retrieval* (COR) to answer SVK queries. This method exploits effective heuristics to prune the search space and construct a data structure called Occlusion-Map. Then the method adopts the best-first strategy to return relevant objects incrementally. Extensive experiments on real and synthetic data sets suggest that our method is effective and efficient when processing SVK queries.

Categories and Subject Descriptors

H.3.3 [**Information Search and Retrieval**]: Search Process

General Terms

Algorithms, Experimentation

Keywords

Location-based query, Keyword search, Visibility, Indexing

1. INTRODUCTION

The wide proliferation of powerful smart phones equipped with multiple sensors, 3D graphical engine, and 3G connection has nurtured the creation of a new spectrum of visual mobile applications. In these applications, users in the real world can be supplied "on the spot" by cyber information that is tightly coupled with the physical surroundings. In what people call *cyber-physical mobile applications*, a user holding a smart phone may be able to perform a 3D walkthrough around her location or issue a reality-augmented Web search in her real-time camera video. Such applications identify new data retrieval problems.

Let us look at one example, a tourist in a city of attractions searches for introductory information about a distant grand church within her eyesight. With a reality-augmented search gadget, she can simply type the keyword "church" and then expect the Web pages about *that* particular church to be displayed on her mobile device, as shown in Figure 1. The most distinguishing characteristic of such applications is the need for What-You-Retrieve-Is-What-You-See (WYRIWYS). Specifically, we need to retrieve spatial Web objects which are both visually conspicuous in physical space and semantically relevant in document space.

Figure 1: An example of WYRIWYS

Unfortunately, the information retrieval community has not realized the importance of supporting WYRIWYS. State-of-the-art spatial access methods are mostly distance-based and thus inapplicable for supporting WYRIWYS. The recent development of spatial keyword query (SKQ) processing techniques [3, 12, 8, 5, 2] along with several variants [19, 1] can be utilized to support location-based keyword search. However, none of these works can provide WYRIWYS for the following reasons: (1) First, most SKQ techniques overlook the visibility of objects. These techniques model an object as an entity with location and keywords. A typical SKQ processor computes the similarity between an object and the query by combining their spatial proximity and semantic relevancy. Objects that are spatially close to the query location are inclined to be returned, whether they are visible to the user or not. Considering our example of reality-augmented search, a SKQ may retrieve numerous unwanted churches which are close but invisible to the tourist. (2) Second, the previous methods consider each object as a *point of interest*. Such a simplification fails to utilize the extent data of spatial objects, which are readily available among map service providers[1]. Thus, visually conspicuous objects have no privilege over inconspicuous ones when being retrieved.

Motivated by the absence of effective retrieval techniques when developing a cyber-physical mobile search prototype [16], we study a novel query called the *spatio-visual keyword (SVK)* query. Given a collection C of spatial Web objects and a query q, a SVK query returns a list of k objects in C with the largest scores, where the s-core of each object is computed by combining its physical visibility and semantic relevancy with respect to q. Note that the SVK query is different from simply imposing visible judgment on distance-based spatial keyword queries, since the visual conspicuousness of objects should be quantitatively measured, based on human visual perception. For this purpose, we propose a novel visibility metric, which measures the visible parts of an object in a cumulative way.

The SVK query is interesting not only because it is useful in real applications, but also because it introduces several new challenges. To the best of our knowledge, no state-of-the-art technique exists for the handling of SVK queries. On one hand, instead of being independent, each object may be partially or totally occluded by other objects. Therefore, the processing of SVK queries is much more challenging than that of distance-based spatial keyword queries, considering the complex correlations among the objects. On the other hand, existing works [10, 9, 15] on visible spatial queries employ Boolean judgment to deal with visibility analysis. The major drawback of such a mechanism is that the degree of being visible cannot be distinguished for visible objects. Thus, the existing visible query techniques are not applicable for SVK queries either.

To address the above problems and effectively process SVK queries, we propose the *Complete Occlusion-map based Retrieval* (COR) method. This method employs the hybrid index IR-tree [5] and works in a two-step manner. In the first step, a dynamic structure called *Complete Occlusion-Map* (COM) is built, which partitions the surrounding space of the query point into a number of angular ranges and maintains visibility information for each range. In the second step, COR computes the accurate visibilities for object-s, as well as the tightest visibility upper bounds for IR-tree nodes. By taking advantage of the best-first search, the search space is effectively pruned and the top-k relevant objects are returned in an incremental manner.

The main contributions of this paper are:

1. We propose a novel query, namely the SVK query, to retrieve spatial Web objects that are both visually conspicuous and semantically relevant. To the best of our knowledge, it is the first work supporting WYRIWYS for spatial Web objects.

2. We present a quantitative visibility metric, which captures the analytical visual angle and distance of an object with s-patial extent.

3. We propose an incremental method, namely COR, to handle SVK queries. And we conduct extensive experiments on both real and synthetic data sets to evaluate the performance of this method.

The rest of this paper is organized as follows. Section 2 reviews existing works on spatial keyword queries and visible spatial queries. Section 3 conducts visibility analysis for spatial Web objects, and formally defines the SVK query. Section 4 provides a baseline solution for SVK query processing. Section 5 presents the detailed COR method. Section 6 empirically evaluates the performance of the proposed solutions. Finally, Section 7 concludes the paper.

[1] http://www.automotiveit.com/bosch-navigation-app-features-3d-"artmap"/news/id-00851

2. RELATED WORK

In this section, we review existing works related to SVK queries, including spatial keyword queries and visible spatial queries.

2.1 Spatial Keyword Queries

Spatial keyword queries have been extensively studied recently. To retrieve objects relevant to the query keywords within a pre-specified region, Chen et al. [3] utilize separate indexes for spatial and textual features. A set of candidate objects is retrieved using the index upon one attribute, which is then refined with the index upon the other attribute. The major drawback of such a mechanism is that the candidate set obtained based on one feature may be too huge. To address this problem, Hariharan et al. [12] propose a hybrid index KR*-tree by augmenting each R*-tree node with a set of keywords appearing in the corresponding subtree. At query time, KR*-tree is traversed, objects containing query keywords and intersecting with the query region are returned. Felipe et al. [8] propose another hybrid index: the IR^2-tree, which integrates R-tree [11] with signature files. In the query process, the signature file of an IR^2-tree node is loaded into memory. Thus, nodes that do not contain all the query keywords are pruned early on and relevant objects are returned incrementally.

Limited by the nature of signature files, the IR^2-tree does not support ranking on textual relevancy. Moreover, loading the signature file of all words into the memory may incur substantial I/O cost. In [5], Cong et al. propose the IR-tree index. Different from IR^2-tree, IR-tree augments each R-tree node with an inverted file for the objects contained in the subtree rooted at that node. Based on IR-tree, Cong et al. develop an efficient solution for answering location-aware top-k text retrieval (LkT) query. Unfortunately, the LkT query is essentially distance-based, which fails to consider object visibility. Thus, objects spatially close to the query location are always inclined to be returned, whether they are visible or not. This difference renders their query techniques infeasible for answering SVK queries.

Several other variants of spatial keyword query have also been studied in [19, 1, 18]. However, these works do not take into account visibilities of objects either, and our focus, the integration of physical visibility and cyber information, has not been studied yet.

2.2 Visible Spatial Queries

Visibility analysis has been well studied in the field of computer graphics [4] and computational geometry [6] in various approaches. To the best of our knowledge, all these approaches assume the data are memory-resident. Apparently, this is not a practical assumption for location-based Web search applications, which usually involve extremely massive data.

In the database community, Kofler et al. [13] propose the LoD-R-tree, which exploits spatial proximity to identify visible objects. Shou et al. [17] design the HDoV-tree, which pre-computes visibility information and incorporates it into the nodes of LoD-R-tree. But the genuine purpose of both LoD-R-tree and HDoV-tree lies in accelerating environment rendering in virtual walkthrough applications. Without maintaining semantic features of objects, they are not capable of supporting SVK queries. More recently, Nutanong et al. propose the visible k nearest neighbor (VkNN) query in [15]. The goal is to retrieve k objects with the minimum smallest visible distances (MINVIDIST) to a query point q. Nutanong et al. prove that it is sufficient to determine the MINVIDIST of an objec-t o by considering only objects nearer than o. On the basis of this observation, they demonstrate the Post-Pruning and Pre-Pruning algorithms to obtain visible nearest neighbors. Several extensions of the VkNN query are also studied [10, 9]. These works do consider the presence of obstacles and the occluding correlations among objects. Nevertheless, the developed techniques do not constitute good solutions for our problem. First, as aforementioned, these works employ Boolean visibility judgment and the degrees of being visible are not distinguished. Second, these works only concern the spatial visibilities of objects, whereas our SVK query focuses on the fusion of both visibility and textual relevancy.

3. PROBLEM DEFINITION

Let $C = \{o_1, o_2, ...o_n\}$ be a collection of spatial Web objects kept by a central server (e.g., a map service provider). Each object $o \in C$ is defined by a tuple $(o.pol, o.height, o.doc)$. Here, $o.pol$ is an arbitrarily shaped polygon, representing the projection of o in the horizontal plane; $o.height$ is the vertical height of the 3D object o; and $o.doc$ is o's Web document. Given a query q with the user location and a set of query keywords specified, i.e., $q = (q.location, q.keywords)$, a SVK query retrieves objects in C that are both visually conspicuous and semantically relevant to q. In the following, we first present a quantitative visibility metric in Section 3.1, then combine it with textual relevancy to propose a hybrid ranking mechanism in Section 3.2, based on which we formulate the SVK query in Section 3.3.

3.1 Visibility Analysis

A number of approaches have been proposed in the computer graphic community to efficiently render visible objects in 3D environments. These approaches assume the 3D models of objects are memory-resident, and exploit graphical techniques (e.g., hierarchical Z-buffer) to clip out hidden polygons on the surface of an object so that visible scenes can be rendered vividly on graphical units. However, these approaches are inapplicable for visibility computation in SVK applications: Given the huge number of spatial Web objects, it is extremely difficult, if not impossible, for the server to access all the complex 3D details of objects, and meanwhile ensure instantaneous response to the query launcher. Hence, there is an evident necessity of simplifying occlusion detection among 3D objects, in such a way as to alleviate the computation burden on the server, but simultaneously guaranteeing a considerable precision.

In view of this problem, we employ a strategy which has been widely adopted in walkthrough systems [4]. This strategy consists of two steps to determine the visibility of each object. First, it utilizes the horizontal (2D) projections of objects to determine occlusion. Second, for each unobstructed object, it uses an accurate 3D algorithm to compute visibility. The rationale behind the 2D approximation of the first step is that, in a wide range of SVK scenarios, the heights of objects are actually in the same range of magnitude, and thus play a less important role in determining if an object is visible or not. Just as shown in Figure 2(a), in a typical urban area, it is common that the densely distributed buildings are not significantly distinguishable in height with respect to an observer. Moreover, since nearer buildings always appear taller than faraway ones, it is safe to judge whether an object is visible by examining its horizontal projection (see Figure 2(b)).

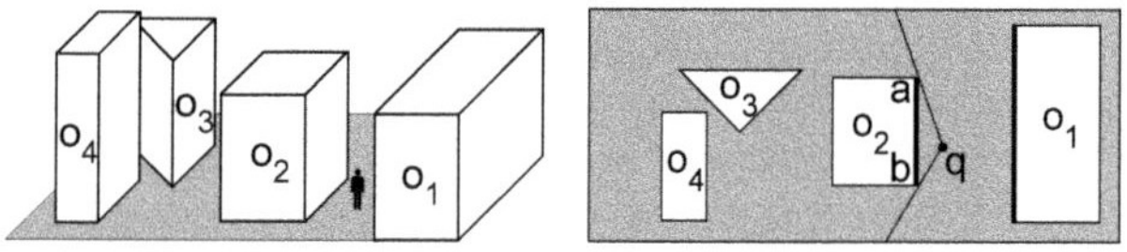

(a) Side view (b) Top view

Figure 2: An urban area with four buildings

Relying on the above assumption, we introduce the concepts of unobstructed segment and unobstructed face to facilitate visibility computation for objects.

DEFINITION 1. *C is a collection of spatial Web objects and q is a query point. For any object $o \in C$, ab is an unobstructed segment of o iff the following two conditions hold: 1) ab is on the boundary of $o.pol$, 2) for any point p on ab, segment pq does not cut the projected polygon of any object.*

Informally, an unobstructed segment is a segment on the boundary of the projected polygon that can be completely seen by the observer. For example, in Figure 2(b), the unobstructed segments of objects $o_1...o_4$ are represented by bold lines. Take object o_2 as a specific example, segment ab is unobstructed because any point on ab is not occluded by obstacles. It is not difficult to find that, each unobstructed segment in the horizontal plane actually determines an unobstructed face of the object in the 3D space. Below, we give the formal definition of unobstructed face.

DEFINITION 2. *Given an object $o \in C$, each unobstructed segment ab of o determines an unobstructed face F_{ab}, which is a vertical rectangle of length $|ab|$ and height $o.height$.*

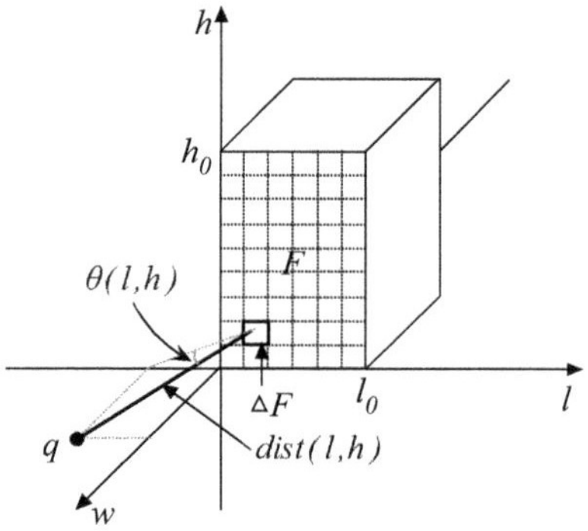

Figure 3: Cumulative face visibility

We proceed to analyze the visibility of an unobstructed face. Intuitively, given an unobstructed face F, F appears more conspicuous if it is *large* and *close* to the observer. However, the challenge is how to define being *large* and *close*, given the fact that different parts on an unobstructed face always have different distances and orientations. To handle this, we develop a cumulative computing approach. As shown in Figure 3, we divide F into numerous infinitesimal grids. For each grid, say ΔF, the distances as well as orientations of all points on ΔF to q are considered to be equal due to its infinitesimal size. Based on this property, we represent the visibility of ΔF as

$$vis(q, \Delta F) = \frac{area_{\Delta F} \cdot \sin \theta_{\Delta F}}{dist^2_{\Delta F}} \quad (1)$$

Here, $area_{\Delta F}$ reflects how *large* ΔF is; $\theta_{\Delta F}$ is the angle between $\overrightarrow{q\Delta F}$ and F, measuring the orientation of ΔF with respect to the observer (when $\theta = 90°$, ΔF right faces q); $dist_{\Delta F}$ is the Euclidean distance between q and ΔF which tells how *close* ΔF is. Since ΔF is a 2D grid, its visibility is inversely proportional to $dist^2_{\Delta F}$ instead of $dist_{\Delta F}$.

Based on Equation 1, the visibility of the entire unobstructed face F can be obtained by summing up the visibilities of all the small grids, as defined in Definition 3.

DEFINITION 3. *Given a query point q and an unobstructed face F, for any point $p = (l, h) \in F$, let $dist(l, h)$ be the Euclidean distance between q and p, and $\theta(l, h)$ be the angle between $\overrightarrow{qp}$ and F, then the visibility of F with respect to q is defined as*

$$vis(q, F) = \iint_F \frac{\sin\theta(l, h)}{dist^2(l, h)} dl dh. \quad (2)$$

The object visibility can then be defined by summing up visibilities of all the unobstructed faces belonging to it.

DEFINITION 4. *Given an object o, let $S(o)$ be the set containing all the non-overlapping unobstructed faces of o, then the visibility of o with respect to query q is defined as*

$$vis(q, o) = \sum_{F \in S(o)} vis(q, F).$$

3.2 Ranking Mechanism

To measure the semantic relevancy between a spatial Web object and a user query, we adopt the classic TF-IDF model, which has been widely used in traditional search engines. According to the TF-IDF model, an object o is assigned a higher ranking value if the query keyword occurs frequently in $o.doc$ and infrequently in documents of other objects. Below, we give the formal definition of semantic relevancy, based on which we derive the weighted ranking score for a spatial Web object.

DEFINITION 5. *Given a collection of spatial Web object C and a query q, for any object $o \in C$, the semantic relevancy between q and o is:*

$$rel(q, o) = \sum_{t \in q.keywords} TF(t, o.doc) \cdot IDF(t, C)$$

where

$$TF(t, o.doc) = 1 + \ln(frequency(t, o.doc))$$

$$IDF(t, C) = \ln \frac{|C|}{1 + |objects\ in\ C\ that\ contain\ t|}.$$

DEFINITION 6. *Given a collection of spatial Web object C, a query q, and a pre-specified value $\alpha \in [0, 1]$, for any object $o \in C$, the weighted ranking score of o with respect to q is:*

$$score(q, o) = \alpha \cdot ||vis(q, o)|| + (1 - \alpha) \cdot ||rel(q, o)||.$$

The weighted ranking score is virtually a linear interpolation that combines physical visibility and semantic relevancy, and α is a parameter used to balance two aspects. Note that both visibility and relevancy of an object are normalized into the range $[0, 1]$.

3.3 The SVK Query

Based on the definition of weighted ranking score, we formulate the SVK query as follows.

DEFINITION 7. *Given a collection of spatial Web objects C, a user query q, and an integer k, the result of SVK query is a list L of spatial Web objects such that, 1)$L \subseteq C$, 2)$|L| = k$ (given that $|C| \geq k$), 3)$\forall o \in L, \forall o' \in C - L, score(q, o) \geq score(q, o')$.*

To specify our previous example query for church, Figure 4 depicts the top view of an area in Rome comprising ten buildings $o_1 \ldots o_{10}$, whose documents are described in Table 1. A tourist in this area may want some introductory information when he faces a grand church o_1, and thus issues a top-1 SVK query at q with the keyword "church". As a result, church o_1 with its cyber information will be returned to the user, since it is both visually conspicuous and semantically relevant. Note that, although another church o_6 is actually nearer than o_1, it is not returned because it is completely occluded by o_7 and is not what the user demands.

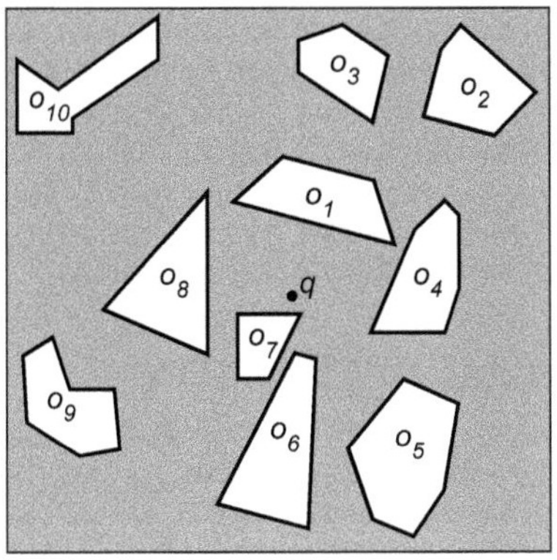

Figure 4: Top view of ten spatial Web objects

Table 1: Documents of objects $o_1 \ldots o_{10}$

	o_1	o_2	o_3	o_4	o_5	o_6	o_7	o_8	o_9	o_{10}
Gothic	5	1	4	2	0	5	0	0	0	0
Church	5	2	0	0	0	5	0	0	0	0
Museum	0	0	0	0	3	0	4	2	4	5

4. A BASELINE SOLUTION

In this section, we provide a baseline solution for answering SVK queries. The idea is quite straightforward. Given a spatial Web object, its ranking score is a combination of its visibility and semantic relevancy. Hence, we can exploit separate spatial and textual indexes of objects, and adapt the threshold algorithm [7] to return top-k results. Algorithm 1 gives an overview of the solution.

Algorithm 1: $Baseline(q, \alpha, k, RTree, InvertedFile)$

1 Build a list L of all spatial web objects;
2 Sort L in the descending order of semantic relevancy;
3 Initialize an empty set A of a fixed size k;
4 **foreach** *object o in L* **do**
5     $threshold$ = the least ranking score in A;
6   **if** $|A| = k$ *and* $score_{max}(q, o) \leq threshold$ **then**
7   **break**;
8   Compute $vis(q, o)$ with $RTree$;
9     $score(q, o) = \alpha \cdot ||vis(q, o)|| + (1 - \alpha) \cdot ||rel(q, o)||$;
10   **if** $|A| < k$ *or* $score(q, o) > threshold$ **then**
11   Update A with o;
12 **return** A

As shown, we first build a list L of all spatial Web objects, which are sorted in the descending order of semantic relevancy. Then we initialize a empty result set A with a fixed size k, and keep track of the least ranking score in A as $threshold$. Next, we scan L sequentially and progressively update A (lines 4-11). Note that L is actually unnecessary to be scanned entirely. For object o currently being processed, if o's score is below $threshold$ even when we set o's visibility to the visibility upper bound (line 6), it is ensured further scanning will not generate top-k results any more and the algorithm safely terminates.

Clear as Algorithm 1 appears, the difficult part lies in the computation of object visibility. In the following, we elaborate line 8 and discuss how to derive object visibility with R-tree. Note that the R-tree only needs to index the projected 2D polygons of objects, with their heights stored as associating features to support visibility computation.

In the horizontal plane, each object o occupies an angular range with respect to the query point q. Apparently, only objects falling in that angular range and nearer than o can potentially occlude o. We retrieve such objects using R-tree and call them *potential occluders*. Next, we need to retrieve o's unobstructed segments, and then sum up the visibilities of their corresponding unobstructed faces. Recall Definition 1, a segment ab is identified as unobstructed when any point on ab is not occluded by other objects in the horizontal plane. In other words, an unobstructed segment is essentially the nearest segment to the observer within its angular range. Thus, the problem is equivalent to comparing edges of $o.pol$ with polygon edges of the *potential occluders*, and obtain the nearest segments that belong to $o.pol$. Suppose e_1 and e_2 are two edges sharing a common angular range $[\theta_{low}, \theta_{high}]$, and their portions in $[\theta_{low}, \theta_{high}]$ are ab and cd respectively. Then, as shown in Figure 5, the relationship of segments ab and cd can be categorized into four cases:

- Case 1: ab and cd completely overlap in $[\theta_{low}, \theta_{high}]$.
- Case 2: ab and cd do not intersect in $[\theta_{low}, \theta_{high}]$.
- Case 3: ab and cd intersect, and the intersecting point is along θ_{low} or θ_{high}.
- Case 4: ab and cd intersect, and the intersecting point is along $\theta \in (\theta_{low}, \theta_{high})$.

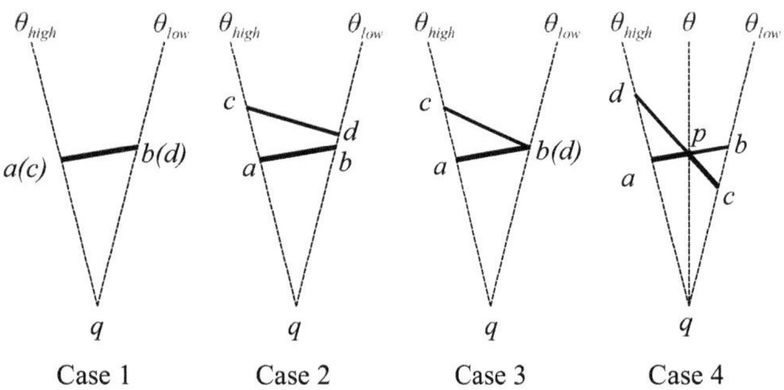

Figure 5: Edge relationships

Case 1, 2 and 3 are actually the same to deal with. In the horizontal plane, as long as one segment is nearer than the other along any direction $\theta \in (\theta_{low}, \theta_{high})$, it is guaranteed that segment will be nearer for the entire angular range. For Case 4, both segments are nearer to the query point but in different sub angular ranges. We need to compute the intersecting point p and split $[\theta_{low}, \theta_{high}]$ along the direction of $\overrightarrow{qp}$. Then the nearer segment in each sub range can be easily obtained.

By comparing the polygon edges of o and o's *potential occluders*, we are able to obtain the nearest segments in o's angular range, and identify o's unobstructed segments. Then the unobstructed faces of o in the 3D space can be constructed. The remaining job is to compute visibility for each unobstructed face and sum them up. For clarity but without loss of generality, we assume the coordinate of the query point q in the 3D space is $(x_q, 0, 0)$ [2]. Given an unobstructed face F constituted by four points $(0,0,0)$, $(0, l_o, 0)$, $(0, l_o, h_o)$ and $(0, 0, h_o)$, the visibility of F with respect to q can be derived as follows.

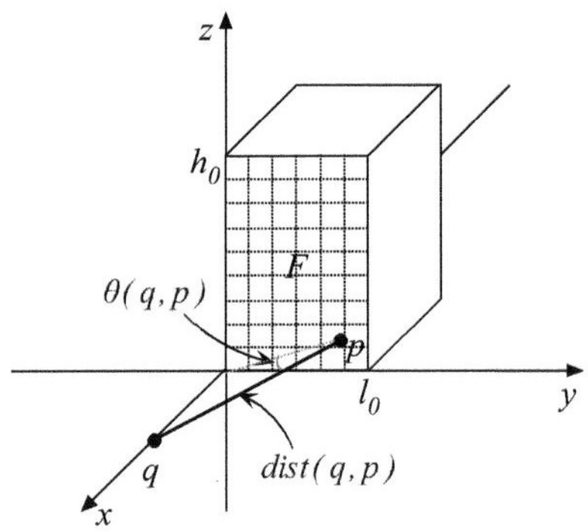

Figure 6: Unobstructed face visibility computation

Refer to Figure 6, for any point $p \in F$, we denote by $\theta(q,p)$ the angle between $\overrightarrow{qp}$ and F, by $dist(q,p)$ the distance between q and p, and by $dist(q,F)$ the perpendicular distance from q to face F. Then the following equation holds.

$$\sin\theta(q,p) = \frac{dist(q,F)}{dist(q,p)} \tag{3}$$

Combining Definition 3 and Equation 3, the visibility of F can be further developed as follows:

$$\begin{aligned} vis(q,F) &= \iint_{\substack{0\le y\le l_0 \\ 0\le z\le h_0}} \frac{dist(q,F)}{dist^3(y,z)} \mathrm{d}y\mathrm{d}z \\ &= \int_0^{h_0}\int_0^{l_0} \frac{x_q}{(x_q^2+y^2+z^2)^{\frac{3}{2}}} \mathrm{d}y\mathrm{d}z \\ &= \int_0^{h_0} \frac{x_q l_0}{(z^2+x_q^2)\sqrt{z^2+x_q^2+l_0^2}} \mathrm{d}z \\ &= \arctan \frac{l_0 h_0}{x_q\sqrt{x_q^2+l_0^2+h_0^2}} \end{aligned}$$

We can see the visibility of an unobstructed face is closely related to: (1) its area, (2)its minimum visible distance to the query point, and (3) its maximum visible distance to the query point. This explains why the cumulative visibility provides an accurate capture of the visual features of an object.

The above discussion addresses the problem of computing object visibility and thus makes Algorithm 1 feasible. Unfortunately, the baseline solution is far from being efficient. On one hand, since an unobstructed segment is the only occluder in its angular range, it is highly redundant to retrieve *potential occluders* repeatedly to compute visibility for each object in L. On the other hand, the separation of indexes fails to closely combine the spatial and textual features of objects, and incurs unnecessary overhead.

5. THE COR METHOD

In this section, we present the COR method to handle SVK queries more effectively. This method employs the hybrid index IR-tree, and performs query processing in two steps. In the first step, a novel structure called Complete Occlusion-Map (COM) is constructed, underpinning the support for high-performance visibility computation. In the second step, the method uses the best-first strategy to retrieve the top-k relevant objects incrementally. In what follows,

[2]Handling the cases where $y_q, z_q \neq 0$ is straightforward using the substitution method for integral.

we first give a brief introduction to the IR-tree index and the COM structure in Section 5.1, then elaborate the two steps in Section 5.2 and Section 5.3, and finally discuss the efficiency of the COR method in Section 5.4.

5.1 Data Structures

5.1.1 The IR-Tree Index

IR-tree [5] is essentially an extension of R-tree by augmenting each node with a pointer to an inverted file. For a leaf node N_L, its inverted file indexes the documents of all objects in N_L. For an intermediate node N_I, its inverted file indexes the pseudo documents of its child nodes. The pseudo document is an important concept to facilitate the computation of textual relevancy upper bound, because it summarizes the terms of all child entries. Figure 7 is an example IR-tree for the spatial Web objects $o_1 ... o_{10}$ shown in Figure 4. The ten polygon-shaped objects are grouped according to their spatial proximity to build up the IR-tree. Similar to the case of R-tree, as we detect object occlusion in the horizontal plane, the IR-tree needs to index only the projected polygons of objects, and stores their corresponding heights as additional feature information. Table 2 lists inverted file contents for all IR-tree nodes.

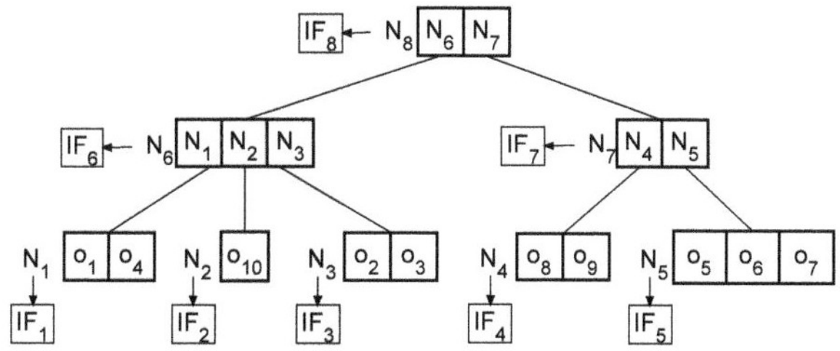

Figure 7: The IR-tree

Table 2: IR-Tree Inverted Files

	Gothic	Church	Baroque
IF_1	$(o_1, 5), (o_4, 2)$	$(o_1, 5)$	
IF_2			$(o_{10}, 5)$
IF_3	$(o_2, 1), (o_3, 4)$	$(o_2, 2)$	
IF_4			$(o_8, 2), (o_9, 4)$
IF_5	$(o_6, 5)$	$(o_6, 5)$	$(o_5, 3), (o_7, 4)$
IF_6	$(N_1, 5), (N_3, 4)$	$(N_1, 5), (N_3, 2)$	$(N_2, 5)$
IF_7	$(N_5, 5)$	$(N_5, 5)$	$(N_4, 4), (N_5, 4)$
IF_8	$(N_6, 5), (N_7, 5)$	$(N_6, 5), (N_7, 5)$	$(N_6, 5), (N_7, 4)$

5.1.2 Complete Occlusion-Map

In the horizontal plane, each unobstructed segment occupies an angular range and causes an invisible region with respect to the observer. Moreover, the angular ranges of different unobstructed segments never overlap. Therefore, given a query point q and a collection C of spatial Web objects, the set of all unobstructed segments from C in fact partitions the space surrounding q into a number of angular ranges, each corresponding to one or zero unobstructed segment.

As shown in Figure 8, $[\theta_{qb}, \theta_{qa}]$ is an angular range occupied by unobstructed segment *ab*. In $[\theta_{qb}, \theta_{qa}]$, it is guaranteed that only the corresponding unobstructed face F_{ab} is visible and all other objects are hidden behind *ab*, i.e., the angular range $[\theta_{qb}, \theta_{qa}]$ is dominated by F_{ab}. We call $[\theta_{qb}, \theta_{qa}]$ a dominated angular range, and define a tuple (SEG, OID, VIS, ANC) to describe it, where, SEG denotes the dominating unobstructed segment, VIS is the visibility of the unobstructed face F_{SEG}, OID is the id of the object that SEG belongs to, and ANC is an array storing the ancestor node ids of object o_{OID} in the IR-tree. Later in Section 5.3 we will see, these attributes facilitate the visibility computation in the dominated angular range.

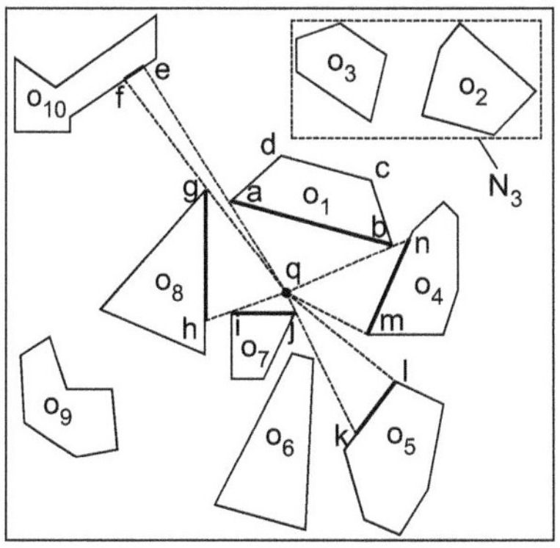

Figure 8: Partitioning the surrounding space of q into angular ranges

In Figure 8, $[\theta_{ql}, \theta_{qm}]$ is an angular range empty of unobstructed segment. Such an angular range indicates no object from C lies in it. We call it a dummy angular range.

In summary, given a collection of spatial Web objects C and a query point q, let $S(C)$ be the set of all unobstructed segments from C, then the COM of q is a partition of the space by $S(C)$ into a set of angular ranges, each angular range is either dominated or dummy. Table 3 illustrates the COM for the ten objects shown in Figure 8.

Table 3: Complete Occlusion-Map

AR	SEG	OID	VIS	ANC
$[\theta_{qb}, \theta_{qa}]$	ba	1	$vis(q, F_{ba})$	(8, 6, 1)
$[\theta_{qe}, \theta_{qf}]$	ef	10	$vis(q, F_{ef})$	(8, 6, 2)
$[\theta_{qg}, \theta_{qh}]$	gh	8	$vis(q, F_{gh})$	(8, 7, 4)
$[\theta_{qi}, \theta_{qj}]$	ij	7	$vis(q, F_{ij})$	(8, 7, 5)
$[\theta_{qk}, \theta_{ql}]$	kl	5	$vis(q, F_{kl})$	(8, 7, 5)
$[\theta_{ql}, \theta_{qm}]$	null	null	0	$\emptyset$
$[\theta_{qm}, \theta_{qn}]$	mn	4	$vis(q, F_{mn})$	(8, 6, 1)

5.2 Construction of Complete Occlusion-Map

In this subsection, we discuss the construction of COM. The idea is to traverse the IR-tree and retrieve all the unobstructed segments to partition the space. A simple search process is described as following: 1) Initialize COM with a large dummy angular range covering the entire plane. 2) Create a priority queue PQ with the IR-tree root node. For each entry in PQ, its MINDIST to the query point q is used as its key. 3) If the head entry of PQ is a node, dequeue it and insert all its child entries into PQ. 4) If the head of PQ is an object, dequeue it and update current COM. To be more specific, each projected polygon edge of the object is compared with the current COM components to produce nearer segments. 5) Repeat step 3) and 4) iteratively. When PQ is empty, the construction finishes.

Unfortunately, the above process needs to access all IR-tree nodes and examine every polygon edge of an object. In the following, we elaborate the construction process by presenting three heuristics to effectively prune the search space.

Firstly, when incorporating an object o to update COM, one can verify that some edges are in fact hidden by other edges of $o.pol$ itself. As a concrete example, for o_2 in Figure 8, its edges *bc*, *cd*, and *da* are occluded by edge *ab*. Apparently, these edges cannot be unobstructed and it is safe to skip them. Based on this observation, we introduce the concept of back edge, and derive Heuristic 1 to avoid unnecessary edge comparisons.

DEFINITION 8. *Given a spatial Web object o and a query point q, an edge e of o.pol is a back edge iff for any point p on e, segment pq cuts at least one other edge of o.pol.*

HEURISTIC 1. *C is a collection of spatial Web objects and q is a query point. For any object $o \in C$, none of the back edges of o can be unobstructed to q.*

The second optimization aims to avoid unnecessary node expansions. Refer to Figure 8 again, N_3 is an IR-tree node bounding $o_2.pol$ and $o_3.pol$. During the construction of COM, due to a smaller MINDIST, $o_1.pol$ is examined before N_3 and segment ab is retrieved. As a result, N_3's MBR is completely occluded by segment ab. Thus, neither o_2 nor o_3 can be visible and N_3 can be pruned.

HEURISTIC 2. *During the construction of COM, if N is an IR-tree node satisfying the following two conditions: 1) the query point q stays outside N's MBR, and 2) N's MBR is completely occluded by current COM. Then no object in N may have unobstructed segment.*

In the horizontal plane, each unobstructed segment in COM could be interpreted as an enhanced nearest surrounder [14], which is associated with visibility and ancestor IR-tree nodes. Therefore, a condition designed in [14] to early terminate nearest surrouder query also applies in COM construction.

HEURISTIC 3. *The construction of COM can terminate when the following two conditions hold: 1) current COM does not have dummy angular ranges, 2) the MINDIST of the head entry in PQ is larger than the minimum bounding radius of current COM.*

Algorithm 2: $Construct\ COM(q, IRTree)$

```
Initialize COM to be dummy;
Initialize a priority queue PQ with IRTree.root;
while !PQ.isEmpty() do
    r = minimum bounding radius of COM;
    if !COM.hasDummy() and PQ.head().key ≥ r then
        break;
    E=PQ.pophead();
    if E is an object then
        Update COM with non-back edges of E.obj;
    else
        foreach entry e in E do
            if e.MBR is not completely occluded then
                key = MINDIST(q, e.MBR);
                newEntry=(e,key);
                Insert newEntry into PQ;
return COM
```

With the above three heuristics, we give the elaborated process for COM construction in Algorithm 2. As shown, entries of the IR-tree are accessed in the ascending order of their minimum distances to q. In this way, nearby objects, which may bring about larger invisible space, are given priority. Hence, the prunable area keeps shrinking and a large number of upcoming entries are pruned (Heuristic 2). Moreover, so long as the currently retrieved segments completely surround q and that their bounding radius is smaller than the MINDIST of the head entry in PQ. The construction terminates successfully according to Heuristic 3.

5.3 Incremental Object Retrieval

In this subsection, we discuss the computation of accurate ranking scores for objects and ranking score upper bounds for IR-tree nodes, then propose an efficient algorithm to retrieve top-k objects incrementally.

5.3.1 *Object Ranking Score*

Given an object o, its ranking score is the linear combination of its visibility and semantic relevancy. The semantic relevancy is quite straightforward to derive by Definition 5, as the terms of $o.doc$ are all maintained in the IR-tree. Below, we mainly discuss the computation of its accurate visibility.

The basic idea is to use the COM structure to select all unobstructed faces that belong to o, and then add up their visibilities. Relying on the OID attribute, the selection is easy, as exemplified in the following using Figure 8. In the horizontal plane, object o_{10} intersects with three COM angular ranges: $[\theta_{qb}, \theta_{qa}]$, $[\theta_{qe}, \theta_{qf}]$, and $[\theta_{qg}, \theta_{qh}]$. In $[\theta_{qb}, \theta_{qa}]$, the value of OID is 1, indicating that the unobstructed face must belong to object o_1 and o_{10} is occluded. The case is similar in $[\theta_{qg}, \theta_{qh}]$ where $OID = 8$. However, in $[\theta_{qe}, \theta_{qf}]$, OID is 10. We conclude that the corresponding unobstructed face F_{ef} must belong to o_{10}, and thus return $vis(q, F_{ef})$ as o_{10}'s visibility.

5.3.2 *Node Ranking Score Upper Bound*

We proceed to discuss visibility upper bound computation for IR-tree nodes. The key is to utilize the attribute ANC of the COM structure. Given an IR-tree node N and a dominated COM angular range intersecting N's MBR, the corresponding unobstructed face belongs to N if and only if N's id is contained in ANC. Hence, the computation of visibility upper bound for node N is performed as following: 1) Obtain all COM components that intersect N's MBR. 2) Find the dominated components whose ANCs contain N's id, and suppose they are called $candidates$. Please note that all dummy components are ignored here, because no object in N can actually lie in the dummy angular ranges and the occupation must be caused by MBR expansion. 3) Group the $candidates$ by their OIDs, thus unobstructed faces of the same object are gathered into the same group. 4) Aggregate the VIS in each group to obtain the group visibility. 5) Find the maximum visibility among all groups and return it as the visibility upper bound of N, which is denoted by $vis(q, N)$.

THEOREM 1. *The visibility obtained from the above process is a tightest visibility upper bound for node N.*

PROOF. Step 1), 2), and 3) actually find all the visible objects in N. By computing their visibilities in step 4) and comparing them in step 5), it is guaranteed that no object in N has a larger visibility than $vis(q, N)$, but at least one object reaches it. □

The semantic relevancy between q and N can be derived from N's pseudo document. Recall that for any term t, the weight of t in N's pseudo document is no smaller than that of any object in N.

Combining the visibility upper bound $vis(q, N)$ and relevancy upper bound $rel(q, N)$, N's weighted ranking score upper bound is given by:

$$score(q, N) = \alpha \cdot ||vis(q, N)|| + (1 - \alpha) \cdot ||rel(q, N)|| \quad (4)$$

THEOREM 2. *The score computed from Equation 4 is a ranking score upper bound for N.*

PROOF. For any object o contained in N, the following inequality holds according to Theorem 1:

$$vis(q, N) \geq vis(q, o)$$

And according to the property of pseudo document, we have:

$$rel(q,N) \geq rel(q,o)$$

Thus:

$$score(q,N) \geq \alpha\cdot||vis(q,o)||+(1-\alpha)\cdot||rel(q,o)|| = score(q,o)$$

which completes the proof. □

5.3.3 *Retrieval Algorithm*

Theorem 2 ensures a hierarchical order of IR-tree nodes' ranking scores. Now, we present the algorithm for object retrieval, which adopts the best-first strategy and returns top-k objects in an incremental manner. As shown in Algorithm 3, a priority queue PQ is maintained to store objects and IR-tree nodes to be visited, and is initialized with the root node of IR-tree. The ranking score of each entry is used as its key in PQ. If the head entry of PQ is possessed by an IR-tree node, we expand it and elaborate the ranking scores of its children. If the head entry is occupied by a spatial Web object o, it indicates that all the objects in PQ do not have a larger score than o, thus it is safe to report o as the next most relevant object. When the top-k objects are obtained or PQ becomes empty, the algorithm terminates successfully.

Algorithm 3: *Object Retrieval*$(q,\alpha,k,COM,IRTree)$

Initialize an empty result set A;
Initialize a priority queue PQ with $IRTree.root$;
while *!PQ.isEmpty() and* $|A|<k$ **do**
  E=PQ.pophead();
  if E *is an object* **then**
    Insert $E.obj$ into A;
  else
    foreach *entry e in* E **do**
      $score=\alpha\cdot||vis(q,e)||+(1-\alpha)\cdot||rel(q,e)||$;
      $newEntry$=$(e,score)$;
      Insert $newEntry$ into PQ;
return A

5.4 Discussion

In the COR method, the cost of the first step is closely related to the environment around the query point q. If q lies in a dense area, the COM construction will be quite efficient. This is because unobstructed segments can be retrieved early to surround q, thus most IR-tree nodes can be pruned with Heuristic 2 and 3. On the contrary, if q lies in an extremely sparse area, a considerable number of IR-tree nodes may need to be accessed. The cost of the second step is expected to be small. On one hand, as proved in Theorem 1, the visibility upper bound for IR-tree node is optimal. On the other hand, the tightness of the upper bound for semantic relevancy depends on the number of query keywords. Since fewer keywords indicate tighter upper bound for semantic relevancy and in most applications a query contains only limited number of keywords, the relevancy upper bound is also expected to be tight.

6. EXPERIMENTS

In this section, we empirically evaluate the effectiveness and efficiency of the Baseline and COR methods. We implement both algorithms in JAVA and conduct the experiments on an Intel Core 2 Duo 2.93Ghz PC with 2GB memory.

6.1 Data Sets

Our experiments are based on both real and synthetic data sets. Similar to [5], the real spatial data set LA[3] is used. LA contains 131,461 MBRs, representing street objects in Los Angeles. We normalize all MBRs in LA into the [0,10000]×[0,10000] horizontal space, and assign a height within [10,20] to each MBR. Meanwhile, we have crawled a real textual data set from Gowalla[4], which is a location-based social network providing checking-in and commenting services. The crawled Gowalla set consists of 28,867 Web documents. Each document is a collection of user-generated comments that aim to describe a point of interest in Los Angeles. By randomly selecting a document from the Gowalla set for each spatial object in the LA set, we obtain a spatial-textual data set, named REALDATA.

We also exploit four synthetic data sets to evaluate scalability of the methods, with a cardinality of 100k, 200k, 500k, and 1,000k. Each object in a synthetic data set is described by a tuple $(o.mbr, o.height, o.doc)$. Here, $o.mbr$ is generated uniformly in the horizontal space with a size no larger than 4.00×4.00 (length×width), $o.height$ is within [10,20], and $o.doc$ is selected randomly from the Gowalla set.

We use disk-based R-tree (for Baseline) and IR-tree (for COR) to index these data sets. The page size is fixed at 4KB and the maximum number of branches per node is 100.

6.2 Query Result Demonstration

We first issue some test queries, and see if the proposed methods can indeed retrieve spatial Web objects that are both conspicuous and relevant. For comparison, we also implemented the LkT algorithm [5], which is designed for distance-based spatial keyword retrieval. Figure 9 and Table 4 report the results of three test queries on REALDATA. Specifically, Figure 9(a) shows the 131461 objects in REALDATA as well as the locations of the three queries. Figure 9(b), 9(c) and 9(d) are the respective zoomed-in results of each query, where the green rectangles are the top-5 SVK query results with the inside letters denoting object ids. And we use blue rectangles to highlight objects that are in the top-5 LkT query results but not in the top-5 SVK list.

As shown, the SVK query can retrieve objects that are physically visible and semantically relevant. Taking the first query as a concrete example, the returned five objects are all within the user's eyesight (see Figure 9(b)) and closely related to "coffee" (see Table 4). Such query results can serve the user with useful cyber information regarding the physical world that the user sees, and thus provide an immersive searching experience. Please note that although object f is semantically relevant, it does not appear in the top-5 SVK query results due to low visibility. In contrast, the LkT query always tends to retrieve objects that are close to the user, even if they are totally invisible. This is because LkT does not take into account object visibility and thus cannot provide WYRIWYS.

6.3 Efficiency Study

In this subsection, we report the efficiency of Baseline and COR under various parameter settings. Table 5 shows the parameter ranges, where the numbers in bold denote the default settings. For each experiment set, we evaluate the effect of one parameter while the others are fixed at their default values, and run 100 randomly generated queries with their average cost reported. Two performance metrics are employed, i.e., the query time and the number

[3]http://www.rtreeportal.org

[4]http://en.wikipedia.org/wiki/Gowalla

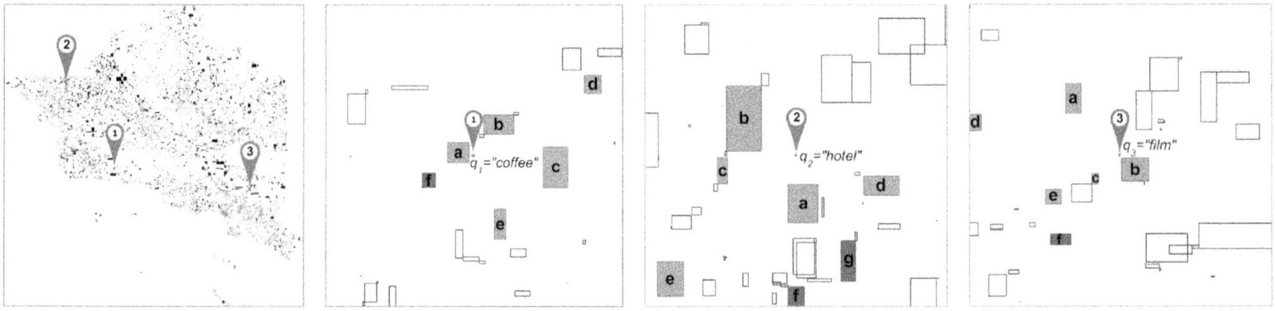

(a) 3 queries on REALDATA (b) Query result 1 (c) Query result 2 (d) Query result 3

Figure 9: Three test SVK queries on REALDATA and their results

Table 4: A Comparison of SVK and LkT Query Results ($\alpha = 0.5$ $k = 5$)

Query	Top-5 SVK Query Results			Top-5 LkT Query Results		
	Object ID	Object Name	SVK Score	Object ID	Object Name	LkT Score
q_1="coffee"	a	Frances Bakery & Coffee	0.806	f	Starbucks	0.985
	b	McDonald's	0.729	a	Frances Bakery & Coffee	0.966
	c	Strawberry Restaurant	0.636	b	McDonald's	0.818
	d	Costa Coffee	0.529	d	Costa Coffee	0.798
	e	Cole's Restaurant	0.519	c	Strawberry Restaurant	0.743
q_2="hotel"	a	Radisson Hotel	0.946	a	Radisson Hotel	0.975
	b	Rose Bowl Motel	0.874	b	Rose Bowl Motel	0.948
	c	Holiday Hotel	0.817	c	Holiday Hotel	0.853
	d	Pasadena Inn	0.649	g	Traveler Motel	0.840
	e	Vegabond Hotel	0.521	f	Hudson Hotel	0.759
q_3="film"	a	Pacific Theater	0.791	a	Pacific Theater	0.846
	b	Park Hotel	0.619	e	Nunavo Cinema	0.797
	c	Highland Club	0.518	f	Alex Theater	0.764
	d	Keda Entertainment	0.512	c	Highland Club	0.619
	e	Nunavo Cinema	0.508	b	Park Hotel	0.613

of IOs. In the following, we present the efficiency results and our findings. Unless stated explicitly, REALDATA is used.

Table 5: Parameter ranges and default values

Parameter	Range
k	5, **10**, 20, 30, 50
α	0.1, 0.3, **0.5**, 0.7, 0.9
number of keywords	**1**, 2, 3, 4

6.3.1 *Effect of* k

In the first set of experiments, we study the effect of k on the performance of the two methods, and Figure 10 shows the results. Since COR works in a two-step manner, its cost is broken into two parts: COR-1 denotes the cost of occlusion-map construction and COR-2 denotes the cost of top-k objects retrieval. As expected, COR significantly outperforms Baseline in terms of both query time and I/O cost. The total cost of both methods increase with k, since a larger k causes a larger search space to obtain relevant objects. But for COR, the cost of occlusion-map construction is irrelevant to k. Another interesting finding for COR is that, although the I/O cost of object retrieval step is larger than that of occlusion-map construction step, the computation cost is smaller. It is explained by the cheap CPU cost of the most frequently used id-comparison operations in the retrieval step.

6.3.2 *Effect of* α

In the second experiment set, we study the effect of α and report the results in Figure 11. Again, we can see COR performs much better than Baseline. Moreover, Baseline deteriorates dramatically as α increases, whereas COR performs well stably. The reason behind is that, a large α means more emphasis is put on visibility.

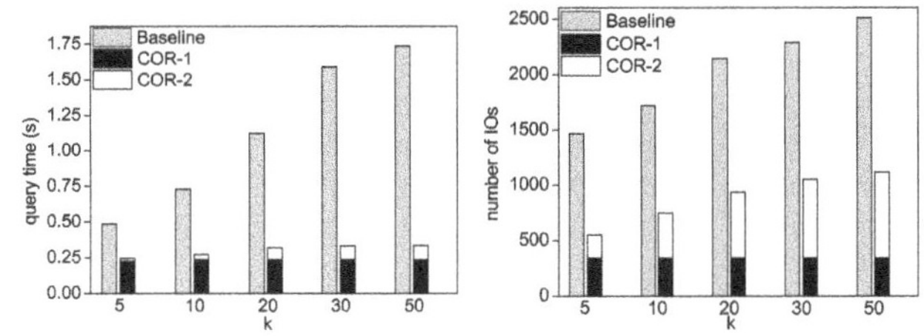

(a) query time (b) IO cost

Figure 10: The effect of k

However, Baseline sequentially scans all objects based on semantic relevancy, and thus suffers from a large number of visibility computations.

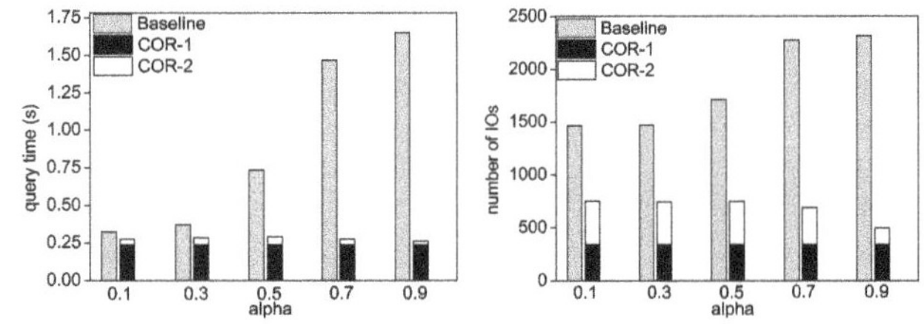

(a) query time (b) IO cost

Figure 11: The effect of α

6.3.3 *Effect of number of keywords*

In the third experiment set, we look into the effect of the number of query keywords. As shown in Figure 12, both methods perform worse with an increasing number of query keywords. For Baseline, a large number of query keywords implies that many objects are not distinguished in terms of semantic relevancy, thus the threshold algorithm terminates later and more objects need to be examined. For COR, although the cost of occlusion-map construction is not related to the number of query keywords, the retrieval step incurs additional overhead. Specifically, as the number of keywords increases, the relevancy upper bound becomes looser. Therefore, more IR-tree nodes need to be accessed, which elevates the number of IOs. Fortunately, as the ranking score computation is quite cheap, the query time increases slowly.

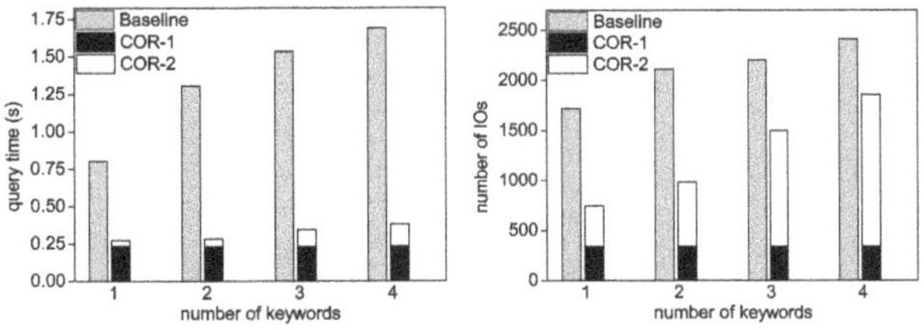

(a) query time (b) IO cost

Figure 12: The effect of number of keywords

6.3.4 *Results for synthetic data sets*

We have also carried out extensive experiments on the synthetic data sets to evaluate the effects of different parameters. We observe that the tendencies are quite similar to that of REALDATA. Thus, we only report a subset of them to demonstrate the scalability of the two methods. Figure 13 shows the query time and IO cost for experiments on different data sets, when all parameters are fixed at their default values. We observe that, Baseline performs worse with an increasing data set size, whereas COR benefits from it. This is expected, the performance improvement is from the occlusion-map construction step. When the number of objects is large, the query point is more likely to lie in a dense area, thus unobstructed segments can be retrieved early to surround it. As a result, most IR-tree nodes are pruned early on and few edge comparison operations are involved.

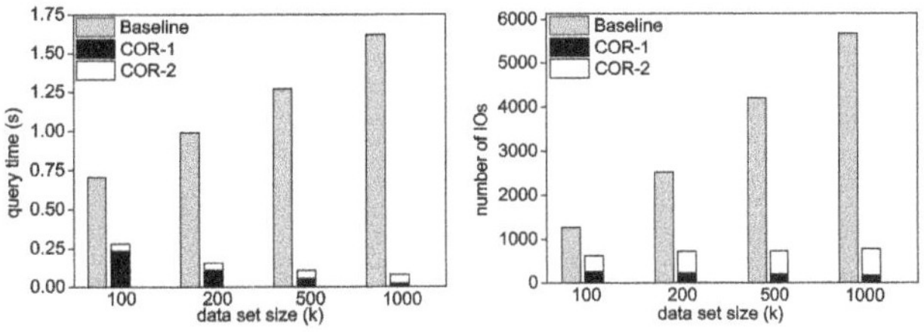

(a) query time (b) IO cost

Figure 13: The effect of data set size

7. CONCLUSIONS

This paper reported a novel study on spatio-visual keyword queries to support WYRIWYS applications. Combining the visual angles and distances of spatial objects analytically, we proposed a quantitative visibility metric for objects with extents, relying on which we derived a hybrid ranking mechanism. To effectively process SVK queries, we proposed the COR method which consisted of two steps in the query processing and was capable of retrieving relevant objects incrementally. The experimental results confirmed the effectiveness and efficiency of our method when processing SVK queries.

8. ACKNOWLEDGMENTS

This work was supported in part by the National Science Foundation of China (Grant No. 60970124, 60903038, and 61170034).

9. REFERENCES

[1] X. Cao, G. Cong, and C. S. Jensen. Retrieving top-k prestige-based relevant spatial web objects. *PVLDB*, 3(1):373–384, 2010.

[2] X. Cao, G. Cong, C. S. Jensen, and B. C. Ooi. Collective spatial keyword querying. In *SIGMOD Conference*, pages 373–384, 2011.

[3] Y.-Y. Chen, T. Suel, and A. Markowetz. Efficient query processing in geographic web search engines. In *SIGMOD Conference*, pages 277–288, 2006.

[4] D. Cohen-Or, Y. Chrysanthou, C. T. Silva, and F. Durand. A survey of visibility for walkthrough applications. *IEEE Trans. Vis. Comput. Graph.*, 9(3):412–431, 2003.

[5] G. Cong, C. S. Jensen, and D. Wu. Efficient retrieval of the top-k most relevant spatial web objects. *PVLDB*, 2(1):337–348, 2009.

[6] M. de Berg, M. van Kreveld, M. Overmars, and O. Cheong. *Computational Geometry: Algorithms and Applications*. Springer, second edition, 2000.

[7] R. Fagin, A. Lotem, and M. Naor. Optimal aggregation algorithms for middleware. In *PODS*, 2001.

[8] I. D. Felipe, V. Hristidis, and N. Rishe. Keyword search on spatial databases. In *ICDE*, pages 656–665, 2008.

[9] Y. Gao, B. Zheng, G. Chen, W.-C. Lee, K. C. K. Lee, and Q. Li. Visible reverse k-nearest neighbor queries. In *ICDE*, pages 1203–1206, 2009.

[10] Y. Gao, B. Zheng, W.-C. Lee, and G. Chen. Continuous visible nearest neighbor queries. In *EDBT*, pages 144–155, 2009.

[11] A. Guttman. R-trees: a dynamic index structure for spatial searching. In *SIGMOD*, pages 47–57, 1984.

[12] R. Hariharan, B. Hore, C. Li, and S. Mehrotra. Processing spatial-keyword (sk) queries in geographic information retrieval (gir) systems. In *SSDBM*, page 16, 2007.

[13] M. Kofler, M. Gervautz, and M. Gruber. R-trees for organizing and visualizing 3d gis databases. *Journal of Visualization and Computer Animation*, 11(3):129–143, 2000.

[14] K. C. K. Lee, W.-C. Lee, and H. V. Leong. Nearest surrounder queries. *IEEE Trans. Knowl. Data Eng.*, 22(10):1444–1458, 2010.

[15] S. Nutanong, E. Tanin, and R. Zhang. Incremental evaluation of visible nearest neighbor queries. *IEEE Trans. Knowl. Data Eng.*, 22(5):665–681, 2010.

[16] L. Shou, K. Chen, G. Chen, C. Zhang, Y. Ma, and X. Zhang. What-you-retrieve-is-what-you-see: a preliminary cyber-physical search engine. In *SIGIR*, pages 1273–1274, 2011.

[17] L. Shou, Z. Huang, and K.-L. Tan. Hdov-tree: The structure, the storage, the speed. In *ICDE*, pages 557–568, 2003.

[18] B. Yao, F. Li, M. Hadjieleftheriou, and K. Hou. Approximate string search in spatial databases. In *ICDE*, pages 545–556, 2010.

[19] D. Zhang, Y. M. Chee, A. Mondal, A. K. H. Tung, and M. Kitsuregawa. Keyword search in spatial databases: Towards searching by document. In *ICDE*, pages 688–699, 2009.

Placing Images on the World Map: A Microblog-based Enrichment Approach

Claudia Hauff*
Delft University of Technology
Delft, The Netherlands
c.hauff@tudelft.nl

Geert-Jan Houben
Delft University of Technology
Delft, The Netherlands
g.j.p.m.houben@tudelft.nl

ABSTRACT

Estimating the geographic location of images is a task which has received increasing attention recently. Large numbers of images uploaded to platforms such as Flickr do not contain GPS-based latitude/longitude coordinates. Obtaining such geographic information is beneficial for a variety of applications including travelogues, visual place descriptions and personalized travel recommendations. While most works in this area only exploit an image's textual meta-data (tags, title, etc.) to estimate at what geographic location the image was taken, we consider an additional textual dimension: the image owner's traces on the social Web. Specifically, we hypothesize that information extracted from a person's microblog stream(s) can be utilized to improve the accuracy with which the geographic location of the images is estimated. In this paper, we investigate this hypothesis on the example of Twitter streams and find it to be confirmed. The median error distance in kilometres decreases by up to 67% in comparison to existing state-of-the-art. The best results are achieved when tweets that were posted up to two days before and after an image was taken are considered. Moreover, we also find another type of additional information useful: population density data.

Categories and Subject Descriptors: H.3.3 Information Storage and Retrieval: Information Search and Retrieval
General Terms: Human Factors, Experimentation
Keywords: image location estimation, image placing

1. INTRODUCTION

Estimating the geographic location of images (also referred to as geotagging, georeferencing or image placement on the world map) is a task which has received increasing attention in recent years. Large numbers of images uploaded to platforms such as Flickr[1] do not contain GPS-based latitude/longitude coordinates. Placing those images on a world map by obtaining geographic information is not only important to aid people in the browsing and organizing of their personal image archives, but it also plays a role in application scenarios for large geographically tagged image corpora such as the automatic illustration of travelogues [16] and personalized travel recommendations [6, 7, 8].

While GPS-enabled cameras are beginning to reach the mainstream market (where an image's latitude/longitude coordinates are automatically recorded as meta-data), this technology is not yet in widespread use. As an example, consider the test set of images we crawled from the photo sharing platform Flickr to test our hypotheses. Of the images that were taken within the last year, more specifically between November 2010 and September 2011, only twenty percent are geo-tagged- since Flickr allows users to manually add geo-information to images after uploading them, this number can be considered as an upper bound to the use of GPS-enabled devices in our data set.

Thus, there are vast amounts of images which are not geographically tagged. A number of approaches, e.g. [21, 22, 23, 13], have been developed that estimate the geographic location of images based either on the textual meta-data that is available for each image (most often the tags that users assign to images), the visual features derived from the image itself, or a combination of the two. These works exploit the very popular image sharing and organizing platform Flickr which we consider here as well. While to our knowledge the existing approaches only consider information derived directly from elements within Flickr (the image itself or meta-data attached to the image), we look beyond this single platform and investigate if location estimation can be improved when considering traces of the image owner/uploader on other social Web platforms. We consider the exploitation of user traces across platforms an important step forward, as a myriad of social Web platforms exist and users are often active on a number of these.

In this work, we consider microblogs, and here more specifically we focus on the microblogging platform Twitter[2]. We hypothesize that we can improve the accuracy of the geographic location estimation when we not only consider the tags the user has assigned to the image but when we also consider the utterances the user has made on Twitter in approximately the same time frame.

*This research has received funding from the European Union Seventh Framework Programme (FP7/2007-2013), grant agreement no ICT 257831 (ImREAL project).

[1]Flickr, `http://www.flickr.com/`
[2]We chose Twitter as it is in wide-spread use around the world.

Imagine a user Alice who for her holidays travelled to North America for a week in the summer. Alice visited Vancouver and Seattle. Alice is also very active on the social Web, having among others a Flickr and a Twitter account which she uses regularly to stay in touch with friends and family. She later uploads the pictures she took during the trip to Flickr. Instead of tagging every single picture with the correct name of the town or monument visited, to safe time, Alice decides to use the same set of tags for all images that describe the entire holiday {*northamerica, seattle, vancouver, holiday*}. During the holiday, Alice regularly tweeted about what she was doing and where she was going, e.g.:

– *"Vancouver this weekend :)"*
– *"Day 1 in Seattle - Been to the Space Needle. Sunny day."*
– *"Sitting in a cafe in Georgetown drinking wine with friends."*

Since posts on Twitter are always time-stamped, we can easily determine which tweets Alice posted around the time of a particular image being taken (information that is readily available for images). We hypothesize that such tweets, where a user mentions place names, particular shops or monuments she has visited or is planning to visit, can improve the accuracy of the location estimation process. Eventually, our goal is the development of a framework, that automatically estimates latitude/longitude of each image, based on the image tags Alice provided *and* the traces Alice left on the social Web. Since various applications, that rely on geographically tagged images are beneficial to the end user (Alice), we expect Alice to provide her online personas and user names willingly.

In this paper, we formulate and investigate the hypothesis that a user's traces on Twitter can increase the accuracy of the image location estimation process. In particular, in this work we make the following contributions:

- We developed an extension to an existing state-of-the-art tag-based approach to location estimation [21] which is based on the language modeling framework for information retrieval. Our extension makes it possible to exploit the information extracted from the user's tweets in a natural way.
- We show that exploiting a user's Twitter stream when estimating the location an image was taken at decreases the median error distance by up to 67%. We also find that the best results are obtained when tweets within two days before and after the image was taken are exploited.
- We find that images, which have fewer than two tags with a geographic scope (see Sec. 3.1.1) assigned to them, benefit the most from our cross-system approach. In our experiments, the median error distance decreases by 40% (57%) for images without tags (with one tag) when the user's Twitter stream is employed as alternative source of information.
- Lastly, we also performed an investigation into the added value of using non-uniform priors in the language modeling approach. We utilized prior information about the population density and the climate. Our results show that a prior based on population density also improves the accuracy of the location estimation.

In the remainder of this paper we first outline previous research (Sec. 2) in the areas of image location estimation and users' motives for using Twitter. The methodology of our approach is presented in Sec. 3. The experimental setup and the data sets used are described in Sec. 4, followed by the results and their discussion in Sec. 5. We conclude the paper in Sec. 6 and outline some avenues for future work.

2. RELATED WORK

Approaches proposed to solve the task of placing images on the world map by determining their latitude and longitude, have been relying on a variety of sources that are based on the image and its meta-data, the user uploading the image or external knowledge bases. Textual features exploited from the image are mostly the assigned tags and the title as well as the description. Visual features derived from the images include a variety of types, such as color histograms or edge histograms [17]. Since photo sharing platforms such as Flickr contain a social network component as well, it is also possible to exploit such information by for example considering the friends of a user or the location of the users commenting on an image. Finally, external knowledge bases, in particular gazetteers (geographic dictionaries), may also be utilized in this task to classify terms as either being geographic in scope or not.

In [21] the tags assigned to images on Flickr are exploited. A grid is placed over the world map which results in equally sized cells. Each training image (with known location) is assigned to its correct grid cell. For each cell, a language model is created from the tags assigned by the user, and a test image is assigned to the geographic cell that produces the highest probability for generating the image's tag set. In contrast to our approach, the cells are of fixed size, which may not be optimal as some regions (e.g., large cities such as London and Paris) will have a larger density of pictures than relatively remote places. We use dynamically sized grid cells, to account for these differences. To determine whether a tag is geographic in nature, in [21] GeoNames[3] is exmployed, a large gazetteer of geographic entities. Speficically, the weights of tags that appear in the English part of GeoNames are boosted.

Also based on tags is the approach proposed in [22]. In contrast to [21], the location estimation is performed on different levels of granularity (city granularity, street level granularity, etc.) and the evidence obtained over the different granularities is combined in order to output the best match granularity location estimate. The authors evaluate their approach by creating a data set with 54 distinct locations (cities in Europe) and classifying test images according to the city they were taken in. This setup is more restricted than the one we investigate in this paper: we attempt to place test images as closely to their true geographic location as possible; we are not restricted by a set of classes.

Instead of determining the correct grid cell and returning the latitude/longitude of the cell's center, a text-based two-step approach is proposed in [23]: first, the most likely area is found by a language modeling approach and within the found cell, the best match images are determined by a similarity search. A test image with unknown location is then assigned the location found by interpolating the locations of the most similar images.

An approach that not only exploits textual information but also visual features was proposed in [13]. Here, textual information (tags) is the primary source of information, and visual features are used as fall-back option in instances where

[3]GeoNames, `http://www.geonames.org/`

tags do not provide meaningful information. The approach works in different stages: first, the image tags are evaluated for the occurrence of at least one known geographic location (geographic lookup). If no location is found, PLSA [10] is performed on the tag data of the corpus. A failure here results in the exploitation of visual features which are used as input to a support-vector machine based classifier.

Georeferencing has not only been applied to images or videos. It has also been utilized to determine the geo-location of the subjects of Wikipedia articles (e.g. [25]) and the geo-location of Twitter messages as well as the respective home location of Twitter users [14, 4]. In [4] it was found that for 51% of Twitter users their home location on the city level could be identified within 161 kilometres (100 miles) of their true location. Based on a large training corpus of Twitter message, the authors trained models (term distributions) for a large number of cities in the USA. While this approach yields one location per user, we are concerned in our work with estimating one location per item (in our case an item is an image).

Finally, we also note a number of works that have considered the questions of why people use Twitter and what they tweet about. Java et al. [12] developed a number of tweet categories: daily chatter (most common use of Twitter), shared information and hyperlinks, conversations and news. In [18] the majority of users (80%) were found to focus on themselves in their tweets, while only a minority of users are driven by the sharing of information. Lastly, Zhao et al. [28] conducted interviews asking users about their motivations for using Twitter; several major reasons surfaced including keeping in touch with friends and colleagues and collecting useful information for one's work and spare time. Overall, these studies show that a lot of tweets are concerned with the user herself; we hypothesize that among these user-centred tweets, there are also useful ones for the derivation of the location of images that were taken by the user.

Our method is similar in spirit to the just described tag-based image location estimation approaches; differences are pointed out in detail in Sec. 3. We would like to stress that in this paper our main focus is on the question of whether a user's traces on the social Web platform Twitter can offer valuable information for the image location estimation task. Such cross-system exploitations have recently begun to attract interest in a number of applications, e.g., [1, 3, 11]. In [1] for example, it has been investigated how users use tags on different social Web platforms (Flickr, Twitter and Delicious) in the context of personalized tag and resource recommendation. It was found that a cross-platform approach can lead to a considerable improvement of the recommendation quality.

In a preliminary study [9] we investigated the research question posed here on a very small data set in a coarse setup: we utilized the most recent tweets and most recent images (instead of aligning tweets and images according to publishing dates) in an oracle setting (instead of an automatic setup to combine both information sources) and found first evidence that this combination improves the image location estimation quality.

3. METHODOLOGY

Previous works have shown that geographic location estimation approaches exploiting textual meta-data provided by the image owner (such as image tags, title, etc.), outperform approaches that rely mainly on visual features. Here, we investigate two additional sources of information: (i) the image owner's traces on the microblogging platform Twitter, and, (ii) prior information about the world, in particular population density and climate. We investigate two hypotheses with our experiments:

- In cases where little (or no) textual meta-data is available for an image, considering a user's tweets as a source of additional textual information will improve the accuracy of the location estimation.
- Adding world knowledge as prior information will improve the estimation accuracy.

We first outline the baseline approach, which is grounded in the language modeling approach to information retrieval and then we turn to describing our proposed extensions.

3.1 Baseline Approach: World Regions as Language Models

Our baseline approach, which is a state-of-the-art approach we compare our Twitter-based extension against, draws inspiration from a number of recently published works. Following [21], we employ the language modeling approach to information retrieval [19, 15, 27, 26]. Instead of documents and queries though as in retrieval, we deal with world regions and image tags. A language model θ_R, which in the retrieval setting is derived for each document, is derived for each region R of the world. Given a test image $\Im$ with tags $T_\Im = \{t_1, ..., t_n\}$ and unknown latitude/longitude, the tags are considered as query terms and the region language models are ranked with respect to the probability $P(\theta_R|T_\Im)$, which according to the Bayes theorem can be expressed as:

$$P(\theta_R|T_\Im) = \frac{P(T_\Im|\theta_R)P(\theta_R)}{P(T_\Im)} \quad (1)$$

$$\propto P(\theta_R) \prod_{t_i \in T_\Im} P(t_i|\theta_R). \quad (2)$$

This is the standard query likelihood based language modeling setup which assumes term independence. Usually, the prior probability of a region $P(\theta_R)$ is considered to be uniform, that is, each region in the world is equally likely. The language models are multinomial probability distributions over the textual meta-data of all training images that were taken in region R, that is, the textual information of all these images is concatenated and treated analogously to a single document.

Since a maximum likelihood estimate of $P(t_i|\theta_R)$ would result in a zero probability of any region that misses one or more of the tags in $T_\Im$, the estimate is usually smoothed with a background language model, generated over all documents in the training corpus. In accordance with [21], we found Dirichlet smoothing [26] to yield the most accurate results when evaluated on our data:

$$P(t_i|\theta_R) = \frac{c(t_i, R) + \mu P(t_i|\theta_C)}{|R| + \mu}. \quad (3)$$

Here, μ is the smoothing parameter, $c(t_i, R)$ is the count of tag t_i in R and $|R|$ is the length of the region document (derived by concatenating all tags of all training images in the region). The probability $P(t_i|\theta_C)$ is the maximum likelihood probability of tag t_i occurring in the collection language model θ_C (derived by concatenating all region documents).

Having identified the most likely region θ_R given test image $\Im$ is only the first step, as such regions often cover hundreds of kilometres and simply assigning the center of the region as estimated latitude/longitude to image $\Im$ is not sufficient. Thus, similar to [23], in a second step we only consider the training images occurring within R. A language model is generated for each of these training images, which are then ranked according to their probability of generating $T_\Im$. The latitude/longitude of the top ranked training image within R is assigned to test image $\Im$.

In contrast to [21], we do not partition the world map into regions (or cells) of fixed size. Instead, we found cells of varying size to yield more accurate results: starting with a grid cell that spans the entire world map (if viewed as a graph, this cell is the root node), the training items are added to the cell one at a time. Once the number of items in a cell exceeds the set limit ℓ_{split}, the cell is split into four equally sized cells, each covering a quarter of the original cell (four children nodes are added) and the training items are re-distributed to these cells. To avoid too many splits in areas where large amounts of training data are available, a cell may not be split any further if its latitude/longitude range reaches a lower limit ℓ_{lat_lng}. This process yields cells of small size in areas where the training data is dense, and cells of large size in areas where the training data is sparse (e.g. regions covering oceans).

If a test image $\Im$ contains no textual elements (or all terms were removed during the filtering steps described in Sec. 3.1.1), the terms in the user location are used instead, which has been proposed in [5]: if a user does not tag an uploaded item with its location, it may have been taken at the user's home location. In contrast to [5], we add the user location terms to $\Im$, instead of relying on an external resource to convert the user location to geographic coordinates which is also often inaccurate due to the ambiguity of place names. Finally, if none of these steps yield a non-empty set $T_\Im$, the test image is assigned the latitude/longitude coordinates of the most frequently occurring location in the training data.

3.1.1 User-Based and Geographic Spread Filtering

In exploratory experiments, we found two strategies that filter terms from the test images' tag sets $T_\Im$ to lead to more robust and considerably more accurate estimations. Firstly, terms are removed from $T_\Im$ that were utilized as tags by less than U users in the training corpus, in line with [22], and secondly, terms are removed that appear in many different geographic areas in the training data. Whether a term is likely to have a geographic scope can either be determined by matching the term against a geographical dictionary such as GeoNames as done in [21] or by considering how localized the term occurs in the training data. We follow the latter approach here. For example, while in our training data the term "sydney" occurs primarily in one particular region (the area containing the location of Sydney, Australia), the term "bowling" appears in many different regions. This observation leads to a simple yet effective filtering method: given a term t_i whose spread is to be determined, a grid is placed over the world map (1 degree latitude/longitude range per cell) and the number of training items in the cell that contain t_i are recorded. Neighbouring grid cells with a non-zero count are merged (to avoid penalizing geographic terms that cover a wide area) and the number of non-zero connected components are determined. This score is normalized by the maximum count. Thus, the smaller the score, the more localized t_i occurs in the training data. While yielding comparable results, our approach is considerably simpler than the χ^2 feature selection based geo-term filtering [23], which determines the geographic score for the tags in each cell separately.

3.2 Adding Additional Knowledge

We consider the language model approach with user-based and geographic spread filtering as our baseline and attempt to improve upon it by relying on additional sources of information. When considering Equation 1, additional information can be added in this framework in three ways:

- **The set of terms $T_\Im$:** The bag-of-words that describe an image can be extended by not only including the tags that are assigned to image $\Im$, but by also including terms from the user's traces on the social Web, in particular the user's Twitter stream.
- **The prior probability $P(\theta_R)$:** Instead of a uniform prior probability, we include knowledge about the world and, for instance, assign a higher prior probability to regions of high population density or regions of moderate climate.
- **The region language model θ_R:** The language model of a region R can be expanded by adding additional information, for example, information extracted from Wikipedia.

In the work presented here, we investigate the first two aspects, expanding the term set used for image location estimation and adding informative priors. We leave the third aspect for future work. Discussed next are the usage of terms extracted from a user's tweets and the usage of informative priors.

3.2.1 Terms Extracted from Tweets

The hypothesis we investigate in this work is that traces a user leaves on Twitter can aid us in estimating the geographic location of the user's images on Flickr. Location estimation based on an image's textual meta-data is based on the assumption that a user who uploads an image or video also spends some time on adding tags, possibly also a title and a description. Not every user though has the time or the patience to do this. In particular in instances where a user adds no or just very little extra information, we expect the user's traces on Twitter to be valuable.

On Twitter, users post short messages (tweets) with up to 140 characters about anything they choose. They can be followed by other users and themselves follow users in order to receive their tweets. Tweets can be directed (at *@user*) and tweets can contain hashtags (*#sigir2012* or *#portland*)[4]. The microblogging service Twitter was chosen due to its popularity and wide-spread use today. Given the date $\mathcal{D}$ (day, month, year) a test image $\Im$ was taken at, we extract the tweets by the user who posted the image to Flickr. We consider only those tweets by the user that were posted within d days of $\mathcal{D}$. After the removal of URLs and user names (*@user*), we are left with a bag-of-words $\mathcal{W}_\Im = \{w_1, ..., w_n\}$

[4]We also note, that Twitter allows tweets to be geo-tagged directly, though this feature is rarely enabled by users and only available when using Twitter from certain devices. In [4] only 0.42% of tweets were found to be geo-tagged.

The world regions are no longer only ranked according to their probability of generating the image tags (Equation 2), but also according to their probability of generating the twitter terms. In our implementation, we interpolate both scores for the final ranking of each world region. Formally:

$$P(\theta_R|T_{\Im}, \mathcal{W}_{\Im}) \propto P(\theta_R) \times \quad (4)$$

$$\left(\lambda \prod_{t_i \in T_{\Im}} P(t_i|\theta_R) + (1-\lambda) \prod_{w_i \in \mathcal{W}_{\Im}} P(w_i|\theta_R) \right) \quad (5)$$

Both, $P(t_i|\theta_R)$ and $P(w_i|\theta_R)$ are determined according to Equation 3. This interpolation approach naturally includes the original image-tag only approach when the parameter λ is set to $\lambda = 1.0$. Conversely, at $\lambda = 0.0$, the image tags of an image are ignored an only the terms extracted from the user's tweets are used to estimate $P(\theta_R|T_{\Im}, \mathcal{W}_{\Im})$.

We chose this interpolation approach due to its simplicity. More elaborate combinations of image tags and tweet terms will be investigated in future work. Note that the term filtering steps (Sec. 3.1.1), if employed, are now not only performed on terms $T_{\Im}$ but also on $\mathcal{W}_{\Im}$. This means effectively, that only a small number of terms that originate from a user's Twitter stream will be included in $\mathcal{W}_{\Im}$.

3.2.2 Region Priors

Instead of a uniform prior, we investigate two informative priors, one based on population information and one based on climate information.

In the case of the population based prior, which we base on the population density of a region, we hypothesize that images are more likely to be taken in areas of high population density than in areas of low population density. This intuitively makes sense, we would expect that people take more images in and around New York City than in the Great Victoria Desert of Australia[5], simply because a greater number of people live or visit the former than the latter. Given a set of places (towns, cities) $\wp = \{p_1, p_2, .., p_m\}$ with their geographic location and number of inhabitants (population pop), for each region R, we sum up the population of all places that are situated within R as well as of those places that are situated within a distance of 100km (according to the Haversine formula hs) of the region's center R_c. To avoid undue influence of major cities (with millions of inhabitants), we use the square root of the population. This yields the following population prior (Z is the normalization constant):

$$P_{pop}(\theta_R) = \frac{1}{Z} \times \left(1 + \sum_{\substack{p \in R \vee \\ hs(p,R_c) \leq 100km}} \sqrt{pop_p} \right).$$

As a second prior, we exploit climate data. Our assumption is that it is more likely that people live in or travel to regions with a moderate climate than regions of extreme weather conditions. We derived the climate prior by collecting a number of geo-tagged images and recording the average temperature in the region where the image was taken at the month the image was taken. We then fitted a Weibull distribution[24][6] to the data; this resulted in a prior which, given the climate (av. temperature) in a region R at month m returns the prior probability of an image being taken in R.

[5]On February 11, 2012, a search on `http://flickr.com` with the query "New York City" returned 3,672,535 results while the query "Great Victoria Desert" returned 115 images.

#Training data (in total)	3,195,474
#Training data with acc. $\geq$ 11	2,974,635
#Terms (data with acc. $\geq$ 11)	21,557,411
#Unique terms (data with acc. $\geq$ 11)	1,095,561

Table 1: Overview of training data.

4. EXPERIMENTAL SETUP

In Sec. 4.1 we first describe the training data and the setting of the parameters used to derive the language models of the world regions. Then, in Sec. 4.2 we introduce our methodology for deriving the test images and the Twitter messages belonging to the users who uploaded these images.

4.1 Training Data

We rely on a publicly available Flickr data set for training: the MediaEval 2011 Placing Task data set [20]. The MediaEval Placing Task data set is a benchmark that tackles the same question we address in this work, namely the estimation of the geographic location of an uploaded Flickr item. It consists of approximately 3.2 million Flickr images and 10,000 Flickr videos. Meta-data is provided for all training images and videos, including their geo-location as well as the accuracy with which they were geo-tagged. There are 16 accuracy levels, ranging from 1 (world level) to 16 (street level). We utilize all training items with accuracy 11 (city level) or higher. We indexed[7] all available tags (available for the images and videos) and title terms (videos only). Each image/video is considered to be a document and the tags and title terms are considered to be the document's content.

In preliminary experiments we found that an index which is neither stemmed nor has stopwords removed yields the best results. Table 1 provides the basic statistics of the index created from the training data.

4.2 Test Data

Although the MediaEval benchmark also provides a test set (a set of Flickr items for which to estimate their latitude/longitude), we created our own for two reasons:

- It is very difficult to determine for arbitrary Flickr users whether they have a Twitter account unless they provide it in their Flickr user profile.
- To investigate our approach, we need to consider a user's tweets for a substantial period of time as the average user does not take photos every day. Due to the limits imposed by the Twitter API, in our investigation we cannot for an arbitrary Twitter user retrieve all the user's tweets at once, only the most recent ones are available.

Taking the above limitations into account we derived our test data by considering an existing long-term Twitter data set (TWD) and finding matching Flickr accounts. In previous work [2] the TWD data set was created by monitoring

[6]We chose this distribution as empirically it yielded the best fit to the data.

[7]For indexing and retrieval we utilized the Lemur Toolkit, `http://lemurproject.org/`.

the tweets posted by 21,102 users over a period of eleven months (November 2010 to September 2011). Having access to such a long term profile of users suits our purposes very well. The question then remains for us, how to determine the Flickr accounts of these users (if they have one).

We approached this issue in two ways: (i) by performing a crawl of the social Web aggregator site FriendFeed and (ii) by manually assessing a subsets of the tweets posted by these users.

First, we conducted a crawl of FriendFeed[8], a social Web aggregator website, which allows users to create a unified feed of the entries on the social Web across a multitude of platforms including Twitter and Flickr. We started the extraction process with one highly connected FriendFeed user and crawled the profiles of all his subscribers and subscriptions. This process was conducted recursively, until no further profiles were discovered. In total, we found 444,226 profiles with at least one public entry in the feed. Of those users, 14.69% have listed in their profiles (among others) at least one Twitter and one Flickr account. We matched these discovered FriendFeed users with a Twitter and Flickr account against the users in the TWD data set and found 131 FriendFeed profiles that listed one of the TWD Twitter accounts with at least 10 public tweets and 5 or more publicly accessible images in their Flickr stream.

As a second strategy, we consider the tweets of the TWD data set, accumulated within the first five month of monitoring and extracted all tweets containing the string "flickr.com". Our intuition is, that Twitter users who tweet a link to Flickr, are likely to tweet about their own Flickr account. Since this is an overly strong assumption, one of the paper's authors judged for each tweeted link whether it indeed links to the user's Flickr account. This could either be inferred from the text (e.g.,"Check out the pics of my recent trip to France") or from the similarity of the Twitter profile and the Flickr profile (same avatar image, the same or similar user name, etc.). Among the tweets we found 3,260 with a "flickr.com" string[9]. After manually investigating them, we found a total of 135 users in TWD that had tweeted their Flickr account and had posted at least 10 tweets and 5 images to Flickr.

The profiles found through these two approaches have little overlap. In total, our test data set consists of 252 users of whom we have recorded their Twitter as well as Flickr account. For these 252 users, we have collected a total of 1,892,168 tweets over the eleven month period. From the users' Flickr accounts we collected a total of 153,773 images, after filtering out batch uploads[10]. Not all images were taken within the eleven month time frame of our TWD data set and not all images contain latitude/longitude values. Table 2 shows the split of the Flickr image data: there are 7,477 images which were taken within the time frame and have a latitude/longitude of sufficient accuracy. Since for our evaluation we can only rely as ground truth on images for which we have a geo-location, we used these 7477 images as our test set of images.

[8]FriendFeed, `http://www.friendfeed.com/`

[9]Note, we did not expand shortened URLs such as `bit.ly`.

[10]We consider a set of images by the same user as a batch, if the images are identical in terms of assigned tags, the date (day/month/year) they were taken, the hour they were taken and the latitude and longitude.

#Non-batch images	153,773
of those:	
#Images within Nov '10-Sept '11	27,879
#Images with latitude/longitude	30,951
#Images within Nov '10-Sept '11 & latitude/longitude	7,477

Table 2: Flickr data set.

4.3 Parameter Settings & Runs

The following subsections describe the parameter settings and runs we investigate. We tuned the parameters for our experiments in a grid-search manner on the 5,347 test items that were provided for the MediaEval 2011 benchmark. There is no overlap to our test set. We found the following parameter settings to yield the best results with respect to the median distance error metric: indexing without stopword removal and without stemming, Dirichlet smoothing with $\mu = 10000$, $U = 2$ (filtering terms used by less than two users in the training data), $\theta_{geo} = 0.1$ (filtering terms with a geo-spread score above 0.1), $\ell_{split} = 5000$ and $\ell_{lat\_lng} = 0.01$. Apart from the geo-filtering, these settings were fixed in all experiments reported in the result section. For the sake of showing the influence of geographic scope filtering, we present results for both types: with geo-filtering and without geo-filtering.

In this setup, there are a total of 1786 non-empty world regions. The maximum extent in terms of latitude and longitude are 22.5 and 45.0 degrees respectively, in areas of the world map where the training data is extremely sparse. The most frequently occurring location in the training data (2834 items) was found to be at latitude/longitude 40.7/−73.9 (New York City, USA).

Baselines. We report the results for two runs: $BaseLine_{geo}$ and *BaseLine*. The first is our primary baseline (geographic spread filtering is employed), while in the latter case, the terms in $T_{\Im}$ are not geo-filtered. In both cases, the mixture parameter is $\lambda = 1$ (Equation 4), i.e. only the image tags ($T_{\Im}$) are utilized to estimate the images' location.

Terms Extracted from Tweets. For the Twitter-based approach (Sec 3.2.1), we extract all tweets from a given user's Twitter stream that were posted $\pm d$ days within the day the test image was taken on. For $d = 0$, we only consider tweets taken at the same day as the image's creation date and we label that run *SameDay*. We also tested $d = \{1, 2, 3, 5, 10, 20, .., 50\}$. Due to space constraints we only report the results for $d = \{2, 10, 20, 50\}$ (labelled *± 2 Days* for $d = 2$ and so on). Recall, that for instance $d = 2$ means that tweets of a total of five days are considered: the two days before the image was taken, the image creation date day itself and the two following days.

The extracted tweets are pre-processed: re-tweets are removed (we consider them as useful for inferring something about a user's interests but not about a user's travels or actions), URLs and *@names* are stripped. Apart from these steps, no further processing is performed. In particular, to align the Twitter-based $\mathcal{W}_{\Im}$ with our training data index, we performed neither stemming nor did we remove stopwords. If a user posts no tweets within the d days before/after the image's creation date, $\mathcal{W}_{\Im}$ will be empty.

	λ	Geo-Filter	1km	10km	50km	100km	1000km	ME km	With respect to $BaseLine_{geo}$ #Better	#Worse	#Same
$BaseLine_{geo}$	1.0	yes	7.24%	34.96%	48.64%	52.67%	61.35%	60.97	–	–	–
BaseLine	1.0	no	7.46%	27.87%	34.87%	36.32%	42.29%	2513.15	2521 $\Delta_{\overline{km}} = -1715$	3017 $\Delta_{\overline{km}} = +4941$	1939
					Informative Priors						
Population (Pop)	1.0	yes	7.10%	34.72%	48.40%	52.59%	70.43%	62.17	1015 $\Delta_{\overline{km}} = -4800$	252 $\Delta_{\overline{km}} = +248$	6210
Population	1.0	no	7.65%	28.25%	35.27%	36.55%	44.66%	2217.60	2692 $\Delta_{\overline{km}} = -1986$	3051 $\Delta_{\overline{km}} = +5276$	1734
Climate	1.0	yes	7.25%	34.98%	48.54%	52.54%	61.16%	60.97	460 $\Delta_{\overline{km}} = -2045$	48 $\Delta_{\overline{km}} = +4783$	6969
					Terms Extracted from Tweets Only						
±2 Days	0.0	yes	4.25%	16.91%	25.21%	28.97%	41.78%	1974.25	2360 $\Delta_{\overline{km}} = -4318$	4446 $\Delta_{\overline{km}} = +5402$	671
±2 Days	0.0	no	1.82%	4.47%	6.42%	8.40%	23.63%	5717.71	1557 $\Delta_{\overline{km}} = -3573$	5611 $\Delta_{\overline{km}} = +5836$	309
					Interpolation: Image Tags and Terms Extracted from Tweets						
SameDay	0.8	yes	9.21%	37.68%	54.09%	59.32%	70.27%	22.04	2064 $\Delta_{\overline{km}} = -4180$	742 $\Delta_{\overline{km}} = +2089$	4671
±2 Days	0.8	yes	9.03%	38.16%	54.66%	59.93%	71.18%	20.13	2180 $\Delta_{\overline{km}} = -4055$	848 $\Delta_{\overline{km}} = +1914$	4449
±10 Days	0.8	yes	8.53%	36.83%	53.98%	59.26%	70.74%	23.36	2355 $\Delta_{\overline{km}} = -3678$	1143 $\Delta_{\overline{km}} = +1967$	3979
±20 Days	0.8	yes	8.31%	36.72%	53.64%	58.84%	70.75%	27.34	2469 $\Delta_{\overline{km}} = -3681$	1353 $\Delta_{\overline{km}} = +2001$	3655
±50 Days	0.8	yes	8.48%	36.39%	51.97%	56.91%	68.02%	33.97	2464 $\Delta_{\overline{km}} = -3368$	1695 $\Delta_{\overline{km}} = +2340$	3320
					Combining Informative Priors with the Interpolation Approach						
±2 Days+Pop	0.8	yes	9.00%	37.87%	54.59%	59.62%	75.98%	20.92	2520 $\Delta_{\overline{km}} = -4245$	959 $\Delta_{\overline{km}} = +1756$	3998

Table 3: Overview of the results across different setups. The column *Geo-Filter* indicates whether the experiment was run on the geo-filtered term set only (yes) or on all terms (no) from $\mathcal{T}_{\Im}$ and/or $\mathcal{W}_{\Im}$. Column 2 contains the interpolation parameter λ. Three evaluation measures are reported: (i) the percentage of test images within $\{1, 10, 50, 100, 1000\}$km of the ground truth location in columns 4-8, (ii) the median error (ME) in kilometres in column 9, and, (iii) the number of test images that were located with better, worse or the same accuracy (columns 10-12) as $BaseLine_{geo}$. For the test images with better/worse accuracy than $BaseLine_{geo}$, we provide the average change in error distance in kilometres $\Delta_{\overline{km}}$ - it is negative when the error decreases and positive when the error increases. In total, the test set consists of 7477 images. In gray, improvements over $BaseLine_{geo}$ are shown for columns 4-9 (note that in column 9, a smaller error distance indicates a better performance).

Two types of runs are investigated, those with mixture parameter $\lambda = 0$ (only information from the tweets is utilized to estimate the image's location) and those with $0 < \lambda < 1$. For the bulk of the interpolation experiments we set $\lambda = 0.8$.

Region Priors. For the population based region prior, labelled *Population*, we utilize population data available from GeoNames[11]. It contains an overview of the latitude, longitude and population numbers for a total of 113,816 towns and cities across the world (places with more than 1,000 inhabitants). For the climate based region prior (labelled *Climate*), we collected 100,000 geo-tagged images from Flickr (no overlap with our training/test data) and determined the average temperature in the region on the month the image was taken by relying on global historical climate data available from the National Climatic Data Center[12]. It provides data from 7278 weather stations around the world. The majority of those images were taken at temperatures between 10° and 28° Celsius. The lowest and highest temperature found were −38° and 37° Celsius respectively. Since the Weibull distribution is only defined for positive values, we shifted the temperatures by +50 which resulted in a maximum likelihood fit of the Weibull distribution with parameters $\lambda = 68$ and $k = 9.578$.

4.4 Evaluation Measures

The accuracy of estimating the geographic location of images is commonly evaluated by reporting the percentage of test items whose estimated location is within a distance of x kilometres (km) according to the Haversine formula from the ground truth geographic location of the image. As in [21, 23], we report the accuracy for different ranges of x: $\{1, 10, 50, 100, 1000\}$km. We also report the median error distance (ME) in kilometres, that is, the error distance that no more than half of the test items exceed.

Additionally, we introduce two more measurements: to offer a comparison to the primary baseline $BaseLine_{geo}$ which we attempt to improve upon, we report the number of test images for which the adapted approach performed better (i.e. the error distance decreased), worse (the error distance

[11] The data is available at `http://download.geonames.org/export/dump/cities1000.zip`, accessed 09/2011.

[12] The data is available at `ftp://ftp.ncdc.noaa.gov/pub/data/ghcn/v3/`, accessed 09/2011.

increased) or exactly the same as the baseline. We also determine the average change in error distance in kilometres ($\Delta_{\overline{km}}$) for the test items that perform better or worse than $BaseLine_{geo}$. A positive change indicates that the error distance *increases* on average by $\Delta_{\overline{km}}$ kilometres, while a negative change indicates that the error distance *decreases* on average by $\Delta_{\overline{km}}$ kilometres.

5. RESULTS

We first discuss the main results and then turn to investigation particular parameters and particular subsets of the test images.

The main results of our experiments are reported in Table 3. For each run, the interpolation parameter is given and it is indicated whether geographic spread based filtering was employed. Shown in gray are improvements over $BaseLine_{geo}$ for the distance cut-off evaluation measures and the median error.

To give an example of how to interpret the numbers, we compare the two baselines now in detail: both, *BaseLine* and $BaseLine_{geo}$ neither include informative priors nor information derived from tweets (thus, $\lambda = 1$). When comparing the results across the various distance cut-offs, the influence of the geo-spread filtering on the accuracy becomes visible. While at the 1km cut-off there is little difference between the two runs, at the 50km cut-off already, $BaseLine_{geo}$ outperforms *BaseLine* considerably with 48.6% accuracy compared to 34.9% of *BaseLine*. The results are similar for the median error distance in kilometres: while for $BaseLine_{geo}$, the median error is 61km, the median error increases to 2513km for *BaseLine*. However, not all test images are estimated with a greater accuracy when geo-filtering is employed. In fact, for 2521 test images *BaseLine* yields a more accurate estimate than $BaseLine_{geo}$. Conversely, for 3017 test images, $BaseLine_{geo}$ yields better estimation than *BaseLine*. These numbers do not explain the big difference observed in median error though; for this reason, we also report the average change in error distance $\Delta_{\overline{km}}$. For the 2521 test images, *BaseLine* outperforms $BaseLine_{geo}$, the error decreases on average by 1715km, whereas for the 3017 test images where *BaseLine* performs worse than $BaseLine_{geo}$, the error increases by 4941km on average.

Informative Priors. Next, let us consider the impact of the informative priors in Table 3. Since these priors are determined over regions (which may span hundreds of kilometres), we do not expect an impact in accuracy in the 1-100km error distance cut-offs. If we however consider the accuracy within 1000km, the population based prior improves considerably over the baseline: while $BaseLine_{geo}$ achieves 61.4% accuracy, adding a population based prior yields 70.4% accuracy. For the 1015 test images that yield a decreased error with this prior, the error distance decreases on average by 4800km, while for the 252 test images that yield a larger error in this setup, the error distances increases on average by only 248km. The climate prior on the other hand has very little effect overall. One reason could be, that monthly average temperatures do not not provide a signal that is fine-grained enough.

Terms Extracted From Tweets. Let us now turn to the main research question of this paper: can the accuracy of estimating the geographic location of images be improved when taking the user's utterances on Twitter in the same time period into account? We first discuss a set of experiments where the information provided in the image tags was ignored and only the terms extracted from the user's Twitter stream is exploited, i.e., $\lambda = 0$. We report the results for $d = 2$, as this setting resulted in the highest accuracy in our experiments. We present the results both for runs with and without geo-filtering employed. When geo-filtering is not applied to $\mathcal{W}_{\Im}$, the accuracy of the estimation is extremely poor with a median error of 5718km. When geo-filtering is employed, the results improve, though the median error is still high at 1974km compared to $BaseLine_{geo}$. These results can be explained by the fact that users do not exclusively tweet about their personal experiences and actions but may also comment on news. We note, that again, there are test images which benefit from relying on Twitter information instead of image tags: 2360 test images have a lower error distance when using Twitter terms compared to $BaseLine_{geo}$.

While relying on Twitter alone to estimate an image's location overall does not yield an improved accuracy, the information contained in a user's Twitter stream is very helpful when combined with the textual meta-data obtained from the image. Consider the results that interpolate both sources with $\lambda = 0.8$. Across a range of time periods, the accuracy in all distance cut-offs increases and the median error decreases with respect to $BaseLine_{geo}$. Overall, the best setting is to consider tweets that were posted up to two days before and after the time the image was taken at: at the 1km cut-off, the accuracy improves from 7.2% to 9%, at 50km the accuracy improves from 48.6% to 54.7% and at the 100km cut-off the accuracy increases again from 52.7% to 59.9%. The median error on the other hand decreases sharply from 61km to 20.1km. Including tweets from a wider time interval (more than two days before and after the image was taken), decreases the accuracy again, though the results are still outperforming $BaseLine_{geo}$. When considering the split of the test images into better/worse/same as $BaseLine_{geo}$, we notice that the inclusion of a wider set of tweets increases the number of test images that either benefit or are harmed by the inclusion of the Twitter data. This is to be expected, since not all images had tweets that were posted within d days of the time the image was taken.

Combining Priors and Twitter Terms. Finally, we consider a combination of the well performing population density based prior and the best performing Twitter setup ($d = 2$, $\lambda = 0.8$). The result of this combination is shown in the last row in Table 3. Recall, that we can only expect the prior to influence the accuracy at the 1000km cut-off. The results show that indeed at the 1000km cut-off using the informative prior increases the accuracy, from 71.2% (run ±2 Days) to 76%.

In Figure 1 we present an overview of the total number of *unique* terms used to estimate the locations of the 7477 test images. In case of *BaseLine*, for instance, all 5600 unique terms found as tags within the test images are utilized, whereas in the case of $BaseLine_{geo}$, 466 unique terms remain after employing geo-filtering. Shown is also the development of including Twitter terms from various days: the vast majority of terms are considered to be non-geographic and thus they do not play a role. The number of geographic terms for instance for ±2 *Days* is 1983, compared with 41,101 unique terms that are not geographic in scope (this high number is the result of neither employing stemming nor stopwording).

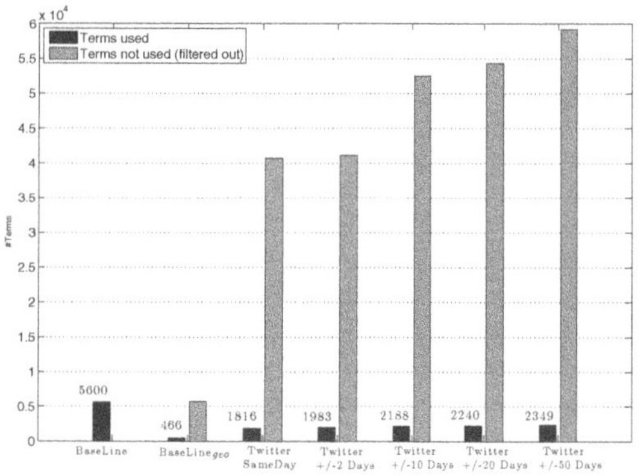

Figure 1: Number of *unique* terms appearing in the tags of the 7477 test images.

5.1 Interpolation Parameter λ

In the results just described, we had fixed $\lambda = 0.8$ for the interpolation experiments. We chose this value as it gave robust results across a range of settings. Now, we only consider the best performing setup ($\pm$ *2 Days*) and plot the results when λ is varied from 0 (no Twitter information is used) to 1 (no image information is used) in steps of 0.1. In Figure 2 we show the development of the accuracy for 1km and 50km. Please note that the two y-axes are on different scales: on the left (right), the results for the 1km (50km) distance cut-off are shown. The horizontal lines indicate the accuracies of $BaseLine_{geo}$ ($\lambda = 1$) for both cut-offs.

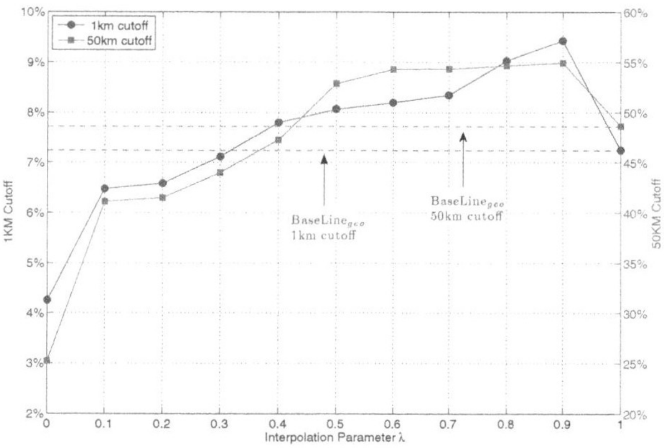

Figure 2: Interpolation parameter λ varied from $[0, 1]$ in steps of 0.1. Results are shown for $\pm$*2 Days* with $\lambda = 0.8$ and geo-filtering employed. Note, the y-axes are on different scales.

The increase in accuracy is similar for both evaluation measures, at $\lambda > 0.3$ (1km cut-off) and at $\lambda > 0.4$ (50km cut-off), the interpolation approach outperforms the baseline. For this particular setup, $\lambda = 0.9$ yields the most accurate results with 55% of the test images being placed within 50km of their true location (compared to 49% in $BaseLine_{geo}$).

5.2 What Images Benefit from $\mathcal{W}_{\Im}$?

Finally, we turn to the question of what images do (not) benefit from adding information from the user's Twitter stream. We consider two dimensions: (i) the number of tags

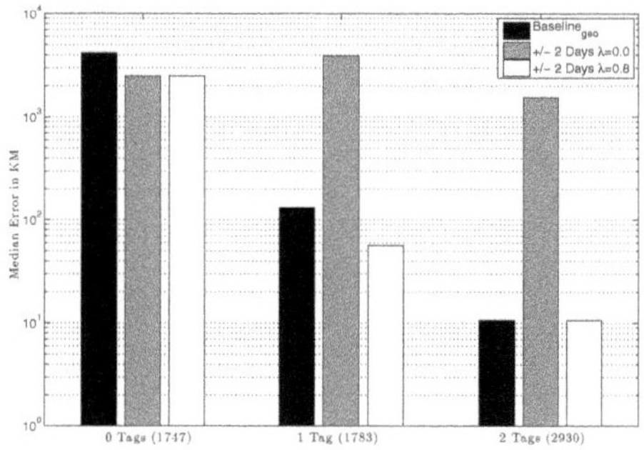

Figure 3: Test set split according to the number of tags $T_{\Im}$ *after* employing geo-filtering. Compared are $BaseLine_{geo}$ ($\lambda = 1$), $\pm$*2 Days* with $\lambda = 0$ and $\pm$*2 Days* with $\lambda = 0.8$. In brackets, the size of each partition is shown.

in $T_{\Im}$ after applying geographic scope filtering, and, (ii) the distance of the image from the user's home location.

Number of Tags. To investigate the impact of the number of tags on the estimation accuracy, we plotted the median error in kilometres for different settings in Figure 3 for the three cases of a test image having 0, 1 or 2 tags in $T_{\Im}$. Please note, that the plot is on a logarithmic scale (y-axis) and that we consider the size of $T_{\Im}$ *after* having employed geographic scope filtering.

Let us first focus on $BaseLine_{geo}$. As can be expected, if no tags are present, the median error distance is highest (with 4142km), as either the most frequent location in the training data is assigned to the test image or, if available, the user's home location is added to $T_{\Im}$. Since the given home location may be geographically ambiguous (.e.g.,"Perth" may refer to a city in Australia or the UK), underspecified (e.g.,"USA") or plainly inaccurate (e.g.,"Mars"), there is often little additional value in it. If one tag is available, the median error distance decreases to 131km, at $|T_{\Im}| = 2$, the median error has fallen to 11km. The interpolation approach $\pm$*2 Days* with $\lambda = 0.8$ improves over $BaseLine_{geo}$ if $T_{\Im}$ contains either zero or one tag only. At zero tags, the median error distance decreases by 40%, for the test images with one tag, the median error decreases by 57%.

For the cases where $|T_{\Im}| \geq 3$, adding information from a user's Twitter stream does not yield any more improvement in accuracy. This confirms our original hypothesis: extracting terms from a user's tweets is valuable for images which contain less than three tags (after geographic filtering).

Distance to Home Location. In [4] it was found that a user's home location can be estimated based on the user's tweets. In our experiments we found that even if tweets from a large number of days ($\pm$50) around the test images are used to extract terms for $\mathcal{W}_{\Im}$, the results still improve over $BaseLine_{geo}$. One potential explanation is that this Twitter based information enables us to mostly estimate those images, that are close to a user's home location with greater accuracy. To evaluate this hypothesis we conducted the following analysis. We manually transcribed/disambiguated the home location that the users who contributed the test images gave on their Flickr profile and description fields and converted them into latitude/longitude. For 4515 of the test images, we could determine the corresponding user's home lo-

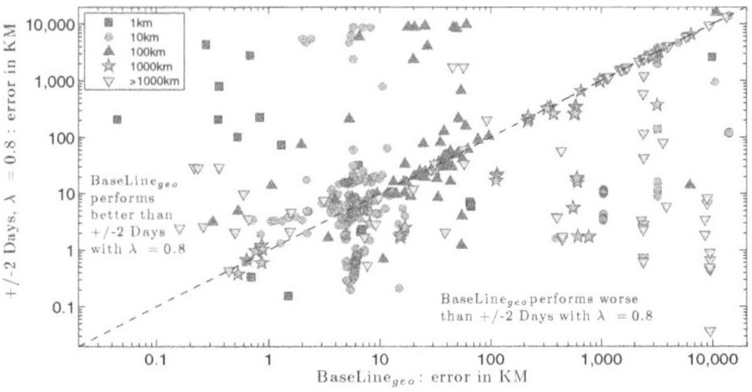

Figure 4: Scatter plot with test data split according to the distance, the images were taken at with respect to the corresponding user's home location. Each marker stands for one image.

cation with city level accuracy. We then removed all images where *BaseLine$_{geo}$* and the run ± 2 *Days* ($\lambda = 0.8$) yield the same error distance. The remaining 1330 images were partitioned according to how far away from the user's home location they were taken: within $\{1, 10, 100, 1000, > 1000\}$km of the user's home location.

In Figure 4 we show a scatter plot for these 1330 images: the error in kilometres at *BaseLine$_{geo}$* vs. the error at ± 2 *Days* ($\lambda = 0.8$). The images belonging to each partition are marked with different markers/colors. Many images were taken within 100km of the respective users' home location. While for these types of images, adding information from a user's Twitter stream sometimes improves and sometimes decreases the error, a clearer pictures emerges for images that were taken a greater distance from the user's home location: the the vast majority of images improve when utilizing information extracted from Twitter.

6. CONCLUSIONS

In this paper, we have presented an approach to image location estimation that exploits a user's traces on the social Web across platforms. We hypothesized that information extracted from a person's Twitter stream can be utilized to improve the accuracy of the image location estimation. Our investigation was motivated by the fact that people often tweet about themselves, and it is likely that they post messages which refer to their activities or travels. Furthermore, we investigated the usage of informative priors, based on population data and on climate data. We developed an extension to an existing state-of-the-art tag-based approach to location estimation [21] which is based on the language modeling framework for information retrieval. Our extension makes it possible to exploit the information extracted from the user's tweets in a natural way. In this work, we presented a number of findings:

- Exploiting a person's Twitter stream when estimating the location of an image decreases the median error distance by up to 67% in comparison to a state-of-the-art approach. The best results are obtained when tweets within two days before and after the image was taken are exploited.
- Images, that were assigned less than two tags after geographic scope filtering (Sec. 3.1.1), benefit the most from terms extracted from Twitter. Specifically, we showed a 40% (57%) decrease in median error distance for images without tags (with a single tag).
- We also investigated the value of informative priors in the language modeling approach. The population density prior improves the accuracy of the location estimation.

These results leave a lot of potential for future work. One possibility is to not only consider the traces a user leaves on Twitter, but also on other social Web platform such as Facebook or LinkedIn. Another area of future work is to classify users' tweets as either being about personal experiences and activities or about local vs. global news: tweets discussing global news (e.g. *"Japan announced meltdown yesterday; situation grim."*) are often adding noise for our purposes, while tweets discussing local news (e.g. *"Here in Toronto the police made multiple arrests today"*) are useful as they can serve as indicators of the user's home location. Lastly, we also consider an investigation into the similarities/differences between (estimated) travel patterns of different users and user groups an interesting avenue of further work.

7. REFERENCES

[1] F. Abel, S. Araújo, Q. Gao, and G.-J. Houben. Analyzing cross-system user modeling on the social web. In *ICWE '11*, pages 28–43, 2011.

[2] F. Abel, Q. Gao, G.-J. Houben, and K. Tao. Analyzing user modeling on Twitter for personalized news recommendations. In *UMAP '11*, pages 1–12, 2011.

[3] F. Abel, N. Henze, E. Herder, and D. Krause. Interweaving public user profiles on the web. In *UMAP '10*, pages 16–27, 2010.

[4] Z. Cheng, J. Caverlee, and K. Lee. You are where you tweet: a content-based approach to geo-locating twitter users. In *CIKM '10*, pages 759–768, 2010.

[5] J. Choi, A. Janin, and G. Friedland. The 2010 ICSI Video Location Estimation System. In *MediaEval 2010 Workshop*, 2010.

[6] M. Clements, P. Serdyukov, A. P. de Vries, and M. J. T. Reinders. Finding wormholes with flickr geotags. In *ECIR '10*, pages 658–661, 2010.

[7] M. Clements, P. Serdyukov, A. P. de Vries, and M. J. T. Reinders. Using flickr geotags to predict user travel behaviour. In *SIGIR '10*, pages 851–852, 2010.

[8] M. De Choudhury, M. Feldman, S. Amer-Yahia, N. Golbandi, R. Lempel, and C. Yu. Automatic construction of travel itineraries using social breadcrumbs. In *HT '10*, pages 35–44, 2010.

[9] C. Hauff and G.-J. Houben. Geo-location estimation of flickr images: Social web based enrichment. In *ECIR '12*, pages 85–96, 2012.

[10] T. Hofmann. Probabilistic latent semantic analysis. In *UAI âĂŹ99*, pages 289–296, 1999.

[11] T. Iofciu, P. Fankhauser, F. Abel, and K. Bischoff. Identifying users across social tagging systems. In *ICWSM '11*, 2011.

[12] A. Java, X. Song, T. Finin, and B. Tseng. Why we twitter: understanding microblogging usage and communities. In *9th WebKDD / 1st SNA-KDD 2007 Workshop on Web mining and Social Network Analysis*, pages 56–65, 2007.

[13] P. Kelm, S. Schmiedeke, and T. Sikora. Multi-modal, multi-resource methods for placing flickr videos on the map. In *ICMR '11*, pages 52:1–52:8, 2011.

[14] S. Kinsella, V. Murdock, and N. OHare. "i'm eating a sandwich in glasgow": Modeling locations with tweets. In *SMUC '11*, pages 759–768, 2011.

[15] V. Lavrenko and W. B. Croft. Relevance based language models. In *SIGIR '01*, pages 120–127, 2001.

[16] X. Lu, Y. Pang, Q. Hao, and L. Zhang. Visualizing textual travelogue with location-relevant images. In *LBSN '09*, pages 65–68, 2009.

[17] M. Lux and S. A. Chatzichristofis. Lire: lucene image retrieval: an extensible java cbir library. In *MM '08*, pages 1085–1088, 2008.

[18] M. Naaman, J. Boase, and C.-H. Lai. Is it really about me?: message content in social awareness streams. In *CSCW '10*, pages 189–192, 2010.

[19] J. Ponte and W. B. Croft. A language modeling approach to information retrieval. In *SIGIR '98*, pages 275–281, 1998.

[20] A. Rae, V. Murdock, P. Serdyukov, and P. Kelm. Working Notes for the Placing Task at MediaEval 2011. In *MediaEval 2011 Workshop*, 2011.

[21] P. Serdyukov, V. Murdock, and R. van Zwol. Placing flickr photos on a map. In *SIGIR '09*, pages 484–491, 2009.

[22] O. Van Laere, S. Schockaert, and B. Dhoedt. Combining multi-resolution evidence for georeferencing Flickr images. In *SUM '10*, pages 347–360, 2010.

[23] O. Van Laere, S. Schockaert, and B. Dhoedt. Finding locations of flickr resources using language models and similarity search. In *ICMR '11*, pages 48:1–48:8, 2011.

[24] W. Weibull. A statistical distribution function of wide applicability. *J. Appl. Mech.-Trans. ASME*, 18(3):293–297, 1951.

[25] B. P. Wing and J. Baldridge. Simple supervised document geolocation with geodesic grids. In *Proceedings of the 49th Annual Meeting of the Association for Computational Linguistics: Human Language Technologies - Volume 1*, pages 955–964, 2011.

[26] C. Zhai and J. Lafferty. A study of smoothing methods for language models applied to ad hoc information retrieval. In *SIGIR '01*, pages 334–342, 2001.

[27] C. Zhai and J. Lafferty. Two-stage language models for information retrieval. In *SIGIR '02*, pages 49–56, 2002.

[28] D. Zhao and M. B. Rosson. How and why people twitter: the role that micro-blogging plays in informal communication at work. In *GROUP '09*, pages 243–252, 2009.

Where Is Who: Large-Scale Photo Retrieval by Facial Attributes and Canvas Layout

Yu-Heng Lei, Yan-Ying Chen, Bor-Chun Chen, Lime Iida, Winston H. Hsu
National Taiwan University, Taipei, Taiwan
{ryanlei, yanying}@cmlab.csie.ntu.edu.tw,
{siriushpa, limeiida}@gmail.com, winston@csie.ntu.edu.tw

ABSTRACT

The ubiquitous availability of digital cameras has made it easier than ever to capture moments of life, especially the ones accompanied with friends and family. It is generally believed that most family photos are with faces that are sparsely tagged. Therefore, a better solution to manage and search in the tremendously growing personal or group photos is highly anticipated. In this paper, we propose a novel way to search for face photos by simultaneously considering attributes (e.g., gender, age, and race), positions, and sizes of the target faces. To better match the content and layout of the multiple faces in mind, our system allows the user to graphically specify the face positions and sizes on a query "canvas," where each attribute combination is defined as an icon for easier representation. As a secondary feature, the user can even place specific faces from the previous search results for appearance-based retrieval. The scenario has been realized on a tablet device with an intuitive touch interface. Experimenting with a large-scale Flickr[1] dataset of more than 200k faces, the proposed formulation and joint ranking have made us achieve a hit rate of 0.420 at rank 100, significantly improving from 0.036 of the prior search scheme using attributes alone. We have also achieved an average running time of 0.0558 second by the proposed block-based indexing approach.

Categories and Subject Descriptors

H.3.3 [**Information Search and Retrieval**]: Query formulation; H.5.2 [**User Interfaces**]: Input devices and strategies

[1]All of the face images presented in this paper except for those by Google Image Search in Fig. 2 (b) and Fig. 4 attribute to various Flickr users under a Creative Commons License.

SIGIR'12, August 12–16, 2012, Portland, Oregon, USA.

Figure 1: Example queries and top 5 retrieval results from our photo search system. (a) specifies two arbitrary faces with the larger one on the left and the smaller one on the right. (b) further constrains that the left face has attributes "female" and "youth" and the right face has attribute "kid." (c) specifies two faces of "male" and "African" on the left and right, in addition to an arbitrary face on the center. (d) specifies a particular face in the database at the desired position and in the desired size. (e) specifies the previous database face on the left, and a face of "female" and "youth" on the right.

Keywords

Face attributes, Face retrieval, Touch-based user interface, Block-based indexing

1. INTRODUCTION

The ubiquitous availability of digital cameras has made it easier than ever to capture moments of life, especially the ones accompanied with friends and family. It is generally believed that most family photos are with faces that are sparsely tagged. Therefore, a better solution to manage and search in the tremendously growing personal or group photos is highly anticipated.

Psychology research in perception shows that images with certain kinds of subjects attract more attention of the eyes [8]. Among these subjects, human faces are the most memorable, followed by images of human-scale space and close-ups of objects [11]. The phenomena becomes more obvious in consumer photos because most of them contain family

Figure 2: Illustration of searching for a face image that the user remembers. The search intention is indicated in the cloud icon in (a), where there are a boy's face on the left and a larger girl's face on the top right of it. Four types of approaches are shown. (b) is Google's text-based image search with advanced options of searching only face images. (c) is facial-attribute-based image search with text-based queries, similar to the scheme proposed by [15]. (d) is image search based on face positions and face sizes. (e) is performed by simultaneously considering facial attributes, face positions, and face sizes. Images squared in green solid lines (blue dashed lines) are believed to be highly (partially) relevant by an average user. The results in (e) best match the search intention, showing the power of multimodal fusion in retrieval systems.

members or close friends that the user cares about and usually keeps in mind. Therefore, they are able to make use of the face content and the face layout that they remember to effectively formulate their search intentions. Furthermore, viewing the retrieved images probably recalls more scenes in the user's memory, so they expect to be able to refine their query interactively. For example, "viewing a photo of Alice standing next to me, it reminds me of another photo with an African kid sitting in the middle of us." Although consumer photos generally lack annotations, automatic face analysis techniques would make the scenario economical and scalable.

In this paper, we propose a novel system for searching consumer photos by automatically analyzing "wild photos" (without tag information at all) through facial attribute detection (Sec. 4.1) and appearance similarity estimation (Sec. 4.2). To better match the content and layout of the multiple faces in mind, rather than laboriously sketching detailed outline or typing text, our system allows the user to graphically specify the face positions and sizes on a query "canvas," where each attribute combination is defined as an icon for easier representation. The query can be simply finding arbitrary faces in the desired layout (Fig. 1 (a)), or further constrained by facial attributes (Fig. 1 (b) and (c)). As a secondary feature, the user can even place specific faces from the previous search results for appearance-based retrieval (Fig. 1 (d)), combined with other attributed faces (Fig. 1 (e)). Other complicated search intentions also apply.

The scenario has been realized on a tablet device with an intuitive touch interface where the user can easily refine their query by interacting with the real-time search results. To provide effective matching in a large-scale Flickr dataset of more than 200k faces, the proposed formulation and joint ranking have made us achieve a hit rate of 0.420 at rank 100, significantly improving from 0.036 of the search scheme proposed by [15] using attributes alone. To provide efficient retrieval, we have also achieved an average running time of 0.0558 second by the proposed block-based indexing approach. The numbers are scalable to even larger photo collections.

The contributions of this paper are as follows:

- Propose the problem in how to formulate search intentions for face images as tangible search queries, i.e., by graphically specifying face content and layout on a query "canvas." We also provide an intuitive touch-based interface for refining the search results interactively.

- Propose a formulation for matching multiple faces between the query canvas and the target image (Sec. 5.1) and effectively match a single face by simultaneously considering attributes, appearances, positions, and sizes (Sec. 5.2).

- Propose a block-based indexing approach for efficient retrieval (Sec. 5.4).

2. OBSERVATIONS AND RELATED WORK

In this section, we review various query formulations and query modalities in image search systems and their applicabilities to face photo search. Fig. 2 is an illustration of such a scenario. The target image in the user's mind (Fig. 2 (a)) is a boy's face on the left and a larger girl's face on the top right of it. The user vaguely remembers the face content and layout, but not the exact image file in the collection.

Existing commercial image search engines mostly rely on matching the query keywords with the surrounding text or manual tags of the target images. Fig. 2 (b) is obtained by Google Image Search using the keywords "boy girl" with advanced options of searching only face images. Directly matching text not only reveals little about the image content, but in this particular case, it also happens to match the movie title "It's a Boy Girl Thing" and retrieves some irrelevant images in the scene. What's worse, tags are often inaccurate, incorrect, or ambiguous [12]. Due to the complex motivations behind tag usage [2], tags do not necessarily describe the content of an image [13].

In content-based image retrieval, Kumar [15] proposes facial attribute classification by SVM and AdaBoost, and uses the confidence scores for image retrieval. Fig. 2 (c) is produced in a similar way by enabling only the attribute modality in our system. The corresponding attributes specified are "male + kid" for boy and "female + kid" for girl. While the attributes (especially the age) are mostly correct, this approach does not consider the face layout in the user's mind at all. On the other hand, Fig. 2 (d) is produced by enabling only the position and size modalities in our system. While the face layouts are highly relevant due to accurate face detection, this approach does not consider about the face content. To utilize both the content and layout information, Fig. 2 (e) is produced by the full version of our system that combines all of these three modalities. The results in Fig. 2 (e) best match the user's search intention in terms of finding highly relevant (squared in green solid lines) and partially relevant (squared in blue dashed lines) images. The above illustration shows the power of multimodal fusion in retrieval systems.

Some efforts also attempt to capture the user's search intention by visually describing both the image content and layout on a query canvas. Thanks to the growing popularity of touch devices, it has become more intuitive and convenient than ever to formulate such queries. [3] revisits the problem of sketch-based image search for scene photos. However, the gap between the user's mind and their specified query can still be large even in such a system. For instance, users with poor drawing skills may have a hard time describing their intention accurately. In addition, some object details are naturally difficult to sketch, and many concepts are even more difficult to describe by sketching, such as the age of a face. Therefore, the practicability of sketch-based retrieval for photo management is questionable, especially for face photos.

To deal with this sketching difficulty, [19] allows the user to formulate a 2-D "semantic map" by placing text boxes of various search concepts at desired positions and in desired sizes. However, it is intended for generic objects, not for faces of different individuals. To apply to face photo management, [14] also allows the user to specify face positions, and face sizes on a canvas. These faces are further described by tagging names and even drawing social relationships [17]. However, non of these efforts proposes an efficient indexing method for large-scale photo retrieval. Meanwhile, typing text is not the most intuitive operation on touch devices even though these efforts aim for better user experience.

Specifically for photo management, some commercial services (e.g., Picasa [18] and iPhoto [10]) that exploit face recognition technologies to help face annotation in a semi-supervised or supervised manner have been shown promising. However, people are mostly reluctant to annotate their photos, especially when photos are taken enormously due to the ubiquitous availability of digital cameras. Also, many of consumer photos are group photos, which makes the face annotation task even more tedious. In our work, we further consider spatial layout, attributes, and appearance for face photo retrieval. We believe it can be complementary[2] to existing face annotation solutions.

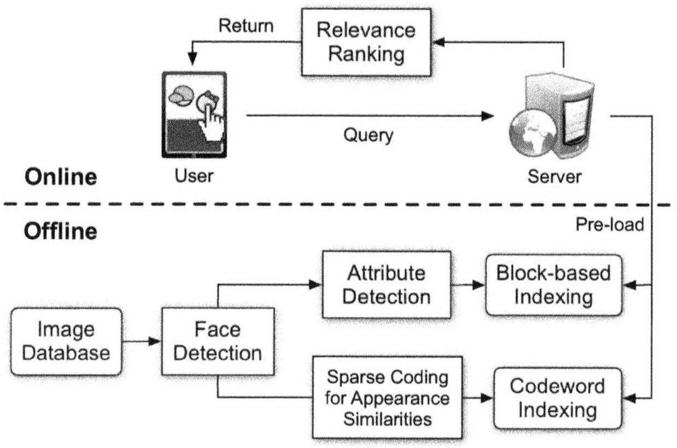

Figure 3: An overview of our proposed system. Photos are analyzed offline through face detection, facial attribute detection, and sparse coding for appearance similarities. The results are incorporated into the proposed block-based index and codeword index for efficient retrieval.

3. SYSTEM OVERVIEW

Fig. 3 is an overview of our proposed system named "Where is Who." In the offline process, the image database first goes through face detection to identify and locate frontal faces in the images. These faces are then analyzed through facial attribute detection (Sec. 4.1) and sparse coding for appearance similarities (Sec. 4.2). Finally, the attribute scores along with the position and size information are incorporated into the block-based index (Sec. 5.4). The sparse codes of faces are also stored in the codeword index. These indices are pre-loaded for rapid online response. In the online process, the server retrieves candidate images in inverted lists, ranks them by relevance (Sec. 5.2), and returns the search results back to the user. Note that appearance-based retrieval is treated as a secondary feature and is not evaluated throughout this paper.

4. IMAGE ANALYSIS

4.1 Detecting Facial Attributes

Facial attributes possess rich information about people and have been shown promising for seeking specific persons

[2]Face recognition or face annotation information can be exploited as another source of the "face content" considered in this work.

Table 1: The 3 attribute types and 8 corresponding attributes detected in our system.

Type	Attribute
Gender	male, female
Age	kid, youth, elder
Race	Caucasian, Asian, African

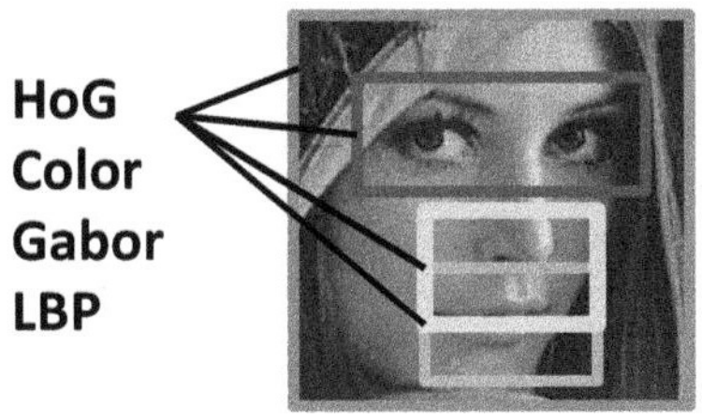

Figure 4: For each of the four face components (whole face, eyes, nose, and mouth), four low-level features (HoG, grid color moments, Gabor, and LBP) are extracted. Each of 16 combinations (e.g., <mouth, LBP>) is treated as a mid-level feature for which an SVM is learned.

in face retrieval and surveillance systems. In this work, we utilize 8 facial attributes (Table 1) including 2 of gender (male, female), 3 of age (kid, youth, elder) and 3 of race (Caucasian, Asian, African) to profile faces in large-scale photos.

In the training phase, each attribute classifier is learned separately through a combination of Support Vector Machines (SVMs) and Adaboost [9] similar to [15]. Firstly, we crawl user-contributed photos from Flickr and extract facial regions by a face detector. The face images are annotated manually with positive and negative class labels. As illustrated in Fig. 4, the faces are then automatically decomposed into four different face components, i.e., whole face, eyes, nose, and mouth. From each of these components, four low-level features, i.e., histogram of oriented gradients (HoG) [6], grid color moments, Gabor filter, and local binary patterns (LBP) [1] are extracted.

A mid-level feature learned is an SVM with a specific low-level feature extracted from a specific face component, e.g., an SVM for <mouth, LBP>. Finally, the optimal weighting of the 16 (4×4) mid-level features for this attribute is determined through Adaboost. The combined strong classifier represents the most important parts of that attribute. For example, <whole face, Gabor> is most effective for the female attribute while <whole face, color> is most effective for the African attribute.

Experimenting with the benchmark data [15], the approach can effectively detect facial attributes and achieve an accuracy of more than 80% on average. Meanwhile, the training framework is generic for various cases thus providing a potential to extend to more attributes[3].

4.2 Sparse Coding for Appearance Similarities

To enable search through face appearance, we adopt the face retrieval framework of [5]. The advantage of this framework includes: (1) efficiency, which is achieved by using sparse representations of face image with inverted indexing, and (2) leveraging identity information, which is done by incorporating the partially-tagged identity information into the optimization process of codebook construction. Both of the above two points are suitable for our system. In details, detected faces are first aligned into canonical position, and then component-based local binary patterns [1] are extracted from the images to form feature vectors. After feature extraction, sparse representations are computed from these feature vectors using an L1-regularized least square objective function. Non-zero entries of sparse representations are considered as visual words for inverted indexing.

[3]For example, the work of [16] has trained as many as 73 attribute classifiers.

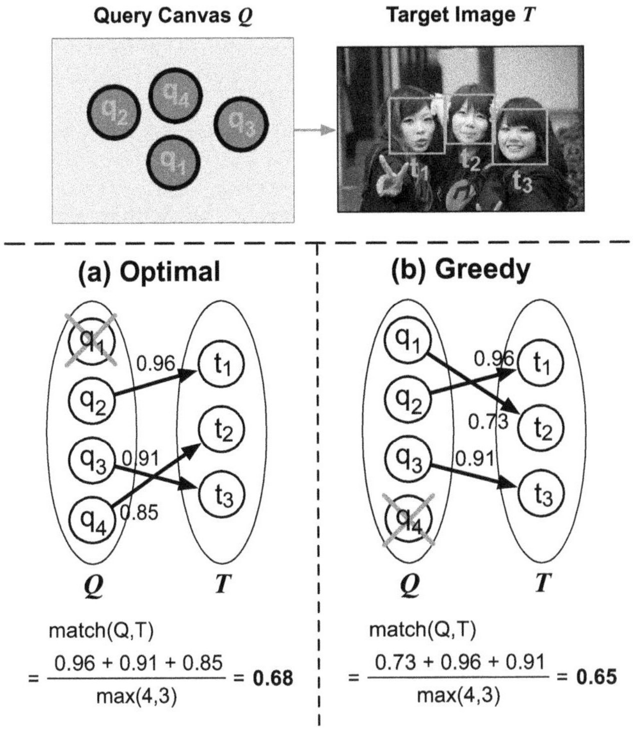

Figure 5: The image ranking problem as a maximum weighted bipartite matching between the query canvas (set Q) and the target image (set T). The numbering in the query canvas implies the order in which the faces are specified. The optimization in Eq. 1 can be carried out by (a) the optimal solution or (b) the greedy approximation. A red cross indicates a mismatched face, and $match(Q, T)$ means the overall matching score between Q and T.

Due to the nature of faces, images of the same individual may have high intra-class variation. To leverage the partially-tagged identity information, a regularization term is added to the objective function to force images of the same identity (tag) to have similar sparse representations. These images will propagate visual words to each other, and the query image will be able to find all images of the same individual if it is similar to at least one of them.

By incorporating such framework into our system, in addition to attributes, the user can also use a face image itself as the face content.

5. IMAGE RETRIEVAL

5.1 Problem Formulation

5.1.1 Maximum Weighted Bipartite Matchings

As illustrated in Fig. 5, for a (query canvas, target image) pair, denoted as (Q, T), the image ranking problem is formulated as a maximum weighted bipartite matching between the two sets Q and T. The objective function $match(Q, T)$, or the overall matching score between Q and T, is defined as the sum of the individual face matching scores $match(q, t)$ (defined in Sec. 5.2) divided by $\max(|Q|, |T|)$. The formulation is as the following constraint optimization problem:

$$match(Q,T) = \frac{\max\left[\sum_{q\in Q}\sum_{t\in T} match(q,t)\delta(q,t)\right]}{\max(|Q|,|T|)} \quad (1)$$

$$\text{subject to: } \delta(q,t) \in \{0,1\} \qquad \forall q \in Q, t \in T \quad (2a)$$

$$\sum_{t\in T}\delta(q,t) \le 1 \qquad \forall q \in Q \quad (2b)$$

$$\sum_{q\in Q}\delta(q,t) \le 1 \qquad \forall t \in T \quad (2c)$$

$$match(q,t) > 0 \qquad \forall q \in Q, t \in T \quad (2d)$$

$$\delta(q,t) = \begin{cases} 1, & \text{if } (q,t) \text{ is matched} \\ 0, & \text{otherwise,} \end{cases} \quad (3)$$

where $\delta(q, t)$ (Eqs. 2a and 3) is an indicator variable of whether (q, t) is matched.

Note that the matching ensures each query face $q = q_1, ..., q_{|Q|}$ matches at most one target face $t = t_1, ..., t_{|T|}$ (Eq. 2b), and each t is matched at most once (Eq. 2c). We add the subscripts here to explicitly denote the individual faces in Q and T.

The numerator of Eq. 1 is the objective function in maximum weighted bipartite matchings. Note the $\max(|Q|, |T|)$ in the denominator. The positive weights (Eq. 2d) ensure that the number of matching pairs equals $\min(|Q|, |T|)$. If the numbers of faces in Q and T are the same, dividing by $|Q|$ or $|T|$ is like averaging. But if $|Q|$ and $|T|$ are different, the overall matching score will be divided by a larger number. Thus, this formulation much favors target images that have the same number of faces as the query canvas.

Fig. 5 shows an illustration of matching 4 query faces with 3 target faces. The optimal solution, by the above formulation, always comes up with the highest $match(Q, T)$ among all the possible matches. As in Fig. 5 (a), $match(Q, T) = 0.68$ for this example. However, computing the optimal solution (e.g., by the Bellman-Ford algorithm) is inefficient if we have to repeat for all target images.

5.1.2 Greedy Approximation

The inefficiency in solving Eq. 1 can be compromised by the proposed greedy approximation. By greedy, we mean the first query face q_1 is the first to match by choosing the best matching face remaining (i.e., the unmatched t^* for which $match(q_1, t^*)$ is maximized), followed by q_2, q_3, etc.. The numbering in Q implies the order in which the faces are specified on the query canvas. The procedure is summarized in Algorithm 1.

In the example of Fig. 5 (b), the greedy approximation allows the first query face q_1 to match first, choosing t_2 to get face matching score of 0.73. The second query face q_2 chooses t_1 of 0.96, followed by q_3 choosing the last target face t_3 remaining to get 0.91. q_4 then becomes a mismatched face (indicated by a red cross in Fig. 5 (b)), but it could have matched t_2 of 0.85 if specified in the first place. Eventually, $match(Q, T) = 0.65$ in the greedy approximation.

Algorithm 1 The procedure in greedy approximation.

Input: The query canvas Q and the target image T.
Output: The overall matching score $match(Q, T)$.

```
match(Q,T) ← 0
/* Maintain a remaining set R. */
R ← T
for q ← q_1, q_2, ..., q_|Q| do
    t* ← max_{t∈R} [match(q,t)]
    match(Q,T) ← match(Q,T) + match(q,t*)
    R ← R − {t*}
end for
match(Q,T) ← match(Q,T) / max(|Q|,|T|)
```

In general, although the greedy approximation has a lower $match(Q, T)$ than the optimal solution, it significantly reduces the computational cost and reflects the idea that the first face coming to the user's mind is the most important.

5.2 Face Matching Scores

Our work uses multimodal fusion to determine the face matching score $match(q, t)$ between a query face q and a target face t. It is defined as a linear combination of the matching scores for facial attributes, appearance similarity, face position, and face size:

$$\begin{aligned} match(q,t) = {} & w_{attr}\left(\prod_{\tau} Attr(q_\tau, t_\tau)\right)^{1/|\tau|} \\ & + w_{app}App(q,t) \\ & + w_{pos}Pos(q,t) + w_{size}Size(q,t) \end{aligned} \quad (4)$$

$$Attr(q_\tau, t_\tau) = \begin{cases} t_{\tau k}, & \text{if } q_\tau = k \\ 1.0, & \text{if } q_\tau = \text{not specified,} \end{cases} \quad (5)$$

where w_{attr}, w_{app}, w_{pos}, and w_{size} are the weights for these four modalities.

The first term in Eq. 4 weights the geometric mean of the matching scores $Attr(q_\tau, t_\tau)$ for all of the attribute types τ, i.e., gender, age, and race ($|\tau| = 3$). As in Eq. 5, if q_τ, or the attribute specification of the query face for type τ, is some attribute k, then $Attr(q_\tau, t_\tau) = t_{\tau k}$, the attribute score of k in type t. For instance, if q specifies the age "youth", then $Attr(q_{age}, t_{age})$ takes the attribute score for youth of t. In notation, if for τ = age, q_{age} = youth, then $Attr(q_{age}, t_{age}) = t_{age,youth}$.

In contrast, if for τ, the attribute is not specified, then $Attr(q_\tau, t_\tau) = 1.0$, the perfect score. The choice of geometric means rather than arithmetic means is to avoid outliers for some attribute type. The second term in Eq. 4 weights the appearance similarity score between q and t, obtained in Sec. 4.2. Note that in our user interface (Sec. 6.1), attributes and appearance similarity (by a specific face instance) of a query face are not specified at the same time.

5.3 Score Normalization

The real-valued scores of each of the four query modalities, that is, attributes, appearances, positions, and sizes, are normalized into the range (0, 1) for late fusion. 0 and 1 represent the worst score and the best score of a modality.

For an attribute score $t_{\tau k}$, we first normalize the strong classifier's output to zero mean and unit variance for each attribute k. Then we apply a sigmoid function to map it to

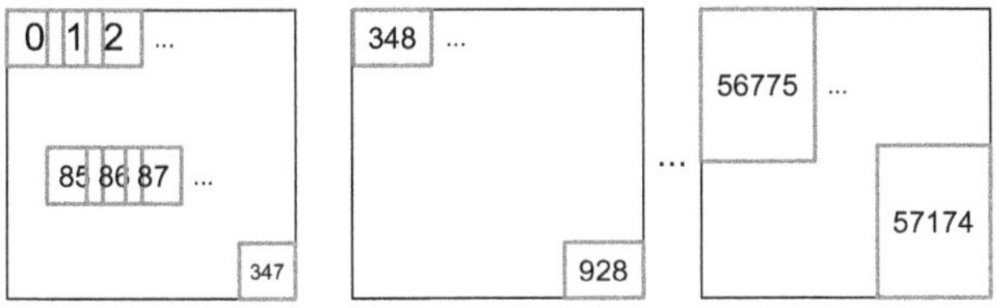

Figure 6: Quantization of (x', y', w', h') into overlapping blocks of various positions and sizes, where the four variables represent the already quantized horizontal and vertical positions, width, and height. The mapping between a (x', y', w', h') combination and a block ID should be unique throughout the system.

$(0, 1)$. The appearance similarity scores $App(q, t)$ are normalized in a similar way.

For the matching scores for face position $Pos(q, t)$ and face size $Size(q, t)$ between a query face q and a target face t, first note that in our system, coordinates are always represented as fractions of the width or height of the image (canvas). This fractional representation allows the computation to be adapted to the various aspect ratios in the the target images (query canvas). The definitions of $Pos(q, t)$ and $Size(q, t)$ are based on the distance errors between q and t as follows:

$$Pos(q, t) = 1 - \frac{d_{center}}{\sqrt{2}} \tag{6}$$

$$Size(q, t) = 1 - \frac{d_{width} + d_{height}}{2}, \tag{7}$$

where d_{center} is the L2 distance between the face centers, and d_{width} and d_{height} are the L1 differences between the face widths and heights. The denominators $\sqrt{2}$ and 2 in Eqs. 6 and 7 indicate the maximum (worst) distance between the face centers and the maximum width plus height differences between the faces, i.e., the diagonal line and the whole width plus whole height. Therefore, each term subtracted from 1 is now normalized into the range $(0, 1)$.

5.4 Block-based Indexing

We apply a block-based method to spatially index all the database faces. Since the face center coordinates, width and height, denoted as x, y, w, and h, are fractions, the infinitely many numbers in the interval $(0, 1)$ make indexing computationally infeasible and quantization too sensitive. Therefore, we first uniformly quantize each of the four variables into L levels, denoted as x', y', w', and h', each in the range $[0, L-1]$. We then quantize the valid (x', y', w', h') combinations uniquely into overlapping blocks of various positions and sizes, as illustrated in Fig. 6. Note that not all the L^4 combinations are valid (within-boundary) blocks. The mapping between an (x', y', w', h') tuple and a block ID should be unique throughout the system. One such mapping is easily achieved by representing the block ID as an L-nary number of 4 digits. For example:

$$BlockID = x' + y'L + w'L^2 + h'L^3. \tag{8}$$

The ordering of digits does not matter as long as it is consistent. The mapping[4] in Eq. 8 is not only unique but also reversible and storage-free (no table lookup).

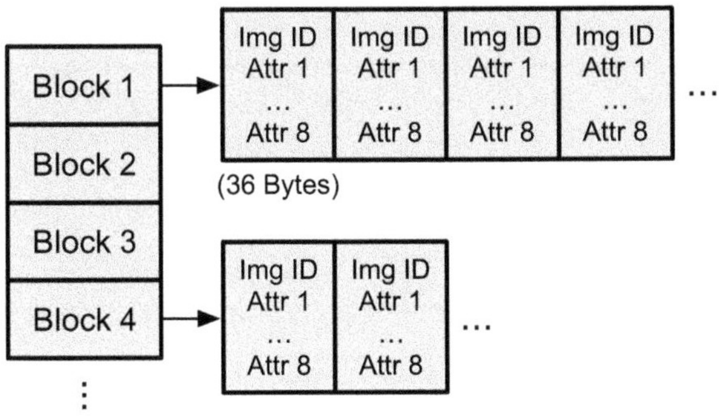

Figure 7: The indexing structure in the proposed system. The block IDs are treated as the visual words in typical inverted indexing. Each of them corresponds to an inverted list of structures, each being a tuple of (image ID, the 8 attribute scores) that requires 36 bytes in the implementation.

To build the index, the block IDs are treated as visual words in typical inverted indexing. Each block then corresponds to an inverted list of structures, each being a tuple of (image ID, the 8 attribute scores), as in Fig. 7. In other words, each list contains all the faces and their attribute scores within this particular block.

Since retrieving only faces in the block of the query face is still too sensitive, in the online search, a query face runs a "sliding window" to retrieve faces in W neighboring blocks. These neighbors are found by adjusting each of the (x', y', w', h') up and down for various quantization levels to produce new combinations. An example neighbor may be $(x' - 2, y' + 1, w' + 3, h')$. Then, we apply the mapping in Eq. 8 to get the neighboring block IDs and retrieve the corresponding inverted lists. The range of the sliding window, denoted by parameters tol_{pos} and tol_{size}, controls the level of tolerance in positions and sizes.

For multiple-face queries, each query face is processed separately to collect relevance scores from inverted lists according to Eq. 4. The greedy manner still applies that the first query face scans the inverted lists first. Finally, the results are merged into a ranking list according to Eq. 1. The retrieval results of block-based indexing and linear scan differ mostly by the quantization errors and the faces skipped by the sliding windows.

6. EXPERIMENTS

In this section, we describe the touch-based user interface of the proposed system named "Where is Who" (short for WiW), followed by the dataset and implementations. We also conduct an estimation on storage cost. For a video demonstration of the system, please visit our project page: `http://www.csie.ntu.edu.tw/~winston/projects/face/`

6.1 User Interface

The user interface of our system is shown in Figure 8. The user can drag faces from the top-right area onto the canvas

[4]As an example, suppose $L = 20$ levels, each being 0.05. An (x, y, w, h) combination of (0.11, 0.28, 0.42, 0.67) will be quantized into (x', y', w', h') = (2, 5, 8, 13). The block ID is then $2 + 5 \cdot 20 + 8 \cdot 20^2 + 13 \cdot 20^3 = 107302$. The reverse mapping can restore (x', y', w', h') from the block ID.

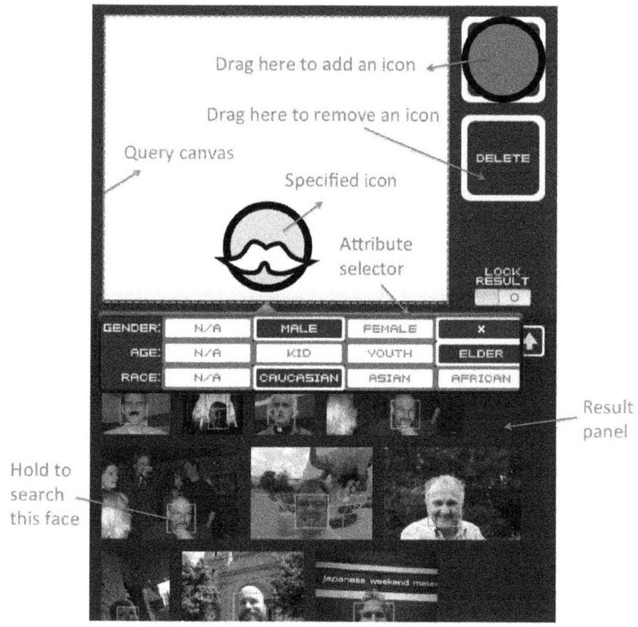

Figure 8: The touch-based interface of our system. The user can formulate a query by dragging face icons from the top-right area onto the canvas at desired positions. They can also pinch their fingers to adjust the sizes of the icons and the canvas. When holding an icon, a pop-up menu will show up for attribute selection. When browsing the search results on the bottom, they can also hold a face and use the changed icon on the top-right to find similar faces (appearance-based) in other photos. For every canvas modification, the system performs a search so that the user can refine their search intention interactively.

at desired positions. They can also pinch their fingers to adjust the sizes of the icons and the canvas. Holding an icon invokes a popup attribute selector. We have designed a total of 48 face icons ($3 \times 4 \times 4$) to represent the various attribute combinations. For appearance-based retrieval, the user can hold a face in the result panel and use the changed icon on the top-right to find similar faces in other photos. For every canvas modification, the system performs a search and shows the results on the bottom so that the user can refine their search intention interactively viewing the current results. Since our system is naturally suitable for a touch-based interface, we have implemented the UI on a tablet device.

6.2 Dataset and Implementations

The dataset is composed of two portions. As mentioned in Sec. 4.1, we crawl a large number of user-contributed photos from Flickr as the first (main) portion. For appearance-based retrieval, 732 daily photos containing 1,248 faces are added to the dataset as the second portion. After face detection by a public API [7], together there are $N = 115,487$ images in the dataset where the average number of faces per image is $F = 2.117$, so the dataset contains $N \times F = 244,491$ faces.

Since appearance-based retrieval is intended as a secondary feature of our system, we only estimate the appearance similarity scores in the second portion. Therefore, faces in the first portion always have zero appearance similarity scores if they are specified on the canvas.

In attribute detection, we adopt the LIBSVM software package [4] for learning the mid-level features. For the fusion weights in Eq. 4, we conduct a sensitivity test to select w_{attr}, w_{pos}, and w_{size} (that sum to 1) to optimize the evaluation criterion in Sec. 7.2. For block-based indexing, we empirically select the number of quantization levels as $L = 20$, and the tolerance (range) of the sliding window as $tol_{pos} = \pm 4$ levels and $tol_{size} = \pm 4$ levels[5].

The server part of WiW is implemented on a 16-core, 2.40GHz Intel Xeon machine with 48GB of RAM.

6.3 Storage Estimation

Since appearance-based retrieval is considered as a secondary feature, the storage cost of codeword index is not considered in this estimation. Following the format of the index structure in Fig. 7, for an inverted list structure, we require 4 bytes for an image ID and $4 \times 8 = 32$ bytes for the eight floating-point attribute scores. That is, 36 bytes for indexing a face. The cost of headers (block IDs and counts) can be neglected in the calculation. Multiplied by $N \times F$, it requires approximately $244.5K \times 36B = 8.8$MB in optimal implementations. Reusing $F = 2.117$ in our dataset, an 1-million image dataset requires a storage cost of around $1M \times 2.117 \times 36B = 76.2$MB.

7. PERFORMANCE EVALUATION

In this section, we evaluate the performance of several variants of our proposed system. We have conducted an experiment to evaluate known-item search, in which the user tries to search for a specific target image in mind. Since appearance-based retrieval is treated as a secondary feature, refer to [5] for the corresponding evaluation. We also evaluate the efficiency of indexing by measuring the running time and the number of visited faces.

7.1 Compared Methods

To the best of our knowledge, our system is the first work to address the problem of face image retrieval based on both facial attributes and face layout. So we compare four variants of the proposed system: (1) "Attr," by enabling only w_{attr} in Eq. 4 with linear scan in order to resemble the search scheme in [15], (2) "Pos + Size (index)," by enabling w_{pos} and w_{size} with block-based indexing (Sec. 5.4), (3) "Attr + Pos + Size," by enabling w_{attr}, w_{pos}, and w_{size} with linear scan, and (4) "Attr + Pos + Size (index)," same as (3) but with block-based indexing. (4) is the full version of WiW except for the appearance-based component.

[5]Therefore, a sliding window visits $W = (4 \cdot 2 + 1)^2 \cdot (4 \cdot 2 + 1)^2 = 6,561$ neighboring blocks. Many of the blocks may be out-of-boundary or empty.

Table 2: Distribution of the number of faces in the 500 query tasks.

# faces	1	2	3	4	5+	Total
# query tasks	249	147	55	22	27	500

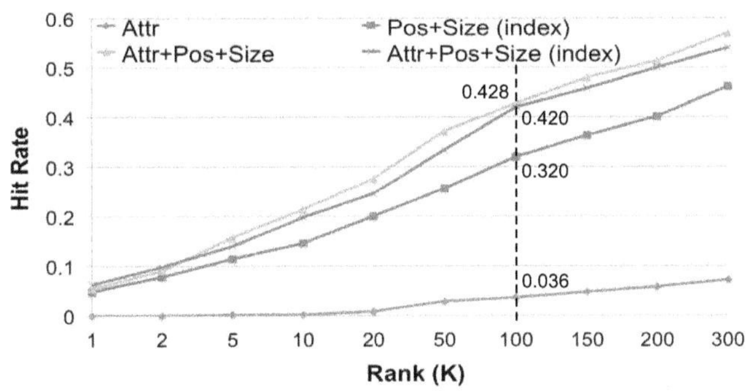

Figure 9: Hit rates@K of different methods over the 500 query tasks for known-item search. Adding layout information achieves a hit rate of 0.420 at rank 100 (purple line). This significantly outperforms 0.036 of using attributes alone (blue line), the search scheme proposed by [15]. In addition, adding attribute information improves the hit rate from 0.320 (red line) to 0.420 (purple line).

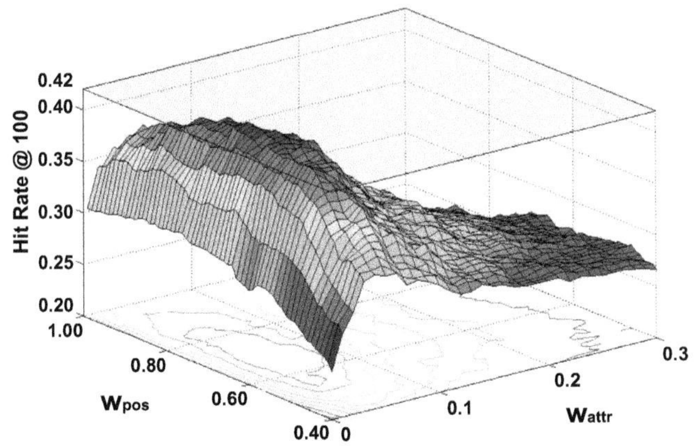

Figure 10: The fusion weight selection to maximize hit rate. The three axes represent w_{attr}, w_{pos} (in Eq. 4), and hit rate@100, respectively. The non-negative weights are constrained by $w_{attr} + w_{pos} + w_{size} = 1$.

7.2 Performance of Known-Item Search

7.2.1 *Evaluation Setup*

In known-item search (KIS), the user aims to search for a specific target image that they have seen. To simulate such a scenario in a large-scale dataset, 500 target images, each containing at least one face (985 faces in total), were randomly selected from our dataset (portions 1 and 2) as query tasks. The distribution of the number of faces is summarized in Table 2. These query tasks were equally distributed among the participants of 20 subjects invited to the experiment.

For each query task, the subject was asked to first carefully observe the target image, and then formulate a query canvas by graphically placing attributed icons at the corresponding positions and in the corresponding sizes for each query face. The subjects were asked to specify the positions and sizes according to the bounding boxes detected by the system in order to minimize the effect of face detection errors. The attributes were specified according to their "strengths" to the subject. If either the gender, age, or race of the face was not obvious enough, the attribute would be "not specified" for this type. Finally, the 500 submitted query canvases were collected for later evaluations.

Although this simulation does not reflect the reality that the user may not accurately remember the face layout or the face content in a large image collection over a long time, our user interface makes it easy to gradually refine the canvas by providing a real-time re-query for every canvas modification. This is useful in reality because the user usually performs several trials in the same way in typical retrieval systems.

7.2.2 *Gain from Layout Information*

To evaluate how well the target image is ranked in the results, we measure the "hit rate@K" as in [3][6], the proportion of the 500 query tasks where the system can retrieve the target image within the top K search results (within rank K).

Fig. 9 shows the performance of the four compared methods for all query tasks. Apparently, all three methods considering face layout significantly outperform "Attr," achieving hit rates of 0.320, 0.428, and 0.420 at rank 100[7] that are 8.8 to 11.8 times higher than 0.036 (blue line) of using attributes alone, the search scheme proposed by [15]. This clearly explains that when the user has the face layout in mind, specifying the positions and sizes on a canvas provides much more information than specifying only the face content.

Also, the hit rate of "Attr + Pos + Size (index)" (purple line) is slightly lower than its linear-scan variant "Attr + Pos + Size" (green line). This is due to the quantization errors introduced by the block-based indexing, where the exact positions and sizes are quantized into nearby blocks.

7.2.3 *Gain from Attribute Information*

We can also observe in Fig. 9 that "Attr + Pos + Size (index)" outperforms "Pos + Size (index)." In other words, adding attribute information can further improve the hit rate@100 from 0.320 (red line) to 0.420 (purple line), although in the fusion weight selection (Fig. 10), the contribution of w_{attr} is only 5% of the total weight. The small weight can be explained by the fact that attribute detection is less robust than face detection and localization.

As reported in Sec. 4.1, a single attribute detector has an average accuracy of around 80%, but when three attributes are specified in a query face, we can expect only $(0.80)^3 = 51\%$ of the target faces to have all correctly de-

[6]In KIS, the performance is often measured by mean reciprocal rank. However, because there may be numerous other images with similar face content and face layout, especially images of 1 or 2 faces (Table 2), many of our target images are ranked up to number several thousand. Averaging by those near-zero reciprocal ranks would make it difficult to compare different methods.

[7]Although a hit rate of 0.420 at rank 100 may not be high enough for practical photo management, the images returned by the system are often relevant to the query canvas, as illustrated in Fig. 13. This high precision enables casual photo browsing when the user does not have a specific target in mind.

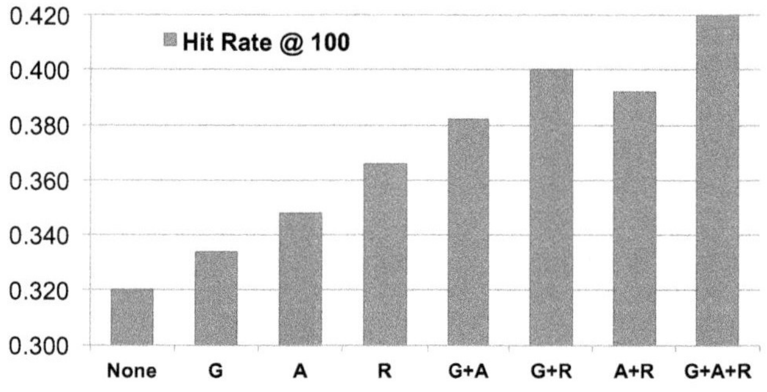

Figure 11: Breakdown of the improvement of hit rate@100 from 0.320 to 0.420 (Fig. 9) by enabling different combinations of attribute types. G, A, and R stand for gender, age, and race, respectively. Starting from 0.320 of no attributes, we can observe that enabling more attribute types improves the hit rate towards the highest 0.420 (G+A+R).

tected attributes. This is challenging for a system supporting multi-attribute queries. Also, in the experiment of KIS, the subjects were instructed to specify the positions and sizes according to the bounding boxes returned by the face detector. This accurate layout information has compromised the contribution of attributes in the multimodal fusion.

7.2.4 Breakdown by Attribute Combinations

Following Sec. 7.2.3, we break down the improvement of hit rate@100 from 0.320 to 0.420 (Fig. 9) by enabling different attribute combinations. In Fig. 11, G, A, and R stand for the three attribute types gender, age, and race, respectively. "A + R," for example, enables attributes in faces in the query tasks where the user specified any age attribute *or* any race attribute.

Starting from 0.320 of no attributes, we can observe that enabling more attribute types improves the hit rate towards the highest 0.420 (G + A + R). Again, this shows the power of multi-modality in retrieval systems. With more attributes available, such as the 73 detected attributes in [16], we can expect such a system to achieve even better performance for practical usage.

It is also interesting to discuss the effect of using some attributes together in a query canvas. Fig. 12 shows the hit rates@100 by *simultaneously* enabling (hence the "&" symbol) any gender attribute (G) *and* one age attribute. A red dot counts the percentage of faces with attributes that meet this requirement.

Generally, the higher the red dot, the more faces with attributes enabled, which is expected to raise the hit rate. However, we can observe that "G & kid" performs the worst among all alternatives, even worse than "G & elder" that has fewer faces with attributes. It reflects the intuition that it is relatively hard to tell the gender among kids.

7.3 Efficiency of Indexing

From the 500 query tasks, we also record the average running time and the average number of visited faces, including repetitive visits, in the search. Table 3 shows the efficiency comparison between linear scan and block-based indexing. In both manners, block-based indexing speeds up

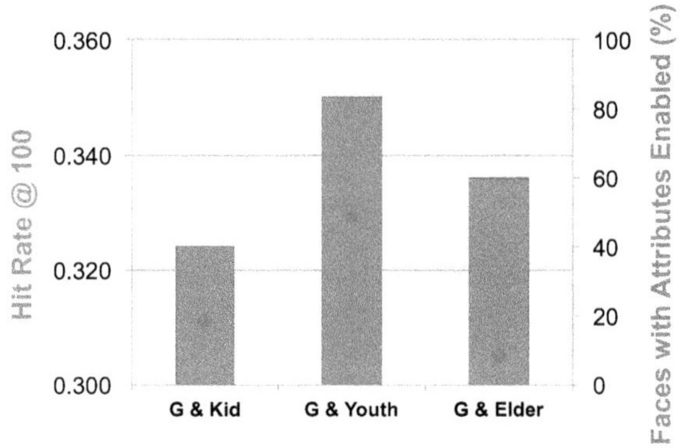

Figure 12: Hit rates@100 by *simultaneously* enabling any gender attribute and one age attribute. A red dot represents the percentage of query faces with such attributes enabled. We can observe that "G & kid" performs the worst among all alternatives, even worse than "G & elder" that has fewer faces with attributes enabled. This reflects the intuition that it is relatively hard to tell the gender among kids.

Table 3: The efficiency comparison between linear scan and block-based indexing, measured by the average running time and the average number of visited faces (including repetitive visits) in the search.

	Running time (sec)	# Visited faces
Linear scan	0.2089	331,225
Block-based index	0.0558	111,303
Indexing speedup	3.74x	2.98x

around 3 times and requires only 0.0558 second in a dataset of more than 200k faces. Although there is still room for improvement (e.g., incorporating attribute scores into the visual words, or better quantization and search methods for the (x,y,w,h) information), we believe the proposed indexing method can be extended to a million-scale dataset.

8. CONCLUSIONS AND FUTURE WORK

Our work proposes a novel way to effectively organize and search for consumer photos by placing attributed face icons on a query canvas at desired positions and in desired sizes. With the help of automatic facial attribute detection and appearance similarity estimation in the offline process, we are able to analyze wild photos without tagging at all. In the online process, the system simultaneously considers attributes, appearances, positions, and sizes of the target faces.

The scenario has been realized on a tablet device with a touch interface. Experimenting with a large-scale Flickr dataset of more 200k faces, we have achieved a hit rate@100 of 0.420, significantly improving from 0.036 of prior search scheme [15] using attributes alone. We have also achieved a fast retrieval response of 0.0558 second by the proposed block-based indexing approach. Experimental results from extensive search tasks (Fig. 13) reveal the potential for effective and efficient photo management.

In the future work, we will exploit more facial attributes for the proposed search system. We will also include more

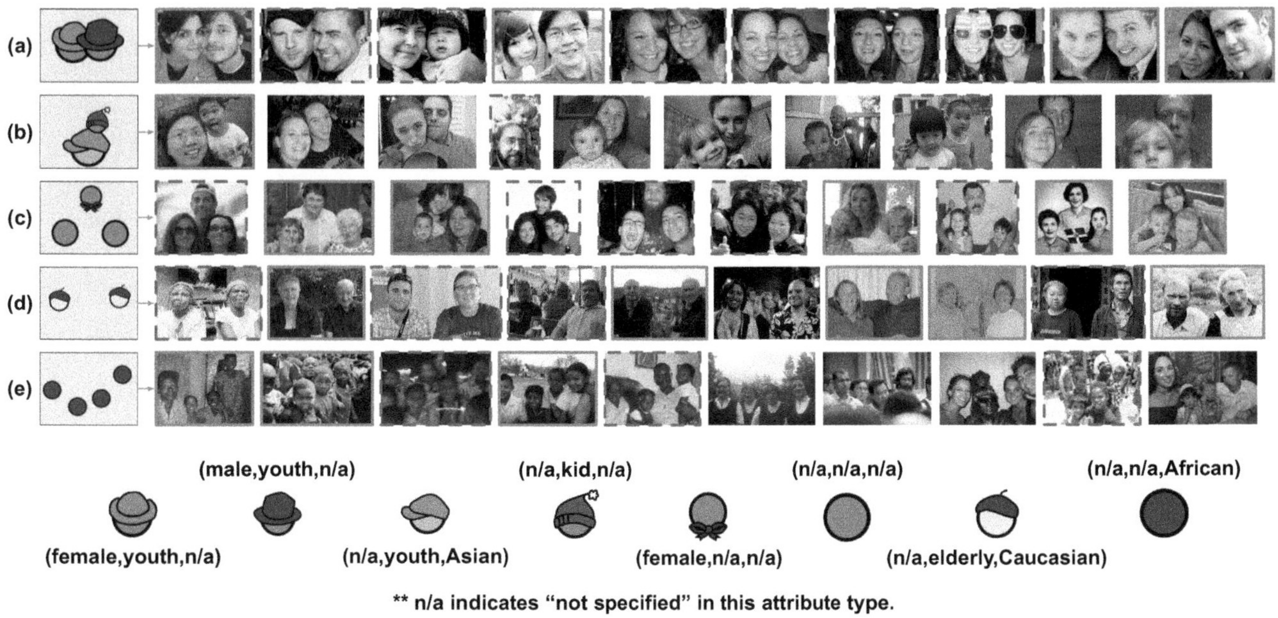

Figure 13: Example query canvases and the corresponding top 10 search results. The figure demonstrates extensive search tasks ranging from very close faces ((a) and (b)) to faces spread in various ways ((c), (d), and (e)). The icons representing the attribute combinations are shown in the bottom. Images squared in green solid lines (blue dashed lines) are believed to be highly (partially) relevant by an average user.

context cues (e.g., time, geo-locations, etc.) for consumer photo management. Meanwhile, the human factors will be considered more in the integration with mobile devices.

9. REFERENCES

[1] T. Ahonen, A. Hadid, and M. Pietikainen. Face description with local binary patterns: Application to face recognition. *PAMI*, 2006.

[2] M. Ames and M. Naaman. Why we tag: Motivations for annotation in mobile and online media. *ACM CHI*, 2007.

[3] Y. Cao, C. Wang, L. Zhang, and L. Zhang. Edgel index for large-scale sketch-based image search. *CVPR*, 2011.

[4] C.-C. Chang and C.-J. Lin. LIBSVM: A library for support vector machines. *ACM Transactions on Intelligent Systems and Technology*, 2011. Software available at `http://www.csie.ntu.edu.tw/~cjlin/libsvm`.

[5] B.-C. Chen, Y.-H. Kuo, Y.-Y. Chen, K.-Y. Chu, and W. Hsu. Semi-supervised face image retrieval using sparse coding with identity constraint. *ACM Multimedia*, 2011.

[6] N. Dalal and B. Triggs. Histograms of oriented gradients for human detection. *CVPR*, 2005.

[7] face.com API. `http://developers.face.com/`.

[8] M. Freeman. *The Photographer's Eye: Composition and Design for Better Digital Photos*. Focal Press, 2007.

[9] Y. Freund and R. E. Schapire. A decision-theoretic generalization of on-line learning and an application to boosting. *Computational Learning Theory*, 1995.

[10] iPhoto from Apple Inc. `http://www.apple.com/ilife/iphoto/`.

[11] P. Isola, J. Xiao, A. Torralba, and A. Oliva. What makes an image memorable? *CVPR*, 2011.

[12] L. Kennedy, M. Naaman, S. Ahern, R. Nair, and T. Rattenbury. How flickr helps us make sense of the world: Context and content in community-contributed media collections. *ACM Multimedia*, 2007.

[13] L. S. Kennedy, S.-F. Chang, and I. V. Kozintsev. To search or to label?: Predicting the performance of search-based automatic image classifiers. *ACM MIR Workshop*, 2006.

[14] H.-N. Kim, A. E. Saddik, K.-S. Lee, Y.-H. Lee, and G.-S. Jo. Photo search in a personal photo diary by drawing face position with people tagging. *IUI*, 2011.

[15] N. Kumar, P. N. Belhumeur, and S. K. Nayar. Facetracer: A search engine for large collections of images with faces. *ECCV*, 2008.

[16] N. Kumar, A. C. Berg, P. N. Belhumeur, and S. K. Nayar. Describable visual attributes for face verification and image search. *PAMI*, 2011.

[17] K.-S. Lee, J.-G. Jung, K.-J. Oh, and G.-S. Jo. U2mind: Visual semantic relationships query for retrieving photos in social network. *ACIIDS*, 2011.

[18] Picasa from Google Inc. `http://picasa.google.com`.

[19] H. Xu, J. Wang, X.-S. Hua, and S. Li. Image search by concept map. *SIGIR*, 2010.

Mining the Web for Points of Interest

Adam Rae
Yahoo! Research
Barcelona, Spain
adamrae@yahoo-inc.com

Vanessa Murdock
Yahoo! Research
Barcelona, Spain
vmurdock@yahoo-inc.com

Adrian Popescu*
CEA, LIST
Vision & Content Engineering Laboratory
Gif-sur-Yvette, France
adrian.popescu@cea.fr

Hugues Bouchard
Yahoo! Research
Barcelona, Spain
bouchard@yahoo-inc.com

ABSTRACT

A *point of interest* (POI) is a focused geographic entity such as a landmark, a school, an historical building, or a business. Points of interest are the basis for most of the data supporting location-based applications. In this paper we propose to curate POIs from online sources by bootstrapping training data from Web snippets, seeded by POIs gathered from social media. This large corpus is used to train a sequential tagger to recognize mentions of POIs in text. Using Wikipedia data as the training data, we can identify POIs in free text with an accuracy that is 116% better than the state of the art POI identifier in terms of precision, and 50% better in terms of recall. We show that using Foursquare and Gowalla checkins as seeds to bootstrap training data from Web snippets, we can improve precision between 16% and 52%, and recall between 48% and 187% over the state-of-the-art. The name of a POI is not sufficient, as the POI must also be associated with a set of geographic coordinates. Our method increases the number of POIs that can be localized nearly three-fold, from 134 to 395 in a sample of 400, with a median localization accuracy of less than one kilometer.

Categories and Subject Descriptors

H.3.1 [**Information Storage and Retrieval**]: Content Analysis and Indexing

Keywords

geographic information extraction, geo-localisation, location-based applications, points of interest

*Work performed while the author was a visitor at Yahoo! Research

SIGIR'12, August 12–16, 2012, Portland, Oregon, USA.

1. INTRODUCTION

A *point of interest* (POI) is a focused geographic entity such as a landmark, a school, an historical building, or a business. Many POIs are permanent structures such as statues, or buildings. Others are semi-permanent, such as restaurants which may open one year and close the next. Still others are temporal or periodic, such as the location of an annual festival.

Points of interest are the basis for most of the data supporting location-based applications. They are displayed on online maps, and are provided to users of location-based mobile applications such as Foursquare[1] and Gowalla.[2] POIs are often displayed in the local search results or in sponsored listings related to a user's search, or are presented to users of recommender systems such travel booking websites.

In this paper we address the question of whether it is possible to automatically identify POIs without manual intervention, given their broad definition, and the lack of consistency in their naming. Further, as knowing the name of a POI is not useful without knowing its location, we address the question of how accurately POIs can be localized using automatic methods.

To curate POI data, companies such as Navteq[3] and TeleAtlas[4] send a surveyor to a location to identify, verify and record POIs. This process yields high-quality and accurate data, although the process is very expensive, and it is difficult to scale to large geographic areas, or hard-to-reach locations. Furthermore, the frequency with which the locations can be surveyed is limited by the expense of gathering the data, so the process focuses on POIs that are more likely to be permanent, in areas of high commercial value. This creates a bias in the data towards POIs such as landmarks, schools, hospitals and other stable, stationary items that are unlikely to change significantly within a short time frame. Other types of POIs, such as restaurants, may change more quickly than human geographers can be sent out to update

[1]`http://www.foursquare.com` visited June 2012

[2]`http://www.gowalla.com` visited January 2012. Gowalla has been purchased by Facebook, and the site is no longer available.

[3]`http://www.navteq.com/` visited June 2012

[4]`http://www.teleatlas.com/` visited June 2012

their records, and hence would become stale. For this reason they are not typically covered in this type of curated data.

A second method for curating POIs is to create a directory of sponsored listings. Directories of this type are used in local search engines and mapping products such as those that display restaurants and businesses. This second type of data is dependent on businesses that have the budget and inclination to pay to be included in the directory. Very small, independent businesses may be less likely to be listed, and in countries where Internet usage is low, the sponsored listings may be non-existent or sparse, or dominated by large businesses and national chains. As a result, the representation of the place in terms of local businesses will be far from the user's perception in real life.

A third technique is crowd-sourcing, such as the OpenStreetMap Project[5], in which users themselves contribute to the representation of the place by uploading location data. This helps address the bias toward large businesses and permanent POIs, but crowd-sourcing introduces other issues such as the provenance of the data, and its reliability. For example, the New York Times reported that Google erroneously labeled businesses as "closed" on their maps, as a result of spamming by competing businesses [18].

In this paper we propose to curate POIs from online sources by bootstrapping training data from Web snippets, seeded by POIs gathered from social media. This large corpus is used to train a sequential tagger to recognize mentions of POIs in text. The features of the sequential tagger are generic, and as such are designed to recognize points of interest from their context. This allows the tagger to tag previously unseen POIs. Furthermore, the evaluation data is taken from a completely different sample of data (news articles as opposed to Web snippets or mentions in social media), and many of the POIs annotated by assessors are not present in gazetteers.

Using Wikipedia data as the training data,[6] we can identify POIs in free text with an accuracy that is 120% better than the state of the art POI identifier in terms of precision, and 48% better in terms of recall. The points of interest represented in Wikipedia resemble curated data found in gazetteers, and focus on official names for permanent structures. Businesses, restaurants and venues are underrepresented in Wikipedia, but are well-covered in online checkin services such as Foursquare and Gowalla. We show that using Foursquare and Gowalla checkins as seeds to bootstrap training data from Web snippets, we can improve precision between 16% and 52%, and recall between 48% and 187% over the state-of-the-art.

The name of a POI is not sufficient, as the POI must also be associated with a set of geographic coordinates. We localize the POI mentions using location models inferred from Flickr data. The result is a method for discovering POIs previously not found in sponsored listings or online gazetteers. Our method increases the number of POIs that can be localized nearly three-fold, from 134 to 395 in a sample of 400, with a median localization accuracy of less than one kilometer.

To summarize, our contributions are as follows:

- A method to identify mentions of POIs in online data that is significantly better than the state-of-the-art in terms of both recall and precision. Our method does not require editorial labeling of data, and allows for the discovery of temporary or ephemeral POIs, in addition to more permanent structures.
- A method to increase the amount of training data by bootstrapping from Web snippets, that is language independent, and can be targeted to a particular region of the world. This allows for vast amounts of training data to be collected, without the overhead of manual labeling.
- A method to localize POIs that is highly precise, with a recall of nearly three times that of the state-of-the-art. The method is language independent, and does not depend on a database of sponsored listings, or human surveyors.

We present an overview of the related work in Section 2, followed by a description of the model for identifying POIs in text in Section 3. While the models are trained on data that is automatically generated, the evaluation is conducted on data labeled by human assessors. Section 4 presents the creation of manually annotated evaluation data, as well as training data gathered from Wikipedia. We present the bootstrapping system in Section 5 to extract POI mentions from social media data, and use those as seeds to create training data from Web snippets. The localization component is presented in Section 6, and the work as a whole is discussed in Section 7. We lay out our conclusions and reflect on our findings in Section 8.

2. RELATED WORK

To the best of our knowledge there is no other work that aims to discover points of interest from unstructured text on the web. This section discusses related work that leverages the location of a user and his interaction with a map to improve the metadata associated with a point of interest. Although the literature on Named Entity Recognition is certainly relevant here, we included the related work on NER in the section describing the models. The localization component is based on the work of O'Hare and Murdock [16] and Serdyukov et al. [19], but there are other similar works that are also relevant to the localization of place mentions.

Mummidi and Krumm discover points of interest from pushpins placed on maps by users [15], mining the annotations of the pushpins for terms with a high TF·IDF value. The authors propose the map data as a reliable source of data from users, because the users have explicitly indicated a point of interest on the map, and after processing the data yields a textual characterisation of the point, plus its geographic coordinates. Evaluating a data discovery system is always a difficult task and the authors address this by conducting a user study in which 100 users assess points of interest shown on a map in their neighbourhood and are asked to indicate whether the POI is identified correctly or not.

In related, more recent work, Zheng et al. [27] propose a method to mine GPS data to recommend locations to users wanting to do an activity and to recommend activities to users at a particular location. Their data is obtained from an interactive mapping application, with 162 users, who have generated roughly 12,000 trajectories in Beijing

[5] `http://www.openstreetmap.org` visited June 2012
[6] `http://www.wikipedia.org` visited June 2012

over the past 2.5 years. In their data, the points of interest from a database of POIs are associated with geographic coordinates.

Both of these works rely on users' interactions with a map and are based on a small-scale user study. This is a key difference between our work and theirs as they rely on users to annotate maps with POI data. Our work discovers the mentions of POIs in Web snippets and does not rely on users interacting with any particular application. This allows us to potentially gather vast amounts of training data, independent of any given application. Although the POIs discovered in Web data are less structured and consistent than those entered by users on a map application, we expect that the vast amount of data will compensate for the noise.

In the case of Zheng et al., their system is restricted to the city of Beijing, whereas we consider any place in the world. Finally, Zheng et al. populate their list of points of interest with a categorised POI database. Thus users can comment on existing POIs, but no previously unseen POIs are introduced into the system. The focus of their work is to recommend known POIs to users who are in a given place, which is distinctly different than discovering previously unknown POIs.

Yin et al. [26] do not extract points of interest, but rather model the topics in a given location. In their system a topic is a "spatially coherent meaningful theme". They create a data set based on seven concepts: Landscape, Activity, Manhattan, National Park, Festival, Car and Food, using the topics as keywords to crawl the Flickr API for images associated with those concepts. They propose latent geographical topic analysis to discover sub-topics related to the seven parent concepts. In a second task they identify the regions associated with a given topic. Their system relates to ours in the sense that a POI could be considered a subtopic of a region and a system that is designed to find topic mentions in Flickr data may discover POIs, along with other topics. However, they have constrained their system to regions in the U.S. and allow for the discovery of a wide range of topics.

Our localization component is based on the work of O'Hare and Murdock, described in [16]. We discuss this work in more detail in Section 6. In similar work, Crandall et al. [6] propose a system to predict among ten landmarks in a given city, within 100 meters, in Flickr images. Their experiments are limited to a specific set of landmarks in a fixed set of cities, as there are no images in their test or training sets that represent places outside of this set of locations. This differs significantly from our task, as we are trying to predict the location of a landmarks and other POIs, anywhere in the world. Furthermore, their work focuses primarily on images, and leverages image features, whereas we work entirely with text.

Yi et al. [25] use language modeling to determine the locations implicit in queries. They use Placemaker to identify location mentions in queries, which they then remove. The resulting queries are intended to contain implicit locations. However, the way in which they use Placemaker is likely to leave mentions of neighborhoods and POIs, as they remove only the primary locations in the queries, in the case that there is more than one location mentioned. This represents an explicit mention of a location, rather than an implicit one. Furthermore, their evaluation is limited to predicting locations that exist in Placemaker. They do not create an independent ground truth.

The work of Hollenstein and Purves [9] seeks to identify vernacular regions in Flickr[7] data. Vernacular regions include mentions such as "Downtown" or "CBD", which are not as granular as POIs, but are significantly smaller than cities, and represent non-official locations that are not typically included in gazetteers. They present a case study of six cities in the U.S. and Europe. This is one of the few studies that attempts to identify regions smaller than a city.

Other work that does not seek to localize geographic entities, but rather to assign a geographic scope to a document includes work to build location topic models from blog data [13, 24], and finding the geographic focus of web pages [7, 4, 28].

3. SEQUENTIAL TAGGING MODEL

Named-entity recognition has been well-studied for a number of years. The Message Understanding Conference [1] (MUC) ran from 1987 to 1999. More recently the Automatic Content Extraction Program (ACE) [2] ran from 2000–2008. The CoNLL Shared Tasks for 2002 [20] and 2003 [21] provides a reasonable overview of the standard data and benchmarking tasks for NER.

Conditional Random Fields (CRF) were introduced by Lafferty et al. [11], for text classification and sequence labelling. The CRF was proposed for NER by McCallum and Li [12], and we borrow this approach for POI detection. They report identifying location mentions in the CoNLL English data set with 87% precision and recall. The locations in the CoNLL data refer only to cities, states and countries and the entire data set is composed of news articles. It represents a much simpler problem, in part because of the nature of the location mentions, and the presence of towns, states and countries in gazetteers and because the news data is more semantically rich and cleaner than social media data and Web data.

The conditional random field computes the probability of a label sequence, y, given an observation sequence x, according to:

$$p(Y|X, \lambda) = \frac{1}{Z(X)} \exp\Big(\sum_j \lambda_j F_j(Y, X)\Big) \qquad (1)$$

where $Z(X)$ is a normalising factor, and $F(Y, X)$ is the set of feature functions computed over the observations and the label transitions. The learning process selects the set of feature weights Λ which maximise the label sequence probability $P(Y|X)$:

$$argmax_{\Lambda}\Big\{\frac{1}{Z(X)} \exp\Big(\sum_j \lambda_j F_j(Y, X)\Big)\Big\} \qquad (2)$$

More information about CRFs are given in Wallach [23]. We use Okazaki's implementation of the CRF [17] from the CRFsuite project[8] as it has been shown to outperform other implementations in terms of training speed for sparse data and implements a number of training methods capable of handling large amounts of data - an important consideration for a system designed to learn over large-scale web snippet

[7] `http://www.flickr.com` visited June 2012

[8] `http://www.chokkan.org/software/crfsuite/` visited June 2012

data. We use the Averaged Perceptron training method [5] with a maximum number of iterations of 10. We limited the iterations in training because it made training over large amounts of data tractable. Our data is labelled in BI0 notation, as is standard for NER tasks; that is, a token is labeled as the beginning of a POI mention (B), the continuation of a POI mention (I), or not part of a POI mention (0).

3.1 Features

Each example sentence in our data is treated as a sequence of tokens, represented by a vector of binary features (described in Table 1). The observation features fall into one of four classes: lexical, geographic, grammatical and statistical. Lexical features are computed over the surface text of the token stream. They represent standard NER lexical features, and include the word identity, word shape, position in the sentence, the prefix and suffix of the token.

Geographic features were computed using Yahoo! Placemaker[9], a geographic parsing service, to provide data for tokens that match a POI name. For a token that matches, Placemaker provides information that includes a list of candidate places to which the token may refer and for each, contextual information like name variants in different languages, and colloquial names. Characterising statistics are computed over this list.

To encode the grammatical function of each token, part-of-speech tagging was done for each token within a sentence using the Apache OpenNLP[10] implementation of a max-ent POS tagger, using the Penn English Treebank POS tag dictionary[11] that comprises of 36 tags.

Normalized pointwise mutual information (*npmi*) was computed over token bigrams appearing in a random sample from the Yahoo![12] mobile search query logs. For each bigram, the normalised point-wise mutual information of a token x and its subsequent token y was computed as:

$$\begin{aligned} pmi(x;y) &\equiv log\frac{p(x,y)}{p(x)p(y)} \\ npmi(x;y) &= \frac{pmi(x;y)}{-log\left[max\left(p(x),p(y)\right)\right]} \end{aligned} \quad (3)$$

To convert the (*npmi*) into a binary feature, the output values were discretized by applying a greater-than threshold test at each 0.1 interval between -1 and +1, resulting in 20 binary features per bigram.

For the state transition features, we consider the previous state and the next state for all features, except for the word identity and word shape features, which are computed over the previous two, and the next two states (this helps in the common case of longer formulaic POI names such as "Church of Saint Martin" of "the Museum of Natural History").

4. POI EXTRACTION

For the extraction task, we created a manually annotated data set composed primarily of news articles from the U.S. and the U.K., but also included a small number of examples from Yahoo! Answers[13] and a small number of queries submitted to a search engine. The POIs represented in this data include businesses, services, landmarks and public buildings such as schools, hospitals, airports and prisons.

Ground Truth Assessor	Precision	Recall	F-Measure
1	0.749	0.792	0.770
2	0.814	0.716	0.762

Table 2: The result of identifying location boundaries, if one assessor is used as the ground truth labelling and the other assessor is used as the test labelling.

Our data was annotated by two assessors, both native English speakers (annotating data in English), one from the U.S. and one from the U.K. They were shown random examples from multiple sources, and were instructed to highlight all locations in the text. The inter-assessor agreement was 73.9%. In total 1,337 of the examples they annotated contained POIs, which yielded 1,066 unique POIs.

In addition to measuring the inter-assessor agreement, we measured the precision, recall, and F-measure of one assessor, using the other assessor's data as the ground truth. The results of this is shown in Table 2. This provides a reasonable upper bound on the performance of the POI detection. The results shown in Table 2 are much lower than those reported on the named-entity recognition benchmarking tasks, where the location mentions are entirely composed of cities, states, and countries, and all of the data is news data. The results indicate that identifying POIs in data is not straightforward, even for human assessors. We trained a model using this data with 10-fold cross validation and a 90/10 split. The results are shown in Table 3 in the row labeled "Manual Annotations". The performance of the model is almost as good as that of the human assessors in terms of precision, on the same task.

To create the Wikipedia data set, we selected pages in Wikipedia whose topic was a POI. We determined which Wikipedia pages relate to POIs as follows. The Geonames[14] database encodes geographic entities with a feature code that classifies entities according to an entity taxonomy. These codes are grouped into 9 classes, labelled with a class code letter. The Yago2 ontology gives a concordance between Wikipedia articles and Geonames geographic entities [8]. We selected English language Wikipedia articles which have been identified with the Geonames "S" class, which corresponds most closely to the definition of POIs used in this paper, containing entities such as airports, buildings, facilities and historical and industrial sites. From this set of articles, the title text is used as a surrogate for the name of the POI. The abstract of the article is segmented into sentences and filtered for those that contain the title text. This process gave us 2,896 unique POIs with a total of 5,186 examples of their use in context.

The results of training a model on the Wikipedia data (with 10-fold cross-validation) are better than the results for the manually annotated data. This reflects the lack of noise in the data, and the use of official names for the POIs. The

[9] `http://developer.yahoo.com/geo/placemaker/` visited June 2012
[10] `http://incubator.apache.org/opennlp/` visited June 2012
[11] `http://www.ling.upenn.edu/courses/Fall_2003/ling001/penn_treebank_pos.html` visited June 2012
[12] `http://www.yahoo.com` visited June 2012
[13] `http://answers.yahoo.com/` visited June 2012
[14] `http://www.geonames.org/` visited June 2012

Feature	Description
Word Identity	The raw text representation of the token
Normalised Word Identity	The lower case version of *Word Identity*
Word Shape	Indicates capitalisation, and hyphens
Word Capitalisation	The first letter of the token is a capital letter
Word Position (First)	The token is at the beginning of a sentence
Word Position (Last)	The token is at the end of a sentence
Word Prefix	First three characters of the token
Word Suffix	Last three characters of the token
Part-Of-Speech	OpenNLP English language maxent labelling
Bi-Gram	Normalised point-wise mutual information of token and next token
Related Location Probability	Probability that token represents a place
Related Location Match	True if token matches a place name
Related Location Size	Number of place matches including variants
Related Location Unique	Place matches where variants are conflated
Related Location Unique Ratio	(*Related Location Size*)/(*Related Location Unique*)

Table 1: Lexical, grammatical, statistical and geographic features used by the CRF tagger.

Data Set	Precision	Recall
Placemaker Baseline Manual Annotations	0.238	0.233
Manual Annotations (10-fold c.v.)	0.686	0.467
Placemaker Baseline Wikipedia	0.133	0.209
Wikipedia Article Sentences (10-fold c.v.)	0.872	0.742

Table 3: Results of training and evaluating on the data using 10-fold cross-validation. The baseline is the result of using Placemaker to identify POIs in the manual annotations data, and the Wikipedia data. The systems trained on either manual annotations, or wikipedia, give significantly better results than Placemaker, which is the state-of-the- art.

results are shown in Table 3 in the row labeled "Wikipedia Article Sentences".

The baseline results (in Table 3 , the rows labeled "Placemaker Baseline") were obtained by processing the two data sets with the Placemaker service to extract points of interest mentioned in the text. We expanded the valid place types returned by Placemaker to include airports, and land features which are not POIs in the Placemaker classification, but are in the Geonames classification.

It is important to note that the Wikipedia data is labeled according to whether it is a POI or some other type of entity, but it has not been labeled with sequence labeling (such as the BI0 notation described above) that would be needed for NER. For the purpose of detecting mentions of POIs with a sequential tagger, the data is unlabeled. Thus, this result represents a first system to recognize geographic points of interest, entirely from unlabeled data. Both the system trained on manual annotations, and the system trained on Wikipedia data performed significantly better than the Placemaker baseline.

5. BOOTSTRAPPING FROM THE WEB

Both the Wikipedia and the manual annotation data sets are very small, which means geographic coverage, as well as their coverage in terms of the types of POIs mentioned is limited. In addition, the mentions of POIs vary greatly from one data source to another. For example, the University of Buffalo might be referred to as **#UBuffalo**, or **University of Buffalo** depending on the data source and the context of the mention. Creating enough manually annotated data to learn patterns from this amount of variation would be a major undertaking. In this section we show that increasing the amount of training data by bootstrapping from the Web yields a signficant improvement in the learned POI extraction.

5.1 Bootstrapping Data

The Wikipedia title text was used as seed queries to the Bing search engine via their web-based API[15] to retrieve snippets or web page abstracts relevant to those queries. We retrieved up to 10 web snippets per Wikipedia title. The snippets provide a small amount of text to contextualize the POI. The idea is to provide a context in which a POI is used, to enable the model to learn a more general representation of the POI. The resultant list of POIs from Wikipedia is relatively clean, but there is no guarantee that the POI will be mentioned in the proper context in the search engine snippets. For example in this scenario the POI "The White House" might retrieve a web snippet about white houses. This process gave data for 2,896 total unique POIs and 21,228 examples of their use in context.

As stated earlier, the POIs mentioned in Wikipedia are largely mentions of permanent structures such as landmarks and government buildings, usually represented by their official name. For Web applications, the definition of POI also includes more ephemeral places such as restaurants and local businesses. Location check-in services such as Foursquare and Gowalla generate a large number of such POIs. An ad-

[15]`http://www.bing.com/toolbox/bingdeveloper/` visited June 2012

Dataset	Total Sample Sentences	Total POIs	Avg. Sentences per POI
Manual Annotations	1,337	1,066	1.25
Wikipedia Article Sentences	5,186	2,896	1.79
Wikipedia Bootstrapped Snippets	21,228	2,896	7.33
Gowalla Web Snippets	50,000	40,152	1.25
Foursquare Web Snippets	50,000	47,858	1.04

Table 4: Characteristics of the experimental data sets

Source Data	Precision	Recall
Foursquare	0.058	0.044
Gowalla	0.075	0.054
Wikipedia	0.153	0.182

Table 5: Results of evaluating each web snippet-based data set using Yahoo! Placemaker

vantage of this data is that it has high coverage of places the users of these applications actually visit.

Both Foursquare and Gowalla provide public APIs that allow their data to be crawled, within a rate limit. The POIs in this data consist largely of mentions of businesses, but also include landmarks and public buildings such as libraries. Users may select from lists of known POIs (mostly sponsored listings, or licensed data), or they may create their own POI. The majority of check-ins in our data are to pre-existing POIs. They are relatively clean, because the formulaic way in which they appear in the data allows them to be extracted reliably. Although the POIs in this data could be used to create a lexicon of POIs, the POI check-ins cannot be used directly to train or evaluate a sequential model because they contain no textual context. Furthermore, mining this data directly for the POIs would simply be reconstructing an existing database, which is not the aim of this work. Rather we seek to model the way in which POIs are mentioned, to allow discovery of previously unseen POIs.

Once the elements that represent POI names are extracted from the checkin, they are used as seed queries to the Bing search API. These snippets contain sentences where the POI has been used in context (as opposed to the terse, formulaic mentions in the checkins). It should be noted however that this mechanism does not guarantee the snippets' relevance to the seed POI query. Nor does it ensure that all possible POIs present in web snippets are correctly labelled.

This process was carried out for all check-ins, with 10 snippets being retrieved from each seed POI query. This generated millions of sample sentences that could be used for training. For each check-in service, we randomly sampled a subset of 50,000 examples, giving the data set characteristics shown in Table 4. These samples were selected with the criteria that they contained the POI as an exact substring and that the sample contained only unextended ASCII characters. Table 5 shows the bootstrapped snippets tagged for POIs using Placemaker, which represents the state-of-the-art in POI detection. The baseline for the manual annotations was shown in Table 3.

The results of training and testing on this data using 10-fold cross validation, as well as training on the checkin data and evaluating on the manual annotations are shown in Table 6. Note that bootstrapping the data improved the results for the checkin data, whereas the bootstrapped Wikipedia results are much lower than simply training on the original Wikipedia POI mentions.

6. POI LOCALIZATION

In order for the discovery of a point of interest to be useful in an application, it must be associated with a location. We employ the location modeling approach proposed by O'Hare and Murdock [16] to predict the location of the POIs in a sample of the manually annotated data set. We evaluate our approach in terms of the distance in kilometers from the ground truth location of each POI. The Placemaker service is our baseline, as it is the current state-of-the-art. Finally, we use our model and Placemaker in a cascade architecture to improve the results over either system alone.

The location models described in Serdyukov et al. [19] and in O'Hare and Murdock [16] are built by quantizing the coordinate system into one kilometer, 10 km or 100 km cells. For the work in this paper, we choose one kilometer grid cells because we are predicting geographic entities that are mostly smaller than one square kilometer. As in [19] and [16], each cell is associated with the geo-tagged Flickr images that were taken within the cell boundaries. We estimated the models from the raw tags associated with ten million geotagged Flickr images, uploaded to Flickr before October 2010. The cell is represented by the distribution of tags associated with its images. The problem of predicting a location can then be reduced to a standard information retrieval ranking problem where cells are "documents" and the image tags are the terms in the document. In [19] the terms in the cell-documents are weighted by their term frequency. This produces a model that might be biased toward the tags applied to a set of images by a single user. To remediate this, in our models we weight the terms in the cell-documents according to the user frequency, as in [16], the number of users who have applied that tag to that cell, rather than the number of times the tag has been applied in that cell. More specifically,

$$P(t|\theta_L) = \frac{c_{user}(t, L)}{|L|}, \quad (4)$$

where $c_{user}(t, L)$ is the number of unique users who use the term in the location (cell). $|L|$ is calculated as the sum of the user frequency of all terms in the location:

$$|L| = \sum_{t_i \in L} c_{user}(t_i, L). \quad (5)$$

Weighting the terms according to the user frequency, rather than the term frequency, reduces the effects of bulk uploading, or of applying near-duplicate tag sets to multiple images. It has been proposed before for choosing representative

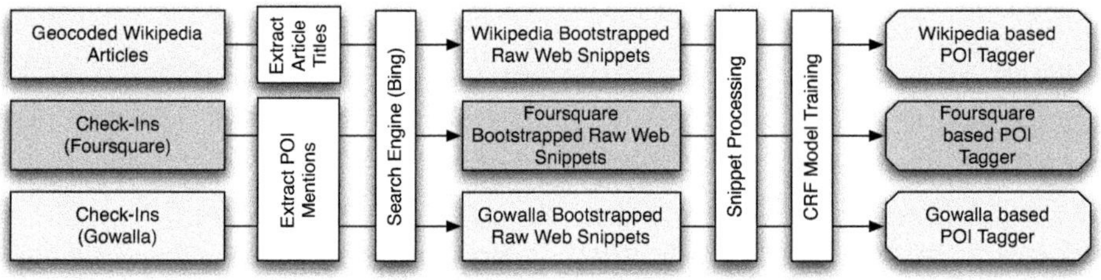

Figure 1: The process to generate a sequential tagger involves extracting mentions of POIs in social media and using these as seed data to generate web snippets.

Training Data	Testing Data	Precision	Recall
Yahoo! Placemaker	All Manual Annotations	0.2372	0.2281
Wikipedia †	All Manual Annotations	0.514	0.337
Wikipedia	Known Manual Annotations	0.447	0.397
Wikipedia	New Manual Annotations	0.521	0.324
Foursquare †	All Manual Annotations	0.276	0.655
Foursquare	Known Manual Annotations	0.215	0.735
Foursquare	New Manual Annotations	0.288	0.638
Gowalla †	All Manual Annotations	0.360	0.414
Gowalla	Known Manual Annotations	0.314	0.510
Gowalla	New Manual Annotations	0.362	0.393
Wikipedia	(10-fold c.v.)	0.879	0.955
Foursquare	(10-fold c.v.)	0.689	0.468
Gowalla	(10-fold c.v.)	0.857	0.868

Table 6: Results of POI tagger trained on bootstrapped web snippet data, evaluated on both human annotated data and using cross validation (c.v.). When each of the three trained models (marked with †) are compared with the baseline Yahoo! Placemaker evaluation, they are found to be significantly different with p-value $<$ 0.001 according to McNemar's χ^2 test.

tags for a given location [3, 10], and for suggesting tags for photos [14].

To evaluate the system, we created a ground truth data set. Although the coordinates given by Placemaker for POIs are derived from curated data sources, and are as accurate as reasonably can be expected, Placemaker does not identify every POI in the data, and when comparing Placemaker to other approaches, both must be compared to a common ground truth. We sampled 400 examples from the manually annotated data described in Section 4. The ground truth locations of the POIs were determined by identifying the address (or geographic coordinates when they were available) of the POI from its official web page. We located the address on a map, and the POI was verified visually by zooming in on the satellite view of the map. POIs were discarded in cases where the POI could not be visually verified on the map, or where the exact address of the POI was not available on its official web page. In our data, out of 400 examples of POIs, 291 represented unique locations according to the geographic coordinates, and 327 were unique mentions of POIs. All of the POIs in our example were mentioned in unique contexts, and the context was used to limit the set of candidate locations.

We measured the Vincenty Distance [22] in kilometers from the predicted location of the POI to its true location. Our localization method predicts the centroid of a one-kilometer grid cell, so our system can be at most accurate within 500 meters at the equator, and more accurate toward the poles. We use the median distance as the metric instead of the average, because a single location that is predicted incorrectly to be on the opposite side of the globe will skew the average distance in such a way as to make the results difficult to interpret.

Our evaluation considers three subsets of the data. The first consists of the subset of examples which are identified by Placemaker as points of interest. We call these "known" locations. The second is the set of examples that Placemaker identifies as some other type of location (such as a city, or a country - the "other" locations). The third consists of locations identified by Placemaker as not containing a location. We call these "new" locations, although they are only new in the sense that they are not in the curated data used by Placemaker. Table 7 shows that placemaker is able to identify 265 locations out of 400, of which 134 are identified as POIs, and 131 are identified as other types of locations. This represents a recall of roughly 33%. Our system localizes 395 out of 400 POIs, a recall of roughly 98%.

When Placemaker identifies a point of interest in text, it localizes it with very high accuracy (roughly 300 meters), thus it makes sense to use Placemaker to find as many POIs as it can. In the cascade model, Placemaker is used first to identify any POIs in the data. For examples that Placemaker does not find a POI, if it finds a location of another type, the bounding box of that location is used to constrain the search for the location in the Location Model, by taking the first result in the ranked list of results returned by the Location model that falls within the bounding box of the location returned by Placemaker.

	265 Locs	134 POIs	131 Other
Placemaker	1.17	0.29	4.19
Location Model	1.77	0.72	3.45
Cascade Model	0.82	0.29	2.90

Table 7: The distance, in kilometers, from the true location to the location predicted by the experimental systems. The 265 locations included in this table were identified by Placemaker, out of 400 total examples. Of the locations found by Placemaker, 134 were identified by Placemaker as points of interest, as opposed to other types of lcoations such as cities, or states.

The Location Model performance in localizing POIs that Placemaker identified as other types of locations is an improvement over the Placemaker result. Using the location information returned by Placemaker, even when Placemaker fails to identify the POI, improves the result further.

For the 130 POIs localized by our system that were determined to contain no place mention by Placemaker, the median distance from the true location was a somewhat depressing 439 kilometers. Clearly, having location information to constrain the search improves performance. The Placemaker system was designed to provide information about the mentions of each individual location in free text, but also to provide information about the text as a whole, such as its geographic scope (the minimum bounding box enclosing most of the locations mentioned in the text). In our data, for the 130 POIs that were deemed non-locations by Placemaker, we took the geographic scope of the textual context from which the POI was originally extracted from (the news article, or query or question-answer pair), and used it to constrain the search in our system. Table 8 shows the results over all examples of the median distance from the predicted location to the true location, when the search in the Cascade model is constrained by the geographic scope.

For locations that are identified by Placemaker, it is clear that other disambiguators in the POI mention improves performance. For example, in the POI "MGM Grand Garden Arena, Las Vegas, NV" Placemaker is unable to identify the arena as the POI, and instead returns the city of Las Vegas. The Location Model ranks the locations associated with the terms mentioned in the POI. In the Cascade Model, after ranking the locations by their score, the list is scanned for the locations that are contained in the bounding box for Las Vegas, NV, and the first location within the bounding box is returned as the correct location of the POI. In the Geo Scope Model, rather than return a bounding box for "Las Vegas, NV", Placemaker returns the geographic scope of the article the POI mention originally appeared in to constrain the search. It is important to note that there is no guarantee that a given POI in an article will be within the geographic scope of the article.

7. DISCUSSION

This work has identified the significant difference between traditional location NER and the task of POI recognition. Such recognition is non-trivial, as demonstrated in Section 4, in which we showed that even with POI labelling undertaken in a strictly controlled environment, consensus was difficult among human assessors.

The subjectivity of POIs also highlights their diverse nature and how their definition is closely dependent on the application in which they are used. It also makes it hard to generate sufficient quantities of manually annotated data for training robust models.

To tackle these problems, we first used Wikipedia as a source of POI mentions and their usage in context. This produced models that performed well at recognizing POIs in Wikipedia articles. However, the POIs found in such text do not reflect the range and variety of those that are used in location-based social media and mobile applications, such as businesses and restaurants.

Social media data, such as location checkins, are an extensive and easily accessible source of POIs, but they lack the textual context required for training sequential models. Extending POIs mentioned in social media with web search engine snippets improves performance over the state of the art. The data itself is not manually labeled, so there is the potential to train on vast amounts of this data cheaply. Furthermore, by being an entirely automatic process run on dynamic data from the Web, models can be continually trained and updated, to capture ephemeral and temporary POIs.

We see that amplifying the Wikipedia data with web snippet data degrades performance. Wikipedia is a very clean data source, and the POIs mentioned in Wikipedia are usually in their canonical form, and in the proper context. Although the data set is small, it is sufficient to predict the entity boundaries for these POIs. It is important to note that such a system can be trained from unlabeled data. Adding web snippet data, however, only makes the data noisier, without adding information.

By contrast, the checkin data benefits greatly from bootstrapping with web snippets. This type of data is an excellent source of POI mentions, but even when there is textual context surrounding the POI mention in the checkin, it is not sufficiently informative to estimate a model from it. Other types of social media data, such as Twitter, may be a good source of information about places that people visit, but it is extremely noisy, and contains abbreviations and textual shortcuts inherent to the constraints of the application itself. Bootstrapping from the web allows the POIs to be placed in a natural language context, which, while noisy, is considerably less noisy than the Twitter data itself.

One reason for lower results on large amounts of data compared to the smaller data sets from Section 4 is the variation in the POIs themselves. They represent different classes of entities and it may be necessary to learn them as distinct classes. It is possible that a mention of a local business in text is not sufficiently similar to a mention of a landmark or library or public school. Since we did not canonicalize the POI mentions or aggregate them according to their geographic coordinates, we do not have equivalences among the POIs. Since the evaluation relies on an exact match of the POI entities, the system is penalized for correct mentions that do not match exactly. For example, if the ground truth assessor marked the POI "The New School" and the system instead tagged the POI "New School," the tagging is completely wrong. Partial credit is not given for correctly matching one boundary but not the other.

With regard to localization, we have shown that we can determine the location of the POI with high accuracy, less than one kilometer for most POIs. In the evaluation, we

	Placemaker	Cascade Model	Geo Scope Model	Number of Examples
Placemaker POIs	0.29	0.29	0.29	134
Placemaker Other Locations	4.19	2.90	2.12	131
All Known Locations	1.17	0.82	0.79	265
New Locations	–	439.0	5.88	130
All Data	–	1.20	0.96	395

Table 8: The distance, in kilometers, from the true location to the location predicted by the Cascade Model, constrained by the geographic scope of the document in which the location mentions appear. The Placemaker results are repeated for the sake of comparison

did not evaluate the end-to-end performance of the entire system, because if a set of tokens is erroneously tagged as a POI, it is not meaningful to try to localize it. The system may correctly guess the location, but if the input to the system is not valid, the evaluation will not be meaningful. The evaluation on the ground-truth tagging gives an upper-bound on the localization performance, as errors generated in the tagging phase will propagate to the localization phase. It may be possible to leverage the localization, either as a filter step, or as a feature in the tagger, to improve the performance of the tagging, but this is left to future work.

The localizer is built on Flickr data, specifically tag sets. The tag sets in Flickr are unique in that they contain mostly nouns, and a few adjectives, and very little noise. Many of the images that are geotagged and uploaded to Flickr portray POIs and tourist destinations. This makes Flickr ideal for localizing POIs in the places where Flickr has coverage. For locations with no Flickr coverage, it is not possible to predict the location. This is a limiting factor that affects all systems built on social media.

The Placemaker system localizes POIs within a median distance of 1.1 kilometers for the locations it identifies (which is just over half of the examples). For the POIs that Placemaker identifies as such, the median distance from the ground truth is around 300 meters. This gives a reasonable bound on the performance of any localization system because the Placemaker system is built upon surveyed, curated data. The differences in the distance from the ground truth can partially be accounted for by the fact that some POIs (such as airports, and university campuses) are larger than one kilometer, and it is not clear how to express the location with a latitude/longitude point.

8. CONCLUSIONS

Points of interest form the basis of content for a growing number of mobile and social media applications. Local search and recommender systems rely on knowing the points of interest in a city in order to understand a user's geographic context, to better serve relevant results. Automatically detecting POIs allows us to develop systems that are dynamic and that reflect the services and places people visit in a city in the course of their daily lives. In this paper we presented a system for detecting POIs in unstructured text from labelled and unlabelled data. We showed system performance on manually annotated data composed mostly of news articles, on Wikipedia articles and on mentions of POIs bootstrapped from social media. We can achieve a precision of up to 87% training and testing on unlabelled data. For half of the POIs, we can identify their location within one kilometer of the true location.

For future work we would like to introduce a more lenient evaluation metric that allows for small variations in the name of a POI. We also intend to refine the learning algorithm to leverage social media data more effectively and to incorporate physical information about the POI such as its relationship to the geography in which it is situated. Finally, as the research community builds more systems on social media data, the credibility of this data must be better understood to determine which data examples are most suitable for training and evaluation.

9. ACKNOWLEDGMENTS

This work was supported in part by the European Commission FP7 programme: (FP7/2011-14) under grant agreement no. 287615 (PARLANCE).

10. REFERENCES

[1] `http://www.itl.nist.gov/iaui/894.02/related_projects/muc/index.html` visited October 2011.

[2] `http://www.itl.nist.gov/iad/mig//tests/ace/` visited October 2011.

[3] S. Ahern, M. Naaman, R. Nair, and J. Yang. World Explorer: Visualizing aggregate data from unstructured text in geo-referenced collections. In *JCDL '07*, 2007.

[4] E. Amitay, N. Har'El, R. Sivan, and A. Soffer. Web-a-where: geotagging web content. In *SIGIR '04*, pages 273–280, New York, NY, USA, 2004. ACM.

[5] M. Collins. Ranking algorithms for named-entity extraction: Boosting and the voted perceptron. In *Proceedings of the Annual Meeting of the Association of Computational Linguistics (ACL)*, 2002.

[6] D. Crandall, L. Backstrom, D. Huttenlocher, and J. Kleinberg. Mapping the world's photos. In *Proceedings of the 18th International Conference on World Wide Web*, pages 761–770. ACM, 2009.

[7] J. Ding, L. Gravano, and N. Shivakumar. Computing geographical scopes of web resources. In *VLDB '00*, pages 545–556, San Francisco, CA, USA, 2000. Morgan Kaufmann Publishers Inc.

[8] J. Hoffart, F. Suchanek, K. Berberich, E. Kelham, G. de Melo, G. Weikum, F. Suchanek, G. Kasneci, M. Ramanath, and A. Pease. Yago2: A spatially and temporally enhanced knowledge base from wikipedia. *Commun. ACM*, 52(4):56–64, 2009.

[9] L. Hollenstein and R. Purves. Exploring place through user-generated content: using Flickr to describe city cores. *Journal of Spatial Information Science*, (1), 2010.

[10] L. Kennedy, M. Naaman, S. Ahern, R. Nair, and T. Rattenbury. How flickr helps us make sense of the world: context and content in community-contributed media collections. In *Proceedings of the 15th international conference on Multimedia*, MULTIMEDIA '07, pages 631–640, New York, NY, USA, 2007. ACM.

[11] J. Lafferty, A. McCallum, and F. Pereira. Conditional random fields: Probabilistic models for segmenting and labeling sequence data. In *Proceedings of the 18th International Conference on Machine Learning (ICML)*, pages 282–289, 2001.

[12] A. McCallum and W. Li. Early results for named entity recognition with conditional random fields, feature induction, and web-enhanced lexicons. In *Proceedings of CoNLL*, 2003.

[13] Q. Mei, C. Liu, H. Su, and C. Zhai. A probabilistic approach to spatiotemporal theme pattern mining on weblogs. In *WWW '06*, 2006.

[14] E. Moxley, J. Kleban, and B. S. Manjunath. Spirittagger: a geo-aware tag suggestion tool mined from flickr. In *Proceeding of the 1st ACM international conference on Multimedia information retrieval*, MIR '08, pages 24–30, New York, NY, USA, 2008. ACM.

[15] L. Mummidi and J. Krumm. Discovering points of interest from users' map annotations. *GeoJournal*, 72:215–227, 2008.

[16] N. O'Hare and V. Murdock. Modeling locations with social media. *Journal of Information Retrieval*, 2012. DOI: 10.1007/s10791-012-9195-y.

[17] N. Okazaki. Crfsuite: a fast implementation of conditional random fields (crfs), 2007.

[18] D. Segal. "Closed, Says Google, but Shops' Signs Say Open". *The New York Times*, September 5, 2011.

[19] P. Serdyukov, V. Murdock, and R. van Zwol. Placing Flickr Photos on a Map. In *Proceedings of the 32nd International ACM SIGIR Conference on Research and Development in Information Retrieval*, pages 484–491. ACM, 2009.

[20] E. F. Tjong and K. Sang. Introduction to the conll-2002 shared task: Language-independent named entity recognition. In *COLING-02 proceedings of the 6th Conference on Natural Language Learning*, 2002.

[21] E. F. Tjong, K. Sang, and F. de Meulder. Introduction to the conll- 2003 shared task. In *CoNLL '03 Proceedings of the Seventh Conference on Natural Language Learning at HLT-NAACL 2003*, 2003.

[22] T. Vincenty. Direct and inverse solutions of geodesics on the ellipsoid with application of nested equations. *Survey Review*, XXIII(176), April 1975.

[23] H. Wallach. Conditional random fields: An introduction. Technical Report Technical report MS-CIS-04-21, University of Pennsylvania, 2004.

[24] C. Wang, J. Wang, X. Xie, and W.-Y. Ma. Mining geographic knowledge using location aware topic model. In *GIR '07*, 2007.

[25] X. Yi, H. Raghavan, and C. Leggetter. Discovering users' specific geo intention in web search. In *WWW '09: Proceedings of the 18th International Conference on World Wide Web*, pages 481–490, New York, NY, USA, 2009. ACM.

[26] Z. Yin, L. Cao, J. Han, C. Zhai, and T. Huang. Geographical topic discovery and comparison. In *Proceedings of the 20th International World Wide Web conference (WWW'11)*, 2011.

[27] V. W. Zheng, Y. Zheng, X. Xie, and Q. Yan. Collaborative location and activity recommendation with gps history data. In *Proceedings of the 19th International World Wide Web conference (WWW'10)*, 2010.

[28] W. Zong, D. Wu, A. Sun, E.-P. Lim, and D. H.-L. Goh. On assigning place names to geography related web pages. In *JCDL '05*, pages 354–362, New York, NY, USA, 2005. ACM.

TwiNER: Named Entity Recognition in Targeted Twitter Stream

Chenliang Li[*1], Jianshu Weng[2], Qi He[3], Yuxia Yao[2], Anwitaman Datta[1], Aixin Sun[1], and Bu-Sung Lee[1,2]
[1] School of Computer Engineering, Nanyang Technological University, Singapore
{lich0020,anwitaman,axsun,ebslee}@ntu.edu.sg
[2] Services Platform Lab, HP Labs, Singapore
{jianshu.weng,yuxia.yao,francis.lee}@hp.com
[3] Almaden Research Center, IBM, USA
heq@us.ibm.com

ABSTRACT

Many private and/or public organizations have been reported to create and monitor targeted *Twitter* streams to collect and understand users' opinions about the organizations. Targeted *Twitter* stream is usually constructed by filtering tweets with user-defined selection criteria (*e.g.,* tweets published by users from a selected region, or tweets that match one or more predefined keywords). Targeted *Twitter* stream is then monitored to collect and understand users' opinions about the organizations. There is an emerging need for early crisis detection and response with such target stream. Such applications require a good named entity recognition (NER) system for *Twitter*, which is able to automatically discover emerging named entities that is potentially linked to the crisis. In this paper, we present a novel 2-step unsupervised NER system for targeted *Twitter* stream, called *TwiNER*. In the first step, it leverages on the *global context* obtained from Wikipedia and Web N-Gram corpus to partition tweets into valid segments (phrases) using a dynamic programming algorithm. Each such tweet segment is a candidate named entity. It is observed that the named entities in the targeted stream usually exhibit a *gregarious* property, due to the way the targeted stream is constructed. In the second step, *TwiNER* constructs a random walk model to exploit the *gregarious* property in the *local context* derived from the *Twitter* stream. The highly-ranked segments have a higher chance of being true named entities. We evaluated *TwiNER* on two sets of real-life tweets simulating two targeted streams. Evaluated using labeled ground truth, *TwiNER* achieves comparable performance as with conventional approaches in both streams. Various settings of *TwiNER* have also been examined to verify our *global context + local context* combo idea.

[*]The work was partially done when Chenliang Li was an intern at HP Labs Singapore.

SIGIR'12, August 12–16, 2012, Portland, Oregon, USA.

Categories and Subject Descriptors

H.3.4 [**Information Systems**]: Content Analysis and Indexing—*Linguistic processing*

Keywords

Twitter, Tweets, Named Entity Recognition, Wikipedia, Web N-Gram

1. INTRODUCTION

Twitter, as a new type of social media, has seen tremendous growth in recent years. It has attracted great interests from both industry and academia. Many private and/or public organizations have been reported to monitor *Twitter* stream to collect and understand users' opinions about the organizations. Nevertheless, due to the extremely large volume of tweets published every day[1], it is practically infeasible and unnecessary to listen and monitor the whole *Twitter* stream. Therefore, targeted *Twitter* streams are usually monitored instead; each such stream contains tweets that potentially satisfy some information needs of the monitoring organization. Targeted *Twitter* stream is usually constructed by filtering tweets with user-defined selection criteria depends on the information needs. For example, the criterion could be a region so that users' opinions from that particular region are collected and monitored; it could also be one or more predefined keywords so that opinions about some particular events/topics/products/services can be monitored.

There is also an emerging need for early crisis detection and response with such target stream. For example, a cosmetic company is interested in automatically discovering any new named entities (e.g. person names, competitor names, or location names) in a targeted stream it creates for the company and its products, which may link to a potential PR crisis. By doing this, the company is able to acquire first-hand information about the crisis and make early response. Such applications require a good named entity recognition (NER) system for *Twitter*, which is the focus of this paper.

Nevertheless, the nature of tweets brings new challenges. Traditional NER methods on well-formatted documents heavily depend on a phrase's local linguistic features [14], such as capitalization, part-of-speech (POS) tags of previous words, etc. However, tweets are usually informal in nature and short (up to 140 charac-

[1]There are more than 200 million tweets published per day, according to `http://blog.twitter.com/2011/06/200-million-tweets-per-day.html`.

ters). They often contain grammatical errors, misspellings, and unreliable capitalizations. These unreliable linguistic features cause traditional methods to perform poorly on tweets. We use the real examples below to illustrate the challenges when applying traditional NER on tweets.

Table 1: Example Named Entities in Tweet

1	**PAP** POSTERS ARE EVERYWHERE! AND FOR SOME LAMP POLES THERE ARE BOTH **NSP** AND **PAP** POSTERS! #whathappentosavingtheearth
2	ya la!! some of them gg to **potong pasir**. I'm gg to **yio chu kang**

Table 1 shows two real tweets collected during a political event. A POS tagger would fail due to the tweets' abnormal capitalization and grammatical errors. For example, in the first tweet, all words (except "PAP" and "NSP")[2] are mislabeled as *NNP* (singular noun). Similarly, in the second tweet, "potong" and "yio" are mislabeled as *JJ* (adjective) and *VB* (verb) respectively, although both are a part of location names ("potong pasir" and "yio chu kang"). This kind of noisy POS labels would make NER tagger fail to recognize named entities.

To address the above challenges caused by tweets' error-prone and short nature, this paper presents a novel unsupervised NER system for targeted tweet streams, called *TwiNER*. Based on the *gregarious* property of named entities in targeted tweet stream, *TwiNER* recognizes named entities collectively from a batch of tweets in unsupervised manner. More formally, let T be the collection of tweets in question. *TwiNER* receives tweets from T in a batch manner. A batch is the set of tweets posted in the targeted *Twitter* stream within one fixed time interval (e.g. a second). So, $T = \{T_1, T_2, .., T_n\}$ and T_i is the batch of tweets posted in the ith interval. *TwiNER* then recognizes all possible named entities in T_i regardless of their types.

It is noted that currently *TwiNER* does not categorize the type of named entity (*e.g.,* person, location). As conventional NER methods fail to address the new challenges posed by emerging social media like *Twitter*, it is more pressing to be able to discover the presence of named entities in targeted *Twitter* stream before we could categorize their types. Furthermore, even without categorizing the types of named entities, *TwiNER* already enable us to make early crisis response. For example, a cosmetic company may be interested in discovering any new named entity which may directly/indirectly link to the company and subsequently causes a PR crisis, be it a person name, product name, or company name. Moreover, as a targeted Twitter stream is constructed for a particular information need, we assume that the user who constructs the stream has the background knowledge in interpreting the named entities detected. In the following subsections, we give an overview of *TwiNER*.

Figure 1 shows the general system architecture of *TwiNER*, which has two main components, namely *tweet segmentation* and *segment ranking*.

1.1 Tweet Segmentation

As shown in Table 1, traditional linguistic features (e.g., capitalization) are unreliable in tweets. Is there any other feature in tweets we can utilize for the task of NER?

In the same examples in Table 1, people spell "yio chu kang" rather than "chu kang yio" or "kang chu yio". In other words, the *correct collocation of a named entity* is still preserved in tweets. This observation holds stronger if a larger set of tweets are aggregated together. This motivates us to learn a weak phrase segmenter for tweets first.

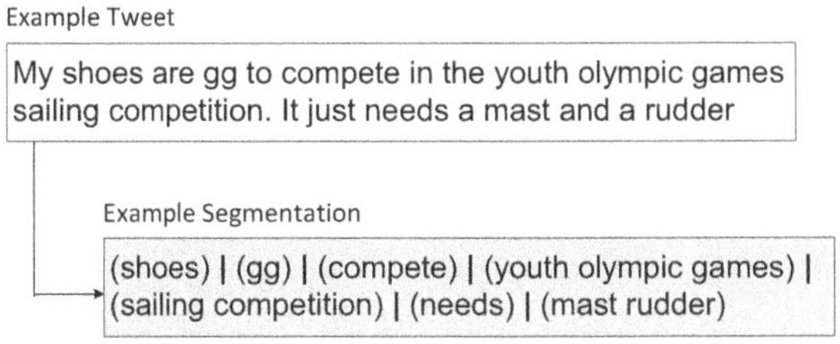

Figure 2: Example of Tweet Segmentation

The idea is to segment an individual tweet into a sequence of consecutive phrases[3], each of which appears "more than chance" [2, 18]. Figure 2 gives an example. In this example, after removing the stop words, a tweet "*My shoes are gg to compete in the youth olympic games sailing competition. It just needs a mast and a rudder*" is segmented into seven parts.

More formally, given a tweet of four words $w_1w_2w_3w_4$, we segment it as $w_1w_2||w_3w_4$ rather than $w_1||w_2w_3w_4$, if $C(w_1w_2)+C(w_3w_4) > C(w_1) + C(w_2w_3w_4)$, where $C(\cdot)$ basically captures *the probability being a valid phrase* of a segment.

A straightforward idea of computing $Pr(\cdot)$ is to count a segment's appearance in a very large corpus. The ideal case is that we use the entire collection of tweets published in *Twitter* to compute the $Pr(\cdot)$ for all possible segments. Unfortunately, to the best of our knowledge, such corpus never exists. Instead, we turn to Microsoft Web N-Gram corpus[4] [19]. This N-Gram corpus is based on all the documents in the World Wide Web indexed by Microsoft Bing in the EN-US market; it provides a good estimate of the statistics of commonly used phrases in English.

Another idea of computing $Pr(\cdot)$ is to look up the segments in a knowledge base where valid segments are more easily recognized. We exploit *Wikipedia* for this purpose, which is by far the largest online encyclopedia in the World Wide Web. We take a snapshot of English *Wikipedia*[5], and build a dictionary by extracting all the article titles, disambiguation pages, redirect pages (synonyms), and wikilinks [8]. If a segment matches any entry in the dictionary, it has a higher prior probability of being a true named entity.

TwiNER combines both ideas in a dynamic programming algorithm to efficiently test various segmentation combinations. Note that in this step, we do not use any local linguistic features of a segment, such as its capitalization. Instead, we leverage on the World Wide Web to derive the segmentation. For ease of presentation, information captured from the World Wide Web for a given segment is called its *global context.*

1.2 Segment Ranking

Each segment extracted in Step (1) is a candidate named entity, e.g. "youth olympic games" and "mast rudder". We now have a huge pool of candidate named entities. Undoubtedly, this pool has a high recall but a very poor precision in identifying the true named entities. For example, among the seven segments extracted in Figure 1, only "youth olympic games" can be considered as a true named entity.

Can we automatically identify the true entities from non-entities in the pool? To address this problem, we learn a function that as-

[2] "PAP" and "NSP" are short forms of political party names. Hashtags such as "#whathappentosavingtheearth" are not considered in this paper.

[3] A segment basically contains a phrase. In the rest of this paper, "segment" and "phrase" are used interchangeably.

[4] http://web-ngram.research.microsoft.com/info/

[5] http://dumps.wikimedia.org/enwiki/

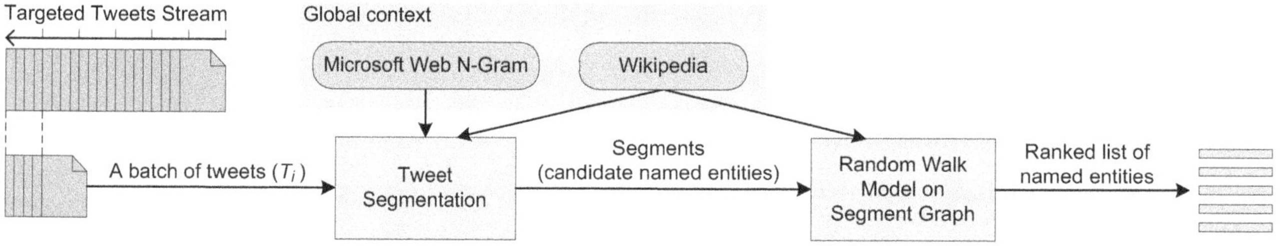

Figure 1: System Architecture of *TwiNER*

signs a confidence score of being a true named entity to each candidate named entity. Candidate named entities are then ranked according to this score. By setting a threshold, we can easily remove the long tails of non-entities with low scores.

Recall there are two types of global context for a given segment in *TwiNER*: Web N-Gram and *Wikipedia*. The former apparently has no clear clue about such score because many common word combinations with high frequency are not named entities, like "there is" and "such a". The latter, on the other hand, provides some hints because many named entities either have corresponding *Wikipedia* pages or have been referenced in *Wikipedia*. However, *Wikipedia* is not as *real-time* as *Twitter*. It usually takes a while for a new named entity appeared in tweets to be captured by *Wikipedia*. For example, in the tweets we use in the experiments, "Vincent Wijeysingha" is the name of a political figure, which appeared in tweets in the early April 2011. Before end of April 2011, there was no mention about this person at all in *Wikipedia*. Furthermore, there is also no guarantee that all named entities in tweets would appear in *Wikipedia* later.

Since the *global context* is insufficient to identify the true named entity, is there any local feature in tweets themselves that we can utilize? It is observed that there exists a *gregarious* property among the named entities in the targeted tweet stream, since the tweets in the targeted tweet stream are normally about similar or related topics/events. Formally, *gregarious* refers to the interaction of named entities with each other and to their collective co-existence in the targeted tweet stream. For example, "Barack Obama" is a named entity. It often co-occurs with other named entities like "United States" and "Michelle Obama" in a targeted stream about *United States*, but seldom co-occurs with "please look", a valid segment extracted from tweets but a non-entity. It is also uncommon that same set of non-entities appear together often.

This *gregarious* property of named entities in *Twitter* motivates us to design a "recursive" algorithm to compute the score of a segment being a named entity. The idea is: an undirected *segment graph* using all the segments extracted in Step (1) is built first, in which nodes are segments and edges are weighed proportional to the co-occurrence similarity; then, a *random walk model* is applied on this graph to derive the probability of a segment being a named entity. Because a segment's confidence is affected by its neighbors in the graph, which only depends on the tweets themselves, we call the *segment graph* as the *local context* of a segment in the tweets. Note that, not only has the *local context* been considered in this model, but also the *global context* is integrated to overcome the limitation of random walk model. Finally, the output of the model is used as the score of a segment being a named entity.

One may wonder that building *local context* (i.e. the *segment graph*) defeats the real-time nature of *Twitter*. Indeed, a buffer of tweets is necessary to construct the local *segment graph*, making *TwiNER* not completely real time (response in a "tweet by tweet" manner). Nevertheless, there are more than 2,000 tweets generated every second[6] in *Twitter*, which is already a big enough buffer to build the *local context* in Step (2). Therefore, *TwiNER* is able to give "near real-time" response practically (in a "second by second" manner).

1.3 Contributions

To sum up, we made the following contributions in the paper:

1. We proposed an unsupervised NER system without explicit human label efforts. Our system does not rely on any linguistic features, making it suitable for tweets and potentially other social text streams with unreliable linguistic features.

2. To the best of our knowledge, our *TwiNER* system is the first to exploit both the *local context* (in *tweets*) and the *global context* (from World Wide Web) together for named entity recognition task in Twitter.

3. The proposed system has been successfully evaluated on two different collections of real-life tweets, simulating two types of targeted twitter streams. A region-based stream for tweets published by users from a particular geographical region; and a topic-based stream for tweets potentially relevant for a political event.

The rest of this paper is organized as follows. A review of related work is given in Section 2. Sections 3 and 4 present the design of *TwiNER* in detail. Following that, experimental results are presented in Section 5 to evaluate the correctness and effectiveness of *TwiNER*. Finally, Section 6 concludes this paper with discussion of future work.

2. RELATED WORK

Tweets are infamous for their error-prone and short nature. This leads to failure of many conventional NLP techniques, which heavily depend on local linguistic features, such as capitalization, POS tags of previous words, etc. Also acknowledging the error-prone nature of tweets, Han and Baldwin [6] proposed to normalize ill-formed words in tweets to make the contents more formal. However, this work does not address the problem of NER. NER has attracted renewed interests recently, due to the challenges posed by tweets. Conventionally, NER studies are mainly conducted in a supervised manner. In most of the cases, they depend on the Part-of-Speech (POS) tags, which again need a tagger to be trained with supervised approach based on linguistic features[14, 20, 21].

There are attempts that design linguistic features to capture tweets' unique characteristics and train tweet-specific models. Gimpel et. al trained a POS tagger with the help of a new labeling scheme and a feature set that captures the unique characteristics of tweets [5]. It was reported to outperform the state-of-the-art Stanford

[6] *200 million Tweets per day*: `http://blog.twitter.com/2011/06/200-million-tweets-per-day.html`.

POS tagger on tweets. In [16], Ritter et. al presented an tweet-based NLP framework which contains tweet-specific NLP tools: POS tagger (*T-POS*), shallow parsing (*T-CHUNK*), capitalization classifier (*T-CAP*), and named entity recognition (*T-NER*). *T-POS* and *T-CHUNK* are trained by using condtional random field (CRF) model with conventional and tweet-specific features. These tweet-specific features include retweets, @usernames, hashtags, URLs, and Brown clustering results. Both *T-POS* and *T-CHUNK* were reported with better performance compared to the state-of-the-art methods. *T-NER* is separated into two task: named entity segmenting (*T-SEG*) and named entity classification (*T-CLASS*). *T-SEG* is trained with a CRF model. The features include orthographic, contextual, dictionary features, and the output by *T-POS*, *T-CHUNK*, and *T-CAP*. *T-CLASS* is implemented by applying Labled-LDA [13] with the external knowledge base Freebase[7]. Liu et. al [9] applied a KNN-based classifier to conduct word-level classification, leveraging the similar and recently labeled tweets. Those pre-labeled results, together with other conventional features (e.g. orthographic and lexical features), were then fed into a CRF model to conduct finer-grained NER.

Due to their supervised nature, those approaches require the availability of labeled data, which is usually expensive to come by. Finin et. al. presented a crowd-sourcing way (using services like Mechanical Turk and CrowdFlower) of preparing labeled data for NER studies in *Twitter* [3]. However, it did not propose a solution for NER.

Similar to *TwiNER*, Downey et. al also proposed a *collocation*-based approach, called *LEX* to detect the boundaries of named entities [2]. Nevertheless, it is not designed for tweet-like informal text. It assumes that named entities are either continuous capitalized words or mixed case phrases beginning and ending with capitalized words, which is apparently too strong to hold in tweets. Silva et. al. [1] studied five different types of *collocation* measurements and their variations for phrase extraction task. Besides SCP measurement used in both *TwiNER* and *LEX*, there are another four types of *collocation measure*. And SCP performs the best among others.

Wikipedia is exploited as a source of *global context* in this paper. *Wikipedia* has been utilized in many text mining and NLP tasks, such as text categorization, topic detection, etc. For NER task, *Wikipedia* is mainly used to derive the category label for phrases, including [7] and [15]. [7] only looks for phrases of no more than eight words that start with a word containing at least one capitalized letter in a sentence, and treats phrases with corresponding *Wikipedia* page as named entities. The head noun of the noun phrase just after *be* in the first sentence of the *Wikipedia* page is picked as the phrase's category. This method is not suitable for informal texts such as tweets due to its heavy dependence on local linguistic features. [15] focused on multilingual NER. It depended on the *Category* information in each English *Wikipedia* page to categorize an English named entity. For a non-English phrase, the *Category* information in its corresponding English *Wikipedia* page, if any, is used for categorization. Nevertheless, it is not clear how named entity candidates are identified in this paper [15].

Existing attempts that exploit *Wikipedia* usually assume that named entities should have corresponding *Wikipedia* pages. This assumption makes them unable to identify emerging named entities which are frequently observed in tweets. However, there are many new named entity mentioned in tweets. In *TwiNER*, information in tweets' *local context* and *global context* are aggregated to calculate the probability that a phrase is a named entity. By doing so, *TwiNER* is able to recognize new named entities which may not appear in *Wikipedia* yet. To the best of our knowledge, it is the first to exploit both the *local context* (in *tweets*) and the *global context* (from World Wide Web) together for NER task in Twitter.

[7]`http://www.freebase.com/`

3. TWEET SEGMENTATION

In this section, we detail our solution for tweet segmentation. Given an individual tweet $t \in T_i$, the problem of tweet segmentation is to split t into m consecutive segments, $t = s_1 s_2 ... s_m$; each segment contains one or more words. To obtain the optimal segmentation, we use the following objective function, where C is the function that measures the *stickiness* of a segment or a tweet defined based on word collocation:

$$\arg\max_{s_1,\ldots,s_m} C(t) = \sum_{i=1}^{m} C(s_i), \tag{1}$$

A high *stickiness* score of segment s indicates that it is not suitable to further split segment s, as it breaks the correct word *collocation*. In other words, a high *stickiness* value indicates that a segment cannot be further split at any internal position.

If the word length of tweet t is l, there exists 2^{l-1} possible segmentations. It is inefficient to iterate all of them and compute their stickiness. We therefore design a dynamic programming algorithm to tackle the problem, which is presented in the following.

3.1 A Dynamic Programming Algorithm

Algorithm 1 outlines our dynamic programming algorithm for tweet segmentation. The basic idea is to recursively conduct binary segmentations and then evaluate the *stickiness* of the resultant segments. More formally, given any segment s from t (s can be t itself or a part of t) and suppose $s = w_1 w_2 ... w_n$, our solution is to conduct a binary segmentation by splitting it into two adjacent segments $s^1 = w_1 ... w_j$ and $s^2 = w_{j+1} ... w_n$ by satisfying:

$$\arg\max_{s^1,s^2} C(s) = C(s^1) + C(s^2). \tag{2}$$

The complexity of Algorithm 1 is $O(lue \log(ue))$, where l is the average tweet length, u is the upper bound of segment length, and e bounds top sub-segments of a segment. Long segments are rare in tweets because each tweet is limited to 140 characters. We observed that in our data, $u = 5$ is a proper bound as the maximum length of a segment, which largely reduces the number of possible segmentations. We also set $e = 5$ so that the segmentation only focuses on top-quality segments and are not stuck by trivial ones, which leads to a complexity of $O(l)$.

3.2 Segment Stickiness Function

In Algorithm 1, one key factor is the *stickiness* function C. A high *stickiness* score of segment s indicates that further splitting segment s would break the correct word *collocation*. There are a number of *collocation* measurements [10, 12]. However, all these measures were defined for two arguments. That is, they were designed to measure the collocation of the bigram or the n-grams with the particular binary partition. A variety of studies have been conducted to extend these binary collocation measures to the n-grams case (where n is greater than 2) [1, 2, 17]. We define the *stickiness* functions by using the generalization framework proposed in [1]. Specifically, the generalized collocation measures of Point Mutual Information (PMI) and Symmetric Conditional Probability (SCP) are studied here.

```
Algorithm 1: Tweet Segmentation
input :
    A tweet: t = w1 w2...wl;
    u: the maximum length of a segment s;
    e: top e segmentations set S for each segment s;
output:
    An optimal tweet segmentation t = s1 s2...sm;
for i = 1 : l do
    initialize a set S_i = {} to store possible segmentation of segment
    s_i = w1 w2...wi;
    if i <= u then
        /* do not split s_i */
        calculate C(s_i);
        add s_i to S_i as a possible segmentation of s_i;
    /* try different possible ways to segment s_i */
    for j = 1 : i - 1 do
        if i - j <= u then
            form two shorter segments of s_i: s_i^1 = w1...wj and
            s_i^2 = w_{j+1}...wi;
            calculate C(s_i^2);
            foreach S_j ∈ S_j do
                /* S_j contains the top e possible
                segmentations of s_i^1, and S_j is one of
                them; */
                concatenate S_j and s_i^2 to form a new segmentation S
                of s_i;
                add S to S_i;
                C(S) = C(S_j) + C(s_i^2)
        Sort S_i and keep only the top e segmentations;
return S ∈ S_l with the highest score as the optimal segmentation;
```

3.2.1 *PMI based Stickiness*

PMI measures the degree that two words occur together more often than by chance. Mathematically, PMI for bigram w_1w_2 is defined as follows:

$$PMI(w_1w_2) = \log \frac{\Pr(w_1|w_2)}{\Pr(w_1)} = \log \frac{\Pr(w_1w_2)}{\Pr(w_1)\Pr(w_2)} \quad (3)$$

Given a segment, $s = w_1...w_n$, PMI is then extended by averaging all binary partitions as follows:

$$PMI(s) = \log \frac{\Pr(w_1...w_n)}{\frac{1}{n-1}\sum_{i=1}^{n-1}\Pr(w_1...w_i)\Pr(w_{i+1}...w_n)} \quad (4)$$

If segment s only contains one word w, we have $PMI(s) = \log \Pr(w)$.

Note that PMI defined above falls into the range of $(-\infty, +\infty)$. The *stickiness* of segment s is then defined by mapping the value of Equation 4 to the range of $[0, 1]$ as follows:

$$C(s) = \frac{1}{1 + e^{-PMI(s)}} \quad (5)$$

3.2.2 *SCP based Stickiness*

Symmetrical Conditional Probability (SCP) was proposed in [1] to measure the "cohesiveness" of bigram w_1w_2 by considering both conditional probabilities for the bigram given each single term:

$$SCP(w_1w_2) = \Pr(w_1w_2|w_1)\Pr(w_1w_2|w_2) = \frac{\Pr(w_1w_2)^2}{\Pr(w_1)\Pr(w_2)} \quad (6)$$

Given a segment, $s = w_1...w_n$, SCP of s is defined similarly as follows:

$$SCP(s) = \frac{\Pr(s)^2}{\frac{1}{n-1}\sum_{i=1}^{n-1}\Pr(w_1...w_i)\Pr(w_{i+1}...w_n)} \quad (7)$$

Here, we smooth SCP value by taking logarithm calculation, Equation 7 is then updated as follows:

$$SCP(s) = \log \frac{\Pr(s)^2}{\frac{1}{n-1}\sum_{i=1}^{n-1}\Pr(w_1...w_i)\Pr(w_{i+1}...w_n)}, \ SCP(s) \in (-\infty, 0) \quad (8)$$

Similarly, we define SCP for any segment s of unit length as $SCP(s) = 2\log \Pr(w)$. We then define the *stickiness* of s by using the sigmoid function as follows:

$$C(s) = \frac{2}{1 + e^{-SCP(s)}} \quad (9)$$

3.3 Enhanced Stickiness by World Wide Web

By now, the calculation of the stickiness is reduced to estimating $\Pr(s)$, $\Pr(s^1)$, and $\Pr(s^2)$ for any segment $s \subset t$, which are prior probabilities of segments. To accurately estimate these prior probabilities, we need a large enough corpus as the *global context* of each segment. The ideal global context is the entire collection of tweets published in *Twitter*. But unfortunately, to the best of our knowledge, such corpus is not available.

Instead, we exploit the one provided by Microsoft Web N-Gram Services [19] as approximation. This corpus is based on the web documents indexed by Microsoft Bing search engine in the EN-US market. The spam and other low quality documents are excluded. Each indexed document is parsed, tokenized, and the text is lowercased with the punctuations removed. No stemming, spelling correction or inflections are performed [19], which provides a large enough English corpus to estimate prior probabilities of segments.

One problem of segmentation based on the lexical statistics derived from such corpus is its preference towards frequent patterns. Figure 3 illustrates such an example, with a portion of tweet and three possible segmentations.

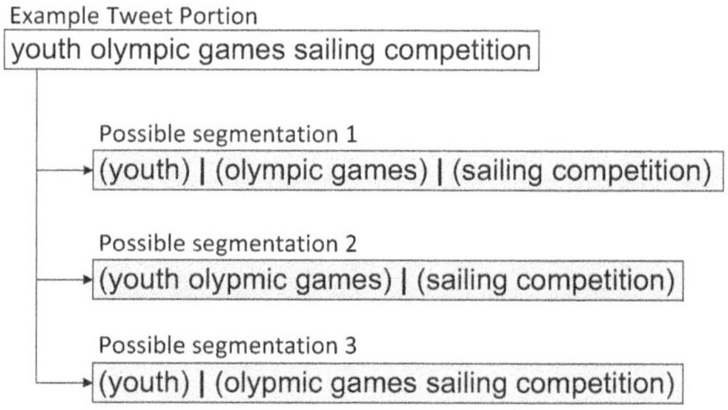

Figure 3: Different Segmentations of a Portion of Tweet

If only Web documents are used as a priori knowledge, then "*youth olympic games sailing competition*" would be segmented into "*youth*" and "*olympic games sailing competition*" (*i.e.*, the possible segmentation 3 in the figure), because both "*youth*" and "*olypmic games sailing competition*" are frequent in Web documents. Nevertheless, this tweet is in fact referring to "Youth Olympic Games" held in Singapore in 2010.

We therefore leverage a knowledge base in the World Wide Web, *Wikipedia*, as another source of *global context* to tackle this problem. There are several reasons for the choice of *Wikipedia*. It provides rich a priori knowledge about entity information and is publicly available. Article titles, references to other *Wikipedia* pages, and the disambiguation pages, have often been used as named entity candidates [7, 15]. In detail, we build a large *Wikipedia* dictionary by extracting from a snapshot of *Wikipedia* on January 30, 2010 all the English article titles, disambiguation pages, redirect pages as well as hyperlinks [8]. Articles isolated from the rest are removed. Finally, we have a *Wikipedia* dictionary of 4,342,732 entries as well as their polysemes, synonyms.

Let $Q(s)$ be the probability that s appears as anchor text in its mentioning *Wikipedia* article, which is the number of *Wikipedia* articles containing s as anchor text divided by the number of *Wikipedia* articles s appears in. A segment appearing as anchor text with a high probability in *Wikipedia* is a strong indication that it is a valid name entity[8]. The *stickiness* function is now defined as follows:

$$C'(s) = C(s) \cdot e^{Q(s)} \tag{10}$$

$C(s)$ is measured by exploiting the *global context* captured in Microsoft Web N-Gram. The second component of Equation 10 is introduced so that segments appearing in Wikipedia as anchor texts are attributed with higher *stickiness*.

3.4 Length Normalization

So far, we treat segments of various lengths equally. However, in Twitter NER task, there are only a few long named entities. And it is observed that longer valid segments have higher chances of being named entities than shorter ones. Note that the Web N-gram data has already had a strong preference for short segments. Given this, we introduce length normalization $\mathcal{L}(s)$ to Equation 10 to favor moderately long segments in both Web N-gram and *Wikipedia*. Finally, we have the following *stickiness* function:

$$C''(s) = \mathcal{L}(s) \cdot e^{Q(s)} \cdot C(s) \tag{11}$$

The length normalization factor $\mathcal{L}(s)$ is empirically defined as:

$$\mathcal{L}(s) = \begin{cases} \frac{|s|-1}{|s|}, \text{ for } |s| > 1 \\ 1, \text{ for } |s| = 1 \end{cases} \tag{12}$$

4. SEGMENT RANKING

Section 3 extracts a large number of segments which are valid in the sense of word collocation by leveraging segments' *global context* in the World Wide Web. However, not all segments extracted are named entities. For example, "please look" is a valid segment but not a named entity. In this section, a set of strategies have been developed to rank segments according to their likelihood of being named entities.

4.1 Noise Filtering

We first remove three types of segments which are obviously *not* named entities.

1. Segments containing well-known slang words, e.g. "lol" and "tmr". We use a compilation of Internet slangs provided by `http://www.noslang.com/dictionary/full`.
2. Segments containing words with consecutive repeating characters, e.g."hahahaha", "nooooo", and "gooooood". These words are frequently used in tweets to represent exaggerative emotions. Regular expressions are used to recognize them.
3. Segments containing words with "#" as prefix. Those words are usually *hashtags* in tweets, which are created by users to highlight keywords/topics. They are not considered named entities in this paper, and can be easily removed by locating the "#" prefix.

4.2 Local Segment Graph

The *global context* alone is insufficient to recognize a named entity. We therefore utilize the *local context* of a segment in tweets to tackle this problem. One intuitive solution is to weigh a segment using its frequency in tweets. However, this method would wrongly favor phrases like "please look", which is not only frequent in World Wide Web, but also frequent in Twitter.

As we discussed in Section 1, there exists a *gregarious* property among named entities in targeted tweet streams. A good example is "Barack Obama". It is a true named entity, and it often co-occurs with other named entities like "United States" or "Michelle Obama" in tweets, but seldom co-occurs with "please look", a valid segment but non-entity. It is also uncommon that same set of non-entities would appear together often.

Based on this property, we propose a "segment graph". At the ith interval (recall that *TwiNER* recognizes named entities in a batch mode), we build an undirected *segment graph* $G(V, E)$ using all segments V extracted from the tweet set T_i on the fly. In this graph, each node is a valid segment after noise filtering, and the edge $e_{ab} \in E$ between two nodes (segments) s_a and s_b is weighed by the *Jaccard Index*:

$$w_{ab} = w(e_{ab}) = \frac{|M(s_a) \cap M(s_b)|}{|M(s_a) \cup M(s_b)|}, \tag{13}$$

where $M(s)$ is the set of tweets in T_i containing segment s.

The *segment graph* $G(V, E)$ provides a good *local context* for each segment in T_i. It does not use the unreliable local linguistics features of tweets but relies on the relations among segments. Because all segments have been parsed once by their *global context* and then filtered with heuristic rules, these relations are relatively more reliable than local linguistics features.

4.3 Random Walk Model

A *random walk model* is then applied on graph $G(V, E)$ to compute the stationary probability of each segment being a true named entity, by considering the graph bidirectional. While random walking, the probability of transiting from node s_a to node s_b (denoted as P_{ab}) is given by

$$P_{ab} = \frac{w_{ab}}{\sum_{c \in V} w_{ac}}. \tag{14}$$

All transition probabilities are then aggregated to form a nonnegative transition matrix P for the whole graph.

To overcome the "dangling links" while conducting a random walk on graph $G(V, E)$, a teleportation vector $\mathbf{e}$ is also introduced to make the random walker jump from a node to any other node in the *segment graph* with a small probability [11]. We observe that $Q(s)$, the probability that s appears as anchor text in *Wikipedia*, is a good teleportation a priori. In other words, we favor those segments that are valid hyperlinks in *Wikipedia*, i.e. those segments are more likely to be named entities. Accordingly, we define the following teleportation probability for node (segment) s:

$$\mathbf{e}_s = \frac{Q'(s)}{\sum_{s_j \in V} Q'(s_j)}, \ \textit{where } Q'(s) = e^{Q(s)}. \tag{15}$$

The exponential function is used here to avoid the situation that the segment is *new* to *Wikipedia* so that its $Q(s) = 0$ and will never be teleported to.

The *Wikipedia*-based teleportation can be considered as an injection of global context into the random walk model of the local context. With the transition matrix P and the *Wikipedia*-based teleportation vector $\mathbf{e}$, the stationary eigenvector π^T of P is calculated iteratively using power method as below:

$$\pi = (\gamma P^T + (1 - \gamma)\mathbf{e}\mathbf{1}^T)\pi, \tag{16}$$

where γ controls the probability of teleportation. The lower γ is, the higher probability the random walk will teleport according to $\mathbf{e}_s$.

Then, π^T is used as probabilities of segments being named entities in the local context.

Finally, for balancing the advantages of *global context* and *local context*, given an input segment s, *TwiNER* multiples its stationary probability $\pi(s)$ in the *segment graph* mainly learned from the local context with its teleportation probability learned from Wikipedia:

$$y(s) = \mathbf{e}_s \cdot \pi(s). \quad (17)$$

Equation 17 is used to rank all segments, and only the top K segments are retained as named entities.

5. EVALUATION

In this section, we conduct extensive experiments to evaluate *TwiNER*. In Section 5.1, datasets simulating two targeted twitter streams are described, and performance metrics are introduced. Section 5.2 compares *TwiNER* with existing methods. We then present a performance analysis of *TwiNER* in different settings in Section 5.3.

5.1 Tweets Data and Performance Metrics

Tweets collections. Two collections of tweets are used in the experiments to simulate targeted twitter streams.

The first collection (*SIN*) was collected to simulate targeted twitter stream of one particular geolocation by monitoring a number of Singapore-based[8] users' tweets published in June 2010. The set of users to be monitored was populated by first getting the top-1000 Singapore-based *Twitter* users with the most number of followers from `http://twitaholic.com`, and then expanding the list by including the top users' followers and friends in *Twitter* within two hops. There are a number of real-life events in the data collection period, such as the flash flood in Orchard Road (a premium shopping belt in Singapore), FIFA World Cup 2010 and WWDC 2010, etc. Collection *SIN* contains 4,331,937 tweets.

The second collection (*SGE*) was collected to simulate targeted twitter stream of one particular event by monitoring a set of predefined keywords related to Singapore General Election 2011. Similar to collection *SIN*, only tweets published by Singapore-based users were collected. The data collection started on April 13, 2011 and ended on May 13, 2011, which covered the duration of Singapore General Election 2011 (nomination day on April 27, 2011, and polling day on May 7, 2011). Collection *SGE* contains 226,744 tweets.

It is observed that, by collecting tweets based on users, topics covered in collection *SIN* are diverse in nature. Topics covered in collection *SGE*, on the other hand, are more concentrated since most of the discussions are about the general election. Another observation is that, twitter users are more formal in political discussions than casual discussions. In other words, tweets in *SGE* are more formal than those in *SIN*.

Manual Annotation. For both collections, 5,000 tweets are randomly sampled from the tweets published on one random day. Each tweet is then labeled by two human annotators, who have strong background knowledge about Singapore-related named entities. The BILOU schema is used [9, 14]. After discarding retweets and tweets with inconsistent annotations, we get 4,422 tweets for *SIN* and 3,328 tweets for *SGE*. We denote these two randomly sampled tweets collections with groundtruth labeling as *SIN_g* and *SGE_g* respectively. Observe that the annotating agreement is relatively low for collection *SGE*. This is mainly due to the disagreement between the human annotators about the way how to handle the concept *GRC*[9] and *SMC*[10], which refer to different types of electoral divisions in Singapore. Annotators did not have an agreement on whether a GRC/SMC should be labeled as part of a location name. For example, some may label "*aljunied grc*" as "*<U>aljunied</U> grc*", while some may label as "*<B>aljunied</B> <L>grc</L>*".

Performance Metric. Performance metrics used throughout the experiments include: Precision(*Prec*), Recall(*Recall*), and *F1*. *Prec* quantifies the percentage of the extracted phrases that are true named entities. *Recall* quantifies the percentage of the true named entities that are correctly recognized. *F1* is the harmonic mean of *Prec* and *Recall*, *i.e.*, $F1 = 2 \cdot \frac{Prec \cdot Recall}{Prec + Recall}$.

Note that different values of K (the parameter in the *segment ranking* step) would result in different performance of *TwiNER*: larger K will increase *Recall* but decrease *Prec*, and vice versa. *TwiNER*'s performance reported in the following sections are the ones with the highest *F1* score *TwiNER* can achieve using SCP-based *stickiness* function, and various values of K. For a fair comparison, K is set to be larger than 50 (*i.e.*, $K > 50$). The maximum iteration for the random walk is fixed at 500.

5.2 Comparison with Other Methods

In this section, we compare *TwiNER* with two conventional NER systems trained on tweets. Specifically, we train Stanford-NER and LBJ-NER with the labeled tweet data and evaluate their performance[11]. Moreover, we also compare with a tweet-specific NER system (T-NER)[12] proposed in [16] on the two tweet collections.

- LBJ-NER: A NER system based on the regularized averaged perceptron approach which uses gazetteers extracted from *Wikipedia*, word class models derived from unlabeled text, and expressive non-local features [14]. It is reported to have achieved the best result (F1-Measure of 0.908) on the CoNLL 2003 test set.

- Stanford-NER: A NER system based on CRF model which incorporates long-distance information [4]. It achieves good performance consistently across different domains.

- T-NER: a supervised NER system uses CRF model for learning and inference. A set of widely-used effective features are used in T-NER, including orthographic, contextual, and dictionary features [16].

Note that, other than the proposed *TwiNER*, the three methods listed above (*i.e.*, LBJ-NER, Stanford-NER and T-NER) are supervised methods and require labeled examples. For performance comparison, we randomly split both *SIN_g* and *SGE_g* in the ratio of 6 : 4 as training and evaluation sets. Stanford-NER and LBJ-NER are trained with default feature settings[13]. While LBJ-NER requires development set for the parameter tuning, we further split the training set in the ratio of 5 : 1 for training and development. All the methods are evaluated on the same evaluation set.

[8] A user is considered Singapore-based if she specifies Singapore in the *location* field of her profile.

[9] `http://en.wikipedia.org/wiki/Group_Representation_Constituency`

[10] `http://en.wikipedia.org/wiki/Single_Member_Constituency`

[11] Note that as the entity type classification is not the focus of this paper, we do not differentiate the entity types when both LBJ-NER and Stanford-NER are trained.

[12] `https://github.com/aritter/twitter_nlp`

[13] We use the same settings for training as in the CoNLL-2003 shared task. `http://www.cnts.ua.ac.be/conll2003/ner/`

Table 2: Different NER systems' performance on tweets

System	Dataset	Prec	Recall	F1
LBJ-NER	*SGE_g*	0.933	0.595	0.727
Stanford-NER	*SGE_g*	**0.950**	**0.880**	**0.913**
T-NER	*SGE_g*	0.713	0.359	0.478
TwiNER	*SGE_g*	0.929	0.660	0.772
LBJ-NER	*SIN_g*	**0.764**	0.265	0.393
Stanford-NER	*SIN_g*	0.762	0.293	0.423
T-NER	*SIN_g*	0.429	**0.509**	**0.466**
TwiNER	*SIN_g*	0.419	0.329	0.419

Table 2 shows the evaluation results of different NER systems. It can be observed from Table 2 that:

1. As observed in Table 2, the overall performance on *SGE_g* is much better than on *SIN_g* by all methods. For the case of LBJ-NER and Stanford-NER, the main reason is the adverse impact of error-prone local context of tweets, since *SIN_g* has more tweets of informal style. This results in a low quality of training set based on the linguistic features. *TwiNER* extracts named entities by exploiting the *local context*. Since *SIN_g* is collected by monitoring twitter users of Singapore, diverse topics are collected. This makes *gregarious* property relatively weaker in this collection, which results in the relatively lower performance of *TwiNER* on *SIN_g*.

2. T-NER performs consistently across the two evaluation sets. Since it was developed by taking into consideration tweets' error-prone context, it outperforms Stanford-NER and LBJ-NER and achieves the best performance on *SIN_g* in terms of $F1$. However, the decrease of *Prec* on *SIN_g* from that on *SGE_g* (0.713 → 0.429) indicates that it still suffers a lot from tweets' error-prone nature.

3. No system outperforms the others on both collections. Stanford-NER performs much better the other systems on *SGE_g*, with F1 performance more than 0.91. However, it only achieves a slightly better $F1$ performance than LBJ-NER and *TwiNER* on *SIN_g*. LBJ-NER performs the worst on *SIN_g* and the third best on *SGE_g* in terms of $F1$. Moreover, the supervised system evaluated here, Stanford-NER, LBJ-NER, and T-NER, achieve relatively lower *Recall* across both collections. This indicates that supervised methods relying on local linguistical features may not generalize well for tweet's error-prone and dynamic nature.

4. *TwiNER*, an unsupervised approach, achieves comparable $F1$ performance with the other supervised systems. *TwiNER* performs much better than LBJ-NER and T-NER on *SGE_g*. It also outperforms LBJ-NER and achieves a comparable performance with Stanford-NER on *SIN_g* in terms of $F1$, where *gregarious* property is relatively weak.

As this set of experiments show, performance of LBJ-NER and Stanford-NER deteriorate significantly when they are applied on tweets, due to tweets' error-prone context. To further illustrate the adverse impacts of tweets' error-prone context, we trained LBJ-NER and Stanford-NER with formal text corpus using the CoNLL-2003 shared task data, and then directly apply the trained models on the evaluation sets of *SIN_g* and *SGE_g*. To distinguish the methods trained using tweet data, we denote the two methods trained on formal text LBJ-NER^F and Stanford-NER^F respectively.

Table 3: Conventional NER systems' performance on tweets

System	Dataset	Prec	Recall	F1
LBJ-NER^F	*SGE_g*	0.674	0.400	0.502
Stanford-NER^F	*SGE_g*	0.691	0.642	0.666
TwiNER	*SGE_g*	**0.929**	**0.660**	**0.772**
LBJ-NER^F	*SIN_g*	0.314	0.314	0.314
Stanford-NER^F	*SIN_g*	0.256	**0.461**	0.329
TwiNER	*SIN_g*	**0.419**	0.329	**0.419**

The results of LBJ-NER^F, Stanford-NER^F and *TwiNER* are summarized in Table 3. It is observed that the performance of LBJ-NER^F and Stanford-NER^F deteriorate significantly with F1-measure of lower than 0.5 on both *SIN_g* and *SGE_g*.

5.3 Analysis of TwiNER

In this section, we investigate the impact of different *TwiNER* components on its performance.

5.3.1 Performance of Tweet Segmentation

Tweet segmentation is used to extract the named entity candidates from tweets, or in other words, to identify the correct boundary of potential named entities in tweets. It is a critical component because the performance of *TwiNER* is heavily affected by the effectiveness of tweet segmentation.

Two *stickiness* functions are defined by using two collocation measures, PMI and SCP, for tweet segmentation. The tweet segmentation algorithm described in Section 3 also incorporates an external knowledge base *Wikipedia*. Further, we normalize the segment length to favor long named entities. In this section, we study the impact of the collocation measures (*PMI* or *SCP*), the *Wikipedia* dictionary (*Wiki*), and the length normalization (*Norm*), based on the ground truth in *SIN_g* and *SGE_g*. We use tweet segmentation with only PMI or SCP measures as the baseline (Equation 5 and 9). We measure the percentage of named entities that are correctly extracted (i.e. split as a segment) as the performance metric, which is denoted as *Prec* as well. The experimental results are listed in Table 4. From Table 4, we observe that:

1. *SCP* significantly outperforms *PMI* for tweet segmentation. We believe this is because PMI returns disproportionately high values for frequent items. This property makes PMI prefer longer segments, which is confirmed by manual investigation of the segmentation result. For example, we observe that "*sdp*" cannot be extracted from "*vote sdp*" by PMI, since PMI-based *stickiness* returns 0.397 for "*vote sdp*", and only 0.017 and 0.004 for "*vote*" and "*sdp*". While SCP-based *stickiness* returns only $5.76E-5$ for "*vote sdp*", and $6.51E-4$ for "*vote*"+"*sdp*".

2. Length normalization (*Norm*) is effective and improves the accuracy of tweet segmentation in the two collections for SCP-based *stickiness*. For example, given a long segment like "*java programming language*", *SCP+Norm* is able to fairly treat it as a named entity, while *SCP* split it as "*java*" and "*programming language*". Since PMI prefers longer segments, further preference introduced by *Norm* does aggravate the problem.

3. *Wikipedia*'s broad coverage and high quality knowledge help reclaim incorrect decisions made by the lexical statistics or reinforce the correct decisions. For instance, *SCP* cannot extract "*pap*" from "*pap team*" given the latter is a frequent

Table 4: Impacts of Tweet Segmentation by SCP

Scheme	Prec@*SIN_g*	Prec@*SGE_g*
SCP	0.721	0.830
SCP+Norm	0.737	0.861
SCP+Wiki	0.739	0.841
SCP+Norm+Wiki	**0.758**	**0.874**
PMI	0.317	0.288
PMI+Norm	0.297	0.288
PMI+Wiki	**0.344**	**0.319**
PMI+Norm+Wiki	0.332	0.308

phrase. With the priori knowledge from *Wikipedia*, where "*pap*" has a $Q(s)$ value of 0.181, "*pap*" is successfully extracted by *SCP+Wiki*.

4. The combination of *Wikipedia* dictionary and length normalization further boosts up the performance of tweet segmentation of SCP-based *stickiness*. This indicates that *Wiki* and *Norm* are complementary to each other. For example, we observe a tweet part "*pap give free iphones*" in a tweet. All of *SCP*, *SCP+Wiki*, and *SCP+Norm* fail to split "*free*" and "*iphones*" apart due to the frequent usage of "*free iphones*" in web documents. However, by combining the both *Wiki* and *Norm*, "*iphones*" is successfully extracted. Also, positive improvement from *PMI+Norm+Wiki* compared to *PMI+Norm* shows the ability of reclaiming incorrect decisions by exploiting *Wikipedia* dictionary.

5.3.2 Impact of Random Walk on Segment Ranking

A *random walk* model is applied to exploit the *gregarious* property of named entities in tweets. The final segment ranking output is an aggregation from the stationary probability of the *random walk* model (*local context*) and the segment's *Wikipedia*-based teleportation *Wiki* probability (*global context*). We analyze their impact on the performance of segment ranking in this section. Specifically, we investigate the following schemes for segment ranking:

- *MFS*: A naive method that ranks the segments based on their frequency in the collection. That is, the most frequent segments are ranked higher.
- *Wiki*: A naive method that ranks the segments based on their *Wikipedia*-based teleportation probability.
- *RW*: A simple random walk with uniform teleportation. The segments are then ranked based on the stationary probability $\pi(s)$.
- *RWW*: A random walk with *Wikipedia*-based teleportation. The segments are then ranked based on the stationary probability $\pi(s)$.
- *RWW+Wiki*: A random walk with *Wikipedia*-based teleportation, while the segments are ranked based on Equation 17.

Table 5 lists the experimental results based on the ground truth in *SIN_g* and *SGE_g*. From Table 5, it can be seen that:

1. While MFS works considerably well on *SGE_g*, its performance degrades significantly on *SIN_g*. The tremendous difference in performance is mainly due to the difference between the nature of the two collections *SGE_g* and *SIN_g*. As discussed earlier, *SGE_g* are tweets published in one day during Singapore General Election 2011. Thus, most of the tweets are about the election and related named entities frequently appear in these tweets. Thus, MFS achieves decent performance. However, MFS hardly recognizes any named entities due to the diverse topics covered on *SIN_g*. This also reflects the degrees of *gregarious* property of the two collections.

Table 5: Impacts of *local context*, *global context* and *random walk* on segment ranking

Scheme	Prec@*SIN_g*	Recall@*SIN_g*	F1@*SIN_g*
MFS	0.039	**0.753**	0.074
Wiki	0.433	0.398	0.415
RW	0.039	0.752	0.074
RWW	0.048	0.336	0.084
RWW+Wiki	**0.576**	0.335	**0.423**
	Prec@*SGE_g*	Recall@*SGE_g*	F1@*SGE_g*
MFS	0.736	0.565	0.639
Wiki	0.738	**0.688**	0.712
RW	0.856	0.536	0.659
RWW	**0.985**	0.536	0.694
RWW+Wiki	0.929	0.646	**0.762**

2. *RW* outperforms *MFS* significantly on *SGE_g* in terms of $F1$. This validates our assumption that named entities are more likely to co-occur with one another than with non-entities. Since *SIN_g* is very diverse, *gregarious* property is too weak to improve the segment ranking. *RWW* significantly outperforms MFS and RW in terms of *Prec* and $F1$ in *SIN_g* and *SGE_g*. The *Wikipedia*-based teleportation priori positively influences the random walk process.

3. An impressive performance is achieved by *Wiki*. It obtains the second best performance in both of the two collections, in terms of $F1$ measure. *RWW+Wiki* achieves the best performance in both *SIN_g* and *SGE_g* in terms of $F1$. We can see that it obtains a large improvement for *Prec*. We believe that the usage of *Wikipedia*-based priori in Equation 17 is the main contributing factor for the improvement of *Prec* compared to *Wiki*. Furthermore, the random walk with *Wikipedia*-based teleportation boost up many named entities that may not be covered by *Wikipedia*, by leveraging the co-occurrence of local context. This results in further improvement of *Prec*.

5.3.3 Impact of K Value

TwiNER's performance is related to the choice of K. Larger K will increase *Recall* and decrease *Prec*, and vice versa. In reality, what matters is rather how many real named entities are in the top list, so that the user can gain direct understanding on what the targeted tweets/Twitter users are concerning about. Thus, we calculate *Prec@K* for each K value from 1 to 200[14]. Here, *Prec@K* is the percentage of top K segments returned by *TwiNER* that are real named entities. Figure 4 shows *Prec@K* curves of *TwiNER* on *SGE_g* and *SIN_g*. Major proportion of segments returned when $K < 50$ are true named entities. *TwiNER* achieves a stable *Prec* performance when K is in the range of $[50, 100]$. After 100, *Prec@K* starts to degrade slowly on *SGE_g*, while *Prec@K* is still stable at

[14]We believe $K <= 200$ is a good range for the tweet collections we studied here.

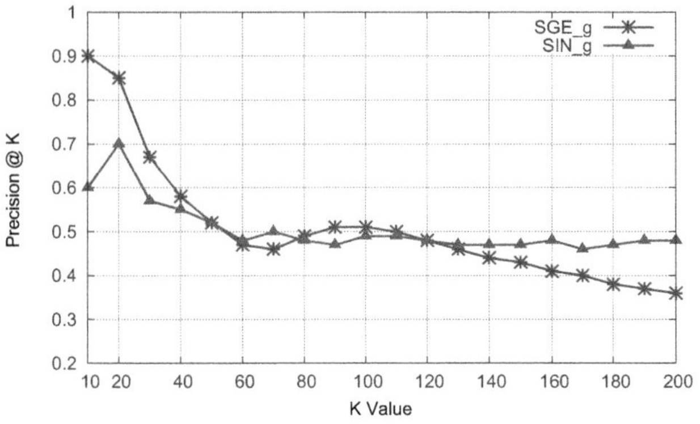

Figure 4: Precision of top K named entities

around 0.5 on *SIN_g*. A good strategy of choosing the suitable K value in various scenarios is planned for future work. Nevertheless, it is observed that the choice of K value depends on the nature of targeted tweet streams, such as topic cohesiveness, *gregarious* property, and size of the tweet collections.

Based on the extensive experiments conducted above, we see that by incorporating the encoded intelligence of World Wide Web and local context of tweets, *TwiNER* shows a promising performance. It provides an unsupervised approach for named entity recognition for Twitter, especially for targeted tweet streams with high *gregarious* property.

6. CONCLUSIONS AND FUTURE WORK

Twitter, as a new type of social media, has attracted great interests from both industry and academia. Many private and/or public organizations have been reported to monitor *Twitter* stream to collect and understand users' opinions about the organizations. Nevertheless, it is practically infeasible and unnecessary to listen and monitor the whole *Twitter* stream, due to it extremely large volume. Therefore, targeted *Twitter* streams are usually monitored instead. Targeted *Twitter* stream is usually constructed by filtering tweets with user-defined selection criteria. There is also an emerging need for early crisis detection and response with such target stream.

Nevertheless, the error-prone and short nature of *Twitter* has brought new challenges to named entity recognition. In this paper, we present a NER system for targeted *Twitter* stream, called *TwiNER*, to address this challenge. Unlike traditional methods, *TwiNER* is unsupervised. It does not depend on the unreliable local linguistics features. Instead, it aggregates information garnered from the World Wide Web to build robust *local context* and *global context* for tweets. Experimental results show promising results of *TwiNER*. It is also shown to achieve comparable performance with the state-of-the-art NER systems in real-life targeted tweet streams.

Despite its promising results, there is still space for improvement. First of all, we plan to study *TwiNER*'s performance in a larger scale. Second, we plan to study the strategy to identify suitable K value. Last but not least, this paper does not address the problem of entity type classification. As discussed earlier, this is because we feel this problem is not as pressing as the problem to correctly locate and recognize presence of named entities in tweets, which existing methods largely fail. Extension of *TwiNER* for entity type classification is also planed for future work.

7. REFERENCES

[1] J. F. da Silva and G. P. Lopes. A local maxima method and a fair dispersion normalization for extracting multi-word units from corpora. In *Proc. of the 6th Meeting on Mathematics of Language*, 1999.

[2] D. Downey, M. Broadhead, and O. Etzioni. Locating complex named entities in web text. In *Proc. of IJCAI*, 2007.

[3] T. Finin, W. Murnane, A. Karandikar, N. Keller, J. Martineau, and M. Dredze. Annotating named entites in twitter data with crowdsourcing. In *Proc. of the Workshop on Creating Speech and Language Data With Mechanical Turk at NAACL-HLT*, 2010.

[4] J. R. Finkel, T. Grenager, and C. Manning. Incorporating non-local information into information extraction systems by gibbs sampling. In *Proc. of ACL*, 2005.

[5] K. Gimpel, N. Schneider, B. O'Connor, D. Das, D. Mills, J. Eisenstein, M. Heilman, D. Yogatama, J. Flanigan, and N. A. Smith. Part-of-speech tagging for twitter: Annotation, features, and experiments. In *Proc. of ACL*, 2011.

[6] B. Han and T. Baldwin. Lexical normalisation of short text messages: Makn sens a #twitter. In *Proc. of ACL*, 2011.

[7] J. Kazama and K. Torisawa. Exploiting wikipedia as external knowledge for named entity recognition. In *Proc. of EMNLP-CoNLL*, 2007.

[8] C. Li, A. Sun, and A. Datta. A generalized method for word sense disambiguation based on wikipedia. In *Proc. of ECIR*, 2011.

[9] X. Liu, S. Zhang, F. Wei, and M. Zhou. Recognizing named entities in tweets. In *Proc. of ACL*, 2011.

[10] C. D. Manning and H. Schütze. *Foundations of statistical natural language processing*. MIT Press, 1999.

[11] L. Page, S. Brin, R. Motwani, and T. Winograd. The PageRank citation ranking: Bringing order to the web. Technical Report 1999-66, Stanford InfoLab, November 1999.

[12] P. Pecina and P. Schlesinger. Combining association measures for collocation extraction. In *Proc. of the COLING/ACL on Main conference poster sessions*, 2006.

[13] D. Ramage, D. Hall, R. Nallapati, and C. D. Manning. Labeled lda: a supervised topic model for credit attribution in multi-labeled corpora. In *Proc. of EMNLP*, 2009.

[14] L. Ratinov and D. Roth. Design challenges and misconceptions in named entity recognition. In *Proc. of CoNLL*, 2009.

[15] A. E. Richman and P. Schone. Mining wiki resources for multilingual named entity recognition. In *Proc. of ACL*, 2008.

[16] A. Ritter, S. Clark, Mausam, and O. Etzioni. Named entity recognition in tweets: An experimental study. In *Proc. of EMNLP*, 2011.

[17] P. Schone and D. Jurafsky. Is knowledge-free induction of multiword unit dictionary headwords a solved problem? In *Proc. of EMNLP*, 2001.

[18] J. Silva, Z. Kozareva, V. Noncheva, and G. Lopes. Extracting named entities. a statistical approach. In *Proc. of TLAN*, 2004.

[19] K. Wang, C. Thrasher, E. Viegas, X. Li, and P. Hsu. An overview of microsoft web n-gram corpus and applications. In *Proc. of NAACL-HLT*, 2010.

[20] Y. Wang. Annotating and recognising named entities in clinical notes. In *Proc. of the ACL-IJCNLP 2009 Student Research Workshop*, 2009.

[21] G. Zhou and J. Su. Named entity recognition using an hmm-based chunk tagger. In *Proc. of ACL*, 2002.

Adaptive Context Features for Toponym Resolution in Streaming News*

Michael D. Lieberman Hanan Samet
Center for Automation Research, Institute for Advanced Computer Studies,
Department of Computer Science, University of Maryland
College Park, MD 20742
{codepoet, hjs}@cs.umd.edu

ABSTRACT

News sources around the world generate constant streams of information, but effective streaming news retrieval requires an intimate understanding of the geographic content of news. This process of understanding, known as *geotagging*, consists of first finding words in article text that correspond to location names (*toponyms*), and second, assigning each toponym its correct lat/long values. The latter step, called *toponym resolution*, can also be considered a classification problem, where each of the possible interpretations for each toponym is classified as correct or incorrect. Hence, techniques from supervised machine learning can be applied to improve accuracy. New classification features to improve toponym resolution, termed *adaptive context features*, are introduced that consider a window of context around each toponym, and use geographic attributes of toponyms in the window to aid in their correct resolution. Adaptive parameters controlling the window's *breadth* and *depth* afford flexibility in managing a tradeoff between feature computation speed and resolution accuracy, allowing the features to potentially apply to a variety of textual domains. Extensive experiments with three large datasets of streaming news demonstrate the new features' effectiveness over two widely-used competing methods.

Categories and Subject Descriptors

H.3.1 [**Information Storage and Retrieval**]: Content Analysis and Indexing

General Terms

Algorithms, Design, Performance

Keywords

Toponym resolution, geotagging, streaming news, adaptive context, machine learning

*This work was supported in part by the National Science Foundation under Grants IIS-10-18475, IIS-09-48548, IIS-08-12377, and CCF-08-30618.

SIGIR'12, August 12–16, 2012, Portland, Oregon, USA.

1. INTRODUCTION

Today's increasingly informed and connected society demands ever growing volumes of news and information. Thousands of newspapers, and millions of bloggers and tweeters around the world generate constant streams of data, and the demand for such data is skyrocketing as people strive to stay up-to-date. Also, Internet-enabled mobile devices are increasingly common, which expands the requirement for location-based services and other highly local content—information that is relevant to where users are, or the places in which they are interested. News itself often has a strong geographic component, and newspapers tend to characterize their readership in terms of location, and publish news articles describing events that are relevant to geographic locations of interest to their readers. We wish to collect these articles and make them available for location-based retrieval queries, which requires special techniques.

To enable news retrieval queries with a geographic component, we must first understand the geographic content present in the articles. However, currently, online news sources rarely have articles' geographic content present in machine-readable form. As a result, we must design algorithms to understand and extract the geographic content from the article's text. This process of extraction is called *geotagging* of text, which amounts to identifying locations in natural language text, and assigning lat/long values to them. Put another way, geotagging can be considered as enabling the spatial indexing of unstructured or semistructured text. This spatial indexing provides a way to execute both feature-based queries ("Where is X happening?") and location-based queries ("What is happening at location Y?") [5] where the location argument is specified textually rather than geometrically as in our related systems such as QUILT [34] and the SAND Browser [31]. Geotagging methods have been implemented in many different textual domains, such as Web pages [3, 23, 27], blogs [28], encyclopedia articles [14, 36], tweets [33], spreadsheets [2, 17], the hidden Web [19], and of most relevance for us, news articles [8, 11, 18, 20, 21, 29, 32, 37]. Particular domains such as blogs and tweets may pose additional challenges, such as having few or no formatting or grammatical requirements. The methods in this paper were applied in the NewsStand system [37], which uses a geotagger to assign geographic locations to clusters of news articles based on their content, which allows users to visually explore the news in NewsStand's interactive map interface. Also, several commercial products for geotagging text are available, such as

MetaCarta's Geotagger[1], Thomson Reuters's OpenCalais[2], and Yahoo!'s Placemaker[3], the latter two of which we investigate here.

Geotagging consists of two steps: finding all textual references to geographic locations, known as *toponyms*, and then choosing the correct location interpretation for each toponym (i.e., assigning lat/long values) from a *gazetteer* (database of locations). These two steps are known as *toponym recognition* and *toponym resolution*, the second of which we investigate here, and are difficult due to ambiguities present in natural language. Importantly, both these steps can be considered as *classification* [10] problems: Toponym recognition amounts to classifying each word in the document's text as part of a toponym or not, and toponym resolution amounts to classifying each toponym interpretation as correct or incorrect. With this understanding, and with appropriately annotated datasets, we can leverage techniques from supervised machine learning to create an effective geotagging framework. These techniques take as input sets of values known as *feature vectors*, along with a class label for each feature vector, and learn a function that will predict the class label for a new feature vector. Many such techniques for classification, and other machine learning problems, exist and have been used for geotagging purposes, including SVM [4, 13, 24], Bayesian schemes [9, 12, 41], and expectation maximization [6].

The effectiveness of such techniques for a given problem domain depends greatly on the design of the input *features* that comprise each feature vector. One common feature used for geotagging is the population of each interpretation, since larger places will tend to be mentioned more frequently and are more likely to be correct. However, using population alone or overly relying on it, as many methods do, resulted in greatly reduced accuracy in our experiments, especially for toponym recall. Instead, in this paper, we consider a new class of features to improve the accuracy of toponym resolution, termed *adaptive context features*. These features construct a window of variable size around each toponym t, and use the other toponyms in the window to aid in resolving t correctly by considering the geographic relationships between interpretations l_t of t and those of other toponyms in the window. In particular, we search for interpretations that are geographically *proximate* to l_t, or are *siblings* of l_t in terms of a geographic hierarchy (e.g., cities in the same state). The more such relationships appear in the window, the greater evidence there is that l_t is the correct interpretation of t. These window features are a natural extension of other *context-sensitive* features which depend on other words nearby the toponym, such as *object/container* and *comma group* [20] evidence, as well as pairing notions such as *pair strength* [19].

We call these features *adaptive* because the window's parameters can be varied for different domains, or to achieve different ends. Some relatively small windows can contain a significant number of highly ambiguous toponyms, especially for toponyms at fine scales [26], and considering all possible combinations of interpretations places inhibitive penalties on feature computation speed. For example, consider Figure 1, which is an excerpt from a press release [25] published in the Earth Times newspaper, with toponyms highlighted and the numbers next to each toponym indicating the number of interpretations in our gazetteer for the toponym. If

> ...in and around [*Louisville* $_{17}$] and [*Lexington* $_{31}$], [*Kentucky* $_{6}$], [*Nashville* $_{27}$] and [*Cordova* $_{55}$], [*Tennessee* $_{5}$], [*Richmond* $_{69}$], [*Virginia* $_{42}$], [*Fort Lauderdale* $_{1}$] and [*Orlando* $_{9}$], [*Florida* $_{96}$], [*Indianapolis* $_{3}$], [*Indiana* $_{8}$] and [*Atlanta* $_{22}$], [*Georgia* $_{12}$].

Figure 1: Excerpt from an Earth Times press release [25] with toponyms and their number of interpretations highlighted, showing the extreme ambiguity of these toponyms and illustrating the need for adaptive context features.

we consider all possible combinations of resolutions for these toponyms, this results in about $3{\cdot}10^{17}$ possibilities, an astonishingly large number for this relatively small portion of text, which is far too many to check in a reasonable time. Instead, we can set parameters which we term the window's *breadth* and *depth*, named analogously to breadth-first and depth-first search, which control the number of toponyms in the window and the number of interpretations examined for each toponym in the window, respectively. The adaptive context features thus afford us flexibility since by varying these parameters, we can control a tradeoff between feature computation time and resolution accuracy. The more toponyms and toponym interpretations we examine, the more likely we are to find the correct interpretation, but the longer resolution will take, and vice versa. Some textual domains such as Twitter, where tweets arrive at a furious rate, demand faster computation times, while in other, offline domains, the time constraint is relaxed and we can afford to spend more time to gain higher accuracy. While window-like features and heuristics have been used in other work related to geotagging (e.g., [15, 16, 24, 30, 35, 42]), these features' adaptive potential has not been explored.

As we pointed out, in this paper our focus is on toponym resolution, while toponym recognition makes use of our previous work [18]. Our work differs from that of others in a number of ways, including our focus on streaming data, and most importantly the size of the domain of the data used in our evaluation. In particular, in our evaluation we make use of articles from a large set of news sources, many of which are from small localities, and the domain of locations is very large, as evidenced by our gazetteer containing 8.1M location interpretations, in contrast to systems such as Web-a-Where [3] which contains only about 30,000 location interpretations. The rest of this paper is organized as follows: Section 2 introduces the geotagging framework that enables us to test our adaptive context features, and describes our toponym recognition and resolution processes as a whole. We also introduce several other features that complement our adaptive context features and serve as baselines for comparison. Section 3 describes our new adaptive context features, as well as algorithms for their computation. Section 4 details extensive experiments showing our methods' performance benefits over OpenCalais and Placemaker, that also test various feature combinations and parameters. Finally, Section 5 offers potential avenues of future work and concludes.

2. GEOTAGGING FRAMEWORK

In this section, we present the framework that enables testing of our geotagging methods. This framework was originally developed for and is an integral component of the NewsStand [37] and TwitterStand [33] systems. We describe our toponym recognition (Section 2.1) and resolution (Sec-

[1]`http://metacarta.com`
[2]`http://opencalais.com`
[3]`http://developer.yahoo.com/geo/placemaker`

tion 2.2) procedures, as well as a set of baseline features (Section 2.3) that we use in combination with our adaptive context features, which will be presented in Section 3.

2.1 Toponym Recognition

Our toponym recognition procedure is designed as a multifaceted process involving many types of recognition methods, both rule-based and statistics-based. After an initial tokenization step, our method proceeds by performing lookups into various tables of entity names, including location names and abbreviations (e.g., "Maryland", "Md."), business names (e.g., "Apple", "Toyota"), person names (e.g., "Chad", "Victoria"), as well as cue words for the above types of entities (e.g., "*X* County", "Mr. *X*", "*X* Inc."). We also refactor geographic names by shifting particular cue words (e.g., "*X* Lake" to "Lake *X*").

In addition to the above rule-based methods, we leverage statistical NLP tools. We use an NER package to recognize toponyms and other entities, and perform extensive postprocessing on its output to ensure higher quality. We also perform part-of-speech (POS) tagging to find phrases of proper nouns, since names of locations (and other types of entities) tend to be composed of proper nouns. The POS tagging also provides a means of recognizing additional grammatical forms that hint at entities' types, including active verbs and noun adjuncts, which we use as signals to adjust entity types. Furthermore, we incorporate evidence from other documents in the document's news cluster. After the above recognition steps, we establish groups of entities to be resolved at the same time, by grouping similar entities together.

This multifaceted recognition procedure is designed to be flexible to capture variations that appear in streaming news, and also to be as inclusive as possible when recognizing toponyms, to maximize toponym recall, which comes at the cost of lower precision. Our recognition procedure's high recall is also corroborated by experimental results in Section 4.3. Since toponym recognition is only the first step in a two-part geotagging process, our toponym resolution methods will serve to restore precision to the entire process.

2.2 Toponym Resolution

As mentioned earlier, geotagging can be understood as a classification problem, and we use methods from supervised machine learning to implement toponym resolution. Specifically, we cast it as a *binary* classification problem, in that we decide for a given toponym/interpretation pair (t, l_t), whether l_t is correct or incorrect. These location interpretations are drawn from a *gazetteer*, which is a database of locations and associated metadata such as population data and hierarchy information. Our gazetteer, which is based on GeoNames[4], is vastly larger than many gazetteers typically used in geotagging methods, which both increases our methods' utility as well as geotagging's difficulty. We characterize our gazetteer further in our experiments in Section 4.1.

For our classifier, we use a decision tree-based ensemble classifier method known as *random forests* [7], which has state-of-the-art performance for many classification tasks. Briefly, given an annotated training dataset, the random forests method constructs many decision trees based on different random subsets of the dataset, sampled with replacement. In addition, each decision tree is constructed using random subsets of features from the training feature vectors. Because the features and subsets are chosen randomly, a variety of trees will be in the forest. Classifying a new feature vector is relatively simple: each tree in the forest votes for the vector's class, and the consensus is taken as the result. Note that individual trees may be excellent or poor class predictors, but as long as some features allow better-than-random classification, the forest taken as a whole will be a strong classifier. Another useful aspect of random forests is that the number of trees that vote for a given class can be used as a confidence score for the classification, and provides a means of tuning the precision/recall balance of the classifier. Assuming the score is an accurate estimate of the method's predictability, accepting classifications with a lower score will result in lower precision but higher recall, and vice versa. For our implementation, we used the fast random forest implementation[5], integrated with the Weka machine learning toolkit[6].

As an alternative to classification, Martins et al. [24] considered the use of SVM *regression* to estimate a distance function based on feature vector values that is intended to capture the distance between a given l_t, and t's ground truth interpretation. They use the resulting distance values to rank the interpretations, essentially using them as confidence scores, and select the one with smallest distance value as the interpretation for t. However, a significant drawback of this technique is that it assumes that all toponyms input to the toponym resolution process are not erroneous, i.e., that the toponym recognition procedure is perfect in identifying toponyms, while in reality, no such procedure is perfect. The distance measures they compute, while useful for ranking, are not necessarily meaningful as confidence scores for deciding whether a given l_t has strong enough evidence to consider it correct. For example, an inferred distance of "10" may indicate strong evidence for a given l_t, but weak evidence for another. On the other hand, our framework using random forests and their confidence scores provide consistent and meaningful scores for deciding classification strength.

2.3 Resolution Features

In addition to the adaptive context features introduced in the next section, we use several baseline toponym resolution features in our methods. To borrow terms from linguistics, these features, which will be computed for each toponym/interpretation pair (t, l_t), can be loosely classed as what we term *context-sensitive* and *context-free* features. Put simply, context-sensitive features depend on t's position in relation to other toponyms in the document, while context-free features do not. Note that our adaptive context features subsume and generalize context-sensitive features, so we will describe them in the next section. On the other hand, the context-free features we use include the following:

I: `interps`. Number of interpretations for t; more interpretations means more opportunities for errors.

P: `population`. The population of l_t, where a larger population indicates that l_t is more well-known.

A: `altnames`. Number of alternate names for l_t in various languages. More names indicates greater renown of l_t.

D: `dateline`. Geographic distance of l_t from an interpretation of a *dateline* toponym, which establishes a general location context for a news article.

L: `locallex`. Geographic distance of l_t from the newspaper's *local lexicon* [21], the expected location of its primary audience, expressed as a lat/long point.

[4]`http://geonames.org`

[5]`http://code.google.com/p/fast-random-forest`

[6]`http://www.cs.waikato.ac.nz/ml/weka`

The **interps**, **population**, and **altnames** features are domain independent, i.e., they can be used in any textual domain, while the **dateline** and **locallex** features are specific to the news domain. In our experiments in Section 4.4, we consider these features alone and in various combinations to understand each feature's relative utility.

3. ADAPTIVE CONTEXT FEATURES

In this section, we present our adaptive context features to aid in the resolution of toponyms. These features reflect two aspects of toponym coocurrence and the evidence that interpretations impart to each other, which include:

1. *Proximate* interpretations, which are both nearby in the text as well as geographically proximate, and
2. *Sibling* interpretations, which are nearby in the text and share containers in a geographic hierarchy.

We capture these interpretation relationships and encode them in features. To compute these features, we examine for each toponym t a window of text around t, and compare interpretations of toponyms in the window with the interpretations of t. That is, a given interpretation l_t of t is promoted if there are other interpretations of toponyms in the window that are geographically proximate to it, or are sibling interpretations. In addition, we vary two parameters of the window termed *window breadth* and *window depth*, which control a tradeoff between computation speed and discriminative utility for the features by changing the number of toponyms in the window, and the number of interpretations per toponym, respectively.

Figure 2 is a schematic representation of the algorithm used to compute our features. Each box represents a toponym, and the lines under the boxes represent location interpretations for each toponym. Different toponyms have different levels of ambiguity, as measured by the number of interpretations for the toponyms. In Figure 2, we are computing adaptive context features for the highlighted toponym and its interpretations in the middle. We compute these features for all toponyms at a document distance of less than the window breadth w_b, and we compare the first few interpretations of each toponym in the window, up to a maximum of w_d interpretations, the window depth.

Note that our proximity and sibling features subsume and generalize other commonly-used features in toponym resolution. In particular, these features generalize *context-sensitive* features, which compute a toponym interpretation's likelihood of correctness based on the other toponyms nearby to it in the document. One example of these context-sensitive features includes the *object/container* pair (e.g., *Paris, Texas, Dallas in Texas*), consisting of two toponyms, one of which contains the other. Authors use them when their audiences are not familiar with the location in question, and use the containing toponym to provide a geographic context for the toponym. Object/container pairs are a particularly common type of evidence used in many types of documents, and much research has investigated its utility (e.g., [3, 16, 21, 30, 35]). This type of evidence can be understood as an extreme case of our sibling feature, in the case where the window is restricted to the immediately next or preceding toponym. More general than object/container pairs is the *comma group* [20], which consists of a sequence of toponyms adjacent to each other separated by connector tokens (e.g., "*Paris, Dallas, San Antonio* and *Houston*") that share geographic characteristics (in our example, all cities in Texas), and hence provide mutual evidence for each others' correct interpretations. These relationships can be captured using our features with a window of appropriate size to contain all the toponyms. Another difference between these sources of evidence and our adaptive context features is that we do not assume any meaning for the specific position of toponyms within the window. For example, we do not consider the grammatical structure involved, or the tokens present between toponyms in the window. This increases the flexibility of our features as compared to, e.g., comma groups, whose recognition depends on specific wording and organization of the toponyms. As noted by Lieberman et al. [20], comma groups in particular can be constructed in various ways that can mislead rule-based heuristics, such as in our original example in Figure 1.

The following sections describe our proximity (Section 3.1) and sibling (Section 3.2) features, and the algorithms we use to compute them (Section 3.3). We also describe a strategy for propagating significant feature values for a toponym to its other instances in the same document (Section 3.4).

3.1 Proximity Features

The *proximity* features we use are based on geographic distance. Because this distance is continuous, appropriate thresholds for what is considered "near" and "far" are not apparent. Thus, it behooves us to defer their definitions to learning algorithms that can learn appropriate and meaningful distance thresholds.

To compute our proximity features for a toponym/interpretation pair (t, l_t), we find for each other toponym o in the window around t the closest interpretation l_o to l_t. Then, we compute the proximity feature for (t, l_t) as the average of the geographic distances to the other interpretations. Thus, a lower feature score indicates a higher level of overall geographic proximity for toponyms within the window. This feature strategy also balances fairness with optimism, in that it allows all toponyms in the window to contribute to (t, l_t)'s feature score, while each toponym in the window contributes its best (i.e., geographically nearest) interpretation to the feature score. It has the additional benefit that no distance thresholds are hard-coded into the feature. Instead, the learning procedure can learn appropriate distance thresholds from its training data.

3.2 Sibling Features

Our second class of adaptive context features are those based on *sibling* relationships between interpretations in a geographic hierarchy. In other words, this feature will capture the relationships between textually proximate toponyms that share the same country, state, or other administrative division. The sibling feature is intended to capture interpretations that are at the same level in the hierarchy (e.g., states in the same country, cities in the same state) as well as interpretations at different levels (e.g., a state and its containing country, a city inside its containing state). The first case captures "true" sibling relationships, while the second case captures containment relationships, which can be considered siblings at a coarse granularity (e.g., *College Park* and *Maryland* are siblings at a state level of granularity).

We compute sibling features in a similar way as the proximity features. For each toponym/interpretation pair (t, l_t), we use as our sibling feature value the number of other toponyms o in the window around t with an interpretation that is a sibling of l_t at a given resolution. We consider three levels of resolution, which correspond to three sibling features for each (t, l_t): country-level, state-level, and county-level.

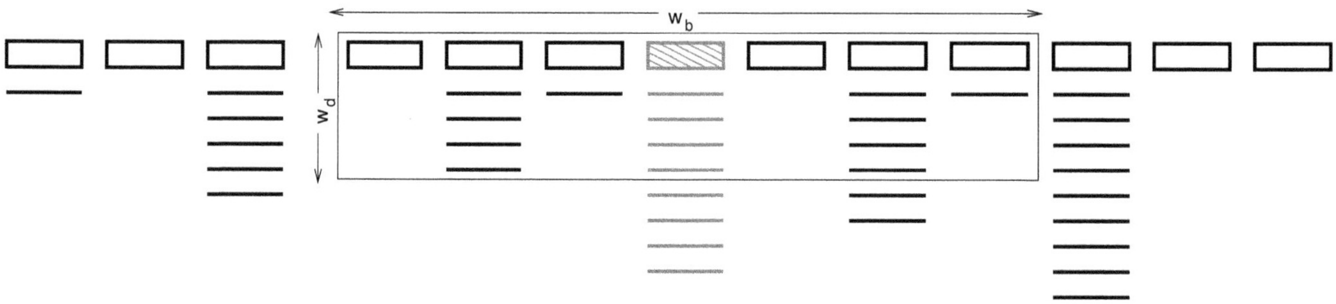

Figure 2: Computing adaptive context features, illustrating the window breadth w_b and window depth w_d.

Given that the sibling features are so related to the proximity features, at first glance, the sibling feature appears to be redundant in that some toponym interpretations that are siblings will tend to be geographically proximate as well (e.g., *Paris, Texas* and *Dallas, Texas*). However, in some cases the sibling feature will prove helpful in distinguishing toponym relationships. For example, cities that are positioned at opposite ends of a given state might be too far to be considered geographically proximate, but would still be considered siblings. Similarly, the notion of geographic distance for area objects such as countries and states depends on their representation. If we represent, e.g., a country by a single point, such as its centroid or the location of its capital city, it might be considered geographically distant from many cities contained in it, while the sibling feature would correctly capture these relationships. Another difference between the proximity and sibling features is that the geographic hierarchy is discrete, while geographic distances are continuous values. As a result, we do not have the same thresholding problem as for the proximity features, as our "thresholds" are effectively the same as the hierarchy levels.

3.3 Feature Computation

As noted earlier, our adaptive context features are based on computing features within a *window* of context around each toponym t. We can consider two variables related to the search for a correct interpretation of t:

1. *Window breadth*, denoted w_b, which corresponds to the size of the window around t to be considered.
2. *Window depth*, denoted w_d, which is the maximum number of interpretations to be considered for each toponym in the window.

The window breadth w_b controls how many toponyms around a given toponym t are to be used in aiding the resolution of t. With a larger w_b, more toponyms will be used to resolve t, thus reducing the resolution algorithm's speed but hopefully increasing its accuracy. Similarly, the window depth w_d controls the number of interpretations to be considered for each toponym in the window. A larger w_d means that more interpretations will be checked, with a resulting decrease in speed, but with more potential for finding corroborating evidence for a correct interpretation of t.

Because the window depth may preclude examination of all interpretations for a given toponym, the order in which the interpretations are examined is important. Ideally, interpretations would be ordered using context-free attributes of each interpretation. In a sense, the ordering is based on an apriori estimate of each interpretation's probability of being mentioned in a given document, though we do not formalize this notion here. We order or rank these interpretations using various factors, which include, in order of importance:

1. Number of alternate names for the location in other languages. GeoNames, being a multilingual gazetteer, contains alternate names and the number of names can indicate the place's renown.
2. Population of the location, where a larger population generally indicates a more well-known place.
3. Geographic distance from a local lexicon location.

These ranking factors can be considered context-free, in that the ordering of interpretations for a given toponym is independent of its position in the document. We could use additional factors such as each interpretation's geographic distance from a dateline toponym interpretation, but because we include these factors as separate features we do not need to include them in the ranking here.

One seeming drawback with regard to the window depth is that it may not seem effective in that most toponyms in our gazetteer have only one or two possible interpretations, as our experiments in Section 4.1 show. However, toponyms that are well-known by virtue of having a well-known interpretation (for example, *Paris*, widely known as the French capital), will tend to be mentioned more frequently in documents, and these will be more ambiguous. This is also reflected in measurements made on the toponyms present in our experimental datasets (Section 4.2).

In addition, rather than using all toponyms in the window around each t, we perform some pre-filtering to remove toponyms that detract from the usefulness of our adaptive context features. For example, we do not use toponyms in the window that have the same name as t, since they will have the same set of interpretations as t, which will impart no useful information. In addition, and more generally, we may not be sure which of the words in the window correspond to toponyms, due to ambiguities in toponym recognition. Our toponym recognition process (described in Section 2.1) is designed for high recall and as a result we will consider many words which are not true toponyms. In other cases, we may not be sure of the appropriate interpretation for a given toponym. For example, consider the phrase "University of Maryland", which could be interpreted as a whole, *University of Maryland*, referring to the school, or as *Maryland*, the state. Rather than immediately deciding on one of these toponyms, our recognition process keeps both, even though they overlap. Thus, we can keep and consider all of them in toponym resolution, though they must be appropriately filtered when processing toponyms in the window.

Our algorithm for computing adaptive context features, called AdaptiveContext, is shown in Algorithm 1. It takes as input the toponyms T in the document being processed, as well as the window breadth w_b and window depth w_d under consideration. The algorithm proceeds by iterating over all toponyms $t \in T$ (line 2). For each t, an array

Algorithm 1 Compute adaptive context features.

1: **procedure** ADAPTIVECONTEXT(T, w_b, w_d)
   input: Topos T, window breadth w_b and depth w_d
   output: Proximity and sibling features
2: **for** $t \in T$ **do**
3: $P \leftarrow \{\}$
4: $O \leftarrow \{o \in T : \text{NAME}(t) \neq \text{NAME}(o) \wedge \text{DOCDIST}(t, o) \leq w_b\}$
5: **for** $o \in O$ **do**
6: $L_o \leftarrow \text{LOCS}(o)[1 \ldots \min\{w_d, |\text{LOCS}(o)|\}]$
7: **for** $l_t \in \text{LOCS}(t)$ **do**
8: $d_{min} \leftarrow \min\{\forall l_o \in L_o, \text{GEODIST}(l_t, l_o)\}$
9: $P[l_t] \leftarrow P[l_t] \cup \{d_{min}\}$
10: **for** $lev \in \{country, admin1, admin2\}$ **do**
11: **if** $\exists l_o \in L_o : \text{SIBLING}(l_t, l_o, lev)$ **then**
12: Increment $\text{SIBFEATURE}(t, l_t, lev)$
13: **end if**
14: **end for**
15: **end for**
16: **end for**
17: **for** $l_t \in \text{LOCS}(t)$ **do**
18: $\text{PROXFEATURE}(t, l_t) \leftarrow \text{AVG}(P[l_t])$
19: **end for**
20: **end for**
21: **end procedure**

P is initialized which will hold minimum distances to interpretations of toponyms in the window around t, which will be used in computing the proximity features for t (3). Next, other toponyms O within the window around t are collected by finding toponyms $o \in T$ whose document distance is smaller than the window breadth w_b, and also have a different name than t (4). We then loop over each toponym $o \in O$ to begin comparing interpretations of t and o (5). First, we collect the location interpretations associated with o, up to a limit of w_d interpretations, the window depth (6). Then, we loop over each interpretation l_t of t (7), and find the interpretation l_o of o with minimum geographic distance from l_t (8). We add the interpretation l_o to the location set $P[l_t]$ associated with l_t which will be used for computation of the proximity feature for l_t (9). Next, we compute the sibling features for each level lev of our geographic hierarchy (10) by checking whether there exists an interpretation l_o of o with l_t as its sibling (11). If so, we increment the sibling feature for that level (12). Finally, after looping over all toponyms of O, the sibling features are fully computed for each interpretation l_t of t, but the proximity feature remains to be completed. We do so for each l_t (17) by averaging the geographic distances computed for l_t, which results in the final proximity feature values (18). We use the median geographic distance as our averaging measure.

3.4 Feature Propagation

Oftentimes, documents will mention the same toponyms multiple times. When considering pairs of toponyms for use in computing adaptive context features, described in the previous section, these toponym repetitions are ignored because they impart no useful information, since the interpretations for each pair will be the same. However, we can still make use of toponym repetition within a single document because the toponyms appear in different contexts (i.e., at different offsets) within the document. Since our adaptive context features are context-sensitive, we can apply stronger feature values computed for the toponym in one context to the same toponym in other, weaker contexts.

To leverage these repetitions, as a final processing step, we compute additional features for each (t, l_t) pair by *propagating* feature values among toponyms in the document that share the same name. We propagate feature values that indicate strong evidence that a given toponym interpretation is correct. For the proximity feature, this corresponds to the lowest average distance values, while for the sibling features, we propagate the largest sibling counts for each level of resolution we consider.

4. EXPERIMENTS

In this section, we describe the extensive experiments performed on our own and competing geotagging methods. We first establish the general difficulty of geotagging using our large gazetteer, due to a large amount of toponym ambiguity (Section 4.1), and then introduce the datasets to be used for measuring geotagging performance, and characterize the toponyms present in them (Section 4.2). In terms of geotagging accuracy, we compare our own adaptive method, referred to as "Adaptive", against two existing prominent competing methods: Thomson Reuters's OpenCalais, and Yahoo!'s Placemaker. Both OpenCalais and Placemaker are closed-source commercial products, but they do provide public Web APIs which allow for automated geotagging of documents, and hence they have been used extensively in state-of-the-art geotagging and entity recognition research (e.g., [1, 24, 28, 38, 40]). In addition to not being able to make direct algorithmic comparisons due to their black box nature, neither OpenCalais nor Placemaker offer a means of tuning the precision/recall balance, so we could not explore this aspect of the systems. We discuss how well these systems fare against our own methods in terms of toponym recognition (Section 4.3) and toponym resolution (Section 4.4). For the latter, we also consider various combinations of features and show how they affect resolution accuracy, and use a feature ranking method to measure the importance of each feature when used in resolving toponyms. Finally, we vary the adaptive context parameters of window breadth (w_b) and depth (w_d), and show how they affect the feature computation time and accuracy of the Adaptive method (Section 4.5).

Note that in all our accuracy experiments, we measure performance using *precision* and *recall* as measured over the correct interpretations. We also used 10-fold cross validation to avoid misleading performance numbers due to potential overfitting. Also, we used 100 trees in our random forests, with 5 attributes for each tree, and accepted classifications with at least 0.5 confidence score (i.e., at least half of the trees voted for the interpretation). All experiments were conducted on a Dell Precision 470 workstation with a dual core Intel Xeon 3GHz CPU and 8G RAM.

4.1 Gazetteer Ambiguity

First, we examined our gazetteer to understand the level of ambiguity of toponyms present in it. The gazetteer contains a total of 8.1M location interpretations, 5.1M distinct names, and 7.0M alternate names in languages other than English. The gazetteer's large size ensures a high level of ambiguity and ensuing greater difficulty in performing geotagging correctly, when compared to gazetteers used by other systems such as Web-a-Where [3]. For each toponym in the gazetteer, we counted the number of interpretations associated with it, and plotted the results. Results are shown in Figure 3. Toponyms in the gazetteer exhibit a power-law relationship in terms of the number of interpretations, in that

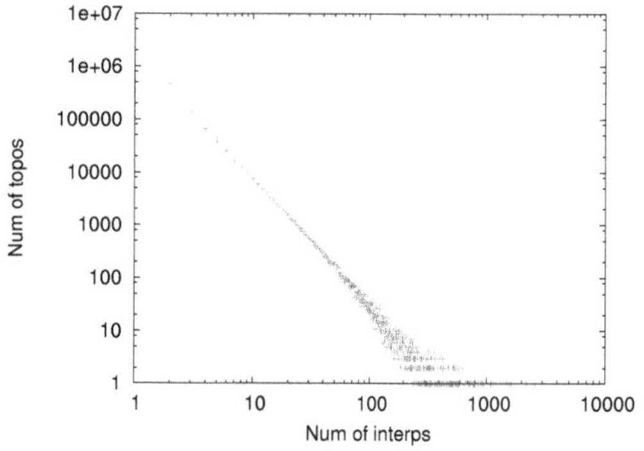

Figure 3: Toponyms and the number of interpretations they have exhibit a power-law relationship.

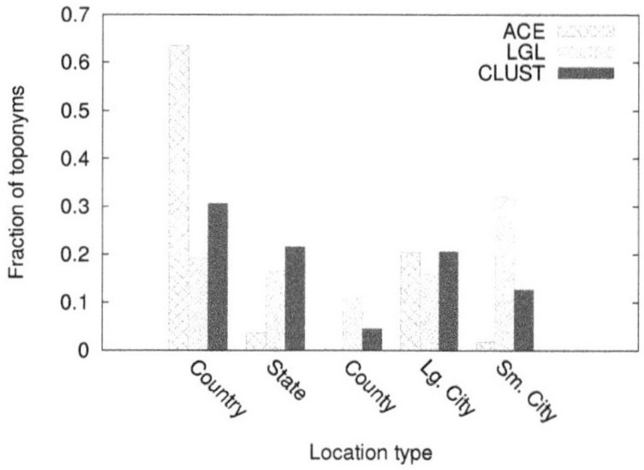

Figure 4: Breakdown of location types within each of our test corpora.

Table 1: Corpora used in evaluating geotagging.

	ACE	*LGL*	*CLUST*
Documents	104	621	13327
Median doc word count	236	242	309
News sources	4	114	1607
Annotated docs	104	621	1080
Annotated topos	2359	4765	11564
Distinct topos	295	1177	2320
Median topos per doc	12	6	8
Median topo ambig per doc	3	14	7

the vast majority of toponyms a small number of interpretations, while a few toponyms have a very large number of interpretations. Of course, most of these unambiguous toponyms will not be mentioned in a given document, and in our datasets, described in the next section, the documents' toponyms have higher levels of ambiguity.

4.2 Datasets

In choosing the datasets for our evaluation, we wanted news data from a variety of sources, and for a variety of audiences. To achieve this end, we used three datasets of news in our evaluation: *ACE*, *LGL*, and *CLUST*. The first, *ACE* [22], consists of articles from four large news sources: Agence France-Presse, Associated Press World, New York Times, and Xinhua. These articles tend to have a broad world interest and concern topics such as international diplomacy and trade, so they tend to mention large, well-known places. Thus, *ACE* serves in our evaluation as a test of the geotagging methods' capability for correctly recognizing and resolving well-known, prominent places. On the other hand, to test smaller places, we used the *LGL* [21] dataset, which consists of articles from about 100 smaller, more local news sources. These articles are intended for more geographically localized audiences, and concern local events that mention small places. Our third dataset, *CLUST* [18], contains a variety of articles from both large and small news sources.

Table 1 presents statistics that broadly illustrate characteristics of our three test corpora. *ACE* is relatively small compared to *LGL* and *CLUST*, both in terms of number of documents and news sources. However, *ACE* tends to have more toponyms per article, which may be due to the content consisting of generally international news involving many different countries and other locations, which would all be mentioned in the articles. In addition, we measured toponym ambiguity in the articles by checking, for each document, the median number of gazetteer interpretations for the toponyms in the document. the median number of interpretations present for toponyms in each document. *LGL* has the largest amount of toponym ambiguity, followed by *CLUST* and *ACE*. This is not overly surprising, given that *LGL* was constructed deliberately focusing on highly ambiguous toponyms [21]. However, the measurements show a high level of ambiguity in all three datasets.

We also classified the annotated locations present in the documents according to their types, which are shown in Figure 4. We normalized the type counts for each corpus to illustrate the fractions of each type within each corpus. For cities, we further divided the locations into large cities (over 100k population) and small cities (less than 100k population). These location types clearly show the important differences between the three corpora. The vast majority of *ACE*'s toponyms, 83%, consist of countries and large cities, indicating *ACE*'s broad geographic scope. This is not overly surprising given that it consists of newswire, which is usually intended for a broad geographic audience. In contrast, 60% of *LGL*'s toponyms are small cities, counties, and states, and among all three datasets, *LGL* contains the smallest fraction of countries and large cities, showing that *LGL* mainly concerns smaller, more local places, with a correspondingly smaller geographic audience. *CLUST* falls in the middle, with the largest fraction of states among the three datasets, and in between the other two in terms of countries, counties, and small cities. Bearing these observations in mind, in terms of overall geographic relevance, *ACE* and *LGL* can be said to have wide and narrow relevance respectively, while *CLUST* falls in the middle, illustrating our three datasets' utility in testing geotagging at coarse, middle, and fine-grained geographic scopes.

4.3 Recognition Accuracy

Though the main focus of this paper is improved toponym resolution, for completeness, we tested each system's toponym recognition performance when isolated from the subsequent toponym resolution step. Note that OpenCalais and Placemaker also provide lat/long values with each toponym, but we disregard these when testing toponym recognition using these systems because it is more information than we need for this experiment. Table 2 shows the performance results for each method's toponym recognition step. For all three datasets, the Adaptive method shows higher recall performance than either OpenCalais or Placemaker, which as we discussed earlier is the crucial measure to consider for toponym recognition used before toponym resolution, as well as a higher overall F_1-score for *LGL* and *CLUST*. While OpenCalais and Placemaker do have higher precision, this

Table 2: Recognition performance.

	P	R	F_1
ACE			
Adaptive	0.748	0.867	0.804
OpenCalais	0.883	0.681	0.769
Placemaker	0.899	0.767	0.828
LGL			
Adaptive	0.671	0.723	0.696
OpenCalais	0.588	0.222	0.322
Placemaker	0.675	0.658	0.666
CLUST			
Adaptive	0.732	0.861	0.791
OpenCalais	0.759	0.425	0.545
Placemaker	0.798	0.692	0.741

Table 3: Resolution accuracy of various methods.

	P_{Resol}	$R_{Recog+Resol}$
ACE		
Adaptive	1635/1659 = 0.986	1635/2359 = 0.693
OpenCalais	1062/1080 = 0.983	1062/2359 = 0.450
Placemaker	1161/1219 = 0.952	1161/2359 = 0.492
LGL		
Adaptive	2799/2970 = 0.942	2799/4765 = 0.587
OpenCalais	1260/1632 = 0.772	1260/4765 = 0.264
Placemaker	2516/3466 = 0.726	2516/4765 = 0.528
CLUST		
Adaptive	7143/7440 = 0.960	7143/11564 = 0.618
OpenCalais	5397/6352 = 0.850	5397/11564 = 0.467
Placemaker	7524/8642 = 0.871	7524/11564 = 0.650

is mitigated by their relative lack of recall. Also, Adaptive's precision is restored by its toponym resolution processing, which will be shown in the next section. These results are also consistent with previously-reported performance [18].

4.4 Resolution Accuracy

In the next experiment, we measured the accuracies of each method's toponym resolution in isolation—that is, if each method were given a set of toponyms, how well the method would select the correct lat/long interpretation for each toponym. Because OpenCalais and Placemaker do not allow for the specification of ground truth toponyms, it is not possible to make direct comparisons of toponym resolution's recall for these systems. Instead, we report the precision for the resolution process in isolation (P_{Resol}), and the recall for the combined recognition and resolution processes ($R_{Recog+Resol}$). For P_{Resol}, we only report accuracy for toponyms that were correctly recognized by each system. Also, for the Adaptive method, we used a window breadth w_b of 80 tokens and unlimited window depth w_d. To determine whether a given interpretation is correct, we check the geographic distance between the interpretation's lat/long values and the ground truth lat/long values, and if it lies within a small threshold (10 miles) we consider it correct. This method allows for the inevitable minor variations between the tested systems, due to their having selected interpretations from different gazetteers.

Table 3 shows the performance results. Of all three methods, the Adaptive method has the best overall precision, especially so for the *LGL* and *CLUST* datasets. Adaptive also maintains this high precision while having high toponym recall. This is best seen for the *LGL* dataset where Adaptive has a 17% advantage over OpenCalais, and a 22% advantage over Placemaker, along with a recall advantage of 32% over OpenCalais and 6% advantage over Placemaker. These performance numbers indicate our method's superior performance in terms of the toponym resolution task. Examining performance for all the methods across the three datasets, the methods performed best on *ACE*, worst on *LGL*, and in the middle for *CLUST*. These results follow our intuition that correctly geotagging documents containing smaller, less well-known locations (*LGL*) is more difficult than for larger, more well-known locations (*ACE*).

Table 4: Toponym resolution accuracy for different feature combinations.

	ACE			*LGL*			*CLUST*		
	P	R	F_1	P	R	F_1	P	R	F_1
I	0.91	0.41	0.57	0.96	0.26	0.40	0.93	0.30	0.45
I,P	0.97	0.59	0.74	0.96	0.47	0.63	0.98	0.38	0.55
$I,P,A{=}B_1$	0.99	0.84	0.91	0.96	0.61	0.75	0.98	0.71	0.82
B_1,D	0.99	0.90	0.94	0.96	0.62	0.75	0.98	0.72	0.83
B_1,L	0.98	0.86	0.92	0.95	0.90	0.93	0.97	0.77	0.86
$B_1,D,L{=}B_2$	0.99	0.90	0.94	0.95	0.90	0.93	0.97	0.76	0.86
$B_1,W_{80,\infty}$	0.98	0.88	0.93	0.94	0.65	0.77	0.96	0.71	0.82
$B_2,W_{80,\infty}$	0.99	0.88	0.93	0.94	0.88	0.91	0.96	0.73	0.83

Our next set of experiments tested various combinations of features used in the Adaptive method, to illustrate each feature's overall utility. We used different combinations of the features described in Section 2.3, as well as the adaptive context features described in Section 3. Table 4 contains the performance results, with feature abbreviations corresponding to those used in Section 2.3, and feature combinations indicated with commas (e.g., I,P combines `interps` and `population`). In addition, we considered two baseline feature combinations B_1 and B_2. B_1 tested only the domain-independent features (I,P,A), while B_2 also included those features tailored for the news domain (D,L). We again used our adaptive context feature ($W_{80,\infty}$) with window breadth of 80 tokens and unlimited window depth. In general, resolution precision was high for all feature combinations, so the main difference was resolution recall. For *ACE* and *CLUST*, the `dateline` and `locallex` features did not improve B_1 much, but `locallex` did make a large difference for *LGL*. Our adaptive context features in general improved B_1, for *LGL* in particular. However, in combination with B_2, the adaptive context features showed little improvement and in some cases lower performance, which is not overly surprising in that domain-specific features will exhibit domain-specific performance, and sometimes, adding features to a model will decrease performance. However, taken as a whole, the results illustrate our adaptive context features' utility for general geotagging purposes, especially over more simplistic features such as `population`.

We also conducted an experiment to measure the importance or utility of our features for classifying toponym interpretations. This process, also known as *feature selection* or *dimension reduction* [10], ranks the individual features in terms of their overall utility. For our feature importance measure, we used the *gain ratio* [10], a commonly-used, entropy-based measure for decision tree construction. We computed the gain ratio for each feature, and normalized the resulting importance values within each dataset. Results are presented in Figure 5. Interestingly, for each dataset, the `interps` and `altnames` features outranked `population`.

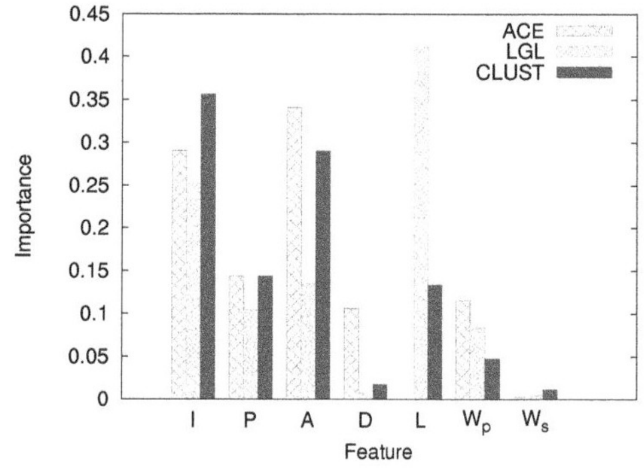

Figure 5: Importance of features used in the Adaptive method, as measured by the gain ratio.

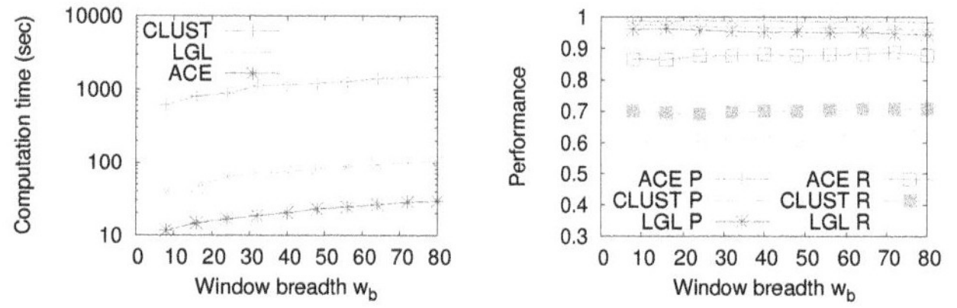

(a) (b)

Figure 6: Performance results when varying window breadth, showing changes in (a) time and (b) accuracy.

The `locallex` feature was highly important for *LGL*, though this is not too surprising considering the dataset's content of smaller, local news articles. The **windowprox** and **windowsib** have lower importance values, but interestingly, the `windowprox` feature has almost the same feature value as `population`. `windowsib`'s low importance value may be due to it being little-used in the three datasets.

4.5 Adaptive Parameters

In our final set of experiments, we tested how varying the adaptive parameters of our window features, namely the window breadth w_b and window depth w_d, would affect the speed and accuracy tradeoff for our methods. We used our adaptive context features in combination with our first baseline comparison method, B_1, described in the previous section, which is a combination of the **interps**, **population**, and **altnames** features. First, we varied the window breadth between 1–80 tokens and measured the resulting tradeoff. Figure 6a and Figure 6b show the results in terms of computation time and method accuracy, respectively. As the window breadth increases, the computation time increases linearly, which is to be expected. The computation time for *CLUST* is larger than for the other datasets due to its size. Interestingly, even with a small window breadth, precision remains high, and recall is respectable for all three datasets, giving evidence that the features are applicable even for domains where little time is allocated for geotagging. Also, while increasing the window breadth, recall also increases for the datasets, showing the time/accuracy tradeoff as expected. Results are similar for when varying window depth, shown in Figure 7a and Figure 7b.

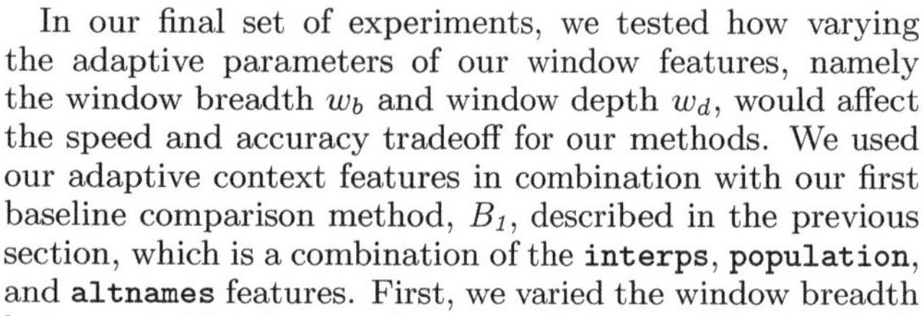

(a) (b)

Figure 7: Performance results when varying window depth, showing changes in (a) time and (b) accuracy.

5. CONCLUSION

Our investigations of adaptive context features have shown their utility and flexibility for improving the geotagging of streaming news. In future work, we plan to test different weightings of toponyms in the window to judge their effect on resolution accuracy. For example, toponyms that are further away in the window could be given less weight, using linear or Gaussian weighting schemes, essentially leveraging Tobler's law [39] which states that "Everything is related to everything else, but near things are more related than distant things". In addition, we could consider clusters of news articles about the same topic, which are collected in the NewsStand system, and design other features using these clusters. For example, we might examine other documents in a cluster to get additional toponyms for consideration in geotagging the current document. This can be thought of as creating one large virtual document consisting of some or all of the documents in a cluster, and then extending the window to include toponyms in those other documents. As before, with large clusters, we may not want to consider all toponyms or all interpretations in other documents in the cluster, due to inhibitive performance penalties. In summary, adaptive context features serve as a flexible, useful addition to geotagging algorithms for streaming news and other textual domains.

6. REFERENCES

[1] R. Abascal-Mena and E. López-Ornelas. Geo information extraction and processing from travel narratives. In *ELPUB'10: Proceedings of the 14th International Conference on Electronic Publishing*, pages 363–373, Helsinki, Finland, June 2010.

[2] M. D. Adelfio, M. D. Lieberman, H. Samet, and K. A. Firozvi. Ontuition: Intuitive data exploration via ontology navigation. In *GIS'10: Proceedings of the 18th ACM SIGSPATIAL International Conference on Advances in Geographic Information Systems*, pages 540–541, San Jose, CA, Nov. 2010.

[3] E. Amitay, N. Har'El, R. Sivan, and A. Soffer. Web-a-Where: Geotagging web content. In *SIGIR'04: Proceedings of the 27th Annual International ACM SIGIR Conference on Research and Development in Information Retrieval*, pages 273–280, Sheffield, UK, July 2004.

[4] I. Anastácio, B. Martins, and P. Calado. Classifying documents according to locational relevance. In *EPIA'09: Proceedings of the 14th Portuguese Conference on Artificial Intelligence*, pages 598–609, Aveiro, Portugal, Oct. 2009.

[5] W. G. Aref and H. Samet. Efficient processing of window queries in the pyramid data structure. In *PODS'90: Proceedings of the 9th ACM SIGACT-SIGMOD-SIGART Symposium on Principles of Database Systems*, pages 265–272, Nashville, TN, Apr. 1990.

[6] P. N. Bennett, F. Radlinski, R. W. White, and E. Yilmaz. Inferring and using location metadata to personalize web search. In *SIGIR'11: Proceedings of the 34th International ACM SIGIR Conference on Research and Development in Information Retrieval*, pages 135–144, Beijing, China, July 2011.

[7] L. Breiman. Random forests. *Machine Learning*, 45(1): 5–32, Oct. 2001.

[8] D. Buscaldi and B. Magnini. Grounding toponyms in an Italian local news corpus. In *GIR'10: Proceedings of the 6th Workshop on Geographic Information Retrieval*, Zurich, Switzerland, Feb. 2010.

[9] R. O. de Alencar, C. A. Davis, Jr., and M. A. Gonçalves. Geographical classification of documents using evidence from Wikipedia. In *GIR'10: Proceedings of the 6th Workshop on Geographic Information Retrieval*, Zurich, Switzerland, Feb. 2010.

[10] R. O. Duda, P. E. Hart, and D. G. Stork. *Pattern Classification*. John Wiley & Sons, New York, second edition, 2001.

[11] E. Garbin and I. Mani. Disambiguating toponyms in news. In *HLT/EMNLP'05: Proceedings of the Human Language Technology Conference and Conference on Empirical Methods in Natural Language Processing*, pages 363–370, Vancouver, Canada, Oct. 2005.

[12] Y.-H. Hu and L. Ge. A supervised machine learning approach to toponym disambiguation. In A. Scharl and K. Tochtermann, editors, *The Geospatial Web*, pages 117–128. Springer, London, 2007.

[13] U. Irmak and R. Kraft. A scalable machine-learning approach for semi-structured named entity recognition. In *WWW'10: Proceedings of the 19th International World Wide Web Conference*, pages 461–470, Raleigh, NC, Apr. 2010.

[14] W. Kienreich, M. Granitzer, and M. Lux. Geospatial anchoring of encyclopedia articles. In *IV'06: Proceedings of the 10th International Conference on Information Visualization*, pages 211–215, London, July 2006.

[15] J. L. Leidner. *Toponym Resolution in Text: Annotation, Evaluation and Applications of Spatial Grounding of Place Names*. PhD thesis, University of Edinburgh, Edinburgh, Scotland, 2007.

[16] H. Li, R. K. Srihari, C. Niu, and W. Li. InfoXtract location normalization: a hybrid approach to geographic references in information extraction. In *Proceedings of the HLT-NAACL 2003 Workshop on Analysis of Geographic References*, pages 39–44, Edmonton, Canada, May 2003.

[17] M. D. Lieberman and J. Lin. You are where you edit: Locating Wikipedia users through edit histories. In *ICWSM'09: Proceedings of the 3rd International AAAI Conference on Weblogs and Social Media*, pages 106–113, San Jose, CA, May 2009.

[18] M. D. Lieberman and H. Samet. Multifaceted toponym recognition for streaming news. In *SIGIR'11: Proceedings of the 34th International ACM SIGIR Conference on Research and Development in Information Retrieval*, pages 843–852, Beijing, China, July 2011.

[19] M. D. Lieberman, H. Samet, J. Sankaranarayanan, and J. Sperling. STEWARD: Architecture of a spatio-textual search engine. In *GIS'07: Proceedings of the 15th ACM International Symposium on Geographic Information Systems*, pages 186–193, Seattle, WA, Nov. 2007.

[20] M. D. Lieberman, H. Samet, and J. Sankaranarayanan. Geotagging: Using proximity, sibling, and prominence clues to understand comma groups. In *GIR'10: Proceedings of the 6th Workshop on Geographic Information Retrieval*, Zurich, Switzerland, Feb. 2010.

[21] M. D. Lieberman, H. Samet, and J. Sankaranarayanan. Geotagging with local lexicons to build indexes for textually-specified spatial data. In *ICDE'10: Proceedings of the 26th International Conference on Data Engineering*, pages 201–212, Long Beach, CA, Mar. 2010.

[22] I. Mani, J. Hitzeman, J. Richer, and D. Harris. *ACE 2005 English SpatialML Annotations*. Linguistic Data Consortium, Philadelphia, PA, Jan. 2008. LDC Catalog Number LDC2008T03.

[23] B. Martins, H. Manguinhas, and J. Borbinha. Extracting and exploring the geo-temporal semantics of textual resources. In *ICSC'08: Proceedings of the 2nd IEEE International Conference on Semantic Computing*, pages 1–9, Santa Clara, CA, Aug. 2008.

[24] B. Martins, I. Anastácio, and P. Calado. A machine learning approach for resolving place references in text. In *AGILE'10: Proceedings of the 13th AGILE International Conference on Geographic Information Science*, pages 221–236, Guimarães, Portugal, May 2010.

[25] NTS Realty Holdings. NTS Realty Holdings limited partnership announces refinancing of debt on eight multifamily properties. URL `http://www.earthtimes.org/articles/show/nts-realty-holdings-limited-partnership,1062375.shtml`. Accessed 16 Jan 2010.

[26] R. C. Pasley, P. D. Clough, and M. Sanderson. Geo-tagging for imprecise regions of different sizes. pages 77–82.

[27] R. S. Purves, P. Clough, C. B. Jones, A. Arampatzis, B. Bucher, D. Finch, G. Fu, H. Joho, A. K. Syed, S. Vaid, and B. Yang. The design and implementation of SPIRIT: a spatially aware search engine for information retrieval on the Internet. *IJGIS: International Journal of Geographical Information Science*, 21(7):717–745, Aug. 2007.

[28] T. Qin, R. Xiao, L. Fang, X. Xie, and L. Zhang. An efficient location extraction algorithm by leveraging web contextual information. In *GIS'10: Proceedings of the 18th ACM SIGSPATIAL International Conference on Advances in Geographic Information Systems*, pages 53–60, San Jose, CA, Nov. 2010.

[29] G. Quercini, H. Samet, J. Sankaranarayanan, and M. D. Lieberman. Determining the spatial reader scopes of news sources using local lexicons. In *GIS'10: Proceedings of the 18th ACM SIGSPATIAL International Conference on Advances in Geographic Information Systems*, pages 43–52, San Jose, CA, Nov. 2010.

[30] E. Rauch, M. Bukatin, and K. Baker. A confidence-based framework for disambiguating geographic terms. In *Proceedings of the HLT-NAACL 2003 Workshop on Analysis of Geographic References*, pages 50–54, Edmonton, Canada, May 2003.

[31] H. Samet, H. Alborzi, F. Brabec, C. Esperança, G. R. Hjaltason, F. Morgan, and E. Tanin. Use of the SAND spatial browser for digital government applications. *CACM: Communications of the ACM*, 46(1):61–64, Jan. 2003.

[32] H. Samet, B. E. Teitler, M. D. Adelfio, and M. D. Lieberman. Adapting a map query interface for a gesturing touch screen interface. In *WWW'11: Proceedings of the 20th International World Wide Web Conference*, pages 257–260, Hyderabad, India, Mar. 2011.

[33] J. Sankaranarayanan, H. Samet, B. Teitler, M. D. Lieberman, and J. Sperling. TwitterStand: News in tweets. In *GIS'09: Proceedings of the 17th ACM SIGSPATIAL International Conference on Advances in Geographic Information Systems*, pages 42–51, Seattle, WA, Nov. 2009.

[34] C. A. Shaffer, H. Samet, and R. C. Nelson. QUILT: a geographic information system based on quadtrees. *IJGIS: International Journal of Geographical Information Science*, 4(2):103–131, Apr. 1990.

[35] D. A. Smith and G. Crane. Disambiguating geographic names in a historical digital library. In *ECDL'01: Proceedings of the 5th European Conference on Research and Advanced Technology for Digital Libraries*, pages 127–136, Darmstadt, Germany, Sept. 2001.

[36] J. Strötgen, M. Gertz, and P. Popov. Extraction and exploration of spatio-temporal information in documents. In *GIR'10: Proceedings of the 6th Workshop on Geographic Information Retrieval*, Zurich, Switzerland, Feb. 2010.

[37] B. E. Teitler, M. D. Lieberman, D. Panozzo, J. Sankaranarayanan, H. Samet, and J. Sperling. NewsStand: A new view on news. In *GIS'08: Proceedings of the 16th ACM SIGSPATIAL International Conference on Advances in Geographic Information Systems*, pages 144–153, Irvine, CA, Nov. 2008.

[38] R. Tobin, C. Grover, K. Byrne, J. Reid, and J. Walsh. Evaluation of georeferencing. In *GIR'10: Proceedings of the 6th Workshop on Geographic Information Retrieval*, Zurich, Switzerland, Feb. 2010.

[39] W. Tobler. A computer movie simulating urban growth in the detroit region. *Economic Geography*, 46(2):234–240, 1970.

[40] A. Weichselbraun. A utility centered approach for evaluating and optimizing geo-tagging. In *KDIR'09: Proceedings of the 1st International Conference on Knowledge Discovery and Information Retrieval*, Madeira, Portugal, Oct. 2009.

[41] B. P. Wing and J. Baldridge. Simple supervised document geolocation with geodesic grids. In *ACL'11: Proceedings of the 49th Annual Meeting of the Association for Computational Linguistics*, pages 955–964, Portland, OR, June 2011.

[42] A. G. Woodruff and C. Plaunt. GIPSY: Automated geographic indexing of text documents. *JASIS: Journal of the American Society for Information Science*, 45(9): 645–655, Oct. 1994.

Structural Relationships for Large-Scale Learning of Answer Re-ranking

Aliaksei Severyn
Department of Computer Science and Information Engineering
University of Trento
38123 Povo (TN), Italy
severyn@disi.unitn.it

Alessandro Moschitti
Department of Computer Science and Information Engineering
University of Trento
38123 Povo (TN), Italy
moschitti@disi.unitn.it

ABSTRACT

Supervised learning applied to answer re-ranking can highly improve on the overall accuracy of question answering (QA) systems. The key aspect is that the relationships and properties of the question/answer pair composed of a question and the supporting passage of an answer candidate, can be efficiently compared with those captured by the learnt model. In this paper, we define novel supervised approaches that exploit structural relationships between a question and their candidate answer passages to learn a re-ranking model. We model structural representations of both questions and answers and their mutual relationships by just using an off-the-shelf shallow syntactic parser. We encode structures in Support Vector Machines (SVMs) by means of sequence and tree kernels, which can implicitly represent question and answer pairs in huge feature spaces. Such models together with the latest approach to fast kernel-based learning enabled the training of our rerankers on hundreds of thousands of instances, which previously rendered intractable for kernelized SVMs. The results on two different QA datasets, e.g., Answerbag and Jeopardy! data, show that our models deliver large improvement on passage re-ranking tasks, reducing the error in Recall of BM25 baseline by about 18%. One of the key findings of this work is that, despite its simplicity, shallow syntactic trees allow for learning complex relational structures, which exhibits a steep learning curve with the increase in the training size.

Categories and Subject Descriptors

I.2.7 [**Natural Language Processing**]: [Language parsing and understanding, Text analysis]

General Terms

Algorithms, Experimentation

Keywords

Question Answering, Kernel Methods, Large-Scale Learning, Support Vector Machines, Structural Kernels

1. INTRODUCTION

A critical step for the design of Question Answering (QA) systems is the passage retrieval and ranking module as even the most powerful approach to answer extraction would inevitably fail if applied to an input passage that either contains no correct answer or simply is not adequate for supporting its correctness. Traditional approaches exploit similarity measures between a question and an answer passage but of course they show obvious limitations, e.g., the passage: *Ron Paul is not the president of the U.S.*, is neither the correct passage nor contains the right answer to the question, *Who is the president of the U.S.?* but it would be easily ranked in the first position according to word overlap measures. TREC QA track [1] has shown that models using syntactic structures can help to overcome the limitations of pure similarity-based models. Unfortunately, syntactic representations are difficult to design when the answer is supported by multiple sentences as (i) discourse processing still requires development to reach a sufficient level of performance and (ii) language models taking into account the dependencies between words spanning several sentences (i.e., long distance dependencies) are rather difficult to model. For example, let us consider a real question-answer pair from the Answerbag community-based QA collection[2] (we will use it as a running example throughout the rest of the paper):

Q1: *Is movie theater popcorn vegan?*

A1: *Any movie theater popcorn that includes butter and therefore dairy products is not vegan. However, the popcorn kernels alone can be considered vegan if popped using canola, coconut or other plant oils which some theaters offer as an alternative to standard popcorn.*

An individual analysis of the two answer sentences produces both a positive and a negative piece of evidence making the answer passage candidate unreliable (and thus it would be ranked lower[3] than other candidates). In contrast, the availability of the cross-sentential structure *pocorn is not vegan, however* would suggest that the candidate is promising as it solves the contradiction. Unfortunately, handcrafting these patterns or rules is not cost-effective and typically requires to replicate the effort when the application domain changes.

A viable alternative is to apply supervised methods to learn answer/passage rerankers, e.g., [35, 15]. Nevertheless,

[1]http://trec.nist.gov/data/qa.html
[2]http://www.answerbag.com
[3]Very simple models would unawarely rank it in top position for the repeated presence of the words popcorn and vegan.

machine learning algorithms applied to similarity scores between questions and answers would not be able to learn patterns such as the one above. In contrast, in [23], we proposed to apply structural kernels [28] to the syntactic representation of question/answer passage pairs. However, such model could only take into account very short passages composed of only one sentence and the experiments were carried out on a small dataset of about 2,000 examples. Most importantly, we did not considered the relational information linking question and answer passages.

In this paper, we define novel relational structural models for passage re-ranking in QA systems based on supervised machine learning. We train our models using structural representations of question and answer passages, which can include multiple sentences. We utilize an off-the-shelf shallow syntactic parser to group words in sentences' constituents, which in turn are organized in a tree structures. Based on the naïve syntactic matching between the word lemmas of a given question and its candidate answer, we mark the corresponding constituents in the resulting tree to capture similar semantic relationships between the two. This way mutual structural relationships between a question and its answer is made available in the tree nodes. To effectively and efficiently use such structures in Support Vector Machines (SVMs), we apply structural kernels, e.g., sequence and tree kernels.

We experimented with our models and the fast SVM algorithm for structural kernels, which allowed us to train our rerankers on datasets up to hundreds of thousands instances. The results on two different QA datasets: Answerbag and Jeopardy! show that our models deliver significant improvements on passage re-ranking tasks, highly improving two different baselines, i.e., reducing the error in Recall by about 18-20% of BM25 and Watson primary search [11], respectively. The very interesting aspect is that the learning curves show that (i) complex relational structures can be learned using large data and (ii) further improvement is possible using more data.

In the remainder of the paper, Section 2 reports on the related work, Section 3 introduces kernel methods for structured data, Section 4 presents our models for re-ranking passages/answers, including the question/answer relational model, Section 5 illustrates our experiments and finally Section 6 derives our conclusions.

2. RELATED WORK

The study carried out in this paper primarily focuses on the use of shallow syntactic/semantic structures for training answer re-ranking with large data. Early related work on the use of syntax and semantics in Information Retrieval was carried out in [38, 39, 32] and in [34, 33]. The results showed that the use of advanced linguistic information was not effective for document retrieval. In contrast, QA work shows that semantics and syntax are essential to retrieve concise answers, e.g., [14, 40, 31]. However, successful approaches in TREC-style systems were based on several interconnected modules exploiting complex heuristics and fine tuning. The effective combination of such modules was strongly dependent on manual setting, which often remained undisclosed.

In our study, we focus on passage re-ranking that can be plugged into virtually any QA system. It can also be directly used as a back-end reranker for ranking non-factoid answers. Reranking can be seen as a typical text categorization task, i.e., the classification of pairs of text fragments constituted by a question and an answer or pairs of questions, e.g., [25, 15]. In this context, a large body of work regards definition/description questions, e.g., [4, 6, 29, 1, 23, 35].

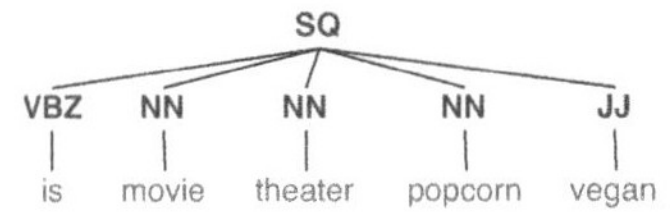

Figure 1: A shallow syntactic tree

In [6], answer ranks were computed based on the probabilities of bigram language models generating candidate answers. Language modeling was also applied to definitional QA in [9] to learn soft pattern models based on bigrams. Other related work, such as [26, 36], was also very tied to bag-of-words features. Our approach is different from the above as we are able to automatically learn structural relationships between a question and candidate answer passages. Such relationships have also been targeted in [10] by creating ad-hoc joint question-answer representations. Additionally, [29, 1, 35] report significant improvement by exploiting expensive linguistic approaches, e.g., predicate argument structures, for re-ranking candidate answer lists. Our work in [23, 21] was the first to exploit kernel methods for modeling answer re-ranking using syntactic and shallow semantic tree kernels based on predicate argument structures. However, our method lacked the use of important relational information between a question and a candidate answer, which is essential to learn accurate relational patterns. Additionally, the low computational efficiency of such approach prevented its application to large datasets. In contrast, we integrate our shallow tree re-ranking models within a much more efficient training algorithm for SVMs with structural kernels, which allows us to carry out experiments on much larger datasets (several hundred thousands examples). Along with our relational representation this appears to be the key aspect for the high improvement over basic models. Finally, models for factoid questions using linguistic structures has been carried out in [2, 3]. Again, the proposed methods rely on manual design of features whereas our approach is more general for passages and/or answer re-ranking.

In summary, the main distinctive property of our approach with respect to the previous work adopting syntactic and semantic structures is that we can define the latter without requiring neither a tedious manual linguistic analysis nor computationally expensive linguistic processors. We do not carry out feature engineering since we simply let kernel functions automatically generate very large feature sets (tree fragments or substrings) to effectively represent structural syntactic/semantic information found in the question/answer pairs. Moreover, our models can be trained on larger datasets, which allows for high improvement over the basic QA system.

Finally, structural kernels have been applied for several natural language tasks, e.g., syntactic parsing [8, 17], Semantic Role Labeling [19, 12, 13, 22], Relation Extraction [24, 42], Pronominal Coreference [37], Recognizing Textual Entailment (RTE) [18] and text categorization [5].

3. KERNELS FOR STRUCTURED DATA

Kernel methods and structural kernels, in particular, are

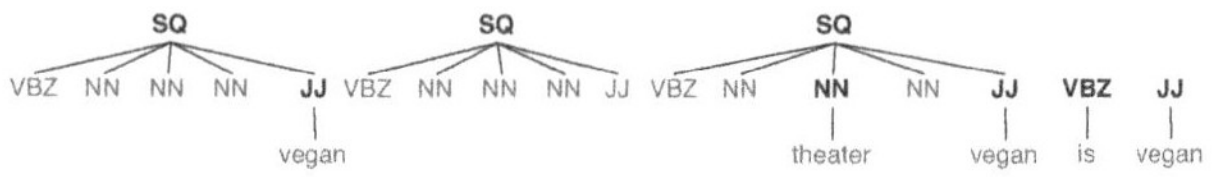

Figure 2: Some tree fragments generated by STK

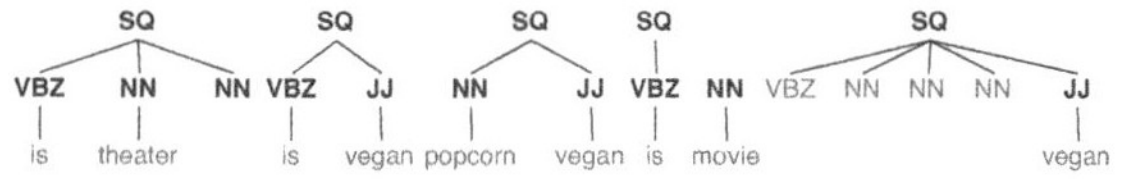

Figure 3: Some tree fragments generated by PTK

very effective means for automatic feature engineering for natural language texts. In kernel machines both learning and classification algorithms only depend on the ability to evaluate an inner product between instances, which corresponds to computing a similarity score. In several cases, the latter can be efficiently and implicitly handled by kernel functions by exploiting the following dual formulation: $\sum_{i=1..l} y_i \alpha_i \phi(o_i)\phi(o)+b = 0$, where o_i and o are two objects, ϕ is a mapping from the objects to feature vectors $\vec{x_i}$ and $\phi(o_i)\phi(o) = K(o_i, o)$ is a kernel function implicitly defining such mapping. In case of structural kernels, K determines the shape of the substructures describing the objects above. The most general kind of kernels used in NLP are string kernels (SKs), e.g., [28], the Syntactic Tree Kernels (STKs) [8] and the Partial Tree Kernels (PTKs) [20].

3.1 String Kernels

The String Kernels (SK) that we consider count the number of subsequences shared by two strings of symbols, s_1 and s_2. Some symbols during the matching process can be skipped. This modifies the weight associated with the target substrings as shown by the following SK equation:

$$SK(s_1, s_2) = \sum_{u \in \Sigma^*} \phi_u(s_1) \cdot \phi_u(s_2) =$$

$$= \sum_{u \in \Sigma^*} \sum_{\vec{I_1}: u = s_1[\vec{I_1}]} \sum_{\vec{I_2}: u = s_2[\vec{I_2}]} \lambda^{d(\vec{I_1})+d(\vec{I_2})} \qquad (1)$$

where, $\Sigma^* = \bigcup_{n=0}^{\infty} \Sigma^n$ is the set of all strings, $\vec{I_1}$ and $\vec{I_2}$ are two sequences of indexes $\vec{I} = (i_1, ..., i_{|u|})$, with $1 \leq i_1 < ... < i_{|u|} \leq |s|$, such that $u = s_{i_1}..s_{i_{|u|}}$, $d(\vec{I}) = i_{|u|} - i_1 + 1$ (distance between the first and last character) and $\lambda \in [0, 1]$ is a decay factor.

It is worth noting that: (a) longer subsequences receive lower weights; (b) some characters can be omitted, i.e., gaps; (c) gaps determine a weight since the exponent of λ is the number of characters and gaps between the first and last character; and (c) the complexity of the SK computation is $O(mnp)$ [28], where m and n are the lengths of the two strings, respectively and p is the length of the largest subsequence we want to consider.

SK applied to a sequence can derive useful dependencies between its elements. For example, from the sequence of words, of the question Q1, we can define the sequence `[[is] [movie] [theater] [popcorn] [vegan]]`, which generates the subsequences, `[[is] [movie]]`, `[[is] [theater] [vegan]]`, `[[is] [vegan]]`, `[[movie] [popcorn] [vegan]]` and so on. Note that this corresponds to a language model over words using skip n-grams.

3.2 Tree Kernels

Convolution Tree Kernels compute the number of common substructures between two trees T_1 and T_2 without explicitly considering the whole fragment space. For this purpose, let the set $\mathcal{F} = \{f_1, f_2, \ldots, f_{|\mathcal{F}|}\}$ be a tree fragment space and $\chi_i(n)$ be an indicator function, equal to 1 if the target f_i is rooted at node n and equal to 0 otherwise. A tree-kernel function over T_1 and T_2 is

$$TK(T_1, T_2) = \sum_{n_1 \in N_{T_1}} \sum_{n_2 \in N_{T_2}} \Delta(n_1, n_2),$$

where N_{T_1} and N_{T_2} are the sets of the T_1's and T_2's nodes, respectively and $\Delta(n_1, n_2) = \sum_{i=1}^{|\mathcal{F}|} \chi_i(n_1)\chi_i(n_2)$. The latter is equal to the number of common fragments rooted in the n_1 and n_2 nodes. The Δ function determines the richness of the kernel space and thus different tree kernels. Hereafter, we consider the equation to evaluate STK and PTK[4].

3.2.1 *Syntactic Tree Kernels (STK)*

To compute STK is enough to compute $\Delta_{STK}(n_1, n_2)$ as follows (recalling that since it is a syntactic tree kernels, each node can be associated with a production rule): (i) if the productions at n_1 and n_2 are different then $\Delta_{STK}(n_1, n_2) = 0$; (ii) if the productions at n_1 and n_2 are the same, and n_1 and n_2 have only leaf children then $\Delta_{STK}(n_1, n_2) = \lambda$; and (iii) if the productions at n_1 and n_2 are the same, and n_1 and n_2 are not pre-terminals then $\Delta_{STK}(n_1, n_2) = \lambda \prod_{j=1}^{l(n_1)}(1 + \Delta_{STK}(c_{n_1}^j, c_{n_2}^j))$, where $l(n_1)$ is the number of children of n_1 and c_n^j is the j-th child of the node n. Note that, since the productions are the same, $l(n_1) = l(n_2)$ and the computational complexity of STK is $O(|N_{T_1}||N_{T_2}|)$ but the average running time tends to be linear, i.e., $O(|N_{T_1}| + |N_{T_2}|)$, for natural language syntactic trees [20].

For example, Figure 1 shows the shallow syntactic tree of the question Q1. This is a flat tree encoding part-of-speech tags and words. Figure 2 shows some of its fragments generated by STK, highlighting an important limitation on the type of substructures it can generate: production rules, i.e., children of a node cannot be split in the substructures.

3.2.2 *The Partial Tree Kernel*

The computation of PTK is carried out by the following Δ_{PTK} function: if the labels of n_1 and n_2 are different then $\Delta_{PTK}(n_1, n_2) = 0$; else $\Delta_{PTK}(n_1, n_2) =$

$$\mu\Big(\lambda^2 + \sum_{\vec{I_1}, \vec{I_2}, l(\vec{I_1}) = l(\vec{I_2})} \lambda^{d(\vec{I_1})+d(\vec{I_2})} \prod_{j=1}^{l(\vec{I_1})} \Delta_{PTK}(c_{n_1}(\vec{I_{1j}}), c_{n_2}(\vec{I_{2j}}))\Big)$$

where $d(\vec{I_1}) = \vec{I}_{1l(\vec{I_1})} - \vec{I}_{11}$ and $d(\vec{I_2}) = \vec{I}_{2l(\vec{I_2})} - \vec{I}_{21}$. This way, PTK penalizes both larger trees and child subsequences with gaps. PTK is more general than STK, e.g., the shared subsequences containing all children of nodes implement STK. The computational complexity of PTK is $O(p\rho^2|N_{T_1}||N_{T_2}|)$ [20], where p is the largest subsequence of children that we want consider and ρ is the maximal outdegree observed in the two trees. However, the average running time again tends to be linear for natural language syntactic trees [20].

PTK can generate any subset of connected nodes of a tree T, whose edges are in T. For example, Fig. 3 shows the fragments of the tree in Fig. 1. Note that each fragment

[4]To have a similarity score between 0 and 1, a normalization in the kernel space, i.e. $\frac{TK(T_1,T_2)}{\sqrt{TK(T_1,T_1) \times TK(T_2,T_2)}}$ is applied.

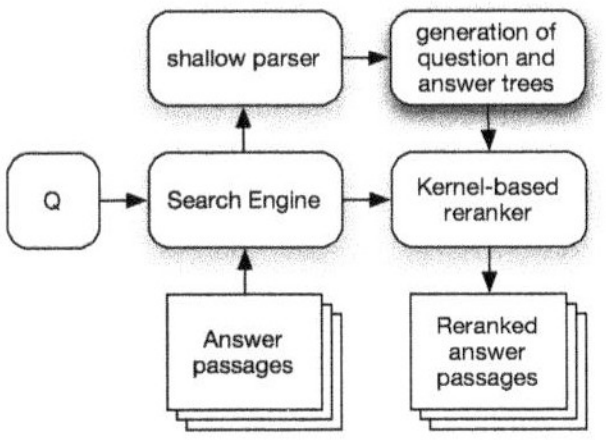

Figure 4: Kernel-based Answer Passage Reranking System

captures dependencies between different groups of word categories and words. This can generalize the language model over words using POS-tags.

4. ANSWER PASSAGE RANKING WITH STRUCTURAL RELATIONSHIPS

The architecture of our system is rather simple as displayed in Figure 4: given a question Q, a search engine retrieves a list of passages ranked by their relevancy. The answer passage retrieval component is fully unsupervised and relies on some scoring model to retrieve most relevant answer passages for a given question. Next, the question together with its candidate answers are processed by a shallow parser that produces a set of annotations, e.g., POS-tags and chunks, for each sentence. These annotations are then used to convert question/answer pairs into various tree structures presented in Sec. 4.2. The obtained pairs are then fed as an input to the kernel based reranker described in the next section. The system outputs a reordered list of answer passages that is supposed to improve the original ranking obtained from the search engine.

4.1 Preference Ranking

Our re-ranking model is an SVM trained to select the best candidate from a given candidate set. To use kernels we apply preference learning [25]. In the preference kernel approach [30], the re-ranking problem – learning to pick the correct candidate h_1 from a candidate set $\{h_1, \ldots, h_k\}$ – is reduced to a binary classification problem by creating *pairs*: positive training instances $\langle h_1, h_2\rangle, \ldots, \langle h_1, h_k\rangle$ and negative instances $\langle h_2, h_1\rangle, \ldots, \langle h_k, h_1\rangle$. This training set can then be used to train a binary classifier. At classification time, pairs are not formed (since the correct candidate is not known); instead, the standard one-versus-all binarization method is applied. Within this kernel-based learning framework offered by SVMs, we can use kernel functions that provide effective means to model the *differences* between the objects representing question/answer pairs. If we have a valid kernel $K(\cdot,\cdot) = \langle\phi(\cdot), \phi(\cdot)\rangle$ over the candidate space $\mathcal{T}$, we can construct a preference kernel P_K over the space of pairs $\mathcal{T} \times \mathcal{T}$ as follows: $P_K(x, y) = P_K((x_1, x_2), (y_1, y_2)) =$

$$\begin{aligned} &= \langle \phi(x_1) - \phi(x_2), \phi(y_1) - \phi(y_2)\rangle = \\ &= K(x_1, y_1) + K(x_2, y_2) - K(x_1, y_2) - K(x_2, y_1), \end{aligned} \quad (2)$$

where $x, y \in \mathcal{T} \times \mathcal{T}$. It is easy to show [30] that P_K is also a valid Mercer kernel. This makes it possible to use kernel methods to train the reranker. We explore innovative kernels K to be used in Eq. 2: $K(x_i, y_j) = r(x_i) \times r(y_j) + DK(x_i, y_j)$, where $r(\cdot)$ is the inverse of the position to which an answer is ranked by the base model (e.g., a search engine) and DK is the summation of a structural kernel, i.e., SK, STK or PTK,

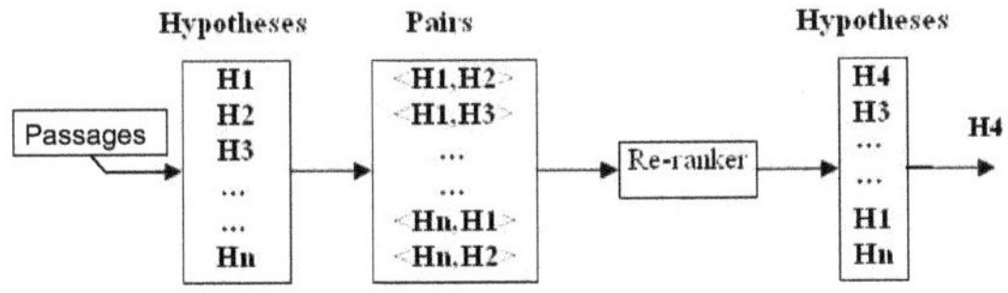

Figure 5: Preference Reranking

applied to both question and answer, respectively. More formally, given $x_i = (a_{x_i}, q_{x_i})$ and $y_j = (a_{y_j}, q_{y_j})$ the representations of two question and answer pairs, $DK(x_i, y_j) = S(a_{x_i}, a_{y_j}) + S(q_{x_i}, q_{y_j})$, where S is SK, STK or PTK.

The structural kernels applied individually to a given question and a candidate answer passage would generate many structural features, yet fail to capture important features relating the question/answer pair as one object. Hence, it is important for the learning algorithm that exploits the expressive power of structural kernels to have a representation where it can also learn the important features relating a question and an answer as a single pair. In the next sections we discuss a simple strategy to establish such a link between a question and an answer using computationally efficient and robust methods.

4.2 Shallow Syntactic/Semantic Models for Relation Learning

The goal of this paper is to learn rerankers that are accurate, robust to noise and scale well with the size of the data available for training. To fulfill these requirements this section introduces several efficient and robust representations for a question and answer pairs.

4.2.1 Shallow Parsing and Semantic Tagging

We derive our representations with a shallow syntactic parser by only considering part-of-speech (POS) tagging and chunking. The former associates words with their grammatical categories (e.g., *movie* → *noun* → NN, *is* → *verb* → VBZ) whereas a chunker groups the words in a sentence into syntactic constituents without specifying their internal structure and their syntactic role (e.g., *can be considered* → *verbal phrase* → VP).

Our representations exhibit the following important characteristics: (i) the pre-processing stage for extracting features from questions and answers is efficient; (ii) manual feature engineering is avoided by using expressive structural kernels; and (iii) our approach is easily adaptable to diverse QA collections, domains and languages as it only relies on shallow syntactic parsers. For example, state-of-the-art POS-taggers and chunkers are also available in special domains, e.g., biomedicine and many languages other than english.

Additionally, we explore the use of semantic information extracted by named entity recognizers (NERs) or by Wordnet super sense (WNSS) taggers. NER can detect sequences of words constituting predefined categories such as names, organizations, locations, etc. (e.g., *Paul McCartney* → *person*, *U.S.* → *location*). WNSS assigns words to one of 41 broad semantic categories derived from Wordnet super sense classes[5]. Typically, NERs implement Conditional Random Field sequence models, while WNSS taggers are Naïve Bayes or Maximum Entropy classifiers. Hence, both NERs and

[5]http://wordnet.princeton.edu/man/lexnames.5WN.html

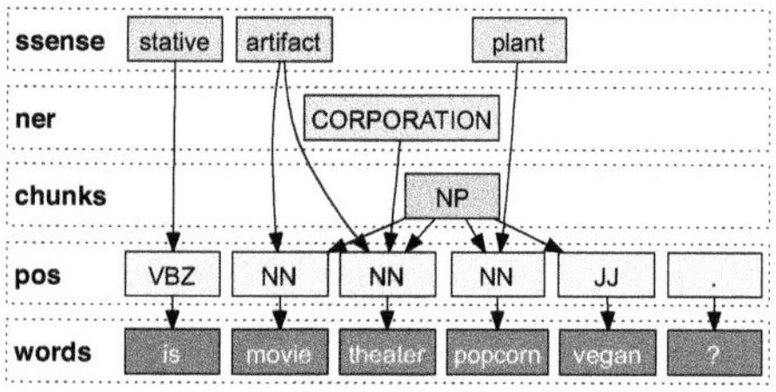

Figure 6: Annotation graph obtained from a shallow parser for the example question Q1.

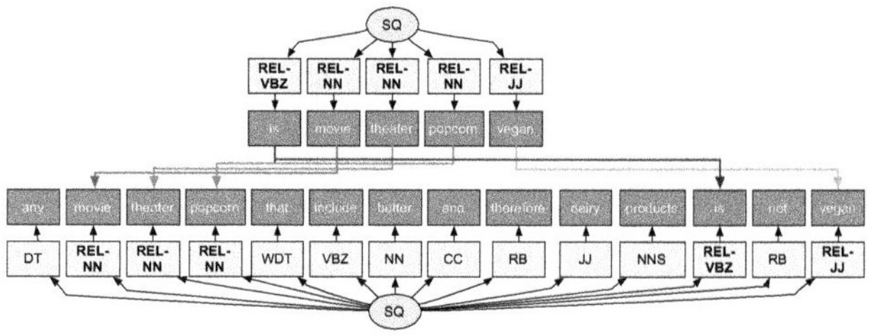

Figure 8: Question and answer sequences aligned by lexical matching on word lemmas. Matched nodes are marked with a special REL marker.

WNSS taggers are more computationally demanding preprocessing tasks. Below, we describe a variety of models for representing question-answer pairs that rely only on the shallow syntactic and semantic analysis described above.

4.2.2 Shallow representations of questions and answer passages

As the first preprocessing step, each question and its answer passage are split into sentences and tokenized. Next, we run a shallow parser, which annotates each token in the sentence with four types of tags: POS, chunks, NER and WNSS tags. As a shallow parser we used SST-light [7] tagger[6], which carries out tokenization, POS-tagging, NER, WNSS tagging and lemmatization, which is useful to increase the matching probability between the words in the question and the answer.

An example of annotation graph obtained for the question of our running example Q1 is provided in Fig. 6. Each word is tagged with its POS tags. Words in the phrase `movie theater popcorn vegan` are organized into a single chunk `NP`. Also the parser finds an NE, `theater`, which is annotated with the tag `CORPORATION`. Typically, NER tags are fairly scarce, while WNSS has better coverage of words in a sentence on average, but many of its semantic categories are rather general. A similar graph can be obtained for each sentence in the answer. It conveniently allows for experimenting with different representations of question-answer pairs.

When structural kernels are applied to the shallow tree in Fig. 6 (we consider a tree root connecting the top POS-tag nodes or the top chunk nodes), they can generate rich features, i.e., n-grams combining tags and words, from the question or from the answer passages. However, to allow kernels capture relations between a question and its answer passage, we need to establish relational links between them. For this purpose, we adopt the following simple strategy: we mark the parent node (POS-tags) of matching leaf nodes (i.e., lemmas) with a special placeholders `REL` in both question and all the sentences of its corresponding answer passage. This way, we are able to derive a joint representation of the question and the answer, where the `REL` nodes represent the most essential parts of the pair.

An example of this procedure between the question Q1 and the first sentence of its answer is shown on the Fig. 8. The `REL` nodes provide the means for the structural kernels, especially STK and PTK, to generate highly discriminative features that carry an extra cue about the structural relations between the question and the answer. For example, PTK can extract the question pattern, `is noun`$^+$`-REL adj-REL` together with the answer pattern[7] `any noun`$^+$`-REL is not adj-REL`. These two patterns, when found together in a new question/answer pair, may indicate that the answer is relevant to the question, e.g., `any BMW series is not cheap` may be an answer for `Is BMW series one cheap?`. Additionally, meaningful pairs of grounded adjectives (related but not identical), i.e., (adj_1, adj_2), can be generally learned since the substructure POS-tag node and its child (i.e., the word) is part of the PTK space (although they are sparser patterns). For example, `any BMW series is not cheap` can be used to answer the question `Is BMW series one expensive?` if patters like `any noun`$^+$`-REL is not cheap` and `is noun`$^+$`-REL expensive` co-occur in answer/question pairs of training data.

4.2.3 Structure Pruning

Providing an efficient representation for the answer passages that contain multiple sentences is not a trivial task. We deal with this problem by simply putting trees representing individual sentences of the passage under a single common root. Since answer passages typically consist of more than two sentences each 10 to 20+ words long the resulting shallow tree may be very large. This makes structural kernels that consider all possible substructures inefficient for such large trees. To alleviate such problem, we propose a simple yet efficient pruning strategy, which reduces the size of the tree down to a manageable size, thus gaining substantial computational savings while preserving the accuracy.

A straightforward approach is to prune away all the nodes that are not marked by the `REL` tag, as they presumably play insignificant role in relating question and its answer passage. However, intuitively, the nodes that surround the relational nodes may carry important contextual information, which can help the learning algorithm to generalize better. Hence, we also keep the nodes that are within a specified distance from the relational nodes (i.e., the ray of pruning is an additional parameter of our models). An example of pruning with ray equal to 1 between example question Q1 and the first sentence of the answer is shown in Fig. 9. The result is a shorter version of the original sentence while preserving the most essential parts (nodes marked with `REL` tag) that encode relational information between the answer and the question. Additionally, the nodes that surround the `REL` tag within the specified distance can serve as a source of additional contextual features. Since questions are typically one sentence long and contain fewer words than answers, we only apply pruning on answer passages.

---

[6] http://sourceforge.net/projects/supersensetag/

[7] $^+$ is the operator of a regular expression meaning at least one occurrence.

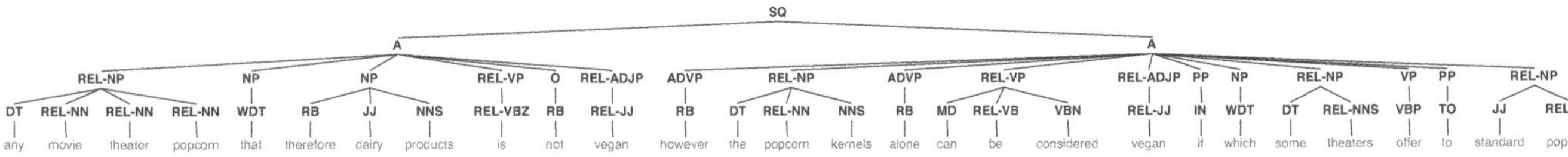

Figure 7: Representation of the entire answer passage using CH+REL model with pruning (ray=1)

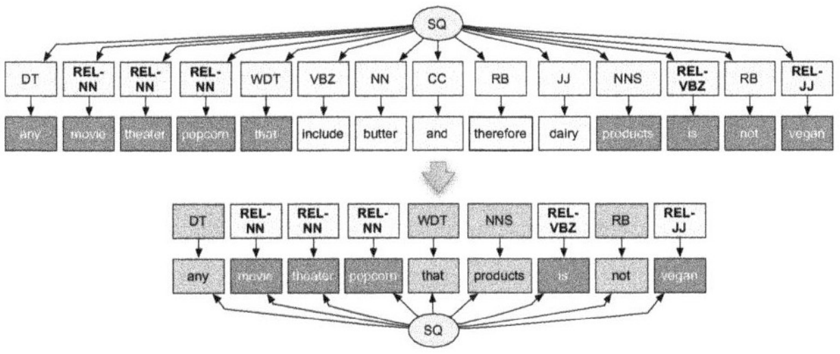

Figure 9: Pruning with ray 1. Original sentence (top) and its pruned version (bottom). Nodes in the middle of the top sequence are pruned away, while the gray-shaded nodes of the bottom sentence are kept as the context.

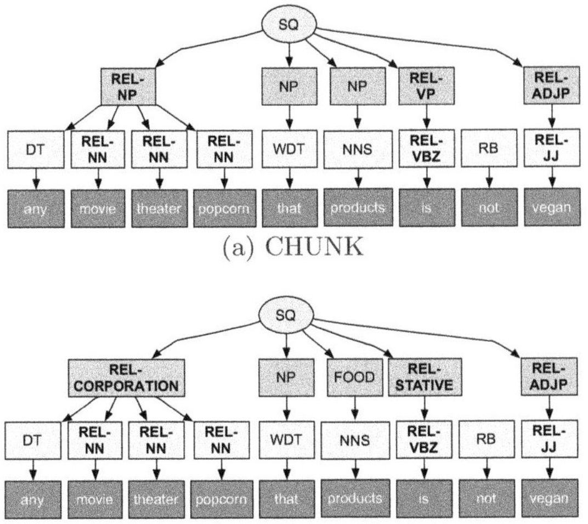

(a) CHUNK

(b) NER+WNSS

Figure 10: (a) Pruned answer trees with constituents re-organized in chunks. REL marker is propagated up from POS to chunk nodes. (b) Enhanced representation with additional semantics from NER and WNSS.

4.2.4 Chunked Representation

Next, we consider the model using chunker tags (CH). Chunks introduce additional level into the shallow tree hierarchy by organizing syntactically related words into constituents. We propagate the REL tag from the relational POS-tags up to their parent chunk nodes. Here we prune the tree on the chunk level, i.e., we keep only the chunk nodes and its subtrees that are within the specified distance from the chunks marked with REL. This results in fewer nodes being pruned compared to POS-tags based pruning, but at the same time, it preserves all contextual words that appear in the same chunk as the matched words. Another very important advantage is that the tree kernel can generate more effective features to characterize the role of relational constituents. For example, Fig. 10(a) reports the shallow tree for the answer sentence reorganized into chunks. The noun phrase *any movie theater popcorn* generalizes the patterns exemplified above thus allowing longer dependency patterns, e.g., `NP is not adj`. Fig. 7 demonstrates the entire answer passage organized in a shallow tree after pruning with radius 1. Thanks to the effective pruning, which allows for preserving important properties and at the same time reducing the size of the inter-sentence structure, our kernels can extract important long distance dependency patterns such as: `NP not adj however alone can be considered adj`, which encode shallow discourse relations.

4.2.5 Semantic Tags

We also consider shallow structures enhanced with additional semantics from NER, and WNSS tags (Fig. 10(b)). If any of the words in a chunk have a NER tag, we propagate it up to the parent chunk tag. If there are multiple words having NER tags inside the same chunk we use the last one. Since NER tags are fairly scarce, we also consider the model where NER tags are augmented with additional WNSS tags (see Fig. 10(b)). For example, when the super sense is used (and considering the adjective grounded in *vegan*), the following pattern is also automatically generated `food not vegan however alone can be considered vegan`.

4.3 Efficient training of the relational ranking model

As discussed in Section 4.1, the task of learning a kernel-based re-ranker using supervised classifiers such as SVMs can be reduced to a problem of binary classification. While this approach allows for the application of a wide range of binary classifiers it may require to carry out learning on very large datasets, since for each question in the training set we need to form all combinations of question answer pairs between the correct and candidate answer passages. Even when the number of candidate answers per question is relatively small, for example 10, the number of training examples generated for the binary classifier increases by an order of magnitude.

Hence, to learn a re-ranker on medium sized datasets (from thousands to tens of thousands of questions) would require to train binary classifiers on datasets of hundreds of thousands to millions of examples. While this poses little limitation for the SVMs with linear kernels for which efficient $O(n)$ learning algorithms have been recently introduced, using SVMs with non-linear kernels, structural kernels in particular, can represent a major computational challenge.

Kernelized SVMs scale quadratically with the number of training examples which prohibits their application on large data. This is why previous research that focused on application of non-linear kernels to question-answer re-ranking tasks has reported experiments on very small datasets (several thousands of examples).

The major bottleneck for the application of SVMs with structural kernels stems from the necessity to carry out learning in the dual space. Training can be seen is an iterative process that requires to compute an inner product between the current model represented by the weight vector $\vec{w}$ and a training example $\vec{o}_i$. It can be shown (see, for example, [27]) that this involves quadratic number of kernel evaluations (Eq. 2) at each iteration, which makes the overall scaling behavior of the learning algorithm $O(n^2)$. In this paper, we adopt a Cutting Plane Algorithm with sampling originally introduced in [41]. The algorithm uses sampling to effectively reduce the number of kernel evaluations while preserving theoretical bounds on accuracy and convergence. We follow the method in [27] developed for SVM learning with structural kernels, which has been shown to provide substantial speedups in training over conventional training methods for non-linear kernels. The Cutting Plane Algorithm also allows for easy parallelization, which makes it possible to experiment with larger data.

5. EXPERIMENTS

To test the efficacy of our re-ranking approach based on relational features, we conduct experiments on two diverse QA collections: Answerbag and Jeopardy!. For the Answerbag dataset, we built the entire answer passage re-ranking system as outlined in Fig. 4. Unlike the Answerbag collection, the Jeopardy! dataset already comes with ranked answer passages for each questions.

5.1 Setup

To train our re-rankers we used uSVM-TK software, which implements highly efficient Cutting Plane Algorithm with sampling [27] within the framework of SVM-Light-TK [20, 16]. This enables the use of structural kernels, e.g., SK, STK and PTK (see Sec. 3.2). We extended the software to handle re-ranking on pairs of multiple trees corresponding to question-answer pairs. We used default parameters to favor replicability of our results.

We ran all the experiments on a machine equipped with 12 CPUs Intel® Xeon® 2.93GHz CPUs carrying 98Gb of RAM under Linux. The uSVM-TK software allows for training and testing in parallel mode; the reported runtimes refer to the use of four CPUs.

To measure the accuracy of our re-ranker system, we used two metrics: Recall of 1 at rank=1 (R1@1) i.e., the percentage of questions with at least a correct answer ranked at the top position of the candidate list, and Mean Reciprocal Rank (MRR) computed as follows: $MRR = \frac{1}{|Q|}\sum_{i=1}^{|Q|}\frac{1}{rank_i}$, where $rank_i$ is the position of the correct answer in the candidate list.

5.2 Corpora

Answerbag. The first corpus we experimented with represents a large sample of Answerbag QA collection[8]. This community-driven Web QA collection is very active and is similar to other popular QA sites such as Yahoo! Answers[9] and WikiAnswers[10]. One of the reasons that makes this site attractive for its users is that it contains a very large portion of questions tagged as "professionally researched". For this type of questions, website moderators provide succinct and exhaustive answers, which makes it ideal for building a high quality question answering corpus. We scraped 180,000 question-answer pairs from 20 different categories. As an answer retrieval component for this collection, we use an off-the-shelf search engine: Terrier[11] using BM25 scoring function with other settings set to default. We retain top 15 candidates for each question. We omit questions for which the search engine failed to retrieve a correct answer in the top 15 positions, since these cases carry no value for training or evaluation of our re-ranker models. This leaves us with roughly 60% of the questions from the original data for which the correct answer is found in the top 15 positions. From this set of questions we form training sets of increasing size starting from 25k and up to 750k pairs. For testing, we use 30k re-ranking examples which corresponds to roughly 2k questions.

Jeopardy! The second dataset represents a small subset of the output from the Primary Search retrieval component of IBM Watson QA system[12] built specifically to provide answers for questions from the Jeopardy! challenge[13]. Different from the setting for the Answerbag collection, where we had to use our own passage retrieval system, here each question is provided together with the set of answer passages ranked by Watson. This allows us to compare our re-ranker to a very strong baseline (IBM Watson is a state-of-the-art QA system). The collection is composed of 517 questions where each question comes with 50 candidate passages. Unlike the Answerbag dataset, most of the questions in this collection have more than one relevant answer passage. On average there are 6 relevant out 50 candidate passages for each question. We use 70% (259 questions) for training and 30% (116 questions) for testing. Since each question has multiple correct answer passages, to create a training set, we paired up each correct answer with all incorrect candidates. As a result we obtain 63,361 examples for training and 5,706 testing.

5.3 Accuracy on Answerbag

Table 1 summarizes the results for various models described in the Section 4.2 trained on the set of 25,000 examples (1,676 questions). W stands for bag-of-words, POS - bag-of-POS-tags, REL - bag-of-REL nodes, CH indicates models with sentence constituents organized in chunks, PR-1 indicates pruning with ray 1. NER corresponds to tags obtained from named-entity recognizer and WNSS are tags from homonymous tagger.

Bags of features. As expected models that are based on just bags of features (W, POS, W+POS) perform poorly showing negative or no improvement over the baseline. Interestingly, we notice that introducing a relational REL tag to mark the matched nodes in the question and its answer (models: POS+REL, W+POS+REL) provides a small increase in accuracy compared to the models that do not exploit such relational information. Even for completely unstructured features, relational nodes can serve as a useful cue to discriminate between the correct and incorrect question-answer pairs. Surprisingly, the model combining all of the features including additional features from NER and WSSN taggers (W + POS + NER + WSNN + REL) results in severe over-fitting. After performing manual inspection, we concluded that, since the search engine (SE) already sets a very strong baseline for this QA collection (MRR: 71.63% and REC1@1: 59.14%), using features similar to those of

[8]http://www.answerbag.com
[9]http://answers.yahoo.com
[10]http://wiki.answers.com
[11]http://terrier.org/
[12]http://www-03.ibm.com/innovation/us/watson/index.html
[13]http://www.j-archive.com.

Table 1: Experiments with different models.

MODEL	MRR	R1@1
BASELINE (BM25)	71.63	59.14
BAGS OF FEATURES		
W	68.23	54.83
POS	69.61	56.38
W+POS	69.79	56.78
W+REL	69.21	55.63
POS+REL	71.25	58.85
W+POS+REL	71.88	59.02
W+POS+NER+WNSS+REL	65.66	52.01
SEQUENCES OF FEATURES		
POS (SK)	67.40	52.24
POS+REL (SK 1)	71.25	58.85
POS+REL (SK 2)	72.54	60.86
POS+REL (SK 3)	72.99	61.08
POS+REL (SK 4)	72.74	61.26
POS+REL (SK 5)	72.91	61.32
STRUCTURAL FEATURES		
POS+REL (STK)	71.99	59.08
POS+REL (PTK)	73.50	61.32
CH+REL (PTK)	75.14	63.68
CH+REL (STK)	73.09	63.52
TRANSLATION	71.55	59.01

the SE for re-ranking cannot provide improvement. Additionally, NER and WSNN taggers that assign words to very general categories are not helpful for discriminating between the similar answer passages retrieved by the SE.

In summary, the top part of the Table 1 provides a clear indication that using unstructured features gives little to no benefit for the re-ranker. To confirm this behavior does not change on larger data, we also carried out training on larger samples of the training set but observed essentially flat learning curves, which means that the models relying only on the bags of features do not improve with more data.

Linear sequence models. In contrast, using SK applied to POS tags generates all possible skip n-grams. Coupled with the relational information captured by the REL marker (POS+REL) it provides interesting improvement over the baseline. At the same time, when applied on the sequence of POS-tags without relational information (POS), we observe no improvement. We also show the results using different values for the maximum subsequence length in SK: (SK 1), (SK 2), (SK 3), (SK 4), and (SK 5). For example, (SK 3) will consider all skip n-grams up to the length 3. The results show that complex features up to 5 elements provide the highest accuracy. This suggests that the modeled structures provide an adequate generalization level for SK to extract effective 5-grams (constituted by POS-tags and words).

Structural features. Next, we consider the application of structural kernels, e.g. STK and PTK, to shallow trees (POS+REL). We first note, that STK does not work well on shallow representations, due to its limited expressive power as discussed in Section 3.2.1. Conversely, PTK that generates all possible tree fragments is able to pick up the relevant features showing significant improvement over the baseline. To make STK more efficient and effective, we consider chunked representation, which allows STK to generate richer feature sets. Indeed, STK on CH+REL gets a higher accuracy.

Translation-based features. To compare with previous work, e.g., [15, 35], we experimented with question-to-answer translation models that have been reported to provide one of the most important features for re-ranking question-answer

Table 2: Chunk models with different levels of pruning ("-" is no pruning, time is in minutes).

MODEL	RAY	TRAIN	TEST	MRR	R1@1
SK					
POS+REL	0	3	2	72.9	61.3
POS+REL	1	6	6	72.7	61.0
POS+REL	-	5	3	72.9	61.3
PTK					
POS+REL	0	19	8	74.1	62.1
POS+REL	1	40	16	74.7	63.4
POS+REL	-	50	20	74.7	63.4
CH+REL	0	27	16	75.0	63.6
CH+REL+NER	0	13	7	73.6	61.5
CH+REL	1	39	23	74.2	62.1
CH+REL+NER	1	21	13	75.0	64.0
CH+REL+NER+WNSS	1	18	11	73.4	61.3
CH+REL	2	53	46	74.3	62.3
CH+REL	-	90	61	75.1	63.7
STK					
CH+REL	0	4	4	73.4	60.9
CH+REL+NER	0	3	13	71.9	59.0
CH+REL	1	7	6	73.7	61.1
CH+REL+NER	1	5	5	73.5	61.9
CH+REL+NER+WNSS	1	5	6	72.5	59.8
CH+REL	2	10	12	73.8	61.8
CH+REL	-	13	13	73.1	60.5

pairs. Translation-based models exploit word translation probabilities to compute a similarity score between a question Q and an answer A: $sim(Q, A) = \prod_{q \in Q} P(q|A)$. The word translation probabilities can be learnt using word alignment toolkits such as Giza++[14] or Berkeley Aligner[15]. To build word translation probabilities we used Berkeley Aligner without any parameter tuning except for increasing the default number of iterations from 2 to 10. To train the word alignment model we used 70% of the data reserved for the training and then used the obtained alignment model to compute the similarity score between a question and the answer for both training and test re-ranking datasets. We added translation features to all the models mentioned in this section and observed little to no improvement independent of the dataset size used for training a reranker. This suggests that only structural features extracted by STK and PTK from POS+REL and CH+REL structures exhibit high discriminative power.

5.4 Efficiency analysis - large scale learning

As discussed in Sec. 4.2 pruning is an effective way to reduce the size of a tree by removing less pertinent nodes. This is essential to speed up kernel evaluations, which would allow for better scaling to larger data. The study of runtime savings for different levels of pruning is presented in Table 2.

We first observe that applying pruning with rays $\in \{0, 1\}$ on POS+REL trees for both SK and PTK results in runtime speedups up to 2x. A similar picture is observed for the CH+REL tree representations. Interestingly, models with the most aggressive pruning using ray=0, such that no context nodes are preserved, demonstrate slightly higher accuracy than other models with softer levels of pruning. This can be explained by the fact that keeping additional context nodes around the relational nodes produces richer fea-

[14]http://code.google.com/p/giza-pp/

[15]http://code.google.com/p/berkeleyaligner/

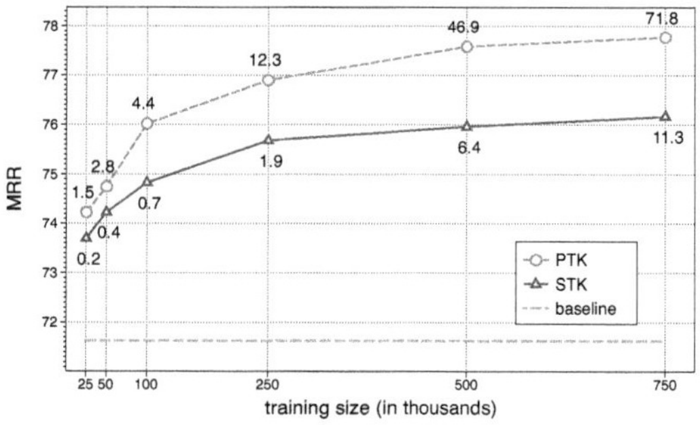

Figure 11: Learning curve for MRR using PTK and STK. Labels along the curves correspond to the training time in hours.

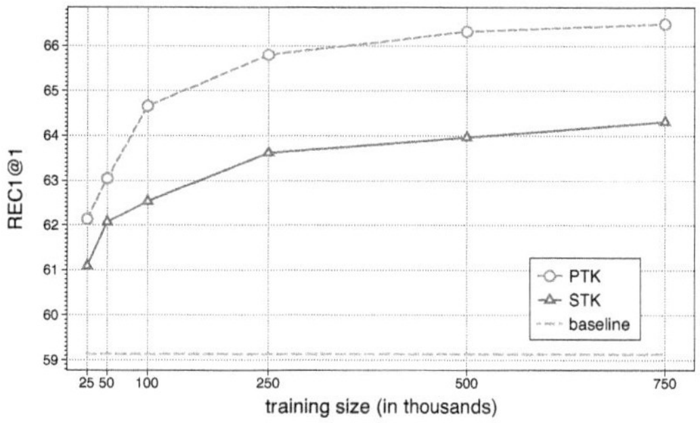

Figure 12: Learning curve for REC1@1 using PTK and STK.

ture spaces (especially with PTK), which may result noisy on relatively small datasets. Hence we studied the learning curves for these models on 50k and 100k training sets and found that CH+REL with pruning at ray=1 provided the steepest learning curve, while maintaining the optimal tradeoff between the training time and accuracy. We also prefer a simpler CH+REL model, which only requires to perform POS-tagging and chunking, over more refined models with NER and WNSS tags, which require additional preprocessing. Thus, we build learning curves for the CH+REL models using STK and PTK reporting MRR (Fig. 11) and REC1@1 (Fig. 12). The plots demonstrate nice scaling behavior when training CH+REL re-ranker model on larger data. For example, the PTK-based rerankers improve BM25 by about 6 absolute points in MRR, i.e., 71.6 vs. 77.8, and about 7 points in R1@1, i.e., 59.1 vs. 66.5, for a relative error reduction of about 18-20% in R1@1.

5.5 Jeopardy! experiments

Since the size of Jeopardy! dataset does not allow for building a meaningful learning curve we report the plot of R1@x, which measures the percentage of questions with at least one correct answer in the first x positions. We experimented with PTK applied to CH+REL structures also encoding NER and WNSS. Figure 13 shows that for any rank position, the simplest model outperforms semantic models. Most importantly, the Primary Search of Watson is improved up to 5 points for an error reduction of 20%.

6. CONCLUSIONS AND FINAL REMARKS

The key aspect in learning to rank answer passages for QA systems is the use of relationships between the question and the supporting passages of its answer candidates.

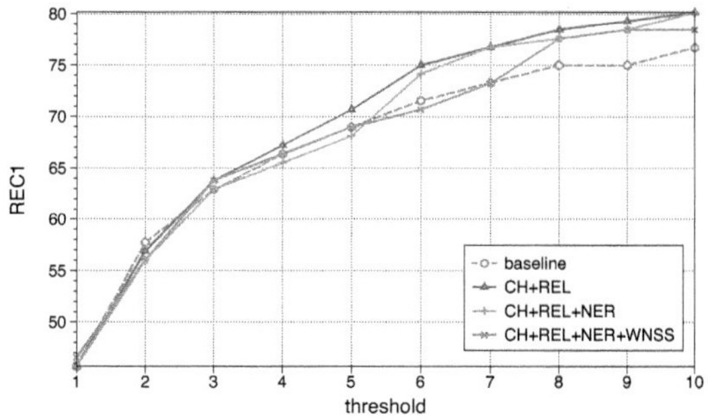

Figure 13: Recall of 1 at different rank positions for the Jeopardy! dataset.

Supervised methods can generalize the properties found in different question/answer pairs and use them to evaluate the validity of new candidates. In this perspective, the most difficult aspect is the design of relational features that can enable the learning algorithm to learn the properties above. In this paper, we propose robust and simple models to learn such properties from large datasets. On one hand, we use shallow syntactic and semantic (at lexical level) representations, which can be efficiently and automatically derived with high accuracy. On the other hand, we exploit the power of structural kernels for automatic engineering of a huge number of structural features. Applied to large training sets (hundreds of thousands) our models allow for efficient learning of complex question/answer relationships.

Our experiments with Support Vector Machines (SVMs) and various shallow models on two datasets: Answerbag and Jeopardy! show that: (i) bag-of-features of question and answer passages, ranging from words to POS-tags or translation probabilities are not effective; (ii) relational features, i.e., encoding pair properties, become effective only when used in structures, e.g, using SK; and (iii) the best compromise between efficiency and accuracy is given by the pure shallow syntactic tree structures as NER or WNSS may introduce noise. Additionally, large scale experiments show significant improvement - about 18-20% of reduction in Recall error, on two strong baselines for passage re-ranking, i.e., BM25 and IBM Watson primary search.

It should be noted that the above baselines are just the first module of QA systems. The latter at the end of their pipeline can produce better rank of passages (also exploiting the answer candidates). However, our rankers use orthogonal information with respect to QA systems, i.e., (i) similarity between relational pairs of questions and answer passages rather than between questions and their answer passages and (ii) complex patterns learned using supervised methods on large data. This kind of information will most likely improve any QA system: verifying this claim is one of our short-term future research directions.

ACKNOWLEDGEMENTS

We thank the IBM Watson team and in particular Jennifer Chu-Carroll for providing us with the Jeopardy! dataset. Many thanks to the SIGIR reviewers. This work has been supported by the IBM's Open Collaboration Research (OCR) awards program. Partial support has been also received by the EC framework FP7/2007-2013 under the grants #247758: EternalS – Trustworthy Eternal Systems via Evolving Software, Data and Knowledge, and #288024: LiMoSINe – Linguistically Motivated Semantic aggregation engiNes.

7. REFERENCES

[1] M. Bilotti, P. Ogilvie, J. Callan, and E. Nyberg. Structured retrieval for Question Answering. In *Proceedings of ACM SIGIR*, 2007.

[2] M. W. Bilotti, J. L. Elsas, J. Carbonell, and E. Nyberg. Rank learning for factoid Question Answering with linguistic and semantic constraints. In *Proc. of CIKM*, 2010.

[3] M. W. Bilotti and E. Nyberg. Improving text retrieval precision and answer accuracy in question answering systems. In *Proc. of IR4QA at COLING*, 2008.

[4] S. Blair-Goldensohn, K. R. McKeown, and A. H. Schlaikjer. Answering definitional questions: A hybrid approach. In *Proc. of AAAI*, 2004.

[5] N. Cancedda, E. Gaussier, C. Goutte, and J. M. Renders. Word sequence kernels. *JMLR*, 2003.

[6] Y. Chen, M. Zhou, and S. Wang. Reranking answers from definitional QA using language models. In *Proc. of ACL*, 2006.

[7] M. Ciaramita and Y. Altun. Broad-coverage sense disambiguation and information extraction with a supersense sequence tagger. In *Proc. EMNLP*, 2006.

[8] M. Collins and N. Duffy. New Ranking Algorithms for Parsing and Tagging: Kernels over Discrete Structures, and the Voted Perceptron. In *Proc. of ACL*, 2002.

[9] H. Cui, M. Kan, and T. Chua. Generic soft pattern models for definitional QA. In *Proc. of SIGIR*, 2005.

[10] A. Echihabi and D. Marcu. A noisy-channel approach to question answering. In *Proc. of ACL*, 2003.

[11] D. Ferrucci. Build watson: an overview of deepqa for the Jeopardy! challenge. In *Proc. of PACT*, 2010.

[12] A.-M. Giuglea and A. Moschitti. Knowledge Discovering using FrameNet, VerbNet and PropBank. In *In Proc. of Ontology and Knowledge Discovering at ECML 2004, Pisa, Italy*, 2004.

[13] A.-M. Giuglea and A. Moschitti. Semantic Role Labeling via Framenet, Verbnet and Propbank. In *Proc. of ACL*, Sydney, Australia, 2006.

[14] A. Hickl, J. Williams, J. Bensley, K. Roberts, Y. Shi, and B. Rink. Question answering with LCC chaucer at trec 2006. In *Proc. of TREC*, 2006.

[15] J. Jeon, W. B. Croft, and J. H. Lee. Finding similar questions in large question and answer archives. In *Proc. of CIKM*, NY, USA, 2005.

[16] T. Joachims. Making large-scale SVM learning practical. In B. Schölkopf, C. Burges, and A. Smola, editors, *Advances in Kernel Methods*, 1999.

[17] T. Kudo and Y. Matsumoto. Fast methods for kernel-based text analysis. In *Proc. of ACL*, 2003.

[18] Y. Mehdad, A. Moschitti, and F. M. Zanzotto. Syntactic/semantic structures for textual entailment recognition. In *HLT-NAACL*, 2010.

[19] A. Moschitti. A study on convolution kernels for shallow semantic parsing. In *Proc. of ACL*, 2004.

[20] A. Moschitti. Efficient convolution kernels for dependency and constituent syntactic trees. In *Proceedings of ECML*, 2006.

[21] A. Moschitti. Kernel methods, syntax and semantics for relational text categorization. In *Proc. of CIKM*, NY, USA, 2008.

[22] A. Moschitti and C. Bejan. A semantic kernel for predicate argument classification. In *Proc. of CoNLL*, Boston, MA, USA, 2004.

[23] A. Moschitti, S. Quarteroni, R. Basili, and S. Manandhar. Exploiting syntactic and shallow semantic kernels for question/answer classification. In *Proc. of ACL*, 2007.

[24] T.-V. T. Nguyen and A. Moschitti. Joint distant and direct supervision for relation extraction. In *Proc. IJCNLP*, Chiang Mai, Thailand, 2011.

[25] F. Radlinski and T. Joachims. Query chains: Learning to rank from implicit feedback. *CoRR*, 2006.

[26] Y. Sasaki. Question answering as question-biased term extraction: A new approach toward multilingual QA. In *Proc. of ACL*, 2005.

[27] A. Severyn and A. Moschitti. Large-scale support vector learning with structural kernels. In *ECML/PKDD*, 2010.

[28] J. Shawe-Taylor and N. Cristianini. *Kernel Methods for Pattern Analysis*. Cambridge Univ. Press, 2004.

[29] D. Shen and M. Lapata. Using semantic roles to improve question answering. In *Proc. of EMNLP-CoNLL*, 2007.

[30] L. Shen, A. Sarkar, and A. Joshi. Using LTAG Based Features in Parse Reranking. In *EMNLP*, 2003.

[31] S. Small, T. Strzalkowski, T. Liu, S. Ryan, R. Salkin, N. Shimizu, P. Kantor, D. Kelly, and N. Wacholder. Hitiqa: Towards analytical question answering. In *Proc. of COLING*, 2004.

[32] A. F. Smeaton. Using NLP or NLP resources for Information Retrieval tasks. In T. Strzalkowski, editor, *Natural Language Information Retrieval.* Kluwer Ac. Pub., Dordrecht, NL, 1999.

[33] T. Strzalkowski, J. P. Carballo, J. Karlgren, A. H. P. Tapanainen, and T. Jarvinen. Natural Language Information Retrieval: TREC-8 report. In *Proc. of TREC*, 1999.

[34] T. Strzalkowski, G. C. Stein, G. B. Wise, J. P. Carballo, P. Tapanainen, T. Jarvinen, A. Voutilainen, and J. Karlgren. Natural Language Information Retrieval: TREC-7 report. In *Proc. of TREC*, 1998.

[35] M. Surdeanu, M. Ciaramita, and H. Zaragoza. Learning to rank answers on large online QA collections. In *Proc. of ACL-HLT*, 2008.

[36] J. Suzuki, Y. Sasaki, and E. Maeda. SVM answer selection for open-domain Question Answering. In *Proc. of Coling*, 2002.

[37] Y. Versley, A. Moschitti, M. Poesio, and X. Yang. Coreference systems based on kernels methods. In *Coling*, Manchester, England, 2008.

[38] E. M. Voorhees. Using Wordnet to disambiguate word senses for text retrieval. In *Proc. of SIGIR*, 1993.

[39] E. M. Voorhees. Query expansion using lexical-semantic relations. In *Proc. of SIGIR*, 1994.

[40] E. M. Voorhees. Overview of the trec 2004 question answering track. In *Proc. of TREC 2004*, 2004.

[41] C.-N. J. Yu and T. Joachims. Training structural SVMs with kernels using sampled cuts. In *KDD*, 2008.

[42] D. Zelenko, C. Aone, and A. Richardella. Kernel methods for relation extraction. *JMLR*, 2003.

Top-k Learning to Rank: Labeling, Ranking and Evaluation

Shuzi Niu, Jiafeng Guo, Yanyan Lan, Xueqi Cheng
Institute of Computing Technology, Chinese Academy of Sciences, Beijing, P.R. China
niushuzi@software.ict.ac.cn, {guojiafeng, lanyanyan, cxq}@ict.ac.cn

ABSTRACT

In this paper, we propose a novel top-k learning to rank framework, which involves labeling strategy, ranking model and evaluation measure. The motivation comes from the difficulty in obtaining reliable relevance judgments from human assessors when applying learning to rank in real search systems. The traditional absolute relevance judgment method is difficult in both gradation specification and human assessing, resulting in high level of disagreement on judgments. While the pairwise preference judgment, as a good alternative, is often criticized for increasing the complexity of judgment from $\mathcal{O}(n)$ to $\mathcal{O}(n \log n)$. Considering the fact that users mainly care about top ranked search results, we propose a novel top-k labeling strategy which adopts the pairwise preference judgment to generate the top k ordering items from n documents (i.e. top-k ground-truth) in a manner similar to that of HeapSort. As a result, the complexity of judgment is reduced to $\mathcal{O}(n \log k)$. With the top-k ground-truth, traditional ranking models (e.g. pairwise or listwise models) and evaluation measures (e.g. NDCG) no longer fit the data set. Therefore, we introduce a new ranking model, namely FocusedRank, which fully captures the characteristics of the top-k ground-truth. We also extend the widely used evaluation measures NDCG and ERR to be applicable to the top-k ground-truth, referred as κ-NDCG and κ-ERR, respectively. Finally, we conduct extensive experiments on benchmark data collections to demonstrate the efficiency and effectiveness of our top-k labeling strategy and ranking models.

Categories and Subject Descriptors

H.3.3 [**Information Search and Retrieval**]: Retrieval models

General Terms

Algorithms, Performance, Experimentation, Theory

Keywords

Learning to Rank, Top-k, Preference Judgment, Evaluation

1. INTRODUCTION

In the past few years, learning to rank has been widely recognized as an important technique for information retrieval (IR). A vital part to employ learning to rank in real search systems is the acquisition of reliable and high quality labeled datasets, both for training and evaluation. In traditional IR literature, assessors are requested to determine the relevance of a document under some pre-defined gradations, which is called *absolute relevance judgment* method. However, there are some significant drawbacks for this evaluation process. Firstly, the specifics of the gradations (i.e. how many grades to use and what those grades mean) must be defined, and it is not clear how these choices will affect relative performance measurements [26]. Secondly, the assessing burden increases with the complexity of the relevance gradations; the choice of label is not clear when there are more factors to consider, leading to high level of disagreement on judgments [4].

Recently *pairwise preference judgment* has been investigated as a good alternative [20, 26]. Instead of assigning a relevance grade to a document, an assessor looks at two pages and judges which one is better. Compared with absolute relevance judgment, the advantages lie in that: (1) There is no need to determine the gradation specifications as it is a binary decision. (2) It is easier for an assessor to express a preference for one document over the other than to assign a pre-defined grade to each of them [7]. (3) Most state-of-the-art learning to rank models, pairwise or listwise, are trained over preferences. As noted by Carterette et al. [7], "by collecting preferences directly, some of the noise associated with difficulty in distinguishing between different levels of relevance may be reduced." Although preference judgment likely produce more reliable labeled data, it is often criticized for increasing the complexity of judgment (e.g. from $\mathcal{O}(n)$ to $\mathcal{O}(n \log n)$ [20]), which poses a big challenge in wide use. Do we actually need to judge so many pairs for real search systems? If not, which pairs do we choose? How to choose? These questions become the original motivation of this paper.

As we know, in real Web search scenario, it is well accepted that users mainly care about the top results [30]. In other words, the ordering of the top results (typically the results on the first one or two pages) is critical for users' search experience. It indicates that a labeling strategy shall take effort to figure out the top results and judge the preference orders among them, but pay less attention to the exact preference orders among the rest results. Based on this observation, we propose a novel top-k labeling strategy which adopts the pairwise preference judgment to generate the top k ordering items from a set of n items in a manner similar to that of HeapSort. The obtained ground-truth from this top-k labeling strategy is a mixture of the total order of the top k items, and the relative preferences between the set of top k items and the set of the rest $n-k$ items, referred as top-k ground-truth. With this top-k labeling strategy, we can not only capture enough information for learning to rank [30], but also largely reduce the complexity of judgment to $\mathcal{O}(n \log k)$.

With top-k ground-truth, we find that traditional ranking models, either pairwise or listwise, are no longer suitable for the labeled data set. It is natural to introduce a mixed ranking model, with the listwise model capturing the total order of the top k items and the pairwise model capturing the relative preference between the set of top k items and the set of the rest $n-k$ items. Such a mixed model can thus combine the advantages of both pairwise and listwise approaches to fully exploit the information in the top-k ground-truth. We refer such a mixed ranking model as FocusedRank, since it emphasizes more on the ordering of the top items.

For evaluation, traditional IR evaluation measures (e.g., MAP, NDCG and ERR), which are mainly defined on the absolute judgment, cannot be directly applied to the top-k ground-truth. To address this problem, we extend NDCG and ERR to κ-NDCG and κ-ERR by taking a function of the position of items as the absolute relevance label. The proposed evaluation measures thus emphasize the importance of the ordering of the top k items. Unlike the evaluation measures based on preference judgments [6], κ-NDCG and κ-ERR keep the same form as NDCG and ERR thus enjoy all the merits of traditional IR evaluation measures.

Finally, we conduct extensive experiments on benchmark data collections. Major experimental findings include: (1) With top-k labeling strategy, the time cost on labeling one pair is much less than that on one item in absolute relevance judgment, and the overall time cost is comparable with that in absolute relevance judgment. (2) With top-k labeling strategy, the level of agreement on judgments is higher than that on absolute relevance judgment. (3) With FocusedRank, the ranking performance is significantly better than the state-of-the-art pairwise and listwise ranking models.

To sum up, we propose a top-k learning to rank framework[1], a novel and complete framework including labeling strategy, ranking model and evaluation measures. Our main contributions are as follows:

1. We propose a novel top-k labeling strategy which adopts pairwise preference judgment to obtain reliable ground-truth for learning to rank. As a result, the complexity of judgment is reduced to $\mathcal{O}(n \log k)$.

2. We introduce a new ranking model named FocusedRank to capture the characteristics of the top-k ground-truth, and it outperforms the state-of-the-art pairwise and listwise ranking models on benchmark datasets.

3. We derive two new evaluation measures named κ-NDCG and κ-ERR applicable to the top-k ground-truth. They both emphasize the importance of top-k ordering and enjoy the merits of traditional IR measures with the similar formulation.

[1]Note that Xia et al. also mentioned the top k ranking problem in [30]. The difference is that they focus on the ranking models under the circumstances of traditional labeling strategy and evaluation measure.

2. RELATED WORK

In this section, we briefly review some related work on labeling strategy, ranking model and evaluation measure in learning to rank literature.

2.1 Labeling Strategy

In learning to rank, labeling strategies can be divided into two categories: absolute judgment and relative judgment [21, 26, 32, 7].

In absolute judgment, assessors are usually requested to assign a graded score to an item independent of the other items [15, 4, 27, 28, 29] under some pre-defined gradations. Such a labeling strategy has been widely adopted in both industry and academia to construct benchmark datasets in IR, e.g. TREC data sets (since 2000), Microsoft learning to rank datasets [18] and Yahoo! Learning to Rank challenge 2010 data set. One difficult problem in using absolute judgment is to clearly define the specifics of the gradations, i.e. how many grades to use and what those grades mean. Some previous studies tried to figure out the proper number of relevance gradations [22, 19]. However, as noted by Cox [12], "there is no single number of response alternatives for a scale which is appropriate under all circumstances". If the descriptions of each degree are not clearly defined, a multi-grade judgment method can be easily misused in the evaluation process [34]. Moreover, the assessing burden in absolute judgment increases with the complexity of the relevance gradations. When there are more factors to consider, the choice of label is not clear, resulting in high level of disagreement on judgments [4].

In contrast, relative judgement aims to directly judge the relative order of a set of items [26]. As a typical form of relative judgment, pairwise preference judgment asks assessors to express a preference for one item over the other [6]. One concern of using this strategy is the complexity of judgment since the number of item pairs is polynomial in the number of items. Carterette et al. [7] attempted to reduce the number of pairs for judging by using transitivity of relevance among documents. Nir Ailon [1] proposed a formal pairwise method based on QuickSort which can reduce the number of preference judgments from $\mathcal{O}(n^2)$ to $\mathcal{O}(n \log n)$. Compared with $\mathcal{O}(n)$ in absolute judgment, this is still not affordable for assessors. To increase the efficiency of relative judgment, R. Song et al. [26] further proposed to select the best one each time from the remaining items, which is only applicable to small datasets. Different from the above related work, we propose a novel top-k labeling strategy to largely save the effort of preference judgment, by exploiting what Web search users actually care about on ranking.

2.2 Ranking Model

So far learning to rank has been mainly addressed by pointwise, pairwise, and listwise ranking models. In pointwise models [17], ranking is transformed to regression or classification on individual items to represent the absolute label on each item. In pairwise models [14, 11, 3], ranking is transformed to classification on item pairs to represent the preference between two items. In listwise models [33, 31, 5], instances as document lists are generated through the comparison over item pairs, and it is superior in modeling more discriminative judgments. Therefore, we can conclude that, pointwise models is well suited for absolute relevance judgment; while both pairwise and listwise models are applicable in either absolute or relative judgment scenario.

In previous work [30], Xia et al. extended three listwise ranking models, namely top-k ListMLE, top-k ListNet and top-k RankCosine, to fit the top-k scenario. Note that they addressed this scenario under the circumstances of traditional labeling strategy and evaluation measure. They conducted experiments on the top-k ListMLE, and claimed that the top-k ListMLE can outperform traditional pairwise and listwise ranking models. However, it cannot avoid the computational complexity on the entire permutation such as that in top-k ListNet.

In our paper, we take the above ranking models as the baselines to show the superiority of FocusedRank.

2.3 Evaluation Measure

To evaluate the effectiveness of a ranking model, many IR measures have been proposed. Here we give a brief introduction to several popular ones which are widely used in learning to rank. See also [16] for other measures.

Precision@k [2] is a measure for evaluating top k positions of a ranked list using two grades (relevant and irrelevant) of relevance judgment. With Precision as the basis, Average Precision (AP) and Mean Average Precision (MAP) [2] are derived to evaluate the average performance of a ranking model.

While Precision considers only two graded relevance judgments, Discounted Cumulated Gain (DCG) [13] is an evaluation measure that can leverage the relevance judgment in terms of multiple ordered categories, and has an explicit position discount factor in its definition. By normalizing DCG@k with its maximum possible value, we will get another popular measure named Normalized Discounted Cumulated Gain (NDCG).

To relax the additive nature and the underlying independence assumption in NDCG, another evaluation measure, Expected Reciprocal Rank (ERR), is proposed in [8]. It implicitly discounts documents which are shown below very relevant documents, and is defined as the expected reciprocal length of time that the user will take to find a relevant document.

Although MAP, NDCG and ERR are widely used in IR, they all adopt absolute relevance labels in their formulation, which imposes restrictions on direct application in the scenario of relative judgment. Therefore, new measures such as $bpref$, $ppref$, and $nwppref$ [6] have been proposed. However, these measures have not been widely accepted by IR community. In this paper, we extend traditional IR evaluation measures to our relative judgment scenario with similar formulation.

3. TOP-K LEARNING TO RANK

In this section, we will introduce our top-k learning to rank framework in detail, which involves the labeling strategy, the ranking model and the evaluation measure.

3.1 Top-k Labeling Strategy

According to previous work and the above discussions, pairwise preference judgment is superior to traditional absolute relevance judgment in the acquisition of reliable judgments from human assessors. However, it is often criticized for increasing the complexity of judgment. In this section, we propose a novel top-k labeling strategy by exploiting what Web search users actually care about on ranking. Our labeling strategy can not only capture enough information for learning to rank, but also largely save the effort of preference judgment.

3.1.1 Motivation

In real Web search applications, users usually pay more attention to the top-k items [9, 25, 10]. For example, according to a user study [30], in modern search engines, about 62% of search users only click on the results within the first pages, and 90% of search users click on the results within the first three pages. It shows that the ordering of the top k results is critical for users' search experience. Two ranked lists of results will likely provide the same value to users (and thus suffer the same loss), if they have the same ranking results for the top positions [30]. Moreover, a good ranking on the top results is much more important than a good ranking on the others. Therefore, a labeling strategy shall take effort to figure out the top k results, judge the preference orders among them carefully, but pay less attention to the exact preference orders among the rest results.

3.1.2 Labeling Strategy

Based on the above analysis, we propose a novel top-k labeling strategy using the pairwise preference judgment as the basis. The basic assumption for our labeling strategy is the transitivity of preference judgments of relevance [24, 7]. That is, if i is preferred to j and j is preferred to k, the assessor will also prefers i to k. With this assumption, our labeling strategy generate the top k ordering items from a set of n items in a manner similar to that of HeapSort. It mainly takes the following three steps:

Step1 Randomly select k items from the set of n items and build a min-heap with t as the root based on the pairwise preference judgments by assessors. Here a min-heap is a complete binary tree with the property: if B is a child node of A, A is less relevant than B.

Step2 Randomly select an item r from the rest $n-k$ items and the preference judgement is conducted between t and r by assessors. We then update the heap if necessary and obtain a new min-heap with the k most relevant items up till now. It is repeated until all the items have been selected.

Step3 Sort the final k items in the min-heap in a descending order, and append the rest items after the k items.

The detailed labeling algorithm is shown in Algorithm1. With the above top-k labeling strategy, the obtained ground-truth is a mixture of the total order of the top k items and the relative preference between the set of top k items and the set of the rest $n-k$ items, referred to as top-k ground-truth.

3.1.3 Complexity Analysis

Here we consider the judgment complexity of each step in top-k labeling strategy:

(1)The judgment complexity of building a min-heap with k items in **Step 1** is $O(k)$;

Algorithm1: Top-k Labeling based on HeapSort

```
Input: (1) D, an item set; (2) k, top item number.
begin
  randomly select k items from D denoted as D_k.
  construct a min-heap H_k over D_k with preference
judgment.
  for each item d in D − D_k do
    obtain preference judgment over pair (d, D_k[1]).
    if the judgment is d more relevant than D_k[1]
      D_k[1] = d,
      update H_k over D_k with preference judgment.
    end if
  end for
  sort H_k to obtain top k items in descending order
denoted as L_D.
  append D − D_k to L_D.
end
Output: L_D.
```

(2)The judgment complexity in **Step 2** is $O((n-k)\log k)$ according to the complexity analysis for HeapSort;

(3)The judgment complexity in **Step 3** is $O(klogk)$.

Therefore, the total judgment complexity of top-k labeling strategy is about $O(n \log k)$. Compared with QuickSort strategy adopted by Nir Ailon [1] for preference judgment, our top-k labeling strategy significantly reduces the complexity from $O(n \log n)$ to $O(n \log k)$, where usually $k \ll n$. The judgment complexity of our strategy is nearly comparable with that of the absolute judgment (i.e. $O(n)$). Experimental results in the following section also verify the efficiency of our labeling strategy which is consistent with the theoretical analysis.

3.2 Top-k Ranking Model

With the top-k ground-truth obtained from our labeling method, traditional ranking models no longer fit the labeled dataset. On one hand, pairwise ranking models can capture the information of the relative preference, but fail to model the total order of the top k items since they ignore the position information. On the other hand, listwise ranking models can capture the information of the total order, but suffer from the great computational complexity due to a large undifferentiated item set in top-k ground-truth. To address this problem, we propose FocusedRank, a mixed ranking model with listwise ranking model capturing the total order of the top k items and pairwise ranking model capturing the relative preference between the set of top k items and the set of the rest $n-k$ items. Such a mixed model can thus combine the advantages of both pairwise and listwise approaches to fully exploit the information in the top-k ground-truth.

3.2.1 Notations

Given m training queries $\{q_i\}_{i=1}^m$, let $\mathbf{x}_i = \{x_1^{(i)}, \cdots, x_{n_i}^{(i)}\}$ be the items associated with q_i, where n_i is the number of documents of this query, T_i be the set of top k items and F_i be the set of other $n_i - k$ items. Denote the total order of T_i as a permutation π_i, where $\pi_i(x_j^{(i)})$ stands for the position of item $x_j^{(i)} \in T_i$. Denote $P_i = \{(x_u^{(i)}, x_v^{(i)}) : x_u^{(i)} \in T_i, x_v^{(i)} \in F_i\}$ as the set of pairs constructed between the set of top k items and the set of the rest $n-k$ items. We relate the top-k ground-truth to relevance labels by defining $\mathbf{y}_i = \{y_1^{(i)}, \cdots, y_{n_i}^{(i)}\}$ as position-aware relevance labels of the corresponding items, and $\mathbf{y}_i^{(T)} = \{y_j^{(i)} : x_j^{(i)} \in T_i.\}$. In our paper, we use $y_j^{(i)} = k + 1 - \pi_i(x_j^{(i)})$, if $x_j^{(i)} \in T_i$, and $y_j^{(i)} = 0$, otherwise. That is, suppose $k = 10$, the relevance labels for the top 10 items are defined in a descending order from 10 to 1, while the relevance labels for the rest items are defined as 0.

3.2.2 FocusedRank

In FocusedRank, we adopt a listwise loss to model the total order of top k items, and a pairwise loss to model the preference of top k items to the other items. The general loss function of FocusedRank on a query q_i is presented as follows[2].

$$L(f;q_i)=\beta \times L_{list}(f;T_i,\mathbf{y}_i) + (1-\beta)\times L_{pair}(f;P_i,\mathbf{y}_i), \quad (1)$$

where L_{list} stands for a listwise ranking model and L_{pair} stands for a pairwise ranking model, β is a trade-off coefficient to balance the two terms. As examples, we combine three popular listwise ranking models (i.e. SVM^{MAP}, AdaRank and ListNet) with three popular pairwise ranking models (i.e. RankSVM, RankBoost and RankNet) respectively to get three specific forms of FocusedRank, namely FocusedSVM, FocusedBoost and FocusedNet accordingly.

(1) FocusedSVM: RankSVM plus SVM^{MAP}

Both RankSVM [14] and SVM^{MAP} [33] apply the SVM technology to optimize the number of misclassified pairs and the average precision, respectively. Therefore, we combine these two ranking models together to get a new FocusedRank method, named FocusedSVM. Specifically, RankSVM is adopted to model the pairwise preference of P_i, and SVM^{MAP} is employed to model the total order of T_i. Therefore, L_{list} and L_{pair} in Eq. (1) has the following specific form, respectively.

$$L_{list}=\max_{\mathbf{z}_i^{(T)}}(1-AP(\mathbf{z}_i^{(T)},\mathbf{y}_i^{(T)})+w^T\Psi(\mathbf{z}_i,T_i)-w^T\Psi(\mathbf{y}_i^{(T)},T_i))$$

$$L_{pair}=\sum_{(x_u^{(i)},x_v^{(i)})\in P_i}\max\{0,1-(y_u^{(i)}-y_v^{(i)})(w^Tx_u^{(i)}-w^Tx_v^{(i)})\}.$$

Like RankSVM and SVM^{MAP}, FocusedSVM can then be formulated as an optimization problem as follows.

$$\begin{aligned}
&\min \frac{1}{2}\|w\|^2 + C\sum_{i=1}^m[\beta\zeta^{(i)} + (1-\beta)\sum_{(x_u^{(i)},x_v^{(i)})\in F_i}\xi_{u,v}^{(i)}]\\
s.t.: &(y_u^{(i)} - y_v^{(i)})(w^Tx_u^{(i)} - w^Tx_v^{(i)})\geq 1-\xi_{u,v}^{(i)}, \forall(x_u^{(i)},x_v^{(i)}) \in P_i,\\
&w^T\Psi(\mathbf{y}_i^{(T)},T_i)-w^T\Psi(\mathbf{z}_i,T_i)\geq 1-AP(\mathbf{y}_i^{(T)},\mathbf{z}_i^{(T)})-\zeta^{(i)}, \forall \mathbf{z}_i^{(T)},\\
&\xi_{u,v}^{(i)} \geq 0, \quad \zeta^{(i)} \geq 0, i=1,...,m,
\end{aligned}$$

where $\mathbf{z}_i^T$ stands for any incorrect label and Ψ is the same as that in SVM^{MAP}. Similar to SVM, $\frac{1}{2}\|w\|^2$ controls the complexity of the model w, and C is a trade-off parameter between the model complexity and hinge loss relaxations.

(2) FocusedBoost: RankBoost plus AdaRank

Both RankBoost [11] and AdaRank [31] adopt the boosting technology to output a ranking model by combining the week rankers, where the combination coefficients are determined by the probability distribution on document pairs and ranked lists respectively. Hence we combine these two

[2]In application, L_{list} and L_{pair} should be normalized to a comparable range, and we adopt this trick in our experiments.

Algorithm2: Learning Algorithm for FocusedBoost

Input: training data in terms of top-k ground-truth.
Given: initial distribution D_1 on T_i and D'_1 on P_i, $i=1,\cdots,m$.
For $t = 1, \cdots, T$
  train weak ranker f_t to minimize: $r_t=\beta\sum_{i=1}^{m}D_t(T_i)L_{list} +(1-\beta)\sum_{i=1}^{m}\sum_{(x_u^{(i)},x_v^{(i)})\in P_i} D'_t(x_u^{(i)},x_v^{(i)})L_{pair}$.
  choose $\alpha_t = \frac{1}{2}\log(\frac{1+r_t}{1-r_t})$.
  update
  $D_{t+1} = \frac{1}{Z_{t+1}}D_t(T_i)\exp(-E(\sum_{s=1}^{t}\alpha_s f_s, T_i, \mathbf{y}_i^T))$,
  $D'_{t+1} = \frac{1}{Z'_{t+1}}D'_t(x_u^{(i)},x_v^{(i)})\exp(\alpha_t(w^T x_u^{(i)} - w^T x_v^{(i)}))$,
  where,
  $Z_{t+1}=\sum_{i=1}^{m}D_t(T_i)\exp(-E(\sum_{s=1}^{t}\alpha_s f_s, T_i, \mathbf{y}_i^T))$.
  $Z'_{t+1}=\sum_{i=1}^{m}\sum_{(x_u^{(i)},x_v^{(i)})\in P_i}D'_t(x_u^{(i)},x_v^{(i)})\exp(\alpha_t(w^T x_u^{(i)} - w^T x_v^{(i)}))$.
Output: $f(x) = \sum_t \alpha_t f_t(x)$.

ranking models together to get a new FocusedRank method, named FocusedBoost. Specifically, RankBoost is adopted to model the preference of P_i, and AdaBoost is to model the total order of T_i. Therefore, L_{list} and L_{pair} in Eq. (1) has the following specific form, respectively.

$$L_{list} = \exp(-E(f, T_i, \mathbf{y}_i^T)),$$
$$L_{pair} = \exp(-(y_u^{(i)} - y_v^{(i)})(w^T(x_u^{(i)} - x_v^{(i)}))),$$

where $E(f, T_i, \mathbf{y}_i^{(i)})$ stands for the IR evaluation to optimize.

As in RankBoost and AdaRank, the detailed algorithm is shown in Algorithm2.

(3) FocusedNet: RankNet plus ListNet

Both RankNet and ListNet aim to optimize a cross entropy between the target probability and the modeled probability. The probability of the former is defined based on the exponential function of difference between the scores of any two documents in all document pairs given by the scoring function f. The probability of the latter is the permutation probability of a ranking list using Plackett-Luce model [23], which is also based on the exponential function. Hence we combine these two ranking models together to get a new FocusedRank method, named FocusedNet. Specially, RankNet is adopted to model the pairwise preference of P_i, and ListNet is to model the total order of T_i. Therefore, L_{list} and L_{pair} in Eq. (1) has the following specific form, specifically.

$$L_{list} = -\sum_{\sigma\in\Sigma_i} P_{\mathbf{y}_i^{(T)}}(\sigma)\log P_{\mathbf{z}_i^{(T)}}(\sigma),$$
$$L_{pair} = -\bar{P}_{u,v}\log P_{u,v}(f) - (1-\bar{P}_{u,v})\log(1-P_{u,v}(f)),$$

where, $\bar{P}_{u,v} = 1$, if $y_u^{(i)} \geq y_v^{(i)}$, and $\bar{P}_{u,v} = 0$, otherwise. In addition, we have that

$$\mathbf{z}_i^{(T)} = \{z_j^{(i)} = w^T x_j^{(i)}, x_j^{(i)} \in T_i\},$$
$$P_{u,v}(f) = \frac{\exp(w^T x_u^{(i)} - w^T x_v^{(i)})}{1+\exp(w^T x_u^{(i)} - w^T x_v^{(i)})},$$
$$P_s(\sigma) = \prod_{j=1}^{|T_i|}\frac{\phi(s_{\sigma(j)})}{\sum_{l=j}^{|T_i|}\phi(s_{\sigma(l)})}, s = \mathbf{y}_i^{(T)}, \mathbf{z}_i^{(T)},$$

where $s_{\sigma(j)}$ denotes the score of the object at position j of permutation σ.

3.3 Top-k Evaluation Measure

As aforementioned, traditional IR evaluation measures (e.g., MAP[3], NDCG and ERR) are mainly defined on the absolute judgment, thus cannot be directly applied to the top-k ground-truth. To address this problem, we extend NDCG and ERR to κ-NDCG and κ-ERR by taking the position of items as the absolute label using the way defined in Section 3.2.1. As a result, the derived evaluation measures actually emphasize the importance of the ordering of the top k items.

3.3.1 κ-NDCG

We first give the precise definition of NDCG as follows.

$$NDCG@l = \frac{1}{N_l}\sum_{j=1}^{l}\frac{2^{r_j}-1}{\log_2(1+j)},$$

where r_j is the relevance label of the item with position j in the output ranked list, and N_l is a constant which denotes the maximum value of NDCG@l given the query.

Using the notations in Section 3.2.1, we can extend NDCG to κ-NDCG with the following definition.

$$\kappa - NDCG@l = \frac{1}{N'_l}\sum_{j=1}^{l}\frac{2^{y_j^{(i)}}-1}{\log_2(1+j)}, \quad (2)$$

where N'_l is a constant which denotes the maximum value of κ-NDCG@l given the query.

3.3.2 κ-ERR

We first give the precise definition of ERR as follows.

$$ERR = \sum_{i=1}^{n}\frac{1}{n}R(r_i)\prod_{j=1}^{i-1}(1-R(r_j)),\ R(r) = \frac{2^r-1}{2^{r_{max}}},$$

where n is the document number of a query, and r_{max} is the highest relevance label in this query.

Similar as κ-NDCG, we can extend ERR to κ-ERR with the following definition.

$$\kappa - ERR = \sum_{s=1}^{n}\frac{1}{n_i}R(y_s^{(i)})\prod_{t=1}^{s-1}(1-R(y_t^{(i)}),\ R(r) = \frac{2^r-1}{2^{y_{max}^{(i)}}}, \quad (3)$$

where $y_{max}^{(i)}$ is the relevance label in the top position, as defined in Section 3.2.1.

4. EXPERIMENTAL RESULTS

In this section, we empirically evaluate our proposed top-k labeling strategy and ranking model. Firstly, we conducted user studies to compare the effectiveness and efficiency of our top-k labeling strategy with traditional absolute judgment based on the dataset from the Topic Distillation task of TREC2003. Secondly, we compared FocusedRank with its corresponding traditional ranking models and top-k ListMLE [30] based on both the ground-truths from the absolute judgment and the top-k ground-truths. The experimental results show the superiority of our labeling strategy and ranking model to previous work.

[3]Since MAP is mainly designed for binary judgment scenario, we omit the modification on it.

Table 1: Comparison results of time efficiency

Method	Time per judgment(s)	Time per query(min)	Judgment complexity	#Judgments per query
Top-k labeling	5.51	13.13	$\mathcal{O}(n \log k)$	142.76
Five-grade judgment	13.87	11.78	$\mathcal{O}(n)$	50

4.1 Top-k Labeling

To study whether top-k labeling is "easier" to make than absolute relevance judgments, we compare the Top-k labeling strategy (i.e., $k = 10$) with the popular five-graded ("bad", "fair", "good", "Excellent", "perfect") absolute relevance judgment method. We investigate which one is a better judgment method under two basic metrics, namely time efficiency [26], and agreement among assessors [7].

4.1.1 Experiment Design

We describe our experimental design from the following four aspects:

Data Set: We adopted all the 50 queries from the Topic Distillation task of TREC2003 as our query set. For each query, we then randomly sampled 50 documents from its associated documents for judgment. Existing Web pages in corpus of TREC2003 were employed in labeling to avoid the time delay in downloading content from Internet. In TREC topics, most of the queries have clear intent in the form of query descriptions, which are also exhibited along with the queries in labeling for better understanding.

Labeling Tools: We designed labeling tools for two judgment methods separately, i.e., the top-k labeling tool $T1$ and the traditional five-graded relevance judgment tool $T2$. In $T1$, a query with its description is shown at the top, and two associated Web pages are placed at the main area. An assessor is then asked to decide which one is more relevant. In $T2$, a query with its description is shown at the top followed with five grade buttons, and a Web page is placed at the main area. An assessor is asked to decide which grade should be assigned to that page. A timer is introduced to both tools for computing time per judgment. Assessors can click the clock button to stop the timer if they want to have a break or leave for a while. This will ensure the computing accuracy.

Assessors: There are five assessors participating our user study. These assessors are all graduate students who are familiar with Web search. They all received a training in advance on how to use the tools and on the specifications of the five grades.

Assignment: To make the comparison valid, the assignment should meet the following requirements. Firstly, for each method, all the selected documents should be judged at least once to obtain a complete data set. Secondly, for each assessor, he/she is most likely to memorize some information on the documents for a given query after judging. Therefore, to compare the methods independently, we shall ensure that each assessor will not see the same query under different tools to minimize the possible order effect. Finally, each tool has to be utilized by all the assessors to avoid the possible differences between individuals. Therefore, we adopted the following assignment to satisfy all the requirements: (1) all the 50 queries are divided into five folds $\{Q_i\}_{i=1}^5$, where each fold has 10 queries; (2) for $i = 1, \ldots, 4$, each assessor U_i judges Q_i with $T1$ and Q_{i+1} with $T2$, and the assessor U_5 judges Q_5 with $T1$ and Q_1 with $T2$. At least such two different assignments are needed to compute the agreement among assessors.

	A≻B	A∼B	A≺B
A≻B	0.6749	0.2766	0.0485
A∼B	0.1138	0.8198	0.0664
A≺B	0.1047	0.3779	0.5174

Table 2: Assessor agreement for preference judgments in top-k labeling results

	A≻B	A∼B	A≺B
A≻B	0.6272	0.2913	0.0815
A∼B	0.2825	0.5232	0.1944
A≺B	0.1534	0.3826	0.4640

Table 3: Assessor agreement for inferred preference judgments in five-graded labeling results

4.1.2 Evaluation Results and Discussions

Two basic metrics are utilized to evaluate the labeling strategies.

(1) Time efficiency: Time efficiency [26] is used to measure the cost of labeling. It is dependent on the time per judgment and the complexity of judgment (the total number of judgments for each query). Statistically, less time per judgment suggests easier judgment.

(2) Agreement: Here we measure the agreement between two assessors over all judgments as [7] to average out differences in expertise, prior knowledge, or understanding of the query. For comparison, we inferred preferences from the absolute judgements: if the judgment on item A was greater than the judgment on item B, we inferred that A was preferred to B (denoted by A≻B). A tie between A and B is denoted by A∼B.

As shown in Table 1, it is obvious that the average time per judgment in absolute judgments is longer than that of the preference judgments in top-k labeling strategy, e.g. about $2 \sim 3$ times. The results verifies the common sense that the preference judgment is easier than absolute judgment. Meanwhile, from the average number of judgments conducted on each query, we can find that the top-k labeling strategy will take more judgments than the absolute judgments, at a scale around the theoretical value $\log k$ (i.e. k=10). Most importantly, we can see that the total judgment time spent on each query is comparable between the two methods. The results indicate that by adopting the top-k labeling strategy, the complexity of pairwise preference judgment becomes similar to that of the absolute judgment. Therefore, it is feasible to use top-k labeling in practice.

The agreement among assessors for preference judgment

Graded MQ2007 (Three-grade relevance judgments)

Methods	N@1	N@2	N@3	N@4	N@5	N@6	N@7	N@8	N@9	N@10	ERR
SVM^{MAP}	0.4006	0.4039	0.4111	0.4128	0.4165	0.4217	0.4266	0.4322	0.4363	0.4419	0.3146
RankSVM	**0.4118**	0.4058	0.4051	0.4099	0.4173	0.4216	0.4267	0.4320	0.4380	0.4447	0.3178
FocusedSVM	0.4060	0.4083	0.4077	0.4079	0.4123	0.4179	0.4234	0.4299	0.4351	0.4400	0.3196
AdaRank	0.3789	0.3941	0.3955	0.4024	0.4066	0.4119	0.4169	0.4225	0.4287	0.4345	0.3061
RankBoost	0.3972	0.4051	0.4062	0.4095	0.4150	0.4197	0.4260	0.4316	0.4374	0.4438	0.3101
FocusedBoost	0.3947	0.4098	0.4110	0.4132	0.4164	0.4235	0.4282	0.4317	0.4368	0.4422	0.3199
ListNet	0.4114	**0.4110**	**0.4134**	**0.4153**	**0.4204**	0.4243	0.4300	0.4332	0.4389	0.4442	0.3206
RankNet	0.4013	0.4086	0.4076	0.4118	0.4156	0.4211	0.4267	0.4330	0.4379	0.4451	0.3157
FocusedNet	0.3968	0.4103	0.4126	0.4153	0.4191	0.4245	**0.4301**	0.4341	**0.4403**	**0.4459**	**0.3223**
Top-k ListMLE	0.4057	0.4091	0.4115	0.4143	0.4188	**0.4247**	0.4293	**0.4346**	0.4392	0.4443	0.3168

Top-k MQ2007 (Top-k judgments)

Methods	κ-N@1	κ-N@2	κ-N@3	κ-N@4	κ-N@5	κ-N@6	κ-N@7	κ-N@8	κ-N@9	κ-N@10	κ-ERR
SVM^{MAP}	0.4530	0.5023	0.5389	0.5702	0.5951	0.6178	0.6346	0.6479	0.6591	0.6690	0.6227
RankSVM	0.4545	0.4932	0.5315	0.5664	0.5930	0.6135	0.6306	0.6445	0.6564	0.6655	0.6205
FocusedSVM	0.4539	0.5087	0.5448	0.5773	0.6024	0.6224	0.6404	0.6527	**0.6646**	**0.6739**	0.6287
AdaRank	0.3896	0.4438	0.4745	0.5062	0.5358	0.5575	0.5777	0.5952	0.6089	0.6190	0.5637
RankBoost	0.4438	0.4825	0.5243	0.5567	0.5850	0.6066	0.6234	0.6361	0.6476	0.6571	0.6131
FocusedBoost	0.4529	0.4943	0.5312	0.5633	0.5918	0.6123	0.6288	0.6420	0.6523	0.6628	0.6187
ListNet	0.4541	0.4937	0.5314	0.5669	0.5922	0.6132	0.6299	0.6419	0.6530	0.6613	0.6195
RankNet	0.4490	0.4875	0.5269	0.5586	0.5865	0.6077	0.6249	0.6390	0.6512	0.6603	0.6143
FocusedNet	**0.4623**	**0.5108**	**0.5460**	**0.5783**	**0.6028**	**0.6240**	**0.6409**	**0.6529**	0.6633	0.6735	**0.6336**
Top-k ListMLE	0.4570	0.4991	0.5356	0.5719	0.5969	0.6176	0.6339	0.6476	0.6585	0.6673	0.6228

Table 4: Performance comparison on Graded MQ2007 and Top-k MQ2007

in top-k labeling and for inferred preference judgment in absolute judgment is shown in Table 2 and Table 3, respectively. Each cell (X_1,X_2) is the probability that one assessor would say X_2(column) given that another assessor said X_1(row). Therefore, they are row normalized. From the results, we can see that by adopting preference judgment, top-k labeling can largely improve the agreement among assessors over the absolute judgment. The overall agreement among assessors reaches 74.5% under top-k labeling, while it is only 54.7% under absolute judgment. We conducted χ^2 test to compare the ratio of the number of pairs agreed on to the number disagreed on for both top-k labeling and absolute judgment. The difference is significant ($\chi^2 = 420.7, df = 1, p < 0.001$). We also investigate the agreement among assessors only on preference pairs (by ignoring ties), where the agreement ratio is 89.7% under top-k labeling, and 83.1% under absolute judgment. We test the difference between the two methods using the ratio of agreed preference pairs to disagreed preference pairs, which is also significant ($\chi^2 = 28.5, df = 1, p < 0.001$).

From the above results, we can conclude that the top-k labeling strategy is both efficient and effective to obtain reliable judgments from human assessors, as compared with traditional absolute judgment.

4.2 Performance of FocusedRank

In this section, we empirically evaluate the performance of our proposed ranking model, i.e. FocusedRank. Specially, we conducted extensive experiments to compare FocusedRank with different state-of-the-art ranking models based on both the ground-truths from the absolute judgment and the top-k ground-truths. Note that k is set to 10 in our experiments. Besides, we also investigated the impact of the balance factor β in our proposed FocusedRank.

4.2.1 Experimental Settings

For comparison, we constructed two datasets, each with both the absolute judgment and top-k labeling. One dataset comes from the benchmark LETOR4.0 collection. There are two homologous datasets with different labeling in LETOR4.0, one is referred to as MQ2007 with three-graded relevance judgments, and the other is MQ2007-list with the total order judgments as the ground-truth. The two datasets share the same queries. The only difference lies in that the documents of a query in MQ2007 is the subset of the documents of the corresponding query in MQ2007-list. Thus the intersection of two document sets on each query is adopted. Those from MQ2007 comprise the ground-truth with absolute judgments, referred as Graded MQ2007. While those from MQ2007-list become the top-k ground-truth by only preserving the total order of top k documents on each query, referred as top-k MQ2007.

The other dataset is the one manually constructed in previous user study experiments with 50 queries from the TREC-2003 Topic Distillation task. The one with the five-graded absolute relevance judgments is denoted as Graded TD2003, and the one with top-k labeling is denoted as Top-k TD2003.

We divided each dataset into five subsets, and conducted 5-fold cross-validation. In each trial, three folds were used for training, one fold for validation, and one fold for testing. For RankSVM and SVM^{MAP} the validation set in each trial was used to tune the coefficient C. For RankNet and ListNet it was used to determine the number of iterations. For our FocusedRank, the validation set was used to tune the balance factor β.

Graded TD2003 (Five-grade relevance judgments)

Methods	N@1	N@2	N@3	N@4	N@5	N@6	N@7	N@8	N@9	N@10	ERR
SVM^{MAP}	0.5055	0.5356	0.5335	0.5374	0.5515	0.5584	0.5669	0.5743	0.5763	0.5801	0.5102
RankSVM	0.5019	0.5409	0.5446	0.5657	**0.5816**	**0.5829**	0.5867	0.5847	0.5905	0.5991	0.5072
FocusedSVM	0.5126	0.5505	0.5498	0.5633	0.5642	0.5656	0.5642	0.5761	0.5840	0.5885	0.5129
AdaRank	0.5278	0.5436	0.5619	**0.5740**	0.5774	0.5797	0.5845	0.5872	0.5944	0.5982	0.5132
RankBoost	0.5230	0.5094	0.5179	0.5362	0.5456	0.5507	0.5555	0.5623	0.5640	0.5750	0.5119
FocusedBoost	**0.5486**	0.5275	0.5356	0.5532	0.5554	0.5706	0.5790	0.5856	0.5876	0.5955	0.5466
ListNet	0.5229	0.5480	0.5514	0.5663	0.5736	0.5804	**0.5885**	**0.5949**	0.5944	0.5985	0.5225
RankNet	0.4971	0.5304	0.5612	0.5638	0.5642	0.5765	0.5817	0.5837	0.5895	0.5983	0.5059
FocusedNet	0.5265	**0.5660**	**0.5642**	0.5706	0.5780	0.5804	0.5848	0.5898	**0.5948**	**0.6082**	**0.5660**
Top-k ListMLE	0.4994	0.5190	0.5356	0.5504	0.5540	0.5717	0.5746	0.5798	0.5861	0.5885	0.5083

Top-k TD2003 (Top-k judgments)

Methods	κ-N@1	κ-N@2	κ-N@3	κ-N@4	κ-N@5	κ-N@6	κ-N@7	κ-N@8	κ-N@9	κ-N@10	κ-ERR
SVM^{MAP}	0.2248	0.2822	0.2884	0.2973	0.3271	0.3359	0.3459	0.3606	0.3769	0.3858	0.3839
RankSVM	0.2246	0.2893	0.2921	0.3083	0.3253	0.3387	0.3561	0.3703	0.3794	0.3872	0.4025
FocusedSVM	0.2243	0.2965	0.2958	0.3192	0.3235	0.3415	0.3662	**0.3801**	0.3819	0.3886	0.4041
AdaRank	0.2029	0.2979	0.2995	0.3116	0.3289	0.3379	0.3427	0.3574	0.3656	0.3766	0.3777
RankBoost	0.2082	0.2931	0.2921	0.3103	0.3255	0.3365	0.3576	0.3654	0.3782	0.3789	0.3970
FocusedBoost	0.2583	0.3168	0.3124	0.3191	0.3346	0.3517	0.3634	0.3732	0.3861	0.3980	0.4214
ListNet	0.2685	0.2731	0.2694	0.2789	0.3044	0.3142	0.3252	0.3404	0.3514	0.3624	0.3962
RankNet	**0.2776**	0.2946	0.2946	0.3021	0.3227	0.3372	0.3470	0.3688	0.3763	0.3813	0.4199
FocusedNet	0.2473	**0.3268**	**0.3237**	**0.3223**	**0.3507**	**0.3605**	**0.3705**	0.3769	0.3849	**0.4058**	**0.4603**
Top-k ListMLE	0.2389	0.2861	0.3055	0.3222	0.3480	0.3552	0.3668	0.3702	**0.3913**	0.4007	0.4028

Table 5: Performance comparison on Graded TD2003 and Top-k TD2003

Besides, in our experiments, when applying traditional ranking models on top-k ground-truths, we relate the top-k ground-truth to absolute labels as defined in Section 3.2.1. While applying top-k ranking models (i.e. FocusedRank and top-k ListMLE) on absolute judgment datasets, we randomly generate a total order of the documents according to graded labels and preserve the top-k order for learning.

To measure the effectiveness of ranking performance, NDCG [13] and ERR [8] are used on ground-truths from absolute judgments, while κ-NDCG and κ-ERR are adopted on top-k ground-truths.

4.2.2 Comparison results

The performance comparison between different ranking models on the two datasets is shown in Table 4 and Table 5, respectively.

From the results on the Graded MQ2007 as shown in the upper part of Table 4, we can see that the overall performance of FocusedRank is comparable with traditional pairwise and listwise ranking models in terms of both NDCG ($N@j$) and ERR. It shows that even though FocusedRank is proposed for the top-k ground-truth, it can work quite well on traditional absolute judgment datasets under traditional IR measures. Such results also reveals that, learning the ordering of the top items well is critical for the success of a learning to rank algorithm. Similar results can also been found on the Graded TD2003 datasets as shown in the upper part of Table 5.

From the results on top-k ground-truths in both tables (i.e. the bottom parts), we can find that FocusedRank can significantly outperform the corresponding pairwise and listwise ranking models in terms of both κ-NDCG (κ-$N@j$) and κ-ERR. For example, considering FocusedBoost, the relative improvement over AdaRank and RankBoost is about 7.08% and 0.87% in terms of κ-NDCG@10, respectively, and the relative improvements in terms of κ-ERR is about 9.76% and 0.91%, respectively. Besides, we can also observe that under all the metrics, the best performance is almost reached by our FocusedRank (The best performance is denoted by number in bold). The results indicate that FocusedRank is particularly suitable for the top-k ground-truth. By combining the advantages of both pairwise and listwise approaches, FocusedRank can fully exploit the information in the top-k ground-truth and thus outperforms each single model.

Moreover, when we compare FocusedRank with the state-of-the-art top-k ranking model, i.e., top-k ListMLE, we can see comparable performances on both absolute judgment datasets and top-k ground-truths. In fact, some of our FocusedRank model, e.g. FocusedNet, can consistently outperform top-k ListMLE on Top-k MQ2007 in terms of both κ-NDCG and κ-ERR. The results demonstrate that FocusedRank, as a mixed ranking model, can effectively cope with the top-k learning to rank problem.

4.2.3 The impact of the balance factor β

Here we investigate the impact of the balance factor β in FocusedRank. By varying β from 0 to 1 with a step of 0.05, the curves of the ranking performance of FocusedRank in terms of κ-NDCG[4] and κ-ERR are shown in Figure 1 and Figure 2. Each performance value on test sets shown in the figures is averaged using five-fold cross validation as the same way used in LETOR.

In Figure 1, the performance variations on graded MQ2007 are represented as curves with open symbols while that on

[4]For space limitation, we just show the results of @5,@10 for NDCG and κ-NDCG.

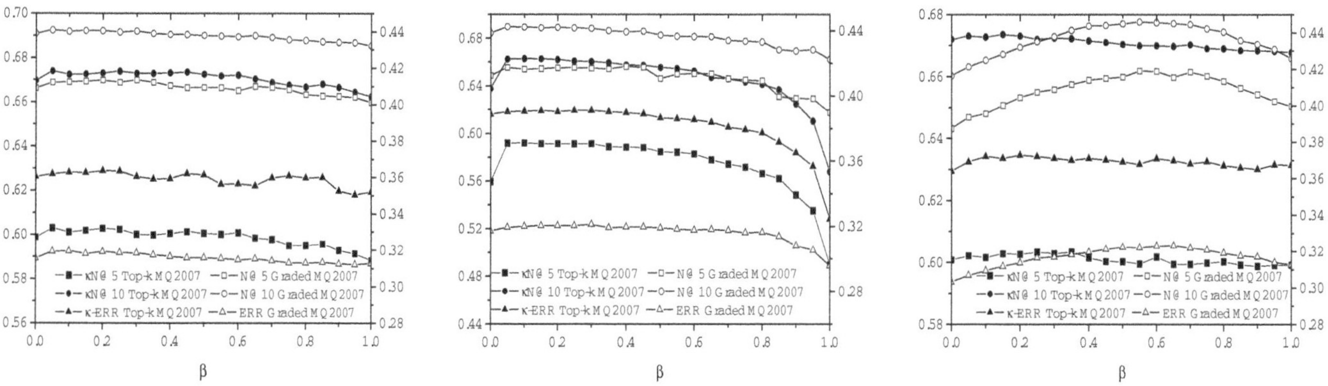

(a) FocusedSVM (b) FocusedBoost (c) FocusedNet

Figure 1: Performance variation of FocusedRank with β on Graded MQ2007 and Top-k of MQ2007 under corresponding evaluation measures.

Top-k MQ2007 are represented as curves with filled symbols. The results of FocusedSVM, FocusedBoost and FocusedNet are shown in Figure 1(a), (b) and (c), respectively. To make the variation trend more clear, each figure adopts double y-axes, where the black curves of κ-NDCG@5 (κ-N@5), κ-NDCG@10 (κ-N@10) and κ-ERR use the left y axis, while the other blue curves of NDCG@5 (N@5), NDCG@10 (N@10) and ERR utilize the right y axis. Similarly, in Figure 2 we also use double y-axes. The performance variations on graded TD2003 are represented as curves with open symbols while that on Top-k TD2003 are represented as curves with filled symbols. The results of FocusedSVM, FocusedBoost and FocusedNet are shown in Figure 2(a), (b) and (c), respectively.

From the results shown in Figure 1 and Figure 2, we find that: (1) There is a consistent trend[5] for the three types of FocusedRank on the two groups of different datasets. That is, as β increases, the ranking performance first grows to reach its maximum, and then drops. (2) The overall variation of each performance curve is small. Take the most varied curves for example, the variance of the mean is 2.7% for the performance curve of κ-NDCG@5 on Top-k MQ2007, and the variances of the mean is 6.2% for that on Top-k TD2003.

Thus, we come to a conclusion that the performance of FocusedRank is relative stable with respect to β.

5. CONCLUSIONS

In this paper, we propose a novel top-k learning to rank framework, including labeling, ranking and evaluation, which can be effectively adopted for real search systems. Firstly, a top-k labeling strategy is proposed to obtain reliable relevance judgments from human assessors via pairwise preference judgment. With this labeling strategy, we can largely reduce the complexity of pairwise preference judgment to $\mathcal{O}(n \log k)$. Secondly, a novel ranking model FocusedRank is presented to capture the characteristics of the top-k ground-truth. Thirdly, two new top-k evaluation measures are derived to fit the top-k ground-truth. We verify the efficiency and reliability of the proposed top-k labeling strategy through user studies, and demonstrate the effectiveness of top-k ranking model by comparing with state-of-the-art ranking models.

There are many interesting issues for further investigation under our top-k learning to rank framework. (1) The top-k labeling strategy could be improved to further reduce the judgment complexity. For example, we may introduce the "Bad" judgment like [7] for pages that are clearly irrelevant to further save labeling effort. (2) With top-k ground-truth, the design for new ranking models remains a valuable problem to investigate. (3) It is also possible to find new top-k based evaluation measures for better comparison between different systems.

[5] The small size of the datasets may be the reason for the non-smooth variation curves with 50 queries on Graded TD2003 and Top-k TD2003, compared with more than one thousand queries on Graded MQ2007 and Top-k MQ2007.

6. ACKNOWLEDGMENTS

This research work was funded by the National Natural Science Foundation of China under Grant No. 60933005, No. 61173008, No. 61003166 and 973 Program of China under Grants No. 2012CB316303.

7. REFERENCES

[1] N. Ailon and M. Mohri. An efficient reduction of ranking to classification. COLT '08, pages 87–98, 2008.

[2] C. Buckley and E. M. Voorhees. *Retrieval system evaluation*, chapter TREC: experiment and evaluation in information retrieval. MIT press, 2005.

[3] C. Burges, T. Shaked, and et al. Learning to rank using gradient descent. ICML '05, pages 89–96, 2005.

[4] R. Burgin. Variations in relevance judgments and the evaluation of retrieval performance. *IPM*, 28:619–627, 1992.

[5] Z. Cao, T. Qin, T.-Y. Liu, M.-F. Tsai, and H. Li. Learning to rank: from pairwise approach to listwise approach. ICML '07, pages 129–136, 2007.

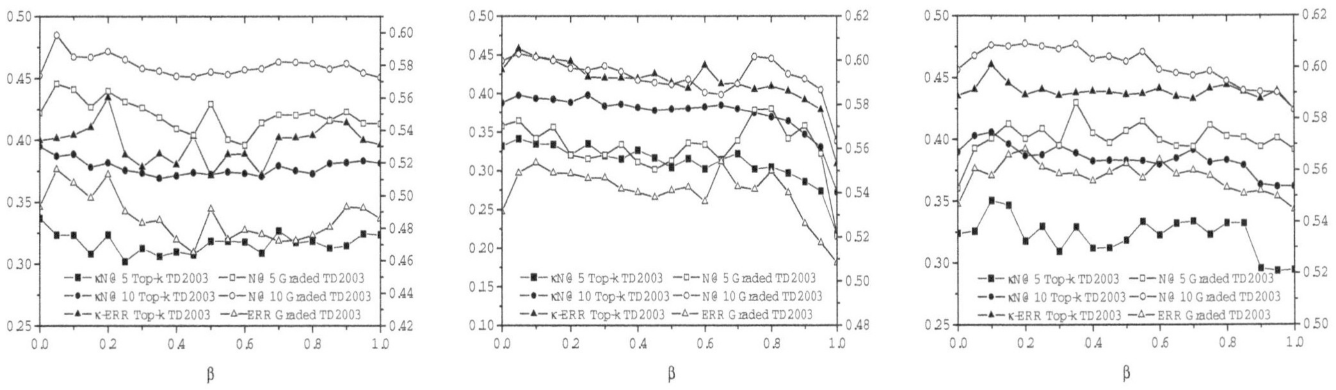

(a) FocusedSVM (b) FocusedBoost (c) FocusedNet

Figure 2: Performance variation of FocusedRank with β on Graded TD2003 and Top-k TD2003 under corresponding evaluation measures.

[6] B. Carterette and P. N. Bennett. Evaluation measures for preference judgments. SIGIR '08, pages 685–686, 2008.

[7] B. Carterette, P. N. Bennett, D. M. Chickering, and S. T. Dumais. Here or there: preference judgments for relevance. ECIR'08, pages 16–27, 2008.

[8] O. Chapelle, D. Metlzer, Y. Zhang, and P. Grinspan. Expected reciprocal rank for graded relevance. CIKM '09, pages 621–630. ACM, 2009.

[9] S. Clémençon and N. Vayatis. Ranking the best instances. *JMLR*, 8:2671–2699, 2007.

[10] D. Cossock and T. Zhang. Subset ranking using regression. *Learning theory*, 4005:605–619, 2006.

[11] Y. Freund, R. Iyer, R. E. Schapire, and Y. Singer. An efficient boosting algorithm for combining preferences. *JMLR*, 4:933–969, 2003.

[12] E. P. C. III. The optimal number of response alternatives for a scale: A review. *Journal of Marketing Research*, 17, No. 4:407–422.

[13] K. Järvelin and J. Kekäläinen. Ir evaluation methods for retrieving highly relevant documents. SIGIR '00, pages 41–48, 2000.

[14] T. Joachims. Optimizing search engines using clickthrough data. KDD '02, pages 133–142, 2002.

[15] J. Kekäläinen. Binary and graded relevance in ir evaluations-comparison of the effects on ranking of ir systems. *IPM*, 41:1019–1033, 2005.

[16] A. Moffat and J. Zobel. Rank-biased precision for measurement of retrieval effectiveness. *ACM Trans. Inf. Syst.*, 27:2:1–2:27, 2008.

[17] L. P., B. C., and W. Q. Mcrank: learning to rank using multiple classification and gradient boosting. In *NIPS2007*, pages 845–852.

[18] T. Qin, T.-Y. Liu, and et al. Letor: A benchmark collection for research on learning to rank for information retrieval. *Information Retrieval*, 13:346–374, 2010.

[19] T. R., S. W. Jr., and V. J.L. Towards the identification of the optimal number of relevance categories. *JASIS*, 50:254–264, 1999.

[20] K. Radinsky and N. Ailon. Ranking from pairs and triplets: information quality, evaluation methods and query complexity. WSDM '11, pages 105–114, 2011.

[21] F. Radlinski and T. Joachims. Query chains: learning to rank from implicit feedback. KDD '05, pages 239–248, 2005.

[22] F. G. Rebecca and N. Melisa. The neutral point on a likert scale. *Journal of Psychology*, 95:199–204, 1971.

[23] P. R.L. The analysis of permutations. *Applied Statistics*, 24(2):193–202, 1974.

[24] M. Rorvig. The simple scalability of documents. *JASIS*, 41:590–598, 1990.

[25] C. Rudin. Ranking with a p-norm push. In *COLT*, pages 589–604, 2006.

[26] R. Song, Q. Guo, R. Zhang, and et al. Select-the-best-ones: A new way to judge relative relevance. *IPM*, 47:37–52, 2011.

[27] E. M. Voorhees. Variations in relevance judgments and the measurement of retrieval effectiveness. SIGIR '98, pages 315–323. ACM, 1998.

[28] E. M. Voorhees. Variations in relevance judgments and the measurement of retrieval effectiveness. *IPM*, 36:697–716, 2000.

[29] E. M. Voorhees. Evaluation by highly relevant documents. SIGIR '01, pages 74–82. ACM, 2001.

[30] F. Xia, T.-Y. Liu, and H. Li. Statistical consistency of top-k ranking. In *NIPS*, pages 2098–2106, 2009.

[31] J. Xu and H. Li. Adarank: a boosting algorithm for information retrieval. SIGIR '07, pages 391–398, 2007.

[32] Yao. Measuring retrieval effectiveness based on user preference of documents. *JASIS*, 46:133–145, 1995.

[33] Y. Yue, T. Finley, F. Radlinski, and T. Joachims. A support vector method for optimizing average precision. SIGIR '07, pages 271–278, 2007.

[34] B. Zhou and Y. Yao. Evaluating information retrieval system performance based on user preference. *JIIS*, 34:227–248, 2010.

Robust Ranking Models via Risk-Sensitive Optimization

Lidan Wang
Dept. of Computer Science
University of Maryland
College Park, MD
lidan@cs.umd.edu

Paul N. Bennett
Microsoft Research
One Microsoft Way
Redmond, USA
pauben@microsoft.com

Kevyn Collins-Thompson
Microsoft Research
One Microsoft Way
Redmond, USA
kevynct@microsoft.com

ABSTRACT

Many techniques for improving search result quality have been proposed. Typically, these techniques increase average effectiveness by devising advanced ranking features and/or by developing sophisticated learning to rank algorithms. However, while these approaches typically improve average performance of search results relative to simple baselines, they often ignore the important issue of robustness. That is, although achieving an average gain overall, the new models often hurt performance on many queries. This limits their application in real-world retrieval scenarios. Given that robustness is an important measure that can negatively impact user satisfaction, we present a unified framework for jointly optimizing effectiveness and robustness. We propose an objective that captures the tradeoff between these two competing measures and demonstrate how we can jointly optimize for these two measures in a principled learning framework. Experiments indicate that ranking models learned this way significantly decreased the worst ranking failures while maintaining strong average effectiveness on par with current state-of-the-art models.

Categories and Subject Descriptors

H.3.3 [**Information Retrieval**]: Retrieval Models

Keywords

Re-ranking, robust algorithms, machine learning

1. INTRODUCTION

Many approaches for learning highly effective ranking models for search have been proposed in recent years [19, 5, 25]. Most commonly, they apply well-developed machine learning algorithms to construct ranking models from training data by optimizing a given IR metric. While the learned ranking models can be highly effective, these approaches have mostly ignored the important issue of robustness – in addition to performing well on average, the model should, with high probability, not perform very poorly for any individual query. Often effectiveness and robustness are competing forces that counteract each other: models optimized for effectiveness alone may not meet the strict robustness requirement for individual queries.

This paper introduces learning robust ranking models for search via risk-sensitive optimization, by exploiting and optimizing the tradeoffs between model effectiveness and robustness. At a basic level, this framework learns ranking models whose effectiveness and robustness can be explicitly controlled. While effectiveness and robustness can be thought of in terms of absolute performance, one can specialize these concepts to a case where we desire to perform well relative to a particular baseline – for example a personalized system vs. the non-personalized baseline, query expansion vs. no expansion, or a learned model vs. a retrieval formula. In this case, we can specialize the notions of effectiveness and robustness to say that we wish to have high average gain relative to the baseline (*i.e.*, positive change in performance) while at the say time incurring low risk relative to the baseline (*i.e.*, low probability of performing worse than the baseline for any particular query).

We develop a unified learning to rank framework for jointly optimizing both gain and risk by introducing a novel tradeoff metric that decomposes gain into reward (upside) and risk (downside) relative to a baseline. While this objective could be integrated into many learning models, we show how to extend and generalize a state-of-the-art algorithm LambdaMart [6] to optimize the new objective. We empirically demonstrate that models learned this way outperform both a selective personalization approach and standard learning to rank models in terms of achieving an optimal balance between gain and risk. Moreover, our results also provide important insights into why our learned models are more robust in terms of the learning convergence property of the new model as compared to standard effectiveness-centric models.

2. RELATED WORK

Multi-objective learning to rank has received much attention in recent years [31, 13]. This is because, in many practical settings, the performance of a ranking model is evaluated by multiple measures of interest (e.g., NDCG, MAP, freshness, efficiency). Multi-objective learning to rank trains ranking models to simultaneously optimize multiple IR measures. Svore *et al.* [31] use a standard web relevance measure, NDCG, as the primary optimization metric and a relevance derived from click-data is used as the secondary metric; the performance of the primary measure is maintained

SIGIR'12, August 12–16, 2012, Portland, Oregon, USA.

constant while the algorithm tries to improve the secondary measure. Dai *et al.* [13] develop a multi-objective learning to rank algorithm for freshness and relevance by extending a state-of-the-art divide and conquer ranking approach [3]. The key differences between these and our work is that we treat both risk and reward, which are potentially competing measures, as first-class metrics during optimization, unlike the "tiered" approach [31]; however, more importantly, our risk measure is inherently different from the previous multi-objective learning to rank metrics – instead of capturing just another facet of web search [31, 13], risk evaluates the fitness of the ranking model *with respect to* a baseline model under a specific metric. In other words, risk is orthogonal to the previous multi-objective metrics – risk is defined on top of these metrics with respect to a baseline model.

Although other risk-aware algorithms have been proposed for ad-hoc retrieval [35, 39] and query expansion [26, 10], our problem differs from them in three important dimensions. First, we focus on designing new learning to rank algorithms to create robust state-of-the-art ranking models using boosted regression trees, rather than focusing on risk-minimization for language models or simple term-based models [35, 39, 34]. Second, unlike [10, 26], the source of risk in our setting comes from the fact that users and queries are diverse, so that a single model cannot serve all users or queries well. Thus we design a new risk-sensitive algorithm that effectively leverages query-dependent features to build models that are highly robust and effective for individual queries. Finally, these previous problems represent particular strategies for ranking, hence their solutions cannot be trivially extended to the more general problem of learning robust ranking models for large-scale retrieval.

Risk can be indirectly addressed by building query-dependent models to better adapt to individual queries. This line of work resulted in recent papers that consider query-specific loss functions [4], where queries of different types (e.g., navigational, information) are optimized with different loss functions. Geng *et al.* [18] proposed a k-Nearest Neighbor based method which trains a query-dependent ranking function for each query based on its nearest neighbors in the training set. Bian *et al.* [3] proposed a clustering-based divide-and-conquer approach for building query-dependent ranking models. However, it is important to note that query-dependent models are *not* perfect – just like any other models, query-dependent models incur risk (*e.g.*, reduced performance for some queries and gains for other queries), and this fact has been largely ignored as well. In a sense, our proposed framework generalizes and complements this thread of work by learning risk-sensitive query-dependent models.

There has been a great deal of research devoted to developing effective retrieval models that have high average retrieval quality. This has given rise to a steady stream of techniques for effective ranked retrieval. Examples include learning to rank [19, 5, 25], learning to re-rank [22], numerous term proximity models [27, 8, 32], and search personalization [1, 36, 11]. However, unlike our work, they ignore the important issue of model robustness – while many queries see performance improvements, other queries are often hurt by the new and complex models as compared to simple alternatives such as BM25 [29] and language models for information retrieval [28].

Our work also has connections to query difficulty and performance prediction for Web search [38], as well as selective personalization [33]. These techniques mitigate risk in re-ranking by using a query performance prediction method to selectively re-rank queries whose baseline effectiveness is expected to be low, and avoid re-ranking for queries where the baseline effectiveness is already high. We note these techniques are robustness-centric, which may lead to overly reduced effectiveness due to unreliable decision in applying the model. In Section 5 we compare our approach to the use of selective re-ranking using performance variables.

It seems reasonable to assume that users tend to remember the singular, spectacular failures of a search engine rather than the many successful searches that preceded them. However, we are not aware of many user studies that have looked at the effect of IR robustness (or the lack thereof) on users' perceptions of system quality. One exception is a recent user study of recommender systems [23] that showed how optimizing the accuracy of a system is not enough: among other interesting findings, they found that high-variance recommendation algorithms can create a bad user experience. Informally, significant errors can have a large negative impact on the perceived quality of the system, even if the system frequently does well.

Finally, the term *robust ranking* has been used previously in the literature, but with somewhat different meaning. For example, Li *et al.* [24] call ranking functions 'robust' that account for volatility in ranker scores, and thus, document ordering, over time, by taking into account the distribution of ranking scores over results. Others have used 'robust ranking' to refer to ranking algorithms that are less vulnerable to spam or noise in the training data [2].

3. MOTIVATION

Before proceeding, it is important to identify sources of uncertainty that contribute to low robustness in ranking models. In most search settings and especially Web search, both users and information needs are highly diverse, thus, it is unlikely a common set of ranking features and the same model learned from these features can optimally work for all users and queries. For instance, it has been shown that: queries with low click entropies typically will not benefit from search personalization [1, 36, 11]; queries with low query clarity will not benefit from query expansion techniques as much [16]. Ignoring these facts during model training leads to a highly risky model. Although previous work has studied whether and when a learned model should be applied to a given query based on the aforementioned query-specific meta-features [33], the average effectiveness that results from the robust application of the ranking model is generally ignored – which means the robustness is typically improved but at an overly aggressive cost in reduced average effectiveness. We take a principled learning to rank approach that directly optimizes multiple requirements.

For instance, Figure 1 illustrates the improvements and degradations of a proposed model (tuned for average effectiveness) with respect to a baseline ranking across queries. The plots shows a high variance of the new results – the performance of a number of queries is improved (right side) at the expense of degraded results for other queries (left side). Directly optimizing for variance is a challenging task – variance is inherently a set-based measure defined on the distribution of results quality over queries, but typically, learning to rank algorithms are not directly applicable to optimizing

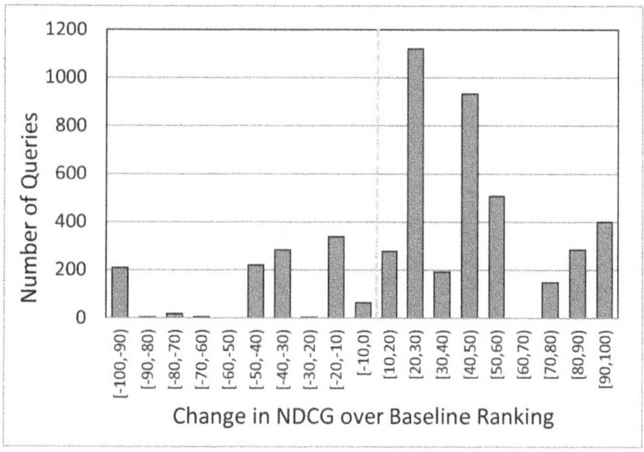

Figure 1: Typical helped-hurt histogram of re-ranking gains and losses compared to a given baseline ranking.

set-based measures. We instead adopt a simple approach suggested by this figure.

Informally, when compared to an alternative or baseline ranking, the probability of decreasing performance is related to the mass on the left-hand side of the figure. In fact the expectation of the left-hand side, which we call risk, is the amount we can expect to decrease retrieval quality on average if we pick a query at random. Likewise, the expectation of the right-hand side, which we call reward, is the amount we can expect to improve retrieval quality on average. By defining each average relative to the total number of queries rather than dividing reward by the number of improved queries and risk by the number of hurt queries, we control for issues of coverage. Typical methods optimize overall performance, $Reward - Risk + Baseline$, but since the baseline is fixed from the optimization point of view, this is equivalent to optimizing the difference, $Reward - Risk$. In order to control the risk or probability of harm, this suggests introducing a weight on the risk term that is user tunable. This is precisely what we do. In the next section, we formalize this intuition before demonstrating how to optimize the objective in practice.

4. A LEARNING TO RANK APPROACH FOR CREATING ROBUST MODELS

4.1 Problem setting

In this section, we present the formal setup for learning robust ranking models for Web search. Given a baseline ranking M_b we would like to construct a new ranking model M_m with high average effectiveness across queries, without degrading the performance of individual queries too much with respect to M_b. The exact instantiation of the baseline M_b depends on the specific application of our general framework. For personalization, M_b might be the initial non-personalized ranking (e.g., optimized for the average user). In a production environment, M_b might represent the results from an earlier release of the ranker. In learning to rank, M_b might be simpler models such as BM25 that are known to be effective on a particular subset of queries. Our framework is applicable to these and any other ranking-based applications where a risk/reward tradeoff may exist.

4.2 Measuring risk and reward

One way to measure risk is by measuring the variance of the new ranking model with respect to baseline results. We instead adopt a variant of this approach, by introducing a risk function $F_{RISK}(Q_T, M_b)$ to capture characteristics of the variance with respect to model M_b over a training set Q_T. We are interested in the downside risk of the new model, defined as the average reduction in effectiveness due to using the new model M_m compared to the baseline model M_b [1].

$$F_{RISK}(Q_T, M_b) = \frac{1}{N} \sum_{Q \in Q_T} \max\left[0, M_b(Q) - M_m(Q)\right] \quad (1)$$

where N denotes the total number of queries in the training set Q_T, and $M_b(Q)$ and $M_m(Q)$ denote the effectiveness of the baseline model and new model for a given query Q, respectively. We note that effectiveness can be measured by any commonly-used IR metrics (e.g. precision@k, recall, average precision, and NDCG@k). Thus, the downside risk accounts for the negative aspect of the retrieval performance across queries.

Similarly we defined reward in relative terms as the positive improvement in effectiveness over baseline model M_b, averaged across all queries in a training set Q_T:

$$F_{REWARD}(Q_T, M_b) = \frac{1}{N} \sum_{Q \in Q_T} \max\left[0, M_m(Q) - M_b(Q)\right] \quad (2)$$

where notations N, M_b, and M_m are defined as before. Thus, the reward function accounts for the positive aspects of the retrieval performance across queries. For any arbitrary baseline, M_b, the overall gain for training set Q_T can then be written:

$$F_{GAIN}(Q_T) = F_{REWARD}(Q_T, M_b) - F_{RISK}(Q_T, M_b). \quad (3)$$

Our goal is to automatically learn ranking models that better adapt to individual queries by optimally trading off between risk and reward. However, before we can learn such a well-balanced model, we must define a new metric that captures the tradeoff. Our objective function, which we call Risk-Reward tradeoff T, is defined as a weighted linear combination of gain (which includes risk and reward) and risk:

$$\begin{aligned} T_\alpha(Q_T, M_b) &= F_{GAIN}(Q_T) - \alpha \cdot F_{RISK}(Q_T, M_b) \quad (4) \\ &= F_{REWARD}(Q_T, M_b) - (1+\alpha) \cdot F_{RISK}(Q_T, M_b) \end{aligned}$$

where $\alpha \geq 0$ is a key *risk-sensitivity parameter* that controls the tradeoff between risk and reward. We chose this formulation so that the case $\alpha = 0$ corresponds to the standard learning-to-rank objective to maximize average F_{GAIN} alone. Note that T is not a single measure, but a family of measures, parameterized by the tradeoff parameter α. By varying α we can capture a full spectrum of risk/reward tradeoffs: from $\alpha = 0$ (standard default ranking) to larger values of α that lead to lower-risk models, or small values of α that lead to higher gain models.

The most common approach to optimizing multiple objectives [30] is to linearly combine objectives, as we have done with the risk and reward functions. While many other ways for combining metrics exist, such as by multiplication, division, geometric or harmonic means, optimizing an arbitrary

[1] For simplicity of notation, in the remaining of the paper M_b will refer to both the baseline model and the effectiveness of the baseline model. A similar convention is used for M_m.

optimization objective can be problematic in many learning algorithms. In contrast, linearly combined objectives are often easily optimized. For our purposes, we will extend the objective of the LambdaMart algorithm [37]. In Sec. 4.3, we prove that our tradeoff measure T satisfies a desirable consistency property [6].

4.3 Constructing robust ranking models

In this section, we describe how to learn models that directly optimize the proposed tradeoff metric T_α in the previous section. The basic assumption is that queries are different, thus requiring potentially different ranking functions to be individually effective. Previous query-dependent models [4, 18, 3] ignore risk. We devise learning to rank algorithms that directly optimize the tradeoff metric in the context of LambdaMart boosted regression trees framework [37].

4.3.1 Model and optimization algorithm

We choose to extend LambdaMart [37] for our ranking model. Boosted regression trees have been shown to be one of the best learning to rank models. In the recent Yahoo! Learning to Rank Challenge [9], boosting (and ensemble methods) have been a dominant technique used by winning entries. Boosted regression trees are a type of non-linear model that can capture the potentially complex interactions between various types of ranking features.

LambdaMart is derived from the tree-boosting optimization MART [17] and the listwise LambdaRank [7]. LambdaMart improves an effectiveness metric by fitting a sequence of boosted regression trees using an approximation to the derivative of a cost function by accumulating pairwise gradients weighted by the total change from the current ranking to a desired ranking.

We now present a brief overview on LambdaMart objective function as it serves as a foundation for deriving the learning algorithm for the tradeoff metric. The objective function of list-wise LambdaMart is based on the cross-entropy objective function used by RankNet [5]. Let r_i denote the relevance grade of a document D_i, so that $R_{ij} = 1$ if $r_i > r_j$, and $R_{ij} = -1$ when $r_j > r_i$. Let s_i denote the score assigned to D_i by the model. For documents D_i and D_j, the cross-entropy is expressed as follows:

$$C = \frac{1}{2}(1 - R_{ij})\beta(s_i - s_j) + \log\left(1 + e^{-\beta\cdot(s_i - s_j)}\right) \quad (5)$$

where β is a shape parameter for the sigmoid function. This cost function assigns zero penalty if two documents are correctly ranked, and asymptotically, assigns linear penalty if they are ranked incorrectly. The derivatives of C with respect to score difference between s_i and s_j is:

$$\lambda_{ij} = \beta\left(\frac{1}{2}(1 - R_{ij}) - \frac{1}{1 + e^{\beta(s_i - s_j)}}\right) \quad (6)$$

LambdaRank [7] and LambdaMart [37] modify this gradient defined on pairwise loss to optimize for list-wise IR measures. The new gradient λ_{ij}^{new} captures the desired change of document scores with respect to the IR metric after the documents have been sorted by their scores, in addition to capturing the original λ_{ij} value. The new gradient under the list-wise optimization is simply defined to be λ_{ij} multiplied by the absolute change in IR measure M due to swapping documents i and j:

$$\lambda_{ij}^{new} = \lambda_{ij}|\Delta M_{ij}| \quad (7)$$

The gradient for each document D_i is obtained by summing λ_{ij} over all pairs that D_i participates in for query Q:

$$\lambda_i^{new} = \sum_{j \neq i} \lambda_{ij}|\Delta M_{ij}| \quad (8)$$

The gradients λ_i^{new} defined on each document for each query are modeled and optimized by LambdaMart regression trees. In principle, LambdaMart can be extended to optimize any standard IR metric by simply replacing ΔM_{ij} in Eq. 8 by the corresponding change $\Delta M_{ij}^{\star}$ in the optimized metric $M^{\star}$. However, it is generally considered desirable for $M^{\star}$ to satisfy the *consistency property*: any pairwise swap between correctly ranked documents D_i and D_j must lead to decrease in $M^{\star}$, i.e., $\Delta M_{ij}^{\star} < 0$ if $r_i > r_j$. Generally consistency is desired since LambdaMart's approximation to the overall gradient is derived from the pairwise gradients.

Unlike standard IR metrics, the tradeoff measure is defined relative to a baseline ranking and it is a meta-measure – a combination of multiple measures. Despite its importance, little existing literature has provided insight into how to optimize meta-measures in a principled way. Next, we prove the consistency property of the tradeoff metric T and show how it can be optimized by boosted regression trees.

4.3.2 Consistency of Risk-Reward Tradeoff T_α

While LambdaMart is a list-wise optimization scheme and can optimize a wide range of IR measures – including NDCG, MAP, and MRR – it is often desirable for an objective measure to satisfy the *consistency property* [6] stated above: when swapping ranked positions of two documents, d_i and d_j, in a sorted document list where d_i is more relevant than d_j, and ranks before d_j, the objective should decrease. While most IR measures easily satisfy this property, in general an arbitrary objective measure M will not always satisfy the consistency property. For example, suppose measures A and B are NDCG@5 and NDCG@10, respectively, and we define a meta-measure $M = A - B$. It is easy to see that M does *not* satisfy the consistency property, because as a correct swap is made, the gain in NDCG@5 is offset by gain in NDCG@10, which may result in a negative change for the overall measure M, causing M to be inconsistent. In general, it is not straightforward to see whether a meta-measure, defined as a combination of different measures, can ensure the consistency property.

We now show that the tradeoff metric T, defined as a weighted linear combination of risk and reward in Eq. 4, satisfies the consistency property.

THEOREM 1. *The tradeoff metric T in Eq. 4 satisfies the consistency property.*

PROOF. Let M_m and M_b be the effectiveness of the LambdaMart model and baseline model respectively. After swapping documents d_i and d_j, denote the resulting change in tradeoff by Δ_T, change in effectiveness by Δ_M, change in reward by Δ_γ and change in risk by Δ_σ. Let Rel(d) be the relevance of document d. To show T is consistent we show that swapping documents d_i and d_j, where d_i is more relevant than d_j and ranks before d_j, results in a decrease of T or equivalently $\Delta_T < 0$. We consider two scenarios as new trees are added to the current LambdaMart ensemble: 1) $M_m \leq M_b$ and 2) $M_m > M_b$. We show T is consistent in both cases.

Scenario A: $M_m \leq M_b$

Case A1) Swap d_i and d_j, where $\text{Rel}(d_i) > \text{Rel}(d_j)$ and $i < j$. In this case $\Delta_\gamma = 0$ and $\Delta_\sigma = \Delta_M < 0$. Thus $\Delta_T = (1+\alpha) \cdot \Delta_M < 0$ as desired.

Case A2) Swap d_i and d_j, where $\text{Rel}(d_i) > \text{Rel}(d_j)$ and $i > j$. Then there are two subcases:

If $M_b > M_m + \Delta_M$ then $\Delta_\gamma = 0,\ \Delta_\sigma = \Delta_M$ and $\Delta_T = (1+\alpha) \cdot \Delta_M > 0$.

If $M_b \leq M_m + \Delta_M$ then $\Delta_\gamma = M_m + \Delta_M - M_b$ $\Delta_\sigma = M_b - M_m$ and $\Delta_T = \alpha \cdot (M_b - M_m) + \Delta_M$.

Then $\Delta_T > 0$, as desired.

Scenario B: $M_m > M_b$

Case B1) Swap d_i and d_j, where $\text{Rel}(d_i) > \text{Rel}(d_j)$ and $i < j$. Then there are two subcases:

If $M_b > M_m - |\Delta_M|$ then $\Delta_\sigma = -M_b + (M_m - |\Delta_M|) < 0$ $\Delta_\gamma = M_b - M_m < 0$ and $\Delta_T = \alpha \cdot (M_m - M_b) - (1+\alpha) \cdot |\Delta_M|$

If $M_b \leq M_m - |\Delta_M|$ then $\Delta_\sigma = 0$ and $\Delta_T = \Delta_M$.

Then $\Delta_T < 0$, as desired.

Case B2) Swap d_i and d_j, where $\text{Rel}(d_i) > \text{Rel}(d_j)$ and $i > j$. There is no risk and $\Delta_M > 0$, so $\Delta_T > 0$ as desired.

Thus, in all cases the tradeoff measure T satisfies the required consistency property. □

We note that NDCG, MRR, and MAP (Mean Average Precision) have all been shown to satisfy consistency [14], and thus Theorem 1 applies generally to risk-reward tradeoff measures based on these widely-used IR measures, as well as any others that have been proven consistent.

4.3.3 *Risk-sensitive LambdaMart optimization*

The details of the proof for Theorem 1 above also tell us how to compute the Δ_T's used in the LambdaMart gradients for optimizing T. We observe that by optimizing the tradeoff metric, the LambdaMart puts more emphasis on the "risky" queries, by modifying the gradient of such queries so that incorrect results for risky queries hurt the tradeoff metric more, and the algorithm learns to optimally utilize query-dependent features in order to be more risk-averse. To illustrate this point, we see that when the current model effectiveness is less than the baseline's and a correct swap is made (i.e., Case A2), the optimizer assigns a larger positive change to the tradeoff if the swap erases the performance difference between the model and baseline (i.e., $\Delta_T = \alpha \cdot (M_b - M_m) + \Delta_M > (1+\alpha) \cdot (M_b - M_m)$); otherwise, it assigns a *smaller* positive tradeoff change to the query ($\Delta_T = (1+\alpha) \cdot \Delta_M < (1+\alpha) \cdot (M_b - M_m)$). As another example, in the case where the current model has a better effectiveness than the baseline and when two documents are incorrectly swapped (i.e., Case B1), the algorithm assigns a non-zero risk to the query if the swap causes the model to degrade below the baseline effectiveness; otherwise, it assigns no penalty. Such risk-sensitive optimization is in sharp contrast to the standard LambdaMart algorithm which treats all queries identically, without paying extra attention to high-risk queries. Thus, our risk-sensitive framework generalizes standard learning-to-rank algorithms like LambdaMart that only optimize for average effectiveness gain without accounting for risk.

5. EXPERIMENTS

We now show the benefits of augmenting the standard average-gain maximization ranking objective with our risk-sensitive objective. We emphasize that our key learning goal is not to maximize NDCG gains alone, or to minimize variance alone, but *to achieve the best possible joint tradeoff between change in risk and change in reward.* The ability to control such tradeoffs can be important in operational decisions, and in giving a better picture of the achievable performance space of a ranking algorithm. We also analyze the effect of the risk-aversion parameter α on the convergence rate of the learning algorithm and on characteristics of risk-averse rankings.

5.1 Datasets

We report results using two datasets, one public and one proprietary. These datasets were chosen to illustrate different applications of risk-sensitive ranking for different types of queries and Web applications. For clarity, we will use "baselines" to refer to the models used to relativize loss in our risk-reward optimization. The model without any risk sensitivity (i.e., $\alpha=0$), we will call the *gain-only model.*

5.1.1 *MSLR learning-to-rank dataset*

We use MSLR-WEB10K, a widely-used publicly released dataset from Microsoft Research[2]. MSLR is a sampling of 10,000 Web search queries and their results from a major commercial search engine that includes graded relevance judgments for supervised learning-to-rank experiments. This dataset is pre-partitioned into five folds, each with train, test, and validation subsets. We use and report results using these same folds in our experiments. We report NDCG@1 and NDCG@10 since both measures are of importance in Web search evaluation. Since our optimization is performed relative to a baseline, we have taken the ranking obtained from sorting by BM25 using the `BM25.whole.document` feature as a baseline. Thus, on this dataset, the goal is to make a more robust tradeoff relative to a well-motivated IR formula for ranking.

5.1.2 *Location personalization dataset*

We use a proprietary dataset for learning to personalize Web results by user location, with details and baseline results as described in [1]. That work introduced a methodology for automatically learning a location distribution to associate with a search result with the goal of promoting results when the user's search location matches the search result's location distribution. The data consists of logs from a competitive top commercial search engine and labels based on a single binary *last satisfied click* by the user per query impression as an implicit relevance judgment. We follow the same methodology as [1] and report average change across test folds in MRR relative to the search engine's original ranking for the last satisfied click. Thus, on this dataset, the goal is to learn both how to personalize and when to personalize simultaneously.

We next define some key evaluation terms used in our experiments.

[2]`research.microsoft.com/en-us/projects/mslr/`

5.2 Evaluation measures

A *retrieval quality* measure for a ranked result list is simply a standard statistic that measures some aspect of relevance. The retrieval quality measures we use to report results on the Web data sets in our study are Non-Discounted Cumulative Gain (NDCG) and Mean Reciprocal Rank (MRR).

Given a baseline ranking, the *reward* of using a retrieval algorithm over a set of queries is the total *positive changes* in retrieval quality compared to the baseline ranking divided by the total number of queries (Eq. 2). The *risk* of using a retrieval algorithm is the total negative changes (losses) in retrieval quality compared to the baseline ranking divided by the total number of queries (Eq. 1). Visually, risk corresponds to the total mass on the left of the vertical zero line in Figure 1 normalized by the total number of queries, while reward is the total mass on the right half normalized by the total number of queries. We call the *overall gain* – or simply gain – of an algorithm the average combined gain over *all* queries, so that *Gain* = *Reward* – *Risk*. There is typically a *risk-reward* tradeoff for retrieval algorithms [10].

Taken together, the $(risk, gain)$ tradeoff pair provides a more complete picture of a ranker's performance profile than simply reporting average NDCG gain. Often, algorithms that appear similar in NDCG gain can differ greatly in their risk-sensitivity, for example. This is evident in some of our results later in Sec. 5.6.

5.3 Query Performance Selective Strategies

Query-dependent features such as click entropy [15], query clarity [21], query length [12], and the maximum of BM25 scores [20] have been shown to be highly indicative of individual query performance and can be used to differentiate performance between different kinds of queries. An alternative approach to attempting to learn a model is simply to selectively apply a learned model by leveraging the insights from query performance prediction. We provide two such selective methods for comparison points. For the MSLR dataset, we use insights regarding the maximum BM25 score from [20] and use the max of the `BM25.whole.document` feature to predict when the baseline (the ranking obtained from the same feature) will perform well. We can then simply sweep out thresholds by using the gain-only learned model when the max BM25 score is low and the BM25 ranking otherwise. We then vary this threshold in an analogy to varying the α parameter. We refer to this as *maxBM25*.

For the location dataset, we also present a selection strategy. For each search result in the location dataset, the entropy of the result's location distribution measures how location-specific a single search result is. When the minimum of this feature over all search results is low, it means that at least one search result has a very location-specific meaning, and therefore, location personalization is more likely to succeed. We again vary the threshold using the personalized gain only model when the minimum is low and using the baseline original ranking of the search engine otherwise. We refer to this as *minEntropy* below.

5.4 Learning methodology

To ensure all methods have the same information available, both the gain-only models and the risk-sensitive models also have the features (max BM25 for MSLR and minimum entropy for location) that are used by the selective methods. In the case of MSLR, in order to ensure strong gain-only model performance, we performed sweeps on LambdaMart parameters using the validation sets. On the MSLR data, for $\alpha = 0$ (i.e. standard optimization), for each fold we used performance on the validation data to do a grid search for parameter settings. The parameter ranges we experimented with were: minimum documents in leaf $m \in 500, 1000, 1500$; number of leaves $l \in 10, 25, 50$; number of trees in ensemble $t \in 50, 100, 200, 400, 800$ and learning rate $r \in 0.025, 0.05, 0.07$. For three folds the optimal values were $m = 1000$, $l = 50$, $t = 800$ and $r = 0.075$, and for the two remaining folds, the values were identical except $m = 500$. For the models learned using $\alpha > 0$, we used these same parameters to keep other variables constant. For consistency of comparison we used the same parameter setting for the Location dataset experiments as in [1].

5.5 Summary statistics

Tables 1 and 2 show summary retrieval quality and robustness statistics for ranking on the MSLR and Location datasets. The gain over baseline effectiveness is broken down into its constituent Risk and Reward components. (Recall that *Gain* = *Reward* – *Risk*.) Unless otherwise noted, other summary stats are based on the top 10 results. The Wins/Losses row shows the counts of queries that contributed to the Reward vs Risk respectively.[3] The 'Loss > 20%' statistic counts queries whose relative NDCG change over baseline NDCG was worse than -20%. Thus, smaller Loss numbers are better.

Risk, reward and wins/losses are relative to the baseline ranking. The NDCG@10 score for the BM25 baseline was 30.869. The ΔMRR score for the Location minEntropy baseline is zero, since we report relative gains on that dataset for proprietary reasons.

As expected, there is a clear trade-off between overall retrieval effectiveness and amount of risk reduction for both collections. As the risk-aversion parameter α is increased, the Wins/Losses row shows consistent reduction in losses, with a small decline in overall effectiveness (NDCG or ΔMRR). Note in particular that for the Location data, the chance of a query being hurt by more than 20% loss in ΔMRR compared to the baseline vanishes almost to zero, while still retaining significant overall effectiveness gains.

5.6 Risk-reward tradeoff

Finding a re-ranking strategy that reduces variance compared to the baseline is easy - simply avoid re-ranking and always use the baseline ranking. In this case, the ΔMRR will be zero, with zero risk. However, this obviously loses all the benefits of the re-ranking for queries that are actually helped by re-ranking. Our goal is to find optimal tradeoff strategies that *dominate* other possible strategies for trading risk for reward.

Figure 2 shows our risk-sensitive objective in LambdaMart indeed dominates alternative effective strategies for selective re-ranking, as measured by the tradeoff curve for risk vs. gain for each collection. This tradeoff curve for the selective re-ranking strategy is produced as a function of the feature threshold (the minEntropy feature for Location queries, and maxBM25 feature for MSLR queries). As the feature threshold is lowered, more and more queries have the feature

[3] We ignore queries with zero NDCG@10 difference from the baseline, with gains over baseline being a 'Win', and losses being a 'Loss'.

Collection/Statistics		All features			
		$\alpha = 0$	$\alpha = 1$	$\alpha = 5$	$\alpha = 10$
MSLR ($N = 10000$)	NDCG@1	46.166	45.835	44.615	43.658
	NDCG@10	47.272	47.221	46.312	45.540
	Risk	2.239	1.974	1.722	1.540
	Reward	18.642	18.327	17.165	16.282
	Wins/Losses	7512/1972	7630/1845	7613/1838	7645/1776
	Loss > 20%	740	684	630	573

Table 1: Summary of generalization performance over test folds for the MSLR dataset.

Collection/Statistics		All features			
		$\alpha = 0$	$\alpha = 1$	$\alpha = 5$	$\alpha = 10$
Location ($N = 541958$)	ΔMRR	1.451	1.144	0.784	0.555
	Risk	0.4725	0.193	0.080	0.051
	Reward	1.923	1.337	0.864	0.606
	Wins/Losses	43616/24499	32253/14952	23598/8041	19818/8090
	Losses > 20%	2539	718	266	14

Table 2: Summary of generalization performance over test folds for the Location dataset.

value above the threshold and are re-ranked according to the baseline ranking. The tradeoff curve for the risk-sensitive re-ranking strategy is a function of α. At $\alpha = 0$, the risk-sensitive ranking coincides with the gain-only ranking. As α is increased, the learned model exhibits a stronger preference for the baseline, which acts like an increasing 'soft' query selection for the baseline ranking. The dotted Break Even line shows the break-even point where the tradeoff objective $T = 0$, and any result above the dashed Proportional Reduction line has the desirable property that it reduces risk proportionally more than it reduces reward. The "near-optimal hull" curve represents an envelope of achievable tradeoffs that results from incorporating an automatic stopping strategy for α, details of which are given in Sec. 5.7.

For both collections it is notable that the selective threshold re-ranking method performs significantly better than the break-even point. Additionally, since it lies above the Proportional Reduction line, it reduces risk proportionally more than it reduces gain at almost all points of the curve. This is most evident at high values of the respective threshold features, when the 'best' queries amenable to that method are most likely to be selected. At much lower threshold values, it is clear that most queries do not benefit from re-ranking with the baseline feature, giving performance closer to break-even. Furthermore, while other selective personalization approaches could be taken, it is clear based on performance that the selective threshold method here provides an informative comparison point.

In turn, for the Location data, the risk-gain tradeoff achieved by risk-sensitive ranking completely dominates that of selective threshold re-ranking. For any given risk level, risk-sensitive ranking achieves significantly higher gain, and conversely, for any given level of gain, it achieves that gain at much lower risk than the selective method. The results also show that the near-optimal hull dominates the selective method for both collections.

5.7 Guidance for setting the α parameter

A natural question is how to set α, or where one should stop trying new α's. While α is a user-set parameter to control risk, the question of where to stop can be approximated. For any model, the risk can always be reduced by flipping a coin with probability p and applying the method given "heads" and the baseline given "tails". Varying p naturally both reduces the gain and the risk (e.g., p=0.20 yields 20% risk and 20% reward). Since we can apply the same logic to the gain only model, this leads to natural guidance in terms of the gain-to-risk ratio of the gain only model (GOM): when $\alpha = Gain_{GOM}/Risk_{GOM}$ the original gain only model would yield a tradeoff objective T=0. Furthermore, randomly reducing the gain only model for greater values of α than this will continue to ensure the tradeoff objective remains non-negative. Thus, solutions with $T > 0$ in the segment $\alpha \in [0, Gain_{GOM}/Risk_{GOM}]$ are interesting non-trivial tradeoffs relative to the original gain-only model.

To find the size of this segment of interest, we used performance over the training data. For MSLR, this yielded a value of α=27.9±1.3 and for Location α=4.0±0.04. Then starting from the maximal nearest computed α points (30 and 4 respectively) in the segment, we simulate the random reduction from there toward the origin and call this the "Near-Optimal Hull" line on the curves. This gives a more realistic picture of achievable tradeoffs.

5.8 Convergence rates

We discussed in Sec. 4.3.3 how adding our risk-sensitive objective to LambdaMart results in modifying the LambdaMart gradient in such a way that its magnitude is amplified as α increases, accelerating the learning rate for queries where baseline effectiveness is already high. Thus, we hypothesized that on average across all training queries, we would see faster convergence rates at high values of α compared to low values of α.

Figure 4 demonstrates that this phenomenon actually occurs on both collections, comparing the ranker convergence when $\alpha = 0$ to setting $\alpha = 5$. The x-axis indicates number of iterations; the y-axis shows the overall NDCG@10 achieved at any given iteration (up to a maximum of 100 iterations), averaged across all validation folds. Although the algorithm ultimately converged to very similar NDCG@10

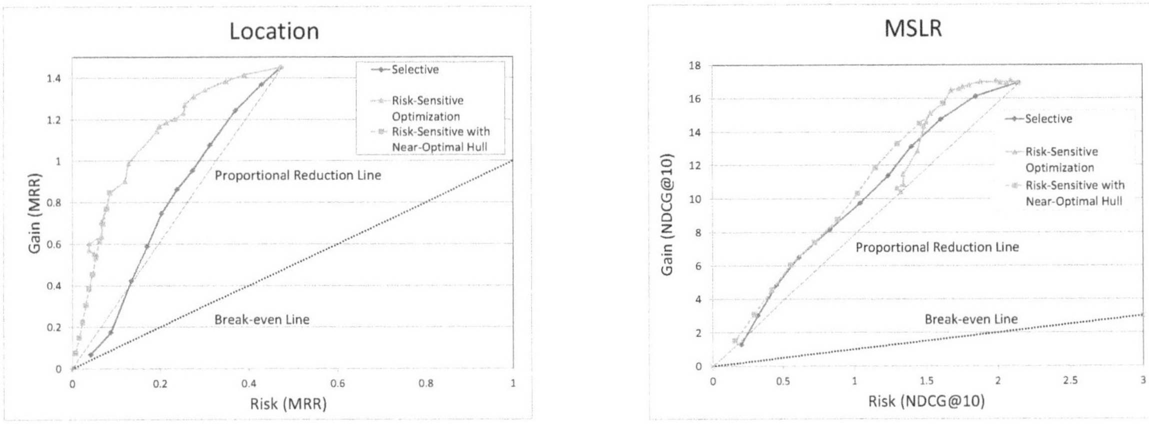

(a) Location: risk vs. gain

(b) MSLR: risk vs. gain

Figure 2: Risk/gain tradeoffs achieved by risk-sensitive LambdaMart learning vs. selective re-ranking for Location dataset (left), and MSLR dataset (right).

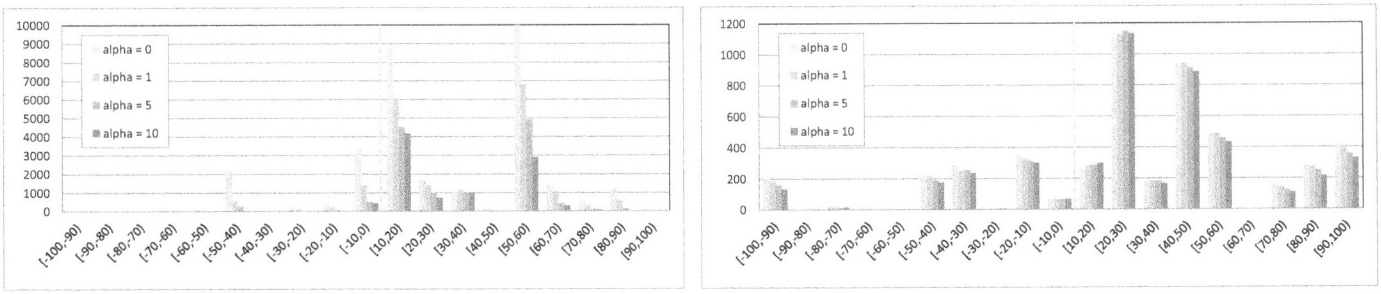

(a) Location: $\alpha = 0, 1, 5, 10$

(b) MSLR: $\alpha = 0, 1, 5, 10$

Figure 3: Helped-hurt histograms, showing how variance around baseline (dotted line) shrinks as the risk-aversion parameter α is increased from $\alpha = 0$ (lightest bars) to $\alpha = 10$ (darkest bars), for Location dataset (left), and MSLR dataset (right). Each histogram bucket corresponds to a different 10% range of loss/gain in effectiveness compared to that collection's baseline, and contains four bars, corresponding to the number of queries helped or hurt for the four risk-reward tradeoff settings $\alpha = 0, 1, 5, 10$. For clearer scaling the large spike of queries for the [0, 10) bucket has been omitted in both charts.

for both settings, the $\alpha = 5$ runs converged faster for all folds on both collections. In the case of the Location data, the speed improvement was dramatic – learning with $\alpha = 5$ took an average of 10.2 iterations to achieve 95% of the final convergence effectiveness, compared to 41.5 with $\alpha = 0$. The improvement was smaller but still consistent across folds for the MSLR data: for example, learning with $\alpha = 5$ reached NDCG@10 gain of 0.42 in an average of 25.4 iterations, compared with 33.4 iterations for $\alpha = 0$.

5.9 Model consistency across risk levels

We now examine how rankings change with respect to the baseline results as the risk-aversion parameter α is increased. To measure change between rankings, we use Kendall's tau distance, a standard distance between two ranked lists that corresponds to the (normalized) number of pairwise swaps required to move from one ranking to another. A large Kendall distance indicates low similarity to the baseline ranking, and conversely a small Kendall distance indicates a ranking that is very similar to the baseline ranking.

For illustration purposes, we binned Kendall distance values into 10 bins from 0 to 9. Queries whose re-ranking is the same or very similar to the baseline ranking are put in Bin 0, while queries with re-rankings that are very different from the baseline are put into Bin 9, or an intermediate bin according to the Kendall distance.

Figure 5 shows, for each value of α, a distribution over Kendall bins using the location personalization dataset. It shows that as the permitted risk increases – alpha changes from high to low – more and more queries start to deviate significantly from the baseline. For example, the lower-risk model learned with $\alpha = 9$ has 85% of the queries staying close to the baseline (bin 0), while the higher-risk model learned with $\alpha = 1$ has only 42% of the queries close to the baseline ranking, with the remaining queries dispersed over much more diverse rankings with much larger Kendall distances from the baseline. This behavior can be explained in terms of risk/reward tradeoff. The higher-risk models have the incentive to deviate significantly from the baseline in exchange for more drastic improvement in effectiveness (which is val-

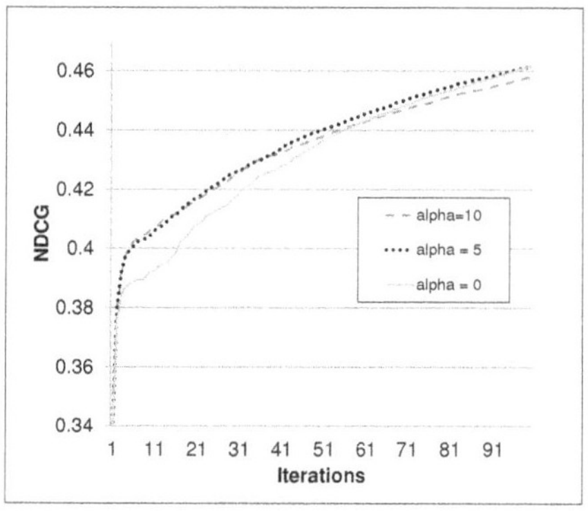

(a)

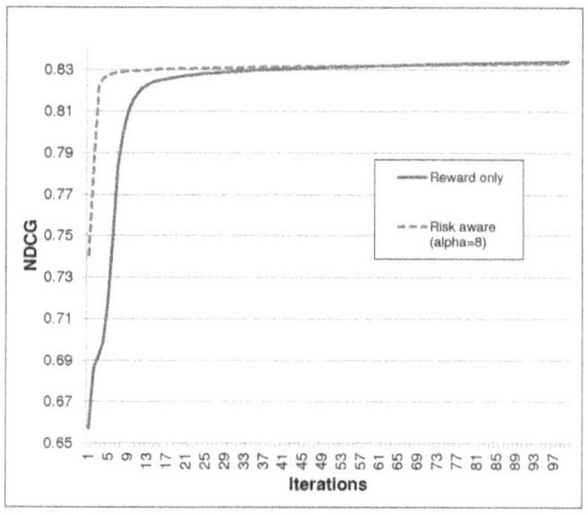

(b)

Figure 4: Risk-sensitive model (high α) consistently converges faster than reward-only objective ($\alpha = 0$), for both the MSLR dataset (top) and Location dataset (bottom). Each iteration point is averaged over all validation folds.

ued more by the tradeoff metric under a low α value); while low-risk models (high α value) tend to stay close to baseline, since risk is aggressively penalized by the tradeoff metric under large α and there is no incentive to significantly deviate from baseline (even if that means a higher gain) due to the potentially large penalty incurred from it. This fact is also confirmed by results shown in Table 2, where the higher-risk model trades off more robustness for effectiveness.

Moreover, in models that heavily penalize risk, the re-ranked results for a particular query may deviate significantly from baseline, but only under the condition that the reward (NDCG gain) acquired as a result of the deviation must be high enough to outweigh the increased risk. We can see this behavior in the risk-sensitive model $\alpha = 9$. Although a majority of the queries are in Bin 0 (near baseline), the overall NDCG gain is moderate and the overall risk is the lowest among all models. Also interesting is that as Kendall distance increases, the safe model tends to have the largest reward among other models under same kendall distance. For safe model ($\alpha = 9$), reward is 0.00371 under kendall bin 2, which is the highest among other models in the same Kendall bin 2. Thus, one potential application of this type of cross-model analysis might be to use the consistency across different models to produce the best reranking model for each query.

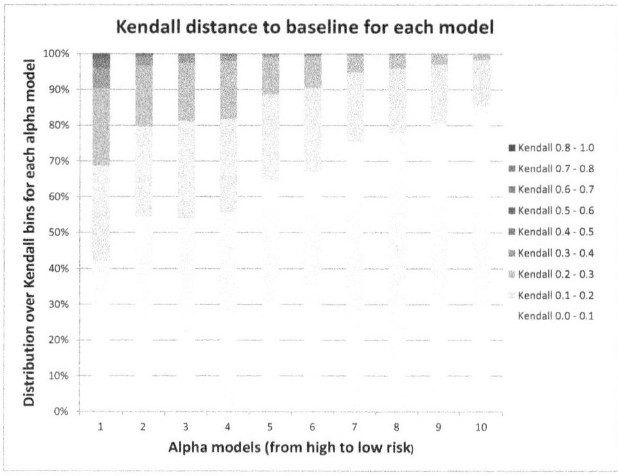

Figure 5: Distributions of Kendall distances to baseline ranking, for increasing values of the risk parameter α (location dataset). For high-risk models ($\alpha = 1$), only 42% of queries have re-ranked results that remain very close to the baseline ranking (Bin 0), compared to low-risk ($\alpha = 10$) models having 90% of queries with results very close to the baseline.

6. DISCUSSION AND FUTURE WORK

In this study we gave a definition of 'risk' in terms of the size of the downside tail of a distribution over a specific performance measure: NDCG. However, our framework is not limited to that choice and can address a much broader family of scenarios.

First, the risk and reward parts of the ranking objective may address other performance aspects of the results ranking, as long as the combined measure is consistent.

Second, we can look beyond strictly performance-related definitions of risk to include other properties of result sets. For example, the *churn* of a set of results for a given query refers to undesirable and unexpected volatility in a given query's results after re-ranking, even (or especially) when the rankings of the best relevant documents - and thus overall performance - might be unchanged or only minimally reduced. All things being equal, given two rankings with the same retrieval performance, we may prefer the one that gives less churn compared to a baseline ranking. Thus, the 'risk' of ranking might be defined using a ranking dissimilarity measure such as Kendall's tau compared to the baseline, instead of the strictly performance-based difference in NDCG we used here.

Third, another assumption we made was that reducing downside variance was a desirable goal. In general, this is true. However, there may be some retrieval tasks where it is beneficial to have an objective that tries to *increase upside variance*, even if this leads to an increased chance of large errors. Typically this will be in cases where a greater diversity of retrieval hypotheses is desirable as part of a larger precision-oriented system. For example, a search engine, acting as one source among several that provides candidate documents to a question-answering application, may be more likely to find high-reward documents if it does more aggressive promotion from deep in the original ranking.

Finally, we note that our use of an objective that minimizes negative outcomes with respect to a baseline is a special case of regret-based learning. In particular, we could generalize our risk-reward objective to minimize the average loss over the worst $X\%$ tail of negative outcomes, instead of all negative outcomes, and this could be viewed as a minimax regret objective - with connections to the widely-used Conditional Value-at-Risk objective from financial optimization. Beyond ranking, we believe this family of robust objectives deserves wider consideration in IR, with potential applicability to tasks such as query rewriting, federated resource selection, meta-search and others, where risk-reward scenarios exist and finding the highest-quality operational tradeoffs is critical.

7. CONCLUSIONS

We presented a general approach for improving the robustness of learned rankers by performing risk-sensitive optimization of ranking models. Our optimization adds a novel additional ranking objective that minimizes downside risk relative to a given baseline, in addition to the standard objective factor that maximizes average effectiveness across queries. Our approach can be viewed as a way to control the robustness/effectiveness tradeoff in learning-to-rank approaches. Thus, it generalizes the standard learning to rank approaches as special cases that do not consider robustness. Our robustness metric is orthogonal to previous multi-objective learning to rank metrics for capturing different facets for search, since robustness is defined *using* standard facet-based and IR performance measures *with respect to* a baseline model. We proved the theoretical consistency of the proposed tradeoff measure and designed a principled learning to rank approach, using boosted regression trees, to optimize it. Our approach can be potentially applied to a wide range of applications in learning-to-rank by plugging in different baseline models. Furthermore, by performing an extensive empirical evaluation using both public and proprietary datasets we demonstrated that our robust models achieve significant benefits in learning rate, robustness, and reliability over existing methods.

8. REFERENCES

[1] P. N. Bennett, F. Radlinski, R. W. White, and E. Yilmaz. Inferring and using location metadata to personalize web search. In *SIGIR*, pages 135–144, 2011.

[2] R. Bhattacharjee and A. Goel. Algorithms and incentives for robust ranking. In *SODA 2007*.

[3] J. Bian, X. Li, F. Li, Z. Zheng, and H. Zha. Ranking specialization for web search: a divide-and-conquer approach by using topical ranksvm. In *WWW*, pages 131–140, 2010.

[4] J. Bian, T.-Y. Liu, T. Qin, and H. Zha. Ranking with query-dependent loss for web search. In *WSDM*, pages 141–150, 2010.

[5] C. Burges, T. Shaked, E. Renshaw, A. Lazier, M. Deeds, N. Hamilton, and G. Hullender. Learning to rank using gradient descent. In *ICML*, pages 89–96, 2005.

[6] C. J. C. Burges. From RankNet to LambdaRank to LambdaMART: An Overview. Technical report, Microsoft Research, 2010.

[7] C. J. C. Burges, R. Ragno, and Q. V. Le. Learning to Rank with Nonsmooth Cost Functions. In *NIPS*, pages 193–200. MIT Press, 2006.

[8] S. Büttcher, C. L. A. Clarke, and B. Lushman. Term proximity scoring for ad-hoc retrieval on very large text collections. In *SIGIR*, pages 621–622, 2006.

[9] O. Chapelle and Y. Chang. Yahoo! learning to rank challenge overview. *Journal of Machine Learning Research - Proceedings Track*, 14:1–24, 2011.

[10] K. Collins-Thompson. Reducing the risk of query expansion via robust constrained optimization. In *CIKM 2009*, pages 837–846.

[11] K. Collins-Thompson, P. N. Bennett, R. W. White, S. de la Chica, and D. Sontag. Personalizing web search results by reading level. In *CIKM*, pages 403–412, 2011.

[12] S. Cronen-Townsend, Y. Zhou, and W. B. Croft. Predicting query performance. In *SIGIR*, pages 299–306.

[13] N. Dai, M. Shokouhi, and B. D. Davison. Learning to rank for freshness and relevance. In *SIGIR*, pages 95–104, 2011.

[14] P. Donmez, K. M. Svore, and C. J. C. Burges. On the local optimality of lambdarank. In *SIGIR*, pages 460–467, 2009.

[15] Z. Dou, R. Song, and J.-R. Wen. A large-scale evaluation and analysis of personalized search strategies. In *WWW*, pages 581–590, 2007.

[16] E. N. Efthimiadis. Chapter: Query expansion. *Annual Review of Information Science and Technology*, 31:121–187, 1996.

[17] J. H. Friedman. Greedy function approximation: A gradient boosting machine. *Annals of Statistics*, 29:1189–1232, 2000.

[18] X. Geng, T.-Y. Liu, T. Qin, A. Arnold, H. Li, and H.-Y. Shum. Query dependent ranking using k-nearest neighbor. In *SIGIR*, pages 115–122, 2008.

[19] F. Gey. Inferring probability of relevance using the method of logistic regression. In *Proc. 17th SIGIR Conference*, 1994.

[20] Q. Guo, R. W. White, S. Dumais, J. Wang, and B. Anderson. Predicting query performance using query, result, and user interaction features. In *RIAO*, 2010.

[21] C. Hauff, D. Hiemstra, and F. de Jong. A survey of pre-retrieval query performance predictors. In *CIKM*, pages 1419–1420, 2008.

[22] C. Kang, X. Wang, J. Chen, C. Liao, Y. Chang, B. L. Tseng, and Z. Zheng. Learning to re-rank web search results with multiple pairwise features. In *WSDM'11*, pages 735–744, 2011.

[23] B. Knijnenburg, M. C. Willemsen, Z. Gantner, H. Soncu, and C. Newell. Explaining the user experience of recommender systems. *J. of User Modeling and User-Adapted Interaction (UMUAI)*, 22, 2011.

[24] F. Li, X. Li, S. Ji, and Z. Zheng. Comparing both relevance and robustness in selection of web ranking functions. In *SIGIR '09*, pages 648–649, 2009.

[25] T.-Y. Liu. Learning to rank for information retrieval. *Foundations and Trends in Information Retrieval*, 3(3), 2009.

[26] Y. Lv, C. Zhai, and W. Chen. A boosting approach to improving pseudo-relevance feedback. In *SIGIR*, pages 165–174, 2011.

[27] D. Metzler and W. B. Croft. A Markov Random Field model for term dependencies. In *Proc. 28th SIGIR Conference*, pages 472–479, 2005.

[28] J. Ponte and W. B. Croft. A language modeling approach to information retrieval. In *Proc. 21st SIGIR Conference*, pages 275–281, 1998.

[29] S. Robertson, S. Walker, S. Jones, M. M. Hancock-Beaulieu, and M. Gatford. Okapi at TREC-3. In *Proc. 3rd TREC Conference*, pages 109–126, 1994.

[30] R. Steuer. *Multiple Criteria Optimization: Theory, Computation and Application.* John Wiley, 1986.

[31] K. M. Svore, M. N. Volkovs, and C. J. Burges. Learning to rank with multiple objective functions. In *WWW*, pages 367–376, 2011.

[32] T. Tao and C. Zhai. An exploration of proximity measures in information retrieval. In *Proc. 30th SIGIR Conference*, 2007.

[33] J. Teevan, S. T. Dumais, and E. Horvitz. Potential for personalization. *ACM TOCHI*, 17(1), 2010.

[34] E. M. Voorhees. The trec robust retrieval track. *SIGIR Forum*, 39(1):11–20, June 2005.

[35] J. Wang and J. Zhu. Portfolio theory of information retrieval. In *SIGIR*. ACM, 2009.

[36] R. W. White, P. N. Bennett, and S. T. Dumais. Predicting short-term interests using activity-based search context. In *CIKM*, pages 1009–1018, 2010.

[37] Q. Wu, C. J. Burges, K. M. Svore, and J. Gao. Adapting boosting for information retrieval measures. *Information Retrieval*, 13:254–270, June 2010.

[38] Y. Zhou and W. B. Croft. Query performance prediction in web search environments. In *Research and Development in Information Retrieval*, pages 543–550, 2007.

[39] J. Zhu, J. Wang, I. J. Cox, and M. J. Taylor. Risky business: modeling and exploiting uncertainty in information retrieval. In *SIGIR*. ACM, 2009.

Dual Role Model for Question Recommendation in Community Question Answering

Fei Xu[1,2], Zongcheng Ji[1,2], Bin Wang[1,3]
[1]Institute of Computing Technology, Chinese Academy of Sciences, Beijing, China
[2]Graduate University of Chinese Academy of Sciences, Beijing, China
[2]{feixu1966, jizongcheng}@gmail.com
[3]wangbin@ict.ac.cn

ABSTRACT
Question recommendation that automatically recommends a new question to suitable users to answer is an appealing and challenging problem in the research area of Community Question Answering (CQA). Unlike in general recommender systems where a user has only a single role, each user in CQA can play two different roles (dual roles) simultaneously: as an asker and as an answerer. To the best of our knowledge, this paper is the first to systematically investigate the distinctions between the two roles and their different influences on the performance of question recommendation in CQA. Moreover, we propose a Dual Role Model (DRM) to model the dual roles of users effectively. With different independence assumptions, two variants of DRM are achieved. Finally, we present the DRM based approach to question recommendation which provides a mechanism for naturally integrating the user relation between the answerer and the asker with the content relevance between the answerer and the question into a unified probabilistic framework. Experiments using a real-world data crawled from Yahoo! Answers show that: (1) there are evident distinctions between the two roles of users in CQA. Additionally, the answerer role is more effective than the asker role for modeling candidate users in question recommendation; (2) compared with baselines utilizing a single role or blended roles based methods, our DRM based approach consistently and significantly improves the performance of question recommendation, demonstrating that our approach can model the user in CQA more reasonably and precisely.

Categories and Subject Descriptors
H.3.3 [**Information Search and Retrieval**]: Information Filtering

General Terms
Algorithms, Design, Experimentation

Keywords
Community Question Answering, Role Analysis, Question Reommendation, Dual Role Model, PLSA

SIGIR'12, August 12–16, 2012, Portland, Oregon, USA.

1. INTRODUCTION
Community Question Aswering (CQA) is a web service where people can seek information (posting a question and getting the answer of it from others) and share knowledge (answering a question). Yahoo! Answers[1] and Baidu Zhidao[2] are two typical examples of CQA system. Compared with the traditional information retrieval, CQA bases on the community, which is a form of social network, so it can make best of user's collective wisdom to meet the information needs of users more easily and accurately.

In CQA system, there are a large number of questions posted every day. Take Yahoo! Answers for example, there are about 207 thousands new questions asked daily [1]. If we can automatically recommend the new question to appropriate users to answer, it will help the question be resolved as soon as possible, which will improve the CQA system's performance. In addition, it will meet the answerers' needs to answer questions. As we can see, question recommendation is a very important component in a CQA system.

The core issue of question recommendation is how to represent the users' interests (profile) and the questions, which is called the representation model. Based on that, we can assess the match between a question and each user, and then recommend the question to top N users who are the most consistent with it. Of course, we can solve question recommendation from another perspective, which is matching a user with each question and recommending the appropriate questions to him. Both of these types of recommendation tasks aim to make new questions answered as early as possible and satisfy the user better. Essentially, the key issues of both of them are the representation models for users and questions. As our target is recommending a new question to the appropriate users to answer, this paper focuses on the first type of recommendation task. At present, a lot of representation models have been proposed. Dror et al [5] represented the user and question as vectors consisting of multi-channel features and casted question recommendation as a classification problem. Other methods [2, 4, 6] utilized latent semantic models (PLSA, LDA, etc.) to model the user and question as the distribution of several topics.

As we can see, each user in CQA plays two different roles (dual roles) simultaneously: the asker and the answerer. That is, a user not only posts his questions, but also is able to answer someone else's questions. Intuitively, the profiles of the two roles of users are different from each other, which existing methods have not paid attention to. For example, a piano teacher wants to learn some computer knowledge which he is not familiar with. Thus he is most likely to ask lots of questions related to computer, and answer many piano-related questions based on his specialty. As an asker, a user may post some questions in

[1] http://answers.yahoo.com/

[2] http://zhidao.baidu.com/

the field that he is not familiar with. In contrast, as an answer, the user will solve the question which he is good at and interested in.

Are there distinctions between users' roles? How do different roles affect the performance of question recommendation? Whether we can legitimately combine the characteristics of different roles to improve the effectiveness of the recommendation system? All of these important issues are worthy of our concern. However, current recommendation methods have not in-depth studied the different characteristics of users' roles and their different influences on question recommendation. All of previous methods only modeled the user using a single role, or simply mixed the two roles together to represent the user without considering the distinctions between roles.

This paper systematically investigates the distinctions between users' dual roles and how they affect the performance of question recommendation differently. To the best of our knowledge, this is the first work on studying these important issues. While Nam et al. [30] observed that users in CQA are divided into askers and answerers and only a few of them both ask and answer in the same category through statistics, they have not theoretically analyzed the distinctions between users' different roles and their different influences on question recommendation. Moreover, we propose the Dual Role Model (DRM) to model the dual roles of users effectively. Finally, we present the DRM based approach to question recommendation, which takes full advantage of users' different roles to improve the effect of question recommendation. There are three primary contributions of our work.

First, DRM which considers the two different roles of users separately provides a more precise and appropriate user representation model for question recommendation in CQA. Specifically, we utilize DRM to analyze the latent topic information of different roles for modeling the user. According to different independence assumptions, two variants of DRM are achieved: (1) independent DRM that assumes that users are independent of each other and models each user individually; (2) dependent DRM which considers the dependence between users.

Next, we carried out systematic experiments on a real-world data to explore the distinctions between users' roles and compare the effects of recommendation methods that are based on asker role, answerer role or blending both of these roles. The results show that not only the two roles but also their influences on question recommendation are different from each other distinctly. In addition, simply mixing the roles together will impair the performance of recommender methods.

Finally, our DRM based recommendation approach allows us to naturally integrate the user relation between the answerer and the asker with the content relevance between the answerer and the question into a unified probabilistic framework, which is more interpretable. Most previous methods only consider the content relevance. There have been several approaches that make use of the user relation [3, 5], however in these approaches, the user relation is either obtained through somewhat heuristic statistics outside of the model or combined with the content relevance by a linear interpolation.

The remainder of this paper is organized as follows: Section 2 introduces some prior work related to our approach. Section 3 is the preliminary description of question recommendation in CQA. Section 4 discusses our dual role model and how to use it in question recommendation. Experimental results are presented in Section 5. At last, we conclude the paper and discuss about the future work in Section 6.

2. RELATED WORK

In this part, we review previous work which is related to our approach: recommender system, question recommendation.

2.1 Recommender System

Because question recommendation is a type of recommender system, we first review general recommender systems. Recommender systems can be divided into three stages based on how recommendations are made: content-based recommendations, collaborative filtering and hybrid approaches [18]. In content-based recommendations, the user will be recommended items similar to the ones the user preferred in the past. In collaborative filtering, the user will be recommended items that people with the similar tastes and preferences liked in the past, that is, user will help each other find what they may like. In order to combine the advantage of both previous methods together, hybrid approaches are proposed. All these recommender systems firstly attempt to profile user preferences based on his history logs, and then recommend items according to the relevancy between him and items. Different kinds of methods are used to capture the model of users, such as classifying [24, 28], PLSA [13], matrix factorization [29], and ranking-oriented approach [17]. However, the user in these general recommender systems only plays one single role, which is significantly different from question recommendation. Therefore, we should pay close attention to this difference as we have mentioned in the above section.

2.2 Question Recommendation

With CQA system becoming popular in recent years, many people turn their attention to question recommendation in CQA, e.g., [2, 3, 4, 5, 6, 16]. Overall, there are two main lines to solve this problem in previous work.

On one hand, question recommendation is consider as a classifier problem which is similar to [5]. In [5], Dror et al. proposed a representation model based on multi-channel vector space model, where the user and question are represented as the vector with multiple dimension features from multi-channel data. Then, the matching degree between a user and a question is learned from their respective features using a binary classifier. Although this model treats user attributes in the answered-channel and asked-channel as two groups of features respectively, all the features are integrated into a single vector space model to represent the user's dual roles without considering the distinctions between user's different roles and their different influences on question recommendation.

On the other hand, we can learn a ranking model to generate a recommendation list for question recommendation. In these earlier works, various extensions of Probabilistic Latent Semantic Analysis (PLSA) or other topic models are developed. Wu et al. [2] presented an incremental automatic question recommendation framework based on PLSA. Question recommendation in their work considered both the users' interests and feedback. Guo et al. [4] developed a general generative model based on basic Latent Dirichlet Allocation (LDA) model for questions and answers in CQA. In this approach, they combined topic-level information about questions and users with word-level information to improve question recommendation. In order to deal with the data sparsity, Qu et al. [6] used a user-word aspect model instead of direct aspect model [9] to model user preferences. However, all of these methods have used a single role, or simply blended roles to represent the user, which have not distinguished user's different roles and considered how they affect the performance of question recommendation differently.

3. PRELIMINARIES

Given the question set $Q = \{q_1 ... q_{|Q|}\}$ and the user set $U = \{u_1 ... u_{|U|}\}$, where $|Q|$ is the number of questions and $|U|$ is the number of users. Each question in Q is denoted as a triple $q =< t, u^a, u^q >$. The t is the text content of the question. For instance, t may include the title or the detailed description of the question. If we assume that words are independent, t can be denoted as a bag of words $\{w_1 ... w_{|t|}\}$, where $|t|$ is the number of words in t. The u^a denotes the answerer of the question (it is also the answerer role of user u). The u^q denotes the asker of the question (it is also the asker role of user u). If there are multiple answerers in the question, all answerers will be separated. If the question is not answered, u^a is null.

Based on the previous discussion in the section of related work, we choose the idea of ranking to solve the problem of question recommendation. For a new posted question, the question answerer recommendation task is to suggest a ranked list of users who are suitable to answer it. To tackle with this problem, we need to resolve the two sub-problems: question and user representation, the method of ranking recommendation candidates.

Since Probabilistic Latent Semantic Analysis (PLSA) [20] can effectively mines the latent semantic information of users and questions, it has been widely used to obtain the question and user representation in question recommendation, e.g., [2, 3, 4, 6]. PLSA assumes that users and questions are generated from a mixture of some latent topics. We can compute the consistency between the distribution on topics of a user and a question to determine whether to recommend the question to the user. We summarized the previous PLSA based methods for question recommendation and discovered that they can be divided into two main categories: (1) methods that model the user indirectly. Similarly to [2], it takes a question as one document and use PLSA to model the question to gain its distribution on topics at first. Then the user can be represented as the average of topic distributions of all the questions that he accesses; (2) methods that obtain the model of the user directly. In these methods, all the questions that a user accesses are treated as one document. Then PLSA is used directly to get the topic information of the user. A typical approach is the user-word aspect model applied by Qu et al. [6]. This model is proposed by Popescul et al. [7], which improves Hofmann's aspect model [9] for collaborative filtering.

However, when these PLSA based methods modeling the user, they did not pay attention to the user's dual roles and their distinctions. In order to effectively analyze characteristics of different roles and make use of both of user roles to improve the performance of question recommendation, we propose a Dual Role Model (DRM) based on PLSA to model the user in CQA precisely. According to different independence assumptions, we implement two variants of DRM. In the next section, we will detail generation processes of these variants and describe the DRM based method for question recommendation.

4. MODEL DESCRIPTION

4.1 Independent DRM

With the assumption that all users are independent of each other in independent DRM (IDRM), we separately model the dual roles of each user. As Figure 1 illustrates, the IDRM can be divided into two steps. First, we employ the PLSA to analyze the topic information of all the questions, and then model the answerer role and asker role of each user based on questions which he answers or asks.

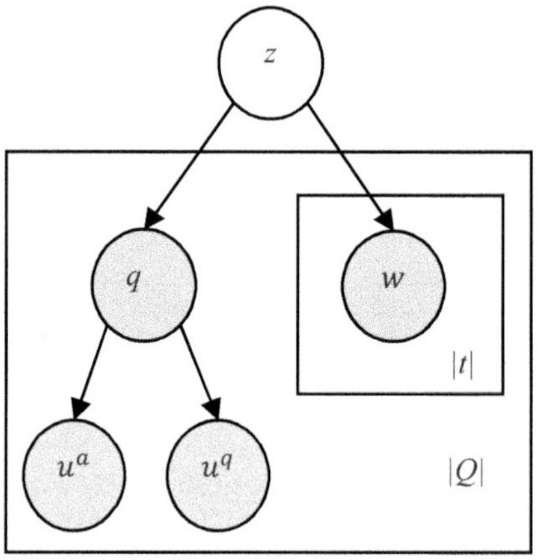

Figure 1: Independent DRM.

We introduce the latent variable $z \in Z = \{z_i\}$ to indicate each topic under users and questions. The model of user's answerer role can be represented as its topic distribution $P(u^a|z)$. Similarly, the asker role is characterized by $P(u^q|z)$ and the latent topic information of the question is $P(q|z)$. According to the first step of IDRM in the Figure 1, the generative model for question/word co-occurrences is defined as: a latent topic z is obtained with probability $P(z)$, and then a question q is generated with probability $P(q|z)$ and a word w is generated with probability $P(w|z)$. Therefore, we can compute the joint probability $P(q, w)$ of observing a question q together with a word w based on topic variable z as follows:

$$P(q, w) = \sum_z P(z)P(q|z)P(w|z)$$

Then considering all question/word pairs $< q, w >$ in question set Q, the log likelihood L is

$$L = \sum_{q,w} c(q, w) \log P(q, w)$$

where $c(q, w)$ is the frequency of word w in the question q.

We use the Expectation Maximization (EM) method to learn the model parameters $P(z)$, $P(q|z)$ and $P(w|z)$:

E-Step,

$$P(z|q, w) = \frac{P(z)P(q|z)P(w|z)}{\sum_{z'} P(z')P(q|z')P(w|z')}$$

M-Step,

$$P(z) \propto \sum_{q,w} c(q, w)P(z|q, w)$$

$$P(q|z) \propto \sum_{w} c(q, w)P(z|q, w)$$

$$P(w|z) \propto \sum_{q} c(q, w)P(z|q, w)$$

After obtaining all questions' representations, we perform the second step to get the representations of users' different roles. The user's answerer role is defined as the combination of topic distributions of all questions that he answers, and the modeling method is similar for the asker role. Intuitively, we can give an example to illustrate the feasibility of this approach. For example, if a user answers lots of questions related to using computer, so the profile of his answerer role is very likely to be related to this topic. Specifically, the role models $P(u^a|z)$ and $P(u^q|z)$ are estimated as:

$$P(u^a|z) = \frac{\sum_{q \in Answer(u)} P(q|z)}{\sum_{z'} \sum_{q \in Answer(u)} P(q|z')}$$

$$P(u^q|z) = \frac{\sum_{q \in Ask(u)} P(q|z)}{\sum_{z'} \sum_{q \in Ask(u)} P(q|z')}$$

where, $Answer(u)$ is the set of questions that the user u answers, and $Ask(u)$ is the set of question he asks.

4.2 Dependent DRM

Different from the IDRM, the assumption made in dependent DRM (DDRM) is that there is dependence between users. As we can see in Figure 2, DDRM assumes that the answer and the asker are dependent on each other when not observing the latent variable. The assumed generative model is as follows. We first pick a latent topic to some prior $P(z)$. We then generate the answerer u^a, the asker u^q, and the content $t = \{w_i\}$ of question q with corresponding probability $P(u^a|z)$, $P(u^q|z)$, and $\prod_{w \in t} P(w|z)^{c(w,t)}$. Thus, the joint probability distribution of a triple $< t, u^a, u^q >$ of question q is defined as:

$$P(t, u^a, u^q) = \sum_z P(z)P(u^a|z)P(u^q|z) \prod_{w \in t} P(w|z)^{c(w,t)}$$

In the above equation, $c(q, w)$ is the frequency of word w in the content t.

Accordingly, the log likelihood L in DDRM is

$$L = \sum_{t,u^a,u^q} \log P(t, u^a, u^q)$$

and we can also train the model using EM method as follows:

E-step,

$$P(z|t, u^a, u^q) = \frac{P(z)P(u^a|z)P(u^q|z) \prod_{w \in t} P(w|z)^{c(w,t)}}{\sum_{z'} P(z')P(u^a|z')P(u^q|z') \prod_{w \in t} P(w|z')^{c(w,t)}}$$

M-step,

$$P(z) \propto \sum_{t,u^a,u^q} P(z|t, u^a, u^q)$$

$$P(w|z) \propto \sum_{w \in t,u^a,u^q} c(w,t)P(z|t, u^a, u^q)$$

$$P(u^a|z) \propto \sum_{t,u^q} P(z|t, u^a, u^q)$$

$$P(u^q|z) \propto \sum_{t,u^a} P(z|t, u^a, u^q)$$

The IDRM and the DDRM respectively model the user's dual roles from different perspectives. Compared with previous models that do not take the dual roles and their distinctions into account, DRM provides a more precise and appropriate user representation model for question recommendation. Apart from different independence assumptions between users, we can see that the IDRM is a type of method modeling user role indirectly while the DDRM is a method which learns the role model directly.

4.3 Question Recommendation

Based on any one of the above DRM variants, we build the DRM based method for question recommendation that takes full advantage the characteristics of different user roles. When a new question q arriving, we compute posterior probability $P(u_i|q)$ for each candidate user u_i, and then recommend this question to the top N users. $P(u_i|q)$ is obtained by:

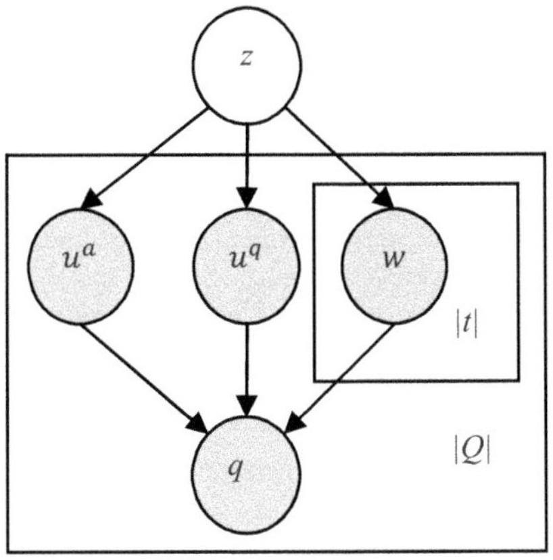

Figure 2: Dependent DRM.

$$P(u_i|q) \propto P(u_i, q)$$

$$= P(u_i^a, u^q, t)$$

$$= \sum_z P(z)P(u_i^a|z)P(u^q|z)P(t|z)$$

$$= \sum_z P(z)P(u_i^a|z)P(u^q|z)[\prod_{w \in t} P(w|z)^{c(w,t)}]^{1/|t|}$$

where, the first step uses the Bayesian formula for an equivalent transformation. In the second step, the question q is decomposed into its content t and its asker u^q. In addition, we only need to consider the candidate's answerer role when we evaluate whether he is suitable to answer this question. Therefore, the u_i is represented as his answerer role u_i^a. The third step and fourth step is based on the role models and the question model obtained in DRM, where the generation probability $P(t|z)$ is normalized by the length of question content $|t|$.

In this recommendation approach, $P(u_i^a|z)P(u^q|z)$ denotes the consistency of the answerer and the asker over topics, which models the user relation between the answerer and the asker. Correspondingly, $P(u_i^a|z) \prod_{w \in t} P(w|z)^{c(w,t)}$ measures the consistency of the answerer and the question content over topics, which models the content relevance between the answerer and the question. As we can see, our DRM based method takes full advantage of users' dual roles to improve the performance of question recommendation. Moreover, this method utilizes a unified probabilistic framework to naturally associate the user relation with the content relevance together, which is more interpretable.

Compared with the DRM, both the methods described in [2] and [6] employed a single role model to represent the user and ignored the user relation when recommending question to users. In the next section, these methods will be used as two groups of baselines in our experiments.

5. EXPERIMENTS

We evaluate the proposed approach using a real-world data from Yahoo! Answers and conduct different experiments to address the following questions: (1) Are there any distinctions between users' dual roles and how they affect the result of question recommendation? (2) Does the proposed DRM improve the effectiveness of question recommendation compared with other baseline methods? (3) Which of the two variants of DRM for question recommendation, namely IDRM and DDRM, is more effective?

5.1 Data Sets

In order to obtain the data sets for experiments, we used Yahoo! Answers API[3] to crawl 246490 resolved questions posted in 2011 from Yahoo! Answers. All the questions are lowercased and all stop words are removed from questions using a standard list of 418 common terms before further experiments.

In our question set Q, we divide the whole question set and user set (Q, U) into three subsets according to the user participation degree. For each subset, we split it into the training set and the testing set based on the asked time of questions. The training set is used solely for parameter estimation and the test set is used for evaluation purposes. In each subset, we take about 9/10 of questions as training set, and the rest as testing set. The data set statistics of all subsets are listed in Table 1. Each dataset contains a question set and a user set. For instance, the question set and user set of User-10 are Q_{10} and U_{10}. We selected users who asked or answered more than 10 questions as the user set U_{10} and then collected questions which were asked or answered by users in U_{10} as the question set Q_{10}. Other subsets are similar to User-10.

	Question Number	Answer Number	User Number
User-10	32009	97911	2515
User-15	28404	89144	1339
User-20	25690	80677	870

Table 1: Statistic of Yahoo! Answers data set.

5.2 Evaluation Metric

In traditional recommender systems, precision is a commonly used measure to evaluate the performance. However, precision is not suitable in the CQA context. There are so many questions asked in a CQA community every day [1] that the user can only access a very small portion of all questions. While the questions one accessed are those he is interested in, we can not guarantee that the remaining unaccessed questions are those he does not like. That is, in some cases, a user did not access a question just because he had no chance to see the question in CQA system. Therefore, we employ a new metric proposed in [6] to evaluate the effectiveness of question recommendation in CQA.

For a question in testing set, the user who provides the best answer (named the best answerer, Adamic et al. [27] have verified that answers selected as the best ones are mostly indeed the most suitable for the questions.) of this question is seemlier to answer it compared with other answerers, so it is more reasonable to recommend this question to the best answerer than other answerers. Based on this intuition, we only recommend the question to the users who actually answered it instead of all possible users in the whole dataset. Then the recommendation accuracy for this question is defined according to the rank of the user who provides the best answer. (We only keep the questions which have more than one answer and are already labeled with the best answers in the testing set.) Therefore, according to the evaluation metric applied in [6], we utilize the best answerer's rank as the ground truth of our evaluation metric:

$$accuracy = \frac{|R| - R_{best} - 1}{|R| - 1}$$

where $|R|$ is the length of recommending list, which is equally the number of answers, and R_{best} is the rank of the best answerer.

5.3 Role Analysis

We first discuss an interesting subject: the distinction between the user's two roles. Based on latent topic analysis of user roles in DRM, the distinction between the answer role and the asker role is defined as the difference between their topic distributions. The larger the difference between the topic distributions is, the greater the distinction between roles is. In information theory, the Kullback-Leibler divergence (KL divergence) is a commonly used non-symmetric measure of the difference between two probability distributions. We apply the KL divergence to assess the distinction between user roles. According to the modeling results of user roles in DRM, we obtain the latent topic distributions of each user role:

$$P(z|u^a) = \frac{P(u^a|z)P(z)}{P(u^a)} = \frac{P(u^a|z)P(z)}{\sum_{z'} P(u^a|z')P(z')}$$

$$P(z|u^q) = \frac{P(u^q|z)P(z)}{P(u^q)} \frac{P(u^q|z)P(z)}{\sum_{z'} P(u^q|z')P(z')}$$

Based on the above two equations, the distinction between answer role and asker role of the user u is

$$D(u^a||u^q) = \sum_z P(z|u^a) \log \frac{P(z|u^a)}{P(z|u^q)}$$

In DRM, the number of topics is a parameter that has siginificant impact on the performance. We utilize cross-validation to estimate the parameters. Based on experiments of tuning parameter, we empirically set topic number to 70 to train our DRM.

First, we analyze the average of KL divergence of all users in the user set of each subset to measure the overall distinction between user roles. The results are summarized in Table 2. Across data subsets , the overall role distinction in IDRM is about 1.3 to 1.5, and that in DDRM is about 2.4. Compared with IDRM, the role distinction in DDRM is greater and relatively more stable over different data subsets.

	User-10	User-15	User-20
IDRM	1.349	1.379	1.502
DDRM	2.440	2.467	2.441

Table 2: The overall distinction between user roles.

Furthermore, we take User-10 as an example to detail the distribution of role distinction, which is illustrated in Figure 3. For the DDRM, role distinction of 65.5% of users is more than 1.0, and most of them is in the range of [0.5, 3.5]. For the DDRM, role distinction of 74.3% of users is more than 2, most of which is in the range of [1.5, 4.5]. This shows that there are clear differences between different roles of most of users in CQA.

Another important result to note is that the role distinction in DDRM is more obvious and relatively more stable than that in IDRM, which can be observed in both of overall and detailed role analysis. This result may be due to that DDRM models the depen-

[3] http://developer.yahoo.com/answers

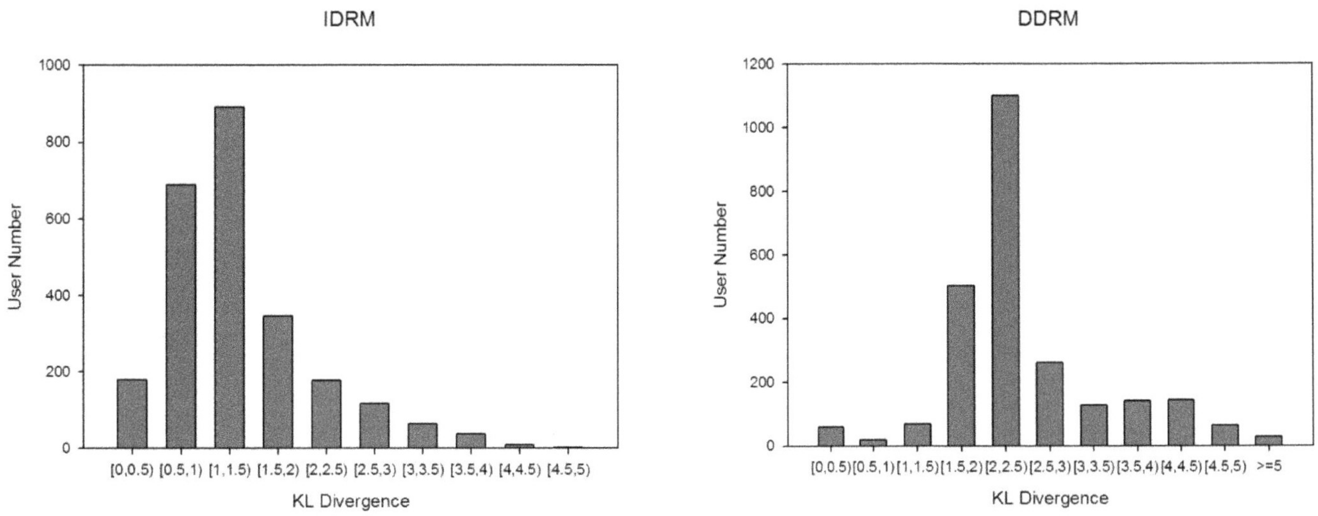

Figure 3: Distribution of the role distinction.

User Role	Topic ID	Top Words
Answerer	41 (using computer)	free, best, windows, antivirus, virus, anti, software, spyware, download, program, xp, vista, hard, drive
Asker	30 (programming)	c, program, file, java, programming, write, language, convert, system, net, code, array, php, number

Table 3: An example of the difference between user roles.

Role	VSM	PLSA1 (modeling user indirectly)	PLSA2 (modeling user directly)
Answerer Role	VSM-an	PLSA1-an	PLSA2-an
Asker Role	VSM-as	PLSA1-as	PLSA2-as
Blended Roles	VSM-bl	PLSA1-bl	PLSA2-bl

Table 4: All versions of baselines considering users' different roles.

dence between users which is more effective to capture the peculiarities of different user roles.

After discussing the role analysis of all users, we take a typical user in DDRM as an illustrative example to show the modeling results of user roles. Table 3 lists the topic with maximum probability and corresponding top words of the topic for both of user roles. As the result shows, this user is most likely to be a junior programmer (such as junior college students from school of computer science). He has some basic knowledge of computer and is familiar with using computer, so he solved many questions about that topic. While he may be just getting started with computer programming, a lot of questions he asked are related to programming.

5.4 Question Recommendation

5.4.1 Result Comparison

In this section, we explored how different roles of users affect the result of question recommendation. Moreover, we compared our DRM-based question recommendation method with other methods.

The models proposed in previous work are classified into two main categories. The first one is the word-level Vector Space Model (VSM) which is directly used to compute the similarity between users and questions. VSM only make use of word-level information to model users and questions. For example, the user and question are represented as vectors with tf.idf word weights, and then cosine similarity between them is defined as:

$$similarity(u,q) = \frac{\vec{u}\cdot\vec{q}}{||\vec{u}||\cdot||\vec{q}||}$$

$$= \frac{\sum_w tf.idf(w,u)\, tf.idf(w,q)}{\sqrt{\sum_w tf.idf(w,u)^2}\sqrt{\sum_w tf.idf(w,q)^2}}$$

where $tf.idf(w,q)$ is the word w's tf.idf weight in question q, and $tf.idf(w,u)$ is the sum of w's tf.idf weights in questions that u asks or answers.

The second one is PLSA based methods. As we have specified in section 3, these methods model the user either indirectly or directly. For the former, we took the model in [2] (PLSA1) as

		User-10	User-15	User-20
VSM	VSM-an	<u>0.555</u>	<u>0.600</u>	<u>0.612</u>
	VSM-as	0.456	0.492	0.466
	VSM-bl	0.541	0.591	0.581
PLSA1	PLSA1-an	<u>0.639</u>	<u>0.650</u>	<u>0.671</u>
	PLSA1-as	0.445	0.482	0.448
	PLSA1-bl	0.622	0.642	0.628
PLSA2	PLSA2-an	<u>0.638</u>	<u>0.651</u>	<u>0.674</u>
	PLSA2-as	0.447	0.485	0.441
	PLSA2-bl	0.619	0.647	0.622
DRM	IDRM	0.669*	0.675*	0.683*
	DDRM	**0.685***	**0.690***	**0.697***
		7.2%	**6%**	**3.4%**

Table 5: Recommendation accuracies of different methods for question recommendation. Each underlined value means the best result for each baseline group. '*' means the corresponding improvement over all baselines is statistically significant.

baseline. For the latter, we implemented the "user-word aspect model" presented in [6] (PLSA2) as another baseline. The details of PLSA1 and PLSA2 have been described in section 3.

In order to explore the impact of different user roles on question recommendation, we implemented the different versions of the three groups of baselines. These versions are based on the answerer role, the asker role, or the blended roles. Table 4 shows the labels of all baseline methods. Each version of a baseline is trained on the question set that users access under the corresponding role. Specifically, the blended roles mean all the question that each user answers or asks are simply mixed together as one set.

Based on cross-validation, we selected the best topic number for PLSA1 and PLSA2. The recommendation results of baselines and our DRM are summarized in Table 5, where the best result for each baseline group is underlined and the best result in each data subset is highlighted.

We first compare the performances of different roles in each baseline group. From Table 5, we observe that the answerer role always wins the best result in all baseline groups across data subsets. Especially, the answerer role is obviously better than the asker role over all the recommendation results. When data sets become denser and denser from User-10 to User-20, the effect of the answerer role becomes better and better as we expect. On the contrary, the result of the asker role appears an unexpected decrease in User-20. Furthermore, we examine the recommendation results of blended roles. As we can see, simply mixing the asker role into the answerer role not only fails to improve but worsens recommendation results of answerer role instead. According to above experiments, we conclude that different user roles reflect the different aspects of the user, moreover, there are clear distinctions between their influences on question recommendation. When modeling the user in CQA, we must distinguish the different user roles. When recommending new questions to users, it would be more appropriate to use the answerer role model to represent the candidate users.

Since the recommendation methods based on blended roles do not work well, whether our DRM based method can make full use of user's dual roles to improve the recommendation result? Tested on each data subset, our model exhibits good performance, significantly outperforming all baselines. The relative improvement of DDRM over the best baseline result is 7.2% for User-10, 6% for User-15, and 3.4% for User-20. In addition, DDRM is significantly better than IDRM across data sets, which means considering the dependence between uses is more effective to model user roles. This result is also consistent with the above role analysis.

Another interesting result to note is that the PLSA1 which models the user indirectly is almost equivalent to PLSA2 which models the user directly on three data subsets, suggesting that it is feasible to model the user indirectly by combining the topic information questions that he accesses. Additionally, it is clear that all methods based on latent topic analysis (PLSA1, PLSA2, and DRM) always perform better than word-level VSM, which demonstrates that the latent topic based model can be more effective to represent the profile of user. And this result also verifies the conclusion drew in [6]. Moreover, it is part of the reason for that Guo et al. [4] introduced topic-level model to improve heuristic word-level methods.

5.4.2 Parameter Sensitivity

We note that the topic number K is an important parameter in our proposed DRM. Therefore, we are interested in analyzing the sensitivity of the recommendation performance of DRM with respect to the topic number. We tested these two DRM variants with 8 different values of K, which is illustrated in Figure 4. Like previous role analysis, we only present the final results in data subset User-10. The results for other subsets are similar. As we can see from Figure 4, the recommendation accuracy gradually increases when the topic number varies from 10 to 40. Then we observe that the effectiveness of both DRM based recommendation approaches begins to be relatively stable when topic number is more than 40.

6. CONCLUSION & FUTURE WORK

The user in CQA plays two different roles (dual roles) simultaneously, which is different from the user in a general recommender system. In this paper, we have systematically investigated the

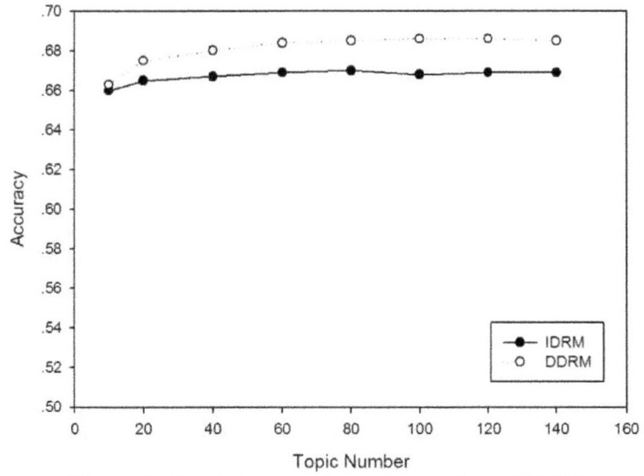

Figure 4: Sensitivity to the topic number of DRM.

distinctions between users' dual roles and how they affect the performance of question recommendation differently. Moreover, in order to represent the user in CQA with dual roles more reasonably and precisely, we proposed a Dual Role Model (DRM) to model the user's different roles. With different independence assumptions, two variants of DRM were achieved, which were independent DRM (IDRM) and dependent DRM (DDRM). Finally, we presented the DRM based approach to question recommendation which can take full advantage of the particularities of users' different roles. Based on a unified probabilistic framework, our DRM based method naturally combines the user relation between the answerer and the asker with the content relevance between the answerer and the question.

Our experiments were carried out on a real-world data crawled from Yahoo! Answers. First, the results of user role analysis showed that there are evident differences between the answerer role and asker role of users in CQA. Comparing the effects of the two roles on question recommendation, we discovered that the answerer role model is more appropriate to represent the candidate users when recommending new questions to users. Additionally, an interesting result was that simply mixing the asker role into the answerer role not only failed to improve but impaired recommendation results of answerer role instead. Furthermore, we compared our DRM based recommendation methods with baseline methods based on a single role or blended roles. Experiment results on three data subsets showed our DRM significantly outperforms all baselines, where the relative improvement of DRM over the best baseline result is 7.2% for User-10, 6% for User-15, and 3.4% for User-20. In addition, DDRM is more effective than IDRM across data subsets, suggesting it is more effective to model users' dual roles. Finally, the parameter sensitivity analysis showed our DRM approach is robust.

There are two interesting future research directions to explore. One of the most interesting directions is to further study how the roles of users will vary over time, and whether that will have influence on question recommendation. The other interesting direction is how to diversify the recommendation results to satisfy users better.

7. ACKNOWLEDGMENTS

We thank the anonymous reviewers for their useful comments. This work is supported by the National Science Foundation of China under Grant No. 61070111.

8. REFERENCES

[1] L. Rao. Yahoo mail and im users update their status 800 million times a month. TechCrunch, Oct282009. http://techcrunch.com/2009/10/28/yahoo-mail-and-im-usersupdate-their-status-800-million-times-a-month/.

[2] Hu Wu, Yongji Wang and Xiang Cheng. Incremental Probabilistic Latent Semantic Analysis for automatic question recommendation. In *RecSys'08*, pages 99-106, 2008.

[3] Damon Horowitz and Sepandar D. Kamvar. The anatomy of a large-scale social search engine. In *WWW'10*, pages 431-440, 2010.

[4] Jinwen Guo, Shengliang Xu, Shenghua Bao, and Yong Yu. Tapping on the potential of Q&A community by recommending answer providers. In *CIKM'08*, pages 921-930, 2008.

[5] Gideon Dror, Yehuda Koren, Yoelle Maarek and Idan Szpektor. I want to answer, who has a question? Yahoo! Answers recommender system. In *SIGKDD'11*, pages 1109-1117, 2011.

[6] Mingcheng Qu, Guang Qiu, Xiaofei He, Cheng Zhang, Hao Wu, Jiajun Bu, and Chun Chen. Probabilistic question recommendation for question answering communities. In *WWW'09*, pages 1229-1230, 2009.

[7] Alexandrin Popescul, Lyle H. Ungar, David M. Pennock and Steve Lawrence. Probabilistic models for unified collaborative and content-based recommendation in sparse-data environments. In *UAI'01*, pages 437-444, 2001.

[8] Baichuan Li, Irwin King and Michael R. Lyu. Question routing in community question answering- putting category in its place. In *CIKM'11*, pages 2041-2044, 2011.

[9] Thomas Hofmann and Jan Puzicha. Latent class models for collaborative filtering. In *IJCAI'99*, pages 688–693. 1999.

[10] Thomas Hofmann. Probabilistic latent semantic indexing. In *SIGIR'99*, pages 50-57, 1999.

[11] Luo Si and Rong Jin. Flexible mixture model for collaborative filtering. In *ICML'03*, 2003.

[12] David M. Blei , Andrew Y. Ng and Michael I. Jordan. Latent dirichlet allocation. In *Journal of Machine Learning Research*, pages 993-1022, 2003.

[13] Thomas Hofmann. Collaborative filtering via gaussian probabilistic latent semantic analysis. In *SIGIR'03*, pages 259-266, 2003.

[14] Tom Chao Zhou, Chin-Yew Lin, IrwinKing, Michael R. Lyu, Young-In Song and Yunbo Cao. Learning to suggest questions in online forums. In *AAAI'11*, pages 1298-1303, 2011.

[15] Qiaoling Liu and Eugene Agichtein. Modeling answerer behavior in collaborative question answering systems. In *ECIR'11*, pages 67-79, 2011.

[16] Ke Sun, Yunbo Cao, Xinying Song, Young-In Song, Xiaolong Wang and Chin-Yew Lin. Learning to recommend questions based on user rating. In *CIKM'09*, pages 751-758, 2009.

[17] Nathan N. Liu and Qiang Yang. EigenRank: A ranking-oriented approach to collaborative filtering. In *SIGIR'08*, pages 83-90, 2008.

[18] Adomavicius G., and Tuzhilin A. Toward the next generation of recommender systems: A survey of the state-of-the-art and possible extensions. In *IEEE Trans. on Knowledge and Data Engineering*, 17(6), 2005.

[19] P. Kantor, F. Ricci, L. Rokach, and B. Shapira. Recommender Systems Handbook: A complete guide for research scientists and practitioners. Springer, 2010.

[20] Thomas Hofmann. Unsupervised learning by probabilistic latent semantic analysis. *Maching Learning Journal*, Vol. 42, No. 1-2, pages. 177-196, 2001.

[21] Jiwoon Jeon, W. Bruce Croft, Joon Ho Lee and Soyeon Park. A framework to predict the quality of answers with non-textual features. In *SIGIR'06*, pages 228-235, 2006.

[22] Jiwoon Jeon, W. Bruce Croft and Joon Ho Lee. Finding semantically similar questions based on their answers. In *SIGIR'05*, pages 617-618, 2005.

[23] G. Linden, B. Smith, and J. York. Amazon.com recommendations: Item-to-item collaborative filtering. In *IEEE Internet Computing*, 07(1):76-80, 2003.

[24] Jiahui Liu, Peter Dolan, Elin Rønby Pedersen. Personalized news recommendation based on click behavior. In *IUI'10*, pages 31-40, 2010.

[25] Y. Cao, H. Duan, Chin-Yew Lin, Y. Yu and Hsiao-Wuen Hon. Recommending questions using the MDL-based tree cut model. In *WWW'08*, pages 81-90, 2008.

[26] S. Deerwester, S. Dumais, T. Landauer, G. Furnas, and R. Harshman. Indexing by latent semantic analysis. *Journal of the American Society for Information Science*, 41(6):391-407, 1990.

[27] J. Zhang, L. A. Adamic, E. Bakshy and Mark S. Ackerman. Every-one knows something: Examining knowledge sharing on Yahoo! Answers. In *WWW'08*, pages 665-674, 2008.

[28] M. Pazzani and D. Billsus. Learning and revising user profiles: The identification of interesting web sites. *Machine Learning*. vol. 27, pages 313-331, 1997.

[29] Y. Koren, R. M. Bell, and C. Volinsky. Matrix factorization techniques for recommender systems. *Journal of Computer*, 42(8):30-37, 2009.

[30] Kevin K. Nam, Mark S. Ackerman, Lada A. Adamic. Questions in, knowledge in? A study of Naver's question answering community. In *CHI'09*, pages 779-788, 2009.

[31] Pawel Jurczyk, Eugene Agichtein. Discovering authorities in question answer communities by using link analysis. In *CIKM'07*, pages 919-922, 2007.

Vote Calibration in Community Question-Answering Systems*

Bee-Chung Chen
LinkedIn
Mountain View, CA
bchen@linkedin.com

Anirban Dasgupta
Yahoo! Labs
Sunnyvale, CA
anirban@yahoo-inc.com

Xuanhui Wang
Facebook
Menlo Park, CA
xuanhui@fb.com

Jie Yang
Google
Mountain View, CA
cnjieyang@gmail.com

ABSTRACT

User votes are important signals in community question-answering (CQA) systems. Many features of typical CQA systems, e.g. the best answer to a question, status of a user, are dependent on ratings or votes cast by the community. In a popular CQA site, Yahoo! Answers, users vote for the best answers to their questions and can also thumb up or down each individual answer. Prior work has shown that these votes provide useful predictors for content quality and user expertise, where each vote is usually assumed to carry the same weight as others. In this paper, we analyze a set of possible factors that indicate bias in user voting behavior – these factors encompass different gaming behavior, as well as other eccentricities, e.g., votes to show appreciation of answerers. These observations suggest that votes need to be calibrated before being used to identify good answers or experts. To address this problem, we propose a general machine learning framework to calibrate such votes. Through extensive experiments based on an editorially judged CQA dataset, we show that our supervised learning method of content-agnostic vote calibration can significantly improve the performance of answer ranking and expert ranking.

Categories and Subject Descriptors: H.2.8 [**Database Management**]: Database Applications – Data Mining.

Keywords: Reputation, user modeling, crowdsourcing, community question-answering.

1. INTRODUCTION

Community question answering (CQA) systems form the crowdsourced alternative to search engines for providing information. Popular and effective CQA systems such as Yahoo! Answers [1] provide an environment for people to share knowledge and experience, which complement search engines by allowing questions to be posed in natural language and be answered by human beings through active content (i.e., answers) creation, instead of mining existing Web pages. Since the basis of CQA systems is the wide participation, the hurdle for users to proffer answers is typically minimal. Hence, CQA systems are also prone to spam and other kinds of abuse. Commercial spam itself is a widespread problem, and one that can mostly be tackled by conventional machine learning. Other forms of abuse, e.g., low quality content, willfully wrong answers are difficult for machines to detect, and again crowdsourcing quality content identification is an engaging, scalable way of ensuring that high quality questions and answers are identified and the creators appropriately rewarded. Different CQA systems have thus implemented different kinds of voting mechanisms coupled with user reputation systems in order to surface high quality content and discourage undesired behavior.

In this paper, we focus on *votes* in CQA sites. Take Yahoo! Answers for example, which is heavily dependent on the best answer voting scheme. An asker (user who asks a question) can vote for the best answer to his/her question. If the asker does vote, the best answer is declared and the question is labeled as resolved. If the asker does not vote for the best answer within certain period of time, other users in the community can vote for the best answer to that question. The answer that receives the largest number of best-answer votes within a certain period of time is then declared as the best answer to this question, and the question is declared resolved. Other than best-answer votes, users can also demonstrate their quality or opinion preferences by casting thumb-up or thumb-down votes on each individual answer.

Although such voting mechanisms are designed with the intuition that they should be able to identify high quality answers and the corresponding answerers, there has been little study on the actual effectiveness of these systems in achieving this goal. On the other hand, many studies [1, 6, 15, 3, 8, 17, 10] have treated the user-voted best answers as the ground truth source of high quality answers and have developed models to predict whether an answer would be voted as the best answer based on features extracted from the answer, past activities of the answerer, etc. As a counter-point, other studies, e.g., [14, 9], report best answers not to be entirely high quality ones. In fact, as part of this work, we also observe that user-voted best answers do not always have high quality, possibly because of bias in users' voting behavior. A few examples of potential bias are:

- Users may vote more positively for their friends' answers.

*This work was conducted when all authors were affiliated with Yahoo!

[1]answers.yahoo.com

SIGIR'12, August 12–16, 2012, Portland, Oregon, USA.

Even users who have interacted with each other in the CQA before might have a positive or negative bias depending on their past experience.

- Users may use votes to show their appreciation to answerers instead of trying to identify high quality content.
- Users who are trying to game the system in order to obtain high status can create multiple accounts and vote for one another.
- For questions about opinions, users tend to vote for the answers that share same opinions as theirs, but not necessarily of high quality.

Thus, instead of treating users' best-answer votes as the ground truth for answer quality, we ask trained human editors to judge answers based on a set of well-defined guidelines. Our first observation is that raw user votes have low correlation with editorial judgment. Based on this finding, we ask *"is it possible to calibrate the votes to mitigate the effects of potential bias, in order to increase the correlation between votes and editorially judged answer quality?"*

Contributions: We make the following contributions.

- We propose the novel problem of *vote calibration* in CQA systems. The basic idea is to associate every vote with a weight. Intuitively, votes from reputable voters who consistently vote for high quality answers should carry more weight, while votes susceptible to bias should carry less weight.
- In Section 5, based on exploratory data analysis we identify a variety of potential factors that possibly bias the votes.
- We develop a novel model for vote calibration based on supervised learning in Section 4. Intuitively, with each vote k we associate a feature vector $\boldsymbol{x}_k$ which includes features capturing potential bias. Then, the importance weight of vote k is a function of the weighted sum of feature values, i.e., $f(\boldsymbol{x}_k'\boldsymbol{\beta})$, where $\boldsymbol{\beta}$ is a vector of regression coefficients, $\boldsymbol{x}_k'\boldsymbol{\beta}$ is the inner product of $\boldsymbol{x}_k$ and $\boldsymbol{\beta}$, and $f(\cdot)$ is a monotone function. Based on a set of editorially labeled answers, $\boldsymbol{\beta}$ is determined by minimizing the error of using calibrated votes $f(\boldsymbol{x}_v'\boldsymbol{\beta})$ to predict the editorial labels.
- In Section 7, we experimentally show that the proposed vote calibration model outperforms a number of alternative methods for the answer ranking problem and the expert ranking problem. In particular, our model significantly outperforms the state-of-the-art SVM model [12] for expert ranking.

We note that since our focus is on vote calibration, we take a content-agnostic approach (i.e., no use of features extracted from answer content) similar to [12]. This makes our model applicable to votes on other types of content. Also, although we use Yahoo! Answers as the example CQA system throughout the paper, our model can be easily applied to other CQA systems. In fact we believe that our approach has the following useful properties – (i) it is robust to vote gaming, having incorporated a variety of such gaming behavioral features, and (ii) it provides a general framework for calibrating user votes in general crowdsourced rating platforms.

2. RELATED WORK

Although there have been many studies on CQA, to our knowledge, the problem of how to calibrate user votes to improve the correlation between votes and answer quality has not been systematically studied before. The related work can broadly be categorized into three threads.

Predicting user-voted best answers: There is a large body of work on building models to predict user-voted best answers (e.g., [1, 6, 15, 3, 8, 17, 10]). The assumption behind this line of work is that quality judgments of answers are expensive to obtain and it seems to be reasonable to use the readily available user-voted best answers as the target to predict. Different from this line of work, we do not try to predict user-voted best answers, but show that user-voted best answers may not be high quality ones because of potential bias in users' voting behavior. Our focus is on how to calibrate votes to minimize the discrepancy between votes and quality.

Predicting editorial judgments: Along with [2, 7, 16, 9, 14, 12], we define answer quality by a set of guidelines and obtain the ground-truth quality scores through an editorial process. For example, Agichtein et al. [2] used features extracted from text, user interaction graphs and votes to predict editorial judgments. Suryanto et al. [16] developed a number of graph-based methods to estimate user expertise, and evaluated these methods using editorially judged quality and relevance. Sakai et al. [9, 14] noticed bias in users' voting behavior that can cause user-voted best answers to be unsuitable for model evaluation, and proposed a number of evaluation methods based on editorial judgments. Similar to these studies, we also want to predict editorially labeled quality scores. Although user votes have commonly been used as features, calibration of each individual vote has not be studied.

Content-agnostic user expertise estimation: User expertise score estimation is an important use case of vote calibration. In the Section 7, we will show that using a simple average of the calibrated votes of a user as his/her expertise score can outperform the best methods reported in Liu et al. [12], where a variety of methods, such as PageRank-based method, HITS-based methods, competition-based methods, are empirically compared based on editorial judgments. Earlier work on user expertise is described in the following. Zhang et al. [18] proposed a PageRank-style algorithm for online forums. Jurczyk et al. [11] leveraged the HITS algorithm. Pal et al. [13] exploited the observation that experts usually answer questions that have not yet received good answers. Bouguessa et al. [4] developed a method to identify the number of users to be considered as experts based on a mixture of two Gamma distributions.

3. DATASET

Our dataset consists of editorial data and voting data.

3.1 Editorial Data

To determine the quality of an answer, we designed a set of guidelines together with a set of carefully selected examples for each quality grade and ask a human editor to judge it. We randomly sampled around 10,000 resolved questions in five popular categories (4.2K from each of "Sports" and "Entertainment and Music", 1.2k from each of "Business and Finance" and "Consumer Electronics", and 500 from "News and Events") from US Yahoo! Answers and, for each question, sampled three answers. These questions were selected by a diffusion process first starting with a random seed of 'active users – those who have answered at least 10 questions and provided 5 best answers; we then sampled resolved questions that these users answered, and then again from all answers to that question. For construction of features when modeling, we however looked at our entire dataset.

When judging an answer, an editor first read the question and answer, and then gave a quality *grade* to the answer according to a

	Editorial Quality Grade				
Type	Excellent	Good	Fair	Bad	#Ans
ABA	4.1%	22.9%	65.3%	7.8%	3,086
CBA	4.9%	24.5%	60.4%	10.3%	4,263
Non-Best	2.6%	18.2%	65.7%	13.5%	14,176
#Ans	698	4,337	13,899	2,591	21,525

Table 1: Best Answer vs. Editorial Quality

pre-determined set of editorial guidelines. In the interest of space, we only give a high-level description of the guidelines.

- *Excellent*: The answer provides a significant amount of useful information, fully answering the question.
- *Good*: The answer provides a partial but not entirely persuasive answer to the question. Minor typos and grammatical problems are acceptable.
- *Fair*: The answer fails to add much value to the knowledge base and is neither good nor bad — it's simply not sufficiently useful, interesting or entertaining to promote.
- *Bad*: The answer is either abusive, not germane to the question or so poor in substance or style.

Each answer was judged by one editor only. We ignored all the non-English questions and answers and also ignored all the answers that the editors could not make a confident judgement on. In total, we obtain 21,525 editorially judged answers on 7,372 questions (note that some questions do not have three answers).

User-voted best answers vs. quality: Table 1 shows the distribution of editorial quality grades for three types of answers: **ABA** denotes the asker-voted best answer, while **CBA** denotes the community-voted best answer through the majority rule. On Yahoo! Answers, CBA votes happen only when the asker of a question does not pick the best answer within certain period of time. **Non-Best** denote the answers that are not best answers. Notice that these three types of answers are disjoint. Each row of Table 1 sums up to one. The numbers of answers of the three types and the four editorial grades are reported in the last column and row. We make the following observations.

- The distribution of editorial grades for best answers are not very different from that of non-best answers, although the percentage of excellent or good best answers is slightly higher than that of excellent or good non-best answers. This indicates low correlation between users' best-answer votes and answer quality.
- A significant percentage (> 70%) of best answers are not even good (i.e., fair or bad). Anecdotally, users sometimes give best-answer votes to show appreciation, instead of identifying good answers. Also, a fair answer is in fact the best answer among other bad answers. These observations show the need to calibrate votes in order to use them to identify good content.
- Many non-best answers are actually good or excellent. This is due to the fact that only one answer can be selected as the best answer to each question even when there are many excellent ones.

Numeric quality scores: To build our vote calibration model, we give a numeric score to each editorial grade: Excellent = 1, Good = 0.5, Fair = 0, Bad = -0.5. We note that slight changes of assignments of numeric scores to editorial grades do not make a significant difference for the results as long as the order is preserved. They also do not affect the evaluation metrics in any way, since we use ranking metrics.

3.2 Voting Data

We collect the voting data in the following manner. We start with the set of answerers of the editorially judged answers and collect all of the resolved questions that were answered by this set of answerers in a one-year period. We then collect all of the answers to this set of questions, together with all of the votes on these answers. As a result, our voting data includes 1.3M questions, 7.0M answers, 0.5M asker best answer votes, 2.1M community best answer votes and 9.1M thumb up/down votes.

Uniqueness of our data: Voters' identities are important to calibrate their votes. To our knowledge, no public CQA dataset releases the identities of the voters. Thus, we were not able to evaluate our methods based on public datasets. Instead, we collect our own data, where each vote is associated with the anonymized IDs of the voter and recipient. Due to user confidentiality agreements, our data is not publicly available.

4. VOTE CALIBRATION MODEL

We present our vote calibration model in this section. Let $z_k \in \{+1, -1\}$ denote the value of vote k. The basic idea is simple. We associate each vote k with an importance weight w_k so that the calibrated value $z_k w_k$ of a vote would have higher correlation with answer quality. In order to determine these importance weights, we define a set of features to capture potential bias in users' voting behavior. Let $\boldsymbol{x}_k$ denote the feature vector of vote k. Then, we predict importance weight w_k using its corresponding features; i.e., $w_k = f(\boldsymbol{x}'_k\boldsymbol{\beta})$, where $\boldsymbol{\beta}$ is a vector of regression coefficients, $\boldsymbol{x}'_k\boldsymbol{\beta}$ is the inner product of the two column vectors ($\boldsymbol{x}'_k$ is the transpose of $\boldsymbol{x}_k$), and $f(\cdot)$ is a monotone function to calibrate the value $\boldsymbol{x}'_k\boldsymbol{\beta}$ (for example, to constrain w_k to be between 0 and 1). The parameter that needs to be determined is $\boldsymbol{\beta}$. Based on a set of answers labeled with ground-truth quality scores and the votes on these answers, we estimate $\boldsymbol{\beta}$ by minimizing the error of predicting quality scores using the calibrated votes.

In the rest of this section, we first introduce the notations and describe how to generate $+1$ and -1 vote values from the three kinds of votes on Yahoo! Answers, then explain how to predict quality scores using calibrated votes, and finally present a training algorithm for estimating the model parameters.

4.1 Notations

We use q to denote a question ID and u to denote an answerer ID. Since each user can provide at most one answer to each question in Yahoo! Answers, (q, u) form the ID of the answer to q provided by answerer u. We use v to denote a voter ID and t to denote a vote type. In Yahoo! Answers, there are three types of votes:

- **Asker votes:** These are the best answer votes by the asker of questions.
- **CBA votes:** These are the best answer votes by users in the community, called community best answer (CBA) votes.
- **Thumb votes:** These are the thumb-up and thumb-down votes on each individual answers.

Since a user can provide at most one vote for each answer and vote type, we use $z^{(t)}_{quv} \in \{+1, -1\}$ to denote the value of the type-t vote that voter v gives the answer provided by answerer u to question q. Let $\boldsymbol{x}_{quv}$ denote the feature vector associated with the vote that voter v gives answer (q, u). Notice that we did not add a superscript t on $\boldsymbol{x}_{quv}$ to reduce notational cumbersome; our method can easily handle features defined specifically for a particular vote type. Let y_{qu} denote the ground-truth numeric quality score of answer (q, u). We discuss how we convert editorial grades into numeric scores in Section 3.1. Finally, we use $\mathcal{V}_{qu}^{(t)}$ to denote the set of all the voters who cast type-t vote on answer (q, u), and $\mathcal{Q}_u^{(t)}$ to denote the set of questions to which answerer u provides answers that receive type-t votes.

4.2 Vote Value before Calibration

In this paper, we focus on binary votes. Extension to numeric ratings is future work. We generate binary votes for the three vote types in the following way.

- **Asker votes:** If the asker of a question votes for an answer as the best answer, then that answer gets a $+1$ vote from the asker and all the other answers get -1 votes from the asker.
- **CBA votes:** Similar to asker votes, if a voter votes for an answer as the best answer, then that answer gets a $+1$ vote from the voter and all the other answers get -1 vote from the voter.
- **Thumb votes:** If a voter thumbs up an answer, then the answer gets a $+1$ vote from the voter. If a voter thumbs down an answer, then the answer gets a -1 vote from the voter.

4.3 Calibrated Vote Aggregation

We now describe how to predict the quality scores using calibrated votes. Intuitively, we predict the quality score y_{qu} of an answer by a weighted sum of (1) the average vote value of the answer (q, u) and (2) the average vote value of the answerer u. Because there are multiple types of votes, we compute average vote value for each type separately and then do a weighted average, where the weight on each type will be learned from a training dataset.

Calibrated vote value: Using the notations defined in Section 4.1, the value of calibrated type-t vote that voter v gives answer (q, u) is $z_{quv}^{(t)} f(\boldsymbol{x}'_{quv} \boldsymbol{\beta}_t)$, where $z_{quv}^{(t)}$ is the vote value before calibration, $\boldsymbol{x}'_{quv}$ is the feature vector associated with this vote and $\boldsymbol{\beta}_t$ is a vector of regression coefficients for type t. Notice that we have a type-specific $\boldsymbol{\beta}_t$, which gives us the flexibility to calibrate votes of different types differently. Although $f(\cdot)$ can be any differentiable monotone function, for concreteness, in this paper we use the sigmoid function: $f(x) = \frac{1}{1+e^{-x}}$. For comparison purposes, we also consider $f(\cdot)$ as the identity function; i.e., $f(x) = x$. We call the votes calibrated through the sigmoid function **sigmoid-calibrated votes** and call the votes calibrated through the identity function **linearly-calibrated votes**.

It is instructive to compare sigmoid calibration with linear calibration based on their definitions.

- Sigmoid calibration is based on a nonlinear function of the features, while linear calibration is based on a linear function of the features. Thus, sigmoid calibration has the potential to capture nonlinear characteristics in vote features.
- The range of the sigmoid function is between 0 and 1. Thus, the calibrated vote value is bounded by -1 and $+1$. The effect of a single vote is always bounded. This is not the case for linear calibration, where a vote may have unreasonably large value when some features take large values.

In Section 7, we will compare these two kinds of calibration experimentally and show the benefit of using the sigmoid function.

Average vote value of an answer: When there are multiple votes on an answer, we use the average calibrated vote value on the answer to predict its quality. The choice of average instead of the sum is prompted by the fact that the total number of votes received is often biased severely by the age of the answer, how prominently it is displayed etc. To make this average stable, we add some number γ_t of "pseudo votes" to the average. Specifically, using the notations defined in Section 4.1, the average type-t vote value of answer (q, u) is computed as

$$\mathit{AnsValue}_{qu}^{(t)}(\boldsymbol{\beta}_t) = \frac{\mu_t \gamma_t + \sum_{v \in \mathcal{V}_{qu}^{(t)}} z_{quv}^{(t)} f(\boldsymbol{x}'_{quv} \boldsymbol{\beta}_t)}{\gamma_t + |\mathcal{V}_{qu}^{(t)}|}, \quad (1)$$

where μ_t and γ_t are two tuning parameters. In this paper, we set $\gamma_t = 1$ and $\mu_t =$ the average uncalibrated vote value over all type-t votes, which is computed by the sum of all type-t uncalibrated vote values divided by the total number of type-t votes in the system. Notice that μ_t is computed based on a large number of votes and should be a quite stable constant. If an answer receives no vote, its *AnsValue* would be exactly μ_t. Thus, μ_t can be thought of as the "prior mean" of *AnsValue*. If an answer receives a small number of votes, its *AnsValue* would still be close to μ_t, where how close they are depends on γ_t — the larger γ_t is, the closer they are. However, if an answer receives many votes, then its *AnsValue* would not be influenced much by μ_t.

Average vote value of an answerer/user: When an answer receives no vote or a small number of votes, we can also use the average value of the votes received by the answerer to predict the quality of the answer. Similar to Equation 1, the average type-t vote value of user u is computed as

$$\mathit{UsrValue}_{u}^{(t)}(\boldsymbol{\beta}_t) = \frac{\mu_t \gamma_t + \sum_{q \in \mathcal{Q}_u^{(t)}} \sum_{v \in \mathcal{V}_{qu}^{(t)}} z_{quv}^{(t)} f(\boldsymbol{x}'_{quv} \boldsymbol{\beta}_t)}{\gamma_t + \sum_{q \in \mathcal{Q}_u^{(t)}} |\mathcal{V}_{qu}^{(t)}|}. \quad (2)$$

Notice that this formula is almost the same as Equation 1, except that here we sum over all of the type-t votes received by answerer u in the numerator and compute the total number of type-t votes received by answerer u in the denominator.

Quality prediction function: Given the answer-level and user-level average vote values of all types on an answer, its quality is predicted by a weighted sum of these average vote values. Specifically, we predict the quality score y_{qu} of answer (q, u) by

$$\mathit{Score}_{qu}(b, \boldsymbol{\alpha}, \boldsymbol{\beta}) = b + \sum_t \alpha_{t,0}\, \mathit{AnsValue}_{qu}^{(t)}(\boldsymbol{\beta}_t) + \alpha_{t,1}\, \mathit{UsrValue}_{u}^{(t)}(\boldsymbol{\beta}_t),$$

where b is a bias term, $\boldsymbol{\alpha} = \{\alpha_{t,0}, \alpha_{t,1}\}_{\forall t}$ consists of the weights of different components, and $\boldsymbol{\beta} = \{\boldsymbol{\beta}_t\}_{\forall t}$ consists of all of the regression-coefficient vectors. Since answer quality is predicted by aggregating calibrated votes, we call this model **calibrated vote aggregation** model. When sigmoid calibration is used, we call it **sigmoid-calibrated vote aggregation (SVA)** model. When linear calibration is used, we call it **linearly-calibrated vote aggregation (LVA)** model. Notice that b, $\boldsymbol{\alpha}$ and $\boldsymbol{\beta}$ are the model parameters that need to be learned from a training dataset.

User expertise: To estimate the expertise score of a user, we simply use the average calibrated vote values of that user. Specifically, the expertise score of user u is $\mathit{Expertise}_u(b, \boldsymbol{\alpha}, \boldsymbol{\beta}) = b + \sum_t \alpha_{t,1}\, \mathit{UsrValue}_u^{(t)}(\boldsymbol{\beta}_t)$. Since this is a special case of the full model, we do not specifically discuss this special case.

4.4 Training Algorithm

Given a training dataset consisting a set of answers together with ground-truth quality scores and votes on them, we determine the model parameters $\boldsymbol{\Theta} = (b, \boldsymbol{\alpha}, \boldsymbol{\beta})$ by minimizing the following loss function

$$\ell(\boldsymbol{\Theta}) = \frac{1}{2}\sum_{qu}(y_{qu} - \mathit{Score}_{qu}(\boldsymbol{\Theta}))^2 + \frac{\lambda_1}{2}\|b\|^2 + \frac{\lambda_2}{2}\|\boldsymbol{\alpha}\|^2 + \frac{\lambda_3}{2}\|\boldsymbol{\beta}\|^2,$$

where $\|\boldsymbol{\alpha}\|^2$ denotes the sum of squares of individual elements in $\boldsymbol{\alpha}$, which serves as a regularizer to prevent potential overfitting. λ_1, λ_2 and λ_3 are the regularization weights of each regularizer. We minimize this loss function using gradient descent.

Gradients: The formulas of the gradients are as follows. Let $e_{qu}(\boldsymbol{\Theta}) = y_{qu} - \mathit{Score}_{qu}(\boldsymbol{\Theta})$ denote the difference between the ground-truth quality score and the predicted quality score.

$$\frac{d}{db}\ell(\boldsymbol{\Theta}) = -\sum_{qu} e_{qu}(\boldsymbol{\Theta}) + \lambda_1 b$$

$$\frac{d}{d\alpha_{t,0}}\ell(\boldsymbol{\Theta}) = -\sum_{qu} e_{qu}(\boldsymbol{\Theta})\, \mathit{AnsValue}_{qu}^{(t)}(\boldsymbol{\beta}_t) + \lambda_2\, \alpha_{t,0}$$

$$\frac{d}{d\alpha_{t,1}}\ell(\boldsymbol{\Theta}) = -\sum_{qu} e_{qu}(\boldsymbol{\Theta})\, \mathit{UsrValue}_{u}^{(t)}(\boldsymbol{\beta}_t) + \lambda_2\, \alpha_{t,1}$$

$$\frac{d}{d\boldsymbol{\beta}_t}\ell(\boldsymbol{\Theta}) = -\sum_{qu} e_{qu}(\boldsymbol{\Theta})\big[\alpha_{t,0}\, \tfrac{d}{d\boldsymbol{\beta}_t}\mathit{AnsValue}_{qu}^{(t)}(\boldsymbol{\beta}_t) + \alpha_{t,1}\, \tfrac{d}{d\boldsymbol{\beta}_t}\mathit{UsrValue}_{u}^{(t)}(\boldsymbol{\beta}_t)\big] + \lambda_2\, \boldsymbol{\beta}_t,$$

where

$$\frac{d}{d\boldsymbol{\beta}_t}\mathit{AnsValue}_{qu}^{(t)}(\boldsymbol{\beta}_t) = \frac{\sum_{v\in\mathcal{V}_{qu}^{(t)}} z_{quv}^{(t)} f'(\boldsymbol{x}'_{quv}\boldsymbol{\beta}_t)\, \boldsymbol{x}_{quv}}{\gamma_t + |\mathcal{V}_{qu}^{(t)}|}$$

$$\frac{d}{d\boldsymbol{\beta}_t}\mathit{UsrValue}_{u}^{(t)}(\boldsymbol{\beta}_t) = \frac{\sum_{q\in\mathcal{Q}_u^{(t)}}\sum_{v\in\mathcal{V}_{qu}^{(t)}} z_{quv}^{(t)} f'(\boldsymbol{x}'_{quv}\boldsymbol{\beta}_t)\, \boldsymbol{x}_{quv}}{\gamma_t + \sum_{q\in\mathcal{Q}_u^{(t)}} |\mathcal{V}_{qu}^{(t)}|}.$$

If $f(\cdot)$ is the sigmoid function in sigmoid calibration, its derivative $f'(x)$ is $f(x)(1-f(x))$. For linear calibration, $f'(x) = 1$ always. However, it can be shown that linear calibration can be transformed into a regular linear regression problem. Thus, we solve linear calibration by using a standard linear regression package.

Loss minimization: There are many gradient descent algorithms, which can be easily applied to minimize our loss function. In our implementation, we use L-BFGS [5].

5. EXPLORATORY ANALYSIS

Before we define the features to be used in our calibration model, we discuss a range of potential indicators of voting bias in this section. In the interest of space, we mainly use community best-answer (CBA) votes to show our analysis. Many of the insights also apply to other types of votes.

Characteristics of CBA votes: First, the importance of CBA votes is seen in Figure 1, which plots the fraction of questions resolved by CBA votes as a function of the number of answers to the question. On average around 61% of the total number of questions in our corpus get resolved by CBA votes, and this fraction reaches its peak for questions with smaller number of answers (being near 70% for questions with less than three answers). One possible explanation for the U-shaped curve of Figure 1 could be that the number of answers being too small indicates that the question is probably not interesting, likely posed by a casual user who is less inclined to give a best answer vote herself – and thus the community has to step in.

Furthermore, CBA votes are rarely unanimous. Figure 2 shows how many answers to a question on average receive at least one CBA vote as a function of the number of answers to the question.

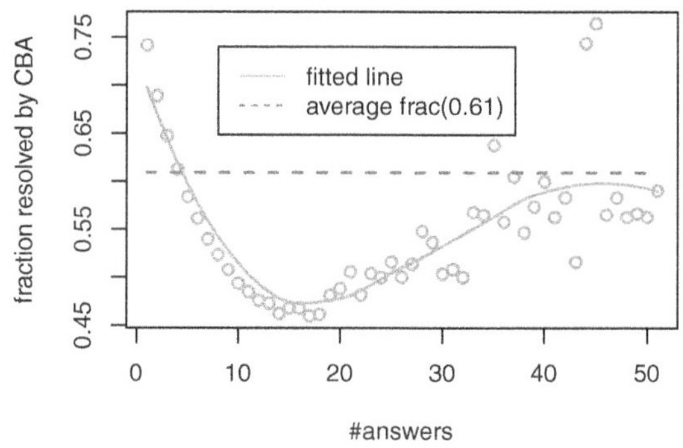

Figure 1: Fraction of questions resolved by CBA votes

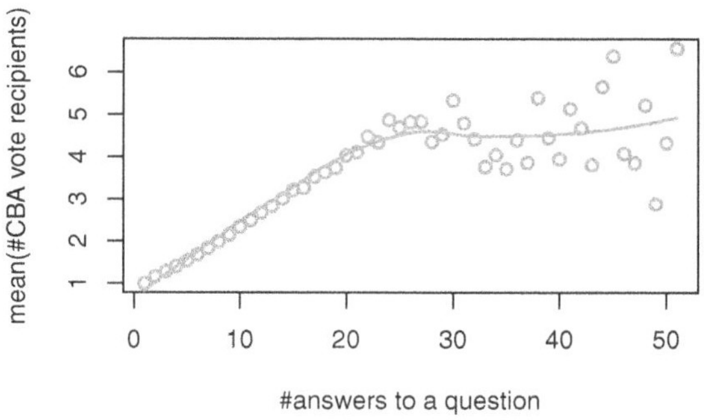

Figure 2: Number of answers receiving CBA votes

The y-axis shows the number of answers that receive at least one CBA vote, averaged over all questions that have the same number of answers. There is a clear linear trend up for questions with ≤ 30 answers. Beyond that, the trend is almost flat and noisier. Sparsity of data is likely the main reason behind the noise. The flatness of the trend can be possibly explained by the fact that a community member looking to vote an answer as CBA is likely only to look at the top few answers in the page; some answers can also be submitted after the CBA deadline passes.

In the following, we discuss our observations about some potential sources of bias that we see in our dataset. For each of these sources, it is important to note that we are not claiming that this bias immediately implies that the corresponding CBA votes provide no signal to predict answer quality. Our goal here is to identify a variety of indicators of potential bias, so that our model can use them to calibrate votes.

Self Voting: Figure 3 shows the extent of self voting (where a user votes for his/her own answers) in our dataset. Self votes contribute to 33% of the total CBA votes, and when we consider users who cast at least 20 votes, the percentage of self votes goes even above 40%. Self votes are certainly unlikely to represent any quality judgment, they can at most be taken as a signal of the user's familiarity with the voting mechanism of the CQA site, which in itself could provide a useful signal.

Vote Spread and Reciprocity: We define *in/out spread* of a user u as the ratio between the number of distinct users who cast/receive a vote to/from u and the number of votes that go into/out of u, which measures the spread of u's incoming/outgoing votes over different users. This measure could capture potential biased behavior in which users are either receiving most of their votes from a small number of users, or are themselves casting the votes in a concentrated manner. This phenomenon might be due to gaming, a user's

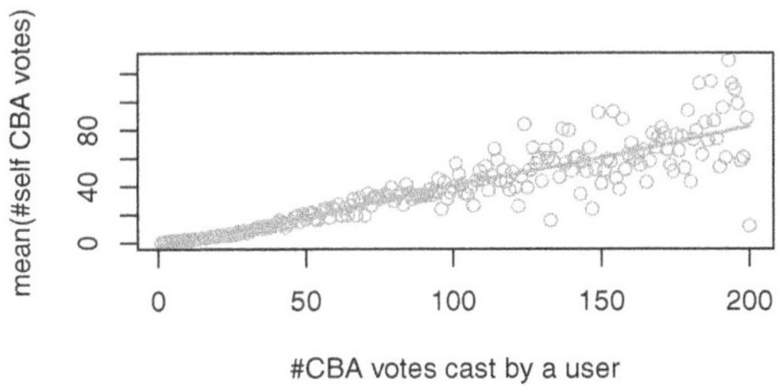

Figure 3: Number of self CBA votes by a user, along with fitted curve showing the trend.

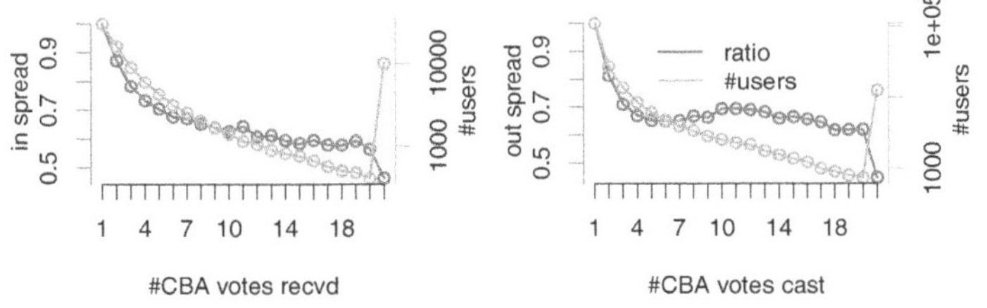

Figure 4: (a) In Spread and (b) Out Spread of CBA votes. The right end point of the x-axis includes all users with > 20 votes

narrow interests, or a scenario where only a small number users provide high quality answers. We report *out spread* and *in spread* in the Figure 4. The red curve together with the left hand y-axis represents in/out spread as a function of the number of votes that go into/out of a user. The green curve with the right hand y-axis shows, in log-scale, the number of users who received/cast a certain number of CBA votes. The spread decreases with increasing number of CBA votes cast/received. It is lowest on average for users who have cast/received more than 20 votes – which could indicate gaming by a small number of active users.

One interesting user-user interaction, almost a "quid pro quo" action, is when two users cast CBA votes on each other thereby creating a reciprocal relation between the two. We call a vote a *reciprocal* vote if the recipient also vote back for an answer authored by the voter. We define *in/out reciprocity* of user u as the fraction of incoming/outgoing votes that are reciprocal. Figure 5 shows in/out reciprocity as a function of the total number of incoming and outgoing CBA votes of a user. Both the curves are concave, and stabilize around 0.46 for users with large number of votes – again indicating potential gaming by heavy users. The number of users involved in such a reciprocal voting pattern is also seen in Figure 6 – over 20K users in our dataset are involved in at least 10 reciprocal votes. Considering this pattern as a feature when calibrating CBA votes certainly seems advisable.

Other Interaction Bias: In the remaining part of the section, we investigate whether CBA votes are independent of previous interaction between the voter and recipient. Our strategy is to use a hypothesis testing framework to analyze whether the null hypothesis — that CBA voting is independent of previous interaction — holds true individually for different interaction types. The different types of interaction we consider are the following: Whether one user answered another's question, whether they thumbed up/down each other, and whether they gave CBA/ABA votes to each other (recall that ABA denote asker best-answer). We represent each of these by a formal relation as follows. Let t be a time point. ANS_t denotes the set of all pairs (u, v) of users such that u answered a question posed by v before time t. TU_t denotes the set

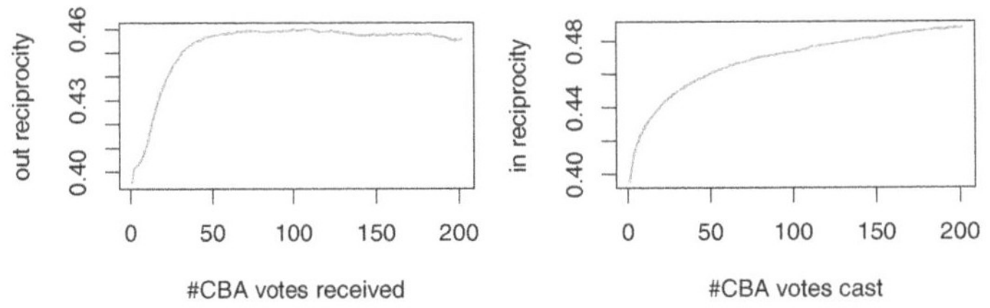

Figure 5: (a) Out Reciprocity and (b) In Reciprocity of CBA votes.

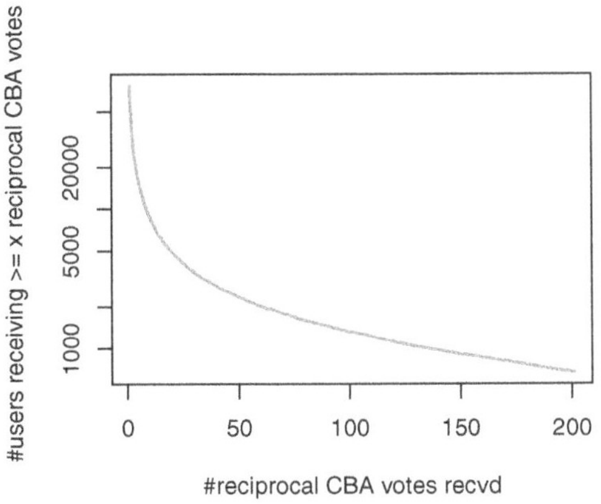

Figure 6: Number of users having at least x reciprocal votes

of the pairs (u, v) such that u thumbed up an answer by v before time t. TD_t, CBA_t, ABA_t are similarly defined based on thumb-down votes, CBA votes and ABA votes that user u gives user v. Our goal is to investigate whether a CBA vote that v gives to u at time $t+1$ is independent of whether $(u, v) \in R_t$ for $R \in \{\mathsf{ANS}, \mathsf{TU}, \mathsf{TD}, \mathsf{CBA}, \mathsf{ABA}\}$. Before describing our observation, we briefly describe our methodology.

Chi-squared Statistic: Let $CBA(u)$ denote the set of recipients of the CBA votes cast by user u. Let R be any of the relation described above. Then, the chi-squared statistic for measuring independence of R and $CBA(u)$ can be computed based on the following counts, show in Table 2. Let $N = a + b + c + d$. Then, the chi-squared statistic $X^2(CBA, R)$ is defined as

$$X^2(CBA, R) = \frac{N(ad - bc)^2}{(a+b)(c+d)(a+c)(b+d)}$$

For measuring the effect of previous interaction on a CBA vote, we will compute this statistic based on the dynamic interaction stream. We go through the list of user actions performed in increasing order of time, and maintain the current set of user pairs who are in relation R. At any point, when we are processing a CBA vote, we use the relation R constructed up until this point to find which of the above cells we should increment the counts of. The X^2 statistic is computed after the entire stream is processed – this is then used for the test.

Randomization Tests: In order to get the confidence interval of the

	$(u,v) \in R$	$(u,v) \notin R$
$v \in CBA(u)$	a	b
$v \notin CBA(u)$	c	d

Table 2: Table for chi-squared statistic.

	empirical ($\hat{X}$)	max random	min random	$\frac{\hat{X}-\mu}{\sigma}$
TU	66941.65	35718.70	35263.40	261.76
TD	5830.44	7369.88	7046.85	-18.81
CBA	55515.30	29976.85	29360.74	168.97
ANS	13391.79	8677.06	8496.51	103.60
ABA	9616.96	5921.43	5755.67	82.56

Table 3: Effect of previous interaction (row indicates type) on CBA.

above X^2 value under the null hypothesis, we resort to randomization of the data. The way the data is randomized is as follows – for each question, we first decide on a list of candidate answers who are eligible to receive CBA votes. We select these to be the answerers who have received at least one CBA vote for this question. The randomized version of the X^2 statistic is then computed by the following process – we again traverse the list of interactions in increasing order of time. Each CBA vote is now replaced by a random choice from the list of candidates to this question – the updates to the counts in Table 2 are now made according to this random choice. Finally, the X^2 statistic is computed at the end.

Effect of Interaction: The above randomization was performed 20 times. In Table 3, we present the statistics obtained. The four columns present the X^2 statistic obtained on our data, the maximum and minimum over the 20 randomizations, and the normalized value of the statistic based on the empirical mean and variance. Based on the 20 randomizations, the null hypothesis of the CBA being independent of the relation was rejected with probability 0.1 for each of the relation TU, TD, CBA, ANS and ABA. Note that this only means that there is some correlation between CBA votes and past interaction of any of the above types – it does not establish a direct bias. Such correlation could, for instance, occur if active users are also experts. Nevertheless, this result suggest past interaction could be useful features for vote calibration.

6. FEATURES

Based on the exploratory analysis, in this section we define the features that we use to calibrate votes. We consider two types of features: voter features, which try to capture a user's voting behavior, and relation features, which try to capture potential bias associated with the relation between the voter and the answerer (vote recipient).

Definitions: We say that user v gives user u a vote if v gives a vote to an answer authored by u. In this relation, v is the voter and u is the answerer. A vote from v to u is a *reciprocal* vote if u has given v a vote before. A vote from user v on an answer is a *majority* vote if the answer receives at least one additional vote and has the largest number of votes among other answers to the same question.

Notations: We will use the following notations.

- $nVotes(v, u)$ = # of votes from user v to user u.
- $nVotesBy(v)$ = # of votes cast by user v.
- $nVotesTo(u)$ = # of votes given to user u.
- $nUsersBy(v)$ = # of unique users receiving votes cast by v.
- $nUsersTo(u)$ = # of unique users who give votes to user v.
- $nRecVotes(v)$ = # of *reciprocal* votes cast by user v.
- $nMajVotes(v)$ = # of *majority* votes cast by user v.
- $nVotersQ(q)$ = # voters voting for any answer to question q.
- $ratio(x, y, n) = \frac{x+\mu n}{y+n}$ is a smoothed ratio between two counts x and y, where n is a pseudo count to stabilize the ratio and μ denote the average of x/y over all of the (x, y) pairs for which we want to compute the ratio with $y \geq n$.

Voter features: We define the following features for voter v, for each vote type separately (when appropriate).

- **Vote volume**: $nVotesBy(v)$, $nVotesTo(v)$, $nUsersBy(v)$ and $nUsersTo(v)$.
- **Vote spread**: $ratio(nUsersBy(v), nVotesBy(v), 3)$, which measures the spread of the votes of v over different users.
- **Vote reciprocity**: $ratio(nRecVotes(v), nVotesBy(v), 3)$, which measures how often v casts reciprocal votes. We also include the raw count $nRecVotes(v)$ as a feature.
- **Self vote**: % of times v votes for his/her own answers.
- **Majority vote**: $ratio(nMajVotes(v), nVotesBy(v), 3)$ and the raw count $nMajVotes(v)$.

Relation features: We define the following features for each pair (v, u) of users, where v is the voter and u is the answerer, for each vote type separately.

- **Voting probability**: $ratio(nVotes(v, u), nVotesBy(v), 3)$, which measures the probability that v would vote for u.
- **Receiving probability**: $ratio(nVotes(v, u), nVotesTo(u), 3)$, measuring the probability that u would receive votes from v.
- **Vote-back probability**: $ratio(nVotes(u, v), nVotesBy(u), 3)$, which measures the probability that u would vote back to v.
- **Voter contribution**: Average of $\frac{1}{nVotersQ(q)}$ over all of the questions on which v vote for u, where $\frac{1}{nVotersQ(q)}$ represents the contribution of v among all the voters who vote for any answer to question q.

Feature transformation: For each of the features C that are counts, we consider $\log(1 + C)$ as an additional feature. For ratio features R, we also include a quadratic term R^2.

Intercept: Same as in linear regression, we always include a feature, called intercept, which value is always 1.

7. EXPERIMENTAL RESULTS

With the above features, we evaluate our methods based on our editorially labeled dataset described in Section 3.

7.1 Evaluation Setup

We evaluate our models at two different levels:

- **User-level expert ranking**: User expertise score estimation is a much studied topic [12, 18, 11]. As described in Section 4.3, our models can be used to estimate such expertise scores for each user. Here, we evaluate how well we rank users based on the predicted user-level scores.
- **Answer ranking**: Our models can be used to predict the quality of each individual answer based on calibrated votes on the answer (if any) and answerer. Here, we evaluate how well we rank answers based on the predicted answer-level scores.

Note that our focus is on vote calibration. Thus, we take a content-agnostic approach to the above two ranking problems. Since the most related work [12] on content-agnostic methods is in the expert ranking setting, this forms our main comparison setting. Next, we compare variants of our methods based on both user-level and answer-level score estimation.

An ideal way to evaluate user-level scores is to collect a ground-truth data which has the expertise grade for each user. As noted by a few research studies, such as [12], obtaining such a dataset by human judgment is very costly because all the activities of a user need to be examined in order to assess her expertise. An alternative approach is to use certain heuristics to define experts (e.g., users with the "top contributor" badge on Yahoo! Answers), which are also prone to have biases or be abused. Thus in our paper, we take an indirect approach similar to [12] in using the editorially judged (question, answer) pairs to evaluate user-level expertise. The evaluation hypothesis is that the answers provided by a user with higher expertise should have higher quality. Thus, we rank all the answers to a question using the user-level expertise scores of the answers and use the standard ranking metrics for evaluation.

Data: We try to predict the editorial quality scores on answers using either user-level or answer-level scores. We obtain 21,525 editorially judged answers as described in Section 3.1. All of the methods to be compared have access to the voting data described in Section 3.2.

Cross-validation: We use 10-fold cross validation to evaluate our models. We randomly split users into 10 groups. We use the editorially judged answers authored by users in 9 groups to train a model and then use this model to predict the user-level scores of the users in the remaining group and the answer-level scores for the answers they authored. This process is repeated 10 times to obtain the predicted scores for all the users and answers. It is important to note that the score of each user is predicted by a model that does not use any label information about that user.

Evaluation Metrics: In Yahoo! Answers, a resolved question has 3.6 answers on average. When creating our editorial dataset, we sampled at most 3 answers for each question. Thus, the ranked list per question is short in our evaluation and the ability to distinguish the performance of different methods is limited. In order to overcome this limitation, we proposed three types of evaluation schemes as follows.

- **Question Level**: For each question, we rank the $\leq$ 3 answers to this question and evaluate using NDCG metrics. The NDCG metrics are sensitive to the highly ranked answers and thus are more suitable for question level evaluation. The NDCG@k is defined to be

$$\text{NDCG@}k = \frac{1}{Z_k}\sum_{i=1}^{k}\frac{G_i}{\log_2(i+1)}$$

where G_i is computed based on the label of the i-th ranked answer and Z_k represents a normalization factor to guarantee that the NDCG@k for the perfect ranking (among all the permutations) is 1. In our paper, we set $G_i = 3, 1, 0, 0$ for Excellent, Good, Fair, Bad.

- **Global Level**: In the global level evaluation, we pool all the (question, answer) pairs together and rank all of them according to a model. After obtaining this ranked list f, we compare it to the ground-truth ranked list g, ranked according to editorial grades, using the Kendall τ rank correlation:

$$\frac{|\{(u,v) : u \succ_f v \& u \succ_g v\}| - |\{(u,v) : u \succ_f v \& u \prec_g v\}|}{\frac{1}{2}n(n-1)}$$

which combines both concordant and discordant pairs in the evaluation. It is important to note that the editorial grade of an answer is on an *absolute scale* across all answers, instead of being relative to other answers to the same question. Thus, it makes sense to pool all (question, answer) pairs together in to a single ranked list. A positive number means that two rank have a positive correlation. The higher the number, the better.

- **Category Level**: Between the above two levels, we have the category level evaluation. In Yahoo! Answers, each question belongs to a category. The category level evaluation is to pool all the questions belonging to the corresponding category together. Each method provides a ranked list of (question, answer) pairs for each category. Here, the ranked lists are much longer than per-question ranked lists. We thus adopt the commonly used Mean Average Precision (MAP) and Precision at 10 (P@10) for evaluation by treating Excellent and Good as relevant but Fair and Bad as irrelevant labels.

Methods for Comparison: The variants of our methods to be compared include (1) **SVA.Full**: SVA model with both voter and relation features; (2) **SVA.Voter**: SVA model with only voter features; (3) **LVA.Full**: LVA model with both voter and relation features; (4) **LVA.Voter**: LVA model with only voter features; (5) **NoCalib**: SVA model that only uses the intercept feature (which value is always one, thus no calibration for individual votes; however, different vote types are weighted differently). All these methods can be applied for either answer ranking or user-level expert ranking. We compare with the following baseline methods:

- Smoothed Best Answer Rate (**BAR**) estimates the probability that an answer provided by a user u would be a best answer. Let Ans(u) be the number of answers that u provided and BA(u) be the number of the best answers that u received in our voting data. We estimate best answer rate by

$$\text{BAR}(u) = \frac{\text{BA}(u) + \mu\text{BAR}_{\text{avg}}}{\text{Ans}(u) + \mu}$$

where BAR_{avg} is the probability of a randomly chose answer to be a best answer and μ is the smoothing parameter.

- Smoothed Competition Win Rate (**CWR**) is based on the competition defined in [12]. In this model, an answerer whose answer is the best answer for a question win a competition over each of other answerers to the same question, as well as the asker. Thus, we have (winner, loser) pairs from our data. The CWR is the rate that a user is the winner in all the pairs that the user appeared. Similarly, we also have a smoothing parameter μ for this method.

- **SVM** is the model proposed in [12]. It computes a single score for each user based on the competition pairs. Let the score vector be $\mathbf{w}$. The problem is formulated in the SVM format

$$\text{minimize } \frac{1}{2}||\mathbf{w}||^2 + C\sum \xi_{ij}$$
$$\text{s.t. } w_i - w_j \geq 1 - \xi_{ij}, \xi_{ij} \geq 0 \text{ for } i \succ j$$

where $i \succ j$ means user i wins over user j in a competition.

- **BAR+BA**: All the above methods are for user-level scores, which can be applied on expert ranking. For the answer ranking evaluation, we combine BAR with a binary score indicating whether the answer is the best answer based on a weighted sum of the two.

7.2 Experiment Results

7.2.1 *Overall comparison*

We compare our methods with all the baselines in Table 4. In this table, we show the three types of evaluation setting for both user-level expert ranking and answer-level ranking. All the parameters, μ for BAR and CWR, C for SVM, and a coefficient for BAR+BA, are tuned and we report their optimal results. In our methods, all the regularization parameters are set to 1.

Significance test: We use the paired t-test to assess the significance of the performance difference in NDCG@k, P@10 and MAP between two methods. Each query (i.e., question or category) gives a point in the significance test. For Kendall's rank correlation, each

Table 4: Overall comparison. Symbol $^+$ indicates significant improvement over BAR, BAR+BA, CWR and SVM; * indicates significant improvement over NoCalib (p-value < 0.05).

		Expert Ranking					Answer Ranking		
	Metric	BAR	CWR	SVM	NoCalib	SVA.Full	BAR+BA	NoCalib	SVA.Full
Question Level	NDCG@1	0.675	0.675	0.676	0.694^+	**0.701^+**	0.690	0.701^+	**0.712^{+*}**
	NDCG@2	0.748	0.752	0.752	0.760^+	**0.765^+**	0.760	0.766^+	**0.769^+**
	NDCG@3	0.800	0.801	0.802	0.808^+	**0.811^+**	0.807	0.811^+	**0.814^{+*}**
Category Level	P@10	0.336	0.315	0.307	0.383^+	**0.407^+**	0.365	0.475^+	**0.501^+**
	MAP	0.366	0.353	0.354	0.386^+	**0.396^{+*}**	0.381	0.425^+	**0.444^{+*}**
Global	Kendall	0.147	0.144	0.143	0.182+	**0.203+***	0.152	0.185+	**0.209+***

method generates a single number which makes t-test inapplicable. In this case, we use bootstrap sampling to construct the distribution of Kendall's correlation and assess significance based on that.

We analyze our results from the following perspectives:

Supervised vs Unsupervised: For either expert ranking or answer ranking methods, we have supervised methods (NoCalib and SVA.Full) and unsupervised methods (all others). In Table 4, the best results are highlighted. SVA.Full outperforms all other methods by a large margin. For example, for expert ranking, SVA.Full improves over BAR by 3.8% on NDCG@1, 8.0% on MAP and 38% on Kendall; for answer ranking, SVA.Full improve over BAR+BA by 3.2% on NDCG@1, 16% on MAP and 37% on Kendall. All these improvement are statistically significant. Among the unsupervised methods, BAR is slightly worse than SVM and CWR on NDCG metrics but consistently better on MAP and Kendall metrics. This shows that BAR is a robust baseline to for expert ranking. Also, NoCalib (which uses three types of votes) consistently outperforms BAR. This shows that in CQA systems, considering all types of voting information is helpful, which has been unfortunately ignored in previous work. Our methods are effective to combine all the votes to improve the utility of CQA.

Effect of Calibration: We analyze the effect of calibration in Table 4 by comparing NoCalib and SVA.Full. From this table, we can see that SVA.Full is significantly better than NoCalib on most of the metrics, especially for answer ranking. For example, the improvement is 1.5% for NDCG@1 and 4.5% on MAP for the answer ranking. All these improvement are statistically significant at p-value < 0.05. Together with Section 5, this result confirms the existence of bias in the current voting data and shows that vote calibration using our methods is effective.

7.2.2 *Comparison of Calibration Models*

In this section, we compare different models of vote calibration and different sets of features. In Figure 7(a), we compare variants of SVA and LVA together with the NoCalib using the category-level metrics on two sets of users: a set with all users and a set with heavy users who have more than 50 answers in our voting data (there are 11 such users). We again see SVA and LVA outperform NoCalib. Furthermore, we have the following observations:

SVA vs LVA: From both figures, we can that SVA (SVA.Full and SVA.Voter) is consistently better than LVA (LVA.Full and LVA.Voter) on both expert ranking and answer ranking. The difference is more significant in the answer ranking setting. This shows that proper normalization is important for the vote calibration in our models.

Full vs Voter: By comparing different set of features, full and voter, we see that the models with full features are also better than those with only voter features. This shows that the relation features are useful in vote calibration.

7.2.3 *Impact on Heavy Users*

We conducted a stratified study on heavy users by selecting them according to their level of activities in our dataset. Specifically, we set a threshold t and select only those users who have at least t answers in our voting data set. We vary t from 2 to 50 and plot the results in Figure 8. In this figure, the larger t is, the more active the set of users are. Clearly, both figures show that accuracy increases as user activity level increases. This makes intuitive sense because we have more information about heavy users and thus their expertise scores and the quality of the answers they provide can be better estimated. On both expert ranking and answer ranking, our models are consistently better than NoCalib and the relative order of different methods stay the same. Furthermore, for expert ranking, we see a larger margin between models with calibration and NoCalib. This suggests that calibration is more important for heavy users.

7.2.4 *Feature Importance and Tuning Parameters*

Feature importance: We now investigate the importance of different features defined in Section 6. To assess the importance of a set of features, we use that set of features alone to build our vote calibration model and compute the Kendall's correlation as the importance score of that set of features. The top 5 sets of features in the order of their importance are: Majority vote, vote spread, self vote, vote reciprocity and voting probability.

Tuning parameters: Recall that our model has two sets of tuning parameters γ_t and λ_k. To prevent overfitting, all the above results are based on simply setting $\gamma_t = 1$ and $\lambda_k = 1$ without tuning. Here, we investigate the sensitivity of SVA.Full to these tuning parameters. We use Kendall's correlation as the evaluation metric.

Setting	0.01	0.1	1	10
Fix $\gamma_t = 1$, vary λ_k	0.209	0.209	0.209	0.205
Fix $\lambda_k = 1$, vary γ_k	0.208	0.209	0.209	0.200

As can be seen, our model is not sensitive to tuning parameter settings.

8. CONCLUSION

In this paper, we introduce vote calibration to CQA systems. By analyzing potential bias in users' voting behavior we propose a set of features to capture such bias. Using supervised models we show that our calibrated models are better than the non-calibrated versions on both user expertise and answer quality estimation.

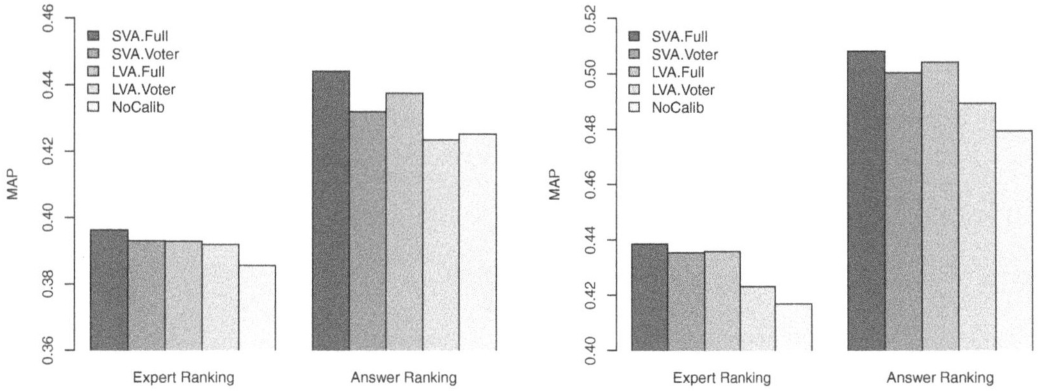

(a) All users

(b) Heavy users with ≥ 50 answers

Figure 7: Comparison of Calibration Models

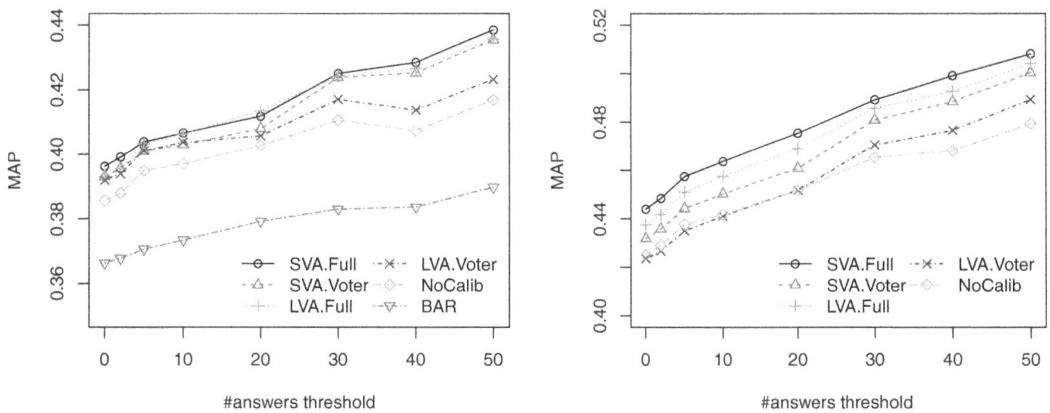

(a) Expert ranking

(b) Answer ranking

Figure 8: Results on heavy users

9. REFERENCES

[1] L. A. Adamic, J. Zhang, E. Bakshy, and M. S. Ackerman. Knowledge sharing and yahoo answers: everyone knows something. In *WWW*, 2008.

[2] E. Agichtein, C. Castillo, D. Donato, A. Gionis, and G. Mishne. Finding high-quality content in social media. In *WSDM*, 2008.

[3] J. Bian, Y. Liu, D. Zhou, E. Agichtein, and H. Zha. Learning to recognize reliable users and content in social media with coupled mutual reinforcement. In *WWW*, 2009.

[4] M. Bouguessa, B. Dumoulin, and S. Wang. Identifying authoritative actors in question-answering forums: the case of yahoo! answers. In *KDD*, 2008.

[5] R. H. Byrd, P. Lu, and J. Nocedal. A limited memory algorithm for bound constrained optimization. *SIAM Journal on Scientific and Statistical Computing*, 1995.

[6] B. Dom and D. Paranjpe. A bayesian technique for estimating the credibility of question answerers. In *SDM*, 2008.

[7] F. M. Harper, D. Raban, S. Rafaeli, and J. A. Konstan. Predictors of answer quality in online q&a sites. In *CHI*, 2008.

[8] L. Hong, Z. Yang, and B. D. Davison. Incorporating participant reputation in community-driven question answering systems. In *SIN*, 2009.

[9] D. Ishikawa, N. Kando, and T. Sakai. Ntcir-8 community qa pilot task. *The 8th NTCIR Workshop*, 2010.

[10] B. John, C. A. Yeow-Kuan, and G. D. Hoe-Lian. What makes a high quality user-generated answer? *IEEE Internet Computing*, 2010.

[11] P. Jurczyk and E. Agichtein. Discovering authorities in question answer communities by using link analysis. In *CIKM*, 2007.

[12] J. Liu, Y.-I. Song, and C.-Y. Lin. Competition-based user expertise score estimation. In *SIGIR*, 2011.

[13] A. Pal and J. A. Konstan. Expert identification in community question answering: exploring question selection bias. In *CIKM*, 2010.

[14] T. Sakai, D. Ishikawa, N. Kando, Y. Seki, K. Kuriyama, and C.-Y. Lin. Using graded-relevance metrics for evaluating community qa answer selection. In *WSDM*, 2011.

[15] M. Surdeanu, M. Ciaramita, and H. Zaragoza. Learning to rank answers on large online qa collections. In *ACL-HLT*, 2008.

[16] M. A. Suryanto, E. P. Lim, A. Sun, and R. H. L. Chiang. Quality-aware collaborative question answering: methods and evaluation. In *WSDM*, 2009.

[17] X.-J. Wang, X. Tu, D. Feng, and L. Zhang. Ranking community answers by modeling question-answer relationships via analogical reasoning. In *SIGIR*, 2009.

[18] J. Zhang, M. S. Ackerman, and L. Adamic. Expertise networks in online communities: structure and algorithms. In *WWW*, 2007.

Category Hierarchy Maintenance: a Data-Driven Approach

Quan Yuan[†], Gao Cong[†], Aixin Sun[†], Chin-Yew Lin[‡], Nadia Magnenat-Thalmann[†]
[†]School of Computer Engineering, Nanyang Technological University, Singapore 639798
{qyuan1@e., gaocong@, axsun@, nadiathalmann@}ntu.edu.sg
[‡]Microsoft Research Asia, Beijing, China 100080
{cyl@microsoft.com}

ABSTRACT

Category hierarchies often evolve at a much slower pace than the documents reside in. With newly available documents kept adding into a hierarchy, new topics emerge and documents within the same category become less topically cohesive. In this paper, we propose a novel automatic approach to modifying a given category hierarchy by redistributing its documents into more topically cohesive categories. The modification is achieved with three operations (namely, *sprout*, *merge*, and *assign*) with reference to an auxiliary hierarchy for additional semantic information; the auxiliary hierarchy covers a similar set of topics as the hierarchy to be modified. Our user study shows that the modified category hierarchy is semantically meaningful. As an extrinsic evaluation, we conduct experiments on document classification using real data from Yahoo! Answers and AnswerBag hierarchies, and compare the classification accuracies obtained on the original and the modified hierarchies. Our experiments show that the proposed method achieves much larger classification accuracy improvement compared with several baseline methods for hierarchy modification.

Categories and Subject Descriptors

H.3.3 [**Information Storage and Retrieval**]: Information Filtering

Keywords

Category Hierarchy, Hierarchy Maintenance, Classification

1. INTRODUCTION

With the exponential growth of textual information accessible, category hierarchy becomes one of the most widely-adopted and effective solutions in organizing large volume of documents. Hierarchy provides an organization of data by different levels of abstraction, in which each node (or category) represents a topic that is shared by the data in it. The connection between two nodes denotes supertype-subtype relation. Examples include Web directories provided by Yahoo! and Open Directory Project (ODP), hierarchies for community-based question-answering services by Yahoo! Answers (YA) and AnswerBag (AB), product hierarchies by online retailers like Amazon and eBay, as well as the hierarchies for news browsing at many news portal websites. Figure 1 shows a small portion of Yahoo! Answers hierarchy. Questions in the same category are usually relevant to the same topic.

Hierarchy enables not only easy document browsing, but also searching of the documents within user defined categories or subtrees of categories. Additionally, hierarchy information can be utilized to enhance retrieval models to improve the search accuracy [4]. On the other hand, users' information needs can only be satisfied with *the documents* accessible through the hierarchy (but not the category hierarchy itself). That is, the usefulness of a hierarchy heavily relies on the effectiveness of the hierarchy in properly organizing the existing data, and more importantly accommodating the newly available data into the hierarchy. Given the fast growth of text data, continuously accommodating large volume of newly available text data into a hierarchy is nontrivial. Automatic text classification techniques are often employed for efficient categorization of newly available documents into category hierarchies. However, hierarchy often evolves at a much slower pace than its documents. Two major problems often arise after adding many documents into a hierarchy after some time.

- *Structure Irrelevance.* A category hierarchy may well reflect the topical distribution of its data at the time of construction. However, as new topics always emerge from the newly coming documents, there is no proper category in the hierarchy to accommodate these new documents, leading to putting these documents in less relevant categories. As the result, some categories contain less topically cohesive documents. Moreover, some categories become less discriminative with respect to the current data distribution. One example is the two categories Printers and Scanners in YA, for there emerged many questions about multi-functional devices which are related to both printers and scanners, leading to ambiguity between these two categories.

- *Semantics Irrelevance.* Semantics may change over time which calls for a better organization of the documents [17]. For instance, when creating the hierarchy, experts are more likely to put category Petroleum under Geography. However, after the disaster of BP Gulf Oil Spill, a lot of news articles in category Petroleum are about the responsibility of the Obama Administration. These documents have stronger connection to category Politics than Geography. It is therefore more reasonable to put these documents under Politics for better document organization.

These two problems not only hurt user experiences in accessing information through the hierarchy, but also result in poorer classification accuracy for the classifiers categorizing newly available documents because of the less topically cohesive categories [15].

SIGIR'12, August 12–16, 2012, Portland, Oregon, USA.

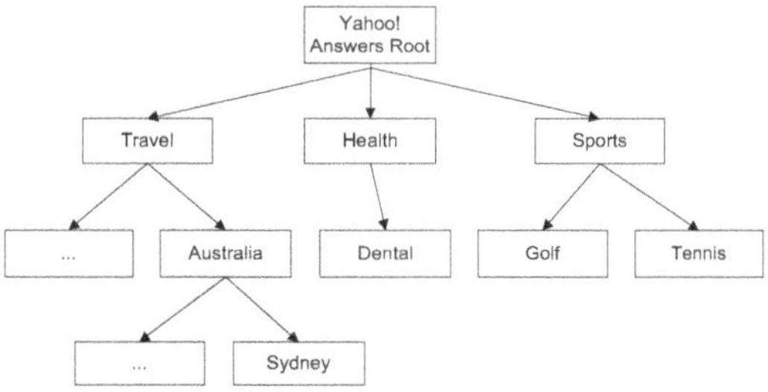

Figure 1: Portion of Yahoo! Answers Hierarchy

Consequently, the poorer classification accuracy further hurts user experience in browsing and searching documents through the hierarchy. This calls for ***category hierarchy maintenance**, a task to modify the hierarchy to make it better reflect the topics of its documents, which in turn would improve the classification accuracy.* Although a category hierarchy is relatively stable, many websites have modified or adjusted their hierarchies in the past. In May 2007, Yahoo! Answers added a new category Environment into her hierarchy, and added several categories like Facebook and Google under Internet later. By comparison, eBay adjusted her hierarchy more frequently, because there always emerge new types of items, like tablets and eReaders.

Hierarchy modification is nontrivial. Manual modification of category hierarchy is a tedious and difficult task, because it is hard to detect the semantic changes as well as the newly emerged topics. This motivates the *data-driven automatic modification* of a given hierarchy to cope with semantic changes and newly emerged topics. This is a challenging task because of at least two reasons, among others. First, the *resultant modified category hierarchy* (hereafter called **modified hierarchy** for short) should largely retain the semantics of the existing hierarchy and keep its category labels semantically meaningful. Second, the categories in the modified hierarchy shall demonstrate much higher topical cohesiveness, which in turn enables better classification accuracy in putting new documents into the modified hierarchy.

To the best of our knowledge, very few work has addressed the hierarchy modification problem (see Section 2). Tang *et al.* propose a novel approach to modifying the relations between categories aiming to improve the classification accuracy [17]. However, their proposed method does not change the leaf categories of the given hierarchy, and thus cannot solve the aforementioned problems. For example, the method may move the leaf category Petroleum to be child category of Politics. However, it is more reasonable to partition the documents in Petroleum into two categories: one being the child category of Geography, and the other child category of Politics. The method [17] fails to do so since it is unable to detect the newly emerged hidden topic "Petroleum politics".

In this paper, we propose a data-driven approach to modify a given hierarchy (also called as the original hierarchy) with reference to an auxiliary hierarchy using three operations (namely, *sprout*, *merge*, and *assign*). An auxiliary hierarchy is a category hierarchy that covers a similar set of topics as does the given hierarchy (*e.g.*, the Yahoo! hierarchy and ODP can be used as auxiliary hierarchy to each other). Similar to the concept of bisociation [8], our approach discovers finer and more elaborate categories (also known as hidden topics) by projecting the documents in the given hierarchy to the auxiliary hierarchy. This operation, similar to a cross-product operation between the categories from the given hierarchy and the categories from the auxiliary hierarchy, is named *sprout* [1]. The similar hidden topics are then *merged* to form new categories in the modified hierarchy. The *assign* operation rebuilds the parent-child relations in the modified hierarchy. The category labels in the modified hierarchy are either borrowed from or generated based on both the original and the auxiliary hierarchies. We emphasize that the reuse of category labels from original and auxiliary hierarchies largely ensures semantically meaningful category labels in the modified hierarchy. When such an auxiliary hierarchy is unavailable, the given hierarchy can be used as an auxiliary hierarchy. Because of the three operations (*i.e., sprout, merged*, and *assign*), we name our approach the *SMA* approach. The main contributions are summarized as follows.

1) We propose a novel data-driven approach *SMA* to automatically modify a category hierarchy making it better reflect the topics of its documents. The proposed approach exploits the semantics of the given hierarchy and an auxiliary hierarchy, to guide the modification of the given hierarchy.

2) We evaluate the proposed approach using data from three real-world hierarchies, Yahoo! Answers, Answerbag, and ODP. The user study shows that the modified hierarchy fits with the data better than the original one does. As we argue that the categories in the modified hierarchy are more topically cohesive compared to the original hierarchy, we employ text classification as an extrinsic evaluation. Our experimental results show that the classifiers trained on the modified hierarchy achieve much higher classification accuracy (measured by both macro-F_1 and micro-F_1), than the classifier built on the original hierarchy, or the classifiers modeled on the hierarchies generated by three baseline methods, including the state-of-the-art method in [17] and the hierarchy generation method in [2].

The rest of this paper is organized as follows. Section 2 surveys the related work. We describe the research problem and overview the proposed approach in Section 3. The three operations are detailed in Section 4. The experimental evaluation and discussion of the results are presented in Section 5. Finally, we conclude this paper in Section 6.

2. RELATED WORK

Hierarchy Generation. Hierarchy generation focuses on extracting a hierarchical structure from a set of categories, each containing a set of documents. The generation process can be either fully automatic [2, 5, 11] or semi-automatic [1, 7, 22]. The semi-automatic approaches involve interaction with domain experts in the hierarchy generation process. In the following, we review the fully automatic approaches in more detail.

Aggarwal *et al.* use the category labels of documents to supervise hierarchy generation [2]. They first calculate the centroids of all categories and use them as the initial seeds. Similar categories are merged and clusters with few documents are discarded. The process is iterated to build the hierarchy. User study is employed to evaluate the quality of the generated hierarchy.

Punera *et al.* utilizes a divisive hierarchical clustering approach, which first splits the given set of categories into two sets of categories, and each such set is partitioned recursively until it contains only one category [11].

An algorithm for generating hierarchy for short text is proposed by Chuang *et al.* [5]. They first create a binary-tree hierarchy by hierarchical agglomerative clustering, and then construct a multi-way-tree hierarchy from the binary-tree hierarchy. They use both classification measurement and user evaluation to evaluate the generated hierarchy.

Recently, Qi *et al.* employ genetic algorithms to generate hierarchy [12]. Given a set of leaf categories, a group of hierarchies are randomly generated as seeds, and genetic operators are applied

[1] We would like to thank an anonymous reviewer for suggesting the connection with bisociation [8] and the name *sprout*

to each hierarchy to generate new ones. The newly generated hierarchies are evaluated and the hierarchies with poor classification accuracy are removed. The process is repeated until the classification accuracy is not improved.

Different from hierarchy generation which assumes a set of categories as input, our hierarchy modification method takes a hierarchy as the input. Hierarchy generation does not change the given categories hence it cannot solve the structure irrelevance problem.

Hierarchy Modification. Tang *et al.* present a method of modifying a hierarchy to improve the classification accuracy [17]. The method introduces three operations. The *promote* operation lifts a category to upper level; the *merge* operation generates a new parent for a category and its most similar sibling; the *demote* operation either demotes a category as a child of its most similar sibling, or makes the sibling a child of the category. For each category in the given hierarchy, promote operation is tested, followed by merge and demote operations, in a top-down manner. The operation comes into effect if it can improve the classification accuracy. The approach iterates the process until no improvement can be observed or some criterion is met. In experiments, this method outperforms clustering-based hierarchy generation method in terms of classification accuracy. However, this method does not change the leaf categories, leaving the topically incohesive leaf categories untouched. In addition, the method [17] has a high time-complexity. Due to the high time complexity of the method [17], Kiyoshi *et al.* propose an approach [10] to addressing the efficiency issue.

Discussion. With the existing work on either hierarchy generation or hierarchy modification, the leaf categories in the modified hierarchy (*i.e.*, either generated or modified) remain unchanged. Clearly, without changing leaf categories, the topical incohesiveness among documents in the same leaf category remains unaddressed. Consequently, the likely poorer classification accuracy for these topically incohesive categories results in poorer document organization in the hierarchy. In this paper, we therefore propose an automatic approach to modify a given hierarchy where the leaf categories could be split or merged so as to better reflect the topics of the documents in the hierarchy.

3. SMA APPROACH OVERVIEW

We observe that each category in a hierarchy may contain several "hidden topics", each of which is topically cohesive, *e.g.*, category Computer contains hidden topics like Internet Programming, Operating Systems, etc. With more documents adding to a category hierarchy, new "hidden topics" emerge within a single category leading to topical incohesiveness among its documents (see Section 1). Our proposed approach, therefore, aims to find the hidden topics within each category and then *sprout* categories based on its hidden topics, *merge* similar hidden topics to form new categories, and then *assign* the parent-child relation among categories. We name our approach ***SMA*** after its three major operations.

The key challenges in the approach include: (i) How to detect the "hidden topics" at the appropriate granularity? (ii) How to evaluate the similarity between "hidden topics"? and (iii) How to assign the parent-child relation between the unmodified and modified categories? Further, recall from Section 1, the modified hierarchy has to largely retain the semantics of the existing hierarchy, with meaningful category labels and topically cohesive categories. In the following, we give a high-level overview of the SMA approach and then detail the three major operations in the next Section.

The framework of our SMA algorithm is illustrated in both Figure 2 and Algorithm 1, where $\mathcal{H}_c$ is the category hierarchy to be modified, $\mathcal{H}_n$ is the modified hierarchy, $\mathcal{H}_n'$ is the intermediate hierarchy during the modification process, and $\mathcal{H}_a$ is the auxiliary hierarchy.

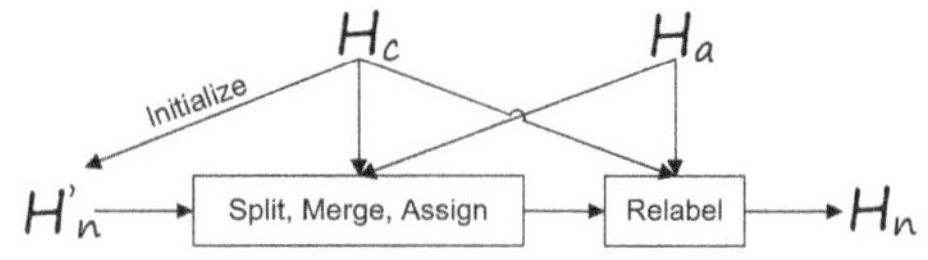

Figure 2: Overview of SMA

Algorithm 1: SMA algorithm for hierarchy modification

Input: $\mathcal{H}_c$: category hierarchy to be modified
$\mathcal{H}_a$: auxiliary hierarchy
λ: minimum coverage ratio
θ: maximum loss ratio
Output: $\mathcal{H}_n$: modified category hierarchy

1 $\mathcal{H}_n' \leftarrow \mathcal{H}_c$;
2 $h \leftarrow$ number of levels of $\mathcal{H}_c$;
3 **foreach** *Level ℓ from 2 to h of $\mathcal{H}_n'$* **do**
4   **foreach** *Category C_i of $\mathcal{H}_n'$ on level ℓ* **do**
5     $\Phi_{C_i} \leftarrow$ `ProjectedCategories`$(C_i, \mathcal{H}_a, \lambda, \theta)$;
6   `Sprout`$(C_i, \Phi_{C_i}, \mathcal{H}_n', \mathcal{H}_a)$;
7   $n_\ell \leftarrow$ number of categories on level ℓ of $\mathcal{H}_c$;
8   Merge$(\ell, n_\ell, \mathcal{H}_n')$;
9   `Assign`$(\ell, \mathcal{H}_n')$;
10 $\mathcal{H}_n \leftarrow$ `Relabel`$(\mathcal{H}_c, \mathcal{H}_a, \mathcal{H}_n')$;
11 **return** $\mathcal{H}_n$

Auxiliary Hierarchy. Briefly introduced in Section 1, an auxiliary hierarchy $\mathcal{H}_a$ is a hierarchy covering similar topics as the given hierarchy $\mathcal{H}_c$. For example, Yahoo! hierarchy and ODP hierarchy can be auxiliary hierarchy to each other. Similarly, Yahoo! Answers and AnswerBag can be auxiliary hierarchy to each other.

The auxiliary hierarchy $\mathcal{H}_a$ plays an essential role in finding hidden topics. Note that the hidden topics are not readily present in the auxiliary hierarchy, and our approach does not simply use the structure of auxiliary hierarchy as part of the modified hierarchy. Instead, they contain semantics from both the original hierarchy and the auxiliary hierarchy. We use the following example to illustrate. Suppose that the original hierarchy has two categories, Action movie and Comedy movie, and the auxiliary hierarchy contains two categories America and Asia. Our approach will find that Action movie has two hidden topics, namely American action movie and Asian active movie; Comedy movie also has two hidden topics, namely American comedy movie and Asian comedy movie.

The auxiliary hierarchy also plays an important role in guiding the merge operation, which is to merge similar hidden topics to generate the categories of the modified hierarchy. Continue with the earlier example, after merging the generated hidden topics, we may get new categories–American movie and Asian movie (if "action vs. comedy" is evaluated to be less discriminative compared with "American vs. Asian"). The semantics of the hierarchy to be modified, together with the semantics of the auxiliary hierarchy, will be exploited to define the similarity between hidden topics.

Validated in our experiments (Section 5), our approach is equally applicable when the original hierarchy $\mathcal{H}_c$ is used as the auxiliary hierarchy to itself.

Algorithm Overview. Shown in Figure 2 and Algorithm 1, $\mathcal{H}_n'$ is first initialized to $\mathcal{H}_c$ (line 1). In a top-down manner, the SMA algorithm modifies the hierarchy level by level. Note that the root category is the only category at level 1. Starting from level 2, for each category C_i in this level, the documents contained in C_i is projected to the auxiliary hierarchy $\mathcal{H}_a$. A set of categories from $\mathcal{H}_a$ each of which contains a reasonable number of documents originally from C_i is identified to represent C_i's hidden topics (line 5). The two parameters, minimum coverage ratio λ and maximum loss ratio θ, adjust the number of hidden topics. New finer categories are then *sprouted* from C_i according to the hidden topics and the documents in category C_i are assigned to these finer categories (or hidden topics) (line 6). Given the expected number of categories n_ℓ on level ℓ (line 7), the *merge* operation forms n_ℓ number of new categories on level ℓ of the intermediate hierarchy $\mathcal{H}'_n$ (line 8). If the current level is not the lowest level in the hierarchy, the parent-child relations between the modified categories and the unmodified categories on the next level are assigned (line 9). The last step in the SMA algorithm is to generate category labels with reference to both the original and auxiliary hierarchies (line 10).

4. SPROUT, MERGE, AND ASSIGN

We detail the three operations to address the challenges in the SMA framework (*i.e.,* to identify hidden topics, evaluate the similarity between hidden topics, and assign the parent-child relation).

4.1 Sprout Operation

The sprout operation first discovers the hidden topics for the documents in a category C_i and then sprouts the category. Without loss of generalization, a leaf category is represented by all documents belonging to the category; a non-leaf category is represented by all documents belonging to any of its descendent categories.

4.1.1 Discovery of Hidden Topics

Ideally, for a category we find a set of its hidden topics, which are comprehensive and cohesive, and have no overlap. This is however a challenging task. We proceed to give an overview of the proposed method. Given a category C_i in the intermediate hierarchy $\mathcal{H}'_n$ during the modification process (see Algorithm 1), we assign all its documents into the categories of the auxiliary hierarchy $\mathcal{H}_a$, and get a set of candidate categories from $\mathcal{H}_a$ in a tree-structure. Each candidate category contains a number of documents from C_i. Then, with the consideration of both cohesion and separation, we select a set of categories from the tree as hidden topics. The selection process is modeled as an optimization problem. We now elaborate the details.

Document Projection. To assign documents from C_i to $\mathcal{H}_a$, we represent a document by its word feature vector, and a category in $\mathcal{H}_a$ by its centroid vector. Based on cosine similarity between the document and the centroids, we recursively assign each document $d \in C_i$ to $\mathcal{H}_a$ from its root to a leaf category along a single path of categories. If a good number of documents from C_i are assigned to a category C_a in $\mathcal{H}_a$, then the topic of C_a is relevant to C_i, and the semantics of C_a can be used to describe a hidden topic of C_i. Thus, multiple categories in C_a can be identified to describe all hidden topics of C_i. For example, large number of documents from category Programming assigned into two categories Security and Network in an auxiliary hierarchy, implies that Programming has two hidden topics: Network Programming and Security Programming. We have also tried to build a classifier on $\mathcal{H}_a$ to assign documents from C_i to $\mathcal{H}_a$ using Naive Bayes and support vector machine, respectively, and the set of generated hidden topics is almost the same.

The process of assigning documents from a category C_i in $\mathcal{H}'_n$ to categories in $\mathcal{H}_a$ is called *projection*. We denote the set of documents *projected* from category C_i to category C_a by $\pi(C_i \to C_a)$. If C_a is a leaf category, then $\pi(C_i \to C_a)$ denotes the set of documents from C_i that are projected into C_a; if C_a is a non-leaf category, then $\pi(C_i \to C_a)$ denotes the set of documents projected into any of the descendent leaf categories of C_a in $\mathcal{H}_a$.

Candidate Topic Tree. Based on the projection, we select categories from $\mathcal{H}_a$ to represent the hidden topics of C_i. A selected category can be either a leaf category or a non-leaf category. Before describing the selection process, we introduce the notions of *major category* and *minor category*. Let λ denote the *minimum coverage ratio* parameter.

Definition 1 **(Major Category).** *A category C_a from $\mathcal{H}_a$ is a major category for category C_i if $|\pi(C_i \to C_a)|/|C_i| \geq \lambda$.*

Definition 2 **(Minor Category).** *A category C_a from $\mathcal{H}_a$ is a minor category for category C_i if $|\pi(C_i \to C_a)|/|C_i| < \lambda$.*

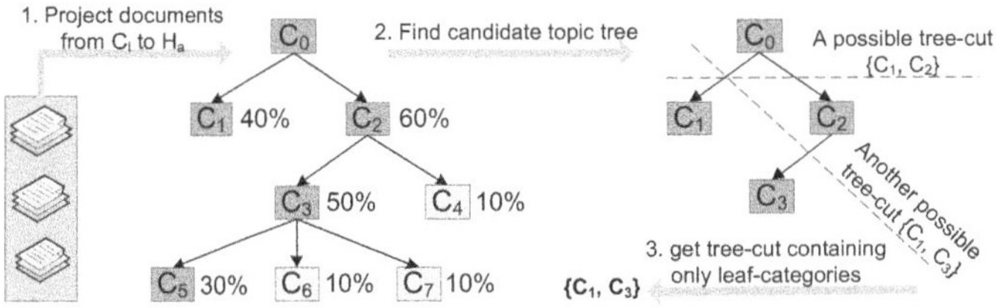

Figure 3: Generate candidate topic tree for C_i using $\mathcal{H}_a$

For example, suppose $\lambda = 15\%$. As shown in Figure 3, category C_i is projected to the categories in $\mathcal{H}_a$. In the left tree, in which each number besides a node represents the percentage of documents of C_i projected to the node, the nodes in dark color are major categories while the others are minor categories.

Naturally, only the major categories are considered candidate categories to represent hidden topics of C_i because a good number of documents in C_i are projected into them. However, not all major categories need to be selected because of two reasons. First, let C_p be the parent of a major category C_a. By definition, the parent of a major category is also a major category. Selecting both C_a and C_p would lead to semantic overlap. Second, assume all C_p's other child categories are minor categories, but altogether those minor categories contain a large number of documents. Then selecting C_a but not C_p would lead to a significant loss of documents from C_i (hence semantic loss). We therefore define the notion of *loss ratio*.

Definition 3 **(Loss Ratio).** *The loss ratio of a leaf category is defined as 0. For a non-leaf category C_a, let C_a^μ be the set of minor categories among C_a's child categories. The loss ratio of C_a with respect to C_i, the category being projected, is the ratio between the projected documents in all its child minor categories and C_a's projected documents,* i.e., $\frac{\sum_{C' \in C_a^\mu} |\pi(C_i \to C')|}{|\pi(C_i \to C_a)|}$.

We set a threshold *maximum loss ratio* θ. After projecting documents from C_i to categories in $\mathcal{H}_a$, we only keep the major categories whose parent's loss ratio is smaller than θ. Note that, if a non-leaf category is not selected in the above process, the subtree rooted at this category is not selected. After the selection, we obtain a sub-hierarchy from $\mathcal{H}_a$ containing only eligible major categories, which is called *candidate topic tree* for C_i, denoted by $\mathcal{T}_{C_i}$.

For example, suppose $\theta = 30\%$. The *candidate topic tree* for C_i is shown on the right hand side of Figure 3. Although node C_5 is a major category, it is not part of the *candidate topic tree* since the loss ratio ((10%+10%)/50% = 40%) of its parent node C_3 is larger than θ.

Hidden Topic Selection. We next present how to choose a set of nodes from $\mathcal{T}_{C_i}$ to represent hidden topics of C_i. Ideally, we expect the hidden topics to be comprehensive but not overlap with each other. Hence, we use *tree-cut* to define the selection [18].

DEFINITION 4 (**Tree-Cut**). *A tree-cut is a partition of a tree. It is a list of nodes in the tree, and each node represents a set of all leaf nodes in a subtree rooted by the node. The sets in a tree-cut exhaustively cover all leaf nodes of the tree, and they are mutually disjoint.*

There exist many possible tree-cuts for $\mathcal{T}_{C_i}$ to generate hidden topics. Two example tree cuts for the *candidate topic tree* in Figure 3 are $\{C_1, C_2\}$ and $\{C_1, C_3\}$. Among all possible tree-cuts, we aim to choose the tree-cut such that each resultant hidden topic (category) is cohesive and well separated from other categories in the tree-cut. In the following, we prove that the tree-cut containing only leaf nodes of the *candidate topic tree* satisfies this requirement. Note that a leaf node in $\mathcal{T}_{C_i}$ is not necessary a leaf category in $\mathcal{H}_a$. For example, in Figure 3, C_3 is leaf node of the candidate topic tree, but not a leaf category in the auxiliary hierarchy.

We proceed to show the proof. We first define the Sum of Square Error (SSE) of cohesion for a category C_a.

$$SSE(C_a) = \sum_{d \in C_a} (d - \overline{c_a})^2,$$

where d is a document and $\overline{c_a}$ is the centroid of category C_a.

Given a set of categories $\{C_a\}$ ($1 \le a \le k$), the Total-SSE and Total Sum of Square Between (Total-SSB), denoted by ε_E and ε_B respectively, are $\varepsilon_E = \sum_{a=1}^{k} SSE(C_a)$ and $\varepsilon_B = \sum_{a=1}^{k} |C_a|(\overline{c} - \overline{c_a})^2$, where $\overline{c}$ is the centroid of documents in all categories $\{C_a\}$. It is verified that, given a set of documents, the sum of ε_E and ε_B is a constant value [16]: $\varepsilon_E + \varepsilon_B = \sum_{a=1}^{k} \sum_{d \in C_a} (d - \overline{c})^2$. Thus, maximizing separation is equivalent to minimizing cohesion error. We therefore formulate the problem of selecting categories from $\mathcal{T}_{C_i}$ to represent hidden topics for category C_i as following:

$$\Phi_{C_i} = \arg\min_{S} \sum_{C_a \in S} SSE(C_a), \text{ where } S \text{ is a tree-cut on } \mathcal{T}_{C_i}. \quad (1)$$

This problem can be reduced to the maximum flow problem by viewing $\mathcal{T}_{C_i}$ as a flow network. Thus, it can be solved directly by Ford-Fulkerson method [6]. However, its complexity is relatively high. Note that we need to solve the optimization problem for every category in the original hierarchy, and thus an efficient algorithm is essential.

Lemma 1: The SSE of a category is not smaller than the Total-SSE of its child categories.

Proof: Suppose there is a category C_p with k child categories $\{C_i\}_{i=1}^{k}$. For a child category C_i, the Sum of Square Distance (SSD) of its data to a data point x is: $SSD(C_i) = \sum_{d \in C_i} (d - x)^2$. We get the minimum value when $x = \frac{1}{|C_i|} \sum_{d \in C_i} d = \overline{c}_i$ which let $\frac{\mathrm{d}}{\mathrm{d}x} \sum_{d \in C_i} (d - x)^2 = 0$. Thus, when x is the mean of data in C_i (or $\overline{c}_i$), the SSD of C_i becomes SSE of C_i, and gets its minimum value. One step further, we have

$$\sum_{d \in C_i} (d - \overline{c}_i)^2 \le \sum_{d \in C_i} (d - \overline{c}_p)^2,$$

where $\overline{c}_p$ is the mean of data of C_p. This demonstrates that the SSE of C_i is smaller than the SSD of data of C_i to the overall mean, and this result leads to

$$\sum_{i=1}^{k} \sum_{d \in C_i} (d - \overline{c}_i)^2 \le \sum_{i=1}^{k} \sum_{d \in C_i} (d - \overline{c}_p)^2.$$

This demonstrates that the SSE of a category is not smaller than the Total-SSE of its child categories.

Procedure `ProjectedCategories`

Input: C_i: the category to be sprouted
$\mathcal{H}_a$: the auxiliary hierarchy
λ: minimum coverage ratio
θ: maximum loss ratio

Result: $\Phi_{C_i}[]$: the list of projected categories for C_i

1 $\Phi_{C_i}[] \leftarrow$ {root category of $\mathcal{H}_a$};
2 **repeat**
3 $\quad C_a \leftarrow \Phi_{C_i}[]$.getNextUnprocessedCategory();
4 $\quad$ *C_List*[] ← child categories of C_a;
5 $\quad$ *M_List*[] ← {};
6 $\quad$ **foreach** *Category C of C_List*[] **do**
7 $\quad\quad$ **if** $\frac{|\pi(C_i \to C)|}{|C_i|} \ge \lambda$ **then**
8 $\quad\quad\quad$ *M_List*[].add(C);
9 $\quad$ **if** $1 - \frac{\sum_{C \in M\_List[]} |\pi(C_i \to C)|}{|\pi(C_i \to C_a)|} < \theta$ **then**
10 $\quad\quad \Phi_{C_i}[]$.add(*M_List*[]);
11 $\quad\quad \Phi_{C_i}[]$.remove(C_a);
12 $\quad$ **else**
13 $\quad\quad$ mark C_a as processed
14 **until** *No more unprocessed category in* $\Phi_{C_i}[]$
15 **return** $\Phi_{C_i}[]$

Lemma 1 enables us to use an efficient method to solve Eq.1 as follows. According to Lemma 1, specializing a category by its child categories can reduce Total-SSE. That is, among all possible tree-cuts in $\mathcal{T}_{C_i}$, the cut that contains only leaf categories has the minimum value of Total-SSE.

In summary, for a category C_i in $\mathcal{H}'_n$, we build a candidate topic tree $\mathcal{T}_{C_i}$ and the leaf nodes of $\mathcal{T}_{C_i}$ are used to represent the hidden topics of C_i. The pseudocode is given in Procedure 2 ProjectedCategories. As discussed, according to Lemma 1, we only need the leaf nodes of the candidate topic tree $\mathcal{T}_{C_i}$ as the result. Instead of explicitly building $\mathcal{T}_{C_i}$ and then finding $\mathcal{T}_{C_i}$'s tree cut containing only leaf nodes, we find $\mathcal{T}_{C_i}$'s leaf nodes directly in our procedure. More specifically, we start from the root category of $\mathcal{H}_a$ in a top-down manner (the root node is a major category by definition as its coverage ratio is 1). Each time we get a unprocessed categories C_a from the list of projected categories $\Phi_{C_i}[]$, and check its child categories (lines 3-4). The major categories among the child categories are put into a major category list (lines 6-8) for further testing on loss ratio. If the loss ratio of C_a is smaller than maximum loss ratio θ, then C_a is replaced by its child major categories (lines 9-11); otherwise, C_a is selected as a candidate category (line 13). We iterate the process until all major categories are processed (line 14).

4.1.2 Sprout Category

For a category C_i of $\mathcal{H}'_n$, we sprout it based on the projected categories Φ_{C_i} returned by Procedure ProjectedCategories. Recall that each of the projected category $C_a \in \Phi_{C_i}$ represents a hidden topic of C_i and contains a good number of documents projected from C_i, *i.e.*, $\pi(C_i \to C_a)$. We sprout C_i with $|\Phi_{C_i}|$ number of categories. However, not all documents from C_i are contained in all these newly sprouted categories, *i.e.*, $\sum_{C_a \in \Phi_{C_i}} |\pi(C_i \to C_a)| \le |C_i|$. For those documents in C_i but not contained in any of the newly sprouted categories, we assign them to their nearest sprouted categories. As the result, each document in C_i is now contained in one and only one sprouted category of C_i.

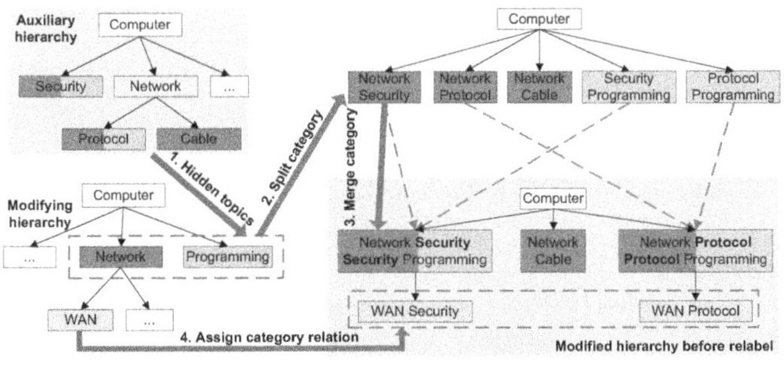

Figure 4: SMA operations by example. The hidden topics and sprouted categories for a category of the original hierarchy are in the same color. The Network and Programming categories have 3 and 2 hidden topics, respectively, leading to 5 sibling sprouted categories. These 5 categories are merged into 3 categories and the category WAN is reassigned to 2 of the merged categories.

Example 4.1: Shown in Figure 4[2], suppose after applying procedure ProjectedCategories, we find Network is projected to Security, Protocol, and Cable. According to the three hidden topics, we sprout Network into three categories Network Security, Network Protocol, and Network Cable. □

The sprout operation may be reminiscent of the work on hierarchy integration, aiming to integrate a category from a source hierarchy into similar categories in the target hierarchy, which has a different purpose from our mapping. Most of proposals (e.g., [3,21]) on hierarchy integration employ a hierarchical classifier built on the target hierarchy to classify each document in the source hierarchy into a leaf node of the target hierarchy, which is too fine a granularity to represent hidden topics as in our approach. Frameworks that can map a category to categories on proper levels in target hierarchy are proposed (*e.g.,* [19]). However, they do not take the cohesion and separation between mapping categories into account, which are essential to find good hidden topics in our approach. Thus, they cannot be applied to our work.

4.2 Merge Operation

The sprout operation in Section 4.1 generates a set of sprouted categories, each representing a hidden topic. The merge operation aims to combine the newly sprouted categories with similar hidden topics.

Suppose we are now working on level ℓ of the intermediate modified hierarchy $\mathcal{H}_n'$ and we have a set of sprouted categories originated from the categories on level ℓ. Our task is to merge some of these sprouted categories such that the number of resultant categories on level ℓ is the same as before (i.e., n_ℓ). Note that the number of resultant categories can also be specified by users. To ease the presentation, the modified hierarchy has the same size as the given hierarchy in our discussion.

During merge, we need to consider an important constraint — we can only merge categories under the same parent category. Thus, existing clustering algorithms need to be modified to accommodate such a constraint. Another key issue here is how to define the similarity between two sprouted categories by considering their semantics enclosed in $\mathcal{H}_c$ and $\mathcal{H}_a$. In the following, we first define a similarity measure and then describe our merge method.

We consider two aspects when defining the similarity for a pair of sprouted categories C_1 and C_2 on level ℓ: (i) the distribution of their documents over categories of $\mathcal{H}_c$ and $\mathcal{H}_a$, and (ii) the similarity between the categories within $\mathcal{H}_c$ and $\mathcal{H}_a$, respectively.

Let $\mathcal{L}_c$ be the set of categories on level ℓ in the original hierarch $\mathcal{H}_c$, $\mathcal{L}_s$ be the set of categories sprouted from $\mathcal{L}_c$, and $\mathcal{L}_a$ be the set of projected categories in auxiliary hierarchy representing the hidden topics of the categories in $\mathcal{L}_c$. That is, $\mathcal{L}_a = \bigcup_{C_i \in \mathcal{L}_c} \Phi_{C_i}$.

For a sprouted category $C_s \in \mathcal{L}_s$, its document distribution over $\mathcal{L}_c$ is defined to be the ratios of its documents in each of the categories in $\mathcal{L}_c$. That is, the document distribution of C_s can be modeled as a $|\mathcal{L}_c|$-dimensional vector $\mathbf{v_{cs}}$. The j-th element of $\mathbf{v_{cs}}$ is $\frac{|C_s \cap C_j|}{|C_s|}$ (*i.e.,* the portion of C_s's documents also contained in C_j), where C_j is the j-th category of $\mathcal{L}_c$. Similarly, we get the data distribution vector $\mathbf{v_{as}}$ for C_s over $\mathcal{L}_a$ based on the ratio of documents in C_s projected to each of the categories in $\mathcal{L}_a$. Because $\mathbf{v_{cs}}$ and $\mathbf{v_{as}}$ usually have different dimensionality for different sprouted category C_s's, we extend $\mathbf{v_{cs}}$ to be $|\mathcal{H}_c|$-dimensional (each category is one dimension) by filling up zeros for corresponding categories in $\mathcal{H}_c$ but not in $\mathcal{L}_c$. Similarly $\mathbf{v_{as}}$ is extended to be $|\mathcal{H}_a|$-dimensional.

We use two matrices $\mathbf{M_c}$, $\mathbf{M_a}$ to represent the similarity between categories of $\mathcal{H}_c$ and $\mathcal{H}_a$, respectively. $\mathbf{M_c}$ is a $|\mathcal{H}_c|$- by-$|\mathcal{H}_c|$ matrix and $\mathbf{M_a}$ is a $|\mathcal{H}_a|$-by-$|\mathcal{H}_a|$ matrix. Each element m_{ij} in a matrix represents the similarity in the corresponding hierarchy between a pair of categories C_i and C_j, which is defined by *Inverted Path Length* [14]: $m_{ij} = \frac{1}{1+path(C_i,C_j)}$, where $path(C_i, C_j)$ is the length of path between C_i and C_j in the hierarchy.

Considering both document distribution and structural similarity from the two hierarchies, the similarity between two sprouted categories C_1 and C_2 on level ℓ of $\mathcal{H}_n'$ is defined as:

$$Sim(C_1, C_2) = (\mathbf{v_{c1}^T} \cdot \mathbf{M_c} \cdot \mathbf{v_{c2}}) + (\mathbf{v_{a1}^T} \cdot \mathbf{M_a} \cdot \mathbf{v_{a2}}).$$

This similarity definition considers both the similarity estimated based on $\mathcal{H}_c$ and the similarity estimated based on $\mathcal{H}_a$. With similarity between two sprouted categories defined, we proceed to detail the merge operation.

We first explain the notion of *sibling sprouted category* through an example. Let C_{i1} and C_{i2} be the two categories sprouted from category C_i, and C_{j1} and C_{j2} be the two categories sprouted from C_j. If C_i and C_j in $\mathcal{H}_m'$ are both children of category C_p, then naturally, all the newly sprouted categories C_{i1}, C_{i2}, C_{j1}, C_{j2} are children of C_p. These four example categories are known as sibling sprouted categories. All the five sprouted categories shown in Figure 4 are sibling sprouted categories.

The merge operation is as follows. We first calculate the similarity between sibling sprouted categories on level ℓ. Then, we pick up the pair of categories with the largest similarity, and merge them into a category, and recompute its similarities with its sibling sprouted categories. The process iterates until the number of remaining categories on ℓ equals n_ℓ, the number of categories on level ℓ of the original hierarchy $\mathcal{H}_c$. When all the sibling sprouted categories under the same parent node are merged into a single category, we shrink the single category into its parent node. Note that we cannot merge two sprouted categories on level ℓ if they have different parent node.

Example 4.2: Recall Example 4.1. We sprout Network into three categories Network Security, Network Protocol, and Network Cable. Suppose there is another category Programming on the same level of Network and sprouted into Security Programming, and Protocol Programming (see Figure 4). Based on the similarity, Network Security and Security Programming are merged together (both are about the Security topic), and Network Protocol and Protocol Programming are merged to generate a new category about protocol. □

[2]For clarity, we recommend viewing all diagrams in this paper from a color copy.

4.3 Assign Operation

After modifying categories (by sprout and merge) on level ℓ of $\mathcal{H}'_n$, the original parent-child relations between the categories on level ℓ and the categories on next level $\ell+1$ do not hold any longer. Hence we need to reassign the parent-child relation.

Based on the fact that a non-leaf category of a hierarchy subsumes the data of all its descendants, we rebuild the children for each of the modified categories on ℓ by checking document containment. If the documents of a category on level ℓ are also contained in a category on level $\ell+1$, then the latter category is assigned to be the children of the former category. In other words, for each category C on ℓ, we calculate the intersection of documents between C and the categories on $\ell+1$. The intersections form new children for category C. Because one category has only one parent category, if a category has intersections with more than one category on level ℓ, the category will be split into multiple categories, each containing the intersection with one category on level ℓ.

Example 4.3: Recall Example 4.2. Suppose WAN was a child category of Network before sprout (see Figure 4). After sprout and merge, Network no longer exists and WAN lost its parent. We compare the documents of WAN and the two newly formed categories after merge (*i.e.,* Network Security & Security Programming and Network Protocol & Protocol Programming). If WAN has overlap with both categories, then WAN have two hidden topics (about security and protocol). Thus, we divide WAN into two categories and assign them to different parent nodes, shown in Figure 4. □

4.4 Relabel

Unlike most of previous work, our approach is able to automatically generate readable labels for every modified category. By projecting documents from $\mathcal{H}'_n$ to $\mathcal{H}_a$, we can consider the three hierarchies $\mathcal{H}'_n$, $\mathcal{H}_c$ and $\mathcal{H}_a$, which contain the same set of data. For every document in $\mathcal{H}'_n$, we trace its labels in $\mathcal{H}_c$ and $\mathcal{H}_a$, and use them together as the label of the document; the semantic of the new label is the intersection of semantics of its two component labels. We then aggregate such labels for all documents in a category of $\mathcal{H}'_n$, and use them as candidate labels for the category. The candidate labels for a category are ranked according to the proportion of documents in their corresponding original categories from $\mathcal{H}_c$ and $\mathcal{H}_a$. In this paper, the top-1 ranked label is chosen.

The labels generated in this way are mostly readable and semantically meaningful, as reflected in our user study (see Section 5.3) and case study (see Section 5.4). Nevertheless, a manual verification of the labels for the newly generated categories can be employed when the proposed technique is used in real applications.

5. EXPERIMENTS

We designed two sets of experiments. The first set of experiment, similar to that in [17], is to evaluate whether the modified hierarchy improves the classification accuracy. Discussed in Section 1, if a category hierarchy better reflects the topics of its contained documents and each category in the hierarchy is topically cohesive, then better classification accuracy is expected than that on a hierarchy with less topically cohesive categories. The second set of experiments employs a user study to manually evaluate the semantic quality of the modified hierarchy following the settings in [2,5]. Finally, we report a case study comparing a part of Yahoo! Answers hierarchy with its modified hierarchy.

5.1 Data Set

We use data from three real-world hierarchies: Yahoo! Answers, AnswerBag, Open Directory Project, denoted by $\mathcal{H}_{YA}$, $\mathcal{H}_{AB}$ and $\mathcal{H}_{ODP}$, respectively. Since the modified category hierarchy contains a different set of leaf nodes, the labels for documents given in the original dataset do not stand in modified hierarchy. Manual annotation of documents in the modified hierarchy is therefore unavoidable. To make the annotation manageable, we selected the documents from two major topics Sports and Computers from these three hierarchies (because the annotators are familiar with both topics). Nevertheless, the number of documents in the two major topics in the three hierarchies ranges from 148,822 to 421,163, and the number of categories ranges from 115 to 558. These numbers are large enough for a valid evaluation. Table 1 reports the statistics on the three hierarchies.

Table 1: Statistics of the three hierarchies

Hierarchy	$\mathcal{H}_{YA}$	$\mathcal{H}_{AB}$	$\mathcal{H}_{ODP}$
Number of documents	421,163	148,822	203,448
Number of leaf nodes	75	195	460
Number of non-leaf nodes	40	70	98
Height	4	5	4

$\mathcal{H}_{YA}$: Obtained from the Yahoo! Webscope datatset[3], $\mathcal{H}_{YA}$ contains 421,163 documents (or questions) from Sports and Computers & Internet categories.

$\mathcal{H}_{AB}$: We collected 148,822 questions from Recreation & Sports and Computers categories from AnswerBag to form $\mathcal{H}_{AB}$. Categories with fewer than 100 questions are pruned and all affected questions are moved to their parent categories.

$\mathcal{H}_{ODP}$: The set of 203,448 documents from Sports and Computers categories are collected[4] in $\mathcal{H}_{ODP}$. Categories containing fewer than 15 documents or located on level 5 or deeper are removed in our experiments.

The preprocessing of the documents in all three hierarchies includes stopword removal and stemming. Terms occurred no more than 3 times across the datasets are also removed.

5.2 Evaluation by Classification

The proposed SMA algorithm modifies a category hierarchy to better reflect the topics of its documents, which in turn should improve the classification performance. Following the experimental setting in [17], we evaluate the effectiveness of hierarchy modification by comparing the classification accuracies obtained by the same hierarchical classification model applied on the original category hierarchy and the modified hierarchy, respectively.

Another three methods for hierarchy modification are employed as the baselines, namely, Bottom Up Clustering (BUC), Hierarchical Acclimatization (HA) [17], and Supervised Clustering (SC) [2]. Table 2 gives a summarized comparison of the three baselines with the proposed SMA, and Section 5.2.1 briefs the baseline methods.

The modified hierarchies by all the methods evaluated in this paper have the same size as the original hierarchy (*i.e.,* same number of levels, and same number of categories in each level). For each hierarchy modification method, we evaluate the percentage of classification accuracy increment obtained by the same classification model (*e.g.,* Support Vector Machine) on the modified hierarchy over the original hierarchy. The classification accuracy is measured by both micro-average F_1 (Micro-F_1) and macro-averaged F_1 (Macro-F_1) [20]. The former gives equal weight to every document while the latter weighs categories equally regardless the number of documents in each category.

We remark that this is a fair evaluation for all the methods, each generating a hierarchy with the same size as that of the original

[3] Available at http://research.yahoo.com/Academic_Relations.

[4] Available at http://www.dmoz.org/rdf.html.

Table 2: Comparison of baseline methods with SMA

Aspect/Methods	BUC	HA [17]	SC [2]	SMA
Utilize original hierarchy	×	√	×	√
Change leaf category	×	×	√	√
Utilize auxiliary hierarchy	×	×	×	Optional

hierarchy, where the same classification method is applied to the modified hierarchies to evaluate the improvement of each modified hierarchy over the original one in terms of classification accuracy.

5.2.1 Baseline Methods

Baseline 1: Bottom Up Clustering (BUC). In this method, each leaf category is represented by the mean vector of its contained documents. The categories are then clustered in a bottom-up manner using K-means to form a hierarchy.

Baseline 2: Hierarchical Acclimatization (HA). The HA algorithm is reviewed in Section 2, In simple words, it employs promote, demote and merge operations to adjust the internal structure, but leaves the leaf nodes unchanged [17].

Baseline 3: Supervised Clustering (SC). Given a set of documents with labels, SC first calculates the mean vector of each category as the initial centroid and then reassigns the documents to the categories based on the cosine similarity with their centroids. Then, similar categories are merged and minor categories are removed. These procedures are repeated, and during each iteration, a constant portion of features with smallest term-frequencies are set to zero (projected out) [2]. The process stops when the number of features left is smaller than a pre-defined threshold. This method cannot generate category labels. We take the most frequent words in a category to name it.

5.2.2 Experiments on Yahoo! Answers

From the data of $\mathcal{H}_{YA}$, we randomly selected 500 questions as test data (used for classification evaluation with manual annotations). To evaluate the possible improvement in classification accuracy, the same set of test documents are classified on the original (or unmodified) $\mathcal{H}_{YA}$, and the modified $\mathcal{H}_{nYA}$'s. Two classifiers, multinominal Naive Bayes (NB) and Support Vector Machine (SVM) classifiers are used as base classifiers for hierarchical classification. We build Single Path Hierarchical Classifier (SPH) [9] as it performs better than other hierarchical classification methods for question classification according to the evaluation [13]. In the training phase of SPH, for each internal node of the category tree, SPH trains a classifier using the documents belonging to its descendent nodes. In the testing phase, a test document is classified from the root to a leaf node in the hierarchy along a single path.

SMA Settings. Recall that SMA uses auxiliary hierarchy in the modification process. We evaluated SMA with three settings, to modify $\mathcal{H}_{YA}$ using $\mathcal{H}_{YA}$, $\mathcal{H}_{AB}$, and $\mathcal{H}_{ODP}$ as auxiliary hierarchy, respectively. The three settings are denoted by $SMA_{YA|YA}$, $SMA_{YA|AB}$, and $SMA_{YA|ODP}$, respectively. The first setting is to evaluate the effectiveness of using the original hierarchy as auxiliary hierarchy, and the last two are to evaluate the effectiveness of using external hierarchies.

Parameter Setting. Before evaluating the test documents on the modified hierarchies, we set the parameters required by SMA for hierarchy modification. Recall that SMA requires two parameters: minimum coverage ratio λ and maximum loss ratio θ. Usually parameters are set using a development set or through cross-validation. In our case, however, there is no ground truth on how good a modified hierarchy is and manual assessment of every modified hierarchy for parameter tuning is impractical. We therefore adopt a bootstrapping like approach described below.

After the test data selected, the remaining data is used for hierarchy modification. We split the remaining data of $\mathcal{H}_{YA}$ into 3 parts: P_1, P_2, P_3, and the proportion of their sizes is 12:3:1. Using P_1 for $\mathcal{H}_{YA}$ and a given auxiliary hierarchy, we obtain a modified hierarchy $\mathcal{H}_{nYA}$. Naturally, all documents in P_1 have category labels from hierarchy $\mathcal{H}_{nYA}$. We then build a classifier using all documents in P_1 and their labels from $\mathcal{H}_{nYA}$. The classifier classifies documents in P_2 and P_3. Assume that the classifier gives reasonably good classification accuracy, then all documents in P_2 and P_3 have their category labels assigned according to $\mathcal{H}_{nYA}$. With these labels, we can evaluate the classification accuracy of documents in P_3 by the classifier built using P_2 on $\mathcal{H}_{nYA}$. Intuitively, if a hierarchy $\mathcal{H}_1$ better organizes documents than another hierarchy $\mathcal{H}_2$, then the classifier trained on $\mathcal{H}_1$ is expected to have higher classification accuracy for P_3 than a classifier built on $\mathcal{H}_2$. We then select the parameters leading to the best classification accuracy for P_3. In our experiments, the parameters (*i.e.*, λ and θ) set for $SMA_{YA|YA}$, $SMA_{YA|AB}$, and $SMA_{YA|ODP}$ are (0.29 and 0.11), (0.17 and 0.17), (0.38 and 0.08), respectively.

Test Data Annotation. With the chosen parameters, each SMA setting generated a modified hierarchy using P_1 as $\mathcal{H}_{YA}$ and its corresponding auxiliary hierarchy. The preselected 500 test questions are used as test data to fairly evaluate the modified hierarchies by the three SMA settings and the baseline methods. Recall that the 500 questions are not included in the three parts (P_1, P_2, and P_3) for parameter setting. Because BUC and HA do not change the leaf categories, the original labels of the 500 questions remain applicable. For SC and SMA, both changing leaf categories, we invited two annotators to label the 500 questions to their most relevant leaf categories in the modified hierarchies. We synthesized the results of the annotators, and assigned the labels for questions. If two annotators conflicted about a label, a third person made the final judgment. The dataset and their annotations are available online [5].

Classification Results. Classification accuracy measured by Micro-F_1 using NB and SVM as base classifiers for the six methods (*i.e.*, three baselines BUC, HA, SC, and the three SMA settings) on modified hierarchies is reported in Figure 5(a). For comparison, the classification accuracy on the original (or unmodified) Yahoo! Answers hierarchy is also reported under column named $\mathcal{H}_{YA}$. Figure 5(b) reports Macro-F_1.

As shown in Figures 5(a) and 5(b), all the three settings of SMA achieve significant improvement over the results obtained on the original hierarchy. For example, using NB as the base classifier, $SMA_{YA|YA}$ improves Micro-F_1 over the results on the original hierarchy by 41.0% and improves Macro-F_1 by 40.3%. NB achieves better accuracy than SVM probably because NB was used as the base classifier for parameter setting. The three baseline modification methods only slightly improve the classification accuracy over the original hierarchy and even deteriorate the accuracy in some cases. Recall that SC and SMA modify leaf categories while BUC and HA only modify internal structures of hierarchy without changing leaf categories. All the methods that change leaf categories outperform the methods that keep leaf categories unchanged. Note that $SMA_{YA|YA}$ significantly outperforms SC. One possible reason could be that $SMA_{YA|YA}$ utilizes the semantics of the original hierarchy in hierarchy modification while SC does not.

We observe that the auxiliary hierarchies employed by SMA have effect on the classification accuracy of the modified hierarchy.

[5]http://www.ntu.edu.sg/home/gaocong/datacode.htm

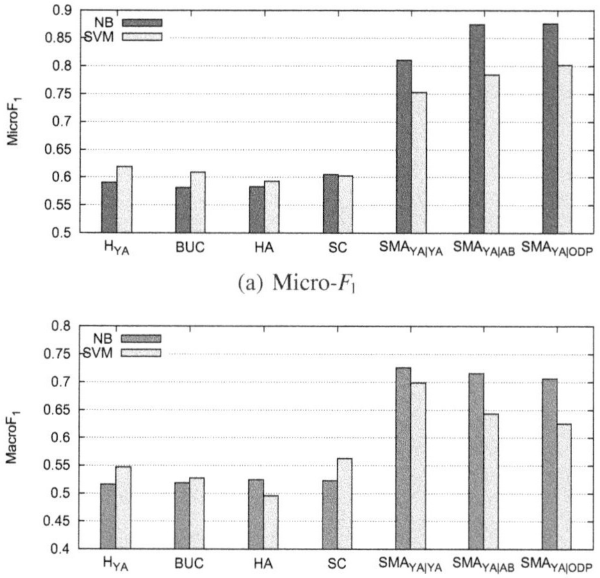

(a) Micro-F_1

(b) Macro-F_1

Figure 5: Micro-F_1 and Macro-F_1 on the modified hierarchies by three baselines and three SMA settings, and on the original Yahoo! Answers hierarchy.

Table 3: Classification accuracy on modifying AnswerBag

Measure/Hierarchy	$\mathcal{H}_{AB}$	$SMA_{AB\|YA}$	Improvement(%)
Macro-F_1 (NB)	0.3444	0.5638	63.7%
Macro-F_1 (SVM)	0.3691	0.4933	33.6%
Micro-F_1 (NB)	0.4671	0.6669	42.8%
Micro-F_1 (SVM)	0.4371	0.5697	30.3%

Measured by Macro-F_1, $SMA_{YA|YA}$ without using an external hierarchy slightly outperforms its counterpart $SMA_{YA|AB}$ or $SMA_{YA|ODP}$, which uses an external hierarchy; while in terms of Micro-F_1, $SMA_{YA|YA}$ performs worse than do its counterparts.

5.2.3 Experiments on AnswerBag

In this set of experiments, SMA is used to modify the AnswerBag hierarchy. The main purpose is to evaluate whether SMA remains effective when the size of the auxiliary hierarchy is smaller than the one to be modified. Specifically, we use $\mathcal{H}_{YA}$ as auxiliary hierarchy to modify $\mathcal{H}_{AB}$ and evaluate the classification accuracy as we did in the earlier set of experiments. Note that the $\mathcal{H}_{AB}$ has 265 categories which is more than twice of the 115 categories contained in $\mathcal{H}_{YA}$. The parameters λ and θ were set as 0.17 and 0.08, respectively, using the parameter setting approach described earlier. The classification accuracy is reported in Table 3. Observe that $SMA_{AB|YA}$ improves the classification accuracy (Macro- and Micro-F_1) by 30% to 63%, compared with the result obtained before hierarchy modification. This demonstrates that the proposed SMA approach is effective for different hierarchies, even if the size of the auxiliary hierarchy is smaller than the hierarchy to be modified.

5.3 User Study

A good category hierarchy must be semantically meaningful: (i) Its category labels should be easy to understand, facilitating data browsing; and (ii) Its category structure should reflect the topics of its data. We would like to note that it is challenging to evaluate these. We evaluate the modified hierarchy by $SMA_{YA|AB}$ through two types of user study by following the methods [2, 5], respectively.

Table 4: Comparison on appropriateness of category labels

Judgement	Number of documents
$\mathcal{H}_{nYA}$ is better than $\mathcal{H}_{YA}$	12
$\mathcal{H}_{nYA}$ is not as good as $\mathcal{H}_{YA}$	1
Both are equally good	81
Neither is good	6

Table 5: Averaged scores of $\mathcal{H}_{YA}$ and $\mathcal{H}_{nYA}$ (by $SMA_{YA|AB}$)

Measure/Hierarchy	$\mathcal{H}_{YA}$	$\mathcal{H}_{nYA}$
Cohesiveness	5.00	6.00
Isolation	4.00	4.67
Hierarchy	5.00	5.33
Navigation Balance	4.50	4.50
Readability	6.00	5.67

Through the study, we aim to quantify both the appropriateness of the category labels and the structure of the modified hierarchy.

Category Labels. Following a similar setting as in [2], we randomly selected 100 questions from the labeled test set originated from Yahoo! Answers. For each question, we gave the path of the categories in $\mathcal{H}_{YA}$ from the second level category to the leaf category, and similarly the category path from $\mathcal{H}_{nYA}$ (by $SMA_{YA|AB}$). We asked three students to annotate which category path better reflects the topic of the question. Which hierarchy a category path was originated from was not provided to the annotators. Given a question, each volunteer is asked to rate each path from 1(lowest) to 5(highest) based on its quality. hen, we select one of the following choices based on the averaged ratings (r_{YA} and r_{nYA} for the two paths, respectively). (1)$\mathcal{H}_{nYA}$ is better than $\mathcal{H}_{YA}$, if $r_{nYA}, r_{YA} \in [3,5]$ and $r_{nYA} > r_{YA}$; (2)$\mathcal{H}_{nYA}$ is not as good as $\mathcal{H}_{YA}$, if $r_{nYA}, r_{YA} \in [3,5]$; (3)Both are equally good, if $r_{nYA}, r_{YA} \in [3,5]$ and $r_{nYA} = r_{YA}$; (4)Neither is good, if $r_{nYA}, r_{YA} \in [1,3)$. The statistics of the labels are reported in Table 4. The table shows that the number of questions having better labels in $\mathcal{H}_{nYA}$ is larger than that in $\mathcal{H}_{YA}$ although for majority of questions, the category paths from the two hierarchy are equally good. This result also suggests that the generated labels well reflects the content of categories.

Category Structure. Following the evaluation approaches in [5], we evaluate the quality of Yahoo! Answers hierarchy and the modified hierarchy by five measures. *Cohesiveness*: Judge whether the instances in each category are semantically similar. Since it is impractical to read all questions in a large category, we randomly select 50 questions from each category for cohesiveness evaluation. *Isolation*: Judge whether categories on the same level are discriminative from each other.We also use the 50 randomly selected questions to represent each category. *Hierarchy*: Judge whether the concepts represented by the categories become finer from top to bottom. *Navigation Balance*: Judge whether the number of child categories for each internal category is appropriate. *Readability*: Judge whether the concept represented by each category is easy to understand.

We invited three students to evaluate the two hierarchies, $\mathcal{H}_{YA}$ and $\mathcal{H}_{nYA}$ (by $SMA_{YA|AB}$) and assigned scores ranging from 0 to 7 on each measure. The mean of the scores is reported in Table 5.

The cohesiveness of the modified hierarchy is better than the original one. A possible reason is that our approach detected the hidden topics and merged the most similar ones together. The isolation of the modified hierarchy is slightly better. This is probably because the proposed method takes isolation into consideration. To find out the reasons that caused the relatively low isolation of the original hierarchy, we get the list of categories with low scores from

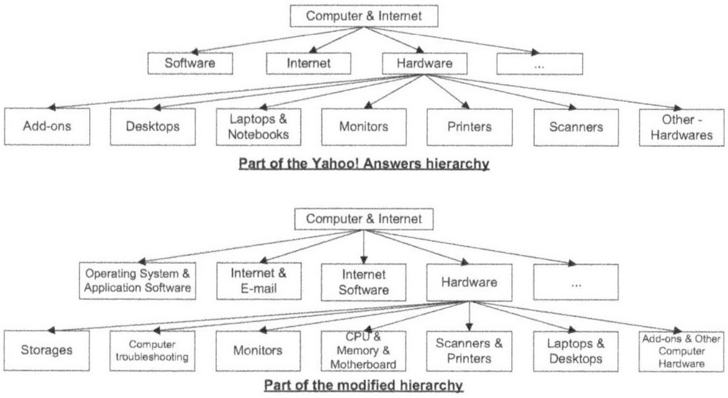

Figure 6: Portion of Yahoo! Answers hierarchy and its modified hierarchy.

the annotators. As an example, a number of questions that are related to motor-cycling were put under Other - Auto Racing by their askers, resulting in low isolation between the two categories. The modified hierarchy does not deteriorate hierarchy quality, navigation balance, and readability of the original hierarchy on average. In summary, the modified hierarchy is of high quality comparable to the original hierarchy generated by domain experts.

5.4 Case Study

As a case study, we select three categories Software, Internet and Hardware from Yahoo! Answers as an example to illustrate the differences before and after modifying $\mathcal{H}_{YA}$. The modified hierarchy $\mathcal{H}_{nYA}$ is by $SMA_{YA|AB}$ utilizing AnswerBag as auxiliary hierarchy.

The two hierarchies are shown in Figure 6. We make the following observations: 1) Different from the original hierarchy, Software and Internet become three categories – Operating System & Application Software, Internet & E-mail and Internet Software. The third category is formed based on the overlapping part of the original two categories, which contains questions about instant messaging (IM) and blog software. This demonstrates that the proposed approach can discover and detach the overlapping hidden topics. 2) Two pairs of categories of the original hierarchy, (Laptops & Notebooks and Desktops), and (Printers and Scanners), are merged into two categories in the modified hierarchy, because of the high similarity between the categories within each pair. This shows that categories with high overlap in semantics are merged. 3) For Hardware, some hidden topics are discovered and new categories are formed, like Storage and CPU & Memory & Motherboard, whose questions come from Desktops, Add-ons and Other - Hardwares in the original hierarchy. These newly formed categories are more isolated from each other.

6. CONCLUSION

Category hierarchy plays a very important role in organizing data automatically (through classifiers built on the hierarchy) or manually. However, with newly available documents added into a hierarchy, new topics emerge and documents within the same category become less topically cohesive. Thus the hierarchies suffer from problems of structure irrelevance and semantic irrelevance, leading to poor classification accuracy of the classifiers developed for automatically categorizing the newly available documents into the hierarchy, which in turn leads to poorer document organization. To address these problems, we propose a novel approach SMA to modify a hierarchy. SMA comprises three non-trivial operations (namely, *sprout*, *merge*, and *assign*) to modify a hierarchy. Experimental results demonstrate that SMA is able to generate a modified hierarchy with better classification accuracy improvement over the original hierarchy than baseline methods. Additionally, user study shows that the modified category hierarchy is topically cohesive and semantically meaningful.

7. ACKNOWLEDGEMENTS

Quan Yuan would like to acknowledge the Ph.D. grant from the Institute for Media Innovation, Nanyang Technological University, Singapore. Gao Cong is supported in part by a grant awarded by Microsoft Research Asia and by a Singapore MOE AcRF Tier 1 Grant (RG16/10).

8. REFERENCES

[1] G. Adami, P. Avesani, and D. Sona. Bootstrapping for hierarchical document classification. In *CIKM*, pages 295–302, 2003.
[2] C. C. Aggarwal, S. C. Gates, and P. S. Yu. On the merits of building categorization systems by supervised clustering. In *KDD*, pages 352–356, 1999.
[3] R. Agrawal and R. Srikant. On integrating catalogs. In *WWW*, pages 603–612, 2001.
[4] X. Cao, G. Cong, B. Cui, C. S. Jensen, and Q. Yuan. Approaches to exploring category information for question retrieval in community question-answer archives. *ACM Trans. Inf. Syst.*, 30(2):1–38, 2012.
[5] S.-L. Chuang and L.-F. Chien. A practical web-based approach to generating topic hierarchy for text segments. In *CIKM*, pages 127–136, 2004.
[6] T. H. Cormen, C. E. Leiserson, R. L. Rivest, and C. Stein. *Introduction to Algorithms, Second Edition*. The MIT Press and McGraw-Hill Book Company, 2001.
[7] S. C. Gates, W. Teiken, and K.-S. F. Cheng. Taxonomies by the numbers: building high-performance taxonomies. In *CIKM*, pages 568–577, 2005.
[8] A. Koestler. *The Act of Creation*. Penguin Books, New York, 1964.
[9] D. Koller and M. Sahami. Hierarchically classifying documents using very few words. In *ICML*, pages 170–178, 1997.
[10] K. Nitta. Improving taxonomies for large-scale hierarchical classifiers of web documents. In *CIKM*, pages 1649–1652, 2010.
[11] K. Punera, S. Rajan, and J. Ghosh. Automatically learning document taxonomies for hierarchical classification. In *WWW (Special interest tracks and posters)*, pages 1010–1011, 2005.
[12] X. Qi and B. D. Davison. Hierarchy evolution for improved classification. In *CIKM*, pages 2193–2196, 2011.
[13] B. Qu, G. Cong, C. Li, A. Sun, and H. Chen. An evaluation of classification models for question topic categorization. *JASIST*, 63(5):889–903, 2012.
[14] G. Siolas and F. d'Alché Buc. Support vector machines based on a semantic kernel for text categorization. In *IJCNN (5)*, pages 205–209, 2000.
[15] A. Sun, E.-P. Lim, and Y. Liu. What makes categories difficult to classify?: a study on predicting classification performance for categories. In *CIKM*, pages 1891–1894, 2009.
[16] P.-N. Tan, M. Steinbach, and V. Kumar. *Introduction to Data Mining*. Addison-Wesley, 2005.
[17] L. Tang, J. Zhang, and H. Liu. Acclimatizing taxonomic semantics for hierarchical content classification from semantics to data-driven taxonomy. In *KDD*, pages 384–393, 2006.
[18] N. Tomuro. Tree-cut and a lexicon based on systematic polysemy. In *NAACL*, 2001.
[19] W. Wei, G. Cong, X. Li, S.-K. Ng, and G. Li. Integrating community question and answer archives. In *AAAI*, 2011.
[20] Y. Yang and X. Liu. A re-examination of text categorization methods. In *SIGIR*, pages 42–49, 1999.
[21] D. Zhang and W. S. Lee. Web taxonomy integration through co-bootstrapping. In *SIGIR*, pages 410–417, 2004.
[22] L. Zhang, S. Liu, Y. Pan, and L. Yang. Infoanalyzer: a computer-aided tool for building enterprise taxonomies. In *CIKM*, pages 477–483, 2004.

When Web Search Fails, Searchers Become Askers: Understanding the Transition

Qiaoling Liu[§], Eugene Agichtein[§],
Gideon Dror[†], Yoelle Maarek[†], Idan Szpektor[†],
[§]Emory University, Atlanta, GA, USA
[†]Yahoo! Research, Haifa, Israel
{qliu26, eugene}@mathcs.emory.edu, {gideondr, idan}@yahoo-inc.com, yoelle@ymail.com

ABSTRACT

While Web search has become increasingly effective over the last decade, for many users' needs the required answers may be spread across many documents, or may not exist on the Web at all. Yet, many of these needs could be addressed by asking people via popular Community Question Answering (CQA) services, such as Baidu Knows, Quora, or Yahoo! Answers. In this paper, we perform the first large-scale analysis of how searchers become askers. For this, we study the logs of a major web search engine to trace the transformation of a large number of failed searches into questions posted on a popular CQA site. Specifically, we analyze the characteristics of the queries, and of the patterns of search behavior that precede posting a question; the relationship between the content of the attempted queries and of the posted questions; and the subsequent actions the user performs on the CQA site. Our work develops novel insights into searcher intent and behavior that lead to asking questions to the community, providing a foundation for more effective integration of automated web search and social information seeking.

Categories and Subject Descriptors

H.3.3 [**Information Systems**]: Information Storage and Retrieval

Keywords

query analysis, community question answering

1. INTRODUCTION

While Web search engines have significantly progressed in effectiveness and efficiency over the last decade, there still exist certain user needs that cannot be satisfied. This could be due to a number of reasons, such as the difficulty of expressing a complex need as a short search query, the lack of existing relevant content on the Web (e.g., for unique or "tail" needs that keep appearing), and for more "social" needs, for which the user prefers to interact with a real human.

SIGIR'12, August 12–16, 2012, Portland, Oregon, USA.

In fact, Hitwise in August 2011 reported that only 66-80% of the searches are successful[1], and Hassan et al. [15] obtained a similar success rate of search goals (73%) via human labeling. We argue that many such unsatisfied searches could be addressed by asking people via Community Question Answering (CQA) services, such as Baidu Knows, Quora, or Yahoo! Answers. It already happens in practice. For example, we have observed that about 2% of web search sessions performed by users who are also members of the Yahoo! Answers community, lead to a question posted to the community. Consider Figure 1a, which depicts a sample search submitted to a major search engine. The searcher is not satisfied with the results, and eventually posts a related question on the Yahoo! Answers site, which is then answered to the searcher's satisfaction. Understanding and improving the synergy between searching and community question answering is at the heart of this work.

Specifically, our goal is to better understand the behavior of these users, as well as characterize the types of Web searches that could be effectively handled by CQA sites. Insights acquired during such analysis should bring multiple benefits to both search engines and CQA systems. On one hand, search engines always need to better understand when searchers are unsatisfied by the returned results. More specifically, Web search engines would find value in analyzing the search session patterns of such unsuccessful queries, the associated underlying query intents, and possibly reflect these findings in search effectiveness metrics. One can even imagine new search experiences that would allow users to turn to the community for certain types of needs better addressed by people than by traditional Web search. Additionally, CQA systems could potentially improve the asking experience by taking advantage of the context provided by unsuccessful queries preceding a posted question. One can imagine several ways to leverage this context, such as automatically giving examples of irrelevant answers to clarify the question to the community.

To the best of our knowledge, our work is the first to perform a large-scale study of the transformation of searchers into askers. That is, we start our analysis with web search sessions, trace the searcher through her visit to a CQA site, and analyze the resulting questions posted for the community.

We focus on one of the most visited, and more mature, CQA systems existing today, namely Yahoo! Answers, which

[1]www.hitwise.com/us/about-us/press-center/press-releases/experian-hitwise-reports-google-share-of-searche/

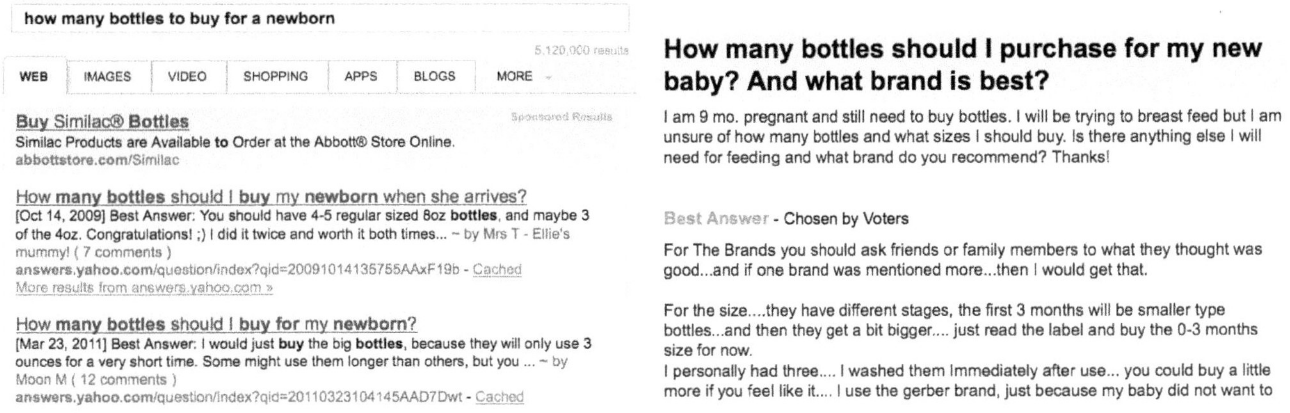

(a) (b)

Figure 1: Example search (a) followed by a question posted by the same user on the Yahoo! Answers site with a satisfactory answer from the community (b).

with more than 1 billion posted answers[2] is highly visible in most search engines result pages. We built a corpus of query-to-question transitions and studied it in order to understand when and why searchers become askers. A privacy-preserving subset of the data has recently been made publicly available through Yahoo's Webscope program[3].

More specifically, our study is organized around the following three research questions, each associated with a set of hypotheses:

Research Question 1: When do searchers turn to CQA for answers?

- **Hypothesis 1:** Queries and information needs of search sessions that lead to posting questions are hypothesized to share common characteristics, and differ from general web searches in words and information needs (Section 3.1).
- **Hypothesis 2:** We hypothesize that searchers who switch to CQA exhibit common search behavior. For instance, they tend to click more on CQA results on the search result page, and their search sessions are longer, allowing to characterize different types of users in the same spirit as [7] (Section 3.2).

Research Question 2: How do search queries relate to the associated questions posted on CQA sites?

- **Hypothesis 3:** Queries and questions follow different word distributions. More specifically, words in queries are hypothesized to follow different distributions than those appearing in questions, and a clear vocabulary gap between these can be observed (Section 4).
- **Hypothesis 4:** Questions are typically more specific than queries and include additional context (e.g., personal background) absent from the original queries. We hypothesize that these differences are reflected in the lexicographic differences between questions and queries, such as occurrence of personal pronouns or sentiment indicators (Section 4).

Research Question 3: How do searchers behave after transferring to the CQA site?

- **Hypothesis 5:** We further hypothesize that the *content* and the *topics* of the questions posted after a search session differ substantially from the general question distribution (Section 5.1).
- **Hypothesis 6:** We hypothesize that the question sessions after switching from searching, exhibit different characteristics than general question sessions and search sessions explored in depth in previous research work [17][10]. We study these different types of sessions in terms of duration and persistence for specific users and examine their behavior over time (Section 5.2).

The rest of this paper is dedicated to answering the above questions and verifying the associated hypotheses.

2. ACQUIRING DATA

In order to understand how searchers become askers, we collected a dataset that contains both the search session part and asking session part of each user who conducted a search session that resulted in posting a question. Our dataset is derived from joining a sample of the query logs of the Yahoo! search engine and the Yahoo! Answers question logs, both for June 2011.

To create this dataset, we first created a mapping of users between the two logs, based on the clicks on the same Yahoo! Answers question page following the same query on the same time frame, as they appear in both logs. Then, we extracted user actions from the query and question logs, *e.g.* posting queries and clicking on results from query logs, as well as posting questions and re-viewing them from the question logs. We constructed search sessions from these extracted actions, with a 30 minutes timeout as a session boundary. Question sessions have no temporal boundary, since every action in the session unambiguously refers to the question posted by the asker.

[2] `http://yanswersblog.com/index.php/archives/2010/05/03/1-billion-answers-served/`

[3] `http://webscope.sandbox.yahoo.com/`

Table 1: Statistics of the constructed datasets.

Description	Number of sessions
Total sampled search sessions	1,287,238 (100%)
SearchOnly sessions	**1,233,279 (95.8%)**
Search sessions that include question sessions	53959 (4.2%)
SearchAsk sessions: search sessions with a single relevant question posted after searching	**21231 (1.65%)**

Once we had search sessions and question sessions, and mapping between some of them, we created two datasets. The first, termed *SearchAsk* dataset, contains search sessions that turned into question sessions. We only kept such sessions that resulted in posting one and only one question for simplicity of analysis later on. In addition, we only kept sessions in which the posted question is "relevant" to a previously issued query (if the query and the question share at least one non-stopword, they were considered relevant). By observing that some users actually searched for Yahoo! Answers to navigate to its home page before they posted a question there, we deleted such special navigational clicks and corresponding queries from the user action sequences. The second dataset, termed *SearchOnly* dataset, consists of search sessions that did not turn into question sessions. In both datasets, we only kept sessions for users that posted at least once in Yahoo! Answers, since these users are aware of the site and know how to post a question there, thus removing the potential investment of effort for newcomers to join the site, and filtering our the users that simply do not know where to ask questions.

Table 1 reports the statistics of the datasets we obtained. As shown in the table, 95.8% of all the search sessions are SearchOnly sessions, while SearchAsk sessions account for 1.65%. Despite the sparsity of the SearchAsk sessions, we still believe that understanding how searchers become askers in such sessions can be helpful for improving the search experience of these users and perhaps more users. Indeed, the two datasets allow us to investigate the differences between sessions in which users posted a question following attempted searches, mainly due to search failure or searcher frustration, and sessions in which users that have experience of asking questions on Yahoo! Answers did not bother or did not need to ask questions at that time. Recall, that the users in these datasets satisfy two conditions: (1) having clicked at least a Yahoo! Answers question page within this month; and (2) having asked at least one question on Yahoo! Answers within the month. Yet, we believe that such users still represent the general, though somewhat experienced, web searchers.

3. FROM SEARCHING TO ASKING: QUERY AND BEHAVIOR ANALYSIS

As a first step, we study the characteristics of queries leading to a question post on Yahoo! Answers (Section 3.1), and the characteristics of searcher behavior before question asking (Section 3.2).

3.1 Characteristics of Queries leading to Questions

The first interesting question is which queries are more likely to be unsuccessful for automated search, but instead are more amenable to be answered by a CQA site. To get such queries, we examine each SearchAsk session, and

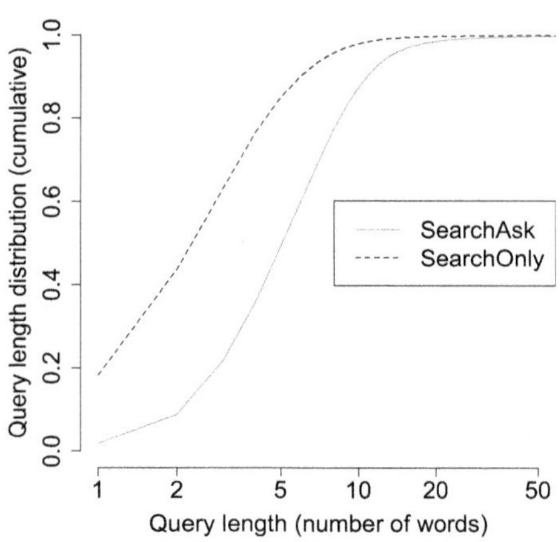

Figure 2: Distribution of query length

Table 2: Statistics of words per query

	Avg # words	Avg # stop-words	Avg % stop-words	Avg word length
SearchAsk queries	6.5	2.4	28%	5.1
SearchOnly queries	3.4	0.72	11%	6.0

extract the queries that are issued before the question is posted, and are relevant to the question. We call such queries *SearchAsk queries*. For comparison, we also extract the queries in each SearchOnly session which are called *SearchOnly queries*. In the following, we explore how SearchAsk queries are different from SearchOnly queries in terms of length, words, frequency, and results.

Query Length Distribution.

Figure 2 compares the distribution of query length (in terms of number of words in the query) for the SearchAsk and SearchOnly queries. We can see that SearchAsk queries tend to be longer than SearchOnly queries, as 85% of the SearchOnly queries contain at most 5 words, while about 50% of the SearchAsk queries contain more than 5 words. Therefore, searchers issuing longer queries are more likely to turn to Yahoo! Answers to post a relevant question.

Table 2 compares the average word length per query and the average number of stopwords for the SearchAsk queries and SearchOnly queries. We can see that, on average, queries turning to questions tend to contain more words (but shorter words) than queries that do not turn to questions. The main reason could be that SearchAsk queries contain more stopwords (which are often short) than SearchOnly queries. Indeed, the percentage of stopwords in SearchAsk queries is over 2.5 times higher than in SearchOnly queries.

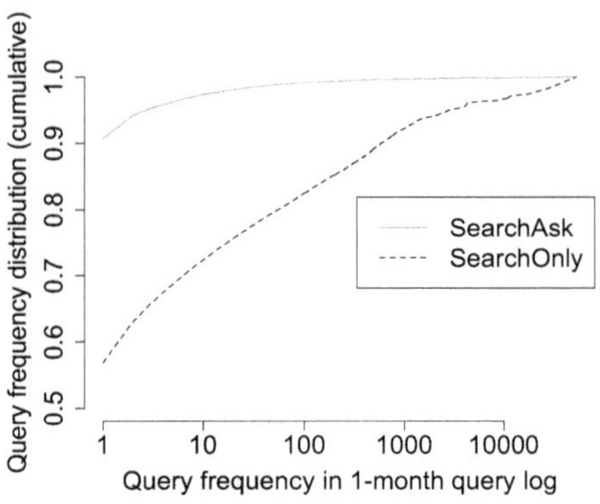

Figure 3: Distribution of query frequency

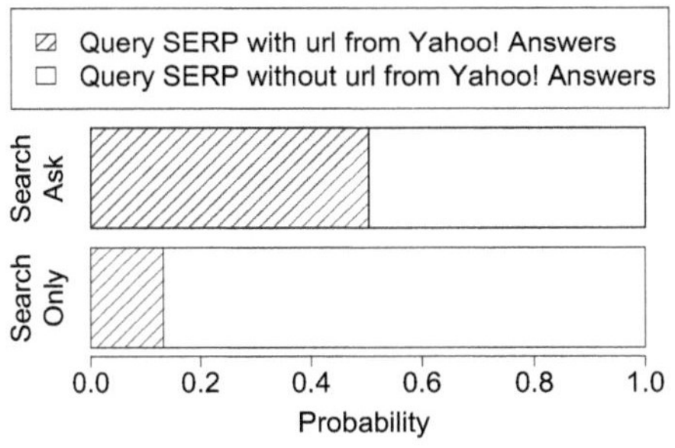

Figure 4: Distribution of query results

Query Words Distribution.

To better understand the difference between the content of SearchAsk queries and SearchOnly queries, we compare their word distributions and show the main difference in Table 3. We can see that SearchOnly queries are more likely to be navigational, e.g., to reach websites like Facebook or YouTube, or to find information related to the searcher's common tasks such as looking up the weather, hunting for coupons, or finding a cooking recipe. In contrast, SearchAsk quries are more likely to start with question words (e.g., 'how', 'what'), and tend to use more verbose natural language to express the needs of the searchers (e.g., 'want', 'to', 'know') rather than using only keywords.

Query Frequency Distribution.

To verify the hypothesis from the above word distribution analysis that SearchAsk queries are more likely to be unique, we compute the frequency[4] of SearchAsk queries and SearchOnly queries in our 1-month query log. Figure 3 shows the results. We can see that over 90% of SearchAsk queries are tail (actually unique) queries, indicating the variety of the needs of searchers and the ways to express them. In contrast, SearchOnly queries contain more popular queries, e.g., around 20% of SearchOnly queries occur in more than 100 search sessions.

Query Results Distribution.

To better understand user needs behind SearchAsk queries, we further examine the results returned in their search engine result pages (SERPs). We found a significant difference between SearchAsk and SearchOnly queries based on whether a SERP contains a Yahoo! Answers question page. As shown in Figure 4, a Yahoo! Answers question page occurs in the SERPs for half of the queries that eventually turn to questions, but for only 13% of SearchOnly queries. It is clear that SearchAsk queries are more likely to have a Yahoo! Answers question page in the SERP. This is not surprising. First, having a Yahoo! Answers question page in search results indicates that the query could be relevant to an existing Yahoo! Answers question. Therefore, answers from a human might be more suitable to address the need behind the query, encouraging the searcher to post a question on Yahoo! Answers. Second, more impressions often leads to more clicks. After landing on the Yahoo! Answers site, the searcher might realize that a community might be able to answer her information need, and try posting a question.

[4]The frequency of a query in this paper is computed as the number of search sessions containing the query.

Summary of Query Characteristics.

As a summary of the above analysis, we conclude that queries that are more likely to fail in search and lead to a question post on Yahoo! Answers tend to be longer, and use more verbose natural language to express the searchers' needs. The needs behind such queries tend to be more unique and complex than those associated with SearchOnly queries.

3.2 Searcher Behavior Before Asking Questions

To understand how searchers become askers, we analyze the searcher behavior in search sessions, with an associated question posted by the same user on Yahoo! Answers.

Last Action Before Question Asking.

First, we examine what searchers do right before they start question asking, i.e., we examine the last user action prior to a question being posted. We found that the last search action before question asking is a click on Yahoo! Answers question result in 47.8% of the sessions, a click on other result in 31.2% of the sessions, and a query in 17.4% of the sessions. We notice that in about half of the sessions, the searcher posts a question right after clicking on a Yahoo! Answers question page from the search engine results. There may be several reasons for this. First, such a click indicates that the query is relevant to the clicked question, and therefore it probably carries an information need that would benefit from a human response. Second, when the clicked Yahoo! Answers question page cannot satisfy the search need, it encourages the user to post a new question on Yahoo! Answers. Of course, it is also possible that a searcher had already decided to post a question when seeing the original SERP, and she then clicked on a Yahoo! Answers question result simply to navigate to the Yahoo! Answers site.

Distribution of Clicks.

To better understand the effects of clicking on a Yahoo! Answers question result on the transformation of searchers into askers, we compute and compare the likelihood of such clicks in SearchAsk and SearchOnly sessions. Figure 5 shows the results. First, 21% of SearchOnly sessions and 81% of SearchAsk sessions contain a Yahoo! Answers question page in the SERPs. Next, after seeing a Yahoo! Answers question page in the SERPs, 81% of the searchers who turned to

Table 3: **Frequent words in SearchAsk queries and SearchOnly queries**

More likely in SearchAsk queries	
Words	to, a, be, i, how, do, my, can, what, on, in, the, for, have, get, with, you, if, yahoo, it
First words	how, what, can, be, why, i, do, my, where, yahoo, if, when, 0000, a, will, 00, best, who, which, should
Content words	yahoo, 00, use, 0, work, song, old, help, make, need, like, change, year, good, long, mail, answer, email, want, know
More likely in SearchOnly queries	
Words	facebook, youtube, google, lyric, craigslist, free, online, new, bank, game, map, ebay, county, porn, tube, coupon, recipe, home, city, park
First words	facebook, youtube, google, craigslist, ebay, the, you, gmail, casey, walmart, amazon, *rnrd, justin, facebook.com, mapquest, netflix, face, fb, selena, home
Content words	facebook, youtube, google, craigslist, lyric, free, bank, map, ebay, online, county, porn, tube, coupon, recipe, anthony, weather, login, park, ca

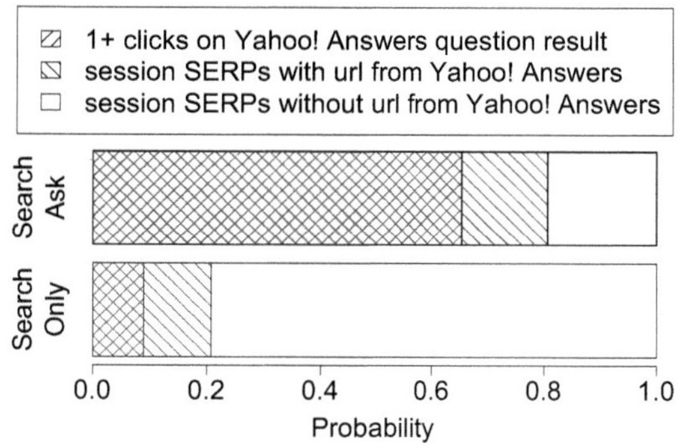

Figure 5: Distribution of clicks

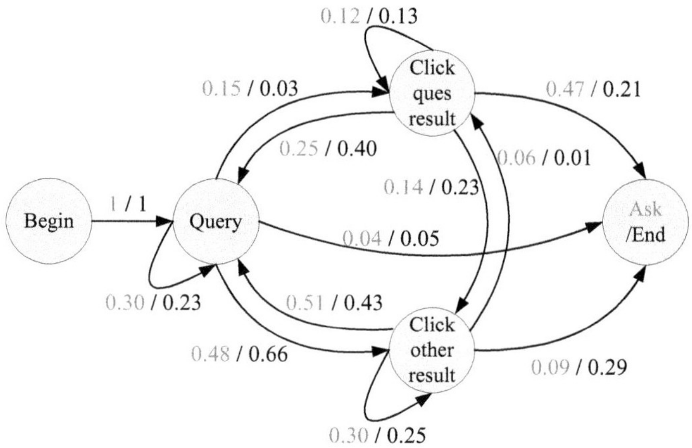

Figure 6: Transition probabilities for actions in SearchAsk (in red, before the slash symbol) and SearchOnly (in black, after the slash symbol) sessions. Note that two other actions (Pagination and Click interface) are ignored for simplicity.

askers had clicked on a Yahoo! Answers question result while 19% of them hadn't; in contrast, 43% of the searchers in SearchOnly sessions seeing a Yahoo! Answers question result clicked on it while 57% of them didn't. Therefore, users in SearchAsk sessions are about twice as likely as in SearchOnly sessions to click on a Yahoo! Answers question page in the search results once seeing it. This indicates that searchers are more likely to post a question once clicking on a Yahoo! Answers question result.

Transitions between Actions.

To better understand searcher actions, we further compute the probability of transitions between actions in SearchAsk and SearchOnly sessions respectively, and compare them in Figure 6. The transition probability between two actions a_i and a_j in SearchAsk (SearchOnly) sessions is computed using Maximum Likelihood estimation: $P(a_i, a_j) = N_{a_i,a_j}/N_{a_i}$, where N_{a_i,a_j} is the number of transitions from action a_i to action a_j in all SearchAsk (SearchOnly) sessions, and $N_{a_i} = \sum_{a_k} N_{a_i,a_k}$. SearchAsk transition probabilities are shown in red before the slash symbol, while SearchOnly transition probabilities are shown in black after the slash symbol. If we look at the transitions for SearchOnly sessions from the figure, we can see that after issuing a query, the searcher is very likely to click on other result, then with perhaps more queries and clicks on other result, and then ends the session. Clicking on a Yahoo! Answers question result is very unlikely. However, in SearchAsk sessions, the searcher has a higher probability on clicking a Yahoo! Answers question result. After the click, the searcher in SearchAsk sessions would post a question on Yahoo! Answers for around half of the time.

Action Sequences Before Question Asking.

To better understand how searchers become askers, we examine the user action sequences in SearchAsk sessions before the question post, and compare them with action sequences in SearchOnly sessions. Table 4 shows a sample of top frequent user action sequences. The top frequent path in SearchOnly sessions indicates navigational needs of the searchers, i.e., they issue a query, click on a search result and leave the session. Such navigational cases account for 30% of total SearchOnly sessions. In contrast, the top frequent path in SearchAsk sessions indicates more "social" needs of the searchers, i.e., they issue a query, click on a search result of Yahoo! Answers question page, and then ask a question on Yahoo! Answers. Yet, the path distribution is more balanced for SearchAsk sessions. Moreover, clicks on Yahoo! Answers question results are common in the paths.

Session Size Distribution.

Finally, we compare the distribution of session sizes for SearchAsk and SearchOnly sessions. Session size can be measured in several ways, e.g., by the number of (unique) queries issued by the searcher in the session, by the number of actions performed in the session, or by the duration that the session lasts. We use the first option in this paper. The results are shown in Figure 7. While only one query

Table 4: Top frequent user action sequences in SearchAsk sessions and SearchOnly sessions (B: Begin a session, Q: Query, C_{qr}: Click on a Yahoo! Answers question result, C_{or}: Click on other result, A: Ask a question, E: End a session)

SearchAsk sessions	Distribution
B Q C_{qr} A	10%
B Q C_{or} A	3.8%
B Q Q C_{qr} A	3.3%
B Q A	2.8%
B Q C_{or} Q C_{qr} A	2.0%
SearchOnly sessions	**Distribution**
B Q C_{or} E	30.2%
B Q C_{or} Q C_{or} E	7.1%
B Q E	6.1%
B Q C_{or} C_{or} E	3.6%
B Q Q C_{or} E	3.6%

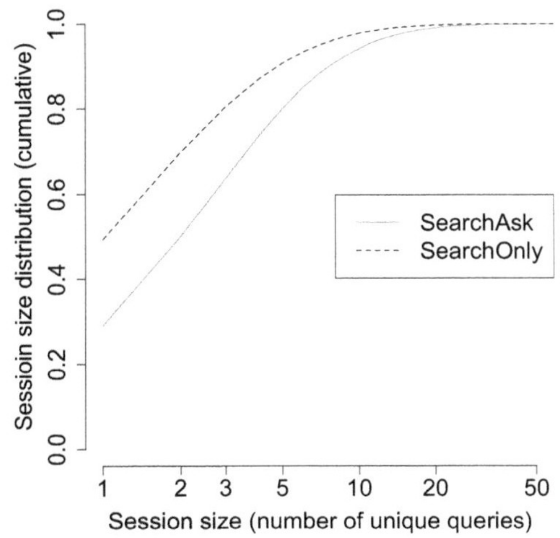

Figure 7: Distribution of session size

is issued in the half of SearchOnly sessions, at least three different queries are issued in the half of SearchAsk sessions. The average session size is 2.5 for SearchOnly sessions and 3.8 for SearchAsk sessions. This shows that searchers tend to issue more queries in SearchAsk sessions, possibly because SearchOnly sessions contain more navigational needs, while SearchAsk sessions are associated with more difficult or complex needs, and thus require more effort in finding answers.

4. QUERIES VS. QUESTIONS: CONTENT ANALYSIS

After discovering the unique attributes of queries that lead to asking a question, we next want to understand better the process of turning a search session, as captured by a query, into a question posted on Yahoo! Answers.

The most expected difference between queries and questions is their length. Table 5 shows these differences. From the table we can see that a question has 66 more words than its associated query on average. This indicates two things: first, as expected, questions are much more verbose, being natural language expressions, compared to the concise queries; second, since Yahoo! Answers questions are not limited in length, additional knowledge of the problem to be solved is added. Interestingly, the subject of the question is very close in length to the query, which shows that searchers still think in search-style writing for the subject. However, the content part of the question is significantly longer, and much more information is added in this question part.

Table 5: Statistics of length difference between a query and its associated question (number of words).

	Median	Avg	Max
|question| - |query|	42	66	1431
|subject| - |query|	3	4	27
|content| - |query|	31	55	1428

Table 6: Overlap of content words (CW) between a query and its associated question.

	?=*question*	?=*subject*	?=*content*
$CW_? \supset CW_{query}$	31.4%	14.6%	14%
$CW_? = CW_{query}$	1.8%	6.2%	0.4%
$CW_? \subset CW_{query}$	0.7%	3.7%	17.1%
$CW_? \not\supset CW_{query}$ $CW_? \not\subset CW_{query}$	66.1%	75.5%	68.5%

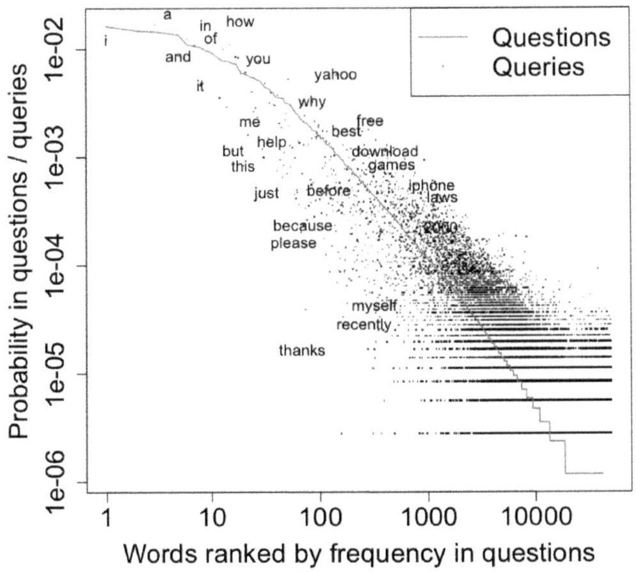

Figure 8: Word distributions over question words

We next look at word distribution differences, since they may point at the lexical gap between queries leading to questions and their associated posted questions. Figure 8 depicts the word occurrence distribution over word ranking by frequency for search-related questions. The most notable difference between the two distributions is that questions tend to be more personal and verbose, as captured by the abundant usage of the pronouns such as '*I*', '*me*', '*it*' and '*this*', connectives such as '*but*', '*because*', '*recently*', and '*just*', as well as sentiment indicators such as '*help*', '*please*', and '*thanks*'. Queries, on the other hand, tend to focus more on the things or actions that are searched for, with content words like '*best*', '*free*', '*download*' and '*games*' as well as question words like '*how*', '*why*' and '*what*' occurring more frequently than in the associated questions corpus. Interestingly, one to four digit figures, such as car model years,

Table 7: Examples showing semantics difference between the query and the question.

ID	Type of context added	Query	Question (Category, Subject, and Content)
1	N/A	what to serve with chicken salad	Food & Drink>Cooking & Recipes **what can you serve with chicken salad?**
2	thought	best nba players without a championship	Sports>Basketball **Greatest NBA players to never win championship?** Patrcik ewing, reggie miller, charles barkley, karl malone? Who else?
3	task	pt cruiser ac fix	Cars & Transportation>Car Makes>Chrysler **how much does it cost to fix an ac system in a pt cruiser?**
4	task	solve n^2-2n-3=5000	Education & Reference>Homework Help **Algebra question, Need Help Pls!!!!?** An owner of a key rings company found that the profit earned (in thousands of dollars) per day by selling n number of key rings is given by n^2 - 2n - 3, where n is the number of key rings in thousands. Find the number of key rings sold on a particular day when the total profit is $5000. Thanx
5	limit	chocolate croissant menlo park	Dining Out>United States>San Jose **Where can I get a good Chocolate Croissant near Menlo Park, CA?** Something with thick, dark chocolate? And please, don't say La Boulanger.
6	situation, task	chicago fried chicken	Dining Out>United States>Chicago **Where can I get really good fried chicken in the Lakeview area in Chicago?** I really want fried chicken after watchin a special on TV. But I cant find any place near me that has decent priced chicken thats not fast food and is homemade and delicious. Any one know of a place?
7	situation, task	douglas az	Education & Reference>Higher Education (University +) **Radiology schools in Arizona?** Does any one know any schools in az that offer radiology degree programs, I moved to Douglas az and don't know any schools near to study radiology. If any one can help that would be great :)
8	attribute, situation, task	how many bottles to buy for a newborn	Pregnancy & Parenting>Newborn & Baby **How many bottles should I purchase for my new baby? And what brand is best?** I am 9 mo. pregnant and still need to buy bottles. I will be trying to breast feed but I am unsure of how many bottles and what sizes I should buy. Is there anything else I will need for feeding and what brand do you recommend? Thanks!

also appear more in question-related queries than in their associated questions, probably since they capture much of the essence of the target information need.

To further understand the semantic difference between composing a query and its related question, we measured the distribution of query-question pairs in which the same words are used for both query and question, the pairs in which one is included in the other, and those pairs in which each contains words that do not occur in the other. Table 6 presents these statistics, while Table 7 provides examples of such pairs, annotated with the type of context added when switching from query to question, as been classified by [23], i.e., task, situation, attribute, limit, and thought.

Some interesting question composition patterns are evident from this analysis. First, in the majority of pairs (66%), both queries and questions contain unique words that do not occur in the other. This is somewhat surprising, since we would expect more complete inclusion of the query terms in the question. However, it seems that with the freedom of writing a free text question, searchers tend to rephrase some of the terms they used in their queries. For example, abbreviations and short terms are turned into their more complete forms, *e.g.* '*AZ*' into '*Arizona*' and '*newborn*' into '*new baby*' (see example 7 and 8 in Table 7). In addition, while 31% of the pairs do show complete inclusion of the query terms in the question, many times the query terms do not all appear in the question's subject or content, but spread in both question parts. Table 7 shows that most of the extensions of the query into a question include additional details that are related to the search task. Yet, many times details of the personal situation are added, such as the state of mind, *e.g.* "*after watching a special on TV*" (example 6 in Table 7).

One interesting future research is to automatically generate questions from queries [25][26]. However, adding context information to the question, such as the situation or limit is a difficult challenge. Still, expanding the query expression to an explicit question form may be possible for many cases, *e.g.* examples 1 and 3 in Table 7.

5. ASKING AFTER SEARCHING: QUESTION ANALYSIS

As our final analysis, we are interested in discovering unique activity patterns in Yahoo! Answers that searchers posting a question have, compared to typical asker behavior in Yahoo! Answers. Specifically, we first examine the differences in lexicon, that is whether different words are used when composing a question (Section 5.1). Then, we analyze the difference in asker *behavior* after posting such questions, in terms of "traditional" CQA activities (Section 5.2).

5.1 Characterizing Questions Posted after a Search Session

As expected, we find that there is a large difference between the word distribution for the corpus of all questions posted in June 2011 and the distribution of the corpus of

Table 8: Categories with largest differences in assignment probability between questions coming from search and general questions

Categories more likely for general questions	Categories more likely for questions following search
Polls & Surveys (Entertainment & Music)	Maintenance & Repairs (Cars)
Singles & Dating	Law & Ethics
Religion & Spirituality	Dogs (Pets)
Politics	Pregnancy
Friends	Maintenance & Repairs (Home & Garden)
Mathematics	Renting & Real Estate
Diet & Fitness	Accounts & Passwords
Lesbian, Gay, Bisexual, and Transgendered	Other - Yahoo! Mail
Other - Beauty & Style	Military
Basketball	Problems with Service
Baby Names	Garden & Landscape
Adolescent	Cooking & Recipes

questions posted by searchers. In addition, the entropy of generating a word from the search-related question corpus is much lower, showing a more focused vocabulary. But what are the reasons for this large difference? It turned out to be mainly topical.

To measure this topical difference between the two types of questions, we looked at the distribution of categories to which the questions in the two compared corpora are assigned. Table 8 shows the categories with largest differences in assignment probability, those that are preferred more in the general question corpus and in the search-related question corpus respectively. These lists show that searchers tend to ask informational questions [14] to get fact- or advice-oriented answers, such as how to fix the car or maintain one's garden, how to bake cookies, but also questions related to Yahoo products, such as Yahoo! Mail. On the other hand, regular askers are more likely to ask conversational questions [14] with a social flavor, such as discussions around music or sports events, politics and religions, and opinions on possible baby names. We manually labeled 100 questions randomly sampled from the search-related question corpus, and found none are conversational, showing a very different distribution compared to that 38% of Yahoo! Answers questions are conversational as reported in [14]. We conjecture that this is because searchers usually turn to search engines to find information instead of starting conversations. Another kind of questions that are less likely searched first over the web are personal questions, in which the asker is interested in adding very personal details. These include topics such as diet and fitness advices, dating and style opinions. Finally, there are questions that are too complex, for which the asker knows the answer cannot be found on the web. A good example are Math questions, such as example 4 in Table 7.

To further investigate the differences between the two question types, we removed the strong bias caused by the different category distributions within the two corpora by sampling questions from the general question corpus based on the category distribution of the search-related question corpus. By comparing the word distribution between the sampled corpus and the search-related question corpus, we found that hardly no topical differences remained. That is, the topical variation in the two corpora is more or less completely captured by the level of assigned categories, without

Table 9: Statistics of words in SearchAsk questions and sampled general questions

Avg. corpus statistics	Sampled general questions	SearchAsk questions
# words	78.3	73.7
# words per sentence	13.5	13.7
# sentences	5.8	5.4
% stopwords	66.3	65.0
word length	4.22	4.17

Table 10: Statistics about user follow-up activities around their posted questions.

	SearchAsk	Ask	Search
Avg duration	30h	32h	19.4m
Median duration	2.2h	3.7h	11.6m
Avg #actions	6.41	7.45	-
Median #actions	5	5	-

more subtle topical differences evident. Still, there may be stylish variations in question composition between searchers and typical askers. Table 9 provides the stylish statistics for the general-sampled and search-related question corpora. The significant difference between the two corpora is the number of words per question: for the same topics, general questions contain 6% more words compared to search-related questions. Yet, interestingly, this attribute is due to more sentences that are written on average per general question, while if we look at the number of words per sentence, we see that surprisingly search-related questions have slightly more words in each sentence. This could be related to more information-focused nature of the questions posted after a search session, and suggests further investigation.

5.2 Asker Follow-up Activity after a Search

As our final question behavior analysis, we wanted to test whether a searcher interacts more or less with Yahoo! Answers after posting the question. To that end, we measured both the number of actions that both searchers and regular askers perform around a specific question they posted, as well as the duration of this set of actions. Follow-up actions after a posted question include: browsing the question page (*e.g.* checking for new answers), adding more details to the question, selecting a best answer, reporting abusive answers, voting for answers, and deleting the question.

Table 10 provides the average statistics of these actions, while Figures 9 and 10 depict the distribution of number of actions and their duration for searchers and regular askers. From the table we can see that searchers perform fewer yet similar number of actions as typical askers do, but in a much shorter duration. As can be seen by Figure 9, in terms of number of actions, the difference of about one more action on average for regular askers is small though constant. For the duration of the interaction, regular askers spend about 7% more time on average around the question, but looking at the median, the difference is substantially larger, with half the searchers spending 2.2 hours or less while the typical askers tend to spend about 68% more time, or 3.7 hours, at the median. As an interesting comparison, we also measured the average time the searchers spent searching before asking questions, to show the substantial difference between

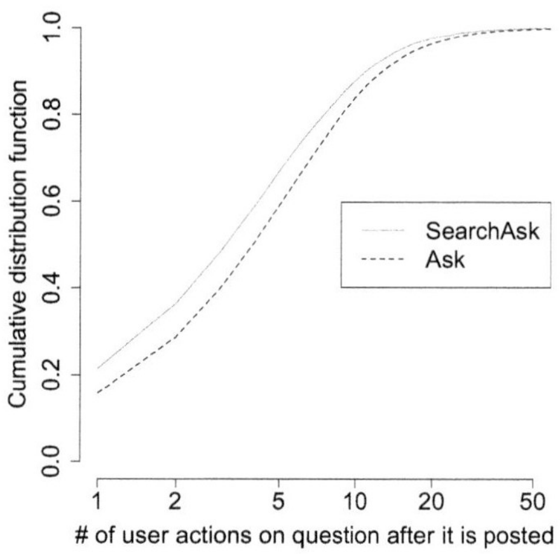

Figure 9: Count of user actions in questions

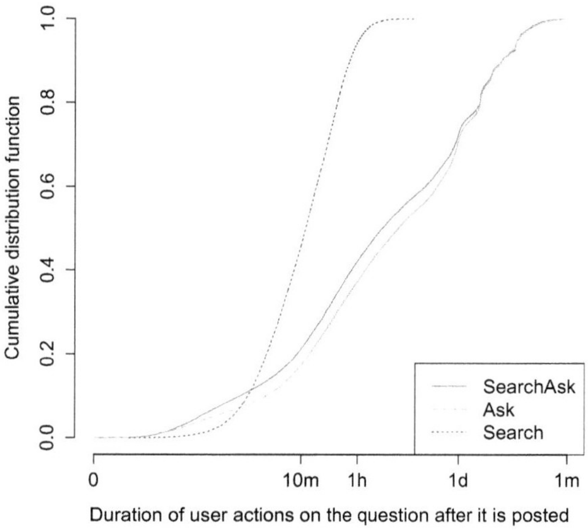

Figure 10: Duration of user actions in questions

an interactive search session and an offline asking session, a difference that is clear to the searchers, since they are willing to spend several hours waiting for an answer to arrive, compared to a few minutes actively searching.

In summary, we showed that searchers are expecting a faster response time for their questions, which often aim to address practical problem solving tasks. On the other hand, general Yahoo! Answers askers are willing to put more effort in following up their questions. One possible reason for this behavior is that Yahoo! Answers site is often viewed by users from a more social perspective, as indicated by many users asking socially-focused (e.g., conversational) questions.

6. RELATED WORK

As we study the transformation of unsatisfied searches into questions posted on a popular CQA site, our work is related to the work on query log analysis, searcher behavior and satisfaction prediction, and CQA question analysis.

On the search side, significant research has been done on analysis of queries and searcher behavior based on query logs. For example, understanding query intent and user goals has attracted much research effort [22][6]. Difficult queries [9][8], long and tail queries [4][5], and question-like queries [21] have also received special research attention. Besides, searcher satisfaction and frustration [11][15][2][16] has also been actively studied, which utilized query log information for satisfaction prediction, such as relevance measures, as well as user behavior during the search session, including mouse clicks and time spent between user actions.

Donato et al. [10] identified the research missions that often associate with complex information needs and require collecting information from many pages. In our work we focused on studying the types of queries that arguably are difficult for a web search engine to satisfy, often require human to answer [19][20][18], and thus could be better handled by CQA sites. Liu et al. [18] argued that some of these needs can be satisfied with existing answers from CQA archives by harnessing the unique structure of such archives for detecting web searcher satisfaction. Our work in this paper further observed that many searchers not satisfied with search results finally posted a related question on a CQA site, which inspired our analysis of how searchers become askers.

White and Dumais [24][12] studied search engine switching behavior and developed models to predict the switching and its rationale. Although different types of searchers are focused on (they focused on searchers who turn to another search engine and issue more queries, while we focused on searchers who turn to CQA sites and post questions), we are both interested in characterizing the types of queries and searcher behavior that lead to the switchings. Our analysis shows both similar (e.g. longer sessions are more likely to involve a switch) and different characteristics (e.g. different last action before switching) compared to their study.

On the CQA side, there is also research effort devoted to question analysis, e.g. distinguishing conversational and informational questions [14], identifying high quality questions [3], and investigating the effects of contexts in questions on answer quality [23]. In our work, we use their classification of contextual factors to analyze the semantic difference between the query and question posted by the same user for the same need. There is also some previous work related to asker behavior analysis. For example, Adamic et al. [1] analyzed the content properties and user interaction patterns across different Yahoo! Answers categories. Gyongyi et al. [13] studied several aspects of user behavior in Yahoo! Answers, including users' activity levels, interests, and reputation. Yet, they did not study the effort that askers spend in tracing their posted questions as we studied in this paper.

7. CONCLUSIONS

Web search needs are becoming increasingly sophisticated, and the expectations have grown accordingly. As a result, quite a few search sessions end in posting a question in a Community Question Answering service, as the searcher realizes that such a service could better answer her need.

This work studies the unique properties of SearchAsk sessions: search sessions that turn into question composition. To the best of our knowledge, this paper presents the first large-scale analysis of the user transition from searching to asking. What makes our work unique is the study of the explicit connection between the search query and the corresponding question from the *same user* for the *same need*. It provides insights into some specific needs that searchers try to express on search engines, yet are not satisfied by search results, and turn to human answerers instead. We analyzed the various aspects of SearchAsk sessions, including the differences between general search-engine queries and those belonging to a SearchAsk session, the transformation of a query into a natural language question and the question composition patterns, as well as other asking behavior of searchers, compared to general askers in a CQA service.

Our findings may contribute both to search-engine optimization, as well as to better user experience in CQA sites. For example, we found out that searchers are not as patient as regular askers when waiting for answers to their questions. This finding may influence CQA sites to promote questions coming from searchers, if they want to retain their engagement. As another example, our analysis of the transitions between user actions in SearchAsk sessions, and especially the fact that question asking is typically preceded by viewing a CQA page, may help search engines. They might decide to detect such cases and explicitly promote the option of asking a question to the searcher, even before she resorts into doing it on her own. Furthermore, as this paper demonstrates, modeling the transformation of a query meant for an automated search engine into a fully specified question meant for human, provides a valuable tool for query intent and satisfaction analysis.

In future work, we intend to develop some of the directions mentioned above. One of the most intriguing ones in our view is for search engines to automatically trigger a dialog for posting questions in the right CQA forum, whenever a SearchAsk need is detected. This is just one application made possible by our study, which lays a foundation for more effective integration of automated web search and social information seeking.

8. ACKNOWLEDGMENTS

This work was supported by the National Science Foundation grant IIS-1018321 and by the Yahoo! Faculty Research and Engagement Program. The authors also would like to thank Elad Yom-Tov for the helpful discussion and the anonymous reviewers for their valuable comments.

9. REFERENCES

[1] L. A. Adamic, J. Zhang, E. Bakshy, and M. S. Ackerman. Knowledge sharing and Yahoo! Answers: everyone knows something. In *WWW*, 2008.

[2] M. Ageev, Q. Guo, D. Lagun, and E. Agichtein. Find it if you can: a game for modeling different types of web search success using interaction data. In *SIGIR*, pages 345–354, 2011.

[3] E. Agichtein, C. Castillo, D. Donato, A. Gionis, and G. Mishne. Finding high-quality content in social media. In *WSDM*, pages 183–194, 2008.

[4] P. Bailey, R. W. White, H. Liu, and G. Kumaran. Mining historic query trails to label long and rare search engine queries. *ACM Trans. Web*, 4:15:1–15:27, September 2010.

[5] M. Bendersky and W. B. Croft. Analysis of long queries in a large scale search log. In *WSCD*, 2009.

[6] A. Broder. A taxonomy of web search. *SIGIR Forum*, 36:3–10, September 2002.

[7] G. Buscher, R. W. White, S. Dumais, and J. Huang. Large-scale analysis of individual and task differences in search result page examination strategies. In *WSDM*, pages 373–382, 2012.

[8] D. Carmel, E. Yom-Tov, A. Darlow, and D. Pelleg. What makes a query difficult? In *SIGIR*, 2006.

[9] S. Cronen-Townsend, Y. Zhou, and W. B. Croft. Predicting query performance. In *SIGIR*, 2002.

[10] D. Donato, F. Bonchi, T. Chi, and Y. Maarek. Do you want to take notes?: identifying research missions in Yahoo! search pad. In *WWW*, pages 321–330, 2010.

[11] H. A. Feild, J. Allan, and R. Jones. Predicting searcher frustration. In *SIGIR*, pages 34–41, 2010.

[12] Q. Guo, R. W. White, Y. Zhang, B. Anderson, and S. T. Dumais. Why searchers switch: understanding and predicting engine switching rationales. In *SIGIR*, pages 335–344, 2011.

[13] Z. Gyongyi, G. Koutrika, J. Pedersen, and H. Garcia-Molina. Questioning Yahoo! Answers. *Evolution*, 2008.

[14] F. M. Harper, D. Moy, and J. A. Konstan. Facts or friends?: distinguishing informational and conversational questions in social q&a sites. In *CHI*, pages 759–768, 2009.

[15] A. Hassan, R. Jones, and K. L. Klinkner. Beyond dcg: user behavior as a predictor of a successful search. In *WSDM*, pages 221–230, 2010.

[16] S. B. Huffman and M. Hochster. How well does result relevance predict session satisfaction? In *SIGIR*, 2007.

[17] R. Jones and K. L. Klinkner. Beyond the session timeout: automatic hierarchical segmentation of search topics in query logs. In *CIKM*, 2008.

[18] Q. Liu, E. Agichtein, G. Dror, E. Gabrilovich, Y. Maarek, D. Pelleg, and I. Szpektor. Predicting web searcher satisfaction with existing community-based answers. In *SIGIR*, pages 415–424, 2011.

[19] M. R. Morris, J. Teevan, and K. Panovich. A comparison of information seeking using search engines and social networks. In *ICWSM*, 2010.

[20] M. R. Morris, J. Teevan, and K. Panovich. What do people ask their social networks, and why?: a survey study of status message q&a behavior. In *CHI*, 2010.

[21] B. Pang and R. Kumar. Search in the lost sense of "query": question formulation in web search queries and its temporal changes. In *HLT*, 2011.

[22] D. E. Rose and D. Levinson. Understanding user goals in web search. In *WWW*, pages 13–19, 2004.

[23] S. Suzuki, S. Nakayama, and H. Joho. Formulating effective questions for community-based question answering. In *SIGIR*, pages 1261–1262, 2011.

[24] R. W. White and S. T. Dumais. Characterizing and predicting search engine switching behavior. In *CIKM*, pages 87–96. ACM, 2009.

[25] S. Zhao, H. Wang, C. Li, T. Liu, and Y. Guan. Automatically generating questions from queries for community-based question answering. In *IJCNLP*, pages 929–937, 2011.

[26] Z. Zheng, X. Si, E. Y. Chang, and X. Zhu. K2q: Generating natural language questions from keywords with user refinements. In *IJCNLP*, 2011.

Content-based Retrieval for Heterogeneous Domains: Domain Adaptation by Relative Aggregation Points

Makoto P. Kato Hiroaki Ohshima Katsumi Tanaka

Kyoto University, Japan
{kato,ohshima,tanaka}@dl.kuis.kyoto-u.ac.jp

ABSTRACT

We introduce the problem of domain adaptation for content-based retrieval and propose a domain adaptation method based on *relative aggregation points* (RAPs). Content-based retrieval including image retrieval and spoken document retrieval enables a user to input examples as a query, and retrieves relevant data based on the similarity to the examples. However, input examples and relevant data can be dissimilar, especially when domains from which the user selects examples and from which the system retrieves data are different. In content-based geographic object retrieval, for example, suppose that a user who lives in Beijing visits Kyoto, Japan, and wants to search for relatively inexpensive restaurants serving popular local dishes by means of a content-based retrieval system. Since such restaurants in Beijing and Kyoto are dissimilar due to the difference in the average cost and areas' popular dishes, it is difficult to find relevant restaurants in Kyoto based on examples selected in Beijing. We propose a solution for this problem by assuming that RAPs in different domains correspond, which may be dissimilar but play the same role. A RAP is defined as the expectation of instances in a domain that are classified into a certain class, e.g. the most expensive restaurant, average restaurant, and restaurant serving the most popular dishes. Our proposed method constructs a new feature space based on RAPs estimated in each domain and bridges the domain difference for improving content-based retrieval in heterogeneous domains. To verify the effectiveness of our proposed method, we evaluated various methods with a test collection developed for content-based geographic object retrieval. Experimental results show that our proposed method achieved significant improvements over baseline methods. Moreover, we observed that the search performance of content-based retrieval in heterogeneous domains was significantly lower than that in homogeneous domains. This finding suggests that relevant data for the same search intent depend on the search context, that is, the location where the user searches and the domain from which the system retrieves data.

Categories and Subject Descriptors

H.3.3 [**Information Storage and Retrieval**]: Information Search and Retrieval

SIGIR'12, August 12–16, 2012, Portland, Oregon, USA.

General Terms

Algorithms, Experimentation

Keywords

Content-based retrieval, domain adaptation

1. INTRODUCTION

Content-based retrieval enables a user to input examples as a query, and retrieves relevant data based on the similarity to the examples. In multimedia retrieval, it is difficult to represent complex search intents by using keywords due to the difference in medium between input and output; thus, content-based retrieval has been successfully applied to a wide range of multimedia retrieval including image retrieval [17] and spoken document retrieval [9], as well as geographic object retrieval [15].

Content-based geographic object retrieval proposed by Kato et al. [15] provides a means by which a user can select geographic objects (e.g. restaurants) as a query in a domain s/he knows well (denoted by *source* domain $\mathcal{D}^{(S)}$) for retrieving objects from a domain s/he does not know well (denoted by *target* domain $\mathcal{D}^{(T)}$). This search method is helpful, especially when the searcher has little knowledge of the target domain, as it is usually difficult to make a concrete query without knowledge on the domain in which the user wants to search [2]. Suppose that a user who lives in Beijing visits Kyoto, Japan, and wants to search for restaurants, say, relatively inexpensive restaurants serving popular local dishes. If the user has little knowledge of Kyoto and no idea about the average cost and what the popular local dishes are there, it might be difficult for him/her to specify attributes (e.g. a category and price range of restaurants), or make a keyword query that represents his/her search intent. By using a content-based geographic object retrieval system, a user is able to make an example query without knowledge of the target domain by selecting familiar source domain examples that are relevant to his/her search intent.

A challenge in content-based geographic object retrieval is to find relevant instances from a target domain $\mathcal{D}^{(T)}$ based on examples selected from a heterogeneous source domain $\mathcal{D}^{(S)}$. When the two domains are dissimilar, examples selected from $\mathcal{D}^{(S)}$ are not always similar to relevant instances from $\mathcal{D}^{(T)}$. For example, assume that the user who visits Kyoto selects relatively inexpensive restaurants serving popular local dishes in Beijing. Such restaurants in Beijing and Kyoto are dissimilar since the average cost and popular local dishes are different in the two domains. Therefore, the content-based geographic object retrieval system has to find instances semantically similar to the given examples against superficial dissimilarity between instances from heterogeneous domains. Although similar problems have been recognized as domain adaptation [20], domain adaptation for content-based retrieval has not been addressed in the literature. We discuss related work on domain adaptation in Section 2, and formalize and characterize domain adaptation for content-based retrieval in Section 3.

We propose a method for accurately predicting relevant instances in a domain based on selected examples in another heterogeneous domain. We assume that different domains include corresponding points that may not be the same in terms of their representation but play the same role in heterogeneous domains. For the Kyoto and Beijing example, both domains include the most expensive restaurant, the average restaurant, and a restaurant serving the most popular dishes there. These kinds of points are identified through aggregation based on relative and domain-independent operation; we call these points *relative aggregation points* (RAPs). We assume that RAPs in different domains correspond, and construct a new feature representation for each instance based on RAPs from the source and target domains. Several kinds of similarities are measured between RAPs and instances, each of which is used to represent instances in the new feature space. Incorporating features represented by RAPs bridges the gap between heterogeneous domains and enables us to capture the place of an instance in a domain.

Our experiment was designed to provide answers to two research questions on domain adaptation for content-based retrieval. The first research question is whether domain adaptation for content-based retrieval is necessary. In other words, are relevant data different for the same search intent in different locations and datasets? We answered this research question based on a test collection developed for content-based geographic object retrieval, which includes relevant data for 100 queries (20 search intents in five domains). Our experimental result showed that mean average precision (MAP) and normalized discounted cumulative gain (nDCG) [12] in out-domain settings ($\mathcal{D}^{(S)} \neq \mathcal{D}^{(T)}$) were significantly lower than those in in-domain settings ($\mathcal{D}^{(S)} = \mathcal{D}^{(T)}$). This finding suggests that relevant data can vary in different search locations and datasets and has important implication for relevance judgment in information retrieval tasks. The second research question is whether domain adaptation based on RAPs can bridge the domain difference and significantly improve the search performance of content-based retrieval in heterogeneous domains. In our experiment based on the aforementioned test collection, our proposed method showed significant improvements on MAP and nDCG over baseline methods.

The remainder of this paper is structured as follows. We describe related work on domain adaptation in Section 2, and formalize and characterize domain adaptation for content-based retrieval in Section 3. In Section 4, we propose a method for domain adaptation based on RAPs. In Section 5, we describe the test collection developed for content-based geographic object retrieval and show experimental results in Section 6. We conclude with a summary of our findings and future work in Section 7.

2. RELATED WORK

Domain adaptation [20] has been addressed in several tasks such as part of speech tagging [5], text classification [4, 16, 27, 28], and learning to rank [7, 11, 26]. The motivation behind domain adaptation is that a model trained in a source domain $\mathcal{D}^{(S)}$ does not work well in a heterogeneous target domain $\mathcal{D}^{(T)}$. The aforementioned content-based retrieval problem is also a domain adaptation problem since it is a process for modeling a search intent from examples selected in a domain, and inferring relevant instances in another by using the model. In this section, we describe related work on domain adaptation and clarify our contributions of this paper.

Blitzer et al. proposed structural correspondence learning (SCL) for domain adaptation [4, 5]. SCL first extracts *pivot* features, which behave in the same way in different domains. The correlation with the pivot features is then used to identify correspondences among features from different domains. Each instance is represented by the correspondence together with its own features. SCL has been successfully applied to part of speech tagging and sentiment classification, and is considered a state-of-the-art method for domain adaptation. Since our proposed method is similar to SCL in terms of incorporating corresponding *points* not corresponding *features*, we included SCL as a baseline and compared it with our proposed method.

Several domain adaptation methods for document classification tasks have been proposed recently. Dai et al. proposed a domain adaptation method based on co-clustering [10]. The method clusters words and documents simultaneously in a target domain, restricting word clusters by labels from a source domain and transferring the labels to documents in the target domain. Ling et al. incorporated spectral clustering for domain adaptation to construct a new feature space based on the clustering results [16]. Spectral clustering is applied to documents in a source and target domain under the source domain supervision, so that documents in the target domain are separated as much as possible. Their method then represents documents by their vector that encodes clusters to which a document belongs. Xue et al. proposed a method based on probabilistic latent semantic analysis (pLSA) for domain adaptation [28]. They assumed that different domains include common latent topics, applied pLSA to documents under the source domain supervision, and classified documents from a target domain using common topics obtained through the pLSA. Wang et al. tackled a problem of cross-language document classification [27]. They argued that cross-language document classification is a challenge because of cultural discrepancies and translation ambiguities. It is an interesting and similar motivation to our geographic object retrieval example in which the cultural discrepancy may prevent training an accurate model.

In addition to document classification tasks, some studies have focused on domain adaptation for learning to rank tasks. Cai et al. proposed active query selection for ranking adaptation, which seeks instances to be labeled in the target domain for an effective training [7]. Wang et al. tackled the problem of learning to rank, assuming that there is a common latent space in different domains, and mapped instances onto the space preserving the label order [26]. Gao et al. proposed a method based on re-weighting labeled instances for learning to rank in heterogeneous domains [11]. The main idea of their approach is that the label information of source domain instances similar to ones from a target domain is more helpful in predicting the label of target domain instances than dissimilar source domain instances. Although we also focus on an information retrieval task, our problem described in the following section uses pairs of an instance and binary label; thus, we cannot simply adapt their methods to our problem and compare them with our proposed method.

Nakajima and Tanaka proposed a relative query processing method [18]. A relative query consists of a set of instances and an instance in the set. Their relative query processing method represents an instance x in a set X as a vector from the centroid of X to x. The differences between domain adaptation for content-based retrieval and the relative query processing method are the following two aspects: (i) a content-based retrieval system returns ranked instances, while the relative query aims to find only a relevant instance, and (ii) domain adaptation for content-based retrieval addresses a problem that the same features may have different meanings in different domains, while the relative query processing method does not and only addresses the relativity of the feature value. Moreover, we included their method as a baseline in our experiment and showed the difference in effectiveness between our proposed method and the relative query processing method.

We assume that different domains include points that play the same role, like the assumption of common features in most of the previous work. However, we would like to emphasize a fundamental difference; we do not assume that common features in different domains correlate with labels in the same way. The reason for this is that even the same features may indicate different meanings in different domains. For example, sushi restaurants in Beijing and Kyoto that are exactly the same may be relevant in Kyoto, but irrelevant in Beijing for a user who wants a restaurant serving local dishes. Moreover, a test collection we developed for the content-based geographic object retrieval is different from commonly used test collections such as 20 Newsgroups[1] in some aspects. Our test collection includes different types of features: continuous, such as the cost and distance from the nearest station, discrete, such as category information, and high-dimensional, such as the description of a restaurant. The label distribution is usually balanced in the sentiment and category classification tasks addressed in previous work, while the amount of relevant instances to a search intent is relatively small in our test collection and is different in different search intents and domains. The unbalanced label distribution might impair the performance of previously proposed methods, as revealed in our experiment.

3. DOMAIN ADAPTATION FOR CONTENT-BASED RETRIEVAL

In this section, we define the problem of domain adaptation for content-based retrieval and discuss domain difference.

A domain consists of a feature space $\mathcal{X}$ and a marginal distribution $P(X)$ [20]; thus, we represent a domain as $\mathcal{D} = (\mathcal{X}, P(X))$. A label space is denoted by Y. Instances $X \subset \mathcal{X}$ are sampled following $P(X)$, and a label $y \in Y$ is assigned to each instance $x \in X$. Label-instance pairs are denoted by $D = \{(x_1, y_1), (x_2, y_2), \ldots\}$.

We set two domains in content-based retrieval: a source domain $\mathcal{D}^{(S)} = (\mathcal{X}^{(S)}, P(X^{(S)}))$, from which instances to be selected as a query are sampled, and a target domain $\mathcal{D}^{(T)} = (\mathcal{X}^{(T)}, P(X^{(T)}))$, from which instances to be retrieved are sampled. From instances $X^{(S)}$ sampled from the source domain $\mathcal{D}^{(S)}$, the user can select a subset $Q \subset X^{(S)}$ that consists of instances relevant to his/her search intent. The example selection can be interpreted as a labeling process on the instances $X^{(S)}$, and label-instance pairs are denoted by $D^{(S)} = \{(x^{(S)}, +1) \mid x^{(S)} \in Q\} \cup \{(x^{(S)}, -1) \mid x^{(S)} \in (X^{(S)} - Q)\}$, where a label space $Y^{(S)}$ comprises -1 (nonselected examples) and $+1$ (selected examples). Therefore, a query in content-based retrieval is represented as the set of label-instance pairs $D^{(S)}$. On another front, instances sampled from the target domain $\mathcal{D}^{(T)}$ are denoted by $X^{(T)}$, and label-instance pairs are denoted by $D^{(T)}$, in which a label represents binary relevance or graded relevance for a search intent; thus, a label space $Y^{(T)}$ is a set of integer values. A content-based retrieval system ranks the instances $X^{(T)}$ based on a ranking function $f : X^{(T)} \to \mathbb{R}$ trained by label-instance pairs $D^{(S)}$ and target instances $X^{(T)}$, where a total order $\prec$ on the instances $X^{(T)}$ is given by $x_i^{(T)} \prec x_j^{(T)} \Leftrightarrow f(x_i^{(T)}) \leq f(x_j^{(T)})$. To evaluate content-based retrieval systems, an arbitrary information retrieval metric is applied to a totally ordered instance set $(X^{(T)}, \prec)$.

For example of content-based geographic object retrieval, a user can select a region (e.g. Beijing) as the source domain $\mathcal{D}^{(S)}$ and another (e.g. Kyoto) as the target domain $\mathcal{D}^{(T)}$. In this case, their feature spaces $\mathcal{X}^{(S)}$ and $\mathcal{X}^{(T)}$ are the same: a set of all possible restaurant instances. A set of restaurant instances in $\mathcal{D}^{(S)}$ is denoted by $X^{(S)} = \{x_1^{(S)}, x_2^{(S)}, x_3^{(S)}\}$, and we assume that the set is obtained by sampling instances following the marginal distribution $P(X^{(S)})$. The user can select a subset $Q = \{x_1^{(S)}, x_2^{(S)}\}$ of $X^{(S)}$, which can be represented as $D^{(S)} = \{(x_1^{(S)}, +1), (x_2^{(S)}, +1), (x_3^{(S)}, -1)\}$. A content-based geographic object retrieval system receives $D^{(S)}$ as a query, and ranks a set of restaurant instances $X^{(T)} = \{x_1^{(T)}, x_2^{(T)}, x_3^{(T)}\}$ sampled from $\mathcal{D}^{(T)}$.

The most important difference from domain adaptation tasks addressed in previous work is that no label information in the target domain is available during the training process in content-based retrieval. Relevant instances in the target domain depend on the user's search intents; thus, it is not realistic to prepare labels for all possible search intents. Note that in many cases all the instances from the target domain are not available for training in ad-hoc information retrieval due to the amount of data. Instead of using all the data, one can sample some data from the target domain or re-rank top ranked instances using them as target instances. For content-based geographic object retrieval, it is feasible to use all the target instances because the size of instances in a region the user focuses on is generally small (1,000 at most).

The difference between domains is characterized by the difference in feature spaces and marginal distributions. In content-based geographic object retrieval, for example, features spaces in different domains are the same, i.e. $\mathcal{X}^{(S)} = \mathcal{X}^{(T)}$. A restaurant instance is represented as three elements in any domain: the price range, category, and description of a restaurant in natural language. On the other hand, marginal distributions in different domains can be different, i.e. $P(X^{(S)}) \neq P(X^{(T)})$. For example, there are many expensive restaurants in Tokyo, many Japanese-style restaurants in Kyoto, and many restaurants serving spicy dishes in Beijing. Recent studies proposed methods for quantifying the domain difference by using $\mathcal{A}$-distance for estimating the learning bound for domain adaptation [3, 21]. In our experiment, we demonstrated the domain difference measured by $\mathcal{A}$-distance $d_{\mathcal{A}}$ for ensuring that domains we used are different from each other. We used the inequation $\mathcal{D}^{(S)} \neq \mathcal{D}^{(T)}$ if and only if the $\mathcal{A}$-distance $d_{\mathcal{A}}(\mathcal{D}^{(S)}, \mathcal{D}^{(T)})$ is greater than a threshold ϵ.

In summary, domain adaptation for content-based retrieval is defined as follows: given label-instance pairs $D^{(S)}$ from a source domain $\mathcal{D}^{(S)}$ and instances $X^{(T)}$ from a target domain $\mathcal{D}^{(T)}$ such that $\mathcal{D}^{(S)} \neq \mathcal{D}^{(T)}$, *domain adaptation for content-based retrieval* is the problem of predicting a ranking function f that maximizes an information retrieval metric of a totally ordered instance set $(X^{(T)}, \prec)$.

4. DOMAIN ADAPTATION BASED ON RELATIVE AGGREGATION POINTS

We propose a domain adaptation method for content-based retrieval in this section. Our assumption is that different domains include corresponding points that may not be the same in terms of their representation, but play the same role in heterogeneous domains. We first introduce RAPs that we believe to be such points and then propose a method for constructing a new feature representation for each instance based on RAPs. We also introduce several

[1] `http://people.csail.mit.edu/jrennie/20Newsgroups/`

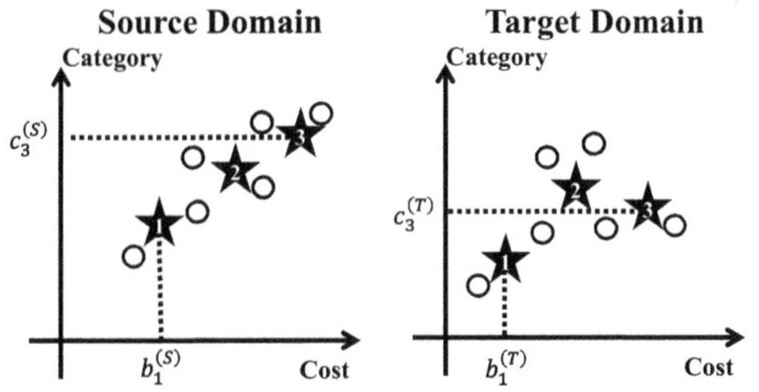

Figure 1: RAPs and construction of a new feature representation. Black stars are RAPs, and white circles are instances. Stars that have the same number are corresponding.

examples of the RAP for geographic object retrieval at the end of this section. Although this domain adaptation method is a framework and can be applied to any type of instances, we use an example of a restaurant instances for simplicity. A simplified restaurant instance x has two attributes: the cost x_b (continuous) and category x_c (a set of category values such as Japanese-style and sushi), and can be represented as a d-dimensional vector $\mathbf{x}$ if needed.

4.1 Feature Representation based on Relative Aggregation Points

A RAP is the expectation of instances in a domain that are classified into a certain class. Let us consider the maximum cost point in a domain $\mathcal{D} = (\mathcal{X}, P(X))$, which is the most expensive restaurant. Given a set of instances X sampled from the domain $\mathcal{D}$, we can easily identify the most expensive restaurants within X, and represent these restaurants as $\psi_{\text{MAX}}(X) = \text{argmax}_{x \in X} x_b$, where x_b is the cost of x. However, a set of instances X might not be representatives sampled from the domain $\mathcal{D}$. For example, the set of instances X may include an extremely expensive out-lier despite the low average cost of the domain. Therefore, we estimate the expectation of the most expensive instances in all possible instance sets sampled from a domain.

Given a domain $\mathcal{D}$ and a subset function $\psi : 2^{\mathcal{X}} \to 2^{\mathcal{X}}$ ($2^{\mathcal{X}}$ is a collection of subsets of $\mathcal{X}$), the RAP a_ψ is defined as follows:

$$a_\psi = \int_{x \in \mathcal{X}} \mathbf{x} P(x|\psi) dx, \quad (1)$$

where $\mathbf{x}$ is the vector representation of an instance x, and $P(x|\psi)$ is the probability that x is sampled from a subset $\psi(X)$ of any instance set X sampled from the domain $\mathcal{D}$. The probability $P(x|\psi)$ is given by marginalizing out a set of instances X:

$$P(x|\psi) = \int_{X \in 2^{\mathcal{X}}} P(x|\psi, X) P(X) dX, \quad (2)$$

where $P(x|\psi, X)$ is the probability that x is sampled from a subset $\psi(X)$. Intuitively, the subset function ψ indicates the deterministic membership of an instance, while probability $P(x|\psi)$ indicates probabilistic membership, which is more stable than the deterministic one.

RAPs are relative because they can vary in different domains for the same subset function ψ. Figure 1 illustrates RAPs as black stars in two domains, where the feature space includes two dimensions: cost and category (e.g. the Japaneseness of a restaurant). Black star 1 is the minimum cost point, star 2 is the average cost point, and star 3 is the maximum cost point, all of which are different between the two domains. We assume that RAPs in different domains correspond and features of RAPs also correspond. In Figure 1, we regard costs of the minimum cost points as the same, i.e. $b_1^{(S)} = b_1^{(T)}$, and categories of the maximum cost points in different domains as the same, i.e. $c_3^{(S)} = c_3^{(T)}$. For the example of Kyoto and Beijing, the maximum cost point in Kyoto and that in Beijing are different: a restaurant serving Kyoto cuisine for 10,000 JPY and one serving Beijing duck for 5,000 JPY. By using the maximum cost point in Kyoto and Beijing, we assume that 10,000 JPY corresponds to 5,000 JPY and Kyoto cuisine corresponds to Beijing duck. Kyoto cuisine in Kyoto is considered the same as Beijing duck in Beijing since those dishes are delicacies in each domain. Based on the above assumption, we can model each instance by the similarity to RAPs, where instances in different domains are similar if their features are similar to ones of RAPs.

We give a concrete feature representation based on RAPs. Let $H = \{h_1, h_2, \ldots h_m\}$ denote a set of similarity functions between two instances, and $A = \{a_1, a_2, \ldots a_n\}$ denote a set of RAPs in a domain $\mathcal{D}$. For example, H includes the similarity in terms of the cost and that in terms of the category. By using a function $\phi : \mathcal{X} \to \mathbb{R}^{mn}$, we transform an instance $x \in \mathcal{X}$ into a mn-dimensional vector $\phi(x)$. The function ϕ is defined as follows:

$$\phi(x) = (\phi_1(x), \phi_2(x), \ldots, \phi_n(x)) \quad (3)$$

where $\phi_i(x) = (h_1(x, a_i), h_2(x, a_i), \ldots, h_m(x, a_i))$ and each dimension corresponds to the similarity to a RAP measured by a similarity function. Combining the vector representation $\mathbf{x}$ of an instance x and the feature representation based on RAPs $\phi(x)$, we obtain an augmented feature representation $(\mathbf{x}, \lambda\phi(x))$, where λ is a parameter that determines the importance of the feature representation based on RAPs. Note that the vector $\mathbf{x}$ and mn-dimensional vector $\phi(x)$ are normalized by their L^2-norm in practice.

RAPs are estimated separately in the source and target domains. Letting $\phi^{(S)}$ denote a function based on RAPs estimated in the source domain and $\phi^{(T)}$ denote one in the target domain, a source instance $x^{(S)} \in X^{(S)}$ is converted into $(\mathbf{x}^{(S)}, \lambda\phi^{(S)}(x^{(S)}))$, while $x^{(T)} \in X^{(T)}$ is converted into $(\mathbf{x}^{(T)}, \lambda\phi^{(T)}(x^{(T)}))$. Thus, our method enables us to take into account ordinary similarity (i.e. the similarity between $\mathbf{x}^{(S)}$ and $\mathbf{x}^{(T)}$), as well as the similarity based on RAPs (i.e. the similarity between $\phi^{(S)}(x^{(S)})$ and $\phi^{(T)}(x^{(T)})$).

The motivating example, relatively inexpensive restaurants serving popular local dishes, is processed by using RAPs in the following way. Relatively inexpensive restaurants should be similar to the minimum cost point in terms of the cost, and restaurants serving local dishes may be similar to restaurants of a category that frequently appears in a domain. It is also possible that expensive or average restaurants serve popular local dishes, and the similarity to such restaurants in terms of the category is helpful to capture what the popular local dishes are. Therefore, we can find relevant restaurants in another heterogeneous domains by calculating the similarity between similarities to those RAPs.

4.2 Examples of Relative Aggregation Point

Our proposed method is a framework, and effective RAPs highly depend on the task. We present some examples of the RAPs that are effective for the content-based geographic object retrieval. Note that methods for estimating RAPs from finite samples are not essential for the purpose of this paper; thus, we describe these methods in Appendix A.

AVG. The most *normal* restaurant may be considered equivalent in different domains. The average (AVG) RAP is the average of instances in a domain. The subset function ψ_{AVG} is defined as $\psi_{\text{AVG}}(X) = \{x | x \in X\}$; thus, the probability $P(x|\psi_{\text{AVG}})$ is equal to the marginal distribution $P(x)$. Therefore, the AVG RAP is defined as follows: $a_{\psi_{\text{AVG}}} = \int_{x \in \mathcal{X}} \mathbf{x} P(x) dx$.

MAX/MIN. The maximum (MAX) (and minimum (MIN)) cost may correspond in different domains as mentioned earlier. The MAX RAP is the expectation of instances that has the maximum cost in a domain. The subset function ψ_{MAX} is defined as $\psi_{\mathrm{MAX}}(X) = \mathrm{argmax}_{x \in X}\, x_b$, where x_b is the cost of an instance x. The probability $P(x|\psi_{\mathrm{MAX}})$ is given by $P(x|\psi_{\mathrm{MAX}}) = \int_{b \in \mathbb{R}} P(x|b)P(b|\psi_{\mathrm{MAX}})db$, using the probability $P(b|\psi_{\mathrm{MAX}})$ of cost b, which is the maximum cost in any instance set, and the probability of x conditioned by b. Therefore, the MAX RAP is defined as follows: $a_{\psi_{\mathrm{MAX}}} = \int_{x \in \mathcal{X}} \mathbf{x} \int_{b \in \mathbb{R}} P(x|b)P(b|\psi_{\mathrm{MAX}})dbdx$.

The MIN RAP is obtained in the same way as the MAX RAP, where the subset function ψ_{MIN} is defined as $\psi_{\mathrm{MIN}}(X) = \mathrm{argmin}_{x \in X}\, x_b$.

FREQ. Relatively frequent (FREQ) categories may correspond in different domains. For example, Japanese-style in Kyoto and Chinese-style in Beijing represent the same meaning, i.e. a popular category in a domain. The subset function ψ_{FREQ} is defined as $\psi_{\mathrm{FREQ}}(X) = \{x | x \in X \wedge (\forall c \in x_c)\mathrm{freq}_X(c) > \mathrm{freq}_A(c)\}$, where $\mathrm{freq}_X(c)$ is the frequency of category value c in a set of instances X, and A is a set of instances sampled from the entire domain (or all the domains we have). This subset function ψ_{FREQ} returns instances with categories that are more frequent in X than those in A. A FREQ RAP is obtained as follows in a similar manner to MAX/MIN: $a_{\psi_{\mathrm{FREQ}}} = \int_{x \in \mathcal{X}} \mathbf{x} \int_{C \in \mathcal{C}} P(x|C)P(C|\psi_{\mathrm{FREQ}})dCdx$, where $\mathcal{C}$ is a collection of subsets of category values.

CLS. RAPs can be automatically defined through clustering. The subset function ψ_{CLS} is defined as $\psi_{\mathrm{CLS}}(X) = \{x | x \in X \wedge x \in S\}$, where a set of instances S is obtained through clustering applied to instances in both the source and target domains. Since $P(x|\psi_{\mathrm{CLS}})$ is independent from a way of samplings, the CLS RAP is simply defined as follows: $a_{\psi_{\mathrm{CLS}}} = \int_{x \in \mathcal{X}} \mathbf{x} P(x|S)dx$.

5. TEST COLLECTION

In this section we describe a method for developing our test collection for content-based geographic object retrieval[2], and show the statistics of the test collection including the degree of differences between domains.

5.1 Instances

Our test collection includes 46,945 restaurant instances crawled from a Japanese restaurant Web site *GourNavi*[3], which is one of the biggest sites that provide restaurant information in Japan. We opted to target at restaurant data for several reasons. Restaurant search is usually conducted with an ambiguous search intent that cannot be easily expressed by using keywords. Moreover, the difference between domains (or regions) is originally derived from the cultural difference and inherits its properties; thus, the difference is generally large and difficult to understand. Therefore, restaurant search is one of the most attractive applications of content-based geographic object retrieval.

Restaurant instances in our test collection include several attributes such as the cost, category, name, genre, and introduction of a restaurant. The name (e.g. Fujiyama), genre (e.g. traditional Japanese sushi bar), and introduction (a detailed description of a restaurant written in natural language, which comprises about 200 words) are text, which were processed by *MeCab*[4], a Japanese morphological analyzer. Only nouns and adjectives were used to construct a text vector $\mathbf{x}_t$ whose elements represent the term frequency in those text attributes. Feature selection was carried out excluding terms that occured less than three times in our test collection. The category attribute is a set of category values, e.g. {bar, sushi, Japanese-style}. We treated the category attribute the same as text attributes (i.e. bag-of-words), and represented a category vector as $\mathbf{x}_c$. Although category values are hierarchically structured in the GourNavi Web service (e.g. top categories include Japanese-style and Western-style, and sub categories under the Japanese-style category include sushi and tempura), we did not use the hierarchical structure for simplicity. The text and category attributes were separately processed and were weighted by the tf-idf method. To be more specific, the i-th element of the text vector $\mathbf{x}_t$ for an instance x is $\mathrm{tf}(t_i)\log(N/\mathrm{df}(t_i))$, where $\mathrm{tf}(t_i)$ is the frequency of a term t_i in the instance x, $\mathrm{df}(t_i)$ is the number of instances that include the term t_i, and N is the number of instances in our test collection. The category vector $\mathbf{x}_c$ is weighted in the same manner. To process the cost attribute together with text and category attributes, we discretized the cost and represented it as a probability distribution on discrete values. The cost b was assumed to follow a normal distribution $\mathcal{N}(z; b, \sigma)$, and was discretized by the probability of each z in a set of real values Z. The cost b was represented by a $|Z|$-dimensional vector $\mathbf{x}_b$ whose element corresponds to each element $z \in Z$ and is $\mathcal{N}(z; b, \sigma)$. In our test collection, Z includes every 500 from $-5{,}000$ to 40,000, and $\sigma = 1{,}000$. This discretization is not essential but is convenient for computation of the similarity between restaurant instances. Through the above processes, an instance was represented as a d-dimensional vector $\mathbf{x} = (\mathbf{x}_t, \mathbf{x}_c, \mathbf{x}_b)$, where d =15,670 in our test collection.

Table 1: The number of instances (#), the average cost (Avg.), and relatively frequent category values in each domain.

Domain	#	Avg. (JPY)	Frequent category values
Kyoto	510	4,530	Japanese-style
Tokyo	511	6,410	Western-style
Sapporo	514	3,490	Seafood
Fukuoka	500	3,760	*Nabe*, Seafood
Nagoya	529	3,590	*Izakaya*

5.2 Domains

We chose five major cities (Kyoto, Tokyo, Sapporo, Fukuoka, and Nagoya) in Japan. We selected a region from each city that contain about 500 restaurant instances, and used the five regions as domains in our test collection. Table 1 shows the number of instances, the average cost, and relatively frequent category values in each domain. The average cost in Tokyo is especially high, that in Kyoto follows, and there is no significant difference across other three domains. There are many Japanese-style restaurants in Kyoto, many Western-style ones in Tokyo, and many *izakaya* ones in Nagoya. The number of seafood restaurants is relatively large in Sapporo and Fukuoka, and that of *nabe* restaurants is slightly large in Fukuoka. Those differences in the average cost and category indicate the difference between marginal distributions, and may affect the performance of content-based geographic object retrieval.

To measure the difference between the five domains and to ensure that domains in our test collection are significantly different from each other, the $\mathcal{A}$-distance $d_{\mathcal{A}}$ was calculated between all the pairs of domains in our test collection. The $\mathcal{A}$-distance was introduced by Ben-David et al. [3], and was defined as the upper bound of the difference between the two marginal distributions $P(X^{(S)})$

[2]The dataset is available at `http://www.mpkato.net/datasets/`.

[3]`http://www.gnavi.co.jp/`

[4]`http://mecab.sourceforge.net/`

and $P(X^{(T)})$. To compute the $\mathcal{A}$-distance from finite samples of the source and target domains, we approximated the distance by a method introduced by Rai et al. [21].

We calculated the $\mathcal{A}$-distance of all the pairs of domains in our test collection, which ranges from 0.537 (Fukuoka-Nagoya) to 0.745 (Kyoto-Tokyo). Rai et al. [21] reported the $\mathcal{A}$-distance across eight types of user reviews in the multi-domain sentiment dataset[5], and the $\mathcal{A}$-distance ranges from 0.0459 (Kitchen-Apparel) to 0.762 (DVD-Book). Comparing the $\mathcal{A}$-distance in our test collection and the multi-domain sentiment dataset, we found that our domains are as different from each other as domains used in some previous work [4, 21], even though all the instances are restaurants and all the domains are domestic cities. Therefore, we will use the inequation $\mathcal{D}^{(S)} \neq \mathcal{D}^{(T)}$ for any pair of the domains hereinafter since it was revealed that any pair of the domains is significantly different, i.e. $d_{\mathcal{A}}(\mathcal{D}^{(S)}, \mathcal{D}^{(T)}) > \epsilon$, as mentioned in Section 3.

5.3 Search Intents

To select relevant instances in our test collection, which were used as a query in the source domain and as the ground truth in the target domain, search intents had to be documented for being understood by subjects. To this end, we manually gathered questions from the *restaurant* category in Yahoo! Chiebukuro [6] (Japanese Yahoo! Answers), where the asker asks restaurants that are relevant to his intents. We opted to use Yahoo! Chiebukuro as the resource of search intents because complex and realistic intents are posted there. A hundred of questions were extracted as search intents from Yahoo! Chiebukuro, and were classified into two types in terms of *domain-dependency* for characterizing each search intent. Domain dependency is the degree of variability of a search intent in different domain, and was subjectively evaluated by two assessors we hired only for this task. We asked them to score the extracted search intent on a scale from one (independent from the domain) to five (dependent on the domain). As their agreement on 100 questions was low: 0.233 in terms of quadratic weighted kappa [24], we separated the labels into *domain-dependent* (a score is three or more) and *domain-independent* (a score is less than three), and excluded all the questions on which the two assessors disagreed. As a result, 57 questions remained, of which 20 (35.1%) questions were domain-dependent and 37 (64.9%) questions were domain-independent. We selected ten questions each from the sets of domain-dependent and domain-independent questions, and included them as 20 search intents in our test collection.

An example of domain-dependent search intents is "I'm going to <v> for business trip with my boss. Do you have any recommendations for dinner? It would be great if you would tell us restaurants for from 3,000 to 5,000 JPY that provide <v>-specific dishes with Japanese sake. We are 30's and 40's. Either meat or fish dish is OK." On the other hand, an example of domain-independent search intents is "Please show me Western restaurants in <v>. I want a Italian or French restaurant that has a lunch course for 5,000 JPY without wine," where the variable <v> is replaced with the name of a domain, or a region (e.g. Kyoto).

5.4 Procedure of Relevance Judgment

We recruited 1,000 subjects living in five regions through an online questionnaire service, and asked them to select instances relevant to each search intent in their home area. The five regions are Kyoto city in Kyoto, 23 special wards in Tokyo, Sapporo city in Hokkaido, Fukuoka city in Fukuoka, and Nagoya city in Aichi, which correspond to the five domains, Kyoto, Tokyo, Sapporo, Fukuoka, and Nagoya. We asked the subjects to select relevant instances in a domain corresponding to their home area because it is difficult to judge the relevance without domain knowledge. Note that the recruitment was controlled so that the number of subjects is uniform for each sex, age, and region combination, i.e. 20 subjects were sampled from each (male and female), (20's, 30's, 40's, 50's, and 60's), and (Kyoto, Tokyo, Sapporo, Fukuoka, and Nagoya) combination. The online questionnaire service we used is hosted by a domestic company, which delivered a mail to users and asked to visit our Web system. Subjects were rewarded through the company if they finished the whole task we instructed.

The task we asked the subjects to work on consists of two steps. In the first step, the subjects were asked to examine 30 restaurant instances randomly sampled from a domain for subjects' better understanding of the domain. To make the subjects carefully examine each restaurant instance, we asked subjects to find a couple of restaurants they wanted to visit. In the second step, two search intents were assigned and presented in random order to each subject. The subjects were asked to select as many restaurants relevant to a presented search intent as possible. The subjects were allowed to use a simple search engine, and can search for restaurants by specifying the upper and/or lower limits of the cost, the top category (e.g. Japanese-style, Western-style, and Chinese-style), and sub category (e.g. sushi, Italian, and French). The search engine returns a list of restaurant instances that satisfy all the specified conditions, and the search result ranking was randomized to reduce the ranking bias. Relevance judgments for each search intent in each domain were conducted by 20 subjects, where two subjects were selected from each sex and age group.

5.5 Post-Processing of Relevance Judgments

As Alonso and Baeza-Yates indicated [1], it is important to keep the quality of relevance judgments when the assessment is conducted through an online service, or crowd sourcing. We ensured the quality of our test collection by conducting the following two steps. First, subjects who finished a task within five minutes were filtered out, as it was supposed to take more than five minutes in a preliminary system test. Second, we manually assessed all the relevant instances for each search intent in each domain, and removed *subjects* who made obviously wrong relevance judgments. For example, we removed a subject who selected a restaurant for 1,000 JPY as relevant when the subject was asked to find restaurants for 5,000 JPY. After the removal of low-quality subjects, there remained 579 subjects and 6,082 relevance judgments. On average, 11.6 subjects worked on each search intent in each domain, and made 121 relevance judgments. Finally, we merged duplicate relevance judgments and generate graded relevance by regarding the multiplicity as the grade. The average number of relevant instances per domain and search intent was 42.1, and the standard deviation was 33.3.

Our test collection contains many subjective search intents and needed as many subjects as possible for avoiding the individual bias, whereas it was difficult to ask individual to evaluate all the restaurant instances due to the cost limitation. To gain the coverage of relevance judgments, we assigned 20 subjects to each search intent and randomized the ranking result returned by the simple search system. However, the relevance judgment we conducted is not always complete since it is not guaranteed that all the restaurant instances in a domain were examined by the subjects. As Buckley and Voorhees's study on retrieval evaluation with incomplete information suggests [6], traditional evaluation metrics such as MAP

[5] `http://www.cs.jhu.edu/~mdredze/datasets/sentiment/`

[6] `http://chiebukuro.yahoo.co.jp/`

and precision at ten are not robust to substantially incomplete relevance judgments.

To assess the completeness of our relevance judgments, we used a method of estimating the population size by multiple census proposed by Schumacher and Eschmeyer [23]. Their method conducts multiple samplings, which correspond to individual's relevance judgments in our case, and estimates the population size, which corresponds to the number of relevant instances in our case. Having estimated the number of relevant instances, we can estimate the fraction of judged relevant instances to all the relevant instances. In our test collection, 62.9% of relevant instances were estimated to be actually judged by the subject. According to the Buckley and Voorhees's work [6], the moderate completeness of our test collection possibly affects the system ranking based on the evaluation metric: the Kendall correlation between the system ranking based on MAP with incomplete relevance judgments and that with complete relevance judgments was 0.9 on average in three test collections from the Text REtrieval Conference (TREC). Although we cannot argue that our test collection is complete and is able to accurately estimate the effectiveness of methods, the effect of the moderate completeness of our test collection is supposed to be small. Moreover, we used an evaluation metric for graded relevance, where relevant instances with a low grade make less impact on the evaluation result than ones with a high grade. As the maximum grade per search intent and region is 4.34 on average in our test collection, relevant instances that were not judged by any subjects are not seriously affect the evaluation metric compared to the binary relevance case.

6. EXPERIMENT

We answer the following two research questions through our experiment: whether domain adaptation for content-based retrieval is necessary, and whether domain adaptation based on RAPs can significantly improve the search performance of content-based retrieval in heterogeneous domains.

6.1 Experimental Settings

We selected a domain as source $\mathcal{D}^{(S)}$ and another as target $\mathcal{D}^{(T)}$ from our test collection. The input in our problem was a set of pairs of a binary label and instance $D^{(S)}$ from the source domain $\mathcal{D}^{(S)}$ as mentioned in Section 3; thus, a label $+1$ was assigned to relevant (selected) source domain instances, while -1 was assigned to irrelevant (nonselected) source domain instances, where the grade for relevance was ignored since the user does not grade but just selects instances as a query in content-based retrieval. A content-based retrieval method receives $D^{(S)}$ and target instances $X^{(T)}$ and predicts an optimal ranking function f to rank instances $X^{(T)}$ from the target domain $\mathcal{D}^{(T)}$. We used both MAP and nDCG [12] in our experiment for evaluating the results in terms of binary relevance and graded relevance. For MAP, relevant instances were defined as ones that were judged as relevant by at least one subject. For nDCG, we set the rank threshold to 10 because it is the common number of search results shown in a search engine result page.

Simple baselines are methods without any knowledge of the target domain: nearest neighbor search (NNS), one-class SVM (OSVM), and SVM. NNS ranks target instances based on the similarity to the centroid of selected instances in $D^{(S)}$. OSVM is a method incorporating the one-class SVM [8, 22], which trains a model for binary classification using only selected instances in $D^{(S)}$, and the ranking function f is defined as $f(x) = \mathbf{w}^T\mathbf{x} - \rho$. Note that $\mathbf{x}$ is a vector representation of an instance x, and $\mathbf{w}$ and ρ are parameters that determine the decision boundary of the one-class SVM. The NNS and OSVM methods do not use nonselected examples, which are considered typical content-based retrieval methods. SVM is a method based on a linear support vector machine using label-instance pairs $D^{(S)}$, which trains a model for binary classification, and the ranking function f is defined as $f(x) = \mathbf{w}^T\mathbf{x} + b$, where $\mathbf{w}$ and b are parameters that determine the decision boundary of the SVM.

Baseline domain adaptation methods are transductive support vector machine (TSVM), structural correspondence learning (SCL), and relative cluster mapping (RCM), all of which use knowledge of both the source and target domains. TSVM proposed by Joachims [13] has been used as a baseline for domain adaptation tasks [16, 28]. The ranking function of this baseline is predicted in the same way as the SVM method. SCL was also compared with our proposed method, which is a state-of-the-art method for domain adaptation [4, 5]. SCL constructs a new feature space and represents each instance with additional features generated based on *pivots* (features that behave similarly in the source and target domains). We applied the SVM method to augmented vectors of instances for predicting the ranking function f. RCM was selected as a baseline since the problem definition and motivation are similar to ours [18]. RCM represents an instance by the vector from the centroid of a set of instances to a vector representing the instance itself. We then applied the SVM in the same manner as SCL.

Our proposed RAP-based domain adaptation method includes a parameter λ, and has variants that use different RAPs. We set $\lambda = 1$ (default) and included all the RAPs mentioned in Section 4.2 for the comparison. The best setting for those factors were explored after comparison. A set of similarity functions involves the cosine of the cost $\mathbf{x}_b$, that of the category $\mathbf{x}_c$, that of the text $\mathbf{x}_t$, and that of $\mathbf{x}$. The CLS RAPs were obtained by using CLUTO[7] with default parameters. The number of clusters was set to 30. The training was conducted using the SVM in the same manner as the baseline domain adaptation methods.

The SVM and TSVM methods were implemented using SVM^{light}[8], and the OSVM was implemented using LIBSVM[9]. All parameters were set to default by the software. SCL was implemented according to the paper authored by Blitzer et al. [4, 5][10]. For SCL, we selected features that occur more than five times in the source and target domains and showed the highest mutual information with respect to labels in the source domain. The number of dimensions h was set to 50 according to a study using SCL for comparison [19], and the number of pivots was set to 100, which is smaller than the one used in the comparison study, due to the lack of frequently occurring features in our test collection.

6.2 Is Domain Adaptation Necessary for Content-based Retrieval?

We first present an answer to the first research question: is domain adaptation for content-based retrieval necessary? The SVM method, which is a baseline that does not use any domain adaptation technique, was applied to all the search intents. In an in-domain setting ($\mathcal{D}^{(S)} = \mathcal{D}^{(S)}$), we used a method similar to k-fold cross validation, where instances in a domain are split into k bins, of which $k - 1$ bins are used as the source and the rest are used as the target. In our study, we set k to 5 and recorded the average

[7]http://glaros.dtc.umn.edu/gkhome/views/cluto/

[8]http://svmlight.joachims.org/

[9]http://www.csie.ntu.edu.tw/~cjlin/libsvm/

[10]To test our implementation of SCL, we applied it to a dataset Blitzer et al. developed [4], which is the one we referred to in Section 5.2. The average accuracy was 0.774, which is close to the average accuracy Blitzer et al. reported.

Table 2: The average nDCG@10 over all the search intents in each combination of the source and target domains. The bold font indicates in-domain settings, while the others are out-domain settings.

		Target				
		Kyoto	Tokyo	Sapporo	Fukuoka	Nagoya
Source	Kyoto	**0.620**	0.463	0.520	0.511	0.431
	Tokyo	0.460	**0.596**	0.449	0.501	0.389
	Sapporo	0.492	0.432	**0.638**	0.524	0.506
	Fukuoka	0.505	0.472	0.510	**0.588**	0.477
	Nagoya	0.476	0.466	0.538	0.527	**0.599**

nDCG@10 over k runs. For an out-domain setting ($\mathcal{D}^{(S)} \neq \mathcal{D}^{(T)}$), we applied a similar method to the in-domain setting for comparison. A domain was used as the source and another was used as the target, where instances in the source and the target domains were split into k bins, of which $k-1$ bins in the source domain were used as input and a bin in the target domain was used as instances to be retrieved. The query in our experiment was different for the combination of the source and search intent. The number of unique queries was 100 (5 domains $\times$ 20 intents). The target domain was selected from the five domains; thus, we conducted 500 runs (5 domains $\times$ 100 queries).

Table 2 lists the average nDCG@10 over all the search intents in each pair of the source and target domains. It is clear that the average nDCG@10 in out-domain settings ($\mathcal{D}^{(S)} \neq \mathcal{D}^{(T)}$) was lower than that in in-domain settings ($\mathcal{D}^{(S)} = \mathcal{D}^{(S)}$). There was a negative correlation between the average nDCG@10 and the $\mathcal{A}$-distance (Pearson's coefficient $r = -0.678$, $p < 0.05$). The negative correlation indicates that the more different domains are, the more difficult it is to achieve high search performance. The average nDCG@10 for the in-domain and out-domain settings are 0.608 and 0.482, respectively. With a Welch's t-test, we found a significant difference between the in-domain and out-domain settings, $t(179) = 5.89, p < 0.001$[11]. Moreover, the effect size of the domain setting was 0.588 in terms of Cohen's d, which is considered medium.

The significant difference in search performance between the in-domain and out-domain settings suggests that domain adaptation for content-based retrieval is necessary. This result also implies that relevant data can vary even for the same search intent when the search context is different. The difference in search context in our case consists of the difference between datasets from which the system retrieves data, the difference between search locations, and the difference between user's home areas. Recently, studies have suggested that relevant data can vary for different users [25] and different search devices [14]. In addition to such hypotheses, our results pose new hypotheses stating that relevant data can vary for different datasets and/or locations where the user searches, which are still open questions since we did not separate the two effects.

6.3 How Effective Is Domain Adaptation based on Relative Aggregation Points?

We compared our RAP-based domain adaptation method with baselines, NNS, OSVM, SVM, TSVM, SCL, and RCM, to demonstrate its effectiveness. We conducted 400 runs (4 out-domains $\times$ 100 queries) in this experiment. Tables 3 and 4 list the average MAP and nDCG@10 for each search intent in the out-domain setting, respectively. "Transductive" methods use knowledge of the target domain, while "Inductive" methods do not. The bold font indicates the highest score per search intent. One-way ANOVA showed a significant effect of methods on MAP and nDCG, $F(6, 2793) = 16.1$, $p < 0.001$ and $F(6, 2793) = 40.0$, $p < 0.001$, respectively. With a paired t-test[12], we found significant differences between baselines and the RAP-based domain adaptation method at $\alpha = 0.05$, which are indicated by a dagger † at the "Total" row in Tables 3 and 4.

Table 3: The average MAP for each search intent in the out-domain setting.

		Inductive			Transductive			
	Intent	NNS	OSVM	SVM	TSVM	SCL	RCM	RAP
Domain-dependent	1	0.539	**0.546**	0.490	0.417	0.482	0.490	0.490
	2	0.387	0.452	0.522	0.439	0.512	0.521	**0.574**
	3	**0.347**	0.319	0.317	0.344	0.321	0.317	0.320
	4	0.409	0.350	0.672	0.558	**0.688**	0.672	0.668
	5	0.488	0.458	0.512	0.506	0.515	0.513	**0.522**
	6	0.198	0.227	0.327	0.329	0.324	0.327	**0.333**
	7	0.078	0.083	**0.155**	0.150	0.153	**0.155**	0.144
	8	0.192	0.219	0.254	0.206	0.251	0.254	**0.260**
	9	0.488	0.491	0.548	0.561	0.548	0.548	**0.570**
	10	**0.261**	0.293	0.335	0.305	0.329	0.335	**0.337**
Domain-independent	11	0.442	0.401	0.630	0.581	0.631	0.630	**0.654**
	12	0.180	0.177	0.280	0.233	**0.284**	0.280	**0.284**
	13	0.586	0.571	**0.645**	0.627	0.638	**0.645**	0.640
	14	0.115	0.114	**0.161**	0.109	**0.161**	**0.161**	0.156
	15	0.354	0.293	**0.545**	0.506	0.541	**0.545**	0.538
	16	0.416	0.399	0.702	0.609	0.686	0.701	**0.705**
	17	0.270	0.270	0.379	0.317	0.384	0.379	**0.385**
	18	0.256	0.226	**0.401**	0.312	0.398	**0.401**	0.399
	19	0.586	0.595	0.641	0.532	**0.646**	0.641	0.645
	20	**0.288**	0.286	0.238	0.203	0.236	0.238	0.239
Total		0.344†	0.338†	0.438†	0.392†	0.436†	0.438†	**0.443**

Table 4: The average nDCG@10 for each search intent in the out-domain setting.

		Inductive			Transductive			
	Intent	NNS	OSVM	SVM	TSVM	SCL	RCM	RAP
Domain-dependent	1	0.191	**0.192**	0.175	0.176	0.171	0.177	0.173
	2	0.173	0.249	0.406	0.277	0.415	0.406	**0.420**
	3	0.149	0.123	0.084	**0.151**	0.103	0.084	0.086
	4	0.145	0.087	0.389	0.315	0.367	0.386	**0.395**
	5	0.182	0.167	0.242	0.250	0.260	0.242	**0.283**
	6	0.118	0.162	0.267	0.213	0.261	0.267	**0.268**
	7	0.024	0.046	**0.174**	0.121	0.170	**0.174**	0.168
	8	0.213	0.251	0.303	0.219	**0.311**	0.303	0.309
	9	0.199	0.184	0.254	0.223	0.258	0.254	**0.282**
	10	0.130	0.178	0.277	0.226	0.269	**0.278**	0.266
Domain-independent	11	0.208	0.172	0.589	0.582	0.617	0.589	**0.631**
	12	0.148	0.121	0.288	0.162	**0.296**	0.288	0.295
	13	0.201	0.198	0.295	0.262	0.283	0.295	**0.325**
	14	0.068	0.056	0.184	0.038	**0.194**	0.184	0.183
	15	0.285	0.230	0.483	**0.513**	0.509	0.483	0.492
	16	0.164	0.136	0.487	0.375	**0.496**	0.486	0.486
	17	0.107	0.135	0.418	0.230	**0.475**	0.418	0.440
	18	0.222	0.174	**0.368**	0.206	0.356	**0.368**	0.323
	19	0.305	0.345	0.492	0.378	0.493	0.492	**0.540**
	20	0.118	0.109	0.127	0.081	**0.128**	0.120	0.121
Total		0.168†	0.166†	0.315	0.250†	0.322	0.315	**0.324**

Our proposed RAP-based domain adaptation method achieved significant improvements over all the baseline methods in terms of MAP, and over NNS, OSVM, and TSVM in terms of nDCG@10. It can be seen that the RAP-based domain adaptation method achieved high MAP and nDCG@10 especially for domain-dependent search intents. SCL achieved comparable nDCG@10 scores but failed to improve the MAP. SCL selected some features as pivots such as "private room" and "seafood," which are considered common in any domains. The MAP and nDCG@10 of

[11] We also tested the difference between the in-domain and out-domain settings in terms of MAP (0.609 vs. 0.479) and found a significant difference, $t(157) = 5.35$, $p < 0.001$, Cohen's $d = 0.585$.

[12] Holm's method was used to adjust the significance level for multiple comparisons.

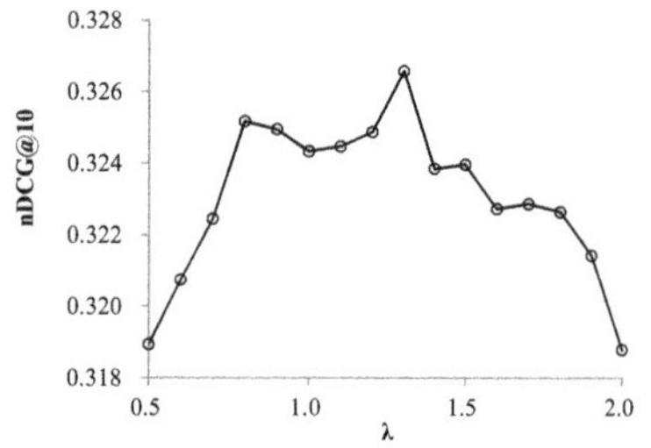

Figure 2: The average nDCG@10 curve for the parameter λ.

RCM was almost the same as SVM, since the centroid vector of instances had small values for all the dimensions in our case: the value distribution was flattened by taking an average over all the instance vectors. The TSVM was worse than SVM in many of the search intents, probably because the number of relevant instances per search intent was not balanced across domains, the same label distribution in the source and target domains is assumed with TSVM. SVM showed higher MAP and nDCG@10 than methods using only selected examples, i.e. NNS and OSVM. The difference between SVM and those methods is that SVM did use nonselected examples. Therefore, this result suggests that using not only selected examples but also nonselected examples can improve the search performance of content-based retrieval when most of the relevant instances are selected in the source domain.

Our proposed RAP-based domain adaptation method showed considerable improvements of nDCG@10 for search intents 5, 11, and 19. Search intent 5 was "Please tell me a tranquil restaurant appropriate for entertaining foreign guests in <v>. Our budget is around 8,000 JPY per person," search intent 11 was "I am looking for Western restaurants in <v> for Christmas dinner for 7,500 JPY per person (but not picky about the cost)," and search intent 19 was "Please show me Japanese restaurants or ones serving meat for celebrating my father's birthday in <v>. He cannot eat Italian dishes or drink alcohol. Our maximum budget is 40,000 JPY for three people." These intents include ambiguous conditions, e.g. a category in search intent 5, and budget in the search intent 11, which can be different in different domains. For example, Japanese restaurants were often judged as relevant in Kyoto for search intent 5, while Western restaurants were usually relevant in Tokyo. As shown in Table 1, Kyoto include many Japanese restaurant and is famous for Japanese-style restaurants because it is one of the oldest cities in Japan. On the other hand, there are many Western-style restaurants in Tokyo because it is a modern international city in Japan. The difference in frequent categories might be lessened by RAPs in our proposed method, which leads to high search performance. Similarly, relevant restaurants were more expensive in Tokyo than those in Kyoto for search intent 11, and the cost difference was probably bridged by RAPs related to the cost.

6.4 Parameter Tuning

There are a parameter λ and choices of RAPs in our proposed RAP-based domain adaptation method. We tested several values for λ using all the RAPs mentioned in the experimental setting. The average nDCG@10 over all the search intents are plotted in Figure 2. The setting $\lambda = 0.5$ was relatively close to the SVM (no RAP was used), while the setting $\lambda = 2.0$ was relatively close to where only features derived from RAPs were used. The best λ was 1.3 in our test collection. These results suggest that both original and domain-dependent features are necessary to better model the similarity between instances in different domains.

We also tested the effectiveness of each RAP. Table 5 lists the relative MAP and nDCG@10 for all combinations of RAPs. The

Table 5: The relative MAP and nDCG@10 for all the combination of RAPs.

	MAP	nDCG@10
CLS, MAX/MIN, AVG	100.0%	98.4%
CLS, MAX/MIN	99.7%	95.4%
CLS, MAX/MIN, Mode	99.4%	94.5%
CLS, MAX/MIN, AVG, FREQ	98.3%	95.9%
MAX/MIN, AVG	96.1%	16.1%
CLS, FREQ	95.2%	97.3%
CLS, AVG, FREQ	93.9%	94.5%
CLS, AVG	92.5%	99.6%
CLS	91.2%	100.0%
AVG	37.7%	-8.7%
(None)	0.0%	0.0%
MAX/MIN, AVG, FREQ	-68.7%	-19.7%
MAX/MIN, FREQ	-139.2%	-27.9%
MAX/MIN	-144.1%	-26.3%
AVG, FREQ	-225.9%	-102.0%
FREQ	-383.6%	-105.8%

percentage indicates the gain from (None), a method with no RAP, normalized by the maximum gain of MAP or nDCG@10. The FREQ RAP was the least effective in our test collection and rather impaired search performance. In contrast, the CLS RAP was the most effective in our experiment and improved search performance even when only CLS was used. The MAX/MIN and AVG achieved high MAP scores when they were used together. The best performance in terms of both MAP and nDCG@10 was obtained by the combination of CLS, MAX/MIN, and AVG. As future work, we will develop a method of finding effective RAPs for a given task.

7. CONCLUSIONS

We introduced the problem of domain adaptation for content-based retrieval, and proposed a domain adaptation method based on RAPs. We developed a test collection for content-based geographic object retrieval, and provided answers to two research questions.

The first research question was whether domain adaptation for content-based retrieval is necessary. Our experimental results showed that evaluation metrics in an out-domain setting ($\mathcal{D}^{(S)} \neq \mathcal{D}^{(T)}$) were significantly lower than those in an in-domain setting ($\mathcal{D}^{(S)} = \mathcal{D}^{(T)}$). Therefore, we conclude that the answer to the first research question is *yes*: search performance without domain adaptation significantly decreases when the source and target domains are heterogeneous, and domain adaptation for content-based retrieval is necessary.

The second research question was whether domain adaptation based on RAPs can bridge the domain difference and significantly improve the search performance of content-based retrieval in heterogeneous domains. Our experimental results answered the second research question by showing significant improvements over baseline methods.

Future work involves applying the RAP-based method to other datasets. In practice, developing a method for finding effective RAPs is the most important part of future work, as it is difficult to find effective RAPs manually. Although we assume that feature spaces in the source and target domains are the same in this paper, it is possible to apply our proposed RAP-based domain adaptation method to heterogeneous feature spaces such as image and music feature spaces. The RAP-based method requires only a within-domain similarity function not a between-domain similarity function for domain adaptation, and enables a user to find popular music by selecting popular pictures. There is also a need to further study the effect of the domain differences, such as the difference between datasets from which the system retrieves data, between search locations, and between user's profiles, on search tasks.

8. ACKNOWLEDGMENTS

This work was supported in part by the following projects: Grants-in-Aid for Scientific Research (Nos. 24240013, 24680008, and 22·4687) from MEXT of Japan, and a Kyoto University GCOE Program entitled "Informatics Education and Research for Knowledge-Circulating Society."

9. REFERENCES

[1] O. Alonso and R. Baeza-Yates. Design and implementation of relevance assessments using crowdsourcing. In *Proc. of ECIR*, pages 153–164, 2011.

[2] N. J. Belkin. Helping people find what they don't know. *Communications of the ACM*, 43:58–61, 2000.

[3] S. Ben-David, J. Blitzer, K. Crammer, and F. Pereira. Analysis of representations for domain adaptation. In *Proc. of NIPS*, pages 137–144, 2006.

[4] J. Blitzer, M. Dredze, and F. Pereira. Biographies, Bollywood, Boom-boxes and Blenders: Domain Adaptation for Sentiment Classification. In *Proc. of ACL*, pages 440–447, 2007.

[5] J. Blitzer, R. McDonald, and F. Pereira. Domain adaptation with structural correspondence learning. In *Proc. of EMNLP*, pages 120–128, 2006.

[6] C. Buckley and E. M. Voorhees. Retrieval evaluation with incomplete information. In *Proc. of SIGIR*, pages 25–32, 2004.

[7] P. Cai, W. Gao, A. Zhou, and K. Wong. Relevant knowledge helps in choosing right teacher: active query selection for ranking adaptation. In *Proc. of SIGIR*, pages 115–124, 2011.

[8] Y. Chen, X. Zhou, and T. Huang. One-class svm for learning in image retrieval. In *Proc. of ICIP*, pages 34–37, 2001.

[9] T. Chia, K. Sim, H. Li, and H. Ng. A lattice-based approach to query-by-example spoken document retrieval. In *Proc. of SIGIR*, pages 363–370, 2008.

[10] W. Dai, G.-R. Xue, Q. Yang, and Y. Yu. Co-clustering based classification for out-of-domain documents. In *Proc. of KDD*, pages 210–219, 2007.

[11] W. Gao, P. Cai, K.-F. Wong, and A. Zhou. Learning to rank only using training data from related domain. In *Proc. of SIGIR*, pages 162–169, 2010.

[12] K. Järvelin and J. Kekäläinen. Cumulated gain-based evaluation of ir techniques. *ACM Transactions on Information Systems*, 20(4):422–446, 2002.

[13] T. Joachims. Transductive inference for text classification using support vector machines. In *Proc. of ICML*, pages 200–209, 1999.

[14] M. Kamvar, M. Kellar, R. Patel, and Y. Xu. Computers and iphones and mobile phones, oh my!: a logs-based comparison of search users on different devices. In *Proc. of WWW*, pages 801–810, 2009.

[15] M. P. Kato, H. Ohshima, S. Oyama, and K. Tanaka. Search as if you were in your home town: geographic search by regional context and dynamic feature-space selection. In *Proc. of CIKM*, pages 1541–1544, 2010.

[16] X. Ling, W. Dai, G.-R. Xue, Q. Yang, and Y. Yu. Spectral domain-transfer learning. In *Proc. of KDD*, pages 488–496, 2008.

[17] Y. Liu, D. Zhang, G. Lu, and W. Ma. A survey of content-based image retrieval with high-level semantics. *Pattern Recognition*, 40(1):262–282, 2007.

[18] S. Nakajima and K. Tanaka. Relative queries and the relative cluster-mapping method. In *Proc. of DASFAA 2004*, pages 843–856, 2004.

[19] S. Pan, X. Ni, J. Sun, Q. Yang, and Z. Chen. Cross-domain sentiment classification via spectral feature alignment. In *Proc. of WWW*, pages 751–760, 2010.

[20] S. Pan and Q. Yang. A survey on transfer learning. *IEEE Transactions on Knowledge and Data Engineering*, 22(10):1345–1359, 2010.

[21] P. Rai, A. Saha, H. Daumé III, and S. Venkatasubramanian. Domain adaptation meets active learning. In *Proc. of the NAACL HLT 2010 Workshop on Active Learning for Natural Language Processing*, pages 27–32, 2010.

[22] B. Schölkopf, J. Platt, J. Shawe-Taylor, A. Smola, and R. Williamson. Estimating the support of a high-dimensional distribution. *Neural computation*, 13(7):1443–1471, 2001.

[23] F. X. Schumacher and R. W. Eschmeyer. The estimation of fish populations in lakes and ponds. *Journal of the Tennessee Academy of Sciences*, 18:228–249, 1999.

[24] J. Sim and C. Wright. The kappa statistic in reliability studies: use, interpretation, and sample size requirements. *Physical therapy*, 85(3):257–268, 2005.

[25] J. Teevan, S. Dumais, and E. Horvitz. Potential for personalization. *ACM Transactions on Computer-Human Interaction*, 17(1):1–31, 2010.

[26] B. Wang, J. Tang, W. Fan, S. Chen, Z. Yang, and Y. Liu. Heterogeneous cross domain ranking in latent space. In *Proc. CIKM*, pages 987–996, 2009.

[27] H. Wang, H. Huang, F. Nie, and C. Ding. Cross-language web page classification via dual knowledge transfer using nonnegative matrix tri-factorization. In *Proc. of SIGIR*, pages 933–942, 2011.

[28] G. Xue, W. Dai, Q. Yang, and Y. Yu. Topic-bridged plsa for cross-domain text classification. In *Proc. of SIGIR*, pages 627–634, 2008.

APPENDIX

A. ESTIMATION OF RELATIVE AGGREGATION POINTS

We approximately estimated RAPs by using finite samples X from a domain. Expectation $E[\mathbf{x}]$ can be approximated as follows: $E[\mathbf{x}] = \int_{x \in \mathcal{X}} \mathbf{x} P(x) dx \approx \frac{1}{|X|} \sum_{x \in X} \mathbf{x}$, where $|X|$ is the number of instances X. This approximation is directly applied to the equation for the AVG RAP.

Similarly, expectation $E[\mathbf{x}|S]$ can be approximated by instances $X_S = X \cap S$ as follows: $E[\mathbf{x}|S] = \int_{x \in \mathcal{X}} \mathbf{x} P(x|S) dx \approx \frac{1}{|X_S|} \sum_{x \in X_S} \mathbf{x}$, which is applied to the equation for the CLS RAP.

The equations for the MAX/MIN and FREQ RAPs are the same form and can be written as follows: $\int_{w \in W} P(w|\psi) \int_{x \in \mathcal{X}} \mathbf{x} P(x|w) dx dw$, where w is an attribute value (i.e. a cost or a category) and W is the entire set of w. By using the approximation for the CLS RAP, we can approximate the equation as follows: $\sum_{w \in W_X} \frac{P(w|\psi)}{|X_w|} \sum_{x \in X_w} \mathbf{x}$, where X_w is a set of instances that have the attribute value w, and W_X is a set of attribute values included in the instance set X.

For the MAX RAP, we assume that the cost follows a normal distribution g, and the number of sampled instances from a domain is constant l. The probability of the cost b that is the maximum cost in a set of sampled instance is then defined as $P(b|\psi_{\mathrm{MAX}}) = \{G(b)\}^l$, where G is the cumulative distribution function of the normal distribution g. For the MIN RAP, the probability $P(b|\psi_{\mathrm{MIN}})$ is defined as $P(b|\psi_{\mathrm{MIN}}) = 1 - \{1 - G(b)\}^l$.

For the FREQ RAP, we assume that the frequency of a category value c follows a binomial distribution B, and is independent from the frequency of other values. In addition, the number of sampled instances from a domain is assumed to be constant l. The probability of a category value c that is more frequent in instances sampled from a domain $\mathcal{D}$ than in ones sampled from another $\mathcal{D}'$ is then defined as $P(c|\psi_{\mathrm{FREQ}}) = \sum_{i=0}^{l} \sum_{j=i+1}^{l} B_{\mathcal{D}}(i) B_{\mathcal{D}'}(j)$, where $B_{\mathcal{D}}(i)$ is the probability that a category value c occurs i times in l instances sampled from $\mathcal{D}$. Thus, $P(C|\psi_{\mathrm{FREQ}})$ is represented as $P(C|\psi_{\mathrm{FREQ}}) = \prod_{c \in C} P(c|\psi_{\mathrm{FREQ}})$ based on the independent assumption.

Mixture Model with Multiple Centralized Retrieval Algorithms for Result Merging in Federated Search

Dzung Hong
Department of Computer Science
Purdue University
250 N. University Street
West Lafayette, IN 47907, USA
dthong@cs.purdue.edu

Luo Si
Department of Computer Science
Purdue University
250 N. University Street
West Lafayette, IN 47907, USA
lsi@cs.purdue.edu

ABSTRACT

Result merging is an important research problem in federated search for merging documents retrieved from multiple ranked lists of selected information sources into a single list. The state-of-the-art result merging algorithms such as Semi-Supervised Learning (SSL) and Sample-Agglomerate Fitting Estimate (SAFE) try to map document scores retrieved from different sources to comparable scores according to a single centralized retrieval algorithm for ranking those documents. Both SSL and SAFE arbitrarily select a single centralized retrieval algorithm for generating comparable document scores, which is problematic in a heterogeneous federated search environment, since a single centralized algorithm is often suboptimal for different information sources.

Based on this observation, this paper proposes a novel approach for result merging by utilizing multiple centralized retrieval algorithms. One simple approach is to learn a set of combination weights for multiple centralized retrieval algorithms (e.g., logistic regression) to compute comparable document scores. The paper shows that this simple approach generates suboptimal results as it is not flexible enough to deal with heterogeneous information sources. A mixture probabilistic model is thus proposed to learn more appropriate combination weights with respect to different types of information sources with some training data. An extensive set of experiments on three datasets have proven the effectiveness of the proposed new approach.

Categories and Subject Descriptors

H.3.3 [**Information Storage and Retrieval**]: Information Search and Retrieval

General Terms

Algorithms, Design, Performance

Keywords

Federated Search, Result Merging, Mixture Model

1. INTRODUCTION

Federated search (also known as distributed information retrieval) [17, 23, 29] is an important research area of information retrieval. Unlike traditional information search systems such as Google or Bing, which index webpages or documents that can be crawled and collected, federated search targets on information distributed in independent information providers. Many contents in this environment may not be arbitrarily crawled and searched by traditional search engines, due to various reasons such as copyright, security and data protection. Only the owners of those documents can provide a full searching service to their set of documents. We refer to a collection of documents with its own and customized search engine as an information source. The size of this type of information (i.e., hidden Web contents) has been estimated to be many times larger than Web contents searchable by traditional search engines [3].

Federated search offers a solution for searching hidden Web contents by building a bridge between users, who have little knowledge about which kind of information sources she is looking for, and the information sources that reveal limited information about their documents through source-specific search engines. To achieve this goal, federated search includes three main research problems: resource representation, resource selection and result merging. Resource representation learns important information about the sources such as their contents and their sizes. Resource selection selects a subset of information sources which are most useful for users' queries. Result merging combines documents retrieved from selected sources into a single ranked list before presenting the list to the end users.

Among the above main problems, result merging substantially suffers from the heterogeneity of information sources. Each information source may adopt a different, customized retrieval model. A query can also be processed in many ways. Even if different sources use similar retrieval algorithms, they may have different source statistics (e.g., different values of inverse document frequencies). All of those make it difficult to compare documents of different sources. A simple solution that downloads all document contents and ranks them with a single method for each user query may yield good results, but it is also costly in an online setting.

Other solutions such as downloading parts of the documents [6] or incorporating scores from the resource selection component into source-specific document scores (e.g., CORI [4]) also suffer when information sources do not provide enough information or vary greatly in their scales of document ranking scores.

The state-of-the-art result merging algorithms merge documents by learning how to map document scores in ranked lists of multiple information sources to comparable document scores. The basic idea is to utilize a centralized sample database created with all sample documents obtained in resource representation. For each query, these algorithms rank documents in the centralized sample database with a single retrieval algorithm, and then build a mapping function between source-specific document scores (or ranks) and comparable document scores. By mapping document scores/ranks returned from all selected sources to a common scale, it is possible to construct the final ranked list. Algorithms of this class such as SSL [27], SAFE [24] and WCF [12] have shown promising results. However, despite using various learning algorithms, those methods still do not fully address the heterogeneity of retrieval algorithms in different information sources. The problem lies in the fact that all these existing methods arbitrarily select a single fixed centralized retrieval algorithm for learning the mapping, which is problematic in a heterogeneous federated search environment, as a single algorithm is often suboptimal for learning comparable scores for different sources.

In this paper, we propose a novel result merging algorithm that utilizes multiple centralized retrieval algorithms. This method can generate more accurate results in result merging due to the flexibility of using multiple types of centralized retrieval algorithms for estimating comparable document scores. In particular, the paper shows that it is not desirable to learn a fixed set of weights (e.g., with a logistic regression approach) for different centralized retrieval algorithms in estimating comparable document scores. A mixture probabilistic model is proposed to automatically learn the appropriate weights for different types of information sources with some training data. The mixture model approach is more flexible in calculating comparable document scores for a heterogeneous set of information sources. Empirical studies have been conducted with three federated search datasets to show the advantages of the proposed result merging algorithm. In particular, one new dataset is created from the Wikipedia collection of ClueWeb data.

The rest of the paper is organized as follows. Section 2 discusses some research work generally related with the work in this paper. Section 3 discusses two specific state-of-the-art results merging algorithms (SSL and SAFE) as they are directly related with the proposed research. Section 4 proposes the novel result merging algorithm with multiple centralized retrieval algorithms. Section 5 introduces experimental methodology. Section 6 presents the detailed experimental results and provides some discussions. Section 7 concludes and points out some future research directions.

2. RELATED WORK

Federated search includes three main research problems: resource representation, resource selection and result merging. There is a large volume of previous research work in all of those research problems. This section first briefly introduces most related prior research in resource representation and resource selection. Then it will provide more details about the literature of result merging.

Resource representation is to collect information about each information source. Such information usually includes sources' sizes, document frequencies, term frequencies, and other statistics. The START protocol [9] is one of the first attempt to standardize the communication between information sources and a broker (or centralized agent) in order to collect, search and merge documents from individual sources. However, this approach can only work in cooperative environments. In an uncooperative environment, it is more practical to collect source statistics with sampling algorithms. The query-based sampling method [4] is a popular algorithm for sampling documents from a set of information sources. In principal, query-based sampling sends randomly generated terms as queries to a source, and downloads the top documents as sample documents for each query. When this process is done, the set of all sample documents can be collected in a *centralized sample database* to build a single index. The centralized sample database is often a good representative of the (imaginary) complete database of all documents in a federated search environment.

Resource selection is to select a subset of information sources most relevant to the user's query. Resource selection has been studied intensively during the last two decades. Many algorithms have been developed, such as GlOSS [10], CORI [4], ReDDE [26], CRCS [22], topic models [2], the classification-based model [1] and many others. The Relevant Document Distribution Estimation (ReDDE) resource selection algorithm and its variants have been shown to generate good and robust resource selection results in different types of federated search environments. ReDDE selects relevant sources by first ranking sample documents in the centralized sample database. Then, each document among the top of the list can contribute a score to its containing source. The magnitude of the score depends on both document's rank and the source's size. Finally, the relevance of a source is measured by the combined score of all of its sample documents.

Result merging is to collect the ranked list of documents from each selected source and combine them into a single ranked list to present to users. Result merging in federated search is similar to data fusion [32, 25], or merging process in multilingual information retrieval [30]. In data fusion, different retrieval models are applied to a single information source, and the problem is to get the best combination of retrieval algorithms. Whereas, in federated search, there are multiple information sources with different (often unknown) retrieval models. Similar to information fusion, multilingual information retrieval also assumes that the whole collection index is available to the merger during the process, which is not always the case in federated search.

One scenario is that the broker can download all returned documents from selected sources, and apply a centralized retrieval algorithm to produce the final ranked list. However, in practice, this method is rarely used since the high cost of communication and time may impair user experience. In another simple case, when all sources implement the same retrieval model, documents' scores (or ranks) returned by the source may be comparable with each other. Thus, merging their scores (or ranks) directly (also known as Raw Score Merging), or in a round-robin fashion may give good results with low cost. However, it is noticed that even if all sources share the same model, some statistics such as document frequency of a term are still different across different sources. It is generally not practical to assume that all independent sources share such a same set of collection statistics.

Some other algorithms in the early generation of federated search also relied on term statistics for making decision. Craswell et al. suggested that by partially downloading a part of the top returned documents, we can approximate term statistics to build the final rank list [6]. Xu and Croft requested that document statistics of query terms should be provided to the broker, in such a way that they can calculate the global inverse document frequencies [34]. However, these algorithms again require some type of collaboration from the independent sources, which is often unavailable.

CORI result merging algorithm [4] is a relatively simple, yet effective algorithm. The intuition is that comparable document scores should depend on two factors: (i) how good a document is compared to other documents from the same source; and (ii) how good the source containing a particular document is compared to other sources. CORI makes a linear combination of those two factors and gets the final score of a document as:

$$D' = \frac{D + 0.4 \times D \times C'}{1.4}$$

where D' is the global score, D is the original score within the source, and C' is the normalized source score from the resource selection step.

The merging algorithm proposed by Rasolofo et al. [19] also explores the combination between document scores and source weights. Unlike CORI, their source weights are not directly related with the sources' relevance scores. Rather, the weight of a source depends on the total number of documents that it returns. The algorithm assumes that a source containing more relevant documents may return a longer ranked list, which is not always the case for information sources using different types of ranking algorithms.

The intuition of combining document and resource scores can also be seen in a variant of the PageRank algorithm in distributed environments [31]. In this work, Wang and DeWitt employed the source's ServerRank and the document's LocalRank to derive the global PageRank values.

Semi-Supervised Learning (SSL) [27] and the Sample Agglomerate Fitting Estimate (SAFE) [24] result merging algorithms offer a better trade-off in efficiency and effectiveness. Both methods try to map source-specific document ranks into comparable document scores generated by a single centralized retrieval algorithm. We will provide more detailed information about SSL and SAFE in the following section as they are directly related with the new research in this paper.

3. RESULT MERGING BY SEMI-SUPERVISED LEARNING & SAMPLE-AGGLOMERATE FITTING ESTIMATE

3.1 Semi-Supervised Learning Merging

Semi-Supervised Learning Merging (SSL) [27] uses curve fitting model to calculate comparable document scores from different sources for result merging. Specifically, given a user's query, SSL sends the query to the centralized sample database and retrieves the sample ranked list with relevance score of each document. Upon receiving documents from a selected information source, SSL checks for overlapping documents exist in the sample database. Those overlapping documents are characterized by two features: the relevance scores in the central sample database, and the relevance ranks in the specific source. The task is to estimate the relevance scores of all non-overlapping documents in the centralized complete database (the imaginary dataset of all documents of all sources). Assume that there is a linear mapping between centralized relevance scores and source-specific document ranks, then that mapping can be inferred by using a regression method on the overlapping documents. Having said that, let R_{ij} be the source-specific rank of document d_i in source C_j, and S_{ij} be the relevance score of document d_i in the centralized sample database, we can build a linear relationship.

$$S_{ij} = a_j \times R_{ij} + b_j$$

where a_j, b_j are two parameters depending on each pair of an information source and a query.

With enough overlapping documents for a source and a query, we can train a regression matrix

$$\begin{bmatrix} R_{1j} & 1 \\ R_{2j} & 1 \\ \cdots & 1 \\ R_{nj} & 1 \end{bmatrix} \times \begin{bmatrix} a_j \\ b_j \end{bmatrix} = \begin{bmatrix} S_{1j} \\ S_{2j} \\ \cdots \\ S_{nj} \end{bmatrix}$$

In the above equation, let us denote the first matrix by X, the second matrix by W, and the third matrix by Y. By minimizing the square loss error, we can derive the solution to the parameters W as

$$W = (X^T X)^{-1} X^T Y$$

One main problem of SSL is that if there is not enough overlapping documents (three requested in the original SSL work) for building a linear mapping, the model will back off to the CORI result merging formula, which is often much less effective.

3.2 Sample-Agglomerate Fitting Estimate Merging

Sample-Agglomerate Fitting Estimate (SAFE) [24] overcomes the SSL's problem of not having enough overlapping documents by estimating the ranks of unoverlapping documents in the centralized sample database. If we assume that the sampling process is uniform, then each sample document will represent the same number of unseen documents in the selected information source. Therefore, a sample document ranked at position i-th in the source-specific sample ranked

Table 1: Transformation Functions

Name	$f(x)$	Model
LIN	$f(x) = x$	$S = a \times R + b$
SQRT	$f(x) = \sqrt{x}$	$S = a' \times \sqrt{R} + b'$
LOG	$f(x) = \log x$	$S = a'' \times \log R + b''$
POW	$f(x) = 1/x$	$S = a''' \times \frac{1}{R} + b'''$

list will have an approximate rank $i \times \frac{|C|}{|C_s|}$ in the source-specific full rank, where $|C|$ is the source's estimated size, and $|C_s|$ is the source's sample size. By using the estimated source-specific ranks together with true centralized ranks (of overlapping documents), SAFE could apply regression with more information than SSL. A problem may occur when there are not enough sample documents of a selected information source in the centralized sample database. However, this is rarely the case, if ReDDE (or its variants) is used for selecting information sources, since this method usually selects a source if it has a significant number of documents in the centralized ranked list with respect to the query.

Another contribution of SAFE to SSL is that, instead of using the raw rank information of documents, SAFE applies different transformation functions to the rank, in order to find the best regression. More specifically, there are four different transformations as in Table 1. Each transformation function is applied to the source-specific ranked list to learn the set of parameters (a_{ij}, b_{ij}). Then, SAFE selects the best transformation by comparing the goodness of curve-fitting of all models based on their coefficient of determination R^2 values [11]. Specifically, for a linear regression equation $X \times w = Y$, the coefficient of determination is calculated as follows.

$$R^2 = \frac{||\hat{Y}||^2}{||Y||^2} = \frac{Y^T P Y}{Y^T Y}$$

where $P = X(X^T X)^{-1} X^T$

4. MIXTURE OF RETRIEVAL MODELS FOR RESULT MERGING

SSL and SAFE are state-of-the-art algorithms for result merging in federated search. However, because of their choosing of a single centralized retrieval algorithm for calculating comparable document scores, these algorithms still do not fully address the heterogeneity of different information sources in federated search environments . A single centralized retrieval algorithm may have good curve-fittings for some information sources, but may also be less fit for some others. This paper proposes to use multiple centralized retrieval algorithms to retrieve a set of ranking scores for each document. Moreover, rather than assigning a fixed set of weights to combine the above scores, our model learns a more appropriate combination of weights with respect to different types of information sources. We assume that there is an underlying distribution (i.e., latent groups) of sources according to their adopted retrieval models. Learning the proposed model thus becomes learning the distribution of groups and the combination weights associated with each group. This model is called the *Mixture of Retrieval Models* (MoRM) for result merging. MoRM is related with SSL and SAFE in the way that it uses the centralized sample database to learn the comparable document scores by curve-fitting. However, unlike SSL and SAFE, MoRM employs multiple retrieval algorithms for the centralized sample database. Therefore it is more flexible to address the heterogeneity of information sources in federated search environments for improving the accuracy of result merging.

4.1 MoRM's Framework

In this section, we describe the general framework of MoRM for document merging. The following steps are applied when a query comes:

- A resource selection algorithm such as ReDDE [26] selects a subset of information sources that are most relevant to the user's query.
- The query is then forwarded to the selected information sources. Each source will return a ranked list of documents. Scores of the returned documents will help the model's performance but are not required. Document ranks are usually sufficient for the next step.
- MoRM also issues the query to the centralized sample database and retrieves documents using a set of predetermined algorithms. At the end of this step, it obtains a set of ranked lists of sample documents.
- For each ranked list, MoRM tries to learn a mapping between source-specific document ranks and the centralized document scores. Ranks of sample documents that are not in the source-specific ranked list are estimated in a similar way as in the SAFE algorithm. All transformation functions as listed in Table 1 are tested in order to find the best curve fitting parameters. The best transformation function is applied to predict the comparable scores of all returned documents.
- All comparable scores of a document are combined using a set of combination weights learned from a training dataset. These final scores are used to rank documents.

In the following sections, we will propose a simple logistic regression model (for learning a single set of combination weights) and then propose the mixture of retrieval models (for learning multiple sets of combination weights) for the task of estimating documents' comparable scores.

4.2 Logistic Regression for Learning Comparable Scores

A learning algorithm such as logistic regression may address the problem of combining different document scores seamlessly. We chose logistic regression to demonstrate the approach of learning a single set of combination weights for ranking documents. Logistic regression is a discriminative model that models the probability that a binary event happens by a sigmoid function. In this case, our predictive functions are:

$$P(y^q_{cd} = 1|\vec{w}, \vec{x}^q_{cd}) = \frac{1}{1 + \exp(-\vec{w} \cdot \vec{x}^q_{cd})} = \sigma(\vec{w} \cdot \vec{x}^q_{cd}) \quad (1)$$

and

$$P(y^q_{cd} = -1|\vec{w}, \vec{x}^q_{cd}) = 1 - P(y^q_{cd} = 1) = \sigma(-\vec{w} \cdot \vec{x}^q_{cd}) \quad (2)$$

where our notations for this model are as follows: let the superscript q refer to the query q, and the subscript cd refer to the d-th document of source c (such a document is called D_{cd}). We also use $\vec{x}^q_{cd}$ to denote the feature vector of document D_{cd} (the set of comparable scores of D_{cd} according to different centralized retrieval algorithms), and $\vec{w}$ for the set of weights associated with $\vec{x}^q_{cd}$. Our target is to predict y^q_{cd}, which is the relevance of document D_{cd} with respect to the query q. The possible values of y^q_{cd} are:

$$y^q_{cd} = \begin{cases} 1 & \text{if document } D_{cd} \text{ is relevant to query } q \\ -1 & \text{otherwise} \end{cases}$$

Finally, in the equations (1) and (2) above, we also use $\sigma(z)$ to indicate the sigmoid function

$$\sigma(z) = \frac{1}{1+\exp(-z)}$$

and apply this property: $\sigma(-x) = 1 - \sigma(x)$.

Given $\mathcal{C}$, the number of sources; Q, the number of queries, and all the returned documents D_{cd} with respect to the training queries, we can write the likelihood function of the model as

$$\mathcal{L}(\vec{w}) = \prod_{q=1}^{|Q|}\prod_{c=1}^{\mathcal{C}}\prod_{d=1}^{D_c} P(y^q_{cd}|\vec{w}, \vec{x}^q_{cd}) = \prod_{q=1}^{|Q|}\prod_{c=1}^{\mathcal{C}}\prod_{d=1}^{D_c} \sigma(y^q_{cd}\vec{w}\cdot\vec{x}^q_{cd})$$

where we have combined equations (1) and (2) above. Learning the combination weight $\vec{w}$ can be done by maximizing the log-likelihood function using the iterative re-weighted least squares method [8].

4.3 Mixture of Retrieval Models for Learning Comparable Document Scores

We now describe the mixture model of retrieval algorithms (MoRM) for result merging. MoRM offers more prediction capability by automatically learning multiple sets of combination weights, each of them is associated with a "soft" information source cluster. The word "soft" means that we use probability to assign a source to its cluster, rather than fixing a hard assignment. Specifically, assuming that there are K of such clusters, and let π_{ck} be the probability that the source c belongs to group k, then the following constraints must be hold:

$$\textstyle\sum_{k=1}^{K}\pi_{ck} = 1 \quad \text{for } c = 1, 2, \cdots, \mathcal{C}$$

To make our formulations simpler, in this section, we will first derive the formulations for only one query, and drop the superscript q of y_{cd} and $\vec{x}_{cd}$. At the end of this section, we will extend the formulations for the set of training queries. Furthermore, we will denote σ_{cdk} for $P(y_{cd}|\vec{w}_k, \vec{x}_{cd})$ (the probability that the document D_{cd} has relevance y_{cd} to the query in question, given that the collection c belongs to cluster k. In short, $\sigma_{cdk} = \sigma(y_{cd}\vec{w}_k \cdot \vec{x}_{cd})$).

Let $\vec{\mathbf{w}} = \{\vec{w}_k | k = 1, \cdots, K\}$, and $\boldsymbol{\pi} = \{\pi_{ck}|c = 1, \cdots, \mathcal{C}; k = 1, \cdots, K\}$. Given a query q, let $\vec{\boldsymbol{\theta}} = \{\vec{\mathbf{w}}, \boldsymbol{\pi}\}$ denote the set of parameters, in which each combination weight $\vec{w}_k$ is associated with the k-th cluster. MoRM assumes the same combination weight for all sources of a cluster for building robust combination model with a limited amount of training data, hence we will set $\pi_k = \pi_{ck} = \pi_{c'k}$ for all sources c, c'.

The probability that a document D_{cd} has relevance y_{cd} given all parameters is calculated as follows.

$$P(y_{cd}|\vec{\boldsymbol{\theta}}, \vec{x}_{cd}) = \sum_{k=1}^{K}\pi_k P(y_{cd}|\vec{w}_k, \vec{x}_{cd}) = \sum_{k=1}^{K}\pi_k\sigma_{cdk} \quad (3)$$

The component π_k acts as the prior of the clusters' distribution, which adjusts the belief of relevance according to each cluster. This equation is also known as the mixture of logistic regression. Given that model, the likelihood function for the training dataset with respect to one query is as follows.

$$\mathcal{L}(\vec{\boldsymbol{\theta}}) = \prod_{c=1}^{\mathcal{C}}\prod_{d=1}^{D_c}\sum_{k}^{K}\pi_k\sigma_{cdk} \quad (4)$$

where D_c is the number of documents returned by the source c.

It is difficult to optimize the above function directly, since taking its logarithm still presents the summation inside the log. Therefore, we will utilize the Expectation Maximization (EM) algorithm [7] to learn the parameters. The derivation of EM algorithm is discussed in the following section.

4.4 Learning MoRM using EM Algorithm

Let $\boldsymbol{z_c}$ be a K-dimensional latent variable associated with source c. $\boldsymbol{z_c}$ has only one element which equals to 1 and the all other elements equal 0 (i.e., a 1-of-K representation). Therefore, $\boldsymbol{z_c}$ must satisfy the following constraints.

$$\textstyle\sum_{k=1}^{K} z_{ck} = 1 \quad \text{for } c = 1, 2, \cdots, \mathcal{C}$$

where z_{ck} is the k-th element of $\boldsymbol{z_c}$.

We then use $\boldsymbol{z_c}$ as the indicator of the membership of source c. If c belongs to cluster k, then $z_{ck} = 1$, and the other elements of $\boldsymbol{z_c}$ equal 0. Given that π_k is the prior distribution of cluster k as above, and note that $\pi_{ck} = \pi_k$ for all c, we can write the prior distribution of z_{ck} as follows.

$$P(z_{ck} = 1) = \pi_k \quad (5)$$

Then the prior distribution of the whole vector $\boldsymbol{z_c}$ can be written as

$$P(\boldsymbol{z_c}) = \prod_{k=1}^{K}\pi_k{}^{z_{ck}} \quad (6)$$

Define another random variable $\boldsymbol{Z} = \{\boldsymbol{z_c}|c = 1, \cdots, \mathcal{C}\}$ associated with all sources. Since each source is independent of each other, the prior of $\boldsymbol{Z}$ is just the multiplication over all sources.

$$P(\boldsymbol{Z}) = \prod_{c=1}^{\mathcal{C}}\prod_{k=1}^{K}\pi_k{}^{z_{ck}} \quad (7)$$

Similarly, if we know that the source c has the membership vector $\boldsymbol{z_c}$, then the probability that the document D_{cd} of that source has relevance y_{cd} is $\prod_{k=1}^{K}\sigma_{cdk}{}^{z_{ck}}$, since σ_{cdk} is the conditional probability with respect to cluster k. Therefore, the likelihood function of the model is obtained by multiplying the above term over all sources and documents.

$$P(\boldsymbol{X}, \boldsymbol{Y}|\boldsymbol{Z}, \vec{\boldsymbol{\theta}}) = \prod_{c=1}^{\mathcal{C}}\prod_{d=1}^{D_c}\Big(\prod_{k=1}^{K}\sigma_{cdk}{}^{z_{ck}}\Big) \quad (8)$$

where $\boldsymbol{X}$ denotes all document feature vectors, and $\boldsymbol{Y}$ denotes the relevance vector of all documents. Multiplying the equations (7) and (8) above, one can calculate the complete likelihood function

$$P(\boldsymbol{X},\boldsymbol{Y},\boldsymbol{Z}|\vec{\boldsymbol{\theta}}) = \prod_{c=1}^{C}\prod_{k=1}^{K}\Big({\pi_k}^{z_{ck}}\prod_{d=1}^{D_c}{\sigma_{cdk}}^{z_{ck}}\Big) \tag{9}$$

Taking the logarithm of the above function yields the complete log-likelihood as follows.

$$\log P(\boldsymbol{X},\boldsymbol{Y},\boldsymbol{Z}|\vec{\boldsymbol{\theta}}) = \sum_{c=1}^{C}\sum_{k=1}^{K} z_{ck}\{\log \pi_k + \sum_{d=1}^{D_c}\log \sigma_{cdk}\} \tag{10}$$

The EM algorithm involves two steps. For the E-step, we need to calculate the posterior probability $P(\boldsymbol{Z}|\boldsymbol{X},\boldsymbol{Y},\vec{\boldsymbol{\theta}})$. Using (9), we can derive the following relation.

$$P(\boldsymbol{Z}|\boldsymbol{X},\boldsymbol{Y},\vec{\boldsymbol{\theta}}) = \frac{P(\boldsymbol{X},\boldsymbol{Y},\boldsymbol{Z}|\vec{\boldsymbol{\theta}})}{P(\boldsymbol{X},\boldsymbol{Y}|\vec{\boldsymbol{\theta}})} \propto \prod_{c=1}^{C}\prod_{k=1}^{K}\Big(\pi_k\prod_{d=1}^{D_c}\sigma_{cdk}\Big)^{z_{ck}} \tag{11}$$

where we can use the proportional sign $\propto$ because the denominator $P(\boldsymbol{X},\boldsymbol{Y}|\vec{\boldsymbol{\theta}})$ does not depend on $\boldsymbol{Z}$.

We wish to calculate the expectation of the variable $\boldsymbol{Z}$ under the above posterior distribution, since that term will be useful in the following M step. Given that all $\boldsymbol{z_c}$ are independent, and the right-hand side of equation (11) can be factorized over c, we can derive the expectation of each variable z_{ck} as

$$\begin{aligned}\mathbb{E}[z_{ck}] &= \frac{\sum_{\{z_{ck}\in\{0,1\}\}} z_{ck}\big(\pi_k\prod_{d=1}^{D_c}\sigma_{cdk}\big)^{z_{ck}}}{\sum_{\{z_{cj},1\le j\le K\}} z_{cj}\big(\pi_j\prod_{d=1}^{D_c}\sigma_{cdj}\big)^{z_{cj}}} \\ &= \frac{\pi_k\prod_{d=1}^{D_c}\sigma_{cdk}}{\sum_{j=1}^{K}\pi_j\prod_{d=1}^{D_c}\sigma_{cdj}} = \gamma(z_{ck})\end{aligned} \tag{12}$$

where we have defined a new variable $\gamma(z_{ck})$.

In the M-step, the updated parameters $\vec{\boldsymbol{\theta}}^{new}$ are calculated according to the following formula

$$\vec{\boldsymbol{\theta}}^{new} = \arg\max_{\vec{\boldsymbol{\theta}}} \mathcal{Q}(\vec{\boldsymbol{\theta}},\vec{\boldsymbol{\theta}}^{old}) \tag{13}$$

where

$$\mathcal{Q}(\vec{\boldsymbol{\theta}},\vec{\boldsymbol{\theta}}^{old}) = \mathbb{E}\big[\log P(\boldsymbol{X},\boldsymbol{Y},\boldsymbol{Z}|\vec{\boldsymbol{\theta}}) \mid P(\boldsymbol{Z}|\boldsymbol{X},\boldsymbol{Y},\vec{\boldsymbol{\theta}})\big]$$

Taking the expectation of $\log P(\boldsymbol{X},\boldsymbol{Y},\boldsymbol{Z}|\vec{\boldsymbol{\theta}})$ (as derived in equation (10)) with respect to the posterior distribution gives us the following objective function for the M-step.

$$\{\boldsymbol{\pi}^{new},\vec{\mathbf{w}}^{new}\} = \arg\max_{\boldsymbol{\pi},\vec{\mathbf{w}}}\sum_{c=1}^{C}\sum_{k=1}^{K}\gamma(z_{ck})(\log\pi_k + \sum_{d=1}^{D_c}\log\sigma_{cdk})$$

To find the new value of π_k, we only need to maximize the first part of the above function

$$\boldsymbol{\pi}^{new} = \arg\max_{\boldsymbol{\pi}}\sum_{c=1}^{C}\sum_{k=1}^{K}\gamma(z_{ck})\log\pi_k$$

subject to the constraint $\sum_{k=1}^{K}\pi_k = 1$

Using Lagrange multiplier and setting the gradient to 0, one can solve the optimal values of π_k as

$${\pi_k}^{new} = \frac{\sum_{c=1}^{C}\gamma(z_{ck})}{\sum_{k=1}^{K}\sum_{c=1}^{C}\gamma(z_{ck})} \tag{14}$$

Searching for the value of $\vec{w}_k^{new}$ is a bit trickier, since we have to solve the following optimization problem.

$$\vec{\mathbf{w}}^{new} = \arg\max_{\vec{\mathbf{w}}}\sum_{c=1}^{C}\sum_{d=1}^{D_c}\sum_{k=1}^{K}\gamma(z_{ck})\log\sigma_{cdk} \tag{15}$$

In fact, the gradient of the above objective function with respect to $\vec{w}_k$ is equal to:

$$\sum_{c=1}^{C}\sum_{d=1}^{D_c}\gamma(z_{ck})(1-\sigma_{cdk})y_{cd}\vec{x}_{cd}$$

Therefore, one can apply a gradient descent algorithm to find the optimal value of $\vec{w}_k$.

In the implementation of the algorithm discussed so far, there is an issue about $\gamma(z_{ck})$. As equation (12) has shown, computing $\gamma(z_{ck})$ involves calculating the product $\prod_{d=1}^{D_c}\sigma_{cdk}$. This could lead to numerical underflow since σ_{cdk} is a probability smaller than 1. Therefore, we need to calculate $\gamma(z_{ck})$ under the log space. Let

$$\gamma(z_{ck}) \propto \pi_k\prod_{d=1}^{D_c}\sigma_{cdk} = \alpha(z_{ck})$$

and $\alpha_{max} = \max_{k=1}^{K}\alpha(z_{ck})$. Therefore

$$\gamma(z_{ck}) = \frac{\alpha(z_{ck})}{\sum_{j=1}^{K}\alpha(z_{cj})} = \frac{\exp\{\log\alpha(z_{ck}) - \log\alpha_{max}\}}{\sum_{j=1}^{K}\exp\{\log\alpha(z_{ck}) - \log\alpha_{max}\}}$$

Since each $\log\alpha(z_{ck})$ is computable under the log space, the above equation will avoid the underflow problem. Finally, we extend our formulations to the set of training queries. In this case, the E-step becomes:

$$\gamma(z_{ck}) = \frac{\pi_k\prod_{q=1}^{|Q|}\prod_{d=1}^{D_c}\sigma_{cdk}^q}{\sum_{j=1}^{K}\pi_j\prod_{q=1}^{|Q|}\prod_{d=1}^{D_c}\sigma_{cdj}^q}$$

In the M-step, the update formula of π_k remains the same (equation (14)), while the optimization function in equation (15) becomes

$$\vec{\mathbf{w}}^{new} = \arg\max_{\vec{\mathbf{w}}}\sum_{c=1}^{C}\sum_{q=1}^{|Q|}\sum_{d=1}^{D_c}\sum_{k=1}^{K}\gamma(z_{ck})\log\sigma_{cdk}^q$$

and the objective gradient with respect to $\vec{w}_k$ is

$$\sum_{c=1}^{C}\sum_{q=1}^{|Q|}\sum_{d=1}^{D_c}\gamma(z_{ck})(1-\sigma_{cdk}^q)y_{cd}^q\vec{x}_{cd}^q$$

5. EXPERIMENTAL METHODOLOGY

In this section, we will describe the methodology and datasets of this work. The experiments were conducted on three datasets: two standard TREC datasets, and one Wikipedia dataset for federated search based on the ClueWeb.

Table 2: Statistics of Three Testbeds

Testbed	Size (GB)	# of inf. sources	# of documents (x1000) Min	Avg	Max	# of queries	# of relevant docs/query Min	Avg	Max
TREC123	3.2	100	0.7	10.8	39.7	100	37	483.7	1,994
TREC4-Kmeans	2.0	100	0.3	5.7	82.7	50	0	127.2	416
ClueWeb-Wiki	252	100	4.4	58.6	434.5	106	1	20.1	93

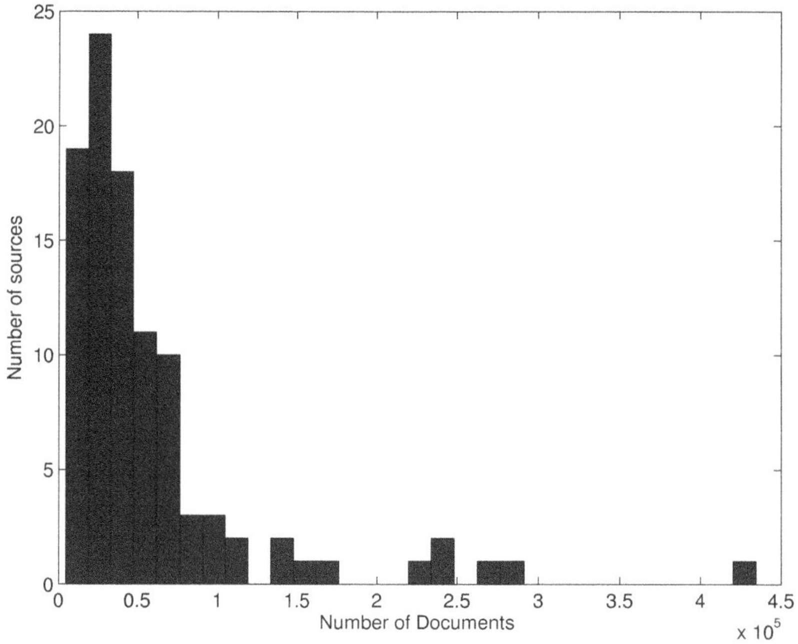

Figure 1: Histograms of the Number of Documents per Information Source in ClueWeb-Wiki. The number of bins is 30, the number of documents ranges from 4,400 to 434,525.

- **TREC123-100col-bysource (TREC123):** 100 collections (information sources) were created from TREC CDs 1,2 and 3 [4]. They are organized by publication source and publication date. This testbed comes with 100 queries (TREC topics 51-150) with judgments.
- **TREC4-100col-Kmeans (TREC4-Kmeans):** 100 collections were created from the TREC 4 data. A two-pass K-means clustering algorithm is used to organize the dataset by topic [33]. This testbed comes with 50 queries (TREC topics 201-250) with judgments.
- **Wikipedia-100col-Kmeans (ClueWeb-Wiki):** 100 collections were created from the Wikipedia dataset of the ClueWeb [13]. Similar to TREC4-Kmeans, we applied clustering algorithm [33] to divide the dataset into 100 collections. This testbed comes with 106 queries with judgments[1].

5.1 ClueWeb Wikipedia Dataset for Federated Search

Table 2 provides more statistics of the three datasets, including sizes, number of information sources; the max, min and average of the number of documents of each source. We also provide the query statistics of each dataset, including the number of queries; the max, min and average of the number of relevant documents per query.

The ClueWeb 09 is a large-scale collection of web documents that was collected in January and February 2009. The entire dataset consists of about one billion web pages in ten languages. For its tremendous size, the ClueWeb has been used in several tracks of the Text REtrieval Conference (TREC), most notably in the Web track. For distributed environment (in a different problem setting), ClueWeb has been used in [15]. It is desired to construct a new dataset based on ClueWeb for experiments in federated search.

Three Web tracks of TREC (from 2009 to 2011) have been using the ClueWeb so far. Each track has provided 50 queries based on which we build the new testbed. Within the full ClueWeb dataset, Wikipedia is the main contributor of relevant documents for Web track queries. The total size of Wikipedia is about 6 million documents, which is reasonable for creating a separate testbed. We extract all Wiki documents, and apply the same K-means algorithm that was used for creating the TREC4-Kmeans. We also select only 106 queries which contain at least one relevant Wikipedia document (out of the 150 provided queries) for training and testing. In the end, we constructed 100 information sources for the testbed ClueWeb-Wiki, with statistics provided in Table 2. The distribution of source sizes is also shown in

[1]The partition assignments are available at http://www.cs.purdue.edu/homes/dthong/clueweb

Figure 1. Most of the sources have less 70,000 documents, and there are 12 sources of more than 100,000 documents.

5.2 Experiment Configuration

Given a set of information sources, we assign each source a retrieval algorithm chosen from a set of: vector space TF.IDF with "ltc" weighting [21], a unigram statistical language model with linear smoothing (with smooth parameter as 0.5) [16] and Okapi [20] in a round robin manner. This choice is based on the fact that those models are commonly and widely used in information retrieval. Each information source is set to return at most 200 documents for each query. At the centralized sample database, we utilize five models: the three above models, the Inquery [5] and the Indri [28] algorithm. All retrieval algorithm implementations use the Lemur Toolkit [14]. We randomly select a set of queries for training, and used the other set for testing. For the TREC123, there are 50 training queries out of 100; those numbers of TREC4-Kmeans and ClueWeb-Wiki are 25 out of 50 and 50 out of 106.

We choose K, the number of latent groups, to be 3 in our main results. Some experimental results with different K values are also presented. For each information source, we sample at most 300 documents for creating the centralized sample database. For each query, we use ReDDE to select the top 5 sources for TREC123, TREC4-Kmeans and ClueWeb-Wiki.

Our metrics for the performance is the high-precision at document level, which is the percentage of the number of relevant documents in the final merged ranked list. Given that list, we measure the precision at top 5, 10, 15, 20 and 30 respectively. In next section, we will present our experimental results of all datasets.

6. EXPERIMENTAL RESULTS

6.1 High-precision Results

We now present the high-precision results on the above three testbeds. Tables 3-5 show the high-precision results on TREC123, TREC4-Kmeans and ClueWeb-Wiki respectively. The first column is our baseline using SAFE algorithm with Indri [18] as the single centralized retrieval algorithm. SAFE has been demonstrated to generate accurate and robust results compared with SSL and other results merging algorithms. We denote this method as SFI. The LR column presents the results using the logistic regression model to learn the combination weights of all centralized retrieval methods. The last column MoRM presents the results using the proposed mixture of retrieval algorithms. All precision results of LR and MoRM are compared with the baseline SFI using paired t-tests at level $p < 0.05$.

For TREC123, the performance of MoRM is significantly better than that of SFI. MoRM is also consistently better than the performance of logistics regression model. In general, both learning methods show improvements over the baseline method of one single feature. For TREC4-Kmeans, MoRM also outperforms SFI, although the differences are not significant as in TREC123. This can be explained as in TREC4-Kmeans, we only train on 25 queries, whereas in TREC123, we trained on 50 queries. These above results have shown the advantage of using multiple centralized retrieval algorithms for learning comparable document scores, over the previous model that uses only one single centralized retrieval algorithm. It also demonstrates the advantage of using the mixture model of multiple sets of weights over the logistic regression model that uses only one single set of combination weights.

For the Wikipedia dataset based on ClueWeb, the proposed model also consistently outperforms SFI and LR. The differences however are not significant. Such a significance may be harder to achieve, since on average, this dataset contains less relevant documents per query than the other datasets, as shown in Table 2.

Table 3: High-precision result on TREC123 with 300 sample documents and top 5 information sources selected for each query. A * denotes a significant difference at level $p < 0.05$ compared to the original SAFE algorithm using Indri as the only centralized retrieval algorithm.

Doc Rank	TREC123 SFI	LR	MoRM
@5	0.268	0.332 (+ 23.88 %)	**0.344** (+ 28.36 %) *
@10	0.246	0.272 (+ 10.57 %)	**0.304** (+ 23.58 %) *
@15	0.229	0.267 (+ 16.31 %)	**0.279** (+ 21.54 %) *
@20	0.208	0.251 (+ 20.67 %) *	**0.261** (+ 25.48 %) *
@30	0.208	0.229 (+ 9.95 %)	**0.232** (+ 11.54 %)

Table 4: High-precision result on TREC4-Kmeans with 300 sample documents and top 5 information sources selected for each query. A * denotes a significant difference at level $p < 0.05$ compared to the original SAFE algorithm using Indri as the only centralized retrieval algorithm.

Doc Rank	TREC4-Kmeans SFI	LR	MoRM
@5	0.272	0.280 (+ 2.94 %)	**0.296** (+ 8.82 %)
@10	0.244	0.252 (+ 3.28 %)	**0.256** (+ 4.92 %)
@15	0.211	**0.227** (+ 7.59 %)	**0.227** (+ 7.59 %)
@20	0.192	0.212 (+ 10.42 %)	**0.216** (+ 12.50 %)
@30	0.177	**0.193** (+ 9.02 %)	0.192 (+ 8.29 %)

Table 5: High-precision result on ClueWeb-Wiki with 300 sample documents and top 5 information sources selected for each query. A * denotes a significant difference at level $p < 0.05$ compared to the original SAFE algorithm using Indri as the only centralized retrieval algorithm.

Doc Rank	ClueWeb-Wiki SFI	LR	MoRM
@5	0.168	0.182 (+ 8.46 %)	**0.204** (+ 21.26 %)
@10	0.146	0.163 (+ 11.00 %)	**0.173** (+ 18.31 %)
@15	0.139	0.164 (+ 17.95 %)	**0.168** (+ 20.53 %)
@20	0.132	0.150 (+ 13.55 %)	**0.153** (+ 15.59 %)
@30	0.111	0.121 (+ 9.67 %)	**0.123** (+ 10.75 %)

6.2 Experiments with Different Number of Latent Variables

In this section, we discuss the experimental results when the number of latent variable K changes. We only report

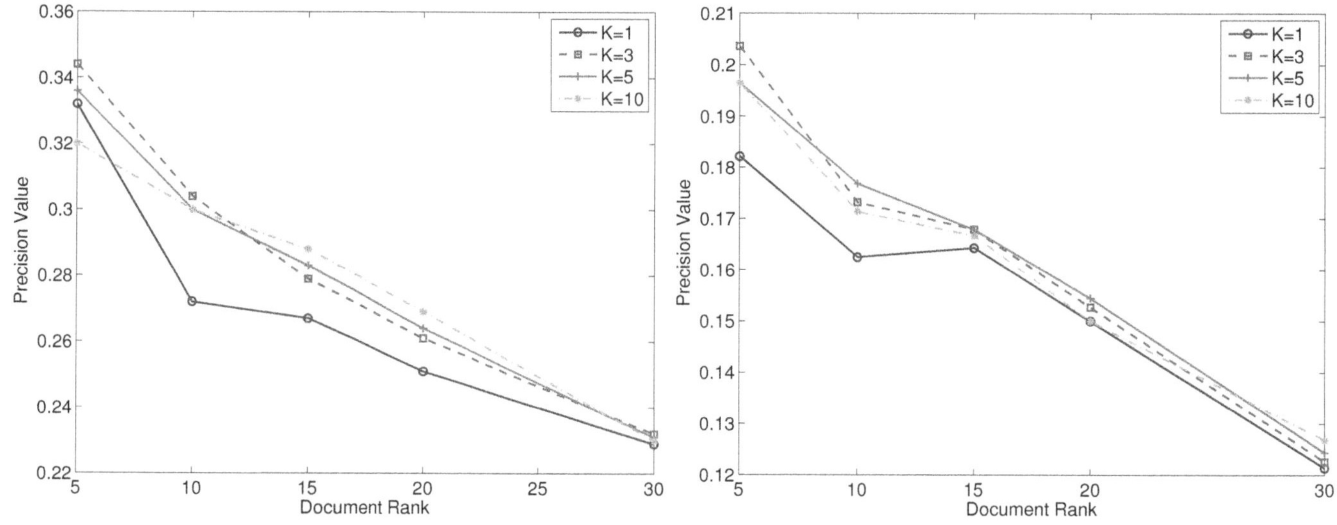

(a) TREC123 (b) ClueWeb-Wiki

Figure 2: High-precision Results of TREC123 and ClueWeb-Wiki with Different Number of Latent Variables

TREC123 and ClueWeb-Wiki for these experiments, and try different configuration of $K = \{1, 3, 5, 10\}$. Similar pattern can be observed on the TREC4-Kmeans. $K = 1$ is actually equivalent to the logistic regression model. Figure 2 shows the results of this experiment. It can be seen that the mixture of retrieval algorithms model is quite consistent with a small range of K values. For ClueWeb-Wiki, the performance of the mixture model with $K > 1$ is at least equal or higher than that of the logistic regression. For TREC123, the performances with different values of K are also stable for most of the test levels.

7. CONCLUSION & FUTURE WORK

This paper proposes a novel method of mixture model with multiple centralized retrieval algorithms for result merging in federated search. Existing result merging algorithms do not fully address the issue of heterogeneity of information sources in federated search. Their arbitrary choices of a single centralized retrieval algorithm suffer from the fact that information sources are inherently different in source statistics, query processing techniques, and/or document retrieval algorithms. The proposed model attempts to combine various evidence from multiple centralized retrieval algorithms in a mixture model framework, in order to map source-specific document ranks to comparable scores for result merging. We have shown that a single set of combination weights of the evidence do not offer enough flexibility in dealing with such a heterogeneous environment. A mixture model that learns multiple sets of combination weights according to the clusters of sources proves to be a better choice. A set of experiments has been conducted with two traditional TREC datasets and a new dataset based on the ClueWeb. The empirical results in three datasets have demonstrated the effectiveness of the proposed mixture model with multiple centralized retrieval algorithms.

This model could be extended in many ways. For instance, we could add more flexibility to the model by customizing the prior distribution π_k independently for each source, which means a source will be associated with a set of combination weights independent of the others. However, this model could require a larger training dataset to learn the parameters. A hybrid model where a cluster of similar sources independently uses multiple sets of weights is more feasible. The similarity between sources will play an important factor in creating those clusters. Another direction is to build a mixture model based on cluster of queries instead of cluster of sources, in which each query will trigger a different set of combination weights of all features. Furthermore, we can combine both of the above methods. It is also interesting to explore other types of evidence, such as the links between documents from different sources and incorporate them into the learning model.

8. ACKNOWLEDGMENTS

This work is partially supported by NSF research grants IIS-0746830, CNS- 1012208 and IIS-1017837. This work also partially supported by the Center for Science of Information (CSoI), an NSF Science and Technology Center, under grant agreement CCF-0939370.

9. REFERENCES

[1] J. Arguello, J. Callan, and F. Diaz. Classification-based resource selection. *Proceeding of the 18th ACM conference on Information and knowledge management*, pages 1277–1286, 2009.

[2] M. Baillie and M. Carman. A multi-collection latent topic model for federated search. *Information Retrieval*, 14(4):390–412, Aug. 2011.

[3] M. Bergman. The deep web: surfacing the hidden value. Technical report, 2001.

[4] J. Callan. Distributed information retrieval. *Advances in Information Retrieval*, pages 127–150, 2000.

[5] J. Callan, W. B. Croft, and S. M. Harding. The inquery retrieval system. In *Proceedings of the Third*

International Conference on Database and Expert Systems Applications, 1992.

[6] N. Craswell, D. Hawking, and P. Thistlewaite. Merging results from isolated search engines. In *Proceedings of the 10th Austrlasian Database Conference*, 1999.

[7] A. P. Dempster, N. M. Laird, and D. Rubin. Maximum likelihood from incomplete data via the em algorithm. *Journal of the Royal Statistical Society*, 39(B):1–38, 1977.

[8] R. Fletcher. *Practical methods of optimization, volume 1*. Wiley, 1987.

[9] L. Gravano, C.-C. K. Chang, H. Garcia-Molina, and A. Paepcke. Starts: Stanford proposal for internet meta-searching. In *Proceedings of the ACM-SIGMOD International Conference on Management of Data (SIGMOD)*. ACM ACM ACM ACM, 1997.

[10] L. Gravano, H. Garcia-Molina, and A. Tomasic. Gloss: text-source discovery over the internet. *ACM Transactions on Database Systems (TODS)*, 24(2):229–264, 1999.

[11] J. Gross. *Linear regression*, volume 175. Springer Verlag, 2003.

[12] C. He, D. Hong, and L. Si. A weighted curve fitting method for result merging in federated search. In *Proceedings of the 34th international ACM SIGIR conference on Research and development in Information Retrieval*, SIGIR '11, pages 1177–1178, New York, NY, USA, 2011. ACM.

[13] http://lemurproject.org/clueweb09/. The clueweb09 dataset.

[14] http://www.lemurproject.org/. The lemur toolkit.

[15] A. Kulkarni and J. Callan. Document allocation policies for selective searching of distributed indexes. *Proceedings of the 19th ACM international conference on Information and knowledge management*, pages 449–458, 2010.

[16] J. Lafferty and C. Zhai. Document language models, query models, and risk minimization for information retrieval. *Proceedings of the 24th annual international ACM SIGIR conference on Research and development in information retrieval*, pages 111–119, 2001.

[17] W. Meng and C. Yu. Advanced metasearch engine technology. *Synthesis Lectures on Data Management*, 2(1):1–129, 2010.

[18] D. Metzler and W. B. Croft. Combining the language model and inference network approaches to retrieval. *Information Processing and Management*, 40(5):735–750, 2004.

[19] Y. Rasolofo, F. Abbaci, and J. Savoy. Approaches to collection selection and results merging for distributed information retrieval. *Proceedings of the tenth international conference on Information and knowledge management*, pages 191–198, 2001.

[20] S. Robertson, S. Walker, S. Jones, M. Hancock-Beaulieu, and M. Gatford. Okapi at trec-3. *NIST SPECIAL PUBLICATION SP*, pages 109–109, 1995.

[21] G. Salton, E. Fox, and H. Wu. Extended boolean information retrieval. *Communications of the ACM*, 26(11):1022–1036, 1983.

[22] M. Shokouhi. Central-rank-based collection selection in uncooperative distributed information retrieval. *Advances in Information Retrieval*, 2007.

[23] M. Shokouhi and L. Si. Federated search. 2011.

[24] M. Shokouhi and J. Zobel. Robust result merging using sample-based score estimates. *ACM Transactions on Information Systems (TOIS)*, 27(3):1–29, 2009.

[25] X. M. Shou and M. Sanderson. Experiments on data fusion using headline information. In *Proceedings of the 25th annual international ACM SIGIR conference on Research and development in information retrieval*, SIGIR '02, pages 413–414, New York, NY, USA, 2002. ACM.

[26] L. Si and J. Callan. Relevant document distribution estimation method for resource selection. *Proceedings of the 26th annual international ACM SIGIR conference on Research and development in informaion retrieval*, pages 298–305, 2003.

[27] L. Si and J. Callan. A semisupervised learning method to merge search engine results. *ACM Transactions on Information Systems (TOIS)*, 21(4):457–491, 2003.

[28] T. Strohman, D. Metzler, H. Turtle, and C. W. B. Indri: A language model-based search engine for complex queries. In *Proceedings of the International Conference on Intelligence Analysis*, 2004.

[29] P. Thomas. Server selection in distributed information retrieval: a survey. *To appear in: Journal of Information Retrieval*, 2012.

[30] M. Tsai, H. Chen, and Y. Wang. Learning a merge model for multilingual information retrieval. *Information Processing & Management*, 47(5):635–646, 2011.

[31] Y. Wang and D. J. DeWitt. Computing pagerank in a distributed internet search system. In *VLDB '04: Proceedings of the Thirtieth international conference on Very large data bases*, pages 420–431. VLDB Endowment, 2004.

[32] S. Wu, Y. Bi, and X. Zeng. The linear combination data fusion method in information retrieval. In *Database and Expert Systems Applications*, pages 219–233. Springer, 2011.

[33] J. Xu and J. Callan. Effective retrieval with distributed collections. *Proceedings of the 21st annual international ACM SIGIR conference on Research and development in information retrieval*, pages 112–120, 1998.

[34] J. Xu and W. B. Croft. Cluster-based language models for distributed retrieval. *Proceedings of the 22nd annual international ACM SIGIR conference on Research and development in information retrieval*, pages 254–261, 1999.

Reactive Index Replication for Distributed Search Engines

Flavio P. Junqueira
Yahoo! Research
Barcelona, Spain
fpj@yahoo-inc.com

Vincent Leroy
Yahoo! Research
Barcelona, Spain
leroy@yahoo-inc.com

Matthieu Morel
Yahoo! Research
Barcelona, Spain
matthieu@yahoo-inc.com

ABSTRACT

Distributed search engines comprise multiple sites deployed across geographically distant regions, each site being specialized to serve the queries of local users. When a search site cannot accurately compute the results of a query, it must forward the query to other sites. This paper considers the problem of selecting the documents indexed by each site focusing on *replication* to increase the fraction of queries processed locally. We propose RIP, an algorithm for replicating documents and posting lists that is practical and has two important features. RIP evaluates user interests in an online fashion and uses only local data of a site. Being an online approach simplifies the operational complexity, while locality enables higher performance when processing queries and documents. The decision procedure, on top of being online and local, incorporates document popularity and user queries, which is critical when assuming a replication budget for each site. Having a replication budget reflects the hardware constraints of any given site. We evaluate RIP against the approach of replicating popular documents statically, and show that we achieve significant gains, while having the additional benefit of supporting incremental indexes.

Categories and Subject Descriptors

H.3.3 [**Information Storage Systems**]: Information Retrieval Systems

General Terms

Design, Experimentation, Performance

Keywords

Multi-site web search engine, distributed index, replication

1. INTRODUCTION

Distributed search engines aim at horizontal scalability for Web search [2, 6]. The search engine is distributed over several search sites deployed in (smaller) data centers spread across the world. Each search site only indexes a fraction of the documents, and receives the queries of the users in its region. When a query cannot be answered locally, it is forwarded to the other sites in order to compute accurate responses [2, 8]. Distributed search engines share the workload among several sites. Thus, deploying an extra site in a new data center increases the capacity of the search engine.

Designing an efficient distributed search engine is a challenging task. Traditional search engine algorithms rely on all the resources being accessed within a single data center. However, in the case of distributed search, the index is split among several distant locations. Accessing data in another search site translates into a higher response time due to network latency. Ideally, a site processes most queries locally to offer low response time and avoid the cost of processing the query in several sites. To enable this property, a careful selection of the documents to index on each site becomes necessary to guarantee that most frequently requested documents can be retrieved locally. A trivial solution is of course to replicate all documents across all sites. This solution, however desirable from a latency perspective, induces a high utilization of computer resources. Consequently, an important goal is to reduce resource utilization while providing low latency to end users through local query processing.

Brefeld *et al.* use machine-learning techniques to assign each document to one or multiple sites [4]. Their approach, however, does not consider the popularity of documents or a resource budget for each site. The popularity of documents becomes important when having to selectively drop documents due to resource constraints. Following a different approach, Blanco *et al.* propose to assign each document to a single site, and later rely on user activity to proceed to documents replication [3]. Their method relies on terms distribution and cache invalidations of a document to predict at which search site it is most likely to be requested. However, they do not propose any replication strategy.

Upon receiving a query, a search site processes it against its local index and then estimates whether other sites may have better documents, in which case the query is forwarded. Several heuristics have been developed for estimating the quality of documents in different sites. They rely on some partial knowledge of the content of the other search sites, either per-term score thresholds [2], or the scores of previously processed queries [8]. These algorithms are conservative: they can generate false positives, but no false negatives. Hence, the results computed by the distributed search engines are always the same as the ones generated by a single-

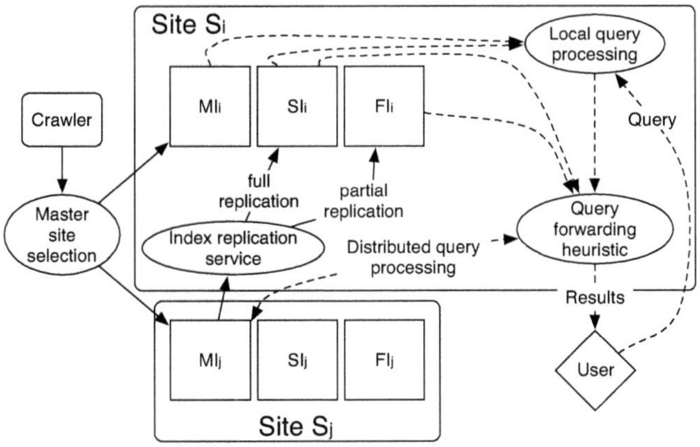

Figure 1: Architecture of a distributed search engine

site search engine. While these two approaches achieve a reasonable precision, they only target static indexes and require offline computation.

Contributions. We make the following contributions in this paper:

- We propose RIP (Reactive Indexing Protocol), a practical algorithm to selectively replicate documents and posting lists across sites in a distributed search engine. The algorithm makes decisions online and locally;
- RIP uses document popularity and user queries to select documents to replicate. Such information is important to ensure locality while respecting resource constraints;
- We evaluate the algorithm and compare it against a baseline that replicates documents statically, as well as a reactive documents replication algorithm. We show that RIP increases query locality by 23% while only increasing the index size of each site by 14%.

Roadmap. The remainder of this paper is organized as follows. We describe the architecture of the distributed search engine in Section 2. In Section 3 we present RIP, and evaluate its performance in Section 4. Finally, we review related work in Section 5 and conclude with Section 6.

2. ARCHITECTURE

We consider a distributed search engine comprising a set of search sites $\mathcal{S}$ deployed across geographically different regions. The collective of the sites forming the search engine indexes a document collection $\mathcal{D}$. We present a global view of the architecture of the distributed search engine in Figure 1, and describe the elements composing it throughout this section.

2.1 Traditional search engine architecture

The architecture of a search engine is typically divided into three components. The *crawler* fetches documents from the Web and discovers new content by following hypertext links. The *indexer* processes $\mathcal{D}$, the collection of documents, to generate an inverted index. For each term t present in the collection, the inverted index contains a posting list, *i.e.*, a list of the documents that contain t. A popular technique for implementing an index is incremental indexing. Incremental indexing enables the addition, deletion, or update of indexed documents without fully regenerating the index. This feature is particularly important in the case of large scale Web search engines where the cost of regenerating the full index to update frequently modified Web pages (*e.g.* news) is prohibitive. Incremental indexes offer a good trade-off between the freshness of the documents and the processing performance. Hence, in this paper, we consider the case of an incremental indexer. The *query processor* receives user queries and processes them against the index. Historically, commercial Web search engines have preferred conjunctive query processing [14]: a document has to contain all the terms in the query to be in the result set. To obtain the result set, the query processor computes the intersection of the posting lists of the query terms, evaluating the scores of the documents using a ranking function. The k (typically 10) results with the highest scores are returned to the user.

2.2 Assignment of documents to sites

In a distributed search engine, each search site has its own index and processes the queries of the users in its region. It is therefore important to carefully select documents to index in each site to tailor the data structures of the sites for their users. For a short response time, a search site must be able to process most of the queries it receives using its local index alone. Indexing documents that are popular in a region enables locality. However, it is also important to limit the number of documents indexed at each site. The query processing latency in fact increases with the size of the index [5]. Furthermore, replicating a large fraction of the documents at each site limits the scalability of the search engine. In this work, we assume that each search site has a fixed index capacity, either due to limited resources, or arbitrarily chosen to reduce the processing time. We express this limit using number of postings, *i.e.*, the sum of the length of all the posting lists in the index.

To the extent of our knowledge, two approaches have been developed to compute an assignment of documents to search sites. The first one relies on machine learning algorithms to analyze new documents upon their discovery and assigns them to one or more search sites [4]. The second one assigns each document to a single *master site* [3]. This assignment results in a minimal index, with each document indexed in a single location. The master site of a document is responsible for maintaining it in its index, which guarantees that the distributed search engine has the same recall as a centralized implementation. Our work builds up on the master selection approach [3]. We assume the existence of an algorithm that assigns each document to a single search site. Hence, the search site S_i has a master index MI_i which indexes all the documents S_i is the master of. Typically, this index represents the majority of S_i's index capacity.

The popularity of Web pages typically follows a power law: while most of the Web pages are unpopular, a few of them are requested very frequently. A Web page might present high locality, being popular in a single region, or be popular across many regions. Distributed search engines work better in a context where documents have a strong locality. Indeed, this means that each document only needs to be indexed by the search site located in the region where it is popular. Fortunately, a large fraction of the popular Web pages exhibit a high divergence in their popularity across regions [3]. Nevertheless, there are still documents which are popular across region boundaries and are requested by users of different search sites. The master selection algorithm, ensures that each document is indexed by its master site.

In this paper, we propose RIP, a Reactive Indexing Protocol. RIP uses part of the remaining index capacity of each search site to replicate documents that are frequently requested locally, but were assigned to a different search site by the master selection algorithm. Contrary to the master selection algorithm, which only relies on the content of the document, RIP is *reactive*: it analyzes the behavior of the users at each site to dynamically adjust replication decisions. These fully replicated documents form the shadow index, denoted SI_i for the site S_i.

2.3 Distributed query processing

In a distributed search engine, a search site indexes locally only a fraction of the documents. To preserve the quality of results, a distributed search engine must generate the same results as a centralized implementation. A query submitted to a site S_i must be evaluated on the full set of documents $\mathcal{D}$, whether they are indexed locally (MI_i and SI_i) or not. So far, the main approach to executing queries in a distributed search engine relies upon query forwarding [2, 8]. When processing a query, a search site first computes results using its local index, and then relies on a forwarding heuristic to determine whether another site may be able to provide higher quality results. If there are such sites according to the evaluation of the heuristic, then the query is forwarded to the relevant search sites for further processing. Finally, the results are then merged and returned to the user.

The forwarding heuristic is conservative with respect to query forwarding, and it can generate false positives, but no false negatives. As already mentioned in Section 2.2, it is preferable to answer a query locally, since it reduces the response time. It is therefore important to devise an accurate forwarding heuristic to reduce the forwarding rate.

Existing forwarding heuristics [2, 8] leverage properties of the search engine ranking function to compute an upper bound on the score of documents which are not indexed locally. This ranking function $s(d|q)$, presented on Figure 2, was introduced by Baeza-Yates *et al.* [2]. The score of a document d is computed by averaging partial scores over the terms of the query q. A document d has a quality score, expressed by $f(d)$, and a relevance score for a term t, computed by $g(d|t)$. The parameters w_f and w_g weight quality and relevance respectively. The partial score of a document d for a term t, expressed as $r(d|t)$, is typically maintained in the posting lists of the index to improve query evaluation performance. Note that distributed search engines are compatible with more complex ranking functions, including positional features, machine learning and diversification. In these cases, the $s(d|q)$ ranking function is used in the first phase of a two-phase ranking [9], which ensures that relevant documents will be known locally before the execution of the second phase of the ranking.

The heuristic we propose here supports the same ranking function. A site S_i may partially replicate the posting lists of the master indexes of other sites in order to estimate the need to forward queries. This forwarding index is designated as FI_i. The posting lists of forwarding indexes are ordered by partial score. For a given term t, S_i replicates the list of documents that have the highest partial score $r(d|t)$. A document whose master is S_j and that contains several terms may only be indexed in one of the posting lists of FI_i, provided its other partial scores are low.

$$s(d|q) = w_f f(d) + \frac{w_g}{|q|} \sum_{i=1}^{|q|} g(d|t_i)$$

$$r(d|t) = w_f f(d) + w_g g(d|t)$$

$$s(d|q) = \frac{1}{|q|} \sum_{i=1}^{|q|} r(d|t_i)$$

Figure 2: Ranking function

2.4 Index structure

In this section, we summarize the different elements of the index of a search site. The index of a site S_i is logically divided into three components:

Master index MI_i: It contains the documents that were assigned to S_i by the master selection algorithm.

Shadow index SI_i: It contains documents that are fully replicated by S_i. They were assigned to one of the other search sites by the master selection algorithm, but are replicated to improve the query processing locality.

Forwarding index FI_i: It contains partial information about documents assigned to the other search sites. For a given term t, the posting list associated to t in FI_i contains the list of documents that have the highest partial scores for t. Documents having high partial scores are also likely to have a high popularity. Hence, SI_i and FI_i may overlap.

These logical indexes represent the data available to S_i for processing queries. The posting lists of search engines are, in most cases, ordered by document ID. This allows high compression rates, and is particularly efficient for conjunctive query processing [14]. In this work, we do not make any assumption on the layout of MI_i and SI_i. However, we present FI_i as an index sorted by impact. This means that the postings are ordered by partial scores. This assumption simplifies the description of the algorithm, but there is, in practice, no reason not to implement these three indexes as a single incremental index relying on document ID ordered posting lists.

3. REACTIVE INDEXING PROTOCOL

3.1 Problem definition

We consider the following problem. In a distributed search engine, each search site is assigned an index budget expressed as the maximum number of posting lists entries a site can accomodate. The collection of documents $\mathcal{D}$ is split across the search sites through an initial master index selection algorithm. The remaining index capacity of each site is freely used to replicate documents and posting lists of the other sites. A sequence of queries is submitted to each search site and the goal is to maximize the amount of queries that are answered locally, without query forwarding. Consequently, a search site updates its index as it processes queries. A search site modifies its index only between query executions, and it does so for a given query only after its results are returned to the user.

Let $res(q)$ be the set of the k documents obtaining the highest scores for the query q according the the search engine's ranking function $s(d|q)$. A site S_i has to fulfill two conditions to answer q locally. First, the documents of $res(q)$ must all be indexed and copied locally. The search site needs a copy of the document data to generate the snippet presented on the results page, and also in the case that it uses using a two-phase ranking [9]. The search site also needs to be able to compute accurate scores for all the top-k results to display them properly ranked. This requirement can be expressed as follows:

$$\forall d \in res(q), d \in \mathrm{MI}_i \vee d \in \mathrm{SI}_i \ .$$

Second, S_i should be able to determine, using local data structures, that no other document could potentially score higher than the lowest score of the results:

$$\forall d \in (\mathcal{D} - res(q)), \forall e \in res(q), scBound(d|q) \leq s(e|q) \ ;$$

where $scBound(d|q)$ is the function that computes an upper bound on the score of the document d for the query q using only local information, *i.e.* the information from MI_i, SI_i and FI_i.

We estimate the future queries Q_i^f of S_i using Q_i, a recent query stream received by S_i. Thus, at any given point, we are trying to maximize the locality of the queries in Q_i to increase the probability that future queries will be answered locally. Let us focus on the first locality condition. The cost of replicating a document is equivalent to the number of posting list entries it requires in the index. To simplify the problem, suppose that all documents contain the same number of terms and therefore have the same cost. The problem we are trying to solve is a particular form of the knapsack problem. The objects we are selecting are queries. The utility of selecting a query is proportional to its frequency, while its cost is equal to the indexing of the results, as well as the partial information ensuring the quality of results.

Given that the search engine aims at serving the k best results for each query, we could make the simplifying assumption that all queries have the same cost: indexing k documents. However, even in this case, the complexity of the problem arises from the fact that many queries share results. Hence, the cost of a selection is not equal to the cost of each query, as some documents would be counted several times. The knapsack problem is NP-hard, but has greedy heuristics that perform reasonably well. In particular, the most common approach consists of selecting the objects in a decreasing order of $\frac{value}{cost}$. In our case, the cost of selecting a query depends on the previously selected ones; hence the costs should be re-evaluated at each step of the algorithm.

3.2 Practical approach

As presented in Section 3.1, a search site has to satisfy two conditions to answer a query locally. The first one is that the results should be indexed locally, and the second one is that the search site should have enough information to guarantee that no other document in $\mathcal{D}$ can score higher. The computation of an exact optimal solution is NP-hard, which leads us towards heuristic solutions. Moreover, we need to consider practical implementation constraints in the design of our algorithm.

This work targets search engines performing incremental indexing. The index of the search engine is regularly updated, and the algorithm must account for the presence of new documents. This eliminates the possibility of relying solely on an offline algorithm executed during the initial index generation. A practical solution should also use a minimal amount of computation and memory, so as to ensure that as many resources as possible are dedicated to query processing. Part of the computational cost of the problem presented in Section 3.1 arises from the fact that the benefit of replicating a document cannot be simply evaluated, it depends on the full selection of replicated documents. From this consideration, it would be tempting to devise a solution based on hypergraphs of documents and queries to model replication dependencies. However, given the scale of the document collections we consider, such data structures do not scale, both with respect to their memory consumption and the processing cost required to exploit them.

Inspired by previous work in Web caches [13], we propose a Reactive Indexing Protocol (RIP). Each search site engine monitors the queries of its users to gather local statistics about the frequency of terms and documents. Based on these observations, our algorithm evaluates the utility of replicating information. A search site S_i may either replicate documents, to ensure that the results are copied locally, or fragments of the posting lists of other sites, to increase its knowledge of their document collection and make more accurate query forwarding predictions by computing tighter score bounds. As introduced in Section 2.4, S_i indexes fully replicated documents in SI_i, while the replicated fragments of posting lists form FI_i.

3.3 Algorithm

Distributed search engines rely on query forwarding heuristics to determine whether a given query q should be evaluated on other search sites to improve the quality of the results. The role of the forwarding heuristic is to compute, for all documents $d \in \mathcal{D}$, a score upper bound $scBound(d|q)$. If the top-k documents are either not fully replicated locally, or cannot be clearly identified, the search engine decides to forward the query to the other sites to guarantee the quality of results. In this work, we introduce a new query forwarding heuristic and RIP, its associated index replication algorithm.

3.3.1 Forwarding heuristic

The forwarding heuristic we propose stems from the NRA top-k processing algorithms [11], with a few adaptations to deal with incomplete posting lists. In NRA, posting lists are sorted by impact and processed from top to bottom. NRA maintains a sorted heap of potential top-k results with upper and lower bounds on their scores. These bounds are updated as the processing progresses down the posting lists. As soon as the upper bound of the $(k+1)^{th}$ document is lower than the lower bound of the kth document, the top-k results are identified and the algorithm terminates. In the worst case, NRA has to process the full posting lists, but, in most situations, it achieves significant performance gains and only processes a small fraction of the index. The forwarding heuristic performs a similar computation. It processes the query over the forwarding index FI_i and computes upper bounds on scores. The posting lists of the forwarding index are only partial, but they are continuous. A posting list replicated by S_i for a term t down to the score value v contains all the documents of $\mathcal{D}$ whose master is different from S_i and whose partial score $r(d|t)$ is higher than v. Therefore, for a given term, FI_i provides either an exact partial score, or an upper bound equal to the score of the last posting list entry. While processing, the forwarding heuristic

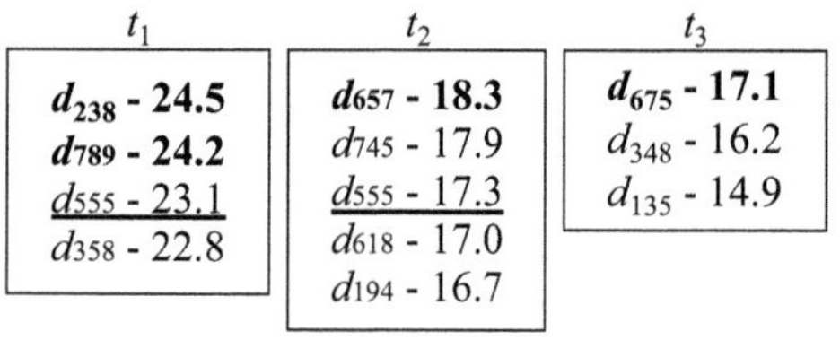

Figure 3: Forwarding heuristic on FI_i

ignores the documents present in the shadow index SI_i, as they are already evaluated by traditional query evaluation and are assigned a precise score.

We illustrate the forwarding algorithm with the example of Figure 3. The query of the user is "t_1, t_2, t_3", and the figure displays the posting lists of FI_i corresponding to those terms which the forwarding heuristic evaluates to decide whether the query should be forwarded. The top documents for t_1 are replicated in SI_i (in bold), so they do not need to be considered. The following document is d_{555}, so we know its exact partial score for this term. This document is also present in the posting list of t_2, so we will also find its exact partial score for t_2 as the top-k execution progresses. However, d_{555} is not represented in the posting list of t_3. The last known document of this posting list is d_{135}. As a consequence, we use its partial score as an upper bound of d_{555}'s partial score for t_3. Hence, the upper bound score computed for d_{555} is (23.1+17.3+14.9)/3=18.4. We can also compute a bound on the score of any document absent from these posting lists using the scores of the last entries (22.8, 16.7 and 14.9 in this example). Using FI_i, the forwarding heuristic computes the highest possible score for a document that is not indexed locally and compares it with the score of local documents (MI_i and SI_i).

As an optimization, when a posting list is fully replicated (*i.e.* replicated down to the 0 score), the forwarding heuristic leverages the conjunctive properties of the ranking function. Any document that is absent from this posting list can be ignored, as it cannot be part of the results.

3.3.2 Replication principle

The replication algorithm works as follows. For each term t, a site maintains two replication thresholds, expressed in partial score values: the document replication threshold td_t and the postings replication threshold tp_t. RIP reactively adjusts these thresholds using the activity of the local users to determine which documents and postings are replicated.

$$\forall d \in \mathcal{D}, r(d|t) \geq td_t \wedge master(d) \neq i \Rightarrow d \in \text{SI}_i$$

$$\forall d \in \mathcal{D}, r(d|t) \geq tp_t \wedge master(d) \neq i \Rightarrow d \in \text{FI}_i$$

For the example described on Figure 3, td_{t_1} is 24.2, while tp_{t_1} is 22.8. By lowering td_t, RIP decreases the highest scores associated to t for a non local document. Lowering tp_t decreases the lowest score associated to t in FI_i. Both these actions increase the information related to the term t and decrease the amount of query forwarding. However, their impact and cost can vary significantly. Fully replicating a document is costly, as it generates one posting entry per unique term in the document. On average, a Web page contains 250 unique terms [15], therefore replicating a document is 250 times more costly than replicating a posting entry. Given that the differences in partial scores between entries are, in most cases, higher among high quality documents, fully replicating a document often has a higher positive impact on query forwarding. RIP's objective is to achieve a good balance between documents and postings replication to use the replication budget as efficiently as possible.

After each query execution, RIP analyses the query results to determine which data should be replicated to ensure that, in the future, this query could be processed locally. Let w be the lowest score of the last document returned as a result for the query $t_1 \ldots t_{|q|}$. If the query only contains one term, then the replication operation is trivial, and the algorithm determines that td_{t_1} should be w. However, if the query contains several terms, then the algorithm has to decide whether it should replicate documents or posting lists. The algorithm we propose relies on a parameter α to balance the replication between documents and postings.

$$td_t = \alpha \times |q| \times w$$

$$tp_t = \frac{(1-\alpha)|q| \times w}{|q|-1}$$

Using the scoring function $s(d|q)$, it is possible to verify that for all the documents present in a single posting list of FI_i, the forwarding heuristic has enough data to compute a score upper bound at most equal to w:

$$\forall t \in q, \frac{1}{|q|}\left(td_t + \sum_{u \in q-\{t\}} tp_u\right) = w$$

By definition, replicating document provides the corresponding postings, so $td_t \geq tp_t$. As a consequence, given that $|q| \geq 2$, $\alpha \geq 0.5$. When α is low, RIP favors replicating documents, which increases the probability of having query results in the local index. However, the forwarding heuristic has less information to ensure that these local results are optimal. On the contrary, a high value of α provides a very accurate forwarding heuristic, but fewer replicated documents.

In practice, some of the documents are present in several posting lists. Hence, they have precise values for several terms, and their score estimations may exceed w. The results of the query, for instance, will be present in all the posting lists matching the query, and will generate scores higher than w. Similarly, other documents present in at least 2 posting lists, such as d_{555} in Figure 3, may have high upper bounds on their score and could trigger the query forwarding mechanism. When these documents are not part of the query results, query forwarding is unnecessary. In order to avoid these cases of false positives, RIP identifies these documents and fully indexes them in SI_i.

3.3.3 Practical algorithm using blocks

RIP needs to estimate the amount of documents or postings a replication decision represents before deciding whether it should be applied or not. Furthermore, taking replication decisions at the level of a single posting may lead to unstable results and generate a high overhead.

Each search site estimates loosely the score distribution for each term by regularly probing the other search sites. This data structure is comprised of blocks, and is illustrated in Figure 4. A block constitutes a unit of replication identified by its index as well as its score bounds. This information

block index/size	t_4	t_5
0/10	**Upper = 15.7, Lower = 12.7**	*Upper = 17.1, Lower = 15.3*
1/20	**Upper = 12.7, Lower = 9.8**	*Upper = 15.3, Lower = 13.7*
2/40	Upper = 9.8, Lower = 7.3	*Upper = 13.7, Lower = 6.4*
3/80	Upper = 7.3, Lower = 4.8	Upper = 6.4, Lower = 1.8

Figure 4: Blocks replication ($k = 10$)

is not required to be perfect, and can be obtained through sampling. The first block has size k, and the size of the following blocks increases exponentially, using a power of 2.

We adapt RIP to apply the replication thresholds td_t and tp_t on blocks of documents and postings instead of single elements. Figure 4 presents the computation of the thresholds for the query "t_4, t_5". The lowest score $w = 8.5$, and $\alpha = 0.6$. RIP determines that td_{t_4} should be $0.6 \times 2 \times 8.5 = 10.2$. Therefore, the first 2 blocks of documents should be replicated (in bold), and dt_{t_4} becomes 9.8, once adjusted to the block limit. tp_{t_5} is evaluated to be $(1-0.6)\times 2\times 8.5/(2-1) = 6.8$, which means that 3 blocks of postings should be replicated (in italics) and tp_{t_5} is adjusted to 6.4. This operation is then repeated for td_{t_5} and tp_{t_4}.

The usage of blocks brings several benefits to RIP. It materializes a small number of well defined replication bounds, which favors clear replication decisions while lowering the amount of memory required to maintain them. In addition, it ensures the continuity of replicated data. A replication decision caused by a given query may, as a side effect, trigger the replication of blocks that contain documents useful for other future queries.

3.3.4 *Space management*

RIP does not directly proceed to the replication of data. Instead, it maintains counters about the number of times a particular piece of information was determined to be useful. We refer to these counters as the temperature of the data. The higher the temperature, the more useful it is. The temperature values are used to determine which data should be replicated within the budget constraint. As explained previously, depending on the data type, the cost of the replication varies. Given that a document has on average 250 distinct terms, the cost of replicating a document is on average 250, the cost of replicating the documents of a block of size n is on average $250n$, and the cost of replicating only the postings of this block is exactly n.

We rely on the cubic selection scheme [13] to decide which elements are selected for replication. This approach was initially designed to cache Web objects. Hence, in this context, the size of an object is always precisely known, and there are no dependencies between objects. In our case, the size of an object is first estimated, and then corrected when a replication decision is actually taken. For instance, RIP first assigns a cost of 250 to a document, and then corrects it upon receiving the content of the document. Similarly, evicting a block whose documents are replicated does not necessarily free $250n$, as some of the documents may remain replicated due to other decisions (*e.g.* replicated blocks of other terms). We also ensure that the continuity of block replication is maintained. It is impossible to evict a block without evicting all the following blocks.

3.3.5 *Dealing with incremental indexing*

Web search engines are often designed to support incremental indexing. This feature is particularly used for popular Web pages that are frequently modified, such as news Websites. Replicating information in several locations poses the problem of data consistency. If a search site does not take into account a new version of a Web page, it will serve stale results to its users.

To ensure that index updates are propagated, a search site keeps track of which other sites replicate the documents it is the master of. In addition, for each term, it maintains the documents and postings replication thresholds of each one of the other sites. When the crawler sends a new version of a document to its master site S_i, MI_i is updated and all the sites replicating any stale data are notified.

4. EVALUATION

To evaluate RIP's efficiency, we simulate a distributed search engine configuration consisting of five search sites $\mathcal{S} = \{S_1 \ldots S_5\}$. We first compute optimal query results through a centralized search engine indexing all documents, and then evaluate each site's ability to generate these results using its master index and the data it replicates. Each search site is associated with a query log originating from neighboring countries and collected from the front-end of a commercial search engine. In total, we sample 7,023,102 consecutive queries, and split them chronologically into a training set and a testing set of equal size. The collection of documents consists of 31,599,910 Web pages randomly sampled from the index of the same search engine.

We rely on the distribution of terms in queries and documents to assign each document to a master site (KL-Q feature), as in the work of Blanco *et al.* [3]. This process creates, for each site, the master index MI, and represents the initial assignment of documents to sites in our evaluation. In this work, the master index creation process is fixed, and these indexes remain constant throughout the experiments. We evaluate RIP's ability to generate SI and FI, and to reduce the query forwarding rate.

Commercial search engines often cache query results to avoid re-evaluating repeated queries. To make our experiment more realistic, we assume that the search engine implements a results cache with a Time-To-Live (TTL): cached results are only served if their TTL has not expired. We use a TTL value of 2 hours. For incremental indexes, it is possible for a results cache to return stale results, which happens when the result set does not reflect accurately the current state of the index. In our setup, the TTL of the cache is 2 hours. Such a TTL value is moderately aggressive: the staleness of the results will never exceed 2 hours.

4.1 Search results diversity

Blanco *et al.* [3] observe that most documents exhibit a high divergence of popularity among the different search sites. They are very popular in a given region, but are rarely requested at other search sites. We confirm this observation by evaluating how the popularity ranking of documents differs across search sites. We execute the training queries on the search engine and count how often each document is returned as part of the top-10 results.

In Figure 5, we present the similarity between the list of documents that are most popular at each individual search site, and the documents that are globally popular, among

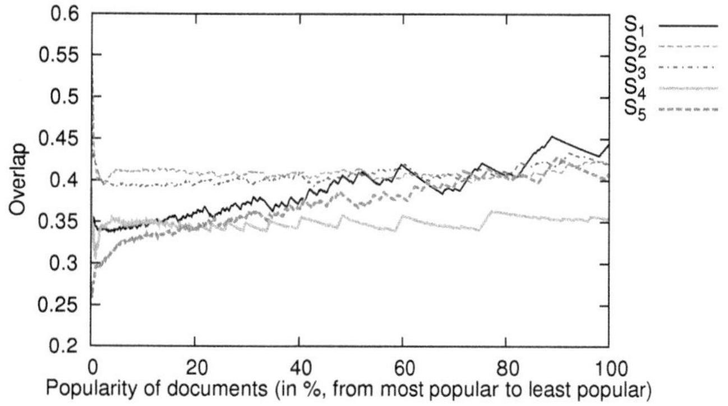

Figure 5: Similarity between documents locally popular and documents globally popular

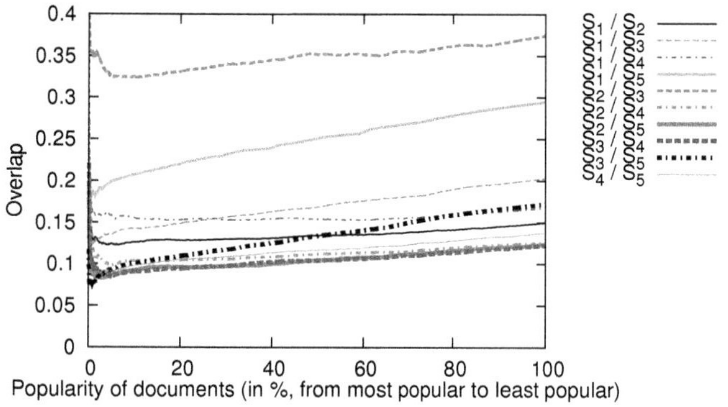

Figure 6: Similarity between locally popular documents at 2 sites

all the search sites taken together. On average, the set of the x documents most popular at a given site and the set of the x documents most popular considering the activity of all sites globally only overlap by 40%. This observation clearly illustrates how users from different regions have diverse interests. This argues in favor of an index replication policy that relies on local user activity and optimizes the replicated data for each site individually.

The comparison of popular documents between pairs of sites, presented in Figure 6, shows even more differences. The pair of sites exhibiting the highest similarity is under 40%. This similarity is due to the language used in queries, as those two regions share the same regional language. Note that the similarity of the very few most popular documents is typically higher. This is due to very few documents being popular across different regions.

4.2 Cache impact

The results cache generates a hit when identical queries are submitted to the search engine within its TTL interval. Longer queries typically present lower frequency compared to short ones [1], and therefore the results cache affects them differently. In our experiments, the average hit rate of the results cache is 48.4%. Figure 7 illustrates the distribution of queries depending on their length. Queries of length 2 represent the largest fraction of the workload, followed by single term queries. As expected, the hit rate of the cache drops

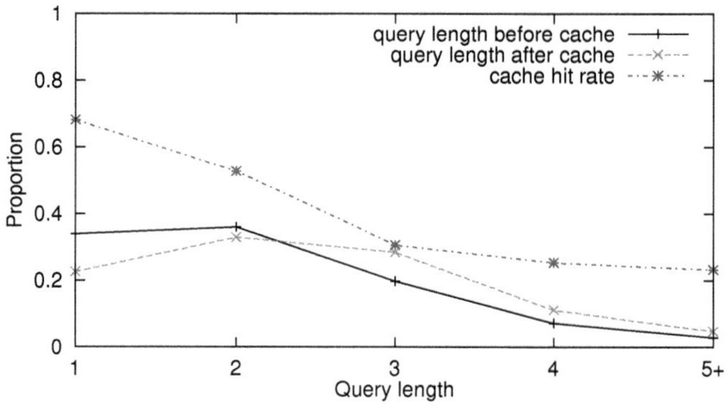

Figure 7: Queries distribution and cache efficiency

as we increase the length of queries; long queries are more likely to be unique. Hence, the workload of a search engine is often dominated by the processing of longer queries. This observation significantly hardens the task of the forwarding heuristic. Indeed, long queries involve more posting lists, and generally have results whose partial scores are lower: they require more replicated data to be indexed locally.

4.3 Replication and query forwarding

We evaluate RIP and its query forwarding heuristic by running queries in our logs against the collection of documents. First, we warm up the replication algorithm and the cache using the training queries. Next, we process the testing queries to evaluate the amount of query forwarding. For these experiments, we use the forwarding heuristic of Section 3.3.1 and one of the following replication schemes:

Static global documents replication (SDR): Using the training queries, we determine which documents are globally popular and replicate this static set across all sites [2, 8]. In this case, FI contains an upper bound per term for non replicated documents, which corresponds to the thresholds of Baeza-Yates *et al.* [2].

Reactive documents replication (RDR): Each search site reactively determines which documents are most frequently part of the results of their users and replicate the most popular ones. This setup computes a different set of replicated documents for each site to match the activities of their users. As with SDR, FI contains one bound per term, dynamically adjusted to reflect document replication.

Reactive Indexing Protocol (RIP): Each site reactively replicates blocks of documents and posting lists, as well as individual documents when they generate false positives. This is the approach we describe in Section 3.3.3. Each site replicates data matching the needs of its users, while preserving the continuity of information in posting lists.

Overall performance.

We evaluate the three different replication schemes using different replication budgets and present the results in Figure 8. The budget is represented as the maximum number of documents replicated, and we assume, as explained in Section 3.3.2, that 250 individual posting list entries use the same space as a fully indexed document. The results clearly indicate that the two algorithms based on local information outperform the static documents replication us-

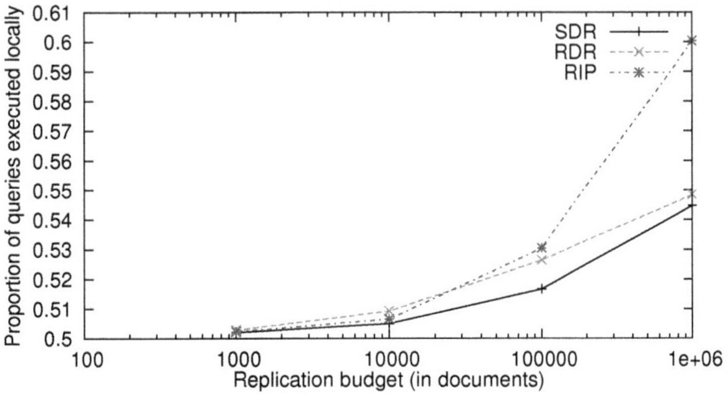

Figure 8: Query locality wrt replication budget

ing global statistics. Indeed, as observed in Section 4.1, the users of each site are interested in different documents.

For a low replication budget, below 100,000, we observe that simply replicating the results of the queries is more efficient than replicating blocks of documents and posting lists. However, as the budget increases, the blocks replication scheme clearly outperforms the replication of individual documents. This difference grows with the amount of space dedicated to replication. With a replication budget of 1,000,000 documents, each search site has an average indexing capacity of 7,119,982 documents (22.5% of the total collection), which represents an overhead of 14% over a setup without any replication. In this configuration, RIP raises the amount of queries processed locally by 23%, while RDR raises it by 13%. Note that the α parameter of RIP, used to compute replication thresholds, is set to 0.6. In practice, any value between 0.55 and 0.65 obtains good performance, above 59.7% with a budget of 1,000,000.

Detailed performance analysis.

We detail the performance of RDR and RIP in Figure 9. With a small replication budget, it is most efficient to focus replication on single term queries. They only require little replicated data to be answered locally, as the results are simply the documents with the highest scores for the query term. RDR performs well for these easy queries. Given that one-term queries are less likely to be unique, the temperature of their results increases over time and they are replicated. However, when the replication budget increases, it becomes more interesting to also replicate data for longer queries. The results show that RDR is unable to answer these queries, even with a large budget. The documents that are part of the results may be replicated. However, given that the corresponding posting lists are not replicated, the search engine is unable to ensure that the query results are optimal, and the forwarding heuristic returns a false positive. RIP can compute low thresholds, even for longer queries, and is able to answer locally over 10% of long queries by replicating continuous blocks of documents and postings.

Query replication cost analysis.

Figure 10 presents the position of the query results in the posting list blocks of RIP's forwarding index, depending on the query length. For a one term query, the result set comprises the documents with the highest partial scores for

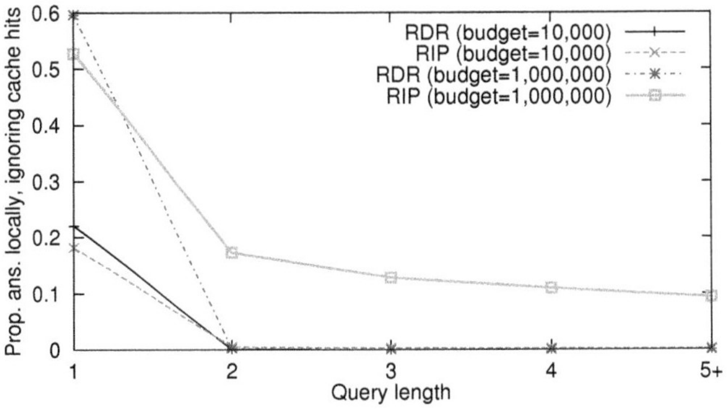

Figure 9: Query locality wrt query length

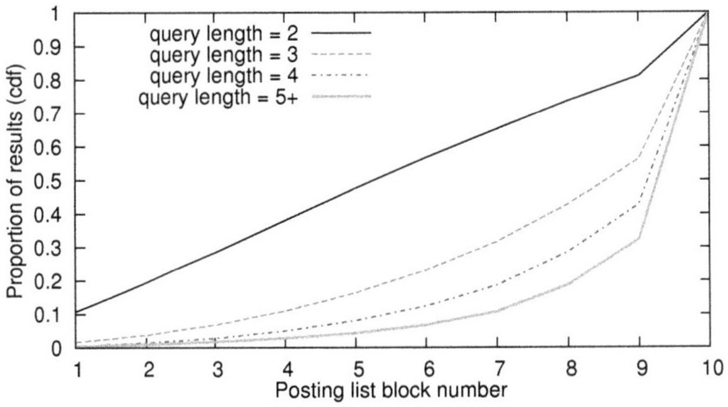

Figure 10: Depth of results in posting lists

the term. Hence, they are all located in the first posting list block, which is a small amount of information for RIP to replicate to answer these queries correctly. However, as the length of the query increases, the matching documents are less frequent, due to the conjunctive nature of the query processing. As a consequence, they are located in deeper blocks, and require more replicated information to enable local processing. For example, 67% of the results of 5-term queries are located in the 10th block. Given that the size of blocks is a power of two, this data is costly to replicate, making forwarding more frequent for long queries.

New queries.

The replication algorithms rely on previous queries to compute a replication scheme and increase the probability of answering future queries locally. When a query is repeated, it can be answered by the results cache, if it falls within the TTL, or by the data replicated upon the first occurrence of the query. New queries however are more challenging. We examine the query processing locality for new queries on Figure 11, with a replication budget of 1,000,000.

SDR is particularly efficient at processing new one-term queries locally, since it benefits from document popularity information from all search sites. A query that is processed for the first time in a site might have been present at another site during the training period. Consequently, the static replication has included it in the computation of the list of replicated documents.

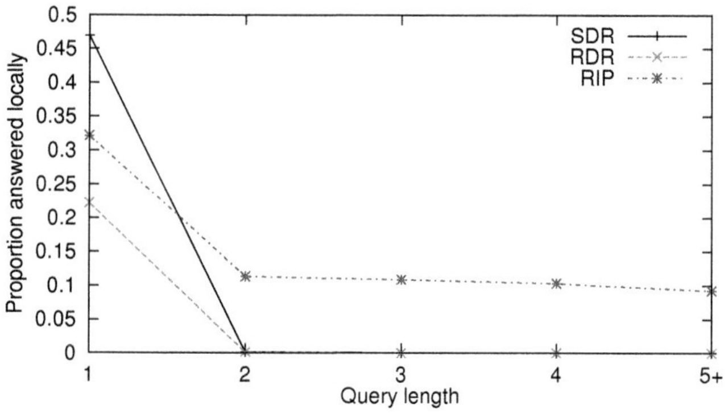

Figure 11: Query forwarding rate for new queries

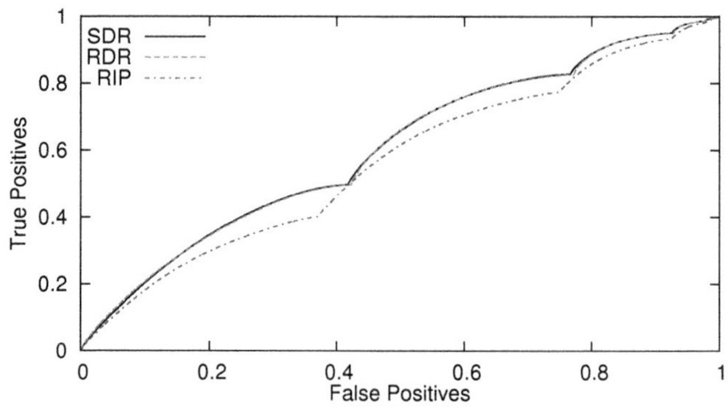

Figure 12: Forwarding ROC curve

RDR has higher overall performance than SDR, since it targets the set of replicated documents for each site. However, since it only relies on the queries processed at a given site to build the list of replicated documents, the performance for new queries is low. New queries can only be processed locally if their data has been replicated due to previous distinct queries executed at this site. As RDR only replicates the documents in result sets, it is unlikely that the site has replicated all the results of the new query and the data necessary to ensure that local results are sufficient.

RIP performs well for new queries. Although it only relies on local knowledge, as it is the case for RDR, the block replication pattern favors new queries. Instead of precisely replicating the documents answering a particular query, RIP transfers blocks of data, which contain additional documents and postings related to the query terms. When a new query arrives, the algorithm is more likely to have replicated a sufficient amount of information for each of the query terms, which increases the probability of processing it locally.

False positives analysis.

Our forwarding heuristic always forwards a query if there another search site may improve its results. As a consequence, the forwarding heuristic does not generate false negatives. For some queries, the search site has the query results in its index but forwards the query nevertheless, because it cannot prove that those are the best results. These cases constitute false positives, as forwarding the query does not modify its results. Considering a setup with a replication budget of 1,000,000, the proportion of false positives among the forwarding decisions is 51%, 53% and 46% for SDR, RDR, and RIP respectively.

Allowing the search engine to return non-optimal results by allowing false negatives reduces the query forwarding rate. The forwarding heuristic computes a score that corresponds to the limits of its knowledge. We use this score, as well as the fact that long queries are more difficult to predict, to rank forwarding decisions. We display, on Figure 12, the distribution of true and false positives (ROC curve [12]). As one-term queries only involve one posting list, making it impossible to generate a false positive, we ignore them in this experiment. The remaining query lengths generate distinctive curve fragments. These fragments remain relatively close to a diagonal, which means that separating true and false positives using solely the knowledge score and query length is difficult. Indeed, scores can vary significantly depending on the query term, and cannot be easily compared. Note that the curve representing RIP is bellow the one of the other algorithms. This is because RIP presents an overall higher performance, and therefore forwards fewer queries. The remaining false positives are therefore harder to detect.

5. RELATED WORK

The problem of assigning documents to sites in distributed search engine has been studied in previous work, and two main approaches have been developed to assign documents to sites. Baeza-Yates *et al.* propose to replicate a set of global, high quality documents to all search sites [2]; Cambazoglu *et al.* follow the same approach [8]. As shown in Section 4.2, the documents users are interested in significantly differ across regions. Thus, it is more efficient to perform fine grain replication, and select different replicated documents for each search site. Our experiments presented in Section 4.3 show that per-site replication algorithms systematically outperform global replication decisions.

Brefeld *et al.* propose to use machine-learning techniques to statically assign documents to search sites [4]. This approach optimizes the replication of documents for each site, but it relies on attributes, such as the language of the document, which are weakly correlated with its popularity. Contrary to this approach, the algorithm we propose is reactive, and only replicates documents when it observes that users actually request them. The algorithm we propose also explicitly prioritizes pieces of replicated data depending on their size and temperature. The approach of Brefeld *et al.* relies on an algorithm that simply assigns documents to search sites, and it does not enable an operator to vary the indexing capacity.

Existing query forwarding algorithms rely on the computation of upper bounds to estimate the score of documents that are not indexed locally. Baeza-Yates *et al.* [2] compute a bound for each term and each search site. Cambazoglu et al. [8] refine this approach and show that maintaining bounds on pairs of terms more precise estimates of scores and can reduce the amount of query forwarding. In the case of a static index, these bounds can easily be computed during the generation of the index, and do not vary at runtime. However, when the index and the set of replicated documents are dynamically selected, these bounds need to be updated. This process can become particularly costly when each site keeps track of many bounds, which is the case in the algorithm of Cambazoglu *et al.* [8]. In that case, one possibility is to maintain these bounds lazily using a sliding window scheme. Yet, it reduces the effectiveness of the results cache, since results computed using these bounds will be time-stamped with the oldest bound used during their computation. The approach we propose explicitly maintains two bounds per term, which is a reasonable trade-off between their accuracy and the maintenance cost.

The main difference between the algorithms we propose and previous work [7, 8] is the interaction between the replication algorithm and the forwarding heuristic. While other algorithms focus on replicating popular documents, our approach also maintains single posting lists elements to ensure the continuity of the information on the scores for a given term. As there is no "hole" in the forwarding index, the upper bounds for each term are lower. In addition, by replicating postings further, we efficiently lower the bounds computed for longer queries. Overall, this significantly reduces the amount of query forwarding.

Ding and Suel [10] developed an algorithm for fast top-k processing on document ID-ordered posting lists. By maintaining upper bounds on the partial scores of compressed posting list segments, they significantly reduce both the amount of computation and the processing time. Our approach for block replication could be adapted to replicate document ID-ordered blocks using these thresholds. However, this would lead to a significant overhead for storing the index, since documents obtaining low scores would also be replicated if they belong to a segment with a high threshold. Consequently, we opted for strictly following the order of partial scores to replicate information.

6. CONCLUSION

We propose RIP, a Reactive Indexing Protocol for distributed search engines. With RIP, the search engine initially indexes each document on a single master site, and monitors the local user activity of each site to generate an index replication scheme. Our scheme replicates documents and fragments of posting lists. RIP enables a significant reduction of the amount of query forwarding between search sites, and consequently, of query processing latency. We show experimentally that, by making local decisions, RIP significantly outperforms previous replication strategies based on global information: in a 5-site setup, when each site has an index capacity of 22.5% of the documents collection, 60% of the queries are processed locally. We also show that replicating fragments of posting lists allows the query forwarding heuristic to compute lower score thresholds on unknown documents, which increases performance. Finally, RIP has by design the additional benefit of being an online approach, supporting both incremental indexing and a precise index capacity configuration, which simplifies operations in a production environment.

Acknowledgments

This work has been partially supported by the COAST project (ICT-248036), funded by the European Community. The authors have been also supported by the INNCORPORA - Torres Quevedo Program from the Spanish Ministry of Science and Innovation, co-funded by the European Social Fund.

7. REFERENCES

[1] R. Baeza-Yates, A. Gionis, F. Junqueira, V. Murdock, V. Plachouras, and F. Silvestri. The impact of caching on search engines. In *Proceedings of the 30th annual international ACM SIGIR conference on Research and development in information retrieval*, pages 183–190, 2007.

[2] R. Baeza-Yates, A. Gionis, F. Junqueira, V. Plachouras, and L. Telloli. On the feasibility of multi-site web search engines. In *Proceedings of the 18th ACM Conference on Information and Knowledge Management*, pages 425–434, 2009.

[3] R. Blanco, B. B. Cambazoglu, F. P. Junqueira, I. Kelly, and V. Leroy. Assigning documents to master sites in distributed search. In *Proceedings of the 20th ACM Conference on Information and Knowledge Management*, pages 67–76, 2011.

[4] U. Brefeld, B. B. Cambazoglu, and F. P. Junqueira. Document assignment in multi-site search engines. In *Proceedings of the Fourth ACM International Conference on Web Search and Data Mining*, pages 575–584, 2011.

[5] E. Brewer. Lessons from giant-scale services. *Internet Computing, IEEE*, 5(4):46–55, 2001.

[6] B. B. Cambazoglu, V. Plachouras, and R. Baeza-Yates. Quantifying performance and quality gains in distributed web search engines. In *Proceedings of the 32nd International ACM SIGIR Conference on Research and Development in Information Retrieval*, pages 411–418, 2009.

[7] B. B. Cambazoglu, V. Plachouras, F. Junqueira, and L. Telloli. On the feasibility of geographically distributed web crawling. In *Proceedings of the 3rd International Conference on Scalable Information Systems*, pages 31:1–31:10, 2008.

[8] B. B. Cambazoglu, E. Varol, E. Kayaaslan, C. Aykanat, and R. Baeza-Yates. Query forwarding in geographically distributed search engines. In *Proceedings of the 33rd International ACM SIGIR Conference on Research and Development in Information Retrieval*, pages 90–97, 2010.

[9] B. B. Cambazoglu, H. Zaragoza, O. Chapelle, J. Chen, C. Liao, Z. Zheng, and J. Degenhardt. Early exit optimizations for additive machine learned ranking systems. In *Proceedings of the third ACM international conference on Web search and data mining*, pages 411–420, 2010.

[10] S. Ding and T. Suel. Faster top-k document retrieval using block-max indexes. In *Proceedings of the 34nd International ACM SIGIR Conference on Research and Development in Information Retrieval*, pages 993–1002, 2011.

[11] I. Ilyas, G. Beskales, and M. Soliman. A survey of top-k query processing techniques in relational database systems. *ACM Computing Surveys (CSUR)*, 40(4):11, 2008.

[12] F. J. Provost, T. Fawcett, and R. Kohavi. The case against accuracy estimation for comparing induction algorithms. In *ICML*, pages 445–453, 1998.

[13] I. Tatarinov. An efficient LFU-like policy for Web caches. Technical report, Computer Science Department, North Dakota State University, 1998.

[14] S. Tatikonda, B. Cambazoglu, and F. Junqueira. Posting list intersection on multicore architectures. In *Proceedings of the 34th international ACM SIGIR conference on Research and development in Information*, pages 963–972, 2011.

[15] J. Zhang and T. Suel. Optimized inverted list assignment in distributed search engine architectures. In *Parallel and Distributed Processing Symposium, 2007. IPDPS 2007. IEEE International*, pages 1–10. IEEE, 2007.

Personalized Diversification of Search Results

David Vallet and Pablo Castells
Universidad Autónoma de Madrid
Escuela Politécnica Superior, Departamento de Ingeniería Informática
{david.vallet, pablo.castells}@uam.es

ABSTRACT

Search personalization and diversification are often seen as opposing alternatives to cope with query uncertainty, where, given an ambiguous query, it is either preferable to adapt the search result to a specific aspect that may interest the user (personalization) or to regard multiple aspects in order to maximize the probability that some query aspect is relevant to the user (diversification). In this work, we question this antagonistic view, and hypothesize that these two directions may in fact be effectively combined and enhance each other. We research the introduction of the user as an explicit random variable in state of the art diversification methods, thus developing a generalized framework for personalized diversification. In order to evaluate our hypothesis, we conduct an evaluation with real users using crowdsourcing services. The obtained results suggest that the combination of personalization and diversification achieves competitive performance, improving the baseline, plain personalization, and plain diversification approaches in terms of both diversity and accuracy measures.

Categories and Subject Descriptors

H.3.3 Information Search and Retrieval – retrieval models, information filtering.

General Terms

Algorithms, Experimentation, Experimentation, Human Factors.

Keywords

Diversity, personalization, search.

1. INTRODUCTION

Maximizing the total returned relevance in response to an information need has been traditionally the main fundamental principle underlying research and development in the Information Retrieval (IR) field. More recently, strands of research in the community considered other angles of the practical effectiveness of the output of retrieval systems, and the role that diversity, in particular, plays along with relevance in delivering effective value to the users of such systems [5,6,22]. The value of IR diversity is motivated by the uncertainty involved in a single query as the only evidence of the user information need [1,7,15,16]. The assumption is that different users may mean slightly (or even quite) different things by the same query expression. In the absence of further knowledge or observations about the actual user need beyond the explicit query, the goal of the diversity approach is to satisfy as many users as possible with a single result set. More specifically, diversification aims to minimize the number of totally unsatisfied users, trading degrees of satisfaction in exchange for increasing the size of the –at least minimally– satisfied population. The implicit assumption is that the loss involved in zero vs. small utility is far more significant than the loss involved between degrees of satisfaction. In other words, relevance follows a diminishing marginal returns pattern, where the gain obtained from increased relevance decreases fast with the number of relevant documents [14,21].

This view contrasts with the principles behind personalization. IR personalization takes the same starting point and addresses the same problem as diversity, where a sole query is viewed as an insufficient expression of the full and precise user need. But in contrast with diversification, the personalization approach strives to get further knowledge beyond the query, so as to explicitly tackle and overcome –to the degree this is possible– the initial uncertainty [9,11,12,18]. The uncertainty is reduced by extracting and exploiting further information from a wide variety of observations and resources, such as session feedback from the user, long-term records of user behavior, user stereotypes, social links, and other sources for user context and interest modeling. While in the diversity approach the system accepts and adapts its behavior to a situation of uncertainty, personalization tries to change this situation by enhancing the system knowledge about the user need. Rather than aiming to satisfy as many users as possible, personalization aims to build, in a way, a sense of who the user is, and maximize the satisfaction for the specific sensed user.

From these considerations, it might seem natural to see diversity and personalization as contradictory approaches. One might understand that by opting for diversity, the adaptation of results to specific users has been implicitly given up on. Conversely, if the query uncertainty is reduced by grasping the user context, the reason for diversification may have been done away with to some extent. In this paper we contend, however, that diversity and personalization are not necessarily incompatible or mutually exclusive goals, but on the contrary they may complement and in fact enhance each other.

Our research is motivated by the understanding that personalization is a process that involves itself a great deal of uncertainty, considerably higher, in fact, than ad-hoc search. The observation of implicit evidence of interest from users involves indeed much higher degrees of ambiguity and incompleteness than regular queries. The interpretation of the input for personalization is an explicit and inherent –and considerably difficult– part of the personalization task. The same observed contextual cues may fit several plausible interpretations whereby, by the same rationale as for search diversification, diversifying the system's assumptions may help minimize the ratio of severe failures in guessing the implicit user interests. Moreover, the observations of user behav-

SIGIR'12, August 12–16, 2012, Portland, Oregon, USA.

ior and preferences available to the system usually cover a small fraction of the full range of user interests, whereby context representations are far more incomplete than queries as expressions of user needs. Furthermore, the same as search diversity considers notions of aspects and facets in user queries and needs, user interests are typically heterogeneous, whereby the consideration of user profile aspects for diversification can be as natural as is the introduction of query aspects.

In this paper we develop a generalization of existing diversification approaches, by adding a personalization component into them. Specifically, we introduce a user random variable in probabilistic diversification models previously developed in the literature on IR diversity [1,16]. We describe in detail a full approach to develop the resulting framework into computable components. We report experiments with real users where our framework is compared to partial approaches that apply either personalization or diversification alone. We also compare our approach to a previous approximation to diversity and personalization combined [13]. Our approach compares favorably to all such alternatives, thus providing an empiric validation of our hypothesis.

The rest of the paper is organized as follows. In section 2, we further discuss the possible complementarity between diversity and personalization. In section 3 we propose the new personalized diversity models. In section 4 we present a possible framework instantiation of the model. In section 5, we describe the evaluation framework. Experimental results are presented in section 6, followed by a brief discussion of related work in section 7. Finally, we conclude in section 8 and indicate possible future directions of the presented work.

2. DIVERSITY AND PERSONALIZATION, AN INTEGRATED VIEW

The vision of combining diversity and personalization opens a rich area for research, barely explored to date. Diversity and personalization are complementary and can play together in different ways. The likes and preferences of people typically comprise quite diverse areas of interest, therefore not all of one's preferences should come into play in a specific retrieval task. The activation of the right preference area is critical for the performance of a personalization technique. Areas of user interest are often related to different contexts (work, leisure, time, tasks, situations, etc.). Choosing the wrong area is the typical cause of personalization intrusiveness – the Achilles' heel of personalization: the inferred preferences may be right, but they are applied at the wrong time.

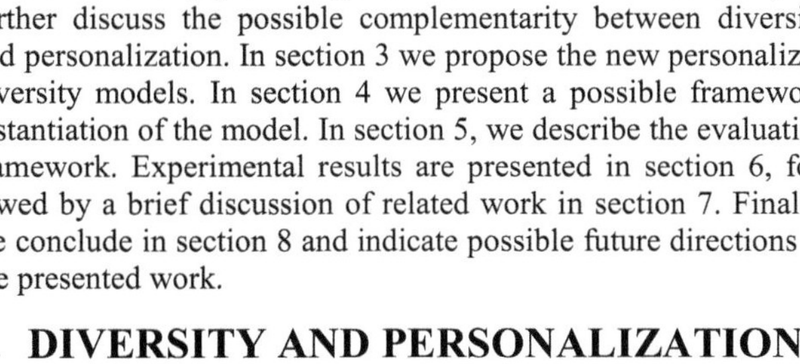

Figure 1. Diversity and personalization as complementary dimensions.

Diversity and personalization may interact and be combined in different ways to enhance each other. For instance, the personalization system may use a diversified selection of user interests, to cope with the uncertainty about which are most pertinent to the current context. Likewise, personalization can improve the effectiveness of aspect weighting in diversification, by favoring query interpretations which are predicted to be more related to each specific user. Besides interacting with each other, personalization and diversification can of course be directly applied to the search system. Which combination of the three components (diversity, personalization, and search system) is more appropriate may depend on a number of factors, including the characteristics of the query, the system knowledge about the user context, and relations between both. For instance, to the extent that user preferences are unrelated to the query, it may be advisable to apply them to the diversification component, and to little or no extent to the accuracy-seeking component. And so forth.

As a noteworthy example of the combination of diversity and personalization, diversity has been an actively researched topic in the Recommender Systems field in the last decade (see e.g. [19,20,23,24]). Recommendation is a genuine personalized retrieval task, but interestingly, one in which the explicitly query is absent, and only implicit evidence of user interests are available to the retrieval system. To this respect, our research vision is new in relation to prior work in that we deal with the problem of handling user preferences, the diversity dimension, and a query, altogether. Also interestingly, recommendation diversity has only been researched by similarity-based methods, devoid of an explicit representation of user intents (with the exception of [23]). In contrast, we shall consider an explicitly intent-oriented approach.

Figure 1 illustrates the complementarity of diversity and personalization in query-based search. Personalization is useful to focus the scope of diversification within a closer scope to general user interests (area 1 in the figure). Still, a fraction of user-neutral diversity beyond this may be appropriate (area 5). This fraction can be made variable and dependent on the degree of uncertainty in the system's knowledge about user preferences. Similarly, depending on this uncertainty, the diversification of user preferences should be more appropriate or less –e.g. diversity of personalization is less appropriate if the area 1 in the figure is much larger than the area labeled 2, and it is more beneficial in the opposite situation.

3. PERSONALIZED DIVERSITY

The approach we investigate here consists of the introduction of the user as an explicit random variable in the diversification models. We take as starting point the original formulations of two representative intent-oriented diversification algorithms, namely IA-Select [1] and xQuAD [15,16], characterized by using an explicit representation of query intents for diversification. Other diversification schemes not explicitly using aquery aspect space [5,6,21,22] might be generalized as well towards personalized versions, which we envision as future work.

As a starting point and general principle in our approach, a user random variable is introduced in every model component as a complement of the query and aspect variables in the representation of user needs. In practical terms, with respect to the original non-personalized methods, the resulting expressions give rise to new and/or additional model terms requiring handling and estimation, as we shall see. We shall deal with and provide approaches for them. On the other hand, the user-based formulation provides for considering independence assumptions at different points, which result in different variants of the framework, standing for different angles on personalized diversification, as we shall see.

3.1 Personalized IA-Select

The IA-Select and xQuAD diversification algorithms greedily rerank search results by maximizing an objective function. Based on the description in [1], the objective function of IA-Select can be expressed as:

$$f_S(d) = \sum_c p(c|q)p(q|d)p(c|d) \prod_{d' \in S} (1 - p(q|d')p(c|d'))$$

where S is the incremental subset of diversified documents from the original result set. We generalize this formulation to a personalized version by introducing the user random variable:

$$f_S(d,u) =$$
$$= \sum_c p(c|q,u)p(q|d,u)p(c|d,u) \prod_{d' \in S} (1 - p(q|d',u)p(c|d',u))$$

In this expression we have three main components involved:

- A personalized search system: $p(q|d,u)$.
- The personalized query aspect distribution: $p(c|q,u)$.
- The personalized aspect distribution over documents: $p(c|d,u)$.

The first component represents a baseline personalized search system. If we only have a non-personalized system, we may develop this term using Bayes' rule as:

$$p(d|q,u) = \frac{p(q|d,u)p(d|u)}{p(q|u)} \sim \frac{p(q|d)p(d|u)}{\sum_{d'} p(q|d')p(d'|u)} =$$
$$= \frac{p(d|q)p(d|u)}{\sum_{d'} p(d'|q)p(d'|u)} = C_1(q,u)\, p(d|q)p(d|u) \quad (1)$$

where we have assumed q and u are conditionally independent given a document, and we assume a uniform document prior. The expression is thus reduced to the combination of a non-personalized search system, represented by $p(d|q)$ –the same as in the original IA-Select–, and a pure personalization factor represented by $p(d|u)$. The latter factor captures how much user u is predicted to like document d (regardless of a specific search task), expressed as how likely it is to observe the document given the user. This is what a personalization system typically provides for, based on some mechanism for extracting or learning user preferences. We shall provide further details for a particular implementation of the baseline search and personalization components in our experiments in section 4.

Now the aspect-document distribution component of personalized IA-Select can be developed as:

$$p(c|d,u) = \frac{p(d|c,u)p(c|u)}{p(d|u)} \sim \frac{p(d|c)p(c|u)}{\sum_{c'} p(d|c')p(c'|u)} =$$
$$= \frac{p(c|d)p(c|u)}{\sum_{c'} p(c'|d)p(c'|u)} = C_2(d,u)\, p(c|d)p(c|u) \quad (2)$$

where we assume a uniform aspect prior, and conditional independence between documents and users given a query aspect.

A natural way to estimate the personalized aspect distribution $p(c|u)$ is by marginalization over the set of documents:

$$p(c|u) = \sum_d p(c|d,u)p(d|u) \sim \sum_d p(c|d)p(d|u)$$

where we assume conditional independence between aspects and users given a document.

Finally, for the personalized query aspect distribution $p(c|q,u)$ several derivations are possible. A convenient one is to develop $p(c|q,u)$ by marginalizing over the set of documents, because it allows taking advantage of the computation of the two previous top-level components in equations 1 and 2:

$$p(c|q,u) = \sum_d p(c|d,q,u)p(d|q,u) \sim \sum_d p(c|d,u)p(d|q,u) \quad (3)$$

where we assume the conditional independence of query aspects and queries given a user and a document. We may also consider $p(c|d,u) \sim p(c|d)$ as a simplified option (assuming conditional independence of aspects and users given a document), using the approximations to $p(c|d)$ discussed in the next section. In appendix A, we offer alternative developments of $p(c|q,u)$, which might be more suitable to specific frameworks.

3.2 Personalized xQuAD

The objective function of the xQuAD algorithm is formulated in [16] as:

$$f_S(d) = (1-\lambda)p(d|q) + \lambda\, p(d,\bar{S}|q) =$$
$$= (1-\lambda)\, p(d|q) + \lambda \sum_c p(c|q)p(d|c) \prod_{d' \in S} (1 - p(d'|c))$$

In the personalized version of this algorithm the objective function is thus generalized to:

$$f_S(d,u) = (1-\lambda)\, p(d|q,u)$$
$$+ \lambda \sum_c p(c|q,u)p(d|c,u) \prod_{d' \in S} (1 - p(d'|c,u)) \quad (4)$$

This expression involves three main components:

- The personalized search system: $p(q|d,u)$.
- The personalized query aspect distribution: $p(c|q,u)$.
- The personalized, aspect-dependent document distribution: $p(d|c,u)$.

The first two terms were already handled in the previous section (equations 1 and 3). Using Bayes' theorem and equation 2, it can be seen that the third term can be approximated by:

$$p(d|c,u) \sim \frac{p(c|d)p(d|u)}{\sum_{c'} p(c'|d)p(c'|u)} = C_2(c,u)\, p(c|d)p(d|u)$$

where –as in equation 2– we are assuming documents and users are conditionally independent given a query aspect. Again, the estimation of $p(d|u)$ admits different approaches depending on the available data, an example of which we develop in our experiments in section 4.

Finally, the term $p(c|d)$ can be estimated in different ways depending on the nature of the query aspect space and available observations. For instance, if c is an Open Directory Project (ODP) category as in [1,14], we may estimate $p(c|d)$ by a text classification method as the probability that document d belongs to class c. Other estimation approaches can be applied for query aspects of a different nature. For instance, $p(c|d)$ can be computed by calling the baseline search system on c and d, as far as c belongs to the space of queries –this is the case in [16], where c are related and suggested queries from a search engine.

3.3 Discussion

The personalized versions of IA-Select and xQuAD provide a framework that supports different views on the combination between diversity and personalization. For instance, the summation $\sum_c p(c|q,u)p(d|c,u)$ in xQuAD can be seen as a marginalization over query aspects for a personalized search model $p(d|q,u)$ (assuming conditional independence of documents and queries given a user and an aspect), that is, a means to diversify user preferences over a query aspect space. This can be seen as a means to tackle the uncertainty about implicit user interests by a diversification strategy, as motivated earlier in section 2.

Conversely, $p(c|q,u)$ can be seen as an enhancement in the estimation of the aspect distribution $p(c|q)$ for diversification, by exploiting available information about user preferences for aspects, in order to improve the effect of diversity by making it more user-specific. Furthermore, $p(d'|c,u)$, in the novelty component, enhances the redundancy model by personalizing the utility estimation of seen documents. With slight variations in the formulation, analogous effects can be identified in IA-Select.

On the other hand, the framework flexibly supports different configurations by selectively removing the user variable (i.e. adding user-independence assumptions) from some of its components. This selective removal results into different combinations and views on personalization and diversity. For instance, if we remove personalization from the external baseline system $(1-\lambda)\,p(d|q,u)$ in xQuAD, the result is a personalized diversification of a non-personalized search system. We may do the opposite in order to have a non-personalized diversification of a personalized retrieval system. At a finer granularity, we may combine a personalized aspect distribution $p(c|q,u)$ with a non-personalized redundancy component $p(d'|c)$. And so forth. The variations could even be dynamic and selective, depending e.g. on the reliability of the system knowledge about implicit user interests, the degree of relatedness between recorded preferences and the query at hand, the vagueness of the query, and so forth.

In our experiments, we compare five framework configurations, as we shall see: a) fully personalized diversification, b) non-personalized diversification, c) non-diversified personalization, d) a plain (non-personalized, non-diversified) search system baseline, and e) personalization *after* diversification, the latter in order to compare our framework to a personalized diversification approach reported in prior work [13].

4. FRAMEWORK INSTANTIATION

In this section we introduce a particular instantiation of the proposed personalization and diversification framework. Instantiating our model involves providing estimates for: 1) the personalization component $p(d|u)$; 2) the diversity component $p(c|d)$; and the document relevance component $p(d|q)$. In the following section we offer insight on how to estimate the query relevance component, based on an external search engine, and the personalization component, from a weighted term-based representation of documents and user profiles. In section 4.2, we present estimations more specific to our framework: a social-based representation of documents and users, and the calculation of the diversification component. Finally, section 4.3 addresses a common problem that can arise from the use of external sources to estimate some components, and its implication on the xQuAD approach.

4.1 Model estimations

Similar to e.g. [4], the document generation model can be approximated from a baseline retrieval function by normalizing the score by the sum of all scores of the top k documents being diversified:

$$p(d|q) \sim \frac{\bar{s}(d,q)}{\sum_{d' \in R_q} \bar{s}(d',q)} \quad (5)$$

where R_q is the set of documents to be diversified for query q. In our implementation we make use of an external Web search system, estimating $\bar{s}(d,q)$ as a rank-sim normalization [10] of the baseline retrieval function, that is $\bar{s}(d,q) = 1 - \tau(d,q)/|R_q|$, where $\tau(d,q)$ is the position of document d in the order induced by the retrieval system scores $s(d,q)$ for $d \in R_q$.

The user preference model described by $p(d|u)$ can be obtained in many ways, depending on the available document features and user behavior observations. For instance, for text retrieval, we may marginalize $p(d|u)$ over words:

$$\begin{aligned} p(d|u) &= \sum_w p(d|u,w)p(w|u) \\ &\sim p(d)\sum_w p(w|d)p(w|u)/p(w) \end{aligned} \quad (6)$$

where we assume conditional independence of words and users given a document. The following estimates of the resulting distributions were tested in our experiments:

$$p(w|d) \sim \frac{tf(w,d)}{\sum_{w'} tf(w',d)} \qquad p(w|u) \sim \frac{tf(w,u)}{\sum_{w'} tf(w',u)}$$

$$p(w) \sim \frac{\sum_d tf(w,d)}{\sum_d \sum_{w'} tf(w',d)} \qquad p(d) \sim \frac{1}{|\Delta|}$$

where $tf(w,d)$ is the term count of term w in d, $tf(w,u)$ is the term count in the user profile representation, and Δ is the document collection.

Alternatively, we can estimate the user preference model by an adaptation of the BM25 probabilistic model, similar to the approach presented in [18]:

$$p(d|u) = \sum_{w:tf(w,d)>0} iuf(w)\frac{tf(w,u)\,(k_1+1)}{tf(w,u)+k_1\left(1-b+\frac{b|u|}{\text{avg}_u|u|}\right)} \quad (7)$$

where $iuf(w)$ is the inverse user frequency of term w in the set of users, and $|u|$ is the size of the user profile calculated as $\sum_w tf(w,u)$. We set b and k_1 to the standard values of 0.75 and 2, respectively. In the following section we show how to implement this estimate with user and document profiles based on social annotations.

4.2 Framework-specific estimations

We propose now an instantiation of the personalized and diversification components by exploiting two sources of information. As a source for document and user representations, we use the social bookmarking site Delicious[1], which allows the collective bookmarking of Web pages by user generated tags. This collection of tag-user and tag-document relations, commonly named *folksonomy*, is used in our model to compute the values for $tf(w,u)$ and $tf(w,d)$, where in this case w represents a tag in the folksonomy and the frequency values are, respectively, the number of times a user used the tag in their profile bookmark annotations, and the number of times a tag was used (by any user) to annotate a document. The inverse frequency of a tag, $iuf(w)$ can be computed by counting how many users have a specific tag in their profile. For the latter calculation, we used a small training collection of 3,000 users, randomly sampled from Delicious. The advantages of using a source of this nature for document and user profile representation is threefold: first, it is a simple solution to having user and document profiles represented in the same term space model; second, folksonomies offer a more concise way of representing content, facilitating the computation of our model; and third, it facilitates the evaluation of our approaches, by providing us with a publicly-available user profiling resource, sparing the need for sophisticated profile learning techniques.

Another key element for our model is the estimation of the diversity component $p(c|d)$, which should capture how related a category is to a document. In our experiments we shall follow a content-based approach, by classifying Web pages into the ODP

[1] Delicious, Discover yourself: http://www.delicious.com/

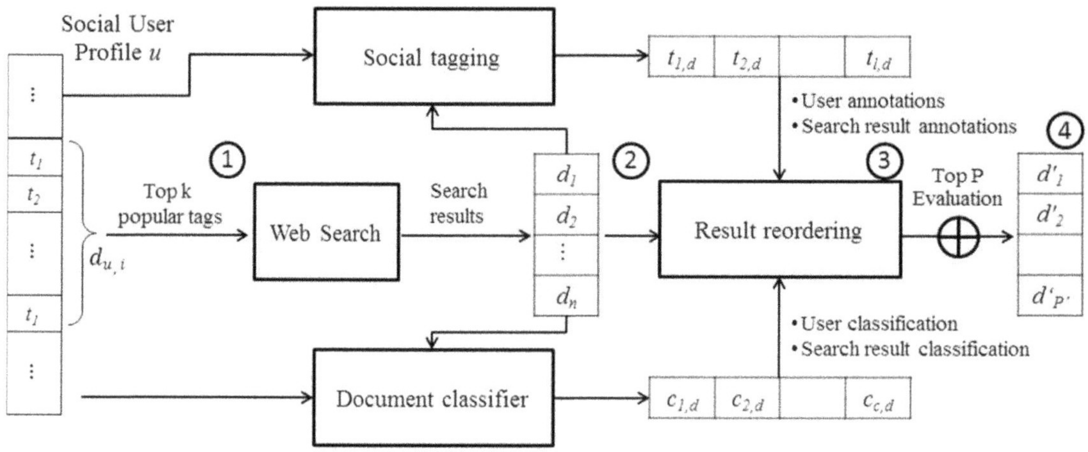

Figure 2. Process of user topic creation, annotation, and evaluation

taxonomy. We first considered a Rocchio-based classification approach, as used by Agrawal et al [1], but after close examination and testing on a development collection, we found it too imprecise to be used as an estimator[2]. As an alternative, we made use of the Textwise[3] ODP classification service which yielded acceptable results on our development collection. The Textwise API returns up to three possible ODP classifications for a document, ranked by a score in [0,1] that reflects the degree of confidence on the classification. We used directly this value as our estimate of $p(c|d)$, after normalization

4.3 Component Normalization

Both the original and the personalized version of the xQuAD scheme use a linear combination of two components, one seeking to procure relevance, and the other seeking diversity (see equation 4). The influence of these two factors can be adjusted by varying the λ parameter. In order for this linear combination to make proper sense, the two components should be comparable –a case of the classic rank fusion problem, which requires a normalization step [10]. Our framework instantiation estimates involve heterogeneous sources and systems, such as an external baseline search system, social annotations, and an external classification service. The use of such third-party tools and resources makes normalization all the more necessary. For this purpose we use a distribution-based normalization approach described by Fernandez et al [8]. Normalization is applied on the two components (relevance and diversity) that are linearly combined, both in the original and the personalized version of xQuAD. The objective function is thus modified to:

$$f_S(d,u) = (1-\lambda)\,\Psi_1\big(p(d|q,u)\big)$$

$$+\lambda\,\Psi_2\left(\sum_c p(c|q,u)p(d|c,u)\prod_{d'\in S}\big(1-p(d'|c,u)\big)\right)$$

where Ψ_1 and Ψ_2 are the score normalization functions. The normalizers use a histogram of output values from the functions to be normalized, sampling from very simple training data (e.g. no relevance judgments required). The reader can refer to [8] for more details on the normalization method.

5. EVALUATION FRAMEWORK

A proper evaluation of personalization techniques is difficult to achieve with offline data only, and in our case indeed requires relevance judgments from real users and potentially real Web search topics, as well as the availability of some form of user profile representation. We used a crowdsourcing service for this purpose, requiring users of this service –known as *workers*– to have a social profile in Delicious in order to evaluate a number of search topics. We provide further details on this in section 5.1.

We first investigated creating a set of fixed ambiguous topics using Wikipedia's disambiguation pages, which indicate concepts or topics that may have multiple meanings. This methodology was used in previous evaluation schemes in the literature [14,15]. However, after an initial analysis of the worker's feedback, we found that workers were sometimes unfamiliar with the selected ambiguous topics, and were as a consequence unable to provide consistent relevance judgments. As a solution to this problem, we investigated an automatic topic creation methodology, which uses the social profile of the worker in order to find test topics known to the worker. In order to extract topics from the Delicious profile, we adapted to our online evaluation setup an offline evaluation technique initially suggested by Vallet et al. [18].

This topic generation technique creates a test topic from a candidate Web page bookmark, randomly chosen from the worker's Delicious profile. Given the candidate bookmark, a query topic is created, using as keywords the top *K* most popular annotations (tags) assigned by all users to the same bookmark, thus obtaining a keyword based topic representation related to the bookmark. We ensured that the topics were generated by somewhat popular bookmarks by only generating topics from documents that had annotations from at least five different users.

By following the above process there is a much higher chance that the evaluation topic is known by the user (as it is related to the document saved in his profile). When analyzing the workers' feedback, we found a much more positive response to this type of profile generated topics, in terms of both knowledge of the topic, and user engagement in the evaluation process.

The complete topic and result generation process is depicted in Figure 2. The first step **(1)** is to generate a topic suitable for the user to evaluate, following the process described above. By setting the number *K* of popular tags used in the topic generation process, we were able to generate somewhat ambiguous topics, since a larger number of keywords would, in general, generate more specific topics. Given our focus on diversification and

[2] Other alternatives such a Naïve Bayes classifier or a probabilistic estimator were considered, obtaining similar results.

[3] Textwise LLC: http://textwise.com

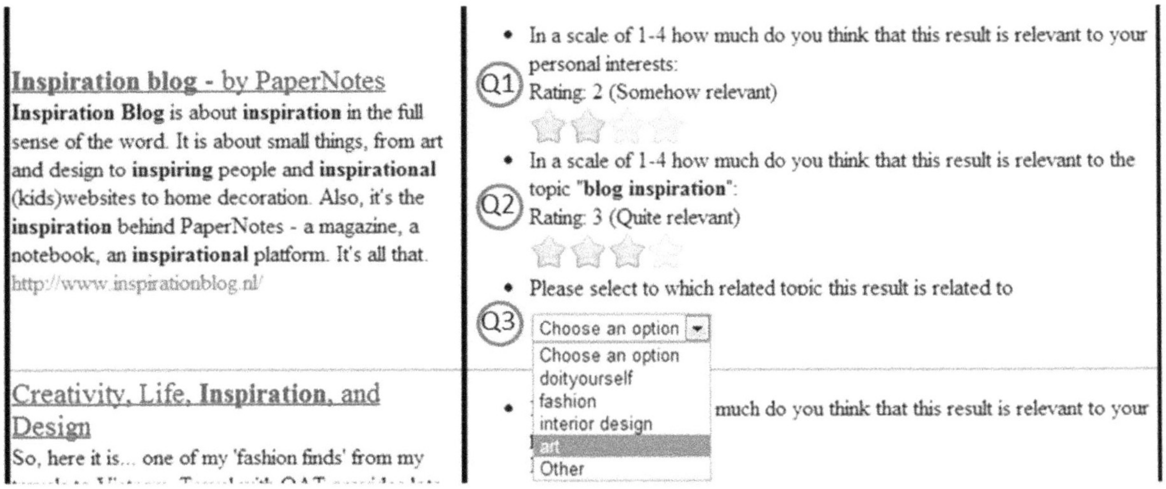

Figure 3. Snapshot of the interactive evaluation interface. Evaluation guidelines have been removed due to space restrictions

personalization on ambiguous topics, we randomly generated an equal amount of topics of size $K = 1$ and $K = 2$, thus focusing on ambiguous topics, and expecting that the latter size, produces, on average, more specific topics. Section 6 further investigates the effect of distinct topic query sizes. The generated query topic was then sent to the Yahoo! Search API[4], from which the top N results were obtained. In our experiments, N was set to 300. We set the location parameter of the search API to the United States, as workers were selected from this region.

In step **(2)**, we extract both social and classification information from each of the documents in the result set. The social annotations were extracted directly from Delicious, by collecting the top 100 most recent annotations given by users. The document topic classification is obtained using the Textwise URL classification service, which returns up to the top 3 ODP most likely categories for each document. The ODP classes were cut down to level 3 in the ODP taxonomy (Top / Level 1 / Level 2 / Level 3). This annotation extraction and document classification process provides the information needed to compute the personalization and diversification estimates of our studied approaches, respectively. It is worth noting that these two services did not provide a complete coverage over the search results. In particular, the Delicious coverage was 57.5% over the top 300 results and went up to a 69.5% coverage over the top 20 results. Textwise had a coverage of 94.7% and returned an average of ~2 categories per document. In order to cope with the incomplete coverage of Delicious, we added a smoothing factor to the computation of $\hat{p}(d|q,u) = \lambda\, p(d|q,u) + (1-\lambda)p(d)$, with $\lambda = 0.5$, so that documents out of coverage would not get a strict zero score.

In step **(3)**, the output of each evaluated approach is used to rerank the Web search results according to personalization and/or diversification features extracted in step 2. The top P documents of each reranking technique are aggregated into a single evaluation list, which is then randomly shuffled and passed onto the evaluation framework. In our experiments, we evaluated the top $P = 5$ results of each algorithm.

5.1 Crowdsourced Evaluation

Crowdsourcing services (e.g. Amazon mechanical turk[5], Crowdflower[6]) are recently proving to be a valuable tool to optimize the necessary resources to evaluate a wide range of information retrieval tasks [2,3]. These evaluations are based on relevance judgments provided by users of the crowdsourcing service. Alonso and Baeza proposed a methodology to obtain relevance assessments for TREC related topics [2] using such crowdsourcing services. In their study, it was concluded that workers can provide relevance judgements with comparable quality to those provided by expert assessors.

Our evaluation framework, however, has to additionally consider the personalization and diversification factors involved in our research. Regarding diversification, Agrawal et al. [1] required workers to manually classify results over a predefined set of ODP categories, representing the subtopics that could possibly be related to a search query. The goal was to obtain a result/topic relevance assessment that could be used to evaluate a diversification approach in terms of both accuracy and diversification metrics. In our setup, in addition to this type of assessment, we also needed to obtain a personal relevance assessment, i.e., to which degree a search result is preferred subjectively by the assessor. This value allows us to measure the accuracy of the personalization techniques with respect to the real interest of the user. Our evaluation framework is based on prior early work [17], which focused on the acquisition of personal assessments from workers, and has been adapted to include diversification factors. The main difference between our evaluation methodology and the one presented by Alonso and Baeza [2,3] is that our assessments are subjective to the worker, thus relevance assessments cannot be compared across workers, as they evaluate specific topics related to their profile, according to their personal interests and their own notion of relevance to the topic.

In prevention for malicious workers, we implemented a simple technique based on the injection of irrelevant results in some of the evaluated topics, which were then used as quality assessment topics to detect workers that were answering questions randomly. This would not detect workers that mark all results as irrelevant, but a close inspection of the gathered results did not show this behaviour.

We also had a number of prerequisites to access the evaluation interface: 1) as mentioned earlier, workers had to have a valid Delicious account;

---

[4] Yahoo! BOSS API: http://developer.yahoo.com/search/boss/

[5] Amazon mechanical turk: http://www.mturk.com/

[6] Crowdflower: http://crowdflower.com/

Table 1: Diversity metric values for the evaluated approaches. Values in bold indicate the best for each metric. Underlined values indicate a statistically significant difference with respect to the baseline, double underlined values indicate, in addition, a statistical significance with respect xQuAD (Wilcoxon, $p < 0.05$).

	Topic relevance									**User relevance**								
	Topic			Topic (K=1)			Topic (K=2)			User			User (K=1)			User (K=2)		
	ERR-IA@5	α-nDCG@5	S-recall@5	ERR-IA@5	α-nDCG@5	S-recall@5	ERR-IA@5	α-nDCG@5	S-recall@5	ERR-IA@5	α-nDCG@5	S-recall@5	ERR-IA@5	α-nDCG@5	S-recall@5	ERR-IA@5	α-nDCG@5	S-recall@5
Baseline	0.274	0.787	0.500	0.268	0.796	0.493	0.281	0.779	0.513	0.254	0.626	0.475	0.240	0.592	0.460	0.273	0.670	0.498
IA-Select	0.262	0.758	0.463	0.251	0.748	0.451	0.274	0.769	0.475	0.237	0.582	0.426	0.211	0.532	0.398	0.268	0.642	0.458
xQuAD	0.275	0.793	0.510	0.272	0.806	0.509	0.279	0.778	0.511	0.257	0.624	0.478	0.244	0.584	0.459	0.273	0.673	0.502
$Pers_{BM25}$	0.267	0.778	0.486	0.266	0.794	0.490	0.267	0.758	0.481	0.262	0.646	0.483	**0.261**	**0.631**	0.481	0.262	0.664	0.486
$xQuAD_{BM25}$	0.272	0.794	0.516	0.266	0.798	0.509	0.279	0.788	0.526	0.258	0.631	0.492	0.244	0.597	0.470	0.273	0.671	0.520
PIA-Select	0.251	0.742	0.489	0.231	0.723	0.478	0.276	0.767	0.503	0.239	0.593	0.481	0.219	0.546	0.457	0.263	0.650	0.512
$PIA\text{-}Select_{BM25}$	0.279	0.803	**0.543**	0.269	0.793	0.515	**0.291**	**0.818**	**0.579**	**0.273**	0.656	**0.521**	0.260	0.613	**0.489**	**0.290**	0.710	**0.562**
PxQuAD	0.275	0.796	0.503	0.268	0.805	0.501	0.285	0.788	0.510	0.268	0.649	0.489	0.255	0.620	0.478	0.286	0.687	0.506
$PxQuAD_{BM25}$	**0.281**	**0.810**	0.519	**0.275**	**0.818**	**0.519**	0.288	0.802	0.520	0.267	**0.658**	0.496	0.249	0.612	0.460	0.290	**0.716**	0.542

2) the Delicious account was validated by asking the worker to add a random bookmark to their public profile; 3) the Delicious profile had to be at least 3 months old, contain at least 30 bookmarks, and the 30th most recent bookmark had to be at least 15 days old. In general, the use of the quality assessment topics and our prerequisites for accessing the evaluation interface were enough to avoid misbehaving workers.

Figure 3 shows a snapshot of the evaluation interface. The aggregated output of the evaluated approaches is presented as a search result list to the worker, who has to provide individual assessments by answering three questions:

- Q1 (user): a 4-grade scale assessment on how relevant is the result to the user's interests.
- Q2 (topic): a 4-grade scale assessment on how relevant is the result to the evaluated topic.
- Q3 (subtopic): workers assign each result to a specific subtopic related to the evaluated topic.

Q1 provides for measuring the accuracy of the evaluated approaches with respect to the user interest. Q2 is used to evaluate how relevant is the result to the overall search topic –a successful reordering technique will place results high that are assessed as both relevant to the topic and to the user's interests. Finally, Q3 provides a subjective classification of the search result to the possible subtopics related to the search topic. The interface is designed to encourage the reuse of introduced subtopics, so as to facilitate workers to provide a more concise categorization of search results. A tutorial was included in the topic description, which was helpful for workers to understand the concepts of subtopics and how this assignment is performed. We decided to take a different approach from Agrawal et al. [1], who used predefined ODP subtopics for result categorization, for the following reasons: 1) we felt that some ODP categories are difficult to understand, often not self-explanatory, and thus can be confusing for workers for annotation; 2) candidate ODP categories need to be automatically selected by the ODP classifier, which could cause difficulties for workers in case of classification errors. In Agrawal et al.'s study this problem was alleviated by having more than one worker evaluating a single topic, but in our personalized setup topics can only be evaluated by a single worker. After analyzing the workers' assessments and open comments feedback, they seemed to be comfortable with providing their own classification scheme. It is also worth noting that our query generation process produced topics that were known to the worker.

The assessment collection process spanned over a period of four weeks. During this period, we were able to collect information from 35 users that satisfied our prerequisites, collecting assessments for a total amount of 180 topics (median of 4 topics per user) and 3,800 individual results. The user profile and relevance assessment information has been anonymized and made publicly available at *http://ir.ii.uam.es/~david/persdivers/*.

6. EXPERIMENT RESULTS

Nine different approaches were evaluated with the approach described in the previous section: the baseline system, namely the original ranking returned by the Web retrieval engine; two state of the art search diversification approaches, IA-Select [1] and xQuAD [16]; a plain (in the sense of "not diversified") personalized search approach based on social tagging profiles and BM25, presented in [18] ($Pers_{BM25}$); a two stage diversification and personalization approach, suggested by Radlinski and Dumais in [13] which, in our implementation, first applies the xQuAD algorithm and then the $Pers_{BM25}$ technique ($xQuAD_{BM25}$); two different personalized versions of IA-Select, one with a probabilistic calculation of $p(d|u)$ –equation 6– (PIA-Select), and the other using BM25 (equation 7) as an alternative calculation ($PIA\text{-}Select_{BM25}$), as described in section 4.1; two different personalized versions of xQuAD, differing on the same alternative as in PIA-Select for the calculation of $p(d|u)$.

In order to evaluate for diversity, we use three well known metrics: the intent aware version of expected reciprocal rank (ERR-IA), α-nDCG [7], and subtopic recall (S-recall) [22]. For accuracy, we use nDCG and precision. User assessments were graded from one to four, where a value greater than one was assumed as relevant. The nDCG metric made use of the graded values for each of these approaches, Since users only evaluated the top 5 results of each of these approaches, all metrics take this cut off point.

Table 2: Accuracy metrics for evaluated approaches. Values in bold indicate the best performing values. Underlined values indicate a statistically significant difference with respect to the baseline, double underlined values indicate, in addition, a statistical significance with respect to xQuAD (by Wilcoxon, p < 0.05 in both cases).

	Topic relevance						User relevance							
	Topic		Topic (*K*=1)		Topic (*K*=2)		User		User (*K*=1)		User (*K*=2)		F(Topic,User)	
	nDCG@5	P@5	nDCG@5	P@5	nDCG@5	P@5	nDCG@5	P@5	nDCG@5	P@5	nDCG@5	P@5	nDCG@5	P@5
Baseline	0.393	0.918	0.401	0.914	0.385	0.923	0.330	0.702	0.318	0.657	0.344	0.755	0.359	0.796
IA-Select	0.363	0.911	0.367	0.905	0.359	0.917	0.294	0.664	0.277	0.617	0.314	0.720	0.325	0.768
xQuAD	0.381	0.911	0.390	0.907	0.370	0.915	0.320	0.670	0.310	0.611	0.332	0.741	0.348	0.772
$Pers_{BM25}$	0.388	0.933	0.410	**0.947**	0.359	0.915	0.357	**0.746**	**0.373**	**0.714**	0.336	0.784	0.372	**0.829**
$xQuAD_{BM25}$	0.375	0.924	0.390	0.931	0.357	0.915	0.334	0.688	0.340	0.642	0.327	0.741	0.354	0.789
PIA-Select	0.331	0.861	0.315	0.840	0.350	0.885	0.306	0.652	0.292	0.590	0.323	0.725	0.318	0.742
$PIA\text{-}Select_{BM25}$	0.363	0.892	0.369	0.897	0.356	0.885	0.345	0.670	0.350	0.625	0.340	0.723	0.354	0.766
PxQuAD	0.395	0.930	0.408	0.928	0.379	0.931	0.337	0.714	0.334	0.674	0.341	0.760	0.364	0.807
$PxQuAD_{BM25}$	**0.405**	**0.939**	**0.414**	0.943	**0.394**	**0.933**	**0.361**	0.730	0.354	0.672	**0.371**	**0.800**	**0.382**	0.821

We compute the metrics in two ways: 1) with the assessments given by workers when replying to Q2 (see section 5.1) where they judge how relevant was the result to the evaluated topic; and 2) metrics that make use of the assessments given by workers when replying to Q1, where they judge how relevant is the result to their personal interests. We also provide a breakdown of the obtained results into topics with single keyword queries ($K = 1$) and topics with two keywords ($K = 2$). The reason is that we expect, on average, the former to represent more ambiguous topics than the latter.

6.1 Diversity Metrics

Table 1 shows the obtained results regarding diversity metrics from which we can conclude the following. In terms of topic relevance (Table 1 left), most approaches, except PIA-Select, are on par with the commercial search engine baseline. $PxQuAD_{BM25}$ has a significantly better performance than the baseline and plain diversification approaches in terms of ERR-IA and α-nDCG@5. In terms of user relevance (Table 1 right) the improvement of personalized diversity over the baseline and plain diversification is increased, indicating that the personalization factors have a positive effect on the overall view of relevance with respect to the user preference and the diversity of results preferred by the user.

Surprisingly, the plain personalization approach did not show a significant decrease in the diversification values with respect to the baseline, although the obtained values are smaller than the diversification approaches. We hypothesize that this is due to this approach taking into account the original ordering of the search results, given by the baseline, which already performs well in terms of diversity. Thus, this diversification approach resembles the two stage diversification and personalization approach implemented in $xQuAD_{BM25}$ [13] in terms of diversity values.

Regarding query size, the best performing version of IA-Select, $PIA\text{-}Select_{BM25}$, seems to provide better results with topic queries of size $K = 2$ (more specific queries), whereas for $K = 1$, the personalized versions of xQuAD –$PxQuAD_{BM25}$ and PxQuAD– seem to perform better regarding topic and user relevance, respectively.

In summary, a general overview of the results indicate that the best performing techniques in terms of diversity metrics are three of our proposed personalized diversification approaches: $PIA\text{-}Select_{BM25}$, PxQuAD, and $PxQuAD_{BM25}$. The latter has a statistically significant difference with respect to the baseline both in terms of topic and user relevance. In subtopic recall, the $PIA\text{-}Select_{BM25}$ approach is the best performing one, as also in terms of topic relevance on more specific topics ($K = 2$). It is worth noting that all of these approaches outperform significantly the plain personalized approach, $Pers_{BM25}$, both in topic and user relevance. The other personalized diversification approach, PIA-Select, is not able to improve the baseline. This might be due to a negative effect of the probabilistic estimate of the personalized factor on the overall behavior of the PIA-Select algorithm. However, the other variation, $PIA\text{-}Select_{BM25}$, which uses BM25 as personalized estimation factor, appears to perform much better. When compared with the best performing full diversification approach, xQuAD, we can observe that either $PxQuAD_{BM2}$ or $PIA\text{-}Select_{BM25}$ achieve statistically significant results in most of the diversity metrics.

6.2 Accuracy

Table 2 shows the accuracy metrics for the different evaluated approaches, from which we may observe the following. In terms of topic relevance (Table 2 left), values are in general close to the baseline: P@5 values are high for all approaches, whereas the nDCG@5 values, which make use of the graded relevance, are more diverse. We see the expected decrease in performance as measured by nDCG values for the plain diversification approaches (IA-Select, xQuAD). It comes as somewhat unexpected that the best value is obtained by a personalized diversification approach, $PxQuAD_{BM25}$, which is supposed to affect diversity negatively, but that even reaches statistical significance with respect to the baseline. The results obtained by this approach seem to be the highest in almost all metrics regarding topic relevance and queries with size $K = 1$ and $K = 2$. These results suggest that there is a further benefit from adding personalized factors to the diversification approach. However, the other personalized diversification approaches do not appear to outperform the baseline, so no definitive conclusion can be drawn from this result.

In terms of user relevance (Table 2 right), there appears to be two clear dominant approaches: $PxQuAD_{BM25}$ and $Pers_{BM25}$. The personalized diversification approach has the best performance in terms of nDCG, outperforming the baseline. It achieves a 9.5% improvement over the baseline, which is statistically significant.

The performance of the plain personalization approach, $Pers_{BM25}$, is on par with the latter, obtaining also a statistical significance with respect to the baseline. It seems that the main difference between these two approaches is that the performance of the $Pers_{BM25}$ approach in more ambiguous queries ($K = 2$) is slightly better than the $PxQuAD_{BM25}$ approach, while on less ambiguous queries ($K = 2$) the latter has better performance.

The last two columns of Table 2 show the F-measure values regarding both the user and topic relevance, in order to assess the combined performance of the approaches taking into account both topic and user relevance. The best values are obtained for the plain personalization approach $Pers_{BM25}$ in terms of P@5 and the diversified personalization approach $PxQuAD_{BM25}$ in terms of nDCG (graded relevance). Both of these approaches achieve statistically significant results with respect to the baseline and the best performing diversity approach, xQuAD.

In summary, while the plain personalization approach, $Pers_{BM25}$, appears to be on par with our best personalized diversification approach $PxQuAD_{BM25}$, in terms of relevance to the user, the former underperforms the baseline in terms of relevance to the topic, while the latter, surprisingly, improves the baseline to this regard, with statistical significance.

6.3 Experiment conclusions

In terms of overall performance, the personalized diversification approach $PxQuAD_{BM25}$ fares best overall: it has the best results in terms of topic-based diversity and is competitive in terms of user-based diversity. Additionally, it has the best accuracy values, together with the plain personalization approach. In most of the obtained values, this approach improves significantly the baseline. Hence, the $PxQuAD_{BM25}$ approach appears to be the best approach to balance both diversification and personalization factors, resulting in competitive values in terms of both diversity and accuracy, with respect to both topic and user relevance.

7. RELATED WORK

To the best of our knowledge, only Radlinski and Dumais [13] have previously investigated a possible combination of personalization and diversification approaches in Web search. They present a two-stage approach: given an initial user query, the search results are first diversified by executing related sub-queries, taken from query reformulations. In a second step, results are personalized using the user profile. Their hypothesis is that by diversifying results there is a higher chance of encountering documents that satisfy the user's interests. In our evaluation, we included a technique based on their two stage approach ($xQuAD_{BM25}$). In our experiments this approach did not achieve significant improvements over plain personalization, and it was outperformed by our personalized diversification approaches. A possible explanation is that the basic personalized approach was applied to the search baseline, which already had competitive diversity performance. Another explanation would be that their approach may further benefit from diversification techniques based on sub-queries, which were not tested in our experiments.

In our work, we exploit social annotation profiles in order to apply personalization factors related to a Web search. The use of a source of information of this type for Web personalization was first suggested by Noll and Meiner [12], who evaluated with real users the use of Delicious user profiles to personalize search, proving the effectiveness of the approach with a simple personalization model. Vallet et al. [18] presented an evaluation framework allowing for offline evaluation of Web search personalization approaches based on social annotations. They tested a number of approaches, including Noll and Meiner's, concluding that the best performing approaches were based either on the BM25 probabilistic model or a simple scalar product. From this work we have adapted the proposed BM25 model as a personalized estimation factor. Our evaluation framework is based on their offline evaluation approach, which has been adapted here to allow for an online evaluation of personalization and diversification methods with real users.

Han et al. [9] presented an improvement over Noll and Meiner [12] and Vallet et al. [18], in which user and document tags are related to the ODP taxonomy. The taxonomy is then exploited to expand tags to related concepts. The authors proposed to use the user's search query to activate concepts within the ODP taxonomy, performing a sort of "contextualization" of user preferences. These preferences are then used to compute the personalization factor to be applied on the search output. Their evaluation, which used the framework presented by Vallet et al., indicated an improvement over the state of the art approaches. In our work, we treated the ODP and tag information as independent sources of information. In future work we will analyze whether relating tags to ODP concepts has a positive impact on personalized diversification approaches.

8. CONCLUSIONS AND FUTURE WORK

In this work we have presented a number of approaches that combine both personalization and diversification components. To this end, we have investigated the introduction of the user as an explicit random variable in two state of the art diversification models: IA-Select [1] and xQuAD [15,16]. Our experiments show that there is a clear benefit in introducing this variable, achieving statistically significant improvements over the baselines that range between 3%-11% in terms accuracy values, and between 3%-8% in terms of diversity values.

These results lead us to conclude that diversification has a case even in the presence of personalization. Personalization in diversity can be seen in two –to some degree equivalent– ways: a) concentrating the extent of diversification in the areas of user interests, and b) seeking relevance to as diverse sides of user preferences as possible. We identify three situations in which our approaches have a potential benefit: 1) user preferences are not necessarily relevant for the query at hand, therefore they may remove uncertainty from it to very variable degrees (from a little to none at all); 2) the system knowledge about user preferences is incomplete (restricted to the observed user activity within the system) and imprecise (evidence of preferences can be implicit, indirect, ambiguous), whereby diversifying the effect of personalization reduces its involved risk; 3) user preferences are themselves diverse, therefore for lack of knowledge about which are most relevant in a given context, it is appropriate to diversify the relevance to the different preference aspects. A similar case as is made for diversification on query intents can thus be made for preference aspects.

We have presented different alternatives to estimate the components that arise from the formal development of our scheme, and we evaluated a number of them. Future work may include further investigation on these alternatives. We have tested two estimation approaches for the user/document and document/category relations, based on social annotations (Delicious) and ODP classification (Textwise), respectively. Other ways of approximating these values could be investigated, such as other sources of social profiles (e.g. Facebook, Twitter) or other sources of user profile information (e.g. query and browsing history). Other alternatives for document classification (e.g. clustering, or query reformulations [16]) might be explored as well. A follow-up evaluation could also take into consideration different values of the combination parameter in xQuAD, which controls the strength of the personalized diversity component on the personalized variation of xQuAD.

The vision of combining diversity and personalization indeed opens a rich array of possibilities. Diversity and personalization can be combined in different ways, some of which we have investigated here, beyond which we see wide room for further research.

9. ACKNOWLEDGMENTS

This work was supported by the national Spanish projects TIN2011-28538-C02-01 and S2009TIC-1542.

10. REFERENCES

[1] Agrawal, R., Gollapudi, S., Halverson, A., and Ieong, S. Diversifying search results. In *WSDM'09*, pages 5-14, 2009.

[2] Alonso, O. and Baeza-Yates, R. Design and implementation of relevance assessments using crowdsourcing. In *ECIR '11*, pages 153-164, 2011.

[3] Alonso, O. and Mizzaro, S. Can we get rid of TREC assessors? using mechanical turk for relevance assessment. In *SIGIR'09 Workshop on The Future of IR Evaluation*, 2009

[4] Bache, R., Baillie, M., and Crestani, F. Language models, probability of relevance and relevance likelihood. In *CIKM'07*, pages 853-856, 2007.

[5] Carbonell, J. G. and Goldstein, J. The Use of MMR, Diversity-Based Reranking for Reordering Documents and Producing Summaries. In *SIGIR'98*, pages, 335-336, 1998.

[6] Chen, H. and Karger, D. R. Less is More. In *SIGIR'06*, pages 429-436, 2006.

[7] Clarke, C. L. A., Kolla, M., Cormack, G. V., Vechtomova, O., Ashkan, A., Büttcher, S., and MacKinnon, I. Novelty and diversity in information retrieval evaluation. In *SIGIR'08*, pages 659-666, 2008.

[8] Fernández, M., Vallet, D., and Castells, P. Probabilistic score normalization for rank aggregation. In *ECIR'06*, pages 553-556, 2006.

[9] Han, X., Shen, Z., Miao, C., and Luo, X. Folksonomy-Based ontological user interest profile modeling and its application in personalized search. In *Active Media Technology*, LNCS, vol 6335 pages 34-46.

[10] Lee, J. H.. Analyses of multiple evidence combination. In *SIGIR '97*, pages 267-276, 1997.

[11] Micarelli, A., Gasparetti, F., Sciarrone, F., and Gauch, S. Personalized search on the World Wide Web. The Adaptive Web, pages 195-230, 2007.

[12] Noll, M. G., Meinel, C. Web search personalization via social bookmarking and tagging. In *ISWC'07*. pages 367-380, 2007.

[13] Radlinski, F. and Dumais, S. Improving personalized web search using result diversification. In *SIGIR'06*, pages 691-692, 2006.

[14] Rafiei, D., Bharat, K., and Shukla, A. Diversifying web search results. In *WWW'10*, pages 781-790, 2010.

[15] Santos, R., Peng, J., Macdonald, C., and Ounis, I. Explicit search result diversification through sub-queries. In *ECIR '10*, pages 87-99, 2010.

[16] Santos, R. L. T., Macdonald, C., and Ounis, I. Exploiting query reformulations for web search result diversification. In *WWW'10*, pages 881-890, 2010.

[17] Vallet, D. Crowdsourced Evaluation of Personalization and Diversification Techniques in Web Search. In CIR' 11 Workshop (SIGIR 2011), 2011.

[18] Vallet, D., Cantador, I., and Jose, J. Personalizing web search with Folksonomy-Based user and document profiles advances in information retrieval. In *ECIR'10*, pages 420-431, 2010.

[19] Vargas, S. and Castells, P. Rank and Relevance in Novelty and Diversity Metrics for Recommender Systems. *In RecSys'11*, pages 109-116, 2011.

[20] Vargas, S., Castells, P., and Vallet, D. Intent-Oriented Diversity in Recommender Systems. In *SIGIR'11*, pages 1211-1212, 2011.

[21] Wang, J. and Zhu, J. Portfolio theory of information retrieval. In *SIGIR'09*, pages 115-122, 2009.

[22] Zhai, C., Cohen, W. W., and Lafferty, J. Beyond independent relevance: Methods and evaluation metrics for subtopic retrieval. In *SIGIR'03*, pages 10-17, 2003.

[23] Zhang, M. and Hurley, N. Avoiding Monotony: Improving the Diversity of Recommendation Lists. In RecSys'08, pages 123-130, 2008.

[24] Ziegler, C-N., McNee, S. M., Konstan, J. A., and Lausen, G. Improving recommendation lists through topic diversification. In WWW'05, pages 22-32, 2005

Appendix A. PERSONAIZED QUERY ASPECT DISTRIBUTION

In this appendix we offer alternative estimations for the personalized query aspect distribution, $p(c|q,u)$, component:

1. $p(c|q,u) \sim \frac{p(q|c)p(c|u)}{\sum_{c'} p(q|c')p(c'|u)} = \frac{p(c|q)p(c|u)}{\sum_{c'} p(c'|q)p(c'|u)}$

   assuming a uniform aspect prior, and conditional independence between queries and users given an aspect. $p(c|q)$ can be estimated as:

   $$p(c|q) = \sum_d p(c|d,q)p(d|q).$$

2. $p(c|q,u) \sim \frac{p(q|c)p(c|u)}{\sum_d p(q|d)p(d|u)} = \frac{p(c|q)p(c|u)}{p(c)\sum_d p(d|q)p(d|u)/p(d)}$

   assuming conditional independence between queries and users given an aspect. Assuming a small aspect overlap (nr. of aspects per document) the ratio of category and document priors can be calculated as

   $$p(c)/p(d) \sim |\{d \in D | c \text{ is covered by } d\}|$$

   where D could be interpreted as the set of documents being reranked, or the whole collection. For higher aspect overlap, all document-aspect pairs should be taken into account, and normalized by the number of pairs.

3. $p(c|q,u) = \sum_d p(c|d,q,u)p(d|q,u) \sim$

   $$\sum_d p(c|d,q)p(d|q,u), \text{ and } p(c|d,q) \sim \frac{p(c|d)p(c|q)}{\sum_{c'} p(c'|d)p(c'|q)},$$

   assuming conditional independence of aspects and queries given a document, and a uniform aspect prior; or $p(c|d,q) \sim \frac{p(c|d)p(c|q)p(d)}{p(d|q)p(c)}$ without the latter assumption.

Combining Implicit and Explicit Topic Representations for Result Diversification

Jiyin He
J.He@cwi.nl

Vera Hollink
V.Hollink@cwi.nl

Arjen de Vries
arjen.de.vries@cwi.nl

Centrum Wiskunde en Informatica
Science Park 123, 1098XG
Amsterdam, the Netherlands

ABSTRACT

Result diversification deals with ambiguous or multi-faceted queries by providing documents that cover as many subtopics of a query as possible. Various approaches to subtopic modeling have been proposed. Subtopics have been extracted internally, e.g., from retrieved documents, and externally, e.g., from Web resources such as query logs. Internally modeled subtopics are often implicitly represented, e.g., as latent topics, while externally modeled subtopics are often explicitly represented, e.g., as reformulated queries.

We propose a framework that: i) combines both implicitly and explicitly represented subtopics; and ii) allows flexible combination of multiple external resources in a transparent and unified manner. Specifically, we use a random walk based approach to estimate the similarities of the explicit subtopics mined from a number of heterogeneous resources: click logs, anchor text, and web n-grams. We then use these similarities to regularize the latent topics extracted from the top-ranked documents, i.e., the internal (implicit) subtopics. Empirical results show that regularization with explicit subtopics extracted from the right resource leads to improved diversification results, indicating that the proposed regularization with (explicit) external resources forms better (implicit) topic models. Click logs and anchor text are shown to be more effective resources than web n-grams under current experimental settings. Combining resources does not always lead to better results, but achieves a robust performance. This robustness is important for two reasons: it cannot be predicted which resources will be most effective for a given query, and it is not yet known how to reliably determine the optimal model parameters for building implicit topic models.

Categories and Subject Descriptors

H.3 [**Information Storage and Retrieval**]: H.3.1 Content Analysis and Indexing; H.3.3 Information Search and Retrieval

General Terms

Algorithms, Experimentation

Keywords

Multi-source, Subtopics, Result diversification, Random walk

1. INTRODUCTION

Queries in Web search are often short and underspecified [2]. For example, the query "python" may refer to a snake as well as a programming language, while the programming language "python" covers a wide range of subtopics, such as tutorials, documentations, and downloads. Without knowing the users' actual intent, result diversification deals with such queries by providing documents that cover as many subtopics of a query as possible, so that the average user's "unhappiness" is minimized [43].

Result diversification has been intensively studied and many diversification algorithms have been proposed [1, 7, 8, 21, 34, 35, 43]. This paper focuses on the discovery of subtopics, also referred to as query intent, facets, and sub-queries in the literature. Subtopics have been extracted internally, e.g., from documents retrieved in response to the query [7, 8, 26, 29], and externally, e.g., from Web resources such as query logs [1, 20, 21, 33, 35]. Internally modelled subtopics are often implicitly represented, e.g., as latent topics or document clusters, while externally modelled subtopics are often explicitly represented, e.g., as reformulated queries[1]. In particular, there has been much work that exploits explicit subtopics using various types of Web resources. Some take suggested queries from commercial search engines as subtopics of a query [35]; others mine the subtopics from resources such as taxonomies [1, 22], query logs[21, 33], anchor text and Web ngrams [20].

While both implicit and explicit subtopics extracted from various Web resources have shown their effectiveness in helping retrieving diverse search results, both topic representations have their limitations. Often, the process of extracting subtopics for a query in a Web resource is focused on finding the subtopics that are relevant to the query, while the relation among the extracted subtopics are not well preserved. For instance, all subtopics discovered in Web resources, e.g., all reformulations of a query, are treated as independent subtopics, regardless the fact that some may be synonymous [21, 35]. In some studies additional steps such as clustering were taken in order to avoid redundancy and find better defined topics [20, 33]. On the other hand, implicitly represented subtopics such as topic models or clusters constructed from document content convey much information about the relations or the structure of the topics present in the documents. Yet, in this case the infor-

[1] Notice that in the context of result diversification, "implicit" sometimes refers to diversification methods such as MMR where no actual topics are modeled and only document similarities are used. In this paper, from a topic modeling perspective, we refer to topic models/clusters as implicit *topic representations*, since no "labels" that indicate the content of the topics are assigned, and refer to subtopics represented with external entities such as query suggestions, anchor text, as explicit topic representations, as such entities present the content of the topic explicitly [25].

mation that can be used is limited to the content of the document. Therefore we are interested in the following question:

- Can we make use of the information from both implicitly and explicitly represented subtopics?

Various resources were shown to provide useful information in subtopic mining, sometimes complementary to each other. Click logs have for example been shown an effective resource for subtopic mining in a number of studies [21, 33], but their availability are mainly limited to commercial web engines. Anchor text has been suggested a good proxy for query information, but it is not clear if one should be preferred over the other. Web ngrams are freely available, but may not provide as high quality subtopics for a query as click logs, partially because of the noise introduced by phrases not relevant to the topic of interest. Given a variety of resources, we are interested in a second question:

- Can we combine multiple external sources to help subtopic modeling?

We seek a principled way to model the subtopics of a query using multiple sources, including implicitly represented topics extracted from document content, as well as explicitly represented subtopics mined from various Web resources. While combining subtopics from multiple sources can be useful, it is non-trivial. Different resources provide evidence that a subtopic is relevant to a query from different perspectives, which leads to different types of measurements to quantify the similarity between subtopics. We propose a graph based approach to combine explicit subtopics from Web resources. More specifically, we construct local graphs over the subtopics extracted from each single resource. The local graphs are interconnected through subtopics that appear in multiple resources. A measure of subtopic similarity within each local graph is converted into random walk transition probabilities, to obtain a probabilistic framework. Subtopics from different sources are combined in a random walk over the resulting graph, that integrates the various external resources. The result of the random walk defines a probability distribution that encodes the similarity between all subtopics from all resources included in the graph. Given the similarities in the explicit subtopic graphs, we exploit these similarities for regularization during the construction of implicitly defined subtopics from the search result list. Using regularized topic models, the similarities among the explicit subtopics serve as additional constraints, that need to be satisfied when constructing implicit subtopics using document content.

Our contribution is two-fold. First, we propose a framework that: i) combines both implicitly and explicitly represented subtopics in a principled way; and ii) allows flexible combination of multiple external resources, in a transparent and unified manner. With respect to the proposed framework, an in-depth investigation on its effectiveness as well as limitations are provided. Second, using this framework, we compare the usefulness of various resources (and their combinations) for identifying diversification subtopics. Our findings provide additional evidence for findings in earlier studies on similar themes, and lay a foundation for future work on selecting useful resources for topic modeling.

The rest of the paper is organized as follows. In Section 2, we discuss the related work on subtopic modeling in result diversification, as well as work related to the techniques employed in this paper. In Section 3, we introduce our proposed framework, referred to as Multi-source subtopics (MSS), to combine explicit subtopics from multiple sources with the implicit ones derived from the initial search result list. In Section 4, we discuss the different types of resources considered for subtopic modeling. We then describe the experiments designed to empirically study the properties of the proposed framework in Section 5, followed by a discussion on the experimental results and their implications in Section 6. Section 7 concludes the paper.

2. RELATED WORK

Search result diversification has a long history [5, 7, 10, 23, 37, 43] and a range of diversification approaches have been proposed previously. Maximum Marginal Relevance (MMR) [7], an early representative diversification method, aims to balance the relevance and diversity of a ranked list. A probabilistic version of MMR has been proposed by Zhai et al. [43], as part of their risk minimization framework. Zhu et al. [44] proposed a ranking method based on random walks in an absorbing Markov chain. By turning ranked items into absorbing states, the method prevents redundant items from receiving a high rank. Yue and Joachims [42] studied a learning algorithm based on a structural Support Vector Machine (SVM) that identifies diverse subsets in a set of documents. Carterette and Chandar [8] proposed a probabilistic model for faceted retrieval, where the facets of a query are modeled with Latent Dirichlet Allocation (LDA) [4], one of the state-of-the-art topic modeling approaches. In most of these studies, the focus has been on the development of ranking algorithms to produce ranked lists that convey both relevant and diverse information about a query. Only limited effort has been made in mining high quality subtopics for a query, and subtopics were usually modeled based on document content.

Recently however, in the context of Web retrieval, a renewed interest in result diversification has emerged. Representative approaches include Intent Aware select (IA-select) [1] and explicit query aspect diversification (xQuAD) [35]. Common to these approaches is the importance of modeling both the subtopics of a query *and* the relevance of a document with respect to the subtopics of a query. Both works exploited Web resources for subtopic mining. In [1], categories in the Open Directory Project (ODP) taxonomy were used as candidate subtopics, and in [35], query suggestions from Web search engines were used as related subtopics of a query. Recently, Dou et al. [21] has first proposed to combine subtopics mined from multiple sources, including query logs, anchor text, document clusters, and web sites of search results. A common assumption among studies where Web resources are used for subtopic extraction is that the extracted subtopics would be independent. However, these assumptions are most likely not true. Anchor text has for instance been shown to be an effective substitute for query logs in generating query reformulations [19], which indicates that these two resources should be correlated. Moreover, within a single resource such as query logs, various reformulations of a query may be synonyms that refer to the same concept. Our approach does not require to assume the independence among mined subtopics. Conversely, we focus on modeling specifically the similarity or relatedness among the subtopics. In our experiments, we employ IA-select as the primary diversification method (see Section 5.3), to indirectly evaluate the effectiveness of using our approach to model subtopics from multiple sources.

A closely related line of research focuses on mining subtopics of a query from various Web resources. Radlinski et al. [33] infer query aspects from query logs, using clicks and session information to model the relations between queries. Dang et al. [20] infer query intent from anchor text and Web ngrams. In both studies, clustering has been applied to the extracted aspects or intents, so that topically redundant or similar entities (queries, anchor text, or Web ngrams) are grouped together. In this paper, we use the same types of Web resources for subtopic mining, and compare their effectiveness in the context of result diversification; although in terms of a query log resource, our data set can only be seen as a very small subset of the log used in [33]. Instead of applying clustering, we incorporate the obtained similarities between the extracted subtopics into the topic models constructed using document content. This way we incorporate the similarity between extracted subtopics into the similarity between documents.

To compute the similarity between subtopics extracted from different Web resource, we construct graphs over these subtopics and compute their associations using Markov random walks. Similar approaches have been studied in a wide range of topic in the context of query log analysis. For example, Craswell and Szummer [16] studied the usage of Markov random walks over the bipartite graph constructed from click logs for document ranking. Fuxman et al. [22] developed a random walk algorithm for keyword generation from query click graphs. This approach was also adopted in [1] to extract subtopics related to a query from the ODP taxonomy. Ma et al. [30] proposed a query suggestion approach based on Markov random walk and hitting time on the query-URL bipartite graph, aimed at suggesting both semantically relevant and diverse queries to Web users. A recent work that is closely related to ours is the Multi-view random walk (MVR) approach proposed by Cui et al. [18], which aims to combine knowledge from different views of an object in a random walk process. We discuss the differences between their work and ours in detail in Section 3.

To balance graph-based and textual similarity between documents, we use regularized topic models [6, 24]. A similar approach was taken in Guo et al. [24], where queries were enriched with document snippets to improve a query similarity model; we however enrich the document content with queries to construct a document similarity model.

3. MULTI-SOURCE SUBTOPICS

3.1 Modeling relation among explicitly represented topics from Web resources

We now detail how we use a Markov random walk based approach to compute the relations between the explicit subtopics of a query in different types of resources. Let $R = \{r_i\}_{i=1}^{N}$ be a resource that contains N subtopics related to a query q. Consider for instance a query log that contains N reformulations of q. For a set of resources $\mathcal{R} = \{R^g\}$, we construct a network consisting of subgraphs on multiple parallel 'planes', as shown in Figure 1. First, for each R^g, we construct a weighted graph $G^g = \{E^g; R^g\}$, where the nodes R^g corresponding to the subtopics in resource g lie on a single plane, and the edges E^g are weighted by the similarity $w(r_i, r_j)$ between the two nodes. For now, we abstract from the specific way the similarity is defined within a plane, aiming for a method that can be applied generically; details of the graphs created for specific resources are deferred to Section 4. In the second step, we interconnect nodes from different planes G^a and G^b with an extra set of edges, where each edge connects the nodes $r_i \in G^a, r_j \in G^b$ that we consider equivalent. Throughout this paper, we consider r_i and r_j equivalent whenever they have exact matching text representations. While it would be interesting to include non-exact matches, we leave this for future investigation.

For each resource considered, the similarity scores computed may encode different semantics, such that they may not be compared directly across different planes. This is the primary reason why we are not in favor of constructing a single graph that mixes up subtopics from different resources. To resolve this problem, we first transform the similarity scores into 1-step random walk transition probabilities. The only assumption behind the resulting transition probability is that the chance to travel from one subtopic to another in a random walk step should depend on the similarity between these subtopics, i.e., the more similar two subtopics are, the more likely the transition from one subtopic to the other can happen.

By applying a t-step random walk over the graphs, we expect to find new associations, in particular between subtopics that were not directly connected in a single graph. Further, the random walk sums up the transition probability of all paths of length t between two nodes. The transition probability will be high if there exist many paths from one node to the other. The higher the transition probability the more similar or closely related the two nodes are. During the random walk, the underlying clustering structure of the nodes emerges [36]. If such a clustering structure exists among the nodes, with longer walks, the probability between nodes within a cluster converges to a value higher than that with any node outside the cluster [16]. The probability distribution that arises can therefore be interpreted as a similarity measure that captures the relations between the subtopics in our graphs.

We use $p_1^{\theta}(r_j|r_i)$ to denote the 1-step transition probability from r_i to r_j within a single plane, which is computed as

$$p_1^{\theta}(r_j|r_i) = w(i,j)/\sum_j w(i,j). \qquad (1)$$

We refer to the nodes connected to nodes in other planes as "teleport points" and the transition from one plane to another as a "between-plane teleport". We use $p_1^{\beta}(r_j|r_i)$ to denote the 1-step between plane transition probability from r_i to r_j. While it is possible to assign a different value for each pair of nodes, e.g., based on additional evidence or the performance on training material, in this paper we only study the simplified situation assuming each plane has a fixed p_1^{β}. p_1^{β} can be viewed as the probability that a plane is chosen as the destination of a teleporting. For simplicity, we use β_g to denote this probability for plane g. In summary, we have

$$p_1^{\beta}(r_j|r_i) = \begin{cases} 0 & \text{if } r_i \text{ is not a teleporting point,} \\ \beta_g & \text{otherwise, where } r_j \in G^g. \end{cases} \qquad (2)$$

Piecing together the within-plane and between-plane transition probability, while conducting the random walk, the 1-step transition probability from r_i to r_j is computed as follows.

$$p_1(r_j|r_i) = \begin{cases} p_1^{\theta}(r_j|r_i) & \text{if } r_i, r_j \in G^g, \\ p_1^{\beta}(r_t|r_i)p_1^{\theta}(r_j|r_t) & \text{otherwise,} \end{cases} \qquad (3)$$

where r_t is the teleport point in the plane of r_j connected with r_i.

A t-step walk from r_i to r_j is defined recursively as

$$p_t(r_j|r_i) = \sum_k p_1(r_j|r_k)p_{t-1}(r_k|r_i), \qquad (4)$$

where r_k's are the intermediate nodes that directly connect to r_j.

At first sight, our proposed representation may look similar to the multi-view random walk (MVR) model [18]. In MVR however, each plane represents a different view of the exact same set of objects; i.e., each object within the network has a corresponding node at each plane. In our setup, this correspondence is not required, and therefore a phrase occuring in, for example, an anchor text collection does not necessarily have to occur in a query log as well. Not requiring such a correspondence allows for a greater diversity of resources used. Also, MVR defines a 1-step cross-view transition only between corresponding nodes. In principle, although we have not yet studied this alternative setting, our representation allows to consider also a between-plane 1-step transition from a node in one plane to multiple nodes in the other plane, i.e., setting the $p_1^{\beta}(j|i)$ with non-zero values to each pair of nodes i and j.

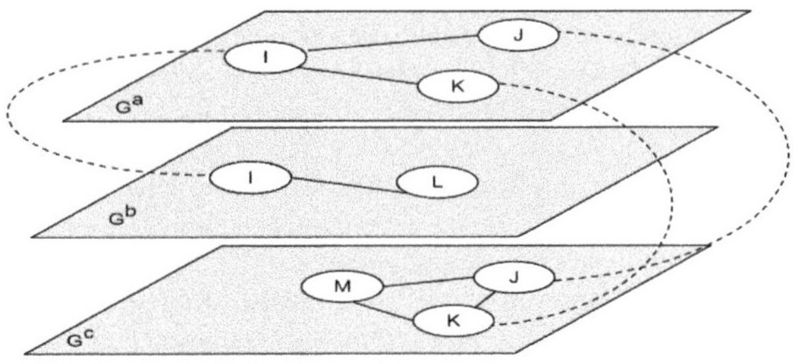

Figure 1: An illustration of the mutli-source subtopic network. Solid lines indicate within plane transitions, and dashed lines indicate the between plane teleporting. Each of the nodes I, K, J, L, M, are possible intents for the same query. Each plane represents intents generated from a single data source.

3.2 Combining implicit and explicit subtopics

Topic models, such as the probabilistic latent semantic analysis (pLSA) [28], are commonly used to model underlying topics associated with a set of documents. The extracted topics are implicitly represented by a set of word distributions. For a query q, we apply pLSA on the set of retrieved documents $D = \{d_i\}_{i=1}^{M}$ to obtain the implicit subtopics associated with q.

Now that we have described our approach to model the relations between subtopics extracted from multiple resources, the next question is: how can we combine the relations between the explicit subtopics with the implicit subtopics? Notice that for diversification, the ultimate goal is to generate a ranked list of *documents* that are both relevant to the query and contain diverse content. Therefore it is necessary to associate the mined subtopics to the documents to be ranked, and convert the relations between subtopics to the relations between documents.

We first translate similarities between explicit subtopics to the similarities between documents as follows.

$$p(d_i|d_j) = \sum_{k,l} p(d_i|r_k)p_t(r_k|r_l)p(r_l|d_j) \tag{5}$$

To obtain $p(r|d)$, we use r as a query and compute the query likelihood score as defined in a language modeling retrieval model [32]. Then following the Bayes' rule, $p(d|r)$ is computed as

$$p(d_i|r_k) = p(r_k|d_i)p(d_i)/p(r_k), \tag{6}$$

where $p(r_k)$ is computed by marginalization as $\sum_{d_i \in D} p(r_k|d_i)$, and $p(d_i)$ as $1/|D|$, assuming a uniform distribution of $d \in D$.

Given these preliminaries, we now combine the similarities between documents, obtained from the explicit subtopics, with the implicit topics. Hereto, we apply Laplacian pLSA [6] (also referred to as regularized topic models [24]), using the document similarities given by Eq. 5 to regularize the implicit topic model. Laplacian pLSA employs a generalized version of EM to maximize the regularized log-likelihood of the topic model, $\mathfrak{L}$:

$$\mathfrak{L} = \mathcal{L} - \gamma\frac{1}{2}\sum_{k}\sum_{i,j}(P(z_k|d_i) - P(z_k|d_j))^2 p(d_i|d_j) \tag{7}$$

Here, $\mathcal{L}$ is the log-likelihood of the implicit topic model as maximized by pLSA. $P(z_k|d_i)$ is the probability of topic z_k given document d_i. γ is a parameter that controls the amount of regularization from external resources.

By maximizing the regularized log-likelihood, Laplacian pLSA (softly) assigns documents to the same cluster if they 1) share many terms *and* 2) belong to the same explicit subtopics. γ allows us to balance these two requirements and combine both implicit and explicit representations of query subtopics in a unified and principled manner. Notice that when no explicit subtopics can be found for a query, the regularized pLSA is reduced to the normal pLSA.

4. RESOURCES

We now describe the implementation of each plane of the network. In this paper, we consider three resources: click logs, anchor text and Web ngrams (summarized in Table 1).

Graph	Nodes	Edge weights
G^C	search queries	coclicked documents
G^A	anchor texts	coocurrence in text passages
G^N	web ngrams	coocurrence in text passages

Table 1: Used resources

4.1 Click logs

Clickthrough data has proven to provide useful information for identifying search intents, or, related topics of queries [24, 33]. In particular, if two queries share many co-clicked documents, it is likely that they convey similar topical information [3, 39].

We construct a graph G^C from click logs, using logged queries as nodes, following a rather standard approach of using the total number of co-clicked documents to set the edge weights for random walk (see e.g. [16]). Since our goal is to find subtopics related to a query, unlike in many other studies where a global graph is constructed over all logged queries, we construct local graphs for a given query. The advantage of using local graphs is two-fold: i) it is computationally efficient, and ii) queries that are not relevant to the original query are effectively pruned. In order to collect related subtopics for a query q, we find the queries that share co-clicked documents with q, and for each of these queries further find its co-clicked queries. We then filter out queries that has a 1-step (or 2-step in the latter case) transition probability less than 0.01 starting from q in order to prevent popular queries such as "yahoo" from connecting to many weakly related queries.

4.2 Anchor texts

Anchor text has proven to be another effective feature for various search tasks, e.g. [19]. We use the anchor texts from the ClueWeb09 collection [27] to construct an anchor text graph G^A, using the method described by Dang et al. [20]. As preprocessing, we remove all anchors that are connected to only one URL. For a given query, we collect the N (N = 100 in our experiments) most frequently occurring anchors that contain all of the query terms. These anchors become the nodes of the graph. The edge weights are computed according to the method that proved most effective in the study of Dang et al. [20]: on the basis of the number of times the anchor phrases co-occur in text passages in the collection.

4.3 Web n-grams

Following Dang et al. [20], we collect Web n-grams using the Microsoft Bing N-gram [38] service to build an n-gram graph G^N. For each query q, we retrieve the M (M = 1000) terms t with the highest probability of seeing t after query q in the body text of the web pages indexed by Bing, $p_{ngram}(t|q)$. As the N-gram service provides n-grams up to length 5, this graph can be constructed for queries consisting of 4 or less terms. Dang et al. [20] use the N terms with the highest $p_{ngram}(t|q)$. However, these often include common terms that are not specific to the queries. Therefore, we

Sample subtopics	Top 3 related subtopics					
G^C	subtopic	score	subtopic	score	subtopic	score
anti spy	windows defender	.2261	microsoft antispyware	.1208	defender	.1122
microsoft spyware	windows defender	.2262	microsoft antispyware	.1208	defender	.1121
antispyware	windows defender	.2265	microsoft antispyware	.1207	defender	.1121
microsoft beta	windows defender	.2260	microsoft antispyware	.1209	defender	.1120
windows defender	microsoft antispyware	.1218	defender	.1141	antispyware	.0995
G^{CA}	subtopic	score	subtopic	score	subtopic	score
space defender 1 0	star defender 4	.1266	star defender 3	.1266	star defender 2	.1266
defender industries	defender industries inc	.2055	defender	.1197	windows defender	.0462
microsoft beta	windows defender	.1062	microsoft defender	.0555	microsoft s windows defender	.0538
a public defender	public defender	.1160	public defender's office	.1040	office of the public defender	.1040
tri state defender	chicago defender	.1035	the chicago defender	.1035	national legal aid defender association	.0352

Table 2: A random sample of 5 subtopics related to the query "defender" from G^C and G^{CA} and the top 3 subtopics related to each of the sample subtopics. The scores are the result of a 5-step random walk on the corresponding graphs.

compute for each retrieved term the lift [41]:

$$lift(t, q) = p_{ngram}(t|q)/p_{ngram}(t) \quad (8)$$

where $p_{ngram}(t)$ is the a priori probability of seeing term t. The N (N = 100) n-grams (= query + term) with the highest lift are included as nodes in the graph. Following Dang et al. [20], the weights of the edges are computed in the same way as in G^A.

4.4 An example of Multi-source subtopics

Having introduced the MSS framework and the target Web resources, now let us see an example that illustrates the result of the random walks on the subtopic graphs.

Table 2 shows an example result of a 5-step random walk on two different graphs, G^C and G^{CA}, i.e., the graphs constructed using click logs, and the combination of click logs and anchor text, respectively. We take the query "defender" and randomly sample 5 subtopics related to this query from each graph. For each sampled subtopic, we list the 3 most similar subtopics (from left to right), where the similarity is measured by the transition probabilities starting from the sampled subtopics as a result of the random walk. In this example, G^C contains 21 subtopics, and G^{CA} contains 118 subtopics. We see that all the subtopics sampled from G^C are closely related to the security software "windows defender", which indicates that this is a dominant topic in G^C. The sample drawn from G^{CA}, on the other hand, covers diverse topics: computer games (space defender, star defender, etc.,), defender industries, windows defender, public defender, and subtopics about the newspapers "tri-state defender" and "chicago defender". On top of that, if we take a close look at the resulting similarity scores, we see that these scores effectively reflect the semantic relatedness between the subtopics. For example, "defender industries" is closely related to "defender industries inc", as both can be interpreted as the marine and boat supply company "Defender Industries Inc."; it is loosely related to "defender", as it is the original query, which is vague and can be interpreted as anything; it is not very likely to be related to "windows defender", and correspondingly, a very weak relation is indicated by the similarity score.

5. EXPERIMENTS

5.1 Research questions and experimental setup

In this section, we empirically investigate the properties of the proposed framework and its impact on result diversification.

Our framework combines different types of resources at two levels. First, it combines the implicitly and explicitly represented subtopics by constructing regularized topic models. It is therefore natural to investigate the following research question.

RQ1 Does regularization with subtopics extracted from external resources help to form better topic models?

Although the question asks whether "better topic models" are formed, it is difficult to access the quality of topic models directly, due to the subjective nature of topics. Instead, by applying the resulting topic models to diversification, we indirectly assess their quality by examining the diversification performance. It is reasonable to assume that better topic models lead to better diversification results.

Further, the framework combines explicit subtopics from multiple external resources, which leads to the following two questions.

RQ2 How do various subtopics from external resources and their combinations compare in terms of diversification performance?

RQ3 Are combinations of subtopics from different external resources more effective in terms of diversification performance than that of single resources?

Particularly, previous studies suggest that anchor text is an effective replacement for query logs (which are often not publicly available), e.g., for query reformulation [19] and inferring query subtopics [20]. Comparison of the two resources within our framework can provide supplementary evidence and validate these findings.

Note that our framework outputs regularized topic models of a query, i.e., an implicit topic representation. Like any topic model based approach, LapPLSA (Laplacian pLSA) depends on a prefixed parameter, the number of topics K. There is no easy solution to find the optimal K without prior knowledge or sufficient training data. In our case, neither is available. However, in reality, "neither is available" is often the practice. Hence, it is useful to investigate the robustness of the framework when K is not optimal.

RQ4 How sensitive is the performance of diversification based on LapPLSA to the choice of K?

5.2 Data

We use the Clueweb09 setB dataset and the topic sets released at TREC2009-2011 Web Track diversity task as our test collection [12–14]. Since the topic sets are designed to be different, e.g., the 2011 topic set is expected to contain "tougher" queries [14] than the others, we experiment with topics from each set separately.

The following data are used as the Web resources that provide query subtopic information. We use the MSN query log [17] to construct G^C. Notice that this log is fairly limited: it contains 15 million queries from US users, sampled over 1 month. Following [20],

Graph	Coverage		
	1-50	51-100	101-150
G^C	39	37	21
G^A	48	47	25
G^N	48	45	34
G^{CA}	48	48	31
G^{CN}	50	48	39
G^{AN}	50	48	39
G^{CAN}	50	48	39

Table 3: Coverage of Web resources over the TREC topic sets

we use the Microsoft Ngram service to construct G^N, and anchor texts extracted from Clueweb09 dataset to construct G^A[27].

Table 3 shows the coverage of the Web resources on the TREC topics. A TREC topic is "covered" by a resource if the corresponding graph of the query is not empty. We see that in terms of individual resources, click logs has the lowest coverage on all three topic sets. In terms of topic sets, the set from TREC 2011 is obviously poorly covered. Combining multiple resources increases the coverage over all three sets, but still, not all topics are covered.

5.3 Diversification method

After pilot experiments with a number of state-of-the-art diversification methods, including IA-select [1], xQuAD[35] and MMR [7][2], we decide to focus on IA-select. Results between IA-select and xQuAD are comparable, while MMR has a lower performance. The advantage of IA-select is that it has no extra parameters to be tuned: both xQuAD and MMR have an extra parameter that linearly combines relevance and diversity. IA-select provides a more transparent way to analyze the behavior of our framework.

Given a set of candidate documents and a set of subtopics related to a query q, IA-select [1] selects a document d to be included in the ranked list base on: the relevance of d to q, and the probability that d covers subtopics that all previously selected documents failed to do so. The key elements used in the algorithm can be reduced to the following quantities: i) $V(d|q,z)$, the probability that d is relevant to q when the intended subtopic is z; and ii) $p(z|q)$, the probability that subtopic z is related to q.

The first quantity is determined by the retrieval score of d given q, weighted by the likelihood that d covers subtopic z, i.e., $p(d|z)$, which can be derived from the resulting topic models.

We compute $p(z|q)$ as follows.

$$p(z|q) = \sum_d p(z|d)p(d|q), \tag{9}$$

where $p(z|d)$ is given by the topic models, and

$$p(d|q) = \sum_r p(d|r)p(r|q). \tag{10}$$

where r are the nodes in the graphs; $p(d|r)$ is calculated using Eq. 6 and $p(r|q)$ is given by the result of random walks. Since our graphs were constructed locally using the original query q as the starting point, all graphs will at least contain the original query as a node. If the external resources do not contain any subtopics related to q, Eq. 10 reduces to the relevance score of d to the original query q.

We use IA-select to re-rank a pre-retrieved set of documents. To create the baseline ranked list, we use the Indri toolkit that implements the retrieval model based on the language modeling framework [31]. We use the spam list released at TREC Web Track [15] for spam filtering, setting the spam threshold to 70%. The top ranked 100 documents are used to construct topic models.

[2]Unlike IA-select and xQuAD, MMR does not actually require subtopics being modeled. Here, when computing the similarities between documents, documents are represented by topic distributions in stead of term distributions.

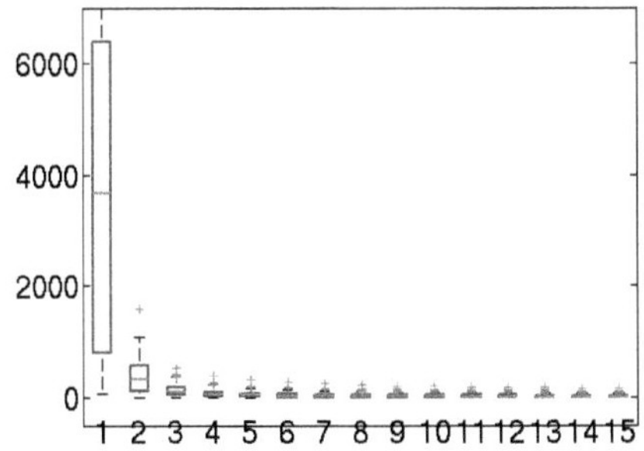

Figure 2: Change of probability distributions during random walks. X-axis shows the number of steps; Y-axis shows the KL-divergence between the states before and after a 1-step walk.

5.4 Parameter settings

Our proposed framework comes with a number of parameters. For random walks, two parameters are involved, namely β, the between plane transition probabilities, and t, the number of steps for the random walks[3]. For LapPLSA, we have: the regularization parameter γ, and the number of topics K.

As discussed in Section 3.1, β is practically the probability that a plane is chosen as the destination of a teleporting. As we do not have evidence or prior knowledge about whether one plane should be preferred over others, we simply assume a uniform distribution over all planes: $\beta_g = 1/|g|$, where $|g|$ is the total number of planes.

Since all our graphs are fairly small due to the fact that they are constructed locally based on subtopics that are closely related to a given query, random walks on these graphs converge very quickly. With a few preliminary experiments, we find that within 5 steps, the changes of the probability distributions over most graphs drop to a level that is almost negligible. Therefore we set t to 5 steps. A typical example is shown in Figure 2, where we use KL-divergence to measure the change of probability distributions over a graph. The graph consists of subtopics from click logs, anchor text and Web ngrams. The box plot is constructed over 150 TREC topics.

Regularization parameter γ can take the value of non-negative real numbers; Researchers have usually set its value empirically [6, 24]. Preliminary experiments with our method suggest that the end-to-end diversification results are relatively stable when varying γ within a range around 10, although fine tuning γ can indeed lead to improved results for a specific experiment. We decide to set γ to a fixed value that generates reasonable diversification results, using $\gamma = 10$ in all our experiments. Finally, note that $\gamma = 0$ makes LapPLSA equivalent to pLSA without regularization.

While results are relatively stable with respect to γ, we find that the performance of diversification with topic models is rather sensitive to the parameter K. In Section 6, we will discuss the impact of K on the diversification results using our framework.

5.5 Evaluation metrics

We evaluate the diversification result in terms of α-nDCG@20 [11] and ERR-IA@20 [9], which are primary evaluation metrics at TREC Web Track for the diversity task [14]. α is set to 0.5 for α-nDCG@20. For significance testing, we use the Wilcoxon sign rank test. When

[3]The implementation of the MSS random walks can be downloaded at http://code.google.com/p/mss-rw/

reporting results, we use $^{\triangle}(^{\blacktriangle})$ to indicate a significant difference with p-value<.05 (.01).

6. RESULTS AND DISCUSSION

We now discuss the experimental results and their indications to the answers to our research questions. In the following discussion, we will first discuss the behavior of LapPLSA regularized by subtopics from different types of external resources in terms of the general trends shown by the results. We then zoom in to a few specific settings of K and examine the effectiveness of the proposed framework, e.g., highlighting the significance of the observed differences between approaches. Although the number of topics K is an important parameter that has an impact on the diversification result, we do not attempt to optimize it. We do investigate the sensitivity of our results to the estimation of K, when discussing RQ4.

6.1 Single resources

We start with the performance of LapPLSA using single resources. Figure 3 shows the result of IA-select using topic models constructed with the following methods: pLSA without regularization and LapPLSA regularized by similarity matrices generated using click logs, anchor text, and Web ngrams, i.e., LapPLSA_C, LapPLSA_A, and LapPLSA_N, respectively. "Baseline" refers to the run without diversification.

First, we see that both pLSA and LapPLSA (with different resources) can outperform the baseline. Compared to pLSA, LapPLSA shows more robust performance: diversification with pLSA can underperform the baseline given an improperly set K, while diversification with LapPLSA regularized by the subtopics from an external resource in general outperforms the baseline irrespective of the choice of K. The only exception is the case where $K = 2$, which is presumably not a sensible choice for K.

Second, judging from Figure 3, the effectiveness of each resource differs on different topic sets. It is noticeable that on topic set 1-50, click logs remarkably outperform the other two resources across all settings of K. A possible explanation is that this topic set is derived from query logs of commercial search engines [12], and therefore the click logs have a relatively high coverage and turn out to be an effective resource for these topics. On topic set 51-100, click logs and anchor text show comparable performance, while Web ngrams are occasionally effective (given a specific settings of K). On topic set 101-150, anchor text generally outperforms click logs. This may due to the fact that the click logs have a very low ($< 50\%$) coverage on this topic set, and that the topic set is rather recent (created in 2011) while the click logs were created in 2006, which may lead to further sparseness: e.g., on average, G^A has 17.1 nodes per query, while G^C only has 7.6 nodes per query on this topic set. In general, click logs and anchor text seem to be more valuable resources for regularization compared to Web ngrams, across different settings of K. Notice that the Web ngrams are primarily derived from document content, so perhaps their lower effectiveness can be explained by lower influence on pLSA, which also uses document content. To some extent, we can consider the Web ngrams more similar to the document content than click logs and anchor text.

As expected, the diversification results of IA-select based on both pLSA and on LapPLSA are sensitive to the change of the parameter K. In particular, there is no clear correlation between the number of clusters and the end-to-end diversification performance, which further suggests the difficulty of finding an optimal K (that would fit for a set of queries). For more detailed analysis on the parameter K, see Section 6.4.

6.2 Combining multiple resources

Figure 4(a)-4(c) show the result of combining subtopics from the two relatively more effective resources, namely click logs(G^C) and anchor text (G^A). While we only show the combination of these two resources, a similar trend can be observed in the other combinations. We see that combining resources does not always lead to improved diversification results over that of the single resources. Such improvement only happens in a few cases where K is likely to be in an optimal setting for the combined resource G^{CA}, i.e., $K = 10$ in Figure 4(b) and $K = 6$ in Figure 4(c). In general, the combination of different resources leads to an "averaged" performance compared to the individual resources that are combined.

This observation is reasonable. Intuitively, combining resources on the one hand increases the coverage of subtopics, e.g., as shown in Table 3, but on the other hand may introduce noise, e.g., if one of the resources contains low quality subtopics. Recall that when constructing the local graphs, their nodes (i.e., subtopics) were selected based on their relation to the original query. In this stage, the relevance of the nodes with respect to the original query was taken into account. However, when combining resources, i.e., during the random walk stage, the goal was to measure the similarities among nodes across resources and no further pruning was conducted. That is, all entries in different graphs were assumed to be equally good. Given our observations on the combined result, a natural step for future work would prune further to prevent low quality resources from deteriorating high quality resources.

6.3 Zoom in on specific settings of K

Now, let us zoom in to the performance of diversification under specific settings of K. Specifically, we aim to examine the answers to the following questions: 1) are the differences between the diversified result and the baseline significant? and 2) are the differences between the LapPLSA regularized by subtopics from different external resources and the non regularized pLSA significant? For the first question, we consider the setting when K is set to the optimal value for a given topic set. For the second question, since both pLSA and LapPLSA are sensitive to K, we set K to the optimal value for each query, so that the impact of K is reduced to the minimum. Note that here by saying "optimal", we mean the best K in the range of $[2, 10]$ in terms of α-nDCG@20.

Table 4 and Table 5 show the results with respect to the first and the second questions, respectively.

From Table 4 we see that with a proper setting of K, in most cases, diversification with pLSA as well as with LapPLSA significantly outperforms the baseline. Again, the effectiveness of each individual resource differs for the three topic sets. For topics 1-50, regularization with click logs is most effective, while regularization with anchor text and with Web ngrams fails to have significant improvement over the baseline. On topic set 51-100, while pLSA based diversification does not result in significant improvement over the baseline in terms of both ERR-IA@20 and α-nDCG@20, all LapPLSA based runs show significant improvement in terms of at least one of the two measures. On topic set 101-150, only the run with LapPLSA using click logs does not achieve significant improvement over the baseline, all others do.

Table 5 shows that LapPLSA regularized with subtopics from external resources does not always lead to significant improvement over pLSA. However, on each of the three topic sets, at least one resource exists that, when used for regularization, outperforms pLSA significantly. Again, regularization with click logs is shown to be most effective, on topic set 1-50. On topic set 51-100, except click logs, regularization with one of the resources or their combinations results in significant improvement over the non-regularized pLSA.

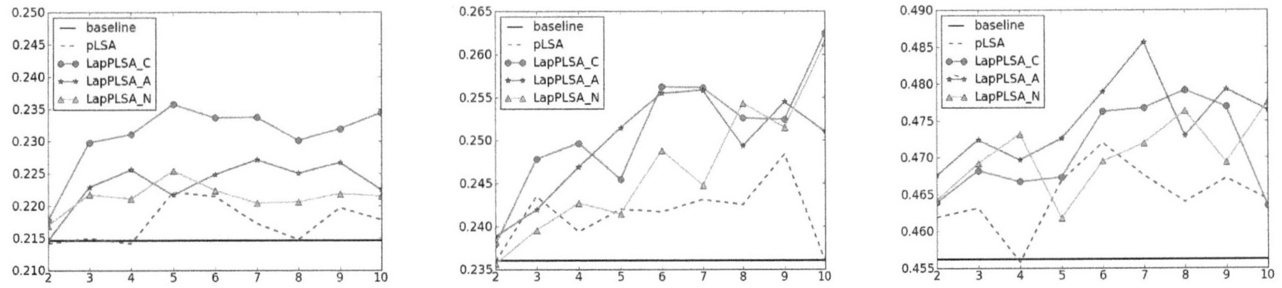

(a) Topics 1-50 (b) Topics 51-100 (c) Topics 101-150

Figure 3: Result of diversification in terms of α-nDCG@20 with topic models constructed using single resources. IA-select is used as the diversification method. The x-axis represents the value of K. The y-axis represents the α-nDCG@20 scores.

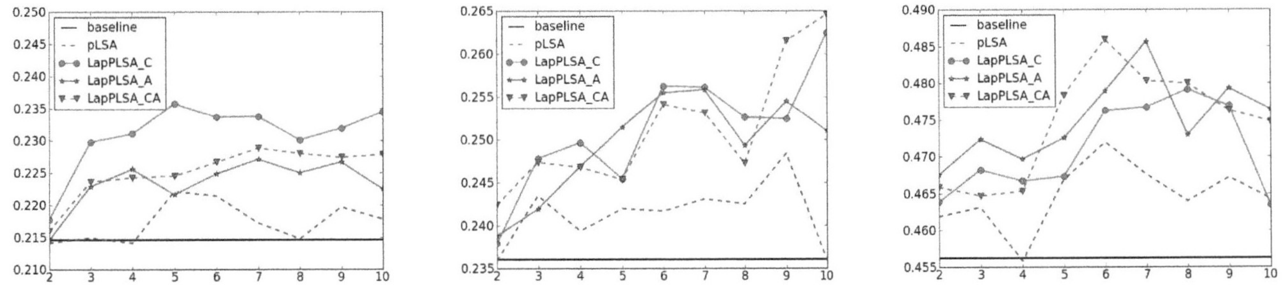

(a) Topics 1-50 (b) Topics 51-100 (c) Topics 101-150

Figure 4: Result of diversification in terms of α-nDCG@20 with topic models constructed using multiple resources. IA-select is used as the diversification method. The x-axis represents the value of K. The y-axis represents the α-nDCG@20 scores.

		Topics 1-50			Topics 51-100			Topics 101-150	
Method	K	E-IA@20	αnD@20	K	E-IA@20	αnD@20	K	E-IA@20	αnD@20
NoDiv	–	.130	.215	–	.161	.246	–	.354	.456
pLSA	5	.136△	.222△	9	.175	.259	6	.365▲	.472△
G^C	5	**.149▲**	**.236▲**	10	.184△	.273	8	.382	.479
G^A	7	.138	.227	7	.182	.266△	7	**.386▲**	**.486▲**
G^N	5	.138	.225	10	.186△	.272▲	7	.379△	.478△
G^{CA}	7	.139△	.229△	10	.186▲	**.276▲**	6	.385▲	**.486▲**
G^{CN}	10	.145	.228	7	.182▲	.267▲	6	.377▲	.481▲
G^{AN}	10	.138△	.224	10	**.187**△	.270△	7	.376▲	.477△
G^{CAN}	7	.135	.224	10	**.187**△	.274△	8	**.386**	.482△

Table 4: Diversification result with pLSA and LapPLSA regularized by different external resources and their combinations. All runs are compared to the baseline NoDiv. Boldface indicates the highest score among all runs.

	Topics 1-50		Topics 51-100		Topics 101-150	
Method	E-IA@20	αnD@20	E-IA@20	αnD@20	E-IA@20	αnD@20
pLSA	.149	.234	.193	.276	.397	.499
G^C	**.164▲**	**.257▲**	.201	.293	.410	.511
G^A	.147	.240	.200	.290△	.410	.509
G^N	.145	.235	.201△	.287▲	.409	.507
G^{CA}	.151	.244	**.207▲**	**.299▲**	.410	.510
G^{CN}	.153	.241	.200	.289△	.402△	.505△
G^{AN}	.144	.234	.196	.283△	.395	.499
G^{CAN}	.148	.240△	.198▲	.289▲	**.413**	**.512**

Table 5: Comparing LapPLSA and pLSA. All runs are compared to pLSA. All the scores are significantly greater compared to the baseline NoDiv in Table 4. Boldface indicates the highest score among all runs.

In fact, the performance of regularization with click logs is still decent; testing for significance of the difference between run G^C and run pLSA has a p-value of 0.077 for ERR-IA@20 and 0.059 for α-nDCG@20. The TREC 2011 topic set seems the most difficult one. Regularization with most resources or their combinations does not lead to significant improvement over the pLSA run. The only exception is the combination of the click logs and the Web ngrams. This result is to some extent consistent with statement in the TREC Web Track guideline that the topic set "*introduces "tougher" topics, ...they can rely less on click/anchor information, and popularity signals like PageRank.*"[14]. Combining all three resources seems to be a relatively safe choice: it improves significantly over the pLSA run on two out of the three topic sets, and on the third topic set, although the difference is not statistically significant (with a p-value of 0.1 for ERR-IA@20 and 0.054 for α-nDCG@20), the highest absolute score is achieved across all settings on this set.

6.4 A robustness analysis on the parameter K

From previous experiments, we have seen that the number of topics K is an important parameter, whose optimal value is difficult to predict. Further, we also see in Figure 3 and Figure 4 that across different settings of K, in most cases the averaged performance of LapPLSA exceeds that of pLSA. Given this observation, we are interested in the question: is regularized pLSA likely to outperform non-regularized pLSA no matter the value of K we select?

The above question can be reformulated as follows. Assume we have two samples of diversification results in terms of α-nDCG@20. Sample 1 is the result of diversification using pLSA for varying K, and sample 2 is the result of diversification using LapPLSA regu-

Resource	1-50		51-100		101-150	
	W	p-value	W	p-value	W	p-value
G^C	122	.0005	117	.0040	107	.0625
G^A	118	.0028	113	.0141	123	.0003
G^N	112	.0188	101	.1902	109	.0400
G^{CA}	**121**	.0007	**118**	.0028	**114**	.0106
G^{CN}	**116**	.0056	**109**	.0400	**118**	.0028
G^{AN}	108	.0503	**110**	.0314	**113**	.0142
G^{CAN}	109	.0400	**112**	.0188	**119**	.0019

Table 6: Comparing performance of LapPLSA and pLSA over random K's. Boldface indicates that the W value of a combined resource is equal or above the lowest W of the single resources that are combined.

Topics	1-50				51-100				101-150			
Method	K	λ	E-IA@20	αnD@20	K	λ	E-IA@20	αnD@20	K	λ	E-IA@20	αnD@20
pLSA	5	.4	.136	.223	3	.1	.179	.258	5	.5	.368	.471
G^C	10	.1	**.167**	**.256**	10	.1	.195	.286	8	.2	.393	.486
G^A	3	.1	.145	.233	9	.1	.195	.286	7	.3	.396	.490
G^N	9	.1	.154	.240	10	.4	.184	.271	10	.3	.384	.482
G^{CA}	5	.1	.145	.240	7	.1	**.202**	**.295**	9	.3	**.397**	**.491**
G^{CN}	7	.1	.152	.243	7	.2	.187	.277	10	.3	.385	.485
G^{AN}	5	.1	.142	.233	10	.1	.192	.283	10	.2	.390	.485
G^{CAN}	3	.1	.148	.236	10	.2	.188	.279	8	.2	.392	.487

Table 7: Performance of xQuAD with pLSA and LapPLSA regularized by different external resources and their combinations. λ and K are optimized with respect to each topic set.

larized by certain external subtopic resource, also for varying K. If we randomly pick a score from each sample, how probable does the score from sample 2 exceed the score from sample 1? This can be tested with a Wilcoxon ranksum test [40][4].

Table 6 shows the result. Each sample contains 9 observations, i.e., for $K = 2, ..., 10$. W is the rank sum statistics , where a larger W indicates a more extreme difference between the two samples. Two observations stand out. First, in all cases but three(G^{AN} on topics 1-50, G^N on topic 51-100, and G^C on 101-150), the differences between pLSA and LapPLSA are significant with a p-value < 0.05. That is, with a random setting of K, LapPLSA regularized with external resources tends to outperform non-regularized pLSA. Second, in most cases, the W value of those combined resources are in between (occasionally above) the resources that are combined. This is consistent with the observation made in Section 6.2. Further, compared to G^C and G^A, G^N has a relatively lower W on all three topic sets, which suggests that with a random K, LapPLSA regularized with G^N is less likely to improve over pLSA compared to G^A and G^C.

6.5 Summary

We conclude the experimental analysis by relating our findings to the research questions formulated before (See Section 5.1).

With respect to RQ1, we find that LapPLSA regularized with explicit subtopics extracted from good resources improves diversification results, which indicates that better topic models are formed.

With respect to RQ2, we find that different resources are effective on different topic sets. Futher, based on the observation in Figure 3 and the results discussed in Section 6.4, we conclude that the effectiveness of Web ngrams is the least robust, or more sensitive to the setting of K compared to anchor text and click logs. As mentioned before, we suspect that the Web ngrams are more similar to the document content than truly external resources, which could explain the observed difference.

For RQ3, we find that combining resources does not always improve the diversification result. The combined resource usually results in a diversification performance in between that of the individual resources combined.

In terms of RQ4, we find that LapPLSA regularized with explicit subtopics tends to outperform the non-regularized pLSA for cases where we do not optimize the setting of K, and simply choose it at random from a reasonable range. We therefore conclude that regularized pLSA has the advantage that it provides a more robust performance in practice (where we will not know the optimal K).

Finally, for completeness, we include the performance of xQuAD in Table 7. With a proper setting of λ and K, xQuAD shows better diversification performance compared to the results of IA-select in Table 4 in most cases. Same as with IA-select, regularization helps in generating better diversification results with xQuAD. Moreover, the usefulness of different resources and their combinations show similar trend compared to that of IA-select.

[4]This includes the assumption that diversification results are independent from each other with respect to different K's. We believe this assumption is sensible, especially given the observation that there is no clear pattern on the change of diversification performance with respect to the change of K.

7. CONCLUSION

We proposed Multi-source Subtopics (MSS), a framework for subtopic modeling that i) uses a random walk based approach to combine and estimate the similarity between subtopics extracted from multiple Web sources, and ii) uses the obtained similarity relations to regularize topic models constructed using document content. MSS combines subtopics from multiple resources transparently, unifying implicit and explicit representations of subtopics.

We have demonstrated how the application of this framework in the context of search result diversification allows us to flexibly combine, analyze and compare subtopics extracted from different resources. Empirical results show that topic models regularized by the topical information extracted from external resources lead to improved and more robust diversification results, supporting our claim that better topic models are formed. Among the Web resources employed in our experiments, anchor text and click logs were shown to be generally more effective than Web ngrams. However, the effectiveness of a resource also depends on the properties of a specific query, and especially whether a resource contains subtopic information related to a query at all. Combining multiple resources could alleviate lack of coverage, but in our current setup leads to a diversification performance in between that of the resources that are combined.

A number of directions are left to be explored in the future. First of all, there is room to improve our method by exploring how to weigh resources by their (expected) quality for a given query. More resources can be analyzed, for example derived from social bookmarking sites, and more sophisticated ways of parameter optimization should be considered. Second, a component wise evaluation may improve our understanding beyond observations on the diversification pipeline as a whole. Hereto, we need to develop a method to evaluate the quality of the constructed subtopics directly through human assessment. This may be especially useful to improve our understanding of the features that make an external resource a good one for a given query. Finally, perhaps the strength of the external resources is not yet exploited in full when we only use them to regularize pLSA. An alternative could be to integrate implicit topics as nodes in the multi-plane random walks, and thus treat both types of topic representations more equally.

Acknowledgements

This research was funded by European Commission FP7 grant 257024, in the Fish4Knowledge project

8. REFERENCES

[1] R. Agrawal, S. Gollapudi, A. Halverson, and S. Ieong. Diversifying search results. In *WSDM '09*, pages 5–14, 2009.

[2] J. Allan and H. Raghavan. Using part-of-speech patterns to reduce query ambiguity. In *SIGIR '02*, pages 307–314, 2002.

[3] D. Beeferman and A. Berger. Agglomerative clustering of a search engine query log. In *KDD'00*, pages 407–416, 2000.

[4] D. M. Blei, A. Y. Ng, and M. I. Jordan. Latent Dirichlet allocation. *J. Mach. Learn. Res.*, 3:993–1022, 2003.

[5] B. R. Boyce. Beyond topicality: A two stage view of relevance and the retrieval process. *Information Processing & Management*, 18(3):105–109, 1982.

[6] D. Cai, Q. Mei, J. Han, and C. Zhai. Modeling hidden topics on document manifold. In *CIKM '08*, pages 911–920, 2008.

[7] J. Carbonell and J. Goldstein. The use of MMR, diversity-based reranking for reordering documents and producing summaries. In *SIGIR '98*, pages 335–336, 1998.

[8] B. Carterette and P. Chandar. Probabilistic models of ranking novel documents for faceted topic retrieval. In *CIKM'09*, pages 1287–1296, 2009.

[9] O. Chapelle, D. Metlzer, Y. Zhang, and P. Grinspan. Expected reciprocal rank for graded relevance. In *CIKM'09*, pages 621–630, 2009.

[10] H. Chen and D. R. Karger. Less is more: probabilistic models for retrieving fewer relevant documents. In *SIGIR '06*, pages 429–436, 2006.

[11] C. Clarke, M. Kolla, G. Cormack, O. Vechtomova, A. Ashkan, S. Büttcher, and I. MacKinnon. Novelty and diversity in information retrieval evaluation. In *SIGIR'08*, pages 659–666, 2008.

[12] C. Clarke, N. Craswell, and I. Soboroff. Overview of the TREC 2009 web track. In *TREC'09*, 2009.

[13] C. Clarke, N. Craswell, and I. Soboroff. Overview of the TREC 2010 web track. In *TREC'10*, 2010.

[14] C. Clarke, N. Craswell, and E. Soboroff, I.and Voorhees. Overview of the TREC 2011 web track. In *TREC'11*, 2011.

[15] G. V. Cormack, M. D. Smucker, and C. L. A. Clarke. Efficient and effective spam filtering and re-ranking for large web datasets. *Information Retrieval*, 14(5):441–465, 2011.

[16] N. Craswell and M. Szummer. Random walks on the click graph. In *SIGIR'07*, pages 239–246, 2007.

[17] N. Craswell, R. Jones, G. Dupret, and E. Viegas, editors. *WSCD'09*, 2009.

[18] J. Cui, H. Liu, J. Yan, L. Ji, R. Jin, J. He, Y. Gu, Z. Chen, and X. Du. Multi-view random walk framework for search task discovery from click-through log. In *CIKM '11*, pages 135–140, 2011.

[19] V. Dang and B. W. Croft. Query reformulation using anchor text. In *WSDM '10*, pages 41–50, 2010.

[20] V. Dang, X. Xue, and B. Croft. Inferring query aspects from reformulations using clustering. In *CIKM '11*, 2011.

[21] Z. Dou, S. Hu, K. Chen, R. Song, and J.-R. Wen. Multi-dimensional search result diversification. In *WSDM'11*, pages 475–484, 2011.

[22] A. Fuxman, P. Tsaparas, K. Achan, and R. Agrawal. Using the wisdom of the crowds for keyword generation. In *WWW '08*, pages 61–70, 2008.

[23] W. Goffman. A searching procedure for information retrieval. *Information Storage and Retrieval*, 2(2):73–78, 1964.

[24] J. Guo, X. Cheng, G. Xu, and X. Zhu. Intent-aware query similarity. In *CIKM'11*, pages 259–268, 2011.

[25] J. He. *Exploring topic structure: Coherence, Diversity and Relatedness*. PhD thesis, University of Amsterdam, 2011.

[26] J. He, E. Meij, and M. de Rijke. Result diversification based on query-specific cluster ranking. *J. Am. Soc. Inf. Sci. Technol.*, 62(3):550–571, 2011.

[27] D. Hiemstra and C. Hauff. MIREX: MapReduce information retrieval experiments. Technical Report TR-CTIT-10-15, University of Twente, 2010.

[28] T. Hofmann. Probabilistic latent semantic indexing. In *SIGIR'99*, pages 50–57, 1999.

[29] Z. Li, F. Chen, Q. Xing, J. Miao, Y. Xue, T. Zhu, B. Zhou, R. Cen, Y. Liu, M. Zhang, Y. Jin, and S. Ma. Thuir at trec 2009 web track: Finding relevant and diverse results for large scale web search. In *TREC*, 2009.

[30] H. Ma, M. R. Lyu, and I. King. Diversifying query suggestion results. In *AAAI'10*, 2010.

[31] D. Metzler and W. B. Croft. Combining the language model and inference network approaches to retrieval. *Inf. Process. Manage.*, 40:735–750, September 2004.

[32] J. M. Ponte and W. B. Croft. A language modeling approach to information retrieval. In *SIGIR '98*, pages 275–281, 1998.

[33] F. Radlinski, M. Szummer, and N. Craswell. Inferring query intent from reformulations and clicks. In *WWW '10*, pages 1171–1172, 2010.

[34] D. Rafiei, K. Bharat, and A. Shukla. Diversifying web search results. In *WWW '10*, pages 781–790, 2010.

[35] R. L. T. Santos, C. Macdonald, and I. Ounis. Exploiting query reformulations for web search result diversification. In *WWW'10*, pages 881–890, 2010.

[36] N. Tishby and N. Slonim. Data clustering by markovian relaxation and the information bottleneck method. In *NIPS*, pages 640–646, 2000.

[37] J. Wang and J. Zhu. Portfolio theory of information retrieval. In *SIGIR '09*, pages 115–122, 2009.

[38] K. Wang, C. Thrasher, E. Viegas, X. Li, and B.-j. P. Hsu. An overview of microsoft web n-gram corpus and applications. In *NAACL HLT'10*, pages 45–48, 2010.

[39] J.-R. Wen, J.-Y. Nie, and H.-J. Zhang. Clustering user queries of a search engine. In *WWW '01*, pages 162–168, 2001.

[40] F. Wilcoxon. Individual comparisons by ranking methods. *Biometrics Bulletin*, 1(6):80–83, 1945.

[41] I. H. Witten and E. Frank. *Data Mining: Practical Machine Learning Tools and Techniques with Java Implementations*. Morgan Kaufmann, 1st edition, 1999.

[42] Y. Yue and T. Joachims. Predicting diverse subsets using structural SVMs. In *ICML '08*, pages 1224–1231, 2008.

[43] C. X. Zhai, W. W. Cohen, and J. Lafferty. Beyond independent relevance: methods and evaluation metrics for subtopic retrieval. In *SIGIR '03*, pages 10–17, 2003.

[44] X. Zhu, A. B. Goldberg, J. Van, and G. D. Andrzejewski. Improving diversity in ranking using absorbing random walks. Technical report, University of Washington, 2007.

Using Preference Judgments for Novel Document Retrieval

Praveen Chandar and Ben Carterette
{pcr,carteret}@udel.edu
Department of Computer and Information Sciences
University of Delaware
Newark, DE, USA 19716

ABSTRACT

There has been considerable interest in incorporating diversity in search results to account for redundancy and the space of possible user needs. Most work on this problem is based on *subtopics*: diversity rankers score documents against a set of hypothesized subtopics, and diversity rankings are evaluated by assigning a value to each ranked document based on the number of novel (and redundant) subtopics it is relevant to. This can be seen as modeling a user who is always interested in seeing more novel subtopics, with progressively decreasing interest in seeing the same subtopic multiple times. We put this model to test: if it is correct, then users, when given a choice, should prefer to see a document that has more value to the evaluation. We formulate some specific hypotheses from this model and test them with actual users in a novel preference-based design in which users express a preference for document A or document B *given* document C. We argue that while the user study shows the subtopic model is good, there are many other factors apart from novelty and redundancy that may be influencing user preferences. From this, we introduce a new framework to construct an ideal diversity ranking using only preference judgments, with no explicit subtopic judgments whatsoever.

Categories and Subject Descriptors: H.3.3 [Information Storage and Retrieval]

Keywords: diversity, user study, preference judgments

1. INTRODUCTION

Research on novelty and diversity aims to improve the effectiveness of search engines by providing results that serve a range of possible user intents for the given query. These problems have been the subject of much interest in IR and web search recently, including the focus of a TREC task[1]. Batch effectiveness evaluation of retrieval systems serves several important purposes: first, giving developers and researchers a measurable objective; second, allowing for failure analysis and troubleshooting; and third, trying to estimate how useful search results will be to users. For the last of these, it is helpful to think of the evaluation measure and relevance judgments as a model of user utility. Measures like precision and recall can be seen as modeling utility in terms of the proportion of retrieved documents that are relevant and the proportion of relevant documents retrieved; measures like discounted cumulative gain or expected reciprocal rank offer a more refined model of user utility that incorporates graded judgments and rank-based discounts.

None of these models capture novelty or redundancy in ranked results. All of them will reward a system for retrieving the same relevant document 10 times in a row, or 10 relevant documents that are only superficially different from each other; while that may be useful for knowing whether retrieval features are working correctly, it is not likely to be very useful to a user. *Diversity evaluation* attempts to model novelty and redundancy in ranked results so as to give a more precise model of user utility.

Current diversity evaluation measures in the literature require judgments of relevance to *subtopics* (also called aspects, facets, or nuggets) of a topic. For example, judgments for the query *Windows* would include binary relevance judgments for each document for the subtopics *window panes*, *windows operating system*, etc. These subtopic judgments are used to determine whether a document is redundant with a previously-ranked document, or whether it contains some new information that a user might find interesting, or whether it is relevant to an alternative intent and perhaps not useful to this user but still useful enough to a different user. Measures like α-nDCG, ERR-IA, subtopic recall, and D-measures [?, ?, ?, ?] all use this same basic model, assigning more value to a document with more novel subtopics and less value to one with more redundant subtopics.

Like any model, the subtopic model surely has shortcomings. Novelty and redundancy are certainly not the only reasons a user might prefer one relevant document over another. Apart from a study by Sanderson et al. that showed that user preferences for rankings correlate with α-nDCG [?], there has not been much work on validating this model against real user preferences. And if the model does *not* track user preferences, then it is hard to justify its continued use: it conflates various aspects of effectiveness in such a way that, if used as an objective function, it can be difficult to understand the precise effect of change in the ranker.

[1] TREC 2009-2011 Web Track Diversity task focuses on novelty and diversity in search results.

SIGIR'12, August 12–16, 2012, Portland, Oregon, USA.

Fortunately these measures produce directly-testable hypotheses about user preferences. In this work we describe a novel user study to test these hypotheses. In Section 2 we start by describing the diversity retrieval problem in more detail and define the model more precisely. In Section 3 we present a user study, including a crowdsourced design; we show that while the model is not perfect, it is certainly not invalid. Section 4 builds on this by presenting a preference-based method for determining a diversity-aware ranking of documents. We conclude in Section 5.

2. NOVELTY RANKING TASK

Consider a user that has an unambiguous but broad information need and goes to a search engine to help satisfy it. This user will input a query and then see a ranked list of results, some of which will be relevant and some of which will not. The user will presumably click the relevant results to view and absorb the information they contain. Ideally, each relevant result would provide some new information that was not provided by previous relevant results; in other words, the relevant results would not be redundant with each other. The idea is that, each time a user clicks on a new relevant document, the amount of knowledge a user gains must be maximized by the novel content in the document.

The goal of ranking documents with novelty is to ensure that each relevant document a user sees as they progress down a ranked list provides new, non-redundant information that will help them satisfy their need. This means that a ranking of documents cannot be based solely on the probability of relevance; the novelty of a document depends to no small degree on the documents that have been ranked above it. Similarly, evaluation of these results cannot be based solely on binary or even graded relevance judgments, since these judgments are made to individual documents independently of all the other documents that might have been ranked. Part of studying the task is defining evaluation measures that can model redundancy and novelty.

2.1 Relationship With Other Tasks

The novelty task has similarities with some existing tasks such as the diversity task studied as part of the TREC Web track. Diversity aims at retrieving a subset of documents that has the maximum coverage of subtopics with the assumption that different users may be interested in different subtopics. In novelty ranking, the goal is to provide a set of documents for a single topic from which the user can get as much information as possible for that particular topic. We assume all users are interested in all of the subtopics, like the standard ad hoc assumption that all users are interested in all of the relevant material.

2.2 Intrinsic vs Extrinsic Diversity

Researchers in the past have identified two types of diversity: extrinsic and intrinsic [?]. Extrinsic diversity addresses the uncertainty in an ambiguous query where the intent is unclear and is best served by a ranking of documents covering several intents. Intrinsic diversity can be described as diversification that focuses on reducing redundancy and providing *novel* information for an unambiguous but still underspecified information need. In our work, we focus on intrinsic diversity which we refer to as *novelty ranking*, as we believe it will be easier for assessors to express preferences when there is no ambiguity of intent.

2.3 Evaluation

Evaluation measures for novelty and diversity must account for both relevance and novelty in the result set. It is important that redundancy caused by documents containing previously retrieved subtopics be penalized and documents containing novel information be rewarded. Most evaluation measures solve this problem by requiring that the subtopics for a query be known and that documents have been judged with respect to subtopics.

2.3.1 *Existing Evaluation Measures*

Subtopic recall. Subtopic recall measures the number of unique subtopics retrieved at a given rank [?]. Given that a query q has m subtopics, the subtopic recall at rank k is given by the ratio of number of unique subtopics contained by the subset of document up to rank k to the total number of subtopics m.

$$S\text{-}recall@k = \frac{\left|\bigcup_{i=1}^{k} subtopics(d_i)\right|}{m} \quad (1)$$

α-nDCG scores a result set by rewarding newly found subtopics and penalizing redundant subtopics. In order to calculate α-nDCG we must first compute the gain vector [?]. The gain vector is computed by summing over subtopics appearing in the document at rank k:

$$G[i] = \sum_{j=1}^{m}(1-\alpha)^{c_{j,i}-1} \quad (2)$$

where $c_{j,i}$ is the number of times subtopic j has appeared in documents up to (and including) rank i. Once the gain vector is computed, a discount is applied at each rank to penalize documents as the rank decreases. The most commonly used discount function is the $log_2(1+i)$, although other discount functions are possible. The *discounted cumulative gain* is given by

$$\alpha DCG@k = \sum_{i=1}^{k} \frac{G[i]}{log_2(1+i)} \quad (3)$$

α-DCG must be normalized to compare the scores against various topics. This is done by finding an "ideal" ranking that maximizes α-DCG, which can be done using a greedy algorithm. The ratio of α-DCG to that ideal gives α-nDCG.

Intent-aware family. Agrawal et al. studied the problem of answering ambiguous web queries, which is similar to the subtopic retrieval problem [?]. The focus of their evaluation measure is to measure the coverage of each intent separately for each query and combine them with a probability distribution of the user intents. They call this the *intent-aware* family of measures. It can be used with most of the traditional measures for evaluations such as precision@k, MAP, nDCG, and so on.

ERR-IA. Expected Reciprocal Rank (ERR) is a measure based on "diminishing returns" for relevant documents [?]. According to this measure, the contribution of each document is based on the relevance of documents ranked above it. The discount function is therefore not just dependent on the rank but also on relevance of previously ranked documents. A weighted average of the ERR measures for each interpretation would give the intent-aware version of ERR [?].

D-Measure. The D and the D# measures described by Sakai et al. [?] aims to combine two properties into a single evaluation measure. The first property is to retrieval documents covering as many intents as possible and the second is to rank documents relevant to more popular intents higher than documents relevant to less popular intents.

2.3.2 *Principles of Existing Evaluation Measures*

All of these measures estimate effectiveness of a system's ranking by iterating over the ranking, rewarding relevant documents containing a unseen subtopic(s) and penalizing relevant documents containing subtopic(s) seen before in the ranking. They are all based on a few principles in general:

1. A document with more unseen subtopics is worth more than a document with fewer unseen subtopics;
2. A document with both unseen and already-seen subtopics is worth more than a document with only the same unseen subtopic;
3. A document with unseen subtopics is worth more than a document with only redundant subtopics.

One of our goals with this work is to test whether these principles hold for real users.

2.4 Data

Our analysis was conducted primarily on the *Newswire* data created by Allan et al. [?] to investigate the relationship between system performance and human performance on a subtopic retrieval task. The data consists of 61 topics, each with a short (3-6 word) query, and judgments of relevance to documents in a subset of the TDT5 corpus. The *Newswire* data includes relevance judgments for the top 130 documents retrieved by a query-likelihood language model for the short query for each query. The judgments consists of binary relevance judgments for each document, and for each relevant document, a list of subtopics contained in that document. This data reflects an intrinsic diversity task and is therefore most appropriate to this work.

3. FACTORS INFLUENCING USER PREFERENCES

In Section 2.3.2, we identified some principles on which the evaluations for diversity are based on. In this section we tests if these principles hold for real users and further study in detail the role of subtopics in influencing user preference. Although in practice the same evaluation measures are used for both intrinsic and extrinsic diversity, our focus is on intrinsic diversity as it is easier for assessors to understand the concept of relevance when there is no ambiguity of intent. We explore the factors that influence user preference for novelty ranking using a preference based framework.

3.1 Triplet Framework

The idea of pairwise preference judgments is relatively new in the IR literature, having been introduced by Rorvig in 1990 [?] but not subject to empirical study until the past several years [?, ?]. Comparison studies between absolute and preference judgments show that preference judgments can often be made faster than graded judgments, with better agreement between assessors (and more consistency with individual assessors) [?]. Also with preferences tassessors can make much finer distinctions between documents.

We propose a preference-based framework to study novelty consisting of a set up in which three relevant documents that we refer to as a *triplet* are displayed such that one of them appears at the top and the other two are displayed as a pair below the top document. We will use D_T, D_L, and D_R to denote the top, left, and right documents respectively, and a triplet as $\langle D_L, D_R | D_T \rangle$. An assessor shown such a triplet would be asked to choose which of D_L or D_R they would prefer to see as the *second* document in a ranking given that D_T is first, or in other words, they would express a preference for D_L or D_R conditional on D_T. For the purpose of this study we will assume we have relevance judgments to a topic, and for each relevant document, binary judgments of relevance to a set of subtopics. Thus we can represent a document as the set of subtopics it has been judged relevant to, e.g. $D_i = \{S_j, S_k\}$ means document i is relevant to subtopics j and k. Varying the number of subtopics in top, left and right documents yields specific hypotheses about preferences for novelty over redundancy.

3.2 Hypotheses

The triplet framework allows us to collect judgments for novelty based on preferences and also enables us to test various hypotheses. As discussed above, varying the number of subtopics in D_T, D_L and D_R it is possible to enumerate various hypotheses concerning the effect of subtopics in a document. We define two types of hypotheses; one very specific with respect to subtopic counts and redundancy, and the other more general.

Hypothesis Set 1 : First we propose the simplest possible hypotheses that capture the three principles above. We will denote a preference between two documents using $\succ$, e.g. $D_L \succ D_R$ means document D_L is preferred to document D_R. Then the three hypotheses stated formally are:

H_1: if $\langle D_L, D_R | D_T \rangle = \langle \{S_2\}, \{S_1\} | \{S_1\} \rangle$, then $D_L \succ D_R$ (novelty is better than redundancy)
H_2: if $\langle D_L, D_R | D_T \rangle = \langle \{S_1, S_2\}, \{S_2\} | \{S_1\} \rangle$, then $D_L \succ D_R$ (novelty+redundancy is better than novelty alone)
H_3: if $\langle D_L, D_R | D_T \rangle = \langle \{S_2, S_3\}, \{S_2\} | \{S_1\} \rangle$, then $D_L \succ D_R$ (novelty+novelty is better than novelty alone)

Hypothesis Set 2 : Here we define a class of hypotheses in which the number of subtopics contained in each document in a triplet is categorized by relative quantity. We identify six variables based on number of subtopics that almost completely describe the novelty and redundancy present in the triplet. The six variable are as follows:

1. Tn - Number of subtopics in D_T;
2. NLn - Number of subtopic in D_L not present in D_T;
3. NRn - Number of subtopic in D_R not present in D_T;
4. Sn - Number of subtopics shared between D_L and D_R;
5. RLn - Number of subtopics in D_L and present in D_T;
6. RRn - Number of subtopics in D_R and present in D_T.

The number of subtopics for each of the six variables are categorized as *low* or *high*. The six variables enable us to test the effect of novelty and redundancy w.r.t the number of subtopics in a triplet. The variables NLn and NRn focus on novelty whereas RLn and RRn focuses on redundancy. For instance, by varying NLn and NRn and holding the other variables constant, it is possible to test the effect of the relative quantity of novel subtopics in a document.

3.3 Experimental Design

In this section we describe the experimental design used to test the hypotheses defined above. Notice that the defined hypotheses are based on the number of subtopics contained in the documents and they fit into the triplet framework which requires conditional preference judgments. Therefore, to test our hypotheses, two kinds of judgments were needed: subtopic level judgments and conditional preference judgments. The subtopic level judgments were obtained from the data described in Section 2.4. Conditional preference judgments were collected using crowd sourcing as it is a fast, easy and a low cost way of collection user judgments [?].

We used Amazon Mechanical Turk (AMT) [?]; an online labor marketplace to collect user judgments. AMT works as follow: requestor create a group of Human Intelligence Task (HITs) with various constraints and worker from the marketplace works on these task to complete the task. In this work we, use a design similar to the one used by Chandar and Cartertte [?]. Designing a user study using AMT involves deciding on the HIT layout and HIT properties.

3.3.1 HIT Layout

In order to collect user judgments for our hypotheses using AMT, we had to organize the triplets satisfying a given hypothesis into HITs. Each HIT consisted of the following (in order of display): a set of instructions about the task, original keyword query, topic description, five preference triplets, and a comment field allowing worker to provide feedback. A brief description about each element is given below:

Guidelines: Workers were provided with a set of instructions and guidelines prior to judging. Guidelines specified that workers should assume that everything they know about the topic is in the top document and are trying to find a document that would be most useful for learning more about the topic. Guidelines did not mention anything about subtopics, or even novelty/redundancy except as examples of properties assessors might take into account in their preferences (along with recency, ease of reading, and relevance).

Query text and topic description: The *query text* described the topic in a few words (we used the topic "titles" in the traditional TREC jargon) and *topic description* provided a more verbose and informative description about the topic. Again, there was no mention of explicit subtopics.

Preference triplet: Figure 1 shows an example preference triplet with the query text and topic description. Each preference triplet consists of *three* documents, all of which were relevant to the topic and the document were picked randomly from the data described in Section 2.4 to meet the constraints of a given hypothesis. One document appeared at the top followed by two documents below it, the triplets were chosen randomly such that the hypothesis constraints were satisfied. A HIT consisted of five preference triplets belonging to the same query shown one below the other.

The triplets were followed by a preference option for the workers to indicate which of the two documents they preferred. The workers were asked to pick the document from the lower two that provided the most new information, assuming that all the information they know about the topic is in the top document. They could express a preference based on whatever criteria they liked; we listed some examples in the guidelines. Note that we do not show them any subtopics, nor do we ask them to try to determine subtopics and make a preference based on that.

Comments Field was provided at the end, so that the workers could to provide a common feedback for all the five triplets, if they chose to do so.

3.3.2 HIT Properties

Workers are paid for each HIT they complete and picking an appropriate amount for each task is always tricky. In our study, workers were paid $0.80 for each completed HIT. Also each HIT had a time limit of three hours before which the HIT had to be completed. While the actual task might not take three hours to complete; the extra time allows them to take breaks if needed, since the workers had to read fifteen documents per HIT. We had five separate workers judge each HIT for the our *first set of hypotheses* and three separate workers judge each HIT for the our *second set of hypotheses.*

3.3.3 Triplets

Triplets were generated by randomly picking the three relevant documents for a given query and representing them as subtopic(s). Triplets for the first set of hypotheses in Section 3.2 were considered such that the constraints are satisfied for each hypothesis. For example, for hypothesis H_1 given a query x the triplet would consist of D_T containing only the subtopic S_1 and D_L containing the subtopics S_1 and S_2. Six queries were used to test the first set of hypotheses with four triplets for each query.

The triplets were generated in a similar way for the second set of hypotheses but the constraints for each hypothesis were based on the six variables described in 3.2. For example, a triplet with a variable setting of Tn = High, Sn = High, NLn = High and NRn = High would contain 5 or more subtopics in the top document D_T and 3 or more subtopics in the left and right documents (D_L and D_R) such that there are 1 or more subtopics shared between D_L and D_R. The details of the number of subtopics for each categories of high and low levels for each variables are provided in the Table 1. Eight queries were used to test the second set of hypotheses with four different triplets for each query.

3.3.4 Quality Control

There are two major concerns in collecting judgments through crowdsourcing platform such as AMT. One is "Do the workers really understand the task?" and the other is "Are they making faithful effort to do the work or clicking randomly?". We address these concerns using three techniques: majority vote, trap questions, and qualifications.

Majority vote: Since novelty judgments to be made by the workers are subjective and it is possible some workers are clicking randomly, having more than one person judge a triplet is common practice to improve the quality of judgments. In our study, each HIT was judged by 5 or 3 different workers (depending on hypothesis set). We look at the individual preferences as well as the majority preference.

Trap questions: Triplets for which answers are obvious were included to assess the validity of the results. We included two kinds of trap questions: "non-relevant document trap" and "identical document trap". For the former, one of the bottom two documents was not relevant to the topic and should never be preferred. For the latter, the top document and one of the bottom two documents were the same. The workers were expected to pick the non-identical document as it provides novel information. One of the five triplets in a HIT was a trap and the type was chosen randomly.

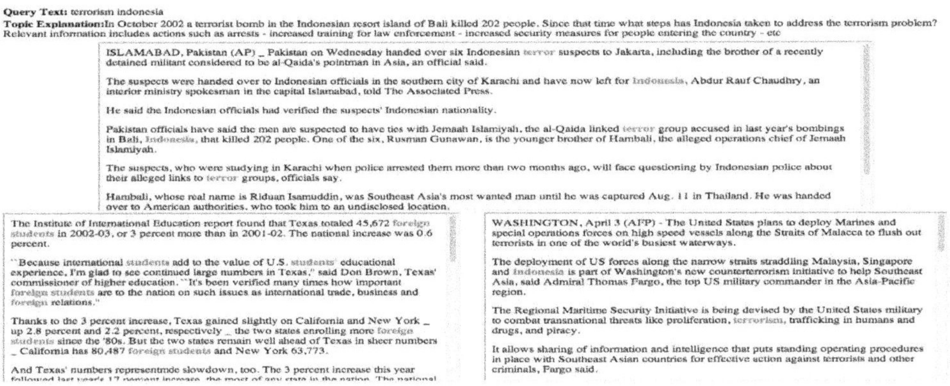

Figure 1: Screenshot of the preference triple along with the query text and description.

variable	number of subtopics	
	low	high
Tn	1-4	5-9
Sn	0	1-2
NLn	0-2	3-6
NRn	0-2	3-6
RLn	0	1-2
RRn	0	1-2

Table 1: Number of subtopics corresponding to the high and low categories for each variable in our second set of hypotheses.

Qualifications: It is possible to qualify workers before they are allowed to work on your HITs in AMT. Worker qualifications can be determined based on historical performance such as percentage of approved HITs. Also, worker's qualification can be based on a short questionnaire or a test. The two qualifications used in are study are explained below:

1. **Approval rate:** HITs can be restricted to workers with an overall minimum percentage of approval. It is commonly used for improving accuracy and reducing spammer from working on your task. An overall approval rate of *95%* was required to work on our HITs.
2. **Qualification test:** Qualification tests can be used to ensure that workers have the required skill and knowledge to perform the task. In our case, workers had to be trained to look for documents that provide novel information given the top document. We created a qualification test having the same design layout as the actual task but had only three triplets. Two of the three triplets were identical document traps and the other was a non-relevant trap with instructions for each triplet aiding in making a preference.

3.4 Results and Analysis

Judgments for a total of 60 triplets (out of which 12 triplets were traps) were obtained for the hypothesis set 1. Since we had each triplet assessed by five separate assessors, a total of 300 judgments were collected out of which 60 were traps. We had 39 unique workers (identified by worker ID) on AMT judge these triplets across six topics.

Table 2 shows results for H_1. It turns out that there is no clear preference for either redundant or novel documents

H_1	all prefs		consensus	
topic	same	new	same	new
childhood obesity	6	14	1	3
terrorism indonesia	8	12	1	3
earthquakes	15	5	3	1
weapons for urban fighting	15	5	3	1
total	**44**	**36**	**8**	**8**

Table 2: Results for H_1: that novelty is preferred to redundancy. The "all prefs" columns give the number of preferences for the redundant and the novel document for all assessors. The "consensus" columns take a majority vote for each triplet and report the resulting number of preferences.

H_2	all prefs		consensus	
topic	new	same+new	new	same+new
kerry endorsement	9	11	2	2
childhood obesity	4	16	0	4
terrorism indonesia	13	7	4	0
libya sanctions	4	16	0	4
total	**30**	**50**	**6**	**10**

Table 3: Results for H_2: that novelty and redundancy together are preferred to novelty alone. The "all prefs" columns give the number of preferences for the redundant+novel document and the novel document for all assessors. The "consensus" columns take a majority vote for each triplet and report the resulting number of preferences.

for the four queries. For two of our queries assessors tended to prefer the novel choice; for the other two they tended to prefer the redundant choice. When we use majority vote to determine a consensus for each triplet, we find that the outcomes are exactly equal. Thus while we cannot reject H_1, we have to admit that if it holds it is much less strong than we expected.

Table 3 shows a clearer (but still not transparent) preference for H_2, novelty and redundancy together over novelty alone. Over all assessors and all triplets, the preference is significant by a binomial test (50 successes out of 80 trials; $p < 0.05$). Still, there is one query ("john kerry endorsement") for which the difference is insubstantial, and one that has the opposite result ("terrorism indonesia"). The latter

H_3	all prefs		consensus	
topic	new	new+new	new	new+new
kerry endorsement	9	11	1	3
childhood obesity	3	17	0	4
terrorism indonesia	2	18	0	4
libya sanctions	8	12	1	3
total	**22**	**58**	**2**	**14**

Table 4: Results for H_3: that two novel subtopics are preferred to one. The "all prefs" columns give the number of preferences for the novel+novel document and the novel document for all assessors. The "consensus" columns take a majority vote for each triplet and report the resulting number of preferences.

topic	high≻low	left≻ right
earthquakes	76 - 20 (79%)	96 - 96 (50%)
terry nichols guilt evidence	75 - 21 (78%)	100 - 92 (52%)
medicare drug coverage	73 - 23 (76%)	86 - 106 (45%)
oil producing countries	65 - 31 (68%)	89 - 103 (46%)
no child left behind	62 - 34 (65%)	81 - 111 (42%)
european union member	61 - 35 (64%)	103 - 89 (54%)
german headscarf court	59 - 37 (61%)	84 - 108 (44%)
ohio highway shooting	51 - 45 (53%)	104 - 88 (54%)
total	522 - 246 (68%)	743 - 793 (48%)

Table 5: Results of preference judgments by the number of new subtopics in D_L, D_R over D_T (variables NLn, NRn). Counts are aggregated over all values of Tn, Sn per query. The first column gives preference counts for the document with more new subtopics over the document with fewer when $NLn \succ NRn$. The second column is the baseline, giving counts for preferences for left over right.

case is particularly interesting because it is the opposite of what we would expect after seeing the results in Table 2: given that assessors preferred redundant documents to novel documents for that query, why would they prefer novel documents to documents with both novelty and redundancy?

Table 4, with results for H_3, is the strongest positive result: a clear preference for documents with two new subtopics over documents with just one. In this case both results are significant (58 successes out of 80 trials and $p < 0.0001$ over all triplets and all assessors; 14 successes out of 16 trials and $p < 0.01$ for majority voting). Nevertheless, there are still queries for which the preference is weak.

Based on this, it seems like *novelty + novelty > novelty*, *novelty+redundancy ≥ novelty*, but not *novelty ≥ redundancy*.

There were a total of 640 triplets (out of which 128 triplets were traps) for the second part of our study. Each of these triplets were judged by three separate assessors, thus a total of 1920 judgments were made out of which 384 were traps. And for this study we had 38 unique workers (identified by worker ID) on AMT working on our triplets. Some of these workers had worked on the first study as well. Almost 70% of the judgments were completed by 15% of the workers and about 93% of the irrelevant traps were passed by the workers. This power law distribution for our task has been observed earlier for other tasks as well [?], we hope to investigate on this issue in the future.

Triplets were generated by controlling four variable: Tn, Sn, NLn and NRn, we obtained sixteen unique settings for the four variable combination as each of the four variables were categorized into *low* and *high* with equal number of triplet in each setting. This allowed us to perform ANOVA such that the number of new subtopics in the left or right document was the primary predictor of preference, with the number of subtopics in the four variables as the secondary predictors. ANOVA indicated that there is a lot of residual variance, suggesting there are various factors influencing preferences that we have not included in the model.

Table 5 analyzes preferences for more new subtopics in D_L or D_R over fewer new subtopics (variables NLn and NRn) by topic. We looked at four cases: the first two (NLn high, NRn low; NLn low, NRn high) can tell us whether users prefer to see more new subtopics over fewer, while the second (NLn high, NRn high; NLn low, NLn low) along with the first two give us a baseline preference for left over right. While we would expect the baseline preference to be 50% (since which document appears on the left versus right is randomized), there may be other unmodeled factors that cause it to be more or less than 50%, so it is useful to compare to this baseline.

It is clear from this table that users as a group prefer to see more new subtopics, just as we saw in the results for H_3 above. Still, there are individual queries for which that preference is not strong, especially when compared to the baseline (e.g. the "Ohio highway shooting" topic), and even when the preference is strong in aggregate there are cases where they do not hold.

There is some effect due to the number of subtopics in D_T, with preferences for more new subtopics stronger when Tn is low. When it is low, the preference for high versus low is 271 to 113 (70%) against a baseline preference for left over right of 347 to 421 (45%)[2]. When Tn is high, the preference for high versus low is 251 to 133 (65%) against a baseline of 396 to 372 (52%). We conjecture that when the top document already has a lot of information about the topic, there is a little less reason to prefer either left or right regardless of how many subtopics they contain.

There is not much effect due to the number of shared subtopics between D_L and D_R. When Sn is low, the preference for more new subtopics over fewer is 268 to 116 (70%) against a baseline of 370 to 398 (48%); when it is high, the preference for more new is 254 to 130 (66%) against a baseline of 373 to 395 (49%). This may be because fewer shared subtopics makes it easier to express a preference. However, the effect is too small to draw any firm conclusion.

There is interesting interaction between the number of new subtopics and the number of redundant subtopics in D_L and D_R. When one has a high number of new subtopics and the other has a low number of new subtopics, number of *redundant* subtopics seems to influence the strength of preference for the one with more new subtopics: if there are more redundant subtopics along with the new subtopics, the preference is 118 to 44 (73%), but when there are fewer redundant subtopics with more new subtopics and more redundant subtopics with fewer new subtopics, the preference is even at 51 to 51 (50%). This suggests again that users *like* redundancy, sometimes enough to overcome a lack of novelty. However we must note that data here is sparse, also the two variables RRn and RLn were not the ones that we controlled for in our experiment.

[2]We presume that the greater-than-expected preference for the right document is just due to random chance.

Topic	Agreement	No. triplets
childhood obesity	0.71	15
weapons for urban fighting	0.92	5
kerry endorsement	0.58	10
libya sanctions	0.62	10
earthquake	0.72	5
terrorism indonesia	0.71	15
Mean	**0.69**	**60**

Table 6: Interassessor agreement scores for each topic for the first study.

Topic	Agreement	No. triplets
oil producing countries	0.63	80
terry nichols guilt evidence	0.72	80
no child left behind	0.61	80
german headscarf court	0.57	80
medicare drug coverage	0.66	80
earthquakes	0.65	80
european union member	0.59	80
ohio highway shooting	0.59	80
Mean	**0.63**	**640**

Table 7: Interassessor agreement scores for each topic for the second study.

3.5 Interassessor Agreement

As described above, each triplet was judged by five different workers for the first study (hypotheses set 1) and by three workers for the second study (hypotheses set 2). We calculated an inter-assessor agreement score for each triplet for the first study as follows. The judgments were considered as 10 pairs of answers given for a single triplet, adding 1 points to the score if the two workers agreed (complete agreement); and adding nothing if they judged different documents (no agreement). The perfect agreement would sum up 10 points, so we divided the score obtained by 10 and normalized from 0 (no agreement at all) to 1 (perfect agreement). Mean agreement for the first study is given in Table 6 for each query. Overall a high mean agreement of 0.7 was found across all triplets and the scores are close to the agreement observed previously [?]. Since the mean agreement was quite high for the first study, it encouraged us to reduce the number of workers for each triplet and increase the number of queries for the second study. Similar mean agreement can be seen for the second study in Table 7.

3.6 Possible Confounding Effects in Display

The way the hits were displayed may introduce some confounding effects, possibly causing assessors to choose documents for reasons other than novelty or redundancy. We investigated two such effects:

Document length A preference towards shorter documents was observed in general, though the preference gets weaker over the three hypotheses. For H_1, assessors preferred the shorter document in 79% of triplets. For H_2, that decreased to 71% of triplets, and for H_3 it dropped steeply to only 44%. However, it is also true that the mean difference in length for the pair of documents they were choosing between was greatest for H_1 triplets and least for H_3 triplets (H_1:158 terms, H_2:126 terms, H_3:47 terms). Therefore its safe to conclude there seems to be a preference towards shorter documents.

Highlighted terms It turns out that assessors tended to prefer the document with *fewer* highlighted query terms. For H_1, assessors preferred the document with more query terms only 35% of the time. For H_2 that drops to 13%, and for H_3 it comes back up to 29%. The mean difference in number of query term occurrences is quite low, only on the order of one additional occurrence on average for H_1 and H_3 documents, and only 0.2 additional occurrences for H_2. While the effect is significant, it seems unlikely that assessors can pick up on such small differences. We think the effect is more likely due to the distribution of subtopics in documents.

3.7 Additional Investigation

While the results suggest that the number of subtopics influences user preferences, it is also clear that from the analysis that other factors are affecting preferences. The results from H_1 and the weaker preference in H_2 were not what we expected. We investigated this more by looking at a number of triplets ourselves and identifying some new hypotheses about why assessors were making the preferences they were. From looking at triplets for the "earthquakes" topic, we identified three possible reasons for preferring a document with a redundant subtopic:

- it updates or corrects information in the top document;
- it significantly expands on the information in the top document;
- despite having a novel subtopic, the other choice provides little information of value.

This suggests to us that there are other factors that affect user preferences, in particular recency, completeness, and value. It may also suggest that there are implicit subtopics (at finer levels of granularity) that the original assessors did not identify, but that make a difference in preferences. None of this is surprising, but there is currently no evaluation paradigm of note that take all of these factors into account in a holistic way. Preference judgments can, and this analysis suggests additional hypotheses for testing with preferences.

4. PREFERENCE JUDGMENTS FOR AN IDEAL NOVELTY RANKING

The user study shows that although users tend to prefer documents containing more novel subtopics, it is also evident that factors other than subtopics play a vital role. The study also shows that the presence of subtopic in a document is taken into account implicitly and preferences are based not only on the number of subtopics but also on several other factors that include subtopic importance, relevance of the subtopic, readability of the document, etc. In this section, we propose an approach that attempts to capture these factors implicitly using a preference based framework to form a full ranking of documents with novelty as an implicit quality.

Our approach involves a series of sets of preference comparisons. Each set is essentially a comparison sort algorithm, with the comparison function a simple preference conditional on information contained in top-ranked documents from prior sets of comparisons, generalizing the triplet framework we introduced above.

The first set of preferences is meant to produce a relevance ranking: given a choice between two documents, assessors select the one they prefer, with topical relevance being the primary consideration in the judgment. Once these comparisons are done for all pairs, it is possible to obtain the best or "most relevant" document, i.e. the most preferred document based on the number of times a document was selected.

For the second set of preferences, the assessor needs to consider the *novelty* of information in the document along with relevance. This leads to exactly the triplet framework we used previously. For this second set, the assessor will see the top-ranked document from the previous set as D_T, then pick from two documents D_L, D_R conditional on that.

The sequence continues by adding more documents to the top. For the third set, the comparison involves information in *two* previously ranked documents along with a pair of documents; for the fourth, it involves information in three previously ranked documents along with a pair. This continues to the final set, in which there are only two documents to compare conditional on $n - 2$ previous top documents.

When complete, the most preferred document in the first set takes rank 1, the most preferred document in the second set takes rank 2, and so on. Observe that the first set of judgments correspond to relevance judgments and sets 2 through $n - 1$ correspond to novelty.

This method asks for a very large number of preferences: if fully judged, there would be $O(n^2)$ preferences in the first set, $O((n-1)^2)$ in the second, and so on, for a total of $O(n^3)$ judgments, which is almost certainly infeasible. We hypothesize that the first two sets of preferences (one for relevance and one for novelty) will provide a near-optimal approximation to the full set and if judgments are transitive (that is, if document A is preferred to B and B is preferred to C, then A should be preferred to C as well), the number of judgements needed can be reduced drastically. We will test both of these hypotheses below.

4.1 Experimental Design

As described above, we asked assessors to make the first two sets of judgments for each topic. The first set of judgments attempts to rank documents by relevance to the topic; intuitively, these judgments could be used to find the most relevant document in the ranked list: that which is preferred to everything else (assuming judgments are transitive) is most relevant. The second set of judgments attempts to rank the remaining documents by the degree of novelty they provide given that we know the document that is ranked at position one from the first set.

For this experiment we elected not to use MTurk. We wanted a single assessor to do all the preferences for a single topic, first so they would be able to build a familiarity with the topic as they judge, and second so we could assess their self-consistency. Thus we asked students at our institution to participate in the study. These students are mostly in computer science, mostly studying NLP and language technologies. Like the workers in the previous section, they were not given explicit instruction regarding subtopics; they were only asked to express a preference. We had 6 assessors complete preferences for at least one topic.

We designed two new web interfaces running on a local server to be used by assessors to collect preferences for both relevance and novelty, the first two sets of preferences described above. Common elements in both interfaces are the original keyword query, topic description, article texts (with query keywords highlighted), preference buttons for indicating which of the two documents the assessor prefers, a progress bar with a rough estimate of the percentage of preferences completed, and a comment field allowing them to say why they made their choice (if they wish). Elements specific to each experiment are described in more detail in the respective sections below.

For this study, we asked assessors to judge all pairs of documents in the first two sets. Topics were chosen from the data described in Section 2.4. We wanted to include all known relevant documents for the topic in the preference experiment. Since we were asking assessors for all pairs, we limited our selection to topics with a relatively small number of relevant documents. We then added a randomly-selected set of nonrelevant documents from among the top-ranked documents for the topic. We kept the total number of preferences in an experiment to less than 200.

The first two documents shown to an assessor were chosen randomly from the set of all documents to be ranked. After that, whichever document the assessor preferred remained fixed in the interface; only the other document changed. This way the assessor only had to read one new document after each judgment, just as they would in normal single-document assessing. Furthermore after the first $O(n)$ judgments we know the top-ranked document for the current set, and thus if transitivity holds it follows that we only need a linear number of preferences at each set.

4.1.1 First Level Judgments: Relevance Preferences

In the first set of judgments, the assessor was shown two documents (news articles) and a statement of an information need (a topic); the task was to pick the most preferred document using the "prefer left" or "prefer right" buttons. A screenshot of the first level judgments is shown in Figure 2

The assessor was provided with a set of instructions and guidelines prior to judging. The guidelines specified that the assessor should assume they know nothing about the topic and are trying to find documents that are topically relevant, that is, that provide some information about it. If a document contains no topical information, the assessor could judge it "not relevant"; if they do so, the system will assume they prefer every other document to that one and remove it from this set as well as all subsequent sets so it will not be seen in future comparisons. Assessors could also judge "both not relevant" to remove both from the set and see a new pair. These buttons can make the task easier by reducing the total number of preference judgments the assessors need to make.

If both documents were topically relevant, the assessor could express a preference based on whatever criteria they liked. Some suggestions included in the guidelines were: one document is more focused on the topic than the other; one document has more information about the topic than the other; one document has more detailed information than the other; one document is easier to read than the other. Assessors could exit for a break as long as they liked and return at the point where they stopped. A progress indicator let them know roughly how close they were to the end

4.1.2 Second Level Judgments: Novelty Preferences

For the second set of preferences, the assessor was shown *three* documents and a statement of an information need (a topic); the task was to pick the most useful document from two of the three to learn more about the topic given what is presented in the third.

The interface for the second level judgment was very similar to the triplet layout shown is Figure 1. One document

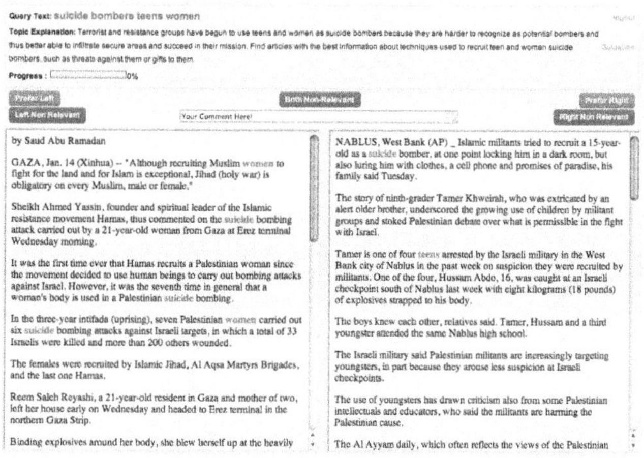

Figure 2: Screenshot of the preference collection interface for relevance preferences.

appeared at the top of the screen; this was the most preferred document as identified by the assessor after the first set of preferences. The assessors were asked to pick a document from a pair of documents (appearing below the top document) that provided the most novel information given that they know all the information in the top document.

Guidelines specified that the assessor should pretend that the top document is the entirety of what they know about the topic, and their goal is now to find the best document for learning *more* about the topic. Beyond that, they could express a preference based on whatever criteria they liked, including those listed above.

There are no nonrelevant judgment buttons in this interface. Any document that was judged nonrelevant in the first set of preferences will not be seen in this set. Anything that was relevant in the first set is assumed to still be relevant; if a relevant documents provides no new relevant information, we assume the assessor's preferences will result in that document being ranked near the bottom of this set.

4.2 Experimental Analysis

As described above, we conducted novelty preference judging with five topics from the data described in Section 2.4. On average, 16.8 documents were judged for each topic. A total of 605 pairs were judged for 4 topics by 6 assessors for experiment levels 1 and 2. We compared these judgments to the original subtopic-based judgments in the data.

Agreement on Relevance. To assess agreement on the relevance of a document, we assume that any document not explicitly judged not relevant must be relevant. We consider the original relevance judgments derived from the subtopic judgments as the ground truth and assess the performance of our assessors relative to that. Table 9 shows the confusion matrix between assessors making preference judgments and the original assessors making subtopic judgments; broad agreement on the two classes is 71%. Preference assessors identified 76% of the relevant documents that the original assessors found, and 60% of the documents judged relevant by at least one assessor were judged relevant by both. This is a high level of agreement for IR tasks; compare to the 40% agreement on relevance reported by Voorhees [?].

topic	Rank Correlation	
	Level 1	Level 2
OPEC actions	0.563	0.534
OPEC actions - Alternate	0.568	0.377
childhood obesity	0.467	0.264
childhood obesity - Alternate	0.403	0.394
suicide bombers teens women	0.320	0.200
foreign students visa restrictions	0.532	0.030

Table 8: Kendall's τ correlations between rankings from real preference judgments and rankings from simulated preference judgments (for the relevance ranking (level 1) and the novelty ranking (level 2)).

Preference Judgments	Subtopic Judgments	
	Relevant	Non-Relevant
Relevant	58	20
Non-Relevant	18	37

Table 9: Confusion matrix for relevance judgments derived from the subtopic judgments in the original Newswire collection and derived from our preference judgments (all queries aggregated).

Rank Correlation. Another way to compare preference judgments to the original subtopic judgments is by using both to construct a ranking of documents, then computing a rank correlation statistic between the two rankings. The subtopic judgments included in the *Newswire* data were obtained by assessors explicitly labeling subtopics for each relevant document. We use the subtopic information to simulate preference judgments that might have been obtained via our experiment. For the first set, we always prefer the document with the greatest number of subtopics. (Except in the case of a tie, when we prefer a random document.) For the second set, the top-ranked document from the first set becomes the "top document", and then for each pair we prefer the document that contains the greatest number of subtopics that are not in that top-ranked document. The final ranking has the most-preferred document from the first set of preferences at rank 1 followed by the ranking obtained from the second set of preferences.

Kendall's τ rank correlation for each topic for both level 1 and level 2 preference judgments is shown in Table 8. Kendall's τ ranges from -1 (lists are reversed) to 1 (lists are exactly the same), with 0 indicating a random reordering. The values we observe are positive and statistically significant (except for level 2 judgments for topic *foreign students visa restrictions*). Kendall's τ is based on pairwise swaps, and thus can be converted into agreement on pairwise preferences by adding 1 and dividing by 2. When doing this we see that agreement is again high for the relevance ranking, and also high for the novelty ranking, well over the 40% observed by Voorhees (except for topic *foreign students visa restrictions*). We believe this validates our second set of preferences, though certainly the question is not closed.

4.2.1 *Transitivity in Preference Judgments*

One issue in using our preference judgments for novelty is that the number of pairwise judgments increases quickly with number of documents. Increase in number of judgments means increase in assessor time, but if the assessors are consistent i.e. if their judgments are transitive, then we can

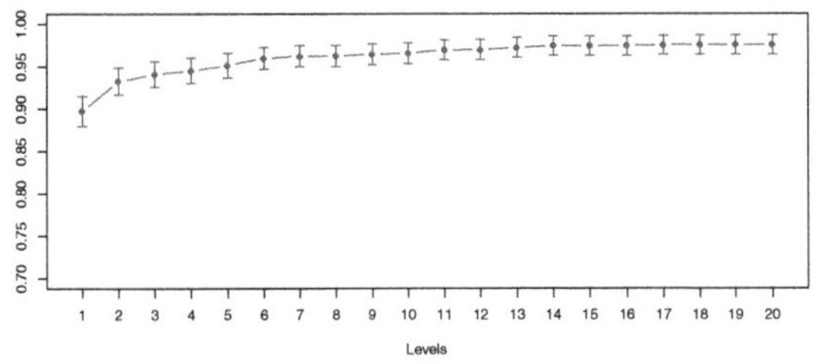

Figure 3: S-recall increases as we simulate deeper levels of preference judgments, but the first set of novelty preferences (level 2) gives an increase that nearly exceeds all subsequent levels combined.

reduce the number of preferences from $O(n^2)$ to $O(n \log n)$ at each level; furthermore, since we really only need the "best" document at each level, transitivity would allow us to reduce the number of preferences to $O(n)$ at each level.

We performed experiments to check for transitivity in the novelty task by looking at triplets of documents. A triplet of documents $\langle i, j, k \rangle$ is transitive if and only if i is preferred to j, j is preferred to k, and i is preferred to k. The ratio of number of triplets found to be transitive to the total number of triplets give a measure of transitivity in the preference judgments. On average transitivity holds for 98% across all queries with each query being transitive 96% of the time. This suggests that the assessors are highly consistent in their judgments; thus using a sorting algorithm with minimum information loss could further reduce the number of judgments required. It also suggests that whatever other features of documents (apart from topical relevance and novelty) the assessors are using in their decision process, they are consistent in their use of those features.

4.2.2 How many levels of judgments are needed?

In this section we show that the first two sets of preferences, i.e. experiments 1 and 2, are approximately sufficient to produce an optimal ranking. We again use preferences simulated from subtopic judgments: a relevance ranking is found by always preferring the document with more subtopics ("level 1"); a first approximation to a novelty ranking is found by always preferring the document with the most subtopics that are not in the top document ("level 2"); a second approximation by always preferring the document with the most subtopics that are not in the first two documents ("level 3"); and so on up to level 20.

Figure 3 shows the S-recall scores increasing as the number of preference sets increases. Clearly the increase in S-recall from level 1 to level 2 is the largest, nearly exceeding the total increase obtained from all subsequent levels put together. This suggests that the first approximation novelty ranking is likely to be sufficient; this has the benefit of reducing the amount of assessor effort needed to produce the data.

5. CONCLUSION AND FUTURE WORK

We have taken initial steps into investigating the use of preference judgments for novelty ranking tasks. We have proposed a novel framework for obtaining preference judgments for the novelty task and explicated the pros and cons of using preference judgments. Preliminary results for comparing explicit subtopic labels with preference judgments suggest that preference judgments can give similar information about both relevance and novelty as the subtopic judgments that are typically used.

Based on this, we proposed a preference-based approach to obtaining a full ranking for relevance, novelty, and all other factors that contribute to user preferences. We showed that rankings obtained in this way correlate well to rankings based on subtopic judgments, and since assessors are highly self-consistent, probably capturing a great deal of other information as well. Of course, if subtopic judgments were replaced with preferences, we would need a new set of evaluation measures. This clearly is a direction for future work.

6. REFERENCES

[1] Amazon mechanical turk. http://www.mturk.com.

[2] R. Agrawal, S. Gollapudi, A. Halverson, and S. Ieong. Diversifying search results. In *Proc. of WSDM*, pages 5–14, 2009.

[3] J. Allan, B. Carterette, and J. Lewis. When will information retrieval be "good enough"? In *Proc. of SIGIR*, pages 433–440, 2005.

[4] O. Alonso, D. Rose, and B. Stewart. Crowdsourcing for relevance evaluation. In *ACM SIGIR Forum*, number 2, pages 9–15, Nov. 2008.

[5] J. Arguello, F. Diaz, J. Callan, and B. Carterette. A methodology for evaluating aggregated search results. In *Proceedings of the 33rd European Conference on Information Retrieval (ECIR*, 2011.

[6] B. Carterette, P. N. Bennett, D. M. Chickering, and S. T. Dumais. Here or there: preference judgments for relevance. In *Proceedings of the IR research, 30th European conference on Advances in information retrieval*, Proceedings of ECIR, pages 16–27, 2008.

[7] P. Chandar and B. Carterette. What qualities do users prefer in diversity ranking. In *Proceedings of the 2nd Workshop on Diversity in Document Retrieval*, 2012.

[8] O. Chapelle, S. Ji, C. Liao, E. Velipasaoglu, L. Lai, and S.-L. Wu. Intent-based diversification of web search results. *Information Retrieval*, pages 1–21, 2011.

[9] O. Chapelle, D. Metlzer, Y. Zhang, and P. Grinspan. Expected reciprocal rank for graded relevance. In *Proceeding of CIKM*, pages 621–630, 2009.

[10] C. L. Clarke, M. Kolla, G. V. Cormack, O. Vechtomova, A. Ashkan, S. Büttcher, and I. MacKinnon. Novelty and diversity in information retrieval evaluation. In *Proceedings of SIGIR*, pages 659–666, 2008.

[11] T. Moore and R. Clayton. Evaluating the wisdom of crowds in assessing phishing websites. In *In 12th International Financial Cryptography and Data Security Conference*, pages 16–30. Springer-Verlag, 2008.

[12] F. Radlinski, P. N. Bennett, B. Carterette, and T. Joachims. Redundancy, diversity and interdependent document relevance. *SIGIR Forum*, 43:46–52, Dec 2009.

[13] M. E. Rorvig. The simple scalability of documents. *JASIS*, 41(8):590–598, 1990.

[14] T. Sakai, N. Craswell, R. Song, S. Robertson, Z. Dou, and C. Y. Lin. Simple evaluation metrics for diversified search results. In *Proc. EVIA*, 2010.

[15] M. Sanderson, M. L. Paramita, P. Clough, and E. Kanoulas. Do user preferences and evaluation measures line up? In *Proceedings of SIGIR*, pages 555–562, 2010.

[16] E. Voorhees. Variations in relevance judgments and the measurement of retrieval effectiveness. In *Proceedings of SIGIR*, pages 315–323, 1998.

[17] C. X. Zhai, W. W. Cohen, and J. Lafferty. Beyond independent relevance: methods and evaluation metrics for subtopic retrieval. In *Proceedings of SIGIR*, pages 10–17, 2003.

Quality through Flow and Immersion: Gamifying Crowdsourced Relevance Assessments

Carsten Eickhoff
Delft University of Technology
Netherlands
c.eickhoff@tudelft.nl

Christopher G. Harris
Padmini Srinivasan
The University of Iowa
USA
{christopher-harris,padmini-srinivasan}@uiowa.edu

Arjen P. de Vries
Centrum Wiskunde & Informatica
Netherlands
arjen@acm.org

ABSTRACT

Crowdsourcing is a market of steadily-growing importance upon which both academia and industry increasingly rely. However, this market appears to be inherently infested with a significant share of malicious workers who try to maximise their profits through cheating or sloppiness. This serves to undermine the very merits crowdsourcing has come to represent. Based on previous experience as well as psychological insights, we propose the use of a game in order to attract and retain a larger share of reliable workers to frequently-requested crowdsourcing tasks such as relevance assessments and clustering.

In a large-scale comparative study conducted using recent TREC data, we investigate the performance of traditional HIT designs and a game-based alternative that is able to achieve high quality at significantly lower pay rates, facing fewer malicious submissions.

Categories and Subject Descriptors

H.1.2 [**Models and Principles**]: User / Machine Systems —*Human Factors*; H.1.2 [**Models and Principles**]: User / Machine Systems —*Human information processing*; H.5.2 [**Information Interfaces & Presentation**]: User Interfaces

Keywords

Crowdsourcing, Gamification, Serious Games, Relevance Assessments, Clustering

1. INTRODUCTION

In the course of the past 5 years, crowdsourcing has advanced from a niche phenomenon to becoming an accepted solution to a wide range of data acquisition challenges [10]. It has been used in the training and test phases of a great number of scientific projects and is firmly integrated into numerous evaluation and data acquisition schemes in academia and industry. One problem, however, seems to be inherent to the field; a significant share of the annotations created on crowdsourcing platforms are fraudsters' attempts to cheat the HIT (Human Intelligence Task) provider into paying them without having properly worked on the HIT. As a consequence, almost every scientific publication that employs crowdsourcing for data acquisition details the authors' tailor-made defense scheme against cheaters and a rising number of publications is exclusively dedicated to the task of detecting these individuals. The range of commonly-observed measures taken includes asking redundant questions to rely on an aggregate of several workers rather than the decisions of just one individual [33], using held-out data to compare with, asking plausibility questions and many more sophisticated methods [16, 13].

In many time-insensitive applications, HIT providers restrict the crowd of workers to certain nationalities (a typical example would be US workers only) who they trust will provide higher quality results. Although the approach is widely accepted and has been shown to significantly reduce the number of spam submissions, we believe that this uptake may be treating symptoms rather than the actual underlying cause. Rather than attributing the confirmed performance differences between the inhabitants of different countries to their nationality, we hypothesize that there are 2 major types of workers with fundamentally different motivations for offering their workforce on a crowdsourcing platform: (1) *Money-driven* workers are motivated by the financial reward that the HIT promises. (2) *Entertainment-driven* workers primarily seek diversion but readily accept the financial incentives as an additional stimulus. We are convinced that the affiliation (or proximity) to one of those fundamental worker types can have a significant impact on the amount of attention paid to the task at hand, and, subsequently, on the resulting annotation quality. We realize, that money-driven workers are by no means bound to deliver bad quality; however, they appear to be frequently tempted into sloppiness by the prospect of a higher time efficiency and therefore stronger satisfaction of their main motivation. Entertainment-driven workers, on the other hand, appear to work a HIT more faithfully and thoroughly and regard the financial reward as a welcome bonus. They typically do not indulge in simple, repetitive or boring tasks. We propose to more strongly focus on entertainment-driven workers by phrasing crowdsourcing problems in an entertaining and engaging way: As games. Csikszentmihalyi's theory of *flow* [12], a state of maximal immersion and concentration at which optimal intrinsic motivation, enjoyment and high task performance are achieved, further encouraged our design.

We intend to increase the degree of satisfaction entertainment-driven workers experience. This can lead to (a) higher result quality, (b) quicker batch processing rates, (c) lower overall cheater rates, (d) better cost efficiency. An additional incentive for delivering high-quality results in a game scenario would be the element of competition and social standing among players. Taking into account recent behavioural analyses of online communities and games [24], entertainment seekers can be expected to put considerable dedication into producing high-quality results to earn more points in a game to progress into higher difficulty levels or a rank on the high score leaderboard.

The novel contributions of this work are 5-fold: (1) We describe a game-based approach to collecting document relevance assessments in both theory and design. (2) Based on NIST-created TREC data, we conduct a large-scale comparative evaluation to determine the merit of the proposed method over state-of-the-art relevance assessment crowdsourcing paradigms. (3) Venturing beyond "hard" quality indicators such as precision, cost-efficiency or annotation speed, we discuss a wide range of socio-economical factors such as demographics and alternative incentives to enhance a fundamental understanding of worker motivation. (4) In a separate study, we demonstrate the generalizability of the proposed game to other tasks on the example of noisy image classification. (5) We create a corpus of relevance assessments of considerable size and quality that we disclose to the research community.

The remainder of this work is structured as follows: Section 2 describes the state of the art of crowdsourcing for document relevance assessments as well as in the domain of games with a purpose (GWAP). Section 3 introduces the theoretical considerations and design decisions that guide our annotation game. In Section 4, we describe the setup as well as the results of a large scale study conducted on several commercial crowdsourcing platforms in order to determine the usefulness of the proposed method. Section 5 demonstrates the generalizability of our method on the task of image classification. Section 6 is dedicated to a discussion of the key insights gained in the course of this work, before concluding in Section 7.

2. RELATED WORK

This section introduces related approaches from three different research areas at the intersection of which this work is situated, namely, relevance assessment, crowdsourcing and games with a purpose.

Document relevance assessments have been playing a central role in IR system design and evaluation since the early Cranfield experiments [42]. Explicit judgements of (the degree of) relevance between a document and a given topic are used as a proxy of user satisfaction. Based on such test collections, the results of retrieval systems can be compared without undergoing numerous iterations of user studies. As a leading actor in IR evaluation and benchmarking, NIST's Text Retrieval Conference (TREC) [43] looks back on two decades of assessing document relevance. In order to be suitable for the evaluation of state-of-the-art Web-scale systems, the requirements in terms of size, topical coverage, diversity and recency that the research community imposes on evaluation corpora have been steadily rising. As a consequence, the creation and curation of such resources becomes more expensive. To further ensure the scalability of test collection-based system evaluation, considerable effort has been invested into designing robust performance measures [6], selecting the right documents for evaluation [8] and inferring judgements from user interaction logs [19].

Crowdsourcing represents an alternative means of collecting and annotating large-scale data sets. By employing a large group of individuals, paid at transaction level, tasks of considerable size can be completed in a timely and affordable manner. Document relevance assessments have been shown to be a task that can reliably be fulfilled by crowd workers [4, 22, 15]. One of the fundamental challenges in crowdsourcing is overcoming malicious and sloppy submissions. Many effective schemes exist, ranging from aggregating the results of independent workers to the use of honey pot questions [17, 18, 14]. Marshall et al. discuss the importance of engaging HIT design on result quality [28]. Recently, several scientific workshops have been dedicated to pursuing how to use crowdsourcing effectively and efficiently [10, 26]. Most notably, TREC 2011 for the first time offered a dedicated crowdsourcing track [25] addressing the crowdsourced collection of document relevance assessments. In this work, we adopt the evaluation scheme and data set used there.

The majority of crowdsourced tasks are plain surveys, relevance assessments or data collection assignments that require human intelligence but very little creativity or skill. An advance into bringing together the communities of online games and crowdsourcing is being made by the platform Gambit [1], that lets players complete HITs in exchange for virtual currency in their online gaming world. This combination, however, does not change the nature of the actual HIT carried out, beyond the fact that the plain HIT form is embedded into a game environment. Instead, we propose using an actual game to leverage worker judgements.

A number of techniques have been designed to make participation in human computation efforts as engaging as possible. Perhaps the most effective technique among these is a genre of serious games called games with a purpose [38] which have been developed with the focus of efficient and entertaining transformation of research data collection into game mechanics. By equating player success in the game with providing quality inputs, the idea is to extract higher-quality data than is currently done with dull repetitive tasks such as surveys. More than half a billion people worldwide play online games for at least an hour a day – and 183 million in the US alone [29]. The average American, for example, has played 10,000 hours of video games by the age of 21 [31]. Channeling some of this human effort to gather data has shown considerable promise. People engage in these GWAPs for the enjoyment factor, not with the objective of performing work. Successful GWAPs include the ESP Game [37], which solicits meaningful, accurate image labels as the underlying objective; Peekaboom [41], which locates objects within images; Phetch [39], which annotates images with descriptive paragraphs; and Verbosity [40], which collects common-sense facts in order to train reasoning algorithms. The typical research objective of these GWAPs is to have two randomly-selected players individually assign mutually-agreed document labels, with the game mechanics designed to reward uncommon labels. In contrast, the game mechanics of our proposed game is to encourage and reward consensus labeling. The Pagehunt game presented players with a web page and asked them to formulate a query that would retrieve the given page in the top ranks on a popular search engine to investigate the findability of web pages [27]. While task-specific games have been shown to be engaging means of harnessing the players' intelligence for a certain research goal, there has not been a formal investigation of the merits of game-based HITs over conventional ones. Additionally, current GWAPs are typically highly tailored towards a certain (often niche) problem at hand and do not lend themselves for application across domains. We will demonstrate the generalizability of our approach in Section 5.

3. METHODOLOGY

In this section, we will introduce the annotation game as well as the necessary pre- and post-processing steps in order to acquire standard topic/document relevance assessments from it. Careful attention will be paid to highlighting motivational aspects that aim to replace HIT payment by entertainment as a central incentive.

3.1 Game Design

The central concept of our proposed game is to require players to relate items to each other. In order to preserve its general applicability, we tried to make as few as possible assumptions about the nature of those items. The game shows $n = 4$ concept buckets $b_1 \ldots b_n$ at the bottom of the screen. From the top, a single item i slides to the bottom, and has to be directed into one of the buckets by the player. Doing so expresses a relationship between i and b_j. Additional information about i can be found in an info box in the top left corner.

In the case of document relevance assessments, the concept buckets b_j display topic titles, item i is a keyword from a document and the info box displays the context in which the keyword appears in that document. Figure 3.1 shows a screenshot of our game. A live version can be found online[1]. For each assigned relation between i and b_j the player is awarded a number of points. The score in points is based on the degree of agreement with other players. In addition to this scheme, the game shows a tree that grows a leaf for every judgement that consents with the majority decision. A full tree awards bonus points. In this way, we reward continuous attention to the game and the task. As a final element, the game is divided into rounds of 10 judgements each. After each round, the speed with which item i moves is increased, making the task more challenging to create additional motivation for paying close attention.

After up to 5 rounds (the player can leave the game at any point in time before that) the game ends and the achieved points as well as the player's position in our highscore leaderboard are shown. Together with the log-in concept, this aims to encourage replaying as people want to advance into the higher ranks of the leaderboard.

3.2 Data Pre-processing

Previously, we described the mechanics and underlying assumptions of the game. Now, we will detail how to set

[1] `http://www.geann.org`

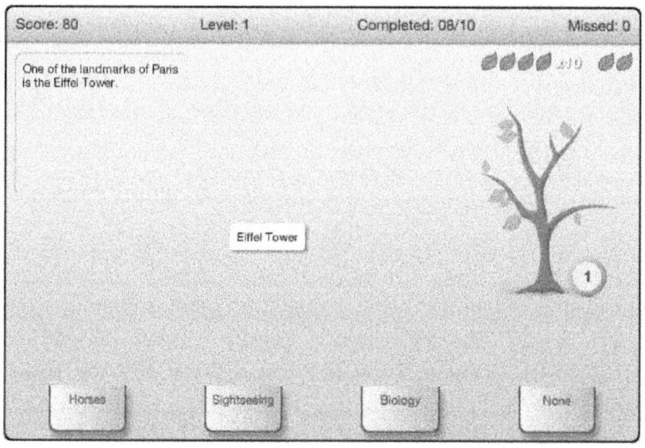

Figure 1: A screenshot of the annotation game in which the keyword "Eiffel Tower" has to be related to one of a number of concepts.

it up with TREC data for relevance assessments. All relevant game information is stored in a relational database from which items, concepts and additional information are drawn and into which user judgements are stored, subsequently. We assume a list of pairs p consisting of a query q and a document d for which we will collect user judgements. For every d, we extract the textual web page content and break it up into a set S of sentences $s_{d,1} \ldots s_{d,|S|}$ using the LingPipe library [5]. In the following step, S is reordered by a ranking function $r(s)$, based on decreasing mean inverse document frequency (idf) of sentences s with a number of $|s|$ constituent terms t_n. $|C|$ denotes the number of documents in the collection and $df(t)$ is the number of documents containing term t. In this way, we promote the most salient and informative sentences in the document. The underlying $idf(t)$ statistics for this step are computed collection-wide.

$$idf(t) = \frac{|C|}{df(t) + 1}$$

$$r(s) = \frac{1}{|s|} \sum_{n=1}^{|s|} idf(t_n)$$

Finally, the k highest-ranking sentences (those with the highest scores of $r(s)$) are selected and used in the game. The concrete setting of k depends on the size of document d and was set to $0.1|S|$ in order to account for different document lengths. Higher settings of k result in a higher judgement density per document. For each of the selected sentences, we extract the single highest-idf term t_n as sliding keyword i, and the full sentence as context information to be shown in the top left corner. The concept buckets b include the original query q, two randomly selected topics from the database, as well as an "other" option to account for none of the offered concepts being related to i. The buckets are shown in random order to prevent selection biases.

3.3 Assessment Aggregation

As a final step, we have to transform the players' conceptual associations into document-wide relevance judgements. Each player annotation a can be understood as a quintuple $a = (p_a, i_a, s_a, c_a, r_a)$ in which player p associated item i occurring in context sentence s with concept c in round r of the game.

In a first step, we map all associations a to relevance votes. We interpret associations of any $s \in d$ to the concept of the original query q as a player's binary relevance vote $v_{p,s,q,r}$ between sentence s and query q as described in Equation 1.

$$v_{p,s,q,r} = \begin{cases} 1 & \text{if } c_a = q \\ 0 & \text{else} \end{cases} \quad (1)$$

In order to account for wrong associations and diversity in personal preference, we aggregate a global sentence-level vote $v_{s,q}$ across all players p. As the game speeds up in higher rounds, players have less time available for making the relevance decision. In a preliminary inspection of annotation results, we noticed significant drops of accuracy across subsequent rounds of the game. In order to account for this effect, we introduce a weighting parameter λ_r representing the confidence that we put into judgements originating from round r of the game being correct. For simplicity's sake, we reduce the confidence by 0.05 per round after the first one. Alternative strategies could for example include learning this parameter as a maximum likelihood estimate across previous observations. Equation 2 details the aggregation to a global sentence-level vote $v_{s,q}$ across the set of players $P_{s,q}$ that had encountered the combination of sentence s and query q.

$$v_{s,q} = \frac{1}{|P_{s,q}|} \sum_{p_i \in P_{s,q}} \lambda_r v_{p_i,s,q,r} \quad (2)$$

Finally, we aggregate across all sentence-level votes $v_{s,q}$ of a document d in order to get one global page-wide judgement that is comparable to well-known (e.g., NIST-created) annotations. Equation 3 outlines this process formally. It should be noted, that omission of this third step may, given the application at hand, be beneficial for the evaluation of tasks such as passage-level retrieval or automatic document summarization.

$$v_{d,q} = \frac{1}{|D|} \sum_{s_i \in D} v_{s_i,q} \quad (3)$$

4. EXPERIMENTATION

4.1 Research Directions

In this section, we describe the setup and results of a large-scale experiment conducted on several major commercial crowdsourcing platforms. Our performance comparison of traditional and game-based HITs will be guided by the following 7 fundamental directions:

Quality. How does the result quality of game-based crowdsourcing HITs relate to that of traditional ones given the same underlying crowd of workers and comparable financial means? We evaluate result quality in terms of agreement with gold standard NIST labels as well as with consensus labels across all participanting groups of the TREC 2011 Crowdsourcing Track [25].

Efficiency. Are game-based HITs more popular, resulting in quicker HIT uptake and completion than conventional ones? We investigate time to completion (for a given batch size) as well as the duration per document and per single vote.

Incentives. How much is fun worth? We investigate the influence of incentives such as fun & social prestige vs. monetary rewards on the uptake rate of HITs. Do users prefer entertaining HIT versions even though they pay less?

Consistency. Does our game encourage a stronger task focus, resulting in better within-annotator consistency? We investigate this dimension using a fixed set of workers (of varying reliability and quality levels) who are exposed to re-occurring HIT questions in a game-based or conventional setting to measure their self-agreement as an estimate of consistency and alertness.

Robustness. Does the share of (alleged) cheaters attracted to our game / attracted to conventional HITs differ? Independent of the overall result quality, the observed cheater rate is a surrogate of how reliable results are and how much sophistication a HIT should dedicate to fraud protection.

Population. Does the use of games lead to a different crowd composition? Offering game-based and conventional HITs, we collect surveys to investigate whether game-based HITs attract different kinds of workers.

Location. State-of-the-art crowdsourcing approaches frequently filter their crowd by nationality in order to improve result quality. We investigate whether there are indeed geographical preferences for game-based or conventional HITs and whether those can be related to the crowd composition in those areas.

4.2 Experimental Setup

In this comparative study, we replicate the setting that was proposed in the TREC 2011 Crowdsourcing Track assessment task [25]. A total of 3200 topic/document pairs (30 distinct topics, 3195 unique documents) were judged for relevance. The documents are part of the ClueWeb09 collection [7], and the topics originate from the TREC 2009 Million Query Track [9]. A comprehensive list of all topics and document identifiers are available from the TREC 2011 Crowdsourcing Track home page[2]. We contrasted the performance and characteristics of our proposed gamified HIT (Section 4.2.2) with those of a traditional one (Section 4.2.1). To attribute for assessment mistakes and personal preference, we collected judgements from at least 3 individual workers per topic/document pair in both settings. All HITs were run in temporal isolation (No more than 1 batch at any given time) to limit mutual effects between the tasks. In the following, we describe the respective task designs in detail.

4.2.1 Traditional HIT

As a performance baseline, we designed a state-of-the-art relevance assessment HIT. Its design follows accepted insights from previous work as detailed in the following. In order to limit the number of context changes, the document is shown in-line on the platform's HIT form as proposed by Kazai [20]. In this way, no distracting opening and closing of windows or browser tabs is required. To further enhance the task, we highlight every occurrence of query terms in

[2]`https://sites.google.com/site/treccrowd2011/`

the document. This technique was reported to be beneficial by several previous approaches, e.g., [36]. Finally, in order to deal with malicious submissions, we measure agreement with NIST gold standard pairs of known relevance. Workers who disagree on more than 50% of the gold labels are rejected from the judgement pool. In the HIT instructions, we briefly introduce the available relevance categories. The definition of relevance was introduced according to the TREC guidelines [25]. The HIT form contains 2 questions:

```
1. Please indicate the relevance of the shown
document towards the topic "<T>".

2. Do you have any remarks, ideas or general
feedback regarding this HIT that you would like to
share?
```

For each HIT, the place holder <T> is replaced by the current topic. Offering the possibility for worker feedback has been frequently reported to improve task quality and track down bugs or design flaws quickly [3]. The HIT was offered at a pay rate of 2 US cents per topic/document pair assessments; a reward level previously found adequate given the task [2].

4.2.2 *Gamified HIT*

The central piece of our proposed gamified version of the relevance assessment HIT is the annotation game that was described in Section 3.1. Instead of having the workers complete tasks locally on the crowdsourcing platform, the technical requirements of our game demanded running it off-site on a dedicated server. In order to verify task completion, workers are provided with a confirmation token after playing one round of the game (10 term associations). Back on the crowdsourcing platform, they enter this token in order to get paid. As a consequence, the actual HIT contained only a brief instruction to the off-site process and two input fields:

```
1. Please enter the confirmation token you
obtained after completing one round of the game.

2. Do you have any remarks, ideas or general
feedback regarding this HIT that you would like to
share?
```

Again, we solicit worker feedback. The HIT was offered at a pay rate of 2 US cents for one round (10 term associations) of the game.

4.3 Evaluation

All experiments described in this section were conducted between December 2011 and February 2012 on two crowdsourcing platforms: Amazon Mechanical Turk [35] as well as all available channels on CrowdFlower [11]. Initial evaluation did not show any significant differences in the work delivered by workers from different platforms. We will therefore not split the pool of submissions along this dimension. In total, 795 unique workers created 105,221 relevance judgements via our game. Additionally, 3000 traditional relevance judgements were collected for comparison. In total, we invested $90 to collect a volume of 108,221 annotations across the two compared experimental conditions. Together with the TREC 2011 Crowdsourcing Track annotations and the original NIST labels, this makes the T11Crowd subset of ClueWeb09 one of the most densely-annotated Web resources known to us. To enable reproducibility of our insights and to further general crowdsourcing research, the complete set of our judgements and the game itself are available to the research community[3].

Table 1: Annotation quality.

HIT type	Accuracy (NIST)	Accuracy (TREC-CS)
Conventional	0.73	0.74
TREC-CS	0.79	1.0
Game (plain)	0.65	0.75
Game (sent)	0.77	0.87
Game (doc)	**0.82**	**0.93**

Table 2: Annotation quality as a function of the game round in which judgements were issued.

Round	Accuracy (NIST)	Accuracy (TREC-CS)
1	0.72	0.81
2	0.67	0.77
3	0.62	0.73
4	0.60	0.69
5	0.54	0.65

4.3.1 *Quality*

As a starting point to our performance evaluation of game-based crowdsourcing of relevance assessments, we investigate the quality of the collected labels. Table 1 details the performance of our game in terms of overlap with gold standard NIST labels as well as the global consensus across all TREC 2011 Crowdsourcing Track participants (TREC-CS). We can note that already the conventional HIT delivers high result quality. Ratios between 65% and 75% are often considered good rules-of-thumb for the expected agreement of faithful human judges given a relevance assessment task [44]. TREC consensus labels show a high overlap with NIST annotator decisions. The third row in Table 1 shows the performance of direct unaggregated sentence-level votes from our game as described in Equation 1. While agreement with the TREC crowd is already substantial, the overlap with high-quality NIST labels lags behind. As we aggregate across multiple workers' annotations of the same sentence (Equation 2) and, finally, across all sentences extracted from the same document (Equation 3), the performance rises significantly, outperforming all compared methods. We used a Wilcoxon signed rank test at $\alpha < 0.05$-level to test significance of results.

In order to confirm the usefulness of our assumption from Section 3 concerning the decline of label quality as the game speeds up and the player has less time to make decisions, we evaluated annotation performance of raw labels according to the round in which they were issued. Table 2 shows a near-linear decline in agreement of plain game scores with TREC consensus as the game progresses. Agreement with NIST scores also consistently shrinks from round to round.

Finally, previous work on prediction in crowdsourcing systems demonstrates that reliability of the average predicted scores by the crowd improves as the size of the crowd in-

[3]`http://sourceforge.net/projects/geann/`

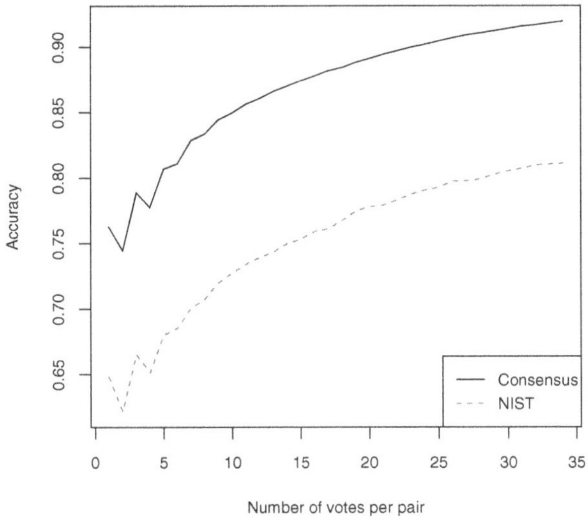

Figure 2: Quality as a function of votes per pair.

creases [34, 30]. The benefit of our game-based HIT is its popularity that allows us to collect more judgements per topic / document pair than traditional HITs. On average, each topic / document pair in the collection received 32 unique user judgements at the sentence level (some of which may originate from the same user as she or he rates different passages of the same document). Figure 2 shows how annotation quality develops as we add more judgements per pair. After initial fluctuation, as single votes have great influence on the overall decision, accuracy consistently improves as we add more votes per pair. The effect levels out as we approach the upper performance limit.

4.3.2 *Efficiency*

The second official performance indicator besides label quality in the TREC 2011 Crowdsourcing Track was the time necessary to collect the required judgements. For many use cases in human computation, low latencies are essential. The particular nature of the game imposed a time limit on players within which they had to make their decisions. As we detailed in the previous section, aggregation across users, weighting votes according to the difficulty level under which they were created, ensured competitive result quality. At the same time, however, a sequence of, individually quick, concept matchings enables workers to be more efficient and motivated than in conventional settings. Table 3 shows how conventional HITs take slightly longer to judge documents even when aggregating the duration of all passage-level votes in the game-based setting. Taking into account the significantly higher uptake rate (number of judgements issued per hour) of the game HITs, this serves for a considerably more efficient batch processing.
Especially in conjunction with the previous section's findings of high degrees of redundancy serving for better result quality, high uptake rates become crucial as they allow for timely, yet accurate decisions.

Table 3: Annotation efficiency.

	Conventional	Game-based
t per vote	40.1 sec	5.2 sec
t per doc	40.1 sec	27.8 sec
Uptake (votes per hour)	95.2	352.1

Table 4: Game-based assessment behaviour.

Criterion	Observation
Games with 2+ rounds	70.9%
Rounds per game	3.5
Players with 2+ games	79.5%
Games per player	4.36
Time between games	7.4 hrs

4.3.3 *Incentives*

The third and final evaluation criterion employed for TREC 2011 was the cost involved in the collection of relevance labels. With our game-based approach, we aim to, at least partially, replace the financial reward of the HIT with entertainment as an alternative motivation. In this section, we will investigate to which degree this change in incentives can be observed in worker behaviour.
In order to be paid via the crowdsourcing platform, workers had to complete at least one round (10 concept matchings) of our game. At that point the required confirmation token was displayed to them and they could return to the platform in order to claim their payment. However, the game offered an additional 4 levels to be played. From a purely monetary-driven perspective there would be no reason for continuing to play at that point. As we can see in Table 4, however, over 70% of games are played beyond the first round. This essentially results in crowdsourcing workers creating judgements free of charge because they enjoy the game experience. Additionally, we can observe players to return to the game after a number of hours to play again and improve their score and their resulting position on the leader board. Subsequent visits often happen directly to the game page, without being redirected from (and paid through) the crowdsourcing platform. Almost 80% of all players (633 out of 795) return after their first round played, with an average time gap of 7.4 hours between games. For regular HITs, we observed a return rate of only 23%.

When inspecting the concrete distribution of judgements across workers, as shown in Figure 3, we see this trend continued. Crowdsourcing tasks often tend to exhibit Power-law distributions of work over unique workers with some strong performers and a long tail of casual workers who only submit single HITs. Here, however, we notice a strong center group of medium-frequency players. We hypothesise that replacing the workers' extrinsic motivation ("*do the HIT to earn money*") by an intrinsic one ("*let's have some fun*"), causes these tendencies.

This has a number of noteworthy consequences: (1) We can attract workers to a HIT at a comparatively low pay rate. Even without playing beyond the first round, 2 US cents for 10 concept associations would roughly result in a prospective hourly pay of $1.20. (2) Furthermore, as most workers continue playing, additional annotations are created with no expectation of financial compensation. (3) Drawn by the competitive aspect of the game, workers re-

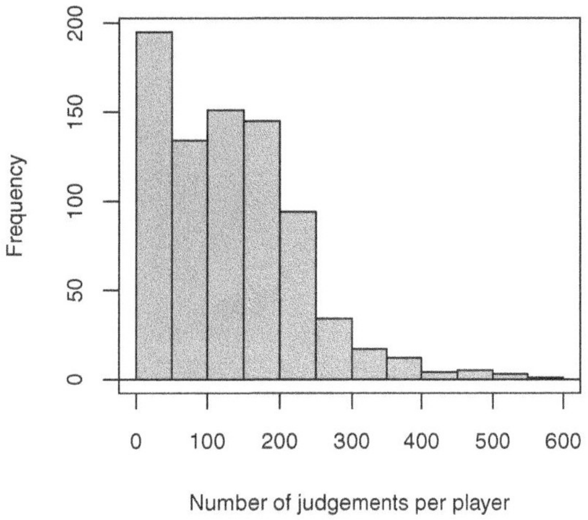

Figure 3: Distribution of judgements across users.

Table 5: Effective annotation cost.

	Conventional	Game-based
Cost per doc	$0.06	$0.0004
Whole corpus	$192	$1.28
Effective hourly rate	$1.80	$0.18

turn and create even more unpaid assessments. As a consequence, the overall amount of money invested into the game-based collection of more than 100,000 sentence-level relevance judgements was $27.74. This includes all administrative fees charged by the crowdsourcing platforms. In comparison, the participants to the TREC 2011 Crowdsourcing Track reported overall costs of $50 - $100 for the collection of significantly fewer labels.

Table 5 shows a final cost comparison of the conventional and game-based versions of the inspected relevance assessment HIT. While all indicators of cost efficiency from a worker's perspective clearly speak for choosing the conventional, better-paying HIT, the previously described figures of HIT uptake rates as well as the high number of alternative HITs available at all times on large-scale platforms such as AMT, indicate, that we reach workers who consider the entertainment potential of a HIT before choosing it. If we consider all judgements made in rounds after the first one and all judgements from revisits that were not paid for on the crowdsourcing platform as free-of-charge judgements, we arrive at a share of 83.7% of all labels having been created free of charge. Additionally, a number of players (39 out of 795) accessed the game without being prompted (and paid) by a crowdsourcing platform. These players were recruited from the authors' professional and private networks or word of mouth of other players. We could not find significant differences in the judgement quality or volume created by this group of players. The invested amount of money can be seen as advertisement costs rather than actual payments. In a traditional setting, collecting the same annotation density would have cost $2104.

4.3.4 *Consistency*

Following Csikszentmihalyi's theory of Flow [12], a state of deep immersion is a good foundation for high performance independent of the concrete task at hand. With our game-based HIT, we aimed to exploit this observation in order to create greater task focus than workers typically achieve on conventional HIT types. The previously shown result quality figures support this hypothesis. As an additional performance indicator, we will measure the workers judgement consistency. Faced with the same passage of text and choice of concepts multiple times, a situation-aware worker is expected to display a high degree of intra-annotator agreement. In the course of our judgement collection, we showed identical assignments to workers 837 times and observed an intra-annotator agreement of 69.8%. We set up a dedicated crowdsourcing experiment in which a portion of the offered topic / document pairs re-occurred. The HIT was set up following the scheme described in Section 4.2.1. Across 500 redundantly issued assignments, we observed an intra-annotator agreement of only 61.3%, a significantly lower ratio (determined using Wilcoxon signed rank test at $\alpha < 0.05$) than in the game-based setting. While the game setting resulted in higher consistency than usual crowdsourcing schemes, we could not match the consistency Scholer et al. [32] report for professional assessors as for example employed by NIST.

4.3.5 *Robustness*

Cheating, spamming and low-quality submissions are well-known and frequently-observed incidents on commercial crowdsourcing platforms. Previously, we demonstrated convincing result quality of gamified document relevance assessments when labels are aggregated across a sufficiently large number of workers. Since our approach appeals more to the entertainment-seeking rather than money-driven workers, we did not include a dedicated cheat detection scheme as would often be considered necessary in state-of-the-art HITs. However, we realise that the observed cheat rate in an assignment can serve as a surrogate for the confidence and reliability of the overall results. To this end, we measure the observed proportion of cheat submissions to our game as well as to the conventional HIT version. Eickhoff et al. [14] suggest categorizing workers who disagree with the majority decision in more than half of all cases as cheaters. In order to deliver a conservative estimate of the rate of cheat submissions, we tighten their definition and consider a worker as cheating if at least 67% of their submissions disagree with the majority vote. This scheme was applied to both, the conventional HIT as well as the gamified version. In the game-based case, we additionally flagged all submissions as cheat that tried using forged confirmation tokens. Overall, this resulted in a share of 13.5% of the conventional HIT's judgements being considered cheated. For the game-based version, the percentage was a significantly lower 2.3%. This finding conforms with [13], who observed innovative, creative tasks being less likely to be cheated on.

4.3.6 *Population*

In this work, we did not make use of any form of *a priori* filtering the pool of workers eligible to access our HITs. We hypothesise, however, that HIT type, financial reward and task phrasing influence the underlying crowd that decides to work on a given assignment. To better understand the com-

Table 6: Composition of the crowd

	Conventional	Game-based
Preference	39%	37%
Female	47%	35%
Age	34	27
Univ. degree	46%	62%
Income	$20k	$45k
English Native Speaker	24%	25%

position of the group of commercial crowdsourcing workers that are interested in games, we accompanied parts of our HITs by surveys in which we asked for high-level participant demographics and their preference for either the conventional or the game-based HIT. Table 6 shows an overview of several salient outcomes of the survey. The split in decisions was roughly equal, with 24% of workers not indicating clear preferences. The entertainment-seeking worker is on average several years younger, more likely to hold a university degree and will typically earn a higher salary. Finally, women were found to be significantly less interested in games than their male co-workers. This conforms with general observations about gender differences made for example by [23]. A worker's language background did not influence his or her likelihood to prefer games.

4.3.7 Location

Many commercial crowdsourcing schemes report performance gains when filtering the crowd by nationality. Due to different expected levels of education, language skills or cultural properties, such steps may influence result quality. As a final dimension of our investigation of games for use on commercial crowdsourcing platforms, we will inspect whether worker origin has an influence on result quality. From our survey, we found Indian workers, with a share of 60%, to be the dominant group in both settings. US workers were consistently the runners-up with a proportion of approximately 25%. There was no significant difference in the likelihood to prefer games over conventional HITs between countries.

Finally, when inspecting result quality from our game, again, no difference in performance or likelihood to cheat could be found. This suggests that filtering workers by nationality may not be ideal. In fact, the underlying worker motivation and HIT type preference may be assumed to have a far greater impact on observed uptake, performance and trustworthiness.

5. IMAGE CLASSIFICATION

In the previous sections, we described and evaluated the performance of the proposed crowdsourcing-powered annotation game for the task of TREC-style document relevance assessments. To demonstrate the generalization potential of the described concept-matching method, we applied the same game in an image classification pilot.

In the course of the Fish4Knowledge project (`http://www.fish4knowledge.eu/`), several underwater cameras have been placed in selected locations in south-east Asian coral reefs. The continuous recordings are supposed to further knowledge about behaviour, frequency and migration patterns of the resident tropical fish species. A key step to coping with the large amounts of image data produced by these cameras is a reliable automatic species classification. In order to train such systems, numerous training examples are required. While the project employs a team of marine biologists, their greater expertise is costly. Using our annotation game, we crowdsource the task of classifying the encountered species. Instead of relating keywords to TREC topics, the objective is now to match a shot of the underwater camera (often low quality) to high-quality examples of resident fish species. By initializing the underlying database with images rather than textual items, no changes to the actual game were necessary. Figure 4 shows a screenshot of this alternative game setting.

Figure 4: GeAnn applied for image grouping.

Our feasibility study encompassed 190 unique underwater camera shots for which known gold standard labels created by the marine biologists existed. Each biologist had classified all images, allowing us to contrast crowd agreement with expert agreement. The HIT was offered in January and February 2012 at the same pay rate (2 US cents per round of 10 associations) as the text-based version. Table 7 shows the results of the experiment in which the degree of agreement with the majority of experts as well as the crowd's inter-annotator agreement are detailed. We can see high agreement with expert labels as well as substantial agreement among workers. The popularity (qualitatively perceived through worker feedback) and uptake rate of this HIT even slightly exceeded those of the game-based one for document relevance assessments. Several workers had mentioned difficulties reading the moving text fragments in the short time available. With images, this does not appear to be an issue.

Methods like this could play an essential role either in the creation of training and evaluation data necessary for the assessment of automatic classification quality, or as part of a hybrid human-computer classification in which automatic methods narrow down the range of potential species before human annotators select the most likely species from the pre-selection. It should be noted, however, that the domain experts are by no means obsolete in this setting. While they annotated fish images simply based on their knowledge of the resident species, players of our game only had to select one out of a range of 4 species by similarity.

6. DISCUSSION

In the previous section, we found convincing results across all inspected performance dimensions, supporting the bene-

Table 7: Image classification performance

	Agreement (exp.)	Inter-annot. Agreement
Experts	0.82	-
Game	0.75	0.68

fit of offering alternative incentives besides the pure financial reward. In this section, we discuss a number of observations and insights that were not yet fully covered by the evaluation.

Firstly, considering the fact that the round concept of the game appears to invite workers to create assessments without payment (by playing on after having received the confirmation token), it is not obvious why we should limit the game to a fixed number of rounds. In the present setting, a game inevitably ends after the fifth round. One might argue that a higher number of rounds or even an open-ended concept would result in even greater cost efficiency. In fact, the opposite seems to be the case. In an initial version of the game, there was no upper limit to the number of rounds per game. As a consequence, some players were frustrated, as the only way to "finish" the game would be to either lose or give up. This resulted in fewer returning players. Additionally, the quality of annotations resulting from higher rounds was highly arguable as the objective of the game became mainly surviving through as many rounds of fast-dropping items as possible, rather than making sensible assessments. In the new, limited, setting, the clear objective is to do as well as possible in 5 rounds. Players who want to improve their score beyond this point have to return and start a new game.

A second key observation to be made is the fact that while we evaluate against the performance of NIST assessors and TREC participants, the tasks our workers face is a significantly different one. In the game, no worker gets to see full textual documents or is even told that the objective is to determine topical relevance of web resources towards given information needs. We deliberately aimed for such a loose coupling between game and task as we wanted to keep the game experience entertaining without the "aftertaste" of working. It is interesting that mere conceptual matching correlates well with actual relevance assessments. Also, in the data pre-processing phase, we do not extract sentences based on query terms but rather focus on pure *idf* figures as described in Section 3.2. In this way, we manage to capture the general gist of a document without artificially biasing it towards the topic.

Finally, the key insight gained from this work was the substantial benefit achieved by offering an alternative incentive to workers. Most of the interesting properties observed in the gamified system, such as workers producing free labels, would not have happened otherwise. This is, however, not necessarily limited to gamified tasks. In this paper we used games as one possible means of showing how a particular incentive (money) can be replaced with another one (entertainment). By doing so, we focus on a certain type of worker, entertainment-seekers, the existence of which we hypothesised based on previous experience with crowdsourcing. We are convinced that a better understanding of worker types and their specific intrinsic motivations is essential in driving the boundaries of current crowdsourcing quality. Kazai et al. [21] proposed an interesting classification of workers into several categories. In their work, a number of performance-based worker types, including e.g., spammers, sloppy and competent workers are described. We believe, that more general worker models which also encompass aspects such as worker motivation capability and interest in certain HIT types, etc. can be of significant benefit for the field. Very similar to the task of advertisement placement, a worker whose motivations we understand, can be targeted with better-suited precisely-tailored HIT types.

The common example of worker filtering by nationality illustrates the practical need for a better understanding of worker motivation. This practice is not only of dubious ethical value, it may additionally address symptoms rather than causes. The original objective of identifying and rejecting such workers that try to game the task and get paid without actually working is often hard to fulfil. Filtering by nationality is straightforward to achieve, but also (at best) only correlated with reliability. This bears the significant risk of artificially thinning the pool of available workers. This work (e.g., Tables 4 and 6), demonstrates that in an entirely unfiltered environment no significant national differences in quality, cheat rates, etc. could be found when focussing on the desired worker type. In this way, we retain a large work force but, by task design, discourage undesired worker types from taking up our work in the first place.

Looking out towards future changes to the game based on lessons learned in this work, we aim for including yet another incentive besides entertainment. The leaderboard concept of the current game tries to spark competition between players and has a moderate success at doing so. However, the workers do not know each other. In a reputation-aware environment, such as a social network, this effect can be expected to have a far greater impact. Having the ability to compare scores and to compete in a direct multi-player game with their friends will create much more compelling incentives for (a) performing well in each game, (b) continuing to play, (c) returning for subsequent matches and (d) recommending the game to their circle of friends. We believe that exploiting these aspects by integrating social reputation into crowdsourcing will create many interesting applications.

7. CONCLUSION

In this work, we demonstrated the benefits of a game-based approach for collecting relevance assessments, exploiting insights from the field of serious games for application in commercial large-scale crowdsourcing. After a description of key design criteria, we evaluated the proposed scheme following the setup of the TREC 2011 Crowdsourcing Track. We achieve confirm high result quality, matching the performance levels of the best TREC participants for the same task at a fraction of the invested cost, while attracting fewer cheaters. In a dedicated experiment, we showed the generalizability of the proposed game, that, without any changes, was applied for the task of image classification and clustering. In summary, we are convinced that alternative incentives besides the actual financial HIT reward can positively influence the outcome of crowdsourced data collection and annotation campaigns. As a tangible outcome of this work, a large-scale set of relevance judgements towards the T11Crowd subset of Clueweb was created and is available to the research community. Furthermore, the described game can be accessed and deployed as an open source project[4]. Future work will further exploit the community aspect to increase the motivation for playing. This could be done by, e.g., introducing a multiplayer mode in which several players are in direct competition or by integrating the game into an identity and reputation-aware environment such as social networks or virtual worlds. More fundamentally, this work has demonstrated the benefit of addressing the specific preferences of entertainment-seeking workers. In the future, however, we should investigate formal worker models of worker motivation and capability to enable an optimal work distribution and representation for arbitrary worker types.

Acknowledgements

We would like to thank Jiyin He and the Fish4Knowledge project for providing us with the fish images and expert judgements.

8. REFERENCES

[1] Gambit - Payment Solutions for Virtual Currency. http://www.getgambit.com/, 2011.

[2] O. Alonso and R. Baeza-Yates. Design and implementation of relevance assessments using crowdsourcing. In *ECIR*, 2011.

[3] O. Alonso and M. Lease. Crowdsourcing 101: putting the WSDM of crowds to work for you. In *WSDM*, 2011.

[4] O. Alonso, D.E. Rose, and B. Stewart. Crowdsourcing for relevance evaluation. In *ACM SIGIR Forum*, 2008.

[5] B. Baldwin and B. Carpenter. LingPipe. *Available from World Wide Web: http://alias-i. com/lingpipe*, 2003.

[6] C. Buckley and E.M. Voorhees. Retrieval evaluation with incomplete information. In *SIGIR 2004*. ACM.

[7] J. Callan, M. Hoy, C. Yoo, and L. Zhao. Clueweb09 data set. *http://boston. lti. cs. cmu. edu*, 2009.

[8] B. Carterette, J. Allan, and R. Sitaraman. Minimal test collections for retrieval evaluation. In *Proceedings of the 29th annual international ACM SIGIR conference on Research and development in information retrieval*, pages 268–275. ACM, 2006.

[9] B. Carterette, V. Pavlu, H. Fang, and E. Kanoulas. Million Query track 2009 overview. In *Proceedings of TREC*, volume 9, 2009.

[10] V.R. Carvalho, M. Lease, and E. Yilmaz. Crowdsourcing for search evaluation. In *ACM SIGIR Forum*, 2011.

[11] CrowdFlower. Crowdsourcing - Labor on demand. http://crowdflower.com/, 2012.

[12] M. Csikszentmihalyi. *Flow: The psychology of optimal experience*. Harper Perennial, 1991.

[13] C. Eickhoff and A. de Vries. How crowdsourcable is your task. In *WSDM Workshop on Crowdsourcing for Search and Data Mining (CSDM)*, pages 11–14, 2011.

[14] C. Eickhoff and A.P. de Vries. Increasing Cheat Robustness of Crowdsourcing Tasks. *Information Retrieval To appear*, 2012.

[15] C. Grady and M. Lease. Crowdsourcing document relevance assessment with Mechanical Turk. In *NAACL HLT Workshop on Creating Speech and Language Data with Amazon's Mechanical Turk*, 2010.

[16] C. Harris. You're Hired! An Examination of Crowdsourcing Incentive Models in Human Resource Tasks. In *WSDM Workshop on Crowdsourcing for Search and Data Mining (CSDM)*, pages 15–18, 2011.

[17] M. Hirth, T. Hoßfeld, and P. Tran-Gia. Cheat-Detection Mechanisms for Crowdsourcing. *University of Würzburg, Tech. Rep*, 2010.

[4] http://sourceforge.net/projects/geann/

[18] P. Ipeirotis. Crowdsourcing using Mechanical Turk: quality management and scalability. In *Proceedings of the 8th International Workshop on Information Integration on the Web: in conjunction with WWW 2011*. ACM, 2011.

[19] T. Joachims. Optimizing search engines using clickthrough data. In *SIGKDD*, 2002.

[20] G. Kazai. In search of quality in crowdsourcing for search engine evaluation. *ECIR*, 2011.

[21] G. Kazai, J. Kamps, and N. Milic-Frayling. Worker Types and Personality Traits in Crowdsourcing Relevance Labels. 2011.

[22] G. Kazai and N. Milic-Frayling. On the evaluation of the quality of relevance assessments collected through crowdsourcing. In *SIGIR 2009 Workshop on the Future of IR Evaluation*, 2009.

[23] C.H. Ko, J.Y. Yen, C.C. Chen, S.H. Chen, and C.F. Yen. Gender differences and related factors affecting online gaming addiction among taiwanese adolescents. *The Journal of nervous and mental disease*, 2005.

[24] J. Lampel and A. Bhalla. The role of status seeking in online communities: Giving the gift of experience. *Journal of Computer-Mediated Communication*, 2007.

[25] M. Lease and G. Kazai. Overview of the TREC 2011 Crowdsourcing Track (Conference Notebook). 2011.

[26] M. Lease and E. Yilmaz. Crowdsourcing for information retrieval. In *ACM SIGIR Forum*, number 2. ACM, 2012.

[27] H. Ma, R. Chandrasekar, C. Quirk, and A. Gupta. Improving search engines using human computation games. In *CIKM 2009*.

[28] C.C. Marshall and F.M. Shipman. The ownership and reuse of visual media. *JCDL*, 2011.

[29] J. McGonigal. *Reality is broken: Why games make us better and how they can change the world*. Penguin Pr, 2011.

[30] David Pennock. The Wisdom of the Probability Sports Crowd. http://blog.oddhead.com/2007/01/04/the-wisdom-of-the-probabilitysports-crowd/, 2007.

[31] C. Richards. Teach the world to twitch: An interview with Marc Prensky, CEO and founder Games2train. com. Futurelab, 2003.

[32] F. Scholer, A. Turpin, and M. Sanderson. Quantifying test collection quality based on the consistency of relevance judgements. In *SIGIR 2011*.

[33] R. Snow, B. O'Connor, D. Jurafsky, and A.Y. Ng. Cheap and fast—but is it good?: evaluating non-expert annotations for natural language tasks. In *EMNLP*, 2008.

[34] J. Surowiecki, M.P. Silverman, et al. The wisdom of crowds. *American Journal of Physics*, 2007.

[35] Amazon Mechanical Turk. Artificial Artificial Intelligence. http://mturk.com, 2012.

[36] J. Urbano, M. Marrero, D. Martín, J. Morato, K. Robles, and J. Lloréns. The University Carlos III of Madrid at TREC 2011 Crowdsourcing Track: Notebook Paper. 2011.

[37] L. von Ahn and L. Dabbish. Labeling images with a computer game. In *SIGCHI*, 2004.

[38] L. von Ahn and L. Dabbish. Designing games with a purpose. *Communications of the ACM*, 2008.

[39] L. von Ahn, S. Ginosar, M. Kedia, and M. Blum. Improving image search with phetch. In *ICASSP*, 2007.

[40] L. von Ahn, M. Kedia, and M. Blum. Verbosity: a game for collecting common-sense facts. In *SIGCHI 2006*.

[41] L. von Ahn, R. Liu, and M. Blum. Peekaboom: a game for locating objects in images. In *SIGCHI 2006*.

[42] E. Voorhees. The philosophy of information retrieval evaluation. In *Evaluation of cross-language information retrieval systems*, 2002.

[43] E. Voorhees, D.K. Harman, National Institute of Standards, and Technology (US). *TREC: Experiment and evaluation in information retrieval*. MIT press USA, 2005.

[44] P. Welinder, S. Branson, S. Belongie, and P. Perona. The multidimensional wisdom of crowds. In *NIPS*, 2010.

An IR-based Evaluation Framework for Web Search Query Segmentation

Rishiraj Saha Roy and Niloy Ganguly
Indian Institute of Technology Kharagpur
Kharagpur, West Bengal, India - 721302.
{rishiraj, niloy}@cse.iitkgp.ernet.in

Monojit Choudhury and Srivatsan Laxman
Microsoft Research India
Bangalore, Karnataka, India - 560025.
{monojitc, slaxman}@microsoft.com

ABSTRACT

This paper presents the first evaluation framework for Web search query segmentation based directly on IR performance. In the past, segmentation strategies were mainly validated against manual annotations. Our work shows that the goodness of a segmentation algorithm as judged through evaluation against a handful of human annotated segmentations hardly reflects its effectiveness in an IR-based setup. In fact, state-of the-art algorithms are shown to perform as good as, and sometimes even better than human annotations – a fact masked by previous validations. The proposed framework also provides us an objective understanding of the gap between the present best and the best possible segmentation algorithm. We draw these conclusions based on an extensive evaluation of six segmentation strategies, including three most recent algorithms, vis-à-vis segmentations from three human annotators. The evaluation framework also gives insights about which segments should be necessarily detected by an algorithm for achieving the best retrieval results. The meticulously constructed dataset used in our experiments has been made public for use by the research community.

Categories and Subject Descriptors

H.3.3 [**Information Search and Retrieval**]: Query formulation, Retrieval models

General Terms

Measurement, Experimentation, Human Factors

Keywords

Query segmentation, IR evaluation, Evaluation framework, Test collections, Manual annotation

1. INTRODUCTION

Query segmentation is the process of dividing a query into individual semantic units [3]. For example, the query `singular value decomposition online demo` can be broken into `singular value decomposition` and `online demo`. All documents containing the individual terms `singular`, `value` and `decomposition` are not necessarily relevant for this query. Rather, one can almost always expect to find the segment `singular value decomposition` in the relevant documents. In contrast, although `online demo` is a segment, finding the phrase or some variant of it may not affect the relevance of the document. Hence, the potential of query segmentation goes beyond the detection of multiword named entities. Rather, segmentation leads to a better understanding of the query and is crucial to the search engine for improving Information Retrieval (IR) performance.

There is broad consensus in the literature that query segmentation can lead to better retrieval performance [2, 3, 7, 9, 13]. However, most automatic segmentation techniques [3, 4, 7, 9, 13, 15] have so far been evaluated only against a small set of 500 queries segmented by human annotators. Such an approach implicitly assumes that a segmentation technique that scores better against human annotations will also automatically lead to better IR performance. We challenge this approach on multiple counts. First, there has been no systematic study that establishes the quality of human segmentations in the context of IR performance. Second, grammatical structure in queries is not as well-understood as natural language sentences where human annotations have proved useful for training and testing of various Natural Language Processing (NLP) tools. This leads to considerable inter-annotator disagreement when humans segment search queries. Third, good quality human annotations for segmentation can be difficult and expensive to obtain for a large set of test queries. Thus, there is a need for a more direct IR-based evaluation framework for assessing query segmentation algorithms. This is the central motivation of the present work.

We propose an IR-based evaluation framework for query segmentation that requires only human relevance judgments (RJs) for query-URL pairs for computing the performance of a segmentation algorithm – such relevance judgments are anyway needed for training and testing of any IR engine. A fundamental problem in designing an IR-based evaluation framework for segmentation algorithms is to decouple the effect of segmentation accuracy from the way segmentation is used for IR. This is because a query segmentation algorithm breaks the input query into, typically, a non-overlapping sequence of words (segments), but it does not prescribe how these segments should be used during the retrieval and ranking of the documents for that query. We resolve this problem

SIGIR'12, August 12–16, 2012, Portland, Oregon, USA.

by providing a formal model of query expansion for a given segmentation; the various queries obtained can then be issued to any standard IR engine, which we assume to be a black box.

We conduct extensive experiments within our framework to understand the performance of several state-of-the-art query segmentation schemes [7, 9, 11] and segmentations by three human annotators. Our experiments reveal several interesting facts such as: (a) Segmentation is actively useful in improving IR performance, even though submitting all segments (detected by an algorithm) in double quotes to the IR engine degrades performance; (b) All segmentation strategies, including human segmentations, are yet to reach the best achievable limits in IR performance; (c) In terms of IR metrics, some of the segmentation algorithms perform as good as the best human annotator and better than the average/worst human annotator; (d) Current match-based metrics for comparing query segmentation against human annotations are only weakly correlated with the IR-based metrics, and cannot be used as a proxy for IR performance; and (e) There is scope for improvement for the matching metrics that compare segmentations against human annotations by differentially penalizing the straddling, splitting and joining of reference segments. In short, the proposed evaluation framework not only provides a formal way to compare segmentation algorithms and estimate their effectiveness in IR, but also helps us to understand the gaps in human annotation-based evaluation. The framework also provides valuable insights regarding the segmentations that can be used for improvement of the algorithms.

The rest of the paper is organized as follows. Sec. 2 introduces our evaluation framework and its design philosophy. Sec. 3 presents the dataset and the segmentation algorithms compared on our framework. Sec. 4 discusses the experimental results and insights derived from them. In Sec. 5, we discuss a few related issues, and the next section (Sec. 6) gives a brief background of past approaches to evaluate query segmentation and their limitations. We conclude by summarizing our contributions and suggesting future work in Sec. 7.

2. THE EVALUATION FRAMEWORK

In this section we present a framework for the evaluation of query segmentation algorithms based on IR performance. Let $\mathbf{q}$ denote a search query and let $\mathbf{s^q} = \langle s_1^{\mathbf{q}}, \ldots, s_n^{\mathbf{q}} \rangle$ denote a segmentation of $\mathbf{q}$ such that a simple concatenation of the n segments equals $\mathbf{q}$, i.e., we have $\mathbf{q} = (s_1^{\mathbf{q}} + \cdots + s_n^{\mathbf{q}})$, where $+$ represents the concatenation operator. We are given a segmentation algorithm $\mathcal{A}$ and the task is to evaluate its performance. We require the following resources:

1. A test set $\mathcal{Q}$ of unquoted search queries.
2. A set $\mathcal{U}$ of documents (or URLs) out of which search results will be retrieved.
3. Relevance judgments $r(\mathbf{q}, u)$ for query-URL pairs $(\mathbf{q}, u) \in \mathcal{Q} \times \mathcal{U}$. The set of all relevance judgments are collectively denoted by $\mathcal{R}$.
4. An IR engine that supports quoted queries as input.

The resources needed by our evaluation framework are essentially the same as those needed for the training and testing of a standard IR engine, namely, queries, a document corpus and set of relevance judgments. Akin to the training examples required for an IR engine, we only require relevance judgments for a small and appropriate subset of $\mathcal{Q} \times \mathcal{U}$ (each query needs only the documents in its own pool to be judged) [14].

Table 1: Example of generation of quoted versions for a segmented query.

Segmented query	Quoted versions
we are | the people | song lyrics	we are the people song lyrics we are the people "song lyrics" we are "the people" song lyrics we are "the people" "song lyrics" "we are" the people song lyrics "we are" the people "song lyrics" "we are" "the people" song lyrics "we are" "the people" "song lyrics"

It is useful to separate the evaluation of segmentation performance, from the question of how to best exploit the segments to retrieve the most relevant documents. From an IR perspective, a natural interpretation of a segment could be that it consists of words that must appear together, in the same order, in documents where the segment is deemed to match [3]. This can be referred to as *ordered contiguity matching*. While this can be easily enforced in modern IR engines through use of double quotes around segments, we observe that not all segments must be used this way (see [10] for related ideas and experiments in a different context). Some segments may admit more general matching criteria, such as *unordered or intruded contiguity* (e.g., a segment `a b` may be allowed to match `b a` or `a c b` in the document). The case of unordered intruded matching may be restricted under *linguistic dependence* assumptions (e.g., `a b` can match `a` *of* `b` or `b` *in* `a`). Finally, some segments may even play non-matching roles (e.g., when the segment specifies user intent, like `how to` and `where is`). Thus, there may be several different ways to exploit the segments discovered by a segmentation algorithm. Even within the same query, different segments may need to be treated differently. For instance, in the query `cannot view | word files | windows 7`, the first one might be matched using intruded ordered occurrence (`cannot` *properly* `view`), the second segment may be matched under a linguistic dependency model (`files` *in* `word`) and the last one under ordered contiguity.

Intruded contiguity and linguistic dependency may be difficult to implement for the broad class of general Web search queries. Identifying how the various segments of a query should be ideally matched in the document is quite a challenging and unsolved research problem. On the other hand, an exhaustive expansion scheme, where every segment is expanded in every possible way, is computationally expensive and might introduce noise. Moreover, current commercial IR engines do not support any syntax to specify linguistic dependence or intruded or unordered occurrence based matching. Hence, in order to keep the evaluation framework in line with the current IR systems, we focus on ordered contiguity matching which is easily implemented through the use of double quotes around segments. However, we note that the philosophy of the framework does not change with increased sophistication in the retrieval system – only the expansion sets for the queries have to be appropriately modified.

We propose an evaluation framework for segmentation algorithms that generates all possible quoted versions of a segmented query (see Table 1) and submits each quoted version to the IR engine. The corresponding ranked lists of retrieved documents are then assessed against relevance judgments available for the query-URL pairs. The IR quality of the best-performing quoted version is used to measure performance of the segmentation algorithm. We now formally specify our evaluation framework that computes what we call a Quoted Version Retrieval Score (QVRS) for the segmentation algorithm given the test set $\mathcal{Q}$ of queries, the document pool $\mathcal{U}$ and the relevance judgments $\mathcal{R}$ for query-URL pairs.

Quoted query version generation

Let the segmentation output by algorithm $\mathcal{A}$ be denoted by $\mathcal{A}(\mathbf{q}) = \mathbf{s}^{\mathbf{q}} = \langle s_1^{\mathbf{q}}, \dots, s_n^{\mathbf{q}} \rangle$. We generate all possible *quoted versions* of the query $\mathbf{q}$ based on the segments in $\mathcal{A}(\mathbf{q})$. In particular, we define $\mathcal{A}_0(\mathbf{q}) = (s_1^{\mathbf{q}} + \cdots + s_n^{\mathbf{q}})$ with no quotes on any of the segments, $\mathcal{A}_1(\mathbf{q}) = (s_1^{\mathbf{q}} + \cdots + \text{“}s_n^{\mathbf{q}}\text{”})$ with quotes only around the last segment $s_n^{\mathbf{q}}$, and so on. Since there are n segments in $\mathcal{A}(\mathbf{q})$, this process will generate 2^n versions of the query, $\mathcal{A}_i(\mathbf{q})$, $i = 0, \dots, 2^n - 1$. We note that if $b_i = (b_{i1}, \dots, b_{in})$ be the n-bit binary representation of i, then $\mathcal{A}_i(\mathbf{q})$ will apply quotes to the jth segment $s_j^{\mathbf{q}}$ iff $b_{ij} = 1$. We deduplicate this set, because $\{\mathcal{A}_i(\mathbf{q}) : i = 0, \dots, 2^n - 1\}$ can contain multiple versions that essentially represent the same quoted query version (when single words are inside quotes). For example, the query versions `"harry potter" "game"` and `"harry potter" game` are equivalent in terms of the input semantics of an IR engine. The resulting set of unique quoted query versions is denoted $\mathcal{Q}_{\mathcal{A}}(\mathbf{q})$.

Document retrieval using IR engine

For each $\mathcal{A}_i(\mathbf{q}) \in \mathcal{Q}_{\mathcal{A}}(\mathbf{q})$ we use the IR engine to retrieve a ranked list $\mathcal{O}_i$ of documents out of the document pool $\mathcal{U}$ that matched the given quoted query version $\mathcal{A}_i(\mathbf{q})$. The number of documents retrieved in each case depends on the IR metrics we will want to use to assess the quality of retrieval. For example, to compute an IR metric at the top k positions, we would require that at least k documents be retrieved from the pool.

Measuring retrieval against relevance judgments

Since we have relevance judgments ($\mathcal{R}$) for query-URL pairs in $\mathcal{Q} \times \mathcal{U}$, we can now compute IR metrics such as normalized Discounted Cumulative Gain (nDCG), Mean Average Precision (MAP) or Mean Reciprocal Rank (MRR) to measure the quality of the retrieved ranked list $\mathcal{O}_i$ for query $\mathbf{q}$. We use @k variants of each of these measures which are defined to be the usual metrics computed after examining only the top-k positions. For example, we can compute nDCG@k for query $\mathbf{q}$ and retrieved document-list $\mathcal{O}_i$ using the following formula:

$$\text{nDCG@}k(\mathbf{q}, \mathcal{O}_i, \mathcal{R}) = r(\mathbf{q}, \mathcal{O}_i^1) + \sum_{j=2}^{k} \frac{r(\mathbf{q}, \mathcal{O}_i^j)}{\log_2 j} \quad (1)$$

where $\mathcal{O}_i^j$, $j = 1, \dots, k$, denotes the jth document in the ranked-list $\mathcal{O}_i$ and $r(\mathbf{q}, \mathcal{O}_i^j)$ denotes the associated relevance judgment from $\mathcal{R}$.

Oracle score using best quoted query version

Different quoted query versions $\mathcal{A}_i(\mathbf{q})$ (all derived from the same basic segmentation $\mathcal{A}(\mathbf{q})$ output by the segmentation algorithm $\mathcal{A}$) retrieve different ranked lists of documents $\mathcal{O}_i$. As discussed earlier, automatic apriori selection of a good (or the best) quoted query version is a difficult problem. While different strategies may be used to select a quoted query version, we would like our evaluation of the segmentation algorithm $\mathcal{A}$ to be agnostic of the version-selection step. To this end, we select the best-performing $\mathcal{A}_i(\mathbf{q})$ from the entire set $\mathcal{Q}_{\mathcal{A}}(\mathbf{q})$ of query versions generated and use it to define our *oracle score* for $\mathbf{q}$ and $\mathcal{A}$ under the chosen IR metric [8]. For example, the oracle score for nDCG@k is as defined below:

$$\Omega_{\text{nDCG@}k}(\mathbf{q}, \mathcal{A}) = \max_{\mathcal{A}_i(\mathbf{q}) \in \mathcal{Q}_{\mathcal{A}}(\mathbf{q})} \text{nDCG@}k(\mathbf{q}, \mathcal{O}_i, \mathcal{R}) \quad (2)$$

where $\mathcal{O}_i$ denotes the ranked list of documents retrieved by the IR engine when presented with $\mathcal{A}_i(\mathbf{q})$ as the input. We note that $\mathcal{Q}_{\mathcal{A}}(\mathbf{q})$ always contains the original unsegmented version of the query. We refer to such an $\Omega_{\cdot}(\cdot, \cdot)$ as the *Oracle*.

This forms the basis of our evaluation framework. We note that there can also be other ways to define this oracle score. For example, instead of seeking the best IR performance possible across the different query versions, we could also seek the minimum performance achievable by $\mathcal{A}$ irrespective of what version-selection strategy is adopted. This would give us a lower bound on the performance of the segmentation algorithm. However, the main drawback of this approach is that the minimum performance is almost always achieved by the fully quoted version (where every segment is in double quotes) (see Table 7). Such a lower bound would not be useful in assessing the comparative performance of segmentation algorithms.

QVRS computation

Once the oracle scores are obtained for all queries in the test set $\mathcal{Q}$, we can compute the average oracle score achieved by $\mathcal{A}$. We refer to this as the Quoted Version Retrieval Score (QVRS) of $\mathcal{A}$ with respect to test set $\mathcal{Q}$, document pool $\mathcal{U}$ and relevance judgments $\mathcal{R}$. For example, using the oracle with the nDCG@k metric, we can define the QVRS score as follows:

$$QVRS(\mathcal{Q}, \mathcal{A}, \text{nDCG@}k) = \frac{1}{|\mathcal{Q}|} \sum_{\mathbf{q} \in \mathcal{Q}} \Omega_{\text{nDCG@}k}(\mathbf{q}, \mathcal{A}) \quad (3)$$

Similar QVRS scores can be computed using other IR metrics such as MAP@k and MRR@k. In our experiments section, we report results using nDCG@k, MAP@k, and MRR@k, for $k = 5$ and $k = 10$ as most Web users examine only the first five or ten search results.

3. DATASET AND ALGORITHMS

In this section, we describe the dataset used and briefly introduce the algorithms compared on our framework.

3.1 Test set of queries ($\mathcal{Q}$)

We selected a random subset of 500 queries from a slice of the query logs of Bing Australia[1] containing 16.7 million queries issued over a period of one month (May 2010). We used the following criteria to filter the logs before extracting a random sample: (1) Exclude queries with non-ASCII characters, (2) Exclude queries that occurred fewer than 5 times

[1] `http://www.bing.com/?cc=au`

in the logs (rarer queries often contained spelling errors), and (3) Restrict query lengths to between five and eight words. Shorter queries rarely contain multiple multiword segments, and when they do, they are mostly named entities that can be easily detected using dictionaries. Moreover, traditional search engines usually give satisfactory results for short queries. On the other hand, queries longer than eight words (only 3.24% of all queries in our log) are usually error messages, complete NL sentences or song lyrics, that need to be addressed separately.

We denote this set of 500 queries by $\mathcal{Q}$, the test set of unsegmented queries needed for all our evaluation experiments. The average length of queries in $\mathcal{Q}$ (our dataset) is 5.29 words. The average query length was 4.31 words in the Bergsma and Wang 2007 Corpus[2] (henceforth, BWC07) [3]. Each of these 500 queries were independently segmented by three human annotators (who issue around 20-30 search queries per day) who were asked to mark a contiguous chunk of words in a query as a *segment* if they thought that these words together formed a coherent semantic unit. The annotators were free to refer to other resources and Web search engines during the annotation process, especially for understanding the query and its possible context(s). We shall refer to the three sets of annotations (and also the corresponding annotators) as H_A, H_B and H_C.

It is important to mention that the queries in $\mathcal{Q}$ have some amount of word level overlap, even though all the queries have very distinct information needs. Thus, a document retrieved from the pool might exhibit good term level match for more than one query in $\mathcal{Q}$. This makes our corpus an interesting testbed for experimenting with different retrieval systems. There are existing datasets, including BWC07, that could have been used for this study. However, refer to Sec. 5.1 for an account of why building this new dataset was crucial for our research.

3.2 Document pool ($\mathcal{U}$) and RJs ($\mathcal{R}$)

Each query in $\mathcal{Q}$ was segmented using all the nine segmentation strategies considered in our study (six algorithms and three humans). For every segmentation, all possible quoted versions were generated (total 4,746) and then submitted to the Bing API[3] and the top ten documents were retrieved. We then deduplicated these URLs to obtain 14,171 unique URLs, forming $\mathcal{U}$. On an average, adding the 9th strategy to a group of the remaining eight resulted in about one new quoted version for every two queries. These new versions may or may not introduce new documents to the pool. We observed that for 71.4% of the queries there is less than 50% overlap between the top ten URLs retrieved for the different quoted versions. This indicates that different ways of quoting the segments in a query does make a difference in the search results. By varying the pooling depth (ten in our case), one can roughly control the number of relevant and non-relevant documents entering the collection.

For each query-URL pair, where the URL has been retrieved for at least one of the quoted versions of the query (approx. 28 per query), we obtained three independent sets of relevance judgments from human users. These users were different from annotators H_A, H_B and H_C who marked the segmentations, but having similar familiarity with search systems. For each query, the corresponding set of URLs was

[2]`http://bit.ly/xoyT2c`

[3]`http://msdn.microsoft.com/en-us/library/dd251056.aspx`

Table 2: Segmentation algorithms compared on our framework.

Algorithm	Training data
Li et al. [9]	Click data, Web n-gram probabilities
Hagen et al. [7]	Web n-gram frequencies, Wikipedia titles
Mishra et al. [11]	Query logs
[11] + Wiki	Query logs, Wikipedia titles
PMI-W [7]	Web n-gram probabilities (used as baseline)
PMI-Q [11]	Query logs (used as baseline)

shown to the users after deduplication and randomization (to prevent position bias for top results), and asked to mark whether the URL was *irrelevant* (score = 0), *partially relevant* (score = 1) or *highly relevant* (score = 2) to the query. We then computed the average rating for each query-URL pair (the entire set forming $\mathcal{R}$), which has been used for subsequent nDCG, MAP and MRR computations. Please refer to Table 8 in Sec. 5.3 for inter-annotator agreement figures and other related discussions.

3.3 Segmentation algorithms

Table 2 lists the six segmentation algorithms that have been studied in this work. Li et al. [9] use the expectation maximization algorithm to arrive at the most probable segmentation, while Hagen et al. [7] show a simple frequency-based method produces a performance comparable to the state-of-the-art. The technique in Mishra et al. [11] uses only query logs for segmenting queries. In our experiments, we observed that the performance of Mishra et al. [11] can be improved if we used Wikipedia titles. We refer to this as "[11] + Wiki" in our experiments (see Appendix A for details). The Point-wise Mutual Information (PMI)-based algorithms are used as baselines. The thresholds for PMI-W and PMI-Q were chosen to be 8.141 and 0.156 respectively, that maximized the *Seg-F* (see Sec. 4.2) on our development set.

3.4 Public release of data

The test set of search queries along with their manual and some of the algorithmic segmentations, the theoretical best segmentation output that can serve as an evaluation benchmark (BQV_{BF} in Sec. 4.1), and the list of URLs whose contents serve as our document corpus is available for public use[4]. The relevance judgments for the query-URL pairs have also been made public which will enable the community to use this dataset for evaluation of any new segmentation algorithm.

4. EXPERIMENTS AND OBSERVATIONS

In this section we present experiments, results and the key inferences made from them.

4.1 IR Experiments

For the retrieval-based evaluation experiments, we use the Lucene[5] text retrieval system, which is publicly available as a code library. In its default configuration, Lucene does not perform any automatic query segmentation, which is very important for examining the effectiveness of segmentation algorithms in an IR-based scheme. Double quotes

[4]`http://cse.iitkgp.ac.in/resgrp/cnerg/qa/querysegmentation.html`

[5]`http://lucene.apache.org/java/docs/index.html`

Table 3: Results of IR-based evaluation of segmentation algorithms using Lucene (mean oracle scores).

Metric	Unseg. query	[9]	[7]	[11]	[11] + Wiki	PMI-W	PMI-Q	H_A	H_B	H_C	BQV_{BF}
nDCG@5	0.688	0.752*	**0.763***	0.745	**0.767***	0.691	**0.766***	**0.770**	0.768	0.759	0.825
nDCG@10	0.701	0.756*	**0.767***	0.751	**0.768***	0.704	**0.767***	**0.770**	**0.768**	**0.763**	0.832
MAP@5	0.882	0.930*	**0.942***	0.930*	**0.945***	0.884	0.932*	**0.944**	**0.942**	0.936	0.958
MAP@10	0.865	0.910*	**0.921***	0.910*	**0.923***	0.867	0.912*	**0.923**	**0.921**	**0.916**	0.944
MRR@5	0.538	0.632*	**0.649***	0.609	**0.650***	0.543	**0.648***	**0.656**	**0.648**	0.632	0.711
MRR@10	0.549	0.640*	**0.658***	0.619	**0.658***	0.555	**0.656***	**0.665**	**0.656**	0.640	0.717

The highest value in a row (excluding the BQV_{BF} column) and those with no statistically significant difference with the highest value are marked in **boldface**. The values for algorithms that perform better than or have no statistically significant difference with the *minimum* of the human segmentations are marked with *. The paired t-test was performed and the null hypothesis was rejected if the p-value was less than 0.05.

Table 4: Matching metrics for different segmentation algorithms and human annotations *with BQV_{BF} as reference.*

Metric	Unseg. query	[9]	[7]	[11]	[11] + Wiki	PMI-W	PMI-Q	H_A	H_B	H_C	BQV_{BF}
Qry-Acc	0.044	0.056	0.082*	0.058	0.094*	0.046	**0.104***	0.086	0.074	0.064	1.000
Seg-Prec	**0.226***	0.176*	0.189*	0.206*	0.203*	**0.229***	0.218*	0.176	0.166	0.178	1.000
Seg-Rec	**0.325***	0.166*	0.162*	0.210*	0.174*	**0.323***	0.196*	0.144	0.133	0.154	1.000
Seg-F	**0.267***	0.171*	0.174*	0.208*	0.187*	**0.268***	0.206*	0.158	0.148	0.165	1.000
Seg-Acc	0.470	0.624	0.661*	0.601	0.667*	0.474	0.660*	**0.675**	**0.675**	0.663	1.000

The highest value in a row (excluding the BQV_{BF} column) and those with no statistically significant difference with the highest value are marked in **boldface**. The values for algorithms that perform better than or have no statistically significant difference with the *minimum* of the human segmentations are marked with *. The paired t-test was performed and the null hypothesis was rejected if the p-value was less than 0.05.

can be used in a query to force Lucene to match the quoted *phrase* (in Lucene terms) exactly in the documents. Starting with the segmentations output by each of the six algorithms as well as the three human annotations, we generated all possible quoted query versions, which resulted in a total of 4,746 versions for the 500 queries. In the notation of Sec. 2, this corresponds to generating $\mathcal{Q}_{\mathcal{A}}(\mathbf{q})$ for each segmentation method $\mathcal{A}$ (including one for each human segmentation) and for every query $\mathbf{q} \in \mathcal{Q}$. These quoted versions were then passed through Lucene to retrieve documents from the pool. For each segmentation scheme, we then use the oracle described in Sec. 2 to obtain the query version yielding the best result (as determined by the IR metrics – nDCG, MAP and MRR computed according to the human relevance judgments). These oracle scores are then averaged over the query set to give us the QVRS measures.

The results are summarized in Table 3. Different rows represent the different IR metrics that were used and columns correspond to different segmentation strategies. The second column (marked "Unseg. Query") refers to the original unsegmented query. This can be assumed to be generated by a trivial segmentation strategy where each word is always a separate segment. Columns 3-8 denote the six different segmentation algorithms and 9-11 (marked H_A, H_B and H_C) represent the human segmentations. The last column represents the performance of the **b**est **q**uoted **v**ersions (denoted by BQV_{BF} in table) of the queries which are computed by ***b**rute **f**orce*, i.e. an exhaustive search over all possible ways of quoting the parts of a query (2^{l-1} possible quoted versions for an l-word query) irrespective of any segmentation algorithm. The results are reported for two sizes of retrieved URL lists (k), namely five and ten. Since we needed to convert our graded relevance judgments to binary values for computing MAP@k, URLs with ratings of 1 and 2 were considered as relevant (responsible for the generally high values) and those with 0 as irrelevant. For MRR, only URLs with ratings of 2 were considered as relevant.

The first observation we make from the results is that human as well as all algorithmic segmentation schemes consistently outperform unsegmented queries for all IR metrics. Second, we observe that the performance of some segmentation algorithms are comparable and sometime even marginally better than some of the human annotators. Finally, we observe that there is considerable scope for improving IR performance through better segmentation (all values less than BQV_{BF}). The inferences from these observations are stated later in this section.

4.2 Performance under traditional matching metrics

In the next set of experiments we study the utility of traditional matching metrics that are used to evaluate query segmentation algorithms against a gold standard of human segmented queries (henceforth referred to as the *reference* segmentation). These metrics are listed below [7]:

1. **Query accuracy (*Qry-Acc*):** The fraction of queries where the output matches exactly with the reference segmentation.

2. **Segment precision (*Seg-Prec*):** The ratio of the number of segments that overlap in the output and reference segmentations to the number of output segments, averaged across all queries in the test set.

Table 5: Performance of PMI-Q and [9] with respect to matching (mean of comparisons with H_A, H_B and H_C as references) and IR metrics.

Metric	nDCG@10	MAP@10	MRR@10	Qry-Acc	Seg-Prec	Seg-Rec	Seg-F	Seg-Acc
PMI-Q	**0.767**	**0.912**	**0.656**	0.341	0.448	0.487	0.467	**0.810**
[9]	0.756	0.910	0.640	**0.375**	**0.524**	**0.588**	**0.554**	**0.810**

The highest values in a column are marked in **boldface**.

3. **Segment recall (*Seg-Rec*):** The ratio of the number of segments that overlap in the output and reference segmentations to the number of reference segments, averaged across all queries in the test set.
4. **Segment F-score (*Seg-F*):** The harmonic mean of *Seg-Prec* and *Seg-Rec*.
5. **Segmentation accuracy (*Seg-Acc*):** The ratio of correctly predicted boundaries and non-boundaries in the output segmentation with respect to the reference, averaged across all queries in the test set.

We computed the matching metrics for various segmentation algorithms against H_A, H_B and H_C. According to these metrics, "Mishra et al. [11] + Wiki" turns out to be the best algorithm which agrees with the results of IR evaluation. However, the average Kendall-Tau rank correlation coefficient[6] between the ranks of the strategies as obtained from the IR metrics (Table 3) and the matching metrics was only 0.75. This indicates that matching metrics are not perfect predictors for IR performance. In fact, we discovered some costly flaws in the relative ranking produced by matching metrics. One such case was rank inversions between Li et al. [9] and PMI-Q. The relevant results are shown in Table 5, which demonstrate that while PMI-Q consistently performs better than Li et al. [9] under IR-based measures, the opposite inference would have been drawn if we had used any of the matching metrics.

In Bergsma and Wang [3], human annotators were asked to segment queries such that segments matched exactly in the relevant documents. This essentially corresponds to determining the best quoted versions for the query. Thus, it would be interesting to study how traditional matching metrics would perform if the humans actually marked the best quoted versions. In order to evaluate this, we used the matching metrics to compare the segmentation outputs by the algorithms and human annotations against BQV_{BF}. The corresponding results are quoted in Table 4. The results show that matching metrics are very poor indicators of IR performance with respect to the BQV_{BF}. For example, for three out of the five matching metrics, the unsegmented query is ranked the best. This shows that even if human annotators managed to correctly guess the best quoted versions, the matching metrics would fail to estimate the correct relative rankings of the segmentation algorithms with respect to IR performance. This fact is also borne out in the Kendall-Tau rank correlation coefficients reported in Table 6. Another interesting observation from these experiments is that *Seg-Acc* emerges as the best matching metric with respect to IR performance, although its correlation coefficient is still much below one.

[6]This coefficient is 1 when there is perfect concordance between the rankings, and −1 if the trends are reversed.

Table 6: Kendall-Tau coefficients between IR and matching metrics *with BQV_{BF} as reference for the latter.*

Metric	Qry-Acc	Seg-Prec	Seg-Rec	Seg-F	Seg-Acc
nDCG@10	0.432	-0.854	-0.886	-0.854	**0.674**
MAP@10	0.322	-0.887	-0.920	-0.887	**0.750**
MRR@10	0.395	-0.782	-0.814	-0.782	**0.598**

The highest value in a row is marked in **boldface**.

4.3 Inferences

Segmentation is helpful for IR. By definition, $\Omega.(\cdot,\cdot)$ (i.e., the oracle) values for every IR metric for any segmentation scheme are at least as large as the corresponding values for the unsegmented query. Nevertheless, for every IR metrics, we observe significant performance benefits for all the human and algorithmic segmentations (except for PMI-W) over the unsegmented query. This indicates that segmentation is indeed helpful for boosting IR performance. Thus, our results validate the prevailing notion and some of the earlier observations [2, 9] that segmentation can help improve IR.

Human segmentations are a good proxy, but not a true gold standard. Our results indicate that human segmentations perform reasonably well in IR metrics. The best of the human annotators beats all the segmentation algorithms, on almost all the metrics. Therefore, evaluation against human annotations can indeed be considered as the second best alternative to an IR-based evaluation (though see below for criticisms of current matching metrics). However, if the objective is to improve IR performance, then human annotations cannot be considered a true gold standard. There are at least three reasons for this:

First, in terms of IR metrics, some of the state-of-the-art segmentation algorithms are performing as well as human segmentations (no statistically significant difference). Thus, further optimization of the matching metrics against human annotations is not going to improve the IR performance of the segmentation algorithms. Thus, evaluation on human annotations might become a limiting factor for the current segmentation algorithms.

Second, the IR performance of the best quoted version of the queries derived through our framework is significantly better than that of human annotations (last column, Table 3). This means that humans fail to predict the correct boundaries in many instances. Thus, there is scope for improvement for human annotations.

Third, IR performance of at least one of the three human annotators (H_C) is worse than some of the algorithms studied. In other words, while some annotators (such as H_A) are good at guessing the "correct" segment boundaries that will help IR, not all annotators can do it well. Therefore, unless

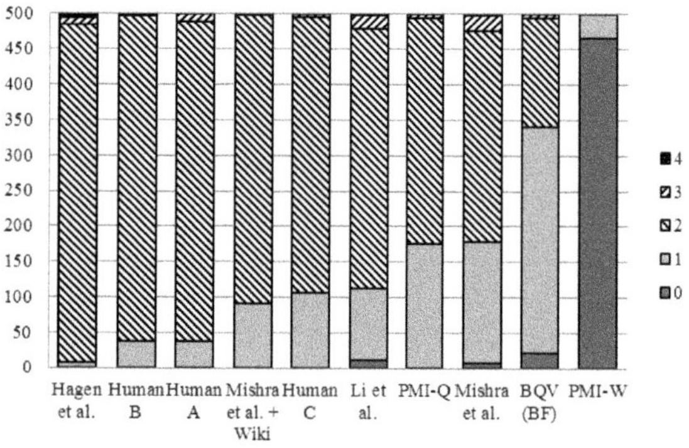

Figure 1: Distribution of multiword segments in queries across segmentation strategies.

the annotators are chosen and guided properly, one cannot guarantee the quality of annotated data for query segmentation. If the queries in the test set have multiple intents, this issue becomes an even bigger concern.

Matching metrics are misleading. As discussed earlier and demonstrated by Tables 4 and 6, the matching metrics provide unreliable ranking of the segmentation algorithms even when applied against a true gold standard, BQV_{BF}, that by definition maximizes IR performance. This counter-intuitive observation can be explained in two ways. Either the matching metrics or the IR metrics (or probably both) are misleading. Given that IR metrics are well-tested and generally assumed to be acceptable, we are forced to conclude that the matching metrics do not really reflect the quality of a segmentation with respect to a gold standard. Indeed, this can be illustrated by a simple example.

Example. Let us consider the query `the looney toons show cartoon network`, whose best quoted version turns out to be `"the looney toons show" "cartoon network"`. The underlying segmentation that can give rise to this and therefore can be assumed to be the reference is:
Ref: `the looney toons show | cartoon network`
The segmentations
(1) `the looney | toons show | cartoon | network`
(2) `the | looney | toons show cartoon | network`
are equally bad if one considers the matching metrics of *Qry-Acc*, *Seg-Prec*, *Seg-Rec* and *Seg-F* (all values being zero) with respect to the reference segmentation. *Seg-Acc* values for the two segmentations are 3/5 and 1/5 respectively. However, the BQV for (1) (`"the looney" "toons show" cartoon network`) fetches better pages than the BQV of (2) (`the looney toons show cartoon network`). So the segmentation (2) provides no IR benefit over the unsegmented query and hence performs worse than (1) on IR metrics. However, the matching metrics, except for *Seg-Acc* to some extent, fail to capture this difference between the segmentations.

Distribution of multiword segments across queries gives insights about effectiveness of strategy. The limitation of the matching metrics can also be understood from the following analysis of the multiword segments in the queries. Fig. 1 shows the distribution of queries having a specific number of multiword segments (for example, 1 in the legend indicates the proportion of queries having *one* multiword segment) when segmented according to the various strategies. We note that for Hagen et al. [7], H_B, H_A and "Mishra et al. [11] + Wiki", almost all of the queries have two multiword segments. For H_C, Li et al. [9], PMI-Q and Mishra et al. [11], the proportion of queries that have only one multiword segment increases. Finally, PMI-W has almost negligible queries with a multiword segment. BQV_{BF} is different from all of them and has a majority of queries with one multiword segment. Now given that the first group generally does the best in IR, followed by the second, we can say that out of the two multiword segments marked by these strategies, only one needs to be quoted. PMI-W as well as unsegmented queries are bad because these schemes cannot detect the one crucial multiword segment quoting which improves the performance. Nevertheless, these schemes do well for matching metrics against BQV_{BF} because both have a large number of single word segments. Clearly this is not helpful for IR. Finally, Mishra et al. [11] performs poorly despite being able to identify a multiword segment in most of the cases because it is not identifying the one that is important for IR.

Hence, the matching metrics are misleading due to two reasons. First, they do not take into account that splitting a useful segment (i.e., a segment which should be quoted to improve IR performance) is less harmful than joining two unrelated segments. Second, matching metrics are, by definition, agnostic to which segments are useful for IR. Therefore, they might unnecessarily penalize a segmentation for not agreeing on the segments which should not be quoted, but are present in the reference human segmentation. While the latter is an inherent problem with any evaluation against manually segmented datasets, the former can be resolved by introducing a new matching metric that differentially penalizes splitting and joining of segments. This is an important and interesting research problem that we would like to address in the future. However, we would like to emphasize here that with the IR system expected to grow in complexity in the future (supporting more flexible matching criteria), the need for an IR-based evaluation like ours' becomes imperative.

Based on our new evaluation framework and corresponding experiments, we observe that "Mishra et al. [11] + Wiki" has the best performance. Nevertheless, the algorithms are trained and tested on different datasets, and therefore, a comparison amongst the algorithms might not be entirely fair. This is not a drawback of the framework and can be circumvented by appropriately tuning all the algorithms on similar datasets. However, the objective of the current work is not to compare segmentation algorithms; rather, it is to introduce the evaluation framework, gain insights from the experiments and highlight the drawbacks of human segmentation-based evaluation.

5. RELATED ISSUES

In this section, we will briefly discuss a few related issues that are essential for understanding certain design choices and decisions made during the course of this research.

5.1 Motivation for a new dataset

TREC data has been a popular choice for conducting IR-based experiments throughout the past decade. Since there is no track specifically geared towards query segmentation, the queries and *qrels* (query-relevance sets) from the ad hoc retrieval task for the Web Track would seem the most rele-

Table 7: IR-based evaluation using Bing API.

Metric	Unseg. query	All quoted for [11] + Wiki	Oracle for [11] + Wiki
nDCG@10	0.882	0.823	**0.989***
MAP@10	0.366	0.352	**0.410***
MRR@10	0.541	0.515	**0.572***

The highest value in a row is marked **bold**. Statistically significant ($p < 0.05$ for paired t-test) improvement over the unsegmented query is marked with *.

vant to our work. However, 74% of the 50 queries in the 2010 Web track ad hoc task had less than three words. Also, when these 50 queries were segmented using the six algorithms, half of the queries did not have a multiword segment. As discussed earlier, query segmentation is useful but not necessarily for all types of queries. The benefit of segmentation may be observed only when there are multiple multiword segments in the queries. The TREC Million Query Track, last held in 2009, has a much larger set of 40,000 queries, with a better coverage of longer queries. But since the goal of the track is to test the hypothesis that a test collection built from several incompletely judged topics is a better tool than a collection built using traditional TREC pooling, there are only about 35,000 query-document relevance judgments for the 40,000 queries. Such a sparse *qrels* is not suitable here – incomplete assessments, especially for documents near the top ranks, could cause crucial errors in system comparisons. Yet another option could have been to use BWC07 as $\mathcal{Q}$and create the corresponding $\mathcal{U}$and $\mathcal{R}$. However, this query set is known to suffer from several drawbacks [7]. A new dataset for query segmentation[7] containing manual segment markups collected through crowdsourcing has been recently made publicly available (after we had completed construction of our set) by Hagen et al. [7], but it lacks query-document relevance judgments. These factors motivated us to create a new dataset suitable for our framework, which has been made publicly available (see Sec. 3.4).

5.2 Retrieval using Bing

Bing is a large-scale commercial Web search engine that provides an API service. Instead of Lucene, which is too simplistic, we could have used Bing as the IR engine in our framework. However, such a choice suffers from two drawbacks. First, Bing might already be segmenting the query with its own algorithm as a preprocessing step. Second, there is a serious replicability issue. The document pool that Bing uses, i.e. the Web, changes dynamically with documents added and removed from the pool on a regular basis. This makes it difficult to publish a static gold standard dataset with relevance judgments for all appropriate query-URL pairs that the Bing API may retrieve even for the same set of queries. In view of this, the main results were reported in this paper using the Lucene text retrieval system.

However, since we used Bing API to construct $\mathcal{U}$and corresponding $\mathcal{R}$, we have the evaluation statistics using the Bing API as well. For paucity of space, in Table 7 we only present the results for nDCG@10, MRR@10 and MAP@10 for "Mishra et al. [11] + Wiki". The table reports results for three quoted version-selection strategies: (i) Unsegmented query only (equivalent to each word being within quotes) (ii) All segments quoted and (iii) *QVRS* (oracle for "Mishra et al. [11] + Wiki"). For all the three metrics, *QVRS* is statistically significantly higher than results for the unsegmented query. Thus, segmentation can play an important role towards improving IR performance of the search engine. We note that the strategy of quoting all the segments is, in fact, detrimental to IR performance. This emphasizes the point that how the segments should be matched in the documents is a very important research challenge. Instead of quoting all the segments, our proposal here is to assume an oracle that will suggest which segments to quote and which are to be left unquoted for the best IR performance. Philosophically, this is a major departure from the previous ideas of using quoted segments, because re-issuing a query by quoting all the segments implies segmentation as a way to generate a fully quoted version of the query (all segments in double quotes). This definition severely limits the scope of segmentation, which ideally should be thought of as a step forward better query understanding.

[7] http://bit.ly/xIhSur

Table 8: Inter-annotator agreement on features as observed from our experiments.

Feature	Pair 1	Pair 2	Pair 3	Mean
Qry-Acc	0.728	0.644	0.534	0.635
Seg-Prec	0.750	0.732	0.632	0.705
Seg-Rec	0.756	0.775	0.671	0.734
Seg-F	0.753	0.753	0.651	0.719
Seg-Acc	0.911	0.914	0.872	0.899
Rel. judg.	0.962	0.959	0.969	0.963

For relevance judgments, only pairs of (0, 2) and (2, 0) were considered disagreements.

5.3 Inter-annotator agreement

Inter-annotator agreement (IAA) is an important indicator for reliability of manually created data. Table 8 reports the pairwise IAA statistics for H_A, H_B and H_C. Since there are no universally accepted metrics for IAA, we report the values of the five matching metrics when one of the annotations (say H_A) is assumed to be the reference and the remaining pair (H_B and H_C) is evaluated against it (average reported). As is evident from the table, the values of all the metrics, except for *Seg-Acc*, is less than 0.78 (similar values reported in [13]), which indicates a rather low IAA. The value for *Seg-Acc* is close to 0.9, which to the contrary, indicates reasonably high IAA (as in [13]). The last row of Table 8 reports the IAA for the three sets of relevance judgments (therefore, the actual pairs for this column are different from that of the other rows). The agreement in this case is quite high.

There might be several reasons for low IAA for segmentation, such as lack of proper guidelines and/or an inherent inability of human annotators to mark the correct segments of a query. Low IAA raises serious doubts about the reliability of human annotations for query segmentation. On the other hand, high IAA for relevance judgments naturally makes these annotations much more reliable for any evaluation, and strengthens the case for our IR-based evaluation framework which only relies on relevance judgments. We note that ideally, relevance judgments should be obtained from the user who has issued the query. This has been referred to as *gold* annotations, as opposed to *silver* or *bronze* annotations which are obtained from expert and non-expert annotators respectively who have not issued the query [1]. Gold annotations are preferable over silver or bronze ones due to relatively higher IAA. Our annotations are silver standard, though very high IAA essentially indicates that they might be as reliable as gold standard. The high IAA might be due to the unambiguous nature of the queries.

6. RELATED WORK

Since its inception in 2003 [12], many algorithms have been proposed for automatic segmentation of Web queries. The approaches vary from purely supervised [3] to fully unsupervised [7, 11] machine learning techniques. They differ widely in terms of resources usage (Table 2) and the underlying algorithmic techniques (e.g., expectation maximization [13] and eigenspace similarity [15]).

6.1 Evaluation on manual annotations

Despite the diversity in approaches to the task, till date there has been only one standard approach for evaluation of query segmentation algorithms, which is to compare the machine output against a set of queries segmented by humans [3, 4, 7, 9, 11, 13, 15]. The basic assumption underlying this evaluation scheme is that humans are capable of segmenting a query in a "correct" or "the best possible" way, which, if exploited appropriately, will result in maximum benefits in IR performance. This is probably motivated by the extensive use of human judgments and annotations as the gold standard in the field of NLP (e.g., parts-of-speech labeling, phrase boundary identification, etc.). However, this idea has several shortcomings, as pointed out in Sec. 4.3. Among those who validate query segmentation against human-labeled data, most [3, 4, 6, 7, 9, 13, 15] report accuracies on BWC07 [3]. The popularity of the BWC07 dataset is partly because it was one of the first human annotated datasets created for query segmentation, and partly because it is the only publicly available dataset of its kind. While BWC07 has provided a common benchmark for comparing various query segmentation algorithms, there are several limitations of this specific dataset. BWC07 only contains noun phrase queries and there is a non-trivial amount of noise in the annotations. See [7] for a detailed criticism of this dataset.

6.2 IR-based evaluation

There has been only a handful of studies that explore some initial ideas about IR-based evaluation [2, 7, 9] for query segmentation. Bendersky et al. [2] were the first to study the effects of segmentation from an IR perspective. They wanted to see if retrieval quality could be improved by incorporating knowledge of query chunks into an MRF-based retrieval system [10]. Their experiments on different TREC collections using popular IR metrics like MAP indicate that query segmentation can indeed boost IR performance. Li et al. [9] examined the usefulness of query segmentation when built into language models for retrieval, in a Web search setting. However, none of these studies propose an objective IR-based *evaluation framework* for query segmentation. Their scope is limited to the demonstration of one particular strategy for exploiting segmentations for improving IR, instead of evaluating and comparing a set of algorithms.

As an excursus to their main work, Hagen et al. [7] examined if submitting fully quoted queries (generated from algorithm outputs) results in fetching better pages by the search engines. They study the top fifty retrieved documents when the following versions of the queries – unsegmented, manually quoted, quoted by the technique in Bergsma and Wang [3], and by their own method – are submitted to Bing. Assuming the pages retrieved by manual quotation as relevant, it was observed that the technique in Bergsma and Wang [3] achieves the highest average recall. However, the authors also state that such an assumption need not hold good in reality and emphasized the need for an in-depth retrieval-based evaluation.

We would like to emphasize here that the aim of a segmentation technique is not to come up with the best quoted version of a query. While some past works have explicitly or implicitly assumed this definition, there are also other works that view segmentation as a purely structural analysis of a query that identifies chunks or sequences of words that are semantically connected as a unit [9, 11]. By quoting all the segments we would be penalizing the latter philosophy of segmentation, which is a more productive and practically useful view.

There have been a few studies on detection of noun phrases from queries [5, 16]. This task is similar to query segmentation in the sense that the phrase can be considered as a single unit in the query. Zhang et al. [16] has shown that such phrase detection schemes can actually help in retrieval, and therefore, is along the lines of the philosophy of the present evaluation framework. Nevertheless, as far as we know, this is the first time that a formal conceptual framework for an IR-based evaluation of query segmentation has been proposed. Our study, also for the first time, compares the effectiveness of human segmentation and related matching metrics to an IR-based evaluation.

7. CONCLUSIONS AND FUTURE WORK

End-user of query segmentation is the retrieval engine; hence, it is essential that any segmentation algorithm should be evaluated in an IR-based framework. In this research, we overcome several conceptual challenges to design and implement the first such scheme of evaluation for query segmentation. Using a carefully selected query test set and a group of segmentation strategies, we show that it is possible to have a fair comparison of the relative goodness of each strategy as measured by standard IR metrics. The proposed framework uses resources which are essential for any IR system evaluation, and hence does not require any special input. Our entire dataset – complete with queries, segmentation outputs and relevance judgments – has also been made publicly available to facilitate further research by the community.

Moreover, we gain several useful and non-intuitive insights from the evaluation experiments. Most importantly, we show that human notions of query segments may not be the best for maximizing retrieval performance, and treating them as the gold standard limits the scope for improvement for an algorithm. Also, the matching metrics extensively used till date for comparing against gold standard segmentations can often be misleading. We would like to emphasize that in the future, the focus of IR will mostly shift to tail queries. In such a scenario, an IR-based evaluation scheme gains relevance because validation against a fixed set of gold standard segmentation may often lead to overfitting of the algorithms without yielding any real benefit.

A hypothetical oracle has been shown to be quite useful, but we realize that it will be a much bigger contribution to the community if we could implement a context-aware oracle that can actually tell the search engine which version of a segmented query should be chosen at runtime.

8. ACKNOWLEDGMENTS

We would like to thank Bo-June (Paul) Hsu and Kuansan Wang (Microsoft Research, Redmond), for providing us with the code for Li et al. [9]. We also thank Matthias Hagen (Bauhaus Universität Weimar), for providing us with the segmentation output of Hagen et al. [7] on our test set at a very short notice. The first author was supported by Microsoft Corporation and Microsoft Research India under the Microsoft Research India PhD Fellowship Award.

9. REFERENCES

[1] P. Bailey, N. Craswell, I. Soboroff, P. Thomas, A. P. de Vries, and E. Yilmaz. Relevance assessment: are judges exchangeable and does it matter. In *SIGIR '08*, pages 667–674. ACM, 2008.

[2] M. Bendersky, W. B. Croft, and D. A. Smith. Two-stage query segmentation for information retrieval. In *SIGIR '09*, pages 810–811. ACM, 2009.

[3] S. Bergsma and Q. I. Wang. Learning noun phrase query segmentation. In *EMNLP-CoNLL'07*, pages 819–826, 2007.

[4] D. J. Brenes, D. Gayo-Avello, and R. Garcia. On the fly query segmentation using snippets. In *CERI '10*, pages 259–266, 2010.

[5] A. L. da Costa Carvalho, E. S. de Moura, and P. Calado. Using statistical features to find phrasal terms in text collections. *JIDM*, 1(3):583–597, 2010.

[6] M. Hagen, M. Potthast, B. Stein, and C. Bräutigam. The power of naive query segmentation. In *SIGIR '10*, pages 797–798. ACM, 2010.

[7] M. Hagen, M. Potthast, B. Stein, and C. Bräutigam. Query segmentation revisited. In *WWW '11*, pages 97–106, 2011.

[8] M. Lease, J. Allan, and W. B. Croft. Regression rank: Learning to meet the opportunity of descriptive queries. In *Proceedings of the 31th European Conference on IR Research on Advances in Information Retrieval*, ECIR '09, pages 90–101, Berlin, Heidelberg, 2009. Springer-Verlag.

[9] Y. Li, B.-J. P. Hsu, C. Zhai, and K. Wang. Unsupervised query segmentation using clickthrough for information retrieval. In *SIGIR '11*, pages 285–294. ACM, 2011.

[10] D. Metzler and W. B. Croft. A markov random field model for term dependencies. In *SIGIR'05*, pages 472–479, 2005.

[11] N. Mishra, R. Saha Roy, N. Ganguly, S. Laxman, and M. Choudhury. Unsupervised query segmentation using only query logs. In *WWW '11*, pages 91–92. ACM, 2011.

[12] K. M. Risvik, T. Mikolajewski, and P. Boros. Query segmentation for web search. In *WWW (Posters)*, 2003.

[13] B. Tan and F. Peng. Unsupervised query segmentation using generative language models and wikipedia. In *WWW '08*, pages 347–356. ACM, 2008.

[14] E. M. Voorhees. Variations in relevance judgments and the measurement of retrieval effectiveness. *Inf. Process. Manage.*, 36:697–716, September 2000.

[15] C. Zhang, N. Sun, X. Hu, T. Huang, and T.-S. Chua. Query segmentation based on eigenspace similarity. In *ACL/AFNLP (Short Papers)'09*, pages 185–188, 2009.

[16] W. Zhang, S. Liu, C. Yu, C. Sun, F. Liu, and W. Meng. Recognition and classification of noun phrases in queries for effective retrieval. In *CIKM '07*, pages 711–720. ACM, 2007.

APPENDIX A: WIKI-BOOST

Algorithm 1 Wiki-Boost(Q', W)

```
W' ← ∅
for all w ∈ W do
    w' ← Seg-Phase-1(w)
    W' ← W' ∪ w'
end for
W'-scores ← ∅
for all w' ∈ W' do
    w'-score ← PMI(w') based on Q'
    W'-scores ← W'-scores ∪ w'-score
end for
U-scores ← ∅
for all unique unigrams u ∈ Q' do
    u-score ← probability(u) in Q'
    U-scores ← U-scores ∪ u-score
end for
W'-scores ← W'-scores ∪ U-scores
return W'-scores
```

In this appendix, we explain how to augment the output of an n-gram score aggregation based segmentation algorithm with Wikipedia titles[8]. Input to *Wiki-Boost* is a list of queries Q' already segmented by the algorithm in Mishra et al. [11] (or any algorithm that meets the above criterion) (say, *Seg-Phase*-1) and W, the list of all stemmed Wikipedia titles (4,508,386 entries after removing one-word entries and those with non-ASCII characters). We compute the PMI-score of an n-segment Wikipedia title w' (segmented by *Seg-Phase*-1) by taking the higher of the PMI scores of the first $(n-1)$ segments with the last segment *and* the first segment and the last $(n-1)$ segments. The frequencies of all n-grams are computed from Q'. Scores for unigrams are defined to be their probabilities of occurrence. Thus, the output of the *Wiki-Boost* is a list of PMI-scores for each Wikipedia title in W.

Following this, we use a second segmentation strategy (say, *Seg-Phase*-2) that takes as input q' (the query q segmented by *Seg-Phase*-1) and tries to further join the segments of q' such that the product of scores of the candidate output segments, computed based on the output of *Wiki-Boost*, is maximized. A dynamic programming approach is found to be helpful in searching over all possible segmentations in *Seg-Phase*-2. The output of *Seg-Phase*-2 is the final segmentation output.

[8] http://dumps.wikimedia.org/enwiki/latest/, accessed April 6, 2011

On Per-topic Variance in IR Evaluation

Stephen E. Robertson
Microsoft Research
7 JJ Thomson Avenue
Cambridge CB3 0FB, UK
stephenerobertson@hotmail.co.uk

Evangelos Kanoulas
Information School
University of Sheffield
Sheffield, UK
ekanoulas@gmail.com

ABSTRACT

We explore the notion, put forward by Cormack & Lynam and Robertson, that we should consider a document collection used for Cranfield-style experiments as a sample from some larger population of documents. In this view, any per-topic metric (such as average precision) should be regarded as an estimate of that metric's true value for that topic in the full population, and therefore as carrying its own per-topic variance or estimate precision or noise. As in the two mentioned papers, we explore this notion by simulating other samples from the same large population. We investigate different ways of performing this simulation. One use of this analysis is to refine the notion of statistical significance of a difference between two systems (in most such analyses, each per-topic measurement is treated as equally precise). We propose a mixed-effects model method to measure significance, and compare it experimentally with the traditional t-test.

Categories and Subject Descriptors: H.3.3 [Information Search and Retrieval]

General Terms: Experimentation, Measurement, Performance

Keywords: information retrieval, evaluation, statistical precision, significance testing, mixed-effects model, simulation

1. INTRODUCTION

In two recent papers, by Cormack and Lynam [3] and Robertson [9], it has been suggested that in Cranfield-style test-collection-based IR evaluations, we should in general consider the document collection used as a sample from a population (in addition to considering the set of topics or queries thus). Such a view suggests (among other things) that each per-topic measurement (such as of Average Precision) should be considered as carrying its own statistical precision, or noise, and that this noise might be different for every topic. This potentially complicates the issue of establishing statistical significance in IR tests. Looked at in a more global way, the set of measurements that we take in a test, averaged over a set of topics, are the result not of a simple sampling of queries/topics, but of the interaction between a sampling of queries/topics and a separate sampling of documents. In [3] this question was investigated in an empirical way, via bootstrap experiments on experimental results; [9] was concerned with more theoretical issues involving the nature of IR evaluation metrics, and appealed only to very limited simulation experiments based on simple models. In some sense the present paper takes a position between these two, with experiments based on a variety of models starting from bootstrapping from empirical results.

The primary question being investigated in this paper is the question of how we should think about the reliability of individual per-topic measurements. The question is tricky, and the paper does not arrive at any firm conclusions. However, it is hoped to shed some light on the question. Specifically, we consider tests of statistical significance for differences between systems. An approach that can make use of per-topic noise is the mixed-effects models. We propose and investigate a linear mixed-effects models approach to significance.

SIGIR'12, August 12–16, 2012, Portland, Oregon, USA.

2. BACKGROUND

2.1 Cormack & Lynam

In this paper [3], a TREC collection of documents was split randomly into two parts. For each topic, the evaluation result (in the form of the value of a metric M such as average precision, AP) in first half of the collection was taken as predicting the value of M in the second half. In order to estimate the variance (or statistical precision) associated with this prediction, the authors took repeated bootstrap samples from the first half of the collection, and re-measured M on each sample. The distribution of M values over samples (single topic, single original set of results) provides an indication of the statistical precision required. They concluded that this procedure does indeed adequately model the variance inherent in an AP estimate for an individual topic in a document collection of a certain size, regarded as a sample from an infinite collection of potential documents (so that the split collection is seen as two independent samples from this population).

Certain technical issues arise: first, it is better to use $M = \text{logit}(AP)$ rather than $M = AP$, as it has better distributional properties; second, in the bootstrap sampling it is necessary to treat very small values of R, the total number of relevant documents in the observed collection, in special ways. These are discussed further below.

2.2 Robertson

In this paper [9], different metrics M are investigated theoretically, with a view to establishing whether it makes sense to pose the infinite-document-population question in terms of each metric. Some metrics turn out not to be understandable in these terms; a metric as defined on a given finite population may not be generalisable to an infinite population. In particular, for example, there appears to be no equivalent to $NDCG$ defined on an infinite population. AP, however, can be so generalised.

Even if it is generalisable, we should ask the question: is the metric value observed on the given finite population a good estimate of its 'true' value in the infinite population? Some limited simulation experiments, using some previously proposed models of score distributions for relevant and non-relevant documents, are made in order to investigate this question. It appears from both theoretical arguments and these simulation experiments that some such metrics may provide biased estimates of their true population values. AP seems to be one of these: AP observed on a given finite document population is likely to be an over-estimate of 'true' AP on the infinite population of which the observed finite population is a sample. The reason postulated for the bias in AP is as follows. The infinite population equivalent is defined as a particular form of integral over (area under) the infinite-population recall-precision curve, which we expect to be smooth. However, in estimating it for an observed sample, we choose to measure the height of the recall-precision curve only at the points in the ranking where relevant documents occur, i.e. exactly at the peaks of the noisy sample curve.

2.3 Topics and documents

The usual approach to system evaluation in IR experiments is to choose a metric defined on the results of searching on an individual topic or query, and take an average of this metric over the set of topics, for the system concerned (there are many such metrics in common use, including AP and $NDCG$). The usual approach to statistical significance is to consider the results for the individual topics as the (indivisible) units of measurement. So suppose, for example, that the measure is RPrec and the significance test is the sign test, the fact that system A performs better than system B by RPrec on topic 1 counts as a definitive result. The significance question arises only at the aggregation-over-topics level ('does system A perform better than system B on significantly more topics?'). We do not ask the question as to whether or in what sense the individual topic 1 result was significant. This approach effectively assumes that the topics were sampled from some population of (possible or actual) topics, but that the document collection is fixed in stone for all time.

Stated like this, it must be clear that this (the document collection part) is a rather drastic assumption. In fact it is in part mitigated by the general view in IR research that a result is only good if it works on multiple test collections. But this is a rather crude approach to the problem. It would be good to have a much better understanding of what each individual topic result is telling us, and of how best to draw general conclusions from the topic sample $\times$ document sample results that we have. A start in exploring these issues is made in the two papers cited above; the present paper attempts to take this analysis a step further.

A basic premise of the approach taken in the two cited papers is that the population of documents looks different from the point of view of each separate topic – in particular, with regard to relevance. The simulations in both papers are based on modelling the document population separately for each topic. An alternative approach would be to model the population of documents independently of the topics, and then model the interaction of each topic with that population. Such an approach would be interesting indeed but very hard. It would also have to model the interaction of each system with the population, separately applied to each topic. The big advantage of the per-topic model of the population is that both relevance and system responses (e.g. scores) can be taken as given. Furthermore, it serves to emphasise an important aspect of the document sample view of IR experiments. While the entire document collection is typically very large (from which one might be tempted to conclude that statistical precision issues do not arise), from the point of view of each topic we see a (typically much smaller) sets of relevant or retrieved documents, on which all the measures depend. Precision at cutoff 5, for example, should be seen as a very imprecise measurement (in the statistical sense) for a single topic.

2.4 Variation between topics

It is well understood in the IR research community that there is a great deal of variation between topics. For example, the analysis of variance in the paper by Banks et al. [1] finds the topic effect to be greater than the system effect (as well as a significant interaction effect). The Robust track at TREC was devoted to investigating hard topics, in the recognition that there are significant numbers of topics that appear to be generally hard for systems to perform well on.

If it is accepted that the document collection should be regarded as sampled in some way from a population, then as indicated above, each per-topic measurement has some built-in error of estimation because the measurement is based on the sample rather than the population. One of the aims of this paper is to get a handle on this estimation error. In particular, we ask the question: does this estimation error vary substantially between topics? If this variation is substantial, should this affect how we analyse test results?

2.5 Scores and simulations

The method of simulation used in [3] is based on bootstrap ideas. We start with a given system and topic and the corresponding set of results (documents retrieved and ranked) from a real test collection of documents. Then we model the process of drawing other samples from the notional infinite population of documents by repeated sampling with replacement from these actual documents. The method used in [9] is a parametric approach based on score distributions. On the back of previous work on fitting distributions to the scores of relevant and non-relevant documents respectively, these distributions are then taken as representing the notional population of documents. We can repeatedly sample from the distributions rather than from any specific documents.

It is clear that the score-distribution approach implies a smoothing effect which the bootstrap method does not have.

Modelling the population as consisting only of instances *exactly* like the ones we have already seen seems to go against at least part of the basic idea of samples and populations – that any sample we take consists only of examples. We should in some sense *expect* the population to include other kinds of examples, not represented directly in the sample we have. On the other hand, the use of score distributions typically involves strong assumptions about the nature of the distributions, and also involves some dependence on the particular scoring methods used by systems. Systems differ greatly not only in the kinds of scores they produce, but also in whether they produce a consistent set of scores at all. For example, some systems may do an implicit AND on the query terms, and then use a scoring function which is defined only within the AND set. Others may rank by rule or on the basis of local comparisons which do not result in an overall score. These facts clearly limit the scope of score-distribution modelling – as against the advantage of smoothness.

In this paper, accepting the limitations of the score distribution approach, we nevertheless use it to investigate the smoothness issues. That is, we try to characterise how assuming a smoother population might affect what we can infer from the sample. But we look at a range of score-distribution methods, of which one extreme (no smoothing) corresponds to the Cormack and Lynam bootstrap method. Thus taking the *scores* of the retrieved real documents as given and performing bootstrap samples on them is equivalent to bootstrapping from the documents themselves[1]. Then we introduce various levels of smoothing, from minimal Gaussian noise to fully-fledged parametric distribution fitting.

An alternative method not pursued in this paper might be to smooth by introducing noise into the documents themselves. Some such methods have been used in the context of query performance prediction [11].

3. MOTIVATING HYPOTHESIS

To restate the hypothesis that motivates this paper, as well as the two earlier ones:

> A test document collection should be thought of as a sample from some hypothetical universe of possible documents.

As is common in statistical analysis of any experimental results, we assume that the sample that we have is in some way representative of the universe, which we take to be large or infinite. The primary object of statistical analysis is to draw inferences about this universe. This is *not* to say that the test collection is representative of other real documents in the world, but that such a view is a prerequisite for basic statistical understanding. If we do not know how to draw inferences correctly for this hypothetical universe, then we certainly do not know how to draw inferences about the real world.

The primary concern of this paper is with the variance (error) associated with each observation that we make (a given metric on a given system-topic pair). Since we cannot normally make multiple repeated observations on different test collections sampled from the same universe, the only way we can discover how such repetitions might be distributed is by simulation.

[1]We note that the assumption that a system would always give the same score to a given document, even in the context of a varying collection, is debatable: there is some discussion in [4]. We do not pursue this question in the present paper.

4. DATA AND METRICS

The document collection used in the experiments reported here is the one contained in TREC Disk 4 and 5, excluding the Congressional Record sub-collection, together with the 50 topics used for the TREC 8 Ad Hoc track. The system runs used are a new set, similar to that used in [6], consisting of a series of 44 runs on the Terrier system. Four different weighting models were used (BM25, the Hiemstra language model, PL2 and TF*IDF), and eleven different query versions (title, title+description, title+description+narrative, and eight query expansion runs using pseudo relevance feedback, expanding the query by between 4 and 512 terms). This set may be characterised in various ways: (a) all the systems (models) generate fairly traditional forms of scores; (b) all runs use the same initial parsing (including Porter stemming and stopword removal); (c) the collection of runs constitutes a systematic matrix of certain variables (weighting schemes and forms of query); (d) all other system variables are held constant.

In the event, four pairs of runs gave the exact same AP values and thus only one run from each pair was used in the experiments while the other was discarded. Thus the analysis below is based on 40 runs.

The primary metric used in this analysis is logit(AP), where AP is average precision. As indicated above, following [3], the distributional properties of logit(AP) seem to be better than those of AP; in particular, because (theoretical) range of logit(AP) is $(-\infty, \infty)$, it makes sense to model distributions of repeated logit(AP) measurements as Gaussian; attempting to do the same with AP measurements results in some logical inconsistencies. In [3], some evidence is presented that such distributions of logit(AP) measurements are indeed approximately Gaussian. However, it should be noted that this does not resolve the issue raised in [9], that of the bias in estimation from finite samples, which applies to logit(AP) as well as to AP. The use of logit necessitates some smoothing, to avoid infinities at either end – we follow previous practice in using an epsilon correction. However, we note that a new more heavily smoothed version of logit(AP), yaAP, is proposed in [8]. This has better distributional properties than logit(AP) itself, and may therefore be a better candidate metric for the work reported here; however, we have not yet rerun the analyses with yaAP.

The 44 runs have MAPs ranging from 0.273 to 0.131, with a significant bunching to the top end (31 of the runs have $MAP > 0.24$). If instead of taking the mean of AP, we take the mean of logit(AP) and then convert it back to the AP scale by reversing the transformation, we see a different ranking of runs and rather lower 'AP' values, ranging from 0.188 to 0.034 (this is consistent with previous reported results using GMAP). Bunching of runs is not quite so strong but still evident.

5. SIMULATION MODELS

5.1 General simulation principles

In general, we take the results from each topic and system run (the scores of the top 1000 ranked documents), split into relevant and non-relevant. This is taken as the results from searching a sample from some (assumed large or infinite) population of documents, and we wish to simulate what the search results from other samples from this same large population of documents would look like. Thus we need to infer a model of the whole population of documents and resample from it. We avoid sampling from the entire supposed population of documents (which would be intractable) by sampling separately for the results of each topic. What follows is a brief description of the method, which is similar to that used in [3], except that it separates the sampling of relevant and non-relevant documents/scores, in order to allow various smoothing methods. It involves a number of approximations that deserve more discussion than is possible in the present paper.

Suppose that the size of the original test collection is N, this topic has R known relevant documents, of which r are retrieved in the top 1000 by this system run. For the purposes of the present experiment, we will assume that all samples from the large population of documents are the same size, N. This assumption is not used directly, but is implicit in what follows. We first take a stochastic decision about how many relevant to include in our sample. This theoretically has two steps: deciding how many reldocs should be in the entire sampled collection, and deciding how many should be in the top 1000 retrieved set. The first step can be based on the observed generality of the topic (proportion of the original test collection that is relevant, R/N), and the second can be based similarly on the proportion of these retrieved by the system (r/R). In practice we combine these two steps, and take a Poisson approximation because R/N at least is assumed to be small. So we take a sample from a Poisson distribution with mean r, to define the number r_s of relevant retrieved for this topic in this simulation run. We ignore instances where this number is zero (further discussion below).

Next we take r_s samples from some model of the distribution of relevant document scores, and $1000-r_s$ samples from some model of the distribution of non-relevant scores. The details of how we do this vary between models. We sort the 1000 resulting scores into descending order, and treat them as the ranked document scores from a new test collection, sampled similarly to the original from the same large population. Since these scores are marked as 'relevant' or 'not relevant', we can apply any IR metric to this ranked list.

5.2 Analysis

For each topic and each run (assume S systems or runs, and T topics), we repeat the process described above some number C of times. This results in C simulated values of the metric M, for each topic and each run. In simulation, these values represent the outcome of C different test collections, all of the same size, all taken from the same infinite population of documents, all searched for the same topic by the same system/run (meaning in this case the same query formulation and the same weighting and scoring method). We note that we could also vary the size of the simulated collection to investigate the effect of such variation on evaluation results.

In what follows, we use these $C \times T \times S$ values of M in two different ways. First, we compare the mean and variance of M over $C = 1000$ samples with the observed value of M for the real test collection. This is used to validate the simulation model as producing reasonable unbiased results; it also serves to demonstrate the large variation between the variances of different topics, thus confirming our initial premise that different topics provide measurements with different associated precision (or estimation error or noise). Second, we take $C = 10$ samples and submit them to an analysis of variance process. This provides us with a way of conducting statistical significance tests which take account of this variation between topics.

5.3 Simulation models

As indicated, the simulation models vary in how they smooth the actual scores obtained from the system in modelling the two required distributions for each topic. In the BST (Bootstrap) simulation, we sample with replacement from the list of actual scores of the top 1000 documents, split into relevant and non-relevant. In this simulation, the scores are in effect labels only; it is therefore more-or-less equivalent to the bootstrap method used in [3]. One difference is in the handling of the zero cases. These turned out to be a problem in [3], because (a) the corpus used (TREC 6) included 5 topics with $R < 5$, and (b) the corpus was split randomly into two parts for their experiments. In the present corpus, there is one topic for which $R = 6$, and the next lowest value is 13; furthermore, we do not split the collection. Therefore it has been assumed to be safe not to treat these cases in any special way, and to simply ignore the bootstrap samples which would have $r_s = 0$.

In the KDE (kernel density estimation) method, we add a small amount of noise (following some simple distributional assumption) to each datapoint, and mix the results into a single smooth distribution. Different noise models may be used, but a common form (used here) is Gaussian – this can therefore be thought of as a Gaussian mixture model with one Gaussian for each observed score. In the present paper, we make use of a Perl module [5], applied separately to the relevant and non-relevant scores for each topic/returned document combination. There are various methods of determining the variance to be applied to the noise model; these are not discussed further in the present paper.

In the GMG (Gaussian Mixture and Gamma) model, developed by Kanoulas et al [6], the relevant distribution is modelled as a mixture of Gaussians (usually 1, 2 or 3 Gaussians, determined by the data), and the non-relevant as a Gamma distribution. Estimated parameters provided by the fitting process are the means and variances of the Gaussians, their relative preponderance, and the shape and scale parameters of the Gamma, as discussed in the cited paper.

As will be clear, simulation of IR evaluation evaluations is a complicated process, deserving of much more discussion. In the present paper, simulation is a means to an end, and such discussion is deferred to a later paper.

6. RESULTS OF THE SIMULATIONS

We present some results, as follows. In Figure 1 (simulation model BST, run 11), each point represents a single topic; the x-axis is the observed logit(AP) on the real test collection, and the y-axis is the value of the same metric in the samples. The points represent the means over all $C = 1000$ samples, and the bars represent one standard deviation either side of the mean. We note that (a) the simulated results are very close to the observed ones; (b), more importantly, the standard-deviation bars are very variable.

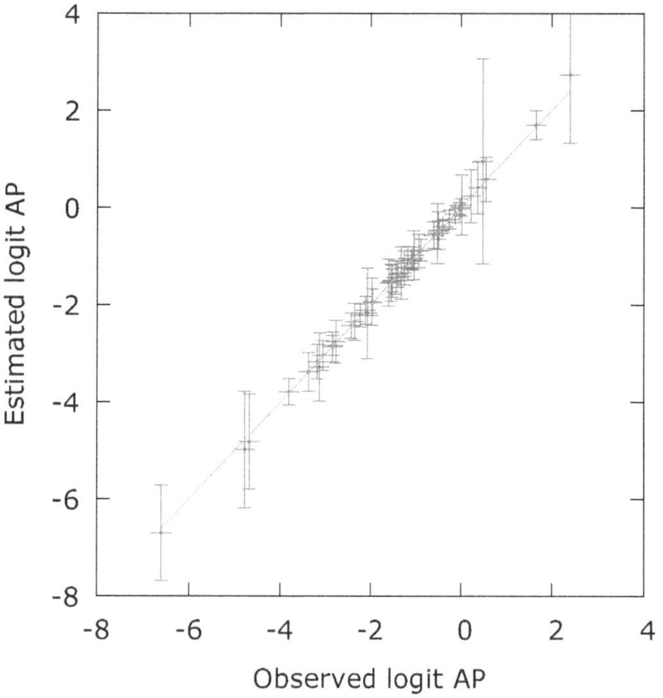

Figure 1: Bootstrap simulation of run 11.

In relation to (a), we note also that this is as expected, since the bootstrap simulation uses the real results very directly; we have made no attempt to prevent overfitting. However, we can clearly see consistency; it is entirely plausible, from the means at least, that the observed results were drawn from the distributions indicated. Once again, we defer more detailed discussion of the fit to observation to a future paper devoted to simulation. Run 11 is the best-performing run according to this metric; Figure 2 shows similar graphs for three more runs, distributed over the ranking of runs, with very similar characteristics.

We note also that the per-topic standard deviation values are similar for different runs. Taking pairwise correlations between runs over the set of topic standard deviations, for the above 5 runs, the correlation values range from 0.60 to 0.97 (the bottom of the range is raised significantly if we ignore the worst-performing run). Thus (on the whole) the same topics have the least precise estimates, or the greatest noise, on the different runs. This result may well be affected by the choice of runs for the present experiment: a more varied set of runs might indicate less commonality in this respect.

Figure 3 shows one run under the Kernel Density simulation and two under the Gaussian Mixture and Gamma simulation. The variation from the observations is slightly greater, though not by very much, as a result of the smoothing; the variances are also broadly similar.

7. COMPARATIVE EVALUATION

So far we have introduced methods to simulate effectiveness measurements over different document corpora, samples from a very large (or infinite) document collection. Hence, the effectiveness of a system/run not only varies across topics but it further varies within each topic. The question that remains to be answered is how can we account for this new source of variability (within topic variability) and distinguish it from the variability across topics when evaluating retrieval systems in a comparative evaluation exercise.

Comparative systems-based evaluation typically uses a statistical hypothesis test such as the t-test to make an inference about the significance of the difference in the effectiveness of two retrieval systems. However, the t-test and similar tests are not adequate to handle multiple sources of variability into a systems-based evaluation. Those tests model a topic sample as a so-called "random effect" that introduces variance to the measure, but they can only model one random effect. On the other hand, mixed-effects models, which will be introduced in this section, can incorporate arbitrary sources of variability into an analysis [7].

In this section we describe how can we express mixed-effects models and then show how to fit them in the statistical programming environment **R**.[2] We start with a simple model of a single source of variance (single effect) and extend it to a model that better corresponds to our experiments of repeated measurements per topic. To illustrate the analysis, we take as example the simulated results for a single pair of systems.

The linear model that accounts only for the topic effect is,

$$y_{ij} = \beta_i + b_j + \epsilon_{ij} \tag{1}$$

$$b_j \sim \mathcal{N}(0, \sigma_1^2), \quad \epsilon_{ij} \sim \mathcal{N}(0, \sigma^2)$$

where y_{ij} is the value of an evaluation measure calculated on topic j for system i, β_i is the effect of system i, b_j is the effect of topic j, and ϵ_{ij} is the residual error. The system effect is a so-called "fixed effect" since the systems we would like to compare are fixed and not a sample from some system distribution. On the other hand the topic effect, as mentioned earlier, is a "random effect", assuming that the topic is actually sampled from a population of topics.

The assumption behind this model is that the random variable, b_j, is independent and identically normally distributed with zero mean and σ_1^2 variance. The residual error is also assumed to be independent and identically normally distributed with zero mean and σ^2 variance.

In **R**, the following procedures fit the same linear effect model (Eq. 1) and result in equivalent inferences:

```
t.test(y ~ system, paired=TRUE, data=data)
aov(y ~ system + Error(topic), data=data)
lme(y ~ system, data=data, random=~1|topic)
```

In all cases our data consists of an evaluation measure calculated over a set of topics for the two systems under comparison. This is stored in a data frame `data` with three fields, the measurement `y`, the system id `system`, and the topic id `topic`. The first line runs a paired t-test while the second one runs an ANOVA analysis; in the latter the response variable y is explicitly written as a function of a fixed effect (`system`) and a random effect (`Error(topic)`). The last line is explicitly fitting a mixed-effects model using the function `lme` in the `nlme` package.

[2]Mixed-effects models have been recently described by Carterette et al. [2]. In their work Carterette et al. considered the variability introduced in measurements when evaluation measure parameters are distributed.

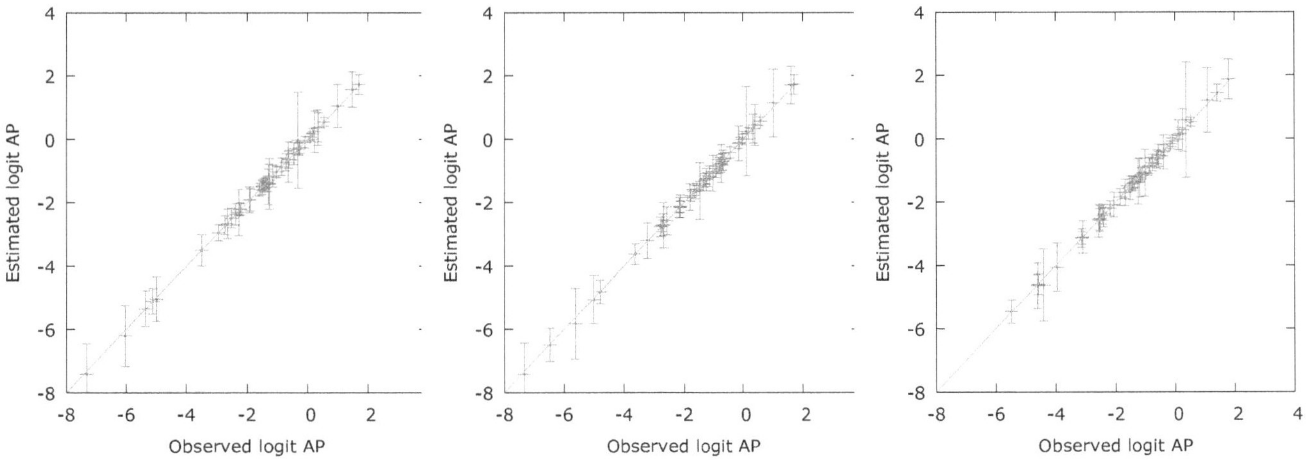

Figure 2: Bootstrap simulation of runs 19, 38, 29

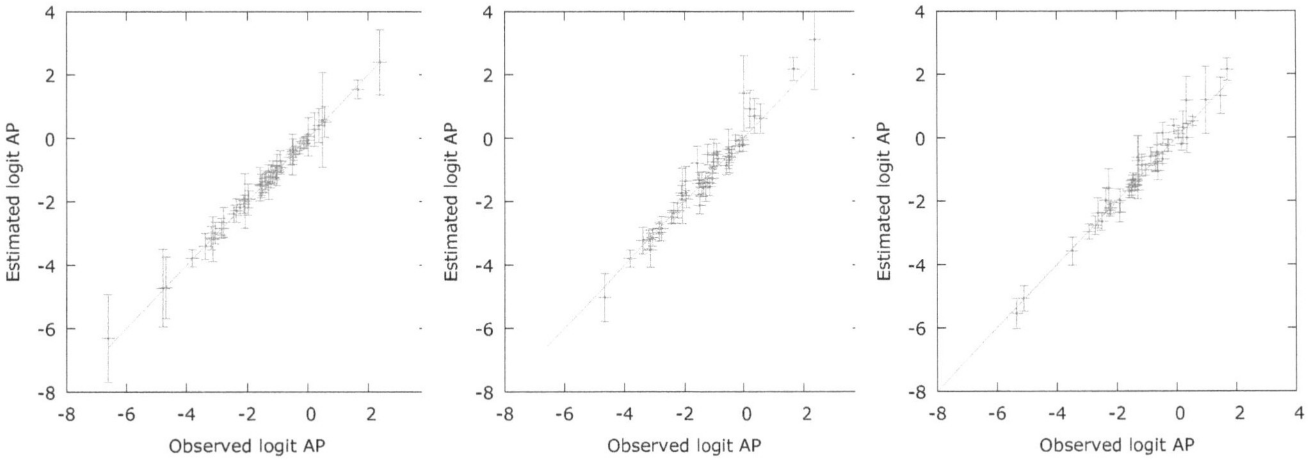

Figure 3: Kernel Density Estimation simulation of run 11, and Gaussian Mixture and Gamma simulation of runs 11, 19

The mixed-effects model in Eq. 1 models the effects of topics over the effectiveness scores of the compared systems. However, it fails to model a far more important effect, that of the interaction between the systems and the topics; that is the fact that a system may find a query hard while the same query is considered easy by a different system. The effect of this interaction in the above model is conflated with the residual error, since we only have one measurement per system-topic. In the case of repeated measurements this interaction effect can be decomposed from the random error and modeled separately,

$$y_{ijk} = \beta_i + b_j + c_{ij} + \epsilon_{ijk} \tag{2}$$

$$b_j \sim \mathcal{N}(0, \sigma_1^2), \quad c_{ij} \sim \mathcal{N}(0, \sigma_2^2), \quad \epsilon_{ijk} \sim \mathcal{N}(0, \sigma^2)$$

where y_{ijk} is the value of an evaluation measure calculated on topic j for system i on the document collection sample k, β_i is the effect of system i, b_j is the effect of topic j, c_{ij} is the interaction effect, and ϵ_{ijk} is the residual error. As it can be seen the interaction effect is a random effect normally distributed with zero mean and σ_2^2 variance. We can fit Eq. 2 in **R** by,

```
> lme1 <- lme(y~system, data=df,
                        random=~1|topic/system)
```

The output of **R**'s `lme` function is,

```
> summary(lme1)
Linear mixed-effects model fit by REML
 Data: df
      AIC      BIC   logLik
   2173.5 2197.719 -1081.75

Random effects:
 Formula: ~1 | topic
        (Intercept)
StdDev:    1.539644

 Formula: ~1 | system %in% topic
        (Intercept)  Residual
StdDev:   0.6191864 0.6386645

Fixed effects: y ~ system
              Value Std.Error  DF   t-value p-value
(Intercept) -1.3445 0.2438470 846 -5.514077  0.0000
system2      0.0999 0.1343512  46  0.744112  0.4606
```

Let's focus on the `Random effects` section of the output. We can observe that σ_1^2, the variance of the topic effect distribution, is estimated to 1.539644, σ_2^2, the variance of the system/topic interaction effect distribution is estimated to 0.6191864, while the variance of the error, σ^2, is estimated to 0.6386645.[3] If we move to the `Fixed effects` section of the above results, we can observe that the effect of the first system is estimated to -1.3445 (`intercept`), while the difference to the second system of the pair under comparison is estimated to 0.0999 (`system2`). The `lme` function, further performs a significance test to examine whether this difference is statistically significant. The p-value over the `system2` line above designates that the difference between the two systems is not statistically significant.

So far, we have assumed that the errors are independent and identically normally distributed, with mean zero and variance σ^2, and they are independent of the random effects. This implies that error over all system/topic pairs are i.i.d. which is the opposite of what we have demonstrated through Figures 1 and 3. To further examine whether this assumption is valid we first plot the boxplots of residual errors grouped by system/topic pairs (Figure 4). This plot is useful for verifying that the errors are centered at zero (i.e., $E[\epsilon] = 0$), have constant variance across groups ($Var(\epsilon_{ijk}) = \sigma^2$), and are independent of the group levels. Figure 4 indicates that the residuals are indeed centered at zero, but that the variability changes with system/topic group.[4]

We can further verify this by plotting the standardized residuals against the fitted values (left hand-side plot in Figure 5). As one can observe residuals vary with different variance across the different groups.

A more general model to better represent our measurements allows different variances by system/topic groups for the errors. We can define such a model by,

$$y_{ijk} = \beta_i + b_j + c_{ij} + \epsilon_{ijk} \tag{3}$$

$$b_j \sim \mathcal{N}(0, \sigma_1^2), \quad c_{ij} \sim \mathcal{N}(0, \sigma_2^2), \quad \epsilon_{ijk} \sim \mathcal{N}(0, \sigma_{ij}^2)$$

This model is called "heteroscedastic", while the model of equal variances per system/topic group (Eq. 2) is call "homoscedastic". The difference between the heteroscedastic model in Eq. 3 and the homoscedastic model in Eq. 2 is the fact that the heteroscedastic model allows for different variances σ_{ij}^2 for each system i topic j group of measurements. This can be expressed in `lme` by a `varIdent` parameter that defines the grouping factors.

```
> lme2 <- lme(y~system, data=df,
            random=~1|topic/system,
            weights=varIdent(form=~1|topic*system))
```

The results of fitting the heteroscedastic model in the data can be viewed below,

```
> summary(lme2)
Linear mixed-effects model fit by REML
 Data: df
      AIC      BIC    logLik
  1080.872 1555.559 -442.4358

Random effects:
 Formula: ~1 | topic
        (Intercept)
StdDev:    1.447164

 Formula: ~1 | system %in% topic
        (Intercept) Residual
StdDev:   0.4537618 0.186183

Variance function:
 Structure: Different standard deviations per stratum
 Formula: ~1 | topic * system
 Parameter estimates:
      1*1       1*2       2*1       2*2  ...
 1.0000000 1.6108387 1.3969085 1.5405710  ...

Fixed effects: y ~ system
              Value  Std.Error  DF   t-value p-value
(Intercept) -1.4385 0.22266286 846 -6.460817  0.0000
system2      0.1834 0.09844907  46  1.863342  0.0688
```

Apart from the random and fixed effects section, there is a `Variance function` section. The values of this section give the ratio of the standard error of each system/topic group to the standard error of the first system/topic group. Thus, for instance, the standard error for the second system when run against the first topic is about 60% more than that of the first system when run against the first topic, while the standard error for the first system run against the second topic is 40% more than the standard error running against the first topic. The standard error of the first system/topic group is itself presented as the `Residual` standard error, in the random effect section (0.186183).

We can confirm the adequacy of the heteroscedastic fit by re-examining plots of the standardized residuals versus the fitted values by system/topic. As expected, the standardized residuals in each block now have about the same variability, Figure 5 (right).

The need for a heteroscedastic model can be formally tested with the anova method.

```
anova(lme1,lme2)
     Model df  AIC  BIC logLik   Test L.Ratio p-value
lme1     1  5 2173 2197  -1081
lme2     2 98 1080 1555   -442 1 vs 2 1278.62  <.0001
```

The anova method compares the two models in terms of *Akaike Information Criterion (AIC)*, *Bayesian Information Criterion (BIC)*, and *Log Likelihood (logLik)*, with the smaller the better in all cases. Further it performs a significance test on the likelihood ratio of the two models. The very small p-value of the likelihood ratio statistic confirms that the heteroscedastic model explains the data significantly better than the homoscedastic model.

8. EXPERIMENTAL ANALYSIS

We have seen that the proposed view of evaluation experiments suggests that not all individual topic measurements have the same status. That is, each one carries its own noise variance, and these vary significantly between topics. This

[3]Note that even though `system %in% topic` appears as a nested effect of the systems within each topic, the function in fact calculates the interaction effect, because of the crossed design of our experiment, in which the two systems under comparison are run against all topics.

[4]For clarity purposes we only plot the residuals of the two systems against the first 10 topics.

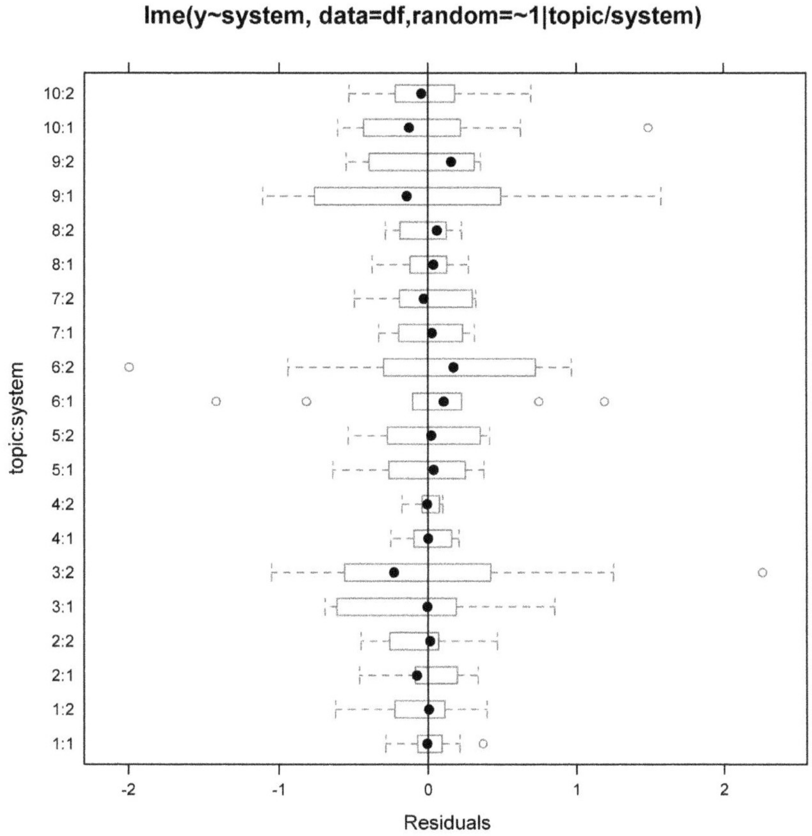

Figure 4: Boxplots of residuals for homoscedastic mixed-effects model by system/topic.

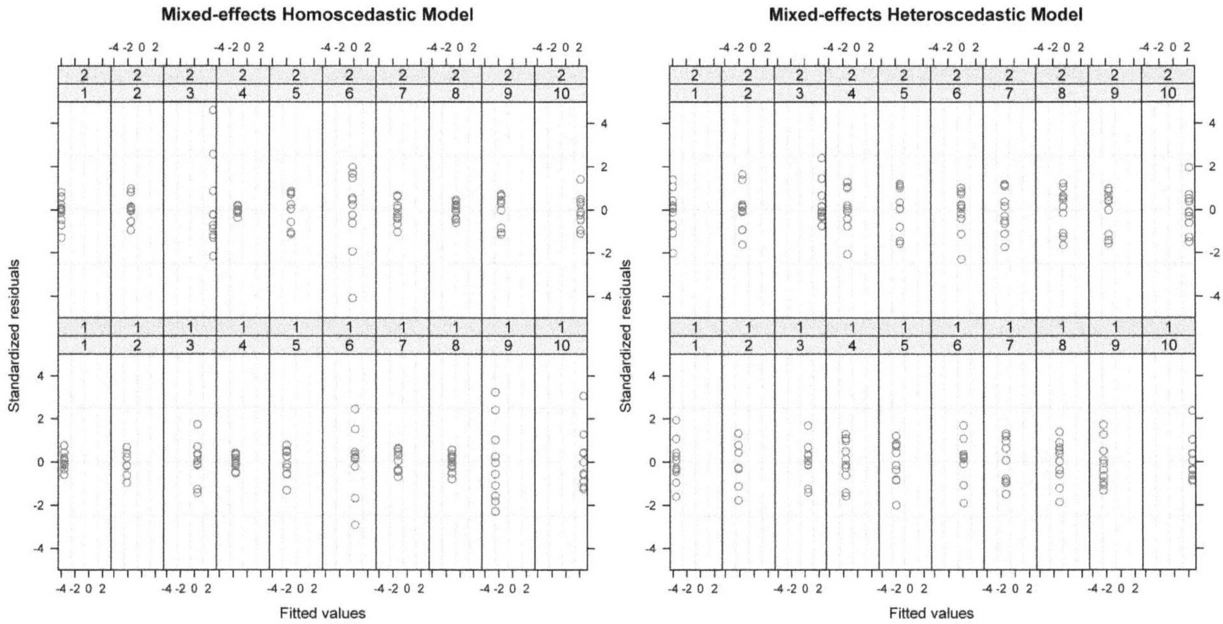

Figure 5: Standardized residuals versus fitted values per system/topic for the homoscedastic (left) and heteroscedastic (right) mixed-effects model.

suggests in turn that the common approaches to statistical significance in comparing systems are over-simplified. Tests like the t-test assign the same status (give the same weight) to every individual topic measurement.

The view proposed by Cormack and Lynam [3] is that each topic should in some sense be regarded as a separate experiment, and that the summarisation of results over sets of topics is analogous to a meta-analysis of a group of experiments. We proposed an approach to statistical significance testing that takes a step in this direction, using mixed-effects models. For each topic/run pair, we run the simulation 10 times, to obtain 10 values of the metric. In mixed-effects terms, we regard these values as repeated measurements, in the sense that the measurements have been taken at random from a population of possible values (i.e. a population of possible test collections). We are not interested in the differences between these individual values within the groups.

The effect of taking multiple values per topic/run combination is to indicate to the mixed-effects model how reliable or unreliable each topic is in determining the effectiveness of this run. One obvious issue is that these measurements are not real – they are the result of simulations. We can appeal to the evidence of Section 6, that they are consistent with the observed results. We need to use the simulations rather than the directly observed results because only here do we have the necessary repetitions.

We compare the (heteroscedastic and homoscedastic) mixed-effects models with the t-test. Since we use simulated data for mixed-effects models, we also use the same data for the t-test: this is performed on the means of the 10 simulated samples for each topic. Again, since this is not the usual way to run a t-test on IR evaluation data, we also run it in the usual way, on the observed results.

In order to measure the power of the test, we follow Sakai [10] in performing all possible pairwise tests, sorting by p-value, and plotting the number of pairs against the p-values: see Figure 6 for the Gaussian Mixture and Gamma simulation; similar plots are obtained by the other two simulation model (note that in this section we focus on the GMG simulations, which show the most discrepancy from the observed results). All these are 2-sided tests. We see that the all four tests appear to be equally powerful, as indicated by how much of the curve is below a significance threshold such as 0.05. Hence, decomposing and separately modeling the precision of each topic separately does not lead to a change in the power of the test.

What is more interesting however is to examine the disagreements between the p-values calculated by the different tests that could lead in disagreements between which system pairs each test consider as significantly different in performance. Figure 7 presents the scatter plot of the p-values for the t-test on the means of the simulated measurements, the homoscedastic mixed-effects model and the heteroscedastic mixed-effects model against the t-test over the actual logit AP values (without any simulation). This again uses the evaluation scores over the Gaussian Mixture and Gamma simulation. Each point is a pair of systems under comparison. As it can be seen from the plots, there is a significant disagreement in the p-values computed by the different tests (but note that the visual effect is somewhat exaggerated because of the large number of superimposed points in the lower left). The t-test over the actual logit AP values agrees best with the heteroscedastic model. This is expected since

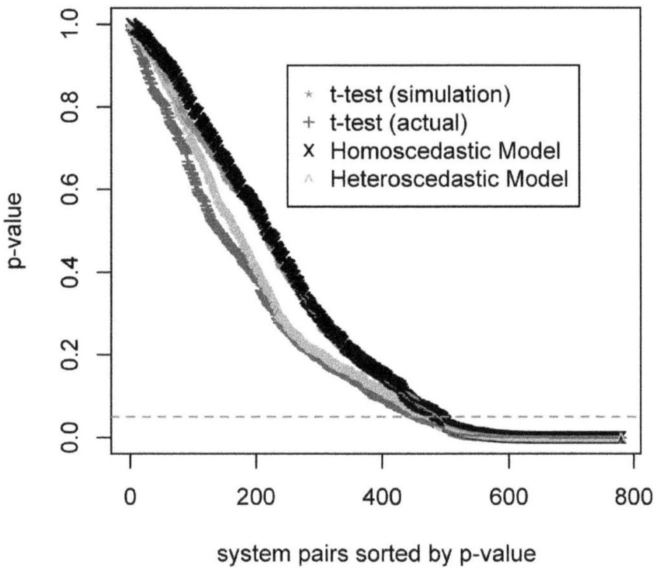

Figure 6: P-values for the different significance tests (GMG simulations).

the t-test over the mean of the repeated measurements per topic and the homoscedastic model do not handle correctly the extra source of variability. The points in the areas to the left and the bottom of the dashed lines in the plots of Figure 7 represent system pairs that have been found significantly different by at least one of the contrasted tests. If we focus at the heteroscedastic model vs t-test plot the percentage of disagreement between the two tests with respect to those system pairs that are found significant by at least one of the tests reaches about 20%. Examining the system pairs for which the two tests disagree is of particular interest; however we leave it as future work.

We also show contingency tables indicating agreement or otherwise between the tests at the threshold of 0.05 (Table 1). The results over all three simulation methods are summarized in these tables. Similarly to the Figures 6 and 7 we see that all test are comparable regarding their power, while there are certain system pairs for which different tests disagree with each other.

9. CONCLUSIONS

The experiments reported here reinforce the notion that we need to worry about the statistical status and validity of evaluation results on individual topics. The usual approach in IR evaluation, of regarding each individual topic measurement as an indivisible atom, is not consistent with our use of particular collections of documents. The size of the document collections we use is actually no insulation against statistical issues, since measurements for individual topics typically depend on the small sets of documents judged relevant.

A good approach to this issue has the potential to inform the measurement of statistical significance in IR evaluations. We provide some evidence that it will affect significance tests and inferences of retrieval quality. The evidence presented is by no means complete, and many other developments and experiments are required. One future direction would be to investigate whether we can characterise the high-variance

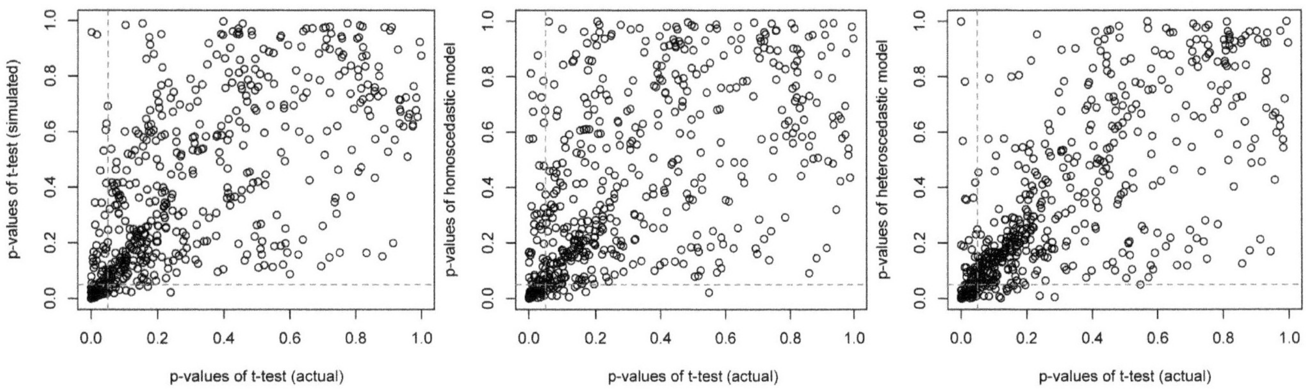

Figure 7: Scatter plots of p-values for the different tests (GMG simulation)

			t-test on actual values $p < 0.05$	t-test on actual values $p \geq 0.05$			t-test on actual values $p < 0.05$	t-test on actual values $p \geq 0.05$
(BST)	Heterosced. 10 samples	$p < 0.05$	287	15	t-test on mean over 10 samples	$p < 0.05$	291	2
		$p \geq 0.05$	16	462		$p \geq 0.05$	12	475
(GMG)	Heterosced. 10 samples	$p < 0.05$	281	20	t-test on mean over 10 samples	$p < 0.05$	281	9
		$p \geq 0.05$	37	435		$p \geq 0.05$	44	446
(KDE)	Heterosced. 10 samples	$p < 0.05$	292	22	t-test on mean over 10 samples	$p < 0.05$	288	3
		$p \geq 0.05$	11	455		$p \geq 0.05$	15	474

Table 1: Contingency table on the agreement of different significance tests for 780 pairs of systems, on 3 simulations: (BST) Bootstrap, (GMG) Gaussian mixture + gamma, (KDE) Kernel Density Estimation.

topics in some simple way. However, the work reported here is seen as a step towards better understanding of this particular source of error in IR evaluation.

Acknowledgments

We would like to thank Jaap Kamps for valuable discussions on an earlier version of this paper. Further, we gratefully acknowledge the support provided by the European Commission grant FP7-PEOPLE-2009-IIF-254562.

10. REFERENCES

[1] David Banks, Paul Over, and Nien-Fan Zhang. Blind men and elephants: Six approaches to TREC data. *Inf. Retr.*, 1(1-2):7–34, 1999.

[2] Ben Carterette, Evangelos Kanoulas, and Emine Yilmaz. Simulating simple user behavior for system effectiveness evaluation. In *Proceedings of the 20th ACM Conference on Information and Knowledge Management, CIKM 2011*, pages 611–620. ACM, 2011.

[3] Gordon V. Cormack and Thomas R. Lynam. Statistical precision of information retrieval evaluation. In *Proceedings of the 29th Annual International ACM SIGIR Conference on Research and Development in Information Retrieval*, pages 533–540. ACM, 2006.

[4] David Hawking and Stephen E. Robertson. On collection size and retrieval effectiveness. *Inf. Retr.*, 6(1):99–105, 2003.

[5] Philipp Jarnet. Statistics-KernelEstimation. `http://search.cpan.org/~janert/Statistics-KernelEstimation/`.

[6] Evangelos Kanoulas, Virgiliu Pavlu, Keshi Dai, and Javed A. Aslam. Modeling the score distributions of relevant and non-relevant documents. In *Proceedings of Second International Conference on the Theory of Information Retrieval, ICTIR 2009*, pages 152–163. Springer, 2009.

[7] Jose C. Pinheiro and Douglas M. Bates. *Mixed-Effects Models in S and S-PLUS*. Statistics and computing. Springer-Verlag New York, Inc., 2000.

[8] Stephen Robertson. On smoothing average precision. In *Proceedings of the 34th European Conference on IR Research, ECIR 2012*, pages 158–169. Springer, 2012.

[9] Stephen E. Robertson. On document populations and measures of ir effectiveness. In *Studies in theory of information retrieval (Proceedings of ICTIR 2007)*, pages 9–12, 2007.

[10] Tetsuya Sakai. Evaluating evaluation metrics based on the bootstrap. In *Proceedings of the 29th Annual International ACM SIGIR Conference on Research and Development in Information Retrieval*, pages 525–532. ACM, 2006.

[11] Vishwa Vinay, Ingemar J. Cox, Natasa Milic-Frayling, and Kenneth R. Wood. On ranking the effectiveness of searches. In *Proceedings of the 29th Annual International ACM SIGIR Conference on Research and Development in Information Retrieval*, pages 398–404. ACM, 2006.

An Uncertainty-aware Query Selection Model for Evaluation of IR Systems

Mehdi Hosseini, Ingemar J. Cox
Computer Science Department
University College, London, UK
{m.hosseini, ingemar}@cs.ucl.ac.uk

Nataša Milić-Frayling, Milad Shokouhi, Emine Yilmaz
Microsoft Research, Cambridge, UK
{natasamf,milads,eminey}@microsoft.com

ABSTRACT

We propose a mathematical framework for query selection as a mechanism for reducing the cost of constructing information retrieval test collections. In particular, our mathematical formulation explicitly models the uncertainty in the retrieval effectiveness metrics that is introduced by the absence of relevance judgments. Since the optimization problem is computationally intractable, we devise an adaptive query selection algorithm, referred to as Adaptive, that provides an approximate solution. Adaptive selects queries iteratively and assumes that no relevance judgments are available for the query under consideration. Once a query is selected, the associated relevance assessments are acquired and then used to aid the selection of subsequent queries. We demonstrate the effectiveness of the algorithm on two TREC test collections as well as a test collection of an online search engine with 1000 queries. Our experimental results show that the queries chosen by Adaptive produce reliable performance ranking of systems. The ranking is better correlated with the actual systems ranking than the rankings produced by queries that were selected using the considered baseline methods.

Categories and Subject Descriptors

H.3 [**Information Storage and Retrieval**]: H.3.4[Systems and Software: Performance Evaluation]

General Terms

Measurements, Algorithms, Theory and Performance

Keywords

Information Retrieval, Test Collection, Query Selection

1. INTRODUCTION

Modern test collections are large, comprising millions of documents and thousands of queries that require relevance judgments in order to calculate metrics of retrieval effectiveness. Constructing a test collection incurs a cost which, in the simplest case, is proportional to the number of queries chosen to evaluate the retrieval systems and the number of documents that need to be judged per query. Hence, the cost can be reduced by: (*i*) query selection that limits the number of queries for which relevance judgments need to be collected, (*ii*) document selection that reduces the number of documents to be judged for each query, and (*iii*) a combination of the two.

Much recent work has been devoted to effective and efficient construction of test collections [1, 5], with the primary focus on document selection [4]. In this paper, we explore methods for query selection as a means of dealing with a budget constraint. As Guiver et al. [10] showed, it is possible to reproduce the results of an exhaustive evaluation of systems by using a much reduced set of queries. However, it is still unclear how to select such a subset when relevance judgments are not available for the queries under consideration.

In our approach, we first formulate query selection as an optimization problem, minimizing the error in systems evaluation based on a subset of queries. In contrast to the previous work which is mostly retrospective and assumes that some relevance judgments are available for each query [10, 15, 17], our model is designed to work in practice and does not require relevance judgments for a query that is not yet selected. The mathematical formulation shows that an optimal subset of queries satisfies the following properties: (*i*) selected queries have a low correlation with one another, thereby maximizing the information we gain from each, (*ii*) selected queries have strong correlation with the remaining queries, as without this correlation there is no predictive capability, and (*iii*) the total uncertainty associated with the selected queries is small. Here the correlation between two queries refers to their similarity in evaluating systems.

Since selecting the optimal subset of queries is a computationally intractable problem, we approximate the solution by an iterative query selection process referred to as Adaptive. The Adaptive algorithm starts by selecting the first query at random, assuming no information about relevance judgments. However, once this query is selected, the relevance judgments are acquired and used to assist with the selection of subsequent queries.

Specifically, at each iteration we use previously selected queries and associated relevance judgments to train a classifier that estimates the relevance of documents pooled for each of the unselected queries. Using the output of the clas-

SIGIR '12, August 12–16, 2012, Portland, Oregon, USA.

sifier we compute the probability of relevance for the pooled documents and used it to estimate the performance metric, e.g. the average precision, and the corresponding approximation variance which we refer to as *uncertainty*.

We evaluate our method by comparing the ranking of systems based on the subset of queries with the ranking over the full set of queries. We report the results in terms of Kendall-τ and Pearson correlation coefficients and show that the query subsets chosen by our models are significantly more effective than those selected by the considered baseline methods.

It is known that using query subsets may lead to poor performance when estimating the performance of previously unseen (new) systems [17]. We conduct experiments to investigate how our method generalizes to new systems. We show that the iterative algorithm can be modified to improve generalizability. Additionally, we consider the query selection problem for multiple metrics. In our experiment we show that a query subset selected based on a particular metric may not provide reliable systems evaluation when another metric is used to measure retrieval performance. Thus, we modify our query selection algorithm to select a query subset that leads to reliable evaluations across multiple metrics.

In summary, the contributions of this paper are threefold: (*i*) we provide a theoretical model for query selection that explicitly models uncertainty in retrieval effectiveness scores, (*ii*) we develop Adaptive, an iterative algorithm, that efficiently implements our theoretical model in practice, and (*iii*) we modify the iterative algorithm to investigate how the selected query subset generalizes to (a) new unseen systems and (b) changes to the evaluation metric.

2. RELATED WORK

The increased size of document corpora and query sets has made the cost of relevance assessments one of the main challenges in creating IR test collections. Spark-Jones and Van Rijsbergen [19] proposed a document pooling technique to select a subset of documents to be judged and the National Institute of Standard and Technology (NIST) adopted this method in most TREC experiments. For example, in the TREC AdHoc task, each participating system adds the top-100 ranked documents per query to the common pool to be judged by human assessors. Documents that are not included in this pool are assumed to be non-relevant. Several alternative approaches to the original pooling method have been suggested in order to judge more relevant documents at the same pool depth, e.g. Zobel [21] and Cormack et al. [7].

On average, NIST assessors judge 2,000 documents per query. This is often sufficient for a reliable evaluation of systems, even for recall-sensitive metrics such as average precision (AP), and increases the reusability of the TREC test collection for other tasks and new systems. Nevertheless, it still demands a considerable human effort and incurs a significant cost when the test collection contains a large number of queries. As a result, most of the existing TREC test collections contain as few as 50 queries.

Using small samples of queries to measure retrieval performance may cause considerable errors in the systems evaluation. Therefore, recent studies have concentrated on the IR evaluation with large set of queries [5]. In order to make relevance assessments feasible, various document selection methods are suggested [2, 4]. These methods reduce the number of documents that need to be judged per query and are often used in conjunction with evaluation metrics [2, 4, 20] designed for shallow sets of relevance judgments.

Following the trend of online search engines with large number of queries, NIST has recently launched the Million Query track [1]. In 2007, the Million Query track used 1800 queries for evaluation. The track mostly focused on (*i*) analyzing the efficiency of document selection methods, and (*ii*) the impact that incomplete relevance judgments have on the measurement accuracy.

Query selection is a complementary approach to document selection and is used to reduce the cost of creating test collections. Guiver et al. [10] have shown that query subsets vary in their accuracy of predicting the average performance of systems. Their results indicate that some subsets of queries, known as representative subsets, are particularly good predictors of the systems average performance as measured over the full set of queries. Mizzaro and Robertson [15] explored the characteristics of individual queries that were beneficial for systems evaluation. They defined the notion of hubness for queries where a higher hubness score indicates that a query is better than others at distinguishing the systems retrieval effectiveness. Robertson [17] later showed that the query selection based on the hubness scores alone does not necessarily result in a reliable prediction of the systems rankings. The work by Guiver et al. [10] shows that, indeed, representative query sets that are effective in approximating the systems ranking, comprise of queries that range in their individual ability to predict the systems performance.

Most studies on query selection are based on retrospective analysis [10, 15, 17] and assume that relevance judgments are available at the time the subset of queries is selected. Typical scenarios involve selecting queries to increase the pool of existing relevance judgments to accommodate evaluation of new systems. For example, Hosseini et al. [14] proposed a query selection approach to enhance the reusability of a test collection. Their focus was on generalizability, i.e. a reliable ranking of systems that did not contribute to the judged pool of documents. They assumed that an initial set of relevance judgments is available for each candidate query, and proposed a budget constrained model to select an optimal subset of queries. The selected queries were then used to expand relevance judgments based on the documents retrieved by new systems. The authors later extended their work [13] by considering a query-document pair selection problem when relevance judgments were to be created iteratively. Yet again, they assumed that the available budget allows for gathering at least a few relevance judgments per each query in the test collection. The authors applied convex optimization with a budget constraint to collect relevance judgments optimally across queries.

3. QUERY SELECTION

Previous research provided valuable insights on framing theoretical models for query selection [13, 14]. It focused on cases where there were judged documents for each query in the pool. The objective was to select a subset of queries to obtain additional relevance judgments for a more robust evaluation. In contrast, we focus on a scenario when no relevance judgments are available until a query is selected. We assume that a large set of queries has been initially compiled to measure the performance of a set of systems. Our goal

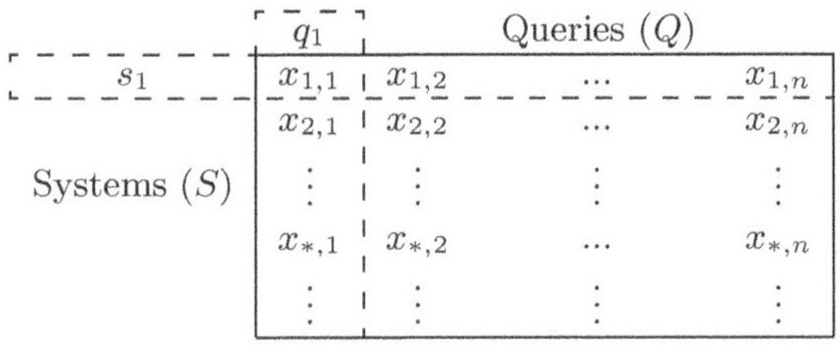

(a) In Theory

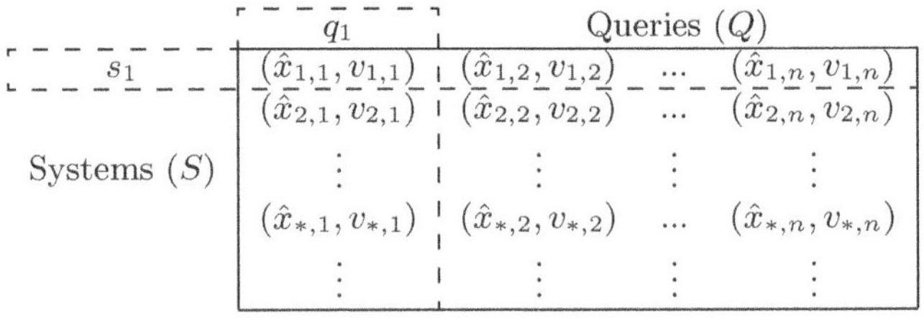

(b) In Practice

Figure 1: (a) The true performance matrix X for systems in S and queries in Q. Each entry indicates the system performance score based on the available relevance judgments. (b) The approximated performance matrix $\hat{X}$, for systems in S and queries in Q. Each pair indicates the estimated performance and associated uncertainty.

is to find a subset of queries that most closely approximates the system evaluation results that would be obtained if we judged documents for the full set of queries.

To that effect we first formulate the query selection problem as in [13], assuming that relevance judgements are available and, thus the performance scores are known. We then relax this assumption and introduce our query selection model in the next section.

Consider a set of n known queries, Q, together with a set of l known systems, S. When relevance judgments are available, we can represent the associated retrieval effectiveness scores of the l systems against the n queries using a $l \times n$ performance matrix $X \in R^{l \times n}$ (Figure 1a). In X, the rows represent systems, the columns represent queries, and the value $x_{s,q}$ shows the performance score, e.g. the average precision, of sth system in S against q^{th} query in Q. We also consider a column vector $M \in R^{l \times 1}$, as the average performance vector. The elements of M represent the average performance scores of individual systems across the set of queries. Thus, when the metric is AP, M represents the mean average precision (MAP) scores for individual systems.

Now, let $\Phi = \{j_1, ..., j_m\}$ be a subset of $\{1, 2, ..., n\}$ with $1 \leq m \leq n$ and Q_Φ be the corresponding query subset. We define $M_\Phi \in R^{l \times 1}$ as the column vector comprising the average performance of systems for the subset of queries, Q_Φ. The aim of a query selection method is to find a subset of m queries such that the corresponding column vector M_Φ closely approximates the M vector.

The approximation is quantified using the mean squared errors between elements of M and M_Φ, if the similarity in terms of the absolute values of performance scores is of interest. Alternatively, we can use Kendall-τ correlation, if the similarity in the ranking of systems is of interest, or Pearson linear correlation, if the similarities in the relative performance scores are of interest. As in [13], we choose Pearson correlation as it is amenable to mathematical optimization. However, we use Kendall-τ as our final evaluation measure for comparing the rankings of systems produced by full set and a subset of queries.

The Pearson correlation between the elements of M and M_Φ is

$$\rho_\Phi = \frac{cov(M, M_\Phi)}{\{var(M)var(M_\Phi)\}^{\frac{1}{2}}} \quad (1)$$

where

$$\begin{aligned} var(M) &= n^{-2} e^T \Sigma e \\ var(M_\Phi) &= m^{-2} d^T \Sigma d \\ cov(M, M_\Phi) &= n^{-1} m^{-1} d^T \Sigma e \end{aligned}$$

where $e = \{1\}^{n \times 1}$ is the vector of n components, each equal to 1; $d \in \{0, 1\}^{n \times 1}$ is a binary vector such that $d_j = 1$ if $j \in \Phi$, and $d_j = 0$ otherwise. Note that this is slightly different from the formulation in [13] as the task is also different. In [13], d is defined as a vector of real values and its role is to establish the proportions of the budget allocated across queries. In this paper, since we are interested in the query selection problem, the vector d is defined, without loss of generality, as a binary vector and considered as an indicator to selected queries.

Following Equation 1, we have $\Sigma = cov(X)$ as the $n \times n$ covariance matrix of the system-query performance scores such that $(i, j)^{th}$ element of Σ is the covariance between i^{th} and j^{th} columns of X. In practice, the covariance matrix Σ calculated based on the l systems is:

$$\Sigma = (l-1)^{-1} \sum_{i=1}^{l} (x_i - \alpha)^T (x_i - \alpha)$$

where $\alpha = l^{-1} \sum_{i=1}^{l} x_i$ and x_i is the ith row of X. The optimum subset maximizes the Pearson correlation ρ_Φ, where substituting for the variances and the covariance we have

$$\rho_\Phi = \frac{(d^T \Sigma e)}{\{(e^T \Sigma e)(d^T \Sigma d)\}^{\frac{1}{2}}}$$

This derivation assumes that the elements of the X matrix are true representatives of the systems performance as computed over the full set of relevance judgments. Of course, in practice this assumption does not hold because of the absence of relevance judgments during query selection. In the following section, we propose an extended model that uses performance predictors for approximating systems true performance. We then extend the model to incorporate explicitly the noise in the measurement of the systems performance.

4. UNCERTAINTY-AWARE SELECTION

We assume that instead of containing the true performance values, each element of X holds a predicted performance estimate with a variance from the true value that we refer to as *uncertainty*. Hence, the noisy $\hat{X}$ matrix can be represented as shown in Figure 1b where each of its elements represents a pair of values: $\hat{x}_{s,q}$ and $v_{s,q} = var(x_{s,q})$. In addition, let $\hat{M}_\Phi \in R^{l\times 1}$ be the vector of l average performance scores computed based on the query subset, Q_Φ, and the performance matrix $\hat{X}$. Thus, in practice we look for a subset that maximizes the Pearson correlation between $\hat{M}_\Phi$ and M. To compute the Pearson correlation we need to compute the variances and the covariance of $\hat{M}_\Phi$ and M.

The variance of $\hat{M}_\Phi$ is due to two sources, the variance across systems and the variance due to the measurement noise. The first variance is expressed by $var(M_\Phi)$ as calculated in Section 3. To compute the second variance we first note that each of the elements in $\hat{M}_\Phi$ has its own variance. If $\hat{\mu}^i_\Phi$ denotes the performance of ith system in $\hat{M}_\Phi$, then the associated variance is

$$var(\hat{\mu}^i_\Phi) = m^{-2}\sum_{j\in\Phi} v_{i,j}$$

Following the law of total variance [3], the variance of $\hat{M}_\Phi$ is given by

$$var(\hat{M}_\Phi) = var(M_\Phi) + E_s(var(\hat{\mu}^s_\Phi)) = \tag{2}$$
$$m^{-2}d^T\Sigma d + m^{-2}\sum_{j\in\Phi} E(v_j) = m^{-2}d^T(\Sigma + U)d$$

where $1 \leq s \leq l$ and $U = diag\big(E(v_1), ..., E(v_n)\big)$ is a diagonal matrix, referred to as the uncertainty matrix. $E(v_q) = l^{-1}\sum_{i=1}^{l} v_{i,q}$ is the mean uncertainty for a query q.

To compute the covariance between $\hat{M}_\Phi$ and M, let us consider an unknown system that is randomly sampled from the l systems, and let x and $\hat{x}$ denote the associated performance row vectors in X and $\hat{X}$. The system's average performance computed based on X and the full set of queries is

$$\mu = n^{-1}xe$$

Also the systems average performance based on the subset of m queries, Q_Φ, and $\hat{X}$ is

$$\hat{\mu}_\Phi = m^{-1}\hat{x}d$$

where e and d are the column vectors as defined in Section 3. The covariance between $\hat{M}_\Phi$ and M is then

$$cov(\hat{M}_\Phi, M) \equiv cov(\hat{\mu}_\Phi, \mu) = m^{-1}n^{-1}cov(\hat{x}d, xe) =$$
$$m^{-1}n^{-1}d^T cov(\hat{x}^T, x)e = m^{-1}n^{-1}d^T\Sigma e \tag{3}$$

where $\hat{x}d = d^T\hat{x}^T$, and

$$cov(\hat{x}^T, x) = cov(x^T + \epsilon, x) =$$
$$E\{\big(x - E(x)\big)^T\big(x - E(x)\big)\} \equiv cov(X) = \Sigma$$

Note that, $\hat{x}^T = x^T + \epsilon$ where $\epsilon \in R^{1\times n}$ is the vector of estimator's noise.

Thus, the Pearson correlation between $\hat{M}_\Phi$ and M is given by

$$\hat{\rho}_\Phi = \frac{(d^T\Sigma e)}{\{(e^T\Sigma e)\big(d^T(\Sigma + U)d\big)\}^{\frac{1}{2}}} \tag{4}$$

Formally, we seek a subset Q_Φ that maximizes $\hat{\rho}_\Phi$. Reordering the correlation above we have

$$\gamma_\Phi \equiv (e^T\Sigma e)^{\frac{1}{2}}\hat{\rho}_\Phi = \frac{(e^T\Sigma d)}{\big(d^T(\Sigma + U)d\big)^{\frac{1}{2}}}$$

Selecting a subset of queries Φ that maximizes $\hat{\rho}_\Phi$ is equivalent to selecting a subset of queries that maximizes γ_Φ since $(e^T\Sigma e)^{\frac{1}{2}}$ is a constant. Let $\sigma_{i,j}$ be the $(i,j)^{th}$ element of Σ and $E(v_j)$ be the jth diagonal element of the uncertainty matrix U. We can then rewrite γ_Φ as

$$\max_\Phi \gamma_\Phi = \frac{\sum_{1\leq i\leq n, j\in\Phi}(\sigma_{i,j})}{\{\sum_{i,j\in\Phi}(\sigma_{i,j}) + \sum_{j\in\Phi} E(v_j)\}^{\frac{1}{2}}} \tag{5}$$

Equation 5 provides valuable insights into the query selection problem. In order to maximize γ_Φ we seek a set of queries that minimizes the denominator and maximizes the numerator.

To minimize the denominator, we need to choose m queries for which the corresponding columns in X are least correlated with one another. This is equivalent to maximizing the information we derive from each query in the subset. Conversely, if the columns of X are perfectly correlated, then all the queries provide the same information and we may as well have a subset of size one. Additionally, the sum of the expected uncertainty, $\{E(v_j)|j \in \Phi\}$, of the selected queries should be a minimum.

The numerator is maximized if the columns in X, associated with the selected queries, have high correlation with the rest of columns in X. This is also intuitively clear. After all, if the selected subset is completely uncorrelated with the remaining queries, then it has no prediction power of the systems performance on the remaining queries. Thus, we seek a subset of queries that are highly correlated with the rest of queries.

5. ADAPTIVE QUERY SELECTION

Thus far, we introduced a theoretical model for query selection that extends the previous work by explicitly modeling uncertainty. The model allows for the elements of the performance matrix to represent predicted rather than actual performance values. Equation 5 shows how the predicted performance values can be incorporated into the optimization process, but does not indicate how they can be computed in practice. We describe in detail the Adaptive query selection algorithm that iteratively selects queries and refines the estimations in $\hat{X}$. This method exploits the supervised prediction and uses the relevance judgments of already selected queries, to train a model for selecting subsequent queries.

The Adaptive method iteratively selects a new query, that in combination with the previously selected queries maximizes Equation 5. The relevance judgments of the previously selected queries are used to predict the relevance judgments of yet non-selected queries. The adaptive method subsequently estimates the performance scores, and updates the $\hat{X}$ matrix by adding the systems performance scores for the selected query, and those predicted for the non-selected queries. This process is repeated until we reach the maximum number of queries to be selected.

In order to predict the relevance of documents for queries that have not been selected yet, we train a classifier using judged documents of previously selected queries as training data. Each query-document pair is represented to the classifier as a vector of 7+l generic features where l refers to the number of systems. These features are:

- The number of systems that retrieved the query-document pair (one feature).

- The average, minimum and maximum ranks given to the query-document pair by the systems (three features).
- For systems that retrieve the query-document pair, we calculate their corresponding past-performance scores based on the subset of queries for which we have relevance judgments. For example, if the metric is AP, we compute a system's MAP based on its AP scores obtained for previously selected queries. We then determine the minimum, maximum and average across systems (three features).
- The l relevance scores provided by l systems for the given query-document pair (l features). If a system does not retrieve the document, the corresponding score is set to the minimum score obtained for the documents retrieved by that system.

We train a linear support vector machine (SVM) as our classifier [8]. For each query-document pair we map the output of the classifier to a probability score using the calibration method proposed in [16]. Briefly, let $f \in [a, b]$ be the output of the SVM classifier. We use a sigmoid function to map f to a posterior probability on [0,1]:

$$p_i = P(r_i = 1|f_i) = \frac{1}{1 + exp(Af_i + B)}$$

where r_i refers to the true relevance value of document i, p_i is its probability of relevance, and A and B are the parameters of the sigmoid function, fitted using maximum likelihood estimation from a calibration set (r_i, f_i). The training data is the same as the training data used by the classifier. Thus, at each iteration we retrain the classifier and fit the sigmoid function to exploit the increase in training data from the new round of relevance judgments.

After each query-document pair is assigned a probability of relevance, we use these probabilities in the family of MTC estimators, proposed by Carterette et al. [4], to provide new estimates for the unknown performance scores in the $\hat{X}$ matrix. For example, when the metric of interest is $P@k$, the expectation and variance are calculated as:

$$\begin{aligned} E[P@k] &= \frac{1}{k}\sum_{i=1}^{k} p_i \\ var[P@k] &= \frac{1}{k^2}\sum_{i=1}^{k} p_i(1-p_i) \end{aligned}$$

where p_i is the calibrated relevance probability of the document retrieved at rank i. The formulations for other metrics, e.g. AP, can be found in [4].

6. EVALUATION SETTINGS

Query selection and document selection methods are often evaluated by considering the systems ranking they produce compared to the ground-truth systems ranking based on all the queries and the full set of relevance judgments. As in previous work [4, 10], we use Kendall-τ and Pearson coefficient as the correlation metrics. Kendall-τ penalizes disordering of high-performance and low-performance system pairs equally. However, in practice, distinguishing between best performing systems is often more important. Therefore, in many of our experiments, we also report separately the results for the subsets of best performing systems in terms of the average precision (AP) and the precision at position 100 ($P@100$).

We run our experiments on both the TREC 2004 Robust track, and the TREC-8 AdHoc track data sets. The TREC 2004 Robust track includes a collection of 249 queries, 14 participants with a total of 110 automatic runs, and 311,410 relevance judgments. The TREC-8 consists of 50 queries, 39 participants with 13 manual runs and 116 automatic runs, and 86,830 relevance judgments. In our experiments, we consider individual runs as different search systems, taking special care when considering runs from the same participant. We also create a Web test collection based on the query logs of a commercial search engine. This dataset comprises 1,000 queries, 50 runs of a learning to rank system trained with different feature sets, and 30,000 relevance judgments. We compare the performance of our query selection against query sets obtained by three baseline methods: random, oracle and iterative query prioritization.

Random: randomly selects a subset of queries. We report the results averaged over 1,000 random trials and consider 95% confidence interval of the sample average.

Oracle(Ideal): selects the best subset of queries by considering the full X matrix constructed from the full set of queries and all the relevance judgments in the test collection. For a given subset size $m < 10$ and $m > (n - 10)$, we perform an exhaustive search to find the best subset. Exhaustive search is computationally expensive for $10 < m < (n - 10)$. Therefore, we estimate the best subset of size $10 < m < (n - 10)$ by randomly generating 10,000 query subsets from which the best subset is selected.[1]

Iterative Query Prioritization (IQP): we consider a modified version of the budget constrained optimization method proposed in [13] as a query selection baseline. The original method, referred to as query prioritization (QP), cannot be used in our experiments because it is defined as a convex optimization that demands a set of initial judgments for all the queries. This assumption is not valid in our experiments. Thus, we consider a modified version of this method that does not rely upon such an assumption and is specialized for the query selection task. We replace the budget vector $\beta \in [0, 1]^{n \times 1}$ with a binary vector $d \in \{0, 1\}^{n \times 1}$ as an indicator to selected queries. Therefore, the optimization function is changed to

$$\max_d f(d) = \frac{d^T \Sigma e}{(d^T \Sigma d)^{\frac{1}{2}}} \quad \text{subject to } \sum_{j=1}^{n} d_j \le m$$

This modified version, (IQP), starts from zero relevance judgments and iteratively selects queries and updates the vector d. Similar to the original method in [13] IQP does not consider the uncertainty in estimating the entries of the X matrix. That is, it uses the same classifier (as in our iterative adaptive method) but directly maps the output of the classifier to 0 or 1, when the relevance judgments are binary, and regards them as the predicted absolute relevance values. Therefore there is no calibration of relevance probabilities involved. As such, it does not use the MTC estimators discussed in Section 5 but, instead, relies upon the standard metrics, e.g. AP, to measure the systems performance. Considering IQP in our experiments helps us investigate the effect of incorporating measurement uncertainty into the query selection.

[1]We considered the oracle subset in our experiments to provide an upper bound for the performance of the query selection algorithms.

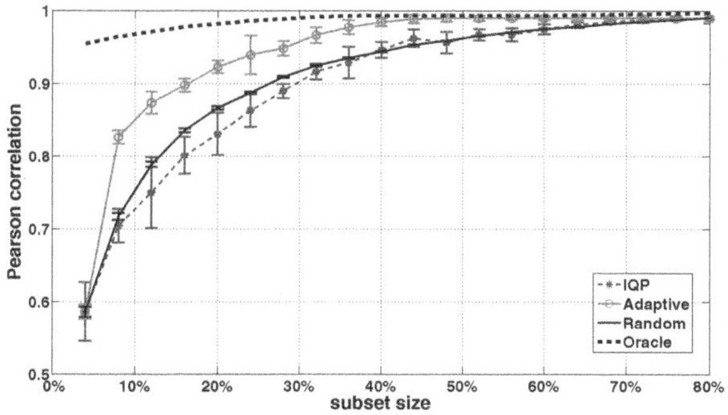

(a)

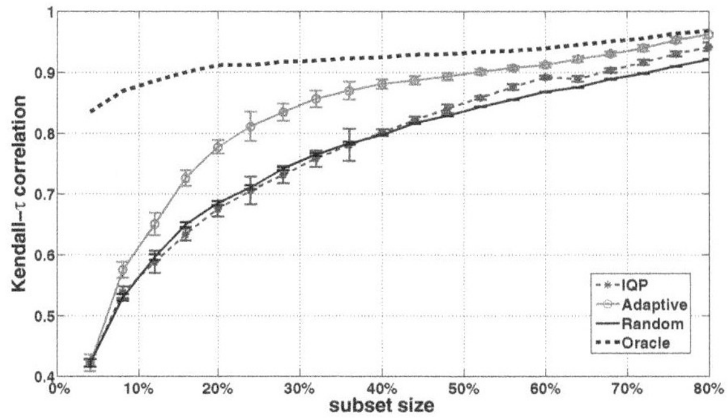

(b)

Figure 2: Selecting queries using (*i*) Oracle, (*ii*) random, (*iii*) *IQP*, (*iv*) Adaptive query selection algorithm, for the Robust 2004 test collections with 249 queries. The first query is randomly selected. The results are averaged over 50 trials with *AP* metric.

7. EXPERIMENTAL RESULTS

In the experiments with TREC test collections, we consider all the official retrieval runs. Each system contributes 100 documents to the pool for each query. After selecting a query, the official TREC judgments are collected and revealed. The Adaptive and *IQP* methods, then add these recently judged documents to their training sets.

On each testbed, we report the results for three different groupings of systems: (*i*) all systems, (*ii*) 30 best performing systems, and (*iii*) only pairs of systems with a statistically significant performance difference, measured by the paired t-test with the significance level of 0.05.

Figure 2 shows the results on the Robust 2004 test collection with 249 queries. The retrieval evaluation metric is *AP*. Pearson and Kendall-τ correlation are used to measure the correlation of a query subset vector $\hat{M}_\Phi$, and corresponding vector M, calculated using the full set of 249 queries. At the initialization step of the Adaptive and *IQP* methods, the first query is randomly selected. To deal with the variation of random sampling, we consider 50 trials. We report the average of 50 trials as the average results for Adaptive and *IQP*. We also consider the 95% confidence interval of the average performance to detect significant differences between the query selection methods. For instance, in Figure 2a when the subset covers 28% of the full query set, the average of 50 Pearson correlation scores obtained by the Adaptive method is 0.94 and the associated standard deviation is 0.07. Thus the 95% confidence interval is: $\left[0.94 \pm 1.96 \times \frac{0.07}{\sqrt{50}}\right]$. The confidence intervals are shown as error bars. In general, the difference between two methods is statistically significant for a particular subset size, if the associated error bars do not overlap. As seen, in Figure 2a and 2b, for both Pearson correlation and Kendall-τ, the Adaptive method significantly outperforms the Random and *IQP* baselines across different subset sizes. From Figure 2b we see that the Adaptive method achieves a Kendall-τ correlation of 0.9 with a subset that covers 50% of the queries (125 out of 249 queries). However, the Random and *IQP* methods require at least 70% of queries to achieve the same Kendall-τ.

Table 1 summarizes the Kendall-τ and Pearson correlation for the four query selection methods when selecting {20, 40, 60}% of queries in the Robust 2004 and the TREC-8 test collections.

The columns labeled 'all' indicates the results for all the systems in a test collection. For both test collections and the three subset sizes, {20, 40, 60}%, the Adaptive method significantly outperforms *IQP* and Random in most cases. For instance, in the Robust 2004 test collection the Adaptive method obtains {15, 10, 5}% average improvements over Random and *IPQ* in Kendall-τ for subsets of {20, 40, 60}% respectively. Similar improvements are observed for the TREC-8 test collection.

The columns labeled 'top' indicates the results for the 30 best performing systems, i.e. those with the highest MAP scores. When calculating Pearson and Kendall-τ correlations, the vectors $\hat{M}_\Phi$ and M are constructed by considering only the top 30 systems. The remaining systems only contribute to the query selection process and are not used for evaluation. Once again, the Adaptive method significantly outperforms the *IQP* and Random methods in most of the cases. Interestingly, the improvements are even larger than the improvements of the full set of systems. For instance, for the Robust test collection, improvement in Kendall-τ is on average 10% for the full set of systems and it rises to 25% for the top 30 best performing systems. Similarly, the average improvement in Pearson correlation rises from 7% to 14% on average. Similar results are observed for the TREC-8 test collection.

The columns labeled 'sig' indicates the results for the pairs of systems whose performances difference is statistically significant. If a difference in average performance scores of two systems is not statistically significant, it is reasonable that they may be ordered differently when evaluated over a subset of queries. Such tied systems increase the probability of a swap and thus may considerably decrease Kendall-τ since the common formulation of Kendall-τ does not distinguish between pairs of systems with and without significant differences. This is, in fact, the case for the Robust and the TREC-8 test collection where about 30% of pairs of systems are tied as measured by the paired t-test with the significance level of 0.05. Thus, we also compute the Kendall-τ of systems with a significant difference in *MAP*. Again, the

Table 1: Comparisons of the four query selection methods for the two TREC test collections based on the *AP* metric. The statistically significant improvements of *Adaptive* over *IQP* and Random are marked by †.

Subset	Method	Robust2004					TREC-8				
		Kendall-τ			Pearson		Kendall-τ			Pearson	
		all	top	sig	all	top	all	top	sig	all	top
20%	**Random**	0.68	0.45	0.75	0.83	0.68	0.72	0.45	0.88	0.92	0.77
	IQP	0.67	0.47	0.78	0.86	0.70	0.74	0.53	0.92	0.93	0.81
	Adaptive	**0.77**†	**0.63**†	**0.85**†	**0.92**†	**0.79**†	**0.83**†	**0.69**†	**0.95**†	**0.95**†	**0.92**†
	Oracle	0.90	0.81	0.90	0.97	0.95	0.88	0.80	0.97	0.97	0.95
40%	**Random**	0.80	0.58	0.82	0.93	0.76	0.77	0.58	0.95	0.95	0.86
	IQP	0.80	0.56	0.85	0.94	0.78	0.81	0.66	0.96	0.95	0.89
	Adaptive	**0.87**†	**0.69**†	**0.89**†	**0.98**†	**0.89**†	**0.90**†	**0.81**†	**0.99**†	**0.97**†	**0.95**†
	Oracle	0.92	0.86	0.95	0.99	0.96	0.93	0.85	1.0	0.98	0.97
60%	**Random**	0.85	0.71	0.88	0.97	0.90	0.87	0.70	0.97	0.97	0.90
	IQP	0.88	0.73	0.90	0.96	0.91	0.88	0.80	0.99	0.98	0.92
	Adaptive	**0.91**†	**0.83**†	**0.95**†	**0.99**†	**0.96**†	**0.93**†	**0.85**†	1.0	0.98	**0.96**†
	Oracle	0.94	0.92	0.97	0.99	0.99	0.95	0.91	1.0	0.99	0.99

Table 2: Comparisons of Random and Adaptive using the Web test collection.

	Method	desired Kendall-τ		
		0.7	**0.8**	**0.9**
#queries	**Random**	167	368	739
	Adaptive	71	207	486
#relevance judgments	**Random**	5010	10235	28804
	Adaptive	2086	5803	15854

Adaptive method significantly outperforms *IQP* and Random in most cases.

We repeated the experiments in Table 1 for *P*@100 metric, and observed similar results for both the test collections.[2]

7.1 Results of the Web Data

We also investigate the performance of Adaptive on a test collection comprising the Web search results from a commercial search engine with 1,000 queries and 50 different search systems. Here, the systems are various rankers (runs) of a learning to rank system that were trained with different feature sets. To generate a ranker we randomly sample $g = \{5, 10, 20, 30 \text{ or } 40\}$ features from a given feature set and optimize the ranker on a common training set (the training details are out of the scope of this paper). For each query, the top 5 web pages returned by the rankers are pooled for relevance assessment. The performance of each ranker is measured according to the precision at the position rank 5 (*P*@5).

Table 2 reports the number of queries, and the number of relevance judgments required to reach Kendall-τ values of {0.7, 0.8, and 0.9} by the Adaptive, and the Random query selection method. We focus on the comparisons between Adaptive and Random because the random sampling is commonly used for selecting candidate queries. Thus, we can observe the cost reduction that can be achieved in practice by the Adaptive method.

The reported results for the Adaptive method are the average over 10 trials. In each trial, the initialization involves 20 queries instead of a randomly selected single query. This ensures a sufficiently large training set for the initial classifier without losing much in the query selection performance.

[2]The results on *P*@100 are not reported due to lack of space.

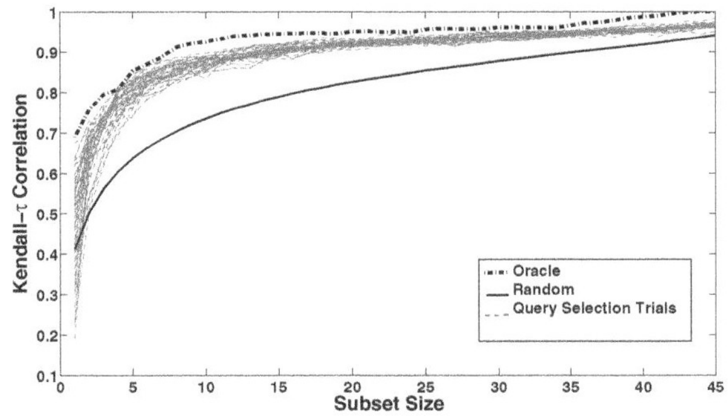

Figure 3: Sensitivity of the query selection to the first query using TREC-8 comprising 50 queries. The subset size varies between 1 and 45.

As seen in Table 2, the required subset sizes for τ={0.7, 0.8, 0.9} are statistically significantly smaller than those required for random sampling. For instance, the random method obtains $\tau = 0.9$ for a subset of size 739 whereas the Adaptive method only requires 486 queries to reach the same τ. This is equivalent to judging 12,950 fewer documents than the Random method. Similar results are observed for τ={0.7 and 0.8}.

7.2 Effects of Initialization

The initialization step of the Adaptive method involves randomly selecting the first query. We now consider the sensitivity of the Adaptive method to the selection of the first query. The choice of the first query could possibly affect the quality of both (*i*) the queries selected in the subsequent stages and (*ii*) the training data for the classifier. Our analysis focuses on (*i*) since the impact on the training data cannot be separated from the characteristics of the classification method and thus is out of the scope of this paper.

In order to isolate the effects of the initial query on the subsequent queries, we assume that the true X matrix is available, i.e. that the estimator has access to all relevance judgments. Using the TREC-8 data set, we randomly select the first query. Subsequent queries are iteratively selected based on the query selection model in Equation 5 but using

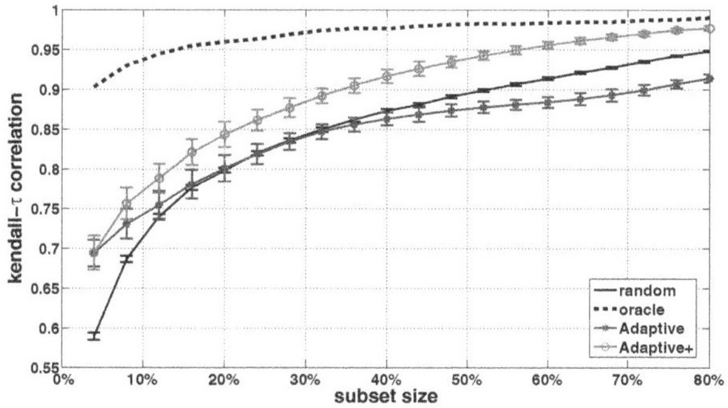

Figure 4: The generalizability test for the query subsets selected by Adaptive and Adaptive$^+$, the modified query selection method.

Table 3: Comparing the generalization of a selected subset using two metrics: $P@100$ and AP.

Subset	Method	kendall-τ			
		Robust 2004		TREC-8	
		P@100	**AP**	**P@100**	**AP**
20%	**Random**	0.77	0.80	0.75	0.78
	Adaptive	0.76	0.82	0.76	0.80
	Adaptive$^+$	**0.84†**	**0.87†**	**0.81†**	**0.85†**
	Oracle	0.91	0.95	0.86	0.89
40%	**Random**	0.82	0.87	0.84	0.85
	Adaptive	0.80	0.85	0.84	0.86
	Adaptive$^+$	**0.89†**	**0.92†**	**0.90†**	**0.90†**
	Oracle	0.93	0.97	0.94	0.93
60%	**Random**	0.89	0.91	0.89	0.90
	Adaptive	0.84	0.88	0.87	0.91
	Adaptive$^+$	**0.93†**	**0.96†**	**0.95†**	**0.95†**
	Oracle	0.96	0.98	0.97	0.97

the true X matrix where the corresponding uncertainty U matrix is zero. Results are shown in Figure 3 for 50 trials. Each trail contains a distinct query for the initialization. As seen, the Kendall-τ scores obtained in all the trials converge to the Kendall-τ for the ideal query set more quickly than the Kendall-τ obtained for Random. The kendall-τ variation across trials decreases as more queries are selected. For the query subsets of size greater than 10 queries the performance is similar across all the trials. This suggests that the query selection model is robust to the selection of the first query.

8. GENERALIZATION

We now consider the generalization of the Adaptive query selection method. In Section 8.1 we discuss the effectiveness of the resulting query set in evaluating new systems that did not contribute to the query selection process. In Section 8.2 we consider the reliability of the query subset for evaluating systems performance using multiple metrics. This is particularly important when systems are compared using various performance metrics.

8.1 Evaluation of New Systems

Previous work [14, 17] has shown that queries selected based on the performance of a particular set of systems may not be effective in evaluating new, previously unseen systems. We observed a similar tendency by the Adaptive query selection. Thus, to avoid over-fitting to the systems used to select the queries we modify the Adaptive algorithm.

The modified algorithm is referred to as 'Adaptive$^+$' and comprises the following changes. When selecting a query we consider $c (c > 1)$ random subsets of the l systems of size $h (h < l)$. We allow overlaps between the subsets and ensure that each system appears in at least one of the subsets. For each subset of systems we choose a query that, in combination with already selected queries in Φ, maximizes γ_Φ (see Equation 5). Finally, we pick the query that is selected by most of the systems subsets, and consider it for relevance assessments.

We test the generalization of the Adaptive$^+$ approach using the two TREC test collections. We first randomly select 50% of systems and treat them as new systems. When selecting new systems, we hold out not only individual runs but the entire set of runs from the same participant. The remaining systems are considered as participating systems and used to select queries. When computing the performance metrics for the participating systems, we also remove documents that are uniquely retrieved by the new (held-out) systems.

The results of the generalization test for the Robust 2004 test collection and Kendall-τ are shown in Figure 4. We created $c = 100$ random system subsets, each of size $h = 0.2 \times l$, where l refers to the number of participating systems. Figure 4 clearly shows that the Adaptive algorithm overfits the set of queries to the participating systems and performs no better than Random when evaluating new systems. In contrast, Adaptive$^+$ significantly outperforms Random across different sizes of the query subsets.

The detailed results of the generalization experiments are shown in Table 3 for both Robust and TREC-8 test collections, and two metrics, AP and $P@100$. In all cases the Kendall-τ obtained by Adaptive$^+$ is significantly larger than the Kendall-τ of the Adaptive and Random algorithm.[3]

8.2 Use of Alternative Performance Metrics

One of the goals of IR test collections is to enable evaluation of systems in terms of various metrics. Ideally, the subset of queries used for systems evaluation should provide reliable estimates of the systems performance regardless of the metrics used. In the following experiments we show that for some methods that may not be the case. Namely, when the metrics used to select queries differs from the metrics used to evaluate systems, the query subset may not provide reliable estimates of the systems performance.

For that reason, we modified the Adaptive algorithm to generalize across multiple metrics. The modified version is referred to as 'Adaptive*'. At each step of the query selection process, for each metrics, and for each non-selected query the Adaptive* computes the associated γ_Φ scores. It averages the scores across different metrics and then selects the candidate query with the maximum average of γ_Φ scores.

We consider four IR metrics: $P@10$, $P@100$, *Recall* and AP and measure the associated Kendall-τ scores (T_1) for query subsets of various sizes selected. Let T_2 be the set of Kendall-τ scores for various subset sizes calculated when the evaluation metric is different from the metric used for query selection – the selection metric. Ideally the Kendall-τ

[3]Similar results were also observed for Pearson correlation but not reported due to lack of space.

Table 4: The average Kendall-τ loss ($mean(T_2)$ - $mean(T_1)$) for four metrics using the TREC 2004 Robust track. Given a metric α, T_1 denotes the set of Kendall-τ scores for various query subset sizes when the metric α is used for both query selection and system evaluation. T_2 denotes the set of Kendall-τ scores when the metric α is used to measure systems performance for a subset of queries selected using another metric.

Selection Metric	Evaluation Metric			
	P@10	P@100	Recall	AP
P@10	0.0	-0.082	-0.065	-0.068
P@100	-0.084	0.0	-0.042	-0.051
Recall	-0.076	-0.063	0.0	-0.073
AP	-0.089	-0.070	-0.062	0.0
Adaptive*	**-0.011**†	**-0.012**†	**-0.018**†	**-0.014**†
Random	-0.114	-0.086	-0.056	-0.078

scores in T_2 would comparable with those in T_1. To measure the distances between T_1 and T_2 set of scores we use $(mean(T_2) - mean(T_1))$, i.e. the average loss Kendall-τ.

Table 4 represents the results of our experiment for the Robust 2004 test collection. Each of the four metrics are used as a selection metric for the Adaptive method and as a system evaluation metric. The Recall metric leads to the smallest average loss for $P@10$ and $P@100$ but not for AP. The best selection metric for AP and Recall is $P@100$. Thus, there is no single selection metric that leads to the minimum loss in Kendall-τ for all of the evaluation metrics.

We also select queries by using the Adaptive* method. As seen from Table 4, the average loss for all the metrics is considerably reduced. The last row of Table 4 represents the results of random sampling averaged over 1000 trials. In order to investigate whether the Adaptive* method significantly outperforms other methods, we measured the differences in average Kendall-τ loss using the paired t-test at the significance level of 0.05. Table 4 shows that Adaptive* leads to average Kendall-τ losses that are significantly smaller than for the Random method and any of the selection metrics.

9. DISCUSSION

Our experiments demonstrated the advantages of the Adaptive query selection method and its variations. Here we consider how they may be practically used to support the query selection and assessment scenarios encountered in the TREC type experiments. In TREC tasks, a set of queries is typically selected in advance and delivered to assessors to collect relevance judgments. This setting ensures that all the assessors are efficiently involved in the construction of relevance judgments, and the full set of judgments is constructed in a reasonable time.

We first investigated if we can use Adaptive to collect a subset of queries before constructing any relevance judgments. We considered the use of the query performance predictors, e.g. [9, 18], to construct the performance matrix $\hat{X}$ and iteratively select a subset of queries in the absence of any relevance judgments. Since no relevance judgments are collected, the elements of $\hat{X}$ are fixed throughout the iterations. Once a set of queries are selected, the associated relevance judgments are collected concurrently.

We used the pseudo-relevance judgments approach proposed by Soboroff et al. [18] to construct $\hat{X}$ since (i) it directly estimates the performance metrics and provides the corresponding variance that is required for our model, and (ii) it is reported to be among the best available performance predictors [11]. However, experiments with the Robust 2004 test collection showed that the accuracy of the performance prediction was not sufficiently high and, as a result, Adaptive failed to perform statistically better than the random sampling of queries.

We then took a different approach and modified Adaptive query selection to construct relevance judgments for multiple queries at a time. Instead of updating $\hat{X}$ at each iteration, we updated $\hat{X}$ after selecting a sequence of $k \geq 1$ queries. Once k queries were selected, the associated relevance judgments were constructed and $\hat{X}$ matrix was updated.

We evaluated this approach on the Robust 2004 test collection with 249 queries and investigated the effect of size k on the performance of the method. We considered three configurations $k = \{1, 10, \text{ and } 50\}$ where the first k queries were randomly sampled. To deal with the sampling variance we repeated the experiments 50 times, every time with a new set of initial queries, and averaged the results across the experiments. For each of the configurations, we calculated Kendall-τ after selecting 60% of the queries. As the value of k increased the associated Kendall-τ decreased. However, for $k = 10$ the Kendall-τ was still statistically larger than the Kendall-τ obtained for the random sampling of queries. As k rose to 50, the Adaptive method performed no better than Random. These results suggest that for some k we can use our iterative method to collect relevance judgments for multiple queries at a time. However, further experiments will be needed to find the optimal setting for k across the iterations, and its relationship with the total number of queries.

10. CONCLUSION

In this paper we considered the task of selecting a representative set of queries and corresponding relevance judgments to achieve an optimal approximation of the systems performance. We started with the premise that no relevance judgments are available for a query before it is selected for the relevance assessment and that only a limited assessment budget is available. Thus, we provided a mathematical model for query selection that explicitly formulated the uncertainty in the performance scores that was due to the absence of relevance judgments. The mathematical formulation showed that the optimal subset of queries should be the least correlated with each other and maximally correlated with the remaining queries. Furthermore, the total uncertainty associated with the selected queries should be a minimum.

Since the optimization problem was intractable, we proposed the Adaptive algorithm in which queries were iteratively selected and their relevance judgments were obtained after they were added to the query set. The relevance judgments of the selected queries were used to train a classifier to facilitate the selection of subsequent queries.

We demonstrated the effectiveness of the Adaptive algorithm using two TREC test collections and a Web test collection of a commercial search engine. For all three test collections, the Adaptive algorithm significantly outperformed the considered baseline methods.

Generally, the query selection methods have been criticized for their lack of generalization to previously unseen systems and multiple evaluation metrics. Our Adaptive algorithm exhibited the same problems. However, we refined the Adaptive algorithm and showed that the selected query subset provides effective evaluations of new systems and can reliably be used with multiple metrics.

One of the main advantages of our query selection model is its extendibility to accommodate different sources of uncertainty in measuring systems performance. In this paper, we focused on the uncertainty of the performance estimator due to lack of relevance judgments for a query. However, other sources of uncertainty could be considered. Recent research is particularly concerned with measuring uncertainty of the systems performance due to (*i*) partial relevance judgments [2, 4, 20] and (*ii*) errors in the relevance judgments made by human assessors [6, 12]. Our future work will expand the theoretical model to incorporate additional sources of uncertainty and explore more general cost models for constructing test collections.

11. REFERENCES

[1] J. Allan, B. Carterette, J. A. Aslam, V. Pavlu, B. Dachev, and E. Kanoulas. TREC 2007 million query track. In *Notebook Proceedings of TREC 2007*. TREC, 2007.

[2] J. A. Aslam, V. Pavlu, and E. Yilmaz. A statistical method for system evaluation using incomplete judgments. In *SIGIR '06: Proceedings of the 29th annual international ACM SIGIR conference on Research and development in information retrieval*, pages 541–548, New York, NY, USA, 2006. ACM.

[3] P. Billingsley. *Probability and Measure*. New York: Wiley, New York, NY, USA, 1995.

[4] B. Carterette, J. Allan, and R. Sitaraman. Minimal test collections for retrieval evaluation. In *SIGIR '06: Proceedings of the 29th annual international ACM SIGIR conference on Research and development in information retrieval*, pages 268–275, New York, NY, USA, 2006. ACM.

[5] B. Carterette, V. Pavlu, E. Kanoulas, J. A. Aslam, and J. Allan. Evaluation over thousands of queries. In *SIGIR '08: Proceedings of the 31st annual international ACM SIGIR conference on Research and development in information retrieval*, pages 651–658, New York, NY, USA, 2008. ACM.

[6] B. Carterette and I. Soboroff. The effect of assessor error on IR system evaluation. In *Proceedings of the 33rd international ACM SIGIR conference on Research and development in information retrieval*, SIGIR '10, pages 539–546, New York, NY, USA, 2010. ACM.

[7] G. V. Cormack, C. R. Palmer, and C. L. A. Clarke. Efficient construction of large test collections. In *Proceedings of the 21st annual international ACM SIGIR conference on Research and development in information retrieval*, SIGIR '98, pages 282–289, New York, NY, USA, 1998. ACM.

[8] C. Cortes and V. Vapnik. Support-vector networks. *Mach. Learn.*, 20(3):273–297, Sept. 1995.

[9] F. Diaz. Performance prediction using spatial autocorrelation. In *Proceedings of the 30th annual international ACM SIGIR conference on Research and development in information retrieval*, SIGIR '07, pages 583–590, New York, NY, USA, 2007. ACM.

[10] J. Guiver, S. Mizzaro, and S. Robertson. A few good topics: Experiments in topic set reduction for retrieval evaluation. *ACM Trans. Inf. Syst.*, 27(4), 2009.

[11] C. Hauff, D. Hiemstra, L. Azzopardi, and F. de Jong. A case for automatic system evaluation. In *Proceedings of the 32nd European conference on Advances in Information Retrieval*, ECIR'2010, pages 153–165, Berlin, Heidelberg, 2010. Springer-Verlag.

[12] M. Hosseini, I. J. Cox, N. Milic-Frayling, G. Kazai, and V. Vinay. On aggregating labels from multiple crowd workers to infer relevance of documents. In *ECIR'12: Proceedings of the 34th European conference on Advances in information retrieval*, ECIR'12, pages 182–194, 2012.

[13] M. Hosseini, I. J. Cox, N. Milic-Frayling, T. Sweeting, and V. Vinay. Prioritizing relevance judgments to improve the construction of IR test collections. In *Proceedings of the 20th ACM international conference on Information and knowledge management*, CIKM '11, pages 641–646, New York, NY, USA, 2011. ACM.

[14] M. Hosseini, I. J. Cox, N. Milic-Frayling, V. Vinay, and T. Sweeting. Selecting a subset of queries for acquisition of further relevance judgements. In *Proceedings of the Third international conference on Advances in information retrieval theory*, ICTIR'11, pages 113–124, Berlin, Heidelberg, 2011. Springer-Verlag.

[15] S. Mizzaro and S. Robertson. Hits hits TREC: exploring IR evaluation results with network analysis. In *Proceedings of the 30th annual international ACM SIGIR conference on Research and development in information retrieval*, SIGIR '07, pages 479–486, New York, NY, USA, 2007. ACM.

[16] J. C. Platt. Probabilistic outputs for support vector machines and comparison to regularized likelihood methods. In *Advances in Large Margin Classifiers*, 2000.

[17] S. Robertson. On the contributions of topics to system evaluation. In *Proceedings of the 33rd European conference on Advances in information retrieval*, ECIR'11, pages 129–140, Berlin, Heidelberg, 2011. Springer-Verlag.

[18] I. Soboroff, C. Nicholas, and P. Cahan. Ranking retrieval systems without relevance judgments. In *Proceedings of the 24th annual international ACM SIGIR conference on Research and development in information retrieval*, SIGIR '01, pages 66–73, New York, NY, USA, 2001. ACM.

[19] K. Sparck Jones and K. van Rijsbergen. Information retrieval test collections. *Journal of Documentation*, 32(1):59–75, 1976.

[20] E. Yilmaz and J. A. Aslam. Estimating average precision with incomplete and imperfect judgments. In *CIKM '06: Proceedings of the 15th ACM international conference on Information and knowledge management*, pages 102–111, New York, NY, USA, 2006. ACM.

[21] J. Zobel. How reliable are the results of large-scale information retrieval experiments? In *SIGIR '98: Proceedings of the 21st annual international ACM SIGIR conference on Research and development in information retrieval*, pages 307–314, New York, NY, USA, 1998. ACM.

Improving Retrieval of Short Texts Through Document Expansion

Miles Efron
University of Illinois at Urbana-Champaign
501 E. Daniel Street, MC-492
Champaign, IL
mefron@illinois.edu

Peter Organisciak
University of Illinois at Urbana-Champaign
501 E. Daniel Street, MC-492
Champaign, IL
organis2@illinois.edu

Katrina Fenlon
University of Illinois at Urbana-Champaign
501 E. Daniel Street, MC-492
Champaign, IL
kfenlon2@illinois.edu

ABSTRACT

Collections containing a large number of short documents are becoming increasingly common. As these collections grow in number and size, providing effective retrieval of brief texts presents a significant research problem. We propose a novel approach to improving information retrieval (IR) for short texts based on aggressive document expansion. Starting from the hypothesis that short documents tend to be about a single topic, we submit documents as pseudo-queries and analyze the results to learn about the documents themselves. Document expansion helps in this context because short documents yield little in the way of term frequency information. However, as we show, the proposed technique helps us model not only lexical properties, but also temporal properties of documents. We present experimental results using a corpus of microblog (Twitter) data and a corpus of metadata records from a federated digital library. With respect to established baselines, results of these experiments show that applying our proposed document expansion method yields significant improvements in effectiveness. Specifically, our method improves the lexical representation of documents and the ability to let time influence retrieval.

Categories and Subject Descriptors

H.3.3 [**Information Storage and Retrieval**]: Information Search and Retrieval; H.3.7 [**Digital Libraries**]: Systems Issues

General Terms

Algorithms, Experimentation, Performance

Keywords

Information retrieval, microblogs, twitter, Dublin Core, document expansion, language models, temporal IR

1. INTRODUCTION

Collections of short documents present a host of challenges to information retrieval (IR) systems. The increasing influence of microblogging platforms such as Twitter[1] makes this challenge especially timely. Twitter search exists alongside other short-text IR problems such as ranking product reviews and advertisement placement. These short documents join more familiar brief texts such as bibliographic and other metadata records.

Faced with a corpus of millions of documents, each of which contains only a few words, traditional IR models run into difficulty. First, the vocabulary mismatch problem becomes especially worrisome. If documents are very brief, the risk of query terms failing to match words observed in relevant documents is large. Second, most IR models rely on some sort of TF-IDF dynamic, with a term's frequency in a document lending evidence to our belief about the document's relevance. In very short documents, most terms occur only once, making simple operations such as language model estimation difficult.

However, we can mitigate these problems. We argue that a massive document expansion improves retrieval effectiveness for short texts. The mechanism that we propose for this expansion is simple. Because the documents that we are concerned with are so brief, each one tends to focus on only a single topic. A topically homogenous document is not very different from a query. Thus we propose submitting each document in a corpus as a pseudo-query. We show that analyzing the results obtained from this pseudo-query improves the models that underpin IR.

This paper proposes and tests two types of document expansion. Given a corpus of N documents $C = D_1 \dots D_N$ and a document of interest D, we augment D's representation in the index by submitting the text of D as a query to a search engine over C. This gives a ranked listed of results $R_1 \dots R_k$. This result set informs two expansions:

1. **Lexical:** We use the terms in $R_1 \dots R_k$ to improve our estimate of the language model for D.
2. **Temporal:** We use the timestamps associated with $R_1 \dots R_k$ to build a "temporal profile" for D–a probability distribution over time. This probability distribution is helpful during time-sensitive document ranking.

Our chief contribution is a novel approach to representing collections of short text. Our methods elaborate on re-

[1] `http://twitter.com`

sults from the well-known language modeling approach to IR, especially the notion of relevance models. But we also show that the single-topic focus of most short documents opens avenues for consideration of information other than language–for example, time.

2. PROBLEM STATEMENT AND MOTIVATION

The growing quantity of information published in small texts such as Twitter posts argues for a sustained analysis of the treatment of brief documents in IR. While this urgency is new, the need for improved retrieval of short texts is not. For instance, many digital libraries manage repositories of terse metadata records. While these repositories (such as the DCC repository we describe in this paper) are nominally searchable, the brevity of their metadata can frustrate effective IR. Other examples of short-text IR include query-specific advertisement and product review ranking.

But retrieval from collections of short documents is difficult for several reasons. First, brief documents attenuate one of the primary signals used by modern IR systems–term frequency. Figure 1 can help us understand why this is the case. The figure shows data from two TREC collections (described in detail in Section 5). The TREC 8 data included a corpus of news articles. Tweets2011 is the collection of Twitter data used for the microblog track at TREC 2011. Figure 1 shows the distributions of the log-probabilities of query terms among the first 100 documents retrieved using a simple query likelihood model. That is, the points that comprise the distributions are the maximum likelihood estimates of $\log P(q|D)$ for each query term q.

Two problematic facts are clear from Figure 1. First, unlike the longer news documents, tweets lead to a distribution of query term probabilities that is strongly peaked. The majority of tweets that contain a query word only contain it once, and tweets are of similar length. Second, in the case of the TREC 8 data, the mean and median log-probability of a query term are higher in relevant documents than in non-relevant documents. This is not the case for the Twitter data. Median $\log P(q|D)$ for relevant TREC 8 documents is -6.92, with median -7.17 for non-relevant documents. The difference in log-probability in relevant versus non-relevant TREC8 documents is statistically significant (Mann-Whitney $p \ll 0.001$ one-sided). But $\log P(q|D)$ for relevant Twitter documents has median -7.82 and -7.80 for non-relevant (Mann-Whitney $p = 1$ one-sided). To the extent that TREC 8 presents a "typical" statistical picture, Figure 1 shows that Twitter data are qualitatively different than more familiar TREC collections.

The impact of this difference is easy to see if we consider the language modeling approach to IR [21]. In the language modeling approach, we assume that each document in our collection was generated by a probability distribution–a language model–over terms in the vocabulary. We rank documents against a query Q by the likelihood that their corresponding language models generated the query:

$$P(D|Q) \propto P(Q|D)P(D). \tag{1}$$

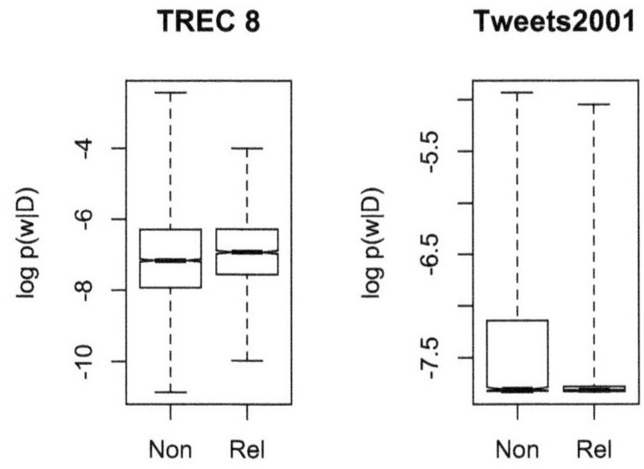

Figure 1: log-Probabilities of Query Terms in Relevant and Non-Relevant Documents in Two Corpora.

If we assume uniform priors over documents and term independence we have:

$$P(Q|D) = \prod_{i=1}^{|Q|} P(w_i|D) \tag{2}$$

where $|Q|$ is the number of word tokens in the query.

Key to language modeling is the estimation of $P(w|D)$. Using multinomial language models, the maximum likelihood estimator $P_{ml}(w|D) = \frac{n(w,D)}{|D|}$. But when confronted with a corpus of brief documents, estimating language models is difficult because the maximum likelihood estimator is not very expressive. Since $|D|$ is small, $n(w, D)$ cannot be large and is very often 1. We refer to this as the "headroom problem:" in brief documents there is little chance for important terms to stand out via repeated usage. Coupled with a small domain of observed document lengths, the headroom problem has the effect of making many documents' estimated language models look nearly identical.

To improve our estimates, we typically smooth language models, re-allocating probability mass away from the maximum likelihood estimator by reference to a background model, such as $P(w|C)$, the language model of the collection as a whole as described by Zhai and Lafferty in [28]. Though several smoothing techniques are common in the IR literature, in this paper we select Bayesian updating with Dirichlet priors. The form of a Dirichlet-smoothed language model is:

$$P(w|D) = \frac{|D|}{|D| + \mu} P_{ml}(w|D) + \frac{\mu}{|D| + \mu} P(w|C) \tag{3}$$

for $\mu \geq 0$. Smoothing in this way improves our estimated probabilities. But smoothing does little to alleviate the headroom problem.

Our goal is to improve the representation of short documents in IR. We argue that short text representation can be improved by an aggressive document expansion. In Section 4.1, we use this expansion to induce improved document language models. However, document expansion has a role to play in IR for short texts that goes beyond language model estimation. As an example of an alternative use of expansion information, Section 4.2 extends our results to allow temporal factors to influence retrieval.

3. RELATED WORK

The problematic nature of IR on short documents has seen little sustained research (though [22, 27] do treat the topic explicitly). However, recent interest in social media has drawn attention to this problem [22, 10]. Familiar operations such as measuring inter-document similarity, scholars have found, is difficult given the brevity of many documents in collections of user-generated content [20].

Though corpora of brief documents are increasingly common, the estimation problems that our proposed expansion methods address are not new. Most similar to our own work are results from research on cluster-based IR. Clusters have been applied to various points in the IR process, including relevance feedback [14, 9], rank fusion [12], and as a separate factor used during document ranking [13]. Clusters are appealing insofar as they afford a level of information about documents that resides at a level higher than intra-document word counts, but below the generalities of the collection at large. For instance, Liu and Croft applied clusters during document language model smoothing [18]. Ramage, Dumais and Leibling address the vocabulary mismatch problem in microblog text using latent Dirichlet allocation (LDA) [23], allowing the LDA model to supplement observed term probabilities in document representation. Other methods of document expansion have also seen sustained work (e.g. [24]), though in contexts different from those that we study here.

The most similar work to ours was given by Tao et al. [26]. In their work, Tao et al. proposed smoothing document language models by analyzing their lexical neighborhoods. That is, the model for document D was smoothed with counts obtained from its k nearest neighbors $D_1, \ldots, D_k$, with each document's influence in the smoothed model being proportional to its cosine similarity with D. Like Tao et al. we propose improving the representation D by an analysis of similar documents. However, the approach we outline in Section 4.1 differs from Tao et al. in its basic theoretical orientation, couching the estimation problem in the generative semantics of language modeling. Tao et al. define the neighborhood of a document in geometrical terms, relying on the cosine similarity. With an explicit assumption of normality, they smooth the model of D based on this neighborhood and this metric. On the other hand, we assume that D arises from an unseen model $\mathcal{D}$, much as relevance modeling assumes the influence of an unseen model of relevance. To estimate $P(w|\mathcal{D})$ we combine evidence from other documents, where the influence that some document D_j exerts on the final model is the likelihood that D_j's language model generated D.

Our work also relies on findings from recent studies on information retrieval and microblogs [6, 19, 2]. The field of microblog retrieval is relatively new, but has seen increasing interest, most noticeably in the 2011 TREC microblog track.

Unlike the methods described in this section, our document expansion technique also invites extension to non-linguistic features. As we show in Section 4.2, aspects of relevance such as temporality fit naturally into our approach.

4. DOCUMENT EXPANSION FOR SHORT TEXTS

Let D be a document consisting of $|D|$ word tokens $d_1, \ldots, d_{|D|}$. Also let C be a corpus of N documents. Using to Eq. 2, we can calculate the likelihood of D given the language model of each document in the collection, $P(D|D_1), \ldots, P(D|D_N)$. We propose analyzing these probabilities to make an augmented representation D' that provides a better basis for estimation and prediction than the original D affords.

From a practical standpoint, this amounts to submitting each document as a pseudo-query and ranking all documents using the standard query likelihood method. As we shall show, the analysis of $P(D|D_1), \ldots, P(D|D_N)$ can play a role similar to relevance feedback, though how literally this comparison holds is variable.

With this in mind, we offer two definitions related to a document D:

> **Definition 1. Pseudo-query of D:** The pseudo-query Q_D is a representation of the text in D that we may submit to an IR system.

> **Definition 2. Result set of D:** By submitting Q_D as a query against the corpus C, we derive a ranking $\mathcal{R}_D = R_{D1}, \ldots, R_{Dk}$. $\mathcal{R}_D$ consists of the top k documents retrieved for Q_D and their retrieval status value scores. In this paper we use query likelihood for retrieval, so the scores are the probabilities $P(D|D_1), \ldots, P(D|D_k)$.

The use of Q_D and $\mathcal{R}_D$ stems from our hypothesis that most short texts discuss only a single topic. If Q_D treats a coherent topical domain, we anticipate that analyzing the documents in $\mathcal{R}_D$ will yield information about the topic that the document of interest D is about.

4.1 Lexical Evidence

Following Lavrenko and Croft's exposition of relevance-based language models [16], we use $\mathcal{R}_D$ to induce D', a language model associated with D. In typical language modeling, we estimate a document's language model by combining evidence from the document itself with information from a background distribution such as the collection. Given $\mathcal{R}_D$, however, we can improve this estimate.

The language model D' is

$$P(w|D') = P(w|d_1, \ldots, d_{|D|}) = \frac{P(w, d_1, \ldots, d_{|D|})}{P(d_1, \ldots, d_{|D|})}. \quad (4)$$

The denominator $P(d_1, \ldots, d_{|D|})$ does not depend on w, leaving the joint probability as the quantity of interest. This joint probability is

$$P(w, d_1, \ldots, d_{|D|}) = \sum_{D_i \in C} P(D_i) P(w, d_1, \ldots, d_{|D|}|D_i). \quad (5)$$

If we further assume that

$$P(w, d_1, \ldots, d_{|D|}|D_i) = P(w|D_i) \prod_{j=1}^{|D|} P(d_j|D_i) \quad (6)$$

then we have

$$P(w, d_1, \ldots, d_{|D|}) = \sum_{D_i \in C} P(D_i) P(w|D_i) \prod_{j=1}^{|D|} P(d_j|D_i). \quad (7)$$

The last factor in Eq. 7 reminds us that most of the probability mass in this joint distribution will derive from documents that are lexically similar to the document D. Thus we can obtain a good estimate of $P(w|D')$ by performing the summation in Eq. 7 over only the k documents with the highest likelihood of generating D. Thus the probability of word w under the augmented model is a weighted average of the observed probabilities of w in the top k documents retrieved by submitting D as a pseudo-query, where the weights are the likelihoods of D given the retrieved documents' language models.

Having obtained our augmented representation, we may then rank documents by the likelihood that their augmented language models generated the query, $P(Q|D')$ which we calculate using the query likelihood model as usual, substituting $P(w|D')$ for the maximum likelihood estimator into Eq. 3. We refer to this method by the abbreviation LExp, for lexical expansion.

As is common when using relevance models for relevance feedback, interpolating the expanded model with the originally observed text is likely to be "safer" than relying on the expanded model alone. Thus we define another lexically expanded model:

$$P_{\lambda}(w|D') = (1-\lambda)P_{ml}(w|D) + \lambda P(w|D') \quad (8)$$

for a parameter λ in [0, 1]. We may then substitute $P_{\lambda}(w|D')$ for the maximum likelihood estimator in Eq. 3 for retrieval. We refer to rankings based on this estimator as LExpλ. For simplicity, when discussing LExpλ we set $\lambda = 0.5$ throughout this paper.

4.2 Temporal Evidence

In addition to supplementing the lexical evidence that we store about documents, the expansion method described above can create new, extra-lexical features. For example, information in $\mathcal{R}_D$ yields actionable information related to temporal aspects of relevance. Indeed, incorporating temporal evidence into IR entails a research area in its own right (cf. [1]). We pursue temporality here as an example of extra-linguistic information that our document expansion method allows.

We assume that for each document D_i, we have a corresponding timestamp t_i which is the time at which the document was published. We also define t_0 as the earliest timestamp in the collection. In this paper we measure time in fractions of days, such that t_i is how many days elapsed between the initial time t_0 and the publication of D_i.

The observed timestamp t_i provides useful information for IR. But our goal is to learn additional temporal information about each document D_i. We hypothesize that the empirical distribution of timestamps related to D_i via document expansion helpfully supplements direct use of t_i.

Working under a similar scenario, Jones and Diaz defined the notion of a query's "temporal profile" [11, 5]. The temporal profile of a query Q is a probability distribution over time, $P(t|Q)$. Analyzing the empirical distribution of documents retrieved for Q gives information helpful in estimating $P(t|Q)$, as shown in [4].

Our discussion above suggests that temporal profiles may be defined not only on queries, but also on documents. For each document D, we define a temporal profile $P(t|D)$. This probability distribution expresses the extent to which D is associated with events that were discussed at various moments in time. Estimating $P(t|D)$ follows the same logic that we use for query temporal profiles; we submit the text of D as a query, yielding $\mathcal{R}_D = R_{D1}, \ldots, R_{Dk}$. Each of the documents R_i in $\mathcal{R}_D$ contains a timestamp t_i. From the empirical distribution of $t_1, \ldots, t_k$ we may estimate the underlying distribution $P(t|D)$.

To estimate $P(t|D)$ we imagine the following generative process. A person interested in D samples documents according to $P(D_1|D), \ldots, P(D_N|D)$. If this choice yields document D_i with timestamp t_i, we choose time t with probability $P(t|t_i)$. We let this probability follow an exponential distribution on $|t_i - t|$.

The probability of choosing document D_i in our generative process is simply the likelihood of D given D_i. To derive a proper density, we normalize the k likelihoods in $\mathcal{R}_D$ to sum to one:

$$s_i = P(D_i|D) = \frac{P(D|D_i)P(D_i)}{\sum_{j \in \mathcal{R}_D} P(D|D_j)P(D_j)}.$$

We then have:

$$\hat{P}(t|D) = \sum_{t_i \in \mathcal{R}_D} s_i \cdot r \cdot e^{-r \cdot |t_i - t|}. \quad (9)$$

The exponential rate parameter r governs the temporal influence; a large r strongly favors times near t_i. It is worth noting that Eq. 9 is similar to a weighted kernel density estimate [25]. It allocates probability mass mostly around the timestamps of those documents that have a high likelihood of having generated D.

For each document and query we observe lexical evidence (i.e. their textual content) and temporal evidence. Let W_Q and W_D be the lexical representations of the query and a document, respectively, and T_Q and T_D be vectors of timestamps retrieved by submitting Q as a query or D as a pseudo-query. It is intuitive to rank on the joint probability $P(W_Q, W_D, T_Q, T_D)$. If we assume conditional independence between lexical and temporal information and a uniform distribution over temporal profiles we have:

$$P(W_Q, W_D, T_Q, T_D) \propto P(W_Q|W_D) \cdot P(T_Q|T_D). \quad (10)$$

This is simply the query likelihood multiplied by the likelihood that the timestamps returned by Q were generated by the same distribution that generated the timestamps observed in the result set of the pseudo-query for D. Using our estimate of the temporal profile of D, the likelihood of T_Q given D is:

$$P(T_Q|T_D) = \prod_{i=1}^{k_Q} P(t_{Qi}|D) \quad (11)$$

where k_Q is the number of timestamps in the query's temporal profile; we set this to $k_Q = 10$. We then obtain a temporally informed retrieval by multiplying Eqs. 2 and 11. In the following discussion, we refer to this model as TExp (temporal expansion). Runs labeled TExp use documents' unexpanded text for W_D. We will compare this method to a baseline using temporal document priors described by Li and Croft [17] (which we call TPrior). TPrior uses an exponential distribution on the age of documents as the prior in Eq. 2. Both methods–TExp and TPrior–rely on a rate parameter r for the exponential. Following Li and Croft, unless otherwise specified we set $r = 0.01$.

5. EXPERIMENTAL DATA

In the discussion that follows we rely mainly on two data sets. First, we use Tweets2011, the collection used for the

TREC 2011 microblog task. Second, we use a collection of metadata records describing holdings in a large digital library. Both of these collections consist mostly of brief documents, though as we shall show, they have many differences.

5.1 Microblog Data

The Tweets2011 collection uses a corpus of posts (called "tweets") made available by the microblogging service Twitter. Instead of distributing the microblog corpus via physical media or a direct download, TREC organizers distributed approximately 16M unique tweet ID numbers. Users of the collection downloaded these ID's, along with software that allowed them to fetch the tweets directly from Twitter. We obtained our data using the supplied HTML scraping tools on May 25–26, 2011. Our corpus contained 15,653,612 indexable tweets, each containing: the screen name of the author, the time at which the tweet was posted, and the tweet text itself.

Our microblog data was preprocessed in several ways. First, in conformance with the track's guidelines all "retweets" were removed by deleting documents containing the string `RT`. Second, we made a simple pass at removing non-English tweets. We deleted tweets containing more than four characters with byte values greater than 255. We also defined a list of 133 words that are common in Spanish, French and German. Tweets containing any of these were removed. After these operations, the corpus contained 8,320,421 documents.

The 2011 microblog track involved a real-time search problem. Track organizers created 50 test topics[2], each of which contained query text Q and a timestamp t_Q. Only documents posted prior to t_Q were assessed for relevance (all others are non-relevant). Aside from returning only documents published before query-time, for the sake of simplicity, in this paper we drop additional real-time strictures defined by the track organizers.

5.2 Digital Library Metadata Collection (IMLS DCC)

The Institute for Museum and Library Studies Digital Collections and Content (IMLS DCC) is a large, federated digital library offering access to the aggregated holdings of a broad spectrum of digital collections at distributed cultural heritage institutions[3]. In collaboration with IMLS DCC, we obtained a collection of 578,385 brief descriptions of cultural heritage resources. IMLS DCC administrators regularly harvest descriptions of several hundred participating institutions' digital resources via the Open Archives Initiative Protocol for Metadata Harvesting (OAI-PMH) [15]. Each of the 578,385 harvested documents is a Dublin Core metadata record describing a single item such as a photograph, manuscript, sound recording. Details of the process by which this corpus was built are given in [8].

To enable IR experimentation, we sampled 53 queries taken from the DCC search engine query logs. It must be stressed that these were not chosen at random. We used care in selecting queries to assure that no query returned zero relevant documents. Because many highly specific queries returned zero or very few items – making changes in IR performance difficult to test – queries with fewer than five relevant documents (as gauged by the following process) in the collection were omitted.

Initial assessments of query suitability for our experiments were made by one of the authors, who is a former DCC administrator with significant experience in collection evaluation and user interactions. When choosing queries for inclusion on our test collection, this judge assessed potential relevance generously; if there seemed to be a reasonable chance that a document could satisfy a query, the document was considered potentially relevant. If a query accumulated at least five plausibly relevant documents, the query was included. Redundant queries and queries submitted by DCC administrators were also culled from the sample. Altogether we retained 53 queries.

We completed this collection by soliciting relevance judgments via Amazon's Mechanical Turk[4] (AMT) service. To accomplish this, the same author wrote relevance criteria for each query. The process of writing relevance criteria is of course subjective and entails obvious limitations. However, without explicit knowledge of the information needs of people who created the queries, the author wrote these criteria to enhance the AMT workers' understanding of the queries and results without unduly limiting or biasing their sense of relevance. For example, relevance criteria for the query *USS Monitor* were given as, "Highly relevant documents should link to photographs or documentation about the Civil-War-era warship, the USS Monitor. Somewhat relevant documents will describe or provide photographic evidence of US Navy ships from the same era."

While the process of choosing and describing queries introduced subjectivity into our study, we pursued this method because we felt that using queries from the DCC's search logs was more realistic than writing queries of our own. Without attendant clickthrough data, this intervention was necessary to give AMT judges sufficient information for relevance assessment.

Documents to be assessed via AMT were gathered from pools created by running several retrievals over all 53 queries. Pools contained results from five of the conditions discussed in Section 6, as well as a run using BM25 ranking. All together, six runs contributed to the judging pools which were held to depth of 100.

Judgments were reconciled with two-thirds majority voting. After the first run of AMT ratings, we found that agreement was low with Fleiss kappa=0.24. However, the majority AMT ratings yielded a kappa=0.724 when compared to a set of oracle ratings by the study authors, suggesting that the problem of low inter-rater agreement was not systematic but due to scattered unreliable workers. To address this issue, we identified unreliable raters based on the proportion of each worker's judgments that were in agreement with the majority. Using an admittedly arbitrary agreement threshold of 0.67, we divided our workers into "good" and "bad" categories. 28 of 131 workers fell into the "bad" category. We removed all work done by these workers and re-submitted their tasks to AMT.

After the second judging round we recomputed reliability scores, this time finding only four bad workers whose sum proportion of ratings was 0.01. Only two workers who were good in round one became bad during round two. After round two, Fleiss kappa was 0.40. While this is lower than

[2]NIST created relevance judgments using the standard TREC pooling method. Because it lacked relevant documents, one topic was removed from the final task.

[3]`http://imlsdcc.grainger.uiuc.edu/`

[4]`http://mturk.com`

Table 1: Summary Statistics for Experimental Corpora. From left to right, columns give total number of documents, observed word types, observed word tokens, median document length, mean document length, standard deviation of document length, and the number of test queries.

Corpus	Indexed Docs	Unique Terms	Tokens	Median Doc Len	Mean Doc Len	SD Doc Len	# Queries
Tweets2011	8,320,421	19,449,151	6,506,465,256	20	21.92	7.30	49
DCC	578,385	2,793,371	114,453,512	45	197.89	556.90	53

we would like, it marks a significant improvement over the initial work quality.

5.3 Data Statistics

Table 1 summarizes length-related aspects of our two test data sets. Not surprisingly, documents in the microblog corpus are very short (median=20, compared to median=328 in TREC 8), with a compressed distribution of lengths. Most DCC documents are a bit longer than microblog posts (median=45), and their lengths vary more than tweet lengths do. The corpora analyzed here are similar insofar as their documents are much shorter than documents in more standard IR collections. But the collections are also different from each other.

6. EXPERIMENTAL ASSESSMENT

All experiments were done using the Indri search engine and the Lemur toolkit[5]. For efficiency, we used the standard Indri stoplist and a custom Twitter-specific stoplist when forming document pseudo-queries. But subsequent retrievals used no stoplists or stemming except to mitigate common words' influence in the baseline relevance feedback condition–feedback models were stripped of words in the Indri stoplist. Unless otherwise specified, all retrieval (both queries and pseudo-queries) used the Indri defaults of Dirichlet smoothing with $\mu = 2500$. For each Tweets2011 query we retrieved 100 documents. We retrieved 50 documents per DCC query. To assess the merit of our proposed expansion methods we tested the conditions shown in Table 2.

6.1 The Effect of Lexical Expansion

Tables 3 and 4 list four effectiveness metrics for the conditions described above, on both of our test data sets[6]. The clearest result from the tables is the improvement over the QL baseline offered by our lexical expansion methods. Except for one case (P10 for LExp on DCC), the lexical expansion methods always outperform the QL baseline. The positive effect of document expansion is especially strong when we interpolated the expanded model with the observed document model (i.e the TExpλ condition).

We can see the positive effect of document expansion in Figure 2. Each panel in the figure schematizes the distribution of query terms in relevant and non-relevant documents, over a variety of data sets. Besides our two short document collections, as a point of reference we show the TREC 8 data described above and the small WT10g web collection. As we discussed earlier, the figure shows that query terms tend to

[5]`http://lemurproject.org`

[6]Reported metrics are mean average precision (MAP), R-precision (Rprec), NDCG over all positions (NDCG) and precision at 10 (P10).

Table 2: Baseline and Experimental Retrieval Names and Parameters.

	Abbr.	Details
Baselines	QL	Basic query likelihood. Dirichlet smoothing, $\mu = 2500$
	FB	Relevance feedback using relevance models. 20 feedback docs; 15 terms. Interpolation with original query $\lambda = 0.5$
	TPrior	Temporal priors to promote recent documents. Exponential rate parameter $r = 0.01$.
Experimental	LExp	Lexical document expansion. $k = 50$ expansion documents.
	LExpλ	Lexical document expansion with linear interpolation of expansion model with MLE. $k = 50$ expansion. Expansion-MLE mixing proportion $\lambda = 0.5$.
	TExp	Temporal document expansion. $k = 50$ expansion documents.
	LTExp	Both lexical and temporal document expansion. i.e. A combination of LExpλ and TExp.
	TBoth	Two types of temporal evidence are used: the prior of TPrior and the expansion method of TExp. No lexical expansion.

Table 3: Observed IR Effectiveness on TREC 2011 Microblog Data. The †symbol indicates $p < 0.05$ on a permutation test against the baseline QL. The ‡symbol indicates $p < 0.01$.

	MAP	Rprec	NDCG	P10
QL	0.187	0.275	0.360	0.398
FB	0.189	0.273	0.361	0.394
TPrior	0.198†	0.284†	0.372	0.427
LExp	0.216†	0.301†	0.404‡	0.380
LExpλ	0.226‡	0.319‡	0.415‡	0.431
TExp	0.204†	0.289	0.373	0.414
TBoth	0.206†	0.289†	0.378†	0.427†
LTexp	**0.235‡**	**0.324‡**	**0.428‡**	**0.451‡**

Figure 2: log Probabilities of Query Terms in Relevant and Non-Relevant Documents in Four Corpora.

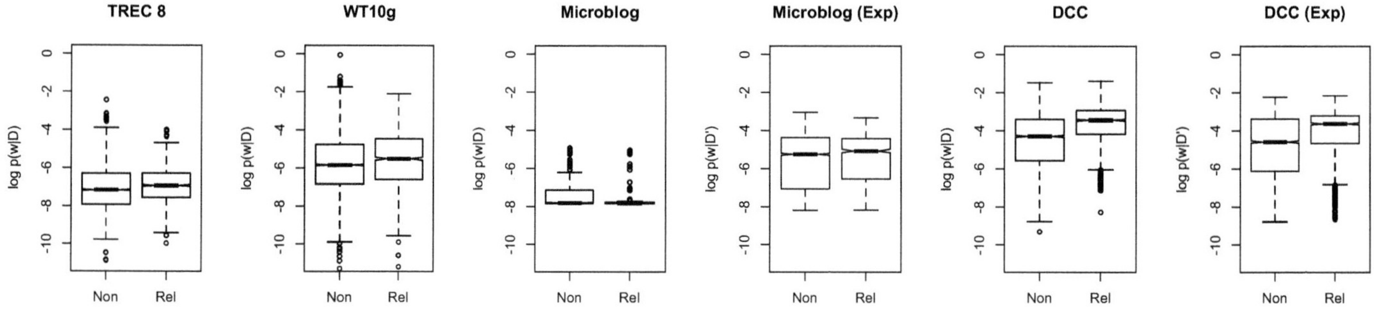

Table 4: Observed IR Effectiveness on DCC Data. The †symbol indicates $p < 0.05$ on a permutation test against the baseline QL. The ‡symbol indicates $p < 0.01$.

	MAP	Rprec	NDCG	P10
QL	0.215	0.287	0.398	0.329
FB	0.205	0.256	0.366	0.300
LExp	0.227	0.292	0.414	0.304
LExpλ	**0.302‡**	**0.359‡**	**0.502‡**	**0.402‡**

have a higher probability in relevant documents than in non-relevant documents. The difference is especially stark for the standard (TREC 8 and WT10g) corpora. Observed query term probabilities in the unexpanded microblog corpus give no consistent evidence of relevance (among retrieved documents). The value of query term probabilities in the unexpanded DCC data is higher than in the Twitter data, but less so than in TREC 8 and WT10g. However, the panels labeled *Microblog (Exp)* and *DCC(Exp)* show query term probabilities in expanded document models. In these cases the estimated probability of query terms in relevant documents is significantly greater than the corresponding probability in non-relevant documents (Mann-Whitney $p \ll 0.001$ one-sided).

A surprising result of our experiments is the poor performance of feedback using relevance models. Inspection of the expanded queries that led to these results showed that the induced query models contained very idiosyncratic terms such as user names (Twitter) and administrative vocabulary (DCC). We include the feedback results because it is worth noting that the expanded document models are capturing semantics that expanded query models cannot, given the conditions encountered in these data. We hypothesize that this effect arises because, in addition to alleviating the vocabulary mismatch problem, our expansion method yields more data for estimating language models. Expanded queries alleviate vocabulary mismatch and improve estimates of the query model, but expanded documents improve our estimates of the document models. In the context of short document retrieval, this effect seems to be crucial.

Figure 3 shows performance over a range of values (from 5 to 50) for k, the number of expansion documents used to fit an augmented language model D' (cf. Eq. 7). Contrary to our expectations, there appears to be little risk in adding many documents to an expanded model. While a small decline in performance is visible for the LExp condition on the DCC data after $k = 35$, when we interpolate with the original model (LExpλ), the performance does not decrease over the range from 5–50 documents. We suspect that this is due to the very small probabilities associated with documents deep in the retrieved set for D.

Figure 3: Mean Average Precision Observed Over Varied Values of k. The x-axis is the number of documents used to fit the expansion model D'.

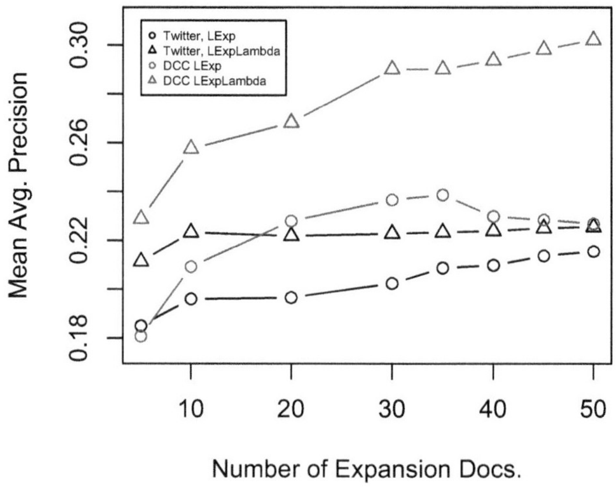

Our reliance on the retrieved sets of documents' pseudo-queries raises the issue of language model smoothing. How aggressively should we smooth when performing IR for document pseudo-queries? Table 5 shows that during document pseudo-query retrieval, previous studies of smoothing's critical role apply [28]. The table shows retrieval effectiveness statistics at three settings of the Dirichlet smoothing parameter μ during retrieval with document pseudo-queries. Our experiments use $\mu = 2500$. This setting is the default in the Indri search engine (we chose it because it obviated the need for training data) and it has been shown to be effective. Table 5 shows that in this choice we were lucky. It is clear that 250 leads to under-smoothing, while 5000

Table 5: Comparison of Retrieval Effectiveness with Different Selections of μ, the Dirichlet Smoothing Parameter, Applied During Retrieval Based on Document Pseudo-Queries.

	Tweets2011			DCC		
Metric	$\mu = 250$	$\mu = 2500$	$\mu = 5000$	$\mu = 250$	$\mu = 2500$	$\mu = 5000$
REL RET	858	1032	796	441	661	633
MAP	0.1810	0.2155	0.1792	0.1702	0.2269	0.1990
Rprec	0.2764	0.3008	0.2584	0.2255	0.2919	0.2526
NDCG	0.3452	0.4034	0.3454	0.3310	0.4136	0.3787
P10	0.3735	0.3796	0.3694	0.2264	0.3038	0.2906
P30	0.3014	0.3190	0.2871	0.1987	0.2994	0.2780

is too high. All declines in MAP, Rprec, and NDCG from $\mu = 2500$ are statistically significant. This suggests that document expansion carries some risk. We hypothesize that much of this risk comes from the conjunctive and disjunctive semantics of aggressive smoothing. Weak smoothing pushes retrieval towards a Boolean AND'ing of query terms, while strong smoothing allows the predominance of only a few query terms to promote a document. Balancing this economy is clearly important. However, it is also the case that Table 5 shows very extreme values for μ. Because computational constraints kept us from performing a full parameter sweep, we chose to test very high and very low smoothing parameters. In future work we plan to examine the "safe" region for smoothing in more depth.

6.2 The Effect of Temporal Expansion

Of our two data sets only Tweets2011 has a temporal component; the DCC documents lack any measurable chronology. Thus we tested the temporal expansion described in Section 4.2 only on the Twitter data. As a baseline we compared our method against the use of temporal priors introduced by Li and Croft. Effectiveness results for each condition are shown in Table 3. Both the baseline method (TPrior) and our temporal expansion (TExp) gave statistically significant improvements over the non-temporally informed QL baseline. However, the difference in effect between TPrior and TExp are small in Table 3, with both methods scoring nearly identically (the differences between them are not statistically significant).

Combining lexical and temporal expansion improves effectiveness further. in Table 3 the method using both expansion sources, LTExp, outperforms all other runs. For completeness, we compared LTExp against a run using the LExpλ condition modified with a temporal prior. LTExp improved on this baseline for all metrics shown in Table 3, with $p < 0.05$ for MAP and P10.

An interesting result is visible in Figure 4. The bar plot shows the difference in mean average precision (between TExp and TPrior) on a query-by-query basis. Though a few queries have near-identical scores under both TPrior and TExp, the majority of queries fare differently under each method. Both the baseline and proposed methods improve aggregate effectiveness on these data. But they appear to do so quite differently, suggesting that they are not interchangeable. The run in Table 3 labeled TBoth uses both temporal priors and temporal expansion. Though its performance is similar to temporal expansion alone, TBoth does see consistent improvement over TExp (p is 0.83, 0.12, 0.01, 0.15 for MAP, Rprec, NDCG and P10, respectively), suggesting that the prior introduces information distinct from temporal expansion.

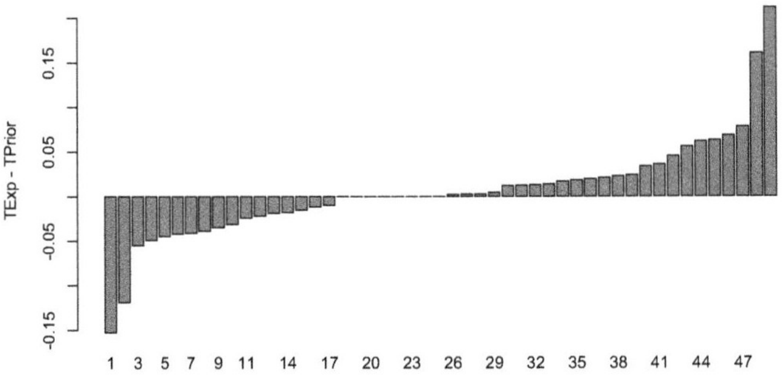

Figure 4: Comparison of Two Methods of Temporal Influence. Each bar is the difference in Mean Average Precision between TExp and TPrior (i.e. MAP$_{TExp}$−MAP$_{TPrior}$ on one the the 49 Tweets2011 Queries.

In earlier work [7] it was shown that choosing the rate parameter r for the exponential distribution when applying temporal priors has a strong effect on retrieval. However, we found that a broad range of exponential parameterizations yielded little difference in performance from the data reported in Table 3. The same was true for the parameter in our temporal expansion; a broad sweep yielded no statistically significant change. We hypothesize that this robustness is due to the short temporal span of the Tweets2011 corpus (two weeks). If we repeated our experiments on collections spanning months or years, we anticipate seeing more sensitivity to setting r in both the baseline approach and our own.

7. DISCUSSION

In our previous exposition we treated temporal and lexical expansion as two distinct operations. But the same rationale and the same mechanism underpin both operations. In both cases, information gleaned from a document's result set is used to derive new information about that document. The influence of each member of the result set is proportional to $P(D|D_i)$. Thus in addition to lexical and temporal expansion, we could apply this operation on arbitrary features of documents. For instance, if each document had geolocation information, we could use the methods presented here to make an expanded location profile. Our main contribution is a way to create, for each document, an empirical distribution of features of whatever type. Our results suggest that for the feature types explored here (lexical and temporal), these distributions convey useful information for IR.

A notable advantage of the temporal expansion method proposed here is its flexibility with respect to the semantics of a query. For instance, the temporal prior method can account only for "recency queries" where the user seeks new information. However, our TExp approach assesses the similarity between the timestamps of documents retrieved by Q and those obtained from the pseudo-query of a document D. If Q retrieves documents clustered around a window of time in the past, TExp will reward documents whose pseudo-queries' results occupy the same window.

One issue that we have not addressed in this paper is the transformation of a document into a pseudo-query. In the interest of simplicity, we omitted any transformation other than removal of stopwords to improve retrieval speed. However, our results suggest room for improvement by a more thoughtful approach. In particular, we consider the difference between LExp and LExpλ on the DCC data evocative on this matter. Interpolation with the original document model helped retrieval to a great extent in this case, a fact emphasized by Figure 3. We suspect that this is due to the length of some DCC documents. Many of these documents are more verbose than, for example, tweets. These results suggest that longer documents do not lead to suitable pseudo-queries without some improvement.

8. CONCLUSION

We have proposed expanding document representations to improve retrieval effectiveness on corpora of very brief texts. Our contribution starts with the idea that short documents often make productive pseudo-queries. Because brief documents tend to discuss at most one topic, the retrieved set for a document D is informative with respect to making predictions about the relevance of D. We proposed two methods of document expansion based on analysis of document pseudo-queries' result sets. First, we augment the language model of D, obtaining an expanded language model D'. Second, we induce a model of the temporal affinity of D by analyzing the temporal profile of D's result set. We find that the likelihood that this density generated the timestamps retrieved by a query Q yields an effective mechanism for letting time inform ranking.

In future work we plan to address several issues raised by this study:

- Self-retrievability and document priors. We hypothesize that the extent to which D is distinguishable from other documents in its result set is an indicator of topical coherence. This intuition could inform a prior over documents.
- Use of longer documents. Though short documents stand to gain significantly from expansion, there is no reason the gains we have seen in this study would not carry over to more standard collections.
- Query expansion vs. document expansion. Studying more conventional corpora will help us assess the differences between query and document expansion more thoroughly. We also plan to compare our approach to other document expansion methods such as Berger and Lafferty's translation model [3].
- Other settings. Short documents arise in many IR applications. Searching for relevant advertisements or product reviews are both domains that we believe could benefit from the approaches outlined here.
- Other expansion data. In future work we hope to examine the value of expansion methods for information such as geolocation data or user-created content.
- Scalable implementation. An efficient way to store and use document expansion data is crucial for our methods' viability in a production setting. In particular, future work will address the matter of changing documents' expansion data as the collection grows.

Despite these unexplored ideas, the results of this study show that document expansion is a compelling method for improving retrieval in corpora of short texts. As people's engagement with social media increases the pervasiveness of abbreviated documents, this problem will grow in importance. Considering short documents as pseudo-queries provides needed traction on this difficult task.

9. ACKNOWLEDGEMENTS

This work was supported by a Google academic research award and Institute of Museum and Library Services LG-06-07-0020. Expressed opinions are those of the authors, not the funding agencies. The project is hosted by the Center for Informatics Research in Science and Scholarship (CIRSS).

10. REFERENCES

[1] Omar Alonso, Michael Gertz, and Ricardo Baeza-Yates. On the value of temporal information in information retrieval. *SIGIR Forum*, 41:35–41, December 2007.

[2] Gianni Amati, Alessandro Celi, Cesidio Di Nicola, Michele Flammini, and Daniela Pavone. Improved stable retrieval in noisy collections. In Giambattista Amati and Fabio Crestani, editors, *Advances in Information Retrieval Theory*, volume 6931 of *Lecture Notes in Computer Science*, pages 342–345. Springer Berlin, Heidelberg, 2011.

[3] Adam Berger and John Lafferty. Information retrieval as statistical translation. In *SIGIR '99: Proceedings of the 22nd annual international ACM SIGIR conference on Research and development in information retrieval*, pages 222–229, New York, NY, USA, 1999. ACM.

[4] Wisam Dakka, Luis Gravano, and Panagiotis G. Ipeirotis. Answering general time-sensitive queries. *IEEE Transactions on Knowledge and Data Engineering*, 24(2):220–235, 2012.

[5] Fernando Diaz and Rosie Jones. Using temporal profiles of queries for precision prediction. In *SIGIR '04: Proceedings of the 27th annual international ACM SIGIR conference on Research and development in information retrieval*, pages 18–24, New York, NY, USA, 2004. ACM.

[6] Miles Efron. Information search and retrieval in microblogs. *Journal of the American Society for Information Science and Technology*, 62(6):996–1008, 2011.

[7] Miles Efron and Gene Golovchinsky. Estimation methods for ranking recent information. In *Proceedings*

of the 34th international ACM SIGIR conference on Research and development in Information, SIGIR '11, pages 495–504, New York, NY, USA, 2011. ACM.

[8] Miles Efron, Peter Organisciak, and Katrina Fenlon. Building topic models in a federated digital library through selective document exclusion. In *Proceedings of the Annual Meeting of the American Society for Information Science and Technology*, 2011.

[9] Inna Gelfer Kalmanovich and Oren Kurland. Cluster-based query expansion. In *Proceedings of the 32nd international ACM SIGIR conference on Research and development in information retrieval*, SIGIR '09, pages 646–647, New York, NY, USA, 2009. ACM.

[10] Giacomo Inches, Mark Carman, and Fabio Crestani. Investigating the statistical properties of user-generated documents. In Henning Christiansen, Guy De Tr, Adnan Yazici, Slawomir Zadrozny, Troels Andreasen, and Henrik Larsen, editors, *Flexible Query Answering Systems*, volume 7022 of *Lecture Notes in Computer Science*, pages 198–209. Springer Berlin / Heidelberg, 2011.

[11] Rosie Jones and Fernando Diaz. Temporal profiles of queries. *ACM Transactions on Information Systems*, 25(3):14, 2007.

[12] Anna Khudyak Kozorovitsky and Oren Kurland. Cluster-based fusion of retrieved lists. In *Proceedings of the 34th international ACM SIGIR conference on Research and development in Information Retrieval*, SIGIR '11, pages 893–902, New York, NY, USA, 2011. ACM.

[13] Oren Kurland and Lillian Lee. Clusters, language models, and ad hoc information retrieval. *ACM Trans. Inf. Syst.*, 27:13:1–13:39, May 2009.

[14] Oren Kurland, Lillian Lee, and Carmel Domshlak. Better than the real thing?: iterative pseudo-query processing using cluster-based language models. In *Proceedings of the 28th annual international ACM SIGIR conference on Research and development in information retrieval*, SIGIR '05, pages 19–26, New York, NY, USA, 2005. ACM.

[15] Carl Lagoze and Herbert Van de Sompel. The Open Archives Initiative: building a low-barrier interoperability framework. In *JCDL '01: Proceedings of the 1st ACM/IEEE-CS joint conference on Digital libraries*, pages 54–62, New York, NY, USA, 2001. ACM.

[16] Victor Lavrenko and W. Bruce Croft. Relevance based language models. In *SIGIR '01: Proceedings of the 24th annual international ACM SIGIR conference on Research and development in information retrieval*, pages 120–127, New York, NY, USA, 2001. ACM.

[17] Xiaoyan Li and W. Bruce Croft. Time-based language models. In *CIKM '03: Proceedings of the twelfth international conference on Information and knowledge management*, pages 469–475, New York, NY, USA, 2003. ACM.

[18] Xiaoyong Liu and W. Bruce Croft. Cluster-based retrieval using language models. In *Proceedings of the 27th annual international ACM SIGIR conference on Research and development in information retrieval*, SIGIR '04, pages 186–193, New York, NY, USA, 2004. ACM.

[19] Kamran Massoudi, Manos Tsagkias, Maarten de Rijke, and Wouter Weerkamp. Incorporating query expansion and quality indicators in searching microblog posts. In *Proceedings of the 33rd European conference on Advances in information retrieval*, ECIR'11, pages 362–367, Berlin, Heidelberg, 2011. Springer-Verlag.

[20] Donald Metzler, Susan Dumais, and Christopher Meek. Similarity measures for short segments of text. In *Proceedings of the 29th European conference on IR research*, ECIR'07, pages 16–27, Berlin, Heidelberg, 2007. Springer-Verlag.

[21] Jay M. Ponte and W. Bruce Croft. A language modeling approach to information retrieval. *Research and Development in Information Retrieval*, pages 275–281, 1998.

[22] Haoliang Qi, Mu Li, Jianfeng Gao, and Sheng Li. Information retrieval for short documents. *Journal of Electronics (China)*, 23:933–936, 2006. 10.1007/s11767-006-0044-2.

[23] Daniel Ramage, Susan Dumais, and Dan Liebling. Characterizing microblogs with topic models. In *ICWSM*, 2010.

[24] Nico Schlaefer, Jennifer Chu-Carroll, Eric Nyberg, James Fan, Wlodek Zadrozny, and David Ferrucci. Statistical source expansion for question answering. In *Proceedings of the 20th ACM international conference on Information and knowledge management*, CIKM '11, pages 345–354, New York, NY, USA, 2011. ACM.

[25] B. W. Silverman. *Density Estimation for Statistics and Data Analysis.* Monographs on Statistics and Applied Probability. Chapman & Hall, Boca Raton, 1996.

[26] Tao Tao, Xuanhui Wang, Qiaozhu Mei, and Chengxiang Zhai. Language model information retrieval with document expansion. In *Human Language Technology Conference of the North American Chapter of the ACL*, pages 407–414, New York, 2006.

[27] Fulai Wang and Jim E. Greer. Retrieval of short documents from discussion forums. In *Proceedings of the 15th Conference of the Canadian Society for Computational Studies of Intelligence on Advances in Artificial Intelligence*, AI '02, pages 339–343, London, UK, UK, 2002. Springer-Verlag.

[28] Chengxiang Zhai and John Lafferty. A study of smoothing methods for language models applied to information retrieval. *ACM Transactions on Information Systems*, 2(2):179–214, 2004.

Extending BM25 with Multiple Query Operators

Roi Blanco
Yahoo! Research
Barcelona, Spain
roi@yahoo-inc.com

Paolo Boldi
Dipartimento di Informatica
Università degli Studi, Milano, Italy
boldi@dsi.unimi.it

ABSTRACT

Traditional probabilistic relevance frameworks for informational retrieval refrain from taking positional information into account, due to the hurdles of developing a sound model while avoiding an explosion in the number of parameters. Nonetheless, the well-known BM25F extension of the successful Okapi ranking function can be seen as an embryonic attempt in that direction. In this paper, we proceed along the same line, defining the notion of *virtual region*: a virtual region is a part of the document that, like a BM25F-field, can provide a (larger or smaller, depending on a tunable weighting parameter) evidence of relevance of the document; differently from BM25F fields, though, virtual regions are generated implicitly by applying suitable (usually, but not necessarily, positional-aware) operators to the query. This technique fits nicely in the eliteness model behind BM25 and provides a principled explanation to BM25F; it specializes to BM25(F) for some trivial operators, but has a much more general appeal. Our experiments (both on standard collections, such as TREC, and on Web-like repertoires) show that the use of virtual regions is beneficial for retrieval effectiveness.

Categories and Subject Descriptors

H.3.3 [**Information Storage Systems**]: Information Retrieval Systems

General Terms

Performance, Experimentation, Ranking

Keywords

Query processing, ranking, query segmentation, BM25

1. INTRODUCTION

Modern information retrieval ranking functions, like the ones used in today's search engines, employ a large number of features derived from different sources of evidence: matches of query terms in documents, document query-independent quality measures, and click-through information among others. Prevalent among those signals, and central to most standard retrieval approaches such as BM25 and language models, is the term frequency (tf) information (i.e., the number of times a term appears in a document). Approaches derived from the probabilistic retrieval model are implemented as a summation of "weights" of the query terms that appear in the document, where the weight is essentially a normalized version of term frequency.

Traditional probabilistic relevance frameworks for informational retrieval [30] refrain from taking positional information into account, both because of the hurdles of developing a sound model while avoiding an explosion in the number of parameters and because positional information has been shown (somehow surprisingly) to have little effect on average [34]. Recently, though, it has been proved that considering sequences of terms that form *query concepts* is beneficial for retrieval [6]. Those extensions build up on the Markov Random Field retrieval model (MRF) and use a linear combination of different concepts and query-term scores in order to derive a final score for a document. Furthermore, the well-known BM25F extension of the successful Okapi ranking function (the latter of which we are aiming on building upon) can be seen as an embryonic attempt in the same direction: the basic idea there is that each document is made of regions (fields) and some fields may provide stronger evidence of relevance than others.

In this paper, we proceed along the same line, defining the notion of *virtual region*: a virtual region is a part of the document that, like a BM25F-field, can provide a different evidence of relevance of the document (the amount of evidence is, like in BM25F, expressed by a weight). Differently from BM25F fields, though, virtual regions are generated implicitly by applying suitable operators to the query: such operators may (and typically will) use positional information.

The techniques we propose can be seen as a two-stage ranking: in the first stage, a number of operators are applied to the incoming query to individuate virtual regions within the document; in the second stage, the regions are ranked much in the same way as with BM25F, using the weights attached to each operator. The idea is that there are "stricter" operators, that give a stronger evidence (e.g., "I want that at least three of the query terms appear in a span of at most ten words"), but are less likely to appear in document, and other that are "weaker" (e.g., "I want at least one of the query terms appearing somewhere", that is

SIGIR'12, August 12–16, 2012, Portland, Oregon, USA.
Copyright 2012 ACM 978-1-4503-1472-5/12/08 ...$15.00.

the standard bag-of-words requirement) and contribute to recall.

The operator-based technique that we propose fits nicely in the usual eliteness model behind BM25 and provides a principled explanation to BM25F; it specializes to BM25(F) for some trivial operators, but we believe it has a more general appeal.

Abstracting from the positional aspect, we can think of our method as an attempt to understand more deeply the user's intent underlying a query [2], following the increasing interest in extracting features and learning about the query itself. For example, all major search engines are able to detect entities in queries in order to shortcut the user to an appropriate vertical (e.g., for e-commerce or news), to trigger different visualization schemes or simply to help ranking better the results that are being produced. The basic idea is that of being able to pre-process a plain set of query terms that a user submitted to build a model of the query (possibly with the help of contextual information, e.g., about the query session and/or the user's profile). This model might simply contain spelling corrections, term annotations or may exhibit more sophisticated expansions, obtained through gazetteers, synonym dictionaries or query-logs, just to name a few.

In general, we observe that information retrieval is moving from a document-centric to a query/user-centric approach, and modern search engines are investing large amounts of research in building better, more comprehensive query models. The question that we address in this paper is whether it is possible to extend the classical probabilistic formulation so as to accommodate in a natural way these extended query models for enhancing ranking, in both Web search and more classical TREC-like retrieval settings.

Contribution.

Summing up, this paper aims at proposing an extension of the probabilistic retrieval framework [30] that accounts for the information coming from queries and documents. Our approach can be seen as a principled way of integrating query-document features into a BM25-based model [32], by extending the event space using a number of *operators* that derive from a query model [7]. For instance, both BM25 and BM25F [33] could be regarded as a special case of the method presented here. The framework operates in a general manner by means of a set of operators that are materialized using query-derived information; each operator determines a (possibly empty) virtual region within the document, that is treated as a (weighted) field; query-term frequencies in each virtual region are used to compute the final score of the document. We shall frame our technique as an extension of BM25(F) and describe how it can be implemented efficiently. Finally, we provide experimental evaluation of our approach showing that the usage of operators outperforms state-of-the-art ranking that use just matching of query terms and is especially helpful for *difficult* queries. The software implementing our technique and used for the experiments will be made available at `http://mg4j.dsi.unimi.it/`.

2. RELATED WORK

Some lines of research attempt at addressing the issue of adding semantic information to documents and queries [22]. The model that we present (which could indeed encode [22] as a special case) can be seen as a template for grounding different graphical model instances, in the spirit of Markov Logic Networks [18, 29], even though in this paper we make no attempt to generalize the learning procedure of the probabilities involved in the model, and the inference we perform is restricted to one particular formulation and combination. However, the very structure of our method allows one to extend it to different combinations and aggregation functionals over probability distributions. Robertson *et al.* [33] introduced BM25F, a variation of BM25 that is able to deal with matches of query terms in different fields of the document, boosting them differently. Our framework stems from the same fundamental notions of BM25F and BM25 (term eliteness, re-weighting of term matches) and it is able to extend/accommodate both.

There are several recent papers that deal with spans of terms in ranking. Svore et al. [35] show that introducing spans of terms as a further feature for machine learning to rank model gives improvements over BM25. Other authors have dealt with the issue of incorporating these spans of terms into the language model framework, the first one being the Markov Random Field (MRF) model of Metzler and Croft [26], extending the language modeling framework for information retrieval [27, 39] to handle term dependencies. Some other approaches [11] compute the aggregated distance of matches and add it to the BM25 score, or define a kernel-like distance [23, 24] that can be successfully used for ranking by plugging it into a language-model divergence between the query and document estimation. One remarkable model close to ours is that of Bendersky *et al.* [5], who weight different query concepts using a parameterized combination of diverse importance features: those concepts can be single query keyword, phrases matching in the document, or matches of keywords that span a window of a certain size. The amount of matching concepts in the document are later integrated into the MRF ranking model. In our case we focus on extending BM25 and not the language modeling framework, the core difference being in the way information is aggregated for each term during ranking.

Besides taking spans into account, it may be beneficial to adopt some additional query segmentation technique, trying to grasp which words in a query should appear in shorter spans (or even consecutively), as successfully attempted in [28, 19].

3. GOALS AND GUIDING EXAMPLES

As explained in the introduction, the basic approach of this paper is to extract, from a given query, a number of regions in the document using suitable operators. Alternatively, you can think that a given *input query* is refined in a number of different ways using some refinement operators, that may (and typically will) use positional information; virtual regions are then the regions matching each of the refined queries.

As a concrete example, consider the following two operators:

- Φ_1 requires that at least any two words in the query appear either consecutively or with an extra word between them;
- Φ_2 just requires that at least one of the query words appears.

One could think of them as query-refinement operators; for example, using the query language syntax of MG4J [9], Φ_1 applied to the query `young nice girl` gives rise to the query:[1]

```
(young nice)~3 OR (young girl)~3 OR (nice girl)~3.
```

When a document is considered against this query, all the areas where at least two of the three queried word appear either consecutively or one word apart are selected. This will determine a (possibly empty) sub-document, in which we can count the frequency of each of the three query words.

Operators Φ_2, instead, applied to the same query will produce

```
young OR nice OR girl;
```

and would just extract the occurrences of either of the three query words from the document.

Clearly, a large frequency in the virtual region determined by Φ_1 would be far more predictive of relevance than that determined by Φ_2 (the latter would amount to actually counting the usual term frequency in the whole document).

To gain some experimental support for this intuition we performed the following experiment: we considered the topics 701-850 from the TREC GOV2 collection, and built queries using the words in their title. To each query, we applied three operators: the plain `or` operator (corresponding to the usual bag-of-words interpretation of the query), the `2-and` operator (satisfied only by documents that contain at least any two of the query terms) and the `2-gram` operator (satisfied by documents that contain two terms consecutively).

Then, for each matching document, we computed the frequency of the query terms within the virtual region and we determined if the document was relevant or not; the fraction of relevant documents is plotted against term frequency. Figure 1 shows the results of the experiment, and provides two fundamental evidences: first of all, stricter operators (2-grams, for instance) provide for the same term frequency a larger probability of relevance, as expected; secondly, the behavior shows in all cases the well-known phenomenon of saturation — as the frequency increases, relevance also increases but at a slower and slower pace, giving rise to the typical sigmoid-shaped function.

Our approach is blind with respect to the operators being considered, which is part of its generality. In our experiments, among other operators, we employ a supervised phrase and entity detection algorithm and feed the different query chunks through the model in order to produce a document score.

Most previous works have addressed the combination of scores in a linear fashion: Bendersky *et al.* [5, 6] and Li *et al.* [20] focused on extensions of the language modeling framework. Linear combinations of features are able to bring increased performance; however, when taking into account evidence coming from the same source of information it is beneficial to understand the distributional properties of the signal the model has to deal with. In these cases, the information employed for ranking is always taken from the number of times one term or a sequence of terms matches a document. In contrast, if one was to incorporate other features, like query-independent document quality [17], or click-based information [1], a linear combination might be

[1]In MG4J, the ~ operator restricts matches to a span of words of a given maximum length.

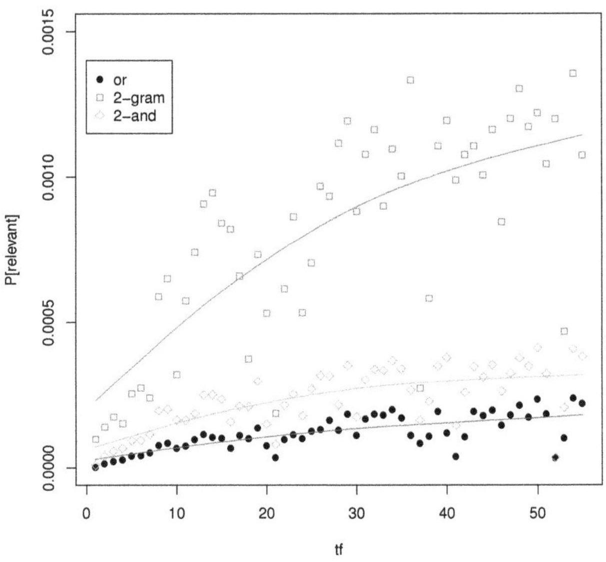

Figure 1: Term frequency versus probability of being relevant, depending on the operator applied to the query. Curves are obtained fitting the points through a spline with three degrees of freedom.

good enough, as long as the features integrated into the model are not correlated. Note however that (somehow surprisingly) even link-based features such as PageRank [10] and BM25 [32] turn out to be non-independent, given the presence of query terms in the anchor text of Web pages [17].

Not assuming feature independence is especially important when devising more complex ranking models that embody a large number of features, such as those employed in learned ranking functions [21]. In case of machine learning frameworks, this dependence is somehow captured by the complexity of learned functions, which in general might incorporate an over-engineering of features.

4. THE OPERATOR-BASED FRAMEWORK

Traditional probabilistic models, like BM25, assume that the relevance of a document to a query can be determined by aggregating individual contributions of the query terms. That is, given the binary random variable R representing relevance, and the vectors of random variables representing the document D and query Q, we want to rank documents according to their increasing odds-probability [30]. Here Q is (or can be thought of as) a set of terms, while D_t is a multi-state variable that encodes the features about the occurrence of term t in D (term frequency, position, etc.); we assume that those features contain a natural zero, corresponding to the absence of t and represented by $\mathbf{0}$. We let d and q denote two actual realizations of D and Q, and r ($\overline{r}$) represent the event $R = 1$ ($R = 0$, respectively), i.e., the document being relevant (irrelevant, respectively). Then, within the probabilistic framework, documents are ranked

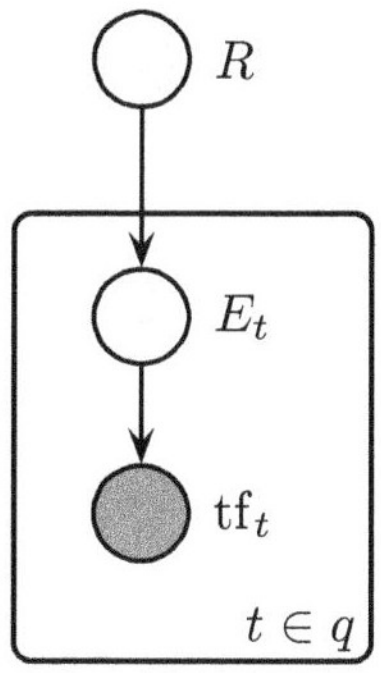

Figure 2: BM25 plate diagram representing the assumptions over variable independence

according to $p(r \mid Q = q, D = d)$, or equivalently

$$\frac{p(r \mid Q=q, D=d)}{p(\overline{r} \mid Q=q, D=d)} \propto_q \frac{p(D=d \mid r, Q=q)}{p(D=d \mid \overline{r}, Q=q)}$$
$$\propto_q \prod_{t \in q} \frac{p(D_t = d_t \mid r)}{p(D_t = d_t \mid \overline{r})}$$
$$\propto_q \sum_{t \in q, d_t > 0} \log \frac{p(D_t = d_t \mid r) \cdot p(D_t = \mathbf{0} \mid \overline{r})}{p(D_t = d_t \mid \overline{r}) \cdot p(D_t = \mathbf{0} \mid r)}$$
$$\propto_q \sum_{t \in q, d_t > 0} w_{t,d},$$

where $w_{t,d}$ is the weight assigned for term t in document d, and you can think of d_t as being the term frequency of t in d, later on denoted by $\mathtt{tf}_{t,d}$.

In the derivation above, we assumed the terms to be *conditionally independent*, that is, $p(D_t = x, D_{t'} = y \mid r, Q) = p(D_t = d_t \mid r, Q) \cdot p(D_{t'} \mid r, Q)$ and $p(D_t = x, D_{t'} = y|\overline{r}, Q) = p(D_t = d_t|\overline{r}, Q) \cdot p(D_{t'}|\overline{r}, Q)$ for any pair of terms t and t'; this is a weaker assumption than term independence, in that we only require terms to be independent for each fixed query and relevance; this assumption is fundamental in practice, because it leads to tractable models, but it also has a deeper justification: as [16] proved, conditional term independence can be obtained when, for any given query, terms are statistically correlated but the correlation is the same on relevant and on non-relevant documents. Empirical evidence on retrieval performances of BM25 suggests that this indeed is often the case. For example, it is true that query terms `New` and `York` are correlated in relevant documents for the query `New York pizza`, but they are also correlated in the whole collection.

Further, the derivation imposes a vague prior assumption over terms not appearing in the query ($p(D_t = x \mid r) = p(D_t = x \mid \overline{r})$ if $t \notin Q$). This can be weakened in the case of query expansion by explicitly linking unseen query terms to relevance.

The final arithmetic trick in the above derivation, known as *removing the zeroes*, is used to eliminate from the final score calculation terms that are not present in the document.

The determination of term weights in BM25 is based on the assumption that there is an *Elite* random variable, which can be cast as a simple topical model that perturbs the distribution of words over the text. That is [30], the author is assumed first to choose which topics to cover, i.e., which are the elite terms and which are not. Furthermore, it is assumed that frequencies of terms on both the elite and the non-elite set follow a Poisson distribution, with two different means; in other words, for a given term t and for $e \in \{0, 1\}$ (denoting whether we are considering the term to be in the elite or not), there is a random variable $E_{t,e}$ that expresses the distribution of the frequencies of the (elite or non-elite) term t in a document, and $E_{t,e} \sim \text{Poisson}(\lambda_{t,e})$; clearly, we expect $\lambda_{t,1} > \lambda_{t,0}$ (i.e., a single term will appear more frequently if it is elite than if it is not). Plugging this assumption in the general formula derived above determines a monotonic weighting function with an horizontal asymptote that may be interpreted as a form of saturation: the probability of relevance increases with term frequency, but the amount of increase is ultimately close zero when the frequency becomes large. In practice, this is well approximated by

$$w_{t,d}^{\text{BM25}} = \frac{\hat{\mathtt{tf}}_{t,d}}{\hat{\mathtt{tf}}_{t,d} + k_1} \cdot w_t^{\text{idf}}$$

where w_t^{idf} is the inverse document frequency for term t (that determines the asymptotic behavior when the frequency goes to infinity), k_1 is a parameter and $\hat{\mathtt{tf}}_{t,d}$ is a normalized term frequency with respect to the document length, i.e.,

$$\hat{\mathtt{tf}}_{t,d} = \frac{\mathtt{tf}_{t,d}}{(1-b) + b \cdot |d|/\text{avdl}}, \tag{1}$$

where $|d|$ is the length of document d, avdl the average length of documents in the collection, and $b \in [0, 1]$ is a tunable parameter. Putting things together, the weight derived from the 2-Poisson elite assumption $w_{t,d}^{\text{BM25}}$ is $U^{\text{BM25}}(\hat{\mathtt{tf}}_{t,d})$ where

$$U^{\text{BM25}}(x) = \frac{x}{x + k_1}.$$

Regions and virtual regions.

In the following derivation we start again from the abovementioned estimation of

$$w_{t,d}^{\text{BM25}} = \log \frac{p(\mathtt{tf}_{t,d} = x \mid r) \cdot p(\mathtt{tf}_{t,d} = 0 \mid \overline{r})}{p(\mathtt{tf}_{t,d} = x \mid \overline{r}) \cdot p(\mathtt{tf}_{t,d} = 0 \mid r)}.$$

Here, the only features that we need to observe are term frequencies; this is a quite mild assumption and stems from the idea that documents are a single body of text with no structure whatsoever. Some earlier refinements of the probabilistic model, however, already introduced the idea that documents may have some structure. In BM25F [33], for example, a notion of region was introduced: each document is made up of regions, or fields, (e.g., title, body, footnotes etc.) and it is possible to observe term frequencies separately in each region. This extension accounts for the fact that some fields may be more predictive for relevance than others (for example, title will be more predictive than footnotes), and fits well in the eliteness model. The idea is that eliteness of terms is decided beforehand, for every given document, and it is the same across fields; term-frequency, instead, will be again modeled as in standard BM25, although it will be influenced by the length of each field—of course, shorter fields (such as title) are expected to contain more elite terms than longer ones.

As said, the present paper extends this idea by defining what we call *virtual regions.* Ideally, suppose that you have some way (as yet unspecified) to single out some parts of the document that you know will provide high-quality information about relevance; then, you may think of that area as a single virtual region, and apply to that region the evaluation described for BM25F. Those virtual regions are actually obtained by the query itself, through a process that we shall now describe.

An *operator* is a function that associates, to a given query and a given document, another document[2] called a "virtual region". We are given a set of such operators, each endowed with a weight, $\{\langle\Phi_j, w_j\rangle\}_{j\in\mathcal{M}}$: for each query q and document d, we individuate the virtual regions $\Phi_j(d,q)$ (the region of document d matching query q according to operator Φ_j), and for each of them we count the term frequency of each term $t \in q$ in that virtual region; such a frequency is denoted by $\mathsf{tf}^{q,j}_{t,d}$ (the term frequency of term t in the virtual region of document d matching query q according to operator Φ_j); as it is customary in the RSJ model [31], we shall omit the query q, and just write $\mathsf{tf}^j_{t,d}$.

To capture this idea, as with BM25F, we proxy the dependence of the eliteness of the occurrences using a set $\{\Theta_j\}_{j\in\mathcal{M}}$ of Bernoulli random variables, which reflect the probability of occurrences in each region generated from a particular operator. De Finetti [8] proved that any set of exchangeable random variables has a representation as a mixture distribution, in general an infinite mixture. Therefore we represent the operators as

$$p(\mathsf{tf}^j_{t,d} = x \mid r) = \sum_{e\in\{0,1\}} p(\mathsf{tf}^j_{t,d} = x \mid e, r)p(e \mid r) =$$

$$\sum_{q\in Q}\ \sum_{e,\theta\in\{0,1\}} p(\mathsf{tf}^j_{t,d} = x \mid \Theta_j = \theta, e, r)p(\Theta_j = \theta \mid e, r)p(e \mid r)$$

and similarly for $p(\mathsf{tf}^j_{t,d} = x \mid \bar{r})$. For $x > 0$, the first of the three factors in the summation is zero if $\theta = 0$, otherwise it is $\lambda^x_{t,e} \cdot \mathrm{e}^{-\lambda_{t,e}}/x!$ (for the Poisson-mixture assumption). The second factor for $\theta = 1$ is just β_j, the parameter that governs the j-th Bernoulli Θ_j. The last factor is the probability that the document is elite for the term if it is relevant.

Let us write λ (μ) for $\lambda_{t,1}$ ($\lambda_{t,0}$, respectively) and let p (q) be the probability that a document is elite for the term, given that it is relevant (irrelevant, respectively).

So

$$p(\mathsf{tf}^j_{t,d} = x \mid r) = \frac{\lambda^x}{x!}\mathrm{e}^{-\lambda}\beta_j p + \frac{\mu^x}{x!}\mathrm{e}^{-\mu}\beta_j(1-p),$$

and similarly

$$p(\mathsf{tf}^j_{t,d} = x \mid \bar{r}) = \frac{\lambda^x}{x!}\mathrm{e}^{-\lambda}\beta_j q + \frac{\mu^x}{x!}\mathrm{e}^{-\mu}\beta_j(1-q).$$

Now following Robertson [30], we can divide both probabilities by $\lambda^x\mathrm{e}^{-\lambda}/x!$ getting

$$\frac{p(\mathsf{tf}^j_{t,d} = x \mid r)}{p(\mathsf{tf}^j_{t,d} = x \mid \bar{r})} = \frac{\beta_j p + \left(\frac{\mu}{\lambda}\right)^x \mathrm{e}^{\lambda-\mu}(1-p)}{\beta_j q + \left(\frac{\mu}{\lambda}\right)^x \mathrm{e}^{\lambda-\mu}(1-q)}.$$

Observe that, since $\lambda > \mu$, the latter tends to p/q as $x \to \infty$, as in [30].

[2]As explained in the next section, technically the operator produces a set of queries that is then matched against the document to obtain a virtual region, but the difference is immaterial for the moment.

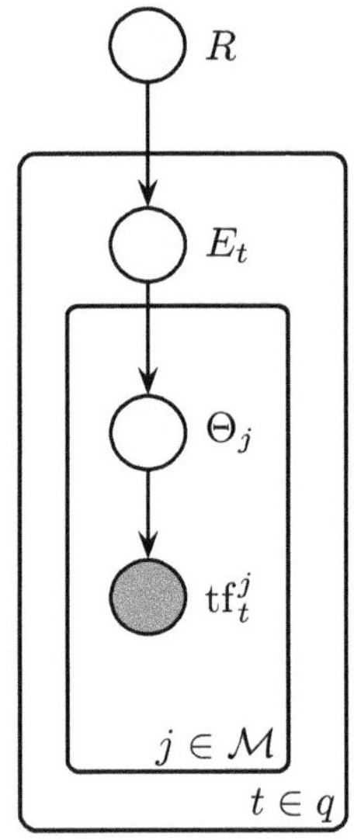

Figure 3: Plate diagram with the extended event space.

The treatment for the case $x = 0$ is slightly more involved, because

$$p(\mathsf{tf}^j_{t,d} = 0 \mid r) = \mathrm{e}^{-\lambda}\beta_j p + \mathrm{e}^{-\mu}\beta_j(1-p) + (1-\beta_j)$$

and similarly for the case of irrelevant documents: the last summand depends on the fact that a term can have zero occurrences in a region simply because of Θ_j; so

$$\frac{p(\mathsf{tf}^j_{t,d} = 0 \mid \bar{r})}{p(\mathsf{tf}^j_{t,d} = 0 \mid r)} = \frac{\mathrm{e}^{-\lambda}\beta_j q + \mathrm{e}^{-\mu}\beta_j(1-q) + (1-\beta_j)}{\mathrm{e}^{-\lambda}\beta_j p + \mathrm{e}^{-\mu}\beta_j(1-p) + (1-\beta_j)}$$

or equivalently

$$\frac{\mathrm{e}^{\mu-\lambda}q + (1-q) + \frac{1}{\beta_j} - 1}{\mathrm{e}^{\mu-\lambda}p + (1-p) + \frac{1}{\beta_j} - 1}.$$

This term behaves like $(1-q)/(1-p)$, under the usual assumption [30] that $\mu - \lambda$ is small, and assuming further that β_j is sufficiently close to 1.

4.1 Implementation of the system

We observe that our underlying retrieval system has a rich query language, the set of whose queries is denoted by Q. Every document d can be matched against the query $q \in Q$ producing a sub-document $M(d,q)$ (i.e., a subsequence of the words the document d is made of).[3] This function is naturally extended to sets of queries, by letting $M(d,A)$ be the union of all sub-documents $M(d,q)$ for $q \in A$.

Conversely, a *raw query* is just a sequence of terms $r = \langle t_1, \ldots, t_u\rangle$: this is what we suppose that the user inputs to the system; the set of all raw queries is denoted by R.

An *operator* is a function $\Phi : R \to 2^Q$ mapping a raw query to a set of queries. Here are some simple examples of operators that we will be using in our experiments:

[3]The exact semantics of the match depends on the query language and on the retrieval system used and will be not described further, but see [9, 13] for two examples.

- $\Phi_{\text{bag-of-words}}$: maps a raw query $\langle t_1, \ldots, t_u \rangle$ to the set of queries whose element are the single terms (i.e., to $\{t_1, \ldots, t_u\}$);
- $\Phi_{p\text{-grams}}$: maps a raw query $\langle t_1, \ldots, t_u \rangle$ to the set of all p-grams of p consecutive terms in the query (i.e., to $\{$"$t_1 \cdots t_p$", "$t_2 \cdots t_{p+1}$", ..., "$t_{u-p+1} \cdots t_u$"$\}$);
- $\Phi_{p\text{-AND}}$: maps a raw query $\langle t_1, \ldots, t_u \rangle$ to the set of all conjunctions of p arbitrary terms in the query (e.g., for $p = 2$, to $\{t_i \text{ AND } t_j \mid i \neq j\}$);
- Φ_{phrasal}: maps a raw query $\langle t_1, \ldots, t_u \rangle$ to the single phrasal query "$t_1 \cdots t_u$";
- Φ_{segments}: maps a raw query to the set of consecutive terms that make up a concept (see Section 5 for a complete description).[4]

Let now $\{\langle \Phi_j, w_j \rangle\}_{j \in \mathcal{M}}$ be a set of operators and weights; for a fixed raw query $r = \langle t_1, \ldots, t_u \rangle$, let $\mathsf{tf}^j_{t,d}$ be the number of occurrences of term t in $M(d, \Phi_j(r))$. The average term frequency of term t in document d is then defined to be[5]

$$\hat{\mathsf{tf}}_{t,d} = \sum_{j \in \mathcal{M}} \frac{w_j \cdot \mathsf{tf}^j_{t,d}}{(1 - b_j) + b_j \cdot |d| / \text{avdl}}.$$

The score of document d for query q is then computed as

$$\sum_{t \in q} \frac{\hat{\mathsf{tf}}_{t,d}}{\hat{\mathsf{tf}}_{t,d} + k_1} \cdot w_t^{\text{idf}},$$

where the latter is the standard term idf.

BM25(F) as a special case.

Note that using a single bag-of-words operator reduces our scoring formula to the usual BM25 score. Conversely, suppose your collection has G fields, and let $\Phi_1, \ldots, \Phi_G$ are operators that work like a standard bag-of-words, but where Φ_i tries to find matches only in field i. So, for example, $M(d, \Phi_{\text{title}}(t))$ would return the sub-document of the title made only by the occurrences of term t. Then, an application of the above formula would reduce to the standard BM25F score.

4.2 Remarks and variants

BM25, following the original probabilistic relevance framework, adopts a disjunctive semantics, that is, there is no need for a document to contain *every* query term in order to receive a non-zero score. The key point behind this assumption is that we need an external mechanism to decide which eliteness models we want to take into account for each query, and this will simplify the number of estimations and scores we need to compute. After that, it is important to decide what is an appropriate shape of the functional estimating relevance probability as a function of term scores: in Section 3 we showed empirically that conjunctive and proximity operator produce the same shape as in the 2-Poisson eliteness model.

An issue raised by our model, and that we must take into account, is the fact that the very same occurrence of a term within a document will be counted more than once, because virtual regions (differently from BM25F fields) may overlap. For instance, if we want to score separately matches of stemmed query terms and matches of unstemmed query terms we would be double-scoring some of the occurrences. This remark calls for discounting signals coming from the same source; one way to obtain this result would be to establish some dependence between the operators Φ_j: in the example above, we might correct the estimation using a $p(\Theta^{\text{st}}_j \mid \Theta^{\text{ex}}_j, r)$ correction factor (here, and in the following, the superscripts st and ex stand for "stemmed" and "exact", respectively).

In practice, however, we can avoid this estimation by recalibrating the different weights. We empirically know that both exact and stemmed matches should contribute to the score on which the saturation function is applied, and we want to aggregate those contributions together, using the proper weights. We can then correct the double counting and substitute accordingly in equation (1) as

$$\hat{\mathsf{tf}}_{t,d} = \frac{w^{\text{ex}} \cdot \mathsf{tf}^{\text{ex}}_{t,d} \cdot w^{\text{ex}}_{\text{idf}}}{1 - b_0 + b_0 \cdot |d^{\text{ex}}| / \text{avdl}^{\text{ex}}} + \frac{w^{\text{st}} \cdot \mathsf{tf}^{\text{st}}_{t,d} \cdot w^{\text{st}}_{\text{idf}}}{1 - b_1 + b_1 \cdot |d^{\text{st}}| / \text{avdl}^{\text{st}}}$$

Some observations about possible variants of our model are worth being remarked here:

- We could have used a different saturation function at the eliteness level; in fact, as with BM25, we could in principle learn the real function shape using an appropriately large dataset (but we would run the risk of over-fitting, though). The one we adopted $\hat{\mathsf{tf}}/(\hat{\mathsf{tf}} + k)$ is appealing: it resembles a logistic function passing through the origin and when the class conditional distributions $p(x|r)$, $p(x|\bar{r})$ belong to the same exponential family, the log-odds ratio of the class posteriors $\log\left(\frac{p(r|x)}{p(\bar{r}|x)}\right)$ will belong to a logistic family [4] (see also [25] for a connection of the log-logistic model and the term frequency normalization of BM25).
- We could have tackled the problem of incorporating positional information within the probabilistic framework by coming up with a higher-order model adding the positions of terms as variables; as noticed, though, this approach would lead either to an *ad-hoc* kernel-like method or to an exponential number of parameters to estimate. Given the scarcity of publicly available training data, and for the sake of domain transparency, we believe that the proposed framework provides an acceptable solution and a good trade-off between learning requirements, complexity and performance.
- The operators that form the basis upon which our system builds can be introduced in many ways: a set of operators can be fixed and applied silently to all queries introduced by the user, as a form of multilevel enrichment (this is what we are assuming in the rest of the paper), or it can be defined externally on a

[4]Both the p-gram, the phrasal and the segment operators can be endowed with an enlargement factor that allows for some extra word to sneak in—also this point will be fully explained in Section 5.

[5]The length-normalization factor here might actually be different for each virtual region, but this solution turns out to be extremely expensive to implement, because the average region length is unknown unless the whole collection is examined. A good approximation can be obtained by using the standard document length as a measure of "verbosity" of all the virtual regions it contains.

per-query basis, or on a per-query-type basis; we may instead think that it is the user herself to introduce operators in the query, which may be sensible and may find applications in some contexts where users are expected to adopt a richer query language. Finally, it is certainly possible to mix the two approaches, having some operators introduced directly by the user and others added automatically by the system.

5. QUERY CONCEPT SEGMENTATION

Albeit today's search engines offer a limited number of operators (phrasal, proximity etc.) most users tend to stick at introducing plain queries, typically a sequence of few words (about 3.08 on average, according to recent studies [36]). Nonetheless, as observed previously [37], many queries are actually made up by some basic conceptual units, each of them being formed possibly by many words. For example, the query `indian summer victor herbert` is clearly formed by two conceptual elements ("indian summer" and "victor herbert", the former referring to a meteorological phenomenon, the second to a person); breaking such conceptual units apart, or inverting the order of the words that label them, would produce information loss—of course, many documents will contain both the words "indian" and "summer" without referring to "indian summer"; also "summer indian" will also probably appear in some document, for example in reference to summer indian food, without any relevance to the concept sought. In some cases, it may be wise to allow for one spurious word to be inserted within a segment (so that, for example, `san jose airport` can also match the sequence "San Jose international airport", or `george bush` match "George W. Bush").

Among our goals, we would like the model to accommodate for query term-dependence, or concept-detection, at the query level. For example, if there is evidence that the query `san jose aiport` consists of two concepts, one referring to a city and the other one denoting a place or an action, we would like the model to be able to weight differently documents that only match one concept from those that match both, taking also into account the distance between the terms making up the concepts. To this end, one of our operators will employ query segmentation, an emerging NLP task that aims at identifying sub-sequences of strings that refer to a single unit or concept [7, 37], as described above. There have been limited attempts to integrate segments into ranking [5, 6, 20] in the context of the language modeling framework [39], but to the best of our knowledge this is the first time that a similar attempt is being applied to BM25-like techniques.

In the experimental section, we use both a segmentation operator based on generative language models and Wikipedia (as described in [37]) and a simple operator extracting p-grams of consecutive terms: the latter is of course less precise (because some p-grams do not correspond to concepts), and is given a lower weight — it serves the purpose of identifying possible word-sequences that for some reason the segmentation algorithm failed to guess. Moreover, for both types of operators we allowed for a variety of amount of spurious words appearing in the segment: this is obtained by introducing different *enlargement factors* μ (a multiplicative factor determining the maximum allowed ratio between the length of the span found and the length of the segment); an enlargement factor $\mu = 1$ corresponds to accepting only exact matches, whereas for example allowing for an enlargement $\mu = 2$ corresponds to accepting at most one extra word for every single word in the segments (e.g., if the segment is made up of two words, it is still acceptable if we find them two words apart). Different enlargement factors are used in the experiments, of course assigning larger weights to smaller enlargements.

Collection	Size	Documents	Topics
TERA04	436G	25M	TREC 701-750
TERA05	436G	25M	TREC 751-800
TERA06	436G	25M	TREC 801-850
WEB	100G	10M	1000
WEB-Phrasal	100G	10M	400

Table 1: Data collections

6. EXPERIMENTAL RESULTS

We tested the usefulness and accuracy of the operators described in Section 4.1 and 5 in a series of experiments. We posit that query segments will only affect to a limited number of queries in the data-set; however the working question is whether combining them has some positive retrieval effect or not. Retrieval performance is optimized iteratively using MAP as a target metric. We sweep one parameter at a time over the allowed parameter range, holding every other parameter fixed, in a similar fashion to the method of Metzler and Croft [26]. Each operator introduces two parameters: a weight w_j controlling the relative importance of the operator, and a factor b_j determining the impact of term-frequency normalization with respect to the corresponding operator. Different *enlargement factors* μ (for segments, p-grams and phrasal operators) are reported in separate rows of the table, as well as different values for the number p of consecutive terms that are considered while building p-grams.

We report on MAP and P@10 and check for statistical significance using a one-sided t-test with $p < 0.05$. The operators are trained on two different Web collections: GOV2, TREC's Terabyte track collection [14, 15, 12], and a subsample of the Web from 2011. The collections are described in Table 1. Training and testing is performed on different topic sets; for TREC topics, we train and test on different years (train on TERA04, test on TERA05/06; train on TERA05, test on TERA04), and for the Web collection we perform 10-fold cross validation across the whole topic set. For the TREC collection, we used the topic title as raw query.

Table 2 presents the results of applying one single operator, combined with BM25 (that is, with the bag-of-words operator). Experiments show that all the operators are able to improve the performance on their own to a reasonable extent. The impact of single operators, specially the segments, is limited. However, it is worth noting that the methods using a single operator that restrict the semantics of the matching (like AND or segments) perform comparably to the best values reported at TREC for early precision (P@20) [14, 15, 12]. Table 3 presents the results of combining segment and p-gram operators with BM25 and BM25F. The different operators have been chosen using various enlargement factors; we further enriched the segment combination with a 2-gram

		TERA04			TERA05			TERA06		
		MAP	P@10	P@20	MAP	P@10	P@20	MAP	P@10	P@20
BM25		0.2648	0.5327	0.5071	0.3228	0.6140	0.5600	0.2928	0.5380	0.5140
BM25F		0.2697	0.5510	0.5143	0.3284	0.6200	0.5570	0.2935	0.5460	0.5160
p-AND	$p = 2$	0.2679	0.5429	**0.5286**	**0.3396***	0.6260	**0.5920**	0.3069	0.5900	0.5300
phrasal	$\mu = 3$	0.2673	0.5306	0.4939	0.3369*	0.6060	0.5790	0.3082*	0.5720	0.5290
segment	$\mu = 1$	0.2685*	0.5143	0.4970	0.3274	0.6080	0.5580	0.3180*	0.5860	0.5350
segment	$\mu = 1.5$	0.2695*	0.5347	0.5010	0.3272	0.6140	0.5620	0.3122*	**0.5940**	0.5460
segment	$\mu = 3$	0.2690*	0.5143	0.5204	0.3295*	**0.6300**	0.5840	**0.3277***	**0.5940**	0.5460
p-grams	$p = 2, \mu = 1$	**0.2786***	**0.5530**	0.5120	0.3294	0.5860	0.5470	0.3137*	0.5860	0.5470
p-grams	$p = 3, \mu = 1$	0.2670	0.5060	0.4950	0.3272	0.5980	0.5560	0.3198*	0.6160	**0.5600**

Table 2: Performance of single operators (* = statistical significance at $p < 0.05$ using a one-sided t-test with respect to BM25, MAP only).

operator. The purpose of this experiment is to determine whether the sigmoid-like term-frequency normalizing function is able to accommodate for different features which stem from the same source of evidence (matches of the query term in the document). Results are significantly better than the baseline and outperform state-of-the-art ranking functions that just use matching of query terms (note we are not adding query-independent evidence, like link information, click-through data, etc.). For instance, the best MAP value for TREC 2004 at TERA04 [14] was 0.2844, the sequential dependence model of the Markov random field for IR peaks at MAP 0.2832 [26] and the two-stage segmentation model of Bendersky *et al.* had an average MAP of 0.2711 over the 150 topics [5].

In order to explore further the usefulness of query segmentation and *p*-grams for *difficult* queries, we selected a sub-sample of 1000 queries taken from Yahoo! Search; the data corpus was a 100GB sub-sample of the Web. The queries had been evaluated by a trained editorial team, with about 130 judged documents per query on average: relevance was assigned on a 4-level scale, from *Bad* to *Excellent*; given that we had graded relevance available, we report on NDCG (gain values at the relevance level, from 0 to 4) and MAP. The average query length was 3.14. We report the performance of BM25 and BM25F as baselines. In addition, we selected a sub-sample of 400 queries where the user herself had employed query segments (i.e., phrasal queries), and removed the segmentation information. This experiment was aimed at establishing if a more elaborate query interpretation mechanisms is able to be of help in these cases.

Table 4 shows that segmentation and *p*-grams, when mixed with the operator combination are able to improve the performance of a large number of Web queries. When looking at the differences between the regular and phrasal queries, we observe that gains, even if consistent over the two different sets, are slightly higher in the second group ($\approx$ 12.3% vs. $\approx$ 7.1% in MAP for *p*-grams vs. BM25F). This fact indicates that the method is helpful for queries that contain *difficult* concepts, as they have been expressed by users manually, whereas maintaining the performance of queries in which identifying concepts is not so critical and standard bag-of-word approaches perform as well.

Anecdotal study.

It is useful to look into the reasons behind the increased retrieval performance we observed in our experiments; with this goal, we considered separately the mean average precision on each of the TREC topics 701-850 and examined the ten queries that produced the largest difference in precision between our system and the BM25 baseline. Table 5 shows the queries that obtained the greatest benefit from the use of segmentation and/or *p*-gram operators: in the rightmost column of the table, we identified the segments (or the *p*-grams) that most contributed to the increased precision, allowing to retrieve relevant documents that BM25 missed (because they were ranked too low).

7. CONCLUSIONS AND FUTURE WORK

In this paper we proposed a way to extend the probabilistic relevance framework with a notion of *virtual region* based on the use of operators applied to the query. Our experiments (both on standard collections, such as TREC, and on other Web-like repertoires) show that the use of virtual regions is especially beneficial for hard queries where positional information is actually precious. The method has room for improvements and further study should be undertaken to understand which operators are more useful and under which circumstances. Even if we explored a reasonable number of combinations, we have not made any systematic attempt to develop a method to select the individual best operators; we just limited ourselves to handpick a few—it was out of the scope of this paper to analyze automated operator selection. In contrast, a machine learning approach [3] would derive features for as many operators as possible and try to combine them optimizing a loss function of MAP or NDCG [38]. One might even envisage the adoption of a query-classification tool to decide which operators should be used, based on the presumed nature of the query. In any case, our experiments show the practical usefulness of the non-linear operator score combination for retrieval [33]. As a final remark, it is interesting to observe that most of the studied operators (actually, all of them except for segments) do not employ *any* source of external information, and still produce a significant performance improvement.

8. REFERENCES

[1] E. Agichtein, E. Brill, S. Dumais, and R. Ragno. Learning user interaction models for predicting web search result preferences. In *Proceedings of the 29th annual international ACM SIGIR conference on Research and development in information retrieval*, volume 1, pages 3–10. ACM, 2006.

[2] R. Baeza-Yates. Query intent prediction and recommendation. In *Proceedings of the fourth ACM*

	TERA04			TERA05			TERA06		
	MAP	P@10	P@20	MAP	P@10	P@20	MAP	P@10	P@20
BM25	0.2648	0.5327	0.5071	0.3228	0.6140	0.5600	0.2928	0.5380	0.5140
BM25F	0.2697	0.5510	0.5143	0.3284	0.6200	0.5570	0.2935	0.5460	0.5160
BM25 + *p*-grams	0.2898*	0.5939	0.5531	0.3368*	0.6260	0.5800	0.3361*	0.6000	0.5048
BM25 + segment	0.2866*	0.5653	0.5306	0.3285	0.5980	0.5710	0.3188	0.5720	0.5100
BM25F + *p*-grams	**0.2908***	**0.5959**	**0.5541**	**0.3398***	**0.6280**	**0.5830**	**0.3319***	**0.5940**	**0.5350**
BM25F + segment	0.2869*	0.5653	0.5306	0.3282*	0.5920	0.5510	0.3315*	**0.5940**	**0.5350**

Table 3: Performance of a combination of operators (* = statistical significance at $p < 0.05$ using a one-sided t-test with respect to BM25, MAP only). Configuration for *p*-gram is $p = 2, \mu = \{1, 2, 3\}$, and for segment is $\mu = \{1, 2, 3\}$.

	WEB			WEB-phrasal		
	MAP	NDCG	P@10	MAP	NDCG	P@10
BM25	0.1553	0.2728	0.3892	0.1350	0.2345	0.3133
BM25F	0.1722*	0.3008	0.4285	0.1575*	0.2842	0.3747
BM25 + *p*-grams	0.1822*	0.3126	0.4390	0.1750*	0.3078	0.4010
BM25 + segment	0.1810*	0.3126	0.4344	0.1725*	0.3029	0.4040
BM25F + *p*-grams	**0.1854***	**0.3216**	**0.4400**	**0.1769***	**0.3123**	**0.4101**
BM25F + segment	0.1842*	0.3190	0.4392	0.1749*	0.3165	0.4005

Table 4: Performance of a combination of operators on the WEB collection (* = statistical significance at $p < 0.05$ using a one-sided t-test with respect to BM25, MAP only). Configuration for *p*-gram is $p = 2, \mu = \{1, 2, 3\}$, and for segment is $\mu = \{1, 2, 3\}$.

conference on Recommender systems, pages 5–6. ACM, 2010.

[3] B. Bai, J. Weston, D. Grangier, R. Collobert, K. Sadamasa, Y. Qi, O. Chapelle, and K. Weinberger. Learning to rank with (a lot of) word features. *Information Retrieval*, 13:291–314, 2010. 10.1007/s10791-009-9117-9.

[4] A. Banerjee. An analysis of logistic models: exponential family connections and online performance. In *SIAM International Conference on Data Mining*, 2007.

[5] M. Bendersky, B. Croft, and D. a. Smith. Two-stage query segmentation for information retrieval. *Proceedings of the 32nd international ACM SIGIR conference on Research and development in information retrieval - SIGIR '09*, page 810, 2009.

[6] M. Bendersky, D. Metzler, and W. Croft. Learning concept importance using a weighted dependence model. In *Proceedings of the third ACM international conference on Web search and data mining*, pages 31–40. ACM, 2010.

[7] S. Bergsma and Q. Wang. Learning noun phrase query segmentation. In *Proc. of EMNLP-CoNLL*, number June, pages 819–826, 2007.

[8] D. M. Blei, A. Y. Ng, and M. I. Jordan. Latent dirichlet allocation. *J. Mach. Learn. Res.*, 3:993–1022, Mar. 2003.

[9] P. Boldi and S. Vigna. MG4J at TREC 2005. In E. M. Voorhees and L. P. Buckland, editors, *The Fourteenth Text REtrieval Conference (TREC 2005) Proceedings*, number SP 500-266 in Special Publications. NIST, 2005. `http://mg4j.dsi.unimi.it/`.

[10] S. Brin and L. Page. The anatomy of a large-scale hypertextual Web search engine. *Computer Networks and ISDN Systems*, 30(1-7):107–117, Apr. 1998.

[11] S. Büttcher, C. L. A. Clarke, and B. Lushman. Term proximity scoring for ad-hoc retrieval on very large text collections. In *Proceedings of the 29th annual international ACM SIGIR conference on Research and development in information retrieval*, SIGIR '06, pages 621–622, New York, NY, USA, 2006. ACM.

[12] S. Büttcher, C. L. A. Clarke, and I. Soboroff. The TREC 2006 terabyte track. In *TREC*, 2006.

[13] C. L. A. Clarke, G. V. Cormack, and F. J. Burkowski. An algebra for structured text search and a framework for its implementation. *The Computer Journal*, 38:43–56, 1995.

[14] C. L. A. Clarke, N. Craswell, and I. Soboroff. Overview of the TREC 2004 terabyte track. In *TREC*, 2004.

[15] C. L. A. Clarke, F. Scholer, and I. Soboroff. The TREC 2005 terabyte track. In *TREC*, 2005.

[16] S. Cooper. Some Inconsistencies and Misnomers Retrieval in Probabilistic Information of Library taken Effective. *Proceedings of the 14th annual international ACM SIGIR conference on Research and development in information retrieval*, pages 57–61, 1991.

[17] N. Craswell, S. Robertson, H. Zaragoza, and M. Taylor. Relevance weighting for query independent evidence. In *Proceedings of the 28th annual international ACM SIGIR conference on Research and development in information retrieval*, volume 1, pages 416–423. ACM, 2005.

[18] P. Domingos, S. Kok, H. Poon, M. Richardson, and P. Singla. Unifying logical and statistical AI. In *Proceedings of the Twenty-First National Conference on Artificial Intelligence*, pages 2–7, 2006.

[19] M. Hagen, M. Potthast, B. Stein, and C. Braeutigam. The power of naive query segmentation. In *Proceeding of the 33rd international ACM SIGIR conference on*

Topic no.	BM25 MAP	Operators MAP	Query	Which segment / *p*-gram helped?
810	0.2759	0.5243	Timeshare resales	"Timeshare resales"
750	0.0903	0.3251	John Edwards womens' issues	"John Edwards" and "womens' issue"
806	0.1279	0.3446	Doctors Without Borders	"Doctors Without Borders"
834	0.2819	0.4859	Global positioning system earthquakes	"Global positioning"
745	0.1801	0.3828	Doomsday cults	"Doomsday cult"
835	0.1306	0.3222	Big Dig pork	"Big Dig"
732	0.1438	0.3309	U.S. cheese production	"U.S." and "cheese production"
723	0.1187	0.3030	Executive privilege	"Executive privilege"
843	0.2420	0.4228	Pol Pot	"Pol Pot"
785	0.2717	0.4323	Ivory billed woodpecker	"Ivory billed"

Table 5: The ten queries that produced the largest gap between standard BM25 and our operator-based scoring. The methods in this table use a combination of BM25, segments and 2-grams.

Research and development in information retrieval, pages 797–798. ACM, 2010.

[20] Y. Li, B.-j. P. Hsu, C. Zhai, and K. Wang. Unsupervised Query Segmentation Using Clickthrough for Information Retrieval. *Proceedings of the 34th international ACM SIGIR conference on Research and development in Information Retrieval*, pages 285–294, 2011.

[21] T.-Y. Liu. Learning to Rank for Information Retrieval. *Information Retrieval*, 3(3):225–331, 2009.

[22] Y. Lu, F. Peng, G. Mishne, X. Wei, and B. Dumoulin. Improving web search relevance with semantic features. In *Proceedings of the 2009 Conference on Empirical Methods in Natural Language Processing Volume 2 - EMNLP '09*, number August, page 648, Morristown, NJ, USA, 2009. Association for Computational Linguistics.

[23] Y. Lv and C. Zhai. Positional language models for information retrieval. In *Proceedings of the 32nd international ACM SIGIR conference on Research and development in information retrieval*, pages 299–306. ACM, 2009.

[24] Y. Lv and C. Zhai. Positional relevance model for pseudo-relevance feedback. In *Proceeding of the 33rd international ACM SIGIR conference on Research and development in information retrieval*, pages 579–586. ACM, 2010.

[25] Y. Lv and C. Zhai. A log-logistic model-based interpretation of TF normalization of BM25. In *Proceedings of the 34th European Conference on Information Retrieval*, ECIR'12, 2012.

[26] D. Metzler and B. Croft. A Markov random field model for term dependencies. *Proceedings of the 28th annual international ACM SIGIR conference on Research and development in information retrieval - SIGIR '05*, page 472, 2005.

[27] J. Ponte and W. B. Croft. A language modeling approach to information retrieval. *Proceedings of the 21st annual international ACM SIGIR conference on Research and development in information retrieval*, pages 275–281, 1998.

[28] L. Ramshaw. Text chunking using transformation-based learning. *of the Third ACL Workshop on Very*, pages 82–94, 1995.

[29] M. Richardson and P. Domingos. Markov logic networks. *Machine Learning*, 62(1):107–136, 2006.

[30] S. Robertson. The probability ranking principle in IR. *Journal of documentation*, 1977.

[31] S. Robertson. On event spaces and probabilistic models in information retrieval. *Information Retrieval*, 8(2):319–329, 2005.

[32] S. Robertson and S. Walker. Some simple effective approximations to the 2-poisson model for probabilistic weighted retrieval. *Proceedings of the SIGIR conference on Research and development in information retrieval*, (1), 1994.

[33] S. Robertson, H. Zaragoza, and M. Taylor. Simple BM25 extension to multiple weighted fields. In *Proceedings of the thirteenth ACM international conference on Information and knowledge management*, CIKM '04, pages 42–49, New York, NY, USA, 2004. ACM.

[34] S. E. Robertson and H. Zaragoza. The probabilistic relevance framework: BM25 and beyond. *Foundations and Trends in Information Retrieval*, 3(4):333–389, 2009.

[35] K. Svore, P. Kanani, and N. Khan. How good is a span of terms?: exploiting proximity to improve web retrieval. In *Proceeding of the 33rd international ACM SIGIR conference on Research and development in information retrieval*, pages 154–161. ACM, 2010.

[36] M. Taghavi, A. Patel, N. Schmidt, C. Wills, and Y. Tew. An analysis of web proxy logs with query distribution pattern approach for search engines. *Computer Standards and Interfaces*, 34(1):162 – 170, 2012.

[37] B. Tan and F. Peng. Unsupervised query segmentation using generative language models and wikipedia. In *Proceeding of the 17th international conference on World Wide Web*, pages 347–356. ACM, 2008.

[38] M. Taylor, J. Guiver, S. Robertson, and T. Minka. Softrank: optimizing non-smooth rank metrics. In *Proceedings of the international conference on Web search and web data mining*, WSDM '08, pages 77–86, New York, NY, USA, 2008. ACM.

[39] C. Zhai and J. Lafferty. A study of smoothing methods for language models applied to information retrieval. *ACM Transactions on Information Systems*, 22(2):179–214, Apr. 2004.

Rhetorical Relations for Information Retrieval

Christina Lioma
Computer Science
University of Copenhagen
Denmark
c.lioma@diku.dk

Birger Larsen
Royal School of Library and Information Science
Copenhagen Denmark
blar@iva.dk

Wei Lu
School of Information Management
Wuhan University China
reedwhu@gmail.com

ABSTRACT

Typically, every part in most coherent text has some plausible reason for its presence, some function that it performs to the overall semantics of the text. Rhetorical relations, e.g. `contrast, cause, explanation`, describe how the parts of a text are linked to each other. Knowledge about this so-called discourse structure has been applied successfully to several natural language processing tasks. This work studies the use of rhetorical relations for Information Retrieval (IR): Is there a correlation between certain rhetorical relations and retrieval performance? Can knowledge about a document's rhetorical relations be useful to IR?

We present a language model modification that considers rhetorical relations when estimating the relevance of a document to a query. Empirical evaluation of different versions of our model on TREC settings shows that certain rhetorical relations can benefit retrieval effectiveness notably ($> 10\%$ in mean average precision over a state-of-the-art baseline).

Categories and Subject Descriptors

H.3.3 [**Information Search and Retrieval**]: Retrieval Models; H.3.1 [**Information Storage and Retrieval**]: Content Analysis and Indexing—*linguistic processing*

Keywords

Rhetorical relations, discourse structure, retrieval model, probabilistic retrieval

1. INTRODUCTION

According to discourse analysis, every part in most coherent text tends to have some plausible reason for its presence, some function that it performs to the overall semantics of the text. Rhetorical relations, e.g. `contrast, explanation, condition`, are considered critical for text interpretation, because they signal how the parts of a text are linked to each other to form a coherent whole [23]. Unlike grammatical relations, which are generally explicitly manifest in

SIGIR'12, August 12–16, 2012, Portland, Oregon, USA.

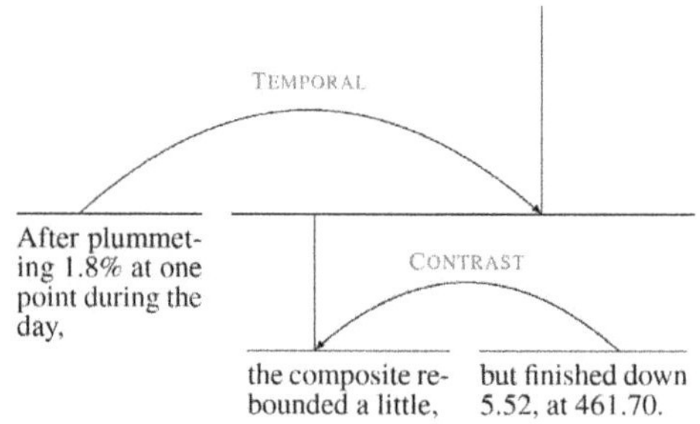

Figure 1: Rhetorical relations example (from [11]).

language, rhetorical relations may be unstated. The goal of discourse analysis is therefore to infer rhetorical relations, and specifically to identify their span, constraints and function.

There is a large body of research on both descriptive and predictive models of rhetorical structure and discourse analysis in natural language text. For instance, annotation projects have taken significant steps towards developing semantic [12, 18] and discourse [5] annotated corpora. Some of these annotation efforts have already had a computational impact, making it possible to automatically induce semantic roles [15] and to automatically identify rhetorical relations [14], achieving near-human levels of performance on certain tasks [27]. In addition, applications of discourse analysis to automatic language processing tasks such as summarisation or classification (overviewed in section 2) indicate that rhetorical relations can enhance the performance of well-trained natural language processing systems.

Motivated by these advances, this work brings perspectives from discourse analysis into Information Retrieval (IR) with the aim of investigating if and how rhetorical relations can benefit retrieval effectiveness. Is there a correlation between certain rhetorical relations and retrieval performance? Can knowledge about a document's rhetorical relations be useful to IR? For example, consider the rhetorical relations of the text shown in Figure 1 (borrowed from [11]). Should some of the terms in this sentence be given extra weight by an IR system, according to their rhetorical relations? Can some rhetorical relations be considered more informative and hence more useful for IR ranking than others? These questions have been posed before (see discussion in section 2), however to our knowledge this is the first time that a principled integration of rhetorical relations into a probabilistic IR model improves precision by $> 10\%$.

Reasoning about query - document relevance using the language modeling formalism [9], we present a model that conditions the probability of relevance between a query and a document on the rhetorical relations occurring in that document. We present an application of this model to an IR re-ranking task, where, given a list of documents initially retrieved for a query, the goal is to improve the ranking of the documents by refining their estimation of relevance to the query. Experimental evaluation of different versions of our model on TREC data and standard settings demonstrates that certain rhetorical relations can be beneficial to retrieval, with notable improvements to retrieval effectiveness (> 10% in mean average precision and other standard TREC evaluation measures over a state-of-the-art baseline).

2. RELATED WORK

Discourse analysis and rhetorical structures have been studied in the context of several automatic text processing applications. This has been partly enabled by the availability of discourse parsers - see [11, 14] for up-to-date overviews of discourse parsing technology. Studies of discourse analysis in relation to IR and its broader applications are briefly overviewed below. For a more general overview of discourse analysis approaches, see Wang et al. [33], section 2.

Sun & Chai [28] investigate the role of discourse processing and its implication on query expansion for a sequence of questions in scenario-based context question answering (QA). They consider a sequence of questions as a mini discourse. An empirical examination of three discourse theoretic models indicates that their discourse-based approach can significantly improve QA performance over a baseline of plain reference resolution.

In a different task, Wang et al. [33] parse Web user forum threads to determine the discourse dependencies between posts in order to improve information access over Web forum archives. They present three different methods for classifying the discourse relationships between posts, which are found to outperform an informed baseline.

Heerschop et al. [16] perform document sentiment analysis (partly) based on a document's discourse structure. They hypothesise that by splitting a text into important and less important text spans, and by subsequently making use of this information by weighting the sentiment conveyed by distinct text spans in accordance with their importance, they can improve the performance of a sentiment classifier. A document's discourse structure is obtained by applying rhetorical structure theory on a sentence level. They report a 4.5% improvement in sentiment classification accuracy when considering discourse, in comparison to a non-discourse based baseline. Similarly to this study, Somasundaran et al. [26] report improvements to opinion polarity classification when using discourse, and Morato et al. [24] report a positive dependence between classification performance and certain discourse variables. An overview of discourse analysis for opinion detection can be found in Zhou et al. [36].

In the area of text compression, Louis et al. [21] study the usefulness of rhetorical relations between sentences for summarisation. They find that most of the significant rhetorical relations are associated to non-discriminative sentences, i.e. sentences that are *not important* for summarisation. They report that rhetorical relations that may be intuitively perceived as highly salient do not provide strong indicators of informativeness; instead, the usefulness of rhetorical relations is in providing constraints for navigating through the text's structure. These findings are compatible with the study of Clarke & Lapata [7] into constraining text compression on the basis of rhetorical relations. For a more in-depth look into the impact of individual rhetorical relations to summarisation see Teufel & Moens [30].

In domain-specific IR, Yu et al. [34] focus on psychiatric document retrieval, which aims to assist users to locate documents relevant to their depressive problems. They propose the use of high-level discourse information extracted from queries and documents, such as negative life events, depressive symptoms and semantic relations between symptoms, to improve the precision of retrieval results. Their discourse-aware retrieval model achieves higher precision than the vector space and Okapi models.

Closer to our work, Wang et al. [31] extend an IR ranking model by adding a re-ranking strategy based on document discourse. Specifically, their re-ranking formula consists of the original retrieval status value computed with the BM11 model, which is then multiplied by a function that linearly combines inverse document frequency and term distance for each query term within a discourse unit. They focus on one discourse type only (`advantage-disadvantage`) which they identify manually in queries, and show that their approach improves retrieval performance for these queries. Our work differs on several points. We use an automatic (not manual) discourse parser to identify rhetorical relations in the documents to be retrieved (not queries). We consider 15 rhetorical relations (not 1) and we study their impact to retrieval performance using a modification of the IR language model.

Finally, Suwandaratna & Perera [29] also present a re-ranking approach for Web search that uses discourse structure. They report a heuristic algorithm for refining search results based on their rhetorical relations. Their implementation and evaluation is partly based on a series of ad-hoc choices, making it hard to compare with other approaches. They report a positive user-based evaluation of their system for ten test cases.

3. RANKING WITH RHETORICAL RELATIONS

There may be various ways of considering rhetorical relations in an IR setting. In this work, we view rhetorical relations as non-overlapping text spans, rather than a graph or a tree with structure and overlapping nodes [27]. We select a principled integration of rhetorical relation information into the retrieval model that ranks documents with respect to queries. The goal is to enable evidence about the rhetorical relations in a document to have a quantifiable impact upon the estimation of relevance of this document to a query, and to study that impact.

3.1 Model Derivation

Let q be a query, d a document, D a collection of documents, and ψ_g a rhetorical relation in the collection (so that $\sum_{\psi_g} p(\psi_g|d) = 1$). In probabilistic IR, each d in D can be ranked by its probability $p(d|q)$ of being relevant to q. Using Bayes' law:

$$p(d|q) = \frac{p(q|d)p(d)}{p(q)} \stackrel{rank}{=} p(q|d) \qquad (1)$$

where the right-hand side of Equation 1 is derived as follows: $p(q)$ is dropped because it is fixed for all documents, and $p(d)$ can be dropped on the assumption that it is uniform in the absence of any prior knowledge about any document. Using the language modeling approach to IR [9], $p(q|d)$ can be interpreted as the probability of generating the terms in q from a model induced by d, or more simply how likely it is that the document is about the same topic as the query. $p(q|d)$ can be estimated in different ways, for instance using Dirichlet, Jelinek-Mercer, or two-stage smoothing [35].

We introduce into Equation 1 the probability of generating the query terms from a model induced by d and by its rhetorical relations $\psi_g \in d$ as follows:

$$p(q|d) = \sum_{\psi_g} p(q|d,\psi_g)p(\psi_g|d) \tag{2}$$

We now explain the two components in Equation 2. The first component, $p(q|d,\psi_g)$, can be interpreted as the probability of generating the query terms from a model induced by d and ψ_g. We estimate $p(q|d,\psi_g)$ as a simple mixture of the probabilities of generating q from d and ψ_g:

$$p(q|d,\psi_g) = (1-\kappa)\cdot p(q|d) + \kappa \cdot p(q|\psi_g) \tag{3}$$

where $p(q|d)$ is the (baseline) probability of relevance between q and d mentioned in the beginning of this section, κ is a free parameter, and $p(q|\psi_g)$ can be interpreted as the probability of generating q from a model induced by the rhetorical relation ψ_g, or more simply, the 'likelihood of relevance' between the terms in the query and the terms in the rhetorical relation.

The second component of Equation 2, $p(\psi_g|d)$, is the probability of the rhetorical relation given the document. Similarly to above, this can be interpreted as the probability of generating the terms in ψ_g from a model induced by d, or more simply the likelihood of relevance between the terms in the rhetorical relation and the terms in the document.

3.2 Model Induction

To make Equations 2-3 operational we need to compute $p(q|\psi_g)$ and $p(\psi_g|d)$. One simple way of doing so is using the respective maximum likelihood estimations:

$$\log p(q|\psi_g) = \sum_{i=1}^{|q|} \frac{f(q_i,\psi_g)}{|\psi_g|} \tag{4}$$

where $f(q_i,\psi_g)$ is the frequency of the query term q_i in ψ_g, and $|\psi_g|$ is the number of terms in ψ_g.

$$\log p(\psi_g|d) = \sum_{j=1}^{|\psi_g|} \frac{f(\psi_{gj},d)}{|d|} \tag{5}$$

where $f(\psi_{gj},d)$ is the frequency of the rhetorical relation term ψ_{gj} in d, and $|d|$ is the number of terms in d. In this work, we use the above equations and, to compensate for zero-frequency cases, we apply add-one smoothing.

Alternative principled estimations of Equations 4-5 are possible (e.g. Dirichlet, Good-Turing) and could potentially improve the performance reported in this work. For instance, one could discount the frequencies in Equations 4-5 by a respective collection model using Dirichlet smoothing: $\log p_s(q|\psi_g) = \sum_{i=1}^{|q|} \frac{f(q_i,\psi_g)+\mu\cdot p(q_i|\Psi)}{|\psi_g|+\mu}$ where μ would be the smoothing parameter and Ψ would be the collection of all rhetorical relations in D. A similarly Dirichlet smoothed alternative estimation of Equation 5 would be: $\log p_s(\psi_g|d) = \sum_{j=1}^{|\psi_g|} \frac{f(\psi_{gj},d)+\mu\cdot p(\psi_{gj}|D)}{|d|+\mu}$. We choose to use maximum likelihood instead of Dirichlet to avoid introducing the extra Dirichlet smoothing parameter μ when investigating the effect of rhetorical relations upon retrieval.

Another alternative would be to use Good-Turing smoothing, however doing so would scale down the maximum likelihood estimations in Equations 4-5 by a factor of $1-\frac{E(1)}{|\psi_g|}$ and $1-\frac{E(1)}{|d|}$ respectively, where $\frac{E(1)}{|\psi_g|}$ (resp. $\frac{E(1)}{|d|}$) is the estimate of how many items in the numerator of Equation 4 (resp. Equation 5) have occurred once in the sample of the denominator (see Gale & Sampson [13] for more on Good-Turing smoothing). In effect, for Equation 4 this scaling down would reduce the probability of the query terms that we have seen in ψ_g, making room for query terms that we have not seen. For our setting this would not be necessary, because in practice most queries and most rhetorical relations correspond to rather short text spans. Good-Turing smoothing might be better suited for larger samples [13].

Overall, the model presented in this section can be seen as a 'basic model' for ranking documents (partly) according to their rhetorical relations. Different variations on this basic model are certainly possible, however we choose to use the simple maximum likelihood version of this model for this exploratory investigation into the potential benefits of using rhetorical relations for IR.

4. EVALUATION

4.1 Experimental Setup

We evaluate our model on the task of re-ranking an initial list of documents, which has been retrieved in response to a query. Re-ranking is a well-known IR practice that can enhance retrieval performance notably [19]. The baseline of our experiments consists of the top 1000 documents retrieved for each query using a state-of-the-art retrieval model (language model with Dirichlet smoothing[1] [9]). Our approach reranks these documents using Equation 2.

4.1.1 Dataset and Pre-processing

We experiment with the TREC datasets of the Web 2009 (queries 1-50) and Web 2010 (queries 51-100) tracks, that contain collectively 100 queries and their relevance assessments on the Clueweb09 cat. B dataset[2] (50,220,423 web pages in English crawled between January and February 2009). We choose these datasets because they are used widely in the community, allowing comparisons with state-of-the-art. We remove spam using the spam rankings of Cormack et al. [8] with the recommended setting of percentile-score < 70 indicating spam[3].

We consider a subset of this collection, consisting of the top 1000 documents that have been retrieved in response to each query by the baseline retrieval model on tuned settings

[1]We also experimented with Jelinek-Mercer and two-stage smoothing for the baseline retrieval model. Dirichlet and two-stage gave higher scores. We chose Dirichlet over two-stage because it includes one less parameter to tune.

[2]http://lemurproject.org/clueweb09.php/

[3]Note that removing spam from Clueweb09 cat B. is known to give overall lower retrieval scores than keeping spam [3].

Table 1: Examples of the 15 rhetorical relations (in bold italics) of our dataset, identified by the SPADE discourse parser [27]

Rhetorical relation	Example sentences with rhetorical relations italicised and bold
attribution	... the islands now known as the Gilbert Islands were settled ***by Austronesian-speaking people*** ...
background	... many whites had left the country ***when Kenyatta divided their land among blacks*** ...
cause-result	... ***I plugged "wives" into the search box and came up with the following results*** ...
comparison	... so for humans, ***it is stronger than coloured*** to frustrate these unexpected numbers ...
condition	... Conditional money ***based upon care for the pet*** ...
consequence	... voltage drop with the cruise control switch ***could cause erratic cruise control operation*** ...
contrast	... ***Although it started out as a research project***, the ARPANET quickly developed into ...
elaboration	... order accutane ***no prescription required*** ...
enablement	... The project will also ***offer exercise programs and make eye care services accessible*** ...
evaluation	... such advances will be reflected in an ever-***greater proportion of grade A recommendations*** ...
explanation	... the concept ***called as "evolutionary developmental biology" or shortly "evo-devo"*** ...
manner-means	... Fill current path ***using even-odd rule, then paint the path*** ...
summary	... Safety Last, Girl Shy, Hot Water, The Kid Brother, Speedy ***(all with lively orchestral scores)*** ...
temporal	... Take time out ***before you start writing*** ...
topic-comment	... ***Director Mark Smith expressed support for greyhound adoption*** ...

(described in section 4.1.2) using the Indri IR system[4] for indexing and retrieval. For this subset, we strip HTML annotation using our in-house WHU-REAPER crawling and web parsing toolkit[5]. Rhetorical relations are identified using the freely available SPADE discourse parser [27]. Table 1 shows the 15 types of rhetorical relations identified by this process, with examples taken from the re-ranking dataset.

4.1.2 Parameter Tuning

Two parameters are involved in these experiments: the Dirichlet smoothing parameter μ of the retrieval model (used by both the baseline and our approach) and the mixture parameter κ of our model. Both parameters are tuned using 5-fold cross validation for each query set separately; results reported are the average over the five test sets. μ is tuned across {100, 500, 800, 1000, 2000, 3000, 4000, 5000, 8000, 10000} (using the range of Zhai & Lafferty [35]) and κ is tuned across {0.1, 0.3, 0.5, 0.7, 0.9}.

Performance is reported and tuned separately for Mean Average Precision (MAP), Binary Preference (BPREF), and Normalised Discounted Cumulated Gain (NDCG). These measures contribute different aspects to the overall evaluation: BPREF measures the average precision of a ranked list; it differs from MAP in that it does not treat non-assessed documents as explicitly non-relevant (whereas MAP does) [4]. This is a useful insight, especially for a collection as large as Clueweb09 cat. B where the chances of retrieving non-assessed documents are higher. NDCG measures the gain of a document based on its position in the result list. The gain is accumulated from the top of the ranked list to the bottom, with the gain of each document discounted at lower ranks. This gain is relative to the ideal based on a known recall base of relevance assessments [17]. Finally, we test the statistical significance of our results using the t-test at 95% and 99% confidence levels [25].

4.2 Findings

Figure 2 shows the distribution of the rhetorical relations in our re-ranking dataset as a percentage of the total number of rhetorical relations. `Elaboration`, `attribution` and `background` are the most frequent rhetorical relations, whereas `topic-comment` is the most infrequent. This happens because quite often in text a topic forms the nucleus of the discourse, which is then linked by a number of different rhetorical relations, for instance about its background, elaborating on an aspect, or attributing parts of it to some entity. As a result, several types of other rhetorical relations can correspond to a single `topic-comment`. Note that the distribution of rhetorical relations reported here is in agreement with the literature, e.g. Teufel & Moens [30] also report a 5% occurrence of `contrast`, albeit in the domain of scientific articles.

[4]http://www.lemurproject.org/

[5]Freely available by emailing the third author.

4.2.1 Retrieval-Enhancing Rhetorical Relations

Table 2 shows the performance of our model against the baseline, for each rhetorical relation and evaluation measure. The baseline performance is among the highest reported in the literature for these setings; for instance Bendersky et al. [3] report MAP=0.1605 for a tuned language model baseline with the Web 2009 track queries on Clueweb cat. B without spam.

We observe that different rhetorical relations perform differently across evaluation measures and query sets. The four rhetorical relations that improve performance over the baseline consistently for all evaluation measures and query sets (shaded rows in Table 2) are: `background`, `cause-result`, `condition` and `topic-comment`. `Topic-comment` is one of the overall best-performing rhetorical relations, which in simple terms means that boosting the weight of the topical part of a document improves its estimation of relevance.

A closer look at which rhetorical relations decrease performance presents a more uneven picture as no relations consistently underperform for all measures and query sets. Some relations, such as `explanation` and `enablement` for Web 2009, and `summary` and `evaluation` for Web 2010, are among the lowest performing, but are not under the baseline across all measures and both query sets. This implies that separating rhetorical relations into those that generally can enhance retrieval performance and those that cannot may not be straight-forward. Even though exploring the family likeness between useful relations and ones that give no mileage is an interesting discussion, in the rest of the pa-

Table 2: Retrieval performance with rhetorical relations and without (baseline). * (**) marks stat. significance at 95% (99%) using the t-test. Bold means > baseline. % shows the difference from the baseline. Shaded rows indicate consistent improvements over the baseline at all times.

rhetorical relation	Web 2009 (queries 1-50) MAP		BPREF		NDCG		Web 2010 (queries 51-100) MAP		BPREF		NDCG	
none (baseline)	0.1625		0.3230		0.3893		0.0986		0.2240		0.2920	
attribution	**0.1654***	+1.8%	**0.3275****	+1.4%	**0.3927****	+0.9%	0.0924	-6.2%	**0.2549****	+13.8%	**0.3008****	+3.0%
background	**0.1646**	+1.3%	**0.3291****	+1.9%	**0.3910**	+0.4%	**0.1086***	+10.2%	**0.2623****	+17.1%	**0.3070****	+5.1%
cause-result	**0.1626**	+0.1%	**0.3255****	+0.8%	**0.3900**	+0.2%	**0.1015**	+2.9%	**0.2491***	+11.2%	**0.3079**	+5.4%
comparison	0.1610	-0.9%	**0.3251***	+0.6%	0.3877	-0.4%	**0.1017**	+3.1%	**0.2282**	+1.9%	**0.3040****	+4.1%
condition	**0.1632**	+0.5%	**0.3258****	+0.9%	**0.3903**	+0.3%	**0.0999**	+1.3%	**0.2470****	+10.3%	**0.2936**	+0.5%
consequence	0.1602	-1.4%	**0.3250**	+0.6%	0.3874	-0.5%	0.0945	-4.1%	**0.2377***	+6.1%	**0.2840****	-2.7%
contrast	0.1549*	-4.6%	**0.3269****	+1.2%	**0.3897**	+0.1%	**0.1103***	+11.8%	**0.2531****	+13.0%	**0.3069****	+5.1%
elaboration	0.1556*	-4.2%	**0.3292****	+1.9%	0.3866	-0.7%	0.0951	-3.5%	**0.2598****	+16.0%	**0.3005****	+2.9%
enablement	0.1601	-1.4%	**0.3240**	+0.3%	0.3869*	-0.6%	**0.1010**	+2.4%	**0.2316***	+3.4%	**0.2992***	+2.5%
evaluation	**0.1632**	+0.5%	**0.3242**	+0.4%	0.3886	-0.2%	0.0814**	-17.4%	**0.2313***	+3.3%	**0.2902**	-0.6%
explanation	0.1546	-4.9%	**0.3259***	+0.9%	0.3813	-2.1%	**0.1034**	+4.9%	**0.2645****	+18.1%	**0.3069****	+5.1%
manner-means	0.1623	-0.1%	**0.3253***	+0.7%	0.3884	-0.2%	0.0986	-	**0.2324***	+3.7%	**0.2897**	-0.8%
summary	**0.1626**	+0.1%	**0.3241**	+0.3%	0.3879	-0.4%	0.0862	-12.6%	0.2220*	-0.9%	**0.2928**	+0.3%
temporal	0.1615	-0.6%	**0.3262****	+1.0%	0.3887	-0.2%	0.0921	-6.6%	**0.2546****	+13.7%	**0.3052**	+4.5%
topic-comment	**0.1673**	+3.0%	**0.3375**	+4.5%	**0.3976***	+2.1%	**0.1090***	+10.5%	**0.2476***	+10.5%	**0.3009**	+3.1%

Table 3: Effect of the rhetorical relation to the retrieval model as indicated by parameter κ (see Equation 3), for the tuned runs of Table 2. Shaded rows indicate rhetorical relations that consistently improve performance over the baseline at all times.

rhetorical relation	Web 2009 (queries 1-50) MAP	BPREF	NDCG	Web 2010 (queries 51-100) MAP	BPREF	NDCG
attribution	0.1	0.5	0.1	0.3	0.5	0.3
background	0.2	0.6	0.2	0.3	0.7	0.3
cause-result	0.3	0.7	0.3	0.5	0.7	0.5
comparison	0.4	0.7	0.4	0.3	0.5	0.3
condition	0.3	0.7	0.3	0.3	0.5	0.3
consequence	0.5	0.7	0.5	0.5	0.7	0.5
contrast	0.3	0.7	0.3	0.3	0.5	0.3
elaboration	0.1	0.5	0.1	0.3	0.5	0.3
enablement	0.1	0.9	0.1	0.3	0.5	0.3
evaluation	0.5	0.7	0.5	0.5	0.7	0.5
explanation	0.5	0.7	0.5	0.5	0.7	0.5
manner-means	0.5	0.7	0.5	0.5	0.7	0.5
summary	0.5	0.7	0.5	0.3	0.7	0.3
temporal	0.1	0.7	0.1	0.3	0.5	0.3
topic-comment	0.5	0.5	0.5	0.5	0.7	0.5

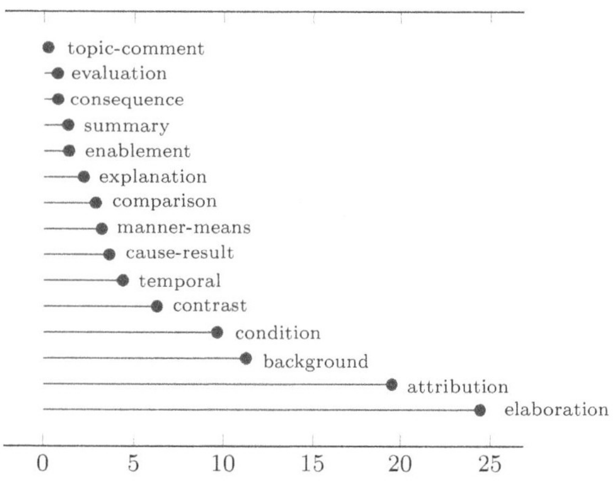

Figure 2: % distribution of rhetorical relations in our dataset.

per we focus on those rhetorical relations that consistently improve retrieval performance (for these datasets).

Improvements over the baseline are generally higher for Web 2010 than Web 2009, possibly because the former baseline is weaker, with potentially more room for improvement. An interesting trend is that more rhetorical relations improve performance according to BPREF than according to MAP and NDCG. As BPREF is the only of these evaluation measures that does not consider non-assessed documents as non-relevant, this indicates the presence of non-assessed documents in the ranking.

The scores shown in Table 2 are averaged over tens of queries, meaning that they can be affected by outliers. Figure 3 presents a detailed per-query overview of the performance of each query in relation to the baseline for each of the 15 rhetorical relations[6]. The plotted points represent the difference in MAP between our approach and the baseline. Positive points indicate that our approach outperforms the baseline. The points are sorted.

We observe that although the overall performance of the Web 2010 query set is lower than that of the Web 2009 query set, the improvements over the baseline of the 2010 set are consistently larger. Only in one case, `topic-comment`, do the plotted points clearly cross. Overall both query sets show similar plots with outliers at both ends of the scale. However, the 2009 query set tends to have a somewhat larger proportion of negative outliers, which goes some way towards explaining the lower improvements over the baseline observed for Web 2009. The Web 2010 set shows improvements over the baseline for most of the rhetorical relations and for the majority of the queries.

4.2.2 *Quantifying the Contribution of Rhetorical Relations to the Ranking*

Exactly how much impact each rhetorical relation has on the ranking can be seen in Table 3. The table lists the κ values for the best performing tuned runs from Table 2, where high κ values mean that the rhetorical relations are given more weight in the ranking (see Equation 3). We see that none of the values are above 0.5 for MAP and NDCG, indicating that too much emphasis on the rhetorical rela-

[6]Similar trends are observed in the corresponding figures for BPREF and NDCG, which are not included here for brevity.

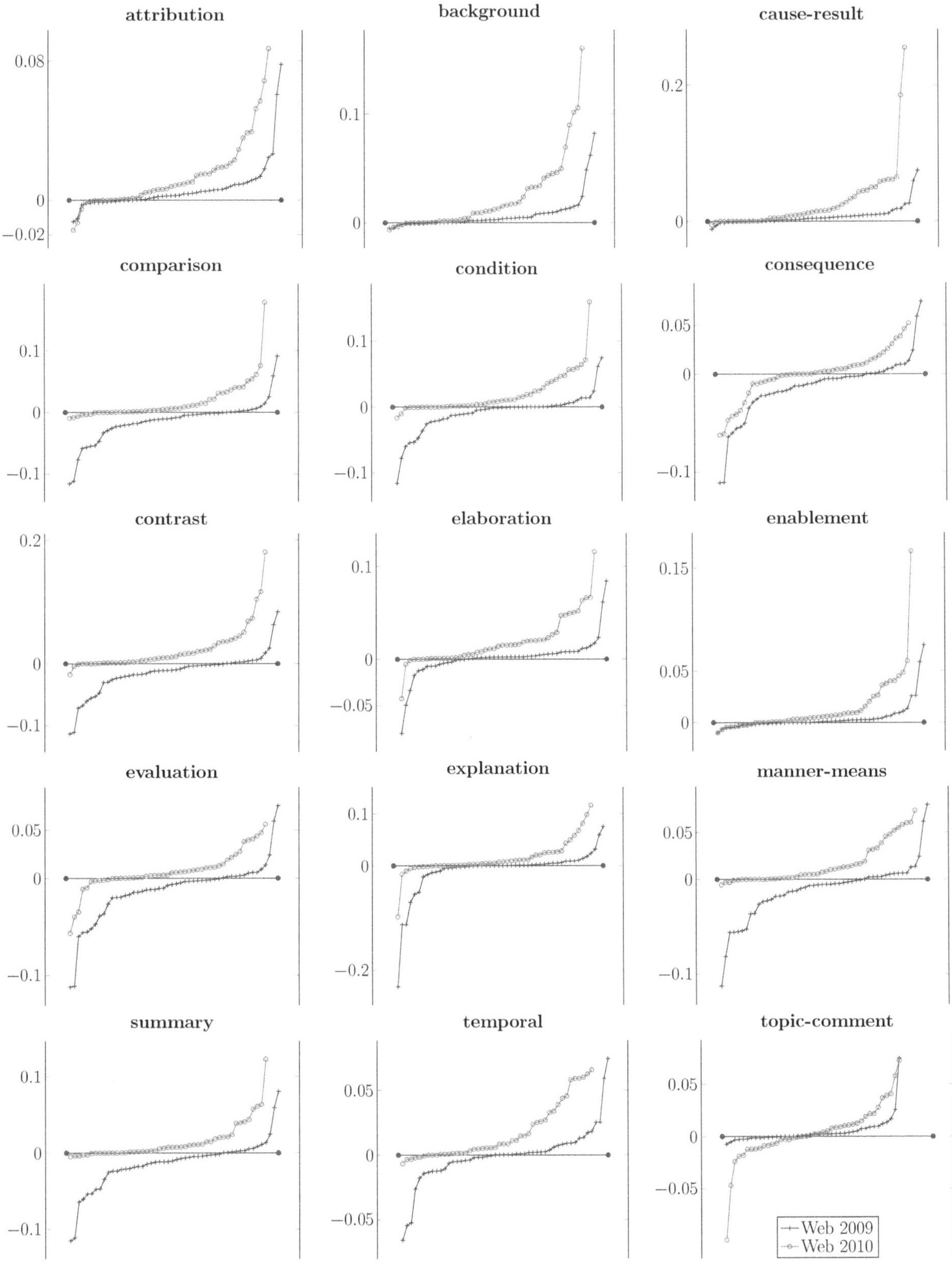

Figure 3: Sorted per-query difference in MAP between the baseline and our model (y-axis), for each rhetorical relation. The horizontal line marks the baseline. + and *o* mark the 2009 and 2010 query sets.

tions may not be beneficial to performance. Consistent with Table 2, BPREF follows a different trend than MAP and NDCG, which could be due to the fact that it is a different type of evaluation measure as discussed above in section 4.1.2. With BPREF, non-assessed documents are not explicitly penalised in the evaluation (as in MAP and NDCG) - resulting in overall higher κ values for best performing runs, typically of around 0.5-0.7.

Further we observe that the rhetorical relations that consistently improve performance over the baseline, as indicated in Table 2, differ in κ values for their best performing runs. For example, $\kappa = 0.2$ - 0.3 for `background` and $\kappa = 0.5$ for `topic-comment`. This implies that, to use rhetorical relations successfully for IR, it is not sufficient to know which rhetorical relations should be considered in the ranking and which not; also knowledge about how much emphasis to put on each rhetorical relation is needed for optimal IR performance.

Finally, note that the frequency of rhetorical relations does not affect their impact to retrieval. For instance, the three best performing rhetorical relations, `topic-comment`, `background` and `cause-result` constitute respectively approximately ~1%, 11% and 5% of all rhetorical relations, as shown in Figure 2.

5. OPTIMISED RANKING WITH RHETORICAL RELATIONS

5.1 Rhetorical Relation Selection

The findings in section 4.2 show that some rhetorical relations can be more beneficial to retrieval performance than others. An ideal solution would not consider the lexical statistics of all rhetorical relations in a document, but rather it would select to include in the ranking only those rhetorical relations that have a higher likelihood of enhancing retrieval performance. This can be formulated as finding the optimal rhetorical relation ψ_g that maximises the expected retrieval scores according to an evaluation measure (e.g. MAP) for a query-document pair:

$$\hat{\psi_g} = \arg\max_{\psi_g \in \Psi} E[y|q,d] \tag{6}$$

where E denotes the expectation and y the retrieval score (rest of notation as defined in section 3).

Bayesian decision theory allows to reason about this type of expectation, for instance see [32]. In this work, we treat this as a problem of Bayesian posterior inference, where the goal is to estimate the retrieval performance associated with a rhetorical relation, given the observed retrieval scores it fetches on a number of queries. Then, we can consider the rhetorical relation associated with the highest retrieval performance as optimal. For this estimation, we split our dataset into different parts so that we use the observations from one to make inferences about the other (see section 5.2 for details).

Let $n = 15$ be the rhetorical relations shown in Table 2, and x_j be the number of queries for which retrieval with the jth rhetorical relation gets a retrieval score y_j. For now we assume that all rhetorical relations may be expected to have similar retrieval performance, with the jth rhetorical relation having an average performance ratio per query λ_j (estimated as $\frac{y_j}{x_j}$). Various densities can be used to fit similar data [22], one of which is the Poisson distribution. Let us assume that, conditional on λ_j, the retrieval scores y_j have independent Poisson distributions with means $\lambda_j x_j$. Let us further assume that the λ_j are independent realisations of a gamma variable with parameters α and β, and that β itself has a prior gamma distribution with parameters ν and ϕ. Thus

$$f(y|\lambda) = \prod_{j=1}^{n} \frac{(x_j\lambda_j)^{y_j}}{y_j!} e^{-x_j\lambda_j}$$

$$\pi(\lambda|\beta) = \prod_{j=1}^{n} \frac{\beta^{\alpha}\lambda_j^{\alpha-1}}{\Gamma(\alpha)} e^{-\beta\lambda_j}$$

$$\pi(\beta) = \frac{\phi^{\nu}\beta^{\nu-1}}{\Gamma(\nu)} e^{-\phi\beta}$$

so that the joint probability density of the retrieval scores y, the average performance ratios λ, and β is

$$f(y|\lambda)f(\lambda|\beta)\pi(\beta) = c\prod_{j=1}^{n}\{\lambda_j^{y_j+\alpha-1}e^{-\lambda_j(x_j+\beta)}\}.\beta^{n\alpha+\nu-1}e^{-\phi\beta} \tag{7}$$

where c is a constant of proportionality.

The conditional density of β can be computed by various numerical approximations, one of which is the Laplace method [2], which we use here. To find the conditional density of β we integrate over the λ_j to obtain

$$f(y,\beta) = c\prod_{j=1}^{n}\{(x_j+\beta)^{-(y_j+\alpha)}\Gamma(y_j+\alpha)\}.\beta^{n\alpha+\nu-1}e^{-\phi\beta} \tag{8}$$

from which the marginal density of y is obtained by further integration to give

$$f(y) = c\prod_{j=1}^{n}\Gamma(y_j+\alpha)\cdot\int_0^{\infty} e^{-h(\beta)}d\beta \tag{9}$$

where $h(\beta) = \phi\beta - (n\alpha+\nu-1)log\beta + \sum(y_j+\alpha)log(x_j+\beta)$. Let I denote the integral in this expression. In this work, we take an uninformative prior for β, with $\nu = 0.1$ and $\phi = 1$ and use $\alpha = 1.8$[7]. We then apply Laplace's method to I, resulting in the approximate posterior density for β, $\tilde{\pi}(\beta|y) = \tilde{I}^{-1}e^{-h(\beta)}$.

To calculate approximate posterior densities for λ_j we integrate Equation 7 over λ_i, $i \neq j$ and then we apply Laplace's method to the numerator and denominator integrals of

$$\pi(\lambda_j|y) = \frac{\lambda_j^{y_j+\alpha-1}e^{-\lambda_j x_j}\int_0^{\infty}e^{-h_j(\beta)}d\lambda}{\Gamma(y_j+\alpha)\int_0^{\infty}e^{-h(\beta)}d\beta}$$

where

$$h_j(\beta) = (\phi+\lambda_j)\beta - (n\alpha+\nu-1)log\beta + \sum_{i\neq j}(y_i+\alpha)log(x_i+\beta)$$

The resulting denominator is again $\tilde{I}_1$, while the numerator must be recalculated at each of a range of values for λ_j. The output is the (posterior) expected retrieval performance associated with each rhetorical relation.

5.2 Experiments

[7]These values are not tuned; they are the default values of this approach as illustrated in [10], chapter 11.3, pages 603-604.

Table 4: Retrieval performance with optimal rhetorical relations (inferred, observed) and without rhetorical relations (baseline). (1)-(5) refers to the five randomised samplings used to infer the optimal rhetorical relations. Bold marks better than baseline.

rhetorical relation	Web 2009 (queries 1-50)						Web 2010 (queries 51-100)					
	MAP		BPREF		NDCG		MAP		BPREF		NDCG	
none (baseline)	0.1625		0.3230		0.3894		0.0967		0.2198		0.2890	
optimal$_{inferred}$ (1)	**0.1879**	+15.6%	**0.3503**	+8.5%	**0.4224**	+8.5%	**0.1355**	+40.1%	**0.2859**	+30.1%	**0.3347**	+15.8%
optimal$_{inferred}$ (2)	**0.1948**	+19.9%	**0.3585**	+11.0%	**0.4202**	+7.9%	**0.1285**	+32.9%	**0.2841**	+29.3%	**0.3394**	+17.4%
optimal$_{inferred}$ (3)	**0.1984**	+22.1%	**0.3532**	+9.3%	**0.4169**	+7.1%	**0.1358**	+40.0%	**0.2906**	+32.2%	**0.3388**	+17.2%
optimal$_{inferred}$ (4)	**0.1952**	+20.1%	**0.3479**	+7.7%	**0.4282**	+10.0%	**0.1360**	+40.6%	**0.2874**	+30.8%	**0.3336**	+15.4%
optimal$_{inferred}$ (5)	**0.1950**	+20.0%	**0.3528**	+9.2%	**0.4287**	+10.1%	**0.1340**	+38.6%	**0.2865**	+30.3%	**0.3322**	+14.9%
optimal$_{observed}$	**0.2157**	+32.7%	**0.3660**	+13.3%	**0.4412**	+13.3%	**0.1474**	+52.4%	**0.2978**	+35.5%	**0.3569**	+23.5%

5.2.1 Setup

The observations required to make the above inference are triples of *rhetorical relation - query number - retrieval score*. To avoid overfitting, we pool randomly 50% of the observations from the 2009 Web query scores and 50% of the observations from the 2010 Web query scores. We use this pool to infer the expected retrieval performance of each rhetorical relation. We repeat this randomised pooling five times, each time randomly pertrubing the data, producing five different sets of observations. We then use each set to infer the expected best performing rhetorical relation per query, in accordance to Equation 6. Following this, we use the model introduced in section 3, Equation 2, to rank documents with respect to queries only for optimal (as inferred) rhetorical relations. We evaluate the above method using the same experimental settings described in section 4.1.

5.2.2 Findings

Table 4 shows the runs corresponding to the five different inferences of the best rhetorical relation that use our model (optimal$_{inferred}$ (1)-(5) respectively). We also report the optimal retrieval performance actually observed in the dataset when using the best rhetorical relation per query (optimal$_{observed}$). Optimal here means with respect to the choice of rhetorical relation, not with respect to the Dirichlet μ parameter of the baseline retrieval model.

Table 4 shows that our optimised ranking model for rhetorical relations is better than the baseline for any of the five random inferences on all three evaluation measures. The probability of getting such a positive result by chance is $\frac{1}{2^5} < 0.05$, and thus the improvements are statistically significant. The improvements over the baseline are considerable, a very promising finding given the relatively low number of observations used for optimising the choice of rhetorical relations. Experiments involving larger query sets can be reasonably expected to perform on a par with state-of-the-art performance.

More generally, the improvements in Table 4 signal that rhetorical relations (derived automatically as shown in this work) could potentially be useful features for 'linguistically-uninformed' learning-to-rank approaches.

6. DISCUSSION

6.1 Rhetorical Relation Distribution

The distribution of the 15 rhetorical relations we identified in our dataset is not the same for all rhetorical relations (see Figure 2). Some types, e.g. `topic-comment`, tend to be very sparse, whereas relations such as `elaboration` prevail. This has no impact on the model presented in section 3, but it can bias the optimised inference of the model presented in section 5. The lower the occurrence of a rhetorical relation in the dataset, the fewer the observations of retrieval performance associated with it, and hence the weaker the predictions we can infer about whether it is optimal or not. A fairer setting would be to have the same number of 'query - retrieval performance' observations for all rhetorical relations - however that would imply fiddling with the document distribution of our dataset significantly, potentially harming its quality as a test collection.

6.2 Limitations

A general limitation of discourse analysis is that not all types of text are susceptible to it. For instance, legal text, contracts, or item lists often lack rhetorical structure. In this work, we made no effort to identify and exempt such types of text from the discourse parsing. We reasoned that, as the SPADE parser includes a first-step grammatical parsing, the initial grammatical parsing of these types of text would flag out ill-formed parts (e.g. missing a verb, or consisting of extremely long sentences), which would then be skipped by the discourse analysis. This was indeed the case, however at a certain efficiency cost. Overall processing speed for SPADE was approximately 19 seconds per document (including the initial grammatical parsing), on a machine of 9 GB RAM, 8 core processor at 2.27GHz. One way of improving this performance would be to update the first-step grammatical parsing. Currently this depends on the well-known Charniak parser [6], which is one of the best performing grammatical parsers, however no longer supported. Other state-of-the-art faster grammatical parsers, e.g. the Stanford parser[8], could be adapted and plugged into SPADE instead.

The choice of applying our model for re-ranking as opposed to ranking all documents was closely related to the efficiency concerns discussed above. Our model is not specific to re-ranking only, however, using SPADE on approximately 50 million documents was too expensive at this point. Improving the discourse parser's efficiency is something we are currently working on, with the aim to apply our model for full ranking and see if the conclusions drawn from this work hold.

Finally, the accuracy of the discourse parser was not considered in this work, apart from indications in the literature that SPADE is a generally well-performing parser [27]. Given that the default version of the parser we used is trained on news articles, one may reason that its accuracy could improve if we train it on the retrieval collection, or on doc-

[8]http://nlp.stanford.edu/software/lex-parser.shtml

uments of the same domain. Note that, parsing accuracy aside, rhetorical relations assignment is not an entirely unambiguous process, even to humans [23]. For the purposes of this work, this type of fine-grained ambiguity may however not be important to retrieval performance.

6.3 Future Extensions

Future extensions include primarily making SPADE scalable on large collections of documents as discussed above, as well as using more than one rhetorical relation per document. For instance, the posterior probabilities estimated in section 5.1 could be used to weight the text in each rhetorical relation. If those posteriors are too flat, an exponent could make them peakier. As the exponent goes to infinity, the maximum relation model presented in section 5.2 would be recovered. In addition, we intend to refine the discourse analysis by considering the nucleus (i.e. central) versus satellite (i.e. peripheral) rhetorical relations for IR, as well as to improve the effectiveness of the discourse parser by training it on data of the same domain. As discussed in section 3.2, we will also investigate alternative estimations of Equations 2-3.

An interesting future research direction is the potential relation between rhetorical relations and user context: for instance, in a search session including several query reformulations, is there a correlation between the progression of the information need of the user and the rhetorical relations that the retrieval system should boost in a document (e.g. `elaboration`), as indicated by Sun & Chai [28]? Another interesting future extension of this work is in relation to evaluation measures of graded relevance measures on an inter-document level, as investigated in XML retrieval [20] for instance. If parts of a document can be regarded as more or less relevant, this may be reflected to their discourse structure. This might be especially useful for multi-threaded documents, such as multiple-user reviews and opinions, where the discourse relations tend to shift markedly. Finally, the current operationalisation of our model is simplistic in the sense that the term 'rhetorical relation' is coerced into meaning 'non-overlapping text fragment' and the actual relation between bits of text is discarded in the process. In future work we could apply fielded XML retrieval models in order to investigate nested structuring among rhetorical relations.

7. CONCLUSIONS

Rhetorical relations, e.g. `contrast, explanation, condition`, indicate the different ways in which the parts of a text are linked to each other to form a coherent whole. This work studied two questions: Is there a correlation between certain rhetorical relations and retrieval performance? Can knowledge about a document's rhetorical relations be useful to IR? To address these, we presented a retrieval model that conditions the probability of relevance between a query and a document on the rhetorical relations occurring in that document. We applied that model to an IR re-ranking scenario for Web search. Experimental evaluation of different versions of our model on TREC data and standard settings demonstrated that certain rhetorical relations can be beneficial to retrieval, with >10% improvements to retrieval precision. Furthermore, we showed that these improvements over the baseline can improve significantly, when the optimal rhetorical relation per document is selected for retrieval.

Overall, three rhetorical relations were found to benefit retrieval performance notably and consistently for different evaluation measures and query sets: `background, cause-result` and `topic-comment`. In retrospect, this is perhaps not surprising, since these are among the most salient discourse relations on an intuitive basis: the main topic or theme of a text, its background, causes and results [21]. Future extensions and research directions of this work include considering more than one rhetorical relation per document, applying our model for ranking all documents (as opposed to re-ranking only) and experimenting with alternative estimations of its components.

8. ACKNOWLEDGMENTS

We thank Kasper Hornbæk, Jakob Grue Simonsen, Raf Guns, Qikai Cheng and the anonymous reviewers for helping improve this paper. Work partially funded by the Danish International Development Agency DANIDA (grant no. 10-087721) and the National Natural Science Foundation of China (grant no. 71173164).

9. REFERENCES

[1] *Proceedings of the 2011 Conference on Empirical Methods in Natural Language Processing, EMNLP 2011, 27-31 July 2011, John McIntyre Conference Centre, Edinburgh, UK, A meeting of SIGDAT, a Special Interest Group of the ACL*. ACL, 2011.

[2] A. Azevedo-Filho and R. D. Shachter. Laplace's method approximations for probabilistic inference in belief networks with continuous variables. In R. L. de Mántaras and D. Poole, editors, *UAI*, pages 28–36. Morgan Kaufmann, 1994.

[3] M. Bendersky, W. B. Croft, and Y. Diao. Quality-biased ranking of web documents. In I. King, W. Nejdl, and H. Li, editors, *WSDM*, pages 95–104. ACM, 2011.

[4] C. Buckley and E. M. Voorhees. Retrieval evaluation with incomplete information. In M. Sanderson, K. Järvelin, J. Allan, and P. Bruza, editors, *SIGIR*, pages 25–32. ACM, 2004.

[5] L. Carlson, D. Marcu, and M. E. Okurowski. Building a discourse-tagged corpus in the framework of rhetorical structure theory. In *Current Directions in Discourse and Dialogue*, pages 85–112. Kluwer Academic Publishers, 2003.

[6] E. Charniak. A maximum-entropy-inspired parser. In *Proceedings of the first conference on North American chapter of the Association for Computational Linguistics*, pages 132–139, San Francisco, CA, USA, 2000. Morgan Kaufmann Publishers Inc.

[7] J. Clarke and M. Lapata. Discourse constraints for document compression. *Computational Linguistics*, 36(3):411–441, 2010.

[8] G. V. Cormack, M. D. Smucker, and C. L. A. Clarke. Efficient and effective spam filtering and re-ranking for large web datasets. *CoRR*, abs/1004.5168, 2010.

[9] W. B. Croft and J. Lafferty. *Language Modeling for Information Retrieval*. Kluwer Academic Publishers, Norwell, MA, USA, 2003.

[10] A. C. Davison. *Statistical Models*. Cambridge University Press, New York, 2009.

[11] D. A. duVerle and H. Prendinger. A novel discourse parser based on support vector machine classification.

In *Proceedings of the Joint Conference of the 47th Annual Meeting of the ACL and the 4th International Joint Conference on Natural Language Processing of the AFNLP: Volume 2 - Volume 2*, ACL '09, pages 665–673, Stroudsburg, PA, USA, 2009. Association for Computational Linguistics.

[12] C. J. Fillmore, C. F. Baker, and S. Hiroaki. The framenet database and software tools. In *Proceedings of the 3rd International Conference on Language Resources and Evaluation (LREC)*, pages 1157–1160, 2002.

[13] W. A. Gale and G. Sampson. Good-turing frequency estimation without tears. *Journal of Quantitative Linguistics*, 2(3):217–237, 1995.

[14] S. Ghosh, R. Johansson, G. Riccardi, and S. Tonelli. Shallow discourse parsing with conditional random fields. In *Proceedings of the 5th International Joint Conference on Natural Language Processing (IJCNLP)*, pages 1071–1079, Chiang Mai, Thailand, 2011.

[15] D. Gildea and D. Jurafsky. Automatic labeling of semantic roles. In *ACL*. ACL, 2000.

[16] B. Heerschop, F. Goossen, A. Hogenboom, F. Frasincar, U. Kaymak, and F. de Jong. Polarity analysis of texts using discourse structure. In *Proceedings of the 20th ACM international conference on Information and knowledge management*, CIKM '11, pages 1061–1070, New York, NY, USA, 2011. ACM.

[17] K. Järvelin and J. Kekäläinen. Cumulated gain-based evaluation of ir techniques. *ACM Trans. Inf. Syst.*, 20(4):422–446, 2002.

[18] P. Kingsbury and M. Palmer. From treebank to propbank. In *Proceedings of the 3rd International Conference on Language Resources and Evaluation (LREC)*, pages x–x, 2002.

[19] E. Krikon and O. Kurland. A study of the integration of passage-, document-, and cluster-based information for re-ranking search results. *Inf. Retr.*, 14(6):593–616, 2011.

[20] M. Lalmas. *XML Retrieval*. Synthesis Lectures on Information Concepts, Retrieval, and Services. Morgan & Claypool Publishers, 2009.

[21] A. Louis, A. K. Joshi, and A. Nenkova. Discourse indicators for content selection in summarization. In R. Fernández, Y. Katagiri, K. Komatani, O. Lemon, and M. Nakano, editors, *SIGDIAL Conference*, pages 147–156. The Association for Computer Linguistics, 2010.

[22] R. Manmatha, T. M. Rath, and F. Feng. Modeling score distributions for combining the outputs of search engines. In W. B. Croft, D. J. Harper, D. H. Kraft, and J. Zobel, editors, *SIGIR*, pages 267–275. ACM, 2001.

[23] W. C. Mann and S. A. Thompson. Rhetorical structure theory: Toward a functional theory of text organization. *Text*, 8:243–281, 1988.

[24] J. Morato, J. Llorens, G. Genova, and J. A. Moreiro. Experiments in discourse analysis impact on information classification and retrieval algorithms. *Inf. Process. Manage.*, 39:825–851, November 2003.

[25] M. D. Smucker, J. Allan, and B. Carterette. Agreement among statistical significance tests for information retrieval evaluation at varying sample sizes. In J. Allan, J. A. Aslam, M. Sanderson, C. Zhai, and J. Zobel, editors, *SIGIR*, pages 630–631. ACM, 2009.

[26] S. Somasundaran, G. Namata, J. Wiebe, and L. Getoor. Supervised and unsupervised methods in employing discourse relations for improving opinion polarity classification. In *EMNLP*, pages 170–179. ACL, 2009.

[27] R. Soricut and D. Marcu. Sentence level discourse parsing using syntactic and lexical information. In *HLT-NAACL*, 2003.

[28] M. Sun and J. Y. Chai. Discourse processing for context question answering based on linguistic knowledge. *Know.-Based Syst.*, 20:511–526, August 2007.

[29] N. Suwandaratna and U. Perera. Discourse marker based topic identification and search results refining. In *Information and Automation for Sustainability (ICIAFs), 2010 5th International Conference on*, pages 119–125, 2010.

[30] S. Teufel and M. Moens. Summarizing scientific articles: Experiments with relevance and rhetorical status. *Computational Linguistics*, 28(4):409–445, 2002.

[31] D. Y. Wang, R. W. P. Luk, K.-F. Wong, and K. L. Kwok. An information retrieval approach based on discourse type. In C. Kop, G. Fliedl, H. C. Mayr, and E. Métais, editors, *NLDB*, volume 3999 of *Lecture Notes in Computer Science*, pages 197–202. Springer, 2006.

[32] J. Wang and J. Zhu. On statistical analysis and optimization of information retrieval effectiveness metrics. In F. Crestani, S. Marchand-Maillet, H.-H. Chen, E. N. Efthimiadis, and J. Savoy, editors, *SIGIR*, pages 226–233. ACM, 2010.

[33] L. Wang, M. Lui, S. N. Kim, J. Nivre, and T. Baldwin. Predicting thread discourse structure over technical web forums. In *EMNLP* [1], pages 13–25.

[34] L.-C. Yu, C.-H. Wu, and F.-L. Jang. Psychiatric document retrieval using a discourse-aware model. *Artif. Intell.*, 173:817–829, May 2009.

[35] C. Zhai and J. D. Lafferty. Two-stage language models for information retrieval. In *SIGIR*, pages 49–56. ACM, 2002.

[36] L. Zhou, B. Li, W. Gao, Z. Wei, and K.-F. Wong. Unsupervised discovery of discourse relations for eliminating intra-sentence polarity ambiguities. In *EMNLP* [1], pages 162–171.

Modeling Higher-Order Term Dependencies in Information Retrieval using Query Hypergraphs

Michael Bendersky
Dept. of Computer Science
Univ. of Massachusetts Amherst
Amherst, MA
bemike@cs.umass.edu

W. Bruce Croft
Dept. of Computer Science
Univ. of Massachusetts Amherst
Amherst, MA
croft@cs.umass.edu

ABSTRACT

Many of the recent, and more effective, retrieval models have incorporated dependencies between the terms in the query. In this paper, we advance this query representation one step further, and propose a retrieval framework that models higher-order term dependencies, i.e., dependencies between arbitrary query concepts rather than just query terms. In order to model higher-order term dependencies, we represent a query using a hypergraph structure – a generalization of a graph, where a (hyper)edge connects an arbitrary subset of vertices. A vertex in a query hypergraph corresponds to an individual query concept, and a dependency between a subset of these vertices is modeled through a hyperedge. An extensive empirical evaluation using both newswire and web corpora demonstrates that query representation using hypergraphs is highly beneficial for verbose natural language queries. For these queries, query hypergraphs significantly improve the retrieval effectiveness of several state-of-the-art models that do not employ higher-order term dependencies.

Categories and Subject Descriptors

H.3.3 [**Information Storage and Retrieval**]: Information Search and Retrieval

General Terms

Algorithms, Experimentation

Keywords

Query hypergraphs, query representation, retrieval models

1. INTRODUCTION

Over the past decade, information retrieval research has undergone a gradual shift of focus from retrieval models that use bag-of-words query representations to retrieval models that incorporate term dependencies. Some recent examples of retrieval models that incorporate term dependencies include, among others, Markov random fields [27], linear discriminant model [14], dependence language model [13], quasi-synchronous dependence model [30], and positional language model [26].

In this paper, we propose a novel retrieval framework that takes a further step toward a more accurate modeling of the dependencies between the query terms. Rather than modeling the dependencies between the *individual query terms*, our framework models dependencies between *arbitrary concepts* in the query.

We broadly define a query concept as a syntactic expression that models a dependency between a subset of query terms. Query concepts may model a variety of linguistic phenomena, including n-grams, term proximities, noun phrases, and named entities. Therefore, a dependency between query concepts represents *a dependency between term dependencies*, i.e., a *higher-order term dependency*[1].

To the best of our knowledge, there is little prior work on modeling this type of higher-order term dependencies for information retrieval. Most retrieval models limit their attention to either pairwise term dependencies [11, 26] or, at most, dependencies between multiple terms [2, 27]. In contrast, the retrieval framework proposed in this paper can model dependencies between arbitrary concepts, e.g., a dependency between a phrase and a term. We hypothesize that an accurate modeling of concept dependencies is especially important for verbose natural language queries. This is due to the fact that the grammatical complexity of these queries often challenges the capabilities of the current retrieval models [2, 20].

As an example, consider the natural language query in Figure 1:

> "Provide information on the use of dogs worldwide for law enforcement purposes."[2]

Figure 1(a) shows an excerpt from the top document retrieved by a sequential dependence model [27], a state-of-the-art retrieval model that incorporates term dependencies. As evident from this excerpt, the top-retrieved document is *non*-relevant with respect to the query. Even though it contains many instances of the phrase *"law enforcement"* as well as the terms *provided* and *information* it does not mention the use of dogs.

On the other hand, an excerpt from the document in Figure 1(b) clearly indicates the relevance of the top document

[1] In the remainder of this paper, we shall use the definitions *"higher-order term dependency"* and *"concept dependency"* interchangeably.

[2] A description of the TREC topic #426.

SIGIR'12, August 12–16, 2012, Portland, Oregon, USA.

*...linking **law enforcement** duties to the definition of "**law enforcement** officer" for retirement purposes....must be handled within the context of...FEPCA and **law enforcement** retirement law and regulations....Adding a discussion of these issues would add unnecessarily to the complexity...of **information** already **provided**...definitions of "**law enforcement** officer" in these regulations should provide guidance...*

(a)

*...Simi Valley, West Covina and Los Angeles police departments were among the first **law enforcement** agencies to receive money through the forfeiture program....a narcotics-sniffing **dog** in a Simi Valley police investigation...led to the largest seizure of cocaine ever by authorities from Ventura County...**dog**'s efforts are expected to yield a substantial amount of money...for the 21-officer department...*

(b)

Figure 1: Excerpts from (a) the top document retrieved by the sequential dependence model [27], and (b) the top document retrieved using a query hypergraph in response to the query: *"Provide information on the use of dogs worldwide for law enforcement purposes"*. Non-stopword query terms are marked in boldface.

retrieved by our method with respect to the query. Even though this excerpt matches *less* of the query terms than the excerpt in Figure 1(a), it contains a relationship between the term *dog* and the phrase *"law enforcement"*, which is highly indicative of its relevance. This relationship cannot be modeled without accounting for higher-order term dependencies.

As Figure 1 shows, the evidence of the concepts co-occurring within a passage of text is a strong indicator of their dependency. This is somewhat akin to term dependencies, which are often modeled based on the frequency of the terms co-occurring next (or close) to each other in the document [27, 39, 26].

In the case of concept dependency, however, instead of relying on the entire document, we only examine a single document passage that is deemed to be the most relevant with respect to the query. This focused evidence can distinguish between relevant documents and documents which simply contain many repeated concept instances, as in Figure 1(a). This approach is reminiscent of the passage retrieval models that often make use of the evidence from the highest-scoring document passage [3, 9, 8, 16, 41].

In contrast to the approach presented in this work, most passage retrieval methods are based on a conjunctive retrieval model and treat a query as a bag of words. However, as the excerpts in Figure 1 demonstrate, such a simple conjunctive retrieval model is not sufficient, especially for verbose, natural language queries.

Instead, the proposed retrieval framework distinguishes between the concepts and the dependencies that are crucial for conveying the query intent, and the concepts and the dependencies of lesser importance. For instance, in the case of the query in Figure 1, the dependency (*dog*, *"law enforcement"*) in Figure 1(b) is crucial for expressing the query intent, while the dependency (*information* and *"law enforcement"*) in Figure 1(a) is not.

To summarize, unlike any of the current retrieval models, the retrieval framework proposed in this paper integrates three main characteristics that we believe are crucial for improving the effectiveness of retrieval with verbose queries. First, it models arbitrary term dependencies as concepts. Second, it uses passage-level evidence to model the dependencies between these concepts. Finally, it assigns weights to both concepts and concept dependencies, proportionate to the estimate of their importance for expressing the query intent. In this paper, we show that by integrating these characteristics, the proposed retrieval framework can significantly improve the effectiveness of several current state-of-the-art retrieval models.

Structure $\boldsymbol{\sigma}$	Concepts $\{\kappa : \kappa \in \boldsymbol{\sigma}\}$
Terms	["members", "rock", "group", "nirvana"]
Bigrams	["members rock", "rock group", "group nirvana"]
Noun Phrases	["members", "rock group nirvana"]
Named Entities	["nirvana"]
Dependencies	["members nirvana", "rock group"]

Table 1: Examples of the possible structures and the concepts they might contain for the query "members of the rock group nirvana" (stopwords removed).

The proposed retrieval framework is based on a query representation using a *hypergraph* structure – a generalization of a graph, where an edge can connect more than two vertices. A vertex in a query hypergraph corresponds to an individual query concept. The vertices are grouped by structures, which model various linguistic phenomena. For instance, as shown in Table 1, a structure can group together terms, n-grams or noun phrases. Finally, any subset (rather than just a pair as in a standard graph) of vertices can be connected via a *hyperedge*, which models concept dependencies.

We use the query hypergraph representation to derive a ranking function that incorporates concepts and concept dependencies in a principled manner, based on the factorization of the hypergraph. We then propose two approaches for the parameterization of the ranking function. The first parameterization approach assigns weights to the concepts and the concept dependencies based on their respective structures. The second parameterization approach assigns weights based on a set of importance features associated with each concept and concept dependency.

The remainder of this paper is organized as follows. First, in Section 2 we provide the theoretical underpinnings of the query hypergraph representation and ranking with query hypergraphs. Then, in Section 3 we describe the related work and its connection to query representation using hypergraphs. In Section 4 we report the details of the empirical evaluation of the proposed framework. Section 5 concludes the paper.

2. QUERY HYPERGRAPHS

2.1 Query Representation with Hypergraphs

In this paper, we base the query representation on two modeling assumptions. First, we assume that given a query Q, we can model it using a set of linguistic structures

$$\Sigma^Q \triangleq \{\boldsymbol{\sigma}_1, \ldots, \boldsymbol{\sigma}_n\}.$$

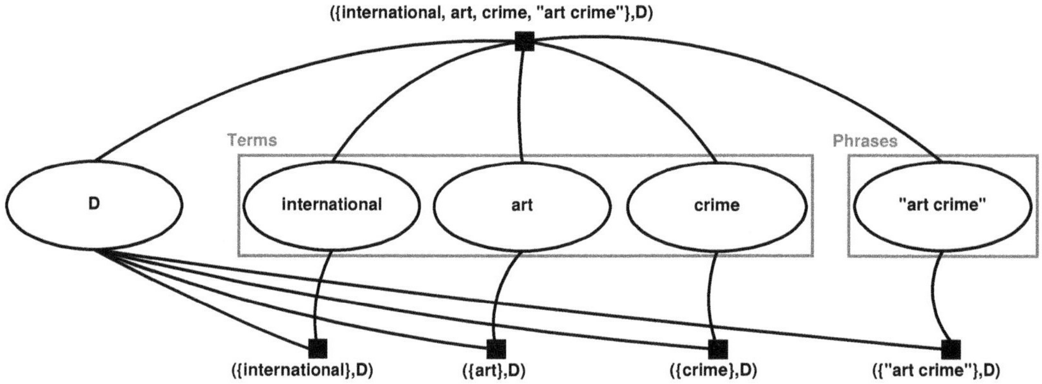

Figure 2: Example of a hypergraph representation for the query "international art crime".

The structures in the set Σ^Q are both *complete* and *disjoint*. The *completeness* of the structure implies that it can be used as an autonomous query representation. The *disjointness* of the structures means that there is no overlap in the linguistic phenomena modeled by the different structures. In other words, each structure groups together concepts of a single type (e.g., terms, bigrams, noun phrases, etc.).

Second, within each structure, arbitrary term dependencies can be modeled as concepts. In other words, each structure $\boldsymbol{\sigma}_i \in \Sigma^Q$ is represented by a set of concepts

$$\boldsymbol{\sigma}_i \triangleq \{\kappa_i^1, \kappa_i^2, \ldots\}.$$

Each such concept is considered to be an atomic unit for the purpose of query representation. In addition, for convenience, we adopt the notation

$$\mathcal{K}^Q \triangleq \bigcup_{i=1}^{n} \boldsymbol{\sigma}_i,$$

to refer to the union of all the query concepts, regardless of their respective structures.

These modeling assumptions, while conceptually simple, create an expressive formalism for hierarchical query representation. This formalism is flexible enough to specify a wide range of specific instantiations. Table 1 shows that it can model a wide spectrum of linguistic phenomena that are often encountered in natural language processing and information retrieval applications.

For instance, as we can see in Table 1, a structure can contain single terms as concepts, resulting in a bag-of-words query representation. A structure can also contain adjacent bigrams or noun phrases. Concepts need not be defined over contiguous query terms, as is demonstrated by the last structure in Table 1, which models a set of linguistic dependency links between the query terms.

For the purpose of information retrieval, we are primarily interested in using the resulting hierarchical query representation to model the relationship between a query Q and a document D in the retrieval corpus. Specifically, given a set of query structures Σ^Q and a document D, we construct a hypergraph $H(\Sigma^Q, D)$[3].

A *hypergraph* is a generalization of a graph where an edge can connect an arbitrary set of vertices. A hypergraph H is represented by a tuple $\langle V, E\rangle$, where V is a set of elements or *vertices* and E is a set of non-empty subsets of V, called *hyperedges*. In other words, the set $E \subseteq \mathcal{PS}(V)$ of hyperedges is a subset of the powerset of V [18].

Specifically for the scenario of document retrieval, we define the hypergraph H over the document D and the set of query concepts $\mathcal{K}^Q$ as

$$\begin{aligned} V &\triangleq \mathcal{K}^Q \cup \{D\} \\ E &\triangleq \{(\mathbf{k}, D) \colon \mathbf{k} \in \mathcal{PS}(\mathcal{K}^Q)\}. \end{aligned} \quad (1)$$

Figure 2 demonstrates an example of a hypergraph H for the search query "international art crime". In this particular example, we have two structures. The first structure contains the query terms denoted i, a, and c, respectively. The second structure contains a single phrase, ac. Over these concepts, we can define a set of five hyperedges – four hyperedges connecting document D and *each of* the concepts, and one hyperedge connecting D and *all of* the concepts.

Formally, for the hypergarph H in Figure 2, the vertices and the hyperedges are defined as follows

$$\begin{aligned} V_{\text{Fig.2}} &= \{D, i, a, c, ac\} \\ E_{\text{Fig.2}} &= \{(\{i\}, D), (\{a\}, D), (\{c\}, D), \\ &\quad (\{ac\}, D), (\{i, a, c, ac\}, D)\}. \end{aligned}$$

Note that this hypergraph configuration is just one possible choice. In fact, any subset of query terms can serve as a query concept, and similarly, any subset of query concepts can serve as a hyperedge, as shown by Equation 1.

2.2 Ranking with Query Hypergraphs

In the previous section, we defined the query representation using a hypergraph $H = \langle V, E\rangle$. In this section, we define a global function over this hypergraph, which assigns a *relevance score* to document D in response to query Q. This relevance score is used to rank the documents in the retrieval corpus.

A factor graph, a form of hypergraph representation which is often used in statistical machine learning [6], associates a factor ϕ_e with a hyperedge $e \in E$. Therefore, most generally, a relevance score of document D in response to query Q represented by a hypergraph H is given by

$$sc(Q, D) \triangleq \prod_{e \in E} \phi_e(\mathbf{k}_e, D) \overset{rank}{=} \sum_{e \in E} \log(\phi_e(\mathbf{k}_e, D)). \quad (2)$$

[3] For conciseness, we use the abbreviation $H \triangleq H(\Sigma^Q, D)$ in the remainder of this paper.

It is interesting to note that Equation 2 is reminiscent of the recently proposed log-linear retrieval models, including the Markov random field model [27] and the linear discriminant model [14]. Similarly to these models, Equation 2 scores a document using a log-linear combination of factors $\phi_e(\mathbf{k}_e, D)$.

However, an important difference from these retrieval models is related to the fact that the factors $\phi_e(\mathbf{k}_e, D)$ in Equation 2 are defined over *concept sets*, rather than *single concepts*, as in previous work [14, 27]. This definition enables the modeling of higher-order dependencies between query terms. Higher-order term dependencies cannot be easily modeled by the existing retrieval models that incorporate term dependencies [4, 14, 26, 27, 30, 39].

Thus far, we have provided only the most abstract definition of the query representation and ranking with query hypergraphs. In the remainder of this section, we provide an in-depth discussion of the query hypergraph induction and a detailed derivation of the ranking function.

First, in Section 2.3, we fully specify the structures, concepts, and hyperedges in the query hypergraph H. Then, in Section 2.4, we instantiate the factors $\phi_e(\mathbf{k}_e, D)$ in the ranking function in Equation 2 using these specifications. Finally, in Section 2.5, we examine the different parameterizations of the ranking function.

2.3 Query Hypergraph Induction

2.3.1 Hypergraph Structures

There are many potential ways in which we could define the set of structures Σ^Q in the query hypergraph. In this work, we focus on three types of structures that are successfully used in previous work on modeling term dependencies for information retrieval [4, 5, 27, 32]. We leave a further exploration of other possible hypergraph structures to future work.

(1) *QT-structure.* The query term (QT) structure contains the individual query words t_i as concepts. Terms are the most commonly used concepts in information retrieval, both in bag-of-words models [33, 34] and models that incorporate term dependencies [27, 29, 14].

(2) *PH-structure.* The phrase (PH) structure contains the combinations of query terms that are matched as *exact phrases* in the document. Exact phrase matching has often been used for improving the performance of retrieval methods [12, 42]. Most recently, it has been shown that using query bigrams for exact phrase matching is a simple and efficient method for improving the retrieval performance in large scale web collections [4, 5, 27, 29, 32]. Following this finding, we define the concepts in the PH-structure as adjacent query word pairs $(t_i t_{i+1})$.

(3) *PR-structure.* Unlike the PH-structure, the proximity (PR) structure can contain arbitrary subsets of query terms of the form $\{t\colon t \in Q\}$ as concepts. The PR-structure also differs from the PH-structure in the way the concepts in the structure are matched in the document. In order to match the document, the individual terms in a concept in the PR-structure may occur in *any order* within a *window of fixed length.* In this paper, we fix the window size to $4|t|$ terms, where $|t|$ is the number of terms in the concept. This approach follows the definition of term proximity as defined by Metzler and Croft [27].

2.3.2 Hyperedges

As described in Section 2.1, a naïve induction approach may result in an exponential number of hyperedges in a query hypergraph. Instead, for the purpose of this paper, we limit our attention to two types of hyperedges, which have an intuitive appeal from an information retrieval perspective.

(1) *Local hyperedges.* For each concept $\kappa \in \mathcal{K}^Q$, we define a hyperedge $(\{\kappa\}, D)$. This local edge[4] represents the contribution of the concept κ to the total document relevance score, regardless of the other query concepts. As we show in the next section, the factors defined over the local edges are akin to the functions that are usually employed in the existing log-linear retrieval models [14, 27].

(2) *Global hyperedge.* In addition to the local edges, we define a *single* global hyperedge $(\mathcal{K}^Q, D)$ over the entire set of query concepts $\mathcal{K}^Q$. This global hyperedge provides the evidence about the contribution of each concept $\kappa \in \mathcal{K}^Q$ given its dependency on the entire set of query concepts $\mathcal{K}^Q$. Unlike in the case of local edges, the factors defined over the global hyperedge cannot be easily expressed using the existing log-linear retrieval models.

Figure 2 provides a simple example of these two types of hyperedges. The hyperedges at the bottom of the hypergraph in Figure 2 are the local edges, while the hyperedge at the top is the global hyperedge.

2.4 Factors $\phi_e(\mathbf{k}_e, D)$

Following the hyperedge induction process described in Section 2.3.2, in this section we define two types of factors. The local factors – corresponding to the local edges – are defined in Section 2.4.1; the global factor – corresponding to the global hyperedge – is defined in Section 2.4.2.

Both local and global factors incorporate a *matching function* $f(\kappa, X)$, which assigns a score to the occurrences of the concept κ in a text fragment X. As a matching function, following some previous work on log-linear retrieval models [4, 14, 27], we use a log of the language modeling estimate for concept κ with Dirichlet smoothing [45], i.e.

$$f(\kappa, X) \triangleq \log \frac{tf(\kappa, X) + \mu \frac{tf(\kappa, \mathcal{C})}{|\mathcal{C}|}}{\mu + |X|}, \tag{3}$$

where $tf(\kappa, X)$ and $tf(\kappa, \mathcal{C})$ are the number of occurrences of the concept κ in the text fragment and the collection, respectively; μ is a free parameter; $|X|$ is the number of terms in X, and $|\mathcal{C}|$ is the total number of terms in the collection.

2.4.1 Local Factors

The local factors are defined over the local edges $(\{\kappa\}, D)$. A local factor assigns a score to the occurrences of concept κ in the document D, regardless of the other query concepts. Therefore, a local factor is defined similarly to the previously proposed log-linear retrieval models [4, 14, 27]

$$\phi(\{\kappa\}, D) \triangleq \exp\Big(\lambda(\kappa) f(\kappa, D)\Big), \tag{4}$$

[4]From now on, we refer to the local hyperedges simply as *edges*, since they are defined over a vertex pair, rather than an arbitrary set of vertices.

where $\lambda(\kappa)$ is an importance weight assigned to the concept κ, and $f(\kappa, D)$ is a matching function between the concept κ and the document D.

2.4.2 The Global Factor

The global hyperedge $(\mathcal{K}^Q, D)$ described in Section 2.3.2, represents a dependency between the entire set of query concepts. In this section, we present a global factor that is defined over this hyperedge.

A common way to estimate a dependency between query terms is using a measure of their proximity in a retrieved document [11, 26, 27, 39]. Analogously, we may simply choose to estimate a dependency between query concepts using similar proximity measures. However, there are two notable difficulties that impede an application of this approach to concept dependency.

First, the existing term proximity measures usually capture close, sentence-level, co-occurrences of the query terms in a retrieved document [27, 32, 39]. The dependency range is much longer for concept dependencies. For instance, in the example in Figure 1(b), the concepts *dog* and *law enforcement* do not ever appear in the same sentence. However, the dependency between them is revealed when examining their co-occurrences in a larger text passage.

Second, since concepts can be arbitrarily complex syntactic expressions, the probability of observing a *concept co-occurrence* is much lower than the probability of observing a *term co-occurrence*, even in large collections. For instance, most documents in the retrieved list for the query in Figure 1, do not contain both of the concepts *dog* and *law enforcement* in a context of a single passage.

Therefore, instead of estimating the dependency between query concepts using the standard proximity measures, we leverage a long history of research on passage retrieval [3, 8, 9, 25, 16, 40, 41] for the derivation of the global factor.

In the passage retrieval literature, a document is often segmented into overlapping passages of text of fixed size [16, 17]. The document is then scored using some combination of document-level and passage-level scores. One of the most successful and frequently-used score combinations is the **Max-Psg** combination, which uses the highest scoring passage to assign a score to the document [3, 8, 16, 24, 41].

Similarly to the **Max-Psg** retrieval model, we define the global factor using a passage π, which receives the highest score among the set Π_D of passages extracted from the document D. Formally,

$$\phi(\mathcal{K}^Q, D) \triangleq \exp\Big(\max_{\pi \in \Pi_D} \sum_{\kappa \in \mathcal{K}^Q} \lambda(\kappa, \mathcal{K}^Q) f(\kappa, \pi)\Big), \quad (5)$$

where $\lambda(\kappa, \mathcal{K}^Q)$ is the importance weight of the concept κ in the context of the entire set of query concepts $\mathcal{K}^Q$, and $f(\kappa,\pi)$ is a matching function between the concept κ and a passage $\pi \in \Pi_D$.

Intuitively, the global factor in Equation 5 assigns a higher relevance score to a document that contains many important concepts in the confines of a single passage. Note that the importance weight $\lambda(\kappa, \mathcal{K}^Q)$ of a concept in the global factor is determined not only by the concept itself – as in the case of the importance weights $\lambda(\kappa, D)$ in the local factors – but also by the concepts that co-occur together with the concept in the passage π.

Feature	Description
GF(κ)	Frequency of κ in Google n-grams
WF(κ)	Frequency of κ in Wikipedia titles
QF(κ)	Frequency of κ in a search log
CF(κ)	Frequency of κ in the collection
DF(κ)	Document frequency of κ in the collection
AP(κ)	A priori constant weight (=1)

Table 2: Concept importance features Φ.

2.5 Query Hypergraph Parameterization

In the previous section, we introduced two types of concept weights that parameterize the ranking function in Equation 2. First, there are the independent importance weights $\lambda(\kappa)$ that parameterize the local factors (see Equation 4). Second, there are the importance weights $\lambda(\kappa, \mathcal{K}^Q)$ that assign weight to a concept, while taking into account the rest of the concepts in the query (see Equation 5).

In this section, we consider two possible parameterization schemes for these concept weights. In Section 2.5.1, we consider parameterization by structure. Conversely, in Section 2.5.2, we examine parameterization by concept.

2.5.1 Parameterization By Structure

A simple way to parameterize the importance weights $\lambda(\kappa)$ and $\lambda(\kappa, \mathcal{K}^Q)$, is to make the assumption that the weights of all the concepts in the same structure are tied. Formally:

$$\begin{aligned} \forall \kappa_i, \kappa_j \in \boldsymbol{\sigma} &: \lambda(\kappa_i) = \lambda(\kappa_j) = \lambda(\boldsymbol{\sigma}) \\ \forall \kappa_i, \kappa_j \in \boldsymbol{\sigma} &: \lambda(\kappa_i, \mathcal{K}^Q) = \lambda(\kappa_j, \mathcal{K}^Q) = \lambda(\boldsymbol{\sigma}, \Sigma^Q) \end{aligned}$$

This assumption has the benefit of significantly reducing the number of free parameters in the retrieval model, thereby greatly simplifying the estimation process. Due to its simplicity, parameterization by structure is often used in the log-linear retrieval models [14, 27, 32].

Using parameterization by structure and the definitions of local and global factors in Section 2.4, we can explicitly rewrite the ranking function in Equation 2 as

$$\begin{aligned} sc(Q, D) &= \sum_{\boldsymbol{\sigma} \in \Sigma^Q} \lambda(\boldsymbol{\sigma}) \sum_{\kappa \in \boldsymbol{\sigma}} f(\kappa, D) + \\ &+ \max_{\pi \in \Pi_D} \sum_{\boldsymbol{\sigma} \in \Sigma^Q} \lambda(\boldsymbol{\sigma}, \Sigma^Q) \sum_{\kappa \in \boldsymbol{\sigma}} f(\kappa, \pi). \end{aligned} \quad (6)$$

2.5.2 Parameterization By Concept

The main drawback of parameterization by structure is the fact that it implies that all the concepts in the same structure are equally important for expressing the query intent. This implication is not always true, especially for more verbose, natural language queries, which may benefit from assigning varying concept weights [2, 4, 22].

Therefore, we may wish to remove the restriction imposed in the previous section, and parameterize the concept weights based on the concepts themselves rather than their respective structures. Assigning a single weight to each concept is clearly infeasible, since the number of concepts is exponential in the size of the vocabulary. Therefore, we take a parameterization approach proposed in recent work on query modeling [2, 4, 5, 22, 35, 38], and represent each concept using a combination of *importance features*, Φ, described in Table 2. These importance features are based on concept frequencies, and can be efficiently computed and cached, even for large-scale collections.

Using these importance features, we can explicitly rewrite the ranking function in Equation 2 as

$$sc(Q,D) = \sum_{\sigma\in\Sigma^Q}\sum_{\varphi\in\Phi}\lambda(\varphi,\sigma)\sum_{\kappa\in\sigma}\varphi(\kappa)f(\kappa,D) + \max_{\pi\in\Pi_D}\sum_{\sigma\in\Sigma^Q}\sum_{\varphi\in\Phi}\lambda(\varphi,\sigma,\Sigma^Q)\sum_{\kappa\in\sigma}\varphi(\kappa)f(\kappa,\pi). \quad (7)$$

2.5.3 *Parameter Estimation*

To estimate the free parameters $\lambda(\cdot)$ in Equation 6 and Equation 7, we rely on a large and growing body of literature on the learning to rank methods for information retrieval (see Liu [23] for a survey). As a base algorithm for parameter optimization we make use of the coordinate ascent (CA) algorithm proposed by Metzler and Croft [28].

The CA algorithm iteratively optimizes a target metric (in our case, retrieval metric such as MAP) by performing a series of one-dimensional line searches. It repeatedly cycles through each of the parameters $\lambda(\cdot)$, while holding all other parameters fixed. This process is performed iteratively over all parameters until the gain in the target metric is below a certain threshold.

We use the CA algorithm primarily for its simplicity, efficiency and effectiveness, as demonstrated by the previous work [4, 5, 27]. However, any other learning to rank approach that estimates the parameters for linear models such as RankSVM [15] or RankNet [7] can be adopted as well.

To ensure the scalability of our retrieval model, we compute the global factor (Equation 5) only for the top thousand documents retrieved by the local factors (Equation 4). Therefore, the setting of the importance weights $\lambda(\kappa)$ will affect the document ranking, which, in turn, will affect the choice of the highest-scoring passages and subsequently the setting of the importance weights $\lambda(\kappa, \mathcal{K}^Q)$.

Accordingly, we perform the optimization in two stages. We decompose $sc(Q, D)$ into its *local* and *global* components. First, we optimize the local component (i.e., the weights $\lambda(\kappa)$). Then, we fix the weights of the local component, and optimize the global component (i.e., the weights $\lambda(\kappa, \mathcal{K}^Q)$). Each of these optimizations is done using the standard CA algorithm.

3. RELATED WORK

In this paper we describe a general retrieval framework that models dependencies between arbitrary query concepts using a query hypergraph. It is important, therefore, to examine the connections between some of the well known retrieval models and query hypergraphs.

3.1 Bag-of-Words Models

As Zobel and Mofat [46] point out, the majority of the standard bag-of-words models in IR can be generally expressed by the following summation:

$$sc(Q,D) \triangleq \sum_{t\in Q}\lambda(t,Q)f(t,D),$$

where $\lambda(t, Q)$ and $f(t, D)$ are some arbitrary functions (which may include normalization constants) defined over a query term t and its occurrences in the query and the document, respectively. Examples of such models include, among others, the query likelihood model [33], BM25 [34] and divergence from randomness [1].

Therefore, it is easy to show that all of these bag-of-words models can be straightforwardly modeled using a query hypergraph. To induce such a hypergraph, we simply need to define a single QT-structure $\boldsymbol{\sigma}_t = \{t_1, t_2, \ldots\}$, and a set of local edges

$$E = \{(t, D) : t \in \boldsymbol{\sigma}_t\}.$$

3.2 Passage Retrieval

There is a long history of passage-based retrieval models in information retrieval [3, 8, 9, 16, 41, 40, 24]. These retrieval models are typically defined using vector space models [9, 16, 17] or language models [2, 24, 40], and employ a simple bag-of-words query representation. One of the most common passage retrieval techniques is Max-Psg, which uses the passage with the highest score for document score derivation [3, 8, 16, 24, 41].

Max-Psg with the bag-of-words query representation is a special case of the general query hypergraph described in this paper. Our model combines the recent advances in retrieval models that go beyond the bag-of-words query representations with passage retrieval models.

In addition, it is important to mention some recent work on query expansion [21] and query reformulation [43] using passage-based evidence, which uses hierarchical graphical representation of the query, similar to the one presented in this paper. This work is orthogonal to ours, as it uses passage evidence to augment the query with new concepts, rather than to model the query and the retrieval function. Combining this work on query expansion and reformulation with the retrieval models based on query hypergraphs is a promising direction for future work.

3.3 Term Dependencies

The advent of large-scale web corpora encouraged the development of retrieval models that employ phrases and proximity matches to model term dependencies [27, 29, 39, 14, 26, 32]. Most of these retrieval models take a log-linear form, and can be modeled using a query hypergraph with the structures described in Section 2.3.1, but *without* the inclusion of the global hyperedege.

Retrieval models that employ term dependencies usually resort to parameterization by structure [27, 14, 39, 32] (as described in Section 2.5.1). While this assumption significantly reduces the number of the free parameters in the retrieval model, it may be detrimental to the performance of verbose natural language queries that may contain concepts of variable importance.

Recently, researchers started to examine retrieval models that employ parameterization by concept. To avoid learning a separate weight for each concept, these models represent a concept using a set of features [4, 5, 22, 35, 38]. This approach significantly outperforms parameterization by structure, especially for verbose natural language queries. Accordingly, we also employ parameterization by concept in the retrieval with query hypergraphs (see Section 2.5.2).

3.4 Higher-Order Term Dependencies

To the best of our knowledge, there is very little prior work on retrieval with higher-order term dependencies (i.e., dependencies between arbitrary concepts rather than terms). One notable exception is an early work on generalized term dependencies by Yu et al. [44], which derives higher-order dependencies from pairwise term dependencies. However, the model proposed by Yu et al. [44] is infeasible for large-scale collections, since it requires an explicit computation of the probability of relevance for each individual query term, as well as pairs and triples of query terms.

A more recent retrieval model that attempts to incorporate higher-order term dependencies is the Full Dependence (`FD`) variant of the Markov random field model proposed by Metzler and Croft [27]. The `FD` model, however, is only able to capture dependencies between multiple terms, rather than multiple concepts. For instance, it can model a dependency between the terms in the triple *(dog, law, enforcement)*, but it cannot model a dependency between the pair of concepts *(dog, "law enforcement")*.

4. EVALUATION

4.1 Experimental Setup

All the empirical evaluation described in this section is implemented using Indri, an open-source search engine [37]. The structured query language implemented in Indri natively supports multiple types of concepts, including exact phrases and proximity matches, as well as customizable concept weighting schemes. As a result, Indri provides a flexible and convenient platform for evaluating the retrieval performance of query hypergraphs.

Table 4 presents a summary of the TREC corpora used in our experiments. The corpora vary both by type (*Robust04* is a newswire collection, *Gov2* is a crawl of the .gov domain, and *ClueWeb-B* is a set of pages with the highest crawl priority derived from a large web corpus), number of documents, and number of available topics, thereby providing a diverse experimental setup for assessing the robustness of retrieval with query hypergraphs.

Name	# Docs	Topic Numbers
Robust04	528,155	301-450, 601-700
Gov2	25,205,179	701-850
ClueWeb-B	50,220,423	1-100

Table 4: Summary of the TREC collections and topics used for evaluation.

For the *Robust04* and *Gov2* collections, a standard Porter stemmer is used. In contrast, the *ClueWeb-B* collection is stemmed using the Krovetz stemmer, which is a "light" stemmer, as it makes use of inflectional linguistic morphology [19] and is especially suitable for web collections where aggressive stemming can decrease precision at top ranks [31]. Stopword removal is performed on both documents and queries using the standard INQUERY stopword list. The free parameter μ in the concept matching function $f(\kappa, X)$ (see Equation 3) is set according to the default Indri configuration of the Dirichlet smoothing parameter.

Since query hypergraphs attempt to capture complex dependencies between query concepts, we apply them to the *description* portions of the TREC topics. TREC topic descriptions express the information needs behind the topics using verbose natural language queries. For instance, a description portion of the TREC topic entitled "hydrogen energy" is a question "What is the status of research on hydrogen as a feasible energy source?". As shown by previous work, these queries are more likely to benefit from complex representation and weighting schemes than their keyword counterparts [2, 20, 22].

In order to compute the global factor (Equation 5), we segment each document into semi-overlapping passages of 150 words (i.e., the overlap between the passages is 75 words). As shown in previous work on passage retrieval [3, 9, 8, 16], this passage configuration leads to improved effectiveness on most TREC collections.

The optimization of the free parameters for all the baselines and the proposed retrieval methods is done using three-fold cross-validation with mean average precision (MAP) as the target metric. In addition to MAP, we also report ERR@20, an early precision metric that was adopted as the official retrieval performance metric at the TREC 2010 Web Track [10]. The statistical significance of differences in the performance of the proposed retrieval methods with respect to their respective baselines is determined using a two-sided Fisher's randomization test [36] with 25,000 permutations and $\alpha < 0.05$.

4.2 Retrieval Performance Evaluation

In this section, we compare the performance of the retrieval with query hypergraphs to a number of state-of-the-art baselines that incorporate exact phrase matches, proximities, and concept weight parameterization. These baselines do not, however, incorporate concept dependencies.

The query hypergraph representation, proposed in this paper, further extends each of these baselines with higher-order term dependencies via the inclusion of the global hyperedge and the corresponding global factor $\phi(\mathcal{K}^Q, D)$ (see Equation 5). In the remainder of this section, we examine the improvements in the retrieval performance (or lack thereof) of these baselines when they are extended with the query hypergraph representation.

4.2.1 Query Likelihood Baseline

Query likelihood [33] is a popular retrieval method that employs a bag-of-words query representation. In this section, we juxtapose the retrieval performance of the query likelihood baseline (denoted `QL`) to the performance of a query hypergraph that includes a single `QT`-structure (structure that contains the individual query terms as concepts). We denote this hypergraph representation $\mathcal{H}$-`QL`. This juxtaposition demonstrates the contribution of the global factor $\phi(\mathcal{K}^Q, D)$ (see Equation 5) to the retrieval performance.

Table 3(a) shows the comparison between the `QL` and the $\mathcal{H}$-`QL` methods. The results in Table 3(a) demonstrate that the addition of the global factor $\phi(\mathcal{K}^Q, D)$ into a bag-of-words representation significantly improves its retrieval effectiveness in all the cases.

Note that the $\mathcal{H}$-`QL` method is equivalent to the `Max-Psg` method proposed in the previous work [3, 8, 9, 16, 41], which ranks the documents in the collection by a combination of the document score and the score of its highest-scoring passage. The improvements in retrieval performance shown in Table 3(a) are in line with the improvements attained by the `Max-Psg` method reported in this previous work.

4.2.2 Markov Random Fields Baselines

Markov random fields for information retrieval (MRF-IR) is a state-of-the-art retrieval framework that incorporates

	Robust04		*Gov2*		*ClueWeb-B*	
	ERR@20	**MAP**	**ERR@20**	**MAP**	**ERR@20**	**MAP**
QL	11.44	24.24	15.06	25.66	7.32	12.75
$\mathcal{H}$-QL	**11.66**	**25.49**$_q$ *(+5.2%)*	**15.33**	**27.24**$_q$ *(+6.2%)*	**7.63**	**13.07**$_q$ *(+2.5%)*

(a) Query likelihood (QL) and its hypergraph representation ($\mathcal{H}$-QL).

	Robust04		*Gov2*		*ClueWeb-B*	
	ERR@20	**MAP**	**ERR@20**	**MAP**	**ERR@20**	**MAP**
SD	11.76	25.62	15.73	27.97	7.58	12.99
$\mathcal{H}$-SD	**11.93**	**26.65**$_s$ *(+4.0%)*	**15.93**	**28.63**$_s$ *(+2.4%)*	**7.78**	**13.08** *(+0.7%)*

(b) Sequential dependence model (SD) and its hypergraph representation ($\mathcal{H}$-SD) parameterized by structure.

	Robust04		*Gov2*		*ClueWeb-B*	
	ERR@20	**MAP**	**ERR@20**	**MAP**	**ERR@20**	**MAP**
FD	11.87	25.69	**16.10**	28.25	**8.21**	13.28
$\mathcal{H}$-FD	**11.94**	**26.50**$_f$ *(+3.1%)*	16.02	**28.70**$_f$ *(+1.6%)*	8.15	**13.35** *(+0.5%)*

(c) Full dependence model (FD) and its hypergraph representation ($\mathcal{H}$-FD) parameterized by structure.

	Robust04		*Gov2*		*ClueWeb-B*	
	ERR@20	**MAP**	**ERR@20**	**MAP**	**ERR@20**	**MAP**
WSD	12.04	27.41	16.52	29.36	**8.58**	14.56
$\mathcal{H}$-WSD	**12.34**$_w$	**27.79**$_w$ *(+1.4%)*	**16.56**	**29.82**$_w$ *(+1.6%)*	8.31	**14.68** *(+0.8%)*

(d) Weighted sequential dependence model (WSD) and its hypergraph representation ($\mathcal{H}$-WSD) parameterized by concept.

Table 3: Evaluation of the performance of the retrieval with query hypergraphs. Best result per column is marked in boldface. Statistically significant differences with a non-hypergraph baseline are marked by the first letter in its title. The numbers in the parentheses indicate the percentage of improvement in MAP over the baseline.

term dependencies. It was first proposed by Metzler and Croft [27], and was shown to be highly effective, especially for large-scale web collections.

Metzler and Croft propose two instantiations of the general MRF-IR framework. The first instantiation is the sequential dependence model (denoted SD), which incorporates only dependencies between adjacent query terms. The second instantiation is the full dependence model (FD), which incorporates dependencies between all query term subsets[5].

The SD and FD baselines can be extended with a respective hypergraph that includes three structures: QT, PR and PH (refer to Section 2.3.1 for the exact definitions of these structures). We denote these hypergraph representations $\mathcal{H}$-SD and $\mathcal{H}$-FD, respectively. These hypergraphs are parameterized by structure, and their ranking functions are derived according to Equation 6.

Table 3(b) compares the performance of the sequential dependence baseline (SD) and its corresponding hypergraph $\mathcal{H}$-SD. As evident from Table 3(b), in most cases (except for the *ClueWeb-B* collection) the retrieval effectiveness (in terms of MAP) is significantly improved by the hypergraph extension. However, these improvements are smaller than in the case of the QL baseline.

Similarly, Table 3(c) compares the performance of the full dependence baseline (FD) and its corresponding hypergraph $\mathcal{H}$-FD. Comparing Table 3(b) and Table 3(c), we can see that in most cases the FD baseline slightly outperforms the SD baseline. However, these differences were not found to be statistically significant.

When comparing the performance of the FD baseline and its corresponding hypergraph $\mathcal{H}$-FD, Table 3(c) demonstrates that the inclusion of the global factor results in an improved retrieval effectiveness (in terms of MAP) for all collections, and in statistically significant improvements for the *Robust04* and *Gov2* collections.

In addition, we can compare between the retrieval performance of the hypergraphs $\mathcal{H}$-SD and $\mathcal{H}$-FD. Similarly to the case of the baselines SD and FD, no statistically significant differences were found in the performance of these hypergraphs. $\mathcal{H}$-FD is slightly more effective for the *ClueWeb-B* and the *Gov2* collections, while being slightly less effective for the *Robust04* collection.

4.2.3 Weighted Sequential Dependence Model

A major drawback of the SD and the FD baselines is that they use the parameterization-by-structure approach (see Section 2.5.1), which ties the importance weights $\lambda(\cdot)$ of all the concepts that belong to the same structure (i.e., all the terms, phrases and proximities get the same respective weights). This parameterization can be detrimental, especially for longer, more verbose queries that may mix concepts of differing importance.

Recently, Bendersky et al. [4] proposed a weighted variant of the sequential dependence mode (denoted WSD) that overcomes this drawback. The concept weights in the WSD method are parameterized using a set of importance features, associated with each concept based on its respective structure, as described in Section 2.5.2.

We extend the WSD baseline with a query hypergraph $\mathcal{H}$-WSD. The $\mathcal{H}$-WSD includes the global factor $\phi(\mathcal{K}^Q, D)$, which is also parameterized by concept. The ranking function for the $\mathcal{H}$-WSD hypergraph is presented in Equation 7.

Table 3(d) compares the retrieval performance of the WSD baseline and its corresponding hypergraph $\mathcal{H}$-WSD. While the retrieval improvements that stem from this hypergraph extensions are not as pronounced as in the cases of the QL, SD

[5]Due to the verbosity of the description queries, in this paper, we limit our evaluation to query term subsets with at most three terms.

and FD baselines, the addition of the global factor to the WSD baseline still results in effectiveness gains for all the collections and most of the metrics. For instance, for the *Gov2* collection, the $\mathcal{H}$-WSD method improves the performance (in terms of MAP) for 60% of the queries compared to the WSD baseline, while hurting only 30% of the queries. For 7% of the queries MAP is improved by more than 25%, while there is a 25% drop in performance for only 2% of the queries.

4.2.4 Further Analysis

In addition to comparing each individual query hypergraph model to its respective baseline, some general trends can be observed in Table 3. First, it is interesting to compare the relative differences in gains across the baselines, when the global factor is added. The gains are the largest for the QL baseline, which does not include any term dependencies, and decrease as more term dependencies are added by the SD and the FD baselines. As an example, for the *Gov2* collection, the effectiveness gain as a result of the global factor inclusion decreases from 6.2% for the QL baseline to 1.6% for the FD baseline.

These diminishing returns demonstrate that there is some degree of overlap between the effect of term dependencies and higher-order term dependencies on the retrieval effectiveness. The overlap is not complete, however, since the addition of the global factor still has a statistically significant impact on the retrieval performance in most cases. This is true even for the FD baseline, which includes term dependencies between all query term pairs and triples.

Finally, we note that the parameterization of the ranking function by concept (as in the WSD baseline) (a) significantly improves the retrieval performance of the ranking function parameterized by structure (as in the SD baseline), and (b) further diminishes the gains obtained through the inclusion of the global factor. While $\mathcal{H}$-WSD is the best-performing retrieval method (in terms of MAP) in Table 3, its average effectiveness gain over the WSD baseline is only 1.3%. For comparison, the average effectiveness gain of the $\mathcal{H}$-QL method over the QL baseline is 4.7%.

4.3 Parameterization Analysis

In this section we analyze the parameterization of the query hypergraph. We examine both parameterization-by-structure and parameterization-by-concept regimes, which are described in detail in Section 2.5.1 and Section 2.5.2, respectively.

Recall that the parameters of the query hypergraph are optimized using the coordinate ascent algorithm such that the ranking function is decomposed into local and global factors (see Section 2.5.3). In this section, due to the space constraints, we focus our attention on the resulting parameterization for the *Robust04* collection. We choose this collection, since it has the largest number of queries, and the learned parameterization is stable across all folds. However, it is important to note that the findings in this section hold for the other two collections as well.

4.3.1 Parameterization by Structure

Table 5 shows the hypergraph parameters for the local factors ($\lambda(\boldsymbol{\sigma})$) and the global factor ($\lambda(\boldsymbol{\sigma}, \Sigma^Q)$), averaged across folds, when the parameterization-by-structure approach is used (see Equation 6). These parameters correspond to the $\mathcal{H}$-SD model, the results for which are shown in Table 3(b).

	$\lambda(\boldsymbol{\sigma})$	$\lambda(\boldsymbol{\sigma}, \Sigma^Q)$
QT	+0.520	+0.322
PH	+0.065	+0.017
PR	+0.065	−0.011

Table 5: Query hypergraph parameterization by structure (*Robust04* collection).

	$\lambda(\varphi, \boldsymbol{\sigma})$		$\lambda(\varphi, \boldsymbol{\sigma}, \Sigma^Q)$	
φ	QT	PR+PH	QT	PR+PH
GF	−0.007	0	−0.005	−0.001
WF	+0.017	+0.007	+0.002	+0.002
QF	+0.012	0	+0.007	+0.008
CF	−0.021	0	−0.008	0
DF	−0.018	0	−0.001	0
AP	+0.540	+0.029	+0.298	+0.003

Table 6: Query hypergraph parameterization by concept (*Robust04* collection).

Note that both for the local and the global factors the weights assigned to the term structure (QT) are the highest, which is in line with other models that incorporate term dependencies [27]. This demonstrates that despite the importance of term dependencies, individual term occurrences are still the most important indicators of relevance.

In addition, in Table 5, the parameters of the local factors are weighted higher than the parameters of the global factor. Recall that the global factor is defined over the highest-scoring passage in the document. Thus, the lower weight of the global factor parameters is in line with previous work, where passage evidence is typically weighted lower than the document evidence [3, 41, 16].

Finally, note the *negative* weight assigned to the proximity (PR) structure in the global factor. While small, this negative weight is consistent across folds, as well as in the other collections. Intuitively, this negative weight indicates that in the highest-scoring passage of the relevant document we expect to encounter exact phrase concepts, rather than unordered proximity concepts.

4.3.2 Parameterization by Concept

Table 6 shows the hypergraph parameters for the local factors ($\lambda(\varphi, \boldsymbol{\sigma})$) and the global factor ($\lambda(\varphi, \boldsymbol{\sigma}, \Sigma^Q)$), averaged across folds, when the parameterization-by-concept approach is used (see Equation 7). These parameters correspond to the $\mathcal{H}$-WSD model, the results for which are shown in Table 3(d). For the convenience of presentation and to reduce weight sparsity, we combine the weights of the PH and PR structures in the PR+PH column.

Note that a priory constant importance feature AP generally receives the highest weight. This is due to the fact that setting all the other feature weights to zero yields exactly the parameterization-by-structure approach.

Features such as document frequency (DF), collection frequency (CF) and Google frequency (GF) receive, as expected, negative weights in most cases. In contrast, the query frequency (QF) and the Wikipedia title frequency (WF) features get positive weights, which indicates that the appearance of the concept in page title or in a search query is positively correlated to the concept importance.

5. CONCLUSIONS

The retrieval framework proposed in this paper represents a query by means of a hypergraph. In the query hypergraph, each vertex corresponds to a concept, and these concepts are grouped into disjoint structures. A hyperedge in the query hypergraph represents a concept dependency. We describe a principled derivation of a ranking function based on the factorization of the query hypergraph. We then propose two parameterization regimes for the derived ranking function, based on either structures or concepts.

The proposed retrieval framework exhibits three important characteristics. First, it models term dependencies as concepts. Second, it models dependencies between these concepts (i.e., higher-order term dependencies). Finally, it assigns weights to concepts and concept dependencies, proportionate to their importance for expressing the query intent. For verbose natural queries, the proposed retrieval framework significantly improves the retrieval effectiveness of several state-of-the-art retrieval methods that do not incorporate higher-order term dependencies.

6. ACKNOWLEDGMENTS

This work was supported in part by the Center for Intelligent Information Retrieval and in part by ARRA NSF IIS-9014442. Any opinions, findings and conclusions or recommendations expressed in this material are those of the authors and do not necessarily reflect those of the sponsor.

7. REFERENCES

[1] G. Amati and C. J. Van Rijsbergen. Probabilistic models of information retrieval based on measuring the divergence from randomness. *ACM Transactions on Information Systems*, 20(4):357–389, October 2002.

[2] M. Bendersky and W. B. Croft. Discovering key concepts in verbose queries. In *Proc. of SIGIR*, pages 491–498, 2008.

[3] M. Bendersky and O. Kurland. Utilizing passage-based language models for document retrieval. In *Proc. of ECIR*, pages 162–174, 2008.

[4] M. Bendersky, D. Metzler, and W. B. Croft. Learning concept importance using a weighted dependence model. In *Proc. of WSDM*, pages 31–40, 2010.

[5] M. Bendersky, D. Metzler, and W. B. Croft. Parameterized concept weighting in verbose queries. In *Proc. of SIGIR*, 2011.

[6] C. M. Bishop. *Pattern Recognition and Machine Learning*. Springer, 2006.

[7] C. Burges, T. Shaked, E. Renshaw, A. Lazier, M. Deeds, N. Hamilton, and G. Hullender. Learning to rank using gradient descent. In *Proc. of ICML*, pages 89–96, 2005.

[8] D. Cai, S. Yu, J.-R. Wen, and W.-Y. Ma. Block-based web search. In *Proc. of SIGIR*, pages 456–463, 2004.

[9] J. Callan. Passage-level evidence in document retrieval. In *Proc. of SIGIR*, pages 302–310, 1994.

[10] C. L. A. Clarke, N. Craswell, I. Soboroff, and G. V. Cormack. Overview of the TREC 2010 Web Track. In *Proc. of TREC-10*, 2011.

[11] R. Cummins and C. O'Riordan. Learning in a pairwise term-term proximity framework for information retrieval. In *Proc. of SIGIR*, pages 251–258, New York, NY, USA, 2009.

[12] J. Fagan. Automatic phrase indexing for document retrieval. In *Proc. of SIGIR*, pages 91–101, 1987.

[13] J. Gao, J.-Y. Nie, G. Wu, and G. Cao. Dependence language model for information retrieval. In *Proc. of SIGIR*, pages 170–177, 2004.

[14] J. Gao, H. Qi, X. Xia, and J.-Y. Nie. Linear discriminant model for information retrieval. In *Proc. of SIGIR*, pages 290–297, 2005.

[15] T. Joachims. Optimizing search engines using clickthrough data. In *Proc. of KDD*, pages 133–142, 2002.

[16] M. Kaszkiel and J. Zobel. Passage retrieval revisited. In *Proc. of SIGIR*, pages 178–185, 1997.

[17] M. Kaszkiel and J. Zobel. Effective ranking with arbitrary passages. *Journal of the American Society for Information Science*, 52:344–364, February 2001.

[18] M. Kaufmann, M. van Kreveld, and B. Speckmann. Subdivision Drawings of Hypergraphs. In *Graph Drawing*, pages 396–407. Springer, 2009.

[19] R. Krovetz. Viewing morphology as an inference process. In *Proc. of SIGIR*, pages 191–202, 1993.

[20] G. Kumaran and V. R. Carvalho. Reducing long queries using query quality predictors. In *Proc. of SIGIR*, pages 564–571, 2009.

[21] H. Lang, D. Metzler, B. Wang, and J.-T. Li. Improved latent concept expansion using hierarchical markov random fields. In *Proc. of CIKM*, pages 249–258, 2010.

[22] M. Lease, J. Allan, and W. B. Croft. Regression rank: Learning to meet the opportunity of descriptive queries. In *Proc. of ECIR*, pages 90–101, 2009.

[23] T.-Y. Liu. Learning to Rank for Information Retrieval. *Foundations and Trends in Information Retrieval*, 3(3), 2009.

[24] X. Liu and W. B. Croft. Passage retrieval based on language models. In *Proc. of CIKM*, pages 375–382, 2002.

[25] X. Liu and W. B. Croft. Cluster-based retrieval using language models. *Proc. of SIGIR*, pages 186–193, 2004.

[26] Y. Lv and C. Zhai. Positional language models for information retrieval. In *Proc. of SIGIR*, pages 299–306, 2009.

[27] D. Metzler and W. B. Croft. A Markov random field model for term dependencies. *Proc. of SIGIR*, pages 472–479, 2005.

[28] D. Metzler and W. B. Croft. Linear feature-based models for information retrieval. *Information Retrieval*, 10(3):257–274, 2007.

[29] G. Mishne and M. de Rijke. Boosting Web Retrieval Through Query Operations. In *Proc. of ECIR*, pages 502–516, 2005.

[30] J. H. Park, W. B. Croft, and D. A. Smith. A quasi-synchronous dependence model for information retrieval. In *Proc. of CIKM*, pages 17–26, 2011.

[31] F. Peng, N. Ahmed, X. Li, and Y. Lu. Context sensitive stemming for web search. In *Proc. of SIGIR*, pages 639–646, 2007.

[32] J. Peng, C. Macdonald, B. He, V. Plachouras, and I. Ounis. Incorporating term dependency in the DFR framework. In *Proc. of SIGIR*, pages 843–844, 2007.

[33] J. M. Ponte and W. B. Croft. A language modeling approach to information retrieval. In *Proc. of SIGIR*, pages 275–281, 1998.

[34] S. E. Robertson and S. Walker. Some simple effective approximations to the 2-Poisson model for probabilistic weighted retrieval. In *Proc. of SIGIR*, pages 232–241, 1994.

[35] L. Shi and J.-Y. Nie. Using various term dependencies according to their utilities. In *Proc. of CIKM*, pages 1493–1496, 2010.

[36] M. D. Smucker, J. Allan, and B. Carterette. A comparison of statistical significance tests for information retrieval evaluation. In *Proc. of CIKM*, pages 623–632, 2007.

[37] T. Strohman, D. Metzler, H. Turtle, and W. B. Croft. Indri: A language model-based search engine for complex queries. In *Proc. of IA*, 2004.

[38] K. M. Svore, P. H. Kanani, and N. Khan. How good is a span of terms?: exploiting proximity to improve web retrieval. In *Proc. of SIGIR*, pages 154–161, 2010.

[39] T. Tao and C. Zhai. An exploration of proximity measures in information retrieval. In *Proc. of SIGIR*, pages 295–302, 2007.

[40] M. Wang and L. Si. Discriminative probabilistic models for passage based retrieval. In *Proc. of SIGIR*, pages 419–426, 2008.

[41] R. Wilkinson. Effective retrieval of structured documents. In *Proc. of SIGIR*, pages 311–317, 1994.

[42] J. Xu and W. B. Croft. Query expansion using local and global document analysis. *Proc. of SIGIR*, pages 4–11, 1996.

[43] X. Xue, W. B. Croft, and D. A. Smith. Modeling reformulation using passage analysis. In *Proc. of CIKM*, pages 1497–1500, 2010.

[44] C. T. Yu, C. Buckley, K. Lam, and G. Salton. A Generalized Term Dependence Model in Information Retrieval. Technical report, Cornell University, 1983.

[45] C. Zhai and J. Lafferty. A study of smoothing methods for language models applied to information retrieval. *ACM Transactions on Information Systems*, 22(2):179–214, 2004.

[46] J. Zobel and A. Moffat. Exploring the similarity space. *SIGIR Forum*, 32(1):18–34, 1998.

Confidence-Aware Graph Regularization with Heterogeneous Pairwise Features

Yuan Fang*
Univ. of Illinois at Urbana-Champaign
201 N Goodwin Avenue
Urbana, IL 61801, USA
fang2@illinois.edu

Bo-June (Paul) Hsu
Microsoft Research
One Microsoft Way
Redmond, WA 98052, USA
paulhsu@microsoft.com

Kevin Chen-Chuan Chang
Univ. of Illinois at Urbana-Champaign
201 N Goodwin Avenue
Urbana, IL 61801, USA
kcchang@illinois.edu

ABSTRACT

Conventional classification methods tend to focus on features of individual objects, while missing out on potentially valuable pairwise features that capture the relationships between objects. Although recent developments on graph regularization exploit this aspect, existing works generally assume only a single kind of pairwise feature, which is often insufficient. We observe that multiple, heterogeneous pairwise features can often complement each other and are generally more robust in modeling the relationships between objects. Furthermore, as some objects are easier to classify than others, objects with higher initial classification confidence should be weighed more towards classifying related but more ambiguous objects, an observation missing from previous graph regularization techniques. In this paper, we propose a Dirichlet-based regularization framework that supports the combination of heterogeneous pairwise features with confidence-aware prediction using limited labeled training data. Next, we showcase a few applications of our framework in information retrieval, focusing on the problem of query intent classification. Finally, we demonstrate through a series of experiments the advantages of our framework on a large-scale real-world dataset.

Categories and Subject Descriptors

H.3.3 [**Information Storage and Retrieval**]: Information Search and Retrieval

General Terms

Algorithms, Design, Experimentation, Performance

Keywords

graph regularization, pairwise features, confidence, query intent classification, applications in information retrieval

*Work done during an internship at Microsoft Research.

1. INTRODUCTION

Many applications in information retrieval (IR) call for effective classification techniques. For instance, the problem of text categorization is fundamental to a myriad of real-world tasks, such as automated email organization, spam detection, and information filtering. As another example, fine-grained query intent classification enables a search engine to direct users to the intended search verticals, greatly enhancing user experience.

While any conventional machine learning algorithm can be used for classification in IR applications, straightforward adaptation is generally unfruitful, since there exist challenges beyond traditional classification tasks. One prominent issue is the sparsity of feature vectors. For instance, in our query intent classification dataset, about 95% of the queries contain no more than five words.

Recent developments in graph-based regularization [20, 18, 2, 3] somewhat tackles the problem of feature sparsity. Instead of object-level features that are independently extracted from each object, we now consider pairwise features that are extracted from each *pair* of objects. Hence, each object can potentially be paired with any other object for feature extraction. In this work, we employ pairwise features derived from similarity functions between objects, such that a graph can be constructed by linking similar objects with edges. The edges can be used to propagate classification evidence from one object to another based on the key assumption of *consistency*—similar objects are likely to have similar class labels [20]. In other words, the classification of an object can be "helped" or regularized by its neighbors on the graph. In comparison, conventional classification algorithms cannot easily incorporate pairwise features without blowing up the parameter space and subsequently requiring more labeled training data.

Given the above benefits, graph-based regularization has also been adopted in IR applications, most notably through the use of a click graph [12, 7, 11] in query intent classification. A click graph usually consists of queries and websites as its vertices. A query q and a website w are connected by an edge if q results in a click landing on w. Intuitively, two queries connected to the same website are related, and thus should share a similar prediction.

While making the same assumption of consistency, we are motivated by two core observations, which entail key intuitions towards a more effective graph-based regularization framework.

First, most existing regularization framework only deals with a single kind of pairwise feature. However, heterogeneous pairwise features often exist. For instance, in query intent classification, queries can be related through not only clicks, but also other pairwise features, including lexical similarity ("acer laptop" and "laptop" are related due to word overlap), co-session (the second query could be a refinement of the first in the same session), and the similarity of search result pages (two queries that retrieve similar pages may be similar themselves). These different pairwise features potentially complement each other, as some may only cover a small fraction of all queries (*e.g.*, not all shopping queries have associated product clicks). In addition to sparsity, some pairwise features may lack the robustness to capture similarities between two objects. *E.g.*, while both queries "hp 3 in 1" and "canon printer" refer to printers, they contain no common words and thus their similarity cannot be represented by lexical pairwise features. To support heterogeneous pairwise features, the challenge lies in how different similarity functions can be aggregated to optimize the regularization, which is missing from previous regularization frameworks.

Second, in existing graph regularization, the extent to which the classification of an object o influences o' only depends on their similarity. Greater similarity between o and o' means that they have stronger influences on each other. While this is reasonable, a second factor, largely overlooked by previous work, is the confidence of classification. If we are more confident about the prediction on o, we expect it to influence its neighbors on the graph more. On the other hand, if we are unsure about the prediction on o, we should minimize its influence. In other words, we use objects that are easier to classify (with higher classification confidence) to help predict harder ones (with lower classification confidence), but less so the other way round. Existing regularization works do not provide for a mechanism to incorporate classification confidence. In contrast, our modeling of objects with Dirichlet priors allows us to interpret the observation counts as confidence.

Finally, another challenge of classification lies in the requirement of a large amount of labeled training data, especially in real-world IR applications with a large number of classes. Our experiments on query intent classification involve 2043 classes, and thus require much more labeled training queries than, say, a binary classification task. Our framework deals with the shortage of labeled training data in two ways. To begin with, like other graph-based regularization frameworks (*e.g.*, [20, 18]), classification evidence is propagated across the graph along the edges. By using more unlabeled data, we generally obtain a denser graph that promotes such propagation, and hence improve the performance. Our experiments show that adding more unlabeled data yields superior results, despite using the same set of labeled training data. Next, our framework allows for fewer parameters, independent of the number of classes. Hence, even with limited training data and a large number of target classes, our technique is effective.

In this paper, we propose a regularization framework that can be applied to different applications, hinged on our insights above. To summarize, we make the following contributions:

- **Motivation:** We recognize the need for heterogeneous pairwise features that complement each other, and confidence-aware regularization that distinguishes objects of different initial classification confidence. (Sect. 1)
- **Framework**: We develop a generic graph-based regularization framework. The framework supports arbitrary heterogeneous pairwise features, is confidence-aware, and works with a limited amount of training data. (Sect. 3)
- **Applications**: We showcase how our framework can be applied to a few applications in IR, primarily focusing on query intent classification in the shopping domain. (Sect. 4)
- **Experiments**: We conduct extensive experiments on a real-world dataset for query intent classification. Our approach substantially outperforms traditional regularization methods which do not consider heterogeneous pairwise features or confidence, validating our observations. (Sect. 5)

2. RELATED WORK

Pairwise features. Many IR classification tasks are plagued by feature sparsity. Thus, a significant amount of research has studied augmenting the feature vector (*e.g.*, [4, 16, 15, 5] for query-intent classification). Unfortunately, these techniques are generally not universal to other classification tasks. Driven by the hypothesis that "similar objects share similar labels" [20], we consider pairwise features that allow for feature extraction from any pair of objects, potentially expanding the feature space.

Although it is difficult to incorporate pairwise features in conventional classification algorithms without blowing up the parameter space, they have been used in recent graph-based regularization frameworks [20, 18, 2, 3] and related random walk approaches [17, 7]. Examples of their applications in IR include the use of click graphs [12, 10, 7, 11] in query intent classification, and document affinity matrices [8, 9] in text retrieval. However, unlike this paper, most of these works do not consider heterogeneous pairwise features, which complement each other and thus play an important role in improving classification accuracy. While a recent work [11] explores a content-based pairwise feature in addition to co-clicks, its treatment is limited as it lacks a mechanism to effectively aggregate arbitrary pairwise features. In particular, their parameters are manually selected, making it difficult to extend to more pairwise features. In comparison, we learn the parameters via an iterative optimization process.

Confidence. Existing regularization frameworks [20, 18, 2, 3] and their task specific realizations (*e.g.*, [12, 10, 7, 11] for query intent classification and [8, 9] for text retrieval) do not recognize the importance and hence take advantage of the classification confidence associated with objects. We observe the need of confidence-aware regularization, and exploit it to improve classification accuracy. Specifically, we are more confident about objects that are easier to classify, which should have a larger influence towards the prediction of their neighbors.

Limited training data. To deal with the shortage of labeled training data, many task specific techniques exist (*e.g.*, [1, 12, 13, 15] for query-intent classification). However, they are often highly tailored and cannot be easily extended to a generic framework. In our framework, we benefit from using more unlabeled data by exploiting the relationships between objects, leveraging the semi-supervised nature of graph-based regularization [20, 18, 2, 3]. In addition, our framework involves a small parameter space independent of the number of target classes, and thus performs well even with limited training data and thousands of target classes.

3. REGULARIZATION FRAMEWORK

In this section, we develop our graph regularization framework. It is universal to different classification tasks, including our example application on query intent classification in Sect. 4.

Given a set of objects O and a set of classes C, each object $o \in O$ has some distribution over C. We regularize the class distribution of o by the class distributions of objects similar to o, *i.e.*, adjust the prediction on o according to objects similar to it. To start, we capture objects and their pairwise similarity features using a graph. Next, based on the graph, we introduce our regularization model.

3.1 Object-Relationship Graph

We model objects and their pairwise features with a graph $G = (O, R)$. O is the set of objects that define the *vertices*. R is the set of relationships between objects that describe the *edges* of the graph, which are derived from the pairwise features between ob-

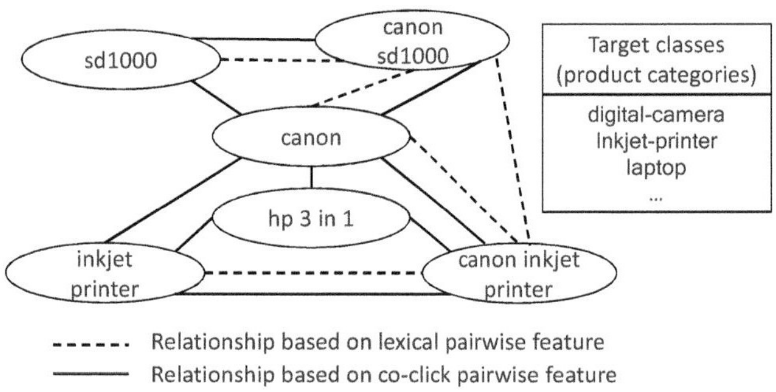

Figure 1: Example graph for classification of shopping queries.

jects. We use the toy graph in Fig. 1 for the task of query intent classification in the shopping domain as our running example.

Vertices. Each object or the target entity of classification is a vertex on the graph. For example, the query "canon" in Fig. 1 is a vertex to be classified as a digital camera or inkjet printer, among others.

Edges. An edge on the graph is represented as a triplet $(o, o', \tau) \in R$, which models the relationship between two objects o and o' based on a pairwise feature τ. Unlike traditional object-level features that are independently extracted from each object (*e.g.*, words in each document in text classification), τ is in fact a feature defined on a *pair* of objects that describes their mutual similarity. Conceptually, τ can be understood as a particular similarity function on two objects. For instance, as Fig. 1 illustrates, it can be the cosine similarity between the word vectors of two queries (lexical pairwise feature), or the number of co-clicks for two queries (co-click pairwise feature). Thus, there can exist as many edges between two objects as the number of pairwise features, such as between "canon" and "canon sd1000" in Fig. 1.

The strength of a relationship is encoded as the non-negative weight of its corresponding edge (o, o', τ), and is thus a function of the two objects o, o' and the pairwise feature τ, denoted as $W(o, o', \tau)$. $W(o, o', \tau)$ can be understood as the similarity between o and o' with respect to τ. By convention, $W(o, o', \tau) = 0$ iff the edge $(o, o', \tau) \notin R$. In this paper, we consider bi-directional, symmetric relationships, which have equal strengths in both directions, *i.e.*, $W(o, o', \tau) = W(o', o, \tau)$.

3.2 Regularization Model

Given K target classes $\{1, \ldots, K\}$, each object $o \in O$ has an underlying probability distribution over the K classes that captures the possible user intents. *E.g.*, in Fig. 1 the distribution for the query "canon" could be (digital-camera:0.3, inkjet-printer:0.2, ...), indicating that the user may be looking for a digital camera with probability 0.3, an inkjet printer with probability 0.2, *etc.*

As such a distribution is inherently latent, we undertake a "distribution over distributions" instead. Specifically, we model the class distribution of each object o using a Dirichlet prior $Dir(\boldsymbol{\alpha}_o)$, parameterized by a vector $\boldsymbol{\alpha}_o = (\boldsymbol{\alpha}_o[1], \ldots, \boldsymbol{\alpha}_o[K])$. Informally, it describes the distribution over all possible latent class distributions of o, given that each class $i \in \{1, \ldots, K\}$ has been observed $\boldsymbol{\alpha}_o[i] - 1$, potentially fractional, times. The Dirichlet prior also conveniently allows us to treat the total count of observations σ_o as the classification confidence—we are more confident in the prior if σ_o is larger. We call σ_o the prior *confidence* of o:

$$\sigma_o \triangleq \sum_{i=1}^{K} (\boldsymbol{\alpha}_o[i] - 1) = \sum_{i=1}^{K} \boldsymbol{\alpha}_o[i] - K \tag{1}$$

In particular, we only consider unimodal Dirichlet priors, *i.e.*, $\forall i \in \{1, \ldots, K\}, \boldsymbol{\alpha}_o[i] > 1$, such that $\sigma_o > 0$. As we shall describe later, such a prior may be derived from an initial object-level classifier or previous iterations of the regularization algorithm.

3.2.1 Regularization by Neighbors

Given a prior over possible class distributions for an object o, we can treat its neighbors as additional evidence to support its classification. In particular, we consider the neighbors as observation data, weighted by their similarity, from which we can compute a posterior distribution over possible class distributions for o. Alternatively, we can interpret this as a form of regularization in that the original belief on o is regularized by the belief on its neighbors.

Let $N(o)$ denote the set of neighbors of o on the graph. Specifically, for each neighbor $o' \in N(o)$, we can interpret its Dirichlet prior $Dir(\boldsymbol{\alpha}_{o'})$ as observing $\boldsymbol{\alpha}_{o'}[i] - 1$ instances of class i for each of the K classes when drawing $\sigma_{o'}$ instances from the underlying multinomial distribution for o'. Under the assumption that similar objects share similar labels and hence observations, we deem that each neighbor o' contributes to the classification of o an observation of $S(o, o')(\boldsymbol{\alpha}_{o'}[i] - 1)$ counts for each of the K classes, weighted by the similarity $S(o, o')$ between o and o'. As o can be connected to o' via multiple pairwise features, we define the similarity between the two objects as a linear combination of their similarity $W(o, o', \tau)$ across all pairwise features:

$$S(o, o') \triangleq \sum_{\tau} \lambda_\tau W(o, o', \tau), \tag{2}$$

where each λ_τ is a parameter specifying the overall influence of τ towards $S(o, o')$. We will learn these parameters in Sect. 3.3 to optimize the regularization.

Since the Dirichlet distribution is *conjugate* to the multinomial distribution, factoring in additional multinomial observations still results in a Dirichlet posterior. Specifically, given a Dirichlet prior $Dir(\boldsymbol{\alpha})$, the posterior distribution after observing $\boldsymbol{\beta}[i]$ counts in each class i is simply $Dir(\boldsymbol{\alpha} + \boldsymbol{\beta})$, where $\boldsymbol{\beta} = (\boldsymbol{\beta}[1], \ldots, \boldsymbol{\beta}[K])$. Hence, for an object o with prior $Dir(\boldsymbol{\alpha}_o)$, the additional weighted observation data from each neighbor o' would give us the Dirichlet posterior $Dir(\widehat{\boldsymbol{\alpha}}_o)$, where:

$$\widehat{\boldsymbol{\alpha}}_o = \boldsymbol{\alpha}_o + \sum_{o' \in N(o)} S(o, o')(\boldsymbol{\alpha}_{o'} - \mathbf{1}) \tag{3}$$

Similar to the prior confidence (Eq. 1), we can compute the posterior confidence for the object o as below:

$$\widehat{\sigma}_o = \sum_{i=1}^{K} \widehat{\boldsymbol{\alpha}}_o[i] - K = \sigma_o + \sum_{o' \in N(o)} S(o, o')\sigma_{o'} \tag{4}$$

However, since all observations are potentially noisy in practice, having more neighbors and hence more observation data does not necessarily imply a higher posterior confidence. As a heuristic, we normalize the observation data by the number of contributing objects weighted by their similarity, $S_o = 1 + \sum_{o' \in N(o)} S(o, o')$. This results in a normalized Dirichlet posterior $Dir(\widetilde{\boldsymbol{\alpha}}_o)$ and a normalized posterior confidence $\widetilde{\sigma}_o$ for each object o:

$$\widetilde{\boldsymbol{\alpha}}_o - \mathbf{1} = \frac{\widehat{\boldsymbol{\alpha}}_o - \mathbf{1}}{S_o} = \frac{1}{S_o}\left(\boldsymbol{\alpha}_o - \mathbf{1} + \sum_{o' \in N(o)} S(o, o')(\boldsymbol{\alpha}_{o'} - \mathbf{1})\right) \tag{5}$$

$$\widetilde{\sigma}_o = \frac{\widehat{\sigma}_o}{S_o} = \frac{1}{S_o}\left(\sigma_o + \sum_{o' \in N(o)} S(o, o')\sigma_{o'}\right) \tag{6}$$

Intuitively, this normalization step causes observations from neighbors of o to "adjust" our confidence in o (Eq. 6), rather than to raise it monotonically in the unnormalized version (Eq. 4).

We can understand Eq. 5 as a form of regularization. Informally, our original belief on object o, as prescribed by its prior $Dir(\boldsymbol{\alpha}_o)$, is regularized by its neighbors, which change our belief and produce the regularized distribution $Dir(\widetilde{\boldsymbol{\alpha}}_o)$. Note that in the special case that o has no neighbors ($N(o) = \emptyset$), Eq. 5 would give us $\widetilde{\boldsymbol{\alpha}}_o = \boldsymbol{\alpha}_o$, *i.e.*, no regularization is done.

Confidence-aware prediction. Given the regularized Dirichlet distribution $Dir(\widetilde{\boldsymbol{\alpha}}_o)$ for an object o, we can make a prediction on o by first choosing the most likely class distribution, *i.e.*, the mode distribution $\widetilde{\mathbf{m}}_o$ of $Dir(\widetilde{\boldsymbol{\alpha}}_o)$. Subsequently, we assign classes to o according to $\widetilde{\mathbf{m}}_o$, say, by taking the top k classes with the largest probabilities in $\widetilde{\mathbf{m}}_o$, or all classes above a given probability threshold. Since $\widetilde{\boldsymbol{\alpha}}_o[i] > 1, \forall i$, the mode has a closed form solution:

$$\widetilde{\mathbf{m}}_o = (\widetilde{\boldsymbol{\alpha}}_o - \mathbf{1})/\widetilde{\sigma}_o, \tag{7}$$

where $\widetilde{\sigma}_o$ is the normalized posterior confidence of o in Eq. 6.

Unlike previous regularization frameworks [20, 18, 2, 3], the prediction by $\widetilde{\mathbf{m}}_o$ is *confidence-aware*, as we will now demonstrate. Dividing both sides of Eq. 5 by $\widetilde{\sigma}_o$, we obtain:

$$\frac{\widetilde{\boldsymbol{\alpha}}_o - \mathbf{1}}{\widetilde{\sigma}_o} = \frac{\boldsymbol{\alpha}_o - \mathbf{1} + \sum_{o' \in N(o)} S(o,o')(\boldsymbol{\alpha}_{o'} - \mathbf{1})}{\widetilde{\sigma}_o S_o} \tag{8}$$

In Eq. 8, the left hand side is simply $\widetilde{\mathbf{m}}_o$. On the right hand side, $\boldsymbol{\alpha}_o - \mathbf{1} = \sigma_o \mathbf{m}_o, \forall o \in O$, where $\mathbf{m}_o$ is the mode distribution of $Dir(\boldsymbol{\alpha}_o)$. Moreover, taking Eq. 6 into consideration, Eq. 8 can be further expressed as:

$$\widetilde{\mathbf{m}}_o = \frac{\sigma_o \mathbf{m}_o + \sum_{o' \in N(o)} S(o,o')\sigma_{o'}\mathbf{m}_{o'}}{\sigma_o + \sum_{o' \in N(o)} S(o,o')\sigma_{o'}} \tag{9}$$

Similar to the harmonic method [20], Eq. 9 implies that the regularized mode $\widetilde{\mathbf{m}}_o$ is a weighted average of the original (unregularized) modes $\mathbf{m}_o$ and $\mathbf{m}_{o'}, \forall o' \in N(o)$. However, unlike [20], the weight on each neighbor o' is $S(o,o')\sigma_{o'}$, which factors in both the similarity $S(o,o')$ and the confidence $\sigma_{o'}$. Hence, our model is confidence-aware, *i.e.*, objects with higher confidence $\sigma_{o'}$ will be weighed more in the regularization. As motivated in Sect. 1, such a property is desirable, since an object with low confidence would potentially introduce noise and thus its influence should be downplayed. On the other hand, [20] and other regularization models [18, 2, 3] only assign weights according to the similarity between the objects, without utilizing the confidence.

Alternative interpretation. Our regularization (Eq. 5) is equivalent to the minimization of a cost function, the essence of many graph-based regularization frameworks [20, 18, 2, 3]. Specifically, we minimize the following function over $\widetilde{\boldsymbol{\alpha}}_o, \forall o \in O$:

$$\mathcal{E} = \frac{1}{2}\sum_{o \in O}\left(\|\widetilde{\boldsymbol{\alpha}}_o - \boldsymbol{\alpha}_o\|^2 + \sum_{o' \in N(o)} S(o,o')\|\widetilde{\boldsymbol{\alpha}}_o - \boldsymbol{\alpha}_{o'}\|^2\right), \tag{10}$$

where $\|\cdot\|$ is the Euclidean distance. Intuitively, the regularization should not change the original belief on o too much, *i.e.*, we want $Dir(\widetilde{\boldsymbol{\alpha}}_o)$ to be close to the prior $Dir(\boldsymbol{\alpha}_o)$. Additionally, $Dir(\widetilde{\boldsymbol{\alpha}}_o)$ should be close to the prior $Dir(\boldsymbol{\alpha}_{o'})$ of each neighbor $o' \in N(o)$, from which observations are contributed towards o.

To see the equivalence, we minimize $\mathcal{E}$ by setting its derivative with respect to $\widetilde{\boldsymbol{\alpha}}_o$ to zero:

$$\frac{\partial \mathcal{E}}{\partial \widetilde{\boldsymbol{\alpha}}_o} = \widetilde{\boldsymbol{\alpha}}_o - \boldsymbol{\alpha}_o + \sum_{o' \in N(o)} S(o,o')(\widetilde{\boldsymbol{\alpha}}_o - \boldsymbol{\alpha}_{o'}) = \mathbf{0}, \tag{11}$$

which is algebraically equivalent to Eq. 5.

3.2.2 *Regularization by Indirectly Related Objects*

In the above model (Eq. 5), an object o is only regularized by its neighbors on the graph. In most scenarios, indirectly related objects, such as "neighbors of neighbors", also provide additional evidence for o. The evidence from "neighbors of neighbors" can be captured by regularizing $Dir(\widetilde{\boldsymbol{\alpha}}_o)$ again. In general, we propose an iterative regularization algorithm, which can potentially model the evidence from any object with a path to o on the graph.

Iterative regularization. As our regularized distribution $Dir(\widetilde{\boldsymbol{\alpha}}_o)$ is also Dirichlet, we can feed it back as input for regularization again in the exact same way as we have done in Sect. 3.2.1, treating $Dir(\widetilde{\boldsymbol{\alpha}}_o)$ as the new Dirichlet prior for o. The process can be repeated for any number of iterations.

Let $\boldsymbol{\alpha}_o^{(0)} \triangleq \boldsymbol{\alpha}_o$ denote the Dirichlet parameter of the initial prior for an object o. Furthermore, let $\boldsymbol{\alpha}_o^{(t)}$ be the regularized Dirichlet parameter after t iterations, $\forall t > 0$. Similar to Eq. 5, it is easy to see that $\forall t \geq 1$,

$$\boldsymbol{\alpha}_o^{(t)} - \mathbf{1} = \frac{1}{S_o}\left(\boldsymbol{\alpha}_o^{(t-1)} - \mathbf{1} + \sum_{o' \in N(o)} S(o,o')\left(\boldsymbol{\alpha}_{o'}^{(t-1)} - \mathbf{1}\right)\right) \tag{12}$$

As shown, we only need to know the Dirichlet parameters from the previous iteration to compute $\boldsymbol{\alpha}_o^{(t)}$. To start the iterative process, we bootstrap from $t = 0$ by specifying $\boldsymbol{\alpha}_o^{(0)}, \forall o$, for the initial prior of each object. How they are initialized is an orthogonal issue to our regularization framework. Different strategies may be applied based on the application, as we will discuss in Sect. 4.

Finally, we make predictions using the mode distributions after t iterations of regularization, $\mathbf{m}_o^{(t)} = (\boldsymbol{\alpha}_o^{(t)} - \mathbf{1})/\sigma_o^{(t)}$, in the same manner as discussed in Sect. 3.2.1.

Number of iterations. The iterative regularization process can be interpreted as a form of information propagation on the graph. In each iteration, information is propagated from each object to its neighbors. The propagation is repeated such that indirectly related objects are also affected through longer-range dependencies.

The total number of iterations T is an important parameter to decide, with similar effects as the length parameter in random walks [17, 7]. In particular, when $T = 1$, it reduces to a simple weighted voting by neighbors. But as $T \to \infty$, $\boldsymbol{\alpha}_o^{(T)}$ becomes the same for every object o in each connected component of the graph, similar to what have been discussed in [17, 7].

Intuitively, if T is too small, only very short-range dependencies can be captured, ignoring potentially useful long-range ones. On the other hand, if T is too large, all dependencies regardless of its range will be captured, making the result less discriminative. Thus, an optimal T would ensure a desirable trade-off between short and long-range dependencies. While the optimal T can be selected either manually [7] or heuristically [17], we propose to learn it in the next subsection.

3.3 Parameters Learning

In addition to the total number of iterations T, each pairwise feature τ has a parameter λ_τ that specifies the overall influence of τ towards the similarity between two objects (Eq. 2). Thus, our parameters are T and Λ, where $\Lambda \triangleq \{\lambda_\tau : \forall \tau\}$.

We propose to learn the parameters with a heuristic objective function defined on only T and Λ. Since $|\Lambda|$ is generally small as restricted by the number of possible pairwise features between objects (in our experiments $|\Lambda| = 2$), only a few labeled objects are needed for learning. In comparison, traditional supervised classification techniques train a model for each target class. In real-world applications where the number of target classes is large ($K = 2043$ in our experiments), an enormous amount of training data would be required, as we would expect at least a few labels for each class. On the other hand, with our heuristic objective function, we require far fewer than K to achieve good classification accuracy.

Our first attempt defines a global error function to optimize the parameters. However, due to computational challenges, we subsequently propose a local error function for the dynamic selection of parameters in each iteration. As the parameters are chosen to minimize the error functions, any existing numerical optimization technique can be used. In particular, we apply Powell's method [14] to solve the optimization problem.

3.3.1 Global Optimization

Given a labeled training set $O_L \subset O$, and an initialization for the Dirichlet parameters $\Omega = \{\boldsymbol{\alpha}_o^{(0)} : o \in O\}$ at $t = 0$, we can define an error function as the minimization objective:

$$G_{\text{err}}(O_L, \Omega, \Lambda, T) = \frac{1}{|O_L|} \sum_{o \in O_L} \left\| \mathbf{m}_o^{(T|\Omega,\Lambda)} - \mathbf{u}_o^* \right\|^2, \quad (13)$$

where $\mathbf{m}_o^{(T|\Omega,\Lambda)}$ denotes the mode after T iterations of regularization (using Eq. 12), with the initialization Ω and parameters Λ. $\mathbf{u}_o^*$ is the "gold standard" distribution derived from the labels of o. $\|\cdot\|$ is the Euclidean distance. (Note that alternative distance measures such as KL-divergence may also be used.) We select parameters that minimize this global error, *i.e.*, $\{\Lambda^*, T^*\} = \arg\min_{\Lambda,T} G_{\text{err}}(O_L, \Omega, \Lambda, T)$.

When $T = 1$, $\mathbf{m}_o^{(T|\Omega,\Lambda)}$ can be computed for all $o \in O_L$ using only the neighbors of objects in the labeled training set O_L. When $T = 2$, we need to consider "neighbors of neighbors" as well. For larger T's, we potentially need to compute iteratively over the entire graph of labeled and unlabeled objects. This makes the computation of the error function very costly. As many optimization techniques require repeated computation of $G_{\text{err}}(\cdot)$ for different values of Λ and T, such an error function is computationally infeasible.

3.3.2 Iterative Optimization

As an efficient alternative to minimizing the global error, we propose an algorithm where we regularize the Dirichlet parameters $\boldsymbol{\alpha}_o^{(t)}$ (Eq. 12) and update the parameters Λ in alternating fashion. In each iteration, we regularize the classification using the Λ learned from the previous iteration. As the Dirichlet distribution on every object changes after regularization, we update Λ by minimizing the error function for the next iteration. This is similar in spirit to the Expectation-Maximization (EM) algorithm. However, unlike EM which maximizes the likelihood function of the parameters, we are minimizing an error function. Our approach involves the following two steps in each iteration $t, \forall t \geq 0$:

(1) **Regularization step.** If $t = 0$, initialize $\boldsymbol{\alpha}_o^{(0)}, \forall o \in O$, according to the given $\Omega^{(0)} = \{\boldsymbol{\alpha}_o^{(0)} : \forall o \in O\}$. If $t > 0$, compute $\Omega^{(t)} = \{\boldsymbol{\alpha}_o^{(t)} : \forall o \in O\}$ from $\Omega^{(t-1)}$ (Eq. 12), using parameters $\Lambda^{(t)}$. Note that $\Omega^{(t-1)}$ and $\Lambda^{(t)}$ are already computed from the previous iteration.

(2) **Minimization step.** To update Λ for the next iteration, we minimize a local error function over Λ:

$$L_{\text{err}}^{(t+1)}(O_L, \Lambda) \triangleq G_{\text{err}}(O_L, \Omega^{(t)}, \Lambda, 1), \quad (14)$$

which is the global error for $T = 1$ with initialization $\Omega^{(t)}$. We find $\Lambda^{(t+1)} = \arg\min_\Lambda L_{\text{err}}^{(t+1)}(O_L, \Lambda)$ for the next iteration. We continue the iteration until the minimum error converges.

Although in the regularization step, we still need to update the entire graph, it is acceptable as it is done only once per iteration. In contrast, to solve the optimization problem in each minimization step, the error function has to be computed numerous times. Thus it is important the error function involves only light-weight computation. Our local error function (Eq. 14) is defined using the global error function (Eq. 13) with $T = 1$, which can be easily computed using only the neighbors of the objects in the training set O_L, where typically $|O_L| \ll |O|$. *E.g.*, in most of our experiments, $|O_L|$ is less than 0.1% of $|O|$.

Another distinction in our iterative optimization is that we do not explicitly learn T, the maximum number of iterations. Instead, we terminate the iterations when the minimum local error $\min_\Lambda L_{\text{err}}^{(t)}(\cdot)$ converges. Although such convergence is guaranteed as established below, similar to EM, there is no guarantee that the global minimum $\min_{\Lambda,T} G_{\text{err}}(\cdot)$ can be achieved.

Proposition 1: As defined in Eq. 14, the sequence of local minimum errors $\{\min_\Lambda L_{\text{err}}^{(t)}(O_L, \Lambda)\}_{t=1}^{\infty}$ converges to a finite limit. ∎

PROOF: Let Λ_0 denote that all parameters λ_τ are zero. Then,

$$\min_\Lambda L_{\text{err}}^{(t)}(O_L, \Lambda) \leq L_{\text{err}}^{(t)}(O_L, \Lambda_0) \overset{*}{=} \min_\Lambda L_{\text{err}}^{(t-1)}(O_L, \Lambda).$$

Note that $(*)$ holds since Λ_0 implies that no regularization is done—we get the same error as the minimum error of the previous iteration. Thus, the sequence is monotonically non-increasing. Additionally, the minimum error is bounded from below by zero. Any bounded monotone sequence converges to a finite limit. ∎

4. APPLICATIONS IN IR

We now discuss the applications of the regularization framework on real-world classification tasks in information retrieval. We first formalize what components of the regularization framework must be realized in any application. Next, we showcase a specific application on query intent classification in the shopping domain, followed by brief discussions of applications on other tasks. Finally, we describe the target scenarios of our applications.

4.1 Realization of the Framework

Realizing our regularization framework requires a *vertex model* and one or more *edge models*.

Vertex model. As we see in Eq. 12, to enable iterative regularization, we need an initial model for $t = 0$, characterized by the Dirichlet parameters $\boldsymbol{\alpha}_o^{(0)}, \forall o \in O$. Since each object o is a vertex in the graph, we call this initialization a *vertex model*. As $\boldsymbol{\alpha}_o^{(0)} = \sigma_o^{(0)} \mathbf{m}_o^{(0)} + \mathbf{1}$, which entails both the mode distribution and the confidence, we can equivalently set $\boldsymbol{\alpha}_o^{(0)}$ by initializing $\mathbf{m}_o^{(0)}$ and $\sigma_o^{(0)}$ separately, as we do in Sect. 4.2.

Edge model. In Sect. 3, the strength of a relationship between two objects o, o' is abstracted into a weight function $W(o, o', \tau)$, where τ is the pairwise feature that induces the relationship. Since relationships are edges on the graph, we call the realization of the weight function $W(q, q', \tau)$ for a pairwise feature τ an *edge model*.

4.2 Example Applications

4.2.1 Query Intent Classification

We address the problem of query intent classification in the shopping domain. Given a query $q \in Q$ from a query log of an e-commerce website, and a set of K predefined product categories, the task is to map the query to a product category, with a limited amount of labeled queries. Additional resources such as existing product metadata may also be leveraged. In the following, we present how we can realize the vertex and edge models for this task. Note that the set of queries Q in the given query log form the vertices on the graph instead of the generic objects O in Sect. 3.

Vertex models. Any conventional query classification algorithm can be used to initialize the mode $\mathbf{m}_q^{(0)}$ for each query $q \in Q$, as long as the output of the algorithm can be converted to a probability distribution over the K categories, which is taken as the most likely distribution, *i.e.*, the mode distribution $\mathbf{m}_q^{(0)}$. We first introduce a vertex model based on unigram language models, followed by possible alternatives.

Language Vertex Model. As input, we leverage existing product metadata from online shopping sites such as Bing Shopping[1]. Each product is associated with metadata that include attributes such as name, brand and description, as well as the category to which the product belongs. From this data, we build a unigram language model θ_i for each category $i \in \{1, \ldots, K\}$ based on all observed words from the attribute values of the products in that category, weighted by product popularity. Given a query q, to estimate $\mathbf{m}_q^{(0)}$, we evaluate the query likelihood $p(q|\theta_i), \forall i$, and convert it to a probability distribution over categories by applying Bayes' rule: $p(\theta_i|q) \propto p(q|\theta_i)p(\theta_i)$, using the prior of the categories as estimated by the total popularity of all products in each category.

On the other hand, to initialize the confidence, we build a background model θ_b by considering all products in our metadata. The intuition is that queries with a lower background model likelihood are easier to classify, as a low likelihood means that the words in the query are rare and more likely to be identified as belonging to those few categories that contain these rare words, resulting in higher classification confidence. On the other hand, a high likelihood implies that the query words are very common and appear in many categories, leading to lower confidence classification. Empirical study shows that the probability of a correct classification of a query is fairly correlated with its negative log likelihood. Thus, we initialize the confidence as follows:

$$\sigma_q^{(0)} = -\log p(q|\theta_b) \tag{15}$$

The language vertex model only requires a weak supervision from the product metadata, which is available from shopping websites. No training labels for individual queries are needed.

Alternative Vertex Models. To initialize the mode distribution, we can also use supervised but substantially more accurate classifiers. The disadvantage of using a supervised classifier is that it requires a large amount of labeled training queries to achieve good classification accuracy. However, after applying our regularization framework, using the weakly supervised unigram models can achieve comparable results to using a well-trained fully supervised classifier for the vertex model, as we shall observe in the experiments.

Eq. 15 is only a simple heuristic for the purpose of initializing the distribution confidence. Other heuristics can be used, such as the query length (longer queries provide additional features to guide its classification), or the consistency of the outputs from multiple classifiers (queries with more consistent outputs are arguably easier to classify). However, developing more theoretical confidence estimation methods, such as those explored by works on query difficulty [6], is beyond the scope of this paper.

Edge models. Among many possible pairwise features between queries, we focus on the lexical (τ_{lex}) and co-click (τ_{click}) features.

[1]http://www.bing.com/shopping

Lexical Edge Model. Given two queries q and q' from a query log, we can view each as a set of words, denoted by $\phi(q)$ and $\phi(q')$, respectively. We can then define the lexical edge model as follows:

$$W(q, q', \tau_{\text{lex}}) = \begin{cases} 1 & \phi(q) \subseteq \phi(q') \text{ or } \phi(q') \subseteq \phi(q) \\ 0 & \text{else} \end{cases} \tag{16}$$

This edge model is a symmetric, binary similarity measure: we draw an edge between two queries if one of them contains all words in the other. *E.g.*, W("canon", "canon camera", τ_{lex}) $= 1$, whereas W("canon printer", "canon camera", τ_{lex}) $= 0$.

Although this edge model is simple, it is more effective in preliminary experiments than other more sophisticated models such as cosine similarity. One possible explanation is that our binary similarity results in less noise than cosine similarity.

Co-click Edge Model. We can also establish relationships between queries using co-click pairwise features. Intuitively, if two queries have more clicks that land on product pages belonging to the same category, they are more closely related. In many cases, we may only be able to deduce that two clicks lead to the same category (*e.g.*, they land on the same URL, or URLs with the same prefix such as example.com/digital_camera/...), but we may not know the actual category, or how to map the vendor category to ours. Formally, we define the co-click edge model as follows, adapted from the co-citation/click measures in [19, 10]:

$$W(q, q', \tau_{\text{click}}) = \log \left(1 + \sum_c \#(q, c)\#(q', c)\frac{N}{N_c}\right) \tag{17}$$

In this edge model, each c is a category, which could be a "virtual category" with no direct correspondence to a target category, for reasons discussed above. $\forall q \in Q$, $\#(q, c)$ denotes the number of clicks associated with query q that leads to category c. N is the total number of clicks across all queries, whereas N_c is the number of total clicks that lead to category c. Thus, N/N_c has an effect similar to inverse document frequency, *i.e.*, more popular categories contribute less to the similarity between two queries. We also use a logarithm function to model a sublinear growth of the similarity with respect to the number of clicks.

Additional Edge Models. The following pairwise features can also be considered, although they are not used in our experiments.

- User sessions. In the same user session, the second query is often a refinement of the first. Thus, whether two queries co-occur in the same session and the frequency of such co-occurrence can be another pairwise feature.
- Search results. On an existing e-commerce system, a query can retrieve a set of related products (*i.e.*, the search results). A pairwise feature between two queries could be the similarity of their search results. Alternatively, search results from a generic search engine can also be used, where similarity between retrieved pages can be measured instead.

4.2.2 Other Applications

We briefly discuss how we can realize our regularization framework on other applications in IR. As discussed in Sect. 4.2.1, the vertex model is often easy to realize using an existing classifier for the initial mode distribution and various heuristics for the initial confidence. Hence, for the following applications, we only discuss the choice of the pairwise features for their edge models, which are often neglected in conventional classification.

Offer classification. Given a product offer from a vendor, which is presented as a list of attribute-value pairs (*e.g.*, product name, brand, image, description, as well as product-specific attributes such as focal length for cameras), the task is to map it to our predefined categories. (Imagine we are an e-commerce website receiving feeds on offers from different vendors, whose attribute schemas and category taxonomies vary.) The following pairwise features could be used: (i) the graphical similarity between two product images; (ii) the overlap of product-specific attribute names, since products from the same category often share similar attribute names even across vendors; (iii) lexical similarity between the names and descriptions of two products.

Text classification. This is a classic task in IR that assigns each document to a class. With additional resources such as access statistics, social media and embedded hyperlinks, we suggest the following pairwise features: (i) co-readership, the number of readers who accessed both of the two documents within some time window; (ii) social tagging, the distributional similarity of the user tags on social sharing sites; (iii) hyperlinks in the documents, where similar documents likely point to similar pages; (iv) lexical similarity in the contents of two documents.

4.3 Target Application Scenarios

As our regularization framework requires multiple iterations over the entire graph $G = (O, E)$, it is not intended for online classification. Instead, it is designed for offline computation, where the precomputed predictions for each object in O is stored in an index. Given a seen object o (*i.e.*, $o \in O$), its precomputed prediction is directly fetched from the index. If o is previously unseen (*i.e.*, $o \notin O$), we can use the vertex model to classify it on-the-fly. Alternatively, we may potentially look up o's neighbors on the graph using an inverted index, locality sensitive hash, or other means, and subsequently regularize the classification of o using its neighbors for one iteration online.

As an example, let us consider a real scenario involving a live search system on the task of query intent classification. In this situation, as time passes, the live system collects a growing amount of data, including queries and clickthroughs. Thus, it is ideal if our regularization framework can be applied periodically offline (say, on a daily or weekly basis), in order to leverage more data and update the precomputed index accordingly. As our experiments show (Sect. 5.3), our approach runs fast enough on a single machine to be computed daily for at least tens of millions of queries.

Alternatively, we can apply our framework and take objects with highly confident predictions as labeled training data. Using these automatically generated training data, we can iteratively train a supervised classifier, extending the approach described in [12].

5. EXPERIMENTS

To analyze the performance of our regularization framework, we conduct extensive experiments on our showcase application of query intent classification, using a large scale real-world dataset.

The objective of our experiments is to validate that the proposed framework can utilize heterogeneous pairwise features as well as classification confidence to improve the performance, especially in a scenario with limited training data. This objective cannot be accomplished by comparing our approach with existing state-of-the-art techniques for query intent classification. Instead, we choose different schemes of our framework as the baselines (*e.g.*, using the same framework, but we assume only one kind of pairwise feature or uniform confidence). Note that in each iteration, our framework makes a similar form of updating on the predictions (Eq. 9) as the well-known graph regularization method Harmonic [20]. Hence, different schemes of our framework are well represented baselines for existing graph regularization techniques.

(a) "canon 35"
canon 35 mm lens
canon 35 f 2
35 mm wide angle 1.4 canon lens

(b) "hp laptop hard drive"
hard drive 1tb
seagate harddrive
western digital 2tb external

Figure 2: Examples of (a) lexical and (b) co-click neighbors.

5.1 Experimental Setting

Dataset. We obtain a hierarchy of product categories from Bing Shopping. As our regularization framework targets generic classification problems, which may not have hierarchical categories as labels, we use only the most detailed 2043 leaf categories (*i.e.*, $K = 2043$), instead of taking advantage of the category taxonomy. Thus, our task is to predict the leaf category for each query.

In our experiments, we use a query log containing four million distinct queries. Some of these queries have been labeled by human judges, which we split into two disjoint subsets for training and testing. Specifically, the training set consists of 10K labeled queries for parameter learning, and the test set consists of over 10K labeled queries for evaluation. Although we reserve 10K labeled queries for training, we only use 1K of them in all experiments except in Sect. 5.2.4, where we vary the number of training queries.

We also use clickthrough data to build the co-click edge model. There are about 11 million clicks associated with about $1/4$ of all queries. The fact that most queries do not have any click motivates the necessity of heterogeneous pairwise features.

Vertex model. Unless otherwise stated, we use the *language vertex model* (Sect. 4.2.1) in all experiments, which is weakly supervised and requires no labeled training queries. However, to demonstrate the robustness of our framework, we also compare it with an alternative vertex model in Sect. 5.2.2.

Evaluation metrics. For each query, we sort the categories according to their predicted probabilities, from which we can apply the following metrics.

- Top-k accuracy: the fraction of test queries which contain a correct result within the top k hypothesized categories;
- Precision-recall plot: a plot of precision against recall while varying the prediction cut-off threshold.
- Optimal f-score: the best f-score achievable among all points in the precision-recall plot.
- Precision @ 0.5 recall: precision at a recall level of 0.5. In practical scenarios, higher precision is usually more important than higher recall—we would rather not predict than suggest a wrong category.

5.2 Accuracy Study

5.2.1 Case Study

We first present some illustrative results, providing insights on why our approach works.

Query 1: "canon 35". This query is misclassified as camcorder by the unigram language model, since both words in the query are not sufficiently discriminative. However, its lexical neighbors reveal some interesting information, as illustrated in Fig. 2(a). Given these neighbors, it is not surprising that our approach can correctly classify this query as camera-lens.

Query 2: "hp laptop hard drive". This query is misclassified as laptop by the unigram model, since the words "hp laptop" strongly suggest laptops. This time, its co-click neighbors, as shown in Fig. 2(b), allow our approach to correctly classify it as hard-drive.

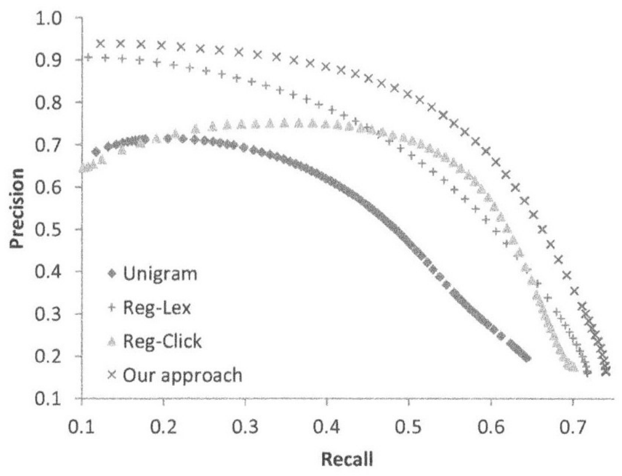

Figure 3: Precision-recall plot.

5.2.2 *Effect of Heterogeneous Pairwise Features*

We compare our approach to the vertex model and regularization baselines that only consider one kind of pairwise feature.

- Unigram: The unigram model used in our vertex model.
- Reg-Lex: The same framework as ours, but with only the lexical pairwise features (*i.e.*, the lexical edge model).
- Reg-Click: The same as Reg-Lex but with co-click pairwise features instead (*i.e.*, the co-click edge model).

Overall results. The results are reported in Fig. 3 and 4. While all regularization methods generally outperform the unigram model especially at high recall levels, we make two further observations.

First, neither Reg-Lex nor Reg-Click clearly dominates the other, which only uses lexical and co-click features, respectively. Normally we would expect Reg-Click to perform much better than Reg-Lex, since the former uses co-click pairwise features, a form of user feedback that may be more indicative than pairwise lexical features. For instance, many queries may be lexically similar yet unrelated (*e.g.*, "laptop" and "laptop bag"), or related but exhibit no lexical similarity (*e.g.*, "hp 3 in 1" and "canon printer"). Instead, our results can be explained by the sparsity of the click-through data, where only $1/4$ of the queries have received at least one click, but almost all queries have lexically similar neighbors.

Second, by using both pairwise features, our approach performs substantially better than Reg-Lex and Reg-Click. One reason is that a single kind of pairwise feature cannot cover all queries. A second reason is that the combined evidence of both pairwise features is more informative than any single one alone, thus directly improving queries that have both features and indirectly improving queries that connect to neighbors with both features.

Result breakdown. We further analyze the performance on two subsets of queries—queries with clicks and ones without—as shown in Fig. 5. As expected, Reg-Click performs well for queries with clicks, but has no effect on queries without clicks. On the other hand, Reg-Lex improves the accuracy for both subsets of queries. It is not surprising that our approach outperforms both Reg-Click and Reg-Lex for queries with clicks, since in this subset, both pairwise features improve the classification accuracy. However, we also outperforms all baselines for queries without clicks, although using co-click pairwise features alone has no effect on this subset. In this case, because classification evidence is iteratively propagated across all edge models in our approach, improvements to queries with clicks will influence their lexical neighbors, not all of which may have clicks. By combining heterogeneous pairwise features, we can extend the reach of each individual pairwise feature to influence and improve the performance of more queries via heterogeneous long-range dependencies.

Algorithm	Top-3 accuracy	Optimal f-score	Prec @ 0.5 recall
Unigram	0.663	0.564	0.465
Reg-Lex	0.735 (+10.8%)	0.660 (+17.1%)	0.676 (+45.4%)
Reg-Click	0.731 (+10.1%)	0.659 (+16.9%)	0.712 (+53.3%)
Our approach	**0.763** (+15.0%)	**0.728** (+29.2%)	**0.821** (+76.7%)

Figure 4: Accuracy comparison.

(a) Queries with clicks

Algorithm	Top-3 accuracy	Optimal f-score	Prec @ 0.5 recall
Unigram	0.721	0.609	0.593
Reg-Lex	0.795 (+10.2%)	0.704 (+15.6%)	0.780 (+31.6%)
Reg-Click	0.832 (+15.3%)	0.798 (+30.9%)	0.920 (+55.1%)
Our approach	**0.836** (+15.9%)	**0.801** (+31.5%)	**0.925** (+56.0%)

(b) Queries without clicks

Algorithm	Top-3 accuracy	Optimal f-score	Prec @ 0.5 recall
Unigram	0.573	0.495	0.238
Reg-Lex	0.641 (+11.9%)	0.583 (+17.9%)	0.445 (+87.2%)
Reg-Click	0.573 (+0.0%)	0.495 (+0.0%)	0.238 (+0.0%)
Our approach	**0.648** (+13.1%)	**0.592** (+19.7%)	**0.483** (+102.9%)

Figure 5: Accuracy comparison for queries with/without clicks.

Alternative vertex model. To demonstrate the robustness of our framework, we also evaluate our approach with an alternative *regression vertex model*. Specifically, we initialize the modes using a supervised logistic regression model (Regression) trained from a large number of labeled queries, with query words as features. To initialize the confidence, we use the query length as a heuristic, as empirical study suggests a correlation between longer queries and better classification accuracy of the regression model—longer queries contain more word features to guide the classification.

The results of using the regression vertex model are shown in Fig. 6. Similar to using the language vertex model as reported in Fig. 4, our approach outperforms the baselines by a clear margin, even though the improvements are not as substantial. We expect such results, since the regression model is a much stronger model than the unigram model, and is thus harder to improve upon. This is analogous to ensemble methods in machine learning, where it is generally easier to improve over weak learners than strong learners. Interestingly, despite initializing from a much stronger vertex model, the final results from regularizing the regression model is only slightly better than those from regularizing the unigram model. Thus, subsequent experiments use the language vertex model, which enjoys the additional benefit of being weakly supervised.

5.2.3 *Effect of Confidence*

Next, we investigate the effect of the confidence initialization on regularization. Specifically, we compare our heuristic method in Eq. 15 (Heuristic) with the following two strategies.

We call the first strategy NoConf, which uses the same framework as ours, except that no confidence information is applied. In other words, uniform confidence is used to initialize each query.

We label the second strategy Simulated, which also uses the same framework as ours. However, we initialize the confidence differently, since our confidence estimation (Eq. 15) is only a simple heuristic. To minimize the adverse effect of weak confidence

Algorithm	Top-3 accuracy	Optimal f-score	Prec @ 0.5 recall
Regression	0.719	0.680	0.739
Reg-Lex	0.746 (+3.9%)	0.697 (+2.5%)	0.773 (+4.6%)
Reg-Click	0.773 (+7.5%)	0.722 (+6.2%)	0.809 (+9.5%)
Our approach	**0.784** (+9.1%)	**0.729** (+7.3%)	**0.823** (+11.4%)

Figure 6: Accuracy comparison with regression vertex model.

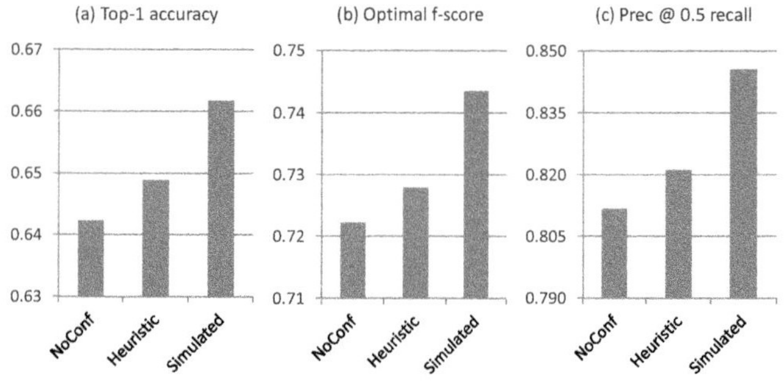

Figure 7: Accuracy with different confidence initializations.

estimation, we generate more reliable confidence values via a simulation. Specifically, for each labeled query, we sample a random value x from two Gaussian distributions. If the top-1 category predicted by the unigram model is correct, then $x \sim N(0.8, 0.1)$; otherwise, $x \sim N(0.2, 0.1)$. Subsequently, we initialize the confidence of the labeled query with x, clipped to the range $[0, 1]$. For each unlabeled query, we initialize its confidence to 0.512, which is the top-1 accuracy of the unigram model on the test queries.

The results of the different confidence initialization strategies are presented in Fig. 7. Although Heuristic only uses a simple heuristic (Eq. 15) to initialize the confidence, it performs better than NoConf, which is not confidence-aware. On the other hand, Simulated performs the best, since it initializes confidence in a more reliable way. Thus, with more sophisticated confidence estimation, we can expect even better results from our framework.

5.2.4 Effect of Varying Amount of Data

In the following experiments, we vary the amount of data in three aspects: the number of labeled training queries, total queries, and clickthroughs. It is important to study the effects of varying the amount of data, since in practical scenarios, data is collected from a live system gradually.

Number of training queries. Recall from Sect. 3.3, we require some labeled queries as training data in order to learn the parameters Λ. We examine the number of training queries needed to reach convergence on accuracy. Varying from 10 to 10K training queries, we record the corresponding performance in Fig. 8(a). The results reveal that with merely 10 training queries, we can already achieve a substantial improvement over the unigram baseline. Furthermore, with as few as 100 training queries, the performance has nearly converged. Considering that 100 is much smaller than the 2043 categories in this classification task, we demonstrate that our model requires very few training queries indeed. This is not surprising as we are not directly modeling the categories, which would require 2000+ training queries at the minimum, one for each category. Instead, we use the training queries only to learn Λ, the weights of pairwise features. Coupled with the weakly supervised language vertex model, our approach reaches convergence with very few training queries in total.

Number of total queries. The majority of our queries are unlabeled and not directly used for parameter learning. However, as we increase the number of unlabeled queries, we also improve the connectivity of the graph. To evaluate the effect, we randomly sample a subset of all queries, and apply our approach using this subset as the total set of queries. The sample size varies between 1% and 100% of all queries. To eliminate any differences due to labeled training queries, our samples include the same set of 1K training queries throughout. The results are presented in Fig. 8(b). Despite using the same set of training queries, the accuracy of our approach increases as the amount of total queries used increases. Although

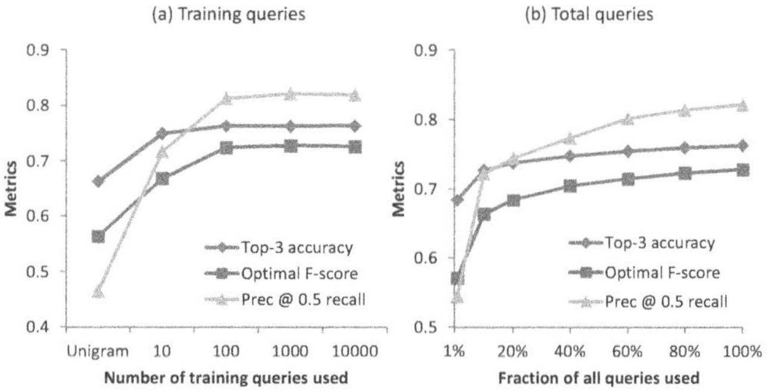

Figure 8: Accuracy versus amount of training/total queries.

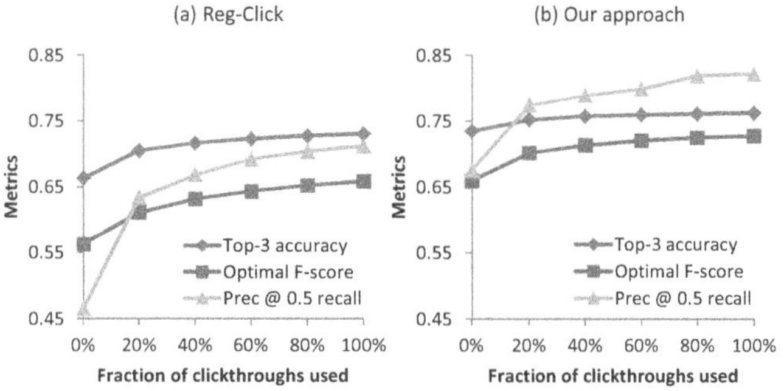

Figure 9: Accuracy versus the amount of clickthroughs.

most of the improvement is achieved when the amount of queries is initially increased from 1% to 20%, further increases result in smaller but continual improvements. From this trend, we expect that the accuracy can be further improved, but to a lesser extent, with an even larger query set.

Number of clickthroughs. Finally, we investigate the effect of varying the number of clickthroughs. Specifically, we randomly sample between 0% and 100% of clickthroughs from our query log, while using all queries and the same set of training queries. Fig. 9(a) and (b) illustrate the effect the amount of clickthroughs has on Reg-Click and our approach[2], respectively. In both methods, using a larger number of clickthroughs improves accuracy. Similar to the effect of increasing the number of total queries, the improvements diminish as more clickthroughs are used. Nevertheless, the improvements have not converged, suggesting that additional clickthrough data will further increase performance.

5.3 Efficiency Study

Although our regularization framework is designed to be applied offline periodically (Sect. 4.3), efficiency is still important. For instance, to apply it daily, it shall not take longer than a day. The following experiments evaluate the efficiency of our approach.

5.3.1 Rate of Convergence

As our approach is iterative, the number of iterations required to achieve convergence is crucial to efficiency. Our experiments show that convergence is fast, with 2 to 4 iterations in most settings. In particular, when using all available data, Fig. 10(a) illustrates the convergence of classification accuracy with a precision-recall plot. Iteration-0 corresponds to the initial vertex model. Regularization in Iteration-1 results in a larger improvement, whereas Iteration-2 shows smaller improvement. There is virtually no improvement from Iteration-3 (not shown in the figure), which indicates that the

[2]The number of clickthroughs does not affect the performance of Reg-Lex, which only utilizes lexical pairwise features.

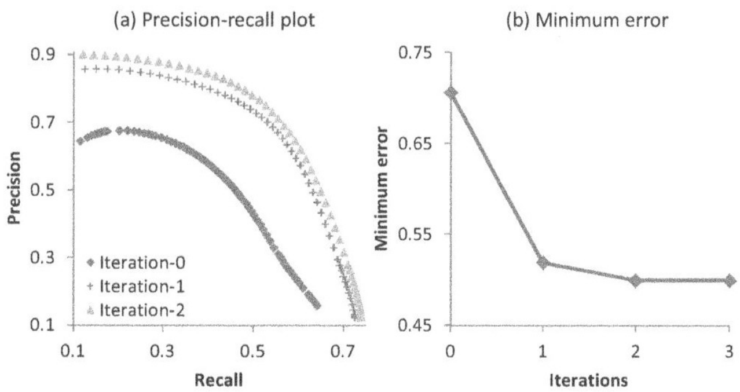

Figure 10: Convergence of (a) accuracy; (b) minimum error.

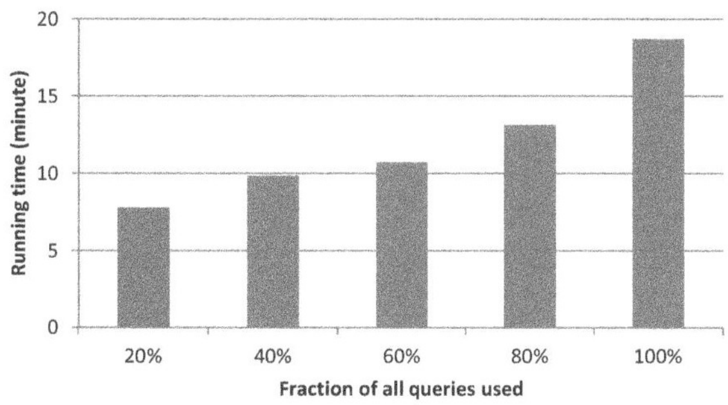

Figure 11: Execution time versus amount of total queries.

accuracy has converged. From another perspective, Fig. 10(b) illustrates the sequence of minimum errors in each minimization step (Eq. 14), which converges after only 3 iterations.

5.3.2 Execution Time

We start with a simple complexity analysis. As we scan all edges and vertices of the graph once in each iteration, the complexity is $O((E+V)T)$, where T is the number of iterations, E is the number of edges and V is the number of vertices (*i.e.*, queries). E potentially increases faster than V—the number of edges introduced by a new query potentially grows with the number of existing queries. Hence, the overall execution time would grow faster than a linear rate as we introduce more queries. Note that we do not consider the time to build the graph, which can be incrementally constructed whenever a new query is collected. Thus, it is unnecessary to build the graph from scratch every time.

In Fig. 11, we record the execution time on a single 8-core PC with 32GB memory. Consistent with our analysis above, the execution time grows slightly faster than a linear rate against the number of total queries. Nevertheless, when all four million queries are used, the execution time is just under 20 minutes. This is a reasonable time frame for our framework to be applied frequently (*e.g.*, on a daily basis), at least on the scale of tens of millions of queries. Furthermore, as the number of new queries within a fixed time interval tends to decrease over time, the total number of queries should grow sublinearly. Lastly, as Sect. 5.2.4 shows, including more queries brings in gradually less boost in accuracy. Thus, we do not expect to handle an arbitrarily large number of queries, since it would not achieve a noticeable benefit beyond a certain point.

6. CONCLUSION

In this paper, we proposed a Dirichlet-based graph regularization framework, driven by our key observations on heterogeneous pairwise features and confidence-aware classification. Building on the proposed framework, we discussed example realizations of several real-world IR tasks, particularly query intent classification in the shopping domain. Finally, we conducted extensive experiments on a large-scale real-world dataset to verify our observations. With limited training data, our approach effectively leverages heterogeneous pairwise features and classification confidence.

7. REFERENCES

[1] S. Beitzel, E. Jensen, O. Frieder, D. Lewis, A. Chowdhury, and A. Kolcz. Improving automatic query classification via semi-supervised learning. In *ICDM*, pages 42–49, 2005.

[2] M. Belkin, I. Matveeva, and P. Niyogi. Regularization and semi-supervised learning on large graphs. *Learning Theory*, pages 624–638, 2004.

[3] M. Belkin, P. Niyogi, and V. Sindhwani. Manifold regularization: A geometric framework for learning from labeled and unlabeled examples. *J. of Machine Learning Research*, 7:2399–2434, 2006.

[4] A. Broder, M. Fontoura, E. Gabrilovich, A. Joshi, V. Josifovski, and T. Zhang. Robust classification of rare queries using web knowledge. In *SIGIR*, pages 231–238, 2007.

[5] H. Cao, D. Hu, D. Shen, D. Jiang, J. Sun, E. Chen, and Q. Yang. Context-aware query classification. In *SIGIR*, pages 3–10, 2009.

[6] D. Carmel and E. Yom-Tov. Estimating the query difficulty for information retrieval. *Synthesis Lectures on Information Concepts, Retrieval, and Services*, 2(1):1–89, 2010.

[7] N. Craswell and M. Szummer. Random walks on the click graph. In *SIGIR*, pages 239–246, 2007.

[8] F. Diaz. Regularizing query-based retrieval scores. *Information Retrieval*, 10(6):531–562, 2007.

[9] F. Diaz. Improving relevance feedback in language modeling with score regularization. In *SIGIR*, pages 807–808, 2008.

[10] X. He and P. Jhala. Regularized query classification using search click information. *Pattern Recognition*, 41(7):2283–2288, 2008.

[11] M. Ji, J. Yan, S. Gu, J. Han, X. He, W. Zhang, and Z. Chen. Learning search tasks in queries and web pages via graph regularization. In *SIGIR*, pages 55–64, 2011.

[12] X. Li, Y. Wang, and A. Acero. Learning query intent from regularized click graphs. In *SIGIR*, pages 339–346, 2008.

[13] X. Li, Y. Wang, and A. Acero. Extracting structured information from user queries with semi-supervised conditional random fields. In *SIGIR*, pages 572–579, 2009.

[14] W. Press, S. Teukolsky, W. Vetterling, and B. Flannery. *Numerical Recipes*. Cambridge Univ. Press, 3rd edition, 2007.

[15] D. Shen, Y. Li, X. Li, and D. Zhou. Product query classification. In *CIKM*, pages 741–750, 2009.

[16] D. Shen, J. Sun, Q. Yang, and Z. Chen. Building bridges for web query classification. In *SIGIR*, pages 131–138, 2006.

[17] M. Szummer and T. Jaakkola. Partially labeled classification with markov random walks. In *NIPS*, volume 14, pages 945–952, 2001.

[18] D. Zhou, O. Bousquet, T. Lal, J. Weston, and B. Schölkopf. Learning with local and global consistency. In *NIPS*, pages 595–602, 2004.

[19] D. Zhou, B. Schölkopf, and T. Hofmann. Semi-supervised learning on directed graphs. *NIPS*, 17:1633–1640, 2005.

[20] X. Zhu, Z. Ghahramani, and J. Lafferty. Semi-supervised learning using Gaussian fields and harmonic functions. In *ICML*, pages 912–919, 2003.

A Utility-Theoretic Ranking Method for Semi-Automated Text Classification*

Giacomo Berardi, Andrea Esuli, and Fabrizio Sebastiani
Istituto di Scienza e Tecnologie dell'Informazione
Consiglio Nazionale delle Ricerche
56124 Pisa, Italy
[firstname.lastname]@isti.cnr.it

ABSTRACT

In *Semi-Automated Text Classification* (SATC) an automatic classifier $\hat{\Phi}$ labels a set of unlabelled documents $\mathcal{D}$, following which a human annotator inspects (and corrects when appropriate) the labels attributed by $\hat{\Phi}$ to a subset $\mathcal{D}'$ of $\mathcal{D}$, with the aim of improving the overall quality of the labelling.

An automated system can support this process by ranking the automatically labelled documents in a way that maximizes the expected increase in effectiveness that derives from inspecting $\mathcal{D}'$. An obvious strategy is to rank $\mathcal{D}$ so that the documents that $\hat{\Phi}$ has classified with the lowest confidence are top-ranked. In this work we show that this strategy is suboptimal. We develop a new utility-theoretic ranking method based on the notion of *inspection gain*, defined as the improvement in classification effectiveness that would derive by inspecting and correcting a given automatically labelled document. We also propose a new effectiveness measure for SATC-oriented ranking methods, based on the expected reduction in classification error brought about by partially inspecting a list generated by a given ranking method. We report the results of experiments showing that, with respect to the baseline method above, and according to the proposed measure, our ranking method can achieve substantially higher expected reductions in classification error.

Categories and Subject Descriptors

I.5.2 [**Pattern Recognition**]: Design Methodology—*Classifier design and evaluation*; H.3.3 [**Information Storage and Retrieval**]: Information Search and Retrieval—*Information filtering; Search process*; I.2.7 [**Artificial Intelligence**]: Natural Language Processing—*Text analysis*

Keywords

Text classification, supervised learning, semi-automated text classification, cost-sensitive learning, ranking

*In order to correctly interpret the plots in Figures 1 and 2, this document should be printed in colour.

1. INTRODUCTION

Suppose an organization needs to classify a set $\mathcal{D}$ of textual documents under classification scheme $\mathcal{C}$, and suppose that $\mathcal{D}$ is too large to be classified manually, so that resorting to some form of automated text classification (TC) is the only viable option. Suppose also that the organization has strict accuracy standards, so that the level of effectiveness obtainable via state-of-the-art TC technology is not sufficient. In this case, the most plausible strategy to follow is to classify $\mathcal{D}$ by means of an automatic classifier $\hat{\Phi}$ (which we assume here to be generated by training a supervised learner on a training set Tr), and then to have a human editor inspect the results of the automatic classification, correcting misclassifications where appropriate[1]. The human annotator will obviously inspect only a subset $\mathcal{D}' \subset \mathcal{D}$ (since it would not otherwise make sense to have an initial automated classification phase), e.g., until she is confident that the overall level of accuracy of $\mathcal{D}$ is sufficient. We call this scenario *semi-automated text classification* (SATC).

An automatic TC system may support this task by ranking, after the classification phase has ended and before the inspection begins, the classified documents in a such a way that, if the human annotator inspects the documents starting from the top of the ranking and working down the list, the expected increase in classification effectiveness that derives from this inspection is maximized. This paper is concerned with devising good ranking strategies for this task.

One obvious strategy is to rank the documents in ascending order of the confidence scores generated by $\hat{\Phi}$, so that the top-ranked documents are the ones that $\hat{\Phi}$ has classified with the lowest confidence[2]. The rationale is that an increase in effectiveness can derive only by inspecting *misclassified* documents, and that a good ranking method is simply the one that top-ranks the documents with the highest probability of misclassification, which (in the absence of other information) we may take to be the documents which $\hat{\Phi}$ has classified with the lowest confidence.

In this work we show that this strategy is, in general, suboptimal. Simply stated, the reason is that, when we deal with imbalanced TC problems (as most TC problems indeed

[1]In the rest of this paper we will simply write "inspect" to actually mean "inspect and correct where appropriate".

[2]We call this strategy "obvious" because of the evident similarities between SATC and active learning (see Section 6), where this strategy is an often-used baseline. However, to the best of our knowledge, the application of this ranking method (or of any other ranking method, for that matter) to SATC has never been discussed in the literature.

are) and, as a consequence, choose an evaluation measure – such as F_1 – that caters for this imbalance, the improvements in effectiveness that derive from correcting a false positive or a false negative may not be the same.

The contributions of this paper are the following. First, we develop a new utility-theoretic ranking method for SATC based on the notion of *inspection gain*, i.e., the improvement in effectiveness that would derive by correcting a given type of mistake (i.e., false positive or false negative). Second, we propose a new evaluation measure for SATC, and use it to evaluate our experiments on a standard dataset. The results show that, with respect to the confidence-based baseline method above, our ranking method is substantially more effective.

The rest of the paper is organized as follows. Section 2 sets out preliminary definitions and notation. Section 3 describes our utility-theoretic strategy for ranking the automatically labelled documents, while Section 4 describes the effectiveness measure we propose for this task. Section 5 reports the results of our experiments in which we compare the different ranking strategies by simulating the work of a human annotator that inspects variable portions of the classified test set. Section 6 reviews related work, while Section 7 concludes by charting avenues for future research.

2. PRELIMINARIES

This paper focuses on semi-automated (multi-class) *multi-label* TC. Given a set of textual documents $\mathcal{D}$ and a predefined set of classes $\mathcal{C} = \{c_1, \ldots, c_m\}$, multi-label TC is usually defined as the task of estimating an unknown *target function* $\Phi : \mathcal{D} \times \mathcal{C} \rightarrow \{-1, +1\}$, that describes how documents ought to be classified, by means of a function $\hat{\Phi} : \mathcal{D} \times \mathcal{C} \rightarrow \{-1, +1\}$ called the *classifier*[3]. Here, $+1$ and -1 represent membership and non-membership of the document in the class. Each document may thus belong to zero, one, or several classes at the same time. Multi-label TC is usually accomplished by generating m independent binary classifiers $\hat{\Phi}_j$, one for each $c_j \in \mathcal{C}$, each entrusted with deciding whether a document belongs or not to a class c_j.

In this paper we will restrict our attention to classifiers $\hat{\Phi}_j$ that, aside from taking a binary decision $D_{ij} \in \{-1, +1\}$ on a given document d_i, also return a *confidence estimate* C_{ij}, i.e., a numerical value representing the strength of their belief in the fact that D_{ij} is correct (the higher the value, the higher the confidence). We formalize this by taking a binary classifier to be a function $\hat{\Phi}_j : \mathcal{D} \rightarrow (-\infty, +\infty)$ in which the sign of the returned value $D_{ij} \equiv sgn(\hat{\Phi}_j(d_i)) \in \{-1, +1\}$ indicates the binary decision of the classifier, and the absolute value $C_{ij} \equiv |\hat{\Phi}_j(d_i)|$ represents its confidence in the decision.

For the purposes of this paper we also assume that

$$F_1(\hat{\Phi}_j(Te)) = 2TP_j/(2TP_j + FP_j + FN_j) \qquad (1)$$

(the well-known harmonic mean of precision and recall) is the chosen evaluation measure, where $\hat{\Phi}_j(Te)$ indicates the result of applying $\hat{\Phi}_j$ to the test set Te and TP_j, FP_j, FN_j, and TN_j indicate the numbers of true positives, false positives, false negatives, and true negatives in Te. Note that F_1 is undefined when $TP_j = FP_j = FN_j = 0$; in this case we take $F_1(\hat{\Phi}_j(Te)) = 1$, since $\hat{\Phi}_j$ has correctly classified all documents as negative examples.

We also use $TP(ij)$ as a shorthand to indicate that $\hat{\Phi}_j(d_i)$ is a true positive, and use $FP(ij)$, $FN(ij)$, and $TN(ij)$ with analogous meanings. In this paper the set of unlabelled documents that the classifier must automatically label (and rank) in the "operational" phase will be represented by the test set Te.

[3]Consistently with most mathematical literature we use the caret symbol (ˆ) to indicate estimation.

3. A RANKING METHOD FOR SATC BASED ON UTILITY THEORY

3.1 Ranking by utility

For the moment being, let us concentrate on the binary case, i.e., let us assume there is a single class c_j that needs to be separated from its complement $\overline{c}_j$. The policy we propose for ranking the automatically labelled documents in $\hat{\Phi}_j(Te)$ makes use of a function $U_j(d_i)$ that estimates the utility, for the aims of increasing $F_1(\hat{\Phi}_j(Te))$, of manually inspecting the label D_{ij} attributed to d_i by $\hat{\Phi}_j$.

Given a set Ω of mutually disjoint events, a *utility function* is defined as a sum $\sum_{\omega \in \Omega} P(\omega)G(\omega)$, where $P(\omega)$ represents the probability of occurrence of event ω and $G(\omega)$ represents the *gain* obtained if event ω indeed occurs.

Upon submitting document d_i to classifier $\hat{\Phi}_j$, a positive or a negative decision can be returned. If a positive decision is returned (i.e., $D_{ij} = +1$) then the mutually disjoint events $TP(ij)$ and $FP(ij)$ can occur, while if this decision is negative (i.e., $D_{ij} = -1$) then the mutually disjoint events $FN(ij)$ and $TN(ij)$ can occur. We thus naturally define the two utility functions

$$\begin{aligned} U_j^+(d_i) &= P(TP(ij)|D_{ij} = +1) \cdot G(TP(ij)) + \\ &\quad + P(FP(ij)|D_{ij} = +1) \cdot G(FP(ij)) \\ U_j^-(d_i) &= P(FN(ij)|D_{ij} = -1) \cdot G(FN(ij)) + \\ &\quad + P(TN(ij)|D_{ij} = -1) \cdot G(TN(ij)) \end{aligned} \qquad (2)$$

with $U_j^+(d_i)$ addressing the case of a positive decision and $U_j^-(d_i)$ the case of a negative decision. We also define

$$U_j(d_i) = \begin{cases} U_j^+(d_i) & \text{if } D_{ij} = +1 \\ U_j^-(d_i) & \text{if } D_{ij} = -1 \end{cases} \qquad (3)$$

as a function embracing both positive and negative decisions.

3.2 Inspection gains

We equate $G(FP(ij))$ in Equations 2 with the average increase in $F_1(\hat{\Phi}_j(Te))$ that would derive by manually inspecting the label attributed by $\hat{\Phi}_j$ to a document in FP_j. We call this the *inspection gain* of a member of FP_j. From now on we will write $G(FP_j)$ instead of $G(FP(ij))$ so as to reflect the fact that the inspection value is the same for all members of FP_j. Analogous arguments apply to $G(TP(ij))$, $G(FN(ij))$, and $G(TN(ij))$.

Quite evidently, $G(TP_j) = G(TN_j) = 0$, since when the human annotator inspects the label attributed to d_i by $\hat{\Phi}_j$ and finds out it is correct, she will not modify it, and the value of $F_1(\hat{\Phi}_j(Te))$ will thus remain unchanged. This means that Equations 2 simplify to

$$\begin{aligned} U_j^+(d_i) &= P(FP(ij)|D_{ij} = +1) \cdot G(FP_j) \\ U_j^-(d_i) &= P(FN(ij)|D_{ij} = -1) \cdot G(FN_j) \end{aligned} \qquad (4)$$

$G(FP_j)$ (resp., $G(FN_j)$) evaluates instead to the average increase in $F_1(\hat{\Phi}_j(Te))$ obtained by correcting a false positive (resp., a false negative). It is easy to see that, in general, $G(FP_j) \neq G(FN_j)$. In fact, if a false positive is corrected, the increase in F_1 is the one deriving from removing a false positive and adding a true negative, i.e.,

$$\begin{aligned} G(FP_j) &= \frac{1}{FP_j}(F_1^{FP}(\hat{\Phi}_j) - F_1(\hat{\Phi}_j(Te))) \\ &= \frac{1}{FP_j}(\frac{2TP_j}{2TP_j + FN_j} \\ &\quad - \frac{2TP_j}{2TP_j + FP_j + FN_j}) \end{aligned} \tag{5}$$

where by $F_1^{FP}(\hat{\Phi}_j)$ we indicate the value of F_1 that would derive by correcting all false positives of $\hat{\Phi}_j(Te)$, i.e., turning them into true negatives. Conversely, if a false negative is corrected, the increase in F_1 is the one deriving from removing a false negative and adding a true positive, i.e.,

$$\begin{aligned} G(FN_j) &= \frac{1}{FN_j}(F_1^{FN}(\hat{\Phi}_j) - F_1(\hat{\Phi}_j(Te))) \\ &= \frac{1}{FN_j}(\frac{2(TP_j + FN_j)}{2(TP_j + FN_j) + FP_j} \\ &\quad - \frac{2TP_j}{2TP_j + FP_j + FN_j}) \end{aligned} \tag{6}$$

where by $F_1^{FN}(\hat{\Phi}_j)$ we indicate the value of F_1 that would derive by turning all the false negatives of $\hat{\Phi}_j(Te)$ into true positives.

3.3 Estimating the probabilities

We derive the probabilities $P(\cdot)$ in Equations 4 by assuming that the confidence scores C_{ij} generated by $\hat{\Phi}_j$ can be trusted (i.e., that the higher C_{ij}, the higher the probability that D_{ij} is correct), and by applying to C_{ij} a *generalized logistic function* $f(z) = e^{\sigma z}/(e^{\sigma z} + 1)$. This results in

$$\begin{aligned} P(FP(ij)|D_{ij} = +1) = 1 - \frac{e^{\sigma C_{ij}}}{e^{\sigma C_{ij}} + 1} \\ P(FN(ij)|D_{ij} = -1) = 1 - \frac{e^{\sigma C_{ij}}}{e^{\sigma C_{ij}} + 1} \end{aligned} \tag{7}$$

The generalized logistic function has the effect of monotonically converting scores ranging on $(-\infty, +\infty)$ into real values in the [0.0,1.0] range. When $C_{ij} = 0$ (this happens when $\hat{\Phi}_j$ has no confidence at all in its own decision D_{ij}), then $P(TP(ij)|D_{ij} = +1) = P(FP(ij)|D_{ij} = +1) = 0.5$ and $P(FN(ij)|D_{ij} = -1) = P(TN(ij)|D_{ij} = -1) = 0.5$, i.e., the probability of correct classification and the probability of misclassification are identical. Conversely, we have

$$\begin{aligned} \lim_{C_{ij} \to +\infty} P(FP(ij)|D_{ij} = +1) &= 0 \\ \lim_{C_{ij} \to +\infty} P(FN(ij)|D_{ij} = -1) &= 0 \end{aligned}$$

This means that, when $\hat{\Phi}_j$ has a very high confidence in its own decision D_{ij}, the probability that D_{ij} is wrong is taken to be very low.

The reason why we use a *generalized* version of the logistic function instead of the standard version (which corresponds to the case $\sigma = 1$) is that using this latter within Equations 7 would give rise to a very high number of zero probabilities of misclassification, since the standard logistic function converts every positive number above a certain threshold (≈ 36) to a number that standard implementations round to 1 even by working in double precision. By tuning the σ parameter (the *growth rate*) we can tune the speed at which the right-hand side of the sigmoid asymptotically approaches 1, and we can thus tune how evenly Equations 7 distribute the confidence values across the [0.0,0.5] interval. How we optimize the σ parameter is discussed in Section 5.1.

3.4 Smoothing contingency cell estimates for computing $G(FP_j)$ and $G(FN_j)$

One problem that needs to be tackled in order to compute $G(FP_j)$ and $G(FN_j)$ is that the contingency cell counts TP_j, FP_j, and FN_j are not known, and thus need to be estimated[4]. In order to estimate $\alpha_j \in \{TP_j, FP_j, FN_j\}$ we make the assumption that the training set and the test set are independent and identically distributed. We then perform a k-fold cross-validation on the training set: if by TP_j^{Tr} we denote the number of true positives for class c_j resulting from the k-fold cross-validation on Tr, the maximum-likelihood estimate of TP_j is $\hat{TP}_j^{ML} = TP_j^{Tr} \cdot |Te|/|Tr|$; the same holds for $\hat{FP}_j^{ML}$ and $\hat{FN}_j^{ML}$.

However, these maximum-likelihood cell count estimates (noted $\hat{\alpha}_j^{ML}$) need to be smoothed, so as to avoid zero counts. In fact, if $\hat{TP}_j^{ML} = 0$, it would derive from Equation 5 that there is nothing to be gained by correcting a false positive, which is counterintuitive. Similarly, if $\hat{FP}_j^{ML} = 0$, the very notion of $F_1^{FP}(\hat{\Phi}_j)$ would be meaningless, since it does not make sense to speak of "removing a false positive" when there are no false positives; the same goes for $\hat{FN}_j^{ML}$.

A second reason why the $\hat{\alpha}_j^{ML}$ need to be smoothed is that, when $|Te|/|Tr| < 1$, they may give rise to negative values for $G(FP_j)$ and $G(FN_j)$, which is obviously counterintuitive. To see this, note that the $\hat{\alpha}_j^{ML}$ may not be integers (which is not bad per se, since the notions of precision, recall, and their harmonic mean intuitively make sense also when we allow the contingency cell counts to be nonnegative reals instead of the usual integers), and may be smaller than 1 (this happens when $|Te|/|Tr| < 1$). This latter fact is problematic, both in theory (since it is meaningless to speak of, say, removing a false positive from Te when "there are less than 1 false positives in Te") and in practice (since it is easy to verify that negative values for $G(FP_j)$ and $G(FN_j)$ may derive).

Smoothing has extensively been studied in language modelling for speech processing [3] and for ad hoc search in IR [24]. However, the present context is slightly different, in that we need to smooth contingency tables, and not (as in the cases above) language models. In particular, while the $\hat{\alpha}_j^{ML}$ are the obvious counterpart of the document model resulting from maximum-likelihood estimation, there is no obvious counterpart to the "collection model", thus making the use of, e.g., Jelinek-Mercer smoothing problematic. A further difference is that we here require the smoothed counts not only to be nonzero, but also to be ≥ 1 (a requirement not to be found in language modelling).

Smoothing has also been studied specifically for the pur-

[4]We will disregard the estimation of TN_j since it is unnecessary for our purposes, given that $F_1(\hat{\Phi}_j(Te))$ does not depend on TN_j.

pose of smoothing contingency cell estimates [1, 21]. However, these methods are inapplicable to our case, since they were originally conceived for contingency tables characterized by a small (i.e., ≤ 1) ratio between the number of observations (which in our case is $|Te|$) and the number of cells (which in our case is 4); our case is quite the opposite. Additionally, these smoothing methods do not operate under the constraint that the smoothed counts should all be ≥ 1, which is a hard constraint for us.

For all these reasons, rather than adopting more sophisticated forms of smoothing, we adopt simple *additive smoothing* (also known as *Laplace smoothing*), a special case of Bayesian smoothing using Dirichlet priors [24] which is obtained by adding a fixed quantity to all the $\hat{\alpha}_j^{ML}$. As a fixed quantity we add 1, since it is the quantity that all our cell counts need to be greater or equal to for Equations 5 and 6 to make sense. We thus leave the study of more sophisticated smoothing methods to future work.

However, it should be noted that we apply smoothing in an "on demand" fashion, i.e., we check if the contingency table needs smoothing at all (i.e, if any of the $\hat{\alpha}_j^{ML}$ is < 1) and we smooth it only if this is the case.

3.5 Ranking by total utility

Our function $U_j(d_i)$ of Section 3.1 is thus obtained by plugging Equations 5 and 6 into Equations 4.

At this point, it would seem sensible to propose ranking, for each $c_j \in \mathcal{C}$, all the automatically labelled documents in Te in decreasing order of their $U_j(d_i)$ value. Unfortunately, this would generate $|\mathcal{C}|$ different rankings, and in an operational context it seems implausible to ask a human annotator to scan $|\mathcal{C}|$ different rankings of the same documents (this might mean reading the same document $|\mathcal{C}|$ times in order to validate its labels). As suggested in [6] for active learning, it seems instead more plausible to generate a *single* ranking, according to a score $U(d_i)$ that is a function of the $|\mathcal{C}|$ different $U_j(d_i)$ scores. In such a way, the human annotator will scan this single ranking from the top, validating all the $|\mathcal{C}|$ different labels for d_i before moving on to another document. As the criterion for generating the overall utility score $U(d_i)$ we use *total utility*, corresponding to the simple sum

$$U(d_i) = \sum_{c_j \in \mathcal{C}} U_j(d_i) \tag{8}$$

Our final ranking is thus generated by sorting the test documents in descending order of their $U(d_i)$ score.

From the standpoint of computational cost, this technique is $O(|Te| \cdot (|\mathcal{C}| + \log |Te|))$, since the cost of sorting the test documents by their $U(\cdot)$ score is $O(|Te| \log |Te|)$, and the cost of computing the $U(\cdot)$ score for $|Te|$ documents and $|\mathcal{C}|$ classes is $O(|Te| \cdot |\mathcal{C}|)$.

4. EXPECTED NORMALIZED ERROR REDUCTION

No measures are known from literature for evaluating the effectiveness of a SATC-oriented ranking method ρ. We here propose such a measure, which we call *expected normalized error reduction* (noted $ENER_\rho$).

4.1 Error reduction at rank

Let us first introduce the notion of *residual error at rank n* (noted $E_\rho(n)$, which we assume to range on [0,1]), defined as the error that is still present in the document set Te after the human annotator has inspected the documents at the first n rank positions in the ranking generated by ρ. The value of $E_\rho(0)$ is the initial error generated by the automated classifier, and the value of $E_\rho(|Te|)$ is 0. We will hereafter call n the *inspection length*.

We next define *error reduction at rank n* to be

$$ER_\rho(n) = \frac{E_\rho(0) - E_\rho(n)}{E_\rho(0)} \tag{9}$$

i.e., a value in [0,1] that indicates the error reduction obtained by a human annotator who has inspected the documents at the first n rank positions in the ranking generated by ρ; 0 stands for no reduction, 1 stands for total elimination of error.

Example plots of the $ER_\rho(n)$ measure are displayed in Figures 1 and 2, where different curves represent different ranking methods $\rho', \rho'', \ldots$, and where, for better convenience, the x axis indicates the fraction $n/|Te|$ of the test set that has been inspected rather than the number n of inspected documents. By definition all curves start at the origin of the axes and end at the upper right corner of the graph. Higher curves represent better strategies, since they indicate that a higher error reduction is achieved for the same amount of manual inspecting effort.

The reason why we focus on error reduction, instead of the complementary concept of "increase in accuracy", is that error reduction has always the same upper bound (i.e., 100% reduction), independently of the initial error. In contrast, the increase in accuracy that derives from inspecting the documents does *not* always have the same upper bound. For instance, if the initial accuracy is 0.5 (with accuracy values ranging on [0,1]), then an increase in accuracy of 100% is indeed possible, while this increase is not possible if the initial accuracy is 0.9. This makes the notion of increase in accuracy problematic, since different datasets and/or different classifiers give rise to different initial levels of accuracy. So, using error reduction instead of increase in accuracy "normalizes" our curves, i.e., allows a meaningful comparison of curves obtained on different datasets and after different classifiers have been used.

Since (as stated in Section 2) we use F_1 for measuring effectiveness, as a measure of classification error we use $E_1 \equiv (1 - F_1)$. In order to measure the overall effectiveness of a ranking method across the entire set $\mathcal{C}$ of categories, we compute two versions of $ER_\rho(n)$, one based on *microaveraged* E_1 (denoted by E_1^μ) and one based on *macroaveraged* E_1 (E_1^M). E_1^μ is obtained by (i) computing the class-specific values TP_j, FP_j and FN_j, (ii) obtaining TP as the sum of the TP_j's (same for FP and FN), and then (iii) applying the formula $E_1 = 1 - \frac{2TP}{2TP+FP+FN} = \frac{FP+FN}{2TP+FP+FN}$. E_1^M is instead obtained by computing the class-specific E_1 values and averaging them across the c_j's. The two versions of $ER_\rho(n)$ will be indicated as $ER_\rho^\mu(n)$ and $ER_\rho^M(n)$.

4.2 Normalized error reduction at rank ...

One problem with $ER_\rho(n)$, though, is that the expected $ER_\rho(n)$ value of the random ranker is fairly high[5], since it

[5]That the expected $ER_\rho(n)$ value of the random ranker is $\frac{n}{|Te|}$ is something that we have not tried to formally prove. However, that this holds is supported by intuition *and* is unequivocally shown by Monte Carlo experiments we have

amounts (for both $ER^{\mu}_{\rho}(n)$ and $ER^{M}_{\rho}(n)$) to $\frac{n}{|Te|}$. The difference between the $ER_{\rho}(n)$ value of a genuinely engineered ranking method ρ and the expected $ER_{\rho}(n)$ value of the random ranker is particularly small for high values of n, and is null for $n = |Te|$. This means that it makes sense to factor out the random factor from $ER_{\rho}(n)$. This leads us to define the *normalized error reduction* of ranking method ρ as $NER_{\rho}(n) = ER_{\rho}(n) - \frac{n}{|Te|}$, with the two versions noted as $NER^{\mu}_{\rho}(n)$ and $NER^{M}_{\rho}(n)$.

4.3 ... and its expected value

However, $NER_{\rho}(n)$ is still unsatisfactory as a measure, since it depends on a specific value of n (which is undesirable, since our human annotator may decide to work down the ranked list as far as she deems suitable). Following [18] we assume that the human annotator stops inspecting the ranked list at exactly rank n with probability $P_s(n)$. We can then define the *expected normalized error reduction* of ranking method ρ on a given document set Te as

$$ENER_{\rho} = \sum_{n=1}^{|Te|} P_s(n) NER_{\rho}(n) \tag{10}$$

with the two versions indicated as $ENER^{\mu}_{\rho}$ and $ENER^{M}_{\rho}$.

Different probability distributions $P_s(n)$ can be assumed. In order to base the definition of such a distribution on a plausible model of user behaviour, we here make the assumption (along with [15]) that a human annotator, after inspecting a document, goes on to inspect the next document with probability p (also called *persistence* in [15]) or stops inspecting with probability $(1-p)$, so that

$$P_s(n) = \begin{cases} p^{n-1}(1-p) & \text{if } n \in \{1, \ldots, |Te|-1\} \\ p^{n-1} & \text{if } n = |Te| \end{cases} \tag{11}$$

It can be shown that, for a sufficiently large value of $|Te|$, the expected number of documents that the human annotator will inspect as a function of p asymptotically tends to $\frac{1}{1-p}$. The value $\xi = \frac{1}{|Te|(1-p)}$ thus denotes the expected fraction of the test set that the human annotator will inspect as a function of p.

Using this distribution entails the need of determining a realistic value for p. A value $p = 0$ corresponds to a situation in which the human annotator only inspects the top-ranked document, while $p = 1$ indicates a human annotator who inspects each document in the ranked list. Unlike in ad hoc search, we think that in a SATC context it would be unrealistic to take a value for p as given irrespective of the size of Te. In fact, given a desired level of error reduction, when $|Te|$ is large the human annotators need to be more persistent (i.e., characterized by higher p) than when $|Te|$ is small.

Therefore, instead of assuming a predetermined value of p we assume a predetermined value of ξ, and derive the value of p from the equation $\xi = \frac{1}{|Te|(1-p)}$. For example, in a certain application we might assume $\xi = .2$ (i.e., that the average human annotator inspects 20% of the test set). In this case, if $|Te| = 1,000$, then $p = 1 - \frac{1}{.2 \cdot 1000} = .9950$, while if $|Te| = 10,000$, then $p = 1 - \frac{1}{.2 \cdot 10000} = .9995$. In the experiments of Section 5 we will test all values of p corresponding to values of ξ in $\{.05, .10, .20\}$.

run on our datasets; see Figures 1 and 2 for a graphical representation.

Note that the values of $ENER_{\rho}$ are bounded above by 1, but a value of 1 is not attainable. In fact, even the "perfect ranker" (i.e., the ranking method that top-ranks all misclassified documents, noted *Perf*) cannot attain an $ENER_{\rho}$ value of 1, since in order to achieve total error elimination all the misclassified documents need to be inspected anyway, which means that the only condition in which $ENER_{Perf}$ might equal 1 is when there is just 1 misclassified document. We do not try to normalize $ENER_{\rho}$ by the value of $ENER_{Perf}$ since $ENER_{Perf}$ cannot be characterized analytically, and depends on the actual labels in the test set.

5. EXPERIMENTS

5.1 Experimental protocol

Let Ω be a dataset partitioned into a training set Tr and a test set Te. In each experiment reported in this paper we adopt the following experimental protocol:

1. For each $c_j \in \mathcal{C}$
   (a) Train classifier $\hat{\Phi}_j$ on Tr and classify Te by means of $\hat{\Phi}_j$;
   (b) Run k-fold cross-validation on Tr, thereby
      i. computing TP^{Tr}_j, FP^{Tr}_j, and FN^{Tr}_j;
      ii. optimizing the σ parameter of Equations 7;
2. For every ranking policy ρ tested
   (a) Rank Te according to ρ;
   (b) Scan the ranked list from the top, correcting possible misclassifications and computing the resulting values of $ENER^{\mu}_{\rho}$ and $ENER^{M}_{\rho}$ for different values of ξ.

For Step 1b we have used $k = 10$.

The optimization method we use for Step 1(b)ii consists in picking the value of σ that minimizes the average (across the $c_j \in \mathcal{C}$) absolute value of the difference between Pos^{Tr}_j, the number of positive training examples of class c_j, and $E[Pos^{Tr}_j]$, the *expected* number of such examples as resulting from the probabilities of membership in c_j computed in the k-fold cross-validation. That is, we pool together all the training documents classified in the k-fold cross-validation, and then we pick

$$\arg\min_{\sigma} \frac{1}{|\mathcal{C}|} \sum_{c_j \in \mathcal{C}} |Pos^{Tr}_j - E[Pos^{Tr}_j]| =$$

$$\arg\min_{\sigma} \frac{1}{|\mathcal{C}|} \sum_{c_j \in \mathcal{C}} |Pos^{Tr}_j - \sum_{d_i \in Tr} \frac{e^{\sigma \hat{\Phi}_j(d_i)}}{e^{\sigma \hat{\Phi}_j(d_i)} + 1}|$$

This is a much faster parameter optimization method than the traditional method of picking the value that has performed best in k-fold cross-validation since, unlike the latter, it does not depend on the ranking method ρ. Therefore, this method spares us from the need of ranking the training set several times, i.e., for each combination of a tested value of σ and a ranking method ρ.

As the learner for generating our classifiers $\hat{\Phi}_j$ we use a boosting-based learner called MP-Boost [5]. Boosting-based methods have showed very good performance across many learning tasks and, at the same time, have strong justifications from computational learning theory. MP-Boost

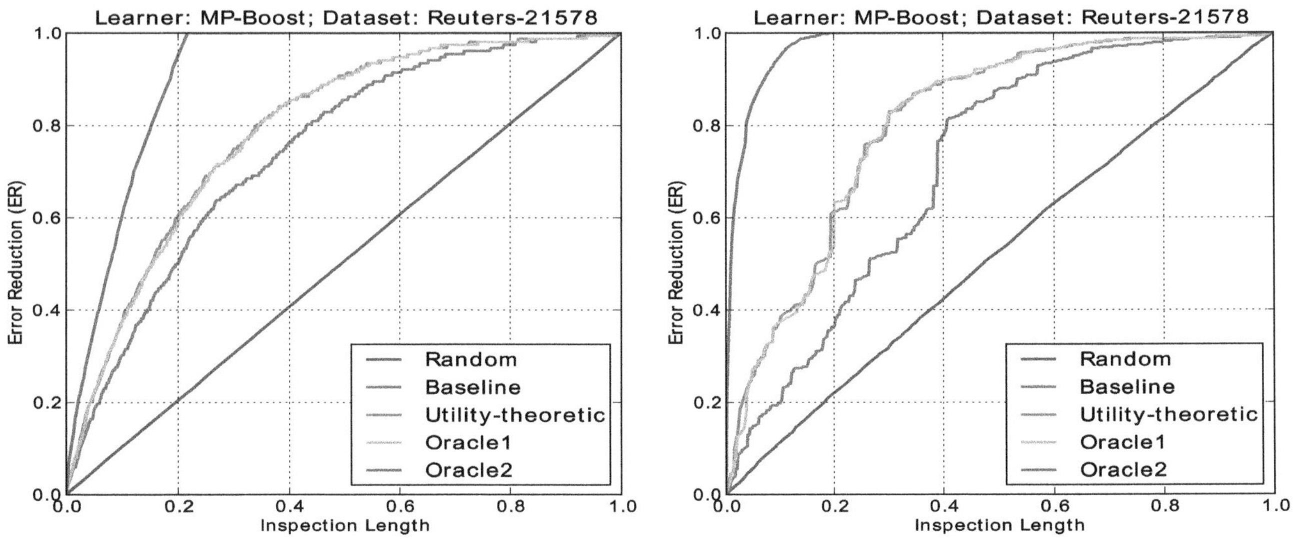

Figure 1: Error reduction as a function of the fraction of the test set that the human annotator has inspected. The dataset is the Reuters-21578 collection. Error reduction is measured as ER_ρ^μ (left) and ER_ρ^M (right). The Random curve indicates the results of our estimation of the expected performance of the random ranker via a Monte Carlo method with 50 random trials. Higher curves are better.

is a variant of AdaBoost.MH [19] optimized for multi-label settings, which has been shown in [5] to obtain considerable effectiveness improvements with respect to AdaBoost.MH. MP-Boost generates a classifier $\hat{\Phi}_j$ where $sgn(\hat{\Phi}_j(d_i))$ represents the binary decision as to whether d_i belongs to c_j and $|\hat{\Phi}_j(d_i)|$ represents the confidence in this decision. In all our experiments we set the S parameter of MP-Boost (representing the number of boosting iterations) to 1000.

As dataset we have used the Reuters-21578 corpus. It consists of a set of 12,902 news stories, partitioned (according to the "ModApté" split we have adopted) into a training set of 9,603 documents and a test set of 3,299 documents. The documents are labelled by 118 categories; the average number of categories per document is 1.08, ranging from a minimum of 0 to a maximum of 16; the number of positive examples per class ranges from a minimum of 1 to a maximum of 3964. In our experiments we have restricted our attention to the 115 categories with at least one positive training example. This dataset is publicly available[6] and is probably the most widely used benchmark in text classification research, which allows other researchers to easily replicate the results of our experiments.

In all the experiments discussed in this paper stop words have been removed, punctuation has been removed, all letters have been converted to lowercase, numbers have been removed, and stemming has been performed by means of Porter's stemmer. Word stems are thus our indexing units. Since MP-Boost requires binary input, only their presence/absence in the document is recorded, and no weighting is performed.

[6]http://www.daviddlewis.com/resources/testcollections/~reuters21578/

5.2 Results and discussion

5.2.1 Lower bounds and upper bounds

As the baseline for our experiments we use the confidence-based strategy discussed in Section 1, which corresponds to using our utility-theoretic method with both $G(FP)$ and $G(FN)$ set to 1. As discussed in Footnote 2, while this strategy has not explicitly been proposed before, it seems a reasonable, common-sense strategy anyway.

While the confidence-based method will act as our lower bound, we have also run "oracle-based" methods aimed at identifying upper bounds for the effectiveness of our utility-theoretic method, i.e., at assessing the effectiveness of "idealized" (albeit non-realistic) systems at our task.

The first such method (dubbed Oracle1) consists of "peeking" at the actual values of TP_j, FP_j, and FN_j in Te, using them in the computation of $G(FP_j)$ and $G(FN_j)$, and running our utility-theoretic method as usual. Oracle1 thus indicates how our method would behave were it able to "perfectly" estimate TP_j, FP_j, and FN_j. The difference in effectiveness between Oracle1 and our method will thus be due to (i) the performance of the smoothing method adopted, and (ii) possible differences between the distribution of the documents across the contingency table cells in the training and in the test set.

In the second such method (Oracle2) we instead peek at the true labels of the documents in Te, which means that we will be able to (a) use the actual values of TP_j, FP_j, and FN_j in the computation of $G(FP_j)$ and $G(FN_j)$ (as in Oracle1), *and* (b) replace the probabilities in Equations 4 with the true binary values (i.e., replacing $P(x)$ with 1 if x is true and 0 if x is false), after which we run our utility-based ranking method as usual. The difference in effectiveness between Oracle2 and our method will be due to factors (i) and (ii) already mentioned for Oracle1 *and* to our method's

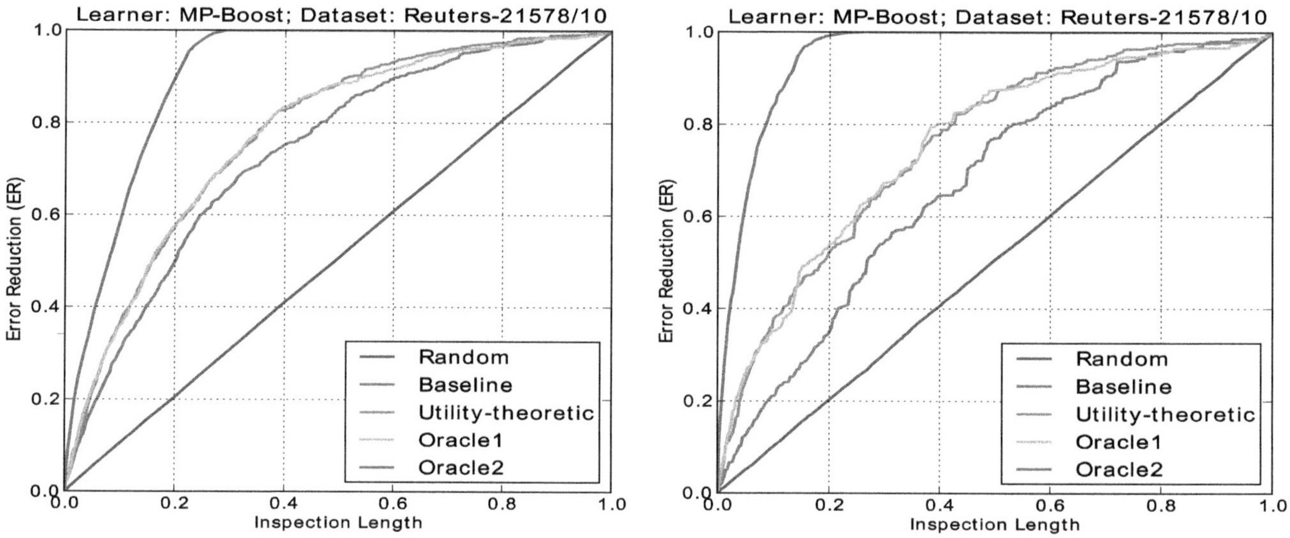

Figure 2: Results obtained by (a) splitting the Reuters-21578 test set into 10 random, equally-sized parts, (b) running the analogous experiments of Figure 1 independently on each part, and (c) averaging the results across the 10 parts.

(obvious) inability to perfectly predict whether a document was classified correctly or not.

5.2.2 *Large test sets*

Figure 1 illustrates the results of our experiments on the REUTERS-21578 dataset in terms of $ER^{\mu}_{\rho}(n)$ and $ER^{M}_{\rho}(n)$; the results of the same experiments in terms of $ENER^{\mu}_{\rho}$ and $ENER^{M}_{\rho}$ as a function of the chosen value of ξ are instead reported in Table 1. The initial error generated by the automatic classifier is $E^{\mu}_1 = .152$ and $E^{M}_1 = .383$. The optimal value of σ returned by the k-fold cross-validation phase is .420.

The first insight we can draw from these results is that our utility-theoretic method outperforms the baseline in a very substantial way. For instance, for $\xi = .10$ (corresponding to $p = .996$) it obtains a relative improvement over the baseline of +30% in terms of $ENER^{\mu}_{\rho}$ and of +119% in terms of $ENER^{M}_{\rho}$. Improvements obtained for the two other tested values of ξ are qualitatively similar.

A second insight is that, surprisingly, our method hardly differs in terms of performance from Oracle1. The two curves can be barely distinguished in Figure 1, and in terms of $ENER_{\rho}$ Oracle1 is even outperformed by our utility-theoretic method, albeit by a narrow margin (.221 vs. .217 for $ENER^{\mu}_{\rho}$ and .233 vs. .224 for $ENER^{M}_{\rho}$, both for $\xi = .10$; the other tested values for ξ give similar results). This shows that (at least judging from this experiment) Laplace smoothing is nearly optimal, and there is likely not much we can gain from applying alternative, more sophisticated smoothing methods. This is sharply different from what happens in language modelling, where Laplace smoothing has been shown to be an underperformer [9]. The fact that our method slightly (and strangely) outperforms Oracle1 is probably due to accidental, "serendipitous" interactions between the probability estimation component (Equation 7) and the contingency cell estimation component of Section 3.4.

Note that in Figure 1 the ER^{μ}_{ρ} curves (left) are smoother than the ER^{M}_{ρ} curves (right). This is due to the fact that E^{μ}_1 is evaluated on a single, global contingency table, so that correcting an individual document always has a small effect on E^{μ}_1. By contrast, even correcting a single document may have a major effect on a class-specific value of E_1 (especially if the class is infrequent), and this may bring about a relatively major effect on E^{M}_1 too.

5.2.3 *Small (and tiny) test sets*

We have run a second batch of experiments in which we randomly split the REUTERS-21578 test set in 10 equally-sized parts (about 330 documents each), we run each ranking method on each such part individually, and we average the results across the 10 parts. We call this scenario REUTERS-21578/10. The relative results in terms of $ER^{\mu}_{\rho}(n)$ and $ER^{M}_{\rho}(n)$ are shown in Figure 2, while the results of the same experiments in terms of $ENER^{\mu}_{\rho}$ and $ENER^{M}_{\rho}$ are reported in Table 2.

The rationale of these experiments is checking how the methods fare when ranking test sets much smaller that the REUTERS-21578 test set. This is *more* challenging than ranking larger sets, since in this case Laplace smoothing (i) can seriously perturb the relative proportions among the cell counts, which can generate poor estimates of $G(FP_j)$ and $G(FN_j)$, and (ii) is performed for more classes, since we smooth "on demand" only and since the likelihood that the $\hat{\alpha}_j$ are smaller than 1 is higher with small test sets.

Figure 2 confirms that our utility-theoretic method substantially outperforms the baseline also in this context. Note that the E^{M}_1 curves (left) are smoother than the analogous curves of the full REUTERS-21578. This is due to the fact that the curves in Figure 2 result from averages across 10 different experiments, and the increase brought about at rank n is actually the average of the increases brought about at rank n in the 10 experiments.

That our utility-theoretic method substantially outperforms the baseline also in this experiment can be seen also

Table 1: **Results of various ranking methods on Reuters-21578 in terms of EER_ρ; the notation $EER^x_\rho(y)$ indicates EER_ρ values obtained by using x as an averaging method (micro- or macro-averaging) for E_1 and y as a value for ξ. Improvements listed for the various methods are relative to the baseline.**

	$ENER^\mu_\rho(0.05)$	$ENER^\mu_\rho(0.10)$	$ENER^\mu_\rho(0.20)$	$ENER^M_\rho(0.05)$	$ENER^M_\rho(0.10)$	$ENER^M_\rho(0.20)$
Baseline	.109	.169	.224	.070	.106	.155
Utility-theoretic	.145 (+32%)	.221 (+30%)	.285 (+27%)	.162 (+133%)	.233 (+119%)	.298 (+92%)
Oracle1	.142 (+29%)	.217 (+28%)	.281 (+25%)	.151 (+116%)	.224 (+111%)	.292 (+88%)
Oracle2	.277 (+153%)	.401 (+137%)	.480 (+113%)	.671 (+864%)	.725 (+582%)	.701 (+351%)

Table 2: **As in Table 1, but with Reuters-21578/10 instead of Reuters-21578.**

	$ENER^\mu_\rho(0.05)$	$ENER^\mu_\rho(0.10)$	$ENER^\mu_\rho(0.20)$	$ENER^M_\rho(0.05)$	$ENER^M_\rho(0.10)$	$ENER^M_\rho(0.20)$
Baseline	.110	.169	.222	.063	.097	.136
Utility-theoretic	.141 (+27%)	.212 (+25%)	.272 (+22%)	.150 (+138%)	.210 (+116%)	.257 (+88%)
Oracle1	.144 (+30%)	.215 (+26%)	.273 (+23%)	.163 (+158%)	.220 (+126%)	.264 (+94%)
Oracle2	.288 (+161%)	.403 (+138%)	.477 (+114%)	.480 (+662%)	.585 (+503%)	.612 (+349%)

from Table 2. For $\xi = .10$ (corresponding to $p = .969$) the relative improvement over the baseline is +25% for $ENER^\mu_\rho$ and +116% for $ENER^M_\rho$. Similarly substantial improvements are obtained for the two other values of ξ tested.

Note also that in this case our method underperforms Oracle1 (.212 vs. .215 for $ENER^\mu_\rho$, .210 vs. .220 for $ENER^M_\rho$), and this points to a possible, small suboptimality of the smoothing method adopted. We leave the investigation of more sophisticated smoothing methods to a future paper.

In further experiments that we have run, we have split the REUTERS-21578 test set even further, i.e., into 100 equally-sized parts of about 33 documents each, so as to test the performance of Laplace smoothing methods in even more challenging conditions. The $ENER^\mu_\rho$ and $ENER^M_\rho$ results for this REUTERS-21578/100 scenario are reported in Figure 3; we do not report the detailed $ER^\mu_\rho(n)$ and $ER^M_\rho(n)$ plots for reasons of space. Our utility-theoretic model still outperforms the baseline, with a relative improvement of +18% on $ENER^\mu_\rho$ and +48% on $ENER^M_\rho$ with $\xi = .10$, corresponding to $p = .696$; qualitatively similar improvements are obtained with the other tested values of ξ.

However, we consider the REUTERS-21578/100 scenario less interesting than the two previously discussed ones, since applying a ranking method to a set of 33 documents only is of debatable utility, given that a human annotator confronted with the task of inspecting just 33 documents can arguably check them all without any need for ranking.

Incidentally, note that the REUTERS-21578/10 and REUTERS-21578/100 experiments model an application scenario in which a set of automatically labelled documents is split (e.g., to achieve faster throughput) among k human annotators, each one entrusted with inspecting a part of the set. In this case, each annotator is presented with a ranking of her own document subset, and works exclusively on it.

5.2.4 A note on (micro- or macro-) averaging

It is important to note that both the baseline and our utility-theoretic method are *explicitly optimized* for $ENER^M_\rho$, and not for $ENER^\mu_\rho$. To see this, note that the $U(d_i)$ function of Equation 8 is based on an unweighted sum of the class-specific $U_j(d_i)$ scores, i.e., it pays equal importance to all classes, irrespective of frequency considerations. This means that it is optimized for metrics that also pay equal attention to all classes, as all macroaveraged measures such as $ENER^M_\rho$ do.

By contrast, $ENER^\mu_\rho$ pays attention to classes proportionally to their frequency. Therefore, a ranking method that optimizes for $ENER^\mu_\rho$ should instead do away with class-specific utility functions and use a utility function that (similarly to what happens for E^μ_1) is directly computed on a single, global contingency table obtained by the cell-wise sum of the class-specific contingency tables. In such a method, $G(FP)$ and $G(FN)$ would be global to $\mathcal{C}$, i.e., they would be the same for all $c_j \in \mathcal{C}$. We leave the investigation of ranking methods optimized for $ENER^\mu_\rho$ to a future paper.

All this shows that the measure according to which both the baseline and our utility-theoretic method should be evaluated is $ENER^M_\rho$, and not $ENER^\mu_\rho$, since it is $ENER^M_\rho$ that these methods were designed for[7]. However, we have also reported results measured according to E^μ_1 for completeness, and in order to show that, while our methods were not meant for use with E^μ_1 as the yardstick, they still perform well even in this context.

It should thus come as no surprise that the improvements displayed by our method (and the oracles) over the baseline are always higher, or much higher, for $ENER^M_\rho$ than for $ENER^\mu_\rho$, as is apparent from all the figures and tables in this paper.

6. RELATED WORK

Many researchers have tackled the problem of how to use automated TC technologies in application contexts in which the required accuracy levels are unattainable by the generated automatic classifiers.

A standard response to this problem is to adopt *active learning* (AL – see e.g., [11, 22]), i.e., use algorithms that optimize the informativeness of additional training examples provided by a human annotator. Still, providing additional training examples, no matter how carefully chosen, may be insufficient, since in many applicative contexts high

[7] The baseline we have used is, as specified in Section 5.2.1, our utility-theoretic method with $G(FP_j)$ and $G(FN_j)$ set to 1; it is thus also optimized for E^M_1. A baseline method optimized for E^μ_1 would be the method outlined in the last paragraph with $G(FP)$ and $G(FN)$ set to 1.

Table 3: As in Table 1, but with Reuters-21578/100 instead of Reuters-21578.

	$ENER^{\mu}_{\rho}(0.05)$	$ENER^{\mu}_{\rho}(0.10)$	$ENER^{\mu}_{\rho}(0.20)$	$ENER^{M}_{\rho}(0.05)$	$ENER^{M}_{\rho}(0.10)$	$ENER^{M}_{\rho}(0.20)$
Baseline	.102	.158	.207	.073	.117	.158
Utility-theoretic	.119 (+16%)	.187 (+18%)	.244 (+17%)	.115 (+56%)	.173 (+48%)	.221 (+39%)
Oracle1	.170 (+66%)	.241 (+52%)	.292 (+41%)	.153 (+108%)	.208 (+77%)	.249 (+57%)
Oracle2	.306 (+198%)	.417 (+163%)	.482 (+132%)	.362 (+395%)	.473 (+304%)	.527 (+233%)

enough accuracy levels cannot be attained, irrespectively of the quantity and quality of the available training data. Similar considerations apply when active learning is carried out at the term level, rather than at the document level [10, 17].

A related response to the same problem is to adopt *training data cleaning* (TDC – see e.g., [7, 8]), i.e., use algorithms that optimize the human annotator's efforts at correcting possible labelling mistakes in the training set. Similarly to the case of AL, in many applicative contexts high enough accuracy levels cannot be attained even at the price of carefully inspecting the entire training set for labelling mistakes.

Both AL and TDC are different from the task we deal with, since we are not concerned with improving the quality of the *training* set. We are instead concerned with improving the quality of the automatically classified *test* set, typically after all attempts at injecting quality in the automatic classifier have proved insufficient; in particular, no retraining / reclassification phase is involved in SATC.

Active learning. As remarked above, SATC certainly bears strong relations with active learning. In both SATC and in the *selective sampling* – also known as *pool-based* – approach to AL [13, 14], the automatically classified objects are ranked and the human annotator is encouraged to correct possible misclassifications by working down from the top of the ranked list. However, as remarked above, the goals of the two tasks are different. For instance, in active learning we are interested in top-ranking the unlabelled documents that, once manually labelled, would maximize the information fed back to the learning process, while in SATC we are interested in top-ranking the unlabelled documents that, once manually inspected, would maximize the expected accuracy of the automatically classified document set. As a result, the optimal ranking strategies for the two tasks may be different too.

Semi-automated TC. While AL (and, to a much lesser degree, TDC) have been investigated extensively in a TC context, semi-automated TC has been completely neglected by the research community. While a number of papers (e.g., [12, 20, 23]) have evoked the existence of this scenario, we are not aware of any published papers that either discuss ranking policies for supporting the human annotator's effort, or that attempt to quantify the effort needed for reaching a desired level of accuracy. For instance, while discussing a system for the automatic assignment of ICD9 classes to patients' discharge summaries, Larkey and Croft [12] say "We envision these classifiers being used in an interactive system which would display the 20 or so top ranking [classes] and their scores to an expert user. The user could choose among these candidates (...)", but do not present experiments that quantify the accuracy that the inspecting activity brings about, or methods aimed at optimizing the cost-effectiveness of this activity.

7. CONCLUSIONS AND FUTURE WORK

We have presented a method for ranking the documents labelled by an automatic classifier. The documents are ranked in such a way as to maximize the expected reduction in classification error brought about by a human annotator who inspects a subset of the ranked list and corrects the labels when appropriate. We have also proposed an evaluation measure for such ranking methods, based on the notion of expected normalized error reduction. Experiments carried out on a standard dataset show that our method substantially outperforms a state-of-the-art baseline method. To the best of our knowledge, this is the first paper in the literature that addresses semi-automated text classification as a task in its own right, and which presents methods explicitly devised for optimizing it; this is obviously the reason of the very substantive improvements obtained by our method with respect to the baseline.

It should be remarked that the very fact of using a utility function, i.e., a function in which different events are characterized by different gains, makes sense here since we have adopted an evaluation function, such as F_1, in which correcting a false positive or a false negative indeed brings about different benefits to the final effectiveness score. If we instead adopted *accuracy* (i.e., the percentage of binary classification decisions that are correct) as the evaluation measure, utility would default to the probability of misclassification and our method would coincide with the baseline, since correcting a false positive or a false negative would bring about the same benefit. The method we have presented is justified by the fact that F_1 is the standard evaluation function for text classification, while accuracy is a deprecated measure in a text classification context since it is not robust to class imbalance. See e.g., [20, Section 7.1.2] for a discussion of this point.

The method we have proposed is obviously valid also when a different instantiation of the F_β function (i.e., with $\beta \neq 1$) is used as the evaluation function. This may be the case, e.g., when classification is to be applied to a recall-oriented task (such as e-discovery [16]), in which case values $\beta > 1$ are appropriate. In these cases our utility-theoretic method can be used once the appropriate instance of F_β is used in Equations 5 and 6 in place of F_1. The same trivially holds for any other evaluation function, even different from F_β and even multivariate and non-linear, provided it can be computed from a contingency table. We also remark that this technique is obviously not limited to *text* classification, but can be useful in any classification context in which class imbalance [2], or cost-sensitivity in general [4], suggest using a measure (such as F_β) that caters for these characteristics.

Note that, by using our method, it is also easy to provide the human annotator with an estimate of how accurate the labels of the test set are as a result of her inspecting all the documents until rank n. In fact, if the contingency cell estimates $\hat{TP}_j$, $\hat{FP}_j$, and $\hat{FN}_j$ (see Section 3.4) are updated (adding and subtracting 1 where appropriate) after each correction made by the human annotator, at any point in the inspection activity these are up-to-date estimates of how well the test set is now classified, and from these estimates F_1 (or other) can be computed as usual.

In the next future we plan to carry our more experiments, using additional datasets, learners, and (when the test sets are small) smoothing methods. We are also currently testing an improved ranking method that we have recently designed. Essentially, this "dynamic" method is based on the observation that inspecting a document misclassified for c_j brings about changes in at least one of TP_j, FP_j, and FN_j (and in $G(FP_j)$ and/or $G(FN_j)$ and $U_j(\cdot)$ as a consequence). This dynamic version of our ranking strategy consists of updating (after each correction has been performed) $\hat{TP}_j$, $\hat{FP}_j$, and $\hat{FN}_j$ by adding and subtracting 1 where appropriate, re-estimating $G_j(FP)$, $G_j(FN)$ and $U_j(\cdot)$, and bringing to bear these new estimates when selecting the document that should be presented next to the human annotator.

8. REFERENCES

[1] P. Burman. Smoothing sparse contingency tables. *The Indian Journal of Statistics*, 49(1):24–36, 1987.

[2] N. V. Chawla, N. Japkowicz, and A. Kolcz. Editorial: Special issue on learning from imbalanced data sets. *ACM SIGKDD Explorations*, 6(1):1–6, 2004.

[3] S. F. Chen and J. Goodman. An empirical study of smoothing techniques for language modeling. In *Proceedings of the 34th Annual Meeting on Association for Computational Linguistics (ACL 1996)*, pages 310–318, Santa Cruz, US, 1996.

[4] C. Elkan. The foundations of cost-sensitive learning. In *Proceedings of the 17th International Joint Conference on Artificial Intelligence (IJCAI 2001)*, pages 973–978, Seattle, US, 2001.

[5] A. Esuli, T. Fagni, and F. Sebastiani. MP-Boost: A multiple-pivot boosting algorithm and its application to text categorization. In *Proceedings of the 13th International Symposium on String Processing and Information Retrieval (SPIRE 2006)*, pages 1–12, Glasgow, UK, 2006.

[6] A. Esuli and F. Sebastiani. Active learning strategies for multi-label text classification. In *Proceedings of the 31st European Conference on Information Retrieval (ECIR 2009)*, pages 102–113, Toulouse, FR, 2009.

[7] A. Esuli and F. Sebastiani. Training data cleaning for text classification. In *Proceedings of the 2nd International Conference on the Theory of Information Retrieval (ICTIR 2009)*, pages 29–41, Cambridge, UK, 2009.

[8] F. Fukumoto and Y. Suzuki. Correcting category errors in text classification. In *Proceedings of the 20th International Conference on Computational Linguistics (COLING 2004)*, pages 868–874, Geneva, CH, 2004.

[9] W. Gale and K. Church. What's wrong with adding one? In N. Oostdijk and P. de Haan, editors, *Corpus-Based Research into Language: In honour of Jan Aarts*, pages 189–200. Rodopi, Amsterdam, NL, 1994.

[10] S. Godbole, A. Harpale, S. Sarawagi, and S. Chakrabarti. Document classification through interactive supervision of document and term labels. In *Proceedings of the 8th European Conference on Principles and Practice of Knowledge Discovery in Databases (PKDD 2004)*, pages 185–196, Pisa, IT, 2004.

[11] S. C. Hoi, R. Jin, and M. R. Lyu. Large-scale text categorization by batch mode active learning. In *Proceedings of the 15th International Conference on World Wide Web (WWW 2006)*, pages 633–642, Edinburgh, UK, 2006.

[12] L. S. Larkey and W. B. Croft. Combining classifiers in text categorization. In *Proceedings of the 19th ACM International Conference on Research and Development in Information Retrieval (SIGIR 1996)*, pages 289–297, Zürich, CH, 1996.

[13] D. D. Lewis and J. Catlett. Heterogeneous uncertainty sampling for supervised learning. In *Proceedings of 11th International Conference on Machine Learning (ICML 1994)*, pages 148–156, New Brunswick, US, 1994.

[14] A. K. McCallum and K. Nigam. Employing EM in pool-based active learning for text classification. In *Proceedings of the 15th International Conference on Machine Learning (ICML 1998)*, pages 350–358, Madison, US, 1998.

[15] A. Moffat and J. Zobel. Rank-biased precision for measurement of retrieval effectiveness. *ACM Transactions on Information Systems*, 27(1), 2008.

[16] D. W. Oard, J. R. Baron, B. Hedin, D. D. Lewis, and S. Tomlinson. Evaluation of information retrieval for E-discovery. *Artificial Intelligence and Law*, 18(4):347—386, 2010.

[17] H. Raghavan, O. Madani, and R. Jones. Active learning with feedback on features and instances. *Journal of Machine Learning Research*, 7:1655–1686, 2006.

[18] S. E. Robertson. A new interpretation of average precision. In *Proceedings of the 31st ACM International Conference on Research and Development in Information Retrieval (SIGIR 2008)*, pages 689–690, Singapore, SN, 2008.

[19] R. E. Schapire and Y. Singer. Boostexter: A boosting-based system for text categorization. *Machine Learning*, 39(2/3):135–168, 2000.

[20] F. Sebastiani. Machine learning in automated text categorization. *ACM Computing Surveys*, 34(1):1–47, 2002.

[21] J. S. Simonoff. A penalty function approach to smoothing large sparse contingency tables. *The Annals of Statistics*, 11(1):208–218, 1983.

[22] S. Tong and D. Koller. Support vector machine active learning with applications to text classification. *Journal of Machine Learning Research*, 2:45–66, 2001.

[23] Y. Yang and X. Liu. A re-examination of text categorization methods. In *Proceedings of the 22nd ACM International Conference on Research and Development in Information Retrieval (SIGIR 1999)*, pages 42–49, Berkeley, US, 1999.

[24] C. Zhai and J. Lafferty. A study of smoothing methods for language models applied to information retrieval. *ACM Transactions on Information Systems*, 22(2):179—214, 2004.

Improving Tweet Stream Classification by Detecting Changes in Word Probability

Kyosuke Nishida, Takahide Hoshide
NTT Service Evolution Laboratories,
NTT Corporation, Kanagawa, Japan
{nishida.kyosuke, hoshide.takahide}
@lab.ntt.co.jp

Ko Fujimura
Otsuma Women's University
Tokyo, Japan
fujimura@otsuma.ac.jp

ABSTRACT

We propose a classification model of tweet streams in Twitter, which are representative of document streams whose statistical properties will change over time. Our model solves several problems that hinder the classification of tweets; in particular, the problem that the probabilities of word occurrence change at different rates for different words. Our model switches between two probability estimates based on full and recent data for each word when detecting changes in word probability. This switching enables our model to achieve both accurate learning of stationary words and quick response to bursty words. We then explain how to implement our model by using a word suffix array, which is a full-text search index. Using the word suffix array allows our model to handle the temporal attributes of word n-grams effectively. Experiments on three tweet data sets demonstrate that our model offers statistically significant higher topic-classification accuracy than conventional temporally-aware classification models.

Categories and Subject Descriptors

H.2.8 [**Database Management**]: Database Applications—*Data mining*; H.3.3 [**Information Storage and Retrieval**]: Information Search and Retrieval

General Terms

Algorithms, Experimentation

Keywords

Twitter, Document classification, Data streams, Concept drift, Control charts, Suffix arrays

1. INTRODUCTION

Twitter, a micro-blogging service, has emerged as a new information infrastructure. Over 300 million status messages, called tweets, are posted per day by users all over the world. The demand for classifying tweets in order to organize the massive volume of tweets has become more urgent.

Classifying document streams is a challenging problem because their statistical properties will change over time. This characteristic is called *concept drift*, and it is one of the hottest topics in data mining [2, 13]. There are multiple types of changes, and the effectiveness of strategies for building classifiers depends on the types of changes.

For classifying tweet streams, the trade-off between quick response to bursty words and accurate learning of stationary words is a significant problem. Conventional methods conduct temporal selection or weighting on documents; so, they cannot handle the different time-scale changes expected for each word. We propose a probabilistic classification model, P-Switch, as an extension of the multinomial naive Bayes classifier. In order to resolve the trade-off, our model switches between the two probability estimates based on full and recent data for each word, by monitoring changes in the probability of word occurrence. It implements monitoring by using a control chart [20], which is a statistical process control tool.

We then describe an implementation method that uses a word suffix array [7]. Our classification model can be formalized as searching the positions of word n-grams of a new tweet, in the training documents that are concatenated chronologically. We, therefore, regard the construction of full-text search indexes as a learning procedure. This approach can effectively handle word n-grams, which are highly important information given the 140 character limit of tweets.

Experiments on topic classification were conducted on three real-world tweet data sets that have different characteristics in terms of topics, languages, and changes. Results show that our model offers statistically significant improvements over the standard multinomial naive Bayes classifier and conventional document weighting and selection methods in terms of accuracy and macro F_1 measures.

Contributions: (i) analysis of the changes in tweet streams, (ii) proposal of a probabilistic classification model that adapts to and detects changes at word-level, (iii) an implementation approach that uses word suffix arrays for effectively learning temporal factors in word n-grams, and (iv) significantly improved topic classification accuracy for tweet streams.

Outline: §2 describes the problem definitions on document stream classification. §3 presents the results of our analysis and preliminary experiments on tweet streams. §4 explains our proposed model. §5 describes the implementation method. §6 presents the results of the experiments. §7

SIGIR'12, August 12–16, 2012, Portland, Oregon, USA.

describes related work and §8 summarizes the contributions of this study.

2. CLASSIFYING DOCUMENT STREAMS

We address previous work on document stream classification and explain the scope of this study.

2.1 Problem Definitions

Problem definitions for document stream classification can be roughly classified into three types depending on how the training and test examples are presented:

[P1] Test-Then-Train (Incremental) [6, 35, 11, 38]

At each time step $t = 1, 2, \ldots$, a classifier is given a new document d_t, and outputs a class prediction, $\hat{c}_t$, for d_t. It then updates itself based on the true class label, c_t.

[P2] Test-Then-Train (Chunk) [17, 16, 15, 30, 18, 12]

At each $t = 1, 2, \ldots$, a classifier is given a new document set, $D_t = \{d_{t,1}, d_{t,2}, \ldots\}$, and outputs a class prediction, $\hat{c}_{t,j}$, for each $d_{t,j} \in D_t$. It then updates itself based on the true class label set, $C_t = \{c_{t,1}, c_{t,2}, \ldots\}$.

[P3] Train-Then-Test [8]

At each $t = 1, 2, \ldots$, a classifier is given a new training document set, $D_t^* = \{(d_{t,1}^*, c_{t,1}^*), \ldots\}$, and a new test document set, $D_t = \{d_{t,1}, d_{t,2}, \ldots\}$. It updates itself based on D_t^* and then outputs $\hat{c}_{t,j}$ for each $d_{t,j} \in D_t$.

Temporally-aware classification methods for batch learning have also been proposed [21, 5, 28, 29]: a classifier is given D_t^* and D_t for all $t = 1, 2, \ldots, T$. It outputs a class prediction, $\hat{c}_{t,j}$, for each $d_{t,j} \in D_t$, based on $(\forall t) D_t^*$.

2.2 Concept Drift

Concept drift means that the statistical properties of data change over time [36, 34], and it creates the most difficult situation in document stream classification. There are three major types of concept drift: **[C1]** sudden shift, **[C2]** gradual drift, and **[C3]** recurring themes.

One example of concept drift is found in the spam mail filtering problem because mail is characterized by skewed and changing class distributions, users' dynamic and growing interests, recurring and periodic themes (e.g., Christmas-related spam), and intelligent and adaptive adversaries.

2.3 Learning Strategies

Previous studies on handling concept drift in document streams employ instance selection, instance weighting, ensemble, and feature selection methods.

Instance selection methods select and adapt to previous training examples [16, 15, 11, 38]. Sliding window is a typical approach that is used to select the most recent previous examples. Klinkenberg et al. proposed a method for automatically deciding the size of window and demonstrated high classification performance in the topic classification of news articles [15].

Instance weighting methods assume that newer instances are more essential for classifying the current instance [15, 18, 5, 11, 28, 29]. Lebanon et al. proposed a naive Bayes classifier with a weighting scheme for handling temporal document streams [18].

These instance selection and weighting methods will adapt well to C2, but often fail to handle C1, because learning with old data worsens the classification of most recent data when sudden changes occur. There is a trade-off between response quickness, needed for C1, and learning accuracy, needed for C2. For example, using a short window improves response quickness but fails to offer good learning accuracy.

Ensemble methods use a set of classifiers adapted to the current concept [8, 35, 30, 12]. New models are added, and old or poor models are removed, in a fixed period of time or when a decrease in classification accuracy is observed. Ensemble methods are effective for C2 and C3; e.g., Katkis et al. proposed a general framework for tracking recurring contexts using ensemble classifiers and improved email filtering accuracy [12].

Feature selection methods dynamically select the most valuable feature (word) set in order to respond to concept drift, which is characterized by changes to the underlying feature space [6, 35, 11]. Feature selection methods are frequently combined with other methods; e.g., Wenerstrom et al. [35] proposed a feature-adaptive ensemble approach, which uses multiple classifiers with different features.

2.4 Scope of this Study

This study handles the incremental test-then-train problem definition P1, the most basic problem definition, and tackles the trade-off between responding to sudden shift (C1) and gradual drift (C2). We propose a classification model, a new weighting method at the *word* level, for tweet streams. While conventional instance weighting methods use temporal weighting functions on *documents*, our model is able to respond to changes in each word. Extending our model to suit ensemble and dynamic feature selection methods in order to handle recurring themes (C3) is our future work.

3. TWEET STREAMS

This section provides the results of analysis and preliminary experiments on the topic classification of tweets, where topics are defined by hashtags.

3.1 Data set

We collected three tweet data sets as shown in Table 1: tweets on 12 Nippon (Japanese) professional baseball teams (**NPB**), tweets on 7 Japanese television networks (**TV**), and tweets on 30 major league baseball teams (**MLB**), by searching hashtags via the Twitter Streaming API (statuses/filter), from 13 September 2011 to 26 September 2011.

These data sets consist of tweets that include a single hashtag; that is, a tweet belongs to a single class. Classes are hashtags on baseball teams for the NPB and MLB data sets, and hashtags on television networks for the TV data set. Retweets (including the tweets containing the string "RT" or "QT"), replies, mentions are not included in these data sets. In the problem definition P1, document d means a tweet text without any hashtags, and class label c means a hashtag. For the NPB and TV data sets, we selected noun, verb, and adjective words by using MeCab 0.98 with IPA dictionary[1] for Japanese word segmentation and part of speech labeling. For the MLB data set, we removed stop words and treated punctuation and other non-alphabetic characters as separate tokens.

[1] http://mecab.sourceforge.net

Table 1: **Tweet data set. We collected tweets that included a single hashtag from 13 to 26 September 2011 by using Twitter Streaming API. Classes are hashtags on "baseball teams" for NPB and MLB data sets, and hashtags on "television networks" for TV data set. Each hashtag corresponds to a class label.**

Data	# Tweets	# Classes	Language	Track Keywords (Hashtags)
NPB	314,210	12	Japanese	#dragons, #hanshin, #giants, #swallows, #carp, #baystars, #sbhawks, #seibulions, #chibalotte, #lovefighters, #orix_buffaloes, #rakuteneagles
TV	249,080	7	Japanese	#nhk, #etv, #ntv, #tvasahi, #tbs, #tvtokyo, #fujitv
MLB	200,521	30	English	#angels, #astros, #athletics, #bluejays, #braves, #brewers, #cubs, #dbacks, #dodgers, #indians, #mariners, #marlins, #mets, #nats, #orioles, #padres, #phillies, #pirates, #rangers, #rays, #reds, #redsox, #rockies, #royals, #sfgiants, #stlcards, #tigers, #twins, #whitesox, #yankees

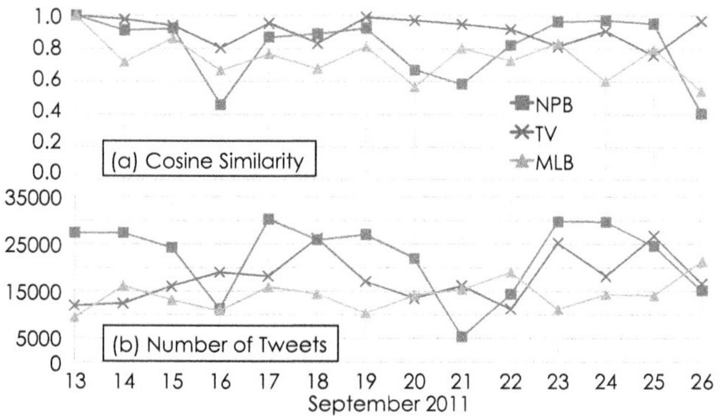

Figure 1: (a) Cosine similarities between class distributions on 13 September 2011 and all other days. (b) Total number of tweets for each day.

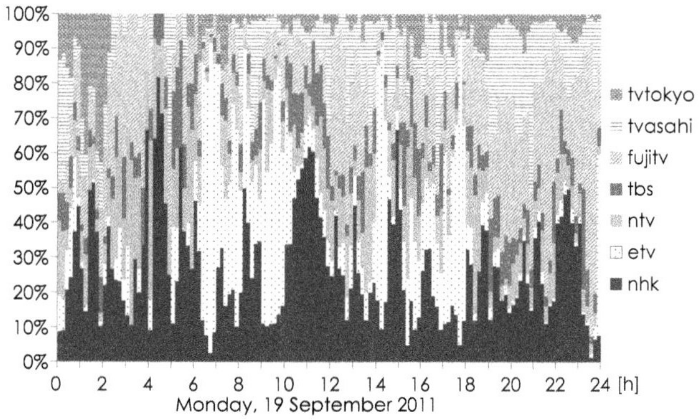

Figure 2: Class distribution (ten minute periods) for TV data set, Monday, 19 September 2011.

3.2 Analysis Results

We analyzed tweet streams in terms of the changes in class distribution and word probability, the occurrence of new words, and the effectiveness of considering word n-grams.

3.2.1 Changes in Class Distribution

Fig. 1 shows (a) the cosine similarities between class distributions on 13 September 2011 and all other days and (b) the total number of tweets for each day. We can see that the class distribution on the NPB and MLB data sets fluctuate more than that on the TV data set. The TV data set also fluctuates dramatically as shown in Fig. 2, which shows the class distribution over ten minute periods.

In summary, the class distributions in tweet streams fluctuate constantly and dramatically at micro and macro time

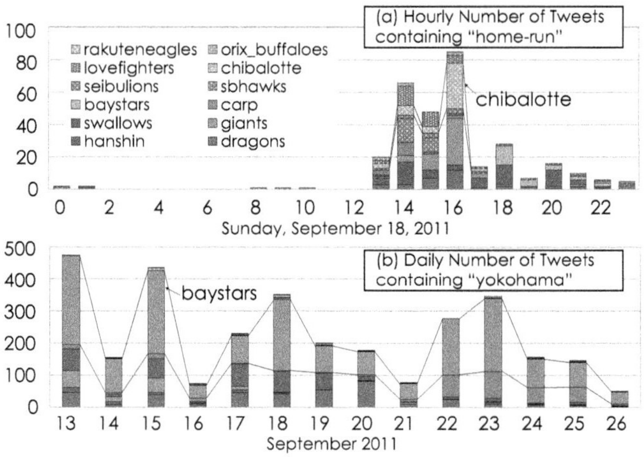

Figure 3: (a) Hourly number of tweets containing "home-run" and (b) Daily number of tweets containing "yokohama" from NPB data set.

scales. Classification models have to respond to these abrupt and gradual changes in class distribution.

3.2.2 Changes in Word Probability

Fig. 3 shows (a) the hourly number of tweets containing "home-run" and (b) the daily number of tweets containing "yokohama" from the NPB data set. "Home-run" is a bursty word since its relevant classes change rapidly. For example, a player of the team #chibalotte hit a home-run at 4PM and the word probability for "home-run" increased suddenly (Fig. 3a). On the other hand, "yokohama" is a relatively stationary word. The most relevant class #baystars, referring to the baseball team that has its home ground in Yokohama, does not change (Fig. 3b).

In summary, the statistical properties of tweet topics change at different rates for different words. Conventional instance weighting and selection methods cannot handle these differences.

3.2.3 Occurrence of New Words

In order to analyze the occurrence and change of effective words for classifying tweets, we calculated the chi-squared statistics χ_c^2 (see details in [39]) of all words for each class c in each day, and got the daily top 100 words in terms of χ_c^2 for each class.

Fig. 4 shows (a) the cosine similarities between the daily top 100 words on 13 September 2011 and all other days and (b) the cumulative number of distinct daily top 100 words. The results of Fig. 4 are averaged over classes.

We can see from Fig. 4b that effective words for classifying

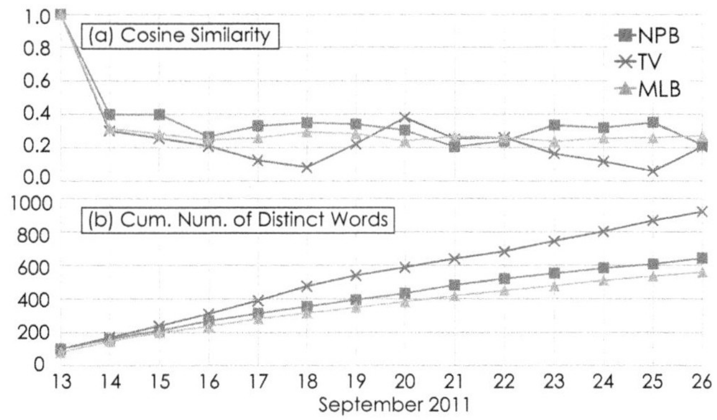

Figure 4: (a) Cosine similarities between daily top 100 words on 13 September 2011 and all other days. (b) Cumulative number of distinct daily top 100 words. These results are averaged over classes.

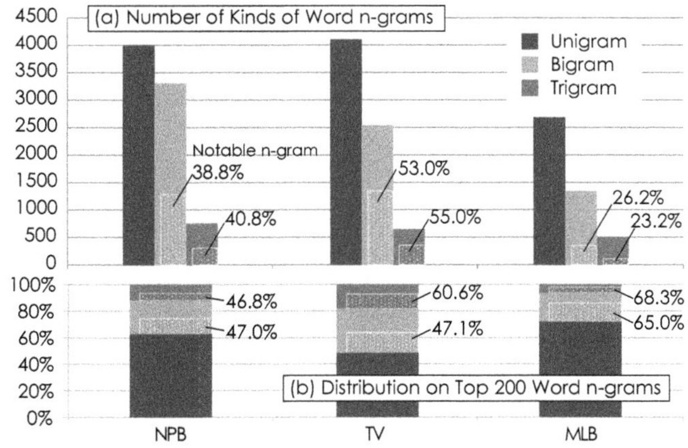

Figure 5: (a) Number of kinds of word n-grams that occur more than five times in each day. (b) Distribution of top 200 word n-grams in terms of $\max_c\{\chi_c^2\}$. These results are averaged over days. Chi-squared statistics $\max_c\{\chi_c^2\}$ of a notable n-gram is greater than that of the first word of the notable n-gram.

tweets emerge continuously. In particular, the words on the TV data set changes dramatically. Moreover, the daily top 100 words in the TV data set change periodically because of the influence of the day of the week, as shown in Fig. 4a.

In summary, classification models have to handle emerging words as well as recurring and periodic themes effectively.

3.2.4 *Effects of Word n-grams*

The word context of the tweet—which is highly important information given the 140 character limit—is lost in the bag-of-words model, which assumes that word order is unimportant.

Accordingly, we investigated whether word n-grams were useful for classifying tweets or not. We first calculated the chi-squared statistics $\max_c\{\chi_c^2\}$ of all word unigrams, bigrams, and trigrams that occurred more than five times in each day. We then found some notable word n-grams, where the $\max_c\{\chi_c^2\}$ value of a notable word n-gram is greater than that of the first word of the word n-gram (Fig. 5a). For example, from the MLB data set, "white sox" is more suitable for identifying the class #whitesox than "white". Moreover, Fig. 5b shows that the distribution on top 200 word n-grams in terms of $\max_c\{\chi_c^2\}$ contains word bigrams and trigrams (37.6%, 52.0%, 28.1% for the NPB, TV, and MLB data sets).

In summary, considering word sequences can be effective for classifying tweets because tweets are short and limited to 140 characters.

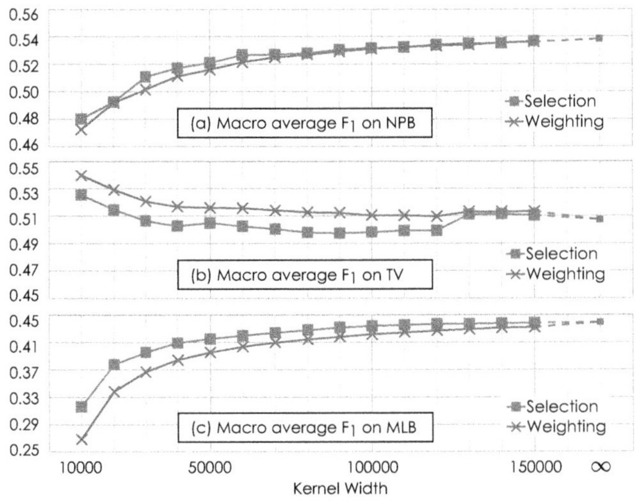

Figure 6: Macro F_1 vs. kernel width of instance selection and weighting methods with multinomial naive Bayes classifier (Eqs. (1)–(5))

3.3 Preliminary Experiments

We applied a temporally-aware multinomial naive Bayes classifier, which was proposed by Salles et al. [29], and independently, by Lebanon et al. [18], to problem definition P1.

The temporally-aware multinomial naive Bayes classifier is given by:

$$\hat{c}_t \leftarrow \arg\max_c\{\, p_{\mathrm{K}}(c|t) \prod_{w_i \in W(d_t)} p_{\mathrm{K}}(w_i|c,t)\,\}, \tag{1}$$

$$p_{\mathrm{K}}(c|t) = \frac{\sum_{\tau=1}^{t} K_h(t-\tau)[\![c_\tau = c]\!]}{\sum_{\tau=1}^{t} K_h(t-\tau)}, \tag{2}$$

$$p_{\mathrm{K}}(w_i|c,t) = \frac{\sum_{\tau=1}^{t} K_h(t-\tau) f_{c,\tau}(w_i)}{\sum_{\tau=1}^{t}\sum_{w\in d_\tau} K_h(t-\tau) f_{c,\tau}(w)}, \tag{3}$$

where $[\![\cdot]\!]$ is 1 if the predicate is true and 0 otherwise, $W(d_t)$ is the set of selected words in document d_t, and $f_{c,\tau}(w)$ is the frequency of word w in d_τ. $K_h(t-\tau)$ is a kernel function such that:

$$K_h(t-\tau) = [\![t-\tau < h]\!], \tag{4}$$

$$K_h(t-\tau) = (1-(t-\tau)/h)\cdot[\![t-\tau < h]\!], \tag{5}$$

where h is the width of the kernel. Using Eq. (4) means adopting an instance selection method and using Eq. (5) means adopting an instance weighting method. The proposal of Salles et al. [29] learns a kernel function with a training data set; however, its learning cost for P1 is extremely high. Accordingly, we used the above kernel functions in this preliminary experiment. We note that Lebanon et al. reported that Eq. (5) was the best kernel function in their experiments [18].

We evaluated the macro F_1 measure of the instance selection and weighting methods while changing the value of h (Fig. 6). Feature selection was conducted by using the chi-squared statistics χ_c^2 based on documents $\{d_\tau \mid t-h < \tau < t\}$: that is, $W(d_t) = \{w \mid \max_c\{\chi_c^2(w)\} > 30.0\}$.

For the TV data set, decreasing kernel width h improved classification accuracy. This data set exhibited significant and frequent changes in class and word probabilities and new and important words emerged constantly (see Figs. 2 and 4); therefore, learning from newer tweets was important. The instance weighting method achieved better classification accuracy than the instance selection method in which all data within the kernel are equivalent. We note that macro F_1 is not a monotonic function of kernel width because of the existence of recurrent themes, as shown in Fig. 6b.

For the NPB and MLB data sets, decreasing the kernel width worsened classification accuracy. The instance selection and weighting methods cannot learn stationary words fully if the kernel width is small. These data sets contained sudden and significant shifts in some words at micro time scales, as shown in Fig. 3a. Responding to such shifts is important for achieving further improvements in classification accuracy.

3.4 Data Characteristics Considered

From the results of data analysis and preliminary experiments, an ideal classification model for handling concept drift in tweet streams should be able to: [**A1**] respond to changes in class distribution, [**A2**] respond to changes in word probability, [**A3**] handle the emergence of new words effectively, [**A4**] resolve the trade-off between quick response to bursty words and accurate learning of stationary words, [**A5**] consider word n-grams, and [**A6**] treat recurring themes effectively. We propose a method that realizes the first five abilities, A1 to A5. A6 lies outside the scope of this study.

4. PROPOSED MODEL

We propose a classification model of tweet streams in which statistical properties will change over time. Our model, called P-Switch, is based on the analysis results shown in §3.

4.1 Outline

At each time step $t = 1, 2, \ldots$, our proposed model outputs a class prediction, $\hat{c}_t$, for a new given document, d_t, as follows:

$$\hat{c}_t \leftarrow \arg\max_c \{ p(c|t) \prod_{w_i \in W(d_t)} p(w_i|c, w_{i-n+1}^{i-1}, t) \}, \tag{6}$$

where w_i is the i-th word in d_t, w_{i-n+1}^{i-1} is the word sequence from the $(i-n+1)$-th to $(i-1)$-th word in d_t, and $W(d_t)$ is the set of selected words in d_t. Our model then updates itself based on the true class label c_t.

Our model, Eq. (6), is a temporally-aware version of the multinomial naive Bayes classifier. The following sections describe three essential components: class distribution, word probability, and word n-gram probability.

4.2 Class Distribution

To acquire ability A1, our model incrementally updates the class distribution, $p(c|t)$, based on c_t:

$$p(c|t) = (1-\gamma)\, p(c|t-1) + \gamma [\![c_t = c]\!], \tag{7}$$

where $[\![\cdot]\!]$ is 1 if the predicate is true and 0 otherwise.

Eq. (7) is the class distribution estimated using an exponentially weighted moving average (EWMA), where γ is a smoothing parameter that represents the degree of weighting decrease ($0 < \gamma < 1$). The weighting for each older data point decreases exponentially, it never reaches zero.

4.3 Word Probability

To acquire abilities A2, A3, and A4, our model estimates the temporally-aware word probability for each word.

First, our model chronologically concatenates documents given until t for each class c, $\mathcal{D}_{c,t}$.

A standard multinomial naive Bayes classifier estimates the word probability of w_i in class c with the maximum likelihood (ML) method,

$$p_{\mathrm{ML}}(w_i|c,t) = \frac{f_c(w_i)}{\sum_{w \in \mathcal{D}_{c,t}} f_c(w)}, \tag{8}$$

where $f_c(w)$ is the frequency of w in $\mathcal{D}_{c,t}$.

Additionally, our model estimates the word probability with the EWMA method,

$$p_{\mathrm{EWMA}}(w_i|c,t) = \sum_{j \in J_c(w_i)} (1-\lambda)^{|\mathcal{D}_{c,t}|-j} \lambda, \tag{9}$$

where $J_c(w_i)$ is the position of word w_i in $\mathcal{D}_{c,t}$, $J_c(w_i) = \{j \mid \mathcal{D}_{c,t}[j] = w_i, 1 \le j \le |\mathcal{D}_{c,t}|\}$, and λ is a smoothing parameter of EWMA ($0 < \lambda < 1$). Eq. (9) is a closed-form expression of EWMA.

Our model monitors the two probability estimates for each word w_i in class c, and switches between them as follows:

$$p(w_i|c,t) = \begin{cases} p_{\mathrm{EWMA}} & \text{if } p_{\mathrm{EWMA}} > p_{\mathrm{ML}} + L\,\sigma_{c,t} \\ p_{\mathrm{ML}} & \text{otherwise} \end{cases}, \tag{10}$$

$$\text{where} \quad \sigma_{c,t} = \sqrt{p_{\mathrm{ML}}(1-p_{\mathrm{ML}})}\sqrt{\lambda/(2-\lambda)}. \tag{11}$$

Note that Eqs. (10) and (11) mean monitoring the statistical process of w_i occurring in $\mathcal{D}_{c,t}$ with a Bernoulli EWMA control chart[31]. EWMA charts are generally used for detecting small shifts in the process mean [20]. The value of L in Eq. (10) determines the upper control limit of the chart, $p_{\mathrm{ML}} + L\sigma_{c,t}$. As long as p_{EWMA} is within the control limit, the word occurrence process is assumed to be currently stable (i.e., our model uses p_{ML}).

Fig. 7 clarifies that Eq. (9) preserves the probabilistic interpretation. We can see that the EWMA value, p_{EWMA}, tracks the changes in true probability. The EWMA method is able to respond to sudden shifts quickly. On the other hand, the ML method is able to estimate the probability for stationary words more accurately. The ML method, however, is apt to underestimate the probabilities of bursty words. This switching of the two probability estimates for each word enables our model to resolve the trade-off between quick response to bursty words and the accurate learning of stationary words.

4.4 Word n-gram Probability

To acquire ability A5, our model extends the bag-of-words model to the n-gram language model [26]. It uses the absolute discounting method [22, 4] as the smoothing method

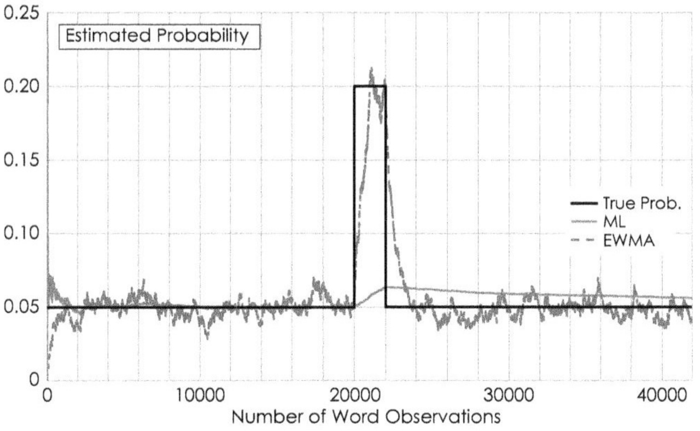

Figure 7: Simulation of estimating probabilities of word occurrence with ML (Eq. (8)) and EWMA (Eq. (9), $\lambda = 0.002$) methods.

used in estimating the word n-gram probability:

$$p(w_i|c, w_{i-n+1}^{i-1}, t) = \frac{\max\{f_c(w_{i-n+1}^{i}) - \kappa, 0\}}{f_c(w_{i-n+1}^{i-1})} + \frac{\kappa \cdot r_c(w_{i-n+1}^{i-1})}{f_c(w_{i-n+1}^{i-1})} p(w_i|c, w_{i-n+2}^{i-1}, t), \quad (12)$$

where $r_c(w_{i-n+1}^{i-1})$ is the number of distinct words following word sequence w_{i-n+1}^{i-1}. The lowest order model in this linear interpolation is $p(w_i|c,t)$; therefore, Eq. (12) retains the temporal effects.

The smoothing of Eq. (8) is also calculated according to the absolute discounting method:

$$p_{\mathrm{ML}}(w_i|c,t) = \begin{cases} \frac{\kappa}{\sum_{w \in \mathcal{D}_{c,t}} f_c(w)} & \text{if } f_c(w_i) = 0 \\ \frac{f_c(w_i)}{\sum_{w \in \mathcal{D}_{c,t}} f_c(w)} & \text{otherwise} \end{cases}, \quad (13)$$

and Eq. (13) is used instead of Eq. (8).

5. IMPLEMENTATION

We can implement our model by constructing full text search indexes (e.g., suffix arrays [19]) for each $\mathcal{D}_{c,t}$. This study uses the word suffix array (WSA) [7]. WSA enables our model to efficiently get $J_c(w_{i-n+1}^{i})$, the positions of w_{i-n+1}^{i} in $\mathcal{D}_{c,t}$, for each word n-gram w_{i-n+1}^{i} in each class c.

5.1 Summary of WSA

Let $T[1,\ldots,l]$ be a text of length l over a constant-sized alphabet Σ, tokenized into k words by word-delimiters, and let I be the set of alphabet positions at which new words start. The word suffix array $A[1,\ldots,k]$ is a permutation of I such that $T[A[i-1],\ldots,l] < T[A[i],\ldots,l]$ for all $1 < i \leq k$; i.e., the A array represents the lexicographic order of all suffixes, as shown in Fig. 8 (see details in [7]). The set of word positions, B, is obtained as a by-product of constructing WSA. Our model uses B to find $J_c(w_{i-n+1}^{i})$ in $\mathcal{D}_{c,t}$.

WSA can be constructed in $O(l)$ time and $O(k)$ space when using the linear-time construction algorithms for suffix arrays (*e.g.*, [23]). It can search w_{i-n+1}^{i} (alphabet length of m) quickly with a binary search in $O(m \log k + f_c(w_{i-n+1}^{i}))$, as in suffix arrays.

T = "ab#a#aa#a#ab#baa#aab#a#aa#baa#"

i	A	B	Word-aligned Suffix
1	4	2	a#aa#a#ab#baa#aab#a#aa#baa#
2	22	8	a#aa#baa#
3	9	4	a#ab#baa#aab#a#aa#baa#
4	6	3	aa#a#ab#baa#aab#a#aa#baa#
5	24	9	aa#baa#
6	18	7	aab#a#aa#baa#
7	1	1	ab#a#aa#a#ab#baa#aab#a#aa#baa#
8	11	5	ab#baa#aab#a#aa#baa#
9	27	10	baa#
10	14	6	baa#aab#a#aa#baa#

Figure 8: Word suffix array. '#' is a word boundary. Columns A and B are the set of alphabet and word positions at which word-aligned suffixes start.

Algorithm 1 Learning word n-gram probability with word suffix arrays.

Require: $\{d_t, c_t\}$, document stream
1: **for each** (d_t, c_t) **do**
2: $\mathcal{D}_{c_t,t} \leftarrow \mathcal{D}_{c_t,t-1} + d_t$ // append d_t after $\mathcal{D}_{c_t,t-1}$
3: construct WSA_{c_t} from $\mathcal{D}_{c_t,t}$
4: **end for**

5.2 Learning and Classification Procedures

This section shows the learning and classification procedures for word n-gram probability (Eqs. (8)–(13)).

Learning constructs WSAs for each class. Algorithm 1 shows the learning algorithm for a document stream, $\{d_t, c_t\}$. The sequential update of WSA is not supported, so, it reconstructs the WSA of class c_t when given a new tweet (d_t, c_t). (lines 2–3)

For reducing the learning time, it is effective to divide tweets into periods and reconstruct the newest WSA on the most recent tweets, while retaining old WSAs. We note that it is able to obtain $J_c(w_{i-n+1}^{i})$ from the divided WSAs by storing the offset position of each WSA and adding it to the positions of w_{i-n+1}^{i} found by each WSA.

Classification needs the $f_c(w_j^i)$, $J_c(w_j^i)$, and $r_c(w_j^i)$ values ($0 \leq i-j < n$) to calculate the word n-gram probability for each word n-gram, w_{i-n+1}^{i}, in class c. Algorithm 2 shows the pseudo-code that acquires the above values from a WSA.

Our model uses three heuristics for speed enhancement: (1) caching search results (lines 6–11, 13), (2) caching the initial search interval for the first alphabets [19] (line 3), and (3) reducing the number of character comparisons by remembering the number of matching characters [19] (line 9). Caching the search results of $(n-1)$-grams enables our model to narrow the initial interval when searching n-grams. The worst case of our approach is $O(m \log k + f_c(w_{i-n+1}^{i}))$ time; however, Ferragina et al. reported in [7] that the $O(m \log k + f_c(w_{i-n+1}^{i}))$ algorithm, which includes heuristics 2 and 3, is faster than the $O(m + \log k + f_c(w_{i-n+1}^{i}))$ [19] and $O(m|\Sigma| + f_c(w_{i-n+1}^{i}))$ [1] algorithms.

5.3 Implementation Details

We used the original implementation of the WSA construction algorithm[2] by Fischer [7] and the sais library[3],

[2]http://ab.inf.uni-tuebingen.de/people/fischer/wordSA.tgz
[3]http://sites.google.com/site/yuta256/sais

Algorithm 2 Acquiring classification parameters for class c.

Require: $d = \text{“}w_1\#w_2\#\cdots\#w_z\#\text{”} = w_1^z$, new document
Require: $R(a)$, search range of WSA for each alphabet a
Require: $W(d)$, set of selected words in d

```
for i = 1 to z do
    next if w_i ∉ W(d)
    R ← R(w_i[1])
    for j = i to i + n − 1 do
        s ← w_j^i // word (i − j + 1)-gram.
        if is_cached?(s) = true then
            ⟨f_c(s), J_c(s), r_c(s), R(s)⟩ ← get_cache(s)
        else
            ⟨f_c(s), J_c(s), r_c(s), R(s)⟩ ← search_by_WSA(s, R)
            set_cache(s, ⟨f_c(s), J_c(s), r_c(s), R(s)⟩)
        end if
        break if f_c(s) < 0
        R ← R(s) // narrow next search range.
    end for
end for
return {f_c(w_j^i), J_c(w_j^i), r_c(w_j^i) | 1 ≤ i ≤ z, 0 ≤ i−j < n}
```

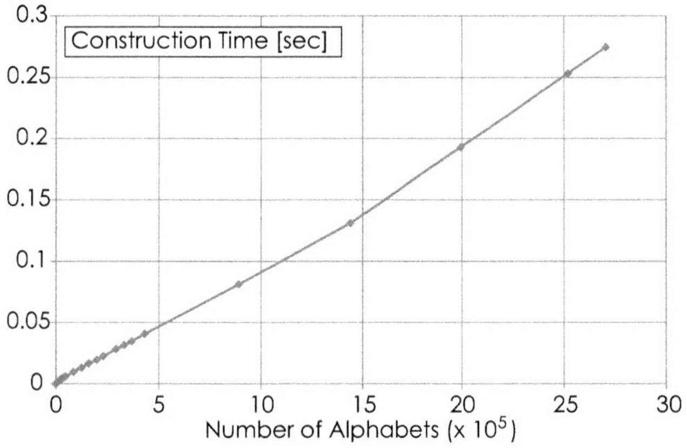

Figure 9: Construction time of word suffix array on tweets of class #dragons on NPB data set. Total 53,000 tweets, 399,825 words, 2,701,985 alphabets. CPU: Xeon X5680 3.33GHz, Memory: 192GB.

which implements Nong et al.'s induced sorting algorithm [23], as the suffix array construction algorithm used by WSA. We also used Kasai et al.'s algorithm [10] for calculating the longest common prefixes. The character encoding of tweets was UTF-8, and the number of alphabets was 256; i.e., a three-byte Japanese character consisted of three alphabets. Fig. 9 shows the results of constructing WSA on the tweets in class #dragons for the NPB data set: the construction time of WSA was linear to the number of alphabets.

6. EXPERIMENTS

In order to evaluate the impact that our proposed model has on the incremental test-then-train problem definition P1 (see §2), we first evaluated our model components and then compared our model against three conventional versions of multinomial naive Bayes classifiers (standard, instance weighting, and instance selection), by using the three tweet data sets shown in Table 1.

The classifiers used the chi-squared statistics feature selection method [39]: that is, $W(d_t) = \{w | \max_c\{\chi_c^2(w)\} > 30.0\}$, and conducted the smoothing of Eq. (13): $\kappa = 0.9$.

6.1 Effects of Individual Contributions

Our model, P-Switch, is also a temporally-aware version of multinomial naive Bayes. The following sections demonstrate the effects of our model's components.

6.1.1 Class Distribution

In order to evaluate the effects by introducing the temporally-aware class distribution described in Eq. (7), we evaluated the Proposal1 model:

$$\hat{c}_t \leftarrow \arg\max_c\{\, p(c|t) \prod_{w_i \in W(d_t)} p_{\mathrm{ML}}(w_i|c,t)\,\}, \qquad (14)$$

which extends the standard multinomial naive Bayes classifier, MNB:

$$\hat{c}_t \leftarrow \arg\max_c\{\, p(c) \prod_{w_i \in W(d_t)} p_{\mathrm{ML}}(w_i|c,t)\,\}, \qquad (15)$$

while changing smoothing parameter γ from 0.001 to 0.5.

We can see from Fig. 10 that the Proposal1 model, where $\gamma = 0.01$, performed statistically significantly better than MNB (McNemar's test; $p < .001$). We note that the multinomial naive Bayes classifier that assumes a uniform class distribution performed poorly.

6.1.2 Word Probability

In order to evaluate the effects of switching between the two probability estimates described in Eq. (10), we evaluated the Proposal2 model:

$$\hat{c}_t \leftarrow \arg\max_c\{\, p(c|t) \prod_{w_i \in W(d_t)} p(w_i|c,t)\,\}, \qquad (16)$$

which extends the Proposal1 model, while changing smoothing parameter λ from 0.0001 to 0.01. Other parameter settings were: $\gamma = 0.01$ and $L = 0.5$ for all data sets.

Fig. 11 shows that the Proposal2 model, when $\lambda = 0.002$, performed statistically significantly better than the Proposal1 model for all data sets (McNemar's test; $p < .001$). The switching of the two probability estimates: p_{EWMA}, which is based on recent data, and p_{ML}, which is based on data that cover long-term period, enables the Proposal2 model to resolve the trade-off between quick response to bursty words and the accurate learning of stationary words. Moreover, treating class distribution and word probability at different time scales (γ and λ), unlike instance selection and weighting methods, is effective in classifying tweet streams.

We also note that the best value for λ is the same for all three data sets, which have different change characteristics as shown in Figs. 1 and 4.

6.1.3 Word n-gram Probability

In order to evaluate the effects of introducing the temporally-aware word n-gram probability described in Eq. (12), we evaluated our P-switch model defined in Eq. (6), while changing the value of n from 1 (corresponds to the Proposal2 model) to 5. Other parameters settings were: $\gamma = 0.01$, $\lambda = 0.002$, $L = 0.5$ for all data sets.

We can see from Fig. 12 that our model performed best when $n = 2$, and there were statistical differences (McNemar's test; $p < .001$) between $n = 1$ and $n = 2$ on NPB and

Table 2: Overall accuracy and macro F_1 results. Bold-faced results were statistically significantly better than other results (McNemar's test; $p < .001$).

Methods	NPB		TV		MLB	
	Accuracy [%]	MacroF$_1$ [%]	Accuracy [%]	MacroF$_1$ [%]	Accuracy [%]	MacroF$_1$ [%]
MNB	55.87	53.81	50.61	50.71	48.29	43.92
MNB-W	50.57 (−5.396)	47.24 (−6.573)	54.77 (+4.160)	53.96 (+3.256)	33.82 (−14.47)	26.85 (−17.06)
MNB-S	51.57 (−4.298)	48.02 (−5.785)	53.26 (+2.649)	52.53 (+1.822)	38.29 (−10.00)	31.60 (−12.32)
Proposal1	60.52 (+4.652)	56.61 (+2.805)	62.82 (+12.21)	62.11 (+11.40)	56.05 (+7.751)	47.03 (+3.119)
Proposal2	65.87 (+9.998)	61.46 (+7.654)	**70.77** (+20.16)	**70.22** (+19.52)	60.26 (+11.97)	50.59 (+6.671)
P-Switch	**66.90** (+11.04)	**62.88** (+9.072)	**70.80** (+20.19)	**70.31** (+19.60)	**60.86** (+12.56)	**51.40** (+7.480)

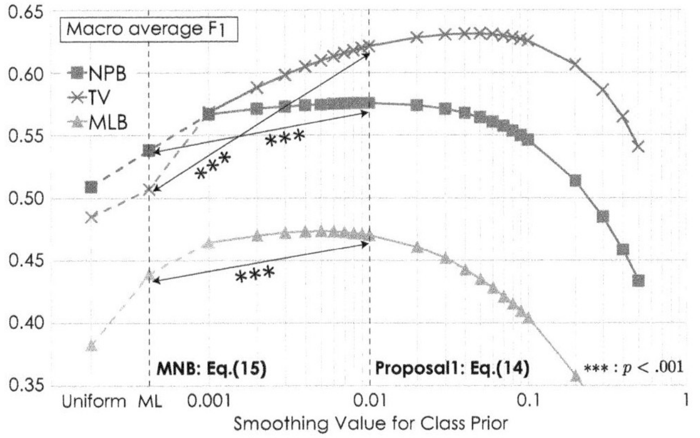

Figure 10: Effects of introducing temporally-aware class distribution, $p(c|t)$. "Uniform" means the multinomial naive Bayes classifier that assumes a uniform class distribution.

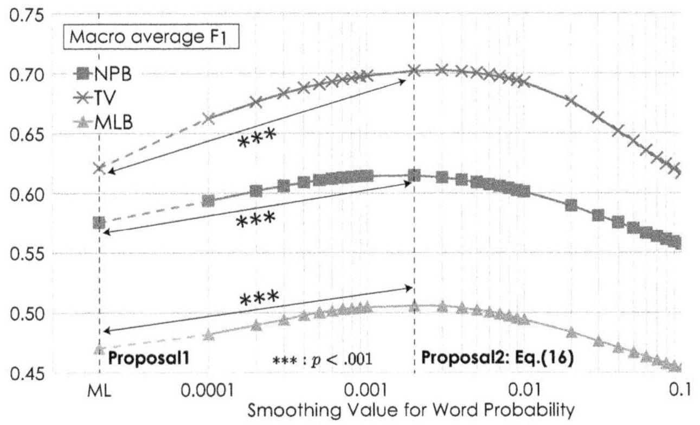

Figure 11: Effects of introducing temporally-aware word probability, $p(w_i|c,t)$. $\gamma = 0.01$ and $L = 0.5$.

MLB data sets. Larger values of n worsened classification accuracy because the zero frequency problem is serious in higher-order n-gram models [37].

6.2 Overall Results

§6.1 demonstrated that all of our individual contributions are effective in handling concept drift in tweet streams.

We next compared the whole P-Switch model against conventional methods for handling concept drift: a temporally-aware multinomial naive Bayes classifier with the instance weighting method (MNB-W; Eqs. (1) and (5)), and with

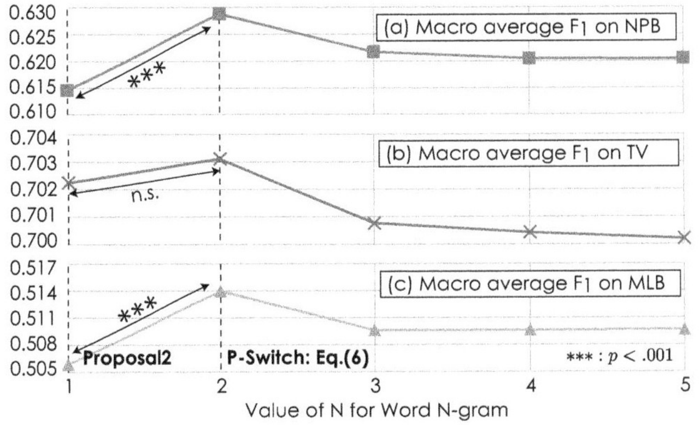

Figure 12: Effects of introducing temporally-aware word n-gram probability, $p(w_i|c, w_{i-n+1}^{i-1}, t)$. $\gamma = 0.01$, $\lambda = 0.002$, and $L = 0.5$.

the instance selection method (MNB-S; Eqs. (1) and (4)) (see details in §3.3 and [29, 18]). Parameter settings were: $\gamma = 0.01$, $\lambda = 0.002$, $L = 0.5$, and $n = 2$. The kernel width of MNB-W and MNB-S was $h = 10{,}000$, which was the best value for the TV data set. Note that the best value of h for the NPB and MLB data sets was ∞ (corresponds to MNB) as shown in Fig. 6.

Fig. 13 plots macro F_1 of the classifiers vs. the training number of tweets (time steps). Table 2 is the overall accuracy and macro F_1 of the classifiers after learning all data.

Although the NPB and MLB data sets contain various changes, MNB performed better than MNB-W and MNB-S; that is, learning stationary words with sufficient data is more important than responding to bursty words for these data sets. Our model resolved the trade-off between quick response and accurate learning by switching between the two probability estimates for each word. It offered a statistically significant improvement over MNB, up to 11.04% and 12.56% in terms of overall accuracy, and up to 9.072% and 7.480% in terms of macro F_1, for the NPB and MLB data sets, respectively (McNemar's test; $p < .001$).

Considering temporal effects enabled MNB-W and MNB-S to perform better than MNB on the TV data set; however, increasing the number of training tweets is not effective for achieving their higher classification accuracy, as shown in Fig. 13b. This is because using the small kernel width yields rapid dropping of old data. MNB, which learns all data, performed worst because the TV data set contained sudden and significant shifts as shown in Fig. 2. Our P-Switch model was able to respond to both the sudden shift and gradual drift; therefore, it achieved statistically signifi-

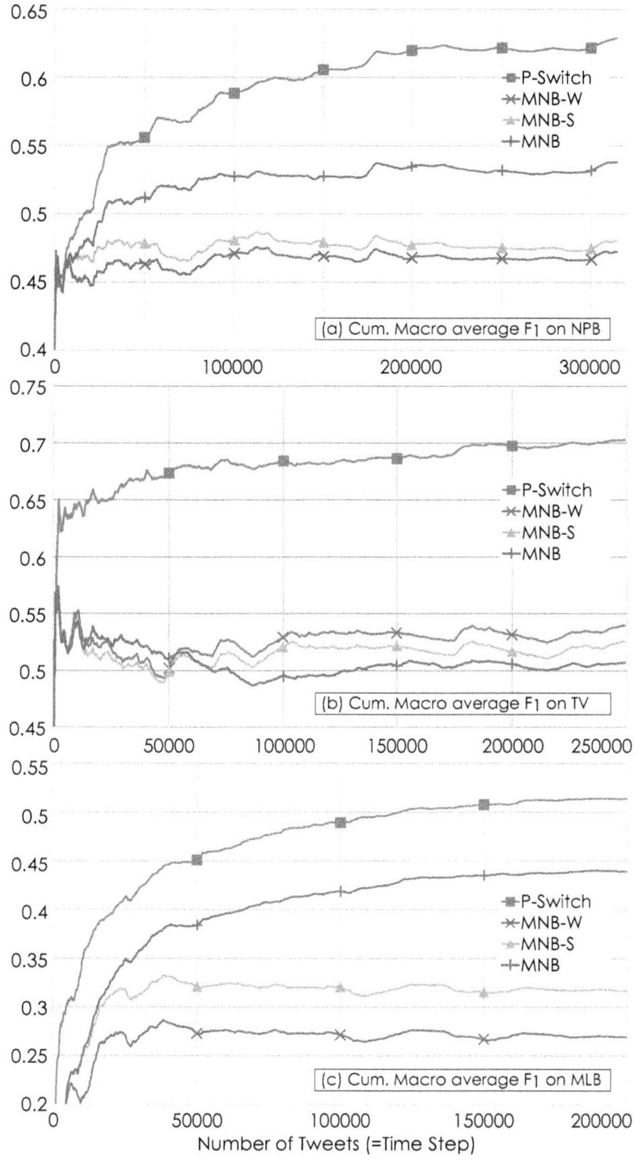

Figure 13: Number of tweets vs. cumulative macro F_1 on (a) NPB, (b) TV, and (c) MLB data sets. $\gamma = 0.01$, $\lambda = 0.002$, $L = 0.5$, $n = 2$, and $h = 10000$.

cant improvements over MNB, up to 20.19% and 19.60% in terms of overall accuracy and macro F_1, respectively (McNemar's test; $p < .001$).

7. RELATED WORK

As related work on classification of tweets, Sriram et al. devised a naive Bayes classifier for identifying tweet types such as news, events, opinions, deals, and private messages based on author information and tweet texts [32]. Sakaki et al. devised a support vector machine for finding tweets related to an event (*e.g.*, earthquake) [27]. Kinsella et al. uses metadata from hyperlinked objects to improve topic classification [14]. The above studies, however, employ batch learning and do not consider concept drift. While sentiment classification methods have been proposed most recently [9, 3, 25], they also do not consider temporal effects.

Some studies that use suffix arrays (SAs) for document classification have been proposed. Teo and Vishwanathan proposed fast and space efficient string kernels based on SAs and used the kernel with the support vector machine [33]. Okanohara and Tsujii proposed a logistic regression model with all-effective substrings, which are found with SAs [24]. These studies target the finding of effective feature spaces for batch learning; our model, on the other hand, uses lazy learning for streaming documents—generalization beyond the training data is delayed until a new document is given.

Salles et al. proposed temporally-aware versions of Rocchio and k-nearest neighbors classifiers that conduct temporal weighting on documents [29], in addition to the multinomial naive Bayes classifier described in Eq. (1). Their experiments showed that there were no significant differences among the classifiers. We find that responding to changes at the word level is more important than model selection for classifying document streams.

8. CONCLUSIONS

We proposed a classification model of tweet streams, which are representative of document streams whose statistical properties change over time.

We analyzed tweet streams by examining the changes in class distribution and word probability, the occurrence of new words and recurring themes, and the effectiveness of considering word n-grams. In particular, we demonstrated that tweet streams change significantly at the word level—the word occurrence probability changes at different rates for different words.

Our model solves this problem by detecting changes in word occurrence probability for each word. It switches between two probability estimates, the maximum likelihood and exponentially weighted moving average estimates, by using a control chart and is very effective in achieving both accurate learning of stationary words and quick response to bursty words. Also, it handles the changes in class distributions and extends the bag-of-words model to cover the n-gram language model. It preserves the probabilistic interpretation of the multinomial naive Bayes classifier.

We then presented an implementation method that uses a word suffix array. This approach enables our model to effectively handle word n-grams, which are highly important information given the 140 character limit of tweets. This new idea, searching the positions of words in documents concatenated chronologically, allows consideration of the temporal effects on changing word streams.

Experiments on topic classification were conducted using three real-world tweet data sets: tweets about Japanese baseball teams, television networks in Japan, and major league baseball teams. Results demonstrated that our model performed statistically significantly better than conventional instance weighting and selection models. In particular, our model was superior to the multinomial naive Bayes classifier with an instance weighting method by up to 16.33% and 16.35% in terms of accuracy and macro F_1, for the television network data set.

9. REFERENCES

[1] M. I. Abouelhoda, S. Kurtz, and E. Ohlebusch. Replacing suffix trees with enhanced suffix arrays. *J. Discrete Algorithms*, 2(1):53–86, 2004.

[2] A. Bifet, J. Gama, M. Pechenizkiy, and I. Zliobaite. Handling concept drift: Importance, challenges and solutions. In *PAKDD Tutorial*, 2011.
[3] S. Brody and N. Diakopoulos. Cooooooooooooooollllllllllllll!!!!!!!!!!!!!! using word lengthening to detect sentiment in microblogs. In *EMNLP*, pages 562–570, 2011.
[4] S. F. Chen and J. Goodman. An empirical study of smoothing techniques for language modeling. *Computer Speech & Language*, 13(4):359–393, 1999.
[5] L. C. da Rocha, F. Mourão, A. M. Pereira, M. A. Gonçalves, and W. Meira Jr. Exploiting temporal contexts in text classification. In *CIKM*, pages 243–252, 2008.
[6] S. J. Delany, P. Cunningham, and B. Smyth. ECUE: A spam filter that uses machine learning to track concept drift. In *ECAI*, page 627, 2006.
[7] P. Ferragina and J. Fischer. Suffix arrays on words. In *CPM*, pages 328–339, 2007.
[8] G. Forman. Tackling concept drift by temporal inductive transfer. In *SIGIR*, pages 252–259, 2006.
[9] L. Jiang, M. Yu, M. Zhou, X. Liu, and T. Zhao. Target-dependent twitter sentiment classification. In *ACL*, pages 151–160, 2011.
[10] T. Kasai, G. Lee, H. Arimura, S. Arikawa, and K. Park. Linear-time longest-common-prefix computation in suffix arrays and its applications. In *CPM*, pages 181–192, 2001.
[11] I. Katakis, G. Tsoumakas, E. Banos, N. Bassiliades, and I. P. Vlahavas. An adaptive personalized news dissemination system. *J. Intell. Inf. Syst.*, 32(2):191–212, 2009.
[12] I. Katakis, G. Tsoumakas, and I. Vlahavas. Tracking recurring contexts using ensemble classifiers: an application to email filtering. *Knowl. Inf. Syst.*, 22:371–391, 2010.
[13] L. Khan, M. Pechenizkiy, and I. Zliobaite, editors. *2nd International Workshop on Handling Concept Drift in Adaptive Information Systems*, 2011.
[14] S. Kinsella, A. Passant, and J. G. Breslin. Topic classification in social media using metadata from hyperlinked objects. In *ECIR*, pages 201–206, 2011.
[15] R. Klinkenberg. Learning drifting concepts: example selection vs. example weighting. *Intell. Data Anal.*, 8:281–300, 2004.
[16] R. Klinkenberg and T. Joachims. Detecting concept drift with support vector machines. In *ICML*, pages 487–494, 2000.
[17] R. Klinkenberg and I. Renz. Adaptive information filtering: Learning in the presence of concept drifts. In *ICML/AAAI-98*, pages 33–40, 1998.
[18] G. Lebanon and Y. Zhao. Local likelihood modeling of temporal text streams. In *ICML*, pages 552–559, 2008.
[19] U. Manber and E. W. Myers. Suffix arrays: A new method for on-line string searches. *SIAM J. Comput.*, 22(5):935–948, 1993.
[20] D. C. Montgomery. *Introduction to statistical quality control.* John Wiley & Sons, 6th edition, 2008.
[21] F. Mourão, L. C. da Rocha, R. B. Araújo, T. Couto, M. A. Gonçalves, and W. M. Jr. Understanding temporal aspects in document classification. In *WSDM*, pages 159–170, 2008.
[22] H. Ney, U. Essen, and R. Kneser. On structuring probabilistic dependences in stochastic language modeling. *Computer Speech & Language*, 8:1–38, 1994.
[23] G. Nong, S. Zhang, and W. H. Chan. Linear suffix array construction by almost pure induced-sorting. In *DCC*, pages 193–202, 2009.
[24] D. Okanohara and J. ichi Tsujii. Text categorization with all substring features. In *SDM*, pages 838–846, 2009.
[25] A. Pak and P. Paroubek. Twitter as a corpus for sentiment analysis and opinion mining. In *LREC*, 2010.
[26] F. Peng, D. Schuurmans, and S. Wang. Augmenting naive bayes classifiers with statistical language models. *Inf. Retr.*, 7(3-4):317–345, 2004.
[27] T. Sakaki, M. Okazaki, and Y. Matsuo. Earthquake shakes twitter users: real-time event detection by social sensors. In *WWW*, pages 851–860, 2010.
[28] T. Salles, L. C. da Rocha, F. Mourão, G. L. Pappa, L. Cunha, M. A. Gonçalves, and W. Meira Jr. Automatic document classification temporally robust. *JIDM*, 1(2):199–212, 2010.
[29] T. Salles, L. C. da Rocha, G. L. Pappa, F. Mourão, W. Meira Jr., and M. A. Gonçalves. Temporally-aware algorithms for document classification. In *SIGIR*, pages 307–314, 2010.
[30] M. Scholz and R. Klinkenberg. Boosting classifiers for drifting concepts. *Intell. Data Anal.*, 11(1):3–28, 2007.
[31] S. E. Somerville, D. C. Montgomery, and G. C. Runger. Filtering and smoothing methods for mixed particle count distributions. *Int. Journal of Prod. Res.*, 40(13):2991–3013, 2002.
[32] B. Sriram, D. Fuhry, E. Demir, H. Ferhatosmanoglu, and M. Demirbas. Short text classification in twitter to improve information filtering. In *SIGIR*, pages 841–842, 2010.
[33] C. H. Teo and S. V. N. Vishwanathan. Fast and space efficient string kernels using suffix arrays. In *ICML*, pages 929–936, 2006.
[34] A. Tsymbal. The problem of concept drift: definitions and related work. Technical Report TCD-CS-2004-15, Trinity College Dublin, 2004.
[35] B. Wenerstrom and C. Giraud-Carrier. Temporal data mining in dynamic feature spaces. In *ICDM*, pages 1141–1145, 2006.
[36] G. Widmer and M. Kubat. Learning in the presence of concept drift and hidden contexts. *Machine Learning*, 23(1):69–101, 1996.
[37] I. H. Witten and T. C. Bell. The zero-frequency problem: Estimating the probabilities of novel events in adaptive text compression. *IEEE Trans. Inf. Theory*, 37(4):1085–1094, 1991.
[38] E. S. Xioufis, M. Spiliopoulou, G. Tsoumakas, and I. P. Vlahavas. Dealing with concept drift and class imbalance in multi-label stream classification. In *IJCAI*, pages 1583–1588, 2011.
[39] Y. Yang and J. O. Pedersen. A comparative study on feature selection in text categorization. In *ICML*, pages 412–420, 1997.

Predicting Quality Flaws in User-generated Content: The Case of Wikipedia

Maik Anderka
Bauhaus-Universität Weimar
99421 Weimar, Germany
maik.anderka@gmail.com

Benno Stein
Bauhaus-Universität Weimar
99421 Weimar, Germany
benno.stein@uni-weimar.de

Nedim Lipka
Bauhaus-Universität Weimar
99421 Weimar, Germany
lipka.nedim@gmail.com

ABSTRACT

The detection and improvement of low-quality information is a key concern in Web applications that are based on user-generated content; a popular example is the online encyclopedia Wikipedia. Existing research on quality assessment of user-generated content deals with the classification as to whether the content is high-quality or low-quality. This paper goes one step further: it targets the *prediction of quality flaws*, this way providing specific indications in which respects low-quality content needs improvement. The prediction is based on user-defined cleanup tags, which are commonly used in many Web applications to tag content that has some shortcomings. We apply this approach to the English Wikipedia, which is the largest and most popular user-generated knowledge source on the Web. We present an automatic mining approach to identify the existing cleanup tags, which provides us with a training corpus of labeled Wikipedia articles. We argue that common binary or multiclass classification approaches are ineffective for the prediction of quality flaws and hence cast quality flaw prediction as a *one-class classification problem*. We develop a quality flaw model and employ a dedicated machine learning approach to predict Wikipedia's most important quality flaws. Since in the Wikipedia setting the acquisition of significant test data is intricate, we analyze the effects of a biased sample selection. In this regard we illustrate the classifier effectiveness as a function of the flaw distribution in order to cope with the unknown (real-world) flaw-specific class imbalances. The flaw prediction performance is evaluated with 10 000 Wikipedia articles that have been tagged with the ten most frequent quality flaws: provided test data with little noise, four flaws can be detected with a precision close to 1.

Categories and Subject Descriptors

H.3.3 [**Information Storage and Retrieval**]: Information Search and Retrieval; H.5.3 [**Information Interfaces and Presentation**]: Group and Organization Interfaces—*Evaluation/methodology*

Keywords

User-generated Content Analysis, Information Quality, Wikipedia, Quality Flaw Prediction, One-class Classification

1. INTRODUCTION

Web applications that are based on user-generated content come under criticism for containing low-quality information. This applies also to Wikipedia, the largest and most popular user-generated knowledge source on the Web; Wikipedia contains articles from more than 280 languages, the English version contains more than 3.9 million articles, and wikipedia.org ranks among the top ten most visited Web sites. The community of Wikipedia authors is heterogeneous, including people with different levels of education, age, culture, language skills, and expertise. In contrast to printed encyclopedias, the contributions to Wikipedia are not reviewed by experts before publication. These factors make clear that the most important, but probably the most difficult challenge for Wikipedia pertains to the quality of its articles. Wikipedia founder Jimmy Wales announced in a recent interview: "Our goal is to make Wikipedia as high-quality as possible. [Encyclopædia] Britannica or better quality is the goal." [36] However, the size and the dynamic nature of Wikipedia render a comprehensive manual quality assurance infeasible. This is underlined by the fact that only a small number of articles are labeled as *featured*, i.e., are considered as well-written, comprehensive, well-researched, neutral, and stable.[1]

The existing research on automatic quality assessment of Wikipedia articles targets the classification task "Is an article featured or not?" Although the developed approaches perform nearly perfect in distinguishing featured articles from non-featured ones, they provide virtually no support for quality assurance activities. The classification is based on meta features that correlate with featured articles in general, but cannot (and were not intended to) provide a rationale in which respects an article violates Wikipedia's featured article criteria. This goal, however, is addressed in this paper where we try to predict the flaws of an article that need to be fixed to improve its quality. We exploit the fact that Wikipedia users who encounter some flaw (but who are either not willing or who don't have the knowledge to fix it) can tag the article with a so-called cleanup tag. The existing cleanup tags give us the set of quality flaws that have been identified so far by Wikipedia users. The tagged articles are used as a source of human-labeled data that is exploited by a machine learning approach to predict flaws of untagged articles.

1.1 Research Questions and Contributions

Our contributions relate to the fields of user-generated content analyses, data mining, and machine learning and focus on the following research questions:

What cleanup tags exist in Wikipedia? Cleanup tags are realized by templates, which are special Wikipedia pages that can be included into other pages. The identification of templates that define

[1]At the time of this writing, less then 0.1% of the English Wikipedia articles are tagged with the "featured" label.

cleanup tags is a non-trivial task since there is no dedicated qualifier for cleanup tags and Wikipedia contains nearly 320 000 different templates. We hence implement an automated mining approach to extract the existing cleanup tags from Wikipedia. Altogether 388 cleanup tags are identified.

How to model quality flaws? A large body of features—allegedly predicting article quality—has been proposed in previous work on automatic quality assessment in Wikipedia. We have compiled a comprehensive breakdown, implement more than 100 features from previous work, and introduce 13 new features that directly target particular quality flaws. Moreover, we distinguish two modeling paradigms: intensional and extensional. The former allows for an efficient and precise prediction of certain flaws based on rules, the latter resorts to the realm of machine learning.

How to predict quality flaws? To the best of our knowledge, an algorithmic prediction of quality flaws in Wikipedia has not been operationalized before. We suggest to cast quality flaw prediction in Wikipedia as a one-class problem: Given a sample of articles that have been tagged with flaw f, decide whether or not an article suffers from f. We adapt a dedicated one-class classification machine learning approach to tackle this problem.

How to assess classifier effectiveness? A representative sample of Wikipedia articles that have been tagged to *not* contain a particular quality flaw is not available. To assess the effects of a biased sample selection our analysis is performed on both an optimistic test set, using featured articles as outliers, as well as a pessimistic test set, using random untagged articles as outliers. Given the optimistic test set and a balanced class distribution, four flaws can be detected with a precision close to 1. Since the true flaw-specific class imbalances in Wikipedia are unknown, we illustrate the classifiers' precision values as functions of the class size ratio.

The paper is organized as follows. Section 2 discusses related work on quality assessment in Wikipedia. Section 3 describes our cleanup tag mining approach. Section 4 presents the quality flaw model. Section 5 gives a formal problem definition and describes the employed one-class classification approach. Section 6 presents the evaluation and discusses the results. Finally Section 7 concludes this paper and gives an outlook on future work.

2. RELATED WORK

From its debut in 2001 till this day Wikipedia is subject of ongoing research in different academic disciplines.[2] This section surveys the research related to information quality, whereas the focus is on automatic quality assessment. We start with a discussion of the general concept of information quality.

Information quality is a multi-dimensional concept and combines criteria such as accuracy, reliability, and relevance. A good deal of the existing research focuses on the mapping between criteria sets and classification schemes [20], for which Madnick et al. [24] give a comprehensive overview. A widely accepted interpretation of information quality is the "fitness for use in a practical application" [33]: the assessment of information quality requires the consideration of context and use case. In Wikipedia the context is well-defined, namely by the encyclopedic genre. It forms the ground for Wikipedia's information quality ideal, which has been formalized—better: made communicable and quantifiable—within the so-called featured article criteria[3]. That the relation between information quality and organizational outcome can be measured is reported by Slone [28]. It stands also to reason that incorporating information quality metrics into information retrieval approaches can significantly improve the search effectiveness of Web search environments [7, 26, 38, 39].

The machine-based assessment of information quality is becoming a topic of enormous interest. This fact is rooted, among others, in the increasing popularity of user-generated Web content [6] and the (unavoidable) divergence of the delivered content's quality. Most of the prior research on automatic quality assessment deals with the identification of high-quality content, see for instance [2]. The relevant literature mentions a variety of approaches to automatically assess quality in Wikipedia. These approaches differ in their document model, i.e., the feature number, the feature complexity, and the rationale to quantify the quality of an article. We have compiled a comprehensive overview of the proposed article features, organized along the four dimensions content, structure, network, and edit history; see Table 3 in Appendix A.

Lih [21] models quality by the number of edits and the number of unique editors; the higher these values are the higher shall be an article's quality. However, an analysis whether the proposed metrics correlate with high-quality articles is missing. Stvilia et al. [29] use exploratory factor analysis to group 19 article features into 7 quality metrics. By classifying 236 featured articles and 834 random articles under these metrics they achieve an F-measure of 0.91 for the featured set and 0.975 for the random set. Hu et al. [19] model the quality of an article via the mutual dependency between article quality and author authority. They perform several quality ranking experiments and show that their model is superior to a baseline model that relies on word counts. Wilkinson and Huberman [34] show that featured articles can be distinguished from non-featured articles by the number of edits and distinct editors. They also find that featured articles are characterized by a higher degree of cooperation, which is quantified by the number of revisions of the particular Wikipedia discussion pages. Blumenstock [8] shows that still a single word count feature can compete with sophisticated features when classifying 1 554 featured articles and 9 513 random articles. Dalip et al. [13] classify the articles along six abstract quality schemes. Their comparison of different feature sets shows that textual features perform best. Lipka and Stein [22] employ character trigrams, originally applied for writing style analysis, to classify a balanced set of featured and non-featured articles. They achieve an F-measure value of 0.964 for featured articles. They also show that character trigrams are superior to part of speech trigrams, word counts, and bag of words models.

Although the mentioned approaches differ in their robustness and complexity, they perform nearly perfect in distinguishing featured articles from non-featured ones or, stated generally, high-quality articles from low-quality articles. As already motivated, the practical support for Wikipedia's quality assurance process is marginal. A first step towards automatic quality assurance in Wikipedia is *the detection* of quality flaws, which we proposed in previous research [3, 4]. Here, we push this idea further and extend our previous work with (1) a comprehensive breakdown of prior work on quality assessment, (2) an in-depth discussion of the cleanup tag mining approach, (3) a description of the quality flaw model, and (4) a detailed analysis of the one-class problem. The cleanup tag mining approach has also been used in [5], were we analyzed the incidence and the extent of quality flaws in the English Wikipedia.

There is also notable research that relates indirectly to quality in Wikipedia: trust and reliability of articles [12, 37], accuracy and formality [14, 16], author reputation [1, 32], and automatic vandalism detection [27].

[2]Academic studies of Wikipedia: `http://en.wikipedia.org/wiki/Wikipedia:Wikipedia_in_academic_studies`.

[3]Featured article criteria: `http://en.wikipedia.org/wiki/Wikipedia:Featured_article_criteria`.

3. MINING CLEANUP TAGS

Cleanup tags provide a means to tag flaws in Wikipedia articles. As shown in Figure 1, cleanup tags are used to inform readers and editors of specific problems with articles, sections, or certain text fragments. However, there is no silver bullet to compile a complete set of all cleanup tags. Cleanup tags are realized with templates, whereas templates in turn are special Wikipedia pages that can be included in other pages. Although templates can be separated from other pages by their namespace (the prefix "Template:" in the page title), there is no dedicated qualifier to separate templates that are used to implement cleanup tags from other templates. A complete manual inspection is infeasible as Wikipedia contains about 320 000 different templates. To cope with this situation we developed an extraction approach that exploits several sources within Wikipedia containing meta information about cleanup tags (Section 3.2). In this regard we also analyzed the frequency and nature of the extracted tags (Section 3.3). At first, we describe the data underlying our mining approach (Section 3.1).

3.1 Data Base and Preprocessing

To ensure reproducibility, the analyses in this paper are based on a snapshot instead of investigating Wikipedia up-to-the-minute. Wikipedia snapshots are provided by the Wikimedia Foundation in monthly intervals. Because of its size and popularity we consider the English language edition most appropriate, and we use the English Wikipedia snapshot from January 15, 2011.[4] A Wikimedia snapshot comprises a complete copy of Wikipedia. The wikitext sources of all pages (and of all revisions) are available as a single XML file that is enriched by some meta information. In addition, several tables of the Wikipedia database are available in the form of SQL dumps, totaling about 40GB. In a preprocessing step, we create a local copy of the Wikipedia database by importing the SQL dumps into a MySQL database. Since we do not target a content analysis, a processing of the XML dumps is not necessary. The local copy of the Wikipedia database allows for efficient parsing and mining without causing traffic on the Wikimedia servers. Note that all of our analyses can be performed on the original Wikipedia database as well.

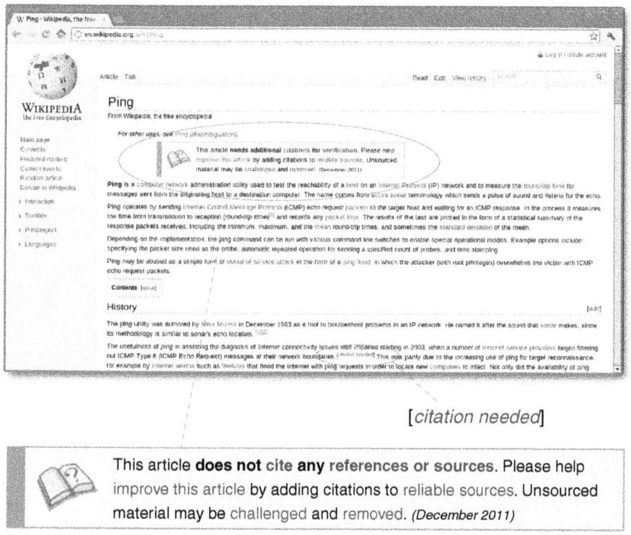

Figure 1: The Wikipedia article "Ping" with two cleanup tags. The tag box *Unreferenced* refers to the whole article while the inline tag *Citation needed* refers to a particular claim.

[4]Wikimedia downloads: `http://download.wikimedia.org`.

3.2 Method

We employ a two-step approach to compile the set of cleanup tags: (1) an initial set of cleanup tags is extracted from two meta sources within Wikipedia, and (2) the initial set is further refined by applying several filtering substeps.

Step 1: Extraction The first meta source that we employ is the Wikipedia administration category *Category:Cleanup_templates*, which comprises templates that are used for tagging articles as requiring cleanup. The category also has several subcategories to further organize the cleanup tags by their usage, e.g., inline cleanup templates or cleanup templates for WikiProjects. The page titles of those templates linking to the category or some subcategory are obtained from the local Wikipedia database, which results in 272 different cleanup tags. The second source is the Wikipedia meta page *Wikipedia:Template_messages/Cleanup*, which comprises a manually maintained listing of cleanup templates that may be used to tag articles as needing cleanup. From a technical point of view, the page is a composition of several pages (transclusion principle). For each of these pages, the content of the revision from the snapshot time is retrieved using the MediaWiki API.[5] A total of 283 different cleanup tags are extracted from the wikitexts of the retrieved pages using regular expressions. Merging the findings from both sources gives 457 different cleanup tags.

Step 2: Refinement A cleanup tag may have several alternative titles linking to it through redirects. For example, the tag *Unreferenced* has the redirects *Unref*, *Noreferences*, and *No refs* among others. We resolve all redirects using the local Wikipedia database. Moreover, we discard particular subtemplates from the initial set of cleanup tags. Subtemplates are identified by a suffix in the page title, and they are used for testing purposes (suffixes "/sandbox" and "/testcases") or provide a template description (suffix "/doc"). We also discard meta-templates, i.e., templates that are solely used either as building blocks inside other templates or to instantiate other templates with a particular parameterization. Meta-templates are derived from the Wikipedia categories *Wikipedia_metatemplates* and *Wikipedia_substituted_templates*. Altogether we collect a set of 388 cleanup tags.

Discussion To evaluate our mining approach, we manually inspected all documentation pages of the 388 cleanup tags. They give information about purpose, usage, and scope of a template, and our analysis reveals that all tags are indeed related to a particular cleanup task. I.e., each of the 388 cleanup tags defines a particular quality flaw. Our mining approach does not guarantee completeness though, since the true set of cleanup tags is unknown in general. However, from a quantitative point of view we are confident that we identify the most common cleanup tags, and hence the most important quality flaws.

3.3 Analysis

The Wikipedia snapshot comprises 3 557 468 articles, from which 979 299 (27.53%) are tagged with at least one quality flaw. Some articles are tagged with multiple flaws (multi-labeling). The number of flaws per article ranges from 1 to 17. However, the majority (74.95%) of the tagged articles are tagged with exactly one flaw. The number of tagged articles is an underestimation of the true frequencies of the quality flaws, since due to the size and the few control mechanisms in Wikipedia it is more than likely that many flawed articles are still not identified. From the 388 cleanup tags 18 merely state that some cleanup is required at all but do not

[5]We use the API in favor of parsing the XML dumps. MediaWiki API: `http://www.mediawiki.org/wiki/API`.

Table 1: **The ten most frequent quality flaws of English Wikipedia articles along with a description and the number of articles that have been tagged with the respective cleanup tag.**

Flaw name	Description	Tagged articles
Unreferenced	The article does not cite any references or sources.	273 230
Orphan	The article has fewer than three incoming links.	166 933
Refimprove	The article needs additional citations for verification.	89 686
Empty section	The article has at least one section that is empty.	46 184
Notability	The article does not meet the general notability guideline.	32 396
No footnotes	The article's sources remain unclear because of its inline citations.	26 920
Primary sources	The article relies on references to primary sources.	21 836
Wikify	The article needs to be wikified (internal links and layout).	14 333
Advert	The article is written like an advertisement.	7 186
Original research	The article contains original research.	6 630

provide further information. Moreover, 307 cleanup tags refer to the whole article (e.g., *Unreferenced* in Figure 1), whereas 81 refer to particular claims (e.g., *Citation needed*). In this paper, we target the prediction of specific flaws referring to the whole article, and hence we discard the 18 unspecific tags as well as the 81 inline tags.[6] Note in this respect that only 2,01% of the tagged articles are tagged with one of the 18 unspecific tags and that the majority (80.02%) of tagged articles are tagged with a flaw that refer to the whole article. 289 cleanup tags remain that define specific article flaws; the ten most frequent are listed in Table 1. 896 953 articles are tagged with the 289 quality flaws, out of which 76.41% are tagged with the ten flaws shown in Table 1.

4. QUALITY FLAW MODEL

The modeling of quality flaws can happen intensionally or extensionally, depending on a flaw's nature and the knowledge that is at our disposal.[7] An intensional model of a flaw f can be understood as a set of rules, which define, in a closed-class manner, the set of articles that contain f. An extensional model is given by a set of positive examples, and modeling means learning a classifier that discriminates positive instances (containing the flaw) from all other instances. Of course, the basis of both modeling paradigms are expressive features of Wikipedia articles.

4.1 Features

To this day a large body of article features—allegedly quality predicting—has been proposed; we have compiled a comprehensive breakdown, see Table 3 in Appendix A. Within our implementation all ticked features are employed, i.e., we capture the state-of-the-art with respect to feature expressiveness and information quality research. Some features are omitted since their implementation effort exceeds the expected benefit by far. In addition we devise several new features, which are marked with an asterisk. The features are organized along four dimensions: content, structure, network, and edit history. The source of information that is required for feature computation as well as the computational complexity differs for each dimension. Our model can be adjusted with respect to its transferability to other text documents than Wikipedia articles as well as to its computational complexity, by restricting to the features from a subset of the four dimensions.

Content features rely on the plain text of an article and are intended to quantify aspects like writing style and readability. Also, the new feature "special word rate", introduced to measure the presence of certain predefined words, provides evidence of unwanted content and article neutrality. E.g., peacock words, such as legendary, great, and brilliant, may be an indicator of advertising or promotional content; similarly, the presence of sentiment-bearing words can be considered as an indicator of missing neutrality. The content features can be computed with a complexity of $O(|d|)$, where $|d|$ denotes the length of an article d in characters.

Structure features are intended to quantify the organization of an article. We employ features which measure quantity, length, and nesting of sections as well as of subsections. Special attention is paid to the lead section, also called intro, as several flaws directly refer to it. Moreover, the usage of images, tables, files, and templates is quantified, as well as the categories an article belongs to; the usage of lists is quantified for the first time. Other features quantify the usage of references, including citations and footnotes and shall target flaws related to an article's verifiability. We introduce new features that check the presence of special sections that are either mandatory, such as "References", or that should be avoided, such as "Trivia". Wikiprep is used to determine the number of related pages, i.e., pages that are linked in special sections like "See also" and "Further reading".[8] The computation of structure features is governed by the complexity of parsing an article's markup, which is in $O(|d|)$.

Network features quantify an article's integration by means of hyperlinks. Here we distinguish the following types of outgoing links:

- Internal links, which point to articles in the same language.
- Inter-language links, which point to the same article in a different language.
- External links, which point to sources outside of Wikipedia.

These features count the number of outgoing links as well as their frequency relative to the article size. We introduce the feature of incoming links, where the origin has to be an article (i.e. links from disambiguation, redirect, and discussion pages are excluded). The in-link count targets the flaw *Orphan*, and the out-link counts target the flaw *Wikify*. The computation of network features is based on the link graph and is in $O(|d| \cdot |D|)$, where D denotes the set of all Wikipedia articles.

Edit history features model article evolution, which pertains to the frequency and timing of revisions as well as to the community of editors. These features have been proven valuable to classify featured articles [13, 21, 29, 34]; they address aspects like stability, maturity, and cooperation. The computation of edit history features is in $O(|d| \cdot r_d)$, where r_d denotes the number of revisions of an article d.

4.2 Intensional Modeling

The flaw descriptions in Table 1 show that three flaws from the set of the ten most frequent flaws, namely *Unreferenced*, *Orphan*, and *Empty section* can be modeled with rules based on the aforementioned features.

[6]Our prediction approach can be applied to inline flaws as well, by breaking the articles into paragraphs or sentences.

[7]For special cases also a hybrid model is conceivable, where a filtering step (intensional) precedes a learning step (extensional).

[8]`http://sourceforge.net/apps/mediawiki/wikiprep.`

An article suffers from the flaw *Unreferenced* if it does not cite any references or sources. Wikipedia provides different ways of citing sources, including inline citations, footnotes, and parenthetical referencing.[9] Here, we summarize all types of citations under the term "references". Using the structure features "reference count" and "reference sections count" we define the predicate $unreferenced(d)$:

$$unreferenced(d) = \begin{cases} 1, \text{ if } & reference\text{-}count(d) = 0 \\ & \text{and } reference\text{-}sections\text{-}count(d) = 0 \\ 0, \text{ else} & \end{cases}$$

An evaluation on $D^-_{Unreferenced}$, the set of articles that have been tagged to be unreferenced, reveals that the $unreferenced$-predicate is fulfilled for 85.3% of the articles. We analyzed the remaining 14.7% and found that they actually provide references, and hence are mistagged. This observation shows a well-known problem in the Wikipedia community, and there is a WikiProject dedicated to cleanup mistagged unreferenced articles.[10] The fact that there is no such WikiProject for other quality flaws suggests that this problem is not considered to be serious for other flaws.

The *Orphan* flaw is well-defined: an article is called orphan if it has fewer than three incoming links. In this regard the following page types are not counted: disambiguation pages, redirects, soft redirects, discussion pages, and pages outside of the article namespace.[11] Using the network feature "in-link count" we define the predicate $orphan(d)$:

$$orphan(d) = \begin{cases} 1, & \text{if } \; in\text{-}link\text{-}count(d) < 3 \\ 0, & \text{else} \end{cases}$$

An evaluation on D^-_{Orphan} reveals that the $orphan$-predicate is fulfilled for 98.4% of the articles.

An article suffers from the flaw *Empty section* if it has a section that does not contain content at all. Using the structure feature "short section length" we define the predicate $empty\_section(d)$:

$$empty\_section(d) = \begin{cases} 1, & \text{if } \; short\text{-}section\text{-}length(d) = 0 \\ 0, & \text{else} \end{cases}$$

An evaluation on $D^-_{Empty\_section}$ reveals that the $empty\_section$-predicate is fulfilled for 99.1% of the articles.

The intensional modeling paradigm is very efficient since no training data is required and since the computation relies on few basic features. Moreover, as the above evaluations show, it is effective at the same time. Note however, that if the definition of a flaw changes, an explicit model needs to be adapted as well.

4.3 Extensional Modeling

The majority of quality flaws is defined informally and cannot be modeled by means of explicit rules (see Table 1); the knowledge is given in the form of examples instead. For an article $d \in D$ we model these flaws as a vector $\mathbf{d}$, called document model. The dimensions of $\mathbf{d}$ quantify the features ticked in Table 3, and, for a set D of Wikipedia articles, $\mathbf{D}$ denotes the set of associated document models. By means of machine learning a mathematical decision rule is computed from $\mathbf{D}$ that discriminates between elements from D^- and $D \setminus D^-$ (see Figure 2).

[9]Guidelines for citing sources: http://en.wikipedia.org/wiki/Wikipedia:Citing_sources.

[10]WikiProject: http://en.wikipedia.org/wiki/Wikipedia:Mistagged_unreferenced_articles_cleanup.

[11]Criteria for orphaned articles: http://en.wikipedia.org/wiki/Wikipedia:Orphan#Criteria.

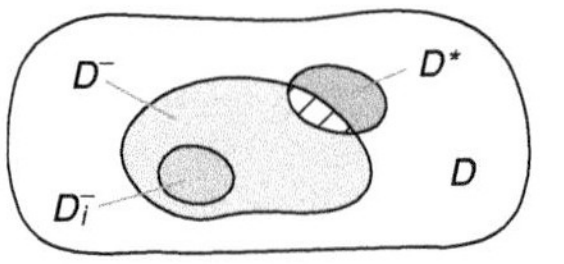

Figure 2: Sets of Wikipedia articles distinguished in this paper. Without loss of generality we assume in our experiments that the hashed area $D^- \cap D^*$ is empty, i.e., featured articles are flawless.

5. PREDICTING QUALITY FLAWS

We argue that the prediction of quality flaws is essentially a one-class problem. This section gives a formal problem definition (Section 5.1) and devises a tailored one-class machine learning approach to address the problem (Section 5.2).

5.1 Problem Statement

Let D be the set of Wikipedia articles and let F be a set of quality flaws. A document $d \in D$ can contain up to $|F|$ flaws, where, without loss of generality, the flaws in F are considered as being uncorrelated. A classifier c hence has to solve the following multi-labeling problem:[12]

$$c : \mathbf{D} \rightarrow 2^F,$$

where 2^F denotes the power set of F. Basically, there are two strategies to tackle multi-labeling problems:

1. by multiclass classification, where an individual classifier is learned on the power set of all classes, and
2. by multiple binary classification, where a specific classifier $c_i : \mathbf{D} \rightarrow \{1, 0\}$ is learned for each class $f_i \in F$.

Since the high number of classes under a multiclass classification strategy entails a very large number of training examples, the second strategy is favorable.

In most classification problems training data is available for all classes that can occur at prediction time, and hence it is appropriate to train a classifier c_i with (positive) examples of the target class f_i and (negative) examples from the classes $F \setminus f_i$. When spotting quality flaws, an unseen document can either belong to the target class f_i or to some unknown class that was not available during training. I.e., the standard discrimination-based classification approaches (binary or multiclass) are not applicable to learn a class-separating decision boundary: given a flaw f_i, its target class is formed by those documents that contain (among others) flaw f_i—but it is impossible to model the "co-class" with documents *not* containing f_i. Even if many counterexamples were available, they could not be exploited to properly characterize the universe of possible counterexamples. As a consequence, we model the classification $c_i(\mathbf{d})$ of an document $d \in D$ with respect to a quality flaw f_i as the following one-class classification problem: Decide whether or not d contains f_i, whereas a sample of documents containing f_i is given.

As an additional illustration consider the flaw *Refimprove*, which is described in Table 1. An even large sample of articles that suffer from this flaw can be compiled without problems (89 686 articles have been tagged with this flaw). However, it is impossible to compile a representative sample of articles that have a reasonable number of proper citations for verification. Although many articles with sufficient citations exist (e.g., featured articles), they cannot be considered as a *representative sample*. The fact that featured articles are not representative for typical Wikipedia articles becomes

[12]Possibly existing correlations among the flaws in F will not affect the nature of the multi-labeling problem.

clear when looking at Figure 3, which shows a sample of Wikipedia articles represented under the first two principle components. Figure 3 also shows that quality flaw prediction is a significantly harder problem than discriminating featured articles. Training a binary classier using featured articles and flawed articles would lead to a biased classifier that is not able to predict flaws on the entire Wikipedia. Also, using random articles and flawed articles to train a binary classier is unacceptable because, as already mentioned, it is more than likely that many flawed articles are not yet identified. Stated another way, quality flaw prediction is a one-class problem.

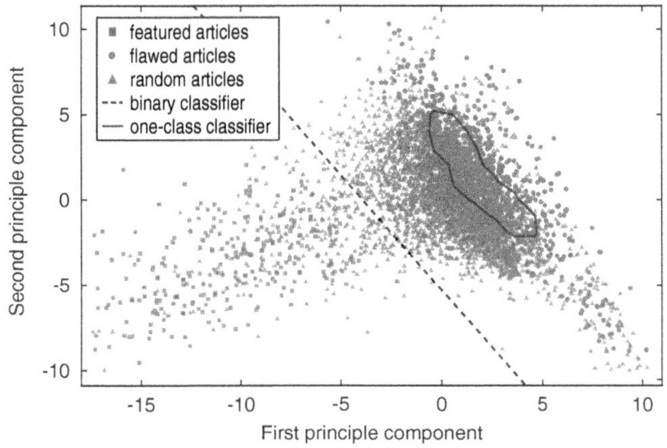

Figure 3: Distribution of featured articles, articles that are tagged with the flaw *Refimprove*, and random articles in the English Wikipedia, represented under the first two principle components. The binary classifier is trained using featured articles and flawed articles, the one-class classifier is trained solely on the set of flawed articles.

5.2 Method

Following Tax [31], three principles to construct a one-class classifier can be distinguished: density estimation methods, boundary methods, and reconstruction methods. Here we resort to a one-class classification approach as proposed by Hempstalk et al. [17], which combines density estimation with class probability estimation. There are two reasons for using this approach: (1) Hempstalk et al. show that it is able to outperform state-of-the-art approaches, including a one-class SVM, and (2) it can be used with arbitrary density estimators and class probability estimators. Instead employing an out-of-the-box classifier we apply dedicated density estimation and class probability estimation techniques to address the problem defined above.

The idea is to use a reference distribution to model the probability $P(\mathbf{d} \mid f_i')$ of an artificial class f_i', and to generate (artificial) data governed by the distribution characteristic of f_i'. For a flaw f_i let $P(f_i)$ and $P(f_i \mid \mathbf{d})$ denote the a-priori probability and the class probability function respectively. According to Bayes' theorem the class-conditional probability for f_i is given as follows:

$$P(\mathbf{d} \mid f_i) = \frac{(1 - P(f_i)) \cdot P(f_i \mid \mathbf{d})}{P(f_i) \cdot (1 - P(f_i \mid \mathbf{d}))} \cdot P(\mathbf{d} \mid f_i')$$

$P(f_i \mid \mathbf{d})$ is estimated by a class probability estimator, i.e., a classifier whose output is interpreted as probability. Since we are in a one-class situation we have to rely on the face value of $P(\mathbf{d} \mid f_i)$. More specifically, $P(\mathbf{d} \mid f_i)$ cannot be used to determine a maximum a-posterior (MAP) hypothesis among the $f_i \in F$. As a consequence, given $P(\mathbf{d} \mid f_i) < \tau$ with $\tau = 0.5$, the hypothesis that d suffers from f_i could be rejected. However, because of the approximative nature of $P(f_i \mid \mathbf{d})$ and $P(f_i)$ the estimation for $P(\mathbf{d} \mid f_i)$ is not a true probability, and the threshold τ has to be chosen empirically. In practice, the threshold τ is derived from a user-defined target rejection rate, trr, which is the rejection rate of the target class training data.

The one-class classifier is built as follows: at first a class with artificial examples is generated, whereas the feature values obey a Gaussian distribution with $\mu = 0$ and $\sigma^2 = 1$. We employ the Gaussian distribution in favor of a more complex reference distribution to underline the robustness of the approach. The proportion of the generated data is 0.5 compared to the target class. As class probability estimators we apply bagged random forest classifiers with 1 000 decision trees and ten bagging iterations. A random forest is a collection of decision trees where a voting over all trees is run in order to obtain a classification decision [18, 10]. The decision trees of a forest differ with respect to their features. Here, each tree is build with a subset of $log_2(|features|) + 1$ randomly chosen features, i.e., no tree minimization strategy is followed at training time. The learning algorithm stops if either all leaves contain only examples of one class or if no further splitting is possible. Each decision tree perfectly classifies the training data—but, because of its low bias the obtained generalization capability is poor [35, 25]. However, the combination of several classifiers in a voting scheme reduces the variance and introduces a stronger bias. While the bias of a random forest results from several feature sets, the bias of the bagging approach results from the employment of several training sets, and it is considered as being even stronger [9].

6. EVALUATION

We report on experiments to assess the effectiveness of our modeling and classification approach in detecting the ten most frequent quality flaws shown in Table 1. As already mentioned, 76.41% of the tagged Wikipedia articles suffer from these flaws (see Section 3.3). The evaluation treats the following issues:

1. Since a bias may not be ruled out when collecting outlier examples for a classifier's test set, we investigate the consequences of the two extreme (overly optimistic, overly pessimistic) settings (Section 6.1).

2. Since users (Wikipedia editors) have diverse expectations regarding the classification effectiveness given different flaws, we analyze the optimal operating point for each flaw-specific classifier within the controlled setting of a balanced class distribution (Section 6.2).

3. Since the true flaw-specific class imbalances in Wikipedia can only be hypothesized, we illustrate the effectiveness of the classifiers in different settings, this way enabling users (Wikipedia editors) to assume an optimistic or a pessimistic position (Section 6.3).

Preprocessing We use the same data basis that underlies our cleanup tag mining approach, i.e., the English Wikipedia snapshot from January 15, 2011. The articles' plain texts and wikitexts are extracted from the "pages-articles" dump, which is included in the Wikimedia snapshot and which comprises the current revisions of all articles in a single XML file of about 25GB size. The plain texts and the wikitexts form the basis to compute the content features and the structure features. Our local copy of the Wikipedia database, which is described in Section 3.1, is used to compute the network features. The computation of the history features is based on the "pages-meta-history" dump, which is included in the Wikimedia snapshot and which comprises the content of each revision in a single XML file of about 7.3TB size. The XML dumps are processed on an Apache Hadoop cluster using Google's MapReduce.

6.1 Outlier Selection

Recall that no articles are available that have been tagged to *not* contain a quality flaw $f_i \in F$. Thus a classifier c_i can be evaluated only with respect to its recall, whereas a recall of 1 can be achieved easily by classifying all examples into the target class of f_i. In order to evaluate c_i with respect to its precision one needs a representative sample of examples from outside the target class, so-called outliers. As motivated above, in a one-class situation it is not possible to compile a representative sample, and a way out of the dilemma is the generation of uniformly distributed outlier examples [31]. Here, we pursue two strategies to derive examples from outside the target class, which result in the following settings:

1. *Optimistic Setting.* Use of featured articles as outliers. This approach is based on the hypothesis that featured articles do not contain a quality flaw at all, see Figure 2.[13] Under this setting one introduces some bias, since featured articles cannot be considered as a representative sample of Wikipedia articles (see Figure 3).

2. *Pessimistic Setting.* Use of a random sample from $D \setminus D_i^-$ as outliers for each f_i. This approach may introduce considerable noise since the set $D \setminus D_i^-$ is expected to contain untagged articles that suffer from f_i.

The above settings address two extremes: classification under laboratory conditions (overly optimistic) versus classification in the wild (overly pessimistic). The experiment design is owing to the facts that "no-flaw features" cannot be stated and that the number of false positives as well as the number of false negatives in the set D^- of tagged articles are unknown.

6.2 Effectiveness of Flaw Prediction

Experiment Design The evaluation is performed for the set $F' \subset F$ of the ten most frequent quality flaws. In the optimistic setting 1 000 outliers are randomly selected from the 3 128 featured articles in the snapshot. In the pessimistic setting 1 000 outliers are randomly selected for each flaw $f_i \in F'$ from $D \setminus D_i^-$. We evaluate our approach under both settings by applying the following procedure: For each flaw $f_i \in F'$ the one-class classifier c_i is evaluated with 1 000 articles randomly sampled from D_i^- and the respective 1 000 outliers, applying tenfold cross-validation. Within each run the classifier is trained with 900 articles from D_i^-, whereas testing is performed with the remaining 100 articles from D_i^- plus 100 outliers. Note that c_i is trained exclusively with the examples of the respective target class, i.e., the articles in D_i^-. The training of c_i is neither affected by the class distribution nor by the outlier selection strategy that is used in the respective setting.

Operating Point Analysis For the major part of the relevant use cases precision is the determining measure of effectiveness; consider for instance a bot that autonomously tags flawed articles. The precision of the one-class classifier is controlled by the hyperparameter "target rejection rate". We empirically determine the optimal operating point for each of the ten flaws under both the optimistic and the pessimistic setting. Here, the optimal operating point corresponds to the target rejection rate of the maximum precision classifier. Figure 4 illustrates the operating point analyses exemplary for the flaw *Unreferenced*: with increasing target rejection rate the recall value decreases while the precision values increase. Observe that the recall is the same in both settings, since it

[13]The hypothesis may hold in many cases but not always: the snapshot comprises 13 featured articles that have been tagged with some flaw. We discarded these articles in our experiments.

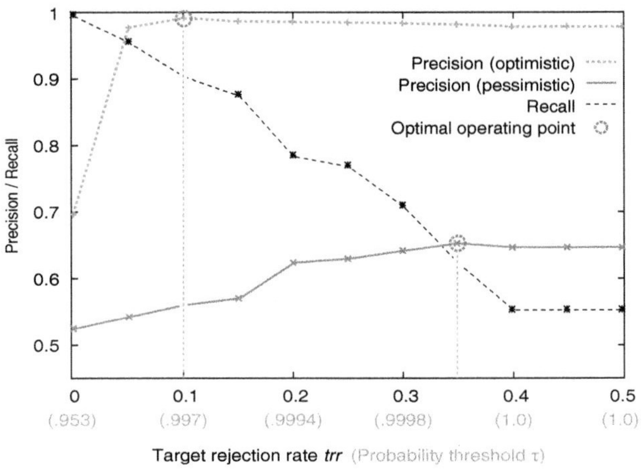

Figure 4: Precision and recall over target rejection rate for the flaw *Unreferenced*. The figure illustrates the difference in terms of precision under the optimistic setting, using featured articles as outliers, and the pessimistic setting, using random articles as outliers. The recall is the same under both settings. The optimal operating points correspond to the target rejection rates that maximizes classifier precision.

solely depends on the target class training data. For the flaw *Unreferenced* the optimal operating points under the optimistic and the pessimistic setting are at a target rejection rate of 0.1 and 0.35 respectively (with precision values of 0.99 and 0.63).

The precision of a one-class classifier cannot be adjusted arbitrarily since the target rejection rate controls only the probability threshold τ for the classification decision. For instance, a target rejection rate of 0.1 means that a τ is chosen such that 10% of the target class training data will be rejected, which results in a classifier that performs with an almost stable recall of 0.9. Increasing the target rejection rate entails an increase of τ. However, if τ achieves its maximum no further examples can be rejected, and hence both the precision and the recall remain constant beyond a certain target rejection rate (which is 0.4 for the flaw *Unreferenced*, see Figure 4).

Results Table 2 shows the performance values for each of the ten quality flaws. The values correspond to the performance at the respective optimal operating point. The performance is quantified as precision (*prec*) and recall (*rec*). We also report the area under ROC curves (AUC) [15], which is important to assess the tradeoff between specificity and sensitivity of a classifier: an AUC value of 0.5 means that all specificity-sensitivity-combinations are equivalent, which in turn means that the classifier is random guessing.

Under the optimistic setting four flaws can be detected with a nearly perfect precision. As expected, the precision values for the flaws *Unreferenced*, *Orphan*, and *Empty section* are very high; recall that these flaws can also be modeled intensionally. For the flaw *Notability* even the achieved recall value is very high, which means that this flaw can be detected exceptionally well. As expected, the effectiveness of the one-class classifiers deteriorates under the pessimistic setting. However, the classifiers still achieve reasonable precision values, and even in the noisy test set the flaw *Orphan* can be detected with a good precision. Notice that the expected performance in the wild lies in between the two extremes. For some flaws the effectiveness of the one-class classifiers is pretty low under both settings, including *Original research*. We explain this behavior as follows: (1) Either the document model is inadequate to capture certain flaw characteristics, or (2) the hypothesis class of the one-class classification approach is too simple to capture the flaw distributions.

Table 2: Individual performance values for each of the ten most frequent quality flaws at the optimal operating point, using featured articles as outliers (optimistic setting) and using random articles as outliers (pessimistic setting). The class distribution is balanced under both settings. The flaw ratio 1:n (flawed articles : flawless articles) corresponds to the estimated actual frequency of a flaw.

	Flaw name	Optimistic setting			Pessimistic setting			Flaw
		prec	*rec*	AUC	*prec*	*rec*	AUC	ratio
f_1	Unreferenced	0.99	0.90	0.95	0.63	0.63	0.63	1:3
f_2	Orphan	1.00	0.90	0.95	0.72	0.59	0.68	1:5
f_3	Refimprove	0.83	0.87	0.85	0.57	0.56	0.57	1:10
f_4	Empty section	0.90	0.70	0.82	0.74	0.70	0.72	1:21
f_5	Notability	0.99	0.96	0.98	0.66	0.61	0.65	1:30
f_6	No footnotes	0.82	0.87	0.84	0.59	0.59	0.58	1:36
f_7	Primary sources	0.94	0.90	0.92	0.61	0.59	0.61	1:44
f_8	Wikify	0.96	0.87	0.92	0.64	0.58	0.63	1:68
f_9	Advert	0.86	0.91	0.88	0.65	0.58	0.63	1:136
f_{10}	Original research	0.76	0.64	0.71	0.56	0.80	0.59	1:147

6.3 Flaw-specific Class Imbalances

The performance values in Table 2 presume a balanced class distribution, i.e., the one-class classifiers are evaluated with the same number of flawed articles and outliers. The real distribution of flaws in Wikipedia is unknown, and we hence report precision values as a function of the class imbalance. Given the recall and the false positive rate (*fpr*) of a classifier for the balanced setting, its precision for a class size ratio of 1:n (flawed articles : flawless articles) computes as follows:

$$prec = \frac{rec}{rec + n \cdot fpr}$$

The false positive rate is the ratio between the detected negative examples and all negative examples, and hence it is independent from the class size ratio; the same argument applies to the recall. Figure 5 shows the precision values as a function of the flaw distribution under the optimistic setting.

We make two assumptions in order to estimate the actual frequency of a flaw f_i:

1. each article in D^- is tagged completely, i.e. with all flaws that it contains (Closed World Assumption), and
2. the distribution of f_i in D^- is identical to the distribution of f_i in D.

Based on these assumptions we estimate the actual frequency of a flaw f_i by the ratio of articles in D_i^- and articles in D^-. Table 2 lists the estimated flaw ratio for each of the ten most frequent flaws. For example, the ratio of the flaw *Unreferenced* is about 1:3 (273 230 : 979 299). In other words, about every fourth article is expected to contain this flaw.

Figure 5 shows that the expected precision values for the flaws *Unreferenced*, *Orphan*, and *Notability* are still high. The flaw ratio of the flaw *Unreferenced* is 1:3, and thus the expected precision is close to that of the 1:1 ratio. The flaw *Orphan* can be detected with a precision of 1, i.e., the false positive rate is 0, and hence the prediction performance is independent of the class imbalance. Although the flaw ratio of the flaw *Notability* is 1:30, the expected precision is still about 0.9, which shows that the respective one-class classifier captures the characteristics of the flaw exceptionally well. The expected precision values for those flaws with a flaw ratio 1:n where n > 40 are lower than 0.2. Aside from conceptual weaknesses regarding the employed document model, the weak performance indicates also that the training set of the one-class classifiers may be too small.

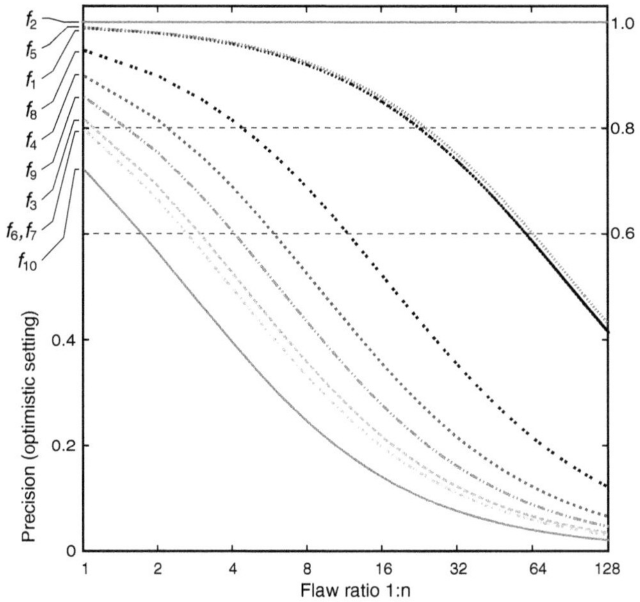

Figure 5: Precision in the optimistic setting over flaw ratio for the ten most frequent quality flaws: 1:n (flawed articles : flawless articles) with n ∈ [1; 128]. The figure puts the classification performances reported in Table 2 into perspective, since it considers imbalances in the test sets that might occur in the wild.

7. CONCLUSIONS AND OUTLOOK

We treat quality flaw prediction as a process where for each known flaw an expert is asked whether or not a given Wikipedia article suffers from it; the experts in turn are operationalized by one-class classifiers. The underlying document model combines several new features with the state-of-the-art quality assessment features. Our evaluation is based on a corpus comprising 10 000 human-labeled Wikipedia articles, compiled by utilizing cleanup tags. We report on precision values close to 1 for four out of ten important flaws—presuming an optimistic test set with little noise and a balanced flaw distribution. Even for a class size ratio of 1:16 three flaws can still be detected with a precision of about 0.9.

We are convinced that the presented or similar approaches will help to simplify Wikipedia's quality assurance process by spotting weaknesses within articles without human interaction. We plan to operationalize our classification technology in the form of a Wikipedia bot that autonomously identifies and tags flawed articles. Our approach also supports the principle of *intelligent task routing* [11], which addresses the automatic delegation of particular flaws to appropriate human editors. Though the proposed quality flaw prediction approach is evaluated in the Wikipedia context, it is also applicable to other user-generated Web applications where cleanup tags are used.

Our current research targets the development of knowledge-based predictors for individual quality flaws. Instead of resorting to a single document model, we develop a flaw-specific view that combines feature selection, expert rules, and multi-level filtering. In this respect, we analyze in detail which features prove essential for the prediction of a certain quality flaw and how effective the newly introduced features are. Moreover, instead of resorting to a single learning approach, we investigate the amenability of different one-class classification approaches with respect to the different flaws. We are also investigating whether a learning approach can benefit from the untagged articles, e.g., using partially supervised classification or PU-learning [23].

8. REFERENCES

[1] B. Adler and L. de Alfaro. A content-driven reputation system for the Wikipedia. In *Proc. of WWW'07*, pages 261–270, 2007.

[2] E. Agichtein, C. Castillo, D. Donato, A. Gionis, and G. Mishne. Finding high-quality content in social media. In *Proc. of WSDM'08*, pages 183–194, 2008.

[3] M. Anderka, B. Stein, and N. Lipka. Towards automatic quality assurance in Wikipedia. In *Proc. of WWW'11*, pages 5–6, 2011.

[4] M. Anderka, B. Stein, and N. Lipka. Detection of text quality flaws as a one-class classification problem. In *Proc. of CIKM'11*, pages 2313–2316, 2011.

[5] M. Anderka and B. Stein. A breakdown of quality flaws in Wikipedia. In Proc. of WebQuality'12, pages 11–18, 2012.

[6] R. Baeza-Yates. User generated content: how good is it? In *Proc. of WICOW'09*, pages 1–2, 2009.

[7] M. Bendersky, W. B. Croft, and Y. Diao. Quality-biased ranking of Web documents. In *Proc. of WSDM'11*, pages 95–104, 2011.

[8] J. Blumenstock. Size matters: word count as a measure of quality on Wikipedia. In *Proc. of WWW'08*, pages 1095–1096, 2008.

[9] L. Breiman. Bagging predictors. *Machine Learning*, 24(2):123–140, 1996.

[10] L. Breiman. Random forests. *Machine Learning*, 45(1):5–32, 2001.

[11] D. Cosley, D. Frankowski, L. Terveen, and J. Riedl. Using intelligent task routing and contribution review to help communities build artifacts of lasting value. In *Proc. of CHI'06*, pages 1037–1046, 2006.

[12] T. Cross. Puppy smoothies: improving the reliability of open, collaborative wikis. *First Monday*, 11(9), 2006.

[13] D. Dalip, M. Gonçalves, M. Cristo, and P. Calado. Automatic quality assessment of content created collaboratively by Web communities: a case study of Wikipedia. In *Proc. of JCDL'09*, pages 295–304, 2009.

[14] W. Emigh and S. Herring. Collaborative authoring on the Web: a genre analysis of online encyclopedias. In *Proc. of HICSS'05*, 2005.

[15] T. Fawcett. Roc graphs: Notes and practical considerations for researchers. Technical report, HP Laboratories, 2004.

[16] J. Giles. Internet encyclopaedias go head to head. *Nature*, 438(7070):900–901, 2005.

[17] K. Hempstalk, E. Frank, and I. Witten. One-class classification by combining density and class probability estimation. In *Proc. of ECML'08*, pages 505–519, 2008.

[18] T. K. Ho. Random decision forests. In *Proc. of ICDAR'95*, pages 278–282, 1995.

[19] M. Hu, E. Lim, A. Sun, H. Lauw, and B. Vuong. Measuring article quality in Wikipedia: models and evaluation. In *Proc. of CIKM'07*, pages 243–252, 2007.

[20] Y. Lee, D. Strong, B. Kahn, and R. Wang. AIMQ: a methodology for information quality assessment. *Information and Management*, 40(2):133–146, 2002.

[21] A. Lih. Wikipedia as participatory journalism: reliable sources? Metrics for evaluating collaborative media as a news resource. In *Proc. of ISOJ'04*, 2004.

[22] N. Lipka and B. Stein. Identifying featured articles in Wikipedia: writing style matters. In *Proc. of WWW'10*, pages 1147–1148, 2010.

[23] B. Liu, Y. Dai, X. Li, W. S. Lee and P. Yu. Building text classifiers using positive and unlabeled examples. In *Proc. of ICDM'03*, pages 179–186, 2003.

[24] S. Madnick, R. Wang, Y. Lee, and H. Zhu. Overview and framework for data and information quality research. *Journal of data and information quality*, 1(1):1–22, 2009.

[25] T. Mitchell. *Machine Learning*. McGraw-Hill Higher Education, 1997.

[26] A. Pirkola and T. Talvensaari. A topic-specific Web search system focusing on quality pages. In *Proc. of ECDL'10*, pages 490–493, 2010.

[27] M. Potthast, B. Stein, and R. Gerling. Automatic vandalism detection in Wikipedia. In *Proc. of ECIR'08*, pages 663–668, 2008.

[28] J. Slone. *Information quality strategy: an empirical investigation of the relationship between information quality improvements and organizational outcomes*. PhD thesis, Capella University, 2006.

[29] B. Stvilia, M. Twidale, L. Smith, and L. Gasser. Assessing information quality of a community-based encyclopedia. In *Proc. of ICIQ'05*, pages 442–454, 2005.

[30] B. Stvilia, M. Twidale, L. Smith, and L. Gasser. Information quality work organization in Wikipedia. *Journal of the american society for information science and technology*, 59(6):983–1001, 2008.

[31] D. Tax. *One-Class Classification*. PhD thesis, Delft University of Technology, 2001.

[32] F. Viégas, M. Wattenberg, and K. Dave. Studying cooperation and conflict between authors with history flow visualizations. In *Proc. of CHI'04*, pages 575–582, 2004.

[33] R. Wang and D. Strong. Beyond accuracy: what data quality means to data consumers. *Journal of management information systems*, 12(4):5–33, 1996.

[34] D. Wilkinson and B. Huberman. Cooperation and quality in Wikipedia. In *Proc. of WikiSym'07*, pages 157–164, 2007.

[35] D. Wilson and R. Randall. Bias and the probability of generalization. In *Proc. of IIS'97*, pages 108–114, 1997.

[36] The Wall Street Journal. Jimmy Wales on Wikipedia quality and tips for contributors. November 2009. URL: `http://blogs.wsj.com/digits/2009/11/06`.

[37] H. Zeng, M. Alhossaini, L. Ding, R. Fikes, and D. McGuinness. Computing trust from revision history. In *Proc. of PST'06*, 2006.

[38] Y. Zhou and B. W. Croft. Document quality models for Web ad hoc retrieval. In *Proc. of CIKM'05*, pages 331–332, 2005.

[39] X. Zhu and S. Gauch. Incorporating quality metrics in centralized/distributed information retrieval on the World Wide Web. In *Proc. of SIGIR'00*, pages 288–295, 2000.

APPENDIX

A. SURVEY OF ARTICLE FEATURES

A variety of features has been proposed in the literature on automatic quality assessment of Wikipedia articles (the relevant literature is reviewed in Section 2). Table 3 gives a comprehensive overview of the proposed features, organized along the four dimensions content, structure, network, and edit history (the dimensions are described in Section 4.1). The overview is intended as a resource for other researcher, and we consider it as the first complete compilation of this kind.

Table 3: Overview of Wikipedia article features, classified along four dimensions: content, structure, network, and edit history. Features that are employed within our document model are marked with ticks (✓), new features that are used for the first time are marked with asterisks (*).

Feature	Description	Reference
Content		
Character count	Number of characters	[8, 13, 29] ✓
Word count	Number of words	[8, 19, 22] ✓
* Word length	Average word length in characters	✓
Syllables count	Number of syllables	[8] ✓
* Word syllables	Average syllables per word	✓
One-syllable word count	Number of one-syllable words	[8] ✓
* One-syllable word rate	Percentage of one-syllable words	✓
Sentence count	Number of sentences	[8, 13] ✓
* Sentence length	Average sentence length in words	✓
Long/short sentence rate	Percentage of long sentences (at least 48 words) and short sentences (at most 33 words)	[13] ✓
Question rate	Percentage of questions	[13] ✓
Passive sentence rate	Percentage of passive voice sentences	[13] ✓
* Long/short sentence length	Number of words of the longest and shortest sentence	✓
Paragraph count	Number of paragraphs	[13] ✓
Paragraph length	Average paragraph length in sentences	[13] ✓
Readability indices	Flesh, Kincaid, Lix, ARI, SMOG-Grading, Gunning Fog, Coleman-Liau, Bormuth, Dale-Chall, Miyazaki	[8, 29] ✓
Word usage rate	Percentage of auxiliary and "to be" verbs, conjunctions, pronouns, prepositions, normalizations	[13] ✓
Sentence beginning rate	Percentage of sentences beginning with a pronoun, interrogative pronoun, article, conjunction, subordinating conjunction, preposition	[13] ✓
* Special word rate	Percentage of weasel-, peacock-, doubt-, editorializing-, long- (> 7 characters), easy- (in Dale-Chall word list), difficult- (not in Dale-Chall word list), complex- (> 3 syllables), stop words, idioms, aphorisms, proverbs	✓
Information-to-noise ratio	Vocabulary size / word count	[29] ✓
Trigrams	Character and part of speech trigrams	[22]
Structure		
Section count	Number of (sub-, subsub-) sections and total number of sections	[8, 13] ✓
Section length	Average (sub-, subsub-) section length in words	[13] ✓
Long/short section length	Number of words of the longest and shortest (sub-, subsub-) section	[13] ✓
Section nesting	Average number of (sub-) subsections per (sub-) section	[13] ✓
Heading count	Total number of sub-, subsub-, and section headings	[8, 13] ✓
Lead length	Number of words / characters of the lead section	[13] ✓
Lead rate	Percentage of words in the lead section	[13] ✓
Image count	Number of images	[8, 13, 29] ✓
Table count	Number of tables	[8] ✓
File count	Number of files (videos, pdfs etc.)	[8] ✓
Category count	Number of Wikipedia categories the article belongs to	[8] ✓
* Template count	Number of (different) Wikipedia templates	✓
* List ratio	Number of words in lists / word count	✓
Reference count	Number of references (*ref*-tags and citation templates)	[8, 13] ✓
Reference rates	Reference count / word count and reference count / section count	[13] ✓
* Reference sections count	Number of reference sections, e.g., "References", "Footnotes", "Sources", "Bibliography", "Citations"	✓
* Trivia sections count	Number of trivia sections, e.g., "Trivia", "Miscellanea", "Facts", "Other facts"	✓
* Mandatory sections count	Number of mandatory sections, e.g., "Further reading", "See also"	✓
* Related page count	Number of related pages, based on "See also", "Further reading", etc. (Wikiprep)	✓
Network		
Internal link count	Number of outgoing internal links	[8, 29] ✓
Broken internal link count	Number of outgoing internal broken links	[29] ✓
Language link count	Number of outgoing inter-language links	[13] ✓
External link count	Number of outgoing external links	[8, 13, 29] ✓
Out-link rate	Number of all out-links / word count	[13] ✓
* In-link count	Number of incoming internal links (from articles)	✓
PageRank	Google PageRank of an article	[13] ✓
Citation measures	In- and out-degree, associativity, clustering coefficient, reciprocity	[13]
Edit history		
Age	Age in days	[29] ✓
Currency	Days between last update and now (date of the snapshot)	[29] ✓
Edit count	Number of edits	[13, 21, 29, 34] ✓
Editor count	Number of distinct editors	[21, 29, 34] ✓
Editor role	Number of registered, anonymous, and admin editors	[13, 29] ✓
Editor rate	Number of edits per editor	[13, 34] ✓
Revert count	Number of reverts	[29]
Revert time	Median revert time in minutes	[29]
Edit rates	Ratio between age and edit count, percentage of edits per day	[13] ✓
Connectivity	Number of articles with common editors	[29] ✓
Cooperation	Revisions of the discussion page	[13, 34] ✓
Edit amount	Number of modified lines, compared to an older revision	[13] ✓
Edit currency rate	Percentage of edits made in the last 3 months	[13] ✓
Special editor rates	Percentage of edits of infrequent editors, percentage of edits made by the top 5% editors	[13] ✓

A Knowledge-based Approach for Summarising Opinions

Marco Bonzanini
Queen Mary University of London
marcob@eecs.qmul.ac.uk

ABSTRACT

The popularity of on-line resources, which allow users to review products or services, is motivating new interest in the area of Sentiment Analysis [3]. An important task is the classification of documents according to the overall sentiment, i.e. whether positive or negative. A common behaviour among reviewers is to summarise the overall sentiment of the review in a single sentence, or in a short passage. On the other hand, the rest of the review can express a feeling which is different from the overall judgement. This can be explained by the presence of several aspects or features that the reviewers want to comment on. Traditional summarisation techniques [2] are not always suitable for building opinion-based summaries, and more sentiment-oriented approaches are needed. In this research, we investigate the use of summarisation techniques applied to reviews, and we propose a knowledge-based approach to summarisation, in the context of sentiment analysis. The proposed research is focused on three different aspects.

Firstly, we investigate the use of summarisation techniques for sentiment classification. Capturing the key passage of a review can be beneficial for both a sentiment classifier, and for a user who could understand the polarity of a review without reading the full text. Secondly, we investigate how to combine knowledge extracted from the reviews or integrated from external sources, with the purpose of producing opinion-oriented summaries. A knowledge-based approach enables to build aspect-based summaries, i.e. summaries which are focused on a specific aspect of the item under analysis. Thirdly, we analyse the possibility of generating personalised (user-oriented or query-biased) opinion-based summaries.

Knowledge extraction tools can be used in order to generate classifications and relationships. Given a representation of a document consisting of the terms, classifications, and relationships extracted from the genuine document, the question is how to generate a summary from the knowledge-based representation. We view term, classification and relationships as *propositions*. In traditional knowledge-based representations, only classifications and relationships are considered. A proposition-context-based representation that combines terms, classifications, and relationships is proposed in [1]. Sentiment adds an extra dimension to this representation. For example, in the sentence "Maximus is a *brave* general", the term "brave" is expressing a positive polarity on the class, while in the sentence "Peter is a *good* friend of Mary" the sentiment is related to the relationship. In a knowledge-oriented approach the sentiment dimension would be inferred to the correct class, leading to the understanding of the sentiment carried by the review. One of the advantages of such a knowledge representation consists in the possibility of augmenting the knowledge through its integration with external knowledge bases. Resources like WordNet[1], DBpedia[2] or other domain-specific ontologies can be exploited for this purpose. In feature-based sentiment analysis, a knowledge-based approach is particularly suitable, as the description of complex domains can benefit from the knowledge representation. Complex objects made of different components and attributes can be described in the knowledge base, and linked to opinion terms and phrases. We view knowledge-based summarisation as a key technology, since it enables reasoning over retrieval results. Entity summarisation is a further application of this technology, as the knowledge about a specific entity can be used to create entity profiles.

A knowledge-based approach to summarisation can be exploited to produce personalised summaries. In the multi-document context, a user can be interested in a specific aspect of topic. For example, given a set of reviews of a movie, the user might want to read all the comments about a specific actor. This can be also extended for multiple topics. The generation of personalised summaries can be triggered explicitly, i.e. through a specific query, or it can take advantage of a user profile. A user model can be based on explicit keywords selected by the user, or on implicit feedback. A user-oriented study is needed to test the efficacy of a personalised summarisation system.

SIGIR'12, August 12–16, 2012, Portland, Oregon, USA.
ACM 978-1-4503-1472-5/12/08.

Categories and Subject Descriptors

H.3.m [**Information Search and Retrieval**]: Miscellaneous

General Terms

Design, Experimentation

Keywords

Summarisation, Sentiment Analysis, Knowledge Extraction

1. REFERENCES

[1] N. Fuhr, N. Goevert, and T. Roelleke. Dolores: A system for logic-based retrieval of multimedia objects. In *SIGIR*, pages 257–265, 1998.

[2] A. Nenkova and K. McKeown. Automatic summarization. *Foundations and Trends in Information Retrieval*, 5(2-3):103–233, 2011.

[3] B. Pang and L. Lee. Opinion mining and sentiment analysis. *Foundations and Trends in Information Retrieval*, 2(1-2):1–135, 2008.

[1]http://wordnet.princeton.edu/wordnet/
[2]http://dbpedia.org

Adaptive IR for Exploratory Search Support

Daniel T. J. Backhausen
University of Hagen
58084 Hagen
Germany
daniel.backhausen@fernuni-hagen.de

Categories and Subject Descriptors

H.3.3 [**Information Search and Retrieval**]: Information filtering, Query formulation, Relevance feedback, Search process, Selection process

Keywords

Interactive information retrieval, exploratory search, personalization, adaptation, recommendation, awareness

ABSTRACT

Most Information Retrieval (IR) software is designed to fit a general user where users are submitting queries and the retrieval system returns a ranked list of results. Regardless of the user, the query always returns the same list of results. Individual aspects like age, gender, profession or experience are often not taken into account, for example the difference in searching between children and adults. Although long challenged by works such as Bates' berrypicking model [1], common systems still assume that the user has a static information need which remains unchanged during the seeking process. Moreover many systems are strongly optimized for lookup searches, expecting that the user is only interested in facts and not in complex problem solving.

But in many everyday situations people search for information to gain knowledge which allows them to fulfill a specific work task (e.g., [3]), like answering research questions, investigating for a publication or thesis, comparing different products or learning a language. Such complex tasks can be divided into sub-tasks and generally include multiple exploratory search sessions, in which the user strongly interacts with the system. This is a longitudinal process where the searcher necessarily gathers, collects, aggregates, interprets, processes, and evaluates information objects from one or more sources. In such complex search scenarios all three activities lookup, learn, and investigate are used in conjunction with one another to bridge the users knowledge gap [2]. In each step of this process, the user faces a new situation in which knowledge and information need changes. This influences the relevance of information objects and may direct the user to different topics, domains, or also tasks.

The goal of this research is to effectively assist at fulfilling complex (work) tasks consisting of multi-session exploratory search activities. To achieve this, information retrieval needs personalization and has to close the gaps between the different search sessions. This can be done by enabling the user to collect information objects into a personal reference library and visualizing past search activities in a kind of breadcrumb or time line.

Thinking one step further, a personalized IR system (PIR) has to adapt to relevant factors and commit itself to the specific user and the personal search behavior. This means the system needs to guide the user through the searching process, suggesting useful search actions like effective search strategies or query formulations and has to recommend information objects relevant to the work task and the users current situation. Thereby the system has to be aware of the user and specific contextual circumstances. General information about the user like gender or age can be fetched explicitly, allowing to adapt in a more coarse grained way (i.e. decide the way of presenting results based on the user group). Moreover integrating used applications or providing other ways to let the user explicitly manage tasks will help to understand the goal of the users search activities and will provide much better ways of user assistance.

To close the gap between user and system, both behavioral and contextual information are necessary. Information about the search behavior and indirectly the users knowledge and expertise can be conveyed by logging (e.g. query logs) and examining system interactions. The fetched data should be made transparent to the user, showing what kind of information has been gathered so far. The implicit information has to be refined with other contextual information collected implicitly from different interfaces or sensors (e.g. time, location) and explicitly by direct user input from e.g. relevance feedback interactions. This will allow a more fine grained way of system adaption and offers new options in assisting the user during the long-term search activities showing personalized search strategies and possible next steps appropriate to the information need and level of experience.

SIGIR'12, August 12–16, 2012, Portland, Oregon, USA.
ACM 978-1-4503-1472-5/12/08.

REFERENCES

[1] M. J. Bates. The design of browsing and berrypicking techniques for the on-line search interface. *Online review*, 13(5):407–431, 1989.
[2] G. Marchionini. Exploratory search: from finding to understanding. *Communications of the ACM*, 49(4):41–46, April 2006.
[3] P. Vakkari. A theory of the task-based information retrieval process: a summary and generalisation of a longitudinal study. *Journal of Documentation*, 57(1):44–60, 2001.

Adversarial Content Manipulation Effects

Fiana Raiber
Faculty of Industrial Engineering and Management
Technion – Israel Institute of Technology
Haifa 32000, Israel
fiana@tx.technion.ac.il

ABSTRACT

We address a question that has been somewhat overlooked throughout the transition from classical ad hoc retrieval to Web search: *how is the performance of classical retrieval approaches affected by the presence of content manipulation?* Our initial experiments have shown that the relative performance patterns of some classical retrieval strategies might change in the transition from non-manipulated to manipulated corpora. A natural future venue to explore is how to mix these strategies and make (some of) them more robust under presumed content manipulation conditions.

Categories and Subject Descriptors: H.3.3 [Information Search and Retrieval]: Retrieval models

General Terms: Algorithms, Experimentation

Keywords: ad hoc retrieval, keyword stuffing, content manipulation, cluster-based retrieval, passage-based retrieval

1. INTRODUCTION

Classical ad hoc (query-based) retrieval approaches focus on the document content for determining relevance to queries. On the other hand, the abundance of information over the Web has driven the utilization of additional information sources such as anchor text [9] and hyperlink structure [2]. Such information sources can potentially help search engines to cope, for example, with the *adversarial* nature of Web search. That is, the fact that some Web-page creators manipulate the content of pages so as to have them ranked high in response to popular queries, even if the pages do not pertain to the expressed information needs. However, as is typical in adversarial settings, manipulation with respect to these additional information sources, e.g., artificial creation of hyperlinks, has emerged [4]. Indeed, various forms of manipulation have been acknowledged as among the main challenges that search engines have to address [5]. Naturally, then, there is a large body of work on automatically detecting and handling different forms of manipulation [1, 3].

Throughout this ever evolving process of an adversarial search setting, a highly interesting question has been somewhat overlooked: how do classical retrieval methods that depend solely on the content of documents and some corpus-based term statistics perform in the presence of content manipulation? Intuitively, such approaches, which heavily rely on within-document term-frequency information, can be easily "mislead" by the simplest form of manipulation — *keyword stuffing* of popular query terms [4]. Indeed, early experiments in the Web setting have shown that the performance of classical retrieval methods is inferior to that of Web search engines that utilize, among others, hyperlink information [10].

Our initial experiments have shown that the relative performance patterns of some classical retrieval strategies can change in the transition from clean (non-manipulated) corpora to corpora containing content-manipulated documents. More specifically, we contrasted standard document-based retrieval with (i) passage-based document retrieval [7], (ii) cluster-based document retrieval [8], and (iii) pseudo-feedback-based retrieval [6].

There are numerous research challenges that rise from our findings. For example, improving the performance of (some of) these classical retrieval methods under presumed content manipulation conditions, and combining the different strategies and making them more robust to content manipulation. Developing new content-based retrieval methods that are resistant to manipulation and are better suited for the adversarial nature of the Web is another interesting research direction.

Acknowledgments This research is based upon joint work with Oren Kurland and Moshe Tennenholtz, and is supported in part by the Technion-Microsoft Electronic-Commerce Research Center and the Miriam and Aaron Gutwirth Memorial Fellowship.

2. REFERENCES

[1] *Proceedings of the AIRWeb workshop:adversial information retrieval on the Web*, 2005-2009.

[2] S. Brin and L. Page. The anatomy of a large-scale hypertextual web search engine. In *Proceedings of WWW*, pages 107–117, 1998.

[3] C. Castillo, D. Donato, L. Becchetti, P. Boldi, S. Leonardi, M. Santini, and S. Vigna. A reference collection for web spam. *SIGIR Forum*, 40(2):11–24, 2006.

[4] Z. Gyöngyi and H. Garcia-Molina. Web spam taxonomy. In *Proceedings of AIRWeb*, pages 39–47, 2005.

[5] M. R. Henzinger, R. Motwani, and C. Silverstein. Challenges in web search engines. *SIGIR Forum*, 36(2):11–22, 2002.

[6] V. Lavrenko and W. B. Croft. Relevance-based language models. In *Proceedings of SIGIR*, pages 120–127, 2001.

[7] X. Liu and W. B. Croft. Passage retrieval based on language models. In *Proceedings of CIKM*, pages 375–382, 2002.

[8] X. Liu and W. B. Croft. Cluster-based retrieval using language models. In *Proceedings of SIGIR*, pages 186–193, 2004.

[9] O. A. McBryan. GENVL and WWWW: Tools for taming the Web. In *Proceedings of WWW*, 1994.

[10] A. Singhal and M. Kaszkiel. A case study in web search using TREC algorithms. In *Proceedings of WWW*, pages 708–716, 2001.

SIGIR'12, August 12–16, 2012, Portland, Oregon, USA.
ACM 978-1-4503-1472-5/12/08.

Building Reputation and Trust Using Federated Search and Opinion Mining

Somayeh Khatiban
City University London
School of Informatics
Northampton Square
London, EC1V 0HB
+44 7860760426
Somayeh.khatiban.1@city.ac.uk

ABSTRACT

The term online reputation addresses trust relationships amongst agents in dynamic open systems. These can appear as ratings, recommendations, referrals and feedback. Several reputation models and rating aggregation algorithms have been proposed. However, finding a trusted entity on the web is still an issue as all reputation systems work individually. The aim of this project is to introduce a global reputation system for electronic product reviews that aggregates people's opinions from different resources (e.g. e-commerce websites, and review) with the help federated search techniques and generate a high quality and trusted result. The first step is to choose a range of product review collections from e-commerce review systems (e.g. Amazon), online review sites (e.g. Epinions), social networks (e.g. Facebook), question and answering sites (e.g. Yahoo! Answers), and blog (e.g. My Nokia Blog) resources. By using a federated search approach the query (product name) will be broadcasted to the selected resources and the result will be a list of reputation data with various formats including star rating, text reviews, voting, video, and so on. The focus of this work is on review text data and star ratings.

A number of challenges including comparison issues (e.g. scale of star ratings: five-star vs. ten-star), hierarchical reviews (e.g. comments about reviews), choice of resources (e.g. choosing relevant sources deepens upon query), display issue (e.g. easy for the user), generalization issue (e.g. apply it on other domains), synchronization problem (e.g. generate up-to-date results), and high quality and trusted reviews will be addressed.

A sentiment analysis approach is subsequently used to extract high quality opinions and inform how to increase trust in the search result. The extracted opinions will be used to generate facets for the global reputation system.

Categories and Subject Descriptors

H.3.3 [**Information Storage and Retrieval**]: Information Search and Retrieval - *Information filtering*; I.2.7 [**Artificial Intelligence**]: Natural Language Processing - *Text analysis*

Keywords

Reputation system, review system, information retrieval, federated search.

SIGIR'12, August 12–16, 2012, Portland, Oregon, USA.
ACM 978-1-4503-1472-5/12/08.

REFERENCES

[1] M. Brzozowski, WaterCooler: exploring an organization through enterprise social media, Proceedings of the ACM 2009 international conference on Supporting group work, ACM, Sanibel Island, Florida, USA, 2009, pp. 219-228.

[2] N. Dalvi, R. Kumar, B. Pang, and A. Tomkins, Matching reviews to objects using a language model, Proceedings of the 2009 Conference on Empirical Methods in Natural Language Processing: Volume 2, Association for Computational Linguistics, Singapore, 2009, pp. 609-618.

[3] L. Dey, and M. Haque, Opinion mining from noisy text data, Proceedings of the second workshop on Analytics for noisy unstructured text data, ACM, Singapore, 2008, pp. 83-90.

[4] F. Diaz, M. Lalmas, and M. Shokouhi, From federated to aggregated search, Proceeding of the 33rd international ACM SIGIR conference on Research and development in information retrieval, ACM, Geneva, Switzerland, 2010, pp. 910-910.

[5] D. Gregg, and S. Walczak, The relationship between website quality, trust and price premiums at online auctions. Electronic Commerce Research 10 (2010) 1-25.

[6] C.W.K. Leung, and S.C.F. Chan, Sentiment Analysis of Product Reviews. in: J. Wang, (Ed.), Encyclopedia of data warehousing and mining, IGI Global, 2009, pp. 6.

[7] M. Morris, J. Teevan, and K. Panovich, What do people ask their social networks, and why?: a survey study of status message Q&A behavior, Proceedings of the 28th international conference on Human factors in computing systems, ACM, Atlanta, Georgia, USA, 2010, pp. 1739-1748.

[8] F. Rohrer, The perils of five-star reviews, 2009, <http://news.bbc.co.uk/1/hi/magazine/8118577.stm> [16th February 2012]

[9] J. Sabater, and C. Sierra, REGRET: reputation in gregarious societies, Proceedings of the fifth international conference on Autonomous agents, ACM, Montreal, Quebec, Canada, 2001, pp. 194-195.

Enhancing Knowledge Base with Knowledge Transfer

Si-Chi Chin
Information Science
The University of Iowa
Iowa City, Iowa, USA
si-chi-chin@uiowa.edu

ABSTRACT

A Knowledge Base (KB) stores, organizes, and shares information pertinent to entities (i.e. KB nodes) such as people, organizations, and events. A large KB system, such as Wikipedia, relies on human curators to create and maintain the content in the systems. However, it has become challenging for human curators to sift through the rapidly growing amount of information and filter out the information irrelevant to a KB node. The area of Knowledge Base Enhancement (KBE) aims to explore and identify automatic methods to assist human curators to accelerate the process. KBE can be viewed as a special case of Information Filtering (IF). However, the lack of high-quality labelled data introduces a major challenge to train a satisfying model for the task. Transfer learning provides solutions to the problem and has explored applications in the area of text mining [3], whereas direct application to KBE or IF remains absent.

Transfer learning is a research area in machine learning, emphasizing the reuse of previously acquired knowledge to another applicable task [2]. The intuition of transfer learning comes from that one may find it easier to learn Spanish having learned French; or to perform ballroom dancing having already practiced figure skating. The method is particularly useful in the situations where labeled instances are absent or difficult to obtain. To accelerate the growth of a KB, a transfer learning approach enables leveraging the heuristics and models learned from one KB node to another. For example, reusing the learned filtering models from Willie Nelson, a famous country singer, to Eddie Rabbitt, another country singer.

Transfer learning requires three components: the target task (e.g. the problem to be solved), the source task(s) (e.g. auxiliary data, previously studied problem), and criteria to select appropriate source tasks. The objectives of my dissertation are twofold. First, it explores methods to identify informative source nodes from which to transfer. Second, it constructs a knowledge transfer network to represent the transfer learning relationship between KB nodes.

This proposed research applies a transfer learning method – *Segmented Transfer (ST)* [1]– and a knowledge representation – *Knowledge Transfer Network (KTN)* – to approach the area of KBE. The primary research questions include: What are the transferable objects in information filtering algorithms? What are the KB nodes of high transferability? What are the factors that determine the transfer learning relationship? Does it manifest on a knowledge transfer network representation? A transfer learning approach can alleviate the cold-start problem in a KB system, leveraging knowledge from more popular KB nodes to nodes of limited or empty profiles. A representation of transfer learning relationships among KB nodes may reveal their hidden ontological connections.

This interdisciplinary research crosses the study area of information filtering, machine learning, knowledge representation, and network analysis. This proposal motivates the problem of KBE, discusses the research methodology and proposed experiments, and reviews related works in information filtering and transfer learning. This line of research hopes to extend the application of transfer learning to KBE and to explore a new dimension of IF. The proposed ST and KTN intends to bring interdisciplinary approaches in the emerging field of KBE.

SIGIR'12, August 12–16, 2012, Portland, Oregon, USA.
ACM 978-1-4503-1472-5/12/08.

Categories and Subject Descriptors

H.4 [**Information Systems Applications**]: Miscellaneous; H.3.3 [**Information Search and Retrieval**]: Information filtering

Keywords

Knowledge transfer, Transfer network, Knowledge base enhancement, Information filtering

Acknowledgments

This work was made possible by Grant Number UL1RR024979 from the National Center for Research Resources (NCRR), part of the National Institutes of Health (NIH). Its contents are solely the responsibility of the authors and do not necessarily represent the official views of the CTSA or NIH.

1. REFERENCES

[1] S.-C. Chin and W. N. Street. Divide and transfer: an exploration of unsupervised knowledge transfer. In *Proc. The 28th Int. Conf. on Machine Learning (ICML-2011): Workshop on on Unsupervised and Transfer Learning*, 2011.

[2] S. J. Pan and Q. Yang. A survey on transfer learning. *IEEE Transactions on Knowledge and Data Engineering*, 22(10):1345–1359, 2010.

[3] W. Pan, E. Zhong, and Q. Yang. Transfer learning for text mining. In C. C. Aggarwal and C. Zhai, editors, *Mining Text Data*, pages 223–257. Springer US, Boston, MA, 2012.

Improving E-Discovery using Information Retrieval

Kripabandhu Ghosh
Information Retrieval Lab
Indian Statistical Institute
203, B.T. Road, Kolkata - 700108, India
kripa_r@isical.ac.in, kripa.ghosh@gmail.com

ABSTRACT

E-discovery is the requirement that the documents and information in electronic form stored in corporate systems be produced as evidence in litigation. It has posed great challenges for legal experts. Legal searchers have always looked to find "any and all" evidence for a given case. Thus, a legal search system would essentially be a recall-oriented system. It has been a common practice among expert searchers to formulate Boolean queries to represent their information need. We want to work on three basic problems:

1. Boolean query formulation - Our primary goal is to study Boolean query formulation in the light of the E-discovery task. This will include automatic Boolean query generation, expansion and learning the effect of proximity operators in Boolean searches.
2. Data fusion - We would also like to explore the effectiveness of data fusion techniques in improving recall.
3. Error modeling - Finally, we will work on error modeling methods for noisy legal documents.

Boolean query formulation

The Boolean queries have traditionally been created manually and on a trial-and-error basis. It can be useful for the lawyers if some system can automatically generate Boolean query suggestions from specific information needs. Perhaps the most relevant work in this line is by Kim et al. [2], but it was done for patent retrieval and the medical domain. No such work has been reported on the legal domain. We believe, therefore, that it is worthwhile to investigate this problem on legal data. The TREC Legal dataset can be used for this purpose.

To start with, our aim is to form an *ideal Boolean query*, i.e., the query that retrieves all and only the relevant documents for the given information need. This will be created from the available set of relevance judgements. Any automatically generated Boolean query can be compared with the ideal query which will act as the upper limit of the performance achievable by any Boolean query. One approach to preparing an ideal query can be to choose the top k terms in each relevant document based on *tf*idf* values. The ideal Boolean query may be difficult to achieve in practice. In such a case, we will try to form a *pseudo ideal query* which will retrieve all relevant documents and at the same time, minimize the number of non-relevant documents in the result set.

An E-discovery topic is different from conventional TREC Ad Hoc topics, so using them straightaway in retrieval produces poor baseline results. Therefore, we plan to generate the baseline run using sample relevant assessments. Thereafter, our endeavor will be to select terms on the basis of the baseline run using the traditional query expansion techniques[1] and try to impose a Boolean structure on these terms based on relations among them.

Data fusion

We look to combine the goodness of runs based on the estimated values of different evaluation measures in improving recall. The values of the evaluation measures are based on a small fraction of the relevant information. We will try to devise an algorithm which will enable us to choose the candidate runs whose fusion will lead to an improvement in recall. We will test our method on the TREC Legal Ad Hoc datasets.

Error modeling

OCR error modeling is crucial while performing retrieval from noisy OCRed legal documents. So, we will try out new error modeling techniques on such data.

Categories and Subject Descriptors

H.3.3 [**Information Storage and Retrieval**]: Information Search and Retrieval—*Information filtering, Query formulation*

General Terms

Algorithms, Legal Aspects, Performance

Keywords

E-Discovery, Boolean query

1. REFERENCES

[1] C. Carpineto and G. Romano. A survey of automatic query expansion in information retrieval. *ACM Comput. Surv.*, 44(1):1:1–1:50, Jan. 2012.

[2] Y. Kim, J. Seo, and W. B. Croft. Automatic boolean query suggestion for professional search. In *Proceedings of the 34th international ACM SIGIR conference on Research and development in Information Retrieval*, SIGIR '11, pages 825–834, New York, NY, USA, 2011. ACM.

Opinion Influence and Diffusion in Social Network

Dehong Gao
The Hong Kong Polytechnic University
Hung Hom, Kowloon, Hong Kong
csdgao@comp.polyu.edu.hk

ABSTRACT

Nowadays, more and more people tend to make decisions based on the opinion information from the Internet, in addition to recommendations from offline friends or parents. For example, we may browse the resumes and comments on election candidates to determine if one candidate is qualified, or consult the consumer reports or reviews on special e-commercial websites to decide which brand of computer is suitable for one's needs. Though opinion information is rich on the Internet, [2] points out that 58% of American Internet users deem that online information is irretrievable, confusing, or conflicting with each other. Early works on opinion mining help to classify opinion polarity, to extract specific opinions and to summarize opinion texts. However, all these works are usually based on plain texts (reviews, comments or news articles). With the explosion of Web 2.0 applications, especially social network applications like blogs, discussion forums, micro-blogs, the massive individual users go to the major media websites, which leads to much more opinion materials posted on the Internet by user-shared experiences or views [3]. These opinion-rich and social network-based applications bring new perspectives for opinion mining as well. First, in addition to plain texts (reviews, newswire) in traditional opinion mining, we see new types of cyber-based text, like personal diary blogs, cyber-SMS tweets. Second, if we regard the opinions in plain text as static, the dynamic change of opinions in the social network is a new promising area, and catch increasing attention of worldwide researchers. In the social network, the opinion held by one individual is not static, but changes, which can be influenced by others. A serial of changes among different users forms the opinion propagation or diffusion in the network.

This paper and my doctoral work focus on the opinion influence and diffusion in the social network, which explore the detailed process of one-to-one influence and the opinion diffusion process in the social network. The significance of this work is it can benefit many other related researches, like information maximum, viral marketing. Now some pioneering works have been conducted to investigate the role of social networks in information diffusion and influencers in the social network. These works are usually based on information diffusion models, like the *cascade* model (CM) or *epidemic* model (EM). However, we argue that it is not enough to simply apply these models to opinion influence and diffusion. 1) For both CM and EM, status shift is along specific directions, from *inactive* to *active* (CM) or from *susceptible* to *infectious*, and then, to *recovered* (EM). But opinion influence is more complex. A new opinion can be identical to, or opposite to existing opinions and even the current opinions from one individual can also be different from his previous ones; 2) CM has some partial focus on either influencer or influencee(persons who are influenced by influencers) views, which cannot fully consider the impacts of two sides. Considering these two drawbacks, we propose a new *Read-Write* model to describe the detailed processes of opinion forming, influence and diffusion.

The Read-Write Model (RWM) assumes that the *opinion forming* can have two ways: forming after observing the information outside the network, and forming by being influenced by one's own previous opinion and/or the others' inside the networks. The behavior of writing one piece of opinion material is based on his reading, and the reading material can be from outside and inside the network. Considering the importance of temporal information in influence [1], we regard all the information posted before one opinion as having certain level of influence. The *opinion influence* can be modeled and inferred from the time-stamped reading and writing behaviors between users. The *opinion diffusion* can be observed by a serial of opinion influence among two different users.

The proposed RWM can accurately describe the whole processes (forming, influencing, and diffusing) of one opinion from its origin node to its end nodes. However, there are three main issues which need further consideration. 1) The model requires many parameters to be inferred, like the reading and writing probabilities. 2) Another issue of opinion influence and diffusion in social network is the collection of datasets. As a pioneering work in opinion influence, we are in lack of available benchmark datasets. According to our model, the requirement of our dataset is higher than that of traditional research on information diffusion. We plan to use the Twitter data, which provides publicly available APIs [1] to crawl data, though with rate limit. 3) We need to investigate the evaluation metrics which are suitable for our task. My ongoing and further study will focus on these issues.

Categories and Subject Descriptors

J.4 [**SOCIAL AND BEHAVIORAL SCIENCES**]: Sociology; I.2.7 [**Natural Language Processing**]: Text analysis

General Terms: Algorithms, Design, Experimentation.

Keywords: Opinion Influence, Opinion Diffusion, Social Network.

ACKNOWLEDGMENTS

The work presented in this paper is supported by a Hong Kong RGC project (No. PolyU 5230/08E).

1. REFERENCES

[1] L. AKRITIDIS, D. KATSAROS and P. BOZANIS. 2009. Identifying Influential Bloggers: Time Does Matter. *In Proceedings of the Web Intelligence*, 76-83. Milano, Italy.

[2] COMSCORE and K. GROUP. 2007. Online consumer-generated reviews have significant impact on offline purchase behavior.

[3] J. ZABIN and A. JEFFIERIES. 2008. Social media monitoring and analysis: Generating consumer insights from online conversation. *Aberdeen Group Benchmark Report.*

SIGIR12, August 12-16, 2012, Portland, Oregon, USA.
ACM 978-1-4503-1472-5/12/07.

[1] https://dev.twitter.com/

Relevance as a Subjective and Situational Multidimensional Concept

Carsten Eickhoff
Delft University of Technology
Delft, Netherlands
c.eickhoff@tudelft.nl

Categories and Subject Descriptors

H.3.3 [**Information Storage and Retrieval**]: [Search Process]; H.1.2 [**Models and Principles**]: [Human Factors]

Keywords

Relevance Models, Personalisation, Score Combination

Abstract

Relevance is the central concept of information retrieval. Although its important role is unanimously accepted among researchers, numerous different definitions of the term have emerged over the years (e.g., [1, 2]). Considerable effort has been put into creating consistent and universally applicable descriptions of relevance in the form of relevance frameworks. Examples of such frameworks are given by [2, 4]. Across these various formal systems of relevance, a wide range of relevance criteria has been identified. The probably most frequently used single criterion, that in some applications even becomes a synonym for relevance, is *topicality*. It expresses a document's topical overlap with the user's information need. For textual resources, it is often estimated based on term co-occurrences between query and document. There is, however, a significant number of further noteworthy relevance criteria. Prominent specimen as for example compiled by [7, 5] are: **(Currency)** determines how recent and up to date the document is. Outdated information may have become invalid over time. **(Availability)** expresses how easy it is to obtain the document. Users might not want to invest more than a threshold amount of resources (e.g., disk space, downloading time or money) to get the document. **(Readability)** describes the document's readability and understandability. A document with a high topical relevance towards a given information need can become irrelevant if the user is not able to extract the desired information from it. **(Credibility)** contains criteria such as the document author's expertise, the publication's reputation and the document's general trustworthiness. **(Novelty)** describes the document's contribution to satisfying an information need with respect to the user's context. E.g., previous search results or general knowledge about the domain.

It is evident that these criteria can have very different scopes. Some of them are static characteristics of the document or the author, others depend on the concrete information need at hand or even the user's search context. Currently, state-of-the-art retrieval models often treat relevance (regardless which interpretation of the term was chosen) as an atomic concept that can be expressed through topical overlap between document and query or a plain linear combination of multiple scores [6]. Considering the broad audiences a web search engine has to serve, such a method does not seem optimal as the concrete composition of relevance will vary from person to person depending on social and educational context. Furthermore, each individual can be expected to have situational preference for certain combinations of relevance facets depending on the information need at hand. We investigate combination schemes which respect the dimension-specific relevance distributions. In particular, we developed a risk-aware method of combining relevance criteria inspired by the economic Portfolio theory. As a first stage, we applied this method for result set diversification across dimensions.

To evaluate our methods, we will work with 2 large-scale standard corpora: (1) The Blogs'08 corpus [3], which contains blog posts and related user comments. At the example of this collection, we will investigate criteria such as topicality and currency for satisfying informational queries. (2) The upcoming ClueWeb'12 corpus that is currently being compiled is envisioned to be annotated with additional labels and scores such as the well-known readability measures. Combining readability scores and topicality, we will investigate the use case of inexperienced readers who prefer easy-to-read resources while depending on topical relevance. The evaluation will be based on the notion of usefulness of shown results for users. Starting off from simulated audiences with given preference patterns, we will finally conduct a real-life study with different participant types (e.g., adults and children).

SIGIR'12, August 12–16, 2012, Portland, Oregon, USA.
ACM 978-1-4503-1472-5/12/08.

1. REFERENCES

[1] M.J. Bates. Information search tactics. *JASIS*, 30(4), 1979.
[2] P. Borlund. The concept of relevance in IR. *JASIST*, 2003.
[3] C. Macdonald, I. Ounis, and I. Soboroff. Overview of the trec blog track 2009. In *TREC 2009, Proceedings*, 2009.
[4] S. Mizzaro. Relevance: The whole history. *JASIS*, 1997.
[5] T.K. Park. The nature of relevance in information retrieval: An empirical study. *The library quarterly*, 63(3), 1993.
[6] S. Robertson, H. Zaragoza, and M. Taylor. Simple BM25 extension to multiple weighted fields. In *CIKM 2004*.
[7] L. Schamber and J. Bateman. User criteria in relevance evaluation: Toward development of a measurement scale. In *American Society for Information Science*, 1996.

Exploiting Temporal Topic Models in Social Media Retrieval

Tuan A. Tran
L3S Research Center
Hannover, Germany
ttran@l3s.de

ABSTRACT

Many of user generated contents in the Web 2.0 center around real-world incidents such as Japanese tsunami, or general concerns such as recent economic downturn. Such type of information is always of interest to users. For instance, when a user reads a news article about a tsunami in Japan, she wants to see related Flickr photos or more tweets about it. Conventional keyword-based search is inappropriate, since it is not always trivial to formulate ad-hoc interests about the event and material. In some cases, the user might want to explore emerging topics that *dominate different sources.* Present systems fail to connect topically documents across media, and the user has to examine individual sources to infer the topics herself.

In this work, we address a special type of user information need, *temporal topic*, which refers to any abstract matter active within some points or periods of time. A temporal topic can be a real-world event, e.g. the Arab Spring revolution, but can also be a less conceivable subject, e.g. the study of vacuum tube computers in 1950s. Topics can also be recurrent such as the US presidency campaigns. There are extensive studies on how to detect topics from a collection of documents, but little uses temporal topics as part of user interest to retrieve documents. We believe that temporal topic-based retrieval is a one solution to improve user experience of present IR systems, as well as to benefit other applications (e.g. topic-sensitive online advertisement).

Our research goal can be defined in three research questions. The first question involves finding latent temporal topics in a social media stream, where documents are well equipped with meta-data (timestamps, geo-spatial data, etc.). Following mixture models such as LDA, we treat each document as a mix of different temporal topic models, each model is incorporated with time. A temporal topic consists of at least two types of attributes - time and representing words, as similar to [4]. The dynamics of temporal topics can be characterized in a timeline fashion [4], or using hierarchical structures [1]. The challenge lies in devising a model flexible enough to diverse and rapidly changing data without many parameter assumptions. For this, we see *Bayesian nonparametrics* [3] as one promising solution, and will extend it to temporal dimension.

The second research question is how to retrieve and rank documents from different social media sites, based on their relevance to one or several given temporal topics. We identify some following challenges. The first one is representing temporal topics as queries: although there have been attempts using keywords and time window separately [2], we aim to unify time and (topical) words in a single query model. The second challenge is integrating temporal topic models into ranking models. Inspired by our previous work [4], we will use language models to capture the relevance scores between documents and topics, and investigate advanced methods to index the scores effectively.

Our last question involves connecting a given document to documents in other sources (data streams or corpora) that shared one of its latent temporal topics. This task does not only provide unified insight into different social media sites, but also help improve the quality of models by data in diverse sources. However, formalizing the semantics of "similarity" for documents in different settings based on temporal topcis is tricky. One baseline method is to apply Kullback-Leibler divergence on comparable features (TF-IDF, n-grams, photo tags, timestamps,..). We can also use language models [5] to construct a language model for each candidate document, then estimate how likely it generates the document of interest within a given temporal topic.

SIGIR'12, August 12–16, 2012, Portland, Oregon, USA.
ACM 978-1-4503-1472-5/12/08.

Categories and Subject Descriptors

H.3.3 [**Information Storage and Retrieval**]: Information Search and Retrieval

Keywords

Topic model, ranking, social media, temporal data analysis

1. REFERENCES

[1] A. Ahmed, Q. Ho, J. Eisenstein, E. Xing, A. J. Smola, and C. H. Teo. Unified analysis of streaming news. In *WWW*, 2011.

[2] P. Haghani, S. Michel, and K. Aberer. Efficient monitoring of personalized hot news over web 2.0 streams. *Journal of Computer Science*, Vol. 27(1), February 2012.

[3] P. Orbanz and Y. W. Teh. Bayesian nonparametric models. *Encyclopedia of Machine Learning*, 2010.

[4] T. A. Tran, S. Elbassuoni, N. Preda, and G. Weikum. Cate: context-aware timeline for entity illustration. In *WWW*, 2011.

[5] M. Tsagkias, M. de Rijke, and W. Weerkamp. Linking online news and social media. In *WSDM*, 2011.

The Essence of Time: Considering Temporal Relevance as an Intent-Aware Ranking Problem

Stewart Whiting
School of Computing Science
University of Glasgow, UK
stewh@dcs.gla.ac.uk

ABSTRACT

Real-time news and social media quickly reflect large-scale phenomena and events. As users become exposed to this information, time plays a central role in prompting both information authorship and seeking activities.

The objective of this research is to develop a retrieval system which can anticipate a user's likely temporal intent(s), considering recent or ongoing real-world events. Such a system should not only provide recent news when relevant, but also higher rank non-timestamped or even older documents which are temporally pertinent as they cover aspects related to recent event topics.

Key challenges to be addressed in this work include: a suitable source and method for event detection and tracking, an intent-aware ranking approach and an evaluation methodology.

Categories and Subject Descriptors: H.3.3 [Information Storage and Retrieval] - *Information Search and Retrieval - Retrieval Models*

General Terms: Algorithms, Experimentation

Keywords: Temporal, Time, Event, Relevance, Intent

1. INTRODUCTION

In this work we propose a notion of temporal relevance, whereby recent events related to the query topic influence the relevance of non-timestamped or older documents during retrieval.

Previous analysis suggests a great deal of information seeking activity is likely to arise from interaction with media as users wish to learn more about *trending* or *hot* topics. As such, many search topics have a temporal affinity, affecting not only query volume but also in many cases, intent at different periods in time [2].

Users may first wish to find out more about the event itself. News articles are undoubtedly most relevant for these initial needs. However, further information needs may arise from knowledge of the event, in order to answer more in-depth related questions such as: *who*, *where*, *why* and *how?* Each topic is likely to have documents considered *temporally pertinent*, that is, they refer to aspects most involved with the event. Conversely, when an event is no longer prominent, documents covering these typically less popular aspects will become no longer temporally pertinent and therefore less important.

To model temporal relevance we treat it as an intent-aware ranking [3] problem. For each intent, during ranking we compute a measure of temporal intent pertinence, thus higher ranking intents that refer to aspects related to recent events. Using Topic Detection and Tracking (TDT) techniques [1], Wikipedia article revision history and viewing counts can be mined for event-driven signals for many real-life topics, allowing the measurement of various temporal characteristics. Early analysis suggests Wikipedia provides an effective source of event-based evidence for TDT tasks. Effectiveness evaluation of such a system in real-time poses a number of challenges. We propose an evaluation methodology based on query-log mining and crowdsourcing for on-going relevance assessment.

SIGIR'12, August 12–16, 2012, Portland, Oregon, USA.
ACM 978-1-4503-1472-5/12/08.

2. RESEARCH PROPOSAL

We propose four research questions (RQ) which this thesis will investigate, following each is an underlying hypothesis:

RQ1: Can search topics with recent event-related temporal intent be detected?

If there is a chance that a user's query has an intent that was prompted by a recent event, then it is appropriate to consider temporal relevance in document ranking.

RQ2: Can the temporal sensitivity of a query topic (or, *intent*) be computed using historic and recent Wikipedia article revision history, and page view statistics?

Wikipedia provides large-scale coverage of article creation/edit history and page view statistics for real-life topics. This temporal evidence is accurate and extensive enough for mining user behaviour and editing trends driven by events.

RQ3: Given the temporal sensitivity of a query topic, can intent ranking be improved by incorporating temporal intent pertinence?

An intent's temporal pertinence may change as the trending topic changes. Increasing the ranking of aspects that are temporally pertinent will improve relevance ranking for a user that is looking for information relating to a temporally-prompted intent.

RQ4: If a query topic itself is not temporally sensitive, yet, an aspect is related to a recent event, can intent ranking be improved by incorporating temporal intent pertinence?

Similar to the previous hypothesis, although a query topic may not be itself directly temporally sensitive, the user's intent may be prompted because it is related to a recent event.

3. REFERENCES

[1] J. Allan. *Introduction to topic detection and tracking*, pages 1–16. Kluwer Academic Publishers, Norwell, MA, USA, 2002.

[2] A. Kulkarni, J. Teevan, K. M. Svore, and S. T. Dumais. Understanding temporal query dynamics. In *ACM WSDM '11*, pages 167–176, New York, NY, USA, 2011. ACM.

[3] C. Zhai, W. W. Cohen, and J. D. Lafferty. Beyond independent relevance: methods and evaluation metrics for subtopic retrieval. In *SIGIR '03*, pages 10–17, 2003.

A Framework for Manipulating and Searching Multiple Retrieval Types

Marc-Allen Cartright, Ethem F. Can, William Dabney, Jeff Dalton,
Logan Giorda, Kriste Krstovski, Xiaoye Wu, Ismet Zeki Yalniz,
James Allan, R. Manmatha, and David Smith

Center for Intelligent Information Retrieval
Dept. of Computer Science
Univ. of Massachusetts
Amherst, MA 01003

ABSTRACT

Conventional retrieval systems view documents as a unit and look at different retrieval types within a document. We introduce Proteus, a frame-work for seamlessly navigating books as dynamic collections which are defined on the fly. Proteus allows us to search various retrieval types. Navigable types include pages, books, named persons, locations, and pictures in a collection of books taken from the Internet Archive. The demonstration shows the value of multi-type browsing in dynamic collections to peruse new data.

Categories and Subject Descriptors

H.3.3 [**Information Storage and Retrieval**]: Information Search and Retrieval—*Search Process*; H.5.4 [**Information Storage and Retrieval**]: Hypertext/Hypermedia—*Navigation*

General Terms

Design, Human Factors, Standardization

Keywords

Proteus, object search, navigation

The idea of browsing over different types of information has been explored by various web sites and researchers for some time [1, 2]. Most efforts to date either collapse the types into one retrieval list or only use boolean-matching queries. These systems provide no way to maintain the separation between the types while performing boolean or ranked search while switching between types – for example, starting from a set of books discussing the trek of Marco Polo between Europe and Asia, then requesting ranked locations mentioned in that set of books and, from there, change to the people who are prominent at those locations, switching to books that discuss those people, and so on. We believe the next step in information systems is to afford seamless movement between boolean and ranked retrieval of such different retrieval types enabling users to easily negotiate this complex information space.

SIGIR'12, August 12–16, 2012, Portland, Oregon, USA.
ACM 978-1-4503-1472-5/12/08.

We introduce Proteus, a data model for representing, searching, and browsing objects extracted from book collections. The Proteus model defines an API for potential data sources to implement and use to provide and exchange information using that data model. Implementing this API allows Proteus to use the items from the system as part of the retrievable set of items, enabling horizontal movement between the "vertical" data types.

We demonstrate the value of Proteus with an implementation of the framework we have developed at the Center for Intelligent Information Retrieval. We have indexed a set of books from the Internet Archive. We use focused collections centered on topics such as William Shakespeare, the westward migration of American settlers, and the American Revolution. In each instance we provide the ability to retrieve pages, books, named persons, locations, and images from these collections, and navigate between them. We also integrate information from DBPedia to provide an existing ontology for the identified objects in the books.

We see the demonstration as an opportunity for users to browse a collection in a new way and discover information that would otherwise be difficult or impossible to deduce through previous navigation systems. The demonstration will be available at `http://books.cs.umass.edu` website.

Acknowledgements This work was supported in part by the Center for Intelligent Information Retrieval and in part by NSF grant #IIS-0910884. Any opinions, findings and conclusions or recommendations expressed in this material are the authors' and do not necessarily reflect those of the sponsors.

REFERENCES

[1] S. Dumais, E. Cutrell, J. Cadiz, G. Jancke, R. Sarin, and D. C. Robbins. Stuff i've seen: a system for personal information retrieval and re-use. In *Proc. SIGIR 2003*, pages 72–79, New York, NY, USA, 2003. ACM.

[2] C. Lagoze, S. Payette, E. Shin, and C. Wilper. Fedora: an architecture for complex objects and their relationships. *International Journal on Digital Libraries*, 6:124–138, 2006.

A Visual Tool for Bayesian Data Analysis: The Impact of Smoothing on Naïve Bayes Text Classifiers

Giorgio Maria Di Nunzio
Dept. of Information Engineering
University of Padua
dinunzio@dei.unipd.it

Alessandro Sordoni
Dépt. d'Informatique et Recherche Opérationnelle
Université de Montréal
sordonia@iro.umontreal.ca

ABSTRACT

Naïve Bayes (NB) classifiers are simple probabilistic classifiers still widely used in supervised learning due to their tradeoff between efficient model training and good empirical results. One of the drawbacks of these classifiers is that in situations of data sparsity (i.e. when the size of training set is small) the maximum likelihood estimation of the probability of unseen features in these situations is equal to zero causing arithmetic anomalies. To prevent this undesirable behavior, a number of smoothing techniques have been proposed [4]. Among these, the Bayesian approach incorporates smoothing in terms of prior knowledge about the parameters of the model usually called *hyper-parameters*. Our research question is: can a visualization tool help researchers to quickly assess the goodness of the performance of NB classifiers by setting optimal smoothing parameters?

Categories and Subject Descriptors: H.3.3 [Information Search and Retrieval]: Retrieval Models

General Terms: Theory, Algorithms, Experimentation

Keywords: Visual Analytics, Bayesian Inference, Smoothing, Text Classification

1. DEMONSTRATION

Our demo aims to record and visualize the effect of different combinations of choices of NB classifiers and smoothing approaches. Inspired by the work of [2, 3, 4], this tool addresses researchers who want to (i) compare different smoothing variants with a manual optimization of the parameters by means of the two-dimensional visual approach [1] and (ii) investigate the differences between Bayesian prior smoothing and the fixed coefficient interpolation method [4]. Moreover, the graphical visualization may be helpful for educational purposes or research projects that consider to employ NB classifiers.

Three NB classifiers — multivariate Bernoulli model, Multinomial model, Poisson model — can be selected and the relative priors' hyper-parameters (Beta, Dirichlet, and Gamma prior respectively) can be tuned to produce different smoothing effect on different standard test collection (Reuters, 20-Newsgroups, Oshumed). The visualization tool allows the user to (i) direct input the values of the hyper-parameters to compare standard smoothing variants, (ii) recall specific settings of actual systems implemented in literature and (iii) perform a visual search of best hyper parameter settings by analyzing their impact on the decision frontier on-the-fly. The visualization tool was designed following the *Model-View-Controller* pattern and was fully implemented in Java 1.6. This architecture is fully modular and allows for easy integration of new models and views. The source code can be found at `https://bitbucket.org/2dpm/2dpm`.

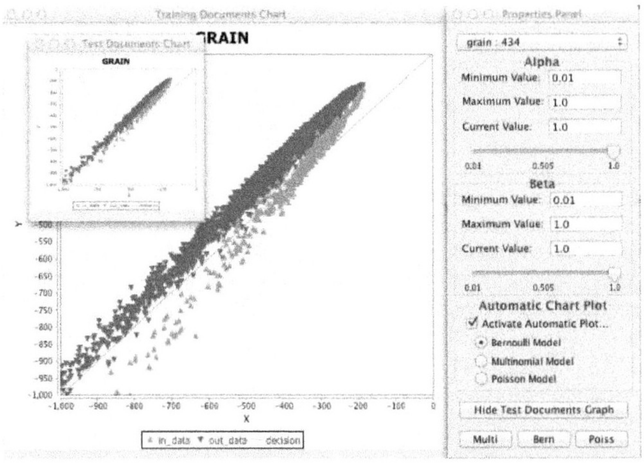

Figure 1: Two of the main panels are shown: the properties panel has been set to recall the multivariate Bernoulli model with Laplacian smoothing.

2. ACKNOWLEDGMENTS.

The authors would like to thank Prof. Jian-Yun Nie for the useful discussions. This work has been partially supported by the QONTEXT project under grant agreement N. 247590 (FP7/2007-2013).

3. REFERENCES

[1] G. Di Nunzio. Using scatterplots to understand and improve probabilistic models for text categorization and retrieval. *Int. J. Approx. Reasoning*, 50(7):945–956, 2009.

[2] S. Eyheramendy, D. D. Lewis, and D. Madigan. On the Naive Bayes Model for Text Categorization. In C. Bishop and B. Frey, editors, *Proceedings of the Ninth International Workshop on Artificial Intelligence and Statistics*, 2003.

[3] A. McCallum and K. Nigam. A comparison of event models for naive bayes text classification. In *AAAI-98 workshop on learning for text categorization*, volume 752, pages 41–48, 1998.

[4] C. Zhai and J. D. Lafferty. A study of smoothing methods for language models applied to information retrieval. *ACM Trans. Inf. Syst.*, 22(2):179–214, 2004.

SIGIR'12, August 12–16, 2012, Portland, Oregon, USA.
ACM 978-1-4503-1472-5/12/08.

ALF: A Client Side Logger and Server for Capturing User Interactions in Web Applications

Myles Doolan, Leif Azzopardi
School of Computing Science
University of Glasgow
United Kingdom
{ 0805976D@student, leif@dcs }.gla.ac.uk

Richard Glassey
School of Computing
Robert Gordon University
United Kingdom
r.j.glassey@rgu.ac.uk

EXTENDED ABSTRACT

Modern day websites offer applications with sophisticated user interfaces and dynamically interactive data [1]. Understanding how a user interacts with a search service, in particular, is an effective way to determine the usability and quality of the search experience [1, 2]. Gathering the necessary data to analyse user interactions with a web based search application can be done either server side and/or client side. Server side solutions provide a course grained approach to logging specific discrete events such as when a query is issued, a web page is viewed, etc. Client side solutions, however, can provide a much richer set of data regarding the specific micro interactions performed by a user given the web application interface (i.e. when there is a mouse over, a scroll, a click, a key press, etc). While a number of logging applications have been previously developed, such as UsaProxy [1], MLogger [2] and Wrapper [3], there are number of issues with these loggers. UsaProxy only intercepts calls between a client/web browser and the webserver and requires the client to set up a proxy. While this is appropriate for lab based studies, it does not work well in less controlled setups. No implementation of MLogger is available (and it is based on Moschkit which is no longer supported), while Wrapper is a Windows/IE6 logger and requires client side installation. Other notable loggers require client side setup (e.g. Lemur Query Log Toolbar and CrowdLogger both require browser plug-ins), do not provide any facilities to remotely capture interaction data or are not freely available to download/use (e.g. Morea and Camtasia).

This demonstration paper introduces ALF which provides a light-weight client side logging application and a server for collecting user interaction data. ALF has been designed as a loosely coupled independent service that runs in parallel with the IR web application that requires logging. Figure 1 shows how the services are related, where (1) the IR application requests ALF to log interactions, this set ups (2) a record of the applications currently being logged, and returns a piece of Javascript (alf.js) to be included in the client interface (with certain parameters). When the Web Search interface is used, the ALF Javascript on the web interface client sends interaction data to the ALF Server. On receipt of the data an acknowledgment is send back (4), if there is no acknowledgment the data is re-sent. Once received the interaction data for that application is checked and then logged

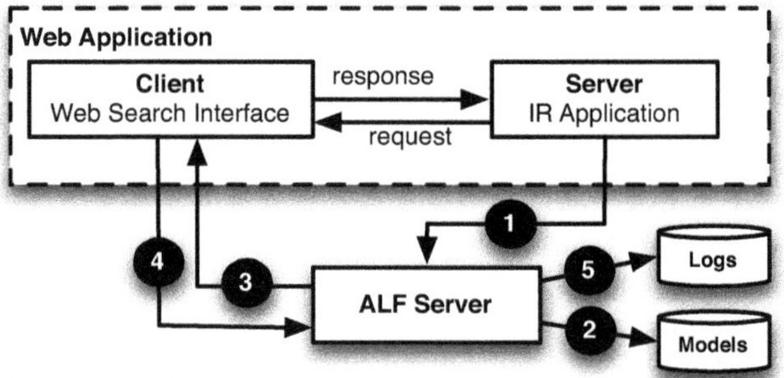

Figure 1: How ALF fits with an Web Application.

(5). The ALF javascript added to the client is parameterized with the application's name along with which interactions on the client side to log. Currently, ALF supports the logging of: Cursor entering/leaving elements, mouse clicks, key presses, scrolling within the page and within elements.

On the server side, ALF receives and then logs the datetime, IP address, the username (if a cookie called username exists), the event, and any associated data with the event i.e. the DOM id of the element in the page, the (x,y) coordinates on the page, the key pressed, etc. All the data is stored in JSON files for easy subsequent processing and analysis. ALF provides some basic visualizations of the data collected through a web interface so that researchers can inspect the data as it is collected. The client side scripts and back-end server is available for download along with an example web search interface called MySe (short for MySearch) that connects to a Bing backend[1]. In sum, ALF provides developers and researchers with the tools to log client side interactions without the need to install any client side software and to remotely collect and store interaction data via an ALF server.

Categories and Subject Descriptors:
H.3.3 [**Information Storage and Retrieval**]: Information Search and Retrieval
General Terms: Design, Human Factors
Keywords: Information Retrieval, Implicit Logging

REFERENCES

[1] R. Atterer, M. Wnuk, and A. Schmidt. Knowing the user's every move: user activity tracking for website usability evaluation. In *Proc. of the 15th WWW*, pages 203–212, 2006.
[2] A. Edmonds, R. W. White, D. Morris, and S. M. Drucker. Instrumenting the dynamic web. *J. Web Eng.*, 6:244–260, 2007.
[3] Ramadoss R. Zhang M. Jansen, B. J. and N. Zang. Wrapper: An application for evaluating exploratory searching. In *SIGIR 2006 Workshop on Evaluating Exploratory Search Systems*.

Acknowledgements: PuppyIR is funded by the EC's FP7 2007-2013 under grant agreement no. 231507.

[1] See `http://www.dcs.gla.ac.uk/access/alfproject/`

SIGIR'12, August 12–16, 2012, Portland, Oregon, USA.
ACM 978-1-4503-1472-5/12/08.

ChatNoir: A Search Engine for the ClueWeb09 Corpus

Martin Potthast Matthias Hagen Benno Stein
Jan Graßegger Maximilian Michel Martin Tippmann Clement Welsch
Bauhaus-Universität Weimar
99423 Weimar, Germany
<first name>.<last name>@uni-weimar.de

ABSTRACT

We present the ChatNoir search engine which indexes the entire English part of the ClueWeb09 corpus. Besides Carnegie Mellon's Indri system, ChatNoir is the second publicly available search engine for this corpus. It implements the classic BM25F information retrieval model including PageRank and spam likelihood. The search engine is scalable and returns the first results within three seconds, which is significantly faster than Indri. A convenient API allows for implementing reproducible experiments based on retrieving documents from the ClueWeb09 corpus. The search engine has successfully accomplished a load test involving 100 000 queries.

Categories and Subject Descriptors: H.3.3 [Information Search and Retrieval]: Search process

General Terms: Experimentation

Keywords: search engine, TREC, ClueWeb09

1. INTRODUCTION

Many of the current TREC tracks and TREC style retrieval performance experiments are based on the ClueWeb09 corpus—a collection of 1 billion web pages crawled and provided by the Carnegie Mellon University. As indexing and searching such a large corpus requires a decent amount of hardware probably not available to all researchers interested in TREC style experiments or TREC participation, a public search engine has been provided with the release of the corpus.[1] So far, this is the only publicly available search engine for the ClueWeb09 and it has been used in many TREC runs over the last years. However, the engine is rather slow (answer time of about 10 seconds or more) and only offers the Indri retrieval model (language modeling combined with an inference network). As an alternative, we provide a faster public search engine—ChatNoir.

2. CHATNOIR SEARCH

The ChatNoir search engine is based on the classic BM25F retrieval model [4] including the anchor text list provided by the University of Twente [3], the PageRank list provided by the Carnegie Mellon University,[2] and the spam rank list provided by the University of Waterloo [1]. ChatNoir also incorporates an approximate proximity feature with variable width buckets as described by Elsayed et al. [2]. The text body of each document is divided into 64 buckets such that neighboring buckets have a half-bucket overlap. For each keyword, not the exact position is stored in a 1-gram index but occurrence in the individual buckets is indicated via a bit flag. Hence, for each document and each occurring keyword, a 64-bit vector is used in ChatNoir's approximate proximity feature.

The web interface of ChatNoir is similar to that of commercial search engines (snippets, phrasal search, etc.). As for query processing, non-phrasal queries are handled by a 1-gram index of the ClueWeb09 built with Hadoop. Phrasal queries are handled by a 2-gram index and a 3-gram exact position index. For phrase queries containing only 2-grams, the 2-gram index suffices. For phrase queries with longer phrases, the 2-gram index is used to identify documents that contain all 2-grams of a longer phrase while merging the postlists with the 3-gram positional index finally identifies the documents that contain the exact searched phrase. To ensure fast answer times, long queries with more than 2 keywords or phrases are treated in a divide-and-conquer manner. The long query is split into sub-queries for which a parallel retrieval is conducted. The parallel results are then merged into just one list.

The ChatNoir engine runs on a cluster of 10 standard quad-core PCs and 2 eight-core servers. It comes with a web interface and a developer API at `chatnoir.webis.de`. This is the first public alternative to Carnegie Mellon's Indri search for reproducible experiments on the ClueWeb09 without the need of an own cluster for indexing/searching. A load test with 100 000 unique queries from a commercial search engine log showed the robustness and scalability of ChatNoir. The first ten results are typically shown within three seconds compared to more than ten seconds for an Indri search.

3. CONCLUSION AND OUTLOOK

With our ChatNoir search engine we provide the second public API for reproducibly searching the ClueWeb09 corpus in TREC style experiments. ChatNoir's much faster BM25F based search offers an alternative to the available Indri retrieval model.

A first use case we are currently handling with ChatNoir is the international PAN competition for automatic plagiarism detection. Therefore, paid human individuals write short reports on TREC topics plagiarizing parts from ClueWeb09 documents found via ChatNoir searches. The competition participants are supposed to find the most likely plagiarism sources also using ChatNoir.

4. REFERENCES

[1] Cormack, Smucker, and Clarke. Efficient and effective spam filtering and re-ranking for large web datasets. *Inf. Retr.* 14(5):441–465, 2011.

[2] Elsayed, Lin, and Metzler. When close enough is good enough: approximate positional indexes for efficient ranked retrieval. *CIKM 2011*, pp. 1993–1996.

[3] Hiemstra and Hauff. MIREX: MapReduce information retrieval experiments. Tech. Report TR-CTIT-10-15, Universiteit Twente, 2010.

[4] Robertson, Zaragoza, and Taylor. Simple BM25 extension to multiple weighted fields. *CIKM 2004*, pp. 42–49.

[1] lemurproject.org/clueweb09.php/index.php#Services

[2] boston.lti.cs.cmu.edu/clueweb09/wiki/tiki-index.php?page=PageRank

SIGIR'12, August 12–16, 2012, Portland, Oregon, USA.
ACM 978-1-4503-1472-5/12/08.

CrowdTerrier: Automatic Crowdsourced Relevance Assessments with Terrier

Richard McCreadie, Craig Macdonald, and Iadh Ounis
firstname.lastname@glasgow.ac.uk
School of Computing Science
University of Glasgow
G12 8QQ, Glasgow, UK

Categories and Subject Descriptors: H.3.3 [Information Storage & Retrieval]: Information Search & Retrieval

General Terms: Experimentation, Performance

Keywords: Crowdsourcing, Relevance Assessment, Terrier

ABSTRACT

Information retrieval (IR) systems rely on document relevance assessments for queries to gauge their effectiveness for a variety of tasks, e.g. Web result ranking. Evaluation forums such as TREC and CLEF provide relevance assessments for common tasks. However, it is not possible for such venues to cover all of the collections and tasks currently investigated in IR. Hence, it falls to the individual researchers to generate the relevance assessments for new tasks and/or collections. Moreover, relevance assessment generation can be a time-consuming, difficult and potentially costly process. Recently, *crowdsourcing* has been shown to be a fast and cheap method to generate relevance assessments in a semi-automatic manner [1]. In this case, the relevance assessment task is outsourced to a large group of non-expert workers, where workers are rewarded via micro-payments.

In this demo, we present *CrowdTerrier*, an infrastructure extension to the open source Terrier IR platform [2][1] that enables the semi-automatic generation of relevance assessments for a variety of document ranking tasks using crowdsourcing. The aim of CrowdTerrier is to reduce the time and expertise required to effectively Crowdsource relevance assessments by abstracting away from the complexities of the crowdsourcing process. It achieves this by automating the assessment process as much as possible, via a close integration of the IR system that ranks the documents (Terrier) and the crowdsourcing marketplace that is used to assess those documents (Amazon's Mechanical Turk (MTurk)).

As illustrated in Figure 1, CrowdTerrier is comprised of three components. *CrowdControl* handles the conversion of ranked results from Terrier as well as the administration of the MTurk tasks. The *JSP Interface* is responsible for the presentation of the pages to be assessed and the assessment interface. Finally the *Validator* performs quality assurance on the assessments produced, possibly with human input. Each of these components is fully customisable to facilitate tackling different tasks and collections.

[1] `http://terrier.org`

SIGIR'12, August 12–16, 2012, Portland, Oregon, USA.
ACM 978-1-4503-1472-5/12/08.

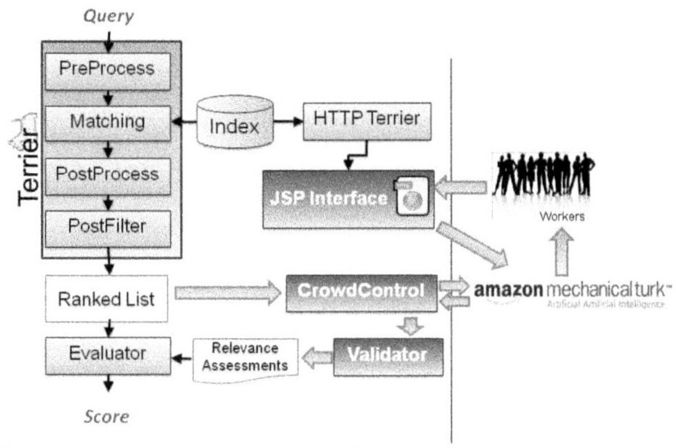

Figure 1: CrowdTerrier relevance assessment generation process.

In comparison to crowdsourcing document relevance assessments from scratch, CrowdTerrier[2] makes the following four key contributions:

- It abstracts away from the assessment task design and implementation, by providing out-of-the-box assessment interfaces driven by Terrier's document presentation capabilities.
- Once configured, it automatically spreads documents ranked by Terrier across multiple assessment tasks, according to best crowdsourcing practises.
- It supplies tools to monitor and summarise the progress of each relevance assessment task once launched.
- It supports both automatic and semi-automatic work validation strategies out-of-the-box for performing quality assurance on the assessments produced.

In summary, we believe that CrowdTerrier provides a useful toolkit for creating relevance assessments by researchers.

1. REFERENCES

[1] R. McCreadie, C. Macdonald and I. Ounis. Identifying Top News using Crowdsourcing. *Information Retrieval*, 2012. DOI: 10.1007/s10791-012-9186-z.

[2] I. Ounis, G. Amati, V. Plachouras, B. He, C. Macdonald and C. Lioma. Terrier: A high performance and scalable information retrieval platform. In *Proc. OSIR Workshop 2006*.

[2] CrowdTerrier is available from `http://terrier.org/crowdterrier/`.

Distilling and Exploring Nuggets from Corpus

Vittorio Castelli, Hema Raghavan, Radu Florian, Ding-Jung Han, Xiaoqiang Luo, Salim Roukos
IBM T.J Watson Research Center, Yorktown Heights, NY 10598
{vittorio,hraghav,raduf,dbhan,xiaoluo,roukos}@us.ibm.com

Categories and Subject Descriptors

H.3.1 [**Information Systems**]: Information Storage and Retrieval—*Content Analysis and Indexing*

General Terms

User Interfaces, Natural Language Processing, Automatic Content Extraction, Summarization

1. EXTENDED ABSTRACT

This paper describes a live and scalable system that automatically extracts *information nuggets* for entities/topics from a continuously updated corpus for effective exploration and analysis. A nugget is a piece of semantic information that (1) must be mapped semantically to the transitive closure of a pre-defined ontology, (2) is explicitly supported by text, and (3) has a natural language description that completely conveys its semantic to a user. Fig. 1 shows a type of nugget "involvement in events" for a person entity (Leon Panetta): each nugget has a short description ("meeting", "news conference") with a list of supporting passages.

Our key contributions are (1) We extract nuggets and remove redundancy to produce a summary of salient information with supporting clusters of passages. (2) We present an entity/topic centric exploration interface that also allows users to navigate to other entities involved in a nugget. (3) We use the statistical NLP technologies developed over the years in the ACE[6] ,GALE [5] and TAC-KBP[7] programs, including parsing, mention detection, within and cross document coreference resolution, relation detection and slot filler extraction. (4) Our system is flexible and easily adaptable across domains as demonstrated on two corpora: generic news and scientific papers. Search engines such as Google News and Scholar[1, 2] do not retrieve nuggets, and only remove redundancy at document level. News aggregation applications such as Evri[3] categorize news articles based on the entities of topics but do not extract nuggets. Other systems extract richer information, but not all of it has clear semantics; e.g., Silobreaker[4] presents results as "the relationship between X and Y in the context of [keyphrase]", leaving users with the task of interpreting the semantics as it is not tied to a clear ontology. In contrast we remove redundancy, summarize results and present nuggets that have clear semantics.

SIGIR'12, August 12–16, 2012, Portland, Oregon, USA.
ACM 978-1-4503-1472-5/12/08.

1.1 User Interface

One entry point to our system is via our news search engine, which generates hyperlinks to the Entity Pages (EPs) of entities appearing in displayed news articles. Users can also select EPs by name or by browsing popular entities. The left pane in Fig. 1 contains a picture and biographical information from wikipedia. The right pane contains a set of tabs that categorize nuggets by the information they convey. The content in each tab is the output of statistical extraction modules. The Figure shows two tabs – *Related People* and *Involvement in Events*. The *Related People* nuggets are people names, and the *Event* ones describe events, like *meetings* and *talks*. Nuggets are sorted by their relevance score. Each nugget has a supporting passage where the evidence is highlighted in context. We also provide hyperlinks to other EPs that appear in the passages. All tabs have graphical content summaries like a network of related people or a word cloud.

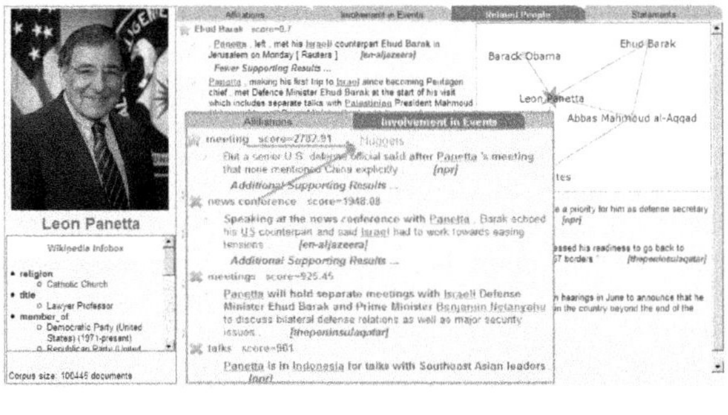

Figure 1: Entity page for *Leon Panetta*

EPs for a collection of Scientific Papers have information organized as *co-Authors, Technology, Cited Papers, Authored Papers*. Unlike DBLP or Google Scholar we detect nuggets for *technology* and *software*, etc.

2. REFERENCES

[1] http://news.google.com/.
[2] http://scholar.google.com/.
[3] http://www.evri.com/.
[4] http://www.silobreaker.com/.
[5] R. Florian, J. Olive, C. Christianso, and J. McCary. *Handbook of Natural Language Processing and Machine Translation*, chapter 4. Springer, 2011.
[6] G. Doddington, et al. The ACE program–tasks, data, and evaluation. In *LREC-2004*, pages 837–840.
[7] *TAC Knowledge Base Population (2010) Track*, 2010.

Integrative Online Research-Data Management

Michael Huggett and Edie Rasmussen
University of British Columbia
Suite 470, 1961 East Mall, Vancouver, BC V6T 1Z1
(1-604) 827-5486
{m.huggett, edie.rasmussen}@ubc.ca

ABSTRACT

In support of our research projects in information retrieval, we have developed an integrated multi-process software system that shepherds research data from induction through aggregation, analysis, and presentation. We combine public-domain code libraries with our own software to provide a flexible, easily-configured modular system that exposes data online for easier collaboration. The goal is to create a single online infrastructure that allows colleagues to submit, process, analyze and visualize data, and discuss and prioritize issues through a single integrated interface. We demonstrate our system within the context of the large data set provided by the *Indexer's Legacy* project [1].

Categories and Subject Descriptors

H.5.2 [**Information Interfaces and Presentation**]: User Interfaces – *evaluation/methodology, prototyping*

Keywords

Digital collections, visualization, user interfaces.

1. RESEARCH-DATA MANAGEMENT

Given a server that can support common research practices, online research collaboration presents several advantages. Data is stored in a central canonical easily-accessed repository, guaranteed to be the most current available. Versioning, automated backups and redundant storage prevent data loss. Tests and processes can be uploaded to the server and run on the data where it is stored, obviating the need to download all and run it on a team member's local machine. Tests and results can be double-checked directly online and confirmed by other members of the research team. If desired, data, processes, and results can also be shared with the world online, as befitting calls within the research community for easier replicability and an "open data" ethos [2].

Web crawlers, user studies, and surveys are administered directly from the server through a web browser, and the accumulated data is stored directly on the same machine where it will be analyzed, reducing upload time and cost. Databases that store related meta-data can also be configured and edited through a web browser, and accessed as needed from any process within the server. Discussions of team members can also be centralized and shared: critical issues can be raised, discussed, assigned, and prioritized using a text-based issue-tracking module (as for bug-tracking).

In our system, we demonstrate an integrative approach that combines all of these abilities in a single, easy-to-use software platform. Such centralization of research data and meta-data helps ensure that all team members are talking about the *same thing*, and also the *right thing*.

SIGIR'12, August 12-16, 2012, Portland, Oregon, USA.
ACM 978-1-4503-1472-5/12/08.

2. OVERVIEW OF THE PROTOTYPE

The prototype manages the data life cycle in four key modules:

Data is *inducted* by parsing input data streams. Our prototype provides a raw-text parser, a table parser, and a web scraper. The *aggregation* module combines data from multiple sources to create summary tables and data objects, which once created can be re-used for further analyses. The *analysis* module is configured with user-selected filter algorithms to find descriptive trends in input data. Our prototype includes a SOLR search engine [3] and the R statistics package [4]. The *display* module automatically generates web pages of result tables and graphs to be shared with other project members.

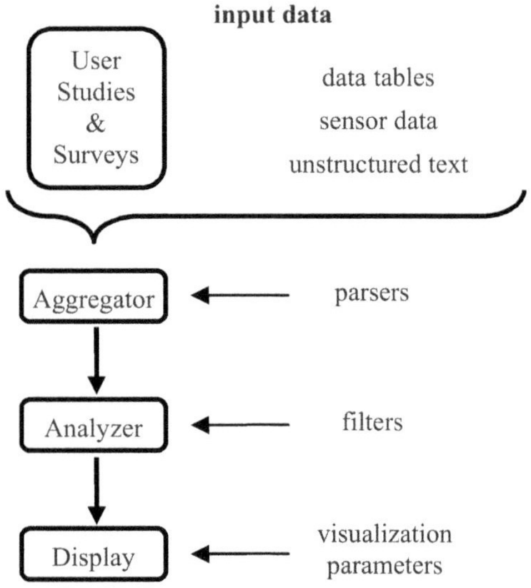

Figure 1: Data flow through the integrated system. System modules are in boxes.

The server uses embedded technology, can be run immediately on any Java-enabled machine, and requires only simple port forwarding to expose its services to the internet.

3. REFERENCES

[1] Huggett, M. & Rasmussen, E. The Indexer's Legacy: Promoting Access to a Million Books, *ICDL 2010*.

[2] Kauppinen, T. & Espindola, G. M. D. 2011. Linked Open Science-Communicating, Sharing and Evaluating Data, Methods and Results for Executable Papers. *Procedia Computer Science* 4: 726.

[3] Apache SOLR, http://lucene.apache.org/solr/

[4] The R Project for Statistical Computing, http://www.r-project.org/

MaSe: Create Your Own Mash-Up Search Interface

Leif Azzopardi, Douglas Dowie, Kelly Ann Marshall
School of Computing Science
University of Glasgow
United Kingdom
{leif, doug, kellym}@dcs.gla.ac.uk

Richard Glassey
School of Computing
Robert Gordon University
United Kingdom
r.j.glassey@rgu.ac.uk

Categories and Subject Descriptors:
H.3.3 [**Information Storage and Retrieval**]:
Information Search and Retrieval
General Terms: Design, Human Factors
Keywords: Information Retrieval, Children

EXTENDED ABSTRACT

MaSe provides a sandbox environment for high school students to create their own personalised search interface. It has been designed with two major goals in mind: (1) as a hands-on tutorial for school children, to excite them about programming and computing science through the development of a practical application, and (2) to enable children to design and create their own search interface without extensive programming knowledge or prior experience. Consequently, MaSe provides a way to ascertain what children would like from a search engine interface in an exploratory and creative way as they can create a working prototype. This approach contrasts with previous work on exploring children's requirements of IR systems which attempts to directly elicit user needs through more traditional methods (i.e. surveys, interviews, focus groups, etc) [2, 3]. However, we have attempted to incorporate the design guidelines for children as identified by [2, 3] into MaSe, where: we make use of bright colours, large text fonts, spell checking and the use of icons to represent search services, as well as including a thematic experience as suggested by [2], with the use of a puppy avatar and puppy dog footprints.

MaSe[1] is built using the PuppyIR framework [1], which utilises a pipe and filter architecture. The framework provides a number of query and document processing components to filter and modify the content (i.e. to filter out inappropriate words, expand queries, simplify snippets and more) and has connections to a wide range of back end search services such as Bing, YouTube, Twitter, Flickr, etc. During the tutorial, students connect these components together to create various search services, which teaches them about: (1) how information flows through a pipe and filter architecture, and (2) how they can configure different search services and their associated pipelines for their search interface. Students can then select and customise the set of search services that they would like within their search interface. As discussed

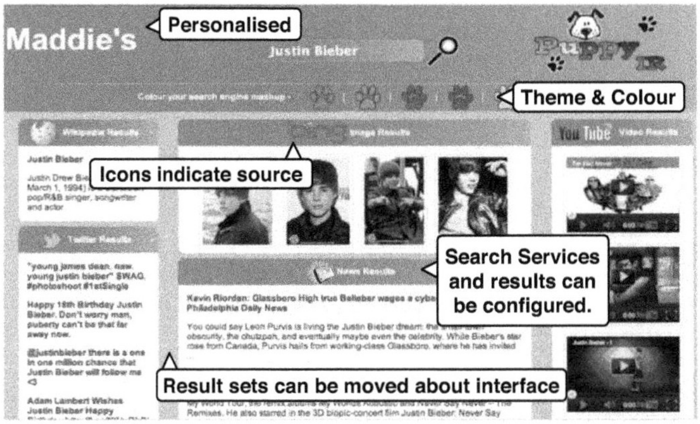

Figure 1: Maddie's search interface using MaSe.

in [2, 3], it is theorised that by allowing children to personalise their own search interface this will lead to a greater sense of ownership over their design and a greater sense of accomplishment. This should not only result in an enjoyable and positive experience of programming, but also provide an engaging experience of designing search interfaces. To this end, the interface can be easily customised. MaSe allows for the selection of a colour scheme, naming of the search engine, custom arrangement of search results using drag and drop, and the customisation of search services (by creating and customising the PuppyIR components in the code so the type of results, number of results and search services to be presented can be manipulated).

To date we have evaluated MaSe with approximately 100 university students, where even students with minimal programming experience were able to successfully complete the tutorial in about an hour with minimal assistance. Overall, their feedback was positive and that they enjoyed creating their own search interface. Next we plan to conduct studies with high school students to see what kinds of interfaces that they would like and what they design.

REFERENCES

[1] R. Glassey, T. Polajnar, and L.Azzopardi. PuppyIR Unleashed: A Framework for Building Child-Oriented Information Services. In *In Proc. of the 11th Dutch-Belgian IR Workshop*, 2011.
[2] A. Large, J. Beheshti, V. Nesset, and L. Bowler. Web portal design guidelines as identified by children through the processes of design and evaluation. In *Procs. of the 69th ASIST*, 2006.
[3] A. Large, J. Beheshti, and T. Rahman. Design criteria for children's web portals: The users speak out. *Journal of the ASIST*, 53(2):79–94, 2002.

Acknowledgements: PuppyIR is funded by the EC's FP7 2007-2013 under grant agreement no. 231507. We would also like to thank Catriona Dowie for the puppy cartoons.

[1]See `http://puppyir.sourgeforge.net` for the list of the underlying technologies used and the tutorial documentation.

SIGIR'12, August 12–16, 2012, Portland, Oregon, USA.
ACM 978-1-4503-1472-5/12/08.

myDJ: Recommending Karaoke Songs From One's Own Voice

Kuang Mao, Xinyuan Luo, Ke Chen, Gang Chen, Lidan Shou
College of Computer Science and Technology
Zhejiang University
Hangzhou, China
{mbill, wisp, chenk, cg, should}@zju.edu.cn

Categories and Subject Descriptors

H.3.3 [**Information Systems**]: Information Retrieval

Keywords

VRP, Learning to rank, Song recommendation

1. EXTENDED ABSTRACT

Singing is a worldwide activity across all walks of life. Many of us have had Karaoke defeats of singing a beloved song but making the others plug their ears. A major reason for such failure is that the songs one loves might not fit his/her personal laryngeal anatomy which determines the capacity of one's voice source.

myDJ is a karaoke recommendation system which recommends proper songs based on the pitch and intensity that one can nicely produce. Unlike most state-of-the-art recommendation systems, which rely on the similarity defined for the contents of songs, the listening habits of users, or the listening patterns, myDJ is the first prototype which recommends songs according to one's physical phonation area. The key challenge in this approach is to connect the singer's phonation model, which is typically described as a Vocal Range Profile (VRP)[1] in clinical quantitative voice assessments, to the music database, so that a given profile retrieves suitable songs. Unfortunately, a VRP is not enough to retrieve songs, as it only describes the minimum and maximum sound pressure levels (dB) across the singer's vocal range (Hz) without evaluating the voice quality. Our work focuses on techniques to build such connection for retrieval.

myDJ consists of four modules: (1) The singer profiler, which creates a profile for each singer via a tranditional musical test known as Messa di voce. The singer profile consists of two parts, the VRP which is depicted as a 2D region, and the Overall Voice Quality (OVQ)[3]combining multiple voice quality features as a distribution over the 2D region defined by VRP. (2) The Midi Song Database. We consider each song in the database as a document, and the notes in a song at the same pitch or intensity as a pitch term (PT) or an intensity term(IT) respectively. The duration of each IT and the TF-IDF weighted duration of each PT, which are accumulated by the note duration in a song, are the major factors affecting the fitness of a song. Thus, we define a song's profile as the combination of the TF-IDF weights, the PT and IT durations, and the pitch and intensity values of all notes in it. (3) The learning to rank module, where algorithm Listnet[2] is applied. (4) The song recommendation module, where songs are recommended using the ranking function learned by Listnet.

SIGIR'12, August 12–16, 2012, Portland, Oregon, USA.
ACM 978-1-4503-1472-5/12/08.

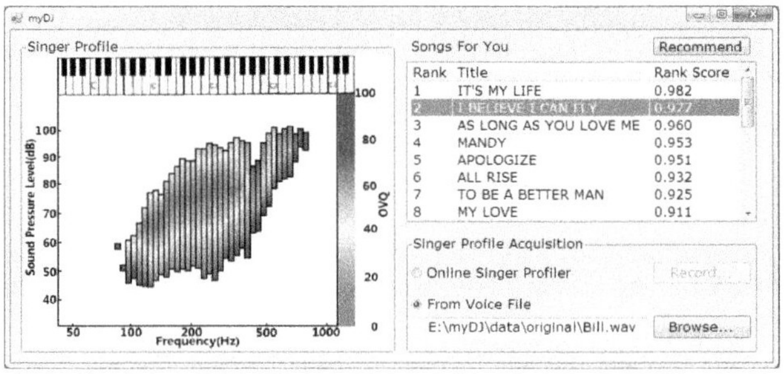

Figure 1: myDJ Interface

myDj works in two phases:

- *The offline training phase:* The learning algorithm uses (1) the singer profiles, and (2) the five-level fitness scored song profiles which are manually labeled by the singers for themselves, as the training data. During the training process, each singer profile is considered as a query and the song profiles as the documents. Thus, the features are extracted from all (query, document) pairs, and Gradient Descent is applied to calculate the parameters in the ranking function.
- *The online phase:* First, the test subject has to take the musical test to acquire the singer profile. Next, feature extraction will be conducted for all (query, document) pairs. To expedite this process, we utilize a document index to prune documents (songs) before any feature extraction. Finally, the rank score of each song is calculated using the ranking function learnt in the first step.

Figure 1 shows a screen shot of myDJ. The left part of the interface shows a singer profile, where the 2D region indicates the VRP and the color of each pixel indicates the OVQ value (Red for good and blue for poor). The top right screen shows a ranked list of songs being recommended for this subject.

2. ACKNOWLEDGMENTS

The work is supported in part by the National Science Foundation of China (GrantNo. 61003050, 60970124, and 61170034).

3. REFERENCES

[1] P. P. Anick Lamarche, Sten Ternström. The singer's voice range profile: female professional opera soloists. *Journal of voice*, 24:540–555, 2010.

[2] Z. Cao, T. Qin, T.-Y. Liu, M.-F. Tsai, and H. Li. Learning to rank: from pairwise approach to listwise approach. In *ICML*, pages 129–136, 2007.

[3] Y. Maryn, P. Corthals, P. V. Cauwenberge, N. Roy, and M. D. Bodt. Toward improved ecological validity in the acoustic measurement of overall voice quality: combining continuous speech and sustained vowels. *Journal of voice*, 24:410–426, 2010.

PageFetch: A Retrieval Game for Children (and Adults)

Jim Purvis, Leif Azzopardi
School of Computing Science
University of Glasgow
United Kingdom
{0801303P@student, leif@dcs} .gla.ac.uk

Richard Glassey
School of Computing
Robert Gordon University
United Kingdom
r.j.glassey@rgu.ac.uk

EXTENDED ABSTRACT

Children often struggle with information retrieval tasks as searching for information often requires a developed vocabulary and strong categorisation skills; neither of which are particularly developed in children under the age of 12 [1]. In a study conducted by Druin *et al* [2], it was found that in an experimental setting many children are often uninterested in searching for information online or are only interested in searching for information that is relevant to their personal interests. Consequently, children who were unmotivated were the least successful in completing information retrieval tasks in their study. It was suggested that a more effective means of engaging child participants in search studies must be developed in order to gain further insights into the searching behaviours of children. To this end we have developed a game called *PageFetch* which aims to engage children (aged 8 to 80) in completing search tasks through a fun and interactive search-like interface.

PageFetch is quite similar to other Human Computation Games developed in IR, i.e. PageHunt [3] and Fu-Finder [4], which have been used to improve search engines and study querying behavior, respectively. In these games, players are presented with a web page, and they need to enter in a query that retrieves the page. Players have three minutes to try and find as many of the pages as possible. However, PageFetch is novel, in a number of respects: (1) PageHunt and Fu-Finder used a similar set of pages (a mixture of hard and easy to find pages given Bing's search engine at the time), in PageFetch pages from six different categories were used (cartoons, music, sports, politics, actors and news) to provide a range of genres for children and adults[1]. (2) Thus, players are given a choice of category from which pages are presented (rather than random categories/pages). The choice of categories provides more focused game play and lets players pick a genre that is of interest. (3) Unlike PageHunt, PageFetch assigns points according to how high the results page is returned (i.e. the higher the rank the more points), and unlike Fu-Finder, PageFetch uses only one search engine (Bing), as opposed to three. Finally, (4) PageFetch was designed to encourage players to focus on entering successful queries for each page, which is achieved by providing a "no pass" bonus. If a player can find each page presented, regardless of how many query attempts for a particular page, the player receives bonus points (where the more pages they find in a row the higher the bonus). This feature tries to stimulate query re-formulations and was included to see whether we could encourage players to improve their searching abilities i.e. helping them to learn to search better. It is envisaged that through repeated gameplay that children (as well as adults) would be able to improve their performance as they refine their search strategies to retrieve pages. Currently, we undertaking a number of evaluations with school children and general web gamers/users[2], where we hope that these studies will establish a better understanding of the search proficiency of younger information seekers.

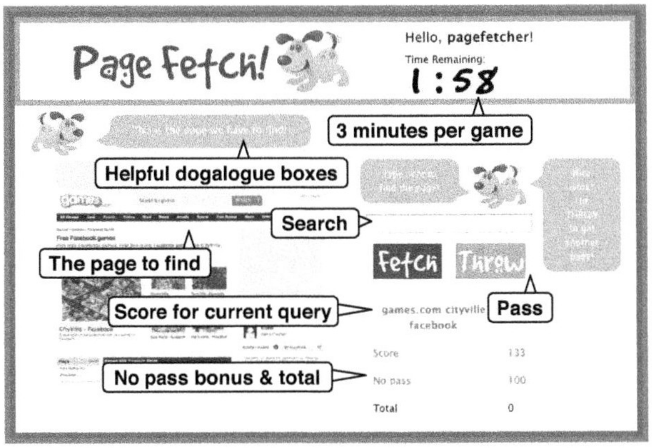

Figure 1: In game PageFetch screenshot.

Categories and Subject Descriptors:
H.3.3 [**Information Storage and Retrieval**]: Information Search and Retrieval

General Terms: Design, Human Factors

Keywords: Human Computational Games

REFERENCES

[1] Large A., Nesset V., and Beheshti J. Children as information seekers: what researchers tell us. *New Review of Children's Literature and Librarianship*, 14(2):121–140, 2008.

[2] A. Druin, E.h Foss, H. Hutchinson, E. Golub, and L. Hatley. Children's roles using keyword search interfaces at home. In *Proceedings of the 28th SIGCHI*, pages 413–422, 2010.

[3] H. Ma, R. Chandrasekar, C. Quirk, and A. Gupta. Improving search engines using human computation games. In *Proceeding of the 18th CIKM*, pages 275–284, 2009.

[4] C. O'Neil, J. Purvis, and L. Azzopardi. Fu-finder: a game for studying querying behaviours. In *Proceedings of the 20th ACM CIKM*, pages 2561–2564, 2011.

Acknowledgements: PuppyIR is funded by the EC's FP7 2007-2013 under grant agreement no. 231507. We would like to thank Doug Dowie and Carly O'Neil for their help and assistance.

[1] Pages were selected using trending search terms for under-12s, under-16 and adults from 2011.

[2] See http://www.dcs.gla.ac.uk/access/pagefetch/

SIGIR'12, August 12–16, 2012, Portland, Oregon, USA.
ACM 978-1-4503-1472-5/12/08.

Pictune: Situational Music Recommendation from Geotagged Pictures

Ke Chen Gang Chen Lidan Shou Fei Xia
College of Computer Science and Technology
Zhejiang University
Hangzhou, China
{chenk, cg, should}@zju.edu.cn xiafei648822481@163.com

Categories and Subject Descriptors: H.3.3 Information Systems: Information Retrieval
Keywords: Music Recommendation, Geo-tag, Image

1. EXTENDED ABSTRACT

We propose a music recommendation prototype named Pictune. Pictune utilizes location-based image retrieval and other Web services to recommend music for users virtually located at any position where such services are available. Our study is theoretically supported by two psychological findings. First, the need for music is driven by diverse motives, such as the leisure, informative, self-educational or experiential motives [2]. Interestingly, such motives are also spotted in photography. Second, the perception of the environment can significantly influence the expectation of music [4]. For example, when a person sees a landmark, its concept may be stimulated, evoking the expectation of other connection related to it, such as music and pictures. On the other hand, the melody of a song can facilitate learning and recall of the situation.

The main objective of this work is to develop a mobile Web application which acquires the user's *ambience* and retrieves music by it. The ambience of a user, as she accesses the application, is defined by her *location*, *time-of-day* (TOD), *day-of-year* (DOY), and the *weather*. These elements can be easily acquired from either the terminal or the Web. The main challenge is to explore the correlation between user ambience and the online rich photos, which are associated with numerous tags describing not only the facts (such as the ambience and the object being shot) but also subjective feelings, sensings, perceptions, and intuitions.

Pictune contains the following components: (1) A music database where each music is associated with a set of tags. (2) An image database indexed by ambience vector. Each ambience is associated with a set of tagged images. These data are retrieved from Flickr API and an online weather service. The components of the ambience vector are represented in discretized form for ease of computation. (3) A tag-by-ambience matrix M_{ta} (precomputed from the image database) where each element indicates the weight of a tag for a particular ambience. Given the current ambience of a new query, we first compute a vector of relevant tags (denoted by T) with weights. Then we perform an *emotion enhancement* process on T, which uses an emotional WordNet category to expand T so that more emotional terms are added and their weights be boosted [1]. T will then be mapped onto the music tag vocabulary relying on a distributional similarity tool [3], which produces another tag vector T' in the music tag space. T' will then be used to retrieve the music via tag-space similarity.

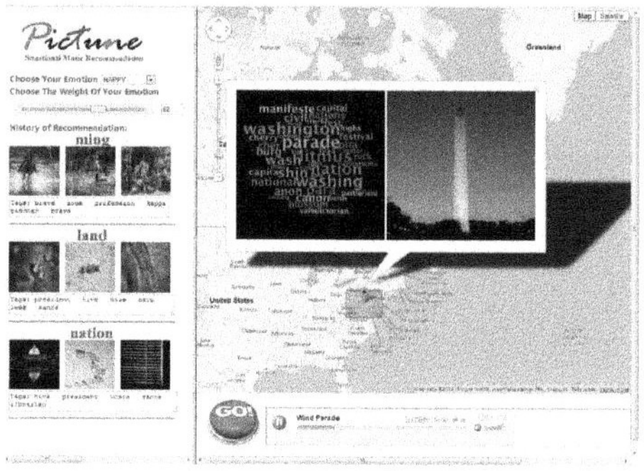

Figure 1: The recommendation results of Pictune

Figure 1 illustrates a Pictune screen with a few points-of-interest in a browser. The main window displays the recommended songs in the pop-ups. Each pop-up also contains a tag cloud showing a part of the T vector and a representative photo which is associated with the most occurrences of tags in T. The left side-bar lists all points being recommended, each showing the respective pictures and tags selected by the ambience. The bottom-bar contains a large button for music recommendation and the music player.

Pictune is distinguished from existing music recommendation systems as it exploits people's situational stimuli contained in social media. Hence, Pictune is not only a gadget to facilitate music discovery, but also a situational audio bridge toward the perception and emotion of the others.

Acknowledgments The work is supported by National Science Foundation of China (Grant No. 60970124, 61170034).

2. REFERENCES

[1] Wordnet-affect. http://wndomains.fbk.eu/wnaffect.html.

[2] C. Gibson and J. Connell. *Music and tourism: on the road again.* Channel View Publications, 2005.

[3] P. Kolb. Disco: A multilingual database of distributionally similar words. In *Proc. KONVENS*, 2008.

[4] W. Wallace. Memory for music: Effect of melody on recall of text. *Jnl. of Experimental Psychology: Learning, Memory, and Cognition*, 20:1471–1485, 1994.

SIGIR'12, August 12–16, 2012, Portland, Oregon, USA.
ACM 978-1-4503-1472-5/12/08.

Political Search Trends

Ingmar Weber
Yahoo! Research Barcelona
ingmar@yahoo-inc.com

Venkata Rama Kiran Garimella
Yahoo! Research Barcelona
gvrkiran@yahoo-inc.com

Erik Borra
University of Amsterdam
Amsterdam, Netherlands
borra@uva.nl

ABSTRACT

We present Political Search Trends, a browser based web search analysis tool that (i) assigns a political leaning to web search queries, (ii) detects trending political queries in a given week, and (iii) links search queries to fact-checked statements. In terms of methodology, it showcases the power of analyzing queries leading to clicks on selected, annotated web sites of interest.

Categories and Subject Descriptors

H.3.5 [**Information Storage and Retrieval**]: Online Information Services

Keywords

query log mining, political blogs, partisanship, fact-checking

1. WHAT IT DOES

Political Search Trends (PST)[1] analyzes anonymized web search queries submitted to Yahoo! that lead to clicks on political blogs. For a given week it shows trending *political* queries. E.g., the query "9 11 coloring book"[2] was found to be trending during Aug. 29-Sep. 4. As its main feature PST assigns a (fractional) political leaning to queries, such as "cost of obamacare" which is determined to be 99% right-leaning. Finally, it links queries to fact-checked statements on politifact.com such that "obama's aunt" is matched to `http://tinyurl.com/politifact-about-obamas-aunt`.

2. HOW IT WORKS

The starting point of PST is a set of blogs annotated as either left-leaning (387) or right-leaning (644). These labels are obtained by combining the work of Benkler and Shaw [1] with the Wonkosphere[3] blog directory. For the demo only queries leading to clicks on these blogs are considered. Obvious navigational queries are detected using string similarity and removed from consideration. Similarly, queries that within a given week only lead to clicks on one or two blogs are removed as they are generally not wide political issues. To improve the precision of detecting "political" queries, we compare the original number of web search results for a query with the number of results when the search term (i) "political" or (ii) "celebrity" is added. In the first case, the difference must not be too large, and in the second it must not be too small. These checks remove a small number of queries such as "whitney houston's death", which lead to clicks on several borderline political blogs. Trends are detected using relative increases in search volume [2]. Queries are annotated as left- or right-leaning, on a 0-to-1 scale, according to the fraction of times a query leads to clicks on a particular leaning. To limit volume-induced leaning biases, we use *normalized* volumes where, conceptually, each leaning is given the same number of "votes" in a given week. To address the problem of sparsity, where a query with a small number of queries could prematurely be assigned an extreme leaning, we use appropriate smoothing. Queries are matched to fact-checked statements by first indexing both the statements, usually one sentence, and Politifact's short summary and then performing basic term-based matching, allowing incomplete fuzzy matches for long queries.

3. RELATED DEMOS

The tool most closely related to PST was Political Insights[4], also developed by us and now obsolete. The methodology for assigning a leaning to a query is the same for both tools [3]. However, PST includes the notions of time and "trending" and shows results for continuously updated fresh data. In terms of write-up, [3] focuses on the methodology and findings derived from the data, whereas here we focus on the demo. Apart from Political Insights, we are not aware of any "political" web search analysis tool. General search analysis tools[5] could be used to obtain historic volume information and a geographical distribution as well as, for Yahoo! Clues, demographic information about the users issuing the particular query. However, such tools do *not* present the political leaning of a query and the queries to explore need to be pre-defined by the user. PST on the other hand provides the user with a list of queries to explore for a given week or for a given search string. Media Cloud[6] uses partisan blogs but does not align them with search logs.

4. REFERENCES

[1] Y. Benkler and A. Shaw. A tale of two blogospheres: Discursive practices on the left and right, 2010. `http://tinyurl.com/Benker-and-Shaw`.

[2] I. Subasic and C. Castillo. The effects of query bursts on web search. In *Web Intelligence*, 2010.

[3] I. Weber, V. R. K. Garimella, and E. Borra. Mining web query logs to analyze political issues. In *Web Science*, 2012.

[1] `http://politicalsearchtrends.sandbox.yahoo.com`
[2] `http://abcn.ws/MyqKgU`
[3] `http://wonkosphere.com/directory.htm`

[4] Screenshots available at `http://bit.ly/KM9ieA`.
[5] `http://yhoo.it/lKSQ7t` or `http://bit.ly/tBzI`
[6] `http://www.mediacloud.org/`

SIGIR'12, August 12–16, 2012, Portland, Oregon, USA.
ACM 978-1-4503-1472-5/12/08.

RDF Xpress: A Flexible Expressive RDF Search Engine

Shady Elbassuoni
Qatar Computing Research Institute
Doha, Qatar
selbassuoni@qf.org.qa

Maya Ramanath
IIT-Delhi
New Delhi, India
ramanath@cse.iitd.ac.in

Gerhard Weikum
Max-Planck Institute for Informatics
Saarbrucken, Germany
weikum@mpii.de

ABSTRACT

We demonstrate RDF Xpress, a search engine that enables users to effectively retrieve information from large RDF knowledge bases or Linked Data Sources. RDF Xpress provides a search interface where users can combine triple patterns with keywords to form queries. Moreover, RDF Xpress supports automatic query relaxation and returns a ranked list of diverse query results.

Categories and Subject Descriptors

H.3.3 [**Information Storage and Retrieval**]: Information Search and Retrieval—*Query formulation, Retrieval models*

Keywords

RDF, SPARQL, entity relationship search

1. INTRODUCTION

RDF data is typically searched using triple-pattern-based query languages such as SPARQL. For example, to find a list of singers who have won an Academy Award, the following two triple-pattern query can be issued: ?x isA Singer . ?x won Academy_Award where ?x denotes a variable. In principle, this allows precise querying in the database spirit. However, RDF data may be highly diverse and queries such as the one above may return way too many results, and thus ranking by informativeness measures is crucial to avoid overwhelming the users. Moreover, as the triples are usually extracted from textual contexts or have community-provided annotations, it can be beneficial to also consider keywords for formulating search requests. For example, to find singers who have won an Academy Award and suffered from drug abuse issues, we can issue the same triple-pattern query as above and associate it with the keywords: *drug* and *abuse*. Finally, to improve the recall of queries with too few or even no results, which happens often due to the Boolean-match semantics of SPARQL queries, automatic query relaxation must be performed. For example, in the second triple pattern of our example query, we can relax Academy_Award to Golden_Globe_Award or won to nominatedFor to retrieve a list of singers who have won a Golden Globe Award or were nominated for an Academy Award, respectively.

2. SYSTEM COMPONENTS

RDF Knowledge Base: Our RDF knowledge base consists of a set of RDF triples. Moreover, each triple is associated with a bag of words which contains any keywords that are associated with that triple (i.e., present in the source from which the triple was extracted). In addition, each triple is associated with a witness count which is the number of sources from which the triple was extracted. Similarly, each triple-keyword pair is associated with a witness count reflecting the number of witnesses for the triple that contain the keyword. The witness counts are used as features that are used to rank query results.

Search Interface: RDF Xpress provides a user-friendly form-based interface to search the underlying RDF knowledge base. The search interface allows users to easily generate triple patterns by using an auto-complete feature for subjects, predicates and objects. Moreover, next to each generated triple pattern, there is a text field where users can freely type any keyword conditions.

Retrieval Engine: The retrieval engine processes the user's query and retrieves a set of ranked results where the results are ranked based on a language modeling approach that utilizes the witness counts of triples as a ranking feature [2] .

Query Relaxer: In case there are no sufficient results for a given query, we generate a set of relaxed queries which are close in spirit to the given query, execute them and rank their results taking into consideration how well a result matches the original query [3].

Result Diversifier: To ensure that the top ranked results are highly relevant to the query and diverse from each other, we re-rank the top-k highest-ranked results using a Maximal-Marginal Relevance approach [1].

3. DEMONSTRATION SCENARIO

RDF Xpress (`http://www.mpi-inf.mpg.de/yago-naga/rdf-express/`) runs over two RDF knowledge bases. The first is constructed from a subset of the Internet Movie Database (IMDB) and automatically linked with YAGO [4]. The second is based on LibraryThing which is an online book catalogue and tagging community. The audience will get a chance to interact with the system and issue their own queries that combine both structured triple patterns with keywords and investigate the ranked list of results returned for their queries.

4. REFERENCES

[1] J. Carbonell and J. Goldstein. The use of MMR, diversity-based reranking for reordering documents and producing summaries. In *SIGIR*, 1998.

[2] S. Elbassuoni, M. Ramanath, R. Schenkel, M. Sydow, and G. Weikum. Language-model-based ranking for queries on RDF-graphs. In *CIKM*, 2009.

[3] S. Elbassuoni, M. Ramanath, and G. Weikum. Query Relaxation for Entity-Relationship Search. In *ESWC*, 2011.

[4] F. Suchanek, G. Kasneci, and G.Weikum. YAGO: A Core of Semantic Knowledge Unifying WordNet and Wikipedia. In *WWW*, 2007.

SIGIR'12, August 12–16, 2012, Portland, Oregon, USA.
ACM 978-1-4503-1472-5/12/08.

Sketch-based Image Similarity Search with a Pen and Paper Interface

Ihab Al Kabary Heiko Schuldt
Databases and Information Systems Group
Department of Mathematics and Computer Science
University of Basel, Switzerland
ihab.alkabary@unibas.ch, heiko.schuldt@unibas.ch

ABSTRACT

We present a novel and innovative user interface for query-by-sketching based image retrieval that exploits emergent interactive paper and digital pen technology. Users can draw sketches with a digital pen on interactive paper in a user-friendly way. The pen is able to capture the stroke vectors and to interactively stream them to the underlying content-based image retrieval (CBIR) system via the pen's Bluetooth interface. We present the integration of interactive paper/digital pen technology with QbS, our CBIR system tailored to Query-by-Sketching, and we demonstrate the use of the paper and pen interface together with QbS for three different collections: MIRFLICKR-25K, a cartoon collection, and a collection of medieval paper watermarks.

Categories and Subject Descriptors

H.5.2 [**Information Interfaces and Presentation**]: User Interfaces; H.3.3 [**Information Storage And Retrieval**]: Information Search and Retrieval

Keywords

digital pen, interactive paper, query-by-sketch, CBIR

1. QUERY-BY-SKETCHING

Content-based image retrieval (CBIR) allows to search in image databases even when no descriptive metadata is attached to the individual objects. To overcome the problem of finding appropriate query objects in CBIR, Query-by-Sketching allows users to contribute sketches (mainly edge drawings) as query objects. However, Query-by-Sketching has suffered in the past from the limitations of existing user interfaces. Drawing sketches with a mouse is a highly inexact method, and even using graphic tablets involves constantly looking away from the hand. Methods that combine the functionalities of graphic tablets with those of a monitor (e.g., the iPad) are best suited for rather simple gestures and thus do not meet the precision necessary for providing exact sketches. Therefore, the intuitively most promising approach to drawing sketches is to just use a (conventional) pen and paper interface [2].

SIGIR'12, August 12–16, 2012, Portland, Oregon, USA.
ACM 978-1-4503-1472-5/12/08.

Figure 1: Execution of Pen-based CBIR Query

2. PEN AND PAPER INTERFACE

Digital pens are designed for drawing on normal paper on which a proprietary Anoto dot pattern is printed. The pens which are equipped with an infrared LED camera can localize the position on paper by reading a 6×6 dot area on paper (approx. 1.8×1.8 mm in size). Each dot is subject to one of four displacements from a regular grid position, leading to 4^{36} different combinations of the 6×6 dot area, which is read to identify the pen tip coordinates. The pens store the pattern information in the form of pen stroke data, which are continuous curves made up of coordinates and which are interactively transmitted to the back-end CBIR application (our QbS system, see Figure 1) via Bluetooth.

The QbS system exploits angular radial partitioning for the extraction of features in the user-provided sketch, and also supports the image distortion model and edge histogram descriptors. This combination provides several highly relevant invariances that allow the query sketch to slightly deviate from the searched image in terms of rotation, translation, relative size, and/or unknown objects in the background. The pen and paper interface for the QbS system has been subject to evaluations and user studies [1] with three different collections: i.) the MIRFLICKR-25K photo collection, ii.) a collection of cartoon images, and iii.) a collection of medieval paper watermarks which are used in the humanities to date ancient documents.

3. ACKNOWLEDGMENTS

This work has been partly supported by the Swiss National Science Foundation, projects PAD-IR and MM-DocTable.

4. REFERENCES

[1] R. Kreuzer, M. Springmann, I. A. Kabary, and H. Schuldt. An Interactive Paper and Digital Pen Interface for Query-by-Sketch Image Retrieval. In *Proc. ECIR'12*, pages 317–328, Barcelona, Spain, Apr. 2012.

[2] G. Kurtenbach. Pen-based Computing. *ACM Crossroads*, 16(4):14–20, 2010.

Task-Aware Search Assistant

Henry Feild & James Allan
Center for Intelligent Information Retrieval
Dept. of Computer Science
University of Massachusetts
Amherst, MA 01003
{hfeild,allan}@cs.umass.edu

Categories and Subject Descriptors

H.3 [**Information Storage and Retrieval**]: Miscellaneous

Keywords

Search task identification, search history

Extended abstract

When users search the web, their goal is to accomplish something, which we call a *search task*. Previous studies have observed an average of 2.6–3.3 queries per search task [2, 3, 4] and Jones and Klinkner [2] found 16% of tasks were revisited over a three-day span of Yahoo! logs. These statistics suggest that a task-aware search assistant may aid users in continuing previous search tasks as well as new ones.

There are several existing tools that are related or similar in nature to a task-aware search assistant, the most basic of which are built-in browser histories and extensions that make them easier to navigate. Both Google and Bing provide search histories over their respective services. However, these lack a task-oriented view of searches. The most closely related work that we are aware of is Yahoo's Search Pad, which attempts to automatically identify that a user is conducting research (e.g., planning a vacation). It then notifies the user and begins tracking queries and result clicks in an interface, to which the user can add and remove content. However, like Bing and Google's search histories, Search Pad only works with Yahoo! search. In addition, the interface is built for automatically detected research tasks, whereas we would like to provide assistance across all varieties of tasks.

Our approach to aiding users during search—both for new and continuing tasks—is to present them with an easy to use sidebar implemented as a browser extension. The interface consists of a collapsible sidebar in the browser with multiple panes that can be paged through using streamlined navigation buttons. The primary pane displays three key groupings: (1) a list of the most recent search tasks, (2) a list of related queries entered in the past, and (3) a list of related tasks conducted in the past. Note that a task consists of a cluster of queries and visited documents. This primary pane is updated with each new query and page visit, adjusting for new tasks as they are detected. A second pane allows users to search and browse their entire task history as a chronologically ordered list. A third pane provides similar functionality, but without task clustering. We expect these functionalities to aid users in orienting themselves among their current and past tasks, and aid them in pulling in information from previous tasks, whether for refinding or for recalling vocabulary. As a browser extension, the interface can extract search tasks from the existing browser history, making the tool useful right out of the box. Unlike many of the search assistant tools describe above, this interface has access to searches from virtually all search engines and web pages visited at any point during a user's search—not just results clicked from a search results page.

The underlying technology relies on performing same-task classification between pairs of queries. Following previous work [1, 2], we use logistic regression models, which are well-suited for binary classification. We also use many of the same lexical features: Jaccard coefficient, tri-gram character overlap, and Levenshtein distance. We borrow a feature presented by Lucchese et al. [4], which computes the semantic similarity between two queries by the cosine similarity between vectors of tf-idf scores over Wikipedia documents. We also use their weighted connected components clustering method once the pair-wise classifications have been made.

In summary, our prototype provides a novel interface for providing users with information about current and past search tasks. The underlying task-classification is based on a fusion of existing methods.

Acknowledgments. This work was supported in part by the Center for Intelligent Information Retrieval and in part by NSF grant #IIS-0910884. Any opinions, findings and conclusions or recommendations expressed in this material are those of the authors and do not necessarily reflect those of the sponsors.

References

[1] P. Boldi, F. Bonchi, C. Castillo, D. Donato, A. Gionis, and S. Vigna. The query-flow graph: model and applications. In *Proc. of CIKM'08*, pages 609–618. ACM, 2008.

[2] R. Jones and K. Klinkner. Beyond the session timeout: automatic hierarchical segmentation of search topics in query logs. In *Proc. of CIKM'08*, pages 699–708. ACM, 2008.

[3] T. Lau and E. Horvitz. Patterns of search: analyzing and modeling web query refinement. In *Proc. of User Modeling'99*, pages 119–128. Springer-Verlag New York, Inc., 1999.

[4] C. Lucchese, S. Orlando, R. Perego, F. Silvestri, and G. Tolomei. Identifying task-based sessions in search engine query logs. In *Proc. of WSDM'11*, pages 277–286. ACM, 2011.

SIGIR'12, August 12–16, 2012, Portland, Oregon, USA.
ACM 978-1-4503-1472-5/12/08.

TweetSpector: Entity-based retrieval of Tweets

Surender Reddy Yerva, Zoltán Miklós, Flavia Grosan, Alexandru Tandrau, Karl Aberer
Swiss Federal Institute of Technology (EPFL)
Lausanne, Switzerland
{surenderreddy.yerva,zoltan.miklos,flavia.grosan,alexandru.tandrau,karl.aberer}@epfl.ch

Categories and Subject Descriptors

H.3.1 [**Information Systems Applications**]: Content Analysis and Indexing; H.3.5 [**Information Systems Applications**]: Online Information Services

Keywords

Entity, Disambiguation, Profiles, Twitter

1. EXTENDED ABSTRACT

People readily express their opinions about the various products, companies, TV shows etc., on Twitter[1]. These tweet messages are thus a rich source of information that can be exploited to understand the sentiments about the concerned products or services. Retrieving the tweets related to given entities is however a challenging task as their names are often (deliberately) ambiguous, e.g. Apple, Blackberry, Friends, etc. Nevertheless, identifying the relevant entities is an essential first step to develop reliable sentiment analysis techniques that is not considered in existing systems, for example TweetFeel[2], TwitterSentiment[3].

While there is a number of techniques for identifying named entities in unstructured text, they are often not directly applicable in this case, as tweet messages are very short (maximal 140 characters). This demonstrator introduces TweetSpector, a tool that addresses this retrieval task and enables to link tweet messages to a given entity. Our retrieval methods rely on classification techniques that exploit our concise descriptions of entity-relevant information, also called entity profiles.

The demonstrator presents the following features of TweetSpector:

-*Entity Profile Creation:* TweetSpector supports automatic profile creation, where we apply named-entity recognition, NLTK, wordnet and Web data extraction techniques to construct profiles for an entity, given a relevant Webpage. TweetSpector also enables manual profile construction, where users can construct arbitrary entity profiles, as well as manual and automatic updates for initially constructed profiles (thus the profiles are dynamic). The profiles can also be visualized using Word Clouds.

[1]`http://www.twitter.com`
[2]`http://www.tweetfeel.com`
[3]`http://twittersentiment.appspot.com`

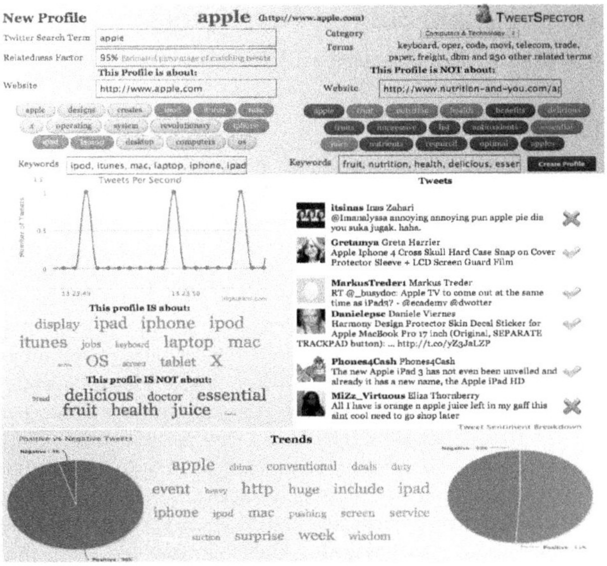

Figure 1: TweetSpector: Various Features

-*Tweet Classification:* TweetSpector displays in real-time the classification results (see Figure 1). For example, a stream of tweets is displayed and it is indicated whether or not the messages shall be related to the company Apple Inc.. The classification techniques are widely extended versions of our earlier work [1].

-*User Feedback:* The users can indicate whether the proposed classification is correct or not. This feedback is taken into account by the algorithms. TweetSpector can also take human input through crowdsourcing (through an interface to Amazon Mechanical Turk).

-*Dashboard:* TweetSpector can display performance metrics and statistical information on a dashboard related to the entity.

2. ACKNOWLEDGEMENTS

This work was partly funded by the NisB project (FP7-ICT-256955) and the European Commission in the PlanetData NoE (contract nr. 257641).

3. REFERENCES

[1] Surender Reddy Yerva, Zoltán Miklós, and Karl Aberer. Entity-based Classification of Twitter Messages. *International Journal of Computer Science & Applications*, 9(1):88–115, 2012.

YooSee: A Video Browsing Application for Young Children

Leif Azzopardi, Douglas Dowie, Kelly Ann Marshall
School of Computing Science
University of Glasgow
United Kingdom
{leif, doug, kellym}@dcs.gla.ac.uk

Categories and Subject Descriptors:
H.3.3 [**Information Storage and Retrieval**]:
Information Search and Retrieval
General Terms: Design, Human Factors
Keywords: Video Browser, Children

EXTENDED ABSTRACT

Nowadays children as young as two years old can easily interact with mobile touch screen devices and personal computers to watch online videos through services such as YouTube. However, such services present a number of challenges for young children (e.g. fine grain gestures/interactions and good typing/literacy skills). In addition, when children use such services there is a risk that they may stumble upon content that is inappropriate. YooSee[1] is a web-based application developed using the PuppyIR framework [1] and designed for children aged between two and six years old. YooSee enables children to: (1) search and browse through video content using an engaging, novel interaction paradigm, and (2) be able to safely enjoy moderated video content.

The application was motivated by a desire to address the issues that children have with text based searching. In [2], Druin *et al* show that children face a number of problems associated with formulating queries, such as: spelling, selecting the right words, and the use - or not - of natural language. Additionally, in [3], it was found that children prefer to browse through content. YooSee avoids the problems associated with querying by providing a novel interaction paradigm based around a *globe* of videos for children to explore. Conceptually the globe can be thought of as a series of carousels containing videos: where the interaction paradigm allows two forms of browsing/scrolling:

1. **in carousel** to access similar and related content, and,
2. **between carousels** to access different content.

Providing content around a globe allows the child to have seamless and continuous interaction with the content provided i.e. as they with move around the carousels, or move between carousels, they will eventually loop around the globe.

YooSee also adopts a minimilist interface in response to concerns raised in [2] about the information overload experienced by children. Consequently, only a small part of the content space is presented at once as shown in Figure 1,

[1]See `http://www.dcs.gla.ac.uk/access/yoosee/`.

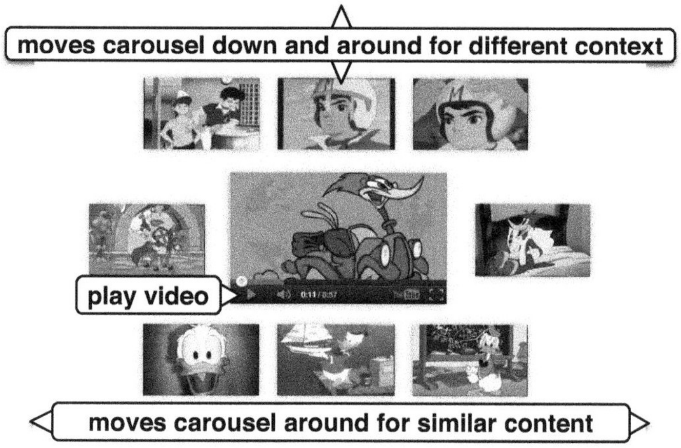

Figure 1: YooSee in action.

where a 3x3 grid of thumbnails is presented except for the central thumbnail which is larger and enables the child to watch the embedded video inline. The child is able to navigate through the space browsing up or down, i.e. *between carousels*, or left and right i.e. *in carousel*, or they can watch the video that is currently in focus.

The moderation of the content is controlled by the parent/guardian of the child. This is accomplished via an administrative section of the application. In this section parent/guardians can manage the various carousels available (adding content by searching for YouTube clips, adding / deleting carousels, etc). While this step is manual, it provides the parent with complete control, and means they only have to find the items that their child likes once, rather than repeatedly searching for the content that their child enjoys. Once setup, children can enjoy their favourite content in a moderated and safe environment. In future work, we will explore how children engage with this novel interaction paradigm, and whether they can easily and quickly navigate to their desired content (over other possible interaction paradigms).

REFERENCES

[1] R. Glassey, T. Polajnar, and L.Azzopardi. PuppyIR Unleashed: A Framework for Building Child-Oriented Information Services. In *In Proc. of the 11th Dutch-Belgian IR Workshop*, 2011.

[2] A. Druin, E. Foss, L. Hatley, E. Golub, M. L. Guha, J. Fails, and H. Hutchinson. How children search the internet with keyword interfaces. In *Proc. of the 8th Int. Conf. on Interaction Design and Children*, pages 89–96, 2009.

[3] A. Large, V. Nesset, and J. Beheshti. Children as information seekers: what researchers tell us. *New Review of Children's Literature and Librarianship*, 14(2):121–140, 2009.

Acknowledgements: PuppyIR is funded by the EC's FP7 2007-2013 under grant agreement no. 231507.

Multi-Platform Image Search using Tag Enrichment

Jinming Min[1], Cristover Lopes[2], Johannes Leveling[1], Dag Schmidtke[3] and Gareth J. F. Jones[1]
[1]:School of Computing, CNGL, Dublin City University, Dublin, Ireland
[2]:Trinity College Dublin, Dublin, Ireland
[3]:Microsoft Ireland, Dublin, Ireland
{jmin, jleveling, gjones}@computing.dcu.ie, lopesc@tcd.ie, dags@microsoft.com

Categories and Subject Descriptors:
H.3.3 [INFORMATION STORAGE AND RETRIEVAL] Information Search and Retrieval—*Query formulation*

General Terms: Algorithms, Experimentation

Keywords: Image retrieval, Query formulation, Relevance feedback, Document expansion

1. EXTENDED ABSTRACT

The number of images available online is growing steadily and current web search engines have indexed more than 10 billion images. Approaches to image retrieval are still often text-based and operate on image annotations and captions. Image annotations (i.e. image tags) are typically short, user-generated, and of varying quality, which increases the mismatch problem between query terms and image tags. For example, a user might enter the query *wedding dress* while all images are annotated with *bridal gown* or *wedding gown*. This demonstration presents an image search system using reduction and expansion of image annotations to overcome vocabulary mismatch problems by enriching the sparse set of image tags.

Our image search application accepts a written query as input and produces a ranked list of result images and annotations (i.e. image tags) as output [2]. The system integrates methods to reduce and expand the image tag set, thus decreasing the effect of sparse image tags. It builds on different image collections such as the Wikipedia image collection[1] and the Microsoft Office.com ClipArt collection[2], but can be applied to social collections such as Flickr as well. Our demonstration system runs on PCs, tablets, and smartphones, making use of advanced user interface capabilities on mobile devices.

Figure 1 presents an overview of the complete system for Document Expansion (DE) using Wikipedia as an external resource. Important terms in the original image annotation are used as a query to retrieve Wikipedia articles and extract DE terms from the top-ranked documents. These terms are added to the original image tags to form the enriched tag set. The expanded annotations are indexed in the retrieval system. The key stage here is to select key terms from the documents prior to expansion in a process we refer to as Document Reduction (DR). The objective of DR is to focus the DE "query" on the most important elements in the tag set.

The system is implemented as a client-server architecture, where the client realizes the graphical user interface and handles query processing. The image annotation index resides on the server side. Users can try general queries on the system to observe the results for different system settings, e.g. with document expansion or without document expansion. Under the document expansion setting, the expanded annotation terms are displayed with the image results. The demo also includes evaluation results on a Wikipedia image collection for *120* queries. For mean average precision, we obtain *16%* improvement compared to a standard retrieval baseline.

In the future, we plan to investigate a combination of the annotation modification approach with a feedback term selection technique from our previous research work [1]. This method classifies feedback terms by supervised learning and has proven to improve feedback term selection in several retrieval tasks.

[1]http://www.imageclef.org/wikidata
[2]http://office.microsoft.com/

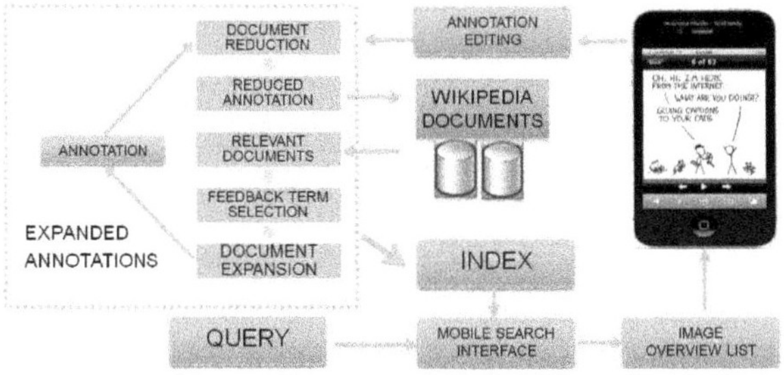

Figure 1: System overview.

Figure 2: Image search system on a PC (left) and on smartphone and tablet (middle and right).

Acknowledgments

This research is supported by the Science Foundation of Ireland (grant 07/CE/I1142) as part of CNGL (http://www.cngl.ie/).

2. REFERENCES

[1] J. Leveling and G. J. F. Jones. Classifying and filtering blind feedback terms to improve information retrieval effectiveness. In *RIAO '10*, pages 156–163. CID, 2010.

[2] J. Min, J. Leveling, D. Zhou, and G. J. F. Jones. Document expansion for image retrieval. In *RIAO '10*, pages 65–71, 2010.

IR Paradigms in Computational Advertising

Andrei Z. Broder
Google
1600 Amphitheatre Parkway
Mountain View, CA 94043
broder@acm.org

ABSTRACT

The central problem in the emerging discipline of computational advertising is to find the "best match" between a given user in a given context and a suitable advertisement. The context could be a user entering a query in a search engine ("sponsored search"), a user reading a web page ("content match" and "display ads"), a user streaming a movie, and so on. In some situations, it is desirable to solve the "dual" optimization problem: rather then find the best ad given a user in a context, the goal is to identify the "best audience", i.e. the most receptive set of users and/or the most suitable contexts for a given advertising campaign. The information about the user can vary from scarily detailed to practically nil. The number of potential advertisements might be in the billions. Thus, depending on the definition of "best match" and "best audience" these problems lead to a variety of massive optimization problems, with complicated constraints, and challenging data representation and access issues.

In general, the direct problem is solved in two stages: first a rough filtering is used to identify a relatively small set of ads to be considered as potential matches, followed by a more sophisticated secondary ranking where economics considerations take center stage. Historically, the filtering has been conceived as a database selection problem, and was done using simple Boolean formulae, for instance, in sponsored search the filter could be "all ads that provide a specific bid for the present query string or a subset of it". Similarly for the dual problem (audience definition) for, say, a sports car ad, the filter could be "all males in California, aged 40 or less".

This "database approach" for the direct problem has been recently supplanted by an "IR approach" based on a similarity search between a carefully constructed query that captures the advertising opportunity and an annotated document corpus that represents the potential ads. Similarly, in the dual problem, the newer approach is to devise an efficient and effective representation of the users, then form a query that represents a prototypical ideal user, and finally find the users most similar to the prototype. The aim of this talk is to discuss the penetration of the IR paradigms in computational advertising and present some research challenges and opportunities in this area of enormous economic importance.

Categories and Subject Descriptors

H.3.5 [**Information Storage and Retrieval**]: Online Information Services—*Web based services*; H.4.3 [**Communications Applications**]: Information browsers; I.7.5 [**Document and Text Processing**]: Document Capture—*Document analysis*

General Terms

Algorithms, Design, Economics, Performance

Keywords

Computational advertising, Similarity search, Audience targeting

SIGIR'12, August 12–16, 2012, Portland, Oregon, USA.
ACM 978-1-4503-1472-5/12/08.

Watson: The *Jeopardy!* Challenge and Beyond

Eric W. Brown
IBM T.J. Watson Research Center
19 Skyline Dr.
Hawthorne, NY 10532
+1-914-784-7708
ewb@us.ibm.com

ABSTRACT

Watson, named after IBM founder Thomas J. Watson, was built by a team of IBM researchers who set out to accomplish a grand challenge—build a computing system that rivals a human's ability to answer questions posed in natural language with speed, accuracy and confidence. The quiz show *Jeopardy!* provided the ultimate test of this technology because the game's clues involve analyzing subtle meaning, irony, riddles and other complexities of natural language in which humans excel and computers traditionally fail. Watson passed its first test on *Jeopardy!*, beating the show's two greatest champions in a televised exhibition match, but the real test will be in applying the underlying natural language processing and analytics technology in business and across industries. In this talk I will introduce the *Jeopardy!* grand challenge, present an overview of Watson and the DeepQA technology upon which Watson is built, and explore future applications of this technology.

Categories and Subject Descriptors

H.0 [Information Systems]: General

General Terms

Algorithms, Design

Keywords

Questioning Answering

SIGIR '12, August 12–16, 2012, Portland, Oregon, USA.
ACM 978-1-4503-1472-5/12/08.

Putting Context into Search and Search into Context

Susan T. Dumais
Microsoft Research
One Microsoft Way
Redmond, WA 98052
sdumais@microsoft.com

Categories and Subject Descriptors

H.3.3 [**Information Storage and Retrieval**]: Information Search and Retrieval – *query formulation, retrieval models, search process.*

General Terms

Algorithms, Experimentation, Human Factors, Measurement.

Keywords

Industry keynote, context and search, personalization, potential for personalization, evaluation.

ABSTRACT

It is very challenging task to understand a short query, especially if that query is considered in isolation. Luckily, queries do magically appear in a search box – rather, they are issued by real people, trying to accomplish a task, at a given point in time and space, and this "context" can be used to aid query understanding. Traditionally search engines have returned the same results to everyone who asks the same question. However, using a single ranking for everyone, in every context limits how well a search engine can do. In this talk I outline a framework to quantify the "potential for personalization", that can be used to characterize the extent to which different people have the same (or different) intents for a query. I then describe several examples of how we represent and use different kinds of context to improve search quality. Finally I conclude by highlighting some important challenges in developing such systems at Web scale including system optimization, evaluation, transparency and serendipity.

SIGIR'12, August 12–16, 2012, Portland, Oregon, USA.
ACM 978-1-4503-1472-5/12/08.

CloudSearch and the Democratization of Information Retrieval

[Extended Abstract]

Daniel E. Rose
A9.com
danrose@a9.com

ABSTRACT

Amazon CloudSearch is a new hosted search service, built on top of many cloud-based AWS services, and based on the same technology that powers search on Amazon's retail sites. Because of its ease of configuration and scalability, CloudSearch represents the next step in the democratization of information retrieval. This democratization process, increasing access to search for both end users and potential search providers, has continued over several decades, through technologies like early online metered search services, enterprise search software, web search, and open source search tools. CloudSearch further reduces barriers to entry, allowing a person or organization to basically say "make my content searchable" and have it happen automatically. CloudSearch may also offer an opportunity to overcome the stagnation that has occurred in search user experiences over the past 15 years. When you no longer need to be a search expert to make your content available, you're not stuck with ten blue links. Instead, you can focus on providing the kind of interaction that makes sense for your application and your users. CloudSearch enables a flowering of search applications that need not be tied to the web, and an opportunity to explore new ways of interacting with information retrieval technology.

Categories and Subject Descriptors

H.3.3 [**Information Storage and Retrieval**]: Information Search and Retrieval; H.3.4 [**Information Storage and Retrieval**]: Systems and Software; C.2.4 [**Computer-Communication Networks**]: Distributed Systems—*Cloud computing*; H.5.2 [**Information Interfaces and Presentation**]: User Interfaces

General Terms

Human Factors, Experimentation

Keywords

cloud search, cloud computing, access to search, search interfaces

SIGIR'12, August 12–16, 2012, Portland, Oregon, USA.
ACM 978-1-4503-1472-5/12/08.

1. AMAZON CLOUDSEARCH

Amazon CloudSearch is a new hosted search service from AWS (currently in beta as of this writing). CloudSearch is based on the product search technology developed by A9 for use by Amazon. This engine was designed from the ground up with semistructured data in mind, including support for faceted metadata and numeric range searches. And since *tf·idf*-style text matching isn't always the most important ranking feature for many real-world applications, CloudSearch provides relevance functions based on a configurable mix of query-dependent and query-independent features. In addition, the engine was designed for memory-resident indexes, with internal data structures that take advantage of this architecture.

CloudSearch relies on many proven AWS services, not only for raw computation (EC2) and storage (S3), but also for important process components. For example, Elastic MapReduce (EMR) is used for index construction, Simple Workflow Service (SWF) for coordinating customer actions, and Elastic Load Balancing (ELB) for routing traffic.

2. IMPACT ON SEARCH ACCESS

The history of information retrieval is one of increased access, or what we call the *democratization* of search. This process has two aspects: increased access by end-users and increased access for potential search providers. New generations of search technology were often accompanied by improvements in one or the other of these kinds of access.

- *Online services.* Search first became commercially available in the early 1970s with online services like DIALOG and ORBIT, which provided access to important research collections. These services charged end users by the hour — $50 per hour was a typical fee — and in some cases required the customer to rent a special terminal installed in his or her office. Due to these limitations, the services were used by only a few people, typically in law offices or university research libraries.
- *Enterprise search.* The 1980s and 1990s saw the appearance of search engine products such as Verity Topic, Excalibur RetrievalWare, and Fulcrum SearchServer that for the first time let an organization make its *own* chosen set of data searchable. Due to both the expense of the software (often tens or hundreds of thousands of dollars per instance per year), the large servers needed to run it, and the skilled people needed to install, configure, and maintain it, customers tended to be limited to large businesses.

- *Web search.* The rise of web search in the mid-to-late 1990s brought search to the general public for the first time. Eventually, end users could search the web from nearly any location and at no incremental cost. While this was a huge step forward in terms of end-user access to search, in some sense it offered less flexibility and control to organizations who had searchable content.
- *Open source search.* The past 10 years have seen the growth and adoption of high-quality open source search tools such as Lucene/Solr and Indri in a variety of domains. Like enterprise search, these tools allow their users to decide what data to make searchable, but without the licensing fee. However, they still require a fair degree of skill to configure and maintain, as well as hardware to run on.

CloudSearch represents the next stage in the process of democratization, particularly for potential search providers. With CloudSearch, people or organizations who want to make their data searchable no longer have to choose between putting it on the web and becoming search engine experts. Instead, they can essentially say "make this collection searchable," and the service does the rest. There are several attributes of CloudSearch that make this possible:

- *Ease of configuration.* To set up a CloudSearch domain, clients provide data in XML or similar format, answer a few questions about the structure of the data via a simple dashboard interface, and they are done. In some cases CloudSearch can automatically deduce the correct configuration from a sample of documents. If the client wants to experiment with the configuration — for example, to change which fields should be facets or how stemming is applied — this can be easily done from the dashboard, without the need to upload documents again.
- *No hardware or software management.* This is one of the most obvious benefits of a cloud-based solution, but it is no less important for being so. The amount of effort required to install and operate a stable service running on one's own hardware is nontrivial; keeping it up 24 x 7 while protecting against a variety of threats, both malicious and natural, requires a serious investment. CloudSearch customers don't have to worry about these issues. Furthermore, CloudSearch automatically upgrades the system with new software without incurring any downtime.
- *Scalability and Elasticity.* Perhaps the most important benefit of CloudSearch is its ability to automatically scale in multiple dimensions. As the size of the data grows, the CloudSearch service will automatically repartition the index across multiple servers, providing horizontal parallelism. As the amount of query traffic grows, the service will automatically replicate the query servers, providing vertical parallelism. Furthermore, the elastic nature of the service means servers will be added at peak times to handle the increased traffic, then removed later so customers aren't paying for capacity they don't need.

3. IMPACT ON USER EXPERIENCE

The early days of commercial search were characterized by the use of text-based interfaces and complex Boolean query syntax. As computers shifted from command-line to graphical user interfaces, interaction with search systems became much simpler. The widespread adoption of unstructured queries also made a huge difference in search usability. Unfortunately, there has been little further improvement in search interfaces, at least those available to the general public, since 1995.

In the intervening years, a typical user's computing power has increased by more than a factor of 50 and her bandwidth by a factor of 200. Operating systems such as Mac OS X and Windows 7 provide dramatically richer interaction, with photorealistic graphics, animation, and so on. Internet services allow multiuser video chat, immersive game environments, and streaming HD video. Yet search interfaces, and web search interfaces in particular, have barely changed.

The reasons for this are complex, but one of them is that the web search market quickly became dominated by a small number of players who stayed with the now-familiar design. Many users have never seen a search engine other than a web search engine and assume this is just the way search is supposed to work.

CloudSearch offers an opportunity to overcome this stagnation. First, it dramatically lowers the barrier of entry for a person or organization that wants to provide search as part of their application or service. A small business or organization that didn't have the resources to offer search before now can. So there will be an explosion of new applications and content sources, filling small niches other than general web search and aimed at a variety of devices. Second, search providers no longer need to be search experts. Instead, they'll be experts in their own applications and their own ways of interacting with their content. Search interfaces will be designed by and for photographers and music lovers and literature scholars, and the results will reflect the different needs of their diverse domains.

Entity Sentiment Extraction Using Text Ranking

John O'Neil
Attivio, Inc.
275 Grove Street
Newton, MA USA
joneil@attivio.com

ABSTRACT

Entity extraction and sentiment classification are among the most common types of information derived from documents, but the problem of directly associating entities and sentiment has received less attention. We use TextRank on a graph linking entities and sentiment-laden words and phrases. We extract from the resulting eigenvector the final sentiment weights of the entities. We then explore the algorithm's performance and accuracy, compared to a baseline.

Categories and Subject Descriptors

H.3.3 [**Information Storage and Retrieval**]: Text Mining

General Terms

Algorithms, Experimentation

Keywords

Entity extraction, sentiment classification

1. OVERVIEW

Entity extraction and sentiment classification are both the focus of extensive research and of numerous applications. However, there's been less research into assigning sentiment to entities directly based on their context within documents. Most documents are neither uniformly positive or uniformly negative, nor are they usually about only one thing. Consider the following snippet (from [1]):

> *I already hated AT&T. It's my fixed telephony and internet provider (because it has something of a monopoly on such services). I go through periods where my internet becomes intermittent, which AT&T refuses to acknowledge... I love love love my iPhone. It's my mini-computer on the go. I use it for texting, social sharing, photography, editing, keeping track of my calendar, storing contacts, finding directions, listening to music and podcasts, watching videos, reading, and blogging. Sometimes, I even make a phone call.*

This document doesn't have a strong, consistent sentiment, but the entities *iPhone* and *AT&T* do. Clearly, we'd like to be able to distinguish the article's opinions about each entity, beyond the overall sentiment of the document or the mere presence of entities in it.

Before we extract entity sentiment, we need to be able to extract entities and to have a sentiment model that associates tokens (and optionally phrases) with a positive or negative sentiment.

There are many approaches to entity extraction. Almost any type of entity extraction can be used with the algorithm presented in this paper. For the experiments reported here, we combined the results of a dictionary-based entity extractor and a statistical entity extractor. For increased accuracy, entity mention tracking can be used, as well as pronoun resolution. When multiple references to the same entity are discovered, we combine their sentiment contexts.

For the algorithm presented here, the sentiment model must be able to map words (and optionally longer n-grams) to a sentiment score. Any approach that yields such a model, like [3], will be satisfactory. In particular, we used a standard supervised document classifier trained on documents labeled *positive* and *negative* to derive the sentiment weights.

To blend the sentiment scores in the neighborhood of entities, we use the *TextRank* algorithm described in [2]. Inspired by Page Rank and similar graph-based algorithms, it describes a general approach to any natural language task that can be reduced to a graph.

For the entity sentiment problem, we make the sentiment-bearing words and all the entities into graph vertices. When any sentiment-bearing word is with a configurable distance from a entity (or one of its mentions), an edge is added to the graph, with the sentiment weight being the edge weight. Then, we use a version of power iteration, which finds the eigenvector with the greatest eigenvalue. When power iteration has converged, we read the final sentiment weights off the entity vertices.

2. REFERENCES

[1] Cosette. Using my beloved iPhone in Australia. `http://stumbledownunder.com/2012/01/07/using-my-beloved-iphone-in-australia/`.

[2] R. Mihalcea and P. Tarau. Textrank: Bringing order into texts. In D. Lin and D. Wu, editors, *Proceedings of EMNLP 2004*, 2004.

[3] B. Pang, L. Lee, and S. Vaithyanathan. Thumbs up? Sentiment classification using machine learning techniques. In *Proceedings of EMNLP 2002*, pages 79–86, 2002.

SIGIR'12, August 12–16, 2012, Portland, Oregon, USA.
ACM 978-1-4503-1472-5/12/08.

A Hybrid Model for Ad-hoc Information Retrieval

Zheng Ye, Jimmy Xiangji Huang
Information Retrieval and Knowledge Management Research Lab
School of Information Technology
York University
Toronto, Canada
{yezheng, jhuang}@yorku.ca

Jun Miao
Information Retrieval and Knowledge Management Research Lab
Department of Computer Science & Engineering
York University
Toronto, Canada
jun@cse.yorku.ca

ABSTRACT

Many information retrieval (IR) techniques have been proposed to improve the performance, and some combinations of these techniques has been demonstrated to be effective. However, how to effectively combine them is largely unexplored. It is possible that a method reduces the positive influence of the other one even if both of them are effective separately. In this paper, we propose a new hybrid model which can simply and flexibly combine components of three different IR techniques under a uniform framework. Extensive experiments on the TREC standard collections indicate that our proposed model can outperform the best TREC systems consistently in the ad-hoc retrieval. It shows that the combination strategy in our proposed model is very effective. Meanwhile, this method is also re-useable for other researchers to test whether their new methods are additive to the current technologies.

Categories and Subject Descriptors

H.3.3 [**Information Search and Retrieval**]: Retrieval models, Relevance feedback

General Terms

Algorithms, Performance, Experimentation

Keywords

Hybrid Model, Rocchio's Relevance Feedback

1. INTRODUCTION

In the past thirty years, researchers make great progress in the Information Retrieval (IR) area. A plenty of new technologies, e.g., stemming, query expansion and smoothing methods, have been introduced and help to obtain better performance in retrieving relevant documents. Some attempts to combine these technologies show that the strategy of combination is very important because one technology can counteract the affects of others. However, how to make an effective combination is still largely unexplored, especially under a unified framework.

In this paper, we propose a hybrid model to incorporate three different retrieval techniques that have proven to be effective for the ad-hoc retrieval on the TREC collections.

SIGIR'12, August 12–16, 2012, Portland, Oregon, USA.
ACM 978-1-4503-1472-5/12/08.

We analyze the best TREC systems for ad-hoc retrieval, and extend the Rocchio's feedback method by incorporating three kinds of IR techniques, which are proximity, feedback document quality estimation and query performance prediction techniques, under the pseudo relevance feedback (PRF) framework to boost the overall performance. We mainly focus on how to refine the representation of the query under the PRF framework in order to avoid the drawbacks of traditional PRF methods. Experimental results on various TREC datasets show that our hybrid model consistently obtains better results over the best TREC systems. Because our proposed model is component-based, it is very flexible to import different techniques in the future. Meanwhile, the hybrid model can help researchers to test whether their methods are additive to improve the overall performance of ad-hoc retrieval which was mentioned in [1].

2. A HYBRID RETRIEVAL MODEL

Rocchio's algorithm [4] is a classic framework for implementing (pseudo) relevance feedback via improving the query representation. When the negative feedback documents are ignored, the traditional Rocchio's model is as follows:

$$Q_1 = \alpha * Q_0 + \beta * \sum_{r \in R} \frac{r}{|R|} \quad (1)$$

where Q_0 and Q_1 represent the original and first iteration query vectors, R is the set of (pseudo) relevance documents, and r is the expansion term weight vector.

Although the Rocchio's model has been introduced for many years, it is still effective in obtaining relevant documents. According to [7], "BM25 term weighting coupled with Rocchio feedback remains a strong baseline which is at least as competitive as any language modeling approach for many tasks". Meanwhile, it is very flexible to adapt additional components. However, the traditional Rocchio's model can still be reformed to be better. First, the query term proximity information which has proven to be useful is not considered. Second, Rocchio's algorithm views terms from different feedback documents equally. Intuitively, a candidate expansion term in a document with better quality is more likely to be relevant to the query topic. Third, the interpolation parameter α is always fixed across a group of queries. In fact, for a well expressed query, the candidate feedback documents are always more reliable for relevance feedback. In this paper, we use a regression model to predict this interpolation parameter. In order to alleviate influence of these problems, we extend Rocchio's algorithm which re-

Table 1: Direct comparison with the best MAP results in each TREC year. In the Hybrid (Fixed) method, proximity and feedback document quality are utilized. In the Hybrid (Regression) method, all the three techniques are adapted. A "*" indicates a statistically significant improvement when a component technique is added in our algorithm.

Method	TREC1	TREC2	TREC3	TREC6	TREC7	TREC8	TREC2004	TREC2005	TREC2006
BM25	0.2292	0.2058	0.2787	0.2397	0.1819	0.2471	0.2672	0.3403	0.2965
BM25+Prox	0.2461*	0.2111*	0.2929*	0.2507*	0.1936*	0.2582*	0.3148*	0.3661*	0.3459*
Hybrid-Fixed	0.2938*	0.2913*	0.3811*	0.2763*	0.2576*	0.2909*	0.3375*	0.4083*	0.3944*
Hybrid-Reg	0.3012	0.2971	0.3912*	0.2886*	0.2611	0.3103*	0.3431*	0.4193*	0.3921
BEST TREC	0.2062	0.2475	0.3231	0.2876	0.2614	0.3063	0.3052	0.4056	0.3737

fines the query representation as follows.

$$Q_1 = \alpha * (\beta * Q_0 + (1-\beta) * Q_p) + (1-\alpha) * \sum_{r \in R} \frac{r * q(d_r)}{|R|} \quad (2)$$

where β controls how much we rely on the query term proximity information [5], α controls how much we rely on the original query, Q_p is an n-gram of original query terms and $q(d_r)$ is the quality score of document d.

As we can see from Equation 2, our proposed algorithm is very flexible and can evaluate different techniques. In this paper, we adopt the co-occurrence interpretation of term proximity to compute Q_p, where the proximity among query terms is represented by the n-gram frequencies and BM25 is used as the weighting model [2].

Full dependencies of query terms are taken into account. For the document quality factor $q(d_r)$, we simple use the scores from the first-pass retrieval for approximation as in [6]. For the prediction to α, we use the same features as in [3] to train the regression model. The difference is that we do it within Rocchio's framework.

3. EXPERIMENTS AND ANALYSIS

We conduct experiments on three representative test collections: disk1&2, disk4&5, and GOV2, which are used in different TREC years. We present the results for each TREC year such that we can directly compare our results with the best TREC systems. Detailed information about the TREC datasets and the evaluation criteria, please refer to http://trec.nist.gov. For the preprocessing of the collections, we use the Porter Stemmer and a stopword list. In addition, we only use the *title* part of the topics to retrieve.

In our experiments, we first empirically evaluate different combinations of our implemented component techniques, then evaluate how these techniques perform when they are integrated in our hybrid model. We set the parameters to fixed values in a parsimonious way such that each component technique gets considerable improvements on most collections. In other words, there is still room for improvement if the parameters are tuned on a collection-by-collection basis. Particularly, for the basic retrieval model, we use the Okapi BM25 model, and set b in BM25 to 0.3. When only the query term proximity technique is added, denoted as "BM25+Prox", we set β to 0.3. In addition, when query expansion and document quality estimation techniques are added, denoted as "Hybrid-Fixed", we empirically set α, $|R|$ to 0.5 and 30. However, when the query performance prediction technique is used, denoted as "Hybrid-Reg", α is not fixed. But it is obtained from a regression model that is trained as in [3]. When evaluating our hybrid model for a particular TREC year, the queries in the remainder TREC years on the same collection are used as training data.

From Table 1, we can see that our hybrid model with different component techniques can significantly outperforms the basic retrieval model, which reconfirms the effectiveness of these techniques. In addition, when all these component techniques are used in our hybrid model, the retrieval performance can be further improved. It indicates that performance gains from these two component techniques can be added up in our proposed hybrid model. However, when we use a regression component to predict α, the performance gain is not very obvious compared with other components. We conjecture the main reason is as follows: when the feedback document set is more reliable for relevance feedback, the regression component is less useful.

When compared with the best TREC systems, our proposed model obviously outperforms the best TREC systems on most collections . It is of note that the results in our paper are obtained in a uniform setting across all collections while the best TREC results were from different participants independently. We believe the significant improvement is mainly from our successful integration of different IR techniques in the proposed model. In addition, according to Armstrong et al.'s survey, very few published results are better than the best TREC systems, mostly below medium systems. Our proposed model is promising, which provides a good avenue for future IR research, especially for evaluating the overall performance of a system (not a particular component of a system).

4. CONCLUSIONS

In this paper, we propose a hybrid model which can successfully integrate three effective techniques in a uniform model. Extensive experiments show that our approach obviously outperforms the best TREC systems in most cases. In the future, we will investigate more effective techniques in IR and incorporate them into our framework to conduct this research in details.

5. ACKNOWLEDGMENTS

This research is supported by the research grant from the Natural Sciences & Engineering Research Council (NSERC) of Canada and the Early Researcher Award/ Premier's Research Excellence Award, Zhejiang Provincial Natural Science Foundation, Q12F020016.

6. REFERENCES

[1] T. G. Armstrong, A. Moffat, W. Webber, and J. Zobel. Improvements that don't add up: ad-hoc retrieval results since 1998. In *CIKM*, pages 601–610, 2009.

[2] B. He, J. X. Huang, and X. Zhou. Modeling term proximity for probabilistic information retrieval models. *Inf. Sci.*, 181(14):3017–3031, 2011.

[3] Y. Lv and C. Zhai. Adaptive relevance feedback in information retrieval. In *CIKM*, pages 255–264, 2009.

[4] J. Rocchio. *Relevance feedback in information retrieval*, pages 313–323. Prentice-Hall Englewood Cliffs, 1971.

[5] C. J. van Rijsbergen. A theoretical basis for the use of co-occurence data in information retrieval. *Journal of Documentation*, 1977.

[6] Z. Ye, B. He, X. Huang, and H. Lin. Revisiting rocchio's relevance feedback algorithm for probabilistic models. In *AAIRS*, pages 151–161, 2010.

[7] C. Zhai. Statistical language models for information retrieval a critical review. *Found. Trends Inf. Retr.*, 2:137–213, 2008.

Exploiting Paths for Entity Search in RDF Graphs

Minsuk Kahng and Sang-goo Lee
Department of Computer Science and Engineering
Seoul National University
Seoul, South Korea
{minsuk, sglee}@europa.snu.ac.kr

ABSTRACT

The field of entity search using Semantic Web (RDF) data has gained more interest recently. In this paper, we propose a probabilistic entity retrieval model for RDF graphs using paths in the graph. Unlike previous work which assumes that all descriptions of an entity are directly linked to the entity node, we assume that an entity can be described with any node that can be reached from the entity node by following paths in the RDF graph. Our retrieval model simulates the generation process of query terms from an entity node by traversing the graph. We evaluate our approach using a standard evaluation framework for entity search.

Categories and Subject Descriptors: H.3.3 [Information Search and Retrieval]: Retrieval models

General Terms: Algorithms, Experimentation

Keywords: Entity Search, RDF Graphs, Object Retrieval, Semantic Search, Structured Data, Semantic Web

1. INTRODUCTION

As the amount of Semantic Web (RDF) data published in the form of Linked Data[1] has been increasing recently, many researchers have been exploiting the RDF data for retrieval tasks [1]. We address the problem of retrieving entities relevant to a keyword query by using only RDF data [8]. This area has gained popularity recently, leading to the consideration of several retrieval models [2, 6, 4, 3].

Unfortunately, existing retrieval models do not fully reflect the characteristics of RDF data. RDF triples can be represented by a graph[2], thus the nodes in the RDF graph are somewhat related to each other even if they are not directly linked through a single triple (distance=1). For example, given a movie entity node `<../movie/35>`, we can find the node with the name of its director by following two triples (`<../movie/35>`, `<../director>`, `<../person/928>`) and (`<../person/928>`, `<../name>`, `"James Cameron"`) as depicted in Table 1 and Figure 1. However, most existing models do not capture this kind of case because they assume that the descriptions of an entity exist only at the nodes that are directly linked to the entity node. Therefore, the entity `<../movie/35>` cannot be described by the name of its director. So, if a user issues a query 'movie james cameron' to find movies that are directed by James Cameron, they fail to retrieve relevant movies. This issue can be partially tackled by tokenizing URIs of resources itself [3, 2, 4]. However, it becomes problematic when URIs are made up of meaningless strings like `<../928>`, rather than `<../James_Cameron>`.

In this paper, we propose a probabilistic entity retrieval model that can capture indirect relationships between nodes in the RDF graph. We design the model based on the assumption that the descriptions of an entity exist at any literal node that can be reached from the resource (entity) node by following the paths in the graph.

Table 1: Examples of RDF triples

Subject	Predicate	Object
<..//a.b/movie/35>	<../title>	"Avatar"
<..//a.b/movie/35>	<../director>	<..//a.b/person/928>
<..//a.b/person/928>	<../name>	"James Cameron"
<..//a.b/movie/19>	<../director>	<..//a.b/person/928>

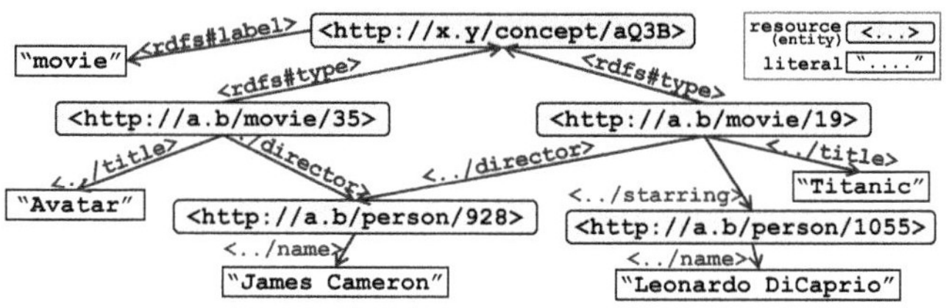

Figure 1: Graph representation of RDF data

2. PROBLEM DEFINITION

The RDF data consists of a set of *triples*, where each *triple* has three components: (`subject`, `predicate`, `object`). Both the *subject* and *predicate* are *resources*, and the *object* is either a *resource* or a *literal*. A *resource* represents any entity or concept (e.g. a movie), and is identified by URI (e.g. `<../movie/35>`). A *literal* contains textual information (e.g. `"Avatar"`). Our problem is to rank resources E according to their probability of being relevant given a keyword query Q, denoted by $P(E|Q)$.

3. RETRIEVAL MODEL

We propose a novel RDF resource retrieval model *PathLM* based on the language modeling. It simulates the generation of query Q by following paths from a resource node E to several related literal nodes L_j. Using Bayes' Rule, we have:

$$P(E|Q) \overset{rank}{=} P(Q|E)P(E), \quad (1)$$

[1]`http://www.w3.org/standards/semanticweb/data`
[2]A triple can be thought of as a directed edge from the subject node to object node in the RDF graph.

SIGIR'12, August 12–16, 2012, Portland, Oregon, USA.
ACM 978-1-4503-1472-5/12/08.

where $P(Q|E)$ is query likelihood, $P(E)$ is resource prior. Assuming independence between query terms, we have:

$$P(Q|E) = \prod_{i=1}^{|Q|} P(q_i|E). \tag{2}$$

A resource can generate terms by passing through literal nodes since only literal nodes contain textual information used to match the query terms. We have:

$$P(q_i|E) = \sum_{j=1}^{m} P(q_i|L_j)P(L_j|E), \tag{3}$$

where L_j is a j-th literal node that can be reached from the resource node E. There are m literal nodes related to E, and the sum of $P(L_j|E)$ is 1 ($\sum_{j=1}^{m} P(L_j|E) = 1$).

Finally, we obtain:

$$P(E|Q) = P(E) \prod_{i=1}^{|Q|} \sum_{j=1}^{m} P(L_j|E)P(q_i|L_j). \tag{4}$$

The details of three probability terms in Eq. 4 are as follows.

$P(E)$: *Resource Prior.*

$P(E)$ is the prior probability of a resource. The value can be assumed to be uniform or determined using the number of literal nodes related to the resource node.

$P(L|E)$: *Select Paths to Literals given Resource.*

$P(L_j|E)$ is the probability of selecting a path to literal L_j given a resource E. It indicates the importance of the path from the resource node E to the literal node L_j in the RDF graph. The value can be either assigned manually based on the path (e.g. $E \xrightarrow{\text{<director>}} \circ \xrightarrow{\text{<name>}} L_j$), or learned.

$P(q|L)$: *Query Likelihood given Literal.*

We use the language modeling approach to simulate the generation of query terms given a literal node. $P(q_i|L_j)$ is estimated by dividing the term frequency of q_i in the literal L_j by the length of L_j. It is smoothed using a Dirichlet prior μ with the collection language model. We have:

$$P(q_i|L_j) = \frac{tf(q_i, L_j) + \mu \frac{c_{q_i}}{|C|}}{|L_j| + \mu}. \tag{5}$$

4. EVALUATION

We evaluate our approach using the evaluation framework used in the *Semantic Search Challenge 2010*[3]. The dataset is the *Billion Triple Challenge 2009* collection. After deduplication, there are about 886 million triples, 175 million resources, and 296 million literals. We index literals using *Indri* with the Krovetz stemmer and no stopwords. The query set has 92 queries extracted from the query logs of search engines. The relevance judgments are made with three-point scale. We add judgments if they are not available. For each query, the model returns top-100 resources, and is evaluated with MAP, P@10, and NDCG. We conduct a series of two-tailed paired t-tests of 99% confidence.

We compare our *path*-based approach to three baseline approaches: 1) *Plain text*, 2) *Attribute with uniform weights*, and 3) *Attribute with different weights*. First, for the *Plain text* approach, a pseudo-document is built for each resource by concatenating literals that are directly linked to the resource node [4, 6]. Two standard retrieval models, *BM25* and *Language Model with Dirichlet smoothing (LM)*, are used. The parameters in the models, such as b and μ, are tuned empirically. Next, the *attribute*-based models are designed by defining attributes as literal nodes whose distances from the resource node are 1. We employ *BM25F* [2, 3] and *Mixture of Field LM (MFLM)* [7, 6, 4]. We note that our *PathLM* can be thought of as a type of the *MFLM*. The weights of attributes are assigned uniformly at first, then we assign them differently by defining some important predicates manually [2]. Lastly, for our *path*-based approach, we consider several selected paths from the resource node to literal nodes where distances between them are 1 or 2.

[3] `http://km.aifb.kit.edu/ws/semsearch10/`

Table 2: Retrieval performance. $*$ indicates significant difference between the BM25- and LM-based models within the same approach. †, ‡ indicate significance over the corresponding models of *Plain* and *Attr(uni)*, respectively. ▽ indicates significantly worse results compared to *PathLM*.

Approach	Ret.Model	MAP	P@10	NDCG
Plain text	BM25	0.2366 ▽	0.4293 ▽	0.4288 ▽
	LM	0.2426 ▽	0.4272 ▽	0.4438 ▽
Attr. (uniform w)	BM25F	0.2014 ▽	0.4380	0.3886 ▽
	MFLM	0.2711 $*$†▽	0.4783	0.4765 $*$†▽
Attr. (different w)	BM25f	0.2523 ‡▽	0.4826 †‡	0.4484 ‡▽
	MFLM	0.2889 $*$†‡▽	0.5076 †	0.4913 $*$†‡▽
Path	**PathLM**	0.3268 †‡	0.5033 †	0.5245 †‡

Table 2 shows experimental results. The LM-based models generally perform better than the BM25-based ones. We also observe that the *MFLM* outperforms the original *LM*. When more weights are given to some important attributes, both *BM25F* and *MFLM* perform better. The proposed path-based approach outperforms all baselines in terms of MAP and NDCG ($p < 0.001$). Moreover, it outperforms all previous work that used the same collection [6, 2, 3]. A possible explanation is that it can retrieve more relevant resources by exploiting some relations like `sameAs` [3].

As future work, we plan to conduct more detailed evaluation based on the proposed model, such as 1) determining resource prior in various ways, 2) learning which kinds of paths have greater effect on performance, and 3) applying different smoothing methods. After further research, we expect to better understand the properties of our path-based retrieval model which enables us to incorporate indirect relationships in the RDF graph [5].

Acknowledgments: This work was supported by the National Research Foundation of Korea(NRF) grant funded by the Korea government(MEST) (No. 20110030812).

5. REFERENCES

[1] K. Balog, P. Serdyukov, and A. P. de Vries. Overview of the trec 2010 entity track. In *TREC*, 2010.

[2] R. Blanco, P. Mika, and S. Vigna. Effective and efficient entity search in rdf data. In *ISWC*, 2011.

[3] S. Campinas, R. Delbru, N. Rakhmawati, D. Ceccarelli, and G. Tummarello. Sindice bm25mf at semsearch 2011. In *SemSearch*, 2011.

[4] J. Dalton and S. Huston. Semantic entity retrieval using web queries over structured rdf data. In *SemSearch*, 2010.

[5] M. Kahng, S. Lee, and S.-g. Lee. Ranking objects by following paths in entity-relationship graphs. In *PIKM (at CIKM)*, 2011.

[6] R. Neumayer, K. Balog, and K. Nørvåg. On the modeling of entities for ad-hoc entity search in the web of data. In *ECIR*, 2012.

[7] P. Ogilvie and J. Callan. Combining document representations for known-item search. In *SIGIR*, 2003.

[8] J. Pound, P. Mika, and H. Zaragoza. Ad-hoc object retrieval in the web of data. In *WWW*, 2010.

A Study of Term Weighting Schemes Using Class Information for Text Classification

Youngjoong Ko
Dept. of Computer Engineering, Dong-A Univ., 840, Hadan 2-dong, Saha-gu, Busan, 604-714, Korea
yjko@dau.ac.kr

Categories and Subject Descriptors: I.5.4 [Pattern Recognition]: Applications – Text processing

General Terms: Experimentation, Performance

Keywords: Text Classification, IDF, Term Weighting

1. INTRODUCTION

Text classification is the task of automatically assigning unlabeled documents into predefined categories. In text classification, text representation transforms the content of textural documents into a compact format so that the documents can be recognized and classified by a classifier. In the vector space model, a document is represented as a vector in the term spaces, $d = (w_1,\ldots,w_{|V|})$, where $|V|$ is the size of vocabulary. The value of w_i between [0,1] represents how much the term w_i contributes to the semantics of the document *d*. Text classification has borrowed the traditional term weighting schemes from information retrieval field, such as *tf*, *tf.idf* [1] and its variants.

This research starts with a question, "Can we make a better term weighting scheme than ones of information retrieval for text classification?" We believe that text classification should utilize class information better than information retrieval because supervised learning based text classification has labeled training data. However, inverse document frequency, *idf*, is a measure of general importance of a term; there is no use of class information. Therefore, this paper focuses on how we can improve text classification by effectively applying class information to a term weighting scheme.

Recently, researchers have attempted to use this prior information, class information, for term weighting. There are two representative term weighting schemes: *rf (relevance frequency)* [2] and *Delta tf.idf* [3,4]. The former was proposed to use the ratio of term occurrences of the positive class and the negative class for calculating term weights. However, they did not discuss how they make the representation of test documents. Since a test document does not have any prior class information, it is hard to represent the test document using class information. The latter provided a solution to use class information for sentiment classification by localizing the estimation of *idf* to the documents of one or the other class and subtracting the two values. However, this approach is limited to classification problems with only two classes just like sentiment classification.

This paper proposes new term weighting schemes for multi-class text classification, which include term weighting methods for test documents. Then it was compared to the previous studies [2,3,4] and *tf.idf*. As a result, the proposed schemes achieved the best performance on all of data sets and classifiers.

2. NEW TERM WEIGHTING SCHEMES

Unlike the previous work, the *idf* part of new term weighting schemes is replaced by using the probability estimations on a relevant class (positive class) and other classes (negative classes), and the log-odds ratio of them as follows:

$$tw_i = (\log(tf_i)+1)\cdot\log\left(\frac{P(w_i \mid c_j)}{P(w_i \mid \bar{c}_j)}+\alpha\right) \tag{1}$$

where tf_i is the number of times term w_i occurs in a document, *d*, c_j is a class of the document, *d*, $\bar{c}_j$ is all of other classes of c_j, and α is a constant value of the base of this logarithmic operation because it makes the logarithmic value a positive value.

This new *idf* part is called *Term Relevance Ratio* (*TRR*). *TRR* can be estimated by the following two different ways.

$$P(w_i \mid c_j) = \frac{\sum_{k=1}^{|T_{c_j}|} tf_{ik}}{\sum_{l=1}^{|V|}\sum_{k=1}^{|T_{c_j}|} tf_{lk}},\quad P(w_i \mid \bar{c}_j) = \frac{\sum_{k=1}^{|T_{\bar{c}_j}|} tf_{ik}}{\sum_{l=1}^{|V|}\sum_{k=1}^{|T_{\bar{c}_j}|} tf_{lk}} \tag{2}$$

where V denotes the vocabulary set of total training data and T_{c_j} is the document set of positive class, c_j, and $T_{\bar{c}_j}$ is the document set of negative classes, $\bar{c}_j$. To resolve zero divisor problem, we assign the smallest probability value, which can be estimated in training data set, to the divisors of both equations.

This is maximum likelihood estimation (MLE) and this estimation misses term distribution in a document. Thus we reform these equations as follows:

$$P(w_i \mid c_j) = \sum_{k=1}^{|T_{c_j}|} P(w_i \mid d_k)\cdot P(d_k \mid c_j),\quad P(w_i \mid \bar{c}_j) = \sum_{k=1}^{|T_{\bar{c}_j}|} P(w_i \mid d_k)\cdot P(d_k \mid \bar{c}_j) \tag{3}$$

where $P(w_i \mid d_k)$ is estimated by MLE like equation (2) and $P(d_k \mid c_j)$ is estimated as a uniform distribution.

The next issue is how to represent test documents. We need to develop a document representation method because test documents do not have any class information and our term weighting schemes require it. A test document can be first represented as $|C|$ different vectors by using estimated distribution of each class, c_j, and then it has to be represented as one vector that well describes the document in our proposed vector space; $|C|$ is the number of classes. We consider the following three solutions for this problem and you can see experimental evidences in the next section.

1. Word Max (*W-Max*): the term weight of each word is chosen by the maximum value among |C| estimated term weights.
2. Document Max (*D-Max*): the sum of all term weights in each vector is first calculated and then one vector with the maximum sum value is selected by a representative vector.
3. Documents Two Max (*D-TMax*): the sum of all term weights in each vector is calculated and then two vectors with the highest and second highest sum values are selected. Then a vector is created by choosing the term weight with the higher score between two term weights of selected vectors for each term.

3. EXPERIMENTS

Two widely-used data sets were used as the benchmark data sets: Reuters and 20 Newsgroups data sets, and two promising learning algorithms, which have shown better performance than other algorithms, were chosen in the experiments: *k*NN and SVM. The one-against-the-rest method was used for setting up positive examples and negative examples for each class.

The *Reuters 21578* data set (*Reuters*) was split as training and test data according to the standard ModApte split and the top 10 largest categories were used in the experiments. The 20 *Newsgroups* data set (*NG*) is a collection of approximate 20,000 newsgroup data evenly divided among 20 discussion groups. For fair evaluation, we used five-fold cross validation.

These data sets have quite different characteristics. *Reuters* has a skewed class distribution and many documents have two or more class labels. On the other hand, *NG* has uniform class distribution and its documents have only one class label. Thus, two different measures were used to evaluate various term weighting schemes on two classifiers for our experiments. For *Reuters*, we used the micro-averaging Break Even Point (BEP) measure which is a standard information retrieval measure for binary classification and, for *NG*, the performances are reported by the micro-averaging F1 measure.

3.1 Experimental Results

3.1.1 Comparison of the proposed schemes and idf

First of all, the proposed term weighting schemes (*TRR*) are compared with the traditional *idf* scheme. All of these schemes did not use any *tf* information. As a result, the proposed schemes achieved better performances than the *idf* scheme. We here need to discuss the results of *TRR* because *TRR* has two different estimation methods (*Cat-MLE* by equation (2) and *Doc-MLE* by equation (3)) and they showed different performance aspects in each data set; *Cat-MLE* obtained the best performances in *Reuters* while *Doc-MLE* the best performances in *NG*. It can be caused by the skewed distribution of the document length in *Reuters*; many documents in *Reuters* consist of small number of sentences such as just two or three. It could make a bad probability estimation in the *Doc-MLE* scheme. We can also observe the same results in the following experiments; *Cat-MLE* is better in *Reuters* while *Doc-MLE* in *NG*.

Table 1. Comparison of *TRR (Cat-MLE & Doc-MLE) and idf*

		idf	*Cat-MLE*	*Doc-MLE*
Reuters	*k*NN	92.86	***94.22***	93.93
	SVM	94.11	***94.69***	94.29
NG	*k*NN	86.39	86.93	***87.20***
	SVM	87.61	87.39	***87.77***

3.1.2 Term weighting schemes for test data

Table 2 shows the performances of three different term weighting methods for test documents: *W-Max*, *D-Max* and *D-TMax*. *D-TMax* achieved the best performance in *Reuters* while *D-Max* the best performance in *NG*. We think it is very natural results because many documents in Reuters have two or more labels. For example, if a document with two labels is represented by using only one class distribution between two labels, classifiers could has some difficulty to classify it in the other class.

Table 2. Comparison of term weighting schemes for test data

			W-Max	*D-Max*	*D-TMax*
Reuters	*k*NN	*Cat-MLE*	94.33	94.51	***94.90***
		Doc-MLE	94.54	93.97	**94.72**
	SVM	*Cat-MLE*	94.83	94.83	***95.30***
		Doc-MLE	94.72	94.65	**95.12**
NG	*k*NN	*Cat-MLE*	84.19	**87.15**	86.03
		Doc-MLE	84.30	***87.75***	86.36
	SVM	*Cat-MLE*	86.60	**87.93**	87.54
		Doc-MLE	86.24	***88.42***	87.75

3.1.3 Comparison of the proposed scheme and other term weighting schemes

Table 3 shows the final experimental results and comparison of the proposed scheme and other schemes. The proposed scheme achieved better performance than other schemes. Note that *tf.idf* used raw term frequency while *log tf.idf* used *log(tf)+1* like equation (1). *Delta and rf* also used the proposed document representation methods for test data and their best performances were chosen and shown in Table 3.

Table 3. Final experiment results

		tf.idf	*log tf.idf*	*rf*	*Delta*	*Proposed*
Reuters	*k*NN	92.46	93.29	92.07	91.96	***94.90***
	SVM	94.87	94.86	94.40	93.00	***95.30***
NG	*k*NN	81.20	85.17	83.60	86.01	***87.75***
	SVM	87.07	87.74	87.46	86.64	***88.43***

4. CONCLUSIONS AND FUTURE WORK

In this work, we utilized class information for term weighting for text classification. As a result, the proposed schemes performed consistently well on the two benchmark data sets and *k*NN and SVM classifiers.

In the future, we would like to explore these schemes to apply and evaluate it on different classifiers and different data sets.

5. REFERENCES

[1] G. Salton and C. Buckley. Term-weighting approaches in automatic text retrieval. *Inf. Process. Manage.* 24(5):513-523.

[2] M. Kan, C.-L. Tan and H.-B. Low. Proposing a new term weighting scheme for text categorization. In *AAAI 2006*, pp. 763-768.

[3] J. Martineau and T. Finin. Delta TFIDF: an improved feature space for sentiment analysis. In *AAAI 2009*.

[4] G. Paltoglou and M. Thelwall. A study of information retrieval weighting schemes for sentiment analysis. In *ACL 2010*, pp. 1386-1395.

A Topic Model of Clinical Reports

Corey Arnold, PhD and William Speier, MS
Medical Imaging Informatics Group, UCLA
924 Westwood Blvd Ste 420
Los Angeles, CA 90024
cwarnold@ucla.edu, speier@mii.ucla.edu

ABSTRACT

Clinical narrative in the medical record provides perhaps the most detailed account of a patient's history. However, this information is documented in free-text, which makes it challenging to analyze. Efforts to index unstructured clinical narrative often focus on identifying predefined concepts from clinical terminologies. Less studied is the problem of analyzing the text as a whole to create temporal indices that capture relationships between learned clinical events. Topic models provide a method for analyzing large corpora of text to discover semantically related clusters of words. This work presents a topic model tailored to the clinical reporting environment that allows for individual patient timelines. Results show the model is able to identify patterns of clinical events in a cohort of brain cancer patients.

Categories and Subject Descriptors

H.3.3 [**Information Search and Retrieval**]: Information filtering.

General Terms

Algorithms.

Keywords

Topic model, clinical reports, brain cancer.

1. INTRODUCTION

Due to the complexity of language, the variability in author reporting styles, and differences in clinical practice, clinical narrative can be challenging to analyze from a computer's perspective. Topic models, such as latent Dirichlet allocation (LDA), provide a method for indexing large unstructured corpora with inferred semantics [1]. Extensions to the LDA model have been proposed that include modeling time [2], finding correlations between topics [3], learning image-word annotations [4], performing automatic translation [5], and learning topic hierarchies [6]. Additionally, previous work has demonstrated the application of LDA in the clinical domain for case-based reasoning [7]. However, to date there is no model designed specifically for clinical reporting, where each patient has a collection of documents that details the progression of disease. We propose a topic model that captures temporal topic patterns in an individual patient's medical record, while being sensitive to the entire patient population.

2. MODEL DESIGN

Similar to [2], we present a model that links topics to time within a corpus by observing a timestamp for each document and using a beta distribution to model a topic's expression in the collection over time. However, we modify the model for application in the

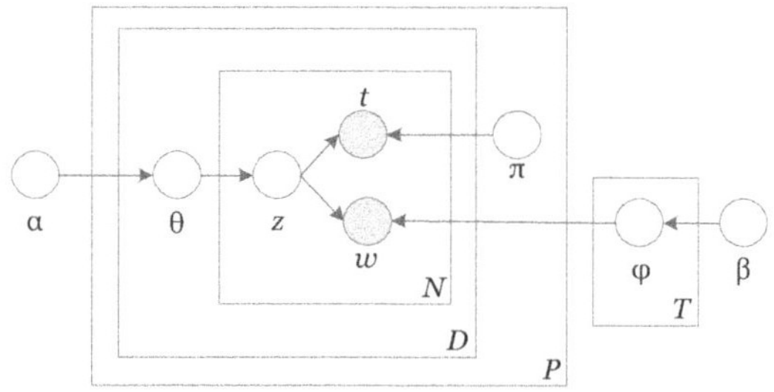

Figure 1: A topic model of clinical reports.

clinical world, where each patient has his or her own timeline that displays only a subset of all possible topics. We introduce a patient plate P to account for variations in topic expression over time between patients. Figure 1 illustrates this extension, denoted by the outermost box, which contains the time modeling beta distributions, π. As denoted by the topic plate T, which falls outside of the patient plate, topics are learned from the entire collection of patient documents. This design fits with our expectation that for a cohort of patients there is a superset of topics, with each patient expressing a subset of topics specific to their individual disease progression. Furthermore, we expect temporal relationships between subsets of topics to generalize across patients (e.g., a patient must first undergo a surgical resection of a tumor before a radiologist notes the resection cavity in a subsequent MRI study). We define the following generative process for the model:

1. For each topic draw $\varphi_t \sim \text{Dirichlet}(\beta)$
2. For each patient p
   a. For each document d from patient p draw $\theta_{pd} \sim \text{Dirichlet}(\alpha)$
   b. For each word i in document pd
      i. Draw a topic $z_{pdi} \sim \mathit{Multinomial}(\theta_{pd})$
      ii. Draw a word $w_{pdi} \sim \text{Multinomial}(\varphi_{z_{pdi}})$
      iii. Draw a timestamp $t_{pdi} \sim \text{Beta}(\pi_{z_{pdi}})$

We fit the model parameters using a Gibbs sampling procedure that calculates the conditional probability of a topic as

$$P(z_{pdi} = j \mid \mathbf{w}, \mathbf{t}, \mathbf{z}_{\neg pdi}, \alpha, \beta, \pi_p) \propto$$
$$\frac{n_{\neg i,j}^{(w_i)} + \beta - 1}{n_{\neg i,j}^{(\bullet)} + W\beta - 1} \frac{n_{\neg i,j}^{(pd_i)} + \alpha - 1}{n_{\neg i,\bullet}^{(pd_i)} + T\alpha - 1} \frac{(1 - t_{pdi})^{\pi_{z_{pdi}1} - 1} t_{pdi}^{\pi_{z_{pdi}2} - 1}}{B(\pi_{z_{pdi}1}, \pi_{z_{pdi}2})}$$

where $n_{\neg i}^{(\bullet)}$ is a count that does not include the assignment for the current word, z_{pdi}, and $B(\ )$ is the beta function. The parameters for a patient's topic beta distributions (π_1 and π_2) are updated after each Gibbs sample using the method of moments.

SIGIR'12, August 12–16, 2012, Portland, Oregon, USA.
ACM 978-1-4503-1472-5/12/08.

Table 1: Example topics learned by the model.

Topic	Label
left brain mass tumor temporal lobe mri contrast cm frontal	"imaging diagnosis"
tumor resection craniotomy head area left flap intraoperative incision scalp	"surgical resection"
radiation treatment therapy cgy total dose physician site oncology outpatient	"radiation treatment"
brain enhancement axial mri contrast cavity resection signal prior scan	"post treatment imaging surveillance"

3. RESULTS

We investigated the use of the proposed topic model in a population of patients with glioblastoma multiforme (GBM), an aggressive brain cancer. For each patient we used any report that conveyed clinical information in natural language (e.g., discharge summaries, radiology reports, pathology reports, etc.). Patients were required to have a minimum of five reports to be included in the model. Reports were preprocessed to remove stop words, rare and common words, and a set of medical stop words, such as "Dr.", "report", "dictated", and "ID". In a general context these medical stop words may prove useful, but limited to the domain of clinical reporting they offer little semantic meaning. The resulting corpus contained 303 patients, 13,028 reports, 2,412,385 words, and 1,374 unique words. Each patient's document collection was normalized to the timespan (0,1) and 100 topics were fit in 1000 iterations. As in [2], we used symmetric Dirichlet priors of $\alpha = 50/T$ and $\beta = 0.1$.

The resulting topics and temporal patterns were reviewed by a neuroradiologist and were found to correlate with valid sequences of clinical events. For example, we observed that the topic describing radiation treatment is generally preceded by the topic describing the surgical resection of a tumor. Table 1 presents several topics learned by the model and Figure 2 shows the topic timeline of a patient from the collection. As expected, because topics are learned across all patients, we found that generally patients exhibit only a subset of all possible topics. For example, some patients have tumors considered inoperable and therefore do not express a surgical resection topic.

4. DISCUSSION

Patients with large numbers of documents can bias the distribution of words in a topic. With a large enough collection of patients these biases may even out, but it is likely that the differences in numbers of documents per patient are systematic (e.g., patients with newly discovered late stage tumors may die quickly and therefore have few documents). This may be corrected by estimating topics through sampling word topic counts from patients as a proportion of their number of documents.

We observed that while general temporal trends were found, there were cases of topic expression that conflicted with actual patient care. For example, we identified patients who began physical therapy before receiving any treatment for a tumor. This discrepancy is due to the fact that although relative temporal topic relationships hold across patients, they are expressed at different points within each patient's timeline. Additionally, due to the

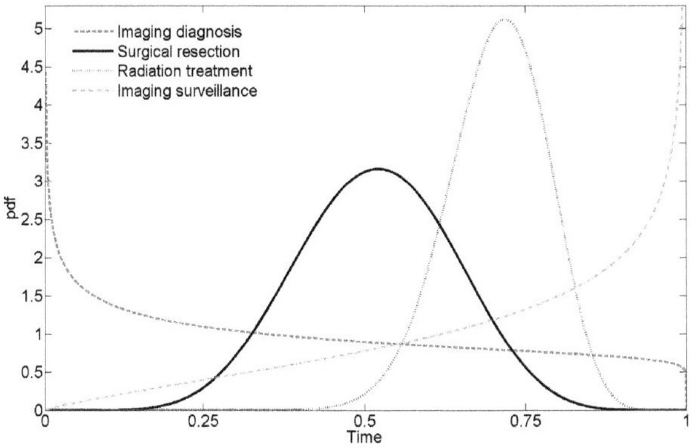

Figure 2: Beta probability density functions (pdf) for four topics in a patient with 48 documents spanning three years.

nature of the clinical corpus, where similar language is used across reports, this problem is compounded as there are a small number of unique words relative to the total number of words.

5. CONCLUSION

The proposed model was able to learn temporal trends between topics in patient records. These topics may be useful for identifying patients based on patterns of temporal-topic expression for predictive purposes or for cohort finding. Topics may also be used for case-based reasoning by comparing topic-time distributions across patients. A metric, such as Kullback-Liebler divergence, may be used for this task. Future work includes pursuing these applications and defining model configurations that allow for more flexible individual topic expression.

6. ACKNOWLEDGEMENTS

This work was supported by R01-LM009961 and T15-LM07536.

7. REFERENCES

[1] Blei, D., Ng, A. and Jordan, M. Latent Dirichlet allocation. *J. of Mach. Learn. Res.* 3 (Jan. 2003), 993-1022.

[2] Wang, X. and McCallum, A. Topics over time: a non-Markov continuous-time model of topical trends. In *Proceedings of the SIGKDD Conference on Knowledge Discovery and Data Mining* (Philadelphia, PA, Aug. 20-23, 2006). SIGKDD '06. ACM New York, NY, 424-433.

[3] Blei, D. and Lafferty, J. A correlated topic model of science. *Ann. Appl. Stat.* 1,1 (Jun. 2007), 17-35.

[4] Blei, D. and Jordan, M. Modeling annotated data. In *Proceedings of the SIGIR Conference on Research and Development in Information Retrieval* (Toronto, Canada, Jul. 28-Aug. 1, 2003). SIGIR '03. ACM New York, NY, 127-134.

[5] Mimno, D., Wallach, H. M., Naradowsky, J., Smith, D. A. and McCallum, A. Polylingual topic models. In *Proceedings of the 14th Conference on Empirical Methods in Natural Language Processing* (Singapore, 2009).

[6] Teh, Y. W., Jordan, M. I., Beal, M. J. and Blei, D. M. Hierarchical dirichlet processes. *J. A. Stat. Assoc.* 101,476 (Dec. 2006), 1566-1581.

[7] Arnold C., El-Saden, S., Bui A. and Taira, R. Clinical case-based retrieval using latent topic analysis. In *Proceedings of the American Medical Informatics Association Annual Symposium* (Nov. 13-17, 2010), AMIA '10, 26-30.

Active Query Selection for Learning Rankers

Mustafa Bilgic
Illinois Institute of Technology, Chicago, IL
mbilgic@iit.edu

Paul N. Bennett
Microsoft Research, Redmond, WA
pauben@microsoft.com

ABSTRACT

Methods that reduce the amount of labeled data needed for training have focused more on selecting which documents to label than on which queries should be labeled. One exception to this [4] uses expected loss optimization (ELO) to estimate which queries should be selected but is limited to rankers that predict absolute graded relevance. In this work, we demonstrate how to easily adapt ELO to work with any ranker and show that estimating expected loss in DCG is more robust than NDCG even when the final performance measure is NDCG.

Categories and Subject Descriptors

H.3.3 [**Information Search and Retrieval**]: Information Search and Retrieval—*active learning*

Keywords

Active learning, query selection

1. INTRODUCTION

Research in information retrieval evaluation has examined how to construct minimal test collections [2], and the balance between the number of queries judged and the depth of judging [3]. With respect to training rankers, most work has focused on document selection [1] or balancing number of queries with depth of documents judged using random query selection [5]. In this paper, we focus on selecting *queries* in order to most rapidly increase ranker retrieval performance.

In particular, we focus on the application of expected loss optimization (ELO) to query selection. Long *et al.* [4] used ELO to select queries for training but relied on having a ranker that estimated absolute graded relevance. We generalize this to work with any ranker – many of which induce a ranking but not absolute labels. To generalize to any ranker, we introduce a calibration phase over validation data.

In addition, although in theory ELO can be used with any performance measure for active learning, we show using DCG loss (as done in [4]) leads to better performance whether DCG or NDCG is used as the final evaluation of ranker performance. We provide evidence this is because ELO using DCG loss tends toward queries that have both more relevant examples *and* many degrees of relevance.

2. APPROACH

ELO suggests that, given a set of candidate queries $\mathcal{C}$, one pick the query $q \in \mathcal{C}$ for labeling where the expected loss is the greatest. Mathematically, we have:

$$\max_{q \in \mathcal{C}} \mathrm{E}_{P(Y \mid X_q, \mathcal{D})} \left[\max_{\pi} \mathrm{M}(\pi(X_q), y) - \mathrm{M}(\mathrm{R}(X_q), y) \right] \quad (1)$$

where $\mathcal{D}$ is the given training data, and $P(Y \mid X_q, \mathcal{D})$ is a distribution over graded relevance labels Y for the documents, X_q, to be ranked for the query q. $\mathrm{M}(r, y)$ is a retrieval performance measure such as DCG that can evaluate the quality of a ranking, r, for a set of documents given a particular labeling of the documents, y. $\pi(X_q)$ is simply a permutation of the documents and $\mathrm{R}(X_q)$ denotes the current ranking of the documents. For most retrieval performance measures, the inner max on the left-hand side of the difference is easily found by sorting from highest relevance to the lowest.

In order to estimate the label distribution $P(Y \mid X_q, \mathcal{D})$ Long *et al.* [4] relied on training an ensemble of models to predict absolute graded relevance. We generalize ELO to work with any ranker by mapping the current ranking model to a distribution over graded labels. To do so, we introduce a calibration phase where a classification model is trained over the labels of the top k documents according to the ranker in the validation data.[1] During active learning, the classification model is used to estimate the $P(Y \mid x_q, \mathcal{D})$ for each document $x_q \in X_q$. The quantity in Eq. 1 is then estimated through sampling of the labels from this distribution.

3. EXPERIMENTS

Like most active learning evaluation settings, we start with some labeled data $\mathcal{D}$ that is randomly chosen, train the models on $\mathcal{D}$, pick a number of queries to be labeled from the candidate set $\mathcal{C}$, add those to $\mathcal{D}$, and repeat this process for a number of iterations. The performance of the active learning strategy in augmenting $\mathcal{D}$ is judged at each iteration by evaluating the current induced rankers on held-out test data. We perform 20 iterations of labeling and based on the findings reported in [5] we label 15 documents per query (or the maximum available). We repeat this process five times, each time starting with a different set of labeled data and report averages. We report both DCG@10 and NDCG@10 (one can use DCG for selection but NDCG for evaluation and so forth).

We use the publicly available Yahoo! LETOR challenge dataset that has 3 splits: we treat the train split as the candidate data $\mathcal{C}$, utilize the validation split for tuning the rankers' parameters and training the calibration models, and use the test split for evaluation. We experiment with two rankers: one that does not produce absolute graded relevance (SVMRank) and one that does (Additive Regression (AR)). SVMRank labels 750 query-document pairs per iteration where AR labels only 150. The difference is due to AR having a steeper learning curve.

We examine four query/document selection methods: (1) select queries and documents randomly (rndQ-rndD); (2) se-

[1] We use the same validation data that is used for model parameter search – this ensures our method does not require any additional labeled data.

SIGIR'12, August 12–16, 2012, Portland, Oregon, USA.
ACM 978-1-4503-1472-5/12/08.

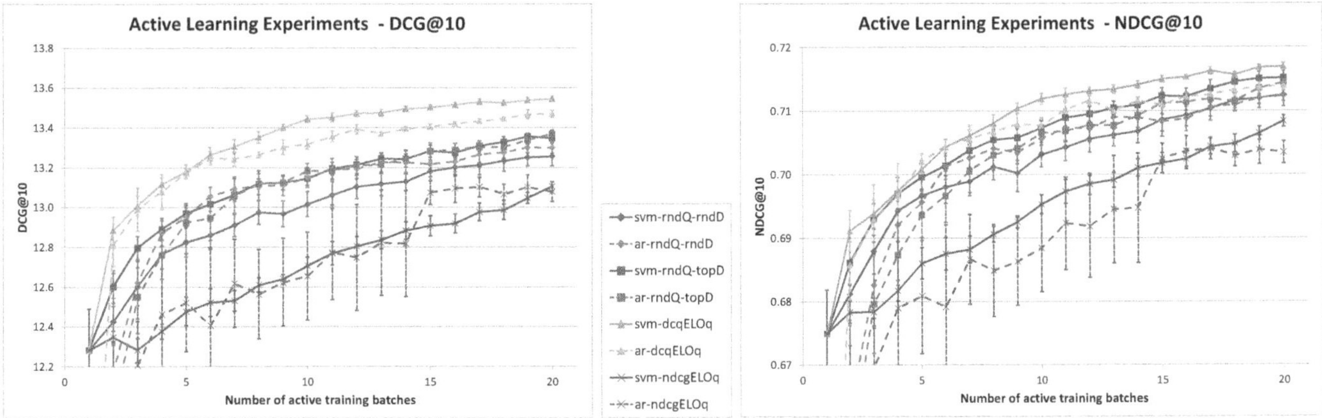

Figure 1: Comparison of query-selection strategies.

lect queries randomly and select the top documents according to the current ranker (rndQ-topD); (3) select queries according to ELO with DCG@10 as the selection measure and the top documents according to the current ranker (dcgELOq); (4) same as 3 but with NDCG@10 instead (ndcgELOq).

4. RESULTS AND DISCUSSION

Figure 1 shows the results for SVMRank (*solid*) and AR (*dashed*) when the evaluation measure is DCG@10 (*left*) and NDCG@10 (*right*).[2] Error bars are standard error about the mean over the five trials. As reported elsewhere [4], selecting the top documents performs as well or better than selecting documents randomly. Note that regardless of whether evaluating by DCG or NDCG, using NDCG for selection (ndcgELOq) leads to the worst performance. In contrast, using DCG for selection leads to the best performance across both rankers and both evaluation measures. Finally, we note that the differences between methods are less significant when evaluated by NDCG than DCG. This suggests that while the learners are more effective – finding more relevant results per query – they are contributing to the marginal relevance for each query according to NDCG. The perceived impact on user utility will likely depend on the scenario and the degree to which the task is recall-oriented.

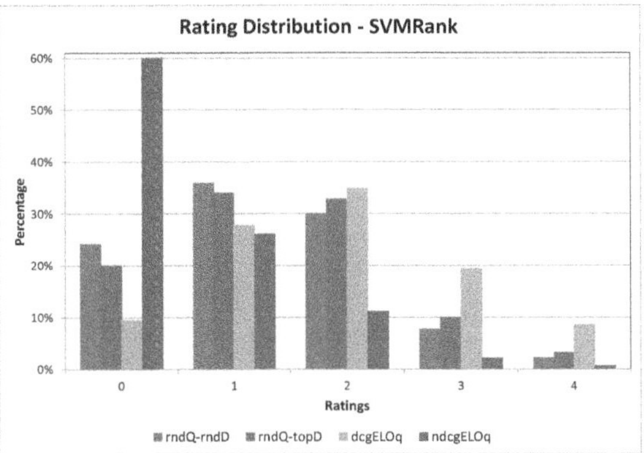

Figure 2: Rating distribution of selected queries.

Figure 2 displays the rating distribution of the training data collected at the last step of active learning as a percentage for the 15,000 labeled instances for SVMRank (the distribution trends for AR were nearly identical). Note that ndcgELOq selects far more irrelevant items than the other methods. This may seem surprising since NDCG selection is the same as DCG but normalized by the max estimate on the left-hand side of Eq. 1. However, for a poorly performing query with a single relevant document, NDCG's max will be 1 but current performance will be near zero. Thus, the selection method often selects queries with very few relevant documents. In contrast, dcgELOq not only obtains the largest percent of documents at the relevant side (labels 3,4) and fewest on the irrelevant side (label 0), it selects queries where a variety of relevance grades exist. This is consistent with the literature that biasing toward relevant documents is not sufficient in itself [1] – one also needs a variety of relevance grades present.

5. SUMMARY

We presented a method that generalizes the applicability of ELO for query selection to any ranker. Our method also has the benefit of being less of a computational burden than training ensembles at each step prior to labeling. We also demonstrated that whether one cares about DCG or NDCG for performance, using DCG provides a more stable query selection method. This is because the nature of NDCG as a ratio pushes the selection toward queries that often have few relevant documents. In contrast, using DCG in the selection mechanism promotes queries that have more relevant documents, and the expected loss component ensures that there will be a variety of relevance grades – since current performance is far below the max. These insights may be useful in developing new query selection methods.

6. REFERENCES

[1] J. Aslam, E. Kanoulas, V. Pavlu, S. Savev, and E. Yilmaz. Document selection methodologies for efficient and effective learning-to-rank. In *SIGIR '09*.

[2] B. Carterette, J. Allan, and R. Sitaraman. Minimal test collections for retrieval evaluation. In *SIGIR '06*.

[3] B. Carterette, V. Pavlu, E. Kanoulas, J. Aslam, and J. Allan. If i had a million queries. In *ECIR '09*.

[4] B. Long, O. Chapelle, Y. Zhang, Y. Chang, Z. Zheng, and B. Tseng. Active learning for ranking through expected loss optimization. In *SIGIR '10*.

[5] E. Yilmaz and S. Robertson. Deep versus shallow judgments in learning to rank. In *SIGIR '09*.

[2] SVMRank and AR are displayed together for space and to emphasize the similarity in trends. We are interested in comparisons within each and not across the two.

Anticipatory Search: Using Context to Initiate Search

Daniel J. Liebling, Paul N. Bennett, Ryen W. White
Microsoft Research
Redmond, WA 98052
{ danl, pauben, ryenw }@microsoft.com

ABSTRACT

Identifying content for which a user may search has a variety of applications, including ranking and recommendation. In this poster, we examine how pre-search context can be used to predict content that the user will seek before they have even specified a search query. We call this *anticipatory search.* Using a log-based approach, we compare different methods for predicting the content to be searched using different attributes of the pre-query context and behavioral signals from previous visitors to the most recent browse URL. Each method covers different cases and shows promise for query-free anticipatory search on the Web.

Categories and Subject Descriptors

H.3.3 [**Information Storage and Retrieval**]: Information Search and Retrieval – *search process, selection process.*

Keywords

Anticipatory search; Pre-search context; Web search.

1. INTRODUCTION

Personalization using recent pre-query context (within session) can improve result quality when combined with existing search result ranking methods [8]. Others have explored methods of biasing search via query expansion and re-ranking results for queries identified as good candidates for contextualization [6]. However, these methods rely on a user issuing a query, limiting their scope.

An alternative approach is to use the context to *generate* queries. Y!Q contextual search generated query augmentations from Web page content and had a "query-less" mode [5] but never presented an evaluation of that mode. Implicit Query [1] studied a similar problem but for a desktop environment using e-mails and other user activity to create queries and proactively find related documents. Henzinger et al. [4] focused on automatically retrieving information alongside live (television) news streams by extracting keywords. However, no one has studied the problem of performing query-less search to anticipate user needs in general Web search and presented a principled evaluation of their methods.

In this work, we attempt to anticipate information needs, and directly predict the results for which users will next search and visit given only the current browse URL. Queries submitted by users following Web browsing have been shown to be related to the most recently browsed document [7]. Therefore, for any URL for likely to be followed by a query (estimated via transitions observed in logs), we aim to predict the page that the user will visit from the result page for that query. This can both help the user in removing the need to type a query as well as potentially provide higher utility by issuing a more effective query than the user may formulate to retrieve the same result. Anticipatory search is a more challenging problem than URL recommendation since the goal is to not only provide URLs of interest but to identify those that the user would have tried to find — a much smaller set.

SIGIR'12, August 12–16, 2012, Portland, Oregon, USA.
ACM 978-1-4503-1472-5/12/08.

We describe and evaluate three methods: (1) a behaviorally-focused method targeting exact-match context, (2) a method that targets higher recall by combining content with a backoff of behavioral context, and (3) a method that combines content with exact-matching behavior context. In addition, we also propose a unique way of evaluating anticipatory search using queries issued to a Web search engine. We now describe each of the methods.

2. SUGGESTING RELATED CONTENT

The data for the study come from users' browse behavior logged anonymously through a popular Web browser's instrumentation over two weeks in November 2011. One week of data is used for aggregation and one week for evaluation. We consider (*browse URL*, *browse title*, *query*, *click URL*) tuples. The *browse URL* is the URL that the user visited prior to initiating a search with the given *query*. The *browse title* is the text which appears in the title bar of the browser. The *click URLs* are all links returned by the search engine for the query that the user clicks. Here, we restrict these to "satisfied" clicks, defined as having a dwell time of ≥ 30 seconds, an effective indicator of satisfaction [3]. Further, we consider only data where the domain of the clicked URL differs from that of the browsed URL. We believe the cross-domain problem is more difficult and more informative.

2.1 Exact–Match Behavioral Context

Method 1 builds a table of (*browse URL*, *click URL*, *Pr*(*click* | *browse*)) tuples using the logs. We use the first week of data to aggregate click URL probabilities conditioned on the browse URL. To help ensure reasonable data quality, we further filter the data to those that appeared for at least five different users, and have conditional probabilities of 0.1 or above. Sorting by probability yields the list of suggested URLs for a given browse URL.

To evaluate the method, we examined the (browse, query, click) tuples in a uniform sample of 100,000 tuples from the test set. For each browsed URL, we score the position of the user's actual click within our sorted list of recommended URLs. For example, the browse URL *aol.sportingnews.com/ncaa-football* is observed in our test set. From our conditional click data we recommend *sportsillustrated.cnn.com/football/ncaa* as the most likely next URL visited since its conditional click probability is 0.13. Following this URL browse, we observe that the user issued the query *sports illustrated*, clicking on the same URL that Method 1 suggests, yielding a reciprocal rank (RR) of 1.0. RR is averaged over all tuples in the test set to compute the mean RR (MRR).

2.2 Content + Backoff Behavioral Context

Our second method uses the title of the browse URL and combines it with the conditional click probabilities of Method 1. We aggregate these click probabilities at the URL domain level, creating a table of (*browse domain*, *click domain*, *Pr*(*click domain* | *browse domain*)) tuples. The method automatically generates a query for each browse URL observed in the test week. The query text is the title of the page located at the browse URL (case folded and sans punctuation) plus a disjunction of "site:" operators which instruct the search engine to restrict results to Web pages on the domain supplied as an argument to the operator. For example, if we observe the browse URL *www.golfdiscount.com/ping-putters*

titled *Putters*, and in the prior week found the distribution of click domains for *golfdiscount.com* to be {(*bizrate.com*, 0.14), (*global-golf.com*, 0.14), (*golfgalaxy.com*, 0.14), …} then our constructed query becomes [*putters* (*site:bizrate.com OR site:globalgolf.com OR site:golfgalaxy.com*)]. As in Method 1, we drop low probability domains, omitting the domain of the browse URL, if present. We then issue the constructed query to a search engine and retrieve at most the top 100 relevant results. This yields a (*browse URL*, *result set*) mapping. To evaluate the method, we examine each tuple in the sampled test set and find the rank position (if any) of the actual click URL in the results from our constructed query. Continuing the above example, we observe a user click on *www.golfgalaxy.com/putters/search* at position 2, for RR of 0.5.

2.3 Content + Exact–Match Behavior

The third method combines concepts from the previous two methods. To formulate the search query, we use only the normalized title of the browsed URL. As above, we issue the constructed query and retrieve results. We then combine the conditionally-clicked URLs from Method 1 with the results from this query by using a stable sort on the results using the click probability when available. That is, we prefer the rank from our click probability table to the rank of the search engine. The evaluation method is the same as Method 2. To illustrate, the browse URL *drugs.com/prednisone.html* is titled *Prednisone*. We use this term as our query, which returns *en.wikipedia.org/wiki/Prednisone* in position 6 for a RR of 0.17.

3. EVALUATION

Table 1 compares the MRR and recall relative to the 1,810 cases where at least one method suggested the clicked URL. All differences are significant by a Wilcoxon Signed Rank test (p=0.01).

Table 1. Coverage and overall accuracy.

Method	n (%) covered	Relative Recall	MRR
1	509 (28.1%)	0.281	0.222
2	973 (53.8%)	0.537	0.289
3	627 (34.6%)	0.346	0.098

Method 2 has both higher recall and precision than the other two methods. This may be because domain-level aggregation increases coverage, while the title and site: operators scope the results. Method 3 can be applied for almost any URL with a title, but its overall firing rate is therefore also high. Figure 1 shows the number of clicked recommended URLs per positional bin (zero-indexed and five rank positions per bin). As shown, Method 2 tends to return relevant results in the top rank positions, like all methods, tailing off exponentially. Methods 1 and 2 seem especially promising since the clicked URL is in top rank of one of the two nearly 40% of the time that is found by any method (with Method 2 accounting for nearly 60% of those). Though Methods 1 and 2 require observing URLs from a log, we believe aggregating by topic can produce similar results. Table 2 shows that that the overlap between the methods is only around 10-20%, suggesting that combining the methods could lead to marked coverage gains over any of singular method. Navigational queries performed poorly; clicked results were almost exclusively the navigational target whose rank was harmed by these methods.

Table 2. Overlap between successfully predicted browse URLs in each method. The diagonal gives the number of distinct successful browse URLs in each method.

	M1	M2	M3
M1	447	–	–
M2	109	922	–
M3	123	138	516

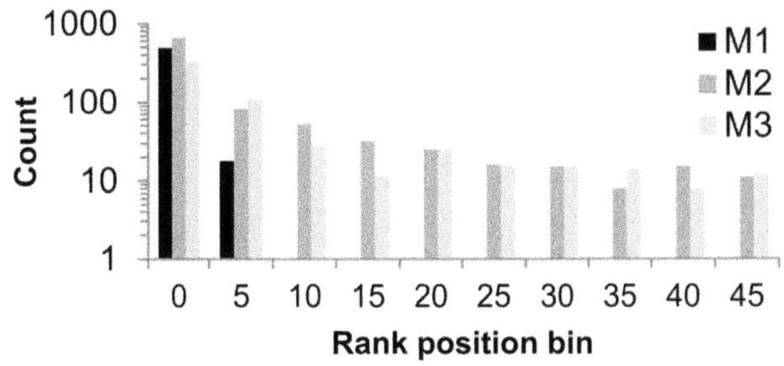

Figure 1. Count of clicked recommended URLs by position.

4. CONCLUSIONS

In this work we considered predicting the URL a user clicks from a set of search results. Instead of waiting to receive the user's query to generate the results, we used the pre-search browse URL coupled with existing clickthrough data and/or the browsed page title. We find that although coverage is low, the user's click URL most often appears in the top few results generated by our methods. Since these searches and clicks represent real information needs, one may surmise that the information need was not completely met by the browse URL prior to the search. Web content maintainers could use these URLs to find content that their site is not exposing, or expand their site content.

Search engines could leverage the pre-search context to present relevant URLs without requiring that the user issue a query. In practice, large advertising and search companies already cover much of the browsed Web via contextual ad matching, e.g., [1]. Future work will compare our methods with such models, increase coverage by exploiting method combinations, use other sources of pre-search context such as topic distributions and alternative page features, and examine whether recommendations other than the clicked URLs have utility to users. The goal is a learned selective application of anticipatory search capable of determining when pre-search context is relevant, increasing precision so that invocation happens such that users receive help only when needed.

REFERENCES

[1] Broder, A., Fontoura, M., Josifovski, V., and Riedl, L. (2007). A semantic approach to contextual advertising. *Proc. SIGIR*, 559-566.

[2] Dumais, S.T., Cutrell, E., Sarin, R., and E. Horvitz. (2004). Implicit queries for contextualized search. *Proc. SIGIR*, 594.

[3] Fox, S., Kuldeep, K., Mydland, M., Dumais, S., and White, T. (2005). Evaluating implicit measures to improve Web search. *ACM TOIS*, 23(2): 147-168.

[4] Henzinger, M., Chang, B., Milch, B., and Brin, S. (2005). Query-Free News Search. *World Wide Web: Internet and Web Information Systems*, 8(2):101-126.

[5] Kraft, R., Mahoul, F., and Chang, C.C. (2005). Y!Q: contextual search at the point of inspiration. *Proc. CIKM,* 816-823.

[6] Rahurkar, M. and Cucerzan, S. (2008). Using the current browsing context to improve search relevance. *Proc. CIKM*, 1493-1494.

[7] Rahurkar, M. and Cucerzan, S. (2008). Predicting when browsing context is relevant to search. *Proc. SIGIR*, 841-842.

[8] Teevan, J., Dumais, S.T., and Horvitz, E. (2005). Personalizing search via automated analysis of interests and activities. *Proc. SIGIR*, 449-456.

[9] Xiang, B., Jiang, D., Pei, J., Sun, X., Chen, E., and Li, H. (2010). Context-aware ranking in Web search. *Proc. SIGIR*, 451-458.

BReK12: A Book Recommender for K-12 Users

Maria Soledad Pera
Computer Science Department
Brigham Young University
Provo, Utah, U.S.A.
mpera@cs.byu.edu

Yiu-Kai Ng
Computer Science Department
Brigham Young University
Provo, Utah, U.S.A.
Ng@compsci.byu.edu

ABSTRACT

Ideally, students in K-12 grade levels can turn to book recommenders to locate books that match their interests. Existing book recommenders, however, fail to take into account the readability levels of their users, and hence their recommendations may be unsuitable for the users. To address this issue, we introduce *BReK*12, a recommender that targets K-12 users and prioritizes the reading level of its users in suggesting books of interest. Empirical studies conducted using the Bookcrossing dataset show that *BReK*12 outperforms a number of existing recommenders (developed for general users) in identifying books appealing to K-12 users.

Categories and Subject Descriptors

H.3.3 [**Information Search and Retrieval**]: Information filtering, retrieval models

Keywords

Recommendation system, book, readability, K-12

1. INTRODUCTION

Reading, an essential skill required for acquiring knowledge, is an integral part of the educational system. It is imperative to encourage the reading habit of K-12 students early on, since research studies have confirmed the enormous influence of reading on students' development as learners and members of the society [7]. Finding books that children/youth are interested in, however, is not a trivial task due to the diversity of topics covered in books, needless to say the huge volume of books available these days.

A recommendation system on books that assists children/ youths in finding books of interest to them is a valuable asset to the age group. Existing book recommenders, however, are developed with a general audience in mind and ignore the *literacy skill* of each individual user. As a result, even if (the topic of) a book B recommended to a user U matches U's interests, B might include complex (basic, respectively) content, which is beyond (below, respectively) the literary level of U and thus is unappealing, i.e., irrelevant, to U.

To address the design fault on excluding the literary issue in existing book recommendation systems, we introduce *BReK*12, a unique recommender tailored to K-12 users. Besides considering diverse content descriptors and item-item similarity to identify books appealing to U, *BReK*12 determines the readability level of books to be recommended based on well-known readability formulas.

We have conducted an empirical study to verify that by considering the readability level of books and its users, in addition to the content and item-item similarity measures, *BReK*12 recommends books that are more suitable for K-12 users than the ones suggested by existing recommenders.

2. THE PROPOSED RECOMMENDER

*BReK*12 recommends books for a K-12 user U based on U's interest on a given book B and the following measures:

Content Similarity: *BReK*12 computes the *content similarity* between B and each candidate book CB to be considered for recommendation, denoted $C_{Sim}(CB, B)$, as defined in Equation 1. B (CB, respectively) is represented as a set of keywords[1] S_B (S_{CB}, respectively) that appear in either the *title*, *description*, or *tag cloud* of B (CB, respectively). Each keyword in the set is associated with its corresponding frequency of occurrence in the title, description, and tag cloud of the book. The title of B (CB, respectively) characterizes its subject matter, whereas its tag cloud captures user-defined keywords posted under social bookmarking sites that describe the content of B (CB, respectively) and its description provides an overview of its content, which is often created by its author(s).

$$C_{Sim}(CB, B) = \frac{\sum_{i=1}^{n} \sum_{j=1}^{m} wcf(CB_i, B_j) \times \#_{CB_i} \times \#_{B_j}}{n} \quad (1)$$

where n (m, respectively) is the number of distinct keywords in S_{CB} (S_B, respectively), CB_i (B_j, respectively) is a keyword in S_{CB} (S_B, respectively), $wcf(CB_i, B_j)$ is the word correlation factor of CB_i and B_j [4], and $\#_{CB_i}$ ($\#_{B_j}$, respectively) denotes the frequency of occurrence of CB_i in S_{CB}(B_j in S_B, respectively).

$\#_{CB_i}$ ($\#_{B_j}$, respectively) is considered in computing C_{Sim} (CB, B), since the *larger* $\#_{CB_i}$ ($\#_{B_j}$, respectively) is, the *more significant* CB_i (B_j, respectively) is in characterizing the content of CB (B, respectively). *BReK*12 employs wcfs to analyze the *content similarity* between CB and B, since they reflect keywords in S_{CB} that are analogous to, but do not exactly match, the keywords in S_B.

Item-item Similarity: *BReK*12 considers the item-item similarity between B and CB, denoted $II_{Sim}(CB, B)$, in making recommendations. In computing $II_{Sim}(CB, B)$,

[1]From now on, unless stated otherwise, (key)words/tags refer to *non-stop*, *stemmed* (key)words/tags.

B (CB, respectively) is represented as an u-dimensional vector, where u is the number of users who have bookmarked either B or CB at a social bookmarking site such that users who bookmarked B (CB, respectively) are assigned a "1" in the corresponding components of the vector. The *cosine metric* is applied on the vectors of B and CB so that the larger the number of users who have bookmarked both B and CB is, the more likely CB is a relevant recommendation for U [1], as indicated by the metric.

Readability Similarity: $BReK12$ recommends books that correlate with the reading level of U (inferred by the readability level of B). The readability level of a book can be determined using various readability formulas, e.g., SMOG or Fog [3, 5]. Each formula measures a different aspect of a text T, such as the length of each word in T or the popularity of words in T, and yields a different readability score for T. $BReK12$ considers multiple readability formulas in tandem to avoid any bias on using one or the other formula. A combined score, which reflects the similarity in readability levels between B and CB, can be computed by applying the *Stanford Certainty Factor* on a number of readability scores.

$$R_{Sim}(CB, B) = \frac{RF_1 + ... + RF_n}{1 - Min\{RF_1, ..., RF_n\}} \quad (2)$$

where $RF_i = 1 - \frac{(|f_i(B) - f_i(CB)|)}{Max}$ $(1 \leq i \leq n)$ is the degree of similarity between the readability levels of B and CB computed using the ith readability formula f_i, $f_i(B)$ ($f_i(CB)$, respectively) is the readability score of B (CB, respectively), and Max, which is a normalization factor, is the largest difference between the readability scores of B and each candidate book to be considered for recommendation.

Ranking: $BReK12$ computes a ranking score for each candidate book CB with respect to B and recommends to U the top-10 candidate books with the highest *Rank* scores.

$$Rank(CB, B) = \frac{C_{Sim}(CB, B) + II_{Sim}(CB, B) + R_{Sim}(CB, B)}{1 - Min\{C_{Sim}(CB, B), II_{Sim}(CB, B), R_{Sim}(CB, B)\}} \quad (3)$$

3. EXPERIMENTAL RESULTS

Dataset and evaluation strategy: To evaluate the performance of $BReK12$, we use a portion of the Bookcrossing dataset (informatik.uni-freiburg.de/~cziegler/BX). The resultant dataset includes 1,173 distinct K-12 users and 8,737 distinct books bookmarked by the users. The description and tag cloud of each book (not provided by the dataset) were extracted from Alibris.com and Librarything.com, respectively. The readability levels computed by using the Flesch-Kincaid and Fog readability formulas for each book in the dataset are available on Amazon.com.

Since $BReK12$ suggests books for a user based on his/her interest on a particular book, we evaluate the recommendations generated by $BReK12$ for each of the 14,014 user-book pairs in the resultant dataset. We treat a recommendation as *relevant* for a user-book pair, if the book has been bookmarked by the user on Bookcrossing and *non-relevant* otherwise, which is a common protocol in evaluating a recommender.

Empirical Study: To validate the effectiveness of $BReK12$, we compare its performance with two newly-introduced recommenders, TVS [2] and Cos [6], which were originally developed as document recommenders and were adapted to recommend books for comparison purposes. While TVS represents the content of each book as a TF-IDF tag profile vector, *Cos* considers the weighted frequency of each keyword in the description or title of the book. TVS and *Cos* compute the similarity of books using the cosine metric.

Table 1: Performance metrics computed for Cos, TVS, and $BReK12$ on 14,014 user-book pairs

Recommenders	$P@1$	$P@10$	MRR	$nDCG$
Cos	0.18	0.12	0.26	0.30
TVS	0.23	0.17	0.32	0.36
$BReK12$	0.75	0.68	0.81	0.83

As shown in Table 1, $BReK12$ outperforms other existing recommenders considered in the empirical study. Based on the computed Mean Reciprocal Rank (MRR), on the average, $BReK12$ users are required to browse through close to *one* ($\cong \frac{1}{0.81} = 1.23$) recommended book before locating a relevant one, whereas users employing TVS and *Cos* are required to scan through close to *three* ($\cong \frac{1}{0.32} = 3.12$) and *four* ($\cong \frac{1}{0.26} = 3.84$) recommended books, respectively. In addition, the *Precision*@1 ($P@1$) achieved by $BReK12$ is significantly higher than the $P@1$ value achieved by TVS or *Cos*. The same applies to the *Precision*@10 ($P@10$) values. The high Normalized Discounted Cumulative Gain ($nDCG$) score of $BReK12$ indicates that $BReK12$ is more effective than *Cos* and TVS in retrieving relevant books to be recommended and positioning them *higher* in the list of suggested books.

4. CONCLUSION

We have introduced $BReK12$, a book recommender tailored to K-12 users. Unlike existing recommenders, $BReK12$ explicitly considers the reading level of a user U and locates books matching not only a book U is interested in, but most importantly, the reading ability of U. We have empirically verified that $BReK12$ outperforms various recommenders in suggesting books suitable for users in K-12 grade levels.

5. REFERENCES

[1] T. Bogers and A. van den Bosch. Fusing recommendations for social bookmarking websites. *IJEC*, 15(3):33–75, 2011.

[2] Z. Guan, C. Wang, J. Bu, C. Chen, K. Yang, D. Cai, and X. Hei. Document recommendation in social tagging services. In *WWW*, pages 391–400, 2010.

[3] R. Gunning. *The Technique of Clear Writing*. McGraw-Hill, 1952.

[4] J. Koberstein and Y.-K. Ng. Using word clusters to detect similar web documents. In *KSEM*, pages 215–228, 2006.

[5] G. McLaughlin. Smog grading: A new readability formula. *Journal of Reading*, 12:639–646, 1969.

[6] C. Nascimento, A. Laender, A. da Silva, and M. G.-. calves. A source independent framework for research paper recommendation. In *JCDL*, pages 391–400, 2011.

[7] R. Slavin, C. Lake, B. Chambers, A. Cheung, and S. Davis. Effective reading programs for the elementary grades: A best-evidence synthesis. *Review of Educational Research*, 79(4):1391–1466, 2009.

Clarity Re-Visited

Shay Hummel, Anna Shtok,
Fiana Raiber, Oren Kurland
Faculty of Industrial Engineering and
Management, Technion, Haifa 32000, Israel
{hummels,annabel,fiana}@tx.technion.ac.il,
kurland@ie.technion.ac.il

David Carmel
IBM Research Lab, Haifa 31905, Israel
carmel@il.ibm.com

ABSTRACT

We present a novel interpretation of **Clarity** [5], a widely used query performance predictor. While Clarity is commonly described as a measure of the "distance" between the language model of the top-retrieved documents and that of the collection, we show that it actually quantifies an additional property of the result list, namely, its diversity. This analysis, along with empirical evaluation, helps to explain the low prediction quality of Clarity for large-scale Web collections.

Categories and Subject Descriptors: H.3.3 [Information Search and Retrieval]: Retrieval models

General Terms: Algorithms, Experimentation

Keywords: query-performance prediction, Clarity

1. INTRODUCTION

Many query performance predictors were proposed over the years [2]. Clarity [5] is a well known, commonly used, state-of-the-art predictor that measures the "coherence" of the top-retrieved documents with respect to the collection. Specifically, the more distinguishable the language used in the retrieved documents from the general language used in the collection, the better the retrieval is assumed to be[1]. Clarity was shown to be highly effective for most TREC benchmarks [6]. However, low prediction quality is observed when using Clarity for large scale, noisy, Web corpora [1].

We present a novel formal analysis of Clarity that sheds some light on its underlying components and the properties of the result list of top-retrieved documents that it quantifies. While Clarity is commonly described as a measure of the "distance" between a language model induced from the result list and that induced from the collection, we show that Clarity actually quantifies an additional property of the result list, namely, its diversity. Our empirical analysis shows that the diversity of the result list has a negative correlation with retrieval performance for older TREC benchmarks and a positive correlation for the new ClueWeb collection. These findings, along with the formal analysis, help to explain the poor prediction quality of Clarity over ClueWeb.

[1]There are are several variants of clarity, among which is a pre-retrieval method (SCS [7]) that considers only the query and the corpus and not the retrieved documents.

SIGIR'12, August 12–16, 2012, Portland, Oregon, USA.
ACM 978-1-4503-1472-5/12/08.

In addition, the novel interpretation we present suggests new integration approaches of Clarity's building blocks.

2. INSIDE CLARITY

Let q and $\mathcal{D}$ denote a query and a corpus of documents, respectively. In what follows we use $p(w|x)$ to denote the probability assigned to term w by a unigram (smoothed) language model induced from x.

The query likelihood (QL) retrieval method scores document d by $\log p(q|d) \stackrel{def}{=} \log \prod_{q_i \in q} p(q_i|d)$, where q_i is a term in q. Let $\mathcal{D}_q^{[k]}$ denote the result list of the k highest ranked documents. The assumption behind Clarity is that the higher the divergence of a model of $\mathcal{D}_q^{[k]}$ from that of the corpus, the higher the effectiveness of $\mathcal{D}_q^{[k]}$ is, and thereby, the better the quality of the QL-based retrieval. The KL divergence between a relevance language model, R, induced from $\mathcal{D}_q^{[k]}$, and a language model induced from $\mathcal{D}$, is used to quantify this divergence. R is a weighted linear mixture of the models of documents in $\mathcal{D}_q^{[k]}$ [5]. Accordingly, the Clarity of q is defined as:

$$Clarity(q) \stackrel{def}{=} KL\left(p(\cdot|R) \;\middle|\middle|\; p(\cdot|\mathcal{D})\right) = \sum_w p(w|R) \log \frac{p(w|R)}{p(w|\mathcal{D})}.$$

As is the case for any two probability distributions, we can write the KL divergence as follows:

$$KL\left(p(\cdot|R) \;\middle|\middle|\; p(\cdot|\mathcal{D})\right) = CE\left(p(\cdot|R) \;\middle|\middle|\; p(\cdot|\mathcal{D})\right) - H\left(p(\cdot|R)\right);$$

CE is the cross entropy between R and $\mathcal{D}$,

$$CE\left(p(\cdot|R) \;\middle|\middle|\; p(\cdot|\mathcal{D})\right) \stackrel{def}{=} -\sum_w p(w|R) \log p(w|\mathcal{D});$$

H is the entropy of the relevance model,

$$H\left(p(\cdot|R)\right) \stackrel{def}{=} -\sum_w p(w|R) \log p(w|R).$$

Under this decomposition, Clarity integrates two measures (building blocks). The first is the "distance" of R from the corpus, as measured by the cross entropy. The more distant R from $\mathcal{D}$, the higher the cross entropy is. We use **CDistance** (for "corpus distance") to refer to the cross entropy between R and $\mathcal{D}$.

The second measure used by Clarity is the entropy of R. High entropy means that R assigns relatively low weights (i.e., probabilities) to a large number of terms; thereby, $\mathcal{D}_q^{[k]}$ is highly diverse. In contrast, low entropy means that only a few terms are highly weighted, hence $\mathcal{D}_q^{[k]}$ is more focused. We use **LDiversity** (for "list diversity") to refer to R's entropy. Next we study the prediction quality of each of these building blocks and compare it with that of Clarity which amounts to their equal-weight linear interpolation:

$$Clarity(q) = CDistance(q) - LDiversity(q). \quad (1)$$

3. EXPERIMENTS

We conducted experiments using the following TREC benchmarks (disks and topics are indicated in the parentheses): TREC4 (disks 2-3; 201-250), TREC5 (disks 2,4; 251-300), WT10G (WT10G; 451-550), Robust (disks 4-5 - {CR}; 301-450, 601-700), GOV2 (GOV2; 701-850), and the ClueWeb collection (category B). Two sets of topics were used for ClueWeb: Clue09 (1-50) and Clue10 (51-100). We applied Porter stemming and stopword removal upon queries and documents using the Lemur/Indri toolkit.

Previous work hypothesized that the low prediction quality of Clarity over Web collections is due to the large amount of noise (e.g. spam) [6]. To address spam effects in ClueWeb, we filtered out the spammiest documents from the result lists (those assigned a spam score below 50 by Waterloo's classifier [4]) and retained the original ranking for the residual corpus. Thus, we get two additional experimental setups for ClueWeb: Clue09+SpRM and Clue10+SpRM.

We use the predictors to predict the performance of the QL retrieval method specified above; unigram Dirichlet-smoothed document language models are used with the smoothing parameter set to 1000. We study three predictors: CDistance, LDiversity, and Clarity which interpolates the two (see Equation 1). Following the common practice to evaluating prediction quality [2], we report Pearson's correlation between the values assigned by the predictor and retrieval effectiveness measured by average precision computed using TREC's relevance judgments. The size of the result list, k, was set to 500 following previous recommendations [6]. The relevance models were clipped to use only the 100 highest weighted terms. The language models of documents used to construct the relevance model were not smoothed.

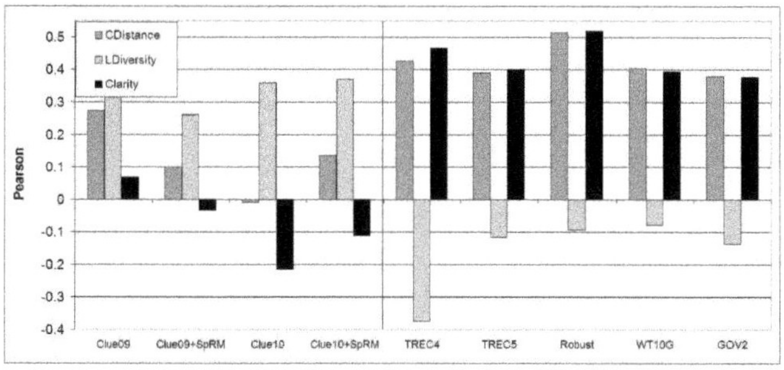

Figure 1: Comparing the prediction quality of Clarity and its building blocks.

Figure 1 presents our main results. To simplify the presentation, we refer to the ClueWeb benchmarks as "ClueWebs" (on the left of the graph) and to all the other benchmarks as "SmallScales" (on the right). The differences of the patterns observed for "ClueWebs" and "SmallScales" are as follows. First, CDistance is not very effective over "ClueWebs" in comparison to "SmallScales". We attribute this finding to the low quality of the collection statistics in a noisy Web setup that affects the estimation of the corpus language model. Evidently, spam removal did not improve prediction quality over ClueWeb.

Second, LDiversity and retrieval performance have positive correlation for "ClueWebs", yet negative correlation is observed for "SmallScales". We presume that list coherence can attest to improved retrieval effectiveness, as is implied by the findings for "SmallScales", which are mainly composed of unambiguous (coherent) queries. On the other hand, list diversity might correspond to improved retrieval performance, as is implied by the findings for "ClueWebs", for ambiguous queries, if it attests to coverage of various query aspects. It was found that for Clue09 topical diversity and retrieval performance are strongly correlated [3].

Following the observations made above, we can explain the low effectiveness of Clarity for "ClueWebs"; Clarity, as presented in Equation 1, is the **subtraction** of prediction values assigned by two predictors which are both positively correlated with retrieval effectiveness. Usually, two predictors that are positively correlated with retrieval performance are integrated by multiplication or summation [2]. Thus, the **subtractive** integration of CDistance and LDiversity, as implemented by Clarity, yields low quality prediction over "ClueWebs".

4. SUMMARY

We showed that Clarity amounts to an equal weight interpolation of two predictors; one measures the "distance" of the result list from the collection, while the second measures the list's "diversity". We used this formal finding to help explain the low prediction quality of Clarity over ClueWeb, in contrast to its high effectiveness over other TREC benchmarks. Preliminary results of using non-equal weights for the interpolation mentioned above, and independently optimizing free-parameter values for each predictor, attest to the merits of these future directions. (Actual numbers are omitted due to space considerations.)

Acknowledgments. We thank the reviewers for their comments. This paper is based upon work supported in part by the Israel Science Foundation under grant no. 557/09, by IBM's SUR award, by an IBM Ph.D. Fellowship and by Miriam and Aaron Gutwirth Memorial Fellowship. Any opinions, findings and conclusions or recommendations expressed in this material are the authors' and do not necessarily reflect those of the sponsors.

5. REFERENCES

[1] N. Balasubramanian, G. Kumaran, and V. R. Carvalho. Predicting query performance on the web. In *Proceedings of SIGIR*, pages 785–786, 2010.

[2] D. Carmel and E. Yom-Tov. *Estimating the Query Difficulty for Information Retrieval.* Synthesis lectures on information concepts, retrieval, and services. Morgan & Claypool, 2010.

[3] C. L. A. Clarke, N. Craswell, and I. Soboroff. Overview of the TREC 2009 Web track. In *Proceedings of TREC*, 2009.

[4] G. V. Cormack, M. D. Smucker, and C. L. A. Clarke. Efficient and effective spam filtering and re-ranking for large web datasets. *CoRR*, abs/1004.5168, 2010.

[5] S. Cronen-Townsend, Y. Zhou, and W. B. Croft. Predicting query performance. In *Proceedings of SIGIR*, pages 299–306, 2002.

[6] C. Hauff, V. Murdock, and R. Baeza-Yates. Improved query difficulty prediction for the web. In *Proceedings of CIKM*, pages 439–448, 2008.

[7] B. He and I. Ounis. Inferring query performance using pre-retrieval predictors. In *Proceedings of SPIRE*, pages 43–54, 2004.

Cluster-Based One-Class Ensemble for Classification Problems in Information Retrieval

Nedim Lipka
lipka.nedim@gmail.com

Benno Stein
benno.stein@uni-weimar.de

Maik Anderka
maik.anderka@gmail.com

Bauhaus-Universität Weimar
99421 Weimar, Germany

ABSTRACT

A number of relevant information retrieval classification problems are one-class classification problems at heart. I.e., labeled data is only available for one class, the so-called target class, and common discrimination-based classification approaches, be them binary or multiclass, are not applicable. Achieving a high effectiveness when solving one-class problems is difficult anyway and it becomes even more challenging when the target class data is multimodal, which is often the case. To address these concerns we propose a cluster-based one-class ensemble that consists of four steps: (1) applying a clustering algorithm to the target class data, (2) training an individual one-class classifier for each of the identified clusters, (3) aggregating the decisions of the individual classifiers, and (4) selecting the best fitting clustering model. We evaluate our approach with four datasets: an artificially generated dataset, a dataset compiled from a known multiclass text corpus, and two datasets related to one-class problems that received much attention recently, namely authorship verification and quality flaw prediction. Our approach outperforms a one-class SVM on all four datasets.

Categories and Subject Descriptors: H.3.3 [Information Storage and Retrieval]: Information Search and Retrieval—*clustering, information filtering*

Keywords: One-class Classification, Ensemble, Clustering

1. ONE-CLASS CLASSIFICATION IN IR

In a one-class problem one is given information of the target class only. The task is to define a boundary that encloses as many target objects as possible while minimizing the chance of accepting objects from outside the target class, so-called outliers [8]. An example for a one-class problem is authorship verification [4], where we are given writing examples for a single author T, and we are asked whether a text of unknown authorship was written by T as well. Notice that, despite the fact that a sheer endless number of outliers are at our disposal, we are not able to define a closed outlier class with texts from other authors. Specialized one-class classifiers shall cope with this setting; however, there is no cure-all for one-class problems, and additional constraints may render the classification task even more challenging. Two of which are pretty common in information retrieval: a highly diverse target class, i.e., a target class with a complex, multimodal data distribution, and, the presence of noise in the application situation of the one-class classifier. In this paper we present a cluster-based one-class ensemble that is able to effectively alleviate both problems.

Combining binary or multiclass classifiers within an ensemble has been proven to increase accuracy in many applications, compared to the best individual classifier in the ensemble [3]. With regard to one-class problems only few ensemble strategies have been proposed, which can be distinguished into two categories. First, approaches that divide the feature space and train individual one-class classifiers on the different feature subsets [9, 5]. Second, approaches that divide the target class data and train individual one-class classifiers on the different object subsets [10, 7]. Our approach belongs to the second category and is related to the work of Wang et al. [10], who employ an agglomerative hierarchical clustering strategy in order to partition target class data. By contrast, we employ a more suitable clustering technology, apply our approach to real-world information retrieval tasks, and empirically demonstrate its advantage compared to a common one-class SVM.

2. CLUSTER-BASED ONE-CLASS ENSEMBLE

Let $\mathbf{D}_T = \{\mathbf{x}_1, \ldots, \mathbf{x}_n\}$ denote the set of n feature vectors when given n target objects. The construction of the ensemble classifier happens within four steps:

Step 1: Clustering. $\mathbf{D}_T$ is clustered using the k-means algorithm [2]. The algorithm aims to find an exclusive clustering $\mathcal{C} = \{C_1, \ldots, C_k\}$, $C_j \subseteq \mathbf{D}_T$, $j \leq k \leq n$, such that the variance in each cluster C_j is minimized. The only free parameter in this step is the cluster number k. Figure 2 shows an example clustering.

Step 2: One-Class Classification. For each cluster $C_j \in \mathcal{C}$ a one-class SVM $c_j : \mathbf{x} \rightarrow \{1, -1\}$ is learned. Similar to a binary SVM a kernel function ϕ is used to map the objects into a higher-dimensional space. The goal is to find a maximum-margin hyperplane in the kernel space that separates $(1 - v) \cdot n$ target objects from the origin. This is formulated as optimization problem [6]:

$$\min_{\mathbf{w},\xi,\rho} \tfrac{1}{2}||\mathbf{w}||^2 + \tfrac{1}{v \cdot n} \textstyle\sum_{i=1}^{n} \xi_i - \rho$$
$$\text{s.t.} \quad (\mathbf{w} \cdot \phi(\mathbf{x}_i)) \geq \rho - \xi_i \text{ with } \xi_i \geq 0,\ i = 1, .., n,$$

where $\mathbf{w}$ denotes the normal vector of the hyperplane, ρ the margin, and ξ_i the slack variables. The value $v \in (0, 1]$ is specific to a one-class SVM: it defines the fraction of target objects outside the target class and controls the number of

SIGIR'12, August 12–16, 2012, Portland, Oregon, USA.
ACM 978-1-4503-1472-5/12/08.

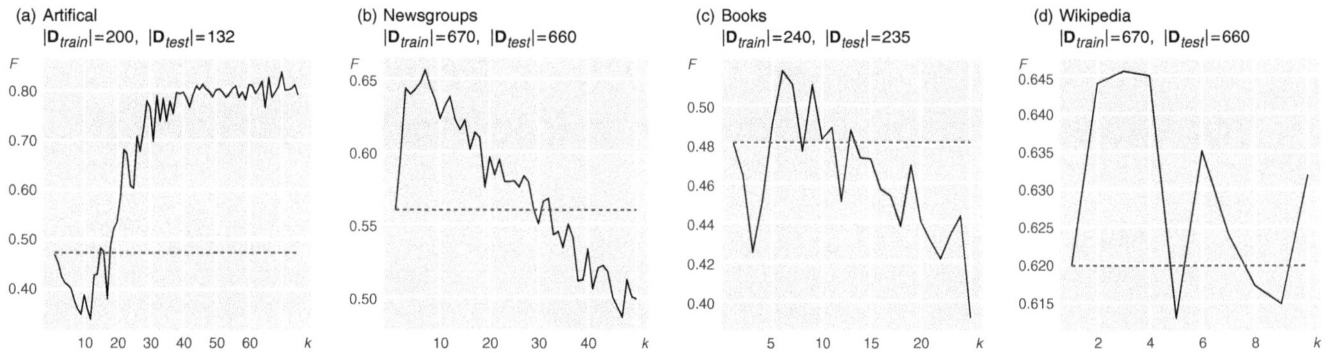

Figure 1: Effectiveness of the cluster-based one-class ensemble approach in terms of F-measure over cluster number k on four datasets. The dotted line shows a one-class SVM, trained with all target class data.

support vectors. The decision function c_j is of the following form:

$$c_j(\mathbf{x}) = sign((\mathbf{w} \cdot \phi(\mathbf{x})) - \rho)$$

Step 3: Aggregation. The ensemble classifier e_k combines the decisions of the k single classifiers for a vector $\mathbf{x}$ as follows:

$$e_k(\mathbf{x}) = \begin{cases} 1 & \text{if } \exists\, c_j(\mathbf{x}) > 0, j = 1, \ldots, k \\ -1 & \text{otherwise.} \end{cases}$$

Step 4: Model Selection. The clustering parameter k runs from 1 to l, and altogether $l(l+1)/2$ one-class SVMs are constructed. We choose the classifier e_k that performs best on holdout validation data in terms of the classification error.

3. ANALYSIS AND RESULTS

We use a random subset $\mathbf{D}_{train} \subset \mathbf{D}_T$ for the training phase; the test set $\mathbf{D}_{test}$ is comprised of a balanced number of outliers and examples from $\mathbf{D}_T \setminus \mathbf{D}_{train}$. Each experiment is repeated 15 times. The effectiveness of the classifier is reported as averaged F-measure and for varying values of the cluster number k. In all experiments a one-class SVM with a non-linear RBF kernel is used. The parameters of classifier c_j are optimized on the respective training set $C_j \subseteq \mathbf{D}_{train}$; clusters with less than five elements are discarded. Figure 1 illustrates the results on four different datasets: artificially created objects with three clusters (plot in Figure 2), documents from the 20 Newsgroups dataset with category "computer" in the role of the target class, books from different authors for which the authorship is to be verified [4], and Wikipedia articles tagged with certain quality flaws that are to be detected [1]. All documents are represented under a vector space model with a tf-idf weighting except for Wikipedia articles where quality-specific features [1] are employed. On all four datasets our approach outperforms a one-class SVM that has been trained with all target objects, or equivalently, where $|\mathcal{C}| = 1$. Table 1 summarizes the achieved improvements (significant) over the baseline. Note that our approach is a meta-classifier. Thus, arbitrary clustering and one-class classification technology can be applied. Both k-means and density estimation can be computed in parallel, so our approach is applicable on huge data as well.

Table 1: Percentage of improvement over the baseline for each dataset and for the optimum cluster number k.

Artificial	Newsgroups	Books	Wikipedia
+34% ($k = 70$)	+10% ($k = 8$)	+3.5% ($k = 6$)	+2.6% ($k = 3$)

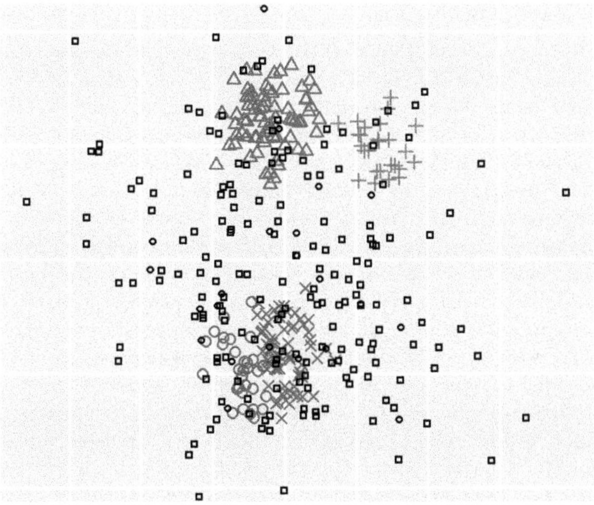

Figure 2: Artificially generated dataset with a diverse target class, constructed as a mixture of Gaussians with one mode for the outlier class and three for the target class. The black squares are outliers, all other objects belong to the target class. The shape and color of the objects indicate a k-means clustering with $k = 4$.

4. REFERENCES

[1] M. Anderka, B. Stein, and N. Lipka. Predicting quality flaws in user-generated content: The case of wikipedia. In *Proc. of SIGIR*, 2012.

[2] J. A. Hartigan and M. A. Wong. Algorithm as 136: A k-means clustering algorithm. *J. R. Stat. Soc. Series C (Applied Statistics)*, 1979.

[3] J. Kittler, M. Hatef, R. P. W. Duin, and J. Matas. On combining classifiers. *IEEE Trans. Pattern Anal. Mach. Intell.*, 1998.

[4] M. Koppel and J. Schler. Authorship verification as a one-class classification problem. In *Proc. of ICML*, 2004.

[5] R. Perdisci, G. Gu, and W. Lee. Using an ensemble of one-class svm classifiers to harden payload-based anomaly detection systems. In *Proc. of ICDM*, 2006.

[6] B. Schölkopf, J. C. Platt, J. C. Shawe-Taylor, A. J. Smola, and R. C. Williamson. Estimating the support of a high-dimensional distribution. *Neural Comp.*, 2001.

[7] A. Shieh and D. Kamm. Ensembles of one class support vector machines. In *Proc. of MCS*, 2009.

[8] D. M. J. Tax. *One-Class Classification.* PhD thesis, Delft University of Technology, 2001.

[9] D. M. J. Tax and R. P. W. Duin. Combining one-class classifiers. In *Proc. of MCS*, 2001.

[10] D. Wang, D. S. Yeung, and E. C. C. Tsang. Structured one-class classification. *IEEE Trans. Syst. Man. Cybern. Part B Cybern.*, 2006.

Collaborative Filtering with Short Term Preferences Mining

Diyi Yang Tianqi Chen Weinan Zhang Yong Yu
Shanghai Jiao Tong University
800 Dongchuan Road, Shanghai, China
{yangdiyi, tqchen, wnzhang,yyu}@apex.sjtu.edu.cn

ABSTRACT

Recently, recommender systems have fascinated researchers and benefited a variety of people's online activities, enabling users to survive the explosive web information. Traditional collaborative filtering techniques handle the general recommendation well. However, most such approaches usually focus on long term preferences. To discover more short term factors influencing people's decisions, we propose a short term preferences model, implemented with implicit user feedback. We conduct experiments comparing the performances of different short term models, which show that our model outperforms significantly compared to those long term models.

Categories and Subject Descriptors

H.3.3 [**Information Systems**]: Information Search and Retrieval—*Information Filtering*

General Terms

Algorithms, Models, Experiments

Keywords

Collaborative Filtering, User Feedback, Recommender Systems

1. INTRODUCTION

Collaborative filtering (CF) has been widely used in web services, such as products recommendation at Amazon[1] and music recommendation at Pandora[2]. There are two canonical approaches to attack this problem. Latent factor models, like singular value decomposition (SVD), map users and items into the same low-dimensional space and predict users' interest on items based on the relations between mapped vectors. The second are neighborhood models, which concentrate on detecting the correlations or similarities between items/users. Both approaches focus on users' long term interests, and do recommendation based on those stable preferences.

However, people's interests are likely to change over time. Long term interests, stay stable for a long time, but short term preferences are volatile. They may depend more on the current situation, users' mood at present, or his/her recent actions. For example, John might suddenly change from his favorite Jazz to light songs just because he had an unexpected guest who required it. It is hard to capture, but better performances will be achieved if considered. We extract this preference, and integrate it with the classical SVD++ model. Experiments conducted on Yahoo! Music dataset show that our model achieves better performances than the baseline SVD++, which proves that short term information does help capture users' changing preferences. We present our models in Section 2, and experimental results in Section 3. In Section 4, we conclude our work.

[1]http://www.amazon.com/
[2]http://www.pandora.com

SIGIR'12, August 12–16, 2012, Portland, Oregon, USA.
ACM 978-1-4503-1472-5/12/08.

2. SHORT TERM MODELS

We introduce our models for short term preferences mining in this section, and characterize short term property through users' implicit feedback. Implicit feedback, i.e. the users' rating history, as an indicator of user preferences, refers to all kinds of behaviors that users have performed on items. The traditional matrix factorization model with implicit feedback, called SVD++, predicts user u's rating $\widehat{r}_{ui}$ on item i as follows[2]:

$$\widehat{r}_{ui} = b_u + b_i + \left(p_u + \frac{\sum_{j \in N(u)} y_j}{\sqrt{|N(u)|}} \right)^T q_i \qquad (1)$$

Here, $N(u)$ is the item set of implicit feedback of user u. b_u is the users' bias and items' bias denotes as b_i. Each user u is related to p_u, and each item i are associated with vectors $q_i, y_j (p_u, q_i, y_j \in \mathbb{R}^k)$.

2.1 Incorporate Short Term Implicit Feedback

Even though global implicit feedback performs effectively, it only captures users' long term preferences by using the users' whole rating history. Since users' interests vary with time, we also need to take the short term, especially the current interest, into consideration. Therefore, we propose a novel short term model as follows:

$$\widehat{r}_{ui}(t) = b_u + b_i + \left(p_u + \frac{\sum_{j \in N(u)} y_j}{\sqrt{|N(u)|}} + \frac{\sum_{j \in N(u,t)} \xi_j}{\sqrt{|N(u,t)|}} \right)^T q_i \qquad (2)$$

Here $N(u,t)$ is user u's short term implicit feedback during time interval t. t is a time indicator that could be week, day, hour, or even minute. $\xi_j (\in \mathbb{R}^k)$ is an item revelent vector. By limiting the original global implicit feedback to a short time t like a minute/an hour, it can capture those fac-

Models	Average RMSE
GSVDP	23.233
Clock.GSVDP	**22.673**
Hour.GSVDP	22.814
Day.GSVDP	22.922
Week.GSVDP	22.972

Table 1: RMSE of different short term implicit feedback models

tors that influences people's decisions directly. For example, an Elsevier[3] user may start to download some CF relevant papers because of confusion in recommendation techniques that a biological paper he is reading refers to. This model captures users' short term interests through their behaviors during a certain period, and does not require extra parameters when we need t to be finer granularity, differing from the traditional temporal dynamics model[3].

3. EXPERIMENT

3.1 Experiment Setup

We use the Yahoo! Music Track 1 dataset[1] introduced in the KDDCup 2011. It contains about 250 million ratings rated by 1 million users for about 0.6 million items with time stamps. We use the official training and validation dataset for training, and report RMSE (Rooted Mean Square Error) on test dataset. To investigate the effectiveness of short term implicit feedback, we utilize five kinds of information, whose implicit feedback comes from the whole history, current week, current day, current hour and current minute(the least time granularity in dataset). We call the model which uses all of the users' rating history as GSVDP. The others are Week.GSVDP, Day.GSVDP, Hour.GSVDP and Clock.GSVDP. Moreover, since we want to test whether the short term preferences help enhance GSVDP, those four models are all implemented with GSVDP as Equation 2. As well as comparing overall performance of the five versions, we also discuss the resolution at which time granularity contributes most. Finally, to further analyze the consistency of short term preferences, we conduct experiments and present each category's differences between GSVDP and Clock.GSVDP.

3.2 Experiment Results

The results of our experiments are presented in Table 1. We find that short term implicit feedback models outperform basic GSVDP significantly. From GSVDP's 23.233 to each short term models' 22.x, different degree of improvements have been given. For example, Clock.GSVDP gives 22.673, achieving the greatest improvement among all the short term models. The runner up result is given by Hour.GSVDP(22.814). Week.GSVDP produces 22.972, and Day.GSVDP is a little better than week model with a RMSE of 22.922. Therefore, it is reachable that short term implicit feedback models assure big improvement overall in contrast to GSVDP.

It is naturally discovered that as time granularity increases, short term models give less satisfying performances. Since Clock.GSVDP is superior to Hour.GSVDP, and Hour.GSVDP outperforms Day.GSVDP with day model superior to Week.GSVDP, we consider that relative large time granularity cannot preserve the short term property, i.e. latest users' activities affects their future's decisions powerfully. Week model performs the nearly same RMSE as day model, that is, when reaching certain time granularity, models forfeit the ability of precisely capturing such preferences. Thus, clock short term implicit feedback is more predictive than hour, day and week granularity, consisting with our experimental results. Implemented with GSVDP which captures the users' long term preferences, our short term models have both long term and short term capabilities to fully capture users' interest.

[3] www.elsevier.com

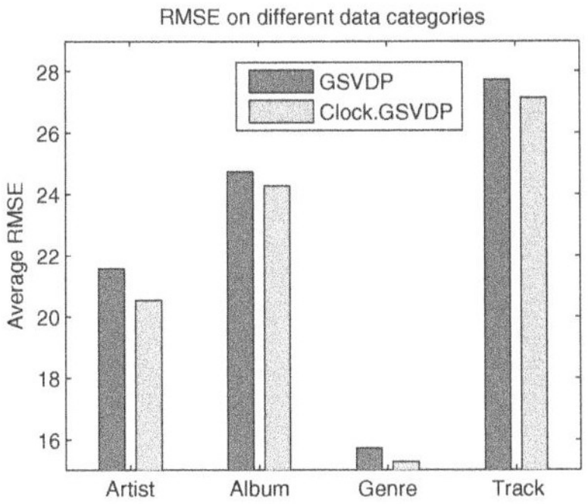

Figure 1: Performance Comparison on Different Categories

To investigate whether the short term model produces the consistency of improvement or not, we present each category's RMSE changes between GSVDP and Clock.GSVDP in Figure 1. There are four categories, artist, album, genre and track, in Yahoo! Music dataset. As we can see, short term implicit feedback models give decreased RMSE on all categories. This consistency of improvement emphasizes again that mining short term information will do well in enhancing a model's overall performance.

4. CONCLUSION

In this work, we extract the short term preferences to enhance our model, and implemented experiments are conducted in different short term settings. We conclude that short term performs well in capturing users' perdue interests and predicts changing preferences more precisely. In the future, we are determined to explore short term preferences further and improve our model systematically.

5. ACKNOWLEDGEMENT

Yong Yu is supported by grants from NSFC-RGC joint research project 60931160445.

6. REFERENCES

[1] G. Dror, N. Koenigstein, Y. Koren, and M. Weimer. The yahoo! music dataset and kdd-cup'11. In *KDD-Cup Workshop 2011*, 2011.

[2] Y. Koren. Factorization meets the neighborhood: a multifaceted collaborative filtering model. In *Proceeding of the 14th ACM SIGKDD international conference on Knowledge discovery and data mining*, KDD '08, 2008.

[3] Y. Koren. Collaborative filtering with temporal dynamics. In *Proceedings of the 15th ACM SIGKDD international conference on Knowledge discovery and data mining*, KDD '09, 2009.

Creating Temporally Dynamic Web Search Snippets

Krysta M. Svore, Jaime Teevan, Susan T. Dumais
Microsoft Research
Redmond, WA, USA
{ksvore, teevan, sdumais}@microsoft.com

Anagha Kulkarni
Carnegie Mellon University
Pittsburgh, PA, USA
anaghak@cs.cmu.edu

ABSTRACT

Content on the Internet is always changing. We explore the value of biasing search result snippets towards new webpage content. We present results from a user study comparing traditional query-focused snippets with snippets that emphasize new page content for two query types: general and trending. Our results indicate that searchers prefer the inclusion of temporal information for trending queries but not for general queries, and that this is particularly valuable for pages that have not been recently crawled.

Categories and Subject Descriptors

H.3.3 [**Information Storage and Retrieval**]: Information search and retrieval – query formulation, search process.

Keywords

Web search, query dynamics, search result snippets.

1. INTRODUCTION

Web content change often drives people to visit webpages to see what is new. For example, people visit news sites, blogs, and social media sites to stay up-to-date. We believe the search experience can be improved if people can quickly understand how a page has changed. Search result snippets typically provide a query-biased summary of the results. For example, Figure 1(a) shows a snippet for the query *tom bosley* that provides background information about the actor. However, people often use search engines to find results that have changed [1]. Someone who searched for *tom bosley* shortly after he died probably already knew who he was and instead wanted to learn more about his death. In cases like this, the availability of time-sensitive information in the snippet (e.g., Figure 1(b)) may help the user make better relevance decisions.

We explore the effectiveness of including new webpage content in search result snippets. We develop a technique for identifying important new content on a webpage, and generate several types of snippets that take advantage of this information. We conducted a study in which people judged these temporal snippets versus baseline snippets for 465 unique query-URL pairs for two types of queries: general and trending. The results demonstrate that for trending queries searchers prefer temporal content over static content. By leveraging temporal webpage information in snippets, we can better indicate the relevance of the page to the query and enhance the searcher's experience.

Researchers have recently studied temporal features of snippets. Alonso et al. [2] identified temporal expressions in webpages, and developed snippet generation algorithms that included explicit temporal expressions in sentence selection. Subjective evaluations of the usefulness of temporal expressions were obtained for 10 queries. Campos et al. [3] examined the extent to which queries and search snippets contained explicit temporal expressions. They found that snippets were a rich source of temporal information and could be used to identify whether queries had a temporal intent. Our research differs in that we focus on changes in page content rather than explicit mentions of time, and we present a more extensive user study with comparisons to a baseline non-temporal snippet.

Researchers have examined how changes in query frequency, document content and user interaction with documents vary over time. Kulkarni et al. [5] developed features to describe changes in query popularity and showed that these features, accompanied by changes in result content, can be a good indicator of a change in query intent. Diaz [4] developed algorithms for identifying queries that are related to breaking news and for blending relevant news results into core search results. We use changes in page content as an indication of the temporal relevance of a sentence when selecting sentences to include in a snippet. We examine how web content dynamics can be used to help users make more informed decisions about the relevance of results.

2. GENERATING TEMPORAL SNIPPETS

The snippets we study are query-focused for a given URL and query. We consider two snippet lengths: long (4 sentences) and short (2 sentences), and two variations of temporal snippets: one that blends new content with the static baseline snippet, and one that only contains new content. To create the snippets for a query-URL pair, we crawl the current version of the page (N for new), and the version of the page that the search engine crawled (C for cached). For each sentence on the webpage we determine its position in the document and the number of total and unique query terms it contains. The *short baseline snippet* is formed by choosing the two earliest sentences from page N that contain the most number of unique query terms. For the *long baseline snippet*, we choose the four earliest sentences with the most number of unique query terms. We do not use the search engine snippets as the baseline since they are of variable length and may be personalized.

For the temporal and blend snippets, we identify the sentences that are the most *changed* from the cached page C. For each sentence on page N, we determine its Dice coefficient with every sentence on page C. The Dice score of the most similar cached sentence is assigned to each sentence on page N, and sentences are ranked by their Dice scores. Ties are broken by the number of

Tom Bosley: Biography from Answers.com
Tom Bosley won a Tony Award in 1958 for his lead role as New York mayor Fiorello LaGuardia in the Broadway musical Fiorello!. But **Tom Bosley** is better remembered for his role on the long-running TV show Happy Days (1974-1984).
www.answers.com/topic/**tom-bosley**

(a) Baseline Snippet

Tom Bosley: Biography from Answers.com
Bosley died at 4:00 a.m. of heart failure on October 19, 2010, at a hospital near his home in Palm Springs, California. His agent, Sheryl Abrams, said **Bosley** had been battling lung cancer.
www.answers.com/topic/**tom-bosley**

(b) Temporal Snippet

Figure 1: Snippets for the same URL for the query *tom bosley*. One (a) is query focused; the other (b) includes new content.

SIGIR'12, August 12–16, 2012, Portland, Oregon, USA.
ACM 978-1-4503-1472-5/12/08.

Table 1. Snippet preference for general and trending queries. (Maximum value for Temporal v. Baseline is shaded.)

Snippet Comparison		General or Trending Queries					
Snippet Length	Temporal Content	General Queries			Trending Queries		
		Temp.	Base.	None	Temp.	Base.	None
Short	New Only	17%	**23%**	60%	18%	**20%**	62%
Short	Blend	17%	**18%**	65%	**23%**	16%	61%
Long	Blend	11%	**14%**	75%	**12%**	12%	76%

Table 2. Trending query snippet preference based on age of the cached page. (Max. value for Temporal v. Baseline is shaded.)

Snippet Comparison		Fresh or Old Cached Page					
Snippet Length	Temporal Content	Fresh Cache			Old Cache		
		Temp.	Base.	None	Temp.	Base.	None
Short	New Only	14%	**21%**	65%	**20%**	19%	61%
Short	Blend	19%	**22%**	59%	**24%**	13%	63%
Long	Blend	10%	**14%**	76%	**13%**	10%	77%

unique query terms, followed by the sentence position. *Short temporal ("new only") snippets* are formed from the two top-ranked temporal sentences. The *short blend snippet* consists of the top-ranked baseline sentence and the top-ranked temporal sentence. *The long blend snippet* is formed from the two top-ranked baseline sentences and the two top-ranked temporal sentences. For all snippets, the selected sentences are shown in order of their original positions on page *N*. Figure 1 shows the short baseline and temporal snippets for a result for the query *tom bosely*. We do not include long temporal snippets since many pages did not contain 4 temporal sentences.

3. STUDYING TEMPORAL SNIPPETS

Sixty-six people, responding to an email request sent to Microsoft employees, participated in a remote study comparing the different search result snippets. Participants were shown a query and asked to indicate a preference for one of two snippets (a baseline snippet and a temporal snippet) for the same URL. We studied three cases for each query-URL pair: 1) Short baseline vs. Short temporal; 2) Short baseline vs. Short blend; 3) Long baseline vs. Long blend. Participants judged all three snippet combinations for 5 distinct URLs for each query; however, combinations with no differences between temporal and baseline snippets were not judged. Placement of each snippet type was randomized to appear on the top or bottom.

Queries were drawn from two sources: 1) a frequency-weighted sample of *general* Bing search engine queries (292 query-URL pairs), and 2) a sample of *trending* Bing queries that had a spike in frequency the prior day (173 query-URL pairs). One challenge in evaluating the temporal nature of a query is that relevance judgments must occur at the time changes happen. Another challenge is that participants not interested in the query topic may not have the background knowledge to understand what is new or interesting about the query. For this reason, judgments collected in an experimental setting are likely to be biased toward background information versus timely information, as compared with real-world situations. To mitigate this, study participants judged snippets the day after events happened (for trending queries) and selected queries to judge from a list of candidate queries, enabling them to select queries that they knew about.

Table 1 shows the snippet preferences for the general and trending queries. For the general queries, baseline snippets were preferred to temporal snippets, between 4% and 32% more often, depending on the condition. This preference is expected since sentences in the baseline snippet are chosen based on the presence of the query terms, and thus are consistently more query-focused than the temporal snippets. For example, in Figure 1, the full query *tom bosely* appears twice in the baseline snippet, while only *bosely* appears in the temporal snippet. Previous work [6] suggests users prefer snippets with many query terms. The baseline snippets may also perform well since they typically provide good background context for the result. This is evidenced by the fact that preferences are less pronounced when there is additional context provided in the blended temporal snippet. Likewise, long snippets result in fewer preferences (75% of the pairs have no preference), perhaps since they enable more background content to be shown. In contrast to the general queries case, for the trending queries, participants preferred snippets with temporal content to the baseline snippets, despite the fact that our judges did not necessarily know that the query had a temporal component. As long as some background context was preserved in the temporal snippets (i.e., the two blended temporal conditions), there was a preference for the temporal snippet. Participants also had fewer preferences in the case of longer snippets. But for the case of the shorter snippets, participants preferred the temporal blended snippet 59% of the time there was a preference.

These results suggest that for trending queries, displaying new content in the snippet can be quite valuable. On manual inspection, we noted that several of the baseline snippets for the trending queries also contained very timely content. In all of these cases, the search engine had recently crawled the page, so the cached version contained very fresh content. To better understand the impact of the time between cache and crawl, we further broke down the data for our trending queries based on the age of the cached page. For 58 of the 173 trending queries, the cached page had been crawled very recently, within one day or less (called *fresh*). For the other 115 queries, the cached webpage was over one day old (called *old*). As can be seen in Table 2, when the cached page was fresh and thus likely similar to the live page, the baseline snippet was preferred over the temporal snippet generated using the difference between the two pages. In contrast, when the cached page was older people were much more likely to prefer the temporal snippet, especially for short blended snippets.

4. CONCLUSION

We performed a user study to determine the impact of including new content in search result snippets for general and trending queries. Our results indicate that users find new content useful for trending queries and when the cached page content is older. A snippet blending static and temporal information also appears beneficial, particularly for trending queries. In future work we hope to study re-finding behavior, which accounts for a significant portion of web search activity. Temporal snippets may be particularly valuable when the user has seen the snippet before.

5. REFERENCES

[1] Adar, E., Teevan, J. & Dumais, S. T. Resonance on the web: Web dynamics and revisitation patterns. *CHI 2009*, 1381-1390.

[2] Alonso, O., Baeza-Yates, R. & Gertz, M. Effectiveness of temporal snippets. *WWW 2009: Workshop on Web Search Results Summarization and Presentation.*

[3] Campos, R., Dias, G. & Jorge, A.M. What is the temporal value of web snippets? *WWW 2011: Temporal Web Analytics Workshop.*

[4] Diaz, F. Integration of news content into web results. *WSDM 2009*, 182-191.

[5] Kulkarni, A., Teevan, J., Svore, K. M. & Dumais, S. T. Understanding temporal query dynamics. *WSDM 2011*, 167-176.

[6] Tombros, A. & Sanderson, M. Advantages of query-biased summaries in information retrieval. *SIGIR 1998*, 2-1.

Dependency Trigram Model for Social Relation Extraction from News Articles

Maengsik Choi
Kangwon National University
1 Gangwondaehak-gil,
Chuncheon-si, Gangwon-do, 200-701, Republic of Korea
mschoi@kangwon.ac.kr

Harksoo Kim
Kangwon National University
1 Gangwondaehak-gil,
Chuncheon-si, Gangwon-do, 200-701, Republic of Korea
nlpdrkim@kangwon.ac.kr

W. Bruce Croft
Dept. of Computer Science
University of Massachusetts
Amherst, MA, 01003, USA
croft@cs.umass.edu

ABSTRACT
We propose a kernel-based model to automatically extract social relations such as economic relations and political relations between two people from news articles. To determine whether two people are structurally associated with each other, the proposed model uses an SVM (support vector machine) tree kernel based on trigrams of head-dependent relations between them. In the experiments with the automatic content extraction (ACE) corpus and a Korean news corpus, the proposed model outperformed the previous systems based on SVM tree kernels even though it used more shallow linguistic knowledge.

Categories and Subject Descriptors
I.2.7 [**Artificial Intelligence**]: Natural Language Processing

Keywords
Social Relation Extraction, Dependency Trigram Kernel, Dependency Kernel, Support Vector Machine

1. INTRODUCTION
In natural language documents, a huge number of social relations are described. Automatic extraction of these social relations from documents would be highly beneficial to social network analysis (SNA) studies on business economics, public administration, and political science. In this paper, we propose a model to automatically extract social relations between people from news articles using support vector machines (SVMs). Table 1 shows the categories of social relations that the proposed model aims to extract from news articles. The proposed model first selects sentences describing social relations between people's names (the names are automatically recognized by a conventional named entity tagger). Then, it classifies the selected sentences into one of the six categories in Table 1.

Recently, kernel-based models based on SVMs have shown good performance on this task. The shortest path kernel model [3] showed the best results in terms of both computational complexity and performance [2]. However, it exhibited low recall rates owing to hard-matching constraints (i.e., two sub-trees should share the same depth or length) between the comparisons of two target sub-trees. To resolve this problem, we propose a dependency trigram kernel to efficiently compute the structural similarity between pairs of dependency trees.

SIGIR'12, August 12–16, 2012, Portland, Oregon, USA.
ACM 978-1-4503-1472-5/12/08.

Table 1. Categories and examples of social relations

Category	Example
EXCHANGE	Present, offer a bribe
CRITICIZE	Blame, make a reckless, censure
MEET	Dispute, introduce, interview
CONGRATULATE	Celebrate, defend, encourage, praise
CONTACT	Call, mail, contact, replay
ASSERT	Request, ask pardon

2. DEPENDENCY TRIGRAM MODEL
Given n words $w_{1,n}$ in a sentence S describing social relations, let w_i denote the i-th word in the sentence, and let "$w_i \rightarrow w_k$" denote that w_i is dependent on w_k. Then, we can define a dependency trigram set S_T as shown in Equation (1).

$$\begin{aligned} &S_T = S_{T_1} \cup S_{T_2}, \\ &\quad \text{where } S_{T_1} = \{w_i \rightarrow w_k \leftarrow w_j \mid i < j\}, \\ &\quad\quad S_{T_2} = \{w_l \rightarrow w_k \leftarrow w_r \mid l < r \text{ and } \forall w_l, w_r = child(w_k)\} \end{aligned} \quad (1)$$

In Equation (1), w_k is the first common head word of w_i and w_j. Further, w_l and w_r are child nodes that are both directly dependent on w_k. Thus, we can design a dependency kernel function that uses the defined dependency trigrams as function inputs, as shown in Equation (2).

$$K(A,B) = \frac{\sum_{i=1}^{n} \max(s(A_T^i, B_T^1), s(A_T^i, B_T^2), ..., s(A_T^i, B_T^j), ..., s(A_T^i, B_T^m))}{n} \quad (2)$$

In Equation (2), A and B are input sentences of the kernel function K that consist of n and m dependency trigrams, respectively. A_T^i is the i-th dependency trigram for sentence A, whereas B_T^j is the j-th dependency trigram for sentence B. The similarity score $s(A_T^i, B_T^j)$ is calculated using the weighted sum of the common attributes between A_T^i and B_T^j, as shown in Equation (3).

$$s(A_T^i, B_T^j) = \prod_{pos} \sum_{q=1}^{r} w_q N_q(pos(A_T^i), pos(B_T^j)) \quad (3)$$

In Equation (3), pos indicates the positions (left, center, or right) of each node in a dependency trigram. In other words, $left(A_T^i)$,

$center(A_T^i)$ and $right(A_T^i)$ are the left, center, and right node of the dependency trigram A_T^i, respectively. Further, $N_q(X)$ is a binary function that returns 0 or 1 depending on whether the q-th attribute of A_T^i is the same as that of. B_T^j. Table 2 shows the attributes used for the comparison of two dependency trigrams.

Table 2. Attributes and their meanings

Attribute	Meaning
Lexeme	The surface form (e.g., money, give)
Part-of-speech	The morphological category (e.g., noun, verb)
Gramm. role	The grammatical category (e.g., sub, obj)

As shown in Table 2, we do not use high-level semantic knowledge such as named entity categories and semantic codes in order to increase domain portability and decrease the effort related to a language change. The weight value w_q for the q-th of the r attributes is assigned according to Equation (4).

$$w_q = 1 + \frac{E_q - MinE}{MaxE - MinE}, \text{ where } E_q = -\sum_{x \in q} p(x) \log_2 p(x) \quad (4)$$

In Equation (4), E_q is the entropy of the q-th attribute, i.e., the total information quantity for all attribute values included in the q-th attribute. Further, $MaxE$ and $MinE$ are normalizing factors denoting the maximum and the minimum of all the entropies of attributes.

3. EVALUATION

To experimentally evaluate the proposed model, we used two types of test collections: One was the well-known automatic content extraction (ACE) corpus [5], and the other was a Korean news corpus that contains 1,540 sentences. The Korean news corpus consists of two groups: One is 770 sentences describing social relations between two people, and the other is 770 sentences containing two people's names, but with no social relations describing them. The first was manually annotated with the category names in Table 1. We implemented a social relation extraction system by replacing the default kernel of LibSVM [4] with the proposed dependency trigram kernel. For experiments with the ACE corpus and the Korean news corpus, we used a Stanford dependency parser, a Korean POS tagger (precision = 95%) based on a hidden Markov model, and a Korean dependency parser (precision = 85%).

Table 3 shows the performance of the proposed model compared with the previous relation extraction systems in the ACE corpus.

Table 3. Comparison of performance in the ACE corpus

Model	Precision	Recall	F1-measure
Bunescu	0.655	0.438	0.525
Wang	0.686	0.513	0.587
Proposed model	0.702	0.554	0.626

In Table 3, Bunescu indicates a relation extraction system using the shortest path kernel [3]. Wang indicates a relation extraction system based on a convolution dependency path kernel, which is known as well relaxing the same length constraints of the shortest path kernel [6]. All systems first selected sentences with relations and then discriminated among the top five classes (i.e., AT, NEAR, PART, ROLE, and SOCIAL) in the ACE corpus. The Bunescu system and the Wang system use named entity categories and semantic code as input features. As shown in Table 4, the proposed model exhibited a considerably higher recall rate than the previous systems. Consequently, their high recall rates resulted in the best F1 scores. Table 4 shows the performance of the proposed model in the Korean news corpus.

Table 4. Performance in the Korean news corpus

Model	Precision	Recall	F1-measure
Bunescu	0.746	0.267	0.394
Proposed model	0.646	0.602	0.623

In Table 4, the Bunescu system uses the same input features with the proposed model. As shown in Table 4, the Bunescu system showed a low recall rate when it does not use high-level semantic knowledge such as named entity categories and semantic codes.

4. CONCLUSION

We presented a social relation extraction model based on a dependency trigram kernel of SVM. In the experiments, we found that the newly designed kernel could relax the hard-matching constraints of the Bunescu system. Moreover, the proposed model showed good performance even though it used only low-level syntactic knowledge.

5. ACKNOWLEDGEMENTS

This research was supported by Basic Science Research Program through the National Research Foundation of Korea(NRF) funded by the Ministry of Education, Science and Technology(No.2010-0009875) This work was also supported in part by the Center for Intelligent Information Retrieval. Any opinions, findings and conclusions or recommendations expressed in this material are those of the authors and do not necessarily reflect those of the sponsor.

6. REFERENCES

[1] Agichtein, E. and Gravano, L. 2000. Snowball: Extracting relations from large plain-text collections. In *Proceedings of ICDL*.

[2] Bach, N. and Badaskar, S. 2007. *A review of relation extraction*. Literature Review for Language and Statistics II, Carnegie Mellon University.

[3] Bunescu, R. C. and Mooney, R. J. 2005. A shortest path dependency kernel for relation extraction. In *Proceedings of HLT / EMNLP*, 724–731.

[4] Chang, C. and Lin, C. 2001. *LIBSVM: a library for support vector machines*. http://www.csie.ntu.edu.tw/~cjlin/libsvm.

[5] NIST 2007. *The NIST ACE evaluation website*. http://www.nist.gov/speech/tests/ace

[6] Wang, M. 2008. A re-examination of dependency path kernels for relation extraction. In *Proceedings of IJCNLP*, 841-846.

Detecting Candidate Named Entities in Search Queries

Areej Alasiry
Birkbeck, University of London
United Kingdom, London
areej@dcs.bbk.ac.uk

Mark Levene
Birkbeck, University of London
United Kingdom, London
mark@dcs.bbk.ac.uk

Alexandra Poulovassilis
Birkbeck, University of London
United Kingdom, London
ap@dcs.bbk.ac.uk

ABSTRACT

The information extraction task of Named Entities Recognition (NER) has been recently applied to search engine queries, in order to better understand their semantics. Here we concentrate on the task prior to the classification of the *named entities* (NEs) into a set of categories, which is the problem of detecting candidate NEs via the subtask of query segmentation.We present a novel method for detecting candidate NEs using grammar annotation and query segmentation with the aid of top-n snippets from search engine results and a web n-gram model, to accurately identify NE boundaries. The proposed method addresses the problem of accurately setting boundaries of NEs and the detection of multiple NEs in queries.

Categories and Subject Descriptors: H.3.3 [Information Storage and Retrieval]: Information Search and Retrieval —*Query formulation*

Keywords: named entity recognition, query logs.

1. INTRODUCTION

The challenges posed by the structure of search engine queries, such as their short length, lack of grammar and orthographic features, imply that classical NER techniques cannot be used without modification. In response, researchers have recently proposed several approaches to address these challenges. A relatively simple yet effective method is to start with a set of seed instances for each NE category, and then scan the query log in order to extract the corresponding contexts, which can then be used to identify new instances for each category. Both Paşca [5] and Guo et al. [2] applied this method, with the context including the prefix and/or suffix surrounding instances that were detected. For example, the word 'lyrics' could be the context for song names; the same context appears in queries such as 'song lyrics', 'James Brown songs lyrics', and 'Music and Lyrics'. The instances extracted could be: (i) 'song', which is not a NE, (ii) 'James Brown songs', where the NE boundaries are incorrect, or (iii) 'Music and', where the context is part of the NE which is a movie name. Thus a problem with this approach is that the queries' structure was not considered. Jain and Pennacchiotti [4] presented an unsupervised approach that utilises the syntactic representation of words such as Capitalisation. Although confidence scores were assigned to each extracted NE based on its presence in a Web corpus, relying on Captilisation will often miss many potential NEs in the query log that were not typed with capital letters.

Here, we present a processing pipeline which overcomes the above drawbacks by: (1) Tagging each query token with its part of speech (POS) and the corresponding orthographic features (ORTH) based on the context in which tokens appear, using top-n query snippets; (2) Finding the most probable query segmentation to accurately set the boundaries of candidate NEs; and finally (3) Using these annotations for NER. The contribution of our work lies in the following: (i) Presenting a NER approach for queries by considering English language structural features; (ii) Using query segmentation to better set the boundaries of candidate NEs, especially in multiple NE queries; and (iii) Fine-grained evaluation of NER for search engine queries.

SIGIR'12, August 12–16, 2012, Portland, Oregon, USA.
ACM 978-1-4503-1472-5/12/08.

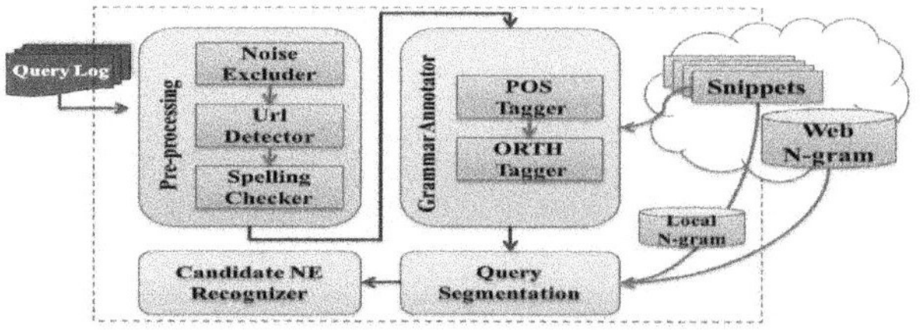

Figure 1: Query Log Candidate NE Recognition

2. CANDIDATE NE RECOGNIZER

Figure 1 presents the processing pipeline we use to identify candidate NEs in a query log. It involves four main stages: (1) Pre-processing the query log; (2) Tagging each query with the corresponding grammatical annotation; (3) Segmenting the query to identify boundaries; and (4) Recognising the candidate NEs with respect to annotations and segmentation.

Pre-Processing: It is important that the query log is processed to exclude *noise*, which is defined as any query that is a sequence of symbols containing no words. *URLs* are also detected in advance before any further natural language processing of the query log. Finally, the *spelling* of each query is checked and corrected.

Grammar Annotation: For each query in the log, the top-n *snippets* are retrieved. Each snippet consists of few sentences from a document retrieved for the query. The advantage of using snippets is that they contain tokens surrounding the query that usually provide enough context to annotate the query, avoiding the cost of parsing complete web documents as in [4]. In addition, the approach we are proposing operates in an offline scenario, therefore snippets are retrieved and stored in advance. The set of grammatical annotations include, parts-of-speech (POS) and orthographic (ORTH) annotations. We assume there are no dependencies between query tokens, adopting the bag-of-words approach as in [1]. It is important to note that we differentiate between common nouns and proper nouns to help identify NEs, and therefore the POS tagging is more specific than that used in [1]. The orthographic features capture the string representation of each query token, such as capital initial, all capital, or mixed letter cases.

Query Segmentation: Many approaches of query segmentations have been proposed in literature. For instance, Hagen et al. [3] used raw n-gram counts and Wikipedia to segment queries. Although their approach achieved high accuracy, in our case we need to segment queries according to their appearance in top-n related snippets. We define query segmentation as follows. For a query Q consisting of tokens $t_1, t_2, ..., t_n$, the set of all possible segmentations is $\mathbf{S(Q)} = \{S_1, ..., S_m\}$, where $m \leq 2^{n-1}$. Each segmentation $S_i \in \mathbf{S(Q)}$ consists of one or more segments, and each segment, say s_{ij}, is a sequence of query tokens that obeys the original order of the tokens. We define the best segmentation S^{β} as the most probable one over all $S_i \in \mathbf{S(Q)}$. The probability of each S_i is calculated as $Pr(S_i) = \prod_{s_{ij} \in S_i} Pr(s_{ij})$, where $Pr(s_{ij})$ is estimated using a *local* n-gram model ($M_{snippet}$) created from the set of retrieved snippets for the query Q. This probability is smoothed by the probability of the segments given a *web* n-gram model (M_{web}) using an empirically set parameter λ between 0 and 1, to obtain

$$Pr(s_j) = \lambda Pr(s_j|M_{snippet}) + (1-\lambda)Pr(s_j|M_{Web}).$$

Recognition of Candidate NEs: A small set of rules was defined by examining a random sample of grammatically annotated and segmented queries as described above. In the sample, three main cases were observed: (1) A sequence of proper nouns contained in a segment (approximately 93%), (2) A conjunction, e.g.'&', or preposition, e.g. 'of' followed and preceded by proper nouns such as 'University of Wisconsin' (approximately 2%), and (3) A sequence of proper nouns that include numbers, such as 'Microsoft Office Professional 2003' (approximately 5%). Hence, rules were created to reflect these cases. Applying these rules with respect to segmentation boundaries will result in, for example, the detection of two NEs from a segmented query "[marriot] [new jersey]".

3. EXPERIMENTAL EVALUATION

Experiment: The approach was applied using a 2006 MSN query log consisting of approximately 15M queries. Removing duplicates and after a further pre-processing stage, approximately 5.5M queries were left. Thereafter, the spelling of each query was checked and corrected using Yahoo API provided through the Spelling Suggestion YQL table. In addition, for each query, the top eight query snippets highlighting the query tokens along with their immediate context were retrieved and stored using Google Custom Search API. Then each snippet was Grammatically annotated using GATE and accordingly each query token was then annotated with the most probable POS and orthographic feature. We used the Bing web n-gram model to find the probability of each distinct segment, and smoothed the probability of the same segment given the local n-gram model with $\lambda = 0.6$ being empirically set. Finally, candidate NEs were extracted using the set of defined NER rules. Table 1 presents examples of segmented queries and corresponding extracted NEs.

Table 1: Sample of Extracted Candidate NEs

Segmented Query	Extracted NE/s
[abc] [dallas]	abc & dallas
[microsoft] [speech to text] [windows xp]	microsoft & windows xp
[leon] [final fantasy]	leon & final fantasy
[mercedes benz] [used parts]	mercedes benz

Table 2: Query Log NER Evaluation

	Accuracy	Precision	Coverage
Evaluation I	0.806	0.794	0.9727
Evaluation II	0.678	0.6431	0.9664

Evaluation and Results Analysis: In previous work, NER was evaluated by manually checking a random sample [4], or the top-n [5][2] of instances extracted for each NE class without considering the NEs they missed or the context of the extracted ones. For example, 'safari' is a NE in the query 'download safari', while it is not in the query 'safari trips'. Since we use hand-crafted rules to extract NEs, the quality of these rules should be reflected in the evaluation. Therefore, we manually checked a uniform random sample of 1000 queries.The performance of our method was assessed at the query-level, which is stricter than the previous evaluation methods at the NE-level. True and False Positives (TP, FP), and True and False Negatives (TN, FN) were counted, and these are defined as follows: **TP**: Query has one or more NEs and all were correctly detected. **TN**: Query has no NE and none were detected. **FP**: One or more query tokens were incorrectly tagged by the rules as NE. **FN**: One or more query NEs were incorrectly missed by the rules. The accuracy was measured using two evaluation methods (see table 2): *Evaluation I*, where NEs detection is tagged as correct regardless of its boundary (with accuracy 80.6%) (e.g. extracting 'Sony PS3 news'), and a stricter version, *Evaluation II*, where NEs boundary must be accurate (with accuracy 67.8%) (e.g. extracting 'Sony PS3').

4. REFERENCES

[1] M. Bendersky, W. B. Croft, and D. A. Smith. Joint annotation of search queries. In Proc. of ACL, pages 102-111, 2011.

[2] J. Guo, G. Xu, X. Cheng, and H. Li. Named entity recognition in query. In Proc. of SIGIR, pages 267-274, 2009.

[3] M. Hagen, M. Potthast, B. Stein, and C. Bräutigam. Query segmentation revisited. In Proc. of WWW, pages 97-106, 2011.

[4] A. Jain and M. Pennacchiotti. Domain-independent entity extraction from web search query logs. In Proc. of WWW, pages 63-64, 2011.

[5] M. Paşca. Weakly-supervised discovery of named entities using web search queries. In Proc. of CIKM, pages 683-690, 2007.

Effect of Dynamic Pruning Safety on Learning to Rank Effectiveness

Craig Macdonald[1], Nicola Tonellotto[2], Iadh Ounis[1]
[1] University of Glasgow, Glasgow, G12 8QQ, UK
[2] National Research Council of Italy, Via G. Moruzzi 1, 56124 Pisa, Italy
{craig.macdonald, iadh.ounis}@glasgow.ac.uk[1], {nicola.tonellotto}@isti.cnr.it[2]

ABSTRACT

A dynamic pruning strategy, such as WAND, enhances retrieval efficiency without degrading effectiveness to a given rank K, known as safe-to-rank-K. However, it is also possible for WAND to obtain more efficient but unsafe retrieval without actually significantly degrading effectiveness. On the other hand, in a modern search engine setting, dynamic pruning strategies can be used to efficiently obtain the set of documents to be re-ranked by the application of a learned model in a learning to rank setting. No work has examined the impact of safeness on the effectiveness of the learned model. In this work, we investigate the impact of WAND safeness through experiments using 150 TREC Web track topics. We find that unsafe WAND is biased towards documents with lower docids, thereby impacting effectiveness.

Categories & Subject Descriptors: H.3.3 [Information Storage & Retrieval]: Information Search & Retrieval

General Terms: Performance, Experimentation

Keywords: Dynamic Pruning, Learning to Rank

1. INTRODUCTION

A search engine deploying learning to rank techniques re-ranks the top K documents retrieved by a standard weighting model, known as the sample [3], as shown in Figure 1. To improve the efficiency of such a deployment, a dynamic pruning strategy such as WAND [1] could easily be used, which omits the scoring of documents that cannot reach the top K retrieved set. In doing so, WAND is *safe-to-rank-K*, which we denote as *safe* for short.

WAND follows a Document-at-a-time retrieval strategy (DAAT), whereby the posting lists for all constituent terms of a query are processed in parallel, allowing immediate decisions as to whether a document has scored high enough to make the current top K retrieved set. In particular, WAND repeatedly calculates a *pivot term*, by comparing the upper bounds $\sigma(t)$ of each query term t to the current score of the K-th ranked document, known as the threshold τ. The next document containing the pivot term is called the *pivot document*, which will be the next document to be fully scored. If the scored document exceeds the threshold τ, then the current K-th ranked document is expelled from the retrieved set, the new document inserted, and τ updated. As the scoring for a query continues, the threshold τ rises, such that more documents can be omitted from scoring.

However, Broder et al. [1] showed that WAND can be made more efficient by relaxing the safeness guarantee. This is achieved by artificially increasing τ by a factor $F \geq 1$. $F = 1$ guarantees safe retrieval, while for $F > 1$, increased efficiency can be achieved without much degradation in effectiveness. However, to the best of our knowledge, no previous work in the literature has addressed how such unsafe document rankings affect retrieval performance within a modern learning to rank setting. This paper provides a first study into the effect of safeness within a learning to rank setting, while providing explanations for the observed inherent bias in unsafe pruning that can improve effectiveness in some settings. Indeed, in contrast to a safe setting, unsafe WAND is dependent on the ordering of the collection, suggesting that further research into addressing the bias is needed.

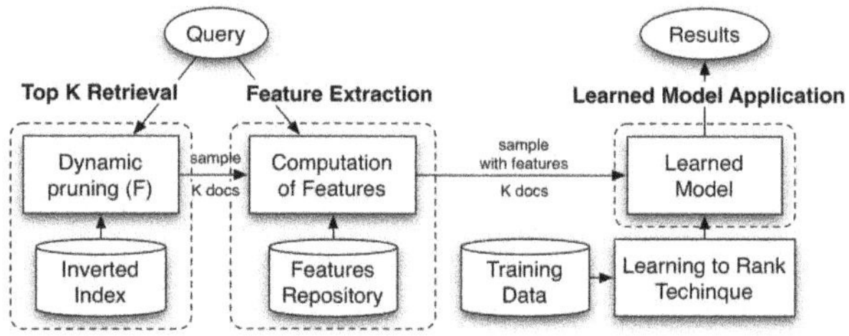

Figure 1: Retrieval phases of a search engine.

2. DATA & METHODS

Our experiments use the ClueWeb09 (cat. B) collection, which comprises 50 million English Web documents, and is aimed to represent the first tier index of a commercial search engine. We use the 150 corresponding topics and relevance assessments from the TREC Web tracks 2009-2011.

We index this collection using the Terrier information retrieval platform[1], with stemming and stopword removal. Following the three phase architecture of Figure 1, the top $K = 1000$ documents are ranked by WAND using the DPH Divergence from Randomness weighting model. We use a total of 33 standard query-dependent features (e.g. term weighting models, proximity features) and query-independent document features (e.g. link analysis, URL length, content quality). To re-rank the documents in the sample, we use the LambdaMART learning to rank technique [2, 4], which represents a state-of-the-art learning to rank technique, as per its recent performance in the 2011 Yahoo! learning to rank challenge. In particular, the 150 TREC topics are randomly split into three sets, namely training, validation and test. In the following, we experiment with the effectiveness of samples and LambdaMART models for various F values, while comparing and contrasting their retrieval effectiveness, in terms of NDCG@20 and relevant documents retrieved.

[1] `http://terrier.org`

SIGIR'12, August 12–16, 2012, Portland, Oregon, USA.
ACM 978-1-4503-1472-5/12/08.

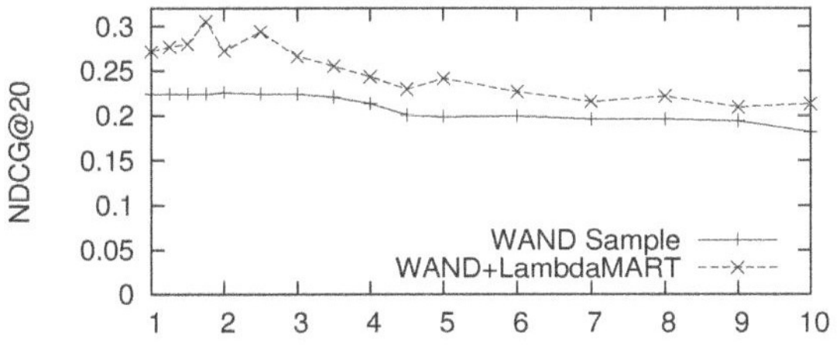

Figure 2: NDCG@20 for the WAND sample, and LambdaMART applied on the WAND sample.

	$F = 1$	$F = 1.75$
LambdaMART NDCG@20	0.2718	0.3055*
Sample NDCG@20	0.2242	0.2242
Relevant Retrieved in Sample	1931	1849
Mean docid of Relevant Retrieved	26.7M	25.6M
	$F = 1$ (A) $\rightarrow$ $F = 1.75$ (B)	$F = 1.75$ (A) $\rightarrow$ $F = 1$ (B)
Mean docid of docs present in sample A not present in sample B	35.8M	11.2M

Table 1: Analysis of safe and unsafe samples and learned models, as well as comparative statistics.

3. RESULTS & ANALYSIS

Figure 2 shows the NDCG@20 effectiveness of both the WAND sample, and LambdaMART applied on the sample document rankings from WAND, as F is varied. Note that as the learned model obtained by LambdaMART may be sensitive to a given F setting, a different model is learned for each F value. From Figure 2, we observe that the effectiveness to rank 20 of the WAND sample is unchanged for $1 \leq F \leq 3$, mirroring the original observations of Broder et al. [1]. However, the LambdaMART performance is much less stable for different F values - indeed, the overall NDCG@20 trend is downward for larger F. This is explained in that the learned model ranks documents from deep in the sample, and hence is affected by degradations in the number of relevant documents retrieved in unsafe samples. Indeed, on analysing $F = 1$, we find that of the top 20 documents ranked by LambdaMART, some were found as deep as rank 935 in the input sample ranking, while the mean rank in the sample of LambdaMART's top 20 documents was 89.

However, for some small F values in Figure 2 ($1 < F < 2$), a learned model obtained from an unsafe sample could improve over the NDCG@20 of the learned model obtained from the safe $F = 1$ sample. To analyse this unexpected characteristic, in Table 1 we compare and contrast four settings: $F = 1$ and $F = 1.75$, with and without the application of LambdaMART. Indeed, $F = 1.75$ is an interesting setting as while it is unsafe, it does not degrade NDCG@20 of the sample ranking obtained from WAND, but significantly improves the effectiveness of LambdaMART, according to a paired t-test ($p < 0.01$). Moreover, $F = 1.75$ is an efficient setting (we find that it reduces the mean response time of 1000 queries from a query log by 19% compared to $F = 1$, while larger F values do not cause further time reductions).

Next, comparing the sample rankings obtained from WAND for $F = 1$ and $F = 1.75$, we note a decrease of 82 relevant documents retrieved across the 50 test queries. Moreover, we examined the docids (in the range 0..50M for ClueWeb09 cat. B) of the documents selected in the safe and unsafe samples. We found that, on average, the safe sample retrieved documents from later in the posting lists (i.e. higher docids) than the unsafe sample (mean docids: 24.3M vs 21.9M). This observation is mirrored in the documents retrieved in one sample and not the other: the mean docid of documents in the safe sample that are missing from the unsafe sample is 35M, while unsafe sample documents missing from safe have a mean docid of 11.2M. Finally, Figure 3 presents the distribution of relevant docids, as well as those retrieved in the safe and unsafe samples. This shows that while there is no docid bias for relevant documents, unsafe WAND is more biased towards low docids than safe WAND. Indeed, the mean docid of the relevant documents retrieved in the safe sample is higher than those found in the unsafe sample (26.7M vs 25.6M in Table 1), explaining the change in retrieval effectiveness. Overall, this shows that aggressive, unsafe pruning by WAND can change the selected documents in a biased manner that is not present in safe pruning.

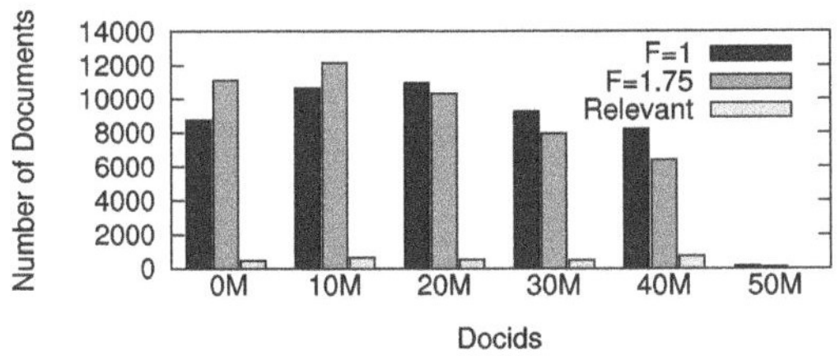

Figure 3: Distribution of relevant documents across the docid range, and for the safe & unsafe samples.

This behaviour of WAND is explained as follows: by artificially increasing the threshold τ by the factor F, the threshold for unsafe WAND causes more documents to be prevented from entering the top K. Early in the traversal of the posting lists, when the τ is lower, documents can still enter into the retrieved set. However as τ gets higher, more pruning occurs, even for documents that would have made the retrieved set for $F = 1$. This explains unsafe WAND's comparative preference for lower docid documents.

4. CONCLUSIONS

We contrasted the effectiveness of safe vs. unsafe rankings from WAND, and its impact on the effectiveness of a learning to rank technique, using ClueWeb09 cat. B and 150 TREC Web track topics. We found that while unsafe retrieval effectiveness has little impact on the top ranked documents directly retrieved by WAND, it does impact deeper down, which can be to the detriment of a learned model applied on that sample. Some unsafe settings were even found to benefit the learned model. Through further analysis, we found that unsafe retrieval has an inherent bias towards documents with lower docids in the applied index ordering.

The observations in this paper can give rise to several further research lines. In particular, static collection orderings may be devised that counteract unsafe WAND's preference for lower docids. On the other hand, it may be possible to devise different manners of changing the threshold for increasing WAND's efficiency in a less biased manner.

Acknowledgements

Craig Macdonald and Iadh Ounis acknowledge the support of EC-funded project SMART (FP7-287583).

5. REFERENCES

[1] A. Z. Broder, D. Carmel, M. Herscovici, A. Soffer, and J. Zien. Efficient query evaluation using a two-level retrieval process. In *Proc. of CIKM 2006*, 426–434.

[2] Y. Ganjisaffar, R. Caruana, and C. Lopes. Bagging gradient-boosted trees for high precision, low variance ranking models. In *Proc. of SIGIR 2011*, 85–94.

[3] T.-Y. Liu. Learning to rank for information retrieval. *Foundations and Trends in IR*, 3(3):225–331, 2009.

[4] Q. Wu, C. J. C. Burges, K. M. Svore, and J. Gao. Ranking, boosting, and model adaptation. Technical Report MSR-TR-2008-109, Microsoft, 2008.

Effect of Written Instructions on Assessor Agreement

William Webber
College of Information Studies
University of Maryland
United States of America
wew@umd.edu

Bryan Toth and Marjorie Desamito *
Eleanor Roosevelt High School
Greenbelt, Maryland
United States of America
bryan.n.toth@gmail.com
magicaura2000@yahoo.com

ABSTRACT

Assessors frequently disagree on the topical relevance of documents. How much of this disagreement is due to ambiguity in assessment instructions? We have two assessors assess TREC Legal Track documents for relevance, some to a general topic description, others to detailed assessment guidelines. We find that detailed guidelines lead to no significant increase in agreement amongst assessors or between assessors and the official qrels.

Categories and Subject Descriptors

H.3.4 [**Information Storage and Retrieval**]: Systems and software—*performance evaluation.*

Keywords

Retrieval experiment, evaluation, e-discovery

General Terms

Measurement, performance, experimentation

1. INTRODUCTION

Assessors frequently disagree on the relevance of a document to a topic. Voorhees [2000] finds that TREC adhoc assessors have mutual F1 scores of around 0.6, while Roitblat et al. [2010] report mutual F1 as low as 0.35 for professional e-discovery reviewers. Such low agreement is of serious practical concern in e-discovery, where large-scale, delegated manual review is still widely used. Possible causes of disagreement include assessor error and ambiguity in instructions. We examine whether detailed relevance guidelines increase agreement amongst assessors and with the guideline author, and find no significant increase in either form of agreement

2. METHODS AND MATERIALS

We measure inter-assessor agreement by Cohen's κ, for which 1 is perfect and 0 is random agreement [Cohen, 1960]. Unassessable documents (too long or misrendered) are ignored. A trial experiment of 75 documents per treatment, on Topic 301 from the TREC 2010 Legal Track, indicated that a sample size of 215 documents per treatment, with even proportions relevant and irrelevant, was required to achieve 80% power for a true κ delta of 0.23, being the difference in agreement with official assessments between first and second tercile assessors in the TREC 2009 Legal Track.

*Work performed while interns at the University of Maryland.

SIGIR'12, August 12–16, 2012, Portland, Oregon, USA.
ACM 978-1-4503-1472-5/12/08.

Message type	Messages	Documents		
		rel	irrel	unass
> 1 relevant document	5	13	12	0
Relevant appealed	170	170	82	4
" unappealed	38	38	7	0
Irrelevant appealed	58	0	78	1
" unappealed returned	32	0	44	1
" " unreturned	16	0	17	1
Total	319	221	240	7

Table 1: Number and types of messages and documents sampled from Topic 204 for re-assessment. A message is classed as "relevant" if it contains a single relevant document (body or attachment). Counts of relevant, irrelevant, and unassessable documents are using the official, post-appeal assessments.

Topic 204 from the interactive task of the TREC 2009 Legal Track [Hedin et al., 2009] was used for the full experiment. The corpus is the EDRM Enron emails. Whole messages were sampled, but each email body and attachment was separately assessed. A stratified sample was taken, as described in Table 1. The strata were divided evenly and randomly into two batches. Each batch was assessed in document id order, with the parts of a message being assessed sequentially, as in TREC.

At TREC, a senior lawyer called the topic authority develops the topic, writes the detailed guidelines, and adjudicates appeals against first-round assessments. The appeals process for this topic was thorough [Webber, 2011], and the majority of sampled documents were appealed; we regard the assessments as an accurate representation of the topic authority's conception of relevance. We measure agreement for each batch between the two experimental assessors and the official, post-appeal assessments.

The latter two authors of this paper acted as experimental assessors. Each assessor assessed all documents in each batch. For the first batch, assessors were given the 42-word topic statement to guide their assessments; for the second, they received the 5-page detailed relevance guidelines. A third pass was then made, in which the two assessors jointly reviewed both batches, in light of the detailed guidelines, and tried to agree on a conception of relevance.

3. EXPERIMENTAL RESULTS

Table 2 shows the results of our experiments. The provision of detailed assessment guidelines (Batch 2) did not improve agreement, significantly or otherwise, over topic-only instructions (Batch 1), either amongst assessors or with the official assessments, in either the full or the trial experiment. Message-level analysis (in

	Full experiment			Trial experiment		
Batch	A v B	A v O	B v O	A v B	A v O	B v O
1	0.519	0.454^{ab}	0.710	0.229	0.557	0.417
2	0.528	0.555	0.637	0.275	0.439	0.294
Jnt-1	*0.992*	0.677^{a}	0.686	–	–	–
Jnt-2	*0.950*	0.665^{b}	0.674	–	–	–

Table 2: Cohen's κ values between official and two experimental assessors, for full and trial experiments, on single-assessed Batch 1 (with topic statement only), single-assessed Batch 2 (with detailed guidelines), and (for full experiment only) joint-assessed Batches 1 and 2 (with topic guidelines and consultation between assessors). Columnar value pairs significantly different at $\alpha = 0.05$ (excepting inter-experimenter joint review) are marked by superscripts.

Assessors	Confidence interval
A v. B	$[-0.155, 0.173]$
A v. Official	$[-0.061, 0.263]$
B v. Official	$[-0.211, 0.065]$

Table 3: Two-tailed 95% normal-approximation confidence intervals on the true change in κ between Batch 1 and Batch 2 amongst different assessor pairs, for the full experiment.

which a message is relevant if any part of it is relevant) gives similar results. Inter-assessor κ values are high for the full experiment's joint assessment, since assessors reached agreement on all save a handful of documents (1 for Batch 1, and 5 for Batch 2). Assessor A's agreement with the official assessments increases significantly under joint review, but this may be due to Assessor A's assessments moving closer to Assessor B's; Assessor A's self-agreement on Batch 1 is 0.399 post-consultation, whereas Assessor B's is 0.739.

Table 3 gives 95% confidence intervals on the true change in κ values with the addition of assessor guidelines. A substantial improvement is still plausible in agreement between Assessor A and the official assessments, but not for Assessor B and official, nor for inter-assessor agreement.

Agreement between the original TREC assessors and the authoritative assessment on the documents examined in our experiment is 0.102 for Batch 1 and 0.024 for Batch 2, much lower than for our experimental assessors; however, this is a biased comparison, since sampling was heavily weighted towards appealed documents. Over the 7,289 documents sampled for assessment at TREC, though, the original assessors achieved a κ of 0.320, still well below that of the experimental assessors. The relatively high reliabilty of the assessor is reflected in their high mutual F1 scores (Table 4).

Qualitatively, the experimental assessors described the full experiment topic description by itself as being clear, and the detailed guidelines as being very clear and easy to relate to the documents. As can be seen in Table 2, agreement for this topic was generally higher than for the trial experiment.

4. DISCUSSION

Our initial, seemingly common-sense, hypothesis was that more detailed instructions would raise agreement between assessors and the authoritative conception of relevance, and therefore amongst assessors themselves. The results of this experiment have failed to confirm this hypothesis, or even to show a general trend in this direction. The only significant improvement occurred when Assessor A consulted with Assessor B, but that may be attributable to the former's assessments moving closer to the latter's. Indeed, confidence intervals indicate that a substantial increase in agreement is not plausible, except possibly between one assessor and the official view. We can conclude that, for this topic and these assessors, the provision of more detailed assessment guidelines did not lead to any marked increase in assessor reliability.

Batch	A v B	A v O	B v O
1	0.679	0.648	0.828
2	0.769	0.791	0.823

Table 4: Assessor mutual F1 scores for the full experiment.

It is also notable that our experimental assessors, who were high school students with no legal training, appear to have produced assessments much more in line with the authoritative conception of relevance than the original TREC assessors, who were legally trained, professional document reviewers.

Our findings are not reassuring for the widespread practice of using delegated manual review in e-discovery. If assessors do no better with detailed guidelines than with a general outline of the topic, then there is an irreducible loss of signal in transmitting the relevance conception of an authoritative reviewer into the minds of other assessors. E-discovery practice is moving towards the use of statistical classification tools [Grossman and Cormack, 2011]; it may well be that the lawyer overseeing a case is better able to convey their conception of relevance by personally training a machine classifier, than by instructing delegated human reviewers.

Acknowledgments.

Venkat Rangan of Symantec eDiscovery provided the TIFF images of Enron documents used in the TREC 2009 Legal Track assessments. Maura Grossman and Gord Cormack advised on the choice of TREC topics. This material is based upon work supported by the National Science Foundation under Grant No. 1065250. Any opinions, findings, and conclusions or recommendations expressed in this material are those of the authors and do not necessarily reflect the views of the National Science Foundation.

References

Jacob Cohen. A coefficient of agreement for nominal scales. *Educational and Psychological Measurement*, 20(1):37–46, 1960.

Maura R. Grossman and Gordon V. Cormack. Technology-assisted review in e-discovery can be more effective and more efficient than exhaustive manual review. *Richmond Journal of Law and Technology*, 17(3):11:1–48, 2011.

Bruce Hedin, Stephen Tomlinson, Jason R. Baron, and Douglas W. Oard. Overview of the TREC 2009 legal track. In Ellen Voorhees and Lori P. Buckland, editors, *Proc. 18th Text REtrieval Conference*, pages 1:4:1–40, Gaithersburg, Maryland, USA, November 2009. NIST Special Publication 500-278.

Herbert L. Roitblat, Anne Kershaw, and Patrick Oot. Document categorization in legal electronic discovery: computer classification vs. manual review. *Journal of the American Society for Information Science and Technology*, 61(1):70–80, 2010.

Ellen Voorhees. Variations in relevance judgments and the measurement of retrieval effectiveness. *Information Processing & Management*, 36(5): 697–716, September 2000.

William Webber. Re-examining the effectiveness of manual review. In *Proc. SIGIR Information Retrieval for E-Discovery Workshop*, pages 2:1–8, Beijing, China, July 2011.

Effects of Expertise Differences in Synchronous Social Q&A

Ryen W. White
Microsoft Research
Redmond, WA 98052
ryenw@microsoft.com

Matthew Richardson
Microsoft Research
Redmond, WA 98052
mattri@microsoft.com

ABSTRACT

Synchronous social question-and-answer (Q&A) systems match askers to answerers and support real-time dialog between them to resolve questions. These systems typically find answerers based on the degree of expertise match with the asker's initial question. However, since synchronous social Q&A involves a dialog between asker and answerer, differences in expertise may also matter (e.g., extreme novices and experts may have difficulty establishing common ground). In this poster we use data from a live social Q&A system to explore the impact of expertise differences on answer quality and aspects of the dialog itself. The findings of our study suggest that synchronous social Q&A systems should consider the relative expertise of candidate answerers with respect to the asker, and offer interactive dialog support to help establish common ground between askers and answerers.

Categories and Subject Descriptors

H.3.3 [**Information Storage and Retrieval**] – Information Search and Retrieval: *search process, selection process.*

Keywords

Synchronous social Q&A; Expert finding; Expertise location.

1. INTRODUCTION

Synchronous social question answering (Q&A) systems match askers to answers in real time and facilitate dialog between them, usually via instant messaging (IM) [3][9]. These systems typically use expert finding methods (e.g., [1]) to identify candidate answerers based on the match between their profile and the initial question. However, since synchronous social Q&A systems initiate direct dialog between askers and answerers, the ability of askers and answerers to converse with each other effectively may also affect the outcome. Indeed, psychologists and human-computer interaction researchers have shown that expertise differences can hinder dialog between domain novices and experts [4][6] and that IM is a difficult medium for establishing the common ground that is important in successful dialog [5]. Understanding the effect of expertise differences on synchronous Q&A can help in designing better social Q&A systems, perhaps by including relative expertise when selecting candidate answerers [7], or providing support to help ground the Q&A dialog.

In this poster we present a study of expertise differences in synchronous social Q&A. We use data from a live synchronous social Q&A system, *IM-an-Expert*, deployed to a community of over two thousand users [9]. IM-an-Expert receives questions via IM, identifies candidate answerers by ranking all users according to the match between their expertise and the question, routes questions only to those available to answer, and mediates the dialog between the asker and answerer. In IM-an-Expert, all users ask or answer questions; to ask, users must be willing to answer. We use the data from the system to study the effect of expertise differences on answer ratings (assigned by askers and indicating answer quality) and the dialog.

SIGIR'12, August 12–16, 2012, Portland, Oregon, USA.
ACM 978-1-4503-1472-5/12/08.

2. IM-AN-EXPERT

The asker poses the question to IM-an-Expert via IM. The system selects (using BM25 [8]) users who seem to be most likely able to answer a question using profile information from three sources: (i) *self-reported knowledge:* a Web interface lets users create and update a profile comprising keywords and URLs of pages about them or their interests; (ii) *email sent to mailing lists:* archives of email sent to internal mailing lists, available on a range of topics. Email is preprocessed to exclude headers and quoted text so that each profile contains only the user's authored text, and; (iii) *history*: each user is associated with questions they answered, allowing the system to improve over time. Other factors such as elapsed time since a user was last asked a question are also considered. A small group of experts who are currently available (not busy, away, etc. via presence data from the IM client) are contacted via IM three at a time, in descending order of expertise, to determine whether they can help answer the question. If and when an answerer accepts, other requests are canceled. If a candidate answerer does not respond in time or rejects the question, the service asks others. Once an answerer accepts, IM-an-Expert mediates the conversation. When the conversation ends, the asker can optionally rate answer quality from one (not helpful) to five (very helpful).

3. STUDY

3.1 Data

IM-an-Expert is deployed within Microsoft and thousands of employees use it to find answers to their questions. We use a set of 1,725 questions from 937 users. 1,144 (66%) of the questions were answered, of which 908 (79%) were rated. 527 users asked at least one question and 573 users answered at least one question. For each question we have the text, the asker and answerer identity, and the full-text of the IM dialog. We also have the profiles of askers and answerers, not including questions that they answered well ((iii) above), which varied based on *when* the question was asked and excluding it simplified our analysis. On average, users provided 8.0 unique keywords and 2.7 unique URLs. The average profile length was 8,930 words (after removing HTML tags).

3.2 Estimating Expertise

To study the effect of differences in the expertise levels on the question outcomes and the dialog itself, we devised a way to estimate the expertise of the asker and the answerer with respect to the question. Following removal of stopwords from the question and from user profiles, we represent each as term vectors with term frequency counts. We then compute the cosine similarity between the question and the profile. We do this on a per-question basis since expertise may vary by question topic. Cosine was used since it gave us a normalized measure of expertise, in the range [0,1], that could be computed for both askers and answerers and easily compared to estimate expertise differences. It also has the advantage of estimating expertise relative to the question at hand, rather than using measures such as reputation or answer history, which are question independent. We use the difference (d) between the similarities of the asker and the answer as a proxy for differences in expertise. Reassuringly, the results show that for 76% of questions, the answerer is at least as expert as the asker and in most cases (58%), is more expert. It is worth noting that using the cosine similarity as the measure of expertise penalizes people whose profiles span multiple areas of expertise. Since such profiles may indicate less expertise in the question than someone whose profile focuses only on that topic, it is unknown whether this is a concern. We could also have focused on asynchronous media such as stackoverflow.com or quora.com. However, targeting synchronous Q&A better aligned with our research focus and let us study dialog dynamics.

3.3 Findings

We focused our analysis of the effect of expertise differences on two important aspects of the synchronous social Q&A process: (i) outcome (answer rating) and (ii) dialog (balance of conversation).

3.3.1 Expertise Difference and Answer Ratings

We were interested in the relationship between the difference in expertise and the quality of the answer. Answer quality is a measure of the benefit to the asker of the dialog. The top row of Table 1 presents the average answer rating depending on whether the answerer was less, equally, or more expert than the asker.

Table 1. Average answer rating and percentage of dialog from question asker, given expertise differences. *Ask*=asker, *Ans*=answerer.

Metric	Expertise differences		
	Ans < Ask	*Ans = Ask*	*Ans > Ask*
Average answer rating	3.66	4.05	4.27
% dialog from asker	54.8	54.7	59.3

Table 1 shows differences in the answer rating as answerers become more expert than askers. All differences in ratings are statistically significant with an independent measures analysis of variance (ANOVA), ($F(2,905) = 4.63$, $p = .01$) and post-hoc testing as appropriate. Figure 1 shows a more granular breakdown of rating by d. Error bars denote standard error of the mean (SEM).

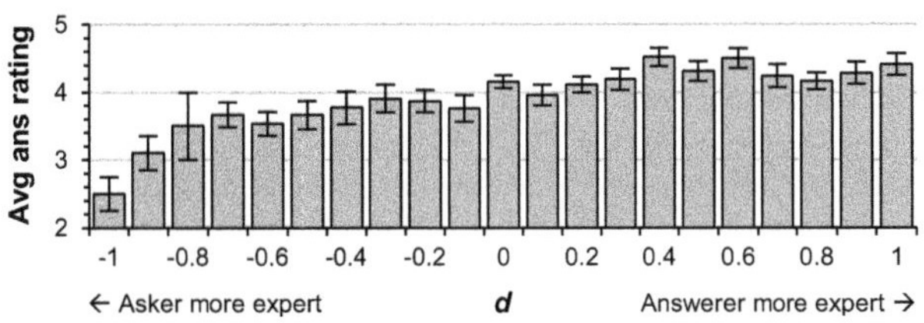

Figure 1. Average answer rating given expertise differences (± SEM).

Figure 1 shows that there is a slight increase in answer rating as answerers become increasingly more expert than askers. However, we can make more interesting observations about the figure:

1. It is not until the answerer is significantly less expert than the asker ($d \leq -0.8$) that the outcome suffers significantly. The rating is pretty robust to expertise differences (ranging from 3.7 at $d = -0.7$ to 4.4 at $d = 1.0$). One possible explanation for this is that the ability to clarify and discuss the problem via IM may lessen the importance of the expertise differences.
2. The asker just needs to have a level of expertise equivalent to the answerer to get an average answer rating of four or more.
3. More expertise is not always valuable. There is no additional asker benefit (at least in terms of answer rating) after $d \geq 0.4$. One possible explanation for this is that askers with little or no expertise on their question topic (required for such high values of *d*) may be easily satisfied with any help received, regardless of how beneficial the help was. Since our measure of answer quality is subjectively provided by the asker, we cannot distinguish between an asker receiving genuinely better answers vs. an asker who is more easily satisfied with mediocre answers.

The third observation in particular motivated us to explore the Q&A process itself for an alternative objective measure. We focus on the dialog balance, representing the relative fraction of the dialog that askers and answerers perform. This can be viewed as a measure of the fraction of the work (the relative cost) to each party of engaging in the conversation.

3.3.2 Expertise Difference and Dialog Balance

To measure the effect of expertise differences on the balance of the conversation, we computed the number of messages from each user for each IM dialog. The average percentage of each dialog coming from the asker, given differences in expertise levels, is shown in Table 1. Large differences are observed when answerers have more topic expertise than the asker ($F(2,1141) = 6.24$, $p < .01$, and $p < .02$ with Tukey post-hoc tests). One possible explanation for this phenomenon is that the asker is spending more time clarifying their question. Possible reasons for this include differences in vocabulary between novices and experts [2] and the tendency of novices to underspecify their goals in dialog with experts [6], both of which may result in more messages. In this case, it may be beneficial if the Q&A system was a more active intermediary and suggested strategies to establish common frames of reference, something that is important in successful novice-expert dialog [4]. Alternatively, it may be the case that the answerer, by being much more expert, is able to rapidly answer the question.

4. CONCLUSIONS AND FUTURE WORK

We have demonstrated the effect of expertise differences on the outcomes and dialog in synchronous social Q&A. As expected, we showed that when askers engage in dialog with those who are more expert on the question topic, they are more satisfied with the answer they receive. However, the benefit does not seem to increase beyond a certain expertise difference. In fact, beyond a difference of 0.4, the average answer rating no longer increases yet the dialog continues to become more and more imbalanced. Synchronous social Q&A systems should consider both asker and answerer topic knowledge during expert finding. In these systems it may be worth finding answerers slightly more knowledge than the asker, and reserve the most expert answerers for the most knowledgeable askers. There are opportunities for future work in better understanding the underlying causes of the observed dialog imbalance, in determining whether the imbalance is positive or negative, and in developing mitigation strategies if negative.

REFERENCES

[1] Balog, K. *et al.* (2006). Formal models for expert finding in enterprise corpora. *SIGIR*, 43-50.
[2] Falzon, P. (1991). Cooperative dialogues. In Rasmussen, J., Brehmer, B. and Leplat, J. *Distributed Decision Making: Cognitive Models for Cooperative Work*, 145-189.
[3] Horowitz, D. and Kamvar, S.D. (2010). The anatomy of a large social search engine. *WWW*, 431-440.
[4] Issacs, E.A. and Clark, H. (1987). References in conversations between experts and novices. *J. Exp. Psych.*, 116(1): 26-37.
[5] McCarthy, J.C *et al.* (1991). An experimental study of common ground in text-based communication. *SIGCHI*, 209-215.
[6] Pollack, M.E. (1985). Information sought and information provided: an empirical study of user/expert dialogues. *SIGCHI*, 155-159.
[7] Smirnova, E. and Balog, K. (2011). A user-oriented model for expert finding. *ECIR*, 580-592.
[8] Spärck-Jones, K. *et al.* (2000). A probabilistic model of information retrieval. *IP&M*, 36(6): 779-840.
[9] White, R.W. *et al.* (2011). Effects of community size and contact rate in synchronous social Q&A. *SIGCHI*, 2837-2846.

Efficient Estimation of Aspect Weights

Jon Parker, Andrew Yates, Nazli Goharian
Department of Computer Science
Georgetown University
{jon, andrew, nazli}@ir.cs.georgetown.edu

Wai Gen Yee
Orbitz Worldwide
Chicago IL, 60661
waigen.yee@orbitz.com

ABSTRACT
Many websites encourage people to submit reviews of various products and services. We present and evaluate a novel approach to efficiently model and analyze the text within user reviews to estimate how much reviewers care about different aspects of a product (i.e., amenities, food, location, room, etc. of a hotel). Our approach performs statistically quite similar to the best existing method. However, our method for computing aspect weights is a linear time method while the current state of the art solution requires cubic time at best.

Categories and Subject Descriptors
I.2.7 [**Natural Language Processing**]: Text Analysis

General Terms
Algorithms, Performance, Experimentation

Keywords
Aspect ranking, opinion and sentiment analysis, review mining.

1. INTRODUCTION
The proliferation of websites that collect user reviews has increased the value of a methodology that can mine these reviews for customer preference data. The Latent Aspect Rating Analysis (LARA) method introduced in [1] and expanded in [2] estimates aspect weights, (i.e. customer preferences) from user reviews. This is the only work we are aware of, besides the work of Xu et al. [3], which tries to determine what customers think about aspects. LARA assumes a review's overall star rating is a linear combination a of the review's aspect star ratings. The coefficients in this linear combination represent the weights a reviewer places on the aspects. Given this assumption, a latent rating regression is performed to simultaneously estimate each individual review's aspect ratings as well as the underlying aspect weights using just the individual review's text and overall rating.

We present a significantly more efficient method for estimating aspect weights that generates very similar results. The Force of Commentary (FoC) method introduced here models the impetus that prompts people to write the text portion of a review. We hypothesize that this impetus is well modeled as a mixture of what users are surprised about and what users care about. FoC estimates customer preference using solely the text within reviews. This enables FoC to be used when ordinal rating data (e.g., star rating) is not reliable or not available. While we perform our experiments on a hotel review data set, our method is not domain-specific and should work for other types of reviews.

SIGIR'12, August 12–16, 2012, Portland, Oregon, USA.
ACM 978-1-4503-1472-5/12/08.

2. METHODOLOGY

2.1 The Force of Commentary Curve
We assume people write about aspects they find important and/or surprising. This assumption suggests a generic functional form for what we call the Force of Commentary (FoC) curve. For each aspect we have the generic equation:

$$E[n_i] = w_i \cdot \int Prob(x_i) \cdot Surprise(x_i)\, dx_i$$

where E[n_i] is the expected value of n_i, the number of comments written about aspect i, w_i is the importance of aspect i, $Prob(x_i)$ is the probability a hotel provides an x_i level of service, and $Surprise(x_i)$ is a function that specifies how much a customer notices receiving an x_i level of service. For convenience, we require *Surprise* to be decreasing from $-\infty$ to 0, increasing from 0 to ∞, and equal to 0 at 0. This requirement ensures that the above integral can be cleanly split into one integral (from 0 to ∞) that corresponds to positive comments and a second integral (from $-\infty$ to 0) that corresponds to negative comments.

Assuming for simplicity that the performance level x_i is Normal(μ_i, 1) and *Surprise* is abs(x_i), the equation becomes:

$$E[n_i] = w_i \cdot \frac{1}{\sqrt{2\pi}} \cdot \int e^{-\frac{(x-\mu_i)^2}{2}} \cdot |x_i|\, dx_i$$

2.2 Processing the Hotel Review Data
The Orbitz hotel review dataset contained 609,884 individual human authored reviews that rated 30,621 hotels. Each review contained an overall experience "star rating", multiple aspect "star ratings", and a review text. The review text typically contains 1 to 5 sentences that detail the customer's thoughts about a hotel property.

Processing the reviews begins by gathering the text portion from every review of a specific hotel property into one large macro-review. Macro-reviews that do not contain 100 sentences are thrown out because they do not contain enough information to estimate our 6 selected aspect weights well.

We selected 6 aspects which we believe are sufficient to characterize hotels and whose themes occur frequently in the reviews. They are food, room, cleanliness, amenities, value, and location. These aspects correspond closely with the aspect ratings available in our dataset as well as the aspects used by Wang et al [1].

We used the χ^2 bootstrapping method described in [1] to expand a list of seed words used to determine which aspect each sentence in a macro-review is addressing. Once a sentence is associated with an aspect its polarity is determined using SentiWordNet[4]. The sentence's polarity is the polarity of the majority of its words. We discard neutral sentences.

To compute the aspects' weights, we begin by finding the μ_i values for which the ratio between the expected number of positive comments and the expected number of negative comments matches the ratio between the observed number of positive comments and the observed number of negative comments. Next, we find the vector of w_i values, for which the relative distribution between the computed $E[n_i]$ values matches the observed distribution of comments. The computed weight vector contains a valuable synthesis of information about the average hotel customer's preferences and expectations as well as what the hotel actually provides.

Notice, the method described herein does not make use of either the overall "star rating" or any of the aspect "star ratings". Relying on ratings presents two problems. First, a non-trivial fraction of reviewers seem to misinterpret the star rating scale. These reviewers write scathing remarks and then leave 5-star ratings, and vice versa. Second, humans vary on how generously they award stars. One reviewer's 5-star experience could be another reviewer's 3-star experience. This bias is well-known in user review research [5]. Ignoring human assigned ratings also allows this method to be deployed where numeric or ordinal ratings are unavailable.

3. RESULTS & EVALUATION

The aspect weight vector was computed twice for each of the 111 hotels with a macro-review of at least 100 sentences. The first weight vector was computed using the Force of Commentary method outlined in Section 2. The second weight vector was computed using the LARA method from Wang et al. [1,2] as the state-of-the-art.

Table 1. Average Aspect Weight Vector by Method

	Food	Room	Cle.	Ame.	Val.	Loc.
FoC	0.06	0.34	0.36	0.11	0.02	0.11
LARA	0.11	0.27	0.23	0.14	0.11	0.14

The average aspect weight vector for all 111 hotels is shown in Table 1. This table suggests the aspect weights computed using FoC are similar to the aspect weights computed using LARA. The correlation coefficients shown in Table 2 confirm a relationship does indeed exist. In fact, the median Spearman's rank correlation coefficient is .829 and the mean Spearman's rank correlation is .699. Given these correlations coefficients, it is clear that these methods are generating answers that are well within the same ballpark.

Table 2. Pearson Correlation Coefficients Between FoC and LARA Aspect Weights

Food	Room	Cle.	Ame.	Val.	Loc.
.614	.567	.534	.617	.217	.733

All 111 hotels were clustered into 6 groups according to their FoC aspect weights. The goal of this clustering was to determine if hotels with similar customer populations were assigned to the same cluster. After all, if FoC aspect weights do indeed characterize customer preferences then this regularity should appear. As expected, 4 of the 6 clusters had clear hotel tier effects. For example, one cluster contained high-end hotels like the ARIA and Wynn (both of Las Vegas) while another cluster contained Quality Suites, Holiday Inn, Ramada, and Best Western chains. The 2 remaining clusters contained hotels with a significant number of cleanliness complaints and location praise respectively.

A human evaluation of the FoC clusters was also performed. However, there was very little agreement among the evaluator comments. We believe this is due to the subjectivity and high dimensionality of the task.

4. EFFICIENCY ANALYSIS

LARA includes a non-linear optimization problem that is solved using a conjugate gradient interior point method. Applying this method to a linear programming problem requires $O(n^3/log(n))$ bit operations. LARA is actually a non-linear optimization problem, thus its computational complexity is higher. We ignore this fact because we can show that FoC is more efficient than the linear optimization problem.

FoC consists of three separate stages performed in succession: sentence aspect assignment, sentence polarity assignment, and weight vector computation. All three rely on lookup tables that can be computed offline. We do not include the cost of computing these tables when determining the final computational complexity.

Both the sentence aspect assignment and sentence polarity assignment stages of FoC require $O(n)$ time (where n is number of words in all the macro reviews) due to the table lookups within each stage. The final weight computation stage is linear in number of macro-views. Thus, the $O(n)$ stages of FoC dominate the computation complexity and FoC is $O(n)$.

Computing the FoC weights listed in the paper took less than 5 minutes while computing the LARA weights took 36 hours.

5. CONCLUSION

We demonstrated that the FoC aspects weights are: (1) vastly more efficient to compute than LARA weights, with FoC's computation taking linear time and LARA's computation taking cubic time (2) statistically very similar to LARA weights and (3) accurate enough to generate hotel clusters that appear natural.

6. REFERENCES

[1] H. Wang, Y. Lu, and C. Zhai. 2010. Latent aspect rating analysis on review text data: a rating regression approach. In KDD '10. ACM, New York, NY, USA, 783-792.

[2] H. Wang, Y. Lu, and C. Zhai. 2011. Latent aspect rating analysis without aspect keyword supervision. In KDD '11. ACM, New York, NY, USA, 618-626.

[3] J. Xu, Z. Zha, M. Wang, and T. Chua. 2011. Aspect ranking: identifying important product aspects from on-line consumer reviews. In *ACL '11*. ACL, Stroudsburg, PA, USA, 1496-1505.

[4] S. Baccianella, A. Esuli, and F. Sebastiani. 2010. SentiWordNet 3.0: An enhanced lexical resource for sentiment analysis and opinion mining. In LREC'10. ELRA, Paris, France, 2200-2204.

[5] Koren, Y. 2009. Collaborative filtering with temporal dynamics. In KDD '09. ACM, New York, NY, USA, 447-456.

Emotion Tagging for Comments of Online News by Meta Classification with Heterogeneous Information Sources*

Ying Zhang
Dept. of Computer Science
Nankai University
zhangying@dbis.nankai.edu.cn

Yi Fang
Dept. of Computer Science
Purdue University
yfang.purdue@gmail.com

Xiaojun Quan
Dept. of Computer Science
City University of Hong Kong
xiaoquan@student.cityu.edu.hk

Lin Dai
Dept. of Computer Science
Beijing Institute of Technology
dailiu@bit.edu.cn

Luo Si
Dept. of Computer Science
Purdue University
lsi@cs.purdue.edu

Xiaojie Yuan
Dept. of Computer Science
Nankai University
yuanxj@nankai.edu.cn

ABSTRACT

With the rapid growth of online news services, users can actively respond to online news by making comments. Users often express subjective emotions in comments such as sadness, surprise and anger. Such emotions can help understand the preferences and perspectives of individual users, and therefore may facilitate online publishers to provide users with more relevant services. This paper tackles the task of predicting emotions for the comments of online news. To the best of our knowledge, this is the first research work for addressing the task. In particular, this paper proposes a novel Meta classification approach that exploits heterogeneous information sources such as the content of the comments and the emotion tags of news articles generated by users. The experiments on two datasets from online news services demonstrate the effectiveness of the proposed approach.

Categories and Subject Descriptors: H.3.3 [**Information Storage and Retrieval**]: Information Search and Retrieval
General Terms: Algorithms, Experimentation
Keywords: Emotion Tagging, Meta Classification, Online News

1. INTRODUCTION

The emergence of social media is reshaping the way how people consume news. Online readers can actively respond to online news by making comments. Users often express subjective emotions in the comments such as sadness, surprise and anger. Such emotions can help understand the preferences and perspectives of individual users, and therefore may facilitate online publishers to provide users with more personalized services. It is a challenging and practical research problem to automatically assign emotion tags to users' comments of online news. One natural approach to achieving the goal is to classify users' comments into different emotion tags based on the contents of the comments. On the other side, an increasing number of social news websites provide a novel service via which users can share their emotions after reading news articles by selecting emotion tags. Figure 1 shows an example from a popular Chinese news website (i.e., Sina News[1]). The user-generated emotion tags for news articles can naturally provide guidance for assigning emotion tags to individual comments.

This paper focuses on the research problem of emotion tagging for comments of online news. As far as we know, this is the first research work for addressing the problem. Some prior work tries to predict emotions of online news articles [2, 4]. Most of these techniques for news articles mainly analyze the content information [1, 3]. This paper proposes novel research to exploit heterogeneous information sources with a Meta classification approach by utilizing both the content of comments and available user-generated emotion tags of news articles. In particular, a content-based classifier is built with a text categorization approach, which is combined with the information of emotion tags of news articles within a Meta classifier by a probabilistic combination method.

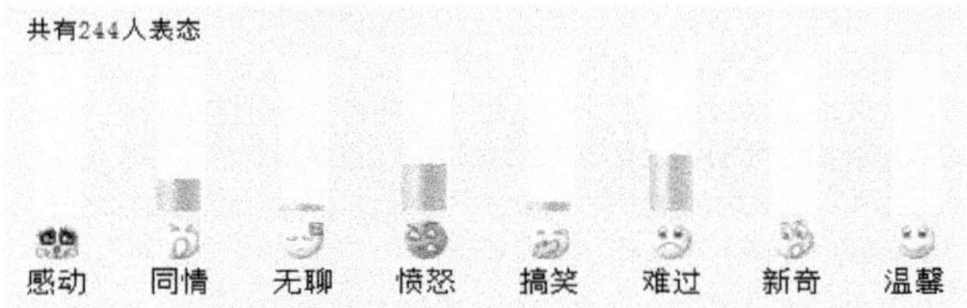

Figure 1: An example of emotion tags voted by 244 users for a Sina news article. The emotion labels (from left to right) are: touched, sympathetic, bored, angry, amused, sad, surprised and fervent.

2. METHODS

In this paper, we adopt two heterogeneous information sources of users' comments of online news. The first one is based on a text categorization approach with contents of the comments, namely Content-based Model (CM). Formally, the probability that the ith comment will be tagged as a predefined emotion $e_k \in E(k = 1, 2, ..., N_E)$ by this method, referred as c_{ik}, can be expressed as follows in terms of softmax function over a linear function of features,

$$c_{ik} = P(e_k|\phi_i) = \frac{\exp(\omega_k^T \phi_i)}{\sum_{r=1}^{N_E} \exp(\omega_r^T \phi_i)} \tag{1}$$

*This research is partially supported by NSF of China research grants 61170184, and also partially supported by NSF research grants IIS-0746830, CNS-1012208 and IIS-1017837.

[1]http://news.sina.com.cn/society/

SIGIR'12, August 12–16, 2012, Portland, Oregon, USA.
ACM 978-1-4503-1472-5/12/08.

Here the feature vector ϕ_i is composed by the count of each term in the ith comment. ω_k denotes the combination parameters for each term with emotion e_k, and can be estimated by maximizing log-likelihood function with L2 (i.e., ridge) regularization. It is worth noting that $\sum_{k=1}^{N_E} c_{ik} = 1$.

The second one is derived from the emotion tags of news articles generated by users, namely User Emotion Tags Model (UM). We can follow the ratio of votes of each emotion to all emotions for tagging emotion for comments. Let u_{ik} denote how likely the ith comment will be tagged by emotion e_k according to the information of emotion tags.

To better integrate the two heterogeneous information sources, a Meta classifier approach is utilized for emotion tagging of users' comments, called Meta Classification Model (MCM). We use the outputs of the above models as features, and also add a constant feature as the bias. Therefore, the probability that emotion e_k will be assigned to the ith comment can be estimated as below,

$$P(e_k|c_i, u_i) = \frac{\exp(\alpha_k + \sum_{l=1}^{N_E} \beta_{lk} c_{il} + \sum_{l=1}^{N_E} \gamma_{lk} u_{il})}{\sum_{r=1}^{N_E} \exp(\alpha_r + \sum_{l=1}^{N_E} \beta_{lr} c_{il} + \sum_{l=1}^{N_E} \gamma_{lr} u_{il})}$$

where α, β and γ denote the combination parameters for bias, the source of comments content and the source of emotion tags of news articles respectively. These parameters can be determined by maximizing the log-likelihood function (i.e., Quasi-Newton optimization method in this paper).

3. EXPERIMENTAL EVALUATION

We collected most-viewed news articles and their some most popular comments and emotion tags, in one month of 2011 from the society channel of Sina News and the entertainment channel of QQ News[2]. Both Sina and QQ are among the largest news portals in China. We use these Chinese datasets since we have not found similar services in English yet, but the proposed model is language independent. We then sample 200 news articles from each news service to construct our two datasets. All news articles and users' comments are segmented to terms by a Chinese word segmentation software: ICTCLAS[3]. The two datasets contain 8,794 distinct terms in 3,593 comments and 9,401 distinct terms in 3,623 comments respectively. For each dataset, one person was asked to label an emotion tag for each comment from 8 predefined emotion categories which are the same as the emotion tags in news services. The distributions of labeled comments on the 8 emotions are shown in Figure 2.

We compare the performances of emotion tagging using CM, UM and MCM with 10-fold cross validation on two dataset. Two measures are adopted: mean reciprocal rank (MRR) and accuracy ($A@n$). Given a comment c, its labeled emotion e_c and predicted emotion set E_{nc} including n top-ranked emotions, $A_c@n$ is defined as,

$$A_c@n = \begin{cases} 1, & e_c \in E_{nc} \\ 0, & e_c \notin E_{nc} \end{cases} \tag{2}$$

Thus, $A@n$ for the collection C is: $A@n = \sum_{c \in C} A_c@n/|C|$.

Table 1 shows MRR and $A@n (n = 1, 2, 3)$ in each dataset. $A@n (n = 1, 2, ..., 8)$ is shown in Figure 3. Based on these results, we can make the following observations: 1) CM performs much better than UM. This seems to indicate that content of comments is more effective and reliable than users' emotion tags of news articles, as a single data source to tag emotions for comments. 2) MCM consistently outperforms CM and UM in terms of all evaluation measures. A paired t-test shows that all improvements of MCM over CM are statistically significant with p-value < 0.001. This indicates that it is more effective that exploiting heterogeneous information sources with a Meta classification approach by utilizing both the content of comments and users' emotion tags of news articles than the methods using either single source, as each source provides its own insight on tagging emotions for the comments of online news.

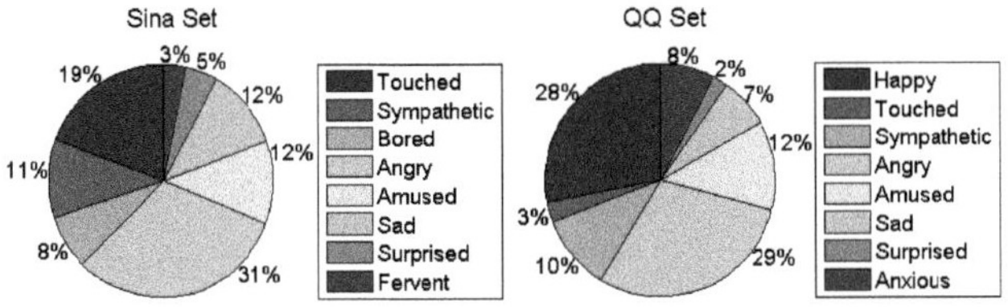

Figure 2: The distributions of labeled comments on 8 predefined emotions in each dataset.

Table 1: MRR and accuracy@1,2,3 of each dataset.

	Sina set				QQ set			
	MRR	A@1	A@2	A@3	MRR	A@1	A@2	A@3
UM	0.54	0.35	0.50	0.62	0.52	0.32	0.46	0.61
CM	0.65	0.47	0.66	0.78	0.65	0.49	0.65	0.76
MCM	0.69	0.53	0.70	0.82	0.67	0.50	0.67	0.79

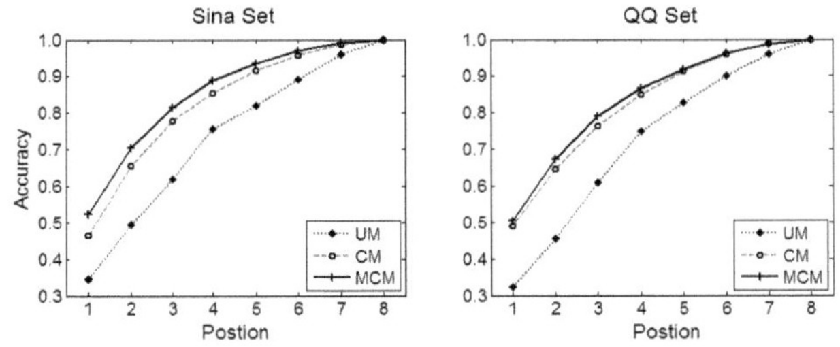

Figure 3: Accuracy at all positions of each dataset.

4. CONCLUSION AND FUTURE WORK

This paper focuses on emotion tagging for users' comments of online news by considering heterogeneous information sources. The empirical results on two testbeds have shown the effectiveness of the proposed approach. This work is an initial step towards a promising research direction. The learned feature weights in Meta classification model are fixed for all comments. In the future work, we will propose more sophisticated probabilistic models by enabling the feature weights to be adaptive to specific users or comments. We will also explore to incorporate other information sources.

5. REFERENCES

[1] C. Alm, D. Roth, and R. Sproat. Emotions from text: machine learning for text-based emotion prediction. In *EMNLP*, pages 579–586, 2005.

[2] S. Bao, S. Xu, L. Zhang, R. Yan, Z. Su, D. Han, and Y. Yu. Mining social emotions from affective text. *IEEE TKDE*, 2011.

[3] D. Das and S. Bandyopadhyay. Sentence to document level emotion tagging–a coarse-grained study on bengali blogs. *Advances in Pattern Recognition*, 2010.

[4] K. Lin, C. Yang, and H. Chen. What emotions do news articles trigger in their readers? In *SIGIR*, pages 733–734, 2007.

[2]http://ent.qq.com/.
[3]http://www.ictclas.org.

Estimating the Magic Barrier of Recommender Systems: A User Study

Alan Said, Brijnesh J. Jain, Sascha Narr, Till Plumbaum, Sahin Albayrak, Christian Scheel
Technische Universität Berlin
Berlin, Germany
{alan, jain, narr, till, sahin, scheel}@dai-lab.de

ABSTRACT

Recommender systems are commonly evaluated by trying to predict known, withheld, ratings for a set of users. Measures such as the Root-Mean-Square Error are used to estimate the quality of the recommender algorithms. This process does however not acknowledge the inherent rating inconsistencies of users. In this paper we present the first results from a noise measurement user study for estimating *the magic barrier* of recommender systems conducted on a commercial movie recommendation community. The magic barrier is the expected squared error of the optimal recommendation algorithm, or, the lowest error we can expect from any recommendation algorithm. Our results show that the barrier can be estimated by collecting the opinions of users on already rated items.

Categories and Subject Descriptors

H.3.3 [**Information Storage and Retrieval**]: Information Search and Retrieval - Information filtering, Retrieval models

Keywords

recommender systems, evaluation, noise

1. INTRODUCTION & RELATED WORK

Recommender Systems (RS) are usually evaluated in offline settings [4], meaning on previously collected transactional data between users and items, such as movie ratings, product purchases etc. Evaluation of RSs is commonly performed in one of two scenarios; *top-N* or *rating prediction*. In the first scenario, the recommended list of probable items is compared to a set of withheld transactions. The quality of the recommendation is then expressed through an accuracy metric such as Precision or Recall based on the withheld transactions. The second scenario, rating prediction, attempts to estimate the ratings of a number of withheld items. Accuracy is measured in terms of prediction errors, such as the Root-Mean-Square Error (RMSE), or Normalized Discounted Cumulative Gain (NDCG). The presumption is that the lower the error measure is, the better the RS performs.

These two evaluation methods have been the de facto standard in the RS community, and common optimization approaches aim at either raising the precision values, or lowering the error measures, or a combination of both [4]. However, none of these methods address the concept of the *magic barrier* introduced by Herlocker et al. [4]. The magic barrier is a theoretical boundary for the level of optimization that can be performed on a recommender algorithm on known transactional data. The evaluation models assume that recorded transactions, whether ratings on movies, purchases of items, etc., reflect a *ground truth*; that the historical transactions users have performed are *free of noise*. These concepts have been addressed previously by Amatriain et al. [1,2] in a user study performed in a synthetic environment, where a service was set up for the purpose of capturing this noise. To our knowledge, the first to mention this phenomenon in a RS setting, Hill et al. [5], discussed the reliability of users in terms of rating consistency already in 1995.

Since then, great advances have been made in the field of RS in terms of algorithmic development [3], much of it thanks to challenges such as the Netflix Prize[1], and yearly versions of the KDD Cup[2]. However, evaluation methodologies have not had a similar evolution, and most RS evaluation still uses traditional information retrieval measures and methods, even though these might not always reflect the actual quality of the recommendation [6].

In this paper, we present a user study, performed on a *real-life* movie RS. The study is intended to capture the natural level of noise in users' ratings. The initial results from the study confirm the notion that users' ratings are inherently noisy, and that the ratings should not be seen as an absolute truth. Based on this we propose a method for estimating a maximum optimization level for RSs based on error measures in a rating prediction scenario.

2. ESTIMATING THE MAGIC BARRIER

RMSE is commonly used for evaluating the accuracy of a rating function f on a set R of ratings

$$E(f|R) = \sqrt{\frac{1}{|R|} \sum_{(u,i)\in R} \left(f(u,i) - r_{ui}\right)^2}, \qquad (1)$$

where the sum runs over all user-item pairs (u, i) where $r_{ui} \in R$.[3]

Assuming the availability of additional transactions for (u, i) given at a different point in time, hereafter *opinions*, the error between an opinion o_{ui} and a rating r_{ui} of a user u for an item i is defined by $\varepsilon_{ui} = o_{ui} - r_{ui}$. We can suppose there is an unknown true rating function f_* that knows the true opinions o_{ui} of each user u about any item i. We derive an estimate of the the RMSE of f_* on the basis of R as

$$E(f_*|R) = \sqrt{\frac{1}{|R|} \sum_{(u,i)\in R} \left(o_{ui} - r_{ui}\right)^2}. \qquad (2)$$

which is equal to the standard deviation of E where $\varepsilon_{u,i} \in E$. It is possible that there are rating functions f with lower RMSE on R

[1] http://www.netflixprize.com
[2] http://www.sigkdd.org/kddcup/
[3] For the sake of brevity, we abuse notation and write $(u, i) \in R$ for user-item pairs (u, i) for which $r_{ui} \in R$.

SIGIR'12, August 12–16, 2012, Portland, Oregon, USA.
ACM 978-1-4503-1472-5/12/08.

than f_*. Those functions, however, tend to overfit the given rating set R and are likely to degrade on the complement of R.

3. USER STUDY

In order to empirically estimate the magic barrier, a user study on the real-life commercial movie recommendation community moviepilot[4] was performed. moviepilot provides its users with personalized movie recommendations based on their previous ratings. The community counts its users in hundreds of thousands, ratings in dozens of millions and movies in tens of thousands. Information about the study was circulated to users through newsletters and on the community forums. The purpose was withheld so to not affect the outcome. The study was performed through a webpage mimicking the look-and-feel of the moviepilot website, on this page users were presented with a random selection of movies they had previously rated, with the ratings withheld. Users who chose to participate in the study were asked to give *opinions* on movies, the term opinion was used in order to mitigate the implicit meaning of *re-rating*, e.g. changing one's mind. A "next" button allowed for loading additional movies, not imposing users to give opinions on any movies shown at a specific page in order to not force users' opinions on movies they did not remember. After 20 opinions were collected the next button terminated the study.

(a) moviepilot (b) Opinion collecting interface

Figure 1: moviepilot's rating interface and the opinion interface used in the study. The opinion interface mimics the look-and-feel of moviepilot in order to create a feeling of familiarity lowering the level of UI-induced noise.

The study, which ran during April and May 2011, resulted in a dataset consisting of 6,299 opinions by 306 users on 2,329 movies.

4. RESULTS AND DISCUSSION

Figure 2 summarizes the opinion polling study. It shows the standard deviation of the error for (a) the deviation between opinion and ratings over all collected opinions, (b) for ratings above each user's average rating value, and (c) for ratings below the personal average rating value. The deviations are shown with respect to the internal rating scale of moviepilot (0 to 100 in steps of 5).

The estimated magic barrier of moviepilot is ± 12.01, as shown in Figure 2, which implies that improvements of predictions differing on average about 25 rating steps or less, on the $0, \ldots, 100$ scale, from the actual ratings are likely to be meaningless. The RMSE of 12.01 is an early stage approximation of the barrier. The study collected only one opinion per user-movie pair, which could introduce potential noise in the opinion values. In a more thorough study collecting several opinions of a user about the same item, we expect to reach a lower estimate of the magic barrier due to lower noise when averaging several user-opinion pairs.

When calculating the RMSE, we performed a temporal analysis, comparing the RMSE between rating and opinions based on the time which had passed between the rating event and the opinion event. The results showed that only if the rating and opinion had

[4]http://www.moviepilot.de

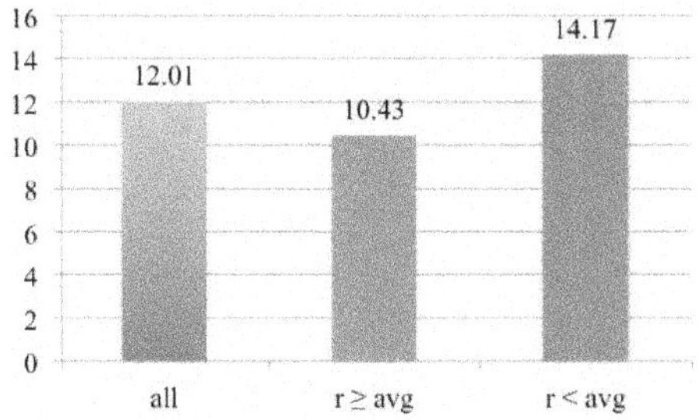

Figure 2: Standard deviation of the error, where *all* refers to the deviation over all opinions; $r \geq avg$ and $r < avg$ refer to the deviation over all ratings above and below average.

been performed within a very short timespan of each other (a few days) did the RMSE become (little) lower. In other cases, the RMSE stayed at a constant level. Due to the temporal aspect being of little difference in terms of RMSE, the results of the study argue for the fact that difference between ratings and opinions were not introduced by time (e.g. users' tastes changing).

5. CONCLUSION & FUTURE WORK

In this paper we have presented a study on the inherent noise found in the rating values given by users in a commercial movie recommendation system. Our assumption, that the so-called *magic barrier* of recommender systems can be better assessed by noise estimation in scenarios similar to ours, seems to hold. Based on the collected data, we have presented an early model for the magic barrier and the level of accuracy a recommender systems can achieve without over-fitting to the noise in the data.

We are currently in the process of processing the data from the study, and preparing a larger scale study in a similar environment in order to gain enough empirical data for a final model for magic barrier estimation.

6. ACKNOWLEDGMENTS

The authors would like to thank the moviepilot team for their support. The presented work was conducted in the scope of the KMulE project, which was sponsored by the German Federal Ministry of Economics and Technology (BMWi).

7. REFERENCES

[1] X. Amatriain, J. M. Pujol, N. Tintarev, and N. Oliver, 'Rate it again: increasing recommendation accuracy by user re-rating', in *3rd ACM conf. on Recommender systems*. ACM, (2009).

[2] Xavier Amatriain, Josep M. Pujol, and Nuria Oliver, 'I like it... i like it not: Evaluating user ratings noise in recommender systems', in *Proc. of 17th Intl. Conf. on User Modeling, Adaptation, and Personalization*. Springer-Verlag, (2009).

[3] Robert M. Bell and Yehuda Koren, 'Lessons from the netflix prize challenge', *SIGKDD Explor. Newsl.*, **9**, (12/2007).

[4] Jonathan L. Herlocker, Joseph A. Konstan, Loren G. Terveen, and John T. Riedl, 'Evaluating collaborative filtering recommender systems', *ACM Trans. Inf. Syst.*, **22**, (2004).

[5] Will Hill, Larry Stead, Mark Rosenstein, and George Furnas, 'Recommending and evaluating choices in a virtual community of use', in *Proc. SIGCHI conf. on Human factors in computing systems*, New York, NY, USA, (1995). ACM.

[6] G. Shani and A. Gunawardana, 'Evaluating recommendation systems', in *Recommender Systems Handbook*, (2011).

Explaining Neighborhood-based Recommendations

Sergio Cleger-Tamayo
Departamento de Informática.
Universidad de Holguín, Cuba
sergio@facinf.uho.edu.cu

Juan M. Fernández-Luna
Departamento de Ciencias de la Computación e I.A.
CITIC– UGR. Universidad de Granada, 18071. Spain
jmfluna@decsai.ugr.es

Juan F. Huete
Departamento de Ciencias de la Computación e I.A.
CITIC– UGR. Universidad de Granada, 18071. Spain
jhg@decsai.ugr.es

ABSTRACT

Recommender Systems (RS) attempt to discover users' preferences, and to learn about them in order to anticipate their needs. The main task normally associated with a RS is to offer suggestions for items. However, for most users, RSs are black boxes, computerized oracles that give advice, but cannot be questioned. In order to improve the quality of predictions and the satisfaction of the users, explanations facilities are needed. We present a novel methodology to explain recommendations: showing predictions over a set of observed items. Our proposal has been validated by means of user studies and lab experiments using MovieLens dataset.

Categories and Subject Descriptors

H.3 [**Information Storage and Retrieval**]; H.5 [**Information Interfaces and Presentation**]

Keywords

Explanation, Effectiveness, Collaborative Filtering

1. INTRODUCTION

Usually, when working with RSs, the users do not have another option to trust. The need of justifications and explanations has started to gain attention during the last decade, being nowadays more crucial due to shilling attacks favoring a given item [1, 2]. Although we can find several alternatives for explaining recommendations, it has been widely accepted the use of simple interfaces (generally, because they can be well understood by ordinary users): For example, it can be used explanations as "users with similar tastes rate this product as ...", "customers who bought this item also bought ...", etc. These simple explanations might be useful when recommending in low-risk domains (such as movies, songs or books), but they are not of much help in a domain where the cost of a wrong decision is high, as electronics, holiday packages or investments portfolios. In such domains, an explanation interface given understandable, effective and acceptable information will be preferred.

In this paper we investigate the use of more informative explanation interfaces that could assist the users to make decisions. Having in mind that the proposed approach must be generalizable, and in order to mitigate the domain dependence, we will only consider collaborative information (nowadays widely available) in the explanations.

SIGIR'12, August 12–16, 2012, Portland, Oregon, USA.
ACM 978-1-4503-1472-5/12/08.

The idea motivating our proposal is that by showing explicitly predictions of `this` system for some items previously observed, the user can understand the reasoning behind the recommendations. Besides, we also show that the information presented in the interface can be useful also for improving the recommendations. As far as we know there is no explanation approach that used this information, which is an example of hybrid Human/Item explanations [2].

2. EXPLANATION INTERFACE

We are looking for an effective explanation that would help the user to evaluate the quality of the recommendation, according to their own preferences. Obviously, this explanation strongly depends on the used recommendation model. In this paper we will assume a neighborhood-based RS predicting how an active user, a, might rate a target item, t. In general, user-based rating prediction is a process in which each neighbor, v, suggests a rating for the target item, $sg(v,t)$, which are combined by weighting the contribution of each one, i.e. $\hat{r}_{a,t} \propto \sum_{v \in N} w(a,v)sg(v,t)$.

Figure A shows a classical interface (bar chart histogram[1]) to explain the predicted rating. This interface is the most convincing explanation of why a movie was recommended in MovieLens [1]. In this case the explanation says that "the system suggest 3$\star$ because it has been rated by other similar users as ...". Although this interface explains in some way *how* the predicted rating is computed, there is a second problem that we are going to consider in this paper: *"Why I shall believe the system's 3$\star$ prediction?"*.

In case of asking to my friend, I believe (or not) her recommendations because usually I know her preferences over a set of common rated items. We will try to include this simple idea in our explanations. A simple approach, also explored in [1], would be to say "because the system made correct predictions in over x% of all products". This explanation is independent of the target item, moreover in a neighborhood-based approach, these predictions may be obtained with quite different neighbors. So, what we propose is to ask `this` neighborhood for their prediction for some items in the active user's profile. This information can give an idea of the quality of `this` neighborhood and must be

[1]We use a bar chart for each possible category (1$\star$ to 5$\star$) plus an additional bar (denoted by "?") representing that we have had some problems when finding a minimum set of neighbors who rated the target item.

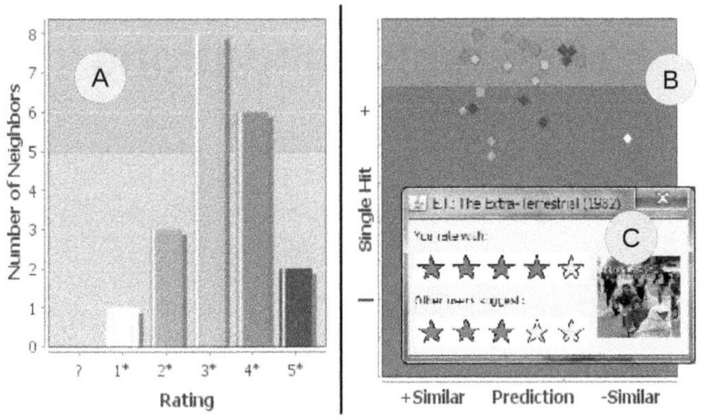

showed to the user in a graphical way, but there exists some questions that remain to be solved.

Q1. *What items can be used in the explanation?* This point is particularly important because if we show many items the user might suffer for information overload whereas if we show a few of them, it might be useless. Particularly, in this paper we show the predictions for those items rated by at least 70% of **these** neighbors. These items represent the support of the explanations[2], denoted as $\mathcal{S}$, in our experimentation a mean of 20.6 movies were selected.

Q2. *How to show the selected items, $\mathcal{S}$?* They will be disposed as points in a two-dimensional graph (Figure B): On the one hand, the x-axis relates each item, $i \in \mathcal{S}$, with the target one, t. Since we do not use content information, this relationships is obtained by considering how far are their predictions in such a way that those items with similar suggestions will be placed at the left. In order to measure this criterion we use a distance measure $d(i,t) \propto \sum_{v \in N} |sg(v,i) - sg(v,t)|$. On the other hand, the y-axis represents the quality of the suggestions, i.e. whether the neighbors suggestions match the rating given by the active user to the target item, $r(a,i)$. Particularly, we compute $h(i) \propto \sum_{v \in N} |r(a,i) - sg(v,i)|$ for each item $i \in \mathcal{S}$. In this way, those items predicted properly by all the members of the neighborhood will be disposed in top positions of the y-axis. For these items we aware of a consensus among the individuals predictions.

Q3. *What information is showed for each item in $\mathcal{S}$?* To show the quality of a prediction we use squares □, or diamond ◇, to represent that **this** particular neighborhood hits, or not, the given rating, respectively, and the color used to fill these figures represents the rating given by the active user to each movie (we use the same colors as the ones used in Figure A). By hovering within these figures, an informational balloon (Figure C) appears showing the particular movie, the real user's rating (4⋆) and the prediction proposed by the system (3⋆).

By means of this explanation the user has information about a wide spectrum of situations, ranging from those that reinforce the system prediction to those explaining a wrong one. For instance, in our example the user can figure out the trend of **these** neighbors to underestimate the rating, and move the decision towards a 4⋆ value.

Evaluation. In order to evaluate this approach we follow a dual-strategy: Firstly, a classical user study[3] using 40 users who rated at least 60 movies in the 100M-MovieLens dataset. After a training step, each user has to judge the explanations for 20 anonymous predictions[4]. Then, they have to confirm whether they agree with the predicted rating or not (in this case, we asked for an alternative). The main conclusions from this experimentation are (i) that our interface gives more information to the user (it helps to reconsider the given rating the 34% of the times whereas the bar histogram helped in the 26%), and (ii) that this information is more useful because it helps to predict the given rating (the original MAE of the system was 0.76, using the histogram it increases to 0,79 and with our proposal it is reduced to 0.71). We have also recommended for each user 10 unobserved movies (in this case we show the title of the movies) and asked then if they would watch the movie. For this purpose, our explanation interface was useful to the user (changing a previous decision the 17% of the times).

We also asked the user for their opinion about the interfaces. The results are consistent with our hypothesis: Explanations facilities are necessary in a RS and users definitively have a look at them. Besides, although in the users' opinions prevails subjective elements associated with the simplicity of the histograms, they prefer to consult the most informative interface (joining both approaches) in case of doubts.

Secondly, we have performed an empirical study trying to evaluate if the information showed might give some trends about the quality of the proposed recommendation. In order to find tendencies, we have decided to correlate the explaining information with the error obtained in the prediction for all the users in 100M-MovieLens. We found that there is no a global pattern that can be applied, the trends depend on the user (what is valid for a user does not have to be good for a different user). Nevertheless, we found significant trends ($p > 0.05$) for the 53% of the users. We consider these results interesting since represents a different piece of information that can be included in recommending models.

Acknowledgements. This work was supported by the Spanish Ministerio de Educación y Ciencia (TIN2008-06566-C04-01 and TIN2011-28538-C02-02) , Spanish Research Program Consolider Ingenio 2010: MIPRCV (CSD2007-00018) and Junta de Andalucía Excellence Project TIC-04526.

3. REFERENCES

[1] J. L. Herlocker, J. A. Konstan, and J. Riedl. Explaining collaborative filtering recommendations. In ACM conference CSCW'00, 241–250, 2000.

[2] A. Papadimitriou, P.Symeonidis and Y. Manolopoulos. A generalized taxonomy of explanations styles for traditional and social recommender systems. Data Min Knowl Disc, 2011.

---

[2]In case of considering a model-based RS we can use predictions for items related to the target one and/or those items that best describe the user's tastes, but how to select the best ones in this approach remains as open problem.

[3]In this paper we only present an snapshot of our study.

[4]The users neither know that they rated these movies nor that we show the same movies in both interfaces.

Exploiting Term Dependence while Handling Negation in Medical Search

Nut Limsopatham[1], Craig Macdonald[2], Richard McCreadie[2], Iadh Ounis[2]
nutli@dcs.gla.ac.uk[1], firstname.lastname@glasgow.ac.uk[2]
School of Computing Science
University of Glasgow, Glasgow, UK

ABSTRACT

In medical records, negative qualifiers, e.g. no or without, are commonly used by health practitioners to identify the absence of a medical condition. Without considering whether the term occurs in a negative or positive context, the sole presence of a query term in a medical record is insufficient to imply that the record is relevant to the query. In this paper, we show how to effectively handle such negation within a medical records information retrieval system. In particular, we propose a term representation that tackles negated language in medical records, which is further extended by considering the dependence of negated query terms. We evaluate our negation handling technique within the search task provided by the TREC Medical Records 2011 track. Our results, which show a significant improvement upon a system that does not consider negated context within records, attest the importance of handling negation.

Categories and Subject Descriptors: H.3.3 [Information Storage & Retrieval]: Information Search & Retrieval

General Terms: Experimentation, Performance

Keywords: Medical Retrieval, Negation, Term Dependence

1. INTRODUCTION

Search in the medical domain is notable for its extensive use of negated language within medical records [2]. However, recently Koopman et al. [2] asserted that the use of term frequency in document weighting models such as BM25 automatically alleviates the problems of negated language. Notably, they argue that terms in negative contexts typically appear once per medical record while, in contrast, terms indicating the presence of a medical condition (positive terms) appear frequently. In this paper, we argue that a dedicated negation handling approach will outperform traditional retrieval models for medical domain queries. Additionally, prior works have focused almost exclusively on negated language in queries rather than documents (e.g. boolean retrieval models or vector negation [7]). For example, for the query 'NOT chest pain AND shortness of breath', the boolean model will find documents not containing 'chest pain', thereby not considering any negation occurring within the records. Moreover, most words indicating negation (e.g. no, not) are stopwords, which are not typically indexed [1].

To cope with negation in medical search, we propose a two-step process: a term representation approach, *NegFlag*, to facilitate the handling of negative context in medical records; and a novel term dependence approach to demote medical records containing query terms in a negated context. We evaluate our proposed approach using the TREC 2011 Medical Records track [6] test collection. As our results exhibit significant improvement over a baseline where negation is not handled, we conclude that negated language should be explicitly handled for effective medial records search.

SIGIR'12, August 12–16, 2012, Portland, Oregon, USA.
ACM 978-1-4503-1472-5/12/08.

Original record	Patient reports palpitations but does not have fever
Negation detection	Patient reports palpitations but does *not have fever*
Removing stopwords	Patient reports palpitations *fever*
NegFlag representation	Patient reports palpitations *n0fever*

Table 1: The NegFlag process for a medical record - italicised terms occur in a negative context.

2. THE NEGFLAG APPROACH

Our negated term representation approach, *NegFlag*, modifies the indexing process to distinguish between positive and negative context terms in medical records, which are identified using the NegEx algorithm [1]. Identified negated terms are replaced with special negated versions of those terms. Table 1 shows how an example sentence is processed using NegFlag, such that the term 'fever' is replaced with its negated version, 'n0fever'.

Hence, given the query 'find patient with fever', without NegFlag, a retrieval model might erroneously rank the original record in Table 1 highly, because it contains all of the query terms. However, after NegFlag processing, as 'fever' has become 'n0fever', the record would not score as highly.

However, while NegFlag only helps to retrieve records containing query terms with positive contexts, it does not prevent records with the negated occurrences from being retrieved. For example, the NegFlag processed example in Table 1 might still be retrieved for the query 'find patient with fever and palpitations', when the patient is known not to have a fever. To alleviate this, in the next section, we propose the use of term dependence to demote medical records containing query terms within negative contexts.

3. TERM DEPENDENCE FOR NEGATION

Term dependence (e.g. Markov Random Fields [4]) has been used to improve effectiveness by scoring higher documents containing many occurrences of pairs of query terms in close proximity. In contrast, we propose to use term dependence to *demote* records containing the *negated* form of neighbouring terms occurring in the queries. For example, given a query 'chest pain', documents containing the pair of terms 'n0chest n0pain' should be demoted. To this effect, we score medical record r for a query Q, taking negation into account, as follows:

$$score(r,Q) = \sum_{t \in Q} score(r,t) - \sum_{\langle t_1,t_2 \rangle \in Q'} score(r, \langle t_1, t_2 \rangle) \quad (1)$$

There are two components in Equation (1), namely the positive scoring of positive query terms, and the negative term dependence score for the negated forms of the query terms. $score(r,t)$ is the score assigned to a query term t in medical record r using any term weighting model, Q' is the set of negated forms of the positive query terms in Q, and $\langle t_1, t_2 \rangle$ is a pair of negated terms in Q'. Two types of term dependence are possible [4, 5]: for full dependence (FD), $\langle t_1, t_2 \rangle$ is the set that contains unordered pairs of neighbouring terms; for sequential dependence (SD), $\langle t_1, t_2 \rangle$ is the set that contains ordered pairs of neighbouring terms. For $score(r, \langle t_1, t_2 \rangle)$, we use the binomial randomness model pBiL [5] from the Divergence from Randomness (DFR) framework to score the occurrences of a pair of terms within *window_size* tokens in a medical record r.

4. EXPERIMENTAL RESULTS

We evaluate our negated term representation and the term dependence approaches using the 34 topics from the TREC 2011 Medical Records track [6]. In this track, the task is to identify relevant patient *visits* for each topic, where a visit contains all of the medical records associated with that patients' admission to the hospital. For indexing and retrieval, we use Terrier[1], applying Porter's English stemmer and removing stopwords. The parameter-free DFR DPH term weighting model is used to rank medical records. The expCombSUM voting technique [3] is then used to rank visits based on the scores of their associated medical records. The number of voting medical records is limited to 5,000 as this was found to be effective in preliminary experiments. We hypothesise that negation should be explicitly handled, hence we compare our approach with a baseline where negation is not explicitly handled, as suggested in [2].

Figure 1 shows the bpref retrieval performance comparing NegFlag, as well as the SD and FD variants of term dependence with NegFlag, and the baseline where negation is not handled. From Figure 1, we observe that our approach employing either only NegFlag or both NegFlag and term dependence outperforms the baseline (bpref 0.4871), by up to 4%. Indeed, NegFlag alone markedly improves the retrieval performance over the baseline, while term dependence for *window_size* = 3 using either SD or FD results in statistically significant improvements over the baseline (paired t-test, $p < 0.05$).

For SD, small *window_size*s are more effective, but performance is generally stable across different *window_size*s, suggesting that the presence of negated ordered pairs anywhere in a medical record is sufficient to ascertain if it should be demoted. For FD, *window_size* > 3 degrades performance compared to NegFlag, but still outperforms the baseline.

Next, we further evaluate the effectiveness of our approach after applying a query expansion (QE) technique (namely DFR Bo1 from Terrier). Table 2 shows the retrieval performances (in terms of bpref, precision@10, and R-precision) of NegFlag, with SD and FD term dependence *window_size* = 3 (identified best settings in Figure 1), as well as without term dependence, compared to a baseline applying only QE. The performances of the top 3 best systems at TREC 2011 are also reported. We observe that the QE baseline is outperformed by NegFlag for all the measures, however,

[1]http://terrier.org

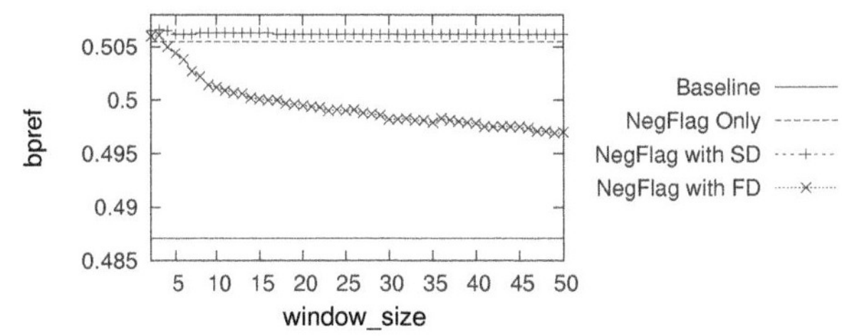

Figure 1: bpref performances of the baseline and our approach, while varying *window_size*.

Approach	QE	bpref	P@10	R-prec
Baseline	Bo1	0.5264	0.6147	0.4290
NegFlag	Bo1	**0.5436**	**0.6324**	**0.4351**
NegFlag with SD *window_size* = 3	Bo1	0.5420	**0.6324**	0.4337
NegFlag with FD *window_size* = 3	Bo1	0.5433	0.6235	0.4332
CengageM11R3	N/A	**0.5520**	**0.6560**	**0.4400**
SCAIMED7	N/A	0.5520	0.6030	0.4250
UTDHLTCIR	N/A	0.5450	0.6030	0.4220

Table 2: Performances of NegFlag and negative term dependence with QE, and the top 3 best systems from TREC 2011.

the combination of term dependence and query expansion when using NegFlag remains challenging. In addition, comparing with the best systems reported at TREC 2011, we find that NegFlag performs better than the second ranked group in terms of precision@10 and R-precision, while for bpref, it is comparable with the third ranked group. Importantly, this is despite our approach not requiring any of the domain-specific ontologies that are exploited in those systems. Overall, our results are very promising, particularly if term dependence and query expansion can be successfully combined in future work.

5. CONCLUSIONS

We have proposed a novel approach to handle negation in medical search using our NegFlag term representation and a novel use of term dependence to demote documents containing the query terms in a negative context. Our approach is shown to be effective on the Medical Records track test collection, across a range of window sizes. Moreover, it verifies our stance that negation should be explicitly handled in medical search. Our proposed approach could also work with queries that contain negative contexts; however, as the available topics in the TREC 2011 test collection do not contain any negated terms, we leave this evaluation for future work.

6. REFERENCES

[1] W. Chapman, W. Bridewell, P. Hanbury, G. Cooper, B. Buchanan. A simple algorithm for identifying negated findings and diseases in discharge summaries. *J. of Biomedical Informatics*, 5:301–310, 2001.

[2] B. Koopman, P. Bruza, L. Sitbon, M. Lawley. Analysis of the effect of negation on information retrieval of medical data. In *ADCS*'10.

[3] C. Macdonald, I. Ounis. Voting for candidates: adapting data fusion techniques for an expert search task. In *CIKM*'06

[4] D. Metzler, W. B. Croft. A Markov random field model for term dependencies. In *SIGIR*'05.

[5] J. Peng, C. Macdonald, B. He, V. Plachouras, I. Ounis. Incorporating term dependency in the DFR framework. In *SIGIR*'07.

[6] E. Voorhees, R. Tong. Overview of the TREC 2011 Medical Records Track. In *TREC*'11.

[7] D. Widdows. Orthogonal negation in vector spaces for modelling word-meanings and document retrieval. In *ACL*'03.

Exploring Example-Based Person Search in Email

Tan Xu[1,3] and Douglas W. Oard[1,2,3]
[1]College of Information Studies/[2]UMIACS, University of Maryland, College Park
[3]Human Language Technology Center of Excellence, Johns Hopkins University
{tanx|oard}@umd.edu

ABSTRACT

This paper describes an entity ranking model for example-based person search in email. Evaluation by comparison to manually resolved named references in Enron email yield results that correspond to typically placing the correct entity in the first or second rank.

Categories and Subject Descriptors

H.3 [**Information Storage and Retrieval**]: Information Search and Retrieval

General Terms

Experimentation, Measurement

Keywords

Entity retrieval, name resolution, email

1. INTRODUCTION

The usual formulation of the *person search* task requires finding a unique page (e.g., the principal home page) for a named person, where the name is provided in isolation as the query [1, 2], but other formulations are possible. In this paper we focus on resolving named mentions in context, a task that we refer to as *example-based person search*. We model our task in a manner similar to the entity linking task in the Text Analysis Conference (TAC),[1] but with a specific mention in an email messages as the "query," and automatically constructed entity models as the items to be ranked. Specifically, given an email message d where a person's name m is mentioned, and a collection of person entities E, find the entity $e \in E$ to which m refers. We report Mean Reciprocal Rank (MRR) rather than TAC's modified B-Cubed score as our principal evaluation measure because our focus is on formative rather than summative evaluation (thus preferring a ranked measure) and because in our present work we test only with mentions that human annotators are able to resolve (obviating the need to score what TAC calls "NILs").

[1]http://nlp.cs.qc.cuny.edu/kbp/2011/

SIGIR'12, August 12–16, 2012, Portland, Oregon, USA.
ACM 978-1-4503-1472-5/12/08.

2. A PROBABILISTIC RANKING MODEL

Our task is to rank all $e \in E$ in decreasing order of the probability of e being the correct resolution given m and d: $P(e \mid m, d)$. By applying the chain rule, this can be inferred as in Formula 1:

$$P(e \mid m, d) = \frac{P(e, m, d)}{P(m, d)} \propto P(d) \cdot P(e \mid d) \cdot P(m \mid e, d) \quad (1)$$

where the prior probability of an email message $P(d)$ can be assumed to be uniform, and $P(e \mid d)$ is the probability of entity e being mentioned in email message d. There are several types of complementary evidence that could help us to estimate $P(e \mid d)$, suggesting a log-linear model:

$$P(e \mid d; \lambda) \propto \exp \sum_{k=1}^{K} \lambda_k f_k(e, d) \quad (2)$$

where, $f_k(e, d)$ is one of K ways of estimating $P(e \mid d)$ and λ_k is some weight for $f_k(e, d)$. In this paper we allocate uniform weights to all λ_k, but in general these weights can and should be learned from training data.

To compute $P(m \mid e, d)$, we simplify it as $P(m \mid e)$ by assuming that the probability of seeing some form of mention for an entity will not be affected by its surrounding email. Of course, this may not be true. For example, when writing to a family member, people might refer to another family member using a nickname that they would not normally use to refer to that same person in an email sent to a business colleague. We leave accounting for that factor to future work.

We estimate $P(m \mid e)$ from normalized occurrence counts in the entity model $C'(l_m)$, which count the number of times each lexical form is observed in a header, salutation or signature. We use the Dice coefficient $s(l_m, m)$ to account for partial string matches between the actual mention m and canonical lexical forms l_m:

$$P(m \mid e) := \sum_{l_m \in e} C'(l_m) \cdot s(l_m, m) \quad (3)$$

3. EXPERIMENTS

We take the Enron email collection [5] hosted by CMU[2] as our email collection; this collection contains messages but no

[2]http://www.cs.cmu.edu/~enron/

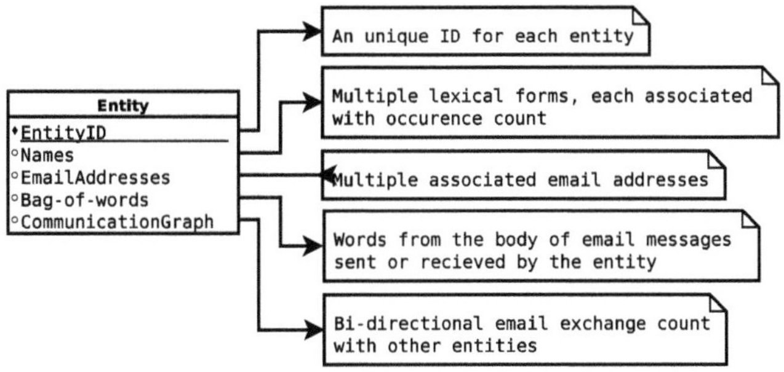

Figure 1: Data Structure for Entity e.

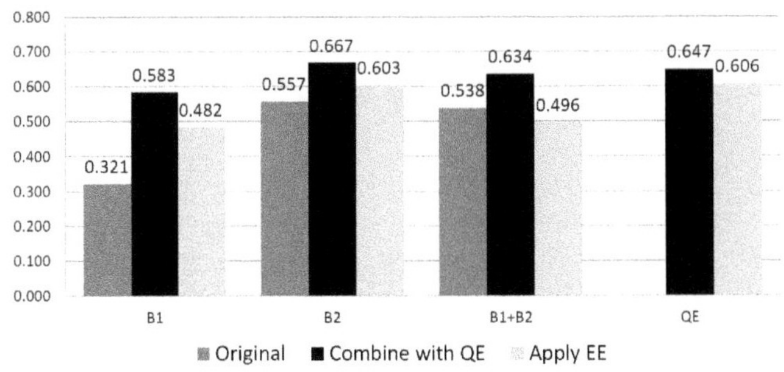

Figure 2: Evaluation Results (MRR)

attachments. We obtained the identity models built automatically for this collection by Elsayed and Oard [4], which includes 123,773 unique entities. Figure 1 shows the data structure for each entity. The bag-of-words representation is stored separately for words in the body of messages sent, received-as-*to* by the entity, and received-as-*cc* by the entity (with quoted text removed). The communication graph contains a list of all entities e' with whom entity e exchanged at least one message in each direction (i.e., at least one message sent as "to" or "cc" to e' and at least one message received as "to" or "cc" from e').

As ground truth we use a publicly available set of 470 single-token mentions (in 285 unique messages) that have been manually resolved to email addresses.[3] The reported inter-annotator agreement is 81% and the median lexical ambiguity (i.e., the number of identity models with an exact string match) is 116 [3].

We tried four ways of estimating $f_k(e,d)$. Method (*B1*), based on Balog's "model 1" [1], finds entities who typically use similar words, regardless of whether those words are used together in one email. The words in the body of d are taken as query terms (with no removal of quoted text), and Lucene's standard analyzer and index searcher are used to score each entity. Method (*B2*), based on Balog's "model 2" [1] works similarly, but indexing individual messages rather than the concatenation of all messages sent or received by each entity. For the top-scoring 50 messages d_r retrieved for d_q, each entity in the "from", "to" or "cc" field of d_r receives an equal portion of d_r's retrieval score and these partial scores are then summed over all 50 documents. Method (*QE*) directly uses d_q's "from" "to" and "cc" fields, assigning each such entity e equal weight. These entities are later used in the communication graph to retrieve their one-hop neighbors e', with each valued by their normalized number of messages exchanged with e. Using this same communication graph, Method (*EE*) is constructed by projecting weights to entities that are directly connected by any ranked entity collected from the three previous methods. Each method's results are first renormalized to sum to 1, and then combined as described in equation (3). Contributions to the same entity are summed, and the final results are renormalized to sum to 1.

4. RESULTS AND CONCLUSIONS

As Figure 2 shows, combining Methods (*B2*) and (*QE*) does rather well, achieving an MRR of 0.667. Since our ultimate goal is to use this as the first stage of an automated entity resolution system (which will also leverage intra-document consistency evidence in subsequent iterative steps), we interpret this as a promising result. Our processing requires an average of 0.78 seconds per query (one core, 2.66 GHz CPU, 4 GB RAM), which meets our efficiency requirements for a preprocessing stage. Elsayed, using different techniques, similarly found the communication graph to be the best source of evidence (MRR=0.785), but at the cost of the substantially greater computational cost to simultaneously resolve all 1.3 million named references to people in the Enron collection [3].

Comparing Methods (*B1*) and (*B2*), our results parallel those Balog et al report for other content types, with (*B2*) markedly better than (*B1*) [1]. Combining evidence from Methods (*B1*) and (*B2*) yields no improvement over Method (*B2*) alone, suggesting that further work on combination methods is called for. Zaragoza et al found the entity graph to be useful for ranking relevant entities [6]; our failure to replicate that by Method (*EE*) suggests that we should exlore graph-based entity ranking measures and that learned weights are likely needed for a log-linear combination in this application. We plan to explore those ideas in future work.

[3] `http://www.cs.umd.edu/~telsayed/research.htm`

5. ACKNOWLEDGMENTS

We appreciate the advice and suggestions of Tim Finin, Tim Oates, Dawn Lawrie, Paul McNamee, Jim Mayfield, Ves Stoyanov and William Webber.

6. REFERENCES

[1] K. Balog, L. Azzopardi, and M. de Rijke. A language modeling framework for expert finding. *Information Processing & Management*, 45(1):1–19, 2009.

[2] A. P. de Vries et al. Overview of the INEX 2007 entity ranking track. In *INEX*, pages 245–251. 2007.

[3] T. Elsayed. *Identity resolution in email collections.* PhD thesis, University of Maryland, 2009.

[4] T. Elsayed and D. Oard. Modeling identity in archival collections of email: A preliminary study. In *Conference on Email and Anti-Spam*, pages 95–103. 2006.

[5] B. Klimt and Y. Yang. The Enron corpus: A new dataset for email classification research. In *ECML*, pages 217–226. 2004.

[6] H. Zaragoza, H. Rode, P. Mika, J. Atserias, M. Ciaramita, and G. Attardi. Ranking very many typed entities on wikipedia. In *CIKM*, pages 1015–1018. 2007.

Exploring Tag Relevance for Image Tag Re-ranking

Jie Xiao
Department of Computer Science
The University of Texas at San Antonio
jxiao@cs.utsa.edu

Wengang Zhou
Department of Computer Science
The University of Texas at San Antonio
zhwgeeis@gmail.com

Qi Tian
Department of Computer Science
The University of Texas at San Antonio
qitian@cs.utsa.edu

ABSTRACT

In this paper, we propose to explore the relevance between tags for image tag re-ranking. The key component is to define a global tag-tag similarity matrix, which is achieved by analysis in both semantic and visual aspects. The text semantic relevance is explored by the Latent Semantic Indexing (LSI) model [1].For the visual information, the tag-relevance can be propagated by reconstructing exemplar images with visually and semantically consistent images. Based on our tag relevance matrix, a random-walk approach is leveraged to discover the significance of each tag. Finally, all tags in an image are re-ranked by their significance values. Extensive experiments show its effectiveness on an image dataset with a large tags vocabulary.

Categories and Subject Descriptors

H.3.3 [**Information Storage and Retrieval**]: Search process

General Terms

Algorithms, Measurement, Performance.

Keywords

Tag re-ranking, random walk, latent semantic indexing.

1. INTRODUCTION

Recently, millions of tagged images are available online in social community. However, tags are labeled in a random order and cannot accurately describe the image content. Therefore, it hinders the applications in the real world. Image tag re-ranking becomes an interesting topic in research community [2] and industry. In this paper, to tackle this problem, we explore the latent semantic relevance among tags from text and visual perspectives.

In sum, this paper has three main contributions: (1) we propose a new scheme to measure tag relevance by integrating a subset of images sharing the same target tag into a global tag-tag similarity matrix; (2) we adopt Latent Semantic Indexing to measure tag-tag text similarity and integrate them with different schemes; and (3) we design a three-step approach to propagate the tag relevance from trustable images that are visually similar to the representative exemplar image.

2. ALGORITHM FRAMEWORK

Given an image with several tags, our goal is to re-rank those tags, so that the more relevant the tag is to the image, the higher it is ranked. We exploit the tag-tag relevance from the perspective of text similarity and visual similarity, respectively.

SIGIR'12, August 12–16, 2012, Portland, Oregon, USA.
ACM 978-1-4503-1472-5/12/08.

Denote **I** as an image dataset with n images, and **T** as tag vocabulary with m tags. We explore tag-tag semantic relevance in a tag-specific manner. Each image I_i is labeled with a set of tags, denoted as S_i. For each tag t_i, we find all images from **I** that contain t_i. We denote such image set as $U(t_i)$, and a tag-image matrix can be constructed as follows,

$$D_{t_i}(j,k) = \begin{cases} 1 & if\ image\ I_k\ contains\ tag\ t_j \\ 0 & otherwise \end{cases}$$

For each tag t_i, we study $\boldsymbol{D_{t_i}} \in \boldsymbol{R}^{m \times n_t}$, a tag-image matrix with n_t images in $U(t_i)$ sharing the same tag t_i and all the tags occurred in those n_t images. $D_{t_i}(j,k)$ denotes the occurrence of tag t_j on image I_k. In Section 2.1, we study the tag-tag text similarity matrix $P_t^{t_i}$ by Latent Semantic Indexing [1] on tag occurrence. And a tag-tag visual similarity matrix $\boldsymbol{P_v^{t_i}}$ is formulated by the propagated tag relevance from trustable images in Section 2.2. We further apply integration functions below to obtain global tag-tag visual similarity $\boldsymbol{P_v}$ and text similarity $\boldsymbol{P_t}$

$$\boldsymbol{P_t} = f_t(\boldsymbol{P_t^{t_i}}) \quad (1)$$

$$\boldsymbol{P_v} = f_v(\boldsymbol{P_v^{t_i}}) \quad (2)$$

$$\boldsymbol{P} = \lambda \boldsymbol{P_v} + (1-\lambda)\boldsymbol{P_t} \quad (3)$$

Then, we embed the global tag-tag similarity $\boldsymbol{P}$ into a random walk based framework for image tag re-ranking.

$$\boldsymbol{R} = \alpha \boldsymbol{P} \boldsymbol{R} + (1-\alpha)\boldsymbol{V} \quad (4)$$

where $\boldsymbol{R}$ is the relevance score vector, $\boldsymbol{P}$ is a transition matrix, P_{ij} indicates the probability of the transition from tag t_i to tag t_j, $\boldsymbol{V}$ describes the relevance between the image and a labeled tag. α is a damping factor ranging from 0 to 1. The process can be illustrated as each tag t_i gives a score with the probability of $(1-\alpha)$ *or* gives a score to other tags based on transition probabilityP_{ij}. Eventually, it converges and the tags with high relevance score will be re-ranked to the top.

2.1 Latent Semantic Tag-Tag Similarity

Given images sharing the same tag t_i in the form of tag-image matrix $\boldsymbol{D_{t_i}}$. We apply Latent Semantic Indexing [1] to estimate the similarity among these tags. More specifically, we do Singular Value Decomposition on $\boldsymbol{D_{t_i}}$,

$$\boldsymbol{D_{t_i}} = \boldsymbol{U\Sigma V'} \quad (5)$$

where $\boldsymbol{U}$ and $\boldsymbol{V}$ are the left and right singular vector, $\boldsymbol{\Sigma}$ is the diagonal matrix of singular values. By keeping the top k largest singular value in $\boldsymbol{\Sigma}$, and set the remaining as zeros, we can obtain $\boldsymbol{\widehat{D}_{t_i}}$.The similarity matrix between two terms is $\boldsymbol{P_t^{t_i}} = \boldsymbol{\widehat{D}_{t_i}\widehat{D}_{t_i}}'$.

We design different integration functions f_t in Eq. (1). $f_t^{(1)}$ is a row-based selection. For tag t_i and its tag-tag similarity matrix $\boldsymbol{P}_t^{t_i}$, we copy the row where t_i lies to the global tag-tag similarity matrix $\boldsymbol{P}_t^{(1)}$. $\boldsymbol{P}_t^{(2)}$ is the summation of $\boldsymbol{P}_t^{t_i}$ with weighting function $f_t^{(2)}$.

$$f_t^{(2)} = sqrt\left(\log\left(\frac{n}{n_t}\right) \times \frac{n_t}{n}\right) \quad (6)$$

2.2 Tag-Tag Visual Similarity

It is a common way to visually represent a tag by images containing it. It unavoidably introduces noise while comparing visual similarity since images contain multiple objects. Therefore, we divide the images containing the same tag into groups so that images within the same group are more visually similar. For a given tag t_i and $\boldsymbol{D}_{t_i}$, we propose a three-step approach to collect propagated tags from trustable images:

(1) Clustering images sharing the same tag into groups by Affinity Propagation algorithm [3]. Each group consists of an exemplar image and group member images.

(2) Applying Locality-constrained Linear Coding (LLC) [4] to reconstruct exemplar image by group members. The members with high contribution should be semantically similar to the exemplar, because they lie in the same group sharing the same latent sub-concept and they all strongly agree with the exemplar. We consider those images as trustable images.

(3) Propagating weighted tag information from the trustable images to form tag relevance vector for a certain group. The aggregated tag relevance vectors from groups are used to describe the similarity between t_i and other tags.

As illustrated in Figure 1, all of beach images are first clustered into groups. A red triangle represents the exemplar of each group. The green dots are member images with high contribution for the reconstruction and their tag information will be propagated with certain weight.

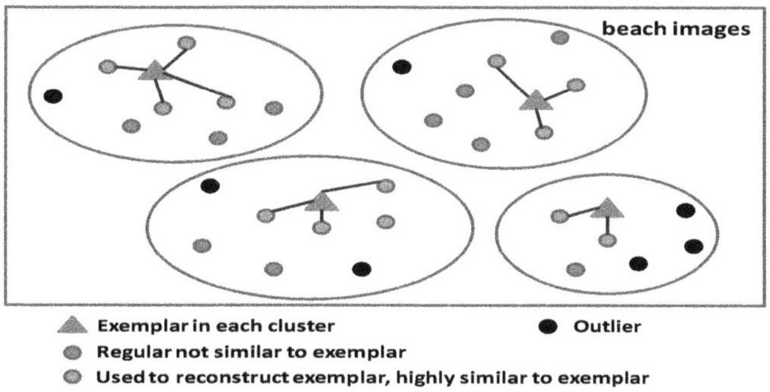

Figure 1. A toy case of reconstructing exemplar by similar images

3. EXPERIMENTS

We evaluate the proposed approaches on NUS-WIDE dataset [5] with 269,648 images. A challenging tag set with 4,926 unique tags is obtained by filtering the noisy tags and tags with less than 30 images in the training set. The ranking accuracy is measured by NDCG@5, which measures the consistency between the top-**N** ranked tags and the ground truth. To build the ground-truth dataset, 150 images are manually labeled with the relevance for each tag on a scale of 5. For each image, we extract a 712-dimension feature, including 225-dimension block-wise color moment feature and 512-dimension GIST feature. In experiment, we estimate image and tag similarity by kernel density estimation. We use all images in each group to reconstruct the exemplar image and integrate the tag relevance from all groups with L_2 norm.

Baseline We implement Liu's method [2] for comparison and use raw data as baseline. In terms of accuracy, Liu's result is 73.36% and the baseline is 65.98%. Another baseline is to use Google distance in [2] as P_t in PageRank, and its accuracy is 68.37%.

We conduct extensive experiments with different integration schemes and combinations for visual similarity and text similarity in Table 1. P_v, $P_t^{(1)}$ and $P_t^{(2)}$ indicate the performance purely based on itself. 'G' refers to the Google distance used in Liu [2]. 'P_v+G' refers to Google distance combined with our visual tag-tag similarity. $P_t^{(1)}$ and $P_t^{(2)}$ are tag-tag text similarity based on integration functions $f_t^{(1)}$ and $f_t^{(2)}$ mentioned in section 2.1

Table 1. Comparison on accuracy (%)

raw	G[2]	Liu[2]	P_v + G	$P_v + P_t^{(1)}$	$P_v + P_t^{(2)}$	P_v	$P_t^{(1)}$	$P_t^{(2)}$
65.98	68.37	73.36	78.47	78.56	78.58	78.37	77.87	77.96

Accuracy As shown in Table 1, our best performance is 78.58%. It improves 5.22% over Liu [2], improves 12.6% over the raw data baseline, and 10.21% over the Google distance. In our approach, we apply all images to reconstruct exemplar image with L_2 norm among groups of image for each tag, α = 8, λ= 4. P_v, $P_t^{(1)}$and $P_t^{(2)}$can work well individually, and their combinations also have some improvement.

Efficiency Our approach is 8% faster than Liu's approach [2], because in Liu's work the visual similarity is calculated online by K-NN search for every tag. Ours is estimated by the aggregated vote for representative images as well as the weighted image cluster groups. It considers the general cases and is efficient in run-time.

4. CONCLUSION

In this paper, we propose a new approach for image tag re-ranking by exploiting tag-tag relevance using Latent Semantic Indexing on tag occurrence. We also study the tag-tag visual relevance by propagating tags based on their contribution to exemplar reconstruction. We evaluate our approach on a large scale vocabulary dataset with 4,926 tags. Extensive experiments demonstrate the superiority of our approach over others.

5. ACKNOWLEDGEMENT

This work was supported in part to Dr. Qi Tian by ARO grant W911BF-12-1-0057, NSF IIS 1052851, Faculty Research Awards by Google, NEC Laboratories of America and FXPAL, respectively.

6. REFERENCES

[1] Deerwester, S., Dumais, S. T., Furnas, G. W., Landauer ,T. K., Harshman , R., Indexing by latent semantic analysis, *Journal of the American Society for Information Science*, 1990

[2] Liu , D., Hua, X.S., Yang, L.,Wang, M., Zhang, H.J., Tag ranking, In *Proc. of WWW*, 2009

[3] Frey, B. J. and Dueck, D , Clustering by Passing Messages Between Data Points, Science, vol. 315, 2007

[4] Wang, J., Yang, J., Yu, K., Lv, F., Huang, T. and Gong, Y., Locality-constrained Linear Coding for image classification, In *Proc. of CVPR*, 2010

[5] Chua, T., Tang, J., Hong, R., Li,H., Luo,Z., and Zheng,Y. NUS-WIDE: a real-world web image database from National University of Singapore, In *Proc. of CIVR*, 2009

Fast On-line Learning for Multilingual Categorization

Michelle Kovesi
Interactive Language Tech.
National Research Council
283 Alexandre-Taché
Gatineau, QC, Canada

Cyril Goutte
Interactive Language Tech.
National Research Council
283 Alexandre-Taché
Gatineau, QC, Canada
Cyril.Goutte@nrc.ca

Massih-Reza Amini
Lab. d'Informatique de Paris 6
Université Pierre & Marie Curie
4, place Jussieu
75252 Paris, France
amini@poleia.lip6.fr

ABSTRACT

Multiview learning has been shown to be a natural and efficient framework for supervised or semi-supervised learning of multilingual document categorizers. The state-of-the-art co-regularization approach relies on alternate minimizations of a combination of language-specific categorization errors and a disagreement between the outputs of the monolingual text categorizers. This is typically solved by repeatedly training categorizers on each language with the appropriate regularizer. We extend and improve this approach by introducing an on-line learning scheme, where language-specific updates are interleaved in order to iteratively optimize the global cost in one pass. Our experimental results show that this produces similar performance as the batch approach, at a fraction of the computational cost.

Categories and Subject Descriptors

I.2.7 [**Artificial Intelligence**]: Natural Lang. Processing

Keywords

Multilingual text categorisation, on-line learning

1. INTRODUCTION

Large annotated multilingual corpora are massively produced by many national or supra-national initiatives and are now available for various purposes, e.g. machine translation [4], semantic web [6] or classification [1]. For the latter, multiview learning was shown to be a natural and efficient framework for supervised or semi-supervised learning of multilingual document categorizers [2].

We propose a new online learning algorithm for multilingual document categorization that is as efficient as, and much faster than, state-of-the-art multilingual categorization algorithms. Our approach operates by learning two language-specific categorizers, iteratively adjusting their parameters on the basis of the prediction error on each language and the disagreement between the predictions on either language. The main difference with previous co-classification work is that we leverage the structure of perceptron updates in order to learn both categorizers simultaneously instead of alternatingly. Experiments carried out on `Reuters` RCV1/RCV2 multilingual documents show that our approach performs at least as well as state-of-the art strategies, while being consistently and significantly faster.

SIGIR'12, August 12–16, 2012, Portland, Oregon, USA.
ACM 978-1-4503-1472-5/12/08.

2. FRAMEWORK

We consider the representation of a *bilingual document* as a pair of two vectors $\mathbf{x} \stackrel{def}{=} (x^1, x^2)$, where each *vector* x^v provides the representation of the same document in a given vectorial space $\mathcal{X}_v, v \in \{1, 2\}$ associated to each language. Our goal is to learn languages-specific categorizers $h^1(x^1)$ and $h^2(x^2)$ that minimize prediction error over new documents in either language. Original work [1] solved this by minimizing a global loss on a training set $S = \{(\mathbf{x}_i, y_i)\}_{i=1}^N$:

$$\mathcal{L}(h^1, h^2, S) = \underbrace{\mathcal{C}(h^1, S) + \mathcal{C}(h^2, S)}_{\text{misclassification}} + \underbrace{D(h^1, h^2)}_{\text{disagreement}} \qquad (1)$$

using either logistic regression or Boosting. These are optimized in turn on each language by minimizing the misclassification loss for that language and the disagreement, and alternating between languages until convergence[1, 2].

3. ALGORITHM FOR ONLINE LEARNING

When many examples are available, online learning has been shown to provide an efficient way to train models. Instead of optimizing the model over the entire training set, online learning randomly picks one example and adjusts the model based on that example alone. Although it doesn't directly optimize the full cost function, it can handle large datasets very efficiently[3].

We consider two linear binary categorizers with parameters $w^v \in \mathcal{X}_v, v \in \{1, 2\}$ associated to each of the two languages. Each may be trained independently by on-line learning in the co-classification framework outlined above. However, we propose to jointly train both models in the same stochastic online learning process. At each iteration t, a multilingual document $(\mathbf{x}_t, y_t)$ is picked randomly from the training set and presented to both model. If it is misclassified by classifier v (i.e. $\langle w^v, x_t^v \rangle . y_t < 0$), the categorizer is updated using the following rule:

$$w^v \leftarrow w^v + \eta \left(y_t x_t^v + \lambda \frac{\partial \mathcal{D}}{\partial w^v}(\mathbf{x}_t, w^v, w^{\overline{v}}) \right) \qquad (2)$$

where $w^{\overline{v}}$ stands for the categorizer on the other language, and η is the learning rate, while λ weighs the influence of the disagreement term (part of D in eq. 1). Following [1], we set the disagreement function $\mathcal{D}$ to the Kullback-Leibler divergence between the outputs of the categorizers on each view,

h^v and $h^{\bar{v}}$, mapped to $[0;1]$ with a sigmoid transformation ($\sigma(x) = 1/(1+e^{-x})$). We then get:

$$\frac{\partial \mathcal{D}}{\partial w^v}(\mathbf{x}, w^v, w^{\bar{v}}) = x^v \left(\sigma(\langle w^v, x^v \rangle) - \sigma(\langle w^{\bar{v}}, x^{\bar{v}} \rangle) \right) \quad (3)$$

The algorithm is summarized as follows:

Algorithm: Online co-classification

repeat
  for $i = 1, ..., m$ **do**
    Pick example $(\mathbf{x}_t, y_t) \in \mathcal{Z}_l$ at random;
    Update w^1 for example $\mathbf{x}_t$ (eq. 2-3);
    Update w^2 for example $\mathbf{x}_t$ (eq. 2-3)
  end
until *Convergence of global loss* ;

4. EXPERIMENTAL RESULTS

We illustrate our method on data from a large extract of the RCV1 corpus [5], processed and made freely available for multiview multilingual learning experiments [2].[1]

We used the entirety of the English and French documents ($N = 111,740$ documents), comprised of both originals and machine-translated Reuters newswire stories covering 6 categories: C15, CCAT, E21, ECAT, GCAT and M21. In these experiments, we randomly sampled 20 different training sets of 10,000 documents from the full corpus, each with a corresponding (non-overlapping) test set of 90,000 documents. All results are averaged over these 20 samples. For each category, we measured the performance using the F-score, and the training time (in seconds), excluding data load.

Table 1 shows the experimental results obtained using the state-of-the-art batch algorithm as well as using online approaches with interleaved updates. As observed in the original work of [1], the performance achieved by the English and French categorizers are very similar, within one point in F-score. This is due to the fact that we minimize the disagreement between the categorizers, therefore biasing them to provide the same categorization (and therefore reach similar scores) in either languages. We see also see that the F-scores are very close for both algorithms, apart from ECAT where the online version does about 1 point better. This is expected as both algorithms learn similar, linear models minimizing the same cost using similar updates. We do not expect large differences in performance, we expect large differences in training time [3]. Here, the online approach provides a very clear and consistent speedup (rightmost column). It is about three times faster, completing training within 11 to 27 seconds depending on the category, while the original batch approach requires 34-71 seconds.

In a typical scenario, convergence is achieved by the online approach (at the chosen convergence threshold) using 7 to 10 epochs over the entire training set. By contrast, the batch algorithm performed as little as 2 (but usually more) alternate otimizations of the models in each view, each composed of several epochs on the training set. This therefore multiplies the overall training time. The following figure shows that the speedup of the online vs. batch algorithm actually increases as the training set size increases.

[1]http://multilingreuters.iit.nrc.ca

Table 1: Online vs. batch results (F-score and time).

	Perf. English		Perf. French		Time (s)		
Cat.	batch	online	batch	online	bat	onl	×
C15	79.9	79.8	78.8	78.7	51	17	3.0
CCAT	70.0	70.0	69.1	69.0	65	27	2.4
E21	72.8	72.7	71.9	72.0	56	17	3.3
ECAT	68.7	69.6	67.8	68.9	71	27	2.7
GCAT	78.1	78.1	77.1	77.0	53	17	3.2
M11	88.5	88.3	87.5	87.6	34	11	3.0

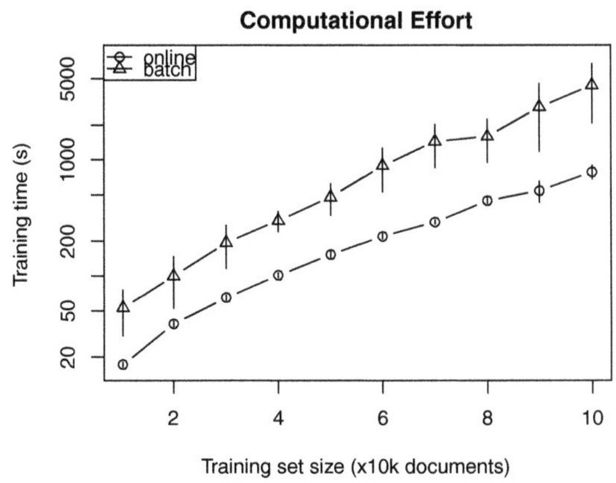

5. DISCUSSION AND CONCLUSIONS

We propose a novel online algorithm that builds on the co-classification work of [1], but leverages the structure of online perceptron learning in order to simultaneously update the models on both views at each example presentation, yielding a clear and consistent speedup while providing similar performance.

This provides a natural way to learn multiple categorizers in a multiview learning framework, without the need to resort to alternating optimizations of regularized view-specific losses as in the original co-classification approach. In addition, although we have not yet obtained evidence for that, we expect that it will scale up better to more than 2 languages, because all models can be updated simulatneously at each iteration, instead of alternating view-specific optimizations. We expect that further work will shed light on the scalability to larger corpora and more languages.

6. REFERENCES

[1] M.-R. Amini and C. Goutte. A co-classification approach to learning from multilingual corpora. *Machine Learning*, 79(1-2), 2010.

[2] M. R. Amini, C. Goutte, and N. Usunier. Combining coregularization and consensus-based self-training for multilingual text categorization. In *SIGIR'10*, 2010.

[3] L. Bottou and Y. LeCun. Large scale online learning. In *NIPS 16*, 2004.

[4] A. Eisele and Y. Chen. MultiUN: A multilingual corpus from united nation documents. In *LREC'10*, 2010.

[5] D. D. Lewis, Y. Yang, T. Rose, and F. Li. A new benchmark collection for text categorization research. *J. Machine Learning Research*, 5:361–397, 2004.

[6] B. Pouliquen, R. Steinberger, and C. Ignat. Automatic annotation of multilingual text collections with a conceptual thesaurus. *CoRR*, abs/cs/0609059, 2006.

Finding Interesting Posts in Twitter Based on Retweet Graph Analysis

Min-Chul Yang†, Jung-Tae Lee‡, Seung-Wook Lee†, and Hae-Chang Rim†
†Dept. of Computer & Radio Communications Engineering, Korea University, Seoul, Korea
‡Research Institute of Computer Information & Communication, Korea University, Seoul, Korea
{mcyang, jtlee, swlee, rim}@nlp.korea.ac.kr

ABSTRACT

Millions of posts are being generated in real-time by users in social networking services, such as Twitter. However, a considerable number of those posts are mundane posts that are of interest to the authors and possibly their friends only. This paper investigates the problem of automatically discovering valuable posts that may be of potential interest to a wider audience. Specifically, we model the structure of Twitter as a graph consisting of users and posts as nodes and retweet relations between the nodes as edges. We propose a variant of the HITS algorithm for producing a static ranking of posts. Experimental results on real world data demonstrate that our method can achieve better performance than several baseline methods.

Categories and Subject Descriptors: H.3.3 [Information Storage and Retrieval]: Information Search and Retrieval

General Terms: Algorithms, Design, Experimentation

Keywords: Twitter, tweet ranking, HITS, social network

1. INTRODUCTION

Twitter is a social networking service that enables its users to share their status updates, news, observations, and findings in real-time by creating short-length posts known as *tweets*. The service rapidly gained worldwide popularity as a communication tool, with millions of users generating millions of tweets per day. Although many of those tweets contain valuable information that is of interest to many people, many others are mundane tweets that are of interest only to the authors and their *followers* (*i.e.*, subscribers). Finding tweets that are of potential interest to a wide audience from large volume of tweets being accumulated in real-time is a crucial but challenging task. One straightforward way is to use the numbers of times tweets have been *retweeted* (*i.e.*, re-posted). [3] proposes to regard retweet count as a measure of popularity and presents classifiers for predicting whether and how often new posts will be retweeted in the future. However, mundane tweets by very popular users, such as celebrities, with huge numbers of followers can record high retweet counts. [1] uses crowdsourcing to categorize a set of tweets as "only interesting to author and friends" and "possibly interesting to others" and reports that the presence of a URL link is a single, highly effective feature for distinguishing interesting tweets with more than 80% accuracy. This simple rule, however, may incorrectly recognize many interesting tweets as not interesting, simply because they do not contain links. In this paper, we follow the definition of interesting tweets provided in [1] and focus on automatic methods for finding tweets that may be of potential interest to not only the authors and their followers but a wider audience. Specifically, we model Twitter as a graph of user and tweet nodes connected by retweet links (edges) and present a variant of the HITS algorithm [4] based on the retweet graph for producing a static ranking of tweets. Our premise is that an interesting tweet attracts users not only in but beyond the author's own network and impels them to retweet as a sign of recommendation; thus, such a tweet can be found by analyzing the retweet relations in the graph. We conduct experiments on real world tweet data and demonstrate that our method achieves better performance than the simple retweet count approach and a similar recent work [2] that uses supervised learning with a broad spectrum of features.

SIGIR'12, August 12–16, 2012, Portland, Oregon, USA.
ACM 978-1-4503-1472-5/12/08.

2. PROPOSED METHOD

We treat the problem of finding interesting tweets as a ranking problem where the goal is to derive a scoring function which gives higher scores to interesting tweets than to uninteresting ones in a given set of tweets. Instead of running the HITS algorithm on the tweet side of the network right away, we run it on the user side first. Our intuition is that the authority of a user is an important prior information to infer the score of the tweets that the user published.

Graph modeling. Formally, we model the Twitter structure as directed graph $G = (N, E)$ with nodes N and directional edges E. We consider both users $U = \{u_1, \dots, u_{n_u}\}$ and tweets $T = \{t_1, \dots, t_{n_t}\}$ as nodes and the retweet relations between these nodes as directional edges. For instance, if tweet t_a, created by user u_a, retweets t_b, written by user u_b, we create a retweet edge e_{t_a,t_b} from t_a to t_b and another retweet edge e_{u_a,u_b} from u_a to u_b.

On user-level. We first run HITS on the user nodes in G. For all user nodes, the scores are updated iteratively as:

$$A(u_i) = \sum_{\forall j: e_{u_j,u_i} \in E} \frac{|\{u_k \in U : e_{u_j,u_k} \in E\}|}{|\{k : e_{u_j,u_k} \in E\}|} \times H(u_j) \quad (1)$$

$$H(u_j) = \sum_{\forall i: e_{u_j,u_i} \in E} \frac{|\{u_k \in U : e_{u_k,u_i} \in E\}|}{|\{k : e_{u_k,u_i} \in E\}|} \times A(u_i) \quad (2)$$

Note that unlike the standard HITS, the authority and hub scores are influenced by the retweet behaviors of users; the idea here is to dampen the influence of users in case they devote most of their retweet activity toward a very few other users like celebrities. After each iteration, the authority and hub scores are normalized by dividing each of them by the square root of the sum of the squares of all authority values and all hub values respectively. This user-level procedure ends after iterating m_U times. After this stage, the algorithm outputs a function $S_{U_A} : U \rightarrow [0, 1]$, which represents the user's final authority score, and another function $S_{U_H} : U \rightarrow [0, 1]$, which represents the user's final hub score.

On tweet-level. When the user-level stage is ended, we compute the authority and hub scores of the tweet nodes. In each iteration, we start out with each tweet node initially inheriting the authority and hub scores of the user who published the tweet. If C is a function that returns the creator of a given tweet, then the scores are updated iteratively as:

$$A(t_i) = S_{U_A}(C(t_i)) + \alpha \sum_{\forall j: e_{t_j,t_i} \in E} F(e_{t_j,t_i}) \times H(t_j) \quad (3)$$

$$H(t_j) = S_{U_H}(C(t_j)) + \alpha \sum_{\forall i: e_{t_j,t_i} \in E} F(e_{t_j,t_i}) \times A(t_i) \quad (4)$$

where $\alpha > 1$ is a weight for hops in retweet chain. If a tweet retweets another tweet which has already been retweeted, it is more likely that the tweet is useful. Thus, tweets are accumulated bonus score, as much as α, for each retweet hop. F is a function that returns $\beta > 1$ if the creator of tweet t_j is not a follower of the creator of tweet t_i and 1 otherwise. It is intuitive that if the users retweet other users' tweets even if they are not friends, then it is more likely that the such tweets are interesting. After each iteration, the authority and hub scores are normalized as done in the user-level. After the iterations are run m_T times, the algorithm finally outputs a scoring function $S_T : T \rightarrow [0, 1]$, which represents the tweet node's final authority score. We use this function S_T to rank a given set of tweets based on interestingness.

3. EXPERIMENTS

We use real world tweets collected during 31 days of October 2011, containing 64,107,169 tweets and 2,824,365 users. For evaluation, we generated 31 initially ranked lists of tweets, each consisting of top 100 tweets created on a specific date of the month with highest retweet counts accumulated during the next 7 days. Two annotators were asked to categorize each tweet as interesting or not by inspecting its content, as done in [1]. In case of disagreement (about 15% of all cases), a final judgment was made by consensus between the two. We observe that the ratio of tweets judged to be interesting is about 36%. The goal of this evaluation is to demonstrate that our approach is able to produce better ranked lists of tweets by re-ranking interesting tweets highly. Table 1 reports the ranking performance of various methods in terms of Precisions at 10 and 20, R-Precision, and MAP. We compare our method to several baselines. The first baseline, denoted as #RT, is obviously based on absolute retweet counts; tweets with higher retweet counts is ranked higher than those with lower retweet counts. The second baseline, HITS_{orig}, is the standard HITS algorithm in which an authority value of a node is computed as the sum of the hub values that point to it, and a hub value is the sum of the authority values of the nodes it points to. No other influential factors are considered in the calculations. Lastly, we choose one recent work [2] that addresses a related problem, which aims at learning to classify tweets as credible or not. Although interestingness and credibility are two distinct concepts, the work presents a wide range of features that may be applied for assessing interestingness of tweets. For re-implementation, we train a SVM classifier using features proposed in [2], which include message-, user-, and propagation-based features[1]; then, we use the probability estimates of the learned classifier for re-ranking. We use leave-one-out cross validation for this learning approach, denoted as ML_{all}. ML_{rt} is a variant that is learned only with propagation-based features observed from retweet trees [2].

Table 1: Performance of individual methods

Method	P@10	P@20	R-Prec	MAP
#RT	0.294	0.313	0.311	0.355
HITS_{orig}	0.203	0.387	0.478	0.465
ML_{rt}	0.658	0.566	0.474	0.551
ML_{all}	0.819	0.795	0.698	0.763
HITS_{prop}	**0.852**	**0.807**	**0.735**	**0.778**
HITS_u	0.823	0.732	0.648	0.732
HITS_t	0.545	0.576	0.536	0.549

We observe that #RT alone is not a sufficient measure for finding interesting tweets. HITS_{orig} performs better than #RT across most metrics but does not perform well in general. ML_{rt}, which uses more features induced from retweet information, demonstrates significantly better results. The results of ML_{all} show that more reasonable performance can be achieved when message- and user-based features are combined with propagation-based features. The proposed method, HITS_{prop} ($\alpha = 2$, $\beta = 3$), shows significantly better performance than #RT and HITS_{orig} and also comparable performance to that of ML_{all}. This result is significant, since our method is based on unsupervised method and does not require complex training as supervised learning approaches do. We lastly compare the contribution of the user-level procedure, denoted as HITS_u against the tweet-level procedure, HITS_t. We observe that the user-level procedure is much more important than the tweet-level procedure. This confirms our intuition described earlier that user authority is a valuable prior information to infer interestingness of tweets.

4. ACKNOWLEDGMENTS

This work was supported by the South Korea Ministry of Knowledge Economy, under the title "Development of social web issue detection-monitoring and prediction technology for big data analytic listening platform of web intelligence" (No. 10039158).

5. REFERENCES

[1] O. Alonso, C. Carson, D. Gerster, X. Ji, and S. U. Nabar. Detecting uninteresting content in text streams. In *SIGIR CSE Workshop*, 2010.

[2] C. Castillo, M. Mendoza, and B. Poblete. Information credibility on twitter. In *WWW*, 2011.

[3] L. Hong, O. Dan, and B. D. Davison. Predicting popular messages in twitter. In *WWW*, 2011.

[4] J. M. Kleinberg. Authoritative sources in a hyperlinked environment. *J. ACM*, 46(5), 1999.

[1]We do not use some topic-based features in [2] since such information was not available in our case.

Finding Readings for Scientists from Social Websites

Jiepu Jiang, Zhen Yue, Shuguang Han, Daqing He
School of Information Sciences, University of Pittsburgh
jiepu.jiang@gmail.com, zhy18@pitt.edu, shh69@pitt.edu, dah44@pitt.edu

ABSTRACT
Current search systems are designed to find relevant articles, especially topically relevant ones, but the notion of relevance largely depends on search tasks. We study the specific task that scientists are searching for worth-reading articles beneficial for their research. Our study finds: users' perception of relevance and preference of reading are only moderately correlated; current systems can effectively find readings that are highly relevant to the topic, but 36% of the worth-reading articles are only marginally relevant or even non-relevant. Our system can effectively find those worth-reading but marginally relevant or non-relevant articles by taking advantages of scientists' recommendations in social websites.

Categories and Subject Descriptors
H.2.8 [**Database Applications**]: scientific databases.

General Terms
Algorithms, Measurement, Performance, Experimentation.

Keywords
Scientific articles; scientific readings; social search.

1. INTRODUCTION
Scientists in nowadays not only read articles closely related to their main research fields but also those from other fields. This makes automatically finding useful readings more difficult than simply matching articles with queries because: 1) many useful readings could come from topics that the scientists do not have adequate knowledge to formulate effective queries; 2) not all topically relevant articles are worth reading; and 3) some useful readings may not contain query terms.

We believe that a useful search system for solving this problem should have the following key features: 1) the scientists are not required to formulate queries related to the topics of the readings, but rather queries about the problems or research topics they are working on, which should be a relatively easier task; 2) the system can find not only readings that are topically relevant, but also those beyond the topics that the scientists are working on. Here we propose a method of finding readings by looking at what scientists' peers are reading about in social websites, which generates a list of candidate readings not limited to topically relevant articles. Specifically, we study the following research questions:

(1) What are the relations between users' perception of relevance and preference of reading?

(2) Can peer scientists' libraries help find worth-reading articles beyond the queries' topics?

2. EXPERIMENT DESIGN
2.1 Dataset
We built a dataset [1] based on articles and users' libraries in CiteULike, a social reference management website. In CiteULike, each user can maintain a collection of articles as the user's personal library. Here we assume CiteULike users are scientists and their personal libraries are their collections of useful readings. Previous studies found co-occurrences of articles in users' libraries can be used for clustering articles into research fields [2]. Our dataset includes titles and abstracts for 913,846 unique articles posted to CiteULike by users in 2010 (99.2% of all articles posted by users in 2010) and 54,402 users' personal libraries.

2.2 Algorithms
Let R be an article (reading). Given a query q, we rank readings by $P(R|q)$, which is equivalent to $P(R, q)$ in ranking. Further, we model $P(R, q)$ as: what is the probability that a scientist working on the problems described by q will read a reading R? $P(R, q)$ is calculated by two steps. First, we find a list of peer scientists by $P(q|u)$ and $P(u)$: $P(u)$ is considered equal for all users, i.e. $1/|\{u\}|$; $P(q|u)$ is calculated as (2) using expert finding "model 2" in [3]. In (2), L_u is the list of articles in u's personal library, which is used to model u's expertise. Second, we let each peer scientist u vote for reading R by the probability $P(R|u, q)$. We assume a peer scientist u will vote for R as a worth-reading article for q if R is in both L_u and the search results of query q (referred to as S_q), as in (3). The whole method is referred to as RUL, which is summarized in (1). We can further set a cutoff value n in (3) so that only the top n retrieved results for query q are considered for voting (referred to as RUL_n). We use two ad hoc search models for comparison: sequential dependence model (SDM) and relevance model 3 (RM3 [4]). We also merge rankings of RUL_n and SDM/RM3 by (4).

RUL: $$P(R,q) = \sum_u P(R,q|u)P(u) = \frac{1}{|\{u\}|}\sum_u P(q|u)P(R|u,q) \quad (1)$$

Finding peer scientists: $$P(q|u) = \sum_{d \in L_u} P(q|d,u) \cdot P(d|u) \quad (2)$$

Voting for articles: $$P(R|u,q) = \begin{cases} 1 & \text{if } R \in L_u \text{ and } R \in S_q \\ 0 & \end{cases} \quad (3)$$

Merge rankings: $$Score(R) = \frac{1}{rank(\mathrm{RUL}_n)} + \frac{1}{rank(\mathrm{SDM/RM3})} \quad (4)$$

2.3 User Judgments
We recruited 10 subjects in academia for judgments (1 faculty member, 1 postdoc and 8 PhD students). Every participant was asked to generate 3 queries, each of which described a research problem related to his/her research. Seven runs were pooled (depth=10) for each query: SDM, RM3, RUL, and RUL_n with n = 20, 50, 100, and 200. On average 31 articles were pooled for each query. The participants need to answer the following questions:

Q1. Do you think this article is relevant to your query? (1-not relevant, 2-somewhat relevant, 3-relevant)

Q2. Do you want to read this article? (1-I already read it, 2-yes, I want to read it, 3-no, I don't want to read it)

Q3. (If Q2=1) I already read it (1-I like it, 2-netural, 3-I don't like it)

For each query, after judging all pooled articles, we asked the participant to select at most 3 articles he/she wanted to read first if he/she is only given limited time. We assign relevance scores (*rel*) to articles based on answers to Q1 (*rel* = 2 for "relevant"; *rel* = 1 for "somewhat relevant"; and *rel* = 0 for "not relevant"). For read-

SIGIR'12, August 12–16, 2012, Portland, Oregon, USA.
ACM 978-1-4503-1472-5/12/08.

ing preference score (*read*), we consider two cases: if the participant has read the article (Q2=1), we assign *read* score based on Q3 (*read* = 2 for "I like it"; *read* = 1 for "neutral"; and *read* = 0 for "I don't like it"); if the participant has not read the article, we assign *read* = 2 to the three articles the participant selected to read first, and *read* = 1 to other articles the participant would like to read (Q2=2). Table 1 shows statistics of participants' judgments. For the 477 articles judged as worth-reading (*read* ≥ 1), 173 (36%) are only marginally relevant or not relevant to the queries' topics (*rel* ≤ 1). After removing 370 articles that are neither relevant to the topic nor worth-reading (*rel* = 0; *read* = 0), we find a moderate correlation (r = 0.357) between articles' *rel* and *read* scores. This indicates the fact that good readings are not necessarily relevant to the queries' topics and vice versa.

Table 1. Article judgments statistics.

	rel = 2	rel = 1	rel = 0	sum
read = 2	166	40	6	212
read = 1	138	111	16	265
read = 0	13	76	370	459
sum	317	227	392	936

3. RESULTS AND DISCUSSIONS

Our evaluation includes two stages:

(1) At the first stage, we use readings that are highly relevant (*rel* = 2; *read* ≥ 1) for evaluation (**HRelRead**). As shown in Table 1, over 90% of the highly relevant articles (*rel* = 2) are also worth-reading (*read* ≥ 1). Current search systems (SDM and RM3) may perform well in finding HRelRead articles because the HRelRead readings are mostly also highly relevant articles. We also evaluate by article relevance (**QRel**) for comparison.

Left and center parts of Figure 1 show the results using QRel and HRelRead for evaluation. Ad hoc search models (SDM and RM3) performed very effectively (nDCG@10 ≥ 0.6 and 0.5). In comparison, RUL_n performed worse than ad hoc search models, but is still very effective (when n = 20, nDCG@10 ≥ 0.45). This is not surprising considering *read* and *rel* scores are highly correlated in HRelRead readings. RUL_n does not explicitly model topical relevance, but SDM and RM3, as two of the best ad hoc search models, model topical relevance very well. Thus, in general, ad hoc search models can effectively find the HRelRead readings, but their success may come from better modeling of topical relevance rather than better modeling the task of finding readings.

(2) At the second stage, we use readings that are marginally relevant or not relevant for evaluation (referred to as **MRelRead**; *rel* <= 1, *read* >= 1). Since such readings are not necessarily relevant, ad hoc search models may not perform effectively. The right part of Figure 1 shows evaluation results for MRelRead readings. It indicates that ad hoc search algorithms (SDM and RM3) cannot perform as effectively as they did in finding HRelRead readings (nDCG@10 < 0.35). In comparison, when n = 20, RUL_n can perform significantly better than SDM (nDCG@10+13.36%; p<0.05). Combining RUL_n with SDM/RM3 further improved performance.

As expected, ad hoc search models cannot effectively solve the problems of finding MRelRead readings because in such cases article relevance and user's preference of reading diverge a lot. It seems unlikely to solve the problem by query expansion, as RM3 performed not much better than SDM. The reasons can be: 1) if the original query is not effective, it is unclear whether or not pseudo-relevance feedback can produce high quality expanded terms; and 2) expanded terms may enrich representations of the query's topic, but do not necessarily help matching of cross-disciplinary articles.

Figure 2 shows per topic differences of nDCG@10 between SDM, RM3, RUL_{20}, and RUL_{20}+SDM/RM3. It shows that RM3 improves and hurts nearly the same number of topics compared with SDM, but RUL_{20} (+SDM/RM3) can not only improve topics hurt by RM3, but can also get as much as improvements in topics improved by RM3. We find the reasons are related to the voting mechanisms in RUL_n. On the one hand, voting can reduce wrong expansions of topics. For example, for topic 28 "science mapping intellectual structure", SDM performs effective but RM3 wrongly emphasizes on "mapping" and matches articles such as "Genetic mapping in human disease". However, since peers found by RUL_n do not read and vote for the article, it is still lower ranked in results of RUL_n. On the other hand, voting is also a useful way of finding good readings beyond topical level. Still, for topic 28, the user wants to read the article titled "Scholarly research and information practices: a domain analytic approach", which is not ranked in top position by SDM or RM3 for the lack of query terms in title and abstract. Instead, RUL_n votes a high score for this article because it has been read by many scientists. We also find, however, RUL_n works poorly if the topic is associated with peers with diversified interests, e.g. topic 7 "collaborative information seeking".

To conclude, our evaluation results demonstrate that current search models can effectively find readings that are also topically relevant, because in such cases article relevance and preference of reading are highly correlated. In comparison, our system can more effectively find readings beyond the query's topic by taking advantages of peer scientists' recommendations in social websites.

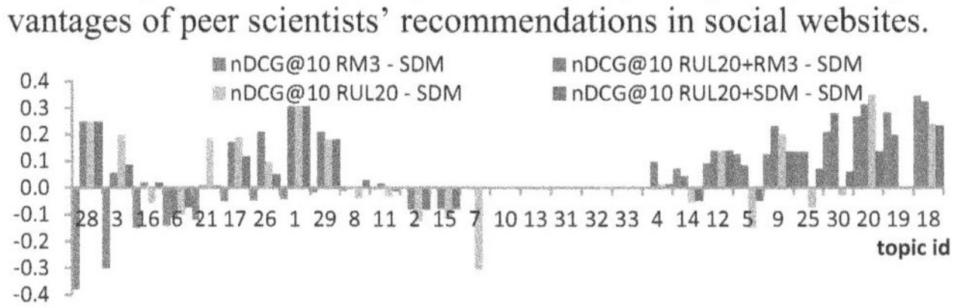

Figure 2. Per topic nDCG@10 differences of algorithms.

4. ACKNOWLEDGMENTS

This work was supported in parts by National Science Foundation grant IIS-1052773 and III-COR 0704628.

5. REFERENCES

[1] http://www.sis.pitt.edu/~jjiang/data/rul/

[2] J. Jiang, D. He, C. Ni. 2011. Social reference: aggregating online usage of scientific literature in CiteULike for clustering academic resources. In JCDL '11: 401-402.

[3] K. Balog, L. Azzopardi, M. de Rijke. 2006. Formal models for expert finding in enterprise corpora. In SIGIR '06: 43-50.

[4] Y. Lv, C. Zhai. 2009. A comparative study of methods for estimating query language models with pseudo feedback. In CIMK '09: 1895-1898.

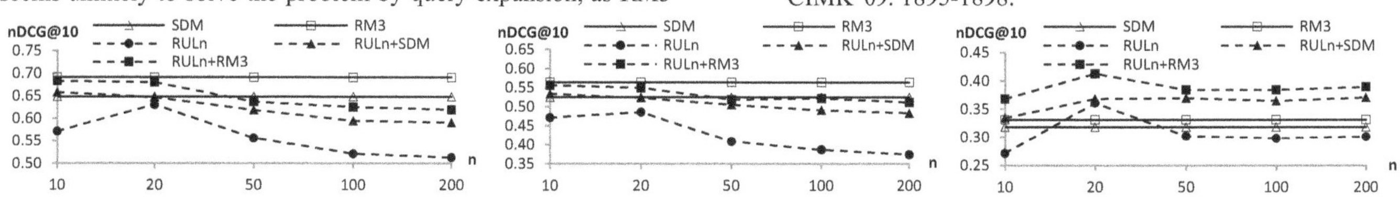

Figure 1. nDCG@10 of SDM, RM3, and RUL_n (+SDM/RM3) evaluated by QRel (left), HRelRead (center), and MRelRead (right).

Finding Web Appearances of Social Network Users via Latent Factor Model *

Kailong Chen[†‡] Zhengdong Lu[‡] Xiaoshi Yin[♮‡] Yong Yu[†] Zaiqing Nie[‡]

† Dept. of Computer Science & Engineering
Shanghai Jiao Tong University
Shanghai, China
{chenkl,yyu}@sjtu.edu.cn

‡ Microsoft Research Asia
49 Zhichun Rd.
Beijing, China
zhengdol@microsoft.com
znie@microsoft.com

♮ School of Computer Science & Engineering
Beihang University
Beijing, China
xiaoshiyin@cse.buaa.edu.cn

ABSTRACT

With the rapid growing of Web 2.0, people spend more time on social networks such as Facebook and Twitter. In order to know the people they are interacting with, finding the web appearances of them will help the social network users to a great extent. We propose a novel and effective latent factor model to find web appearances of target social network users. Our method solves the name ambiguity problem by simultaneously exploring the link structure of social networks and the web. Experiments on real-world data show the superiority of our method over several baselines.

Categories and Subject Descriptors

H.4.0 [**Information Systems**]: Information Systems Applications—*General*

General Terms

Algorithms, Experimentation

Keywords

Name Disambiguation, Social Network, Latent Factor Model

1. INTRODUCTION

Searching web pages related to a person in search engines is a common experience of web users [2]. This is because the web is a rich knowledge base of people and web users would like to search the web appearances of their friends or acquaintances to know more about them. With the rapid growing of social networks, web users spend more time on social networks to join in activities via interacting with other people. Finding web appearances of other users on social networks will meet the user demands to a great extent, because this will help them know more about each other and have better communications and interactions. In this paper, we propose a novel and effective model to find the web appearances of targeting social network users.

*This work was done when Kailong Chen and Xiaoshi Yin were visiting Microsoft Research Asia.

Name ambiguity is a major obstacle of finding web appearances for specific persons, especially the unknown average Joes. Fortunately, social networks like Facebook provide rich user information such as user profiles, friends relations, which are very useful for disambiguating web appearances. Here we propose a novel and effective latent factor model to find the low dimensional representations of users and web pages then measure the relevance between them as a key element for judgement. Our method not only utilizes the information provided by social networks, but also considers the link structure of web pages. Our experiments show all these considered elements combined help improve targeting the web pages of a specified social network user.

Past related research about finding web appearances has focused much on name disambiguation by grouping web pages into clusters, each corresponding to a real person [4, 6, 5]. Han [3] enhanced name disambiguation by exploiting the semantic knowledge existed in multiple knowledge sources. Bekkerman [1] disambiguated a group of people in a mail list based on clustering models.

2. LATENT FACTOR MODEL FOR FINDING WEB APPEARANCES

In latent factor model, we try to determine the low dimensional representations for social network users and web pages. In the first step, we format queries by combining each user's information such as names, colleges, occupations then use them to retrieve in a search engine. All the retrieved web pages are web appearances candidates of targeting users because they contain their names. W is defined as the initial relevance score between social network users and web pages. This matrix can be regarded as a noisy observation of the grant truth and it actually provides a lower bound of the name disambiguation performance. Many strategies can be used to define W, such as the text similarity between a user profile and a web page, or the retrieval score returned by the search engine, etc. In our experiment, $W_{i,j}$ is simply defined as a binary indicator of whether the name of user i appears in web page j. To consider the observed entries in W, the latent factors are designed to meet the following requirement:

$$U^\top V \approx W \tag{1}$$

where $U = [u_1, u_2, \cdots, u_N], V = [v_1, v_2, \cdots, v_M]$. $u_i \in \mathbb{R}^d$ and $v_i \in \mathbb{R}^d$ are latent factors of user i and page j respectively. N is the number of users and M is the number of web pages. d is the dimension of latent factors.

To consider the social relations in disambiguation, we try to smooth a user's latent factors by considering his neighborhoods. The smoothing strategy can be expressed as below:

$$U^\top U \approx \lambda_e E \tag{2}$$

Here λ_e is a constant for scaling, E is the adjacent matrix of the social network. This is based on an intuitive assumption that if two users have neighbor relationships like friends, they are tend to be more similar than others. Similarly, we also smooth the web pages' latent factors by meeting the following requirement:

$$V^\top V \approx \lambda_p P \tag{3}$$

Here P is the adjacent matrix of web pages. However, the relations between web pages are not explicitly defined as social relations. Here we assume that if two web pages contain a hyperlink to the same page or one of them link to the other, there is a link between them. This is also based on an intuitive assumption that if two web pages are close on the web, the content of them will be more relevant than others.

Considering all the elements mentioned above, we use Frobenius norm and a linear combination strategy to express the requirements as the following optimization problem:

$$\min_{U,V} \|U^\top U - \lambda_e E\|^2 + 2\|U^\top V - W\|^2 + \|V^\top V - \lambda_p P\|^2. \tag{4}$$

Mathematically, solving this optimization problem can be equivalently written as optimization over C as

$$\min_{C} \|C - C_0\|_F \quad s.t. \quad rank(C) \leq d, \tag{5}$$

where $C = \begin{bmatrix} U^\top \\ V^\top \end{bmatrix} \begin{bmatrix} U & V \end{bmatrix}$, $C_0 = \begin{bmatrix} \lambda_e E & W \\ W^\top & \lambda_p P \end{bmatrix}$. The global optimal solution to C can be obtained by performing singular value decomposition on C_0. λ_e and λ_p specify the influence strength of social relations and the web link structure on latent factor model respectively. After getting the latent factors, we obtain the relevance score between a user and a web page by calculating the inner product of their factors. These relevance scores indicates the probability of a web page is the web appearance of a specified user and we use them to rank the web pages for each user as the final displayed results.

3. EXPERIMENTS

Two social network data sets are derived from a popular social network site in our experiments. We begin with a single user and expanded the user-base by following their friends' links. To ensure there are enough neighbors for each person, we remove the nodes whose degree is less than five in the base. With two different seeds, we get two user sets, an academia set containing 271 researchers from the areas of information retrieval, bioinformatics, and an industry set containing 254 employees in a software company. For each data set, 20 users with serious name ambiguities are used to format queries and retrieve the top 100 web pages from a search engine, and finally there are 4000 web pages for evaluation. Pages with no links and pdf files are disregarded while evaluation. Each web page is manually labeled as relevant or non-relevant to the given user and the performance are measured by using mean average precision and P@10. For comparison, the first baseline is that pages are ranked the same as in the order returned by search engine. The second baseline, co-occurrence method ranks the pages by counting the names of a user's friends appeared in each page. In another baseline we identify the largest connected subgraph in all retrieved pages as the central cluster G, then rank web pages according to the Euclidean distances to the center of G. Here the links of web pages is the same as the ones in latent factor model. This is based on an intuitive assumption that the web pages in central cluster are more likely to be web appearances of the social network users, as mentioned in [1]. Table 1 shows the performances of the baselines and the latent factor model. The low performance of search engine results indicate the seriousness of name ambiguity. The co-occurrence method greatly improves upon the search engine results on both data set. This shows that the social relations provide valuable context information for name disambiguation, even with a relatively naive model. Using the link structure of the web as context knowledge, the result of the clustering model is substantially better than co-occurrence method. Compared to the clustering baseline, latent factor model achieves 7.0% and 13.8% improvement on two data sets in terms of MAP and performs the best. Our experiments show that the performance is relatively insensitive to λ_e and λ_p. According to the overall best performance these parameters are set as $\lambda_e = 1$ and $\lambda_p = 1$. Similarly the dimension of latent factors d is set as 20. In summary, evaluation results indicate that both the social network structure and the link structure of the web can help reduce name ambiguity, and our proposed latent factor model makes effective use of these information and performs superior to all the competing models.

	Academia		Industry	
	MAP	P@10	MAP	P@10
SEARCHE ENGINE	0.3613	0.2900	0.3419	0.2850
CO-OCCURRENCE	0.4049	0.4550	0.4825	0.4350
CLUSTERING	0.6546	0.6400	0.6652	0.6150
LATENT FACTOR	0.7007	0.6650	0.7391	0.7001

Table 1: Evaluation Results on Both Data Sets

4. REFERENCES

[1] R. Bekkerman and A. McCallum. Disambiguating web appearances of people in a social network. In *WWW*, pages 463 – 470, 2005.

[2] R. V. Guha and A. Garg. Disambiguating people in search. In *WWW*, 2004.

[3] X. Han and J. Zhao. Structural semantic relatedness: a knowledge-based method to named entity disambiguation. In *ACL*, pages 50–59, 2010.

[4] D. Kalashnikov, R. Nuray-Turan, and S. Mehrotra. Towards breaking the quality curse.: a web-querying approach to web people search. In *SIGIR*. ACM, 2008.

[5] J. Tang, Q. Lu, T. Wang, J. Wang, and W. Li. A bipartite graph based social network splicing method for person name disambiguation. In *SIGIR*, 2011.

[6] M. Yoshida, M. Ikeda, S. Ono, I. Sato, and H. Nakagawa. Person name disambiguation by bootstrapping. In *SIGIR*, pages 10–17. ACM, 2010.

Fixed versus Dynamic Co-Occurrence Windows in TextRank Term Weights for Information Retrieval

Wei Lu
School of Information Management
Wuhan University, China
reedwhu@gmail.com

Qikai Cheng
School of Information Management
Wuhan University, China
chengqikai0806@gmail.com

Christina Lioma
Computer Science
University of Copenhagen, Denmark
c.lioma@diku.dk

ABSTRACT

TextRank is a variant of PageRank typically used in graphs that represent documents, and where vertices denote terms and edges denote relations between terms. Quite often the relation between terms is simple term co-occurrence within a fixed window of k terms. The output of TextRank when applied iteratively is a score for each vertex, i.e. a term weight, that can be used for information retrieval (IR) just like conventional term frequency based term weights.

So far, when computing TextRank term weights over co-occurrence graphs, the window of term co-occurrence is always fixed. This work departs from this, and considers dynamically adjusted windows of term co-occurrence that follow the document structure on a sentence- and paragraph-level. The resulting TextRank term weights are used in a ranking function that re-ranks 1000 initially returned search results in order to improve the precision of the ranking. Experiments with two IR collections show that adjusting the vicinity of term co-occurrence when computing TextRank term weights can lead to gains in early precision.

Categories and Subject Descriptors

H.3.3 [**Information Storage and Retrieval**]: Information Search and Retrieval

Keywords

TextRank, term co-occurrence

1. INTRODUCTION

Associative networks have long been used to represent units of text and their interconnecting relations [5]. The symbolic structures that emerge from these representations correspond to graphs, where text constituents are represented as vertices and their interconnecting relations as edges. Graph ranking algorithms, such as the TextRank [5, 6] variant of PageRank, have been used successfully in keyword extraction [6], classification [3] and information retrieval [2] to compute term weights from graphs of individual documents, where vertices represent the document's terms, and edges represent term co-occurrence within a fixed window. Using these computations iteratively, the weight of a term can be estimated with respect to the terms that fall in its vicinity and their respective term weights. An underlying assumption in these approaches is that the vicinity of term co-occurrence is fixed for all terms. To our knowledge, there is no theoretical or intuitive basis for this assumption.

SIGIR'12, August 12–16, 2012, Portland, Oregon, USA.
ACM 978-1-4503-1472-5/12/08.

Fixed-window term co-occurrence may not be optimal for TextRank term weights. Lexical affinities may span across more words in longer sentences than they do in shorter sentences. Hence, adjusting the co-occurrence window according to the discourse span of the text might be a better choice. Based on this intuition, in this work we look at the effect of dynamically adjusted windows of term co-occurrence upon their resultant TextRank term weights. We experiment with co-occurrence windows that follow the document structure on two levels of granularity: sentences and paragraphs. For each of these, we compute term weights using TextRank, and use them for retrieval using the ranking model of [2], i.e. linearly combined with inverse document frequency (idf). Experiments using these TextRank term weights for re-ranking the top 1000 search results show that sentence-based co-occurrence can outperform fixed-window co-occurrence in terms of early precision.

2. CO-OCCURRENCE WINDOWS

2.1 Methodology

We experiment with two datasets: Reuters RCV1 from TREC 2002 (2.5GB, 50 title-only queries) and INEX 2005 (764MB, 40 content-only queries). We build a separate graph for each document: terms are represented as vertices (initially unweighted), and term co-occurrence within a window is represented as an undirected edge linking the vertices of the co-occurring terms. We use TextRank [6] to compute iteratively the score of each vertex v_i:

$$s(v_i) = (1 - \delta) + \delta \times \sum_{j \in V(v_i)} \frac{S(v_j)}{|V(v_j)|} \qquad (1)$$

where $s(v_i)$ is the TextRank score of vertex v_i, $V(\cdot)$ denotes the set of vertices connecting with a vertex, $|\cdot|$ marks cardinality, and $0 \leq \delta \leq 1$ is a damping factor that integrates into the computation the probability of jumping randomly from one vertex to another. We iterate the formula 200 times, using the default $\delta = 0.85$ [6]. The final score of each vertex represents a term weight where the higher the number of different words that a given word co-occurs with, and the higher their weight, the higher the weight of this word. It has been shown that a nonlinear correlation exists between such TextRank term weights and term frequency based term weights [5].

We use these term weights to compute the score of a document for a query ($s(d, q)$) according to [2]:

$$s(d, q) = \sum_{i \in q} \log idf_i \times \log s(i) \quad (2)$$

where i is a query term, and $s(i)$ is the corresponding TextRank score for vertex v_i. No document length normalisation is used. We use Porter's stemmer for the documents and queries.

To compare fixed versus dynamically adjusted windows of term co-occurrence, we use a baseline where the window of term co-occurrence is fixed to the best values reported in the IR literature (albeit for other datasets)[1][2]: k =5 & 6. We compare this baseline against term co-occurrence that is dynamically adjusted to the length of each (a) sentence and (b) paragraph[2], separately. The sentence/paragraph term statistics are displayed in Table 1. We evaluate this comparison in a re-ranking scenario, where the task is to re-rank an initially retrieved set of 1000 documents. For the INEX collection (where relevance assessments apply to document sections) we consider a document relevant if any of its containing sections is assessed relevant.

2.2 Findings

Table 2 shows different metrics of retrieval performance when using fixed versus sentence- and paragraph-length windows of term co-occurrence. We see that results vary[3]. For average precision (NDCG) fixed co-occurrence is best for RCV1, and sentence-based co-occurrence is best for INEX. The reverse happens for precision in the top 10 retrieved documents (P@10): fixed co-occurrence is best for INEX, and sentence-based co-occurrence is best for RCV1. The only consistent trend is in the precision of the single top retrieved document (MRR), which benefits more from dynamically adjusted co-occurrence consistently for both collections. This finding is novel, considering the earlier position of [6] that the larger the window of co-occurrence, the lower the precision. This finding indicates that larger window sizes may lead to gains in precision, if however they are not fixed but rather dynamically adjusted to text units like sentences.

Finally, sentences appear to be an overall better boundary of term co-occurrence than paragraphs, with the exception of NDCG for INEX where paragraph-based co-occurrence slightly outperforms sentence-based co-occurrence (and they both outperform fixed co-occurrence). This could be due to the fact that INEX paragraphs are relatively short and focused content-wise [4].

	sent (RCV1)	para (RCV1)	sent (INEX)	para (INEX)
min length	1	1	1	1
max length	1731	31696	7920	111136
min tokens	1	1	1	1
max tokens	250	4662	2447	17379
average tokens	19.87	20.35	15.73	58.51

Table 1: Sentence (sent) and paragraph (para) statistics per retrieval dataset.

Re-ranking top 1000 retrieved documents								
co-occurrence window		RCV1			INEX		
		NDCG	MRR	P@10	NDCG	MRR	P@10
fixed	5 terms	**0.5238**	0.6736	0.4300	0.5541	0.6865	**0.4750**
	6 terms	0.5025	0.6559	0.4280	0.5540	0.6966	0.4714
dynamic	sentence	0.5119	**0.6811**	**0.4340**	0.5543	**0.7021**	0.4743
	paragraph	0.5178	0.6574	0.4160	**0.5545**	0.6975	0.4714

Table 2: Retrieval performance with TextRank term weights using fixed vs. dynamic co-occurrence windows, on two datasets. Bold font marks best scores.

3. CONCLUSION

We modelled individual documents as separate graphs where vertices represent terms, and co-occurrence relations among terms represent edges. Using the TextRank model of Mihalcea et al. [5, 6] we computed vertex weights corresponding to term weights, which we used for retrieval using the ranking of Blanco et al. [1, 2]. Unlike all these existing approaches where term co-occurrence is fixed to a window of k terms at all times, we reasoned that term co-occurrence should be varied according to sentence or paragraph length. Our motivation was that meaningful term relations may span across more words in longer sentences than they do in shorter sentences, hence fixing term co-occurrence may not be optimal for all terms.

Preliminary experiments in a re-ranking scenario with two retrieval datasets showed that sentence-based co-occurrence can lead to early precision gains over fixed term co-occurrence at 5 and 6 terms, which are optimal values in the IR literature. More experiments with larger datasets and full-ranking (as opposed to re-ranking) documents are needed to investigate the optimal term co-occurrence vicinity. This small-scale work contributes a novel comparison between fixed versus dynamically adjusted co-occurrence windows for TextRank term weights, and the initial finding that sentence-based co-occurrence can improve early precision.

Acknowledgments. Work partially funded by DANIDA (grant no. 10-087721) and the National Natural Science Foundation of China (grant no. 71173164).

4. REFERENCES

[1] R. Blanco and C. Lioma. Random walk term weighting for information retrieval. In W. Kraaij, A. P. de Vries, C. L. A. Clarke, N. Fuhr, and N. Kando, editors, *SIGIR*, pages 829–830. ACM, 2007.

[2] R. Blanco and C. Lioma. Graph-based term weighting for information retrieval. *Inf. Retr.*, 15(1):54–92, 2012.

[3] S. Hassan, R. Mihalcea, and C. Banea. Random walk term weighting for improved text classification. *Int. J. Semantic Computing*, 1(4):421–439, 2007.

[4] S. Malik, G. Kazai, M. Lalmas, and N. Fuhr. Overview of inex 2005. In N. Fuhr, M. Lalmas, S. Malik, and G. Kazai, editors, *INEX*, volume 3977 of *Lecture Notes in Computer Science*, pages 1–15. Springer, 2005.

[5] R. Mihalcea and D. Radev. *Graph-Based Natural Language Processing and Information Retrieval.* Cambridge University Press, 2011.

[6] R. Mihalcea and P. Tarau. Textrank: Bringing order into text. In *EMNLP*, pages 404–411. ACL, 2004.

[1] In non-IR literature, optimal fixed values are: k =2,4 for classification [3] and k =2 for keyword extraction [6], however these values consistently underperform for IR [1, 2].
[2] We treat these elements as paragraphs: `p` (for RCV1) and `ilrj, ip1, ip2, ip3, ip4, ip5, item-none, p, p1, p2, p3, Bib, Bm, St` (for INEX).
[3] Results were not stat. significant when the t-test was used.

Gender-aware Re-ranking

Eugene Kharitonov
Yandex, LLC & Moscow Institute of Physics and Technology
16, Leo Tolstoy st
Moscow, Russia
kharitonov@yandex-team.ru

Pavel Serdyukov
Yandex, LLC
16, Leo Tolstoy st
Moscow, Russia
pavser@yandex-team.ru

ABSTRACT

In this paper we study usefulness of users' gender information for improving ranking of ambiguous queries in personalized and non-contextual settings. This study is performed as a sequence of offline re-ranking experiments and it demonstrates that the proposed gender-aware ranking features provide improvements in ranking quality. It is also shown that the proposed personalized features exhibit performance superior to non-contextual ones.

Categories and Subject Descriptors

H.3.3 [**Information Search and Retrieval**]: Information Search and Retrieval

General Terms

Algorithms, Measurement

Keywords

web search, personalization, gender-aware ranking

1. INTRODUCTION

Web search personalization and utilization of a search context in ranking received a lot of interest in the research community. For instance, the geographical context was discussed in the paper by Bennett et al. [1], Collins-Thompson et al. [2] proposed a method to provide users with results personalized by their reading proficiency level. Both papers demonstrated that the search context is especially useful in case of ambiguous and underspecified queries. Several studies (e.g., [4, 5, 6]) suggested that enriching the search context with the user's gender data has potential to improve retrieval quality. But, to the best of our knowledge, specific attempts to quantitatively assess possible usefulness of gender data in the large-scale web search setting were not yet made.

However, we consider the goal of this paper to be a little broader: we want to investigate how information about user's gender can be used to improve ranking quality of "hard", ambiguous queries not only in personalized, but in non-contextual setting, too. The main contribution of the paper is two-fold: 1) Introduction of two groups of gender-aware features: non-contextual and personalized; 2) Comprehensive study of both groups of features in off-line re-ranking experiments with respect to queries of different level of ambiguity.

SIGIR'12, August 12–16, 2012, Portland, Oregon, USA.
ACM 978-1-4503-1472-5/12/08.

2. GENDER-AWARE RE-RANKING

We organize our study as a comparison of non-contextual and personalized gender-aware settings in terms of retrieval quality improvements. The comparison is performed in a set of re-ranking experiments performed in an offline setup, following the evaluation scenario proposed in [1] and [2].

We build a dataset of user sessions and augment it with proposed features. Secondly, we learn a function which predicts a document with a user-specific positive judgement in each query session. Finally, documents are re-ranked according to their probability of being relevant. The re-ranking quality is measured by the inverse of the rank of the relevant document (mean reciprocal rank, MRR). The original ranking produced by the search engine serves as a baseline.

2.1 Dataset

Firstly, we build a set of search sessions (session is a sequence of actions separated with time intervals not longer than 20 minutes) that took place during a four-week period and were performed by users from a 44mln anonymized set of users whose gender is known with a high degree of confidence[1]. The sessions from the first two weeks were used to calculate gender-aware query and document features. The rest of the sessions were used to train and evaluate the re-ranking algorithm. From the latter subset we removed sessions associated with 15 most popular queries and all queries which were asked less than 100 times by either female or male users.

To proceed, let us introduce the necessary terminology. A click is called *satisfied* if it is the last click in the session or it has dwell time not less than 30 seconds [1, 2]. We refer to a query result as *examined* in a session if it was clicked or there is a click on the result below or a user clicked on the "next page" button.

Since labelling relevance judgements to evaluate personalized search is impractical, we use a user's click behaviour instead. With each session we assign a positive judgement to one of the top 10 urls if it corresponds to the last click

[1]A user's gender is determined by a proprietary classifier. This classifier was trained to separate users of both genders using their genders and full names (often gender-specific) specified in their personal accounts at the search engine or in their accounts at popular social networks outlinked from the search engine account. The accuracy of the classifier on the considered set of users is 80%.

in the session and this click was satisfied (the last click in a session is not necessarily satisfied due to possible additional queries without clicks). All other documents from the top-10 results are considered as irrelevant, even if they were not examined. Sessions without positive judgements were removed from the dataset. Labelling non-examined documents as irrelevant provides us with the lower bound on the re-ranking performance. As a result we have the dataset of 15,021,054 sessions with 30,329 unique queries. Due to the filtering performed while constructing the dataset, it constitutes 18% of the whole query stream. The dataset was uniformly divided into two approximately equal parts: training and test sets.

Learning to rank was performed by the Generalized Boosted Regression Models R package [3], with its parameters tuned on a subset of the training data. The number of iterations was set to 3000, learning rate to 0.005, exponential (adaboost) loss function was selected.

2.2 Features

Let us consider features used to rank document D for a query Q asked by a user U of gender G. These features can be divided into two groups:

G1: Non-contextual group of gender-aware features includes features which do not take the gender of the current user U into account: 1) Two features characterize symmetrised Kullback-Leibler Divergences between gender distributions of users who submit query Q and users a) who click on the documents from the same site[2] as D b) for whom these clicks are satisfied. 2) Entropy of the gender distribution of users who submit Q: $H(G|Q)$; 3)Usefulness of the G attribute to predict clicked documents in sessions with query Q, calculated as information gain ratio:

$$IGR(G,Q) = \frac{1}{H(G|Q)}\left[H(U|Q) - \sum_{G} p(G) \cdot H(U|Q,G)\right]$$

where $H(U|Q)$ - entropy of distribution of clicks over documents, $H(U|Q,G)$ - click entropy calculated using only clicks of users of gender G. Information gain ratio is widely used as a feature selection criterion in decision tree algorithms.

G2: Personalized feature set include the following features: 1) probability that result D for query Q will be clicked after examination by a user of gender G; 2) probability that a user of gender G will be satisfied with the document D for query Q after clicking on it;

The original (baseline) ranking algorithm uses features similar to **G2**, but calculated on the whole population of the users. The reciprocal of the document's original rank was included as an additional feature in all the experiments.

3. RESULTS

It should be emphasized that the baseline ranking is a very competitive one since it represents a default ranking of a commercial search engine. We do not report absolute values of quality metrics due to proprietary nature of the system, but report relative improvements over the baseline instead (in accordance with previous studies, e.g. [1, 2]). We use click entropy $H(U|Q)$ to sample subsets of queries with different levels of ambiguity: higher values of entropy

Table 1: Re-ranking results for subsets of the test data. Higher values of $H(U|Q)$ correspond to higher level of query ambiguity

	G1, %	G2, %	G1+G2, %	share
$H(U\|Q) \geq 3$	+0.8 △	+1.2 ▲	+1.9 ▲	5.5%
$H(U\|Q) \geq 2$	+0.2 △	+0.4 ▲	+0.6 ▲	33.3%
$H(U\|Q) \geq 1$	+0.03	+0.3 ▲	+0.3 ▲	66.1%
Entire set	+0.04 △	+0.05 ▲	+0.1 ▲	100 %

are believed to correspond to more ambiguous queries (for instance, in [1]). Symbols ▲ and △ denote improvements statistically significant according to Wilcoxon paired signed-rank test at the $p < 0.01$ and $p < 0.05$ levels, respectively. The last column shows which part of the test set is covered with queries of the specific ambiguity level. This ratio was estimated using the first two-week part of the dataset.

4. CONCLUSIONS AND FUTURE WORK

As we hoped, described features are especially useful for ranking "hard", ambiguous and underspecified queries. Also, we see that the relative usefulness of the gender context increases as query ambiguity grows. The performance demonstrated on high-entropy queries is comparable to reported in other papers on personalization [1, 2]. It should be noticed that personalized features exhibit superior improvements in comparison with non-personalized ones on every subset of queries.

However, there is a variety of reasons for query ambiguity and, surely, only a part of ambiguous queries can be disambiguated be means of gender information.

As a natural direction of the future work we consider extending the search context to include more socio-demographic user attributes (e.g., age). Furthermore, it is tempting to learn user latent attributes automatically from their search behaviour and add them to the search context afterwards.

5. REFERENCES

[1] P. N. Bennett, F. Radlinski, R. W. White, and E. Yilmaz. Inferring and using location metadata to personalize web search. SIGIR, 2011.

[2] K. Collins-Thompson, P. N. Bennett, R. W. White, S. de la Chica, and D. Sontag. Personalizing web search results by reading level. CIKM, 2011.

[3] G. Ridgeway. Generalized boosted models: A guide to the gbm package, 2007.

[4] J. Teevan, M. R. Morris, and S. Bush. Discovering and using groups to improve personalized search. WSDM, 2009.

[5] I. Weber and C. Castillo. The demographics of web search. SIGIR, 2010.

[6] I. Weber and A. Jaimes. Who uses web search for what: and how. WSDM, 2011.

[2]Aggregation at the document level did not result into any improvement. The reasons could be: 1) gender-specific interest has site-level granularity 2) increased sparsity.

Genre Classification for Million Song Dataset Using Confidence-Based Classifiers Combination

Yajie Hu
Department of Computer Science
University of Miami
Coral Gables, Florida, USA
yajie.hu@umail.miami.edu

Mitsunori Ogihara
Department of Computer Science
University of Miami
Coral Gables, Florida, USA
ogihara@cs.miami.edu

ABSTRACT

We proposed a method to classify songs in the Million Song Dataset according to song genre. Since songs have several data types, we trained sub-classifiers by different types of data. These sub-classifiers are combined using both classifier authority and classification confidence for a particular instance. In the experiments, the combined classifier surpasses all of these sub-classifiers and the SVM classifier using concatenated vectors from all data types. Finally, the genre labels for the Million Song Dataset are provided.

Categories and Subject Descriptors

I.5.2 [**Design Methodology**]: Classifier design and evaluation; H.5.5 [**Sound and Music Computing**]: Methodologies and techniques

General Terms

Algorithms, Experimentation

Keywords

Classifier Combination, Song Genre Classification

1. INTRODUCTION

In music information retrieval, many methods see song genre as important metadata for retrieving songs. As the largest currently available dataset, the Million Song Dataset (MSD) is a collection of audio features and metadata for a million contemporary popular music tracks. However, none of records have any genre labels. The goal of this paper is to automatically classify songs in the MSD according to genre.

Some papers have discussed the importance of multiple data sources in genre classification and proposed methods to use them. Most of these methods [3] concatenated features from different data sources into a vector to represent the song. However, for a huge scale dataset, it is impossible that every instance will have valid data in all data sources. It is inevitable for the classification results to be demoted due to data missing influence in the concatenated vector.

If we imagine classifiers as experts in voting, the accuracy of each classifier represents the authority of the expert. Because the types of input data are different, the views of experts are not same. Therefore, the confidences to make a correct decision regarding a particular item are also different. Hence, the voting result of an instance is related to both the authority of the classifier and the confidence of the classifier to classify the particular instance.

In this paper, we extract features from audio, artist terms, lyrics and social tags to represent songs and train sub-classifiers. The trained sub-classifiers are combined to classify song genre. The songs with missing data in certain data types are classified by the remaining data without any negative influence by the missing data.

SIGIR'12, August 12–16, 2012, Portland, Oregon, USA.
ACM 978-1-4503-1472-5/12/08.

2. METHOD

We apply each data source to train a sub-classifier and we assume that classifier set C contains n sub-classifiers, namely, $C = \{c_1, c_2, \ldots, c_n\}$. Furthermore, we assume that songs are distributed into m genres, $G = \{g_1, g_2, \ldots, g_m\}$. The voting result is shown in Equation 1.

$$\mathrm{G}\left(I_k\right) = \arg\max_{g_j} \left\{ \sum_{i=1}^{|C|} \left[\mathrm{Auth}\left(c_i\right) \cdot \mathrm{Conf}\left(c_i, g_j, I_k\right)\right] \right\} \quad (1)$$

$\mathrm{Auth}\left(c_i\right)$ denotes the authority of the classifier c_i from 0.0 to 1.0. $\mathrm{Auth}\left(c_i\right)$ is estimated by the accuracy of the classification in the validation test.

$\mathrm{Conf}\left(c_i, g_j, I_k\right)$ is the confidence of the classifier c_i to classify the instance I_k to genre g_j. For Naïve Bayes, the posterior probability is seen as the confidence for a class. Neural Net has normalized real value output from -1.0 to 1.0. A positive value means the confidence to assign the instance to a positive label. We employ the method proposed by Lee [2] to estimate the confidence for logistic regression. The margin from the instance location to the classification hyperplane is considered to be the confidence of the SVM classifier. The confidences of classifiers are normalized into $[0.0, 1.0]$. The confidence for invalid data is set to 0.0, in order to avoid negative effect caused by invalid data.

3. EXPERIMENT

In our experiment, we applied MSD, MusiXmatch and Last.fm tag datasets to extract features, as shown in Table 1. The records in these data sources are matched via `trackID`.

AllMusic.com provides genre taxonomy, which consists of 10 major genres with sample songs. 1,138 songs are collected from AllMusic.com and they have valid records in MSD as the ground truth. The distribution of the songs according to genre is shown in Figure 1.

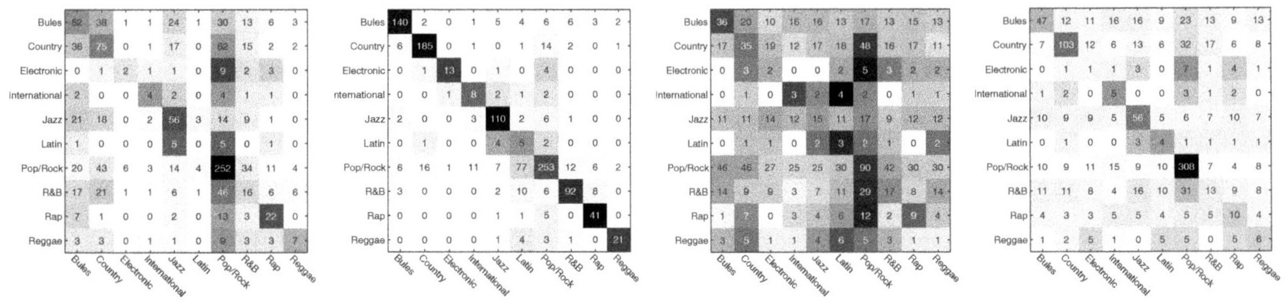

(a) Neural Net by audio features (b) Neural Net by artist terms (c) Logistic Regression by lyrics (d) Naïve Bayes by social tags

Figure 2: Confusion matrixes of four sub-classifiers

Table 1: Data sources

Name	Extracted information	Number of records
MSD	Audio features, artist terms	1,000,000
MuisXmatch	Lyrics features	237,662
Last.fm tags	Social tags	505,216

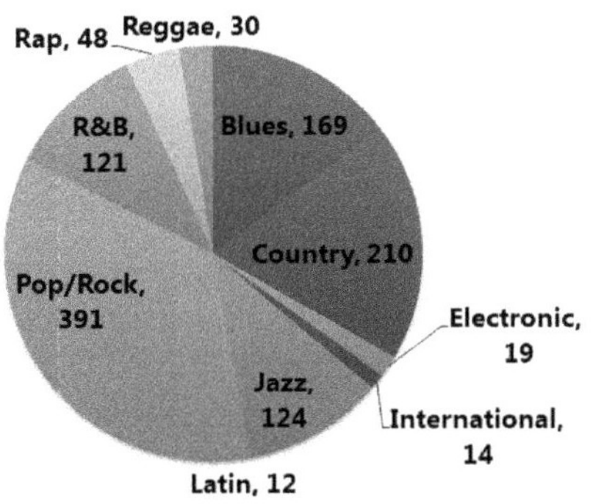

Figure 1: Genre Samples in AllMusic.com

In order to improve classification performance, we convert genre classification into a series of binary classifications. Thus, the classification result of a song is a vector of confidence to classify the song into a genre. The predicted genre is the one whose confidence is highest.

We extract features from different data sources and trained individual classifiers by each type of features using Naïve Bayes, Rule Induction, LDA, Neural Net, Logistic Regression and SVM, respectively. The classifiers' performances are evaluated by 5-folder cross validation. The best performance classifiers in different types of features are shown in Figure 2.

The four sub-classifiers are combined based on classification authority and confidence. The resultant combined classifier is significantly better than sub-classifiers and the SVM classifier using concatenated vectors from four data sources as shown in Figure 3 and Table 2. The result is encouraging regarding to the result of genre classification task in MIREX [1]. Furthermore, we apply the combined classifier to classify all of the songs in the MSD and the result is available at `http://web.cs.miami.edu/home/yajiehu/resource/genre`.

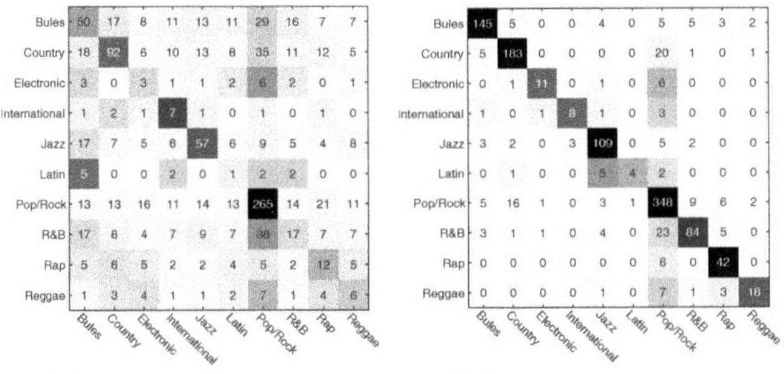

(a) SVM by long vector (b) Combined classifier

Figure 3: Confusion matrixes by all data

Table 2: Experiment result comparison

Data	Method	Accuracy
Audio	Neural Net	42.70%
Artist terms	Neural Net	76.27%
Lyrics	Logistic Regression	18.54%
Social Tags	Naïve Bayes	48.59%
All data	SVM	44.82%
All data	Combined classifiers	**83.66%**

4. CONCLUSION

Based on classifier authority and classification confidence, the combined classifier integrates sub-classifiers, which are good at classification of certain data sources. The combined classifier performs with higher accuracy than sub-classifiers and the SVM classifier using concatenated vectors.

5. REFERENCES

[1] `http://www.music-ir.org/mirex/wiki/2009`.

[2] C.-H. Lee. Learning to combine discriminative classifiers: confidence based. In *Proceedings of the 16th ACM SIGKDD*, KDD '10, pages 743–752, New York, USA, 2010.

[3] C. McKay, J. A. Burgoyne, J. Hockman, J. B. L. Smith, G. Vigliensoni, and I. Fujinaga. Evaluating the genre classification performance of lyrical features relative to audio, symbolic and cultural features. In *Proceedings of the 11th ISMIR*, ISMIR '10, pages 213–718, Utrecht, Netherlands, 2010.

GLASE 0.1: Eyes Tell More than Mice

Viktors Garkavijs[*†], Mayumi Toshima[*], and Noriko Kando[†*]

[*]Department of Informatics, The Graduate University for Advanced Sciences, [†]National Institute of Informatics

2-1-2 Hitotsubashi, Chiyoda-ku, Tokyo 101-8430, Japan

{gvb,mamitako,kando} @ nii.ac.jp

ABSTRACT

This paper proposes a prototype system called Gaze-Learning-Access-and-Search-Engine 0.1 (GLASE), which can perform image relevance ranking based on gaze data and within-session learning. We developed a search user interface that uses an eye-tracker as an input device and employed a relevance re-ranking algorithm based on the gaze length. The preliminary experimental results showed that using our gaze-driven system reduced the task completion time an average of 13.7% in a search session.

Categories and Subject Descriptors

H.3.3. [**Information Search and Retrieval**]: Relevance feedback
H.5.2. [**User Interfaces**]: Input devices and strategies

General Terms

Experimentation, Measurement

Keywords

Image search, gaze-based interaction, within session learning

1. INTRODUCTION

The interactivity of most search user interfaces (UI) is mostly supported by a keyboard and a mouse. Our prototype system, GLASE 0.1, provides a gaze-driven search UI and personalizes the search results based on within-session learning.

Gaze data can be used as feedback for learning to rank and re-rank based on the dynamic interest and attention of users. Since the provided data are continuous, compared to discrete mouse click events, learning can be performed in continuous time rather than by discrete iterations. Gaze conveys information that mouse clicks don't, including the gaze length, the direction, and the speed of movements. The data are more accurate and can capture the user attention and interest toward the items that were not clicked on; (this phenomena is called "good abandonment" [4]) and can also convey such information as whether users are actually looking at the screen while they are performing multiple tasks. Mouse "dwell time" fails to track this. Gaze-driven navigation is a great support when a user's hands are occupied during the search process. Finally, such input can greatly benefit people with sensory system, motor system, or cognitive disorders.

The search process has a high cognitive load, especially during query formulation and relevant document tagging [1]. Using implicit feedback, which requires nothing more from users than looking at items on a search engine results page (SERP), may lower the cognitive load and simplify the search task. Users are freed from clearly formulating their intents, if the system can learn them fast during within-session interaction. This can be especially effective in exploratory search for images.

Many related researches exist that prove that eye-tracking is an effective means both as an input device in an interactive UI as well as a data source for determining object relevance [2,3,5].

SIGIR'12, August 12–16, 2012, Portland, Oregon, USA.
ACM 978-1-4503-1472-5/12/08.

Our developed prototype system bases its relevance ranking on learning from gaze data. The experiment results show that it satisfied user needs 13.7% faster than two mouse-driven baseline systems and obtained 39% more feedback data from interaction with users.

2. SYSTEM

The system's UI was designed to be simple and concise. It includes a standard query box, a *search* button, and a *stop* button to stop eye tracking. The images are displayed as thumbnails with a maximum edge size of 150 pixels. Right clicking on the SERP brings a context menu with an option to reset the index.

Clicking on a thumbnail produces a pop-up window with the image title a list of its tags and a zoomed-up version of an image, which can be closed by a mouse click anywhere on the screen. For gaze-driven version, a user can instead fix his gaze on a thumbnail for more than 800 ms to bring the pop-up, which can be closed by moving the gaze outside the pop-up window area.

Data set. We indexed 786126 images extracted from the MIRFLICKR-1M image collection, which has 1 million Flickr images. For the tags, we used a "tags_raw" fileset that contains original tags obtained from users. To narrow the index tree breadth, we discarded the tags that don't exist in the ispell-enwl-3.1.20 dictionary fileset. This resulted in removing 213874 image files from the index.

Engine. Images are indexed by tags. We implemented a trie-like structure to access the image IDs faster. The trie branches store tag characters, and the leaves store lists of image IDs and the scores generated for respective tags. The initial scores of the tags are 0.

We employed two scoring mechanisms: "dwell-time" and "binary". The former is used in both mouse-driven and gaze-driven UIs. In this mechanism, the scores are being added to the image tags based on the time in milliseconds the image pop-up was opened, distributed among the tags equally on each iteration: $s_i = \frac{l_i}{|T_x|}$, where i is iteration, s is score, l is the length of the time interval the preview was open, and T_x is a set of tags of image x.

The "binary" mechanism adds a score to each tag, $s_i = \frac{1}{|T_x|}$, regardless of the time the pop-up was shown. This mechanism is used only in binary version of a mouse-driven UI.

To adapt to user interactions, we introduced an overlapping sliding window. In preliminary experiments, we determined that a window size of 5 is optimal for most cases; however this will be investigated in future studies. The total tag score thus can be calculated like this: $\begin{cases} S_i = \sum_{j=1}^{i} s_j, & \text{if } i \le w \\ S_i = S_{i-1} + s_i - s_{i-w} & \text{if } i > w \end{cases}$, where w is the window size and S is the total score after the i-th iteration.

Based on these scores we calculate the relevance score of image x: $R_x = \sum_q \sum_{t \in T_{X_q}} S_t$, where R is the relevance score, x is the image, q is the query term, X_q is a set of images that include tag q and T_X is a set of tags that occur for image set X. After calculating the scores for every image in X_q, we sort the images in descending order and present them on the UI.

3. EXPERIMENT

3.1 Setup

An experiment explored the effects of using eye-tracker as an input device in an image search user interface.

Six Japanese university students from various majors were recruited for the experiment; two were female.

Each participant performed four search tasks: 2 with an eye-tracker-driven (ET) UI and 2 with a mouse-driven UI. We used two types of relevance recalculation methods for the mouse-driven interface: "binary" and "dwell-time". The experiment organizers assigned the participants to either the "binary" (MB) or "dwell-time" (MD) interfaces. The tasks were counterbalanced among the participants.

Before performing the tasks, the system was briefly explained and a training session was held. After that the participants performed search tasks. The participants were asked to search for the images, that are similar to the sample images (these are the images from MIRFLICKR with the following IDs: 859626, 585623, 926255, 781859). The search session started with an input of a query. Depending on the task, the navigation had to be performed using gaze or a mouse. There was no time restriction for the tasks; however the participants were told that the tasks should not take longer than five minutes and that the overall experiment duration should not exceed 1 hour.

3.2 Results

The task completion time means and standard deviations, shown in the Table 1 are floored down to the nearest integer. The task completion time for ET is smaller than for the mouse-driven UI by 13.7%.

Table 1. Means and standard deviations of task completion times and pop-up show lengths, in seconds.

Measure	Mouse	ET	p-value
Task completion time	131 (48)	113 (24)	0.26
Pop-up show length	1.7 (2.0)	1.0 (1.3)	< 0.01

We generated heat maps of pop-up-counts and pop-up-view-lengths of the images on the UI (Fig. 1). The SERP consisted of five lines of images, seven images per line.

The total number of pop-ups on gaze-driven UI was 1.35 times bigger than on the mouse UI, but the total duration of the pop-ups was 1.24 times smaller on the gaze-driven UI. The cases of "good abandonment," when users looked at the images without clicking on them were captured by the gaze-driven UI. So the system learned this action; however the mouse-driven UI failed to capture these events. Thus, the system satisfied the information needs of users in a shorter time.

The total time effort of the users is smaller on the gaze-driven UI, but the computational cost required for relevance recalculation is slightly bigger due to the larger number of iterations. This increase is, however, negligible and was not noticed by the users during the experiment.

4. CONCLUSION

Using an eye-tracker as a relevance feedback input device can help save time in image search tasks. The information of relevance that is otherwise lost due to the phenomena of "good abandonment" can be retrieved during search sessions and used to learn the user's search intent. User experiments showed that the total duration of a search session can be decreased by an average of 13.7% using our proposed system, the gaze-driven UI of GLASE 0.1.

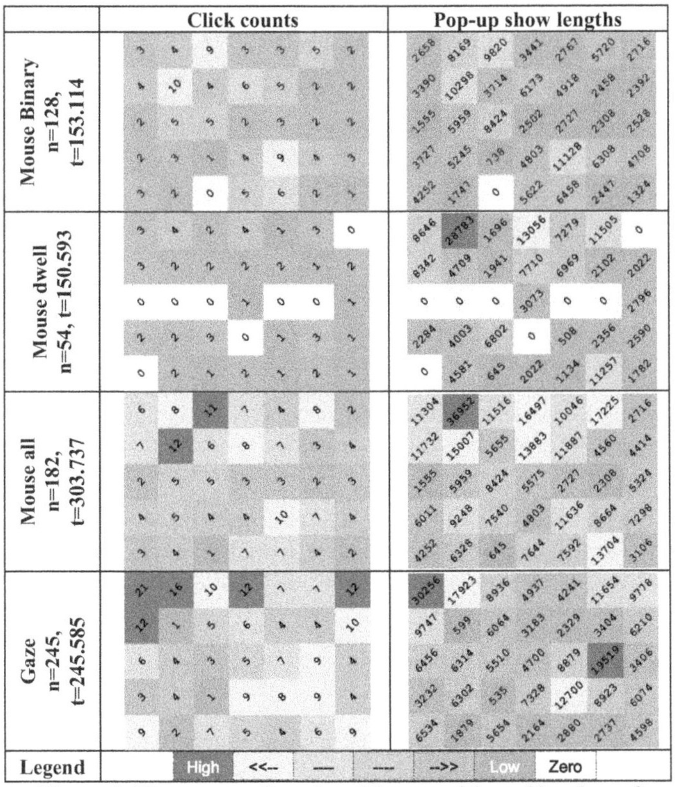

Figure 1. Heat maps of retrieved item positions. Number of pop-ups is n, and pop-up show length sum is t.

Even though out of all kinds of the rich gaze data, we used only gaze length to learn user's intents, the task completion time was shorter comparing to that of a conventional mouse-driven UI. In the future it is worth investigating if it is possible to use brain-wave data for relevance calculation, as well as using other gaze information to infer user intentions. We are also considering implementation of negative feedback handling feature for one of the future versions of our prototype as well as conducting experiment with a larger number of users.

5. REFERENCES

[1] Gwizdka, J. 2010. Distribution of Cognitive Load in Web Search. In *JASIST, vol. 61, issue 11*, (Nov. 2010), 2167-2187.

[2] Kandemir, M., Saarinen, V.-M., Kaski, S.. 2010. Inferring object relevance from gaze in dynamic scenes. In *Proceedings of the 2010 Symposium on Eye-Tracking Research Applications* (ETRA '10). ACM, New York, NY, USA, 105-108.

[3] Kumar, M., Paepcke A., and Winograd, T. 2007. EyePoint: Practical Pointing and Selection Using Gaze and Keyboard. In *Proceedings of the SIGCHI conference on Human factors in computing systems (CHI '07)*. ACM, New York, NY, USA, 421-430.

[4] Li, J., Huffman, S., and Tokuda, A. 2009. Good abandonment in mobile and PC internet search. In *Proceedings of the 32nd international ACM SIGIR conference on Research and development in information retrieval* (SIGIR '09). ACM, New York, NY, USA, 43-50.

[5] Oliveira, F. T.P., Aula, A., and Russell, D. M. 2009. Discriminating the relevance of web search results with measures of pupil size. In *Proceedings of the 27th international conference on Human factors in computing systems* (CHI '09). ACM, New York, NY, USA, 2209-2212.

How Query Extensions Reflect Search Result Abandonments

Aleksandr Chuklin
Yandex & Moscow Institute of Physics and Technology
Moscow, Russia
chuklin@yandex-team.ru

Pavel Serdyukov
Yandex
Moscow, Russia
pavser@yandex-team.ru

ABSTRACT

It is often considered that high abandonment rate corresponds to poor IR system performance. However several studies suggested that there are so called *good abandonments*, i.e. situations when search engine result page contains enough details to satisfy the user information need without necessity to click on search results. In this work we propose to look at query extensions. We will show that an extension by itself might motivate abandonment type (*good* or *bad*) for the underlying query to some degree. We also propose a way to find *potentially good abandonment* extensions in an automated manner.

Categories and Subject Descriptors

H.3.3 [**Information Storage and Retrieval**]: Information Search and Retrieval

General Terms

Experimentation, Verification, Human Factors

Keywords

query log analysis, query reformulation, search result abandonments

1. INTRODUCTION

Abandonment rate is one of the most broadly used online user satisfaction metrics to evaluate the quality of information retrieval (IR) system. It is often considered that high abandonment rate corresponds to poor IR system performance. However in [4] it was suggested that some abandonments might be *good*: user decided not to click on search results because her information need were satisfied with a search engine result page (SERP) itself. Such situations were further studied in [3] where cursor movements were proposed to measure user satisfaction when no clicks had been issued. In all previous works authors relied on human judgements to decide whether particular query resulted in a good abandonment or not without evaluating actual user behavior. Work [1] even suggested that users tend to go to the original document (click on the page/URL) even if the snippet shows the information they were needed. So, we wanted to find real-world evidence for these good abandonments.

SIGIR'12, August 12–16, 2012, Portland, Oregon, USA.
ACM 978-1-4503-1472-5/12/08.

2. METHOD

We started with the query log of a large commercial search engine. We extracted queries that were issued at least 10 times in 10-days period and calculated abandonment rate. We say that the query q was abandoned if it was not followed by any click on a search result item's url/image. If we had some clickable ads or Answers[1] present we counted these clicks as usual. If the query was followed by another search request and user did not return to the query q we still mark q as abandoned.

After that we performed automated extraction of query extensions. If query q' matched pattern "s q" or "q s" for some query q and some suffix/prefix s (s consists of one or more words) and queries q and q' were both present in our dataset D, we said that q' is an extended query for q: $q' = e(q)$, where function e is parametrized by either suffix or prefix. Then we compared abandonment rates a for the query q and its extended variant q'. For each extension e we calculated the following value:

$$\gamma(e) = Median\left\{ \frac{a(e(q))}{a(q)} \middle| q \in D \;\&\; e(q) \in D \right\} \qquad (1)$$

If the value is greater than 1 we may claim that this particular extension e increases abandonment rate, being applied to the query. We have an intuition that some query extensions may correspond to very specific information needs that can easily be answered directly on a search engine result page. The top and the bottom γ values are presented in Table 1.

We performed hand labeling of 190 popular query extensions found in our dataset[2]. The question was similar to that used in [4] to find *potential good abandonment* queries: "Given an extension e is it true that queries with such an extension have a dominant information need that could theoretically be achieved by an internet search engine result page?". As in [4] possible answers were "yes", "no" or "maybe". In order to confirm correlation of γ value and *potential good abandonment* label we sorted all extensions according to γ (in descending order) and split them to 10 bins of equal size. Label distribution in each bin is visualized in the Figure 1. We can see that the portion of *potential good abandonments* decreases with decrease of γ while the portion of *potential bad abandonments* increases. Some deviations from this trend may be motivated by poor search

[1] As in [2] we use the notion of *Answers*: specially designed search result items.

[2] Queries with such extensions represent 4% of all search engine traffic.

Table 1: Query Extensions (translated)

extension	γ
Finnish (translate)	2.584
Polish (translate)	2.150
author (who is the author of ...?)	2.014
English (translate)	1.758
qt (programming)	1.727
Schengen	1.705
post code	1.649
Tatar (translate)	1.519
capital (what is the capital of ...?)	1.410
credit (credit program)	1.363
...	...
visual basic (programming)	0.551
dating	0.550
auto	0.540
map	0.520
official site (of some company/person)	0.508
Kazakh (translate)	0.504
c# (programming)	0.494
points of interest	0.387
ipod (soft)	0.304
top 40	0.293

result quality, unusual user behavior or the expert's uncertainty.

It is important to note that we did not perform labeling of the SERPs (we labeled extensions only). As it was shown in [1] user behavior on good-looking SERPs may not necessarily result in abandonment: 68% of participants said that they still click on the page/URL even if the snippet shows the information they were looking for. So we decided to have clean assessors instructions in order to avoid problems with rating process.

We also experimented with a somewhat different task. We provided assessors not only with extension itself but also with a small sample of extended queries[3] with this extension. That different task resulted in almost identical labeling and we decided not to include the results to this work. It was interesting finding that information contained in an extension itself is generally sufficient to determine potential abandonment type.

CORRELATION. In order to compute numerical representation of the results shown in the Figure 1 we calculated correlation value of *potential abandonment type* and γ. For each extension e_i we computed $x_i = \gamma_i - 1$ and

$$y_i = \begin{cases} 1 \text{ if } e_i \text{ was marked as } \textit{potentially good} \\ 0 \text{ if } e_i \text{ was marked as } \textit{maybe} \\ -1 \text{ if } e_i \text{ was marked as } \textit{potentially bad} \end{cases}$$

Once we have two vectors x and y we can compute correlation coefficient:

$$Corr(x,y) = \frac{\sum_{i=1}^{n} w_i(x_i - \mu_x)(y_i - \mu_y)}{\sqrt{\sum_{i=1}^{n} w_i(x_i - \mu_x)^2}\sqrt{\sum_{i=1}^{n} w_i(y_i - \mu_y)^2}}$$

$$\mu_x = \frac{\sum_{i=1}^{n} w_i x_i}{\sum_{i=1}^{n} w_i},\ \mu_y = \frac{\sum_{i=1}^{n} w_i y_i}{\sum_{i=1}^{n} w_i}$$

where w is a weight vector.

[3]we used 10

Figure 1: γ and Potential Good Abandonments

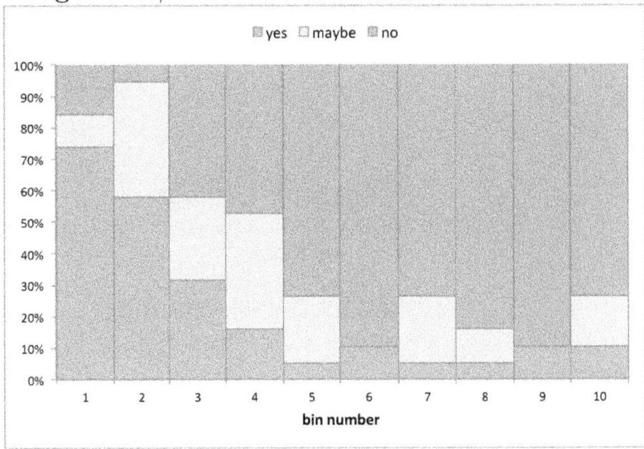

If we used unit weight vector, we got correlation equal to **0.507**. When we set w_i equal to the number of different queries used with the extension e_i we got correlation equal to **0.518**.

3. DISCUSSION

In this paper we performed analysis of query extensions and their effects on query abandonments. We found that some extensions usually result in higher abandonment rate while others decrease abandonment rate dramatically. By performing hand labeling we found that median abandonment ratio is correlated with *potential abandonment* type of the extension: *potentially bad* extensions decrease abandonment rate while *potentially good* extensions increase it. These results may be exploited by search engines to improve *Answers* quality[4]. Now rules to fire an *Answer* are usually selected by humans and do not necessarily reflect actual user needs. In this work we showed that queries with several extensions (with high γ value) are very likely to be good abandonments and therefore are good candidates to be presented with *Answers*. For this task we need to filter out queries with *Answer* already present and sort the extensions according to the γ value. We did not show the results here, but they look very similar giving us weighted correlation with *potential good abandonment* equal to **0.588** and unweighted correlation equal to **0.469**.

4. REFERENCES

[1] O. Alonso, R. Baeza-Yates, and M. Gertz. Effectiveness of temporal snippets. In *WWW'09*.

[2] L. Chilton and J. Teevan. Addressing people's information needs directly in a web search result page. In *WWW'11*.

[3] J. Huang, R. R. W. White, and S. Dumais. No clicks, no problem: using cursor movements to understand and improve search. In *CHI'11*.

[4] J. Li, S. Huffman, and A. Tokuda. Good abandonment in mobile and PC internet search. In *SIGIR'09*.

[4]See [2] for a detailed analysis of *Answers*.

Identifying Entity Aspects in Microblog Posts

Damiano Spina
UNED NLP & IR Group
damiano@lsi.uned.es

Edgar Meij
ISLA, University of Amsterdam
edgar.meij@uva.nl

Maarten de Rijke
ISLA, University of Amsterdam
derijke@uva.nl

Andrei Oghina
ISLA, University of Amsterdam
oghina@science.uva.nl

Minh Thuong Bui
ISLA, University of Amsterdam
mbui@science.uva.nl

Mathias Breuss
ISLA, University of Amsterdam
mbreuss@science.uva.nl

ABSTRACT

Online reputation management is about monitoring and handling the public image of entities (such as companies) on the Web. An important task in this area is identifying *aspects* of the entity of interest (such as products, services, competitors, key people, etc.) given a stream of microblog posts referring to the entity. In this paper we compare different IR techniques and opinion target identification methods for automatically identifying aspects and find that (i) simple statistical methods such as TF.IDF are a strong baseline for the task, significantly outperforming opinion-oriented methods, and (ii) only considering terms tagged as nouns improves the results for all the methods analyzed.

Categories and Subject Descriptors

H.3.1 **[Information Storage and Retrieval]**: Content Analysis and Indexing

Keywords

Microblog posts, entity profiling, aspects

1. INTRODUCTION

Online reputation management (ORM) deals with monitoring and handling the public image of entities such as people, products, organizations, companies, or brands on the web. In the field of ORM, much of the effort is focused on analyzing mentions on social web streams (such as tweets) that are relevant to the entity of interest. An important task in this area is to identify not only posts that are relevant for a given entity, but also the specific *aspects* that people discuss.

Aspects refer to "hot" topics that people talk about in the context of an entity and are of particular interest for companies. Aspects can cover a wide range of issues and include (but are not limited to) company products, key people, other entities, services, and events. They are typically nouns, but can also be verbs, and (rarely) adjectives. They can change over time as public attention shifts from some aspects to others. For instance, for a company releasing its quarterly earnings report, its earnings can become a topic of discussion for a certain period of time and, hence, an aspect. Identifying aspects not only helps reputation analysts in determining what people say about an entity of interest, but it also facilitates a more fine-grained sentiment analysis than is typically possible, since opinions pertaining to aspects rather than to the entity can be identified [4]. Although aspects have been investigated in the context of, e.g., discussion fora [9], automatically determining aspects in streams of microblog posts remains an unsolved problem.

We study the following scenario. Given a stream of microblog posts related to a company [1, 7], we are interested in a ranked list of aspects that are being discussed with respect to the company. We formulate our scenario as an information retrieval (IR) task, where the goal is to provide a ranking of terms, extracted from tweets that are relevant to the company.[1] We compare different methods that address this task with three main goals: (i) to analyze how state-of-the art IR approaches perform, (ii) to see how methods tailored specifically to identifying opinion targets perform, and (iii) to create a publicly available, humanly annotated dataset to facilitate follow-up research [8].[2]

2. IDENTIFYING ENTITY ASPECTS

We evaluate four models for identifying aspects, given an entity and a stream of microblog posts related to that entity. All models work according to the same principle: comparing a pseudo-document D built from entity-specific tweets with a background corpus C. This comparison allows us to score a term t using a function $s(t, D, C)$.

We compare four methods for identifying entity aspects: TF.IDF, the log-likelihood ratio (LLR) [2], parsimonious language models (PLM) [3] and an opinion-oriented method (OO) [5] that extracts targets of opinions to generate a topic-specific sentiment lexicon; we use the targets selected during the second step of this method. Table 1 describes how the scoring function is computed by each method. As usual, $tf(t, D)$ denotes the term frequency of term t in pseudo-document D; $cf(t)$ denotes the term frequency in the collection C and $df(t)$ denotes the total number of pseudo-documents $D_i \in C$ in which the term t occurs at least once.

3. EXPERIMENTS

Determining aspects of an entity in streams of microblog posts involves two tasks. In the first task, tweets relevant to a given entity need to be identified; in the second, these tweets need to be analyzed in order to identify aspects. We focus on the second task and base our annotations on the data used for the WePS-3 ORM Task [1]. Here, the task that participating systems need to solve is to decide which tweets containing a company name are actually related to the company. In total, 99 companies are used for testing, with around 450 tweets (manually annotated for relevance) on average for each company. In our experiments we only consider the tweets that are related to a company, adding up a total of 94 companies and 17,775 tweets with an average of 177 tweets per company.

SIGIR'12, August 12–16, 2012, Portland, Oregon, USA.
ACM 978-1-4503-1472-5/12/08.

[1]We only consider unigrams. When a unigram is an obvious constituent of a larger, relevant aspect it is considered relevant.
[2]Available at `http://bit.ly/profilingTwitter`

Table 1: Scoring functions for identifying entity aspects.

Method	Scoring function
TF.IDF	$s(t, D, C) = tf(t, D) \cdot \log \frac{N}{df(t)}$ N = number of pseudo-documents D_i in C $df(t) = \sum_i^N tf(t, D_i) > 0, D_i \in C$
LLR	$s(t, D, C) = 2 \cdot ((a \cdot \log(\frac{a}{E_1})) + (b \cdot \log(\frac{b}{E_2})))$ $E_1 = \frac{c \cdot (a+b)}{c+d} \quad E_2 = \frac{d \cdot (a+b)}{c+d}$ $a = tf(t, D) \quad b = cf(t)$ $c = \sum_i tf(t_i, D) \quad d = \sum_i cf(t_i)$
PLM	$s(t, D, C) = P(t\|D)$ (when model converges) E-step: $e_t = tf(t, D) \cdot \frac{\lambda \cdot P(t\|D)}{(1-\lambda) \cdot P(t\|C) + \lambda \cdot P(t\|D)}, \lambda = 0.1$ M-step: $P(t\|D) = \frac{e_t}{\sum_t e_t}$ initial $P(t\|D) = \frac{tf(t,D)}{\sum_i tf(t_i,D)} \quad P(t\|C) = \frac{cf(t)}{\sum_i cf(t_i)}$
OO	$s(t, D, C) = \chi^2(target(t, D), target(t, C))$ $\chi^2(o, e) = \frac{(o-e)^2}{e}$ $target(t, D)$ = freq. of potential target t in tweets D $target(t, C)$ = freq. of potential target t in background C

We lowercase, remove punctuation, and tokenize the tweets. We do not perform stopword removal or stemming, but only keep terms occuring at least 5 times in the corpus to remove noisy terms.

We evaluate the methods for ranking aspects using a pooling methodology [10]; the 10 highest ranked terms from each method are merged and randomized. Then, three human assessors consider each term and determine relevance in the context of the company; relevant aspects can include terms from compound words, mentions, or hashtags and should provide insight into the hot topics discussed regarding a company. We compute the inter-annotator agreement using both *Cohen's* and *Fleiss' kappa* and compare the annotators' pairwise and overall. All obtained kappa values are above 0.6, indicating a substantial agreement.

Table 2 (upper part) shows the results of all methods for identifying aspects. Since TF.IDF is the simplest approach, it is considered as the baseline. We use Student's t-test to test for statistical significance and indicate a significant difference with $\alpha = 0.01$ using $^\blacktriangle$ (or $^\blacktriangledown$) and $^\triangle$ (or $^\triangledown$) for $\alpha = 0.05$.

First, we observe that TF.IDF is a strong baseline. In terms of precision, it significantly outperforms PLM and OO, while differences between TF.IDF and LLR are not significant. The results for OO are much lower than for the other methods. Since terms that are (part of) the name of the entity were also annotated as aspects, and these terms are very frequent in the tweets related to the entity, they are often in the top of the ranking returned by the methods. This explains the high MRR values in the results.

When manually inspecting the results, we observe that the results for the frequency-based methods (TF.IDF, LLR and PLM) are very similar, while OO tends to return more subjective terms as aspects (e.g., *haha*, *pls*, *xd*, *safety*, *win*), probably because of errors in the syntactic parsing of tweets. Moreover, this approach has more difficulty to filter out generic terms (e.g., *new*, *use*, *today*, *come*).

Most of the true aspects are nouns (89.72%). Hence, in addition to the preprocessing steps detailed above, we experiment with applying a part-of-speech filter and only consider terms tagged as nouns (Penn Treebank's N* tags) [6]. Table 2 (lower part) shows the results when non-noun terms have been filtered out from the vocabulary. For all methods, MAP and precision values are slightly higher than in the all words condition: considering only nouns helps to identify aspects. Interestingly, the relative order of the approaches (as determined by the scores they achieve) changes with respect to the upper part. PLM now outperforms TF.IDF for two of the four metrics (significantly so for P10).

Table 2: Aspect identification results. Best results in boldface; significant changes are w.r.t. the TF.IDF All words baseline.

	Method	MAP	P5	P10	MRR
All words	TF.IDF	**0.3953**	**0.6957**	**0.6426**	0.7908
	LLR	0.3879	**0.6957**	0.6309	**0.7979**
	PLM	$0.3685^\blacktriangledown$	$0.6723^\triangledown$	$0.6096^\blacktriangledown$	**0.7979**
	OO	$0.1537^\blacktriangledown$	$0.4596^\blacktriangledown$	$0.2915^\blacktriangledown$	0.7021
Noun filter	TF.IDF	0.4015	**0.7213**	0.6436	**0.7979**
	LLR	0.4055	0.7128	0.6511	**0.7979**
	PLM	**0.4097**	0.7106	$\mathbf{0.6617}^\triangle$	**0.7979**
	OO	$0.1635^\blacktriangledown$	$0.4809^\blacktriangledown$	$0.3000^\blacktriangledown$	0.7021

4. CONCLUSION

We addressed the task of identifying *aspects* that people discuss in a stream of microblog posts related to an entity, a task at the heart of online reputation management. We modeled this task as a ranking problem and compared IR techniques and opinion target identification methods for automatically identifying aspects. We used a pooling methodology to evaluate the methods. Simple statistical methods such as TF.IDF are a strong baseline for the task. Moreover, it is difficult to identify aspects by extracting opinion targets mainly because the language used in tweets is often non-standard, hampering the performance of such techniques. Future work includes considering n-grams as aspects and applying topic modeling techniques.

5. ACKNOWLEDGMENTS

This research was supported by the European Union's CIP ICT-PSP under grant agreement nr 250430, the European Community's FP7 Programme under grant agreements nr 258191 (PROMISE Network of Excellence) and 288024 (LiMoSINe), the Netherlands Organisation for Scientific Research (NWO) under project nrs 612.-061.814, 612.061.815, 640.004.802, 380-70-011, 727.011.005, the Center for Creation, Content and Technology (CCCT), the Hyperlocal Service Platform project funded by the Service Innovation & ICT program, the WAHSP project funded by the CLARIN-nl program, under COMMIT project Infiniti, the Spanish Ministry of Education (FPU grant nr AP2009-0507), the Spanish Ministry of Science and Innovation (Holopedia Project, TIN2010-21128-C02), the Regional Government of Madrid and the ESF under MA2VICMR (S2009/TIC-1542) and the ESF Research Network Program ELIAS.

References

[1] E. Amigó, J. Artiles, J. Gonzalo, D. Spina, B. Liu, and A. Corujo. WePS-3 evaluation campaign: Overview of the online reputation management task. In *CLEF '10*, 2010.

[2] T. Dunning. Accurate methods for the statistics of surprise and coincidence. *Comput. Linguist.*, 19, 1993.

[3] D. Hiemstra, S. Robertson, and H. Zaragoza. Parsimonious language models for information retrieval. In *SIGIR '04*, 2004.

[4] L. Jiang, M. Yu, M. Zhou, X. Liu, and T. Zhao. Target-dependent twitter sentiment classification. In *ACL '11*, 2011.

[5] V. Jijkoun, M. de Rijke, and W. Weerkamp. Generating focused topic-specific sentiment lexicons. In *ACL '10*, 2010.

[6] D. Klein and C. D. Manning. Accurate unlexicalized parsing. In *ACL '03*, 2003.

[7] E. Meij, W. Weerkamp, and M. de Rijke. Adding semantics to microblog posts. In *WSDM '12*, 2012.

[8] D. Spina, E. Meij, A. Oghina, M. T. Bui, M. Breuss, and M. de Rijke. A Corpus for Entity Profiling in Microblog Posts. In *LREC Workshop on Language Engineering for Online Reputation Management*, 2012.

[9] T. Thet, J. Na, and C. Khoo. Aspect-based sentiment analysis of movie reviews on discussion boards. *J. Inf. Sci.*, 36(6):823, 2010.

[10] E. M. Voorhees and D. K. Harman. *TREC: Experiment and Evaluation in Information Retrieval*. The MIT Press, 2005.

Impact of Assessor Disagreement on Ranking Performance

Pavel Metrikov Virgil Pavlu Javed A. Aslam*
College of Computer and Information Science
Northeastern University, Boston, MA, USA
{metpavel, vip, jaa}@ccs.neu.edu

ABSTRACT

We consider the impact of inter-assessor disagreement on the maximum performance that a ranker can hope to achieve. We demonstrate that even if a ranker were to achieve perfect performance with respect to a given assessor, when evaluated with respect to a different assessor, the measured performance of the ranker decreases significantly. This decrease in performance may largely account for observed limits on the performance of learning-to-rank algorithms.

Categories and Subject Descriptors: H. Information Systems; H.3 Information Storage and Retrieval; H.3.3 Information Search and Retrieval:Retrieval models

General Terms: Experimentation, Measurement, Theory

Keywords: Inter-assessor Disagreement, Learning-to-Rank, Evaluation

1. INTRODUCTION

In both Machine Learning and Information Retrieval, it is well known that limitations in the performance of ranking algorithms can result from several sources, such as insufficient training data, inherent limitations of the learning/ranking algorithm, poor instance features, and label errors. In this paper we focus on performance limitations due solely to label "errors" which arise due to inter-assessor disagreement.

Consider a *training* assessor A that provides labels for training data and a *testing* assessor B that provides labels for testing data. Even if a ranker can produce a *perfect* list as judged by A, its performance will be suboptimal with respect to B, given inevitable inter-assessor disagreement. In effect, no ranking algorithm can simultaneously satisfy two or more disagreeing assessors (or users). Thus, there are inherent limitations in the performance of ranking algorithms, independent of the quality of the learning/ranking algorithm, the availability of sufficient training data, the quality of extracted instance features, and so on.

We model inter-assessor disagreement with a *confusion matrix* C, where c_{ij} corresponds to the (conditional) probability that a document labeled i by testing assessor B will be labeled j by training assessor A, for some given set of label grades such as $\{0, 1, 2, 3, 4\}$. Given such a model of inter-assessor disagreement, we ask the question, "What is the expected performance of a ranked list optimized for training assessor A but evaluated with respect to testing assessor B?" We approach this question in two ways, via *simulation* and *closed form approximation*. In the former case, we use the confusion matrix C to probabilistically generate training labels A from testing labels B, optimally rank documents according to A, and evaluate with respect to B. In the latter case, we analytically derive a closed-form approximation to this limiting performance, as measured by nDCG.

Given a confusion matrix C modeling inter-assessor disagreement, one can apply our results to any learning-to-rank dataset. The limiting nDCG values obtained correspond to reasonable upper bounds on the nDCG performance of any learning-to-rank algorithm, even one given unlimited training data and perfect features. Considering the performance of existing algorithms on these datasets, and comparing with the upper bounds we derive, one can argue that learning-to-rank is approaching reasonable limits on achievable performance.

2. ASSESSOR DISAGREEMENT MODEL

Much research in the IR community has focused on addressing the problem of system evaluation in the context of missing, incomplete, or incorrect document judgments [1]. Soboroff and Carterette [4] provide an in-depth analysis of the effect of assessor disagreement on the Million Query Track evaluation techniques. Both assessors and users often disagree on the degree of document relevance to a given query, and we model such disagreement with a confusion matrix C as described above. On data sets with multiple assessments per query-document pair, such as the TREC Enterprise Track [2], these confusion matrices can be directly estimated from data, and they can be obtained from user studies as well [3, 5].

For any ranked list returned by a system, the expected limiting nDCG due to assessor disagreement can be formulated as a function of (1) the disagreement model C and (2) the number of assessed documents and their distribution over the label classes. One way to compute this expected nDCG is numerical simulation: For every document d having testing label i_d in the ranked list, we randomly draw an alternative label j_d with the probability c_{ij}; we then sort the ranked list in decreasing order of $\{j_d\}$ and evaluate its nDCG performance with respect to labels $\{i_d\}$. This simulation is repeated multiple times and the results averaged to obtain an accurate estimate of the expected limiting nDCG.

In our first experiment, we test whether the inter-assessor confusion matrix C alone can be used to estimate the limiting nDCG value. We do so by considering data sets that have multiple judgments per query-document pair, such as were collected in the TREC Enterprise Track where each

9*This work supported by NSF grant IIS-1017903.

SIGIR'12, August 12–16, 2012, Portland, Oregon, USA.
ACM 978-1-4503-1472-5/12/08.

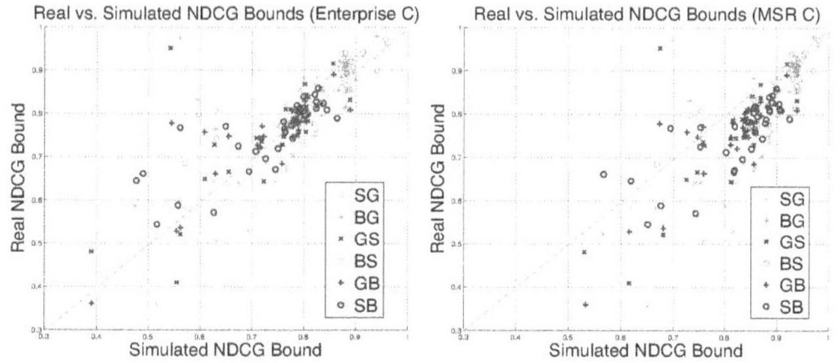

Figure 1: Applying C_ENT model (left) and C_MSR model (right) to TREC enterprise data. X-axis is the simulated nDCG upper bound, while Y-axis is the actual nDCG assessor disagreement measured between 2 TREC assessors; pairs of assessor type ("Gold-Silver" as GS) are indicated by colors.

topic was judged by three assessors: a gold assessor G (expert on task and topic), a silver assessor S (expert at task but not at topic), and a bronze assessor B (expert at neither). Each G, S, and B set of assessments can take on the role of *training* or *testing* assessor, as described above, giving rise to six possible combinations: GS, GB, SG, SB, BG, BS. For each such combination, such as GS, the optimal ranked list can be computed with respect to G and evaluated with respect to S, resulting in a *real* suboptimal nDCG. The GS confusion matrix can also be computed from the data given and the simulation described above performed, yielding an *estimated* limiting nDCG. These actual and estimated limiting nDCG values can then be compared.

Using the TREC Enterprise data, Figure 1 compares the estimated limiting nDCG obtained through simulation with a confusion matrix (x-axis) with the real suboptimal nDCG (y-axis) obtained from different assessors. The left plot uses a confusion matrix C_{ENT} obtained from the TREC Enterprise data itself, as described above, while the right plot uses a confusion matrix C_{MSR} obtained from a user study conducted by Microsoft Research [3]. Note that the more accurate confusion matrix yields better simulated results, as expected, and that the confusion matrix alone can be used to accurately estimate limiting nDCG values in most cases.

Given that a confusion matrix alone can be used, via simulation, to estimate limiting nDCG performance, we next consider other data sets and their associated real or estimated confusion matrices. Yandex [5] conducted user studies to obtain confusion matrices specific to Russian search (C_{YanR}) and to Ukrainian search (C_{YanU}), and these were shown to improve learning-to-rank performance if the learner was given such models as input. Table 1 presents the estimated limiting nDCG values when applying three different confusion matrices to two learning-to-rank data sets. For comparison, the last column in the table presents the actual best known performance of a learning algorithm on these data sets. Consider the difference between the estimated limiting nDCG bounds (middle three columns) and known ranking performance (last column): If C_{MSR} is a good model of assessor disagreement for these data sets, then the known learning-to-rank performance is reasonably close to the limiting bound, and little improvement is possible. On the other hand, if C_{YanU} is a better model of inter-assessor disagreement, then learning algorithms have room for improvement.

3. CLOSED FORM APPROXIMATION

Let $\mathcal{L} = \{0, 1, 2, 3, 4\}$ be the set of relevance grades, n_k the number of documents with reference label $k \in \mathcal{L}$, n the total

Collection	C_MSR	C_YanR	C_YanU	LearnToRank
MSLR30K(SIM)	0.780	0.867	0.900	0.741
MSLR30K(CFA)	0.794	0.869	0.898	
Yahoo(SIM)	0.861	0.920	0.944	0.801
Yahoo(CFA)	0.887	0.919	0.938	

Table 1: nDCG upper bounds derived from disagreement models C applied to popular learning-to-rank data sets. SIM rows are simulated values; the CFA rows are closed form approx. Last column is best known learning-to-rank performance.

number of documents in the rank-list, and $P_{rank}(i,r)$ the probability that the rank of a given document with reference label i is r, as ordered by the alternative labels j. One can then show that the expected nDCG as measured by reference labels is

$$E[nDCG] = \frac{1}{IdealDCG} \cdot \sum_{i \in \mathcal{L}} \left[n_i \cdot gain(i) \cdot \sum_{r=1}^{n} \frac{P_{rank}(i,r)}{discount(r)} \right]$$

where $P_{rank}(i,r) = \sum_{j \in \mathcal{L}} \left[c_{ij} \cdot \left(\sum_{h=0}^{r-1} \sum_{s=r-1-h}^{n-h-1} \frac{\Psi_{ij}(h,s)}{s+1} \right) \right]$ and $\Psi_{ij}(h,s)$ is the probability that other s documents have the same alternative label j, and other h documents have alternative label higher than j, given that a particular document with reference label i has alternative label j. Computing $\Psi_{ij}(h,s)$ straightforwardly is inefficient for even moderately long rank-lists, with a running time of $\mathcal{O}(n^{2|\mathcal{L}|})$.

We instead employ a closed form approximation (CFA) based on approximating Ψ, a sum-product of binomial conditional distributions, with a Gaussian joint distribution of two variables $(h+s, s)$. This approximation becomes more accurate as rank-lists get longer. For a fixed i and j we have $\binom{h+s}{s} \sim \mathcal{N}^{ij}(\mu, \Sigma)$, $\mu = \binom{\mu_{h+s}}{\mu_s}$, and $\Sigma = \begin{pmatrix} \sigma^2_{h+s} & cov_{h+s,s} \\ cov_{s,h+s} & \sigma^2_s \end{pmatrix}$ where (1) $a_{ij} = \sum_{k \geq j} c_{ik}$, (2) $\mu_{h+s} = -a_{ij} + \sum_{k \in \mathcal{L}} n_k \cdot a_{kj}$, (3) $\mu_s = -c_{ij} + \sum_{k \in \mathcal{L}} n_k \cdot c_{kj}$, and

$$\begin{aligned} \sigma^2_{h+s} &= -a_{ij} \cdot (1 - a_{ij}) + \textstyle\sum_{k \in \mathcal{L}} n_k \cdot a_{kj} \cdot (1 - a_{kj}) \\ \sigma^2_s &= -c_{ij} \cdot (1 - c_{ij}) + \textstyle\sum_{k \in \mathcal{L}} n_k \cdot c_{kj} \cdot (1 - c_{kj}) \\ cov_{s,h+s} &= -c_{ij} \cdot (1 - a_{ij}) + \textstyle\sum_{k \in \mathcal{L}} n_k \cdot c_{kj} \cdot (1 - a_{kj}). \end{aligned}$$

We can approximate $E[nDCG]$ in $\mathcal{O}(n^2)$ time given that the "spread" of the Gaussian grows as $\mathcal{O}(\sqrt{n})$ per component. The CFA rows of Table 1 show closed form approximations for comparison with simulated nDCG upper bounds.

4. CONCLUSION

We present a simple probabilistic model of assessor disagreement and results which indicate that the performance of learning-to-rank algorithms may be approaching inherent limits imposed by such disagreement.

5. REFERENCES

[1] P. Bailey, N. Craswell, I. Soboroff, P. Thomas, A. P. de Vries, and E. Yilmaz. Relevance assessment: Are judges exchangeable and does it matter? SIGIR, 2008.

[2] P. Bailey, A. P. De Vries, N. Craswell, and I. Soboroff. Overview of the TREC-2007 Enterprise Track.

[3] B. Carterette, P. N. Bennett, D. M. Chickering, and S. T. Dumais. Here or there: Preference judgments for relevance. In *ECIR*, 2008.

[4] B. Carterette and I. Soboroff. The effect of assessor error on ir system evaluation. In *SIGIR*, 2010.

[5] A. Gulin, I. Kuralenok, and D. Pavlov. Winning the transfer learning track of Yahoo!'s learning to rank challenge with YetiRank. *Journal of Machine Learning Research*, 2011.

Incorporating Statistical Topic Information in Relevance Feedback

Karla Caballero*
UC, Santa Cruz
Santa Cruz CA, USA
karla@soe.ucsc.edu

Ram Akella
UC, Santa Cruz
Santa Cruz CA, USA
akella@soe.ucsc.edu

ABSTRACT

Most of the relevance feedback algorithms only use document terms as feedback (local features) in order to update the query and re-rank the documents to show to the user. This approach is limited by the terms of those documents without any global context. We propose to use statistical topic modeling techniques in relevance feedback to incorporate a better estimate of context by including global information about the document. This is particularly helpful for difficult queries where learning the context from the interactions with the user is crucial. We propose to use the topic mixture information obtained to characterize the documents and learn their topics. Then, we rank documents incorporating positive and negative feedback by fitting a latent distribution for each class of documents online and combining all the features using Bayesian Logistic Regression. We show results using the OHSUMED dataset for 3 different variants and obtain higher performance, up to 12.5% in Mean Average Precision (MAP).

Categories and Subject Descriptors

H.3.3 [**Information Storage and Retrieval**]: Information Search and Retrieval—*Relevance Feedback, Document Filtering*

General Terms

Algorithms, Experimentation

Keywords

Relevance Feedback,Topic Models, Language Models

1. INTRODUCTION

Relevance feedback has been studied extensively in Information Retrieval as a form of incorporating feedback from the user to refine the results retrieved. The authors in [5] concluded that negative feedback is also valuable to improve the ranking. However, the need to capture broader context in difficult queries is still a challenge. The authors in [2] have showed that including global features and using clusters can improve the retrieval performance significantly. Thus, statistical topic modeling provides a robust and automatic method to incorporate context to the user feedback.

Previous approaches have used statistical topic models to represent documents according to their latent topic content and use this representation in information retrieval [1, 4]. Authors in [4], use topics as a form of smoothing the Language Model used in retrieval. However, this approach does not address the incorporation of relevance feedback. Recent work from [1] explores the use of topics as a form to perform the query expansion for relevance feedback. However, this action might make the query noisier because the top topic terms might not contribute to a better discrimination of the relevant documents. In addition, these terms might not be distinctive across different topics.

We propose to include the topic information as feedback using the document topic mixture instead of the document word mixture. We first estimate the topic mixture for each document in the corpus using LDA and save it as meta data. Given an initial query we use a standard retrieval engine, Language Models for this case, to show the first set of documents to the user and obtain relevance judgments. Then, we assume that topic mixtures for feedback documents are observed. We then define two latent Dirichlet distributions: one for relevant documents and another for non-relevant documents. We fit these distributions iteratively, by finding a sufficient statistic and maximizing the likelihood of observing this statistic. To score the documents, we use Bayesian Logistic Regression. This function results in a very efficient scoring function, and incorporates the benefits of active learning. Under this model, we incorporate positive and negative feedback, and context based on topics in the interaction without changing the query. We also provide efficient updates of the latent distributions based on topics.

2. METHODOLOGY

In this section we describe how we incorporate the topic mixture of feedback documents as a global measure in contrast to query expansion. To achieve this, we estimate the topic mixtures of the documents, θ_i, for K topics in the corpus using LDA off-line. Given a initial ranking, the user provides relevance feedback which is used to fit the latent relevant/non-relevant distributions of topic mixtures. Thus, we assume two Dirichlet distributions: one for the relevant set of documents α_R, and one for the non-relevant documents $\alpha_{\bar{R}}$. Therefore, we have:

$$P(\theta_i|\alpha_R) \sim Dirichlet(\alpha_R) = \frac{\Gamma(\sum_{k=1}^{K} \alpha_{k,R})}{\prod_{k=1}^{K} \Gamma(\alpha_{k,R})} \prod_{k=1}^{K} \theta_{i,k}^{\alpha_{k,R}-1}$$

for α_R and $\alpha_{\bar{R}}$. Then, we calculate the log-probability of the document being generated by those distributions:

*Main contact.

SIGIR'12, August 12–16, 2012, Portland, Oregon, USA.
ACM 978-1-4503-1472-5/12/08.

$$\text{Log}P(\theta_i|\alpha) = \log\Gamma(\sum_{k=1}^{K}\alpha_k) - \sum_{k=1}^{K}\log\Gamma(\alpha_k) + \sum_{k=1}^{K}(\alpha_k - 1)\log(\theta_{i,k})$$

We denote these scores as PR_i and $P\bar{R}_i$ respectively. To update the latent distributions of the relevant α_R and non-relevant topics $\alpha_{\bar{R}}$, we use the topic content from the documents labeled by the user as relevant, θ_R, and non-relevant, $\theta_{\bar{R}}$, after each interaction. The Dirichlet distribution guarantees a unique maximum when the Maximum Likelihood (ML) is estimated for α. Moreover, a sufficient statistics, SS, can be estimated to update this distribution as more observations are available. We can update SS efficiently without keeping previous document feedback. The initial value of the sufficient statistic $SS_{k,R}^{(0)}$ for the relevant topic k and its update from the interaction j is described by:

$$SS_{k,R}^{(0)} = \frac{1}{N_R^{(0)}} \sum_{i \in R_0} \log\theta_{i,k}$$

$$SS_{k,R}^{(j)} = \frac{N_R^{(j-1)}}{N_R^{(j)}} SS_{k,R}^{(j-1)} + \frac{1}{N_R^{(j)}} \sum_{i \in R_j} \log\theta_{i,k}$$

where $N_R^{(j)} = N_R^{(j-1)} + |R_j|$, and $|R_j|$ is the total number of relevant documents at the j-th interaction. Given $SS_R^{(j)}$ and $SS_{\bar{R}}^{(j)}$, we use the method proposed in [3] to calculate the ML estimator for $\alpha_R^{(j)}$ and $\alpha_{\bar{R}}^{(j)}$. In addition to these distributions, we use the topic-based Language Model P_{TW} for document i as follows:

$$P_{TW,i}(w|\theta_i, \hat{\phi}) = \sum_{k=1}^{K} P(w|z=k, \hat{\phi}_k)P(z=k|\theta_i)$$

where $\hat{\phi}$ are the word mixture for the topics obtained from LDA. Thus, the score $S_{TW,i}$ for query Q with terms q is defined as:

$$S_{TW,i} = \prod_{q \in Q} P_{TW,i}(w = q|\theta_i, \hat{\phi})$$

To combine the scores from the latent relevant/non-relevant topic mixtures and the topic-based Language Model, we use the Bayesian Logistic Regression approach [5]. Let $y_i = \{+1, -1\}$ be the relevant/non-relevant label for document, we have the score function:

$$P(y_i|\beta, \mathbf{d}_i) = \frac{1}{1 + \exp(-\beta^T \mathbf{d}_i y_i)}$$

where $\mathbf{d}_i$ is the feature vector scores: PR_i, $P\bar{R}_i$, $S_{TW,i}$. β is a parameter vector assumed to be normally distributed and updated in a Bayesian form. Here, the distribution of β from the j-th iteration is taken as prior distribution for the next iteration. To approximate the posterior distribution we use the Laplace approximation as discussed in [5].

3. RESULTS

We test our method using the OHSUMED dataset which consists of 196,000 medical abstracts and 3,506 relevance labels for 63 queries from the Document Filtering Track from TREC 4. As suggested in the track, we assume unobserved labels as non-relevant. We fit the LDA model using $K = 50$ topics, which is the number of topics with highest performance based on Empirical Likelihood. To test the impact of topic information, we use standard Language Model (LM) with Dirichlet smoothing described in [4] as baseline. This score is used with Bayesian Logistic Regression. We test 3 variants of the model and the baseline: LM as baseline; LM+S_{TW}; LM+S_{TW}+PR; LM+S_{TW}+PR+$P\bar{R}$. We calculate the initial ranking using LM and asked for feedback until we have at least one relevant and one non-relevant documents. We use 10 feedback documents and estimate precision at 10 (P@10), Mean Average Precision (MAP), and Discounted Gain (DiscGain). There are two relevance level labels available in the dataset, $\{1, 2\}$, that are assumed equally, $\{+1\}$ for P@10 and MAP. However for DiscGain, we use both labels in the evaluation.

Table 1: Results of Topic feedback using 50 topics in the OHSUMED dataset

Method	P@10	MAP	DiscGain
LM	0.3968	0.4286	0.5660
LM+S_{TW}	0.4206	0.4557	0.6315
LM+S_{TW}+PR	0.2968	0.3307	0.5590
LM+S_{TW}+PR+$P\bar{R}$	**0.4698**	**0.5141**	**0.6580**

Table 1 shows the results for the variants tested. We observe that the LM+S_{TW} performs better than the baseline. This score is similar to the LDA-based retrieval proposed in [4] but the value of the linear combination parameters β is fitted based on the feedback as opposed to a corpus-wide parameter. When we incorporate only the score from the relevant distribution of topics PR, the performance decreases. However, when the score for the non-relevant distribution $P\bar{R}$ is incorporated, the performance is the highest. This shows the value of negative feedback reported previously in [5]. We notice that, the combination of PR and $P\bar{R}$ is equivalent to the log of the likelihood ratio test (probabilistic ranking principle) weighted by β. This also explains why both scores should be included in the model.

We observe that the combination of the four scores improves the general performance by: **11.6%** P@10, **12.8%** MAP, and **4.6%** DiscGain respect topic-based language model (LM+S_{TW}). This demonstrates, the power of statistical topic modeling in relevance feedback.

4. CONCLUSION AND FUTURE WORK

We have presented a method to incorporate statistical topic information in relevance feedback without changing the query. Results show that including the mixture of topics in relevance feedback improves the performance by pruning the search space, and adding context to the query. As future work, we plan to incorporate a policy to decide when to update the parameters of the relevant and non-relevant topic distribution optimally.

5. ACKNOWLEDGMENTS

This work is partially funded by CONACYT grant 207751 and SAP Gift Support

6. REFERENCES

[1] D. Andrzejewski and D. Buttler. Latent topic feedback for information retrieval. In *Proceedings of the 17th ACM SIGKDD conference*, KDD '11, pages 600–608, 2011.

[2] K. S. Lee, W. B. Croft, and J. Allan. A cluster-based resampling method for pseudo-relevance feedback. In *Proceedings of the SIGIR conference*, pages 235–242, 2008.

[3] T. Minka. Estimating a dirichlet distribution. Technical report, 2003.

[4] X. Wei and W. B. Croft. Lda-based document models for ad-hoc retrieval. In *Proceedings of the 29th ACM SIGIR conference*, SIGIR '06, pages 178–185, 2006.

[5] Z. Xu and R. Akella. A bayesian logistic regression model for active relevance feedback. In *Proceedings of the 31st ACM SIGIR conference*, SIGIR '08, pages 227–234, 2008.

Inferring Missing Relevance Judgments from Crowd Workers via Probabilistic Matrix Factorization

Hyun Joon Jung
Dept. of Electrical and Computer Engineering
University of Texas at Austin
hyunJoon@utexas.edu

Matthew Lease
School of Information Science
University of Texas at Austin
ml@ischool.utexas.edu

ABSTRACT

In crowdsourced relevance judging, each crowd worker typically judges only a small number of examples, yielding a sparse and imbalanced set of judgments in which relatively few workers influence output consensus labels, particularly with simple consensus methods like majority voting. We show how probabilistic matrix factorization, a standard approach in collaborative filtering, can be used to infer missing worker judgments such that all workers influence output labels. Given complete worker judgments inferred by PMF, we evaluate impact in unsupervised and supervised scenarios. In the supervised case, we consider both weighted voting and worker selection strategies based on worker accuracy. Experiments on crowd judgments from the 2010 TREC Relevance Feedback Track show promise of the PMF approach merits further investigation and analysis.

Categories and Subject Descriptors

I.2.6 [**Artificial Intelligence**]: Learning

General Terms

Algorithms, Design, Experimentation, Performance

Keywords

Crowdsourcing, label aggregation, matrix Factorization

1. INTRODUCTION

Crowdsourced relevance judging offers potential to reduce time, cost, and effort of relevance judging [1] and benefit from greater diversity of crowd judges. However, quality of judgments from non-workers continues to be a concern, motivating continuing work in quality assurance methods based on statistical label aggregation methods or greater attention to human factors. A common approach is to collect multiple, redundant judgments from workers and aggregate them via methods like majority voting (MV) or expectation maximization (EM) to produce consensus labels [4].

Because each crowd worker typically judges only a small number of examples, collected judgments are typically sparse and imbalanced, with relatively few workers influencing output consensus labels. MV is completely susceptible to this problem. EM addresses this indirectly: while only workers labeling an example vote on it, global worker judgments are used to infer class priors and worker confusion matrices.

SIGIR'12, August 12–16, 2012, Portland, Oregon, USA.
ACM 978-1-4503-1472-5/12/08.

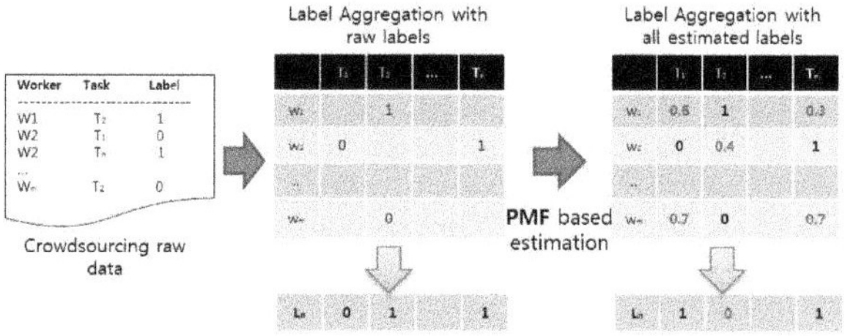

Figure 1: Crowdsourcing workers judgments (Left) are copied to a sparse worker-task matrix (Middle). Missing judgments are inferred via PMF (Right).

We propose to tackle this issue directly by adopting a collaborative filtering approach, which routinely deals with the issue of each user rating only a small number of items (e.g., movies, books, etc.) vs. the complete set. In particular, we employ probabilistic matrix factorization (PMF), which induces a latent feature vector for each worker and example [6] in order to infers unobserved worker judgments for all examples. **Figure 1** depicts our approach graphically.

We are not familiar with any prior work investigating PMF, or collaborative filtering approaches more generally, toward crowdsourcing quality assurance. Related prior work has investigated other ways to infer bias corrected labels in place of raw labels [4], as well as inference of missing labels by estimating a unique classifier for each worker [3].

Probabilistic Matrix Factorization (PMF). Suppose we have M tasks (examples to be labeled), N workers, and a label matrix R in which R_{ij} indicates the label of worker i for task j. Let $U \in \mathbb{R}^{D*M}$ and $V \in \mathbb{R}^{D*N}$ be latent feature matrices for workers and tasks, with column vectors U_i and V_j representing D-dimensional worker-specific and task-specific latent feature vectors, respectively. The conditional probability distribution over the observed labels $R \in \mathbb{R}^{N*M}$ is given by Equation 1. Indicator I_{ij} equals 1 *iff* worker i labeled task j. We place zero-mean spherical Gaussian priors on worker and task feature vectors (Equations 2 and 3).

$$p(R|U,V,\sigma^2) = \prod_{i=1}^{N}\prod_{j=1}^{M}[\mathcal{N}(R_{ij}|U_i^T V_j, \sigma^2)]^{I_{ij}} \quad (1)$$

$$p(U|\sigma_U^2) = \prod_{i=1}^{N}[\mathcal{N}(U_i|0, \sigma_U^2 \mathrm{I})] \quad (2)$$

$$p(V|\sigma_V^2) = \prod_{j=1}^{M}[\mathcal{N}(V_j|0, \sigma_V^2 \mathrm{I})] \quad (3)$$

Method	Supervised	Worker Labels	Label Aggregation	ACC	Rank	RMSE	Rank	SPE	Rank
1	No	raw (sparse)	MV	0.603	4	0.63	4	0.332	6
2	No	raw (sparse)	EM	**0.644**	**3**	**0.596**	**3**	0.418	**4**
3	No	PMF (complete)	MV	**0.643**	**3**	**0.598**	**3**	**0.440**	5
4	Yes	raw (sparse)	WV	0.642	3	0.598	3	**0.900**	**1**
5	Yes	raw (sparse)	Filtering(α=0.67)	**0.752**	**1**	**0.498**	**1**	0.838	2
6	Yes	raw (sparse)	WV & Filtering(α=0.67)	**0.750**	**1**	**0.500**	**1**	0.848	2
7	Yes	PMF (complete)	WV & Filtering(α=0.7)	0.673	2	0.571	2	0.542	3

Table 1: Results of PMF-based inference of missing worker labels. For the unsupervised case, majority voting (MV) with PMF (Method 3) is compared to MV and EM approaches using input (sparse) worker labels (Methods 1-2). With supervision, we compare weighted voting (WV) and/or filtering with and without PMF. Ranks shown indicate statistically significant differences at $p <= 0.05$ using a two-tailed paired t-test.

To estimate model parameters, we maximize the log-posterior over task and worker features with fixed hyper-parameters. Maximizing the posterior with respect to U and V is equivalent to minimizing squared error with L2 regularization:

$$\frac{1}{2}\sum_{i=1}^{N}\sum_{j=1}^{M} I_{ij}(R_{ij} - U_i^T V_j)^2 + \frac{\lambda_U}{2}\sum_{i=1}^{N}\|U_i\|_F^2 + \frac{\lambda_V}{2}\sum_{i=1}^{M}\|V_j\|_F^2$$

where $\lambda_U = \sigma_U/\sigma, \lambda_V = \sigma_V/\sigma$, and $\|\boldsymbol{.}\|_F^2$ denotes the Frobenius Norm. We use gradient descent to find a local minimum of the objective for U and V. Finally, we infer missing worker judgments in the worker-task matrix R by taking the scalar product of U and V. Note that as in [4], we also replace actual labels with bias-corrected inferred labels.

Label Aggregation. Given the complete set of inferred worker relevance judgments in matrix R, we next aggregate worker judgments to induce consensus labels. We consider both unsupervised supervised scenarios. In the former, we consider majority voting with raw (sparse) labels (Method 1), expectation maximization with raw labels (Method 2), and PMF-based MV (Method 3). In the supervised case, we measure each worker's accuracy based on expert judgments, with labels of anti-correlated workers flipped such that accuracy is always $\geq 50\%$. We use supervision in two distinct ways: weighted voting (WV) and worker filtering, in which only workers with accuracy $\geq \alpha$ participate in voting.

2. EVALUATION

Experiments are performed on crowd judgments collected in the 2010 TREC Relevance Feedback Track [2] from Amazon Mechanical Turk. 762 crowd workers judged 19033 query-document tasks (examples), and 89624 judgments were collected. Our worker-task matrix thus has 762 columns (workers) and 19,033 rows (tasks); only 89,624 out of 14,503,146 labels (0.6%) are observed, so data is extremely sparse. 3,275 expert relevance judgments by NIST are partitioned into training (2,275) and test (1,000) sets. The test set is evenly-balanced between relevant and non-relevant classes.

Parameters. For dimensionality of task and worker latent feature vectors, we consider $D \in 10, 30, 50$ and select $D = 30$ based on cross-validation on the entire set of labels (unsupervised). We similarly tune regularization parameter $\lambda \in \{0.001, 0.01, 0.1, 0.5\}$ and select $\lambda = 0.1$. We tune the worker filtering threshold $\alpha \in [0.6, 0.99]$ by cross-validation on the training set using a linear sweep with step-size 0.01.

Metrics and Results. Table 1 reports accuracy (ACC), RMSE, and specificity achieved by each method.

Unsupervised Methods. Method 2 of PMF with majority voting (MV) outperforms the MV baseline (Method 1) and performs equivalently to EM (Method 2).

Supervised vs. Unsupervised Methods. While supervised methods tend to dominate, unsupervised EM and PMF both match performance of the supervised weighted voting (WV) method without filtering or PMF (Method 4).

Supervised Methods. Worker filtering is clearly seen to provide the greatest benefit, and surprisingly performs better without PMF than with PMF (Methods 6 vs. 7). When filtering is used, use of WV is not seen to further improve performance (Methods 5 vs. 6). We do see PMF-based modeling outperform non-PMF modeling when worker filtering is not employed (Methods 7 vs. 4).

3. CONCLUSION

While unsupervised consensus labeling accuracy with PMF only matched EM performance, PMF is advantageous in that once complete worker judgments are inferred, they might be used for a variety of other purposes, such as better routing or recommending appropriate tasks to workers.

Intuitively, an accurate worker's empirical label distribution should resemble the actual class prior. This suggests an alternative, more weakly supervised scenario to consider in which class priors are known while example labels are not. In the unsupervised case, we might instead simply examine the distribution of empirical priors for each worker and detect outliers [5]. In future work, we plan to investigate these ideas further in combination with those described here.

4. REFERENCES

[1] O. Alonso, D. Rose, and B. Stewart. Crowdsourcing for relevance evaluation. *SIGIR Forum*, 42(2):9–15, 2008.

[2] C. Buckley, M. Lease, and M. D. Smucker. Overview of the TREC 2010 Relevance Feedback Track (Notebook). In *Proc. of the 19th Text Retrieval Conference*, 2010.

[3] S. Chen, J. Zhang, G. Chen, and C. Zhang. What if the irresponsible teachers are dominating? a method of training on samples and clustering on teachers. In *24th AAAI Conference*, pages 419–424, 2010.

[4] P. Ipeirotis, F. Provost, and J. Wang. Quality management on amazon mechanical turk. In *Proceedings of the ACM SIGKDD workshop on human computation*, pages 64–67. ACM, 2010.

[5] H. J. Jung and M. Lease. Improving Consensus Accuracy via Z-score and Weighted Voting. In *AAAI Workshop on Human Computation (HComp)*, 2011.

[6] R. Salakhutdinov and et al. Probabilistic matrix factorization. In *NIPS 2008*, volume 20, January 2008.

Investigating Performance Predictors Using Monte Carlo Simulation and Score Distribution Models

Ronan Cummins
Department of Information Technology
National University of Ireland, Galway
ronan.cummins@nuigalway.ie

ABSTRACT

The standard deviation of scores in the top k documents of a ranked list has been shown to be significantly correlated with average precision and has been the basis of a number of query performance predictors [8, 6, 3]. In this paper, we outline two hypotheses that aid in understanding this correlation. Using score distribution (SD) models with known parameters, we create a large number of document rankings using Monte Carlo simulation to test the validity of these hypotheses.

Categories and Subject Descriptors: H.3.3 [Information Storage and Retrieval]: Information Search and Retrieval: Retrieval models

Keywords: Monte Carlo Simulation, Score Distributions

1. DOCUMENT SCORE DISTRIBUTIONS

Many works [2, 1] have shown that document scores can be modelled using score distributions (SD), while others [5] have shown that unexpected observations in large collections can be explained using SD models. Therefore, and in particular, we assume document scores can be drawn from an SD model comprised of two-lognormal distributions, where $f(s|1)$ and $f(s|0)$ are the probability density function of the relevant (1) and non-relevant (0) document scores respectively, and where λ is the mixing parameter (i.e. $f(s) = \lambda \cdot f(s|1) + (1 - \lambda) \cdot f(s|0)$). As a consequence of the recall-fallout convexity hypothesis (RFCH) [7], each lognormal SD model can be described using four parameters $\{\mu_1, \mu_0, \sigma_1 = \sigma_0, \lambda\}$ where $\mu_1 > \mu_0$ and $\sigma_1 = \sigma_0$. Recent research [4] has shown that the RFCH implies the following relationship[1] between the moments in a two-lognormal model:

$$\frac{E[s_1]}{E[s_0]} = \frac{\sqrt{Var(s_1)}}{\sqrt{Var(s_0)}} \quad (1)$$

where $E[s_1]$, $E[s_0]$, $Var(s_1)$, $Var(s_0)$ are the expected value (E) and variance (Var) of relevant (1) and non-relevant (0) document scores respectively. It can be seen that the RFCH implies that the standard deviation of relevant scores (monotonically related to variance) is proportional to the expected value of the relevant scores. All else being equal, it is intuitive to assume that the larger the expected value of the relevant scores is (i.e. $E[s_1]$), the higher average precision will be.

1.1 Hypotheses

We now outline two hypotheses that aim to explain the correlation between average precision and the standard deviation in the head of a ranked list:

H1: As a consequence of the RFCH, the standard deviation at the head of a ranked list is positively correlated with the mean score of relevant documents, which in turn is positively correlated with average precision.

H2: A lower standard deviation of document scores in the head of a ranked list indicates that the separation between the relevant and non-relevant distributions is low, and therefore there is a higher contamination of non-relevant documents in the head of the list. This leads to a lower average precision.

2. MONTE CARLO SIMULATION

We now investigate these hypotheses using Monte Carlo simulation. We simulate rankings by drawing samples of document scores from SD models with known parameters. In particular, to test the first hypothesis (**H1**), we simulate rankings returned for 50 queries. Each ranking is drawn from an SD model with a different μ_1 value **(variable μ_1)** ranging uniformly from 1.5 to 2.5, while $\mu_0 = 1.5$, $\sigma_0 = 0.25$, and λ remains fixed[2]. This experimental setting changes the distribution (i.e. the mean score) of relevant documents while keeping the other parameters constant. The Kendall-τ correlation of average precision with the standard deviation-at-k documents for the 50 rankings is recorded. We repeat this process 50 times to ensure that the resultant correlation coefficients are not spurious. The average Kendall-τ is reported.

To test the second hypothesis (**H2**), we simulate rankings for another 50 queries. Each of these rankings is drawn from an SD model with a different μ_0 value ranging uniformly from 1.5 to 2.5 **(variable μ_0)** while $\mu_1 = 2.5$, $\theta_0 = 0.25$, and λ remains fixed. This experimental setting changes the distribution (i.e. the mean score) of non-relevant documents

[1] A two-gamma model is another suitable SD model that yields similar results to those in this paper. The moment relationship is similar for a two-gamma SD model that adheres to the RFCH. In that model, the variance replaces the standard deviation (i.e. $\frac{E[s_1]}{E[s_0]} = \frac{Var(s_1)}{Var(s_0)}$).

[2] These values were chosen by fitting a two-lognormal SD model to scores returned by a Language Model run on actual TREC data (disks 4 and 5)

SIGIR'12, August 12–16, 2012, Portland, Oregon, USA.
ACM 978-1-4503-1472-5/12/08.

while keeping the remaining parameters static. This essentially increases the contamination of non-relevant documents in the head of a ranking. Again we record the Kendall-τ correlation of average precision with the standard deviation-at-k documents and average the correlation for 50 simulations.

We perform both of these experiments, (**variable** μ_1) and (**variable** μ_0) for different values of λ (i.e. the parameter controlling the portion of relevant documents drawn). We wanted each sample ranking to contain approximately 50 relevant documents[3] (R) and so we drew different sample sizes (N) from each SD model so that we simulate returned sets of various sizes. In particular, we set $N = \{250, 500, 1000, 2000, 4000, 8000, 16000, 32000, 64000, 128000\}$ and so the mixing parameters was $\lambda = 50/N$ for each value of N.

3. RESULTS

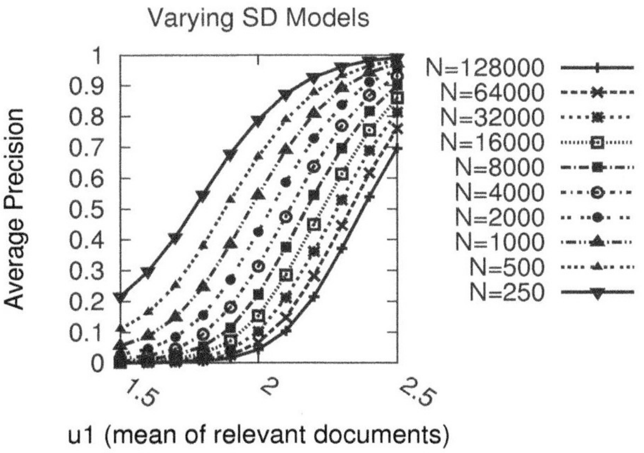

Figure 1: Average precision of rankings drawn from SD models with $\sigma_0 = 0.25$, $\mu_0 = 1.5$ and variable μ_1 for various mixing levels $\lambda = 50/N$.

Each point in Figure 1 shows the mean average precision of 50 simulated rankings drawn from an SD model. Plotted are SD models for various μ_1 and λ values. Intuitively, we can see that the average precision of the rankings increase as both λ and μ_1 increase. This shows that our simulated rankings cover a large range of average precision values.

Table 1 shows the average Kendall-τ correlation of average precision with the standard deviation-at-k for the simulated rankings for both experimental settings (**variable** μ_1 and **variable** μ_0). We can see that when only **varying** μ_1, the correlation coefficient is high and significant for all values of λ. This is a consequence of the RFCH (equation 1) and is similar for many values of k (not shown due to space limitations).

We can also see that there is a significant correlation between standard deviation-at-100 and average precision when **varying** μ_0 for most settings of λ. By examining our simulated rankings, we have determined that this is because the standard deviation is measured at a value $k = 100$, which is higher than the number of relevant documents (R) in the average ranking. Therefore, the standard deviation-at-k has the potential to measure the score of all relevant documents but also includes the score of several non-relevant documents when $k > R$. Thus, the lower the score of these non-relevant documents compared to the relevant documents, the better the query (i.e. the degree of separation between μ_1 and μ_0 is measured when $k > R$). It can be seen that the correlation of standard deviation with average precision is lower when $k = 25$. Also shown is the correlation when $k = 400$, which shows that including too many documents in the standard deviation calculation leads to a lower correlation when only varying μ_0. A high deviation can in some cases indicate that the non-relevant documents have contaminated the relevant documents to a high degree, due to the right-skewed nature of score distributions. This can lead to a negative correlation between standard deviation-at-k and average precision when λ is low and k is high.

[3]For TREC disks 4 and 5 and for many TREC collections, this is approximately the average number of relevant documents per topic.

Table 1: Average Kendall-τ correlation of average precision of simulated rankings with the standard deviation of scores for top k documents

R=50		Ave. Kendall-τ			
		variable μ_1	variable μ_0		
N	λ	$k = 100$	$k = 400$	$k = 100$	$k = 25$
250	0.2000	0.838	-	0.663	0.238
500	0.1000	0.833	0.230	0.629	0.297
1000	0.0500	0.828	0.295	0.586	0.331
2000	0.0250	0.803	0.225	0.523	0.349
4000	0.0125	0.780	0.138	0.463	0.326
8000	0.0063	0.762	0.045	0.384	0.325
16000	0.0031	0.729	-0.058	0.312	0.298
32000	0.0016	0.708	-0.147	0.217	0.291
64000	0.0008	0.686	-0.250	0.144	0.251
128000	0.0004	0.660	-0.335	0.058	0.229

4. CONCLUSION

We have presented two hypothesis regarding the relationship between average precision and the standard deviation in the head of a ranking. Furthermore, we performed an analysis using SD models that indicates the conditions under which these hypotheses can be deemed true.

Acknowledgments

The author is funded by the Irish Research Council for Science, Engineering and Technology (IRCSET), co-funded by Marie-Curie Actions under FP7.

5. REFERENCES

[1] Avi Arampatzis and Stephen Robertson. Modeling score distributions in information retrieval. *Inf. Retr.*, 14(1):26–46, 2011.

[2] Ronan Cummins. Measuring the ability of score distributions to model relevance. In *AIRS*, pages 25–36, 2011.

[3] Ronan Cummins, Joemon Jose, and Colm O'Riordan. Improved query performance prediction using standard deviation. In *SIGIR 2011*, pages 1089–1090, New York, NY, USA, 2011. ACM.

[4] Ronan Cummins and Colm O'Riordan. On theoretically valid score distribution in information retrieval. In *ECIR 2012*, pages 1089–1090, Barcelona, Spain, 2012. ACM.

[5] David Madigan, Yehuda Vardi, and Ishay Weissman. Extreme value theory applied to document retrieval from large collections. *Inf. Retr.*, 9:273–294, June 2006.

[6] Joaquín Pérez-Iglesias and Lourdes Araujo. Standard deviation as a query hardness estimator. In *SPIRE*, pages 207–212, 2010.

[7] Stephen Robertson. On score distributions and relevance. In *ECIR*, pages 40–51, 2007.

[8] Anna Shtok, Oren Kurland, and David Carmel. Predicting query performance by query-drift estimation. In *ICTIR*, pages 305–312, 2009.

Learning to Select a Time-aware Retrieval Model

Nattiya Kanhabua
L3S Research Center
Leibniz Universität Hannover
Hannover, Germany
kanhabua@L3S.de

Klaus Berberich
Max-Planck Institute for Informatics
Saarbrücken, Germany
kberberi@mpi-inf.mpg.de

Kjetil Nørvåg
Dept. of Computer Science
Norwegian University of Science and Technology
Trondheim, Norway
noervaag@idi.ntnu.no

ABSTRACT

Time-aware retrieval models exploit one of two time dimensions, namely, (a) *publication time* or (b) *content time* (temporal expressions mentioned in documents). We show that the effectiveness for a *temporal query* (e.g., illinois earthquake 1968) depends significantly on which time dimension is factored into ranking results. Motivated by this, we propose a machine learning approach to select the most suitable time-aware retrieval model for a given temporal query. Our method uses three classes of features obtained from analyzing distributions over two time dimensions, a distribution over terms, and retrieval scores within top-k result documents. Experiments on real-world data with crowdsourced relevance assessments show the potential of our approach.

Categories and Subject Descriptors H.3.3 [Information Storage and Retrieval]: Information Search and Retrieval
General Terms Algorithms, Experimentation
Keywords temporal queries, time-aware ranking prediction

1. INTRODUCTION

Previous work [1, 4] has shown that the retrieval effectiveness of temporal queries can be significantly improved by modeling and taking into account *publication time* (i.e., when a document was published) or *content time* (i.e., what time a document refers to). The right choice of time-aware retrieval model can make a huge difference for a given temporal query, as we observe empirically. Thus, the model based on publication time proposed in [4] (labeled *PT-Rank*) performs best for temporal queries like iraq 2001 and mac os x 24 march 2001, whereas the model based on content time from [1] (labeled *CT-Rank*) performs best for temporal queries like sound of music 1960s and michael jackson 1982.

Our contribution in this work is *a novel machine learning approach to select the most suitable time-aware retrieval model for a given temporal query* – to the best of our knowledge the first approach tackling this objective. It uses three classes of features obtained from analyzing distributions over two time dimensions, a distribution over terms, and retrieval scores within top-k result documents. We further present experimental results, showing the significance of the problem addressed and the effectiveness of our approach.

2. MODEL

A document d consists of a textual part d_{text} (a bag of words) and a temporal part d_{time} composed of its publication time $PubTime(d)$, and temporal expressions $\{t_1, \ldots, t_k\}$ mentioned in d, denoted $ContentTime(d)$. A temporal query q consists of keywords q_{text}, and temporal expressions q_{time}. *PT-Rank* and *CT-Rank* both employ a mixture model that linearly combines *textual similarity* and *temporal similarity* between q and d as $S(q,d) = (1-\alpha) \cdot S'(q_{text}, d_{text}) + \alpha \cdot S''(q_{time}, d_{time})$ using a mixing parameter α. The *textual similarity* S' can be determined using any existing term-based retrieval model (e.g., tf.idf or a unigram language model). The *temporal similarity* S'' is determined assuming that temporal expressions in the query are generated independently from a two-step generative model, i.e.:

$$S''(q_{time}, d_{time}) = \prod_{t_q \in q_{time}} \frac{1}{|d_{time}|} \sum_{t_d \in d_{time}} P(t_q|t_d) \; .$$

For *CT-Rank* [1] the probability $P(t_q|t_d)$ is estimated according to the LMTU method based on *content time*. For *PT-Rank* [4] $P(t_q|t_d)$ is estimated based on *publication time* using an exponential decay function. For both methods Jelinek-Mercer smoothing eliminates zero probabilities.

3. SELECTING A RETRIEVAL MODEL

Given a temporal query q, we will predict which time-aware retrieval model achieves the best effectiveness by learning a prediction model using three classes of features:

Temporal KL-divergence, originally proposed in [3], measures the difference between the distribution of publication time within a set of top-k result documents D_q and their distribution in the overall document collection C. This definition thus only considers publication time, and we further refer to it as KL_{PT}. While it gives a strong signal, for instance, when all relevant documents were published around the occurrence of an important *real-world event* (e.g., a sports tournament), it does not capture when they all refer to a common time period (e.g., the 19th century). We therefore adapt temporal KL-divergence to also consider *content time* as $KL_{CT}(D_q||C,q) = \sum_{t \in T_C} P(t|q) \cdot \log \frac{P(t|q)}{P(t|T_C)}$, where T_C is a set of all temporal expressions in C. $P(t|T_C)$ is the probability of a temporal expression t in C. $P(t|q)$ is the probability of generating a temporal expression t given q: $P(t|q) = \sum_{d \in D_q} P(t|d) \cdot \frac{P(q|d)}{\sum_{d' \in D_q} P(q|d')}$, where $P(q|d)$ is a retrieval score of d wrt. a particular retrieval model. Since a document can contain more than one temporal expression, $P(t|d) = \frac{c(t,d)}{\sum_{t' \in d} c(t',d)}$, where $c(t',d)$ is the number of occurrences of t' in d. Again, we employ Jelinek-Mercer smoothing when estimating $P(t|d)$ to avoid zero probabilities.

SIGIR'12, August 12–16, 2012, Portland, Oregon, USA.
ACM 978-1-4503-1472-5/12/08.

As suggested in [3], temporal features alone could not achieve high accuracy for query classification. Thus, we also employ a **clarity score** [2] for measuring the KL-divergence between the distribution of terms within top-k results D_q and their distribution in the overall document collection C. A clarity score can be computed as $Clarity = \sum_{w \in V} P(w|q) \cdot \log \frac{P(w|q)}{P(w|C)}$, where w is a term from the vocabulary V of all distinct terms in C. $P(w|q)$ is the probability of generating w given q and $P(w|C)$ is the probability of w in C.

Retrieval scores can also be exploited to select a retrieval model, as proposed in [5]. We employ different features obtained from analyzing/comparing the retrieval scores of a term-based baseline model that is *not* time-aware, *PT-Rank*, and *CT-Rank*, namely: 1) average score of the baseline (AVG_{base}), 2) average score of *PT-Rank* ($AVG_{PT\text{-}Rank}$), 3) average score of *CT-Rank* ($AVG_{CT\text{-}Rank}$), and 4) the divergence of retrieval scores according to *PT-Rank* and *CT-Rank* from those produced by the baseline ($JS_{PT\text{-}Rank}$ and $JS_{CT\text{-}Rank}$). We employ Jensen-Shannon divergence to measure the extent to which the time-aware models alter the scores of the baseline retrieval model, formally:

$$JS(S_b||S_r, q) = \sum_{d \in D_q} S_b(q,d) \cdot \log \frac{S_b(q,d)}{\frac{1}{2} \cdot S_b(q,d) + \frac{1}{2} \cdot S_r(q,d)} .$$

where $S_b(q,d)$ is the retrieval score of d according to the baseline S_b. $S_r(q,d)$ is the score of d when ranked using a time-aware retrieval model $S_r \in \{PT\text{-}Rank, CT\text{-}Rank\}$.

4. EXPERIMENTS

We conducted two sets of experiments: 1) evaluate our prediction model as classification accuracy, and 2) demonstrate how an accurate choice of the retrieval model can improve retrieval effectiveness. We used the New York Times Annotated Corpus containing 1.8M documents published between 1987 and 2007, and the 40 temporal queries and relevance assessments from [1]. Temporal expressions were extracted using the TARSQI Toolkit. Documents were indexed and retrieved with Apache Lucene 2.9.3 using its default similarity function as a baseline retrieval model. We consider both *inclusive* and *exclusive* modes of evaluating queries, described in [1], that differ in whether temporal expressions are also treated as textual query terms. The mixture parameter α was determined empirically: $\alpha = 0.5$ for *PT-Rank* and $\alpha = 0.6$ for *CT-Rank* in *inclusive*, and $\alpha = 0.5$ for *PT-Rank* and $\alpha = 0.1$ for *CT-Rank* in *exclusive*. The parameters for TSU were: $DecayRate = 0.5$, $\lambda = 0.5$, and $\mu = 6$ months. For LMTU, smoothing γ was 0.75. For temporal KL-divergence, smoothing was set to 0.1.

For classification, each query was labeled according to whether *PT-Rank* or *CT-Rank* performs best on it. More precisely, we assumed the model with the best MAP as a *query label*. We excluded queries with a small difference in MAP of two time-aware models. We learned a prediction model using several algorithms: decision tree, Naïve Bayes, neural network and SVM, using 10-fold cross-validation with 10 repetitions. We measured statistical significance using a t-test with $p < 0.05$. In the tables, bold face indicates statistically significant difference from the respective baseline.

Classification results. The baseline method for query classification is the majority classifier. The accuracy of the baseline is 0.54 for *exclusive* and 0.60 for *inclusive*. Table 1 shows the accuracy of the best-performing classifiers, i.e., SVM for *exclusive* and decision tree for *inclusive*. The

Table 1: Accuracy of query classification.

Feature	*exclusive*		*inclusive*	
	100	*500*	*100*	*500*
Clarity	0.51	0.53	0.59	0.60
KL_{PT}	0.53	0.53	0.60	0.59
KL_{CT}	0.53	0.53	0.60	0.60
AVG_{Base}	0.53	0.53	0.63	0.56
$AVG_{PT\text{-}Rank}$	0.53	0.53	0.60	0.60
$AVG_{CT\text{-}Rank}$	0.53	0.53	0.60	0.59
$JS_{PT\text{-}Rank}$	**0.72**	0.42	**0.74**	0.64
$JS_{CT\text{-}Rank}$	0.38	0.42	0.60	0.60
$Clarity+KL_{PT}+KL_{CT}$	0.54	**0.65**	0.61	0.61
$Clarity+JS_{PT\text{-}Rank}+JS_{CT\text{-}Rank}$	0.42	**0.65**	**0.75**	0.61

Table 2: Effectiveness of different retrieval models.

Method	*exclusive*			*inclusive*		
	P@1	*P@5*	*MAP*	*P@1*	*P@5*	*MAP*
CT-Rank	0.55	0.50	0.53	0.58	0.55	0.56
PT-Rank	**0.63**	0.53	0.55	0.63	0.58	0.61
PR	**0.68**	0.53	**0.59**	**0.70**	0.58	**0.64**
MAX	**0.83**	**0.61**	**0.64**	**0.78**	**0.62**	**0.67**

results show that prediction accuracy tends to be better when using $k = 100$ rather than $k = 500$. One reason for this is that with the larger number of top-k documents, more irrelevant documents are introduced into the analysis. The performance among different feature classes shows that $JS_{PT\text{-}Rank}$ performs well in most case. For *exclusive*, using a small number of top-k documents is better than a large number of top-k documents. For top-100, $JS_{PT\text{-}Rank}$ outperforms the baseline classifier and other features significantly (accuracy=0.72). For top-500, all single features perform worse compared to the baseline classifier. For *inclusive*, the performance of top-100 is better than top-500. For top-100, the best performing feature is the combination of *Clarity*, $JS_{PT\text{-}Rank}$ and $JS_{CT\text{-}Rank}$, which achieves an accuracy of 0.75.

Retrieval results. For each query, we determined retrieval results using a model chosen according to the best prediction model determined in the previous experiment, such as, 1) $JS_{PT\text{-}Rank}$ for retrieval in *exclusive*, and 2) *Clarity*+ $JS_{PT\text{-}Rank}$+$JS_{CT\text{-}Rank}$ for retrieval in *inclusive*. Table 2 shows the effectiveness of different retrieval models, where *PR* is the retrieval model based on our prediction model. *MAX* is the maximum (or optimal) effectiveness that can be achieved, that is, if a prediction model performs accurately 100%. The retrieval results are compared with the baseline method *CT-Rank*. The results show that our prediction-based retrieval model (*PR*) outperforms the baseline significantly in P@1 and MAP. However, we note that it is difficult for *PR* to achieve the optimal effectiveness because of the classification accuracy as explained above.

5. CONCLUSIONS

We have demonstrated that selecting the right time-aware retrieval model can have a significant impact on the retrieval effectiveness of temporal queries. We proposed a novel machine learning approach to do so automatically and demonstrated its effectiveness through extensive experiments.

6. REFERENCES

[1] K. Berberich, S. Bedathur, O. Alonso, and G. Weikum. A language modeling approach for temporal information needs. In *Proceedings of ECIR'2010*, 2010.

[2] S. Cronen-Townsend, Y. Zhou, and W. B. Croft. Predicting query performance. In *Proceedings of SIGIR'2002*, 2002.

[3] R. Jones and F. Diaz. Temporal profiles of queries. *ACM Trans. Inf. Syst.*, 25, July 2007.

[4] N. Kanhabua and K. Nørvåg. Determining time of queries for re-ranking search results. In *Proceedings of ECDL'2010*, 2010.

[5] J. Peng, C. Macdonald, and I. Ounis. Learning to select a ranking function. In *Proceedings of ECIR'2010*, 2010.

Learning-Based Time-Sensitive Re-Ranking for Web Search

Po-Tzu Chang, Yen-Chieh Huang, Cheng-Lun Yang, Shou-De Lin, Pu-Jen Cheng
Graduate Institute of Computer Science and Information Engineering
Graduate Institute of Network and Multimedia
National Taiwan University
{r98922102, r98944011, r99944042, sdlin, pjcheng}@csie.ntu.edu.tw

ABSTRACT

To model time-dependent user intent for Web search, this paper proposes a novel method using machine learning techniques to exploit temporal features for effective time-sensitive search result re-ranking. We propose models to incorporate users' click through information for queries that are seen in the training data, and then further extend the model to deal with unseen queries considering the relationship between queries. Experiment shows significant improvement on search result ranking over original search outputs.

Categories and Subject Descriptors

H.3.3[**Information Search and Retrieval**]:Information Search and Retrieval

General Terms: Algorithms, Design

Keywords: Time sensitive query, temporal features

1. INTRODUCTION

Traditional search engine uses keyword matching with link-based strategies, such as PageRank, to improve search results without considering users' intent. We have observed through web query logs that the ideal ranking of search results does depend on query intent, which usually vary with time. For the same query, the users may want to find different web pages in different time of the day. For example, from AOL dataset, we found that users who enter the query term "aa" prefer visiting substance control website (www.alcoholics-anonymous.org) from 7am to 2pm, but the visiting preference changes to American Airline website (www.aa.com) from 3pm to 3am next day (see Figure 1). The aim of this paper is to re-rank search results based on user intents at different time of a day.

2. RELATED WORK

Several researchers have observed that query popularity changes over time. Beitzel et al. [7] show changes in popularity of topically categorized queries across different hours of a day. Anagha et al. [6] explore how queries, their associated documents, and the query intent change over the course of 10 weeks by analyzing query log data. Dong et al. [2] propose ideas of "recency ranking", which refers to ranking documents by relevance which takes freshness into account. They use multiple recency features to provide temporal evidence which effectively represents document recency. Li and Croft [4] identify a type of query that favors very recent documents, and propose a time-based language model to retrieve these queries. However, above works do not focus on exploiting queries intent with time to improve the search quality.

3. METHODOLOGY

We use the users' temporal click information from query logs as training data to re-rank the search results at different time period. We design models to handle queries with click history, *existing queries (see 3.1)*, and queries with few or no click information, *missing queries (see 3.2)*. Finally, we use a learning-based method to build an ensemble of our predictions for search result re-ranking. The training data contains the aggregated user click counts, with time stamp, of top URLs returned for each query. We use several different models to generate a raw score for each <query, URL> pair at each time period. Then, we exploit a learning approach to combine the scores from different models and rank each URL for each given query. Finally, such ranking is linearly combined with the original (or baseline) ranking results through the following re-ranking formula, $Score(u) = \frac{\alpha}{original\_rank(u)} + \frac{(1-\alpha)}{predicted\_rank(u)}$, *where* α *is a weighting parameter varied from 0.0 to 1.0.*

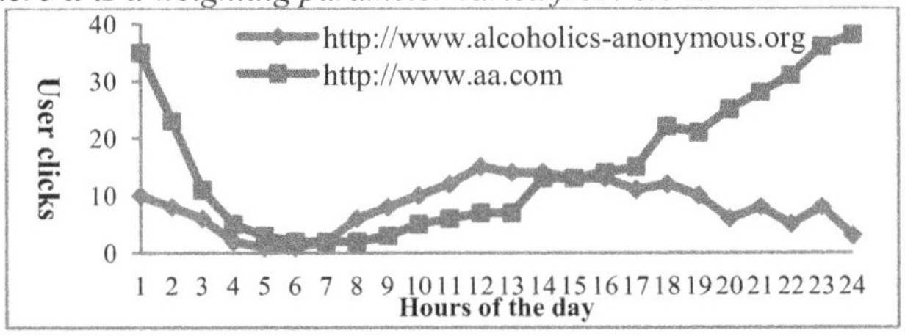

Figure 1. Example of time-sensitive query. For the same query, "aa", user preference changes during the day.

3.1 Models for Existing Queries

Given the query and time, we propose several models to estimate the quality of each returned documents for the re-ranking task.

Temporal Prior: The relevance of a document/URL u to an existing query q issued at time t is defined as: $P(u|q,t) = \frac{f_t(q,u)}{\sum_{\forall u_i} f_t(q,u_i)}$, where $f_t(q,u)$ is the frequency of users visiting URL u when searching query q at time t. This stands for u's prior clicking frequency probability given query q at time t in training data. This can be considered as a maximum-likelihood model.

Time-sensitive Content Model: Previous model only works for URLs that has been seen in the training set. To overcome such limitation, we propose to exploit the similarity between unseen documents. The relevance of a URL u to query q issued at time t is defined as: $P(u|q,t) \fallingdotseq \sum_{\forall q'} Sim(u,u') * P_{click}(u'|q,t)$ where u' repre-sents the URL that are already in the training corpus and $Sim(u,u')$ is the context similarity of u and u'. Sim(u,u') can be estimated from comparing the difference between the n-gram distributions generated from u and u', and $P(u'|q,t)$ is the temporal prior of u'.

Temporal PageRank: PageRank is a popular model to assess the authority of a page. Unfortunately, the original PageRank algorithm does not consider temporal information. Here we propose temporal PageRank to incorporate such information by adding time information (click count of each URL u at time t) into PageRank. To facilitate such idea, we first build a directed graph of all URLs in the dataset. There is a link connecting two webpages if the content of one URL contains a hyperlink to another URL. Then, we assign a click number for each webpage which is the total number of user clicks for that URL at time t. Temporal PageRank function is defined below.

$$R(t) = \begin{bmatrix} (1-d)/N \\ \vdots \\ (1-d)/N \end{bmatrix} \begin{bmatrix} P(u_1|U,t) \\ \vdots \\ P(u_n|U,t) \end{bmatrix} + d \begin{bmatrix} l(u_1,u_1) & \dots & l(u_1,u_n) \\ \vdots & \ddots & \vdots \\ l(u_1,u_n) & \dots & l(u_n,u_n) \end{bmatrix}$$

$l(u_i,u_j)$ is the adjacency function of these URLs, N is the total number of URLs, and d is the damping factor. The main difference from the original PageRank equation lies in $P(u_i|t) = \frac{f(u_i,t)}{f_{\forall u_i \in U \max}(u_i,t)}$, which represent the click opportunity of URL u at time t. Note that this model measures the temporal authority of pages, and thus is query independent (similar to PageRank).

SIGIR'12, August 12-16, 2012, Portland, Oregon, USA.
ACM 978-1-4503-1472-5/12/08.

3.2 Dealing with Missing Queries

Missing queries presents a more difficult challenge because of the insufficient temporal click information to learn from. To solve this problem, we propose to exploit click information from *extended queries* which we have sufficient click information. First, we build a bi-partite graph of all queries and URLs as shown in Figure 3. We eliminate popular hub URLs such as Amazon.com, to avoid the interference from hub sites. Then, we define a query set Q', which contains queries q' that are 2 steps away from missing query q, as the extended queries, and generate new $f_t(q,u)$ by combining user clicks of q and q' as defined in the following equation, $f_t'(q,u) = f_t(q,u) + \sum_{q' \in Q'} f_t(q',u)$. Note that $f_t(q,u)$ is either 0 or a very small number based on the definition of missing query.

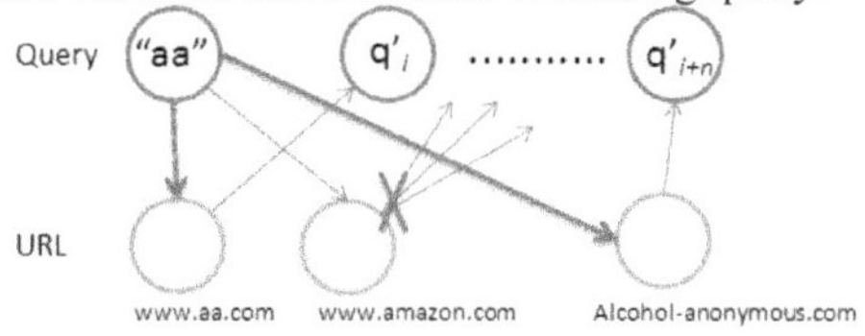

Figure 3. Query Expansion after removing hub URLs

Since extended queries may have different degree of resemblance to the missing query, we propose to weight click counts based on the similarity between them. We define two similarity measures:

1. $\text{Sim}(q,q') = \sum_{u \in U, u' \in U'} LM(u,u')$ where $LM(u,u')$ is the content similarity of u and u' using character-based Language Model described in [10] while U and U' are the set of URLs returned by search engine for query q and q' respectively.
2. We further consider the click count of users using: $\text{Sim}_{wgt}(q,q') = \sum_{u \in U, u' \in U'} LM(u,u') * P_{click}(u'|q')$.

We use the similarity measures defined in this section as features in Support Vector Regression for missing query dataset.

3.3 Model-Ensemble through Regression

Eventually we want to combine the results from proposed models with global features, including query term, query time, click count, and target URL. Instead of manually choosing the ensemble weights, we propose to learn them through a regression model. We choose epsilon-SVR with linear kernel for its superior performance.

4. EXPERIMENTS

We collect data from the AOL query log, which contains click-through records from March 1, 2006 to May 31, 2006, representing the search behavior of 650,000 users generating 20 million queries. Each record has five fields, user id, query, query time, URL, and the relevance rank of each URL. The relevance rank is the default ranking of URLs for a query given by AOL search engine. Note that here we assume the query time in AOL dataset reflects the local time zone instead of an adjusted global time. To verify our hypothesis, we compare it with the query log from Sogou, a popular search engine in China, as China uses one time zone throughout the country. The result shows similar searching behavior over time (see Figure 4), and support our hypothesis that AOL data reports local time zone, where there are fewer records from midnight to early morning. If the time were converted to a global time zone in AOL, it is likely we would have seen more evenly distributed graph throughout the day.

We merge the clicks within four-hour interval starting from 2am, resulting in six time periods. Then 70% raw data are selected at random as training with the remaining 30% as testing and the process repeats 10 times. Existing queries are defined as queries containing two or more URLs whose cumulative click counts are greater than 50 in the training data. Missing queries are those containing two or more URLs whose cumulative click counts are greater than 25 in testing data, but do not appear in the training data. The baseline is determined by the original search ranking given in the AOL query log. For ground truth, we use the click number rankings from testing data. We calculate the Kendall's tau value between the ground truth and the ranking we predicted. Note that the baseline (i.e. without re-ranking, $\alpha = 1$) reaches Kendall's tau value 0.570.

Existing Queries: The first row of Table 1 shows a decent improvement of 9.1% on content model over the baseline. Note that the temporal prior model is not listed as it cannot be generated with missing URLs. The final row of Table 1 shows using all features achieves the best result of 10.3% over the baseline when α=0.2.

Table 1. Kendall's tau of proposed models.

α	0	0.2	0.5	0.7	0.9
Time-sensitive Content Model	0.658	0.661	0.629	0.589	0.574
Temporal PageRank	0.594	0.607	0.618	0.596	0.585
SVR w/Time-sensitive Content Model	0.657	0.661	0.626	0.590	0.573
SVR w/ All Models	0.669	0.673	0.634	0.590	0.573

Missing Queries: On top of the global features, our learner adds similarity scores obtained from Section 3.2 for ensemble. The Kendall's tau value of the original order is 0.189, much lower than that of existing queries. The baseline is not as good because these queries usually contain typos or unpopular combinations of terms, which causes problems for a search engine due to lack of training data. Our model achieves Kendall's tau value of 0.309, a significant improvement of 12%. The results show that considering users' temporal intent can bring relatively more information to missing queries than to existing ones.

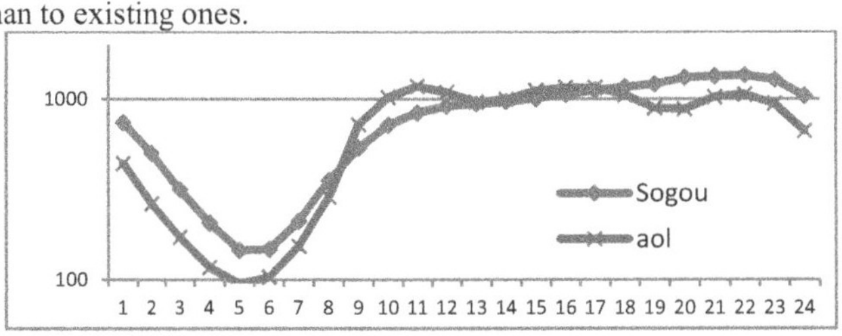

Figure 4. Number of searches by the hour. X-axis is hour of the day. Y-axis is log (number of searches)/1000.

5. CONCLUSION

This study verifies that understanding how users' search intents change over time is critical for a search system. The consistent improvement with a wide range of α, together with the fact that better improvement can be achieved when α decreases (i.e. the weight of our model increases) show the effectiveness of this framework. Future work includes exploiting advanced models (e.g. probabilistic graphical model) and design more temporal features for learning.

6. ACKNOWLEDGEMENT

This work was supported by National Science Council, National Taiwan University and Intel Corporation under Grants NSC 100-2911-I-002-001, and 101R7501.

REFERENCES

[1] Elsas, J. and Dumais, S. T. 2010. Leveraging temporal dynamics of document content in relevance ranking. In *Proc. of ACM WSDM Conference*, 2010.

[2] Dong, A., Chang, Y., Zheng, Z., Mishne, G., Bai, J., Buchner, K., Zhang, R., Liao, C. and Diaz, F. 2010. Towards recency ranking in Web search. In *Proc. of ACM WSDM*, 2010.

[3] Kulkarni, A., Teevan, J., Svore, K., and Dumais, S. Under-standing temporal query dynamics. In *Proc. of WSDM*, 2011.

[4] Li, X. and Croft, W. B. 2003, Time-based language models. In *Proc. of ACM CIKM Conference*, 2003.

[5] Zhang, R., Chang, Y., Zheng, Z., Metzler, D. and Nie, J.-Y. 2009. Search result re-ranking by feedback control adjustment for time-sensitive query. In *Proc. of NAACL*, 2009.

[6] Anagha K., Jaime T., Krysta M. S. and Susan T. D. 2011. Temporal Query Dynamics. In *Proc. of ACM WSDM*, 2011.

[7] Beitzel, S. M., Jensen, E. C., Chowdhury, A., Grossman, D. and Frieder, O. 2004. Hourly analysis of a very large topically categorized Web query log. *In Proceedings of SIGIR 2004*.

[8] Zhao, Q., Hoi, C.H., Liu, T.Y., Bhowmick, S.S, Lyu, M.R., Ma, W.Y. 2006. Time-Dependent Semantic Similarity Measure of Queries Using Historical Click-Through Data. In *Proc. of WWW*, 2006.

[9] Baraglia, R., Castillo, C., Donato, D., Nardini, F.M., Perego, R. 2010. The Effects of Time on Query Flow Graph-based Models for Query Suggestion. *In Proceedings of RIAO*.

[10] Carpenter, B. 2005. Scaling high-order character language models to gigabytes. *Proceedings of the 2005 Association for Computational Linguistics Software Workshop*.

Lightweight Contrastive Summarization for News Comment Mining

Gobaan Raveendran Charles L. A. Clarke
University of Waterloo, Canada

ABSTRACT

We develop and discuss a news comment miner that presents distinct viewpoints on a given theme or event. Given a query, the system uses metasearch techniques to find relevant news articles. Relevant articles are then scraped for both article content and comments. Snippets from the comments are sampled and presented to the user, based on theme popularity and contrastiveness to previously selected snippets. The system design focuses on being quicker and more lightweight than recent topic modelling approaches, while still focusing on selecting orthogonal snippets.

Categories and Subject Descriptors: H.3.3 [Information Search and Retrieval]: Information filtering; I.2.7 [Natural Language Processing]: Language Models
General Terms: Algorithms, Experimentation
Keywords: Summarization, Comments, Opinion

1. INTRODUCTION

The study of blogs and other news sources has proved useful for both governments and companies looking to improve the quality of their services[3]. News sources, however, draw from a small set of expert users who drive all the discussion in an area. Thus, these sources may not necessarily represent public opinion. Recently, microblogging sites have provided a rich source of user opinion which has been heavily researched. Unfortunately, this data can be noisy due to length restrictions, which limit what can be expressed.

Alternatively, news portals may provide the ability to comment on articles directly from their websites. These comments are attached to an article and are relatively unrestricted, allowing for a much wider range of opinion. Commentors also highlight both errors and interesting facets about articles on any given topic. However, on a highly debated topic it becomes time consuming to read all the comments and to understand the distinct perspectives.

Thus, the problem of multidocument comment ranking or comment mining requires some attention. Our goal should be to create a system that, given a set of articles and comments on those articles, extracts a set of interesting snippets from the comments. These snippets should be representative of the different views of the commentors.

SIGIR'12, August 12–16, 2012, Portland, Oregon, USA.
ACM 978-1-4503-1472-5/12/08.

2. RELATED WORK

The problem of comment mining is somewhat similar to the concept of review summarization, in which the goal is to generate summaries of the opinions on a given product. In contrastive review summarization we wish to also highlight the differences in multiple products. The work in contrastive review summarization largely focuses on extracting sentiment and opinion[4]. The problem of extracting sentiment is somewhat eased by the fact that reviews are often associated with a rating system that provides supervised data. Furthermore, for news stories, sometimes sentiment extraction may add unnecessary overhead, and highlight unimportant aspects, as the objective facts of the story may be more interesting.

General multidocument summarization has also provided a rich source of tools for comment mining. However, much of this work focuses on creating a single overall summary, which may not be plausible with comments representing a lengthy discussion or argument. Furthermore, this work often attempts to create natural language models that are able to stitch together information in order to ensure that summaries are human readable and coherant[6]. This overhead is unnecessary and expensive for individuals wishing to get an overall understanding of user opinion. Topic modeling approaches employing PLSA have also been used to extract latent themes within a set of articles[5], however this approach is heavyweight and may incorrectly cluster important terms causing them to be missed. For example, in our data it was shown that conservatives preferred writing "Barrack Hussein Obama" over the liberal "Obama".

Some work has recently been invested into comment sentence extraction[2]. This work focuses on extracting interesting sentences from a single blogs comments using models that explicitly model different types of comments and topic mixtures. The term-term graph was deemed too heavyweight for the multidocument snippet extraction.

Our final algorithm takes a lightweight approach to review captioning building on simple language models. This approach attempts to explicitly extract orthogonal sentences that represent the most discussed points, and is explained in section 3. This lightweight approach was taken due to its ability to process our corpus containing over 5 million comments and over 2 million distinct terms within an hour. In contrast, implementations on PLSA discuss 50,000 by 8,000 term-doc matrices, and execute in about half an hour[1].

In order to understand the data analyzed, we briefly describe the framework used to implement the lightweight comment summarizer.

Internet founding father Vinton Cerf opposes SOPA http://www.examiner.com/intern... The existing laws are being enforced everyday, without the need for SOPA or PIPA, as was illustrated by last weeks actions. Why do we need new internet piracy laws like SOPA and PIPA? http://www.examiner.com/intern...
Especially since Google is opposing the bill because it is the world's biggest copyright infringer. It has copied millions (and this is not an exaggeration) of books without permission and seeks to put them all up on the Net without compensating the copyright holders. And it makes big money from copyright infringing material on its sites, such as YouTube.
If Hollywood wants to try to protect their profit margins by eliminating online entertainment they are fighting the wind. Hollywood needs to embrace the web or go the way of the horse and buggy. There are already websites offering original content that employs more people, more regularly than movies ever would.
Another reason to not support the bill is simply because the RIAA and MPAA don't understand tech. Hell, RIAA still doesn't understand digital distribution of music and the MPAA would still keep us on VHS tapes if it meant less pirating. Right here just crosses the line.

Table 1: Top four snippets for SOPA in 2012

3. SYSTEM OVERVIEW

The input of the system is a query and a date range, for example "SOPA 01/2012 02/2012". The system then uses metasearch techniques to extract the hundred most relevant articles from each of over forty-five different news portals. An associated rule scraper is then used to extract news article and comment data from each link. The comments and articles are fed to a snippet extractor that attempts to extract a finite set of interesting sentences from the corpus.

The primary innovation comes from applying a known algorithm to a different domain, and the implementation of a lightweight comment extraction framework.

3.1 Example

To illustrate the scoring algorithm, we present the results of extracting four snippets from articles about the internet regulatory legislation nicknamed "SOPA". The snippets highlight multiple opinions such as the existence of competing laws, and perceived copyright infringement by Google.

Initially, we assume a background set of comments C and a target set of comments $C_q \subset C$, that are commenting about articles relevant to the query q. C is generated by executing the comment mining engine on as many different queries as time allows, twenty seven in our case. We can estimate a language model for each term t in the collection as follows:

$$p(t) = \frac{\text{number of comments in C containing t} + \delta}{\text{number of comments in C} + \delta} \quad (1)$$

$$p_q(t) = \frac{\text{number of comments in } C_q \text{ containing t} + \delta}{\text{number of comments in } C_q + \delta} \quad (2)$$

Here we use the additive smoothing parameter δ, with δ = 1 for our tests. Given this model we can use the K-L divergence to calculate *score(t)*

$$score(t) = \begin{cases} p_q(t) log(p_q(t)/p(t)) & p_q(t) > p(t) \\ 0 & otherwise \end{cases} \quad (3)$$

We select snippets using the following algorithm.

1. Find a snippet S of at least l contigious words, rounding up to the nearest sentence boundary. We choose l=50, allowing for human readable snippets.
2. Compute a snippet score as follows:

$$score(S) = \frac{\sum_{unique(t) \in S} score(t)}{length(S)} \quad (4)$$

3. Present the highest scoring snippet S' to the user.
4. Set $score(t) = 0 \ \forall t \in S'$
5. Repeat step 1-4 while the score is above a threshold ϵ. $\epsilon = 0.05 * l$ in our case.

4. CONCLUSION

The ability to quickly and effectively extract comments from articles opens up a large corpus of data for analyzing and extracting opinion. By using K-L divergence and a bag of words model we are able to quickly isolate interesting opinions and present analysts' feedback on how users generally feel about a given topic. As ongoing research, we are comparing the results with more heavyweight topic modelling approaches to summarization. Using the current work as a baseline, we hope to evaluate both algorithms and compare the benefits of each method.

5. REFERENCES

[1] M. Blondel. LSA and pLSA in Python, June 2010.

[2] M. Hu, A. Sun, and E.-P. Lim. Comments-Oriented Blog Summarization by Sentence Extraction. In *16th CIKM*, pages 901–904, 2007.

[3] L.-W. Ku, L.-Y. Lee, and H.-H. Chen. Opinion Extraction, Summarization and Tracking in News and Blog Corpora. In *Proceedings of AAAI-2006 Spring Symposium on Computational Approaches to Analyzing Weblogs*, 2006.

[4] K. Lerman and R. McDonald. Contrastive Summarization: An Experiment with Consumer Reviews. In *NAACL*, pages 113–116, 2009.

[5] Y. Lu and C. Zhai. Opinion Integration Through Semi-supervised Topic Modeling. In *17th WWW Conference*, pages 121–130, 2008.

[6] D. R. Radev and K. R. McKeown. Generating Natural Language Summaries from Multiple On-Line Sources. *Computational Linguistics*, 24:470–500, Sept. 1998.

Looking Inside the Box: Context-Sensitive Translation for Cross-Language Information Retrieval

Ferhan Ture[1], Jimmy Lin[2,3], Douglas W. Oard[2,3]
[1]Dept. of Computer Science, [2]College of Information Studies, [3]UMIACS
University of Maryland
fture@cs.umd.edu, jimmylin@umd.edu, oard@umd.edu

ABSTRACT

Cross-language information retrieval (CLIR) today is dominated by techniques that use token-to-token mappings from bilingual dictionaries. Yet, state-of-the-art statistical translation models (e.g., using Synchronous Context-Free Grammars) are far richer, capturing multi-term phrases, term dependencies, and contextual constraints on translation choice. We present a novel CLIR framework that is able to reach inside the translation "black box" and exploit these sources of evidence. Experiments on the TREC-5/6 English-Chinese test collection show this approach to be promising.

Categories and Subject Descriptors: H.3.3 [Information Storage and Retrieval]: Information Search and Retrieval

Keywords: machine translation, context

1. INTRODUCTION

Query translation approaches for cross-language information retrieval (CLIR) can be pursued either by applying a machine translation (MT) system or by using a token-to-token bilingual mapping. These approaches have complementary strengths: MT makes good use of context but at the cost of producing only one-best results, while token-to-token mappings can produce n-best token translations but without leveraging available contextual clues. This has led to a small cottage industry of what we might refer to as "context recovery" in which postprocessing techniques are used to select or reweight translation alternatives, usually based on evidence from term co-occurrence in a comparable collection.

We argue that this false choice results from thinking of MT systems as black boxes [5]. Inside an MT system we find not alternative translations for individual tokens, but rather for entire sentences. In state-of-the-art MT systems, these alternative "readings" are based on Synchronous Context-Free Grammars (SCFG) and pieced together from units of varying size with complex hierarchical dependencies. Reducing these to context independent token translation probabilities discards potentially useful contextual constraints. An elegant solution, which we explore in this work, is to perform translation in context using a full SCFG MT system and then to reconstruct context-sensitive n-best token translation probabilities by tokenizing each reading and accumulating translation likelihood evidence, which can then be renormalized as estimates of probabilities. This technique is now routinely used in speech retrieval [7], but we are not aware of its prior use for CLIR.

These context-sensitive token translation probabilities can then be used in the same way as context-independent probabilities. We use a technique based on mapping term statistics before computing term weights [8, 2] to establish a strong context-independent baseline. Experiments on the TREC-5/6 English-Chinese CLIR task show that our new approach yields promising (although not statistically significant) improvements over that baseline.

2. APPROACH

We consider the technique presented by Darwish and Oard [2] as the baseline. Given a source-language query s, we represent s in the target language as a probabilistic structured query, where weights are derived from word-to-word bilingual translation probabilities that are learned automatically from parallel text ("bitext"):

$$\text{Score}(D|s) = \sum_{j=1}^{\#\text{ tokens}} \text{bm25}(\text{tf}(s_j, D), \text{df}(s_j)) \quad (1)$$

$$\text{tf}(s_j, D) = \sum_{t_i, Pr_{\text{bitext}}(t_i|s_j) > L} \text{tf}(t_i, D) Pr_{\text{bitext}}(t_i|s_j) \quad (2)$$

$$\text{df}(s_j) = \sum_{t_i, Pr_{\text{bitext}}(t_i|s_j) > L} \text{df}(t_i) Pr_{\text{bitext}}(t_i|s_j) \quad (3)$$

where L is a lower bound on conditional probability. We also impose a cumulative probability threshold, C, so that translation alternatives are added (starting from most probable ones) until the cumulative probability has reached C. We use the Okapi BM25 term weighting function, although in principle any other weighting function can be substituted.

Compared against this baseline, we show how we can take advantage of a full MT decoder to better estimate translation probabilities. A decoder uses a translation model (TM) and language model (LM) to find all possible derivations of a source text, and the corresponding translations in the target language, along with associated derivation scores. We use cdec [3], a state-of-the-art MT system which provides fast "decoding" using *Hiero*-style synchronous grammars [1] for representing the translation model in a way that can model distant dependencies within a sentence.

As a point of comparison, we might use only the best translation:

$$\text{Score}(D|s) = \sum_{j=1}^{m} \text{bm25}(\text{TF}(t_i^{(1)}, D), \text{DF}(t_i^{(1)})) \quad (4)$$

where $t^{(1)}$ is the most probable translation of s, computed by:

$$t^{(1)} = \arg\max_t \ell(t|s) = \arg\max_t \text{TM}(s,t)\text{LM}(t) \quad (5)$$

where ℓ is the likelihood function, a mapping learned by the decoder, which scores each derivation using the TM and LM.

Decoders produce a set of candidate sentence translations in the process of computing equation (5), so we can generalize our model to consider the n candidates with highest likelihood, for some $n > 1$. In this case, the score of document D would be a weighted average of scores with respect to each candidate translation:

$$\text{Score}(D|f) = \sum_{k=1}^{N} \text{Score}(D|e^{(k)}) Pr_{\text{cdec}}(e^{(k)}|f) \quad (6)$$

where Pr_{cdec} is the normalized likelihood value.

In order to compute tf and df statistics for tokens, we start by tokenizing each candidate sentence translation. For each token s_j of source query s, we use word alignments in the grammar rules to determine which target tokens it is associated with. By doing this, we are constructing a probability distribution of possible translations of s_j based on the n query translations. Specifically, if source token s_j is aligned to (i.e., translated as) t_i in the kth best translation, it receives a weight equal to $Pr_{\text{cdec}}(t^{(k)}|s)$.[1] As a result, we can map tf and df statistics by replacing Pr_{bitext} with Pr_{nbest} (see below, φ is the normalization factor) in Equations 2 and 3.

$$Pr_{\text{nbest}}(t_i|s_j) = \frac{1}{\varphi} \sum_{k=1}^{N} \sum_{\substack{t_i \\ s_j \text{ aligned to } t_i \text{ in } t^{(k)}}} Pr_{\text{cdec}}(t^{(k)}|s) \quad (7)$$

This new probability distribution (i.e., Pr_{nbest}) is based only on the n translations that the decoder scores highest for the source query. Therefore, the distribution is informed by the query context and its derivation by the translation model. From this we would expect the distribution to be better biased in favor of appropriate translations, but perhaps at the cost of some reduction in variety due to overfitting. Finally, we can combine the two probability estimates to mitigate overfitting using simple linear interpolation: $Pr_c(s_j) = \lambda Pr_{\text{nbest}}(s_j) + (1 - \lambda) Pr_{\text{bitext}}(s_j)$.

3. EVALUATION

We evaluated our system on the TREC-5/6 CLIR task, using a corpus of 164,778 Chinese documents and titles of the 54 English topics as queries. The evaluation metric is Mean Average Precision (MAP). The English-to-Chinese translation model was trained using the FBIS parallel text collection, which contains 1.6 million parallel sentences. The Chinese collection was tokenized using the Stanford segmenter for Chinese, the Porter stemmer was used for English, and alignment was performed using GIZA++ [6]. A SCFG was extracted from these alignments using a suffix array [4]. A Chinese token 3-gram model serves as the LM.

Results are summarized in Figure 1. At the left edge of the graph, at $\lambda = 0$, we have the approach in equation (2) with context-independent translation probabilities (call this A).[2] At the right edge of the graph, at $\lambda = 1.0$, we rely exclusively on context-sensitive probabilities (call this B). Effectiveness peaks at $\lambda = 0.78$ (call this C).[3] For reference, the horizontal line represents simply taking the one-best translation from the MT system (call this D). We also tried one-best context-independent translation for each token, and the MAP score was 0.2431. A randomization test shows that this is significantly below A, B, C and D ($p < 0.05$). On the other hand, A, B, C, and D are statistically indistinguishable on this test collection. Yet, results are still promising: when C is compared to A and D, the p-value is approximately 0.15 and 0.18, respectively. Also, a

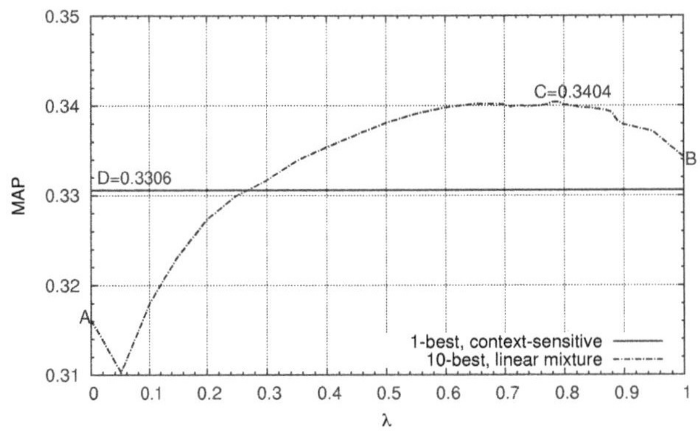

Figure 1: Evaluation on TREC-5/6 English-Chinese CLIR task.

topic-specific analysis shows that C yields better average precision than D on 36 of the 54 topics (which actually is significant by a two-tailed sign test at $p < 0.05$).

4. CONCLUSIONS AND FUTURE WORK

In this work, we have introduced an approach that combines the representational advantage of probabilistic structured queries with the richness of the internal representation of a translation model. We introduced a novel way to learn term translation probabilities from the top scoring "readings" of alternative query translations, as generated by the decoder. We evaluated our approach on the English-Chinese CLIR task of TREC-5/6: although we did not observe significant improvements, we feel that this approach is nevertheless promising. In future work we plan to try this approach for document translation (where we would expect greater benefit from context, although with higher computational cost, at least in experimental settings). Replications on test collections with larger numbers of topics, and with a greater variety of query and topic languages, can also be expected to yield additional insights.

Acknowledgements. This work was supported in part by DARPA BOLT under contract HR0011-12-C-0015. Any opinions, findings, conclusions or recommendations expressed in this paper are those of the authors and do not necessarily reflect the view of DARPA.

5. REFERENCES

[1] D. Chiang. Hierarchical phrase-based translation. *Computational Linguistics*, 33:201–228, 2007.

[2] K. Darwish and D. W. Oard. Probabilistic structured query methods. In *SIGIR*, 2003.

[3] C. Dyer, J. Weese, H. Setiawan, A. Lopez, F. Ture, V. Eidelman, J. Ganitkevitch, P. Blunsom, and P. Resnik. cdec: a decoder, alignment, and learning framework for finite-state and context-free translation models. In *ACL Demos*, 2010.

[4] A. Lopez. Hierarchical phrase-based translation with suffix arrays. In *EMNLP*, 2007.

[5] W. Magdy and G. Jones. Should MT systems be used as black boxes in CLIR? In *ECIR*, 2011.

[6] F. Och and H. Ney. A systematic comparison of various statistical alignment models. *CL*, 29(1):19–51, 2003.

[7] J. Olsson and D. Oard. Combining LVCSR and vocabulary-independent ranked utterance retrieval for robust speech search. In *SIGIR*, 2009.

[8] A. Pirkola. The effects of query structure and dictionary-setups in dictionary-based cross-language information retrieval. In *SIGIR*, 1998.

[1]Since a source term may be aligned to multiple target terms in the same query translation, we still need to normalize the final weights.

[2]We selected $C = 0.95$ and $L = 0.005$ for baseline model parameters after manually trying a range of values.

[3]We selected $N = 10$ for conditions B and C, but $N = 5$ also yields similar results, peaking at a MAP score of 0.3387.

Making Results Fit Into 40 Characters: A Study in Document Rewriting

Johannes Leveling and Gareth J. F. Jones
School of Computing, CNGL
Dublin City University
Dublin, Ireland
{jleveling, gjones}@computing.dcu.ie

ABSTRACT

With the increasing popularity of mobile and hand-held devices, automatic approaches for adapting results to the limited screen size of mobile devices are becoming more important. Traditional approaches for reducing the length of textual results include summarization and snippet extraction. In this study, we investigate document rewriting techniques which retain the meaning and readability of the original text. Evaluations on different document sets show that i) rewriting documents considerably reduces document length and thus, scrolling effort on devices with limited screen size, and ii) the rewritten documents have a higher readability.

Categories and Subject Descriptors

H.3.1 [**INFORMATION STORAGE AND RETRIEVAL**]: Content Analysis and Indexing—*Abstracting Methods, Linguistic Processing*

General Terms

Experimentation, Measurement

Keywords

Document rewriting, Summarization, Result presentation

1. INTRODUCTION

With the increasing popularity of handheld devices, making effective use of the limited screen size becomes more important. Showing textual information retrieval (IR) results still predominates on mobile devices with small screens. Documents are often laid out for presentation on desktop displays. Access to these documents from mobile devices can result in a poor or unusable experience, because only a limited amount of material is visible to the user and context and overview are lost due to the limited screen size.

We investigate document rewriting, which comprises adding, deleting, or modifying phrases, words, or characters in text to reduce the number of lines needed to render the text while retaining its meaning and readability. The objective of rewriting is to use the display area on mobile devices more effectively, which can have many benefits: elder people or visually impaired people can use an increased font size for better readability; the decision if a document is actually relevant can be made more easily by showing more or longer document snippets; the user effort in scrolling through results is reduced; the list of results can be read faster if shorter words are used; results are easier to understand when more consistent vocabulary is used; and there is less loss of meaning which can result when a full document is summarized. In this paper, we investigate document rewriting and its effect on document length and readability to adapt result presentation to mobile devices.

2. RELATED WORK

McKay and Watter [4] discuss four different approaches to migrate data to mobile devices: 1. direct migration (i.e. unmodified content), 2. data modification (e.g. summarization), 3. data suppression (i.e. removed content), and 4. data overview (i.e. imposing a hierarchical structure in content to display smaller chunks). Our proposed approach is a mixture of direct migration (keeping unmodified text), data modification, and data suppression. Note that these techniques do not include inserting data (e.g. hyphenation), which is used in the experiments described in this paper.

Traditional summarization and snippet extraction has focused on extracting key sentences from a text [5]. Snippet extraction is a popular method for search engines and question answering systems to show some context for query terms or the exact answers [3]. Most often, snippets are not grammatically correct sentences and include triplets of periods ("...") to indicate sequences of omitted words. Summarization for mobile devices can even limit the result presentation to a single sentence or key phrase [2, 1], which results in the loss or change of meaning.

In contrast, our proposed approach focuses on keeping the meaning and removing only irrelevant or redundant parts of the text in order to shorten it. Document rewriting can even be applied on an already summarized text to shorten it even further. Thus, our goal is not to summarize a text, but to make it fit into a limited display.

A related problem is the reduction of text to make it fit into a given character limit by introducing abbreviations or omitting characters e.g. SMS or Tweets. However, this typically results in text which is more difficult to comprehend (i.e. so-called "textese").

To the best of our knowledge, the application of document rewriting techniques for adaptation of result presentation to mobile devices has not been investigated.

3. DOCUMENT REWRITING

We view document rewriting of text as the insertion, deletion, or modification of characters, words, or phrases of text. (Eliminating full sentences would result in summarization). We investigate the following rewriting methods in our experiments:

Synonyms: replace a word with its shortest synonym from WordNet 3.0[1], generating the correct full word form based on the CMU English morphology database (e.g. "vehicle" →"car").

[1] http://wordnet.princeton.edu/

SIGIR'12, August 12–16, 2012, Portland, Oregon, USA.
ACM 978-1-4503-1472-5/12/08.

Acronyms: replace an expanded acronym with the shorter acronym, based on the Vera acronym database[2] (e.g. "United Nations" →"UN").

Simplifications: apply substitution rules compiled from stylistic guidelines and data from the classic Unix tool "diction"[3] (4019 rules), which provides support for simplifying and shortening text (e.g. "in fact" →" ", "red in color" →"red").

Parentheses: delete expressions enclosed in parentheses (e.g. "Smyth (age 43) ..." →"Smyth ...").

Numbers: strip commas from numbers and abbreviate numbers (e.g. "thirteen" →"13", "100,000" →"100K").

Whitespace: remove double or redundant whitespace (e.g. space before a comma).

Hyphens: hyphenate words at end of line, based on TeX hyphenation patterns (e.g. "libraries" →"li-\nbraries").

For our experiments, we assume that a monospaced font is used (e.g. the characters "m" and "i" will take up the same width), with 40-80 characters per line. We think that this is a realistic assumption for phones with limited graphics capabilities and even for modern smartphones, because images or advertisements could take up additional space.

We employ a greedy algorithm for text wrapping, inserting a linebreak when adding a word to the current line would exceed the maximum number of characters per line.

For simplicity, we assume that the first word sense (typically the most frequent one) is correct. We presume that the accuracy of word sense disambiguation is unrelated to the number of lines or the average word length which is used in the computation of readability scores. However, we employ morphologic information to generate the correct word form of the replacement. For example, if the word "added" in the sense of "respond" is encountered in the text, the morphological information includes the base form "add", the part of speech, person, number, gender, case, and tense. The WordNet synonym with the shortest full form matching the morphologic information of the original word (i.e. "say") is then selected as a replacement (i.e. "said").

4. EXPERIMENTS AND RESULTS

We evaluate our proposed approach to document rewriting using two types of metrics: readability scores, which indicate how easy a text is to understand, and the amount of text, which indicates how much user effort is required to scroll through a list of results. We calculate Flesch Reading Ease (FRE, where higher values correspond to better readability), Coleman-Liau grade level (CLGL), and SMOG index[4]. FRE is the standard readability formula and is widely by government agencies, including the US Department of Defense. SMOG and CLGL both estimate the grade level (i.e. years of education) a person needs to understand a text, but CLGL relies on computing the number of characters instead of syllables per word (which can be computed more accurately than the syllable count or sentence length).

In addition, we compute the number of lines (# lines) required to render the text for the original and the rewritten document using 40, 60, and 80 characters per line.

The evaluation is based on three datasets which have been used for summarization evaluations: a sample of texts from the Brown corpus (30 documents), a set of full articles from JAIR (141 documents), and a random set of Wikipedia articles (512 documents). Evaluation results for original (O) and rewritten documents (R) are shown in Table 1. The asterisk (∗) indicates a significant improvement over the corresponding metric for the original text (Wilcoxon test with 95% confidence measure). Note that improvement means a higher FRE score and lower values for the other metrics. In general, rewriting the text reduces the amount of text while increasing readability. The number of lines is reduced by 7.4-13.3% for the tested documents. This can be partially attributed to hyphenation, which reduces unused whitespace before linebreaks. Surprisingly, document rewriting also results in increased readability, because rewriting typically involves removing redundant words and selecting shorter words with fewer characters or syllables. Readability scores such as FRE are based on average word or sentence length, which are decreased by document rewriting.

Table 1: Readability scores for rewriting documents.

Corpus	FRE	CLGL	SMOG	#lines @ 40/60/80 chars		
Brown O	56.84	11.84	12.62	9495	/6226	/4634
Brown R	63.83*	10.20*	11.49*	8694*	/5746*	/4291*
Wiki O	44.93	13.24	13.04	111156	/72804	/54158
Wiki R	51.79*	11.93*	12.32*	96707*	/63874*	/47726*
JAIR O	48.59	11.82	13.72	282132	/184682	/137270
JAIR R	54.34*	10.74*	12.90*	244570*	/161429*	/120513*

5. CONCLUSIONS AND OUTLOOK

We have shown that applying document rewriting can considerably reduce the amount of text (up to 13.3% compared to the original) while improving the readability of documents. This makes document rewriting a viable approach to adapting result presentation to devices with limited display size, which can be applied in addition to summarization to further increase the compression rate.

Future work will include conducting user studies (e.g. measuring reading time and understanding of rewritten documents, when more aggressive document rewriting techniques such as leaving out vowels are applied), integrating more advanced natural language processing (e.g. including NLP for word sense disambiguation, named entity recognition, and coreference analysis), and investigating the effect of document rewriting on other areas of IR such as indexing or summarization.

Acknowledgments

This research is supported by the Science Foundation of Ireland (grant 07/CE/I1142) as part of the Centre for Next Generation Localisation (`http://www.cngl.ie/`).

6. REFERENCES

[1] O. Buyukkokten, O. Kaljuvee, H. Garcia-Molina, A. Paepcke, and T. Winograd. Efficient web browsing on handheld devices using page and form summarization. *ACM TOIS*, 20(1):82–115, 2002.

[2] M. Jones, G. Buchanan, and N. Mohd-Nasir. An evaluation of WebTwig - a site outliner for handheld web access. In *HUC'99*, volume 1707 of *LNCS*, pages 343–345. Springer, 1999.

[3] Q. Li, K. S. Candan, and Q. Yan. Extracting relevant snippets for web navigation. In *AAAI'08*, pages 1195–1200. AAAI, 2008.

[4] B. Mackay and C. Watters. The impact of migration of data to small screens on navigation. *IT & Society*, 1(3):90–101, 2003.

[5] M. Sanderson. Accurate user directed summarizatiion from existing tools. In *CIKM 1998*, pages 45–51. ACM, 1998.

[2] `ftp://prep.ai.mit.edu/pub/gnu/vera/`

[3] `http://ftp.gnu.org/gnu/diction/`

[4] `http://www.readabilityformulas.com/`

New Assessment Criteria for Query Suggestion*

Zhongrui Ma
Renmin University of China
zhongrui.ma@gmail.com

Yu Chen
Microsoft Research Asia
yu.chen@microsoft.com

Ruihua Song
Microsoft Research Asia
rsong@microsoft.com

Tetsuya Sakai
Microsoft Research Asia
tesakai@microsoft.com

Jiaheng Lu
Renmin University of China
jiahenglu@ruc.edu.cn

Ji-Rong Wen
Microsoft Research Asia
jrwen@microsoft.com

ABSTRACT

Query suggestion is a useful tool to help users express their information needs by supplying alternative queries. When evaluating the effectiveness of query suggestion algorithms, many previous studies focus on measuring whether a suggestion query is relevant or not to the input query. This assessment criterion is too simple to describe users' requirements. In this paper, we introduce two scenarios of query suggestion. The first scenario represents cases where the search result of the input query is unsatisfactory. The second scenario represents cases where the search result is satisfactory but the user may be looking for alternative solutions. Based on the two scenarios, we propose two assessment criteria. Our labeling results indicate that the new assessment criteria provide finer distinctions among query suggestions than the traditional relevance-based criterion.

Categories and Subject Descriptors

H.3.3 [**Information Search and Retrieval**]: query formulation

General Terms

Measurement

Keywords

Assessment criteria, query suggestion

1. INTRODUCTION

Query suggestion is widely adopted in commercial search engines to supply alternative queries and assist users to achieve their search goals. When evaluating the effectiveness of query suggestion methods, some previous works [1, 4, 6] assign relevant or irrelevant labels to the suggestion queries, and then compute metrics such as precision, recall, MAP.

This evaluation method, however, is too rudimentary to capture users' requirements precisely, and various refinements have been proposed in the literature. For example, Jain et al. [5] require a *good* suggestion to be not only relevant but also useful. The suggestions return zero search results or are synonyms of the input query are treated as *bad*. Bhatia et al. [3] also regard suggestions that are almost duplicate to the input query as irrelevant. Yang et al. [7] adopt a five-point score to distinguish suggestions from "Precisely related" to "Clearly unrelated". Baraglia et al. [2] define a suggestion as *useful* if it "can interpret the possible intent of the user better than the original query".

We argue that we should emphasize the *usefulness* instead of *relevance* because a *relevant* suggestion is not necessarily *useful* to the user. Therefore, we attempt to describe the usefulness of a suggestion by our proposed assessment criteria.

2. THE ASSESSMENT CRITERIA

Whether a suggestion is useful or not depends on the situation that the user encounters in her/his search session. We believe there exists at least two different scenarios:

Scenario 1 The search result of the input query is unsatisfactory. In this case, the user expects a suggestion that can return better search results to meet his/her information need. For example, for an input query q ="aol instant mess", two suggestion queries q_1="aol instant messenger" and q_2="aol aim" (here, "aim" is the acronym of "AOL Instant Messenger") are both labeled as relevant to q by the assessor. When we submit these three queries to a search engine and checked their results, we found that q_1's result matches q's intention better than the results of both q and q_2. Therefore, q_1 is more useful than q_2 in terms of retrieving relevant documents.

Scenario 2 The search result of the input query already contains desirable documents. In this case, the user expects a suggestion that is related to the input query, but has some difference in topics, in order to broaden his/her knowledge. For example, when the input query is "aol instant messenger", whose search result is good enough, returning "windows live messenger" and "yahoo! messenger" as alternative solutions might be more useful than returning "aol aim".

According to the two scenarios, we propose two judgment guidelines for human assessors.

2.1 Utility Judgment

The utility judgment address scenario 1 by measuring whether a suggestion query q_s can retrieve more relevant web documents than the input query q, based on the information need described by q. To decide the utility judgment of q_s for q, an assessor must compare the search results of both q and q_s. Then she can put q_s into one of the following three categories, based on the comparison:

- **Better**: q_s retrieves more relevant documents than q;
- **Worse**: q_s retrieves fewer relevant documents than q;
- **Same**: The quality of q_s's search result is similar to that of q.

Although some of the existing works, e.g. [6], also require assessors to read the search results of q and q_s, the search results are

*The work was done when the first author and the fifth author were visiting Microsoft Research Asia.

SIGIR'12, August 12–16, 2012, Portland, Oregon, USA.
ACM 978-1-4503-1472-5/12/08.

only for understanding the intention of q and q_s in order to decide whether they are relevant. To the best of our knowledge, none of them compare the quality of the two search results.

2.2 Relationship Judgment

The desirable suggestions in scenario 2 should be related to the input query and have some difference in topic. Instead of using this vague expression directly, we ask assessors to classify the relationship between q and q_s into one of the following five categories:

- **Same intention**: If q_s has the same search goal with q. E.g., q="msn messenger" (also for all the following examples), and q_s="windows live messenger";
- **Generalization**: If q_s is more general than q. E.g., q_s="instant messenger";
- **Specialization**: If q_s is more special than q. E.g., q_s="msn download";
- **Peer**: If q_s and q are about two different things, but belong to a common topic. E.g., q_s="yahoo! messenger". Both q and q_s belong to the class of instant messenger software;
- **No association**: q and q_s are irrelevant to each other.

Suggestions in generalization, specialization, and peer are the desirable ones, because they are related to the input queries and have some differences in topic. Suggestions in same intention are less useful as they have no difference in topic. Suggestions in no association are irrelevant to their input queries and hence are useless.

3. LABELING EXAMPLES

Using our proposed criteria, we hired three assessors to label 17,053 suggestions for 200 queries, which are sampled from a recent one month search log of Bing search engine. We will show some examples to demonstrate the advantages of our new assessment criteria in this section.

No.	Suggestion	Utility	Relationship
1	aol instant messenger	better	same intention
2	aim messenger	same	same intention
3	aim instant mess	worse	same intention
4	msn messenger 2011 beta	worse	peer
5	yahoo messenger express	worse	peer

Table 1: Suggestions "aol instant mess" and their labels

Table 1 shows the suggestions of the query "aol instant mess" and their labeling results. Although suggestions 1 to 3 are all in the same intention category, 1 can retrieve better documents while 2 and 3 cannot. Therefore, users in scenario 1 would prefer suggestion 1 rather than 2 or 3. Traditional assessments cannot reflect their differences. Suggestion 4 and 5 are peers of the input query. Although their search results do not satisfy the input query's intention, users in scenario 2 would be interested in them because they help to broaden the knowledge.

No.	Suggestion	Utility	Relationship
1	juicer blender machines	same	peer
2	juicer machine	same	same intention

Table 2: Suggestions "juicer" and their labels

There are also cases that suggestions not in the same intention category can return better results, such as suggestion 1 in Table 2 and all the suggestions in Table 3. In these cases, the peer suggestions retrieve better search results because they introduce better query keywords. In traditional assessments, they are likely to be labeled as irrelevant and query suggestions algorithms are discouraged to return them. Therefore, our assessment criteria are more precise at describing the usefulness of query suggestions.

No.	Suggestion	Utility	Relationship
1	consumer reports best teeth whitening	better	peer
2	best whitening toothpastes	better	peer
3	crest whitestrips directions	better	peer
4	how does baking soda work	better	peer

Table 3: Suggestions "top 5 teeth bleaching treatments" and their labels

4. CONCLUSION

In this paper, we identify two user scenarios of query suggestion and introduce corresponding assessment criteria. The first criterion addresses the scenario that the input query fails to return satisfactory search result. It requires assessors to compare the search results of the suggestions to that of the input query and awards those suggestions having better search results. To the best of our knowledge, this is the first criterion that compares the search result quality of the input query and its suggestions. The second criterion considers different kinds of relationships between an input query and its suggestions. It assumes the input query already returns good search result, and awards the suggestions that help to broaden the user's knowledge.

Our assessment can be applied to different types of evaluation by assigning a suitable score value to each category depending on the evaluation purpose. Then precision, recall, MAP, and even DCG/NDCG can be applied to measure the effectiveness of a suggestion list.

5. REFERENCES

[1] R. A. Baeza-Yates, C. A. Hurtado, and M. Mendoza. Query recommendation using query logs in search engines. In *EDBT Workshops*, pages 588–596, 2004.

[2] R. Baraglia, C. Castillo, D. Donato, F. M. Nardini, R. Perego, and F. Silvestri. Aging effects on query flow graphs for query suggestion. In *CIKM*, pages 1947–1950, New York, NY, USA, 2009. ACM.

[3] S. Bhatia, D. Majumdar, and P. Mitra. Query suggestions in the absence of query logs. In *SIGIR*, pages 795–804, New York, NY, USA, 2011. ACM.

[4] B. M. Fonseca, P. B. Golgher, E. S. de Moura, B. Pôssas, and N. Ziviani. Discovering search engine related queries using association rules. *J. Web Eng.*, 2(4):215–227, 2004.

[5] A. Jain, U. Ozertem, and E. Velipasaoglu. Synthesizing high utility suggestions for rare web search queries. In *SIGIR*, pages 805–814, New York, NY, USA, 2011. ACM.

[6] Y. Song and L. wei He. Optimal rare query suggestion with implicit user feedback. In *WWW*, pages 901–910. ACM, 2010.

[7] J.-M. Yang, R. Cai, F. Jing, S. Wang, L. Zhang, and W.-Y. Ma. Search-based query suggestion. In *CIKM*, pages 1439–1440, New York, NY, USA, 2008. ACM.

On Automatically Tagging Web Documents from Examples

Nicholas Woodward
Texas Advanced Computing Center
The University of Texas at Austin
nwoodward@utexas.edu

Weijia Xu
Texas Advanced Computing Center
The University of Texas at Austin
xwj@tacc.utexas.edu

Kent Norsworthy
The University of Texas Libraries
The University of Texas at Austin
kentn@mail.utexas.edu

Abstract

An emerging need in information retrieval is to identify a set of documents conforming to an abstract description. This task presents two major challenges to existing methods of document retrieval and classification. First, similarity based on overall content is less effective because there may be great variance in both content and subject of documents produced for similar functions, e.g. a presidential speech or a government ministry white paper. Second, the function of the document can be defined based on user interests or the specific data set through a set of existing examples, which cannot be described with standard categories. Additionally, the increasing volume and complexity of document collections demands new scalable computational solutions. We conducted a case study using web-archived data from the Latin American Government Documents Archive (LAGDA) to illustrate these problems and challenges. We propose a new hybrid approach based on Naïve Bayes inference that uses mixed n-gram models obtained from a training set to classify documents in the corpus. The approach has been developed to exploit parallel processing for large scale data set. The preliminary work shows promising results with improved accuracy for this type of retrieval problem.

Categories and Subject Descriptors

H.3.3 **[Information Search and Retrieval]**: Retrieval models

General Terms

Algorithms, Document Representation, Information Retrieval.

Keywords

Web archive, Naïve Bayesian classification

1. INTRODUCTION

Information is frequently gathered from internet for various research fields. A common task in the social sciences is to identify a set of web documents belonging to an abstract concept. For example, a researcher may be interested in collecting all available transcripts of the presidential speeches from a set of web documents across multiple countries and a wide time span. Since the content of those documents varies greatly, with term index based on content, a researcher has to try multiple combinations of keyword searches and manually sift through search results. Still, the approach often yields incomplete results with very low accuracy. In this poster, we investigate how to develop a computational method to automatically tag documents of interest based on a training set that is capable of effectively processing large-scale data in a reasonable amount of time.

In this case study, the corpus for our experiment comes from the Latin American Government Documents Archive (LAGDA[1]) that contains over 70 million of documents, totaling more than 5.8 terabytes, gathered from government websites of 18 Latin American and Caribbean countries. Because the corpus is comprised of web-archived data culled from numerous sources over the course of several years, it presents several challenges to traditional content-based approaches for document representation. For example, variations in subject matter limit the effectiveness of using named entities to compare documents. Metadata such as file or folder naming conventions, as well as titles and descriptions of the documents, are extremely limited. And finally, links and anchor text, where they can be ascertained, tend to vary greatly across country, administration and department.

Our problem is then an issue of finding documents that may be of the same type despite the fact that they contain different content. We attempt to solve this problem with a hybrid approach that uses multiple n-grams to find the terms that correlate to the functions of documents in a training set and then compare them to documents in the larger corpus. By tagging the documents in the training set using words related to their function, we can create a model for classifying other documents. Our implementation divides and distributes computations across multiple nodes for parallel processing.

2. BACKGOUND AND CHALLENGES

Traditional webpage classification assigns categorical labels to each webpage, which is often treated as a text document of the same text content [1]. Among these approaches, while different classification algorithms might be used, only textual information is used as the feature of each webpage. Although state-of-art full text-based web classification can achieve relatively high accuracy, it is not suitable for our practical needs. In this particular problem, the documents of interest often do not share a high similarity in terms of their overall text content.

Another general approach for improving web page classification is to utilize link information. In this approach, the neighbor pages, which are pages linked from and to the page, are used to enhance classification. Research efforts have been made on how neighbor pages can be used. [2]. The overall effectiveness of those approaches is limited for our problem. First, many web documents are generated dynamically from a source such as a relational database. Therefore, all URLs of a website that are pulled from the same source are similar and only differ by some unique identifier. Secondly, most documents of interest in our experiment are terminal documents in the form of Microsoft Office or PDF-formatted documents, and they generally do not have any outgoing links. The anchor text and pages that may lead to the document of interests are sometime created dynamically

SIGIR'12, August 12–16, 2012, Portland, Oregon, USA.
ACM 978-1-4503-1472-5/12/08.

[1] http://lanic.utexas.edu/project/archives/lagda/

and can vary across different governments, departments and time periods.

Therefore, existing web page classification methods are not very effective in meeting our challenges. Our proposed approach seeks alternative feature representation of each webpage in order to improve the performance. Our approach uses selected n-grams of variable length as a representation of the document. Strotgen et al proposed a novel document similarity model based on events extracted from the document. In their approach, a document can be represented as a set of events extracted from the document and compared based on geological and spatial references [3, 4]. Mladenic first proposed a document representation consisting of n-grams where n is up to 5 [5]. In this approach, each web document is first processed with all unigram to select a subset of unigram as features. In a subsequent step, the length of n-gram is increased by 1 and features of the set of n-gram are selected based on the previous results. The process continues until the 5-gram is used. The features that were selected at each step are combined as a vector representation of the web document.

3. PRELIMINARY WORK

The corpus for this experiment comes from a single LAGDA crawl taken from August 16th-19th, 2006. It is a subset of the crawl, consisting of 109 ARC files (14GB). The training documents are divided among four types of documents: presidential speeches, ministerial documents, ministerial reports and annual state of the union speeches.

The corpus contains 160,638 entities pulled from the web, 96,423 of which we consider as documents (HTML, Word and PDF). The documents represent approximately 26 different languages, though the vast majority documents are in Spanish (83%). Document length in the general corpus ranges from a few hundred terms (in HTML files) to more than 60,000 terms (Word and PDF files), with an average of approximately 850 terms per document.

The training documents are divided into two groups: 90% of them are used to create a model and 10% are set aside to test the performance of the model. With the corpus text prepared, we iterate over the training documents, creating separate structures to store n-grams from one to five terms. We measure the frequency of each n-gram, *t*, in the training set and the general corpus, and its relative importance to the training model is determined by the equation (1). We use the log function to smooth the effects of differences between n-gram frequencies.

$$\text{score (t)} = \log\left(\frac{frequency\ of\ t\ in\ model}{frequency\ of\ t\ in\ corpus} * \frac{\#\ of\ n\text{-}gram\ in\ corpus}{\#\ of\ n\text{-}gram\ in\ model}\right) \quad (1)$$

Using the most relevant n-grams as tags related to the function of the training set documents, we can then calculate a probabilistic measure for every document in the larger corpus. We iterate over the entire collection, computing the score of document *D* as the sum of all n-gram, t_i in *D* (equation 2) and then normalize all scores, dividing them by the document's length to dampen the effects of longer documents.

$$Score\ (D) = \sum\nolimits_{t\ in\ D} score(t_i) \quad (2)$$

Documents from the corpus are ranked separately by their score for each n-gram model, and we search for the remaining 10% of the training set. These training documents are labeled as true positives, while all other documents are false positives. We then calculate the ROC score for the highest ranked 25 and 50documents from each n-gram model, and compare these scores to determine the most effective model for classification[6].

We used our approach to identify potential presidential speeches in the general corpus, dividing the training documents into 90% used to create classification models with n-grams from length one to five and 10% set aside for testing purposes. The models were used to rank all documents in the collection according to their probability scores. For scalability of the processing, our implementation uses a divide-and-conquer strategy to distribute the corpus over multiple computing nodes for parallel processing. We compared our rankings to rankings obtained from the Naïve Bayesian classifier in the Apache Mahout library by calculating the ROC scores of the two result sets. However, the Mahout classifier was unable to rank any of the documents set aside in the first 1,000 results for any n-gram of length one to five during our test runs. Our method can return true positive results as early as within the first seven results, on average. Table-1 details average accuracy results of identifying five presidential speech records using our approach over 10 runs. In terms of performance, our approach uses multiple strategies (limited I/O, single pass through text, reusing data structures to store n-gram models) to achieve a superior runtime to that of Mahout, finishing in approximately 55%-60% of the time.

Table 1. Accuracy of using various n-grams

	N=1	N=2	N=3	N=4	N=5
ROC25	0	.192	.288	.224	.296
ROC50	.088	.396	.596	.596	.620

4. CONCLUSION

We have presented a case study that represents an increasingly common search problem: locating documents by function rather than content. Our hybrid approach based on Bayes inference that uses models derived from multiple n-grams is a first step towards solving this type of research task in a manner that is well-suited for parallel implementation to handle large-scale data. We are continuing to refine our approach to utilize the structure information and limited metadata available with each document to improve the results.

This project has been supported by National Science Foundation (NSF-OCI-0504077 and NSF-DBI-0735191).

5. REFERENCES

[1] X. Qi, and B. D. Davison, "Web page classification: Features and algorithms," *ACM Comput. Surv.*, vol. 41, no. 2, pp. 1-31, 2009.

[2] M. Richardson, and P. Domingos, "The Intelligent surfer: Probabilistic Combination of Link and Content Information in PageRank," in Advances in NIPS 14, 2002, pp. 1441-1448.

[3] J. Strotgen, M. Gertz, and C. Junghans, "An event-centric model for multilingual document similarity," in Proceedings of the 34th international ACM SIGIR, Beijing, China, 2011, pp. 953-962.

[4] H. Wang, H. Huang, F. Nie *et al.*, "Cross-language web page classification via dual knowledge transfer using nonnegative matrix tri-factorization," in Proceedings of the 34th international ACM SIGIR, Beijing, China, 2011, pp. 933-942.

[5] D. MLADENIC, "Turning Yahoo into an automatic Web-page classifier," in 13th European Conference on Artificial Intelligence (ECAI), 1998, pp. 473-474.

[6] T. Fawcett, "An introduction to ROC analysis," *Pattern Recogn. Lett.*, vol. 27, no. 8, pp. 861-874, 2006.

On Building a Reusable Twitter Corpus

Richard McCreadie[1], Ian Soboroff[2], Jimmy Lin[3],
Craig Macdonald[1], Iadh Ounis[1], Dean McCullough[2]

[1] University of Glasgow, Glasgow G12 8QQ, UK
[2] National Institute of Science and Technology, MD 20899, USA
[3] University of Maryland, MD 20742, USA

{richard.mccreadie, craig.macdonald, iadh.ounis}@glasgow.ac.uk[1],
{ian.soboroff, dean.mccullough}@nist.gov[2], jimmylin@umd.edu[3]

ABSTRACT

The Twitter real-time information network is the subject of research for information retrieval tasks such as real-time search. However, so far, reproducible experimentation on Twitter data has been impeded by restrictions imposed by the Twitter terms of service. In this paper, we detail a new methodology for building and distributing Twitter corpora, developed through collaboration between the Text REtrieval Conference (TREC) and Twitter. In particular, we detail how the first publicly available Twitter corpus – referred to as Tweets2011 – was distributed via lists of tweet identifiers and dedicated tweet crawling software. Furthermore, we analyse whether this distribution approach remains robust over time, as tweets in the corpus are removed by users. Tweets2011 was successfully used by 58 participating groups for the TREC 2011 Microblog track, and our results attest to the robustness of the crawling methodology over time.

Categories and Subject Descriptors: H.3.3 [Information Storage & Retrieval]: Information Search & Retrieval

General Terms: Experimentation, Performance

Keywords: Twitter, Corpus Creation, Reproducibility

1. INTRODUCTION

Twitter is a communications platform on which users can send short, 140-character messages, called "tweets", to their "followers" (other users who subscribe to those messages). Conversely, users can receive tweets from people they follow via a number of mechanisms, including web clients, mobile clients, and SMS. As of Spring 2011, Twitter has over 140 million active users worldwide, who collectively post over 340 million tweets per day. Twitter is an active research area in the information retrieval (IR) field [1]. However, previously it has not been possible to build and distribute reusable tweet corpora due to restrictions placed upon researchers by Twitter's terms of service.[1] Indeed, this has resulted in two prior unsuccessful attempts to share Twitter data by Stanford and Edinburgh universities.

The Text REtrieval Conference (TREC) is a workshop series that aims to improve the state of the art in information access task effectiveness through building sharable *test collections*. Beginning in 2011, TREC ran the Microblog track

[1] `twitter.com/tos`

SIGIR'12, August 12–16, 2012, Portland, Oregon, USA.
ACM 978-1-4503-1472-5/12/08.

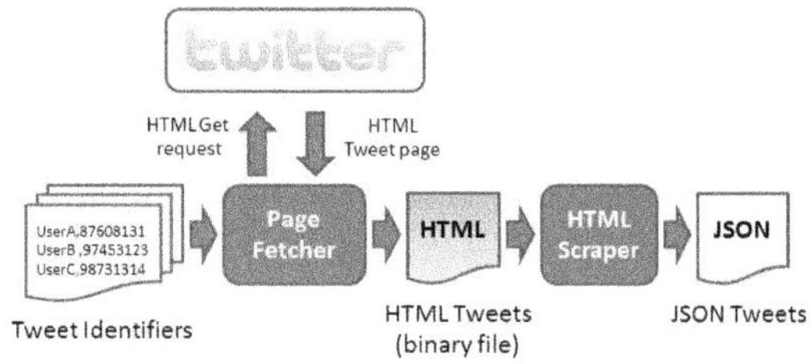

Figure 1: Illustration of tweet crawling.

that investigated tweet search and ranking [2]. In line with the TREC aims and in collaboration with Twitter, a new methodology was developed to build and distribute a publicly available Twitter dataset, known as *Tweets2011*. In this paper, we describe this new methodology, whereby a corpus like Tweets2011, is distributed as a set of tweet identifiers and a tweet crawling tool for downloading the identified tweets. However, since researchers separately download the tweets themselves at different times, and the set of tweets available is not static (as tweets can be deleted), the exact composition of the corpus will vary depending upon when it is downloaded. We also examine how robust the distribution methodology is over time, by comparing crawls of Tweets2011 made at different points in time. Our results show that over the time period tested, the changes in the corpus over time had no noticeable effect on the systems that participated in the TREC 2011 Microblog track.

2. DISTRIBUTION METHODOLOGY

The Twitter terms of service forbids third parties from data redistribution, which means that researchers that have gathered tweets cannot share them. To overcome these constraints, a compromise had to be reached. In particular, a collection would not consist of the tweets themselves, but rather (username, tweet id) pairs and associated software for reconstructing the tweets.

The Twitter REST API provides flexible access to any available tweet; nearly all common Twitter capabilities can be programmatically accessed, e.g., posting new tweets, retweeting, following a user, searching, etc. The API is generally available to the public, although by default it is rate limited; the most common unauthenticated connection places a limit of 150 requests per hour. This restriction makes it impractical to gather large number of tweets for offline processing. Historically, Twitter has lifted the API request limit for some clients based on a particular IP address or an authentication token, but this capability is no longer offered.

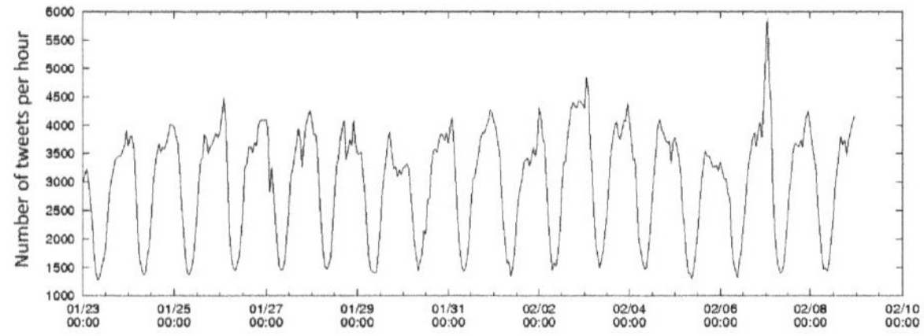
Figure 2: Tweets2011 tweet distribution over time.

The software for reconstructing tweets is an asynchronous HTTP fetcher that downloads each tweet individually. For researchers that had access to the REST API without rate limit restrictions, that can be used to download each tweet in JavaScript Object Notation (JSON) format. However, for researchers without this access, the fetcher instead crawls raw HTML pages from the `twitter.com` site and reconstructs the tweets in JSON format, as shown in Figure 1.

3. TWEETS2011 AND TREC 2011

We used the above methodology to distribute the Tweets2011 collection to the participants of the TREC 2011 Microblog track, which is now available to everyone.[2] To create Tweets2011, we identified a common set of tweets (username, tweet id pairs), for distribution. In particular, we created a sample from tweets posted during the period from January 23rd to February 8th, 2011 (inclusive). It was important to sample, as even for users who were not rate limited, downloading billions or more tweets in a sequential manner would not be practical. Instead, some spam removal was performed and then approximately 1% of the remaining tweets were sampled for the corpus, resulting in a set of approximately 16 million tweets. The distribution of these tweets over the two week period is shown in Figure 2. The chosen time period includes the Egyptian revolution as well as the US Superbowl, and a spike of tweeting activity on February 6th is easily observed. Moreover, to ensure the corpus was representative of the multi-lingual tweet retrieval environment, no language filtering was performed.

For the evaluation of TREC 2011 participating systems, 49 topics were created. From the pool of 50,324 tweets formed from the participants runs for these topics, 2,965 were judged relevant.

4. COLLECTION DEGRADATION

Tweets2011 is unique in the history of information retrieval test collections in that it will degrade over time. Twitter users can delete their tweets, or mark their accounts as private, and after that point, these tweets will not be part of the collection. This is an experimental challenge because system effectiveness may be affected by missing tweets even if those tweets are not relevant, for example due to altered collection statistics. If two systems are compared on different versions of the collection, we worry that those comparisons may not be valid.

Figure 3 illustrates the effect as we have been able to observe it in the short lifetime of the collection so far. When someone downloads the collection in HTML format, which was the case for nearly all participants, each tweet has an HTTP status code associated with it. HTTP 404 indicates a deleted tweet, 403 indicates a protected tweet, and 302 indicates a retweet. Status 301 represents a new report code from the Twitter API and we are not entirely certain what

[2] `trec.nist.gov/data/tweets/`

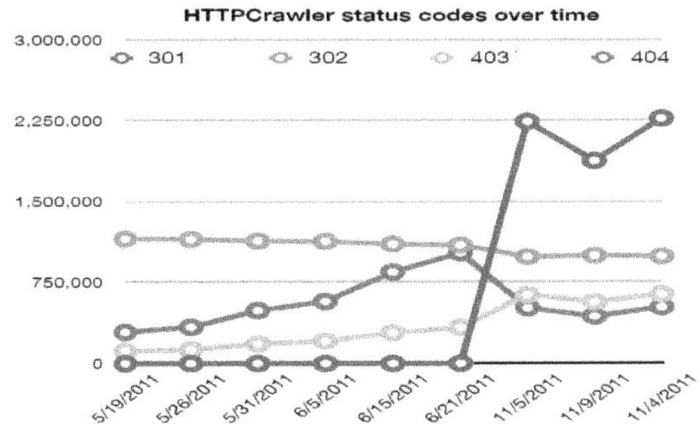

Figure 3: HTTP statuses of participant crawls of the Tweets2011 collection over time.

it indicates; preliminary investigations suggest that it occurs for users that have changed their screen name since the tweets were originally sampled, but the frequency seems much too high for that to be the only explanation. For the 4th of November 2011 crawl, 3,424,155 (21.2%) of the original 16,141,809 tweets were unavailable. Note that for some status codes, the number of missing tweets is not monotonically increasing. This behavior can result from crawler (download) errors, as well as when users mark their accounts as private and subsequently open them again.

We measured the effect of this collection decay by recrawling the collection after all participants had done so, and removing 200 tweets that were pooled and judged for the 49 topics, but which were subsequently deleted or protected. We then computed the precision at rank 30 of all participating runs, and compared the ordering of runs by P@30 to the official results using Kendall's τ. The correlation was 0.99, indicating that missing tweets seemed to affect all participating systems equally if at all.

Further decay in the collection may render it unusable at some point in the future. We do not recommend comparing evaluation scores done after TREC to the official TREC results, because of decay concerns. Rather, experimenters should compare multiple systems (or versions of the same system) that all use the same crawl, or closely contemporaneous crawls. This is not a concern for the official TREC results since participants all crawled the collection during a short window of time.

5. CONCLUSIONS

We detailed a new methodology for building and distributing tweet corpora, developed through collaboration between the Text REtrieval Conference (TREC) and Twitter. In particular, we described how tweet corpora can distributed via lists of tweet identifiers in tandem with tweet crawling software. This distribution approach will work for any collection of tweets. We detailed the first corpus to be distributed in this manner, Tweets2011. We recognized that the corpus may change over time as tweets are deleted, and through an analysis of different versions of the Tweets2011 corpus downloaded by TREC participants, we showed that the distribution method, at least to date, is robust to changes in the underlying corpus.

6. REFERENCES

[1] M. Busch, K. Gade, B. Larson, P. Lok, S. Luckenbill and J. Lin. Earlybird: Real-Time Search at Twitter. In *Proc. of ICDE'12*.

[2] I. Ounis, C. Macdonald, J. Lin and I. Soboroff. Overview of the TREC-2011 Microblog Track In *Proc. of TREC'11*.

On Judgments Obtained from a Commercial Search Engine

Emine Yilmaz, Gabriella Kazai
Microsoft Research Cambridge, UK
{eminey,v-gabkaz }@microsoft.com

Nick Craswell, S.M.M. Tahaghoghi
Microsoft, Bellevue, WA, USA
{nickcr,saied.tahaghoghi}@microsoft.com

ABSTRACT

In information retrieval, relevance judgments play an important role as they are used for evaluating the quality of retrieval systems. Numerous papers have been published using *judgments obtained from a commercial search engine* by researchers in industry. As typically no information is provided about the quality of these judgments, their reliability for evaluating retrieval systems remains questionable. In this paper, we analyze the reliability of such judgments for evaluating the quality of retrieval systems by comparing them to judgments by NIST judges at TREC.

Categories and Subject Descriptors

H.3 [**Information Storage and Retrieval**]: H.3.3[Information Search and Retrieval]

General Terms

Experimentation, Human Factors, Measurement

Keywords

Crowdsourcing, Evaluation, Test Collection

1. INTRODUCTION

In information retrieval (IR), test collections are typically used to evaluate and optimize the performance of IR systems. The quality of a test collection can impact the conclusions of the evaluation, where the quality of the relevance judgments is a key factor. For example, evaluation outcomes are shown to be affected by using different judge populations [1] and different judging guidelines [3]. On the other hand, using different judges from the same population of NIST judges employed by TREC has been shown to lead to relatively stable conclusions as to which retrieval algorithm beats another [4].

In recent years, several papers using *judgments obtained from a commercial search engine* have been published [2]. Most of these papers use such judgments (which are typically not publicly available) to validate the superiority of their proposed methods over existing algorithms. Since judges employed by commercial search engine companies are likely to come from different populations than NIST judges and are likely to be subjected to different training and judging procedures, we may reason that judgments from a commercial search engine are likely to lead to different conclusions than judgments from NIST judges.

We analyze whether judgments obtained from a commercial search engine are reliable, in terms of leading to the same evaluation conclusions as when using NIST judgements.

SIGIR'12, August 12–16, 2012, Portland, Oregon, USA.
ACM 978-1-4503-1472-5/12/08.

2. EXPERIMENTAL RESULTS

We use the test collection from the TREC Web Track Adhoc tasks from 2009 and 2010. This dataset consists of nearly 50K NIST relevance labels, roughly 25K in each year, for 50 topics in each year. We took these 100 topics and using the topic titles as queries we scraped the top 10 search results from Google and Bing for each query. This gave us a total of 1603 unique query-URL pairs for the 100 topics.

We constructed three different collections by obtaining judgments from three judge groups : judges from (1) the TREC Web track ad-hoc task (**NIST**), (2) a commercial search engine (**ProWeb**), and (3) crowdsourcing (**Crowd**). ProWeb judges were experienced and highly trained judges, employed by the search engine company, while crowd workers, recruited via Clickworker, received no prior training on relevance assessing.

The NIST judgments differ across the two years. In 2009, three relevance levels were used (Highly Relevant, Relevant, and Not Relevant), while in 2010, five grades of relevance were used (Navigational, Key, Relevant, Non-relevant, and Junk). The ProWeb and Crowd judgments were obtained using a simple interface that asked judges to rate a search result's usefulness to a query using a five point scale that can be viewed as a variation of the 2010 Web Track scale (Ideal, Highly Relevant, Relevant, Somewhat Relevant, Non-relevant). Unlike the ProWeb and Crowd judges, the NIST judges were given descriptions (topic narrative) about what information need is associated with a particular query.

Using the different sets of judgments and the NDCG measure, we evaluate the effectiveness of the runs submitted to the TREC 2009 and 2010 Web Track ad-hoc task. Since we only have labels for a subset of the retrieved documents, we remove unjudged documents from the runs. To avoid variance due to having different documents labeled across the different judge groups, we only consider documents that were judged by all three groups.

To remove the inconsistency across different judge groups due to the different levels of relevance scales used, we converted all the judgments to the Web Track 2009 scale using the following mapping:*Navigational* (or *Ideal*) judgments to *Highly Relevant*, *Key* and *Relevant* (or *Highly Relevant* and

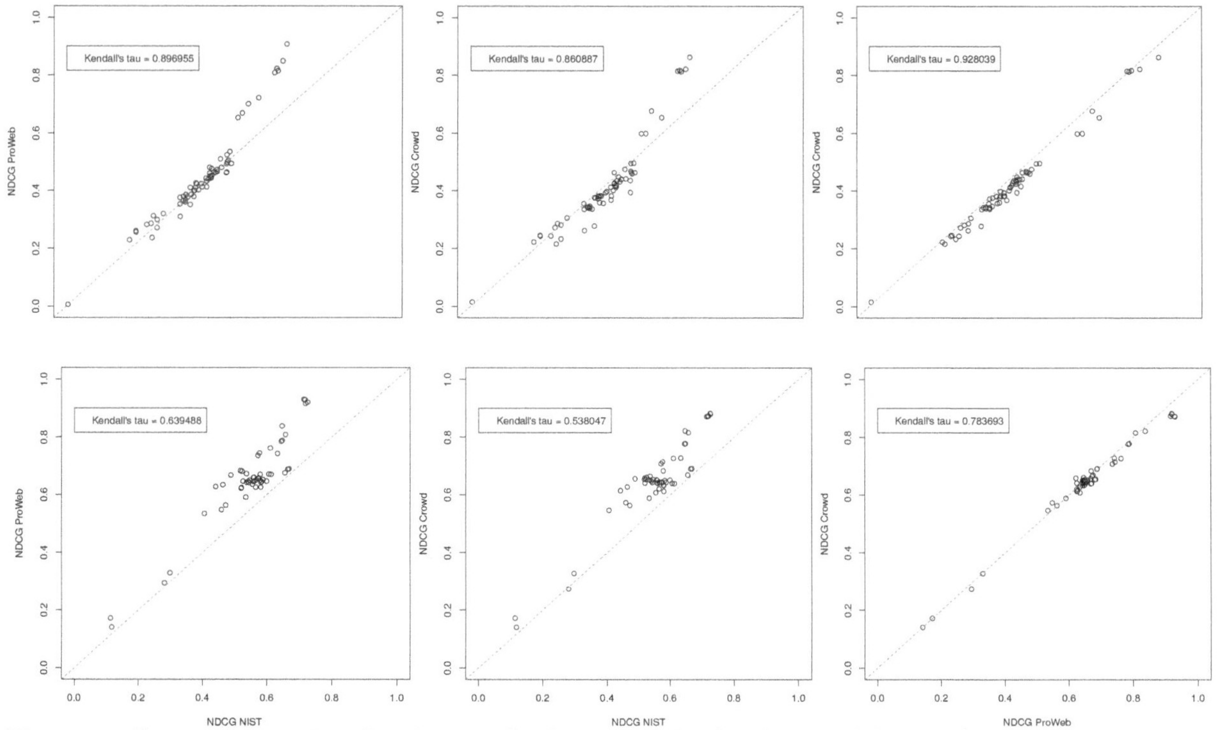

Figure 1: Comparisons of evaluation results for runs submitted to TREC 2009 (top) and TREC 2010 (bottom) using three different sets of judges and their judgements

Relevant) to *Relevant*, and *Non-relevant* and *Junk* (or *Somewhat Relevant* and *Non-relevant*) to *Not Relevant*. We have also experimented with various other mappings but all supported the same conclusions of this poster.

Figure 1 shows the obtained scatter plots: TREC 2009 results in the top row and TREC 2010 in the bottom row. For each year, we plot the results obtained from evaluating the runs using the NIST vs ProWeb (left plot), NIST vs. Crowd (middle plot) and Crowd vs. ProWeb (right plot) judgments. In each plot, we also include the Kendall's τ correlation between the resulting system rankings, obtained using the two respective sets of judgments.

We see that for TREC 2009, evaluations using the NIST, ProWeb and Crowd judgments mostly agree with each other (Kendall's τ of 0.86-0.93). This suggests that the judgments obtained from a commercial search engine are more or less consistent with NIST: using them will not cause major differences in the evaluation. Crowd judgments may be somewhat noisier, but still lead to stable evaluations. The differences in the three plots could be caused by the consistency in the number and description of relevance grades between the Crowd and ProWeb judges as compared to the NIST judges.

On the other hand, for TREC 2010, evaluations using the ProWeb and NIST judgments are quite different (Kendall's $\tau = 0.639$). At first glance, one might think that ProWeb judgments are not reliable at evaluating the systems and the high agreement on the TREC 2009 data is due to chance. However, if we compare the agreements between the evaluations using the Crowd and ProWeb judgments, we also see low agreements. This suggests that the low correlation is specific to this particular TREC. As the figure suggests, systems that were submitted to this particular TREC have very similar performance. Hence, the Kendall's τ statistic may be affected by these systems. Furthermore, when we considered the cases where NIST judgments highly disagree with the Crowd and ProWeb judgments, we found that there are quite a few documents that got the best rating by the Crowd and ProWeb judges but were labeled as non-relevant by the NIST judges. When we analyzed the disagreement cases, we realized that these differences could be caused by the specific topic description that was given to the NIST judges, which limited the possible intents associated with a query. Since the Crowd and ProWeb judges were not given such topic descriptions, they would have considered all possible intents for a query when assigning labels to the documents.

Overall, our conclusion is that even though judgments from a commercial search engine could lead to slightly different conclusions than NIST judges in some settings, evaluations using the two judge groups seem mostly consistent.

3. REFERENCES

[1] Peter Bailey, Nick Craswell, Ian Soboroff, Paul Thomas, Arjen P. de Vries, and Emine Yilmaz. Relevance assessment: are judges exchangeable and does it matter. In *Proc. of ACM SIGIR Conference*, pages 667–674. ACM, 2008.

[2] Christopher J. C. Burges, Robert Ragno, and Quoc Viet Le. Learning to rank with nonsmooth cost functions. In *NIPS*, pages 193–200. MIT Press, 2006.

[3] Charles L.A. Clarke, Nick Craswell, Ian Soboroff, and Azin Ashkan. A comparative analysis of cascade measures for novelty and diversity. In *Proc. of ACM WSDM Conference*, pages 75–84. ACM, 2011.

[4] Ellen M. Voorhees. Variations in relevance judgments and the measurement of retrieval effectiveness. In *Proc. of ACM SIGIR Conference*, pages 315–323. ACM, 1998.

On the Mathematical Relationship between Expected n-call@k and the Relevance vs. Diversity Trade-off

Kar Wai Lim
ANU & NICTA
Canberra, Australia
karwai.lim@anu.edu.au

Scott Sanner
NICTA & ANU
Canberra, Australia
ssanner@nicta.com.au

Shengbo Guo
Xerox Research Centre Europe
Grenoble, France
shengbo.guo@xrce.xerox.com

ABSTRACT

It has been previously noted that optimization of the n-call@k relevance objective (i.e., a set-based objective that is 1 if at least n documents in a set of k are relevant, otherwise 0) encourages more result set diversification for smaller n, but this statement has never been formally quantified. In this work, we explicitly derive the mathematical relationship between *expected n-call@k* and the *relevance vs. diversity trade-off* — through fortuitous cancellations in the resulting combinatorial optimization, we show the trade-off is a simple and intuitive function of n (notably independent of the result set size $k \geq n$), where diversification increases as $n \to 1$.

Categories and Subject Descriptors

H.3.3 [**Information Search and Retrieval**]: Retrieval Models

Keywords

diversity, set-based relevance, maximal marginal relevance

1. RELEVANCE VS. DIVERSITY

Subtopic retrieval — "the task of finding documents that cover as many *different* subtopics of a general topic as possible" [5] — is a motivating case for diverse retrieval. One of the most popular result set diversification methods is Maximal Marginal Relevance (MMR) [1]. Formally, given an *item set* D (e.g., a set of documents) where retrieved items are denoted as $s_i \in D$, we aim to select an optimal subset of items $S_k^* \subset D$ (where $|S_k^*| = k$ and $k < |D|$) *relevant* to a given query $\mathbf{q}$ (e.g., query terms) with some level of *diversity* among the items in S_k^*. MMR builds S_k^* in a greedy manner by choosing the next optimal selection s_k^* given the set of $k-1$ optimal selections $S_{k-1}^* = \{s_1^*, \ldots, s_{k-1}^*\}$ (recursively defining $S_k^* = S_{k-1}^* \cup \{s_k^*\}$ with $S_0^* = \emptyset$) as follows:

$$s_k^* = \mathop{\arg\max}_{s_k \in D \setminus S_{k-1}^*} [\lambda(\mathrm{Sim}_1(\mathbf{q}, s_k)) - (1-\lambda) \max_{s_i \in S_{k-1}^*} \mathrm{Sim}_2(s_i, s_k)]. \quad (1)$$

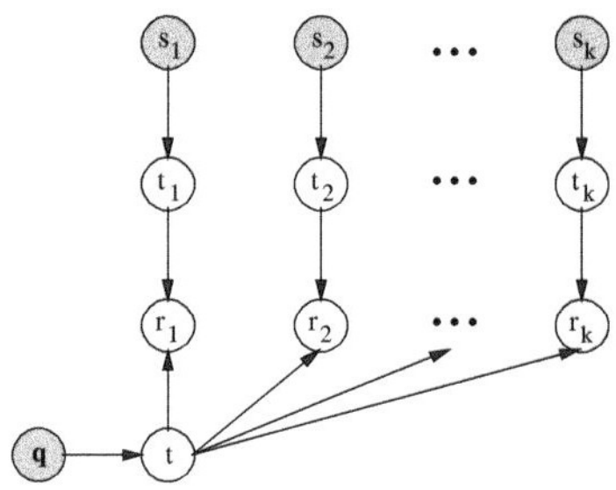

Figure 1: Latent subtopic binary relevance model.

Here, $\lambda \in [0, 1]$, metric Sim_1 measures query-item relevance, and metric Sim_2 measures the similarity between two items.

Presently, little is formally known about how a particular selection of λ relates to the overall *set-based relevance objective* being optimized. However, it has been previously noted that the n-call@k set-based relevance metric (which is 1 if at least n documents in a set of k are relevant, otherwise 0) encourages diversity as $n \to 1$ [2, 4]. Indeed, Sanner *et al.* [3] have shown that optimizing *expected n-call@k* for $n = 1$ corresponds to $\lambda = 0.5$ — we extend this derivation to show that $\lambda = \frac{n}{n+1}$ for arbitrary $n \geq 1$ (independent of result set size $k \geq n$). This result precisely formalizes a relationship between n-call@k and the relevance vs. diversity trade-off.

2. RELEVANCE MODEL AND OBJECTIVE

We review the *probabilistic subtopic model of binary relevance* from [3] shown as a directed graphical model in Figure 1. Shaded nodes represent observed variables, unshaded nodes are latent. Observed variables are the query terms $\mathbf{q}$ and selected items s_i (where for $1 \leq i \leq k$, $s_i \in D$). For the subtopic variables, let T be a discrete subtopic set. Then $t_i \in T$ represent subtopics for respective s_i and $t \in T$ represents a subtopic for query $\mathbf{q}$. The r_i are $\{0, 1\}$ variables that indicate if respective selected items s_i are relevant ($r_i = 1$).

The conditional probability tables (CPTs) are as follows: $P(t_i|s_i)$ and $P(t|\mathbf{q})$ respectively represent the subtopic distribution for item s_i and query $\mathbf{q}$. For the r_i CPTs, using $\mathbb{I}[\cdot]$ as a $\{0, 1\}$ indicator function (1 if $\cdot$ is true), item s_i is deemed *relevant iff its subtopic t_i matches query subtopic t*:

$$P(r_i = 1|t, t_i) = \mathbb{I}[t_i = t]$$

We next define $R_k = \sum_{i=1}^{k} r_i$, where R_k is the number of relevant items from the first k selections. Reading $R_k \geq n$ as $\mathbb{I}[R_k \geq n]$, we express the *expected n-call@k* objective as

$$\text{Exp-}n\text{-Call@}k(S_k, \mathbf{q}) = \mathbb{E}[R_k \geq n | s_1, \ldots, s_k, \mathbf{q}].$$

3. MAIN DERIVATION AND RESULT

Taking MMR's greedy approach, we select s_k given S^*_{k-1}:[1]

$$s^*_k = \arg\max_{s_k} \mathbb{E}[R_k \geq n | S^*_{k-1}, s_k, \mathbf{q}]$$
$$= \arg\max_{s_k} P(R_k \geq n | S^*_{k-1}, s_k, \mathbf{q})$$

This query can be evaluated w.r.t. our latent subtopic binary relevance model in Figure 1 as follows, where we marginalize out all non-query, non-evidence variables T_k and define $T_k = \{t, t_1, \ldots, t_k\}$ and $\sum_{T_k} \circ = \sum_t \sum_{t_1} \cdots \sum_{t_k} \circ$:

$$= \arg\max_{s_k} \sum_{T_k} \Big(P(t|\mathbf{q})\, P(t_k|s_k) \prod_{i=1}^{k-1} P(t_i|s^*_i) \cdot P(R_k \geq n | T_k, S^*_{k-1}, s_k, \mathbf{q}) \Big)$$

We split $R_k \geq n$ into two disjoint (additive) events $(r_k \geq 0, R_{k-1} \geq n)$, $(r_k = 1, R_{k-1} = n-1)$ where all r_i are D-separated:

$$= \arg\max_{s_k} \sum_{T_k} P(t|\mathbf{q})\, P(t_k|s_k) \prod_{i=1}^{k-1} P(t_i|s^*_i) \cdot \Big(\underbrace{P(r_k \geq 0 | R_{k-1} \geq n, t_k, t)}_{1} P(R_{k-1} \geq n | T_{k-1}) + P(r_k = 1 | R_{k-1} = n-1, t_k, t) P(R_{k-1} = n-1 | T_{k-1}) \Big)$$

We distribute initial terms over the summands noting that $\sum_{t_k} P(t_k|s_k) P(r_k = 1 | t_k, t) = \sum_{t_k} P(t_k|s_k) \mathbb{I}[t_k = t] = P(t_k = t | s_k)$:

$$= \arg\max_{s_k} \Bigg(\sum_{T_{k-1}} \underbrace{\Big[\sum_{t_k} P(t_k|s_k) \Big]}_{1} P(R_{k-1} \geq n | T_{k-1}) P(t|\mathbf{q}) \prod_{i=1}^{k-1} P(t_i|s^*_i) + \sum_t P(t|\mathbf{q}) P(t_k = t | s_k) \sum_{t_1, \ldots, t_{k-1}} P(R_{k-1} = n-1 | T_{k-1}) \prod_{i=1}^{k-1} P(t_i|s^*_i) \Bigg)$$

Next we proceed to drop the first summand since it is not a function of s_k (i.e., it has no influence in determining s^*_k):

$$= \arg\max_{s_k} \sum_t P(t|\mathbf{q}) P(t_k = t | s_k) P(R_{k-1} = n-1 | S^*_{k-1}) \quad (2)$$

By similar reasoning, we can derive that the last probability needed in (2) is recursively defined as $P(R_k = n | S_k, t) =$

$$\begin{cases} n \geq 1, k > 1: & (1 - P(t_k = t|s_k)) P(R_{k-1} = n | S_{k-1}, t) \\ & + P(t_k = t | s_k) P(R_{k-1} = n-1 | S_{k-1}, t) \\ n = 0, k > 1: & (1 - P(t_k = t|s_k)) P(R_{k-1} = 0 | S_{k-1}, t) \\ n = 1, k = 1: & P(t_1 = t | s_1) \\ n = 0, k = 1: & 1 - P(t_1 = t | s_1) \end{cases}$$

We can now rewrite (2) by unrolling its recursive definition. For expected n-call@k where $n \leq k/2$ (a symmetrical result holds for $k/2 < n \leq k$), the explicit unrolled objective is

$$s^*_k = \arg\max_{s_k} \sum_t \Bigg(P(t|\mathbf{q})\, P(t_k = t|s_k) \cdot \sum_{j_1, \ldots, j_{n-1}} \prod_{l \in \{j_1, \ldots, j_{n-1}\}} P(t_l = t | s^*_l) \prod_{\substack{i=1 \\ i \notin \{j_1, \ldots, j_{n-1}\}}}^{k-1} (1 - P(t_i = t | s^*_i)) \Bigg) \quad (3)$$

where $j_1, \ldots, j_{n-1} \in \{1, \ldots, k-1\}$ satisfy that $j_i < j_{i+1}$ (i.e., an ordered permutation of $n-1$ result set indices).

[1] We present a derivation summary; A full derivation may be found in an online appendix at the authors' web pages.

If we assume each document covers a single subtopic of the query (e.g., a subtopic represents an intent of an ambiguous query) then we can assume that $\forall i\ P(t_i|s_i) \in \{0, 1\}$ and $P(t|\mathbf{q}) \in \{0, 1\}$. This allows us to convert a $\prod$ to a max

$$\prod_{\substack{i=1 \\ i \notin \{j_1, \ldots, j_{n-1}\}}}^{k-1} (1 - P(t_i = t|s^*_i)) = 1 - \Bigg(1 - \prod_{\substack{i=1 \\ i \notin \{j_1, \ldots, j_{n-1}\}}}^{k-1} (1 - P(t_i = t | s^*_i)) \Bigg)$$
$$= 1 - \Big(\max_{\substack{i \in [1, k-1] \\ i \notin \{j_1, \ldots, j_{n-1}\}}} P(t_i = t | s^*_i) \Big)$$

and by substituting this into (3) and distributing, we get

$$= \arg\max_{s_k} \sum_t \Bigg(P(t|\mathbf{q}) P(t_k = t|s_k) \sum_{j_1, \ldots, j_{n-1}} \prod_{l \in \{j_1, \ldots, j_{n-1}\}} P(t_l = t | s^*_l) - P(t|\mathbf{q}) P(t_k = t|s_k) \sum_{j_1, \ldots, j_{n-1}} \prod_{l \in \{j_1, \ldots, j_{n-1}\}} P(t_l = t|s^*_l) \max_{\substack{i \in [1, k-1] \\ i \notin \{j_1, \ldots, j_{n-1}\}}} P(t_i = t|s^*_i) \Bigg).$$

Assuming m selected documents S^*_{k-1} are relevant then the top term (specifically $\prod_l$) is non-zero $\binom{m}{n-1}$ times. For the bottom term, it takes $n-1$ relevant S^*_{k-1} to satisfy its $\prod_l$, and one additional relevant document to satisfy the $\max_i$ making it non-zero $\binom{m}{n}$ times. Factoring out the max element from the bottom and pushing the $\sum_t$ inwards (all legal due to the $\{0, 1\}$ subtopic probability assumption) we get

$$= \arg\max_{s_k} \binom{m}{n-1} \underbrace{\sum_t P(t|\mathbf{q}) P(t_k = t|s_k)}_{\text{relevance: } \mathrm{Sim}_1(s_k, \mathbf{q})} - \binom{m}{n} \underbrace{\max_{s_i \in S^*_{k-1}} \sum_t P(t_i = t|s_i) P(t|\mathbf{q}) P(t_k = t|s_k)}_{\text{diversity: } \mathrm{Sim}_2(s_k, s_i, \mathbf{q})}.$$

From here we can normalize by $\binom{m}{n-1} + \binom{m}{n} = \binom{m+1}{n}$ (Pascal's rule), leading to fortuitous cancellations and the result:

$$= \arg\max_{s_k} \frac{n}{m+1} \mathrm{Sim}_1(s_k, \mathbf{q}) - \frac{m-n+1}{m+1} \max_{s_i \in S^*_{k-1}} \mathrm{Sim}_2(s_k, s_i, \mathbf{q})$$

Comparing to MMR in (1), we can clearly see that $\lambda = \frac{n}{m+1}$. Assuming $m \approx n$ since Exp-n-Call@k optimizes for the case where n relevant documents are selected, then $\lambda = \frac{n}{n+1}$.

Acknowledgements

NICTA is funded by the Australian Government via the Dept. of Broadband, Comm. and the Digital Economy and the Australian Research Council through the ICT Centre of Excellence program.

4. REFERENCES

[1] J. Carbonell and J. Goldstein. The use of MMR, diversity-based reranking for reording documents and producing summaries. In *SIGIR-98*. ACM, 1998.

[2] H. Chen and D. R. Karger. Less is more: Probabilistic models for retrieving fewer relevant documents. In *SIGIR-06*. ACM, 2006.

[3] S. Sanner, S. Guo, T. Graepel, S. Kharazmi, and S. Karimi. Diverse retrieval via greedy optimization of expected 1-call@k in a latent subtopic relevance model. In *CIKM-11*. ACM, 2011.

[4] J. Wang and J. Zhu. Portfolio theory of information retrieval. In *SIGIR-09*. ACM, 2009.

[5] C. Zhai, W. W. Cohen, and J. Lafferty. Beyond independent relevance: Methods and evaluation metrics for subtopic retrieval. In *SIGIR-03*. ACM, 2003.

On Real-time Ad-hoc Retrieval Evaluation

Stephen E. Robertson
Microsoft Research
7 JJ Thomson Avenue
Cambridge CB3 0FB, UK
stephenerobertson@hotmail.co.uk

Evangelos Kanoulas *
Information School
University of Sheffield
Sheffield, UK
ekanoulas@gmail.com

ABSTRACT

Lab-based evaluations typically assess the quality of a retrieval system with respect to its ability to retrieve documents that are relevant to the information need of an end user. In a real-time search task however users not only wish to retrieve the most relevant items but the most recent as well. The current evaluation framework is not adequate to assess the ability of a system to retrieve both recent and relevant items, and the one proposed in the recent TREC Microblog Track has certain flaws that quickly became apparent to the organizers. In this poster, we redefine the experiment for a real-time ad-hoc search task, by setting new submission requirements for the submitted systems/runs, proposing metrics to be used in evaluating the submissions, and suggesting a pooling strategy to be used to gather relevance judgments towards the computation of the described metrics. The proposed task can indeed assess the quality of a retrieval system with regard to retrieving both relevant and timely information.

Categories and Subject Descriptors

H.3.4 [**Information Storage and Retrieval**]: Systems and Software—*Performance Evaluation*

General Terms

Experimentation, Measurement

Keywords

evaluation, measures, pooling, real-time retrieval, microblog

1. INTRODUCTION

Lab-based evaluations typically assess the quality of a retrieval system with respect to its ability to retrieve documents that are relevant to the information need of an end user. There are retrieval tasks however for which relevance is only one of the dimensions on which we want to evaluate retrieval systems. In particular, we consider a real-time ad-hoc retrieval task, where the user wishes to retrieve information that is not only relevant, but also recent – the focus of the recent TREC Microblog Track [1]. The corpus for the task was composed of about 16 million tweets with time-stamps. Information needs were represented by queries at specific time-stamps. Systems were expected to respond to each query with the most recent relevant tweets, prior to the query time.

Evaluating a system over a real-time ad-hoc task clearly requires a measure that accounts both for relevance and recency. Instead of inventing a new measure the TREC Microblog Track chose to use traditional set-based evaluation measures on a time-ordered ranked list of the submitted by participants ranked lists of tweets/runs. Each participant was asked to submit a set of up to 1000 tweets, submitted tweets were then ordered by reverse time, the top 30 were pooled, handed to NIST assessors to be assessed with respect to relevance ("interestingness"), and each system was then evaluated by precision@30 over these 30 time-ordered tweets.

What became immediately apparent was that such an experiment could not properly measure the effectiveness of a system to provide both timely and relevant tweets. A system could achieve optimal performance by returning just 30 relevant tweets, ignoring the time dimension. Hence, the optimal strategy for each run was to return a set of the top-30 tweets ordered by a probability (score) of relevance, even if these were not the most recent relevant tweets. An intuitive explanation of the flaw in this evaluation experiment is that runs were not evaluated against a single global target set of tweets (the most relevant, recent tweets) and thus the evaluation measure was only aware of the relevant and non-relevant tweets returned by each individual system separately. The aim of this poster is to correct this flaw by redefining a real-time ad-hoc task experiment, in a form suitable for the Microblog track, in which systems are evaluated for their ability to return both relevant and timely information.

2. REAL-TIME AD-HOC TASK

In what follows we define the following elements of the task:

- general description of the task
- submission requirements
- metric(s)
- pooling/assessment strategy

As in the Microblog Track [1] we assume that there is an effective timeline for items, and queries are time-specific.

*We gratefully acknowledge the support provided by the European Commission grant FP7-PEOPLE-2009-IIF-254562.

SIGIR'12, August 12–16, 2012, Portland, Oregon, USA.
ACM 978-1-4503-1472-5/12/08.

To simplify the evaluation of runs we assume that judgments are binary, i.e. items are either relevant or not relevant to a query. We briefly discuss graded relevance in Section 3 that follows.

General description of the task: The aim for each system is to retrieve the 30 most recent relevant items.

Submission requirements: Participants will need to submit (a) a set of not more than 30 items; (b) a ranked list of 1000 top previous items by relevance only. Evaluation will be based on the set only (see Metrics below), but the ranked list will be used in constructing the assessment pools (see pooling/assessment strategy below).

Metric(s): For each topic, we define a single Target Set, consisting of the 30 most recent relevant items known. Basic metrics will be recall and precision in relation to the target set. Further metrics might include e.g. F1. Defining a single target set informs the metrics of the optimal behaviour of a retrieval system, which is to retrieve the most recent 30 relevant items, allows the observation of suboptimal behaviour of submitted systems when the items they return in the submitted set are either irrelevant or too old, and makes scores comparable across all submitted runs.

Pooling/assessment strategy: The pooling process is iterative rather than one-off – involving further additions to pools after initial items have been judged. The goal of the pooling process is to identify the items in the target set, that is the 30 relevant recent items. The iterative process follows:

1. Pool all sets of the 30 items submitted, together with the top 1 ranked item from all the ranked lists. Judging all sets avoids having holes in the sets of the 30 items over which runs are evaluated and thus enforces fairness across all submissions.
2. Obtain judgments for the current pool.
3. Identify the 30 most recent relevant items so far in the pool and set a time window from the time of the 30th most recent to the time of the query. This time window allows pruning of the space of items to be judged. Any item with a time stamp out of this time frame, i.e. older than the 30th most recent relevant item, does not need to be judged for relevance.
4. Take the next item from each result list which falls within the window, add it to the pool, judge unjudged documents. If additional relevant documents are found, iterate.

As mentioned this method guarantees to evaluate all submissions fairly according to the metric, and also provides good material for participants to do diagnostic work on their mixture of relevance and time-like criteria for retrieval. For future use, it identifies what is likely to be a good approximation to the true target set, and also labels for relevance a reasonable number of older items, again helpful for diagnostic work.

3. DISCUSSION

So far we have only considered binary relevance assessments; often multiple grades are used. In the Microblog Track tweets were judged as non-relevant, relevant, or vital (highly relevant) [1]. A simple way to account for graded relevance in the proposed framework is to define the target set to contain not only the 30 most recent relevant items but also all previous vital items known. This is a rather crude balance between the importance of relevance and time but it allows the measurement process to remain quite simple.

Note that the current set up does not prohibit a future definition of a measure that combines relevance and time through some gain function for instance. Under such a development, the submission requirements, as described here, should remain similar with participants submitting an auxiliary list of items ranked by relevance only to allow the construction of a target set/ranking. Further, pruning of the judgment space during pooling should also be possible in a way similar to the one described in the proposal above.

Further it should be also possible to consider giving extra weight to the retrieval of all vital items, but that complicates the metrics somewhat and a discussion on this is out of the scope of the current poster. An extension of set measures to graded relevance can be found in Robertson et al. [2].

Another point regarding the proposed experiment is that one could continue adding items to the pool even if no relevant documents are found for a small number of iterations, so that any recent relevant items that appear low in the ranked list by all systems gets a chance to be pooled. The number of iterations that would be required is a point of further investigation on the implementation of the proposed experiment and out of the scope of this poster.

Last, note also that set retrieval typically requires ranking and thresholding; thresholding is known to be hard. However, for the task as defined, participants will be able to get away with thresholding at fixed rank (20 or 25 or 30) without disastrously damaging effectiveness. There will be room for more sophisticated thresholding methods to be used.

4. CONCLUSION

In this poster we proposed a experiment to test the effectiveness of retrieval systems towards returning both relevant and timely information. We discussed a rather simple case, where relevance is binary and the only measures considered are set measures. Extensions of the proposed experiment for graded relevance, ranking measures are possible and follow the general principles of the proposed framework with somewhat more complex details on the implementation side. The proposed framework resolves the flaw of the current evaluation framework used by the TREC Microblog Track.

5. REFERENCES

[1] Craig Macdonald, Iadh Ounis, Jimmy Lin, Abdur Choudhury, and Ian Soboroff. TREC Microblog Track. `https://sites.google.com/site/microblogtrack/`, 2011.

[2] Stephen E. Robertson, Evangelos Kanoulas, and Emine Yilmaz. Extending average precision to graded relevance judgments. In *SIGIR '10: Proceeding of the 33rd international ACM SIGIR conference on Research and development in information retrieval*, pages 603–610, New York, NY, USA, 2010. ACM.

Opinion Summarisation through Sentence Extraction: an Investigation with Movie Reviews

Marco Bonzanini, Miguel Martinez-Alvarez and Thomas Roelleke
Queen Mary University of London
{marcob,miguel,thor}@eecs.qmul.ac.uk

ABSTRACT

In on-line reviews, authors often use a short passage to describe the overall feeling about a product or a service. A review as a whole can mention many details not in line with the overall feeling, so capturing this key passage is important to understand the overall sentiment of the review. This paper investigates the use of extractive summarisation in the context of sentiment classification. The aim is to find the summary sentence, or the short passage, which gives the overall sentiment of the review, filtering out potential noisy information. Experiments on a movie review data-set show that subjectivity detection plays a central role in building summaries for sentiment classification. Subjective extracts carry the same polarity of the full text reviews, while statistical and positional approaches are not able to capture this aspect.

Categories and Subject Descriptors

H.4.m [**Information Systems Applications**]: Miscellaneous

General Terms

Algorithms, Experimentation

Keywords

Summarisation, Sentiment Classification, Opinion Mining

1. INTRODUCTION

New interest in the area of Sentiment Analysis is pushed by the popularity of on-line resources, which allow users to review products and services. One of the main tasks in this field is the classification of documents according to the overall polarity, i.e. either positive or negative. A common behaviour among reviewers is to summarise the overall sentiment of the review in a short passage, or even in a single sentence. However, the rest of the review can express different feelings from the overall judgement. Moreover, often a review contains sentences which do not provide any information about opinions, i.e. they are not subjective. This is the case of movie reviews, where a short picture of the plot can be given to open the review, without commenting on it. Previous work has shown how the detection of subjective sentences can improve the sentiment classification [3].

This poster investigates how summarisation techniques can be applied in the context of sentiment classification of on-line reviews. More specifically, the aim is to capture the summary passage, i.e. the short passage which gives the overall sentiment of the review. From the user's perspective, the advantage of having a summarised review consists in a reduced effort to understand the message of the document, given that the key information is preserved. Traditional summarisation techniques can be applied for this task, although a more opinion-oriented approach is needed, since the goal is not to better describe the topic of the review in a single sentence, but to capture its overall polarity. In order to verify whether the summarisation task preserves the information about the sentiment of reviews, text classification is performed on the original documents and on the produced summaries.

The contributions of this work are two-fold: firstly, we show how the summaries based on subjectivity well represent the polarity of the full-text review; secondly, we investigate different techniques for identifying the key passage of a review with respect to polarity. Experiments on a movie review data-set show the importance of subjectivity detection for polarity classification.

SIGIR'12, August 12–16, 2012, Portland, Oregon, USA.
ACM 978-1-4503-1472-5/12/08.

2. EXTRACTIVE SUMMARISATION

Different sentence selection techniques can be applied to produce various kinds of extractive summaries. This section outlines the different approaches taken into account for the experimental study.

2.1 Luhn's Approach

Firstly, the traditional Luhn's approach [1] is used to score the sentences according to their significance. The top-n sentences are selected to create the summary. The results for this approach are labelled as *Luhn-n*, where n is the number of sentence used to create the summary. The significance score of a sentence is based on clustering of sentence tokens using a distance threshold (5 is the distance used in this poster). The significant words are chosen according to their frequency, i.e. the terms with higher tf, excluding stop words, are considered significant. The significance score for a sentence will be the maximum score for any of its clusters.

2.2 Position-based Approaches

A second family of summarisers is built on top of an empirical observation: often reviewers tend to summarise their overall feeling in a sentence or in a short paragraph, placed either at the beginning or at the end of the review. In this case, a summary can be created simply selecting the n opening, or closing, sentences. Results for these approaches are labelled as *First-n* and *Last-n*, respectively.

2.3 Subjectivity Detection

The previous approaches do not consider the subjective nature of the reviews. To overcome this issue, a classifier can be used to identify and filter subjective sentences. A specific data-set, described in Section 3, is used to train the classifier. Filtering out the objective sentences and aggregating only the subjective ones can already be seen as a summarisation approach. The average compression rate of the data under analysis is around 60%. Results for this approach are labelled as *Subjective-Full*.

2.4 Summarising Subjective Extracts

One of the first two approaches can be applied to subjective extracts, in order to increase the compression rate. In the results, this family of approaches is labelled as follows: *Subjective-Luhn-n* for the summaries produced using Luhn's approach on the subjective sentences, *Subjective-First-n* and *Subjective-Last-n* for the summaries based on the subjective sentence positions.

3. EXPERIMENTAL STUDY

The evaluation of summarisation systems is a research issue in itself [2]. The purpose of this work is observing how summarisation preserves the opinion of a document, so the evaluation is performed w.r.t. the polarity classification, i.e. a good summary is ideally able to carry the same polarity of the full document. Full text reviews and summaries are classified according to their overall polarity. Traditional machine learning approaches can be applied for this classification task. Specifically, Naive Bayes (NB) and Support Vector Machine (SVM) classifiers are considered, using unigram-presence as features. The feature selection for NB is based on document frequency, being a commonly used selection strategy.

For the subjectivity detection, a data-set of subjective and objective sentences is used to train the classifiers [3]. This data-set contains 5000 subjective sentences, taken from RottenTomatoes[1] snippets, and 5000 objective sentences, taken from IMDb[2] plots. The classifiers can be considered reliable enough for the subjectivity detection task which leads to the generation of subjective extracts (micro-average F_1 results on this data-set, with a five-folding cross validation, are 88.85 for NB and 88.68 for SVM).

The sentiment classification has been evaluated on a different movie review data-set firstly used in [3], containing reviews taken from IMDb and annotated as positive or negative. The data-set contains 2000 documents, evenly distributed between the two classes. Table 1 reports the results of the micro-averaged F_1 scores [4] on the review data-set. The macro-averaged results are very similar to the micro-averaged ones, given the data-set is well balanced.

Table 1: Micro-averaged F_1 results of sentiment classification

	NB	SVM
Full Review	83.31	87.10
Luhn-1	70.12	70.28
Luhn-3	75.47	74.96
First-1	68.94	68.82
Last-1	70.61	70.49
First-3	70.81	70.43
Last-3	75.58	76.57
Subjective-Full	84.61	86.82
Subjective-Luhn-1	71.02	70.50
Subjective-Luhn-3	74.92	74.91
Subjective-First-1	69.33	68.90
Subjective-Last-1	70.90	71.15
Subjective-First-3	71.12	71.07
Subjective-Last-3	75.49	76.26

[1] http://www.rottentomatoes.com
[2] http://www.imdb.com

4. DISCUSSION AND CONCLUSION

The first observation is that statistical and positional summarisation approaches do not provide any improvement to the sentiment classification results. In fact, the performances are substantially worse for both NB and SVM. The explanation behind this behaviour is that these approaches are not explicitly opinion-oriented, so they are not able to capture the sentiment behind a review. The quality of sentiment classification for subjective extracts is instead in line with the full review classification. Subjective extracts through NB achieves a 1.5% better result compared to the classification of full text. On the SVM side, the classification of subjective extracts is performed slightly worse than the full text. In other words, the subjectivity detection step preserves the most important information about polarity, and this aspect is captured by both classifiers. In order to further analyse this finding, experiments on objective extracts classification have been also performed. The objective sentences have been aggregated, building the counterparts of the subjective extracts. The micro-averaged F_1 values for the objective extracts classification were below 75% for both classifiers, hence significantly worse than both the full review and subjective extract classification. When further summarisation is performed on the subjective extracts, the results drop again. In Table 1, we can observe a similar behaviour between summaries created from the full text and summaries created from the subjective extracts. As further analysis, we also examine the classification of the summaries with respect to the full documents. In other words, we verify if a full text and its respective summary are classified under the same label, without considering whether this is the correct answer or not. In 91% of the cases, the subjective summaries are assigned to the same label of the correspondent full text. For all the other summarisation approaches, this value drops below 80%, and in some cases below 70%. This is further evidence of the connection between subjectivity and polarity.

Sentence extraction techniques purely based on statistical or positional approaches do not capture the subjectivity of a review, and hence are inadequate to summarise the sentiment of the document. On the contrary, subjectivity detection produces results which are comparable to the full text classification. Further summarisation on top of subjectivity detection, again fails to capture the polarity of documents, as more opinion-oriented approaches are needed. Showing a subjective extract instead of the full text, a potential user would need to read about 60% of a review, or even less, in order to understand its polarity.

5. REFERENCES

[1] H.P. Luhn. The automatic creation of literature abstracts. *IBM Journal of research and development*, 2(2):159–165, 1958.

[2] A. Nenkova and K. McKeown. Automatic summarization. *Foundations and Trends in Information Retrieval*, 5(2-3):103–233, 2011.

[3] B. Pang and L. Lee. A sentimental education: Sentiment analysis using subjectivity summarization based on minimum cuts. In *Proceedings of the 42nd Annual Meeting on Association for Computational Linguistics*, pages 271–278. Association for Computational Linguistics, 2004.

[4] Fabrizio Sebastiani. Machine learning in automated text categorization. *ACM Comput. Surv.*, 34(1):1–47, 2002.

Optimizing parameters of the Expected Reciprocal Rank

Yury Logachev, Pavel Serdyukov
Yandex
Leo Tolstoy st. 16, Moscow, Russia
ylogachev@yandex-team.ru, pavser@yandex-team.ru

ABSTRACT

Most popular IR metrics are parameterized. Usually parameters of these metrics are chosen on the basis of general considerations and not adjusted by experiments with real users. Particularly, the parameters of the Expected Reciprocal Rank measure are the normalized parameters of the DCG metric, and the latter are chosen in an ad-hoc manner. We suggest an approach for adjusting parameters of the ERR metric that allows to reach maximum agreement with the real users behavior. More exactly, we optimized the parameters by maximizing Pearson weighted correlation between ERR and several online click metrics. For each click metric we managed to find the parameters of ERR that result into its higher correlation with the given online click metric.

Categories and Subject Descriptors

H.3.3 [**Information Storage and Retrieval**]: Information Search and Retrieval

General Terms

Metrics, Experimentation, Performance

Keywords

information retrieval measures, evaluation

1. INTRODUCTION

One of the most challenging problems in the field of Web Search is choosing an appropriate metric for learning and evaluating retrieval algorithms. Chapelle et al. suggested the Expected Reciprocal Rank (ERR) metric [1], which received wide recognition in the community. They calculated a correlation of the ERR and other IR measures with online click metrics to prove significance of the ERR metric. Chapelle et al. discovered that correlation of the ERR (and other measures) with click metrics varies for different types of queries (Navigational vs. Non-navigational, queries of various lengths) and different markets. It implies that for different tasks and different purposes different measures (or different parameters of the same measure) should be used. We suppose that one way to set a purpose of an IR system is to choose the target click-metric. For example, if we want our users not to visit a competitor's search engine, then abandonment rate is an adequate click metric. If the focus is on the fast satisfaction of the users, then the position of the first click is an appropriate metric.

The ERR metric has a set of parameters. Each parameter (weight) means the probability of getting completely satisfied after reaching a document with a certain relevance grade. Chapelle et al. suggested a method of setting these parameters using the gain parameters of the DCG metric: $R(g) = \frac{2^g-1}{2^{g_{max}}}$ where $g \in \{0, \ldots, g_{max}\}$ are the relevance grades. Thereby, commonly used parameters of the ERR metric for a 5-grade scheme with grades *Perfect*, *Excellent*, *Good*, *Fair*, *Bad* are respectively $\approx 0.94, 0.44, 0.19, 0.06, 0$. The same set of parameters (also for a 5-grades scheme) was used at TREC 2010/2011 [2] and de facto became a standard. We argue that these parameters should be adjusted more accurately and depend on the purpose (target click-metric) and market. Thus we suggest a method for optimizing these parameters by maximizing Pearson correlation between ERR and a target online click metric.

2. PARAMETERS OPTIMIZATION

We followed Chapelle et al. and optimized weighted Pearson correlation. Suppose that there are N configurations (a configuration is a query and an ordered set of results). For the i-th configuration, let x_i be the value of ERR metric, y_i the value of the click metric, and n_i the number of times this configuration is present in the data set. Then, the weighted correlation is computed as following:

$$C(x, y, n) = \sum_{i=1}^{N} \frac{n_i(x_i - m_x)(y_i - m_y)}{\sqrt{\sum_{i=1}^{N} n_i(x_i - m_x)^2}\sqrt{\sum_{i=1}^{N} n_i(y_i - m_y)^2}},$$

where m_x and m_y are the weighted averages:

$$m_x = \frac{1}{\sum_{i=1}^{N} n_i} \sum_{i=1}^{N} n_i x_i, m_y = \frac{1}{\sum_{i=1}^{N} n_i} \sum_{i=1}^{N} n_i y_i.$$

x_i as the value of ERR metric may be considered as a function of five variables: $x_i = x_i(P, E, G, F, B)$, where $params = (P, E, G, F, B)$ corresponds to the weights of the

SIGIR'12, August 12–16, 2012, Portland, Oregon, USA.
ACM 978-1-4503-1472-5/12/08.

Target click metric:	MaxRR	MinRR	MeanRR	UCTR	SS	PLC	NDCG-based
Bad	0.	0.01	0.	0.02	0.	0.0	0.0
Fair	0.21	0.21	0.20	0.10	0.03	0.20	0.06
Good	0.21	0.22	0.20	0.29	0.38	0.21	0.19
Excellent	0.26	0.30	0.28	0.29	0.38	0.27	0.44
Perfect	0.98	0.94	0.97	1.0	0.93	0.97	0.94
C_{opt}	**0.83**	**0.89**	**0.89**	**0.21**	**0.44**	**0.86**	
C_{old}	0.82	0.88	0.86	0.17	0.34	0.84	

Table 1: Results of the experiment. In each column optimal parameters for the given metric are presented. In C_{opt} and C_{old} rows presented values of correlation of target click metric with ERR with optimized and original parameters respectively.

Perfect, Excellent, Good, Fair, Bad documents respectively. Thus $C(x, y, n)$ may be considered as $C_{x,y,n}(params)$. So the optimization problem is formulated as following:

$$Q(params) \to \max_{params} \text{ subject to } P, E, G, F, B \in [0; 1],$$

where

$$Q = C_{x,y,n}(params) - \sum_{i=0}^{3} a \cdot 10^{k \cdot (params[i+1] - params[i])}.$$

We added an extra summand to the target function Q to encourage the following essential requirement:

$$P \geq E \geq G \geq F \geq B.$$

This requirement follows from the nature of the parameters (P, E, G, F, B). Parameters $a = 100, k = 400$ were selected experimentally to meet the latter requirement.

Any click metric may be used to optimize the correlation with. We examined the same 6 metrics as Chapelle et al.: MinRR, MaxRR, MeanRR, UCTR, SS and PLC [1] (Section 6.2).

2.1 Data collection.

We used query logs of a popular search engine for three months period. Queries generated by search bots were filtered using a proprietary bot filtering algorithm. We followed Chapelle et al. and considered only one-query sessions (60 minutes period was used to delimit sessions), that did not have clicks on additional SERP elements (such as ads). We sampled random 13,755 unique queries and filtered such of them for which click rate on additional SERP elements is higher than 0.10. We were guided by the following reasons: if the CTR on the additional elements is high, then the cases with no such clicks (as mentioned we consider only such queries) are probably outliers. We then asked our judges to assess all result documents (with the common 5-grade system) that were actually shown to the users. As a result we got 10,134 queries (32,239 configurations) in 9,500,687 search sessions.

2.2 Optimization method.

For each configuration from the data set the value of the target click metric y_i was calculated as the average over all the sessions belonging to the given configuration. Next, for each configuration the ERR@10 measure was calculated and stored as the polynomial $x_i(params)$. For example, if the i-th configuration looks like < *Perfect, Good, Bad* > (we take 3 documents instead of the 10 in this example for the simplicity) then according to the definition of ERR:

$$x_i(params) = P + \frac{1}{2}(1 - P)G + \frac{1}{3}(1 - P)(1 - G)B.$$

Thus each configuration specifies the pair $(x_i(params), y_i)$. That allows to calculate $Q(params)$ as a function of $params$. Finally that function was optimized by the truncated Newton algorithm (SciPy.optimize package [1] was used). The results are presented in Table 1.

3. DISCUSSION AND CONCLUSION

We described a method of tuning parameters of the ERR measure. For each target click metric the correlation of ERR with new parameters is higher. The most noticeable improvement was obtained for the SS (Search Success) click metric. The reason is probably that this metric takes less noisy clicks into account and consequently it is easier to optimize correlation with it.

We demonstrated that for different purposes (i.e. target click metric) there are different optimal parameters of the ERR measure. It is clear that the parameters that we obtained in the experiment are not universal and depend on the market and other specifics of the search engine under study. However, we believe that it is worthwhile to tune them in each case, if online click metrics are assumed to be indicators of search engine user satisfaction. In the future, we plan to experiment with other metrics and markets, different types of queries. Besides, we are going to develop a method to optimize correlation with several click metrics simultaneously.

4. REFERENCES

[1] O. Chapelle, D. Metlzer, Y. Zhang, and P. Grinspan. Expected reciprocal rank for graded relevance. CIKM '09, 2009.

[2] C. L. A. Clarke, N. Craswell, N. Craswell, and G. V. Cormack. Overview of the trec 2010 web track. TREC '10, 2010.

[1] docs.scipy.org/doc/scipy/reference/tutorial/optimize.html

Ousting Ivory Tower Research: Towards a Web Framework for Providing Experiments as a Service

Tim Gollub, Benno Stein, Steven Burrows
Bauhaus-Universität Weimar
99421 Weimar, Germany
<first name>.<last name>@uni-weimar.de

ABSTRACT

With its close ties to the Web, the IR community is destined to leverage the dissemination and collaboration capabilities that the Web provides today. Especially with the advent of the software as a service principle, an IR community is conceivable that publishes experiments executable by anyone over the Web. A review of recent SIGIR papers shows that we are far away from this vision of collaboration. The benefits of publishing IR experiments as a service are striking for the community as a whole, and include potential to boost research profiles and reputation. However, the additional work must be kept to a minimum and sensitive data must be kept private for this paradigm to become an accepted practice. To foster experiments as a service in IR, we present a Web framework for experiments that addresses the outlined challenges and possesses a unique set of compelling features in comparison to existing solutions. We also describe how our reference implementation is already used officially as an evaluation platform for an established international plagiarism detection competition.

Categories and Subject Descriptors: H.5.3 [Information Systems]: Information Interfaces and Presentation—Group and Organization Interfaces
Keywords: Open Evaluation, Experiment Management, Result Dissemination

1. MOTIVATION AND SURVEY

Within IR research, the integration of previous work in one's experiments is significantly simplified if the data and software assets are published together with the papers. In this respect, Armstrong et al. [1] pointed out the verification problems that arise if research assets are not streamlined with the latest publications. In our view, the most convenient way to enhance comparability in experiments is to publish experiments as an online service where researchers can verify experimental results and explore alternate parameter settings.

To explore how IR research is published today, we reviewed all 108 full papers from the SIGIR 2011 proceedings concerning experiment assets. The results in Figure 1 show the extent to which the authors published their *data*, their *software*, and whether the experiments were hosted as a *service*. All three aspects need to be addressed to make publishing data and software more widespread. The questions we posed when examining the proceedings and our findings are given as follows.

Data. *Are any of the datasets used in the research publicly available?* We observe that 51% of the papers use a publicly available dataset for experiments. In this respect, evaluation initiatives

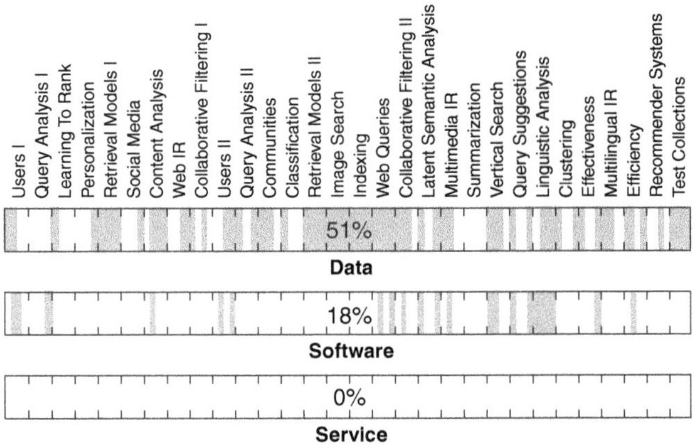

Figure 1: Assessment of the 108 full papers at SIGIR 2011 with respect to the publication of data, software, and experiments hosted as a service. The papers are ordered as they appear in the conference proceedings, and the labels on the horizontal axis denote the 30 sessions. The gray bars denote papers that meet the respective criteria.

such as TREC do a great job in supplying researchers with open datasets. The papers from the Image Search, Indexing, Retrieval Models, Test Collections, and Web Queries sessions all used public datasets. Other datasets such as search engine query logs require *non-disclosure* due to commercial and sensitivity reasons, which accounts for much of the unavailability of data. Correspondingly, only two of eight Query Analysis papers used public datasets, which was second lowest and only ahead of the Summarization papers, where no public datasets were used.

Software. *Are any of the software assets used in the research publicly available?* We observe that 18% of the papers use shared software contributions, and hence publishing software is currently a minority practice in IR research.[1] Only the Linguistic Analysis papers published software with their papers in all cases. One explanation for this low ratio is the *lack of acknowledgment* researchers receive for publishing software. To foster software release, new incentives must be created that turn invested time in developing reusable software into reputation gain for the researchers.

Service. *Are any of the experiments in the research provided as an online service?* We observe that providing experiment software as a service is not practiced at all in the examined papers. The application closest to a web service is the online demonstration of ViewSer [2]. The lack of a *compelling web framework* that researchers can use to easily transform their experiments into a web service is a plausible explanation.

[1] A further 17% of researchers instead published algorithms in their papers as a compromise.

2. PROPOSED FRAMEWORK

Motivated by the observations from the paper study above, we propose the development of an online framework to foster publishable IR experiments. The proposal is based on the needs for local installation, web dissemination, platform independence, result retrieval, and peer to peer collaboration. Our assessment of existing experimentation frameworks with respect to these goals is depicted in Table 1, which shows that none of the systems fully comply.

Table 1: Assessment of existing experimentation frameworks with respect to our five proposed design goals.

Tool	URL	Domain	1	2	3	4	5
evaluatIR	1	IR	×	✓	✓	✓	×
expDB	2	ML	×	×	×	✓	×
MLComp	3	ML	×	✓	×	✓	×
myExperiment	4	any	×	✓	✓	✓	×
NEMA	5	IR	×	✓	×	✓	×
TunedIT	6	ML, DM	✓	✓	×	✓	×
Yahoo Pipes	7	Web	×	✓	×	×	×

[1] http://www.evaluatir.org/
[2] http://expdb.cs.kuleuven.be/expdb/
[3] http://www.mlcomp.org/
[4] http://www.myexperiment.org/
[5] http://www.music-ir.org/
[6] http://www.tunedit.org/
[7] http://pipes.yahoo.com/

1. *Local Instantiation.* If data must be kept confidential, the framework must be able to reside with the data, hence the framework must be locally installable. Unlike centralized experiment platforms like MLComp and myExperiment, local instantiation allows experiments on sensitive data to be published as a service from a local host. External researchers can then use the service for comparison and evaluation of their own research hypotheses, whilst the experiment provider is in full control of the experiment resources.

2. *Web Dissemination.* URLs are definitive identifiers for digital resources. If all runs of an experiment are accessible over a unique URL, researchers can conveniently link the results in a paper with the experiment service used to produce them. Especially for standard pre-processing tasks or evaluations on private data, such a web service can become a frequently cited resource. In addition, attention can be attracted to one's work through integration of the service into home pages and blog articles. To address the issue of digital preservation, URLs should encode all information needed to recompute a resource, such as program and input parameter specifications, in case stored data is lost.

3. *Platform Independence.* The sophisticated and varying software and hardware requirements of information retrieval experiments as well as individual coding preferences of software developers render any development constraints imposed by the web framework critical for its success. Ideally, software developers can deploy experiments as a service unconstrained by the utilized operating system, parallelization paradigm, programming language, or data formats. Local instantiation is one key to realize this goal. Furthermore, the web framework must operate as a layer strictly on top of the experiment software and should use, instead of close intra-process communication such as in TunedIT, standard inter-process communication on the POSIX level and the file system to exchange information. This way, any running software can be deployed as a web service without internal modifications.

4. *Result Retrieval.* Especially for computationally expensive retrieval tasks, the maintenance of a public result repository can become a valuable asset of a research group. For example, experiment services that can index datasets with state-of-the-art natural language processing technology have the potential to raise the comparability of retrieval model research to a higher level. For clustering and result diversification research, comparability is enhanced by establishing static snapshots of the search results from major search engines regularly. The persistent storage of experiment results by the web framework is key to achieve this goal. Even if the public release of an experiment service is not desired, the framework is still useful if it assumes responsibility for managing the raw experiment results and making them available across a research team.

5. *Peer to Peer Collaboration.* Consider a scenario where a consortium of service providers become renowned *gatekeepers* for various streams of research, and maintain the community-wide repository of state-of-the-art algorithms, datasets, and experiment results on their web site. The gatekeepers drive the standardization of data formats and can, by utilizing the retrieval facility, stage competitions in a semi-automated fashion. A mechanism for connecting the local framework instances to a network of experimentation nodes has to be provided to achieve this scenario. Note that currently none of the experimentation platforms implements peer to peer collaboration.

3. REFERENCE IMPLEMENTATION

The reference implementation[2] of our proposal has been developed as a RESTful J2EE servlet. This implementation is also the official training and evaluation platform for the detailed comparison task of the PAN 2012 plagiarism detection competition[3] as part of the PAN series [3]. For the training phase, an evaluation service is provided where the participants upload their results and receive the performance score. For the final performance assessment, the participants submit their detection algorithms as executable software on either a Windows 7 or Linux based virtual machine. All submissions are automatically evaluated on the holdout test set with the reference implementation. This method is required since the organizers evaluate the detection approaches using real data that is subject to non-disclosure. The proposed method also allows the runtime of the submitted approaches to be recorded for the first time. The participants also have the possibility to opt-in for a public release of their plagiarism detection software as a service.

4. SUMMARY

In this paper, we proposed a web framework for IR experiments as a service motivated by low trends in sharing data and software in recent IR research. The fundamental design decisions concerning local instantiation, web dissemination, platform independence, result retrieval, and peer to peer collaboration address the specific needs of IR research. A reference implementation has been developed complying with these design rules that has been put to widespread use as part of the PAN competition series in 2012.

References

[1] T. G. Armstrong, A. Moffat, W. Webber, and J. Zobel. Improvements that don't add up: Ad-hoc Retrieval Results since 1998. In CIKM '09, pages 601–610, Hong Kong, China, 2009.

[2] D. Lagun and E. Agichtein. ViewSer: Enabling Large-Scale Remote User Studies of Web Search Examination and Interaction. In SIGIR '11, pages 365–374, Beijing, China, 2011.

[3] M. Potthast. *Technologies for Reusing Text from the Web.* PhD Thesis, Bauhaus-Universität Weimar, Weimar, Germany, 2011.

[2] `http://tira.webis.de`

[3] `http://pan.webis.de`

Parallelizing ListNet Training using Spark

Shilpa Shukla
School of Information
University of Texas at Austin
shilpa@ischool.utexas.edu

Matthew Lease
School of Information
University of Texas at Austin
ml@ischool.utexas.edu

Ambuj Tewari
Dept. of Computer Science
University of Texas at Austin
ambuj@cs.utexas.edu

ABSTRACT

As ever-larger training sets for *learning to rank* are created, scalability of learning has become increasingly important to achieving continuing improvements in ranking accuracy [2]. Exploiting independence of "summation form" computations [3], we show how each iteration in ListNet [1] gradient descent can benefit from parallel execution. We seek to draw the attention of the IR community to use *Spark* [7], a newly introduced distributed cluster computing system, for reducing training time of iterative learning to rank algorithms. Unlike MapReduce [4], Spark is especially suited for iterative and interactive algorithms. Our results show near linear reduction in ListNet training time using Spark on Amazon EC2 clusters.

Categories and Subject Descriptors

H.3.3 [**Information Search and Retrieval**]

Keywords

Learning to Rank, Distributed Computing

1. INTRODUCTION

A potentially easy way to improve learning to rank accuracy is to simply train on more data. The challenge, of course, is scalability [2]. Prior work showed that many machine learning algorithms, such as those based on a "summation form", can be easily parallelized [3]. While summation terms can be independently computed via MapReduce, MapReduce is not well-suited to computing iterative learning algorithms and relatively inefficient for such usage.

Instead, we adopt the recently developed *Spark*[1] cluster computing system [6]. Spark is not only well-suited to such iterative (and interactive) algorithms such as gradient descent, but it runs on existing Hadoop[2] clusters. Spark supports reuse of a working set of data across multiple parallel operations via a distributed memory abstraction called Resilient Distributed Datasets (RDDs), which support parallel, in-memory computations on large clusters while retaining similar fault tolerance as MapReduce to reconstruct a lost partition whenever faults occur. As with Hadoop, the same Spark program can be run *stand-alone* on a single node or distributed on a compute cluster.

ListNet [1] uses gradient descent to minimize the loss between gold relevance scores and predicted scores. Scores can then be sorted to produce document ranking. Suppose there are m queries in the training set. Denoting gold relevance scores and predicted scores on query i by $y^{(i)}$ and $z^{(i)}$ respectively, the total loss is given in "summation form" by:

$$\text{TotalLoss}(w) = \sum_{i=1}^{m} L(y^{(i)}, z^{(i)}) \quad (1)$$

We sum loss over queries in the dataset. ListNet attempts to minimize this loss using gradient descent:

$$w \leftarrow w - \alpha \nabla_w \text{TotalLoss}(w) \quad (2)$$

where α is a *step-size parameter* and $\nabla_w \text{TotalLoss}(w)$ is the gradient of the loss (1) evaluated at w. Since we have:

$$\nabla_w \text{TotalLoss}(w) = \sum_{i=1}^{m} \nabla_w L(y^{(i)}, z^{(i)}) \ . \quad (3)$$

the gradient is in "summation form" and its computation can be parallelized. Optimization of w iteratively alternates between (2) and (3). We are not aware of any existing work that parallelizes ListNet training on commodity clusters. There is some recent work [5] on parallelizing learning to rank for information retrieval but it proposed a new algorithm based on evolutionary computation.

Figure 1 shows our implementation of "vanilla" gradient descent for ListNet using Spark. Using `SparkContext`, we create an RDD by reading in the training set from a file in Amazon S3. This RDD is parsed to populate a datastructure using the `map` transformation, creating a list such that each element in the list consists of a query, documents to be ranked, gold relevance labels, and feature vectors. We then call a `cache` function to advise Spark to keep the RDD in memory of the worker nodes to improve performance. Further, we use a shared variable `gradient` which is a Spark *accumulator*, similar to Hadoop counters. The `gradient` accumulator is used to sum up the contributions to the gradient calculated by all the worker nodes for computing the weight vector in the driver code.

EVALUATION. We use the Microsoft Learning to Rank datasets[3] MSLR-WEB10K and MSLR-WEB30K. There is a trade-off involved in choosing the step size α. If it is too small, the convergence will be slow. If it is too large, we may not have convergence. We tried α values in the

[1] `http://www.spark-project.org`
[2] `http://hadoop.apache.org`
[3] `http://research.microsoft.com/en-us/projects/mslr/`

SIGIR'12, August 12–16, 2012, Portland, Oregon, USA.
ACM 978-1-4503-1472-5/12/08.

```
for (i <- 1 to ITERATIONS) {
          val gradient = sparkContext.accumulator(spark.examples.Vector.zeros(dim))
          val loss = sparkContext.accumulator(0.0)
          for (q <- queries) {
              val expRelScores = q.relScores.map(y => math.exp(beta*y.toDouble))
              val ourScores = q.docFeatures.map(x => w dot x); val expOurScores = ourScores.map(z => math.exp(z))
              val sumExpRelScores = expRelScores.reduce(_ + _); val sumExpOurScores = expOurScores.reduce(_ + _)

              val P_y = expRelScores.map(y => y/sumExpRelScores); val P_z = expOurScores.map(z => z/sumExpOurScores)

              var lossForAQuery = 0.0; var gradientForAQuery = spark.examples.Vector.zeros(dim)
              for (j <- 0 to q.relScores.length-1) {
                  gradientForAQuery += (q.docFeatures(j) * (P_z(j) - P_y(j)))
                  lossForAQuery += -P_y(j) * math.log(P_z(j))
              }
              gradient += gradientForAQuery; loss += lossForAQuery
          }
          w -= gradient.value * stepSize
      }
```

Figure 1: Parallel implementation of ListNet algorithm in Scala (`www.scala-lang.org`) using Spark. The code `for(q <- queries){body}` is equivalent to `queries.foreach(q => {body})`. As `foreach` is a parallel operation in Spark, all queries will be processed in parallel. The variables `gradient` and `loss` are *accumulators* that support only "add" operations and are used to sum values obtained by various worker nodes.

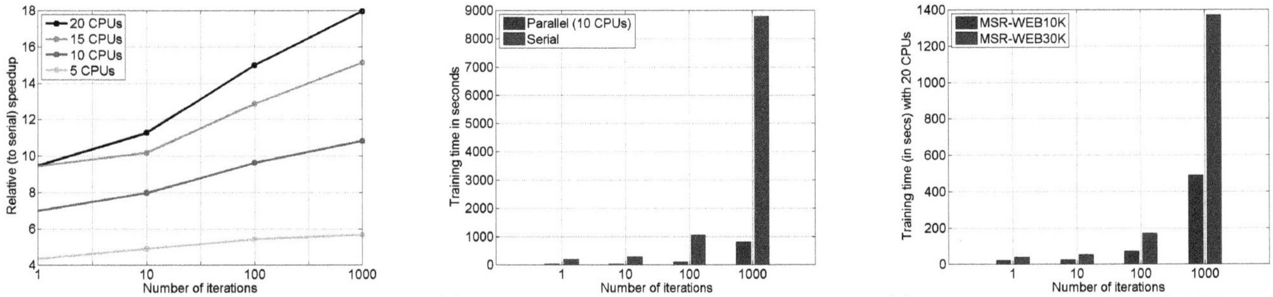

(a) Relative speedups on the 10K training set as more CPUs are used.

(b) Training times for MSLR-WEB10K for serial (1 CPU) vs. parallel (10 CPUs).

(c) Run times on 10K and 30K training sets with 20 CPUs.

Figure 2: Performance improvement in ListNet training time enabled by parallelization.

range 10^{-4} to 10^{-2} and chose the largest one that did not lead to divergence. Standard MSLR dataset partitioning of queries facilitates computation of NDCG accuracy using five-fold cross-validation. Average NDCG@10 ranking accuracy achieved over all five test folds of MSLR-WEB10K is 0.252; greater NDCG accuracy might be achieved by using more sophisticated line search procedures in the gradient descent algorithm shown in Figure 1.

Figure 2(a) shows that as the number of iterations increases, the overhead of using Spark reduces, achieving linear speedup in training time. Figure 2(b) shows that with a parallelism of 10 we achieve roughly 11x speedup on the MSLR-WEB10K dataset as compared to serial implementation. When the degree of parallelism is 1 and the cache is insufficient, some recomputations might become inevitable leading to slightly super-linear speedup. Figure 2(c) shows that training times for MSLR-WEB30K, which has 3x as many queries as MSLR-WEB10K, is actually less than 3x the corresponding times for MSLR-WEB10K, showing greater benefit from parallelization as the training size increases.

2. REFERENCES

[1] Cao, Z., Qin, T., Liu T.-Y., Tsai M.-F., and Li, H.: Learning to Rank: From Pairwise Approach to Listwise Approach. In: ICML '07, (2007).

[2] Chapelle, O., Chang, Y., and Liu, T.-Y.: Future Directions in Learning to Rank. In: JMLR Workshop and Conference Proceedings 14, pp. 91-100, (2011).

[3] Chu, C.T., Kim, S.K., Lin, Y.A., Yu, Y., Bradski, G., Ng, A., and Olukotun, K.: Map-reduce for machine learning on multicore. In: NIPS '06, (2007).

[4] S. Ghemawat and J. Dean.: MapReduce: Simplified data processing on large clusters. In: OSDI '04, pages 137–149 (2004).

[5] Wang, S., Gao, B. J. and Wang, K. and Lauw, H. W.: Parallel learning to rank for information retrieval. In: SIGIR '11, (2011).

[6] Zaharia M., Chowdhury, M., Das, T., Dave, A., Ma J., McCauley, M., Franklin, M., Shenker S. and Stoica, I.: Resilient Distributed Datasets: A Fault-Tolerant Abstraction for In-Memory Cluster Computing. In: NSDI '12 (2012).

[7] Zaharia M., Chowdhury, M., Franklin, M. J., Shenker S. and Stoica, I.: Spark: Cluster Computing with Working Sets. In: HotCloud '10, (2010).

Predicting Lifespans of Popular Tweets in Microblog

Shoubin Kong and Ling Feng
Tsinghua National Laboratory for Information Science and Technology
Dept. of CS&T, Tsinghua University
Beijing, China
kongsb09@mails.tsinghua.edu.cn
fengling@tsinghua.edu.cn

Guozheng Sun and Kan Luo
Tencent, SOSO
Beijing, China
gordonsun@tencent.com
raymondluo@tencent.com

ABSTRACT

In microblog like *Twitter*, popular tweets are usually retweeted by many users. For different tweets, their lifespans (i.e., how long they will stay popular) vary. This paper presents a simple yet effective approach to predict the lifespans of popular tweets based on their static characteristics and dynamic retweeting patterns. For a potentially popular tweet, we generate a time series based on its first-hour retweeting information, and compare it with those of historic tweets of the same author and post time (at the granularity of hour). The top-k historic tweets are identified, whose mean lifespan is estimated as the lifespan of the new tweet. Our experiments on a three-month real data set from Tencent Microblog demonstrate the effectiveness of the approach.

Categories and Subject Descriptors: H.3.3 [Information Storage and Retrieval]: Information Search and Retrieval

General Terms: Algorithms, performance.

Keywords: Tweet, popularity, lifespan, prediction, time series.

1. INTRODUCTION

Nowadays, microblog has become one of the most popular social network services, used by billions of people all over the world. In microblog, popular information usually spreads incredibly rapidly through users' retweeting behaviors. Predicting tweets' popularity is desirable for a large scope of applications like burst events detection, microblog advertisement and real-time recommendation, etc. Such popularity prediction involves two issues: 1) *how popular a tweet will be* (i.e., popularity degree) and 2) *how long a tweet will stay popular* (i.e., popularity lifespan). A bundle of research has recently been carried on to address the first issue. Hong *et al.* [2] predicted tweets' popularity using a classification method. Cui *et al.* [1] proposed an HF-NMF approach to predict how many friends of a user in a Facebook-like social network service would share the same content as the user forwarded.

This paper examines the second issue, aiming to predict lifespans of tweets in microblog. To our knowledge, this is the first attempt in the literature to address the prediction problem of tweets' lifespans. Different from traditional microblog analysis methods, we do not focus on semantic understanding of tweets and social graphs of microblog users. Instead, we explore the use of historic tweets with similar static and dynamic characteristics for prediction. After a tweet is posted, we collect its retweeting amount within the first one hour. If the amount is greater than a certain threshold (say 100), it is regarded as a popular tweet, and we then formulate its retweeting amounts at different time intervals of the first one hour into a time series. We identify a set of historic tweets with the same author and post time (at the granularity of hour), and find from them the top-k tweets with similar retweeting patterns. The mean lifespan of the top-k tweets is computed as the estimated lifespan of the new tweet. We evaluate our method on the real data set from Tencent Microblog, which has the largest number of users (over 200 millions) in China. The experimental results show our approach outperforms the baseline approaches.

2. PROBLEM AND SOLUTION

To predict the lifespans of popular tweets, we first define the notions of popular tweets and lifespan based on the following observations. We investigated a two-month collection of tweets in 2011 and observe that

- after a tweet is posted, its retweeting amount at the beginning hours reflects whether the tweet is popular or not within the next few days.
- almost 100% of tweets are rarely retweeted after 72 hours since they are posted. In other words, the retweeting amount of tweets almost achieves the maximum within the first 72 hours after posted.

Definition 1. A tweet is a **popular tweet** if its retweeting amount within the first 1 hour is no less than a certain threshold.

Definition 2. For a popular tweet, its **lifespan** is the hours that have passed when its retweeting amount reaches 95% of the total retweeting amount. In this study, the retweeting amount in 72 hours is approximately taken as the total retweeting amount.

For a popular tweet, we predict its lifespan based on historic tweets with similar characteristics.

First, candidate tweets with similar static characteristics are identified. Two aspects are considered in the study. 1) *Post time of the tweet.* The time when a tweet is posted impacts its retweeting pattern. For example, the retweeting pattern of a tweet posted at 5 am is different from that posted at 5 pm. 2) *Author of the tweet.* Different microblog users have different followers with diverse characteristics in terms of retweeting behavior, active involvement, follower composition, interest, etc. We gather historic tweets with the same author and post time as the one to be predicted.

Second, top-k historic tweets are found from the candidate tweet set based on the similar dynamic retweeting pattern. To do that, we partition the first one hour into N number of equal time intervals, where $N = 2n + 1$ $(n = 0, 1, \ldots)$. We then count the retweeting amount of the tweet during each time interval. The tweet's retweeting amounts at consecutively different time intervals thus formulate a time series $RTS = \langle RC_1, RC_2, \ldots, RC_N \rangle$.

The distance between two time series is defined as the Euclidian distance:

$$dist(RTS, RTS') = \sqrt{\sum_{m \leq N} (RC_m - RC'_m)^2}.$$

Note that influential time intervals with more contribution to the similarity could be picked up and enforced with different weights here. For instance, we could pick up the first, middle, and last time intervals of RTS, $\langle RC_1, RC_n, RC_{2n+1} \rangle$, to characterize the retweeting trend of the tweet.

Third, after obtaining the top-k similar historic tweets $\{T_1, T_2, \ldots, T_k\}$, their mean lifespan is calculated as the estimated lifespan of the tweet to be predicted:

$$LifeSpan_p(T) = 1/k * \sum_{i=1}^{k} LifeSpan(T_i).$$

3. PERFORMANCE

We evaluated our lifespan prediction approach on the real data set from Tencent Microblog. We collected the retweeting information of all the tweets from October 1, 2011 to December 31, 2011, and filtered out potentially unpopular tweets whose first-hour retweeting amounts are less than 100. We took the tweets of the first two months, total 229666, as the historic tweet set, and the tweets of the third month, total 118471, as the test set.

The **Root Mean Square Error** ($RMSE$) is used as the evaluation metric. The smaller $RMSE$ is, the better the performance is. Let X be the total number of tweets for prediction, $LifeSpan_p(T_i)$ and $LifeSpan_t(T_i)$ be the predicted and real lifespan of the i-th tweet.

$$RMSE = \sqrt{1/X * \sum_{i=1}^{X} (LifeSpan_p(T_i) - LifeSpan_t(T_i))^2}.$$

The value of k is set to 5, because our experiments show that the improvement is not obvious when k is over 5. *fhrc* (**first-hour retweeting count**) is the retweeting amount of a tweet during the first hour after it is posted.

The Q-Q plot [3] of the predicted lifespan and real lifespan is shown in Fig.1. As illustrated in Fig.1, the distribution of predicted lifespan matches that of the real lifespan well, especially when the lifespan lasts for 20-40 hours. Due to the insufficient number of historic tweets and the average method, the predicted value is less than the real one for tweets with over 50-hour lifespan in the data set, which will be considered in our future work.

We further compare our approach with three baseline algorithms, which are kNN (k-Nearest Neighbors), SVR (Support Vector Regression), and LR (Linear Regression). ATR-kNN approach considers identical author, similar post time and retweeting pattern, AR-kNN approach considers identical author and retweeting pattern, and TR-kNN approach considers similar post time and retweeting pattern. Table 1 shows the prediction performance in $RMSE$ by different methods.

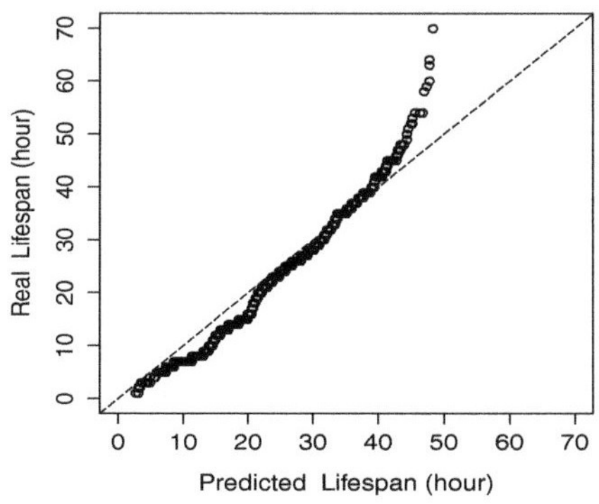

Figure 1: The Q-Q plot of the predicted lifespan and real lifespan for tweets with *fhrc*>=1000

Table 1: Performance Comparison (*RMSE*)

	tweets with *fhrc*>=100	tweets with *fhrc*>=500	tweets with *fhrc*>=1000
ATR-kNN	9.22	7.39	6.60
AR-kNN	9.34	7.79	6.97
TR-kNN	11.60	11.00	10.86
kNN	11.94	11.36	11.22
SVR	13.01	10.71	9.67
LR	29.14	17.99	15.73

From Table 1, three conclusions can be made. 1) The proposed ATR-kNN approach outperforms the baseline algorithms (kNN, SVR and LR), achieving the best performance under different *fhrc* values. 2) The two static characteristics emphasized in our approach do contribute to the prediction performance, and the author requirement plays a more important role than the post time of the tweets. 3) The more the *fhrc* is, the better performance our approach achieves. This demonstrates that our approach is effective to deal with popular tweets.

Acknowledgments

The work is supported by National Natural Science Foundation of China (60773156, 61073004), Chinese Major State Basic Research Development 973 Program (2011CB302203-2), Important National Science & Technology Specific Program (2011ZX01042-001-002-2), and the research fund of Tsinghua-Tencent Joint Laboratory for Internet Innovation Technology.

4. REFERENCES

[1] P. Cui, F. Wang, S. Liu, M. Ou, S. Yang, and L. Sun. Who should share what? item-level social influence prediction for users and posts ranking. In *SIGIR*, pages 185–194, 2011.

[2] L. Hong, O. Dan, and B. Davison. Predicting popular messages in twitter. In *WWW*, pages 57–58, 2011.

[3] M. Wilk and R. Gnanadesikan. Probability plotting methods for the analysis for the analysis of data. *Biometrika*, 55(1):1–17, 1968.

Preliminary Study of Technical Terminology for the Retrieval of Scientific Book Metadata Records

Birger Larsen
Royal School of Library and Information Science, Copenhagen, Denmark
blar@iva.dk

Christina Lioma
Computer Science, University of Copenhagen, Denmark
c.lioma@diku.dk

Ingo Frommholz
Computer Science and Technology, University of Bedfordshire U.K.
ingo.frommholz@beds.ac.uk

Hinrich Schütze
Institute for Natural Language Processing, University of Stuttgart, Germany

ABSTRACT

Books only represented by brief metadata (*book records*) are particularly hard to retrieve. One way of improving their retrieval is by extracting retrieval enhancing features from them. This work focusses on scientific (physics) book records. We ask if their technical terminology can be used as a retrieval enhancing feature. A study of 18,443 book records shows a strong correlation between their technical terminology and their likelihood of relevance. Using this finding for retrieval yields >+5% precision and recall gains.

Categories and Subject Descriptors

H.3.3 [**Information Storage and Retrieval**]: Information Search and Retrieval

Keywords

Book Records, Technical Terminology

1. INTRODUCTION

Information retrieval (IR) systems often can rely on having full texts available for processing. However, there are cases when full text is not available, e.g. in commercial online bookstores or traditional libraries where material may only be available in print, or where using optical character recognition is difficult. Access to these materials is primarily realised through the supplier or the library catalogue, where documents are represented by short *book records* of metadata information, e.g. author, title, etc. The problem is that book records provide very little information, and hence they are very hard to retrieve. As a consequence, the accessibility of potentially relevant books is restricted for users. This work focuses on such books from the physics domain.

We ask whether we can increase the retrievability of physics book records by focussing on the special language in this scientific domain, as used by searchers and authors. Specifically, we model separately the technical/non-technical terminology of physics book records, motivated by the intuition that technical terminology may make a good retrieval enhancing feature. Our intuition that this modelling may benefit book record retrieval is experimentally confirmed: we find a strong correlation between the technical terminology contained in book records and their likelihood of relevance. Applying this to the retrieval of book records yields notable improvements in retrieval precision and recall.

2. TECHNICAL TERMINOLOGY AND RELEVANCE

Preprocessing. We use a collection of 18,443 physics book records with 53 queries and relevance assessments (qrels) from the iSearch dataset[1]. These book records contain basic Machine-Readable Cataloging information, e.g. title, key phrases. To identify technical terms, we part-of-speech (POS) tag the collection (including queries) with the TreeTagger[2]. We extract all terms tagged as nouns, verbs, adjectives and participles, which are the most salient POS classes, hence the most likely to be technical terms. This results in a list of 12,548 terms, which we submit to Amazon Mechanical Turk (AMT) as isolated tokens (without any context) for classification into technical/non-technical terms. Using 3 AMT users per annotation ($\geq$95% approval rate, paid approximately \$0.33 per hour), 34.7% of all terms were annotated as technical, and 65.3% as non-technical, with strong inter-annotator agreement (Fleiss' $\kappa \approx 0.8$).

Technical terminology density analysis. We count the number of technical terms in each book record (referred to as document henceforth) normalised by their length - this gives the document's *terminological density*. We sort all documents by their terminological density, and we divide them into 34 bins: 33 equal-sized bins of 300 documents each, and 1 bin of the remaining 253 documents. We estimate the probability that a randomly selected relevant document belongs to a certain bin as: $p(d \in b_i|rel.) = \frac{|rel.\ d \in b_i|}{|rel.\ d|}$ and the probability that a randomly selected retrieved document belongs to a certain bin as: $p(d \in b_i|ret.) = \frac{|ret.\ d \in b_i|}{|ret.\ d|}$, where

[1] http://itlab.dbit.dk/~isearch

[2] http://www.ims.uni-stuttgart.de/projekte/corplex/TreeTagger

SIGIR'12, August 12–16, 2012, Portland, Oregon, USA.
ACM 978-1-4503-1472-5/12/08.

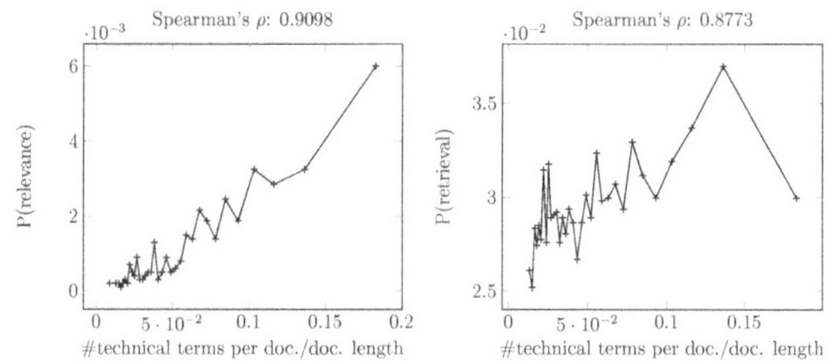

Figure 1: Normalised number of technical terms per document vs. probability of relevance (LEFT) & retrieval (RIGHT), with rank correlation coefficients.

$(rel./ret.)\, d$ is a (relevant[3]/retrieved[4]) document, b_i is the ith bin, and $|\cdot|$ denotes cardinality.

Fig. 1 shows the plots of these probabilities (y axis) vs. the average terminological density in a bin (x axis). We see that $p(d \in b_i|rel.)$ varies non-randomly across bins - terminological density is positively correlated to probability of relevance ($\rho = 0.9098$). Hence, boosting the ranking of documents of higher terminological density may boost retrieval performance. The differences between how $p(d \in b_i|rel.)$ and $p(d \in b_i|ret.)$ vary across bins shows the document groups for which the retrieval model underperforms: the retrieval model has a weaker correlation to the documents' terminological density ($\rho = 0.8773$), with some instability in its performance for documents of low terminological density, and fails for documents of the highest terminological density.

Ranking model. If a user submits the query `design of biexcitonic models`, and we know that `biexcitonic` is a technical term, we hypothesise that boosting the weight of documents that contain `biexcitonic` will improve retrieval performance. We implement this boosting using Indri[5]'s combination of the Language Modeling (LM) and inference network approaches [1], which allows assigning degrees of belief to different parts of the query. This belief can be drawn from any suitable external evidence of relevance - in our case the knowledge that a search term is technical terminology. Using the *#weight* and *#combine* operators for combining beliefs, the relevance of a document d to a query q is computed as the probability that d generates q: $p(q|d) = \prod_{t \in q} p(t|d)^{\frac{w_t}{W}}$, where $W = \sum_{t \in q} w_t$, t is a term and w_t is the term's belief weight. The higher w_t is, the higher the rank of documents containing t. We apply the above equation separately for non-technical common query terms with belief weight w_{com}, and for technical query terms with belief weight w_{tec}, ($w_{com}, w_{tec} \in w_t$, $w_{com} + w_{tec} = 1$). To boost the ranking of documents containing technical terms, we increase w_{tec} at the expense of w_{com}.

Experiments. The baseline matches the documents to queries without any treatment of technical terminology using LM with Dirichlet smoothing. Our approach boosts the weight of technical terms using the same retrieval model but enhanced with belief weights as described above (TEC). We also use a pseudo-relevance feedback (FB) baseline (Indri's default FB implementation), against which we compare our approach combined with FB (TEC+FB). We measure performance with the standard TREC metrics shown in Table 1, averaged over all queries for the top 1000 results (apart from the number of relevant retrieved documents (REL.RET.) which is summed). For each metric we tune: Dir's $\mu \in \{100, 500, 800, 1000, 2000, 3000, 4000, 5000, 8000, 10000\}$; the belief weights $w_{com}, w_{tec} \in \{0.1 - 0.9\}$ in steps of 0.1 with $w_{com} + w_{tec} = 1$ at all times; FB's number of feedback documents $\in \{1, 2, 5, 10, 20\}$ and number of feedback terms $\in \{3, 5, 10, 20, 40\}$.

[3]according to qrels

[4]in top 1000 for any query by the baseline (see *Experiments*)

[5]http://www.lemurproject.org

	BPREF	NDCG	MRR	P@100	REL.RET.
BASE	28.67	23.84	28.74	02.67	185
TEC	33.97 +18.5	25.17 +5.6	29.21 +1.6	02.88 +7.9	234 +26.5
FB	36.60 +27.7	27.71 +16.2	32.46 +12.9	02.92 +9.4	222 +20.0
TEC+FB	38.24 +33.4	27.77 +16.5	32.85 +14.3	03.07 +15.0	261 +41.1

Table 1: Retrieval of our method (TEC) vs. the baseline (BASE) & pseudo-relevance feedback (FB). +% shows percent difference from the baseline.

Table 1 shows that boosting the weight of technical terminology improves retrieval at all times[6]. The biggest improvement is for REL.RET., indicating that our approach introduces to the ranking relevant documents that neither the baseline nor FB retrieve. This finding is positive, considering that our approach does not add new terms to the query - it just boosts the weight of existing query (technical) terms. Average precision benefits more when non-assessed documents are ignored in the ranking (BPREF) than when using graded relevance assessments (NDCG), possibly because NDCG gives a lower score to relevant documents that occur in the low ranks (and hence 'penalises' non-relevant documents or non-assessed documents that occur in the high ranks). Our approach benefits early precision for both the top 100 retrieved documents (P@100) and the first relevant retrieved document (MRR). We can also report that our approach outperforms the baseline and FB across the whole tuning range of μ and for $w_{tec} = 0.1 - 0.5$ (plots not included for brevity) without any outliers. The values $w_{tec} = 0.1 - 0.5$ practically correspond to applying a moderate boost to the weight of technical terminology.

3. CONCLUSION

We asked whether the retrieval of scientific books represented only by limited metadata can be improved by using their technical terminology, motivated by the empirical finding that the proportion of technical terms they contained was positively correlated with their probability of being relevant. To our knowledge this is a novel finding. We integrated this finding into the retrieval model successfully by boosting the ranking of documents containing technical terms, hence showing that our approach benefits the retrieval of book records. Future work includes using the technical term annotations to train an automatic classifier, comparing our approach against an automatic way for determining term relevance (e.g. ontologies, wikipedia pages), and testing the generality of our approach on more scientific domains.

4. REFERENCES

[1] D. Metzler and W. B. Croft. Combining the language model and inference network approaches to retrieval. *IPM*, 40(5):735–750, 2004.

[6]Results were not stat. significant when the t-test was used.

Queries Without Clicks: Evaluating Retrieval Effectiveness Based on User Feedback

Athanasia Koumpouri
Department of Computer Engineering and Informatics
University of Patras
26500, Patras, Greece
+30 2610 996991
koumpour@ceid.upatras.gr

Vasiliki Simaki
Department of Computer Engineering and Informatics
University of Patras
26500, Patras, Greece
+30 2610 996994
simaki@ceid.upatras.gr

ABSTRACT
Until recently, the lack of user activity on search results was perceived as a sign of user dissatisfaction from retrieval performance. However, recent studies have reported that some queries might not be followed by clicks to the content of the retrieved results, because the search task can be satisfied in the list of retrieved results the user views without the need to click through them. In this paper, we propose a method for evaluating user satisfaction from the results of searches that are not followed by clickthrough activity to the retrieved results. We found that there is a strong association between some implicit measures of user activity and user's explicit satisfaction judgments. Moreover, we developed a predictive model of user satisfaction based on implicit measures, achieving accuracy up to 86%.

Categories and Subject Descriptors
D.3.3 [**Queries and Query Analysis**]: Question answering [**Evaluation**]: Effectiveness measures, experimental design.

General Terms
Measurement, Design, Experimentation, Human Factors.

Keywords
positive search abandonment, implicit feedback, explicit feedback, user satisfaction, retrieval effectiveness, user activity.

1. INTRODUCTION
Recently, researchers highlighted the need to discriminate between successful and failed searches that are not followed by clicks to the content of the retrieved results [3], [4]. They have reported that the user's inactivity on search results should not be interpreted as a sign of dissatisfaction from retrieval performance. To this respect, we conducted a user study in order to identify the search intentions of queries without follow-up clicks to any of the results returned. We also attempt to identify the search tasks that can be accomplished successfully based entirely on information provided on the results page. Additionally, we developed an instrumented browser, QWC Browser, to collect various measures indicative of user activity after the query submission. Moreover, we examine whether explicit judgments of user satisfaction are associated to implicit measures of user interest in order to understand which implicit measures are most strongly associated to user satisfaction. Finally, we use Bayesian modeling techniques to develop predictive models in order to capture user satisfaction from searches that are not followed by clicks to the retrieved results.

SIGIR'12, August 12–16, 2012, Portland, Oregon, USA.
ACM 978-1-4503-1472-5/12/08.

2. METHODOLOGY
2.1 Implicit user feedback
In order to gather the data required for this study (both implicit measures and explicit feedback), we developed a web browser, called QWC Browser. We recruited 18 participants that represented the average web searcher and we installed the QWC Browser on their computers. Then, we asked participants to conduct their web searches as they would normally do and use Google as search engine. We explained to them that we would record their searches respecting their privacy and anonymity. Our data collection lasted 4 weeks.

The idea of utilizing the searcher post-query activity on the returned results as an indicator of implicit relevance judgments is not new [1],[2]. QWC Browser allows us to record users' actions as they conduct their searches on the Web. Actions included scrolling (both vertical and horizontal), time spent on results page, bookmark, print, move to next results page, time spent moving mouse and copy text from titles or snippets.

2.2 Explicit user feedback
At the same time, we conducted a user study to identify search tasks related to queries that are not followed by clicks on the retrieved results. Therefore, we examined for which search tasks the user's information needs can be satisfied in the contents of the displayed results. For every query recorded, we asked the participants to answer in four questions presented to them via pop-up questionnaire during their search. The first question attempts to capture the user's search goal from a defined list of possible web search tasks. The second one aims to capture user's intention of clicking or not. The third question asks the user if he did click on the displayed results or not. Finally, the last question (prompt only if the answer in previous question is no) captures the reason for not clicking.

2.3 Predictive models
We examined whether there is an association between implicit measures of user activity and user's explicit satisfaction judgments. Our objective is to model which implicit measures best predict user satisfaction from queries not followed by clicks. Based on previous studies on this field [2], we built a Bayesian network model using the collected implicit interest indicators as input to predict user's explicit judgment of satisfaction/dissatisfaction.

3. EXPERIMENTAL RESULTS
Our findings indicate that in 29.32% of the queries users did not click on any of the retrieved results, either because they were looking for a quick answer to their question in titles and/or snippets retrieved or because their information needs were satisfied by the functionality that the predefined search engine

offers (image, news, linguistics). Moreover, we observed that in some cases the search task has a strong association with the user's predetermined intention to click or not (42% of informational task intent not to click, 27% of quick answer intent to click). Additionally, user satisfaction from queries without click, summarized in Table 1, indicates that the lack of clickthrough activity on retrieved results for some types of searches (informational, navigational, transactional and repeat) is a strong sign of user dissatisfaction.

Search Tasks	% Satisfaction
Informational	0.41%
Navigational	1.05%
Transactional	0.66%
Image	60.31%
News	67.48%
Person	52.21%
Linguistic	99.5%
Quick answer	87.12%
Update	31.22%
Repeat	1.76%

Table 1. The user satisfaction in several search tasks

As an example, let "*convert 233.50 usd to euros*", "*Robert Pattinson*" be two queries submitted by our participants and their search task were defined as *Quick answer* and *Image* relatively. In both cases, the user had no intention to click on the retrieved results and he did so, declaring his satisfaction about the search results. We found that time spent on results page, total time scrolling and copying text from titles and/or snippets are the indicators mostly associated with user's explicit satisfaction judgments.

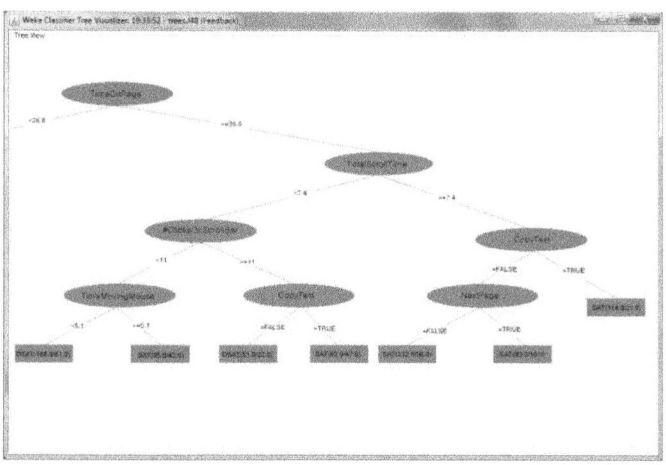

Picture 1. Decision Tree for queries without clicks

As shown in Picture 1, in 81.5% of the cases that a user spends more than 26 seconds in results page, scrolls more than 7.4secs and copies text from snippets/titles, the retrieved results satisfy his information needs without clicking. We also noticed that there were implicit measures such as *print*, *bookmark* and *move to next page* highly correlated with satisfaction (almost 100% accuracy), but very infrequent (less than 2% of the dataset cases). As described above, we learned a Bayesian model to predict user's satisfaction by using the implicit measures as input variables. The learned model combining all the implicit measures, described in Section 2.1, was able to predict satisfaction in 86% of cases.

4. CONCLUSIONS

The objective of our research is to show that search abandonment should not uniformly be considered as a negative signal of user satisfaction about retrieval performance. Our findings indicate that in nearly 80% of all searches conducted with initial intention not to click, the user's information need was successfully addressed by the displayed results. In addition, about 45% of all searches not followed by clicks, achieve to find the desired information in the search results' list.

Furthermore, we found that time spent on the results page, the total scrolling time and copying text from titles and/or snippets are the best predictors of user satisfaction. We plan to conduct additional studies using different search engines in order to generalize our findings. Moreover, we aim to measure explicit user satisfaction more accurately by using a 1-5 rating scale and detect additional implicit measures, such us query-title overlap, query-snippet overlap, etc. in order to capture user activity more precisely.

5. ACKNOWLEDGMENTS

We would like to acknowledge the help of Lecturer Sofia Stamou for motivating and encouraging us, as well as the participants of our survey.

6. REFERENCES

[1] Claypool, M., Lee, P., Wased, M., and Brown, D. 2001. Implicit interest indicators. In Proceedings on the International Conference on Intelligent User Interfaces. Santa Fe, NM.

[2] Fox, S., Karnawat, K., Mydland, M., Dumais, S. and White, T. 2005. Evaluating implicit measures to improve Web search. ACM Transactions on Information System.

[3] Li, J., Huffman, S. B., and Tokuda, A. 2009. Good abandonment in mobile and PC internet search. In Proceedings of the 32nd Annual International ACM SIGIR Conference on Research and Development in Information Retrieval, Boston, MA, USA.

[4] Stamou, S. and Efthimiadis, E. 2010. Interpreting user inactivity on search results In Proceedings of the Advances in Information Retrieval, 32nd European Conference on IR Research, volume 5993 of Lecture Notes in Computer Science, 100-113.

Retrieval Evaluation on Focused Tasks

Besnik Fetahu
Graduate School of Computer Science,
Saarland University
Saarbrücken, Germany
bfetahu@mmci.uni-saarland.de

Ralf Schenkel
Saarland University
Saarbrücken, Germany
schenkel@mmci.uni-saarland.de

ABSTRACT

Ranking of retrieval systems for focused tasks requires large number of relevance judgments. We propose an approach that minimizes the number of relevance judgments, where the performance measures are approximated using a Monte-Carlo sampling technique. Partial measures are taken using relevance judgments, whereas the remaining part of passages are annotated using a generated relevance probability distribution based on result rank. We define two conditions for stopping the assessment procedure when the ranking between systems is stable.

Categories and Subject Descriptors

H.3 [**Information Storage and Retrieval**]: H.3.4 Systems and Software: Performance Evaluation

Keywords

Information Retrieval, Evaluation, Ranking, Algorithms

1. INTRODUCTION

We consider the problem of comparing retrieval systems for focused tasks, where not complete documents, but focused fragments of documents are retrieved. For building existing benchmark collections such as INEX [3], relevance judgments on the level of passages are created by human annotators or, recently, using crowdsourcing [1, 5]. A large number of documents are considered for assessment for each topic (500-750 at INEX), which makes the assessment procedure very work intensive (and expensive if done with crowdsourcing). Recent results [6] indicate that much smaller pools yield largely similar rankings of systems, but still in the order of 50 documents per topic need to be assessed.

For document-level retrieval, an interesting idea to reduce assessment effort was proposed in [2], which proposes to determine a minimal set of documents (MTC) that have the highest impact on average precision at a given rank. However, focused tasks are often not evaluated with rank-based quality metrics, but with recall-based measures such as interpolated precision (iP) [4] evaluated at a fixed set of recall levels. Unlike precision at a rank, iP is not monotonic in the number of assessments, i.e., the iP of a run can decrease when additional relevant passages are identified even outside the run. Figure 2 shows an example for this, where an initial iP[0.01] of 1.0 (1) first drops to 0.7 (2) when another relevant passage is found (and recall grows), and then increases again (3) with the next relevant passage.

SIGIR'12, August 12–16, 2012, Portland, Oregon, USA.
ACM 978-1-4503-1472-5/12/08.

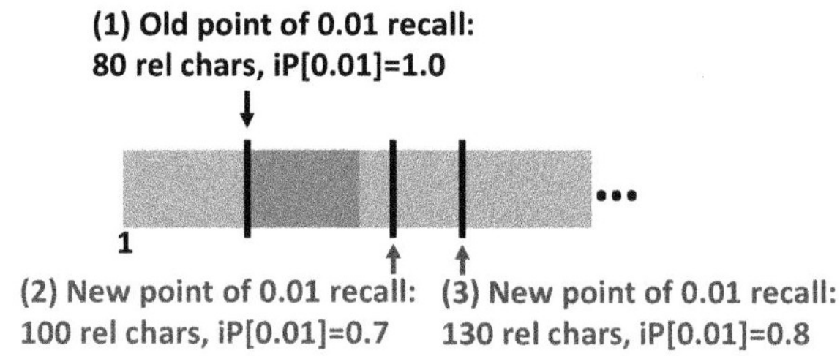

Figure 1: Example for non-monotonicity of iP

In this poster we extend the idea of MTC towards focused retrieval and recall-based metrics, and show that comparable system rankings can be computed with much less assessments that currently done.

2. EVALUATION METRICS

We use ***interpolated precision (iP)*** at different recall levels, a standard evaluation measure for Focused Tasks [4]. Here, the recall base is the set of all relevant characters for a topic (collected during assessment), and each rank of the result list is assigned recall (fraction of all relevant characters retrieved up to this rank) and precision (ratio of retrieved relevant to all retrieved characters up to this rank). The metric is evaluated at recall levels $x \in \{0, 0.01, \ldots, 1.0\}$, and the value at recall level x is the highest precision at any rank with recall at least x. Additionally, average precision AiP over all recall points and mean average precision $MAiP$ over all topics are defined. Please see [4] for the full formal definitions.

3. OUR METHOD

We now present our method that, given a set of runs $A, B, \ldots, N$ for a set of topics, selects passages from these runs to assess and finally builds a ranking of the runs.

3.1 Document Selection

We want to assess only the passages that have most impact on system ranking. To achieve this we first create, a pool of unique passages retrieved from all systems on all topics. We then compute the impact on iP of assessing each passage for each run where it appears (considering other non-assessed passages as non-relevant). If a passage appears in multiple systems $(A \ldots N)$ its weight is constructed by the pairwise difference of each individual weight (as the precision of a system up to that point) in all systems, shown here for some system c (n is the number of systems in which the passage does not appear). The highest weight is assigned to a passage (from the passage weights computed at other systems):

$$\Delta iP = |iP_A - iP_B| + \cdots + |iP_{N-1} - iP_N| + n * iP_c$$

We then select a number k of passages for each topic, sorted by the weight defined above. This is repeated until all systems are marked as stable by one of the stopping conditions.

3.2 Approximated Metrics

We now explain how to compute an approximated value for interpolated precision when only a subset of all passages have been assessed. A first alternative would be to consider *partial iP*, where unassessed passages are set to not relevant, but this is too simplistic since many passages at early ranks will be unassessed in the initial rounds of our method. Instead, we use Monte Carlo sampling to compute an estimated iP value. Here, the relevance of unassessed passages is considered a random variable, with a probability of relevance based on the rank on which they appear. The number of samples N was specified using the absolute ϵ-approximation, which approximates the measures with probability at least $1-\delta$, where $\epsilon = 0.1$, and $\delta = 0.9$. An initial analysis with the INEX'08 runs (considering a passage as relevant when it contained at least one relevant character) showed that this probability is exponentially decaying with increasing rank.

3.3 Stopping Conditions

Our method runs in iterations where in each iteration, k documents from each non-stable system are chosen for assessment. After each iteration, partial and approximated *iP* are computed, and we check if we can stop based on two stopping conditions:

- **Test Statistics:** We statistically compare partial iP to approximated iP, where we test the hypothesis if they are approximately similar to each other. H_0 : $\mathbf{AiP} = \mathbf{E}[AiP]$, and H_1 : $\mathbf{AiP} \neq \mathbf{E}[AiP]$. It is expected that the null hypothesis is rejected in most cases due to the difference in partial and approximated measures.
- **Pairwise Measure Comparison:** We compare if partial and approximated iP agree pairwise on the ranking of a system compared to all other systems. If that is the case, that system is marked as stable. We can stop if all systems are marked as stable, i.e., if the ranking computed from the partial measure agrees with the ranking computed from the approximated measure.

4. RESULTS & DISCUSSIONS

We evaluated our method with data from the Focused Task of the INEX 2009 AdHoc track [3], which consisted of ***68*** topics. The comparison performance of systems on topic level was measured based on ***AiP***. The rank probability distribution was constructed using INEX'08 data. In total only 4080 relevance judgments, with approx.60 per topic, were needed until the stopping condition fired after 3 iterations (we stopped when more than half of the systems were marked as stable). We compared the produced ranking to the ranking with full INEX assessments (restricted to a standard pool of size 500 built for the considered runs) using Kendall's τ correlation. Figure 2 shows the correlation for all recall points, and Table 1 shows the correlation at four selected recall points after each iteration, and for PoolSize-55 (which uses 60 assessments per topic). It is evident that our method reaches an agreement level of 0.9. It is also more effective than standard INEX pooling with 50 documents per topic, which achieves a correlation slightly below 0.9 (Figure 2).

iteration	iP[0.00]	iP[0.01]	iP[0.05]	iP[0.10]
iter-1	87.66	88.87	87.54	91.17
iter-2	92.38	90.8	89.59	92.62
iter-3	93.71	**91.65**	**90.44**	**93.35**
PoolSize-55	**93.80**	90.64	88.31	90.64

Table 1: τ-coefficient on official recall points.

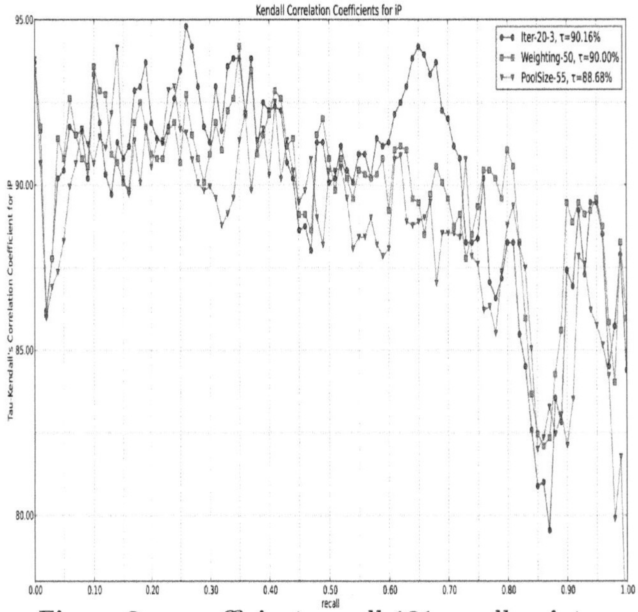

Figure 2: τ-coefficient on all 101 recall points.

5. CONCLUSIONS

The main goal of our was to rank multiple systems with minimal number of relevance judgments for focused retrieval. We proposed a new algorithm for selecting passages for assessment under recall-based evaluation metrics such as interpolated precision. We iteratively pick new passages to assess until all systems achieved a stable ranking, based on two stopping conditions.

6. REFERENCES

[1] Omar Alonso, Ralf Schenkel, and Martin Theobald. Crowdsourcing assessments for xml ranked retrieval. In *ECIR*, pages 602–606, 2010.

[2] Ben Carterette, James Allan, and Ramesh K. Sitaraman. Minimal test collections for retrieval evaluation. In *SIGIR*, pages 268–275, 2006.

[3] Shlomo Geva, Jaap Kamps, Miro Lehtonen, Ralf Schenkel, James A. Thom, and Andrew Trotman. Overview of the inex 2009 ad hoc track. In *INEX*, pages 4–25, 2009.

[4] Jaap Kamps, Jovan Pehcevski, Gabriella Kazai, Mounia Lalmas, and Stephen Robertson. Inex 2007 evaluation measures. In *INEX*, pages 24–33, 2007.

[5] Gabriella Kazai, Jaap Kamps, Marijn Koolen, and Natasa Milic-Frayling. Crowdsourcing for book search evaluation: impact of hit design on comparative system ranking. In *SIGIR*, pages 205–214, 2011.

[6] Sukomal Pal, Mandar Mitra, and Jaap Kamps. Evaluation effort, reliability and reusability in xml retrieval. *JASIST*, 62(2):375–394, 2011.

Rewarding Term Location Information to Enhance Probabilistic Information Retrieval

Jiashu Zhao[1], Jimmy Xiangji Huang[2], Shicheng Wu[2]
Information Retrieval and Knowledge Management Research Lab
[1]Department of Computer Science & Engineering, [2]School of Information Technology
York University, Toronto, Canada
jessie@cse.yorku.ca, {jhuang, scwu}@yorku.ca

ABSTRACT

We investigate the effect of rewarding terms according to their locations in documents for probabilistic information retrieval. The intuition behind our approach is that a large amount of authors would summarize their ideas in some particular parts of documents. In this paper, we focus on the beginning part of documents. Several shape functions are defined to simulate the influence of term location information. We propose a Reward Term Retrieval model that combines the reward terms' information with BM25 to enhance probabilistic information retrieval performance.

Categories and Subject Descriptors

H.3.3 [**Information Storage & Retrieval**]: Information Search & Retrieval

Keywords

BM25-RT, Influence Shape Function

1. INTRODUCTION

Using document semantic information is usually regarded as an effective approach for improving Information Retrieval (IR) performance. In this paper, we propose to reward terms according to their location information in documents.

Human beings do not treat each word equally when reading a document. People pay more attention on certain parts of the document. This is due to the fact that many authors would summarize their ideas in some particular locations, e.g. the beginning and/or the end. It particularly fits articles that have abstract and introduction at the beginning and conclude the summary in the end. In this paper, we focus on the situation that the beginning of the documents should be rewarded during retrieval.

Many researchers have studied using semantic information in some particular domains in IR. For example, Ontology Web Language and Information Retrieval (OWLIR) system [4] is designed for Semantic Web documents, using several techniques such as information extraction, annotation and inference. Wang and Li [5] investigated semantically annotated Wikipedia XML corpus to improve retrieval performance. Zhao and Callan [6] utilized query structure expansion to enhance structured retrieval in a question answering (QA) application. Gao and Toutanova [1] learned semantic models from large amounts of query-title pairs constructed from clickthrough data. Compared with the above approaches, our approach does not require any domain-specific knowledge.

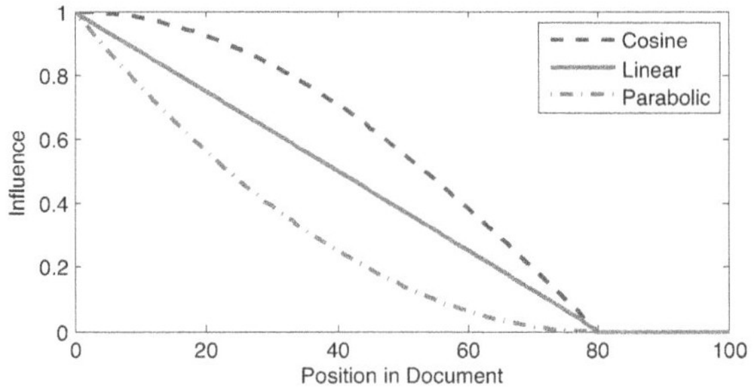

Figure 1: Influence Shape Functions

For structured data, different fields could be given different weights. Robertson and Zaragoza [3] proposed an extension of BM25 to weight multiple fields separately, such as title text, body text, and anchor text. However, each part of a document is treated equally for unstructured documents. Compared to their approach, our approach rewards terms smoothly according to their locations in documents, and doesn't incorporate any field information.

The remainder of this paper is organized as follows. In Section 2, we propose several Influence Shape functions and extend BM25 by rewarding terms according to their locations in documents. Section 3 presents the experimental results and parameter sensitivity in ISF function. Section 4 concludes the findings in this paper and discusses possible future directions.

2. OUR APPROACH

We firstly build the Influence Shape Functions (ISF) that could represent the term influence at the locations closer to the beginning part, and then integrate the influence into BM25 by adding an extra part to term frequency. Under our assumption, when a term occurs closer to the beginning part in the document, it would be more likely to reveal the meaning of the document. Therefore, an ISF should have the highest value at the first position and gradually decreases. We build three functions with different gradients which satisfy this property.

$$ISF_{Parabola}(p, D) = (\frac{p}{\lambda \cdot |D|} - 1)^2, \ when\ p < \lambda \cdot |D|$$

$$ISF_{Linear}(p, D) = 1 - \frac{p}{\lambda \cdot |D|}, \ when\ p < \lambda \cdot |D|$$

$$ISF_{Cosine}(p, D) = cos(\frac{\pi \cdot p}{2 \cdot \lambda \cdot |D|}),\ when\ p < \lambda \cdot |D|$$

where p is the position that a term occurs, $|D|$ is the length of the document, and λ is a parameter controlling the percentage of the document that should be considered as the beginning part. It ranges from 0 to 1. When $\lambda = 0$, p is always greater than $\lambda \cdot |D|$. Therefore the value of each ISF is always 0. It becomes a special case that ISFs do not affect the retrieval process. The above ISFs are normalized to 0 to 1, and their shapes are shown in Figure 1. In this figure, the document length |D| is 100 and λ is 0.8.

In [3], the field information is integrated into BM25 by using weighted term frequency on each field. Here we enhance the within-document term frequency of a query term by the ISFs to reward query terms occurring closer to the beginning of the document. The within-document query term frequency is linearly combined with the accumulation of a term's ISF value.

$$tf_{RT}(i, D) = tf(i, D) + \sum_{j=1}^{tf(i)} ISF(p_j, D) \quad (1)$$

where ISF could adopt any of the above defined shape function. The only parameter that is affected is k_1, which controls the non-linear tf function.

$$k_1^{RT}(i) = k_1 \cdot \frac{\sum_{D \in Index} tf_{RT}(i, D)}{\sum_{D \in Index} tf(i, D)} \quad (2)$$

The weighting function of BM25 with Rewarded Terms (BM25-RT) is as follows.

$$w_{RT}(q_i, D) = \frac{(k_1^{RT} + 1) * tf_{RT}}{K + tf_{RT}} * \frac{(k_3 + 1) * qtf}{k_3 + qtf} * \log \frac{N - n + 0.5}{n + 0.5}$$

where N is the number of documents in the collection, n is the number of documents containing q_i, tf_{RT} is within-document term frequency, qtf is within-query term frequency, dl is the length of the document, $avdl$ is the average document length, nq is the number of query terms, k_3 is tuning constant defaulted to be 8, K equals to $k_1^{RT} * ((1 - b) + b * dl/avdl)$. In this paper, we set $b = 0.75$ and $k_1 = 1.2$, which are regarded as default parameter settings in many BM25 applications [2].

3. EXPERIMENTAL RESULTS

We evaluate the proposed approach on three data sets: WT2G (topic 401-450), TREC8 (topic 401-450), and Blog06 (topic 851-950). The WT2G collection is a 2G size crawl of Web documents. The TREC8 contains 528,155 newswire articles from various sources, such as Financial Times (FT), the Federal Register (FR) etc., which are usually considered as high-quality text data with little noise. The Blog06 collection includes 100,649 blog feeds collected over an 11 week period from December 2005 to February 2006. For all test collections used, each term is stemmed using Porter's English stemmer, and standard English stopwords are removed. We use the MAP and P@10 as measurements in our experiments.

Table 1 shows the result of BM25-RT on the above three data sets using Cosine ISF, Linear ISF, and Parabolic ISF. We compare BM25-RT with BM25, since BM25-RT doesn't incorporate any field or annotation information. Significant improvement is observed on all the data sets.

Figure 2 shows how the parameter λ in ISF affects the retrieval performance. We have discussed in Section 2 that

	WT2G		TREC8		Blog06	
	MAP	P@10	MAP	P@10	MAP	P@10
BM25	0.2694	0.4400	0.2410	0.4460	0.2966	0.6033
Cosine	0.2812*	**0.4500**	**0.2467***	**0.4580**	0.2968	0.6173*
Linear	**0.2814***	0.4440	0.2460*	**0.4580**	0.2874	**0.6200***
Parabola	0.2787	0.4460	0.2460*	0.4560	**0.2982***	0.6180*

Table 1: MAP and P@10 for BM25-RT with different ISFs (* indicates significant improvements compared to BM25)

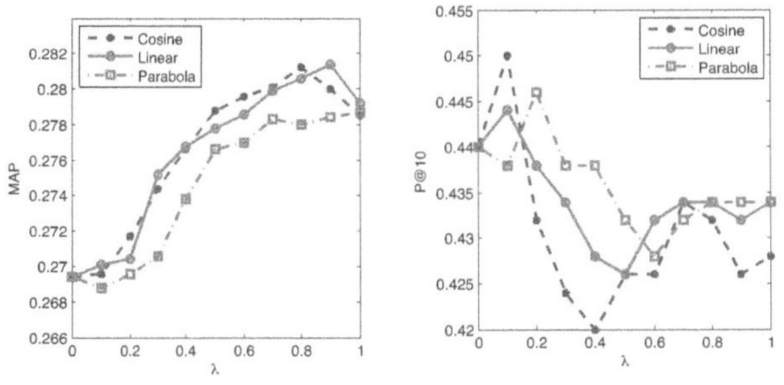

(a) MAP (b) P@10

Figure 2: Parameter Sensitivity of λ on WT2G for BM25-RT with Cosine ISF, Linear ISF, and Parabola ISF.

BM25-RT becomes BM25 when $\lambda = 0$. When λ is increasing, it means BM25-RT takes into more proportion of document into account. We can see that MAP and P@10 of BM25-RT increase at first when λ increments from 0. It means the term rewarding technique boosts BM25-RT's performance. As λ keeps incrementing, both MAP and P@10 decrease after reaching optimal values.

4. CONCLUSIONS AND FUTURE WORK

In this paper, we propose a BM25-RT model which tries to reward terms according to their location information during retrieval. A term occurrence is regarded to be more important when it is closer to the beginning of the document. In the future, we plan to discuss more possible document distributions, for instance, to reward the endings of documents.

5. ACKNOWLEDGEMENTS

This research is supported in part by the research grant from the Natural Sciences & Engineering Resarch Council (NSREC) of Canada and the Early Researcher/Premier's Research Excellence Award.

6. REFERENCES

[1] J. Gao, K. Toutanova, and W. Yih. Clickthrough-based latent semantic models for web search. In SIGIR'11, pages 675–684, New York, NY, USA, 2011. ACM.

[2] S. Robertson, S. Walker, and M. Beaulieu. Okapi at TREC-7: automatic ad hoc, filtering, vlc and interactive track. In TREC'99, pages 253–264, 1999.

[3] S. Robertson, H. Zaragoza, and M. Taylor. Simple BM25 extension to multiple weighted fields. In CIKM'04, pages 42–49, New York, NY, USA, 2004. ACM.

[4] U. Shah, T. Finin, A. Joshi, R. S. Cost, and J. Matfield. Information retrieval on the semantic web. In CIKM'02, pages 461–468, New York, NY, USA, 2002. ACM.

[5] Q. Wang, Q. Li, S. Wang, and X. Du. Exploiting semantic tags in xml retrieval. In INEX'09, pages 133–144, Berlin, 2010.

[6] L. Zhao and J. Callan. Effective and efficient structured retrieval. In CIKM'09, pages 1573–1576, New York, NY, USA, 2009. ACM.

Scheduling Queries Across Replicas

Ana Freire[1], Craig Macdonald[2], Nicola Tonellotto[3], Iadh Ounis[2], Fidel Cacheda[1]
[1] University of A Coruña, Campus de Elviña s/n, 15017 A Coruña, Spain
[2] University of Glasgow, G12 8QQ Glasgow, UK
[3] National Research Council of Italy, Via G. Moruzzi 1, 56124 Pisa, Italy
{ana.freire, fidel.cacheda}@udc.es[1], {craig.macdonald, iadh.ounis}@glasgow.ac.uk[2], {nicola.tonellotto}@isti.cnr.it[3]

ABSTRACT

For increased efficiency, an information retrieval system can split its index into multiple shards, and then replicate these shards across many query servers. For each new query, an appropriate replica for each shard must be selected, such that the query is answered as quickly as possible. Typically, the replica with the lowest number of queued queries is selected. However, not every query takes the same time to execute, particularly if a dynamic pruning strategy is applied by each query server. Hence, the replica's queue length is an inaccurate indicator of the workload of a replica, and can result in inefficient usage of the replicas. In this work, we propose that improved replica selection can be obtained by using query efficiency prediction to measure the expected workload of a replica. Experiments are conducted using 2.2k queries, over various numbers of shards and replicas for the large GOV2 collection. Our results show that query waiting and completion times can be markedly reduced, showing that accurate response time predictions can improve scheduling accuracy and attesting the benefit of the proposed scheduling algorithm.

Categories & Subject Descriptors: H.3.3 [Information Storage & Retrieval]: Information Search & Retrieval

General Terms: Performance, Experimentation

Keywords: Query Scheduling, Simulation

1. INTRODUCTION

A distributed information retrieval (IR) system consists of several query servers, each of them storing the index *shard* for a subset of the documents in the corpus. New queries arrive at the *broker*, which routes them to each shard, before collating and merging the results for presentation to the user. The efficiency of each query server can be improved by deploying a dynamic pruning strategy, such as WAND [1], which aims to avoid the scoring of postings for documents that cannot make the top K retrieved set.

While multiple shards increase efficiency compared to a monolithic ("single shard") retrieval system, the throughput of a distributed retrieval system can be further enhanced by *replicating* shards, so that one of multiple query servers can provide the results for a single shard [6]. The problem tackled in this work is how a broker should select (*schedule*) the most suitable replica of a given shard in order to reduce the queue waiting time. For example, the replica with the minimum number of queued queries can be selected.

However, the response time for different queries can vary widely, particularly if dynamic pruning is employed [5]. Hence, the accurate choice of replica is made more difficult, as the number of queries queued by a given query server does not accurately predict the processing backlog of the server. A recently proposed technique for *query efficiency prediction* [5] offers a plausible manner to estimate the workload of a replica. Hence, we hypothesise that query efficiency prediction [4] can permit accurate query scheduling in a distributed/replicated IR system. Indeed, to the best of our knowledge, this work contributes the first study to applying query efficiency predictors for scheduling in a distributed/replicated IR system. Using a simulated distributed/ replicated search environment, based on actual query response times, we experiment to determine how different scheduling algorithms can be deployed for replica selection. Our results show that by using query efficiency prediction, we can improve the selection of replicated query servers, and hence the average query completion times are reduced. For instance, using predicted response time to select between 4 replicas of a 2 shard index results in a 42% reduction in mean completion time compared to selecting replicas by considering only the length of their queues.

2. SIMULATING REPLICATION

In comparing different scheduling algorithms, we experiment with a various numbers of shards and replicas. To facilitate such experiments without exhaustive hardware resources, we build a simulation framework that supports different distributed settings. Indeed, Cacheda et al. [2] showed that a simulation framework could accurately model the efficiency of a real distributed IR system, including the network delays, the queue waiting and processing time for queries and the time for merging the results. Following this, we implement a simulation framework[1], extended to encapsulate the presence of multiple shards each with multiple replicas as well as several scheduling algorithms for selecting replicas. The constants for network delays follow [2], in order to achieve a proven realistic simulation environment.

The baseline scheduling algorithms implemented for selecting replicas are: Random (the replica is chosen randomly); Round Robin (modulo the number of replicas, if replica i was selected for this query, replica $i+1$ is used for the next query); Queue Length (the replica with the fewest queries waiting to be processed is selected). In addition to these baselines, we propose Predicted, where the replica with the current shortest queue in terms of predicted response times is selected. We use query efficiency predictions [5]

[1]Built using JavaSim: `http://javasim.codehaus.org/`

SIGIR'12, August 12–16, 2012, Portland, Oregon, USA.
ACM 978-1-4503-1472-5/12/08.

Replicas	Random		Round Robin		Queue Length		Prediction		*Oracle*	
	ACT	AWT	ACT	AWT	ACT	AWT	ACT	AWT	*ACT*	*AWT*
2 Shards										
2	9617	9382	10061	9826	8897	8662	**613**	**362**	*610*	*359*
4	902	667	409	174	434	199	**253**	**3**	*253*	*3*
8	410	175	263	28	428	193	**250**	**0**	*250*	*0*
5 Shards										
2	375	237	241	103	247	109	**158**	**4**	*159*	*5*
4	265	126	155	16	231	93	**154**	**0**	*154*	*0*
8	192	54	**140**	2	231	93	154	**0**	*154*	*0*
10 Shards										
2	168	69	120	22	145	47	**114**	**1**	*114*	*1*
4	139	41	**101**	3	144	46	114	**0**	*114*	*0*
8	123	25	**98**	**0**	144	46	114	**0**	*114*	*0*

Table 1: ACTs and AWTs (in milliseconds) for different settings and scheduling algorithms.

for estimating the response time of a query. Moreover, as the predicted response time is dependent on statistics of the query terms on that index shard, our framework accounts for the time to calculate the prediction at the selected replica and transmit it back to the broker, such that the expected workload of the replica can be updated.

Finally, as the selection of replicas is based on predicted response times, we additionally implement an Oracle scheduling algorithm, which knows the actual response time of a query before it is executed, but still accounts for the calculating the predicted response time. In this way, Oracle represents a best-case scenario for Predicted scheduling.

3. EXPERIMENTAL SETUP

We hypothesise that using predicted response times can increase overall efficiency compared to other scheduling algorithms. To address this hypothesis, we conduct experiments by indexing TREC GOV2 corpus using Terrier[2], applying Porter's English stemmer and removing standard stopwords. We experiment with three different index configurations: 2, 5 and 10 shards. For retrieval on each query server, we use a set of 2200 queries of the TREC 2005 Terabyte track Efficiency task. We sample real arrival times of a set of queries from an Excite query log and assign them to our TREC queries (query arrival rates vary from 20 to 180 per second). We use the WAND dynamic pruning strategy [1] to retrieve $K = 1000$ documents, scored by the DPH Divergence from Randomness document weighting model. Timings are made using an Intel Xeon 2.66GHz.

To obtain the response time predictions, we follow Tonellotto et al. [5], by calculating various term-level statistics, such as the IDF, maximum score, number of postings, number of postings with scores > 95% maximum score. These are then aggregated across terms by sum, max, min, mean, median, stddev, variance and range functions, to form a total of 113 features (14 statistics * 8 aggregations + query length). Predicted response times are obtained by gradient boosted regression trees [3], trained on a separate subset of 2500 Efficiency task queries. Finally, to compare the five scheduling algorithms, we use two measures: average waiting time (AWT) and average completion time (ACT) over all the queries, in milliseconds (ms). Note that the average completion time is inclusive of the average waiting time.

4. EXPERIMENTAL RESULTS

From Table 1, we note that increasing both the numbers of shards and the number of replicas reduces both ACTs and AWTs. Indeed, in general, 2 shards with only 2 replicas is insufficient for a low completion time for this query workload, as queries can spend 8 seconds waiting for an available query server. For 5 or more shards, more than 4 replicas is sufficient for eliminating any *contention* for query servers (i.e. AWTs close to 0).

Next, comparing the scheduling algorithms, we note that Random obtains the highest ACTs and AWTs, because it can choose replicas that are busy, whist other replicas for that shard are idle. Queue Length is superior to Round Robin under high contention (i.e. 2 shards, 2 replicas). In other settings, Round Robin appears to better balance load than Queue Length. However, across different numbers of shards and replicas, Prediction always achieves the smallest AWT. For instance, with 4 replicas of the 2 shard index, Prediction can reduce AWT to 3ms, compared to 199ms for Queue Length and 174ms for Round Robin. Under settings with very little contention (e.g. 10 shards, 4 or 8 replicas), Round Robin has slightly lower ACTs than Prediction and even Oracle, due to the expense of predicting the response time (typically 6-40ms, depending on query length). Finally, Prediction obtains ACTs and AWTs that are almost identical to the best-case Oracle algorithm, based on actual response times. Overall, we find that using predicted response times to select the suitable replica for each query results in improved efficiency.

5. CONCLUSIONS

We proposed that using the predicted response time (obtained using query efficiency prediction) could enhance replica selection within a distributed/replicated IR system, compared to other scheduling algorithms. Indeed, experiments using the GOV2 corpus showed that the proposed Prediction algorithm could attain marked reductions in the query waiting times, across different number of shards and replicas. In future work we will investigate if query response times within a shard are correlated, and hence if the number of replicas required for a given shard can be predicted in advance.

6. ACKNOWLEDGEMENTS

Ana Freire acknowledges the support from the Spanish Government (Project TIN2009-14203). Craig Macdonald and Iadh Ounis acknowledge the support of EC-funded project SMART (FP7-287583).

7. REFERENCES

[1] A. Z. Broder, D. Carmel, M. Herscovici, A. Soffer, and J. Zien. Efficient query evaluation using a two-level retrieval process. In *Proc. CIKM 2003.*

[2] F. Cacheda, V. Carneiro, V. Plachouras, and I. Ounis. Performance analysis of distributed information retrieval architectures using an improved network simulation model. *Information Processing and Management*, 43:204–224, 2007.

[3] J. H. Friedman. Greedy function approximation: A gradient boosting machine. *Annals of Statistics*, 29:1189–1232, 2000.

[4] C. Macdonald, N. Tonellotto, and I. Ounis. Learning to Predict Response Times for Online Query Scheduling. In *Proc. SIGIR 2012.*

[5] N. Tonellotto, C. Macdonald, and I. Ounis. Query efficiency prediction for dynamic pruning. In *Proc. LSDS-IR 2011.*

[6] F. Cacheda, V. Carneiro, V. Plachouras and I. Ounis. Performance Comparison of Clustered and Replicated Information Retrieval Systems. In *Proc. ECIR 2007.*

[2]http://terrier.org

Re-Examining Search Result Snippet Examination Time for Relevance Estimation

Dmitry Lagun
Emory University
dlagun@emory.edu

Eugene Agichtein
Emory University
eugene@mathcs.emory.edu

ABSTRACT

Previous studies of web search result examination have provided valuable insights in understanding and modelling searcher behavior. Yet, recent work (e.g., [3]) has been developed based on the assumption that the time a searcher spends examining a particular result abstract or snippet, correlates with result relevance. While this idea is intuitively attractive, to the best of our knowledge it has not been empirically tested. This poster investigates this hypothesis empirically, in a controlled setting, using eye tracking equipment to compare search result examination time with result relevance. Interestingly, while we replicate previous findings showing examination time to be indicative of whole-page relevance, we find that viewing time of individual results alone is a poor indicator of either absolute result relevance or even of pairwise preferences. Our results should not be taken as negating the usefulness of modeling searcher examination behavior, but rather to emphasize that snippet examination time is not in itself a good indicator of relevance.

Categories and Subject Descriptors

H.4 [**Informational storage and retrieval**]: evaluation, search process.

Keywords

Web search snippet examination; web search behavior; search evaluation.

1. MOTIVATION AND OVERVIEW

As terabytes of search log data are being generated daily, correct interpretation of patterns in these data becomes ever more challenging. Mining of click data has become a fertile area for many applications, including result relevance estimation, automatic query suggestion, and many others. One interesting application of using search logs to infer result examination behavior on Search Result Pages (SERP) was introduced by He et al. [3]. Another successful application of examination data is identification of relevant sub-parts of documents, which can be used for query expansion or term re-weighting (see Buscher et al. [1] for more details). Yet, while result examination data is likely to provide rich contextual information for machine learning algorithms for accurate user modeling and interpretation of past clicks, to our knowledge, the examination behavior on the SERP itself as a predictor of relevance has not been empirically evaluated in prior research [3].

This poster reports preliminary results on analyzing whether viewing time of a search result snippet can be directly used to estimate its relevance label. Using eye tracking equipment, we confirm that previously suggested measures of viewing behavior (e.g., the distribution of viewing time across all result ranks) indeed correlate with overall result quality. However, we also find that examination time alone is unlikely to be a good indicator of relevance of *individual results*, primarily due to severe position bias in the examination behavior. Our results are consistent with and complement the findings of Guan and Cutrell [2], where users were observed to spend more time finding relevant results placed in the bottom of the result list, as opposed to the original result ordering. Next, we describe the details of eye tracking user study that we conducted, after what we present our findings on correlating result viewing time and relevance, both for the whole set of results and for individual search results.

SIGIR'12, August 12–16, 2012, Portland, Oregon, USA.
ACM 978-1-4503-1472-5/12/08.

2. USER STUDY

Our study used 25 benchmark search tasks selected from the Web Track of the TREC 2009 competition. The goal for each task (the description) was provided to the participants. For example, the goal of the query "toilet" was stated as: "Find information on buying, installing, and repairing toilets". For each task, the query keywords were submitted to the Google search engine, and the Search Engine Result Pages (SERPs), as well as all the result URLs linked from each SERP, were cached. We did not remove non-organic results such as ads, embedded image results, news or local results, etc. - thereby recreating a realistic search experience for the subjects. Paid annotators rated every search result for relevance, with at least five ratings per document, on a three-point scale ("Bad", "Partially Relevant" and "Perfect"). We retained the majority opinion as the final result relevance label. For the rest of the details about user study we refer to [5].

3. RESULTS AND DISCUSSION

While our main goal is to investigate whether snippet examination time can be used as a proxy for result relevance, we first confirm that our data are in correspondence with prior work on studying user examination behavior on the search result page.

Figure 6(a) of [5] reports the fraction of the examination time of the snippets, broken down by the result rank. Specifically, the values were computed for each subject and query (that is, the viewing time for each result abstract by a subject was divided by the total viewing time of the corresponding SERP) for an individual query, and then averaged across all queries. The decaying shape of the viewing time distribution is similar to that reported in prior work (e.g., by Joachims et al. [4]). The fact that web search users tend

	Viewing time (rel.)	*Viewing time (abs.)*
Pooled (all)	0.157	0.107
Pairwise - All	**0.194**	**0.148**
Pairwise - Above	0.119	0.063
Pairwise - Adjacent	0.007	0.003

Table 1: Pearson correlation between individual result examination time and relevance labels.

to spend more time reading top results irrespective to the result relevance is well known and typically referred as position bias (sometimes called presentation bias). However, when considering viewing time for individual queries, the effect of the position bias is smaller. In fact, for some of the queries in our dataset, the viewing time does not peak at rank one, and actually can be used to estimate the *whole page relevance*, as we discuss below.

Viewing time vs. individual result relevance: we now investigate whether variation in snippet examination time, as measured per result or by entire distribution, could be attributed to result relevance. Figure 1 reports the box plot of relative viewing time, broken down by relevance labels, where the boxes correspond to 25th and 75th percentiles, and the median is marked with a red line. As Figure 1 reports, there is a substantial overlap in values of viewing time for different relevance levels. Statistical tests on differences of result viewing time between *Bad* and *Partially Relevant* groups, and *Bad* and *Perfect* groups fail to reject the null hypothesis, leading us to conclude that *snippet examination time alone can not be used to infer individual result relevance.* To verify our findings, we pool viewing time and relevance labels from all queries, and compute Pearson correlation between them. Overall, we find that there is only a weak correlation (0.157) between snippet viewing time and relevance. In order to mitigate the effects of position bias, we also compared relative *result preferences* based on relevance vs. based on the difference in examination time. Specifically, we compared the differences of snippet viewing time per result to the differences in relevance levels, in three ways: *Pairwise-All*, pairwise preferences derived based on all (usually 10) results on the SERP; *Pairwise-Above*, pairwise preferences between each result and only the results ranked above it; *Pairwise-Adjacent*, pairwise preferences between adjacent results only. Surprisingly, as reported in Table 1, we find that even pairwise preferences do not exhibit a stronger correlation with viewing time, except for *Pairwise-All*, where pairwise preferences have a higher correlation with viewing time compared to using the absolute document relevance. Additionally, we re-calculated these correlation coefficients using absolute viewing time, instead of the relative viewing time. Finally, we repeated our computations and considered only the results viewed at least once, without finding significantly higher correlation levels. We omit details on these experiments due to space constraints.

Viewing time distribution vs. whole page relevance: while viewing time on individual results is a poor predictor of relevance, we also investigated whether we can relate viewing behavior on the SERP as a whole, with result relevance of the whole result set. To quantify overall page quality we calculated standard information retrieval metrics, namlely: Mean Average Precision (*MAP*), Normalized Discounted Cumulative Gain (*NDCG*) and Expected Reciprocal Rank (*ERR*). Intuitively, when the result ranking is poor, the users are expected to spend more time reading

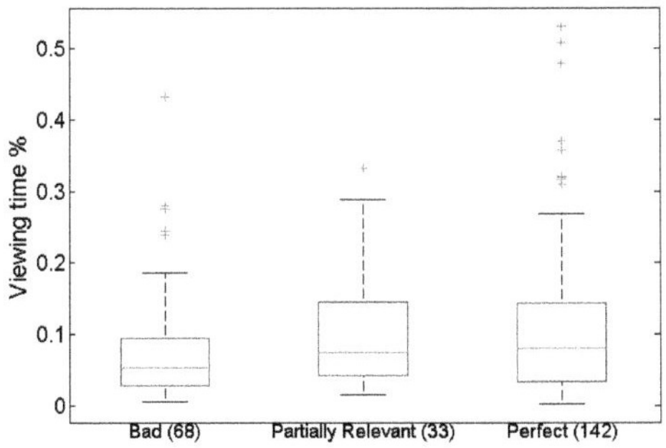

Figure 1: Viewing time on search results broken down by relevance label.

	MAP	NDCG	ERR
Views@1	**0.452**	**0.249**	**0.102**
Mean Rank	0.162	0.041	-0.042

Table 2: Pearson correlation between viewing time and whole page relevance.

result abstracts at lower ranks. To validate our intuition we compute correlation between relative viewing time at rank one (*Views@1*) and mean rank of viewing time distribution (analog of distribution mean). Note that the relative *Views@1* is linearly depended on viewing time at lower ranks (due to normalization constraint), hence when more attention is spent on lower ranks, the value of *Views@1* decreases. Table 2 reports Person correlation between *Views@1* and mean rank and whole page quality represented by one of the three metrics above. We find that *Views@1* has substantial correlation of 0.452 with the *MAP* metric, while exhibiting smaller, but non-negligible correlation with *NDCG* (0.249) and to a smaller degree with ERR (0.102). **Summary**: to our knowledge, we performed the first empirical examination of the *result examination hypothesis*, disproving the intuition that longer snippet examination times indicate higher relevance of individual results. Surprisingly, this was the case both for absolute relevance levels, and for pairwise result preferences, under commonly observed strategies of result examination (i.e., the "Skip-Above" and "Skip-Next" strategies in reference [4]). However, we confirmed that the *distribution* of the viewing times on the SERP does correlate with ranking quality of the SERP as a whole, suggesting a more promising direction for further research. In our future work we plan to conduct more thorough analysis on result examination behavior and associated relevance that would account for consistent biases in result perception such as abstract length and judgeability.

4. REFERENCES

[1] G. Buscher, A. Dengel, R. Biedert, and L. V. Elst. Attentive documents: Eye tracking as implicit feedback for information retrieval and beyond. *ACM Trans. Interact. Intell. Syst.*, 1(2):9:1–9:30, 2012.

[2] Z. Guan and E. Cutrell. An eye tracking study of the effect of target rank on web search. In *Proc. of CHI*, pages 417–420, 2007.

[3] Y. He and K. Wang. Inferring search behaviors using partially observable markov model with duration (pomd). In *Proc. of WSDM*, pages 415–424, 2011.

[4] T. Joachims, L. Granka, B. Pan, H. Hembrooke, F. Radlinski, and G. Gay. Evaluating the accuracy of implicit feedback from clicks and query reformulations in web search. *ACM TOIS*, 25(2):7, 2007.

[5] D. Lagun and E. Agichtein. Viewser: enabling large-scale remote user studies of web search examination and interaction. In *Proceedings of the 34th international ACM SIGIR conference on Research and development in Information*, pages 365–374. ACM, 2011.

Sentiment Identification by Incorporating Syntax, Semantics and Context Information

Kunpeng Zhang, Yusheng Xie, Yu Cheng, Daniel Honbo
Doug Downey, Ankit Agrawal, Wei-keng Liao, Alok Choudhary
EECS Department, Northwestern University
2145 Sheridan Road, Evanston IL,USA
{kzh980,yxi389,ych133,dkh301,ddowney,ankitag,wkliao,choudhar}@eecs.northwestern.edu

ABSTRACT

This paper proposes a method based on conditional random fields to incorporate sentence structure (syntax and semantics) and context information to identify sentiments of sentences within a document. It also proposes and evaluates two different active learning strategies for labeling sentiment data. The experiments with the proposed approach demonstrate a 5-15% improvement in accuracy on Amazon customer reviews compared to existing supervised learning and rule-based methods.

Categories and Subject Descriptors

H.4 [**Information Systems Applications**]: Miscellaneous; D.2.8 [**Software Engineering**]: Metrics—*complexity measures, performance measures*

Keywords

Sentiment, Syntax, Semantic, CRF, Active Learning

1. INTRODUCTION

Understanding the sentiment of sentences allows us to summarize opinions which could help people make informed decisions. All of the state-of-the-art algorithms perform well on individual sentences without considering any context information, but their accuracy is dramatically lower on the document level because they fail to consider context and the syntactic structure of sentences at the same time. There are many difficulties owing to the special characteristics and diversity in sentence structure in the way people express their opinions, including mixed sentiments in one sentence, sarcastic sentences, and opinions expressed indirectly through comparison, etc. In addition, complicated sentence structure and Internet slang make sentiment analysis even more challenging. In this work, we not only consider syntax that may influence the sentiment, including newly emerged Internet language, emoticons, positive words, negative words, and negation words, but also incorporate information about sentence structure, like conjunction words and comparisons. The context around a sentence also plays an important role in determining the sentiment. Therefore, we employ a conditional random field (CRF) [2] model to capture syntactic, structural, and contextual features of sentences. Our experiment results on customer reviews and Facebook comments show better accuracy compared to supervised and rule-based methods. Furthermore, we also employ active learning to help collect more labeled data. We propose two different strategies to select data with high uncertainty for human beings to label, and our experimental results on customer reviews show faster convergence compared to baselines.

SIGIR'12, August 12–16, 2012, Portland, Oregon, USA.
ACM 978-1-4503-1472-5/12/08.

2. METHODOLOGY AND EXPERIMENTS

CRF and Features Different subjectivity can generate different or even reversed sentiments for sentences. Therefore, the input is a set of m documents: $\{d_1, d_2, \dots, d_m\}$ along with the specified subject: $\{sub_1, sub_2, \dots, sub_m\}$. Each d_i contains n_i sentences $S^i : \{s_1^i, s_2^i, \dots, s_{n_i}^i\}$. The output for all documents is that for the jth sentence in the ith document s_j^i, it will assign a sentiment $o_j^i \in \{P : positive, N : negative, O : objective\}$. Conditional Random Fields (CRF) provides a probabilistic framework for calculating the probability of label sequences Y globally conditioned on sequence data X to be labeled. Parameters $\Theta = \{\lambda_k, \mu_l\}$ are estimated by maximizing the conditional log-likelihood function $\mathcal{L}(\Theta)$of the training data.

$$\mathcal{P}(Y \mid X) = \frac{1}{Z_X} exp(\sum_{i,k} \lambda_k f_k(y_{i-1}, y_i, X) + \sum_{i,l} \mu_l g_l(y_i, X))$$

where Z_X is the normalization constant.

$$\mathcal{L}(\Theta) = \sum_{j=1\dots M} log(\mathcal{P}(Y^{(j)} \mid X^{(j)};\Theta)) - \sum_k \frac{\lambda_k^2}{2\sigma_k^2} - \sum_l \frac{\mu_l^2}{2\sigma_l^2}$$

Various features have been widely extracted from sentences for sentiment classification and can be leveraged through CRF model. In this paper, we use features based on two aspects: syntactic and semantic structure of sentences (listed in the Table 1).

Data Collection Table 2 shows the data collected from Amazon Mechanical Turk (AMT). For each of these reviews, we asked 10 different workers from AMT to label the sentences as positive, negative, or objective. We used majority vote to determine the final label for each sentence. We also randomly selected 500 sentences from each of the camera and TV reviews and checked the labeling accuracy. The average response accuracy for all workers for the camera and TV reviews was 0.66 and 0.62 respectively. We also manually labeled 500 Facebook comments. We did some preprocessing tasks on the original data, including word correction (e.g., changing "luv" to "love") and part-of-speech (POS) tagging.

Experimental Results We compare our proposed method against the following rule-based algorithms and supervised

Table 1: Features used for this sequence labeling problem.

Semantic Features	
n_pos_words	Number of positive words (a positive word list: 1948 words)
n_neg_words	Number of negative words (a negative word list: 4550 words)
if_pos_emo	Existence of positive emoticons (a positive emoticon list: 52 emoticons)
if_neg_emo	Existence of negative emoticons (a negative emoticon list: 35 emoticons)
if_comp_sent	A sentence is comparative if it contains comparative parts-of-speech (JJR, JJS,RBR, RBS), or comparative phrases ("compare to", "in contrast", etc.)
type_conjunction_words	Type of conjunction words: subordinating, coordinating, and correlative
Syntactic Features	
sent_post	Sentence position. If the sentence is within first 20% of the sentences, it's a beginning sentence; an end sentence if within the last 20%, and middle for all others
post_pos_words	Position of positive words occurring. 0: no positive words occur; 1: only exist in the first part of a sentence; 2: only exist in the second part; -1: exist in both parts (mixed).
post_neg_words	Position of negative words occurring. Same as above.
post_negation_words	Position of negation words. Same as above.
comp_sub	Comparison subject: If the subjectivity is the same as the input subjectivity.
cos_sim_neigh_sent	cosine similarity score to neighboring sentences (previous sentence and next sentence).
LSI_sim_neigh_sent	LSI similarity score to neighboring sentences (previous sentence and next sentence).

Table 2: Data distribution. nrc|ns|nps|nns|nos: # of reviews/comments | sentences | positive sentences | negative sentences | objective sentences

Data	nrc	ns	nps	nns	nos
Camera	300	5156	2524	1185	1447
TV	300	5036	2364	1252	1420
Facebook	500	723	313	157	253

Table 3: Accuracy results of CRF model comparing to other methods (CSR, SVM, LR, and HMM) with semantic features only (SO) and with semantic and syntactic features (SS).

Data+Feature	CSR	SVM	LR	HMM	CRF
Camera (SO)	0.57	0.633	0.615	0.631	0.654
Camera (SS)	0.57	0.640	0.648	0.651	**0.72**
TV (SO)	0.54	0.612	0.60	0.629	0.630
TV (SS)	0.54	0.622	0.619	0.633	**0.665**
Overall (SO)	0.55	0.622	0.610	0.627	0.634
Overall (SS)	0.55	0.632	0.637	0.640	**0.693**
Facebook (SO)	**0.72**	0.60	0.610	0.607	0.612
Facebook (SS)	**0.72**	0.60	0.612	0.61	0.614

methods: compositional semantic rules (CSR) [1], support vector machine (SVM), logistic regression (LR), and hidden Markov models (HMM). Table 3 shows that CRFs outperform the other four methods in all cases on the Amazon review dataset. Using our CRF-based method with semantic and syntactic features is 5-15% more accurate than the other methods tested. However, CSR performs the best on the Facebook comments dataset, while all other methods generated similar results. We believe that this result is due to the length of the Facebook comments, which provide little to no context for our CRF-based method, as well as the use of emoticons, which convey sentiments directly.

Active Learning Since collecting labeled data is expensive, we use active learning to collect the most valuable labeled examples. The fundamental step of active learning procedure is to choose what data to present to the oracle. When we apply our trained model on inferring unlabeled data, we get a sequence of label probabilities for a document which has m sentences : $\{p_1, p_2, \ldots, p_m\}$. Each p_i is the probability for the most probable label. In Strategy 1 (S1), we rank documents based on the average probability: $\frac{1}{m}\sum_{i=1}^{m} p_i$ and select the document with the smallest value

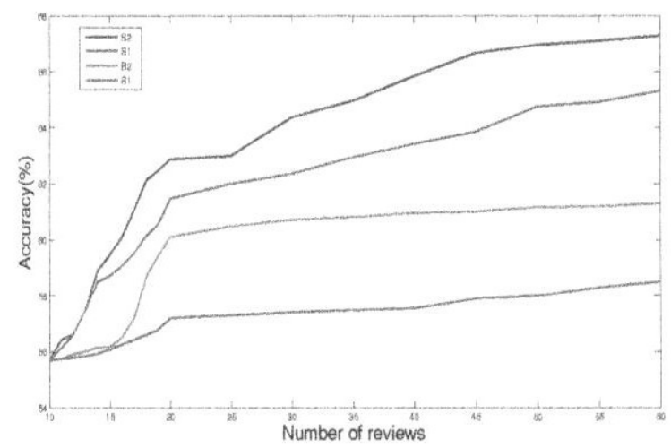

Figure 1: The convergence speed of classification accuracy (10-fold cross validation).

to present to oracle. In Strategy 2 (S2), we rank sentences based on the probability in an ascending order and calculate the average of the probabilities in the smaller half $\mathcal{P}$. We then rank the document based on $\mathcal{P}$ and present the document with the smallest $\mathcal{P}$ to oracle. We start from a training size of 10 documents and add one document at a time. We compare these strategies against two baselines, (B1) selecting a document at random and (B2) selecting a document based on the minimum probability of its sentences. In this paper, we use customer reviews to test the convergence speed. Figure 1 shows that S2 achieves the same accuracy faster than S1. Because documents with the smallest average probability may have some sentences with high probability, which do not need to be disambiguated.

3. ACKNOWLEDGEMENT

This work is supported in part by NSF award numbers: CCF-0621443, OCI-0724599, CCF-0833131, CNS-0830927, IIS-0905205, OCI-0956311, CCF-0938000, CCF-1043085, CCF-1029166, and OCI-1144061, and in part by DOE grants DE-FG02-08ER25848, DE-SC0001283, DE-SC0005309, DE-SC0005340, and DE-SC0007456.

4. REFERENCES

[1] Y. Choi and C. Cardie. Learning with compositional semantics as structural inference for subsentential sentiment analysis. EMNLP '08, pages 793–801, 2008.

[2] J. D. Lafferty, A. McCallum, and F. C. N. Pereira. Conditional random fields: Probabilistic models for segmenting and labeling sequence data. ICML '01, pages 282–289, 2001.

Short Text Classification Using Very Few Words*

Aixin Sun
School of Computer Engineering, Nanyang Technological University, Singapore
axsun@ntu.edu.sg

ABSTRACT

We propose a simple, scalable, and non-parametric approach for short text classification. Leveraging the well studied and scalable Information Retrieval (IR) framework, our approach mimics human labeling process for a piece of short text. It first selects the most representative and topical-indicative words from a given short text as query words, and then searches for a small set of labeled short texts best matching the query words. The predicted category label is the majority vote of the search results. Evaluated on a collection of more than 12K Web snippets, the proposed approach achieves comparable classification accuracy with the baseline Maximum Entropy classifier using as few as 3 query words and top-5 best matching search hits. Among the four query word selection schemes proposed and evaluated in our experiments, term frequency together with clarity gives the best classification accuracy.

Categories and Subject Descriptors

H.3.3 [**Information Storage and Retrieval**]: Information Search and Retrieval—*Information filtering*

Keywords

Short Text Classification, Search and Vote

1. INTRODUCTION

We are now dealing with much more short texts. Examples are snippets in search results, tweets, status updates, comments, and reviews from various social platforms. Short texts are in general much shorter, nosier, and sparser, which calls for a revisit of many fundamental text mining techniques including text classfiication.

Short text classification is to assign a piece of short text one or more predefined categories. Most existing approaches try to *enrich* the representation of a short text using additional semantics. The semantics could be derived internally from the short text collection [3], externally from a collection of much longer documents in a similar domain as the short texts [5], or from much larger external sources such as Wikipedia and WordNet [1,3,4]. In [1,4], the classification accuracy is significantly improved by enriching short text feature vector with relevant hidden topics derived from Wikipedia pages using topic model.

In the opposite direction of enriching short text representation, we propose to *trim* a short text representation to get a few most representative words for topical classification. This approach is to

*This work was supported by MINDEF-NTU-DIRP/2010/03.

SIGIR'12, August 12–16, 2012, Portland, Oregon, USA.
ACM 978-1-4503-1472-5/12/08.

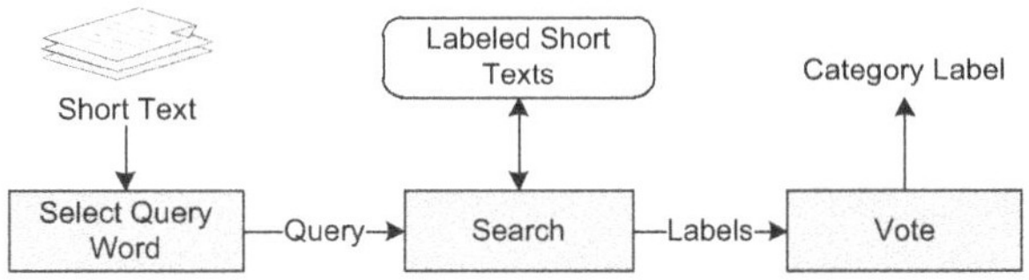

Figure 2: The search and vote framework

mimic the human labeling process. Due to the length of short text (*e.g.*, a search result snippet is usually fewer than 20 words, a tweet has at most 140 characters), one finishes reading a piece of short text at a glance; the category label is assigned mainly based on the few keywords observed from the short text. More specifically, given a short text, we identify one or more words that best represent the short text and formulate a weighted word query using each selected word and its associated weight. Illustrated in Figure 2, this query is submitted to a local search engine for the best matching labeled examples. Analogous to the widely used k-nearest-neighbor (kNN) classifier, the predicted category is the one receiving highest votes from the search results (*i.e.*, labeled short texts).

Leveraging the well studied IR techniques, the proposed approach is extremely scalable. More importantly, the lazy and non-parametric approach well accommodates fast updating of labeled examples, changes to the classification scheme (*e.g.*, adding a new category), as well as giving specific attention to certain groups of labeled examples by changing the scoring function in the search (*e.g.*, a search may favor more recently added labeled examples). Note that, different from kNN classifiers, our approach requires no computation of the nearest neighbors in the labeled data. Instead, we search for the top-H best hits using few query words.

2. SEARCH AND VOTE

Query Word Selection. The most critical step in the proposed approach is the selection of representative words from a short text as query words. Ideally, the query words should be (i) well representing the main content of the short text, and (ii) topically indicative. A word is topically indicative if it is about a specific topic.

With bag-of-words representation, the most widely used TF or $TF.IDF$ weighting scheme is sufficient for the first requirement. For the second requirement, we propose to use *clarity* to measure the topical-specificity of a word. Proposed for predicting query performance in [2], the clarity score of a query is the Kullback-Leibler (KL) divergence between the query language model (*i.e.*, unigram distribution of word occurrences) and collection language model. The former is inferred from a set of documents best matching a given query and the latter from the entire collection. Given a short text data collection $\mathcal{D}$. Let word w be a candidate word for selection, we use w as a single-term query to retrieve its top-N most

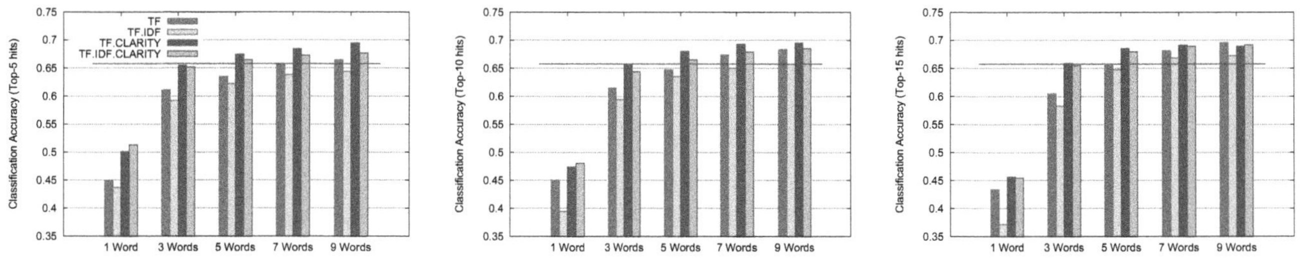

(a) Category voting by top-5 hits (b) Category voting by top-10 hits (c) Category voting by top-15 hits

Figure 1: The classification accuracy voted by top-{5, 10, 15} hits respectively using {1, 3, 5, 7, 9} words as query

Table 1: Number of training/test snippets in the 8 categories.

Category	#Train	#Test	Category	#Train	#Test
Business	1200	300	Culture-Arts-Ent	1880	330
Computer	1200	300	Education-Science	2360	300
Health	880	300	Engineering	220	150
Sports	1120	300	Politics-Society	1200	300

relevant documents ($N = 20$ in our experiments[1]), denoted by Q_w. The clarity score of word w is computed using the equation below, where $\mathcal{V}$ denotes the vocabulary.

$$Clarity(w) = \sum_{w' \in \mathcal{V}} P(w'|Q_w) \log \frac{P(w'|Q_w)}{P(w'|\mathcal{D})}$$

Intuitively, if w is specific to a topic, then the documents matching w share a common topic indicated by a few words with very high probabilities of occurrences against their probabilities in the entire collection. On the other hand, if the documents matching w do not share a common topic, then this set of documents is analogous to a random sample from the document collection, with similar distributions of word occurrences.

Scoring and Voting. In literature, many scoring functions for relevance ranking have been proposed for document search. To search for the most relevant labeled examples for a given query, we use the default scoring function implemented in Lucene[2]. Note that, Lucene allows query word boosting, *i.e.,* to assign weight to each query word in a multi-term query. The score computed in query word selection step is used to weigh each selected query word. After query execution, each category label of the returned documents serves as an evidence that supports the likelihood of the querying document belonging to that category. Majority voting shows better results than its weighted counterpart in our experiments.

3. EXPERIMENTS

We conducted experiments on the Web snippet dataset that has been used in [1,4]. The dataset consists of 10,060 train and 2,280 test snippets from 8 categories, shown in Table 1. On average, each snippet has 18.07 words after indexing by Lucene.

We evaluate four schemes to select query words: *TF*, *TF.IDF*, *TF.CLARITY*, and *TF.IDF.CLARITY*. The latter two are the product of *TF* and *TF.IDF* respectively with clarity score. For each scheme, the top {1, 3, 5, 7, 9} words with highest scores are selected as query words. The category label of a test snippet is voted by the top-{5, 10, 15} hits respectively. The classification accuracies are reported in Figures 1(a), 1(b), and 1(c). Note that, as each snippet has exactly one category label, the reported accuracy is the same as Micro-Precision/Recall/F_1. For comparison, the horizontal line plotted in the three figures indicates the accuracy of 0.6575 achieved by Maximum Entropy (MaxEnt) classifier as baseline [4].

From the results, we make the following observations. First, more words (from 1 word to 5 words) in query generally lead to better classification accuracy. The improvement becomes very minor when more than 5 words are used in query. Observe that using 3 words, the classification accuracy voted by top-5 hits matches MaxEnt, an advanced model that has shown good classification accuracies in many applications. Second, using 1 word in query, more hits lead to poorer results. When more than 3 words are selected in query, more hits yield slightly better accuracy. Third, among all word selection schemes, *TF.CLARITY* outperforms the others in most runs when 3 or more words are used in query. For one word query, *TF.IDF.CLARITY* is the best scheme.

We note that the best classification accuracy achieved is better than MaxEnt, but poorer than the results reported on the same dataset using enriched short text representation [1]. The enriched representation is a combination of *word feature* from the short text, and *topic feature* from a topic space derived from Wikipedia. We argue that our approach is directly applicable to any enriched representation because each enriched feature (*e.g.,* a topic feature) can be selected as a query word. That is, our approach complements the approach enriching text representation.

4. SUMMARY AND FUTURE WORK

We propose a simple, scalable, and non-parametric approach for short text classification. Using the simple *TF.CLARITY* to select as few as 3 words, the default Lucene scoring function, and majority voting from 5 search hits, our approach achieves comparable classification accuracy with MaxEnt classifier. We also note that our approach complements the research on enriching short text representation. Moreover, the non-parametric approach offers much more flexibility in handling updates in labeled examples and classification schemes.

The proposed approach has great potential to achieve much better results with more research on (i) query word or phrase selection, (ii) relevance ranking techniques specifically for short texts, and (iii) short text representation enrichment.

5. REFERENCES

[1] M. Chen, X. Jin, and D. Shen. Short text classification improved by learning multi-granularity topics. In *IJCAI*, pages 1776–1781, 2011.

[2] S. Cronen-Townsend, Y. Zhou, and W. B. Croft. Predicting query performance. In *SIGIR*, pages 299–306, 2002.

[3] X. Hu, N. Sun, C. Zhang, and T.-S. Chua. Exploiting internal and external semantics for the clustering of short texts using world knowledge. In *CIKM*, pages 919–928, 2009.

[4] X. H. Phan, M. L. Nguyen, and S. Horiguchi. Learning to classify short and sparse text & web with hidden topics from large-scale data collections. In *WWW*, pages 91–100, 2008.

[5] S. Zelikovitz, W. W. Cohen, and H. Hirsh. Extending WHIRL with background knowledge for improved text classification. *Information Retrieval*, 10(1):35–67, 2007.

[1] If a word appears in fewer than 20 documents, its clarity score is set to 1.0.

[2] http://lucene.apache.org/core/

Summarizing the Differences from Microblogs

Dingding Wang
University of Miami
1365 Memorial Drive
Coral Gables, FL 33146
d.wang1@miami.edu

Mitsunori Ogihara
University of Miami
1365 Memorial Drive
Coral Gables, FL 33146
ogihara@cs.miami.edu

Tao Li
Florida International University
11200 SW 8th ST
Miami, FL 33199
taoli@cs.fiu.edu

ABSTRACT

With the rapid growth of social media websites, microblogging has become a popular way to spread instant news and events. Due to the dynamic and social nature of microblogs, extracting useful information from microblogs is more challenging than from the traditional news articles. In this paper we study the problem of summarizing the differences from microblogs. Given a collection of microblogs discussing an event/topic, we propose to generate a short summary delivering the differences among these microblogs, such as the different points of view for a news topic and the changes and evolution of an ongoing event.

Categories and Subject Descriptors

H.3.3 [**Information Storage and Retrieval**]: Information Search and Retrieval; I.2.7 [**Artificial Intelligence**]: Natural Language Processing

Keywords

Summarizing differences, Microblogs

1. INTRODUCTION

Nowadays, microblogs provide a new communication channel for users to share information and report news. Compared to regular blogs and traditional media, microblogging spreads first-hand reports on real-life events faster and more widely. For a hot event, thousands even millions of individuals join the discussion and express their opinions through popular microblogging web sites such as Twitter. A natural and interesting question is what are the differences among the discussion. In this paper, we explore the problem of generating a short summary of the differences among microblogs.

This problem is related to document summarization which aims to extract sentences from documents to form a brief summary. However, traditional document summarization usually selects sentences delivering the majority of information or query-relevant information from the documents, while in our task the differences need to be addressed. Recently there are some research works on comparative document summarization [7, 5] which also try to summarize the differences from news articles. However, all of the existing research focuses on traditional news articles, few attempts have been made to the newly emerging microblogs. Different from traditional news reports, microblogs are short noisy text streams and are of the dynamic and social natures. In this paper, we propose a framework to generate short summaries capturing the differences from microblogs. The proposed framework consists of three modules: keyword selection, query expansion, and sentence selection. First of all, discriminant keywords are selected via an unsupervised approach which combines document clustering and keyword selection. Then the keywords are used as the original query to perform query expansion, which is important to deal with the unique characteristics of microblogs. Finally, a query-based sentence selection is conducted using a strategy of maximizing the relevances between the selected sentences and the expanded query and at the same time minimizing the redundancy.

2. THE METHODOLOGY

2.1 Keyword Selection via Weighted Feature Subset Non-negative Matrix Factorization

In order to find the differences among microblogs, we use weighted feature subset non-negative matrix factorization (WFS-NMF) proposed in [6] to cluster the microblogs into different topics and simultaneously extract discriminant keywords for these topics. This is an unsupervised approach to combine data clustering and feature selection. Unlike the keywords selected from co-clustering or latent semantic analysis which usually strongly associate with one cluster, the keywords selected by WFS-NMF are the most representative and discriminant terms among the topics.

Given a term-microblog matrix X, let G represent the cluster indicator matrix for terms and F be the cluster indicator matrix for microblogs. WFS-NMF can be formalized as follows.

$$\min_{W\geq 0, F\geq 0, G\geq 0} ||X - FG^T||_W^2, s.t. \sum_j W_j^\alpha = 1 \quad (1)$$

where W is a diagonal matrix indicating the weights of the terms in X, and α is a parameter. The terms with the highest weights are the most discriminant keywords.

2.2 Query Expansion using Pseudo Relevance Feedback

The original query is usually short and vague, to enhance the query expressibility, query expansion is used to replace the original query by a high-quality query. In this paper, we adopt the pseudo relevance feedback methods implemented in the Terrier information retrieval platform [3]. The methods extract informative terms from the top-ranked documents retrieved using the original query and use them for query expansion.

Here we model each microblog m in the corpus C as θ_m, and model each query Q as θ_Q. The expanded query is defined as Q'. In a pseudo relevance manner, suppose the few top-ranked microblogs $m+$ by the initial query Q build a relevant model θ_F. We set the new query to be a linear combination of original query Q and relevant model θ_F:

$$p(w|\theta_{Q'}) = (1-\alpha)p(w|\theta_Q) + \alpha p(w|\theta_F), \tag{2}$$

where α controls the degree of coherence of the new query to the pseudo relevance. The relevance model method approximates θ_F as the query model, and each pseudo relevant microblog is a sample from the query model. Therefore the relevance model method defines term distribution in θ_F as the likelihood of generating terms from the pseudo relevance:

$$p(w|\theta_F) \propto \sum_{m+\in F} p(m+)p(w|m+)p(Q|m+), \tag{3}$$

where $p(Q|m+) = \prod_{q\in Q} p(q|m+)$.

2.3 Query-based Sentence Selection

Once we obtain the expanded query, we perform a query-based sentence selection under the max-relevance and min-redundancy framework [4]. The sentences are selected one by one, and each selected sentence should be highly related to the query and be dissimilar to the other selected sentences so that to remove the redundancy. This problem then becomes an optimization problem as follows.

Suppose set S represents the set of sentences and we already have V_{k-1}, the selected sentence set with k-1 sentences, then the task is to select the k-th sentence from the set $\{S - V_{k-1}\}$. In the following formula, we see that minimizing the redundancy and maximizing the relevance can be achieved concordantly [4].

$$\max_{s_j \in S - V_{k-1}} [Sim(s_i; query) - \frac{1}{k-1} \sum_{s_i \in G_{k-1}} Sim(s_j; s_i)], \tag{4}$$

where Sim is the cosine similarity between a pair of sentences. The computational complexity of this incremental sentence selection method is $O(|V| \times |S|) = O(km)$.

3. EXPERIMENTS

3.1 Data Annotation and Preprocessing

First of all, we select 10 hot topics of world news and technology such as "Japanese earthquake and Fukushima nuclear disaster", "swine flu outbreak", and "Siri for iphone 4s", etc. For each topic, we collect 1000 tweets which have the most replies and retweets from Twitter. Three human labelers manually create reference summaries describing the differences of the tweets for each topic. The length of each summary is limited to 250 words.

In the preprocessing, mentions (@somebody) are removed from the vocabulary. Non-English tweets containing less than one English word with more than 2 characters are filtered. Explicit re-tweets, empty tweets, and forbidden tweets are also filtered.

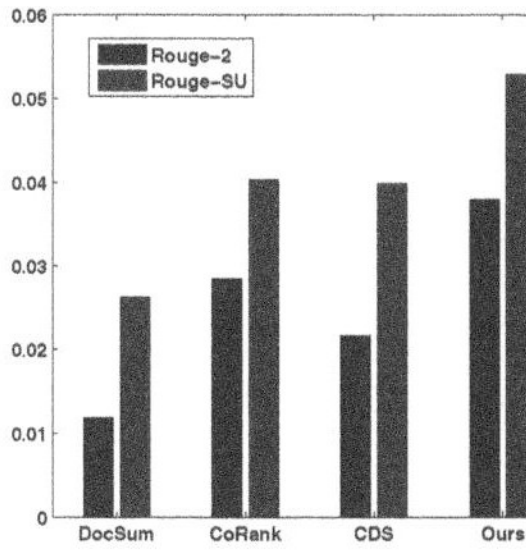

Figure 1: Comparison of different summarization systems.

3.2 Implemented Systems and Evaluation Measures

We compare our proposed method with the following existing summarization systems: (1) DocSum - one of the most widely used traditional document summarization methods [1]; (2) CoRank - a method summarizing the differences from multilingual news articles [5]; (3) CDS - a comparative document summarization proposed in [7]. We compare the human created summaries with the summaries generated by different systems using the ROUGE toolkit (version 1.5.5) [2].

3.3 Experimental Results

Figure 1 shows the Rouge scores of different systems. From the results, we observe that (1) DocSum achieves the poorest results since it focuses on delivering the major information in the tweets and can not handle the requirement of finding differences; (2) CoRank and CDS outperform DocSum because they are designed to extract different themes from documents and the common aspects among the documents are removed; (3) our proposed method achieves the highest scores because we consider the unique characteristics of microblogs which are usually short and noisy, and the discriminant keyword selection, query expansion, and the optimization based sentence selection schemes used in our method can effectively address the problem.

4. ACKNOWLEDGMENTS

This work is in part supported by NIH/NIA 1P30DA027828-01A1 and NSF grants DBI-0850203 and CNS-1126619.

5. REFERENCES

[1] G. Erkan and D. R. Radev. Lexpagerank: Prestige in multi-document text summarization. In *EMNLP*, 2004.

[2] C. Y. Lin. ROUGE: A package for automatic evaluation of summaries. In *Proceedings of the Workshop on Text Summarization Branches Out (WAS)*, 2004.

[3] I. Ounis, G. Amati, V. Plachouras, B. He, C. Macdonald, and D. Johnson. Terrier information retrieval platform. In *ECIR*, 2005.

[4] H. Peng, F. Long, and C. Ding. Feature selection based on mutual information: criteria of max-dependency, max-relevance, and min-redundancy. *IEEE Transactions on Pattern Analysis and Machine Intelligence*, 2005.

[5] X. Wan, H. Jia, S. Huang, and J. Xiao. Summarizing the differences in multilingual news. In *SIGIR*, 2011.

[6] D. Wang, T. Li, and C. H. Q. Ding. Weighted feature subset non-negative matrix factorization and its applications to document understanding. In *ICDM*, 2010.

[7] D. Wang, S. Zhu, T. Li, and Y. Gong. Comparative document summarization via discriminative sentence selection. In *CIKM*, 2009.

Survival Analysis of Click Logs

Si-Chi Chin
Information Science
The University of Iowa
Iowa City, Iowa 52242
si-chi-chin@uiowa.edu

W. Nick Street
Department of Management Sciences
The University of Iowa
Iowa City, Iowa 52242
nick-street@uiowa.edu

ABSTRACT

Click logs from search engines provide a rich opportunity to acquire implicit feedback from users. Patterns derived from the time between a posted query and a click provide information on the ranking quality, reflecting the perceived relevance of a retrieved URL. This paper applies the Kaplan-Meier estimator to study click patterns. The visualization of click curves demonstrates the interaction between the relevance and the rank position of URLs. The observed results demonstrate the potential of using click curves to predict the quality of the top-ranked results.

Categories and Subject Descriptors: H.4 [Information Systems Applications]: Miscellaneous

General Terms: Theory

Keywords: Clickthrough Logs, Kaplan-Meier Survival Analysis, Click Curve Visualization

1. INTRODUCTION AND DATASET

Ranking is a major concern to information retrieval applications such as document ranking on search engines. Implicit feedback from click logs can be used to approximate relevance judgements and improve rank results [7, 5]. This paper adopts Kaplan-Meier survival analysis [8] to examine clicking patterns, accounting for relevance labels and rank position of the URLs on a search engine result page (SERP). In medical research, the Kaplan-Meier estimator approximates the survival function, measuring the probability of patients surviving for different time points after treatment. We use the estimator to create click curves, showing the probability of URLs remaining unclicked across time. In both cases, the data is often right-censored, i.e. final outcomes are not observed for some instances. In click logs, censoring occurs when a search session ends or a query is replaced by the succeeding query. Figure 1(a) illustrates the definitions for clicked and censored time in one session. Click times are derived from the immediately previous query, and censored times include the time from the first Q_A to Q_B, and from second Q_A to the end of the session.

The visualization of click curves can show the interaction between relevance and position bias, making the knowledge of clicks more explicit. We expect that if a search engine returns a relevant URL on top of the ranked list, its click curve will drop drastically at the beginning and eventually approach zero, e.g., in Figure 1(b), URL 3808 is relevant to Query 5771. Our goal is to quantify and visualize the effects of relevance and ranking on the probability and speed of user clicks. To our knowledge, this is the first work that applying survival analysis to study click patterns.

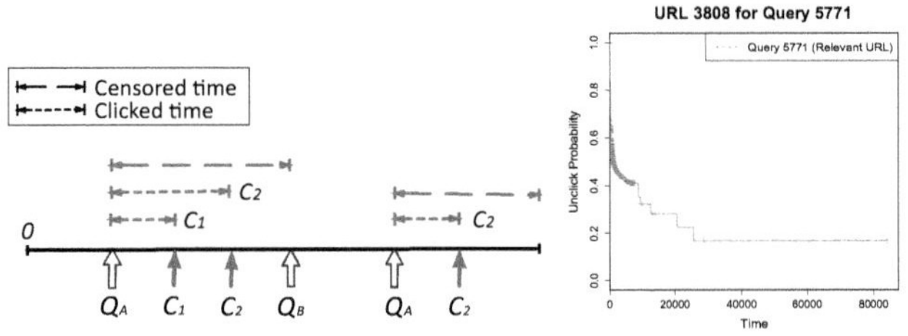

(a) Clicked and Censored Times (b) URL 3808

Figure 1: Times and click curves.

We use the Yandex click log dataset provided by the Relevance Prediction Challenge and Workshop on Web Search Click Data (WSCD 2012). The goal of the challenge is to rank URLs by relevance based on user search behavior. The click log is grouped by sessions, containing query IDs, ranked URLs from the Yandex SERP for each query, and a sequence of click actions. Yandex assigned binary labels ("relevant" and "not relevant") to a subset of URLs appearing in the log. There are 5,191 unique queries in the original training set. We selected Query 5771 (Q5771), Query 222491 (Q222491), to test our approach. Q5771 and Q222491 each have 3468 and 2179 unique sessions, and have 14 and 13 judged URLs. As shown in Table 1, Q5771 has stronger performance in ranking than Query 222491. The top 10 ranked list in the table is sorted by the average rank for each labeled URLs displayed on SERP, showing the overall performance for the two queries. However, the top 10 URLs in actual session logs can be different from the table.

Table 1: Summary statistics for Q5771 and Q222491.

	Query 5771	Query 222491
Rank 1-10	{1,1,1,1,0,1,0,0,1,0}	{1,0,0,1,1,1,1,1,1,1}
NDCG@5	0.88	0.54
NDCG@10	0.73	0.69

2. CLICK CURVE ANALYSIS

Click curve analysis and visualization was performed using the R (http://www.r-project.org) survival package. Figure 2 shows the click curves for Q222491 and Q5771, grouping

SIGIR'12, August 12–16, 2012, Portland, Oregon, USA.
ACM 978-1-4503-1472-5/12/08.

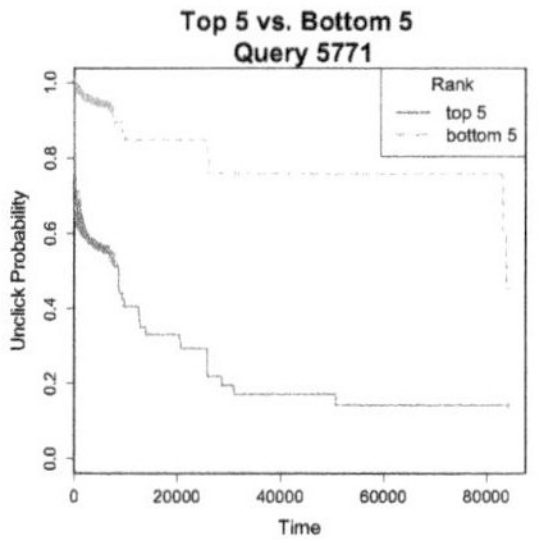

(a) Rank:Q5771

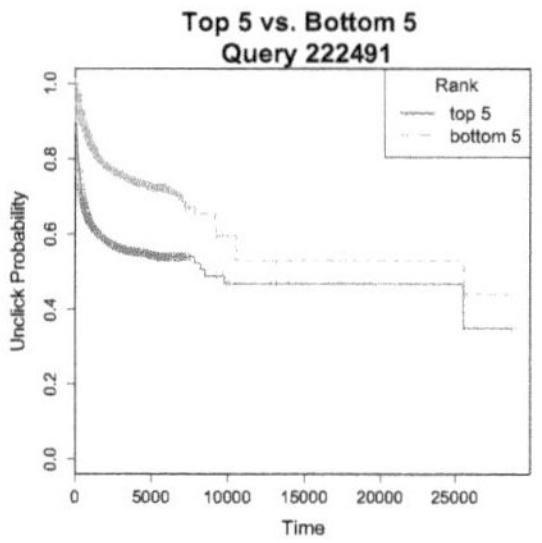

(b) Rank:Q222491

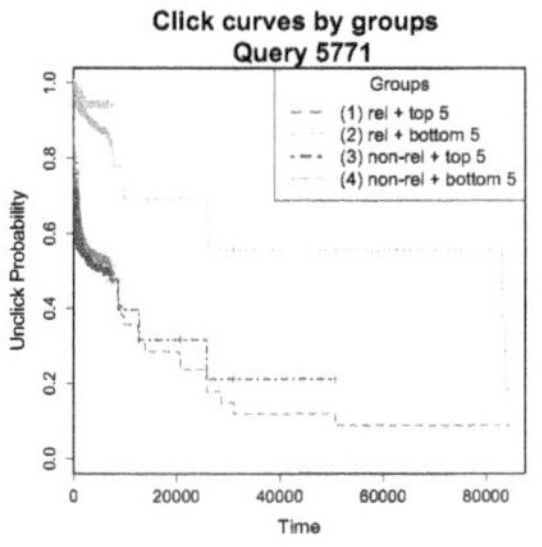

(c) Group:Q5771

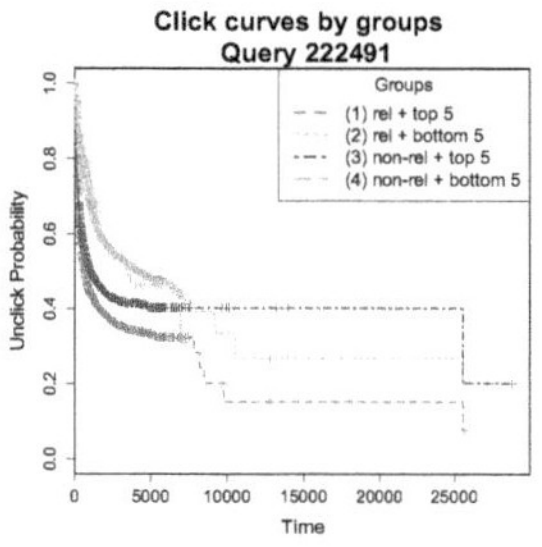

(d) Group:Q222491

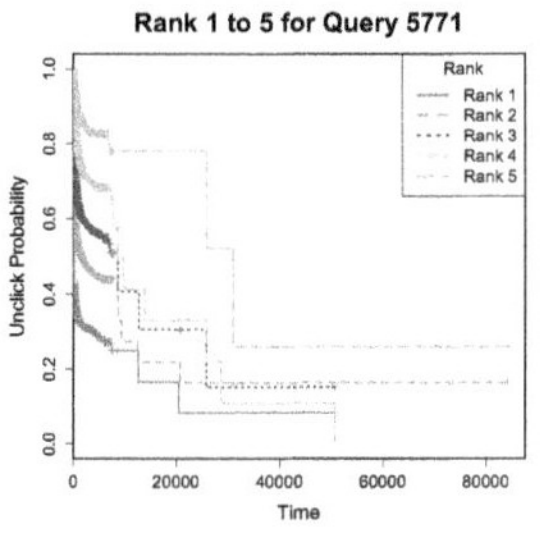

(e) Top 5:Q5771

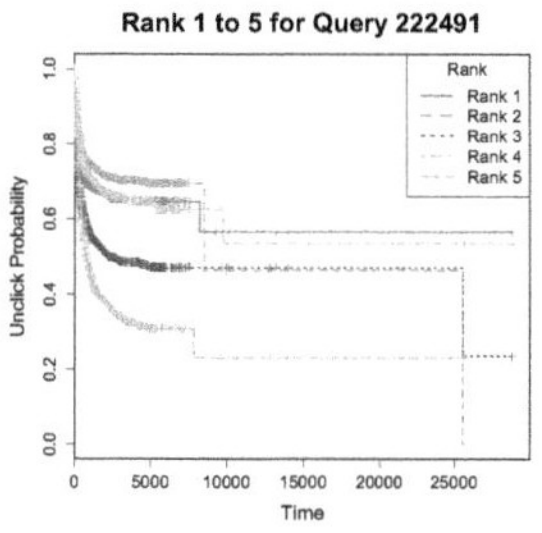

(f) Top 5:Q222491

Figure 2: Click curves for various groupings of the URLs from the two queries.

URLs by rank and relevance. Log-rank tests ($p = 0.05$) were performed on all pairs of curves.

Both Figures 2(a) and 2(b) show significantly different clicking patterns for URLs in the top 5 on the SERP. However, the distance between the two curves diminishes as more relevant URLs were ranked lower for Q222491. The results indicate that the effect of position bias may vary among queries. To further study the interaction between relevance and rank, we divide URLs into four groups as shown in Figure 2(c) and 2(d). Group 1 contains relevant URLs ranked in the top 5; Group 2, relevant URLs in bottom 5; Group 3, irrelevant URLs in top 5; Group 4, irrelevant URLs in bottom 5. The pair-wise tests on groups are significant except in two cases: between Group 2 and 4 for Q222491, and between Group 1 and 3 for Q5771. Figure 2(c) indicates that the irrelevant URLs mixed in the top 5 can become hard to discover as Q5771 has evident position bias. On the other hand, since Q222491 has better ranking at the bottom, the differences between Group 2 and 4 diminish. In Figure 2(d), since the ranking on the top 5 for Query 222491 is imperfect, the click patterns for relevant and irrelevant URLs are distinct. Moreover, both Figure 2(c) and 2(d) show that, even given the position bias, the click curve for relevant URLs ranked at the bottom is still lower than irrelevant URLs on the top.

Figure 2(e) and 2(f) explore the effect of position bias on click curves at the position 1 to 5. As the ranked results are ideal for Q5771, we observed distinct clicking patterns on the top 5 results for Q5771 in Figure 2(e). Figure 2(f) shows a sharp drop on rank 5, implying the URL at rank 5 is more relevant than URLs at rank 2 and 3, which are judged not relevant to the query.

3. DISCUSSION AND CONCLUSION

Position bias is a primary concern in click logs. The probability of a click depends not only on its relevance, but on its position in the results page. Several papers formalized position bias using probabilistic models, such as the Cascade model [2], dynamic Bayseian network click model [1], Click Chain model [6], and user browsing model [3]. Unlike these models, we incorporate the time from a query to a click to model and visualize the unclicked probability of URLs. We believe that although top-ranked URLs may be clicked faster, a lower ranked but relevant URL may still be quickly discovered and clicked. The proposed click curve analysis exhibits distinct patterns between groups with various combinations of relevance and rank positions.

Although the time to first click was considered by Fox et al. [4], opportunities remain for exploring the use of activity time as a source of implicit feedback to judge the relevance of search results [5]. Compared to [4], we expand the scope from time to first click to time to *all* clicks. We adopted survival analysis to examine click patters in click logs, investigating the inter-related effect of relevance and rank positions.

This paper demonstrates the potential of applying survival analysis to determine the quality of ranked results. Visualizing click curves helps understand the interaction between the rank positions and the relevance of the retrieved URLs. The proposed approach can also be personalized to model individual users. Future work can focus on deriving functions for click curves to predict relevance labels for individual URLs. Click curves can also be included as an informative feature for learning to rank.

4. REFERENCES

[1] O. Chapelle and Y. Zhang. A dynamic Bayesian network click model for web search ranking. In *WWW*, pages 1–10, Madrid, Spain, 2009.

[2] N. Craswell, O. Zoeter, M. Taylor, and B. Ramsey. An experimental comparison of click position-bias models. In *WSDM*, pages 87–94, Stanford, CA, 2008.

[3] G. E. Dupret and B. Piwowarski. A user browsing model to predict search engine click data from past observations. In *SIGIR*, pages 331–338, Singapore, 2008.

[4] S. Fox, K. Karnawat, M. Mydland, S. Dumais, and T. White. Evaluating implicit measures to improve web search. *ACM Trans. Inf. Syst.*, 23(2):147–168, Apr. 2005.

[5] X. Fu. Towards a model of implicit feedback for web search. *Journal of the American Society for Information Science and Technology*, 61(1):30–49, Jan. 2010.

[6] F. Guo, C. Liu, A. Kannan, T. Minka, M. Taylor, Y. Wang, and C. Faloutsos. Click chain model in web search. In *WWW*, pages 11–20, Madrid, Spain, 2009.

[7] T. Joachims, L. Granka, B. Pan, H. Hembrooke, and G. Gay. Accurately interpreting clickthrough data as implicit feedback. In *SIGIR*, pages 154–161, Salvador, Brazil, 2005. ACM.

[8] E. L. Kaplan and P. Meier. Nonparametric estimation from incomplete observations. *Journal of the American Statistical Association*, 53(282):457–481, June 1958.

Text Selections as Implicit Relevance Feedback

Ryen W. White
Microsoft Research
Redmond, WA 98052
ryenw@microsoft.com

Georg Buscher
Microsoft Bing
Bellevue, WA 98004
georgbu@microsoft.com

ABSTRACT
Users' search activity has been used as implicit feedback to model search interests and improve the performance of search systems. In search engines, this behavior usually takes the form of queries and result clicks. However, richer data on how people engage with search results can now be captured at scale, creating new opportunities to enhance search. In this poster we focus on one type of newly-observable behavior: text selection events on search-result captions. We show that we can use text selections as implicit feedback to significantly improve search result relevance.

Categories and Subject Descriptors
H.3.3 [**Information Storage and Retrieval**]: Information Search and Retrieval – *search process, selection process.*

Keywords
Text selection; implicit relevance feedback.

1. INTRODUCTION
Searchers express their needs to search engines via query statements. These queries can be augmented by information from prior search activity, such as previous search engine result page (SERP) clicks within the session or across multiple sessions. Indeed, previous research has shown that prior clicks mined from session histories can be effective in modeling search interests [6]. However, search interaction with SERPs and landing pages is richer than simply queries and clicks [4]. A variety of methods have been proposed for gathering implicit feedback based on document examination and retention behaviors [5], but generally such information is not available to search engines at scale. More recently, methods have been proposed to capture richer interactions with SERPs such as cursor movements, scrolls, and text selections [2]. Monitoring these events on the SERPs of search engines affords a range of possibilities to improve retrieval effectiveness by modeling user interests. In this poster, we study the value of feedback gleaned implicitly from one of these behaviors, SERP text selections, where users mark blocks of text for further manipulation.

2. TEXT SELECTION AS FEEDBACK
The source of our implicit feedback is text selection events on SERPs, specifically blocks of text selected from result captions. We refer to the text within which the selection occurs as the *container.* Figure 1 shows an example of a selection event in a result caption, where the user has selected text in the caption snippet.

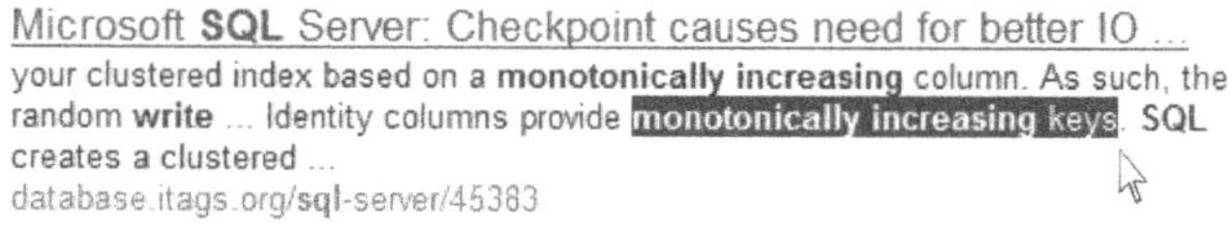

Figure 1: Text selection (blue background) on SERP snippet.

Searchers may select text for a number of reasons, including to copy-and-paste to another application, as a query to a search engine (e.g., via direct functionality available in some browsers or the browser search box), or as a reading aid. Using browser-specific JavaScript functionality similar to that in [2], we can identify when text selections occur and can also determine the bounding box of the immediately surrounding HTML element (e.g., the result snippet).

SIGIR'12, August 12–16, 2012, Portland, Oregon, USA.
ACM 978-1-4503-1472-5/12/08.

We believe that text selection events provide valuable information about searcher interests that could be used to improve search performance on future queries for that user. Specifically, we were interested in determining whether there was value from using text selection events as implicit feedback and using the text associated with a text-selection event (the title, the snippet, or the title plus snippet) to model search interests. For example, in Figure 1, although only some words in the snippet are selected, the full snippet (from "your clustered index" to "creates a clustered") could be used to construct a model of the user's search interests.

We describe a log-based study of one application of such interest models: re-ranking the search results for near-future queries based on their similarity to captions that contained text selections.

3. STUDY
3.1 Data
To perform the analysis required for our study, we used 928 users' queries and SERP interactions over a four-week period in late 2011. Data were gathered as part of a related study of SERP interaction behavior. Participants were employees of Microsoft Corporation and volunteered to participate in the study. Participation involved installing a plugin for the Internet Explorer browser that recorded the Web pages visited. When users were on the SERP of the Microsoft Bing search engine, the plugin injected JavaScript into the page, allowing for it to record cursor movements, scrolling, and text selections using a method similar to that used in [2]. Scalability considerations meant that the actual content or precise position of the selected text were not recorded using this method. However, the full text of every caption on a SERP (title, snippet, URL) could be obtained by mining the Bing search logs, and those captions containing a text selection could be identified.

Participants performed 9,433 search sessions comprising a total of 39,606 queries over the course of the study. 754 (1.9%) of the queries logged had text selections, including in the search box (reformulations) and on inline answers. Since we were focused on re-ranking the organic search results, we restricted the set of queries to the 389 queries A (1.0%) that had at least one text selection on the snippet of an organic result and had a follow-on query B with at least one term in common with the current query A, to help ensure consistency in user information needs. We will be re-ranking the results for query B directly after the query A which contained a text selection, since that gives the search engine an opportunity to include the implicit feedback in the result ranking.

Although 389 queries may seem like a small set by search log analysis standards, there is still sufficient volume to study the value of using text selections in our study. Also, in terms of application, any significant improvement in search performance for 1% of queries to a search engine is still potentially impactful given the amount of investment engines make in improving their performance and the large the number of queries that they process.

3.2 Relevance Judgments and Measures

For evaluation, we required a relevance judgment for each result. Obtaining many relevance judgments directly from end users is impractical and there is no known approach to train expert judges to provide reliable judgments that accurately reflect individual user preferences. Hence we obtained these judgments using a log-based methodology similar to that adopted by [1]. Specifically, we assign a positive judgment to each of the top 10 results for which there was a satisfied (SAT) SERP click. We defined a satisfied click in a similar way to previous work [3], as either a click followed by no further clicks for 30 seconds or more, or the last result click in the session. URLs without a click received a negative judgment. Positive judgments are used to evaluate retrieval performance before and after re-ranking using average precision (AP) across the top 10 results and reporting mean average precision (MAP) over all queries in our set. Queries without a positive judgment for any result in the top 10 are excluded from the evaluation since we needed at least one click to evaluate our method.

3.3 Systems

We compared the performance of three systems:

Original ranking (baseline): The search engine result ranking.

QuerySimilarity: The original search engine results are re-ranked by: (1) Selecting snippets from the directly preceding query A with at least one term in common with the current query B. Note that stopwords such as "and" or "the" are removed prior to this comparison. (2) Building a term-based model of the user's search interests comprising the non-stopword terms in the snippets and the frequency with which they appear in the snippets. (3) Re-ranking the top-10 results for the current query B by the cosine similarity between the interest model and each result snippet. Note that this system serves as an alternative baseline in our study.

SelectionSimilarity: The original search engine results are re-ranked using the same cosine-similarity function as in *QuerySimilarity*. However, rather than building the interest models based on all snippets from the previous query A with at least one shared term, we build models based on the non-stopword terms appearing in snippets with a text selection event from the previous query.

3.4 Method

To ensure that we were comparing the performance of the systems on the same queries, we focused on the 252 queries from 92 users where an interest model could be generated for both *QuerySimilarity* and *SelectionSimilarity* and the next query B had a SERP click (for evaluation). For each query in the set, we built the interest models for each method using the preceding captions and text selections as appropriate, and re-ranked the top 10 search results (as described in the previous section). Once we had the new ranking, we computed AP for that list using the click-based judgments and averaged across all queries to get the MAP value on which we compare system performance. We also retained the individual AP values for each query and used them for statistical significance testing, performed using parametric tests at α=0.05.

4. FINDINGS

4.1 Overall Performance

The performance statistics for the original Bing ranker are proprietary and cannot be shared. However, this is a strong baseline and we can present the percentage change in MAP obtained by re-ranking using our two similarity methods with respect to the original ranking. Figure 2a shows the percentage change in MAP for each method. Error bars denote the standard error of the mean (SEM). The findings suggest that re-ranking based on *SelectionSimilarity* leads to strong gains of around 6% in MAP over the baseline, while those based on *QuerySimilarity* perform much worse than the original ranking. A one-way analysis of variance (ANOVA) revealed that there were significant differences between the three systems (F(2,753)=5.85, p=.003), and Tukey post-hoc tests showed all differences were significant at p<.02. *QuerySimilarity* may underperform because of the added noise from snippets included to increase result diversity, but which in our case hurt retrieval effectiveness.

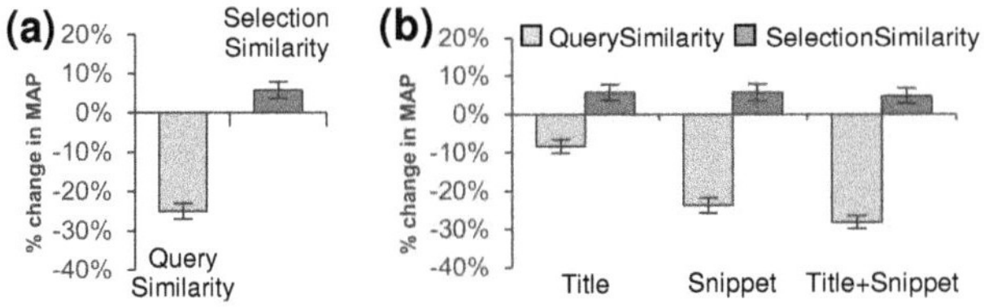

Figure 2: Change in MAP for methods vs. baseline (a) and impact of container on MAP change (b) (± SEM).

4.2 Effect of Container Type

The results presented in the previous section are for snippet only, since that is the container where the user selected the text of interest. However, the title of the result may also be valuable. We varied the container type, using the title, snippet, or title plus snippet to represent the matching results in query A and all results in query B. Figure 2b illustrates the performance of each method using different container types. We can see that *SelectionSimilarity* is largely unaffected by the container type, but *QuerySimilarity* performs much better when title-only is used (perhaps due to reduced noise). A two-way ANOVA, with ranking method and container type as factors, revealed significant differences between the container types for *QuerySimilarity* (F(1,1506)=9.58, p=.001), with title-only outperforming the others (Tukey post-hoc tests, p<.01).

5. CONCLUSIONS AND FUTURE WORK

We presented a novel method for using text selections on SERPs as implicit feedback. Our results are promising and show that we can significantly improve search performance for queries where text selection events are available on immediately-preceding and related SERPs. Although we saw relevance gains from our method, the use of cosine similarity for re-ranking is somewhat simplistic. Features of text highlighting such as the length of the selection and the number of blocks of text selected could be learned to improve our models. Also, recording the selected text, as well as what users did with it post-selection could yield more accurate feedback and larger gains. User studies may also help better understand SERP highlighting and how to use this behavior.

REFERENCES

[1] Bennett, P. et al. (2011). Inferring and using location metadata to personalize web search. *Proc. SIGIR*, 135–144.

[2] Buscher, G. et al. (2011). Large-scale analysis of individual and task differences in search result page examination strategies. *Proc. WSDM*, 373–382.

[3] Fox, S. et al. (2005). Evaluating implicit measures to improve the search experience. *ACM TOIS*, 23(2): 147–168.

[4] Joachims, T. et al. (2007). Evaluating the accuracy of implicit feedback from clicks and query reformulations in web search. *ACM TOIS*, 25(2).

[5] Kelly, D. and Teevan, J. (2003). Implicit feedback for inferring user preference. *SIGIR Forum*, 37(2): 18–28.

[6] White, R.W., Bennett, P.N., and Dumais, S.T. (2010). Predicting short-term interests using activity-based search context. *Proc. CIKM*, 1009–1018.

Time to Judge Relevance as an Indicator of Assessor Error

Mark D. Smucker
Department of Management Sciences
University of Waterloo
mark.smucker@uwaterloo.ca

Chandra Prakash Jethani
Yahoo! Inc.
Sunnyvale, CA, USA
jethani@yahoo-inc.com

ABSTRACT

When human assessors judge documents for their relevance to a search topic, it is possible for errors in judging to occur. As part of the analysis of the data collected from a 48 participant user study, we have discovered that when the participants made relevance judgments, the average participant spent more time to make errorful judgments than to make correct judgments. Thus, in relevance assessing scenarios similar to our user study, it may be possible to use the time taken to judge a document as an indicator of assessor error. Such an indicator could be used to identify documents that are candidates for adjudication or reassessment.

Categories and Subject Descriptors: H.3.3 [Information Storage and Retrieval]: Information Search and Retrieval

Keywords: Relevance judging, assessor error detection

1. INTRODUCTION

We have two motivations for wanting to better understand assessor behavior and assessor error. First, knowledge of assessor behavior should help IR researchers in the construction of more accurate relevance assessing systems. Second, while traditional retrieval metrics are relatively insensitive to assessor error [6], newer metrics that sample documents for judging, can be dramatically affected by assessor error [1, 7]. A single sampled document can represent thousands of documents in the final estimation, and a single document falsely judged to be relevant can greatly inflate the estimated number of relevant documents. Being able to predict which documents might have incorrect judgments could be useful for improving assessor consistency by asking assessors to judge certain documents a second time [1].

We have previously reported on relevance judging errors made by the 48 participants who took part in our user study [5], but we have not previously reported on what behaviors correlate with errors.

In this paper, we present results for a relevance assessing scenario where there was not an incentive for users to work faster. In this scenario, where the assessor is not paid per judgment, but is paid for the time spent, we have found an interesting result: users take more time to make mistakes than they do to make correct relevance judgments.

SIGIR'12, August 12–16, 2012, Portland, Oregon, USA.
ACM 978-1-4503-1472-5/12/08.

2. MATERIALS AND METHODS

The user study presented participants with fixed ranked lists of documents. Given a ranked list, participants were instructed to search for and save relevant documents. The user interface was web-based and consisted of two web pages. The first page showed 10 document summaries in a format similar to a web search engine's results page. Clicking on a summary took the participant to a page that displayed the full document and allowed the participant to save the document as relevant. We did not require relevance judgments to be made. We treat viewing a full a document and not saving it as a decision to judge the document as non-relevant. Participants could view the next 10 results by clicking on a link at the bottom of the document summaries page.

The study used 8 topics from the 2005 TREC Robust track. The documents came from the AQUAINT newswire collection. Each participant searched ranked lists with a uniform precision of 0.6 or 0.3. We use the NIST relevance judgments as truth.

Participants worked on 4 search topics for 10 minutes each. The study used a fully balanced design. Participants were instructed to work as fast as possible while making as few mistakes as possible. We use data from the second phase of the study. All participants had already completed phase 1 of the study and gained experience with relevance judging before participating in the second phase. The result lists contained near-duplicate documents. We use only the first judgment on a set of near-duplicates.

We measured the time the participants spent on the full document page before saving the document as relevant or leaving the page. It is well-known that large variations in behavior are caused by the search topic and the user. To allow comparisons of times across users and topics, we standardized a participant's times on a topic to have a mean of zero and a standard deviation of 1.

We average a participant's times on a topic, and then average across topics for that participant to produce a participant average. We finally average across participants to produce average participant times.

3. RESULTS AND DISCUSSION

When a participant judges a non-relevant document to be relevant, a false positive error is made. Likewise, when a relevant document is judged to be non-relevant, a false negative error is made. Table 1 and Figure 1 show the main results. These results are based on 3614 judgments (2706 correct judgments, 511 false negative errors, 397 false positive errors).

Average Participant Time to Judge Doc. Relevance	Correct	False Positive	p-value	False Negative	p-value
Standardized Times	-0.05 ± 0.01	0.26 ± 0.07	< 0.001	0.13 ± 0.08	0.02
Raw Times in Seconds	28 ± 2	39 ± 4	0.03	33 ± 3	0.16

Table 1: Average participant times to judge document relevance for both standardized times and raw times in seconds. Shown with the average is the standard error of the mean. We used a two-sided, Student's t-test to measure the statistical significance of the difference between the time to make correct judgments and each of the error conditions: false positive and false negative errors. For the standardized times, both types of errors took a statistically significant longer time ($p < 0.05$).

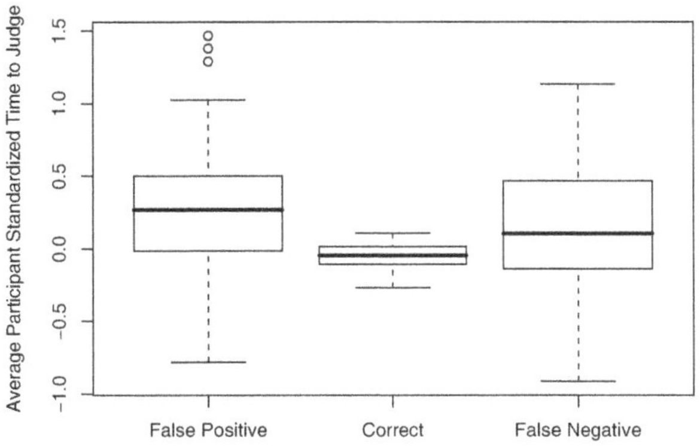

Figure 1: Average participant standardized times to judge document relevance for false positive, correct, and false negative judgments.

We found that on average, participants took significantly longer to judge documents when they made an error compared to when they were correct in their judgment. A priori, one might guess that participants would make errors by not taking enough time, but in contrast, we find here that time appears to indicate difficulty in making a correct judgment.

We hypothesize that the study participants make judgment errors according to the following process. First the participants identify a topically relevant document based on the document's summary and then click on the summary to view the full document. Participants then study the document to determine if it is relevant or not to the specifics of the search topic. The more difficult it is to determine the document's relevance, the longer the participant takes. At some point, the participant decides to save the document as relevant or abandon the document without saving it. False negatives result from not finding the relevant material in the document, and false positives are the result of the final decision being a guess.

There are many other factors that can cause a user to take longer to judge a document. For example, we have shown that the longer a document, the longer it takes to judge its relevance [3]. Is it just that mistakes are being made on longer documents? To investigate this, we modeled the probability that a judgment was an error using logistic regression. For the model, we considered time, document length measured in words, and the rank of the document in the results list. We found that when both time and document length were used together in the model, document length was not a useful predictor of errors. On the other hand, when we included the interaction between time and document length, this interaction was helpful. In other words, if the time to judge is too long given the length of the document, this is an indicator of error. We also found that ranks above about 50 were predictive of making errors. Reaching a rank over 50 in 10 minutes is likely indicative of a participant who is not carefully judging documents. For ranks less than 50, rank was not predictive of errors.

The relevance assessing setup may have a significant effect on assessor behavior. In preliminary analyses of separate studies where assessors had an incentive to work faster [4] and relevant documents were highly prevalent (90% relevant) [2], we have seen false negatives be *long errors* and false positives be *short errors*. In this paper, both types of errors were long errors. In future work we intend to analyze these studies in more detail by using this paper's method of standardizing times.

4. CONCLUSION

We found in a relevance assessing scenario where the assessor is trusted and paid by time spent, and not by number of judgments made, that all things equal, the longer an assessor takes to make a relevance judging decision, the more likely a mistake will be made. We hypothesize that time to judge a document relative to other documents, gives an indication of the difficulty of judging the document.

5. ACKNOWLEDGMENTS

David Hu wrote the software to compute the sets of near-duplicate documents. This work was supported in part by NSERC, in part by Amazon, and in part by the University of Waterloo.

6. REFERENCES

[1] B. Carterette and I. Soboroff. The effect of assessor error on IR system evaluation. In *SIGIR*, pp. 539–546, 2010.

[2] C. Jethani. Effect of prevalence on relevance assessing behavior. Master's thesis, University of Waterloo, 2011.

[3] C. Jethani and M. D. Smucker. Modeling the time to judge document relevance. In *Proceedings of the SIGIR'10 Workshop on the Simulation of Interaction*, 2010.

[4] M. D. Smucker and C. Jethani. The crowd vs. the lab: A comparison of crowd-sourced and university laboratory participant behavior. In *Proceedings of the SIGIR 2011 Workshop on Crowdsourcing for Information Retrieval*, 2011.

[5] M. D. Smucker and C. Jethani. Measuring assessor accuracy: a comparison of NIST assessors and user study participants. In *SIGIR*, pp. 1231–1232, 2011.

[6] E. M. Voorhees. Variations in relevance judgments and the measurement of retrieval effectiveness. *IPM*, 36:697–716, September 2000.

[7] W. Webber, D. W. Oard, F. Scholer, and B. Hedin. Assessor error in stratified evaluation. In *CIKM*, pp. 539–548, 2010.

Towards Alias Detection Without String Similarity: An Active Learning based Approach

Lili Jiang[1], Jianyong Wang[2], Ping Luo[3], Ning An[4], Min Wang[3]
[1]School of Information Science and Engineering, Lanzhou University, Lanzhou, Gansu, China
[2]Department of Computer Science and Technology, Tsinghua University, Beijing, China
[3]HP Labs China, Beijing, China
[4]Anhui Province Key Laboratory of Affective Computing And Advanced Intelligent Machine, School of Computer and Information, Hefei University of Technology, Hefei, China
jianglili06@lzu.cn;
jianyong@tsinghua.edu.cn;{ping.luo, min.wang6}@hp.com;ning.an@hfut.edu.cn

ABSTRACT

Entity aliases commonly exist and accurately detecting these aliases plays a vital role in various applications. In this paper, we use an active-learning-based method to detect entity aliases without string similarity. To minimize the cost on pairwise comparison, a subset-based method restricts the alias selection within a small-scale entity set. Within each generated entity set, an active learning based logistic regression classifier is employed to predict whether a candidate is the alias of a given entity. The experimental results on three datasets clearly demonstrate that our proposed approach can effectively detect this kind of entity aliases.

Categories and Subject Descriptors: H.4[Information Systems Applications]:General

General Terms: Algorithms, Experiment, Measurement

Keywords: Alias Detection, Pairwise Comparison, Active Learning

1. INTRODUCTION

Solving the problem of alias detection is important for a large number of applications including entity identification, terrorist detection, and social network analysis. Some aliases can be detected through string similarity measures, such as "World Trade Organization" and its alias "WTO". While another aliases have a quite low string similarity with their original entities, such as "Bill Clinton" and its nickname "Slick Willie". Detecting the second type of entity aliases turns out to be the aim of this paper.

Some previous work [1][2][4][5] has investigated this problem. These studies hold the same goal with ours but focus on a special domain respectively. This paper tries to detect entity aliases regardless of domains. To solve this problem, we employ an active-learning-based method taking three issues into consideration: picking the potential alias candidates for each given entity, choosing features and labeled samples to train a high-quality classifier. The contributions of this paper include: 1) a subset-based method to reduce the cost of pairwise comparison when picking alias candidates; 2) an active learning method, which selects informative samples in training classifier; 3) experiments on three types of datasets and comparison with other four baseline methods.

SIGIR August 12–16, 2012, Portland, Oregon, USA.
ACM ACM 978-1-4503-1472-5/12/08.

2. THE OVERALL FRAMEWORK

Given a document corpus D and an entity e, the task of alias detection is to extract all the entities from D which denote the same real-world object with e. Firstly, since the given entity may have no/(quite low) string similarity with its aliases, and especially certain type of aliases (e.g., terrorist or ghostwriter) are intentionally hidden from their real identities, the commonly used rules[1] (e.g., "aka", "as well known as", and "also called") will not always work. Secondly, it is difficult to locate entity aliases, since the number of aliases of an entity is rather fewer compared to the millions of strings/entities in the document corpus, let alone the increasing volume of internet. Thirdly, data labeling for training a classifier is time-consuming. To address these challenges, we propose a solution depicted in Figure 1 and describe it in the following subsections.

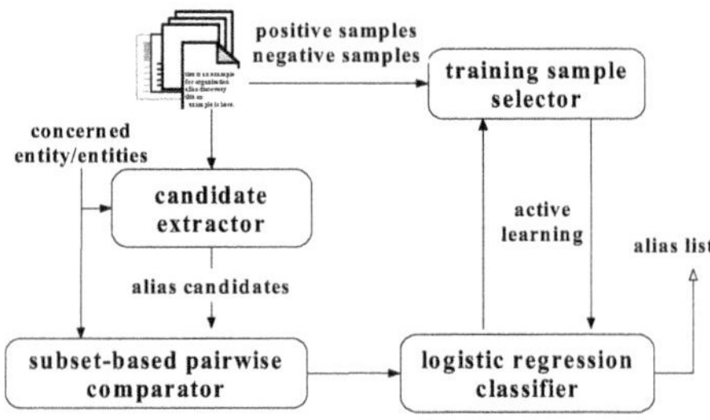

Figure 1: Entity Alias Detection Framework

2.1 The Subset-based Pairwise Comparison

Given a document corpus D and some entities to be resolved, the *candidate extractor* firstly employs a NLP tool (http://alias-i.com/lingpipe/) to extract all the named entities from D as candidates. Considering the first and second challenges mentioned above, the cost for pairwise comparison between entities and their alias candidates is non-trivial, which requires solutions to reduce the cost. The *subset-based pairwise comparator* in Figure 1 is designed to narrow the pairwise comparison scope for each given entity.

It is motivated by the observations that among the entities which are aliases with each other: 1) some ones frequently occur in documents, while others are mentioned infrequently; 2) the document union, where some of the most frequent entities appear, is often the superset of the documents union of the infrequent entities.

Based on these observations, the *subset-based pairwise comparator* is trying to keep each entity and its aliases in the same subset and it runs as follows: 1) builds an entity-document index and extracts the top $N\%$ most frequently used entities in the documents, and 2) for any two entities in the top $N\%$ ones and their corresponding occurring document sets, D_1 and D_2. If D_1 is the subset of D_2, D_1 will be removed. And when the intersection ratio between D_1 and D_2 is larger than a predefined threshold α, they are merged. After such iterations, we get a list of document sets. Finally, all the entities appearing in the documents of the same set are formed as an entity subset. Here, two parameters, α and N are trained using the 10 cross-validation, among which α denotes the entity overlapping ratio deciding whether two document sets are merged.

2.2 Active Learning for Alias Detection

For each given entity, the entities in the same entity subset are its alias candidates. We use a *logistic regression classifier* to output two values, among which p_1 denotes the probability that they are aliases and p_2 denotes the opposite. When p_1 is larger than p_2, we will conclude they may denote the same object. The classifier training is carried out in combination of active user learning, which tries to achieve higher performance with fewer training labels. The *training samples selector* randomly selects a subset of U and get labels for each sample, and then iteratively adds the labeled samples with high uncertainty[6] to the training set and trains a classifier until the trainers satisfy or U is null. The used features in the classifier training are presented as follows.

Co-occurrence relevance Pointwise mutual information(PMI) is used to measure the co-occurrence relevance in the corpus D between entities e_i and e_j, $PMI(e_i, e_j) = log$ $(p(e_i, e_j)/(p(e_i)p(e_j)))$. Herein, $p(e_i) = |D_{e_i}|/|D|$ where D_{e_i} is the occurring document set of e_i. $p(e_i, e_j)$ denotes the co-occurrence probability of e_i and e_j, calculated through dividing the co-occurring document count by the size of document union they appear respectively.

Social relevance Entities can be connected as a network based on their co-occurrence. For example, organization o and its aliases may co-occur with the persons affiliating with o. Thus, the social relevance between e_i and e_j is $CF(e_i, e_j) = (F(e_i) \cap F(e_j))/(F(e_i) \cup F(e_j))$ where $F(e_i)$ is the number of common nodes with e_i in the entity network.

Topic relevance We build an entity-document matrix M and each element in M is computed as $TFIDF(e_i, d_k) = (N_{d_k}^{e_i}/N_{d_k}^{*}) * \log(|D|/|D_{e_i}|)$. Herein, $N_{d_k}^{e_i}$ is the frequency of e_i appearing in document d_k, $N_{d_k}^{*}$ is the total entity count in document d_k, $|D|$ denotes the overall document count, and $|D_{e_i}|$ denotes the number of documents in which entity e_i appears. The similarity between any two entities can be calculated as $LSA(e_i, e_j) = cosine(V(e_i), V(e_j))$, where $V(e_i)$ is the entity-document frequency vector of e_i.

3. EXPERIMENTAL STUDY

We use three datasets to evaluate the proposed approach and compare it with other four methods in terms of F_1. The first dataset[1] contains 50 person names, 50 location names, and their aliases. To extend this dataset, we collected Web pages through issuing these names/aliases as queries to Google. The second dataset[3] contains terrorism data and spam emails. The third dataset was collected from an IT company including about 100k documents, 300k employee names and emails. As each email address can uniquely match one person, thus we regard an email as an alias of the person. We divided these datasets into training dataset and test dataset. The training data is used for parameter setting and classifier training, while the test dataset is used for evaluation. All ground-truth for evaluation is given in these datasets.

Table 1: Efficiency of subset-based method

	Pairwise Comparison Count	
Datasets/Methods	*no_subset*	*subset*
person/location	112, 020	20, 940
terrorism/spam	246, 030	56, 856
person/email	955, 631	187, 433

Table 2: Evaluation of the proposed approach

Datasets/Methods	*BPMI*	*BGraph*	*BLR*	*TLSA*	*Proposed*
person/location	0.21	0.20	0.25	0.19	**0.60**
terrorism/spam	0.43	0.39	0.41	0.35	**0.70**
person/email	0.40	0.24	0.32	0.28	**0.62**

Baselines Four state-of-the-art methods were implemented for comparison, namely, PMI based method(*BPMI*)[5], the graph based method(*BGraph*)[2], the logistic regression based method(*BLR*)[3], and a two-step LSA method(*TLSA*)[4].

Experimental Evaluation In Table 1, we present the optimization results in terms of pairwise comparison counts, which show that the subset-based method can reduce the comparison counts between all the given entities and their alias candidates. According to the experimental study, we found that the documents union in which only the top 50% entities appear can totally cover all the documents of the given corpus. Through parameter training, we choose merge threshold α as 0.2 and N as 50% for all test cases. Table 2 presents the performance of different methods in terms of F_1. We see that our method outperforms the four baseline methods significantly.

4. ACKNOWLEDGMENTS

This work was supported in part by National Basic Research Program of China (973 Program) under Grant No. 2011CB302206 and National High-Tech Research & Development Program of China (863 Program) under Grant No. 2012AA011103, National Natural Science Foundation of China under Grant No. 60833003 and Grant No. 90924025, and an HP Labs Innovation Research Program award.

5. REFERENCES

[1] BOLLEGALLA ET AL. Identification of personal name aliases on the web. In *Proceedings of WWW* (2008).

[2] HÖLZER ET AL. Email alias detection using social network analysis. In *Proceedings of LinkKDD* (2005).

[3] HSIUNG, P. ET AL. Alias detection in link data sets. In *Proceedings of IA* (2005).

[4] OATES, T. ET AL. Using latent semantic analysis to find different names for the same entity in free text. In *Proceedings of the 4th international workshop on Web information and data management* (2002).

[5] PANTEL, P. Alias detection in malicious environments. In *Proceedings of AAAI Fall Symposium on Capturing and Using Patterns for Evidence Detection* (2006).

[6] LEWIS, D. D., AND GALE, W. A. A sequential algorithm for training text classifiers. In *Proceedings of SIGIR* (1994).

Towards Zero-Click Mobile IR Evaluation: Knowing What and Knowing When

Tetsuya Sakai
Microsoft Research Asia, Beijing, P.R.C.
tetsuyasakai@acm.org

ABSTRACT

In this poster, we propose two evaluation tasks for mobile information access. The first task evaluates the system's ability to guess what the user's query should be given a context ("Knowing What"). The second task evaluates the system's ability to decide when to proactively deploy a given query ("Knowing When"). We conduct a preliminary manual analysis of a mobile query log to limit the space of possible queries so as to design feasible and practical evaluation tasks.

Categories and Subject Descriptors

H.3.3 [**Information Storage and Retrieval**]: Information Search and Retrieval

General Terms

Experimentation

Keywords

evaluation, metric, mobile, query log, test collection

1. INTRODUCTION

In February 2012, forty-five IR researchers gathered in Lorne, Australia, to discuss important research areas in IR for the near future. This SWIRL (Strategic Workshop on Information Retrieval in Lorne) workshop[1] identified six important topics, three of which were "Mobile IR", "Zero Query", and "Querying by Walking Around". The latter two were basically the same idea proposed by different discussion groups: in a mobile environment where the user does not (or cannot) necessarily issue a query, can the system provide the user with the right information at the right time? Even though similar ideas have existed for many years, the IR community still lacks an established evaluation methodology for them.

In response to the SWIRL outcomes, we propose a few concrete ideas for evaluating mobile information access. More specifically, we propose two tasks: *Knowing What*, which evaluates the system's ability to guess what the user's query should be given a context, and *Knowing When*, which evaluates the system's ability to decide when to proactively deploy a given query. We conduct a preliminary manual analysis of a mobile query log to limit the space of possible queries so as to design feasible and practical evaluation tasks.

[1] `http://www.cs.rmit.edu.au/swirl12/index.php`

SIGIR'12, August 12–16, 2012, Portland, Oregon, USA.
ACM 978-1-4503-1472-5/12/08.

2. RELATED WORK

Proactive IR is not a new idea. For example, over a decade ago, Rhodes and Maes [4] described *Just-in-Time IR Agents*, "that proactively present information based on a person's context in an easily accessible and non-intrusive manner." In the context of mobile IR, Jones and Brown [2] described *Context-Aware Retrieval*, where the system can be "interactive" (waits for the user to request information) or "proactive" (information to be searched contains a *triggering condition*, and is retrieved automatically when the user's context satisfies the condition). For evaluating such systems, they mention the traditional approach of precision and recall.

More recently, Coppola *et al.* [1] described the *Context-Aware Browser* for mobile IR, where the trigger for the search engine may be events such as "User arrives at Heathrow." Moreover, they built a test collection with ten topics, which resembles TREC ad hoc test collections: the key difference is that each topic contains a short text that describes the context of the user rather than an explicit query. As in traditional IR, nDCG was used for evaluating ranked lists of web pages. The TREC 2012 Context Suggestion Track[2] is currently underway to pursue similar ideas.

Sakai, Kato and Song [5] proposed an information access evaluation framework primarily designed for mobile environments. In their *One Click Access* task, systems are required to return a short multi-document summary instead of a ranked list of web pages. The task is called "One Click" because it aims to satisfy the user immediately after her click on the SEARCH button.

In the present study, we go one step further and address the problem of *Zero Click Access*: instead of waiting for the user to enter a query and click SEARCH, the system decides when and what to provide to the user. In the aforementioned SWIRL workshop, "Zero Query" referred to situations where the user does not provide a query but clicks SEARCH; "Less than Zero" referred to proactive cases where the system does not wait for a search button click.

3. PROPOSED TASKS

We break down the Zero Click Acces problem and propose two tasks: *Knowing What*, which evaluates the system's ability to guess what the user's query should be given a context, and *Knowing When*, which evaluates the system's ability to decide when to proactively deploy a given query. The key here is to isolate these two problems from the problem of finding relevant information for a given a query.

For evaluating Knowing What and Knowing When, we propose to use real mobile query log data, which is of the form:

<timestamp> <query> <context>.

[2] `http://sites.google.com/site/treccontext/`

Here, we define *context* generically as "any piece of information besides a query string that may help identify the user's information need." This could include the user's profile, location, sensor data that reflect the objects and the environment that surround the user, mobile apps the user is using and so on. Clearly, several obstacles exist if we are to release such data to the research community, but here we assume that they can be overcome.

An alternative approach to evaluating mobile IR would be to utilise *clicked URLs* in mobile query logs. However, a study on desktop and mobile query logs by Li, Huffman and Tokuda [3] showed that users are often satisfied without actually clicking and visiting a particular URL: the search engine result page itself suffices for obtaining the desired information; the aforementioned Once Click Access aims exactly at freeing the user from the burden of clicking several times. Moreover, a clicked URL may only partially reflect the user's information need (if relevant at all).

Below, we define two new tasks for Zero-Click mobile IR. using real mobile query logs obtained in the above format.

3.1 Knowing What

Knowing What evaluates the system's ability to guess what the user's query should be given a context. The task is defined as: *Given a mobile query log whose timestamps span* $[1, T]$ *where all queries in the* $[t, T]$ *range have been masked, and a context for timestamp* t' $(t \leq t' \leq T)$*, recover the query string at timestamp* t'. Thus, the system is required to guess the query by observing previous data and the current context. A natural evaluation metric for this task would be *accuracy* (whether each predicted query string is right or wrong), or perhaps *weighted accuracy* which allows partial matches between the true and predicted queries.

If we allow arbitrary queries, this task would be very challenging. We believe that a feasible and practical task setting would be to impose some restrictions on the type of queries and thereby limit the possible space of queries. We shall discuss this in Section 4.

3.2 Knowing When

Knowing When evaluates the system's ability to decide when to proactively deploy a given query. Using the same mobile query log data, this task can be defined as: *Given a mobile query log whose timestamps span* $[1, T]$ *where all queries in the* $[t, T]$ *range have been masked, and a query string sampled from* $[t, T]$*, recover the query's timestamp (i.e. when it was issued by the user).* Thus, if a system is effective in both Knowing What and Knowing When, it should be able to automatically issue an appropriate query for the mobile user at the right moment.

The output of a Knowing When system is a timestamp (or a set of timestamps). Thus, suppose the absolute difference between the true and the predicted timestamps is d. Then, for an allowance parameter Δ, the *timestamp accuracy* could be computed for example as $1 - \min(1, d/\Delta)$. It is one when the predicted timestamp is perfectly accurate; it is zero if the difference exceeds Δ; the system is partially rewarded otherwise for being "close."

4. INITIAL QUERY LOG ANALYSIS

For both Knowing What and Knowing When, we probably need to limit the space of possible queries for designing feasible and practical tasks. For this purpose, we manually examined 5,000 most frequent mobile queries (approximately 472 million queries by volume) sampled between November and December 2011 from the US English market, and manually classified them into major query types. These query types were defined in a bottom-up manner and were revised repeatedly as the author carefully went through the queries.

Table 1: Query types for 5,000 head mobile queries.

type	example	%unique	%volume
WEBSITE	`facebook`	10.74	30.25
VIDEO	`youtube`	17.98	15.11
MUSIC	`romantic song`	19.03	10.99
PERSON	`Obama`	12.35	10.34
GEO	`chicago, IL`	4.92	3.92
SHOP	`starbucks`	5.99	2.99
SPORTS	`nfl scores`	2.59	1.56
ANIMAL	`squirrels animal`	1.54	1.05
WEATHER	`weather`	0.42	0.93
FOOD	`pizza`	0.46	0.63
FACILITY	`Beijing The Egg`	0.66	0.50
MAP	`mapquest`	0.51	0.45
GAME	`games`	0.93	0.40
IMAGE	`funny pictures`	0.56	0.36
NEWS	`msnbc`	0.81	0.32
PRODUCT	`Windows Phone 7`	0.49	0.16
BANKING	`wellsfargo.com`	0.32	0.16
AIRLINE	`southwest airlines`	0.29	0.12
STOCK	`quote GOOG`	0.24	0.10
OTHER	-	19.15	19.66

Table 1 shows the query type distribution after removing pornographic queries (18% of the unique queries; 14% by volume). It can be observed that WEBSITE, VIDEO, MUSIC and PERSON query types constitute about 66% of the head queries by volume. In particular, most of the WEBSITE queries are homepage finding queries such as `facebook` and `bing`. Thus, even though previous work in mobile IR evaluation discussed ranking webpages and evaluating with nDCG etc., perhaps a more important question for mobile users is whether the system can provide the one correct URL to the user at the right time. As a first step to evaluating Knowing What and Knowing When, limiting the query space to homepage finding queries is probably feasible and practical.

Leveraging query types such as the ones shown in Table 1 for *evaluating* Knowing What may also be a good idea, as this may separate the task of collaborative recommendation from that of personalisation. For example, suppose that a "Knowing When and What" system learns from the training data that a certain group of users tend to issue MUSIC queries right after they get off a train. But just because User X likes `romantic songs` (Table 1) does not necessarily imply that User Y, who behaved similarly to X, wants to listen to the same kind of music. Personalisation can be used orthogonally to this Knowing When and What system, so that (say) `techno beats` can be provided to Y.

5. SUMMARY

We defined mobile IR tasks called Knowing What and Knowing When, and identified popular query types in a mobile query log to make the tasks both feasible and practical. We hope to deploy a pilot task at evaluation venues such as NTCIR.

6. REFERENCES

[1] P. Coppola, V. D. Mea, L. D. Gaspero, D. Menegon, D. Mischis, S. Mizzaro, I. Scagnetto, and L. Vassena. The context-aware browser. *IEEE Intelligent Systems*, 25(1):38–47, 2010.

[2] G. J. F. Jones and P. J. Brown. Context-aware retrieval for ubiquitous computing environments. In *Mobile and Ubiquituos Information Access (LNCS 2954)*, pages 227–243, 2004.

[3] J. Li, S. Huffman, and A. Tokuda. Good abandonment in mobile and PC internet search. In *Proceedings of ACM SIGIR 2009*, pages 43–50, 2009.

[4] B. J. Rhodes and P. Maes. Just-in-time information retrieval agents. *IBM Systems Journal*, 39(685-704), 2000.

[5] T. Sakai, M. P. Kato, and Y.-I. Song. Click the search button and be happy: Evaluating direct and immediate information access. In *Proceedings of ACM CIKM 2011*, pages 621–630, 2011.

Twanchor Text: A Preliminary Study of the Value of Tweets as Anchor Text

Gilad Mishne and Jimmy Lin
Twitter, Inc.
@gilad @lintool

Categories and Subject Descriptors: H.3.3 Information Storage and Retrieval: Information Search and Retrieval

General Terms: Algorithms, Experimentation

Keywords: real-time search, document enrichment

1. INTRODUCTION

A common practice in web search is enriching document representations with incoming anchor text, aggregated in some manner [5, 4], so that the anchor text "field" is available at ranking time. In this paper, we present a preliminary investigation of the value of tweets and tweet conversations as anchor text. Twitter is a communications platform on which users exchange 140-characters messages (called tweets). It is often used as a broadcast mechanism to publicize newly-published web pages: for example, the website techcrunch.com might tweet a link (URL) to a breaking technology-related news story as soon as the page is posted on the web, as a way to generate traffic to the site. In a sense, the tweet text itself serves the same role as traditional anchor text to the web page.

For the most part, tweets with links serve primarily to alert followers (recipients) to the presence of new stories and contain little more than article titles. A typical example is:

> ▷ Obama Signs Defense Bill Despite 'Serious Reservations' huff.to/uiGfU4 via @huffingtonpost

However, tweets often generate discussion, providing a rich source of content terms not directly found in the article itself. Consider the following tweets, referencing the same article or responding to a previous tweet that referenced it:

> ▷ The "war on terror" is lost. The terrorists have won: Obama Signs Defense Bill [link] #NDAA #StateTerror
>
> ▷ So now we are suspending habeas corpus? [link]
>
> ▷ @MGhasspoken 1022 in the NDAA exempts US citizens from military detention but not from law enforcement detention

In the case of breaking news stories, anchor text is hard to acquire, primarily because new web pages require time to accumulate inbound links. A notable exception is a news site linking to new articles from other new articles (or from a portal page), but anchor text from this type of linking behavior usually consists only of the title, which is uninteresting. The lack of interesting anchor text means that web search engines cannot take advantage of what is typically a rich relevance signal for ranking. In contrast, for real-time text processing applications, tweet text contains relevance signals that are unlikely to be found anywhere else at the time the tweet was posted.

We present, to our knowledge, the first systematic characterization of the phenomenon of tweets as anchor text, which we dub "twanchor text". Our goal is to convince the reader that there is substantial value in twanchor text for search and other text mining tasks. Due to limited space, we stop short of actual extrinsic evaluation in an end-to-end application, but present our arguments in terms of statistical characterization of twanchor text content.

Related Work. An early study of anchor text—focusing on differences between anchors and the landing page—was presented in [2]. Although tweets have not been used as or compared to anchors, several other similar sources of information have, including social annotations [3] and search queries [1]. Finally, a search system based on indexing tweets *instead* of the linked documents was recently discussed in [6].

2. METHODOLOGY

We've developed SpiderDuck, a high-throughput fetcher that listens to the Twitter firehose (stream of all tweets) and downloads the content of all URLs found in tweets.[1] This itself is a non-trivial engineering challenge due to the high throughput demands and usage of URL shortening services, but these issues are beyond the scope of this paper.

Our collection consists of all links tweeted in the month of January 2012. Many of the tweeted URLs point to photos and other media, which are not relevant for our analysis. Since we are primarily interested in new web pages of high quality, we restrict our attention to a list of approximately 15K news domains, constructed semi-automatically (again, for space constraints we omit the details). Over the entire month, we observe about 7.1 million *unique* resolved URLs, in 123M tweets, from these hosts. Additional statistics are provided in Table 1. We emphasize that this figure is arrived at after resolving the target of shortened links; frequently, especially for popular pages, multiple users independently tweet different shortened URLs to the same page. For each page, we collected the following:

- The title of the web page.
- Text content of the web page (after removing tags, js, etc.)
- Tweets linking to the page.

[1] http://engineering.twitter.com/2011/11/spiderduck-twitters-real-time-url.html

SIGIR'12, August 12–16, 2012, Portland, Oregon, USA.
ACM 978-1-4503-1472-5/12/08.

Table 1: Twanchor text corpus

URLs	7.12M
with titles	7.09M (99%)
with anchor text	717K (10%)
with replies	1.28M (18%)
with 2nd-degree replies	500K (7%)
with 3rd-degree replies	297K (4%)
Tweets	**123M**
with replies	6.84M (5.6%)
with 2nd-degree replies	1.95M (1.6%)
with 3rd-degree replies	1.05M (0.9%)

- Tweet conversations around the link, up to three levels. The first level is defined as all tweets in response to the original tweet containing the link. The second level is defined as all responses to first level tweets, and so on.
- Anchor text to the web page. Note that we are restricted to extracting anchor text from other pages that have been tweeted (SpiderDuck is not a general-purpose web crawler). By definition these anchor texts are limited in scope (but see previous discussion).

To measure the potential contribution of twanchor text in the context of search, we focus on *new terms* introduced through these texts: that is, terms included in the tweets and their replies that are not part of the web page itself (or its title). Our argument is simple: in the case of real-time search (and unlike web search), recall plays as important a role as precision, and so the more relevant terms are available for retrieving the document, the better.

Note that there are other potential gains from using twanchors. For example, although a particular term may already appear in the page text, its inclusion in referencing tweets may signal increased importance. Other more complex approaches (such as measuring the diversity among twanchors) may also prove useful, and while we believe this is the case, it is beyond the scope of this short piece. We note that conversations around an article often expresses sentiment, from which we can gauge users' responses to the content. Finally, twanchor text and conversations often contain hashtags, a Twitter convention that can be treated as topic-labels for semi-supervised machine-learning purposes.

3. RESULTS

Table 2 shows the potential contributions of direct twanchor text, as well as that of surrounding conversations. For each potential content source (anchors, twanchors, and conversations) we show the average number of new terms added to a URL, as well as break down the contribution to the fraction of URLs that has no new terms, the fraction that has fewer than 10 new ones, and the fraction that has 10 or more new terms. Furthermore, we separately show the contribution to three types of URLs: *head*, defined as URLs appearing in 100 or more tweets; *tail*, URLs appearing in 5 or fewer tweets, and *torso*—everything else. The corpus breakdown is 0.5% head, 13.1% torso, and 86.4% tail.

The potential gains from twanchors are substantial: tweets and their replies contribute new terms significantly more than anchor text, consistently across the board. Although the contribution to head URLs is the strongest, we are particularly encouraged by the contribution to torso and tail URLs. Top news pages tend to be discovered and ranked effectively by search engines due to an abundance of incoming links and high-quality hosts; not so for lower-tier articles. Nevertheless, these still engage many users—the number of

Table 2: Twanchor text contribution

	Number of new terms			
Source	0	1–9	10+	Mean
Head				
Anchors	78.5%	20.2%	1.3%	0.98
Twanchors	0.5%	0.4%	99.1%	272.8
Conversations	1.5%	2.6%	95.9%	219.4
Torso				
Anchors	91.5%	7.8%	0.7%	0.37
Twanchors	2.8%	34.9%	62.3%	22.5
Conversations	54.8%	14.5%	30.7%	12.4
Tail				
Anchors	98.1%	1.8%	0.1%	0.05
Twanchors	29.5%	63.5%	7.0%	3.1
Conversations	93.5%	3.4%	3.1%	0.85
All URLs				
Anchors	96.1%	3.6%	0.3%	0.15
Twanchors	22.4%	55.3%	22.3%	12.3
Conversations	82.3%	11.5%	6.2%	7.3

Table 3: Twanchor text contribution; queried terms

	New queried-terms			
Source	0	1–9	10+	Mean
Anchors	97.1%	2.8%	0.1%	0.1
Twanchors	31.2%	53.5%	15.3%	7.4
Conversations	82.7%	7.8%	9.5%	4.8

tweets referencing torso and tail URLs exceeds the number referencing head ones. The paucity of information available to traditional web search engines (without Twitter signals) limits effectiveness in retrieving those pages.

Clearly, not all new terms added are indeed useful in a retrieval setting; stopwords and other function words that are common on Twitter (e.g., "RT", an abbreviation for "retweet") do not contribute much. In Table 3 we repeat our evaluation, this time limiting the new terms to new *queried terms*—that is, terms that appeared in a search query issued by at least 1000 unique users to twitter.com over the same month our data was collected on. We omit the breakdown into head, torso, and tail, but the numbers are proportional to those shown in Table 2: the majority of newly-available terms (about two-thirds, on average) are terms actually found in common queries.

4. CONCLUSIONS

Using a simple proxy—the amount of additional textual content—we demonstrate that, at least in the case of news-centric search, tweets referencing web pages provide a valuable source of content not found in the pages themselves. Using such tweets as "twanchors" improves significantly over using anchors themselves, particularly for long-tail pages that may have few other external information sources. In follow-up work we will show how to utilize twanchors in a full retrieval setup, using additional information present in tweets referencing web pages (e.g., raw counts).

5. REFERENCES

[1] E. Amitay, A. Darlow, D. Konopnicki, and U. Weiss. Queries as anchors: selection by association. In *Hypertext*, 2005.

[2] N. Eiron and K. McCurley. Analysis of anchor text for web search. In *SIGIR*, 2003.

[3] P. Heymann, G. Koutrika, and H. Garcia-Molina. Can social bookmarking improve web search? In *WSDM*, 2008.

[4] M. Koolen and J. Kamps. The importance of anchor text for ad hoc search revisited. In *SIGIR*, 2010.

[5] D. Metzler, J. Novak, H. Cui, and S. Reddy. Building enriched document representations using aggregated anchor text. In *SIGIR*, 2009.

[6] T. Rowlands, D. Hawking, and R. Sankaranarayana. New-web search with microblog annotations. In *WWW*, 2010.

Unsupervised Linear Score Normalization Revisited

Ilya Markov
University of Lugano
Lugano, Switzerland
ilya.markov@usi.ch

Avi Arampatzis
Democritus University of Thrace
Xanthi, Greece
avi@ee.duth.gr

Fabio Crestani
University of Lugano
Lugano, Switzerland
fabio.crestani@usi.ch

ABSTRACT

We give a fresh look into score normalization for merging result-lists, isolating the problem from other components. We focus on three of the simplest, practical, and widely-used linear methods which do not require any training data, i.e. MinMax, Sum, and Z-Score. We provide theoretical arguments on why and when the methods work, and evaluate them experimentally. We find that MinMax is the most robust under many circumstances, and that Sum is—in contrast to previous literature—the worst. Based on the insights gained, we propose another three simple methods which work as good or better than the baselines.

Categories and Subject Descriptors

H.3.3 [**Information Storage and Retrieval**]: Information Search and Retrieval

Keywords

Score Normalization, Distributed Retrieval

1. INTRODUCTION

Merging ranked-lists produced by several engines requires two steps: score normalization and combination. In distributed setups with disjoint collections, the combination step becomes trivial since each document is assigned a single score from one of the participating engines. This makes such setups ideal in isolating the normalization problem. Distributed setups usually include another step before normalization, i.e. resource selection (RS). While useful in improving efficiency, RS has been also shown to improve effectiveness significantly. We argue that this is due to the far-from-perfect quality of state-of-the-art normalization methods: in an ideal normalization, e.g. scores are normalized to probabilities of relevance, any kind of RS will hurt effectiveness by excluding sources with relevant documents; in such an ideal situation, the more systems one combines, the better the effectiveness. Consequently, the theoretical ceiling of effectiveness can only be achieved with an ideal normalization without RS, and distributed setups with disjoint collections are best for experimenting with normalization [1].

Previously proposed normalizations vary from linear to non-linear functions which may require or not training data for their estimation. While there is a rich literature on the subject, most experiments reported do not isolate the problem as we described above [3, 4, 5]. We give a fresh look into the simplest normalization methods: linear functions which do not require any training or search engine cooperation. Being the most practical, they are also the fastest and generally have been proved to be robust and effective. Beyond an empirical comparison, we also give theoretical justifications on their implicit assumptions. To our knowledge, these assumptions have never been made explicit or they are 'lost' in the large volume of the related literature. Based on the gained insights, we propose three alternative linear normalization methods.

In the experiments we use the gov2.1000 and gov2.30 splits of the TREC GOV2 dataset [2]. In gov2.1000 the largest 1000 hosts of the GOV2 dataset are treated as 1000 sources, and the number of sources that contain relevant documents is usually much less than 1000. In gov2.30 the collections of gov2.1000 are clustered into 30 sources; here, relevant documents appear in most of the sources. We use ten retrieval functions implemented by the Terrier toolkit [1], namely, BM25, tf-idf (Terrier and Lemur versions), language modeling (original and with Dirichlet smoothing), and a number of DFR-based functions (BM25, BB2, IFB2, InL2 and PL2). Retrieval functions are randomly assigned to sources. Topics 701-850 are used as queries. Operationally, engines return truncated rankings for efficiency reasons, thus, we only consider either the top 10 or 1000 results. Our results are summarized in Tables 1 and 2, which we will refer to throughout the paper. Statistical significance is measured with a paired t-test. † shows the significantly best baseline (MinMax, Sum or Z-Score) and ‡ marks the modification that is significantly better than any baseline, both at the 0.05 level.

2. LINEAR SCORE NORMALIZATION

The MinMax method [3] scales the output score range per engine to $[0, 1]$. We argue that the most important assumption behind MinMax is that each source contains at least 1 relevant document, and that this document will most-likely get ranked 1st. By assigning the same highest score to all 1st documents, they are ranked before any other in the merged list. Since it is also assumed that these documents are most-likely relevant, a high early precision is achieved which pushes higher other evaluation measures sensitive to early rank positions, e.g. MAP. Thus, MinMax owes its success to getting right the early ranks in the merged list. However, due to fact that the 1st document of each engine is assigned the same highest score, MinMax produces a round-robin effect in merging which may impact effectiveness neg-

[1] http://terrier.org

SIGIR'12, August 12–16, 2012, Portland, Oregon, USA.
ACM 978-1-4503-1472-5/12/08.

atively as the number of engines increases. Indeed, MinMax shows high performance when run on 30 sources that contain sufficient relevant documents, i.e. the above assumption is satisfied. On the contrary, when run on 1000 sources, where the assumption is weakened by the sparseness of relevant documents and additionally the round-robin effect is more prominent, MinMax performance degrades considerably.

The Sum method [5] is similar to MinMax, but without using a fixed highest score eliminating the undesirable round-robin effect: the minimum score is shifted to 0 while the sum of all scores per ranked-list is scaled to 1: $s' = s - min$, $s_{norm} = s' / \sum_i s'_i$. The intuition given in [4] is: under the assumption of exponentially-distributed scores, the normalization is equivalent to setting the means of score distributions of sources to be equal to each other. However, many studies on modeling scores show that the aforementioned assumption of exponentially-distributed scores does not hold in practice, especially for top-ranked documents. Our experimental results show that the Sum method almost always has the worst performance. This contradicts the results of the original work [5], however, the authors in the last-mentioned study used a meta-search setup and evaluated normalization and combination methods together—a setup that does not isolate the normalization problem.

In [5] also the Z-Score method is proposed, which normalizes each score to its number of standard deviations that it is away from the mean score. However, as previously noted in [1], this method rather assumes a bell-like distribution of document scores (e.g. a Normal), where the mean would be a meaningful 'neutral' score. However, in practice score distributions are highly skewed and clearly violate this assumption. Still if only the top documents are considered from each result list, they are likely to be relevant, and therefore the distribution of their scores may be close to that of relevant documents, i.e. likely a Normal. Indeed, our results show that when only the top-10 documents are retrieved from each source, Z-Score usually shows higher performance than when applied on the top-1000 documents.

So far we have seen that methods that assume particular score distribution shapes, such as Sum and Z-Score, are worse, and that MinMax which does not make such assumptions is better. In other words, the sum or the mean of scores do not seem to be a good statistics for normalization, and that we should be looking into the direction of MinMax for developing a better normalization. We also know that using a fixed highest score should be preferably avoided so as to eliminate the round-robin effect, as well as, to be able to down-weigh sources of no relevance (haunting the main assumption of MinMax). Another problem rarely mentioned that all three methods above have is that they are greatly affected by the minimum score seen, or else, the chosen truncation point of the rankings (e.g. the minimum score of top-10 documents is usually very different from the minimum score of top-1000).

We will first try to deal with the minimum-score problem. The lowest theoretical score of many scoring functions is 0. Thus, making the assumption that the most non-relevant documents usually score at 0, the minimum in MinMax function should also be set to 0. This way we obtain the Max method: $s_{norm} = s/max$. Our results show that Max, although simpler, almost always has the same or higher performance than that of the MinMax method.

Let us now try to deal with non-relevant sources which violate the main assumption of MinMax. Scoring functions aim at assigning scores in a way that relevant documents have very different scores from non-relevant documents. Therefore, if the standard deviation σ of scores in a ranked-list is high, the list is likely to contain both relevant and non-relevant documents. If σ is low, the list is likely to contain either only relevant or only non-relevant documents. On one hand, long ranked-lists (e.g. 1000 documents) are likely to contain many non-relevant documents and, therefore, we prefer those that have high standard deviation (i.e. they also contain many relevant documents). In this case, the following linear modification makes sense: $s_{norm} = \sigma \frac{s-min}{max-min}$. We call it MM-Stdv. On the other hand, short ranked lists (e.g. 10 documents) may contain only relevant documents and, therefore, we might prefer the lists with low standard deviation. Unit-variance linear modification (UV) is similar to Z-Score and scale-invariant but does not shift the mean to 0: $s_{norm} = score/\sigma$. Our results support both formulas depending on the situation.

	gov2.30			gov2.1000		
	MAP	p@10	p@100	MAP	p@10	p@100
MinMax	0.0700†	**0.1953**†	0.1674†	0.0027†	**0.0161**†	**0.0140**†
Sum	0.0171	0.0134	0.0292	0.0004	0.0013	0.0019
Z-Score	0.0367	0.0819	0.0935	0.0014	0.0013	0.0054
Max	**0.0722**	**0.1953**	**0.1734**‡	0.0023	**0.0161**	**0.0140**
MMStdv	0.0632	0.1738	0.1348	**0.0038**	0.0114	0.0088
UV	0.0182	0.1248	0.0676	0.0006	0.0013	0.0009

Table 1: Top 1000 documents are retrieved.

	gov2.30			gov2.1000		
	MAP	p@10	p@100	MAP	p@10	p@100
MinMax	0.0372†	0.1966	0.1437†	0.0027	0.0161†	0.0140
Sum	0.0355	0.1785	0.1401	0.0029	0.0013	0.0140
Z-Score	0.0353	0.1839	0.1413	0.0031	0.0007	0.0162
Max	**0.0397**‡	0.1953	**0.1656**‡	0.0028	0.0161	0.0140
MMStdv	0.0366	0.1604	0.1432	0.0025	0.0054	0.0139
UV	0.0381	**0.1980**	0.1498	**0.0049**‡	**0.0228**	**0.0225**

Table 2: Top 10 documents are retrieved.

3. CONCLUSIONS

We isolated the normalization problem and found that MinMax is the most robust method under many circumstances, Z-Score and Sum may perform well when some conditions are met, and Sum is worse than previous literature suggested. Furthermore, we gave theoretical insights on why and when these methods work or fail, and proposed three new methods that work as good or better than the baselines.

4. REFERENCES

[1] A. Arampatzis and J. Kamps. A signal-to-noise approach to score normalization. In *Proceeding of the ACM CIKM*, pages 797–806, 2009.

[2] J. Arguello, J. Callan, and F. Diaz. Classification-based resource selection. In *Proceedings of the ACM CIKM*, pages 1277–1286. ACM, 2009.

[3] J. H. Lee. Analyses of multiple evidence combination. In *Proceedings of the ACM SIGIR*, pages 267–276. ACM, 1997.

[4] R. Manmatha and H. Sever. A formal approach to score normalization for meta-search. In *Proceedings of the HLT*, pages 98–103. MKP Inc., 2002.

[5] M. Montague and J. A. Aslam. Relevance score normalization for metasearch. In *Proceedings of the ACM CIKM*, pages 427–433. ACM, 2001.

User-Aware Caching and Prefetching Query Results in Web Search Engines*

Hongyuan Ma
Institute of Computing Technology, Chinese Academy of Sciences
Graduate University of Chinese Academy of Sciences
Beijing, P.R. China 100190
mahongyuan@foxmail.com

Bin Wang
Institute of Computing Technology, Chinese Academy of Sciences
Beijing, P.R. China 100190
wangbin@ict.ac.cn

ABSTRACT

Query results caching is an efficient technique for Web search engines. In this paper we present User-Aware Cache, a novel approach tailored for query results caching, that is based on user characteristics. We then use a trace of around 30 million queries to evaluate User-Aware Cache, as well as traditional methods and theoretical upper bounds. Experimental results show that this approach can achieve hit ratios better than state-of-the-art methods.

Categories and Subject Descriptors

H.3.3 [**Information Storage and Retrieval**]: Information Search and Retrieval—*Search process*; H.3.4 [**Information Storage and Retrieval**]: Systems and Software—*Performance evaluation (efficiency and effectiveness)*

General Terms

Performance, Experimentation

Keywords

Web search engines, query results, caching, prefetching.

1. INTRODUCTION

Caching is an effective technique to reduce user response time and back-end server workload. Millions of queries are submitted by users daily to Web search engines, and they all expect low latency to receive answers. Results caching and index caching are two basic approaches for improving the performance of large scale Web search engines. Results cache stores the previous search results which were recently computed to resolve future queries, while index cache stores the posting lists of the involved query terms to resolve future query results computing. In addition to these approaches, Web search engines may also prefetch a search engine results page (SERP) which is the listing of Web pages returned by the Web search engines in response to a query that it predicts to be requested in the near future. Lempel and Moran [2] present probability driven cache (PDC) which is based on a probabilistic model of Web search engine query streams, and examine the prefetching of search results with PDC. PDC divides its cache into a segment which caches top-K queries and a priority queue which caches follow-up queries. Fagni et al. [1] present static and dynamic cache (SDC) which is based on historical usage data. SDC divides its cache into a read-only static cache which caches the most popular queries and a dynamic cache which caches the rest together with an adaptive prefetching policy, which is called pre-SDC in this paper.

Web search engine caching and prefetching have been studied by a number of researchers. As we know, most of earlier studies extract query frequency feature from a query log to select the queries to be kept in a cache. We take into consideration the fact that some users who contribute greatly to Web search engines' page views (PV), and pay more attention to these users. This paper concentrates on results caching and prefetching, and in particular discusses the application of user characteristics in the context of Web search engine results caching. Our goal is to design a mechanism for results caching that exploit the characteristics of Web search engine users to achieve a high hit ratio for both requests from the special users group who contributes most to Web search engines and all requests. To do this, we divide results cache into two areas: the first area caches results for the queries submitted by that special users group, while the second area is for the rest of the queries.

2. USER-AWARE RESULTS CACHING & PREFETCHING

2.1 User Data Characterization

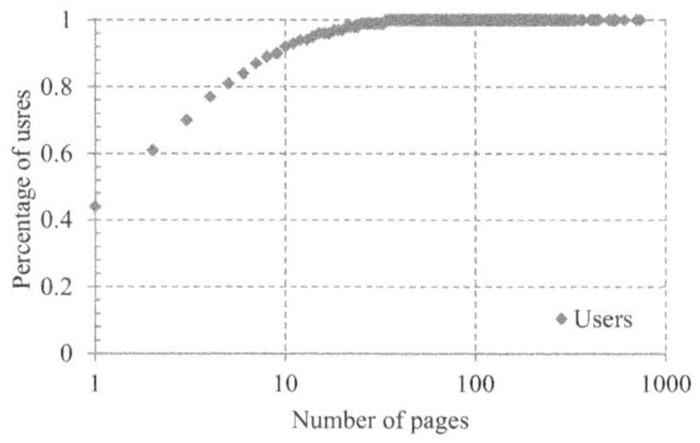

Figure 1: Cumulative percentage of users as a function of requested pages (From a famous Chinese Web search engine [3])

As discussed in the introduction, different user contributes to the PV of Web search engine differently. Figure 1 shows that 80% of

*This work was supported by the National Natural Science Foundation of China (Grant No. 61070111).

SIGIR'12, August 12–16, 2012, Portland, Oregon, USA.
ACM 978-1-4503-1472-5/12/08.

users' requested pages, also termed as PV are within five, and 67% of the requests received by the Web search engines are submitted by only 20% of users. Thus, we can draw the following conclusions: different user's contribution to Web search engine is different.

2.2 User-Aware Cache

Usually, the capacity of a caching system is far less than the volume of requests received by Web search engines, and a user's query results page which is prefetched may be flushed out before the next reference to it, especially for a small size caching system. In order to decrease the impact of caching capacity on those loyal users, we divides a fixed amount of available cache into two parts and use one part as a cache for caching results for the queries submitted by the special users group which is pre-defined by Web search engines and the other part as a cache for the rest of the queries. It is not necessary that both parts of the cache use the same replacement and prefetching policy, but in this study we use the same policy which is LRU replacement and pre-SDC prefetching policy. Note that User-Aware Cache is formed by the two parts as a whole, and a query results page can only exist in one part. When received a query submitted by a user, a results page should first be looked up in the user's corresponding part.

2.3 User Subset Selection

As shown in figure 1, the distribution of number of query results pages browsed by users has significant long tail characteristic. The finding implies that there is a high possibility that some users reference the query results pages frequently. We describe one feature that can be extracted from the dataset and used for selecting a subset of all users for the partition. The feature in this paper is listed below:

User Follow-up Query Frequency (UFQF): The query frequency of a user is defined as the number of queries including follow-up queries submitted by this user. In fact, we sort all user query frequencies in decreasing order and select users who have the most frequent user query frequencies.

3. EXPERIMENTAL RESULTS

We use a query log from a famous Chinese Web search engine [3] which contains around 30 million queries of about 5.8 million people for a period of 2-months (from 09/01/2006 to 10/31/2006). The first 5 million queries constitute the training set to warm up the cache. The remaining about 25 million queries are reserved as the test set. We choose 14,748 users according to UFQF as a special users group and use the cache whose size is 10% of the total capacity of the cache to cache the queries submitted by this group.

The first experiment aims to compare the hit ratio of the user-aware cache with the hit ratio of the cache using local optimal replacement policy which is widely used in the literature and the upper bound [1] which is achieved on the test set of our query log when prefetching is not used. Local optimal replacement policy works as follows: when a results page needs to be evicted, the cache would evict the page whose next reference will occur farthest in the next W times requests. W is the constant length of sliding window, and we set the value of W equal to the cache size in our experiment. Figure 2 shows the result of this experiment.

In Figure 2, cache size is given as the number of queries that are cached. It can be seen that there is a significant hit ratio difference between the cache with local optimal replacement policy and the user-aware cache. Especially when the cache size is larger than 150K, the user-aware cache hit ratio is larger than the upper bound on the hit ratio that is achieved if the availability of the cache is

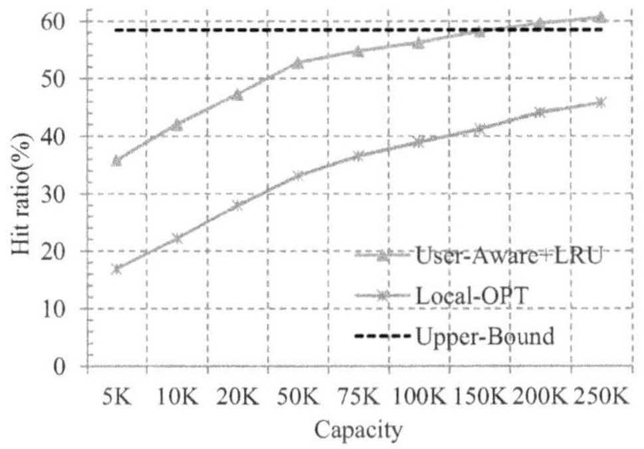

Figure 2: Comparison of the hit ratios for all requests

infinite in size without prefetching. Thus, user-aware cache with prefetching can achieve a high hit ratio.

Table 1 shows the hit ratios of the user-aware cache and the caches which use different prefetching policies without any user characteristics by varying the cache size. These results in table 1 reveal that the proposed user-aware cache with prefetching performs better than the cache using LRU replacement policy with Pre-K1 or Pre-SDC1 prefetching policy.

Table 1: Hit ratios (%) vs. cache sizes

Cache Size	Pre-K1	Pre-SDC1	**User-Aware**
5K	31.58	32.78	**35.81**
10K	37.46	38.55	**42.05**
20K	42.40	43.41	**47.29**
50K	47.62	48.60	**52.73**
75K	49.78	50.65	**54.81**
100K	51.25	52.06	**56.22**
150K	53.29	54.05	**58.20**
200K	54.78	55.47	**59.59**
250K	55.99	56.60	**60.69**

4. CONCLUSIONS

In this study, we introduce a new caching approach which is the user-aware cache and show that it can achieve better hit ratios. The future work involves:

- Combining more policies with the user-aware cache;
- Exploring more features used for selecting the queries for the user-aware cache;
- Analyzing the impact of crawlers and scrapers on the user-aware cache.

5. REFERENCES

[1] T. Fagni, R. Perego, F. Silvestri, and S. Orlando. Boosting the performance of web search engines: Caching and prefetching query results by exploiting historical usage data. *ACM Trans. Inf. Syst.*, 24(1):51–78, Jan. 2006.

[2] R. Lempel and S. Moran. Predictive caching and prefetching of query results in search engines. In *Proceedings of the 12th international conference on World Wide Web*, WWW '03, pages 19–28, New York, NY, USA, 2003. ACM.

[3] Y. Li, S. Zhang, B. Wang, and J. Li. Characteristics of chinese web searching: A large-scale analysis of chinese query logs. *Journal of Computational Information Systems*, 4(3):1127–1136, 2008.

Using Eye-Tracking with Dynamic Areas of Interest for Analyzing Interactive Information Retrieval

Vu T. Tran
Information Engineering
University of Duisburg-Essen
Duisburg, Germany
vtran@is.inf.uni-due.de

Norbert Fuhr
Information Engineering
University of Duisburg-Essen
Duisburg, Germany
norbert.fuhr@uni-due.de

ABSTRACT

Based on a new framework for capturing dynamic areas of interest in eye-tracking, we model the user search process as a Markov-chain. The analysis indicates possible system improvements and yields parameter estimates for the Interactive Probability Ranking Principle (IPRP).

Categories and Subject Descriptors

H.3.3 [**Information Storage and Retrieval**]: Information Search and Retrieval—*Search Process*

Keywords

User Study, Interactive Retrieval, Eye-Tracking

1. INTRODUCTION

Interactive retrieval systems are a commodity today, the theoretic foundation for this type of systems is rather scarce. The IPRP [3] is a probabilistic foundation for this kind of system. However, there has been little work building upon this framework. Although there have been many user studies of search behaviour, none of them provides results that could be used for improving the functional level of an IR system.

In this paper, we present a new methodology for analysing interactive IR, extending current approaches by separating between eye-tracking and action level, and by considering dynamic areas of interest for the former. An example study demonstrates the feasibility of our approach, yielding suggestions for system improvements as well as parameter estimates for the IPRP.

In the following, after giving a survey over related work, we describe our test setting, and then analyse the experimental results, before we come to the conclusion.

The IPRP assumes that a user moves between situations s_i, in each of which the system presents a list of choices, about which the user has to decide, and the first accepted choice moves the user to a new situation. Each choice c_{ij} is associated with three parameters: the effort e_{ij} for considering this choice, the acceptance probability p_{ij}, and the benefit a_{ij} resulting from the acceptance. Below, we show how the first two parameters can be estimated in our setting, while the third one still is an open research issue.

By applying economic theory to IIR Azzopardi modelled the process of interaction between a user and a system and constructed a cost function to measure the user effort [1].

SIGIR'12, August 12–16, 2012, Portland, Oregon, USA.
ACM 978-1-4503-1472-5/12/08.

Cutrell and Guang [4] used eye-tracking to explore the effects of different presentations of search results. Joachims et al. [5] examined the reliability of click-through data for implicit relevance feedback of a web search engine by comparing them to eye-tracking data.

2. EXPERIMENTAL DESIGN

For our experiments, we used a collection based on a crawl of 2.7 million records from the book database of the online bookseller Amazon.com. As test subjects, we recruited 12 students of computer science, cognitive and communication science and related fields. After an introduction into the system, users had to work on three tasks, with a time limit of 20 minutes per task (rotating tasks in a Latin square design). Due to space limitations, we only discuss the results of the 'complex' task type here, where users were asked to find books about one of the following topics: 1) Trustworthy books about 9/11 terrorist attacks, 2) Controversial books discussing the climate change, 3) Highly acclaimed novels about racial discrimination.

The user interface of our system consists of four major areas: a query input field, a list of result items, a detail area showing all available data about the currently selected document, and a basket where users should place documents they deemed relevant. We wanted to collect eye-tracking data for each specific result list item, even when the user is scrolling down in this list; however, standard eye-tracking software allows only for the monitoring of static 'areas of interest' (AOI). Thus, we developed a framework called *AOILog* which automatically keeps track of position, visibility and size of all user interface objects at any point in time. Combining this information with the eye-tracking data, we always know at which object the user is currently looking.[1]

3. RESULTS AND ANALYSIS

Our analysis is based on the combination of logging and eye-tracking data. For the latter, as in other studies, we focus on the so-called fixations, and also consider them only if they last for at least 80 ms, since this is the minimum time required for reading anything on the screen [2].

Corresponding to the four areas of the user interface, we can distinguish four types of user actions: formulating *queries*, looking at a *result item*, regarding document *details*, and looking at the *basket* (which can be viewed as a more strategic action, where the user is thinking about the continuation of her search). Thus, a one-to-one mapping of eye-tracking

[1] *AOILog* is an open source software; it can be easily integrated into any user interface based on Java Swing.

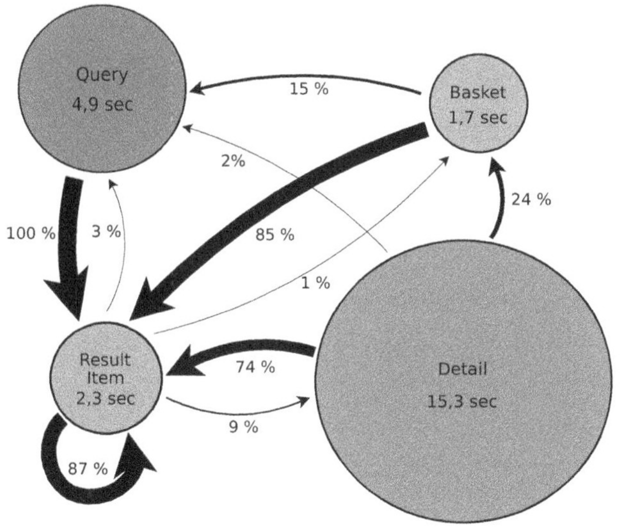

Figure 1: Transition probabilities and user efforts

data and user actions seems to be straightforward. However, a closer analysis showed that this is too simplistic.

First, we noted that users were frequently looking back and forth between the details and the basket. The behaviour was due to the fact that the book database often contains very similar entries (e.g., different editions of a book), thus forcing users to check if the current result item was substantially different from the books already placed in the basket. Occasionally, this also happened for items in the result list. In a similar way, when formulating a new query, users did not only look at the query field, but also checked the details of the current document as well as the items in the basket.

In order to deal with these problems, we separate between two levels, the eye-tracking level and the action level. Then we define a mapping from the former to the latter, which also considers the logging data. By default, the area the user looks at defines the current action, with the following exceptions:

- When the user looks from a result item to the basket and back, without moving the item to the basket, this is counted as part of regarding the item.
- The same holds for looking back and forth between details and the basket.
- Query formulation starts when the user's gaze wanders from the details or the basket to the query field for the first time, even when it returns to the basket/details several times before the query is actually submitted.

Applying these rules resulted in the transition probabilities and average times spent for the different actions displayed in Figure 1. From this data, a number of observations can be made:

1. Query formulation is roughly the same time as looking at two result items.
2. Retrieval quality is surprisingly low—only about 3 % of the items in the result list are relevant. This is mainly due to the complexity of the retrieval tasks.
3. Since only 24 % of the details regarded are judged as relevant, the quality of the result entries could be improved, in order to increase this rate (while the probability of the transition from result to details would decrease, thus leading to a reduction of the overall effort). Furthermore, we also see that click-through data is a poor indicator of relevance.
4. As mentioned above, users often compare the current document with entries from the basket. This could be supported by a similarity search function, which show the current document and similar one from the basket side-by-side.

Now we analyse this data with regard to the IPRP. The timings correspond to the effort e_{ij} for evaluating a choice c_{ij}, while the transition probabilities give the chances p_{ij} of accepting it. As a possible approach for quantifying the benefit a_{ij} of a decision, we can regard the time needed for finding the first (next) relevant document. For that, we compute the expected time for reaching the basket. Here we can apply the method for computing "first passage times" in Markov networks, which leads to a linear equation system. As results, we get 127.9 s for the query, 123.0 s for the result list and 109.5 s for the details stage. The benefits can then be defined as the time differences between the two situations of a transition invoked by accepting a choice. As could be expected, the biggest benefits are achieved when moving to the basket—but the corresponding acceptance probabilities are low. On the other hand, there are also choices with negative benefits (when going back to query reformulation or from detail to result). While the order of the benefits seems ok, negative benefits are in contradiction to the IPRP, which says that the corresponding choices are useless and thus should be avoided. This is a more general problem of parameter estimation for the IPRP: when reformulating the query, users do not really go back to the initial situation, they submit an improved query. For considering that, we would need a more complex Markov model, and a much larger number of observations.

4. CONCLUSION

In this paper, we extended current methodologies for analyzing interactive IR by separating between eye-tracking and action level, and by implementing dynamic areas of interest. Our example study shows the findings point to possible system improvements, and that click-through rates are a poor indicator of relevance. Finally, we can immediately derive parameters for the IPRP, although open problems remain.

5. ACKNOWLEDGEMENT

This work was supported by the German Science Foundation under grant no. FU 205/24-1.

6. REFERENCES

[1] L. Azzopardi. The economics in interactive information retrieval. SIGIR '11, pages 15–24, New York, NY, USA, 2011. ACM.

[2] G. Buscher, A. Dengel, and L. van Elst. Eye movements as implicit relevance feedback. In *CHI '08*, pages 2991–2996, New York, NY, USA, 2008. ACM.

[3] N. Fuhr. A probability ranking principle for interactive information retrieval. *Information Retrieval*, 11(3):251–265, 2008.

[4] Z. Guan and E. Cutrell. An eye tracking study of the effect of target rank on web search. In *CHI '07*, pages 417–420, New York, NY, USA, 2007. ACM.

[5] T. Joachims, L. Granka, B. Pan, H. Hembrooke, F. Radlinski, and G. Gay. Evaluating the accuracy of implicit feedback from clicks and query reformulations in web search. *ACM Trans. Inf. Syst.*, 25(2), 2007.

Using PageRank to Infer User Preferences

Praveen Chandar and Ben Carterette
{pcr,carteret}@udel.edu
Department of Computer and Information Sciences
University of Delaware
Newark, DE, USA 19716

ABSTRACT

Recently, researchers have shown interest in the use of preference judgments for evaluation in IR literature. Although preference judgments have several advantages over absolute judgment, one of the major disadvantages is that the number of judgments needed increases polynomially as the number of documents in the pool increases. We propose a novel method using PageRank to minimize the number of judgments required to evaluate systems using preference judgments. We test the proposed hypotheses using the TREC 2004 to 2006 Terabyte dataset to show that it is possible to reduce the evaluation cost considerably. Further, we study the susceptibility of the methods due to assessor errors.

Categories and Subject Descriptors: H.3.3 [Information Storage and Retrieval]

Keywords: preference judgments, PageRank

1. INTRODUCTION

The idea of pairwise preference judgments is relatively new in IR literature. In the case of preference judgments, an assessor looks at a *pair* of documents and expresses a preference for one over the other instead of assigning a relevance label to a document. Comparison studies between absolute and preference judgments show that preference judgments have various advantages such as reducing the complexity of the task and increasing inter-assessor agreement [3]. Preference judgments tend to help assessors make finer distinctions between documents [5]. Although it is possible to use graded absolute judgments, it is difficult to determine the specifics of the grades, and the burden on assessors is likely to increase with an increase in the number of grades.

A major drawback of using pairwise preference judgments is that as the number of documents in the pool increases, the number of judgments increases polynomially. If there are n documents in the pool, then $n(n-1)/2$ preference judgments would be necessary to ensure that all pairs of documents are judged. This enormous increase in the number of pairwise judgments not only increases evaluation cost but also gives rise to user fatigue and boredom, possibly leading to poor quality of judgments.

SIGIR'12, August 12–16, 2012, Portland, Oregon, USA.
ACM 978-1-4503-1472-5/12/08.

In this work, we describe a novel technique that could be used to reduce the number of pairwise judgments. Firstly, we show that pairwise judgments for each query can be represented in the form of a directed graph on which various graph algorithms can be applied. We study the behavior of PageRank and show that the number of pairwise judgments could be reduced considerably. Further, we show that the PageRank method, although susceptible to assessor error, does significantly better than the majority vote approach that is considered as the baseline.

2. PREFERENCE FRAMEWORK

In this section we describe a novel technique to collect preference judgments at a reduced cost. The technique consists of two steps: graphical representation of pairwise judgments and scoring of each node in the graph. Scoring of nodes can be done using various graph algorithms such as PageRank, HITS, etc.

We describe a typical user interface for collecting preference judgments as follows: the assessor would be shown two documents and a statement of an information need (a topic); the assessor would have to pick the most preferred document using the *prefer left* or *prefer right* buttons. Additionally, both documents could be judged *not relevant* to indicate that all other documents should be preferred to them. The criteria for preference is task dependent and is often explained to the assessor in the form of guidelines.

The collected pairwise judgments are then represented in the form of a directed graph. Each unique document is represented as a vertex in the graph and the edges between vertices corresponds to the pairwise judgments. While there are several ways to do this conversion, we describe a way which worked for us. Let's say there are three judgments a user can make for a pair of documents (Doc_A, Doc_B): prefer Doc_A, both non relevant, and prefer Doc_B. When prefer Doc_A is selected for a pair, this translates to a directed link from Doc_B to Doc_A, similarly a link from Doc_A to Doc_B when Doc_B is preferred and there exists no link between Doc_A and Doc_B in the case of both non relevant.

Now that the pairwise judgments have been represented in the form of a graph, there are several graph algorithms such as PageRank, HITS, etc. that could be used to assign a score. The score represents the relevance of a document and documents are ranked based on these scores. In this work we compare the performance of PageRank with the a baseline majority vote method.

PageRank The PageRank algorithm proposed by Brin and Page [2] is a graph algorithm that assigns a numerical weighting to each vertex in a graph, with the purpose of measuring its relative importance within the graph. We compute the page rank scores for each node in the preference graph and hypothesize that the page rank scores correlate to the degree of relevance of the document.

Majority Vote A common technique used to produce a ranking from pairwise judgments is to sort documents by the number of times the document was preferred. The count of the number of preferences can be obtained from the preference graph by computing the in-degree for each node. We use this method as our baseline.

Both algorithms produce the same ranking when all pairwise judgments are used, *i.e.* if $n(n-1)/2$ pairwise judgments are used to judge n documents. But their behavior changes if some pairwise judgments are removed from the sample of $n(n-1)/2$ pairwise judgments. In order to study this behavior, we simulate preference judgments from graded judgments and evaluate the performance of rankings produced by randomly sampling 1%, 5%, 10%, ..., 100% of $n(n-1)/2$ pairwise judgments. We use the nDCG measure proposed by Jarvelin and Kekalainen [4] to evaluate the performance of each ranking against original graded judgments.

3. IMPLEMENTATION AND RESULTS

Our experiments are conducted on data simulated using the TREC 2004 to 2006 Terabyte dataset. The TREC Terabyte consists of a total of 150 topics with relevance graded judgments on a three-point scale. The corpus is a collection of Web data crawled from websites in the GOV domain during early 2004. The absolute graded judgments are converted to preference judgments by generating all possible pairs for the documents in the qrels file for each topic; the document with a higher grade is preferred in each pair. Aslam et al. [1] presented a meta-search approach known as meta-AP which is a function of the document's position in a set of ranked lists, with higher rankings contributing more to the metaAP score. We employ metaAP scores to resolve ties when the grades of both the documents in a pair are equal (document with higher meta score is chosen). Document pairs containing two non-relevant documents are considered as *both non-relevant* (no link in preference graph).

Figure 1 shows the nDCG scores at rank 20 and 1000 for the PageRank method compared with the majority votes method. The figure includes a run each for various sample sizes of the pairwise judgments and three *Down Sample* runs represented as *DS*. The *Down Samples* were generated by pairing each document in the pool of n documents with another document k times, *i.e.* each document in the pool of n documents is paired with *another* document for *DS1* and *two* other documents for *DS2* and so on. Note that there would be n pairwise judgments in *DS1* and $2n$ pairwise judgments in *DS2*. The nDCG computed from PageRank-based judgments is much higher than that computed from majority vote. Clearly, the PageRank method requires fewer number of pairs of judgments compared to the majority votes method on average and the results suggest that it is possible to collect preference judgments by judging just 5% of the pairs with minimal loss of performance.

Figure 2 shows the performance of majority votes and PageRank methods with error. We added error for each run by sampling 1%, 5% and 10% of the pairs and changing the judgments. The judgments were changed randomly either by deleting the edge or changing the direction of the edge. The PageRank method dominates the majority vote method when more preferences are given (5% and greater), but majority vote tends to do better for smaller samples and when there are a constant number of preference judgments for each document.

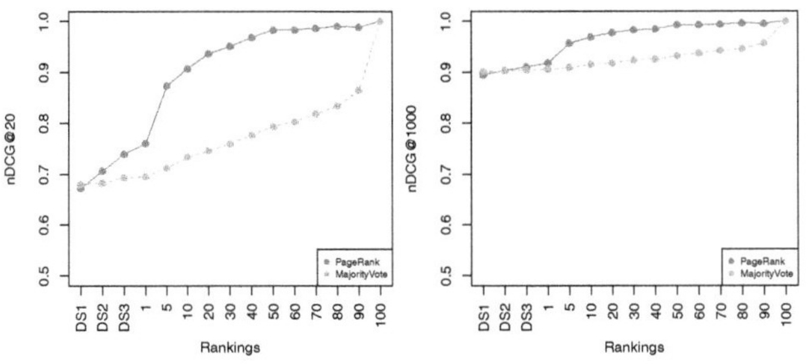

Figure 1: nDCG@20 and nDCG@1000 scores for the PageRank and majority votes method for various sample sizes. DS denotes *Down Sample*.

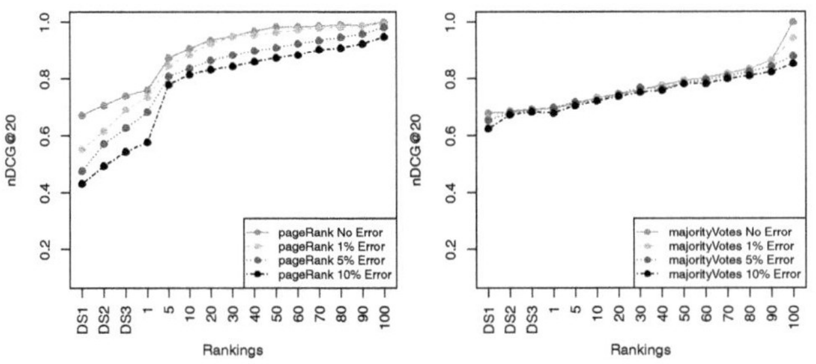

Figure 2: nDCG@20 scores for the PageRank and majority votes method for various sample sizes with assessor errors. DS denotes *Down Sample*.

4. CONCLUSION AND FUTURE WORK

We have presented a novel method to reduce evaluation cost using PageRank. While it is common to use majority vote to score and obtain a ranking from preferences, we have shown that using PageRank might be cost effective. Further, the PageRank method outperforms the baseline while assessor errors are added. Future directions for our work includes studying various other graph methods, picking documents intelligently for pairwise judging.

5. REFERENCES

[1] J. A. Aslam, V. Pavlu, and E. Yilmaz. Measure-based metasearch. In *Proceedings of SIGIR*, SIGIR '05, pages 571–572, NY, USA, 2005. ACM.

[2] S. Brin and L. Page. The anatomy of a large-scale hypertextual web search engine. In *Proceedings of WWW*, pages 107–117, 1998.

[3] B. Carterette, P. N. Bennett, D. M. Chickering, and S. T. Dumais. Here or there: preference judgments for relevance. In *Proceedings of the ECIR*, pages 16–27, 2008.

[4] K. Järvelin and J. Kekäläinen. Cumulated gain-based evaluation of ir techniques. *ACM Trans. Inf. Syst.*, pages 422–446, October 2002.

[5] M. E. Rorvig. The simple scalability of documents. *JASIS*, 41(8):590–598, 1990.

Utilizing Inter-Document Similarities in Federated Search

Savva Khalaman
savvakh@tx.technion.ac.il

Oren Kurland
kurland@ie.technion.ac.il

Faculty of Industrial Engineering and Management
Technion — Israel Institute of Technology
Haifa 32000, Israel

ABSTRACT

We demonstrate the merits of using inter-document similarities for federated search. Specifically, we study a results-merging method that utilizes information induced from clusters of similar documents created *across* the lists retrieved from the collections. The method significantly outperforms state-of-the-art results merging approaches.

Categories and Subject Descriptors: H.3.3 [Information Search and Retrieval]: Retrieval models

General Terms: Algorithms, Experimentation

Keywords: inter-document similarities, federated search

1. INTRODUCTION

Federated search is the task of retrieving documents from multiple (possibly non-overlapping) collections in response to a query [1]. The task is typically composed of three steps: attaining resource (collection) description, selecting resources (collections), and merging the results retrieved from the selected collections [1]. We focus on the results-merging step; specifically, we study the merits of using information induced from inter-document similarities.

While there is much work on utilizing inter-document similarities for the single-corpus retrieval setting, there is little work along that venue for federated retrieval. For example, clustering was used to transform a single-collection retrieval setting into that of multiple collections [8]. Clusters of sampled documents were used for performing query expansion in federated search [5]; yet, inter-document similarities were not used for results merging. Furthermore, it was shown that among the clusters created across the lists retrieved from different collections there are some that contain a high percentage of relevant documents [3]; still, a results merging method exploiting these clusters was not proposed

The only work, to the best of our knowledge, that uses inter-document-similarities for (direct) results merging is based on scoring a document by its similarity with other documents in the retrieved lists [6]. We show that the method we study substantially outperforms this approach.

The method we present for merging results in federated search is adapted from recent work on fusing lists that were retrieved from the *same collection* [4]. In contrast to the non-overlapping collections setting we explore here, the retrieved lists in this work [4] were (partially) overlapping and the merging (fusion) methods used to assign initial scores to documents exploited this overlap. The adapted method that we study integrates retrieval scores assigned by a state-of-the-art results-merging approach (e.g., CORI [1] and SSL [7]) with information induced from clusters created from similar documents across the retrieved lists. Specifically, a document can provide relevance-status support to documents in the same list or in other lists that it is similar to. The resultant retrieval performance is substantially better than that of using only the initial retrieval scores assigned by the state-of-the-art merging approach.

SIGIR'12, August 12–16, 2012, Portland, Oregon, USA.
ACM 978-1-4503-1472-5/12/08.

2. RESULTS-MERGING METHOD

Suppose that some resource (collection) selection method was applied in response to query q [1]. We assume that document lists were retrieved from the selected (non-overlapping) collections and merged by *some* previously proposed results-merging algorithm [1, 7]. Let $D_{init}^{[n]}$ denote the list of the n documents most highly ranked by the merging algorithm that assigns the (initial) score $F_{init}(d;q)$ to document d.

Our goal is re-ranking $D_{init}^{[n]}$ to improve ranking effectiveness. (Documents not in $D_{init}^{[n]}$ remain at their original ranks.) To that end, we study the utilization of inter-document similarities by adapting a method proposed in work on fusing lists retrieved *from the same corpus* [4]. Let Cl be the set of document clusters created from $D_{init}^{[n]}$ using some clustering algorithm; c will denote a cluster. Then, the score assigned to document d ($\in D_{init}^{[n]}$) by the **Clust** method is:

$$F_{Clust}(d;q) \stackrel{def}{=} (1-\lambda)\frac{F_{init}(d;q)}{\sum_{d' \in D_{init}^{[n]}} F_{init}(d';q)} + \lambda \sum_{c \in Cl} \frac{F(c;q)}{\sum_{c' \in Cl} F(c';q)} \frac{\sum_{d_i \in c} Sim(d_i,d)}{\sum_{d' \in D_{init}^{[n]}} \sum_{d_i \in c} Sim(d_i,d')};$$

$F(c;q) \stackrel{def}{=} \prod_{d_i \in c} F_{init}(d_i;q)$; as all the clusters in Cl contain the same number of documents (see details below), there is no cluster-size bias incurred; $Sim(\cdot,\cdot)$ is the inter-document similarity measure used to create Cl; λ is a free parameter.

Thus, d is highly ranked if (i) its (normalized) initial score is high; and, (ii) it is similar to documents in clusters c that contain documents that were initially highly ranked. In other words, similar documents provide relevance-status support to each other via the clusters to which they belong. Note that if $\lambda = 0$, then cluster-based information is not used and $F_{Clust}(d;q)$ is d's normalized initial score.

			Queries: 51-100			Queries: 101-150		
			p@5	p@10	MAP	p@5	p@10	MAP
Uni	CORI	initial	.460	.420	.060	.396	.380	.054
		CRSC	.524	$.474^{i}$	.062	.376	.372	.052
		Clust	$\mathbf{.536}^{i}$	$\mathbf{.498}^{i}$	$\mathbf{.064}^{i}$	$\mathbf{.480}^{i}_{c}$	$\mathbf{.454}^{i}_{c}$	$\mathbf{.059}^{i}_{c}$
	SSL	initial	.432	.410	.060	.412	.396	.055
		CRSC	.492	.458	.062	.400	.346	.052
		Clust	**.504**	$\mathbf{.490}^{i}$	$\mathbf{.064}^{i}$	$\mathbf{.492}_{c}$	$\mathbf{.468}^{i}_{c}$	$\mathbf{.060}^{i}_{c}$
Rel	CORI	initial	.424	.384	.059	.432	.370	.064
		CRSC	.428	.402	.061	.456	.442	$.072^{i}$
		Clust	**.476**	$\mathbf{.442}^{i}$	$\mathbf{.063}^{i}_{c}$	**.496**	$\mathbf{.466}^{i}$	$\mathbf{.073}^{i}$
	SSL	initial	.412	.384	.095	.440	.376	.095
		CRSC	.412	.404	.096	.452	.436	$.103^{i}$
		Clust	$\mathbf{.480}^{i}_{c}$	$\mathbf{.454}^{i}_{c}$	$\mathbf{.099}^{i}_{c}$	**.492**	$\mathbf{.474}^{i}$	$\mathbf{.105}^{i}$
NRel	CORI	initial	.452	.446	.064	.416	.394	.054
		CRSC	.476	.476	.066	.472	.414	.057
		Clust	$\mathbf{.552}^{i}_{c}$	$\mathbf{.516}^{i}_{c}$	$\mathbf{.069}^{i}_{c}$	$\mathbf{.500}^{i}$	**.450**	$\mathbf{.059}^{i}_{c}$
	SSL	initial	.464	.448	.065	.396	.398	.055
		CRSC	.488	.462	.067	.456	.412	.058
		Clust	$\mathbf{.536}^{i}$	$\mathbf{.516}^{i}_{c}$	$\mathbf{.070}^{i}_{c}$	$\mathbf{.504}^{i}$	**.452**	$\mathbf{.060}^{i}$
Rep	CORI	initial	.428	.408	.060	.428	.388	.050
		CRSC	.416	.418	.060	.432	.424	.052
		Clust	$\mathbf{.492}_{c}$	$\mathbf{.474}^{i}_{c}$	$\mathbf{.064}^{i}_{c}$	**.496**	$\mathbf{.474}^{i}$	$\mathbf{.056}^{i}_{c}$
	SSL	initial	.444	.408	.061	.452	.408	.052
		CRSC	.448	.434	.060	.396	.418	.052
		Clust	**.476**	$\mathbf{.470}^{i}$	$\mathbf{.064}^{i}_{c}$	$\mathbf{.508}_{c}$	$\mathbf{.484}^{i}_{c}$	$\mathbf{.058}^{i}_{c}$

			Queries: 201-250		
			p@5	p@10	MAP
KM	CORI	initial	.468	.402	.135
		CRSC	.484	.396	.138
		Clust	**.496**	$\mathbf{.460}^{i}_{c}$	$\mathbf{.147}^{i}$
	SSL	initial	.480	.412	.152
		CRSC	.512	.412	.150
		Clust	**.532**	$\mathbf{.478}^{i}_{c}$	$\mathbf{.165}^{i}_{c}$

Table 1: Results. Boldface: the best result per testbed, evaluation measure, and initial merging method; 'i' and 'c': statistically significant differences with initial and CRSC, respectively.

3. EVALUATION

We conducted experiments with testbeds that are commonly used in work on federated search [1, 2, 5, 8, 7]: (i) **Uni**: Trec123-100col-bysource (Uniform), (ii) **KM**: Trec4-kmeans (K-means), (iii) **Rep**: Trec123-2ldb-60col (Representative), (iv) **Rel**: Trec123-AP-WSJ-60col (Relevant), and (v) **NRel**: Trec123-FR-DOE-81col (non-relevant). Titles of the TREC topics 51-150 served for queries for all testbeds except for KM where the description fields of TREC topics 201-250 were used. Tokenization, Porter stemming, and stopword removal were applied using the Lemur toolkit (www.lemurproject.org), which was used for experiments. To acquire resource (collection) description, we adopt the query-based sampling method from [2] which was also used in [1, 7, 5]. Following common practice [1, 7], the 10 highest ranked collections are selected in the resource-selection phase using CORI's resource selection method. As in previous report [7], 1000 documents are retrieved from each selected collection using the INQUERY search engine. Then, the retrieved lists are merged using either CORI's merging method [1] or the single-model SSL merging approach [7]. The **initial** score, $F_{init}(d;q)$, assigned to d by these methods is used in our Clust method.

To cluster $D^{[n]}_{init}$, we use a simple nearest-neighbors-based clustering approach [4]. For each $d \in D^{[n]}_{init}$ we create a cluster that is composed of d and the $\delta - 1$ ($\delta = 5$) documents d' in $D^{[n]}_{init}$ ($d' \neq d$) that yield the highest $Sim(d, d') \stackrel{def}{=} \exp\left(-D(p^{[0]}_{d}(\cdot)||p^{[\mu]}_{d'}(\cdot))\right)$; $p^{[\mu]}_{x}$ is the Dirichlet-smoothed unigram language model induced from x with the smoothing parameter μ ($= 1000$); D is the KL divergence; the term-counts statistics used for smoothing language models is based on the query-based sampling mentioned above.

The **initial** ranking induced by the CORI and SSL results-merging methods serves for a baseline. Additional reference comparison that we use is the Cross Rank Similarity Comparison (**CRSC**) approach [6] that re-ranks $D^{[n]}_{init}$ here by scoring d with $\sum_{d'(\neq d)\in D^{[n]}_{init}} \frac{Sim(d',d)}{\sum_{d''(\neq d')\in D^{[n]}_{init}} Sim(d',d'')}$. Our Clust method incorporates two free parameters: n ($\in \{10, 30, 50, 100\}$), the number of documents in $D^{[n]}_{init}$, and λ ($\in \{0, 0.1, \ldots, 1\}$), the interpolation parameter; CRSC only depends on n. We set the free-parameter values for each method using leave-one-out cross validation performed over the queries per testbad; MAP@1000 serves as the optimization criterion in the learning phase. In addition to MAP, we also present p@5 and p@10 performance numbers. Statistically significant differences in performance are determined using the two-tailed paired t-test at a 95% confidence level.

Results and Conclusions. We see in Table 1 that Clust always outperforms the initial ranking that was induced by a state-of-the-art results-merging method; often, the improvements are statistically significantly. This finding attests to the merits of integrating the initial results-merging score with information induced from clusters of similar documents. Further exploration reveals that $\lambda \notin \{0, 1\}$ often yields optimal performance. This shows that the integration just mentioned yields performance that is better than that of using each of the two integrated components alone. We also see that Clust consistently outperforms CRSC, which does not utilize the initial results-merging scores, nor uses a cluster-based approach.

Acknowledgments We thank the reviewers for their comments. This paper is based upon work supported in part by the Israel Science Foundation under grant no. 557/09. Any opinions, findings and conclusions or recommendations expressed here are the authors' and do not necessarily reflect those of the sponsors.

4. REFERENCES

[1] J. Callan. Distributed information retrieval. In W. Croft, editor, *Advances in information retrieval*, chapter 5, pages 127–150. Kluwer Academic Publishers, 2000.

[2] J. Callan and M. Connell. Query-based sampling of text databases. *ACM Transactions on Information Systems*, 19(2):97–130, 2001.

[3] F. Crestani and S. Wu. Testing the cluster hypothesis in distributed information retrieval. *Information Processing and Management*, 42(5):1137–1150, 2006.

[4] A. Khudyak Kozorovitsky and O. Kurland. Cluster-based fusion of retrieved lists. In *Proceedings of SIGIR*, pages 893–902, 2011.

[5] M. Shokouhi, L. Azzopardi, and P. Thomas. Effective query expansion for federated search. In *Proceedings of SIGIR*, pages 427–434, 2009.

[6] X. M. Shou and M. Sanderson. Experiments on data fusion using headline information. In *Proceedings of SIGIR*, pages 413–414, 2002.

[7] L. Si and J. Callan. A semisupervised learning method to merge search engine results. *ACM Transactions on Information Systems*, 21(4):457–491, October 2003.

[8] J. Xu and W. B. Croft. Cluster-based language models for distributed retrieval. In *Proceedings of SIGIR*, 1999.

Want a Coffee? Predicting Users' Trails

Wen Li
Delft University of Technology
Delft, Netherlands
wen.li@tudelft.nl

Carsten Eickhoff
Delft University of Technology
Delft, Netherlands
c.eickhoff@tudelft.nl

Arjen P. de Vries
CWI
Amsterdam, Netherlands
arjen@acm.org

ABSTRACT

Twitter and Foursquare are two well-connected platforms for sharing information where growing numbers of users post location-related messages. In contrast to the longitude-latitude geotags commonly used online, e.g., on photos and tweets, new place-tags containing category information show more human-readable high-level information rather than a pair of coordinates. This grants an opportunity for better understanding users' physical locations which can be used as context to facilitate other applications, e.g., location context-aware advertisement. In this paper, we verify the assumption that users' current trails contain cues of their future routes. The results from the preliminary experiments show promising performance of a basic Markov Chain-based model.

Categories: H.2.8 [Database Management] Database applications - Data mining J.4 [Computer Application] Social and Behavioral Science

General Terms: Experimentation

Keywords: Twitter, location-based estimation, text mining, geotagging, mobile applications

1. INTRODUCTION

Twitter is a platform for sharing various kinds of information, such as photos, videos and even users' geo-locations. This is going far beyond what the service was designed for; sending text messages of 140 characters. Originally, user messages, so-called tweets, only contained a pair of geo-coordinates to indicate the location where the user issued his/her tweet. This hardly provides any information about the environment around users at the time of posting. Last year, Twitter extended its API to supporting *Places of Interest* (POI) to facilitate users tagging their tweets with more accurate high-level geo information. This novel kind of geo-tags provides several properties such as names, bounding-boxes, and information about geographically-related entities, giving easy access to the functional aspect of locations.

Foursquare is a dedicated geo-location sharing platform. Users are encouraged to check-in at a POI, that is, to post a message on both Twitter and Foursquare, declaring their visit, upon which they are rewarded with badges, coupons, etc. The service's API provides rich information, such as POI categories and URLs to homepages. This kind of information enables making connections between users, locations and their potential activities. The place level geo-information arising in Twitter and Foursquare facilitates our research on predicting users' likelihoods of visiting a place based on their current and previous visits. With this kind of knowledge, advertisers could display targeted information more accurately to earn more attention and clicks. For example, having known a user would go for a coffee after work, a suggestion of an attractive lately-opened café would be more persuasive before he/she already visited one.

Recently, there were many discoveries in the domain of location-related social information. Backstrom et al. [1] studied the vocabulary gap between users in different areas in the US and proposed a method based on local word filtering to estimate users' hometowns. Kurashima et al. [2] proposed a method of integrating Markov Chains and Topic Models to recommend travel routes based on geo-tagged photos shared online. Sadilek et al. [3] studied the relation between friendships and location visiting patterns and proposed a friend recommendation method. These studies on location-aware applications show an interesting connection between a user's location and his/her characteristics in other aspects.

In this paper, we formalize our task as, given a user's history of visits in a trail, how can we estimate the types of POI in the future part of trail? Here, a trail is defined as a sequence of POIs a user visits during one day. We experimentally validate whether we can predict user behavior represented by the POI type of their next visit based on data from Twitter and Foursquare using a Markov Chain-based model. The method can also be easily integrated into applications on mobile devices which may facilitate a location recommendation or context-aware advertising.

SIGIR'12, August 12–16, 2012, Portland, Oregon, USA.
ACM 978-1-4503-1472-5/12/08.

2. DATA

The data were collected via Twitter's API following a strategy of tracking active users of POI-tagged tweets and the places popular among those users. After 6 months of consecutive crawling, we hold a corpus of 1 277 596 tweets tagged with 236 369 unique POIs. In Figure 1, we can see that the distribution of tweets over POIs approximate a power law distribution and around 90% of POIs are observed less than 10 times.

Twitter has no hierarchic POI categorization in terms of

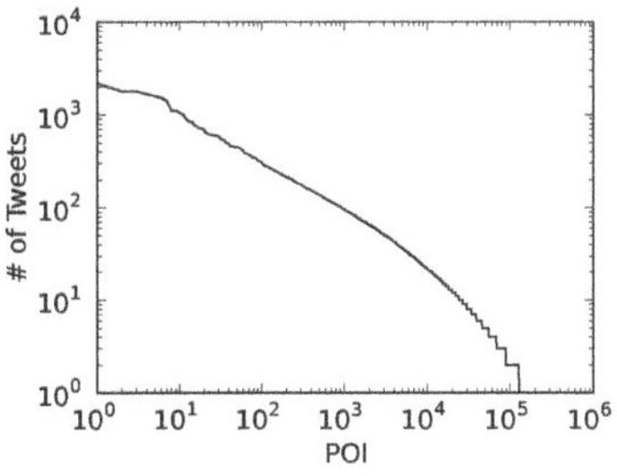

Figure 1: Tweet Distribution over POIs

functionality; Foursquare, on the other hand, does not provide adequate API for crawling data, but offers POI categories organized in a 3-level hierarchy with 9 categories at the top level, such as *food*, *nightlife*, *shops* and 391 subcategories at lower levels, such as *American food*, *bars*, *apparels*. This would enable us to analyze user behavior on different levels of granularity. As no public API exists to map places between the two services, we have to bridge the data from Twitter and Foursquare by using Foursquare's venue search API. This API accepts a query and a pair of coordinates and returns a list of matching places. By carefully mapping places from both sides, we obtain category information (i.e., POI types) for about 85% of the POIs. By grouping tweets into trails as defined in Section 1, and filtering out those trails shorter than 5 visits, we finally have 17 738 trails forming our ground truth. The average length of those trails in terms of visits and places are respectively 7.345 and 5.096. To enable reproduction of our results, we make our anonymous dataset available at `http://homepage.tudelft.nl/9y54n`

3. METHODS AND EXPERIMENTS

Similarly to the work in [2], we assume users' next steps to depend on their current and past locations. Let a trail be a sequence of random variables X_t indicating the categories of POIs, and then simplifying the assumption, we have $P(X_t|X_{t-1}, X_{t-2}, \ldots, X_0) = P(X_t|X_{t-1})$. This fits the definition of Markov Chains. We use them in this exploratory study to verify our assumption of causal dependencies between trail elements. As a baseline, we assume users to stay at their current location type. This is inspired by the observation that users tend to post several times from a single place and its performance is significantly better than random guessing.

The experiments are conducted at two levels of granularity of categories provided by the hierarchy from Foursquare, i.e., the top level categories and sub-level categories. Under both levels of granularity, we repeat the experiment on tweets with POIs located in 4 major US cities, namely, New York (NY), Chicago (CH), Los Angeles (LA) and San Francisco (SF) as well as the whole country, in order to check whether users from the same areas have locally coherent visiting patterns.

The data set in each experiment is split according to 10-fold cross validation. Moreover, our split is based on users, i.e., there is no overlap between training set and testing set in terms of users, which will prevent the methods from overfitting users who have more trails. Due to the sparsity in the data, there are few trails in the test set, e.g., within San Francisco, there are only 200 trails composed of 800 POI-tagged tweets for test. According to the assumption of dependency in the model, we test the method for each consecutive POI pair in each trail. For example, we test (Desserts, Apparel), (Apparel, Record Shop), (Record Shop, Toys&Games) for the trail (Desserts, Apparel, Record Shop, Toys&Games). Due to the setting, there is only *one* true positive in each result list. Accuracy-based measurements would fail distinguishing differences between two rankings having the reference ranked higher than the cut-off. Therefore, Mean reciprocal rank (MRR) is used for evaluation. The results of our experiments are listed in Table 1 and the significance of our results is tested by a Wilcoxon signed rank test ($\alpha < 0.002$).

Table 1: Evaluation in MRR

	Frequency		Subcategory		Category	
	Tweets	Trails	MC	BL	MC	BL
NY	22307	5471	0.400	0.334	0.661	0.618
CH	8313	1835	0.545	0.474	0.750	0.709
LA	9641	2315	0.794	0.777	0.888	0.871
SF	7399	2315	0.591	0.536	0.779	0.733
US	130298	26135	0.469	0.420	0.710	0.668

From Table 1, we can see our trail-causality-based model (MC) outperforming the baseline (BL) significantly in all experiments. On the other hand, the performance of the baseline suggests that there is a strong tendency that users stay at the same POI type for many consecutive postings. By manually checking against the data, we find that there are numerous trails composed of chat with friends posted coherently in both time and space dimensions, i.e., a short burst of tweets from one place. For example, we find one user with two trails full of tweets coming from a single place. The content of those tweets are replies to her friends' tweets. This observation suggests a more thorough study on the time dimension of trails which is left for our future work.

4. CONCLUSION AND FUTURE WORK

We have shown, in our preliminary research, the viability of using Markov Chains to estimate users' next visits in terms of place types based on POI-tagged tweets. By matching places in Twitter and Foursquare, we augment the place information with category information which we would like to share. In the future, we would like to exploit additional sources of evidence such as time of posting or notions of personal preference to further support user tasks that depend on spatial context.

5. REFERENCES

[1] L. Backstrom, E. Sun, and C. Marlow. Find me if you can: improving geographical prediction with social and spatial proximity. In *WWW '10*, pages 61–70, 2010.

[2] T. Kurashima, T. Iwata, G. Irie, and K. Fujimura. Travel route recommendation using geotags in photo sharing sites. In *CIKM '10*, pages 579–588, 2010.

[3] A. Sadilek, H. Kautz, and J. P. Bigham. Finding Your Friends and Following Them to Where You Are Categories and Subject Descriptors. In *WSDM '12*, pages 723–732, 2012.

Will This #Hashtag Be Popular Tomorrow?*

Zongyang Ma
zma4@e.ntu.edu.sg

Aixin Sun
axsun@ntu.edu.sg

Gao Cong
gaocong@ntu.edu.sg

School of Computer Engineering
Nanyang Technological University, Singapore, 639798

ABSTRACT

Hashtags are widely used in Twitter to define a shared context for events or topics. In this paper, we aim to predict hashtag popularity in near future (*i.e.,* next day). Given a hashtag that has the potential to be popular in the next day, we construct a hashtag profile using the tweets containing the hashtag, and extract both *content* and *context* features for hashtag popularity prediction. We model this prediction problem as a classification problem and evaluate the effectiveness of the extracted features and classification models.

Categories and Subject Descriptors

H.3.3 [**Information Storage and Retrieval**]: Information Search and Retrieval—*Information filtering*

Keywords

Twitter, Hashtag, Popularity prediction, Hashtag clarity

1. INTRODUCTION

Micro-blogging services represented by Twitter are changing our way of accessing and disseminating information online. Because of the fast information disseminating rate, various topics emerge within a very short time period, particularly some public relations crises. This calls for effective prediction on what topics would emerge into significant ones in near future. As an important feature in Twitter, hastags (keywords prefixed with # symbols) are widely used to define a shared context for specific events, topics, or meme [1]. We therefore propose to predict hashtag popularity in near future, which could identify topics/events that might be critical for relevant organizations to response earlier.

Hashtag has attracted significant research interest. In [2], the authors analyze hashtags in eight categories (*e.g.,* politics, celebrity) for the differences in the mechanics of information diffusion. The evolution of hashtag popularity over time (*e.g.,* usage patterns before and after bursty peaks) is analyzed in [1]. Different from both studies which perform retrospective analysis of hashtags using historical data, we aim to predict hashtag popularity for newly appearing hashtags in a Twitter stream in the next day.

Most germane to this work is the recent paper on predicting hashtag popularity in weekly basis [3]. Our work is significantly different. First, we predict the *number of users* who adopt a hashtag, but not the *number of tweets* annotated by the hashtag in [3]. We therefore derive 8 features from the virtual community formed by users who adopt a hashtag; these context features are not used in [3]. Second, our content features are derived from *the content of the tweets* annotated by a hashtag whereas almost all content features in [3] are derived from *the hashtag itself* (*e.g.,* number of characters in a hashtag). Third, we target on time critical applications to predict hashtag popularity on daily basis rather than weekly basis, because most bursty hashtags are popular for a few days only [1].

To the best of our knowledge, we are the first to predict hashtag popularity in daily basis, using both content and context features. Additionally, we are the first to utilize clarity and topic modeling as content features for hashtag analysis.

2. HASHTAG POPULARITY PREDICTION

Problem Definition. In our problem setting, all tweets received from a Twitter stream are partitioned into consecutive fixed time-intervals by their time-stamps. The time-interval could be an hour, a few hours, or a day, depending on the number of tweets received as well as the time criticalness of the prediction. We define the *popularity degree* of a hashtag h in time-interval t, denoted by Φ_t^h, to be the number of users who post at least one tweet annotated by h within time-interval t. Given the collection of tweets published in t and a hashtag h of interest, our task is to predict Φ_{t+1}^h.

Note that predicting the *exact value* of Φ_{t+1}^h is extremely hard and is often not necessary. Therefore we relax the problem and predict the *range* of popularity degree. We define 5 ranges: $[0, \phi)$, $[\phi, 2\phi)$, $[2\phi, 4\phi)$, $[4\phi, 8\phi)$, and $[8\phi, +\infty)$, representing *not popular, marginally popular, popular, very popular,* and *extremely popular*, respectively. Note that the ranges are defined following an exponential order and ϕ is application-dependent.

Let T_t^h be the collection of tweets annotated by hashtag h in time-interval t. T_t^h is also known as *hashtag profile*. Next, we detail the content and context features extracted from a hashtag profile.

Content Features. The 6 content features extracted from T_t^h are listed in Table 1. We elaborate *hashtag clarity* and *hashtag topic vector* features in more detail. Hashtag clarity quantifies topical cohesiveness of all tweets in T_t^h. It is computed as the Kullback-Leibler (KL) divergence between the uni-gram language model inferred from T_t^h and the background language model from the entire tweet collection $\mathcal{T}$. If a hashtag refers to a specific topic, then the high probabilities of a few topic-relevant words distinguish its tweets from the background.

$$Clarity(T_t^h) = \sum_{w \in T_t^h} P(w|T_t^h) log_2 \frac{P(w|T_t^h)}{P(w|\mathcal{T})}$$

Hashtags in a similar topic (*e.g.,* political, music) may follow similar popularity trends [1]. We use Latent Dirichlet Allocation (LDA) to identify the topic distribution of a hashtag. Each hashtag profile T_t^h is considered as a document and 20 topics are inferred

*This work was partially supported by Singapore's National Research Foundation's research grant NRF2008IDM-IDM004-036, and Singapore MOE AcRF Tier-1 Grant RG13/10.

SIGIR'12, August 12–16, 2012, Portland, Oregon, USA.
ACM 978-1-4503-1472-5/12/08.

Table 1: The 6 content features and 8 context features

Type	Description
Content Feature	(1) number of tweets in T_t^h, (2) fraction of tweets containing URL, (3) fraction of re-tweet, (4) fraction of tweets with mention "@", (5) hashtag clarity, and (6) 20-dimension hashtag topic vector.
Context Feature	(1) number of users $\|U_t^h\|$, (2) average authority of users, (3) density of G_t^h, (4) fraction of users forming triangles in G_t^h, (5) ratio between the number of connected components and the number of nodes in G_t^h, (6) average edge weights in G_t^h, (7) number of border users, and (8) 15-dimension exposure probability vector.

from all such documents in our data. A 20-dimension topic vector is then assigned to each hashtag profile with the entries quantifying the likelihood of the hashtag belonging to the corresponding topic.

Context Features. We first construct a directed weighted graph $\mathcal{G} = \langle U, E \rangle$ to model user relations in the data collection. In $\mathcal{G}$, a user $u \in U$ is a node and a directed edge $e(u_p, u_q) \in E$ from u_p to u_q is weighted by the number of times u_p mentions u_q in her tweets, similar to that in [2]. The authority scores of users are computed in this global user graph using PageRank algorithm.

We consider all users who post at least one tweet in hashtag profile T_t^h form a virtual community. By extracting their relations from the global user graph, we form a community graph $G_t^h = \langle U_t^h, E_t^h \rangle$. From G_t^h, 8 context features (see Table 1) are derived to capture the current popularity of h, the influential power of its users, the connectivity among these users, and the distribution of the users exposed to h. We elaborate the last two features in Table 1.

Based on the global graph, border users are those each has at least one edge from users in G_t^h but has not adopted hashtag h, *i.e.*, $\{u_q | \exists e(u_p, u_q), u_p \in U_t^h, u_q \notin U_t^h\}$. Exposure probability vector depicts border user distribution in a more detailed manner: $P(k)$ $(1 \leq k \leq 15)$ is the ratio of border users who have k edges from users in G_t^h. A border user with more exposure to a hashtag is expected to be more likely to adopt the hashtag.

3. EXPERIMENTS

Experimental Setting. We used tweets published by Singapore-based users from Jan to Aug 2011. The dataset consists of more than 31M tweets from over 2M users. The global user graph constructed based on mention relation consists of 214K users and 680K edges. Note that, only users participated in mentions are included in this graph. In our experiments, we set the time-interval to be *a day* and set $\phi = 25$. That is, a hashtag used by fewer than 25 users in a day is considered not popular.

A key issue in the experiments is that, among all hashtags appeared at least once in a day, which hastags should be selected for popularity prediction. Figure 1(a) plots the number of popular tags ($\Phi_t^h \geq \phi$) against their popularity duration in number of days. Observe that a large number of tags are popular for only a day. In fact, a much larger number of tags has never been popular. In our experiments, we therefore choose to predict the popularity degree of *newly appearing hashtags* that are *at least marginally popular*, $\Phi_t^h \geq \phi$. A hashtag is considered *new* if it has not gained marginal popularity in the past 7 days. Note that, the same hashtag may gain popularity in different time periods for different reasons. For example, #apple may gain popularity at different time periods for releasing different products.

We conducted experiments using five commonly used classification methods: Naïve Bayes (NB), Decision Tree (C4.5), k-Nearest Neighbor (KNN), Support Vector Machine (SVM) and Maximum Entropy (MaxEnt). Their prediction accuracies are compared with three baseline methods, which do not use any extracted features.

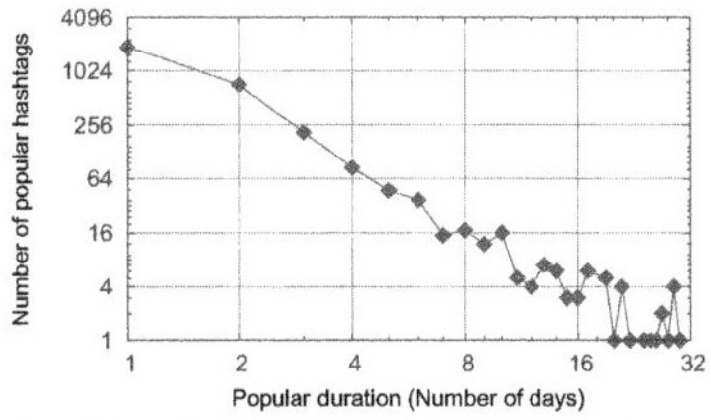

(a) Popular tag vs popular duration

Popularity	No. hashtags
[0, 25)	1609
[25, 50)	614
[50, 100)	353
[100, 200)	211
≥200	111
Total	2898

(b) Hashtag distribution

Figure 1: Popular tag vs duration; and distribution of instances

Table 2: Hashtag popularity prediction accuracy by 8 methods

Method	Micro-F_1	Macro-*Pr*	Macro-*Re*	Macro-F_1
Random	0.197	0.198	0.205	0.163
Lazy	0.254	0.251	**0.450**	0.317
PriorDist	0.385	0.209	0.210	0.209
NB	0.397	0.341	0.390	0.338
KNN	0.500	0.426	0.419	**0.422**
C4.5	0.527	0.413	0.408	0.409
SVM	0.582	0.401	0.329	0.296
MaxEnt	**0.591**	**0.437**	0.387	0.382

The baseline methods are Random (predicts the popularity range of Φ_{t+1}^h randomly), Lazy (predicts the range of Φ_{t+1}^h the same as Φ_t^h), and PriorDist (predicts the range of Φ_{t+1}^h randomly following a prior probability distribution in the 5 ranges).

Results. We conducted 10-fold cross validation and evaluated prediction accuracy using Micro-F_1, Macro-*Pr*ecision, Macro-*Re*call and Macro-F_1. Note that, because each instance has exactly one correct label, Micro-*Pr*ecision/*Re*call is the same as Micro-F_1.

Table 2 reports the prediction accuracies by the 8 methods, in increasing order of Micro-F_1. All baseline methods perform the worst. Observe that MaxEnt achieves the best Micro-F_1 of 0.591 which is triple of Random and 54% of increment over the best baseline PriorDist. SVM is the second best performing method by Micro-F_1; MaxEnt also achieves the best Macro-*Pr* followed by KNN. Surprisingly, Lazy prediction yields the best Macro-*Re*. The main reason is the skewed distribution of our categories (see Figure 1(b)). Because of the small number of instances in *very popular* and *extremely popular* ranges, most classifiers fail to learn effective patterns for accurate prediction. Lazy prediction enjoys high accuracy mainly in these two ranges. By Macro-F_1 KNN is the best performing method.

Our analysis on features reveals that context features are relatively more effective than content features (detailed results not reported due to page limit). The top-5 most effective features are: (1) number of users, (2) number of border users, (3) number of tweets, (4) hashtag clarity, and (5) fraction of users forming triangles.

4. SUMMARY

In this paper, we propose to predict hashtag popularity to identify fast emerging topics attracting collective attention. Our preliminary results demonstrate the effectiveness of both content and context features. In our future work, we will continue to investigate other possible features, and more importantly to investigate effective prediction models specifically for hashtag popularity prediction.

5. REFERENCES

[1] J. Lehmann, B. Gonçalves, J. J. Ramasco, and C. Cattuto. Dynamical classes of collective attention in twitter. In *WWW*, pages 251–260, 2012.

[2] D. M. Romero, B. Meeder, and J. M. Kleinberg. Differences in the mechanics of information diffusion across topics: idioms, political hashtags, and complex contagion on twitter. In *WWW*, 2011.

[3] O. Tsur and A. Rappoport. What's in a hashtag?: content based prediction of the spread of ideas in microblogging communities. In *WSDM*, pages 643–652, 2012.

$100,000 Prize Jackpot. Call Now! Identifying the Pertinent Features of SMS Spam

Henry Tan, Nazli Goharian, and Micah Sherr
Department of Computer Science, Georgetown University
Washington D.C.
ztan@cs.georgetown.edu, nazli@cs.georgetown.edu, msherr@cs.georgetown.edu

ABSTRACT

Mobile SMS spam is on the rise and is a prevalent problem. While recent work has shown that simple machine learning techniques can distinguish between ham and spam with high accuracy, this paper explores the individual contributions of various textual features in the classification process. *Our results reveal the surprising finding that simple is better*: using the largest spam corpus of which we are aware, we find that using simple textual features is sufficient to provide accuracy that is nearly identical to that achieved by the best known techniques, while achieving a twofold speedup.

Categories and Subject Descriptors

H.3.3 [**Information Storage and Retrieval**]: Information Search and Retrieval—*Information filtering*

General Terms

Algorithms, Experimentation

Keywords

SMS, Spam, Short Text, Feature Selection, Messaging

1. INTRODUCTION

Spam detection has historically focused on email spam. More recently, with the ubiquity of mobile phones and the advent of Twitter and other social media, short text spam detection has garnered interest and importance. Our work focuses on SMS spam, which contains on the order of tens of characters. Various spam filtering methods have been examined in the SMS domain – for example, using challenge-response methods such as CAPTCHA [4] and a variety of content-based filters. Content-based filtering has shown significant promise and recent papers suggest that existing filters and methods for email spam are sufficiently accurate for identifying short text spam [1, 2, 5].

However, most of the work in this area operates with large, composite, and complex feature sets (e.g., part-of-speech, n-grams, etc.) without showing the contributions of any subset of the features.

In this paper, *we examine the individual contributions of different sets of text-based features to the classification process.* Our work provides insight into the characteristics of spam and what kinds of features would be good choices for SMS classification. Surprisingly, we find that using simple feature sets instead of those suggested by previous work provides comparable quality at increased speed.

SIGIR'12, August 12–16, 2012, Portland, Oregon, USA.
ACM 978-1-4503-1472-5/12/08.

2. METHODOLOGY

Cormack et al. showed that a variety of supervised learning methods paired with a set of features consisting of orthogonal sparse word grams, character n-grams, and words, works very well for short text spam detection [2]. They composed an English SMS corpus from multiple sources, generated the features mentioned above and showed that standard classifiers such as Naive Bayes and SVM performed extremely well. This dataset was used by Almeida et al. in a baseline study where they showed the performance of a large number of classifiers paired with two simple feature sets [1]. The feature sets used by Almeida et al. were based on simple tokenization of the text (e.g., splitting the text into tokens by punctuation and spaces and using each unique token as a feature).

In this paper, rather than picking a feature set and showing the performance of various classifiers, we examine the effects of various feature sets on the performance of a fixed SVM classifier.

Our work uses the publicly available corpus curated by Cormack et al., which allows us to use their work and the work done by Almeida et al. as a baseline. While the work done by Cormack et al. in creating, curating and hosting the spam corpus is admirable, its usage comes with a few caveats. An examination of the corpus showed a variety of issues which we try to mitigate with preprocessing (described in Section 3).

We generate standard sets of features (e.g., n-grams) suggested in previous work [1, 2]. We additionally experiment with novel "content matching" features (explained below). For all experiments, we measure the *classification quality* (accuracy, recall, precision, and F1 score) and the *computation cost* (the time required to compute the features and perform the classification).

3. EXPERIMENTAL FRAMEWORK

Normalization. We pre-process the corpus used by Cormack et al.[1] which contains 4827 ham messages and 747 spam messages, to change certain terms and characters to mitigate the effects of having spam and ham that were collected from independent geographic regions. Specifically, we converted '£' to '$', converted the words 'uk' and 'uks' (symbolizing the United Kingdom) to 'sg' (in order to standardize country references), and removed word and number-suffix instances of 'p' and 'ppm' (pence and pence per minute).

We then normalize the corpus, which was collected from multiple sources, to be consistent in its treatment of numbers. Certain sources had replaced the numbers with symbolic representations (presumably as a privacy-preserving measure). We replaced these representations, and all remaining numbers, with '⟨#⟩' and '⟨.⟩' to respectively denote numbers and decimal points.

[1] http://www.dt.fee.unicamp.br/~tiago/smsspamcollection/

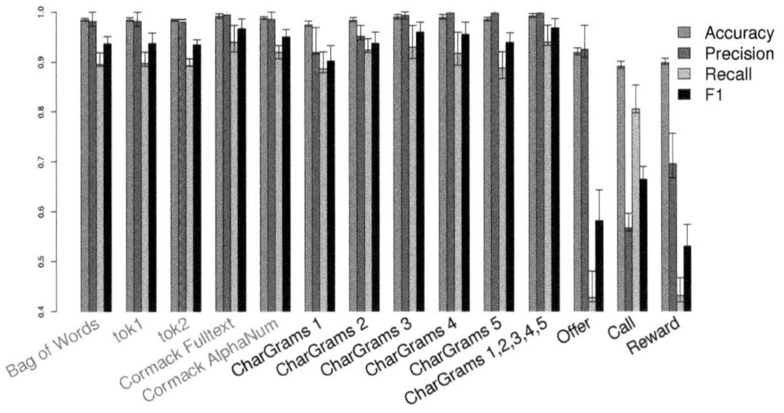

Figure 1: Average classification quality (accuracy, recall, precision, and F1 score) of the various feature sets. The first five feature sets (the baseline) have been suggested in previous work. Error bars indicate the interquartile range.

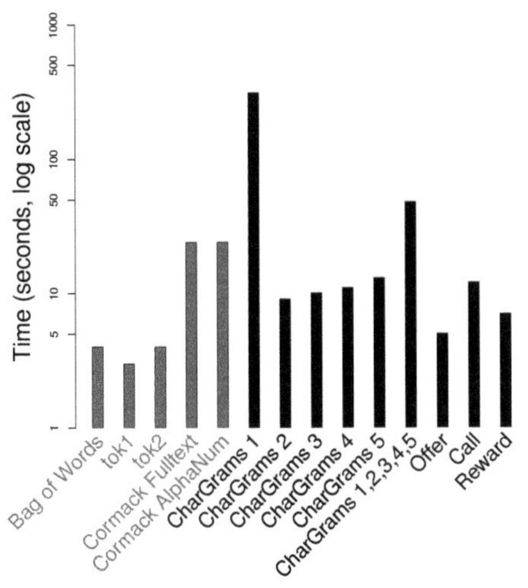

Figure 2: Computation time (in seconds) for computing the features and performing the classification using the various feature sets.

Feature Set Generation. We generate each of the following feature sets separately and in various combinations: word grams; character grams (ranging from $[1,5]$-grams); and alphanumeric versions of the above n-grams (i.e., ignoring all non-alphanumeric characters). We additionally construct features for various regular expressions, which we hypothesized might be indicative of spam:

- **rate:** $(/|per)(\ |)(\mathrm{year}|\mathrm{month}|\mathrm{hour}|\mathrm{week}|\mathrm{call})$
- **reward:** free|award|prize|win|reward
- **website:** .co|.org|.net
- **call:** call|text|txt|msg|contact
- **offer:** **(call$\vee$website)$\wedge$(reward$\vee$rate)**

Note that **offer** is a logical combination of the previous four expressions. The **rate** expression can be interpreted as a percentage (either specified as a fraction or having the sequence `p-e-r`) optionally followed by a space and ending with a listed keyword.

Finally, we test a few statistical features: message length; the proportion of upper-case letters; and the proportion of punctuation.

The feature sets we generate are binary features (i.e., set to 1 iff the feature exists in the text) as recommended by Cormack et al. [2], except in cases in which the feature is inherently quantitative.

As a baseline, we also implement Cormack's feature selection method [2] and Almeida's *tok1* and *tok2* techniques [1].

Classification. We use *SVMLight* with stratified 10-fold cross validation and the recommended settings [3] to classify the corpus and record the resulting accuracy, precision, recall and F1 score.

4. RESULTS

Classification Quality. The classification quality achieved using the various feature sets is presented in Figure 1. Due to space constraints, we omit the features that result in poor classification.

We test two versions of the feature selection method used by Cormack et al. – one that ignores all non-alphanumeric characters and another that considers all characters – respectively labelled *Cormack AlphaNum* and *Cormack Fulltext* in the figure. Since the unstripped version produces slightly better results, we use that as our main baseline. Our results confirm that *Cormack Fulltext* is quite effective. We also note that none of *tok1* (F1: 93.698), *tok2* (F1: 93.409) or the standard bag-of-words model (F1: 93.625) produce classification quality on par with the highest performing feature sets.

Surprisingly, however, many of the simpler techniques achieve classification performance nearly identical to that of Cormack et al. [2]. In particular, using a feature set consisting of 1-, 2-, 3-, 4-, and 5-grams (*CharGrams 1,2,3,4,5*), we obtained an equivalent average F1 score to that of *Cormack Fulltext* (96.75 vs. 96.62). 3-grams (*CharGrams 3*) comes in third with an F1 score of 95.97.

The results also show that the regular expression and statistical features (e.g., proportion of upper case characters) that we tested are not good indicators of spam. The **offer** expression stands out with relatively good precision for a single feature. However, its recall is low due to the rule coverage, leading to an F1 of 58.132.

Computation Cost. Figure 2 plots the computation cost (in seconds) for computing the features and performing the classification across all 10 folds. As expected, the simpler techniques offer lower computation times. In particular, our results show that character 3-grams (*CharGrams 3*) produces comparable performance to *Cormack Fulltext* (F1: 95.97 vs. 96.62) at over twice the speed (9 vs. 24 seconds).

Mutual Information Study. We additionally examined the mutual information values of the various features. The string '$\langle\#\rangle$' offers the greatest mutual information, indicating that the presence of numbers is a very good indicator of spam. We also found that certain words show up in ham but not in spam; these consist mostly of spoken and text slang found in the geographic region of the ham dataset (Singapore). There are also words that show up in spam but not in ham (e.g., 'claim', 'URGENT', 'WON', 'YES' and 'prize'), as one would expect. We surmise that if one were able to obtain good coverage of such words to better formulate an **offer** expression, classification quality would further improve.

References

[1] T. A. Almeida, J. M. G. Hidalgo, and A. Yamakami. Contributions to the Study of SMS Spam Filtering: New Collection and Results. In *ACM DocEng*, 2011.

[2] G. V. Cormack, G. Hidalgo, E. P. Sánz, and J. María. Spam Filtering for Short Messages. In *CIKM*, 2007.

[3] D. Sculley and G. M. Wachman. Relaxed Online SVMs for Spam Filtering. In *SIGIR*, 2007.

[4] M. H. Shirali-Shahreza and M. Shirali-Shahreza. An Anti-SMS-Spam Using CAPTCHA. In *CCCM*, 2008.

[5] D. Sohn, J. Lee, and H. Rim. The Contribution of Stylistic Information to Content-based Mobile Spam Filtering. In *ACL-IJCNLP Conference*, 2009.

Beyond Bag-of-Words: Machine Learning for Query-Document Matching in Web Search

Hang Li
Microsoft Research Asia
No. 5 Danling street, Haidian District
Beijing, China 100080
hangli@microsoft.com

Jun Xu
Microsoft Research Asia
No. 5 Danling street, Haidian District
Beijing, China 100080
junxu@microsoft.com

Categories and Subject Descriptors

H.3.3 [**Information Storage and Retrieval**]: Information Search and Retrieval—*Retrieval models, Query formulation*

General Terms

Algorithms, Theory

Keywords

web search, machine learning, query-document matching

1. INTRODUCTION

In web search, relevance is one of the most important factors to meet users' satisfaction, and the success of a web search engine heavily depends on its performance on relevance. It has been observed that many hard cases in search relevance are due to term mismatch between query and document (e.g., query 'ny times' does not match well with document only containing 'new york times'), and thus it is not exaggerated to say that dealing with mismatch between query and document is one of the most critical research problems in web search. Recently researchers have spent significant effort to address the grand challenge. The major approach is to conduct more query and document understanding, and perform better matching between enriched query and document representations. With the availability of large amount of log data and advanced machine learning techniques, this becomes more feasible and significant progress has been made recently.

In this tutorial, we will give a systematic and detailed presentation on newly developed machine learning technologies for query document matching in search. We will focus on the fundamental problems, as well as the novel solutions for query document matching at word form level, word sense level, topic level, and structure level. We will talk about novel technologies about query spelling error correction [3, 13], query rewriting [1, 4, 6, 7], query classification [2], topic modeling of documents [5, 9], query document matching [8, 10, 11, 12], and query document-title translation. The ideas and solutions introduced in this tutorial may motivate industrial practitioners to turn the research fruits into product reality. The summary of the state-of-the-art methods and the discussions on the technical issues in this tutorial may stimulate academic researchers to find new research directions and solutions.

Matching between query and document is not limited to search, and similar problems can be observed at online advertisement, recommendation system, and other applications, as matching between objects from two spaces. The technologies we introduce can be generalized into more general machine learning techniques, which we call learning to match.

SIGIR'12, August 12–16, 2012, Portland, Oregon, USA.
ACM 978-1-4503-1472-5/12/08.

2. REFERENCES

[1] M. Bendersky, D. Metzler, and W. B. Croft. Parameterized concept weighting in verbose queries. In *SIGIR*, pp. 605–614, 2011.

[2] P. N. Bennett, K. Svore, and S. T. Dumais. Classification-enhanced ranking. In *WWW*, pp. 111–120, 2010.

[3] E. Brill and R. C. Moore. An improved error model for noisy channel spelling correction. In *ACL*, 2000.

[4] A. Broder, P. Ciccolo, E. Gabrilovich, V. Josifovski, D. Metzler, L. Riedel, and J. Yuan. Online expansion of rare queries for sponsored search. In *WWW*, pp. 511–520, 2009.

[5] J. Gao, K. Toutanova, and W.-t. Yih. Clickthrough-based latent semantic models for web search. In *SIGIR*, pp. 675–684, 2011.

[6] J. Guo, G. Xu, X. Cheng, and H. Li. Named entity recognition in query. In SIGIR, pp. 267–274, 2009.

[7] D. Sheldon, M. Shokouhi, M. Szummer, and N. Craswell. Lambdamerge: merging the results of query reformulations. In WSDM, pp. 795–804, 2011.

[8] C. Wang, R. Raina, D. Fong, D. Zhou, J. Han, and G. Badros. Learning relevance from heterogeneous social network and its application in online targeting. In SIGIR, pp. 655–664, 2011.

[9] Q. Wang, J. Xu, H. Li, and N. Craswell. Regularized latent semantic indexing. In *SIGIR'11*, pp. 685–694.

[10] Z. Wang, G. Xu, H. Li, and M. Zhang. A fast and accurate method for approximate string search. In ACL-HLT, pp. 52–61, 2011.

[11] W. Wu, H. Li, J. Xu, and S. Oyama. Learning a robust relevance model for search using kernel methods. *JMLR*, pp. 1429–1458, 2011.

[12] J. Xu, W. Wu, H. Li, and G. Xu. A kernel approach to addressing term mismatch. In *WWW*, pp. 153–154, 2011.

[13] J. Xu and G. Xu. Learning similarity function for rare queries. In *WSDM*, pp. 615–624, 2011.

Methods for Mining and Summarizing Text Conversations

Giuseppe Carenini
Department of Computer Science,
University of British Columbia
Vancouver, B.C., Canada
1(604) 822-5109
carenini@cs.ubc.ca

Gabriel Murray
Department of Computing
and Information Systems
University of the Fraser Valley
Abbotsford, B.C., Canada
gabriel.murray@gmail.com

Categories and Subject Descriptors
I.2 [**Computing Methodologies**]: Artificial Intelligence; I.7 [**Computing Methodologies**]: Document and Text Processing

Keywords
Text Mining, Text Summarization, Text Conversations, Topic Modeling, Opinion Mining, Email, (Micro)Blog, Discussion Forums, Social Media,.

1. INTRODUCTION
More and more today, people are engaging in conversations via email, blogs, discussion forums, text messaging and other social media. A person may want to archive these conversations and later retrieve information about what was discussed, or analyze a conversation in real-time. What topics are covered in these conversations? What opinions are people expressing? Have any decisions been made? Have action items been assigned? This tutorial will present various natural language processing (NLP) techniques that can help answer these questions, thus creating numerous new and valuable applications that can support people in more effectively participating in these conversation. The tutorial is based on a book that we have recently published, Methods for Mining and Summarizing Text Conversations [1].

2. TUTORIAL DETAILS
2.1 Intended audience and prerequisites
This tutorial should be suitable for researchers who have a background in Computer Science, Information Science or Linguistics, but only minimal exposure to Natural Language Processing. We assume the audience to be at least somewhat familiar with basic probability and basic machine learning. If most of the audience will lack such a background, we will be ready to provide a quick and gentle introduction to the key ideas and techniques.

2.2 Course Material
Our tutorial will be based on a book we have recently published:

[1] G. Carenini and G. Murray and R. Ng, *Methods for Mining and Summarizing Text Conversations*, **Morgan Claypool, 2011 –**

The book is freely available online at subscribing institutions (which include most universities and research labs). This is a new tutorial, so we do not already have presentation material for it. However, we have presented related material in several invited talks and university lectures. For instance, Dr. Murray was the invited speaker at the summarization workshop at ACL 2011. Dr. Carenini has recently presented work on mining conversations at the AT&T Labs and at IBM Research.

2.3 Course Objectives
People attending this tutorial will learn about a set of computational methods to extract information from conversational data, and to provide natural language summaries of the data.

(30 mins) The tutorial will start with an overview of basic concepts by examining a simple written conversation. We will clarify fundamental differences; for instance, between topic segmentation and topic labelling and between extractive and abstractive summaries.

After this, students will learn about metrics for evaluating the effectiveness of summarization and various extraction tasks. They will also become familiar with some of the benchmark corpora used in the literature.

(1 hour) In the second part of the tutorial student will learn about extraction and mining methods for performing subjectivity and sentiment detection, topic segmentation and modeling, and the extraction of conversational structure. Our focus will be on clarifying how methods developed for generic text can be extended to work on conversational data, such as meeting transcripts (which exemplify synchronous conversations) and emails (which exemplify asynchronous conversations). Very recent approaches to deal with blogs, discussion forums and microblogs (e.g.,Twitter) will be also discussed by interactively exploring several examples.

(1 hour) In the third part of the tutorial, students will learn about natural language summarization of conversational data. We will initially provide a critical overview of several extractive and abstractive summarizers developed for emails, meetings, blogs and forums. Then, we will describe our own recent attempts for building multi-modal summarizers.

(30 mins) At the end of the tutorial we will engage students in a discussion on the future of the research on mining and summarizing conversations with a special focus on how this research can be informed by and be beneficial to research and applications in information retrieval.

2.4 Course Relevance to Information Retrieval
With the phenomenal growth in the amount of text conversations stored in computer memory comes the need for supporting

SIGIR'12, August 12-16, 2012, Portland, Oregon, USA.
ACM 978-1-4503-1472-5/12/08.

effective search. Generally speaking, the ability to mine and summarize text can benefit any Web search. The more information that can be extracted from text, the more search can be based on the extracted information, rather than on simple matching with the words in the query. For instance, the reader may be very interested in browsing through all the sentences expressing negative opinions, sentences that represent action items, or sentences that describe decisions made.

Moreover, if any document can be effectively summarized, the quality of the presentation of search query results can be improved by presenting a summary as the snippet for each returned documents. Arguably, these advantages would also apply to a search engine for text conversations that relies on the techniques presented in our tutorial. For instance, if it was possible to extract topics and opinions from conversations, a conversational search engine could support queries like: "what messages in the company blogs express opinions on the new budget?". And the output of such search query could be a list of relevant messages summarized in the context of both the query and the conversation.

3. BRIEF BIOGRAPHY OF THE PRESENTERS

Dr. Giuseppe Carenini is an associate professor in computer science at the University of British Columbia, UBC (BC, Canada), with broad interdisciplinary interests. His work on combining natural language processing and information visualization to support decision making has been published in over 70 peer-reviewed papers. Dr. Carenini was the area chair for "Sentiment Analysis, Opinion Mining, and Text Classification" of ACL 2009 and he is currently the area chair for "Summarization and Generation" of NAACL 2012. He has recently co-edited an ACM-TIST Special Issue on "Intelligent Visual Interfaces for Text Analysis". In July 2011, he has published a co-authored book on "Methods for Mining and Summarizing Text Conversations". In his work, Dr. Carenini has also extensively collaborated with industrial partners, including Microsoft and IBM.

Dr. Gabriel Murray has just recently joined as an assistant professor the dept. of CS of the University of the Fraser Valley, UFV, (BC, Canada). His background is in natural language processing as well as theoretical linguistics. Dr. Murray has an established research record in the area of automatic summarization, with particular attention to summarization of noisy genres such as speech and web data, and comparison of abstractive and extractive techniques. He did his graduate studies at the University of Edinburgh under Dr. Steve Renals, was a member of the EU-funded AMI project on studying multimodal interaction. Before joining UFV, Dr. Murray was a researcher at UBC with the NSERC Business Intelligence Network on intelligent data management and decision making. While at UBC, he also gained substantial teaching experience. In July 2011, Dr. Murray has published a co-authored book on "Methods for Mining and Summarizing Text Conversations".

4. TUTORIAL OUTLINE

(A) Introduction

1 The Internet Revolution and The Rise of Text Conversations

2 The Speech Technology Revolution

3 Application Scenarios

4 Mining and Summarizing Text Conversations: An Overview

(B) Background: Corpora and Evaluation Methods

1 Corpora and Annotations (Meetings, Email, Blogs…)

2 Evaluation Metrics for Text Mining

3 Evaluation Metrics for Summarization

(C) MiningText Conversations

1 Topic Modeling of Conversations: Topic Segmentation and Topic Labeling

2 Sentiment and Subjectivity Detection in Conversations

3 Extracting the Dialog Acts and the Conversational Structure

4 Detecting Decision and Action Items

(D) SummarizingText Conversations

1 Assumptions and Inputs, Measuring Informativeness, Outputs and Interfaces

2 Summarizing Conversations in One Domain

3 Summarizing Emails / Meetings /Chats /Blogs

4 Summarizing Multi-Domain Conversations

5 Abstractive Conversation Summarization: A Detailed Case Study

(E) Conclusions / FinalThoughts

1 Future trends in research on mining and summarizing conversations

2 How this research can be informed by and be beneficial to research and applications in information retrieval?

5. REFERENCES

[1] G. Carenini and G. Murray and R. Ng, *Methods for Mining and Summarizing Text Conversations*, **Morgan Claypool, 2011 –** Available online: http://www.morganclaypool.com/toc/dtm/1/1

Crowdsourcing for Search Evaluation and Social-Algorithmic Search

Matthew Lease
School of Information
University of Texas at Austin
ml@ischool.utexas.edu

Omar Alonso
Microsoft Corp.
Mountain View, CA 94043
omar.alonso@microsoft.com

ABSTRACT

The first computers were people. Today, Internet-based access to 24/7 online human crowds has led to a renaissance of research in *human computation* and the advent of *crowdsourcing*. These new opportunities have brought a disruptive shift to research and practice for how we build intelligent systems today. Not only can labeled data for training and evaluation be collected faster, cheaper, and easier than ever before, but we now see human computation being integrated into the systems themselves, operating in concert with automation. This tutorial introduces opportunities and challenges of human computation and crowdsourcing, particularly for search evaluation and developing hybrid search solutions that integrate human computation with traditional forms of automated search. We review methodology and findings of recent research and survey current generation crowdsourcing platforms now available, analyzing methods, potential, and limitations across platforms.

Categories and Subject Descriptors

H.3.4 [**Information Storage and Retrieval**]: Systems and software — performance evaluation

Keywords

Crowdsourcing, human computation.

1. Introduction

Human capabilities continue to exceed state-of-the-art automation in many areas, such as computer vision and language understanding. While automation will certainly continue to improve, strategic use of human computation in tandem with automation enables us to build systems which offer greater capabilities today. Use of human computation offers a wider design space in which researchers and developers can explore tradeoffs between processing time, cost, effort, or accuracy. Whereas the traditional mixed-initiative model of human-computer interaction explores the balance between automation vs. user effort, crowdsourcing generalizes this beyond interactions with an individual user to broader social participation. In addition to human-system interactions being driven by an engaged user, we increasingly see interactions where the crowd is engaged by the system to perform work on its behalf. Specific to Information Retrieval (IR), the rise of online crowds has created new opportunities to leverage social wisdom in order to better address information needs than would be possible using purely automated systems and isolated individuals. Today's vibrant crowdsourcing industry boasts a myriad of vendors offering a wide range of features and workflow models for accomplishing complex, quality work. Researchers and developers can now more easily and effectively create and evaluate search systems with crowds.

While search evaluation is an essential part of the development and maintenance of information retrieval (IR) systems, current approaches for search evaluation face a variety of challenges. Many Web search engines reportedly use large editorial staffs to judge the relevance of web pages for queries in an evaluation set, but his is expensive and has limited scalability. Academic researchers, without access to such editors, often rely instead on smaller test sets than desired, making it harder to detect statistically significant differences in performance. While behavioral data, such as mined from search engine logs of user activity, is much cheaper than the editorial method, it requires access to a large stream of data, something not always available to a researcher testing an experimental system. These challenges provide an ideal setting for demonstrating both the potential and practical challenges for the crowdsourcing paradigm.

2. Target Audience

This tutorial will introduce the opportunities and challenges of human computation and crowdsourcing, including methodology and findings of the latest research, particularly in IR. We will also survey several crowdsourcing platforms, analyzing crowdsourcing methods, potential, and limitations. The tutorial will provide academic and industrial attendees alike with a solid introduction and great start to begin applying crowdsourcing in the context of their own particular research problems or practical tasks.

3. Tutorial Outline

- Introduce crowdsourcing and human computation
- Survey recent "killer apps" of crowdsourcing for search systems (evaluation, training, and crowd-driven search)
- Provide practical "how to" guidance for effectively using several commercial crowdsourcing platforms
- Summarize key best practices for achieving efficient, inexpensive, and accurate work
- Review current opportunities, untapped potential, and open challenges for IR crowdsourcing, particularly evaluation

SIGIR'12, August 12–16, 2012, Portland, Oregon, USA.
ACM 978-1-4503-1472-5/12/08.

SIGIR 2012 Tutorial

(Big) Usage Data in Web Search

Ricardo Baeza-Yates
Yahoo! Research, Barcelona, Spain
rbaeza@acm.org

Yoelle Maarek
Yahoo! Research, Haifa, Israel
yoelle@ymail.com

Categories and Subject Descriptors
H.3.3 [Information Search and Retrieval]

General Terms
Algorithms, Human Factors

Keywords
Web Retrieval, User Interaction

EXTENDED ABSTRACT

Web Search, which takes its root in the mature field of information retrieval, evolved tremendously over the last 15 years. The field encountered its first revolution when it started to deal with huge amounts of Web pages. Then, a major step was accomplished when engines started to consider the structure of the Web graph and leveraged link analysis in both crawling and ranking. Finally, a more discrete, but no less critical step, was made when search engines started to monitor and exploit the numerous (mostly implicit) signals provided by users while interacting with the search engine. In this tutorial we focus on this "revolution" of large scale usage data.

In the first part of this tutorial, we focus on usage data, which typically refers to any type of information provided by the user while interacting with the search engine. It comes first under its raw form as a set of individual signals, but is typically mined after multiple signals have been aggregated and linked to the same interaction event. The two major types of such data are (1) *query streams*, which include the query string that the user issued, together with the time-stamp of the query, a user identifier, possibly the IP of the machine on which the browser runs, and (2) *click data*, which include the reference to the element the user clicked on the page together with the timestamp, user identifier, possibly IP, the rank of the link if it is a result, etc.

Exploiting usage data under its multiple forms brought an unprecedented wealth of implicit information to Web Search. We discuss in the second part of this tutorial some of the key Web search applications that it made possible. One such example is the query spelling correction feature embodied now in all search engines. In fact, after years of very sophisticated spell checking research, simply counting similar queries at a small edit distance would in most cases surface the most popular spelling as the correct one, a beautiful and simple demonstration of the wisdom of crowds principle.

In practice, such a feature clearly uses more sophisticated techniques than direct counting, but this simple example illustrates how even trivial "data crunching" over big *real* data brings more value than sophisticated techniques on small datasets. Query logs have also revolutionized query assistance tools such as related queries (recommended queries after the search was issued) or query completions (suggested queries as the query is being typed). While, in the past, query assistance tools would analyze the document corpus in order to identify phrases that could serve as alternate queries, the tremendous growth in Web search engine traffic allowed these tools to mostly rely on real user-issued queries. Using query logs as the source corpus significantly improved the quality of suggestions, at least as perceived by the user. In practice, query assistance tools are now deployed on all major Web search engines, and their quality improves as query logs grow. An additional revolutionary benefit of usage data is to consider clicks as a measure of satisfaction or at least of interest from the user, as if the user, by clicking, had actually voted in favor of the clicked element. One major reason of the quick pace of innovation in Web search can be credited to these "pseudo-votes". Instead of testing a new feature, or any sort of change, on a small sample of beta-users in a controlled environment, search engines now use real users on a much larger scale. Various metrics are used to verify whether users react positively or not to the change, thus helping search engines to decide whether to deploy the change to all users. After deployment, user behavior is constantly monitored, not only at pre-launch time, and features for which clicks or other metrics are decreasing might be discontinued or retired as it often happens.

In spite of its multiple benefits, adequately leveraging usage data is not always straightforward. We discuss, in the third part of this tutorial, the effects of three major factors that often pull in opposite directions:

- **Size of the data**: Large-scale or big usage data is a key pre-requisite to inferring new insights. As a consequence, the needs of the crowd dominate long-tail needs, which are expressed by definition by very few individuals. Averaging on the more popular needs can dominate so much, in some cases, that it conflicts with some specific needs that personalization should address. More data also brings algorithmic challenges as we need faster and faster algorithms. Hence, we can have a trade-off between the quality of the output and the performance to obtain it.
- **Personalization**: In order for search engines to personalize their services for a specific user, threy obviously need enough data to know more about the persona behind the individual, at the risk of exposing some private aspects. Hence,

SIGIR'12, August 12–16, 2012, Portland, Oregon, USA.
ACM 978-1-4503-1472-5/12/08.

personalization in many cases might conflict with the user's privacy.

- **Privacy**: One key demand of privacy-protecting activists pertains to not accumulate too much data on a single individual over long periods of time, as they want everyone's past to remain private. As big data is typically gathered over a given window of time, the longer the window, the bigger the data. Restricting persistence of data to short periods of time clearly reduces the amount of data that can be mined and thus threatens the effectiveness of data aggregation on a large scale, in particular for personalization.

These conflicting factors impose serious limitations on leveraging big usage data. We discuss some ways to tackle these limitations, in the last part of our tutorial. One solution that we focus on is to aggregate data in the *right* way, depending on the context, the task, the need, so as to increase the amount of relevant data. We show that aggregated data can be generated in a variety of scenarios, as the bulk of user queries belong to a few tasks: users are after all not that different, and many tasks share similarities at some level, for example find a home page, look for information, perform a transaction or download a resource. The main differences among users are not with what they do, but when they do it, how long they do it and how well they do it. We expect to see many types of aggregations arising in the future. Indeed, even social search can be seen as an incarnation of aggregation, where the aggregation is social and formed by the user's friends and other connections rather than by a common need.

We conclude by providing some research directions as well as discuss with the audience the influence of regulation current or future such as the recently proposed privacy "bill of rights" in the US. This tutorial is a sequel of "Web Retrieval: The Role of Users", a tutorial offered at SIGIR'2010 in Geneva and then at WSDM'2011 and ECIR'2011.

Biographies of Presenters

Ricardo Baeza-Yates is VP of Yahoo! Research for Europe and Latin America, leading the labs at Barcelona, Spain and Santiago, Chile. Until 2005, he was the director of the Center for Web Research at the Department of Computer Science of the Engineering School of the University of Chile, and ICREA Professor at the Dept. of Technology of University Pompeu Fabra in Barcelona, Spain. He is co-author of the bestseller textbook Modern Information Retrieval by Addison-Wesley, first published in 1999 with a second edition in 2011, as well as co-author of the second edition of the Handbook of Algorithms and Data Structures, Addison- Wesley, 1991; and co-editor of Information Retrieval: Algorithms and Data Structures, Prentice-Hall, 1992, among more than 200 other publications. He has been PC-Chair of the most important conferences in the field of Web Search and Web Mining. He has given tutorials in most major conferences many times, including SIGIR, WWW and VLDB. He is, both, ACM and IEEE Fellow.

Yoelle Maarek is the Senior Director of Yahoo! Research in Haifa, Israel, leading research activities for Yahoo! Mail and Yahoo! Answers since 2009. Prior to this, Yoelle was the Director of Google Haifa Engineering Center, which she opened in 2006. There, she led the development of "Suggest", Google's query completion feature deployed on google.com and YouTube worldwide. Before this, Yoelle had been with IBM Research, first in the US, and then in Israel, where she led the search and collaboration department and became a Distinguished Engineer. She graduated from the ENPC in Paris, France, and received her DEA in Computer Science from Paris VI University. Yoelle obtained her PhD in Computer Science from Technion. She has served as senior PC member at several SIGIR, WWW and WSDM conferences, and as PC co-chair of WWW'2009, WSDM'2012 and SIGIR'2012. Yoelle is a member of the Board of Governors of Technion, and was appointed ACM Distinguished Scientist in 2010.

A New Look at Old Tricks: The Fertile Roots of Current Research

Paul B. Kantor
Rutgers University and CCICADA
4 Huntington St.
New Brunswick, NJ 08901 USA
732-932-7500 x 8216
paul.kantor@rutgers.edu

ABSTRACT

As we face an explosion of potential new applications for the fundamental concepts and technologies of information retrieval, ranging from ad ranking to social media, from collaborative recommending to question answering systems, many researchers are spending unnecessary time reinventing ideas and relationships that are buried in the prehistory of information retrieval (which, for many researchers, means anything published before they entered graduate school).

Much of today's received wisdom may be nothing more than the fossilized residue of lively debates concerning such things as . estimation of value and evaluation of systems. Returning to those discussions may open the door to genuinely new insights.

On the other hand, of the ideas that surface as "new" in today's super-heated research environment have very firm roots in earlier developments in fields as diverse as citation analysis, statistics, and pattern recognition. The purpose of this tutorial is to survey those roots, and their relation to the contemporary fruits on the tree of information retrieval, and to separate, as much as is possible in an era of increasing commercial secrecy about methods, the problems to be solved, the algorithms for solving them, and the heuristics that are the bread and butter of a working operation.

Among the important new topics whose foundations will be explored are the use of social media in search and advertising, and the growing management of personal image collections for search and for commercial purposes.

While some might think that an examination of the roots is of merely historical interest, it has practical value as well. When you know which earlier research has provided the origins for the things that you are interested in, you can use that fact to trace its other descendents, and often find rich and rewarding ideas in a literature that you would not normally reach, because it was not considered important by your instructors when you were learning about the problems. In addition to pattern recognition and citation analysis, the tutorial will also expose and review some of the relations to the fields of statistics and operations research.

Participants will become familiar with roots in Pattern Analysis, Statistics, Information Science and other sources of key ideas that reappear in the current development of Information Retrieval as it applies to Search Engines, Social Media, and Collaborative Systems. They will be able to separate problems from algorithms, and algorithms from heuristics, in the application of these ideas to their own research and/or development activities. Course materials will be made available on a Web site two weeks prior to the tutorial. They will include links to relevant software; links to publications that will be discussed; and mechanisms for chat among the tutorial participants, before, during and after the tutorial.

Specific Topics will include:

1. The earliest "automated retrieval;
2. Vectors and Logarithms: their pragmatic origins;
3. Probabilistic approaches. A frequentist foundation;
4. The quest for a theoretical foundation;
5. Generative approaches;
6. Network approaches;
7. Binding approaches together.

Certain materials that are very hard to find, including foundational IBM technical reports by H.P. Luhn and I.J. Good will be scanned and placed on a web site for the tutorial. Since this will not be a public site, we will need some information on advance registration to add participants to the site..

Categories and Subject Descriptors
H.3.0 General; H.3.3 Information Search and Retrieval

General Terms
Algorithms, Measurement, Performance, Theory

Keywords
Foundations of Information Retrieval

1. ACKNOWLEDGMENTS

Thanks to John Prager and the Library at IBM for providing the classic papers.

SIGIR'12, August 12–16, 2012, Portland, Oregon, USA.
ACM 978-1-4503-1472-5/12/08.

Aspect-based Opinion Mining from Product Reviews

Samaneh Moghaddam
School of Computing Science
Simon Fraser University
Burnaby, BC, Canada
sam39@cs.sfu.ca

Martin Ester
School of Computing Science
Simon Fraser University
Burnaby, BC, Canada
ester@cs.sfu.ca

ABSTRACT

"What other people think" has always been an important piece of information for most of us during the decision-making process. Today people tend to make their opinions available to other people via the Internet. As a result, the Web has become an excellent source of consumer opinions. There are now numerous Web resources containing such opinions, e.g., product reviews forums, discussion groups, and blogs. But, it is really difficult for a customer to read all of the reviews and make an informed decision on whether to purchase the product. It is also difficult for the manufacturer of the product to keep track and manage customer opinions. Also, focusing on just user ratings (stars) is not a sufficient source of information for a user or the manufacturer to make decisions. Therefore, mining online reviews (opinion mining) has emerged as an interesting new research direction. Extracting aspects and the corresponding ratings is an important challenge in opinion mining. An aspect is an attribute or component of a product, e.g. 'zoom' for a digital camera. A rating is an intended interpretation of the user satisfaction in terms of numerical values. Reviewers usually express the rating of an aspect by a set of sentiments, e.g. 'great zoom'. In this tutorial we cover opinion mining in online product reviews with the focus on aspect-based opinion mining. This problem is a key task in the area of opinion mining and has attracted a lot of researchers in the information retrieval community recently. Several opinion related information retrieval tasks can benefit from the results of aspect-based opinion mining and therefore it is considered as a fundamental problem. This tutorial covers not only general opinion mining and retrieval tasks, but also state-of-the-art methods, challenges, applications, and also future research directions of aspect-based opinion mining.

Categories and Subject Descriptors

H.3.0 [**Information Search and Retrieval**]: General; I.2.7 [**Natural Language Processing**]: Text Analysis

General Terms

Algorithms, Performance, Experimentation

Keywords

sentiment analysis, opinion mining, aspect-based opinion mining, aspect identification, rating prediction

SIGIR'12, August 12–16, 2012, Portland, Oregon, USA.
ACM 978-1-4503-1472-5/12/08.

1. PRESENTERS' BIOS

Samaneh Moghaddam is a PhD candidate in the school of computer science at Simon Fraser University. Her main research interests include information retrieval, text mining, machine learning, natural language processing, and social network analysis. Samaneh is a senior member of SFU Database and Data mining lab under supervision of Dr. Martin Ester. Her PhD thesis is "Aspect-based Opinion Mining from Online Product Reviews". She has proposed some novel techniques for extracting product aspects and estimating their ratings from product reviews. Samaneh Moghaddam has published several papers in top international conferences such as ACM CIKM, ACM SIGIR, and IEEE ICDM. Her publications are mostly related to her research on information retrieval and machine learning models for mining opinion from product reviews.

Martin Ester received a PhD in Computer Science from ETH Zurich, Switzerland, in 1990 with a thesis on knowledge-based systems and logic programming. He has been working for Swissair developing expert systems before he joined University of Munich as an Assistant Professor in 1993. Since November 2001, he has been an Associate Professor, now Full Professor at the School of Computing Science of Simon Fraser University, where he co-directs the Database and Data mining research lab. He has published extensively in the top conferences and journals of his field such as ACM SIGKDD, VLDB, ICDM and ICDE, and his work has been very well-cited. His most famous paper on DBSCAN received more than 2900 citations, and his H-number is 34. His current research interests include social network analysis, recommender systems, opinion mining, biological network analysis and high-throughput sequence data analysis. Martin Ester's interests in applications have resulted in various collaborations with research labs, industry and government agencies.

2. TARGET AUDIENCE

The tutorial will draw information retrieval researchers and students who want to make themselves familiar with opinion mining as well as practitioners who want to develop state-of-the-art methods for different tasks of opinion mining. We expect participants to have a working knowledge of basic information retrieval and machine learning methods. Basic natural language processing techniques used in opinion mining will be discussed during the tutorial.

Experimental Methods for Information Retrieval

Donald Metzler
Google Inc.
Venice, CA, USA
metzler@google.com

Oren Kurland
Faculty of Industrial Engineering and Management
Technion — Israel Institute of Technology
Haifa, Israel
kurland@ie.technion.ac.il

Categories and Subject Descriptors: H.3.3 [Information Storage and Retrieval]: Information Search and Retrieval

General Terms: Experimentation

Keywords: information retrieval, experimental methods, evaluation

1. OVERVIEW

Experimental evaluation plays a critical role in driving progress in information retrieval (IR) today. There are few alternative ways of exploring, in depth, the empirical merits (or lack thereof) of newly devised search techniques. Careful evaluation is necessary for advancing the state-of-the-art; yet, many published papers present work that was ill-evaluated. Indeed, this phenomenon has garnered attention from the community recently, after the publication of a controversial, but eye-opening, study by Armstrong et al. that suggested *ad hoc* search quality has not meaningfully advanced since 1984 [1]. The authors noted that the root of the problem was generally lax evaluation methodologies (e.g., weak baselines, etc.). Furthermore, many submissions to top IR research venues (e.g., SIGIR, CIKM, ECIR, WSDM, WWW, etc.) are rejected primarily due to insufficient or inappropriate evaluation.

There is therefore a strong need to educate students, researchers, and practitioners about the proper way to carry out IR experiments. This is unfortunately not something that is taught in IR courses or covered in IR textbooks. Indeed, to the best of our knowledge, there is very little written work that lays down *some* principles for running an IR experiment [3]. More specifically, there have not been any recent tutorials or written works that have specifically, and comprehensively, addressed the question of "how to run an IR experiment" in terms of effectiveness evaluation. This has potentially yielded a number of detrimental effects, as described above.

The goal of the tutorial is to provide an initial set of training material for researchers interested in rigorous evaluations of information retrieval systems. Although the primary focus is on *ad hoc* retrieval experiments, the principles and concepts described in the tutorial are general and can easily be applied to a wide range of experimental scenarios both within, and beyond, the field of information retrieval.

The tutorial is primarily inteded for graduate students, researchers from other disciplines, and industrial practitioners who are interested in experimentally validating the effectiveness of search engines in a rigorous, scientifically sound manner.

The primary goals of this tutorial are as follows:

- Highlight the importance of experimental evaluation in IR. This will be accomplished by providing a brief explanation of the importance of experimental evaluations as from the early days of IR, and the ramifications of poorly executed experimental studies.
- Provide attendees with an in-depth overview of the fundamental IR evaluation paradigm. The tutorial will explain all of the key "tools" (e.g., test collections, baselines, statistical significance testing, result analysis, etc.) that make up an "experimental toolbox". We will cover a number of case studies and provide specific examples of how the various "tools" can be used to evaluate new *ad hoc* search techniques.
- More broadly, we hope that this tutorial will be an important first step towards developing a culture of strong experimental evaluations within the IR community. We will make our slides publicly available to help fill the gap in knowledge left by the fact the topic is largely ignored within IR courses and textbooks.

It is important to note that this is *not* a tutorial about devising evaluation measures or building test collections. Those issues are orthogonal to the topics covered by this tutorial.

After the tutorial, attendees should be able to distinguish between strong and weak experimental evaluation methodologies and be able to design strong, convincing experimental evaluations for their own projects.

2. MATERIALS

The tutorial material will consist of the following:

- A web page that contains a description of the tutorial and relevant pointers.
- A comprehensive set of (downloadable) slides available in both PowerPoint and PDF format.
- An extensive bibliography that will allow attendees to read more about topics of interest in more detail after the tutorial has concluded.

SIGIR'12, August 12–16, 2012, Portland, Oregon, USA.
ACM 978-1-4503-1472-5/12/08.

3. OUTLINE

- Introduction
  - The critical role of (proper) empirical evaluation in IR [3, 1]
- A high level view of empirical evaluation
  - The fundamental evaluation paradigm (task definition, benchmarks, ground truth, reference comparisons, statistical significance testing, macro and micro analysis of experimental results, etc.)
  - Brief, high level, examples of using the paradigm for several IR applications (e.g., *ad hoc* retrieval, question answering, filtering, text classification)
  - Brief survey of different types of evaluation (crowdsourcing, user studies, online evaluation, TREC-based evaluation, etc.)
- In-depth exploration of the empirical evaluation paradigm
  - Main focus: TREC-based evaluation [7, 4] of *ad hoc* retrieval approaches
  - A running example will be used for demonstrating specific principles (e.g., devising a novel pseudo-feedback-based query expansion method)
  - Devising an experimental setup
    * Full specification (reproducibility)
    * Effectiveness versus efficiency
    * Using open-source toolkits for implementation (e.g., Ivory, Lemur/Indri, Lucene, Terrier)
    * Selecting corpora (newswire versus Web, scale)
    * Selecting queries (titles vs. descriptions, how many queries? [2])
    * Relevance judgments (binary vs. graded)
    * Data pre-processing (tokenization, stemming, stopword removal)
    * Free parameters
    * Reference comparisons (baselines)
    * Evaluation measures
    * Statistical significance tests [5, 6, 8]
  - Analyzing experimental results
    * What counts as a "meaningful" performance difference? [2]
    * Studying the effect of varying free-parameter values
    * Exploring specific instances of the proposed methods (e.g., by using extreme values of free parameters)
    * Micro-analysis (e.g., failure analysis, use cases for specific queries)
- Summary of important evaluation principles

4. CONCLUSIONS

Given the highly applied nature of information retrieval research, this tutorial will take a first step towards developing a broader pedagogical movement that will help instill the importance of rigorous, scientifically sound experimental evaluations. It is also our hope that this tutorial will help inspire others to develop similar training material (e.g., tutorials, courses, books, etc.) in the future.

5. REFERENCES

[1] T. G. Armstrong, A. Moffat, W. Webber, and J. Zobel. Improvements that don't add up: ad-hoc retrieval results since 1998. In *Proceedings of CIKM*, pages 601–610, 2009.

[2] C. Buckley and E. M. Voorhees. Evaluating evaluation measure stability. In *Proceedings of SIGIR*, pages 33–40, 2000.

[3] A. Moffat and J. Zobel. What does it mean to "measure performance"? In *Proceedings of WISE*, pages 1–12, 2004.

[4] M. Sanderson. Test collection based evaluation of information retrieval systems. *Foundations and Trends in Information Retrieval*, 4(4):247–375, 2010.

[5] M. Sanderson and J. Zobel. Information retrieval system evaluation: effort, sensitivity, and reliability. In *Proceedings of SIGIR*, pages 162–169, 2005.

[6] M. D. Smucker, J. Allan, and B. Carterette. A comparison of statistical significance tests for information retrieval evaluation. In *Proceedings of CIKM*, pages 623–632, 2007.

[7] E. M. Voorhees and D. K. Harman. *TREC: Experiments and evaluation in information retrieval.* The MIT Press, 2005.

[8] W. Webber, A. Moffat, and J. Zobel. Statistical power in retrieval experimentation. In *Proceedings of CIKM*, pages 571–580, 2008.

IR Models: Foundations and Relationships

Thomas Roelleke*
Queen Mary, University of London
School of Electronic Engineering and Computer Science

ABSTRACT

In IR research it is essential to know IR models. Research over the past years has consolidated the foundations of IR models. Moreover, relationships have been reported that help to use and position IR models. Knowing about the foundations and relationships of IR models can significantly improve building information management systems.
The first part of this tutorial presents an in-depth consolidation of the *foundations* of the main IR models (TF-IDF, BM25, LM). Particular attention will be given to notation and probabilistic roots. The second part crystallises the *relationships* between models. Does LM embody IDF? How "heuristic" is TF-IDF? What are the probabilistic roots? How are LM and the probability of relevance related? What are the components shared by the main IR models?
After the tutorial, attendees will be familiar with a consolidated view on IR models. The tutorial will be illustrative and interactive, providing opportunities to exchange controversial issues and research challenges.

Categories and Subject Descriptors

H.3.3 [**Information Storage and Retrieval**]: Information Retrieval Models

General Terms

Theory, Algorithms

Keywords

TF-IDF, Language Modelling, BM25, Relationships

1. IR MODELS: FOUNDATIONS (90 MINS)

The introduction of the main IR models includes: TF-IDF, VSM (Vector-Space Model), G-VSM (Generalised VSM), PRF (Probability of Relevance Framework), BIR (Binary Independence Retrieval, RSJ (Robertson-SparckJones) weight, Laplace-like estimation of probabilities), Probabilistic Inference Networks (PIN), Poisson and 2-Poisson, BM25, DFR (Divergence from Randomness), and LM.
This part will consolidate the main foundations following from [15] (probabilistic retrieval, BIR model), [5] (missing relevance), [20, 22, 21, 11] (PIN), [13] (2-Poisson, foundation for the BM25 TF quantification $\mathrm{tf}/(\mathrm{tf}+K)$), [4] (IDF is Poisson approximation, aspects of burstiness), [3] (DFR), [12, 8, 9] (LM).
Moreover, this part will emphasises that IR models are consequent applications of basic techniques from probability theory: Bayes' Theorem, Total Probability Theorem, probability mixtures, and divergence measures (e.g. KL-divergence, mutual information). Particular emphasis will be given to the issue of event spaces [16, 18, 10], and a notation that is consistent across different models.
Finally, the first part will refer to general frameworks such as logic and matrices [23, 25, 17] and PIN's [20].

2. IR MODELS: RELATIONSHIPS (90 MINS)

The second part of the tutorial is dedicated to the relationships between retrieval models. In addition to the aim to look across the boundaries of single models models, i.e. different from "single-model" tutorials, the relationships between models is a differentiator to previous tutorials presented by Hugo Zaragoza, Stephen Robertson, Djoerd Hiemstra, Victor Lavrenko, and Donald Metzler.
There are several relationships between the models, and for selected relationships the tutorial will outline the mathematical proofs while keeping the formalisms minimal. We will look at the following relationships:

- BIR and TF-IDF: BIR can be used to explain TF-IDF; this views IDF as an approximation of the BIR/RSJ weight for the case of missing relevance, [14, 6].
- TF-IDF, LM and Poisson: There are relationships that follow from being precise about the event spaces [16, 18, 10], e.g. probabilities based on document frequencies of terms, or based on token occurrences of terms.
- PRF, TF-IDF and LM: Recently, [2], "Towards a better understanding of the relationship between probabilistic models in IR", investigated some controversial aspects regarding the relationship between PRF (probabilistic odds), TF-IDF and LM.
- PRF and LM: There is an early view on the relationship between LM (language modelling) and the PRF (probability of relevance framework) [9] which is addressed and criticised in [10].
- PIN's and TF-IDF and LM: A relationship between LM and PIN's has been pointed out in [11]; this relationship builds upon the earlier work [20, 22, 21] discussing the relationship between PIN's and TF-IDF;

*Visiting Professor at Yahoo Research Barcelona

SIGIR'12, August 12–16, 2012, Portland, Oregon, USA.
ACM 978-1-4503-1472-5/12/08.

overall, this marks the total probability theorem and PIN's as a binding link between TF-IDF and LM.

- Logical IR, VSM and G-VSM: Based on [25], we can relate the G-VSM to the total probability theorem, leading to geometric and probabilistic IR [24].
- Information theory: Does it explain or relate IR models [1, 14]?
- Axiomatic approach: Models can be characterised by axioms/constraints [7] the models do or do not satisfy.

The tutorial makes explicit that "there is as much LM in TF-IDF as there is TF-IDF in LM". TF-IDF has probabilistic roots. The duality of TF-IDF and LM marks TF-IDF as a model, not just as a weighting scheme in the VSM; the VSM is a "framework" to express models [17].

Also, the tutorial looks at the statement "in LM, the estimate $P(t) := \mathrm{df}(t)/(\sum_{t'} df(t'))$ is wrong; $P(t)$ should be based on the term frequency". Moreover, the tutorial will review that LM is based on $P(q|d)/P(q)$, and what makes the relationship between LM and the probability of relevance $P(r|d,q)$ [9]. Finally, the tutorial will include conducive interpretations of the renown BM25 TF quantification tf/(tf+K) [3, 26, 19]. After the tutorial, the participants will have their view on statements such as "we know *that* LM works, but we do not know *why*"; "TF-IDF is intuitive, LM is not"; "TF-IDF is heuristic, whereas LM has a probabilistic semantics".

In summary, the tutorial is structured as follows:

IR Models: Foundations
TF-IDF, Vector-space Model
PRF, BIR, 2-Poisson, BM25
LM, Relevance
DFR, KL-Divergence
Entropy, Mutual Information
IR Models: Relationships
PIN's, TF-IDF and LM [20, 11]
IDF and BIR [14, 6]
Event spaces [16, 18, 10]
Model axioms/constraints [7]
LM and PRF/BM25: related? [9, 2]
LM and TF-IDF: siblings! [19]

Thomas Roelleke is a senior lecturer at Queen Mary, University of London. His research expertise lies in IR Models & Theory and Probabilistic DB+IR. Currently, Thomas is a visiting scientist at Yahoo Research, Barcelona Media. Thomas has presented IR model tutorials at German summer schools, taught MSc modules on Foundations of IR, and published several IR model & theory papers.

3. REFERENCES

[1] Akiko Aizawa. An information-theoretic perspective of tf-idf measures. *Information Processing and Management*, 39:45–65, January 2003.

[2] R. Aly and T. Demeester. Towards a better understanding of the relationship between probabilistic models in ir. *ICTIR (Intl. Conference on Theory in Information Retrieval), Bertinoro, Italy*, pages 164–175. Springer-Verlag, 2011.

[3] Gianni Amati and C. J. van Rijsbergen. Probabilistic models of information retrieval based on measuring the divergence from randomness. *ACM TOIS*, 20(4):357–389, October 2002.

[4] K. Church and W. Gale. Inverse document frequency (idf): A measure of deviation from Poisson. *Third Workshop on Very Large Corpora*, pages 121–130, 1995.

[5] W.B. Croft and D.J. Harper. Using probabilistic models of document retrieval without relevance information. *Journal of Documentation*, 35:285–295, 1979.

[6] Arjen de Vries and T. Roelleke. Relevance information: A loss of entropy but a gain for IDF? *ACM SIGIR*, pages 282–289, Salvador, Brazil, 2005.

[7] Hui Fang and ChengXiang Zhai. An exploration of axiomatic approaches to information retrieval. *ACM SIGIR*, pages 480–487, New York, 2005. ACM.

[8] Djoerd Hiemstra. A probabilistic justification for using tf.idf term weighting in information retrieval. *International Journal on Digital Libraries*, 3(2):131–139, 2000.

[9] John Lafferty and ChengXiang Zhai. *Probabilistic Relevance Models Based on Document and Query Generation*, chapter 1. Kluwer, 2003.

[10] Robert W. P. Luk. On event space and rank equivalence between probabilistic retrieval models. *Inf. Retr.*, 11(6):539–561, 2008.

[11] Donald Metzler and W. Bruce Croft. Combining the language model and inference network approaches to retrieval. *Information Processing & Management*, 40(5):735–750, 2004.

[12] J.M. Ponte and W.B. Croft. A language modeling approach to information retrieval. *ACM SIGIR*, pages 275–281, New York, 1998. ACM.

[13] S. E. Robertson and S. Walker. Some simple effective approximations to the 2-Poisson model for probabilistic weighted retrieval. *ACM SIGIR*, pages 232–241, London, et al., 1994.

[14] S.E. Robertson. Understanding inverse document frequency: On theoretical arguments for idf. *Journal of Documentation*, 60:503–520, 2004.

[15] S.E. Robertson and K. Sparck Jones. Relevance weighting of search terms. *Journal of the American Society for Information Science*, 27:129–146, 1976.

[16] Stephen Robertson. On event spaces and probabilistic models in information retrieval. *Information Retrieval Journal*, 8(2):319–329, 2005.

[17] T. Roelleke, Theodora Tsikrika, and Gabriella Kazai. A general matrix framework for modelling information retrieval. *Journal on Information Processing & Management (IP&M), Special Issue on Theory in Information Retrieval*, 42(1), 2006.

[18] T. Roelleke and J. Wang. A parallel derivation of probabilistic information retrieval models. *ACM SIGIR*, pages 107–114, Seattle, USA, 2006.

[19] T. Roelleke and J. Wang. TF-IDF uncovered: A study of theories and probabilities. *ACM SIGIR*, pages 435–442, Singapore, July 2008.

[20] H. Turtle and W. B. Croft. Inference networks for document retrieval. *ACM SIGIR*, pages 1–24, New York, 1990. ACM.

[21] H. Turtle and W.B. Croft. Evaluation of an inference network-based retrieval model. *ACM TOIS*, 9(3):187–222, 1991.

[22] H.R. Turtle and W.B. Croft. Efficient probabilistic inference for text retrieval. *Proceedings RIAO 91*, pages 644–661, Paris, France, 1991.

[23] C. J. van Rijsbergen. A non-classical logic for information retrieval. *The Computer Journal*, 29(6):481–485, 1986.

[24] Cornelis J. van Rijsbergen. *The Geometry of Information Retrieval.* Cambridge University Press, 2004.

[25] S.K.M. Wong and Y.Y. Yao. On modeling information retrieval with probabilistic inference. *ACM TOIS*, 13(1):38–68, 1995.

[26] Hengzhi Wu and T. Roelleke. Semi-subsumed events: A probabilistic semantics for the BM25 term frequency quantification. *ICTIR (Intl. Conference on Theory in Information Retrieval).* Springer, 2009.

Patent Information Retrieval

An Instance of Domain-specific Search

Mihai Lupu
Vienna University of Technology
Favoriten Strasse 9-11/188
Vienna 1040, Austria
lupu@ifs.tuwien.ac.at

ABSTRACT

The tutorial aims to provide the IR researchers with an understanding of how the patent system works, the challenges that patent searchers face in using the existing tools and in adopting new methods developed in academia.

At the same time, the tutorial will inform the IR researcher about the unique opportunities that the patent domain provides: a large amount of multi-lingual and multimodal documents, the widest possible span of covered domains, a highly annotated corpus and, very importantly, relevance judgements created by experts in the fields and recorded electronically in the documents.

The combination of these two objectives leads to the main purpose of the tutorial: to create awareness and to encourage more emphasis on the patent domain in the IR community. Table 1 provides details on how the tutorial covers the topics of the SIGIR conference.

Categories and Subject Descriptors

J.1 [**Computer Applications**]: Administrative Data Processing—*Law, Business, Government*; A.1 [**General Literature**]: Introduction and Survey

General Terms

Documentation, Human Factors, Languages, Algorithms

Keywords

Patents

1. TUTORIAL DESCRIPTION

1.1 Intended Audience

PhD Students, junior and senior researchers looking for a new challenge for their algorithms. In terms of general IR, the audience can have any level: beginner, intermediate or advanced. In terms of patent IR, the audience is expected to consist of novices in the domain.

1.2 Agenda Details

Introduction (~30 minutes)

The tutorial starts by introducing the attendees to the patent system. We discuss how it works, international standardization efforts, key players. In doing so, we define some of the terms that we will be using in the rest of this session.

Types of Searches (~30 minutes)

To understand what patent IR is we must understand the tasks that a professional searcher has to solve. While at first sight this may be simply "search for patents", an in-depth look identifies different search tasks, with different types of requests for information and different expectations in terms of the results.

Evaluation (~30 minutes)

The different tasks the professional searcher has to accomplish are crystalized in benchmarking tasks. The domain is particularly suited for large-scale IR evaluation campaigns, since search reports are public information and can be used as relevance judgements. We will talk about the pros and cons of this use of search reports, and about how to run your own tests and create your own test collections.

Contents (~75 minutes)

The largest part of this tutorial will be on the actual content of the patent documents and what we can do with it. First, I will describe the standard metadata available for each patent document. It covers a set of different physical and legal persons, hyper-references between patents, dates, and several types of classifications. From this, we can already extract interesting observation pertaining to the evolution of technologies and their key players.

We can learn even more from the actual text, and I will present here examples of content and describe the current state-of-the-art in using this unstructured information for retrieval. Issues such as the use of different genres and languages, as well as hidden semantic information will be presented.

Finally, I will briefly talk about image search in this domain. The particularity here is that most of the image retrieval methdos, based on colors and textures, are powerless in this domain, where 2-bit color depth images are the rule.

Data Sources (~15 minutes)

In conclusion, I will summarize the further resources available to the researcher interested in the domain, as well as the sources of actual patent data publicly available.

2. REFERENCES

Table 1, with references for each of its claims, is available at `http://mihailupu.net/patentTutorial`.

SIGIR'12, August 12–16, 2012, Portland, Oregon, USA.
ACM 978-1-4503-1472-5/12/08.

Table 1: Patent IR touches on all aspects of IR research

What was *your* paper about?	Did you know that... (and would your method still work in this case)?
Document Representation and Content Analysis (e.g., text representation, document structure, linguistic analysis, non-English IR, cross-lingual IR, information extraction, sentiment analysis, clustering, classification, topic models, facets)	• patent documents are highly structured and cover different genres within the same document? • the global patent collection has manually created relevance judgments across languages? • and that it also has an international classification scheme covering all patents? • a patent has been overthrown in 1997 at the USPTO for prior art disclosed in ancient Sanskrit texts?
Queries and Query Analysis (e.g., query representation, query intent, query log analysis, question answering, query suggestion, query reformulation)	• a patent search process always starts with a multi-page document describing the invention? • patent search professionals are experts in creating large queries with both keywords and metadata? • "a system having a storage for storing data, an output device to display information, a terminal for entering information, and a component that modifies the input data and controls flow of data between different parts" is a computer?
Users and Interactive IR (e.g., user models, user studies, user feedback, search interface, summarization, task models, query logs, personalized search)	• a patent search process can take up to five months • the USPTO publishes the examiner's search strategy and results for each application • an examination division at the EPO always consists of three technical examiners?
Retrieval Models and Ranking (e.g., IR theory, language models, probabilistic retrieval models, feature-based models, learning to rank, combining searches, diversity)	• the most popular model among patent searchers is boolean, because it provides clear evidence as to why a document was in the retrieved list or not? • published search reports can be used to learn to rank and provide significant retrieval improvements? • common search strategies involve different features (inventors, owners, classes, references), whose weights need to be balanced?
Search Engine Architectures and Scalability (e.g., indexing, compression, MapReduce, distributed IR, P2P IR, mobile devices)	• the only source for absolutely reliable patent legal status data are the national patent offices • more and more National Patent Offices publish their data online, creating a de-facto distributed repository of patent data?
Filtering and Recommending (e.g., content-based filtering, collaborative filtering, recommender systems, profiles)	• a patent searcher has to cull through thousands or tens of thousands of patents for a validity search
Evaluation (e.g., test collections, effectiveness measures, experimental design)	• there already exist over 5 test collections dedicated to patent search • patent search includes at least 3 different types of search use-cases, for which different effectiveness measures are needed
Web IR and Social Media Search (e.g., link analysis, social tagging, social network analysis, advertising and search, blog search, forum search, CQA, adversarial IR, vertical and local search)	• patents form an extensive 'social' network • the objective of a patent claim is to provide as wide as coverage as possible, while disclosing as little as possible
IR and Structured Data (e.g., XML search, ranking in databases, desktop search, entity search)	• patents are distributed as XML files? • by their definition, patents' core entities have not previously been seen? • entities are the fundamental way to searching chemical patents?
Multimedia IR (e.g., Image search, video search, speech/audio search, music IR)	• there are 9 types of images in patents? • patent images are black-and-white, not even grayscale? • currently, engineering patent searchers have no option but to manually review thousands of images?

Medical Information Retrieval

An Instance of Domain-Specific Search

Allan Hanbury
Institute of Software Technology and Interactive Systems
Vienna University of Technology
Favoritenstraße 9-11/188
Vienna, Austria
hanbury@ifs.tuwien.ac.at

ABSTRACT

Due to an explosion in the amount of medical information available, search techniques are gaining importance in the medical domain. This tutorial discusses recent results on search in the medical domain, including the outcome of surveys on end user requirements, research relevant to the field, and current medical and health search applications available. Finally, the extent to which available techniques meet user requirements are discussed, and open challenges in the field are identified.

Categories and Subject Descriptors

H.3 [**Information Storage and Retrieval**]: Information Search and Retrieval; J.3 [**Life and Medical Sciences**]: Medical Information Systems

Keywords

Information Retrieval, Domain-Specific Search, Medical Information, End User Requirements

1. TUTORIAL SUMMARY

Search techniques are becoming increasingly important in the medical domain, in particular due to an explosion in the amount of medical information available. This includes both patient-specific information (e.g. electronic health records) and knowledge-based information (e.g. scientific papers). The increasing emphasis on the use of *evidence-based medicine* (using the best evidence from the scientific literature in clinical decision making) also increases the importance of search in medical practice [10]. Furthermore, the secondary use of anonymized electronic health records for facilitating research and improving quality in medical practice is also gaining in importance [7]. This use of health records also requires IR techniques, and has been modelled in the new TREC medical records track in 2011.

All parties involved in medical treatment are regularly faced with an information need that cannot be met from their own store of knowledge. Medical information search is a classic example of a *domain-specific search*, but the medical domain is so complex that simply limiting the target documents to those in the medical domain and indexing with a standard search engine is not sufficient. The range of sources of medical information (primary research sources, secondary research sources, web pages and popular publications, etc.) and the range of end users (members of the general public, general practitioners, specialists, researchers, etc.) lead to complex requirements. Recent work in the Khresmoi project[1] has collected end user requirements for search in the medical domain through online surveys, interviews and observation [17, 9, 3, 14]. The results of the requirement analysis are presented based on a model of domain-specific search, for which the following aspects need to be specified: information sources to restrict the search, search refinements that can improve the access to information in the domain, and end users and their tasks.

Although many groups of people search for information in the medical domain, the analysis in the Khresmoi project has been restricted to three of the most important groups: search by *physicians*, search by *members of the general public* and search by *radiologists* (a subset of physicians for which search in images is of particular importance). Different end users have different requirements based on the technical level (accessibly or technically written), level of specificity (overview or in-depth), type of research paper (primary or secondary), language of the results, etc. Naturally, the trustworthiness of medical information is of particular importance. Analyses of search behaviour based on search engine log files have also been done [4, 18].

For physicians, an unmet information need has been reported as occurring for 2 of every 3 patients seen [11], or for 41% of the questions they pursued [6]. This requires that they attempt to meet this information need by using available resources, which has traditionally involved searching in printed sources and asking colleagues, although searching on the Internet is of increasing importance. The Khresmoi survey has shown that the three most common sources of online information used by physicians (in decreasing order of usage) are: general search engines (e.g. Google, Bing, Yahoo!), medical research databases (e.g. Pubmed) and Wikipedia. Image search is particularly important in the medical domain, especially for radiologists [16]. Internet image search applications are starting to appear (e.g. Goldminer, Yottalook). However, image search within Picture Archiving and Communication Systems (PACS) in hospitals is also being developed [15].

Patients also have regular information needs, illustrated by the fact that 61% of American Adults seek out health advice online [8]. The Khresmoi survey of the general public

SIGIR'12, August 12–16, 2012, Portland, Oregon, USA.
ACM 978-1-4503-1472-5/12/08.

[1] http://khresmoi.eu

revealed that the most common sources of online information used by this group are: general search engines (e.g. Google, Bing, Yahoo!), web sites providing health information (e.g. university, hospital, pharmaceutical company) and Wikipedia. However, as this group has had less training in interpreting the information found, issues such as trustworthiness of the information and *cyberchondria* [20] gain more importance.

A number of publications of work towards meeting the requirements for search in the medical domain have recently appeared. This includes work on estimating the granularity of information in a document [21], estimating the difficulty of a document [5, 12], the quality of documents [19], document summarization [1] and the use of terminology resources for query refinement [13]. Cross-lingual search is of importance for end users at all levels [2]. The tutorial presents how well this work meets the requirements and discusses the remaining challenges for search in the medical domain.

2. ACKNOWLEDGMENTS

The research leading to these results has received funding from the European Union Seventh Framework Programme (FP7/2007-2013) under grant agreement no. 257528 (KHRESMOI).

3. REFERENCES

[1] S. Afantenos, V. Karkaletsis, and P. Stamatopoulos. Summarization from medical documents: a survey. *Artif. Intell. Med.*, 33:157–177, 2005.

[2] S. Bedrick. Improving access to medical literature using multilingual search interfaces. In *Proc. MEDINFO*, 2010.

[3] C. Boyer, M. Gschwandtner, A. Hanbury, M. Kritz, N. Pletneva, M. Samwald, and A. Vargas. Use case definition including concrete data requirements. Technical Report D8.2, Khresmoi project, 2012.

[4] M.-A. Cartright, R. W. White, and E. Horvitz. Intentions and attention in exploratory health search. In *Proceedings of the 34th international ACM SIGIR conference on Research and development in Information Retrieval*, pages 65–74. ACM, 2011.

[5] K. Collins-Thompson, P. N. Bennett, R. W. White, S. de la Chica, and D. Sontag. Personalizing web search results by reading level. In *Proceedings of the 20th ACM international conference on Information and knowledge management*, pages 403–412. ACM, 2011.

[6] J. W. Ely, J. A. Osheroff, S. M. Maviglia, and M. E. Rosenbaum. Patient-care questions that physicians are unable to answer. *Journal of the American Medical Informatics Association*, 14(4):407–414, 2007.

[7] M. A. Feufel, G. Antes, J. Steurer, G. Gigerenzer, J. A. Muir Gray, M. Mäkelä, A. G. Mulley, Jr., D. E. Nelson, J. Schulkin, H. Schünemann, J. E. Wennberg, and C. Wild. What is needed for better health care: Better systems, better patients or both? In G. Gigerenzer and J. A. Muir Gray, editors, *Better Doctors, Better Patients, Better Decisions: Envisioning Health Care 2020*, pages 117–134. MIT Press, 2011.

[8] S. Fox and S. Jones. The social life of health information. Technical report, Pew Internet & American Life Project Report, 2009.

[9] M. Gschwandtner, M. Kritz, and C. Boyer. Requirements of the health professional search. Technical Report D8.1.2, Khresmoi project, 2011.

[10] W. R. Hersh. *Information Retrieval: A Health and Biomedical Perspective*. Springer, 3rd edition, 2009.

[11] W. R. Hersh and D. H. Hickam. How well do physicians use electronic information retrieval systems? A framework for investigation and systematic review. *Journal of the American Medical Association*, 280(15):1347–1352, 1998.

[12] G. Leroy and J. E. Endicott. Combining nlp with evidence-based methods to find text metrics related to perceived and actual text difficulty. In *Proceedings of the 2nd ACM SIGHIT International Health Informatics Symposium*, pages 749–754. ACM, 2012.

[13] G. Luo and C. Tang. On iterative intelligent medical search. In *Proceedings of the 31st annual international ACM SIGIR conference on Research and development in information retrieval*, pages 3–10. ACM, 2008.

[14] H. Müller. Report on image use behaviour and requirements. Technical Report D9.1, Khresmoi project, 2011.

[15] H. Müller and T. M. Deserno. Content-based medical image retrieval. In *Biomedical Image Processing - Methods and Applications*. Springer, 2011.

[16] H. Müller, C. Despont-Gros, W. Hersh, J. Jensen, C. Lovis, and A. Geissbuhler. Health care professionals' image use and search behaviour. In *Proc. Medical Informatics Europe*, pages 24–32, 2006.

[17] N. Pletneva, A. Vargas, and C. Boyer. Requirements for the general public health search. Technical Report D8.1.1, Khresmoi project, 2011.

[18] D. Rubin, A. Flanders, W. Kim, K. Siddiqui, and C. Kahn. Ontology-assisted analysis of web queries to determine the knowledge radiologists seek. *Journal of Digital Imaging*, 24:160–164, 2011.

[19] T. Tang, N. Craswell, D. Hawking, K. Griffiths, and H. Christensen. Quality and relevance of domain-specific search: A case study in mental health. *Information Retrieval*, 9:207–225, 2006.

[20] R. W. White and E. Horvitz. Cyberchondria: Studies of the escalation of medical concerns in web search. *ACM Trans. Inf. Syst.*, 27:23:1–23:37, November 2009.

[21] X. Yan, R. Y. Lau, D. Song, X. Li, and J. Ma. Toward a semantic granularity model for domain-specific information retrieval. *ACM Trans. Inf. Syst.*, 29:15:1–15:46, July 2011.

Visual Information Retrieval using Java and LIRE

Oge Marques
Florida Atlantic University
777 Glades Road
Boca Raton, FL 33431
omarques@fau.edu

Mathias Lux
Klagenfurt University
Universitätsstrasse 65-67
Klagenfurt, Austria
mlux@itec.uni-klu.ac.at

ABSTRACT
Visual information retrieval (VIR) is an active and vibrant research area, which attempts at providing means for organizing, indexing, annotating, and retrieving visual information (images and videos) form large, unstructured repositories. The goal of VIR is to retrieve the highest number of relevant matches to a given query (often expressed as an example image and/or a series of keywords). In its early years (1995-2000) the research efforts were dominated by content-based approaches contributed primarily by the image and video processing community. During the past decade, it was widely recognized that the challenges imposed by the *semantic gap* (the lack of coincidence between an image's visual contents and its semantic interpretation) required a clever use of textual metadata (in addition to information extracted from the image's pixel contents) to make image and video retrieval solutions efficient and effective. The need to bridge (or at least narrow) the semantic gap has been one of the driving forces behind current VIR research. Additionally, other related research problems and market opportunities have started to emerge, offering a broad range of exciting problems for computer scientists and engineers to work on.

In this tutorial, we present an overview of visual information retrieval (VIR) concepts, techniques, algorithms, and applications. Several topics are supported by examples written in Java, using Lucene (an open-source Java-based indexing and search implementation) and LIRE (Lucene Image REtrieval), an open-source Java-based library for content-based image retrieval (CBIR) written by Mathias Lux.

After motivating the topic, we briefly review the fundamentals of information retrieval, present the most relevant and effective visual descriptors currently used in VIR, the most common indexing approaches for visual descriptors, the most prominent machine learning techniques used in connection with contemporary VIR solutions, as well as the challenges associated with building real-world, large scale VIR solutions, including a brief overview of publicly available datasets used in worldwide challenges, contests, and benchmarks. Throughout the tutorial, we integrate examples using LIRE, whose main features and design principles are also discussed. Finally, we conclude the tutorial with suggestions for deepening the knowledge in the topic, including a brief discussion of the most relevant advances, open challenges, and promising opportunities in VIR and related areas.

The tutorial is primarily targeted at experienced Information Retrieval researchers and practitioners interested in extending their knowledge of document-based IR to equivalent concepts, techniques, and challenges in VIR. The acquired knowledge should allow participants to derive insightful conclusions and promising avenues for further investigation.

Categories and Subject Descriptors
H.3.3 [**Information Search and Retrieval**]

General Terms
Algorithms.

Keywords
Content-Based Image Retrieval, Visual Information Retrieval, Image Search, Java.

Bios
Oge Marques is Associate Professor in the Dept of Computer and Electrical Engineering and Computer Science at Florida Atlantic University. He has more than 20 years of teaching and research experience in the fields of image processing and computer vision. He is the (co-) author of five books in these topics, including "Content-Based Image and Video Retrieval" (with Borko Furht) (Springer, 2002), the recently published textbook "Practical Image and Video Processing Using MATLAB" (Wiley, 2011), and the upcoming book "Visual Information Retrieval using Java and LIRE" (with Mathias Lux). He has also published several book chapters and more than 50 refereed journal and conference papers in these fields. He serves as a reviewer and Editorial Board member for several leading journals in computer science and engineering. He is a senior member of both the ACM and the IEEE.

Mathias Lux studied Mathematics at Graz University of Technology. After finishing his Master's studies in 2004, he started his PhD studies in multimedia retrieval based on semantic metadata, also in Graz, which he finished in 2006 with distinction. From 1998 to 2001 he worked in industry in the area of web-based applications, before being employed as a researcher at the Know-Center, a competence center for knowledge- based applications in Graz, focusing on information retrieval. From 2004 to 2006 he worked at the Knowledge Management Institute (KMI) of Graz University of Technology as a university assistant. He is currently working on multimedia retrieval based on metadata and emergent semantics in social computing.

SIGIR'12, August 12–16, 2012, Portland, Oregon, USA.
ACM 978-1-4503-1472-5/12/08.

Large-Scale Graph Mining and Learning for Information Retrieval

Bin Gao
Microsoft Research Asia
No. 5, Danling Street
Beijing, 100080, P. R. China
bingao@microsoft.com

Taifeng Wang
Microsoft Research Asia
No. 5, Danling Street
Beijing, 100080, P. R. China
taifengw@microsoft.com

Tie-Yan Liu
Microsoft Research Asia
No. 5, Danling Street
Beijing, 100080, P. R. China
tyliu@microsoft.com

ABSTRACT

For many information retrieval applications, we need to deal with the ranking problem on very large scale graphs. However, it is non-trivial to perform efficient and effective ranking on them. On one aspect, we need to design scalable algorithms. On another aspect, we also need to develop powerful computational infrastructure to support these algorithms. This tutorial aims at giving a timely introduction to the promising advances in the aforementioned aspects in recent years, and providing the audiences with a comprehensive view on the related literature.

Categories and Subject Descriptors

H.3.3 [**Information Storage and Retrieval**]: Information Search and Retrieval; H.5.4 [**Information Interface and Presentation**]: Hypertext/Hypermedia.

General Terms

Algorithm, Experimentation, Theory

Keywords

Large-scale graph, graph ranking, Markov process, MapReduce.

1. INTRODUCTION

In many information retrieval applications, we need to tackle the problem of ranking on large-scale graphs with rich metadata. For example, to compute page importance ranking for search, one may need to analyze the link structure of the Web graph; to understand Web user behaviors and preferences, one may need to rank the nodes on user-page bipartite graphs extracted from search engine logs; and to make recommendations in online community, one may need to conduct ranking on the social network graph. All these graphs are of very large scale and contain rich information (represented by rich metadata). As a result, it is non-trivial to perform efficient and effective ranking on them. On one aspect, we need to design scalable algorithms. On another aspect, we also need to develop powerful computational infrastructure to support these algorithms. We observe that in recent years, there are some promising advances in the aforementioned aspects, which can potentially enhance many important Web search and data mining applications, and greatly advance the state of the art of the related research. This tutorial aims at giving a timely introduction to these works, and providing the audiences with a comprehensive view on the related literature. We believe many researchers in the Web search and data mining community would have interest in listening to this tutorial, and we hope that they can be motivated to participate in the research of large-scale graph ranking with rich metadata.

SIGIR'12, August 12–16, 2012, Portland, Oregon, USA.
ACM 978-1-4503-1472-5/12/08.

2. TUTORIAL DESCRIPTION

We will organize the tutorial into five parts.

In the first part, a brief introduction of large-scale graphs with rich metadata and their properties will be given. The widely-used mathematical tools and models to represent these graphs and rich metadata will be introduced.

In the second part, we will focus on unsupervised ranking on large-scale graphs. We propose a unified view on the unsupervised graph ranking algorithms, i.e., they are generative models based on some stochastic processes. Specifically, a general ranking framework based on Markov skeleton process [9, 10] will be introduced. The algorithms in the literature are organized in two categories.

- **Graph ranking algorithms on single graph.** To compute page importance ranking in Web graphs, HITS [11] and PageRank [14] were proposed, which are based on the analysis of link structures of Web graphs. These methods can be explained using random walks on a discrete-time Markov process. After that, quite a few link analysis algorithms like TrustRank [8] and PopRank [13] were developed to improve HITS and PageRank to robustly deal with web spam, and to handle heterogeneous graphs. BrowseRank [12] was proposed recently to consider rich metadata (e.g., visiting frequency and staying time) in user behavior data for page importance ranking, which is based on a new mathematical tool - continuous time Markov process. MobileRank [6] and BrowseRank Plus [6] further improved BrowseRank in considering more dependency between different nodes in the graph and more metadata. It has been shown that most of these algorithms can be summarized into a general framework based on Markov skeleton process.
- **Graph ranking algorithms on graph series.** Mining on a time series of graph snapshots also attract much interests in recent years. Basically with the graph series, one can find some trends or to obtain

a more stable ranking results. We will introduce such kind of work like TemporalRank [17].

In the third part, we will introduce supervised large-scale graph ranking algorithms. We propose a unified view on the supervised graph ranking algorithms, i.e., they are discriminative models on some graph-based smoothing function. Specifically, a supervised/semi-supervised graph ranking framework will be introduced.

- **Supervised/Semi-supervised graph ranking algorithms.** Recently people have realized that unsupervised graph ranking sometimes might not be consistent with human intuition. To solve the problem, supervised or semi-supervised graph ranking schemes have been considered. Take importance ranking on graphs as an example, there are several pieces of work along this line. LiftHITS [5] learns from user feedback to realign the eigenvectors of the link matrix in HITS. Adaptive PageRank [16] alters the PageRank scores according to human feedback, using a quadratic programming technique. NetRank [2, 4, 1] provides a uniform framework for learning the parameters of Markov random walks on graphs according to supervision in terms of pairwise preference between nodes. In Laplacian Rank [3, 18, 15], the supervised graph ranking problem was formulated as minimizing the combination of the empirical error and a regularization term represented by graph. Semi-supervised PageRank [7] considers both graph structure and the rich metadata contained in node features and edge features in the ranking process.

In the fourth part, we discuss how to design a distributed system to support large-scale graph ranking algorithms, and how to parallel existing algorithms to better fit into the system. The design principles for such a distributed system will first be discussed, and then a real system will be explained in detail, which has been used in a commercial search engine. This system contains a map-reduce engines specifically optimized for graph operations, as well as a rich pool of graph operators such as graph traverse, graph partitioning, and graph sampling. It is easy to implement a graph ranking algorithm on this platform. We will take Semi-supervised PageRank as an example to make detailed discussion on this process.

In the last part of the tutorial, the future research directions regarding large-scale graph ranking with rich metadata, and open questions and challenges will be discussed.

3. REFERENCES

[1] A. Agarwal and S. Chakrabarti. Learning random walks to rank nodes in graphs. In the proceedings of the 24th International Conference on Machine Learning (*ICML*), pages 9-16, 2007.

[2] A. Agarwal, S. Chakrabarti, and S. Aggarwal. Learning to rank networked entites. In the proceedings of the 12th ACM SIGKDD International Conference on Knowledge Discovery and Data Mining, pages 14-23, 2006.

[3] S. Agarwal. Ranking on graph data. In the proceedings of the 23th International Conference on Machine Learning (*ICML*), pages 25-32, 2006.

[4] S. Chakrabarti and A. Agarwal. Learning parameters in entity relationship graphs from ranking preferences. In the proceedings of the 10th European Conference on Principles and Practice of Knowledge Discovery in Databases (*PKDD*), volume 4213, pages 91-102, 2006.

[5] H. Chang, D. Cohn, and A. K. McCallum. Learning to create customized authority lists. In the proceedings of the 17th International Conference on Machine Learning (*ICML*), pages 127-134, 2000.

[6] B. Gao, T. Liu, Z. Ma, T. Wang, and H. Li. A general markov framework for page importance computation. In CIKM'09, pp, 1835-1838, 2009.

[7] B. Gao, T. Liu, W. Wei, T. Wang, and H. Li. Semi-Supervised Ranking on Very Large Graph with Rich Metadata. In KDD'11, pp, 96-104, 2011.

[8] Z. Gyongyi, H. Garcia-Molina, and J. Pedersen. Combating web spam with trustrank. In *VLDB '04*, pages 576–587. VLDB Endowment, 2004.

[9] Z. Hou and G. Liu. Markov Skeleton Processes and their Applications. Science Press and International Press, 2005.

[10] Z. Hou, Z. Liu, and J. Zou. Markov Skeleton Processes. In *Chinese Science Bulletin*, vol 43, no 11, pages 881-889, June, 1998.

[11] J. M. Kleinberg. Authoritative sources in a hyperlinked environment. In the proceedings of the 9th Annual ACM-SIAM Symposium on Discrete Algorithms (*SODA*), pages 668-677, 1998.

[12] Y. Liu, B. Gao, T. Liu, Y. Zhang, Z. Ma, S. He, and H. Li. BrowseRank: letting users vote for page importance. In *SIGIR '08*, pages 451–458, 2008.

[13] Z. Nie, Y. Zhang, J. Wen, and W. Ma. Object-Level Ranking: Bringing Order to Web Objects. In *WWW'05*, 2005.

[14] L. Page, S. Brin, R. Motwani, and T. Winograd. The PageRank citation ranking: bringing order to the web. Technical report, Stanford Digital Library Technologies Project, 1998.

[15] D. Rao, and D. Yarowsky. Ranking and semi-supervised classification on large scale graphs using map-reduce. In the proceedings of the 4th International Joint Conference on Natural Language Processing of the Asian Federation of Natural Language Processing (*ACL-IJCNLP*), 2009.

[16] A. C. Tsoi, G. Morini, F. Scarselli, M. Hagenbuchner, and M. Maggini. Adaptive ranking of Web pages. In the proceedings of the 12th International World Wide Web Conference (*WWW*), pages 356-365, 2003.

[17] L. Yang, L. Qi, Y. Zhao, B. Gao, and T. Liu Link Analysis using Time Series of Web Graphs. In CIKM'07, pp. 1011-1014, 2007.

[18] D. Zhou, J. Huang, and B. Scholkopf. Learning from labeled and unlabeled data on a directed graph. In the proceedings of the 22th International Conference on Machine Learning (*ICML*), pages 1041-1048, 2005.

SIGIR 2012 Tutorial: Query Performance Prediction for IR

David Carmel
IBM Research - Haifa Labs
Haifa 31905, Israel
carmel@il.ibm.com

Oren Kurland
Faculty of Industrial Engineering and Management
Technion, Haifa 32000, Israel
kurland@ie.technion.ac.il

ABSTRACT

The goal of this tutorial is to expose participants to current research on query performance prediction. Participants will become familiar with state-of-the-art performance prediction methods, with common evaluation methodologies of prediction quality, and with potential applications that can utilize performance predictors. In addition, some open issues and challenges in the field will be discussed.

This tutorial is an updated version of the SIGIR 2010 tutorial presented by David Carmel and Elad Yom-Tov on the same subject [7]. This year we intend to expand on new results in the field, in particular focusing on recently developed frameworks that provide a unified model for performance prediction.

Categories and Subject Descriptors: H.3.3 [Information Search and Retrieval]: Retrieval models

General Terms: Algorithms, Experimentation

Keywords: query-performance prediction

1. OBJECTIVES

Many information retrieval (IR) systems suffer from a radical variance in performance when responding to users' queries. Even for systems that succeed very well on average, the quality of results returned for some of the queries is poor. Thus, it is desirable that IR systems will be able to identify "difficult" queries in order to handle them properly. Understanding why some queries are inherently more difficult than others is essential for IR, and a good answer to this important question will help search engines to reduce the variance in performance, hence serving better their customer needs.

The high variability in query performance has driven a new research direction in the IR field on estimating the expected quality of the search results, i.e., the query difficulty, when no relevance feedback is given. Such an estimation is beneficial for many reasons:

- As feedback to the users: The IR system can provide the users with an estimate of the expected quality of the results retrieved for their queries. The users can then rephrase queries that were found to be "difficult", or alternatively, resubmit the "difficult" query to alternative search resources.
- As feedback to the search engine: The search engine can invoke alternative retrieval strategies for different queries according to their estimated difficulty. For example, heavy query-analysis procedures that are not feasible for all queries due to time response restrictions, may be invoked selectively for difficult queries only.
- As feedback to the system administrator: The administrator can identify queries related to a specific subject that are "difficult" for the search engine, and to expand the collection of documents to better answer poorly covered subjects. Identifying *missing content queries* is especially important for commercial search engines which should better identify, as soon as possible, popular emerging user needs that cannot be answered appropriately due to missing relevant content.
- For IR applications. For example, difficulty estimation can be used by a distributed search application as a method for merging the results retrieved from different datasets by weighing the results according to their estimated quality.

Estimating the query difficulty is a significant challenge due to the numerous factors that impact retrieval performance. Many prediction methods have been proposed throughout the last years. However, as many researchers observed, the prediction quality of state-of-the-are predictors is still too low to be widely used by IR applications. The low prediction quality is due to query ambiguity, missing content, vocabulary mismatch, and many other factors. This complexity burdens the estimation task and calls for new prediction methods that will be able to cope with the complex prediction challenge.

In this tutorial we will first discuss the reasons that cause search engines to fail for some of the queries. Then, we will overview several state-of-the-art approaches for estimating query difficulty. We will also describe common methodologies for evaluating the prediction quality of query-performance prediction methods, and present some experimental results for the prediction quality of some predictors, as measured over several TREC's benchmarks. We will cover a few potential applications that can utilize query difficulty estimators. Finally, we will summarize with a discussion on open issues and challenges in the field.

2. PRESENTERS:

David Carmel. is a Research Staff Member at the Information Retrieval group at IBM Haifa Research Lab. David's

SIGIR'12, August 12–16, 2012, Portland, Oregon, USA.
ACM 978-1-4503-1472-5/12/08.

research is focused on search in the enterprise, query performance prediction, social search, and text mining. David has published more than 80 papers in IR and Web journals and conferences, organized a number of workshops, and taught several tutorials at SIGIR, and WWW. David is co-author of the book "Estimating the Query Difficulty for Information Retrieval". David earned his PhD in Computer Science from the Technion – Israel Institute of Technology in 1997.

Oren Kurland. is a Senior Lecturer in the Faculty of Industrial Engineering and Management at the Technion, Israel Institute of Technology. The information retrieval research group that Oren leads at the Technion focuses on developing formal models for information retrieval. Oren published more than 30 peer-reviewed papers in IR conferences and journals. He served as a senior program committee member (area chair) for the SIGIR and CIKM conferences. Oren also serves on the editorial boards of the Journal of Information Retrieval and the Journal of Artificial Intelligence Research (JAIR).

3. REFERENCES

[1] Giambattista Amati, Claudio Carpineto, and Giovanni Romano. Query difficulty, robustness, and selective application of query expansion. In *Proceedings of ECIR*, pages 127–137, 2004.

[2] Javed A. Aslam and Virgiliu Pavlu. Query hardness estimation using Jensen-Shannon divergence among multiple scoring functions. In *Proceeding of ECIR*, pages 198–209, 2007.

[3] Niranjan Balasubramanian and James Allan. Learning to select rankers. In *Proceedings of SIGIR*, pages 855–856, 2010.

[4] Niranjan Balasubramanian, Giridhar Kumaran, and Vitor R. Carvalho. Exploring reductions for long web queries. In *Proceedings of SIGIR*, pages 571–578, 2010.

[5] Niranjan Balasubramanian, Giridhar Kumaran, and Vitor R. Carvalho. Predicting query performance on the web. In *Proceedigns of SIGIR*, pages 785–786, 2010.

[6] David Carmel and Elad Yom-Tov. *Estimating the Query Difficulty for Information Retrieval.* Synthesis Lectures on Information Concepts, Retrieval, and Services. Morgan & Claypool Publishers, 2010.

[7] David Carmel and Elad Yom-Tov. Estimating the query difficulty for information retrieval. In *Proceedings of the 33rd international ACM SIGIR conference on Research and development in information retrieval*, SIGIR '10, pages 911–911, New York, NY, USA, 2010. ACM.

[8] David Carmel, Elad Yom-Tov, Adam Darlow, and Dan Pelleg. What makes a query difficult? In *Proceedings of SIGIR*, pages 390–397, 2006.

[9] David Carmel, Elad Yom-Tov, and Haggai Roitman. Enhancing digital libraries using missing content analysis. In *Proceedings of JCDL*, pages 1–10, 2008.

[10] Kevyn Collins-Thompson and Paul N. Bennett. Predicting query performance via classification. In *Proceedings of ECIR*, pages 140–152, 2010.

[11] Steve Cronen-Townsend, Yun Zhou, and W. Bruce Croft. Predicting query performance. In *Proceedings of SIGIR*, pages 299–306, 2002.

[12] Steve Cronen-Townsend, Yun Zhou, and W. Bruce Croft. A language modeling framework for selective query expansion. Technical Report IR-338, Center for Intelligent Information Retrieval, University of Massachusetts, 2004.

[13] Steve Cronen-Townsend, Yun Zhou, and W. Bruce Croft. Precision prediction based on ranked list coherence. *Information Retrieval*, 9(6):723–755, 2006.

[14] Ronan Cummins. Predicting query performance directly from score distributions. In *Proceedings of AIRS*, pages 315–326, 2011.

[15] Ronan Cummins, Joemon M. Jose, and Colm O'Riordan. Improved query performance prediction using standard deviation. In *Proceedings of SIGIR*, pages 1089–1090, 2011.

[16] Ronan Cummins, Mounia Lalmas, and Colm O'Riordan. The limits of retrieval effectiveness. In *Proceedings of ECIR*, pages 277–282, 2011.

[17] Fernando Diaz. Performance prediction using spatial autocorrelation. In *Proceedings of SIGIR*, pages 583–590, 2007.

[18] Donna Harman and Chris Buckley. The NRRC reliable information access (RIA) workshop. In *Proceedgins of SIGIR*, pages 528–529, 2004.

[19] Claudia Hauff, Leif Azzopardi, and Djoerd Hiemstra. The combination and evaluation of query performance prediction methods. In *Proceedings of ECIR*, pages 301–312, 2009.

[20] Claudia Hauff, Djoerd Hiemstra, and Franciska de Jong. A survey of pre-retrieval query performance predictors. In *Proceedings of CIKM*, pages 1419–1420, 2008.

[21] Claudia Hauff, Diane Kelly, and Leif Azzopardi. A comparison of user and system query performance predictions. In *Proceedings of CIKM*, pages 979–988, 2010.

[22] Claudia Hauff, Vanessa Murdock, and Ricardo Baeza-Yates. Improved query difficulty prediction for the web. In *Proceedings of CIKM*, pages 439–448, 2008.

[23] Ben He and Iadh Ounis. Inferring query performance using pre-retrieval predictors. In *Proceedings of SPIRE*, pages 43–54, 2004.

[24] Oren Kurland, Anna Shtok, David Carmel, and Shay Hummel. A unified framework for post-retrieval query-performance prediction. In *Proceedings of ICTIR*, pages 15–26, 2011.

[25] Josiane Mothe and Ludovic Tanguy. Linguistic features to predict query difficulty. In *ACM SIGIR 2005 Workshop on Predicting Query Difficulty - Methods and Applications*, 2005.

[26] Joaquín Pérez-Iglesias and Lourdes Araujo. Standard deviation as a query hardness estimator. In *Proceedings of SPIRE*, pages 207–212, 2010.

[27] Daniel Sheldon, Milad Shokouhi, Martin Szummer, and Nick Craswell. Lambdamerge: merging the results of query reformulations. In *Proceedings of WSDM*, pages 795–804, 2011.

[28] Anna Shtok, Oren Kurland, and David Carmel. Predicting query performance by query-drift estimation. In *Proceedings of ICTIR*, pages 305–312, 2009.

[29] Anna Shtok, Oren Kurland, and David Carmel. Using statistical decision theory and relevance models for query-performance prediction. In *Proccedings of SIGIR*, pages 259–266, 2010.

[30] Natali Soskin, Oren Kurland, and Carmel Domshlak. Navigating in the dark: Modeling uncertainty in ad hoc retrieval using multiple relevance models. In *Proceedings of ICTIR*, pages 79–91, 2009.

[31] Stephen Tomlinson. Robust, Web and Terabyte Retrieval with Hummingbird Search Server at TREC 2004. In *Proceedings of TREC-13*, 2004.

[32] Vishwa Vinay, Ingemar J. Cox, Natasa Milic-Frayling, and Kenneth R. Wood. On ranking the effectiveness of searches. In *Proceedings of SIGIR*, pages 398–404, 2006.

[33] E. M. Voorhees. Overview of the TREC 2003 robust retrieval track. In *Proceedings of TREC-12*, 2003.

[34] E. M. Voorhees. Overview of the TREC 2004 robust retrieval track. In *Proceedings of TREC-13*, 2004.

[35] Mattan Winaver, Oren Kurland, and Carmel Domshlak. Towards robust query expansion: Model selection in the language model framework to retrieval. In *Proceedings of SIGIR*, pages 729–730, 2007.

[36] Elad Yom-Tov, Shai Fine, David Carmel, and Adam Darlow. Learning to estimate query difficulty: including applications to missing content detection and distributed information retrieval. In *Proceedings of SIGIR*, pages 512–519, 2005.

[37] Yun Zhou and W. Bruce Croft. Ranking robustness: a novel framework to predict query performance. In *Proceedgins of CIKM*, pages 567–574, 2006.

[38] Yun Zhou and W. Bruce Croft. Query performance prediction in web search environments. In *Proceedings of SIGIR*, pages 543–550, 2007.

Collaborative Information Seeking – Art and Science of Achieving 1+1>2 in IR

Chirag Shah
School of Communication & Information (SC&I)
Rutgers, The State University of New Jersey
4 Huntington St, New Brunswick, NJ 08901, USA
chirags@rutgers.edu

ABSTRACT

The assumption of information seekers being independent and IR problem being individual has been challenged often in the recent past, with an argument that the next big leap in search and retrieval will come through incorporating social and collaborative aspects of information seeking. This half-day tutorial will introduce the student to theories, methodologies, and tools that focus on information retrieval/seeking in collaboration. The student will have an opportunity to learn about the social aspect of IR with a focus on collaborative information seeking (CIS) situations, systems, and evaluation techniques. The course is intended for those interested in social and collaborative aspects of IR (from both academia and industry), and requires only a general understanding of IR systems and evaluation.

Categories and Subject Descriptors

H.3: INFORMATION STORAGE AND RETRIEVAL **H.3.3: Information Search and Retrieval**: *Search process*; **H.5.3 [Information Interfaces and Presentation]**: Group and Organization Interfaces—*Collaborative computing, Computer-supported cooperative work; Theory and models.*

Keywords

Collaborative information seeking (CIS); Tutorial.

1. OVERVIEW AND RATIONALE

Traditionally, IR is considered an individual pursuit, and not surprisingly, the majority of tools, techniques, and models developed for addressing information need, retrieval, and usage have focused on single users. The assumption of information seekers being independent and IR problem being individual has been challenged often in the recent past (e.g., [2,5,12]. This course will introduce such works to the students, with an emphasis on understanding models and systems that support collaborative search or browsing. To put CIS in perspective, the course will show the students how various related concepts, such as collaborative information behavior (CIB), co-browsing, co-search, collaborative filtering, can be placed on the dimensions of human-system and explicitness-implicitness along with CIS and CIR (Figure 1) for exploration and developmental needs, as well as evaluation purposes.

Specifically, the course will (1) outline the research and latest developments in the field of collaborative IR, (2) list the challenges for designing and evaluating collaborative IR systems, and (3) show how traditional single user IR models and systems could be mapped to those for CIS. This will be achieved through introduction to appropriate literature, algorithms and interfaces that facilitate CIS, and methodologies for studying and evaluating them. Thus, the course will offer a balance between theoretical and practical elements of CIS.

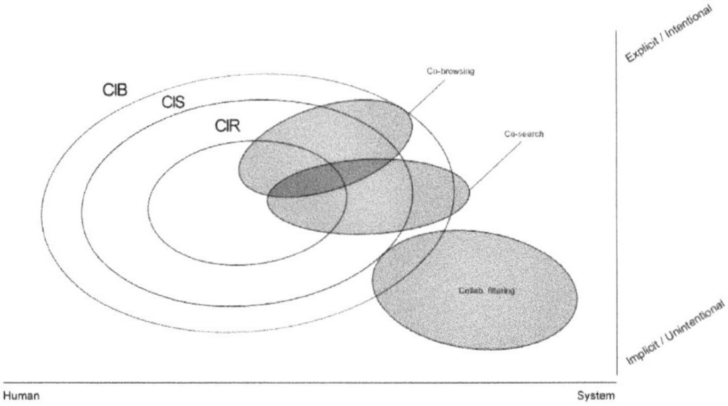

Figure 1: Depiction of CIS and related topics using the dimensions of human-system and explicit-implicit collaboration.

2. COURSE OBJECTIVES

The course will have the following broad objectives:

1. Define collaborative information seeking (CIS) and differentiate it with related terms.
2. Identify situations and motivations for CIS.
3. List various dimensions of collaborative work/systems/method.
4. Discuss system-mediated and user-mediated CIS with examples.
5. Enumerate essential and desired features of CIS systems.
6. Outline an evaluation framework for CIS.

3. RELEVANCE TO THE IR COMMUNITY

With an increasing number of researchers from the fields of IR, HCI, and social media coming together, there has been an unprecedented interest to CIS/CIR and related issues in the recent years. While the concept of people working together in solving IR problems has been explored before, it has made its strong comeback in the past few years. This area has gained significant momentum through a number of workshops and other professional events, as well as special issues of journals. And yet, we have just scratched the surface. With the advent of social media and collaboratively generated content (CGC) everywhere, it is time the IR community takes a serious look at this topic that is increasingly achieving more relevance and importance. With its applicability to numerous domains including education, legal, health, and business, studying various issues relating to CIS/CIR is very timely and relevant to the IR community.

4. OUTLINE OF THE TUTORIAL

The three-hour course will follow a general structure given below.

- *Hour-1*: Discuss situations for CIS; Introduce a few group-based information seeking models and systems (e.g., Grudin's work [4]); Learn about the taxonomy for CIS systems and situations (e.g., [3,8]) and see how existing systems fit into this structure.
- *Hour-2*: Discuss the back-end of CIS systems; Look at the works by Pickens et al. [7] and Shah et al. [9] that focus on algorithmic mediation; Discuss the front-end of collaborative IR systems; Look at the works by Twidale et al. [12] and Morris and Horvitz [6] that focus on interface-based mediation.
- *Hour-3*: Learn about existing approaches to data mining and evaluation for CIS systems (e.g., [1]); See how system-based and user-based measurements could be used for a more holistic analysis (e.g., [10]).

5. COURSE MATERIALS

Course materials will be made available on a Web site hosted under http://collab.infoseeking.org/ two weeks prior to the tutorial. They will include links to relevant software; links to publications that will be discussed; and mechanisms for communication (Twitter hashtags #cis2012 and #sigir2012, blog space, etc.) among the tutorial participants, before, during and after the tutorial.

Since this course is focused on introducing several relevant theories, models, approaches, and findings in the field of CIS/CIR, the participants will also be given an annotated bibliography that represents seminal works in this area.

6. ABOUT THE PRESENTER

Chirag Shah is an assistant professor at the Dept. of Library & Information Science (LIS) within the School of Communication & Information (SC&I) at Rutgers University, USA. He received his PhD from the School of Information & Library Science (SILS) at UNC Chapel Hill (advisor: Gary Marchionini). He holds an MTech, Computer Science & Engineering from IIT Madras, India and an MS, Computer Science from UMass Amherst (advisor: W. Bruce Croft).

His research interests include various aspects of interactive information retrieval/seeking, especially in the context of online social networks and collaborations, contextual information mining, and applications of social media services for exploring critical socio-political issues. At Rutgers, he runs a research group on Information Seeking and Behavior (http://www.infoseeking.org/) as well as special interest groups on Collaborative Information Seeking and Social Information Seeking. He has published numerous papers in journals and conferences relating to these topics, and specific to collaborative information seeking (CIS). His co-authored paper for SIGIR 2008 titled "Algorithmic Mediation for Collaborative Exploratory Search" won the best paper award. He co-organized workshops on CIS at ACM Group 2010 and ASIST 2011 conferences. He has developed Coagmento system (http://www.coagmento.org/), which allows a group of users to search and share information in collaboration. He recently received the Yahoo! Campus Innovation Award for his project titled "Reimagining and Reinvigorating Information Seeking with a Novel Approach to Collaborative Information Seeking". He also taught a short course on collaborative IR at the Russian Summer School of Information Retrieval (RuSSIR) in St Petersburg in Summer 2011, and a tutorial on CIS at WSDM 2012. His book on Collaborative Information Seeking is being published by Springer [11].

7. REFERENCES

[1] Baeza-Yates, R., & Pino, J. A. (1997). A First Step to Formally Evaluate Collaborative Work. *Proceedings of GROUP* (pp. 56-60).

[2] Fidel, R., Bruce, H., Pejtersen, A. M., Dumais, S. T., Grudin, J., & Poltrock, S. (2000). Collaborative Information Retrieval (CIR). *The New Review of Information Behaviour Research*, 235-247.

[3] Golovchinsky, G., Pickens, J., & Back, M. (2008). A taxonomy of collaboration in online information seeking. *Proceedings of JCDL 2008 Workshop on Collaborative Exploratory Search*. Pittsburgh, PA.

[4] Grudin, J. (1994). Groupware and social dynamics: eight challenges for developers. *Communications of the ACM*, *37*(1), 92-105.

[5] Hansen, P., & Jarvelin, K. (2005). Collaborative Information Retrieval in an information-intensive domain. *Information Processing and Management*, *41*, 1101-1119.

[6] Morris, M. R., & Horvitz, E. (2007). SearchTogether: An Interface for Collaborative Web Search. *ACM Symposium on User Interface Software and Technology (UIST)* (pp. 3-12). Newport, RI.

[7] Pickens, J., Golovchinsky, G., Shah, C., Qvarfordt, P., & Back, M. (2008). Algorithmic Mediation for Collaborative Exploratory Search. *Proceedings of the Annual ACM Conference on Research and Development in Information Retrieval (SIGIR)*. Singapore.

[8] Rodden, T. (1991). A Survey of CSCW Systems. *Interacting with Computers*, *3*(3), 319-353.

[9] Shah, C., Pickens, J., & Golovchinsky, G. (2010). Role-based results redistribution for collaborative information retrieval. *Information Processing & Management*, *46*(6), 773-781. doi:10.1016/j.ipm.2009.10.002

[10] Shah, C. (2010). Collaborative Information Seeking: A Literature Review. *Advances in Librarianship*, *32*, 3-33. doi:10.1108/S0065-2830(2010)0000032004

[11] Shah, C. (2012). Collaborative Information Seeking: The Art and Science of Making The Whole Greater Than The Sum of All (The Information Retrieval Series) (p. 212). Springer. Retrieved from http://www.amazon.com/Collaborative-Information-Seeking-Science-Retrieval/dp/364228812X

[12] Twidale, M. B. T., Nichols, D. M. N., & Paice, C. D. (1997). Browsing is a Collaborative Process. *Information Processing and Management*, *33*(6), 761-783.

Advances on the Development of Evaluation Measures

Ben Carterette
University of Delaware
101 Smith Hall
Newark, DE, USA
carteret@cis.udel.edu

Evangelos Kanoulas
Information School
University of Sheffield
Sheffield, UK
ekanoulas@gmail.com

Emine Yilmaz
Microsoft Research
7 JJ Thomson Avenue
Cambridge, UK
eminey@microsoft.com

ABSTRACT

The goal of the tutorial is to provide attendees with a comprehensive overview of the latest advances in the development of information retrieval evaluation measures and discuss the current challenges in the area. A number of topics are covered, including background in traditional evaluation paradigm and traditional evaluation measures, evaluation measures based on user models, advanced models of user interaction with search engines, measures based on these models, measures for novelty and diversity, and session-based measures.

Categories and Subject Descriptors

H.3.4 [**Information Storage and Retrieval**]: Systems and Software—*Performance Evaluation*

General Terms

Experimentation, Measurement

Keywords

evaluation, measures, user models, novelty, diversity, cascade model, sessions

1. TUTORIAL DESCRIPTION

The effectiveness of a retrieval system, i.e. its ability to retrieve items that are relevant to the information need of an end user, is one of the most important aspects of retrieval quality. A number of different experimental frameworks have been designed in IR to measure retrieval effectiveness. The *systems-based* approach of using a test collection comprising canned information needs and static relevance judgments to compute evaluation measures has so far served well IR experimentation. The availability of query logs that can demonstrate the interactions of a user with a retrieval system has led to an increasing interest in better modeling user needs and user interaction with an engine and building measures on the top of such models. This approach has led to measures that are better correlated with the actual *utility* that a system is offering to an end user.

This tutorial focuses on methods of measuring effectiveness, in particular focusing on recent work that more directly models the utility of an engine to its users. We discuss traditional approaches to effectiveness evaluation based on test collections, then transition to approaches based on test collections along with explicit models of user interaction with search results.

SIGIR'12, August 12–16, 2012, Portland, Oregon, USA.
ACM 978-1-4503-1472-5/12/08.

2. TUTORIAL OBJECTIVES

The primary objectives of the tutorial are to

- describe models of user interactions with retrieval systems and measures constructed on the top of such models;
- introduce complex retrieval tasks that require the construction of advanced user models;
- highlight recent advances in the field that has influenced the evaluation measures adopted by forums such as TREC;
- enable attendees to use advanced evaluation measures, tailored to their own tasks;
- identify open questions in modeling user interactions and constructing evaluation measures and motivate work in the field.

3. ANNOTATED OUTLINE

1. Test collections and traditional evaluation measures [17, 18, 19, 20, 16]
2. Basic User Model and Measures
   (a) Cooper's Expected Search Length [7]
   (b) Robertson's Interpretation of Average Precision [14]
   (c) Graded Relevance [15]
3. Cascade User Model and Measures
   (a) Cascade Model
   (b) Ranked Bias Precision [13]
   (c) Normalised Discounted Cumulative Gain [8, 9, 3, 2]
   (d) Expected Reciprocal Rank [5]
   (e) Expected Browsing Utility [22]
4. Models and Measures for Novelty and Diversity
   (a) Information Nuggets
   (b) Subtopic Recall and Precision [23]
   (c) Intent-Aware Family [1]
   (d) α-NDCG[6]

   (e) Intent-aware ERR [4]
5. Models and Measures for Session Evaluation
   (a) TREC Session Track [11]
   (b) Session DCG [10]
   (c) Expected Utility [21]
   (d) Session Precision, Recall and Average Precision [12]

4. BIOGRAPHIES

Ben Carterette is an assistant professor of Computer and Information Sciences at the University of Delaware in Newark, Delaware, US. He completed his PhD in Computer Science at the University of Massachusetts Amherst in 2008. His work on information retrieval evaluation has been recognized with several Best Paper Awards at conferences such as SIGIR, ECIR, and ICTIR. With Evangelos Kanoulas, he has been actively involved in coordination of the TREC Million Query Track and the TREC Session Track.

Evangelos Kanoulas is a postdoctoral research scientist at Google, Switzerland. Prior to that he was a Marie Curie fellow in the Information School at the University of Sheffield. Evangelos received his PhD from Northeastern University, Boston. He has published extensively in the field of information retrieval evaluation in SIGIR, CIKM and ECIR. He was actively involved in coordinating the TREC Million Query and TREC Session Track.

Emine Yilmaz is a researcher at Microsoft Research Cambridge. She obtained her Ph.D. from Northeastern University in 2008. Her main interests are information retrieval and applications of information theory, statistics and machine learning. She has published research papers extensively at major information retrieval venues such as SIGIR, CIKM and WSDM. She has also organized several workshops on Crowdsourcing and served as one of the organizers of the ICTIR Conference.

5. REFERENCES

[1] Rakesh Agrawal, Sreenivas Gollapudi, Alan Halverson, and Samuel Ieong. Diversifying search results. In Ricardo A. Baeza-Yates, Paolo Boldi, Berthier A. Ribeiro-Neto, and Berkant Barla Cambazoglu, editors, *WSDM*, pages 5–14. ACM, 2009.

[2] Chris Burges, Tal Shaked, Erin Renshaw, Ari Lazier, Matt Deeds, Nicole Hamilton, and Greg Hullender. Learning to rank using gradient descent. In *ICML '05: Proceedings of the 22nd international conference on Machine learning*, pages 89–96, New York, NY, USA, 2005. ACM Press.

[3] Ben Carterette. System effectiveness, user models, and user utility: a conceptual framework for investigation. In *SIGIR*, pages 903–912, 2011.

[4] Olivier Chapelle, Shihao Ji, Ciya Liao, Emre Velipasaoglu, Larry Lai, and Su-Lin Wu. Intent-based diversification of web search results: metrics and algorithms. *Inf. Retr.*, 14(6):572–592, 2011.

[5] Olivier Chapelle, Donald Metlzer, Ya Zhang, and Pierre Grinspan. Expected reciprocal rank for graded relevance. In *In Proceedings of the 18th ACM Conference on Information and Knowledge Management (CIKM)*, 2009.

[6] Charles L.A. Clarke, Maheedhar Kolla, Gordon V. Cormack, Olga Vechtomova, Azin Ashkan, Stefan Büttcher, and Ian MacKinnon. Novelty and diversity in information retrieval evaluation. In *SIGIR '08: Proceedings of the 31st annual international ACM SIGIR conference on Research and development in information retrieval*, pages 659–666, New York, NY, USA, 2008. ACM.

[7] William S. Cooper. Expected search length: a single measure of retrieval effectiveness based on the weak ordering action of retrieval systems. *American Documentation*, 19:30–41, 1968.

[8] Kalervo Järvelin and Jaana Kekäläinen. IR evaluation methods for retrieving highly relevant documents. In *SIGIR '00: Proceedings of the 23rd annual international ACM SIGIR conference on Research and development in information retrieval*, pages 41–48, New York, NY, USA, 2000. ACM Press.

[9] Kalervo Järvelin and Jaana Kekäläinen. Cumulated gain-based evaluation of IR techniques. *ACM Transactions on Information Systems*, 20(4):422–446, 2002.

[10] Kalervo Järvelin, Susan L. Price, Lois M. L. Delcambre, and Marianne Lykke Nielsen. Discounted cumulated gain based evaluation of multiple-query ir sessions. In *ECIR*, pages 4–15, 2008.

[11] Evangelos Kanoulas, Ben Carterette, Paul Clough, and Mark Sanderson. Session track overview. In *The Nineteenth Text REtrieval Conference Notebook Proceedings (TREC 2010)*, December 2010.

[12] Evangelos Kanoulas, Ben Carterette, Paul Clough, and Mark Sanderson. Evaluating multi-query sessions. Submitted to the 34th international ACM SIGIR conference on Research and development in information retrieval (SIGIR 2011), 2011.

[13] Alistair Moffat and Justin Zobel. Rank-biased precision for measurement of retrieval effectiveness. *ACM Trans. Inf. Syst.*, 27(1):1–27, 2008.

[14] Stephen Robertson. A new interpretation of average precision. In *SIGIR '08: Proceedings of the 31st annual international ACM SIGIR conference on Research and development in information retrieval*, pages 689–690, New York, NY, USA, 2008. ACM.

[15] Stephen E. Robertson, Evangelos Kanoulas, and Emine Yilmaz. Extending average precision to graded relevance judgments. In *SIGIR '10: Proceeding of the 33rd international ACM SIGIR conference on Research and development in information retrieval*, pages 603–610, New York, NY, USA, 2010. ACM.

[16] Karen Sparck Jones and C. J. van Rijsbergen. Information retrieval test collections. *Journal of Documentation*, 32(1):59–75, 1976.

[17] Jean Tague. The pragmatics of information retrieval evaluation. pages 59–102.

[18] Jean Tague-Sutcliffe. The pragmatics of information retrieval experimentation, revisited. *Inf. Process. Manage.*, 28(4):467–490, 1992.

[19] Jean Tague-Sutcliffe. The pragmatics of information retrieval experimentation, revisited. *Readings in Information Retrievalnformation retrieval*, pages 205–216, 1997.

[20] Ellen M. Voorhees and Donna K. Harman. *TREC: Experiment and Evaluation in Information Retrieval.* MIT Press, 2005.

[21] Yiming Yang and Abhimanyu Lad. Modeling expected utility of multi-session information distillation. In Leif Azzopardi, Gabriella Kazai, Stephen E. Robertson, Stefan M. Rüger, Milad Shokouhi, Dawei Song, and Emine Yilmaz, editors, *ICTIR*, pages 164–175, 2009.

[22] Emine Yilmaz, Milad Shokouhi, Nick Craswell, and Stephen E. Robertson. Incorporating user behavior information in IR evaluation. In *in Understanding the user - Logging and interpreting user interactions in information retrieval. Workshop in Conjunction with the ACM SIGIR Conference on Information Retrieval*, 2009.

[23] ChengXiang Zhai, William W. Cohen, and John D. Lafferty. Beyond independent relevance: methods and evaluation metrics for subtopic retrieval. In *SIGIR*, pages 10–17, 2003.

Information Retrieval for E-Discovery

David D. Lewis,
David D. Lewis Consulting, sigir2012tutorial@DavidDLewis.com

Abstract: This tutorial will introduce the IR issues posed by the "discovery" process in legal cases, i.e. the requirement that parties turn over documents responsive (relevant) to the issues at dispute. The explosion of electronically stored information has created a multi-billion dollar market in technology and services for discovery on electronically stored information (e-discovery).

I will discuss the discovery process, the scale and diversity of materials to be searched, and the economics of identifying and reviewing potentially responsive material. I will then focus on three major IR areas: search, supervised learning (including text classification), and relevance assessment. For each, I will discuss the technologies used in e-discovery, and research results that have not yet seen commercial practice. I will particularly concentrate on evaluation issues, which are crucial to acceptance of these technologies in a legal context. I will also outline research directions in IR for e-discovery, and in particular ones where progress can be made without access to "realistic" test collections. Connections will be drawn with the use of IR in related tasks, such as enterprise search, criminal investigations, intelligence analysis, historical research, truth and reconciliation commissions, and freedom of information (open records or sunshine law) requests.

ACM Categories & Descriptors: H.3.3 Information Search and Retrieval; H.4.1 Office Automation; I.2.1 Artificial Intelligence, Applications and Expert Systems - Law

Keywords: computer forensics, document formats, duplicate detection, machine learning, e-mail, electronic mail, OCR, text mining, sampling, effectiveness, confidence intervals

SIGIR'12, August 12–16, 2012, Portland, Oregon, USA.
ACM 978-1-4503-1472-5/12/08.

Bio: David D. Lewis is an independent consultant working in the areas of information retrieval, text mining, machine learning, natural language processing, and the statistical evaluation of complex information systems. He previously held research positions at AT&T Labs, Bell Labs, and the University of Chicago. Lewis has published more than 75 scientific papers and is an inventor on 8 patents on information retrieval and text mining technology. He has presented over 20 tutorials on topics in machine learning and language processing at a range of conferences, including SIGIR, KDD, ACL, JSM, ASIS, Infonortics, and others, as well as lecturing widely at universities, businesses, and industry events. He was a member of committees that designed and administered the U.S. government MUC and TREC evaluations of language processing technologies. He was elected a Fellow of the American Association for the Advancement of Science in 2006.

Dr. Lewis was one of the founders of the TREC Legal Track, the first large scale open evaluation of information retrieval technology for electronic discovery in legal cases. As part of the Legal Track work, he created the first large scale test collection for experimentation on electronic discovery, the IIT CDIP test collection. Dr. Lewis has also served as a consulting expert or expert witness in a number of legal cases. He was a testifying expert in *Kleen Products, LLC, et al. v. Packaging Corporation of America*, et al., a US Federal Court case involving issues of information retrieval, machine learning, and statistical sampling in e-discovery.

Author Index

www.ingramcontent.com/pod-product-compliance
Ingram Content Group UK Ltd.
Pitfield, Milton Keynes, MK11 3LW, UK
UKHW051455290926
15471UKWH00008B/1220

9 781450 320016